Toward
Understanding
Children

Toward Understanding Children

Judith A. Schickedanz
Boston University

David I. Schickedanz
Regional Educational Assessment and Diagnostic Services, Inc.
Lakeville Hospital, Lakeville, Massachusetts

Peggy D. Forsyth
The Pennsylvania State University, Hazelton

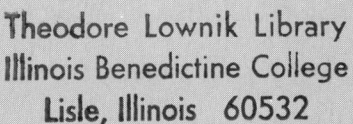

Little, Brown and Company
Boston   Toronto

Library of Congress Catalog Card No. 81-84198
ISBN 0-316-773247

9 8 7 6 5 4 3 2 1

HAL

Published simultaneously in Canada by Little, Brown & Company (Canada) Limited
Printed in the United States of America

Picture research by Tina Schwinder

ILLUSTRATION CREDITS

Cover and title page photo: © 1980 Erica Stone.
 Chapter 1. p. 5: James Holland/Stock, Boston; *p. 7:* © Bruce Roberts/Photo Researchers; *p. 16:* Alan Carey/The Image Works; *p. 18:* Polumbaum/Monkmeyer.
 Chapter 2. p. 20: Lew Merrim/Monkmeyer; *p. 29:* © Bohdan Hrynewych/Stock, Boston; *p. 31:* Mike Mazzaschi/Stock, Boston; *p. 36:* Paul Conklin/Monkmeyer.
 Chapter 3. p. 48: Jean-Claude Lejeune/Stock, Boston; *p. 50:* Gesell Institute; *p. 55:* Clemens Kalischer/Image Photos; *p. 61:* © 1980 Yves de Braine/Black Star.

(continued on p.593)

To J. McVicker Hunt, Eleanor Robinson, and Bernard Spodek,
who introduced the authors to child development and education;
and to Adam and Scott, who brought it all home.

Preface

In our years of teaching introductory child psychology and child development courses we have searched for the ideal book. Despite the large number of texts available, we did not find one that suited our needs. If a text was readable, it often lacked depth. If it was sufficiently substantive, its style was too often burdensome. If it had a sound theoretical and research base, connections to everyday life were missing. If it was an applied text, the theoretical and research ties were often only weakly drawn. If a text was current, it sometimes went to the extreme of being faddish. If it was authoritative, it did not evoke for us the emotions — the sadness, the wonder, the joy, the anger, the surprise — we experienced with children.

We set out to write a more perfect textbook. To trace the fascinating story of development we have adopted a chronological approach. After an introductory section on methods of studying children and the theories underlying the study of child development, we begin our chronology by discussing genetics, prenatal development, birth, and the neonatal period. Each succeeding part of the book dealing with a particular age and stage is divided into five chapters. The first four examine specific areas of development — physical, cognitive, language, and social — always in that sequence. The fifth chapter we call *Knowledge and Action* because in it we discuss applications of the material presented in the preceding four chapters that are of particular interest to teachers, parents, or anyone who works with children and adolescents. If chapters covering a common topic, such as language development, are assigned together, the book can easily be used in courses organized topically. The last section of the text covers the social context of parenting, focusing on changing social conditions and their effects on parents and children.

To construct the story of development we have selected traditional content that is of interest to students of child development. We have also chosen to include new material that is likely to be of enduring interest. As we wrote, we constantly kept in mind that we intended this book for those individuals who are or who will be working with children and adolescents and seeking to apply their knowledge of development. Yet at the same time we realize that wise and successful application rests on a firm knowledge of theory and research. The first four chapters of each part, therefore, cover not only theory and research but also applied material. We then devoted the fifth chapter of each part, the *Knowledge and Action* chapter, entirely to applied concerns linked to the topics presented in the preceding four chapters. Some instructors will be satisfied with the applied material included in the first four chapters of a part and will wish to omit use of the fifth chapter. But for many instructors the material on toys, education, assessment, safety, and parenting found in the *Knowledge and Action* chapters will be just what they need to meet the practical concerns of their students. The organization of the book allows for easy adaptation to these varying needs.

We have paid close attention to writing style. In addition, numerous illustrations and examples make concepts clear and remind the reader that we are talking about real children. We also pose problems, ask questions, and suggest issues to think about in order to engage student interest and to encourage deeper involvement with the text. Some places in this book will make you laugh — and others will surely disturb you. Throughout, we think you will find the material interesting and thought-provoking.

Finally, we have also tried to make this textbook more useful to students and professors alike. For students we have provided detailed chapter summaries, lists of new terms, and suggested readings at the ends of chapters. A glossary and an appendix of student projects are at the end of the book. A study guide that includes study aids, activities, and projects is also available. For professors we have created both an instructor's manual with suggestions for teaching the course and a test bank of objective questions.

About the Authors. How we wrote the book, the content we included, and the goals we had in mind were influenced by our varied educational backgrounds and professional experiences. We hold degrees in the areas of child development and family studies, child psychology, clinical psychology, and early childhood education. Our professional experiences have included roles as teacher of children and of college students (both undergraduate and graduate), parent educator, researcher, administrator, and clinician. The result of our education and experience is a book that reflects the interests and concerns of a number of fields of study and has a richness and completeness not found in many other texts.

Those Who Helped. Throughout the long and intensive process of writing this book, a number of people were most generous with their time and ideas. We wish to thank our reviewers, who made numerous suggestions for improving the manuscript: Linda F. Annis, Ball State University; George M. Bass, Jr., College of William and Mary; Earl M. Caspers, University of Arkansas; Roy P. Doyle, Arizona State University; Barbara N. Flagg, Harvard University; Elaine M. Justice,

Old Dominion University; Alice S. Honig, Syracuse University; Phyllis R. Hughes, Parkland College; Mary Louise Hunley, University of South Carolina–Spartanburg; Suzanne V. La Bregue, North Texas State University; Patricia Miller, University of Florida; Scott A. Miller, University of Florida; Jackie Mize, Purdue University; Lenorah Polk, Central Oklahoma State University; Richard J. Venjohn, West Virginia University; Joel Walters, University of Illinois; Mary York, Portland State University; and Susan Berry.

We wish also to express our appreciation to Dan Otis for his fine efforts in helping us convey our ideas in a smooth and consistent writing style. Additionally, the visual appeal of this book is the result of the imagination and talent of Victor Curran, who designed the cover and interior of the book, and of Tina Schwinder, our art editor. We are also grateful to Billie Ingram for her assistance in all aspects of the project. Lastly, we extend special thanks to our book editor, Dana Norton, for her extraordinary commitment to this project and her attention to detail. Her skill in coordinating the many aspects of the book production process helped bring our work to fruition.

J.S.
D.S.
P.F.

Age-Stage Contents

x

Topical Contents

Contents

Part I

Introduction

The behavior of children sometimes puzzles everyone who lives and works with them — parents, teachers, neighbors, and friends alike. Why do children do what they do, think what they think, say what they say? What should we do, think, or say in response? The following story is a good example of how the perceptions of children can surprise us.

A three-year-old boy was crying hard and rubbing the side of his head. His mother said that this was unusual behavior — the child usually dismissed bumps with a shrug. She expected to find a big lump, but when she searched she found no evidence that the boy was hurt. Finally, she asked him if his head *really* hurt that much. She got no answer. Then the child began to plead with her not to let the doctor take his eye out.

Suddenly the mother realized what was happening. A baby who lived on their block had recently lost an eye because of a tumor on the retina. The mother had explained this to her son when he had asked about the baby's eyepatch. At the time, she had not thought it had worried him, but thinking back she remembered his silence, the absence of his usual three-year-old "why?" He apparently had not understood completely what had been said — all he knew was that when something happens to your eye, the doctor might take it out. His fear was sparked when the wooden handle of his sister's jump rope hit the side of his head near his eye. Now, he thought, the doctor will take *my* eye out, too! The mother realized that she had some more explaining to do, but how could she explain to a three-year-old the difference between a serious injury or illness and a slight bump?

In this book we describe child behavior and provide information about how children understand and how adults can further their understanding. We focus on children's growth and development, but we hope to promote the growth of adults as well. Adults who understand and enjoy children not only add greatly to children's lives, they enrich their own lives, too.

We also discuss the controversial issues related to children and explain some of the many questions that remain unanswered. These goals may seem to contradict our first goal of helping adults know more about children so they can aid

3

their development. How can adults know what to do if there are unanswered questions? The fact is that there are no simple explanations for children's actions or pat methods for handling the situations in which children become involved. Even the knowledge we do have does not translate easily into prescriptions for dealing with individual children. But it would be inaccurate to suggest that we know nothing about child behavior and how to influence it, or that those who spend time with children do not already make decisions based on their own assumptions about why children behave as they do. The best course is to let current understanding of children inform our interactions with them, while realizing that progress in understanding may change our interactions.

We will begin in Chapter 1 with brief discussions of some of the major concerns adults have about children and the major difficulties confronting children in today's world. In Chapter 2 we turn our attention to ways of studying children to collect information about what children are like and what causes them to behave as they do. In Chapter 3 we discuss the major theories of child development. More complete explanations about child behavior and development and suggestions for action are the focus of later chapters.

Chapter 1

Why Study Children?

Concern about children is experienced at two levels. At the first level are parents, teachers, and others who interest with children day in and day out. Their concerns are immediate: How should children be disciplined? What behavior is atypical and what behavior is within the normal range? The second level of concern goes beyond the individual parent or teacher to society in general and its interest in children's welfare: How can society protect children's rights? How can it provide for the education of the next generation? In this chapter we discuss a number of concerns at both of these levels.

Children: Areas of Concern to Parents and Teachers

People who are responsible for children play a variety of roles and are interested in many different aspects of children's behavior. Four areas of concern to almost everyone are helping them develop and learn, communicating with them, disciplining them, and meeting their special needs.

Fostering Children's Development

"She says only three words. How can I encourage her to talk more?"

"Sometimes he writes his name backward. Is something wrong with him?"

"She doesn't want to share her toys. Should I expect more of a three-year-old?"

"He wants to do what his friends do instead of what I want him to do. Why don't children continue to think their parents know what's best?"

Whatever a child's behavior, we are likely to have questions about it. Is it typical of the child's age? How long will it last? Why did it start? How can we get it to continue — or to stop? How do children develop? When should we expect certain behaviors to occur? How can we support development? Teachers, parents, and others who wish to understand the characteristics of children of various ages will be interested in many of the topics discussed in this book. We will discuss in detail the behaviors typical of various ages, the sequences of development, and the circumstances in which a behavior should be considered a problem.

Communicating with Children

We know from research and from our own interactions with children that they rarely see the world as we do. If we assume that their perceptions are the same as ours, we are likely to find that communication has stopped, and that we have lost touch with them. A four-year-old asks her mother, "When are we going to the store?" In a matter-of fact voice, mother says, "At two o'clock." In two minutes, the child asks the question again. With a hint of irritation in her voice, Mother says, "I told you we were going at two o'clock," "But *when* are we going?" "I told you and I won't say it again. Stop pestering!"

The mother might be surprised to learn that the child probably wondered when they were going, not in clock time, which means little to four-year-olds, but in time measured by the familiar sequence of events in her day. "We're going to the store after we eat lunch, and that will be around two o'clock," would have been a helpful, understandable reply. But this mother did not know how a child understands time; she may have assumed that the persistent questioning was a deliberate attempt to annoy her, or that the child was a poor listener.

When adults consistently misinterpret what children say, or use words or concepts that children cannot understand, communication will be limited, and our relationships with them may cease to grow. Children may also stop asking questions, which will limit their understanding of the world. To keep the channels of communication open, we can study development to find out how children's thinking differs from that of adults. We can then better understand their questions and provide answers we are sure they will understand. This can have important effects on children's development. Children who grow up misunderstood and mistreated are likely to pay a high price. They may underachieve, become destructive, drop out of school, escape through drugs and alcohol, or withdraw, too frightened to venture out of themselves.

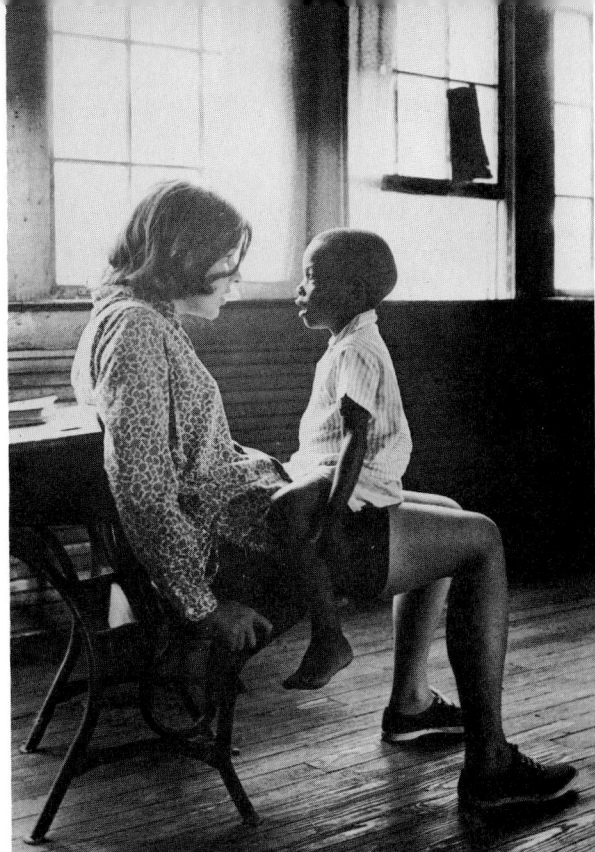

Understanding children involves knowing what children mean by what they say. Adults who have this understanding communicate well with children.

Disciplining Children

> Why did the children put beans in their ears when the one thing we told the children they must not do was put beans in their ears?
>
> Why did the children pour molasses on the cat when the one thing we told the children they must not do was pour molasses on the cat?

— Carl Sandburg

Getting children to do what we want them to do, or what we think they should do, can be a struggle. It is not surprising that one of the most frequently asked questions is "How should I discipline the children?"

Over the years the question has been answered in many different ways. Milton Senn (1977, p. 41), a physician interested in the history of child study, noticed a poster in a toy store window that summarized the changes in answers over the years:

1910 — Spank them   1950 — Love them
1920 — Deprive them   1960 — Spank them lovingly
1930 — Ignore them   1970 — To hell with them?
1940 — Reason with them

Herbert Kohl (1978, p. 25), a popular writer on children and schooling, properly points out that the question of how to discipline children "is not a scientific question but rather a question of how you believe people should treat each other." For us, one thing is clear: people should avoid hitting others, and "others" includes children. But what do you do when you put the paddle away? Do you allow children to create a reign of terror? Do you let them do what you wish they would not and know they should not? Of course not. Eliminating physical punishment does not mean dispensing with all limits and controls, or ceasing to make children understand that we expect certain behaviors and forbid others. It is in the area of disciplining children without using physical punishment that an understanding of children and methods of changing behavior can be helpful. For example, a preschool teacher who has trouble keeping her children from running, even though she constantly tells them to stop, might change their behavior if she understood that (1) young children are always moving and need opportunities to do so; (2) some room arrangements prevent inappropriate running better than others; and (3) attention to appropriate rather than inappropriate behavior can help children do what we want them to do.

In the dictionary, discipline is defined as (1) instruction; (2) training that corrects, molds, strengthens, or perfects; (3) punishment or chastisement; and (4) control gained by enforcing obedience or order, hence orderly conduct. One of our goals in this book is to suggest ways to implement the first two processes without overemphasizing the second two.

Meeting Special Needs

Children who are mentally retarded or have speech impairment, learning problems in some academic areas, behavior problems, or sensory handicaps are now described as *special needs* children. These children comprise between 10 and 20 percent of the school-age population. The estimates vary radically because authorities use different criteria to determine whether a child should be included in a particular category. Some estimates of speech disorders alone run as high as 10 percent when both minor and severe problems are included. We have summarized in Table 1-1 the approximate percentages of school-age children in various special needs categories.

Each child's problems are unique, of course, and categorization is of little use in choosing the best method of helping a child. The categories are useful in an introductory explanation, however, as long as you remember that the children in each category may differ from each other in many important respects.

Another common question concerns the effect of a problem on a child's future. The effects, of course, vary with the seriousness of the problem. Children with major problems such as psychosis, severe antisocial behavior, or severe mental retardation often have serious difficulties as adults (Cass and Thomas, 1979). Nevertheless, many children with these disabilities do recover or vastly improve. That most children in these areas may have special problems for a long

Table 1-1. Percentages of the school-age population with various special needs

Type of exceptionality	Approximate percentage	Description of the exceptionality
Speech impairment	3.5	Articulation (pronunciation of speech sounds) problems make up the largest proportion. Problems range from complete inability to speak to minor problems.
Mental retardation	1.0	Subaverage general intellectual functioning combined with defects in adaptive behavior manifested during the developmental period (Grossman, 1973).
Learning disability	3.0	Academic performance in a specific area (or in several areas) lags significantly behind what is expected for the child's age, and the problem cannot be attributed to mental retardation, emotional disturbance, or a physical handicap (Safford, 1978).
Behavior disorders	2.0	Severe fears, shyness, and withdrawn behavior; neuroses, severe conduct problems, and psychoses.
Physical and sensory handicaps	1.2	Visual and auditory impairment; crippling; palsy.
Gifted	3.0	Advanced ability in several areas.

SOURCE: Percentages were drawn from Bryan, T. H., and Bryan, J. H. *Understanding learning disabilities.* Port Washington, N.Y.: Alfred, 1975; Kirk, S. *Educating exceptional children.* 2d Ed. Boston: Houghton Mifflin, 1972; and Macmillan, D. L. *Mental retardation in school and society.* Boston: Little, Brown, 1977.

time should encourage us to commit more, not fewer, resources to helping them.

Many other special needs children can be expected to improve greatly as they mature. The majority of children whose speech is slow to develop will by adolescence be using well-articulated speech indistinguishable from that of the average child. At least three-quarters of the children described as mentally retarded are only mildly retarded, and the great majority of these will live independently in the community. Studies of children seen at child guidance clinics and other treatment centers for neurosis, excessive shyness, or other problems unrelated to psychosis or antisocial behavior show that these children have no more problems as adults than comparison groups who had no problems as children.

In fact, some of the best-known and best-loved people in the world would have been described as special needs children had such a label been used during their childhood. Albert Einstein did not speak until he was five years old and consistently had trouble in language examinations and courses. He found being a senior in secondary school so intolerable that he obtained a letter from his school doctor stating that he had had a nervous breakdown and must spend time with his parents in Italy. Childhood neighbors and relatives of Thomas Edison suggested that he was abnormal, and his teacher diagnosed him as mentally ill.

Winston Churchill did poorly in school; today he would be considered both hyperactive and in need of a remedial reading class. Eleanor Roosevelt did poorly in spelling, grammar, and arithmetic. She also lied, stole sweets, bit her nails, had a great fear of burglars and the dark, was very shy, and, as an adolescent, was described as "insecure" (Goertzel and Goertzel, 1962).

Like many others, these people matured from childhoods filled with problems to adult lives of outstanding service. It is safe to say that being considered to have a problem at some point during childhood is quite commonplace. According to their mothers, for example, nearly half of all school-age children are overactive, frequently fearful, and lose their tempers at least twice a week. In fact, the average four- to six-year-old behaves in a fashion that parents consider deviant once every four minutes (Johnson et al., 1973). Adults, of course, often consider behaviors to be a problem when in fact they are quite normal in children at certain stages of development.

One reason to study child development and behavior is to become familiar with genuine problems and methods of overcoming them. Another important reason is to develop the ability to distinguish real problems from behavior that may seem problematic to an adult who does not understand it but is normal for the child who exhibits it. We hope this book will help the reader understand that a broad range of behaviors is considered typical or "normal" for children at every age and stage of development.

Children's Issues of National Concern

The questions we have considered thus far are those which might be raised by individual adults. There are other issues, closely related in many respects to those already discussed, that are of concern to our society as a whole. They include the quality of the educational system, children's rights, and problems in family life.

Problems with the Educational System

Why are schools so often under attack? The answers are complex, but the cause is partly the nature of schooling itself. One problem with Western schooling is that instruction is not coupled with meaningful activity. Experiences or lessons are contrived rather than being encountered in daily life. In school one learns math by doing problems in a book rather than by helping mother, father, or an older brother gather the eggs, make candles, weave, or do the marketing.

This problem leads to another, that of relating knowledge acquired in school to action. Children taught through experience know how to relate what they know to what they do, but in a society that has schools, abstract learning and its practical application are often separated. Getting them back together again can be a problem. Because the learner does not always see the value of what he or she is doing, motivation, too, can become a problem.

Deciding what should be taught is another controversial issue. When children were taught at home or learned from an apprentice selected by the parents, a child's parents could control what the child was taught. In today's schools, however, children and parents can form a very diverse group. One group may want children to learn basic skills such as reading, writing, and arithmetic; another might prefer that the children learn how to be creative, plan, and make decisions. The arguments continue.

Opinions differ, not only about what should be taught, but also about how children should be taught. Some people think that information and knowledge should be parceled out by the teacher in sequenced bits, and that children should listen carefully and be drilled repeatedly. Others believe that children should be more active in the learning process, and that knowledge is best acquired through direct experience. The first group charges that the other is too permissive and sets no standards, whereas the second group makes counter-charges — that schools are too rigid and stultifying. Each group's attitudes reflect fundamentally different philosophies about the nature of mankind, how children learn, and the purposes of schools.

Other school-related problems are the result of compulsory education laws that support a prolonged adolescent period. These laws were contrived by Western societies to help ensure a highly educated labor force and to reduce the number of adults seeking employment. We are not suggesting that adolescents should be out of school; we use the example of compulsory attendance until age sixteen to illustrate that in addition to educating children, schools serve as instruments for enforcing social and political policies. Fulfilling these roles can create immense problems. These noneducational objectives of schools, which are rarely stated explicitly in the school curriculum guides, have been called "the hidden curriculum" (Giroux and Penna, 1979; Jackson, 1968).

We cannot discuss at length all of the problems confronting schools today; to do so would require that we venture into sociology, political science, economics, and philosophy. But we will have quite a lot to say in later chapters about how young children understand and learn, and about what Bruner (1978, p. 296) calls *conversion*, or putting the knowledge and skills of adults into a form capable of mastery by a beginner. (Where does one start when helping children learn to read or to understand mathematics?) We will also provide a lengthy discussion of interest, motivation, and the relationship between knowledge and action.

Children's Rights

In Massachusetts recently there was a tragic incident of child abuse. The father of a four-year-old girl knocked her across the room; she hit her head, and the injury proved fatal. The parents kept her body in a room of their house for several weeks. Then the father cut it up with an ax, put the pieces in a bag, and threw it in the trash for the garbage collectors to pick up (WCVB-TV, 1980).

Table 1-2. Children's rights: Two views

Content area	Orientation to children's rights	
	Nurturance	Self-determination
Health	Free health care	Option of refusing treatment
Education-Information	Quality education	Option of not attending school
Economics	Equal pay for equal work	Right to enter into binding contracts
Safety-Care	Safely designed housing	Choice of where to live
Law-Justice-Politics	Due process	Choice of legal counsel

SOURCE: Rogers, C., and Wrightsman, L. Attitudes toward children's rights: Nurturance or self-determination? *Journal of Social Issues,* 34(1978): 59–68.

A public discussion of the incident later revealed that this girl and a younger brother had previously been removed from their parents because of abuse and had lived in a foster home. But the mother had later shown evidence of "rehabilitation" and a social worker had judged her able to care for the children again. They were returned to her care — with disastrous results.

Should children be returned to live with parents who have previously abused them? Some people say they should not. Others contend that they should: "The children are theirs and they have a right to raise them." But do children have rights, too? Those who say they do argue that children's rights must be balanced against the rights of parents. People who work for children's rights in cases of abuse and on other issues are known as *child advocates.*

There are two types of child advocates: (1) those interested primarily in child welfare, and (2) the child liberators (Baumrind, 1978). The first group is concerned with protecting children, with nurturance. The second group is concerned with protecting children's rights and allowing them self-determination. Table 1-2 shows each group's specific concerns regarding certain issues.

Although children's rights have recently been given a renewed emphasis, the issue has been with us for about a hundred years. The fields of early childhood education, pediatrics, child development, and child welfare have all emerged during this time. (See Box 1-1 for a partial listing of events related to the movement for children's rights.) As time passes, however, the specific issues of concern to child advocates change. In the early part of this century, when young infants died from drinking contaminated milk, campaigns to pasteurize milk and make it available as a "right" were undertaken (Takanishi, 1978; Weiss, 1978). Today, the issues of children's right to an education and their right to be free of physical abuse are considered to be of greatest importance.

Right to an Education. In 1975 legislation was passed that ensured the handicapped child's right to an education. Public Law 94-142, the Education for All Handicapped Children Act, forbade schools from excluding children who do not "fit in." The law states that schools must provide for all handicapped children from the age of three. PL 94-142 has changed the lives of thousands of children and has dramatically affected their teachers and parents, too.

> Annie who was almost 9, was in first-grade class. She had silky, reddish hair and was attractively dressed, but she had the unmistakable features of Down's Syndrome. I watched her sitting in a cluster of desks, copying arithmetic examples from the board, counting her fingers to figure out the answers, picking out words on a chart, doing puzzles, reading, and writing. I watched her playfully tap a little boy who stopped at her desk, and then turn to a neighbor with a question. She wasn't the most popular child in the class, but neither was she the least popular. She wasn't as good as some of the other children in arithmetic, but neither was she the worst. She was, by the way, the best reader. And she loved school. . . .
>
> Annie's teacher had said to me, "I never had a child like Annie before. I didn't know what to do with her, how to treat her. I was afraid I couldn't control her." [Cohen, 1977, pp. 124–27]

Because the handicapped child is now entitled to a "suitable" and "appropriate" education in the *least restrictive environment*, many children, like Annie, are receiving education in regular classrooms. They have been *mainstreamed*, which means that they receive all or nearly all of their education along with children who have no handicap (Keogh and Barkett, 1978). Their teachers, like Annie's, may find, to their initial surprise, that such arrangements work out remarkably well. However, not all children can benefit from a placement in a regular classroom. For some children the least restrictive environment may be an institution, a special school, or special classes within a regular school.

The Right to Be Free from Abuse. In 1874 in New York City, a church worker who discovered that a child was being mistreated had to seek help from the Society for the Prevention of Cruelty to Animals, which had been established in the 1860s. At the time, no group existed to protect children from cruelty (Van Stolk, 1974).

The New York Society for the Prevention of Cruelty to Children was founded in 1874, but it was not until physician Henry Kempe discussed the battered-child syndrome at the Annual Meeting of the American Academy of Pediatrics in 1961 that child abuse began to receive widespread attention as a social issue. Even today, as many as five children in the United States die of abuse each day. Obviously, there is still a great need to increase public awareness and understanding of children and to give families more support.

We must also be certain that children removed from abusive families are not subsequently abused by the institutions society makes responsible for their "protection." The abusive mother of the child mentioned earlier, the child who was brutally murdered by her father, had herself been a neglected child. When she was only nineteen months old, she and her four brothers and sisters were placed, at their mother's request, in the care of the state. In the fifteen years that she was a ward of the state, she was in eleven different placements and had been the responsibility of eighteen different social workers. She was beaten and psychologically abused in some of these placements. At seventeen she ran away from her final placement, got married, and soon had children, whom she cared for in the brutal fashion that she herself had experienced while in the care of the state (WCVB-TV, 1980). Clearly, children must be protected from abuse occurring in both family *and* institutional situations. This book will speak to both needs.

BOX 1-1. Key events in the children's rights movement

Date	Event
1873	American Medical Association forms section on Obstetrics and Diseases of Women and Children.
1874	New York Society for the Prevention of Cruelty to Children is organized, ten years after the Society for the Prevention of Cruelty to Animals.
1893	Dr. Henry L. Coit presents "Certified Milk" plan to Practitioners' Club in Newark, N.J., as a strategy for reducing infant mortality rates.
1894	Child Study Department is formed in the National Education Association; G. Stanley Hall is first president.
1897	First municipal milk station is established in Rochester, N.Y.
1899	First juvenile court is established in Rochester, N.Y.
1909	First White House Conference on Children recommends establishment of Children's Bureau, declaring that poverty alone should not be grounds for removing children from families. States that "home life is the highest and finest product of civilization."
1912	Children's Bureau is established to conduct studies and to crusade for infant and maternal welfare — "to investigate and report upon all matters pertaining to the welfare of children and child life among all classes of our people."
1914	U.S. Children's Bureau first publishes best-selling manual, *Infant Care*.
1921	Sheppard-Towner Act of 1921 provides infant and maternal hygiene and welfare programs. "The Sheppard-Towner Act established the national policy that the people of the U.S., through their federal government, share with the states and localities the responsibility for helping to provide community services that children need for a good start in life" (Martha M. Eliot).
1926	National Association for Nursery Education is founded (later became National Association for the Education of Young Children).

Problems of Family Life

The difference between the study of child development and the study of the social context of development is an important one. It is one thing to understand child development and how to support it. Understanding the social conditions that lead to the support of all children's development is another matter.

We generally assume that the family is the crucible in which development occurs, but the family reflects conditions in the rest of society. Urie Bronfenbrenner (1973), a child psychologist, says that parents are largely at the mercy of a society that does not support meaningful family activities. Family life can be influenced by poverty, the demands of jobs, and the hypnotic spell of the televi-

---

BOX 1-1 continued

Date	Event
1929	American Academy of Pediatrics is founded by physicians who disassociated themselves from the American Medical Association, which had lobbied against the renewal of the Sheppard-Towner Act.
1938	Fair Labor Standards Act of 1938 is the first enforceable work law for the protection of children. (Children first began to work in industrial factories in 1817 in Derby, England.)
1959	United Nations adopts Declaration of the Rights of the Child.
1963	Colorado passes first child abuse law requiring physicians to report suspected cases of child abuse.
	National Institute of Child Health and Human Development is established to conduct research and training in maternal and child health, special maternal health requirements, and human development.
	Maternal, Child Health and Mental Retardation Act is enacted to deal with infant mortality, retardation, and neurological disease.
	Mental Retardation and Community Health Centers Act is enacted to improve service, teaching, and research for the mentally retarded.
1969	Office of Child Development (OCD) is established. It incorporated the Children's Bureau and administered Head Start programs.
1975	DHEW requires state agencies administering social services "to provide for the reporting of known and suspected instances of child abuse and neglect" by all caregivers.

SOURCE: Takanishi, R. Childhood as a social issue: Historical roots of contemporary child advocacy movements. *Journal of Social Issues* 34 (1978):8–28.

sion set. The extended family — grandparents, aunts, uncles, and cousins — is likely to be dispersed over a wide area. Business and residential areas are separate, and our high mobility has led to the disappearance of neighborhoods where people know each other. Social groups are segregated by age, and consolidated schools are larger, less personal, and frequently distant from neighborhoods. When you consider all these factors, you can see that being a parent is a formidable job. An added psychological difficulty is that parents are held responsible for their children even when they are powerless to control many of the conditions that can lead to difficulties.

This introductory text is about child development itself, and not about the social and economic factors that influence family life. It provides a somewhat limited view of children because it does not focus on "the 'ecology of childhood' — the overall social and economic system that exerts a crucial influence on what happens to parents and children" (Keniston, 1977, p. xiii). We are concerned with social context, however, and whenever possible we will explain its influence. In addition, we will stress social context in our concluding chapter, which is on parenting. We fall short of providing a comprehensive "sociology of childhood," but we hope to spark enough interest in the topic to prompt readers to explore this important area of study in other courses.

Not many children in the United States today see grandma on a daily basis.

A Word from the Authors

Yet another context is important to understanding this or any book — that of the authors' concerns and attitudes. This introduction would be incomplete without some explicit statements about the themes that seemed important to us as we wrote this book.

One of our chief concerns is related to the responsibility involved in dealing with children. Children cannot grow up on their own; they cannot be expected to accept the burden of making their own way. This is not to say that children should be given little responsibility — quite to the contrary. Our point is that parents and teachers must be willing to devote themselves energetically to the task of nurturing children. A society that considers children important has a similar obligation.

A second concern is that adults comprehend the importance of understanding the world from a child's perspective. Too often, children are expected to do what they cannot and are unjustly accused of wrongdoing because adults assume that children understand the world the same way they do. We think that adults must be able to see the world as children see it if they are to support children's development. We do not wish to imply that children are helpless or unskilled; our point, rather, is that abilities and competence must be assessed in context. An accurate conception of children's competence emerges when one realizes what children can do and how much they learn in a short period of time.

Although we are required to present information objectively, we have also tried to convey our awe of children. We hope, too, that we have communicated our respect for them and our conviction that the lives of adults can be enriched by their presence. Many of us spend a great deal of time with children as parents, teachers, physicians, and in countless other roles. Those who do not enjoy this time together, who do not understand what happens during it, who wish when it is over that they could return and undo the damage, have missed one of life's opportunities. Herbert Kohl puts the adult experience with children into a good perspective:

> Inevitably we will play a modest role in our children's lives; we'll grow apart as they make friends, fall in love, become parents. . . . No matter how painful a moment or a month of our lives together might be, it will pass and our children will have more important things to do in their lives than spend so much time with us. We should take what joy we can together, given the brevity of our lives and the amount of grief there is in the world. [1978, p. 32]

We hope that this book will contribute to an understanding of children, and that by doing so, it will reduce the measure of grief and increase that of joy, both for them and for us.

Each stage of development brings increasing independence. Eventually both child and parent must let go.

Summary

- Although there are no simple explanations for child behavior and no easy formulas for interacting with children, an understanding of children can help determine our actions.

Children: Four Areas of Concern
- Four areas of concern for those who work with children are encouraging development, facilitating communication, using discipline effectively, and meeting special needs.
- To foster children's development adults need to know about the behaviors typical of various ages, the sequences of development, and the circumstances in which a behavior should be considered a problem.
- Effective communication with children requires an understanding of how children think and how they perceive the world from their own perspective.
- Good discipline does not include physical punishment. It is based on understanding what is appropriate behavior and on accepting the child as a person worthy of respect.
- "Special needs" is a term used to describe children with speech impairment, mental retardation, learning disabilities, behavior problems, sensory handicaps, or physical handicaps. But many behaviors that adults perceive as special needs problems are developmental in nature and quite normal for children at certain ages.

Children's Issues of National Concern
- Children's issues of particular interest to our society include the effectiveness of the educational system, children's rights, and problems in family life.

- The educational system is constantly under attack for *what* it teaches — theoretical learning that is too far removed from its practical application — and *how* it teaches — methods that are either too strict or too permissive, depending on the point of view.
- The issues of greatest concern to people who work for children's rights change with the times. The right to an education is one of the major concerns today, and in 1975, the passage of Public Law 94-142 ensured this right for all children. Children's right to be free from physical and psychological abuse has also become a matter of serious concern.
- A study of child development should include attention to the social and economic context in which individual development occurs. This development takes place within the family, but family life and problems are often a reflection of conditions in the rest of society.

A Word from the Authors

- Children need the nurturing and support of both teachers and parents on the personal level, and the support of a society that considers children important.
- Parents and teachers must understand how children perceive the world at each stage in their development, to guide them accurately to the next stage.

New Terms

special needs children
conversion
child advocates

mainstreaming
least restrictive environment

Selected Readings

Greenberg, J. **A Child Called Noah.** *New York: Holt, Rinehart and Winston, 1970.* A father's story about his emotionally disturbed son. Engrossing and heart rending.

Jarolimek, J. **The Schools in Contemporary Society.** *New York: Macmillan, 1981.* An up-to-date and readable overview of the problems and challenges facing today's schools.

Kempe, R. S., and Kempe, C. H. **Child Abuse.** *Cambridge, Mass.: Harvard University Press, 1978.* An overview of the problem of child abuse. Describes types of abuse, characteristics of abusive parents, and methods of treatment. Very readable.

Koocher, G. P. (Ed.). **Children's Rights and the Mental Health Professions.** *New York: Wiley, 1976.* An interesting collec-

tion of twenty papers covering many areas of children's rights and the role of professionals and public policy.

Rasmussen, M. **Listen! The Children Speak: Anecdotes with Interpretation.** *Washington, D.C.: United States Committee, World Organization for Early Childhood Education, 1979.* A book of about 100 quotations, drawings, and anecdotes from children. Stress is on listening to and understanding children. Delightful reading!

Westman, J. C. **Child Advocacy.** *New York: Free Press, 1979.* A book about children's needs and how various educational, health, legal, and social services can meet these needs. A good overview of child advocacy strategies and social policy.

Chapter 2

Methods of
Studying Children

Becoming well informed about child development may seem to be an easy task. Information is readily available from books, television, newspapers, lectures, and discussions. Nevertheless, this information sometimes seems contradictory and incoherent to many people, particularly to those who are just beginning. Many a parent, teacher, and student of child behavior has asked in despair, "How can I know what children are like when even the experts seem so uncertain?" And, they may wonder, "Why can't those who study children use better methods and techniques so that we could know once and for all exactly what children are like and why?" Unfortunately, research, like life, is not quite so simple.

In this chapter we will discuss the major methods used in studying children. In these discussions we will stress the kind of information about children that different research methods yield, and how understanding these differences can help clarify why, on the one hand, we seem to know a lot about children, whereas on the other hand, we seem to know so little. We will also discuss issues involved in conducting research and how these influence the methods that may be selected in a particular situation. As you understand these issues you will see that there are often practical and ethical reasons for our lack of knowledge.

Overall, it is not our goal to make research experts out of our readers. However, we think the information presented later will be better understood if we take the time now to explain how information about children is obtained. This chapter and the next are to serve as background, to set the stage. They may not be understood completely at this point, but they can be compared to a map: although we cannot get where we are going without one, we will understand it fully only after we have explored the terrain it represents. For this reason we recommend that you study the map of methods we present, but that you also remember it is here to refer back to as you journey through the rest of the book. Only in this way will you understand and appreciate the symbols and turns in the road that make each research method unique.

We will start our discussion by placing information gained from research methods — what we will call child development data — in context by explaining how data differ from, or are influenced by, theories, values, and practices. Distinguishing among these terms and concepts is essential to understanding why people are likely to continue to disagree to some extent about what children are like and what we might or should do to influence their behavior. Then we will move on to a discussion of general data-collection procedures that apply no matter what research method we employ. After that, we will discuss the major research methods. We will conclude the chapter with a short discussion about the factors that influence researchers when they select a research method.

Differences Among Data, Theories, Values, and Practices

Discussions about children can take place on several levels. We might talk about *data* (what children do), *theories* (explanations for or hypotheses about why children do what they do and why behavior changes), *values* (what children should do or should be like), and *practices* (what we as adults should do to influence children). It is important to understand how each of these levels of discussion affects the study of child development — its practical application and the disagreements that can arise.

Data

People sometimes disagree about what children are like and what they do. For example, some people claim that babies coo after being fed, cry when hungry, and smile at strangers, but other people disagree. Similarly, many teachers say that three-year-olds cover the entire piece of paper on the easel when they paint, that they are possessive of toys, and that they usually cry on the first day of school; others would contend that these behaviors are atypical of three-year-olds. These differences have several sources, as we shall later see.

Theory

When discussions about children change from what they do to why they do it, disagreements move into the realm of theory, to statements about what data mean, to hypotheses about and explanations for data. For example, a group of parents and teachers, asked why preschoolers sometimes cry on the first day of school, might give a whole range of answers, such as the following:

1. Because they are afraid of the new situation in school and they do not understand exactly what will happen to them there.
2. Because they are spoiled and have learned how to control their parents by crying.
3. Because some previous experience with strange adults has been unpleasant, and they think this one will be, too.
4. Because they want attention from the teacher and do not like sharing it with other children.

Though data and theories are conceptually different, they are closely related: theories determine which data are considered significant and are as a result collected; data collected then influence the construction and modification of theories. Theory and data are also related in another, more subtle way: theories can affect what we see; that is, they can influence not only the questions we ask, and thus the kind of data we set out to collect, but the data we actually collect. For example, there was a controversy in the seventeenth and eighteenth centuries about whether all structures existed preformed in the egg or sperm and merely grew with maturity, or whether structures emerged through successive differentiation during the period of development. Scientific theory of the day held that all structures were preformed. Even after the compound microscope came into use, making it possible to observe differently, scientists still perceived data in terms of the accepted theory. They "saw" tiny horses in the semen of a horse, and tiny roosters in rooster semen. Drawings of what they "saw" appeared in texts of the day (Needham, 1959). It was not until the use of tissue fixatives and work on the larger, and more easily visible chick embryo provided data that was overwhelmingly against the theory that it began to crumble. Subsequently, scientists who looked at ova or spermatozoa under the microscope saw differently — not because what was there had changed, but because their expectations, or theory, had changed.

A more recent example of the same phenomenon is described in a book written by June Goodfield (1981). She describes the work of a woman scientist who wished to remain anonymous. The scientist's work is with lymphocytes, cells that are part of the body's immune system and circulate in the bloodstream. Goodfield tells about the scientist's discovery that there are two types of lymphocytes, not one as everyone before had assumed. She had looked at lymphocytes many times before, but had not seen two types. She describes how she missed seeing them because she had not expected to see them. Then she began to think differently about lymphocytes and how they function. When her thinking changed, what she saw changed: she discovered that there were two types of lymphocytes — and they had been there all the time. For a time her data and its implications were disputed by colleagues: what she claimed could not be true, they thought, for they were seeing things in terms of a different theory. But apparently the new data have held up and might lead to new thinking about diseases such as Hodgkin's, which is a form of cancer affecting the lymphocytes.

Values

People disagree not only about data and theory, but also about what children should do. These are disagreements about values, which are goals or ideals for behavior. Values questions cannot be answered through the study of child development alone; one's philosophy, religion, culture, and experience all influence one's answers.

Values influence what we consider worthwhile to study and what theories we are willing to consider. For example, more people today are willing to consider new theories and data about the emotional development of infants — ones that indicate a mother does not need to devote full time to childrearing. More people want to believe that the ideal mother can both work and raise babies, and that an ideal childhood does not require devotion from a single mothering figure. Of course, others refuse to consider the new theories or data, because they value the more traditional view of what an ideal mother and childhood should be. Overall, however, a change in values has encouraged researchers to construct new theories and conduct new studies about the role of multiple caregivers in a child's development.

The Role of Data, Theories, and Values in Determining Practices

All of the levels of discussions and disagreements we have considered — that is, discussions about what children do, why they do it, and what they should do — lead to a fourth area of discussion and disagreement: What are the best practices to use with children? This is a question about what we should do to promote children's optimum development.

In attempting to influence the practices of others, or to understand the basis for our own practices, we must be aware of the distinction between values, and data and theory. A goal of development for one person may not be valued by another. For example, it would be pointless to use data and theories in trying to persuade a parent to talk to a baby more frequently if the parent's lack of interest in encouraging the child to speak results from a belief that a quiet child is an ideal child. Here there is a conflict in values. This presents what Lillian Katz (1977) has referred to as an *ethical dilemma*. These conflicts, she points out, cannot be resolved by simple recourse to knowledge, because the adults hold different goals for the child's development. We might change the parent's behavior by showing how the development of the child's abilities will affect the child's opportunities later in life. If the parent values opportunities that would be adversely affected by the parent's current behavior, he or she may be willing to change. But unless we address the issue of values in some way it is doubtful that such a parent would be influenced by our recitation of data about how verbal interaction promotes language development in a child.

Box 2-1 contains descriptions of situations in which disagreements occur. Try to determine which of the four factors — data, theories, values, or practices — is the source of each disagreement and decide which can be resolved by the study of child development and which cannot.

BOX 2-1. Why the Disagreement?

1. The doctor told the father that the child would have to wear shoes when playing outdoors to prevent another cut or puncture wound. "Oh, heavens," said the father. "What's a childhood without a few cuts and scrapes, and what's a summer without going barefooted?"

2. Two mothers were overheard as they talked about the language of their preschoolers: "Oh," said one mother, "I don't pay any attention to his mistakes. He'll change in time by listening to how adults talk."

   "Well," said the other mother, "I don't know how a child can correct mistakes if someone doesn't point them out."

3. "I'm sorry," said the nursery school director, "but we do not admit two-year-olds who are not yet toilet trained. If you'd like, you can go home and try to do it in a week, and then we can talk again."

   "I don't think I will," said the father. "There have been so many changes for us lately that I don't want to push toilet training right now."

4. During a conference, a teacher said to a parent: "I understand your concern, and I, too, want your child to learn addition facts; but right now, I think your child needs experience with counting cubes or other concrete objects rather than drill."

5. During a conversation between two parents, one was heard to say to the other, "You'd better not leave the baby so near the edge of the bed like that." The other parent said, "Oh, there's nothing to worry about. It will be a long time before she'll be able to move enough to be in danger of falling off."

(See end of chapter for answers.)

General Data Collection Procedures

Many disagreements about data are due to technical problems rather than to theoretical, philosophical, or valued-based debates. When this is the case, we can resolve the disagreement by attending to the methods and procedures used in data collection. This does not mean that the solutions are always simple; often they are not. It does mean, however, that the solutions are technical and can be worked on in a reasonably straightforward manner. For example, the use of standard methods of data collection encourages agreement about data and the judgments we can make about them. Similarly, understanding the various research methods and the kind of statements that can be made about children when each method is employed can help us greatly in sorting out what at first may appear to be contradictory or conflicting information. We begin with a discussion of good data-collection techniques.

Separating Data and Conclusions

One of the ways we can try to reach agreement about data is to follow certain procedures in recording data so that we can compare the data we collect with data collected by someone else. When the data we are trying to collect consists of descriptions of actual behavior we must be careful to separate what children do (actual descriptions of behavior) from interpretations of behavior (what we can conclude about a child on the basis of what we see the child do).

Suppose we sent two observers into a day-care classroom for four-year-olds to observe a child's behavior and prepare a report about the child's relationships with peers. It would be unrealistic to expect the observers to prepare identical reports, for a variety of reasons. First, an observer cannot record everything a child does. Each observer must record some behaviors and ignore others, and the two observers may make different selections. Second, even if the observers were to agree about what behaviors should be considered significant, their records would probably still reflect differences due to what we might call "physical limitations." One observer might be able to hear what a child says more clearly because the child's head is turned in his or her direction, or to see a child better because of an advantageous location in the room.

If observers agree in advance about which behaviors they will consider significant, and minimize physical limitations, we should expect their observations to be quite similar. Differences might still arise from a third source, however. The observers might fail to distinguish between observations of what children do and conclusions about those observations.

Examples of observations recorded without and with conclusions are given in Box 2-2. Notice that the observer who recorded conclusions as observations used phrases such as "seems *tired*," "seems *not to care*," and "is very *possessive*." This observer has gone beyond simply describing the child to make judgments about the meaning of the child's behavior. He has also provided little detail in his descriptions. Someone looking at his observation would not be able to determine on what basis the conclusions were drawn.

The observer who completed the first observation in Box 2-2 used techniques of observation more skillfully. The times of the observations are carefully recorded, and, more importantly, the detailed descriptions are not mixed with conclusions. These are provided separately (see Box 2-3).

Of course, we can never completely eliminate the influence of human mediation when we collect data. That is, we can never achieve a direct recording of behavior. We always make decisions about what we record, and these decisions will differ from observer to observer. Yet, we can strive to separate what we see from what we think about what we see. Then, disagreements about conclusions

---

BOX 2-2. Sample Observations With and Without Conclusions

**AN OBSERVATION
WITHOUT CONCLUSIONS**

9:10   S arrived at school at 9:05. S's mother came with him into the classroom. Went to cubby, took off coat, hung it up on hook. Smiled and waved goodbye to mother, who said "Have a good day."

9:15   Stood with back toward cubby. Rubbed eyes with right fist. Looked out into room — first in one direction, then in another. Yawned. Walked over to block area where girl was already playing. S entered area. Began taking a block from the top shelf. "You can't take my blocks," the girl said. "I won't," responded S. "I can use these" (gestured toward shelf).

9:20   S placed a long block on the floor away from the girl's building. S obtained another block, same as the first one, bent over, and placed one end of it next to the end of the first block. "I'm making a road," he said as he looked at the girl and then glanced at her building. "Don't make it go this way," she said (points toward her blocks). "I won't," S said. "It's going to be a long road that way" (points in direction away from girl's blocks).

9:25   A boy entered the block area. "Hi, _____," said S. "Want to help me build this road? Then we'll drive on it." "Yeah," the boy said. He began to take blocks from the shelf and place them end to end with S's road. After adding five blocks, he took a truck off the shelf and began to push it along the top of the block road.

9:30   "Hey," said S. "I wanted the truck. You have to use the car. This is *my* road!"

[record continues]

**AN OBSERVATION
WITH CONCLUSIONS**

S arrives at school. He is glad to be at school. He doesn't miss his mother. He seems tired at the beginning of the day. After a while, he decides to play with blocks. He seems not to care about building something with blocks with a girl who is playing there, and he builds a road alone. But he seems to want to build with a boy, and when a boy came close to the area, he invited him to play. S is very possessive of his road and the toy vehicles used with it.

[record continues]

BOX 2-3. Possible Conclusions About a Child's Behavior

1. The child does not prefer boys or girls as friends.
2. The child initiates contacts with other children.
3. The child readily plays with other children.
4. The child shares materials with other children although he protects what is his.
5. The child uses words to communicate wishes to other children.
6. The child offers suggestions for solving problems.

can be resolved by referring to the observations, or they can be seen to reside in the process of drawing conclusions rather than in different recordings of what a child did. It is common for people to disagree in interpreting or summarizing behavior over an entire observation period or in drawing conclusions about probable future behavior. But it is useful to know that is where the disagreement arises and that it is not due to the collection of unreliable data. *Reliability* refers to the agreement between data collected by different observers or between data collected at different times. Recording conclusions adds an additional source of possible differences between records — differences in what the observer at that time thought the behaviors meant. As a result, records that contain conclusions are less likely to be reliable, if they can be compared at all.

Failure to distinguish observations from conclusions can be a source of conflict or confusion not only in research studies, but in discussions between teachers or between parents and teachers as well. "Jerome is an aggressive and unhappy child," one teacher writes in his year-end report. The following year the child's new teacher reads the report hoping to gain information that will help her understand the child. When she reads the statements about Jerome she is startled: she has seen no behavior that would lead her to make similar comments. She wonders what Jerome did during the previous year for his teacher to have drawn those conclusions. "Is Jerome behaving differently this year," she wonders, "or do the other teacher and I differ concerning which behaviors indicate aggressiveness or unhappiness?" The first teacher could have been more helpful by including in his report some detailed descriptions of Jerome's behavior, as well as his conclusions.

Or, in a conversation with a child's teacher, the parent might say the child is "uncooperative, sullen, and stubborn." The teacher says the child is "responsible, cheerful, and easygoing." "Are we speaking about the same child?" the parent asks. "He surely must behave differently here than he behaves at home!"

Unless both parent and teacher share descriptions of the child's behavior rather than conclusions about it, they may have difficulty proceeding. Report cards typically do not help parents and teachers in this respect, for they usually contain conclusions (e.g., "your child is cooperative"; "your child is attentive during story time"; "your child shares with others"; "your child can take turns"). Parent conferences can be used to provide the background information for such conclusions, but teachers and others who work with children should expect questions from parents and be prepared to provide concrete details.

Defining Terms

A second source of disagreement about data concerning children results from possible variation in the meaning of terms used to label behaviors. For example, what does "aggressive" mean? Does it refer only to behavior involving physical harm to another person, or does it also apply to the destruction of inanimate objects? If an inanimate object belongs to the child who destroys it, is the behavior still considered "aggressive"?

If observations are to be collected by checking coded categories of behavior when they occur, rather than by describing behavior itself in detail, then observers must agree beforehand on exactly what the category labels mean. For example, if they are observing a group of children and counting the frequency of aggressive behaviors, then observers would need to agree about the behaviors to be considered as aggressive before they start. Observers typically practice observing using the categories and then compare their data. When they reach a high degree of reliability (that is, when their data agree fairly well), they can assume that they are interpreting "aggressive" in the same or a very similar way.

Earlier we stressed avoiding conclusions when collecting data by recording descriptions of actual behavior. One reason this is important is that different observers may mean different things by labels such as aggressive or friendly. If these differences are not worked out beforehand, there is no way to know if the observers saw different behavior or merely drew different conclusions about the same behavior. Therefore, when we are recording descriptions of actual behavior we must guard against including conclusions with our observations. If, on the other hand, we wish not to record actual descriptions of behavior, but to observe for a specific category of behavior such as aggression or friendliness, then we must agree on the meaning of terms and practice using these to make certain that we agree, before we actually begin a study.

Many studies use previously defined categories for observing behavior, rather than descriptions of behavior, because it is extremely difficult to make detailed recordings of everything a child does. What is lost, of course, is rich detail of what children actually did that resulted in our characterizing them. This loss of detail may not matter when we wish to know if children in group X are as aggressive as children in group Y. But the loss may matter a great deal if we wish to discuss a child's aggressive behavior with his or her parents. Parents are likely to ask us not only what we mean when we use the term "aggressive," but what their child did that made us conclude that he or she should be so characterized.

Specifying Which Children Were Studied

A third way we can try to reach agreement about data is to specify which children were studied. Different investigators considering the same problem may collect different data if they study different groups of children. Disagreement about the extent to which four-year-olds share toys, for instance, might be the result of examining one group of children who had attended nursery school and another group who had not, or of one study considering boys only and another considering both boys and girls. Similarly, children in various studies can differ in their socioeconomic or cultural background, their geographic location, or their family size. If children from many groups are included in a study, the conclusions can be assumed applicable to all or most children. We say that we can *generalize*, or apply the study's findings, to most children, that what is true about the children we studied is true of the typical child as well. The results of studies of only one type of group, however, can only be generalized to children from similar groups. Generalizability is more limited in this case because the results can be assumed to be true only for a specific group of children — those who are like the group studied.

This is also true for conclusions we draw from our own experiences with children. It would be unreasonable for a teacher who has taught the same grade in the same school for ten years to claim that "much of what others say about children is inaccurate" if he or she has had no experience with children from other cultural backgrounds or of different ages.

We could not generalize about the running ability of eight-year-old children if our study included only eight-year-old girls.

FOCUS: Sleep Patterns of Infants in Two Cultures

To ignore the role of the cultural context in describing the child can lead to a lack of differentiation between the structure of the child's own development and the structure of the environment. A case in point is theory related to sleep/wake behavior in infancy (Super and Harkness, 1978). The longest single episode of sleep during a twenty-four-hour period averages around four hours for American babies at one month of age. Over the next three months, there is a sharp increase in maximum sleep episodes, so that at four months the American baby averages a maximum sleep of about eight hours. On the basis of American studies, it has been argued that the increase in maximum sleep over the first few months of life is one of the best behavioral indices of the psychological maturation of the brain.

The development of sleep/wake behavior in rural African infants, however, shows a rather different pattern. The African baby's average maximum sleep at one month is about three hours, and this measure remains stable for at least the first eight months of life.

The differences in sleep patterns between American and African babies can be readily explained by the different contexts for this behavior which each culture provides. American parents generally make major modifications in their living quarters and family life to create a separate space for the baby. At night, the baby sleeps in its own bed — often, in a separate room. Night waking is apt to be inconvenient to parents, especially since it usually involves the complex and highly structured behavior called feeding. Consequently, parents are highly motivated to get the baby to sleep through the night; and this disposition is reinforced by child care experts. The African babies, on the other hand, are constantly in the company of other people, whose activities determine their opportunities to sleep. At night, the baby sleeps in skin-to-skin contact with the mother, and may wake up to nurse at will. The African data suggest a modification in theory related to the development of sleep/wake behavior: the increase of maximum sleep episodes in infancy may be an index of the maturation of the brain only when the environment is pushing it to the limits of its capacities.

SOURCE: Excerpted from Sara Harkness, The cultural context of child development. In C. M. Super and S. Harkness (eds.) Anthropological perspectives on child development, *New Directions for Child Development*, San Francisco: Jossey-Bass Inc., 1980. 8, 7–13.

Number of Children Studied

Just as we cannot generalize from one group of children to a different group, we cannot generalize the results of a study of just a few children to a larger group of children. To make statements about children's behavior, either many studies should be done of a few children each, or a large group should be studied. Studies of a few children can yield constructive results about *those children*, of course; that there are few subjects permits them to be studied very intensively.

Because most parents have experiences with only a few children, they sometimes consider what they read or hear about children from other sources to be inaccurate. "My child never did that," they say. "There's no truth to it." They may not realize that other children are different from their own and that these differences account for the discrepancies.

When and Where the Children Were Studied

Even when the same children or similar groups of children participate as subjects in a number of studies, discrepancies can occur if data are collected at different times or in different situations. In later chapters we will see that research yields conflicting answers to the question of how well very young children get along with each other. Close scrutiny of the research reports reveals that in the different studies different toys were offered, the children were together for varying lengths of time, and the adults in each study were instructed to behave differently. It is not surprising that the researchers reached different conclusions about peer interaction.

Data can also be affected by the time at which they are collected. No teacher would want children's attention spans to be measured only on Friday afternoons or days preceding holidays. Similarly, parents would not want data about their child's social behavior to be gathered only during times when the child is usually

Children's behavior at a birthday party may not be typical of behavior at other times.

tired. In both instances the children's behavior would probably vary from what it is at other times, and would not, therefore, be reliable.

As you can see, the timing and circumstances of data collection can influence the reliability of the information one gathers. If data cannot be gathered at many times to reflect the full range of typical situations, the researcher must clearly explain where and when the data were collected. It is only in this way that a researcher conducting a second study can know if the data he or she gathers can be compared to the data in the first study, or a reader of both studies can know the actual source of any discrepancy between data in one study and another.

The Observer/Child Relationship

The effects of an observer on a child's behavior are revealed when an infant refuses to roll over or wave bye-bye in the presence of company — even though the baby has been doing it for days. A similar effect can occur in testing situations. If someone other than the familiar classroom teacher tests a child, results may indicate that the child knows far less than the teacher judges. If so, it is possible that the strange tester adversely affected the child's behavior.

It is important in any study to indicate exactly who collected the data and what relationship, if any, this observer had with the children. It is also important to indicate whether the children were aware that they were being observed, and what procedures, if any, were used to familiarize them with the observer.

Understanding Research Methods

We will consider three major research methods that overlap somewhat: naturalistic observation, the experimental method, and the case study. For each method we will show what level of information can be gained. Some methods can be used to describe behavior, or to make statements about correlations between behaviors, but not to determine whether one factor causes another. Other methods do permit us to make statements about behaviors and their causes. That is, different methods yield different levels of information: *descriptive, correlational,* or *causal.* Confusion in discussing children sometimes results when statements about causation, for example, are made from only descriptive or correlational data.

Naturalistic Studies

One way to gather information about children is to watch them in their usual environment and record their behavior. In *naturalistic studies,* the researcher does not attempt to manipulate behavior. That is, he or she does not apply a treatment to children to determine its effects. Instead, the researcher observes the behavior children bring to the study (the behavior naturally acquired in all of their encounters with the world), without making any explicit attempt to determine what has led them to behave as they do.

This basic method can be varied in many ways. We can vary the number of children involved in the study, the number of observers collecting the data, the degree to which the behaviors to be noted are determined and defined at the outset, and the extent to which the situation is natural or contrived. These variations determine the extent to which the results can be generalized to other children and whether the data are objective or reliable.

In *systematic observation*, children are observed in their usual environment but only previously determined and defined classes of behavior are noted. Using a method of systematic observation called behavior or *event sampling*, Dawe (1934) performed a classic study of children's quarrels. She observed children during the free-play period of the nursery school day but only recorded behavior related to quarreling:

> In order to view the group as a whole, the observer watched the children from some central spot on the playground or from the doorway between the two main playrooms. When a quarrel developed the observer moved quickly to the scene of action as unobtrusively as possible. (1934, p. 142)

Narrowing the range of behaviors to be observed made more precise and accurate recording possible, increasing the reliability of the data. Defining what was meant by "quarrels" also allowed the observer to collect reliable data, of course. You will recall that reliability of data refers to the extent to which one investigator's observations resemble or agree with another's, or the extent to which observations collected at one time agree with those collected at another time, perhaps a week or month later.

Time sampling can be used to ensure that data on each child are collected across a span of time that reflects the child's full range of behavior. This method involves the use of a specific schedule for data collection — at weekly or monthly intervals, for example. Observations may be scheduled within each observation period as well. One child might be observed for five minutes, then another for five minutes, and so on, until each child in the study has been observed. The cycle is then repeated. If such a schedule were not used, data collected at a nursery school (for example, on one child during outdoor play, on a second during midmorning snack, and on a third during group discussion) might vary, not because the children's behavior varies greatly overall, but because they were observed in different situations.

Parten (1932) used the time-sampling technique to study children's social play patterns. She was interested in whether they played alone (solitary play), alongside other children (parallel play), with other children but without subordinating their own interests to the group (associative play), or cooperatively with others. To determine how frequently various children engaged in each type of play, she set up an observation schedule allowing for one minute of observation of each child each day for several days. The order for observing each child was varied systematically so that each was observed at different times during the free-play period on different days.

Studies in which systematic observation methods are used generally employ several observers so that one observer's data can be checked against another's for accuracy. Behavior is sometimes recorded on audio or video tape so that it can later be coded independently by a number of people. These techniques help ensure that the data collected are reliable.

Many naturalistic studies are carried out in the child's natural environment — home, school, or play area. But sometimes investigators have specifically designed environments to elicit certain classes of behavior and to provide standardized conditions for all the participating children. For example, Wanda Bronson (1975), a psychologist interested in peer interaction among very young children, set up a playroom and invited mothers and their very young children to visit periodically, thereby ensuring herself opportunities to study the situation she was interested in. Such studies are still considered naturalistic because the purpose of the study is not to compare the effects of one situation with the effects of another.

Because there is no attempt to determine and compare the effects of two contrived situations, all naturalistic observation methods, whether systematic or not, yield only descriptive or correlational information. As a result, these methods are entirely appropriate when used to answer questions about what children do, about the association of one behavior to another, or about the relation of a behavior to other events. They cannot, however, be used to answer questions about the causes of behavior, although they can give us some good ideas to test out.

The Experimental Method

In the experimental method, variables are manipulated so that their effects on behavior can be observed. A *variable* is something that changes or is changed to a different value or form. Variables refer both to the quality we are measuring and to possible influences on that quality. The variable being manipulated (the one changed by the researcher), is called the *independent variable*, and the behavior being observed to see if it changes when the independent variable is changed is called the *dependent variable*. If we can demonstrate that the dependent variable is affected by changing the independent variable, we have demonstrated a causal relationship between the two.

In most experimental studies, the independent variable is manipulated in the laboratory and the dependent variable is measured in the laboratory. For example, in a study of the effects of viewing violent TV cartoons on children's behav-

FOCUS: The Difference Between Causation and Correlation

A friend's child once told a story to one of the authors about a hailstorm and the bursting of kitchen pipes. It seems that on one hot August afternoon, there was a severe hailstorm at the child's house. In some cases, the stones were as large as good size pebbles. Any four-year-old would have been intrigued with this rare phenomenon, and this one was no exception.

Also on the evening of the hailstorm, a pipe under the sink in the child's house burst and his parents called a plumber to repair it. The child was fascinated by the plumber's work and tools and watched all of the plumber's actions intently.

After telling the author of both incidents, the child turned to his mother and asked, "Why did the hail make the pipe break?" The child had noted that the two incidents occurred close together, or were correlated, and he had jumped to the erroneous conclusion that one event had caused the other. He did not know that the relationship between the two events was completely coincidental, and that causation cannot be assumed from correlation.

Our adult logic and store of information tell us that a hailstorm could not have caused the kitchen pipes to burst. But when we are confronted with situations for which we have no known explanations, we sometimes make the same error as the four-year-old; we assume that one event is caused by another simply because it is associated with the other; they seem to occur together. But even when events are truly correlated, rather than accidentally occurring together as was the case of the burst pipes and hailstorm, we cannot assume causation. Perhaps a third factor causes both of the observed phenomena. For example, height and weight are highly correlated: people who are taller generally also weigh more than people who are shorter. But we would be incorrect to assume that an increase in height causes an increase in weight or vice versa. Both height and weight are caused by a third factor such as growth hormone.

To know if two correlated events are causally related, we must manipulate variables systematically. That is, we must apply some treatment to one group of individuals and not to a second group and then observe the effect. The experimental design or research method must be used to carry out studies if we are to determine causation. Naturalistic studies do not yield this level of information.

ior, several groups of children may be shown different types of TV programs (the independent variable). Perhaps one group sees a violent cartoon. A second group may watch a program such as "Mr. Roger's Neighborhood" that contains no aggressive episodes and even attempts to teach children positive ways of interacting (teaches prosocial behavior). A third group may view a neutral film showing how to clean a fish tank. The first two groups are the *experimental groups*, which means that they receive the treatment of interest: TV programs varying in aggressive versus prosocial content. The third group is the *control group*, which means that it is like the other groups in every way except that it does not receive the experimental treatment. Notice that this group is also shown a film. This is necessary to make certain that there is nothing about merely seeing a film that influences aggressive versus nonaggressive behavior, that it is the content of the film that has an effect.

Children's aggressive behavior (the dependent variable) might be measured in the laboratory after the various programs had been viewed. If children who saw violent cartoons played more aggressively than children who watched some other kind of film, then we could assume a causal link between watching filmed aggression and aggressive behavior.

In designing such a study, we would need to be sure that the groups of children assigned to each TV condition did not initially differ in any way that might explain variations in aggressive behavior. For example, we surely would not want all boys in the aggressive TV cartoon group and all girls in the group watching the film about cleaning the fish tank. We know that, in general, boys are more aggressive than girls, and starting with groups that differed in this way would make it impossible for us to determine if watching TV cartoons had any effect. We also would not want to place children from different social classes all in one group and not in the others.

The best way to ensure that the groups exposed to different treatments are

Increases in children's height are *correlated* with increases in weight, but one does not *cause* the other. A third factor, growth hormone, causes both increases.

the same to start with is to *randomly assign* large numbers of children to the different groups. For example, we could place all of the names of the children in a box, shake it up, and draw one name at a time. The first name would be placed in group 1, the second name in group 2, and the third name in group 3. Then the fourth name would be placed in group 1, the fifth name in group 2, and the sixth name in group 3. This process would continue until all names had been drawn. We could be fairly certain that all children having certain experiences or characteristics would not end up in the same group but would be evenly distributed. Then any differences found in the groups after treatment could not be attributed to prior differences in the groups.

One of the problems of conducting experimental studies in the laboratory is that we do not know whether children's behavior is affected outside the laboratory. Perhaps a child playing with other children under the watchful eye of a parent who expects nonaggressive behavior would show no aggression regardless of the films watched, whereas in the laboratory with the researcher hidden behind a one-way mirror the child would display aggression. In short, in the world outside the laboratory, many forces influence behavior. Controlled data-collection settings such as a laboratory may make it possible to state that X causes Y under certain conditions, but they do not ensure that X will cause Y under different conditions. Of course, this applies to naturalistic studies as well as to experimental studies: there is no reason to believe that children behave the same way at home as at school, for example.

Urie Bronfenbrenner, a well-known child psychologist, has suggested that too much research in developmental psychology is conducted in contrived situations, calling it "the science of strange behavior in strange situations with strange adults for the briefest possible periods of time" (1977, p. 513). Bronfenbrenner suggests that data be collected in several contexts so that we can be certain that effects are valid and generalizable.

In fact, many experimental studies are not conducted solely in the laboratory. For example, children may be shown a particular type of TV film in the laboratory, but their subsequent behavior may be observed in the schoolyard or classroom, as well as the laboratory. Although the dependent variable in this case is measured in a naturalistic setting instead of or in addition to the laboratory, the study is still experimental, not naturalistic. A variable (type of TV program watched) has still been manipulated, and children assigned to each group are not known to differ in any significant way other than exposure to the TV programs, because they have been randomly assigned to TV-viewing groups. These are the crucial characteristics in an experimental study, not the exact setting in which the dependent variable is measured or the independent variable is manipulated. These are also the characteristics that allow us to make statements about causation when the experimental method has been employed. (You may at this point wish to test your ability to distinguish between descriptive, correlational, and causal statements. Statements of each type are provided in Box 2-4.)

BOX 2-4. Examples of Descriptive, Correlational and Causal Statements

Which of the following statements are descriptive? correlational? causal?
1. On the average, babies weigh about seven pounds at birth.
2. The incidence of Down's syndrome in children increases as maternal age increases.
3. Older children tend to have more diseases than infants.
4. When the drug thalidomide is given to pregnant women early in pregnancy, it prevents the formation of arms and legs in the fetus.
5. Girls mature physically faster than boys.

(See end of chapter for answers.)

The Case Study Method

In the case study method only one child is studied. In the oldest method of child study, the traditional case study, there are no clear guidelines used to describe which behavior should be recorded. The ideal is to record everything of any importance. Since this is impossible, the observer is forced to record only the behavior he or she thinks most important. The observations selected by one observer are likely to be at least slightly different from those selected by another. This is one limitation of the case study method.

A second limitation of case studies that record a broad range of behavior, is the extreme difficulty of providing clear definitions of terms and detailed explanations of all the circumstances surrounding a child's behavior. In the case study of Louis XIII of France by his physician, Heroard, we learn that Louis "knew his letters" by the time he was three and one-half, but we don't know what Heroard meant by this statement. Did "knowing" his letters mean that Louis could point to the correct letter when it was named by an adult, or that he could perform the more difficult task of supplying the correct name when an adult did the pointing? We do not know, because Heroard did not provide this information. Case studies need not suffer from these problems, but because it is difficult to be precise when recording many behaviors, they often do.

A third limitation of the case study method is that generalizations about all children cannot be drawn from the study of one child, especially when there is reason to believe that the child is atypical. We also learn from Heroard's diary that Louis XIII played the violin at the age of seventeen months and played tennis before he was three (Aries, 1962). We do not, however, know if this behavior was typical of the children who were Louis's contemporaries. Since Louis XIII was a king, we might expect that it was rather unusual.

A fourth limitation of the case study method is shared by other research methods, too, but may be particularly troublesome in a case study if the researcher knows the subject very well. This limitation is subjectivity of the observer, or what we call *observer bias*. It is the tendency for the observer to see what he or she would like to see. Recall in our earlier discussion of the influence of theory on data collection, that theory can be a source of observer bias. That is, expectations about what we will see influence what we actually see. In a case study that is conducted by a parent, wanting to see the child in a certain light, or wanting others to see the child in a certain light, can lead to observer bias.

A final limitation of the traditional case study is that only descriptive and correlational statements can be made. Because there is no manipulation of behavior, we cannot make statements about causation.

Variations of the traditional case study method have resolved some of these problems and limitations. By deciding in advance what behaviors are to be observed, by defining terms explicitly, and by adding a second observer for reliability, a researcher can increase objectivity.

Elements of the experimental method can also be injected into the case study method so that researchers can make some reasonably sound statements about causes of the behavior of a child studied. For example, suppose we examine only one behavior of interest (similar to a dependent variable in an experiment), observing it under typical conditions for an extended period of time. These conditions are frequently called *baseline conditions*, and data collected at this time are called *baseline data*. They are referred to as "baseline" because they occur before we introduce any change into the situation.

When a second variable is changed (similar to the independent variable in an experiment) any change in the observed variable may be due to the change in the independent variable. If the independent variable is repeatedly changed, and the dependent variable follows suit, we can increasingly be sure that the independent variable is causing the change in the dependent variable we are observing (Campbell and Stanley, 1963). In fact, when this is done properly, we can be quite sure of the causal relationship between the changing independent variable and the observed variable. These procedures are called "quasi-experimental."

But regardless of how sophisticated a case study is, it will remain limited in generalizability. Overgeneralizing ranks with interpreting correlations as causal relationships as one of the most common mistakes made in interpreting studies of child behavior.

The great advantage of the case study method is that one child can be observed in depth. The case study allows us to collect more detailed information than other methods. Such studies can give us many ideas about development and its sequence, although they do not permit us to know if what we have learned is characteristic of children other than the one studied.

FOCUS: Studying Age-Related Changes in Child Behavior: Longitudinal and Cross-Sectional Research Designs

When we wish to know if child behavior changes over time, or if the effect of an experimental treatment is different when applied at different ages, there are two basic research designs we can use. The *cross-sectional design* utilizes different groups of children varying in age, perhaps groups of two-year-olds, six-year-olds, and ten-year-olds. The *longitudinal design* utilizes the same group of children repeatedly as they pass from age to age, perhaps at two, six, and ten.

There are advantages and disadvantages to both designs. The cross-sectional design allows studies to be completed much faster than does the longitudinal design. We must wait for children to grow up when we use the same group (longitudinal design) to learn about the behavior characteristic of various ages, whereas with the cross-sectional design we simply study at the same time children of different ages.

Not only does the cross-sectional design allow us to obtain knowledge more rapidly, it can prevent *biased sampling* (the inclusion of children who are unique rather than representative). For longitudinal studies, parents must make a long-term commitment and be willing to cooperate with numerous observations of their children; therefore, parents who agree to participate in longitudinal research may be different from parents who refuse to participate. They may be better educated, more interested in their children, or more socially oriented. If they are different from other parents, then the study and its results would not apply to children in general.

A second reason why studies with longitudinal designs sometimes contain nonrepresentative samples is because subjects often withdraw over the course of a study. Families may move or for some other reason stop participating. If the families who remain differ systematically from those who withdraw, then the sample becomes nonrepresentative and we cannot generalize the study's results. Furthermore, if we discover differences in behavior at various ages, we do not know if these are age differences. They may be due to the differing composition of groups we were left with at the various ages.

The longitudinal design, however, allows us (1) to observe changes in one individual's behavior over time and (2) to be fairly certain that differences at different ages are not due to the completely unique histories of different subjects from age to age. The cross-sectional design does not.

An often-cited example of the first advantage is the preadolescent growth spurt. Individual growth is typically rapid, truly a spurt. However, if we use a cross-sectional design, we get, instead, a smooth curve, because the timing of the growth spurt for any individual varies: some experience it at age eleven whereas others experience it at age fourteen. As a result, no abrupt peak appears when we look at group data: there is a gradual increase in height, for example, spanning the entire period from ten and a half to about fifteen. This curve tells us how eleven-year-olds as a group differ in height from fourteen- or fifteen-year-olds as a group, but it does not describe the growth experience for an individual. Group averages may be all that are needed by clothes designers, but a parent or physician also needs to know if a growth spurt, rather than continuous gradual growth, is physically normal. Only longitudinal data that show abrupt, unforeseen changes in each individual's height will reveal that the preadolescent growth spurt is the norm, not some abnormality.

The problem of history and cross-sectional design can be illustrated by the apparent "cumulative deficit in intelligence" reported to occur with age in black children growing up in poverty. Using a cross-sectional design, a psychologist named Arthur Jensen (1974, 1977) reported that the IQs of socioeconomically deprived black children declined as they progressed through elementary school. No such decline occurred in white children. Jensen attributed this decline, at least in part, to genetic differences in mental development curves between blacks and whites. However, this interpretation was criticized because it assumes a *within-subjects effect* where none can be assumed (interprets cross-sectional data as if they were obtained from the same subjects over time, rather than from different subjects, as was the case) (Kamin, 1978). Perhaps the younger children (six-year-olds) were attending better educational programs than the older children (ten- or twelve-year-olds) had attended when they were six. That is, perhaps the older children's IQs at six had not been as high as those of the six-year-olds included in the study. If we assume a gradual improvement in educational opportunity over time, then we might expect an apparent decline in IQ scores with increasing age: the older the children, the poorer their earlier educational opportunities and early IQs may have been. Kamin (1978) suggests that what appears to be a change resulting from age may in fact be only a change resulting from history, or changes in conditions each age group experienced.

Each generation or group of the same age is called a *cohort*. Schaie (1965) has referred to the differences among age groups that are due to their common history, or experiences unique to each cohort, as *cohort effects*. The main difficulty with the cross-sectional design is that it confounds age effects with cohort effects. In the example above, Jensen is said to confound age with educational history.

To avoid the disadvantages and to utilize the advantages of each type of design, the best features of each are sometimes combined. The *cross-sectional/short-term longitudinal design* does just that. Suppose we wish to study the changes occurring in some characteristic between ages eight and sixteen, and we want data for two-year intervals. We could use different groups of children (cross-sectional design feature), but test each group at two successive ages (longitudinal design feature). We would use a group of eight-year-olds and study them again at age ten. We would also observe another group for the first time at age ten and then at age twelve. We would also observe a new group of twelve-year-olds and then observe this group again at age fourteen. Finally, we would include a group observed first at age fourteen, and then again at age sixteen. Such a study would take two years to complete (the time required for the longitudinal aspect of the study), yet the data gathered would cover the ages eight to sixteen. Furthermore, we would have data concerning changes in individual children from each age to the next without having had to study one group for eight years.

Selecting a Suitable Research Method

Suppose you wanted to study some aspect of child behavior and had to select the best method. Which one would it be? Actually, no method is clearly superior to the others for all studies. Which method is the best for a particular study depends on the question being considered, on ethical considerations, and on the circumstances of the investigator.

The Research Question and Research Methods. As we have stated before, there are three types of statement we can make about child behavior after collecting data in a study: descriptive (what children do), correlational (what behaviors occur together or are associated with each other or with certain circumstances), and causal (what effect one variable has on another or what causes a particular behavior). The method to be used will be determined by the question we hope to answer. That is, is it a question about what children do or about what causes them to do what they do? If it is the first, then a naturalistic study will serve our purposes. If it is the second, then we must do an experimental study. As long as the method selected is consistent with the question being pursued, and the only conclusions drawn are those the method allows, the method can be considered a good one for that study.

For example, the traditional case study or a naturalistic study may be more appropriate when an aspect of development is just beginning to be explored and we merely wish to describe behavior and determine which behaviors occur together. The experimental method may be more appropriate later, when we wish to determine if behaviors observed to occur together are causally related. There may be times, however, when we would prefer to employ the experimental method to investigate causation, but cannot because of ethical or practical reasons.

Ethics and Research Methods. Some questions cannot be investigated in the manner that would yield the most conclusive results because manipulation of a variable might harm the research subjects. We would not, for example, deprive a group of infants of protein to test a hypothesis that infants need protein to attain adequate growth. Instead, we would compare the growth of naturally occurring groups of infants who received more or less protein in their diets. Any relationship would be correlational, of course, so we could not be certain that differences in growth were due to variations in the protein in the infants' diets, rather than to some other difference in the naturally occurring groups.

The ethics of research, particularly that which involves children, have been considered by many groups during the past decade (American Psychological Association, 1973; Department of Health, Education and Welfare, 1978; Society for Research on Child Development, 1974). The result has been the development of codes of ethics that state, among other things,

1. Investigators may use no research operations that may harm a child physically or psychologically.

2. *Informed consent* must be obtained from parents or whoever is legally responsible for the child before he or she can be used as a subject in a study. This means that the parent must be given complete and accurate information about the study in understandable language.
3. Consent cannot be obtained by promising that the research will benefit the child.
4. The investigator cannot force a child to participate if it is apparent that the child would prefer not to.

Note that these rules concern the rights of children with regard to research studies. Studies that use observation methods sometimes do not involve manipulation of variables or any direct interaction between child and researcher. Therefore, they are less likely to encounter problems in meeting ethical requirements or in setting to rest the fears of parents.

Circumstances of the Investigator. One's role in children's lives and one's relationship to children also influence the selection of research methods. A teacher who has daily contact with a specific group of children will probably find case studies and other observation methods useful, but a teacher is not in a very good position to study the causes of children's behavior using the experimental method. It is sometimes impossible to create experimental and control groups within a classroom or to obtain the resources necessary to manipulate certain variables.

Consider the case of a teacher who notices that her class is not achieving in reading as well as might be expected. She might think of several possible reasons for the problem: (1) the books being used for reading instruction may be uninteresting and unattractive to the children; (2) reading instruction might seem to be of little worth to the children because it is not tied to practical or meaningful situations; and (3) the children might be too tired to pay attention to reading instruction because it is scheduled right after gym class. To determine which, if any, of the hypothesized conditions is actually affecting reading achievement, the teacher would need to divide the class into two groups, one experimental and one control. Then the three conditions of interest (books, meaningfulness, fatigue), would need to be varied, one at a time, to see if there was an effect.

Conducting such a study would be a long and tedious process. How long would the teacher need to use materials judged to be "very interesting" before expecting to see a change in children's reading achievement? How would the interest level of the materials be judged in the first place? Where would the more interesting materials be obtained if the school budget for reading materials has already been spent? How might a child in the experimental group be prevented from allowing a friend in the control group to read the more interesting book while visiting some evening? How would the teacher explain to the parent of a control group child who was achieving poorly that the child's instruction could not be changed for six months so that the factors influencing reading achievement could be determined? If the teacher really thinks that more interesting materials or a different schedule will help children in their reading, how can he or she rightfully deny these to some children but not to others for the sake of testing an hypothesis?

In practice, teachers must change the conditions they think affect their classroom as soon as they can. Teachers are expected to manipulate the variables in the classroom to produce optimal behavior in children. They can change what they have the resources to change and then note the effect on children's behavior. This would not permit them to pinpoint the exact cause of a behavior, of course, and teachers would have to be careful not to claim that one thing or another was completely responsible for an observed difference.

Tying Things Together

In this chapter we have discussed (1) differences and relationships among data, theories, values, and practices; (2) general techniques of data collection; (3) research methods; and (4) considerations that must be made in selecting a research method. Our goals were to help you see how complicated it is to study children, to help you understand why we do not know as much about children as we would like, and to help you see why people do not always agree about what is known. We will draw on this foundation as we discuss children in the chapters that lie ahead. These discussions should be more meaningful now and lead to greater understanding. For example, you may understand more completely why the effects of a mother's smoking on her unborn child are so hotly debated despite data from numerous studies, when we explain that most of the studies have been correlational, not experimental. You may also understand better why, despite many studies on some aspects of child behavior, our knowledge may still be limited. There is only so much that one study can do, and no matter how well it is conceived and carried out, it is bound to have some limitations. Perhaps for some ethical or practical reason the study is correlational and not experimental. As a result, we might have good descriptions of a behavior and know what other behaviors or circumstances it is correlated with, yet not know what causes it. Or perhaps an experimental study is done by another researcher, but only children from one particular group, perhaps one sex or racial group, participated. Such a study would tell us something about what causes the behaviors we are investigating, but we could not generalize the results to all children. Typically, it takes many studies, conducted over several years, to give us comprehensive information about an area of child behavior. This is why, when we discuss an aspect of child behavior in the chapters that lie ahead, we will often discuss several studies rather than just one or two. Even then, the studies are likely to have been generated from only one theoretical point of view, because it is extremely difficult, if not impossible at times, to integrate data gathered by researchers operating with differing theoretical points of view.

In the next chapter we will discuss the major theories of child development. It will give you some idea of how explanations of and hypotheses about child development data can differ, and will inform you about the theoretical viewpoints underpinning the child development data we have chosen to discuss in the remaining chapters of this book.

Summary

Differences Among Data, Theories, Values, and Practices
- Knowing the relationships between data, theories, values, and practices is helpful in studying child development.
- Child development data refer to information about what children do. Child development theories attempt to provide explanations for and hypotheses about why children do what they do and why behavior changes. Our values concerning children are our ideas about what children should be like. Practices are our actions. They are determined by what we know about children, how we interpret what we know (how we use theories), and what we think children should be like.
- Each of these four factors can influence the other three. For example, theories influence how we see phenomena and, therefore, the data we collect, and values can influence the theories and data we are willing to consider.

General Data Collection Procedures
- If disagreements about data are not due to theoretical or philosophical debates, they can be resolved in part by following standard data collection procedures.
- Good data collection procedures include: (1) separating data and conclusions, (2) defining terms, (3) specifying which children were studied, (4) noting the number of children studied, (5) specifying when and where the children were studied, and (6) specifying the observer's relationship to the child or children.

Understanding Research Methods
- There are three major research methods: (1) naturalistic, (2) experimental, and (3) case study.
- Descriptive and correlational statements can be made when naturalistic or the traditional case study methods are used. Causal statements can be made only when the experimental method is used.

- Time sampling and event sampling can ensure reliable data for naturalistic observation. Other ways to increase objectivity and reliability of data obtained in naturalistic studies include narrowing the range of behaviors being considered, defining terms at the outset of the study, and employing more than one observer.
- In the experimental method, variables are manipulated to determine causation.
- A case study is a study of one person. It is subject to observer bias, which occurs when someone loses objectivity while studying a child. The results of case studies cannot be generalized to other children (unless many case studies indicate that most children behave the same way).
- A research method must be consistent with the type of question the researcher wishes to answer. Each method is appropriate for some situations and problems and less suitable for others. A primary consideration in selecting a research method is being certain that the research subjects cannot be harmed in any way. The circumstances of the researcher also can influence the choice of research method.

Tying Things Together
- Several research studies are sometimes required before much information about an aspect of child development can be accumulated, because often each single study has limitations.
- Despite many studies on an aspect of child development, our knowledge can still be limited in that area. Because it is usually difficult to integrate research data from researchers with different theoretical orientations, a group of studies on one aspect may actually reflect only one theoretical point of view.

New Terms

data
theories
values
practices
ethical dilemma
reliability
descriptive data
correlational data
causal data
naturalistic studies
systematic observation
event sampling
time sampling
variable
independent variable

dependent variable
experimental group
control group
random assignment
observer bias
baseline conditions
baseline data
cross-sectional design
longitudinal design
biased sampling
within-subjects effect
cohort
cohort effect
cross-sectional/short-term
    longitudinal design

Selected Readings

Achenbach, T. M. **Research in developmental psychology: Concepts, strategies, methods.** *New York: The Free Press, 1978.* A good summary of many research designs and strategies. Interesting and useful material on the use of research to solve social problems. Not for the beginner unless motivation is high.

Goodfield, J. **An imagined world.** *New York: Harper & Row, 1981.* The story of a medical scientist interested in the role that lymphocytes play in the body. The story beautifully illustrates how we see what our theory leads us to expect. This scientist saw things differently from other researchers because she went to her microscope with a different theory about lymphocytes. She made new discoveries as a result. Well written and engrossing.

Leiderman, H. P., Tulkin, S. R., and Rosenfeld, A. **Culture and infancy: Variations in the human experience.** *New York: Academic Press, 1977.* For the student seriously interested in knowing about research methodologies used in infancy research. Particularly good coverage of cross-cultural studies.

Van Eyes, J. (Ed.). **Research on children: Medical imperatives, ethical quandaries, and legal constraints.** *Baltimore, Md.: University Park Press, 1978.* A good presentation of some of the issues involved in conducting research with children. Children's rights are stressed. Very readable.

Vasta, R. **Studying children: An introduction to research methods.** *San Francisco: W. H. Freeman and Company, 1979.* A very informative little paperback. Not too technical but very meaty. Excellent examples and illustrations.

Box Answers

Box 2-1
1. *values* — The father and the doctor disagree about what is important for a child to do or what an ideal childhood should be like.
2. *theory* — These mothers disagree about why language changes, about the causes of behavior. If the mothers had said, "My child changed his language without my ever correcting him" or "My child changed his language only after I started correcting his mistakes," then the disagreement would be over data.
3. *values* — The father and nursery school director disagree about what is ideal for this child right now. Toilet-training isn't important to this father right now, even if it could be accomplished in a week.
4. *practice* — The discussion and disagreement are about a practice — what to do to improve the child's mastery of addition facts. The parent and teacher agree that they are concerned about the child learning these (they have the same values), but they disagree about how to accomplish the goal. Underlying the differences in views about practice is a disagreement about theory, or why behavior changes.
5. *data* — These parents disagree about what children do — about child development data.

Box 2-4
1. descriptive   2. correlational   3. correlational   4. causal   5. correlational.

Chapter 3

Theories of
Child Development

The major theories of development are based on groups of hypotheses or tentative explanations about many interrelated aspects of development. Different theories have often emphasized different aspects of development, such as physical, cognitive, or personality. They have also differed in their overall explanations for development in any area. Some theories emphasize the role of genetic inheritance much more than the role of environment, whereas others emphasize the role of environment over that of inheritance. Some emphasize changes in terms of stages of development, whereas others view development as incremental or continuous.

In this chapter we will discuss the major theories of child development and some of the central constructs of each. We will also discuss the people who have contributed to each theory. We will conclude the chapter with a brief discussion about why it is difficult to reach agreement about theories and why competing theories are likely to be around for some time to come.

Maturational Theory

In *maturational theory* one assumes that individual differences in behavior are due to individual differences in the genes inherited. This theory received its original impetus in the mid- and late 1800s from the work of Charles Darwin (1859) on evolution and from his cousin, Francis Galton, a British investigator who found that genetically similar people have comparable abilities. If one member of a family was intelligent, the others tended to be intelligent as well; if one was dull, others were likely to be dull. Galton concluded from his studies that intellectual abilities are fixed by heredity.

Galton's conclusion, of course, was based on correlational data, and as we saw in Chapter 2, causation cannot be inferred from such data. Family members are not only related genetically; they are usually raised under similar conditions as well. Galton's demonstration of family similarities did not control for or eliminate the alternate hypothesis that similar intellectual abilities result from the influence of similar environments. Nevertheless, his thinking spurred interest in the biological or genetic basis for behavior, the underpinning of maturational theory.

According to maturational theory, heredity may have an effect in at least two ways. First, some characteristics believed to be fixed by the genes are the same from the beginning of a person's life. Eye color would be a characteristic of this sort. Second, other characteristics not present at birth may nevertheless be fixed by the genetic code and then unfold according to a timetable for developmental processes. One of these is the onset of puberty. Another is the form of adult characteristics, such as height. This is largely determined from the moment of conception, when an individual receives his or her assortment of genes, even though he or she is not six feet tall at birth.

Maturation is the process of biological change associated with the emergence of many new behaviors. The maturational theory suggests that behavior is biologically determined by the genetic code, and that, within a broad range of normal environmental conditions, time is the crucial factor in making it appear. Environment is thought to play a negligible role.

G. Stanley Hall, an American psychologist of the late 1800s and early 1900s, was an early proponent of maturational theory. He thought that the history of the human race was present in the genes and that successive periods of childhood were a recapitulation of man's evolution. Hall's recapitulation ideas were not accepted widely because, for one thing, they were based on misapplication of Darwin's theory of evolution, which held that humans did not remain the same,

Arnold Gesell

but changed, over time. However, Hall was a tremendously influential person. He was the first president of the American Psychological Association, and he founded the first scientific psychological journal, *The Journal of Genetic Psychology.* In addition, Hall's students adopted his biological or genetic view of behavior with its emphasis on a predetermined unfolding in stages, and some of their contributions were widely accepted and very influential.

One of Hall's students was Arnold Gesell, a physician who described the average ages at which skills such as walking and talking develop. Gesell, whose work was influential in the 1920s and 1930s, believed that behavior changed with age because of maturation, which itself was controlled by the individual's genetic timetable. According to Gesell, learning or experience was not a major determinant of behavior. Learning could occur only after the organism was biologically ready or mature.

Biological *readiness*, a major idea put forth by Gesell, influenced some school practices to a great extent. For example, during the 1930s it was suggested that children should not be exposed to any type of reading instruction before they reached a mental age of 6.5 years (Morphett and Washburne, 1931). This landmark itself was thought to be determined by neural ripening, or maturation of the nervous system. The idea that a child's experiences with language, for example, might influence the development of both readiness for reading and intelligence as measured by intelligence tests (with which mental age was determined), was not seriously considered. We shall see in the discussions in later chapters that this view of readiness has been questioned.

A second student of Hall's who became well known was Lewis Terman. Terman's primary interest was intelligence testing, and he translated the test constructed by the Frenchmen Binet and Simon (1905) into English. Terman was a professor at Stanford University at the time, which is why the test became known as the Stanford-Binet Intelligence Test (Terman, 1916). Terman saw intelligence basically as a genetically fixed characteristic. Although children learned more things the older they became, Terman thought their ability to learn (their IQ) was stable. We shall see in Chapter 22 that this assumption is open to question.

Several historians have remarked that child psychology in the first half of the twentieth century consisted of merely gathering *norms* (age-related changes in behavior) for children, without the guidance of theory. However, to a maturationist, gathering norms *is* generating the details of a developmental theory, one in which maturation determines when behaviors will occur. Gathering norms about the emergence of intellectual abilities, for example, was viewed as gathering data about the maturation of the nervous system, and maturation was the undisputed explanation of the times for the development of intellectual abilities.

Today, few psychologists believe that abilities are fixed by genes for life, regardless of environmental influences. However, despite the relative disfavor of such views, we still come across evidence of their effect periodically (see Box 3-1).

BOX 3-1. Common Statements Based on a Genetic-Maturational Interpretation of Behavior Change

1. "We don't accept children for kindergarten until they are at least five years old."
2. "We don't teach reading in the kindergarten. The children are not ready yet."
3. "Don't worry if your two-year-old is not yet toilet trained; when he or she is ready, bladder control will occur without training."
4. "Oh, she'll grow out of it. Just leave her alone."
5. "Girls will be girls and boys will be boys."

Psychoanalytic Theory

Sigmund Freud

In the first half of this century, while maturation was the dominant explanation of the development of intellectual and physical abilities, social and personality development was being explained by a theory that recognized the importance of biology as it interacted with the environment. That theory was developed by an Austrian physician, Sigmund Freud. Freud was interested in neurology, and this interest, in turn, led him to an interest in nervous disorders. He was advised by a Viennese psychiatrist friend that patients' nervous symptoms improved when they were encouraged to talk about them (Hall and Lindzey, 1970). Freud tried the technique and had some success with it. This marked the beginning of his work to develop the therapy known as *psychoanalysis*.

Freud considered the important biological component of each person's personality to be essentially the same, calling it the instinct. Freud's concept of instinct differs from the instinct as described by other theorists, who use the word to refer to any innate behavior in animals. Freud used *instincts* to mean the mental representations of body states or needs. Hunger and sexual arousal are examples of such needs (Freud, 1925).

An understanding of Freud's idea of instinct is the key to his entire theory. According to Freud, the motivation for all action is to maximize instinctual gratification while minimizing punishment, guilt, and anxiety (Maddi, 1976). These motivations are what drive behavior. Because these needs are basically biological or physical, Freud's theory is a biological theory first of all. However, environment comes into play, too, because personality development depends on how the biologically based needs are met.

According to Freud, three parts of the psyche or personality must develop: the id, the ego, and the superego. The *id* is the inherited and unconscious source of instincts. It constantly propels the organism to resolve tension in or excitation of bodily states, that is, to satisfy needs. Freud contended that the world of the young child is one in which there is a tendency to gratify selfish instincts. However, the *ego*, or the reality-oriented mind, tries to direct the id to seek satisfaction in appropriate ways, ways that are not punished. The rules for appropriate behavior according to society are taught to the child by his or her parents. These become part of the personality, too. This part is known as the *superego*. The superego functions not merely to guide the ego to gratify the id in ways that are not punished, but often to block gratification altogether (Hall and Lindzey, 1970). The ego keeps the id's instincts in check by the use of *ego defense mechanisms*, such as repression and sublimation. In *repression*, the mind blocks out the thought or event leading to the anxiety, as when a child represses the thought of hitting his brother. In *sublimation*, the energy is displaced in some other, acceptable activity, as when the parent invites the child to pound clay after the child has been unpleasant.

Consider the following illustration of how the three parts of the personality work together. Suppose a younger sibling's unconscious source of instincts (the id) tells his conscious and reality-oriented mind (the ego), which directs his action, to eat the food on his older sister's plate to relieve a bodily tension — hunger. If the older sister's id has just told her to eat her food, she may hit her brother as he reaches for her plate. The body tension generated by being hit is greater than that generated by hunger, and the younger brother does not repeat the behavior. After a number of such collisions, little brother eventually acquires a set of rules (the superego) that he knows he must not break for fear of punishment and guilt. All behavior, then, is a function of the id, superego, and ego, with the ego mediating between the other two — that is, trying to find ways to satisfy the id that will not violate the rules of the superego.

The instincts at the center of the child's conflict with the punishing world change their "location" as the child moves from one stage of development to the next. Freud's stages are oral, anal, phallic, latency, and genital. Each is named for the zone of the body Freud thought was the source of troublesome instinctual activity for that period of life. That is, as the child matures biologically, the instincts that are most likely to get the child into trouble change. In the *oral stage*, lasting from birth to about one year of age, the mouth is the center of activity, that is, the center of satisfaction that may be provided (or not) by parents. In the *anal stage*, which lasts from about the end of the first year to the end of the third, the anal region is the center of instinctual activity that comes in conflict with parental values. It is during this period that the child's developing sphincter control encourages the parents to attempt toilet training in spite of the child's urge for immediate gratification of the instincts associated with defecation. In the *phallic stage*, which lasts until about age five, the genitals are the new source of prohibited instinctual activity. These early stages were seen by Freud to be especially important for personality development.

The *latency stage* lasts from age five or six until adolescence. It is a period of no new conflictful instinctual activity. No particular body zone is the center of problem activity. In adolescence, the *genital stage* is entered, and mature love of others and socialized adult behavior emerge. Social rules may be in conflict with desires, of course, and then the superego and ego defenses function to keep the id in check.

If instincts are not under- or overgratified at each stage by parents, the child progressively acquires the ego defenses properly associated with each stage to keep the instincts in check; these ego defenses largely determine the behavior we see. Biological maturation leads the child to the next stage, with its new conflict with society. If at any point instincts are undergratified or overgratified, however, defense mechanisms and behavior become *fixated* at that stage. This means that

---

**BOX 3-2. Common Statements Based on a
Psychoanalytic Interpretation of Behavior**

---

1. "It is better to feed a baby on demand than on a rigid schedule."
2. "Children who suck their thumbs weren't allowed to suck the bottle or breast long enough when they were babies."
3. "Nursery schools should be equipped with a punching bag so that children who tend to quarrel with other children can release their emotions in a constructive way."
4. "Don't interfere with children's dramatic play; it is important that they work out their emotional conflicts."

---

some instinctual energy remains in a previous zone rather than moving on to the next. As a result, the individual as an adult continues to exhibit needs, defenses, and behavior more typical of individuals at an earlier stage. For example, an adult who overeats may be doing so because he or she is fixated at the oral stage.

Although theoretically, either over- or undergratification of instincts (or alternating over- and undergratification) could lead to fixation, Freud's ideas were introduced at a time in history when childrearing practices concerning feeding and toilet training were very rigid. Therefore, much of the application of Freud's theory was oriented toward guarding against undergratification of instincts. Despite little unequivocal research support for much of Freud's theory, it has been influential, and even today it influences how many teachers and parents behave toward children (see Box 3-2).

Erik Erikson

Erik Erikson, whose major works were published in the 1940s, 1950s, and 1960s, also subscribed to a psychoanalytic view of personality development. However, whereas Freud emphasized the determination of behavior by the instincts (especially sex) and unconscious defense mechanisms, Erikson emphasized the ego. That is, Freud's emphasis was more on the unconscious, whereas Erikson's was more on the conscious. Erikson emphasized the effect of society on all ego functions. (The ego is thought to house the unconscious defense mechanisms as well as our conscious thinking.) In addition, Erikson recognized that adaptation to reality varies from society to society and that within a society demands differ according to age. Erikson's theory has been called a psychosocial view of development, indicating that the major crisis at each developmental stage originates in society's demands. Freud's has been called psychosexual, indicating that the crises have their basis in bodily states, such as sexual arousal.

Erikson's theory postulates eight stages of development. Each stage is characterized by a major "crisis" or turning point, which is a time of increased vulnerability as well as potential for psychological growth. In stage 1, which lasts from birth to about eighteen months, the psychosocial conflict or crisis is between trust and mistrust. Depending on how the caregiver responds to the infant's physical needs such as hunger, the infant will decide that he or she is either "all right" or "not all right." Adequate resolution of this as well as of succeeding conflicts does not involve development of complete trust, for if it did the child's behavior would not truly be adaptive. There are situations in which we should mistrust. Appropriate resolution results in more trust than mistrust, but not in complete trust.

In stage 2, which lasts from about eighteen months to three and a half years of age, the crisis is between autonomy and shame and doubt. If toilet training is not

Erik Erikson

Table 3-1. Erikson's eight stages of development

Psychosocial conflict (crisis)	Pivotal events	Age	What a person learns when development proceeds successfully
Trust vs. mistrust	Caregiver response to physical needs of infant, especially in feeding	Birth to 18 months	I am all right.
Autonomy vs. shame or doubt	Toilet-training, locomotion, exploration and touching of objects in environment	18 months to 3½ years	I can make choices.
Initiative vs. guilt	Curiosity resulting from increased language, motor, and cognitive skills	3½ to 6 years	I can do and I can make.
Industry vs. inferiority	School tasks such as learning to read	6 to 12 years	I can join with others in doing and making things.
Identity vs. identity confusion or diffusion	Learning one's vocational and professional orientation	Adolescence	I can be to others what I am to myself.
Intimacy vs. isolation	Love relationship	Young adult	I can risk offering myself to another.
Generativity vs. stagnation	Parenting, nurturing others, civic responsibility	Mature adult	I am concerned for others.
Integrity vs. despair	Reflection on one's life	Older adult	I can accept my life.

SOURCE: Adapted from material in Erikson, E. H., *Identity, youth and crisis*. New York: W. W. Norton, 1968.

severe, and if locomotion, exploration, and touching of objects are not restricted unreasonably, the child learns "I can make choices; I have some control."

The remaining stages are summarized in Table 3-1. Unlike Freud's stages, which continue only until the onset of adulthood, Erikson's stages span the entire life course.

Behavioral Theory

Although psychoanalytic theory suggests that individual differences in development occur as a result of environment or childrearing, psychoanalytic theory, especially Freud's, stresses the biological base of events that set personality development in motion. In contrast, behavioral theorists discuss few of the biological changes that occur within the child over time and concentrate on how a specific environment changes behavior. *Behavioral theory* has been known by various names over the years, including learning theory, S-R theory, and behaviorism. The name *S-R theory* resulted from the fact that learning is considered a process of forming individual connections between a stimulus (S) in an organism's environment and the organism's response (R). These connections are known as "S-R bonds." The name "behaviorism" was derived from the assumption that psychological theories should be based only on observable behavior and stimuli, and should exclude references to consciousness or cognition.

Classical Conditioning

Ivan Pavlov (1849–1936), a Russian physiologist, was the first learning theorist to suggest that an organism's response to a stimulus is "conditional" on the previous pairing of that stimulus with stimuli that reliably produce a particular response. Pavlov's theory has been called *classical conditioning*. The stimulus that initially produces the response reliably is called the *unconditioned stimulus*, and the stimulus that is paired with it (or presented slightly before it) is called the *conditioned stimulus*.

Pavlov's most famous example of classical conditioning involved dogs that were taught to salivate to the sound of a bell. The conditioned stimulus, the sound of the bell, was repeatedly presented at the same time as the unconditioned stimulus, food in the mouth, which naturally produced salivation as an *unconditioned response*. Subsequently, the presentation of the bell alone elicited salivation as a *conditioned response* (or as a substitute stimulus for the food).

Examples of apparent classical conditioning in child development are common. Placing a nipple in an infant's mouth elicits sucking as an unconditioned response. If an infant is fed from a nippled bottle, the sight of the bottle alone may become a conditioned stimulus for sucking. The nipple in the mouth is the unconditioned stimulus with which the sight of the bottle is paired. As a result, sucking becomes a conditioned response to the sight of the bottle. After the initial conditioning, the unconditioned stimulus (nipple) must be presented at least occasionally in conjunction with the conditioned stimulus (bottle) to "reinforce" the conditioned response. The response to the conditioned stimulus may also generalize to other, similar stimuli.

Instrumental Conditioning

Whereas Pavlov studied how behavior was elicited by stimuli that precede it, Thorndike (1905), an American psychologist working early in this century, described how the frequency of essentially voluntary behavior is affected by stimuli (reward and punishment) that consistently follow and are contingent on that behavior. This type of conditioning is called *instrumental conditioning*. Instrumental conditioning provides a theoretical basis for educational programs that try to increase the frequency of performance of academic skills by following them with a reward such as a gold star or a small toy.

Freudians and early S-R theorists agreed that satisfaction of physiological needs or drives plays a large role in determining behavior. According to the early S-R view, each person strives to obtain rewards — objects which alleviate the primary needs of hunger, thirst, sex, and pain. These goal objects are called *primary rewards* to distinguish them from *secondary rewards*, which are learned. The latter become rewards or reinforcers because they are associated with the need reduction which occurs when primary reinforcers are presented. For example, a mother's smile may acquire its reward properties, that is, become a secondary reinforcer, from an initial pairing with food and other primary reinforcers. Present-day behaviorists, however, have some more basic disagreements with Freudians.

B. F. Skinner

B. F. Skinner is considered the most influential contemporary behaviorist. His radical behaviorism rejects completely concepts such as drives that are in some sense inside the organism and unobservable. Instead, he attempts to explain behavior in terms of observable phenomena. For example, the concept of reward of the S-R theorists has been replaced by that of *reinforcement*. A reinforcer is defined as any observable stimulus that increases the frequency of a response when presented contingent on (or following) the response. The process of increasing the frequency of a behavior (a response) by adding a reinforcing stimulus is called *operant conditioning*. This type of learning was first investigated by Thorndike, who called it instrumental conditioning.

Skinner has been interested in explaining, among other things, how new behaviors can be acquired. Skinnerians are best known for teaching new behavior by taking a frequently emitted behavior and reinforcing variations of it that are more and more like the desired behavior. The process of reinforcing successive approximations to the desired behavior until the new behavior finally appears is known as *shaping*. The shaping process is the same regardless of the organism it is applied to, whether it be teaching a rat to press a bar completely or teaching a child to copy letters legibly.

Classical conditioning was originally thought to apply almost exclusively to involuntary behavior (behavior governed by the autonomic nervous system), whereas instrumental or operant conditioning was thought to describe voluntary behavior. However, operant conditioning of autonomic and visceral responses indicates that there are some exceptions to this rule. For example, in *biofeedback*, bodily processes such as heart rate and blood pressure are monitored by machine and the data are given to a patient. The patients are instructed in relaxation techniques, and the feedback from the machine lets them know if they are successfully employing relaxation to lower their heart rate. As a consequence of this reinforcing feedback, patients shape their ability to lower this "involuntary" response until they can do it relatively quickly when they desire.

Social Learning Theorists

Some present-day behaviorists such as Rotter (Rotter, Liverant, and Crowne, 1961), Bandura (1973, 1977) are more willing than others to discuss conscious cognitive phenomena (thinking, reasoning). Bandura, for example, emphasized that many behaviors are not acquired gradually through shaping but rapidly through observation and imitation. For example, it is unlikely that many of us could learn to drive through shaping, which depends so heavily on trial and error. We might not live through the first lesson. Instead, we depend on what we learn cognitively through imitation and verbal instruction.

A recent spokesman for the *social learning* position, Mischell (1976), suggests that we can predict behavior by understanding a situation and which of an individual's competencies, interpretations of events, expectations, values, and plans relate to that situation. These qualities are not directly observable and are essentially cognitive. That is, Mischel notes that the same stimulus — for example, a classroom test — does not produce the same behavior in all individuals. Instead, each person interprets stimuli in a way that will produce a valued outcome. In short, one difference between a social learning theorist and a more radical behaviorist is their view of the effect of a stimulus. The control a stimulus has over the behavior of an individual is thought to be stronger by radical behaviorists than by social learning theorists.

Common practices and statements based on behavioral or learning theory are presented in Box 3-3.

BOX 3-3. Common Statements Based on Behavioral or Learning Theory

1. "You may watch television after you finish your homework."
2. "In our math program children are asked to learn just one small step at a time. Thus success is ensured and children want to continue working with the materials."
3. "When you finish your reading and math assignments, you may paint, play with blocks, or choose a learning game."
4. "Ignore children when they are behaving badly; praise them when they are behaving well."
5. "You'll spoil the baby if you pick him up when he cries."
6. "Here's the box of tokens we use to reward the children who are doing their work. They can trade them in at the end of the day for any of the toys that are in the cabinet. The toys are labeled with their cost in tokens."
7. "Children who answer questions correctly will receive a gold star on their papers."
8. "The baby stops crying now as soon as she hears my footsteps. I guess she knows that she will be fed soon."
9. "If children see you hitting, they will learn to hit."

Cognitive-Developmental Theory

In the 1950s S-R theorists began to accumulate research evidence that behaviors occurred in the absence of S-R drives, external reinforcements, and punishments. Butler (1953), for example, found that monkeys would learn a task when it was followed by an opportunity to look at something outside their cages. Nissen's (1930) earlier work had focused on similar behavior: he found that white rats would endure the pain of passing over an electrified grid to get to a maze filled with new objects. Some theorists (White, 1959) proposed manipulation and exploration drives to explain such behaviors, but many others turned to the study of cognition rather than drives for explanations.

Piaget's Theory

Jean Piaget, a Swiss psychologist and biologist, had been investigating the development of cognition during the 1930s and 40s, and his work proved to be of great importance. He tried to understand the acquisition and nature of adult knowledge by considering the levels of knowledge of children of different ages. He asked two basic questions: Why do children and adults think differently in similar situations? What causes human knowledge to change over time?

According to Piaget, adults and children think differently because they have different levels of understanding. Our response to a situation is determined, not by external conditions alone, but by how we understand the situation as well. This is the crux of *cognitive-developmental theory*.

Piaget's explanation of the changes in knowledge over time is quite complex. Knowledge, he suggests, is constructed or created gradually as people interact with their environment. Thus children are seen as being active in their own development. In maturational theory, you will recall, the child is at the mercy of the genes that determine the rate of maturation. When the child is physically ready for learning (that is, when neural ripening has occurred with respect to a certain area of development), knowledge is assumed to be acquired quite easily from the environment. Behavioral theorists also assume that knowledge is external, but they think it can be acquired as a result of experience and the laws of reinforcement. Piaget, on the other hand, does not assume that knowledge is external, that it exists in the external world to be acquired. Knowledge is instead a creation resulting from interaction between the person and the environment.

Jean Piaget

Piaget used two processes to explain how knowledge is created and changed over time. *Assimilation* refers to the taking in of information about the environment. New information, if assimilated, is always incorporated into an existing knowledge structure or *scheme*. A two-year-old who is familiar with dogs, for example, can be said to possess a dog scheme. The first time the child sees a cat, he or she may say "dog," because that is the most appropriate scheme the child has. The child assimilates "cat" to a dog scheme. But gradually, the child differentiates "dog" from "cat," to develop two schemes, one for dog and one for cat. This change in a knowledge structure is known as *accommodation*.

Piaget (1963) points out that our schemes are consistently inadequate to handle all of our experiences. Thus, assimilation often results in the distortion of information about events in our experience to fit available structures. Eventually, the distortions are corrected because mental structures change to accommodate the new information.

It is through accommodation that schemes are differentiated to conform more closely to the environment. As the two-year-old becomes more familiar with cats, he or she will alter his dog scheme to exclude animals that climb trees and meow, at the same time developing information about cats into a cat scheme. The child will eventually differentiate the two schemes in a way that more accurately reflects all of the characteristics of each type of animal.

Piaget uses the term *equilibration* to describe the process whereby assimilation and accommodation balance each other. At first new information assimilated is accommodated rather slowly. As thinking becomes more developed, however, accommodation occurs more rapidly such that thinking in turn is generally more equilibrated.

Piaget suggests that development progresses through a series of stages. Movement to a new stage occurs when the child's way of thinking, which has re-

Table 3-2. Piaget's developmental stages

Stage	Description
Sensorimotor (0–18 months)	Schemes are sensorimotor rather than symbolic; that is, they involve action.
Preoperational (2–6 years)	Schemes involve symbols, such as words, but they are intuitive rather than logical.
Concrete operational (7–12 years)	Schemes are symbolic *and* logical but are limited to concrete and present objects and events.
Formal operational (12 years and older)	Schemes are symbolic and logical, and hypothetical-deductive ("if, then" thinking can be employed to generate all the possibilities in a particular situation).

mained essentially the same for a relatively long period, changes to the qualitatively different way of thinking of the next stage. In other words, assimilation and accommodation do not lead merely to continuous increases in knowledge, but to reorganizations of knowledge, or to different ways of thinking. The points at which reorganization takes place mark the Piagetian stages, of which there are four. We have outlined these stages briefly in Table 3-2. We will discuss each stage in considerable detail in later chapters.

Implications of Piaget's Theory

Piaget's theory suggests that children favor moderately novel events because these are the events most likely to result in accommodation (Hunt, 1965). Events that are completely familiar will require no change in schemes; as a result the child will find them uninteresting. By the same token, completely novel events produce no accommodation because the child cannot assimilate them to a scheme. Such events may seem "scary" or incomprehensible to the child.

These ideas about the relationship between a child's experience and his or her level of understanding provide a theoretical basis for *intrinsic motivation*, or motivation derived from the demands of information processing (Hunt, 1965). On the basis of Piaget's ideas about assimilation and accommodation, we can predict that children will initiate actions in the absence of classic motives of hunger, thirst, sex, and pain, or of secondary reinforcement related to external rewards and punishments. Children will act in order to understand; when they express interest in something it indicates both that they are trying to understand it and that they are understanding it. But Piaget's theory implies that child and adult interests are likely to differ, because their schemes are different.

The cognitive-developmental perspective is evident in many educational and childrearing practices and beliefs, some of which are listed in Box 3-4.

**BOX 3-4. Common Statements Based on
Cognitive-Developmental Theory**

---

1. "Children learn best when they are interested in what they are doing."
2. "Children are active learners."
3. "When children answer questions incorrectly, ask them why they answered as they did before deciding how to help them arrive at the correct answer."
4. "Children seek stimulation."
5. "Don't put all of the new toys out in the classroom at once; add new ones gradually to renew interest."

Reaching Agreement About Theories

After this lengthy discussion of theories, you might well be wondering which one is the best. Which one truly explains why behavior occurs and why it changes? These are difficult questions to answer, and different people and groups favor competing theories or explanations.

Programs based on all the different theories have been developed for use in fields such as psychological therapy and early childhood education. For example, within the latter, behaviorally oriented programs such as *Behavior Analysis* use tangible objects such as candy, tokens, or special classroom activities to reward on-task behavior relating to academic skills learning. The *Bank Street Program*, on the other hand, is based on cognitive-developmental and psychoanalytic theory. Children are given a wide variety of toys and activities to choose from, such as cooking, blocks, picture books, easel painting, dramatic play, puzzles, and manipulative math and prereading materials. They may select what they will do during much of the day. Teachers interact with children when they feel they can facilitate learning. Concrete rewards are not used to motivate children to learn or to correct misbehavior; instead, attempts are made to provide experiences that interest the children, and to adjust expectations and demands to the children's levels and needs.

But how does one go about choosing one theory over another? One helpful step involves determining what behaviors a theory was developed to explain. Gesell's theory, for example, was not constructed to explain how children acquire the concept of number or how the neuroses of adults develop. Neither Freud nor Piaget was interested in explaining why crawling occurs before walking, or why behavior is displayed consistently in one situation but not in another. No theory addresses all questions. The answer to our question about which theory is best depends in part on which theory is most closely concerned with the behavior we are trying to explain.

If two or more theories relate to the behavior of interest to us, then we must assess their ability to predict and explain behavior by considering the research evidence. This, however, is not an easy task as we learned in the last chapter. Recall the problem of interpreting the data gathered by Jensen (1974, 1977) concerning the changes in the IQs of low-income black children. Jensen considered the change in IQ over time gathered from his cross-sectional sample as evidence for a genetic interpretation of IQ. However, critics such as Kamin (1978) have argued that the methodology used did not eliminate an environmental explanation for the phenomenon observed. These two competing explanations for the data — that genes or heredity versus environment play the essential role — are two major theoretical positions, as we have seen in this chapter. Thus studies often do not clearly support either of two competing theories. It often takes considerable time, and a collection of studies, to shed much light on the validity of one theory versus another.

We hope that you now have a better understanding of some of the ideas used to explain child behavior, and that you recognize some of the sources of disagreement among child developmentalists. You might wonder why we worry about theories at all, since we are so uncertain about them. The fact is, a theory is always implied in our thinking, because our ideas can be analyzed to derive a structure of assumptions about why changes occur. Part of the reason for investigating a field of study is to develop an understanding of the theories that underlie one's own thinking and how they relate to what others think. As we discuss many topics throughout the remainder of this book, we will identify the theories behind the research studies we cite.

Summary

Maturational Theory

- According to the maturational interpretation of development, behavior change is determined by genetic codes that influence the development of the nervous system.
- At the turn of the century, Arnold Gesell was the leading proponent of the maturational view of development. One of his concepts was "readiness" — that a person can learn only when biologically "ready."

Psychoanalytic Theory

- Psychoanalytic theory focuses on social and emotional rather than physical development.
- Freud and Erikson were the two major formulators of psychoanalytic theory.
- Freud and Erikson differed in the importance they attributed to reality or the ego. Freud's theory is termed psychosexual, while Erikson's theory is termed psychosocial.

Behavioral Theory

- The behavioral view of development stresses the influence of the environment in behavior change. Pavlov and Thorndike were important early behaviorists.
- In classical conditioning, behaviors are elicited by stimuli that precede them.
- In instrumental conditioning, behaviors are affected by stimuli (reward and punishment) that follow them.
- B. F. Skinner, an influential contemporary behaviorist, explains behavior in terms of observable phenomena. The concept of "reward," for example, has been replaced by the concept of "reinforcer." A reinforcer is any observable stimulus that increases the frequency of a response when it is applied contingent to that response.

- Social learning theorists such as Rotter and Bandura consider human qualities that are not directly observable.
- All behaviorists have in common an interest in behavior as a function of reinforcement, reward, and punishment in an organism's external environment.

Cognitive-Developmental Theory

- Cognitive-developmental theory grew in popularity because psychologists could not explain all behavior in terms of drives, external reinforcement, and punishment. Jean Piaget was the leading theorist of the cognitive-developmental perspective.
- According to the cognitive-developmental interpretation, behavior is influenced both by what a person brings to a situation (what he or she knows) and by the characteristics of the situation.
- Piaget considered behavior change the result of the interaction between two processes — assimilation and accommodation.

Reaching Agreement About Theories

- It is difficult to assess the value of the various theories conclusively because the necessary research is extremely complicated and hard to conduct. However, because all the major theories of development have been translated into education programs, both understanding and some assessment of them is necessary for educators.

New Terms

maturational theory
maturation
readiness
norms
psychoanalysis
instincts
id
ego
superego
ego defense mechanisms
repression
sublimation
fixation
behavioral theory
S-R theory
classical conditioning
unconditioned stimulus

conditioned stimulus
unconditioned response
conditioned response
instrumental conditioning
primary rewards
secondary rewards
reinforcement
operant conditioning
shaping
biofeedback
social learning theory
cognitive-developmental theory
assimilation
scheme
accommodation
equilibration
intrinsic motivation

Selected Readings

Evans, E. D. **Contemporary influences in early childhood education.** *New York: Holt, Rinehart and Winston, 1971.* Covers the theoretical underpinnings of several early childhood programs. There is a particularly good discussion of the behaviorial view as it has been applied in behavior analysis programs.

Maier, H. **Three theories of child development.** *3rd ed. New York: Harper and Row, 1978.* Discusses and compares three theories: the cognitive theory of Piaget, the behaviorial theory of Sears, and the psychoanalytic theory of Erikson. Part Two discusses application of the theories to the helping process.

Senn, M. J. **Insights on the child development movement in the United States.** *Monographs of the Society for Research in Child Development 40 (1975).* Senn taped interviews with over eighty people prominent in the area of child development to gather material for this hundred-page monograph. Some of those interviewed had been associated with pioneers in child development during the 1920s. Others were younger. The personal reactions to and comments about people included in this history are fascinating and make history come alive.

Erikson, E. **Childhood and society.** *Second edition. New York: Norton, 1963.* This book explains Erikson's theory of psychosocial development. Interesting to read and understandable.

Skinner, B. F. **About behaviorism.** *New York: Knopf, 1974.* Skinner discusses behaviorism and common misunderstandings about it.

Part II
The Beginning

We think of birth as a beginning, yet by the time a child is born events of great significance have already taken place. The genes that determine the child's sex and other physical characteristics began to exert their influence at conception; soon afterward it was determined whether the child would be born singly or as an identical twin. In the remaining nine months, malnutrition, disease, drugs, or irradiation may have played havoc with a perfect genetic plan, or the child may, like most, have received only support and protection as it developed. In Chapter 4 we discuss the crucial early events that influence the lives of children before they are born.

The very beginning of life after birth is a unique period, too. This period can be very precarious, yet it is also remarkable in terms of the child's potential for adaptation and survival. This early period of life after birth — the special time when parents and their child first meet and learn how to live together as individual human beings — is the topic of Chapter 5.

Chapter 4

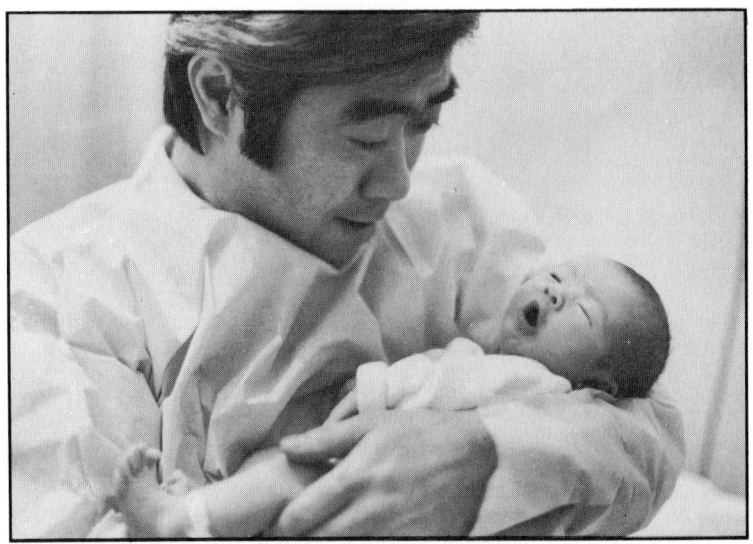

Genetics, Prenatal Development, and Birth

The study of the period of life before birth has resulted in some crucial discoveries. It has enabled prospective parents, with the aid of a genetic counselor and some knowledge of their genetic background, to understand their chances of conceiving a healthy baby. It has helped parents-to-be ensure that their unborn child stays healthy. An understanding of life before birth can benefit others, too. It can help teachers understand why children in their classes have cystic fibrosis or sickle-cell anemia. It can resolve the doubts of a school superintendent who wonders whether a policy barring unimmunized children from class is well-founded. It can inform the decisions of a government policymaker who is considering whether to vote for funding for prenatal care or research into the effects of obstetrical anesthesia. People from a surprising variety of backgrounds can profit from a knowledge of genetics, prenatal development, and birth. These are the topics we will discuss in this chapter.

Genetics

You sit waiting for the parents of your twenty-seven first graders to arrive at the school open house. The parents will meet with you in the classroom while the children go to the gym for some organized games.

Parents arrive and take their places in the chairs you have assembled. To begin the meeting you give some background: what you hope to accomplish during the year, what the parents can expect children to be doing, how you hope you can count on their important help. After a brief talk, you invite the parents to ask questions. As they speak, you try to place their questions in context: Is that Juan's father who wants to know if there will be homework? It must be: he has Juan's dark brown hair and dark eyes. And the question about conferences being held in the evening so that working parents can attend — whose mother is that? By the end of the meeting you think you know which child belongs to each parent, but then the children come into the room. Are you surprised!

Genetics helps explain why children both resemble and differ from their parents.

Juan's father has curly brown hair and a light complexion, but Juan is dark and has straight hair, jet black. Matthew, the biggest kid in the class, has rather small parents. Gretchen has bright blue eyes, but both her parents have brown eyes. Some of the parents are stepparents or adoptive parents — that explains a few of the "mismatches" — but most of them are biologically related to their children. How can the dissimilarities be explained in those cases?

Questions such as these can be answered, at least in part, by *genetics*, which is an area of study in the field of biology. Geneticists investigate how and why similar organisms vary. The basic mechanism of variation is the *gene*, which carries the coded information that determines whether a person will have blue eyes or brown, have freckles or fair skin, or be tall or short. Genes, in turn, are carried on *chromosomes*, threadlike structures found in every cell of the body. These can be seen when a cell is dyed and viewed through an electron microscope.

Humans have twenty-three pairs of chromosomes in each cell, forty-six individual chromosomes altogether. In each pair, the genes on one chromosome have counterparts on the other chromosome. The effect of a particular gene is greatly influenced by the other genes we inherit. A *dominant* gene always expresses its characteristic, whereas a *recessive* gene does so only when paired with another recessive gene.

Cell Division and Conception

A person's genes (there are thousands of them) come from two cells, one from the father, one from the mother. The cells involved in reproduction are called *germ* cells, as distinct from *somatic* cells, which are all the other cells in the body. The germ cells of the female are called *ova* or eggs and those of the male are called *sperm*.

Germ cells differ from body cells in the way they divide, and it is this which makes them unique. First, let us consider what happens when a body cell divides. When we grow new skin or blood cells, each new cell contains forty-six individual chromosomes in twenty-three pairs. The genes on each chromosome are identical to those of the *parent* or original cell that divided in two (see Figure 4-1). This kind of cell division, which exactly duplicates the original cell, is known as *mitosis*.

But consider what would happen if germ cells were created the same way: the ovum and sperm would each contain a full complement of forty-six chromosomes, and when they united, the new organism would have ninety-two! But it only has forty-six. How does this happen?

A special kind of cell division called *meiosis* reduces the number of chromosomes by one-half to prepare a germ cell for conception (see Figure 4-2). During the same process, genes are exchanged between chromosomes before they separate into two sets (step 3, Figure 4-2). This step in the meiotic process is called

Figure 4-1
Mitosis

Original cell (only one of the 23 pairs of chromosomes is shown).

Each chromosome of the pair divides into two identical halves (chromatids), which draw apart.

The chromatids migrate to opposite poles of the cell.

The cell divides.

Two cells are formed. Each contains 23 pairs of chromosomes identical to those of the parent cell.

Figure 4-2
Meiosis

Step 1: Original cell (only one of the 23 pairs of chromosomes is shown).

Step 2: Chromosomes divide into two halves, but the halves do not separate.

Step 3: Duplicated chromosome pairs wrap around each other and exchange genetic material (crossing over).

Step 4: Chromosome pairs unwrap.

Step 5: One chromosome pair goes to each pole and the cell divides.

Step 6: Two new cells are formed, each one different from the original cell and from each other. These two cells then divide and one chromosome goes to each of four new cells.

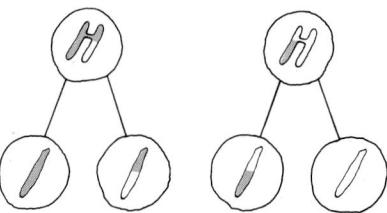

Step 7: Each of the four new cells is different, and each contains a total of 23 *single* chromosomes.

crossing over; it ensures that the twenty-three single chromosomes inherited from each parent will not be identical to any of either parent's chromosomes. Thus, offspring look different from both their parents not only because half of their genes came from each parent, but also because the genes contributed by each parent do not exactly duplicate the genes found in the parent's own cells.

Meiosis provides the biological basis for individual differences. Crossing over of the chromosomes makes the possibilities for unique combinations of genes practically limitless. Brothers may differ greatly from sisters, and children may differ greatly from their parents. These differences may be increased by variations in experience. Teachers, parents, and everyone else can expect that children will not be exactly like their parents, and that brothers and sisters will be different from each other.

Determination of Sex

One of the twenty-three pairs of chromosomes determines whether a fetus will be male or female. Females have a matching pair of sex chromosomes (XX), whereas males have one X chromosome and one Y chromosome (XY). After meiosis, a sperm may contain either an X or a Y chromosome, but the ovum always contains an X chromosome. It is the father, not the mother, who determines the sex of the child. (See Figure 4-3.)

You might expect that exactly half of the babies conceived would be female and half males, but the evidence indicates at least 120 males are conceived for every 100 females. The ratio of male to female births, however, is about 105:100, because more male fetuses die *in utero*. Although not conclusive, research indicates that this is because the genes carried on the X and Y chromosomes determine characteristics other than sex. A defective X chromosome in a female may be kept in check by a healthy gene on the other X chromosome; a female would have to inherit *two* defective chromosomes to be affected. But the Y chromosome is much smaller than the X chromosome, and it is thought to carry fewer genes. This means that a defective gene on the male's X chromosome may not have a corresponding gene to correct its effect on the Y chromosome. Thus, an abnormality is more likely to be expressed in the male than in the female, and this accounts for the male's higher mortality rate. The mortality of males is higher than that of females at every age, so females outnumber males even though there were more males to begin with.

Multiple Births

In some cases two or more ova, rather than the usual single ovum, are released from the ovary at one time. If each is fertilized by a sperm cell two babies will develop, but they will be no more similar genetically than siblings born at dif-

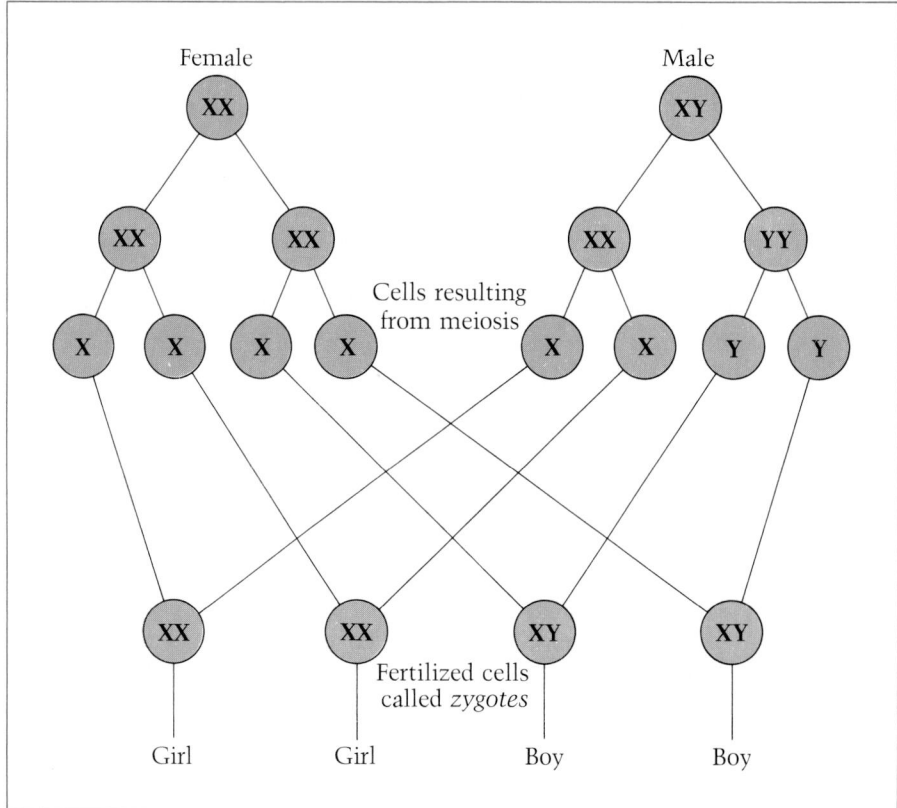

Figure 4-3. Sex determination

ferent times because each came from a different fertilized egg. Twins who develop in this way are called *fraternal*; they may be two girls, two boys, or a boy and a girl.

The simultaneous release of several ova can be triggered by fertility drugs. These are sometimes taken by women who have difficulty becoming pregnant because their body chemistry prevents them from ovulating — releasing an ovum during each monthly cycle. It is hoped that fertility drugs will cause a woman to ovulate normally, but they sometimes overstimulate the ovaries to release more than one ovum. When this occurs a woman is likely to give birth to twins, triplets, or even greater numbers of children.

Multiple births can also result when a single fertilized ovum, known as a *zygote*, divides by mitosis into two separate cells, which develop independently. Because mitosis involves exact replication of the genetic material in the original cell, persons who develop in this way — *identical twins* — are genetically identical and are, naturally, of the same sex. (See Figure 4-4.)

Twinning occurs about once in every eighty-nine births; one-third of the twins born are identical. Triple births, due to multiple ovulation or to a second separation of the original zygote with one of the four cells perishing, occur about once in every 7000 births. Quadruplets are very rare, occurring only once in every 385,499 births (Gedda, 1961).

Figure 4-4. Twinning

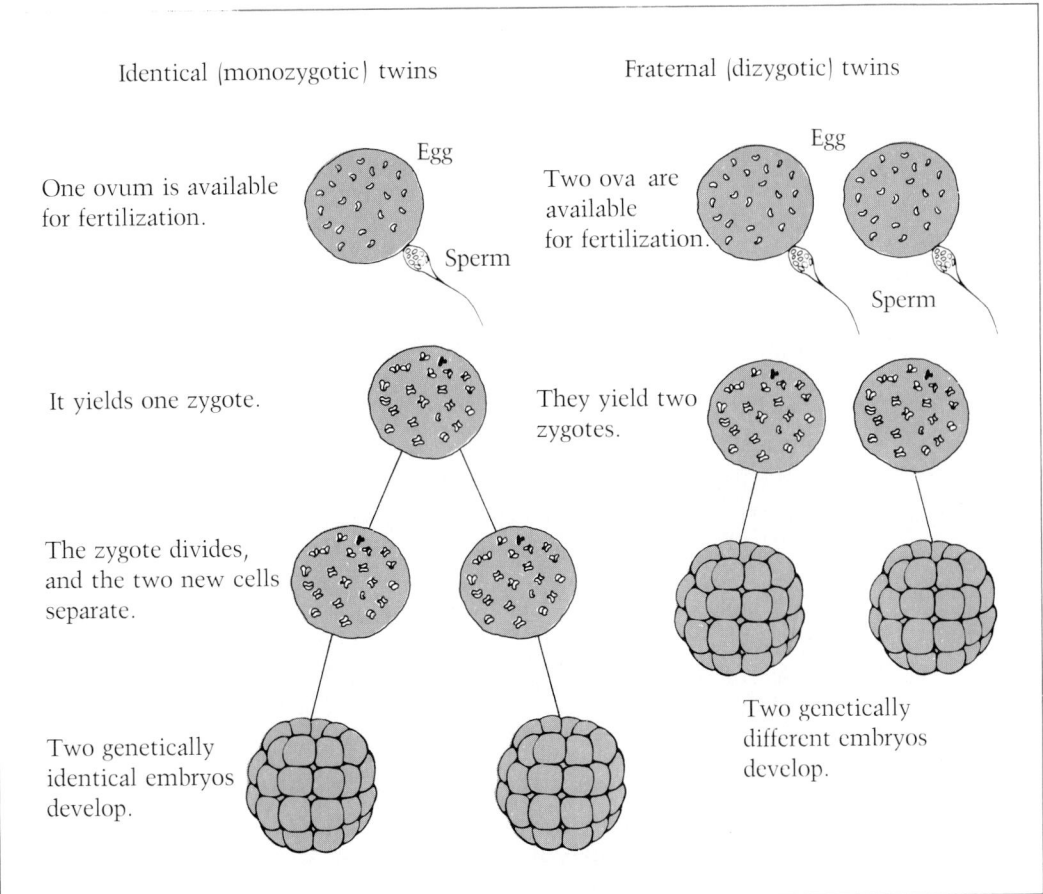

The incidence of multiple births varies among different population groups, being more frequent in Nigerian populations and quite rare in South American, Chinese, and Japanese populations (Stern, 1973). In addition, the incidence of twins increases as the mother's age increases.

Prenatal Development

Early Theories

Aristotle wrote that male semen provides the "form" of the embryo, while the female provides the material that is given form. This stood to reason, according to Aristotle, because the male is active and the female passive (Needham, 1959). Aristotle was not the first to think so. Earlier, a Greek dramatist had written that the woman contributes nothing to the child: the child is merely "sown" in her and the male is its only parent (Needham, 1959). Modern genetics has put such ideas to rest. We now know that the male and female contribute equally to each new life they create.

Today we can look with humor on some of the early ideas about prenatal development, but there was often little humor involved when such ideas were being debated. For centuries a question raised by Aristotle was fiercely debated: Does the embryo exist preformed from the beginning and increase only in size, or does it develop through successive stages? Aristotle favored the developmental, or *epigenic*, theory. As we mentioned in Chapter 2, however, some scientists claimed they could see tiny, preformed embryos in the sperm or egg, even after the microscope came into use. It was not until the late 1700s and early 1800s that preformationism was soundly disputed by work with the chick embryo, whose epigenic development could easily be observed. Preformationism was succeeded by the idea of predeterminism, which argued that although structures were not actually formed at the beginning, the form they would take was predetermined *by the genes*. This concept provided the basis for the maturational interpretation of development discussed in Chapter 3.

Though ideas such as these have changed, the notions of that time invariably influenced policies and practices. For example, during a period when a child's sex was thought to be determined by the woman, husbands could divorce wives who had not borne them a son.

Current Knowledge

Experts in human embryology now can tell us precisely how a new person gets started and how development unfolds. We know the order of formation of the heart, lungs, and brain, and how they change during the prenatal period. These changes are explained in Table 4-1.

Table 4-1. Prenatal development

Age in weeks	Emerging structures	Emerging functions and behaviors	Total weight and length (end of period)	Head length (% of total body length)	Trunk length (% of total body length)	Lower limb length (% of total body length)
0–1	Embryoblast and trophoblast					
1–2	Embryonic disk; tendrils from trophoblast (beginning of placenta)		0.2mm	65	35	
2–3	Neural groove; blood vessels, somites (precursors of muscles); blood cells; head and tail regions		2.7mm			
3–4	Mouth cavity; upper limb buds (arms); heart, brain, and lung buds	Primitive circulation of blood; heartbeat	4mm			
4–6	Eyes; inner nose; lungs; liver; eustachian tube; esophagus; stomach; intestine; kidney; trachea; thyroid; parathyroid and thymus glands; primary tooth buds; bones in inner ear; lower limb buds; tongue and palate		12mm (0.5 in)			

Table continues on following page.

Table 4-1 continued

Age in weeks	Emerging structures	Emerging functions and behaviors	Total weight and length (end of period)		Head length (% of total body length)	Trunk length (% of total body length)	Lower limb length (% of total body length)
6–8	Limb buds differentiate into parts of arms and legs; upper and lower jaw; external structures of nose; external features of ear; eyelids seal eyes; testes and ovaries	Liver produces bile; sex hormones produced by testes	2g (1/14 oz)	39mm (1.5 in)	44	36	20
8–10	Hands and fingers; feet and toes; bone development in head, trunk and limbs; muscles; rapid nerve cell multiplication in brain	Response to touch	20g (5/7 oz)	8cm (3.2 in)			
10–14	Differentiation of male and female genitalia	Liver produces blood cells; kidneys secrete urine; spontaneous movements of arms and legs; sucking movements; extension of trunk	130g (4.6 oz)	15.5cm (6 in)			
14–19	Bronchial branches; body hair (lanugo)	Grasping reflex; tonic neck reflex	400g (14 oz)	24.4cm (9.6 in)	32	36	32

Week	Developments	Weight	Length			
19–22	Hair on head; nails on fingers and toes; enamel crowns on primary tooth buds; tooth buds for permanent teeth; eyelashes and eyebrows; air sacs of lungs	650g (1.5 lbs)	29.2cm (11.5 in)			
	Swallowing; rhythmic contractions of intestines; movement of fluid in and out of lungs (breathing movements)					
22–26	Taste buds; sweat glands; oil glands at base of hair follicles; eyelids open; myelinization of brain begins	1130g (2.5 lbs)	35.2cm (14.2 in)			
	Oil glands produce substance that combines with dead skin cells to form vernix caseosa; opening and closing of eye; crying, if born prematurely, will breathe for a short period					
27–30		1750g (3.9 lbs)	40.7cm (16 in)			
	Eyes respond to light; taste buds sensitive to sweet, sour, and bitter substances; response to touch and pain					
30–34	Fat tissue under skin; mammary gland ducts; terminal air sacs in lungs (alveoli)	2490g (5.5 lbs)	45.8cm (18 in)			
34–38		3330g (7.3 lbs)	50.6cm (19.9 in)	25	42	33
	Surfactant in lung surface necessary for gas exchange is produced; hiccoughs					

SOURCE: Arey, L. D. Developmental anatomy, 7th Ed. Philadelphia: Saunders, 1965.

The first period of prenatal development, called the *period of the ovum*, begins in one of the *fallopian tubes*, which is entered by the ovum when it is released from the ovary (see Figure 4-5). It is here that fertilization takes place; the resulting zygote begins to undergo cell division as it continues to move toward the uterus. In about three days the cluster of twenty to thirty cells enters the uterine cavity, where it organizes itself into a hollow ball. In one area of this single layer of cells is a group of larger cells, called the *embryoblast*, that will develop into the embryo itself. The rest of the layer, the *trophoblast*, will develop into structures such as the *placenta* and *chorion*, which will nourish and support the developing embryo. About six to seven days after fertilization, the embryo attaches itself to the uterine wall. Four or five days later, it becomes embedded in the uterine wall.

In some cases the fertilized ovum does not descend the complete length of the fallopian tube; instead it becomes attached to the fallopian tube wall. A pregnancy that develops outside the uterus is known as an *ectopic* pregnancy. It must be terminated by surgery.

The second period of prenatal development, called the *period of the embryo*, lasts until the end of the eighth week. This period is a time of extremely rapid differentiation and change. All the major structures of the body are formed during this time, and some begin to function. The heart, brain, liver, and lungs appear. The liver begins to produce blood cells and the heart begins to beat.

Because body structures are forming during the period of the embryo, environmental influences such as drugs, infections, and irradiation can have devastating effects. This is the period of prenatal development when the developing organism is most vulnerable to insults from outside agents.

The third and final period of prenatal development, the *period of the fetus*, lasts from the ninth week until birth. During this period, structural development continues until completion. The major part of the fetus's growth takes place, and all body systems begin to function.

It is early in this period that the external genitalia begin to develop. Though the genes inherited at conception determine whether a boy or girl will develop, both boys and girls initially develop as females. The release of male hormones, known as androgens, by the male embryo's testes during the sixth week after conception triggers the development of the external male genitalia. On rare occasions this hormone is not released, and the child who develops is genetically a male, but physically a female.

During this period the expectant mother begins to feel the baby's movements, beginning in the fifth month. These movements become stronger as the pregnancy progresses, until near the end they can keep the mother awake at night. Babies born as early as twenty-eight weeks may survive.

During prenatal development, various body parts grow at different rates and at different times. At first, the head region grows very quickly compared to the trunk and lower limbs. Later these structures grow faster, catching up to a certain extent, but the head is always more fully developed than other parts of the body.

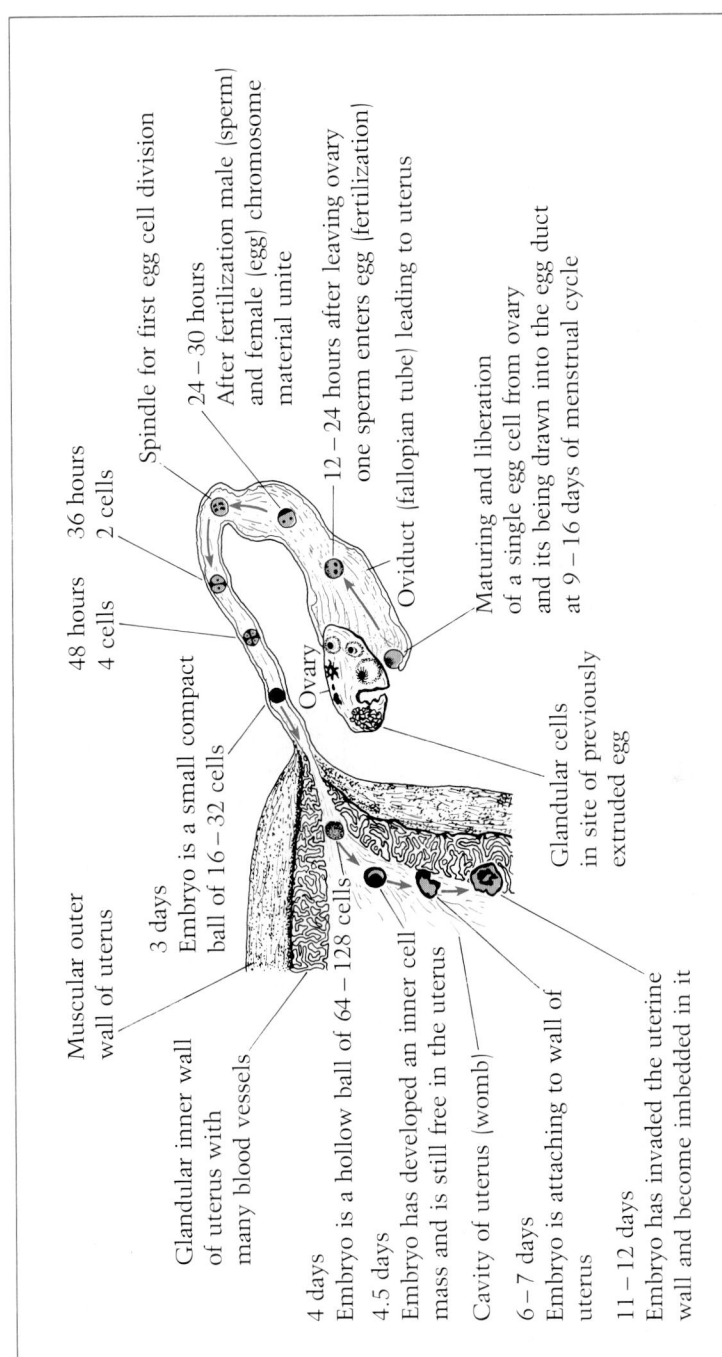

Figure 4-5. Fertilization and cell division in the fallopian tube (period of the ovum)

This is why babies and young children are "top-heavy" compared to older children and adults.

Table 4-1 may give the impression that growth and development proceed in a static, additive fashion, but this is not the case. Growth processes are fluid and dynamic. Structures emerge, disappear, change position, and shrink, as well as grow (Meredith, 1975b). Gill arches and pouches present at three and four weeks of fetal age disappear later, developing into structures such as the bones of the inner ear, the larynx, and the thyroid gland. Long bones increase in size at their ends, but bone tissue is absorbed from their centers to permit the growth of marrow (Meredith, 1975b).

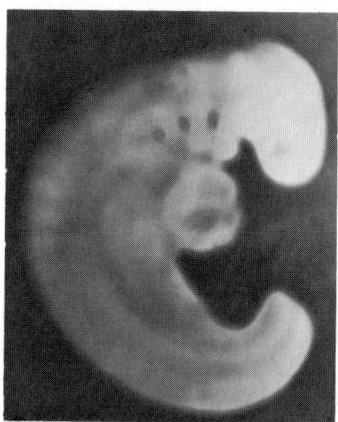

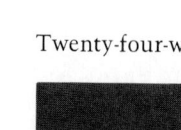
Four-week-old embryo

Twenty-four-week-old fetus

Twelve-week-old fetus

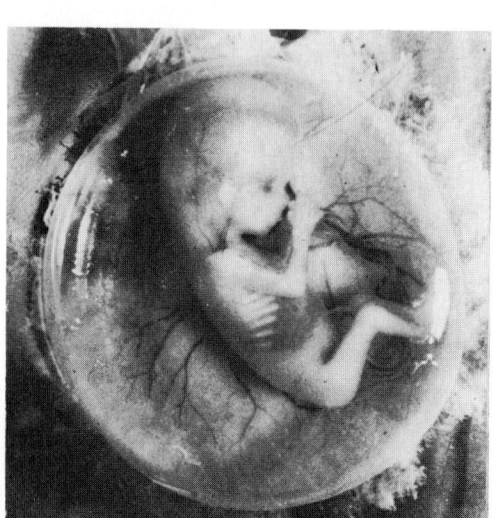

Birth

After about 266 days of prenatal development, the child moves from the uterus into the outside world. Birth is the name given to the process that accomplishes this movement.

The Physical Process

There are three stages in the birth process. During the first and longest, *opening*, the neck of the uterus (cervix) which protrudes into the vagina dilates. During the second, or *expulsion*, stage, the fetus passes out of the uterus through the cervix, on through the vagina, and out of the mother's body. It is during this stage that the child is born. During the final stage, *afterbirth*, the placenta is expelled. The entire process is accomplished by strong uterine contractions. On the average, it takes twelve hours for women having their first baby and seven hours for women having subsequent babies, but average hours can be misleading. The first stage alone can range from eight to twenty hours for a first baby and three to eight hours for a second (Ingalls and Salerno, 1975).

In recent years, the participation of the mother in the birth process has been receiving greater emphasis. This is due in part to the efforts of Dr. Grantly Dick-Read, who suggested in 1932 that the pain of childbirth results from learned fears and anxieties that interfere with the natural processes involved in birth. Dick-Read organized childbirth classes and taught physical and respiratory relaxation.

Another natural childbirth method currently popular in the United States is the Lamaze method, which also teaches mothers and fathers how to participate in the birth process. Lamaze's theory about the pain of childbirth is slightly different from that of Dick-Read. Whereas Dick-Read claimed that childbirth need not involve pain if a mother can rid herself of related fears and anxieties, Lamaze admitted that childbirth can be painful. He also claimed, however, that mothers can learn to concentrate on other activities to keep the brain preoccupied and unreceptive to signals it receives from the uterus (Miller and Brooten, 1977). Lamaze training involves learning breathing exercises that resemble those recommended by Dick-Read. Whichever method is used, medication to the mother can often be reduced or avoided completely. This is an important advantage: the evidence indicates that medication given to the mother during labor and delivery can adversely affect the newborn baby (Aleksandrowicz, 1974; Dodson, 1976).

The Social and Psychological Context of Birth

Giving birth is a physical experience, but it has psychological effects as well. As the emotional aspects of birth have become more widely recognized in recent years, hospital and obstetrical procedures have been altered to provide more support to parents and babies. Some of these arrangements are reviewed below.

Involvement of Fathers. Fathers are increasingly becoming involved in the birth process. This not only enables them to support the mother during delivery, it helps them establish good relationships with their children. Fathers' comments in a British study conducted by Greenburg and Morris (1974) illustrate how strong the effect of experiences with a newborn can be. One father was struck by his newborn daughter's uniqueness:

> There was much more character in the child than I ever thought there was going to be at that stage *in the face*. I mean it didn't remind me of anybody, but it seemed to have a personality immediately. . . . It was absolutely incredible, the sight itself. [p. 523]

Another father, who didn't witness the birth but saw his baby immediately afterward, was taken by his child's abilities:

> I was so surprised to find that it was already, even at this age, doing certain things like moving itself around. I thought it was going to be an object that just was going to be there. And it was looking around and it was gripping. At least I think it was gripping. You put your finger in its hand, and it was holding on . . . and when they just wrapped it up and put it in the cot by the side, it immediately took on somebody — somebody that one could look at and touch; and it was moving immediately. [p. 524]

Other fathers talked about their strong attachment to their newborns:

> I thought if it was going to be a boy and everything were going to be great, we could go out and jump around together and play about together. I was thinking about eighteen months, two years, two-and-one-half years, then we'd start to have a relationship. And I thought for the first eighteen months, it would be for the wife and everything would be fine for her and I'd just take it easy. But it wasn't like that at all. It was completely different. The kid was born — and I was there — and I really had a strong feeling toward her. [p. 525]

> When I come up to see me wife and I say "Hi! How's things, everything all right, you need anything?" And then I pick her up and then I put her down and then I say, "Hi! is everything all right?" And then I go back to the kid. I keep going back to the kid. It's like a magnet. That's what I can't get over, the fact that I feel like that. [p. 526]

You can see that fathers who participate in the hospital birth experience with their infants are not as passive toward them as our stereotype of males has suggested. In one study (Parke, 1975), mothers and fathers were observed with their newborn infants in the hospital on the second and fourth days after birth. They were observed in three situations: father alone with baby, mother alone with baby, and mother and father together with baby. The father's behavior when alone with baby resembled the mother's behavior alone with baby. But, surprisingly, when all three were together, the father held the baby twice as much as the mother, and talked to and touched the baby more, though mothers smiled more often. It appears that fathers who spend time with their newborns are apt to get "hooked." Today, we recognize the importance of permitting this to happen.

Rooming-in, Birthing Rooms, and Early Discharge. Some hospitals encourage parent-child relationships by providing rooming-in arrangements, which allow mother and baby to stay together in one room. Until its effects on the mother-child relationship were realized, the practice of keeping mothers in one room and babies in the hospital nursery was widespread. Some hospitals have a partial rooming-in arrangement, in which the baby stays with the mother throughout the day but is taken to the hospital nursery during the night.

The emotional effect of separating mothers from their newborns is evident in the comments of this mother, who gave birth in a hospital without rooming-in facilities:

> I remember feeling very strange, to have experienced the most re-
> markable of all things, the birth of my first child, and then to be left
> all alone. First they took the baby into the nursery. Then I was
> wheeled into my room, where my husband was able to stay and chat
> for a while. But he had to work the next day, so he needed some
> sleep. I was tired, but too excited to sleep. So there I was, alone,
> remembering the experience full of wonder and amazement that we
> had all shared. But for the next few hours we were not sharing. The
> hospital had separated us. [Bell et al., 1973, p. 204]

Rooming-in nurtures the parent-child relationship.

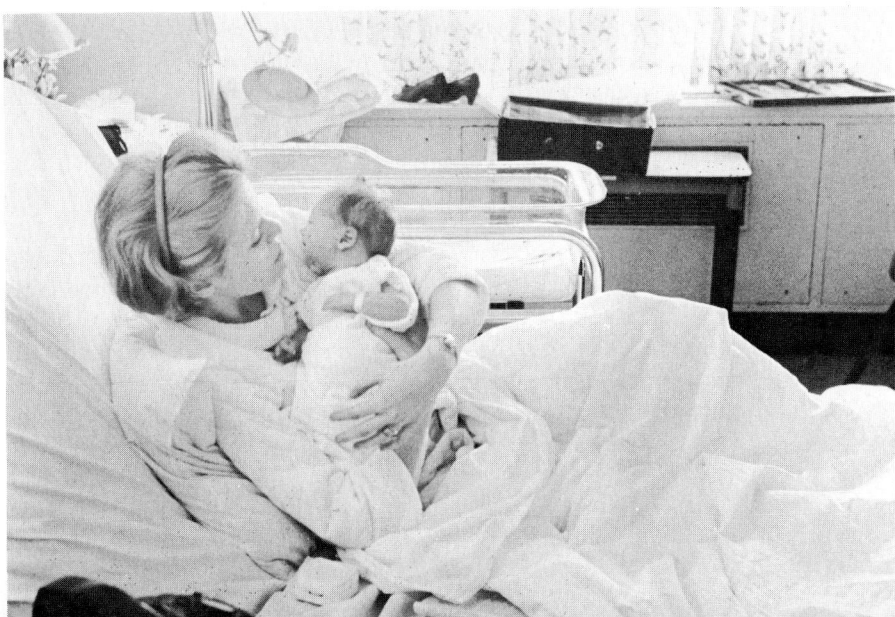

Rooming-in might have diminished this new mother's feelings of isolation and given her relationship with her child a better start (O'Connor et al., 1979). A brief paternity leave for the father might also have helped.

Some hospitals try to render the hospital atmosphere more homelike by providing birthing rooms. As the name suggests, these are rooms where babies are born, but they are furnished comfortably and resemble a room in a home more than a hospital room. In these rooms fathers can be with mothers throughout labor and delivery, and the mother does not have to undergo the inconvenience of being moved from the labor to the delivery room, just at the point when she would prefer to focus her entire attention on the birth process.

The separation traditionally imposed on families by hospitals can also be diminished by allowing mother and baby to go home as soon as possible. If both mother and baby are healthy, there is no need for a long hospital stay. They are sometimes allowed to leave just a few hours after the baby's birth.

Some hospitals have a visiting nurse program connected with their early discharge program. This program provides several days of follow-up medical care to the mother and baby at home rather than in a hospital. It not only permits parent and child to be together during the first few days after birth; it also reduces the cost of giving birth considerably. Double-occupancy hospital rooms can easily cost $200 or more a day, and the newborn nursery charge can be between $60 and $100 a day.

Some people have rejected any type of hospital birthing experience and have decided to have their children at home or in a birthing center, which is similar to an outpatient medical clinic. In fact, these alternative choices may have played a large role in bringing about the changes discussed above in hospital maternity practices.

Changes in Delivery Practices. Delivery practices have also been changed to encourage good parent-child relationships. By decreasing the amount of medication given to the mother during labor and delivery, the hospital reduces physical risks to the infant. The infant is then more alert and responsive immediately after birth, and able to interact with the parent. The recent interest in "natural" childbirth, or childbirth as free of drugs as possible, is due in part to an increased awareness of the effects of drugs on the child's psychological well-being. A mother may react differently to an infant who is alert and calm than she would to a groggy infant (Brazelton, 1961, 1970).

Another change is the "birth without violence" procedure introduced by Frederich Leboyer (1975), a French obstetrician. This method is claimed to result in the birth of calmer, more alert babies. Leboyer argues that newborns need not engage in lengthy crying — that crying is not "normal" or "natural" but the result of being held upside-down and slapped. According to Leboyer, newborns typically emit a few short cries and stop. The procedure he suggests involves dimming the lights and lowering voices when the baby is born. The baby is also given a warm bath.

FOCUS: The Increase in Cesarean Births

Cesarean birth is delivery of the child through an incision in the abdominal wall. This method of delivery is necessary if the mother's pelvis is not large enough to permit passage of the baby, or if the baby is in the breech position — feet or buttocks, rather than head, down. Cesarean delivery is also performed if the placenta covers the cervix (the entrance to the womb), rather than being higher in the uterus (Guttmacher, 1973). Finally, cesarean delivery is performed if the fetus shows signs of distress, such as a slowed heart rate, or if the mother cannot undergo the stress of a normal labor and delivery for some medical reason.

Cesarean deliveries have tripled during the last ten years (Bottoms et al., 1980). In some hospitals as many as 20 percent of all deliveries are by cesarean (Beth Israel Hospital, 1981). Today such deliveries create less risk than fifteen or twenty years ago, because there is better control of infection with antibiotics and there are better methods of anesthesia. In fact, mothers are often given a local rather than a general anesthetic today when undergoing a cesarean; therefore, they can remain conscious during the whole procedure. The increase of cesarean deliveries also reflects more sophisticated techniques for detecting fetal distress. Fetal monitoring, for example, can accurately detect a slowed heart rate due to stress from inadequate oxygen during labor; this condition may lead to a decision to perform a cesarean delivery.

There is some controversy over whether too many cesarean deliveries are being performed. Those who argue in favor of the increase suggest that the greater safety of the procedure makes a cesarean delivery better for the baby and mother than a prolonged and stressful vaginal delivery would be. Those who urge conservative use of cesarean deliveries argue that it is major abdominal surgery, which always carries some risk, and should not therefore be used for convenience or when a vaginal delivery is possible without undue risk.

The debate about cesarean births probably reflects, in part, larger debates about childbirth: naturalness versus technical and mechanical intervention, and participation and control by the mother versus delivery by physicians using sophisticated machines. Perhaps these opposing viewpoints will be resolved when we can better differentiate cases that truly require mechanical and technical intervention and those that do not.

Research on the effects of the Leboyer method yields mixed results. A study by Salter (1978) indicates that babies born by this method cry less in the period following birth than control babies. But in another study (Hamilton, 1979), Leboyer babies actually cried for longer periods than the controls. More research is needed to provide conclusive results.

The possibility that Leboyer's claims may be borne out by research illustrates an important point: We must be careful about referring to a behavior as "natural" or "normal," as if the behavior existed in the child without reference to external events and would occur under any conditions. We think behaviors that appear

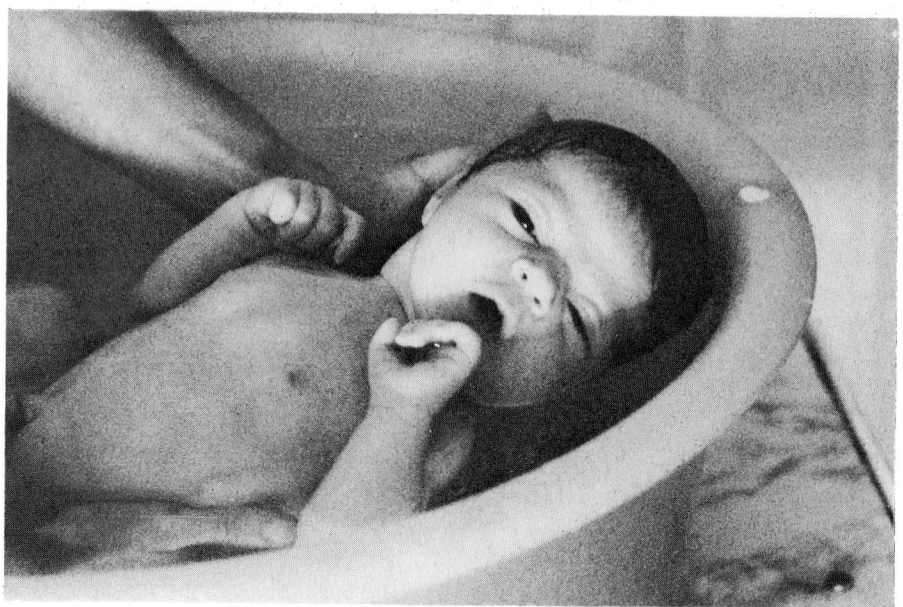

The Leboyer method includes immersion in a warm bath soon after birth.

regularly are inherent in the child, but their appearance may be the result of standardized practices. In this country, we think of vigorous crying at birth as "natural," but it may be common because the procedures that elicit it are widespread.

Another point raised by the Leboyer research was discussed earlier: if we are to agree about data, we must specify the group from which the data are collected. Infants delivered with the Leboyer technique are different from those delivered with more standard American techniques; they have been treated differently and their parents may be different from those who chose other methods. It is important to explain what groups of infants were observed when presenting data on their behavior.

Problems in Early Development

Two types of problems can affect early development. Some can be attributed to genes and chromosomes the child inherited. Others are *congenital;* they are present at birth as if inherited, but they are not inherited. Congenital problems can be caused by factors that influence the developing baby during the prenatal period. Other congenital problems result from the birth process itself. Together, genetic and congenital problems are known as *birth defects.*

Gene-Related Problems

Sickle-cell anemia, cystic fibrosis, phenylketonuria, and Tay-Sachs disease are gene-related disorders. Their effects are apparent at birth or soon after. All are caused by the inheritance of a pair of abnormal recessive genes. Recessive genes, as you may remember, must be inherited in pairs for their trait to be expressed. Traits carried by dominant genes, however, are expressed when only one of the genes is present (see Box 4-1). Another disorder, Rh disease, is due not to the inheritance of abnormal genes, but to incompatibility between proteins in the blood of the fetus and its mother.

Sickle-Cell Anemia. *Sickle-cell anemia* is caused by the abnormal develop-ment of hemoglobin, the oxygen-carrying component in red blood cells (Ingram, 1961). The red blood cells of persons with this abnormality "sickle," or change shape, during periods of infection or stress, when oxygen intake is reduced at high altitudes, and under other conditions. Sickled cells are more susceptible than normal red blood cells to damage and destruction. They also stick together or clump. Clumping impairs the flow of blood, which can result in the death of

BOX 4-1. Probability of inheriting a disease carried by recessive genes

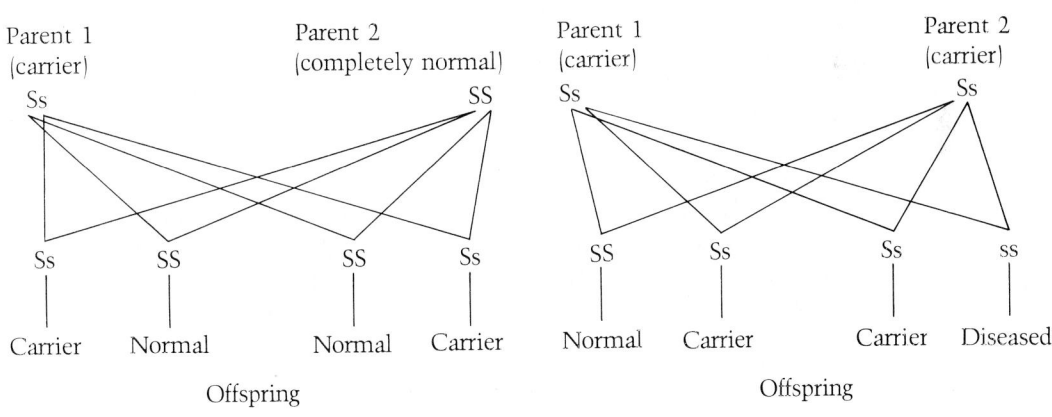

1. If one parent is a carrier for the disease and the other parent neither has the disease nor carries it, what are the chances that a child will (a) get the disease, (b) be a carrier for the disease?

2. If both parents are carriers for the disease, what is the probability that a child will be a carrier? That a child will inherit the disease? (Answers are on p. 103.)

NOTE: Uppercase S indicates a dominant gene. Lowercase s indicates a recessive gene.

tissues due to lack of oxygen. Children who suffer from sickle-cell anemia may be irritable and have poor appetites, swollen abdomens, and yellowish eyes. Few survive to adulthood (Linde, 1972).

The sickle-cell disease afflicts people of African ancestry far more frequently than others. This is probably because sickle cells are resistant to malaria, a disease that has been common in Africa. The trait increased chances for survival, and as a result many people of African ancestry possess it (Livingstone, 1967).

But how can a life-threatening disease protect a person from another disease? The answer is that persons may be *carriers* of the sickle-cell trait and have some sickle-shaped cells, without suffering from the disease. Those who inherit only one gene for the sickle cell are resistant to malaria but do not develop anemia; it is these people whose chances for survival are increased (Lerner, 1968).

About 10 percent of the American black population carry the sickle-cell trait. A blood test will reveal whether a person is a carrier. This information can be useful in genetic counseling.

Cystic Fibrosis. *Cystic fibrosis*, which affects about one child in 1000, also results from the inheritance of two abnormal genes. Victims of the disease develop thick mucus in the lungs and intestinal tract. The mucus causes serious problems such as pneumonia.

The rate of survival for children with cystic fibrosis has improved considerably in recent years. In the 1940s about 70 percent of the children born with cystic fibrosis died during the first year, and 95 percent by age five. By the 1970s more than 25 percent of those affected were living into adulthood as the result of effective antibiotic and enzyme therapy. A recently developed test to detect carriers of the disease can be used in counseling to prevent birth of children afflicted with cystic fibrosis.

Phenylketonuria. Children born with *phenylketonuria* (PKU) are unable to produce an enzyme that is needed to metabolize one amino acid (phenylalanine) into another (tryosine). The toxins that accumulate because of this problem destroy nerve tissue and cause severe mental retardation (Stern, 1973).

PKU can be detected with a urine test. In most states, hospitals must administer this test to all newborns. With early detection, retardation can be minimized by limiting the consumption of foods such as milk and other protein substances that contain high levels of phenylalanine (Fuller and Schuman, 1971).

Tay-Sachs Disease. Another metabolic disorder resulting from the inheritance of two recessive genes is *Tay-Sachs disease.* Children who are afflicted cannot metabolize fat properly, which causes the brain and other nervous tissue to deteriorate. There is no treatment for the condition; it proves fatal by the age of three or four.

Tay-Sachs disease is found predominantly among Jews of eastern European ancestry. Carriers of the recessive gene can be identified with a blood test, and couples in which both persons are carriers can decide if they wish to take the one-in-four chance that a pregnancy will result in an afflicted child. If they take the chance, *amniocentesis* — the procedure of extracting a sample of the fluid surrounding the fetus — can then be used to see if the child conceived does in fact have the disease.

Rh Disease. *Rh disease* is a genetically-related disorder caused by the interaction between a specific factor (protein) in the blood of the fetus and its mother's blood. The factor is called the *Rh* factor because it was first identified in the rhesus monkey. Persons with this factor are Rh positive; persons without it are Rh negative. The problem arises when a child is conceived by an Rh-negative mother and an Rh-positive father. If the baby inherits the Rh-positive characteristic from the father, then the blood of the baby and its mother will be incompatible. If some of the baby's blood enters the mother's bloodstream during delivery, it will cause the mother to develop antibodies just as she might toward a virus. The first child is not harmed, because at that time no antibodies have been produced in the mother's bloodstream. But subsequent Rh-positive children are likely to be harmed, because the antibodies developed in response to the earlier pregnancy will destroy red blood cells of the fetus. The destruction of these oxygen-carrying cells causes jaundice, anemia, and other problems, which can lead to mental retardation or death (Snyder, Schonfeld, and Offerman, 1945).

Fortunately, a serum called Rhogam, which destroys the Rh-positive cells as they enter the mother's body, is now available. It prevents the development of antibodies by the mother if it is given to her within a few hours after she has given birth to an Rh-positive child (Clarke, 1968; Zimmerman, 1973). This vaccine is a major success story in the fight against birth defects. Before it was developed in the 1960s, about 40,000 babies each year were affected with the Rh disorder.

Chromosome-Related Problems

Down's syndrome is one of the most common conditions resulting from chromosome abnormality. Persons with Down's syndrome have three number 21 chromosomes rather than the normal pair. (Down's syndrome is also called trisomy 21, which means "three bodies" 21.) This happens when the halves (chromatids) of the number 21 chromosome do not separate during the last cell division of meiosis. As a result, two of the four cells formed have the usual single twenty-first chromosome, but one of the four has two of these chromosomes, and the fourth cell has none (Kerkay, Zsako, and Kaplan, 1971; Lilienfield, 1969). Ova that lack the twenty-first chromosome do not live, but ova with two do. If an ovum with two of these chromosomes is fertilized, the sperm contributes another, and the child has three. It is this child who has Down's syndrome.

Down's syndrome occurs about once in every 600 births. Women over the age of thirty-five are more likely to give birth to a child with Down's syndrome

A child with
Down's syndrome

than women between the ages of twenty and thirty-five. We do not know exactly why older women carry a higher risk; perhaps it is related to the aging of the ova or accumulated damage to genetic material as a result of environmental conditions such as radiation or chemicals.

Other chromosomal abnormalities are associated with problems in development. Klinefelter's syndrome, for example, results when a male receives an extra X chromosome. Males with this problem are mentally retarded and develop some female characteristics at puberty (Johnson et al., 1970). Males may also inherit an extra Y chromosome, which also seems to impair intellectual functioning (Witkin et al., 1976).

Problems Due to Environmental Factors

Following the epidemic of *rubella* (German measles) in 1964–65 in the United States, nearly 50,000 children died *in utero* or were born with birth defects. A few years earlier, hundreds of European mothers who had taken the tranquilizing drug thalidomide gave birth to babies without limbs (Lenz, 1966). These are just two of the many environmental factors that can impair prenatal development. There are many others, including inadequate diet, irradiation, smoking, and alcohol.

Some of the agents and conditions known to affect prenatal development are listed in Table 4-2. The majority are most dangerous early in pregnancy during the period of rapid differentiation of basic structures. German measles may affect eyes, ears, and brain during the first trimester of pregnancy, but it may cause little harm if it strikes later. Similarly, women who took thalidomide early in pregnancy gave birth to children without arms and legs, but those who took the drug after the fetus's arms, legs, hands, and feet were basically formed, were not affected.

The effects of narcotics and other drugs have been examined more intensively in recent years as drug abuse has increased. Narcotic drugs are usually not

Table 4-2. Environmental factors that adversely affect prenatal development

Agent or condition	Effects
Rubella (German measles)	Blindness; deafness; heart abnormalities; stillbirth
Syphilis	Mental retardation; physical deformities; miscarriage
Addictive drugs	Low birth weight; addiction of infant to drug, with possible death after birth from withdrawal
Smoking	Prematurity; low birth weight and length[a]
Alcohol	Mental retardation; smaller-than-average birthweight; microcephaly (smallness of the head)[a]
Irradiation	Physical deformities and mental retardation
Inadequate diet	Reduction in growth of brain; smaller than average birthweight; decrease in birth length; rickets
Tetracycline	Discoloration of teeth
Quinine	Deafness
Barbiturates	Congenital malformations
Endocrine disorders	Cretinism; microcephaly
Maternal age of less than 18	Prematurity and stillbirth; increased incidence of Down's syndrome
Maternal age of more than 35	Increased incidence of Down's syndrome
DES (diethylstilbestrol)	Increased incidence of vaginal cancer in adolescent girls whose mothers were given DES during pregnancy to prevent miscarriage; impaired reproductive performance in same population

[a]Evidence is correlational.
SOURCE: Berger and Goldstein, 1980; Brown, 1979; Greenburg, Pellituri, and Barton, 1957; Herbst, 1972; Herbst, Scully, and Robbey, 1975; Lenz, 1966; Meredith, 1975a; Naeye, Blanc, and Paul, 1973; Plummer, 1952; Siegel, Fuerst, and Guinee, 1971; Snyder, Schonfield, and Offerman, 1945; Walters, 1975.

teratogenic; that is, they do not cause birth defects such as ill-formed limbs or cleft palate, but about 50 percent of the babies born to narcotic addicts have a low birth weight (Brown, 1979). A period of withdrawal in the mother can kill the fetus, and a fetus that survives will suffer withdrawal itself soon after birth. Such infants usually need to be treated with narcotics for a time to prevent abrupt withdrawal and subsequent vomiting, diarrhea, dehydration, and convulsions (Brown, 1979). Obviously, this is a poor way to start life.

Infants born to women who take methadone, a substitute for heroin, also suffer withdrawal to a certain extent. A recent study of women taking methadone indicates that infants born to women narcotics addicts are more likely than other infants to fall victim to Sudden Infant Death syndrome, the death that occurs during sleep of an apparently healthy infant. This affliction claims the lives of 2.5 percent of the infants born to addicts, whereas the incidence among women who are not addicted is only 0.5 percent (Chavez et al., 1979).

Alcohol is also associated with problems in prenatal development, including mental retardation, smaller than average birthweight, and microcephaly or abnormal smallness of the head (Streissguth, 1979). In addition, alcoholic women are relatively likely to suffer from malnutrition and injuries due to falls, which can also harm a developing fetus.

There is even evidence that caffeine can affect prenatal development. Though caffeine itself may not be teratogenic, it appears to be *coteratogenic* — it increases the risk from other teratogenic agents, such as irradiation (Kihlman, 1977).

Much of the evidence that various agents affect the development of the unborn child is correlational. This is because researchers try to discover common habits among the mothers of children born with a particular problem. They might find, for example, that the mothers of microcephalic babies (babies with abnormally small heads) drink more alcohol than the mothers of normal babies. Correlational evidence such as this does not prove causation, however. The commonalities detected among a group of mothers may not be the causative factors. The experimental studies necessary to prove causation are of course unethical, except with animals.

But the lack of absolutely conclusive proof of causation should not lead us to dismiss research evidence and delay protective action. For example, the 1979 report of the surgeon general and other sources provide strong evidence that smoking by pregnant women injures their unborn children. It is possible that some factor common to the group of women who smoke, other than smoking itself, causes the difficulties we have associated with smoking. But researchers have controlled for so many other possible factors that it seems likely that smoking is indeed the culprit (Naeye, 1981). There is at any rate no evidence that smoking has a positive effect on a fetus. The safest course is to discourage smoking during pregnancy.

Passing on a defective gene or chromosome to a child is largely a matter of chance, and in many cases it is impossible to improve one's probability of conceiving a healthy baby, but when it comes to the factors discussed above, a person can exercise some control. Parents can insist that children be immunized against rubella, and schools can refuse to admit children who have not been immunized. Immunizing children against rubella to prevent outbreaks of the disease is the primary method of preventing pregnant women from contracting the disease. Pregnant women can watch their diet, and we as a society can make an effort to inform young people about the principles of good nutrition. Tobacco, alcohol, and drugs can be avoided, but this is more difficult when a woman enters a pregnancy already addicted. X rays can also be avoided unless serious illness makes them mandatory.

Problems Resulting from the Birth Process

Lack of Oxygen. During birth, the chief danger to the infant is deprivation of oxygen, which can occur in many ways. A difficult delivery can cause the blood vessels in the infant's head to break, interrupting the flow of oxygen to the brain. Premature infants are especially vulnerable to this problem, because they lack the padding of subcutaneous fat characteristic of full-term babies. Oxygen deprivation, or *anoxia*, affects the lower centers of the brain most severely, and can impair motor functioning that these centers control. Cerebral palsy is one syndrome that can result when the lower brain centers are damaged at birth. Because these parts of the brain are not involved in the thinking processes, people with cerebral palsy do not necessarily have impaired intelligence (Denhoff and Robinault, 1960). (See Figure 4-6 for a diagram of brain structure.)

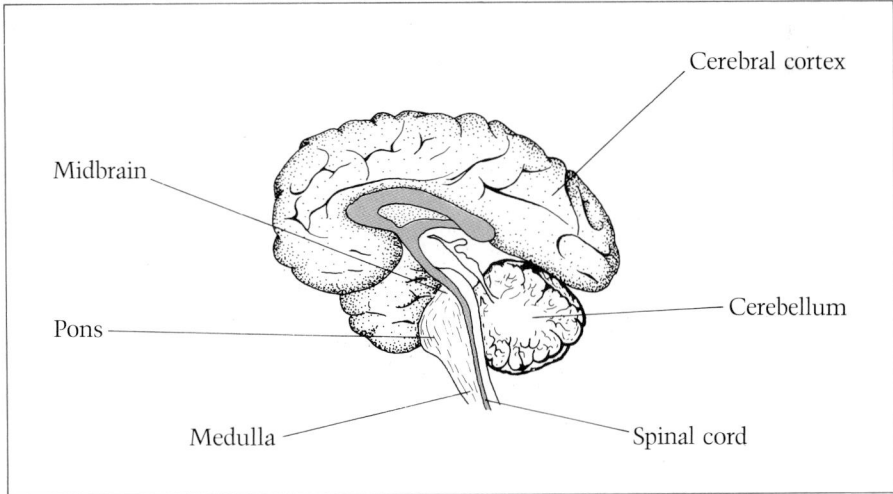

Figure 4-6. The human brain. The cerebral cortex is the center of thinking processes. Lower brain structures, such as the cerebellum, play roles in coordinating motor movements.

Oxygen shortage can also occur immediately after birth if the infant has trouble beginning to breathe. Breathing difficulties are most common among premature babies and those whose mothers were given certain pain-relieving drugs. Almost any drug given to a mother during labor can affect the fetus as well, and can depress the newborn's responsiveness. Drugs that enter our bodies frequently undergo a detoxifying process controlled by an enzyme in the liver before being eliminated. This process proceeds very slowly in the young infant. The mother may be free of the effects of the drugs in a few hours, but the baby may not be free of them for days (Aleksandrowicz, 1974). This drugged condition can impair not only biological functions such as breathing, but social interactions and relationships as well. As we stated earlier, parents may well feel differently about a newborn who is listless and unresponsive than they would about an alert baby.

Risk of Infection. Any infection of the mother's reproductive tract can be contracted by the infant as it is being born, or may infect the fetus before birth. Three infections are particularly serious: syphilis, gonorrhea, and herpes simplex virus. Syphilis can infect the developing fetus and cause it to die. Or if it is born alive, it will be infected with syphilis. Treatment of the mother with penicillin during pregnancy cures the infection in the fetus as well.

The chief danger to the child from gonorrhea is infection during delivery and subsequent blindness due to the infection. Newborns can be protected against gonorrhea infection by the administration of silver nitrate drops in the eyes soon after delivery. This procedure is common practice.

Herpes simplex virus also can be contracted by the baby during delivery from an infected mother if the mother's virus is in an active phase. The infection can cause eye damage and serious brain damage to the baby, and there is no medication to cure the infection. To avoid infecting the baby a cesarean delivery is often performed.

Translating Knowledge into Action

Prenatal Diagnosis and Genetic Counseling

Today, couples can seek information from a genetic counselor about the probability that they will have a child with a genetic disorder. The genetic counselor obtains a detailed medical and family history from the couple and uses this information along with his or her knowledge about the genetic basis of various diseases to determine the likelihood that an afflicted child will be conceived. The couple can then decide whether or not they wish to take the risk.

Some disorders, such as Down's syndrome and Tay-Sachs disease, can be detected in the fetus through amniocentesis, as we mentioned earlier. A sample of the fluid that surrounds a fourteen- to sixteen-week-old fetus is extracted by inserting a needle into the mother's abdomen. This fluid contains cells that have sloughed off the fetus much as dry cells fall off your own skin. After growing these cells in an artificial culture, doctors can perform chromosomal and biochemical analyses on them (Friedman, 1971; Miller and Erbe, 1978). If analyses reveal that the child's chromosomal pattern is defective, then the parents can decide whether to terminate the pregnancy.

Because genes have their effect through the control of enzymes, it is possible that the effects of genetic problems will eventually be counteracted by supplying enzymes chemically (Valenti, 1968). Should that occur, amniocentesis could be used to identify the fetuses that need such treatment. Such procedures must await further knowledge of the enzymes controlled by various genes and how they affect the body.

Genetic counseling and prenatal diagnosis of genetic problems have profound moral, social, and political implications. Consider, for example, the following questions: Which disorders are severe enough to be considered serious

FOCUS: The Use of Ultrasound in Prenatal Diagnosis

Ultrasound is a technique for detecting prenatal problems that was introduced during the last decade. Sound waves at a frequency far beyond the capacity of the human ear to detect are used in ultrasound; in fact, this is where the term, ultrasound, comes from.

Sound waves are absorbed or deflected according to the density of the substance they contact. For example, they bounce off of or create an echo when they strike bone, but they echo much less when they strike soft tissue, water, or blood. This differential deflection can be converted into electrical signals, which can then be converted into a visual image (Garrett and Robinson, 1970).

In prenatal diagnosis using ultrasound, a hand-held transducer that emits pulses of ultrasound is passed over the mother's abdomen. Deflected sound waves are converted into a visual image of the fetus on a TV monitor. Trained personnel read these images and can diagnose or prevent various problems.

Ultrasound is used routinely today in connection with amniocentesis. Before the amniocentesis is performed, ultrasound is used to see exactly where the fetus and placenta are located. By knowing where these structures are, the physician can avoid inserting the needle into them and causing damage.

Ultrasound can also be used to determine if multiple fetuses are present in the uterus, or if a fetus is in a position that will not allow a normal vaginal delivery. For example, a cesarean delivery will be needed if the fetus is lying across the mother's abdomen (transverse position) or if the placenta is partially covering the cervix.

Ultrasound is also used to detect gross problems in fetal anatomy. For example, an abnormally large head or an improperly formed spine can be seen, as can certain abnormalities of the heart.

problems? Can a civilized society decide that persons below a certain level of development are incapable of living a "worthwhile" life? If so, what level of development is sufficient to ensure a worthwhile life? Worthwhile in what terms, and from whose point of view? Who is to decide whether the solution to genetic problems lies in finding ways to treat afflicted individuals or in preventing such births altogether? If treatment methods are to be sought, which disorders should receive top priority? What are the social and political consequences of deciding that research into a disorder that has an especially high incidence in a particular ethnic group should take precedence over research into other disorders? Answers to questions such as these are more a matter of values and ethics than of science. See Milunsky and Annas (1976) for an extensive discussion of this topic.

Prenatal and Natal Health Care

Today, the importance of proper care during prenatal development and during the birth process itself is widely recognized. Adequate care is currently available to many women in this country, and superb care is provided to those who have access to tools such as ultrasound, and amniocentesis. Amniocentesis can be used not only to diagnose various inherited problems but also to determine, for example, the lung maturity of an unborn fetus. If a mother's health is in danger from some reason late in pregnancy, knowing how mature the unborn fetus is can inform an obstetrician about whether it is safe for the baby to be born early by inducing labor or performing a cesarean (Simon, et al., 1981).

Unfortunately, such care is not available to all. In 1975 Betty Caldwell, a well-known child development expert, testified before the United States Senate that "at present our services to children and families are too few, too inaccessible to those who need them most, and all too often, available too late to be of maximum help." The statistics bear her out. The infant mortality rate for white American infants ranks us eighth among industrial nations, but the mortality rate for nonwhites ranks us thirty-first. Babies with low birth weights are twice as likely to be born to nonwhite than to white mothers (*America's Children*, 1976). Seventy percent of all white mothers receive prenatal care during their first three months of pregnancy; only half as many nonwhite mothers receive care during this period (Keniston, 1977).

The discrepancy between our knowledge and our practices often leads to disenchantment among those who have just entered a profession. In the college classroom we discuss what we know how to do, but in the world outside the classroom we must find ways to act on what we know. The discrepancy between what we could do and what we actually do is sometimes enormous. But there have always been people who have worked to diminish the discrepancy, people like Grace Abbott, the second chief of the Children's Bureau. Her 1935 comments about the difficulty of making people aware of the needs of children are inspiring even now:

Sometimes when I get home at night in Washington I feel as though I had been in a great traffic jam. The jam is moving toward the Hill where Congress sits in judgment on all the administrative agencies of the Government. In that traffic jam there are all kinds of vehicles moving up toward the Capitol. . . . There are all kinds of conveyances that the Army can put into the streets — tanks, gun carriers, trucks. . . . There are the hayracks and the binders and the ploughs and all the other things that the Department of Agriculture manages to put into the streets . . . the handsome limousines in which the Department of State rides in such dignity. It seems so to me as I stand on the sidewalk watching it become more congested and more difficult, and then because the responsibility is mine and I must, I take a very firm hold on the handles of the baby carriage and I wheel it into the traffic. [Andrews, 1976, p. 122]

Today, some forty-five years later, a great deal remains to be done to improve the chances that children will be born healthy. Parents who are too young to know firsthand the effects of rubella need to be informed so they will insist that their own children be immunized. More research is needed on the effects of chemicals in the environment and those administered to pregnant women before or during labor and delivery. Services must be provided to young women before they become pregnant, as well as during their pregnancy, to ensure that what is known can be applied to help them have healthy babies. Finally, we must work to reaffirm the belief that children have a right to enter the world as healthy as possible. Although we often hear that "our children are our most precious resource," we continue to act in ways that suggest we do not take this statement seriously.

Summary

- An understanding of life before birth is of vital importance, because many events that will have a lasting effect on the child occur before birth.

Genetics
- Genetics is a branch of biology that deals with the heredity and variation of organisms. Genes are the basic mechanisms of variation; they determine a person's hair color, eye color, height, and many other characteristics. A dominant gene always expresses its characteristic; a recessive gene does so only when paired with another recessive gene.
- Germ cells are cells involved in reproduction. They divide by meiosis, a process that results in extensive genetic variability.
- It is the father, not the mother, who determines whether the fetus will be male or female.
- Multiple births occur when two or more ova are released at one time and are each fertilized by a sperm cell.

Prenatal Development

- Early ideas about reproduction and prenatal development, such as preformationism, affected social customs and standards of conduct. Now, many of these ideas and theories have proved to be incorrect.
- Prenatal development can be divided into three stages or periods: the ovum, the embryo, and the fetus. Fertilization takes place and the resulting zygote undergoes cell division during the period of the ovum. The major differentiation of body structures occurs during the period of the embryo. Most prenatal growth (that is, weight gain) occurs during the period of the fetus.

Birth

- The process of birth can also be divided into three stages: the opening; the expulsion, during which the baby is actually born; and the afterbirth.
- Hospital and obstetrical procedures have been altered in recent years because of recognition that the experience during and immediately after birth may have a long-term effect on the emotional ties that develop between parent and child. These changes include the increasing participation of fathers in the birth process, provision of rooming-in arrangements and birthing rooms, and increased practice of natural childbirth coupled with a decreased use of medication.

Problems in Early Development

- Birth defects are either congenital (present at birth but not inherited) or genetic (caused by genes and chromosomes inherited by the child).
- Sickle-cell anemia, cystic fibrosis, phenylketonuria, and Tay-Sachs disease are gene-related disturbances. Down's syndrome is caused by a chromosome abnormality.
- Environmental factors such as drugs, diseases, X rays, and malnutrition can adversely affect prenatal development and lead to congenital problems such as deformity, mental retardation, blindness and deafness, heart malfunction, and drug addiction.
- Other congenital defects are caused during the birth process itself. Two causes of such defects are infection and oxygen deprivation.

Translating Knowledge into Action

- Prenatal diagnosis and genetic counseling can help parents determine their chances of having a child with a genetic disorder. The decisions they make based on this information have far-reaching moral, social, and political implications.
- Good prenatal and natal care is essential for healthy mothers and babies, and should be available to everyone.

New Terms

genetics
genes
chromosomes
dominant genes
recessive genes
germ cells
somatic cells
ova
sperm
mitosis
meiosis
crossing-over
fraternal twins
identical twins
zygote

epigenic theory
period of the ovum
fallopian tubes
embryoblast
trophoblast
placenta
chorion
ectopic pregnancy
period of the embryo
period of the fetus
opening
expulsion
afterbirth
birth defects
sickle cell anemia

carriers
cystic fibrosis
phenylketonuria (PKU)
Tay-Sachs disease
amniocentesis
Rh disease
Down's syndrome
Klinefelter's syndrome
rubella
teratogenic
coteratogenic
anoxia
cerebral palsy
cesarean

Selected Readings

Bergsma, D. (Ed.). **Birth defects compendium,** 2d ed. *New York: A. R. Liss, 1979.* A comprehensive description of about 1000 birth defects, their origins and risks. Many illustrations.

Brigitte, J. **Birth in four cultures.** *Montreal, Canada: Eden Press, 1980.* A very interesting and readable little book written by an anthropologist. Brings a cultural perspective to the birthing process.

Ewy, D., and Ewy, R. **Preparation for childbirth.** *New York: The New American Library, 1972.* A guide to the Lamaze method of prepared childbirth. Easy to read.

McCauley, C. S. **Pregnancy after 35.** *New York: Pocket Books, 1976.* This nontechnical book discusses risks of pregnancy in the woman who decides to wait to have children. Also discussed are issues such as how a new baby fits into a working mother's life. Many anecdotes from actual cases make this a very interesting book.

Box Answers

Box 4-1:
1. There is a 50 percent chance that a child will be a carrier and a 50 percent chance that a child will be normal. There is no chance that a child will inherit the disease, because a child of this couple could not inherit two recessive genes.

2. There is a 50 percent chance that a child will be a carrier, a 25 percent chance that a child will be normal, and a 25 percent chance that a child will have the disease.

Chapter 5

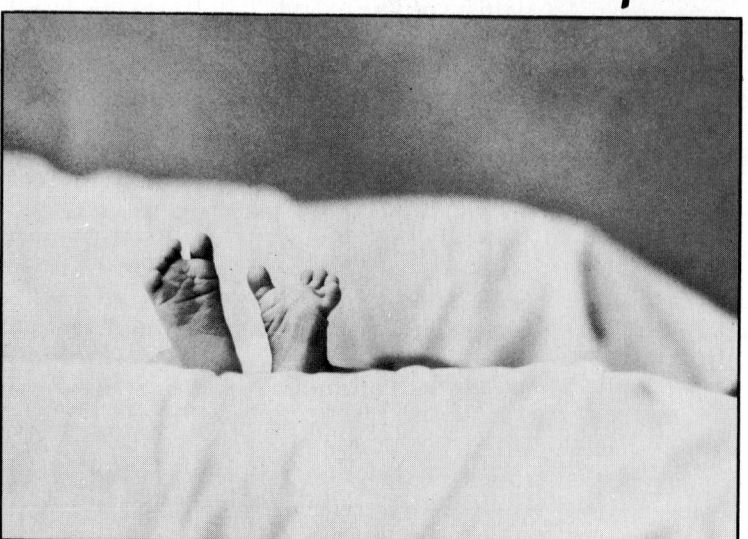

*T*he Neonate

The first few weeks of life are known as the *neonatal period*. During this time the infant's body makes the physiological changes necessary to adjust to life outside the womb. This adjustment can take a few days or a few weeks, depending on the infant's condition at birth — whether it is full-term or premature, for example.

If you ever have spent time with a newborn you may think that new babies sleep most of the time, cry some of the time, and eat the rest of the time — and they do. Ordinarily these might be considered pretty humdrum activities, but to the newborn they are quite novel. Until birth the neonate has relied on its mother for food, oxygen, warmth — all the necessities of life.

To foster development at this stage, you must know the usual sequence of the infant's adaptation to independent existence and how to provide effective support. A knowledge of the symptoms of poor adjustment is also important; intervention can sometimes save a life or prevent mental retardation.

The child's emotional development begins during the neonatal period. Communication also begins at this time, although it takes a different form than it does later in childhood. In fact, relationships formed in this early period appear to influence relationships later in childhood. The concern about the social and emotional aspects of birth (discussed in Chapter 4) grew out of the awareness that emotional attachment between parent and child begins immediately at birth.

In addition to being of practical interest to caregivers, the neonatal period is of theoretical interest to psychologists. Because neonates have had little experience with the environment, investigators of their behavior can help us determine the relative influence of nature (genetic endowment) and nurture (experience). Studies of the simple behavior of this early period can help psychologists understand how behavior is organized and how its organization changes with time and experience.

Physical Characteristics

Appearance

> His skin was wrinkled and quite loose, ready to scale in creased places such as his feet and hands. The hair, matted with vernix, gave an odd, pasted appearance. Louis was obviously no beauty at this point. His ears were pressed to his head in unusual positions — one ear was matted firmly forward on his cheek. His nose was flattened and pushed to one side by the squeeze as he came through the pelvis. [Brazelton, 1969, p. 3]

Puffy face and puffy eyes, wrinkled skin, misshapen head, deep red face, a coat of fine hair (called the *lanugo*), and a covering of a white, greasy substance — these are the characteristics of the newborn. But why do newborns look the way they do?

The white, greasy covering, called *vernix caseosa*, is accumulated sebum, a secretion from glands surrounding the hair follicles in the skin. Sebum produced before birth collects on the skin's surface, forming a protective barrier between the fetus's skin and the fluid that surrounds it. During the birth process itself, it provides lubrication to ease the baby's passage. It also helps protect the skin from infection.

Some of the puffiness in the baby's face and eyes is caused by the accumulation of fluids when the baby is in the head-down position to be born. The swelling of the eyes is increased by the silver nitrate drops used to keep the baby from contracting gonorrhea from an infected mother during delivery.

The newborn may have a misshapen head because the bones of the skull were squeezed together during birth to the point of overlapping. The squeezing together, known as *molding*, is possible because of the open spaces, or *fontanelles*, between the bones in the baby's incompletely developed skull. Molding permits the brain to mature more than would be possible otherwise; the baby's head may be an inch larger than the mother's pelvis, but the molding process permits it to pass through the birth canal. The fontanelles gradually close during the first two years of life.

The infant's skin is red because its capillaries are much more visible than those of older children. This is because the infant's skin, and the layer of fat beneath it, are thin at birth. The redness fades as the infant gains weight.

The neonate's appearance changes during the first few weeks after birth. The head resumes its usual rounded shape; the eyelids lose their puffiness; forceps marks, if present, disappear; the hair that may have covered the newborn's body falls out. Despite these changes, the newborn may still look a little peculiar to most adults because of other, more enduring physical characteristics.

Body Proportions

If you have ever held a tiny baby, you probably know that it cannot hold its head up. If its head fell back, the infant would have trouble bringing it up again; you probably placed one hand behind the baby's head and neck. The baby has this problem for two reasons: the muscles of the neck are not well developed, and the baby's head is very large and heavy compared to the rest of its body, due to differential growth during the prenatal period.

Just as the top of the body is more fully developed than the lower part of the body, the top of the head is more fully developed than the bottom of the head. Infants' jawbones are underdeveloped and they have practically no chin. They have very short necks; the newborn's head sits practically on top of its very narrow shoulders. The newborn's head is about one-fourth of its total body height, whereas the head of an adult is only about one-tenth of his or her height. Growth patterns during childhood gradually change the infant's body proportions, and the characteristic features of babyhood eventually fade.

Physiological Changes

Respiration and Circulation. The fetus gets its oxygen from its mother, through the placenta. The fetus's blood does not even pass through its own lungs, but bypasses them through a vessel known as the *ductus arteriosus*. Immediately after birth, the ductus arteriosus closes as air fills the infant's lungs, and from that point onward the infant obtains its own oxygen (Wennberg, Woodrum, and Hodson, 1973).

The characteristic breathing pattern of the neonate sometimes alarms adults. Periods of regular, rapid, shallow breathing are interspersed with deeper breaths, and sometimes breathing stops altogether for a period of a few seconds, an occurrence known as *apnea*. Although it can certainly upset a parent, this sort of apnea is quite normal and apparently harmless. The neonate's breathing is also punctuated with coughs and sneezes caused by mucus in the airways of the nose and throat.

The change in the source of the child's oxygen supply causes other important changes. The child apparently needs fewer red blood cells outside the uterus, because the oxygen is richer and obtained more directly. As a result, the infant's body destroys some red blood cells. This is a natural process that occurs to a certain extent at all times. The destruction of red blood cells yields a by-product, however, that the infant's body cannot handle as efficiently as the adult body. Problems can arise when the newborn's liver cannot produce enough of the enzyme that converts the byproduct, known as *bilirubin*, into a form that can be excreted. When this happens, the child's bilirubin level rises, which causes a yellowing of the skin known as *physiological neonatal jaundice*. Most infants adapt to the increased demand for the necessary enzyme within a few days, and the condition disappears.

Newborns with jaundice should be observed carefully, however, because serious forms of the condition can overload the bilirubin-binding capacity of the blood. When this occurs bilirubin passes into brain tissue, causing a type of neurological damage known as *kernicterus* (Maisels, 1972).

Serious jaundice can result from Rh incompatability, discussed in Chapter 4. In addition, normal neonatal jaundice can be prolonged and exacerbated by giving a mother heavy doses of obstetrical drugs during delivery. Many of these drugs must be metabolized in the liver before they can be excreted. This can overload the infant's immature liver, which may already be working to capacity making the usual adaptations to postnatal life.

Digestion and Feeding. The fetus receives all of its nutrients from its mother, but at birth the newborn must be able to ingest food and extract nutrients from it. The newborn's digestive system produces enough enzymes to digest efficiently and absorb both proteins and sugars. During the first few months the newborn may absorb saturated fats less efficiently, however (Katz and Hamilton, 1974).

During the first few days of life, it is sometimes difficult to keep a baby from frequently falling asleep while nursing. The infant may also tend to gag on the mucus in the airways of its throat, which can cause it to vomit the milk it has drunk along with the mucus. But most newborns can tolerate a day or two without eating much. They are born with stores of a starch called *glycogen* that can easily be transformed into sugar when the body needs energy. They also have stores of extra fat and fluids, so they are nicely adapted to wait the several days it usually takes for a mother to begin producing milk.

Before a mother begins to produce milk, she produces a substance called *colostrum*. This thin, yellowish liquid is high in protein and low in fat — perfectly suited to the infant's nutritional needs and digestion. Colostrum also contains *immunoglobulins* — antibodies for specific foreign agents that protect the young infant from infectious disease (Kabara, 1980). As a result, some experts suggest that premature infants, who are more vulnerable to disease than full-term infants, be fed human milk (Goldman and Smith, 1973).

Newborns typically lose weight during their first few days of life. Fluid is lost through the urine, lungs, and skin; the vernix caseosa is removed; glycogen and fat stores are used; and the feces present in the intestine at birth are excreted. It is common for a newborn to lose as much as 10 percent of its birth weight. The extent of the loss is determined by the child's condition at birth and by the speed with which the child adjusts to regular feedings. Premature infants can eat little at first, so they tend to gain weight relatively slowly. Breast-fed infants tend to begin their weight gain later, because their mother's milk may not come in for four or five days.

Newborns eat little at first, but they eat often. The frequency of eating depends on such factors as birth weight; small babies eat a little less at each feeding, but they eat a little more often. Most newborns eat once every two and a half to four hours. Today, parents generally recognize the importance of responding to the baby rather than trying to adhere to a strict schedule determined by the clock. A good procedure is to base the schedule on immediate past experience with the baby and then adjust it as needed.

Young infants also need to be fed during the night. Though some parents say their infants slept through the night right from the beginning, most babies need one or more night feedings for a couple of months, and many need them for much longer. This schedule, of course, interferes with parents' sleep. A mother in

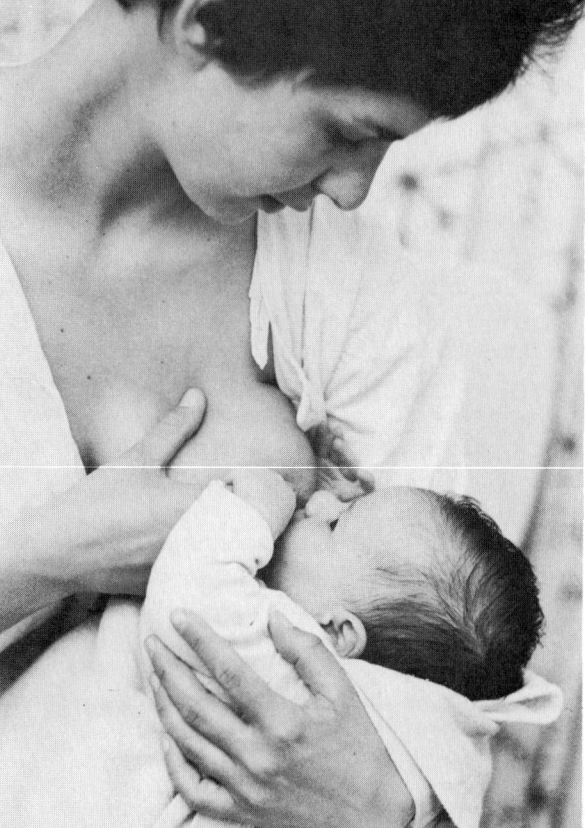

Breast feeding has health benefits for the baby.

one of our classes, when asked what she had missed most since becoming a parent, said that it was sleep:

> When the children were tiny babies, there were the feedings in the middle of the night. When they were older, it was the croup — keeping the vaporizer filled with water and listening to make sure they were breathing all right. A little later, it was bad dreams and wet beds. We're enjoying a peaceful phase right now, but in a few years when the children become teenagers, I suspect I won't be able to sleep because I'll wonder if they'll get home safely. Once you're a parent, you never really sleep soundly again!

The initial nighttime feeding schedule can put considerable stress on parents who work. If both parents work they can alternate feeding the baby to allow each other periods of uninterrupted sleep. If the mother is breast feeding the baby, breast milk can be expressed and collected during the day, refrigerated, and then fed to the baby with a bottle at night by the father.

Temperature Regulation. An adult can run out to the mailbox and back even in very cold weather without putting a coat on. You might shiver a little, but you soon would warm up. But a young baby exposed to the cold for even a brief period might become dangerously cold.

We do not know exactly why newborns have trouble keeping warm. Some researchers think that the mechanism in the brain that controls temperature is immature, or that it works differently than the adult mechanism. Others think the high ratio of the infant's body surface to its mass results in relatively rapid cooling, or that scanty stores of fat beneath the skin offer little insulation (Mestayan and Varga, 1960; Perlstein et al., 1974; Sinclair, 1975). Whatever the cause, the implications for practice are clear: the newborn baby should be kept warm. The baby should be dressed in hat, sweater, and coat for even brief outings in cold weather. To prevent the cooling effect of evaporation, the baby should be quickly wrapped in a towel when it is taken from its bath water. The temperature in the room should be kept comfortably warm.

It is difficult to detect whether a baby is too warm or too cold. A cold baby does not shiver like an adult, and a very young baby perspires little when it is too hot (Klaus and Fanaroff, 1973). Rather than watching for these signs of discomfort, it is best simply to keep the infant's environment comfortably warm.

The Premature Infant

Early Risks

The previous comments about physiological adaptation during the first few weeks of postnatal life apply to babies who are robust and healthy at birth. If a baby is unhealthy, its adaptation period may be more prolonged and difficult. One condition that typically prolongs the neonatal period is prematurity.

A premature baby is one who is born without having spent the usual amount of time in the uterus, although the label is sometimes applied to full-term infants who are *small for date* (under five pounds) due to hereditary factors, maternal malnutrition, or disease. Small-for-date babies adjust to life differently than premature babies (Lubchenco, Delivoria-Papodopoulos, and Searle, 1972).

Physical Problems. The premature infant is more vulnerable during the birth process than the full-term infant. Fat deposits do not form under the fetus's skin until the last few weeks of prenatal life. As a result, the infant's head is more likely to sustain damage during delivery, and the newborn infant has less protection against cooling. Skin sensors are now attached to premature infants to measure temperature accurately and adjust the incubator environment accordingly.

Premature infants are also susceptible to respiratory problems. About 15 percent suffer from a serious breathing problem known as *hyaline membrane disease*. Lung development begins early in the prenatal period, but the air sacs, or alveoli, at the very ends of the lungs are not completely formed until late in the prenatal period. These air sacs are kept from collapsing, when a breath is expelled, by *surfactant*, a substance not present to a normal extent in the premature infant (Brumley, 1970). It is the collapse of air sacs that characterizes hyaline membrane disease. If the condition is severe, the infant can die. The younger the premature infant, the more serious the condition, because surfactant is not produced until the thirty-fourth to thirty-eighth weeks of prenatal life (Wennberg, Woodrum, and Hodson, 1973).

Modern medical techniques have made it possible to save the lives of many premature babies. Brain damage can be averted by providing oxygen-enriched environments to infants who cannot breathe effectively. Unfortunately, it was not known for many years that too much oxygen leads to *retrolental fibroplasia*, a form of blindness. As a result of this condition, there have been more blind children in the last two decades than ever before (Hatfield, 1972). This example emphasizes the fragility of the human body's systems — too little oxygen causes brain damage, but too much destroys the retina of the eye. Modern medicine was able to save the lives of infants who at an earlier time would almost certainly have died, but in doing so it impaired the infants' vision. A delicate balance must be maintained. Today there are continuous monitoring devices available to measure oxygen use precisely at all times, thereby preventing both brain damage and blindness.

Emotional Problems. Premature infants also may suffer from emotional problems. For example, the number of premature children who are later abused by their parents is higher than would be expected. The incidence of prematurity is about 10 percent, but about 21 to 24 percent of all abuse cases involve children who were premature babies. In other words, a disproportionate number of premature children are abused (Klein and Stern, 1971; Stern, 1973). Why is this?

FOCUS: Emotional Risks of Prematurity

Budin, the first *neonatalogist* (specialist in the newborn), issued a warning in 1907 about the effects of separating premature infants and their parents. He designed glass-walled incubators so that mothers could see their infants and become involved in their care. But when Martin Cooney, one of Budin's pupils, introduced incubators into this country in the early 1900s, he disregarded Budin's advice. When he exhibited incubators at the Chicago World's Fair in 1932 he had nurses care for babies in them rather than the infants' mothers. (He did give the mothers free passes!) The separation of the child from its parents had a dramatic effect: Cooney sometimes found it difficult to get mothers to take their babies back when the babies were free to leave the incubator (Klaus and Kennell, 1976).

When incubators became common in American hospitals, isolation of mother and baby was standard practice — not just for premature babies, but for other babies as well. There was great concern over the spread of infection in hospitals, and parents were considered carriers of germs. Full-term babies who stayed in the hospital a short time and were taken on brief excursions out of the nursery to see their mothers were not as seriously affected as premature babies who stayed in the incubator, tended by nurses, for weeks, sometimes for months.

The story of one premature infant and its mother's response after they had been separated for several weeks is told by Klaus and Kennell (1976, p. 10). The baby suffered from respiratory problems and was attached to a respirator for a few days. When it was well enough, it was placed in an incubator and given food through a tube. By the end of two weeks, the infant could be fed by nipple, at which time the mother was taught to care for the baby. But the nurses soon complained that the mother could not get the infant to drink milk, although the nurses themselves could. One day, when she was being observed, the mother "placed the baby on her knees, picked up his head in her hands, looked at his face, and said, 'Are you mine? Are you really mine? Are you alive? Are you really alive?' " Apparently this mother, like many others, had not expected her baby to live and her emotional detachment interfered with effective feeding. Her exclusion from the baby's care for two weeks had kept her from observing the baby's improvement and from developing an emotional bond.

Today, many experts believe strongly that rigid isolation of parents from their premature infants is a poor practice, creating emotional problems in infants who already have physical problems. Guidelines have been developed for parents visiting intensive care units that allow them to provide emotional support without endangering their infants physically. In addition, some hospitals have developed special family-centered care units for premature and other high-risk infants. Infants are moved to these centers when they no longer need intensive care, but need to remain in the hospital. These units are decorated as much as possible to resemble a home-like atmosphere in which parents can interact with their babies (Goldson, 1980).

The risk of later abuse is thought to be related to the way premature infants are cared for in hospitals. Hospital procedures usually require that premature infants be separated from their parents. The baby often stays in the incubator and is cared for by nurses for a few weeks after the mother has gone home. Many health care professionals have now concluded that separating the parent from the care of the infant soon after birth prevents the development of infant-parent bonding or attachment. (Attachment, or the emotional relationship between parents and a baby, is discussed in detail in Chapter 9.)

Later Development

The long-term effects of prematurity on development are an important concern. Do premature babies catch up with their full-term peers? Are they more likely to develop problems later on?

The research indicates that the severity of long-term effects is largely determined by the extent of the prematurity. The lower an infant's birth weight, the greater the chances that it will have lowered intelligence and difficulties in areas such as language learning and reading (Caputo and Mandell, 1970; Drillien, 1963, 1969). The likelihood that premature infants will have long-term difficulties is much greater when they are reared in low socioeconomic circumstances (Broman, Nichols, and Kennedy, 1975). This group has the highest rate of premature birth in the first place. You can see the importance of making good prenatal care and nutritional supplements, both of which decrease the chances of prematurity, accessible to all women. In addition, parents of premature infants need emotional support and encouragement in caring for their infants from the very beginning so that good relationships will develop and the important stimulation that comes from good relationships will be provided.

Motor Capabilities

Reflexive Behavior

As soon as they are born, infants are capable of motor responses that help them survive. If you touch or stroke an infant's mouth or cheek, its lips and tongue will move and its head will turn toward your finger. This behavior, known as the *rooting reflex*, puts the infant in a good position to get the nipple of the breast into its mouth. Once an object is in an infant's mouth, the *sucking reflex*, a complex behavior involving pressure and suction, is triggered.

The infant also has a *gag reflex*. In some newborns this reflex is prompted frequently by mucus in the airways of the throat. Sneezing and coughing are also reflex actions.

A series of reflex actions is set in motion if the infant's nose and mouth are obstructed when it is in a prone position (on its stomach). The movements involve raising and turning the head, extending and flexing the arms and legs in

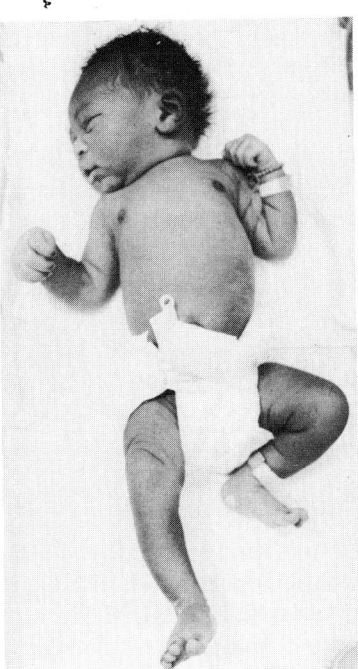 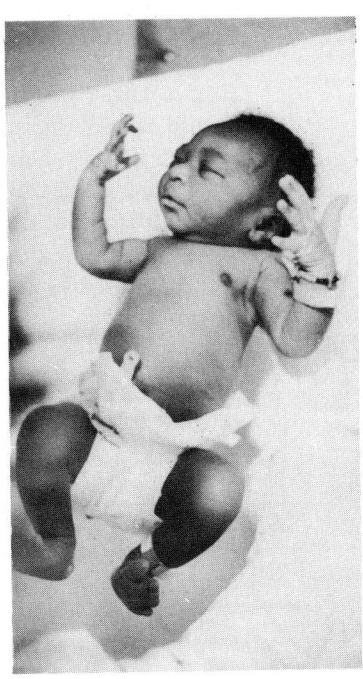

The tonic neck reflex   The Moro reflex

movements like crawling, and raising the shoulders. The knowledge that babies can move this way can be reassuring to parents who fear that their baby might smother if placed on its stomach in bed. This and other "defensive reactions" have been of interest to child development experts attempting to demonstrate that even newborns can protect themselves to a certain extent (Brazelton, 1969).

Other reflexes are apparently less vital to functional adaptation than those just mentioned, but are nevertheless of interest as indicators of neurological well-being. In other words, if the reflexes are present as they should be, it is an indication that the child's nervous system is intact and is functioning normally. The *tonic neck reflex* can be elicited by laying a baby on its back and turning its head to one side. The arm and leg on the side that the baby faces will be stretched out, whereas the other arm and leg will be flexed.

The *Moro*, or *startle reflex*, is a series of movements in which the infant throws out its arms, fans out its fingers, extends its neck, lets out a cry, and then brings its arms back to "embrace" or clasp its chest (Dargassies, 1966). The Moro, triggered when internal receptors sense movement in the neck muscles, can be elicited by a loud sound, or by position changes involving a dropping back of the head. Babies sometimes startle themselves during crying episodes and become even more upset.

There is also a *Babinski reflex*, in which stroking the outer edge of the sole of the foot makes the baby's toes fan out. Both hands and feet have, in addition, a *grasping reflex*. The hand grasp can be elicited by stroking or applying pressure to the palm of the infant's hand. This grasp, known as the *palmar grasp*, is so strong that it will support the infant's weight and can be used to lift the infant up from its back when it is lying on a surface. The toe grasp can be stimulated by pressing the bottom of the infant's foot just below the toes.

Reflex action diminishes during the first few months of life. For example, by six months of age it is difficult to elicit a startle reflex, and by eight or nine months of age it is usually impossible. The Babinski reflex is usually gone by four months of age. As the brain matures, lower brain centers (midbrain, pons, medulla, cerebellum) come under the control of the higher brain center, the cerebral cortex, which inhibits reflex action. If reflexes persist beyond the time when they typically disappear, it is an indication that the brain is not functioning normally.

Voluntary Behavior

The newborn's control over its movements is limited; movements are jerky and limited rather than sustained and smooth. During the last few weeks of prenatal life the newborn's muscles develop a high degree of *tonus*, which is the continuous tension or contraction normal even in muscles at rest (Dargassies, 1966).

The neonate's fists are clenched and its arms are bent at the elbows and raised up. The legs are crossed at the ankles and bent at the knees so that they often touch the abdomen. In the fetal position the baby's legs are bent in this manner and tucked up tightly against the body.

A newborn who starts a movement is unlikely to hit its target. An infant who tries to move its fingers or hand to its mouth sometimes misses. The other parts of the baby's body move, too; in fact, the very young infant's excess movement seems a little like the unwinding of a tightly wound spring. As the infant gradually gains control over its muscle activity, it more frequently hits the targets aimed for and can stop movements with less excess motion.

Sensory Abilities

Vision

When an infant looks at its parents can it see them? Apparently it can; infants are quite competent visually. If an object is held in front of an infant until the infant's eyes fix on it, and then the object is moved, the infant will gaze at the object and track it, that is, move its eyes or both its head and eyes to keep the object in its visual field (Brazelton, 1973; Salapatek, 1968; Wolff, 1959). Newborns can also look at an object with both eyes at the same time, a response known as *binocular fixation*. In some circumstances they do not use binocular fixation, however, as when an object is held very close to their face (Slater and Findlay, 1975). The one visual act that newborns perform poorly is *accommodation*, changing the shape of the lens to bring objects at various distances into focus. They do not, however, see everything as a blur. Objects between seven and eight inches from their faces they see clearly (Haynes, White, and Held, 1965). This is just about the distance an infant is from an adult's face when it is cradled in the arms.

Hearing

If you ring a bell or shake a rattle, a newborn will usually turn toward the sound and look alert, as if searching for its source (Brazelton, 1969; Muir and Field, 1979; Wertheimer, 1961; Wolff, 1959). Infants not only hear sounds, they can distinguish high and low and loud and soft sounds (Hirschman and Katkin, 1974). Researchers have discovered what newborns hear by using a process involving *habituation*. It works this way: The infant is exposed to a sound that it responds to. After a succession of exposures, however, the newborn stops responding — it becomes habituated. If a different sound is introduced at this point, and the baby becomes alert again, it can be assumed that the infant senses the difference between this sound and the previous one. Habituation can be explained by assuming that the infant is building a store of information about the stimulus — a "neuronal" or "mental" model (Cohen and Gelber, 1975; Sokolov, 1963). The child stops paying attention when the model is refined enough to match the incoming stimulus. When a new sound is introduced, however, the incoming information no longer matches the mental model exactly, and the infant begins building a new mental model.

Taste

Newborn infants will drink more of a sweet fluid than of a salty, sour, bitter, or neutral one (water) (Desor, Maller, and Andrews, 1975). They also indicate a preference for a sweeter solution over one that is less sweet (Desor, Maller, and Turner, 1973) by sucking the sweeter one longer and harder. Those who care for young babies are aware of this preference, and hospitals routinely give newborns bottles of sucrose and water. Some authorities have criticized this procedure, suggesting that it causes children to become sugar addicts.

Smell

Habituation studies have also been used to determine that the ability to distinguish odors is present at birth. Infants can also localize odors, that is, tell where they are coming from (Bower, 1974; Self, Horowitz, and Paden, 1972). This was determined in a study by Rieser, Yonas, and Wilner (1976) in which infants turned away from the source of an odor of ammonium chloride.

Pain

Neonates also respond to pain, as from a pinprick or electric shock. As neonates grow older, their sensitivity to pain increases (Lipsitt and Levy, 1959). Girl newborns are more sensitive to pain than boy newborns; this is consistent with the finding that girls are generally more mature than boys at birth.

Visual Perception

We have seen that the newborn's sensory apparatus works well, but knowing that infants can sense stimuli is not the same as understanding how stimuli are perceived after they are sensed. Do newborns have a particular method of organizing stimuli? Do they see things as adults see them? During the last two decades a good deal of research has been devoted to answering these questions.

Perception of Distance

When we gaze out a window or across a room, we can tell which objects are close to us and which are farther away. And when we reach for something, we know exactly how far to extend our hands. We possess these abilities because we have accurate *distance perception*. Do young infants also have this ability?

In an experiment designed to answer this question, ten-day-old infants were seated in the path of a moving object. The object began its journey at a point far from the infant and gradually moved closer. The researchers were interested in whether a baby would react in a situation that, if not stopped by the experimenter, would result in a collision.

The researchers found that even ten-day-old infants opened their eyes wide, pulled back their heads, and put their hands up in front of their faces as the object moved toward them. They apparently did notice the change in the object's distance from them and used a defensive reaction to protect themselves (Bower, Broughton, and Moore, 1974, cited in Bower, 1974, pp. 83–91).

Preference for Pattern and Contrast

Infants not only perceive distance, they can perceive the difference between patterned and unpatterned surfaces. They indicate that they can tell the difference by looking longer at patterns than at nonpatterns. In other words, they show pattern preferences.

The infant's preference for pattern was illustrated during the visit of a one-month-old baby to a seminar on child development and education taught by one of the authors. The baby was a little fussy when she arrived, so the mother held her up to her shoulder in the baby's favorite position. The mother sat with her back to the class so we could see the baby's face. At first the baby seemed to look around the room, her glance lingering, we thought, at a light. After a short time the students began holding up objects they had brought to class, to see if the baby liked to look at them. The baby was not very interested in pieces of red, blue, and yellow construction paper, or in a pastel blue and white rattle. She looked for a relatively long time at a tassle of red and yellow yarn, but her attention was really caught by a piece of paper with black stripes. The baby raised her head up off her mother's shoulder, opened her eyes wide, and furrowed her brow. Her mouth stayed open and she no longer sucked her fist. Everything about her expression asked "What *is* that?" Although she had trouble keeping her head raised, she looked at the striped paper for a long time. As you can see, she demonstrated an obvious preference for patterned visual displays.

Fantz (1963) was the first researcher to demonstrate that newborns (babies ten hours to five days old) notice the difference between patterned and unpatterned visual displays. Fantz used six stimuli, three patterned (a schematic face, concentric circles, and a section of newspaper containing print), and three unpatterned (white, fluorescent yellow, and dark red). Newborns looked at the patterned stimuli longer than they looked at the colored, unpatterned stimuli. Of the patterned stimuli, they liked the schematic face best, followed by the concentric circles and the newsprint.

But why do infants prefer patterned stimuli over unpatterned stimuli, and some patterns over others? A number of researchers thought complexity was the key to catching the newborn's visual attention, and they designed experiments to find out if they were right.

Apparatus used in Fantz's study of infant form perception

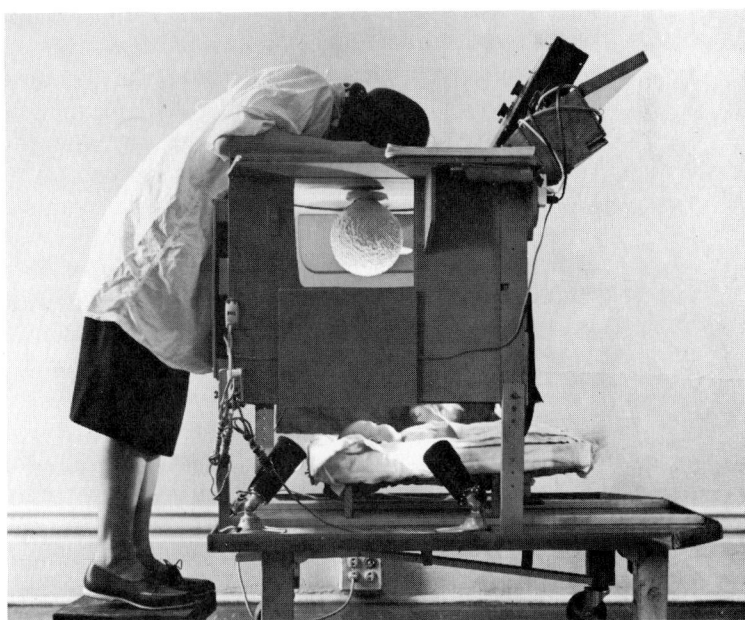

Figure 5-1. Stimuli used in Hershenson's complexity experiment

One study made use of three stimuli shown in Figure 5-1 (Hershenson, 1964). The infants preferred the simplest stimulus, and looked least at the most complex stimulus. Hershenson's results appeared to contradict the results of studies with older infants, which indicated that more complex patterns were preferred (Berlyne, 1958). Could preferences change with age? To test this idea, Brennan, Ames, and Moore (1966) studied three-, eight- and fourteen-week-old infants using checkerboard patterns of 4, 64, and 576 squares. Because infants cannot focus well, Brennan thought the youngest of them might see the most complex pattern only as a patch of gray. For this reason, she also used a fourth stimulus, a plain gray square. If looking time was the same for the most complex pattern and the gray square, it could be assumed that the infants did not perceive the most complex pattern as a pattern.

Brennan found that the three-week-old infants could see the pattern of the most complex stimulus but that it was not their favorite. They liked the least complex pattern best, followed by the intermediate pattern. But eight-week-old infants liked the pattern of intermediate complexity most, whereas fourteen-week-old infants preferred the most complex pattern. As Brennan had suspected, preferences do change with age.

It is not the characteristics of a pattern alone that determine whether an infant will look at it. The infant's experience is also important. A familiar pattern may seem too easy and bore the infant, whereas a completely novel pattern may be beyond the infant's understanding. Patterns that vary slightly from the familiar seem to be preferred. (This interpretation, known as the *discrepancy hypothesis* of visual attention, will be discussed more fully in Chapter 6.) You will recognize that babies' visual behavior is consistent with the cognitive-developmental theory discussed in Chapter 3.

Studies of visual perception indicate that infants also have a preference for contrast. They tend to fix their gaze at the edges of figures (Salapatek and Kessen, 1966). The stimuli used in these studies were white figures on black backgrounds, or black figures on white; the contrast would be greatest where the figure and background meet. The baby in our class who reacted to the black stripes on white paper may have been responding to contrast as well as pattern.

Visual Perception and the Nature-Nurture Issue

It is clear from the research on visual perception that certain characteristics of the infant are "wired in" from the beginning. Infants perceive and prefer patterns long before they have had an opportunity to learn to prefer them.

The infant's innate visual preferences encourage certain adaptations. Infants' attraction to pattern and contrast, for example, motivates them to look at the eyes in the human face. Although the infant does not at first know one adult from another, its parents may interpret the infant's looking at their eyes as a sign of recognition. It is easy to see how this behavior could facilitate the attachment of parents to their child.

Preference for pattern may also be intellectually adaptive. Color and brightness carry little information; that is, they do not help us make fine discriminations between one thing and another. But patterns do provide lots of information. The infant's preference for pattern permits it to take advantage of this fact.

Whether an infant develops an attachment to an adult or learns to distinguish among certain complex patterns depends on social and physical circumstances. Innate structures influence the infant's orientation and the way it uses the environment, but the infant's level of development is also influenced by the environment. This is another way of saying that development depends on the interaction between the infant and its environment, not on either nature or nurture alone.

Behavioral States

Some parents report that their baby is fussy and cries much of the time; others say their infant is calm and alert. Babies differ greatly in the extent to which they are awake, drowsy, irritable, or active. Characteristics such as these are known as *behavioral states*. (Table 5-1 describes various states in the newborn.)

Influences on Behavioral States

We do not know why some infants experience some states more frequently than other infants, but genetic differences seem to be partly responsible. The method of delivery (Leboyer or conventional; medicated or nonmedicated) may also affect a baby's state. We know, for example, that medicated deliveries tend to alter the infant's state, usually by depressing activity and alertness.

Childrearing practices, too, may influence the infant's state. Brazelton (1969) suggests that *swaddling*, or wrapping the baby tightly, calms babies by restraining their arms and legs. The infant has little control over its limbs, and swaddling prevents a baby from startling and upsetting itself. It is a common child-care custom in some cultures.

FOCUS: Effects of Obstetrical Pain-Relieving Drugs on the Neonate and Infant

In 1853 Dr. Jonas Y. Simpson used chloroform anesthesia in obstetrics. Previously, women had been given nothing to relieve the pain of labor and delivery (Butarescu, 1978). Today, the use of medication during labor and delivery is being questioned because of its effects on the newborn (Brackbill et al., 1974). We now know that drugs given to the mother quickly cross the placenta and enter the fetus (Bonica, 1967; Marx, 1961; Morishima et al., 1966; Ploman and Persson, 1957).

We also know something about how medication affects the newborn. Infants born to nonmedicated mothers stay in the alert inactive state (that is, they do not fall asleep) for a longer period immediately after birth than infants born to medicated mothers (Desmond et al., 1963). As we said in Chapter 4, this can have an important influence on parent-child relationships: the alert infant will interact with the parent, but the groggy baby will not.

What is more, infants born to medicated mothers suck less vigorously and for shorter periods than infants born to nonmedicated mothers. The duration of such effects is from four to ten days (Brazelton, 1970; Kron, Stern, and Goddard, 1966; Richards and Bernal, 1972).

In addition, infants born to medicated mothers habituate more slowly to sounds, track objects with their eyes less well, and have poorer muscle tone and reflexive responses (Aleksandrowicz and Aleksandrowicz, 1974; Conway and Brackbill, 1970). Differences in performance on some measures were noticeable for as long as one month after birth. Some effects, in fact, did not peak until the twenty-eighth day after birth, and presumably exerted some effect for an unknown period thereafter.

A study (Brackbill et al., 1974) using the Brazelton Neonatal Scale (see page 125) found that the item that most clearly differentiated the two groups of infants was consolability, or the ease with which the infant stops crying when, for example, it is held and talked to. Infants born to medicated mothers were harder to console. Finally, infants born to nonmedicated mothers were more cuddly than infants born to medicated mothers. These effects have a tremendous potential for influencing the parent-child relationship.

The research methods used in some studies of the effects of maternal medication on the newborn have been criticized (Federman and Yang, 1976), and long-term harmful effects of early behavior changes have not been demonstrated. Nevertheless, it is generally agreed that medication should be administered with caution during delivery. Its effects on the infant should be the subject of rigorous research.

Table 5-1. Behavioral states in the newborn

State	Motor Activity	Muscle tone	Skin	Eyes	Face	Respiration	Vocalization
Regular sleep	No movement of limbs and trunk; startle reflexes present	Relaxed	Pink, but pale	Closed; no movement	Relaxed	Regular; breaths 36 per minute	
Irregular sleep	Movement of trunk and limbs between periods of rest	Moderate degree of tension	Flushed during activity	Closed, but movements present	Grimaces such as smiles and frowns	Irregular rhythm; 48 breaths per minute	
Drowsiness	More movement than during regular sleep but less than during irregular	Moderate degree of tension		Eyes open and close; dull, glazed and unfocused		Generally regular	Occasional high-pitched squeal
Alert inactivity	Inactive	Moderate degree of tension		Eyes are open, bright, shining, attentive; eyes move together in horizontal & vertical plane		Faster than during regular sleep	
Waking activity	Activity occurs in spurts	Higher degree of tension	Flushed during activity	Eyes are open, but not bright and shining		Irregular	Moans, grunts, whining, but no sustained crying
Crying	Very active	Considerable tension	Flushed bright red	May be open or closed; tears in some babies	Grimaces	Fast and irregular	Crying

SOURCE: Wolff, P. The causes, controls, and organizations of behavior in the newborn. *Psychological Issues* 5 (1966), Whole No. 17, 1–105.

All babies apparently progress through a similar series of states during the first few days after birth. Babies are alert for a period of between fifteen minutes and one and a half hours immediately after birth, but they then go into a deep sleep that lasts for a day or longer (Wolff, 1965). Brazelton (1961) suggests that this is an adaptation to the physiological changes the infant is undergoing. After the first few days, the amount of time spent in the alert inactive state gradually increases.

Self-Organization

An infant's states may accurately reflect its capacity for self-organization — the extent to which its nervous system is functioning well (Brazelton, 1973). Irritable infants, for example, may be unable to shut out excessive stimulation from the environment. Infants who can shut out stimulation may be less easily upset.

The theory of self-organization has led to the use of the habituation procedure to assess the functioning of the newborn's central nervous system. Infants react the first time they perceive a stimulus such as a bell, but their responses diminish after repeated presentations. A child who has a long habituation rate — that is, who requires many presentations of the stimulus before becoming habituated — is thought to have poorer nervous system functioning than one who has a short habituation rate. If the infant's normal environment is thought of as rich in stimuli — full of sights and sounds — then an infant's behavioral state could indicate its self-organizing ability.

Behavioral States and Infant Responses

Some researchers think that an infant's state influences its ability to learn (Moss, 1972). The infant is most responsive to sensory stimulation, for example, during the alert inactive state. Since babies learn about the world through their senses, you can see that a baby who sleeps or cries all the time might be at a disadvantage.

State may also affect the mother-child relationship. Many experts believe that the baby's behavior affects the parent's behavior as much as the parent's behavior affects the baby's. If this is true, parents' reactions toward the infant will be influenced by which state predominates in it (Brazelton, 1961). This view is supported by the observations of Klaus et al. (1970) who found that mothers were interested in getting their babies to open their eyes when they first saw them. Some mothers mentioned that they felt closer to their infants after the infant had looked at them. Klaus suspected that a period of alert inactivity in the infant during the first interaction with its mother would facilitate a positive mother-child relationship. A later study indicated that he was right (Klaus and Kennell, 1976). For this reason, some experts recommend that silver nitrate drops not be placed in a newborn's eyes until after the baby and its parents have spent some time together. Klaus's findings have also reinforced the trend of the last decade toward reducing predelivery medication, thereby decreasing babies' grogginess.

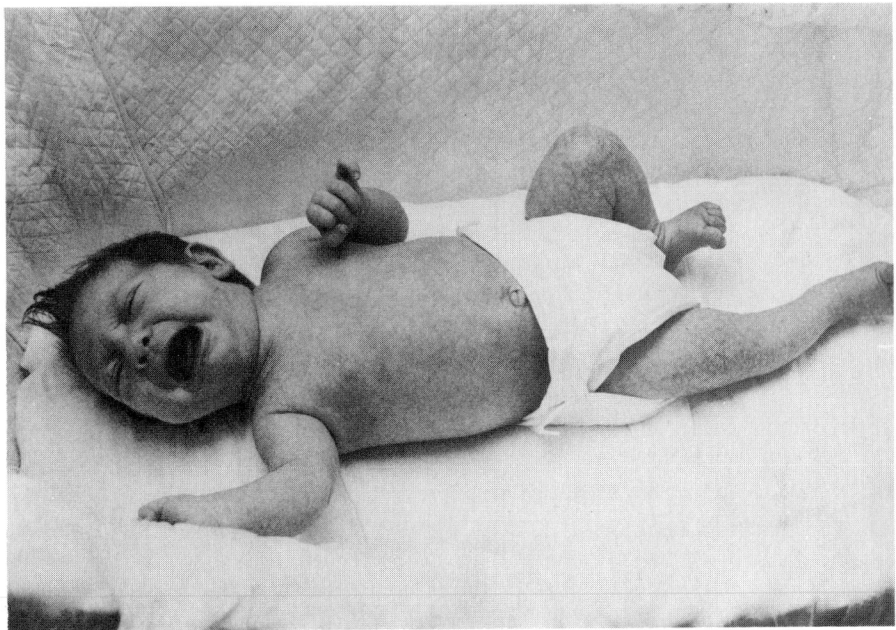

Crying is a common behavioral state in young infants.

The findings also argue for the use of the Leboyer method: in the Hamilton (1979) study, Leboyer babies opened their eyes after delivery in half the time it took for the control group.

Because state influences an infant's response to stimulation, researchers must take it into account if they wish to obtain reliable data from assessment tools. A researcher who checks infants' responses when they are sleepy, and another researcher who checks them while they are alert, are likely to come to different conclusions about the nature and behavior of neonates.

Learning

A Behaviorist View

In our review of psychological theories in Chapter 3, we discussed the environmental view (behaviorism), which is based on ideas about association and reinforcement. These ideas have influenced the design of some of the research conducted with infants. Most attempts to demonstrate learning in young infants using classical conditioning techniques have met with little success, in part because of the difficulty in keeping a neonate alert during the conditioning.

Operant, or instrumental, conditioning (that is, following a response with reinforcement), on the other hand, appears to be possible with newborn infants (Millar, 1974; Sameroff, 1972).

In the initial demonstrations of operant conditioning, elaborations of reflexes present at birth were reinforced. For example, the rooting reflex, when followed by the presentation of the nipple, increased the frequency of significant head turns (Papoušek, 1967; Siqueland and Lipsitt, 1966). Nonreinforcement did not.

Like head turning (rooting), sucking behavior is altered by the presence or absence of nutrient. Sucking consists of two actions: *expression* is related to how hard the infant squeezes the nipple, and *suction* is related to the amount of negative pressure exerted on the nipple. Studies have shown that infants will change the extent of their suction and expression in order to receive nutrient (Sameroff, 1968). They will even stop sucking altogether when nutrient is given solely for expressing. The opposite was not found to occur; it is apparently impossible for the infant to exert suction without also exerting pressure on the nipple. The young infant's ability to alter sucking behavior has an obvious adaptive effect: it allows it to adjust to different types of nipples. As you can see, research indicates that neonates are not just a "bundle of reflexes" but are capable of modifying their behavior as well.

A Piagetian View

Piaget also believes that infants can adapt their behavior, although his cognitive-developmental interpretation differs from the behaviorist view. He stresses how the infant's understanding and knowledge, even at this early stage, affect its response to stimuli.

Piaget (1952) provided some instructive observations of the modification of sucking behavior in one of his own children from birth to about one month of age. During this time, the child sucked various objects, including the nipple and skin of his mother's breast, the corner of a quilt, his own hand, and his father's index finger. The sucking reflexes initiated when one of these objects touched his mouth were soon modified and differentiated. The modifications involved behaviors more complex than sucking when the object provided food, as with a nipple, and ceasing to suck when it did not.

> Sucking of the eider-down quilt, of the coverlet, etc., leads to rejections, that of the breast to acceptance; sucking of the skin (the child's hand, etc.) leads to acceptance if it is only a matter of sucking for the sake of sucking, but it leads to rejection (for example when it involves an area of the breast other than the nipple) if there is great hunger; the paternal index finger is rejected when the child is held against the breast, but is accepted as a pacifier, etc. [Piaget, 1952, p. 31]

According to Piaget, the child continually modifies its behavior on the basis of its experiences. As a result, behavior becomes differentiated — the baby responds differently to different situations. For example, different objects in the mouth may elicit different kinds of sucking. Some things are sucked, and other things are spit out. Or some things are sucked some of the time, and not at other times. This rudimentary "thinking" leads to more complex behavior, although during the first two years of life knowledge or intelligence is sensorimotor in nature. That is, children know about the world only through their physical and sensory interactions with objects; they cannot represent what they know with symbols. (Piaget's stages of sensorimotor intelligence will be discussed in more detail in Chapter 6.) Whether one adopts the behavioral or the cognitive-developmental theory, it is clear that infants learn right from the start. Gentle play and interaction with even the very young baby are important.

Assessing the Neonate

Because some very important events occur during the neonatal period, tools have been developed to assess routinely and objectively the neonate's adjustment and well-being. Let us look at some of the most frequently used instruments.

Assessment Instruments

A newborn's *Apgar score* (named for the physician who developed the assessment procedure) is determined in the delivery room at one and five minutes after the child is born. It indicates the infant's overall physical condition, including heart rate, respiratory effort, muscle tone, reflex irritability, and color, each of which is rated from zero to two and noted on a scoring chart (see Table 5-2). Total scores on the Apgar can range from zero to ten, with higher scores indicating a better condition (Apgar, 1953).

The *Brazelton Neonatal Assessment Scale* is usually administered on the third day of life, and, ideally, on several subsequent days as well. The Brazelton scale indicates the child's neurological well-being, capacity for self-organization, and reactions to a caretaker. Specific items are concerned with state; the major reflexes; habituation to repeated visual, auditory, and tactile stimuli; orientation to the human face and voice; activity level; and muscle tone (Brazelton, 1973). For example, one item involves ringing a bell loudly over the infant when it is awake and lying on a flat surface. The infant will usually startle at the first presentation of the bell. The tester then rings the bell again. Typically, the infant startles again, but perhaps not as much as the first time. The infant habituates to the sound of the bell, so that after a few rings there is little or no reaction. To score the infant on this and similar items, the examiner notes how many presentations are necessary before the infant stops responding. The longer it takes for responses to cease, the poorer the rating the baby receives.

Dr. Brazelton stresses the importance of "bringing the baby up to his or her optimum performance level" on the test. This means that the examiner must be aware of the baby's state and make sure that items are presented when the baby is comfortable and awake. If the baby falls asleep (which certainly happens), the examiner must try gently to awaken the baby or resume testing at a later time when the baby is awake. Similarly, if the baby begins to cry, the examiner must stop the testing and hold the baby or provide comfort in some other way. If the baby becomes less irritable, testing may be resumed. If the baby continues to cry for some time, the tester may have to wait until later to resume testing.

The *Prechtl Neurological Examination* (Prechtl and Beintema, 1964) is designed for assessing infants within ten days after birth. The assessment has two parts: (1) an observation period during which spontaneous movement and posture are noted, and (2) an examination period during which reflexes and other motor behavior are checked.

In addition to instruments that assess overall physical or neurological functioning, specific instruments have been developed to diagnose hearing loss in the neonate. A technique known as the *High Risk Registry* works like this: Mothers are questioned by trained volunteers soon after the birth of the baby to determine if there is any family history of hearing loss, or if the mother was exposed to diseases such as German measles during pregnancy. If the mother's responses indicate that there might be a problem, the baby's hearing is tested in the hospital by administering a *Crib-O-Gram* or by using *Brain Stem Evoked Response* audiometry. These techniques record actual brainwaves with special apparatus (Downs, 1978). Because neonates cannot tell us if they hear a sound, we must watch for their response after a sound is made or measure actual brain activity.

Table 5-2. Apgar scoring chart

	Score		
Sign	*0*	*1*	*2*
Heart rate	Absent	Slow (less than 100 beats/min.)	Over 100
Respiratory effort	Absent	Slow, irregular	Good, crying
Muscle tone	Flaccid	Some flexion of extremities	Active motion
Reflex irritability	No response	Cry	Vigorous cry
Color	Blue, pale	Body pink, extremities blue	Completely pink

SOURCE: Apgar, V. Proposal for a new method of evaluating the newborn infant. *Anesthesia and Analgesia* 52 (1953): 260–267. Reprinted by permission.

Assessment Problems

One purpose of assessing neonates is to identify those who might have problems later or who have life-threatening conditions. The early detection of problems sometimes allows us to change the infant's environment to provide more support for development.

It is sometimes difficult, however, to know which behaviors can be used to predict later consequences. Neurological examinations such as the Prechtl concentrate on measuring reflexive behaviors, noting simply whether or not they occur. New scales such as the Brazelton, on the other hand, test not only for the presence or absence of reflexes, but also for such things as infants' ability to inhibit responses to a repeated stimulus, to escape a stimulus, to quiet or console themselves, and to orient toward or seek out stimulation. This scale has a lower error rate in predicting later functioning than the basic neurological exams, probably because it gives a more complete picture of total central nervous system functioning (Tronick and Brazelton, 1975).

Other difficulties with instruments such as the Apgar are their gross nature (they allow only the most obvious difficulties to be detected) and the possible influence of the time of their administration. The Apgar scale, for example, is administered at one and five minutes after birth. But studies indicate that a baby's functioning two hours after birth may differ considerably from what it was immediately after birth (Desmond et al., 1963). A baby who receives a high score immediately after birth might receive a lower score a few hours later, and the later score might be a better predictor of future behavior. As we mentioned earlier, a baby's state when it is assessed can also influence its behavior.

Living with the Neonate

Although we have reviewed the major areas of early development, some aspects of neonatal behavior remain to be discussed. These are matters of practical concern such as soothing newborns and adjusting to their individual differences.

Soothing the Neonate

Researchers have found that infant crying is disconcerting to adults (Frodi et al., 1978a; Lamb, 1978). In a study of maternal responsiveness to crying, Wolff (1966, 1969) found that newborns engage in three distinct kinds of crying: (1) the basic, or hunger, cry, (2) the angry cry, and (3) the pain cry. All mothers studied responded immediately to the pain cry and seemed worried or alarmed by it. All mothers responded to the angry cry, too, but this kind of cry did not seem to worry them. The basic or hunger cry usually got a quick response from first-time mothers, but experienced mothers sometimes did not respond to it.

What can be done with a crying infant to quiet it? To answer that question, we must ask what makes an infant cry in the first place. Hunger is one cause of crying in the neonate. Wolff (1966) found that feeding the infant is the most effective quieter, rather than holding it or allowing it to suck without getting nutrient. Wolff also found that being undressed can often cause a newborn to cry; covering the infant with a blanket, or dressing it again, usually stops the crying. The crucial factor seems to be contact of cloth with the skin rather than temperature; infants cried when undressed even when their cribs were kept very warm. Perhaps clothing and blankets keep a baby from startling by inhibiting motor activity. We mentioned earlier that swaddling seems to keep a baby from startling, and, not surprisingly, it reduces crying. Finally, physical pain such as a pinprick or colic can make an infant cry.

These procedures reduce crying by directly eliminating its causes, but more general methods can also diminish crying. Sucking on a pacifier appears to have this effect. It may not quiet a very hungry infant at all, or have a consistent quieting effect on an infant who is moderately hungry, but it does seem to quiet the fussy infant by inhibiting diffuse motor activity, which may keep a baby thrashing, upset, and awake (Wolff, 1966).

Events in the child's environment, such as recordings of a heart beating or sounds of the womb (these *are* available) also inhibit crying. A noise from a rattle or a bright light placed in the visual field has the same effect, although it may be brief in the very young infant. By the second or third week, however, an event such as a bright object in the visual field or the sound of the human voice, has a

FOCUS: Effects of Premature Infant Crying on Adults

Recent research about the effect of infant crying and smiling on adult behavior indicates that infant cries are perceived as aversive stimuli by adults, whereas infant smiles are perceived as pleasant (Frodi et al., 1978a; Lamb, 1978). Other studies show that the cry of a premature infant is perceived to be even more aversive than the cry of a full-term infant (Frodi et al., 1978b). Investigators have suggested that this fact may contribute to the high rate of child abuse among premature children. Another factor may be that premature infants smile infrequently (Fontana, 1973; Klein and Stern, 1971).

Klaus and Kennell (1976) have suggested that the reason parental involvement in the care of premature infants nurtures attachment between them is that the parent learns how to respond effectively to the infant's crying. This finding would be consistent with some preliminary research data indicating that maternal attachment is facilitated by teaching parents about their infants.

SOURCE: Davidson, S. M. *An experiment in teaching parenting skills.* Paper presented at the biennial meeting of the Society for Research in Child Development, San Francisco, March 1979.

more prolonged inhibiting effect (Wolff, 1966). Wolff notes that around the second week the kind of event that quiets crying changes. With the very young infant, direct physical interventions such as feeding, swaddling, or offering the baby a pacifier are most effective; psychological interventions such as shaking a rattle or offering the baby a bright object to look at work less well. By the end of the second week, however, infants appear to be more interested in the environment, and auditory and visual events often cause sustained alertness in the infant and keep it from crying. In fact, there seems to be an intricate interplay between mental stimulation and the infant's emotional state.

Maria Montessori, a famous physician who devised a method of educating young children, comments in *The Absorbent Mind* on why crying is a problem with babies in Western countries: "The child is bored. He is mentally starved, kept prisoner in a confined space offering nothing but frustration to the exercise of his powers" (1967, p. 107). Montessori may have been correct to think that emotional state and mental stimulation are related. More recently, researchers have found that picking up an infant is a very effective way to quiet it (Korner and Grobstein, 1966; Wolff, 1966). When infants are picked up, they not only stop crying; they become alert and look around (Korner and Grobstein, 1966; Korner and Thoman, 1972). As Montessori suggested, they "find something to do."

A parent's response to an infant's crying and the method used to soothe the infant may affect its learning. The infant is most receptive to sensory stimulation when it is in the alert inactive state, and during the first weeks of life this state rarely occurs spontaneously in most infants (Wolff, 1965). But if, as Korner suggests, this alert state is induced by picking the infant up, that practice may facilitate its intellectual development.

Adjusting to Individual Differences

Despite the findings discussed above, it is difficult to say exactly how to provide a supportive learning environment and begin a healthy relationship with a particular newborn. Research evidence and everyday observation indicate that newborns differ, right from the beginning. Because the newborn's environment has had little opportunity to influence it, it can be assumed that some individual differences are innate. Some newborns simply cry more than others or respond more readily to soothing or to stimulation (Birns, 1965; Brazelton, 1969; Korner, 1971).

These differences can have an important influence on parent-child relationships and infant learning. A baby who is not easily soothed, for example, can make a parent feel incompetent, anxious, and frustrated. These feelings may in turn affect the parent's approach to the infant, which may affect the infant's future responses.

Because babies differ, it is crucial that their caregivers respond to them as individuals, as Korner indicates in the following passage:

> The finding that infants differ significantly from each other right from the very start suggests that there is more than one way of providing good child care; that, in fact, the only way to do so is to respond flexibly to the individual requirements of each and every child. . . . The prevailing emphasis [today, however] is on the fervent advocacy of one treatment method or another, rather than on the importance of a case-specific choice of treatment. . . . We are thus forever looking for *the* method to raise children, to educate, to cure. . . . In working with parents, it is important that we stress not only their crucial influence on their children's development but also that we free them to see, to hear, to tune in and to trust their own intuition in dealing differentially with what their children present as separate individuals. [1971, pp. 617–18]

One reason some parents can have trouble adapting to their infant is that the infant may not be what they hoped or expected it to be. An active, outgoing mother and father may be disappointed with a quiet, passive baby, and a parent who expected a calm infant might have trouble coping with a lively baby. But if the parents concentrate on the infant that is now theirs and adapt to its requirements, a good relationship is likely to result. Brazelton gives an example of a mother doing just that with his prototype of an active baby, Daniel:

> Daniel was hard to rouse from his deep sleep. He was wheeled in to Mrs. Kay, breathing deeply and noisily, moving little. . . . Then, as if with a start, he shot from sleeping to an unapproachable state of screaming. He cried with a loud, piercing bellow that continued until he was quieted. Quieting him demanded a vigorous approach on the part of Mrs. Kay.
>
> . . . He could not be quieted with her crooning, with quiet rocking and cuddling, or with a bottle alone. His crying could only be broken into by a combination of tight swaddling of his extremities, plus vigorous rocking, plus the bottle nipple held in his mouth at his soft palate until he stopped crying to breathe and felt it there.
>
> His mother felt foolish and unhappy about the means that were necessary to quiet him, but she found they were successful, and after the second day of these maneuvers, she found that he could even be played with and enjoyed after one of his feedings. [1969, p. 21]

This mother was able to adjust to her baby, although he was not exactly what she had expected. Many parents have trouble making such adjustments and need help in learning to relax and understand their infant's messages. Researchers in child development are currently investigating why some parents can make these adjustments easily whereas others cannot.

Summary

- The first month of life is called the neonatal period. It is of theoretical interest to psychologists studying the nature-nurture issue.

Physical Characteristics
- The newborn's appearance immediately after birth reflects conditions during prenatal life and delivery. For example, compared to adult proportions, a young infant's head is large in relation to the rest of its body due to differential growth.
- Physiological neonatal jaundice is thought to be caused by changes necessary for independent respiration.
- For the most part, neonates are well adapted for life outside the womb. Full-term newborns have sufficient stores of food to survive for a few days without eating very much (although they will usually lose weight during their first few days of life). However, newborns cannot regulate their temperatures well enough to keep warm when exposed to cool temperatures.

The Premature Infant
- A premature birth is one that occurs before the usual gestation period of 266 days is completed. Premature infants are more susceptible to postnatal problems. For example, they often suffer from hyaline membrane disease, a result of incomplete development of the lungs.

Motor Capabilities
- An infant is born with a number of adaptive reflexes, including the rooting, sucking, and gag reflexes. These reflexes can indicate its neurological well-being at birth, and indicate normal development as those no longer needed disappear. The neonate has poor control over its voluntary movements, however.

Sensory Abilities
- The "higher" brain centers apparently function from the time of birth and regulate sensory responses.
- Newborns basically can see quite well. They see objects seven to eight inches away most clearly.
- The newborn's adaptive functioning can be assessed with habituation procedures.

Visual Perception
- Newborns can perceive distance, and they prefer to look at patterned versus nonpatterned visual stimuli. Visual perceptual abilities and preferences appear so early in life that one must assume they are innate.

Behavioral States

- Behavioral states describe how alert, awake, or irritable an infant is. Predelivery medication given to the mother can effect the newborn's states for its first month of life.

Learning

- That neonates can learn has been proved by experiments involving the elaboration of reflex behaviors. Piaget believed that the modification of infant reflexes indicates that they possess "knowledge" and can behave "intelligently."

Assessing the Neonate

- Neonatal assessment is used to detect problems, including some that can threaten the infant's life. However, the relationship between the results of neonatal assessment and later development is not well understood. We do not know which early behaviors can be used to predict problems later in life.

Living with the Neonate

- Behavioral states appear to be influenced somewhat by stimulation. Neonates are most sensitive to sensory stimulation during the alert inactive state. Because picking up an infant can stop it from crying and induce the alert inactive state, it may facilitate intellectual development.
- Because babies differ, it is impossible to state hard and fast rules for providing good care, but good development does seem to require that adults adapt to their baby's individual style.

New Terms

neonatal period	retrolental fibroplasia
lanugo	neonatalogist
vernix caseosa	rooting reflex
molding	sucking reflex
fontanelles	gag reflex
ductus arteriosus	tonic neck reflex
apnea	Moro or startle reflex
bilirubin	Babinski or grasping reflex
physiological neonatal jaundice	palmar grasp
kernicterus	binocular fixation
glycogen	habituation
colostrum	distance perception
immunoglobulins	discrepancy hypothesis
small for date	behavioral states
hyaline membrane disease	swaddling
surfactant	Apgar score

Selected Readings

Brazelton, T. B. **Infants and mothers.** *New York: Dell, 1969.* Discusses the entire first year of life, but the first three chapters are devoted to the neonatal period. Stress is on individual differences among babies and on practical issues of caregiving. Interesting, nontechnical, and informative.

Brown, W. A. **Psychological care during pregnancy and the postpartum period.** *New York: Raven Press, 1979.* About one-third of this nontechnical but informative book is about the reactions of parents during the days and weeks immediately following the birth of a child. A unique chapter deals with bereavement reactions when a child is born with a handicap, or dies.

Klaus, M. H., and Kennell, J. H. **Maternal-infant bonding.** *St. Louis: C. V. Mosby, 1976.* Stresses the emotional significance of the period immediately following birth. Includes interesting material on fathers and on parents of premature or sick infants. A chapter is also devoted to dealing with parents whose infants die.

Leboyer, F. **Birth without violence.** *New York: Knopf, 1975.* Describes Dr. Leboyer's "gentle birth" method. About half the book covers infant behavior and care during the first hours after birth.

Reed, D., and Fiona, S., (Eds.). **The epidemiology of prematurity.** *Urban and Schwarzenberg, 1977.* An exhaustive and authoritative work on the factors relating to premature birth and on the consequences of prematurity during the neonatal period.

Spock, B. **Baby and child care.** *New York: Pocket Books, 1968.* This old standby discusses child care throughout childhood, but many topics of interest relate to the newborn. The reader can find information about everything, from infant crying in the early weeks to questions about breast feeding.

Part III
The Infant

The period of time designated by the term *infancy* varies from expert to expert. To some, it is the period between birth and the age of two-and-a-half or three. That is, there is no separate stage of development between infancy and the preschool years. To others, however, infancy lasts only until about eighteen months of age. The period from eighteen months to three years is considered to be a distinct period known as *toddlerhood.*

There are several reasons why the first three years of life are often divided into more than one stage. For one thing, changes occur so rapidly during these early years that there are vast differences between infants who are six months old and those who are eighteen or twenty months old. For example, a six-month-old cannot yet walk, whereas an eighteen-month-old can walk well. A six-month-old also cannot talk, but an eighteen- to twenty-month-old can usually say several words and may even begin to speak in short sentences. These differences have major implications for how to care for and respond to children.

We prefer to divide the first three years of life into the two periods of infancy and toddlerhood. We discussed the first few weeks of infancy, the neonatal period, in the last chapter. In the next five chapters we cover the remaining months of infancy, leaving a discussion of toddlerhood for Part IV.

For a long time little thought was given to what babies could know or do; it was simply assumed that they could do very little. During the last twenty years however, early infancy has been investigated by many child development experts. Their studies have shown that infants do notice the world around them and are capable of learning. In fact, the realization that crucial development occurs during infancy has led many experts to claim that it is the most crucial of all developmental periods. Although we would hesitate to say that one period of development is more important than another — they are all crucial in their own ways — we can say that the accomplishments of infancy seem the most remarkable. Everything adults know and take for granted, an infant must learn from the beginning. In just a few months, as we shall see, a baby begins to talk, think, and form relationships with others.

Chapter 6

Physical Development

To the casual observer, the most obvious changes during infancy are physical. The tiny, helpless newborn becomes an older infant who is heavy to carry about and so quick and agile that he or she is hard to keep up with. What are the changes that result in this transformation? They include rapid growth as well as development of the motor skills leading to reaching and grasping and walking. We discuss these and related topics next.

Growth

Most conspicuously, the infant becomes much bigger. This is the change often noted by relatives who rarely see a baby. "My goodness, but she has grown!" they say in astonishment, and that is no overstatement. Infants usually double their birth weight during their first six months and triple it by their first birthday, their weight changing from about seven to twenty-one pounds. By the time a child is two years old, its birth weight has often quadrupled. Length also changes dramatically during infancy. The typical twenty-inch length of the newborn increases by about five and a half inches during the first half-year, by three more inches at year's end, and by an additional four inches during the second year (Lowrey, 1978).

Of course, some infants grow more than others. This variation is caused by several factors, including heredity and nutrition. If conditions such as poor nutrition or inadequate space in the uterus prevented the fetus from growing as fast as it could have during the prenatal period, it may catch up after the adverse condition is eliminated. Thus, babies who are small at birth are likely to grow the most during infancy, although they may not grow as much as they would have under good conditions.

An apparently harmless situation in which "catch up" growth is common is that of infants who have large fathers and small mothers (Tanner, 1970). Although a child may be destined by genetics to be large, its prenatal growth may be inhibited by a slowing mechanism triggered by crowding in the uterus. The growth of such a child continues toward its genetically determined potential after it is born. This explains not only why some infants grow much more than others during infancy, but why birth length is a poorer predictor of adult height than length at a later age.

Changes in Body Proportions

As mentioned in earlier chapters, all parts of the baby's body do not grow at the same rate. Parents sometimes notice, for example, that pants that fit perfectly when purchased for the child's first birthday come well above the ankles six months later even though they still fit nicely around the child's waist. This is because more of the child's increase in length takes place in the legs than in the trunk. As this differential growth continues, the infant's proportions come to resemble those of an adult.

Tissue Growth

Just as there is a pattern to the growth of the head, trunk, and legs, there is a pattern to tissue growth. These changes affect the baby's appearance, strength, stamina, and control over its movements.

Subcutaneous Fat. The layer of fat that lies just beneath the skin begins to form in the fetus about six weeks before birth. It accumulates rapidly until about nine months after birth; thereafter it accumulates much more slowly. It is this layer of fat that makes an infant look rounded and filled-out — like a baby.

Normal infant plumpness should not be confused with obesity, which is as unhealthy at this stage as at any other. In the past, because many infants suffered from serious infectious diseases that resulted in emaciation and death, fat babies were welcomed because they were considered healthy. Now experts think that

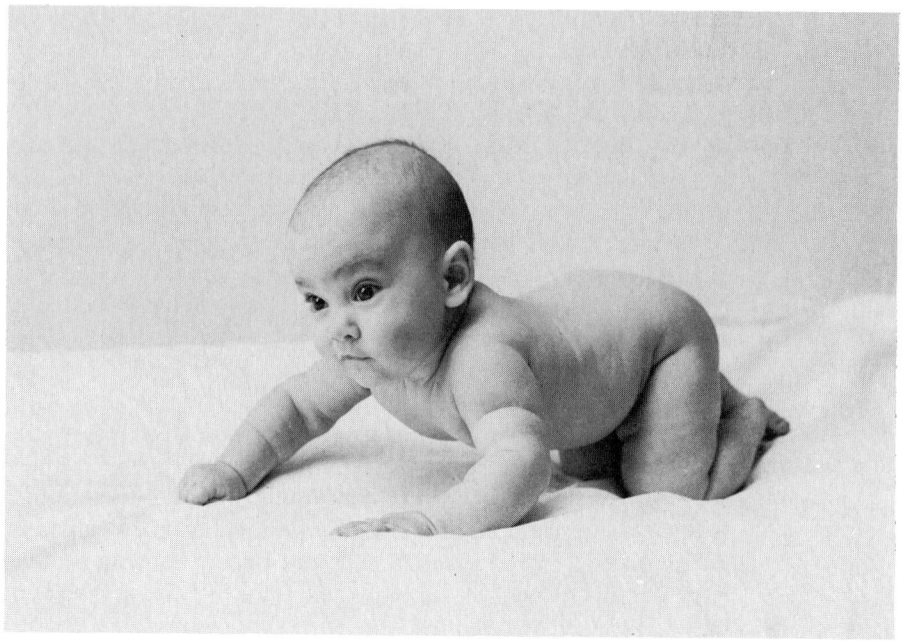

Subcutaneous fat develops rapidly during the first nine months of infancy. This baby is well padded.

the number of fat cells in a person's body is determined by how much he eats in his first year of life. After this time fat cells increase in size but not in number (Winick, 1974). People who have many fat cells because they were overfed as infants may have trouble losing weight as adults, although the number of fat cells formed during infancy does not seem to be the total explanation for later obesity. That is, some fat infants become fat children and adults, but not all fat infants do (Dobbing, 1975; Widdowson and McCance, 1975).

Muscle. Muscle tissue also changes during infancy. Although no new muscle cells are formed after birth, changes do occur in the muscle fibers already present. For example, the proportion of water in the fibers decreases, whereas salts and protein increase. As a result the infant's strength and stamina increase.

Bone. At birth, babies have soft bones composed largely of cartilage. Through a process known as *ossification*, however, minerals are gradually deposited and the cartilage turns to bone. The hardening and fusing of bones eliminates the soft spots or *fontanelles* in the infant's skull, although the large fontanelle at the top of the head does not close completely until the child is about two (Weinnberg, Woodrum, and Hodson, 1973). The growth of bones also changes the support structure of the body such that the child can eventually learn to walk.

Because ossification proceeds in a particular pattern, with some bones and bone parts ossifying before others, it indicates the child's level of maturity. The extent of ossification can be determined with X rays; the ossified areas, being more dense, show up on the film. Research using this technique confirms that girls mature faster than boys. At birth girls are about four weeks ahead of boys in terms of skeletal maturity; by age five or six, the gap has widened to about one year (Tanner, 1970).

Today, x-raying bones to determine maturity would probably be considered unethical because of the harmful effects of irradiation. To use this technique to study maturity, researchers would have to use X rays taken to diagnose conditions such as broken bones.

Brain. Some parts of the brain complete their development before birth, whereas other parts begin to develop prenatally but continue developing during infancy. Nerve cells, which make up about 10 percent of the brain, develop between the second and fifth months before birth. The extensions or fibers from the nerve cell body or nucleus, known as *dendrites* and *axons*, keep growing after the child is born. These fibers carry impulses to and from the cell. The rest of the brain consists of *glial cells*, which begin to appear about three months before birth and continue to multiply for several years after birth. These cells support the nerve cells and may serve nutritional and regulatory functions as well (Thompson, 1967). They also produce *myelin*, which forms a sheath around nerve fibers and greatly increases the speed with which impulses are transmitted (Dobbing, 1974).

At birth the brain is about one-quarter of its adult weight. By six months of age it has achieved 30 percent of its adult weight. By one year of age the brain is 60 percent of its adult weight. By the time the child is thirty months old, the brain has achieved nearly 75 percent of its adult weight. Ninety percent of the adult weight has been achieved by the child's brain by age five (Tanner, 1978). The last three prenatal months and the first year and a half of postnatal life have been called the period of the "brain growth spurt" because more than half of adult brain weight is achieved in this short period (Dobbing, 1974).

Good nutrition is crucial during this period of rapid brain growth, apparently as important as it is during early pregnancy. Poor nutrition can have serious consequences during all of pregnancy and infancy (Winick, 1976). This suggests that the nutritional component of comprehensive programs for preschool children such as Head Start is begun later than is most desirable. A program such as the Women, Infants, and Children (WIC) supplemental feeding program, which becomes available to pregnant women, nursing mothers, and infants who qualify in terms of family income, may have a more beneficial effect.

In addition to adequate nutrition, environmental stimulation also appears to affect proper brain growth and functioning. In studies with rats, it has been demonstrated that the weight of the cortex, the chemistry of the brain, and

FOCUS: The Special Supplemental Food Program for Women, Infants, and Children (WIC)

In 1972 Congress passed legislation authorizing a special food program for women, infants, and children (Section 17 of the Child Nutrition Act). The WIC program is unique in that it is the only nutrition program that provides supplemental food in connection with health services (Egan, 1977).

Eligibility for the program is restricted to pregnant women, nursing mothers, infants, and children under the age of five. Within these groups, risk is determined by income guidelines and by actual assessments of health and nutritional status by health professionals. In other words, recipients must first meet low-income guidelines to be eligible, and then be judged at risk on the basis of health and nutritional assessments.

Only certain foods are made available to program recipients. These include iron-fortified infant formulas, iron-fortified cereal, fruit or vegetable juices high in vitamin C, milk, cheese, and eggs (Egan, 1977). These foods were selected because iron-deficiency anemia, inadequate levels of vitamin C, and low levels of protein intake are common among at-risk populations. In addition, these are the nutrients necessary for good prenatal development, rapid growth during infancy and early childhood, and adequate protection against disease.

Food is distributed to WIC program recipients in a variety of ways. Some local agencies issue vouchers that can be redeemed at certain grocery stores. Other agencies deliver food directly to recipients' homes. Regardless of the method of service delivery, each recipient receives a specified amount of each type of food each month, at a cost of about $20 to $23.

The WIC program is administered by the United States Department of Agriculture. Grants are made by the USDA to the health departments of each state, which, in turn, utilize local health agencies to actually carry out the program.

According to medical evaluations conducted between 1973 and 1976, the program has resulted in the following benefits:

- The program was associated with an acceleration of growth in height and weight in infants.
- There was a consistent increase in the mean blood hemoglobin concentration of the infant participants in the program and a reduction in the prevalence of anemia.
- Pregnant women who participated in the program gained more weight during pregnancy than women like themselves who were not program participants.
- The program was associated with an increase in the mean birth weight of babies. [Egan, 1977, p. 237]

In addition, an evaluation conducted in 1975 indicated that participants utilized medical services to a greater extent than they had prior to the program.

The success of the WIC program was recognized by the Senate Nutrition Subcommittee in June 1980, when it voted to slash $500 million from all child nutrition programs, such as school lunch and breakfast programs, but voted to increase the size of the WIC program by 300,000 participants yearly. However, the committee also decided to lower the income eligibility requirement from a yearly income of $15,990 for a family of four to a yearly income of $14,743 for a family of four. The intent of the proposed legislation was to extend the program within the group of those truly in need of it (Report on Preschool Education, June 17, 1980).

The WIC program, like all publicly funded programs, is reviewed periodically. There is no guarantee that administrations with differing political and social views will consider such a program equally valuable. However, the WIC program is likely to be one of the last of the nutrition programs to be drastically cut back or disbanded. It appears to have been effective in achieving its goals and it is aimed at preventing nutritional problems when they are most likely to lead to serious impairment of physical and mental growth.

problem-solving abilities were influenced by conditions such as whether the rats lived in a stimulating or isolated environment (Rosenzweig et al., 1962).

Different parts of the brain mature at different rates. Lower brain structures such as the midbrain, pons, and medulla develop before higher structures such as the cerebral cortex. Within the cerebral cortex, different parts or areas, such as the motor area, mature at varying rates (Tanner, 1978). These differences in maturation influence the sequence in which a baby masters various physical skills. Babies can hold their heads up, for example, before they can sit up, and can sit up before they can walk.

Motor Development

As an infant's body structures and tissues develop, its abilities change, too. Various muscles gradually come under control during infancy, and the older infant can do things that the younger infant cannot.

Directed Reaching

One skill infants develop is that of reaching toward objects and picking them up. In the sequence of abilities that results in mature reach and grasp, the first behavior to appear is swiping at an object without attempting to grasp it. Babies do this at about two and a half months of age. By the time they are about four and a half months old, babies will reach for and grasp an object if they can see both their hand and the object at the same time. It is not until the age of about five and a half months that infants can reach and grasp an object when their hand is initially out of sight.

How babies use their hands to pick up objects changes as they grow and develop. At first, infants use an awkward, squeezing grasp in which the fingers surround the object and press it into the palm without much help from the thumb. Later, the thumb is more active in helping the fingers grasp objects. By about nine months of age infants can usually grasp small objects using just the thumb and the index or forefinger. This latter type of grasp is called a *pincer grasp.*

Although it is often stated that reaching skills develop through maturation, there is evidence that genetic and environmental conditions interact to affect them. Some evidence comes from studies of reaching and grasping in blind babies. Other evidence comes from studies of the effects of altering sighted babies' environments. We will consider the studies of blind babies first.

Blind babies attempt to reach and grasp early in life when they hear a sound. But the sound from an object does not tell the infant how far away it is; as a result its efforts at grasping are unsuccessful, and the baby stops making them (Bower, 1977). Fraiberg describes the special problems encountered by blind babies and how they can be overcome by altering the environment:

> Localizing an object on sound is normally mediated by vision. Reaching for an object on sound cue alone requires a level of conceptual development other than reach on sight. . . . But sound alone does not confer substantiality or "graspability" on an object; the blind baby must actually acquire a concept of an object in which the sound connotes "the thing." For a perilously long time in the first year of life the blind baby behaves as if the musical toy in his hand is one object and the sound of the musical toy "out there" is another object. . . .
>
> . . . Toys that united tactile and sound qualities were sought out by us and the parents to encourage a sound-touch identity for objects. . . . Through the devices of a special play table and a playpen we created "an interesting space" in which a search or a sweep of the hand would guarantee an encounter and interesting discovery. . . . Even the motor patterns for reaching may not appear in a blind baby who has no incentive to reach.
>
> Then, one day . . . the sound of the bell would motivate the hands. A grasping-ungrasping motion would appear. . . . There was not yet reach, but we knew the idea was emerging. A few days later, a few weeks later . . . without vision, a baby would discover that the sound that we call "a bell," and the bell which he could not experience in his hand were "out there" in space. [1975, p. 48]

Because the biological structures of blind babies differ from those of the typical baby, the environment must be specially adapted to assist their development.

Alterations in the environment can also affect the development of infants who have normal vision. Some of our knowledge on this subject comes from the work of White (1971). He added stimulation to infants' usual visual fields by giving institutional infants who were a few months old multicolored sheets, additional time on their stomachs, and large stabiles (stationary mobiles) above their cribs. One group received the stabile during the infants' second, third, and

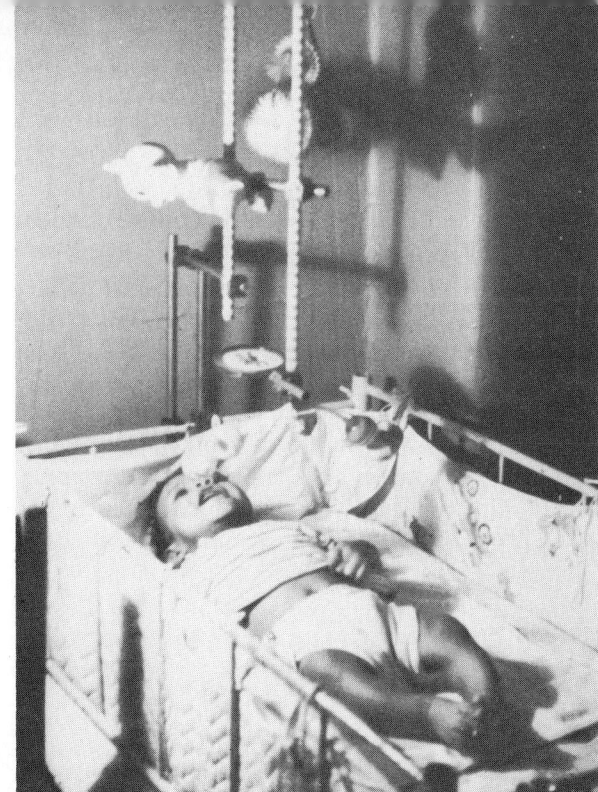

In some of the studies of directed reaching conducted by White, infants were given visual stimulation by placing stabiles above their cribs.

fourth months. A second group received an attractive pacifier centered on a disc at both sides of the crib during the babies' second month, and the stabile during their third and fourth months. Babies in both groups began reaching and grasping with the hand initially out of view in about 100 days, whereas babies in the control group, who had not received any added visual stimulation did not do so until about 140 days. Environmental influences apparently do influence the development of reaching and grasping.

But sometimes an attempt to influence development in one way also affects it in other, unexpected ways. The babies who received the stabile for all three months at first cried more than any other group. They had apparently been given stimulation that was too novel. As you will remember, Piagetian theory suggests that extreme novelty elicits fear; perhaps these infants were afraid.

To avoid frightening a baby, it is helpful to provide stimulation that the baby can choose not to look at. A mobile, for example, could be hung at the side of a crib rather than directly over the infant's head. The baby's reactions are probably the most useful guide to providing stimulation. Expressions of extreme surprise and fear indicate that the stimulation is too novel, whereas continuous looking probably indicates that the stimulation is just right.

Locomotion

Infants also improve their skills in using their legs. These are referred to as *locomotor skills*, because they result in the ability to move from place to place.

The Sequence of Locomotor Development. Walking is preceded by an orderly progression of development. Before an infant walks, it must be able to stand. To stand, it must know how to sit, and to sit, it must be able to hold its head up. The sequence of the development of locomotion is *cephalocaudal*, that is, the head and neck muscles come under control first, and the leg muscles last. The order of development is illustrated in both the detailed account of one locomotor milestone, creeping, shown in Box 6-1 (Ames, 1937), and in Box 6-2, which shows the complete sequence of development that results in walking (Shirley, 1933). Today, infants usually accomplish these locomotor tasks somewhat earlier than the average ages indicated in Shirley's chart because of improved nutrition, but the sequence of development remains the same.

BOX 6-1. Progression of prone development

A detailed account of one motor step, creeping, has been given by Ames (1937). The 14 stages of prone progression begin with movements that result in crawling (number 6) and end with creeping on the hands and feet (number 14).

BOX 6-2. Locomotor development

Rolling over from front to back and from back to front are not included on this chart. Considering the muscles that would be used in these maneuvers, where would you place them?

Factors Influencing Locomotor Development. Is the development of locomotion determined by heredity, or are learning and practice required? The evidence indicates that heredity and environment interact. Fraiberg's work with blind babies provides an excellent example of how the two are intertwined:

> In normal development when control of the trunk is achieved in a stable sitting posture, there is a smooth transition to bridging and creeping. In our sample, most of our babies achieved stability in sit well within the range of sighted babies. Most of our babies demonstrated the ability to support themselves on hands and knees within the range for sighted babies. Then, something that should appear on the developmental timetable did not appear. The baby did not creep!
>
> The sighted child will reach for the out-of-reach toy which propels him forward. It is the visual incentive that initiates the creeping pattern.
>
> At every point where vision would normally intervene to promote a new phase in locomotor development we had to help the blind baby find an adaptive solution. The prone position, for example, is not an "interesting" position for the blind baby. . . . The blind baby, without . . . incentives, may resist the prone position. We build in "interest" in prone through speaking to the baby, through dangle toys or other devices. . . .
>
> Practicing pulling to stand and cruising will be "more interesting" in familiar space of a playpen with favorite toys offering sound-touch incentives. And one day, sometimes between 13 and 19 months, the blind baby steps out into the vast black space to his mother's voice across the room and the news is telegraphed to us that he is walking! [Fraiberg, 1975, p. 48]

Additional evidence that environmental factors influence the development of locomotion skills comes from a study by Dennis (1960) of children in three institutions in Iran. About 600 children lived in Institution I. Almost half were less than one year old, and all were under three years old. One attendant was provided to care for every eight children. Children were bathed every other day. Those who could not yet sit spent their time in their cribs on their backs. They were never propped up or given toys. They were even fed in their cribs with bottles propped on pillows. When children managed to pull themselves into a sitting position, they were placed on the floor while awake, but still they were given no playthings. Not surprisingly, of the children between the ages of one and two, only 42 percent could sit alone, and none could walk; in fact, only 8 percent of the children between two and three could walk.

Children three years old and older lived in Institution II. Conditions there were as bad as in Institution I, where most had lived previously. Behavioral testing indicated that the children were equally delayed in development: only 15 percent of those between three and four could walk alone.

Institution III had been opened to model improved methods of child care. The most retarded children living in Institution I had been transferred to Institution III in very early infancy. The adult-child ratio in this institution was 1 to 4. Children were held when fed, placed prone or propped in a sitting position in their cribs, placed in playpens each day after they reached four months of age, and given toys. In this institution, 90 percent of the children could sit alone by two years of age, and 15 percent could walk alone. By age three, all children could walk alone. Dennis attributed the improved development to better child care, especially to the procedure of placing the babies prone in bed and on the floor.

Whereas there is some evidence that the effects of retarded early development can be overcome if good conditions are established later (Dennis, 1960; Kagan, Kearsley, and Zelazo, 1978), Dennis's study proves conclusively that child care practices influence motor development. Because most parents provide similar experiences that result in rapid motor development, we tend to believe that what we consider normal development occurs spontaneously and almost inevitably. This is not the case, however; children's development depends in part on the conditions we provide in caring for them. (See Pines, 1979 for a discussion of some of the intervention programs J. McV. Hunt used in the same orphanages.)

Some studies have provided data that appear to contradict the finding that environment or experience influences the development of locomotor skills. These studies have used identical twins because they are the same genetically. This makes it possible to attribute differences in behavior to variations in environment.

In Gesell and Thompson's (1929) study of maturation and learning, one twin was given daily practice climbing stairs for six weeks, beginning at forty-six weeks

Climbing up stairs is one milestone in locomotor development.

of age. By the fourth week of practice this twin could climb the stairs alone, and at the end of six weeks he could climb them in just twenty-six seconds. The other twin, introduced to the stairs at fifty-three weeks of age, climbed them in forty-six seconds on his first attempt, and two weeks later in just ten seconds.

The conclusion drawn from this study and similar ones was that maturation alone causes motor development to emerge, and that children's experiences have few consequences. But what if the ability to climb stairs is influenced, not by practice at climbing stairs alone, but also by opportunities to crawl, creep, and walk? If that were true, the twin who was given no practice at climbing stairs would still be able to do so when given the chance because he had crawled, crept, and walked as much as the other twin. Demonstrating that learning a behavior does not require a *specific* experience does not mean that the behavior is unaffected by all experiences (Bower, 1974). We can say, fairly certainly, that experience does influence the development of locomotor skills.

Summary

Growth

- During the first year of infancy children grow very rapidly, although the extent of growth during the first year varies from infant to infant and different parts of the infant's body grow at different rates.
- Babies typically put on a layer of fat during early infancy, but obesity in infancy is unhealthy.
- Infant bones are mostly cartilage at first, but they become harder through the deposit of minerals. The extent of a child's bone ossification indicates its level of maturity. In this respect, girls mature faster physically than boys.
- The nerve cells of the brain are formed early in prenatal development, but nerve fibers develop later in the prenatal period and during infancy. The last three months of prenatal development and the first eighteen months of infancy are a period of "brain growth spurt." Adequate nutrition during this period is essential for proper development. Environmental stimulation also appears to affect brain development.
- Different areas of the brain develop at various rates; this influences the sequence in which infants master motor skills.

Motor Development

- Babies swipe at objects before they can reach and grasp them. They can reach and grasp objects if both the object and their hand are in view before they can reach and grasp an object when their hand is initially out of view.
- Reaching and grasping skills are apparently influenced by experience. Some evidence of this comes from research with the blind. Blind babies must learn to reach by using sound cues alone.

- Locomotor development proceeds in a definite sequence. This sequence is cephalocaudal: it begins at the head and ends at the tail.
- Alterations in the environment can affect infants' motor development. Overstimulation can be avoided by arranging environments in such a way that infants can disregard stimulation if they choose to. Locomotor development also seems to be influenced by experience.

New Terms

subcutaneous fat   **glial cells**
ossification   **myelin**
fontanelles   **locomotor skills**
dendrites   **cephalocaudal development**
axons   **pincer grasp**

Selected Readings

Brazelton, T. B. **Infants and Mothers.** *New York: Dell, 1969.* An interesting and readable book that discusses many aspects of physical and motor development up to twelve months of age.

LaChance, P. A. Save WIC — A program that works. **Mothers Manual** 17 (1981): 20–23. A nontechnical article that gives an overview of the goals and characteristics of the Supplemental Feeding Program for Infants, Women, and Children and provides information about the program's success.

Tanner, J. M. **Education and Physical Growth,** 2d ed. *New York: International Universities Press, 1978.* Provides an overview of all aspects of physical growth from infancy to maturity. It is an authoritative and informative book, but not too technical for the student just beginning to explore this topic.

White, B. L. **The First Three Years of Life.** *Englewood Cliffs, N.J.: Prentice-Hall, 1975.* This book, written primarily for parents, discusses many aspects of physical growth and motor development from birth to three years of age. Covers practical implications of growth and development.

Chapter 7

*C*ognitive Development

Cognition is the act or process of knowing. Our understanding of the development of cognition comes from the study of perception and learning, from the work of Jean Piaget, and from the mental testing movement that became popular at the turn of the century with the invention of the intelligence test. In this chapter we begin by describing how some of the perceptual abilities and tendencies found in the neonate continue to develop during infancy. This is followed by a discussion of infant learning and of Piaget's stages of sensorimotor development.

Visual Perception

Investigators of infant perception have considered a number of important questions. What do infants look at? Why do they prefer to look at some objects more than others? Are infants born with certain visual perception abilities, or do such abilities develop with experience? Although research on these questions continues, we have partial answers to all of them.

Preference for Moderate Novelty

Like the newborn, the infant prefers visual stimuli that have contour and pattern, but the stimuli that elicit a response change as the infant matures. This has been explained in terms of the *discrepancy hypothesis*, which suggests that infants build up mental representations for objects and events in the environment and prefer to look at things that differ slightly from their current model of them (Kagan, 1971). They prefer a moderate level of novelty.

Older infants have had more visual experiences than younger infants, so we would expect them to have more and better-developed models. This suggests that older infants should prefer more complex stimuli than younger ones. As the Brennan study (1966) cited in Chapter 5 illustrated, this is in fact the case. Three-week-olds preferred the least complex of the stimuli shown to them, eight-week-olds preferred the intermediate stimulus, and fourteen-week-olds preferred the most complex stimulus. These results indicate that each group liked the moderately novel stimulus best.

As infants get older, their preferences for various representations of the human face also change. This, too, can be explained with the discrepancy hypothesis. Pictures of the sort used in several studies of infant reactions are shown in Figure 7-1.

Infants less than two months old show no preference among the various drawings. For them, the stimuli are apparently equally novel relative to their undeveloped mental representations of a face. By the age of three or four months, however, infants look longer at a partially scrambled face than at a completely scrambled one, and longest of all at a drawing of a normal face (Haaf and Bell, 1967; Wilcox, 1969). At this age, infants' experiences with people have developed their representations of the face more extensively; the drawing of the face is interesting because it resembles the faces they are familiar with but is slightly different, too. The scrambled face is still different from their model too and is not looked at. For one-year-olds, the ordinary face is so familiar that it presents no novelty, and the scrambled face receives the most attention.

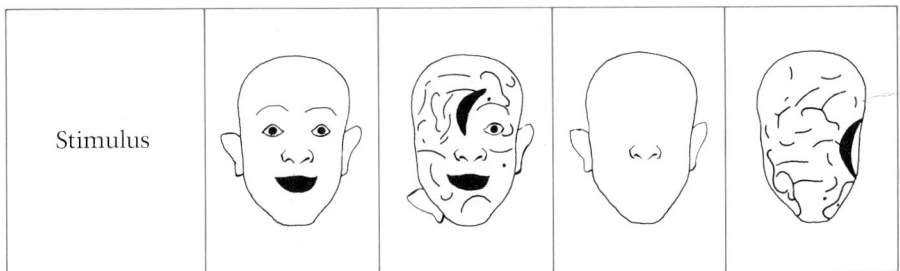

Figure 7-1. Face stimuli used in visual perception studies

Infants' visual attention seems to be influenced by a sort of "thinking" or "hypothesis testing" (Kagan, 1971). When infants look longer at a regular face because their model of a face is not completely developed, they may be wondering how what they see resembles what they know. They may hypothesize that the drawing resembles their developing representation of the face, and then test their hypothesis by matching certain features of what they see with their mental representations. Infants who look longer at the scrambled face may be considering how what they see differs from their mental representation. In this case, the infant may wonder why features are not where it expects them to be, and begin searching for the features not found in their expected places.

Although the moderate novelty principle can often be used to predict infant attention (McCall, 1974), there are times when it apparently does not (Cohen and Gelber, 1975). This is because we cannot currently assess a child's mental representations precisely enough to predict what new stimuli would be novel to exactly the right extent. The principle is nevertheless both general and useful. It helps us understand what motivates children to pay attention to one thing and not another (Hunt, 1965), and improves our knowledge of the conditions necessary for intellectual development. For example, it helps explain why the infants who do well on general tests of development in the first year of life are those who have had floor freedom, responsive mothers, and a variety of toys to play with. The reason, at least in part, is that these babies have been able to discover and explore a novel and socially responsive environment (Ainsworth and Bell, 1973; Beckwith, 1972; Yarrow, Rubenstein, and Pedersen, 1971).

Depth Perception

Depth perception is the understanding of the distance or drop between one plane and another. It is important in avoiding common dangers. A classic study with infants six to fourteen months old was done by Gibson and Walk (1960). The study was designed to determine whether infants perceive a drop-off in surface level. The apparatus used was a crawling surface, half of which was "shallow," while the other half was "deep" but covered with a glass. The mother stood on the deep side and tried to coax the infant to cross over from the shallow side. Infants would not cross over, however, even when they felt the glass over the deep side that told them it was solid. This behavior indicates that infants appreciate depth. Studies have shown that infants as young as ten days old have depth perception, which is a specific form of distance perception (Bower, Broughton, and Moore, 1974, cited in Bower, 1974).

Perception of Color

A third area of visual perception is the perception of color. Adults categorize certain wavelengths of light by hue into red, yellow, blue, and other colors. But are wavelengths placed in the categories we use because these have names, or

Gibson's visual cliff

were the names we use derived from natural color categories determined by the structure of our visual system? In other words, does language influence perception or does perception influence language? This is a very old question in psychology dating back to the work of Gladstone in 1858.

To determine how infants perceive stimuli from adult color categories, Bornstein, Kessen, and Weiskopf (1976) studied infants who were four months old. We will cite just one example to show the method they used. First, they habituated a group of babies to a green-blue stimulus (a green that is near the blue boundary in the spectrum). This color was called the *habituation stimulus* because it was shown to the infants until they no longer responded to it. Then they showed the children three other stimuli. One was the original green-blue color. The other two were equidistant from it in terms of absolute wavelength, but one was toward the green category of the spectrum, while the other was toward the blue category, albeit on the side nearest the green in the spectrum (see Figure 7-2). The greener stimulus was an average green color, and the other color was called blue-green. The question was this: Would infants see both of the new colors, the average green and the blue-green, as different from the habituation

Figure 7-2
Wavelengths shown to infants in the Bornstein study

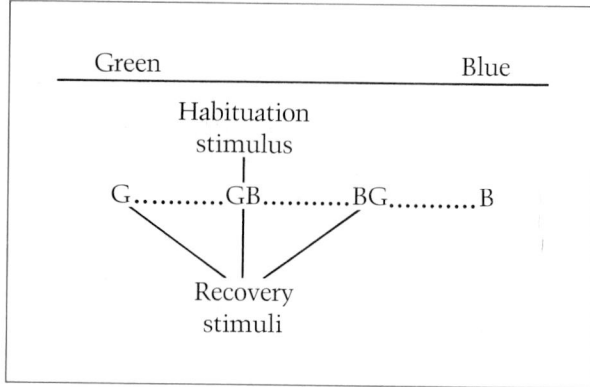

stimulus, the green-blue? Or would they see just the color in the different category of the spectrum, the blue-green, as different?

As it turned out, babies looked at the color in the different category of the spectrum, the blue-green, more than either the average green or the habituation stimulus (the green-blue). The average green and the green-blue were looked at the same amount, which indicates that they were seen as similar.

The results of the Bornstein study mean that even before children have language they perceive stimuli from the *same* adult color category as more similar than stimuli equidistant in wavelength from the habituating stimulus but from a *different* adult color category. We must conclude that the infant's color categories are the same as that of the adult, and that these categories affected by the structure of the visual system determine the color names given to wavelengths. That is, infants apparently bring their perceptual organization to bear on their language learning.

Learning

It was not long ago that people wondered whether infants a few months old could demonstrate any learning ability (Lipsitt, 1963). But since the mid-1960s, a number of studies have indicated that infants can solve problems and master tasks. One difficulty in conducting studies with infants is finding a way for them to show that they have mastered a task. Experimenters have solved this problem by making the appearance of stimulation contingent on responses such as eye fixations, head turning, smiling, sucking, or vocalizing, which young infants are capable of performing. For example, a learning task might require an infant to figure out that its sucking is what brings a visual display into focus or makes a mobile go around. The experimenter wants to find out if the baby learns what it must do to create the stimulation.

Mastering Specific Tasks

In one experiment a light was turned on when the infant turned its head 30 degrees to the right of midline. Young infants learned how to turn the light on by turning their heads but, surprisingly, head turning then declined until the experimenter made the light presentation contingent on more complex head turning, such as a turn to the right followed by a turn to the left. When infants found that the usual head turn did not turn on the light as it had before, they began a flurry of head turning, apparently trying to find out what to do to get the light to come on again. But once they had succeeded in turning on the light several times in succession, head turning declined again. In short, *infants seem to be motivated to learn by opportunities to solve problems*, not simply by primary reinforcement such as milk from a nipple (Papousek and Bernstein, 1969), or by visual stimulation such as seeing a light. This is an important finding for teachers: making learning interesting might be far more effective in keeping children involved in their work than stars or smiley faces pasted to their papers.

One crucial question is how individual learning experiences build on one another to determine a baby's later behavior. Is learning that is acquired during a previous task used in learning something new? Papousek (1967) was one of the first to provide evidence that it is. Babies in Papousek's study were taught a bell indicated that head turns to one side would be reinforced, whereas a buzzer indicated that head turns to the opposite side would be reinforced. Each day, a few trials of this task were given to two groups of infants of the same age. One group had previously mastered a similar discrimination task, whereas the second group had had no previous training in such tasks. The group that had received previous training took only ninety-six trials to learn the discrimination task, whereas the other group took about twice as many trials. Obviously, the first group of babies had learned something during the first training task that helped them learn the second task.

Learning and Environmental Responsiveness

In addition to learning specific methods of influencing the world, children may also learn a more general lesson when they discover that events are contingent on their actions. They learn that their actions can make interesting things happen in the environment. Infants who have not achieved results with their actions — that is, who have not received stimulation contingent on their actions — may learn "helplessness" instead. According to current thought, one or the other of these two attitudes results from a person's history of learning. That is, a lack of response-contingent stimulation leads to helplessness, whereas response-contingent stimulation in a sense immunizes an organism against helplessness (Maier, Seligman, and Solomon, 1969).

That this is true is indicated by at least two correlational studies. In one of them, researchers observed mothers and their five-month-old babies at home.

FOCUS: Is Helplessness Learned?

An interesting phenomenon was reported by Leaf (1964) and Overmier and Leaf (1965) when they were studying inhibition in the laboratory of R. B. Solomon at the University of Pennsylvania. It involved Pavlovian fear conditioning, which is giving an animal electric shocks that it cannot avoid, and avoidance training, which is putting an animal in a situation where there is a way to avoid electric shock. It was found that when fear conditioning was followed in less than two days by avoidance training, the animals had trouble learning how to escape the shock. This "interference phenomenon" was investigated in a number of studies by Maier, Seligman, and Solomon (1969). Most of these studies involved comparing the performance of dogs who had experienced Pavlovian fear conditioning with dogs that had not, on an escape/avoidance learning task. Dogs were conditioned to avoid a shock on one side of a two-way shuttle box by jumping from one compartment to the other after a stimulus was presented. All of the dogs who had not experienced Pavlovian fear conditioning learned this task easily. Nearly two-thirds of the dogs that had previously received uncontrollable shock did not, even after many trials. There were great differences in the avoidance learning of the two groups even when they had only had one fear conditioning session of sixty inescapable shocks.

Both groups of dogs behaved in the same manner when they were initially given avoidance training, running around randomly and howling until the shock ended. The dogs that had been given no fear conditioning, however, eventually fumbled into the other compartment and thereafter quickly learned the avoidance response. The dogs that had been subjected to uncontrollable shocks, on the other hand, grew quiet after a few trials and simply cowered in anticipation when presented with the stimulus that indicated the shock was coming. They seemed to give up and passively accept the shock, which made the probability of fumbling across the barrier low. Even the fear-conditioned dogs that managed to escape the compartment where they were shocked did not seem to realize that the same response (crossing the barrier) would work again.

Maier, Seligman, and Solomon (1969) explain the interference effect in terms of "learned helplessness." They suggest that an animal learns during inescapable shock, not simply that none of the behaviors it has attempted end the shock, but that no response it *can* make will end the shock. That is, it learns that there is no correlation between its behavior and the reinforcement that follows. This belief is then generalized to other situations, even those in which it can influence whether or not it is shocked.

These experiments suggest that raising children in an environment where desired results (such as food) are consistently unrelated to the child's efforts (such as crying) can have far-reaching effects on their motivation (Seligman, 1975) and, as a result, on their development.

The effects of being reared in poorly run orphanages can be explained in terms of "learned helplessness." Why should a child learn to pull itself up if it only gains a look at the same wall-to-wall cribs? Throughout this book we'll discuss the relationship between unresponsive environments and children's development.

They correlated these observations with clusters of items from an IQ test, the Bayley Scales of Infant Development (Yarrow, Rubenstein, and Pedersen, 1971, 1975). The cluster concerning goal orientation included such behaviors as persistent and purposeful attempts to secure objects just out of reach. The cluster concerning reaching and grasping consisted of items emphasizing visual-motor coordination and fine motor skills in actions with play objects. The third cluster, concerning effects of actions on the environment, included items that dealt with repeated behaviors that yielded interesting results, such as banging on something to make sounds. The researchers found significant positive correlations between maternal responsiveness to crying and each of these three clusters. Learning that their crying had an effect may have helped them understand that they could make things happen.

In another study, mothers' responsiveness to babies signals during feeding were found to be positively correlated with the babies' IQ scores (Ainsworth and Bell, 1973). Responsive mothers, for example, gave their babies a rest from feeding when they signaled by turning their heads to the side. As in the Yarrow, Rubenstein, and Pedersen (1971) study, infant development was positively correlated with how much a mother provided interesting results by responding to her infant's signals, as when she picked the infant up or spoke to it when it cried or fussed.

Because the evidence from these studies is correlational, we cannot be certain of the relationship between the responsiveness of the environment and infant development. Experimental studies have shown, however, that receiving response-contingent feedback on one task produces positive effects on the learning of a second, unrelated test task (Finkelstein and Ramey, 1977; Ramey and Finkelstein, 1978). Together these studies suggest that an environment that is generally responsive to baby's efforts may provide the most important of baby's learning experiences. As we shall discuss later, such an environment can also enhance the attachment of an infant to the caregiver who provides interesting results.

Piaget's Description of Sensorimotor Development

Because American psychology was dominated by S-R theory until the mid-1960s, we have many studies that show how babies learn a specific response over short periods in the laboratory, but few studies of how intelligence develops over time. Piaget began to fill this gap with longitudinal descriptions of the behavior of his own three children.

Piaget provided detailed descriptions of the development of several dimensions of infant intelligence, including the development of object permanence, imitation, and new means of achieving desired environmental events. According to Piaget, each of these aspects of intelligence develops in six stages, during a phase of development he called the *sensorimotor period*. During this period behavior consists of simple coordinations between what the child senses and how he or she reacts physically; there is no mediation by representational (symbolic) thought.

We have chosen to describe means of achieving desired environmental events because it is this aspect of infant development that is used in large part to define the six stages of sensorimotor intelligence. We discuss object permanence and imitation because of their importance in determining intelligent behavior, including language. The activities that characterize each sensorimotor stage have been used in infant stimulation and education programs, which we will describe later.

Piaget sees development as a continuous process from Stage 1 to Stage 6 of the sensorimotor period. Old schemes are seldom lost; they are modified to form new ones. The ages associated with each of the six stages by Piaget are only approximate. Individual children may pass through the stages at ages that differ somewhat from those given.

Means of Achieving Desired Environmental Events

Stage 1: Reflexes (roughly 0–1 month). Piaget's first stage is dominated by the use and progressive organization of reflexes. As we described earlier, reflexes change with age. (In Chapter 5 we saw how experience affected the sucking reflex in Piaget's son, Laurent.) The structures used in later sensorimotor stages are modifications of some of these initial hereditary organizations (Piaget and Inhelder, 1969).

Stage 2: Primary Circular Reactions (1–4 months). A circular reaction occurs when an infant's action leads accidentally to an interesting result. The child tries to achieve the result again by repeating the original action, which leads to the interesting result, which causes the child to repeat the action, and so on. The reaction is called "circular" because the action-event-action-event sequence repeats itself over an extended period of time. It is called "primary" because it involves only the infant's own body, not objects in the environment.

Though a primary circular reaction may involve actions that were once reflexive, it develops beyond this kind of primitive behavior. Piaget and Inhelder describe how this happens with thumbsucking:

> Fortuitous or accidental thumbsucking may occur as early as the first day. The more advanced sucking is systematic and dependent upon a coordination of movements of arm, hand, and mouth. . . . It is quite clear that this is a genuine case of acquisition in a broad sense, since there exists no reflex or instinct for sucking one's thumb. (Indeed the appearance of this activity and its frequency are subject to variation.) [1969, pp. 7–8]

Another infant behavior at this stage is repeatedly touching tongue to lips. Having touched tongue to lips once and noticed the sensation, the infant touches tongue to lips again, notices the sensation again, and repeats the sequence.

Cooing, which refers to noncrying vocalizations, can also be considered a primary circular reaction. The baby makes a sound, hears or feels it, and does it again.

Stage 3: Secondary Circular Reactions (4–8 months). The repeated actions seen frequently during this stage are "secondary" because they affect objects in the infant's environment rather than simply the infant's own body. Piaget provides the following example:

> At [3 months] I attached a string to the left arm after six days of experiments with the right. The first shake is given by chance: fright, curiosity, etc. Then, at once, there is coordinated circular reaction: this time the right arm is outstretched and barely mobile while the left swings . . . [1952, p. 161]

A common secondary circular reaction is an infant's shaking its crib to make a mobile move. As was true of primary circular reactions, the infant notices an effect of an action and repeats the action to experience the effect again. But this time the effect is in the environment.

Stage 4: Coordination of Secondary Circular Reactions (8–12 months). During this stage Piaget sees what he considers the first true acts of intelligence, that is, actions instigated intentionally to achieve a goal and pursued after the infant searches for an appropriate means. At this stage the individual schemes are not new, but the coordination of several of them to achieve a new goal is. One familiar scheme serves as the means to an end that involves another familiar scheme. For example,

> Laurent, at 6 months and one day tries to grasp a big piece of paper that I offer him and finally place on the hood of his bassinet (and on the string connecting the hood with the handle of the bassinet). Laurent begins by stretching out his hand; then as soon as the object is placed, he reacts as he always does in the presence of distant objectives: he shakes himself, waves his arms, etc. . . . After having behaved thus for a moment, he seems to look for the string hanging from the hood, then pulls it harder and harder while staring at the paper. At the moment when this is ready to fall off the hood, Laurent lets go the string and reaches toward the objective of which he immediately takes possession. Several sequential attempts have yielded the same result. [Piaget, 1952, p. 214]

Another common example of coordination of secondary schemes is an infant's crawling to an object to pick it up. It crawls, and then reaches, to achieve a goal: grasping an object. An adult can play a game with the infant at this stage by placing a hand in front of a toy. The baby will move the hand away and then reach to grasp the toy.

Stage 5: Tertiary Circular Reactions (12–18 months). Tertiary circular reactions differ from the schemes of Stage 4 in two important ways. First, desired ends are achieved, not by coordination of two familiar schemes, but by creating new schemes from familiar ones. Second, the infant's attention shifts from the goal (getting the rattle) to the means (different ways to get the rattle). In other words, there is active experimentation.

> I place my watch on a big red cushion (of a uniform color and without a fringe) and place the cushion directly in front of the child. Laurent tries to reach the watch directly and not succeeding, he grabs the cushion which he draws toward him as before. But then, instead of letting go of the support at once, as he has hitherto done, in order to try again to grasp the objective, he recommences with obvious interest, to move the cushion while looking at the watch. Everything takes place as though he noticed for the first time the relationship for its own sake and studied it as such. He thus easily succeeds in grasping the watch. [Piaget, 1952, p. 283]

The reaction is still considered circular because the novel schemes are frequently repeated, albeit with variations. The variation is no longer accidental, however; there is a search for novelty as such.

> At [10 months and 11 days] Laurent is lying on his back but nevertheless resumes his experiments of the day before. He grasps in succession a celluloid swan, a box, etc., stretches out his arm and lets them fall. He distinctly varies the positions of the fall. Sometimes he stretches out his arm vertically, sometimes he holds it obliquely, in front of or behind his eyes, etc. When the object falls in a new position (for example on his pillow), he lets it fall two or three times more on the same place, as though to study the spatial relation; then he modifies the situation. At a certain moment the swan falls near his mouth: now, he does not suck it (even though this object habitually serves this purpose), but drops it three more times while merely making the gesture of opening his mouth. [Piaget, 1952, p. 269]

Almost everyone has retrieved objects dropped or thrown by an infant from a highchair tray. The infant drops a spoon and someone picks it up. The infant drops it again, and the adult says, "Now try not to drop it again," when he gives the spoon back to the infant. Less tolerant parents warn, "Don't drop that spoon again!" Many parents apparently think the infant is being clumsy or naughty, but according to Piaget, the behavior indicates intelligent action with the goal of creating novelty.

Stage 6: The Invention of New Means Through Mental Combinations (18–24 months). This stage marks the end of the sensorimotor period and the beginning of the use of mental representation in solving problems. If the child desires a goal but lacks a means of acquiring it, he invents a means. This is not done by physical trial and error or groping as it was in the previous stage; instead, experimentation and "insight" now occur mentally:

> At [1 year, 4 months and 5 days] Laurent is seated before a table and I place a bread crust in front of him, out of reach. Also, to the right of the child I place a stick about 25cm. long. At first Laurent tries to grasp the bread without paying attention to the instrument, and then he gives up. I then put the stick between him and the bread; it does not touch the objective but nevertheless carries with it an undeniable visual suggestion. Laurent again looks at the bread, without moving, looks very briefly at the stick, then suddenly grasps it and directs it toward the bread. But he grasped it toward the middle and not at one of its ends so that it is too short to attain the objective. Laurent then puts it down and resumes stretching out his hand toward the bread. Then, without spending much time on this movement, he takes up the stick again, this time at one of its ends (chance or intention?), and draws the bread to him. He begins by simply touching it, as though contact of the stick with the objective were sufficient to set the latter in motion, but after one or two seconds at most he pushes the crust with real intention. He displaces it gently to the right, then draws it to him without difficulty. Two successive attempts yield the same result. [Piaget, 1954, p. 335]

Imitation

The first events related to imitation occur during Stage 2 (primary circular reactions: 1–4 months). If an adult interrupts vocal play and begins to utter the same "ahs" the baby has been making, the baby may begin its primary circular reaction again. Piaget states that the baby begins vocal play again at this point because it does not distinguish its own sounds from the adult's imitation, so the adult's sounds reinstate the primary circular reaction. Because it is the adult rather than the child who does the real imitating, this phenomenon is called *pseudoimitation*. It occurs only if the adult repeats a sound recently made by the baby. It has been suggested that pseudoimitation explains why one infant will begin to cry if another one does, a phenomenon that has been observed by several researchers (Simner, 1971; Wolff, 1969).

In Stage 3 (secondary circular reactions: 4–8 months), babies can imitate a specific behavior they have never performed before, but it must involve familiar, not novel, schemes. Suppose a particular child sometimes bangs on her highchair tray with a spoon while waiting to be fed. One morning, immediately after

Who is imitating whom?
The father is imitating the baby's frown; imitation of invisible gestures — gestures the baby cannot see itself perform — is difficult for babies prior to Stage 5.

putting the baby in the highchair, the child's father gets a pot and bangs the bottom of it with a spoon. He hands the pot to the child, who then entertains herself by banging her spoon on the pot. That only familiar schemes are imitated is consistent with secondary circular reactions generally, in which only familiar schemes are voluntarily begun.

Imitation of novel behavior increases in Stages 4 (coordination of secondary circular reactions: 8–12 months) and 5 (tertiary circular reactions: 12–18 months), as does the frequency of other novel behavior. For example, if an adult turns up the volume of the TV set by turning a knob, an infant sitting nearby may immediately try to turn the knob in a similar fashion.

In the stages of imitation discussed so far, the child can imitate the act only if an adult has exhibited it immediately before. In Stage 6, however, new mental abilities make deferred imitation possible.

At [1 year, 4 months, and 3 days] Jacqueline had a visit from a little boy of [1 year and 6 months] whom she used to see from time to time, and who, in the course of the afternoon got into a terrible temper. He screamed as he tried to get out of a playpen and pushed it backward, stamping his feet. Jacqueline stood watching him in amazement, never having witnessed such a scene before. The next day, she herself screamed in her playpen and tried to move it, stamping her foot lightly several times in succession. [Piaget, 1954, p. 63]

A friend of ours told a similar story about her two-and-a-half-year-old daughter. The child had watched "Sesame Street" one day when Ernie was searching for a toy in his toy box. His method was to stand in front of the box and throw toys out with both hands until he reached the toy he wanted at the bottom. A few days later, the mother noticed that her daughter, who had previously found a toy she wanted by rummaging around inside her toy box, was tossing her toys out onto the floor in the manner so effectively demonstrated a few days earlier by Ernie.

You can see how babies' imitative repertoires can increase enormously through the ability to defer imitation. You may also understand why some people have labeled this period the "terrible twos." Children sometimes imitate what adults wish they would not, and children's limited linguistic and reasoning skills make it difficult to overcome this influence. Children of this age should not be given this disparaging label, however. Their behavior is perfectly understandable and even delightful when placed in perspective.

Pat-a-cake, an age-old imitation game enjoyed by year-old infants

Object Permanence

A typical six-month-old who watches a favorite toy being covered up with a cloth will not pick up the cloth to get the toy: out of sight, out of mind. But a typical one-year-old in the same situation will search for the hidden toy. The one-year-old has *object permanence:* he or she understands that an object exists even when it cannot be seen. Like other sensorimotor abilities, object permanence develops in stages. Schemes related to object permanence are present from the beginning and become progressively more mature over the course of the sensorimotor period.

In Stage 1 (reflexes), babies can follow a moving object continuously with their eyes over a short arc in attempting to keep it in view. In Stage 2 (primary circular reactions), babies will continue to stare at the place where the object disappeared if it leaves the field of vision. These are both relatively passive attempts to continue to look at the object.

In Stage 3 (secondary circular reactions), however, the child begins to reach and grasp for objects in the environment. Piaget observed that the child at this stage will search manually for a partially hidden object such as a baby bottle covered with a cloth so that only the bottom of the bottle shows. The child's enthusiasm for this task suggests that seeing part of the object tells the child that the whole bottle still exists. A baby does not search for a bottle that is completely covered, however, which suggests that the permanence of screened objects is incomplete. Recent evidence suggests that Stage 3 babies do possess object permanence for objects *behind,* rather than *under,* a screen (Brown, cited in Bower, 1974).

It is in Stage 4 (coordination of secondary schemes) that babies are first likely to find objects under screens. But even at this stage the baby's concept of the object is incomplete. Suppose a large object such as a baseball is placed under a red cloth and a baby finds it several times in succession. If the ball is then placed under a green cloth, the ten-month-old is still likely to search under the red cloth, even if it is lying flat on the table. This Stage 4 perseveration error suggests that the ten-month-old has learned only to make a missing object reappear by pulling on the cloth the object was found under by chance on a previous occasion. The child apparently believes, not that the toy exists under the cloth, but that the object is made to reappear suddenly by pulling the cloth up.

Object permanence improves in Stage 5 (tertiary circular reactions). At this point a baby who previously stumbled onto the first hiding place knows enough to look under a second screen when the object is hidden there. The fifteen-month-old now chooses the screen where the hidden object was last *seen,* not where it was last found. But there are still two situations in which the child has difficulties: (1) If we put two screens in front of the baby, hide a toy under the screen on the left and then switch the screens so that that screen is on the right,

Peek-a-boo, a game en-
joyed by year-old infants
as object permanence
emerges

the baby will look where the object was last seen to disappear, under the left
screen. Before the child can avoid this switching error it must have a mental
representation of the *path* of the hidden object. (2) If you hide a small toy in your
hand so that it can no longer be seen by the fifteen-month-old, then put your
hand under a cloth, leave the toy, and bring your hand back empty, the fifteen-
month-old will probably look in your hand and not know where to search next.
Discovery of an object after this type of invisible displacement also requires a
mental representation of the object's path, which does not develop until Stage 6.

The transition from one stage of object permanence to another provides a
good example of accommodation of schemes. In Stage 3 babies cannot find objects

under horizontal screens, but they can find objects behind vertical screens. Perhaps the Stage 3 baby has trouble with horizontal screens because the baby's place scheme says that two objects cannot be in the same place simultaneously. The place scheme inhibits object permanence when an object is hidden *under* a screen because the screen and object appear to occupy the same location (Bower, 1974). The place scheme does not interfere with finding an object *behind* a screen, however, because the child sees that the objects occupy different locations. Then, as a consequence of greater success using progressively more complex strategies, babies acquire schemes in addition to those in Stage 3. One of these is acquired in Stage 4; if an object is replaced in the same place by an object differing from it in size, shape, and color, the infant searches for the original object where it was *last found.* Then, in Stage 5, if an object is replaced in the same place by an object of a different size, shape, and color, the infant searches for the original object where it *last disappeared.* Then the one-year-old comes into contact with situations where one object is inside another:

> Around [1 year, 2 months, and 18 days] Laurent has begun to put pebbles, small apples, etc., into various pails etc., and to turn them over. This behavior pattern becomes increasingly frequent during the following weeks. Between [1 year, 3 months] and [1 year, 6 months] the sight of a hollow object almost automatically arouses in Laurent a desire to fill it, to displace it, and to empty it shortly afterward. At [1 year, 3 months, and 17 days], for example, he fills a metal cup with grass and pebbles and empties it at a distance, etc. [Piaget, 1954, p. 218]

These situations present a conflict to the child: container and contained move as one, yet they remain potentially separable into two independent objects. Sometime after the concept of "inside" is discovered, it is combined with the place scheme. The place scheme is accommodated, and the infant behaves as though "two objects cannot be in the same place simultaneously *unless* one is *inside* the other." At this point babies have mature object permanence.

An Overview of the Sensorimotor Period

Table 7-1 shows how the three dimensions of sensorimotor development we have described relate to each other. A child may not reach a particular stage at the same time in all of the three dimensions (Uzgiris, 1973). For example, a baby may have Stage 4 object permanence skills, such as uncovering hidden objects, before it has Stage 3 imitation skills, such as imitating familiar sounds (Schickedanz, 1976). However, a review of many studies indicates that, within a particular dimension, few if any babies show behavior characteristic of a higher stage before behavior characteristic of a previous stage (Brainerd, 1978). The few reversals that have been recorded may be the result of misclassification of the behavior.

Table 7-1. Summary of three dimensions of sensorimotor development

Stage	Development of means to achieve desired environmental events	Imitation	Object permanence
1. Reflexes 0–1 mo.	Elaboration of reflexes		Follows object with eyes over short arcs
2. Primary circular reactions 1–4 mo.	Use of means to produce interesting effects involving own body	Pseudo-imitation	Glance lingers where an object disappears
3. Secondary circular reactions 4–8 mo.	Use of means to produce interesting effects involving objects in environment	Imitation of familiar schemes	Uncovers partially hidden object
4. Coordination of secondary circular reactions 8–12 mo.	Novel coordinations of familiar schemes	Imitation of somewhat novel schemes	Uncovers hidden object but shows perseveration error
5. Tertiary circular reactions 12–18 mo.	Progressive modification of familiar schemes to produce novel schemes as means to an end; groping	Imitation of novel schemes	Uncovers hidden object but shows switching error
6. Invention of new means through mental combinations 18–24 mo.	Insight without groping	Deferred imitation	Uncovers object hidden through invisible displacement

The fact that Piaget's description of behavior is accurate does not prove that his theory of behavior change is completely accurate. We will need further evidence before concluding that behavior change always involves significant conflict between current schemes and experience. In addition, the appearance of habituation and a preference for moderate novelty in the first few months of life suggest that some kinds of mental representation are possible before one and a half years of age. Nevertheless, the evidence that discrepancy at least occasionally leads to behavior change (Bower, 1974, 1977) and the dramatic growth of language skills in the second year of life suggest that Piaget's theory is at least partially correct. It is undoubtedly an important theory that is sure to produce much more study and controversy in the 1980s.

Summary

Visual Perception
- The discrepancy hypothesis is one explanation for why infants of different ages respond differently to the same visual stimulus. It also helps explain why optimal intellectual development is apparently related to the responsiveness of the adults who care for a child and the responsiveness of other aspects of the child's environment.
- Studies have shown that infants can perceive depth.
- Infants perceive the color categories labeled with color names by adults. Their color perception appears to provide categories that children use in learning language.

Learning
- Infants appear to be motivated to learn by opportunities to solve problems rather than by primary reinforcers, such as milk.
- When infants' efforts receive no response, they may learn helplessness. Responsive caregiving and responsive toys can therefore help performance on infant intelligence tests.

Piaget's Descriptions of Sensorimotor Development
- Piaget calls the earliest period of intellectual development the sensorimotor period. It consists of six stages, which are often defined in terms of an infant's means of achieving desired environmental events. A circular reaction is one in which an action-event sequence repeats itself over and over. In a primary circular reaction (Stage 2), the action-event sequence involves the infant's own body rather than objects in the environment. A secondary circular reaction (Stage 3) involves an action that has an effect on an object in the infant's environment. Stage 4 of the sensorimotor period signals the first appearance of intentional acts. In Stage 5, tertiary circular reactions, an infant achieves ends by creating new schemes from familiar ones. In Stage 6 the child invents means to ends in his head. He does not have to discover all new means through physical experimentation.
- Imitation first occurs in Stage 2. Pseudoimitation refers to a cycle of events in which an adult first repeats a baby's behavior.
- Object permanence refers to the understanding that objects not seen still exist. Babies are unlikely to search for completely hidden objects under screens until they are in Stage 4 of the sensorimotor period. Until babies are capable of mentally representing the path of an object, they cannot solve the problem of invisible object displacement; this occurs in Stage 6.

New Terms

cognition
discrepancy hypothesis
habituation stimulus
sensorimotor period
cooing
object permanence
place scheme
Stage 1: reflexes

Stage 2: primary circular reactions
Stage 3: secondary circular reactions
**Stage 4: coordination of secondary
  circular reactions**
Stage 5: tertiary circular reactions
**Stage 6: invention: mental
  combinations**
pseudoimitation

Selected Readings

Ginsburg, H., and Opper, S. **Piaget's theory of intellectual development,** 2d ed. *Englewood Cliffs, N.J.: Prentice-Hall, 1979.* Explains all of Piaget's stages of development. One section explains sensorimotor development. For the beginning student.

Kagan, J., Kearsley, R., and Zelazo, P. **Infancy: Its place in human development.** *Cambridge, Mass.: Harvard University Press, 1980.* Discusses many aspects of infant development, with extensive coverage of cognitive development. Authoritative but not too technical for the beginning student.

Hunt, J. McV. **Intelligence and experience.** *New York: Ronald Press, 1961.* For the serious student who is interested in a detailed discussion of Piaget's work. A good portion of the book is devoted to the sensorimotor period.

Chapter *8*

*L*anguage Development

The study of language development in infancy is concerned with describing early language behavior, both what infants "say" and how they understand and respond to what others say to them. Of great interest is how and why language development occurs and what factors aid or impede it.

We begin by discussing theories of language development and then cover early language behavior in detail. We conclude the chapter by examining possible links between sensorimotor intelligence and language behavior and the social conditions necessary to support optimal language development.

Studying Language Acquisition

Suppose you wanted to study language development from its beginning until it has all the characteristics of mature, adult language. How old would children have to be before you began observing them? Would you study newborns, or begin when children utter their first "word" at about the time of their first birthday? Or would you wait until simple sentences of at least two words appear around the age of two? Each choice would be based on assumptions about the nature of language, its origins, and how it changes. In the same manner, experts in language acquisition make assumptions and conduct their research accordingly.

Learning Theory

Before the 1950s, when *learning theory* was the dominant explanation of language learning, researchers studied language development in infancy. They tended, however, merely to catalog the sounds or words produced by infants of different ages. They assumed that these "building blocks" were gradually put together in accordance with the principles of reinforcement and that this process, along with direct imitation of adult models, explained how children learned to talk.

In the late 1950s and early 1960s, psycholinguists and linguists began to criticize the learning theory view. They argued that children do not imitate specific utterances they have heard, but rather learn rules for making up sentences (Chomsky, 1959; 1965). Children use language creatively, the critics suggested. They say things that adults never say, such as "My cat has four feets," by using rules that are never directly taught, such as adding an *s* to the end of a noun to form the plural.

The critics of the learning theory explanation also argued that language acquisition could not be explained in terms of reinforcement, learning theory's central construct. Parents, it was found, rarely reinforce grammatically correct speech. They ignore grammatical errors and pay attention to whether the child is telling the truth, being polite, or acting in accordance with other semantic or pragmatic values:

> In general, the parents fit propositions to the child's utterances, and then approve or not, according to the correspondence between proposition and reality. Thus "Her curl my hair" was approved because mother was, in fact, curling Eve's hair. However, Sarah's grammatically impeccable "There's the animal farmhouse" was disapproved because the building was a lighthouse and Adam's "Walt Disney comes on, on Tuesday" was disapproved because Walt Disney comes on, on some other day. [Brown, Cazden, and Bellugi, 1969, pp. 57–58]

Psycholinguistic View

In the 1960s and early 1970s psycholinguists, such as Roger Brown, concluded that the ability to learn *syntax* — the rules governing how words are put together to form phrases and sentences — is innate. They argued that language is too complex and acquired too young to be accounted for by the learning explanation. This view prevailed for a time, and describing the rules according to which children constructed their early sentences was the focus of research. There was little interest in vocal behavior before the two-word stage for two reasons. First, analysis of formal syntax required at least two words. Second, searching for the roots of language in early vocal behavior was inconsistent with the notion that language acquisition was made possible by an innate structure.

Emphasis on Semantics and Interaction

By the mid-1970s the idea that language acquisition was largely innate was being criticized. Critics suggested that the basis for syntactic understanding was the action schemes of sensorimotor intelligence rather than an innate language acquisition device. Perhaps a child's first level of understanding involved actions, which were later coded linguistically. If so, children know how to "mean" before they know how to "say." As Macnamara stated it, perhaps "infants learn their language first by determining independent of language, the meaning which a speaker intends to convey to them, and by then working out the relationships between the meaning and the language" (1972, p. 1). In this view, *semantics* (the meaning aspects of language) and what it is used for are as important as syntax and can be expected to appear early (Clark and Clark, 1977). The assumption made by those who emphasized syntax was just the opposite: an understanding of syntax, which is assumed to be largely innate, is considered to give the child clues to meaning.

The Implications of Theories

The adoption of one theoretical view or the other has important implications for both the researcher and the practitioner. For example, if you thought that a knowledge of syntax is innate, then you would not study infants incapable of "talking." Similarly, you would not encourage programs designed to support language development until "real" language developed in late infancy. If, on the other hand, you assumed that syntax is learned, you would study very young infants and begin language supporting programs at an earlier age.

Those who hold an interactionist view of language acquisition believe that infancy is an important period, but for different reasons than those who held the earlier, learning theory orientation. Interactionists do not assume, for example, that early vocalizations are necessarily the direct precursors of later words. They are interested instead in the interaction between the child's sensorimotor intelligence and the linguistic environment provided by adults, in the meaning adults give to the child's early vocalizations, in how the situational context helps children learn language, and in how children learn the social conventions of language use, such as taking turns. The relation between the infant's actions and language learning is also of interest. In the following pages we will describe language development and discuss some of the evidence for the interactionist view.

Language Production

Early Vocal Behavior

The first vocalization is made at birth or soon after. Noncrying sounds begin to appear during the first month. P. Wolff (1969) claims that the first noncrying sounds develop out of a "fake cry": "The cry is of low pitch and intensity; it consists of long drawn out moans which occasionally rise to more explicit cries, and then revert to poorly articulated moans" (p. 98). Most parents call this a "fussy cry." Wolff's explanation is consistent with the behavior of the primary circular reaction period: behaviors first discovered are then repeated. Baby emits a sound, apparently feels and hears it, and then emits it again in a circular pattern. Later, infants discover sounds, not when they are crying, but when they are playing (Wolff, 1969).

Cooing (noncrying vocalizations) consists mostly of "open" sounds, what we would call vowels (Cruttenden, 1970; Menyuk, 1977), such as the "aaaaah" you make for the doctor when you have a sore throat, or the "oooooooh!" you make when your favorite baseball player strikes out. The few consonant-like sounds that appear in cooing are produced for the most part by stopping air with the very back of the throat ([k] as in kite; [g] as in goat), or with the lips ([w], [p]) (Cruttenden, 1970). When infants are four or five months old, they begin to make a larger number of both vowel and consonant sounds. Sometime after that, they begin to combine these sounds into consonant-vowel strings, such as "kaka-kakakakaka" or "mamamamama." This vocal behavior is called *babbling*. Near the end of the babbling stage, at about ten to twelve months of age, vocalizations of one syllable, or a syllable repeated twice, are more likely than strings. The infant might say "da-da," rather than "dadada"; or "ma-ma," rather than "ma-mama" (Menyuk, 1977). At this point, the baby's vocalizations begin to sound like words.

Social Interaction and Early Vocal Behavior

Many parents know that talking to a baby encourages it to "talk" back. A mother faces her baby and says something like "Are you going to talk today? Why don't you talk a little? Hmmmm?" Often, a previously quiet and serious-looking infant begins to smile and make sounds.

Researchers, too, have found that social interaction with infants increases their sound making (Lewis, 1951; Rheingold, Gewirtz, and Ross, 1959; Wolff, 1969). But can adults get infants to make certain sounds rather than others? They can, but there are some limitations. During the second or third month, babies sometimes respond to adult sounds with pseudoimitation, which was discussed in Chapter 7. As you will remember, during pseudoimitation the infant reproduces only sounds that he or she has previously made. If the adult makes sounds that are not in the baby's repertoire, the infant will not repeat them. Piaget explains it this way:

> In order to stimulate the baby's voice, the other voices must either reproduce certain familiar sounds already uttered by the child, or certain intonations known to him. . . . The child makes no effort to adapt himself to the sound he hears, but merely has to retain the sound he himself was making a moment earlier. [1954, pp. 10–11]

A different interpretation of this situation is that the baby is taking turns rather than imitating. According to this view, the baby's sounds are original creations.

Vocal Behavior in Later Infancy

Most children stop babbling around the age of one year and enter the single-word stage. One-word utterances have been called *holophrases* because infants seem to be expressing intentions rather than naming objects. Thus, "milk" could mean "Is that milk?" "Give me some milk," or "That is milk" (McNeill, 1970; Menyuk, 1977).

Although the issue of whether children are expressing intentions with their one-word utterances has not been settled conclusively (Dore, 1975), most authorities agree that adults interpret the words as if they are intentional (Bruner, 1975a; Menyuk, 1977). But how does an adult know what a baby is trying to say and how he or she should respond? The most important clues are context and the child's intonation (the rise and fall of the voice). Suppose a child sitting in a high chair reaches toward the cookie jar while saying "ku-ku-ku-ku" to her father, who is standing nearby. Father is likely to say, "Do you want a cookie? Finish your yogurt and then we'll have one." But later, when the child is eating a cookie and holds it up and says "ku," father might say, "Yes, that's a cookie. That's a mmmmm good, chocolate chip cookie."

Bruner (1975a) has reported this kind of parental interpretation of intentions long before the one-word stage. For example, a mother responded differently to a six-month-old child when the child spoke at different pitches. The infant used higher-pitched vocalizations when manipulating objects than when vocalizing to his mother. The mother looked at the infant when the pitch of vocalizations dropped, apparently to see if the infant was "talking" to her. In addition, the child's vocalizations began more sharply when the child was reaching for objects that were out of reach than when he was reaching for accessible objects. The mother responded to the sharper onset by moving the object toward the child.

The cookie example used earlier also illustrates how children's first words do not always follow adult sound patterns. Children's words may be based on approximations of adult sound patterns, as when "ku" is used to refer to cookies. A child may also make up a word that has a different sound sequence than the word adults use for the same object (Carter, 1975; Winitz and Irwin, 1958). Sometimes parents can understand what a young child says when it is incomprehensible to an outsider. "He said 'ah!'" they explain. "That's his word for 'outside.'" The child's sound sequences gradually come to resemble those used by adults (Goldin-Meadow, Seligman, and Gelman, 1976; Menyuk, 1977).

Children's First Words

We remember a child who loved the Muenster cheese her mother often gave her for lunch. Her first word was "cheese," although she did not speak it very clearly. She would sometimes go to the refrigerator door and say "cheese, cheese," or say "cheese" after being put in her highchair for meals.

The first word of another child we know was "light," which he usually said when a light was turned on in the room. "Water" was the choice of a third child. During the hot summer months this child had visited Grandma, who watered the garden with a hose. The child "helped" with this chore and played with the hose for long periods, filling and refilling buckets and pans with water. When inside the house, this child often went to the door, reached for the doorknob, and said "water, water."

What do the words used by these three children have in common? A study by Katherine Nelson (1973), a language researcher, suggests what it might be. She found that the words used first by eighteen children between one and two years old could be categorized into five groups, as shown in Table 8-1.

Table 8-1. Categories of first words observed by Nelson

Word Group	Description
1. Nominals	Words used to refer to things
a. Specific	Words used to refer to one exemplar of a category: a specific person, animal, or object (Mommy, Dusty).
b. General	Words used to refer to all members of a category (car, doggie, key, 2, he, milk, snow).
2. Action words	Words that describe, demand, convey action or express attention or demand for attention (bye-bye, up, hi).
3. Modifiers	Words that refer to properties or qualities of things or events (big, pretty, hot, all gone, outside, mine).
4. Personal-social	Words that express affective states and social relationships (please, ouch, no, thank you, want).
5. Function words	Words that fulfill a solely grammatical function (what, where, is, for).

SOURCE: Adapted by permission from Nelson, K. Structure and strategy in learning to talk. *Monographs of the Society for Research in Child Development* 38 (1973), Serial No. 149. Copyright © The Society for Research in Child Development, Inc.

Nelson noticed that the children she observed used general nominals (ball, clock, dog, cookie) more often than words from other categories. Half of the children's first fifty words were of this sort. Why were these general nominals chosen rather than others such as table, grass, sidewalk, or carpet? When she surveyed the list of general nominals she had collected, she noticed that most of the words were names of things that children act on in some way. This, she concluded, was the key to their importance to children. Children, it seems, ignore things that simply exist, but they pay attention to objects that do something such as roll, run, drive away, or make sounds. Our observations of the use of "cheese," "light," and "water" are nicely consistent with Nelson's idea. All of these things can act or be acted on, or both.

But, you may be asking, why should action matter? The answer may be that action results in changes in stimuli, which in turn produce novelty, the discrepancy between what a child knows and what he or she observes. As discussed earlier, novelty catches children's attention. When a baby hears the call of the cuckoo clock, or sees the numerals change on the digital clock face, its mother notices the direction of the child's gaze, or the sudden cessation of the child's activity accompanied by an expression that indicates listening. Mother says, "Clock? Did you hear the clock? Do you see the clock?" Baby hears the name for the object, and so learns to associate the object with a particular sound.

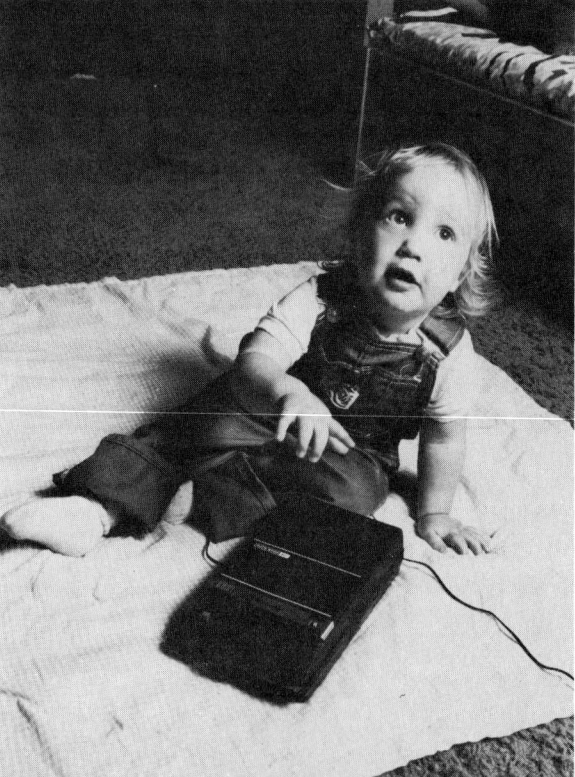

If it moves or makes a noise, an infant is likely to notice it.

There is some evidence that mothers do follow their baby's *line of regard* (that is, they look in the direction the baby looks) when the babies are as young as four months of age (Scaife and Bruner, 1975). This helps ensure that mother and baby are paying attention to the same thing, and that words spoken are attached to the objects to which they refer. It also explains why so many of a child's first words are names of things that act or can be acted on: these are the things that catch a baby's attention.

Speech Perception

Up to this point we have been discussing what infants "say." But what about the receptive side of language? How does an infant respond to the speech it hears? How much does the infant understand?

Perception of Speech Versus Nonspeech Sounds

Infants hear all kinds of sounds, not just speech sounds. There is the hum of the air conditioner, the patter of rain, the creaking of the crib. Is the infant equally sensitive to all sounds, or does the human voice have special significance? Research indicates that by the second week of infancy the human voice quiets a crying infant more effectively than other sounds (Wolff, 1969). Apparently infants are especially attracted to speech, or soon learn to be attracted to it.

Perception of Speech Sounds

But what about speech sounds themselves? Do they resemble each other, or can infants detect differences between one sound and another? Research using the habituation technique suggests that infants begin very early to discriminate between various speech sounds. Infants as young as one month can differentiate the voiced and voiceless stop consonants, /b/ and /p/ (Eimas et al., 1971, 1974). Other studies indicate that young infants can tell the difference between /d/ and /t/, as well as /b/ and /g/ (Moffit, 1971; Trehub and Rabinovitch, 1972). Infants can also differentiate pairs of vowels, whether they are presented in combination with consonants (/pa/, /pi/) or as vowels alone (/a/, /i/) (Trehub, 1973).

It is not clear how this amazing perceptual ability helps children acquire language. The differences detected by infants are not linguistically significant at this early stage; infants do not attach different meanings to them. Nevertheless, it seems very probable that this ability facilitates language learning.

Perception of Intonation and Stress

The sounds within words that we have discussed are called *segmental* features of speech. *Intonation* (the rising and falling of the voice) and *stress* (placing an emphasis on certain words), are called *suprasegmental* features of language. Suprasegmental features help indicate whether someone is angry or friendly, asking a question or making a statement. Notice the differences in your own intonation and stress when you say, "Do I like ice cream!" and "Do I like ice cream?"

We know that adults are sensitive to the suprasegmental features of children's speech. They respond differently when they think children are making a statement and when they think they are asking a question. Can infants detect these differences? In natural situations it is extremely difficult to determine whether infants are sensitive to suprasegmental features, because additional clues to meaning are provided by the expression and gestures of the speaker and by the situation. However, there is some evidence that infants as young as eight months can differentiate between the intonation of statements, in which the voice falls at the end and the intonation of questions, in which the voice rises at the end (Kaplan and Kaplan, 1970). They may not understand the different meanings at this point, but they can hear the difference.

Comprehension of Words

Infants understand more words than they can produce (Goldin-Meadow, Seligman, and Gelman, 1976). At first, however, children may have an incomplete understanding of the words they hear or say. Meanings can be *overextended*, as when a child uses a word in circumstances where it does not apply. For example, a child who thinks anything with four legs and a tail is a dog may say "dog" when shown a picture of a horse. In other instances a child will not apply a word to all examples of the class it names; the child *underextends* the word. Peter Reich (1976), a language researcher, tells how his son, Adam, first responded to the word "shoe" by finding a shoe in his mother's closet. Apparently thinking that the word referred only to objects in a particular place, he would not respond by picking up a shoe outside the closet, or even a shoe in his father's closet. Gradually, Adam extended the meaning to include shoes in any closet, shoes on the floor in front of the closet, and shoes being worn by someone.

This is another example of how children form and test hypotheses. The child at first thinks "shoes" refers to specific objects in his mother's closet. Then someone refers to the same objects in front of the closet as "shoes," and the child revises his hypothesis to include a type of object that can be found either inside or outside the closet. When someone uses "shoes" to refer to the same objects worn on their feet, the hypothesis is again revised, this time to include a particular type of object regardless of location. The hypothesis is changed again when the child hears things on the feet called "boots," and when he hears a discussion about a game of "horseshoes."

Recent research suggests that there may be a third category of discrepancy between adult and child word meanings. In addition to narrower meanings (underextensions) and broader meanings (overextensions), children may simply hold different meanings for some words from those held by adults (Kay and Anglin, 1979). As you can see, providing varied experiences to a child and explaining things to him can encourage language development.

Sensorimotor Foundations
of Early Language Development

When a child asks, "Where ball?" when the ball is not in sight, it is certain that she knows that objects exist even when she cannot see them (Brown, 1973). Sometimes a child acts as she would with an object even when she does not have that object, as when she shakes her hand slightly when seeing a rattle. In such instances the child may be showing an early form of demonstration (*that* rattle; *there* rattle) (Brown, 1973). When an infant applies a series of action patterns to an object (shakes the rattle, bangs the rattle, pokes the rattle, mouths the rattle), or applies a single action to many objects (shakes the spoon, shakes the cup, shakes the box) she is, in a sense, commenting on a topic. In the first case the object is the topic and the actions are the comment; in the second case the action is the topic and the objects are the comments (Bruner, 1975b). Sinclair (1971) suggests that these actions can be compared to grammatical relations, the subject and object of a sentence. These examples illustrate how sensorimotor intelligence may be related to language learning.

Although sensorimotor knowledge may be necessary for language learning, we do not mean to suggest that it is all that is necessary. Cognitive understanding is essential, but so are other conditions (Bloom, Lightbown, and Hood, 1975). Without access to an adult speaker, children are unlikely to learn how to code the relations of their cognitive schemes into language.

Some adults begin very early to provide linguistic coding for children's actions, and for their own actions when interacting with the child. They talk to the baby and interpret the baby's "talk," even though the talk may at first consist only of coos and babbles. Some mothers seem to give their children "turns" at talking, and consider almost any vocalization as legitimate "conversation" (Donahoe, 1978). This type of behavior has been found to be related to social class: Low-income mothers are more likely than mothers of middle income to feel that talking to babies is "silly," and that it only makes sense to talk to babies who can actually speak (Tulkin and Kagan, 1972). Low-income mothers also seem to believe that infants do not attempt to communicate (Tulkin and Kagan, 1972).

Parents can have an important positive effect on a baby by talking to it throughout early infancy. Consider the following example. "Let's have some lunch," father says as he puts the baby into the infant seat. "We'll have peas, applesauce, and beef. Let's get your bib on — under your chin and around your neck. There we are. Now, how about a little applesauce? *Mmm*, isn't that good? Oh, you *are* hungry. How about some peas? Oh, don't spit them out! You're supposed to swallow them, not spit them out. Open up. Come on. Don't you like peas? How about peas with a little applesauce? Let's try that. Is that better? Okay, we'll have peas and applesauce together. Hey, let go of the spoon. I can't feed you if you don't let go of the spoon." (Conversation continues during entire feeding.)

This kind of language-rich environment actively promotes language develop-

"Isn't this cereal good?" Talking to a baby about events of interest while they occur is a good way to promote language development.

ment. Actions involving the baby are coded in language by the adult as they occur. You can imagine how development might suffer if a baby is cared for by adults who rarely talk to it. Some of the differences in language development found between middle- and lower-class children seem to be due to differences in parental verbal interaction with the children when they are young. Middle-class parents talk more to their infants than do lower-class parents.

Summary

Studying Language Acquisition
- Different theories make different assumptions about the nature and development of language. Learning theory was based on assumptions about reinforcement and imitation. However, the principles of reinforcement do not account satisfactorily for some of the facts of language development. A current view of language acquisition suggests that children learn language by first determining a speaker's meaning and then figuring out the meaning's relationship to language.

Language Production

- Infants' earliest noncrying utterance is called cooing. Babbling follows cooing and consists of consonant-vowel combinations. Infant vocalization is increased by social interaction with adults.
- A baby's one-word utterances often seem to express intentions. Adults read the context of these utterances to determine what they mean. The first words infants learn are apparently the names of things that act or can be acted on.

Speech Perception

- Infants can apparently differentiate various consonant sounds as well as various vowel sounds. They can also detect differences in intonation and stress in the language used by others.
- Infants may initially overextend or underextend the meanings of words.
- Sensorimotor intelligence appears to be necessary but not sufficient for language learning. Many of the relationships coded by language must be learned through interaction with an adult.
- There are social class differences in adults' attitudes toward talking with very young children and in the extent to which they use language when interacting with them. A parent who talks to a baby often can help the baby's language development.

New Terms

syntax	**suprasegmental features**
semantics	**intonation**
babbling	**stress**
holophrases	**overextension**
segmental features	**underextension**

Selected Readings

Brown, R. **A first language: The early stages.** *Cambridge, Mass.: Harvard University Press, 1973.* Absolutely essential reading for students seriously interested in learning about early language behavior. The book is technical but understandable even to students with a minimal background.

deVilliers, P. A., and deVilliers, J. G. **Early language.** *Cambridge, Mass.: Harvard University Press, 1979.* These authors discuss major aspects of early language along with the factors that influence language development in nontechnical, easy-to-read style.

Reilly, A. P., and Stark, R. E. (eds.). **The communication game. Pediatric Round Table: 4.** *New York: Johnson and Johnson, 1980.* Written for parents and practitioners in the medical and child care fields, this small book discusses normal language development as well as screening for language difficulties. Includes many short pieces contributed by researchers well known in these fields.

Chapter 9

Social Development

The study of social development is concerned with a child's feelings and behavior toward himself and other people. It includes specific social behaviors such as smiling or crying in response to the behavior of others, and learning to behave in ways that are expected, depending, for example, on the child's sex. It includes as well a child's unique pattern of behavior — his or her personality — which is "made up of those characteristics each person possesses that determine the person's cognitive, emotional and overt behavior" (Lamberth et al., 1978, p. 6). In this chapter we will consider some aspects of social development that are of concern during infancy, and variations in children's patterns of response to various social situations.

Attachment

Attachment refers to the emotional, or *affective*, relationship between a child and other human beings. It is expressed in many different ways, some of which we will discuss.

The First Relationship: The Initial Six Months

In *The First Relationship* Daniel Stern carefully examines what occurs during feeding. He gives the following example of a typical social interaction:

> While talking and looking at me the mother turned her head and gazed at the infant's face. He was gazing at the ceiling, but out of the corner of his eye he saw her head turn toward him and turned to gaze back at her. This had happened before, but now he broke rhythm and stopped sucking. He let go of the nipple and the suction around it broke as he eased into the faintest suggestion of a smile. The mother abruptly stopped talking and, as she watched his face begin to transform, her eyes opened a little wider and her eyebrows raised a bit. His eyes locked on to hers, and together they held motionless for an instant. The infant did not return to sucking and his mother held frozen her slight expression of anticipation. This silent and almost motionless instant continued to hang until the mother suddenly shattered it by saying "Hey!" and simultaneously opening her eyes wider, raising her eyebrows further, and throwing her head up and toward the infant. Almost simultaneously, the baby's eyes widened. His head tilted up and, as his smile broadened, the nipple fell out of his mouth. Now she said, "Well, hello! . . . hello . . . heeelloooo!", so that her pitch rose and the "hellos" became longer and more stressed on each successive repetition. With each phrase the baby expressed more pleasure, and his body resonated almost like a balloon being pumped up, filling a little more with each breath. The mother then paused and her face relaxed. They watched each other expectantly for a moment. The shared excitement between them ebbed, but before it faded completely, the baby suddenly took an initiative and intervened to rescue it. His head lurched forward, his hands jerked up, and a fuller smile blossomed. His mother was jolted into motion. She moved forward, mouth open and eyes alight, and said "Oooooh . . . ya wanna play do ya . . . yeah? . . . I didn't know if you were still hungry . . . no . . . noooooo . . . no I didn't . . ." And off they went. [1977, p. 3]

The pattern of interaction that characterizes this exchange between mother and child can be broken off by either one, although it is usually interrupted by the baby because the stimulation becomes too intense or novel. The baby controls the level of stimulation provided by a sensitive caregiver through the use of signals such as gaze and facial expressions.

Gazing. Babies are born with the ability to avoid excessive visual stimulation. As we said in Chapter 7, they can focus clearly on objects eight to ten inches from their eyes. This is how far away a mother's face is during feeding, regardless of whether the child is breast- or bottle-fed.

The human face is an especially attractive stimulus for the child during its first few months of life. The contrast between light and dark areas in the mother's eyes seems to hold a special appeal. The infant's attention to eyes has an important adaptive function: the caregiver interprets it as evidence that he or she is recognized as a special person. "The baby knows me," a parent is likely to think. Showing "recognition" by gazing appears to elicit a repertoire of caregiver behavior, including looking, exaggerated facial expressions, vocalizations, close facial encounters, and social games such as tickling and peek-a-boo.

As infants get older, they develop other "social" behaviors. At one and a half months, a baby can focus its gaze on its mother's eyes and widen and brighten its own eyes to prolong the interaction. At three months, when the baby's focal range is almost as extensive as that of an adult, the child can track a caregiver moving about the room. By this time the infant can also turn its head from side to side, which makes tracking easier. These abilities are all important because they increase the probability that the caregiver will interact with the baby.

Facial Expression. Because development is cephalocaudal (from head to trunk), infants quickly acquire the ability to communicate with smiles and frowns. The infant's smile, particularly when combined with a gaze from directly in front of the caregiver, is probably the most potent signal the baby has to increase stimulation.

Smiling develops through at least three stages (Bowlby, 1969). The first type of smile appears between birth and about six weeks of age. It consists of a brief grimace of the mouth without the crinkling of the muscles around the eyes seen in later smiles. This type is called the *spontaneous smile*, because it is often unrelated to a specific external stimulation, although it may be elicited by stroking the baby's cheek or stomach, or by various sounds, especially the human voice.

The *social smile* appears next. Beginning in about the sixth week, it lasts until the child is roughly six months old; smiling peaks at about four months. During this period the child will smile quite broadly at either a strange or a familiar face, although it may prefer a familiar face. After six months of age, the baby smiles more selectively, saving smiles for people he knows.

Later Infancy: Six Months Through Two Years

Specific Attachment. During the stage of *differential social responsiveness* (Bowlby, 1969), a baby will no longer smile at strangers. In fact, some six-month-olds stare for a few minutes and then begin to cry. Between the ages of six months and two years, many infants will cry immediately at the approach of a stranger, a phenomenon known as *stranger anxiety*. This is reduced if a parent or familiar adult is present (Kotelchuck et al., 1975). During the same period the child also shows *separation anxiety*: if a familiar caregiver leaves, the child begins to cry. Crying is particularly intense if the child is left in a strange place.

Children react differently, however, when they have an opportunity to enter a strange place on their own. In this situation, children will explore the room without distress, in many instances using their mothers as secure bases from which they make progressively longer excursions into the unknown.

Multiple Attachments. Several months after specific attachments begin, most children smile at and try to be near several familiar adults, such as family members or a babysitter. By eighteen months, only about 10 percent are still attached to a single adult (Schaffer and Emerson, 1964).

Theories of Separation and Stranger Anxiety

Secondary Reinforcement. Several theories have been offered to explain attachment to caregivers and stranger anxiety. The oldest theories came from the psychoanalytic and S-R traditions. Although these theories interpreted development very differently (see pages 52–59), their assumptions about attachment had something in common: both maintained that mother became a *secondary reinforcer* through being present when the child's basic needs (such as feeding) were being met. Mother was thought to become associated with positive feelings in much the same way that a buzzer was associated with food by Pavlov's dogs, because the mother was present when the *primary reinforcement* of food was given.

An eight-month-old experiencing stranger anxiety

Preprogrammed Response. A second major theory about attachment emphasized *preprogrammed biological responses*, which were explained in several ways. Spalding (1954), for example, explained them in terms of imprinting, the tendency for newly hatched chicks to become permanently attached to the first moving thing they see. How this applied to infants was never clearly explained, however. In the 1950s, psychoanalytic theorist John Bowlby suggested that attachment was caused not by secondary reinforcement alone, but by what he called "primary object-clinging." He suggested that the infant's response is innate, since it offers the adaptive advantage of keeping the infant close to its mother, thereby preventing attack by predators. He also suggested that the "maternal instinct" was a similarly adaptive predisposition to be found in mothers.

Also during the mid-1950s researchers at the University of Wisconsin noticed that monkeys raised in the laboratory became attached to the folded gauze diapers on the floors of their cages. The infant monkeys flew into a violent rage when these were removed and changed (Harlow, 1958). An investigator named Harlow designed an experiment to determine whether secondary reinforcement or object-clinging (presumed to be biologically preprogrammed) was responsible for the attachment. He made "surrogate mothers" — some from tubes of terry cloth, others from wire mesh — and placed one of each in the baby monkey's cages. Some of the monkeys were fed only from a bottle placed on the wire

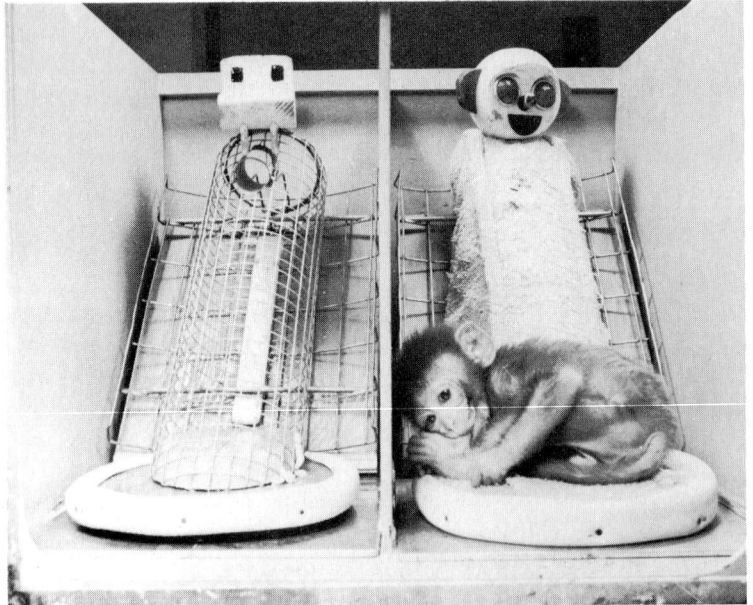

Harlow's surrogate mothers

mother; these monkeys spent an extraordinary amount of time on the cloth mother. Harlow concluded that "the disparity time spent on each surrogate is so great as to suggest that the primary function of nursing as an affectional variable is that of insuring frequent and intimate body contact with the mother" (p. 677). As an explanation for attachment, secondary reinforcement had been dealt a major blow.

Support for the secondary reinforcement hypothesis declined further when Schaffer and Emerson (1964) reported that 30 percent of the infants they observed had a preferred adult other than their primary caregiver, and 22 percent of the infants had a preferred adult who had never performed any primary caregiving activities (feeding, diapering, etc.) for the child.

Cognitive Theory. Some time after the Harlow experiments, a *cognitive theory* was introduced to explain stranger and separation anxiety. This view suggests that before six months of age, the infant is slowly building a scheme for the face of the primary caregiver. When the scheme is complete, the face of a stranger differs from the face scheme for the caregiver enough to evoke fear. Separation anxiety, too, is explained in this theory as a result of discrepancy between the familiar scheme of a face and the unfamiliar face of the caregiver who is present.

Although this theory nicely accounts for the observed reduction of stranger and separation anxiety when infants are with familiar adults in familiar surroundings, it cannot be considered conclusively proven. It cannot be fully tested until we know how novel a stimulus must be to provoke fear, and until the scheme itself can be defined so that we can assess moderate and fear-provoking discrepancies.

Responsive Feedback. A final explanation of attachment behavior makes use of the notion of *responsive feedback*. Mary Ainsworth and her colleagues believe, along with Bowlby, that innate human responses such as crying, gazing, smiling, and later, vocalizing and clinging, are crucial parts of the attachment process. According to Ainsworth, however, the child must receive feedback contingent on his or her signals, or the child will stop sending them (Ainsworth and Bell, 1969).

The importance of responsive feedback in determining attachment has been emphasized by other theorists as well. J. S. Watson (1966, 1972) studied learning and information processing by monitoring infants' reactions to mobiles in their cribs, which they could revolve by moving their heads on an air pillow. When the mobiles were removed from the cribs, the babies cried, and when they were returned the infants frequently smiled and cooed. This behavior resembled the typical baby's reaction to its caregiver, which led Watson to propose that babies become attached to whomever or whatever responds immediately to their signals. He also suggested that the earliest naturally occurring situation in which adults repeat their reactions is the social "game." These games frequently occur when the child is about three to four months old, during Piaget's Stage 3 (secondary circular reactions). For example, a baby gazes at an adult who responds by making a face and vocalizing. The baby then smiles, and the adult responds with another face and more vocalization. These interaction games continue until the baby no longer signals for feedback from the adult. It was this sort of game that Stern described — mothers playing with their babies during feeding.

The Schaffer and Emerson (1964) study of attachment, mentioned earlier, provided further evidence for Watson's thesis. When the person infants were most attached to was not their primary caregiver (30 percent of the cases studied), that person was someone who seemed especially "interesting" to the infant. Harlow's monkeys also support Watson's thesis: monkeys who were raised with a terrycloth mother equipped with a motor (in such a way that clinging to the mother caused movement) were more socially responsive than infants raised with "unresponsive" terrycloth mothers (Mason, 1967).

According to the Watson and Ainsworth theory that attachment is a function of responsive caregiving, stranger anxiety is caused by the unpredictability of strangers. By the time a baby is six months old, the person it is attached to has learned to respond to its signals with moderately novel events. A stranger, however, cannot interpret the baby's signals in the same way. As a result, strangers' responses to the baby are too unfamiliar, and the baby cries. Theories of attachment that emphasize responsiveness and controllability nicely explain why moderately predictable parents or familiar surroundings reduce separation and stranger anxiety.

Of the theories of attachment we have reviewed, secondary reinforcement is the only one that is no longer popular. Preprogrammed biological responses, cognitive theory, and responsive feedback from the caregiver are still considered valid. These theories are quite compatible. For example, an uncontrollable or unpredictable event is certainly discrepant from previous schemes. It is probable that all three theories can contribute to the explanation for attachment.

Individual Differences in Attachment Behavior

Variations in the attachment behavior of children of the same age may be caused by differences in the stimulation provided by caregivers or by different hereditary predispositions. Attachment behaviors are defined as attempts to approach the caregiver.

Caregiver Behaviors. Several investigators have observed that a caregiver's responsiveness to a baby's signals in timing feedings and in face-to-face interactions predicts the child's attachment behavior (Ainsworth and Bell, 1969; Blehar, Lieberman, and Ainsworth, 1977; Clarke-Stewart, 1973). Three kinds of attachment behavior have been described.

In *secure attachment*, children use the caregiver as a base from which to make repeated sojourns into their surroundings. In addition to their attachment to the caregiver, children show an interest in exploring playthings and other aspects of the environment. These behaviors indicate that the children know they can operate on the environment to produce interesting results. They do not believe they are helpless. When left by the caregiver in a strange room, a securely attached child tends to cry at first, then settle down to interact with available playthings. When the caregiver returns, the child approaches the adult.

Stimulating caregivers who are responsive to their children's signals tend to have children who are securely attached to them. Their children also tend to receive high scores on infant IQ tests (Ainsworth and Bell, 1973; Yarrow, Rubenstein, and Pedersen, 1971) and to cry little.

In *anxious attachment*, children consistently cry when their caregivers are absent. Some securely attached infants do this, too. Anxiously attached children, however, have several other behaviors that set them apart. When their caregivers return, they both seek contact and resist interaction, perhaps reaching for their mothers and then pushing away. These children also have a poorer ability to use the mother as a secure base from which to explore the environment.

The third type of child is *unattached*. Under most circumstances, such children show little tendency to try to be physically close to their mothers. Both anxious and unattached infants are likely to have caregivers who are less responsive and provide less novel stimulation than the caregivers of children who are securely attached.

We tend to think of unresponsive caregivers as those who ignore their infants. Some unresponsive caregivers overstimulate them, however, as this example from Stern indicates:

> The dance they had worked out by the time I met them went something like this. Whenever a moment of mutual gaze occurred, the mother went immediately into high-gear stimulating behaviors, producing a profusion of fully displayed, high-intensity, facial and vocal infant-elicited social behavior. Jenny invariably broke gaze rapidly. Her mother never interpreted this temporary face and gaze aversion as a cue to lower her level of behavior. . . . Instead, she would swing her head around following Jenny's. . . . She would reinitiate the same level of stimulation with a new arrangement of facial and vocal combinations. Jenny again turned away. . . . Again, instead of holding back, the mother continued to chase Jenny. . . . She moved closer, in an apparent attempt to break through and establish contact. She also escalated the level of her stimulation even more by adding touching and tickling to the unabated flow of vocal and facial behaviors. . . .
>
> With Jenny's head now pinned in the corner, the baby's next recourse was to rapidly swing her face from one side to the other right past her mother's face. When her face crossed the mother's face, in the face-face zone, Jenny closed her eyes to avoid any mutual visual contact and only reopened them after the head aversion was established on the other side. All of these behaviors on Jenny's part were performed with a sober face or at times a grimace.

The mother followed her to the new side, producing volleys of stimulation that again progressively pushed Jenny's head farther away until she performed another pass-through. After a series of "failures," the mother would pick the infant up from the infant seat and hold her under the armpits, dangling in the face-to-face position. This maneuver usually succeeded in reorienting Jenny toward her, but as soon as she put Jenny back down, the same pattern reestablished itself. After several more repeats of these sequences the mother became visibly frustrated, angry, and confused and Jenny, quite upset. At that point the interaction was terminated and Jenny was put to bed. [1977, pp. 110–11]

This mother was insensitive to the child's indications of interest and did not permit the child to disregard stimuli when she chose to do so. Although the effects of overstimulation on attachment have not been demonstrated, theories that emphasize responsiveness and moderately novel stimulation suggest that they are probably negative.

Infant Contributions. In their initial report, Ainsworth and Bell (1969) suggested that the relationship between maternal responsiveness and attachment could be attributed to hereditary differences in infant temperament. More recent evidence, however, suggests that heredity is not the major cause of the relationship (Blehar, Lieberman, and Ainsworth, 1977). In infants between six and fifteen weeks of age, no differences in the responsiveness to a strange adult were observed between those who would and those who would not later be securely attached. Regarding responsiveness to their mothers, however, those who would be securely attached at age one were more responsive than those who would not later be securely attached. This suggests that attachment is a function of varying maternal behavior, rather than of hereditary differences in infant temperament that influence maternal responsiveness.

This is not to say that an infant's behavior does not affect the responsiveness of some caregivers. An extremely fussy baby may tire many caregivers to the point of apathy. Similarly, it may be hard for a parent to look at, much less interpret signals from, a baby who is in some way abnormal.

A blind baby not only may suffer from its parents' negative reactions, it has to manage without two of the components important in most attachment relationships: (1) looking at objects or people to indicate an interest, and (2) visual stimulation from parents. Fraiberg has taught the parents of blind babies how to understand their babies' signals.

"How will he know me?" is one of the first questions parents may ask us. We could tell the parents because we know the blind baby's language. Some parents were amazed to learn that the blind baby would smile in response to mother's or father's *voice* at around the same time that sighted babies smile at the *sight* of the human face. And, when the smile emerged, as predicted, the baby's parents were slightly more delirious than the parents of sighted babies at the same stage. Then, because we had information from our research on differential smiling in the first quarter, we could initiate a small experiment which was very impressive to parents. We would ask mother and father to speak to the baby and the smile would appear. Then one of the investigators would speak to the baby. No smile. We could repeat the sequence. The baby responded selectively to the sound of mother's or father's voice. It was an eloquent demonstration. The baby "knew" his parents. . . . [1975, p. 45]

In another demonstration, Fraiberg had an observer hold a five-month-old for a few minutes. The baby invariably squirmed and complained. When it was returned to the parents, however, the baby would snuggle down and be comforted. Fraiberg also pointed out to parents that the stranger anxiety shown in response to observer's voices at eight to twelve months and the separation anxiety shown at one year were signs of attachment to the parents. She assured parents that the child's vocalizations indicated that language development was proceeding on schedule, and that it offered important opportunities for parents to make use of the signals common to all children to promote positive interactions.

At the end of eighteen months, half the blind babies in Fraiberg's training program had fulfilled, stage by stage, all the criteria for attachment to the caregiver that are expected of a sighted child.

FOCUS: Crying and Maternal Responsiveness

During their study of attachment behavior, Bell and Ainsworth (1972) observed crying behavior and maternal responsiveness to it. Children were observed extensively, for sixteen hours in each of the four quarters of the first year. The investigation came to several conclusions.

DEVELOPMENTAL CHANGES IN CRYING

Children cried about half as long in the fourth quarter as they did in the first. In the first quarter, the *duration* of crying per hour ranged from zero to twenty-one minutes, with the median child (the one in the middle of the ranged order) crying 7.7 minutes per hour. The median fell to 4.4 minutes per hour in the fourth quarter. The frequency of crying, however, did not decrease, and episodes of crying occurred at a rate of about four per hour throughout the first year.

SEX DIFFERENCES

Boys who are first borns tended to cry more than firstborn girls in the first quarter (Moss, 1967). This difference disappeared in subsequent quarters. If birth order is disregarded, however, there were no significant differences between boys and girls in amount of crying (Bell and Ainsworth, 1972).

(continued on following page)

FOCUS *(continued)*

STABILITY OF INDIVIDUAL DIFFERENCES

The babies who cry most in the first quarter are unlikely to be the same ones who lead the list in later quarters. The only significant correlation of crying durations or frequencies occurs between the third and fourth quarters. These findings argue against the hypothesis that biologically determined individual differences in irritability determine how much various children cry during the first year.

DIFFERENCES IN MATERNAL RESPONSIVENESS

The percentages of crying episodes ignored by the mother in the first quarter ranged from 4 percent by the most responsive mothers to 97 percent by the least responsive mothers, with a median of 46 percent. The duration of maternal unresponsiveness to crying in the first quarter also varied widely, from an average of two minutes by the most responsive mothers to nine minutes by the least responsive mothers, with a median of nearly four minutes. All mothers become somewhat more responsive over the course of the first year, with the median frequency of ignoring crying dropping by about one-third and the median duration of unresponsiveness dropping by about one-half. In contrast to the order of children's irritability, the order of mothers' responsiveness remained stable throughout the first year.

THE RELATIONSHIP BETWEEN CRYING
AND MATERNAL RESPONSIVENESS

A mother's unresponsiveness may increase a baby's crying and irritability over a period of time. Bell and Ainsworth (1972) intercorrelated frequency of crying and episodes of crying ignored by mother in all four quarters. Infants of unresponsive mothers cried more frequently and longer than infants who had responsive mothers. Their findings led Bell and Ainsworth to conclude that "an infant whose mother's responsiveness helps him to achieve his ends develops confidence in his own ability to control what happens to him," and this confidence reduces subsequent crying. In addition, the children of responsive mothers are likely to develop less urgent ways of communicating than crying. This is because these mothers tend to be in close physical contact, which enables them to learn to "read" noncrying signals, and because these mothers tend to reinforce noncrying signals more than other mothers.

Bell and Ainsworth's interpretations of their data have been subject to criticism (Gewirtz and Boyd, 1977a; Parsley and Rabinowitz, 1975). These interpretations do not involve the building of the child's confidence in general control of the environment. It has been suggested, for example, that unresponsive mothers reinforce hard crying, whereas responsive mothers reinforce relatively weak cries, and it is the reinforced cries that are repeated. It has also been suggested that the reinforcement of noncrying signals and their subsequent increase in frequency (1) reduces the appearance of the conditions responsible for crying and (2) replaces crying with noncrying signals when these conditions do occur. In other words, it is the reinforcement of alternatives to crying that is important. As we mentioned before, this kind of controversy is almost inevitable in evaluating correlational research.

EFFECTIVE MATERNAL INTERVENTIONS

A final variable examined by Ainsworth and Bell was the effectiveness of various maternal interventions to stop crying (Ainsworth, Bell, and Stayton, 1972). The table below indicates which interventions were used most frequently and which were most effective. Notice how effective most interventions were, regardless of their nature. Even entering the room was effective 46 to 61 percent of the time. Ainsworth and colleagues (1972) concluded from these and other data that the response per se is important, not the nature of the response. However, this conclusion would be debated by Gewirtz and Boyd (1977b), who point out that within a given quarter mothers who attempt many different kinds of interventions before crying ceases have babies who cry less. In other words, the fact that mothers who tried many interventions were most effective suggests that the nature of a mother's response is important.

As can be seen, it is not easy to draw a conclusion from the various studies done on this subject. A decrease in infant crying may be caused by a mother's responsiveness to crying per se or else by some other characteristic of responsive mothers. We can conclude, however, that mothers who are most responsive to all kinds of signals have children who cry less, not only as an immediate consequence but in the future as well.

Maternal interventions in infant crying and their effectiveness

Maternal intervention	First quarter		Fourth quarter	
	Percent of total interventions	Percent effectiveness	Percent of total interventions	Percent effectiveness
Picking up	38	86	29	84
Interacting	22	40	17	45
Routines (feeding, diapering)	14	77	15	77
Touching	13	41	9	66
Toys, pacifier	7	60	7	55
Entering room	2	46	7	61
Other	4	75	16	54

SOURCE: Ainsworth, M. D. S., Bell, S. M., and Stayton, D. J. Individual differences in the strange-situation behavior of one-year-olds. In H. R. Schaffer (Ed.), *The origins of human social relations*. London: Academic Press, 1972. Reprinted by permission of Bedford College, University of London.

Prolonged Separation Without Responsive Caregiving. Babies who grow up in situations such as hospitals or institutions that provide very little stimulation pass through several stages. At first they protest when parents leave after an occasional visit. After several weeks, they show despair: they protest less and withdraw more when parents leave. Some children at this stage grow hostile to adults, whereas others cling excessively to nurses on the ward. If they fail to receive responsive care consistently for a longer time, they enter a detachment phase marked by lack of interest in parents and interpersonal relationships generally. These stages are found even when children are first deprived of responsive care at age three or four, although such children are less likely to become detached (Robertson and Bowlby, 1952).

Infants raised from birth in physically adequate but psychologically unstimulating environments are consistently retarded in social skills such as clinging, smiling, crying in response to distress, approaching adults, vocalization, and language development. A study of seventy-five children in an orphanage, conducted by Provence and Lipton, showed that by the second half of the first year children were conspicuously helpless and passive in relation to humans and the inanimate environment alike. Below is a description of one such child.

> Outstanding were his soberness, his forlorn appearance, and lack of animation. The interest that he showed in the toys was mainly for holding, inspecting and rarely mouthing. When he was unhappy he now had a cry that sounded neither demanding nor angry — just miserable — and it was usually accompanied by his beginning to rock. The capacity for protest which he had had earlier was much diminished. He did not turn to adults to relieve his distress or to involve them in a playful or pleasurable interchange. He made no demands. The active approach to the world . . . had vanished. [1962, p. 134]

The social behavior of these children parallels that of monkeys who were raised in isolation for their first year. After being removed from isolation, the monkeys commonly engaged in self-clasping and rocking, and they engaged in neither the social nor the exploratory forms of play typical of monkeys of this age (Harlow and Harlow, 1966).

Attachment and Infant Day Care

The social and cognitive deficits of children raised in poorly run institutions have caused some people to question all nontraditional methods of rearing children. Psychoanalytic theorists have suggested that emotional deficits can result from entrusting the care of an infant to more than one adult. They often believe that emotional bonding to one mother figure is necessary for other social relationships to develop properly. This suggestion disregards the fact that poorly run institutions also lack both responsive caregiving and a stimulating environment.

Some of the strongest evidence that multiple caregiver arrangements do not inevitably have a bad effect on social development comes from studies of children raised in Israeli kibbutzim, which are collective communities often devoted to agriculture. Infants are cared for in a common infant house by a caregiver called a *metapelet*. Children also spend Sabbaths, holidays, and a few hours on weekday evenings in the homes of their parents. (Some children live with their parents and go to the children's center much as American children go to day care centers.) Children raised in a kibbutz have no deficits in social skills or in attachments to parents or others (Beit-Hallahmi and Rabin, 1977; Gewirtz, 1965; Maccoby and Feldman, 1972).

Other studies show that no bad effects result from having multiple caregivers in well-run day care centers for infants and toddlers. In a study of day care at the Syracuse University Children's Center, children who had been in day care for a year and a half, after entering at one year of age, were reported to be as attached to their mothers as home-reared children (Caldwell et al., 1970). Doyle (1975) and Kagan, Kearsley, and Zelazo (1980) report similar results. Blehar (1974), on the other hand, studied centers with more children per caregiver (7 to 1 versus 4 to 1) and found that these children showed more unattached and anxious attachment behavior than home-reared peers.

Attending a good infant day care center appears to have none of the harmful effects of attending poorly run institutions. The interest in objects shown by these infants indicates normal development.

Blehar's American day care study and Maccoby and Feldman's kibbutz study made use of similar attachment assessment techniques, and their results have been compared. The differences in attachment behavior in the two groups can apparently be attributed to differences in the quality of care. In the kibbutz, the children's houses tend to be at the center of the community, both literally and figuratively. They are well equipped. The ratio of children to caregivers is about 5 to 1, lower than it was for Blehar's American sample. The child's metapelet stays with the same group of children from birth until they are seven years old; as a result she learns to "read" the child well enough that she can provide the moderately novel and interesting activities needed to foster cognitive and social growth. The children in Blehar's American sample were less likely to have such responsive caregivers; although the children studied had been in day care for an average of only five months, they were likely to be placed in new groups and get new caregivers three times before age six. Furthermore, most caregivers stay at a given day care center only about three years (Blehar, 1974). It is safe to conclude that the quality of care rather than the number of caregivers is what determines the quality of a child's attachment (Cummings, 1980). Where the quality of care is good, the attachment will be too.

Sex-Role Development

Few studies have been designed exclusively to provide information about sex differences in behavior during the first eighteen months. One of the studies (Goldberg and Lewis, 1969) that was undertaken showed that when thirteen-month-olds were placed in a strange playroom with their mothers, the boys were more independent of their mothers, showed more exploratory behavior, and tended to run and bang more in their play than did girls. It took the boys longer to return to their mothers; they returned less frequently; they touched their mothers less; and they vocalized to and looked at their mothers less. When the room was divided in half by a barrier of mesh, and a baby was placed on the side opposite its mother and the toys, girls cried more whereas boys made more attempts to get around the barrier. Finally, boys and girls differed in the objects they preferred to play with and in the manner of their play. Boys played more with objects that were not toys, such as doorknobs, covered outlets, and lights. They also banged their toys more during play.

Why do boys and girls behave differently toward their mothers in the playroom? One possible reason is that when their children were six months old, mothers touched, talked to, and handled their daughters more than their sons. This may be why girls touched and talked to their mothers more at thirteen months.

Sex-typing is the term used for the process by which children acquire behavior more typical of one sex than of the other. Boys and girls are treated differently

Sex-typing begins early in children's lives.

from birth; after learning what society expects of them, they come to see them-selves differently. Some of the differences in treatment are quite obvious, such as dressing girls in pink and boys in blue. Others are less conspicuous: studies in which adults were told that a baby was a boy or girl regardless of the infant's sex indicate that adults interpret facial expressions differently depending on whether they believe an infant is male or female (Haviland, 1976). These differences in treatment and the differences children observe in the stereotypic behavior of men and women influence children's perceptions of what behaviors will be reinforced and what can be appropriately imitated.

Because the differences in treatment are often very subtle and their effects are frequently unknown, it is difficult to tell whether a particular sex-typed behavior is caused by hereditary or environmental factors. As is the case with other behaviors, it is probable that sex-typed behavior is caused by the interaction of hereditary and environmental influences. For example, Moss (1967) reports that boys cry more than girls at six weeks. He attributes this difference to hered-ity — boys are physiologically less advanced than girls at birth. At three months, mothers are less likely to respond to boys' cries than to girls' cries, apparently because they believe girls are more likely to be soothed. This difference in the children's environments originates in differences in mothers' perceptions of a child's heredity (perceptions of what boys and girls are like). In other words, heredity affects parental behavior (Bell, 1971). As you can see, a complex process such as attachment would be influenced by dozens of factors. Distinguishing environmental effects from hereditary influences is an extremely complex and difficult process, so much so that, for the present at least, it may be impossible.

Summary

Attachment
- Attachment refers to the emotional, or affective, relationship between a child and other human beings.
- Gazing and smiling are infant behaviors that appear to elicit adult responses. Smiling behavior changes during an infant's development.
- Infant distress at the approach of an unfamiliar person is known as stranger anxiety. Distress on being left by a familiar caregiver is known as separation anxiety. When infants are allowed to control their separation from familiar caregivers, they often leave them to briefly explore the environment, returning from time to time to the secure adult base.
- The theory of attachment based on ideas about secondary reinforcement has little evidence to support it. Currently accepted theories of attachment are based on ideas about biological preprogramming, cognitive discrepancy, and responsive feedback.
- Responsive caregiving appears to enhance infants' attachment, and babies with responsive mothers cry less than those with unresponsive mothers. Unresponsiveness can involve disregarding an infant's cues as well as simply ignoring an infant. Such cues are more difficult to interpret in a blind baby; its parents must learn to interpret the child's responses to their voices rather than their gazes.
- Quality day care does not appear to be detrimental to the development of infant attachment.

Sex-Role Development
- Sex differences in play behavior of boy and girl infants have been found in some studies.
- Sex differences may not be directly due to the influence of heredity. Knowledge of the child's sex may influence parental behavior, which, in turn, may lead to different treatment of boys and girls. For example, mothers respond less to infant boys' crying at three months than to infant girls' crying, apparently because they feel girls are more likely to be soothed.

New Terms

personality
attachment
affective relationship
spontaneous smile
social smile
differential social responsiveness
stranger anxiety
separation anxiety

primary reinforcement
secondary reinforcement
preprogrammed biological responses
cognitive theory
responsive feedback
secure attachment
anxious attachment
sex-typing

Selected Readings

Kagan, J., Kearsley, R. B., and Zelazo, P. R. **Infancy: Its place in human development.** *Cambridge, Mass.: Harvard University Press, 1980.* Contains a good summary of the issues and research concerning the effects of infant day care.

Klaus, M. H., Leger, T., and Trause, M. A. (Eds.). **Maternal attachment and mothering disorders: A round table.** *New York: Johnson and Johnson, 1975.* This booklet contains twelve interesting and diverse papers about the attachment process. Topics include failure-to-thrive, infant and mother play, father-infant interaction, and parental visitation in the premature nursery.

Stern, D. **The first relationship: Infant and mother.** *Cambridge, Mass.: Harvard University Press, 1977.* A very readable book about the development of attachment. Covers, among other topics, behaviors of the infant and the caregiver and things that can go wrong in mother-infant interactions.

Chapter 10

*K*nowledge and Action

Throughout Part III we have stressed the importance of the development that occurs during infancy. We will now discuss some practical suggestions for educators and parents about encouraging optimal development. We begin with infant education programs and infant assessment. Then we turn to practical issues of caring for infants, including responding to individual differences, keeping a baby safe and healthy, and providing playthings.

Infant Education Programs

Many infant stimulation and education programs have been developed in the past twenty years. Some were designed to help parents prevent the developmental delays in cognition, language, and other areas that are common among poor children. Others were developed in connection with research studies such as those which evaluated the effects of day care on infants. Regardless of a program's goals, program developers have been guided by research studies such as those we have discussed. The importance of moderately novel stimulation and responsive caregivers has been of particular concern in designing things for infants to do, as will be evident in our discussion of some of the best-known infant programs.

The Florida Parent Education
Infant and Toddler Program

The Florida program's emphasis is on parent education. Rather than having teachers of the usual sort, this program trains parents to teach their own infants. That is a common feature of programs designed for very young children.

The Florida program, begun in 1966, was developed by the late Dr. Ira Gordon, who was a professor of education at the University of Florida in Gainesville. Economically deprived families were enrolled in the program, which included children as young as three months old.

Gordon relied heavily on Piaget's conception of sensorimotor intelligence to develop activities sequenced to provide moderate novelty for the infant. He faced a difficulty Hunt (1965) has called "the problem of the match" — the match between the child's schemes and external experiences. A "match" occurs when an experience results in accommodation. You will recall that accommodation is greatest when an experience is related to an existing scheme but provides some new information, too.

Another problem involved helping infants learn that they can make things happen. As we saw in Chapter 7, the lack of response-contingent stimulation can lead to learned helplessness. For this reason Gordon developed activities in which "the child could see what was happening and could see that his behavior was having an effect" (Gordon, Guinagh, and Jester, 1977, p. 101).

A sample activity from the Florida program is called *Look Ma, No Hands*. The instructions are as follows:

> Baby will be delighted to learn he can make some things happen, even when he can't touch them.
>
> You can use either the cradle gym, or you can fasten a mobile to the crib, or you can tie some colorful pieces of cording or other fabrics to the top bar of the crib over the baby's feet, where he can see them.
>
> Bounce the crib mattress with your hand near his feet to make the objects move.
>
> Take one of his feet, and gently tap it on the mattress to set the objects in motion. He'll see that movements on the mattress cause an interesting action, and he can do it on his own, when he wants to. [Gordon, 1970, p. 16]

You can probably see that the behavior elicited with this activity is characteristic of secondary circular reactions, Piaget's Stage 3. The infant uses its own body to create an event in the external environment. To ensure that moderately novel experiences are being provided, the adult is instructed to provide new toys from time to time. One way to determine if good "matches" are being made is to watch for signs that the baby is interested.

Another activity from the Florida program is called *Hide and Seek.* Instructions for this game are as follows:

> Begin with a simple game using a toy and some soft covering material, such as a blanket. Attract his attention to the toy and then partly hide it under the blanket so the baby can still see a part of it.
>
> Then say, "Where did it go?" "Find the toy."
>
> If he's puzzled and doesn't seem to know how to retrieve it, show him how. If he ignores the toy after it is hidden, play with it yourself in front of him, but don't demand his attention or any action. He will, on his own, get interested in what you are doing. Partly hide it again until he's able to get it himself.
>
> Play the same game, but hide the toy completely under the soft materials.
>
> Repeat this for fun a number of times and then leave the child with both toy and blanket. . . .
>
> A third approach to hide-and-seek is to place one of his favorite objects in a box or other container where he can no longer see it. Be sure the container is easy to open. Ask him, "Can you find it?" "Let's look in the box." "There it is!" "Can you get it now?" . . .
>
> Remember, don't tease, don't frustrate and don't force. Watch for the child "turning off."
>
> When he discovers the toy is in the container, he'll enjoy putting it in, closing the box, opening it up, taking it out, and then he can be left to repeat this for his own continued learning and amusement. [Gordon, 1970, pp. 34–37]

This activity involves object permanence. Notice that the instructions stress variation and responsiveness and suggest verbalizations. The Florida program, like most other infant programs, emphasizes the importance of using language when interacting with infants.

The Family Development Research Program

The Family Development program was developed at Syracuse University in 1964 by Dr. Bettye Caldwell under a grant from the Office of Child Development. It, too, was offered to low-income families. Dr. Ronald Lally directed the program in later years; he and Dr. Alice Honig have written many of the descriptions of the program. The infant program was discontinued when funds ran out, but the program continues to serve as a model for other infant programs (Lally and Honig, 1977). The program emphasized family development, but our focus will be on the part that was designed for infants.

The infant curriculum was based on the theories of Piaget and Erikson and on current knowledge about language development. An outline of the formal infant program, for children six to fifteen months old, is given in Box 10-1. You will recognize the strong emphasis on the dimensions of sensorimotor intelligence formulated by Piaget.

BOX 10-1. The Family Development Research Program Infant Curriculum: Selected Items

Development of prehension skills
- Reaching for toys
- Shaking toys
- Grasping and handling objects of different sizes and shapes

Development of object permanence
- Playing peek-a-boo
- Finding toys after visible displacements under screens
- Putting toys into containers and finding toys under containers

Development of means for achieving desired environmental ends
- Reaching over obstacles for toys
- Using a string vertically to obtain a toy tied to the string
- Putting a chain into a box

Development of new schemes in relation to objects
- Hitting two toys together
- Stretching an elastic bracelet
- Adorning oneself (with pop-it bead necklace, for example)
- Drinking from a cup

Development of causality (understanding the distinction between act and external result)
- Ringing a bell to make a sound
- Turning a key to make a mechanical toy run
- Working a jack-in-the-box

Developmental achievement of the construction of the object in space (conceiving of a single, objective space within which all objects are contained and interrelated)
- Finding a toy by its sound
- Bunching a chain and putting it into a box
- Nesting several boxes
- Creeping around a barrier, such as a rocking chair, to retrieve a ball rolled underneath the chair

Development of gestural imitation
- Imitating a familiar visible gesture, such as pat-a-cake
- Imitating a familiar invisible gesture, such as an eye wink

Development of verbal learning
- Imitating baby sounds
- Imitating familiar sounds, such as "la-la"
- Labeling objects, people, feelings, actions, places, times, etc.

Physical development and exercises
- Stretching and flexing legs
- Doing somersaults
- Bouncing body to music
- Bending to pick up objects

Development of sense organs
- Producing and listening to sounds (e.g., music boxes, rattles, wrist bells, records, tapes)
- Producing tactual experiences (e.g., feel boxes, fur collars, nylon net, styrofoam)
- Tasting new foods and new textures of familiar food

SOURCE: Adapted from Lally, R., and Honig, A. The Family Development Research Program, in C. Day and R. Parker (Eds.), *The preschool in action.* Boston: Allyn & Bacon, 1977, pp. 149–194.

The program also stressed the importance of "routine caregiving activities, such as diapering, feeding, and napping, to promote a positive self-concept, joyful emotional encounters, and language experiences" (Lally and Honig, 1977, p. 152). The program attempted to integrate cognitive and socioemotional development — to make the everyday "living" and "loving" environment of the infant a "learning" environment as well. For example, caregivers talked to babies during diapering, and mirrors were attached to the walls next to the changing tables so that infants could see themselves (Lally and Honig, 1977). (See Honig and Lally, 1972, for detailed descriptions of infant activities.)

Another feature was the assignment of a "special" person to handle an infant's feeding, diapering, and comforting. (This program was center-based rather than home-based.) Each caregiver was assigned four babies. Caregivers also interacted with other babies, but each baby had its own caregiver to ensure continuity and emotional attachment.

An Intervention Program for Atypical Infants

The intervention program, located in Marin County, California, is sponsored as part of the community's mental health services. It has been supported by grants from the United Cerebral Palsy Association, which has in turn received funds from the Bureau for the Educationally Handicapped located in the Federal Office of Education. The program serves four categories of infants: (1) physically handicapped, (2) mentally retarded, (3) emotionally disturbed, and (4) infants who were at risk at birth because of factors such as low birth weight or maternal psychosis (Nielsen et al., 1975, pp. 222–23).

The total program is divided into several subprograms. The Home and Individual subprogram involves weekly visits to the homes of the children served. The Parent-Infant Group subprogram, which serves infants less than a year old and their mothers, meets once a week. It includes parent-child interaction, parent discussion, and staff work with children. There is also a Group subprogram for infants between twelve and eighteen months old. The children may attend the program for three hours four mornings a week, but most attend for only two or three days.

All of the subprograms emphasize (1) sensorimotor development, (2) language development, (3) motor development, and (4) feeding and prespeech development. To support sensory development, for example, various tactile experiences are provided. There may be both carpeted and tiled areas in the playroom floor, and children may be taken for walks (or crawls) on grass or foam rubber. Children are also given materials to feel: wet and dry sand, corn meal, or warm and cool water. (Care is necessary to prevent infants from rubbing the sand they have been feeling into their eyes.) For young infants who mouth everything, the program designers recommend tactile experiences with pudding, whipped cream, or mashed potatoes.

Language development experiences include social interaction between adults and infants, and pseudoimitation. New sounds are introduced in the latter activity when baby is ready. Language is associated with actions as they occur, by saying "milk" or "How about some milk?" for example, when giving a baby a drink. Parents are encouraged not to give up when their babies seem unresponsive. As Fraiberg has pointed out, adults must learn to recognize the special ways handicapped infants have of responding.

Motor development experiences vary considerably depending on the infant's handicap. Children may be swung in a blanket or hammock, or given help in exploring a specific space. Feeding and prespeech experiences also vary with the individual child's needs. If an infant lacks the normal rooting and swallowing reflexes, for example, they might be stimulated by touching his cheeks, lips, and tongue. As parents become more assertive about their children's rights, it is likely that many more programs for children with special needs will be developed.

Infants with motor handicaps may be unable to produce sufficient stimulation for themselves. Special programs can provide stimulation for such babies so that intellectual development is not delayed.

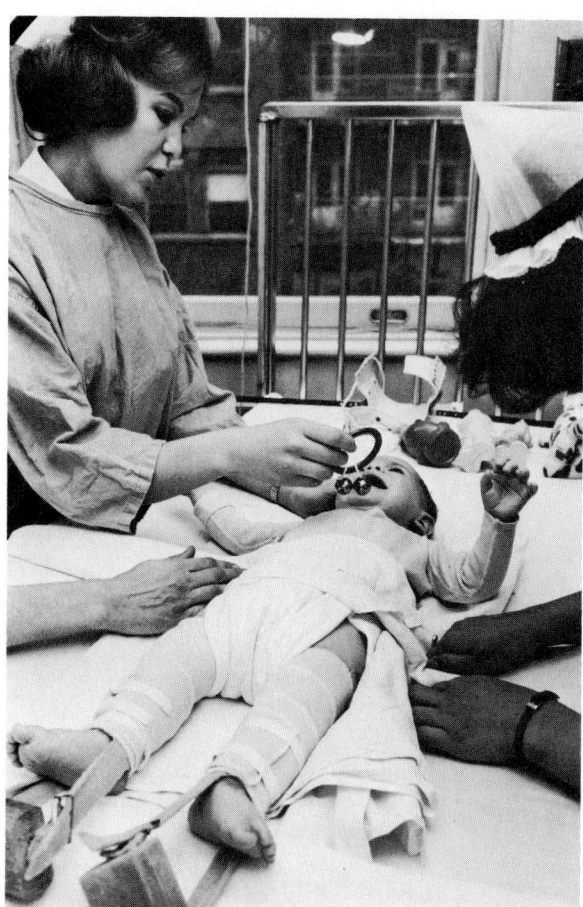

FOCUS: Cerebral Palsy

Cerebral palsy refers to a group of disorders caused by brain damage that results in abnormal positions and motor behavior. There are between 1 and 5 cerebral palsied children per 1000, with the variation due to methods used in identification (Thompson and Quinn, 1979).

Cerebral palsy differs from disorders such as poliomyelitis, in which problems are localized below the brain, in the spinal cord and musculature. In cerebral palsy, problems are localized in the brain. Failure of the brain to develop, or environmentally caused damage to areas of the brain responsible for movement, results in inappropriate voluntary movement and abnormal postures. These abnormal postures occur because muscles remain largely controlled by reflexes rather than by later maturing or higher parts of the brain. When a muscle remains immobile in these reflex postures for long periods, it loses its ability to contract and/or stretch. Physical therapy is necessary to avoid fixed reflex patterns of muscle and bone on which future deformities develop. Such deformities can develop rapidly in the first few years of life, a time of rapid growth (Abroms and Pangakos, 1980).

Cerebral palsy may be caused by a genetic cerebral malformation, by anoxia, or by brain damage due to the bursting of blood vessels in the brain. Severe head injury at birth or later in life also may cause cerebral palsy. The disorder may also result from a prenatal infection such as rubella or syphilis or by postnatal infection such as encephalitis. However, use of the term "cerebral palsy" implies that there is no active disease at the time of diagnosis. That is, damage to the brain is nonprogressive at the time of diagnosis, though physical deformities may continue to develop due to abnormal posturing, especially if the child is untreated.

Most individuals with cerebral palsy exhibit *spastic* syndromes, in which some muscles are consistently involuntarily contracted. If these muscles are limited to one side of the body (for example, the right arm and leg), the condition is called *hemiplegia.* In *diplegia* the legs are primarily affected; note that diplegia is one kind of *paraplegia,* the latter referring to any paralysis of the legs. In *quadriplegia,* all four limbs are involved, with the legs more affected than the arms.

About 50 percent of children with cerebral palsy have mild to severe mental retardation; the greater the amount of cerebral damage, the more likely it is that retardation will occur. But some 25 to 33 percent of these children can be entirely self-supporting as adults (Abroms and Pangakos, 1980).

Identification of all but mild forms of cerebral palsy is possible in the first year of life. Parents of cerebral palsied children may notice a severe delay in purposeful manual, sitting, or locomotor abilities at ages six to twelve months. They may note differential development of either (1) legs and arms, such as inability to sit but precise reaching and grasping skill with thumb and forefinger, or (2) the two sides of the body, such as clear handedness before one year of age.

If cerebral palsy is diagnosed in infancy, child development professionals can help reduce some of its negative effects. A nurse can tell parents how to handle feeding difficulties due to lack of coordination of the oral musculature. A physical therapist can help parents use exercises to prevent loss of range of motion in the joints, reduce the use of abnormal postures that may lead to further deformities, or decrease spasticity by encouraging muscle relaxation. An early childhood educator can recommend sensorimotor experiences for the child who lacks the ability to locomote or reach and grasp objects well.

To coordinate these activities proper diagnosis by the physician is essential. Frequent visits to the physician are often necessary to clearly differentiate the young cerebral palsied child from children with diseases of the nervous system that get progressively worse and from those with simple developmental lags that have no long-range pathological implications. The coordination of these child development personnel is made possible with frequent evaluations not only by a physician but a physical therapist or clinical psychologist who will describe the child's present behavior as it is affected by the disorder.

Assessing the Infant's Cognitive and Language Development

Adults often want to know whether an infant's cognitive development is progressing well, or whether a child is behaving typically for his or her age. Such questions are hard to answer because we do not know how accurate our assessment instruments are in predicting later development. We do not understand the relationship between early behaviors and later development. A discussion of instruments used for infant assessment will indicate why prediction of later development, especially as measured by IQ tests, has been a problem.

The Gesell Developmental Schedules

The Gesell Developmental Schedules were designed at the Yale University Clinic of Child Development. One of the first infant tests to be developed, it is still in use today. The subtests measure motor, adaptive, language, and personal-social behavior, in children between four weeks and five years of age.

The motor scale includes items relating to posture, prehension (reaching and grasping), locomotion, and coordination. The adaptive behavior scale is designed to assess a child's ability to initiate new experiences and learn from past experiences. The language scale assesses various receptive and productive language skills. The personal-social behavior scale is used to evaluate a child's reactions to people and observance of social conventions. An infant's performance is scored in terms of norms; i.e., a particular infant's score is compared to the performances of other infants of the same age (Gesell, 1954).

Although studies have provided conflicting results about how well the Gesell schedules predict a child's later IQ, correlations in general have been rather low. Babies who score high on the scale as infants may very well not get a high score on an IQ test at age three.

Bayley Scales of Infant Development

The Scales of Infant Development were developed by Dr. Nancy Bayley at the University of California at Berkeley during the 1930s; they have been periodically updated and revised. The Bayley tests consist of a motor scale and a mental scale. The mental scale includes items that measure small motor skills such as use of the hands in tower building or pegboard tasks. It also includes assessments of sensory abilities such as response to sound and light as well as items related to language and to adaptability. The motor scale includes items that assess locomotor and large motor skills such as pulling up, creeping, walking, and balancing (Bayley, 1933, 1969).

Like the Gesell scales, the Bayley scales have not been found to predict later IQ with great precision. The Bayley and Gesell scales are similar in that they rely heavily on the assessment of sensorimotor skills. They cannot measure language-related skills that will appear later such as defining words which make up large portions of later IQ tests. Because they measure different skills, the infant scales are rather poor predictors of later IQ scores.

Living with the Infant

Responding to Individual Differences

Children, even as tiny infants, seem to differ from one another. Neonates spend different amounts of time in various states and have different sensory thresholds. Schaffer and Emerson (1964) reported that some infants were "noncuddlers" (they resisted being held close), whereas others were "cuddlers."

For healthy relationships to develop, caregivers must adjust to the style of the infant. The following statements of parents who participated in the Schaffer and Emerson study illustrate the kinds of adaptations they learned to make (1964, pp. 3–4):

NONCUDDLERS

Never has liked sitting on knee. It is easier to play with him sitting beside him on the floor.

You can't calm him by picking him up even when he is teething — wheeling him around in his pram (buggy) is much more effective.

Most easily comforted by walking him around and showing him things.

CUDDLERS

I have to walk him in my arms every night till he falls asleep.

It should be emphasized that both "cuddlers" and "noncuddlers" were attached to their mothers. The "noncuddlers," though resistant to contact that involved restraint, were fond of being kissed, tickled, swung, and bounced. The infants in the two groups had different methods of relating, and parents had to find ways to adapt to them. One of the most important tasks of caregivers is making sensitive adaptations.

Ensuring the Infant's Safety

Infants need to be protected from falls, from accidental poisoning, and from swallowing small objects. They are explorers, and their overwhelming curiosity sometimes leads to trouble.

Preventing Falls and Collisions. Children learning to walk fall quite frequently, and mild tumbles and bumps are common. These are no cause for worry. Once a child begins to move around by itself it can get into dangerous situations, however. Broken bones and head injuries can have serious consequences.

Even when infants perceive danger, they may be unable to avoid hurting themselves. In their study of depth perception, Gibson and Walk (1960) noted that although infants were wary of a "cliff" and refused to cross over, they often lacked sufficient control to have protected themselves had the "deep" side of the experimental apparatus not been covered with glass:

> Many supported themselves on the glass over the deep side as they maneuvered awkwardly on the board; some even backed out onto the glass as they started toward the mother on the shallow side. Were it not for the glass some of the children would have fallen off the board. Evidently infants should not be left close to a brink, no matter how well they may discriminate depth. [Gibson and Walk, 1960, p. 64]

You can make an environment safe for infants by taking some common precautions. Never leave a baby unattended on a table or bed. Keep stairs and floors free of clutter that could trip a child. Use folding gates to block off stairs, and keep high chairs away from tables or walls against which the baby could push itself over.

The most serious collisions usually occur in automobiles. A sudden stop can send a baby hurtling through a windshield to death or serious injury. Statistics indicate that about 1000 children under five are killed in car crashes each year and that many thousands are injured. And surveys have shown that less than 8 percent of children under five are appropriately protected from crash injuries by being placed in infant car seats (Reisinger and Williams, 1978). What is even more alarming is the fact that programs to educate parents about the risks of children riding unrestrained in cars has not led to high levels of car seat use. Even when parents of infants were given free car seats and pamphlets and verbal information about the importance of restraining infants for safety, the use rate

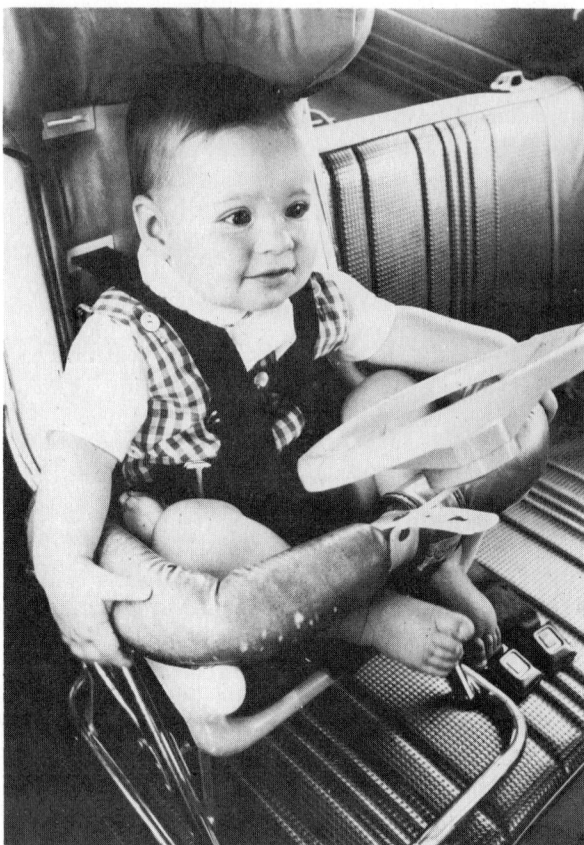

A 7-pound baby becomes the equivalent of a 210-pound weight in a 30-miles-per-hour crash, and a parent cannot possibly hold onto it. The only safe place for a baby in a car is in the back, in an approved infant safety seat.

was only 41 percent (Reisinger and Williams, 1978). The poor outcome of numerous attempts to educate parents on this subject has led some states to consider enacting laws requiring parents to place young children in safe car seats.

Preventing Poisoning. Poisoning is another serious accident. Infants like moderate novelty, and they like to explore with their mouths. Once they can crawl about, medicines and many other common household products become a hazard. Nail polish, nail polish remover, perfumes, hair dyes, furniture polish, detergents, bleach, ammonia, toilet-bowl cleaners, kerosene, gasoline, pesticides, lawn fertilizers — all must be kept out of children's reach (Done, 1970).

Some parents mistakenly think they can teach their infants not to touch household products kept under a sink or in a medicine cabinet. "It's important for him to learn where he can and cannot go," they say. But this is too risky a situation to use for lessons on territoriality or responsibility. The infant's urge to find out is overwhelming and its capacity to understand is limited. The adult must take full responsibility for keeping poisons where children cannot get them.

Preventing Ingestion of Small Objects. Small objects can become lodged in an infant's throat or aspirated into the bronchial tubes or lungs. Because infants like to explore things with their mouths, small objects must simply be kept away from them. Similarly, toys that might come apart and release small pieces should not be given to infants. Rattles, for example, must be very durable because they all have beads or other small objects inside. The eyes of stuffed animals should be sewn on rather than attached with pins; the best animals have embroidered eyes.

Ensuring the Infant's Health

Common Childhood Diseases. Childhood diseases are often grouped into five categories: respiratory, communicable, gastrointestinal, accidents and surgery, and other types. Respiratory illnesses include colds, bronchitis, tonsillitis, and sore throat. Some communicable diseases are measles, chicken pox, mumps, German measles, and whooping cough. Gastrointestinal infections affect the stomach and intestines and usually involve vomiting and diarrhea.

Infancy is a time of relatively good health. In fact, children suffer from fewer illnesses between birth and two years of age than at any other time during childhood. (The highest incidence of illness during childhood occurs during the preschool years.) Illnesses can be more serious in infants than in older children because infants have small air passages that become blocked more easily from respiratory infections. In addition, infants dehydrate (lose water) rapidly when afflicted with vomiting and diarrhea. Prompt medical care for these conditions is essential.

Communicable diseases can be controlled by immunization. Today, immunizations are available for diphtheria (an upper respiratory illness), tetanus (an infection causing contractions of muscles of face, jaw, and neck), pertussis (whooping cough), polio, measles, rubella, and mumps. The first immunizations are given at about two months of age. Others are given at three months, four months, six months, and one year. "Booster" shots are given at around eighteen months, and again when the child is five years old.

Because today's parents are too young to remember the epidemics of communicable diseases common before immunizations were developed, they have grown somewhat lax about having their children immunized. Some school systems have had to bar children from entering to force parents to have their children immunized.

Sudden Infant Death Syndrome (SIDS). Parents often blame themselves for sudden infant death, but they are not to blame for it. Sudden infant death syndrome strikes about 8000 infants each year. The baby usually appears perfectly normal before it is put to bed at night or for a daytime nap, but later it is found dead.

The exact cause of sudden infant death syndrome is not known. It is certain, however, that these babies do not smother in their bedclothes. Researchers have several theories about causes. Some think a virus or a sensitivity to milk is responsible; others think the cause is related to malfunctions in babies' breathing control mechanisms, which may be triggered by stress of infection (Naeye, 1974). The fact is that no one really knows for sure what kills these infants, or if a single cause is responsible for all deaths.

Parents of infants who die in this way often feel that they could have prevented the death if only they had done something differently. Unfortunately, there is nothing we know of that a parent can do. The National Foundation for Sudden Infant Death was formed to help families of victims cope with the tragedy; it now has chapters throughout the United States. (See National Institute of Child Health and Human Development, 1972, for an extensive annotated bibliography of writings about sudden infant death syndrome.)

FOCUS: Use of Apnea Monitoring to Prevent Sudden Infant Death

Research suggests that some infants who die from sudden infant death syndrome (SIDS) may do so because of a malfunction in their breathing mechanism (Naeye, 1974). Before death actually occurs, these infants are observed to have irregular respiratory patterns with apnea (cessation of breathing) occurring more frequently and for more prolonged periods than is normal (Shannon, 1980).

When an infant with breathing irregularities is identified, apnea monitors are sometimes installed in the infant's home. These devices are attached to the baby when it is put to bed. An alarm rings if the infant fails to breathe for more than a few seconds. The alarm alerts the baby's parents who can then awaken the baby and cause it to resume normal breathing. The monitor is used until two months have passed without an alarm being triggered. Apparently, as the baby gets older, the malfunctioning of the breathing mechanism, whatever its cause, corrects itself in such a way that the infant is no longer in danger of dying in its sleep.

Whereas apnea monitoring appears to be a promising technological tool for preventing SIDS, there are practical drawbacks to its use. For example, unless a previous child in a family has died from SIDS, it is difficult for medical personnel or parents to be alert to the possibility that a child is at risk. In addition, the use of monitoring devices has an enormous psychological impact on parents. They are often anxious that they will not hear the alarm, or that the device will malfunction and the alarm will not ring. They are also reluctant to leave the baby with a babysitter for fear that something will happen while they are away and the person left in charge will not respond as necessary. Because of these fears, supportive counseling is recommended for parents whose children are being monitored so that psychological stresses can be lessened (Black et al., 1978).

Play and Playthings for the Infant

Sooner or later most of us have the pleasure of selecting toys for an infant. What makes a toy good for a particular infant or group of infants? Much of the information in this chapter can be used to answer these questions.

Toys for Young Infants. A mobile for the crib is often one of the first playthings purchased for infants. Mobiles have become increasingly popular in the last few decades as research on the infant's abilities has increased. Although manufacturers apparently know that infants like to look at things, they do not seem to understand exactly what is most appealing to them. As you will recall, infants prefer patterns that provide a great deal of contrast, which means that pastels are not as good a choice as dark colors alternated with light colors. By the same token, the infant has little to look at when decorations appear only on the sides of the mobile figures (where an adult buyer is most likely to see them). To interest an infant, the mobile's patterns should appear on the bottoms of the figures.

Rattles are another favorite plaything for infants. A rattle placed in a three-month-old infant's hand will be mouthed, looked at, felt with the other hand, and shaken. The sound created by moving it is appealing to all infants, but especially to those who are blind.

Many other toys are available for the very young infant, and several of them appeal to their preference for the moderately novel. There are soft objects in a variety of shapes — intertwined rings, cubes, barbells, and jacks — that can be looked at, mouthed, and felt.

Toys for Crawlers and Walkers. A colorful ball is a good toy for the infant who has begun to crawl. The ball's movement appeals to the baby, and pushing a striped ball produces a changing pattern and a moderately predictable path of movement.

The musical push toys such as the popular lawnmower are favorites of the infant who can walk. However, pull toys such as the animal that rolls and goes "click-click-clack" as it moves are best saved until the child has completely mastered walking. An infant is still top-heavy due to the relatively large size of its head, and it may still find balancing difficult. The infant compensates by walking with the feet rather wide apart and the arms outstretched. A young infant may find holding an arm down to pull a string and looking around to check on the movements of the toy are too much to manage. A toddler who has mastered walking will enjoy such toys.

Fill and Dump Toys. For the infant who is at least one year old, there are a number of interesting playthings. First, there are the "fill and dump" toys. (See page 164 to review how these toys relate to the child's developing concept of the object.) One of the more popular is the set consisting of a large plastic bottle and large colored pegs. Infants drop the pegs through the large mouth of the bottle, and then dump them out again. Of course, everything is brought to the mouth periodically to be sucked or chewed.

A considerably more difficult "fill and dump" toy is the form box, a hollow, wooden cube with a lid containing holes through which small spheres, cubes, and cylinders can be pushed. Children drop the forms through the holes in the lid and then raise the lid to retrieve them or hold the box upside-down to dump them out. Infants often quickly lose interest in boxes that have many holes of different shapes. Getting an object through any hole is enough of a challenge without the additional problem of matching cylinders to round holes, cubes to square ones, and so on. For this reason the simplest form boxes should be chosen, or all the holes but the round one should be taped over and only cylindrical pegs provided. Most infants do not have sophisticated enough schemes to obtain interesting results with an unmodified form box and will ignore it.

Interactive and Responsive Toys and Games. Older infants begin to enjoy simple picture books, especially when an adult holds both baby and book and talks about the pictures. Books for infants are made of cloth or have very thick cardboard pages; otherwise, they would never withstand baby's newly de-

Even a baby enjoys a good book now and then.

Pots and pans sure are interesting. Mom and dad were thoughtful to put them in this low cupboard where I can get them all by myself.

But somebody forgot to remove the glass bowls and the grater—they're dangerous.

veloped schemes for tearing and crumpling, or baby's very early but persistent mouthing scheme.

Some of the infant's favorite playthings are bowls, pots and pans, and large wooden and metal spoons. When these are combined with other playthings such as the plastic bottle and pegs and the form box and shapes, the possibilities for exploration are endless. The infant can bang the wooden and metal spoons on plastic bowls, the plastic bottle, and the metal pots and pans. The shapes from the form box that only fit through a specific place in the lid go into the other containers easily. The colored pegs can be dumped into a pan and stirred with a spoon. The pegs or form box shapes make different sounds when dropped into different containers. In short, the infant can easily create many moderately novel situations. Is it any wonder that children like to play in the kitchen with these "toys"?

Perhaps the infant's favorite form of play is interacting with familiar adults — what we earlier called "social games." Episodes of pseudoimitation, for example, are enjoyed by many babies. Babies also enjoy being placed in their infant seats in the middle of the kitchen table so they can observe the goings-on. And, of course, an occasional pause by the adults to "chat" with the baby increases its pleasure. Favorite social games for the older infant include peek-a-boo and pat-a-cake. Adults can hold baby's attention at these games indefinitely with moderately novel "peeks" and "pats."

Responsiveness is as important in toys as it is in humans. An object's responsiveness is its potential to change as a stimulus as a result of being handled. Paper is very responsive because with little effort it will crackle and crumple and take a different shape. Studies have demonstrated significant, positive correlations between an infant's access to responsive toys and his or her performance on tests of development such as the Bayley scales (Yarrow, Rubenstein, and Pedersen, 1971). In short, when toys respond to their actions, babies learn more as they play.

Summary

Infant Education Programs
- The Florida Parent Education Infant and Toddler Program is based largely on Piagetian principles. The Family Development Research Program is based on theories of both Piaget and Erikson.
- Special programs have been developed to meet the needs of children with handicaps.

Assessing the Infant's Cognitive and Language Development
- The Gesell Development Schedules and the Bayley Scales of Infant Development are instruments used to assess development in infancy. Infant intelligence tests, however, do not predict later IQ with much accuracy.

Living with the Infant
- One important task of parents is to adapt to their infant's individual needs.
- Parents must "baby-proof" their infant's environment to keep the infant from falling, colliding with something, ingesting poison or small objects, or otherwise hurting herself.
- Although infancy is a time of relatively good health, medical care and immunization are important. Upper respiratory and gastrointestinal illnesses in infants can be serious because infants' air passages are narrow and they may become dehydrated with high fever or vomiting and diarrhea.
- Infants enjoy toys that are responsive to their actions and that relate to their developing schemes. They also enjoy social games such as peek-a-boo.

New Terms

sudden infant death syndrome (SIDS)   **cerebral palsy**

Selected Readings

Caplan, F. (Ed.). **The parenting advisor.** *Garden City, N.Y.: Anchor Press/Doubleday, 1977.* This book, written for parents, includes information about caring for the sick child, selecting playthings, supporting learning in babies, and much more.

Spock, B. **Baby and child care.** *New York: Pocket Books, 1968.* The all-time favorite reference book for parents. Includes descriptions of illnesses and their treatment and ways to prevent accidents and injuries.

United States Public Health Service. **Parents' guide to childhood immunization.** *Washington, D.C.: U.S. Government Printing Office, DHEW Publication No. (OS) 77-50058, 1977.* All the common communicable childhood diseases for which immunization is available are described in this pamphlet, and immunization schedules and records are discussed.

Willis, A., and Ricciuti, H. **A good beginning for babies: Guidelines for group care.** *Washington, D.C.: National Association for the Education of Young Children, 1975.* Describes the components and characteristics of good group programs for babies. The intended audience is child care workers but parents may find the information useful in knowing what to look for in infant care.

Part IV
The Toddler

Toddlerhood is a period of transitions. Toddlers — children between one and a half and three years of age — want to be with their parents and other familiar adults, but they also enjoy meeting new people, especially those of their own age. They still need to be fed, but they want to feed themselves. They begin the period needing two naps a day and often finish it needing only one. They have a great deal to say, but at least at first they are unable to say it.

Living with a toddler can be trying for children and adults alike. It is during this period that adults begin to expect children to behave according to certain standards. Children must acquire a knowledge of acceptable patterns of behavior and the goals and beliefs of their family and society. This process, known as *socialization*, involves learning how to get along with other children, how to feed oneself, and how to use the toilet, among other things. These achievements are made possible by the child's continuing physical and cognitive development. An understanding of the development that occurs during this time can help us support the child's transitions. It also enables us to recognize and enjoy some rather remarkable achievements.

Chapter *11*

*P*hysical Development

We saw in Chapter 6 that infancy is a period when extremely rapid physical development takes place. By toddlerhood, changes are taking place less rapidly. Growth, for example, slows down somewhat, although not as much as it will in a few more years. Motor skills that began to emerge in infancy are consolidated and varied during the toddler period. For example, an infant who has just learned to walk is not very surefooted. During toddlerhood, however, coordination and balance improve considerably, and walking can be done with ease. Furthermore, other locomotor skills that are variations of walking begin to emerge: the toddler begins to learn how to run and to climb. Similarly, fine motor skills continue to expand. We saw that in infancy children learn to use their hands to grasp things. During toddlerhood, they become more skillful in using their hands to manipulate objects grasped. In this chapter we will discuss toddlers' physical development in detail, including body growth and motor skills, as well as eating behavior and readiness for toilet training, both of which are influenced by physical maturity.

Growth

Changes in Height, Weight, and Appetite

Remarks such as, "I no like that!" and "I not hungry!" are familiar to every parent. At mealtime parents often find themselves staring at a piece of toast that has been nibbled in one corner, at a glass of milk from which one tiny gulp has been taken, or at scrambled eggs ingeniously spread over an entire plate to disguise the fact that not a single bite has been taken. Parents frequently worry that the child will be malnourished or will stop growing.

Toddlers do grow, of course, but their rate of growth is slower than it was formerly, and they need less food. Children triple their birth weight during their first year (from seven to twenty-one pounds) and they increase in length by about one-third (from twenty-one to twenty-nine inches). During their second year, however, their weight increases by only a third (from twenty-one to twenty-eight pounds), and their length by about one-seventh (from twenty-nine to thirty-three inches). It is not surprising that children who frequently cried when hungry during infancy sometimes become finicky eaters during toddlerhood.

By age two, adult height can be predicted with a fair degree of accuracy. Garn (1966) has provided multipliers for this purpose. For boys, the multiplier to use at age two is 2.06; for girls, it is 2.01. For example, if a two-year-old boy is 34 inches tall, we would predict his adult height to be 70.04 inches. If a two-year-old girl is 34 inches tall, we would predict her adult height to be 68.34 inches.

Changes in Body Proportions and Shape

At the age of two or two and a half children lose the "baby fat" that accumulated during the first nine months after birth. They do not lose weight, however, because their bone and muscle tissue grows more rapidly. As a result, children appear leaner by late toddlerhood even though they do not lose weight.

Toddlers continue to be chubby around the middle, because the trunk grows slowly during infancy and early toddlerhood and there is little room for the child's relatively large abdominal organs. The underdeveloped muscles of the abdomen offer little resistance as the organs push out the toddler's middle. The abdomen remains distended until the trunk grows enough to provide more room.

Teething

Teething actually begins in infancy, with the child cutting his or her first tooth at around seven or eight months of age. Children often have four teeth on the top and two teeth on the bottom by their first birthday; within the next six months, most children add six more. The remaining eight are cut during the toddler years. These ages, as well as others we cite for growth, are averages, of course. Occasionally, an infant is born with a tooth or two, and some infants do not cut their first one until after seven or eight months of age.

A typical toddler tummy

Although teething begins in infancy, children cannot really chew solid food until they have a full set of teeth, in toddlerhood. Most children do begin to eat chopped rather than strained foods late in their first year, but this is possible because foods that crush easily, such as cooked carrots and apple slices, can be chewed adequately with the gums. Teeth are required to chew meats, however. Prior to toddlerhood, children should have only minced or chopped meats.

It is during toddlerhood that children are usually taught to brush their teeth, although parents and caregivers should begin brushing the baby's teeth as soon as several have appeared. Children should also take their first trip to the dentist between the ages of two and three — 50 percent of all two-year-olds in the United States have one or more decayed teeth (Caplan, 1977).

We have all heard about the effects of thumb sucking on the teeth. Dentists agree that thumb sucking does push the teeth off course; the upper front teeth are pushed forward and the lower teeth are pushed backward. This does not, however, affect the alignment of the permanent teeth. If thumb sucking stops by the age of five or six, no permanent effect on teeth will result (Caplan, 1977). Thumb sucking usually goes away by itself, and it is probably best to ignore it in the young child. A child with a thumb in his mouth clutching the tattered remains of a favorite blanket, or twirling a lock of hair is a pretty common sight, especially at bedtime.

Motor Development

Fine Motor Development

The development of the arms and hands is said to be *proximodistal:* the muscles near the trunk (proximo), which control the shoulders and elbows, mature before the muscles of the extremities (distal), which control the wrists and hands. This sequence is evident in the attempts of twelve- and fifteen-month-old babies to build a "tower" of two cubes: the fifteen-month-old can do it with ease, but the younger child is rarely successful. The younger infant simply does not have enough control of her hand movements to place the cubes in precisely the right place. In addition, she is just beginning to learn how to release objects voluntarily. Infants actually must learn how to let an object go; a child less than six months old finds it difficult if not impossible to do so, because the palmar grasp, which is just beginning to disappear, interferes with letting go. It is not until between one year and eighteen months of age that children actually learn how to release an object voluntarily.

Toddlers make great gains in their coordination, strength, and steadiness in releasing objects. Toddlers can snap pop-beads together, make moderately con-

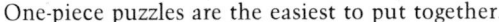

One-piece puzzles are the easiest to put together.

trolled marks on paper with pencil and crayon, and work simple, two- or four-piece puzzles. They can even string large beads if the end of the string is taped for the length of a bead.

Locomotor Skills

The toddler also makes great progress in moving about. The different levels of ability of an infant and a mature toddler are apparent in the following observation made by one of the authors in a carpet store one evening:

> The mother held the door wide open for the baby (about one year old) to walk in. On the pavement beneath the door was a metal strip intended to make the door fit snugly, but in this case it presented a hurdle for the child. The strip was only slightly raised, perhaps one-quarter of an inch; nevertheless, the baby saw it and stopped. She pressed the toes of her bare feet hard against the sidewalk to stop her forward movement. It worked, but then she rocked backward. Even with arms outstretched to help with balance, she could not recover her stability. She blinked as she sat down, kerplop! on the sidewalk.
>
> At the same time there was a child of two and one-half in the store with his sister and mother. This mature toddler was climbing on rolled-up carpets and then jumping off. He walked along the tops of large, thick rolls, only occasionally losing his balance and having to catch himself with his hands. Sometimes he and his older sister chased each other around a carpet display, dashing down one aisle, turning the corner, and dashing up the aisle on the other side.

The infant who was just beginning to walk had to concentrate her full attention on standing up. She held her arms out and placed her feet wide apart to maintain balance. She sometimes failed even at this and fell down. But the more mature toddler moved with abandon and ease. Having mastered balance, he no longer had to hold his arms outstretched. The wide stance used by the beginning walker to offset top-heaviness, had also disappeared. He was really in control: he could vary his movements and use them for his own ends. Toddlers can walk sideways, backward, and up and down stairs, leading with one foot. They can jump up and down, kick a large ball, and sometimes even ride a tricycle.

The toddler's new locomotor skills emerge as a result of maturation of the motor area of the cerebral cortex. As we have seen, locomotor development proceeds in a cephalocaudal, or head to tail, direction — nerve cells that control movements of the upper body, such as sitting, mature before those that control the lower trunk and legs. This pattern of development also influences the ability to control the *sphincters* — the smooth, circular muscles of the bladder and bowel. That is, control of these muscles comes later, with control of the lower trunk and legs, rather than earlier with control of the upper body and arms.

Top-heavy toddlers might fall over if they bent from the waist. Squatting works much better.

Achieving Bladder and Bowel Control

In young children, the sphincter of the rectum or bladder relaxes reflexively, permitting the contents to escape. As children mature, however, they can learn to inhibit these reflex actions. This requires motor control and an awareness of the sensations indicating a full rectum or bladder, both of which depend on the maturation of the cerebral cortex. Just as there is a particular order to the development of the motor area of the cerebral cortex (cephalocaudal), there is order to the development of the sensory area. Sensory development of the leg area is not fully achieved until age two, or even a little later (Tanner, 1978).

Bowel control comes first, usually beginning about midway through the second year. A little later the child begins to gain control of the bladder, first during the day and then also during the night. Boys achieve control later than girls because they are physically less mature. Girls may be toilet trained by age two or two and a half. Boys may not be very reliable until almost age three. Most children learn control over a period of several months, although it sometimes takes much longer; the process of acquiring night control may span several years. Furthermore, all children seem prone to relapse from time to time, when they are ill, tired, in a strange place, or absorbed in play with a new toy. Similarly, a child who has been dry at night for several months, may occasionally have an episode or two of bed wetting.

Toilet training requires more than physical readiness. The child must also be familiar with social expectations and be able to understand what he or she should do. We will have more to say about toilet training in Chapter 15, after we have discussed other aspects of development.

Summary

Growth

- Toddlers' appetites decrease as their growth rate slows, and they tend to lose some of their baby fat, giving them a leaner appearance. Although they eat less, they are able to eat a variety of foods, including meats, because they have a full set of teeth.
- Thumb sucking during toddlerhood does not appear to affect the alignment of the permanent teeth.

Motor Development

- Motor development in the arms and hands is proximodistal — it progresses from the center of the body to the extremities.
- During toddlerhood, the wide-stanced walk of the younger infant gradually disappears.
- Skill in using the hands increases considerably by late toddlerhood.
- Neurological development influences bladder and bowel control.

New Terms

proximodistal development
sphincter muscles

Selected Readings

Caplan, F. (Ed.). **The parenting advisor.** *Garden City, N.Y.: Anchor Press/Doubleday, 1977.* This general reference book written for parents has good discussions of teething, feeding, and toilet training.

Sinclair, C. B. **Movement of the young child: Ages two to six.** *Columbus, Ohio: Charles E. Merrill, 1973.* A thorough but readable overview of many physical skills that develop in young children. Because the book begins with children at age two, some of the discussion is helpful in understanding motor skill development during toddlerhood.

Tanner, J. M. **Education and physical growth.** Second edition. *New York: International Universities Press, 1978.* An authoritative and informative book about physical growth throughout childhood.

Chapter *12*

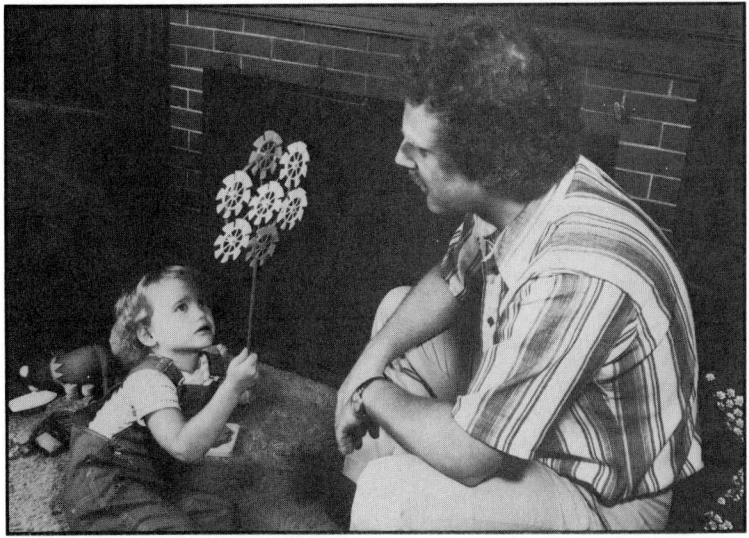

*C*ognitive Development

Because Piaget's period of sensorimotor development spans the period from birth to about two years of age, we have already discussed in Chapter 7 some of the cognitive developments that occur during the period we have defined as toddlerhood. In this chapter we will discuss very young children's views about causality, another area Piaget covered in detail, and then describe play behavior from a cognitive point of view. Mature toddlers are in the beginning of Piaget's next major stage of development, the preoperational stage. But because the preoperational stage spans all the preschool years, we save a full discussion of this topic for Chapter 17, when we discuss cognitive development in the preschool child.

Children's Questions and Explanations: Clues to Their Views of Causality

A child sits outside on a patio painting rocks with water. "Where moon?" he asks. His father is silenced by the question: How does one explain the earth's rotation and the movement of the planets to a two-year-old? But is this actually what the child wants to know? The parent has a hunch that he is actually asking a different question. The child had recently seen the moon in the sky in his book, *Good-night Moon;* could he be wondering where the moon is in the real sky? The adult offers an explanation based on his hunch: "The moon is in the sky at night. You won't be able to find it now."

"Oh," the child replies. Then he checks his understanding: "Moon come at night?"

"That's right; you can see the moon at night."

The child turns back to his rock painting. He continues to ask the question occasionally over the next few days, however, until one evening he looks up and sees a very bright, full moon. The next day he looks up at the sky and says, "Moon come at night; sun sky at day." Then he asks, "Why moon come at night?"

As you can see, explaining things to toddlers can be difficult. Unlike adults, they do not seek physical or mechanical explanations. Children believe everything is both *animate* (alive) and *conscious* (capable of motives and intentions), and they want moral or psychological explanations (Piaget, 1969, 1972). A child who asks, "Where moon?" could be wondering a number of things: Where is the moon now? When is he coming back so that I can see him, or so that he can see me? The question, "Why moon?" may mean, what is the purpose of the moon? The child may think the moon comes and goes at will, as he does.

Sometimes children continue to ask, "But why?" after several careful, thorough explanations. In many instances the problem is not that the child is not paying attention, but rather that the adult has misinterpreted the question. A child who asks why thunder and lightning come probably does not want to know about the nature of electric charges and the relationship between air movements and the production of sound. The real question might be, "Why did the thunder and lightning want to scare me and keep me from playing outside?" The question is asked repeatedly because it is not answered by an explanation of the laws of physics, which adults usually give.

Does that mean that adults should provide answers that perpetuate children's belief in animism and the consciousness of inanimate objects? Probably not. A child learns by having to assimilate unexpected explanations into current understandings. In time, this leads to modification or accommodation of these understandings. Simple, accurate explanations are best, but adults should expect such answers to be greeted by another "Why?"

Children do not fully understand physical causality until they are well into their school-age years. Until then they are likely to get explanations a bit confused. We know of a two-and-a-half-year-old girl who decided to follow her mother to a next-door neighbor's house one winter night. (Her father was home with the children, but he did not notice when the child slipped out.) When the neighbor finally heard the child's faint knocking, she had been out in the cold for five or ten minutes. Interestingly, she had put on her mittens, hat, and boots, but she had not put on her coat. When her mother asked why she had not dressed properly, she replied, "I did! I put on my hat, mittens, and boots." After thinking a bit, the mother figured out why her daughter had behaved as she did. She had frequently reminded her daughter to put on her mittens, hat, and boots because it was so cold outside. The mother meant, of course, that these items were needed *in addition* to the snowsuit, but the child assumed that the mittens, hat, and boots bestowed some kind of protection all by themselves.

Cognition and Play

Young children also reveal their thinking through their play. Some researchers think that changes in play parallel changes in cognition (Chaille, 1978; Greenfield and Smith, 1976).

Defining Play

Although experts differ considerably in their definitions of *play*, many would agree that it has the following characteristics (Garvey, 1977a):

1. Play is pleasurable. Even when there are no signs of enjoyment, it is still gratifying to the player.
2. Play serves no particular or utilitarian purpose. The player enjoys the methods he or she is using for their own sake rather than because they help him or her accomplish a task.
3. Play is spontaneous and voluntary rather than obligatory.
4. Play actively involves the player.

The fact that play serves no utilitarian purpose does not mean that playing is unproductive. Children gain skills and understanding during play that can be applied in other situations. A child who dresses a doll, for example, may have to struggle with tiny buttons. This practice improves the child's small motor skills, and those skills can later be applied to more utilitarian tasks. Good teachers understand this and have no difficulty answering parents who ask, "Why don't you make the children sit down and *learn* something?" They know children are learning constantly while they play.

Whether or not a child is playing is determined, not by what she is doing, but by her "mode of experiencing" (Garvey, 1977b, p. 28). Reality is suspended during play, and the usual consequences of an action do not apply. For example, the inability to button will delay a child's dressing to go to school, but during play it has no problematic result. The child may go on playing "mother" even though the dress put on to indicate the mother's role is not buttoned up the front.

The Function of Play

Several explanations of why children play have been formulated. The *preexercise theory* suggests that play is a preparation for adult activities. Psychoanalytic theorists argue that it is a way of working out the conflicts that arise in daily life.

The child spanks the baby, gives it shots, and tells it to stop crying. Cognitive-developmental theories explain play in terms of cognition: children play because moderate novelty is interesting or because there is satisfaction in reducing the discrepancy between a child's schemes and his or her immediate experiences. That is, a child's ideas about why something happens do not correspond to reality, and the child explores further to find out why. The child might try to find out how a broom works, what it is like to be a mother, what a shot is, or how one gives comfort. The relationship between play and cognition is currently receiving much attention and will be emphasized in our discussion.

Stages in the Development of Play Behavior with Social Materials

In an investigation of the development of play, Fenson et al. (1976) gave tea sets to children between seven and twenty months of age. Each set included two cups, two saucers, two spoons, and a pot with a removable lid. The acts that children could perform with these objects were divided into three types: (1) *relational*, (2) *symbolic*, and (3) *sequential*. These are defined in Table 12-1.

The psychologists found that children of different ages played with the toys differently. At seven months they related objects occasionally, but most of their responses were acts such as banging, shaking, mouthing, and chewing. The nine-month-olds also banged and shook objects a great deal, but in addition they

Table 12-1. Categories for child behaviors in Fenson's study of play

Category	Examples
1. Relational acts (combining or relating two objects).	
a. simple	Touching spoon against base of pot; touching lid against side of cup.
b. accommodative	Appropriate association, such as putting a cup on a saucer, or a lid on a pot.
c. grouping	Putting two cups, spoons, or saucers together.
2. Symbolic acts	Eating, drinking, pouring, stirring, or spooning imaginary substances.
3. Sequential acts	
a. two parallel acts in succession	Putting one cup on one saucer, then a second cup on a second saucer.
b. variations on a theme	Stirring in the pot, then in the cup.

NOTE: A fourth action, banging, was not placed in a category.
SOURCE: Fenson, L., Kagan, J., Kearsley, R., and Zelazo, P. The developmental progression of manipulative play in the first two years. *Child Development* 47 (1976): Copyright © The Society for Research in Child Development, Inc. Reprinted by permission.

A doll becomes a person
and a toy cup becomes a
real one in symbolic play.

performed simple relational acts. The thirteen-month-olds performed relational acts quite often, especially accommodative acts, but they rarely used the materials symbolically. Twenty-month-old infants performed symbolic acts very frequently but sequential acts only occasionally.

The order in which these behaviors appeared is related to the development of sensorimotor intelligence and language behavior. Accommodative acts become common around one year to fourteen months of age, during the beginning of tertiary circular reactions (stage 5 of sensorimotor development). At this stage of sensorimotor development, *accommodation*, or adapting one's behavior to meet the demands of the environment, is occurring more rapidly than in earlier stages when *assimilation*, or taking in or relating experiences to existing schemes or behavior patterns, tends to dominate.

Symbolic (pretend) play emerges during stage 6 of sensorimotor development, at about the same time children begin to acquire language. Both of these behaviors involve representation: in language, words represent things; in symbolic play, one object or action represents another (for example, a toy cup represents a real cup, or a block represents a house). Piaget (1962) refers to this underlying ability to represent as the *symbolic function*.

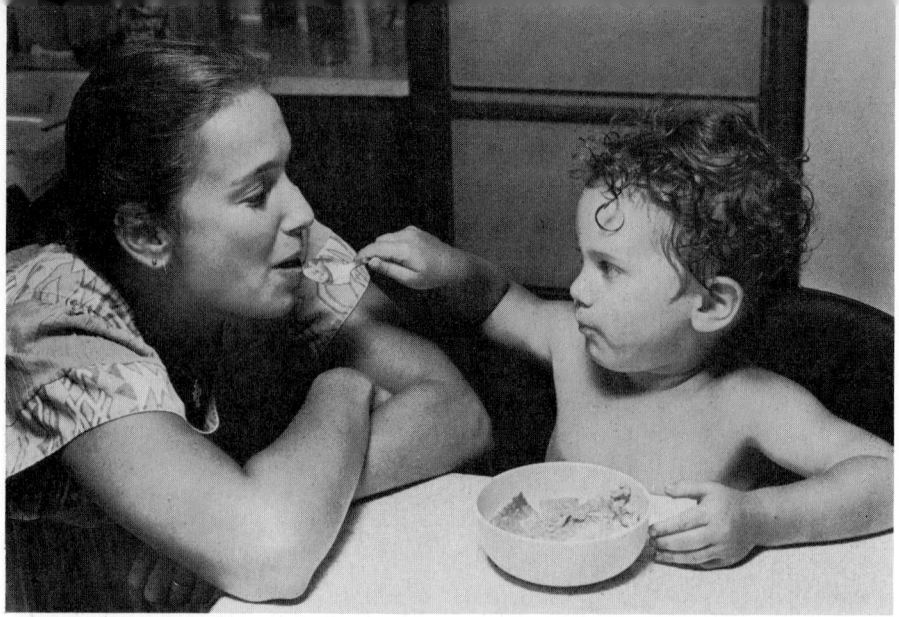

In an early stage of symbolic play, children pretend to do to others what they often do to themselves.

Sequential acts involve variation, which is a frequent behavior during the fifth stage of sensorimotor development, tertiary circular reactions. You might wonder why these behaviors followed symbolic acts in Fenson's study, rather than preceding them as one would expect on the basis of behavior characteristic of each stage of sensorimotor development. The reason may be that the objects involved in the Fenson study were social. That is, the child is varying observed social relationships with these objects, rather than relating the objects to understand their nature or the nature of actions on them *per se.* So, in a sense, what is being varied are pretend or symbolic actions involving objects. Obviously, this behavior cannot emerge until the child can first perform symbolic acts themselves.

The developmental sequence of play has also been described by other researchers. The results of work by Lowe (1975) and Fein (1975) indicate that children progress in the following way:

1. *12 months* — children begin to use objects or actions to enact familiar activities (e.g., pretend to eat or sleep, or uses a toy brush to brush his or her own hair)
2. *18 months* — children begin to focus on others rather than on themselves (e.g., pretend to feed mother, a doll, or a stuffed animal)
3. *24–30 months* — children use one object to represent another even though the objects do not resemble one another (e.g., a block becomes a bed or an airplane)

The ability to use one object to represent another even though they do not resemble each other develops later than other types of pretending. Researchers have found that children become less dependent on having realistic objects for pretend play as they grow older. Fein (1975) suggests that this is because the younger children have trouble making the substitutions necessary for pretend play. If a child who is usually fed by adults pretends to feed another child, a substitution in role is involved. Similarly, substitution is required if a child uses an inanimate object such as a block to represent an animate object (e.g., a dog) or another inanimate object (e.g., a chair).

Fein found that two-year-olds engaged in pretend play the most when they had *prototypical materials* (replicas of real things). They were also capable of pretending when one of the objects was not prototypical if the other one was. For example, a two-year-old could pretend to give a drink from a shell if he had a prototype, such as a doll, to give it to. But without prototypical props, young children engaged in little pretend play. These findings suggest that two-year-olds should be given realistic toys to use in their pretend play. Children three years old

In pretend play, one object often represents another. Here a bristle block becomes a drinking glass.

and older can pretend without realistic toys. Children under eighteen months of age, who are incapable of the symbolic thought involved in pretend play, do not need prototypical objects as toys.

Summary

Children's Questions and Explanations: Clues to Their Views of Causality
- Toddlers attempt to understand physical causality in psychological rather than mechanical terms.
- Children who persistently repeat questions may be doing so because adults do not understand what they are really asking.

Cognition and Play
- Although children do not play for utilitarian purposes, they do learn useful skills while playing.
- Playful activity seems to reflect cognitive understanding. Children's first pretend play behavior involves enactment of their own familiar activities. Around eighteen months of age, children begin to include others in pretend activities. By two to two-and-a-half years of age, children can use one object to represent another, although until they are age three, they have difficulty making many substitutions at once.

New Terms

animism	relational acts	assimilation
consciousness	symbolic acts	symbolic function
play	sequential acts	prototypical play materials
preexercise theory	accommodation	

Selected Readings

Adcock, D., and Segal, M. **Two years old/Play and learning.** *Rolling Hills Estates, Calif.: Nova University Series, B. L. Winch and Associates, 1979.* A readable book about play and playthings for two-year-olds.

Frost, J. L., and Klein, B. L. **Children's play and playgrounds.** *Boston: Allyn and Bacon, 1979.* This book deals primarily with children older than toddlers and with playgrounds. However, the first two chapters present a good discussion of theories of play, and play and culture.

Piaget, J. **The child's conception of physical causality.** *Totawa, N.J.: Littlefield, Adams and Company, 1972.* Any book written by Piaget is not exactly easy to read. However, this is one of the most readable, and it includes interesting observations of young children's limited understanding of physical causality.

Schwartzman, H. B. **Transformations: The anthology of children's play.** *New York: Plenum, 1978.* A thorough and scholarly discussion of play and playthings. For those who wish to know *all* about play.

Chapter *13*

*L*anguage Development

A child's ability to use language as a means of communication blossoms during the toddler period. It is during this time that the child is first able to carry on a conversation using words. By the end of toddlerhood, most children can use language remarkably well.

In this chapter we will discuss the toddler's progress in producing and understanding language. Again, we stress an interactionist view of language development, emphasizing the relationship between the meaning a child intends to convey and what is said, and the relationship between the child's language behavior and his knowledge of the world and specific contexts in which language exchanges occur.

Production

The First Multiword Utterances

We pointed out in our discussion of language development in infancy that children begin to use real words around one year of age and that these often function as holophrases: children intend to express relations with these single

235

words, not just name actions or objects. After using single words for several months, children begin to code more relations in words by stringing words together. For example, they start using language to express location: "lotion tummy" or "car garage"; possession: "dolly hat" or "aunt car"; and negation: "no wash" or "no wet" (Schlesinger, 1974; Braine, 1963).

The relations children can express at this stage have been categorized by language researchers (Bloom, Hood, and Lightbown, 1974, 1975). These categories

Table 13-1. Bloom's semantic-syntactic categories

Action

1. Agent-action-object	*Agent*	*Action*	*Affected Object*
(Peter trying to open box)	my	open	that
(Eric has just reassembled train)	I	made	
2. person or object moves	*Actor*	*Action*	
(Kathryn has just jumped)	Kathryn	jumps	
(Peter watching reels of tape recorder)	tape	go round	

Locative action

1. Agent-action-object-place	*Agent*	*Location*	*Object*	*Place*
(Kathryn throwing car and truck in box)		put		in box
(Eric holds out hand to have Lois put puppet on it)	you	put		a finger
2. Agent and affected object or person were the same	*Mover*	*Location*		*Place*
(Gia wants Mommy to get balloon from ceiling)	Mommy	stand up		a chair
(Peter has been playing piano; he stops and turns around on bench)	I	get down		

Locative state

Object-state-place	*Object*	*Locative state*	*Place*
(Gia looking for toy bag)	the bag	go	
(Eric on Mommy's chair)	I	sitting	

Notice

Attention to a person, object, or event	*Noticer*	*Notice*	*Noticed*
(Lois talking to Gia's Mommy)	Lois	watch	Gia
(Children shouting in hallway)	I	hear	children

are summarized and illustrated with examples in Table 13-1. Although the list of relations is quite extensive, children's utterances still do not resemble those of the older child or adult. Context is still important in figuring out exactly what the child has said; Bloom had to add explanatory comments in her list to tell us exactly what was going on when the child produced a particular utterance. However, less of the message now depends on interpretation of context than was the case earlier, when the child only used one-word sentences or holophrases.

Table 13-1 continued

State	
Transitory states involving persons or other animate beings	
(Peter standing next to cabinet where pretzels are kept)	I want pretzel
(Lois has said she was going to take Eric's book home)	need book
Existence	
Naming or pointing to objects in the environment	
Negation	
References to disappearance or nonexistence of objects	no
	all gone
	no more
Attribution	
1. State of an object	broke
	sharp
2. Specification of an object	red
	big
3. Quantity	two
Possession	
Reference to objects in domains of other persons	Mommy
	Daddy
	my
Recurrence	
Reference to reappearance of an object, or another instance of object	more
	another

SOURCE: For *Action, Locative Action, Locative State, Notice, State:* Bloom, L., Lightbown, P., and Hood, L. Structure and variation in child language. *Monographs of the Society for Research in Child Development* 40 (1975), Serial No. 160. © 1975 The Society for Research in Child Development, Inc. Reprinted by permission. For *Existence, Negation, Attribution, Possession, Recurrence:* Bloom, L., Hood, L., and Lightbown, P. Imitation in language development: If, when and why. *Cognitive Psychology* 6 (1974): 380–420. Reprinted by permission of Academic Press, Inc.

"I play piano." An example of Bloom's "agent-action-object" category.

Children's Telegraphic Speech and Adults' Expansions

When children first put two or more words together to express relations, they often omit words that are not essential to convey their meaning. For example, if an adult says to a child, "It goes in the big box," the child is likely to say, "Big box" or "In big box" (Brown and Fraser, 1964). Speech of this sort, which is also illustrated by most of the utterances listed in Bloom's categories, is called *telegraphic* because it resembles the speech adults use in telegrams when they must pay for every word. The reader, or listener in the case of child language, must read between the lines and embellish the message to construct the total meaning.

Adults respond to children's telegraphic speech in a characteristic way: they put in the words children leave out. This behavior is known as *expansion*. If the child says "Mommy eggnog," her mother might say, "Mommy had her eggnog" (Brown and Fraser, 1964). If the child says, "Throw Daddy," her father might say, "Throw it to Daddy" (Brown and Fraser, 1964). The adult's response is determined by his or her interpretation of what the child means, and it depends heavily on context. The adult may provide expansions as a means of checking to see if the interpretation is indeed the meaning the child intended, or the adult may interact in this way in order to provide the child with information about how sentences could be formed more completely. We do not really know why adults respond to children's speech with expansions, but most adults seem to do it naturally.

The characterization of speech at this stage as telegraphic came from researchers who were interested in a syntactic analysis of language development. The child's language is telegraphic if we take the child at his word; that is, consider what he says only. If, on the other hand, we take the child's meaning, or the total message the child wishes to convey, into account, the child's language is not actually telegraphic. In other words, the term "telegraphic" is a good description if we focus on the speech actually produced by the child, but it is not as useful if we focus also on the message communicated. For this reason many language experts interested in a semantic (meaning) and interactionist view of language do not like the telegraphic characterization. The origin and use of this label illustrates how different language theorists focus on different aspects of language.

Comprehension

Comprehension of Words

Young children rely on context not only to help them get across what they say to others, but to understand the meaning of what others say to them. A study by Clark illustrates this process.

Clark (1978) studied how young children understand "in," "on," and "under." She showed children the objects in Figure 13-1 in pairs chosen to permit only two relations at a time. Objects 1 and 2 allowed the relations "in" and "on," 3 and 4 allowed the relations "in" and "under," and 5 and 6 allowed the relations "on" and "under." She found that children interpreted instructions differently depending on which objects they were shown. If children were shown any kind of container, they always placed something in it, even when they were instructed to put the item "on" or "under" it. Similarly, children interpreted the instruction to mean "on" whenever the object had a supporting surface, even when they were asked to place something "under" or "in" it.

These findings suggest that until children are about two and a half, they do not understand these words — they rely on nonlinguistic strategies (the objects' characteristics) to interpret what has been said. When children actually do begin to understand the words, "in" is learned first, followed by "on" and then "under." It appears, however, that children respond to these words as if they understand them, before they do, basing their responses on the options available to them.

Because children may interpret these words correctly sometimes but not at other times, depending on the situation, adults sometimes erroneously assume

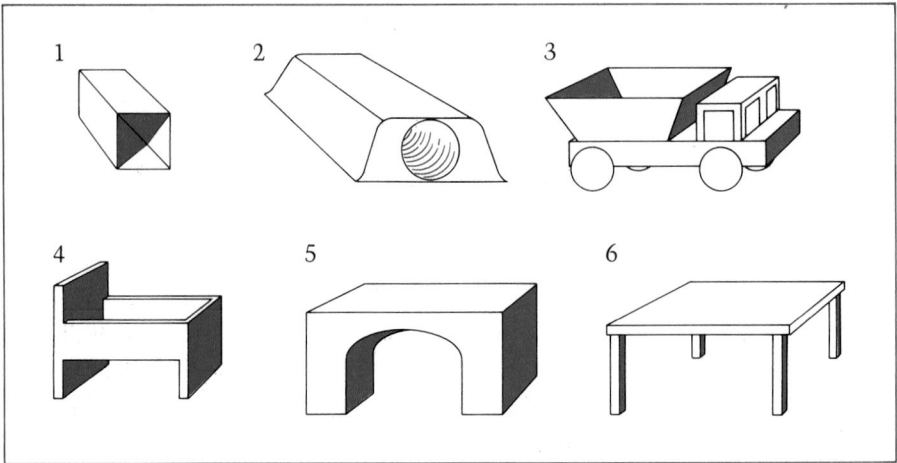

Figure 13-1. The reference point objects used in Clark's experiment: Items 1 and 2 allow the relations IN and ON; items 3 and 4 allow the relations IN and UNDER; items 5 and 6 allow the relations ON and UNDER.

that a child understands the terms completely and makes errors because of obstinacy or poor listening. Actually, the child is probably acting in accordance with his understanding in all situations. The problem is that some situations reveal more about the child's limited understanding of these terms than do other situations.

Children's Understanding of Relations Expressed in Sentences

One way relations are coded in speech is through word order, which indicates what or who is the actor, and what or who is the object of the action. When we say "John hits the ball," we know John is the actor and the ball is the object of his action, even though the ball actually could have hit John.

Do young children understand that word order of sentences functions in this way? Fraser, Bellugi, and Brown (1963) studied two-and-a-half-year-olds to find out. They read sentences such as "The dog bites the cat" and then showed the children two pictures, one of a dog biting a cat, the other of a cat biting a dog. They found that children could pick out the correct picture about 60 percent of the time. In another study, children were asked to act out what the sentence said rather than to select pictures to go with them (Bever, Mehler, and Valian, 1974). Children between the ages of two and three could act out about 95 percent of the sentences.

Another group of researchers investigated whether children's understanding of word order is related to their progress in spontaneous speech. Children in this study were accordingly grouped in terms of the length of their spontaneous utterances, rather than by age (deVilliers and deVilliers, 1974). It was found that children who were just beginning to make multiword utterances did not understand the relations expressed by word order. For example, when the sentence was "Make the truck push the car," some children made the car push the truck; others pushed both the car and the truck. Children who could make longer spontaneous utterances were able to perform the actions expressed by the sentences. These results showed that children begin to understand that relations are coded in word order when they are between two and three years old. They realize that the word representing the actor comes earlier in the sentence than the word representing the object of the action. Linguistic coding in English corresponds nicely to the real sequence of events in this case; an actor initiates actions. Children may use their knowledge of how things occur in the world to figure out how to talk about them.

Some sentences are more complex than this, however. We can, for example, reverse the order of actor and object to make a passive sentence: "The ball was hit by John." Adults still realize that John did the hitting, but young children often misinterpret such sentences. Very young children interpret sentences such as "Peter is washed by Mary" as "Peter washes Mary." Somewhat older children interpret the sentence as if the relationship were reciprocal: "Peter and Mary wash each other." The sentence is interpreted correctly by children about five years old (Sinclair-de-Zwart, 1969).

"The ball was hit by John." A young child hearing this passive sentence may interpret it as "The ball hit John."

Focus: Language Development in Deaf Children

Children who are born deaf, or who become deaf very early in childhood from diseases such as meningitis or encephalitis, are often taught American Sign Language as their first language.

Sign language, as its name implies, uses gestures or signs to indicate words. Each sign consists of a specific configuration of the hand, made in a specific location in space (the cheek or the side of the nose, for example) combined with a specific movement of the hand, such as an upward or a downward sweep.

The questions of interest here are (1) How early do children exposed to sign language learn it? and (2) Is learning sign language similar to or different from learning an oral language?

There have been reports of deaf children who learned to sign before one year of age (Meadow, 1978). Furthermore, deaf infants seem to babble in sign, just as hearing infants babble orally, before they begin to use actual words or signs (Dale, 1976). In addition, deaf children at the one-word or single-sign stage use signs in much the same way hearing children use holophrases — a single sign can have a range of meanings. Schlesinger and Meadow (1972) found the same semantic relations expressed in two-sign strings that researchers such as Bloom have found in the oral language of hearing children. There is evidence, therefore, that deaf children learn sign language at about the same rate that hearing children learn oral language and that the processes are similar.

Dale (1976) summarizes what we know about language learning in deaf children:

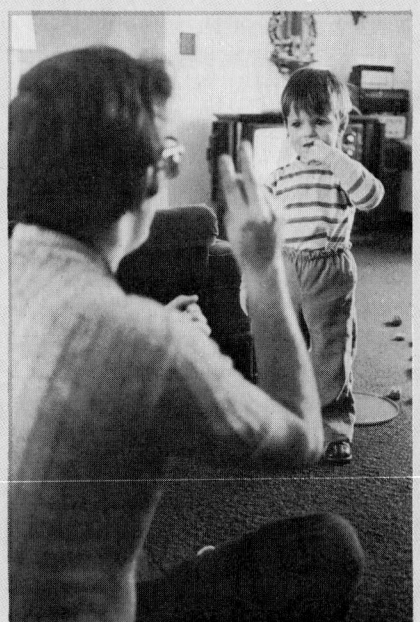

> "The really important aspects of language and the really important abilities the child brings to the problem of language learning are independent of the modality in which the linguistic system operates. Language is a central process, not a peripheral one. The abilities that children have are so general, and so powerful, that they [deaf children] proceed through the same milestones of development as do hearing children. [p. 59]

Because deaf children are so capable of learning language (although in a different mode), it is very important to detect hearing problems early so that appropriate language input can be provided. This is why we stressed in Chapter 10 some of the new techniques for detecting hearing loss in very young infants.

Learning to sign

Even two- and three-year-olds, however, can correctly interpret passive sentences when the events described are highly probable (Strohner and Nelson, 1974). For example, a sentence such as "Babies are fed by mothers" is likely to be understood even though it is passive, because children know from experience that mothers feed babies but babies do not feed mothers. A sentence such as "the dog was chased by the bunny" is unlikely to be interpreted correctly, however, because this situation does not occur in real life. Apparently children at first make little use of syntactic knowledge (knowledge of the relations expressed by words), basing their interpretations instead on a "probable event strategy." This is another example of how children use what they know about the world to figure out what sentences mean.

Children's Understanding of the Social Aspects of Language Use

Part of learning how to talk involves learning how to use language to sustain social interactions. There are rules or common ways to interact when conversing with others. For example, we learn how to signal others that we are finished talking and that they may respond to what we have said. We also learn how to get other people's attention when we have something to say to them. When do young children learn about this aspect of language?

Mueller (1972) found that three- to five-year-olds already understand that if you want someone to respond to your verbal overtures you must; (1) talk about what your listener is doing, ask a question, or give a command; (2) get the listener's attention by looking at him or her; (3) stand relatively close to your listener; and (4) use attention-getting gestures or verbalizations such as "Hey!" or "Guess what?"

To find out when children develop this sort of understanding, Mueller and his colleagues did a second study (1977) using toddlers rather than preschool-age children. They found that children acquire the social conventions of language use between the ages of two and two-and-a-half. They learn, among other things, to talk about the listener's activity rather than their own, and to pay attention to a person who is speaking to them.

Toddlers understand not only how to begin a conversation, but how to continue it as well. This requires more skill than most of us realize. We all inadvertently interrupt people occasionally. What goes wrong in such instances? How do we know when it is our turn to speak? The speaker gives us a number of clues: pauses, the rise and fall of the speaker's voice, and the nature of the speaker's statement. A question, for example, usually indicates that it is the listener's turn to talk.

A study of the "conversations" between young toddlers and their mothers indicates that even young children know how to take turns when they talk to someone (Donahue, 1978). This ability may be based on the experiences with role shifting required in adult-infant games such as peek-a-boo or pushing a ball back and forth (Bruner, 1975a, b), as well as on conversational experience itself. According to Donahue (1978), mothers assume their infants intend to say something, pause to let them "talk," and then answer back. Mothers keep the conversation going — they pause in their own speech to give the child a chance to respond, and begin to speak again even when the child's response is minimal: "Are you a tired baby?" (Mother pauses, child nods.) "Tell daddy goodnight." (The subjects of Donahue's study were middle-class; mothers from other socioeconomic levels might respond differently.) As in interactions with objects, which we will discuss in Chapter 15, children seem to acquire skills during interactions with cooperative and supportive adults and then generalize them to others (Garvey, 1977a; Eckerman et al., 1975).

These social skills call into question Piaget's contention that young children's language is egocentric (Piaget, 1963). Current research suggests that even very young children know something about how to relate their verbal behavior to the verbal behavior of others to keep a social interaction going, and that their verbal behavior is not dominated by *dual monologues* in which children take little account of what another person involved in the conversation is saying.

Summary

Production
- Toddlers combine two or three words to express semantic relations.
- In telegraphic speech, children omit words in sentences they hear, but they preserve word order. Adults respond to these telegraphic utterances with expansions — statements that put in words children leave out.

Comprehension
- The nonlinguistic context apparently influences children's understanding of what is said.
- Children have difficulty understanding many passive sentences until they are about five. But children as young as two or three years of age interpret passive sentences correctly when this interpretation is what makes sense in the real world.

Children's Understanding of the Social Aspects of Language Use
- Social aspects of language development include knowing how to take turns in a conversation and how to get a listener's attention.

- Studies by Mueller indicate that children learn some important social aspects of language use between the ages of two and two and a half.
- New research has called into question Piaget's characterization of young children's speech as egocentric.

New Terms

telegraphic speech
expansion

dual monologues

Selected Readings

deVilliers, P. A., and deVilliers, J. G. **Early language.** *Cambridge, Mass,: Harvard University Press, 1979.* This readable paperback begins with language as it develops in infancy but includes discussions of language development during toddlerhood as well.

Mackey, W. F., and Andersson, T. (Eds.). **Bilingualism in early childhood.** *Rowley, Mass.: Newbury House Publishers, 1977.* Contains interesting material about children who learn a second language before the age of three and about children who grow up in bilingual families.

Schlesinger, H. S., and Meadow, K. P. **Sound and sign.** *Berkeley: University of California Press, 1972.* This book discusses the development of sign language in children. It includes actual case material about language development in four deaf children.

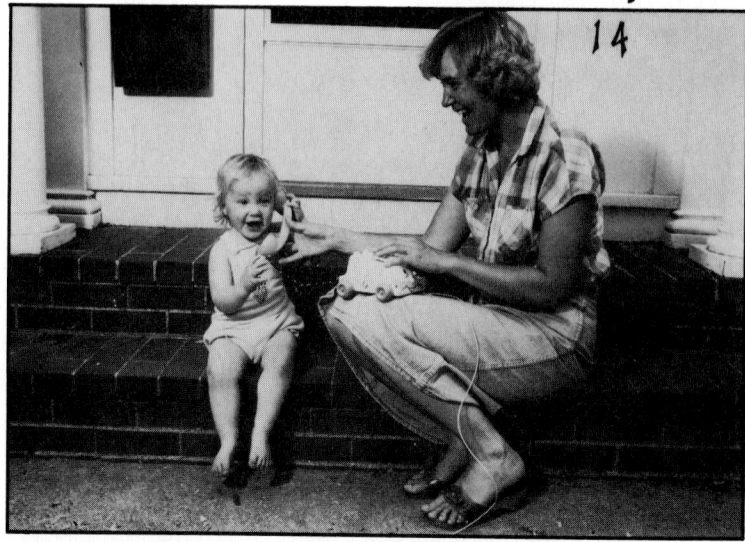

Chapter *14*

*S*ocial Development

As we saw in Chapter 9, most children enjoy social contact from the beginning of infancy. They smile, coo, gurgle, play peekaboo, and gaze at us when we look at them. They also develop strong attachments to one or more persons and may become very distressed when first left alone in the presence of strangers. During toddlerhood social skills develop further: children use objects to make social contacts, they begin to learn to interact with peers, they use language to sustain social interactions, and they learn more about coping with separations from familiar adults.

The Use of Objects in Social Relations with Peers and Adults

It may seem a bit strange for us to associate objects and social relations; we usually think of the social realm as consisting exclusively of people. But objects play a large part in the social lives of children. Adults often shake a rattle or wind up a mechanical toy to engage a child's interest, and then observe the toy with the child. Children use objects in the same way, making contact by showing or giving something to an adult. In short, "The responses we call social do not develop in a context devoid of inanimate objects; similarly those responses toward inanimate objects that we label exploration or play occur often in social context" (Eckerman, Whatley, and Kutz, 1975, p. 48).

Three Ways of Interacting

Research suggests that a toddler uses objects in interactions with others in at least three ways: he or she shows them to others, gives them to others, or uses them to initiate "partner play" (Rheingold, Hay, and West, 1976).

Showing is defined as directing a person's attention to an object by pointing with the index finger or by holding an object up and out while looking at the person. *Giving* is defined as placing an object in a person's hand or lap and letting go of it. *Partner play* is defined as manipulating an object that one has given to another person while the object is in contact with that person.

In a study of fifteen- to eighteen-month-old children and various adults, Rheingold, Hay, and West (1976) found that toddlers shared toys often and under many different conditions. In fact, they shared all but one of twenty-one objects and toys made available for their play.

> The present studies call attention to sharing as a common behavior of infants and young children. They show that children very early share with others on their own initiative — without prompting, direction, or praise. We propose that the sharing behaviors, from the first holding up of objects for others to see, the first offering of an object to another, through all of the behaviors we have recorded here, qualify as developmental milestones. That children so young share contradicts the egocentricity so often ascribed to them and reveals them instead as already able contributors to social life. [pp. 1156–57]

The results obtained by Rheingold and her colleagues contradict the widely held belief that children "need to learn to share." But this comment is usually made in reference to children's behavior toward other children, and the behaviors in the Rheingold study were directed toward adults. Would children behave differently when interacting with other children?

To answer this question, Eckerman and her colleagues (1975) studied the social interaction of ten pairs of children in three age groups, ten- to twelve-month-olds, sixteen- to eighteen-month-olds, and twenty-two- to twenty-four-month-olds. Pairs of children were observed with their mothers in an unfamiliar playroom containing toys. Each child was observed for twenty observation periods on the same day. The observer noted whether or not certain behaviors occurred. Some of the noted behaviors that concerned the presence or activity of

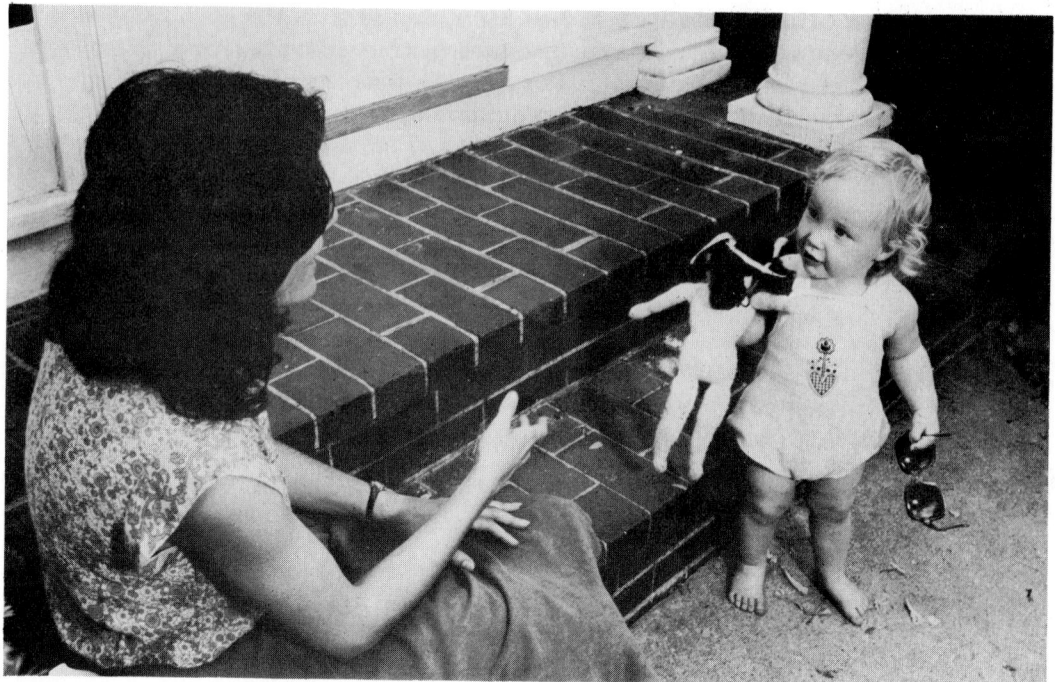

Showing a toy

the peer are listed in Table 14-1. The observers also recorded the child's contact with his mother and his solitary play (that is, contacts with toys that lasted at least three seconds and did not involve the peer or the mother).

The results of the study can be summarized as follows:

1. Children in each age group watched each other.
2. Distant social responses were more frequent than physical contact. The most common distant social responses were vocalizing and smiling.
3. Touching was the most frequent form of physical contact, especially in the youngest group.
4. Play with the same play material and direct involvement in the peer's play increased with age. In the latter category, offering a toy, accepting a toy, taking a toy, taking over a toy, and struggling over a toy accounted for most of the behavior at all age levels. Imitation, taking, struggling, and coordinating activities showed a steady increase with age.
5. When behaviors in all categories were considered, positive reactions far outweighed negative reactions.
6. Both positive and negative behaviors increased with age.

Table 14-1. Behaviors related to the presence or activity of the peer

Category	Definition
Watch	Continuous visual regard of the peer or his activities for at least 3 seconds.
Distant social response	One or more of the following six behaviors occurs.
Vocalize	A vocal sound or series of sounds, that may or may not be distinguishable as words, emitted while watching the peer.
Smile	Pleasant facial expression distinguished by a curved mouth with corners up-turned, while watching the peer.
Laugh	An explosive sound of joy or amusement, while watching the peer.
Fuss	A fretting, whining, complaining sound emitted while watching the peer.
Cry	Loud continuous wailing while watching the peer.
Gesture	Wave at a peer as in greeting or departure; clap hands while watching the peer.
Physical contact	Touch and/or strike occurs.
Touch	Placing a hand upon the peer in a nonforceful manner, including patting, hugging, rubbing.
Strike	Forceful physical contact with the peer by either hand or foot, including hitting, pushing, or kicking.
Same play materials	Contact of the same toy as the peer or its duplicate for at least 3 continuous seconds without any direct involvement in the activities of the peer.
Direct involvement in peer's play	One or more of the following eight behaviors occurs.
Imitate	Duplication of the peer's activity, preceded by visual regard of the peer's activities. The peer's activity usually involves a toy or some other aspect of the inanimate environment, but it might consist of a distinctive motor response such as jumping.
Show a toy	Hold out a toy toward the peer within his reaching distance, while looking and/or vocalizing to the peer.
Offer a toy	Hold out a toy toward the peer within his reaching distance, while looking and/or vocalizing to the peer.
Accept a toy	Take a toy offered by the peer.
Take over a toy	Contact a toy released by the peer not more than 3 seconds previously.
Take a toy	Take an unoffered toy from the possession of the peer without a struggle.
Struggle over a toy	Both children attempt to gain sole possession of the same toy, including pulling, pushing, whining, etc.
Coordinate play	Act together with the peer to perform a common task, such as building a tower of blocks; or each child repeatedly takes turns performing an activity with attention to the other's activity, as when one child builds a tower of blocks, stands back and laughs as the other kicks it down.

SOURCE: Eckerman, C., Whatley, J., and Kutz, S. Growth of social play with peers during the second year of life. *Developmental Psychology* 11 (1975), 42–49. Reprinted by permission.

7. The amount of time sent in solitary play was about the same across all age groups; social play showed a significant increase with age.
8. Play with mother was most frequent in the sixteen- to eighteen-month-old group. It declined dramatically in the twenty-two to twenty-four-month-old group, at the same time that interaction with peers showed a dramatic increase.
9. In all age groups, a child rarely interacted with the other child's mother.

On the basis of this information, one would have to say that these children interacted remarkably well. Though they did sometimes fuss or struggle over a toy, they more often smiled, vocalized, imitated, exchanged toys, and coordinated their play.

Contradictory Studies

The results of this study contradict those of an earlier study by Maudry and Nekula (1939), which concluded that young children treat each other as inanimate objects. Eckerman, Whatley, and Kutz attributed the different results to differences in the conditions of the experiment. The Maudry and Nekula study used fewer toys and activities and encouraged the subjects to interact. Eckerman

Although toddlers often struggle over toys, some studies have found that positive interactions predominate in toddler play.

and her colleagues provided two of each of five different toys and allowed only two children in the playroom at a time, so each child had one of each type of toy.

Other studies have also yielded contradictory results, perhaps because of variations in methodology. A study by Bronson (1975) for example, involved groups of three or four children with their mothers, and observations were carried out over several months. Eckerman, on the other hand, studied pairs of children who were brought together just once. Bronson found that about 45 percent of the toddlers' interactions involved disagreements and struggles. She concluded that toddlers interact more with toys and other objects than with other toddlers, because other toddlers behaved too erratically. Eckerman might have reached the same conclusion if her children had been together longer or if they had encountered each other in larger groups.

As these studies demonstrate, our conclusions about children's behavior may be influenced by the situations in which we observe them. Teachers and parents may think Bronson's conclusion more accurate than Eckerman's because they see toddlers in familiar settings over a long period of time, and because in most situations children have a limited number of toys. Behavior is a function of the child and his or her environment: it does not reside in the child alone.

Social Interaction Through Language

As we discussed in Chapter 13, children begin to understand how to use language to sustain social interactions between the ages of two and two-and-a-half. This skill has a major impact on how children interact with each other and with adults. For example, a child may no longer need to tug on an adult's arm to get the adult's attention but can say "Hey!" instead, and then tell the adult what she wants. In addition, as children begin to play more with other children they can use language to help them coordinate actions. Children do not really play cooperatively until midway into the preschool years, but an understanding of social aspects of language is a prerequisite for being able to do so. For example, if a child wants a row of chairs to be a bus, she must be able to explain this to co-players. To do so, the child must also know how to get the attention of the other players.

Departure Protest and Separation Distress

Toddlers not only must learn how to get along with new people, they must learn to tolerate being away from familiar people. Children often find this very difficult. They first begin to show distress when an attachment figure leaves at around eight months. Distress peaks at about eighteen months and declines sharply by the age of three (Weinraub and Lewis, 1977).

Studies Conducted by Weinraub and Lewis

As in all areas of development, children's reactions to being left vary considerably. The reasons for this variation have been investigated by Weinraub and Lewis (1977). These researchers make a distinction between *departure protest*, which is the child's response at the time a parent is leaving and *separation distress*, which is the child's response after the parent has left. As you will recall, we discussed *separation anxiety* in Chapter 9 in relation to social development in infancy. Separation anxiety is the more common term used to label the child's overall negative reaction to being separated from a familiar caretaker. Weinraub and Lewis have chosen to be more specific in dealing with separation responses by dividing reactions into immediate and more prolonged ones.

To study departure protest and separation distress, Weinraub and Lewis asked two-year-old children and their mothers to visit a laboratory playroom. The mother was instructed to play with her child in a natural manner for fifteen minutes and then leave the room in a manner that was comfortable and natural for her, closing the door behind her. The child was then observed for two minutes while alone in the playroom. If the child began to cry, the experiment was ended immediately; it is unethical to continue experiments in which children show distress.

Weinraub and Lewis found that children's behavior was related to three factors.

1. The child's level of cognitive abilities. Children with advanced abilities were more likely to play in their mothers' absence than less-advanced children.
2. The degree of mother-child interaction immediately before departure. Children whose mothers played with them before leaving cried more often than children whose mothers did not play with them.
3. Maternal departure style. Mothers who explained to their children that they were leaving and would return had children who played more and cried less. Crying was diminished further if the mother suggested activities for the child during her absence.

The researchers realized that, as in any correlational study, factors other than those identified may have been responsible for the children's behavior. Perhaps mothers who knew from previous experience that their children would be upset left unobtrusively, whereas mothers whose children generally did not become upset explained where they were going. If that is true, initial differences in the children, rather than maternal behavior at departure, were responsible for the children's different reactions. To test this possibility, Weinraub (1976) conducted a second study in which children and mothers made two visits to the laboratory and mother departed differently on each occasion. The results indicated that there was a causal relationship between maternal departure style and separation distress: children responded differently when their mothers acted differently. (The Weinraub studies illustrate how researchers change their methodology at different stages of their inquiry. A correlational study is often pursued first, followed by a study to determine whether the variables are causally related.)

Implications of the Weinraub and Lewis Studies

This research has several implications. First, it suggests that parents should explain that they are leaving and will return before they leave their children in an unfamiliar setting. Teachers sometimes discourage this procedure, however, because they have noted that children often settle down as soon as their mothers leave. The sooner the mother leaves, they think, the sooner the child will quiet down. But an explanation does help, because children's reactions to departure and separation are different. The children most likely to protest a parent's departure are those who know what is going to follow, either because they are more advanced cognitively or because they have been told. The same children, however, are likely to have less separation distress. In other words, a caregiver who explains his or her leaving to a child may increase the child's departure protest but decrease the child's separation distress. Children who are going to spend a great deal of time away from their parents, at a day care center, for example, benefit most from a reduction of separation distress.

A mother familiar with this research has pointed out that departure protest might be diminished if parents begin to explain what is going to happen a day before it actually occurs. Although her three-year-old daughter became panicky and impossible to reason with if told of a departure immediately before it occurred, she seemed to be able to adjust if told the previous day. The mother found that this gave the child a chance to ask questions and rehearse the events in her own mind. Her child would say, "You're coming with me, then you're going to go somewhere for a while, and then you'll come back? Melissa and Curt [friends] will be there, too?" By the time her mother left her, she was pretty well prepared, although she did sometimes cry a little. This seems like a sound procedure, although it would be possible only for children who have the language ability and sufficient comprehension to carry it out. It would be a good subject for further investigation, especially with preschool children.

The finding that parent-child interaction before separation increases separation distress is more difficult to interpret. In some nursery schools parents often accompany the child into the playroom and play for a while before leaving for the day. Informal observation suggests that children show less separation distress if the parent helps the child get involved in something. These conflicting conclusions can perhaps be attributed to differences between the playroom and the laboratory. In the nursery school the parent's goal is to get the child involved, not just with toys, but with other children. As a result, the parent's departure does not disrupt the child's play; the child continues with other children. Also, the parent's involvement with the child may actually decrease in this situation.

A parent can ease separation distress in nursery school by helping his child become involved in activities with other children.

Parent and child have probably been interacting with each other on the way to nursery school, but now the child is more involved with other children. In the laboratory, on the other hand, the parent is the only other person present; when the parent leaves, there is no one else for the child to carry on with, and play is disrupted. This is a good example of how a situation contrived for research may not yield results that are completely applicable to a naturally occurring situation. The fact that X affects Y in a research study does not mean that X will affect Y in real situations where other variables come into play.

Summary

The Use of Objects in Social Relations with Peers and Adults

- Inanimate objects are important in social interactions of young children. They are used in showing, giving, and partner play.
- Some studies indicate that children begin to share when they are still quite young.
- Some of the contradictions in the data gathered in different studies of peer interactions may be due to differences in the research methodologies used.

Social Interaction Through Language

- Toddlers learn to be quite good at conversational turn-taking. They also learn to use language to interact and play with other children.

Departure Protest and Separation Distress

- A child may respond to the departure of a familiar adult with departure protest.
- Separation distress is the child's response after the parent has departed. To minimize separation distress, parents should explain that they are leaving and suggest activities the child may do in their absence.

New Terms

showing an object
giving an object
partner play

departure protest
separation distress

Selected Readings

Brazelton, T. B. **Toddlers and parents.** *New York: Delacorte Press, 1974.* Covers some of the social and emotional aspects of the toddler period. Topics include the child's growing independence; sibling rivalry; withdrawn, hyperactive, and demanding children; and becoming aware of self. An interesting and very readable book, written for parents.

Mueller, E., and Vandell, D. Infant-infant interactions. In J. D. Osofsky (Ed.), **Handbook of infant development.** *New York: Wiley-Interscience, 1979.* Mueller and Vandell's chapter provides a summary of the research relating to peer relationships during infancy and toddlerhood.

Rubin, Z. **Children's friendships.** *Cambridge, Mass.: Harvard University Press, 1980.* Chapter 2 of this book is entitled "The earliest friendships." It discusses peer interactions in older infants and toddlers.

Chapter *15*

*K*nowledge and Action

The knowledge we gain through studies on the toddler, such as those discussed in Chapters 11 through 14, has practical applications in many areas. We will discuss just a few of these areas: toddler education programs, encouraging social interactions, toilet training, and teaching the child to feed himself.

Toddler Education Programs

We will consider two intervention programs designed for use with low-income children: (1) the Mother-Child Home Program, and (2) the Infant Education Research Program. (You will recall that some authorities extend the use of the term "infant" to include children whom we refer to as toddlers.)

The Mother-Child Home Program

The Mother-Child Home Program, developed by Phyllis Levenstein, is sponsored by the Family Service Association of Nassau County and the State University of New York at Stony Brook.

As its name indicates, this program is home-based: the staff works with parents and toddlers at home rather than in school. The structure is a reflection of the program's philosophy, which is based on the assumptions that the parent is the child's first and most important teacher, and that learning is influenced by the child's emotional state. Home-based programs are thought to have at least three advantages over school-based programs: (1) parents are encouraged to consider themselves important teachers of their children; (2) parents learn more effective ways of interacting with their children if they are involved in the program; and (3) children may be more receptive to program experiences if they are introduced to them in a familiar setting by familiar people.

Children begin the program at age two and continue until they are four. The curriculum focuses on language and conceptual development. Each year eleven toys and twelve books are provided. The criteria for selecting these items are shown in Tables 15-1 and 15-2. These materials are called Verbal Interaction Stimulus Materials (VISM) because their primary purpose is to promote language development.

Each week the home visitor gives the child a toy or a book, which the child is allowed to keep. The visitor shows the child how to play with the toy or reads the book, encouraging the parents to become involved too (Levenstein, 1977).

Home visits are an integral part of some educational programs.

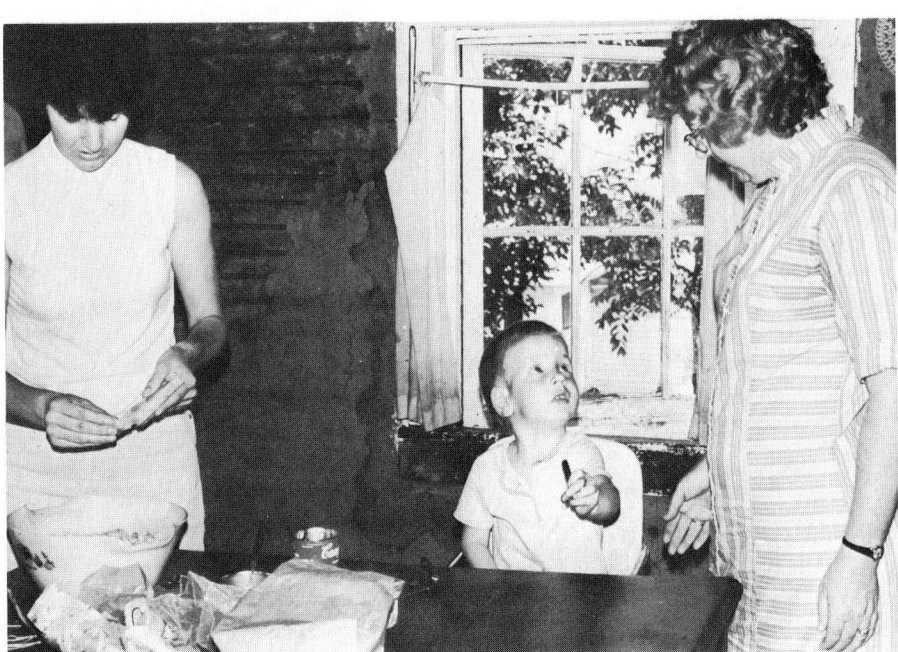

Table 15-1. Criteria for VISM toys, with illustrations from the 1967 Mother-Child Home Program VISM list

Criteria	Names and descriptions of toys	Criteria met by toys
Verbal 1. Induces language 2. Permits language	*Block cart* Wooden wagon, colored blocks with holes, rods that fit into holes	All but 6, 15
Perceptual 3. Strong colors 4. Geometric forms 5. Space organization 6. Size differences 7. Sound differences 8. Tactile differences 9. Form matching	*Hammer and pegs* Pegs fixed into wooden bench can be pounded through to under side; bench can then be reversed	All but 5, 6, 11, 13
	Mail box Copy of corner mail box; colored wood beads are dropped through top holes into bin	All but 15
Motor 10. Specific skills 11. Fitting parts 12. Hitting 13. Pulling 14. Lifting 15. Diffuse motor discharge	*Transportation puzzle* Jigsaw puzzle, each piece a different vehicle	All but 7, 12, 13, 15
	Two plush hand puppets Animals, movable mouths	All but 5, 6, 9, 12, 15
Conceptual 16. Problem solving 17. Intelligible goal 18. Intrinsic reward 19. Imaginative uses 20. Social concepts 21. Sex neutrality 22. Ethnic neutrality	*Circus puzzle* Jigsaw puzzle of circus tent, circus scene beneath	All but 7, 12, 13, 15
	Cash register Simple copy with cash drawer and bell activated by crank	All
Other 23. Low anxiety potential 24. Safety 25. Durability 26. Easy care for mother	*House puzzle* Jigsaw puzzle of street and outside of house, inside of house and buried utilities shown under pieces (fewer pieces than same puzzle used with three-year-olds)	All but 7, 12, 13, 15

SOURCE: Levenstein, P. The mother-child home program. In M. C. Day and R. Parker (Eds.), *The preschool in action: Exploring early childhood programs*, 2d ed. Boston: Allyn and Bacon, 1977, 28–49. Copyright © 1977 Phyllis Levenstein. Reprinted by permission of the author.

Table 15-2. Criteria for VISM books, with illustrations from the 1967 Mother-Child Home Program VISM list

Criteria	Titles and authors of books by subject groups (in order of presentation)
1. Content geared to children's age and interest; interesting to mothers; leads to verbalized associations; widens experience 2. High literary standards 3. Language simple, rhythmic, with some repetition 4. Reading level within ability of all mothers 5. Content, illustrations, and general format attractive to both sexes and any ethnic group 6. Illustrations profuse, large, colorful, detailed, rich source of labeling and classification 7. Low anxiety potential 8. Durability	*Two- and Three-Year-Olds* Kunhardt, D. *Pat the Bunny* Brown, M. W. *Good Night Moon* Rojankovsky, F. (Illus.) *The Tall Book of Mother Goose* Keats, E. J. *The Snowy Day* Zion, G. *All Falling Down* Krauss, R. *The Carrot Seed* Keats, E. J. *Peter's Chair* Eastman, P. D. *Are You My Mother?* Keats, E. J. *Whistle for Willie* *Two-Year-Olds* Tresselt, A. *Rain Drop Splash* Tresselt, A. *Wake Up Farm* Gag, W. *Millions of Cats* *Three-Year-Olds* Brown, M. W. *The Runaway Bunny* Seuss, Dr. *The Cat in the Hat* MacGregor, E. *Theodore Turtle*

SOURCE: Levenstein, P. The mother-child home program. In M. C. Day and R. Parker (Eds.), *The preschool in action: Exploring early childhood programs,* 2d ed. Boston: Allyn and Bacon, 1977, 28–49. Copyright © 1977 Phyllis Levenstein. Reprinted by permission of the author.

The Levenstein program is sound in several respects. First, it emphasizes the parents' interaction with their child, which, as we have seen, can affect cognitive development. Second, it encourages a strong language-learning environment. Adults are urged to describe ongoing events and to interact verbally in other ways. Books and objects are used as vehicles for language learning. Third, the variety of playthings, introduced at reasonable intervals, should keep the situation moderately novel, which is likely to keep a child interested and learning.

We disagree, however, with two of the stated assumptions underlying this program. The most important period of language growth is assumed to be between two and four years of age. Although children do begin mature speech after age two, a child's ability to use language begins to develop much earlier. The second assumption is that attachment develops between the ages of two and four. As we have seen, the basis for attachment is established much earlier.

The fact that both language and attachment begin to develop before children are enrolled in their program does not necessarily mean that the program should start when children are still infants. Parents may be able to nurture language and attachment in early infancy without outside support. The Levenstein program may be successful because it begins at a time when it can help parents sustain their efforts to support the continued development of language and attachment past the second year of life.

The Infant Education Research Project

The Infant Education Research Project was designed by Earl Schaefer and May Aaronson for children between the ages of fifteen and thirty-six months. Like the Levenstein program, it was home-based. The objectives of the program were to "(a) develop a positive relationship with the child and his family, (b) provide the child with varied and increasingly complex experiences, and (c) provide the child with age-appropriate language stimulation" (Schaefer and Aaronson, 1977, p. 55).

The curriculum of the program was flexible. It made use of toys, books, puzzles, games, music and rhythm, and experiences such as walks or playing in the snow. Tutors were instructed:

> (1) to reinforce positive personality characteristics that should help the child to succeed in school, (2) to encourage the child to develop feelings of competence and of human worth and to assert himself in a positive way, (3) to utilize toys, materials, and varied experiences to broaden the child's comprehension and meaningful use of language, and (4) to set aside time, preferably at the beginning of the tutoring session, for varied activities with books. [Schaefer and Aaronson, 1977, p. 57]

A sample activity, water play, and some of the vocabulary that might be used in the activity are given in Box 15-1.

The Infant Education Research Program, like the Levenstein program, appears to be theoretically sound. Schaefer suggests that the program be used with children even younger than fifteen months old, because interests and relationships developed the first year can affect later intellectual development.

Living with the Toddler

As you have seen, children go through many important changes during the toddler period. There are many ways that parents can assist children in making these changes. We will discuss a few of these techniques in the following pages.

Encouraging Social Interactions

Promoting Adjustment to Unfamiliar Places. Toddlers find going to a strange place unsettling, if not downright terrifying, especially when it means being separated from familiar people. What can parents do to make these movements more comfortable?

The Weinraub and Lewis (1977) study cited in Chapter 14 demonstrated that maternal departure style affects separation distress. Parents can diminish distress

Box 15-1. Sample Activity from the Infant Education Research Project

WATER PLAY

Materials. Scissors, several squares of paper toweling to dry child, vessel with water, 2 sponges of size child's hand can squeeze.

Some uses for them (you can probably think of many more). Allow child free play with the 2 sponges in the water. Cut one in half, as child watches. Now you have 3 sponges — 1 big one and two little ones, or 1 whole sponge and 2 half sponges.

Possible vocabulary.
- One sponge.
- Two sponges.
- A whole sponge.
- A half sponge.
- Two halves of a sponge.
- Squeeze one half.
- Squeeze the other half.
- Squeeze the big one.
- Squeeze a little one.
- Squeeze both of the little ones.
- This one is bigger.
- This one is smaller.
- Put one in one hand.
- Put one in the other hand.
- Squeeze the two together.
- Throw one in the bucket.
- Go get it.
- Get it out of the bucket.
- Is it wet?
- Is it dripping?
- Rub your hand with the sponge.
- Are you washing yourself?
- How does it feel?
- Does it feel cool?
- Does it feel good?
- You are all wet.
- We will have to dry you.

Other benefits.
- Fun and cooling off in hot weather.
- Learning to count.

SOURCE: Schaefer, E., and Aaronson, M. Infant education research project: Implementation and implications of a home tutoring program. In M. C. Day and R. Parker eds., *The preschool in action: Exploring early childhood programs,* 2d ed. Copyright © 1977 by Allyn and Bacon, Inc., Boston, 52–71. Reprinted with permission.

by explaining where they are going, when they will return, and what the child can do while they are away.

It may also help to familiarize the child with the new place and people before he or she is left for the first time. Teachers sometimes make home visits to become acquainted with the child in a familiar place before the child begins nursery school. Introducing a child to another child who will be attending the same school can also reduce anxiety; each child will have one friend in the new situation. Another helpful procedure is for a parent to stay with the child on the first visit to the new setting. As we noted in Chapter 9, children will usually explore new places if they have a parent to return to occasionally.

Even when parents use all these techniques, however, many children still become distressed. We know of a five-year-old girl whose mother used all these techniques to prepare the child for kindergarten: (1) she and her daughter visited the kindergarten classroom before the first day; (2) the child knew some of the children in the class from a play group; and (3) the mother stayed a little while on the first day. The child was fine when the mother left and for the first two hours.

Then the school librarian, who knew the mother and child quite well, thought it would be nice to stop by the classroom to say hello to the child, who had been talking for days about going to kindergarten. Unfortunately, the visit did not have the intended effect. As soon as the little girl saw her mother's friend, she was apparently reminded of her mother. The child began to sob, saying, "Take me to my mommy." The librarian assured her that her mother would be there soon, and the child eventually calmed down.

Good teachers know that departure protest and separation anxiety are normal, healthy behaviors in toddlers and even older children. Comments such as "Babies cry; are you a baby?" or "Go over there if you are going to insist on crying; we don't want to listen to you," are demeaning and cruel. They have no place in the repertoire of the skilled teacher or parent.

Supporting Relationships with Peers. As toddlers mature, they begin to interact less often with family members and more often with others. They apparently learn how to relate, at least in part, through playing with cooperative, supportive adults, which suggests that playing a social game with a young child will help him or her interact with others.

But children are learning to expect certain social responses as they play games with adults, and they may be disappointed or annoyed when they begin to play with other children. Adults will return a toy that a child has given to them earlier, but other children are likely to be less cooperative.

Sometimes a child trying to take a toy from another child cries, hits, or bites when the other child does not give it to him or her. Children should be shown how to cope with this type of situation. A parent might say, "No, he has that right now. How about playing with this until he's finished with that?" or "I know you want it, but he wants it too. You'll have to wait." In addition, a child needs to learn to say "No, it's mine," when another child tries to grab something he or she is playing with.

Parents should try to be patient in situations of this sort, when children are likely to be angry and have complex thoughts and feelings that they cannot express. Teaching children how to cooperate can be very time consuming at this stage; some parents even find it necessary to play with children to keep them from fighting. Generally, however, parents do not need to give children their undivided attention. A study by Burton White (1975) indicates that mothers of children who were later judged to be socially and intellectually competent acted as "consultants" to their children in ten- to twenty-second snatches. These mothers used brief interactions to answer questions, encourage exploration, or help a child with a problem, usually by giving just enough information to allow the child to solve the problem her- or himself. These mothers were responsive to their children and could accurately judge their interests and abilities. The children, in turn, learned to use their mothers as resources rather than constant companions in play.

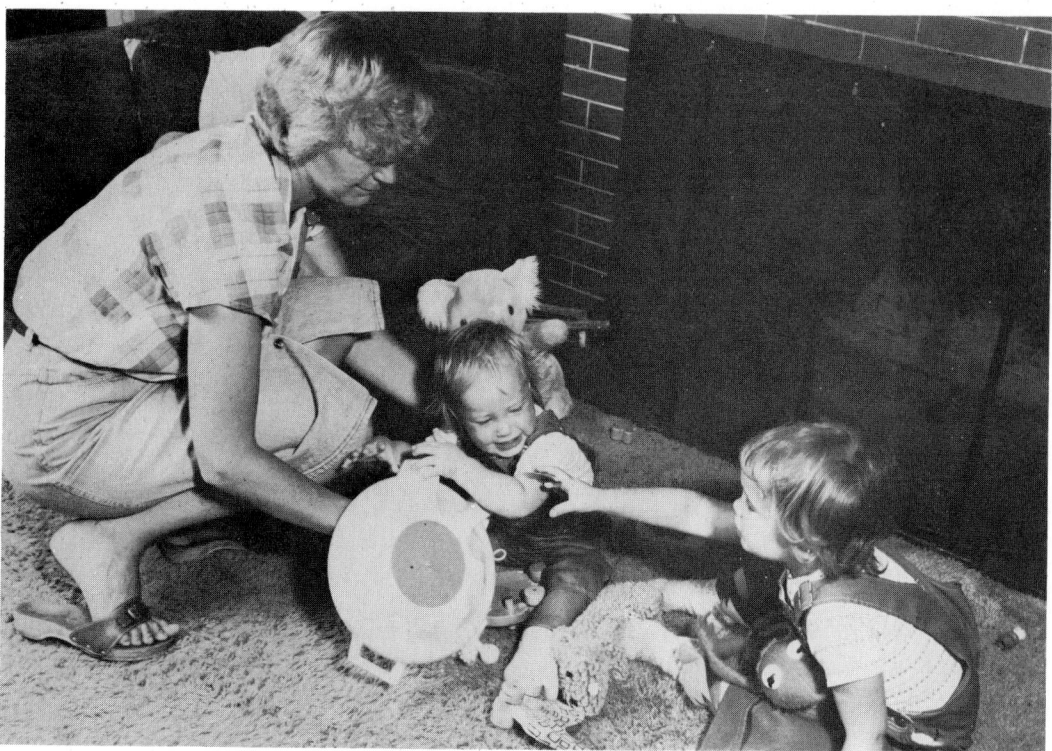

Adults frequently must help young children learn to get along with playmates.

Toilet Training

Sometime between the ages of two and three, most children can learn the socially acceptable behaviors related to elimination. However, the child cannot achieve bladder and bowel control until he or she is capable of inhibiting the reflex that controls the sphincters. This requires a certain level of physical maturity; toilet training before this level is reached is pointless. Most children learn to walk quite some time before toilet training can begin.

Training the Parent or Other Caregiver. Once a child is mature physically and seems able to comprehend verbal explanations about toileting behavior, the first step is to let the child know what is expected of him. This can be accomplished by placing the child on a potty when he is dry but needs to urinate, often just after a nap or a meal. The parent can explain why the child is being placed on the potty and give encouragement. This stage of toilet training could be called "training the parent" because the parent must be able to predict when it is best to place the child on the potty. Once the parent or other caregiver learns how to do this and the child begins to understand that he can urinate in the potty instead of the diaper, it is useful to ask the child to tell the adult when he has to urinate so that the child can be taken to the toilet. At first, a child usually says he needs to use the toilet *after* he has urinated, but the fact that he is telling the adult at all is a sign of progress. The child can then be encouraged to tell the adult *before* the child urinates. And an adult who observes the child holding himself can ask the child if he needs to use the toilet.

When the adult thinks the child can anticipate needing to use the toilet, the diaper can be replaced by training pants (a thick type of underwear) during the day. The adult should be prepared for many accidents, however. It takes most children several months to become consistently reliable. During this time, the adult must continue to encourage, praise, and remind the child.

A Training Technique. A number of techniques have been designed to make toilet training easier on parent and child. One such technique was recently developed by Azrin and Foxx (1974). The procedure makes use of reinforcement and modeling or social-learning techniques. It has several steps:

1. The parent waits until he or she is certain that the child is physically ready to be toilet trained.
2. The parent teaches the child how to lower and raise his pants by demonstrating how to do it and praising the child's efforts.
3. The parent teaches the child toileting procedures by having him teach them step by step to a doll. The child helps the parent "give dolly a drink." Then the parent tells the child that dolly has to "pee-pee," and the child is asked to help dolly sit on the potty. "Helping" involves pulling down the dolly's pants and setting the dolly on the potty. When dolly has finished "urinating" in the potty, the child is asked to give the dolly a piece of candy "for being such a big girl." But, of course, dolly cannot eat the candy, so the parent tells the child that he can eat it if he will be a big boy and go "pee-pee in the potty." The child is then shown how to empty the potty into the big toilet, flush, and replace the potty dish in the potty chair. The child is given clear instructions for each of these steps. Physical help is provided when needed, and the child is praised all along the way.

   Then the parent begins to teach the child how to use the potty. Being a "big boy like daddy" is emphasized. Training continues for a number of hours. The child is given drinks of soda or juice to make sure he needs to urinate frequently. The parent alternately checks to see if the child is dry, and encourages him to use the potty. Dolly is used again several times, and once she is made to have an "accident." The child is asked to feel that dolly is wet; the parent points out that dolly is a "baby," but that the child is a "big boy who will not wet his pants."

Rehearsal with a stand-in can help a child learn toileting behavior.

As the parent continues the practice sessions, he or she uses less prompting for each step and waits to see if the child remembers to pull down his pants, pull up his pants, empty the potty, and so on. The child is praised and given rewards such as candy and potato chips throughout the training.

There are several advantages to the Azrin and Foxx technique. It provides specific directions to follow in the toilet-training process. The procedure does not involve spanking, scolding, or other negative parental reactions. These aspects of the program provide some assurance that toilet training will be a positive experience for the child. Another advantage is that the child is toilet trained in four hours on one day rather than over a long period. Some parents drag toilet training out over many months because they do not devote enough time to it, or they start before the child is physically ready. Finally, the use of the doll gives the child a chance to get instruction and rehearse what is expected of him before he is trained himself.

The method has its drawbacks, too. Some two-year-olds tire of the "game" before four hours have passed, despite the constant praise and rewards. It may also be difficult to determine whether a child is physically mature enough to be trained, and a parent, once set on implementing the technique, may not stop the process even when this would make sense. Another problem is that the technique, although designed to be positive, is loaded with pressure. A child who hears the comments suggested by Azrin and Foxx will certainly get the idea that

FOCUS: Modeling

The type of social learning that involves imitating another person's behavior, is known as *modeling*. Many studies of imitation indicate that children who watch another person receive reinforcement for a specific behavior may model that behavior themselves. According to Bandura (1977) whether a child will imitate a model depends on several conditions: whether she was paying attention, how well she could retain what she observed, whether she had the motor skills to reproduce the action, and whether she had an incentive.

1. *Attention*. The child must attend to what the model is doing. A child's attention is influenced by the characteristics of the model — whether the child perceives the model to be similar to himself and whether the child knows she will later be asked to reproduce the model's actions.

2. *Retention*. The child must remember the model's actions. Verbal rehearsal or verbal description helps her remember.

3. *Motoric reproduction*. The child must be able to reproduce the action of the model. A beginning skater who is four years old cannot reproduce the fancy figure eights of an accomplished adult skater no matter how long she attends or how well she remembers what she saw, because she lacks the physical maturity needed. Similarly, a child cannot be toilet trained until she is sufficiently mature.

4. *Incentive conditions*. A child may not imitate her parents' behavior unless she is motivated to do so. When a child understands that her parents think it is important to do something, she may be motivated by the wish to please them.

Modeling

everybody would like him a whole lot more if only he would do what is being asked of him. In addition, we question the advisability of giving a child so much candy and soda in such a short period of time for any reason. Finally, the method can backfire. Children who realize that going to the potty is rewarded with candy or other goodies may use it as a method of getting rewards. Cantor comments on how the system worked, or rather, did not work, with her daughter, Lauren:

> I read the book and followed the instructions. Lauren had Oscar the Grouch, her doll, urinate in the potty, and we both rewarded Oscar with graham crackers at the appropriate times. Lauren drank large quantities of ginger ale and ate candy and crackers for three days. She loved it. She learned this method so well that she urinated in the potty at least thirteen times every day, expecting a reward not only each time she urinated but also all the times in between, when she remained dry. She was terrific. As the tangible food rewards were diminished, according to the instructions, Lauren's patience with this procedure also diminished. After the fourth day she refused to urinate in the potty; on eight different occasions she chose the floor instead. I then realized that I was asking Lauren's cooperation to accomplish my goal. I was over-eager and Lauren was frustrating me by not cooperating, which was her way of saying "enough." We decided to relax the whole intensive procedure. She now urinates in the potty whenever she is without her diaper and urinates in her diaper whenever she is wearing it (contrary to the Azrin and Foxx instructions which are never to return to a diaper once training has begun). She shows great pride in her accomplishments, and I am sure that in short order or in good time, as Lauren prefers, she will train herself. [1977, p. 100]

Adjusting the Training Methods. Children sometimes have a way of beating even the most cleverly conceived system. Cantor was wise to use her own judgment in modifying the system for her child. Depending on the situation, modifications of other types might be useful. Young children sometimes enjoy imitating older children, so it might be helpful to have an older child take the child being trained to the bathroom. It might also help to make sure the child gets to observe that adults use the bathroom, although it cannot be assumed that children understand that adults use the toilet and will want to imitate them. We know of one instance in which a father often praised his young daughter for using the potty chair when she was being trained. Shortly thereafter, she saw her father come out of the bathroom; she may also have heard the toilet flush. She said, "Good girl, daddy, good girl!" as if he, too, were just mastering using the toilet and needed a little praise and encouragement. Notice that at age two she apparently did not know the difference between a girl and a boy.

A few more facts about toilet training deserve mention. First, it is difficult for toddlers to hold their urine for long when their bladders are full, so they should be dressed in clothes that are easy to remove. For example, slacks with elastic bands at the waist can be pulled down quickly while slacks with a zipper and snap take more time. Easy-to-remove clothing can mean the difference between making it to the potty or not making it. Second, as we mentioned earlier, occasional lapses of control should be expected, especially when a child is very tired or ill. Finally, punishment and scolding for accidents have not been found to be effective (Sears, Maccoby, and Levin, 1957). Perhaps more importantly, they are inhumane reactions.

Feeding

Although they have learned some self-feeding skills much earlier, children develop most of their feeding skills during toddlerhood. A summary of development in this area is presented in Table 15-3.

Parents often worry whether their child is eating enough and eating the right foods. They may also be concerned when the child's appetite diminishes. But it is perfectly normal for toddlers to have varying appetites and to prefer some foods to others. Instead of worrying, parents can ensure that the child has a variety of good foods available. If rich and sugary foods are made inaccessible, the child can be allowed to decide what and how much he or she will eat. Small servings of finger foods encourage tasting and give the child a feeling of success for being able to finish eating the food he has been given. If necessary, the child can request additional servings. Because a toddler's hunger is satisfied by relatively small amounts of food, what is offered must be nutritious. The problem is that we often allow candy, cookies, soda pop, and other sweet snacks between meals and then try to force children to eat good food at mealtime. "You ate all of those cookies this afternoon; you have to eat some vegetables tonight," we say. The child will not be hungry of course, but he does not know that his selection has been poor, and we should not blame him for it. Adults must substitute apples, raisins, cheese, and vegetable or fruit juices for most sugary snacks, and simply acknowledge that many children will not eat, and do not need to eat, large amounts of food at every meal.

Toddlers are not very neat eaters. They are just learning to use utensils, and it takes time to learn to control them completely. In addition, toddlers are interested in the physical characteristics of food. Jello and mashed potatoes are extremely interesting. One jiggles but cannot be stirred, whereas the other can be stirred but not jiggled. The spoon shows through the jello but not the potatoes. Wow! Children should eventually be taught that food is for eating rather than playing, but parents should be tolerant of curiosity, too. It is possible to satisfy curiosity and encourage eating at the same time by saying something like, "Put a bite of that pretty jello in your mouth and see if it is soft and cold." or "Are the potatoes all stirred up? Are they ready to eat now? Okay, try a bite." Providing exploratory play experiences with foods such as dough and water can also help

Table 15-3. Self-feeding: Average age levels

6–9 months	Holds, sucks, and bites finger foods
9 months–1 year	Holds own bottle (or may no longer drink from a bottle); enjoys finger foods; eats most table foods; drinks from cup with help; will hold and lick spoon after it is dipped in food
15 months	Begins to use spoon, but turns it over before it reaches mouth; may no longer need bottle; may hold cup; is likely to tilt cup rather than head, spilling contents
1.5 years	Eats with spoon, often spilling; empties spoon in mouth; requires assistance; holds glass with both hands; can hold only glasses of certain sizes
2 years	Puts spoon in mouth correctly, occasionally spilling; holds glass with one hand; distinguishes between food and inedible materials; plays with food
2–3 years	Feeds self entirely, with occasional spilling; uses fork; pours from small pitcher; can obtain drink of water from faucet without help

SOURCE: Adapted from Caplan, F., ed. *The parenting advisor.* Copyright © 1976, 1977 by The Princeton Center for Infancy and Early Childhood. Reprinted by permission of Doubleday & Company, Inc.

satisfy the child's curiosity so that playing with food at mealtime is not quite so tempting. Similarly, a child can be invited to help prepare food. Even toddlers can help cut cookies out of dough, pour liquids into bread batter (an especially good task for the child who enjoys tipping her cup and watching the milk drip to the floor during mealtime!), scramble eggs, knead bread, or break lettuce into bits.

Encouraging Autonomy

You will recall from our discussion of theories and theorists in Chapter 3 that according to Erikson, children develop a sense of autonomy versus shame and doubt during the toddler period. In providing guidance during this time it is useful to remember that children's emerging skills enable them to do more and more for themselves. In addition, their developing will makes them want to do more for themselves. Of course, children this age still need a great deal of help from time to time: leaving too much up to them so they fail what they attempt can lead to doubts about their ability. The sensitive adult sets up a manageable environment for exploration and decision making and allows the child to do what she can on her own, but the adult also provides help and support when necessary. The adult also sets limits and has expectations — for eating behavior and toilet training, for example — but does not lose sight of the fact that the child's spirit and sense of self must not be sacrificed just for the quick accomplishment of a task.

Summary

Education Programs for Toddlers
- The Mother-Child Home Program and the Infant-Education Research Project were model programs designed for children in the toddler stage of development.
- Home-based education programs utilize home visitors whose goal is to teach parents how to work with their children.
- Education programs for toddlers help promote language development by encouraging the adult to verbalize while the child engages in some activity.

Living with the Toddler
- A child's adaptation to new people and places can be eased by introducing him to other children who will be there, by having the new adult visit the child at home, and by having a familiar person stay with the child on the first visit.
- Parents often need to help young children interact in positive ways with other children.
- Before a child can be toilet trained, he or she must have reached a certain level of physical maturity and understand what behaviors are expected. Because girls are more physically mature they can usually be toilet trained earlier than boys.
- Toddlers often enjoy exploring their food before they eat it. They also enjoy helping prepare food. Involvement in this activity can satisfy some of their curiosity about food and its physical characteristics.
- The sensitive adult understands that the toddler must be guided so as to allow autonomy to develop rather than shame and doubt.

Selected Readings

Caldwell, B. M., and Stedman, D. J. (Eds.). **Infant education: A guide for helping handicapped children in the first three years.** New York: Walker and Company, 1977. This readable paperback discusses the need for early detection of handicapping conditions, infant assessment, and several intervention programs.

O'Brien, M. O., Porterfield, J., Herbert-Jackson, E., and Risley, T. R. **The toddler center: A practical guide to day care for one and two year olds.** Baltimore, Md.: University Park Press, 1979. This comprehensive book, written for child care workers, discusses feeding toddlers, keeping them healthy and safe, providing for play, keeping in touch with parents, and much more.

Sullivan, S. D. **The father's almanac.** Garden City, New York: Doubleday, 1980. This practical book addressed to fathers includes topics such as child-proofing a home, disciplining, and childbirth. Some of the topics relate to issues that arise during infancy, but many others concern the toddler period.

Part V
The Preschool Child

The preschool period begins at about age three and lasts until age six. The term "preschool" can be misleading because many children of this age do attend school. In the United States in 1977, for example, 92 percent of the five-year-olds and 32 percent of the three- and four-year-olds attended some kind of school (Hymes, 1978). But most schools for children under age six do not emphasize instruction in academic skills. They are concerned with the whole child — his or her social, physical, and emotional development as well as intellectual development. Thus, "preschool" makes sense if interpreted as meaning "before formal academic instruction," but it should not be construed as meaning that children of this age are incapable of learning. As we shall see, they learn a great deal.

A larger proportion of the children in this age group have been attending school in the last few decades. This is probably due to four recent trends:

1. More states began to provide kindergarten during the 1970s.
2. The number of women with children under six who work outside the home is increasing. Twenty-nine percent did so in 1970, 36 percent in 1976, and 42 percent in 1977 (*America's Children*, 1976; Hymes, 1978). Between 10 and 15 percent of these parents use group day care centers (R. E. Smith, 1979).
3. More education programs are being provided for children who may be academically disadvantaged because of their parents' economic circumstances (Head Start, for example), than was true two or three decades ago.
4. Recognition of the importance of early childhood in cognitive development has increased.

The preschool years are a time of many accomplishments. Children's reasoning becomes more logical. Physical skills develop rapidly, which makes a new degree of independence possible. The last vestiges of child language begin to disappear and the child begins to use almost completely mature speech. Finally, children make great progress in learning socially appropriate behavior. Six-year-olds are far from being grown up, of course, but in many ways they will never seem like little children again.

Chapter 16

*P*hysical Development

Preschool children are different in appearance from both toddlers and school-age children. The groups are distinguished by physical size and by relative proportions of different parts of the body. Preschoolers also differ considerably from toddlers in terms of body control. By the end of the preschool period, for example, children can perform complicated locomotor tasks such as hopping and skipping, and fine motor tasks such as buttoning small buttons on a shirt or blouse. In this chapter we will discuss the changes in growth and motor skills that occur between the ages of about three and six.

Growth

Children's rate of growth continues to decrease during the preschool years. But because the preschool period is longer than the periods of infancy and toddlerhood, the physical growth that occurs during this stage is still noticeable, and a typical three-year-old looks quite different from a typical six-year-old.

Changes in Weight and Height

Children gain about five pounds a year between the ages of three and nine. This is considerably less than the fourteen pounds children gain during their first year and also less than the six or seven pounds they gain during their second.

Much the same pattern holds for increases in height: About three and a half inches are gained during the third year, followed by about two and a half inches each year until age ten (Lowrey, 1978). Compared to the increase of ten inches during the first year and four and a half during the second, these gains are relatively small.

Changes in Body Proportions

Children's legs and trunks continue to grow faster than their heads. As a result, children continue to thin out. There is no trace of the earlier protruding abdomen by the end of this period.

By age four or five, the protruding abdomen has usually disappeared.

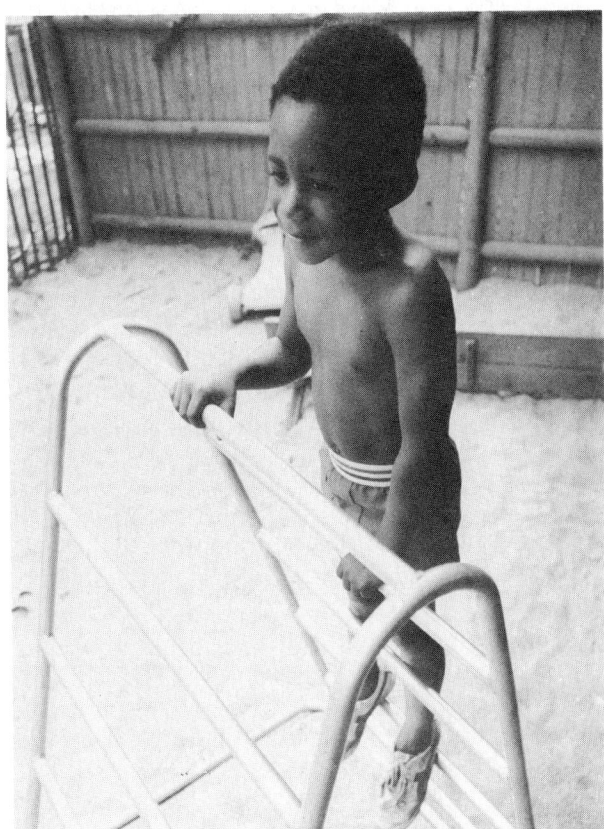

Motor Development

Arms, hands, and legs come under progressively better control throughout early childhood, but it is during the preschool period that complex coordination and skilled control of many movements become possible.

Fine Motor Development

It is not uncommon to see a three-year-old struggling with a button on a coat or a snap on a pair of pants. A big button that must go through a relatively loose buttonhole near the waist of a child's coat may be easy for a three-year-old, but a smaller button near the neck will almost certainly require adult assistance. Similarly, regular snaps can be manipulated by some three-year-olds, but the heavy-duty gripper type used to fasten young boys' trousers often require more strength than even a four-year-old can muster. Zippers that separate completely, such as

Preschoolers like to dress themselves, but tying shoes is difficult. Using scissors is also difficult for preschoolers, but they find a way!

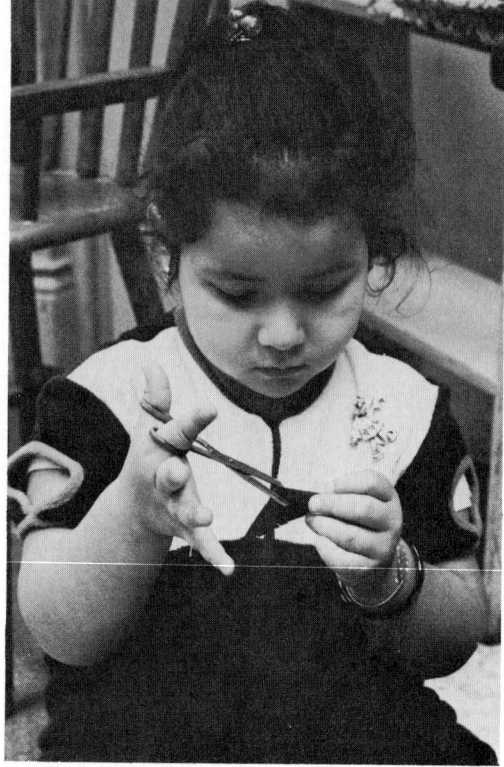

those used in coats, are beyond the abilities of many four-year-olds unless an adult first connects the two sides.

By the end of the preschool period, however, most children can buckle, button, snap, and zip with little difficulty. By that time children have also learned to cut with scissors and to make relatively controlled marks with crayons, pencils, and paintbrushes. At first children grip writing and drawing tools with an over-handed, full-fist grasp, but they later change to a mature grip using the thumb and fingers. Some children also learn to tie a bow by the end of the preschool years, although many children do not. Mastering these skills involves much struggle and practice, but preschoolers do not seem to mind this if adults allow them to proceed at their own speed and in their own way.

FOCUS: Adapting Clothing to Meet the Needs of the Handicapped Child

Most preschoolers learning to dress themselves sometimes encounter difficulties with fasteners, such as buttons, snaps, and zippers. But handicapped children, especially those whose handicap involves motor control or impaired use of limbs due to paralysis, have even greater difficulties. For these children to achieve a measure of independence and self-sufficiency, clothing must be designed to take the handicapping condition into account.

Friend et al. (1973) have suggested that clothing for handicapped children be designed with the following considerations in mind:

1. Clothing must fit bodies that may not be standard size or shape.
2. Clothing must be strong enough to withstand abrasion from appliances (such as leg braces) or mechanical aids.
3. Clothing must permit a person in a wheelchair to move easily. Tight sleeves would be a hindrance, for example.
4. Clothing must have openings and fasteners that can be reached by a person who has limited movement and poorly controlled coordination.

A handicapped preschool child may be able to dress herself if a shirt or blouse is fastened in the front with Velcro rather than with buttons. Similarly, a large ring placed through a zipper may make it easy to get hold of and thus allow a child with limited hand and finger control to zip. A regular zipper may be impossible for the same child to manage.

Unfortunately, special clothing for handicapped children is not available and, even if it were, it would probably be expensive. Therefore, parents must adapt existing clothing to meet the needs of the child. Teachers who work with young handicapped children may want to suggest to parents changes that will make clothing easier for a child to manage. Parents may benefit also from workshops to which they bring items of clothing and learn how to make alterations.

Gross Motor Development

The *center of gravity,* the point in the body around which weight is evenly distributed, is near the bottom of the breastbone in the newborn. As children grow, the center of gravity moves down the body; by the time a child is five or six, it is below the belly button (Lowrey, 1978). As the center of gravity changes, children become much steadier on their feet and become capable of movements that were impossible for the top-heavy infant and toddler.

Locomotor Skills. The preschooler can change the speed and rhythm of his walk, and when he is moving quickly, both his feet may leave the ground for an instant. A true run appears between the ages of two and three. Even younger children appear to run, but their feet never actually leave the ground at the same time. But even though three-year-olds can run, they do not know how to stop and start and to change directions quickly. These skills are mastered by most children by the time they are four and a half or five (Cratty, 1970).

The three-year-old can walk a straight line; by age four, most children can walk a circular path. Walking a balance beam (a board raised off the ground) is still difficult for preschool children: they may have to step to the ground several times in their attempt to cross it (Cratty, 1970).

Before age two, children jump from a low height by stepping off with one foot while keeping the other foot in contact with the ground. A two-footed jump from a short height with neither foot in contact with the ground is accomplished around age two. (This early developmental sequence is illustrated in Figure 16-1.) By age three, children are attaining some height in their two-footed jumps, but they "wing" or throw their arms back as they take off and do not lean their body forward the way a somewhat older child does. By four and a half, children usually move their arms forward and up at take-off for a two-footed jump, and lean forward at the shoulders. Similarly, children begin jumping over obstacles by leading with one foot and later jump with both feet together. Most children can perform a variety of jumps well by age five.

Walking up and down stairs is also mastered during the preschool years. Children first learn to walk up stairs by stepping up with one foot and then the other before attempting the next step. This is known as *marked-time climbing.* Around age three, children learn to walk up stairs alternating feet. They learn to walk down stairs alternating feet at around age four. Ladder climbing progresses through the same stages as stair climbing (Cratty, 1970).

Other locomotor skills that appear during the preschool years are hopping, skipping, and galloping. A hop involves moving by taking off and landing on one foot while keeping the other foot suspended. Children can hop a few steps on their preferred foot at the age of about three and a half. A one-foot hop of four to six steps can be performed by most four-year-olds; by age five the number of steps usually reaches eight or ten. Rhythmic hopping, which involves hopping on alternate feet without breaking pace, is very difficult, and few five-year-olds are capable of it.

Figure 16-1. Developmental sequence of a two-footed jump from a short height. Rows 1 and 2, stepping off an elevation at 17 months of age. Row 3, momentary suspension during a jump made at 18 months. Row 4, signs of incipient two-footed jumping at 21 months. Observe beginning shoulder girdle and arm retraction.

Skipping and galloping are difficult skills. Galloping involves an uneven succession of rhythmic movements using a lead foot. Many children can gallop well by age four. Skipping requires alternation of the feet and coordination of a step forward with a hop. It is more difficult than galloping, and most children cannot do it until they are almost six (Cratty, 1970).

FOCUS: Making Playgrounds Safe

Developing physical skills during the preschool and school-age years inevitably places children at some risk for injury. Bumps, bruises, and tumbles are common, and are part of the growth process. However, serious injury and even death can result if play areas and equipment are not minimally safe, or if children are not taught how to play on equipment safely.

During 1972 almost 160,000 playground-related injuries in the United States required emergency room treatment (National Electronic Injury Surveillance System, 1977). On playgrounds, children suffered the most serious injuries and the greatest number of deaths by falling from a height onto a hard surface. They sustained other serious injuries when hit by a moving object such as a swing seat, getting a body part trapped, or coming into contact with sharp or rough equipment edges or exposed bolts (Consumer Product Safety Commission, 1975).

Safety standards for playgrounds have been proposed by the National Recreation and Park Association, although these have not become mandatory. The association ranks surfaces under equipment in terms of safety. Concrete, asphalt, and packed earth are considered very hazardous. Pea gravel, wood chips, two-inch-thick gym mats and 1 1/8-inch-thick rubber mats are considered marginally acceptable. Sand at a depth of eight to ten inches is considered to be the safest surface and the only one rated acceptable.

The association also suggests that minimum zones surround various types of equipment. For example, a certain area should surround a swing so that children approaching and leaving other equipment will not accidentally come into the path of a swing in use. In addition, structures over a certain height should have protective railings or be completely enclosed to prevent falls.

Safe playground design and equipment can do much to reduce accidents and injuries, but, in addition, children must be taught how to use equipment and playgrounds safely. For example, safety zones around swings can reduce the number of children who might come near a swing while approaching other equipment, but children still must be taught not to enter these zones when swings are in use. Similarly, railings at the tops of climbing structures can prevent falls, but children must learn not to climb while holding objects in their hands. Roughhousing at the top of a slide or on a jungle gym can cause children to fall, and tricycle traffic that is not directed on set paths can lead to collisions. For all these reasons, young children need supervision and instruction to avoid injuries.

At first, preschoolers do not get their bodies behind a throw.

Upper Body and Arm Skills. Throwing or tossing of objects begins in infancy during Stage 5 of the sensorimotor period (see Chapter 4) and continues through the toddler and preschool years. As children get older, their arms become less rigid during the throwing movement. They also change from underhanded to overhanded throwing and learn how to take a step and shift their weight to get it behind the throw. These changes result in throws that are longer, faster, and more accurate (Cratty, 1970).

The first catching behavior is the rigid, passive acceptance of an object placed in a child's arms. This is accomplished at around age one and a half. Catching a large ball thrown very slowly is usually accomplished at about age two and a half. This catch is also almost passive: the thrower must throw the ball into the child's arms and hands rather than expect the child to reach out to grab the ball. Skilled catching of a moving ball with arms in front of the body and elbows bent to absorb the impact does not appear until late in the preschool period, and even then a child cannot successfully catch a small ball thrown with much force (Cratty, 1970).

Reaction time is slower in the preschool child than in older children because the nervous system is less mature. When playing catch with a preschooler, you would probably throw the ball quite slowly and say something like, "Now get ready; here it comes." Even when they are ready, however, preschool children react more slowly than older children and adults.

Summary

Growth

- The growth rate during the preschool years is slower than during infancy and toddlerhood. But because trunk growth is faster, children's protruding abdomens flatten.

Motor Development

- As children grow, the center of gravity moves down the body, which makes preschoolers more stable on their feet than toddlers.
- Preschoolers become quite skillful in manipulating objects with their hands. However, small motor tasks such as drawing, writing, and tying a bow require a certain level of cognitive understanding, and may not be mastered during this period.
- Children first walk up stairs without alternating their feet.
- Skipping is more difficult than galloping, and children may not be able to skip until they are about six years old.
- Early throwing involves more rigid movement of the arms and body than later throwing. Catching begins as passive acceptance of an object into the arms and develops into grabbing a moving object with the hands.

Selected Readings

Engstrom, G. Ed. **The significance of the young child's motor development.** *Washington, D.C.: National Association for the Education of Young Children, 1971.* This 50-page booklet discusses the importance of motor development in the preschool child. Included are useful pictures of sequences of movements young children make in throwing a ball and in jumping from a height. Useful information is provided about how to observe children's motor skills.

Frost, J. L., and Klein, B. L. **Children's play and playgrounds.** *Boston: Allyn and Bacon, 1979.* The authors discuss theories of play, types of playgrounds and play equipment, hazards and safety precautions, and adapting play areas and equipment for use by handicapped children. An interesting and information-packed book.

Sinclair, C. B. **Movement of the young child: Ages two to six.** *Columbus, Ohio: Charles E. Merrill, 1973.* This book provides detailed information about development of all basic movement tasks that appear during the preschool years. These include climbing stairs, bouncing a ball, catching a ball, galloping, hitting, hopping, and many more. Several charts are provided to summarize age norms for skill attainment. This book is highly recommended for the student interested in young children's motor skill development.

Chapter *17*

*C*ognitive Development

Intellectual functioning in the preschool child has been studied from many psychological perspectives, most notably from the behavioral and cognitive orientations. We will discuss only the cognitive view, and specifically the work of Piaget, because we think he explains the important phenomena of the period so thoroughly. We begin with a discussion of preoperational thinking, and then move on to consider development of concepts of number, mass, space, and dreams.

The Preoperational Child

We have seen that between birth and about two and a half years of age children understand the world in terms of sensorimotor *schemes* (action patterns). During the late toddler and early preschool years, children become capable of *representational* or *symbolic thought*. Their ability to think is still limited, however; they cannot think in logical terms, at least not in terms of what adults generally consider to be logical. Piaget calls this prelogical stage the *preoperational period*.

Preoperational thought has several distinguishing characteristics. For example, a child may agree that two rows haye exactly the same number of pennies when the rows are placed directly opposite each other. But if one row of pennies is spread out or gathered into a cluster so that the physical correspondence of the two sets of pennies is destroyed, the preoperational child will assume that the new arrangements contain different amounts of pennies, even though he or she could see that no pennies were added or taken away. Because preoperational children make judgments based on how things look, we say their thinking is *dominated by perception.*

Preoperational thinking is also characterized by certain forms of *egocentrism.* During the sensorimotor period, children learn to differentiate themselves from other objects, but they do not understand that external frames of reference can be imposed on them and on other objects — that they, too, are objects among objects, in space. This new egocentrism is what the preoperational child must overcome. Because preoperational children lack this understanding, they are unaware that there can be many points of view, and they do not realize that their own view is only one of many that are possible. Thus, they assume that an object's existence corresponds to their view of it; they do not consider how it might look to a person whose view of the object was different.

The inability to consider all views is often revealed when very young children play hiding games. They hide so that they cannot see out, but they can be seen from other perspectives. For example, a child might hide under a table sitting next to a wall by facing the wall and covering her eyes with her hands. The child apparently thinks that she cannot be seen if she cannot see anyone, assuming that her view is the only one possible.

Preschool children also think about only one aspect of a relationship at a time. In the situation with the rows of pennies, a child might focus on the length of the rows but disregard their density. As a result, the child does not grasp that the rows are numerically equivalent. This aspect of preoperational thinking is called *centering* or centration.

Another limitation of preschoolers' thinking is its *irreversibility.* After observing an action, preschoolers cannot play it backward in their heads to reconstruct how things were originally. While the action is in progress, they focus more on *states,* or how things look at the end of a particular action, than on *transformations,* or how one state changes to another and is related to it. For example, a child may claim that two rows no longer contain the same number of pennies once the members of one row have been spread out so they are no longer directly opposite the pennies in the other row; this child does not realize tha tthe action of spreading the pennies out could be reversed. If the child watches while someone else performs the action of putting the pennies back, or if the child does it himself when asked, he will then say that the rows once again contain the same number of pennies. The child thinks only about each end state — pennies lined up opposite each other or pennies not directly opposite each other. The transformation, or the action connecting these two states, escapes the preoperational child.

These basic characteristics of preoperational thinking influence how children perform on various intellectual tasks. We will see them revealed in behavior as we discuss tasks related to number, mass, space, and dreams in the pages to follow.

Conservation

Conservation refers to the ability to understand that the distribution of a substance or of objects does not change the quantity of the substance or objects. We will consider two types of conservation situations below: conservation of number or discrete objects and conservation of continuous quantity.

Conservation of Number

To an adult, number is unrelated to the physical arrangement of objects. But young children are likely to confuse number with the distribution of objects in space. To study the development of the number concept in children, Piaget (1965) used conservation tasks. A child is said to be able to conserve number or to be able to solve conservation of number tasks when he or she understands that the quantity of a set of objects remains the same even when the arrangement of the objects is changed.

To begin the task, children are shown a row of several objects and are given additional objects to make a second row with the same number of objects. Three- and four-year-olds are usually unable to construct a second row with the same number of objects as the model. They pay attention to the lengths of the rows and make sure that their row begins and ends just opposite the model, but the number of objects they use is sometimes more than that contained in the model, and sometimes less. Children who do this are said to be at Stage 1 (see Figure 17-1).

If a child creates a second row equal to the first by matching the objects one-to-one, then the experimenter can proceed with the second part of the task. This step involves changing the distribution of objects in one of the rows so that it becomes either longer or shorter than the other (see Figure 17-1, Stage II). At this point the child is asked if the two rows still have the same number of objects. Less-advanced children say that the new row contains a different number of objects. Children who center on the density of the rows believe the shorter row contains more objects; children who center on the lengths of the rows believe the longer row has more objects. Responses such as these indicate that the child is in Stage II, which generally occurs between five and six years of age.

Some children, however, claim that the rearranged rows still contain the same number of items for at least one of three reasons: (1) identity — none was taken away or added; (2) compensation — the longer row has big gaps; (3) reversibility — the displaced row could be put back the way it was in the beginning. Children who give one of these responses can conserve number. Children usually reach this stage when they are six or seven years old. When the child can conserve number, he or she enters the *concrete operational period*, which will be discussed in detail in Part VI.

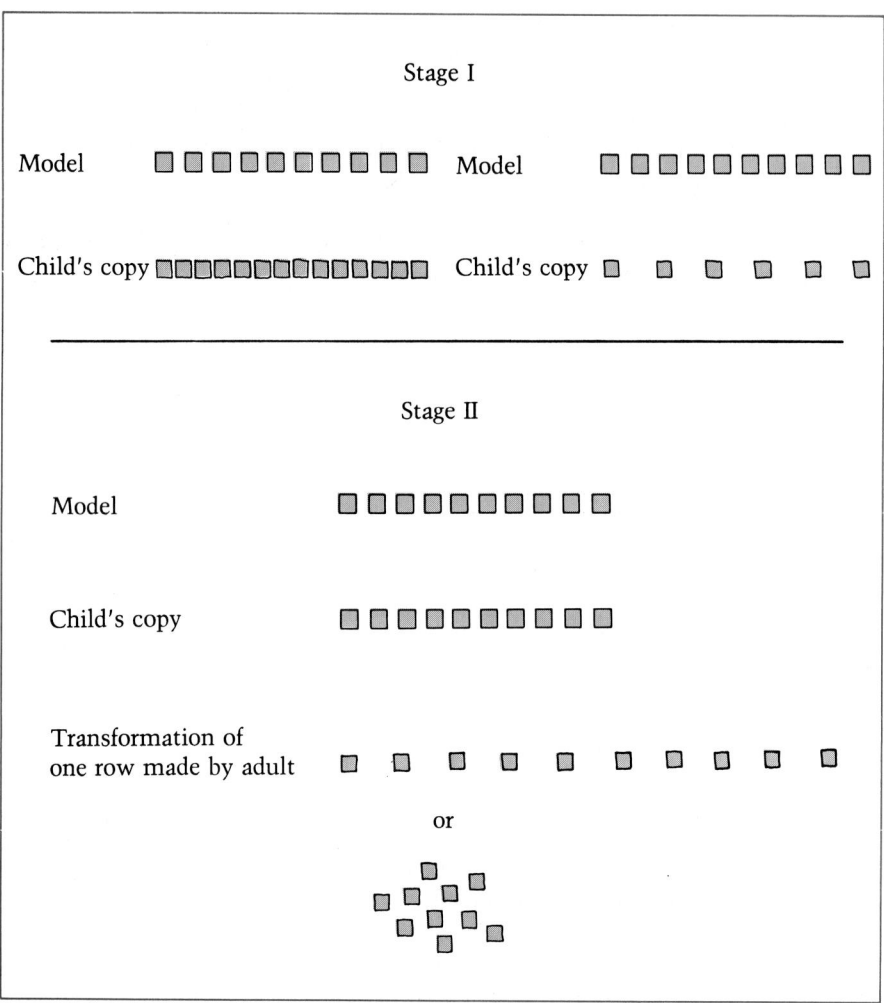

Figure 17-1. Conservation of number task

Conservation of Continuous Quantity

The previous task is also known as the conservation of discontinuous quantity; the quantity is discontinuous because it consists of identifiable units. In a second task, Piaget (1965) assessed continuous quantities — those which do not consist of identifiable units. One task requires two large identical beakers (referred to here as beaker 1 and beaker 2) filled with colored water. The child is asked to look at them to be sure that they contain the same amount of liquid. The child is allowed to pour liquid from one to the other, if necessary, until they are exactly the same. When the child has agreed that the quantities in the two beakers are identical, the experimenter does one of two things: (1) he pours the contents of beaker 2 into a third container, which is either taller and narrower or shorter and wider than the original beakers; or (2) he pours the contents of beaker 2 into a number of small containers resembling medicine cups. In other words, the liquid is transferred to a third container, which is shaped differently, or to several small containers. The child is then asked two questions: Do beaker 1 and beaker 3 contain the same amount of liquid? Do beaker 2 and the series of cups contain the same amount? (See Figure 17-2.)

Stage I children (three to four years of age) think that the liquid that has been displaced has also changed in quantity. When they center on the tallness of the

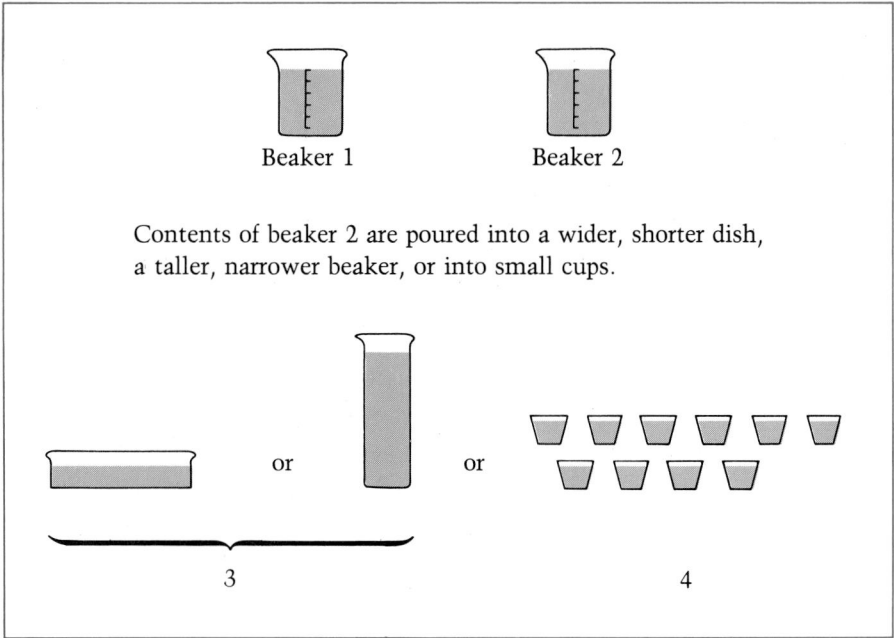

Figure 17-2. Conservation of continuous quantity

liquid in the tall, thin beaker, or on the number of small containers, they say that there is more liquid. When they center on the low height of the liquid in the short, wide beaker, or on the small amount of liquid in each of the cups, they say the amount of liquid has decreased.

Stage II children (five to six years of age) sometimes say the quantity of the transferred liquid is the same as before, but when the perceptual discrepancy between beaker 1 and the displaced liquid from beaker 2 is great, they revert to saying the quantity has changed. Thus, when they are confronted with many small containers holding the contents of beaker 2, they usually say the quantity has increased. As you can see, Stage II children are capable of only partial *decentering*, — the ability to consider two aspects of a relationship at the same time.

Stage III children (six to seven years of age, on the average) judge that the quantity of liquid previously in beaker 2 does not change regardless of the kind or number of containers it is transferred to. They give reasons such as "This container is wider, but it is not as high," "There are more little cups, but they don't hold very much," and "We could pour all of these back into this one." We can see in their comments evidence of decentering, and also the ability to reverse an action mentally. Children no longer rely on an object's appearance to judge its quantity, and are capable of logical thinking.

We can see evidence of the preschool child's inability to conserve quantity in everyday situations. Mother pours juice for her two young children into a plastic cup and a narrow juice glass. Despite the differences in the shapes of the two containers (the cup is shorter but wider), they hold roughly the same amount of liquid. But the older child complains: "You gave him more! His cup is bigger than mine!" Mother may think the child is just behaving badly to cause a commotion, but the child may actually believe that the two glasses hold different amounts of juice and that his mother has favored his brother.

The Child's Construction of Space

To an adult, space resembles a container into which objects can be placed. But to young children, space is the arrangement of the objects themselves; they have no concept of space apart from objects. The relationships young children understand first are *topological* (that is, they think about one object's relationship to another object in approximate terms, but not an object's relationship to an external frame of reference or the exact relationship of one object to another). Topological relationships include proximity (closeness), separation, order (what is placed next to something else), enclosure (what things are surrounded by other things), and continuity (what things are open and what things are closed). The child gradually constructs a notion of space separate from objects and comes to understand that objects can be oriented in space in one of two ways: in terms of either a point of view — *projective space* — or of straight lines, angles, or coordinates — *Euclidean space*. Piaget and Inhelder (1967) used several tasks to study the development of children's concepts of space.

Drawing Geometrical Shapes Based on Models

In one task children are shown models of geometrical shapes and asked to copy them. (All twenty-one models are shown in Figure 17-3.) The models include typical Euclidean shapes such as circles and squares (models 4, 5, 6, 8). Also included are shapes that differ topologically in various ways: whether one part of the drawing is inside or outside another part (*enclosure*; models 1–3); whether two shapes are touching or separated (*proximity* and *separation*; models 9–11); or whether shapes are open (*noncontinuous*; models 20–21) or closed (*continuous*; models 1–19).

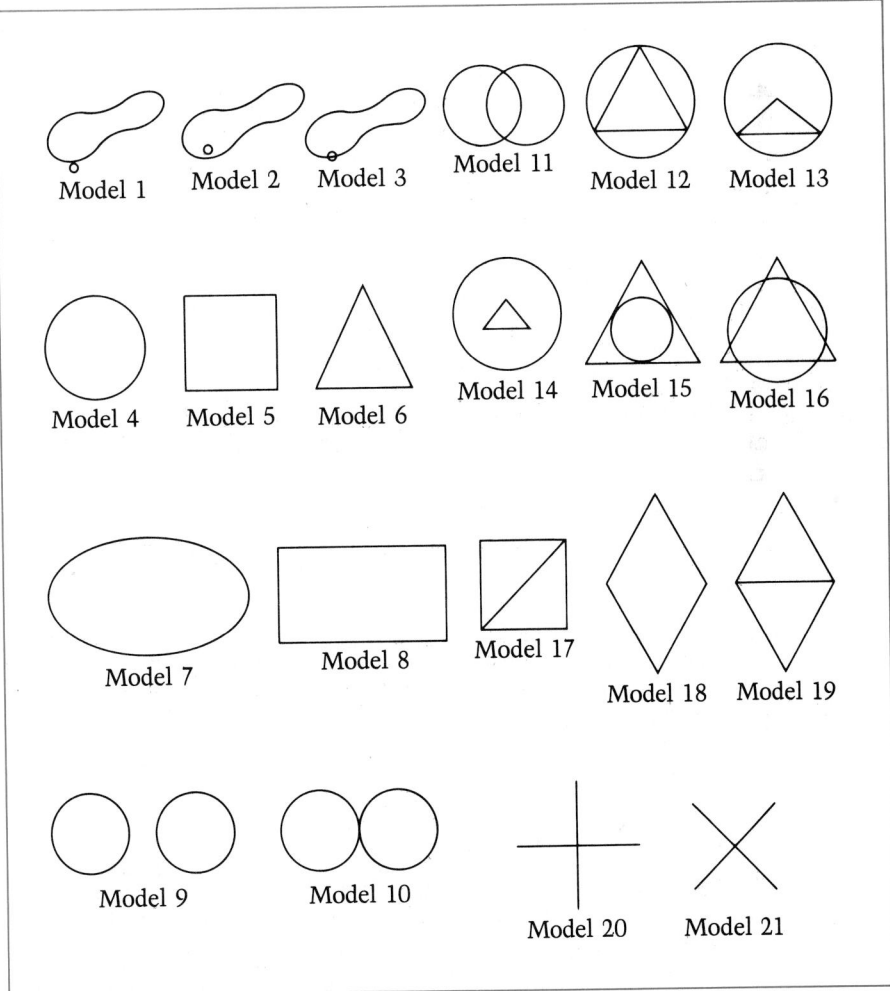

Figure 17-3. Models used in Piaget's geometrical shape task

Children's performance on the shape drawing task indicates that they initially represent shapes in terms of topological relationships, and only gradually come to represent them in terms of Euclidean relationships. (See the sequence of development in Box 17-1.) Even though children had previously drawn straight lines to form a cross and curved lines to form a circle (Stage IB), they did not use these different lines in their first attempts to draw the circle, triangle, and square when shown these closed figures as a group. All were drawn as circles. At first, children apparently center on the fact that these figures are closed rather than open ones, and it is this aspect only that they try to represent in their drawings.

BOX 17-1. Sequence of Development in Differentiating Among Shapes

STAGE 0 (UP TO 2½–3)

Drawings consist only of scribbles. The scribbles bear no resemblance to the model presented.

STAGE I

IA (up to about 3½) .
Scribbles vary depending on whether the model presented is open or closed. A cross may be drawn like this:

while a circle may be drawn like this:

The child does not yet draw an accurate cross or circle, but his drawings indicate that he understands at a representational level that some figures are open while others are closed.

SOURCE: From Jean Piaget and Bärbel Inhelder, *The Child's Conception of Space,* translated by F. T. Langdon and L. L. Luger. First published in France in 1948 by Presses Universitaires de France. First published in England in 1956 by Routledge & Kegan Paul Ltd. Reprinted by permission of Humanities Press Inc., New Jersey 07716.

IB (3½–4)
The child can draw a reasonably accurate circle and cross.

The child cannot represent differences among Euclidean figures. They are all drawn as circles, with lines being added in some cases to indicate placement of angles.

circle   ellipse

triangle   square

The child can accurately represent the inside-outside relationships shown in models 1–3.

model 1   model 2   model 3

Children's performance on this task suggests that difficulty in drawing figures cannot be attributed exclusively to a lack of motor skill, as is sometimes claimed. It is also caused by a conceptual misunderstanding. This distinction between motor and conceptual ability can be useful to teachers who are trying to help children learn to draw circles, triangles, and squares. Stringing beads, working with clay, or other activities that facilitate small muscle control, while worthwhile for that purpose, may not help children develop concepts about shapes. A teacher trying to improve children's understanding of shapes should provide them with opportunities to handle shapes, to draw and paint shapes, and to construct shapes with popsicle sticks or a geoboard.

BOX 17-1 continued

Transition between IB and IIA

The child's representations indicate that he or she makes a distinction between curved and straight lines but does not differentiate different kinds of curved figures or different kinds of straight-line figures.

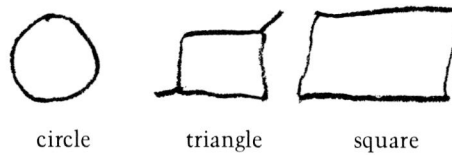

circle   triangle   square

STAGE II

IIA (4–5½)

The child differentiates most Euclidean shapes.

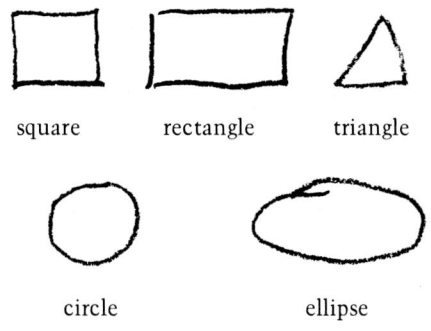

square   rectangle   triangle

circle   ellipse

The child represents the differences between the two types of crosses and understands oblique lines.

The relationship of two circles in models 9–11 is *accurately* represented. (Proximity and separation are indicated more grossly at an earlier stage.)

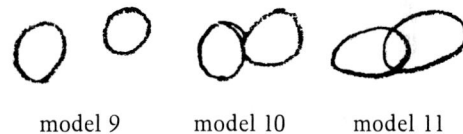

model 9   model 10   model 11

IIB (5½–6½)

The rhombus is drawn correctly and all circumscribed figures are gradually mastered except model 16.

rhombus

STAGE III (6½–7)

All models are drawn accurately.

Pictorial Space

A second method Piaget and Inhelder (1967) used to understand the development of children's concepts of space involved looking at their picture drawings. See Box 17-2 for Piaget's description of the stages of development in this area.

Constructing a Projective Straight Line

Piaget and Inhelder developed a specific task to study the development of concepts of projective space. The materials for the task include matchsticks mounted in clay bases, and two tables, one round and one square. Children are asked to make a straight line on each of the two tables by placing matchsticks between two widely spaced vertical poles placed on the table by the experimenter. In some instances the two end poles are placed so that the child's line would run parallel to the edge of the square table; in other cases they are placed such that the line would form an oblique angle with the table's edge. When the poles are placed on the round table, the line formed will run across a section of it (see Figure 17-4).

The youngest children (four- and five-year-olds) are unable to sight between the two poles. They place the matchsticks side by side, but the line they create is quite irregular, even when the line to be formed is parallel with the edge of the square table. Five- and six-year-olds can form a straight line with the sticks when it runs parallel to a table edge, but they become confused when it runs obliquely. Six- and seven-year-olds realize that from a certain perspective there is a line connecting the two poles, and they disregard completely the lines of the table edge, sighting instead between the poles. Sighting involves adopting a perspective and sticking with it, and adopting a perspective requires the knowledge that there are many perspectives that can be adopted.

Perhaps you can see why preschool children often have trouble forming themselves into a straight line. They usually form a very irregular line with children standing two or three abreast at several points. Teachers may think that their children are just being sloppy, but young children lack the concept of a line

Preschoolers do not understand what it means to "get into line."

BOX 17-2. Stages in the Development of Pictorial Space

STAGE I (3–4)

Even topological relationships are not completely understood. A child may draw a person with arms and legs attached to the head, or a head with eyes, nose, and mouth scrambled. Parts that are connected in reality may not be shown as connected in the child's drawing, as when a cat's tail is not attached to the cat.

A simple baseline may appear, but the child has no concept of planes from foreground to background (Euclidean space).

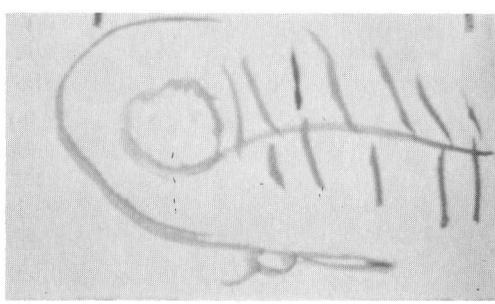

STAGE II (5–9)

Topological relationships are well understood; thus, eyes, nose, and mouth are placed in correct relationship to each other. But proportions and relative distances (Euclidean relationships) are not understood. Thus, people are drawn as big as houses. Perspective (viewpoints in projective space) is not understood either.

Children include conflicting views such as the inside and outside of a house all in the same picture.

STAGE III (8–9)

Drawings take perspective, proportion, and relative distances into consideration. The child understands projective and Euclidean space concepts.

and cannot, as a result, form one themselves. A teacher, of course, sights along an imaginary line he or she has created in his head.

Teachers can help children form lines by placing pieces of tape on the floor to designate where each child is to stand, by having the line form along the wall, or by asking children to place their hands on the shoulders of the person in front of them. These are practical devices, however — the fact that they work does not mean that the children understand the concept of lines.

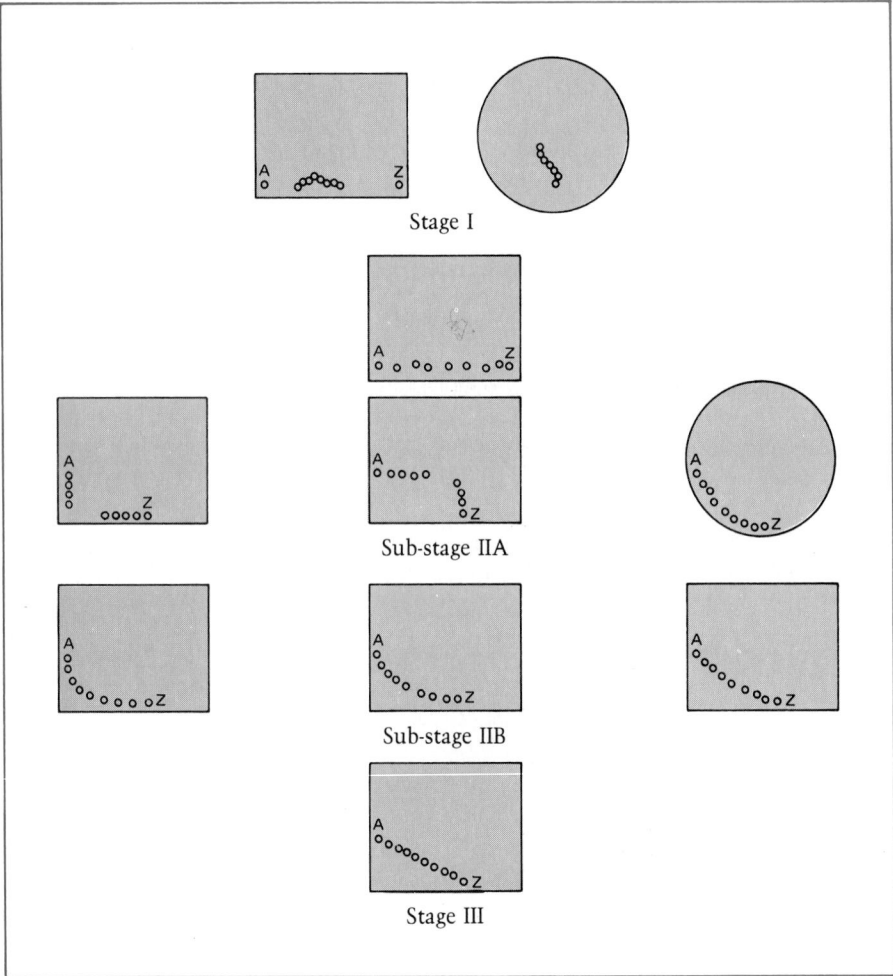

Figure 17-4. Projective straight line task and stages

The Child's Understanding of Dreams

Young children do not understand that thoughts are internal or that they are separate from the things thought about. In fact, children are scarcely aware that they are thinking about things at all, and they confuse thoughts, dreams, labels, and names with the physical things they represent. Young children believe that thoughts are created in the act of speaking, and consider names to be part of the objects named. Piaget refers to this tendency to endow thoughts with substance as *realism*.

It is not, then, surprising that young children misunderstand dreams. Piaget (1969) investigated children's notions about dreams by asking them questions such as these:

1. "Do you know what a dream is?"
2. "Where do dreams come from?"
3. "Where do dreams happen?" "Where is the dream when you are dreaming?"
4. "Could someone else see your dream?"
5. "What do you dream with?"
6. "Why do you dream?" "What sends them?"

Stages in Children's Thinking About Dreams

Children's responses to the above questions vary with age. (The authors have found that children pass through the stages noted by Piaget at ages considerably younger than those Piaget indicated.) In Stage I (four to seven years of age, according to Piaget), children think that dreams are caused by external forces; they also believe that dreams take place outside of their bodies. The following response is typical of behavior at this stage:

Zeng (6): Where do dreams come from? — *They come from the night.* — How? — *I don't know.* — What do you mean by "they come from the night"? — *The night makes them.* — Does the dream come by itself? — *No.* — What makes it? — *The night.* — Where is the dream? — *It's made in the room.* — Where does the dream come from? — *From the sky.* — Is the dream made in the sky? — *No.* — Where is it made? — *In the room.* [Piaget, 1969, p. 94]

Stage II children (seven to nine years of age, approximately) understand that dreams originate in the dreamer, but they still do not understand that dreams occur in their heads. The following response is typical of this stage:

Pig (9½): Where do dreams come from? — *When you are asleep, you think someone is beside you. When you see something in the day, you dream of it at night.* — What is the dream? — *Oh, anything.* — Where does it come from? — *I don't know. It comes by itself.* —

Table 17-1. Summary of developmental stages in children's understanding of dreams

	Origin	Location
Stage I	external	external
Stage II	internal	external
Stage III	internal	internal

> Where from? — *Nowhere. Where is it made? — In the room. —* Where? *— When you are lying down. —* Where is it made, in the room or inside you? *— In me . . . outside. —* Which, do you think? *— Outside.* — Where does the dream come from, from the room or from you? — *From me. —* Where is it, outside or in you? *— Beside me. —* Where? *— In my room. —* How far away? (He points to 30 cm in front of him.) [Piaget, 1969, p. 108]

This child initially states that the dream originates externally, but he later says it comes from him. But he still believes that the dream takes place outside of his body.

Stage III children (nine to eleven years of age, approximately) understand that dreams originate inside them, that dreams consist of thoughts and that dreams occur in their heads.

> Visc (11;1): You dream *"with the head,"* and the dream is *"in the head."* It isn't in front? — *It's as if (!) you could see. —* Is there anything in front of you? — *Nothing. —* What is there in your head? — *Thoughts. —* Do the eyes see anything in the head? — *No.* [Piaget, 1969, p. 119]

A summary of development during these stages is provided in Table 17-1.

Implications of Children's Early Thinking About Dreams

Considering young children's thoughts about dreams, it is not surprising that they sometimes fear sleeping in the dark, and occasionally wander into their parents' room and ask to sleep there. When we recognize that young children think (1) that dreams are made of real things, (2) that dreams take place in their rooms or right beside them, and (3) that they are caused by other people or things, it is easy to understand why they are afraid. We will explain how children's fears about dreams can be diminished when we discuss living with the preschooler in Chapter 20.

A Word of Caution About Piaget's Work

In this discussion of cognitive development, we have relied heavily on the work of Piaget, because his work is more comprehensive and, we believe, more insightful than other interpretations. We should point out, however, that Piaget's work has been criticized.

One valid criticism is that Piagetian tasks may provide a very conservative estimate of a child's cognitive ability because of the social context of task administration. When an adult performs an action that *appears* to result in a change, children think they are expected to notice a change, and they respond accordingly. Thus, they might say that the number of objects in a row has changed even when they do not actually believe it has.

Some recent research indicates that children's behavior on the Piagetian tasks is in fact influenced by their perception of the experimenter's expectations. In a study involving the conservation of number task, a teddy bear named Naughty Teddy rushes in and rearranges the objects in Stage II. (The rearrangement is usually done by the experimenter.) The exasperated experimenter then invites the child to put Naughty Teddy back in his box and resumes the experiment, saying "Now, where were we? Ah yes, is the number in this row the same as in this row?" In the standard experiment, only thirteen four- to six-year-olds out of eighty conserved number, but in the Naughty Teddy experiment, fifty out of eighty did so. Donaldson suggests that "humanly meaningful contexts sustain our thinking" (1978). In other words, children may not perform number tasks as well as they can because they base their answers, not on what they believe is correct, but on what they assume, from previous experience, the experimenter wants to hear.

Summary

The Preoperational Child
- The preschool child's thinking is preoperational; that is, it is not logical. This preoperational thinking is dominated by perception. It is also characterized by egocentrism, centering, and irreversibility.

Conservation
- According to Piaget, the concept of number involves the understanding that quantity is unrelated to the arrangement of objects. When children understand that quantity is unaffected by arrangement, they are said to be able to conserve number.

The Child's Construction of Space
- Preschool children do not think of space as an entity distinct from the objects that occupy it. They understand topological relationships before they understand Euclidean or projective relationships.

- Children's drawings and writings are influenced by their understanding of space.
- Before children can construct a straight line with objects, they must be able to construct a line in their imagination.

The Child's Understanding of Dreams

- Children misunderstand dreams because they have trouble differentiating their thoughts from the objects being thought about.
- One reason young children may be afraid of going to bed at night is because they think their dreams are really happening.

A Word of Caution About Piaget's Work

- The social context of the administration of Piagetian tasks may influence how children respond to the tasks.
- Children's performance on Piagetian tasks may underestimate their actual understanding of certain concepts.

New Terms

representational thought	**conservation**
symbolic thought	**reversibility**
preoperational period	**decentering**
egocentrism	**topological relationships**
centering	**projective space**
irreversibility	**Euclidean space**
states	**realism**
transformations	

Selected Readings

Francks, O. R. Scribbles? Yes, they are art! **Young Children,** 34 (1979): 15–22. The author discusses stages in children's developing ability to draw. She begins by describing the scribbles of two-year-olds and continues with examples up through the pictorial drawings of four- and five-year-olds. A good article for the student unfamiliar with children's early drawing behavior.

Gelman, R., and Gallistel, C. R. **The child's understanding of number.** Cambridge, Mass.: Harvard University Press, 1978. These authors stress the development of counting skills in preschool children. As such, the book is a contrast to Piaget's work and may be interesting to a student who wishes to take a broader look at children's cognitive development in relation to mathematics.

Ginsburg, H., and Opper, S. **Piaget's theory of intellectual development.** Second edition. Englewood Cliffs, N.J.: Prentice-Hall, 1979. A very readable discussion of Piaget's theory and descriptions of stages of development. A large portion of the book is devoted to a discussion of children between the ages of two and eleven — the preoperational and concrete operational periods.

Chapter *18*

*L*anguage Development

Children begin to communicate as soon as they are born, and to talk by their first birthday. At three they are skillful talkers, but early talk is quite different from mature talk. In the preschool years, many changes in language occur, and by the end of the period children's oral language resembles that of adults.

Children also become familiar with written language during the preschool years. Most of us assume that reading and writing do not begin until the child is of school age, but just as children begin to talk long before they can talk like adults, they begin to learn to read and write long before they can read and write like adults. For this reason we will discuss both oral and written language development.

Verbal Language

Production

A child's first sentences are very simple. A very young child says such things as "Mommy sock," "bite finger," and "boot off." At about age three, these give way to sentences such as "Where the wheel?" "He's make it?" and "That not cowboy."

It is during the preschool years that children learn to utter their first grammatically correct sentences: "Where does the wheel go?" "That's mommy's sock," "I can't do this," "That's not a cowboy." (Menyuk, 1969, p. 73).

Acquiring Morphological Rules. Most of the mistakes children make in sentences such as "That mommy sandwich," "He walk fast," or "Two girl played," can be corrected by adding just one or two letters: "That's mommy's sandwich," "He walks fast," and "Two girls played." These one- and two-letter additions, known as *morphemes*, are the smallest units of meaning in a language. "Dog" is one morpheme, for example, and "dogs" is two. Morphemes are used to *inflect* certain words. Verbs are inflected to indicate tense ("walking," "walked," "walks") and person ("I walk," "he walks"); nouns are inflected to indicate plurals ("dogs," "shoes," "houses") and possession ("girl's," "man's"). Knowing how to change words to various forms requires that children learn *morphological rules*. That is, children do not learn each specific word, but learn instead how to change certain classes of words (verbs, nouns) into their different forms.

At first children omit entirely the morphemes needed to create inflections, but later they begin to add them: "There goes one," "That's mommy's sandwich." Curiously, children who are learning morphological rules begin to make a new kind of mistake. The problem is that, in English, the rules for forming plurals of nouns and past tenses of verbs cannot be applied to all words. The plural of "mouse" is "mice," for example; we do not say "mouses." "Foot" and "tooth" are also made plural by using phonologically different words, "feet," and "teeth." Similarly, some verbs are not placed in the past tense by adding *ed*. The past tenses of "teach" and "run," for example, are "taught" and "ran."

Before children learn any morphological rules, they use the correct forms of the common, irregular plurals and verbs (Brown, 1973). For example, they use "came" and "ran" appropriately. But once they learn that most words can be inflected according to certain rules, they *overgeneralize* the rules or apply them even when they are inappropriate. This explains why four-year-olds say "My mommy *teached* me to swing," "My cat has four *foots*," or "I *runned* home fast." Children eventually figure out which words are irregular and which ones are not and then apply the rules correctly, but they may continue to make occasional errors until they are six or seven years old.

Children's Creative Use of Words. Preschool children sometimes create words or use words differently than adults. A child might say "I am claying," "Look! A sweep" (Garvey, 1977, p. 60), or "I seed him brooming" (Branigan and Stokes, 1976, p. 7). Instances such as these reveal that children understand that some words can be used as both nouns and verbs (e.g., "saw" and "sawing," "rake" and "raking," "sled" and "sledding"). As with inflections, however, children do not realize that this formula can be applied to some words but not to others, such as "broom" and "sweeping." This is another example of rule overgeneralization.

Creative usage also occurs when children use words more broadly than adults. Chukovsky (1963) provides some examples:

— a bald man had a "barefoot head"
— a mint candy made a "draft" in your mouth
— "the husband of a grasshopper is a daddyhopper"
— a doll being placed in and out of water was said to be "drowning-in" and "drowning-out" [pp. 2–7]

It has been suggested that language behavior of this kind indicates an understanding of metaphor, that is, a knowledge that one thing can be described in terms of another (Gardner et al., 1978). We think the behavior is more a matter of necessity than of conscious choice. But whatever the reason for its appearance, it is one of the most delightful aspects of young preschoolers' behavior, and it passes all too quickly.

Formulating Sentences. Not only are there rules for creating inflections, but there are rules for creating variations of declarative sentences. For example, we form questions and negative sentences in systematic ways. We do not need to learn how to say each question sentence or each negative sentence we use. What we do instead is learn an underlying rule for formulating such sentences in general, just as we learn a general rule for inflecting words to create plurals or past tense.

Children, however, do not master all aspects of these rules at once, with the result that their early questions and negative sentences are different from ours. The developmental changes involved in forming questions and negative sentences have been described by Menyuk (1969). For example, a *Wh* question (one using "what," "which," "where," "when") might be formulated in the following ways as development proceeds (Menyuk, 1969, p. 73):

1. Where (goes) the wheel?
2. Where the wheel (goes)?
3. Where the wheel go?
4. Where does the wheel goes?
5. Where does the wheel go?

As this example illustrates, children form their first questions by combining a *Wh* word with a primitive sentence: "Where dollie?" "Where man?" Negatives are formed by adding "no": "No break," "No do this." Later, both negative and question sentences are developed further to include a subject and predicate, and sentences such as "Where dollie is going?" "What you did buyed?" and "I no do this" appear. The child eventually learns how to rearrange words within sentences. They also learn how to mark verbs for tense. In the sentence "Where does the wheel go?" for example, "do" rather than "go" should be marked for tense. In the sentence "What did you buy," "do" should be marked for tense and "buy" should not.

Correction of Children's Ungrammatical Sentences. Sometimes adults wonder if they should correct children's grammatical errors. Some language experts say they should not because children do not understand such corrections. Gleason (1967, cited in Cazden, 1972) tells what happened when she tried to correct the grammar of a child who said "My teacher holded the baby rabbits and we patted them." The dialogue went like this:

> I asked, "Did you say your teacher held the baby rabbits?"
> She answered, "Yes."
> I then asked, "What did you say she did?"
> She answered, again, "She holded the baby rabbits and we patted them."
> "Did you say she held them tightly?" I asked.
> "No," she answered, "She holded them loosely." [Cazden, 1972, pp. 4–5]

McNeill (1966) gives an example of a more direct attempt at correction:

> Child: "Nobody don't like me."
> McNeill: "No, say 'Nobody likes me.' "
> Child: "Nobody don't like me."
>   (eight repetitions of this dialogue)
> McNeill: "No. Now listen carefully; say 'Nobody likes me.' "
> Child: "Oh! Nobody don't likes me!" [p. 69]

Most parents concentrate on talking naturally with children, trying to understand their intended meaning and assessing the truth of what is being said. This is probably for the best. This does not mean that children do not benefit from instruction in language, but rather, that instruction should involve more than correcting individual errors. The best type of instruction consists of exposure to natural, meaningful language in which the correct use of rules is constantly demonstrated. It is not useful to correct children's grammatical errors directly and adults should not do so. Developmental errors of this type will gradually be corrected by the child as he or she hears and uses more language.

Comprehension

Comprehending Words. As children grow older, they learn to use words more specifically. For example, it takes quite some time for children to understand the exact meanings of the words "cup" and "glass" (deVos, 1977, quoted in Nelson and Nelson, 1978). Three-year-olds use "glass" and "cup" almost interchangeably without considering features that adults associate exclusively with one type of container or the other. Furthermore, the use of one label or the other by three-year-olds is influenced only very slightly by the context: knowing, for example, whether the container is filled with ice water or hot cocoa. Four- and five-year-olds, on the other hand, apply the word glass to taller containers and containers filled with ice water. They consider both physical form and context in judging the term's meaning. The rules used to differentiate "glass" and "cup" seem to develop as follows:

R1: Some vessels that hold liquid are called "glass." (3 years)

R2: Tall vessels are sometimes called "glass." Vessels that hold cold drinks may be called "glass." (4–5 years)

R3: Vessels that are twice as high as they are wide are called "glass" regardless of what they hold. (6–8 years)

R4: Vessels that are twice as high as they are wide are called "glass" regardless of what they hold, but shorter vessels may be called "glass" when they hold cold drinks. (10 years) [Nelson and Nelson, 1978, p. 244]

As you can see, a mature understanding of these terms is not achieved until the child is well past the preschool years.

It takes several years to acquire a mature understanding of opposites such as "more" and "less." "More" is used correctly from the start, but "less" is used at first as if it were a synonym (Donaldson and Balfour, 1968; Holland and Palermo, 1975; Palermo, 1974). When shown pictures of trees with different numbers of apples, for example, children point to the trees with more apples even when asked to point to the one with less. Clark (1973) suggests that children completely understand neither term, at first, but they do know that both are used to indicate quantity. Because larger amounts are better indicators of quantity, children respond to both "more" and "less" by pointing to the tree with more apples. As a result, the response to the word "more" appears correct, and to the word "less," incorrect, but children do not understand the precise meaning of either term. In Clark's view, children acquire a complete understanding of "more" and "less" at the same time, at the point when they understand that quantity is relative: it can be positive (more) or negative (less). As this example illustrates, it can be very difficult to know for sure what children understand. Even their misunderstandings may be unapparent; they may get the right answer for the wrong reason.

Comprehending Sentences. The fact that a child understands a word's meaning does not necessarily mean that he or she understands how the word can be used in all grammatical constructions. For example, a child may understand the meaning of the words "promise" and "ask," but may nevertheless misinterpret the meaning of certain sentences in which these words appear. The sentence, "John promised Mary to shovel the driveway," is interpreted by five- and six-year-olds to mean that Mary, rather than John, will do the shoveling (Chomsky, 1969, p. 4). Once again the problem seems to be overgeneralization: when verbs such as "coaxed," "begged," "ordered," and "persuaded" are used, the meaning is that Mary will do the shoveling. The child inappropriately uses the same rule for the word "promise."

Misunderstandings of this sort can be very confusing. When the teacher says, "You promised your friend to share that toy," a child may assume that it is his friend who promised to share and continue to play with the toy. This could result in a scolding if the teacher thinks the child is simply refusing to do what he said he would. Adults sometimes think children are behaving badly when they actually just misunderstand what has been said.

Written Language

The teacher was reading *Where the Wild Things Are* (Sendak, 1963) to two four-year-olds in the library corner of the classroom. When she got to the pages with pictures but no print, one child asked her to turn past them, saying, "You can't read these; you have to turn back here where the words start again."

The other child objected. "No!" she said. "She has to read *all* of the pages."

"She can't read those pages," protested the first child. "They don't have words."

"Yes she can!" repeated the second child.

At this point, the teacher suggested that she talk about the pages with pictures but no words, and then begin reading where the words started again. The children accepted her compromise.

One of these children understood that a reader reads words, but the other child, like most young children, thought that it is the pictures that are read. Before they have reached even this point, children seem to think that the reader just *knows* what to say.

Learning about written language has traditionally been considered a secondary linguistic process, something children learn little or nothing about until the "primary" linguistic process, oral language acquisition, has been completed (Mattingly, 1972). It has also been claimed that oral language is natural in that it can be learned without direct instruction, whereas reading and writing must be taught (Mattingly, 1972). As the incident we just described reveals, however, even very young children understand something about written language if they are exposed to it.

Some experts now consider oral and written language acquisition to be parallel processes, and they think children are as naturally inclined to writing as they are to speaking (Doake, 1979; Goodman and Goodman 1977; F. Smith, 1974, 1977). The fact that children have more trouble learning to read than they do learning to talk is usually attributed to two factors; children's written environment is not as meaningful as their oral environment, and many adults are unaware of early reading behavior.

These researchers and educators have criticized the behavioral approach to reading, which emphasizes learning isolated skills beginning with small units of language such as sounds and letters and then moving on to words and sentences. These experts argue that children should be exposed from the beginning to language as a whole and to real reading in meaningful contexts.

The Preschool Child and Reading

Children and Storybooks. Many investigators have found that children who have been read to at home before entering school have greater success when they enter reading programs (Durkin, 1966; Sutton, 1964). This is correlational data, of course, and we cannot be sure that being read to is the cause of the later success; it may be that parents who read to their children also talk to them more, take them on more trips, or interact with them in some other way that improves reading. However, many experts believe that story reading itself contributes directly to children's increased success with reading by helping them learn about the reading process and about print.

As a parent reads to a child, the child learns how books work — where the beginning is and how one goes from page to page until the end. They learn that each book has its own story, and that the pictures in the book serve as clues to where a certain part of the story appears. In one study of children who learned to read before entering first grade, it was found that when parents read to their

Experience with storybooks is not only enjoyable for preschool children but useful in helping them learn about written language.

children often, the children learn the books by heart (Durkin, 1966). One child, Carol, had been read to by both parents since the age of two, and had heard *The Cat in the Hat* so often that she had memorized the story. Once a child has reached that point, he or she may try to match familiar parts of the story (said orally) with the words printed on the page.

Learning to read in this fashion involves much more than mimicking. Children think about reading and develop hypotheses about how it works as they did about spoken language. Among other things, they probably come to realize that words are arranged not randomly, but in terms of meaningful relationships (Smith, 1977). This is an important insight. Although we commonly think of reading as simply translating graphic symbols (letters) into phonemes (sounds), studies of skilled readers have shown that they actually use several integrated strategies (Athey, 1977; Singer, 1979). The skilled reader does not have to read every word, because he or she knows that the words are related to each other in a meaningful way. The context provides clues about what is coming next. In this manner, readers use *syntactic* clues (knowledge of language structure), *semantic* clues (knowledge of the meanings of words), and *graphophonic* clues (knowledge of symbol-sound relationship), and knowledge about the world in general. Being introduced to reading through storybooks may teach children at the outset that a variety of strategies can be used to read and that thinking about what is being read can be as useful as looking at all the graphic clues.

Storybook experience may also encourage children to correlate spoken words with print. Young children do not know that each letter represents a sound; in fact, they find segmenting speech into individual sounds very difficult. This is because the sounds represented by letters do not actually appear separately in speech. Our awareness that words are composed of different, individual sounds is an abstract concept, not a perception based on what we actually hear (McNeill and Lindig, 1973; Savin and Bever, 1970).

When children know what a sample of print says, as in a storybook they have memorized, they try to figure out how the print says it. During this process, they formulate and test hypotheses about the relationship between speech and print. For example, one three-year-old tried to read the title on the cover of the book, *Frosty the Snowman*. She moved her finger along the individual letters of the word "Frosty" as she said: "Frosty the snowman." When her finger came to the "y" she asked, "What does this one say?" As shown in Figure 18-1, the child thought not only that each letter represented a word, but that every syllable in speech was a word. She did not understand that a printed word consists of several letters, or that in English spelling each letter represents a single sound.

As Figure 18-2 illustrates, a four-year-old child understood a little more than the three-year-old, but she still lacked a complete understanding of the relationship between speech and print. She was reading a page from Eric Carle's (1979) book, *The Very Hungry Caterpillar*. This child knew that printed words consist of a collection of letters separated by spaces, but she still assumed that a single

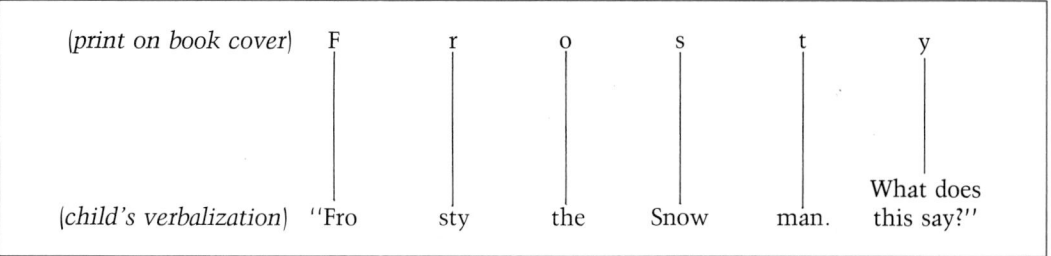

Figure 18-1

syllable in speech was always a whole word. Children who make this mistake run out of words to point to when they are confronted with polysyllabic words in the line of print. This mismatch puzzles children, and they revise their hypotheses or ask for help: "Where does it say 'hungry'?"

Children gradually learn how to recognize word boundaries in both speech and print and to match print and speech correctly. They come to understand that because words consist of collections of letters, they can be thought of as collections of sounds. When the children have this essential insight about the relationship between speech and print, learning the relationship between letters and individual sounds begins to make sense to them. It may be that story reading is useful because it provides an environment in which such insights can develop.

Other Experiences with Print. Experiences with print other than that in storybooks can also help preschool children learn about written language. For example, school-age siblings of preschoolers often teach them about reading by playing school (Durkin, 1966). This can involve using materials such as paper and pencils, chalkboards, books, and word games. The preschooler may also be assigned tasks such as copying words from the older sibling's school papers.

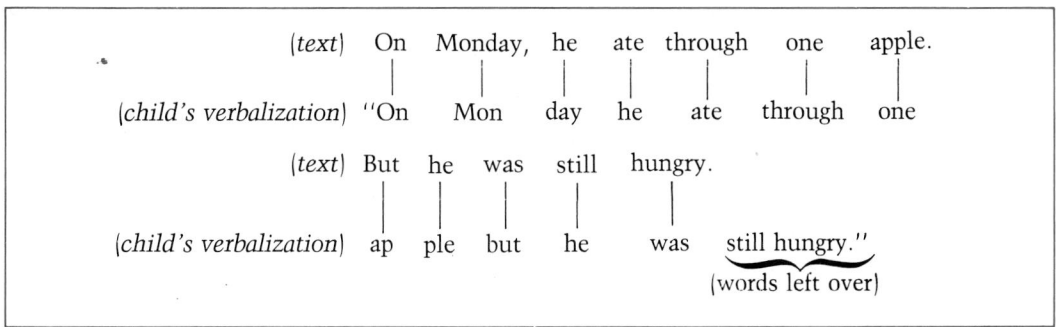

Figure 18-2

Children see print
everywhere.

Preschoolers also learn about reading from the print that surrounds them in the environment — on food containers, the television set, store fronts, billboards, cars, trucks, toys, and even clothes. Print is so prevalent in the everyday environment that researchers have wondered why not all children learn to read. This question prompted Durkin (1966) to conduct a study comparing early readers to a control group of children who did not learn to read early. She found that parental behavior seemed to be the key difference between the two groups. "What is important . . . is the presence of parents who spend time with their children; who read to them; who answer their questions and their requests for help; and who demonstrate in their own lives that reading is a rich source of relaxation, information, and contentment" (Durkin, 1966, p. 136). Print, to be understood, must be socially mediated; that is, it must be used by others in the presence of and with children so that children can see how it works.

Durkin's study revealed that parents whose children learned to read before going to school did not set out to teach their children to read. Their methods were informal and indirect; they intended merely to explain or to entertain, almost always in response to their children's requests. The children themselves were not extraordinary. "Early readers are not some unique species capable of being identified and sorted by tests. Rather, it would seem their preschool achievement in reading is the combined expression of themselves, their parents, and the kinds of environments these parents provided" (p. 110).

Parents of children who learn to read in this way often claim that their children "taught themselves to read" without being instructed. We applaud such parents for recognizing the active nature of learning, but we believe their children did learn to read through their parents' efforts. Teaching does not necessarily entail direct instruction, a process of funneling abstractions formulated by adults into children's heads. Informal teaching is much better, especially when dealing with preschool children, who have not had enough experience to comprehend other people's abstractions. At this level, the most important aspect of teaching is creating an environment in which the child can acquire knowledge at his or her own level of understanding. It is also important to interact with the learner — to read stories, respond to scribbled "letters," and ask and answer questions. In addition, parents should observe their children and listen to them carefully, so that when they are beginning to understand some aspect of the environment intuitively, they can be given direct help, perhaps in abstract form if they are ready for it. The parents of all the early readers in Durkin's study helped their children learn using methods such as these. As you can see, the children did not learn to read by themselves; they had superb help.

The Preschool Child and Writing

If you take out a pencil and paper and begin to write in the presence of a preschooler, the preschooler will probably insist on being given paper and pencil, too, and may pretend to write along with you. The child's markings might seem random and meaningless but, surprisingly, very young children have some accurate (albeit incomplete) notions about what writing is and how people do it.

Understanding the Difference Between Writing and Nonwriting. One of the first steps in learning how to write is learning to differentiate lines of writing and lines of pictures or other markings. In a study by Lavine (1977), children from three to six and a half years of age were shown visual displays of various sorts printed on cards (see Figure 18-3). Each card had only one item printed on it: one picture, or one sample of conventional writing, or one linear arrangement of units, or one multiple unit, etc. "Revolt," for example, appeared by itself on one card, as an example of conventional writing. Children were asked to sort the cards into two piles, one of writing and one of marks that were not writing. Actual writing samples were recognized as such by 80 percent of the three-year-olds, 90 percent of the four-year-olds, and 96 percent of the five-year-olds. Even when children could not name letters or words, they knew that writing was writing. Lavine's analysis of the variables used in her visual displays indicated that children first recognize writing by its linearity and variety (it has nonrepetitive units), and later, by the features of letters.

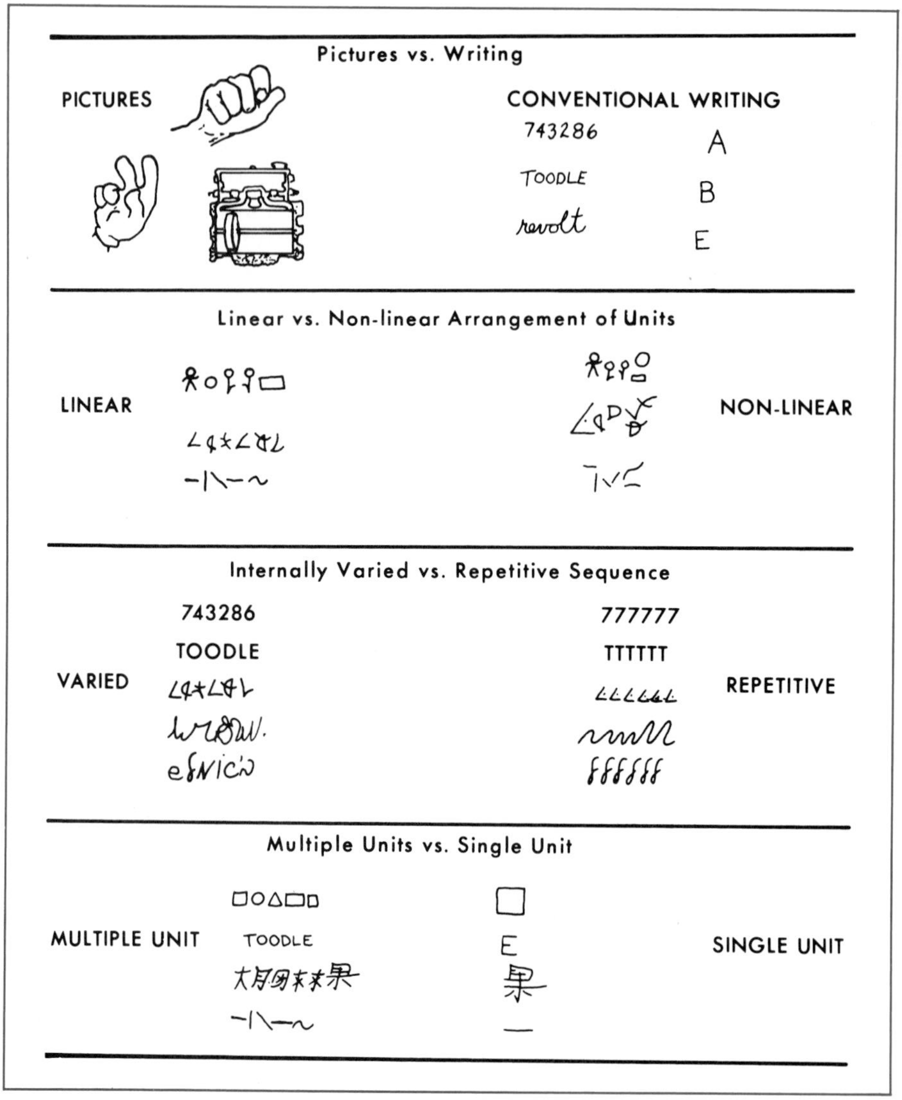

Figure 18-3. Displays contrasting categorical features and nonfeatures of writing as characterized by Lavine

Learning the Distinctive Features of Print. *Distinctive features* are the characteristics of one class that set it apart from other classes. More specifically, they are "the feature contrasts within a set of similar things. All members of the set have some of the features that distinguish this kind of thing from other kinds of things, but different members *within* the set share the features in different combinations and degrees" (Gibson and Levin, 1975, p. 15). Gibson

(1969) proposed that the distinctive features of the English alphabet include such characteristics as whether a line is straight or curved, whether curves are open or closed, and whether straight lines are diagonal or horizontal or vertical.

The first distinctive feature that children notice is whether a line is straight or curved. Round letters (O, C) and other letters with curved lines (B, P, S) are distinguished next, and then curved letters with intersections (B, R) are distinguished from curved letters without intersections (S, J). The distinction between letters with diagonal lines (K, X) and letters with vertical and horizontal lines only (H, L) is recognized very late in the developmental sequence (Gibson and Levin, 1975). Piaget's finding that children first differentiate closed and open shapes, and later differentiate among the closed shapes is consistent with Gibson's findings about distinctive features.

One distinctive feature of letters is their orientation in space. Letters such as *d* and *b* or *p* and *q* differ only in their orientation. Young children often reverse letters until they are well into the elementary grades. Why is orientation so difficult for young children to grasp?

To understand the child's problem, imagine that you are going to a cupboard to get two identical mugs to serve coffee in. There are four mugs on the shelf: (1) a tall, brown, plastic mug sitting upside-down with its handle to the left (2) a short, brown, ceramic mug, sitting upright with its handle to the right; (3) a second, tall, brown, plastic mug, sitting upright with its handle to the right, and (4) a second short, brown, ceramic mug sitting upside-down with its handle to the left.

Chances are you would select mugs 1 and 3 or mugs 2 and 4 as a pair completely ignoring whether or not the mugs were upside-down, or right-side up, or whether their handles were turned to the left or to the right. This task illustrates that the orientation of objects is not one of their distinguishing features. When children first begin to look at print, all of their previous experience has involved objects, and although they see that some letters are reversed versions of others, they do not assume that the differences matter any more than they did with the physical objects. Good teachers emphasize the different orientations of letters and point out that they are important. But even after children realize that orientation matters, it takes a long time to remember how a letter should be oriented when it is written.

The Emergence of Handwriting. Children's first "writing" emerges from their scribbling. This early writing possesses the same features that children considered print-like in the Lavine study discussed earlier.

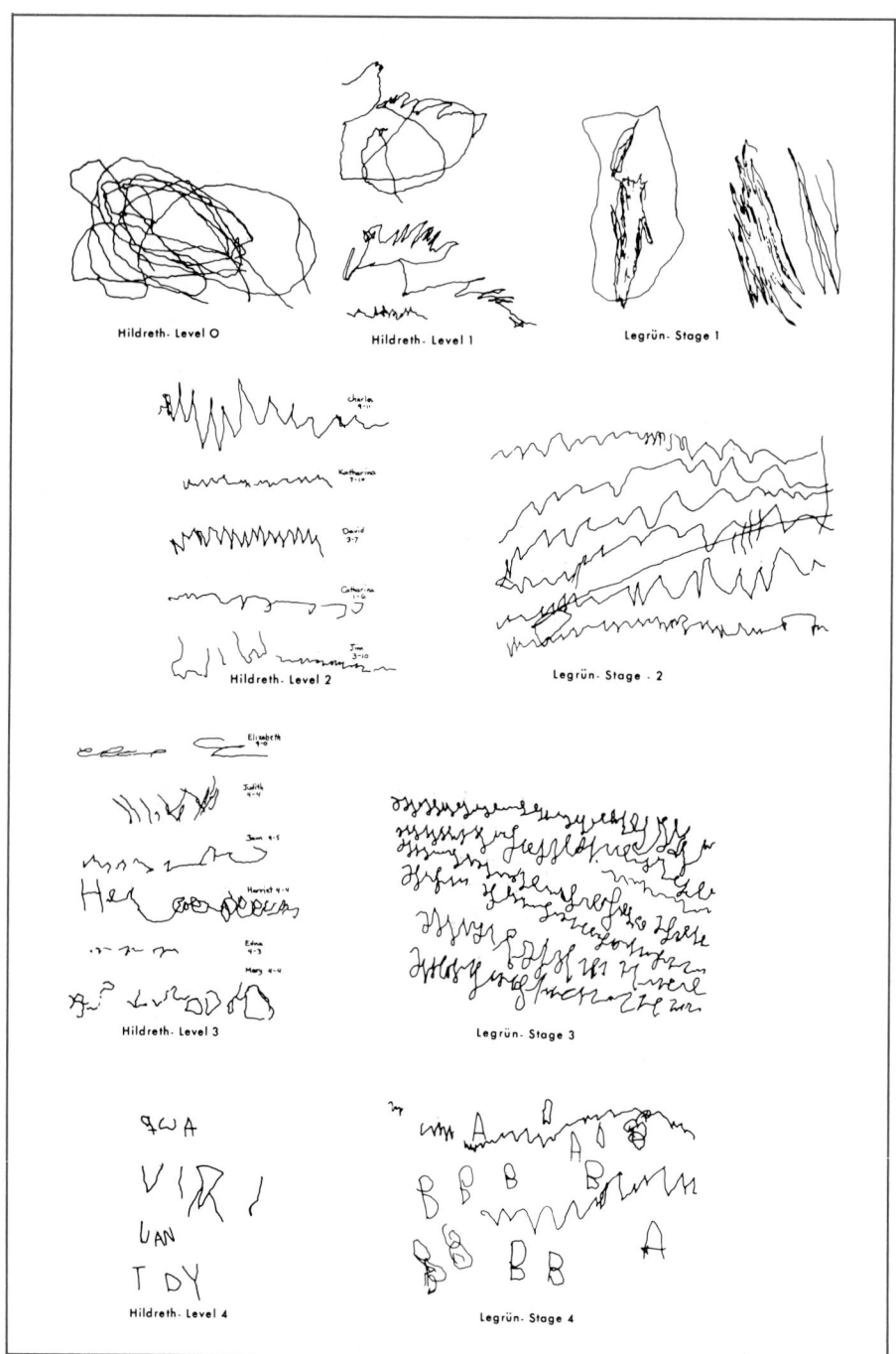

Figure 18-4. Representative samples of "writing" in its early stages of development

Two early researchers, Hildreth (1936) and Legrün (1932), found that children's scribbling passes through four stages or levels (see Figure 18-4). At the first level it has a horizontal orientation. At level 2 it becomes more linear, and by level 3 it begins to include many of the features of real letters, such as straight, curved, diagonal, and intersecting lines. At level 4 good approximations of true letters appear.

Similar observations have been made more recently. Wheeler (1971) found that the errors children make in writing letters resemble those they make in recognizing letters; that is, they involve a failure to perceive a distinctive feature of print. These errors become less frequent even when children are given no formal instruction in how to write letters. It is not surprising that children who spend their preschool years in "literate" environments have an advantage in learning to write.

Organizing Print on the Page: Writing and Concepts of Space. Children's early writing is also influenced by their concepts of space. Look at the attempt of a four-year-old to copy her name under a model in Figure 18-5. The child's rendition reflects an understanding of some topological relationships. The letters are related in terms of proximity, separation, and order. On

Figure 18-5
Name writing by Felicia, age four

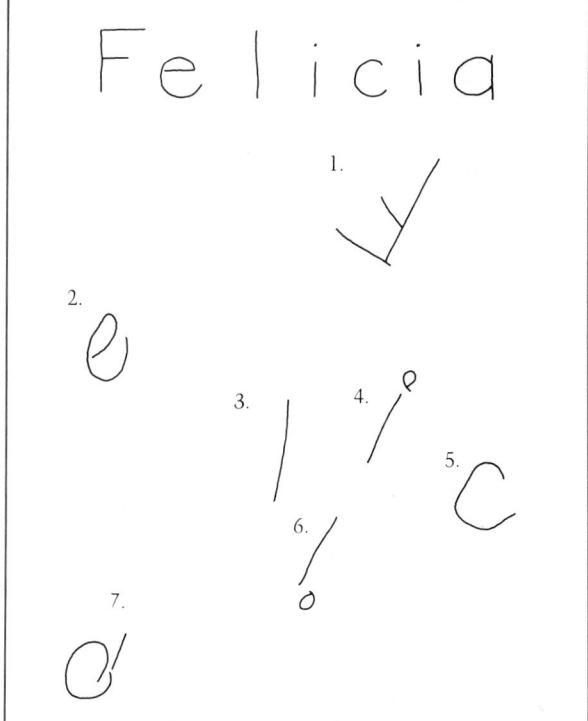

a vertical plane the *e* is located between the *F* and the *l*, and letters *l*, *i*, and *c* are placed in sequence, as are *c*, *i*, and *a*. But the child obviously lacks an understanding of Euclidean space. She wrote in several ways: from top to bottom (*F, e, and l*), from left to right (*l, i*, and *c*) and from right to left (*c, i*, and *a*). The child apparently did not understand the coordinates of space (vertical and horizontal axes), or direction. When an adult writes his name, his understanding of space permits him to create a line in his mind on which the letters are placed. The letters themselves do not make the line.

The child also lacks a concept of projective space (point of view). Various orientations are evident in the child's name: letters are reversed and written upside-down. When adults write, we adopt a particular perspective from which all letters are oriented in the same way. Because children do not understand projective space, they often write or draw from a number of perspectives.

Another example of mixed orientations in a four-year-old's name writing is shown in Figure 18-6. In this sample the child may have turned the paper around after writing the *o* and then moved from left to right when writing the second *t* and the *y*. The child did not consider that turning the paper around would mean that some letters would be upside-down in relation to other letters; they were all right-side-up when he wrote them! This four-year-old understood the topological relationships of order perfectly, but the lack of a concept of space within which objects are placed caused some confusion.

Figure 18-6
Name writing by Scotty, age four

The Preschool Child's Approach to Written Language Acquisition

As we have seen, preschool children learn about many aspects of written language. They often are not yet reading and writing in the conventional ways characteristic of older children and adults, but they are learning about print just the same. It is important to realize that children approach learning about printed language in much the same way they learn about oral language — by experiencing it and by testing out hypotheses and gradually revising them. It should be clear from our discussion that "readiness" for reading and writing does not consist merely of learning to recognize and write letters of the alphabet. Children who are "ready" to read and write in the conventional way have many more skills than these. Furthermore, they acquire even very complicated understandings about printed language without specific tutoring of the sort we typically associate with learning how to read and write. Yet experiences with print and with adults who use it are essential, just as experiences with adults who talk to them is essential if children are to learn to talk.

Summary

Verbal Language

- An important part of language learning during the preschool years is developing an understanding of morphological rules.
- Direct correction of preschool children's grammatical errors does not improve their grammar. They seem to learn language and correct their own errors simply through being exposed to meaningful communication. Some errors can be delightful; for example, preschool children often create words by overextending a rule or a word meaning. Some can be problematic; because they do not fully understand the meanings of many of the words they use or hear, preschoolers may act in such a way that parents assume they are intentionally misbehaving.

Written Language

- Preschool children have traditionally been considered too young to learn how to write, but some current experts think that these children can learn a great deal about written language if they are exposed to it. Reading to children seems to be a good way to help them learn about reading and writing.
- The reading process involves much more than simply translating written symbols into sounds.
- Preschoolers do not at first understand the difference between letters and words, and often believe every syllable spoken to be a word. They may try to figure out the relationship between spoken and written words by matching

parts of a memorized story with print on a page, and they will probably run out of print before they end their reading.

- As young children's writing emerges from their scribbling, it reveals how their understanding of the characteristics of print and the distinctive features of letters emerge.
- The last distinctive feature of letters that children come to understand is their orientation. The fact that physical objects are not changed by varying their orientations makes it difficult for children to understand that letters *do* change if their orientations are altered.

New Terms

morphological rules	**inflection**
overgeneralization of rules	**graphophonic clues**
morphemes	**distinctive features**

Selected Readings

Chukovsky, K. **From two to twelve.** *Berkeley, Calif.: University of California Press, 1968.* This is a delightful book filled with samples of children's language. It is interesting to read and provides an excellent picture of how young children talk.

Clay, M. **What did I write?** *Auckland, New Zealand: Heinemann Education Books, 1975.* Written by a New Zealand educator, this book describes the process of learning to write in a group of five-year-olds. It is loaded with samples of children's writing to illustrate every point. For those interested in a development approach to writing, this is a good place to start.

Durkin, D. **Children who read early.** *New York: Teachers College, Columbia University, 1966.* A report of Durkin's classic study on children who learned to read before they entered school. Interesting reading even for the nonresearcher.

Chapter 19

Social Development

In school one day, Amelia and JoAnn were running around a table playing a chasing game. Their teacher, when he noticed what they were doing, took them by the hand and said, "Let's stop the running. You might hurt somebody or fall down and hurt yourselves. Let's find something else to do. There's clay over at the table, or you can play in the block area or the library corner."

"Let's build with blocks!" said JoAnn. "We can make cages for the animals."

"Okay," said Amelia.

"Good idea," said the teacher as they hurried off.

As this little scene illustrates, children learn to behave the way adults in their society think they should. In our discussion of socialization here we will explain some of the basic socialization processes, including: (1) reinforcement and punishment; (2) classical conditioning; (3) verbal instruction; (4) observational learning; and (5) other cognitive processes. We will also explain how these processes are influenced by biological factors. Later in this chapter we will discuss how these socialization processes are involved in the learning of two types of socialized behavior: control of aggression and prosocial behavior, or behavior that benefits others rather than oneself.

Socialization Processes

Reinforcement and Punishment

When parents are rearing their first child, their thoughts often turn to discipline. How should the child be encouraged to develop good values? How should she be punished when she does something wrong and rewarded when she acts the way we would like? Before we can answer questions such as these, we must understand the nature of reinforcement and punishment and how they exert their influence.

Reinforcement. Let's begin by considering the following scene involving a preschool child and her father. Susan turns the knob of the TV set and watches the screen light up. She finds the consequences of her behavior interesting, and begins to turn the television on and off repeatedly. Her father hears what she is doing and comes in from another room to suggest that she choose some toys to play with outside. He plays with her briefly in the back yard, and then goes to a chair on the back porch to do some reading. From time to time, he looks over at Susan as she plays and makes a comment: "Looks like you're making some cookies with your playdough." The child plays happily for the rest of the afternoon and does not try to return to the TV.

A learning theorist would say that Susan's responses in the situation above were reinforced. *Reinforcement* is defined as providing a consequence to a response that increases the probability that the response will recur in similar situations. In the preceding example, the lighted TV screen and father's attention to play acted as reinforcers for the child. Once the child noted the interesting consequence of turning the knob, she turned it again. Having received attention from her father for playing, she continued to play.

When Susan's father commented on her cookie making, he was using positive reinforcement to encourage a particular behavior. At the same time, he was reducing the frequency of undesirable behavior that was incompatible with the reinforced response: the child could not make cookies and turn the television on and off at the same time.

Punishment. The father in the TV example showed great care and skill in his reaction to his child's behavior. Other parents might have simply punished the child for the inappropriate behavior of turning the television on and off. *Punishment* is defined as providing a consequence to a response that decreases the probability that it will recur in similar situations.

There are two general types of punishing consequences. First, stimuli can be added to the environment following a response. After a child turns on the TV, for example, a parent could yell at the child; the child would subsequently turn on the TV less frequently. Second, stimuli can be removed from the environment following the response. The stimuli that are removed are often those which previously served as positive reinforcers. Taking away a child's favorite toys or a trip to the ice cream shop, for example, might make her turn the TV on less frequently. Such positive reinforcers subtracted from the environment in punishment are described as *response costs* (Reese and Lipsitt, 1970). One kind of removal of positive reinforcement sometimes used in preschool classrooms is that of removing the child from the classroom and seating her in an isolated place. Assuming that the classroom is an environment with a number of positive reinforcers, taking the child from the classroom following misbehavior should punish the misbehavior. Punishment that takes the form of isolating the child by removing her briefly from an environment of positive reinforcement is called *time out from positive reinforcement.*

There is a third way to reduce inappropriate behavior. We could unplug the TV set so that turning the knob did not result in an interesting consequence. This process, known as *extinction*, usually stops any undesirable behavior from occurring.

Problems with the Use of Punishment. There is evidence that punishment may do more harm than good. Punishment may be reinforcing rather than punishing. If a consequence intended to be negative is perceived as being positive it may increase rather than decrease inappropriate behavior. It is sometimes difficult, however, to know whether a particular consequence will be reinforcing or punishing.

Consider the following example of how consequences intended as punishment can backfire: (1) A child approaches the TV set and turns the dial. (2) The father intervenes, telling the child "No!" (3) The child stops playing with the dial; the father returns to his book. (4) The child again turns the TV dial, but this time his father does not notice right away. (5) Father notices again and intervenes, once more telling the child "No!" (6) Father returns to the book; the child begins to play with toys. (7) The child approaches the TV, turning to look at his father; father looks back at the child; the child smiles and reaches for the dial. (8) Father intervenes, says "No!" picks the child up, and puts him down in a different part of the room. "This is *fun*," the child thinks. "When I go to the TV set, I bet Dad will look at me, talk to me, and then come over and carry me across the room." As you can see, the child is no longer approaching the TV because it is interesting, but because he wants his father's attention. After a while, the father may provide a more punishing consequence: he may spank the child or make him stay in his room. The class "clown" is often a child who can get attention only by misbehaving.

Punishment can also cause problems by interfering with teaching the child appropriate behavior. Both the pain caused by physical punishment and the violation of positive expectations caused by time out from reinforcement are distressing to the child. This distress can interfere with attempts to explain why a behavior is inappropriate or what one should do when one makes an error (indicate one's true intent or make restitution, for example). The period following inappropriate behavior is often a unique opportunity for instruction, the effects of which may generalize to other situations. Good opportunities to help children learn are wasted if a child is punished when an explanation might reduce the inappropriate behavior just as well.

Punishment may also reduce exploration and initiative, especially if it comes without warning. A child in a new situation must be given an opportunity to find out what behaviors are considered inappropriate. Children who are punished for behaviors they do not yet know are wrong may learn that the only way to avoid punishment is to avoid new situations altogether. As a result they may become timid, hesitant, and fearful.

Another problem with punishment is that it can create hostility and resentment and make the person administering it an aversive stimulus. This is especially true if the child regards the punishment as harsh, unnecessary, or motivated by anger rather than concern for his or her well-being. This can have a devastating effect on the warmth and responsiveness of parent-child interactions. The destruction of responsive interactions reduces the child's motivation to imitate the parent's otherwise socialized behavior and lowers the reinforcement value of the parent's other actions.

The most serious problem with punishment is that it can lead to child abuse. If physical punishment works, it can reinforce the parent for hitting. This is especially probable when punishment is repeatedly so severe that the parent becomes an aversive stimulus, in which case positive reinforcement of the child's appropriate behavior becomes less effective. This can begin a vicious circle; the parent or teacher begins to regard punishment as the only way to change the child's behavior because it is the only thing that seems to work. Such punishment can become so severe that it constitutes *child abuse*, which is defined as intentional acts of physical force or of omission of care on the part of a parent or caretaker interacting with a child, aimed at hurting, injuring, or destroying that child (Gil, 1970). In a well-known study by Gil (1970), many of the abusive parents interviewed indicated that their acts of abuse began as physical punishment, which they simply took too far. As a result, Gil stressed that the first step in eliminating child abuse is eliminating the use of such physical force with children (1970, 1971).

Finally, physical punishment provides the child with an aggressive model of behavior. A heavily documented positive correlation has been found between parents' use of physical punishment and children's aggressive behavior (Eron, Walder, and Lefkowitz, 1971). Once again the evidence is correlational, so we cannot assume that parental aggression causes children to be aggressive. Perhaps the correlation exists because aggressive children do not respond to reinforcement or other less aversive disciplinary techniques, which forces parents to use physical punishment as a last resort. But the correlation is consistent with the finding that a great deal of aggression can be learned by imitation.

Classical Conditioning

Although it has sometimes received little attention, classical conditioning may also be an important socialization process (Brown, 1965). The beginnings of *empathy*, the ability to feel the way someone else feels, can be explained in terms of classical conditioning principles (Hoffman, 1976). When young children experience pain, the conditions associated with the pain, including crying, become conditioned stimuli which can themselves cause a conditioned response. When another child cries with pain, the cry is thought to elicit the conditioned negative emotional response, similar to pain, in the observer. Of course, cognitive processes like the ability to label one's emotions or to break from one's egocentric point of view and assume another person's view also play a part in a complex emotion like empathy as the child gets older (Hoffman, 1976; Schacter and Singer, 1962).

There is little objective data available about emotional responses in everyday situations, but perhaps classical conditioning plays a part in producing our emotional and other individual reactions to people and events as we are growing up.

Verbal Instruction

As everybody knows, the quickest way to give children some idea of appropriate and inappropriate behaviors and their consequences is to tell them. This can not only discourage undesirable behavior, it can of course be used to teach and encourage positive alternatives.

One situation in which verbal instruction is helpful is when children must resist an immediate reward to get a larger reward later, as in this example: A child enters the kitchen as the parent is preparing dinner and asks for something to eat. The child's mother says that eating now would spoil the child's appetite, and dinner is almost ready. The child complains a bit, but her mother suggests that she go work on her new puzzle while she waits.

Several studies have confirmed that the mother's technique is a good one. Mischel and Ebbeson (1970) observed that those children who could resist small immediate rewards to achieve large, delayed rewards, were able to resist focusing attention on either reward for longer periods than other children. Instead of looking at the rewards in front of them, they did everything from covering their eyes to making up games with their hands and feet. One child even attempted to fall asleep, and succeeded! In a second study children were helped to delay taking rewards such as pretzels and marshmallows by being told to think about the pretzel sticks as little brown logs and the marshmallows as white cotton balls or clouds (Mischel and Baker, 1975). Apparently, children can be diverted from taking immediate rewards by telling them to think about, play with, or do practically anything else. These studies also suggest that, in many common situations, the best procedure of all is simply to remove the temptation.

Verbal instruction can help children delay rewards.

Verbal instruction can be helpful in other ways, too. Though many prescriptions for personality and behavior change emphasize the use of imitation and reinforcement, the most effective techniques combine these with direct instruction. You may recall from our earlier description of modeling (Chapter 15) that children must pay attention to all of the relevant aspects of a model if they are to imitate behavior successfully. Verbal instruction can be used to draw children's attention to important details of the model's behavior. Direct prompting can also be used to help children learn which behaviors will be reinforced (Combs and Slaby, 1977), and explanations of punishment can dramatically increase its effectiveness (Parke, 1972).

But if verbal instruction is to enhance modeling and reinforcement, it must be consistent with actions. When adults are teaching children, actions speak louder than words.

Observational Learning

Some behaviors cannot be learned efficiently through reinforcement or verbalization alone. Children learn many of the ways of society by observing others. Each of the major theories of child development has given us a theory of how and why observational learning occurs. We will consider modeling explanations, which come from learning theory, and identification, which is derived from Freud's psychoanalytic theory.

Imitation and Modeling. Actually, the first explanation of the role of learning in imitation emphasized reinforcement. Children were thought to repeat behaviors they had observed; those which were reinforced continued to be performed, whereas those which were not reinforced dropped out.

This early view of observational learning was criticized by Albert Bandura, a social learning theorist, who claimed that reinforcement as a learning mechanism is simply too inefficient to account for children's observational learning. Children do not stumble onto behaviors one at a time and repeat them simply because they are reinforced. According to Bandura, imitation of a model depends on several processes.

First, the child must *attend* to the behavior to be modeled. Aspects of the behavior that go unnoticed will not be modeled. Second, children must *retain* a model's actions if they are to imitate them. Retention is improved when important aspects of the modeled actions are verbalized (Meichenbaum, 1977), and when the observer tries to teach the actions observed to someone else (Rosenhan, 1969, 1972; Rosenhan and White, 1967). Retention is also influenced by cognitive development and the ability to use symbols: children can copy (or accommodate to) a model only when they can understand the behavior. An adult could model shoe tying to a three-year-old all day, but the child would probably be unable to perform the actions because they involve concepts of space such as enclosure and continuity that the child does not understand.

Third, the child must be able to *reproduce* the behavior motorically. In the Azrin and Fox toilet training procedure, mentioned in Chapter 15, the child's sphincter muscles must be mature before he or she can imitate the doll.

Finally, there must be *incentive conditions* to motivate the child's imitation. These incentives can be of several types. Actions may be imitated because they are interesting or intrinsically rewarding, or because the model was rewarded or punished.

In considering the effects of the reinforcement or punishment of the model, we must distinguish between the performance and the acquisition of the modeled behavior. Children apparently acquire modeled behaviors whether or not the model receives reinforcement. In an important study by Bandura (1965a), preschoolers watched an aggressive adult model, "Rocky," beating up a large Bobo doll. Afterward, Rocky was (1) given candy and 7-Up, (2) spanked, or (3) neither punished nor rewarded. The children who saw the model punished later performed fewer of the aggressive acts than those who saw the model receive rewards or no response. But even these children had acquired Rocky's response: When they were offered rewards for "showing what Rocky did," they modeled the aggression at the same high level as those who had seen the model receive a reward or no consequences. They had apparently acquired the response just as the other groups did, but they did not perform it until they were rewarded for doing so.

Identification. Unlike the behaviorists, Freud developed the construct of identification to explain how children come to be like their same-sex parent. During the phallic stage of psychosexual development, boys compete with their fathers for their mother's attention. This creates what Freud called the Oedipal conflict. The little boy even contemplates killing his father, but because this is too frightening, he decides instead to become like his father — to adopt many of his behaviors, attitudes, and beliefs. It is this process that Freud labeled *identification*.

Freud's explanation of how little girls identify with their mothers was more circuitous than his explanation for little boys, because girls' first love object was assumed to be their mother. However, the little girl was also faced with resolving conflicts about competing with the same-sex parent for the attention of the opposite-sex parent. The competition begins presumably because the little girl blames her lack of a penis on her mother. But her desire for a penis, and thus her positive envy of her father, leads to concern that her mother will reject her. This fear, according to Freud, leads to identification with the mother so that her love can be retained. This conflict was called the Electra complex by Freud.

Learning theorists did not argue the obvious fact that children usually take on the behaviors of the same-sex parent, but they disagreed with the psychoanalytic interpretation of how and why this occurred. As we have seen, they developed explanations based on modeling and the principles of reinforcement.

Other Cognitive Processes

A child's actions in a given situation are influenced not only by the socialization processes, but by the child's level of understanding. For example, even when children have been encouraged and reinforced for helping in the past they are unlikely to help others if they do not understand that help is needed or how they might offer help.

Changes in children's social cognition (their understanding of social situations) are related to their general intellectual development. As children become less egocentric, for example, they are better able to understand other people's problems and feelings; as a result they are likely to respond in a socially appropriate manner. (We will discuss changes in social cognition in detail in Part VI.)

Biological Factors and Socialization Processes

The socialization process is actually affected by a complicated series of interactions between environmental factors, a child's genetic inheritance, and other biological events. Biological characteristics can exert their influence in many different ways, some of them obvious, others very subtle. Genetic problems or prenatal environmental problems can impair intelligence or the ability to communicate. The socialization process is more difficult, for example, for children who are deaf or blind. Heredity also influences a child's temperament (Thomas and Chess, 1977), which affects parental reactions such as responsiveness and the extent to which a child is rewarded or punished. These factors, in turn, influence the extent to which children identify with their parents or respond to intended reinforcement.

We do not mean to suggest that behavior is determined by biology alone; it is not. Biology does influence behavior, but only indirectly: it influences socialization, and socialization affects behavior. This indirect relationship is sometimes misunderstood even by social scientists. For example, some investigators (Glueck and Glueck, 1950; Sheldon, Hartle, and McDermott, 1949) have reported a relationship between a muscular body build and aggressive behavior. They did not point out, however, that possessing a muscular physique increases the probability that physically aggressive responses will be reinforced, or at least not punished by the victim (Bandura and Walters, 1963). Similarly, the behavior of Down's syndrome children may be caused by what we expect of them as much as by the physical effects of retardation. In the same way, the differences in the behavior of boys and girls may be due, not to innate predisposition, but to adults' reactions. (There are instances in which biology may play a major role in determining behavior, such as in the case of the pervasive developmental disorders.)

FOCUS: Pervasive Developmental Disorders

Pervasive developmental disorder is a term introduced by the most recent version of the American Psychiatric Association's Diagnostic and Statistical Manual of Mental Disorders (DSM III), the standard reference book on mental disorders. The term refers to *infantile autism*, which occurs before age two and one-half, and *child onset pervasive developmental disorder*, which occurs after this age. Both include a number of severe disturbances in areas of psychological functioning, including social skills, language use, and attention to and understanding of the world around us (American Psychiatric Association, 1980).

In the past, infantile autism and child onset pervasive developmental disorder were commonly called childhood psychoses. Because a psychosis is a disorder reflecting lack of appropriate contact with reality, this term was too vague to convey much meaning (Ross, 1980). These disorders have also been referred to as variations of childhood schizophrenia. However, they are now differentiated from schizophrenia since that disorder is characterized by hallucinations, delusions (poorly systematized false beliefs), or extreme disturbances in thought or logic (American Psychiatric Association, 1980), and these are seldom seen in children in the form shown by schizophrenic adults. In addition, schizophrenia is generally first seen in the stressful adolescent and early adult years, not in childhood.

(continued on following page)

FOCUS *(continued)*

Infantile autism. Infantile autism is characterized by (1) onset before age two and a half, (2) lack of responsiveness to people, (3) deficiencies in speech and language, and (4) bizarre responses to the environment, such as a preoccupation with twirling objects.

In its original sense, "autism" referred to the normal self-centered thinking thought to take place in infancy. This autism is associated with a lack of responsiveness to adults. Parents often report that their first indication of something wrong with their child was the child's failing to make the continuous eye contact at a few months of age as expected, or arching his body to avoid being held. However, autistic children frequently begin to differentiate themselves most clearly from other children by their deficits in language development. Frequently there is no language at all, or there may be peculiar speech such as immediate parroting of what was said by others, or reversal of the pronouns "me" and "you."

Childhood onset pervasive developmental disorder. There is also a disorder of social relationships, though in some ways it is not quite as extreme as autism. There is lack of appropriate emotional responsiveness (lack of laughter or crying). As in infantile autism, there may be repetitive motor movements such as flickering fingers or waving the arms inappropriately. However, there may be more eye contact than in autism, and frequently there is excessive clinging to adults. Bizarre behavior rather unique to this disorder includes sudden excessive anxiety in response to everyday situations as well as unexplained rage reactions.

Etiology and Prognosis

There has been a long-standing debate as to whether schizophrenia and the pervasive developmental disorders are caused by genetics or environment. Some experts believe that organic dysfunction is central to these disorders, for example, that they are caused by a genetic vulnerability that is activated by a biological crisis, such as infection or damage prenatally, at birth, or in infancy (Bender, 1961). Some psychoanalytic writers, on the other hand, believe that the primary cause is an unresponsive or confusing mother. Several writers think that biological vulnerability, early physiological problems, parental psychopathology, and family stress all contribute to various forms of schizophrenia. Most experts believe that the etiology of infantile autism is different than that of schizophrenia or childhood onset pervasive developmental disorder. Prenatal infection, encephalitis, and meningitis contribute to autism, and biological and genetic factors seem to be especially important, too.

The future for children with these disorders is poor. Most are unable to lead independent lives or to function in school or work in adolescence and adulthood (Lotter, 1978). Behavioral techniques have succeeded in reducing self-stimulation and increasing appropriate speech and social behavior, although spontaneous use of appropriate language in new situations is often difficult for autistic children. Gains, particularly in the latter group, require consistent and long-term reinforcement in order to be maintained (Lovas, Koegel, Simmons, and Long, 1973).

Aggression and Its Control

All of the processes we have discussed play a part in the socialization of preschoolers. One of the most important goals of such socialization is the control of aggression.

During the preschool years children learn how to deal with their anger and aggressiveness in socially acceptable ways. The aggressive behavior of most children peaks when they are two or three years old and declines thereafter (Green, 1933). The drop in *instrumental aggression* — aggression intended to gain some object or privilege — is especially dramatic.

Observational Learning and Aggression

Bandura's important studies clearly demonstrated that children can learn aggressive responses simply through observing an aggressive model. Observation of aggression also influences whether or not children will act aggressively in a given situation (Bandura and Walters, 1963). Even when a model is not reinforced for aggression, the child may learn the response and be aggressive when he or she thinks it will lead to reinforcement. These studies have obvious implications for how aggression may be learned from aggressive friends and family members. In addition, the ease with which children imitate models acting aggressively in films and cartoons suggests that aggression can be learned from violence seen on television.

TV and Reduced Social Interaction with Good Models. Preschool children watch an average of four to five hours of television each day (Friedrich and Stein, 1973; Lyle and Hoffman, 1972). This has an enormous effect on socialization, both directly and indirectly. Indirectly, television can affect the child's intellectual and interpersonal behavior (Winn, 1977). Before TV, parents had to keep one eye on their child as they went about their work. This not only kept the child out of danger, but it familiarized parents with his interests and activities, which enabled them to offer new ideas for the child's play. A study by White and Watts (1973) indicated that behavior of this sort was characteristic of the parents of competent first-graders.

This is only one of many social interactions that has decreased because of television. Social contacts with adults other than parents are less frequent than formerly. Visits and social gatherings both at home and elsewhere, as well as conversation in general, have given way to the television (Liebert and Poulos, 1976). This, in turn, may have led to fewer opportunities for children to observe models of good behavior.

TV and Aggressive Models. Perhaps the greatest cause for concern, however, is the number of violent incidents seen on television. Though the numbers fluctuate somewhat, Gerbner (1972) reported that the average prime-time hour contained eight violent incidents, and the average hour of cartoons, seventeen. It

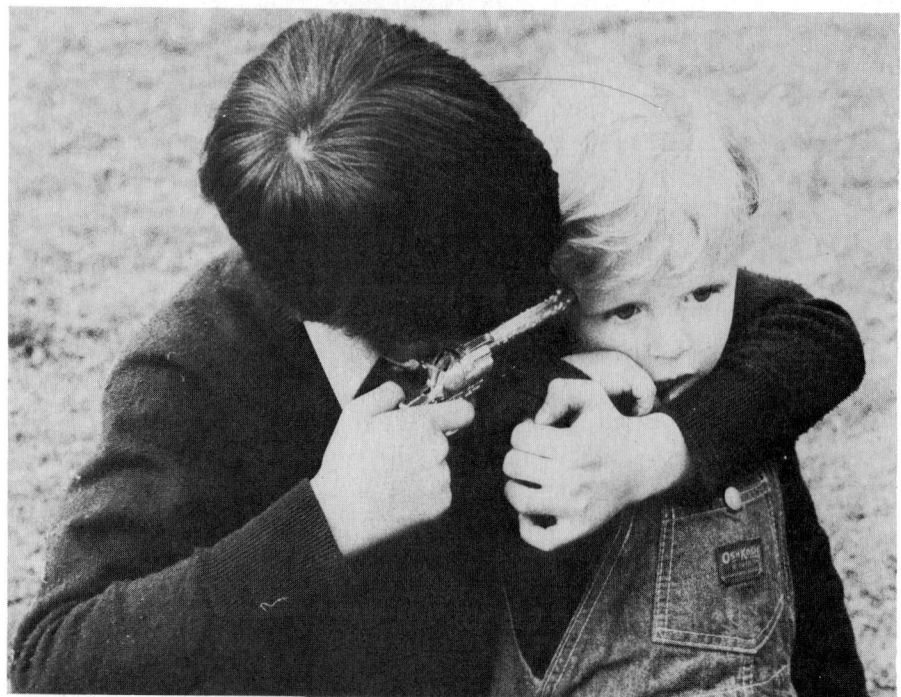

"Don't move or I'll shoot!" Children model the violence they see on television.

was estimated in the mid-1960s that the average child watches the violent destruction of more than 13,000 persons on TV between the ages of five and fifteen (National Association for Better Radio and Television, 1964).

But what is the relationship between watching aggression on TV and developing aggressive behavior? A committee reporting to the Surgeon General of the United States (*Television and growing up: The impact of televised violence,* 1972) concluded that exposure to TV violence is correlated slightly with aggressive behavior in deviant children. Critics contend that television's influence is much stronger, however, arguing that the conclusions were biased because some committee members were associated with the broadcast industry (Liebert, Neale, and Davidson, 1973). This reflects the general state of affairs concerning the effects of TV violence; most investigators agree that it has some influence but disagree about the extent of the influence.

Correlational studies have shown that viewing aggressive models on TV is associated with aggressive behavior (Chaffee, 1972). But the most incriminating evidence comes from experimental studies showing a causal relation between TV violence and viewer aggression.

In an ambitious study of causality, Friedrich and Stein (1973) showed nursery school children twenty-minute television programs of three types: aggressive cartoons such as "Batman" and "Superman," neutral films, and prosocial programs such as "Mister Roger's Neighborhood." The children were divided into three groups, each of which watched only one type of program daily for four weeks. During this time the experimenters observed the preschoolers' behavior each day during free play; baseline data were collected before TV viewing began. Among the children who were initially above average in interpersonal aggression, those who watched aggressive programs showed more interpersonal aggression than those who watched the other programs. The group that saw the aggressive cartoons showed less self-control in waiting for materials or adult attention than the other groups, regardless of their initial level of aggressiveness. The same group was also less obedient to rules.

Less elaborate studies have shown increases in aggression in young children during free play immediately after viewing only one violent TV program (Ellis and Sekyra, 1972). In one study children were shown either a violent sequence from the TV series "The Untouchables" or a neutral athletic competition. Those who had watched the violence were more willing to hurt other children by heating a handle that they believed a child was touching. No child was actually hurt, of course (Liebert and Baron, 1972).

In many television shows the "bad guy" is punished after the last commercial to discourage the modeling of negative behavior, but there is little evidence that this inhibits aggression in children. This is especially true of very young children, whose cognitive abilities are not well enough developed for them to understand the motives and consequences of the violence (Leifer and Roberts, 1972). Even when preschoolers are told that the violence is bad, their imitation of aggression may not be reduced. Studies in which young children watched television with either an adult who criticized the violent character's behavior or with an adult whose response was neutral have shown that adult criticism does not affect aggression levels. All young children showed equal aggression, despite the fact that children who watched with critical adults were more critical in their verbal disapproval of the TV viewing. The aggression of ten-year-olds, however, was affected by the criticisms of adult observers. It appears that the watchful eye of a parent who responds with disapproval to TV violence observed by his or her preschooler may be too late to counter negative effects.

Finally, even if an understanding of the motivation of "bad guys" and what happens to them did reduce imitation of their behavior, there is still plenty of violent behavior by the "good guys" to be modeled. Television heroes tend to use violent means to attain their prosocial ends. In this regard, Liebert and Poulos (1976) in their review of the effects of TV quote Bryan and Schwartz (1971) in concluding that "the aggressive hero who verbalizes socially sanctioned norms may well be teaching the observer how to be brutal and what to verbalize."

TV and Desensitization to Violence. Using TV violence as an electronic babysitter has a final, less visible, consequence. It appears to change the kind of babysitters its charges will in turn become, making them more permissive of violence in others. In one study, third- and fourth-graders shown a violent cowboy movie were less likely than those shown a nonviolent film to seek adult help, as instructed, when younger children they were to observe began to fight (Drabman and Thomas, 1974). These desensitizing effects of observing violence are similar to correlations found by Cline, Croft, and Corrier (1972). They showed that both five- and twelve-year-old boys who were high users of TV showed less emotional reactivity (measured by pulse amplitude and other physiological signs of arousal) to violence observed on film than low users.

The Catharsis Theory. It may surprise you, but it has been suggested that watching filmed violence has some positive effects. Psychoanalytic writers and some ethologists (for example, Lorenz, 1966) believe that watching aggression releases pent-up instincts or drives that might otherwise be expressed in action. This is known as the *catharsis theory* of eliminating interpersonal aggression. This theory has encouraged teachers to allow children to act aggressively toward an inanimate object such as a punching bag or woodworking bench to reduce aggressive behavior toward their peers. Unfortunately, the research evidence is overwhelmingly against the catharsis theory (Bandura, 1973; Berkowitz, 1973). In fact, it appears that children given toy guns and themes for aggressive play are subsequently more aggressive in other forms of play and toward each other (Berkowitz, 1973). In summary, the research suggests that

> "for *some* children under *some* conditions, viewing televised violence may enable the child to discharge some of his or her aggressive feelings, [but] for *many* children under *many* circumstances, viewing aggression on television leads to an increase in aggressive feelings, attitudes, and behavior" (Murray, 1980, p. 38).

Some Final Comments About TV and Aggression. With all of this evidence about the effects of TV violence on children, you might wonder why something more is not done to eliminate violence from television. There is continuing debate about this issue.

Some people believe that it is parents' responsibility to monitor their children's television viewing and that much of the violence seen by children occurs on adult programs not intended for children in the first place. Other arguments about what should be done stem from conflicting data in the research itself. We have stressed in our discussion some of the most compelling research on the detrimental effects of televised violence. However, not all studies have produced results showing that television viewing is related to post-viewing increases in aggression. In addition, the problems we discussed in Chapter 2 about not being able to assume causation from correlational research or to generalize results obtained in contrived settings such as experimental laboratories to real life, have plagued some of the research studies on the effects of televised violence. Those who are against changes in the content of television programs, for whatever reason, cite these problems and conflicting data to prove their case. Furthermore, conflicting values among citizens of a country as large and diverse as ours make it difficult to arrive at a consensus even if everyone could agree about the research data. There are those who deplore censorship for whatever reason, but there are others who would welcome it in spite of some possible negative consequences.

For all these reasons, the debate about television and violence is likely to continue. We can also expect another review of the research on this subject from the U.S. Surgeon General (Pearl, Bouthilet, and Lazar, in press), and continued discussion about its implications.

Reinforcement, Punishment, and Aggression

The extent to which children are reinforced or punished for aggression influences whether they learn to be aggressive or nonaggressive.

Reinforcement. In addition to material rewards, children's aggression sometimes receives *intrinsic reinforcement*. For example, children can often produce many novel changes in the environment with just a little aggression: children cry and run away, leaving the aggressor to play with the toys left behind; objects fly across the room and shatter when they land; adults run and scream excitedly. Aggression may be one of the few means of causing a little excitement when the environment is otherwise boring (Roedell, Slaby, and Robinson, 1977).

Aggression sometimes increases when children are initially formed into a group. This is apparently because aggression is reinforced in such situations. In a study of preschool children's free play, Patterson, Litmann, and Bricker (1967) found that 80 percent of children's aggressive responses were rewarded by victims giving up objects or leaving the field. These rewards made the aggressor more likely to aggress again. Children who were not aggressive at the beginning of the year became more aggressive if they were frequent victims of aggression: they modeled aggression to defend themselves. If their defensive aggression was successful, they began to use aggression themselves. Only initially nonagressive children who were unsuccessful in their first attempts at defensive aggression did not increase their aggression.

Prevention and Intervention. Aggressive behavior in a classroom of preschoolers can quickly get out of hand if the teacher does not prevent it. Planning the environment can be very important. It is a mistake to provide only one of each toy, for example. The waiting time for a turn in a group of eighteen or twenty children is just too long, and children almost inevitably use aggression to get toys they want. Most nursery schools provide several toys of each type. (Note that asking children to wait their turn does not help them learn to share when the waiting time is excessive.)

Even when several toys of every type available are not being used, a child will sometimes try to take a toy from another child. When young preschoolers see a desired toy in the hand of another child, they do not always think of the alternatives to grabbing it. This is a good opportunity for teacher intervention. The toy must be given back to the child who was originally playing with it, and the teacher must explain to the other child that "toys are not to be taken from other people when they are playing with them." Then the child should be shown some alternatives to aggressive behavior. If identical items are available, the teacher can show them to the child and explain that it is a good idea to check there first. If there is only one of a particular type of toy, the teacher can help the aggressor ask the other child to give her the toy when she is done with it, and then help the child find something to do in the meantime. Teacher intervention of this sort keeps aggression from being reinforced with the desired object and develops alternatives to aggression. In addition, appropriate behavior is likely to be rein-

Children need help in learning to share.

forced when the child is immediately involved in something new. This reinforcement can be either intrinsic — that is, coming from within the child, as when the child finds the new activity rewarding — or extrinsic — coming from outside the child, as when the teacher praises the child's appropriate behavior.

Aggression is most common in classrooms where there are (1) few things to do, (2) few items in multiple sets, and (3) few instances of teacher intervention to head off trouble before it occurs or to follow through after it happens. In poorly run classrooms acts of aggression may go unnoticed unless the victim protests. When there is a protest, the teachers are likely to punish the child by yelling at him or making him sit by himself. Teachers rarely suggest alternatives to aggression in advance or help a child make arrangements with another child to play together or transfer a toy at an agreed-on time.

Teachers should be aware that intervention at the time of aggression can reinforce a child for aggression. Some children act aggressively to get a teacher's attention. If a teacher thinks this is occurring, the victim rather than the aggressor should be given attention, and the teacher should make a special effort to involve the child in prosocial interactions *before* he or she has a chance to begin behaving badly. For example, the teacher might greet the child warmly when he or she arrives for the day and casually ask what the child would like to play with. If the toy mentioned is already being used, the teacher can offer alternatives: "Oh, I see that Brian is playing with one hammer, let's see if we can find the other one," or "Brian is playing with the hammer right now. Let's ask him if he will be sure to let you know when he's finished with it. Then we'll see what else we can find to do while you wait." In this manner the child gets off to a good start and the teacher is more likely to be able to provide attention for prosocial behavior.

Finally teachers should not expect a quick, dramatic response from most children. As with other types of learning, learning alternatives to aggression takes time. In our experience, intervention to prevent aggression and suggestions of acceptable alternatives must be made for a number of weeks before children begin consistently to use the alternatives themselves.

Punishment. You may have noticed that we have not suggested using punishment to change children's aggressive behavior. We feel that punishment is the least effective strategy for helping children become nonaggressive. If aggression continues after reinforcement for good behavior is provided, however, we suggest the use of time out from positive reinforcement. For example, suppose a child working at an easel slams her paintbrush hard against the paper so that paint spatters all over her and the floor. If the child continues to slam the brush after being told once that such behavior is unacceptable because it damages the brush and gets paint all over everything, she can be quietly asked to leave the easel and sit in a chair away from the activities for a short time.

Teachers sometimes use time out inappropriately. Denying a child the opportunity to do something planned for later in the day deprives the child of any incentive to behave appropriately. If the activity is something especially enjoyable, the child may become so frustrated that even more aggression and emotional behavior result. To diminish the likelihood that this will happen, the teacher should make it clear when a privilege is introduced that it is contingent on certain behaviors, which should be specified. This is much better than withdrawing a privilege the child has routinely expected. Children should be told, for example, that their being allowed to go on a trip is contingent on other behaviors or that going on future trips is contingent on their good behavior on the first trip. In addition, removal of positive reinforcement that is relevant to the child's behavior is likely to be more effective than removal of positive reinforcement that is unrelated.

We agree with those who suggest that the minimum removal of privileges or rewards — known as the minimum *response cost* — be used when punishment is necessary (Roedell, Slaby, and Robinson, 1977). For example, to make your point it may be necessary only to insist that the child who is slamming the brush at the easel stop painting and find something else to do. This procedure would not technically be time out from reinforcement (the child can do something else that is reinforcing), but it may nevertheless be effective because the child is not allowed to do what he or she wanted to do. Minimum response cost may be more effective than more severe punishment because it minimizes frustration and may actually increase identification with positive standards (Lepper, 1973).

Cognition and Aggression

A young preschooler whose block building is knocked down may retaliate with hitting. Older children, however, are more likely to judge the other person's intentions rather than the damage alone. An older child might still be upset, but he woull be less likely to hit the other child because he would be able to think differently about the situation.

Teachers can help reduce aggression resulting from a limited understanding of intentions by clarifying what the child who caused the damage intended to do. The teacher might also help the child rebuild the block structure or suggest that the child who knocked the blocks down help.

Cognitive processes also influence aggression in other ways. Because their cognitive development is incomplete, young children have a limited ability to generate alternative behaviors, and this can lead to trouble. For example, suppose several children are playing house and Jennifer wishes to join them. When she offers to be the mother, Ann protests: "We already have a mother. Get out. You can't play!" Jennifer doesn't like being rejected: "I can so play here," she says, raising her hand to hit Ann. At this point, an alert teacher enters the scene and says, "Jennifer, it looks like there's already a mother in this family. Could you be the aunt, or the mother who lives next door and comes to visit?" Ann says, "Yeah, you be the mother from next door. Get a baby."

A number of studies indicate that instruction about alternatives does decrease aggression. In a study conducted some time ago, preschool children who discussed alternative solutions to conflicts and watched adults demonstrate alternatives with dolls later showed less aggression and more cooperation in their play (Chittenden, 1942). In a more recent study (Spivack and Shure, 1974), children who had been participating in a program in which stories and puppets were used to encourage them to think of alternatives gave fewer aggressive suggestions and behaved less aggressively in the classroom. Stories read to children in most preschool classrooms can have this effect if teachers choose books wisely, but reading stories in addition to teaching alternatives in actual situations involving the children is likely to be the most effective approach of all.

Prosocial Behavior

Prosocial behavior is behavior that benefits others rather than oneself. It includes such conduct as helping, sharing, comforting, and cooperating. Children learn to be prosocial (1) by watching others model prosocial behavior, (2) by being instructed in how to be prosocial, (3) by being reinforced, and (4) by being with other people so that they can practice prosocial behavior. The ability of children to understand situations and to think about the predicaments of others is also influential.

Observational Learning and Prosocial Behavior

Children are likely to increase their prosocial behavior by watching others model it, but some models and modeling situations are more effective than others. It appears that models who are warm and nurturant are more effective than models who are not. In the same way, models who demonstrate prosocial behaviors in real situations are more effective than those who demonstrate these behaviors in contrived situations — with puppets, for example.

Studies on Nurturance and Helping. These conclusions resulted from a study of preschoolers undertaken by Yarrow, Scott, and Waxler (1973). The experimenters began the study by collecting baseline data on the children's helping behavior. Children were tested individually by an adult during a play session in which they were shown pictures of animals, adults, and children, all in distress. For example, one picture showed a child being hit on the head by a swing. The children were asked, "What's happening in this picture?" and "If you were there and saw that happening, what would you do?" In addition, real incidents of distress occurred during the session. For example, the experimenter "accidentally" knocked a vase of flowers to the floor, and a kitten caught in yarn was brought into the room. The child's responses to the pictures and incidents were recorded and rated in terms of helping behaviors.

In the next phase of study, an adult interacted with groups of eight to ten children in a playroom for half an hour a day on five days over a two-week period. Half of the groups were nurtured during these sessions; the adult offered help, gave praise and attention, and was friendly and sympathetic. The other half were

Children who have seen helping modeled are more likely to lend a helping hand themselves.

not nurtured by the adult; there were no prolonged interactions, achievements were criticized, and so on.

In the following stage, the adult who interacted with the groups modeled prosocial behaviors in one of two ways: (1) symbolically with a diorama (a small box with a scene depicting a situation; for example, a toy monkey was helped to get a banana that had been out of reach); (2) in real-life situations in addition to the diorama. For example, a person entered the room and bumped her head; the model comforted her and asked if she would like to sit down.

In summary, then, there were four sets of conditions:

1. Nurturant adult behavior paired with symbolic modeling.
2. Nonnurturant adult behavior paired with symbolic modeling.
3. Nurturant adult behavior paired with symbolic and real-life modeling.
4. Nonnurturant adult behavior paired with symbolic and real-life modeling.

All groups received the same total amount of modeling, and there was also a control group.

During posttesting (the period when changes in behavior were observed) children were given opportunities to play with the dioramas. They were also taken to a nearby house to visit a mother and baby. During the visit, several "accidents" were made to occur. For example, toys fell outside of the baby's crib. The child's helping behavior was recorded in both the symbolic (diorama) and real-life (baby) situations.

The results indicated that only the children with the nurturant adult who saw modeling in the diorama and real-life situations significantly increased their helping behavior beyond their baseline level in real-life situations. This indicates that nurturant adults are more effective models than nonnurturant adults, but that nurturance alone may not be enough. Apparently, adults must also demonstrate concern for others in real situations. When helping is modeled only in principle, using symbolic materials such as dioramas, children may learn only the principle of helping. For children to learn to help in practice, it may be necessary for them to see helping modeled in real-life situations. Nurturant adults are more effective models of helping in real-life situations than nonnurturant adults.

Similar findings resulted from a study of kindergarten children by Staub (1971). In this study, children played games in a room with the experimenter, who was either nurturing (warm and friendly, smiling often and praising the child's skill at the games) or nonnurturing (task-oriented, and not warm or friendly).

After spending time in the game-playing situation, the experimenter excused himself saying he had to do one of two things. (1) Check on a child in an adjoining room. (2) Respond to a child's crying in the next room, which the child who had been playing games could also hear. (This was the distress modeling situation.) When the experimenter returned from the "crying child," he explained that the child had fallen, but that she was all right because he had helped her get up. Soon after his return, the experimenter explained that he had to go do some work, but that the child could continue playing. The child was also told more crayons could be found in the adjoining room.

After the experimenter left, a second type of crash followed by crying was played to the control children and the modeling condition children. This situation served as the posttest. The child's attempts to help by entering the adjoining room or describe the trouble to the experimenter when he returned were noted. Children who actually went into the adjoining room to help the child they thought would be there saw the tape recorder instead and were told by the experimenter that he had wanted to find out how children felt when they heard another child cry. Children who did not offer direct help were told that the "crying child" had been attended to by someone else and was fine.

The results indicated that children who saw helping modeled were more helpful than children who did not. When the two kinds of helping, giving direct help and telling the experimenter about the trouble, were analyzed separately, nurturance was shown to be extremely important in determining whether a child offered active help. Even children in the nurturant group who had not seen helping behavior modeled provided more active help than children in the nonnurturant modeling condition, although they did not offer more help of both kinds in total.

The experimenters suggest that nurturance helps children learn that they are unlikely to be punished by an adult for initiating actions even if their actions are inappropriate. When they have not observed an adult perform helping behaviors and may not know exactly what to do, they are willing to risk an attempt because they are fairly certain that whatever they do will be acceptable to the adult. In the nonnurturant condition, even children who had seen a model's helping behavior were hesitant to initiate helping behavior themselves, presumably because they were afraid that their efforts would be wrong in some way and the adult would find them unacceptable. Thus, they told the experimenter about the trouble, but they did not try to remedy it themselves.

Studies on Sharing and Nurturance. Sharing is another prosocial behavior that is influenced by modeling. Most studies of the effects of modeling on sharing have been conducted with school-age children (Bryan and Walbek, 1970a, 1970b; Rice and Grusec, 1975; Rushton, 1975), but a few have used younger children as subjects. A study by Elliott and Vasta (1970) involved kindergarteners as well as first- and second-graders. The experimenters considered two questions: (1) Does modeling influence sharing? (2) Are modeling plus reinforcement and verbalization ("symbolization" was the term used by the experimenters) more influential than modeling alone?

The study began with a pretest of sharing behaviors. Each child was taken to a room and asked several simple questions (what was his or her name, age, teacher's name, and so on). When the questioning was completed the child was given a bag of candies and told that it was his to keep. He was also told that the experimenter was collecting candies for a child who had no money; if the child wished to donate to this child, candies could be left in a box in the room. Then the experimenter left.

Next, the modeling conditions were presented on videotape. The tape showed a little boy named Johnny, who was having a birthday. Johnny had received a bag of candies from his mother and father. The narrator explained that Johnny could keep all of the candies for himself, but he added that he knew of another child who was also having a birthday whose parents had no money for presents. Johnny decided to mail some of his candies to the less fortunate child.

After Johnny put four handfuls of candy in the envelope, an adult entered the room and did one of three things:

1. Said "Let's go back to the classroom." (modeling only condition)
2. Gave Johnny a teddy bear and said "That was very nice, Johnny, here's a toy for you to keep." (modeling and reward condition)
3. Gave Johnny a teddy bear and said "That was very nice, Johnny, here's a toy for you to keep. If you do something nice for someone else it means you are a good boy." (modeling, reward, and symbolization condition)

Control children saw no videotape. They were taken to a room and asked several questions, but they did not see sharing modeled.

The results showed that all of the children exposed to the model shared significantly more than the children in the control group, who had seen no model. In addition, children who saw the model being rewarded and told why he was being rewarded shared more candies than children who merely saw the model, or saw the model rewarded without explanation. Sharing increased with age, with five-year-olds sharing the least and seven-year-olds the most. This study is a nice illustration of conditions we discussed in our introductory remarks about observational learning, incentive conditions and verbalization.

You might expect nurturance to increase sharing as it increased helping but this does not seem to be the case (Grusec and Skubiski, 1970; Rosenhan and White, 1967). In some instances, nurturant relationships with the model actually decreased children's sharing. Most explanations of this phenomenon follow this line of reasoning: When children share, they give up control of materials that they would otherwise have all to themselves. Sharing requires some sacrifice. By being nurturing a model may indicate that adult disapproval is unlikely when the child does not act in the socially expected way by sharing. Thus, nurturant models do not encourage children to share more.

Helping a child in distress, on the other hand, is a slightly different matter. We mentioned empathy in our earlier discussion of the effects of classical conditioning. As you will recall, we sometimes feel concern for others because their signals of distress cause distress in us; we remember what we felt like in similar situations. Thus, we increase our own comfort by comforting them and stopping their distress. But children may not know how to help another child in distress, and they may worry that initiating an action will lead to adult disapproval. A nurturant model indicates to the child that he or she need not fear retribution for an inappropriate act, however, so the child does not hesitate to act in his or her own interest. In this instance, it is in the child's interest to relieve the other's distress (Grusec and Skubinski, 1970; Staub, 1971, 1975).

If this explanation is correct, nurturance has the same general effect in both helping and sharing situations: it encourages the child to act in his or her own interest without fear of consequences. Helping and sharing differ, however, in that helping another is usually in the child's own interest because it relieves his or her discomfort as well as the distressed person's, whereas sharing with another is not in the child's interest.

How can we resolve this problem? If we are nurturant, children learn to help others in distress, but they do not learn to share. According to Baumrind (1972), the dilemma can be resolved through keeping firm control of expectations. In laboratory sharing studies, children's sharing occurred in the absence of the experimenter, and the children did not expect to see the experimenter again. In a naturally occurring situation, however, parents would be a continuing presence who could consistently encourage children to share.

Parents and Teachers as Models. Baumrind described three types of parents. The type she characterized as authoritative can encourage sharing, helping, and other prosocial behaviors by acting as nurturant models. Authoritative parents set limits and expect children to follow them, but they react to violations with reasoning rather than with physical punishment. Permissive parents set no limits on behavior and do not set standards they expect children to meet. They reward all behavior equally. Because of their permissiveness, they do not encourage prosocial behavior when they are nurturant. Authoritarian parents, on the other hand, set limits and expectations, but they are harsh in enforcing them, using physical punishment to an extreme. They also make demands of children before the children can reasonably be expected to meet them. Authoritarian models are nonnurturant and do not help children develop prosocial behavior. Children growing up with these models become hostile, resentful, or withdrawn, instead.

In summary, then, we see that several conditions encourage children to develop prosocial behaviors of helping and sharing through modeling. Adults must be nurturant, but not indiscriminately. Modeling prosocial behaviors in real life is more effective than explaining them verbally or demonstrating them in symbolic situations.

What can be done in everyday situations by parents or teachers? Actually, quite a lot. Teachers can be warm and friendly to children by interacting with them during play, by praising their achievements, and by smiling at them or being physically affectionate. But warmth and friendliness should not be extended regardless of how children behave. If Susan hits John over the head with a block, the teacher should tell Susan firmly but not harshly that she must not do it again. She should also make certain that Susan is not reinforced in any way, including getting blocks from John by threatening to hit him again. The teacher might in addition explain other ways to use the blocks, such as trading some of her play people for some of John's blocks, or playing with blocks when fewer children are using them.

The teacher could also increase children's willingness to share by demonstrating how to do it. The teacher might join children at the clay table and start working a piece of clay. When joined by other children the teacher could offer to share: "Here, Johnny, I'll give you some of my clay to play with."

Teachers can also model helping. When Susan's crayons fall to the floor, the teacher might say, "Oh, I'm sorry all of the crayons fell to the floor, Susan. Here, I'll help you pick them up." At cleanup time the teacher might say, "You sure played with a lot of blocks today, Anthony. I'll help you put them all away so you won't be late for snack. I'll get all of the little ones. Can you get all of the big ones?"

We have also found that encouraging helping or sharing in other children as the teacher models is very effective. For example, in the situation with Anthony at cleanup time, the teacher might say, "Michael, Anthony and I sure could use your help over here with these blocks. You're such a good block organizer, could you help us for a little while?" Or when sharing clay, the teacher might say, "Susan, do you think you could give John some of your clay? You have quite a lot and he needs some."

The combination of modeling and enlisting help is effective for several reasons. First, it gives children a chance to practice the modeled behavior, and practice increases the behavior more than modeling alone (Rosenhan and White, 1967; White, 1972). Second, the technique involves verbalizing the behavior involved in the prosocial acts. We saw earlier that retention of modeled behavior is enhanced by verbalization of the salient features of the model's action. Third, the verbalization informs the child of (1) the nature of the problem, (2) the feelings of the person needing the help, and (3) the possible effects of the prosocial behavior being requested. As a result, the child's understanding of the other child's situation is increased, and the child's awareness of the effects of his efforts is heightened. Finally, verbalizations may include praise for the child, as when the teacher told Anthony that he was "a good block organizer." Anthony may help John in the future to show how good he is at organizing blocks and perhaps win another compliment.

Reinforcement, Punishment, and Prosocial Behavior

Adult praise and attention to children's prosocial behavior encourages children to behave similarly in the future (Harris, Wolf, and Baer, 1967; Hart et al., 1968). A teacher who sees Michael and Dan help John carry the ladder to the jungle gym might comment that it was thoughtful of them to help. Similarly, a smile of approval when Susan offers a crayon to Tim may motivate her to share in another situation.

Teachers can reinforce prosocial behavior not only when it occurs spontaneously, but in situations contrived to elicit it. For example, two helpers might be designated each day to prepare the snack for the class. This might involve counting out cups, napkins, and crackers, and making juice. While children are doing this, the teacher can comment on how well they are working together.

As we discussed earlier, we think punishment should be used sparingly. Suppose Emile is using a set of crayons and Karen wants to use the red one. Emile says, "No, they're mine! You can't have any." Some teachers would punish Emile by scolding him or taking his crayons away, saying, "If you can't share the crayons, you can't play with them at all." However, future behavior might be improved more if the teacher explained how to share: "Could she use the red crayon while you use the blue one?" The teacher's effectiveness might also improve if he could model sharing and praise sharing that occurred spontaneously.

Verbalization and Prosocial Behavior

As we saw in the Elliott and Vasta (1970) study, explaining why a model was rewarded increases the observer's modeling of the behavior. Studies show, however, that replacing modeling with verbalization is ineffective. Though most of the research on the effects of verbalization versus modeling has been done with children seven to nine years old, the results are quite clear: telling children what they should do without doing it oneself does not work. When sharing is modeled, children share, but merely telling them to share does not influence subsequent behavior (Bryan and Walbek, 1970a, 1970b; Rushton, 1975). It seems that we cannot expect children to do what we say unless we do it ourselves.

Cognition and Prosocial Behavior

Before children can be expected to act in ways that benefit others, they must be able to understand others' situations and feelings and know how to go about helping them (Roedell, Slaby, and Robinson, 1977).

Because young children are egocentric, they have trouble assuming another person's role; they cannot consider the other person's situation from that person's perspective. Between the ages of three and seven, children do learn to identify whether people feel happy, sad, afraid, or angry when given a description of the situation and shown a picture (Borke, 1973), but some experts believe that at this age they do not really understand how the other person feels. They are thought instead to remember their own feelings in similar situations in the past. If this is true, the children's behavior is a matter of self-description rather than role taking. When unfamiliar situations and people who do not resemble the child (such as adults) are depicted, the accuracy of judgments declines. It is only in middle childhood that children learn to identify the emotions of unfamiliar people in unfamiliar situations (Chandler and Greenspan, 1972; Flapan, 1968). (We will discuss the development of role-taking skills in Chapter 24.)

Another reason younger children do not behave prosocially more often is that they cannot think of alternatives when their desires conflict. The studies conducted by Chittenden (1942) and Spivack and Shure (1974), mentioned earlier, made use of dolls, stories, and puppets to encourage children to think of new ways to resolve conflicts. After practicing, children showed less aggression and more cooperation in their play, and offered fewer aggressive suggestions in response to symbolic situations involving stories and puppets.

The inability of young children to think of alternatives implies that teachers should be specific when suggesting that children behave prosocially. Telling children to share, for example, is not very helpful. A concrete suggestion, such as asking Susan to let Jane use the red crayon while she uses the yellow one, may be more helpful, because it explains exactly how to share. As we saw earlier, however, it is important to model sharing as well as talk about it.

Summary

Socialization Processes

- Children learn to behave in ways that adults consider appropriate through reinforcement and punishment, classical conditioning, verbal instruction, observational learning, and other cognitive processes.
- Reinforcement is providing a consequence to a response that increases the probability that the response will occur in similar situations. Punishment is providing a consequence to a response that decreases the probability that the response will occur in similar situations. Punishment has several harmful effects. It can interfere with a child's chances to learn from his or her mistakes, reduce exploration and initiative in new situations, and lead to child abuse.
- Verbal instruction enhances modeling when it is used to draw children's attention to important details of modeled behavior; thus, explanations of how children should behave should be accompanied by modeling the desired behavior.
- Identification involves assuming the attitudes and beliefs as well as the behaviors of a model.
- Children's cognitive abilities influence the effectiveness of the socialization processes.
- Biological factors can influence what parents expect of a child, which can in turn affect how the child behaves.

Aggression and Its Control

- Studies indicate that watching aggression on TV increases the aggressive behavior of children in the period following their TV viewing. The theory that watching violence on film allows for vicarious venting of aggression is not supported by research.
- Aggression increases when it helps children get what they want. Therefore, adults should make sure that aggression is not reinforced. Also, reinforcements removed for punishment should be related to children's behavior.
- Children must have developed a certain level of cognitive ability before they can think of alternatives to aggression.

Prosocial Behavior

- Nurturance increases helping behavior and decreases sharing behavior, apparently because in both situations nurturance diminishes the child's fear of acting in his or her best interest. However, sharing behavior can be encouraged through a combination of nurturance and firm control of expectations.
- Verbalization alone is not effective in getting children to engage in prosocial behavior.

- A child's level of cognitive development affects her ability to judge feelings and thus be able to judge what kind of help others need. This is why older children may exhibit more prosocial behavior than younger children.

New Terms

reinforcement
punishment
response costs
extinction
child abuse
empathy

identification
instrumental aggression
catharsis theory
intrinsic reinforcement
response cost
prosocial behavior

Selected Readings

Kaye, E. **The family guide to children's television.** *New York: Pantheon Books, 1974.* This book was written under the guidance of Action for Children's Television and in cooperation with the American Academy of Pediatrics. It contains general information on why parents should be concerned about the television programs their children watch, and provides many practical suggestions for controlling television viewing and using television wisely.

Murray, J. P., and Lonnberg, B. **Children and television: A primer for parents.** *Boys Town, Neb.: Boys Town Center for the Study of Youth Development, 1980.* This is a companion volume to **Television and youth** *(Murray, 1980),* cited in this chapter. The volume for parents is much briefer than the volume prepared for scholars, and, of course, less technical.

Roedell, W. C., Slaby, R. G., and Halbert, H. B. **Social development in young children.** *Monterey, Calif.: Brooks/Cole, 1977.* This small paperback contains readable surveys of the research on aggression and prosocial behavior. Most valuable are the discussions of the implications of social development research for teachers.

Chapter *20*

*K*nowledge and Action

In this chapter we will discuss the practical applications of our knowledge of preschool children. We begin with a description of preschool education and some of the instruments used to assess the intellectual functioning of preschool children. We will also have some suggestions for coping with children's increasing motor capabilities and relieving children's fears of dreams and the dark. Some of the considerations involved in selecting toys will also be discussed.

Preschool Education Programs

A Typical Preschool Program

Classroom Design. The classroom is divided into sections designed for specific activities. The *block area* has a good supply of unit blocks and props such as road signs, vehicles, and people. Near the block area is a *climbing box*, a wooden structure with ladder rungs for climbing up and down.

A preschool classroom

There is also a *dramatic play area* with a play refrigerator, stove, sink, table and chairs, doll beds, dishes, dressup clothes, and dolls. The *library area* has a low bookcase filled with storybooks. A rug and some pillows cover the floor in front of the books, and adult- and child-size rocking chairs sit to one side. On the wall nearby are a large felt board and three wicker baskets for felt letters, numerals, and shapes.

The *writing, drawing, construction center* has shelves on two sides and a table and four chairs in the center. The supplies for the center are plentiful and varied. There are many kinds of paper, and a great many different drawing and writing tools, including lead pencils, colored pencils, magic markers, wax pencils, chalk, and crayons. There are also wood and plastic tools for marking magic slates. Several boxes filled with bits of yarn, fabric, and string sit nearby. A hole punch, stapler, small bottles of glue and paste, and a small blackboard are also available.

At the end of the room opposite the library and writing/drawing centers is a *woodworking bench* and a supply of wood. The tools include a drill with various bits, a large and a small hammer, and a saw. There is a pegboard rack mounted on the wall where the tools are hung when not in use; each tool's place is marked with a silhouette of black contact paper. At one end of the rack hang a dustpan and brush for sweeping up sawdust.

Near the sink are two *easels* and a drying rack for paintings; close by is a coffee can filled with brushes of various sizes. A smock hangs on each easel, and between the easels sits another coffee can, which holds a damp sponge for wiping up drips.

Not far from the easels is a table for *water play* that has been filled with contrasting sets of containers — little and big ones, short and tall ones, and round and square ones. In tubs under the table are flour sifters, collanders, strainers, tubes, funnels, syringes, turkey basters, squeeze bottles, and solid objects such as plastic and wooden boats.

Elsewhere in the room there is a *manipulative materials center.* On the shelves surrounding this area are a rack of puzzles, a shape-sorting box, small colored cubes, unifex cubes and tray, pegboards and pegs, a set of attribute blocks, a container of popsicle sticks, and several geoboards. There are also picture dominoes, regular dominoes, beads to string, and lotto games that encourage an understanding of shape, color, or pictures. Each type of plaything has its own box or basket for storage.

Just inside the door is a row of cubbies along the wall. Each has a shelf for belongings at the top and a hook for coat and hat. The cubbies are labeled with the children's names.

Near the cubbies is a wooden divider. Mounted on it are a box of name cards and a pocket attendance chart. Children put their name cards in a pocket on the chart when they enter the room in the morning. On the other side of the divider is a large pegboard on which labels and numerals are hung in the pattern of a calendar. Children's birthdays are noted by hanging cards with birthday cakes on them on the appropriate dates.

This classroom is used by twenty children between three and five years old. It is staffed by three teachers. If you stop by the classroom at midmorning you will find children doing all sorts of things.

Classroom Activities. In the library corner a child is lying on a pillow on the floor looking at a book by himself. A teacher sitting in the rocking chair has a child on her lap. The teacher is reading to her, but the child often stops the reading to ask questions and comment on the story. Sometimes the child says the story along with the teacher.

Three children are building with blocks. They have set up a long line of blocks and are crossing it in several places with other lines of blocks. The pattern resembles a set of intersecting streets, which is apparently what the children have in mind, for a few minutes later they begin running toy cars and trucks over it. A teacher stops to watch and then makes a few comments about what they have constructed. She takes a container of small road signs off the shelf and sets it on the floor, suggesting that the children may wish to use them to direct traffic on their roads. "Oh, yeah!" one child says, searching for a sign. "Here's a stop sign," says another. She places it at an intersection. The teacher leaves the area as the children inspect the other signs and decide where to place them.

At the easel, two children are painting, but one of them has not put on a smock. A teacher stops by and asks, "What should you put on to protect your clothes before you start to paint?" "Oh, a smock," says the child, "I forgot." He gets a smock from the end of the easel and puts it on. The teacher pats him on the back and moves on, saying, "Now you're ready to paint."

As the children paint, they mix colors in a muffin tin or on their paper. They seem to be experimenting with the colors and brushes. One boy holds a wide brush in one hand and a narrow one in the other and moves them across and then down his paper, making a tic-tac-toe pattern. Then he puts the wide brush down and uses the narrow brush to paint a third color in the middle space. When he finishes, he takes the paper from the easel and puts it on the drying rack. Then he attaches a clean piece of paper to the easel. This time he paints a picture of a person, a house, and the sun. When the picture is finished, he hangs it up to dry and takes the brushes from the five containers of paint to the sink to wash them. He puts the stopper in the sink and lets it fill up with colored water. A teacher intervenes before the sink overflows and asks if the brushes are clean. "Other children may want to use them," she says. The child says they are clean and places them in the can on the sink. The teacher then says that other children will need the sink soon and suggests that he go to the water play table if he wants to

Preschoolers enjoy painting with tempera at the easel.

play with water. "Shall we color it blue today?" she asks, as the child heads for the water play table.

In the writing and drawing area, a child has finished a drawing to give her mother as a birthday present. She is working on a card to go with it. When she finishes drawing pictures on the card, she goes to find a teacher to help her write "Happy Birthday." The teacher follows her back to the table and writes the words on a piece of paper. The child then tries to copy the words onto her card. Her version does not match the teacher's but the teacher accepts her version rather than trying to correct her. The little girl puts her card in her cubby to take home.

As this girl wrote, a younger girl who had been drawing with crayons began watching with interest. At one side of her paper are a few linear scribbles, perhaps an attempt to "write" like the older child. When the older child finished writing, the younger child went back to scribbling in circles at the center of her paper.

On the counter beside the sink, two children are counting out crackers, cups, and napkins to put in the three snack baskets. These are the helpers for the day; their names appear on the helpers' chart posted nearby. The children know that eight of each item go into each basket. The teachers deliberately pair a child with good counting skills with a less skillful counter so they can help each other.

Two children are sitting on the floor putting felt shapes on the felt board. They have separated the shapes into groups on the board and are busy counting how many they have of each kind. A teacher who stops to watch points to a group of triangles and says, "Why did you put these together?" "Because they are all triangles," says one child. "They sure are," answers the teacher. Then he asks, "Is there another way to make groups with these felt pieces?" The child says, "No, this is the way we want them." "Okay," says the teacher, "that sure is one good way to do it."

In the manipulative materials area, a child is working a puzzle for the fourth time in succession. Another child is putting pegs in the pegboard. She has filled seven rows and is working on the eighth. Each row is of one color only. A teacher stops by to comment. Pointing to the rows as she talks, she says, "You sure are working hard on the pegboard. I see you've put all of the red pegs together, and all of the yellow pegs together, and all of the green ones, blue ones, and orange ones, too." Another child is building with small colored cubes. She has built several structures. One has two cubes on the bottom and is three cubes high; another has four cubes on the bottom layer and is two cubes high. She is working on the third one, which has six cubes on the bottom layer. The child is currently building the second tier.

Over in the house play area, children have been dressing up, cooking, going to work, cleaning house, and caring for babies. There has been much discussion of what is what and who is who. The teacher had to intervene to help settle an argument: Angela was wearing the favorite pair of dressup shoes, but Susan wanted them, too. The teacher asked "Who had them first?" The children agreed that Angela did. "But *I* want them," said Susan. "But Angela wants them too," pointed out the teacher. "Could you wear one of the other pairs of dress-up shoes?" "No, I want those," Susan said, pointing to the red ones Angela wore. "Do you think you'll want to wear them during the entire activity time today?" the teacher asked Angela. "Yes," she answered. "Okay," said the teacher. To Susan she said, "If Angela finishes with the shoes today before cleanup time, then you can have a turn with them, but if she doesn't, you'll have to wait until tomorrow for your turn. I'll put a note up on the bulletin board over there. That way we'll remember. For today, you'll have to wear one of the other pairs of dressup shoes, but tomorrow you'll have the red ones." As Susan watched, the teacher left the dressup area and put a note on the board. Then Susan began to play again. "I get the red shoes tomorrow, and you can wear one of these," she said, pointing to the other pairs.

During cleanup time the teachers move about the room, helping, praising, and making suggestions. A child who is standing around with nothing to do is asked to make sure the puzzles have all their pieces. "That sure would be a big help," the teacher tells him. Then the teacher goes to the house area and offers to help: "I'll put the dishes away in the cupboard if you hand them to me, Joshua. You'll have to tell me exactly where they go."

After the activity period, children gather at small tables for snacks. They pour their own juice from small pitchers, and take crackers from the basket as it is passed. A teacher sits at each table and enjoys a snack with the children. The children talk among themselves and with the teacher about the morning's activities. Then a girl knocks over her glass of juice and spills it. She grabs the sponge while the teacher goes to the sink for a paper towel. When the teacher returns, he asks another child to take a cup to another table to see if they have extra juice. Then he wipes up the rest of the juice while the girl goes to the sink to squeeze out the sponge. When everyone is back at the table, the teacher asks where cups could be placed so that children would not tip them over when they pass the cracker basket. After some discussion, everyone agrees that people should put them near the center of the table, rather than to the side where an arm or hand might knock them over.

Outdoor play comes after snacks. It is summer, so storybooks are taken out to be read on a blanket under the shade tree. Children also take out cans of water and paintbrushes, which they use to "paint" the fence, the sidewalk, and the side of the building. There are also balls and hoops to play with, as well as swings, climbing bars, a sand box, tricycles, wagons, and a wheelbarrow.

Outdoor play is followed by singing. While most of the children sing, two children help set the tables for lunch. After lunch, there are naps.

The rest of the afternoon is spent in a variety of activities. Sometimes a small group of children cooks something for the next day's snack or lunch. On this day a teacher helps four children make a list of fruit to buy at a nearby grocery. When they return, they make fruit salad.

Two days a week, high school students come to read to children. Sometimes there are other visitors, perhaps a firefighter, nurse, police officer, or mail carrier.

What Makes a Good Preschool Program?

We think the program we have just described is a good one. The variety of materials and the social environment give children many opportunities to learn about written and oral language, the arts, numbers, space, physical objects, and the feelings and views of others. Many activities help children improve their gross and fine motor abilities. The program also encourages (1) decision making — children choose what they will do and how they will do it for much of the day; (2) problem solving — through such tasks as learning how to keep a block tower from toppling, how to keep drips from running down a painting, and how to participate in dramatic play groups; (3) responsibility — children get things out and put them away themselves, clean up, prepare snacks, and help set the table for lunch; and (4) peer and adult interaction. As you have seen, the program touches on many important areas.

Another virtue of the program is that it assumes that children acquire knowledge in an active way. There are no ditto sheets for drill on isolated skills, no outlined pictures to color in. Learning is not reduced to sensory discrimination and matching or perceptual-motor tasks. Rather than telling children about objects and the world, or about space and number, the teachers allow children to have direct experiences. Information, comments, and questions are offered when necessary. Children are taught to care for materials and be responsible.

In addition, the program allows children to learn in ways that are meaningful to them. When shapes are provided, they are diverse enough that they can be assembled in many different ways, not just named or matched with identical shapes. They can be organized according to shape, color, or size. These classification schemes are manifestations of logicomathematical knowledge — that is, knowledge that is constructed mentally as the child acts on objects, as distinct from knowledge inherent in objects themselves (Kamii and DeVries, 1977).

In classrooms such as the one described, number concepts are acquired through counting real objects such as snack items or felt shapes, not by repeating number words or writing numbers on paper. This permits children to discover an important Piagetian concept: as they play with objects, they discover that changing the arrangement of objects does not alter their number. In other words, numbers are treated, not as symbols, but as relationships among objects imposed on the objects by the child.

Written language, too, is learned in a meaningful context. When children try to write, as in the birthday card example, teachers' reactions are influenced by the understanding that children have a limited understanding of space and the distinctive features of print. At first, various errors are expected.

As when the teacher named the colors of the pegs, oral language is demonstrated in the midst of the child's activities. More importantly, language is used for communication. Children talk to each other when they build together with blocks or negotiate for turns.

FOCUS: Types of Knowledge

Piaget differentiated among four different types of knowledge: (1) physical, (2) social, (3) logicomathematical, and (4) symbolic. The distinctions were based on the *source* of the knowledge.

Physical knowledge consists of characteristics inherent in objects, such as color, weight, and temperature. The source of this type of knowledge is the objects themselves.

The source of *social knowledge* is other people. Examples of social knowledge include knowing that we knock before entering someone's house and knowing that Thanksgiving is celebrated on a certain Thursday in November.

Logicomathematical knowledge is created by the learner. This type of knowledge is derived from the actions we perform on objects. It involves our understanding of the relationships among objects. Although objects are necessary to construct logicomathematical knowledge, individual objects are not themselves the source of the knowledge. For example, a classification scheme is not inherent in objects themselves; it is a relationship we impose on objects. In the same way, number is a relationship we impose on a collection of objects; it is not inherent in objects themselves. If you remove a book from a collection of three books, for example, there is nothing about the book you have removed that retains the quality of "threeness."

Symbolic knowledge involves knowing how to represent our other types of knowledge. Symbolic knowledge is partly social (knowing that a pencil is called a pencil, for example) and partly constructed (knowing rules of syntax, for example). The basic ability to represent, known as the symbolic function, can be manifested in forms other than language, such as dramatic play, drawings, or maps. Each form of knowledge shares some sources with other forms and has other sources exclusively. For example, one source of the ability to represent through drawing is logicomathematical knowledge about spatial relations.

The various kinds of knowledge have important implications for teaching. We tend to treat all knowledge as if it were social knowledge, and as a result we try to *tell* children about everything. But, according to Piaget, telling is a poor way of teaching subject matter based on objects or relationships among objects. In such cases it would be far more effective to give children opportunities to act on objects directly.

There also are many opportunities for children to learn physical knowledge, that is, knowledge about objects and substances in the world (Kamii and DeVries, 1977). Children must be able to touch and play with materials for them to learn about them. At the water table, for example, the child will discover that a solid container is different from one that has holes in it such as the flour sifter. At the writing table, writing tools have different characteristics: a lead pencil is different from a crayon or magic marker; you can use your finger or a wooden tool to write on the magic slate, but a different implement is necessary to write on paper. Opportunities to build with blocks, move around the room, draw, write, and paint give children a chance to develop an understanding of spatial relationships.

Dramatic play is useful in several ways. It provides practice with symbols as children use one object to represent another. It permits them to experience unfamiliar roles and new perspectives. It requires verbal explanation when a particular role or action is desired. Finally, dramatic play reduces egocentricity as children come into conflict with peers about dressup clothes or who gets to play what role.

A program of the sort described also gives teachers many opportunities to model prosocial behavior. Teachers can help children find alternatives in conflicts with peers and engage children in tasks that benefit the class. Assigning responsibilities is a good way to promote prosocial behavior. When children do assigned tasks that improve the welfare of others, such as preparing snacks, checking puzzles, or setting the table, they apparently learn to be more thoughtful of others as well (Staub, 1975).

Variations in Preschool Programs

Not everyone agrees about what a good preschool education program consists of. In fact, this is a subject of great controversy. There are profound differences in *what* people think children should learn (values) and *how* people think they learn (theories of development). Underlying the different views of learning are even more fundamental notions about the sources of knowledge. For example, when knowledge is thought to exist outside the learner, the problem is getting it inside the learner. Teachers with this view tend to simplify and sequence learning tasks for children and give them information piecemeal, one "skill" at a time. These teachers often teach verbally rather than giving children experiences with concrete objects. This is the behavioral view of learning: it assumes that the learner is passive.

Many proponents of the maturational view of development also regard children as passive learners. Advocates of this view believe it is important to wait until children are mature enough to understand a subject before introducing it to them. They often believe that preschoolers are too young to learn about written language, for example; as a result, they may object to helping them learn to read. Instead, they tend to select a mental age of six or six and one-half before instruction should begin (see page 390 for a definition of mental age). Once this level of maturity has been reached, there is not too much objection from people adopting this view to the method employed to teach children to read. A behavioral approach is considered about as useful as any other. The key to success of any instructional method is the child's readiness — what the child brings to the instruction. If a child is ready, the child will learn, proponents argue, despite the method.

By contrast, a basic assumption of the program described earlier is that some kinds of knowledge do not exist in the external world. Logicomathematical knowledge, for example, is assumed to be created by the learner. So are the knowledge of the distinctive features of print and the knowledge of concepts of space necessary to write the letters of the alphabet. In this program, which reflects the interactionist point of view, learners are assumed to be mentally active in the sense of creating knowledge. But without experiences out of which such knowledge can be created, no knowledge relating to reading will develop.

These fundamental differences in philosophy lead to differences in the classroom. The organization of the room, the materials available to children, the schedule of the day, the role played by the teacher — all may vary with the program's philosophical orientation. Programs that vary in areas such as these are often characterized as being *structured* or *unstructured*. We find these terms as they are commonly used neither useful nor accurate. Any program that is consistent with stated adult values and a particular learning theory can be considered structured; it has internal integrity. Structured programs can vary widely in terms of their materials, organization, and scheduling. Unstructured programs can also vary, their common characteristic being that what is taught is not consistent with stated values and how it is taught is not consistent with a theory of development. Internally, there are often conflicts between organization and stated goals. For example, the teacher may expect silence in the classroom and yet have arranged seating so that students face each other in small groups as they work.

The Effectiveness of Preschool Programs

Many preschool programs were designed to give poor children the same opportunities to exercise their intellectual abilities as children living in more advantageous circumstances. The best known program of this type is Head Start. Do children who attend such programs do better in school or in tested intellectual functioning than those who do not attend such programs? Unfortunately, this is a difficult question to answer.

Problems in Evaluation. The decision to place a child in a particular type of preschool is of course made by the child's parents. For this reason, it is very difficult to study the relative effectiveness of different programs. It is hard to tell whether differences in abilities are caused by variations in preschool programs, or whether the children who attended different programs were different to begin with.

To overcome this problem, experimenters may initially recruit enough families to fill a control group and a group that will participate in a program. After a total pool has been selected, children may be arbitrarily assigned to one group or the other. This does not necessarily resolve all problems, however, because the parents and children are often from the same community. When the parents of control group children interact with the parents of the program children, they may learn about the experiences the program children are having. If this information influences how the control parents interact with their children, the differences between the groups may be diminished. To solve this problem, some program planners establish control groups and program groups in separate communities.

A second problem is that the actual program may differ from the program that was designed. Some teachers are much better than others at implementing a program according to a plan. Properly conducted studies monitor the program the children actually experience, not the program that exists on paper. If the program is not being implemented properly, it should be put back on course.

Monitoring of this magnitude is tedious and costly. Suppose we wanted to include in a study children from thirty preschools. Before significant differences would be revealed, the program would have to be in operation for at least one year, and preferably two, and monitoring visits might be necessary every two weeks. If the program were not being implemented properly, the staff would need some kind of training, which might consist of anything from an hour's consultation with a teacher about effective room arrangement to a series of workshops on the relationship between manipulative materials and mathematical concepts.

An evaluation effort of this size is terribly expensive. It can involve dozens of people to evaluate programs and help the staff implement the program correctly, and it can cost hundreds of thousands of dollars. You can see why attendance in a program, though often a poor indicator of the actual experience, is often considered evidence that children have experienced a program as it was intended to be.

A third problem concerns what to evaluate and when and how to evaluate it. Should we evaluate progress in social and physical areas, or in intellectual areas exclusively? Should we use tests to collect data, or should we observe children in real situations? Should we evaluate the effects of programs immediately after children have attended them, or should we continue our evaluation for an extended period to judge long-term effects?

Each of these decisions will influence the cost of an evaluation and the reliability of the information it provides. Evaluations done immediately after a program ends do not reveal long-term effects, whereas long-term evaluations can often be criticized on the grounds that the children who moved away and thus could not be evaluated may be the very ones who benefited most. The use of tests that assess only cognitive skills may be criticized because motivation is also important in predicting later success in school.

As you can see, evaluation is a difficult task, and many decisions can influence the outcome. The best one can do is design as thorough and accurate an evaluation as possible with the available resources and then be aware of the problems with the results.

Effects of Model Compensatory Programs. Because of some of the problems we have mentioned, evaluations of preschool programs for children from impoverished backgrounds have yielded mixed results. The effects discussed here were taken from the best studies available.

One way to measure the effects of compensatory programs is by administering IQ tests before and immediately after children have been enrolled in a program. The IQs of program children are then compared with IQs of control children. This procedure indicates the short-term gains, if any, that result from a program.

Long-term evaluation can involve monitoring the progress of children in elementary school for several years. Data on IQ, school achievement, and characteristics such as inventiveness and curiosity can be collected.

Both long- and short-term studies have yielded contradictory results, but in general they can be summarized as follows:

1. The IQs of program children have shown significant increases immediately after program attendance (Bronfenbrenner, 1974; Gray and Klaus, 1970; Weikart, 1970).
2. Children from all types of programs have shown IQ and achievement gains, but children who received direct instruction on school-related tasks have usually shown the highest *initial* gains (Karnes, 1969; Miller and Dyer, 1975).
3. On entering school, program children have usually had higher IQ and achievement scores whereas control children have lower IQs and achievement scores. After two or three years in school, however, the two groups were about the same. The children who attended the programs that resulted in the greatest gains in IQ and achievement also showed the quickest decline after entering elementary school (Bronfenbrenner, 1974).
4. Children in programs involving parent-child intervention (such as the Levenstein program reviewed in Chapter 15) showed significant gains in IQ that persisted in elementary school (Levenstein, 1977).
5. Long-term studies of the children who attended some compensatory programs indicated (1) that they were placed in special classes and retained at grade level *less* frequently than control children, and (2) that they viewed school more positively (Moore, 1978; Royce, 1979; Schweinhart and Weikart, 1980).

As you can see, the results obtained are influenced by the measure used (IQ, school achievement, or retention in grade) and by the time at which data are obtained. The most recent data suggest that high-quality programs do have long-term positive effects on children of poverty (Schweinhart and Weikart, 1980).

Obviously, we still have much to learn about how to help children learn and benefit from schooling. We will need to continue to provide high-quality programs and to mount quality evaluation efforts for some time before we arrive at definitive answers.

Preschool Assessment Instruments

There are many assessment tools available for use with preschoolers. We will discuss only a few of those which are unique or widely used, including (1) the Metropolitan Readiness Tests, (2) the Concepts about Print Test, (3) the Caldwell Preschool Inventory, and (4) Piagetian Tasks. (Intelligence tests will be discussed in Chapter 21.)

Metropolitan Readiness Tests

The Metropolitan (1976) consists of test batteries at two levels. Level I tests are administered to kindergarten children at the beginning and middle of the school year. Level II tests are used at the end of kindergarten or at the beginning of first grade. The tests are administered to groups of children by the classroom teacher over a period of several days. Children are given practice items before testing begins to be certain they understand the directions. Box 20-1 shows sample items in the Level I test. This test includes subtests in the following areas:

1. *Auditory Memory.* Items contain several boxes in a row with a series of pictures. The teacher asks the children to close their eyes, and then he or she names the pictures in one box in the order they appear. The children are then instructed to open their eyes and to mark the box containing the pictures named.

   Example: Teacher says SPOON, BALL, STAR

   The first few items in this subtest contain three pictures. The later, more difficult, items contain four.

2. *Rhyming.* In this subtest, the teacher says a word and asks the children to choose from an array of pictures the one whose name rhymes with the word said. For example, if the teacher says "floor," the children are to mark the picture of a door.

3. *Letter Recognition.* Each item in this subtest consists of a row of four upper- or lowercase letters. The teacher names one letter and children mark it.

4. *Visual Matching.* In this subtest, children are asked to match identical visual displays. They are shown a model shape and then asked to select the one that matches it from a row of several. The matching items consist of individual letters, series of letters, or numerals.

5. *School Language and Listening.* The items in this subtest show pictures or series of pictures that illustrate

   a. The use of prepositions ("The boy is behind the tree.")

   b. The use of verb tenses ("The girl will cut the string.")

   c. The use of passive sentences ("The boy is being carried by the girl.")

   d. A sequence of events described in a short paragraph ("Bob tore a piece of paper out of his notebook and wrote his name on it. Then he crossed out his name and wrote it again.")

BOX 20-1. Sample Items from the Metropolitan Readiness Test, Level I

AUDITORY MEMORY

A. Now put your finger on the little black BIRD. Close your eyes. Don't peek! Listen. CHAIR CUP. Open your eyes. Mark the right box.

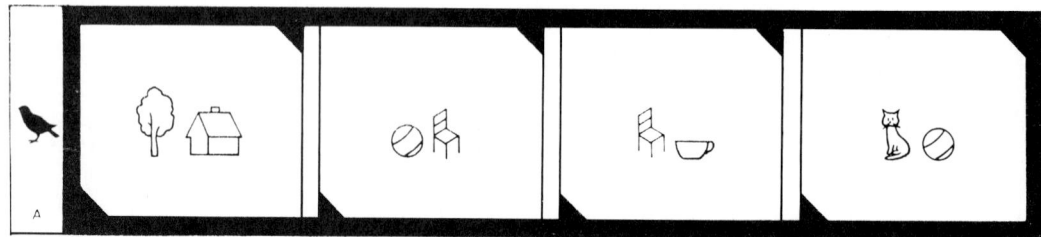

B. Now put your finger on the little black MOON. Close your eyes. Remember not to peek. As soon as I say the words, open your eyes and mark. Don't wait for me to tell you to open your eyes. Listen. SPOON BALL STAR.

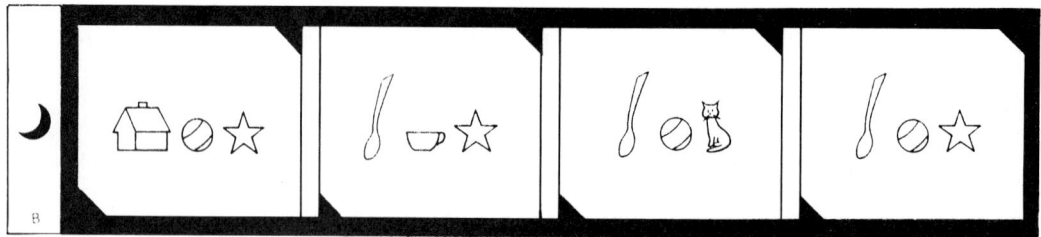

RHYMING

A. Put your finger by the top row. The pictures are MILK, LEAF, TIE, BIKE. Listen to the word I say: LIKE. Mark the one that rhymes with LIKE, the one that rhymes with LIKE.

BOX 20-1 continued

LETTER RECOGNITION

A. Put your finger on the little black SPOON at the beginning of the top
row. Look at the letters in this row. Mark the *S* ... the *S*.

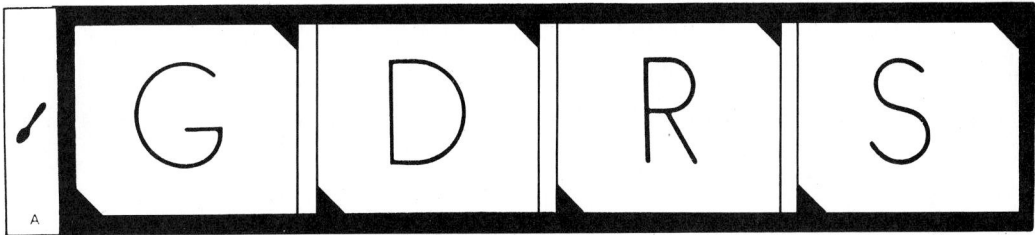

VISUAL MATCHING

B. Put your finger on the little black CUP. Look at what is in the red box.
Then mark the box that has in it just what is in the red box.

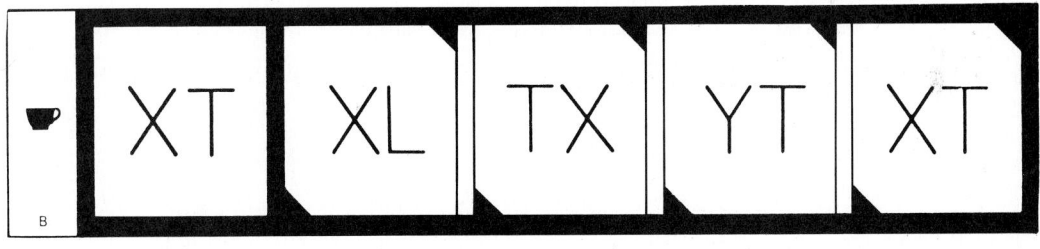

[red box]

Children are asked to choose the picture that illustrates the event described in the sentence the teacher has said.

6. *Quantitative Language.* This subtest assesses the child's understanding of words such as "more" and "less" and "big" and "little." Children are also tested on their ability to (a) count; (b) recognize numerals; (c) match numerals to the numbers they represent; (d) determine the ordinal position of an item ("Mark the fifth turtle."); (e) determine the equality of two sets; (f) match one-to-one the items in two sets; and (g) understand the concept of subtraction ("There were four cookies to start with. A child ate two. Mark the picture showing how many cookies were left.").

The subtests of Level II resemble the Level I subtest in many respects, but they are more complex. The subtests assess understanding in the following areas:

- Beginning consonants
- Sound-letter correspondence
- Visual matching
- Finding patterns
- School language
- Listening
- Quantitative concepts
- Quantitative operations

Concepts About Print Test: The Sand Test

The Concepts About Print Test (1976), developed by an educator from New Zealand named Maria Clay, can be used with kindergarten children and children entering first grade. A picture book entitled *Sand* is the only material needed to administer the test. The tester reads the book and asks the child questions about it. The questions are designed to determine whether children know

1. the front from the back of the book
2. that the reader reads print rather than pictures
3. that print is scanned from left to right and from top to bottom
4. how to match a spoken word with a written word
5. the difference between a letter and a word
6. that print is incorrect when it is inverted

The Denver Developmental Screening Test

The *Denver* test (Frankenburg and Dodds, 1970) can be used with children from infancy to age six. Four types of abilities are tested: (1) personal-social, (2) fine-motor adaptive, (3) language, and (4) gross motor. Children must be tested individually. (See Figure 20-1 for a list of items found on the Denver.)

Figure 20-1. The *Denver Developmental Screening Test.* All of the items included in the four areas of the test are shown in the chart on the facing page. Each item appears in a box. The left end of the box indicates the age at which 25 percent of the children in the standardization sample passed the item. The small line at the top of the box indicates the age at which 50 percent passed the item. The beginning of the shaded portion indicates the age at which 75 percent passed the item and 90 percent of the children passed the item at the age indicated by the right end of the box.

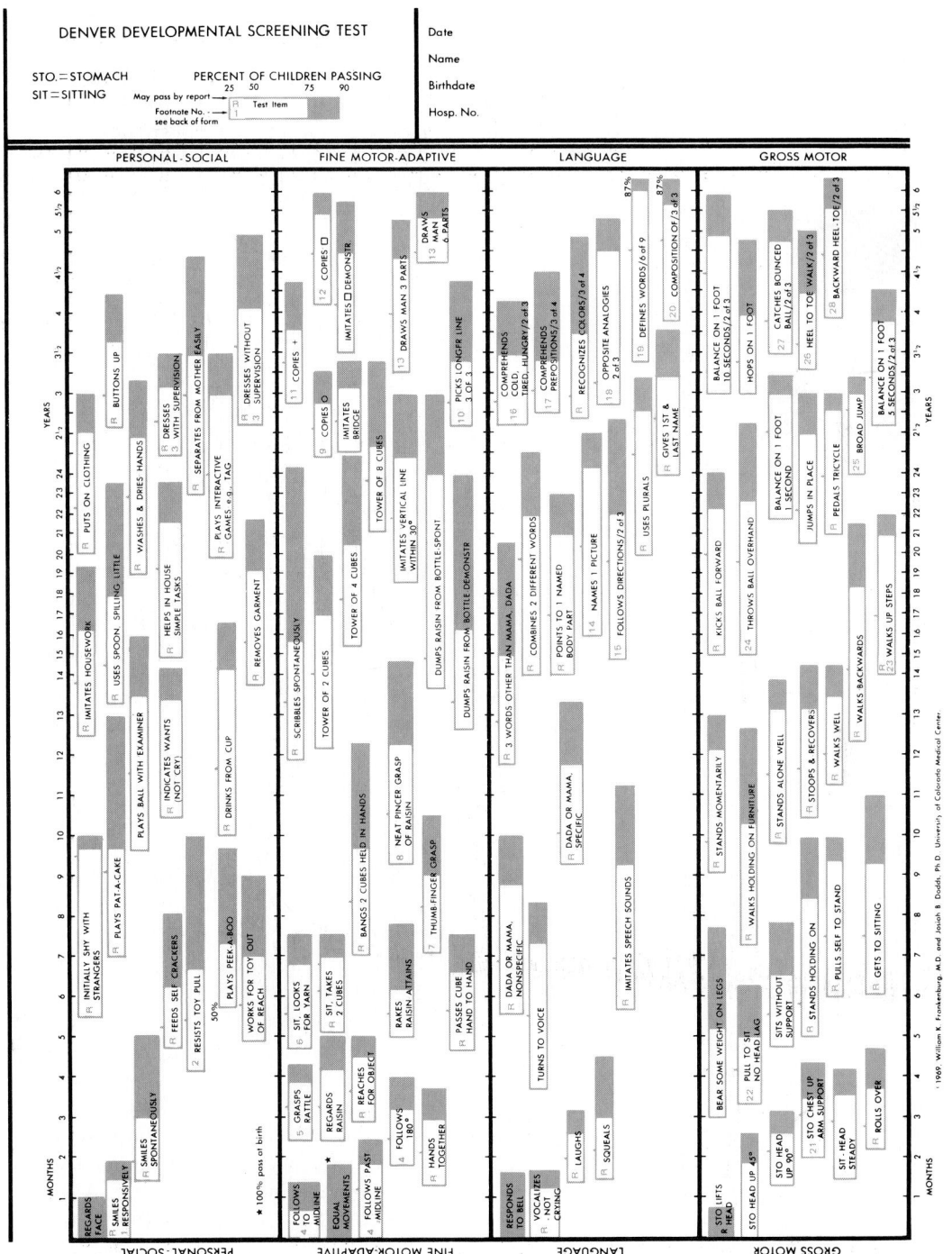

The Caldwell Preschool Inventory

The Preschool Inventory (Caldwell, 1970) is designed for use with individual children between the ages of three and six. This is an achievement test designed to assess the effectiveness of educational intervention programs such as Head Start. Items on the test assess three basic categories of abilities: (1) concept activation ("Copy a circle." "Count to five."), (2) personal-social responsiveness ("What is your name?" "Show me your neck."), and (3) vocabulary ("What color is this crayon?").

The Piagetian Tasks

Piagetian tasks are often used to assess children's intellectual development. For example, a child may be administered the conservation of number task we described in Chapter 17 or the task relating to the construction of a projective straight line. Materials for the conservation of number task would include any kind of discrete object. Materials for the projective straight line task would include two kinds of tables, one round and one square, and objects to represent poles. These could be toothpicks mounted in a clay base, for example.

Piagetian tasks are always administered to children individually; in groups children are likely to copy the actions of other children. Furthermore, the researcher is as interested in *why* a child does what he or she does as in *what* the child does, and discussions of this kind cannot take place in a group.

Issues in Test Construction and Use

The tests we have described differ in important ways. The Denver assesses several areas of development, whereas the Metropolitan, the Concepts About Print, the Preschool Inventory, and the Piagetian Tasks assess intellectual functioning only. Of the intellectual functioning tests, the Concepts About Print Test assesses only readiness for reading instruction, whereas the Preschool Inventory and the Metropolitan assess a child's understanding of language and numbers.

Even tests designed to assess the same area of development may differ significantly. Subtests of the Metropolitan and the Concepts About Print Test assess readiness for reading, but the items reflect different assumptions about the nature of the reading process: the Metropolitan stresses separate skills involving letter-sound associations and visual perception, whereas the Concepts About Print Test stresses book knowledge and concepts about print. Similarly, the Metropolitan and the Piagetian Tasks both deal with mathematical understanding, but the Metropolitan Tests emphasize numeral recognition and counting, whereas the Piagetian Tasks stress an operational understanding of number.

There is nothing sacred about tests. They always reflect the designer's preferred theory of development and what he or she believes children should learn. Teachers and parents sometimes fail to understand this, and as a result tests sometimes "take over" the school curriculum. When this occurs, all instruction is geared toward the test. Test items and items resembling them are taught almost exclusively, regardless of whether they reflect what adults think children should learn. This is another instance of a problem resulting from interpreting correlational data as if they were causal data. The fact that children who do well on tests that assess knowledge of letter names tend to be good readers does not mean that teaching children only letter names leads to success in learning to read. Perhaps children know letter names because their parents have read to them, because they have been given manipulative alphabet materials to play with, because they have played school with siblings, or because their questions about print have been answered by their parents. Children who have had these experiences undoubtedly know more about print than the names of letters. Teachers who merely teach letter names directly through workbooks and verbal drill may be teaching children letter names only — not other skills necessary to learn to read. This instruction may be of little use to children who do not have other experiences with print.

An additional problem associated with "teaching to the test" is that the skills involved in answering some items may not actually be those the test is saying it measures. For example, in the Metropolitan Tests, Level I, the first subtest is labeled "auditory memory." But the ability to remember something depends on the ability to associate and organize what has been heard in a cognitive framework.

Thus, a child who has difficulty with auditory memory may benefit little from direct practice on memory tasks; experience of a more general type might be more beneficial. Similarly, a child who has trouble listening might benefit more from experiences that broaden his or her general understanding of the world than from practice on listening exercises.

We think that erroneous assumptions about the relationship between instruction and testing can lead to some serious problems in education. In far too many preschool classrooms, teachers are concerned with developing specific skills that enable children to do well on tests or in the first-grade curriculum, which is often based on tests. This is not to say that we disapprove of children's learning the skills tested by the instruments we have discussed. We are suggesting rather that children who are educated well will understand much more than these tests indicate, and that acquiring even these skills requires experiences that go far beyond skill-oriented instruction. In our opinion, workbooks and kits cannot give children a good education. Children need to be able to explore rich environments. They also need to interact with adults who are concerned, knowledgeable, and willing to involve themselves with children in a variety of well-chosen ways.

Living with the Preschooler

The Preschooler's Need for Movement

At the beginning of this chapter we described the many physical skills that emerge during the preschool years. We did not mention, however, that children love to practice their new skills. As soon as they learn to hop and skip, they begin to hop and skip all of the time. When they have a skill down pat, they like to vary it and try to do it in new ways. In fact, preschoolers are almost always on the move. Even when they are supposed to sit still, at the dinner table for example, they squirm, wiggle, and get up and down.

Adults sometimes have trouble coping with the preschooler's constant motion. "Sit still!" they demand. "Relax for a minute," they suggest. "Walk instead of run," they instruct. The child may cease his or her activity for a while, but usually not for very long.

Children may also concentrate so completely on a new skill that they fail to move quickly when it is appropriate. More than once we have seen a parent with a preschooler in hand trying to hurry across the street before the light changes, while the child hops or jumps across at his or her own pace!

Knowledgeable adults give children lots of opportunities to move, and then tolerate a certain amount of activity even in situations where relative calm is the adult norm. Children must learn not to get up and down from their chairs at dinnertime, of course, but this can usually be accomplished with simple reminders to "sit down and eat your dinner now."

A preschool child on the move

Adults should accept, however, that most preschoolers find it hard to stop moving, especially when they have nothing else to do. If you have ever watched children at an airport, a supermarket, a doctor's office, or a laundromat, you have seen how active they are. They run up and down aisles, walk on the ledges in front of the windows, swing on the ropes that block the gates, climb on chairs, push shopping carts, and go in and out of swinging doors or around and around in revolving doors. Their parents scold, yell, or punish them, often with little success. To stop the behavior for relatively long stretches of time, it is best to involve the child in activities that are incompatible with the ones considered inappropriate. Giving the child paper and pencil, a magic slate, or a book will often work.

Physical Abilities and Independence

As children acquire motor skills, they can do more by themselves and they often insist on being allowed to do so. Among other things, they learn to dress and undress by themselves. Children learn to undress before they learn to dress, because it takes less skill to unbutton and unzip, for example, than to button and zip. It is also easier to pull garments off than to put them on.

Some skills involved in dressing, such as tying shoelaces, are very difficult. It is unusual for children to master shoe tying before the age of five or six (Coley, 1978). But the problem is not entirely a lack of fine motor skill; tying a bow involves cognitive abilities too. According to Piaget and Inhelder (1967), bow tying requires an understanding of ideas such as enclosure, continuity, order, and separation, all of which are topological relationships.

To encourage independence, it is a good idea to select clothes that are easy to put on and take off. Children should be given plenty of time to button coats, put on mittens, and buckle boots.

The Preschooler's Fear of the Dark

Preschoolers' limited understanding of dreams was mentioned in Chapter 17. Because they think dreams actually take place in their rooms, they are easily frightened, and they may come to fear going to bed or being in the dark. What can be done to comfort children in these situations?

The basic problem is that children cannot differentiate their thoughts from what they think about. This confusion is difficult to sort out, and it takes children several years to develop accurate notions about dreams. Thus, although discussions with the child may be helpful in the long run, we should not expect an explanation of what has occurred to quiet a frightened child. Some steps can be taken to make an upset child more comfortable, however.

Providing a night light can reduce the fear of going to bed and show the child that there is nothing to be afraid of when he or she awakens from a dream. When the child wakes up, the parent can also turn on the room light to help the child see that there is nothing in the room. Helping the child back into bed and

"I'm scared to go to bed. There's monsters in my room!"

offering comforting comments such as "There is nothing in the room; you were just dreaming or imagining things" can help, not because the child understands them completely, but because they help the child comprehend that a trusted person who believes that everything is all right is nearby. Staying close by until the child goes back to sleep can also help, as can the presence of familiar stuffed animals or dolls.

Parents who have tried these procedures may think they do not work, because the child continues to awaken, upset, for a long time. This is to be expected; it takes a long time for a child's ideas about dreams to change. The procedure should be considered successful if it settles the child down reasonably soon after he or she awakens from a bad dream.

In this situation it is probably unwise for the parent to help the child to search the room to see if the "things are still there" and then say "No, they must have gone." This is different from saying, "There is nothing in your room; you were only dreaming" before helping the child look around the room to see that it is safe. In the first instance you are suggesting that there was something in the room before it left; in the second instance you are saying that there was nothing there in the first place. Telling the child that the monsters are gone will not help her understand the nature of dreams, nor will it keep her from being afraid. If monsters were there once, they might return!

Play Materials for the Preschooler

If you have ever walked through a department store toy department, you probably realize how important toys are to most preschool children. There were undoubtedly toys for infants, toddlers, older children, and adults, but the toys for preschoolers probably outnumbered those available to other age groups. In this section we will describe some of the play materials preschoolers enjoy and discuss how they reflect preschoolers' interests and capabilities.

Motor Play Materials. Swing sets, climbing apparatus, tricycles, wagons, and large plastic or rubber balls give children a chance to use their large muscles. Some play materials that require motor skill are puzzles, beads for stringing, blocks, crayons, pencils or magic markers and paper, paints and paintbrushes, scissors, glue, and dolls with clothes having buttons, snaps, and hooks and eyes.

In addition to developing motor skills, motor toys enhance development in other areas. When children draw, for example, they learn about space and think about objects in the world as they try to reconstruct them. Similarly, children learn about space and print when they try to write. When children climb on a jungle gym or climbing box or manipulate the fastenings on doll clothes, they learn basic concepts such as "inside," "outside," "on," "off," "on top of," "around," and "through." When an adult comments on a child's actions during play, the child learns how to express these concepts in words: "I see that you glued a red piece of paper *on top of* the blue piece." "Are you having trouble getting that tiny button to go *through* the buttonhole?"

Materials for Pretend Play. At around age three, children begin to engage in play about social roles and situations. Play of this type, known as *sociodramatic play*, occurs when children are alone as well as when they play with others (Fein, 1978). If playing alone, children often create imaginary companions as play partners (Manosevitz, Prentice, and Wilson, 1973; Pines, 1978).

Certain materials are especially conducive to sociodramatic play. Dolls, stuffed animals, and dressup clothes are good, as are play dishes, appliances, and props such as hats or jewelry. Children also enjoy empty food cartons and detergent bottles, as well as the empty containers of such things as shaving cream, talc, and body lotion. Materials such as paper and pencil or crayons and pieces of fabric come in handy, too, when children wish to make a prop of their own, such as a shopping list for use in pretend trips to the grocery store, a birthday card, tickets, a sign, or a handkerchief for a doll.

Water, Sand, and Dough. Water, sand, and dough are favorites. Children may enjoy them because they offer almost limitless opportunities for exploration and experimentation, especially in combination with utensils such as plastic or metal bowls, cups, pans, spoons, molds, and cookie cutters. A puzzle, on the other hand, can be worked in one way and one way only. Although such a toy is valuable, it may become tiresome soon after it is mastered.

Water, sand, and dough also provide practically unlimited opportunities for learning. For example, children learn the materials' various characteristics and properties. Liquids and granular substances take the shape of their containers, but the dough does not unless it is pressed down. The dough and the sand, when wet, retain the shape of their containers, but the water does not unless it is frozen. The water evaporates if left uncovered, whereas the dough hardens and crumbles, and the sand remains unchanged.

Storybooks. Books are among the most enjoyable and important play materials. In Chapter 18 we discussed how storybooks are thought to contribute to children's understanding of print and the reading process. Storybooks also contribute to language development and provide excellent opportunities for close and positive adult-child interactions.

A good book for a preschooler should have attractive, clear illustrations that go along with the text. The story itself should be simple and of moderate length. The language should be interesting. Children enjoy repeated phrases and rhyming words. The content of the story and the values it expresses should be consistent with the adult's standards.

The Role of the Adult in Children's Play

Should children be left alone to play, or should adults play along? When adults do play with children, how should they go about it? These questions often lead to heated debates among preschool teachers.

Sociodramatic Play. Some authorities state emphatically that adults should not involve themselves in children's sociodramatic play; others argue that adult intervention can sometimes be appropriate and helpful. The conflict is based on differing interpretations of why children play. The prevailing view early in this century, which has its adherents even today, was psychoanalytic. Play was considered a form of catharsis through which children could release anxieties and frustrations. According to this interpretation, adult intervention may interfere with children's emotional lives by causing them to keep their feelings pent up and unresolved.

Other experts regard sociodramatic play as a cognitive and social process (Garvey, 1974; El 'konin, 1969). Proponents of this view believe that children's play reflects what they know, and what they know is thought to be affected by their experiences. One important type of experience consists of interactions with adults, who can be the source of play themes and techniques (Rosen, 1974; Saltz and Johnson, 1974; Smilansky, 1968). Accordingly, adult intervention is thought to enhance play, as long as "the adult is more partner than director and the child is free not to participate" (Fein, 1978). This means that the adult should not dictate the play themes and roles, but should suggest roles and assume roles

Adult participation can enhance a child's play, but the adult should allow the child to control the action.

assigned by the children. In the same way adults should sometimes leave children to themselves, because entering play sometimes disrupts. It is often wise to enter play briefly to introduce new ideas and then leave the play to the children.

Creative Activities. Should adults involve themselves with children when they are painting, drawing with crayons, or building with blocks? Some preschool teachers say yes and show children how to draw figures and tell them what to build with blocks; other teachers would oppose such actions.

At issue here are assumptions about what can be told and shown to children and what they must learn for themselves. As we discussed earlier, children's representational pictures reflect their understanding of concepts of space. Before children can draw or paint representational pictures, they simply manipulate the materials and enjoy the motoric and visual feedback (N. R. Smith, 1979). We think that giving a child a model to copy or an outlined picture to color in deprives him or her of opportunities to conceptualize spatial relationships and to think about details of objects in the world. Self-expression is also reduced. This can make children feel incapable of making acceptable drawings. We think good adult intervention consists of providing experiences that help children understand the nature of real objects and situations, not of specifying how children should represent what they know (or do not know, as the case may be).

Summary

Preschool Education Programs

- People differ in their views about what makes a good preschool program. We think a good program includes opportunities for learning from direct experiences, for decision making, problem solving, assuming responsibility, and interacting with peers and adults.
- Teacher behavior is determined in part by the teacher's assumptions about the nature of knowledge. Piaget classified knowledge into four categories. Physical knowledge is what we know about the characteristics of objects. Social knowledge is gained from other people. Logicomathematical knowledge is acquired through interactions with objects. Symbolic knowledge is knowledge of how we can represent what we know.
- A structured classroom is one in which the teacher's behavior, the daily schedule, the materials available, and the aspects of the classroom are consistent with stated values and a theory of development.
- Evaluation of preschool programs is a difficult process. However, it has been found that compensatory programs that involve parents extensively are usually more successful in the long run than programs that do not involve parents.

Preschool Assessment Instruments

- Common assessment instruments used with preschool children include the Metropolitan Readiness Tests and the Denver Developmental Screening Test. The Concepts About Print Test and the Piagetian tasks provide assessment of very specific areas of development.
- Assessment instruments reflect values and a preferred theory of learning, and their importance can be exaggerated. "Teaching to the test" is a practice based on erroneous assumptions about the relationship between prediction and causation.

Living with the Preschooler

- As children acquire motor skills, they increase their independence. Adults can help by making tasks such as dressing simpler and giving children plenty of time.
- Preschoolers' fear of the dark is probably related to their inability to differentiate thoughts and things thought about.
- Common play materials for preschoolers include motor toys, materials for pretend play; water, sand, and dough; and storybooks.
- Opinions regarding the role of adults in children's play are based on assumptions about development.

- A good approach for intervening in children's dramatic play is to step in with an idea and then step out again, leaving the play to the children. In helping children learn to draw, providing experiences that permit children to know how things look is probably a more useful intervention than providing models for children to copy.

New Terms

physical knowledge
social knowledge
logicomathematical knowledge

symbolic knowledge
sociodramatic play

Selected Readings

Fassler, D. **The young child in the hospital.** *Young Children 35 (1980): 19–25.* Discusses young children's fears about being hospitalized and how these can be alleviated with good preparation and sensitivity to children's needs. Covers orientation programs provided by some hospitals and provides a list of books to use with children.

Forman, G. E., and Hill, F. **Constructive play: Applying Piaget in the preschool.** *Monterey, Calif.: Brooks/Cole, 1980.* This book contains some wonderful ideas for manipulative play in the preschool. These ideas have been tested with real children, and excellent descriptions of children's behavior are provided.

Jones, S. **Learning for little kids: A parent's sourcebook for the years 3 to 8.** *Boston: Houghton Mifflin, 1979.* The author offers many ideas for materials preschoolers can play with at home. She also provides much good information about characteristics of preschool children. There are chapters on teaching self-care, safety, cooking, and nutrition; dealing with illness; and providing experiences with art, nature, wood, mud, sand, water, music, dance, and language. The book also contains many lists of books for children.

Kamii, C., and DeVries, R. **Piaget, children, and number.** *Washington, D.C.: National Association for the Education of Young Children. 1976.* This brief paperback discusses the nature of number according to Piaget. Gives many practical suggestions for experiences that teachers can provide in the preschool setting.

Part VI
The School-Age Child

The period between the ages of six and twelve is known as middle childhood, or the school-age period. During this period children learn to ride bikes, shoot marbles, play jacks, read books by themselves, play the piano, sew on buttons, write their names in script, add columns of numbers, and much more.

To the adult, middle childhood may seem like a relatively tranquil period. The problems of coping with young children are over. Parents no longer must deal with a child who is almost totally dependent on them and thinks very differently than they do. And the problems of adolescence seem far away.

But to the school-age child life is anything but calm. It is filled with challenges, a few traumas, and many new pleasures. It is pleasant to be allowed to ride a bike to a friend's house or to spend a week at camp during the summer, but being left out of activities by children considered friends, or being denied permission to watch the television programs that everybody else is allowed to watch can lead to miserable moments. Being taller or shorter than everyone else in the class can also be upsetting.

There are significant changes in every aspect of development during this stage. We will discuss some of these changes and their effects on children and on the people who interact with them.

Chapter 21

Physical Development

As in previous periods, physical development during the school-age period includes increases in height and weight, changes in body proportions, and the acquisition of both fine and gross motor skills. We will discuss these aspects of development next, along with their implications for child behavior.

Growth

Height and Weight

Growth during the school-age period, or middle childhood, is much slower than it is among younger children. The average six-year-old weighs about forty pounds and is about three and one-half feet tall. The average twelve-year-old weighs about eighty pounds and is about five feet tall. Thus, it takes six years for school-age children to double their weight and increase their height by about one-third. This is about twelve times as long as it takes infants to grow a proportional amount.

By the time children enter middle childhood, they have achieved about two-thirds of their adult height. By the end of middle childhood boys have achieved about 80 percent of their adult height and girls have achieved about 90 percent of theirs (Tanner, 1978). The percentage of adult height achieved by British and American children at various ages is shown in Table 21-1.

Body Proportions

During the school-age period a child's legs grow considerably; the trunk also lengthens. This growth pattern makes school-age children look quite slim compared to younger children. Parents with chubby, short-legged children often have trouble buying pants that fit them. At this stage dresses and shirts are outgrown by becoming short-waisted rather than too tight around the child's middle.

The proportions of the face also change during middle childhood. During the first six years of childhood the head achieves a larger percentage of its total growth than other body parts, but more of this growth occurs in the upper part of the head. During the middle years the lower face and jaw begin to catch up, and the face becomes longer and thinner.

The growth of the lower face influences the position of the *Eustachian tubes*, which connect the middle ear to the throat. During early childhood the tubes are nearly horizontal, but as the lower face grows during the school-age years the tubes become more vertical. This allows them to drain more easily into the throat, and ear infections, which can be quite common in young children, occur much less frequently. Children who suffer from repeated ear infections sometimes need to have tubes placed in their ears to promote drainage and avoid hearing loss. These tubes can usually be removed when the child is six or seven.

Another change that occurs during childhood is the replacement of the baby, or *deciduous*, teeth with permanent teeth. Most of the time school-age children have a tooth coming or going, and toothless smiles are a common sight in grade school.

A toothless smile

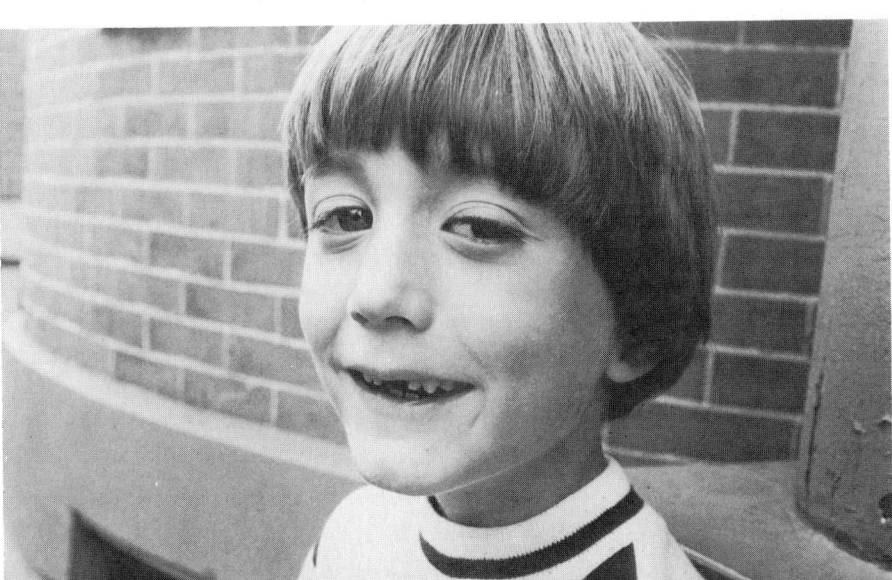

Table 21-1. Percentage of adult height achieved by boys and girls at various ages

Age (yr)	Boys U.K.	Boys U.S.A.	Girls U.K.	Girls U.S.A.
0.08	30.9	30.8	32.7	32.6
0.25	34.7		36.4	
0.50	39.0	38.5	40.4	40.3
0.75	41.6		43.3	
1.00	43.7	43.0	45.7	45.3
1.25	45.4		47.8	
1.50	47.0	46.7	49.7	49.3
1.75	48.4		51.3	
2.00	49.8	49.4	52.8	52.7
2.00	49.2	48.8	52.1	52.7
2.5	51.6		54.8	
3.0	53.9	53.8	57.3	57.4
3.5	56.1		59.7	
4.0	58.2	58.1	61.9	62.0
4.5	60.1		64.0	
5.0	62.0	62.0	66.1	66.4
5.5	63.8		68.0	
6.0	65.6	65.7	69.9	70.0
6.5	67.3		71.8	
7.0	69.0	68.9	73.6	73.6
7.5	70.6		75.3	
8.0	72.2	71.7	77.1	77.2
8.5	73.8		78.8	
9.0	75.4	74.6	80.5	80.6
9.5	76.9		82.2	
10.0	78.3	77.6	83.8	84.5
10.5	79.8		85.5	
11.0	81.3	81.1	87.3	88.4
11.5	82.7		89.5	
12.0	84.1	84.6	92.2	91.1
12.5	85.5		94.7	
13.0	87.1	88.1	96.7	96.1
13.5	89.1		98.0	
14.0	92.0	92.1	98.9	98.0
14.5	94.6		99.5	
15.0	96.6	95.4	99.8	99.1
15.5	97.9		99.9	
16.0	98.8	98.1	100.0	99.2
16.5	99.4		—	
17.0	99.8	99.7	—	99.5
17.5	99.9		—	
18.0	100.0	100.0	—	100.0

SOURCE: From *Fetus into Man* by J. M. Tanner, Copyright © 1978 by J. M. Tanner. Reprinted by permission of the publisher, Harvard University Press.

Variations in Growth Patterns

Children grow at different rates. It is not unusual for children who were tall for their age at eight or nine to be surpassed in height by many of their classmates by the early teens. Variations in growth are particularly apparent during the later years of the school-age period, when the preadolescent growth spurt occurs. The age at which this growth spurt occurs can vary by several years. Girls usually experience it before boys.

The growth spurt and its timing can influence how children feel about themselves. They may feel awkward if they tower over their peers or if they are especially short. The physical changes associated with puberty, such as the growth of breasts and pubic hair, can also affect how children are regarded by their peers (Faust, 1960). Adults who work with older school-age children must be sensitive to how physical growth can influence children's perceptions of themselves.

FOCUS: Deviations from Normal Growth in School-Age Children

Not all children grow normally during the school years. Children may fail to grow or may grow too slowly; they may be heavier than is normal and healthy; or they may undergo precocious puberty (mature sexually early on in the school-age period rather than in adolescence).

Slow growth can have a social-environmental or organic-physical cause. Children whose growth is far below typical growth for their age are known as *failure-to-thrive* children. When this syndrome is the result of parental neglect, it is most often found in infants. However, if conditions in the home are not changed, or if intermittent episodes of crisis and stress continue to affect parenting, failure to thrive can continue throughout childhood (Kempe and Kempe, 1978). A failure-to-thrive child is small for his or her age, often looks undernourished, and may be lethargic or listless. Treatment involves working with the neglectful parents or removing the child to a home setting where proper care can be provided.

One physical problem that may retard growth is a disturbance of the pituitary gland such that the growth hormone it produces is not supplied in normal quantities. Sometimes the disturbance is due to a lesion (injury due to disease or trauma) in the endocrine glands. For example, an infectious disease such as meningeal tuberculosis can cause a lesion and thus damage the functioning of the pituitary. Radiation treatment for tumors of the middle ear or eye or for leukemia can also disturb hormone production. Such malfunctions are known as *organic*. When a lesion is not present, the condition is known as *idiopathic*. Idiopathic pituitary conditions are inherited as recessive characteristics (Frasier, 1979).

(continued on following page)

FOCUS *(continued)*

Children who have low levels of growth hormone are short for their age, although they tend to be overweight for their height. Their chests and abdomens tend to be chubby. Their head size, however, may be typical for their age (Frasier, 1979). Deviation from normal height is the best indicator of the problem, and it has been suggested that height screening of all children on entrance to primary school could result in early diagnosis and treatment of this syndrome (Tanner, 1978).

Precocious development also has organic or genetic causes. A hereditary disorder found in boys results in onset of puberty (reproductive maturity) as early as four years of age or early in the school years. A similar condition has been reported in girls, but it is not thought to be hereditary (Tanner, 1978). Reports of pregnancy in girls as young as five or six are possible due to this rare condition.

Obesity is the most common deviation from normal growth found in the school-age population. Obesity is defined in terms of weight-for-height or weight-for-age that exceeds the standard by 20 percent (Neumann, 1977). Studies vary in their estimates of the number of overweight school-age children, but there are probably around 10 percent in the United States (Rauh and Schumsky, 1968).

Surprisingly, fat children do not always eat more than their normal peers. What almost always distinguishes the two groups, however, is lack of activity and exercise in the overweight group (Neumann, 1977; Winick, 1974). Treatment of overweight children must include daily exercise, such as hikes or active games; restriction of inactive pastimes such as television viewing; and enrollment in organized programs such as YMCA, YWCA, or programs sponsored by park and recreation departments (Neumann, 1977). Not only do such programs increase physical activity, but they encourage the child to make social contacts and thereby reduce loneliness and boredom. Obese children often become obese teens, and obese teens may not eat out of hunger as much as out of boredom and loneliness (Winick, 1974). Development of peer relations during the school-age years can help alleviate the social isolation that can lead to continued weight problems during the teenage years.

Motor Development

During middle childhood children learn to ride bicycles and skateboards, to ski, roller skate, and jump rope. They learn to snap their fingers and spin a top. This is the period when musical instruments are taken up, and writing increases in precision and skill, first in manuscript (printing), then in cursive (script). Hobbies and crafts that require small motor skills, such as painting by number, assembling models, and stitchery are popular, as are games that involve gross physical skills.

It is during the school-age period that organized sports such as Little League and swim teams begin. Although children during this period have the cognitive and motor skills to play sports, their bones and muscles are immature and easily injured. Immature bones are softer than those of teenagers and adults, and they can be deformed from strain or squeezing. In the same way, immature muscles are easily strained and torn. This is why restrictions are placed on the amount of time a child can pitch in a Little League game (Milberg, 1976). No limit has been placed on the number of hours that a Little League pitcher can practice pitching, however (Zimbler, 1980).

In some elementary schools the development of motor skills is a low priority. Schools often teach reading every day for at least an hour but provide physical education only once a week, if at all. Educators should remember that good motor coordination and strength can increase a child's independence and self-esteem, contribute to good health, and promote cognitive development. Physical education can also encourage socialization as children join teams and learn the rules of games.

School-age children are interested in making things.

Summary

- The school-age period, or middle childhood, is the period when children are between six and eleven or twelve years old.

Growth

- Growth is relatively slow during middle childhood. The legs, trunk, lower face, and jaw grow more than other parts of the body during middle childhood. However, children grow at different rates, and the age at which the preadolescent growth spurt occurs varies considerably.

Motor Development

- Hobbies and crafts that require good small motor skills are popular among school-age children.
- School-age children learn many games requiring motor skill. Organized sports, such as Little League, usually begin during the school-age years.
- Motor skill development can contribute to a child's sense of independence and self-esteem, as well as to social and cognitive development.

New Terms

Eustachian tubes
deciduous teeth
failure-to-thrive syndrome
idiopathic growth retardation

organic growth retardation
precocious development
obesity

Selected Readings

Magill, R. A., Ash, M. J., and Smoll, F. L., (Eds.). **Children in sport: A contemporary anthology.** *Champaign, Ill.: Human Kinetics, 1978.* Discusses physical and motor development and its relationship to the child's capacity to participate in various sports.

Riley, M., Barett, K. R., Robertson, M., and Martinek, T. J. **Physical activity and your child's well-being.** *Washington, D.C.: U.S. Government Printing Office, 1979.* This booklet discusses the contribution of physical activity to the child's health and overall well-being.

Tanner, J. M. **Education and physical growth.** *Second edition. New York: International Universities Press, 1978.* This is the same book recommended in our earlier chapters on physical development. It is the best source for information on growth for all stages of childhood.

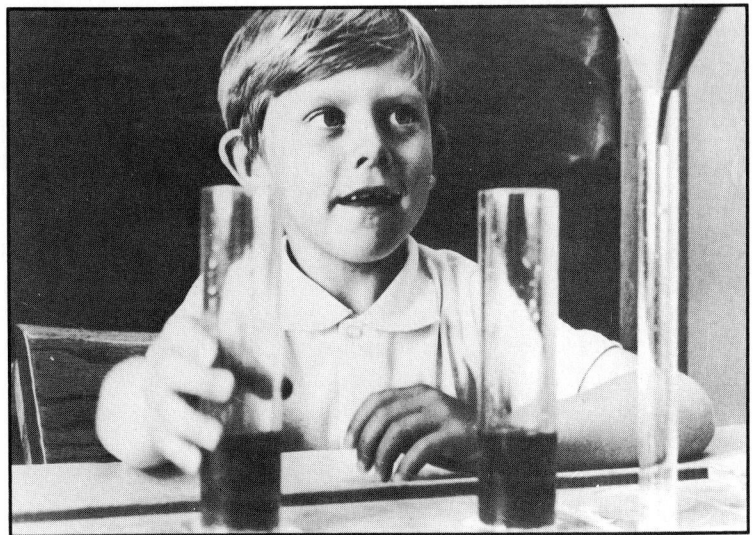

Chapter 22

Cognitive Development

School-age children enter Piaget's *concrete operational stage* of cognitive development. In the following pages we will discuss the characteristics that distinguish concrete operational thinking from preoperational thinking, which precedes it, and from formal operational thinking, which follows it. In addition, we will discuss the development of some of the specific concepts that emerge during the concrete operational stage. Finally, we will examine intelligence and intelligence testing — topics of long-standing interest to psychologists.

The Concrete Operational Child

School-age children think differently than younger and older children. Whereas the thinking of young children is characterized as *preoperational*, and the thinking of older children is called *formal operational*, school-age children have what is called *concrete operational* thought. Unlike that of the preoperational child, the thinking of a concrete operational child is dominated by logic rather than perception. Concrete operational children realize that changing the length of one of two equal rows of objects does not influence the number of objects in the row. "You didn't add any or take any away," the child might say. "They are still the same."

The concrete operational child's thinking, however, is still limited by its reliance on what the child has observed. At this stage children cannot imagine all possible actions or determine which of several variables causes an action. Suppose you were asked to determine the factors that influence how long it takes a pendulum to complete one swing. Several factors could be responsible: the weight of the object at the end of the string, the length of the string, or the height from which the pendulum is let go. You would have to alter each variable systematically, while holding the others constant to determine which variable was responsible, through the process of elimination. This type of reasoning is called *hypothetico-deductive*. It characterizes the stage of formal operations, which begins around age twelve. The school-age child's thinking may be operational, but he or she can perform operations involving only concrete, observable phenomena. The child cannot think of all possible actions.

Concrete operational children also overcome some of the egocentricity characteristic of preoperational children. During the concrete operational stage children begin to understand that what one perceives depends on one's perspective. They also begin to understand that thoughts and things thought about are different. In other words, their realism, or the tendency to endow thoughts with physical substance, diminishes. They begin to realize as well that thoughts and the meanings of words vary from person to person. This leads a child to see that others do not always know what she means. She comes to realize that more complete explanations are necessary if others are to understand her.

In the following pages we will discuss the development of specific concepts during the concrete operational period.

Conservation

Children of six or seven years of age realize that quantity remains the same despite transformations of position: they conserve number. But conservation is not achieved in all areas at the same time. Conservation of number and mass are acquired first, but a child who conserves in these areas may deny that the length of a zig-zag line is the same as that of a straight line (see Box 22-1), or that two plastic horses have the same amount of "pasture" to graze on regardless of whether "barns" are scattered throughout the pastures or lined up neatly at one end (Box 22-2). Children may conserve number, but not length or area. This separation of concepts indicates that some concepts are harder to learn than others. The ages at which various types of conservation emerge are shown in Figure 22-1.

BOX 22-1. Conservation of Length

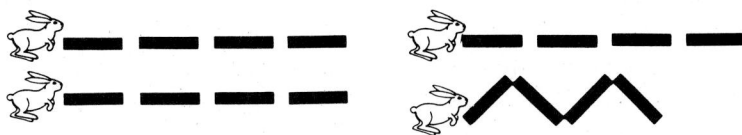

A test used to assess conservation of length starts with two equal straight "roads" constructed from a series of sticks. One road is then bent or curved so that it does not extend as far as the other road. The child is asked if rabbits hopping down the two roads would arrive at the ends of the roads together, or whether one would reach the end ahead of the other.

BOX 22-2. Conservation of Area

A test used to assess conservation of area makes use of two green boards or pieces of construction paper of the same size, which represent pastures. In each pasture is a toy horse. Several barns, represented by small red cubes, are placed either close together or far apart on the two pastures. The child is asked if the horses have the same amount of grass to eat. By age eight or nine, children can conserve area. They realize that changing the positions of the barns does not affect how much grass they cover.

Type of conservation	Dimension	Change in physical appearance	Average age at which invariance is grasped
Number	Number of elements in a collection	Rearranging or dislocating elements	6–7
Substance (mass) (continuous quantity)	Amount of a malleable substance (e.g., clay or liquid)	Altering shape	7–8
Length	Length of a line or object	Altering shape or configuration	7–8
Area	Amount of surface covered by a set of plane figures	Rearranging the figures	8–9
Weight	Weight of an object	Altering its shape	9–10
Volume	Volume of an object (in terms of water displacement)	Altering its shape	14–15

Figure 22-1. Piaget's conservations

Seriation

Seriation is the ordering of objects according to size. The ability to seriate can be assessed by asking children to put ten sticks of varying lengths in order from the smallest to the largest. In Piaget's Stage I, four to five years of age, children cannot make the series. They sometimes place sticks in piles, perhaps separating short sticks and long sticks (see Figurer 22-2a), or make a staircase arrangement by centering on one end of the sticks (Figure 22-2b). These arrangements, however, are not true series.

In Stage II, five to six years of age, children can make a series, but only through trial and error. They are unable to think of two aspects of the relationship at the same time: "The next stick must be longer than the last one, but shorter than the rest." As a result, they often select a stick longer than the last one placed in the series, but also longer than some of the remaining sticks. The error is discovered and corrected in arranging the remaining sticks. Piaget describes this behavior as both intuitive and empirical. The child starts with a vague idea of how to seriate (intuition) and then discovers how to do it exactly when he or she is in the process of arranging the sticks (empirical).

Stage III children, six to seven years old, can solve the problem operationally. They know exactly how to construct the series before they begin. The child thinks, "I must find one that is longer than the last one but shorter than all the others." Note that the preoperational child can consider only one aspect of a relationship at a time, whereas the concrete operational child can consider two.

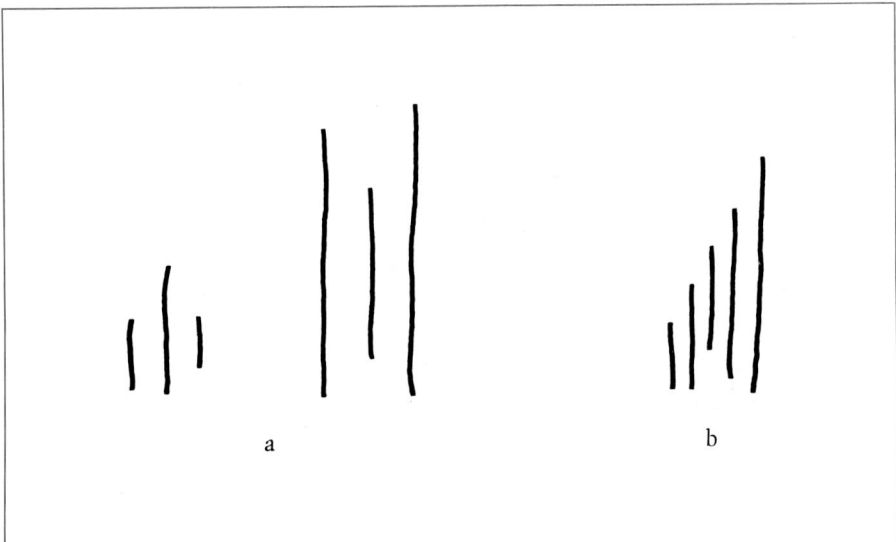

Figure 22-2. Early attempts to seriate

Classification

Suppose you were asked to organize the following materials on a table: a large red circle, a large blue circle, a large blue square, a small red square, a small blue square, a small red circle, a paper clip, an elastic band, and an eraser. To begin, you might separate the geometric figures from the objects. Then you might work within the class of figures to make finer categories. You could put the red figures together and the blue figures together, and then divide these groups further into circles and squares or big figures and little figures. Groupings such as these can be represented schematically as shown in Figure 22-3. This process is known as *hierarchical classification* because subclasses are created within classes.

When we classify, the classes we create exist in our minds. We no longer see the group of figures after forming subgroups of red and blue figures. Similarly, we no longer see a complete group of red and blue, but several groups — red circles and red squares. A classification system is constructed and imposed on objects; it is not inherent in the objects themselves, although objects' attributes determine what classes we can make. (Recall that the ability to classify is a type of logico-mathematical knowledge.)

The classification task no doubt seems simple to you, but it would be difficult for most five- and six-year-olds. Children under four years of age have trouble separating objects into groups with similar attributes, much less organizing groups in relation to each other. They group objects into collections but not into true classes defined by a stable attribute or attributes (Inhelder and Piaget, 1969). Sometimes the defining attributes of their collections change with each figure the child adds. Assume that the child starts with a red square, following it with a red circle, a blue circle, and then a blue square. The child changes the defining attribute from red (the attribute that figures 1 and 2 have in common) to circle (the attribute that figures 2 and 3 have in common) to blue (the attribute that figures 3 and 4 have in common). It is as if the child forgets the defining characteristic of the previous grouping and changes it when he or she notices a different property. You will remember that the thinking of preoperational children is dominated by what they see.

Sometimes children make a picture with figures, perhaps a house, a bridge, or an airplane. In this case children place figures together, not because of a defining characteristic, but because they are a good fit for what children are trying to make. To use Inhelder and Piaget's (1969) terminology, the *intension* of a class (the characteristics defining members belonging to a class) for a child at this stage is not limited to "relations of similarity and difference, as in the case of logical classes. The intension includes relations of affinity or of belonging."

Stage II children, five to seven years old, can form classes with a single defining attribute; for example, all red objects may be separated from all blue ones, or little ones may be separated from big ones. Only when they enter Stage III at age seven or eight can children make hierarchical classes such as those involved in the organizing task shown in Figure 22-3.

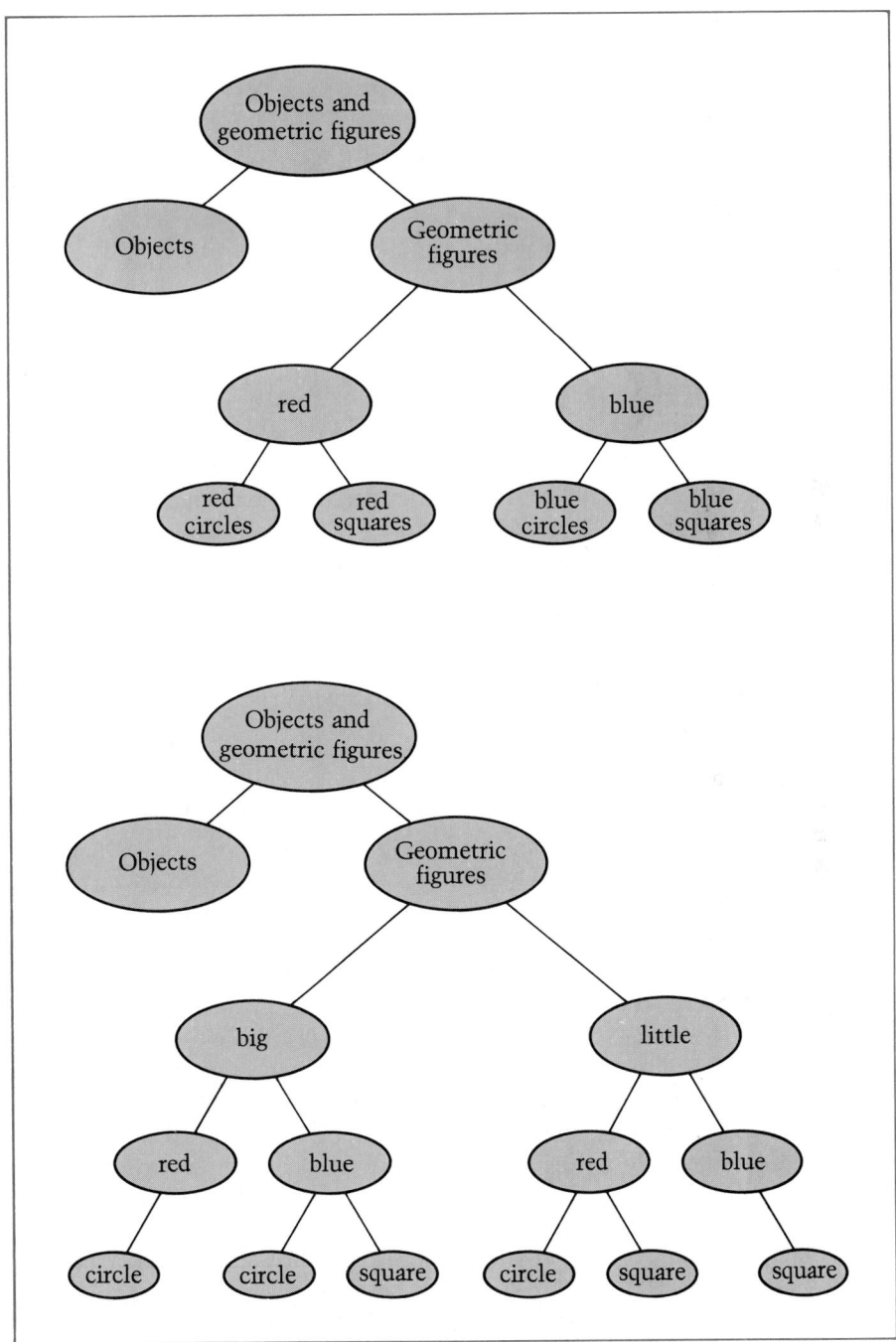

Figure 22-3. Hierarchical classification

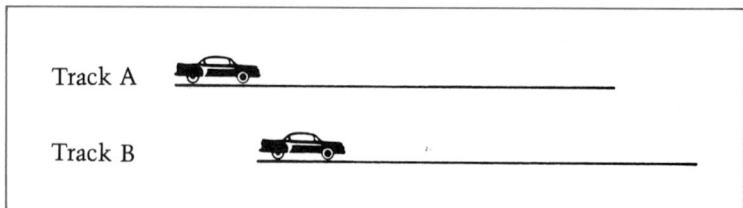

Figure 22-4. Equal tracks placed sequentially in space

The Child's Understanding of Time

Suppose you were asked to observe cars running along the tracks shown in Figure 22-4. The tracks are of equal length, but they begin and end at different places. The cars are to start at the same time, travel at the same speed, and stop at the same time. Would you say that the cars take the same amount of time to make their trips? Of course you would; adults understand that different starting and ending points will not affect how long it takes a car to cover a particular distance. Six-year-olds see the situation differently, however. They claim that the car beginning farthest to the left started first, stopped first, and took less time than the other. They assume that the spatial layouts of the tracks influence the duration of the trips.

A somewhat older child may agree that the cars started and stopped together, but assert at the same time that the car on the track that started and stopped first in space took *less* time. The child admits that the movements are simultaneous but denies that the movements are of equal duration. Conversely, a child sometimes agrees that the movements are equal in duration but then denies their simultaneity. Children who make these type of statements have not yet coordinated the ideas of simultaneity and duration: they center on one idea or the other.

Piaget (1971) used several other tasks to explore children's concepts of time. In one the tracks started at the same point in space but stopped at different points, because one track was longer than the other. By varying the speed of the cars, however, he made them start and stop at the same time. He found that regardless of how the task is varied, the outcome is essentially the same: children do not initially separate their concept of time from their concept of space. Movements beginning and ending at different points in space are assumed to take different amounts of time, regardless of the actual time they take. Not until the age of ten or twelve do children understand that movements that begin and end at the same time take the same amount of time, and that simultaneous movements across unequal distances are possible because speed can vary.

FOCUS: An Information-Processing Approach to Cognitive Development

Some psychologists have been interested in describing very precisely the set of rules for processing information that a child must use to solve the Piagetian Tasks. Typically, the list of rules or operations used is written as a computer program. This means that symbols are used to write statements describing each step of mental operations involved in solving the particular task.

For the conservation-of-number task, the symbols x and y may be used to represent the two collections of materials, such as rows 1 and 2 of pennies. Symbols x' and y' may be used to represent the rows of pennies after a transformation has been made; that is, after a row has been spread out or gathered together in a clump. Q_i may represent a quantification operator, which is a procedure for establishing the quantity of objects in each row. For example, a child might count (Q_c) or estimate (Q_e) to establish quantity.

Once the researcher has created symbols to represent all objects and operations, he or she can write statements for the precise steps involved in failing or succeeding in the conservation-of-number task. The same process, of course, can be used to describe any of the other cognitive tasks, such as class inclusion or seriation (Klahr and Wallace, 1976).

Researchers with an information-processing orientation have also been very interested in short-term and long-term memory, and in attention. *Short-term memory* refers to brief storage of information received visually or auditorily. *Long-term memory* refers to more permanent storage. Information is first entered in short-term memory and then is transferred to long-term memory if it is understood and can be incorporated into a cognitive framework. *Attention* refers to what a person selects to process from all sensorially available information (Simon, 1972).

These three processes — short-term memory, long-term memory, and attention — can be used to describe characteristics of thinking that Piaget has described more globally. For example, centration, or the inability to consider two aspects of a relationship simultaneously, such as the height and width of containers of colored water, may be thought of as a problem of attention. The child eliminates or fails to attend to some of the information available.

There is some debate about the usefulness of the information-processing approach to human thinking. According to Richard Mayer (1977), a computer program may simulate human thinking behavior but not the underlying cognitive processes. Such machine-like views of human thinking, according to Mayer, may limit more useful theoretical thinking about how the human mind works. However, others suggest that the approach is useful because it provides a detailed description of cognitive behavior.

Intelligence

The mental abilities studied by Piaget are common to all children. Children may acquire object permanence or conservation of number at different ages, but all children eventually acquire them. Furthermore, once children acquire these concepts, they acquire them completely. In other words, all children who conserve number conserve it equally well.

A different view has dominated discussions of intelligence, for almost three-quarters of a century. This view is concerned with individual differences in intelligence; people are thought to develop the abilities assumed to indicate intelligence in varying degrees. Intelligence tests like those you probably took in elementary school were developed to measure these abilities.

Measuring Intelligence

The first intelligence test was developed by Alfred Binet and Theodore Simon in the early 1900s. They had been asked to devise a way to differentiate Parisian schoolchildren who could be expected to succeed from those who would probably fail. Binet and Simon chose tasks requiring judgment and reasoning. They determined *norms* (typical or normal ranges) by testing a large number of children of various ages. The *mental age* (MA) of a child was determined by comparing the child's score to the norm for different age levels. For example, a child of ten who passed items typically passed by five-year-olds was said to have a mental age of 5. The problem with using an absolute measure such as mental age is that a child of four with a mental age of 3 and a child of ten with a mental age of 9 would each have an MA one year behind their age group. However, these children would not be equal in intelligence. A difference of one year between a child's MA and *chronological age* (CA) means different things at different age levels. To overcome this problem, Stern (1912) introduced the idea of the *intelligence quotient* (IQ), which is calculated with the following formula:

$$a\frac{MA}{CA} \times 100 = IQ$$

The four-year-old who has an MA of 3 has an IQ of 75:

$$\frac{MA\ (3)}{CA\ (4)} \times 100 = 75$$

The ten-year-old who has an MA of 9 has an IQ of 90:

$$\frac{MA\ (9)}{CA\ (10)} \times 100 = 90$$

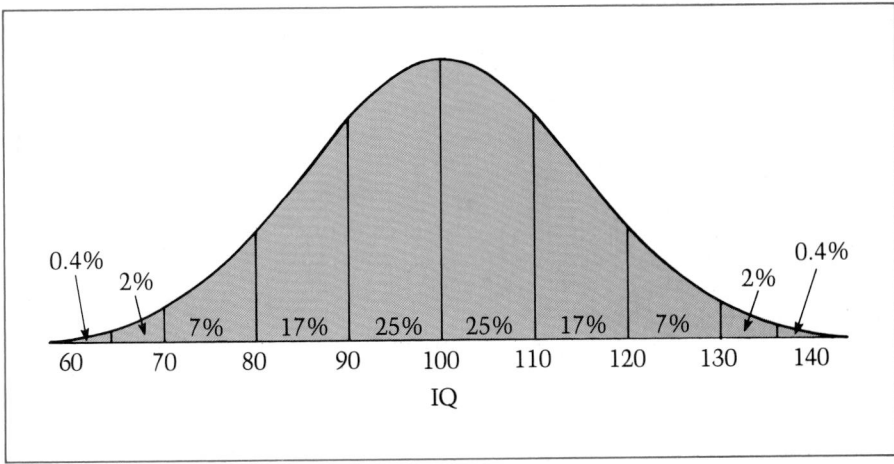

Figure 22-5. The normal theoretical distribution of IQs, showing percentages of the population expected to fall in each IQ range. (Due to rounding, the total is more than 100 percent.)

A child whose mental and chronological ages are the same has an IQ of 100; a child whose mental age is higher than his or her chronological age has an IQ over 100. Today, IQ is calculated by reference to tables of age-group norms; the ratio method is no longer used.

The distribution of IQ scores in the population is shown in Figure 22-5. This curve indicates the frequency of IQ scores. Most people have an IQ of about 100. Only about 3 percent of the population have IQs above 130. An additional 3 percent have IQs below 70 (see FOCUS on mental retardation).

FOCUS: Mental Retardation

Mental retardation is a term that has been used for many years to describe quite a range of mental abilities. According to the American Association on Mental Deficiency (AAMD): "Mental retardation refers to significantly subaverage general intellectual functioning resulting in or associated with impairments in adaptive behavior and manifested during the developmental period." (Grossman, in press) Let us consider what this all means.

"Subaverage general intellectual functioning" is defined as a score of less than 70 on one or more of the individually administered standardized tests of intelligence. "Adaptive behavior" refers to the self-help and social skills needed to get along in everyday life. Deficits in adaptive behavior are harder to identify than is

(continued on following page)

FOCUS *(continued)*

an IQ below 70. Although clinical judgment and experience are usually needed to identify deficits in adaptive behavior, some useful standard tests are available. The best-known of these is the Vineland Social Maturity Scale, which outlines the self-help, social, and occupational skills that should develop at given ages. For example, for ages six to seven, the items of the scale are "uses table of knife for spreading," "uses pencil for writing," "bathes self assisted," and "goes to bed unassisted" (Doll, 1965).

"Manifested during the developmental period" means that the delays in intellectual functioning and adaptive behavior must have taken place at least before age eighteen. If they take place after age eighteen, the diagnosis is that of "dementia," and actual loss of previous intellectual abilities for some organic (biological) reason (American Psychiatric Association, 1980).

DEGREE OF RETARDATION AND EDUCATIONAL PROGRAMS

Four degrees of mental retardation are commonly recognized. In *mild mental retardation*, IQ scores range from 50 to 70. This group comprises about 80 percent of those with mental retardation. Because the retardation is not extreme, these children are often not distinguished from others until they have done poorly in elementary school and have been referred for testing. As adults they usually achieve social and occupational skills needed to support themselves independently (American Psychiatric Association, 1980). Individuals with scores on IQ tests ranging from 35 to 49 are labelled *moderately retarded* and constitute about 12 percent of the population showing mental retardation. It is expected that during their adult years, members of this group will be able to care for themselves with moderate supervision and will be able to contribute to their own economic support by performing primarily unskilled and semiskilled supervised work in sheltered workshops. In *severe mental retardation* (IQ scores from 20 to 34) and *profound mental retardation* (IQ scores below 20), self-care and occupational skills are expected to be extremely limited. These four subcategories are continuous rather than discrete. That is, the general expectations we have described must be modified in each individual case. For example, some adults who are "moderately retarded" will be able to care for themselves independently better than some showing "mild mental retardation."

When we study mentally retarded children in school, we encounter new labels. The special education category of educable mentally retarded corresponds roughly with mild mental retardation, and the special education category *trainable mentally retarded* corresponds roughly with moderate and severe mental retardation. These terms are used to describe educational programs for the mentally retarded and do not refer strictly to IQ levels as in the AAMD categories. Educable mentally retarded children are taught fundamental academic skills needed to function independently as adults. On the other hand, most trainable mentally retarded children are considered unlikely to progress beyond the second grade in academic subjects. Therefore their curriculum emphasizes vocational and adaptive (self-help and social) skills. A trainable mentally retarded child who masters the skills in his or her program can be reassigned to a more academic program.

To maximize each child's development, accurate intellectual and special educational evaluation is needed. It would be tragic to educate a moderately retarded child only in academic skills and then discover at adolescence that he or she has mastered them only minimally. Perhaps the child would have benefitted more had school hours been spent learning self-help and vocational skills necessary for functioning in a supervised setting. In addition to recognizing the need for continuous assessment of intellectual capabilities, we should understand that the very process of labelling children "retarded" and placing them in a special class is likely to lower self-esteem and create self-fulfilling expectations. For example, if we expect retarded children to be unable to live independently as adults and place them in a class for trainable retarded children, this guarantees the absence of academic skills necessary to live and work independently. Recent educational practice is to mainstream retarded children with other children. They are placed in an environment that least restricts their joining the activities of the regular class whenever possible while giving them an educational program appropriate to their present developmental level.

A CASE EXAMPLE

Dawn is a ten-year-old girl with Down's Syndrome (see Chapter 4). Chromosomal studies were done to identify her disorder shortly after birth. City Hospital's Early Intervention Team then assigned a home visitor to instruct Dawn's parents in providing learning experiences of interest to Dawn, and at three she entered the preschool for special needs children sponsored by her local school system. She is presently in a special class for trainable mentally retarded children during most of her school day. Her curriculum emphasizes self-help skills, social skills training, and practical academics in real-life situations, such as using money.

Dawn's parents are active in the City Association for Retarded Citizens (CARC), an affiliate of the National Association for Retarded Citizens. They met with a CARC parents' group when Dawn was a preschooler and Dawn met some playmates there. Dawn frequently goes to CARC's respite care center, providing a needed rest for her parents. CARC also runs recreation groups and a summer camp for the retarded, which Dawn attends. CARC programs are supported in part by the Division of Mental Retardation of the State Department of Mental Health, and continuing CARC's programs is a prime concern of Dawn's parents.

Intelligence and the Nature-Nurture Controversy

It is not uncommon for a teacher or parent to speak of a child as "having an IQ" of a particular number. Although the child's intelligence may have been tested many years earlier, the score is cited as if IQ were stable over long periods of time. There is much debate about whether a child's performance on an intelligence test — the IQ score earned — indicates a potential for intellectual functioning that remains constant.

Traditionally, intelligence has been assumed to be determined primarily through genetics. It has been thought to remain stable throughout one's life. According to this view, a child who receives a score of 90 on an IQ test at age seven should receive a score of about 90 if he or she takes another intelligence test at age ten, regardless of whether the child's environment changed.

Experience obviously influences whether a child will pass any item on an intelligence test. As children grow older they learn new information and the meanings of new words. According to the genetic view of intelligence, however, a child's *capacity* to learn from experience is considered impervious to experience. A child may pass more items on an intelligence test at age ten than at age seven, because he or she has had more experiences to learn from. But a child who inherited more intelligence would be expected to learn more from experience than a child who inherited less, and as a result their IQs would remain unchanged.

Is intelligence determined by nature or nurture? Can the contributions of the two ever be separated? These questions have been the subject of fierce debate for many years. To answer them, researchers have compared the IQs of biologically related people raised in different environments and studied whether improving the environment influences children's IQs.

Studies of IQ and Kinship. In one type of study, researchers compared identical twins (same genetic inheritance), who had been reared in different environments (Burt, 1966; Newman, Freeman, and Holzinger, 1937; Shields, 1962). Presumably, this type of study should be able to assess the relative contributions of genes and environment to intelligence. The results of these twin studies have been interpreted as indicating that genetic inheritance is a stronger determinant of intelligence than environment. Identical twins reared apart, for example, have been found to be closer in intelligence than fraternal twins reared together.

These results have been questioned, however. Critics claim that identical twins reared apart are not assigned to new environments at random. Parents are likely to place the twin they give up with a relative or family similar to themselves in important ways, such as socioeconomic level. If twins are adopted, agencies are likely to place children in homes similar to the home the child would have had with his or her biological parents. In short, the environments of twins reared apart may be quite similar (Kamin, 1974; Schwartz and Schwartz, 1974). Thus, this type of study may not really assess the effects of different environments, and does not resolve the question of which influences intelligence more, genetics or environment.

In a variation of this kind of research, the intelligence of adopted children has been compared to the intelligence of both the biological and adoptive parents. In one study, children of mothers with IQs in the eighties who were placed in good foster homes by six months of age were found to have IQs of around 110

(Skodak and Skeels, 1949). The researchers claimed that the differences between the IQs of the children and their biological mothers indicated that environment plays an important role in determining intelligence.

This study has also been criticized. The first criticism is that children do not inherit a characteristic of the parent to the extent that the parent has it. Children can be expected to differ from their parents in the direction of the mean of the population. If a parent has a very high tested IQ, the children's IQs can be expected to be somewhat less high. If the parent has an exceptionally low tested IQ, as was the case in the Skodak and Skeels study, the children's IQs can be expected to be somewhat less low. This statistical phenomenon is referred to as *regression toward the mean*. Thus, part of the difference between the IQs of children and their biological parents in the Skodak and Skeels study can be attributed to genetics (Jensen, 1973).

A second criticism of the study is based on details of the children's adoption. Apparently, children were selected for adoption in part because they were in good health. In addition, there was a probation period before the adoptions were made final — adoptive parents could reject any child they thought was intellectually limited. The children actually adopted may have been those who were most capable intellectually. The critics contend that the discrepancy between their IQs and the IQs of their biological mothers may be due once again to genetic inheritance as well as improved environmental conditions.

Difficulties such as these with most of the kinship studies designed to assess heritability of intelligence indicate that they may be of little use in settling the nature-nurture controversy (Vernon, 1979).

Studies of Changed Environmental Conditions. In other studies, changes in children's IQs were monitored after their environments were intentionally altered. A classic study of this kind was conducted by Skeels (1966). Two girls from an orphanage where Skeels was working were transferred by chance to a home for retarded children when they were about eighteen months old. There they were cared for by older girls on the ward. The girls took great interest in the babies and gave them attention they had not received in the crowded, unstimulating orphanage. After a few months, to Skeels's surprise, the young girls, who had previously been considered retarded, showed amazing alertness.

As a result of the observation, Skeels designed a study in which thirteen eighteen-month-old children were deliberately transferred from the orphanage to the home for retarded children. A control group remained in the orphanage. After two years the children who had been transferred showed an average increase in IQ of about 28 points, while the IQs of children remaining in the orphanage declined by about the same amount. Because the children who had been transferred no longer showed signs of mental retardation, eleven of them were adopted.

Skeels followed up the two groups after they reached adulthood. All thirteen of the children in his experimental group were self-supporting adults, and many held good jobs. Most had received a high school education. The adults who as infants had remained in the orphanage did not fare nearly as well. Several were still in institutions, and those who were not held unskilled jobs. Most had completed only a few years of schooling. Skeels's study demonstrates that environment can have a major effect on intellectual functioning.

A second study of the effects of altering environmental conditions was conducted at the University of Wisconsin by Heber and Garber (1975). Forty black infants from impoverished homes, all born to mothers with IQs below 80, were selected for the study. Twenty of the children were assigned to a control group that received no intervention except psychological testing. The other twenty children were assigned to an experimental program in which care was provided for five full days a week at the University Training Center for the Mentally Retarded, beginning at age three months. In addition, the infants' mothers attended an educational program that provided information on childrearing and other assistance.

The intelligence of the two groups was assessed with the Gesell scale when the children were infants. The groups were found to be equally intelligent. Beginning in the preschool years, however, group differences of about 30 IQ points began to emerge. These differences continued until the children reached the age of six, at which time the intervention program stopped. When the children were tested again at age eight, the experimental children's IQs were around 104, whereas the control children's IQs were about 80. There were also major differences in the groups' school achievement, with the experimental children doing far better.

Of course, not even strong advocates of the genetic position on intelligence deny that environment affects intelligence. The controversy is over the relative importance of the environment and genetic inheritance, and whether the effects of these sources can be separated at all. Even today there is widespread disagreement about the extent of their influence. One reason that the nature-nurture issue is so controversial is that various groups have different tested IQs.

Group Differences in Intelligence. Differences in group IQs are associated with race and with social class, which is defined by income, education, and occupation. Middle-class children, for example, have higher IQs as a group than poor children; the IQs of black children average about 15 points lower than those of white children (Jensen, 1969). As was true of individual variations in IQ, group differences are attributed by different authorities to either genetic inheritance or environmental factors.

Recent research by Scarr and Weinberg (1978) casts doubt on genetic explanations of group differences in IQ. Two studies of adoption were conducted, one involving white adolescents, the other involving black children adopted into white homes.

The results of the Scarr and Weinberg study suggest that differences in the IQs of black and white children are not genetically based. Black children raised in white, middle-class homes have an average IQ of 110, about 15 points higher than the IQs of the black children raised by their own parents. The average IQ score of both black and white adoptees (110), was higher than the average IQ of their biological parents (which was estimated on the basis of their education level to be about 100). But adoptees did not score as high as the biological children of adoptive parents (116.7) or as the adoptive parents themselves (119).

Scarr and Weinberg concluded that individual differences within a group from similar environments, such as middle-class white children, may be largely genetic in origin, whereas group differences are due largely to differences in environment. Let us look at some environmental influences on intelligence.

Intelligence and Environmental Influences

Environmental influences can affect children's scores on intelligence tests in two general ways. (1) The environment can actually limit the development of a child's intellectual potential. (2) The environment can encourage abilities other than those tested by intelligence tests.

Environmental Correlates of Intelligence. Some environmental factors are associated with variations in the development of intellectual capacity, not just with variations in the way children learn to think or in what they learn to think about. For example, the quality of prenatal care, nutrition, and childrearing practices have been found to vary among different social classes. In middle-class families these factors have generally been associated with an enhancement of mental functioning. In impoverished families, however, prenatal care, nutrition, and childrearing practices have been associated with lowered intellectual development.

We pointed out earlier that mental development is correlated with parental responsiveness and the availability of appropriate play materials (Ainsworth and Bell, 1973; Bradley and Caldwell, 1976; Elardo, Bradley, and Caldwell, 1975; Hamilton, 1976; White and Watts, 1973; Yarrow, Rubenstein, and Pederson, 1971). Although parents from all income groups provide play materials and interact responsively with their children, middle- and upper-income families are likely to provide more play materials and to interact more responsively than low-income families. There is also much evidence that inadequate nutrition can limit mental development (Brockman and Ricciuti, 1971; Stoch and Smythe, 1963; Winick, 1976). The results of some of this research are inconsistent, probably because (1) the ages at which children had been undernourished varied from study to study; (2) the extent of the malnutrition was unknown in some studies, and (3) different tests were used to assess mental functioning in different studies. Nevertheless, the evidence that malnutrition affects mental functioning is strong. The effects are especially serious when malnutrition occurs in a period

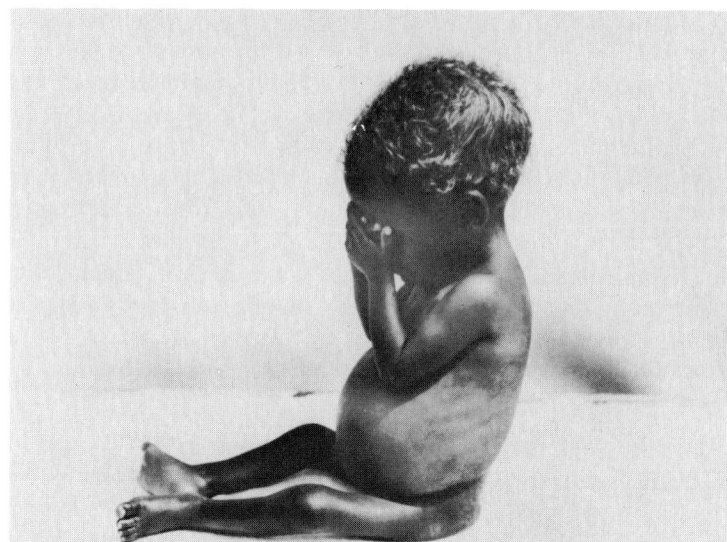

Severe malnutrition is devastating to both body and mind.

of considerable brain growth. The offspring of impoverished parents may be malnourished both prenatally *and* postnatally for extensive periods of time. Sustained malnourishment during childhood can have devastating effects, especially when it occurs in the absence of responsive parental care.

Cultural Differences. Differences in measured intelligence can also result from differences in cultural groups and the abilities that they emphasize. These differences are sometimes obvious; large portions of the American population have a native language other than English, for example. Other cultural differences are more subtle, however. Many cultural groups have a pool of common knowledge that differs from that of the white, urban population on whom intelligence tests are often standardized. In the same way, distinct cultural groups often value different abilities, methods of doing things, and ways of thinking and expressing thoughts. Tests standardized on one cultural group can be expected to yield biased results when used to assess the intelligence of other groups.

Summary

The Concrete Operational Child
- During middle childhood, the thinking of children is concrete operational. Children in this stage develop conservation concepts, but some (length, weight, area, etc.) are acquired later than others.
- School-age children learn seriation (placing objects in order according to size) and classification (relating objects in hierarchical classes).

- In middle childhood, children initially have trouble separating the concept of time from the concept of space. For example, they may confuse the time it takes two objects to travel a specific distance with the spatial placement of the distances.

Intelligence

- A controversial issue in the study of intelligence is whether it is a stable, genetically determined potential or a characteristic capable of being influenced by the environment. Adoption studies indicate that intelligence is greatly affected by environment, but their data are sometimes open to dispute.
- Controversy occurs over the cultural bias of tests. Many of the environmental circumstances that can influence IQ are correlated with social class, and group differences in IQ scores have led some psychologists to question the fairness of intelligence tests.

New Terms

concrete operational stage
hypothetico-deductive reasoning
seriation
hierarchical classification
intension
short-term memory
long-term memory

attention
norms
mental age
chronological age
intelligence quotient (IQ)
regression toward the mean

Selected Readings

Furth, H. G. **Piaget for teachers.** Englewood Cliffs, N.J.: Prentice-Hall, 1970. This short book discusses the major characteristics of Piaget's view about children's thinking. Interesting ideas are presented for thinking games. Piaget's ideas are explained in an understandable and interesting way.

Ginsburg, H., and Opper, S. **Piaget's theory of intellectual development.** 2d edition. Englewood Cliffs, N.J.: Prentice-Hall, 1979. Presents one of the clearest discussions of Piaget's

theory and the various tasks used in studying children's thinking. Covers all periods of development, but includes considerable information on the concrete-operational period.

Vernon, P. E. **Intelligence: Heredity and environment.** San Francisco: Freeman, 1979. Reviews the issues and research relating to the question about the roles of heredity and environment in determining intelligence. Biased in favor of the genetic side, but presents much information in a readable fashion.

Chapter *23*

*L*anguage Development

Although children acquire basic oral language competence by the time they enter the school-age period, they do not understand complex syntactic structures until well into this stage of development. In addition, children become able to think about and manipulate language in ways that previously were impossible. We will discuss these two aspects of oral language development in this chapter as well as dialects and second-language acquisition. We will also discuss written language, teaching reading to speakers of dialects, and the development of writing abilities.

Oral Language

You may wonder why we are discussing oral language development again in this chapter when we stated earlier that children master oral language by the end of the preschool years. Our earlier statements were essentially correct, but school-age children still have trouble with some complex syntactic structures, which will be discussed here.

400

Children develop the ability to think about language during middle childhood. This ability, known as *metalinguistic awareness* (Cazden, 1974), enables them to play with language. Jokes, puns, and riddles are forms of metalinguistic play.

We will also discuss learning a second language after having mastered (or nearly mastered) a first. This topic is important because of the current interest in bilingual education.

Finally, we will discuss dialect. This is important because some children in the United States do not learn Standard English as their first language.

Understanding Complex Syntactic Structures

Carol Chomsky (1969) has investigated why school-age children find certain grammatical structures confusing. An adult understands that the sentence "John is easy to see," means not that John is seeing something, but that someone is seeing John. But young school-age children misinterpret the sentence, thinking that it means John can see easily. They interpret this sentence as they would a sentence such as "John is eager to see," which has a similar sequence of words. However, the way meaning is derived in the two sentences is different, and children do not understand this at first.

Chomsky studied how children understand this type of sentence by seating them at a table on which she had placed a blindfolded doll. Then she asked them, "Is this doll easy to see or hard to see?" If the child answered that the doll was hard to see, Chomsky asked the child to make her easy to see. If the child answered that the doll was easy to see, Chomsky asked the child to make the doll hard to see. Children who answered that the doll was hard to see thought they were being asked if it was hard or easy for *the doll* to see, not if it was hard or easy for them to see the doll.

Consider the behavior of Lisa, aged six years, five months:

Is this doll easy to see or hard to see?
    "Hard to see."
Will you make her easy to see.
    "If I can get this untied."
Will you explain why she was hard to see.
    (To doll): "Because you had a blindfold over your eyes."
And what did you do?
    "I took it off." [Chomsky, 1969, p. 30]

Children who understood the question correctly, on the other hand, responded like Ann, aged eight years and seven months:

This is Chatty Cathy. Is she easy to see or hard to see?
    "Easy."
Would you make her hard to see.
    "So you can't see her at all?"

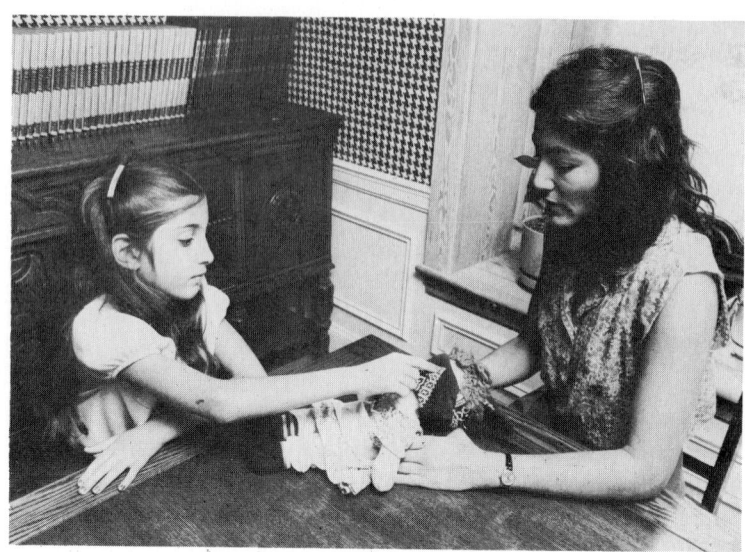

"Is the doll easy to see or hard to see?"

OK.
> (Places doll under table.)
Tell what you did.
> "I put her under the table." [Chomsky, 1969, p. 31]

School-age children also confuse the words "ask" and "tell." Consider the example of Samuel, age eight years, five months:

Ask Ellen what to feed the doll.
> "Feed her hamburgers."
All right now, tell Ellen what to feed her.
> "Again?"
M-hm.
> "Tomato."
Now I want you to *ask* Ellen something. I want you to *ask* her what to
feed the doll.
> "Feed her this thing, whatever it's called."
All right. Now listen very carefully, because I don't want you to *tell*
her anything this time. I want you to ask her a question. I want you
to *ask* her what to feed the doll. Can you do that?
> "Let's see, I don't get it."
OK, just go ahead, and ask her what to feed the doll.
> "Feed her eggs." [Chomsky, 1969, p. 57]

Samuel interpreted "tell" correctly, but interpreted "ask" as "tell." In Chomsky's sample, even nine- and ten-year-olds were confused by "ask" and "tell."

Think of the trouble such a misunderstanding could create. Suppose a child tells his father that he sometimes does not understand a teacher's explanations about schoolwork. "Well," his father advises, "when you don't understand, just ask the teacher what you are to do."

"But I don't know what to do," the child says, interpreting the parent's suggestion to mean that he should *tell* the teacher what to do. "That's why I'm suggesting that you *ask* the teacher what you should do," explains the parent once again. The child still appears puzzled. If the parent realized that the child did not understand his use of "ask," he could instruct the child to raise his hand when he does not understand and ask the teacher to repeat the explanation.

Jokes, Riddles, and Metalinguistic Awareness

> "Knock-Knock."
> "Who's there?"
> "Duane."
> "Duane who?"
> "Duane the tub . . . I'm dwowning."

> "Knock-Knock."
> "Who's there?"
> "Amos."
> "Amos who?"
> "A mosquito bit me."
> "Knock-Knock."
> "Who's there?"
> "Andy."
> "Andy who?"
> "And he bit me again."

School-age children delight in telling jokes and riddles, and anyone planning to spend time with them should be prepared to listen to an extensive repertoire. But children understand language quite well before middle childhood. Why don't they begin to tell jokes earlier?

The reason is that, to understand jokes and riddles, children must not only understand language, they must be able to make the sophisticated mental comparisons characteristic of the concrete operational period (McGhee, 1971; Whitt and Prentice, 1977). The child must be able to "go back and forth in thought between different ideas, meanings, and relationships" (McGhee, 1979). As with any emerging skill, children practice the new language and cognitive skills over and over.

Riddles ask questions that stump the listener so that the listener must ask for the answer. The answer is usually ambiguous in some way, and the listener must determine how it makes sense in relation to the original question. The question in one riddle is

> "Why did the farmer name his hog Ink?"

The answer is

"Because he kept running out of the pen." [Schultz, 1974]

This riddle is based on the double meaning of the word "pen," which can, of course, indicate either a writing tool or an enclosed area for animals. The listener may at first think the answer does not make sense, but then the play on words is detected and the listener understands.

The linguistic ambiguity in this case is *lexical* — it is a play on words. Ambiguity of other types is also used in jokes and riddles. The knock-knock jokes at the beginning of this section are based on *phonological* ambiguity — the sound sequences can be interpreted in more than one way. For instance, "Andy" can be interpreted as "and he." Similarly, *syntactical* ambiguity can be humorous. The sentence "He sent her kids story books," when stated orally, could mean "He sent story books to her kids" or "He sent storybooks suitable for kids to her" (Schultz and Pilon, 1973). The sentence "The duck is ready to eat," could mean that the duck is (1) going to eat, or (2) going to be eaten.

Children appreciate some forms of linguistic ambiguity before others. Phonological ambiguity is understood first, at age six or seven. An understanding of lexical ambiguity appears next, with appreciation increasing steadily for several years. Syntactical ambiguity, however, is not understood until children are eleven or twelve years old (Schultz and Pilon, 1973). The reasons for this progression can be understood by considering the Chomsky (1969) research discussed earlier. Sentences such as "John is easy to see" and "John is eager to see" have the same *surface structure* — the words in the sentence are organized in the same way. Their *deep structure* (the way meanings are derived) is different, however. It is this ambiguity of meaning that is played on in jokes and riddles.

Learning a Second Language

Many children enter school speaking a native language other than English. The goal of bilingual education is to help children maintain their native language while helping them to learn English. But how do children learn a second language? Do they use what they know about their native language, or do they approach the new language as they did their first language?

Developmental Progression. There are three basic theories of how children learn a second language (McNamara, 1976, p. 46):

1. The child acquires the second language in exactly the same way an infant would acquire it as a first language. In other words, learning a second language is *identical in process* to learning the same language as a first language.
2. The child uses the structures from his or her first language to form structures in the second language. This process assumes *interference* between the first and second languages.

3. The child does not make use of the structures of his first language or acquire the structures as a first language learner would. Instead, he or she formulates *unique grammatical structures.*

We will confine our discussion to the first two theories, because the third lacks support from research.

To study second-language acquisition, the researcher must find people who have mastered a first language and are beginning to learn a second. The researcher must also be familiar with the syntax of both languages and understand the typical sequence of development children go through in learning each language as a first language. (You will recall that in English, for example, the first questions and negative utterances children construct are different from those used by mature speakers, and that the patterns undergo several changes before the standard patterns appear.) Then the investigator can compare the developmental patterns of the person learning the second language with the developmental patterns of native speakers of each of the two languages. If the second-language learner's developmental patterns match those of a child learning the language as a first language, the evidence supports the identical process model. If the developmental pattern of the second-language learner matches structures from the child's own first language, then we have evidence for the interference model.

Most research supports the identical processes model, although instances of interference are also observed. For example, Raven (1974) noted that two Norwegian children learning English as a second language did not usually invert the verb and subject when formulating *wh-* questions — even though this was how they formed questions in their native Norwegian. Like children learning English as a first language, they said, "What she is doing?" rather than "What is she doing?" Even when children have mastered a language whose structure could be applied to English, they often do not use what they already know, but pass through the same stages as children acquiring English as a first language. This is also true when the structure of their first language differs from English; they do not apply it, but learn English as children learning a language for the first time. Not until children are ten or twelve years old and have well-developed metalinguistic and cognitive abilities do they begin to apply structures from their own first language when learning a second.

Supporting the Acquisition of a Second Language. Children acquire a second language most quickly when they spend time communicating naturally with native speakers of the language. Social influences are very important (Fillmore, 1976, cited in McLaughlin, 1978, pp. 108–110). This means that children learning a new language should get involved with children who know the language. Strategies used by children learning a second language include the following:

- Join a group and act as if you understand what is going on, even if you don't. (social)

- Assume that people's statements are directly relevant to the situation at hand or to what they or you are experiencing. Metastrategy: Guess! (cognitive)
- Give the impression — with a few well-chosen words — that you can speak the language (e.g., say Look it or Wait a minute). (social)
- Give the impression that you understand, and start talking. (cognitive)
- Look for recurring structures in the formulas you know. (cognitive)
- Rely on your friends for help. (social)
- Make the most of what you've got. (cognitive)
- Work on the big things first; save the details for later. (cognitive)

In summarizing his study, Fillmore said,

> The important thing was to communicate, even if details of the utterances were incorrect. The native-speaking children cooperated by simplifying their speech, by including the non-native speakers in their play, and by directing their speech at objects and activities at hand. Furthermore, they believed that their friends would learn the language, encouraged them, and made an effort to figure out what they were trying to say. [McLaughlin, 1978, p. 110]

The process described by Fillmore resembles that which children go through when learning a first language: meanings are initially determined from context, and then used to figure out the language. Skilled language users (friends in the case of children acquiring a second language, parents in the case of infants acquiring a first language) try to understand what the unskilled speaker is trying to say. They also simplify their own utterances and try to make their meaning known through gestures and facial expressions.

Natural contexts and meaningful communication facilitate second language learning.

Unfortunately, the situations in which language is taught in school are usually far from natural. Children may not use the language to communicate at all, learning it instead through formal instruction. John Macnamara sums up the usual classroom situation quite well:

> The teacher misses the whole point of "natural" language learning, because his or her attention is on the language, whereas the attention of the infant is on the message. Language is for communicating, not for learning, and we learn it best when our conscious attention is on meaning. . . . the language teacher seldom has anything to say that is so important that his pupils will eagerly guess his meaning. And pupils seldom have anything so urgent to say to the teacher that they will improvise with whatever communicative skills they possess to get their meaning across. . . .
>
> Basically, it is the disease we have encountered before. The teacher sees language mainly as something to be learned; the child is interested in what someone can tell him in *using* language.
>
> Probably the teacher's best strategy would be to turn the language class into an activity period. If the students are cooking, or engaged in handicrafts, they need to communicate with one another. The teacher could explain in the new language what needed to be done and allow students to demand further clarification and information. The teacher should be so serious about this that he would allow what is being made to be spoiled if the students fail to understand. The teacher should not fuss about language. Perhaps there would be much to gain by mixing students of various levels and proficiencies in the same activity so as to increase the linguistic resources. This would create an atmosphere that is similar to the family atmosphere in which children learn first languages. [Macnamara, 1976, pp. 51–52]

Dialect

Various groups who speak the same language may use it differently from each other. These minor variations in the use of the same language are called *dialects*. Actually, we all speak several dialects. For example, we may use one type of language when speaking with colleagues (jargon), especially when discussing technical matters, and another type of language to explain the same matter to friends outside our profession (Dale, 1976). There also are dialect differences associated with age, geography, and social class.

Perhaps the most familiar dialect in the United States is one associated with ethnicity. It is known as Black English, but it is not, of course, spoken by everyone who is black. The grammar of Black English and of standard English are quite similar in most respects. They are, after all, forms of the same language. But there are some differences. For example, in Black English, the verbs "come" and "say"

A major dialect in the United States is black English.

are not always marked with morphemes to indicate past tense. So users of this dialect say "He say" rather than "He said." Speakers of this dialect may also drop auxiliary verbs, saying "What you mean?" rather than "What do you mean?" Another difference is that the 's may be left off when possessives are formed, which results in sentences such as "This is Susan sweater" rather than "This is Susan's sweater."

There are also phonological differences between Black English and standard English. It is differences of this sort that usually cause the most difficulty for teachers who speak standard English when they try to understand the speech of children who speak Black English.

It is important to understand that both Black English and standard English are legitimate languages with their own rules and complexities. As languages, neither is better than the other. But different dialects do have varying social currency. Standard English is the accepted language of schools, government, and business, and children who know it may have more social options (such as choice of occupation) than children who do not. Nevertheless, the issue of whether schools should teach children in standard English or in their own dialect is very controversial; in some instances it has led to court battles.

Written Language

It is during the school-age period that children usually become skillful readers and writers. In this section we will briefly review several interpretations of reading and comment on their implications for teaching. We will also discuss methods of teaching reading to children who speak a nonstandard English dialect. Then we will move on to a discussion of writing, considering such topics as invented spelling and mastery of the conventions of print, which include capitalization and punctuation. We will end this unit with samples of children's creative writing.

Reading

How Children Learn to Read: Two Views. We outlined the issues related to the acquisition of written language in Chapter 18. The basic issue was which comes first — form, or meaning and function. The answer a teacher gives will determine how he or she teaches reading. Those who think that form comes first emphasize specific skills related to alphabet recognition and letter-sound correspondence; the assumption is that children who learn to say words correctly when they see them in print will arrive at the correct meaning and function. Others believe teachers should focus on meaning and function from the beginning and give the teaching of "word attack" skills less emphasis. These two viewpoints are based on different assumptions about the strategies involved in reading and about the very nature of knowledge. For instance, does reading involve translating print into sound, or does it involve several strategies based on syntactic, semantic, and graphophonic knowledge? Is distinguishing different sounds simply a matter of perceiving certain vibrations in the air, or does it involve constructing a *concept* of individual sounds?

If a teacher regards the use of graphophonic information as the primary strategy involved in reading and believes the acquisition of this information to be a matter of auditory and visual perception, then his or her reading program will emphasize phonics skills. Children beginning to learn to read may spend little time with whole reading materials, because the teacher assumes that children must learn skills *before* they can read. Instead, the teacher will provide drill on auditory and visual discrimination, visual-motor exercises, and letter names and sounds.

Teachers who assume that children read by using their knowledge of language and the world in addition to their knowledge of letter-sound associations use a different approach. Children may begin by dictating their own compositions to the teacher and then trying to read what the teacher has written. Knowing the language and the context enables them to recognize words without having to sound all of them out. The teacher may also read to children from storybooks, and children may be encouraged to browse through and "read" books that interest them. When children are read familiar storybooks over and over, they learn them by heart and are able to move on to learning some words by sight and discovering how speech and print map onto each other. This approach does not omit word attack skills, but subordinates them to actual reading. It enables children to learn to use other strategies in reading and to develop an intuitive understanding of how phonics skills are derived.

In our discussion of written language acquisition among preschoolers, we sided with those who adhere to the meaning and multiple-strategy views. We think these views also apply to the school-age child. We agree with Smith (1977) that the teacher's task is not to make reading meaningless and difficult by giving children isolated bits and pieces of it, as in workbook exercises, but to make reading easy — meaningful and sensible. "Children who can make sense of instruction should learn to read; children confronted by nonsense are bound to fail. The issue is as simple — and as complicated as that" (Smith, 1977, p. 395). (A few children, for reasons that are not fully understood at present, have difficulty learning how to read, regardless of the approach used — see FOCUS on learning disabilities.)

FOCUS: Learning Disabilities

For a number of years educators have seen a need to identify and serve children who experience continuous and serious school failure in one or more subjects. These are children who are not included in the traditional categories of special needs such as mental retardation, behavior disorders, physical or sensory handicaps, and speech disorders. Today many of these children are referred to as having *learning disabilities* or *specific learning disability* (SLD).

Some authorities writing about children with specific academic problems have defined *specific learning disability* without reference to cause. For example, Kirk (1968) defined SLD as "a specific retardation or disorder in one or more of the processes of speech, language, perception, behavior, reading, spelling, writing, or arithmetic." However, a neurological deficit, neurological delay, or perhaps neurochemical deficit (Wender, 1977) was still implied by the definition of specific learning disability.

Public Law 94-142, the landmark federal law that ensures a free public school education for all handicapped, includes the following definition: "A specific learning disability is a significant discrepancy between intellectual ability and achievement in any of the several areas of oral expression, listening comprehension, basic reading, reading comprehension, written expression, mathematical calculation, or mathematical reasoning." The definition goes on to say that in order for this discrepancy between intellectual ability — as measured by an IQ test — and achievement scores to be called a learning disability, it cannot be primarily due to (1) sensory or a motor handicap, (2) mental retardation, (3) emotional disturbance, or (4) environmental, cultural, or economic disadvantage. That is, when the discrepancy cannot be explained by other known factors, it is assumed to be caused by a specific learning disability (Federal Register, 1977).

The definition of a specific learning disability given in PL94-142 has been roundly criticized to say the least. Critics have objected to the old assumption of a biological cause when the environment may be at fault but the cause hard to isolate. For example, Singer (1979) argues that "they should not only examine *students* to determine 'learning disabilities,' but also *teachers* to discover whether they have 'teaching disabilities.' " Other critics have objected to the idea that an IQ test is a valid indicator of intellectual ability or of learning potential when it is in fact a test of previous learning, namely academic learning.

Public Law 94-142 specifies the general method used to identify a specific learning disability, though some of the details of identification vary at the level of local government. In general, a child's IQ is used to estimate expected performance on academic achievement and cognitive processing tests. This estimate is sometimes called an "expectancy age." If the child's achievement and cognitive processing scores fall below a cutoff percentage of his or her expectancy age, they indicate a specific learning disability. The cutoff percentages used depend on several factors, including how long the child has attended school.

After a child has been identified as learning disabled, an Individualized Educational Program is developed that calls for remediation either in the regular classroom or in the SLD classroom. PL94-142 specifies that handicapped students, including the learning disabled, be educated in the "least restrictive" environment. In addition, they should participate for as much of the school day as possible with their nonhandicapped peers. Remediation strategies have been explicitly proposed to teach academic skills to SLD children. These have included not only teaching academic skills directly but also remediating problems thought to underlie SLD, such as motor problems. In general, it is still too soon for research evidence to have shown the superiority of any one method. Common characteristics of day-to-day instruction include (1) individualized or small-group instruction that allows the child to proceed at his or her own pace and allows the teacher to isolate the child's specific deficiencies, (2) behavioral or task analysis of the deficiency so as to break the task into sequential, manageable subtasks, and (3) presentation of material in a sensory mode the child is strong in as well as in the one in which he or she shows weakness, for example, tactile tracing sandpaper letters with the finger if the child has had trouble visually remembering them. Academic skills are taught in an individualized setting and the child is encouraged to compensate for weak abilities by applying his or her strengths.

There is a great deal still to be learned about specific learning disabilities. As Lynn (1979) points out, "The most difficult question about learning disabilities is how people who are *not* disabled can spell, read, speak, calculate and carry out . . . many other intellectual tasks." Until this question is answered, our knowledge of specific learning disabilities will continue to be unsystematic and controversial.

According to Smith, the beginning stages of the process are those we discussed in the last chapter: reading to children, allowing them to read to you, giving them writing materials, encouraging them to read what they write, supporting and appreciating their work, and answering and asking questions. The same process continues when children begin to read new material independently: they are allowed to read books about topics of interest and encouraged to write. Carol Chomsky sums this view up quite nicely:

> It would seem beneficial to read to children all through elementary school, and to encourage them to read books as complicated as they are willing to tackle. Controlled texts and carefully graded material would seem less to the point than a varied sampling from children's literature. It doesn't matter if they miss some of what is in the book — that is how we all read, after all. . . .
>
> In the long run what the child needs to learn to do, if he is to grow up into a reading adult, is to read for his own purposes. Whether it be for pleasure, or to find out about something, or for whatever reasons, it has to be out of internal motivation and not because someone else requires it. [1976, pp. 20–21]

But what about skills? We suggest that after children have an intuitive understanding of reading and they begin to read independently, teachers can help them understand the relationships between speech and print that they have probably begun to notice for themselves. In other words, skill teaching can be considered a way of encouraging a form of metalinguistic awareness, a method of coding intuitive knowledge into abstractions, which can then be consciously applied to similar situations. This is probably how phonics instruction works anyway. As Smith (1977) has noted, good readers are always good at phonics, because their sense of the text enables them to use letter-sound correspondences effectively. If the child approaches print with any other goal than finding out what the words mean, phonics skills are likely to be of little help.

In addition, it is important to realize that reading does not consist merely of naming every word on a page, a practice referred to as *word calling*. Skilled reading is getting the intended meaning from the text.

> Any fluent reader . . . asked to read a passage quickly, will make errors. . . . But these errors often leave the meaning unchanged. Contractions may be formed, synonyms may be substituted, and compound sentences may be broken up. Good readers are constantly guessing ahead as to what comes next. Only if the guess is clearly wrong (doesn't make sense; doesn't fit with the meaning) will the reader correct himself. Otherwise, he is not aware of any error. [Dale, 1976, p. 292]

One problem with the method of teaching reading we have endorsed is that it takes a great deal of work at the beginning when children do not know how to read independently in the conventional way. This is especially the case when they come to formal schooling without having had much previous experience with written language. How can one teacher read to children individually, listen to them read, take down their dictation, and listen to them read it back, with a class of twenty-five or thirty? It is very difficult, but there are ways to get additional help. Older children can spend time reading to kindergarten children or first graders. We know of one situation in which the younger children made written requests for the books they wanted the older children to bring to them from the library. The older children answered the younger children's letters, brought the books, and read them. This gave both the older and younger children a real purpose for writing and also provided them with interesting reading.

Parents or other volunteers can also come into the classroom to read to children, listen to them read, or help them write. In addition, schools can urge parents to continue to read to their children even after the children have reached the second or third grade and can read on their own.

Before we leave the topic of reading, we should discuss the issues involved in teaching reading to children who speak a dialect other than standard English, such as Black English.

Teaching Reading to Speakers of Nonstandard Dialect. When children who speak Black English read a standard English text, they usually translate the text into dialect. They may understand the text, but they often do not read it as it is printed.

If teachers emphasize exact word calling rather than understanding meaning, they may think that a child who changes standard English into his own dialect has a reading problem. Educators have proposed a number of solutions to this "problem."

One suggestion is that reading materials be provided in the child's own dialect rather than standard English. This does permit more accurate word calling, but it denies black children the chance to familiarize themselves with standard English. This can ultimately exclude them from important opportunities in jobs and education.

Other authorities suggest that standard English be taught initially as a second language. Reading is taught only after standard English has been mastered orally. But it is difficult to teach a second language quickly, especially in schools where the language generally spoken is different from the one that the child hears at home. Another problem is that children's self-concept may be damaged if they are forced to deny their native language on first entering school.

Perhaps the best solution is for teachers to provide material written in standard English but allow children to read it in their own dialect, at least at first (Dale, 1976; Barnitz, 1980). Teachers would have to be familiar with the child's dialect and pay attention to the child's understanding of meaning, rather than the exact words the child is saying. For example, the teacher would need to know that "Trees be pretty" is a dialect translation of "Trees are pretty," and not a change based on a real decoding problem (Barnitz, 1980). When the language experience approach (an approach in which children learn to read by using stories they have dictated) is used in conjunction with frequent readings from children's literature, children have some materials to read in their own language as well. The use of both approaches at the same time exposes children to standard English but also allows them to feel that their own dialect is acceptable. As children are exposed to written and spoken standard English, they learn to talk and read in both Black English and standard English, and this is the ultimate goal.

Writing

Development of Handwriting. The school-age child's improved motor skills and increased understanding of space, the distinctive features of print, and the conventions of print, lead to dramatic changes in handwriting. The changes in a boy's handwriting between the ages of four and eight (see Figure 23-1) indicate how various types of understandings emerge.

The writing is much smaller in Sample 2 than in Sample 1. Although no one watched Scotty write his name, we suspect that he wrote Sample 1 with his hand raised from the surface of the table, holding the pencil rigid in his hand and moving his entire arm. Try writing your name on a piece of paper by holding your hand and arm up off the table and moving your whole arm rather than just your fingers and hand. Then write your name by resting your hand on the table top and moving only your hand and fingers. In the first instance your writing is controlled by the muscles of your upper arm, in the second by the muscles of your hand. The shift from large to small writing probably occurred as Scotty developed fine motor control. Even at age four Scotty had considerable knowledge of the distinctive features of print. Although far from perfect, his efforts are a great improvement on the scribble-writing and use of letter forms characteristic of younger preschool children who are not familiar with print. The only distinctive feature these samples indicate he did not understand is orientation. Reversals do not disappear until Sample 4, written around age five. Reversals persist beyond age five in the writing of many children.

You may have noticed that the *S* is not reversed in the first sample but is reversed in samples 2 and 3. Why did the child orient it correctly at age four and then incorrectly at ages four and one-half and five? Actually, it is a misinterpretation to assume that the child initially understood how to orient the *S* and then underwent a regression. He was probably unaware that the orientation of letters is important and wrote the *S* correctly in the first sample only by accident. It is also possible that Scotty was learning to write numerals at the same time he was learning to write letters; the *S* in sample 2 resembles a *2*, and he may have confused the two symbols.

In sample 1, problems in orientation are apparent not only among individual letters but in the relation of one letter to the others. Before a child can correctly orient letters in relation to each other, he or she must understand concepts of space.

Sample 1: age 4

Sample 2: age 4½

Sample 3: age, early 5

Sample 4: age, early 5

Sample 5: age, late 6

Sample 6: age 7½

Sample 7: age 8¼; with lined paper

Figure 23-1. Changes in handwriting between ages 4 and 8

I liked the pogram today because the lade was beautiful. because the lade taught us to Duw nuw things and the man wus a phony.

Story 1

I caught a buttur fly before and I caught it with a net too.

Story 2

Figure 23-2. A first grader's stories

The samples also reveal how the child gradually comes to understand the rules of capitalization. In the first sample all letters are uppercase. In the second sample, the *t*'s are apparently lowercase, but all the other letters are uppercase. In sample 3, a lowercase *o* is added to the lowercase *t*'s. In samples 4 and 5, the *y* has the characteristics of lowercase (a diagonal rather than vertical main line), but the *t*'s and the *o* are uppercase. In samples 6 and 7, lowercase letters are used for all but the first letter, which is in keeping with the rules of capitalization.

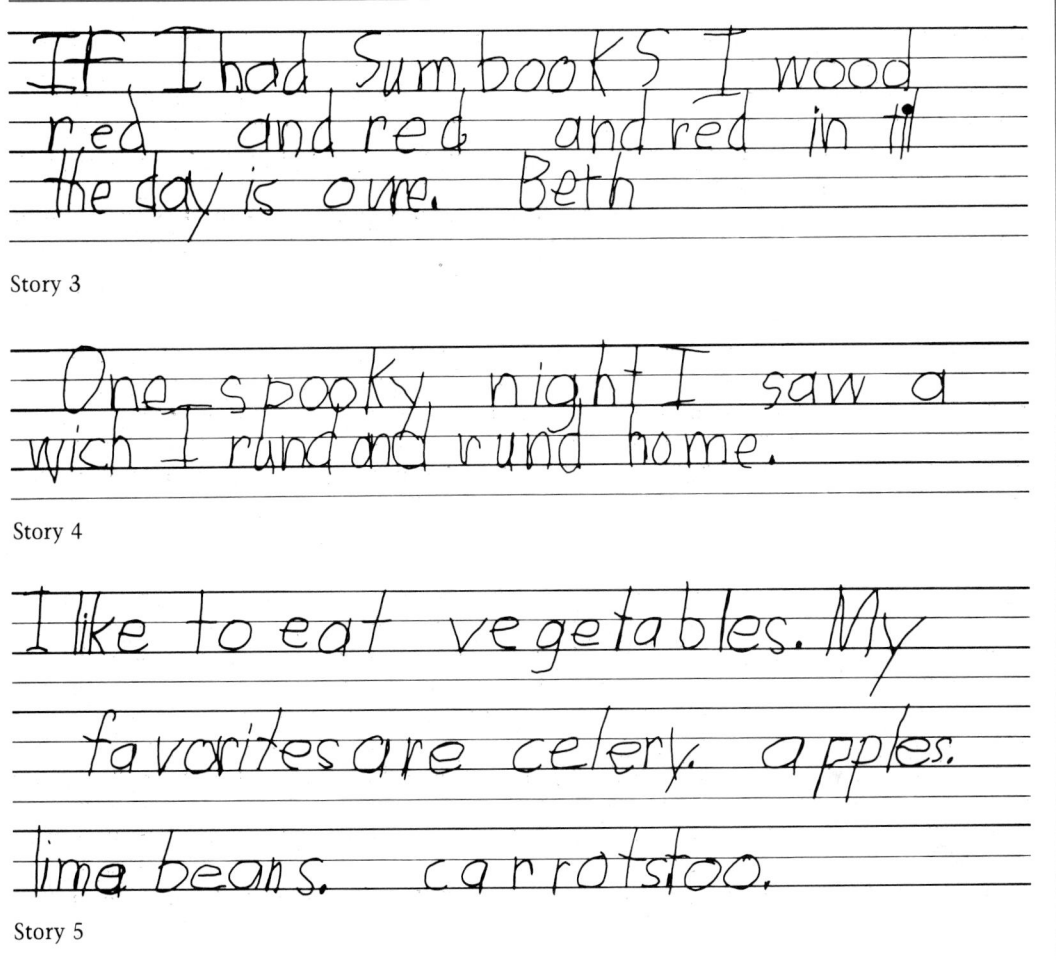

If I had sum books I wood
red and red and red in til
the day is ovre. Beth

Story 3

One spooky night I saw a
wich I rund and rund home.

Story 4

I like to eat vegetables. My
favorites are celery. apples.
lima beans. carrots too.

Story 5

Conventions of Print: Capitalization and Punctuation. Samples of writing done by a first grader are shown in Figure 23-2. These stories are quite short, perhaps because Beth still has trouble with handwriting and spelling; she might be able to create lengthy and elaborate stories if she did not have to write them down.

These stories are of interest here because they contain errors in capitalization and punctuation. In story 1, the child does not capitalize the *b* in the first word in the second sentence, but she does capitalize the word "Duw" in the middle of the sentence. The capitalization and punctuation of story 2 is correct, but this story consists of a single sentence, which greatly reduces the chances for error. In story 3, the *S* in "Sum" is incorrectly capitalized. The punctuation and capitalization are correct in story 4. In story 5, Beth apparently makes a new error: she forgets to capitalize the first word of a sentence (i.e., a word following a period). But we think this mistake represents progress rather than a regression, because Beth is trying to use the periods as commas. The words "celery," "apple," and "lime" (for "lima") were not capitalized. You will notice that the *M* which follows the period at the end of the first sentence *is* capitalized. This story illustrates the importance of considering a child's work carefully before coming to conclusions about it.

All young children have trouble with the types of problems evident in the work of Scott and Beth. Children make frequent errors because they lack the motor skills necessary to write correctly and because their understanding of space and the features and conventions of print is still developing. But adults need not worry that errors will lead to bad writing habits. As children become familiar with writing, they learn the underlying rules that govern how we write, and they will correct their own errors, just as they did when they were learning to talk. Adults can be most helpful by modeling correct writing and by showing interest in what children are trying to communicate.

Handwriting in the School Curriculum. Before leaving this topic we want to express our opinion about the role of handwriting in the school curriculum. We agree with Graves (1978) when he says, "Handwriting is for writing." Too often, writing is emphasized as an end in itself:

> Handwriting was one of those early school experiences I have tried to repress. Images of ink globules racing across white paper from deadly scratch pens still give me a heavy feeling. Recollections of endless circles, precise spacing, and comments about my untidiness take away my energy. I had no idea that handwriting was for writing. . . . Handwriting was punishing, mindless, and mechanical whereas composing with ideas was lofty and worthwhile. [Graves, 1978, p. 393]

We have seen very young children spend long periods trying to write when they want to convey an important message. At such times they use whatever skills they have to get their message across. They do not concern themselves overmuch with technical perfection, and neither should we. They can and do work on technical skills at other times. It is not unusual for four- and five-year-olds to fill page after page with letters and numerals, experimenting, practicing, and developing their understanding and control. They often come to adults during these times to ask questions such as, "How do you make a *Z?*"

We think that allowing children to write in meaningful contexts is an important way to encourage children to sustain their struggles to acquire technical skills. A lack of technical skills will not keep children from writing; in fact, children acquire technical skills through trying to write.

Invented Spellings. At first, children do not spell words correctly. They often invent spellings for the same reasons that they create words such as "feets" and "mouses" in their early talking: they understand rules but apply them differently than adults do. Invented spellings reflect children's incomplete understanding of English phonology, and their inability to distinguish similar physical speech sounds the way adults distinguish them. For example, preschool children often write words containing *tr* with the letters *ch* because when *t* is followed by the *r* the *t* is *affricated* — released slowly with a "shh" sound (Read, 1980, p. 161). On the other hand, *t* in "toy" is not affricated. Adults on the other hand consider both *t*'s to be the same sound and different from *ch* because they are both articulated in the same way, with the tongue just behind the teeth at the roof of the mouth. But young children do not understand how adults categorize sounds, and as a result they sometimes use letters differently than we do. Examples of invented spellings are shown in Box 23-1.

BOX 23-1. Invented Spellings

DA (day)
LADE (lady)
EGLE (eagle)
FEL (feel)
FLEPR (flipper)
SIGIRAT (cigarette)
AODOV (out of)
GRL (girl)
BRD (bird)
  (Read, 1980)

PPL (people)
BCAZ (because)
FRN (friend)
NHR (nature)
TABL (table)
GRIF (giraffe)
HL (hill)
  (Paul, 1976)

GNYS (genius)
TLEFNMBS (telephone number)
KRWSH (car wash)
  (Bissex, 1980)

SOURCES: Read, C. Preschool children's knowledge of English phonology. In M. Wolf, M. K. McQuillan, and E. Radwin (Eds.), *Thought and language/Language and reading.* Reprint Series No. 14, *Harvard Educational Review* (1980): 150–179; Bissex, G. L. *GNYS AT WRK: A child learns to write and read.* Cambridge, Mass.: Harvard University Press, 1980; Paul, R. Invented spelling in kindergarten. *Young Children* 31 (1976): 195–200.

Children also omit silent letters such as the *e* in "kite." In addition, they often omit vowels at first, writing such things as "PPL" for "people" because they have less conspicuous sounds than consonants and are less important in capturing the essential sound of a word (Read, 1980).

Children must not only learn to differentiate and categorize sounds according to the phonetic features adults use; they must realize that English spelling often violates phonetic transcription to retain lexical similarities. In pairs of words such as "quest" and "question," "muscle" and "muscular," and "critic" and "criticize," one word is spelled phonetically, but the spelling of a sound in the other word is ambiguous. For example, the *t* in "question" is not pronounced, and the *c* in "criticize" sounds like an *s*. If the words were spelled phonetically, there would be no evidence that their meanings are related to other forms of the word. Our spelling system takes both phonetics and word meanings into account in a way that is quite remarkable and efficient for a skilled reader but troublesome for the beginner (Chomsky, 1980).

As children listen to language, see it represented in print, and try to write it themselves, they gradually begin to understand how to spell. Good spellers not only learn to categorize sounds appropriately for representation by our alphabet, they understand the relationships among different forms of a word. This permits them to spell words correctly when phonetic transcription is violated; an understanding of one form of a word is used to get clues for spelling another (Chomsky, 1980). It takes some time for children to learn how to spell, and it is not unusual for errors to persist through the primary grades.

Composition. Children also learn how to compose during middle childhood. Graves has investigated how children in the beginning of this stage write. The case of Sarah is fairly typical:

> Usually Sarah does not know what she will write about until she draws. She must write and draw to discover the story. When asked, "What will happen next?" Sarah usually says, "Wait and see," or "I don't know yet. I have to think."
>
> Sarah drew a girl in her room. She had a flower in her hand, a doll in her canopy bed, a refrigerator, a door, a window, and a night light. Sarah wrote:
>
> She loves flowers the best.
> She hates school the worst.

On the next page Sarah drew a similar scene but added a new face with sharp teeth. Sarah seemed startled. She said, "Now wait a dog-gone minute! A bad guy. He's coming to kidnap her."

Sarah composed these sentences aloud before writing:

> She jumped up.
> She was scared.
> She saw the villain.

Then Sarah said, "Wait, the bulb fell out," referring to the night light.

> She turned the page and composed aloud before drawing: "She punched him out."

> The researcher asked about an object in the drawing. "What's that?"

> "A night light falling," she said. "It broke. He's sorry. She punched him."

> Sarah wrote:

> She punched him.

> Sarah composed her last two sentences aloud before writing — "She's so glad" and "She's asleep." [Graves, 1979, p. 833]

As you can see, Sarah discovers her story as she draws and writes — just like adult writers.

By the age of eight or nine, children can produce some remarkable writing if they are encouraged and have many opportunities to write. Calkins (1978) has described the creations of fifth graders whose teachers encouraged them to write frequently. Instead of grading the children's papers, the teacher had children read their papers and then revise them. One child's story started like this:

> When I was skating yesterday I fell down and whacked my head on
> the ice. "Ha, ha," Brian laughed, "You can't even skate...."

After reading the story to other class members and listening to their reactions, the story was revised to begin this way:

> Whack, my head hit the ice.

In the same classroom, a nine-year-old named Rebecca wrote this first draft of a poem:

> My legs spring off the ground
> My back arches
> pulls
> My back stretches
> bends
> Then my feet hit the ground
> with a bounce
> I jump in the air.

When she read her poem, however, she was dissatisfied with it. Her teacher suggested that she go to the hall to do some handsprings; she could pay close attention to her feelings and movements and then write about them. Her final draft went like this:

> *"Back Handsprings"*
>
> I spring from scrunch to stretch
> reaching.
> My back arches,
> pulling.
> My eyes follow my hands,
> straining.
> I reach the ground
> with pushing hands
> and bouncing feet
> I jump in gladness. [Calkins, 1978, p. 707]

Children's writing can be vivid, interesting, and precise when they are encouraged to write about what they know and want to share with others, and when they are given time to think about and revise their first drafts. The reason so many children and adults cannot write may be that they were required to do mechanical exercises and not encouraged to write when they were in school.

Summary

Oral Language
- During the school-age years, children develop metalinguistic awareness — the ability to think about language in the abstract. They also master certain complex syntactic structures.
- Children can appreciate jokes and riddles only after they have acquired certain cognitive and linguistic abilities, because most jokes and riddles are based on some kind of linguistic ambiguity.
- Children learning a second language apparently go through the same patterns of development as children learning the same language as a first language. They learn a second language best in situations in which they are required to communicate in it.
- Dialects are variations in the use of a language. Black English may be the most familiar dialect in this country.

Written Language
- Authorities make different assumptions about the strategies involved in learning to read. Some stress form and skills as prerequisites for deriving meaning. Others stress meaning from the beginning and think skills will be better understood in context.
- The development of mature handwriting involves cognitive and motor abilities as well as an understanding of the distinctive features of print.

- Children sometimes invent spellings based on their understanding of phonology and spelling rules. But as children become more familiar with reading and writing, they begin to correct their own spelling errors.
- An emphasis on meaningful writing rather than just technical skills will encourage good writing. Even young children can compose stories and poems.

New Terms

metalinguistic awareness
lexical ambiguity
phonological ambiguity
syntactical ambiguity
surface structure

deep structure
dialect
word calling
language experience approach
affrication

Selected Readings

Bissex, G. L. **GNYS AT WRK: A child learns to write and read.** *Cambridge, Mass.: Harvard University Press, 1980.* This is the story of Paul from age five to eleven written by his mother. It describes his learning to write and read. Wonderful examples and good commentary are provided throughout. Provides an excellent, in-depth look at a child's written language acquisition.

Christian, D., and Wolfram, W. **Exploring dialects.** *Arlington, Va.: Center for Applied Linguistics, 1979.* Easy to read twenty-page booklet provides an overview of dialect differences. Informative without being technical.

Knapp, M., and Knapp, H. **One potato, two potato: The secret education of American children.** *New York: Norton, 1976.* A book about socialization by peers during the school-age years. A good source of songs, riddles, and jokes popular with this age group.

Wolfram, W., Potter, L., Yanofsky, N. M., and Shuy, R. W. **Reading and dialect differences.** *Arlington, Va.: Center for Applied Linguistics, 1979.* This 20-page booklet discusses the issues surrounding reading and dialect. Excellent examples illustrate the impact of dialect on reading performance and achievement test scores.

Chapter 24

Social Development

In Chapter 19 we discussed the major socialization processes, including observational learning, reinforcement and punishment, and verbal instruction. We also examined two categories of socialized behavior: control of aggression and prosocial behavior. Here we will look at changes in social cognition that occur during the school-age period, and the development of moral judgment, achievement motivation, and sex-role behavior.

Social Cognition

As children mature, their *social cognition* — the way they think about social matters — undergoes a number of changes. They develop a better understanding of other people's thoughts, feelings, and interactions, and learn how to put themselves in another person's position or role. These changes influence how they interact with other people, for example, how aggressive they are and the extent to which they exhibit prosocial behaviors.

Children's Descriptions of Others

One of the changes children undergo during middle childhood involves how they describe others. To discover how the perceptions of children vary with age, Scarlett, Press, and Crockett (1971) asked boys in first, third, and fifth grades to describe four people: a boy and girl they liked and a boy and girl they disliked. The boys' responses were divided into four categories:

1. *Concrete-we-constructs* — The boy focused on the overt actions of the other child and did not differentiate himself from the child he was describing. ("We play together.")
2. *Egocentric-concrete constructs* — The boy focused on the other child's overt actions, but did differentiate himself from the other child. However, the other's actions were still described in terms of their relation to the boy providing the description. ("He gives me things.")
3. *Nonegocentric-concrete constructs* — The boy still focused on the other child's overt actions, but he did not describe the actions only in terms of himself. ("He hits people all of the time.")
4. *Abstract constructs* — The boy focused on dispositions rather than specific actions, and inferred that the other child had a certain type of personality from his or her actions in different contexts. ("He is nice.") [Scarlett, Press, and Crockett, 1971, p. 449]

The researchers found that as a child gets older, his or her descriptions focus less on what others do in specific situations and more on their psychological makeup. The child also begins to base judgments about other people on how they behave with people in general, not simply on how they behave toward him or her.

Other studies (Bigelow and LaGaipa, 1975; Livesley and Bromley, 1973; Peevers and Secord, 1973; Yarrow and Campbell, 1963) confirm the basic results found by Scarlett et al. Young children seem to base their assessments of other people on what they do, what they look like, how they interact with the child her- or himself, and where they are ("John lives in a red house"). As children move into the later school-age years, they begin to describe people in terms of their personalities, which are inferred from actions and persist over time. Rather than talking about specific events ("John is sad right now"), they talk about enduring characteristics ("John is talkative"). They also come to understand that other people have personalities separate from their own interactions with them.

Children's Understanding of Others' Feelings

In Chapter 19 we mentioned that a preschool child can identify with the emotions of other people when these people resemble the child and he or she has experienced a situation similar to the one responsible for the emotions (Chandler and Greenspan, 1972). We also pointed out that children's judgments in these cases may really be based on self-descriptions rather than on an understanding of how others feel.

As children enter middle childhood, they begin to recognize the emotions of persons who are dissimilar to themselves (Flapan, 1968; Rothenberg, 1970). They also begin to understand the causes of other people's emotions, not only when they are caused by a specific circumstance, as when a child is unhappy because someone will not let her use a swing, but when they have a psychological cause, as when a person is sad because someone does not like her. Furthermore, older children begin to see that people change their behavior in response to other people's feelings (Flapan, 1968).

These changes in understanding enable children to adapt their behavior to various situations. They become capable of a level of sensitivity and consideration that was previously impossible. Younger children are not intentionally inconsiderate or insensitive, but they do not understand that others feel differently and, therefore, cannot adapt to their feelings.

Children's Conception of Friendship

Children's understanding of friendship and membership in a peer group also changes during middle childhood. Preschool children assess these relationships in terms of physical involvement: a friend is whoever you are playing with, who does not break your toys. Members of a group are those who play together or hold hands. As children move into the school years, they begin to understand that friendship and membership in a peer group are based on feelings and intentions, not simply on physical interactions. At first, however, they view friendship as a one-way relationship: a friend is someone who does something for you, or you are a friend if you do something for someone else. Later, friendship is recognized as reciprocal: friends do things for each other (Cooney and Selman, 1978). By age nine or ten, people who have similar interests, beliefs, or personalities are regarded as friends, and the things friends do together are seen as acknowledgments of the relationship (Youniss and Volpe, 1978). In short, they realize that doing things together does not make people friends but that being friends leads people to do things together.

Children's understanding of friendship can explain why five- and six-year-olds are sometimes upset when they see someone they consider their friend playing with someone else. "Hey, she's *my* friend," they may assert. Older children, on the other hand, do not get upset when a friend of theirs spends time with other friends. They realize that the person can do things with others and still be their friend. But young children think friendship is determined by physical proximity and may imagine that they have lost a friend when they see someone they have played with earlier playing with another child.

Children's Understanding of Others' Thoughts

A young couple sat in their car staring at the waves splashing onto the beach. They had argued earlier, but now sat in silence. Finally, she turned to him and asked, "What are you thinking?"

"I'm thinking about what you must be thinking," he answered. "You must think I don't care about you because I didn't call last night like I said I would, but went out and had a good time with Ron and Jim instead."

"No, I really think you care," she answered, "but I also think you think I'll put up with being treated that way. You think I care so much about you that you don't have to be considerate. Well, let me tell you something: If you think I'm going to tolerate such treatment, you're wrong. No matter how much I care about you, I won't see you any more if you do that again."

"Well, I didn't think you'd think it was all that terrible," he explained.

"Well, now you know," she said with finality.

It is easy for adolescents and adults to understand how others think, a process known as *recursive thinking* or *metathinking*. Although it is sometimes hard for us to realize, young children are incapable of understanding how other people think. Only gradually do they develop an awareness of their own thoughts and come to realize that other people's thoughts may be different.

Role-taking Stages. Investigators have studied children's ability to understand another person's thoughts by presenting them with games or with social role-taking dilemmas. In a study conducted by DeVries (1970), children were asked to guess in which hand an adult had concealed a penny, and also to take the role of the concealer. This game involves thinking about what the other person is thinking.

DeVries found five stages of role-taking ability. In the first two stages, children do not even understand that the game involves uncertainty, thinking that the penny is always in the same place and that the game simply involves uncovering the penny. When children are asked to hide the penny, they do not understand that they should do it secretly, and it is not uncommon for children to extend only the hand the penny is hidden in, or to say to the guesser, "Pick this hand." Children who play like this do not understand that the two players have different perspectives and different motives: one hopes to find; the other hopes to conceal.

In Stage 3, children realize that the game is competitive; when they hide the penny, they are delighted when the guesser picks the wrong hand. But apparently they do not realize that the guesser is thinking about the concealer's strategy; they hide the penny in a predictable pattern, first in one hand, then in the other. They also assume that the other person uses this strategy.

By Stage 4, children understand that the hider must be unpredictable. They clearly think about what the other is thinking and try to outwit him or her, but only when hiding the penny. They still use a predictable alternating pattern when guessing. They apparently understand that they can think about the thoughts of others, but do not realize that others can think about what they are thinking.

Stage 5 children realize that the other person can think about their thoughts. They realize that an unpredictable pattern is necessary both when hiding the penny and when guessing where the penny has been hidden. DeVries found that many six- and seven-year-olds, and even some bright five-year-olds, were operating at Stage 5.

In other studies of role-taking behavior, children this young have not shown that they know they can think about others' thoughts or that others can think about their thoughts. The differences are probably due to variations in methodology. In these studies children were asked to respond to social dilemmas presented orally rather than to play a game. One such study of role-taking was conducted by Selman (1976). A dilemma involving Holly is given below.

> Holly is an eight-year-old girl who likes to climb trees. She is the best tree climber in the neighborhood. One day while climbing down from a tall tree, she falls off the bottom branch but does not hurt herself. Her father sees her fall. He is upset and asks her to promise not to climb trees any more. Holly promises.
>
> Later that day, Holly and her friends meet Shawn. Shawn's kitten is caught up in a tree and can't get down. Something has to be done right away, or the kitten may fall. Holly is the only one who climbs trees well enough to reach the kitten and get down, but she remembers her promise to her father.

After hearing the dilemma, children are asked the following questions:

1. Does Holly know how Shawn feels about the kitten?
2. How will Holly's father feel if he finds out she climbed the tree?
3. What does Holly think her father will do if he finds out she climbed the tree?
4. What would you do in this situation?

On the basis of this type of research, Selman and his colleagues (Selman, 1976; Selman and Byrne, 1974) concluded that children's role-taking abilities progress through the following five stages:

- Stage 0 (ages four to six) *Egocentric Role Taking*
  At the beginning of this stage, children understand that they are different from others, but they are unaware of different points of view. The child thinks there is only one possible view, and that he or she and everyone else holds it. The child typically answers the question about Holly's father's reaction by saying, "He will feel happy because he likes kittens." Obviously, the child likes kittens and assumes that Holly and her father like kittens. Children are unaware that other people's views can differ from their own until late in this stage.

- Stage 1 (ages six to eight) *Social-Information Role Taking*
  At this stage the child understands that others interpret situations differently, but he or she thinks this happens because they received different information. The child is unaware that one can think about the thinking of another person. He or she cannot assume another person's role. The child answers the question about Holly's father's reaction by saying, "If he didn't know why she climbed the tree, he would be angry. But if Holly tells him why she did it, he would realize that she has a good reason."
- Stage 2 (ages nine and ten) *Self-Reflective Role Taking*
  Children at this level know that others can think about their thoughts and feelings. These children can also think about their own thinking *or* think about another person's thinking about them, but they cannot do these two kinds of thinking simultaneously. In other words, the child can assume another person's role, but cannot take his or her own role at the same time. At this stage children say Holly's father will not be angry: "Holly knows that her father will understand why she climbed the tree, so she knows that he won't want to punish her at all."
- Stage 3 (ages ten to twelve) *Mutual Role Taking*
  At this stage the child can consider his or her point of view and another point of view simultaneously, as a disinterested third party (i.e., the child can speculate about what other people are thinking about other people's thoughts). "Let's see," the child might say about Holly, "Holly wanted to get the kitten because she liked kittens, but she knew that she wasn't supposed to climb trees. Holly's father knew that Holly had been told not to climb trees, but he couldn't have known beforehand about this situation. He'd probably punish her anyway just to enforce his rule."
- Stage 4 (ages twelve to fifteen and older) *Social and Conventional System Role Taking*
  At this stage the child realizes that each person considers the view of the "generalized other" (the social system) to understand the view of a particular person. The perspective of the social group is now taken into account. A child commenting on the fate of Holly might say, "Holly's father would probably get angry and punish her because that's what fathers generally do, or are supposed to do when their children disobey." If the child has moved beyond a conventional view of morality (see the discussion of Kohlberg later in this chapter) the child might respond by saying, "You'd really have to know Holly's father to know if he would get angry. Some fathers would get angry, and others wouldn't."

Effect of Role Taking on Social Behavior. Changes in the ability to assume a role have an effect on children's social behavior. When children can think about what others think they can anticipate reactions to their behavior and alter it before it leads to trouble. One reason children in the egocentric stage may do things their parents have instructed them not to do is that they assume their parents share their affection for the toy, child, or animal involved — that the parent sees things the way they do. Similarly, one reason why six- to eight-year-olds sometimes "talk back" to their parents may be because they believe their parents will see things the way they see them if only they have the right information.

Several attempts have been made to increase children's prosocial behavior through practice in role playing. The assumption (which is apparently correct) is that if children can see things from another person's viewpoint, they will behave more prosocially. In a study by Staub (1971), children were given opportunities to assume a helping role in five situations. Other children were asked only to make helpful suggestions. Role playing had a significant effect on girls' helping behavior and boys' sharing behavior.

Another change resulting from an increased ability to take roles is that children begin to judge the behavior of others in terms of their intentions and their actions, not in terms of their actions alone. Rather than associating degrees of "badness" with the extent of physical damage, children begin to take people's goals and desires into account.

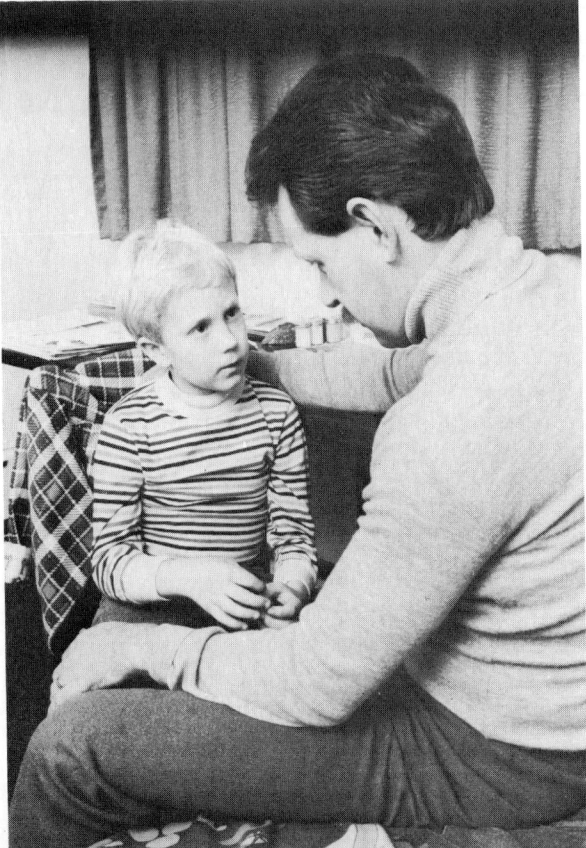

"But, Dad. Just let me tell you why I did it."

Moral Development

During socialization we develop ideas about right and wrong; we learn to make moral judgments. Several elaborate theories and a great deal of research have been based on Piaget's theory of moral development (1965). We will discuss Piaget's work first and then explain the investigations of Lawrence Kohlberg.

Piaget's Research

Children's Judgments about Moral Dilemmas. One method Piaget used to study the development of moral judgment in children was to present them with moral dilemmas in which a person's intentions were at odds with the damage he or she did. The person who caused a great deal of damage usually did so unknowingly, whereas the actor who caused relatively little damage did so on purpose. The following dilemma is fairly typical.

A. A little boy who is called John is in his room. He is called to dinner. He goes into the dining room. But behind the door there was a chair, and on the chair there was a tray with twelve cups on it. John couldn't have known that there was all this behind the door. He goes in, the door knocks against the tray, bang go the twelve cups and they all get broken!

B. Once there was a little boy whose name was Henry. One day when his mother was out he tried to get some jam out of the cupboard. He climbed up on to a chair and stretched out his arm. But the jam was too high up and he couldn't reach it and have any. But while he was trying to get it he knocked over a cup. The cup fell and broke. [Piaget 1965, p. 122]

Piaget asked children whether the characters were equally guilty, which of them was naughtier, and why one was naughtier than the other. Young children ascribed blame in proportion to the damage: their judgments were based on objective events. For example, Geo, age six, answered Piaget's questions as follows:

> Is one of the boys naughtier than the other? — *The first is because he knocked over twelve cups.* — If you were daddy, which one would you punish most? — *The one who broke twelve cups.* — Why did he break them? — *The door shut too hard and knocked them. He didn't do it on purpose.* — Have you got a brother? — *No, a little sister.* Well, if it was you who had broken the twelve cups when you went into the room and your little sister who had broken one cup while she was trying to get the jam, which of you would be punished most severely? — *Me, because I broke more than one cup.* [Piaget, 1965, p. 125]

By middle childhood, however, children were taking subjective intentions into account. Judgments about lying and stealing follow the same trend as judgments about material damage. Younger children judge the seriousness of a lie by how it varies from the truth, not by whether the child who told it was intentionally deceptive. Young children presented with two stories involving lying thought the character whose story was the farthest from the truth was naughtier. A six-year-old said a character was worse because what he said "could never happen." A character who said he saw a dog as big as a cow was judged worse by a seven-year-old because "There's no such thing." A ten-year-old, on the other hand, took motivation into account: "The lie about the teacher was worse because he deceived his mother."

Similarly, stealing is judged in terms of the amount stolen, not in terms of the purpose of the stealing — whether it was self-serving or undertaken to help someone. Presented with a dilemma in which a boy stole a roll to give to a hungry friend and a girl stole a ribbon for herself, six-year-olds said that the boy's theft was worse "because rolls cost more." A nine-year-old, however, said, "The little girl was worse. The little girl took the ribbon for herself. The little boy took the roll too, but to give it to his friend who had no dinner" (Piaget, 1965).

Actually, even the youngest children studied made both objective and subjective judgments on occasion, but between ages five and ten, objective reasoning gave way to subjective reasoning (Lickona, 1976; Piaget, 1965).

Piaget believes that the tendency for younger children to emphasize objective responsibility in these cases results from their egocentric thought and unilateral respect for the authority of adults. We have already shown that children are unaware that other people can have different points of view. If children assume that only one view is possible, they are obviously incapable of considering another person's intentions. Only after children have had extensive experiences with peers do they realize that people can have different points of view. At that stage they begin to evaluate damage in terms of intentions rather than damage alone.

The nature of children's relations with parents also supports objective rather than subjective moral judgments. Piaget (1965) has suggested that younger children's objective morality stems from unilateral respect for adults: the child regards the adult and his or her rules as infallible and, as a result, inflexible. Young children assimilate judgments about moral dilemmas to their experience with their parents, and thus disregard intentions.

More recent studies suggest that children do not hold adults in perfect esteem, as Piaget implied (Epstein, 1965, cited in Lickona, 1976, p. 223). Perhaps young children follow the rule that more damage equals worse behavior, not because they respect adults but because parents present rules to young children, whose understanding is limited, as inflexible commands that ignore the intentions of the actor (Mischel and Mischel, 1976).

Piaget suggests that a family atmosphere that emphasizes democratic reasoning and cooperative interactions with peers will enhance the acquisition of mature moral judgment. Correlational studies support his view, indicating a relationship between democratic discussions of rules in the family and children's moral reasoning and moral behavior (Baumrind, 1972; Hoffman and Saltzstein, 1967; Kohlberg, 1969).

Children's Views About Rules of Games. Piaget began his investigations of moral development by questioning children about the rules of games. Like other rules, the rules of games indicate which behaviors are permissible and which are not. For the game to be played, everyone playing must feel an obligation to obey the rules.

To begin his investigation, Piaget asked children to explain how to play marbles. In this way he determined how children actually used rules to play games. He found that children pass through four stages. In the first play is purely motoric: the child handles the marbles, perhaps dropping them or rolling them on the ground. The child's actions may develop a pattern (he or she may repeat the same actions over and over), but these motor rules are individual rather than social or collective. The child feels no obligation to obey the rules as a condition for collaborating in play with another person and would actually be content to play marbles alone.

The second stage emerges sometime between the ages of two and five, when children have been exposed to others playing a game according to rules, perhaps by watching older siblings play. This stage is known as egocentric, because even though the play involves imitation of rules (for example, marking off a space in which to place the marbles; attempting to shoot with one marble to hit others), children at this stage are often content to play by themselves. If they do play with others, they play to win, but they still think it is possible for everyone to win. Children in this stage have clearly learned some of the rules used by others, but they use them for their own purposes, not to coordinate their actions with the actions of others.

By age seven or eight, in Stage 3, children no longer follow rules egocentrically, and games become truly social. Children try to win or to get the better of others, but they realize that everyone must follow the same rules. They understand, for example, that knocking marbles out of the center does not constitute winning, but that the winner is the person who knocks the most marbles out of the center. In addition, they know that everyone must adhere to certain procedures so that the conditions in which people shoot are similar. This stage is known as incipient cooperation.

In Stage 3, however, children still have only vague knowledge of the details of the actual rules, and they are likely to have different versions of the rules. Disputes arise as they play, and they work out the rules game by game. Thus, children in this stage may not play with the same rules in every game, not because they think the rules can be changed, but because their conception of the right rules varies.

In Stage 4 (eleven to twelve years of age), children are in agreement about the rules, which are understood in great detail. When children disagree, it is usually because they have learned different versions of the rules. They realize that rules can vary and understand that inconsistencies can be cleared up by asking all players which set they wish to follow. They also understand that the rules can be changed if everyone agrees.

Children's consciousness of rules develops differently from their practice of rules. Their consciousness of rules consists of their awareness of the rules' origins and their views about whether rules can be changed and under what circumstances. In the first stage, children do not regard rules as obligatory. They think rules can be disregarded.

In the second stage, which overlaps Stage 2 (egocentricity) and Stage 3 (cooperation) of the practice of rules, children believe rules are inviolate and sacred. They think rules have always existed unchanged, and were devised by God or by the people in the first community. They should not be changed; if they are, the game is not considered the "real" game.

Children's practice of rules seems inconsistent with their beliefs at this stage. Children do not believe that rules can be changed, but when they play a game they may not follow them precisely or use the same rules for two games in succession. They are not actually inconsistent, however. Every time they play a game, they play it in accordance with what they believe the rules to be, but their understanding of the rules changes from game to game.

In the third stage of consciousness of rules, which emerges at around age ten, a child realizes that rules are not products of external authority but are developed through mutual decision. The child understands that rules can be changed as long as everyone agrees to the changes. As Piaget put it, "He no longer relies, as do the little ones, upon an all-wise tradition. He no longer thinks that everything has been arranged for the best in the past and that the only way of avoiding trouble is by religiously repeating the established order. He believes in the value of experiment in so far as it is sanctioned by collective opinion" (1965, p. 65). At this stage children realize that the rules for marbles were developed by children as they played, perhaps at first with rounded pebbles; adults did not develop the rules and impose them on children. This third stage parallels Stage 4 of the practice of rules, observing rules in actual practice.

Piaget characterized the Stage 2 child's view of morality as "morality of constraint," and the Stage 3 child's morality as "morality of cooperation." The differences are due to the same two processes that are responsible for the differences in objective and subjective judgment of moral dilemmas: cognitive development and social interaction.

At first children accept rules because they think they are permanent and not created in people's minds. Then, as their realism and egocentrism diminish, they begin to realize that if rules are created by people, then people can change them. They also realize that people can have different points of view.

Children's ideas about the sacredness of rules also change as a result of their increased social interaction with peers. They begin to realize that rules are not handed down to children by adults, but that children create rules as they play. At first, however, they do not think that children can change all rules. They think it would be okay for children to change the rules of games played with peers but not classroom rules; they think classroom rules can be changed by the teacher but that the teacher should not change school rules made by the principal; they think laws can be changed only by policemen. As children get older, they come to realize that people governed by a rule have a right to influence what it says (Epstein, 1965, cited in Lickona, 1976).

Epstein's work suggests that Piaget's framework is too limited for application to the upper levels of moral development. This suggestion is confirmed by the work of Lawrence Kohlberg.

Kohlberg's Research

Kohlberg's work on moral reasoning is based on the work of Piaget, but there are some important differences. For example, Piaget's work does not differentiate the moral development of adults. By age eleven or twelve, Piaget says, all children are making "mature" moral judgments because they take intentions into account. In Kohlberg's scheme, even adults may not reach the highest stage of moral reasoning.

Kohlberg, like Piaget, studied moral reasoning by analyzing responses to moral dilemmas. One dilemma used by Kohlberg is that of Heinz, a man who was faced with the choice of stealing medicine or letting his wife die:

> In Europe, a woman was near death from cancer. One drug might save her, a form of radium that a druggist in the same town had recently discovered. The druggist was charging $2,000, ten times what the drug cost him to make. The sick woman's husband, Heinz, went to everyone he knew to borrow the money, but he could only get together about half of what it cost. He told the druggist that his wife was dying and asked him to sell it cheaper or let him pay later. But the druggist said "No." The husband got desperate and broke into the man's store to steal the drug for his wife. Should the man have done that? Why? [Kohlberg, 1969, p. 379]

Kohlberg was more interested in the reason given for the judgment than in the judgment itself. In the following example, for instance, the judgments of the two people differ. Nevertheless, their reasoning is basically the same, and Kohlberg classified them in Stage 1 because they were motivated by avoidance of punishment.

> *Pro* — If you let your wife die, you will get in trouble. You'll be blamed for not spending the money to save her and there'll be an investigation of you and the druggist for your wife's death.

> *Con* — You shouldn't steal the drug because you'll be caught and sent to jail if you do. If you do get away, your conscience would bother you thinking how the police would catch up with you at any minute.
> [Kohlberg, 1969, p. 381]

Kohlberg (1976) classified moral judgments into six stages at three levels (see Table 24-1). He thought of these levels as characteristic of a person's relationship to society's rules and expectations. People at Level I are considered preconventional. Level II people are conventional. They have chosen to conform to the

Table 24-1. Kohlberg's moral stages

Level and stage	Content of stage		Social perspective of stage
	What is right	*Reasons for doing right*	
Level I — Preconventional Stage 1 — Heteronomous morality	To avoid breaking rules backed by punishment, obedience for its own sake, and avoiding physical damage to persons and property.	Avoidance of punishment, and the superior power of authorities.	*Egocentric point of view.* Doesn't consider the interests of others or recognize that they differ from the actor's; doesn't relate two points of view. Actions are considered physically rather than in terms of psychological interests of others. Confusion of authority's perspective with one's own.
Stage 2 — Individualism, instrumental purpose, and exchange	Following rules only when it is to someone's immediate interest; acting to meet one's own interests and needs and letting others do the same. Right is also what's fair, what's an equal exchange, a deal, an agreement.	To serve one's own needs or interests in a world where you have to recognize that other people have their interests, too.	*Concrete individualistic perspective.* Aware that everybody has his own interest to pursue and these conflict, so that right is relative (in the concrete individualistic sense).
Level II — Conventional Stage 3 — Mutual interpersonal expectations, relationships, and interpersonal conformity	Living up to what is expected by people close to you or what people generally expect of people in your role as son, brother, friend, etc. "Being good" is important and means having good motives, showing concern about others. It also means keeping mutual relationships, such as trust, loyalty, respect and gratitude.	The need to be a good person in your own eyes and those of others. Your caring for others. Belief in the Golden Rule. Desire to maintain rules and authority which support stereotypical good behavior.	*Perspective of the individual in relationships with other individuals.* Aware of shared feelings, agreements, and expectations which take primacy over individual interests. Relates points of view through the concrete Golden Rule, putting yourself in the other guy's shoes. Does not yet consider generalized system perspective.

Stage	What is right	Reasons for doing right	Social perspective of stage
Stage 4 — Social system and conscience	Fulfilling the actual duties to which you have agreed. Laws are to be upheld except in extreme cases where they conflict with other fixed social duties. Right is also contributing to society, the group, or institution.	To keep the institution going as a whole, to avoid the breakdown in the system "if everyone did it," or the imperative of conscience to meet one's defined obligations (Easily confused with Stage 3 belief in rules and authority.)	*Differentiates societal point of view from interpersonal agreement or motives.* Takes the point of view of the system that defines roles and rules. Considers individual relations in terms of place in the system.
Level III — Postconventional, or principled Stage 5 — Social contract or utility and individual rights	Being aware that people hold a variety of values and opinions, that most values and rules are relative to your group. These relative rules should usually be upheld, however, in the interest of impartiality and because they are the social contract. Some nonrelative values and rights like *life* and *liberty*, however, must be upheld in any society and regardless of majority opinion.	A sense of obligation to law because of one's social contract to make and abide by laws for the welfare of all and for the protection of all people's rights. A feeling of contractual commitment, freely entered upon, to family, friendship, trust, and work obligations. Concern that laws and duties be based on rational calculation of overall utility, "the greatest good for the greatest number."	*Prior-to-society perspective.* Perspective of a rational individual aware of values and rights prior to social attachments and contracts. Integrates perspectives by formal mechanisms of agreement, contract, objective impartiality, and due process. Considers moral and legal points of view; recognizes that they sometimes conflict and finds it difficult to integrate them.
Stage 6 — Universal ethical principles	Following self-chosen ethical principles. Particular laws or social agreements are usually valid because they rest on such principles. When laws violate these principles, one acts in accordance with the principle. Principles are universal principles of justice: the equality of human rights and respect for the dignity of human beings as individual persons.	The belief as a rational person in the validity of universal moral principles, and a sense of personal commitment to them.	*Perspective of a moral point of view from which social arrangements derive.* Perspective is that of any rational individual recognizing the nature of morality or the fact that persons are ends in themselves and must be treated as such.

SOURCE: Kohlberg, L. Moral stages and moralization. In T. Lickona (Ed.), *Moral development and behavior: Theory, research, and social issues.* New York: Holt, Rinehart and Winston, 1976, pp. 34–35. Reprinted with permission.

standards expected of them by society. Level III people are postconventional; they define their values in terms of principles that are not chosen simply because they conform to the will of the majority.

The stages of moral development proposed by Kohlberg always seem to emerge in the same order and tend to appear at certain ages. Young children are incapable of reasoning at the highest level, but progress to the postconventional stages is by no means inevitable. People's experiences influence how they advance. Exposure to moral dilemmas and the values of others can have an important effect, although the progress of young children may be limited by their level of cognitive development. Children between the ages of ten and twelve, for example, may be in Stage 2, 3, or 4. It is not until adolescence that people are capable of the reasoning required in the highest stages, but the fact that a certain person has the capacity to reach Level III (Stages 5 and 6) does not necessarily mean that he or she will attain it.

Efforts have been made to influence how children make moral judgments. The most effective ones help the child understand and value the reasoning behind the moral choices. For example, young children may be capable of basing judgments on intentions but they often fail to do so (Bearison and Isaacs, 1975). It may be that they have to learn to value intentions as a relevant dimension in judging wrongdoing. Lickona (1976) found that even when children appreciate that a character in a moral predicament had good intentions, they sometimes consider him guiltier than a person who was intentionally deceptive. This indicates that simply being able to put oneself in another's place does not ensure that one will behave fairly. One must also learn to value the intentions of the other.

Teachers and parents often instruct children directly on the importance of valuing intentions. When John accidentally hits Mark and Mark begins to hit back, disregarding John's intentions and reacting to his actions alone, an alert teacher might remind Mark that John's behavior was accidental. In doing so, the teacher would emphasize the value that intentions are more important than damage.

Achievement

Some children work hard on school assignments or practice pitching or playing the piano for hours. Others are much less inclined to work at activities of this sort. Even casual observers notice that some children are far more interested than others in meeting prescribed standards to win approval. Activities intended to meet a goal or get approval are known as *achievement behavior* (Crandall, Katkovsky, and Preston, 1962).

What determines whether children engage in achievement behavior in a particular situation? As you might expect, achievement behavior is strongly influenced by ability, but many other factors can also have an effect. We have all met bright children who do not work very hard and children of average ability who try exceptionally hard. Clearly, achievement is influenced by personality as well as ability. We will discuss a number of influential factors, including achievement motivation (the "need for achievement"), expectancy of success, and attribution of success or failure (the child's explanation of why he or she accomplished or failed to accomplish something).

Achievement Motivation

The desire to be successful, to outperform others or meet a standard, is called *achievement motivation* or the *need for achievement.* It is usually assessed by asking a subject to respond to pictures by writing stories. This procedure assumes that what people say about the characters in the pictures reflects how they feel about themselves. Methods of this sort are called *projective techniques* because the subjects supposedly project aspects of themselves onto the picture characters. Among other things, the pictures show (1) two men ("inventors") in a shop working on a machine, (2) a young boy and a violin, and (3) a boy sitting at a desk with an open book in front of him (McClelland et al., 1976, p. 375). Subjects are asked to answer the following four questions:

1. What is happening? Who are the persons?
2. What were the circumstances leading up to the situation in the pictures?
3. What are the characters thinking? What do they want?
4. What will happen? What will be done? [McClelland et al., 1976, p. 98]

Subjects are told that this is a test of creativity, and that there are no right or wrong answers.

Some children are motivated to achieve, while others are not.

The assessment of the stories involves noting references to achievement goals (that is, concern over success in competition with a standard of excellence). Subjects who refer to achievement goals are rated high in achievement motivation; subjects who refer to achievement goals rarely or not at all are rated low.

Achievement motivation is generally found in conjunction with actual achievement behavior (Evans, 1967). Motivation may not be evident in areas the child does not value, however. For example, a child may be highly motivated to achieve, but in something other than school-related tasks. The child's desire to achieve in a situation depends on whether the child values that kind of achievement. In other words, different situations have different *attainment values* for children (Battle, 1966; Stein and Bailey, 1973).

Children who are achievement oriented usually come from environments in which parents provided achievement and independence training. *Achievement training* "stresses competence in situations involving standards of excellence," whereas *independence training* "involves putting the child on his own" (Rosen and D'Andrade, 1975).

Parents of achievement-oriented children encourage children to do well, expect them to do well, and reward good performance warmly. They also disapprove when children perform poorly. Fathers of achievement-oriented children are especially likely to give indirect guidance and advice to help children solve problems, rather than simply telling them the solution. Finally, parents of achievement-oriented children get emotionally involved in their child's performance and react to it rather than expressing indifference (Rosen and D'Andrade, 1975). These research findings are consistent with the informal observations of many teachers, who note that children who do well in school usually have parents who take an active interest in their children's school performance.

Expectancy of Success

Children vary not only in their desire to excel but in whether or not they *expect* to excel. Children's *expectancy of success* is measured in a variety of ways: They may be asked to predict their grades in school, indicate how sure they are that they can solve a particular problem, or select the hardest task they think they can do from a collection of tasks varying in difficulty. In the last-mentioned situation, the easiest task is described as "one that most children your age can do," whereas the hardest task is described as "one that very few children your age can do." Children are asked to indicate the hardest task on the continuum that they think *they* can do.

Children with high expectancies for success on a task usually persist at it longer and perform better than children with low expectancies (Battle, 1965). One study found that children with high IQs and a high expectancy of success in school did in fact get the highest grades, whereas children with high IQs and low expectancies received lower grades than children with low IQs and high expectancies (Battle, 1966). Expectancy of success is so powerful an influence that on a national study of children's achievement, it predicted the success of white children in school better than any other factor (Coleman, 1966).

A child's expectancy of success is related in part to his or her history of success or failure. A child who has been successful in the past expects success in the future, whereas a child who has failed expects failure to continue. These are general findings, however; in some situations children who usually succeed may fail, and children who usually fail may succeed. The actual effect depends in part on how difficult the child thought the task was in the first place: failure on a task perceived to be very easy has a different effect than failure on a task perceived to be very hard. The effects of failure and success may also be influenced by what the child attributes his or her performance to.

Attribution of Success and Failure

People can explain the causes of their success or failure in many different ways. They can attribute their performance (1) to themselves — "We are smart," "We tried hard," "We didn't study hard enough"; (2) to others — "The teacher doesn't explain things very well," "The teacher likes me"; (3) to the situation — "The room is too noisy to study"; or (4) to luck — "Some people do okay, others don't; that's just how it is." Those who attribute causation to their own efforts and abilities are considered to have an *internal locus of control*, whereas those who attribute causation to things outside of themselves are considered to have an *external locus of control* (Rotter, 1954, 1966).

Assessing Children's Locus of Control. Children's locus of control is usually determined by administering the *Intellectual Achievement Responsibility Questionnaire* (Crandall, Katkovsky, and Preston, 1965). This questionnaire contains items that describe instances of success and items that describe instances of failure. For each instance, the child is asked to select one of two probable causes. For example, consider the following items:

> If a teacher passes you to the next grade, would it probably be

I+   a. because she likes you, or
　　 b. because of the work you did?

> When you read a story and can't remember much of it, is it usually

I−   a. because the story wasn't well written, or
　　 b. because you weren't interested in the story?
　　　　　　[Crandall, Katkovsky, and Preston, 1965, p. 95]

Items marked with an I+ are success items: those marked with an I− are failure items. The child receives a total I+ score, the number of items in which success is attributed to an internal cause, and a total I− score, the number of items in which failure is attributed to an internal cause. A child's overall score is determined by combining these two scores. Thus, children who receive high scores have an internal locus of control, and those who receive low scores have an external locus of control.

The Influence of Locus of Control. Although studies have yielded contradictory results, they generally show that children with an internal locus of control do better academically than children with an external locus of control (Phares, 1976). Obviously, children who believe that they can control what happens to them, who know that their effort is related to their achievement, are likely to try harder than children who feel that their actions do not really influence what happens to them.

Locus of control also affects how children modify their expectancy of success after success or failure. Suppose an internally oriented person spends little time on a school assignment and does it poorly. He or she might think, "Doing poorly was my fault. If I study harder the next time, I'll probably do better." This person's expectancy of success in the future is unlikely to be decreased by the failure.

But suppose the same person had studied hard and still did poorly. He or she might think, "I did my best. I tried as hard as I could. I guess I'm not very good at this subject." In some instances, he or she might expect to continue to do poorly in that subject. If the person felt that skills could be learned to increase ability in that subject area, however, he or she might not develop a reduced expectancy of success.

In short, "internals" adjust expectancy on the basis of past successes and failures, taking into account the stability of the trait they believe is responsible for the failures. If they think they can change the responsible characteristic, their expectancy of success is unlikely to decrease, but if they think they cannot, it will probably decrease (Dweck, 1978). Thus, well-adjusted "internals" are likely to have a low expectancy of success in some areas (Phares, 1976).

Children who attribute success and failure to external factors adjust their behavior after success or failure erratically. The adverse effects of occasional failure on these children can sometimes be decreased through attribution retraining — being told that their failure was due to lack of effort. Interestingly, providing successful experiences, unaccompanied by attribution retraining does not help children persist through future failures (Dweck, 1975). Apparently, it is not success or failure per se that influences achievement, but what one attributes success or failure to.

Sex Differences in Attribution of Success and Failure. The school environment seems to have different effects on how boys and girls see themselves in relation to what happens to them. Boys as a group are likely to attribute success to ability and failure to lack of effort, whereas girls as a group are likely to attribute failure to lack of ability and success to effort. In view of our earlier remarks about the influences of success and failure on expectations of future success, it should come as no surprise that girls are more likely than boys to decrease their efforts on tasks they have previously failed. After failing, boys apparently believe that an increase in effort will lead to success in the future, whereas girls think they lack the ability to succeed (Dweck, 1978).

The crucial question is why boys and girls react to failure differently. A study by Dweck (1978) has provided a possible answer. Dweck found that teachers reacting to boys' failure emphasize lack of neatness, failure to follow directions, and other nonintellectual aspects of boys' work. But when they react to the failures of girls, they tend to emphasize their abilities and intelligence. In fact, Dweck found that teachers attributed boys' failures to motivation problems *eight times* as often as they did girls' failures.

These differences in attribution may explain why girls expect to do less well than boys, despite the fact that girls consistently do better than boys in the early elementary grades. In other words, girls' expectancies are lower than actual performance indicates they should be, whereas boys' expectations are higher than performance indicates they should be. The expectations of both boys and girls are somewhat unrealistic, but in opposite directions (Dweck, 1978).

Differences such as these can have important consequences. When confronted with novel tasks at which initial failure is probable, girls may decide that they cannot do the task well whereas boys may simply decide they should try harder. Dweck suggests that this may account for sex differences in mathematics performance. Unlike verbal tasks, mathematical tasks are quite dissimilar. Algebra is quite different from arithmetic, and calculus is quite different from algebra. Thus, children who take mathematics are presented with novel tasks quite often. Dweck suggests that girls may become convinced they are bad at math and fail to stick with it, whereas boys resolve to try harder and succeed.

Dweck's hypothesis about this matter is still speculative, but it does seem to make sense intuitively. As we shall see in the next section, the causes of sex differences are very difficult to determine.

Sex Differences and Sex-Role Development

Every culture makes certain assumptions about what activities, abilities, social positions, and other attributes are appropriate for women and men. Together, these characteristics comprise a *sex role* (Angrist, 1969; Block, 1973). Developing gender identity — the understanding that you are a boy or a girl — is one thing, but adopting a sex-role identity and accepting that girls and boys are supposed to act differently is quite another.

We will begin this section by describing and trying to explain sex differences and similarities as assessed by various measures of cognitive ability and personality. Then we will discuss sex role development — how children adopt behaviors consistent with their understanding of what girls should be like and what boys should be like.

Sex Differences

> "Boys are mechanically inclined; girls are not."
> "Girls are verbal; boys are not."
> "Boys are aggressive; girls are not."
> "Girls are sociable; boys are not."

Some of these statements are true; others are not. Before we begin our discussion of differences, however, we should explain some of the difficulties involved in determining the ways that boys and girls differ.

First, studies that find sex differences are more likely to be published than studies that do not, because evidence of differences is considered more newsworthy by psychological journals. While differences found in one study may be peculiar to the subjects of that study alone they may not hold for the rest of the population. Thus, differences may receive an undeserved emphasis.

Second, there is the problem of definitions. If sociability is defined as making friends or seeking out the company of others, then we would conclude that boys are more sociable (Baumrind and Black, 1967; Whiting and Edwards, 1973), but if we define sociability as including people in drawings or enjoying the company of a few best friends rather than a large group of peers, then girls would be considered more sociable (Goodenough, 1957; Waldrop, cited in Maccoby and Jacklin, 1974, pp. 609–610). To get an accurate picture of sex differences in the general population, we must consider a great many studies. Maccoby and Jacklin (1974), who conducted the most extensive review of the literature on sex differences to date, examined over 2000 books and articles. Reviews of this magnitude discover fewer differences than less exhaustive reviews.

Boys and girls are alike in many respects.

A third problem is that differences are sometimes related to age. A difference apparent during the preschool years may vanish during middle childhood but reappear in adolescence or adulthood. In the same way differences may emerge for the first time during adolescence or adulthood. When discussing sex differences, one should always note in what age group the differences are found.

If, after taking these precautions, we still find sex differences, we must keep one more precaution in mind when interpreting them. The differences found are often small, which means that boys and girls are quite similar in most respects. Individual boys or girls may not fit the general pattern of sex differences. For example, some girls are much better in math than most boys. The fact that group differences exist does not mean that all members of one sex are better in some areas than all members of the other sex.

Cognitive Abilities. Similarities and differences between the cognitive abilities of boys and girls are summarized in Box 24-1. Generally, girls do better than boys in verbal skills, but the differences are slight during the infancy and toddler years. The major differences emerge during adolescence and adulthood.

BOX 24-1. Differences and Similarities Between Boys and Girls in Cognitive Abilities

---

DIFFERENCES

1. Girls have better verbal abilities between birth and age three and after the age of eleven or twelve. They vocalize more and talk earlier. During middle childhood boys and girls have similar verbal abilities.
2. Boys are better in mathematical tasks but not until adolescence.
3. Boys have better spatial abilities, but again the differences do not emerge decisively until adolescence.
4. Girls have fewer problems than boys with reading.
5. Girls get better grades in school than boys of all ages.

6. Boys do better than girls on analytic tasks involving mathematical or spatial abilities (e.g., embedded figures, rod and frame tasks, and Luchin jars).
7. Girls do better than boys on verbal analytic tasks such as making different words from a set of letters.

SIMILARITIES

1. Boys and girls do equally well in reasoning and logic as measured by tasks resembling those used by Piaget.
2. Boys and girls do equally well on tasks involving nonverbal creativity.
3. Boys and girls have the same group IQs.

SOURCES: Bee, H. Overview: Sex differences. In H. Bee (Ed.), *Social issues in developmental psychology.* New York: Harper and Row, 1978; Brooks-Gunn, J., and Matthews, W. S. *He and she: How children develop their sex-role identity.* Englewood Cliffs, N.J.: Prentice-Hall, 1979; Maccoby, E. E., and Jacklin, C. N. *The psychology of sex differences.* Stanford, Calif.: Stanford University Press, 1974; Tavris, C., and Offrir, C. *The longest war: Sex differences in perspective.* New York: Harcourt Brace Jovanovich, 1977.

In mathematics and spatial abilities it is boys who take the lead, but again, the differences become most evident in adulthood. There are no significant differences between girls and boys in IQ or on tasks requiring reasoning, logic, or verbal creativity. Similarly, there is no pattern of superiority in all types of analytic ability: girls are better at verbal analytic tasks, and boys are better at mathematical or spatial tasks. Once again, most differences become evident after childhood.

There are two areas in which differences are found among children of all ages: girls get better school grades, and boys have more problems in school. For example, boys consistently have more trouble reading than girls.

Similarities and Differences in Personality. We want to dispel some myths. Girls are not more sociable, nurturant, timid, fearful, or anxious than

BOX 24-2. Differences and Similarities Between Boys and Girls in Personality

DIFFERENCES

1. Boys are more aggressive than girls at all ages.
2. Boys cry somewhat more than girls between the ages of one and six, especially when frustrated, as when they are separated from their mothers.
3. Boys show more anger and upset behavior than girls between ages one and six, but it is uncertain whether they differ when they are older.
4. Girls between one and six comply with demands from adults more readily than boys, but boys appear to be more susceptible to peer pressure, even in adulthood.
5. Boys appear to be more peer-oriented than girls at all ages, and spend more time with groups of peers than girls do. Girls tend to spend their time with one or two best friends.
6. Girls *report* more fear and anxiety than boys

do, and teachers *report* that girls are more timid and anxious than boys.

7. Boys between one and twelve may be more active than girls, but the data are inconclusive. When boys are alone, they seem no more active than girls, but when they are with groups of boys, they are apparently more active. During infancy girls and boys have the same level of activity.
8. Boys are judged to be tougher and more dominant than girls between the ages of one and twelve. In adulthood men appear to be more dominant than women, but in some situations the reverse may be true.
9. Girls have lower expectancies for success than do boys, especially on novel intellectual tasks.
10. Girls apparently feel they are less in control of what happens to them than boys, but the differences are not consistently apparent until adolescence and adulthood.

SOURCES: Bee, H. Overview: Sex differences. In H. Bee (Ed.), *Social issues in developmental psychology.* New York: Harper and Row, 1978; Brooks-Gunn, J. and Matthews, W. S. *He and she: How children develop their sex-role identity.* Englewood Cliffs, N.J.: Prentice-Hall, 1979; Maccoby, E. E., and Jacklin, C. N. *The psychology of sex differences.* Stanford, Calif.: Stanford University Press, 1974; Tavris, C., and Offir, C. *The longest war: Sex differences in perspective.* New York: Harcourt Brace Jovanovich, 1977.

boys, nor are they less persistent on all tasks or less achievement oriented. Neither is it true that girls have lower opinions of themselves than boys, although boys and girls (and men and women) apparently think well of themselves for different reasons. Girls do have lower expectancies for success than boys, especially on novel intellectual tasks. They also feel less in control of what happens to them than boys, especially as they get older. Boys are more dominant and are judged to be "tougher" during childhood, but this pattern does not hold in all situations in adulthood. Girls are also less aggressive than boys. In addition, boys in groups are more active than groups of girls during childhood (but not during infancy). When boys are playing alone, however, they are no more active than girls. (See Box 24-2 for a summary of personality similarities and differences between boys and girls.)

BOX 24-2 continued

SIMILARITIES

1. Boys and girls appear to be equally sensitive to people and social stimuli. For example, as infants they attend equally to faces and objects. (Studies yield mixed results on this issue, but consistent differences have not been found.)
2. Boys and girls show the same degree of empathy or altruistic behavior, such as helping someone in distress.
3. The data on the nurturant behavior of boys and girls in the United States reveal no differences. A review of cross-cultural studies does indicate that girls are more nurturant than boys. When communities are analyzed separately, however, there were often no differences; when there were, it was sometimes found that boys were more helpful than girls (in Okinawa, for example). One reason cross-cultural data in general show that girls are more nurturant is that girls are more often assigned responsibility for care of younger siblings than boys. Studies of communities in the United States in which girls are not assigned this task indicate that boys and girls do not differ in nurturant behavior.
4. Girls and boys appear to be equally fearful, timid, and anxious when actual *behavior* is observed. You may recall, however, that girls *report* more feelings of fear and anxiety.
5. Girls and boys tend to be equally motivated to achieve in neutral situations. Boys seem to be aroused to achieve by competition to a greater extent than girls.
6. Girls and boys seem to be equal in self-esteem during childhood, but they seem to feel positively about themselves for different reasons. Girls and women seem to think positively of themselves for their social skills, but boys and men seem to think positively of themselves for more individual traits such as ambition or dominance.
7. Girls and boys are equally persistent in most tasks.

Explaining Sex Differences

We have seen that boys and girls are more similar than different, but there are a few areas in which differences are well documented. Why do males and females differ in these areas? Are the differences inborn, the result of genetic differences, or do they result from socialization patterns? Are both biology and environment influential? Let us consider some of the evidence for each of these explanations.

Biology and Sex Differences. There is considerable evidence that sex differences in spatial ability and aggression are biologically based. The occurrence of spatial ability, for example, fits the pattern characteristic of inherited, sex-linked, recessive traits. You may recall from Chapter 4 that males receive an X and a Y chromosome, whereas girls receive two X chromosomes. Suppose the genes for spatial ability are carried only on the X chromosome, and that the recessive gene(s) leads to good spatial ability, whereas the dominant gene(s) suppresses it. Because girls inherit two X chromosomes, they are twice as likely as boys to inherit the dominant gene and poor spatial ability. But the Y chromosome has no gene for spatial ability, so a recessive gene for good spatial ability will always be expressed. As it turns out, about twice as many men as women have good spatial ability, which supports the inheritance model. (Possible gene patterns for both males and females are shown in Box 24-3.)

Additional evidence that spatial ability is inherited comes from studies that show that the spatial abilities of children are correlated more with the abilities of the parent of the opposite sex than with the parent of the same sex. As you know, boys inherit their X chromosome from their mothers. This means that a boy who inherits the recessive gene for spatial ability must have received it from his mother, who may or may not have good spatial ability; the female genetic patterns ss, sS, or Ss could all contribute a recessive gene to a boy. However, a girl who has good spatial ability must have inherited a recessive gene from her mother and her father, and her father must have inherited good spatial ability himself (i.e., he must carry the recessive gene for spatial ability on his single X chromosome). In other words, a girl who inherits the double recessive gene always has a father who has good spatial ability.

Investigations show that boys' spatial abilities are correlated with their mothers' spatial abilities but not with their fathers'. Girls' spatial abilities are correlated with both parents' abilities, but more strongly with their fathers' than with their mothers'. These correlations provide further support for the inheritance model.

Sex differences in aggression may also be biologically based. The male sex hormone, testosterone, is thought to be the responsible factor. During the sixth week after conception, the testes begin to produce male sex hormones, androgens. These hormones trigger the development of the reproductive structures that differentiate males from females physically. If the hormones are not released, the fetus will not develop male genitalia even though it does have the typical XY male chromosomes.

BOX 24-3. Possible Patterns for Spatial Genes in Males and Females

Females	
Chromosomes	*Consequences*

X^1	X^2	
s	s	good spatial ability
s	S	carrier for good spatial ability but performs poorly
S	s	carrier for good spatial ability but performs poorly
S	S	poor spatial ability

This model predicts that one out of four females will inherit good spatial ability.

Males	
Chromosomes	*Consequences*

X	Y	
s	—	good spatial ability
S	—	poor spatial ability

This model predicts that one out of two males will inherit good spatial ability.

SOURCE: From *The longest war: Sex differences in perspective* by Carol Tavris and Carole Offir, © 1977 by Harcourt Brace Jovanovich, Inc. Reprinted by permission of the publisher.

Androgens may also predispose boys to behave more aggressively during childhood. In addition, they may affect the hypothalamus of the brain such that it responds to the same hormones when they appear again during puberty. This may cause the emergence of masculine sexual behavior (Levine, 1966; Phoenix, Goy, and Resko, 1978).

The evidence of a link between the male sex hormone and aggression comes from several sources:

1. Female monkeys given testosterone before birth engage in more aggressive play than females not treated (Young et al., 1964).
2. In humans, prenatal accidents sometimes result in masculinized females. Although their genitalia can be corrected surgically, their mothers reported that they continued to display masculine behavior. They enjoyed outdoor play, thought of themselves as "tomboys," and did not like to play with dolls (Erhardt and Baker, 1974).
3. The administration of testosterone to female animals in infancy increases their fighting behavior (Edwards, 1969; Joslyn, 1971).

This evidence is not conclusive, however. Although the data are suggestive, they present at least two problems. (1) The strongest evidence comes from animal studies. Humans may not be as subject to hormonal influences as lower animals. (2) In the human studies, the masculinized females' parents knew of their children's condition. Although surgery corrected their masculinized genitalia, their parents may have been more tolerant of aggressive behavior in these girls, thinking it appropriate because of their developmental histories. Thus, the biological difference in these girls may have influenced how they were socialized, which could in turn have made the girls more aggressive.

Even if males and females have different biological predispositions toward aggressiveness, "an individual's aggressive behavior is strengthened, weakened, redirected, or altered in form by his or her unique pattern of experiences" (Maccoby and Jacklin, 1974). In other words, the environment has a powerful influence on sex differences.

Environment and Sex Differences. Parents perceive their newborn boys and girls differently. In one study parents interviewed within a day after the birth of their child rated girls as smaller and softer than boys (Rubin, Provenzano, and Luria, 1974). Fathers described their sons as stronger and hardier and their daughters as more delicate. Differences such as these in initial perceptions of the two sexes influence how the babies are treated to some extent. The differences are summarized by Bee:

> Boys are handled more roughly than girls; parents engage in more roughhousing and physical play with boys than girls. Girls are perceived by parents as being more fragile and parents seem to worry more about physical injury to girls. A second consistent difference is that boys are physically punished more than are girls, and this appears to be true from infancy through adolescence. Finally, there is some evidence that parents press for behavior that is consistent with sex-role stereotypes. Particularly in the case of boys, parents of preschoolers or older children seem to be very distressed at the possibility that their son may choose "feminine" toys or activities. Fathers are especially likely to feel strongly about the importance of appropriate sex-role behavior from their sons. Daughters feel some of this pressure, but apparently to a lesser extent. So parents *say* that appropriate sex-role behaviors are important to them, and one can only presume that this sense of importance is in some way(s) reflected in the parents' behavior toward the children. [1978, p. 32]

Despite Bee's findings, Maccoby and Jacklin (1974) concluded after reviewing many studies that parents treat boys and girls the same in most respects. For example, a number of studies indicated that parents do not reward or punish boys and girls differently for aggressive behavior. Parents do not treat boys' aggression more permissively than girls', even though we might expect them to if we thought boys' aggression was influenced by socialization.

Some parents tolerate "tomboy" behavior by girls but consider doll play by boys to be feminine and inappropriate.

You may recall, however, that modeling has an important influence on socialization. Although parents may not be permissive with boys' aggression, they seem to model more aggression with boys than with girls. Their play is rougher with boys, and they are more likely to punish boys physically.

Determining the basis for sex differences is clearly a knotty problem. At present, we simply do not understand precisely how biological and environmental influences interact to affect sex differences, and it is unlikely that we will for some time to come.

Sex-Role Development

We know that boys and girls develop sex-related preferences for toys, clothing, occupations, and family roles. But how do these differences come about? As usual, different schools of thought have offered different theories. Sex-role development has been explained in terms of (1) observational learning, (2) reinforcement, and (3) cognition. You will recognize these explanations as the socialization processes discussed in Chapter 19.

Proponents of observational learning and identification claim that children learn to be like their same-sexed parent by watching him or her. The motivation for doing what the same-sex parent does is different in identification and social learning imitation (observational learning). In the identification view the motivation comes from the Oedipal conflict, whereas in the social learning view motivation comes from rewards and punishments; that is, after imitating same-sex models, children are rewarded and thus continue to exhibit the behavior. After imitating opposite sex models, they are not reinforced, which leads to extinction.

These two theories, however, do not adequately explain sex-role development. The identification theory, which is Freudian in orientation, would have us believe that sex-role identity in boys and girls begins with their realization that boys and girls (and men and women) have different genitalia. Actually, children first distinguish boys and girls by such characteristics as dress and hair style, not genitalia (Brooks-Gunn and Lewis, 1979; Katcher, 1955). Differences in genitalia are not consistently associated with gender identity until age six or seven (Kohlberg and Ullian, 1974).

There are also problems with the social learning theory of imitation, which assumes that children learn to imitate same-sex models as a result of reinforcement for previous imitation. The evidence suggests that children do not pay attention to same-sex models selectively until *after* they understand gender constancy — that is, until they realize that they would continue to be boys or girls despite changes in dress or hair style. Children develop gender constancy between four and five years of age (Slaby and Frey, 1978). In short, children's *concepts* about gender seem to be important in determining the extent to which they imitate same-sex models. This cognitive view of sex-role identity has been advocated most strongly by Kohlberg and Ullian (1974). It indicates that until children have established their *gender identity* (what sex they are), *gender stability* (that their sex will not change as they grow up), and *gender constancy* (that it will not change with changes in dress, hair style, or activity), they will not selectively imitate same-sex models. This seems to be the case (Slaby and Frey (1978). Although imitation and direct reinforcement no doubt directly influence the behavior of young children, it is apparently only after children develop concepts of gender stability that they systematically try to keep their behavior in line with their conceptions of masculinity and femininity. Parental behavior may play only a small part in shaping such behavior, despite the assertions of the identification and social learning theories of imitation (Maccoby and Jacklin, 1974). If this view is correct, then the school-age years and the period following them may be the most important periods of sex-role development.

Sex-Role Stereotyping

Many surveys have shown that children's books are sexually stereotyped; boys and girls are portrayed doing different things (Lee and Gropper, 1974; Saario, Jacklin, and Tittle, 1973; Women on Words and Images, 1972). Furthermore, boys and girls and men and women have been represented unequally, as the following ratios from Women on Words and Images (1972) indicate:

Boy-centered to girl-centered stories	5:1
Adult male to adult female main characters	3:1
Male biographies to female biographies	6:1
Male animal stories to female animal stories	2:1
Male folk or fantasy stories to female folk or fantasy stories	4:1

In addition, as Tavris and Offir point out, the Women on Words and Images study

> found that boys and men in children's readers monopolize the traits that Americans regard highly: ingenuity, bravery, perseverance, achievement, sportsmanship. Boys make things. They rely on their wits to solve problems. They are curious, clever, and adventurous. . . . Girls and women are incompetent and fearful. They ask other people to solve their problems for them. . . . They spend most of their time baking or sewing, and they are constantly concerned about how they look. . . . In story after story, girls are the onlookers, the cheerleaders, speaking such lines as "Oh, Raymond, boys are much braver than girls," and even accepting humiliation and ridicule. [Tavris and Offir, 1977, p. 177]

One of the most obvious differences between portrayal of males and portrayal of females in books is in the area of occupations. In the 136 children's readers surveyed in the study by Women on Words and Images (1972), 147 occupations were filled by males, whereas only 26 were filled by females. (These are listed in Table 24-2.) In only three instances were mothers portrayed as working outside the home.

The representation of the sexes on television traditionally has been no better. Boys fill at least twice as many roles as girls (Stein and Friedrich, 1975; Sternglanz and Serbin, 1974). All the sex-typed characteristics found in print media occur on television as well: Girls and women are portrayed as more deferential and more interested in staying home, and as less competent, aggressive, and effective (except when using magic!). In short, as Tavris and Offir state, "Television stories are children's text books in motion" (1977, p. 180).

Of course the situation in real life is very different from that presented in books and on television. Women do cook, clean, and care for children more often than men, but many men do cook, go to the supermarket, give the children baths, and read bedtime stories. What is more, women cut the grass, solve problems cleverly, become physicians, chemists, and truck drivers, and sometimes make men and boys cry. Many men and women do things once thought appropriate only for the opposite sex. Those who do tend to be less anxious and higher in

Table 24-2. Occupations of adult males and females in grammar-school readers

Male Occupations

airplane builder	electrician	milkman	sheepherder
animal trainer	engineer	miller	sheriff
architect	expert on art	miner	ship builder
artist	explorer	mineralogist	shoemaker
astronaut	fairgroundsman	monk	silversmith
astronomer	farmer	mover	ski teacher
athlete	figure skater	museum manager	soldier
author	film maker	naturalist	space station worker
babysitter	fireman	newspaper owner	stagecoach driver
baker	fisherman	news reporter	statesman
balloonist	foreman	organ grinder	steamshovel operator
band conductor	forest ranger	outlaw	stonecutter
banker	gardener	painter	storeowner
barber	gas station attendant	parent	submarine operator
baseball player	glassblower	peddlar	tailor
blacksmith	guard	pet store owner	taxidermist
botanist	handyman	photographer	teacher
building contractor	humorist	pilot	telephoneman
businessman	hunter	pirate	telephone lineman
bus driver	ice cream man	plumber	TV actor
carpenter	inn keeper	policeman	TV man
circus keeper	inventor	pony herder	TV newsman
clerk	janitor	popcorn vender	TV writer
clockmaker	judge	priest	ticket seller
clown	juggler	principal	train conductor
coach	king	professor	train engineer
computer operator	knight	prospector	trapper
construction worker	landlord	radio reporter	trashman
cook	lifeguard	railroad inspector	trolley driver
cowboy	lighthouse keeper	restaurant owner	truck driver
craftsman	lumberman	roadmaster	veterinarian
decorator	magician	rocket firer	watchman
detective	mailman	sailor	whaler
deliveryman	mathematician	salesman	woodcutter
dentist	mayor	scientist	World War II hero
doctor	m.c. in nightclub	scoutmaster	zookeeper
doorman	merchant	sea captain	

Female Occupations

acrobatist	cook	librarian	school nurse
author	doctor	painter	secretary
babysitter	dressmaker	parent	shopkeeper
baker	fat lady (in circus)	queen	teacher
cafeteria worker	governess	recreational director	telephone operator
cashier	housekeeper	school crossing guard	witch
cleaning woman	ice skater		

SOURCE: Women on Words and Images, *Dick and Jane as victims: Sex stereotyping in children's readers.* Princeton, N.J.: Central New Jersey NOW, 1972, pp. 73–74. Reprinted by permission.

self-esteem, social acceptance, and intellectual ability than those who assess behavior in terms of sexual stereotypes (Bem, 1975).

Story and script writers often still portray women and men in terms of sexual stereotypes. We suggest that they discard the old version of the nursery rhyme that begins "What are little boys made of?" and the attitudes that go along with it, and substitute one that goes like this:

> What are little boys made of, made of?
>   What are little boys made of?
>   Love and care
>   And skin and hair
>   That's what little boys are made of.
>
> What are little girls made of, made of?
>   What are little girls made of?
>   Care and love
>   And (see above)
>   That's what little girls are made of.
>   [Free to Be Foundation, 1974]

Recent Developments. Several publishers of basal readers have attempted to correct the underrepresentation of female characters in stories. In a recent study (Rupley, Garcia, and Longnion, 1981), researchers found that books published in 1977 and 1978 show a significant reduction in the number of stories with male characters and an increase in the number of those containing female characters. For example, of basal readers published between 1974 and 1976, the researchers found that 61 percent had male characters, 16 percent had female characters, and 23 percent had "other" characters (animals, etc.). By 1978, about 26 percent of the stories in basal readers had male characters, about 24 percent had female characters, and about 50 percent had other characters. However, for supplementary reading materials, which are materials teachers use with children who have reading difficulties, male characters still dominated even in 1978 materials (29 percent male characters versus 13 percent female characters). One reason for the imbalance in these materials is probably that more boys than girls experience reading difficulties. Publishers, in attempting to provide materials of interest to boys, may include more male characters in these books.

Of course, a mere counting of male versus female characters does not tell the whole story of whether sex-role stereotyping has vanished from basal readers. How the sexes are portrayed, that is, the roles they fill and the attitudes they express, is critically important, too, but comprehensive studies to determine improvement in these areas have not been numerous. It is to be hoped that improvement in these areas in the 1980s will equal the improvement in balancing male and female characters that took place in the late 1970s.

Summary

Social Cognition

- Social cognition refers to children's ability to think about social matters.
- At first, children describe others in terms of themselves.
- Children's early concepts of friendship are based on physical interaction with others. These early concepts change as children understand the thoughts of and can take the roles of others. The ability to take the role of another person requires cognitive skills that develop during the school-age years.

Moral Development

- Children at first judge the seriousness of a mishap or other action by the damage done, not by the intentions of the actor. As with other social concepts, they make objective judgments about moral dilemmas in part because they are unable to assume other peoples' roles.
- During middle childhood, as role taking becomes possible, children begin to be able to play games according to rules.
- Kohlberg's stages of moral development, unlike those of Piaget, can be used to differentiate levels of moral reasoning among adults.

Achievement

- Achievement is influenced by personality factors as well as ability. Achievement motivation seems to be supported best by parents who emphasize achievement and independence training. A child's expectancy of success also influences his or her achievement motivation.
- Children's achievement behavior is influenced by what factors they attribute their successes and failures to. Girls tend to attribute their failures to lack of ability, whereas boys tend to attribute their failures to lack of effort.

Sex Differences and Sex-Role Development

- Gender identity refers to knowing you are a girl or a boy, whereas sex-role identity refers to knowing what boys and girls are expected to do.
- Extensive reviews of research indicate that sex differences are not very significant. One should also keep in mind that group differences cannot be used reliably to predict individual characteristics.
- Some sex differences occur in mathematical and spatial abilities. Also, boys are more aggressive than girls. Another difference is that girls have lower expectations of success than boys, especially on novel tasks.
- Sex differences in spatial ability seem to be related to genetic factors.

- Some sex differences are environmentally influenced. There is some evidence, for example, that parents think of their infant boys and girls differently and also treat them differently. Evidence for imitation of sex roles is less clear. According to Kohlberg's cognitive theory of sex-role development, children do not selectively imitate same-sex models until after they have developed the concept of gender consistency.

New Terms

social cognition
recursive thinking or metathinking
achievement behavior
achievement motivation (need for
    achievement)
projective techniques
attainment values
achievement training

independence training
expectancy of success
locus of control
sex role
gender identity
gender stability
gender constancy

Selected Readings

Lamb, M. E. (Ed.). **Social and personality development.** *New York: Holt, Rinehart and Winston, 1978.* Contains chapters on topics such as children's peer relations, achievement, the development of gender role and gender identity, and moral development. Not all of the chapters relate to the school-age child, but many do. Includes good reviews of current research in each area.

Rubin, Z. **Children's friendships.** *Cambridge, Mass.: Harvard University Press, 1980.* A very readable little book about friendships during childhood.

Sprung, B. S. (Ed.). **Perspectives on nonsexist early childhood education.** *New York: Teachers College Press, Teachers College, Columbia University, 1978.* A collection of articles on sexism in schools. Parts of the book relate to preschoolers, but others pertain to the school-age child.

Chapter 25

Knowledge and Action

In Chapters 21 through 24 we examined various aspects of development in middle childhood. In this chapter we will discuss ways of applying our knowledge of this development, specifically in the following areas: teaching the elementary school curriculum; intelligence tests and issues in their use; anxieties, fears, and phobias, and how these can be overcome; and play and play materials enjoyed by school-age children.

Cognitive Skills and School Tasks

The teacher is conducting a group meeting in her kindergarten class. She has brought in various red objects: a toy car, a scarf, a pencil, a magic marker, a paper bag, and a glove. She asks how all the objects are alike. "You keep them all in your room," one child says. "No," the teacher answers. "That's not it." (This could be the right answer but it is not what the teacher had in mind.) Another child says, "They're all red."

"That's right," the teacher says. "What are some other red things?"

One child says an apple, another says a cherry lifesaver. A third child says a fire engine. Then Tommy breaks in: "I got one for my birthday. It has a real siren, too, and you can wear the siren hat. But it doesn't work if the batteries are dead. My car has batteries that work."

"Wait a minute!" the teacher says sternly, "We are *not* talking about fire engines and sirens right now, but about things that are red. You need to listen and put your thinking cap on." Then she says, "Now, where were we? Oh, yes, who can think of something else that is *red?*"

Was Tommy really being inattentive? We think not. When he heard the child say "red fire engine," he began thinking, but not about red objects; he focused on fire engines instead. Thoughts of the red fire engine led to thoughts about sirens, then to batteries, and then to the batteries in his car. And all of this led to big trouble for Tommy, because apparently his teacher did not understand that Tommy changed the attribute he was focusing on as different objects were mentioned. He could not keep the central topic in his mind. He associated the objects mentioned, but not in terms of a single characteristic they had in common.

Tommy's behavior is typical of young children, especially those under five. Children learn to focus on a subject during a discussion when they enter the concrete operational period. During the same period they begin to acquire many other abilities that they can apply to school tasks.

Young children have difficulty sticking to a topic during a discussion, perhaps because their classification abilities are limited.

Classification

In addition to enabling children to participate in group discussions, the acquisition of classification skills (at age seven or eight) helps children understand math problems such as the following:

$$4 + 5 = \square$$
$$9 - 5 = \square$$

To recognize the relationship between addition and subtraction, the child must understand part-whole relationships. In this case, nine is the superordinate class and four and five are two subclasses. The child must understand how both parts relate to the whole in order to solve this problem. Mathematically addition and subtraction are inverse operations, and teachers often teach them together for the sake of efficiency. But children incapable of reversing actions in their minds and classifying in hierarchies may find learning to add and subtract at the same time extremely difficult. Until children can conserve, it is probably useless.

Consider some other types of hierarchical relationships: letters, words, and sentences; cities, counties, states, countries, and continents; ducks, birds, and animals. Being able to classify hierarchically allows children to organize information and thus understand and retain it more easily.

Conservation

To understand addition, children must be able to conserve number; that is, they must know that the number of objects in a group is not influenced by the way the group is arranged. For example, the addition facts for the number six are $6 + 0, 5 + 1, 4 + 2, 3 + 3, 2 + 4, 1 + 5, 0 + 6$. Adults realize that $6 + 0$ is the same as $0 + 6$, and that $2 + 4$ is the same as $4 + 2$, so we can eliminate duplicates of this kind. This leaves us with the unique combinations of two numbers which, when combined, equal the number six.

It is much more complicated for a nonconserver. He or she does not realize that different arrangements of objects contain the same number. Such children may not see that addition facts are systematically related to each other. (For example, $5 + 1$ differs from $4 + 2$ in the same way that $4 + 2$ differs from $3 + 3$: one number increases by one, while the other number decreases by one). Similarly, the nonconserver may not realize that $5 + 1$ and $1 + 5$ are the same, because they are arranged differently.

Although we often think that learning addition facts is merely a matter of memorizing them, our ability to remember is influenced by how well we can understand and organize material before we store it (Liben, 1977; Moely, 1977; Piaget and Inhelder, 1973). If we do not see a pattern or relationship in the material, we cannot organize it; the information is not transferred to our long-term memories, and we forget what we thought we learned only seconds earlier.

Piaget and a colleague, Barbel Inhelder (1969), conducted an experiment that demonstrated how cognitive development and memory are related in children.

Groups of three- to eight-year-olds were shown a seriated pattern of ten sticks varying in length from nine to fifteen centimeters. The children were asked to look at the pattern carefully, because they would be asked to remember it. The children were asked to draw the pattern one week later and six months later. They were also given similar sticks to try to recreate the pattern.

Piaget and Inhelder found a relationship between children's memory of the display and their ability to seriate. Even though children were not shown the pattern again during the six-month period, in the interim those whose ability to seriate had improved drew more accurate series. In other words, children who were able to understand seriation seemed to "remember" better. Inhelder concluded that we code memories in accordance with our cognitive understanding.

Space

Picture yourself in an unfamiliar city trying to find your way to a friend's house. You take the map out of the glove compartment of your car, open it up, and then look out the car window to determine which direction you are facing. "That's north," you say to yourself, noticing that the morning sun is to your right, in the east. Then you orient the map so that it corresponds to the directions in reality. You reread the directions your friend wrote for you, tracing your route on the map with your pencil. You find the spot where your friend's house should be and mark it with an X.

Whether you knew it or not, your actions in this situation would have involved an understanding of concepts of Euclidean space: you established coordinates, north-south and east-west, and located yourself in relation to them. Children in the early elementary grades do not understand space well enough to solve such problems. Not until the middle elementary grades do abstract maps of unfamiliar places begin to make sense to children.

Time

Children learn to tell time during the elementary grades. This involves learning to read a clock face and learning the mathematics (counting, fractions) necessary to understand statements of time such as "half-past nine" and "quarter of three." But even after children can understand such things, they may not understand time the way adults do. For example, if you were to ask a six- or seven-year-old at one o'clock if a clock with a large face and a clock with a small face will read two o'clock at the same time, the child is likely to indicate that the little clock will reach two o'clock first. Children who have not acquired a concept of speed cannot understand how different-sized clocks can be synchronized. Children cannot solve problems involving the concept of speed until sixth or seventh grade.

Some of the problems in our schools can undoubtedly be attributed to teachers who do not know how children learn. Whether it be in mathematics, science, or reading, teachers should understand how children think about things.

Intelligence Tests and Issues Associated with Their Use in Schools

Individual Intelligence Tests for Children

Three intelligence tests are commonly used to test children individually. These are the *Stanford-Binet Intelligence Scale*, the *Wechsler Intelligence Scale for Children-Revised* (WISC-R), and the *Wechsler Preschool-Primary Scale of Intelligence* (WPPSI). These tests take between thirty minutes and one hour to administer.

Perhaps the best known of these tests is the *Stanford-Binet (Intelligence Scale)*. Developed at Stanford University, it is a modification of the original Binet and Simon test and is designed for use with preschool and school-age children. The test contains subtests for each age level. These subtests consist of items related to abilities such as logical reasoning, perceptual-motor coordination, and language. For example, a perceptual-motor test item requires the child to place a square, a triangle, and a circle in the correct places on a three-hole form board; a verbal ability test item requires the child to name objects, pictures, or parts of the body.

The WISC-R (Wechsler, 1974) is used with children six to sixteen years old.

A child taking the WISC-R

BOX 25-1. Paraphrased Wechsler-like Questions

GENERAL INFORMATION

1. How many wings does a bird have?
2. How many nickels make a dime?
3. What is steam made of?
4. What is pepper?

GENERAL COMPREHENSION

1. What should you do if you see a man forget his hat when he leaves his seat in a restaurant?
2. Why do some people save sales receipts?
3. Why is copper often used in electrical wires?

ARITHMETIC

1. Sue had two pieces of candy and Joe gave her four more. How many pieces of candy did Sue have altogether?
2. Three children divided eighteen pennies equally among themselves. How many pennies did each child receive?
3. If two pencils cost 15¢, what will be the cost of a dozen pencils?

SIMILARITIES

1. In what way are a lion and a tiger alike?
2. In what way are a saw and a hammer alike?
3. In what way are an hour and a week alike?
4. In what way are a circle and a triangle alike?

VOCABULARY

This test consists simply of asking, "What is a _____?" or "What does _____ mean?" The words cover a wide range of difficulty or familiarity.

PERFORMANCE TESTS

In addition to verbal tasks of the kinds illustrated above, there are a number of performance tasks involving the use of blocks, cut-out figures, paper and pencil puzzles, etc.

SOURCE: Paraphrased questions printed by permission of The Psychological Corporation, 757 Third Avenue, New York, N.Y.

The test has verbal and performance sections, each of which is divided into six subtests. The subtests have different sections for children of different ages. A child receives three scores on this test, a verbal IQ, a performance IQ, and a full-scale IQ, which is based on the other two scores.

The six Verbal Scale subtests test information, comprehension, arithmetic, vocabulary, digit span, and the ability to distinguish similarities. The six Performance Scale subtests test picture completion, picture arrangement, block design, object assembly, coding, and the ability to work mazes. Simulations of items are shown in Box 25-1.

The WPPSI (Wechsler, 1967) is similar to the WISC-R, but it is used with children four to seven years old. Like the WISC-R, it contains verbal and performance scales consisting of six subtests each.

Group Intelligence Tests

Individual tests are expensive because of the time and expertise required to administer them. Group tests are less expensive because many children can be tested together and the tester needs no special training.

One commonly used group intelligence test is the *Otis-Lennon Mental*

Ability Test (Otis and Lennon, 1967). It measures verbal, numerical, and reasoning abilities. Children are given test booklets and answer cards or sheets. When the test is administered to younger children, each item is explained orally. Older children are given general directions orally and then go through the items on their own.

Issues in the Use of Intelligence Tests

As we discussed in Chapter 22, differences in measured intelligence can result from differences in culture. Tests standardized on one cultural group can be expected to yield biased results when used to assess the intelligence of other groups. Because of this problem, many attempts have been made to design non-discriminatory tests. One such test is the *Raven Progressive Matrices Test.* Another is Cattell's test, which assesses reasoning with abstract shapes (Cattell, 1971). Critics contend, however, that there is no such thing as a culture-fair or culture-free test, and argue that performance on any test is influenced by environmental experiences that inevitably vary from group to group (Anastasi, 1976). In fact, some psychologists believe that IQ tests can be used to predict performance only in white-dominated schools; they assume that tests do not indicate children's total mental capacity or functioning. Because this issue has not been settled, some states have enacted laws that prevent schools from giving intelligence tests to children for the purpose of grouping them for instruction. Both the Education for All Handicapped Children Act and other laws require that tests be administered in a child's native language. In general, teachers need to be aware of culture and language as possible sources of bias in intelligence tests and interpret scores accordingly.

Living with the School-Age Child

Anxieties, Fears, and Phobias

> The next morning when it was time for Anne to leave for school, her parents became anxious. Her father was annoyed by what he termed "nonsense"; there was nothing to fear. Anne admitted as much. He had to go to work and he became angry as Anne started to cry and he insisted that she put on her wraps and come along with him to school. When the mother acted as though she felt he was doing the wrong thing, he became more annoyed; the mother's behavior increased his doubts about what he was doing. Realizing that this was no time to change his mind, however, since that would only confuse Anne more, he got into the car with her. Anne cried all the way to school, saying she knew she could not make it. Her father assured her that she would get along well as soon as she was at her desk with all her friends around her. Anne and her father walked up the school steps, but as they approached the entrance, Anne grew pale and vomited. [Lippman, 1956, p. 86]

Anne was suffering from school phobia, a fear so intense that it made her sick. Ordinary fears are quite common among young children. They are a natural reaction. For example, a child who is afraid of snakes may say so when asked. He might flee to the house when he sees a snake in the yard and avoid the reptile house at the zoo. Phobias, on the other hand, are much more severe. They can be quite overwhelming, and a person who suffers from a phobia may have trouble putting it out of his or her mind. In addition, a phobia may focus on a situation that most people regard as perfectly harmless. Most children get through school without developing a real phobia.

Children's Fears. A summary of children's fears is presented in Table 25-1. You will notice that children's fears vary with age. Children under age six tend to be afraid of "spooks" and the dark, but they are not afraid of natural hazards such as storms, deep water, volcanoes, or avalanches. They are also less afraid than older children of people and such things as cars, airplanes, guns, knives, explosions, and tractors. Children's fears vary with age, in part because their understanding matures. Children who do not understand where dreams come from or know the difference between reality and fantasy are relatively likely to fear spooks, "boogeymen," or the dark. At the same time, young children who do not understand death may not be afraid of situations that could kill them.

Fears may also change with age because children have new experiences. Older children often express fears of tests, for example, but younger children have never taken a test. Similarly, older children are more likely to fear people than younger children. This is probably because they have been exposed to more people; younger children have usually encountered only family friends and relatives. Children old enough to leave the house on their own may also have been warned to avoid people: "Don't take candy from strangers." "Don't play with those big kids who hang around on the street corner." It is necessary, of course, to teach children to be appropriately fearful of situations that could lead to harm. Fears are safeguards as long as there is a rational reason to be fearful of a situation.

Table 25-1. Children's fears

Age	Animals	People	Dark	Spooks	Natural hazards	Machinery	Miscellaneous
5–6	80%	20%	20%	33%	0%	20%	0%
7–8	73	17	3	17	34	34	14
9–10	61	42	3	10	35	35	16
11–12	68	42	0	0	26	42	26
13–14	23	39	0	0	31	46	46

SOURCE: Maurer, Adah. What children fear. *The Journal of Genetic Psychology,* 106(1965): 265–277. Reprinted by permission of The Journal Press, Provincetown, Mass.

FOCUS: Children's Understanding of Death

"Are we burying him so he'll die?" asked four-year-old Robbie. The gerbil, dead since early morning, was being buried in the school yard. Robbie's question revealed some uncertainty about the gerbil's state. What does "dead" mean to a four- or five-year-old? To an eight- or ten-year-old?

Until age six or seven, children do not understand that death is final and irreversible. One child, asked how dead things could be brought back to life, said, "No one ever taught me about that, but maybe you could give them some medicine and take them to the hospital to get better" (Koocher, 1974, p. 408). Another child offered these suggestions: "Help them, give them hot food, and keep them healthy so it won't happen again" (Koocher, 1974, p. 408). Children believe that death resembles sleep; they do not think that reing dead one moment precludes being alive the next. According to Kestenbaum, children think that "even while dead, you still 'live,' although perhaps in a more restricted style" (1967, p. 98).

Children over seven, on the other hand, understand that death is permanent. One child said, "If it was a tree you could water it. If it's a person you could rush them to the emergency room, but it would do no good if they were really dead already" (Koocher, 1974, p. 408).

Children's ideas about the *causes* of death also change with age. Younger children's explanations of death are concrete and egocentric. When asked, "What makes things die?" Carol (age seven) said,

> They eat poison and stuff: pills. You'd better wait til your mom gives them to you. [Anything else?] Drinking poison water and stuff like going swimming alone." Naomi (age six-and-a-half) said: "When they eat bad things, like if you went with a stranger and they gave you a candy bar with poison on it. [Anything else?] Yes, you can die if you swallow a dirty bug." [Koocher, 1974, p. 407]

As children get older, their explanations of causes focus more on dangerous weapons, hazards, cars, and specific diseases such as cancer and heart attacks.

Children entering adolescence begin to describe the specific physical processes that result in death: "They get old . . . and their body gets all worn out, and their organs don't work as well as they used to." "When the heart stops, blood stops circulating, you stop breathing and that's it" (Koocher, 1974, p. 407).

Because younger children have trouble comprehending the causes of death, they may misunderstand adult explanations of the deaths of relatives. Parents who say "Grandma died. It was like going to sleep," may find that their child is afraid to go to bed because he thinks he might die, too. Similarly, a child whose friend died at the hospital may be afraid to go to the hospital for fear of dying there. Young children may also believe that they caused another's death, especially if they did something they were specifically forbidden to do.

Because children under age six or seven are easily confused about death, it is best to talk openly with them about any death that occurs. Adults who listen to their questions and comments can detect any gross misunderstandings and correct them.

"What does 'dead' mean?"

In studies of fears conducted by Croake (1969; 1973), third and sixth graders expressed political fears of war or communists more often than any other type, although these fears were not as intense as fears about animals. The researcher suggested that the political fears emerged because of children's increasing exposure to television.

Children learn to be fearful in three different ways: (1) through direct instruction — "If you go swimming alone you might drown"; (2) by actual experience — being bitten by a dog or falling into water; (3) by seeing fear modeled by others — seeing someone scream at the sight of a mouse. The effects of these processes are influenced by the child's level of understanding.

In a recent study (Schwartz, 1979), preschool children watched their mothers react when a toy gorilla walked out of a box. The mothers were randomly assigned to three treatment groups. One group acted frightened, another acted indifferent, and the third group reacted positively. The researcher found that, although the behavior modeled was significantly correlated with children's reactions, their reactions were predicted better by their knowledge of gorillas —

FOCUS: Systematic and In Vivo Desensitization of a School Phobia

A SCHOOL-PHOBIC CHILD

Jimmy had been treated for six months in a traditional psychotherapeutic situation. Treatment was stopped when school was closed for the summer. After summer Jimmy was still unable to attend school. A desensitization procedure was then started. Having obtained the cooperation of the school, the therapist worked with Jimmy for twenty to forty minutes every day. The therapist used the following steps:

1. Sitting in the car in front of the school.
2. Getting out of the car and approaching the curb.
3. Going to the sidewalk.
4. Going to the bottom of the steps of the school.
5. Going to the top of the steps.
6. Going to the door.
7. Entering the school.
8. Approaching the classroom.
9. Entering the classroom.
10. Being present in the classroom with the teacher.
11. Being present in the classroom with the teacher and one or two classmates.
12. Being present in the classroom with a full class.

These steps were carried out over a period of twenty consecutive days. At the end of that time, Jimmy resumed his normal school routine with no return of the symptom during a two-year follow-up period. The authors [Garvey and Hegrenes] explain that:

> since Jimmy and the therapist had a good relationship, the presence of the therapist may be considered as a relatively strong stimulus evoking a positive affective response in the patient. As a consequence, because there was reduced anxiety in the presence of the fear stimulus, instead of an avoidance response, Jimmy was able to make an approach response which was reinforced by the therapist with strong praise.

It was felt that if the child had been forced into the classroom, the therapist might have acquired a negative stimulus value. Garvey and Hegrenes think that their method requires less time but that their results are just as effective as those of the methods of traditional psychoanalysis.

SOURCE: "A School-Phobic Child" (pp. 164–165) in *Behavior Disorders in Children*, Second Edition by Harvey F. Clarizio and George F. McCoy (Thomas Y. Crowell Co.) Copyright © 1970, 1976 by Harper & Row, Publishers, Inc. Reprinted by permission of the publisher.

whether they had negative expectations of gorillas. The influence of a model's fearful reaction to a situation apparently depends on what the observer already knows about the situation.

Helping Children Overcome Fears. A person who is afraid of something can often use a simple procedure to overcome his or her fear (Ulman and Krasner, 1969). A technique known as *systematic desensitization* involves pairing something pleasant such as pleasant thoughts or a pleasant relationship with thoughts about what is feared. This technique is based on the assumption that pleasant experiences cause one to relax and thus relieve the anxiety usually associated with the fear.

Another method, known as *in vivo desensitization,* involves approaching the fearful situation gradually. In this procedure the person has a chance to conquer the fear little by little.

A third technique, overcoming fear by watching others, is called *imitation, modeling,* or *vicarious reinforcement.* This procedure was illustrated in an experiment by Bandura, Grusec, and Menlove (1967). Children unafraid of dogs played with dogs in the presence of children who were afraid of dogs. After observing their "fearless peers," the children who were initially frightened of dogs were much less fearful.

Play and Playthings

Characteristics of Play. Children of school age enjoy games, jokes, riddles, and being silly. They like sports, reading, television, movies, and collecting stamps, coins, insects, or rocks. They are also fond of testing their skills — riding their bikes without holding the handlebars, for example. When they have the chance, they prefer playing with others to playing alone. Unlike preschool children, who need to be closely watched by adults and need adult help with disputes, school-age children often play without close supervision. They may go into a child's bedroom and close the door to keep others out. If a dispute arises, they often settle it themselves. When they cannot, a visiting friend may simply say, "I'm going home" and get on his or her bike and leave.

One of the school-age child's most puzzling behaviors is the fits of silliness, which seem to erupt for no apparent reason. *Everything* seems funny, and the children roll on the floor laughing uncontrollably or they giggle and giggle. When adults ask, "What's so funny?" they are met with more laughter.

School-age children also enjoy pretending, although we usually think of this type of play as characteristic of the preschool child. Young school-age children play with dolls, play school, talk to stuffed animals, and engage in other kinds of fantasy play. For example, one day one of the authors observed a group of neighborhood children, ranging in age from five to eight, walking on the top of a log fence that enclosed a front yard. A misstep that sent a player to the ground was followed by screams and much frantic behavior. The fallen player would flail about and moan for a time, and then play dead. It seems that the ground below was an "alligator pit," and of course, anyone who fell into it was doomed.

Playthings. The skills that emerge during the school years enable children to enjoy many new playthings. Some playthings involve using new skills. These include

- baseball bat, ball, glove
- basketball
- roller skates, and ice skates
- bicycle
- jump rope
- skis
- skateboard
- jacks
- marbles
- hobby and craft kits

There are also many games for school-age children, including

- checkers
- Chinese checkers
- Othello
- Scrabble
- MasterMind
- Battleship
- Stratego

These games all involve strategy, which requires that children assume the role of the other; therefore, they are recommended for children aged eight and older. This is about the age when children acquire the ability to think about what others are thinking. Games for younger children, such as Candyland, Sorry, and Cootie involve simple counting, or matching pictures, shapes, or colors, but do not involve strategy.

Squabbles sometimes arise when a young child wants to play with older children. Young children may be incapable of thinking about others' thoughts, and as a result they may not be able to play the game correctly. Older children find the younger child a bore because his or her strategy is so obvious. They often do not want the younger child to play with them, but the younger child does not understand that he or she is playing incorrectly and wants to play along. Problems of this sort disappear as children grow up, but in the meantime adults may have to help settle many disputes.

School-age children also enjoy a variety of reading materials. Most book stores and libraries have collections of books for the beginning and intermediate reader. There are also magazines written especially for the school-age child. These include:

- *Ranger Rick* — a nature magazine
- *Jack and Jill* — a magazine with stories, puzzles, and poems
- *National Geographic World* — similar to National Geographic, but written for children
- *Crafts 'n Things* — ideas for arts and crafts
- *Cricket* — stories, poems, jokes, and riddles

Adults who care about developing nonsexist and nonracist attitudes in their children may want to supervise their children's book purchases. Guidelines for selecting nonstereotypical children's books have been developed by several organizations, including the Council on Interracial Books for Children (1841 Broadway, New York, New York 10023). Among other things, it is recommended that illustrations be checked for the absence of stereotypical dress such as headdress and loincloth on Native Americans or dresses only on girls and women, and that characters be checked for nonstereotypical assignment of roles.

Industry Versus Inferiority

As we mentioned earlier in Chapter 21, the school-age child's increasing control over fine motor skills leads to interest in various hobbies and crafts such as assembling models and doing stitchery. Many school-age children are very interested in making things, whether from specialized materials, as in the case of many hobbies and crafts, or from bits and pieces of things on hand at home.

According to Erikson, children in middle childhood must face the psychosocial crisis of coming to feel industrious rather than inferior. Industriousness includes coming to view oneself as a worker, a contributor, and as one who can join with others in doing things. The child sees these as characteristics of adult life and enters into learning skills modeled on adult life in order to feel that he or she can in the future contribute as an adult. Failure to learn skills, such as making things with one's hands, can lead to a feeling of inferiority. Of course this does not mean that children must experience only success. In fact, in Erikson's view it is the balance of the two sides of the crisis — the winning out of industry over inferiority — that counts. To have never overcome an initial failure may lead to weaker feelings of industry and worthiness than having experienced a mixture of success and failure and having learned to surmount the latter. Adult reactions to a child's successes and failures are important factors in the child's ability to deal with both. Praise and recognition for success and encouragement and guidance in the face of failure are needed.

Summary

Cognitive Skills and School Tasks

- Children's ability to understand school work such as math, mapping and the measurement of time is determined by their cognitive development. For example, young children may not stay on the topic of conversation selected by a teacher if they cannot classify very well. Overall cognitive development also provides a framework for remembering information.

Living with the School-Age Child

- A phobia is an intense fear of a particular object or situation. Older children have different fears than young children. One reason is that children under six rarely understand the causes or finality of death.
- Systematic desensitization, in vivo desensitization, and vicarious reinforcement are three techniques used to help children overcome their fears.
- Many games for children eight years old and over are strategy games that require the ability to take the role of the other. Younger and older children often squabble when playing strategy games because the younger children cannot play them with the sophistication that would present a suitable challenge for the older child.
- Adults concerned about developing nonsexist and nonracist attitudes in children should look carefully at reading materials they select for children.

New Terms

systematic desensitization   **vicarious reinforcement**
in vivo desensitization

Selected Readings

Arnstein, H. S. **What to tell your child: About birth, illness, death, divorce and other family crises.** New York: Condor, 1978. Advises parents and teachers as to how they might approach the discussion of various crises. Very practical and helpful.

Grollman, E. (Ed.). **Explaining death to children.** Boston: Beacon Press, 1967. An informative collection of papers dealing with how children understand and react to death. Presents interesting cross-cultural information about how death is handled and how this affects children's experiences and understandings.

Milberg, A. **Street games.** New York: McGraw-Hill, 1976. A book of instructions for games that are of interest to school-age children. The historical origin of each game is given and provides some interesting reading. A fun book.

Part VII
The Adolescent

Adolescence is the stage of development during which childhood behaviors are adapted to become adult behaviors. It is the period when children grow up.

Although many people assume that adolescence corresponds to the teenage years, the ages at which pubescence begins and full adult status is attained can vary considerably. Pubescence, the onset of the physiological changes that lead to sexual maturity, can begin as early as age eight and a half or as late as twelve for girls and as early as ten and a half or as late as sixteen for boys (Dusek, 1977). Adult status, which is defined socially, is usually conferred when persons live independently from their parents, support themselves economically, or have children of their own. It may be attained as early as age seventeen or as late as twenty-six. Some persons never fully achieve adult status because they never assume the social duties associated with it.

The replies given by adults to the following questions about their transition from adolescence to adulthood give some idea of what is involved:

> *When did you feel that you became an adult, and what accounted for your own transition from adolescence to adulthood?*
>
> It wasn't a physical change. I became an adult when I felt I was aware of what went on around me and began making intelligent decisions of my own.
>
> The girl I had been going steady with broke off with me. This made me evaluate myself and realize that I was very immature.
>
> It was my second year in college. I had experienced a year of work in industry. I received the added responsibilities of owning a car and had suffered an ulcer.
>
> *Was your maturing, or coming to feel like a man, affected at all by your peer group?*
>
> Yes, my peer group looked on me as being more grown up when I left home to go to college.

Yes, my peer group gave me more confidence in myself.

Yes, I was forced to disagree with them and stand alone in my convictions on certain matters. [Rogers, 1972, p. 191]

Adolescence has not always been recognized as a distinct stage of development, nor has it always been as prolonged as it is now. Even today it is not considered a distinct period of development in many non-Western societies. Adolescence as a period of development is largely a social invention characteristic of highly technical societies in which many years of schooling are required and the number of people entering the labor market must be controlled. In less technical societies children make an abrupt transition from childhood to full adult status without a prolonged intervening period.

Even in a technical society such as ours the number of years a person is considered an adolescent can vary considerably. A boy or girl who marries, enters the work force, and has a child soon after high school may achieve adult status, as commonly defined, by age seventeen or eighteen. Others, such as those who pursue graduate studies, may not achieve adult status until several years later. Adolescence has become such a prolonged period for some persons that substages of early, middle, and late adolescence have been proposed (Muuss, 1975), as well as a new postadolescent period known as "youth."

Adolescence was first portrayed as a period of "storm and stress" by G. Stanley Hall in 1904. For a long time, it was hypothesized that adolescent development is filled with conflict and turmoil, and that it is a period of intense struggles to become free of parental control. Much later, Albert Bandura (1975) suggested that this view of adolescence was largely a myth based on (1) overemphasis of superficial signs of nonconformity, (2) mass media sensationalism, (3) generalization from samples of deviant adolescents, (4) inappropriate generalization from cross-cultural data, (5) overemphasis on the biological determination of heterosexual behavior, and (6) stage theories of personality development.

Several other researchers agree with Bandura that "storm and stress" is not the rule in adolescent development (Adelson, 1979; Keniston, 1963; Offer, Marcus, and Offer, 1970). Conformity appears to be more characteristic of adolescence than rebellion (Douvan and Adelson, 1966). In the following pages, we will discuss all aspects of adolescent development, including the physical, cognitive, emotional, and social changes that occur in this period.

476

Chapter *26*

NISSEN

*P*hysical Development

The physical changes associated with the adolescent period are dramatic. Not only does the child's body grow bigger, but it also becomes capable of sexual reproduction. In this chapter we review the major physical changes that occur during this time and the implications of these changes for adolescents and those who work with them.

Growth

The term *adolescence*, which is derived from Latin, means "to grow into maturity." The most dramatic changes in physical development during adolescence occur during *puberty*, the stage of development that results in the ability to reproduce. In boys, the testes and scrotum grow during puberty and the first ejaculation occurs. For girls, the first menstruation, or menarche, is considered the beginning of puberty.

The period preceding puberty is called *pubescence*. It precedes puberty by approximately two years. During pubescence, physiological changes take place

477

that lead to the development of primary and secondary sex characteristics. *Primary sex characteristics* are those directly involved in reproduction — ovulation and menstruation in the female, the development of testes and production of sperm in the male. These characteristics result from the direct effects of pituitary hormones on the reproductive organs. *Secondary sex characteristics* are not directly involved in reproduction, but they also distinguish the sexes. They are called "secondary" because they are the result of hormone production by the reproductive organs themselves.

The secondary sex characteristics of boys include indentation of the hairline of the upper forehead; appearance of hair on the face, chest, and pubic region; growth of the jawbone; lengthening of vocal cords; and deepening of the voice. In girls, secondary sex characteristics include breast development, growth of pubic hair, and, for some, a slight growth of hair on the upper lip.

The growth spurt associated with adolescence involves increases in height, weight, and skeletal growth, and precedes puberty. The growth spurt for girls as a group begins two to three years earlier than it does for boys as a group, although individual girls may mature later than individual boys. The ages at which physical development begins and ends vary greatly. For boys, it may begin as early as age ten and a half and end as late as sixteen, with the average boy beginning the spurt at thirteen. Growth then peaks at age fourteen and virtually ceases at

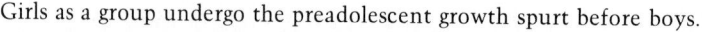

Girls as a group undergo the preadolescent growth spurt before boys.

around fifteen and a half. For the average girl, the onset of the growth spurt can occur anytime between eight and a half and ten and a half. For the average girl the peak of the growth spurt is between twelve and thirteen (Dusek, 1977; Tanner, 1981).

Children in the United States mature about one year earlier than children in Europe, and children in industrial countries in general have been getting larger and maturing earlier during the last 100 years. In 1900, for example, the average age at first menstruation for females in the United States was fourteen years and two months; today it is twelve years (Peterson, 1979; Tanner, 1981). These differences, known as the *secular trend in growth*, are probably due to better nutrition and health. For example, it is known that the first menstruation does not occur until body fat is about 17 percent of body weight (Peterson, 1979). The better nourished the population, the earlier this situation occurs. As nutrition and health reach some optimum level, it is expected that increases in size and decreases in age at maturity will stop.

Effects of Early and Late Maturing

Studies of the effects of early and late maturation on social and emotional development indicate that boys and girls are affected differently. An early-maturing boy may enjoy heterosexual activity on an equal ground with normally maturing girls of his age (remember that girls are about two years ahead of boys), success in sports and school, and acceptance by older late-maturing boys (Gross and Duke, 1980; Jones and Bayley, 1950; Latham, 1951). When rated by adults, early-maturing boys were judged to be more attractive and more masculine than late-maturing boys. When rated by peers, the early maturers again were judged to be more attractive and more masculine than the late maturers.

Early-maturing girls, on the other hand, may feel awkward because they are taller than most boys their age; they may be rejected by other girls and overprotected by parents. Unlike late-maturing boys, late-maturing girls tend to be at an advantage socially (Jones, 1949). This may be because early-maturing boys tend to develop physical qualities (such as muscular build and tallness) that are valued in American society, whereas early-maturing girls tend to be plump, which is not a valued characteristic (Staffieri, 1972).

However, late-maturing girls sometimes suffer anguish about not yet having undergone changes typical of their peers. Judy Blume's book, *Are you there God? It's me, Margaret,* is the story of a girl desperately awaiting one sign of growing up, the onset of menstruation:

> Are you there God? It's me, Margaret. Gretchen, my friend, got her period. I'm so jealous God. I hate myself for being so jealous, but I am. I wish you'd help me just a little. Nancy's sure she's going to get it soon, too. And if I'm last I don't know what I'll do. Oh, please God. I just want to be normal. [1970, p. 100]

Concern for Appearance During Adolescence

Both boys and girls are very interested in their appearance during adolescence, and they often compare themselves with their peers. They are concerned about many physical features, including height, weight, body proportions, and complexion. (Acne can be a problem during adolescence, because hormonal changes increase skin secretions.) Evidence indicates that some of these features are associated with social success. One study found that overweight and underweight adolescents were at a disadvantage in social and educational encounters (Hendry and Gillies, 1978). Physique can affect the adolescent's self-concept and involvement in sports and the peer group.

Sometimes, concern for appearance becomes distorted. In the syndrome are *anorexia nervosa*, adolescent females are convinced they are fat and begin to starve themselves to become, in their view, thin and beautiful. This serious disorder requires extensive psychological therapy, often involving the entire family, to cure.

An anorexia nervosa victim

FOCUS: Anorexia Nervosa

As early as 1689, physician Richard Morton described the syndrome now called *anorexia nervosa*. Morton named the disease "a nervous consumption" and described the appearance of those afflicted as "a skeleton only clad in skin." These descriptions are accurate even today, for we know that the syndrome involves a psychological disturbance that leads the individual to starve herself.

Almost all sufferers from this syndrome are adolescent females. Only very rarely has the disorder been reported in males. Incidence estimates vary, but they are as high as one in 200 for adolescent girls (Crisp, Palmer, and Kalucy, 1976).

The person afflicted with the disorder is preoccupied with her body and often feels out of control of her life. Very often the girl has been a "perfect" child who has done just as her parents have wished. Her parents most likely have a stable marriage. They may appear to have been perfect parents. However, they may need a perfect child to provide proof of their parenting skill and may never have allowed this child much initiative. Thus, the child may have failed to develop a self-directed identity. Becoming slimmer by controlling eating may be the girl's way of feeling in control. And fear of losing control over one's hunger urge may keep the girl from giving in, even a little, to the urge to eat (Bruch, 1979).

Symptoms of anorexia nervosa include a fanatical preoccupation with food and eating. The person may spend hours preparing the tiny portions eaten. She may eat extremely slowly, taking hours to eat a very small amount. Sometimes she eats only late at night and goes to sleep immediately, perhaps to escape guilt about having eaten at all. Despite the extreme loss of weight, the individual tends to see her emaciated body as normal or even fat (Bruch, 1979).

Treatment of the disorder often includes hospitalization to ensure weight gain and to avoid death due to starvation. (Reports of death due to anorexia nervosa range from 5 to 20 percent [Schleimer, 1981]). Sometimes behavior modification (operant conditioning) techniques are used to force the girl to eat. However, weight gain is not a cure, and behavior modification has been shown not to lead to long-term changes in eating behavior (Pertshuck, 1977). Extensive individual and family therapy is usually needed to effect a permanent cure.

Motor Development and Skills

Strength, stamina, and coordination continue to develop during adolescence. Bones harden, becoming more dense due to mineral deposits, and muscles become stronger. It is during adolescence and early adulthood that the physical skills required for athletic events usually reach their peak. Champions in world competitions such as the Olympics are often between the ages of fourteen or fifteen and twenty-six or twenty-eight.

Physical fitness is important for adolescent development, not only to ensure good health, but to ensure psychological well-being. Research indicates, for example, that adolescent self-confidence improves when physical fitness improves

Physical skills peak during adolescence and young adulthood.

(McGowan, Jarman, and Pederson, 1974). Good physical education programs can help build physical fitness and physique, as can programs for such sports as basketball, soccer, field hockey, and track.

Summary

Growth

- Pubescence is the period when the physiological changes that lead to sexual maturity begin. Girls enter pubescence about two to three years earlier than boys. During pubescence both primary sex characteristics (those required for reproduction) and secondary sex characteristics (those not related to reproduction) develop.
- Age at puberty has decreased in industrial countries during the last 100 years because of better nutrition and general health.
- Early maturation benefits the social and emotional development of boys but not of girls, apparently because early-maturing girls tend to be plumper than late-maturing girls, and this physique is not valued in our society.
- Adolescents typically worry a great deal about their appearance, especially about their height, weight, and complexion.

Motor Development and Skills

- Physical skill often reaches its peak during late adolescence and early adulthood.
- Physical fitness contributes to good health and improves self-confidence.

New Terms

adolescence
puberty
pubescence
primary sex characteristics

secondary sex characteristics
secular trend in growth
anorexia nervosa

Selected Readings

Faust, M. S. **Somatic development of adolescent girls.** *Monographs of the Society for Research in Child Development.* 42 (1977). This discussion of physical development of adolescent girls is based on a longitudinal study of ninety-four girls conducted by the Institute of Human Development at the University of California, Berkeley. It is readable but very detailed. Some knowledge of growth patterns that occur during adolescence is helpful in reading this monograph.

Minuchin, S., Rosman, B. L., and Baker, L. **Psychosomatic families: Anorexia nervosa in context.** *Cambridge, Mass.: Harvard University Press, 1978.* Discusses anorexia nervosa as a family problem. Interesting.

Tanner, J. M. **Growth at adolescence.** *Second edition. Oxford: Blackwell Scientific Publications, 1962.* An old but good source of information about physical growth and development in the adolescent. Start here before delving into Faust, above.

Chapter 27

Cognitive Development

Thinking typically moves beyond the concrete operational level to formal operations during adolescence. This change in intellectual capacity causes many changes in behavior, including a new form of egocentricity. First we will discuss formal operational thinking in adolescence and its implications for instruction in school. We then go on to examine the effects of formal operational thinking on adolescent egocentricity.

Formal Operations: Piaget's Fourth Stage of Cognitive Development

It is during adolescence that many persons enter Piaget's fourth stage of cognitive development — *formal operations*. Unlike concrete operational thought, formal operational thought is no longer tied to events observed in the environment. The formal operational thinker considers the possible, not merely the actual. Thinking is abstract, not concrete (Piaget, 1957).

Piaget used several tasks to explore formal operational thinking (Inhelder and Piaget, 1958). Perhaps the best known is the pendulum problem (see Figure 27-1). The child is asked to figure out what determines the pendulum's period — the speed with which it makes one sweep back and forth. Is it the length of the string from which the weight is suspended, the heaviness of the weight, or the height from which the weight is let go?

Piaget was interested in the process children use to approach this problem. Some children change the length of the string and the size of the weight at the same time, but this confounds their results. If a change in the period occurs, they cannot tell which adjustment caused it. Other children systematically hold all but one variable constant. This ability to systematically exclude competing possibilities characterizes formal operational thought.

Some of Piaget's other tasks involve the ability to consider probabilities. One task uses a mixed collection of colored shapes in an opaque bag. An identical set of objects is placed on a table in front of the child. The child must predict which shape is most likely to be drawn from the bag. If the set includes five green squares, two yellow triangles, one red circle, and one orange rectangle, it is most probable that a green square will be drawn. But as the drawing proceeds and the bag's contents are depleted, the probability of drawing the different shapes changes. If four green squares and one red circle have been drawn, the odds are that the next draw will yield a yellow triangle rather than the orange rectangle or

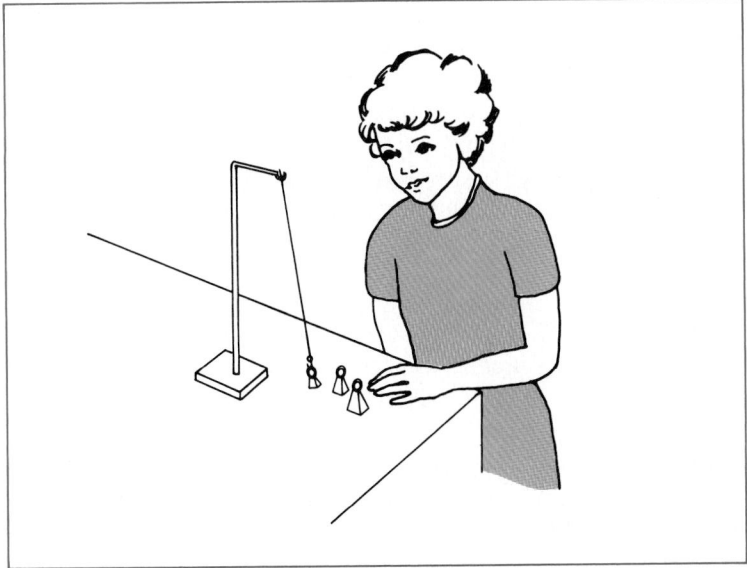

Figure 27-1

the remaining green square. To play the probability game, the child must consider not only what was in the bag to begin with, as represented by the shapes on the table, but what has been taken from the bag in previous drawings. Concrete operational children seem to consider the first rule, that probability is determined by the number of each shape placed in the bag, but to disregard the second, that probability changes as the drawing proceeds. Formal operational thinkers, on the other hand, coordinate the two rules (Brainerd, 1978).

Prevalence of Formal Operational Thinking

Although most children become capable of formal operational thinking during adolescence, some use it more than others and some never achieve it at all. "Situational, motivational and cultural factors all exert an influence on both the rate at which formal thought structures develop and the full extent of their development" (Chandler, 1976, p. 230). According to some experts (e.g., Chiappetta, 1976), most young adults and adolescents have not reached the stage of formal operational thinking. It has been estimated that only 20 to 35 percent of adults and adolescents function at a fully formal level (Dulit, 1975).

Elkind (1978b) has suggested that those who develop formal operational thinking do not have it under complete control at first. "The capacity to conceive many different alternatives is not immediately coupled with the ability to assign priorities and to decide which choice is more or less appropriate than others. Consequently, young adolescents often appear stupid because they are in fact too bright" (pp. 128–129). Elkind, who calls this state *pseudostupidity*, indicates that the obvious often eludes these adolescents. They may, for example, fail at a task because they are approaching it in too complex a fashion, considering too many alternatives.

It has been suggested that some older adolescents and adults develop a kind of thinking that goes beyond formal operations problem solving to a type of thinking called *problem finding*, which is characterized by the creation of ideas (Arlin, 1975, 1977). Research on this level of thinking is rather sparse at present; we need to await further data to understand all of its characteristics and how it relates to formal operations.

Formal Operational Thinking and Schooling

Chiappetta, who is especially concerned with adolescents' learning of science, believes that the concrete level of thinking characteristic of many adolescents must be matched by the content, instruction, and assessment procedures used in high school and college science courses. He suggests that courses be designed to provide two kinds of instruction — a concrete core, in which students can interact directly with real objects and events, and an advanced component, which requires more formal and abstract thinking.

Some experts suggest that instruction in schools may neglect more basic cognitive processes which involve thinking (Nucci and Gordon, 1979). These experts stress the importance of making learning an active process, arguing that "maximum educational growth occurs when students' thinking is challenged with developmentally more adequate ways of viewing the world" (p. 99). They offer guidelines, based on Piaget's perspective, for educating adolescents. Some of these are listed below.

1. Educational content should be coordinated with students' ability to understand. Topics should be slightly more difficult than students understand immediately, but not too complex.
2. Content should be relevant to the student and to his or her future. Memorizing Babylonian numeral systems, as a chapter in a current math text requires, is irrelevant, but an understanding of fractions is usually quite relevant.
3. Students should be encouraged to interact with each other, ask questions, and challenge each other's ideas.
4. Student activity and thinking should be fostered through such means as group discussions, debates, and laboratory activities.
5. To get students to discover inadequacies in their own thinking, teachers should ask them questions designed to resolve issues just beyond their immediate grasp.
6. Both answers and reasons for arriving at answers should be considered in evaluating the student.

To be effective, science instruction must be consistent with the individual's level of thinking.

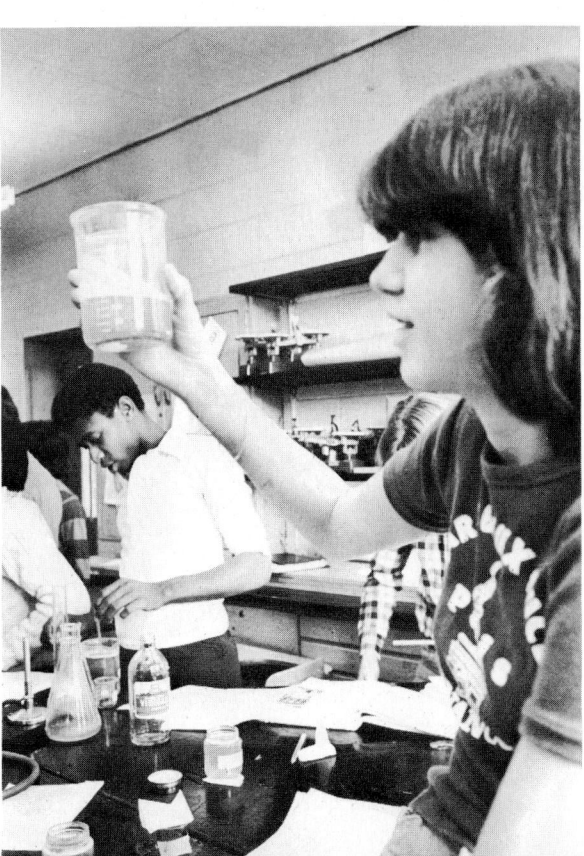

Formal Operations and Egocentricity

Although the development of formal operations is a big step forward in a person's thinking, it brings with it some problems. All stages of cognitive development have their own form of egocentrism, and adolescence is no exception (Elkind, 1976; Enright, Lapsley, and Shukla, 1979). Adolescent egocentricity often involves confusing the concern one has for oneself with the concern that others have for one. Adolescents tend to assume that everyone else is scrutinizing them as carefully as they are scrutinizing themselves. Elkind has suggested that adolescents create and react to an imaginary audience, acting as if others are constantly viewing them. Self-consciousness, concern about dress and looks, mortification at the slightest social mistake — behaviors typical of adolescents — are the result of this adolescent egocentricity.

Adolescents are very concerned about what others think of them and imagine that others look at them as much as they look at themselves.

Elkind also suggests that adolescents believe they are special and think that bad things that happen to others could not possibly happen to them. Elkind refers to this thinking as a "personal fable," a story adolescents believe about themselves that is not true.

> One way the personal fable manifests itself is the failure of the young person to distinguish that which is unique to the self from that which is common to mankind. He or she assumes that what is common to everyone is unique to themselves; and what is unique to themselves is common to everyone. These personal fable confusions . . . account for what appears to be self-destructive behavior but in fact results from a belief that the young person is special and shielded from harm. "It can happen to others, not to me." [Elkind, 1978, pp. 131–132]

Many adolescents feel self-critical, self-conscious, or perhaps self-admiring for some of the reasons Elkind mentions. They may also show off, be loud, and have idealistic and impractical dreams of changing society. Their ideas of personal uniqueness may be helpful in explaining adolescent accidents and pregnancies. Their fantasies of heroic achievement may encourage them to attempt feats without thinking of the consequences. One benefit of some school programs is that they require adolescents to think about possible consequences and receive proper training. Supervised sports programs, for example, might permit an adolescent to dive off a high diving board after proper training rather than off a bridge into shallow water to show off to a friend.

Summary

Formal Operations: Piaget's Fourth Stage of Cognitive Development

- Many persons begin to develop formal operational thinking during adolescence. Such thinking is characterized by the ability to think of the possible rather than the actual. It is abstract, not concrete. Some adolescents and adults never reach the formal operational level of thinking.
- Sometimes adolescents' ability to generate hypotheses leads them to make a problem more complex than it needs to be — they get carried away with thinking of alternatives. This state is called pseudostupidity.
- A stage of thinking called problem finding has been suggested as following the stage of formal operations.
- Some experts think that high school instruction must take levels of adolescent thinking into account if it is to be effective.
- Adolescence has its own form of egocentricity, which involves an imaginary audience and a "personal fable." Both of these traits involve an individual confusing his thoughts about himself with others' thoughts about him.

New Terms

formal operations
pseudostupidity

problem finding

Selected Readings

Elkind, D. **A sympathetic understanding of the child from birth to sixteen.** *Second edition. Boston: Allyn and Bacon, 1978.* Chapter 10 of this small volume deals with mental development in the adolescent. Easy to read.

Ginsburg, H., and Opper, S. **Piaget's theory of intellectual development.** *Second edition. Englewood Cliffs, N.J.: Prentice-Hall, 1978.* An introduction to Piaget's theory and tasks. Chapter 5 covers the adolescent period and formal operations. Informative and readable.

Inhelder, B., and Piaget, J. **The growth of logical thinking from childhood to adolescence.** *A. Parsons and S. Milgram, trans. New York: Basic Books, 1968.* This volume provides extensive discussions of formal thought. It is not for the beginner.

Chapter 28

*L*anguage Development

By adolescence, a child has been using language skillfully for almost a decade. The changes we see in language at this time are more a matter of increased cognitive skills than increased language skills. In other words, changes in cognitive functioning result in changes in the way language is used and understood. In addition, the social milieu of the adolescent influences language behavior. In this chapter we will discuss some aspects of adolescent language behavior and explain how these are related to cognitive and social development.

Increasing Complexity of Language

Adolescent language generally becomes more complex. Vocabularies increase and more complicated sentence structures come into use. The emergence of formal operational thinking makes new language patterns possible. The formal operational thinker's ability to use deductive reasoning and generate hypotheses is reflected in the use of "if-then" sentences and words such as "however" and "therefore."

Hypothetical deductive reasoning influences the ability to discuss things in depth.

Semantics

The adolescent's understanding of semantics, the meanings of words, also progresses. Adolescents continue to add new words to their vocabularies, but they understand word meanings differently and relate word meanings in new ways. They develop a better understanding of the influences of context in choosing one word over another. In addition, concrete and functional definitions of words give way to abstract definitions (Palermo and Molfese, 1973).

Influence of Formal Operational Thinking

The ability to understand written material also changes with the emergence of formal operational thinking. Adolescents develop the ability to understand several levels of meaning. Younger children, in contrast, interpret written material literally or concretely. This new ability is evident in children's interpretations of the following proverbs at different ages. The intended meaning of each proverb is given in parentheses.

1. Never go into deep water until you can swim. (Don't attempt things you don't have the skills for.)

    Age
    5   "Because you'll drown if you don't know how to swim."
    7   "Cause you'll drown."
    9   "Learn how to swim first."
    10   "Wait till you're older."
    11   "Only do what you know you can do."

2. People in glass houses shouldn't throw stones. (Don't criticize others unless you're invulnerable to criticism yourself.)

Age
 5   "Because it breaks the glass."
       "Never throw stones at a house."
 7   "You know people don't live in glass houses. I don't see no glass houses."
 9   "If you buy a glass house, expect to have a broken window."
11   "If you hurt people, you may get hurt yourself."

3. When the cat's away the mice will play. (When the person in charge is absent, people will do what they shouldn't.)

Age
 4½   "Cause the mouse scares the cat."
 6   "When the cat goes, the mice stay."
 7   "Because the cat would eat the mice so they play when the cat is gone."
10   "When parents are away, children will wreck the house." [Saltz, 1979, p. 511]

It is not until children are about eleven years old — on the brink of formal operational thinking — that they begin to understand the meanings of these proverbs.

Adolescents can enjoy several levels of meaning in the books they read.

Adolescents' ability to understand metaphor enables them to appreciate political cartoons and to understand the use of such terms as "rat" or "dog" as applied to people. In addition, they can understand the social messages that go beyond the literal stories in works of literature such as *Gulliver's Travels* (Elkind, 1978).

Communication through the medium of the visual arts also changes at adolescence. No longer is there concern with achieving accurate representation of things as they are in the world. Now pictures are purposely distorted or done in an abstract style in order to convey a message. In addition, works of art created by the adolescent are no longer as much a description of tangible objects as they are a statement about ideas such as love, war, intolerance, injustice, and so on (Lansing, 1970).

Social Influences on Oral Language

Adolescent language is sometimes very specialized, reflecting a person's membership in a particular *clique* (a group of friends with similar backgrounds and interests). Sometimes cliques are formalized into clubs in which leaders and followers emerge. There are often many cliques in a high school, which might be

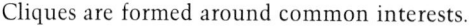

Cliques are formed around common interests.

associated with such interests as sports, cars, or drugs (Leona, 1978). Each group may have a language of its own that reflects its main interest. Leona (1978), for example, found that an uncoordinated member of a sports team was called a "spaz," acceleration of a car at a traffic light was called a "hole shot," and smoking marijuana was called "taking a hit." Adult observers, Leona indicates, might well be perplexed on hearing the following:

> Hey, man, let's go cruisin' and drain some frosties. We'll pull a
> chirper right in front of the pigs then do quarter or find a wicked rat
> race with some Bondo. [Leona, 1978, p. 495]

One reason adolescents may create unique words is to make it difficult for adults to know what they are talking about. A specialized language also builds cohesiveness among group members and serves to exclude those who do not belong. Younger children may simply say "you can't play," or "we don't like you; get out." Adolescents are more subtle: they create a culture and tell its secrets only to those whom they wish to become members.

Summary

Increasing Complexity of Language
- Language development during adolescence is characterized by an increased use and understanding of complex sentences.
- Formal operational thinking enables the adolescent to understand meanings at more than one level.

Social Influences on Oral Language
- Adolescents sometimes develop specialized vocabularies when they belong to cliques. These allow adolescents to build group cohesiveness and to exclude nonmembers.

Selected Readings

Charrow, V. R., and Fletcher, J. D. **English as a second language of deaf children.** *Developmental Psychology, 10 (1974): 463–470.* This article discusses the use of English by children who learn American Sign Language as a first language. Some of the discussion is about language development in deaf adolescents.

Palermo, D. S., and Molfese, D. L. **Language acquisition from age five onward.** *In F. Rebelsky and L. Dorman (Eds.), Child development and behavior. New York: Knopf, 1973, 401–423.* This chapter provides a good summary of language acquisition in older children, including the young adolescent.

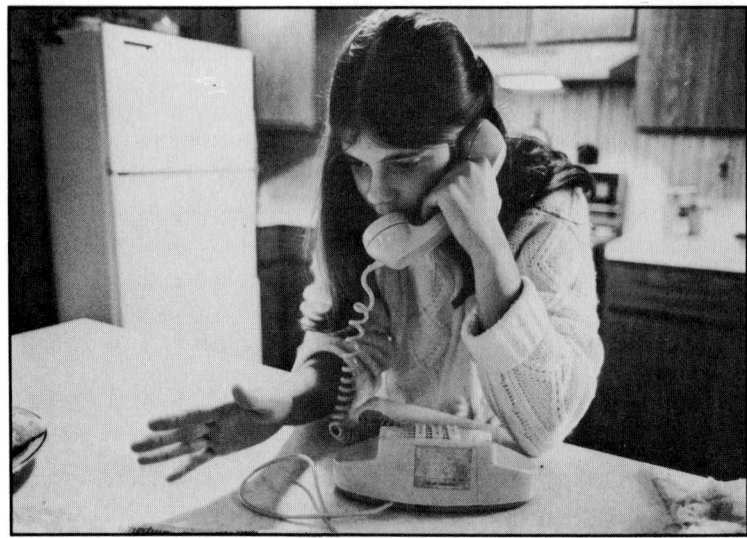

Chapter 29

Social Development

Perhaps no other topic receives as much attention in discussions of adolescent development as does social development. The reason for this may be that adolescence is primarily a period of social transition. In nonindustrial and nontechnical societies there is no adolescent period at all: biological maturity coincides with social adulthood. But our society recognizes the adolescent period and may even prolong it. This can lead to conflicts between the recognized adults of the society and the emerging adults — the adolescents. We discuss next how to minimize such conflict and lead the child with relative ease from adolescence to adulthood.

Theories of Adolescent Social Behavior

Erik Erikson

According to Erikson, the adolescent is striving to "be somebody" — looking for a place among peers, a career, and a role to play. Erickson believes that if an adolescent does not form a positive *ego identity*, "role confusion" will result.

Role confusion may manifest itself in self-doubt and self-destruction, which can lead to personality problems and juvenile delinquency. It is adolescents' striving for identity that leads them to form cliques and to stereotype themselves and their enemies. "To keep themselves together they temporarily overidentify, to the point of apparent complete loss of identity, with the heroes of cliques and crowds" (Erikson, 1963, p. 262). Erikson contends that young adults are ready to fuse their identities with others and commit themselves to concrete affiliations and partnerships only after their individual identities are established. In the intimacy relationship, a person can be him or herself, trust others, and be honest and sharing. Erikson considers it important for adolescents to have a positive sense of who and what they are and for them to evaluate themselves positively. Erikson's psychosocial theory places more emphasis on cultural determinants of development than does original Freudian theory. Freud stressed psychosexual determinants of behavior resulting from the parent-child relationship and the child's changing biological makeup.

Anna Freud

Anna Freud (1948) believed that maturational factors influence psychological functioning directly, leading to stress and anxiety. She suggested that the functioning of the sexual glands in adolescence and other changes in physiological processes lead to sexual disequilibrium. The ego, governed by the reality principle, yields to the id (instinctual impulses), and comes in conflict with the superego, or conscience. The adolescent thus experiences internal frustration because moral standards interfere with the attainment of goals.

Social Learning Theorists

Social learning theorists assume that adolescent behavior is determined mainly by social, cultural, and situational factors. Bandura (1974) contends that adolescent development occurs in response to certain social expectations and cultural conditions. Adolescent behavior is also thought to be influenced by early learning experiences such as childrearing practices, and by childhood behavior as well. In addition, Bandura suggests that modeling is very important in determining adolescent behavior.

Each of these theories undoubtedly makes some contribution to our understanding of the emotional and social development of adolescents. You will see the influence of these theories in our discussion of some specific aspects of adolescent social behavior.

Socialization

Adolescents must acquire the knowledge, skills, and values that will enable them to become effective members of society. Moriatry and Toussieng state that adolescents must "work actively on an identity that will allow them to cope with a world which changes at a dizzying pace and in unpredictable directions" (1976, p. 151). Adolescents must cope with our fast-changing society; the influence of the mass media; cultural ideals; and family, peer, school, and career decisions. Just as in childhood, growth patterns and cognitive abilities influence styles of coping and interactions with other people. The adolescent's experiences with parents and peers are also influential.

Parents

Parents can help or impede the adolescent's transition from child to adult status through their methods of discipline, the models they provide, the values they support, and the autonomy they allow. Some parents hinder adolescent development by refusing to allow a greater measure of independence, perhaps because the misuse of independence may reflect negatively on themselves (Saltzman, 1973). A completely laissez-faire approach by parents, on the other hand, may not give children enough guidance and support.

Parental methods of control influence the level of independence achieved by the adolescent. The relationship between adolescent independence and autocratic, democratic, and permissive parent types has been studied by Elder (1963). The adolescents who rated highest in autonomy and independence had parents who were democratic and who explained the rules they made. Adolescents with the lowest levels of self-confidence and independence tended to have autocratic parents who did not explain their rules. (See Table 29-1.)

Baumrind's (1968) conclusions are consistent with those of Elder. She suggests that for parents and adolescents to avoid conflict and develop a relationship as equal adults, parents must give rational explanations for their control and permit the adolescent to express his or her views.

Peers

Adolescents spend an increasing amount of time with their peer group — practicing adult roles, sharing similar problems and conflicts, and learning to adjust to other people. The activities of peer groups vary considerably, depending on the size of the town and school, the cultural opportunities available, and the community's interest in sports. The school is often the center of activities, providing clubs, interest groups, parties, sports events, plays, and musical events. The junior prom or the senior class play can be very important to the adolescent, as can working on the school yearbook or being on the basketball team.

The adolescent often participates in activities as part of a *clique* or a *crowd*. A crowd is larger than a clique and may involve both sexes or just one sex. Often based in the school or neighborhood, the crowd offers security and a feeling of belonging to its members. The crowd often consists of a collection of cliques, which, as we saw in Chapter 28, are groups of friends, with similar interests and

Table 29-1. Effects of parental power on adolescent independence

| Level of parental power | Parental explanations | N | Types of adolescent dependence-independence behavior | | | | |
| | | | Lack of confidence | | Confidence | | |
			Dependent	Independent	Dependent	Independent	Total
Autocratic	Frequently	139	27.3%	6.5%	37.4%	28.8%	100%
	Infrequently	231	34.2	14.7	20.3	30.3	100
Democratic	Frequently	1233	10.5	6.7	37.6	45.2	100
	Infrequently	194	22.7	9.8	35.6	31.9	100
Permissive	Frequently	729	13.2	7.2	29.8	49.8	100
	Infrequently	177	28.2	13.6	24.9	33.3	100

NOTES: N = number of subjects included in study.

The degree of self-confidence in personal ideas and values was measured by the following item: "How confident are you that your own ideas and opinions about what you should do and believe are right and best for you?" Lack of confidence: (1) not at all confident, (2) not very confident, (3) I'm a little confident. Confidence: (4) I'm quite confident, (5) I'm completely confident.

Self-reliance in problem solving and decision making was measured by the following item: "When you have a really important decision to make about yourself and your future, do you make it on your own, or do you like to get help on it?" Dependent: (1) I'd rather let someone else decide for me, (2) I depend a lot upon other people's advice, (3) I like to get some help. Independent: (4) I get other ideas, then make up my own mind, (5) I make up my own mind without any help.

SOURCE: Elder, G. H. Parental power legitimation and its effect on the adolescent. *Sociometry* 26 (1963): 50–65. Reprinted by permission.

backgrounds. Cliques can revolve around academics, sports, and other activities considered desirable by parents and educators, or they may revolve around norm-breaking, such as using drugs and alcohol.

Peer group acceptance is important to the adolescent, and close friendships may be important in developing a sense of self-worth. Being neglected or rejected by the peer group can lead to feelings of low self-esteem. Cavoir and Dokecki (1973) found that adolescents like peers who resemble themselves and who have similar values. They do not like peers with very different values, backgrounds, and personality characteristics.

Peers and parents both play large roles in adolescent life. It appears that the relative influence of peers and parents may vary. In a study conducted by Brittain (1963), for example, girls' acceptance of either peer or parental reactions to specific dilemmas depended on the situation. Brittain concluded that immediate concerns, such as what to wear or what to do in a current school situation, are often resolved by reference to peer values, but decisions about the future, such as what kind of job to pursue, are more often influenced by parents.

There is a greater degree of intimacy among teens today than was true in the past.

Sexual Behavior

A larger percentage of unmarried young people are sexually active today than in previous generations. According to Peter Scales (1979), 20 percent of all adolescents under age fifteen have had intercourse, and each year one out of every ten adolescent girls becomes pregnant.

Sex Education

Scales suggests that innovative programs of sex education for adolescents should emphasize not just contraception, but also the responsibilities of parenthood, emotions, and the meaning of sex. He believes that sex educators should confront the issues seriously, considering sexuality as part of overall human growth from the perspective of the adolescent. Sex education is still a controversial topic in many communities, however. According to the Alan Guttmacher report (1976), only one-fifth of the states requiring health education mandate sex education. Many states leave decisions about sex education to local school districts, many of which forbid sex education, especially discussions of contraception. Nine out of ten high school teachers consider teaching about birth control to be controversial (Alan Guttmacher, 1976).

Is *not* educating young teens about sex and contraception (perhaps in hopes that they will not engage in sexual activity) worth the price? Shaw, Zelnick, and

Kanter (1975) list the major reasons given by adolescent females for not using contraception:

1. Conception was impossible because sex was too infrequent.
2. Conception could not occur because it was the wrong time of the monthly cycle.
3. The girl was too young to become pregnant.
4. The male claimed sterility.

FOCUS: Adolescent Pregnancy

Approximately 10 percent of the adolescents in the United States become pregnant every year, and about 6 percent give birth (the other 4 percent have spontaneous or induced abortions) (McKenry, Walters, and Johnson, 1979). One-third of the adolescents who give birth have been married more than nine months, one-third are pregnant when they marry, and the final third give birth without being married (Alan Guttmacher Institute, 1976). In 1974 over half of all births to unmarried women were to teenagers (Baldwin, 1976).

A pregnant high school cheerleader

Actually, the birth rate for teenagers in the United States has declined in recent years. Among women aged fifteen to nineteen, the rate was 97.3 births per 1,000 women in 1957 and 58.7 births per thousand in 1974, a decline of one-third (Baldwin, 1976). In the same time period, however, the birth rate for women aged twenty to twenty-four fell by 54 percent, and for women aged twenty-four and twenty-nine, by 43 percent (Baldwin, 1976). Thus, a larger percentage of the total number of current births are to adolescent mothers. In addition, because there are now more women between the ages of ten and nineteen, the actual number of births to women in this age group is greater than before.

Of special concern is the fact that the birth rate has been increasing among the younger teenage group. Between 1970 and 1974 the birth rate among fourteen-year-olds *rose* from 6.6 to 7.2 per 1000 women, an increase of 9 percent. Among fifteen-year-olds, the increase was 3 percent. In the same time period, the rate dropped by 3 percent for sixteen-year-olds, by 11 percent for seventeen-year-olds, by 18 percent for eighteen-year-olds, and by 24 percent for nineteen-year-olds (Baldwin, 1976). It is to be hoped that the dropping birth rates will soon extend to the younger teenagers, because they are the least capable of caring for a baby.

If adolescents had a good background of information about their bodies, birth control, and sex and its consequences, they might make better decisions about sexual behavior. Garcia and Rosenfeld (1977) found that 53 percent of all sexually active adolescents did not use contraceptives the last time they had intercourse.

A program to help prevent adolescent pregnancy has been developed by Schinke, Gilchrist, and Small (1979). Based on cognitive and behaviorial principles, it consists of four steps:

1. Providing access to relevant reproductive and contraceptive information, including accurate and complete information on reproductive biology, contraceptive methods, pregnancy resolution options, and normal sexual development in adolescence.

2. Encouraging accurate perception, comprehension, and storage of the information through small-group study, hypothetical situations, quizzes, and rewards.

3. Encouraging the use of information in decision-making by relating facts to personal attitudes, beliefs, and values, and by translating facts into personal statements. As Schinke, Gilchrist, and Small put it,

   At this point, adolescents must evaluate the consequences of taking knowledge-based action. Since such action usually involves other people, each self-statement includes their anticipated responses. For example, a young man might verbalize the following thoughts: "*Fact:* Unprotected intercourse frequently results in pregnancy; that means: If Ann and I have sex without birth control, she might get pregnant. Since neither of us wants her to get pregnant, we had better start using birth control. She doesn't like the pill, so I guess we better talk about using something else." [1979, p. 86]

4. Helping students implement decisions by using small-group discussions, modeling, role play, feedback, and verbal instruction to help the adolescent practice for real situations.

This program is particularly strong because, rather than merely providing information, it encourages students to think about that information. It also encourages adolescents to think about what to do in specific situations. Such a program may counter the tendency of adolescents to think that what happens to others cannot possibly happen to them (the "personal fable" we discussed in Chapter 27) and cause them to consider their behavior and its possible consequences more seriously.

We know of no data that indicate that increasing adolescents' knowledge of sex leads to increased sexual involvement. Data do indicate, however, that a lack of knowledge leads to more pregnancies.

Parents and Sex Education

Some parents may resist school sex education programs because they hope to provide such education at home. Many parents apparently do want to participate in the sex education of their teenagers (Roberts and Gagnon, 1978), and teenagers express an interest in talking more with their parents about sex (General Mills, 1979). Actual discussions, however, occur infrequently. A recent study indicates that the level of communication between mothers and daughters about sexual behavior during the prime adolescent years can be predicted by (1) their pattern of early communication, and (2) the daughters' rating of the quality of the relationship. Discussion about sex during the prime teen years was related to the frequency of discussion before age twelve and a half and the positiveness and openness of the relationship between mother and daughter (Fox and Inazu, 1980). The researchers concluded that communication about sex during adolescence is difficult if there has has been no history of open communication prior to this time.

The consequences of adolescent pregnancy can involve social, psychological, and medical problems for both the mother and the child. Clearly, adolescent pregnancy is a problem that deserves our concern and attention.

FOCUS: Consequences of Adolescent Pregnancy

Adolescent pregnancy can cause many problems and force the mother and perhaps father to redirect their intended life courses. The social and medical consequences of adolescent pregnancy for teenage parents and their child have been discussed by Garcia and Rosenfeld (1977).

CONSEQUENCES FOR THE PARENT

Social

1. The risk to the mother's health is increased.
2. It is the leading cause of dropping out of school.
3. The parents are required to assume responsibility without being prepared for it.
4. The likelihood of divorce, suicide, and unhappiness is higher.
5. The likelihood that the family will have a low income is increased.

Medical

1. Increased risk during pregnancy and delivery of toxemia, anemia, prolonged labor, and cholecystitis.
2. Undernutrition is common.
3. The intervals between the births of later children are shorter.

(continued on following page)

FOCUS *(continued)*

CONSEQUENCES FOR THE CHILD

1. The rate of infant mortality is higher among babies born to adolescents.
2. The likelihood of premature or low birth weight is increased.
3. The risk of the baby's having poor perceptual abilities and motor coordination is increased.
4. Problems in growth and development associated with fatherless homes and ill-prepared parents are more likely.

Another risk to the child is the increased probability of neurological impairments such as blindness, deafness, and mental retardation (Schinke, Gilchrist, and Small, 1979).

Many of the medical risks to teenage mothers and the physical risks to their children apparently could be reduced with good prenatal and postnatal care. In a special program conducted at the University of Colorado Medical School, an obstetric clinic was established for young pregnant women. Followup care was also provided after delivery. In the group receiving such care, most of the medical risks to mothers and children were greatly reduced (Perkins et al., 1978).

Young teenage mothers often do not seek prenatal care early in their pregnancies because they deny that they are pregnant or wish to keep this pregnancy a secret from parents and peers. In addition, a high school principal has told us that pregnant teenagers sometimes diet in order to stay thinner and hide the pregnancy. Other teenagers do not seek medical care or eat well because they do not have the financial means to do so. These circumstances, of course, would be injurious to the health of both the mother and the unborn child. It would seem wise to provide better supportive services to pregnant teenagers to help prevent some of these problems.

Moral Behavior

Adolescence is a time for thinking about questions of morality: what is right, what is wrong, what is justified or unjustified, and what it means to have "morals."

Social Cognition and Moral Behavior

Kohlberg's theory of moral development, discussed in Chapter 24, suggests that people go through six successive stages, although some persons do not reach the final stages. Kohlberg believes that progression through these stages can be facilitated through role playing and presenting students with moral dilemmas. Adolescents who learn to consider another person's point of view may be more likely to give more advanced moral responses. Chandler (1973) has used this knowledge to reduce the number of arrests among delinquent preadolescent boys. The boys used dramatic techniques and made video films to reduce social egocentrism. Boys in the program were arrested significantly less often than boys in a control group, and the positive effects of the program were still evident more than a year later. The results of Chandler's study suggest that it is useful to consider solving some of the problems of delinquency by approaching them from a sociocognitive perspective. Some delinquent youths may not have learned to think about things from the point of view of someone else. Thus, they may not consider the harm and distress their behavior causes to others.

Adolescents must make moral decisions in many situations and about many different issues — drugs, alcohol, lifestyle, political activity, and sex. Many adolescents seek answers through experimentation. Levine and Kozak (1979) found, for example, that more than 50 percent of eleventh and twelfth graders had used marijuana, and that a substantially higher percentage had used alcohol.

Effect of Family Relationships

An adolescent's choice of experiences and the outcomes of these experiences both seem to be related to family relationships. A classic study by Peck and Havighurst (1960) found significant relationships between family interactions and character development. Their findings are summarized in Table 29-2. Positive character development, described as "rational-altruistic," is associated with consistently democratic and loving family relationships. Amoral and expedient character development, on the other hand, are both associated with rejecting, inconsistent, and permissive family relationships.

Patterns of parental interaction and family relationships may be partially responsible for such rebellious behavior as gang formation and delinquency.

Table 29-2. Family influences and character development

Family Relationships	Character
Rejecting, inconsistent, no rules	Amoral (impulsive, egocentric)
Lenient, unthinking; inconsistent approval	Expedient (concerned about others for personal gain; behaves to obtain rewards or avoid punishment)
Consistent, autocratic, authoritarian	Conforming (follows rules and accepts roles)
Consistent, loving, democratic, lenient; rational discipline	Rational and altruistic (perceptive and concerned with the well-being of others)

SOURCE: Peck, R. F. and Havighurst, R. J. *The psychology of character development.* New York: Wiley, 1960.

Balswick and Macrides (1975) suggest that these behaviors are products of patriarchal homes that are unhappy, very restrictive, or very permissive. Childrearing techniques may be one of several factors responsible for delinquent behavior. To encourage *prosocial* behavior, parents and others should be loving and accepting and should reward prosocial behaviors in the peer group. Role playing and sharing opportunities in the society are also important means of fostering prosocial behavior.

Self-Concept

An adolescent's self-concept is determined by social, cognitive, and biological factors. The adolescent's response to the question, "Who am I?" is influenced by many factors: body build and image, social encounters with peers and adults, successes and failures, and how the adolescent thinks and feels about these circumstances. Dusek suggests that "a positive self-concept, as reflected in self-esteem, is important for the individual's general outlook and mental health; those who have high self-esteem tend to be better adjusted socially than those who have relatively low self-esteem" (1977, p. 329). Adolescents who think they are capable and worthy act in ways that indicate as much. Those who have low self-esteem may behave unacceptably, thereby lowering their self-esteem even further.

A study by Pomerantz (1979) suggests that male and female adolescents derive social satisfaction from different sources. Females in the study reported more interpersonal and physical self-satisfaction, whereas males were oriented more toward performance and external satisfactions. Pomerantz suggests,

> for females, self-worth develops as a result of feedback from others. Thus, how she feels about her body and herself are closely tied to, and in fact, stem from, the ability of the female adolescent to function in her social world. Therefore, while the male's sense of self-worth is based on achievements and carried over to the social world, the female is bound to her audience as a source of identity, self-definition, and self-evaluation. [1979, pp. 60–61]

Erik Erikson suggests that because of the rapid body growth and genital maturity, adolescents are "primarily concerned with what they appear to be in the eyes of others as compared with what they feel they are, and with the question of how to connect the roles and skills cultivated earlier with the occupational prototypes of the day" (1963, p. 261).

Stanley Coopersmith (1967) suggests that the term "success" may have different meanings for different persons, proposing that it may be defined by four kinds of experiences:

1. Power — the ability to influence and control others.
2. Significance — the acceptance, attention, and affection of others.
3. Virtue — adherence to ethical and moral standards.
4. Competence — successfully meeting achievement demands.

Coopersmith contends that adolescents measure their self-worth primarily through competence and significance. He believes, however, that a person can develop high self-esteem by doing well in just one area, as long as he or she considers that area important. One high school student who does very well academically may have a positive self-concept even though he or she is not well accepted by peers and has little or no influence with them. Another student who does well academically but who cares about being accepted may develop a negative self-concept.

Problems in Adolescence

Each of the theories we discussed earlier assumes that problems stem from a different source. Bandura's theory suggests that variables in the parent-child relationship contribute to adolescent aggression. Erickson contends that adolescents who fail in their search for identity experience self-doubt, which can lead to self-destructive tendencies and even suicide. Anna Freud suggests that it is the struggle between the ego and the id that leads to aggression. Elkind argues that adolescent behaviors that adults often attribute to devious motives are actually the result of intellectual immaturity. Some especially common problems during the adolescent years include drug abuse, dropping out of school, and delinquency.

Drugs

Levine and Kozak's data (1979), mentioned earlier, indicate that at least 50 percent of all eleventh and twelfth graders had used alcohol and marijuana. Although adolescents tend to use marijuana and hallucinogenic drugs more than opiates (Rogers, 1972), it is estimated that about 3 percent use cocaine, about 1 percent use heroin or methadone, and about 6 percent use other opiates (Lerner, and Spanier, 1980). Dusek (1977) concludes that adolescents use drugs for several reasons:

1. Curiosity, to see if they will alter consciousness, and in what ways.
2. Social pressure, perhaps to acquire prestige and a reputation for daring, or perhaps because "everybody's doing it."
3. Escape from daily problems and anxieties.
4. Imitation of adult models.

Although earlier researchers found little evidence that casual or moderate use of marijuana is dangerous, a recent article by Richard Hawley (1978) provokes "some unsettling thoughts about settling in with pot." Hawley's summary of researct on the physiological effects of the drug states that it interferes with several processes, including sexual performance, memory, thinking, immunity, hormonal regulating activities, and the cell metabolism responsible for genetic replication. Hawley also suggests that marijuana inhibits one's ability to feel stress and distorts one's sense of time. Archer and Lopata (1979) contend that the studies showing acute effects have major methodological problems, but they agree that an absence of acute effects has not been demonstrated. They also indicate that marijuana can affect memory, intellectual ability, and motor skills. In addition, it can cause users to become more antisocial and independent, and less achievement-oriented than nonusers. The current trend of adding substances such as angel dust, embalming fluid, and other toxic chemicals to marijuana, clearly increases the hazards involved in its use.

Adolescents often use tobacco, of course. In fact, the number of adolescent cigarette smokers continues to increase each year (Dusek, 1977). Adolescents and adults continue to smoke, despite the fact that it is associated with shortness of breath, a lowered tolerance for exercise, and greater risks of lung cancer and heart disease.

The drug most frequently used by young people is alcohol. In fact, the seriousness of the problem may be obscured by the dramatic increase in the use of other drugs (Rogers, 1972). It is estimated that about 85 percent of adolescents have used alcohol (Yancy, Nader, and Burnham, 1972). Alcohol is an anesthetic, and people under its influence cannot function at normal levels. Alcohol depresses the central nervous system, interferes with intellectual functioning, and impairs perception, sensorimotor coordination, and thinking speed.

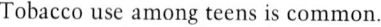
Tobacco use among teens is common.

Dropping Out of School

Roughly 20 percent of all adolescents in the United States fail to complete high school (Gallatin, 1975). It has been estimated that at least half of these dropouts are of average intelligence or above. Adolescents from the lower social classes, underpriviledged sectors, and certain minority groups drop out in disproportionate numbers. This is a serious problem. Adolescents' aspirations are related to their socioeconomic status. Those who have unskilled, unemployed, or uneducated parents may find it difficult to rise above that status. The stress of daily life alone can make it difficult to stay in school. In addition, schools may not relate to these children, all through the school years, as well as they relate to children from other social classes, with the result that the children do not like or see the value of school.

Many middle- and upper-class adolescents also drop out of school. In addition to social class, the overall family situation is important. Affluent under-achievers, for example, may be rebelling indirectly, trying to frustrate their families by flunking out (Gallatin, 1975). Others drop out of school when they run away from home to escape intolerable conditions.

Delinquency

"Juvenile delinquency" is the legal term used to denote lawbreaking by those who are not considered adults (under age sixteen or eighteen depending on the state) (Dusek, 1977). The incidence of juvenile delinquency is rising and has been for some time. Common offenses include theft, vandalism, assault, ungovernability, reckless driving, use of alcohol, and sexual offenses.

Contrary to popular belief, juvenile delinquency is not confined to lower socioeconomic groups, although it is more likely to be recorded by legal authorities when it occurs in this group (Empey, 1975). One study of self-reported delinquency indicated no significant differences in the average number of delinquent acts committed by lower-, middle-, and upper-class high school students (Kratcoski and Kratcoski, 1975).

Empey (1975) estimates that about 75 percent of all delinquent acts are committed by groups or gangs. They are often spontaneous rather than carefully planned. Empey suggests that gang members remain together, not because of feelings of loyalty or solidarity, but because they lose more than they gain by leaving the group.

According to Dusek (1977), delinquency is correlated with heredity, child-rearing techniques, social structure, peer group, self-concept, and personality. Chromosomal aberrations, especially those which occur in the XYY male, may also be related to aggression and criminal behavior. But parental childrearing techniques and the adolescent's relationship with parents are the best predictors of adolescent delinquency, especially for boys. The families of delinquents are characterized by overly strict discipline, parental rejection and neglect, minimal parental aspirations for the child, paternal absence, poor communication, and unaffectionate behavior.

The juvenile delinquency problem has not been solved; it is getting worse. Some advocate "get tough" actions such as imprisonment, but this may only exacerbate psychological problems such as poor self-concept, alienation from family and society, and hostility (Dusek, 1977). Clearly, the answer lies in part in better parenting, beginning when the child is very young.

Suicide

The suicide rate for the age group fifteen to nineteen increased 260 percent between 1950 and 1976 (Wynne, 1979). The rates are substantially higher for males than for females (Marks, 1980).

The suicide rate for adolescents is still lower than the rate for adults, but it is the increase that is alarming. Furthermore, it is estimated that nonlethal suicide attempts peak during adolescence and run as high as 200 per year for every one successful attempt. In adults, the ratio of attempts to successes is about ten to one (Marks, 1980).

Why have adolescents turned increasingly to such drastic and self-destructive measures? Wynne (1979) suggests that the suicide rate is an indicator of the degree of alienation. He cites the work done by Durkheim in Europe in the late nineteenth century to support his position. Durkheim found that the suicide rate was higher among Protestants than Catholics, among urban than rural dwellers, among the well-to-do than the poor, and among persons in the professions than laborers. Wynne summarizes what these data may mean:

> People [are] shielded from suicidal impulses because of the communal intensity of their religion, the stability of life patterns, the predictability of their aspirations, the intensity and complexity of their social commitments, the focus of their responsibilities, and the tangibility of their work products. . . . these forces [place] human beings in complex but predictable patterns of human relations that [move] toward identifiable goals. [p. 4]

According to Wynne, suicide is not so much the outcome of pressure itself, as of pressure without support. "Suicide does not automatically mean that a person has not been loved or cared for. It probably does mean that he was not needed by others in an immediate, tangible fashion. . . . Indeed, the most "pressured" status is that of being left without apparent and immediate responsibilities to help others" (p. 4). If Wynne is correct, then the solution to this problem may lie in our making greater efforts to include adolescents in meaningful ways in activities at home, school, and work. But this will be difficult. Work, especially, is becoming more specialized and complex, which requires an even more prolonged period of preparation — the very reason for a recognized period of adolescence in the first place.

Summary

Theories of Adolescent Social Behavior

- Erikson's theory of adolescent personality development stresses ego identity.
- Anna Freud's theory of adolescent personality development stresses frustrations due to conflict between biologically based sexual impulses and society's moral standards.
- Social learning theorists stress the role of child-rearing and modeling in adolescent development.

Socialization

- Autocratic parents who do not explain the reasons for their rules are likely to have adolescents who are low in self-confidence.
- Peer group affiliations during adolescence include the clique and the crowd.
- Peers seem to influence adolescent decisions about immediate concerns such as dress, while parents influence long-term decisions such as career choices.

Sexual Behavior

- Adolescents are more sexually active today than they were in the past.
- The incidence of pregnancy among younger teenagers is increasing. Teenage pregnancy carries social and medical risks for both parents and baby.
- There is no evidence that sex education increases adolescent sexual activity. Some schools now offer sex education courses, although they are still very controversial in many communities.

Moral Behavior

- The lack of ability to consider another person's point of view is related to delinquent behavior.
- Family interaction patterns and character development seem to be related; for example, rational-altruistic behavior is usually associated with democratic and loving family relationships.

Self-Concept

- Male adolescents tend to derive social satisfaction and self-esteem from performance and achievement, while female adolescents tend to derive social satisfaction from interpersonal relations and physical appearance.
- Coopersmith says that power, significance, virtue, and competence determine self-concept, but that a person need not do well in all areas to have a good self-concept.

Problems in Adolescence

- Many adolescents experiment with drugs such as marijuana. Adolescents use tobacco, too, and its use among adolescents has been increasing in recent years despite publicity about its risks.

- Many adolescents who drop out of school have average or above average intelligence. The drop-out rate among adolescents from lower social classes is greater than the rate among middle- and upper-class youths, probably because of stress at home and lack of understanding at school.
- The best predictor of delinquent behavior is the child-rearing technique of the child's parents. Harsh discipline, parental rejection and neglect, and low parental aspirations for the child are usually associated with delinquency.
- The suicide rate among adolescents has increased dramatically during the past three decades. It has been suggested that the increased rate may be due to a greater degree of alienation.

Selected Readings

Group for the Advancement of Psychiatry, Committee on Adolescence. **Power and authority in adolescence: The origins and resolutions of intergenerational conflict.** *Group for the Advancement of Psychiatry, 1978.* This book discusses the sources of conflict between adolescents and their parents. The book is written for professionals who work with adolescents and their parents, but the information would be useful to anyone.

Haim, A. **Adolescent suicide.** *(Trans. by A. M. Sheridan Smith.) New York: International Universities Press, 1974.* An interesting and In-depth discussion of adolescent suicide. Many French references are cited.

Ross, S. **Youth values project.** *Putney, Vt.: Youth values project, 1979.* A report of teenage sexual behavior and contraceptive use. The volume is unique in that the research was done by teenagers themselves.

Chapter 30

Knowledge and Action

School and family are important to the adolescent, just as they are to the younger child. But the relationships with each are different in adolescence: school and family must provide support but allow increasing autonomy as well. In this chapter we discuss how school and family can realize this difficult balance.

Education and Assessment

Importance of the Teacher

Educational programs for adolescents consist of junior high and high school systems, vocational schools, and special programs. These settings can vary considerably, but they all attempt to improve motivation and encourage learning. Hamachek reviewed teacher variables and found that teachers exceptionally capable of motivating and teaching students have the following characteristics:

1. willingness to be flexible, to be direct or indirect as the situation demands

2. capacity to perceive the world from the student's point of view
3. ability to "personalize" their teaching
4. willingness to experiment, to try out new things
5. skill in asking questions (as opposed to seeing self as a kind of answering service)
6. knowledge of subject matter and related areas
7. skill in establishing definite examination procedures
8. willingness to provide definite study help
9. capacity to reflect an appreciative attitude (evidenced by nods, comments, smiles, etc.)
10. conversational manner in teaching — informal, easy style. [1972, p. 237]

Good teachers are likely to motivate students to finish high school, thereby improving their earning ability, self-esteem, and preparation for life. When students do have academic problems, aid that is provided early in the academic career may be more helpful than later aid (Fitzsimmons et al., 1975). Academic assistance, counseling, and home visitations can decrease the dropout rate. Moriarty and Toussieng (1976), in a study of adolescent coping, found that the adolescents desired a classroom atmosphere of mutual respect and teachers who knew how to take charge of a classroom while retaining the willingness to admit they were wrong.

Individual teachers have a very strong influence on the development of adolescent attitudes toward school. Teacher expectations of student behavior may influence their success in school (Rosenthal and Jacobson, 1968), and students' self-concepts may be determined in part by their interactions with teachers (Davidson and Lang, 1960). In addition to teaching skills and information, teachers also influence adolescent ideas and attitudes.

Assessment Instruments

In assessing students, teachers should carefully consider what they want to test. Testing can be a valuable teaching aid, a means of grouping students for appropriate instruction as well as finding out what students have learned. Often, however, tests are used unwisely:

The status of classroom examinations is contradictory. Even groups that vigorously attack other types of testing generally concede that the measurement of classroom achievement is an essential educational process. Yet, few teachers, either in their college preparation or while practicing their art, take the necessary time to build better tests, analyze the test after it is given, fully utilize the test as a learning tool, or increase their test building skills. Hopefully those of you who plan to become teachers will take the time. [Brown, 1970, p. 281]

Students may be given standardized achievement tests in addition to tests constructed by teachers. Achievement tests are currently used for two major purposes, which are not immediately apparent: (1) to chart the strengths and deficiencies of individual school districts, and (2) to measure varied, goal-related achievements other than the general skills of language, math, reading, science, social studies, and study skills. They can be used, for example, to assess the student's knowledge of health, ecology, or the fine arts; to obtain information about student interests and possible future occupations; and to assess ability in the performing arts (Tuckman, 1975).

Of course, achievement tests are used to assess typical academic skills as well. Many adolescents take the School and College Ability Test (SCAT) and the Scholastic Aptitude Test (SAT). The SCAT predicts academic achievement, yielding verbal, quantitative, and total scores. Anastasi (1976) notes that the SCAT measures developed rather than innate abilities. That is, the SCAT scores actually "reflect the nature and amount of schooling the individual has received rather than measuring 'capacity' independently of relevant prior experiences" (p. 315).

The SAT is used in the admission and placement of college students. It gives separate scores for verbal and mathematics abilities. Most colleges and universities require that all applicants take the SAT, which is administered by the College Entrance Examination Board.

The use of intelligence tests continues to be controversial. Critics claim that intelligence tests add nothing to the educational process, and that they may even impair it. The tests may be a form of self-fulfilling prophecy. That is, students who do poorly may become less motivated to try hard on intellectual tasks, whereas students who do well may try extra hard. Intelligence tests should probably not be used in isolation to make major life decisions. In addition, if used to identify gifted students for special programs, their cultural bias may result in the enrollment of very few minority students (see FOCUS on gifted and talented students).

The assessment instruments used for adolescents are not very different from those used for adults. In addition to achievement and intelligence tests, various instruments are available to assess interests, vocational preferences, attitudes, values, personality, and self-concept. They can be given individually or in groups and may require single or multiple testing sessions. Vocational *interest inventories* in particular are widely used by students and guidance counselors to make decisions about high school courses, colleges and carreers. Two standard interest tests are especially well known: the Strong-Campbell Interest Inventory and the Kuder Vocational Preference Record. The Strong-Campbell Interest Inventory is concerned with six general occupational areas, including realistic, artistic, and social professions. The Kuder Vocational Preference Record indicates interest in a number of broad areas rather than in specific occupations.

FOCUS: Gifted and Talented Students

Gifted and talented individuals are found at every age and show special abilities in almost all areas valued by society. According to the wording of the Gifted and Talented Children's Act of 1978 (PL95-561), the gifted and talented are children in preschool through secondary school who excel or have the potential to excel in "intellectual, creative, specific academic, or leadership ability, or in the performing and visual arts and who, by reason thereof, require services and activities not ordinarily provided by the school." When the "gifted" are distinguished from the "talented," the latter are described as those doing well in a specific area of academic, social, or artistic endeavor, such as mathematics or music, whereas the former are said to possess a broad range of abilities, particularly those tapped by intelligence tests.

The term "gifted" is commonly associated with high IQ. In fact, one of the most famous research studies of gifted individuals was a longitudinal study conducted by Lewis Terman of Stanford University. Terman selected more than 1500 pupils from the California public schools with IQs of 140 and above using the Stanford-Binet test and the Terman Group Test of Mental Abilities. He followed them from 1920 until 1956, and wrote five volumes entitled *Genetic Studies of Genius* (1925–59). As a group, the individuals in the research study did well not only academically but also physically, emotionally, socially, land morally. More than half had mastered the school curriculum to a point more than two grades beyond their grade level. They memorized rapidly, retained what they learned, and had advanced vocabularies. After twenty years, only 10 percent scored below roughly the eighty-fifth percentile on IQ tests and about 80 percent of the gifted men were in the two highest occupational groups — professional, and semiprofessional-higher business — whereas only 14 percent of the men in the general population fell into these groups. The results of the study helped dispel the myth that the gifted are maladjusted or excel only in academic endeavors.

Schools, too, have identified gifted students primarily by their intelligence test scores. Because it has been argued that IQ tests are culturally biased and do not measure abilities such as creativity and leadership, the trend today is to identify gifted children using several sources of information, such as teacher and parent ratings, grades, and achievement and creativity tests, as well as intelligence tests. The identification of talented students, of course, uses primarily ratings and tests related to the student's area of expertise.

Too many bright youngsters spend much of their time in school practicing what they already know, reading books that are too easy for them, and answering questions that require little mental effort. Although gifted and talented children are not always recognized as having special needs, schools are responding to the challenge that they help all students develop their full potential. Programs for gifted children include enrichment, special grouping, and acceleration. *Enrichment* is work such as independent study, which takes place alongside age-mates in regular classrooms. It broadens the number of subjects by adding, for example, astronomy or computer science. *Special grouping* is placement in special schools, classes, or tracks, making it easier to present intellectually appropriate material. It may involve presenting the regular curriculum at a faster rate, as well as broadening the number of subjects. Because it has been argued that grouping stigmatizes both gifted and average children, creates self-fulfilling prophecies, and places barriers between students who should learn to get along, it is often suggested that gifted children spend only part of their day in special classes.

Acceleration shortens the time required to complete a program of study. It may involve, for example, early admission to elementary school, high school, or college. Acceleration places the student with new classmates who are advanced in relation to his or her old classmates, not just academically but physically and socially, too. To cope, the student must be able to advance quickly academically and be advanced enough physically and socially to be on a par with the new classmates. Because of the many changes involved in acceleration, it is important that students themselves want to enter a program rather than simply being encouraged to do so by parents.

Individual educational programs (IEPs) are effective tools for designing and implementing a combination of options for gifted children. IEPs for the gifted ensure that they are not automatically placed in an honors, enrichment, or other special program for part of the day. Instead, each child will have a program designed specifically to fit his or her capabilities.

Living with the Adolescent

How can parents help their adolescents mature into happy, competent, self-assured adults? A good relationship between parents and adolescents is crucial. Parents must begin to treat their adolescents as persons on the brink of adulthood and allow them appropriate independence.

Modeling Desired Behavior

Adults working with adolescents must also provide models of the behavior they wish adolescents to adopt. Parents who, for example, approach problems in an independent, flexible fashion may encourage adolescents to do the same. The teacher who handles conflict in a quiet, positive fashion may encourage adolescents to deal with conflict calmly themselves.

Adolescents are likely to notice discrepancies between what adults say and what they do. As with younger children, this influences their behavior:

"I take life seriously. I want to live ethically. But I am becoming cynical. I have realized that no one expects you to live up to our professed ideals. You are naive if you try. I have discovered that hypocrisy is institutionalized. It is expected at home, in school, and in society. My father is very ethical in personal relations, but he is

Good high school teachers can influence students' motivation.

almost a crook in business. Mother is a liberal in politics, but she prays and hopes that no [Blacks] move into our neighborhood. Our school teaches equality, yet the faculty is all white, and the classes are only tokenly integrated." [Ginott, 1969, pp. 130–131]

Communicating with Adolescents

Thomas Gordon (1970) suggests that parents and teachers use a method called "active listening" to encourage adolescents to accept responsibility for finding their own solutions to problems. The adult using this technique tries to understand what the adolescent is feeling and then restates it in a different form for verification:

1.

CHILD: Boy, do I have a lousy teacher this year. I don't like her. She's an old grouch.

PARENT: Sounds like you are really disappointed with your teacher.

CHILD: I sure am.

2.

CHILD: Daddy, when you were a boy what did you like in a girl? What made you really like a girl?

PARENT: Sounds like you're wondering what you need to do to get boys to like you, is that right?

CHILD: Yeah. For some reason they don't seem to like me and I don't know why. [Gordon, 1970, p. 53]

Talking openly about plans, ideas, and problems can prevent many problems from occurring and help solve them when they do occur. Taubenheim (1979) suggests that reading can help adolescents clarify their goals. Identifying with characters and knowing that others have had the same experiences and feelings can help adolescents approach their problems and find direction for their lives. Taubenheim presents an annotated bibliography of works based on Erikson's ideas about identity versus role confusion.

Including Adolescents in Family Activities

Although adolescents are very involved with school and peer group activities, they also enjoy family activities — playing Monopoly with younger siblings, challenging mom to a ping-pong game, helping little brother with his math, coaching little sister's soccer team, or being a subject for older sister's child development course. Adolescents are usually quite willing to go along with the family for an afternoon of swimming, bowling, bicycling, or tennis, or perhaps to a basketball or soccer game. They also like to debate issues with parents, and they enjoy being a part of the family decision-making team.

Adolescents still have time for family activities.

One family we know with three teenagers plays games one night a week, taken from Raudsepp and Hough's (1977) book *Creative Growth Games*. These games are designed to encourage new ways of thinking, and they provide feedback on how well the players are doing. The authors say, "The games and exercises cumulatively enhance your creative powers and enrich the vigor of your imagination" (p. 11). This family gets intellectual stimulation and has fun at the same time.

Another adolescent we know joins his family on Sunday nights to take turns reading aloud from a book chosen by the family. Although some parents may be yelling at their teenagers for watching too much TV or for turning on the X-rated cable show while they were away from home, others are providing positive alternatives.

Parents are not the only adults who play a role in the adolescent's life. "Parents build the foundation for general development and remain as strong influences, sometimes stronger than they realize, but teachers, coaches, church personnel, camp counselors, work supervisors and others who come in contact with adolescents on a regular basis can have significant effects upon them" (Brophy, 1977, p. 537). These adults often provide a wider range of models than the adolescent's own family, and they can serve as sounding boards for adolescents who wish to discuss their own parents' behavior and attitudes. Unlike the peer group, which may have a somewhat antiadult attitude, other adults can often listen objectively to an adolescent and at the same time consider problems from an adult point of view.

Living and working with adolescents can be enjoyable or agonizing, depending on how adults and adolescents interact. Open communication, discussions of values, and appropriate modeling can be very helpful in making the experience positive for both adults and adolescents. Adults who understand that adolescence

Adults other than a child's parents serve as important role models, especially during adolescence.

is a time of increasing independence when children are testing their wings, and who know that support and limits are also needed, are likely to enjoy it. Adults who insist on telling their children what to do and who blame them for every little mistake may find it difficult.

Summary

Education and Assessment

- Good teachers are flexible, can see the world from the students' point of view, are willing to experiment, are knowledgeable about their subject matter, and teach in a conversational, informal manner. Studies show that adolescents prefer a classroom atmosphere of mutual respect between teacher and students, but that they also like teachers who take charge of the classroom.
- Achievement tests chart student strengths and weaknesses and measure goal-related achievements in areas such as language, math, science, and social science. The SAT (Scholastic Aptitude Test) is an achievement test often used for college admissions and placement.
- Interest inventories are tests that provide information to use in making vocational choices.

Living with the Adolescent

- Good parent-child relations during adolescence require that parents allow the adolescent appropriate independence.
- When adults do not model the behavior they expect adolescents to adopt, adolescents notice the discrepancy.
- Active listening is a technique used in talking with adolescents that encourages them to solve their own problems.
- Adolescents are very involved with peers, but they still enjoy and need involvement with their families.
- Adults other than parents can provide important models for adolescents.

Selected Readings

Cottle, T. J. **Time's children: Impressions of youth.** *Boston: Little, Brown, 1971.* A moving book, relating the author's experiences with youth and his thoughts about this period of life. Descriptions of young people the author has known are vivid. The style is conversational. A personal and thought-provoking book.

Gordon, T. **Parent effectiveness training.** *New York: Peter Wyden, 1970.* This book teaches parents how to communicate with their children using the active listening technique.

Kamin, L. J. **The science and politics of IQ.** *Hillsdale, N.J.: Lawrence Erlbaum Associates, 1974.* This book provides information that suggests caution in the use of IQ tests. It reflects a strong environmental point of view as regards the IQ issue.

Part VIII
The Parent

Throughout our discussion of each successive stage of childhood, we have touched on the relationship between social variables and child behavior. In Chapter 8, for example, we noted the contrasts in attitudes and behavior among parents of different social classes in relation to infant language abilities. We now turn to a detailed discussion of various social phenomena and what we know about their effects on parents and families, and therefore on child rearing.

It is important to know the effects of social phenomena on children, because measures can then be taken by society to support families in various ways. Changes in social conditions affect the roles of family members, for example, and society's role may need to change if it is to provide support to children. Such change is often difficult to bring about, perhaps because it is human nature to first try to return to earlier ways of doing things in an attempt to restore calm in our lives. But rarely can we go back. As much as we would like to hold individual parents and families responsible for the "weakening" of the American family, it seems closer to the truth to suggest that our change from an agrarian to an industrial and technological society has been responsible. It is unlikely that such a basic economic trend can be reversed, or that its social repercussions on family life will cease. What we *can* do is attempt to understand the changes that are occurring and find new ways to help children lead healthy and happy lives under the new conditions.

Chapter 31

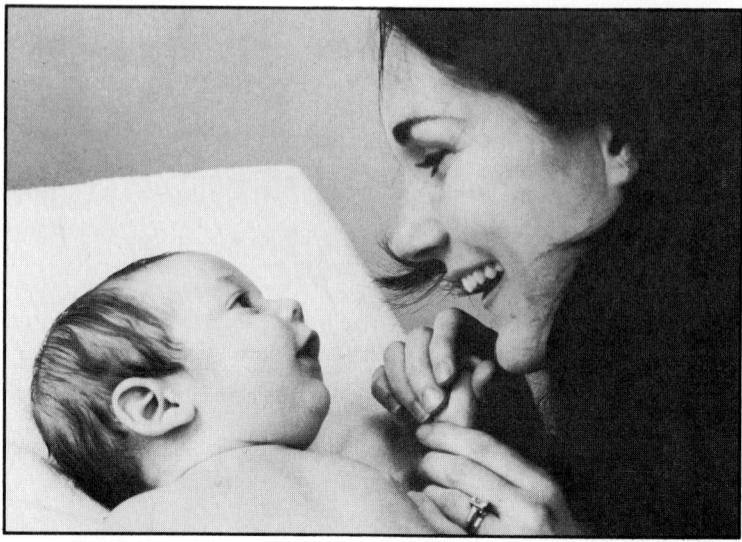

The Social Context of Parenting

American social science habitually has studied the psychological, social, and intellectual development of children in relative isolation from the social context in which they live. Parents have been studied in much the same way.... Experts, lay people, parents, and children themselves seldom think concretely about the impact on children's lives of such things as the jobs parents have and the unemployment rate. [Keniston, 1977, p. xiii]

In this chapter we will discuss the effect of social factors on the family. We will begin by describing how the American family has changed in the last few decades, and how these changes have influenced the care and development of children. We will also discuss how individuals and society in general can support better care for children.

Changes in the Family

Increased Divorce Rate

The divorce rate has never been higher than it is today. Roughly one marriage in three currently ends in divorce. In 1965 the figure was only one in four (Katz, 1979).

Sixty to seventy percent of today's divorces involve families with children under eighteen. About 1 million children *each year* go through the divorce experience. There are about 20 million children of divorced parents in the country today (Jenkins, 1977).

Changes in the Role of Women

A second change in American families is that more women are working outside the home. In 1920 women over sixteen years of age made up 20 percent of the labor force. By 1970 the figure stood at 43 percent, and by 1976 the figure had risen to 49 percent (Pifer, 1979; Smith, 1979).

An increasing number of working women are mothers: 9 percent in 1940, 27 percent in 1955, 35 percent in 1965, and 49 percent in 1976 (U.S. Women's Bureau, 1977). Unlike earlier working mothers, contemporary working mothers often have children under six. In 1948 only 13 percent of mothers with children younger than school age were in the labor force. By 1976 the number had risen to 37 percent (Keniston, 1977). Working was even more common among women with children under six *whose husbands were absent.* Fifty-six percent of these women were in the labor force in 1976 (U.S. Women's Bureau, 1977). It is predicted that these trends of greater participation of mothers in the labor force will continue (Department of Labor, Bureau of Labor Statistics, 1977), and that the largest increase will be among mothers with children under six (Smith, 1979).

One-Parent Families

About 4.5 million American families today are headed by a single parent (Orthner, Brown, and Ferguson, 1976). In 1970 only 11 percent of all families were headed by a single parent, but by 1979 nearly 19 percent fell into this category (National Association of Elementary School Principals, 1980).

Traditionally, most single-parent families have been headed by mothers. For example, in 1975 this was the case for about 88 percent of these families. However, it is estimated that by 1985 as many as 30 percent of all single-parent families may be headed by fathers (Katz, 1979). This increase is probably because views about child custody have changed and because women are increasingly likely to hold jobs that would be jeopardized if they had full responsibility for child care, just as fathers' jobs are more likely to be jeopardized today. In other words, when men earn more than women, it makes better family economic sense to award custody to women and expect fathers to provide child support. When women are paid as much as men, however, it is just as plausible to award custody to fathers and to expect mothers to contribute to child support.

The increase in single-parent families is due not only to the higher divorce rate, but also to the increasing number of unmarried women having children and raising them themselves rather than placing them in adoptive homes. Although the number of unmarried women having children has increased in all age groups, the sharpest rise has occurred among teenage women.

Today, more fathers are awarded custody of their children following a divorce than was true in the past.

FOCUS: A Short History of Child Custody

Prior to 1900 it was fathers rather than mothers who customarily received custody of children following dissolution of a marriage. This practice was based on views about the disposition of family property, not on attitudes about parental competence. Children were considered property and went to their father along with other family possessions.

At the turn of the century, however, psychological literature began to stress the special fitness of the mother for the parenting role. This led to the *"tender years doctrine"* in law, which held that the mother should receive custody of the children unless she was proven unfit. As a result of this doctrine few fathers were awarded custody of their children during the first three-quarters of this century.

Recently, however, the "tender years" doctrine has been changing. Current research on attachment indicates that the biological relationship of a parent and a child is less important than the quality of the adult's interaction with the child. An important consideration in awarding custody is which adult is the child's "psychological parent" — which parent the child has the best relationship with. Fathers are currently being awarded custody more often than they were in the past.

Changing views about sex roles have also encouraged more fathers to seek custody and have influenced the attitudes of judges and society as a whole. It is no longer assumed that fathers are less capable than mothers.

A remaining obstacle to the equal consideration of fathers and mothers for custody is the difference between the incomes of men and women. Because men's incomes are still substantially higher than women's (*America's Children*, 1976; Pearce, 1979), it is usually considered more practical economically for the mother to take custody so that the child care responsibilities do not jeopardize the father's job performance. We are unlikely to see true equality in child custody until men and women receive comparable salaries and participate equally in the labor force.

Decline of the Extended Family and the Close-Knit Community

Experts are not in complete agreement about the changes that have occurred in the *extended family*. Some claim that the *nuclear family* in America has never received extensive support from the extended family (aunts, uncles, grandparents), and that Americans have always moved from place to place because of job changes (Keniston, 1977). Other experts contend that nuclear families now receive less support from other family members than they used to, and that community ties are weaker than they once were. Bronfenbrenner, arguing the latter view, writes:

> To begin with, families used to be bigger — not in terms of more children so much as more adults — grandparents, uncles, aunts, cousins. Those relatives who did not live with you lived nearby. . . . This had its good side and its bad side.

On the good side, some of the relatives were interesting people. . . . And they gave you Christmas presents.

But there was the other side. You had to give them all Christmas presents. Besides, everybody minded your business. . . .

And it wasn't just your relatives. Everybody in the neighborhood minded your business. Again thss had its two aspects.

If you walked on the railroad trestle, the 'phone would ring at your house, and your parents would know what you had done before you got back home. . . . Sometimes you liked it and sometimes you didn't — but at least people *cared*. [1973, pp. 99–100]

Although Bronfenbrenner may be exaggerating the involvement in the nuclear family of the extended family and community, he is probably right in asserting that there was formerly more support from these sources than there is today. Help during crises (unemployment, illness, birth of children, death) and information about one's children are harder to come by than they used to be.

The Effects of Family Changes on Children

The effect of a particular change on a child is difficult to determine. At any time children are likely to be subject to many varying conditions, and the influence of any isolated factor is hard to determine. Suppose a recently divorced mother was getting a job. How could we determine whether a particular change in a child's behavior was caused by the mother's job rather than the divorce? Changes rarely occur in isolation, and this makes it difficult to know their effects.

Researchers encounter other methodological problems when studying family changes, as they do when investigating any subject. There are problems with definitions, for example. What is a "working mother"? Must she work full-time, three-quarters time, or only half-time to be included in a study? What about the question of timing? Should we consider long-term effects, short-term effects, or both?

There are additional problems associated with deciding whether to investigate a phenomenon as a whole or just certain aspects of it. Divorce, for example, is sometimes preceded by turmoil and violence in the home. When it is, children may welcome the divorce, but when it is not children may not feel the divorce is necessary.

Similarly, some divorces allow children to maintain close relationships with both parents, whereas others effectively cut children off from one parent. The two situations are likely to affect children very differently. Thus, the effects of a family change can be accurately assessed only when important conditions associated with the change are considered as well. We summarize our knowledge of the effects of family changes below, but you should keep in mind that our knowledge is limited by the difficulties inherent in studying this sort of phenomenon.

Effects of Maternal Employment

You might expect mothers who do not work to have different attitudes toward their children than mothers who hold jobs, or to differ in the emotional satisfaction they receive from the mother-child relationship. But maternal employment per se is apparently unrelated to patterns of childrearing (Yarrow et al., 1978). Mothers who work outside the home do not differ as a group from nonworking mothers in their philosophy about children, in their relationships with children, or in their practice with children. However, more working mothers are anxious about their role as mother (42 percent versus 24 percent). Much of the anxiety they express is related to the worry that their working will have a bad influence on their children (Yarrow et al., 1978).

Maternal Attitudes Toward Employment. Although a mother's being employed does not influence her childrearing, her attitude toward her role is influential. Working and nonworking mothers who are satisfied with their roles have similar relationships with their children and similar attitudes toward child-rearing. Dissatisfaction with one's role, however, does have a negative influence on mothering. This influence is greatest among mothers who are *not* employed. In the Yarrow et al. study (1978), 67 percent of the unemployed, dissatisfied mothers reported this difficulty. In terms of confidence in their role as mothers, 50 percent of the working dissatisfied mothers reported high confidence, but only 11 percent of the unemployed, dissatisfied mothers reported the same degree of confidence. Finally, more working, dissatisfied mothers expressed emotional satisfaction in their relationship with their children than did nonworking, dissatisfied mothers.

Yarrow et al. summarize their findings as follows:

> Mothers' employment status [work versus nonwork] is not related to child-rearing characteristics [but] mothers' fulfillments or frustrations in non-mother roles are related to child rearing. When mothers' motivations regarding working are taken into account, the nonworking mothers who are dissatisfied with not working (who want to work but, out of a feeling of "duty," do not work) show the greatest problem in child rearing. . . . Working mothers who prefer to work and those who do not wish to work show few group differences in child-rearing practices, probably because the working mothers (of this sample) who prefer not to work are nonetheless achieving certain valued family goals by means of their employment. (1978, p. 128)

Similar data were obtained in a study by Birnbaum (1971, cited in Hoffman, 1978, pp. 141–142), who compared mothers employed in professions with mothers capable of professional work (graduated from college with honors) who became full-time homemakers. Nonworking mothers were found to have lower self-esteem than working mothers. They also had a weaker sense of personal competence (in caring for children, among other things) and considered themselves less attractive. In addition, they reported more loneliness than working mothers. Nonworking mothers tended to note the sacrifice involved in motherhood, whereas working mothers were more likely to say that children enriched their lives or contributed to their self-fullfillment. Nonworking mothers also expressed more ambivalence and regret about their children's growing up and becoming independent.

One would expect the children of the working mothers in Birnbaum's sample to have developed better than the children of nonworking mothers, especially in terms of social adjustment. Unfortunately, however, Birnbaum did not collect data on the children.

Working mothers expect their children to be more independent than nonworking mothers do. Whether their children actually become more independent or are different in other ways has not yet been determined. One would expect them to be more independent and more achievement-oriented; however, studies indicate that independence training is associated with independence and achievement.

Childrearing Practices and Child Behavior. Childrearing in two-parent families with a working mother differs in one important respect from childrearing in families with nonworking mothers: Fathers are more involved in childrearing (Hoffman, 1978). The increased involvement of fathers seems to enhance the development of both boys and girls, especially girls' achievement (Ginzberg, 1971) and boys' social adjustment. The involvement of fathers, along with modeling of the mother, may also contribute to the lower levels of sex-role stereotyping found among children whose mothers work (Hoffman, 1978). The children of working mothers are more likely than the children of nonworking mothers to approve of maternal employment and are less inclined to assume that a mother's working will disrupt a marriage. The children of working mothers also discern more positive traits in the opposite sex, whether it be male or female. The fact that women worked did not decrease these children's evaluations of their warmth (Baruch, 1972; Broverman et al., 1972; King, Abernathy, and Chapman, 1976; Miller, 1975; Stein, 1973).

The children of employed mothers also do more housework than the children of nonworking mothers. This may have a beneficial effect, contributing to greater family cohesion. Whether this occurs depends on the age of the child, whether the parent's expectations are reasonable, and whether the parents continue to carry out their roles while depending on their children for help (Weiss, 1979). There is a difference between leaving children to cook, shop, and take care of their clothes to survive, and planning to cooperate as a family to help all family members meet their own and the family's goals.

In summary, there is no evidence that maternal employment has any adverse effect on childrearing practices on attitudes — or on children. (Recall our discussion in Chapter 9 of the effects of alternate caregiving arrangements such as day care.) Further, the fact that a mother is not employed outside the home is unrelated to significantly more positive childrearing attitudes and behaviors or child outcomes. There are undoubtedly countless mothers who work only at home and spend much of their time not in positive interactions with their children, but in front of the television set or on the phone with a friend. There are probably many mothers at home who are angry, depressed, drunk, drugged, or bored, who yell at their children constantly, ridicule and degrade them, force them to eat or refuse to feed them, or lock them in the house or out of it to avoid dealing with them.

In this country, we have tended to assess a mother's devotion to her family on the basis of whether she stays at home or takes a job. This is clearly a poor measure of effective mothering. Women can demonstrate devotion and commitment to their roles as mothers in a number of ways. There are many methods of executing parental responsibilities. As a society, it would be better for us to support a variety of parenting styles than to try to find a single parenting arrangement that is best for everyone.

Effects of Divorce

A divorce is a major crisis for every member of a family, including the children. The effects of a divorce, however, vary with the situation preceding the divorce and the parent-child relationships that follow the divorce. Before the divorce was there constant conflict between the parents? Did the child have a good relationship with the parent given custody and a poor relationship with the noncustodial parent? Factors such as these can have a crucial influence on the effects of the divorce (Luepnitz, 1979). Divorce in itself does not make a child different from a child in an intact family. In a recent study, *family process variables* such as affective relationships between the child and each parent, contact between the child and the noncustodial parent, and parental harmony were found to predict a child's stress and aggression better that the fact of divorced versus nondivorced status of the family (Hess and Camara, 1979). Again we see that the situation is more complicated than researchers might wish.

In truth, questions about the effects of divorce can only be answered by statements such as the following:

> It depends, and we really don't know; it depends on what kind of divorce it is: a tranquil arrangement in which the interests of the children are one of the foremost considerations, or a rancorous battle in which the children are considered part of the spoils. It depends on the resilience and the personal strength of the children as well as the parents involved. It depends on the circumstances, the age of the child, the economic resources of the family, the stability of the

child's home environment after the divorce, supports which are provided by the departed parent, by relatives and friends. It depends on peer influence upon the child, the mores, the laws and the policies of the community, and the society in which the divorce occurs. [Zill, 1978, p. 3]

Only recently has research been undertaken that takes into account important aspects of the divorce situation, not merely the parents' marital status. We will know much more about the effects of divorce in a few years than we know now. Some of our current knowledge of the effects of divorce can be summarized as follows:

1. Children usually undergo an emotional upset following a divorce. They become angry, depressed, anxious, fretful, or aggressive. They usually mourn the loss of the noncustodial parent or the loss of the mother-father-child family (Hess and Camara, 1979; Toomin, 1974).
2. The effects of a divorce on a child apparently depend on the child's age and level of development (Wallerstein and Kelly, 1975).
3. Children who live with the opposite-sex parent following a divorce show poorer social adjustment than children who live with the same-sex parent (Warshak and Santrook, 1979). This may explain why divorce leads to more serious adjustment problems for boys; mothers have traditionally been given custody of children.

The effects of divorce on a child are influenced in large measure by the child's relationship with the noncustodial parent.

4. Children of divorced parents report more feelings of rejection than children not involved in divorce, but children who considered their parents' marriage "unhappy" reported even higher levels of rejection. The highest levels of rejection were found among children of never-married mothers, but this may be due to low income and limited education rather than marital status (Zill, 1978).

5. The quality of the child's continuing relationship with his or her parents after the divorce is the most important predictor of the child's adjustment to the divorce. Children adjust best when they continue to have a good relationship with both parents; their adjustment is poorest when their relationships with both parents are poor (Hess and Camara, 1979).

6. Children of divorced parents may be given more responsibility in the family after the divorce, and they may have a greater voice in family decisions (Weiss, 1979). This may result in greater growth and self-esteem in children old enough to accept the responsibilities, but too much responsibility can have a negative effect and lead to resentment.

The year immediately following the divorce is the most disruptive. Disruption peaks at about one year. During this period the play of young children is less mature and less imaginative. These children are more aggressive, and seek help, attention, and proximity to adults more often. They also exhibit fewer positive affective behaviors such as smiling and hugging, and more negative affective behaviors, such as pouting and scowling (Hetherington et al., 1979). Boys are especially likely to have difficulties interacting with peers, and they are often rejected by their peer group, probably because of their negative behavior. By the end of two years many families become stable again, although boys may continue to have problems with peers (Hetherington, et al., 1979).

Adults working with children of divorced parents must be sensitive to the turmoil they may experience. Teachers must realize that energy previously devoted to schoolwork may be absorbed in worry about home. Books such as Earl Grollman's *Talking about Divorce* can guide adults trying to help children adjust.

Effects of Single-Parent Family Life

Being raised by one parent rather than two does not inevitably have a detrimental effect on children. Single-parent families do, however, have an unusually large number of potentially problematic characteristics, such as low income and low level of education. These conditions do adversely affect families and children.

As mentioned earlier, most single-parent families are headed by women, who are divorced, separated, or widowed, or who were never married. They have one thing in common: their average income is well below the average income of families headed by males. In fact, about half of all families with incomes at the poverty level or below are headed by women (Bureau of Census, 1974). Since

FOCUS: Child Abuse: Its Incidence and Social Correlates

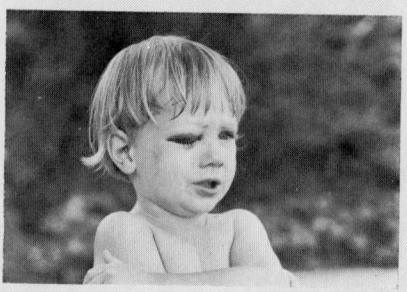

Child abuse victim

It is estimated that more than three out of every hundred children are *at risk* of serious injury from their parents each year. The actual incidence of physical abuse is difficult to determine because some cases go unreported, but it is estimated that the number is between 1.4 and 1.9 million children each year (Gelles and Straus, 1979).

Some experts claim that the incidence of abuse has increased in recent years, but others suggest that the increase can be attributed to the establishment of child abuse hotlines and the public's heightened sensitivity to the problem, which has resulted in more cases being recognized and reported. In California in 1968, 4000 cases of abuse were reported; in 1972 the number stood at 40,000. Similar increases have occurred in Florida (10 cases versus 30,000) and Michigan (721 cases versus 30,000) (Kempe and Kempe, 1978).

According to Kempe and Kempe (1978, p. 24), child abuse is associated with four conditions: (1) parents have a background of emotional and physical deprivation; (2) parents consider a child difficult, unlovable, or disappointing; (3) there is a crisis in the parent's life such as loss of a job or an argument with a boss; and (4) the parent is socially isolated and feels that he or she cannot get help.

Gelles and Straus (1979) have also specified some correlates of child abuse: (1) Parents who as children were abused or who witnessed violence between their own parents are more likely to be abusive themselves. (2) Parents with the lowest incomes have the highest rates of violence although abuse occurs within families at all income levels. Blue-collar workers have a higher rate of abuse than white-collar workers. (3) Unemployed parents or a father who works only part time is more likely to be abusive. (4) Stress, such as trouble with a boss, family illness, or sexual difficulties, can also lead to abuse. Middle-income families are particularly vulnerable to these stresses, perhaps because they interfere with their aspirations. High-income families can apparently shield themselves from many sources of stress with their money. Low-income families are perpetually under stress, which probably accounts for their persistently high rate of abuse. (5) Socially isolated parents are more abusive than parents with ties to other people or to community groups. (6) Cultural norms can also influence abuse. The acceptance of physical punishment as a tool to "teach" children and of physical violence between spouses as is justified in some circumstances is associated with a higher incidence of abuse.

Additional evidence that social context is related to the incidence of abuse comes from a study by Garbarino and Crouter (1978), who also found that income level, social isolation, and other factors were related to levels of abuse.

Low income and social conditions are clearly important factors in child abuse. Until these conditions are eliminated, abuse will not be eradicated.

women head only about 15 percent of all families in the United States, they are disproportionately represented in the ranks of poverty families (*America's Children*, 1976).

There are two major reasons why single-parent families headed by women suffer economically. Women are more likely than men to take part-time jobs and move in and out of the labor force as they balance work with family responsibilities. They have traditionally acquired less education than men in anticipation of filling traditional roles as wives and mothers. As a result, women have not acquired seniority in jobs and have stayed in the lowest-paid and most vulnerable positions. In addition, occupations typically filled by women pay lower wages than occupations filled by men (Pearce, 1979).

Single-parent families headed by women are also influenced by the fact that many of these women started families as teenagers. Women who have children as teenagers have been found to have less education, lower incomes, more children, and a higher rate of divorce than women who delay childbearing. These factors, in turn, disrupt a mother's career and limit her opportunity to further her education (The Alan Guttmacher Institute, 1976; Stevens, 1980).

In earlier chapters of this book, we discussed the effects of low socioeconomic status on various aspects of child development. Language development, cognitive development, social development, and success in school are all closely correlated with social class. The quality of prenatal care and health care during childhood are also correlated with social class (Keniston, 1977). In addition, although child abuse and neglect are found in all socioeconomic strata, abuse and neglect are especially common among children from families of low socioeconomic status (Garbarino and Crauter, 1978; Gelles and Straus, 1979).

In summary, single-parent families are faced with a whole host of difficulties, but these may not be caused by a family's only having one parent. To predict how children are affected in a specific situation, we would need to know many details: (1) the reasons why the family only has one parent; (2) the nature of the relationships between the single parent, the children, and other members of the nuclear and extended family; (3) the parent's level of education; and (4) the employment history and income of the parent.

Support for Parents and Families

Every period of history has seen changes in the organization of society. When farm production became mechanized people moved to the cities. When cities became crowded and beset with problems such as crime, many people moved to the suburbs or the country. (This movement was made possible in large part by the construction of the interstate highway system.) Today, with the high cost of oil and suburban housing, people are moving back to the cities.

Families must adapt to each of these social changes, and society, in turn, makes adaptations to families. Society often changes slowly, however, and families sometimes lack the support they need to function smoothly in novel circumstances. People are always predicting that the breakdown of the stable, caring family has occurred. Our view is that families and children can thrive in many different circumstances. The stress of newer arrangements can be eased by various social adaptations, some of which are discussed below.

Out-of-Home Care for Young Children

The children of working parents must be cared for while their parents are at their jobs. Some parents can find and afford good group day care. Others find good family day care homes — homes licensed by the state to care for a small number of children — or rely on babysitters, who may be family members, neighbors, or friends. In other instances, older siblings are left in charge of the younger children, or young children are simply left at home alone to fend for themselves.

The most common arrangement is to leave children in the care of babysitters in the children's home. Most children cared for outside their own home are in family homes, but only a small proportion of these homes are licensed. In 1975, 777,000 children were cared for in licensed homes, compared to 6,755,000 in unlicensed hou es. Only about 12 percent of the children requiring care currently attend group day care centers — about 850,000 in 1975 (*America's Children*, 1976).

Most of the informal care used by working parents is of very good quality, but some of it is not. Many parents have trouble finding good care. Paying for care is often a problem, too. You will remember that women heads-of-household usually have low incomes, and many of the women in two-parent families who work do so because the family needs money. In fact, it is estimated that the majority of all women who work do so for eco nomic reasons, rather than self-fulfillment (Smith, 1979). Families such as these may have trouble paying for good quality care and meeting other financial needs at the same time. We believe that public policy should support parents and families by helping to fund a range of alternate care options: center-based day care, employer-operated day care, and family day care.

In addition to child care for very young children, there is also a need for a place for school-age children to go after school while their parents are still at work. Many schools and agencies now provide after-school day care for these children (Genser and Baden 1980). In many cases the programs are organized and paid for largely by parents. More programs of this sort are needed if we are to provide for all children who need them. The alternative is to leave young children at home or on the streets for several hours each day without supervision.

One concern about day care arrangements is that they will diminish the family's influence on childrearing. Parents worry that their relationship with their children will be harmed, and that children will actually be raised by the government or by "society." But parents can monitor the care their children receive to be sure it is consistent with their values and beliefs. The alternative is that children will not be reared by anyone except perhaps the television set.

Finally, there is no evidence that part-time separation from parents such as occurs when children attend day care interferes with a close parent-child relationship. Studies indicate that children's attachment to their mothers, for example, is not disrupted by day care attendance (Caldwell et al., 1970; Kagan, 1978; Kilmer, 1979).

Flexible Working Schedules and Other Methods of Assisting Parents

> I make breakfast. [My wife] sits with them while I step in and out of the shower and jump into my clothes. I drink a cup of coffee as I drive them, one to one school and one to the other. I work steadily until noon, when Deb and I have a conference call about the afternoon pickups. At four I pick up Alan at day care and drive on to get Lee at a friend's. We have to stop on the way pome for more sequins for the Halloween costume they are making. At home I bathe them and Deb makes dinner. I clean up dinner, while Deb reads to them, then I practice recorder with Lee for a minute and tell Alan a funny story to make up for the time he resents my spending with Lee. Then after who knows how many drinks of water they are asleep. [Ditzion and Wolf, 1978, p. 61]

Working parents must often work out complicated schedules such as this to fulfill all their responsibilities. Employers can help by allowing flexible scheduling of work hours so that parents can meet children's needs. For example, if one parent starts work early in the day and the other starts later, one parent will be home to get the children off to school, and the other will be home when the children return from school in the afternoon. Flexible scheduling might also permit a single parent to start work late in the morning to take advantage of an afternoon day care program at the child's elementary school.

Another work-related benefit is parental leave when a child is born. Increasingly, women workers are being given maternity leave, but in most cases leave is quite brief and must be taken without pay. Keniston (1977) has suggested that parents be granted twelve weeks of pregnancy leave, which they can split between themselves if they wish. In Sweden, recent legislation grants parents nine months of leave from work. The parents can decide how to divide the time between them, and health insurance reimburses their lost earnings (Gustafsson, 1979).

Parents are under a lot of pressure. We make them choose between work and their children, and often they both suffer. Women are especially vulnerable. One mother made these comments about the pressures she faced when her baby was born:

> When he was born I was determined to show all the people at work that it wouldn't take its toll on me. That I was different. I would stay up until morning, trying to prepare work for the next day, nursing between times. It was a nightmare. . . . Looking back, I think that it

would have been fine to ask a fellow worker to take some of the slack. . . . I think I bought the mentality that in order for a woman with a child not to be looked down upon, she has to be better than anyone else, to overcome other people's expectations that mother's energies are being siphoned off. I think the society should support rather than penalize mothers for taking time off. [Ditzion and Wolf, 1978, p. 48]

A father had this to say:

I took over night feedings. Those moments of feeding and rocking my daughter in the quiet hours of night were extraordinarily precious to me. On the other hand, I woke up each morning to face a hard day at the office feeling wiped out, and slightly irritable as I anticipated facing my colleagues, who had no sympathy for my post-partum stress. [Ditzion and Wolf, 1978, p. 43]

As a society, we could make life easier for new parents by changing our current attitudes and instituting new work arrangements such as job-sharing, flexible schedules, and childrearing leaves.

Parent Education: Before Children Are Born and After

Our expectations do not always correspond to reality. In most areas of our lives we take this into account and try to prepare ourselves for new roles. When we take a new job, for example, we generally undergo a period of training. Preparing for a new role does not necessarily mean we will succeed, but it does familiarize us with the problems we may encounter and possible solutions to them.

The discrepancy between our expectations about becoming parents and its realities is often great. This is especially true today, when the extended family, close-knit communities, and age-integrated neighborhoods cannot always be counted on for help. The "on-the-job training" approach to learning about parenting is often full of surprises, as the parents who made these mistakes discovered:

I grew up with the idea that women have an instinctive way of knowing what a child's needs are and they do it wonderfully and they are always calm and happy and graceful about it. When I discovered that I very often didn't know how to handle the baby, rather than relax and figure out what to do, I felt that I was not a good mother. [Ditzion and Wolf, 1978, p. 45]

When I used to think about having children I imagined us all fitting together neatly — like the parts of a puzzle. Come to find out, often it's more like pieces competing for the same space. You want the last piece of cheese, so do they. You want to read and they want you to read to them. You need to work and they need you — they have fallen down, gotten scared, have something wonderful they have to show you right that minute. [Ditzion and Wolf, 1978, p. 62]

At just the time when you need others for models and information the most, you are often isolated in your own little house with your own little kids and no institutional affiliation. [Ditzion and Wolf, 1978, p. 45]

You think to yourself, "Help her to eat with a spoon and then you can have the space to eat your own dinner." What you don't realize is what comes between — the banging on the metal tray with it, the constant putting it back into her hand, the food-filled spoon dropping to the floor. [Ditzion and Wolf, 1978, p. 55]

In an effort to diminish the surprises involved in parenting, more junior and senior high schools are offering courses that give a realistic picture of childrearing and describe the probable results of making various decisions. Some excellent curriculum materials have been developed for these courses, including the *Exploring Parenthood* materials produced by the Education Development Center in Newton, Massachusetts.

Because the extended family *(below)* is rare today, young parents must obtain information about child rearing from other sources, such as parenting classes *(right)*.

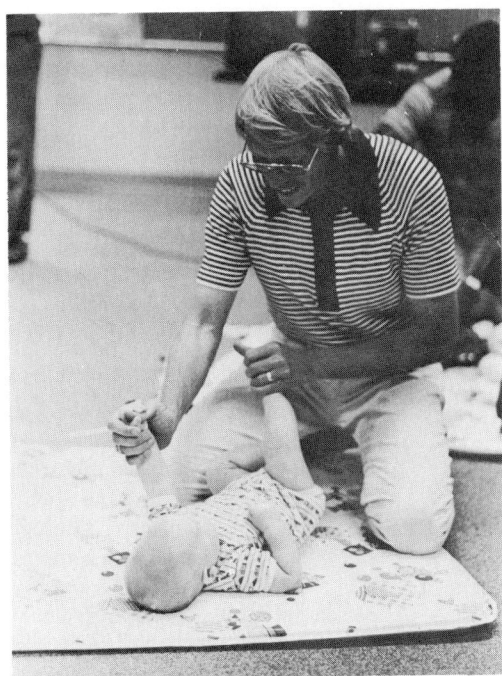

Parent education should also continue after adults have children. Programs of this sort could involve discussion groups where parents could share information and concerns with each other, and seminars with guests such as nurses, educators, or safety experts. Groups such as the Red Cross, the YMCA and YWCA, health clinics, and church and school groups sponsor programs of this sort now, but they are not abundant enough to meet parents' needs. Many federally funded parent education programs, such as Levenstein's mother-child home program and Gordon's Florida Parent Education Program (Chapters 10 and 15) have also been started in the last fifteen years, but these programs are often offered to a particular population such as low-income parents.

Parent hotlines also supply information and emergency advice. Television and radio are another obvious source of information for parents.

Parents of children with special needs often need more support than other parents. Parents of blind or deaf children must be taught special techniques to facilitate their children's development. Sylvia Frailberg's program for blind babies and their parents was described in Chapter 6. The parents of children with special problems may also need relief from the stresses of parenting and opportunities to talk to other parents with similar problems. Sometimes schools conduct programs for handicapped children between birth and three years of age. When the child is a young infant, the program may consist of home visits by a teacher or other specialists such as a physical therapist. As the child gets older, he and other special needs children may be brought together in a classroom setting where they not only receive individual therapy but also participate in small-group activities. Parents may attend the program once a week and discuss observations and questions. Sometimes schools run Saturday sessions to accommodate parents who work during the week. Such programs can be immensely helpful to both children and parents.

Changing Attitudes

Many of the suggestions discussed above require well-organized efforts by a number of people to yield good results. Other changes are easier to accomplish, however, because they involve a change in individual behavior.

> I was shopping in the food co-op late one afternoon. There was a woman there with a child who was screaming with exhaustion. She was trying to weigh vegetables and tend the child all at once. The bag over the handles of the stroller was overloaded and threatened to tip the baby out onto the floor. All around her other adults went about their shopping as if nothing was happening. I don't know how they could ignore her. I'd been there before and could remember what I'd wanted. I went over, and began to get the groceries she still needed, while she picked up the baby and walked him round and round. In two minutes he was asleep and she could be at peace. [Ditzion and Wolf, 1978, p. 68]

We could all help parents by offering our assistance in such situations, but we often ignore parents in distress. A student of one of the authors told of a similar predicament she experienced while registering for classes. She had brought her nine-month-old with her because she could not find a babysitter. As she stood in line, the baby began to cry. She tried the usual means of soothing her — talking, offering her a cracker, picking her up — but nothing worked. The trouble was a soiled diaper. As the baby cried, the other students in line glared at her. The mother had waited in line for an hour and didn't want to lose her place, but she needed to take her baby to the restroom. The mother said she should have asked the student standing behind her to save her place and watch the stroller while she changed the baby, but she sensed such a hostile attitude — "Why don't you and your baby go home where you belong" — that she left without asking and lost her place in line.

We often communicate messages to parents to keep away from us. The message is sometimes overt, as in "adults only" communities, and sometimes more subtle — a hostile stare, perhaps. Another problem occurs in buildings and public transportation, which are often inaccessible to parents with strollers (as well as people in wheelchairs), unless they want to pick up the stroller and baby and lug both up the stairs. Barriers of this sort could be eliminated.

It would also be helpful to provide more play areas for children in stores, banks, and museums. A recent article described the use of such areas in Denmark:

> The Danes have ingeniously seized areas otherwise unused, converting them for play; they have introduced play spaces (sometimes very small) into unusual environments such as banks, stores, shopping centers, and shopping malls. . . . For example, Magasin du Nord (a large department store in central Copenhagen) maintains a playroom, staffed and well-equipped where children may play under supervision at no cost while their parents are shopping. Banks often

A play space for young children in a dentist's office

have a small play table in the lobby with toys attractive to children who have to wait for parents to transact business. On the shopping malls or walking streets, play areas are set up with slides, a tricycle-ring-around, or some other active equipment. . . . Other play areas for children are found in museums and on the ferries. The Modern Art Museum has equipped a room next to the entrance where children may paint, draw, or make collages while adults enjoy a leisurely visit through the museum. [Mitchell and Anderson, 1980, pp. 2–3]

These are just a few of the ways a society can let parents and children know that, rather than being a bother, they are welcome in the mainstream of life. We can all help in small ways. Broader innovations such as the creation of play spaces in places of business can also be accomplished through the efforts of concerned people.

Other people's children should be of interest to all of us, for what happens to them touches our lives as well. They become our neighbors, employees, junior colleagues at work, daughters or sons-in-law, and the parents of our grandchil-

Promoting children's welfare should be everyone's — not only parents' — concern.

dren. In a few years, we will call them to repair our plumbing, work on our automobiles, defend us in court, or operate to save our lives. By supporting parents, we support their children and ensure a better quality of life for ourselves. In addition, people are living longer today, and we often depend for many years on the help of those who once depended on us. Our children's benevolence toward us may be shaped by the care we give them. The frequency of abuse of older parents by their children suggests that we have not done very well. There is no escaping it; the energy we invest in our children can make life better for us all. A refusal to accept our responsibilities to our children today will affect all of us tomorrow. The preferable course seems obvious.

Summary

Changes in the Family

- In the last few decades, the American family has changed greatly. Today, one-third of all marriages end in divorce, and 60 to 70 percent of all divorces currently involve minor children.
- The rising divorce rate and the growing number of unmarried mothers has led to an increase in the number of single-parent families. This, in turn, has caused an increase in the number of women entering the labor force who have young children.
- It is predicted that more single-parent families will be headed by fathers in the future than has been true in the past.

The Effects of Family Changes on Children

- There is no evidence that a mother's working outside the home is detrimental to her children. A mother's attitude toward her role has a stronger influence on her childrearing than her status as a working or nonworking mother.
- Divorce has a strong influence on children, but its effect on a particular child depends on the circumstances of the divorce. Children fare better when they can maintain relationships with both parents after the divorce.
- Most single-parent families are headed by women. Women usually have lower incomes than men, which makes them vulnerable to many stresses. This situation inevitably affects their children. Child abuse is correlated with many negative social factors such as low income level, feelings of isolation, and unemployment.

Support for Parents and Families

- Most children with working mothers are cared for by babysitters in the children's homes. The majority of children cared for outside their own homes are in family homes rather than group day care centers.

- Support for parents and parenting can take many forms, including better day care and flexible working schedules. Also, education for parenthood is needed both before and after people become parents.
- A change in our individual attitudes toward parents and children would provide them with much-needed support.

New Terms

tender years doctrine   nuclear family
extended family   family process variables

Selected Readings

Carlson, N. S., Whiren, A., and Howe, D. **After-kindergarten day care.** *Young Children* 36 (1980): 13–20. Discusses the need for after kindergarten day care and describes the components of an actual program.

Finkelhor, D. **Sexually victimized children.** *New York: Free Press, 1979.* Describes a specific type of child abuse: sexual abuse.

Skeen, P., and McKenry, P. C. **The teacher's role in facilitating a child's adjustment to divorce.** *Young Children* 35 (1980): 3–12. Authors first briefly review what we know about children's reactions to divorce, then discuss how schools and teachers can provide support to children whose parents divorce. Specific suggestions are made about working with children and their parents.

Appendix: Student Projects

Part I: Introduction

1. Arrange to interview a teacher or parent of children between the ages of three and eight. Tell the teacher or parent that you wish to obtain information about children's behavior for a course in child development, and that you will need approximately half an hour of his or her time.

When you begin the interview, tell the teacher or parent that you are particularly interested in hearing about specific situations in which a child's behavior was at first very puzzling, but later made sense when more information was obtained or more thought was given to the situation. You might begin the interview by saying, "Tell me about something a child [or your child] did that really puzzled you at the time — you didn't know what was upsetting the child, what the child was trying to tell you, or what gave the child a certain idea. Then tell me how you solved the puzzle or gained some understanding of the child's behavior. For example, did you ask someone else for information, think back to previous experiences with this child, consult a book, or what?"

This interview should provide you with some good examples of child behavior and the situations with which teachers and parents are confronted. You may wish to keep information obtained from this project and try to explain the child behavior as you gain information through the course. You can then compare your interpretations of the child's behavior with those provided by the teacher or parent at the time of the interview.

2. Check the schedule of TV programs in your newspaper to see if there are any special programs on children's rights, problems with the educational system, special needs, or changes in the family and their effect on children. Watch any such program and keep notes on its content. Write a summary report and comment on the program's quality, indicating why it was good or poor.

3. You will need to do this project with a partner. Arrange to observe one child in a group of at least three children. You might be able to observe a child in a classroom setting, at home, or on a playground. Decide with your partner which child you both will observe. Then observe for five minutes, and attempt to write down everything the child does. At the end of the five minutes, compare observations with your partner. Did both of you write down essentially the same behaviors, or did each of you note things that the other person missed? Check each other's notes for detail and absence of conclusions. Did either of you write down conclusions rather than descriptions of behavior?

Next, decide with your partner on some specific behavior that you wish to observe. This time, you will be observing the frequency of a single behavior. Perhaps you will note the number of times the child talks to another child or acts aggressively. First, you will need to define the behavior you will be observing to make certain that both of you agree. You may also wish to practice observing for the behavior for a short time and compare observations to establish reliability. Then, observe the child for a longer period of time, perhaps fifteen or twenty minutes, noting the behavior of interest. At the end of the observation period, compare your frequency count with that of your partner. Do they agree?

What are the advantages and disadvantages of each way you observed? In what situations might you use each method?

4. Arrange to interview two or three adults who have had extensive experience with children (teachers, parents, social workers, etc.). Prepare a list of child behaviors cast in terms of questions about causation. For example, you might ask:

- "Why do some children know how to read by age six, whereas others do not know how until age eight?"
- "Why do some children walk by the time they are a year old, whereas others do not walk until sixteen or eighteen months?"
- "Why do some children become fearful of new experiences, whereas other children greet new experiences with interest and curiosity?"

You will need about eight or ten questions. Take notes on the explanations given by the people you interview; then try to categorize the responses in terms of the theories discussed in the text. Do some people tend to rely on one theory? Does anyone use a variety of theories as explanations, depending on the behavior in question? Would you have offered different explanations from the ones you obtained? What theory or theories would your explanations have been consistent with?

Part II: The Beginning

1. Contact your local chapter of the March of Dimes. Visit its local office and obtain printed material on birth defects and their prevention. Try to arrange for a brief interview with someone who works in the March of Dimes office to learn about the activities undertaken by this organization to prevent birth defects. Be sure to check with your course instructor if you wish to do this project. If several members of the class are interested in learning about the March of Dimes's activities, divide up the tasks to avoid placing a burden on the March of Dimes personnel. For example, one person might contact the office and collect printed leaflets, another might interview a member of the office staff to gain an overview of the activities of the March of Dimes, and still another might investigate audiovisual materials available from the March of Dimes. Then you could meet as a group to pool information and develop a report.

2. Contact the community relations director at a local hospital to obtain information about the hospital's policies and procedures for allowing fathers to participate in the birth of their children. Most hospitals have brochures on this. You might also ask the community relations director for the name of the head nurse on the maternity floor and try to arrange to talk with this person about fathers' involvement in the birth process. Be sure to prepare a list of questions before your interview.

Most hospitals now provide "expectant parent" classes in order to prepare mothers and fathers for labor and delivery. Ask the community relations director for the name of the person who is in charge of this program at the hospital and contact the person to obtain information about the content of such courses. Be sure to prepare a list of questions before talking with this person. You might ask if it is possible for you to visit such a class for one session.

3. Interview your own mother or grandmother (or both) to learn about their experiences in giving birth. It would be interesting to know if their husbands were allowed to spend any time with them while they were in labor or if the husbands were present for delivery. Also ask them if they received any education about childbirth. Was any anesthesia used during labor and delivery? If yes, what type? Did they have any options with regard to type of anesthesia, or did the physician simply make the decision? How long did they remain in the hospital following delivery? How much contact was permitted with the new baby? Ask any other questions of interest to you. Then compare your mother's and/or grandmother's experiences with what you have learned about the experiences of mothers today. Have things changed very much? How?

4. One of the best-selling government publications is a pamphlet entitled *Infant Care*. It was first published in 1914 and has since undergone many revisions. Try to locate several old issues in your city or school library. Compare the advice from issue to issue. How has it changed over the years? What might account for the changes? Has any advice remained essentially the same for several decades?

5. Contact a local hospital that has a nursery for premature infants. Find out what its policies are concerning parent involvement in the care of premature infants.

If you live in a large city, there may be a hospital with a nursery for high-risk infants (infants born very prematurely or infants with other problems). Contact the hospital, starting with the community relations director, and obtain information about the nursery. Try to arrange to visit the nursery and talk to staff who work in it. (If several students are interested in doing this project, efforts should be coordinated to reduce the burden placed on hospital staff.) You may wish to ask how much parent involvement there is, what problems some of the infants have and what type of care is necessary, how long some infants must stay in the nursery, etc.

Part III: The Infant

1. Visit a toy store or the toy department of a department store. Look at toys marked for use by infants of various ages: birth to three months, three to six months, six months to one year, one year to eighteen months. Compare the toys and think about the physical skills the toys in each age category require. Do the toys for the younger infants require looking and use of hands and arms? Do the toys for older infants require locomotor skills?

Make a list of from eight to ten toys you looked at. Beside each toy list the physical skills you think an infant would need to use it.

2. Arrange to observe an infant who is about one year old. Tell the child's parents that you wish to observe the child for a class project and that you are particularly interested in the child's physical skills. You will want to note the baby's prehension skills (use of hands) and locomotor skills (use of legs). Take notes as you observe and be careful to write down exactly what the baby does. For example, instead of saying "baby picks up red cube," note that "baby picks up a red cube from the floor with his right hand, using only his thumb and index finger to grasp it." Also ask the parent what the baby's birth weight and length were and what the baby's current weight and height are. Decide if this baby's growth rate and motor development are similar to the norms cited in your book.

3. Arrange to observe and interact with an infant between one and one and a half. Present the object permanence task to the baby. You will need some object or objects the baby is interested in and can grasp in its hand. You will also need three opaque cloths, each about one foot square. In addition, if you are testing an older infant (sixteen to eighteen months), you will need a small box for the hidden displacement step.

Get acquainted with the baby first. This will require ten to fifteen minutes of gentle interaction with the parent close by. Then give the baby one of the objects to play with. When the baby has grasped it and seems intent on looking at it, place the object under the cloth. Note the baby's reaction. If the baby finds the toy, allow the baby to play with it for a minute or two. Then hide the object again. If the infant again finds it, allow another brief play period. If the infant's interest in this toy is beginning to wane, offer a new toy. Now place another cloth near the first cloth and when you take the toy away this time, place it under the new, not the old, cloth. Where does the baby search?

If you are observing an older infant (sixteen to eighteen months), switch the placement of the cloths and see what the baby does when you next hide the toy. Also, try the hidden displacement task. (Place the object in the box first, and then place box and object under the cloth, dump the toy, and then show the baby the empty box.)

Decide in what stage of sensorimotor development the baby is.

4. You will need to work with several of your classmates on this project. Each student should arrange to visit the home of an infant who is between six months and one year of age. Tell the parent that you are interested in learning about the types of toys that girl versus boy infants are given to play with and that some of your classmates are visiting boy infants, whereas others are visiting girl infants.

When you visit the infant, make a complete inventory of the baby's toys, noting any important characteristics. For example, squeeze toys come in a variety of shapes and sizes. Some are shaped as animals, others are shaped as footballs or basketballs, and still others are shaped as tools such as hammers.

Try to find out from the baby's parents who gave each toy to the baby. Note this beside the name and description of the toy.

Note: You will need to be careful not to make a parent feel uncomfortable as you do this project. Avoid making any judgmental comments about the types of toys any infant has. After each member of your project team has collected his or her information, meet as a group to organize and analyze the data. You may find it useful to categorize toys on your list into the following groups:

a. Toys Possessed about Equally by Both Boy and Girl Infants
b. Toys Possessed Only by Boy Infants
c. Toys Possessed Only by Girl Infants
d. Toys Purchased for Boys by Males
e. Toys Purchased for Girls by Females
f. Toys Purchased for Girls by Males
g. Toys Purchased for Boys by Females

Try to summarize your findings. Indicate the socioeconomic level or other social context variables important in interpreting your results. For example, were all of the infants whose toys you and your group inventoried from middle-class homes? Were some babies the firstborn in the family whereas others were third or fourth? (These latter infants may have a wider variety of toys simply because they have inherited the toys from older siblings of both sexes.)

Part IV: The Toddler

1. Try to obtain information from your own parents about your height at various ages from two to five. Use Garn's multipliers and see how well your height then predicted your present height. For age two, use 2.06 if you are male, and 2.01 if you are female. For age five, use 1.62 if you are male, and 1.51 if you are female.

2. Review in the text the research on locative prepositions reported by Clark. Work with a toddler. Take along materials such as a box, a block, a small toy table — any objects that allow the positioning of another object on, in, or under them. Also take along small toys to place on, in, or under the target objects. Using two of the target objects at a time, give the child directions to place an object on, in, or under the appropriate target object. Decide beforehand how you are going to present the task, and make a list of your directions in the order you plan to present them. Then note on your paper what the child does.

Did the child's responses to the directions vary depending on the position allowed by the target objects? Was *in* preferred as Clark suggested?

3. Find out from your course instructor or some other source if there are programs in your community for infants or toddlers with special needs. If there are any, arrange to visit one and observe. Note the activities, special equipment, and techniques used. Try to talk with the teacher, director, or physical therapist who works with the program to learn who sponsors it, how often children attend, why certain materials and techniques are used, and so on.

4. Interview a teacher or a director of a day care center or nursery school for toddlers or preschool-age children. Discuss his or her techniques for lessening departure protest and separation distress. It would be a good idea to interview teachers or directors from different schools to see if their ideas and procedures vary. Use your text to evaluate the information you obtain from the people you interview.

Part V: The Preschool Child

1. Arrange to interview two children, one about age four and the other close to six, in order to learn what they understand about dreams. Use the following questions in your interview:

a.   Do you know what a dream is? If the child says no, ask the child if he or she ever dreams while asleep. If the child relates a dream, assume that the child understands what a dream is.

b.   Where do dreams come from? What makes them? Here you are seeking evidence about children's understanding that dreams are created by them, in their heads. Young children typically have no awareness that the dream actually comes from them, and they will say something else creates it.

c.   Where do dreams happen? Where is the dream when you are dreaming? You are probing for the child's understanding that a dream occurs or takes place in his or her head. Young children typically view dreams as "real" things and will say that they take place in the room, under the bed, etc.

d.   Could someone else see your dream? Where would they look? This is another probe about where a dream takes place. A child who knows that dreams take place in the head will deny that anyone else can see the dream.

e.   What do you dream with? This is another probe about the source of the dream. A child who thinks dreams are created in the head will say that you dream with your head or your mind. A younger child may say that you dream with your eyes and your ears, indicating that the dream is outside of you and that dreaming means watching this external creation.

f.   Why do you dream? What sends them? This is another probe about the child's thoughts about where dreams come from.

Note: Children may begin to tell you about a dream they have had. It is best to listen with interest and then go back to the questions.

You will need to write down the child's responses to the questions or record them with a tape recorder. Analyze the child's responses and decide which stage the child's behavior is most consistent with.

2. Arrange to conduct the Piagetian conservation of number task with at least two preschool children, one around the age of five, and one around the age of three. (Try to obtain the exact age of the child in years and months.)

To conduct the task, you will need twenty-five objects, such as small colored cubes, poker chips, or paper shapes. All items should be identical. Begin the task by explaining that you wish to play a game with the child. The game starts when you build a road with cubes, chips, or whatever. (Use eight to ten objects to make your road.) Then ask the child to make a road that has the same number, or just exactly as many cubes, chips, or whatever, as the road you have built. (Make sure the child has at least fifteen objects from which to select to build his or her road.) If the child does not use one-to-one correspondence in making the row, the game ends here. If the child does make a row using one-to-one correspondence, then proceed by saying, "Now I'm going to do something. Watch. I'm going to move the cubes [chips, paper shapes, or whatever] in my road like this. [Lengthen the row or arrange the objects in a clump or circle.] Now, are there still just as many cubes here as there are here, or are there more cubes in one place or the other?" (Gesture toward each group of objects as you ask the question.) If the child says that the number of objects in the two groups is now different, the game ends here. If the child says the number of objects is still the same in the two groups, ask the child to tell you how he or she knows there are still the same number, or to prove to you that there are still the same number in each group.

Analyze each child's responses in terms of the three stages of development for conservation of number. Was there any difference in the performance of the younger and older child?

Compare your results with those of classmates who conducted the task with preschool children the same age as the children you worked with. Did children of the same age perform similarly?

3. Select two Saturday morning cartoon television programs to watch. Make a list of aggressive acts you will observe for. These might include striking another person, destroying property, verbally abusing another, etc. As you watch the programs, tally the frequency of each kind of aggressive behavior. What is your general impression of the aggressive content of the programs you watched? What do you think their effect on young children's behavior might be?

Watch one "Mr. Roger's Neighborhood" program and one "Sesame Street" program. Make a list of prosocial behaviors you wish to observe for. As you watch the programs keep track of each instance in which prosocial behavior is modeled, verbalized, praised, etc. Also keep track of any aggressive behavior modeled. Analyze your results and evaluate the programs.

4. Arrange to work with a preschool child. You will need a pencil, crayons, or magic markers. (Magic markers might be the best writing tool because children like to use these. Get the thin-tipped kind.) You will also need some plain paper. Ask the child to "write everything he or she knows how to write." If the child hesitates, suggest that the child write his or her name. A younger child may be more willing to "write" even though unable to do so conventionally. An older child, who is aware that his or her writing does not resemble that of adults, may say, "I don't know how." Offer help by asking what the child would like to write. Then ask if it would help if you would write it on a piece of paper first. The goal is to collect a sample of a preschool child's writing. Analyze it in terms of material provided in the text on the development of writing. For example, does the child "write" merely by forming jagged linear scribbles, or does the child try to form letters? If the child creates letters, what kinds of errors are included? Also notice how the child organizes the writing on the page. Is a consistent direction used, or is the placement essentially random?

Obtain the child's exact age in years and months. Take your writing sample to class and compare it with the samples collected by your classmates.

5. Visit a nursery school or day care program. Observe for at least two hours, preferably in the morning. Note the physical organization of the classroom, the materials and equipment available to the children, and the activities the children engage in. Compare what you observed with the description of the preschool program in your text. What are the similarities and differences? What is your general opinion of the program you observed? Would you send a child to this program? Why or why not?

Part VI: The School-Age Child

1. In your local library or at a bookstore find a book of jokes and riddles suitable for school-age children. Select jokes and riddles that are based on linguistic ambiguity.

Interview individually two school-age children, one between the ages of six and seven, and one between the ages of eight and nine. Tell several jokes and riddles to each child and note whether he or she responds to them (laughs, for example). Ask the child why the joke or riddle was funny. Note what the child says and then analyze it (did the child explain the humor in terms of ambiguity at the phonological or lexical level?).

Ask each child to tell you some jokes or riddles. Write these down. Are they based on linguistic ambiguity? If yes, what level of ambiguity is used?

Did you notice any differences in the younger and older child's ability to detect and appreciate humor? What were the differences?

2. Consult the text for materials and procedures to use in administering the conservation of length and area tasks. Arrange to work with a child who is between six and eight years of age. Present the tasks and record the child's responses. In addition, show a wristwatch and electric or wind-up alarm clock (not digital). Ask the child what time it will be on the bigger clock face when the wristwatch reads _____ o'clock. Younger children tend to think that the smaller clock will get to a certain time before the larger clock; they fail to realize that clocks can be synchronized and that the hands on a bigger clock move faster than the hands on a small clock. (Be certain that the child you are interviewing can "tell time," that is, can read the time on a clock before you present this task. If the child cannot, the task cannot be presented.)

From your results, comment on the child's ability to conserve length and area, and to understand the concept of speed.

3. Play DeVries' penny-hiding game with three or four children, ranging in age from four to seven or eight. Note how each child both hides the penny and guesses where you have hidden it.

In what stage does each child fall? Do the older children tend to be more skillful in playing the game than the younger children? You might ask the older children why they hid the penny the way they did or why they searched for the penny where they did. Their answers may reflect their awareness that others can think about their thoughts and that they think about what others are thinking.

4. Visit a toy store or the home of someone who has the following games:

Candyland	*MasterMind*
Cootie	checkers
Sorry (or *Aggravation*)	*Othello*

Look carefully at the directions for each game. Compare the thinking skills needed to play *Candyland*, *Cootie*, and *Sorry*, with those needed to play *Master-Mind*, checkers, and *Othello*. For example, which games require strategy, or the ability to think about the thinking of the other player?

Note the ages recommended on the packages for each game. Are they consistent with the ages stated in the text for the emergence of skills necessary to play the games?

Part VII: The Adolescent

1. Arrange to work with a preadolescent (ten- to twelve-year-olds) or an adolescent (over twelve). Gather materials necessary for the probability task described in your text. Explain the task to the child you work with. After each prediction offered by the child, ask *why* the child predicted that a certain shape rather than another was most likely to be drawn. Analyze the child's answers to determine if he or she took into account not only the original contents of the bag, but the contents previously drawn as well. Was the child's thinking more typical of concrete or formal operational thinking?

2. Contact the principal or headmaster of a local high school and explain that you wish to learn about any course the school offers on sex education. If such a course is offered, try to meet with the course instructor to discuss the course content and instructional materials. Be sure to explain to the people you contact that you are doing this project for a course.

Summarize the content of the course and describe how the course is taught. Comment on the course, giving your opinion about its probable effectiveness.

3. Arrange to meet with a high school guidance counselor to learn about problems of youths (drug use, suicide, delinquency, dropping out of school, etc.). Try to get information on the incidence of each problem in this school and on whether certain problems have been increasing or decreasing in recent years. Also get the counselor's opinion about why some youths have problems whereas others do not, and what might be done about it.

Write a summary of what you found out.

Part VIII: The Parent

1. Talk with the personnel director or the director of human resources development of any reasonably large business or industrial concern in your community. Beforehand, construct a list of questions relating to personnel policies affecting family life. For example, you may wish to ask about maternity and paternity leaves for new parents, flexible scheduling for parents, availability of day-care facilities for the children of the company's workers, and so on.

2. Visit a large shopping mall in your community. Scout the entire mall to see if there are any child play spaces. If there are any, describe them. What age children do they seem to be designed for? What opportunities for play do they provide? Are they safe?

Do you have any ideas for additional play spaces? Describe these.

Glossary

accommodation A process basic to Piaget's theory of intellectual development that involves changes in intellectual structures to fit new experiences.

afterbirth The placenta, which is delivered after the birth of the baby.

amniocentesis Analysis of amniotic fluid to determine the presence of various diseases in the fetus.

animism The attribution of life to inanimate objects.

anorexia nervosa A psychological problem afflicting adolescent females that causes them to starve themselves.

anoxia Oxygen deprivation.

anxious attachment An emotional relationship between an infant and caregiver characterized by crying when the caregiver is absent and by clinging mixed with resistance to contact on reunion.

Apgar test A test of various physiological functions used to assess infants at birth.

apnea A period during which breathing stops briefly.

apnea monitor A machine that can detect abnormally long periods of apnea and sound an alarm to warn parents.

assimilation A process basic to Piaget's theory of intellectual development that involves the taking in of new experiences by current intellectual structures or schemes.

attachment The emotional bond between infants and their caregivers, usually their parents.

authoritarian parenting A style of parenting described by Baumrind that involves unreasonable expectations and harsh punishment.

authoritative parenting A style of parenting described by Baumrind that is characterized by reasonable limits and expectations.

axons Nerve fibers that carry impulses away from the cell.

babbling Early vocalization consisting of consonant-vowel combinations.

Babinski reflex A reflex present in young infants characterized by fanning of the toes when the outer edge of the sole is stroked.

baseline conditions The natural or typical conditions that are present before an experimental treatment is introduced by a researcher.

behavioral states The degree of alertness versus sleepiness, and calmness versus agitation that can be observed in infants.

behavioral theory The theory of development that stresses observable behavior and the role of the environment.

biased sampling Including in a study subjects who are not representative of the population as a whole.

bilirubin A byproduct of red blood cell destruction that is excreted from the body.

binocular fixation The ability to look at an object with both eyes at the same time.

biofeedback The process of using machines to provide information about an individual's heart rate or blood pressure to enable him or her to learn to relax and control these functions.

birth defects Genetic or congenital conditions involving physical or mental impairment.

brain stem   A lower part of the brain that modifies, among other things, reflex activity.

carriers   A person who has a recessive gene for a genetic disease but who does not suffer from the disease because he or she has not inherited two recessive genes.

centering   The inability to coordinate two aspects of a relationship, such as the height and width of a container of liquid.

center of gravity   The point around which weight is evenly distributed.

cephalocaudal development   Development that proceeds from the head to the tail.

cerebral palsy   Brain damage that results in abnormal body positions and muscle control.

Cesarean   Delivery of a baby surgically through the abdominal wall.

child advocates   People who work to ensure children's rights.

child development data   Information about children.

child development theories   Explanations for or hypotheses about why children do what they do and why their behavior changes.

chorion   The part of the placenta that embeds in the mother's tissues and surrounds the mother's blood supply.

chromosomes   The structures in cells that carry the genes.

classical conditioning   The pairing of a stimulus with another stimulus that reliably produces a response such that the second stimulus itself begins to elicit the response.

clique   An adolescent friendship group based on a specific interest such as sports or music.

cognitive theory   A theory of development that states that what one knows influences interpretation of stimuli and behavior in response to stimuli.

cohort   A group of people of a particular age.

cohort effect   In cross-sectional studies, a difference that is not due to the effects of age, but to the different histories of the age group studied.

colostrum   A thin, yellowish substance excreted from a mother's breast before breast milk is produced.

communicable diseases   Contagious diseases such as measles, mumps, and the common cold.

concrete operational period   The third of Piaget's stages of intellectual development, which is characterized by the ability to think logically about events observed.

conditioned response   The response elicited by the conditioned stimulus that initially was elicited by the unconditioned stimulus.

conditioned stimulus   The stimulus paired with the unconditioned stimulus in classical conditioning such that it elicits the response initially elicited by the unconditioned stimulus.

conservation   The ability to realize that number, for example, is not altered when objects are rearranged in space.

control group   The subjects in an experimental study who are like the subjects in the experimental groups in every way except that they do not receive the experimental treatment.

cooing   Early vocal behavior consisting of open vowel-like sounds.

coordination of secondary circular reactions   Behavior characteristic of Piaget's fourth stage of sensorimotor development in which one scheme serves as means and another scheme serves as the end.

coteratogen   A substance that itself does not cause birth defects but that interacts with other substances enabling them to cause birth defects.

crossing over   The exchange of genetic material between chromosomes that occurs during meiosis.

cross-sectional design   A research method used to study age-related differences in behavior in which different groups of children of different ages are utilized.

cross-sectional/short-term longitudinal design   A research design that combines features of the cross-sectional and longitudinal designs.

crowd   An adolescent friendship group that is larger than the clique and consists of friends from a neighborhood or school.

cystic fibrosis   A recessively carried genetic disease that affects the mucous membranes of the body and usually results in early death.

decentering   Coordinating two aspects of a relationship.

dendrites   Nerve fibers that carry impulses to the cell.

departure protest   Distress shown by young children as their parent leaves them in a new situation.

dependent variable   The behavior observed by a researcher to see if changes occur as a result of changes made in the independent variable.

differential social responsiveness   The tendency of infants six months of age and older to prefer familiar to unfamiliar adults.

discrepancy hypothesis   The hypothesis that states that infants like to look at patterns that differ somewhat from patterns previously looked at.

distance perception   The ability to judge the distance of an object.

dominant gene   A gene that always expresses its trait.

Down's syndrome   A disease involving mental retardation that is most commonly due to failure of chromosomes to divide correctly during meiosis.

dual monologues   Conversations in which the participants do not acknowledge or adapt to what the other is saying.

ductus arteriosus   The blood vessel through which fetal blood flows to bypass the lungs.

ectopic pregnancy   A pregnancy in which the embryo implants outside the uterus, typically in one of the Fallopian tubes.

ego   A term used by Freud and Erikson to refer to that part of personality that is reality oriented and seeks to satisfy the id in ways that are not punished.

egocentrism   The tendency to see things only from one's own point of view.

ego defense mechanisms   Unconscious processes that Freud suggested are used by the ego to attempt to reduce anxiety and maximize pleasure in handling the instincts of the id.

embryoblast   The part of the ball of cells formed soon after fertilization that will become the embryo itself.

epigenic theory   The theory stating that body structures are not preformed in the sperm and egg, but develop during the prenatal period.

ethical dilemma   A conflict concerning child-care practices that is due to adults' differences in values.

Euclidean space   Spatial relationships involving coordinates, relative distances, angles, and lines.

event sampling   An observation method in which only preselected and predefined behaviors are recorded.

expansion   The tendency of adults to repeat young children's utterances and put in words children omit.

experimental groups   The groups in an experimental study that receive the experimental treatment.

extinction   The disappearance of a behavior due to lack of reinforcement.

finger foods   Foods that are easily eaten with the fingers rather than with silverware.

fixation   The condition that results, according to psychoanalytic theory, when instincts are over- or undergratified such that a person exhibits behavior typical of an earlier stage of development.

fontanelles   Soft places on an infant's skull where the bones have not yet fused.

formal operations Piaget's fourth stage of intellectual development, which is characterized by the ability to think in hypothetical terms.

fraternal twins Genetically dissimilar twins resulting from fertilization of two ova.

gag reflex Reflex that results in expelling mucus or other material from the infant's throat.

genes Cell structures that carry coded information that determines a person's basic characteristics.

genetics The study of inherited characteristics.

germ cells Cells (sperm or ova) involved in reproduction.

glial cells Cells found in the brain that presumably serve a nutritional function.

glycogen A starch that is stored and can easily be converted by the body into energy.

graphophonic clues The information used to read written words that consists of letter-sound associations.

habituation The decrease in responding to repeated presentations of a stimulus.

holophrases One-word utterances that function as statements of intent.

hyaline membrane disease A lung disease that afflicts premature infants whose lungs are immature and lack surfactant.

id A term used by Freud to refer to that part of the personality driven by the inherited and unconscious instincts.

identical twins Genetically similar individuals resulting from separation of a single fertilized ovum.

identification The taking on of behavior and attitudes of the same-sex parent.

imaginary audience Thinking that everyone else looks at one as much as one looks at oneself (a symptom of adolescent egocentrism).

imitation The acquisition of behavior by copying behavior performed by a model.

immunoglobulins A component of breast milk that protects an infant from disease.

independent variable The variable that is manipulated or changed in a study by the researcher.

inflection A change made in a word by the addition of a morpheme.

informed consent Permission researchers must obtain from research subjects or their guardians before a study can begin.

instrumental aggression Aggression performed for the purpose of obtaining a desired goal, such as hitting a peer to grab a toy.

instrumental conditioning Learning in which a response (reward) following a behavior increases the frequency of the behavior.

interest inventories Instruments designed to help adults make vocational decisions.

intonation The rise and fall of the voice in speech.

intrinsic reinforcement Reinforcement that is inherent in information processing.

irreversibility The inability to mentally reverse an action observed with objects.

kernicterus Brain damage caused when an excessive amount of bilirubin in the blood passes into the brain.

lanugo Hair that sometimes covers a newborn's body.

least restrictive environment An educational environment for a special needs child that is as similar as is possible to the educational environment that would be provided for a nonhandicapped child.

locomotor skills Skills that culminate in walking.

logicomathematical knowledge Knowledge created by acting on objects.

longitudinal design   A method for studying age-related differences in behavior in which the same group of children is studied repeatedly over time.

mainstreaming   The placement of special needs children in regular classrooms to be educated.

marked-time climbing   The initial technique used by children to climb stairs or ladders, which is characterized by placing one foot on a rung or stair and bringing the second foot up to meet it.

maturation   Changes in behavior attributed to body changes controlled by a genetic timetable.

maturational theory   The theory of development that explains behavior in terms of genetic endowment and age-related physical growth of the nervous system.

meiosis   Cell division in germ cells that results in reduction of chromosomes in preparation for conception.

mitosis   Cell division occurring in somatic cells.

modeling   A process, described by social learning theorists, in which behavior is learned quickly by observing and copying a model.

molding   The squeezing of an infant's head that occurs as it passes through the birth canal.

Moro reflex   A startle reflex during which the baby stretches its arms out and then clasps them to its chest.

morphemes   The smallest meaningful units of language.

morphological rules   Rules that govern how words are changed into their various forms such as past tense or plural.

myelin   A fatty substance that coats nerve fibers and increases the speed at which impulses can travel.

neonatalogist   A physician who specializes in the care of newborns.

neonatal period   The first few weeks of infancy during which the baby adjusts to postnatal life.

norms   The average ages at which children exhibit certain behaviors.

object permanence   The notion that objects still exist when they cannot be seen.

observer bias   The tendency for a researcher to see what he or she wants or expects to see rather than to see the data objectively.

opening   The first part of the first stage of labor, when the cervix dilates.

operant conditioning   The process of increasing the frequency of a behavior by adding a reinforcing stimulus contingent on the behavior.

ossification   The hardening of the bones that takes place as minerals are deposited in cartilage.

ova   Female germ cells.

overgeneralization of rules   The tendency of young children to apply language rules in situations that are exceptions to the rules.

palmar grasp   A reflex, present in young infants, that is characterized by the curling of the fingers around any object touching the palm of the hand.

partner play   A type of interaction between toddlers and adults in which they share contact with a play object.

period of the embryo   The second stage of prenatal development, lasting from the second to the eighth week.

period of the fetus   The third period of prenatal development, lasting from the eighth week to birth.

period of the ovum   The first period of prenatal development, lasting from conception to implantation in the uterus.

permissive   A style of parenting described by Baumrind that is characterized by an absence of limits and expectations.

personality   A child's unique pattern of behaving toward others.

phenylketonuria (PKU)   A recessively carried genetic disorder that involves the inability to metabolize a certain amino acid and can result in severe retardation.

physical knowledge   Knowledge of the attributes of objects, such as color.

physiological neonatal jaundice   A normal type of jaundice in newborns caused by destruction of red blood cells not needed for extrauterine life.

pincer grasp   A grasp involving only the index finger and thumb.

placenta   The vascular organ that nourishes the fetus prenatally.

preexercise theory   One theory of play, which states that play prepares children for adult tasks.

preoperational period   The second of Piaget's stages of intellectual development, which is characterized by representational thought and the absence of logic characteristic of the concrete operational period.

primary circular reaction   Behaviors characteristic of the second stage of Piaget's sensorimotor stage of development, in which action is focused on the infant's own body.

primary reinforcement   Something such as food that satisfies a primary need such as hunger.

primary sex characteristics   Characteristics involved directly in reproduction, such as ovulation and menstruation and sperm production.

problem finding   A stage of intellectual development that has been proposed to follow Piaget's formal operational period.

projective space   Spatial relationships involving points of view.

prosocial behavior   Behavior directed toward enhancing the welfare of others.

prototypical play materials   Materials for pretend play that bear some physical resemblance to the things they stand for.

proximodistal development   Motor development that proceeds from the center of the body outward toward the hands.

pseudoimitation   Imitation in which the adult first repeats a behavior performed by the baby.

psychoanalytic theory   Freud's theory of personality development.

puberty   The point at which the individual is first capable of biological reproduction.

pubescence   The period preceding puberty during which physical changes leading to sexual maturity and adult stature occur.

punishment   A response that follows a behavior and results in a reduction in the frequency of that behavior.

random assignment   Distribution of subjects to experimental and control groups such that members of each group are not systematically different from each other.

readiness   The ability to utilize opportunities to learn that is attributed to maturation ov the nervous system.

recessive gene   A gene that expresses its trait only when it is paired with another recessive gene.

reflexes   Involuntary responses to specific stimuli.

reinforcement   A response following a behavior that increases the frequency of that behavior.

reliability   The extent to which data collected at one time or by one observer agree with data collected at another time or by a second observer.

responsive feedback   Responses by adults to an infant's efforts and cries for comforting or food.

repression   An ego defense mechanism in which the mind blocks out thoughts and events causing anxiety.

representational thought   The ability to think using symbols rather than having to think through sensorimotor actions.

response costs   Positive reinforcers subtracted from the environment in punishment.

retrolental fibroplasia A type of blindness caused by excessive oxygen in incubators.

reversibility The ability to reverse mentally an action observed.

Rh disease A disease involving clumping of an Rh-positive newborn's blood by antibodies produced by its Rh-negative mother.

rooting reflex Turning of the head toward the stimulus stroking a cheek.

rubella A form of measles that can cause birth defects such as blindness and deafness if contracted by a mother during the first three months of pregnancy.

secondary circular reactions Behaviors characteristic of Piaget's third stage of sensorimotor development in which action is focused on an event in the environment.

secondary reinforcement Something that is present when a primary reinforcer satisfies a primary need such that in time it, too, becomes a reinforcer.

secondary sex characteristics Bodily changes at puberty that are not directly involved in reproduction, such as facial hair and breast development.

secular trend in growth The increase in adult stature and decrease in age at puberty that has occurred during the last 100 years in industrial parts of the world.

secure attachment An emotional relationship between an infant and caregiver characterized by willingness of the infant to leave the caregiver for brief explorations into the environment.

segmental features of language Sound features within words.

self-fulfilling prophecy The tendency for people to live up to expectations.

semantics The study of word meanings.

sensorimotor period Piaget's first major stage of development, which lasts from birth to about age two and is characterized by thinking through action.

separation distress Behavior exhibited by a child who is upset by being away from his or her parent or other primary caregiver.

sex-typing The labeling of certain behaviors and attitudes as appropriate for boys or for girls.

shaping A process described by behaviorists in which successive approximations to a desired behavior are reinforced.

sickle-cell anemia A recessively carried genetic blood disease.

small-for-date baby An infant who has spent the usual amount of time in utero, but who is under five pounds at birth due to maternal malnutrition or other factors.

socialization All of the techniques and procedures used by adults to teach children accepted ways to behave.

social knowledge Knowledge gained from other people.

social learning theory A branch of behaviorism that recognizes conscious cognitive phenomena and suggests that many behaviors are not acquired by shaping but by observing and imitating models.

social smile An infant's smile that is voluntary and can be elicited by social stimulation from almost any person.

sociodramatic play Pretend play that involves the taking on of roles.

somatic cells All body cells.

special needs children Children with any of a number of handicapping conditions such as speech impairment, mental retardation, and learning disabilities.

sperm Male germ cells.

sphincters Smooth muscles at the opening of the bladder and anus.

spontaneous smile The earliest smile present in an infant; it lasts from birth to about six weeks of age and appears unrelated to specific external stimuli.

stranger anxiety Distress shown by infants beginning around six months of age toward unfamiliar adults.

subcutaneous fat The layer of fat that lies just under the skin and becomes quite thick during early infancy.

sublimation   An ego defense mechanism in which the energy leading to anxiety is directed toward some accepted activity.

sucking reflex   A reflex present in young infants that involves suction and expression in response to an object placed in the mouth.

sudden infant death syndrome   Death of an infant during sleep; its causes are unknown.

superego   A term used by Freud to refer to the part of personality that guides the ego to satisfy the instincts in acceptable ways or to block satisfaction altogether.

suprasegmental features of language   Features such as intonation and stress that give clues to the intention of an utterance.

surfactant   A substance that coats the lining of the lung and prevents the alveoli from collapsing when a breath is taken.

swaddling   The practice of wrapping infants tightly.

symbolic knowledge   Knowledge of how to represent knowledge mentally.

syntax   Rules of language that govern how sentences are constructed.

systematic observation   Any of several methods used to increase the reliability of naturalistic observations.

Tay-Sachs disease   A recessively carried genetic disease that involves degeneration of the nervous system.

telegraphic speech   Sentences in which words carrying little meaning are deleted.

teratogenic   A substance that causes a birth defect.

tertiary circular reactions   The fifth stage of Piaget's sensorimotor stage of development, which is characterized by development of new means through experimentation.

time sampling   An observation method in which children are observed in a particular sequence for a specified period of time.

tonic neck reflex   A reflex in young infants characterized by extension of the arm and leg on the side the baby's head faces, and flexion of the other arm and leg.

topological relationships   Relationships among objects, such as *inside* or *outside* and *next to* or *separated from*.

trophoblast   The part of the cluster of cells formed after fertiliztion that will develop into the placenta and chorion.

unconditioned response   The response that reliably follows an unconditioned stimulus.

unconditioned stimulus   A stimulus such as food that reliably produces a response such as salivation.

underextension of language   Young children's use of a word more narrowly than the adult understanding of the word allows.

values   Beliefs about what children do and should be like.

variable   Something that changes or is changed to have a different value or form.

vernix caseosa   The cheeselike substance that coats an infant's skin at birth.

within-subjects effect   A change or difference in the behavior of a group of subjects from one time to another as opposed to a difference between one group of subjects and another group.

zygote   A fertilized ovum.

Bibliography

Abroms, I. F., and Panagakos, P. G. The child with significant developmental motor delay (cerebral palsy). In A. P. Scheiner and I. F. Abroms (Eds.), *The practical management of the developmentally disabled child.* St. Louis, Mo.: C. V. Mosby, 1980.

Adelson, J. Adolescence and the generalization gap. *Psychology Today* 12 (1979): 33–37.

Ainsworth, M. D. S., and Bell, S. M. Some contemporary patterns of mother-infant interaction in the feeding situation. In A. Ambrose (Ed.), *Stimulation in early infancy.* New York: Academic Press, 1969.

Ainsworth, M. D. S. , and Bell, S. M. Mother-infant interaction and the development of competence. In K. Connolly and J. Bruner (Eds.), *The growth of competence.* New York: Academic Press, 1973.

Ainsworth, M. D. S., Bell, S. M. and Stayton, D. J. Individual differences in the strange-situation behavior of one-year-olds. In H. R. Schaffer (Ed.), *The origins of human social relations.* London: Academic Press, 1972.

Alan Guttmacher Institute. *11 million teenagers: What can be done about the epidemic of adolescent pregnancies in the U.S.?* New York: Planned Parenthood Federation of America, 1976.

Aleksandrowicz, M. The effect of pain relieving drugs administered during labor and delivery on the behavior of the newborn. *Merrill-Palmer Quarterly* 20 (1974): 121–41.

Aleksandrowicz, M. K., and Aleksandrowicz, D. R. Obstetrical pain-relieving drugs as predictors of infant behavior variability. *Child Development* 45 (1974): 935–58.

American Psychological Association. *Ethical principles in the conduct of research with human participants.* Washington, D.C.: American Psychological Association, 1973.

America's Children 1976. Washington, D.C.: The National Council of Organizations for Children and Youth, 1976.

Ames, L. B. The sequential patterning of prone progression in the human infant. *Genetic Psychology Monographs* 19 (1937): 409–60.

Anastasi, A. *Psychological testing.* 4th ed. New York: Macmillan, 1976.

Andrews, D. 200 years of child health in America. In E. Grotberg, (Ed.), *200 years of children.* Washington, D.C.: U.S. Department of Health, Education and Welfare, 1976.

Angrist, S. S. The study of sex roles. *Journal of Social Issues* 25 (1969): 215–32.

Apgar, V. Proposal for a new method of evaluating the newborn infant. *Anesthesia and Analgesia* 52 (1953): 260–67.

Archer, J., and Lopata, A. Marijuana revisited. *Personnel and Guidance Journal* 51 (1979): 244–50.

Arey, L. D. *Developmental anatomy.* 7th ed. Philadelphia: W. B. Saunders, 1965.

Aries, P. *Centuries of childhood* (Robert Baldick trans.). New York: Vintage Books, 1962.

Arlin, P. K. Cognitive development in adulthood: A fifth stage? *Developmental Psychology* 11 (1975): 602–06.

Arlin, P. K. Piagetian operations in problem finding. *Developmental Psychology* 13 (1977): 297–98.

Athey, I. Syntax, semantics, and reading. In J. T. Guthrie (Ed.), *Cognition, curriculum, and comprehension.* Newark, Del.: International Reading Association, 1977.

Azrin, N., and Foxx, R. *Mrs. James potty trains*

Mickey. New York: Simon and Schuster, 1974.

Baldwin, W. H. Adolescent pregnancy and child-rearing — Growing concerns for Americans. *Population Bulletin.* Vol. 31, No. 2. Washington, D.C.: Population Reference Bureau, 1976.

Balswick, J. O., and Macrides, C. Parental stimulus for adolescent rebellion. *Adolescence* 10 (1975): 253–66.

Bandura, A. Influence of models' reinforcement contingencies and acquisition of imitative responses. *Journal of Personality and Social Psychology* 1 (1965): 589–95.

Bandura, A. The role of modeling process in personality development. In W. W. Hartup and N. L. Smothergill (Eds.), *The young child: Reviews of research.* Vol. 1. Washington, D.C.: National Association for the Education of Young Children, 1967.

Bandura, A. *Aggression: A social learning analysis.* Englewood Cliffs, N.J.: Prentice-Hall, 1973.

Bandura, A. Behavior theory and the models of man. *American Psychologist* 29 (1974): 859-69.

Bandura, A. The stormy decade: Fact or fiction? In C. Guardo (Ed.), *The adolescent as individual: Issues and insights.* New York: Harper and Row, 1975.

Bandura, A. *Social learning theory.* Englewood Cliffs, N.J.: Prentice-Hall, 1977.

Bandura, A., Grusec, J., and Menlove, F. Vicarious extinction of avoidance behavior. *Journal of Personality* 5 (1967): 16–23.

Bandura, A., and McDonald, F. Influence of social reinforcement and the behavior of models in shaping children's moral judgments. *Journal of Abnormal and Social Psychology* 67 (1963): 274–81.

Bandura, A. and Walters, R. *Social learning and personality development.* New York: Holt, Reinhart and Winston, 1963.

Barnitz, J. G. Black English and other dialects: Sociolinguistic implications for reading instruction. *The Reading Teacher* 33 (1980): 779–86.

Baruch, G. K. Maternal influences upon college women's attitudes toward women and work. *Developmental Psychology* 6 (1972): 32–37.

Battle, E. S. Motivational determinants of academic task persistence. *Journal of Personality and Social Psychology* 2 (1965): 209–18.

Battle, E. S. Motivational determinants of academic competence. *Journal of Personality and Social Psychology* 4 (1966): 634–42.

Baumrind, D. Authoritarian vs. authoritative parental control. *Adolescence* 3 (1968): 255–72.

Baumrind, D. Socialization and instrumental competence in young children. In W. W. Hartup (Ed.), *The young child: Reviews of research.* Vol. 2. Washington, D.C.: National Association for the Education of Young Children, 1972.

Baumrind, D. Reciprocal rights and responsibilities in parent-child relations. *Journal of Social Issues* 34 (1978): 179–96.

Baumrind, D., and Black, A. E. Socialization and practices associated with dimensions of competence in preschool boys and girls. *Child Development* 38 (1967): 291–329.

Bayley, N. Mental growth during the first three years. A developmental study of sixty-one children by repeated tests. *Genetic Psychology Monographs* 14 (1933): 1–92.

Bayley, N. *Bayley Scales of Infant Development: Manual.* New York: The Psychological Corporation, 1969.

Bearison, D. J., and Issacs, L. Production deficiency in children's moral judgments. *Developmental Psychology* 11 (1975): 732–37.

Beckwith, L. Relationships between infants' social behaviors and their mothers' behavior. *Child Development* 43 (1972): 397–411.

Bee, H. Overview: Sex differences. In H. Bee (Ed.), *Social issues in developmental psychology.* New York: Harper and Row, 1978.

Beit-Hallahmi, B., and Rabin, A. I. The kibbutz as a social experiment and as a child-rearing laboratory. *American Psychologist* 32 (1977): 532–41.

Bell, R. D., Pincus, J. K., Swenson, N. M., Sanford, W. C., Pfeufer, R., and Cane, B. *Our bodies, ourselves.* New York: Simon and Schuster, 1973.

Bell, R. W. Stimulus control of parent or caretaker behavior by offspring. *Developmental Psychology* 4 (1971): 63–72.

Bell, S. M., and Ainsworth, M. D. Infant crying and maternal responsiveness. *Child Development* 43 (1972): 1171–90.

Bem, S. L. Beyond androgyny: Some presumptuous prescriptions for a liberated sexual identity. Keynote address for APA-NIMH Conference on Research Needs of Women, Madison, Wis., May 31, 1975.

Berger, M. J., and Goldstein, D. P. Impaired reproductive performance in DES-exposed women. *Obstetrics and Gynecology* 55 (1980): 25–27.

Berkowitz, L. Control and aggression. In B. M. Caldwell and H. N. Ricciuti (Eds.), *Review of child development research.* Vol. 3. Chicago: University of Chicago Press, 1973.

Berlyne, D. E. The influence of the albedo and complexity of stimulation on visual fixation in the human infant. *British Journal of Psychology* 49 (1958): 315–18.

Beth Israel Hospital manual for expectant parent classes. Boston: Beth Israel Hospital, 1981.

Bever, T. G., Mehler, J. H., and Valian, V. Linguistic capacity of very young children. In T. G. Bever and W. Weksel (Eds.), *The acquisition of structure.* New York: Holt, Rinehart and Winston, 1974.

Bigelow, B. J., and LaGaipa, J. J. Children's written descriptions of friendship: A multidimensional analysis. *Developmental Psychology* 11 (1975): 857–58.

Binet, A., and Simon, T. Methodes nouvelles pour le diagnostic du niveau intellectual des anormous. *L'Annee Psychologique* 11 (1905): 191–244.

Birns, B. Individual differences in human neonates' responses to stimulation. *Child Development* 36 (1965): 249–56.

Bissex, G. L. *GNYS AT WRK: A child learns to write and read.* Cambridge: Harvard University Press, 1980.

Black, L., Hersher, L., and Steinschmeider, A. Impact of apnea monitor on family life. *Pediatrics* 62 (1978): 681–85.

Blehar, M. C. Anxious attachment and defensive reactions associated with day care. *Child Development* 45 (1974): 683–92.

Blehar, M. S., Lieberman, A. F., and Ainsworth, M. D. S. Early face-to-face interaction and its relation to later infant-mother attachment. *Child Development* 48 (1977): 182–94.

Block, J. H. Conceptions of sex role: Some cross-cultural and longitudinal perspectives. *American Psychologist* 28 (1973): 512–76.

Bloom, L., Hood, L., and Lightbown, P. Imitation in language development: If, when and why. *Cognitive Psychology* 6 (1974): 380–420.

Bloom, L., Lightbown, P., and Hood, L. Structure and variation in child language. *Monographs of the Society for Research in Child Development* 40 (1975): Serial No. 160.

Blume, J. *Are you there God? It's me Margaret.* Scarsdale, N.Y.: Bradbury Press, 1970.

Bonica, J. J. *Principles and practices of obstetric analgesia and anesthesia.* Vol. I. Philadelphia: Davis, 1967.

Borke, H. The development of empathy in Chinese and American children between 3 and 6 years of age: A cross-cultural study. *Developmental Psychology* 9 (1973): 102–08.

Bottoms, S. F., Rosen, M. G., and Sokol, R. J. The increase in the Cesarean birth rate. *New England Journal of Medicine* 302 (1980): 559–62.

Bornstein, M. H., Kessen, W., and Weiskopf, S. The categories of hue in infancy. *Science* 191 (1976): 201–02.

Bower, T. G. R. The development of reaching in infants. Unpublished manuscript, University of Edinburgh, 1973.

Bower, T. G. R. *Development in infancy.* San Francisco: W. H. Freeman, 1974.

Bower, T. G. R. *A primer of infant development.* San Francisco: W. H. Freeman, 1977.

Bowes, W. A. Obstetrical medication and infant outcome: A review of the literature. *Mono-*

graphs of the Society for Research in Child Development 35 (1970): 3–23.

Bowlby, J. Beginnings of attachment behavior. In J. Bowlby, *Attachment and loss.* Vol. 1. New York: Basic Books, 1969.

Brackbill, Y., Kane, J., Manniello, R. L., and Abramson, D. Obstetric premedication and infant outcome. *American Journal of Obstetrics and Gynecology* 118 (1974): 377–84.

Bradley, R. H., and Caldwell, B. M. Early home environment and changes in children from 6 to 36 months. *Developmental Psychology* 12 (1976): 93–97.

Braine, M. The ontogeny of English phrase structure: The first phase. *Language* 39 (1963): 1–13.

Brainerd, C. J. *Piaget's theory of intelligence.* Englewood Cliffs, N.J.: Prentice-Hall, 1978.

Branigan, G., and Stokes, W. Introduction: A sketch of language development. *Journal of Education* 158 (1976): 4–11.

Brazelton, T. B. Psychophysiologic reactions in the neonate. *The Journal of Pediatrics* 58 (1961): 513–18.

Brazelton, T. B. Psychophysiologic reactions in the neonate II. Effect of maternal medication on the neonate and his behavior. *The Journal of Pediatrics* 58 (1961): 513–18.

Brazelton, T. B. *Infants and mothers.* New York: Delacorte Press/Seymour Lawrence, 1969.

Brazelton, T. B. Effects of prenatal drugs on the behavior of the neonate. *American Journal of Psychiatry* 126 (1970): 95–100.

Brazelton, T. B. *Neonatal assessment scale.* Philadelphia: J. B. Lippincott, 1973.

Brennan, W. M., Ames, E. W., and Moore, R. W. Age differences in infants' attention to patterns of different complexities. *Science* 151 (1966): 354–56.

Brittain, C. Adolescent choice and parent-peer cross-pressures. *American Sociological Review* 28 (1963): 385–91.

Brockman, L. M., and Ricciuti, H. N. Severe protein-calorie malnutrition and cognitive development in infancy and early childhood. *Developmental Psychology* 4 (1971): 312–19.

Broman, S. H., Nichols, P. L., and Kennedy, W. A.

Preschool IQ: *Prenatal and early developmental correlates.* Hillsdale, N.J.: Lawrence Erlbaum, 1975.

Bronfenbrenner, U. *Two worlds of childhood.* New York: Pocket Books, 1973.

Bronfenbrenner, U. *A report of longitudinal evaluations of preschool programs.* Vol. II. Is early intervention effective? Washington, D.C.: U.S. Department of Health, Education, and Welfare, 1974.

Bronfenbrenner, U. Toward an experimental ecology of human development. *American Psychologist* 32 (1977): 513–31.

Bronson, W. Development in behaviors with agemates during the second year of life. In M. Lewis and L. Rosenblum (Eds.), *Peer relations and friendship.* New York: John Wiley and Sons, 1975.

Brooks-Gunn, J., and Lewis, M. Early social knowledge: In H. McGurk (Ed.), *Childhood social development.* London: Methuen, 1979.

Brooks-Gunn, J., and Schempp-Matthews, W. *He and she: How children develop their sex-role identity.* Englewood Cliffs, N.J.: Prentice-Hall, 1979.

Brophy, J. *Child development and socialization.* Chicago: Science Research Associates, 1977.

Broverman, I., Vogel, S. R., Broverman, D. M., Clarkson, F. E., and Rosenkrantz, P. S. Sex role stereotypes: A current appraisal. *Journal of Social Issues* 28 (1972): 59–78.

Brown, R. *A first language.* Cambridge: Harvard University Press, 1973.

Brown, R., Cazden, C. B., and Bellugi, U. The child's grammar from I to III. *Minnesota Symposium on Child Psychology.* Vol. 2. Minneapolis: University of Minnesota Press, 1969.

Brown, R., and Fraser, C. The acquisition of syntax. In U. Bellugi and R. Brown (Eds.), The acquisition of language. *Monographs of the Society for Research in Child Development,* 29 (1964): 43–79.

Brown, R. W. *Social psychology.* New York: Free Press, 1965.

Brown, W. A. *Psychological care during preg-*

nancy and the postpartum period. New York: Raven Press, 1979.

Bruch, H. Anorexia nervosa. In R. J. Wurtman and J. J. Wurtman, Nutrition and the brain. Vol. 3. New York: Raven Press, 1979.

Brumley, G. Biochemical aspects of alveolar function. In Uve Stove (Ed.), Physiology of the perinatal period. Vol. I. Appleton-Century Crofts, 1970.

Bruner, J. S. From communication to language — A psychological perspective. Cognition 3 (1975): 255–87. a

Bruner, J. S. The ontogenesis of speech acts. Journal of Child Language 2 (1975): 1–19. b

Bruner, J. S. The growth of mind. In J. K. Gardner (Ed.), Readings in developmental psychology. Boston: Little, Brown, 1978, pp. 271–93.

Bryan, J. H., and Schwartz, T. Effects of film material upon children's behavior. Psycholingual Bulletin 75 (1971): 50–59.

Bryan, J. H., and Walbek, N. H. Preaching and practicing generosity: Children's actions and reactions. Child Development 41 (1970): 329–53. a

Bryan, J. H., and Walbek, N. H. The impact of words and deeds concerning altruism upon children. Child Development 41 (1970): 747–57. b

Bryan, T. H., and Bryan, J. H. Understanding learning disabilities. Port Washington, N.Y.: Alfred, 1975.

Bureau of the Census, Money income and poverty status. U.S. Government Printing Office, 1974.

Burt, L. The genetic determinants of differences in intelligence: A study of monozygotic twins reared together and apart. British Journal of Psychology 57 (1966): 137–53.

Butarescu, G. F. Perinatal nursing. Vol. 1: Reproductive health. New York: Wiley, 1978.

Butler, R. A. Discrimination learning by rhesus monkeys to visual exploration motivation. Journal of Comparative Physiological Psychology 46 (1953): 95–98.

Caldwell, B. M. Preschool Inventory. Princeton, N.J.: Educational Testing Service, 1970.

Caldwell, B. M., Wright, C. M., Honig, A. S., and Tannenbaum, J. Infant day care and attachment. American Journal of Orthopsychiatry 40 (1970): 397–412.

Calkins. L. M. Writers need readers, not robins. Language Arts 55 (1978): 704–07.

Campbell, D. T., and Stanley, J. C. Experimental and quasi-experimental designs for research. Chicago: Rand McNally, 1963.

Cantor, P. Understanding a child's world: Readings in infancy through adolescence. New York: McGraw-Hill, 1977.

Caplan, F. (Ed). The parenting advisor. New York: Anchor Press/Doubleday, 1977.

Caputo, D. V., and Mandell, W. Consequences of low birth weight. Developmental Psychology 3 (1970): 363–83.

Carle, E. The very hungry caterpillar. New York: Collins, 1979.

Carter, A. The transformation of sensorimotor morphemes into words: A case study of the development of "more" and "mine." Journal of Child Language 2 (1975): 233–50.

Cass, L. K., and Thomas, C. B. Childhood pathology and later adjustment. New York: John Wiley and Sons, 1979.

Cattell, R. B. The structure of intelligence in relation to the nature-nurture controversy. In R. Canco (Ed.), Intelligence: Genetic and environmental influences. New York: Grune and Stratton, 1971, pp. 3–30.

Cavoir, N., and Dokecki, P. R. Physical attractiveness, perceived attitude similarity and academic achievement as contributors to interpersonal attraction among adolescents. Developmental Psychology 9 (1973): 44–54.

Cazden, C. Suggestions from studies of early language acquisition. In C. Cazden (Ed.), Language in early childhood education. Washington, D.C.: National Association for the Education of Young Children, 1972, pp. 3–8.

Cazden, C. B. Play and metalinguistic awareness: One dimension of language experience. The Urban Review 7 (1974): 27–39.

Chaffee, S. H. Television and adolescent aggressiveness (overview). In G. A. Comstock and

E. A. Rubenstein (Eds.), *Television and social behavior.* Vol. III: Television and adolescent aggressiveness. Washington, D.C.: U.S. Government Printing Office, 1972.

Chaille, C. The child's conceptions of play, pretending, and toys: Sequences and structural parallels. *Human Development* 21 (1978): 201–10.

Chandler, M. J. Egocentrism and anti-social behavior: The assessment and training of social perspective-taking skills. *Developmental Psychology* 9 (1973): 326–33.

Chandler, M. J. Social cognition and life-span approaches to the study of child development. In H. W. Reese and L. P. Lipsitt (Eds.), *Advances in child development and behavior.* Vol. 11. New York: Academic Press, 1976.

Chandler, M. J., and Greenspan, S. Ersatz egocentrism: A reply to H. Borke. *Developmental Psychology* 7 (1972): 104–06.

Chavez, C. J., Ostrea, E. M., Stryker, J. C., and Smialek, Z. Sudden infant death syndrome among infants of drug-dependent mothers. *Journal of Pediatrics* 95 (1979): 407–09.

Chiappetta, E. L. A review of Piagetian studies relevant to science instruction at the secondary and college level. *Science Education* 60 (1976): 253–61.

Chittenden, G. E. An experimental study in measuring and modifying assertive behavior in young children. *Monographs of the Society for Research in Child Development* 7 (1942).

Chomsky, C. Creativity and innovation in child language. *Journal of Education* 158 (1976): 12–24.

Chomsky, C. Reading, writing, and phonology. In M. Wolf, M. K. McQuillan, and E. Radwin (Eds.), *Thought and language/Language and reading.* Reprint Series No. 14, *Harvard Educational Review,* 1980, 51–71.

Chomsky, C. S. *The acquisition of syntax in children from 5 to 10.* Cambridge: MIT Press, 1969.

Chomsky, N. *Syntactic structure.* The Hague: Mouton, 1957.

Chomsky, N. A review of *Verbal Behavior,* by B. F. Skinner. *Language* 35 (1959): 26–58.

Chomsky, N. *Aspects of the theory of syntax.* Cambridge: MIT Press, 1965.

Chukovsky, K. *From two to five.* Berkeley: University of California Press, 1963.

Clarizio, H. F., and McCoy, G. E. *Behavior disorders in children.* New York: Thomas Y. Crowell, 1976.

Clark, E. V. Non-linguistic strategies and the acquisition of word meaning. In L. Bloom (Ed.), *Readings in language development.* New York: John Wiley and Sons, 1978.

Clark, E. V. Non-linguistic strategies and the acquisition of word meanings. *Cognition* 2 (1973): 161–82.

Clark, H. H., and Clark, E. V. *Psychology and language: An introduction to psycholinguistics.* New York: Harcourt Brace Jovanovich, 1977.

Clarke, C. A. The prevention of rhesus babies. *Scientific American* 219 (1968): 46–65.

Clarke-Stewart, K. A. Interactions between mothers and their young children: Characteristics and consequences. *Monographs of the Society for Research in Child Development* 38 (1973): Serial No. 153.

Clay, M. *The early detection of reading difficulties: A diagnostic survey.* Auckland, New Zealand: Heinemann Educational Books, 1976.

Cline, V. B., Croft, R. G., and Corrier, S. The desensitization of children to television violence. *Proceedings of the American Psychological Association* 80 (1972): 99–100.

Cohen, L., and Gelber, E. Infant visual memory. In L. B. Cohen and P. Salapatek (Eds.), *Infant perception: From sensation to cognition.* Vol. 1. New York: Academic Press, 1975.

Cohen, S. *Special people.* Englewood Cliffs, N. J.: Prentice-Hall, 1977.

Coleman, J. S. *Equality of educational opportunity.* Washington, D.C.: U.S. Office of Education, 1966.

Coley, I. L. *Pediatric assessment of self-care activities.* Saint Louis: C. V. Mosby, 1978.

Combs, M. L., and Slaby, D. A. Social-skills training with children. In B. Lahey and A. Kazdin (Eds.), *Advances in clinical child psychology.* Vol. 1. New York: Plenum Press, 1977.

Conway, E., and Brackbill, Y. Delivery medication and infant outcome: An empirical study. *Monographs of the Society for Research in Child Development* 35 (1970): 24–34.

Cooney, E. W., and Selman, R. L. Children's use of social conceptions: Towards a dynamic model of social cognition. In W. Damon (Ed.), *Social cognition.* San Francisco: Jossey-Bass, 1978.

Coopersmith, S. *The antecedents of self esteem.* San Francisco: W. H. Freeman, 1967.

Crandall, V., Katkovsky, W., and Crandall, V. J. Children's beliefs in their own control of reinforcements in intellectual-academic achievement situations. *Child Development* 36 (1965): 91–109.

Crandall, V., Katkovsky, W., and Preston, A. Motivational and ability determinants of children's intellectual achievement behaviors. *Child Development* 33 (1962): 643–61.

Cratty, B. J. *Perceptual and motor development in infants and children.* New York: Macmillan, 1970.

Crisp, A. H., Palmer, R. L., and Kalucy, R. S. How common is anorexia nervosa? A prevalence study. *British Journal of Psychiatry* 128 (1976): 549–54.

Croake, J. W. Fears of children. *Human Development* 12 (1969): 239–47.

Croake, J. W. The changing nature of children's fears. *Child Study Journal* 3 (1973): 91–105.

Cruttenden, A. A phonetic study of babbling. *British Journal of Disorders in Communication* 5 (1970): 110–18.

Cummings, E. M. Caregiver stability and day care. *Developmental Psychology* 16 (1980): 31–37.

Dale, P. S. *Language development: Structure and function.* 2nd ed. New York: Holt, Rinehart and Winston, 1976.

Dargassies, S. Neurological maturation of the premature infant of 28 to 41 weeks' gestational age. In Faulkner (Ed.), *Human development.* London: W. B. Saunders, 1966.

Darwin, C. *The origin of species.* London: Murray, 1859.

Davidson, H., and Lang, G. Children's perception of their teachers' feelings toward them related to self-perception, school achievement and behavior. *Journal of Experimental Education* 29 (1960): 107–18.

Davidson, S. M. An experiment in teaching parenting skills. Paper presented at the biennial meeting of the Society for Research in Child Development, San Francisco, March 1979.

Dawe, H. C. An analysis of two hundred quarrels of preschool children. *Child Development* 5 (1934): 139–57.

Denhoff, E., and Robinault, I. *Cerebral palsy and related disorders.* New York: McGraw-Hill, 1960.

Dennis, W. Causes of retardation among institutional children: Iran. *Journal of Genetic Psychology* 96 (1960): 47–59.

Department of Health, Education and Welfare, Protection of human subjects: Research involving children. *Federal Register* 43 (1978): 2084–2114.

Department of Labor, Bureau of Labor Statistics, *U.S. Working Women: A Datebook.* Washington, D.C.: U.S. Government Printing Office, 1977.

Desmond, M. M., Franklin, R. R., Vallbona, C., Hilt, R. H., Plumb, R., Arnold, H., and Watts, J. The clinical behavior of the newly born I. *Journal of Pediatrics* 12 (1963): 307–25.

Desor, J. A., Maller, O., and Andrews, K. Ingestive responses of human newborns to salty, sour, and bitter stimuli. *Journal of Comparative and Physiological Psychology* 89 (1975): 966–70.

Desor, J. A., Maller, O., and Turner, R. Taste in acceptance of sugars by human infants. *Journal of Comparative and Physiological Psychology* 84 (1973): 496–501.

deVilliers, J., and deVilliers, P. Competence and performance in child language: Are children really competent to judge? *Journal of Child Language* 1 (1974): 11–22.

DeVries, R. The development of role-taking as reflected by behavior of bright, average, and retarded children in a social guessing game. *Child Development* 41 (1970): 759–70.

Ditzion, J. S., and Wolf, D. P. Beginning parenthood. In W. C. Sanford (Ed.), *Ourselves and our children: A book by and for parents*. New York: Random House, 1978.

Doake, D. B. Reading: A language learning activity. Paper presented at the University of Victoria International Reading Research Seminar on Linguists Awareness and Learning to Read, Victoria, British Columbia, June 1979.

Dobbing, J. The later development of the brain and its vulnerability. In J. A. Davis and J. Dobbing (Eds.), *Scientific foundations of pediatrics*. Philadelphia: W. B. Saunders, 1974.

Dobbing, J. Fat cells in childhood obesity. *Lancet* 1 (1975): 224-28.

Dodson, W. E. Neonatal drug intoxication: Local anesthetics. *Symposium on Pediatric Neurology, Pediatric Clinics of North America* 23 (1976): 399–410.

Donahue, M. Form and function in mother-toddler conversational turn-taking. Unpublished doctoral dissertation, Boston University, 1978.

Donaldson, M. *Children's minds*. New York: W. W. Norton, 1978.

Donaldson, M., and Balfour, G. Less is more: A study of language comprehension in children. *British Journal of Psychology* 59 (1968): 461–72.

Done, A. K. Poisoning from common household products. *The Pediatric Clinics of North America* 17 (1970): 569–82.

Dore, J. Holophrases, speech acts and language universals. *Journal of Child Language* 2 (1975): 21–40.

Douvan, E., and Adelson, J. *The adolescent experience*. New York: Wiley, 1966.

Downs, M. P. That a child may hear. *Deafness Research Foundation Receiver*, Fall 1978.

Doyle, A. Infant development in day care. *Developmental Psychology* 11 (1975): 655–56.

Drabman, R. S., and Thomas, M. H. Does media violence increase children's toleration of real-life aggression? *Developmental Psychology* 10 (1974): 418–21.

Drillien, C. M. Obstetric hazard, mental retardation and behavior disturbance in primary school. *Developmental Medicine and Child Neurology* 5 (1963): 3–13.

Drillien, C. M. School disposal and performance for children of different birthweight born 1953-1960. *Archives of Diseases in Childhood* 44 (1969): 562–70.

Dulit, E. Adolescent thinking a la Piaget: The formal stage. In R. Grinder (Ed.), *Studies in adolescence*. New York: Macmillan, 1975, pp. 536–56.

Durkin, D. *Children who read early*. New York: Teachers College Press, 1966.

Dusek, J. *Adolescent development and behavior*. Chicago: Science Research Associates, 1977.

Dweck, C. S. The role of expectations and attributions in the alleviation of learned helplessness. *Journal of Personality and Social Psychology* 31 (1975): 674–85.

Dweck, C. S. Achievement. In M. E. Lamb (Ed.), *Social and personality development*. New York: Holt, Rinehart and Winston, 1978, pp. 114–30.

Eckerman, C., Whatley, J., and Kutz, S. Growth of social play with peers during the second year of life. *Developmental Psychology* 11 (1975): 42–49.

Edwards, D. A. Early androgen stimulation and aggressive behavior in male and female mice. *Physiology and Behavior* 4 (1969): 333–38.

Egan, M. C. Federal nutrition support programs for children. *Pediatric Clinics of North America* 24 (1977): 229–39.

Ehrhardt, A. A., and Baker, S. W. Fetal androgens, human central nervous system differentiation, and behavior sex differences. In R. C. Friedman, R. M. Richart, and R. L. Vande Wiele (Eds.), *Sex differences in behavior*.

New York: John Wiley and Sons, 1974, pp. 33–51.

Eimas, P. D. Auditory and linguistic processing of cues for place of articulation by infants. *Perception and Psychophysics* 16 (1974): 513–21.

Eimas, P. D., Siqueland, D. R., Jusczyk, P., and Vigorito, J. Speech perception in infants. *Science* 171 (1971): 303–06.

Elardo, R., Bradley, R., and Caldwell, B. M. The relation of infants' home environments to mental test performance from six to thirty-six months: A longitudinal analysis. *Child Development* 46 (1975): 71–76.

Elder, G. H., Jr. Parental power legitimation and its effects on the adolescent. *Sociometry* 26 (1963): 50–65.

Elkind, D. *Child development and education: A Piagetian perspective.* New York: Oxford University Press, 1976.

Elkind, D. *A sympathetic understanding of the child: Birth to sixteen.* 2nd ed. Boston: Allyn and Bacon, 1978. a

Elkind, D. Understanding the young adolescent. *Adolescence* 13 (1978): 127–34. b

Elliott, R., and Vasta, R. The modeling of sharing: Effects associated with vicarious reinforcement, symbolization, age and generalization. *Journal of Experimental Child Psychology* 10 (1970): 8–15.

El'konin, D. B. Some results of the study of the psychological development of preschool-age children. In M. Cole and I. Maltzman (Eds.), *A handbook of contemporary Soviet psychology.* New York: Basic Books, 1969.

Ellis, G. T., and Sekyra, F. The effect of aggressive cartoons on the behavior of first grade children. *Journal of Psychology* 81 (1972): 37–43.

Empey, L. T. Delinquency theory and research. In R. Grinder (Ed.), *Studies in adolescence.* New York: Macmillan, 1975, pp. 475–90.

Enright, R., Lapsley, D., and Shukla, D. Adolescent egocentrism in early and late adolescence. *Adolescence* 14 (1979): 687–95.

Erikson, E. H. *Childhood and society.* New York: W. W. Norton, 1963.

Erikson, E. H. *Identity, youth and crisis.* New York: W. W. Norton, 1968.

Eron, L., Walder, L., and Lefkowitz, M. *Learning of aggression in children.* Boston: Little, Brown, 1971.

Evans, D. The effects of achievement motivation and ability upon discovery learning and accompanying incidental learning under two conditions of incentive set. *The Journal of Educational Research* 60 (1967): 195–200.

Fantz, R. L. Pattern vision in newborn infants. *Science* 140 (1963): 296–97.

Faust, M. S. Developmental maturity as a determinant in prestige of adolescent girls. *Child Development* 31 (1960): 173–84.

Federman, E. J., and Yang, R. K. A critique of obstetrical pain-relieving drugs as predictors of infant behavior variability. *Child Development* 47 (1976): 294–96.

Fein, G. A transformational analysis of pretending. *Developmental Psychology* 11 (1975): 291–96.

Fein, G. Play revisited. In M. Lamb (Ed.), *Social and personality development.* New York: Holt, Rinehart and Winston, 1978.

Fenson, L., Kagan, J., Kearsley, R., and Zelazo, P. The developmental progression of manipulative play in the first two years. *Child Development* 47 (1976): 232–36.

Finklestein, N. W., and Ramey, C. T. Learning to control the environment in infancy. *Child Development* 48 (1977): 608–19.

Finnie, N. R. *Handling the young cerebral palsied child at home.* New York: Dutton, 1975.

Fitzsimmons, S. J., Cheever, J., Leonard, E., and Macunovich, D. School failures: Now and tomorrow. In R. E. Grinder (Ed.), *Studies in adolescence.* New York: Macmillan, 1975.

Flapan, D. *Children's understanding of social interaction.* New York: Teachers College Press, 1968.

Fontana, V. J. Further reflections on maltreatment of children. *Pediatrics* 13 (1973): 675–78.

Fox, G. L., and Inazu, J. K. Patterns of mother-daughter communication. *Journal of Social Issues* 38 (1980): 7–29.

Fraiberg, S. Intervention in infancy: A program for blind infants. In B. Z. Friedlander, G. M. Sterritt, and G. E. Kirk (Eds.), *Exceptional infant.* Vol. 1. New York: Brunner/Mazel, 1975.

Frankenburg, W. K., and Dodds, J. B. *Denver Developmental Screening Test.* Denver: University of Colorado Medical Center, 1970.

Fraser, C., Bellugi, U., and Brown, R. Control of grammar in imitation, comprehension and production. *Journal of Verbal Learning and Verbal Behavior* 2 (1963): 122–35.

Frasier, S. D. Growth disorders in children. *Pediatric Clinics of North America* 26 (1979): 1–12.

Freda, V. J., Groman, J. G., and Pollack, W. Suppression of Rh immune response. *New England Journal of Medicine* 227 (1967): 1022.

Free to Be Foundation, 1974.

Freud, A. *The ego and the mechanisms of defense* (C. Bains, trans.). New York: International Universities Press, 1948.

Freud, S. Instincts and their vicissitudes. In S. Freud, *Collected Papers.* Vol. 4. London: Institutes for Psycho-analysis and Hogarth Press, 1925.

Friedman, T. Prenatal diagnosis of genetic disorders. *Scientific American* 225 (1971): 34.

Friedrich, L. K., and Stein, A. H., Aggressive and prosocial television programs and the natural behavior of preschool children. *Monographs of the Society for Research in Child Development* 38 (1973), Serial No. 151.

Frodi, A. M., Lamb, M., Leavitt, L. A., and Donovan, W. L. Fathers' and mothers' responses to infant smiles and cries. *Infant Behavior and Development* 1 (1978): 187–98. a

Frodi, A. M., Lamb, M. E., Leavitt, L. A., Wilberta, L., Donovan, C. N., and Sherr, D. Fathers' and mothers' responses to the faces and cries of normal and premature infants. *Developmental Psychology* 14 (1978): 490–98. b

Fuller, R., and Schuman, J. Treated phenylketonuria: Intelligence and blood phenylalanine levels. *American Journal of Mental Deficiency* 75 (1971): 539–45.

Gallatin, J. E. *Adolescence and individuality.* New York: Harper and Row, 1975.

Garbarino, J., and Crouter, A. Defining the community context for parent-child relations: The correlates of child maltreatment. *Child Development* 49 (1978): 604–16.

Garcia, C., and Rosenfeld, D. L. *Human fertility: The regulation of reproduction.* Philadelphia: F. A. Davis, 1977.

Gardner, H., Winner, E., Bechhofer, R., and Wolf, D. The development of figurative language. In K. E. Nelson (Ed.), *Children's language.* Vol. 1. New York: Gardner Press, 1978.

Garrett, W., and Robinson, D. E. *Ultrasound in clinical obstetrics.* Springfield, Ill.: Charles C. Thomas, 1970.

Garvey, C. Some properties of social play. *The Merrill-Palmer Quarterly* 20 (1974): 163–80.

Garvey, C. *Play.* Cambridge: Harvard University Press, 1977. a

Garvey, C. Play with language and speech. In Susan Ervin-Tripp and Claudia Mitchell-Kernon (Eds.), *Child discourse.* New York: Academic Press, 1977, pp. 27–47. b

Gedda, L. *Twins in history and science.* Springfield, Ill: Charles C. Thomas, 1961.

Gelles, R. J., and Straus, M. A. Violence in the American Family. *Journal of Social Issues* 35 (1979): 15–39.

General Mills, Inc. *Family health in an era of stress: The General Mills American Family report.* Minneapolis, Minn.: General Mills, 1979.

Genser, A., and Baden, C. (Eds.). *School-age child care: Programs and issues.* Urbana, Ill.: ERIC Clearinghouse on Elementary and Early Childhood Education, 1980.

Gerbner, G. Violence in television drama: Trends and symbolic functions. In G. A. Comstock and E. A. Rubenstein (Eds.), *Television and social behavior.* Vol. 1, *Media content and control.* Washington, D.C.: Government Printing Office, 1972.

Gesell, A. The ontogenesis of infant behavior. In L. Carmichael (Ed.), *Manual of child psychology.* New York: John Wiley and Sons, 1954, pp. 335–73.

Gesell, A., and Thompson, H. Learning and growth in identical infant twins: An experimental study of the method of co-twin control. *Genetic Psychology Monographs* 6 (1929): 1–124.

Gewirtz, J. L. The course of infant smiling in four child-rearing environments in Israel. In B. M. Foss (Ed.), *Determinants of infant behavior: III.* New York: John Wiley and Sons, 1965.

Gewirtz, J. L., and Boyd, E. F. Does maternal responding imply reduced infant crying? A critique of the 1972 Bell and Ainsworth report. *Child Development* 48 (1977): 1200–07. a

Gerwirtz, J. L., and Boyd, E. F. In reply to the rejoinder to our critique of the 1972 Bell and Ainsworth report. *Child Development* 48 (1977): 1217–18. b

Gibson, E., and Levin, H. *The psychology of reading.* Cambridge: MIT Press, 1975.

Gibson, E. J. *Principles of perceptual learning and development.* New York: Prentice-Hall, 1969.

Gibson, E. J., and Walk, R. P. The "visual cliff." *Scientific American* 202 (1960): 64–72.

Gil, D. G. *Violence against children: Physical child abuse in the United States.* Cambridge: Harvard University Press, 1970.

Gil, D. G. Violence against children. *Journal of Marriage and the Family* 33 (1971): 637–48.

Ginott, H. G. *Between parent and teenager.* New York: Macmillan, 1969.

Ginzberg, E. *Educated American women: Life styles and self-portraits.* New York: Columbia University Press, 1971.

Giroux, H., and Penna, A. N. Social education in the classroom: Dynamics of the hidden curriculum. *Theory and Research in Curriculum* 7 (Spring 1979): 21–42.

Glueck, S., and Glueck, E. *500 Criminal careers.* New York: Knopf, 1950.

Goertzel, V., and Goertzel, M. *Cradles of eminence.* Boston: Little, Brown, 1962.

Goldberg, S., and Lewis, M. Play behavior in the year-old infant: Early sex differences. *Child Development* 40 (1969): 21–31.

Goldin-Meadow, S., Seligman, M., and Gelman, R. Language in the two year old. *Cognition* 4 (1976): 189–202.

Goldman, A. S., and Smith, C. W. Host resistance factors in human milk. *Journal of Pediatrics* 82 (1973): 1082.

Goldson, E. The family care center: A hospital program for the medically high risk infant and his family. Paper presented at the tenth annual Child Abuse and Neglect Symposium at Keystone Resort, Colorado, May 15–18, 1980.

Goodenough, E. Interest in persons as an aspect of sex differences in the early years. *Genetic Psychology Monographs* 55 (1957): 287–323.

Goodfield, J. *An imagined world.* New York: Harper and Row, 1981.

Goodman, K., and Goodman, Y. Learning about psycholinguistic processes by analyzing oral reading. *Harvard Educational Review* 47 (1977): 317–33.

Gordon, I. *Baby learning through baby play.* New York: St. Martin's Press, 1970.

Gordon, I., Guinagh, B., and Jester, R. E. The Florida Parent Education Infant and Toddler Program. In M. C. Day and R. K. Parker (Eds.), *The preschool in action.* Boston: Allyn and Bacon, 1977, pp. 95–128.

Gordon, T. *Parent effectiveness training.* New York: Peter Wyden, 1970.

Graves, D. Handwriting is for writing. *Language Arts* 55 (1978): 393–99.

Graves, D. A six-year-old's writing process. *Language Arts* 56 (1979): 829–35.

Gray, S. W., and Klaus, R. A. The early training project: The seventh year report. *Child Development* 41 (1970): 909–24.

Green, E. H. Group play and quarreling among preschool children. *Child Development* 4 (1933): 302–07.

Greenburg, M., and Morris, N. Engrossment: The newborn's impact upon the father. *American Journal of Orthopsychiatry* 44 (1974): 520–31.

Greenburg, M., Pelliteri, O., and Barton, J. Frequency of defects in infants whose mothers had rubella during pregnancy. *Journal of the American Medical Association* 165 (1957): 675–78.

Greenfield, P. M., and Smith, J. *The structure of communication in early language development.* New York: Academic Press, 1976.

Grollman, E. *Talking about divorce.* Boston: Beacon Press, 1975.

Gross, R. T., and Duke, P. M. The effect of early versus late physical maturation on adolescent behavior. *Pediatric Clinics of North America* 27 (1980): 71–77.

Grossmann, H. J. *Manual on terminology and classification in mental retardation.* Washington, D.C.: American Association on Mental Retardation, 1973.

Grusec, J., and Skubiski, S. Model nurturance, demand characteristics of the modeling experiment, and altruism. *Journal of Personality and Social Psychology* 14 (1970): 352–59.

Grusec, J. E. Effects of co-observer evaluations on imitation: A developmental study. *Developmental Psychology* 8 (1973): 141.

Gustafsson, S. Women and Work in Sweden. *Working Life* 15 (December 1979).

Guttmacher, A. F. *Pregnancy, birth and family planning.* New York: New American Library, 1973.

Haaf, R. F., and Bell, R. Q. A facial dimension in visual discrimination by human infants. *Child Development* 38 (1967): 893–99.

Hall, C. S., and Lindzey, G. *Theories of personality.* 2nd ed. New York: John Wiley and Sons, 1970.

Hall, G. S. *Adolescence.* New York: Appleton, 1904.

Hamachek, D. E. Toward more effective teaching. In D. E. Hamachek (Ed.), *Human dynamics in psychology and education.* Boston: Allyn and Bacon, 1972.

Hamilton, J. S. Crying behavior and the "nonviolent" Leboyer method of delivery. Paper presented at the Society for Research in Child Development Biennial Meeting, San Francisco, 1979.

Hamilton, V. Motivation and personality in cognitive development. In V. Hamilton and M. D. Vernon (Eds.), *The development of cognitive processes.* London: Academic Press, 1976, pp. 451–506.

Harlow, H. F. The nature of love. *American Psychologist* 13 (1958): 673–85.

Harlow, H. F., and Harlow, M. Learning to love. *American Scientist* 54 (1966): 244–72.

Harlow, H. F., and Zimmerman, R. R. Affectional responses in the infant monkey. *Science* 130 (1959): 421.

Harris, F. R., Wolf, M. M., and Baer, D. M. Effects of adult social reinforcement on child development. In W. W. Hartup and N. L. Smothergill (Eds.), *The young child.* Vol. 1. Washington, D.C.: National Association for the Education of Young Children, 1967.

Hart, B. A., Reynolds, N. J., Baer, D. M., Brawley, E. R., and Harris, F. R. Effect of contingent and noncontingent social reinforcement on the cooperative play of a preschool child. *Journal of Applied Behavior Analysis* 1 (1968): 73–76.

Hatfield, E. M. Blindness in infants and young children. *Sight Saving Review* 42 (1972): 69–89.

Haviland, J. M. Sex-related pragmatics in infants' nonverbal communication. Paper presented at the Annual Meeting of the Eastern Psychological Association, New York, April 1976.

Hawkins, R. P., Peterson, R. F., Schweid, E., and Bijou, W. Behavior therapy in the home: Amelioration of problem parent-child relations with the parent in a therapeutic role. *Journal of Experimental Child Psychology* 4 (1966): 99–107.

Hawley, R. Some unsettling thoughts about settling in with pot. *The Education Digest* (March 1978): pp. 26–29.

Haynes, H., White, B. W., and Held, R. Visual accommodation in human infants. *Science* 148 (1965): 528–30.

Heber, R., and Garber, H. Report No. 2: An experiment in the prevention of cultural-familial retardation. In D. A. Primrose (Ed.), *Proceedings of the Third Conference of the International Association for the Scientific study of Mental Deficiency.* Warsaw: Polish Medical Publishers, 1975, pp. 34–43.

Hendry, L., and Gillies, P. Body type, body esteem, school and leisure: A study of overweight, average and underweight adolescents. *Journal of Youth and Adolescence 7* (1968): 181–95.

Herbst, A. L. Vaginal and cervical abnormalities after exposure to stilbestrol in utero. *Obstetrics and Gynecology* 40 (1972): 287–98.

Herbst, A. L., Scully, R. E., and Robboy, S. J. Problems in the examination of DES-exposed females. *Obstetrics and Gynecology* 46 (1975): 353–55.

Hershenson, M. Visual discrimination in the human newborn. *Journal of Comparative Physiological Psychology* 58 (1964): 270–76.

Hess, R., and Camara, K. Post-divorce family relationships as mediating factors on the consequences of divorce for children. *Journal of Social Issues* 35 (1979): 79–96.

Hetherington, E. M., Cox, M., and Cox, R. Play and social interaction in children following divorce. *Journal of Social Issues* 35 (1979): 26–49.

Hildreth, G. Developmental sequences in name writing. *Child Development* 7 (1936): 291–303.

Hirschman, R., and Katkin, E. S. Psychophysiological functioning, arousal, attention, and learning during the first year of life. In H. W. Reese (Ed.), *Advances in child development and behavior.* Vol. 7. New York: Academic Press, 1974.

Hoffman, L. W. Effects of maternal employment on the child: A review of the research. In H. Bee (Ed.), *Social Issues in Developmental Psychology.* 2nd ed. New York: Harper and Row, 1978, pp. 130–71.

Hoffman, M. L. Empathy, role taking, guilt, and development of altruistic motives. In T. Lickona (Ed.), *Moral development and behavior.* New York: Holt, Rinehart and Winston, 1976, pp. 124–43.

Hoffman, M. L., and Saltzstein, H. D. Parent discipline and the child's moral development. *Journal of Personality and Social Psychology* 5 (1967): 45–47.

Holland, V. M., and Palermo, D. S. On learning "less": Language and cognitive development. *Child Development* 46 (1975): 437–43.

Honig, A. S., and Lally, J. R. *Infant caregiving: A design for training.* New York: Media Projects Incorporated, 1972.

Huey, E. B. *The psychology and pedagogy of reading.* Cambridge: MIT Press, 1977.

Hunt, J. M. Intrinsic motivation and its role in psychological development. *Nebraska Symposium on Motivation* 13 (1965): 189–282.

Hymes, J. *Early childhood education. The year in review. A look at 1977.* Carmel, Calif.: Hacienda Press, 1978.

Ingalls, A. J., and Salerno, M. C. *Maternal and child health nursing.* Saint Louis: C. V. Mosby, 1975.

Ingram, V. M. *Hemoglobin and its abnormalities.* Springfield, Ill.: Charles C. Thomas, 1961.

Inhelder, B. Memory and intelligence in the child. In D. Elkind and J. Flavell (Eds.), *Studies in cognitive development.* New York: Oxford University Press, 1969.

Inhelder, B., and Piaget, J. *The growth of logical thinking from childhood to adolescence.* New York: Basic Books, 1958.

Inhelder, B., and Piaget, J. *The early growth of logic in the child.* (E. A. Lunzer and D. Papert, trans.) New York: W. W. Norton, 1969.

Jackson, P. *Life in classrooms.* New York: Holt, Rinehart and Winston, 1968.

Jenkins, J. J., and Palermo, D. S. Mediation processes and the acquisition of linguistic structure. In U. Bellugi and R. Brown (Eds.), The acquisition of language. *Monographs of the Society for Research in Child Development* 29 (1964): 141–69.

Jenkins, R. L. Maxims in child custody cases. *Family Coordinator* 26 (1977): 335–90.

Jensen, A. How much can we boost IQ and scholastic achievement? *Harvard Educational Review* 39 (1969): 1–123.

Jensen, A. *Educability and group differences.* New York: Harper and Row, 1973.

Jensen, A. Cumulative deficit: A testable hypothesis? *Developmental Psychology* 10 (1974): 996–1019.

Jensen, A. Cumulative deficit in IQ of blacks in

the rural south. *Developmental Psychology* 13 (1977): 184–91.

Johnson, H. R., Mykre, S. A., Ruvalcaba, R. H. A., Thuline, H. C., and Kelley, V. C. Effects of testosterone on body image and behavior in Klinefelter's Syndrome: A pilot study. *Developmental Medicine and Child Neurology* 12 (1970): 454–60.

Johnson, S., Wahl, G., Martin, S., and Johansson, S. How deviant is the normal child? A behavioral analysis of the preschool child and his family. In R. Rubin, J. Brady, and J. Henderson (Eds.), *Advances in behavior therapy* Vol. 4. 1973, pp. 37–54.

Jones, H. F. Adolescence in our society. In Anniversary Papers of the Community Service Society of New York: *The family in a democratic society.* New York: Columbia University Press, 1949, pp. 70–82.

Jones, M. C., and Bayley, N. Physical maturing among boys as related to behavior. *Journal of Educational Psychology* 41 (1950): 129–48.

Joslyn, W. D. Androgen induced social dominance in infant female rhesus monkeys. *Journal of Child Psychology and Psychiatry* 84 (1971): 35–44.

Kabara, J. J. Lipids as host-resistance factors of human milk. *Nutrition Review* 38 (1981): 73–85.

Kagan, J. *Change and continuity in infancy.* New York: John Wiley and Sons, 1971.

Kagan, J. Do infants think? *Scientific American* 226 (1972): 74–82.

Kagan, J., Kearsley, R. B., and Zelazo, P. R. *Infancy: Its place in human development.* Cambridge: Harvard University Press, 1980.

Kamii, C., and DeVries, R. Piaget for early education. In M. C. Day and R. K. Parker (Eds.), *The preschool in action.* Boston: Allyn and Bacon, 1977.

Kamin, L. J. *The science and politics of IQ.* Potomac, Md.: Lawrence Erlbaum, 1974.

Kamin, L. J. A positive interpretation of apparent "cumulative deficit." *Developmental Psychology* 14 (1978): 195–96.

Kaplan, E. L., and Kaplan, G. A. The prelinguistic child. In J. Eliot (Ed.), *Human development and cognitive processes.* New York: Holt, Rinehart and Winston, 1970, pp. 358–81.

Karnes, M. B. Research and development program on preschool disadvantaged children: Final report. Washington, D.C., U.S. Office of Education, 1969.

Katcher, A. The discrimination of sex differences by young children. *Journal of Genetic Psychology* 87 (1955): 131–43.

Katz, A. Lone fathers: Perspectives and implications for family policy. *The Family Coordinator* 28 (1979): 521–28.

Katz, L. *Ethical considerations in working with young children.* Urbana, Ill: ERIC Clearinghouse on Early Childhood Education, 1977.

Katz, L., and Hamilton, J. R. Fat absorption in infants of low birth weight less than 1,300 gm. *Journal of Pediatrics* 85 (1974): 6081.

Kay, D. A., and Anglin, J. M. Overextension and underextension in the child's expressive and receptive speech. Paper presented at the biennial meeting of the Society for Research in Child Development, San Francisco, March 1979.

Kempe, R. S., and Kempe, C. H. *Child abuse.* Cambridge: Harvard University Press, 1978.

Keniston, K. Social change and youth in America. In E. H. Erikson (Ed.), *Youth: Change and challenge.* New York: Basic Books, 1963.

Keniston, K. Youth: A "new" stage of life. *American Scholar* 39 (1970): 631–41.

Keniston, K. *All our children.* New York: Harcourt Brace Jovanovich, 1977.

Keogh, B. K., and Barkett, C. J. Children's rights in assessment and school placement. *Journal of Social Issues* 34 (1978): 87–100.

Kerkay, J., Zsako, S., and Kaplan, A. Immunoelectrophoretic serum patterns associated with mothers of children affected with the G_1-trisomy syndrome (Down's Syndrome). *American Journal of Mental Deficiency* 75 (1971): 729–32.

Kestenbaum, R. The child's understanding of death: How does it develop? In E. Grollman

(Ed.), *Explaining death to children.* Boston: Beacon Press, 1967, pp. 89–110.

Kihlman, B. A. *Caffeine and chromosomes.* Amsterdam: Alseveir, 1977.

Kilmer, S. Infant-toddler group day care: A review of research. In L. Katz (Ed.), *Current topics in early childhood education.* Vol. 2. Norwood, N.J.: Ablex Publishing Corporation, 1979, pp. 69–116.

King, K., Abernathy, T. J., and Chapman, A. H. Black adolescents' views of maternal employment as a threat to the marital relationship. *Journal of Marriage and the Family* 38 (1976): 733–37.

Kirk, S. *Educating exceptional children.* 2nd. ed. Boston: Houghton Mifflin, 1972.

Klahr, D., and Wallace, J. G. *Cognitive development: An information-processing view.* Hillsdale, N.J.: Lawrence Erlbaum, 1976.

Klaus, M. H., and Fannaroff, A. A. *Care of the high-risk neonate.* Philadelphia: W. B. Saunders, 1973.

Klaus, M. H., and Kennell, J. H. *Maternal-infant bonding.* St. Louis: Mosby, 1976.

Klaus, M. H., Kennell, B. S., Plumb, N., and Zerehlke, S. Human maternal behavior at the first contact with her young. *Pediatrics* 46 (1970): 187–92.

Klein, M. H., and Stern, L. Low birth weight and the battered child syndrome. *American Journal of Diseases of Childhood* 122 (1971): 15–18.

Kohl, H. *Growing with your children.* Boston: Little, Brown, 1978.

Kohlberg, L. Stage and sequence: The cognitive developmental approach to socialization. In D. A. Goslin (Ed.), *Handbook of socialization theory and research.* Chicago: Rand McNally, 1969, pp. 347–480.

Kohlberg, L. Moral stages and moralization. In T. Lickona (Ed.), *Moral development and behavior: Theory, research, and social issues.* New York: Holt, Rinehart and Winston, 1976, pp. 31–53.

Kohlberg, L. A., and Ullian, D. Z. Stages in the development of psychosexual concepts and attitudes. In R. C. Friedman, R. M. Richart, and R. L. Vande Wiele (Eds.), *Sex differences in behavior.* New York: John Wiley and Sons, 1974.

Koocher, G. Talking with children about death. *American Journal of Orthopsychiatry* 44 (1974): 404–11.

Korner, A. Individual differences at birth: Duplications for early experience and later development. *American Journal of Orthopsychiatry* 41 (1971): 608–10.

Korner, A., and Grobstein, R. Visual alertness as related to soothing in neonates: Implications for maternal stimulation and early deprivation. *Child Development* 37 (1966): 867–76.

Korner, A., and Thoman, E. B. The relative efficacy of contact and vestibular-proprioceptive stimulation in soothing neonates. *Child Development* 43 (1972): 443–53.

Kotelchuck, M., Zelazo, P. R., Kagan, J., and Spelke, E. Infant reaction to parental separations when left with familiar and unfamilair adults. *Journal of Genetic Psychology* 126 (1975): 255–62.

Kratcoski, P. E., and Kratcoski, J. E. Changing patterns in the delinquent activities of boys and girls: A self-reported delinquency analysis. *Adolescence* 37 (1975): 53–91.

Kron, R. E., Stern, M., and Goddard, K. E. Newborn sucking behavior affected by obstetrics sedation. *Pediatrics* 37 (1966): 1012–16.

Lally, R., and Honig, A. The Family Development Research Program. In C. Day and R. Parker (Eds.), *The Preschool in action.* Boston: Allyn and Bacon, 1977, pp. 149–94.

Lamb, M. E. Influence of the child on marital quality and family interaction during the prenatal, perinatal and infancy periods. In R. M. Lerner and G. B. Spanier (Eds.), *Child influences on marital and family interactions: A life span perspective.* New York: Academic Press, 1978.

Lamberth, J., Rappaport, H., and Rappaport, M. *Personality: An introduction.* New York: Knopf, 1978.

Lansing, K. *Art, artists, and art education.* New York: McGraw-Hill, 1970.

Latham, A. J. The relationship between pubertal status and leadership in junior high school boys. *Journal of Genetic Psychology* 78 (1951): 185–94.

Lavine, L. O. Differentiation of letterlike forms in prereading children. *Developmental Psychology* (1977): 89–94.

Leaf, R. C. Avoidance response evocation as a function of prior discriminative fear conditioning under curare. *Journal of Comparative and Physiological Psychology* 58 (1964): 446–49.

Leboyer, F. *Birth without violence.* New York: Knopf, 1975.

Lee, P. C., and Gropper, N. B. Sex-role culture and educational practice. *Harvard Educational Review* 44 (1974): 364–410.

Legrün, A. Wie und was "schreiben" Kindergarten-soglinge? *Zeitschrift Fur Padagpgische Psychologie* 33 (1932): 322–31.

Leifer, A. D., and Roberts, D. F. Children's responses to television violence. In J. P. Murray, E. A. Rubenstein, and G. A. Comstock (Eds.), *Television and social behavior II: Television and social learning.* Washington, D.C.: U.S. Government Printing Office, 1972, pp. 43–180.

Lenz, W. Malformations caused by drugs in pregnancy. *American Journal of Diseases of Children* 112 (1966): 99–106.

Leona, M. H. An examination of adolescent clique language in a suburban secondary school. *Adolescence* 13 (1978): 495–502.

Lepper, M. Dissonance, self-perception, and honesty in children. *Journal of Personality and Social Psychology* 25 (1973): 65–74.

Lerner, M. *Heredity, evolution and society.* San Francisco: W. H. Freeman, 1968.

Lerner, R. M., and Spanier, G. B. *Adolescent development.* New York: McGraw-Hill, 1980.

Levenstein, P. The mother-child home program. In M. C. Day and R. K. Parker (Eds.), *The preschool in action.* 2nd ed. Boston: Allyn and Bacon, 1977.

Levine, E., and Kozak, C. Drug and alcohol use, delinquency, and vandalism among upper middle class pre- and post-adolescents. *Journal of Youth and Adolescence* 8 (1979): 91–101.

Levine, S. Sex differences in the brain. *Scientific American* 214 (1966): 84–90.

Lewis, M. M. *Infant speech.* London: Routledge and Kegan Paul, 1951.

Liben, L. S. Memory from a cognitive-developmental perspective: A theoretical and empirical review. In W. Overton and J. Gallagher (Eds.), *Knowledge and development.* Vol. 1. New York: Plenum Press, 1977.

Lickona, T. Research on Piaget's theory of moral development. In T. Lickona (Ed.), *Moral development and behavior: Theory, research, and social issues.* New York: Holt, Rinehart and Winston, 1976, pp. 219–240.

Liebert, R. M., and Baron, R. A. Some immediate effects of televised violence on children's behavior. *Developmental Psychology* 6 (1972): 469–75.

Liebert, R. M., Neale, J. M., and Davidson, E. S. *The early window: Effects of television on children and youth.* New York: Pergamon Press, 1973.

Liebert, R. M., and Poulos, R. W. Television as a moral teacher. In T. Lickona (Ed.), *Moral development and behavior: Theory, research, and social issues.* New York: Holt, Rinehart and Winston, 1976, pp. 284–98.

Lilienfield, A. M. *Epidemiology of Mongolism.* Baltimore: John Hopkins Press, 1969.

Linde, S. M. *Sickle-cell: A complete guide to prevention and treatment.* New York: Pavilion, 1972.

Lippman, H. S. *Treatment of the child in emotional conflict.* New York: McGraw-Hill, 1956.

Lipsitt, L. P. Learning in the first year of life. In L. P. Lipsitt and C. C. Spiker (Eds.), *Advances in child development and behavior.* Vol. 1. New York: Academic Press, 1963.

Lipsitt, L. P., and Levy, N. Electrotactual threshold in the neonate. *Child Development* 30 (1959): 547–54.

Livesley, W. J., and Bromley, D. B. *Person perception in childhood and adolescence. London. John Wiley and Sons, 1973.

Livingstone, F. B. Abnormal hemoglobin in human populations. Chicago: Aldine, 1967.

Lorenz, K. On aggression. New York: Harcourt, Brace and World, 1966.

Lowe, M. Trends in the development of representational play in infants from one to three years: An observational study. Journal of Child Psychology and Psychiatry 16 (1975): 33–47.

Lowrey, G. H. Growth and development of children. 7th ed. Chicago: Year Book, 1978.

Lubchenco, L. O., Delivoria-Papodopoulos, M., and Searle, D. Long-term follow-up studies of prematurely-born infants II. Influences of birth weight and gestational age on sequelae. Journal of Pediatrics 80 (1972): 509–12.

Luepnitz, Deborah. Which aspects of divorce affect children? The Family Coordinator 28 (1979): 79–85.

Lyle, J., and Hoffman, H. R. Children's use of television and other media. In E. A. Rubenstein, G. A. Comstock, and J. P. Murray (Eds.), Television and social behavior IV. Television in day-to-day life: Patterns of use. Washington, D.C.: U.S. Government Printing Office, 1972.

McCall, R. B. Exploratory manipulation and play in the human infant. Monographs of the Society for Research in Child Development 39 (1974), Serial No. 155.

McClelland, D. C., Atkinson, I. W., Clark, R. A., and Lowell, E. L. The achievement motive. New York: Halsted Press, 1976.

Maccoby, E. E., and Feldman, S. S. Mother-attachment and stranger-reactions in the third year of life. Monographs of the Society for Research in Child Development 37 (1972): Serial No. 146.

Maccoby, E. E., and Jacklin, C. N. The psychology of sex differences. Stanford, Calif.: Stanford University Press, 1974.

McGhee, P. E. Cognitive development and children's comprehension of humor. Child Development 42 (1971): 123–38.

McGhee, P. E. Humor: Its origin and development. San Francisco: W. H. Freeman, 1979.

McGowan, R. W., Jarman, B. O., and Pederson, D. M. Effects of a competitive endurance training program on self concept and peer approval. Journal of Psychology 86 (1974): 57–60.

McKenry, P. C., Walters, L. H., and Johnson, C. Adolescent pregnancy: A review of the literature. The Family Coordinator 28 (1979): 17–28.

McLaughlin, B. Second language acquisition in childhood. New York: John Wiley and Sons, 1978.

Macnamara, J. The cognitive basis of language learning in infants. Psychology Review 79 (1972): 1–13.

Macnamara, J. First and second language learning: Same or different? Journal of Education 158 (1976): 39–54.

McNaught, A. B., and Callander, R. Illustrated physiology. Baltimore: Williams and Wilkins, 1963.

McNeill, D. Developmental psycholinguistics. In F. Smith and G. A. Miller (Eds.), The genesis of language: A psycholinguistic approach. Cambridge: MIT Press, 1966, pp. 15–84.

McNeill, D. The development of language. In P. H. Mussen (Ed.), Carmichael's manual of child psychology. Vol. 1. New York: John Wiley and Sons, 1970.

McNeill, D., and Lindig, K. The perceptual reality of phonemes, syllables, words, and sentences. Journal of Verbal Language and Verbal Behavior 12 (1973): 419–30.

Maddi, S. R. Personality theories. Homewood, Ill.: Dorsey Press, 1976.

Maier, S., Seligman, M., and Solomon, R. Pavlovian fear conditioning and learned helplessness. In B. A. Campbell and R. M. Church (Eds.), Punishment and aversive behavior. New York: Appleton-Century-Crofts, 1969.

Maisels, M. J. Bilirubin. Pediatric Clinics of North America 19 (1972): 447–501.

Manosevitz, M., Prentice, N. M., and Wilson, F. Individual and family correlates of imaginary companions in preschool children. *Developmental Psychology* 8 (1973): 72–79.

Marks, A. Adolescent suicide: Epidemiologic study of recent trends. In F. A. Oski and J. N. Stockman (Eds.), *1980 yearbook of pediatrics.*

Marx, G. F. Placental transfer and drugs used in anesthesia. *Anesthesiology* 22 (1961): 294.

Mason, W. A. Motivational aspects of social responsiveness in young chimpanzees. In H. W. Stevenson, E. H. Hess, and H. L. Rheingold (Eds.), *Early behavior.* New York: John Wiley and Sons, 1967.

Mattingly, I. G. Reading, the linguistic process and linguistic awareness. In J. F. Kavanagh and I. G. Mattingly (Eds.), *Language by ear and by eye.* Cambridge: MIT Press, 1972.

Maudry, M., and Nekula, M. Social relations between children of the same age during the first two years of life. *Journal of Genetic Psychology* 54 (1939): 193–215.

Maurer, A. What children fear. *The Journal of Genetic Psychology* 106 (1965): 265–77.

Mayer, J. *Health.* New York: Van Nostrand, 1974.

Mayer, R. *Thinking and problem solving: An introduction to human cognition and learning.* Glenview, Ill.: Scott, Foresman, 1977.

Meichenbaum, D. *Cognitive-behavior modification: An integrative approach.* New York: Plenum Press, 1977.

Menyuk, P. *Sentences children use.* Cambridge: MIT Press, 1969.

Menyuk, P. *Language and maturation.* Cambridge: MIT Press, 1977.

Meredith, H. V. Somatological development. In B. B. Wolman, (Ed.), *Handbook of general psychology.* Englewood Cliffs, N.J.: Prentice-Hall, 1973.

Meredith, H. V. Relation between tobacco smoking of pregnant women and body size of progeny. *Human Biology* 47 (1975): 451–72. a

Meredith, H. V. Somatic changes during human prenatal life. *Child Development* 46 (1975): 603–10. b

Mestayan, G., and Varga, F. Chemical thermoregulation of full-term and premature newborn infants. *Journal of Pediatrics* 56 (1960): 623–29.

Metropolitan Readiness Tests. New York: Harcourt, Brace Jovanovich, 1976.

Milberg, A. *Street games.* New York: McGraw-Hill, 1976.

Millar, W. S. Conditioning and learning in early infancy. In B. Foss (Ed.), *New perspectives in child development.* Harmondsworth, Eng.: Penguin, 1974.

Miller, L. B., and Dyer, J. L. Four preschool programs: Their dimension and effects. *Monographs of the Society for Research in Child Development* 40 (1975), Serial No. 162.

Miller, M. A., and Brooten, D. A. *The childbearing family: A nursing perspective.* Boston: Little, Brown, 1977.

Miller, S. M. Effects of maternal employment on sex role perceptions, interests, and self esteem in kindergarten girls. *Developmental Psychology* 11 (1975): 405–06.

Miller, W. A., and Erbe, R. W. *Prenatal diagnosis of genetic disorders.* Boston: Massachusetts General Hospital, 1978.

Milunsky, A., and Annas, G., (Eds.) *Genetics and the law.* New York: Plenum Press, 1976.

Mischel, W., and Baker, N. Cognitive transformations of reward objects through instructions. *Journal of Personality and Social Psychology* 31 (1975): 254–61.

Mischel, W., and Ebbesen, E. Attention in delay of gratification. *Journal of Personality and Social Psychology* 16 (1970): 329–37.

Mischel, W., and Mischel, H. A cognitive social-learning approach to morality and self-regulation. In T. Lickona (Ed.), *Moral development and behavior: Theory, research, and social issues.* New York: Holt, Rinehart and Winston, 1976, pp. 84–107.

Mischell, W. *Introduction to personality.* New York: Holt, Rinehart and Winston, 1976.

Mitchell, E., and Anderson, R. T. Play spaces in Denmark. *Young Children* 35 (1980): 2–8.

Moely, B. E. Organizational factors in the development of memory. In R. V. Kail and J. W. Hagen (Eds.), *Perspectives on the develop-*

ment of *Memory and cognition.* Hillsdale, N.J.: Lawrence Erlbaum, 1977.

Moffitt, A. R. Consonant cue perception by twenty- to twenty-four-week-old infants. *Child development* 42 (1971): 717–31.

Montessori, M. *The absorbent mind.* (C. A. Claremont, trans.) New York: Dell, 1967.

Moore, S. M. The persistence of preschool effects: A national collaborative study. *Young Children* 33 (1978): 65–71.

Moriarty, A., and Toussieng, P. *Adolescent coping.* New York: Grune and Stratton, 1976.

Morishima, H. O., Daniel, S. S., Finster, M., Poppers, P. J., and James, L. S. Transmission of mepivocaine hydrochloride (carbocaine) across the human placenta. *Anesthesiology* 27 (1966): 147–54.

Morphett, M. V., and Washburne, C. When should children begin to read? *Elementary School Journal* 31 (1931): 496–503.

Moss, H. A. Sex, age, and state as determinants of mother-infant interaction. *Merrill-Palmer Quarterly* 13 (1967): 19–36.

Moss, H. A. Sex, age and state as determinants of mother-infant interaction. In J. M. Bordwick (Ed.), *Readings on the psychology of women.* New York: Harper and Row, 1972.

Mowrer, O. H. Hearing and speaking: An analysis of language learning. *Journal of Speech and Hearing Disorders* 23 (1958): 143–51.

Mueller, E. The maintenance of verbal exchanges between young children. *Child Development* 43 (1972): 930–38.

Mueller, E., Bleir, M., Krakow, J., Hegedus, K., and Cournoyer, P. The development of peer verbal interaction among two-year-old boys. *Child Development* 48 (1977): 284–87.

Muir, D., and Field, J. Newborn infants orient to sounds. *Child Development* 50 (1979): 431–36.

Murray, J. P. *Television and youth: 25 years of research and controversy.* Boys Town, Neb.: The Boys Town Center for the Study of Youth Development, 1980.

Muuss, R. E. (Ed.), *Adolesence behavior and society: A book of readings.* (2nd ed.) New York: Random House, 1975.

Naeye, R. L. Hypoxemia and the sudden infant death syndrome. *Science* 183 (1974): 837–38

Naeye, R. L. Influence of maternal cigarette smoking during pregnancy on fetal and childhood growth. *Obstetrics and Gynecology* 57 (1981): 18–24.

Naeye, R. L., Blanc, W., and Paul, C. Effects of maternal nutrition on the human fetus. *Pediatrics* 52 (1973): 494–503.

National Association for Better Radio and Television. *Crime on television: A survey report.* Los Angeles: National Association for Better Radio and Television, 1964.

National Association of Elementary School Principals. One-parent families and their children: The school's most significant minority. *Principal* 60 (1980): 31–37.

National Institute of Child Health and Human Development. *Sudden infant death syndrome.* Bethesda, Md.: National Institute of Child Health and Human Development, 1972.

Needham, J. *A history of embryology.* New York: Abelard-Schuman, 1959.

Nelson, K. Structure and strategy in learning to talk. *Monographs of the Society for Research in Child Development* 38 (1973), Serial No. 149.

Nelson, K. E., and Nelson, K. Cognitive pendulums and their linguistic realization. In K. E. Nelson, *Children's language.* Vol. 1. New York: Gardner Press, 1978.

Neumann, C. G. Obesity in pediatric practice: Obesity in the preschool and school-age child. *Pediatric Clinics of North America* 24 (1977): 117–22.

Newman, H. H., Freeman, F. N., and Holzinger, K. J. *Twins: A study of heredity and environment.* Chicago: University of Chicago Press, 1937.

Nielsen, G., Collins, S., Meisel, J., Lowry, M., Engh, H., and Johnson, D. An intervention program for atypical infants. In B. Z. Friedlander, G. M. Sterritt, and G. E. Kirk (Eds.), *Exceptional infant: Assessment and Intervention.* Vol. 3. New York: Brunner/Mazel, 1975.

Nissen, H. W. A study of exploratory behavior in the white rat by means of the obstruction method. *Journal of Genetic Psychology* 37 (1930): 361–76.

Nucci, L. P., and Gordon, N. J. Educating adolescents from a Piagetian perspective. *Journal of Education* 161 (1979): 87–99.

O'Connor, S., Altemeier, W., Cherrod, K., and Sandler, H. How does rooming-in enhance the mother-infant bond? Paper presented at the Society for Pediatric Research, Atlanta, May 1979.

Offer, D., Marcus, D., and Offer, J. L. A longitudinal study of normal adolescent boys. *American Journal of Psychiatry* 126 (1970): 917–24.

Orthner, D., Brown, T., and Ferguson, D. Single-parent fatherhood: An emerging lifestyle. *The Family Coordinator* 25 (1976): 429–37.

Otis, A. S., and Lennon, R. T. *Otis-Lennon Mental Ability Test Primary 1 Level.* New York: Harcourt, Brace and World, 1967.

Overmier, J. V., and Leaf, R. C. Effects of discriminative Pavlovian fear conditioning upon previously or subsequently acquired avoidance responding. *Journal of Comparative and Physiological Psychology* 60 (1965): 213–17.

Palermo, D. S. Still more about the comprehension of "less." *Developmental Psychology* 10 (1974): 827–29.

Palermo, D. S., and Molfese, D. L. Language acquisition from age five onward. In F. Rebelsky and L. Dorman (Eds.), *Child Development and behavior.* 2nd ed. New York: Knopf, 1973, 401–23.

Papoušek, H. Experimental studies of appetitional behavior in human newborns and infants. In H. Stevenson, E. Hess, and H. Rheingold (Eds.), *Early behavior: Comparative and developmental approaches.* New York: John Wiley and Sons, 1967.

Papoušek, H., and Bernstein, P. The functioning of conditioning stimulation in human neonates and infants. In A. Ambrose (Ed.), *Stimulation in early infancy.* New York: Academic Press, 1969.

Parke, R. D. Some effects of punishment on children's behavior. In W. Hartup (Ed.), *The young child: Reviews of research.* Vol. 2. Washington, D.C.: National Association for the Education of Young Children, 1972.

Parke, R. D. Father-infant interaction. In M. H. Klaus, T. Leger, and M. A. Trause (Eds.), *Maternal attachment and mothering disorders: A round table.* New York: Johnson and Johnson, 1975, pp. 61–63.

Parsley, N. J., and Rabinowitz, F. M. Crying in the first year: An operant interpretation of the Bell and Ainsworth (1972) findings. *Child Study Journal* 5 (1975): 83–89.

Parten, M. Social play among preschool children. *Journal of Abnormal and Social Psychology* 27 (1932): 243–69.

Patterson, G. L., Litmann, R. A., and Bricker, W. Assertive behavior in children: A step toward a theory of aggression. *Monographs of the Society for Research in Child Development* 32 (1967): 1–43.

Paul, R. Invented spelling in kindergarten. *Young Children* 31 (1976): 195–200.

Pearce, D. Women, work, and welfare: The feminization of poverty. In K. W. Feinstein (Ed.), *Working women and families.* Beverly Hills, Calif.: Sage, 1979.

Pearl, D., Bouthilet, L., and Lazar, J. (Eds.). *Television and behavior: Ten years of scientific progress and implications for the eighties.* Washington, D.C.: U.S. Government Printing Office, in press.

Peck, R. F., and Havinghurst, R. J. *The psychology of character development.* New York: John Wiley and Sons, 1960.

Peevers, B. H., and Secord, P. F. Developmental changes in attribution of descriptive concepts to persons. *Journal of Personality and Social Psychology* 27 (1973): 120–28.

Perkins, R. P., Nakashima, I. I., Mullin, M. Dubansky, L. S., and Chin, M. L. *Obstetrics and Gynecology* 52 (1978): 179–88.

Perlstein, P. H., Hersh, C., Glueck, C. J., and Sutherland, J. M. Adaptation to cold in the first three days of life. *Pediatrics* 54 (1974): 411.

Pertshuck, M. J. Behavior therapy: Extended follow-up. In R. Vigersky (Ed.), *Anorexia nervosa.* New York: Raven Press, 1977, pp. 305–13.

Peterson, A. C. Can puberty come any earlier? *Psychology Today* 12 (1979): 45.

Phares, E. J. *Locus of control in personality.* Morristown, N.J.: General Learning Press, 1976.

Phoenix, C. H., Goy, R. W., and Resko, J. A. Psychosexual differentiation as a function of androgenic stimulation. In H. Bee (Ed.), *Social Issues in developmental psychology.* 2nd ed. New York: Harper and Row, 1978.

Piaget, J. *Play, dreams and imitation.* (C. Gahego and F. M. Hodgson, trans.) New York: W. W. Norton, 1951. (Originally published, 1945.)

Piaget, J. *The origins of intelligence in children.* (M. Cook, trans.) New York: W. W. Norton, 1952. (Originally published, 1936.)

Piaget, J. *The construction of reality in the child.* (M. Cook, trans.) New York: Ballantine Books, 1954. (Originally published, 1937.)

Piaget, J. *Logic and psychology.* New York: Basic Books, 1957.

Piaget, J. *Play, dreams and imitation* (C. Gattegno and F. M. Hodgson, trans.). New York: W. W. Norton, 1962.

Piaget, J. *The origins of intelligence in young children* (M. Cook, trans.) New York: W. W. Norton, 1963.

Piaget, J. *The child's conception of number.* New York: W. W. Norton, 1965. a

Piaget, J. *The moral judgment of the child.* (M. Gabain, trans.) New York: Free Press, 1965. (Originally published, 1932.) b

Piaget, J. *The child's conception of the world* (J. and A. Tomlinson, trans.). Totowa, N.J.: Littlefield, Adams, 1969.

Piaget, J. *The child's conception of time.* (A. J. Pomerans, trans.). New York: Ballantine Books, 1971. (Originally published, 1927.)

Piaget, J. *The child's conception of physical causality* (M. Gabain, trans.). Totowa, N.J.: Littlefield, Adams, 1972.

Piaget, J., and Inhelder, B. *The child's conception of space.* (F. T. Langdon and J. L. Lunger, trans.) New York: W. W. Norton, 1967. (Originally published, 1948.

Piaget, J., and Inhelder, B. *The psychology of the child.* (H. Weaver, trans.) New York: Basic Books, 1969. (Originally published, 1966.)

Piaget, J., and Inhelder, B. *Memory and Intelligence.* New York: Basic Books, 1973.

Pifer, A. Women working: Toward a new society. In Karen W. Feinstein (Ed.), *Working women and families.* Beverly Hills, Calif.: Sage, 1979.

Pines, M. Invisible playmates. *Psychology Today* 12 (1978): 38–43.

Pines, M. A head start in the nursery. *Psychology Today* 13 (1979): 56–68.

Ploman, L., and Persson, B. On the transfer of barbiturates to the human fetus and their accumulation in some of its vital organs. *Journal of Obstetrics and Gynaecology of the British Empire* 64 (1957): 706–11.

Plummer, G. Anomalies occurring in children exposed *in utero* to the atomic bomb in Hiroshima. *Pediatrics* 10 (1952): 687.

Pomerantz, S. C. Sex differences in the relative importance of self-esteem, physical self-satisfaction, and identity in predicting adolescent satisfaction. *Journal of Youth and Adolescence* 8 (1979): 51–61.

Prechtl, H. F. R., and Beintema, D. J. *The neurological examination of the full-term newborn infant: Clinics in developmental medicine,* No. 12. London: Heinemann, 1964.

Provence, S., and Lipton, R. C. *Infants in institutions.* New York: International Universities Press, 1962.

Ramey, C. T., and Finkelstein, N. W. Contingent stimulation and infant competence. *Journal of Pediatric Psychology* 3 (1978): 89–96.

Raudsepp, E., and Hough, G. *Creative growth games.* New York: Jove, 1977.

Rauh, J. L., and Schumsky, D. A. An evaluation of tricepts skinfold measures from urban school children. *Human Biology* 40 (1968): 263–74.

Raven, R. The development of Wh-questions in 1st and 2nd language learners. In J. C. Richards (Ed.), *Error analysis: Perspectives on second language acquisition.* London: Longmans, 1974.

Read, C. Preschool children's knowledge of English phonology. In M. Wolf, M. K. McQuillan, and E. Radwin (Eds.), *Thought and language/Language and reading.* Reprint Series No. 14, *Harvard Educational Review,* 1980, pp. 150–79.

Reese, H. W., and Lipsitt, L. P. *Experimental child psychology.* New York: Academic Press, 1970.

Reich, P. A. Notes and discussion: The early acquisition of word meaning. *Journal of Child Language* 3 (1976): 117–23.

Reisinger, K. S., and Williams, A. F. Evaluation of programs designed to increase the protection of infants in cars. *Pediatrics* 68 (1978): 280–87.

Rheingold, H. L., Hay, D., and West, M. Sharing in the second year of life. *Child Development* 47 (1976): 1148–58.

Rheingold, H. L., Gewirtz, J. L., and Ross, H. W. Social conditioning of vocalizations in the infant. *Journal of Comparative and Physiological Psychology* 52 (1959): 68–73.

Rice, M. E., and Grusec, J. E. Saying and doing. Effects of observer performance. *Journal of Personality and Social Psychology* 32 (1975): 584–93.

Richards, M. P., and Bernal, J. F. An observational study of mother-infant interactions. In N. B. Jones (Ed.), *Ethological studies of child behavior.* London: Cambridge University Press, 1972.

Rieser, J., Yonas, A., and Wilner, K. Radial localization of odors by human newborns. *Child Development* 47 (1976): 856–59.

Roberts, E. J., and Gagnon, J. *Family life and sexual learning. Volume 1.* Summary Report. Cambridge, Mass.: Population Education, 1978.

Robertson, J., and Bowlby, J. Responses of young children to separation from their mothers. *Courrier: Centre International de l'enfance* 2 (1952): 131–42.

Roedell, W. C., Slaby, R. C., and Robinson, H. B. *Social development in young children.* Belmont, Calif.: Wadsworth, 1977.

Rogers, C., and Wrightsman, L. Attitudes toward children's rights: Nurturance or self-determination? *Journal of Social Issues* 34 (1978): 59–68.

Rogers, D. *Adolescence: A psychological perspective.* Monterey, Calif.: Brooks-Cole, 1972.

Rosen, B. C., and D'Andrade. The psycho-social origins of achievement motivation. In U. Bronfenbrenner and M. H. Mahoney (Eds.), *Influences on human development.* 2nd ed. Hindsdale, Ill.: Dryden Press, 1975, pp. 438–50.

Rosen, C. E. The effects of sociodramatic play on problem-solving behavior among culturally disadvantaged preschool children. *Child Development* 45 (1974): 920–27.

Rosenhan, D. L. Some origins of concern for others. In P. Mussen, J. Langer, and M. Covington (Eds.), *Trends and issues in developmental psychology.* New York: Holt, Rinehart and Winston, 1969.

Rosenhan, D. L. Learning theory and pro-social behavior. In L. Wispe (Ed.), *Positive forms of social behavior. Journal of Social Issues* 28 (1972): 151–63.

Rosenhan, P., and White, G. M. Observation and rehearsal as determinants of prosocial behavior. *Journal of Personality and Social Psychology* 5 (1967): 424–31.

Rosenthal, R., and Jacobson, L. *Pygmalion in the classroom.* New York: Holt, Rinehart and Winston, 1968.

Rosenzweig, M. R., Krech, D., Bennett, E. L., and Zolman, J. F. Variation in environmental complexity and brain measures. *Journal of Comparative and Physiological Psychology* 55 (1962): 1092–95.

Rothenberg, B. Children's social sensitivity and the relationship to interpersonal competence, intrapersonal conflict, and intellectual level. *Developmental Psychology* 2 (1970): 335–50.

Rotter, J. B. *Social learning and clinical psychology*. Englewood Cliffs, N.J.: Prentice-Hall, 1954.

Rotter, J. B. Generalized expectancies for internal versus external control of reinforcement. *Psychological Monographs* 80 (1966), Whole No. 609.

Rotter, J. G., Liverant, B., and Crowne, D. P. The growth and extinction of expectancies in chance controlled and skilled tests. *Journal of Psychology* 52 (1961): 161–77.

Royce, J. M. Effects of preschool on later school outcomes. Paper presented as part of the symposium. Persistence of preschool effects: Evidence of impact. At the meeting of the Society for Research in Child Development, San Francisco, March 1979.

Rubin, J. Z., Provenzano, F. J., and Luria, Z. The eyes of the beholder: Parents' views on sex of newborns. *American Journal of Orthopsychiatry* 44 (1974): 512–19.

Ruch, F. L., and Zimbardo, P. G. *Psychology of life*. 8th ed. Glenview, Ill.: Scott, Foresman, 1971.

Rupley, W. H., Garcia, J., and Longnion, B. Sex role portrayal in reading materials: Implications for the 1980s. *The Reading Teacher* 34 (1981): 786–91.

Rushton, J. P. Generosity in children: Immediate and long term effects of modeling, preaching, and moral judgment. *Journal of Personality and Social Psychology* 31 (1975): 459–66.

Saario, T. N., Jacklin, C. N., and Tittle, C. K. Sex role stereotyping in the public schools. *Harvard Educational Review* 43 (1973): 386–416.

Safford, P. L. *Teaching young children with special needs*. Saint Louis: C. V. Mosby, 1978.

Salapatek, P. Visual scanning of geometric figures by the human newborn. *Journal of Comparative and Physiological Psychology* 66 (1968): 247–58.

Salapatek, P., and Kessen, W. Visual scanning of triangles by the human newborn. *Journal of Experimental Child Psychology* 3 (1966): 155–67.

Salter, L. Birth without violence: A medical controversy. *Nursing Research* 27 (1978): 84–88.

Saltz, E., and Johnson, J. Training for thematic-fantasy play in culturally disadvantaged children. *Journal of Educational Psychology* 66 (1974): 623–30.

Saltz, R. Children's interpretations of proverbs. *Language Arts* 56 (1979): 508–14.

Saltzman, L. Adolescence: Epoch or disease. *Adolescence* 8 (1973): 247–56.

Sameroff, A. The components of sucking in the human newborn. *Journal of Experimental Psychology* 6 (1968): 607–23.

Sameroff, A. J. Learning and adaptation in infancy. In H. W. Reese (Ed.), *Advances in child development and behavior* Vol. 7. New York: Academic Press, 1972.

Savin, H. B., and Bever, T. G. The nonperceptual reality of the phoneme. *Journal of Verbal Learning and Verbal Behavior* 9 (1970): 295–302.

Scaife, M., and Bruner, J. S. The capacity for joint visual attention in the infant. *Nature* 253 (1975): 265–66.

Scales, P. The context of sex education and the reduction of teenage pregnancy. *Child Welfare* 63 (1979): 263–73.

Scarlett, H. H., Press, A. N., and Crockett, W. H. Children's descriptions of peers: A Wernerian developmental analysis. *Child Development* 42 (1971): 439–53.

Scarr, S., and Weinberg, R. A. Attitudes, interests and IQ. *Human Nature* 1 (1978): 29–36.

Schachter, S., and Singer, J. E. Cognitive, social and physiological determinants of emotional states. *Psychological Review* 69 (1962): 379–99.

Schaefer, E. S., and Aaronson, M. Infant education research project: Implementation and implications of a home tutoring program. In M. C. Day and R. K. Parker (Eds.), *The preschool in action*. 2nd ed. Boston: Allyn and Bacon, 1977.

Schaffer, H. R., and Emerson, P. E. The development of social attachments in infancy. *Monographs of the Society for Research in Child Development* 29 (1964), Serial No. 94. a

Schaffer, H. R., and Emerson, P. E. Patterns of response to physical contact in early human development. *Journal of Child Psychology and Psychiatry* 5 (1964): 1–13. b

Schaie, K. W. A general model for the study of developmental problems. *Psychological Bulletin* 64 (1965): 92–107.

Schickedanz, D. I. Effects of an intervention in childrearing on Uzgiris-Hunt scale performance. Paper presented at the Annual Meeting of the New Hampshire Speech and Hearing Association, Portsmouth, N.H., June 1976.

Schinke, S., Gilchrist, L. and Small, R. Preventing unwanted adolescent pregnancy: A cognitive behavioral approach. *American Journal of Orthopsychiatry* 49 (1979): 81–88.

Schleimer, K. Anorexia nervosa. *Nutrition Review* 38 (1981): 99–103.

Schlesinger, I. M. Relational concepts underlying language. In R. Schiefelbusch and L. Lloyd (Eds.), *Language perception: Acquisition, retardation and intervention.* Baltimore: University Park Press, 1974.

Schwartz, J. C. Young children's fears: Modeling or cognition? Paper presented at the Society for Research in Child Development, San Francisco, March 1979.

Schwartz, M., and Schwartz, J. Evidence against a genetical component to performance on IQ tests. *Nature* 248 (1974): 84–85.

Schweinhart, L. J., and Weikart, D. P. *Young children grow up: The effects of the Perry Preschool Program on youths through age 15.* Ypsilanti, Mich.: High/Scope Educational Research Foundation, 1980.

Sears, R. R., Maccoby, E. E., and Levin, H. *Patterns of child rearing.* New York: Harper and Row, 1957.

Self, P. A., Horowitz, F. D., and Paden, L. Y. Olfaction in newborn infants. *Developmental Psychology* 7 (1972): 349–63.

Selman, R. Social-cognitive understanding: A guide to educational and clinical practice. In T. Lickona (Ed.), *Moral development and behavior: Theory, research, and social issues.* New York: Holt, Rinehart and Winston, 1976, pp. 219–240.

Selman, R. L., and Byrne, D. A structural-developmental analysis of levels or role taking in middle childhood. *Child Development* 45 (1974): 803–06.

Senate panel votes to expand WIC. *Reports on Preschool Education* 12 (1980): 5–6.

Sendak, M. *Where the wild things are.* New York: Harper and Row, 1963.

Senn, M. *Speaking out for America's children.* New Haven, Conn.: Yale University Press, 1977.

Shannon, D. C. Sudden infant death syndrome and near miss infants. In S. S. Gellis and B. M. Kagan (Eds.), *Current pediatric therapy.* Philadelphia: Saunders, 1980, pp. 756–57.

Shaw, F., Zelnick, M., and Kanter, J. F. Unprotected intercourse among unwed teenagers. *Family Planning Perspectives* 7 (1975): 39.

Sheldon, W. H., Hartle, E. M. and McDermott, E. *Varieties of delinquent youth.* New York: Harper, 1949.

Shields, J. *Monozygotic twins.* London: Oxford University Press, 1962.

Shirley, M. M. *The first two years: A study of twenty-five babies.* Vol. II. Minneapolis: University of Minnesota Press, 1933.

Shultz, T. R. Development of the appreciation of riddles. *Child Development* 45 (1974): 100–05.

Shultz, T. R., and Pilon, R. Development of the ability to detect linguistic ambiguity. *Child Development* 44 (1973): 728–33.

Siegel, M., Fuerst, H., and Guinee, V. Rubella epidemicity and embryopathy. *American Journal of Diseases of Children* 121 (1971): 469–73.

Simner, M. L. Newborn's response to the cry of another infant. *Developmental Psychology* 5 (1971): 136–50.

Simon, H. A. On the development of the processor. In S. Farnham-Diggory (Ed.), *Information processing in children*. New York: Academic Press, 1972, pp. 5–22.

Simon, N. V., Williams, G. H., Fairbrother, P. F., Elser, R. C., and Perkins, R. P. Prediction of fetal lung maturity by amniotic fluid fluorescence polarization, L:S ratio, and phosphatidyl glycerol. *Obstetrics and Gynecology* 57 (1981): 295–300.

Sinclair, H. Sensorimotor action patterns as a condition for the acquisition of syntax. In R. Huxly and E. Ingram (Eds.), *Language acquisition: Model and methods*. London: Academic Press, 1971.

Sinclair, J. C. The effect of the thermal environment on neonatal mortality and morbidity. In K. Adamsons and H. A. Fox (Eds.), *Preventability of perinatal injury*. New York: A. R. Liss, 1975.

Sinclair-de-Zwart, H. Developmental psycholinguistics. In D. Elkind and J. Flavell (Eds.), *Studies in cognitive development*. New York: Oxford University Press, 1969.

Singer, H. Learning to read and learning from text: A multidimensional process. Paper presented at the International Reading Association/University of Victoria International Reading Research Seminar on Linguistic Awareness and Learning to Read, June 26–30, 1979, Victoria, British Columbia.

Siqueland, E. R., and Lipsitt, L. P. Conditioned headturning in human newborns. *Journal of Experimental Child Psychology* 3 (1966): 356–76.

Skeels, H. M. Adult status of children with contrasting early life experiences. *Monographs of the Society for Research in Child Development* 31 (1966): Serial No. 105.

Skodak, M., and Skeels, H. M. A final follow-up study of one hundred adopted children. *Journal of Genetic Psychology* 75 (1949): 85–125.

Slaby, R. G., and Frey, K. S. Development of gender constancy and selective attention to same sex-models. In H. Bee (Ed.), *Social issues in developmental psychology*. 2nd ed. New York: Harper and Row, 1978.

Slater, A. M., and Findlay, J. M. Binocular fixation in the newborn baby. *Journal of Experimental Child Psychology* 20 (1975): 248–73.

Smilansky, S. *The effects of sociodramatic play on disadvantaged preschool children*. New York: John Wiley and Sons, 1968.

Smith, F. Learning to read by reading: A brief case study. *Language Arts* 53 (1974): 297–99.

Smith, F. Making sense of reading — and of reading instruction. *Harvard Educational Review* 47 (1977): 386–95.

Smith, N. R. How a picture means. *New Directions for Child Development* 3 (1979): 59–72.

Smith, R. E. The movement of women into the labor force. In R. E. Smith (Ed.), *The subtle revolution: Women at work*. Washington, D.C.: The Urban Institute, 1979. a

Smith, R. E. (Ed.). *The subtle revolution: Women at work*. Washington, D. C.: The Urban Institute, 1979. b

Snyder, L., Schonfeld, M., and Offerman, E. The Rh factor and feeble-mindedness. *Journal of Heredity* 36 (1945): 9–10.

Society for Research in Child Development. Ethical standards for research with children. In *Society for research in child development: Directory*. Chicago: Society for Research in Child Development, 1974.

Sokolov, E. N. *Perception and the conditioned reflex*. New York: Macmillan, 1963.

Spalding, D. A. Instinct, with original observations on young animals. *Macmillan's Magazine*, 1893. Reprinted in *British Journal of Animal Behavior* 2 (1954): 6.

Spitz, R. A., and Wolfe, K. M. The smiling response: A contribution to the ontogenesis of social relations. *Genetic Psychology Monographs* 34 (1946): 57–125.

Spivack, G., and Shure, M. B. *Social adjustment of young children*. San Francisco: Jossey-Bass, 1974.

Staffieri, J. R. Body build and behavioral expectancies in young females. *Developmental Psychology* 6 (1972): 125–27.

Staub, E. A child in distress: The influence of

nurturance and modeling on children's attempts to help. *Developmental Psychology* 5 (1971): 124–32.

Staub, E. *The development of prosocial behavior in children*. Morristown, N.J.: General Learning Press, 1975.

Stein, A. H. The effects of maternal employment and educational attainment on the sex typed attitudes of college females. *Social Behavior and Personality* 1 (1973): 111–14.

Stein, A. H., and Bailey, M. M. The socialization of achievement orientation in females. *Psychological Bulletin* 80 (1973): 345–65.

Stein, A. H., and Friedrich, L. K. Impact of television on children and youth. In E. M. Hetherington (Ed.), *Review of child development research*. Vol. 5. Chicago: University of Chicago Press, 1975, pp. 183–256.

Stern, D. *The first relationship: Infant and mother*. Cambridge: Harvard University Press, 1977.

Stern, G. *Principles of human genetics*. 3rd ed. San Francisco: W. H. Freeman, 1973.

Stern, L. Prematurity as a factor in child abuse. *Hospital Practices* 8 (1973): 117–23.

Stern, W. *The psychological methods of testing intelligence*. (G. M. Whipple trans.). Baltimore: Warwick and York, 1912.

Sternglanz, S. H., and Serbin, L. A. Sex role stereotyping in children's television programs. *Developmental Psychology* 10 (1974): 710–15.

Stevens, J. H. The consequences of early childbearing. *Young Children* 35 (1980): 47–56.

Stoch, M. B., and Smythe, P. M. Does undernutrition during infancy inhibit brain growth and subsequent intellectual development? *Archives of Diseases in Childhood* 38 (1963): 546.

Streissguth, A. P. Fetal alcohol syndrome. *Women and Health* 4 (1979): 223–38.

Strohner, H., and Nelson, K. E. The young child's development of sentence comprehension: Influence of event probability, nonverbal context, syntactic form, and strategies. *Child Development* 45 (1974): 567–76.

Suomi, S. J., and Harlow, H. F. Social rehabilitation of isolate-reared monkeys. *Developmental Psychology* 6 (1972): 487–96.

Super, C. M., and Harkness, S. The infant's niche in rural Kenya and metropolitan Boston. Paper presented at the meetings of the American Anthropological Association, Los Angeles, 1978.

Sutton, M. Readiness for reading at the kindergarten level. *The Reading Teacher* 22 (1964): 234–39.

Takanishi, R. Childhood as a social issue: Historical roots of contemporary child advocacy movements. *Journal of Social Issues* 34 (1978): 8–29.

Tanner, J. Physical growth. In P. H. Mussen (Ed.), *Carmichael's manual of child psychology*. 3rd ed. Vol. 1. New York: John Wiley and Sons, 1970.

Tanner, J. M. *Education and physical growth*. 2nd ed. New York: International Universities Press, 1978.

Tanner, J. M. Growth and maturation during adolescence. *Nutrition Review* 39 (1981): 43–55.

Taubenheim, B. Erikson's psychological theory applied to adolescent fiction: A means for adolescent self-clarification. *Journal of Reading* 22 (1979): 517–22.

Tavris, C., and Offir, C. *The longest war: Sex differences in perspective*. New York: Harcourt Brace Jovanovich, 1977.

Television and growing up: The impact of televised violence. Washington, D.C.: U.S. Government Printing Office, 1972.

Terman, L. M. *The measurement of intelligence*. Boston: Houghton Mifflin, 1916.

Thomas, A. T., and Chess, S. *Temperament and Development*. New York: Brunner/Mazel, 1977.

Thompson, R. F. *Foundations of physiological psychology*. New York: Harper and Row, 1967.

Thompson, R. J., and O'Quinn, A. N. *Developmental disabilities: Etiologies, manifestations, diagnoses, and treatments*. New York: Oxford University Press, 1979.

Thorndike, E. L. *The elements of psychology.* New York: Seiler, 1905.

Toomin, M. K. Counseling needs of the child of divorce. In J. C. Coll and R. E. Hardy (Eds.), *Deciding on divorce.* Springfield, Ill.: Charles C. Thomas, 1974, pp. 89–122.

Trehub, S. E. and Rabinovitch, M. S. Auditory-linguistic sensitivity in early infancy. *Developmental Psychology* 6 (1972): 74–77.

Tronick, E., and Brazelton, T. B. Clinical uses of the Brazelton Neonatal Behavior Assessment. In B. S. Friedlander, G. M. Sterritt, and G. E. Kirk (Eds.), *Exceptional infant: Assessment and intervention.* Vol. 3. New York: Brunner/Mazel, 1975.

Tuckman, B. *Measuring educational outcomes: Fundamentals of testing.* New York: Harcourt Brace Jovanovich, 1975.

Tulkin, S., and Kagan, J. Mother-child interaction in the first year of life. *Child Development* 43 (1972): 31–41.

Ullman, L., and Krasner, L. *Psychological approach to abnormal behavior.* Englewood Cliffs, N.J.: Prentice-Hall, 1969.

U.S. Women's Bureau, *Working mothers and their children.* Washington, D.C.: U.S. Government Printing Office, 1977.

Uzgiris, I. C. Patterns of cognitive development in infancy. *The Merrill-Palmer Quarterly* 19 (1973): 181–204.

Valenti, C. The child: His right to be normal. *Saturday Review* 51 (1968): 75–78.

Van Stolk, M. Who owns the child? *Childhood Education* 50 (1974): 259–65.

Vernon, P. E. *Intelligence: Heredity and environment.* San Francisco: W. H. Freeman, 1979.

Wallerstein, J. S., and Kelly, J. B. The effects of parental divorce: Experiences of the preschool child. *Journal of the American Academy of Child Psychiatry* 14 (1975): 600–16.

Walters, J. Birth defects and adolescent pregnancies. *Journal of Home Economics* 67 (1975): 23–27.

Watson, J. S. The development and generalization of "contingency awareness" in early infancy: Some hypotheses. *The Merrill-Palmer Quarterly* 12 (1966): 123–35.

Watson, J. S. Smiling, cooing, and "the game." *The Merrill-Palmer Quarterly* 18 (1972): 323–39.

Warshak, R., and Santrock, J. W. The effects of father and mother custody on children's social development. Paper presented at the Annual Meeting of the Society for Research in Child Development. San Francisco, March 1979.

WCVB-TV, *Denise,* Boston, 1980.

Wechsler, D. *Manual for the Wechsler Preschool and Primary Scale of Intelligence.* New York: Psychological Corporation, 1967.

Wechsler, D. *Manual for the Wechsler Intelligence Scale for Children — Revised.* New York: Psychological Corporation, 1974.

Weikert, D. A comparative study of three preschool curricula. In J. E. Frost and G. R. Hawkes (Eds.), *The disadvantaged child.* Boston: Houghton Mifflin, 1970, pp. 186–96.

Weinraub, M. Children's responses to brief periods of maternal absence: An experimental intervention study. Final report to the Foundation for Child Development, 1976.

Weinraub, M., and Lewis, M. The determinants of children's responses to separation. *Monographs of the Society for Research in Child Development* 42 (1977), Serial No. 172.

Weiss, N. P. The mother-child dyad revisited: Perceptions of mothers and children in twentieth century child-rearing manuals. *Journal of Social Issues* 34 (1978): 29–45.

Weiss, R. S. Growing up a little faster: The experience of growing up in a single-parent household. *Journal of Social Issues* 35 (1979): 97–111.

Wennberg, R., Woodrum, D., and Hodson, A.

The perinate. In D. Smith and E. Bierman (Eds.), *The biologic ages of man.* Philadelphia: W. B. Saunders, 1973.

Wertheimer, M. Psychomotor coordination of auditory-visual space at birth. *Science* 134 (1961): 1692.

Wheeler, M. E. Untutored acquisition of writing skill. Unpublished doctoral dissertation, Department of Human Development, Cornell University, 1971.

White, B. *The first three years of life.* Englewood Cliffs, N.J.: Prentice-Hall, 1975.

White, B. L. *Human-infants: Experience and psychological development.* Englewood Cliffs, N.J.: Prentice-Hall, 1971.

White, B. L., Castle, P., and Held, R. Observations on the development of visually-directed reaching. *Child Development* 35 (1964): 349-64.

White, B. L., and Watts, J. C. *Experience and environment: Major influences on the development of the young child.* Englewood Cliffs, N.J.: Prentice-Hall, 1973.

White, G. M. Immediate and deferred effects of model observation and guided and unguided rehearsal on donating and stealing. *Journal of Personality and Social Psychology* 21 (1972): 139–48.

Whiting, B., and Edwards, C. P. A cross-cultural analysis of sex differences in the behavior of children aged three through eleven. *The Journal of Social Psychology* 91 (1973): 171–88.

Whitt, J. K., and Prentice, N. M. Cognitive processes in the development of children's enjoyment and comprehension of joking riddles. *Developmental Psychology* 13 (1977): 129–36.

Widdowson, E. M., and McCance, P. A. New thoughts on growth. *Pediatric Research* 9 (1975): 154–59.

Wilcox, B. M. Visual preferences of human infants for representation of the human face. *Journal of Experimental Child Psychology* 7 (1969): 10–20.

Winick, M. Childhood obesity. *Nutrition Today* 9 (1974): 6–12.

Winick, M. *Malnutrition and brain development.* New York: Oxford University Press, 1976.

Winitz, H., and Irwin, O. Syllabic and phonetic structure of infants' early words. *Journal of Speech and Hearing Research* 1 (1958): 250–56.

Winn, M. *The plug-in drug.* New York: Bantam Books, 1977.

Witkin, H. A., Mednick, S. A., Scholsinger, F., Bakkestrøm, E., Christiansen, K. O., Goodenough, D. R., Hirschhorn, K., Lundsteen, C., Owen, D. R., Philip, J., Rubin, and Stocking, M. Criminality in XYY and XXY men. *Science* 193 (1976): 547-55.

Wolff, P. Observations of newborn infants. *Psychosomatic Medicine* 21 (1959): 110–18.

Wolff, P. The development of attention in young infants. *Annals of the New York Academy of Sciences* 118 (1965): 815–30.

Wolff, P. The causes, controls, and organizations of behavior in the newborn. *Psychological Issues* 5 (1966): 1–105.

Wolff, P. H. The natural history of crying and other vocaliztions in early infancy. In B. Foss (Ed.), *Determinants of infant behavior.* Vol. IV. London: Methuen, 1969.

Women on Words and Images. *Dick and Jane as victims: Sex stereotyping in children's readers.* Princeton, N.J.: Central New Jersey NOW, 1972.

Wynne, E. A. Facts about the character of young Americans. *Character* 1 (1979): 1–7.

Yancy, W. S., Nader, P. R., and Burnham, K. L. Drug use and attitudes of high school students. *Pediatrics* 50 (1972): 739–45.

Yarrow, L. J., Rubenstein, J. L., and Pedersen, F. A. Dimensions of early stimulation: Differential effects on infant development. Paper presented at the Biennial Meeting of the Society for Research in Child Development, Minneapolis, April 1971.

Yarrow, L. J., Rubenstein, J. L., and Pedersen, F. A. *Infant and environment: Early cognitive and motivational development.* New York: John Wiley and Sons, 1975.

Yarrow, M. R., and Campbell, J. S. Person perception in children. *The Merrill-Palmer Quarterly 9* (1963): 57–72.

Yarrow, M. R., Scott, P., Leeuw, L. D., and Heenig, C. Child-rearing families of working and nonworking mothers. In H. Bee (Ed.), *Social Issues in Developmental Psychology.* 2nd ed. New York: Harper and Row, 1978, pp. 112–29.

Yarrow, M. R., Scott, P. M., and Waxler, C. Z. Learning concern for others. *Developmental Psychology 8* (1973): 240–60.

Young, W. C., Goy, R. W., and Phoenix, C. H. Hormones and sexual behavior. *Science* 143 (1964): 212–18.

Youniss, J., and Volpe, J. A relational analysis of children's friendship. In W. Damon (Ed.), *Social cognition.* San Francisco: Jossey-Bass, 1978.

Zill, N. Divorce, marital conflict, and the mental health of children: Findings from a national survey of children. Paper presented at the symposium on "Children and divorce," Wheelock College, Boston, Mass., November 3–4, 1978.

Zimbler, S. Injuries related to sports and recreation. In S. S. Gellis and B. M. Kagan, *Current pediatric therapy.* Philadelphia: W. B. Saunders, 1980, pp. 700–03.

Zimmerman, D. R. *Rh: The intimate history of a disease and its conquest.* New York: Macmillan, 1973.

Chapter 4. p. 70: Mimi Forsyth/Monkmeyer; *p. 71:* Anna Kaufman Moon/Stock, Boston; *Fig. 4-5, p. 83:* From Jean Mayer, *Health* (New York: D. Van Nostrand, 1974). Reprinted by permission of Brooks/Cole Publishing Company, Monterey, California 93940; *p. 84:* Landrum B. Shettles, M.D.; *p. 87:* Suzanne Szasz; *p. 90:* Leboyer, F., *Birth Without Violence.* Random House, N.Y., 1975; *p. 94:* © Bruce Roberts/Photo Researchers.

Chapter 5. p. 104: Suzanne Szasz; *p. 108:* Ken Heyman; *p. 113:* Emily Burrows; *p. 117:* David Linton; *Fig. 5-1, p. 118:* From Maurice Hershenson, "Visual discrimination in the human newborn," *Journal of Comparative Physiological Psychology* 58 (1964). Copyright 1964 by the American Psychological Association. Reprinted by permission of the publisher and author; *p. 123:* © 1977 Erika Stone/Photo Researchers.

Chapter 6. p. 136: Michael Weisbrot/The Image Works; *p. 138:* Suzanne Szasz; *p. 143:* Reprinted from White, B. L., *Human Infants: Experience and Psychological Development,* Englewood Cliffs, N.J., Prentice Hall, 1971; *p. 147:* Lew Merrim/Monkmeyer.

Chapter 7. p. 150: Bob Bouchal; *Fig. 7-1, p. 151:* From R. A. Haaf and R. Q. Bell, "A Facial Dimension in Visual Discrimination by Infants," *Child Development,* 1967, 38, 893–899. © 1967 The Society for Research in Child Development, Inc. Reprinted by permission; *p. 153:* William Vandivert; *p. 162:* Mimi Forsyth/Monkmeyer; *p. 163:* Suzanne Szasz; *p. 165:* Michael Weisbrot/The Image Works.

Chapter 8. p. 170: James Holland/Stock, Boston; *p. 176:* Bob Bouchal; *p. 180:* Hanna Schreiber/Photo Researchers.

Chapter 9. p. 182: Peter Vandermark; *p. 185:* Suzanne Szasz; *p. 186:* Harry F. Harlow, University of Wisconsin Primate Laboratory; *p. 195:* Bob Bouchal; *p. 197:* Bob Bouchal.

Chapter 10. p. 200: © 1973 Erika Stone/Photo Researchers; *p. 205:* Ken Heyman; *p. 210:* Bob Bouchal; *p. 214:* Jean-Claude Lejeune/Stock, Boston; *p. 215:* Suzanne Szasz.

Chapter 11. p. 220: Gabor Demjen/Stock, Boston; *p. 222:* © Frank Siteman/The Picture Cube; *p. 223:* Suzanne Szasz; *p. 225:* © Alice S. Kandell/Photo Researchers.

Chapter 12. p. 227: Bob Bouchal; *p. 231:* © 1973 Margot Granitsas/Photo Researchers; *p. 232:* Fredrik D. Bodin; *p. 233:* Fredrik D. Bodin.

Chapter 13. p. 235: © Paul Fortin/Picture Group; *p. 238:* © 1979 Erika Stone; *p. 240:* From E. Clark, "Non-Linguistic Strategies and the Acquisition of Word Meanings," in L. Bloom, ed., *Readings in Language Development,* John Wiley & Sons, 1978. Reprinted by permission. *p. 241:* © Ken Robert Buck; *p. 242:* Alan Carey/The Image Works.

Chapter 14. p. 246: Bob Bouchal; *p. 248:* Bob Bouchal; *p. 250:* Peter Vandermark; *p. 254:* Bob Bouchal.

Chapter 15. p. 256: Bodin/Faneuf photo; *p. 257:* Elaine Wickens; *p. 263:* Bob Bouchal; *p. 265:* Michael Weisbrot/Stock, Boston; *p. 266:* Jean-Claude Lejeune/Stock, Boston.

Chapter 16. p. 274: Peter Vandermark; *p. 275:* Bob Bouchal; *p. 276 (left):* © Peter Menzel; *p. 276 (right):* Karyl Gatteño/Taurus Photos; *Fig. 16-1, p. 279:* From F. A. Hellebrandt, G. L. Rarick, R. Glassow and M. L. Carns, "Physiological Analysis of Basic Motor Skills. 1. Growth and Development of Jumping," *American Journal of Physical Medicine,* 40, 14–25, 1961. © 1961 The Williams & Wilkins Co., Baltimore. Reprinted by permission; *p. 281:* Ginger Chih/Peter Arnold.

Chapter 17. p. 283: © Jean-Claude Lejeune; *Fig. 17-3, p. 289:* From Jean Piaget and Bärbel Inhelder, *The Child's Conception of Space,* translated by F. T. Langdon and L. L. Luger. First published in France in 1948 by Presses Universitaires de France. First published in England in 1956 by Routledge & Kegan Paul Ltd. Reprinted by permission of Humanities Press Inc., New Jersey 07716; *p. 292:* © 1976 Elizabeth Hamlin/Stock, Boston; *p. 293, top right:* Kellogg, R. and O'Dell, S., *The Psychology of Children's Art.* Random House, N.Y., 1967. p. 86.; *p. 293, bottom right:* Lansing, *Art, Artists and Art Education,* 1926. Reprinted with permission of Kendall/Hunt Publishing Company; *Fig. 17-4, p. 294:* From Jean Piaget and Bärbel Inhelder, *The Child's Conception of Space,* translated by F. T. Langdon and L. L. Luger. First published in France in 1948 by Presses Universitaires de France. First published in England in 1956 by Routledge & Kegan Paul Ltd. Reprinted by permission of Humanities Press Inc., New Jersey 07716.

Chapter 18. p. 299: James Holland/Stock, Boston; *p. 305:* © 1978 George Malave/Stock, Boston; *p. 308:* Ken Heyman; *p. 310:* From L. O. Lavine, "The Development of Writing in Pre-Reading Children: A Cross-Cultural Study." Unpublished doctoral dissertation, Department of Human Development, Cornell University, 1972. Reprinted by permission; *p. 312:* © 1936 The Society for Research in Child Development, Inc. Reprinted by permission; *p. 312:* © The Society for Research in Child Development, Inc.

Chapter 19. p. 317: Bob Bouchal; *p. 322:* Bob Bouchal; *p. 328:* © 1978 John Garrett/Woodfin Camp; *p. 332:* ©1981 Suzanne Szasz/Photo Researchers; *p. 336:* Photograph by Gary Easter, High/Scope Educational Research Foundation.

Chapter 20. p. 345: Bob Bouchal; *p. 346:* Elizabeth Hamlin/Stock, Boston; *p. 348:* Elaine M. Ward; *p. 364:* Bob Bouchal; *p. 361:* © 1969, William K. Frankenburg and Josiah B. Dodds, University of Colorado Medical Center.

p. 366: Radie Medlin/Leo de Wys; *p. 369:* Bob Bouchal.

Chapter 21. p. 374: © Mike Kelly/Picture Group; *p. 375:* Bob Bouchal; *p. 379:* David S. Strickler/The Picture Cube.

Chapter 22. p. 381: The New York Times; *Fig. 22-2, p. 384:* From Jean Piaget and Bärbel Inhelder, *The Child's Conception of Space,* translated by F. T. Langdon and L. L. Luger. First published in France in 1948 by Presses Universitaires de France. First published in England in 1956 by Routledge & Kegan Paul Ltd. Reprinted by permission of Humanities Press Inc., New Jersey 07716; *p. 398:* World Health Organization.

Chapter 23. p. 400: Paul Conklin/Monkmeyer; *p. 402:* Bob Bouchal; *p. 406:* Bob Bouchal; *p. 408:* Bob Bouchal.

Chapter 24. p. 424: Michael Weisbrot/Stock, Boston; *p. 430:* © 1980 Michal Heron/Woodfin Camp; *p. 439:* Jean-Claude Lejeune/Stock, Boston; *p. 444:* Mimi Forsyth/Monkmeyer; *p. 451:* Bob Bouchal.

Chapter 25. p. 458: © Peter Menzel; *p. 459:* © Elizabeth Crews; *p. 462:* Judith Sedwick; *p. 467:* Vivienne della Grotto/Photo Researchers.

Chapter 26. p. 477: Peter Vandermark/Stock, Boston; *p. 478:* © Donald Dietz/Stock, Boston; *p. 480:* Neal Boenzi/The New York Times; *p. 482:* © 1979 Joel Gordon.

Chapter 27. p. 484: Joseph Schuyler/Stock, Boston; *p. 487:* Sybil Shelton/Peter Arnold; *p. 488:* Cynara/DPI.

Chapter 28. p. 491: Fredrik D. Bodin; *p. 492:* Sybil Shelton/Peter Arnold; *p. 493:* Peter Vandermark/Stock, Boston; *p. 494:* Sybil Shelton/Peter Arnold.

Chapter 29. p. 496: © 1976 Joel Gordon; *p. 500:* Ken Heyman; *p. 501:* © Arthur Tress/Photo Researchers; *p. 508:* Paul Fusco/©Magnum.

Chapter 30. p. 513: Ann Hagen Griffiths/Omni-Photo Communications; *p. 518:* Fredrik D. Bodin/Picture Group; *p. 519:* © Elizabeth Crews; *p. 520:* © Jim Anderson/Woodfin Camp.

Chapter 31. p. 524: Suzanne Szasz; *p. 526:* © 1981 Peter Menzel; *p. 532:* © Jack Spratt/Picture Group; *p. 534:* James Holland/Stock, Boston; *p. 539 (left):* © 1978 Joanne Leonard/Woodfin Camp; *p. 539 (right):* Dr. Athol Packer, University of Florida; *p. 541:* © Paul Fortin/Picture Group; *p. 542:* © Elizabeth Crews.

TEXT CREDITS

Chapter 4, p. 86: From Martin Greenberg and Norman Morris, "Engrossment: The Newborn's Impact Upon the Father." Reprinted, with permission, from the *American Journal of Orthopsychiatry;* copyright 1974 by the American Orthopsychiatric Association, Inc.

Chapter 7, pp. 158, 159, 160: From Jean Piaget, *The Origins of Intelligence in Children,* translated by M. Cook, by permission of International Universities Press, Inc. Copyright 1952 by International Universities Press, Inc.; *pp. 161–163, 166:* From Jean Piaget, *The Construction of Reality in the Child,* translated by M. Cook. Copyright © 1954 by Basic Books, Inc. By permission of Basic Books, Inc. and Routledge & Kegan Paul Ltd.

Chapter 9, pp. 189, 190: From Daniel Stern, *The First Relationship: Infant and Mother,* pp. 3, 110–111. Copyright © 1977 by Daniel Stern. Reprinted by permission of the publisher, Harvard University Press.

Chapter 10, pp. 201, 202: From Ira J. Gordon, *Baby Learning Through Baby Play: A Parent's Guide for the First Two Years.* Copyright © 1970 by Ira J. Gordon. Reprinted by permission of St. Martin's Press, Inc.

Chapter 23, pp. 401, 402: From Carol Chomsky, *Acquisition of Syntax in Children from Five to Ten.* Copyright © 1969 by The Massachusetts Institute of Technology. Reprinted by permission of the MIT Press; *pp. 404–407:* From J. Macnamara, "First and Second Language Learning: Same or Different?" *Journal of Education,* 158 (2), 1976. Reprinted by permission; *pp. 418, 420, 421:* From Donald Graves, "A Six-Year-Old's Writing Process," *Language Arts,* Vol. 56, No. 7 (1979). Copyright © 1979 by the National Council of Teachers of English. Reprinted by permission of the publisher and the author; *pp. 422:* From L. M. Calkins, "Writers Need Readers, Not Robins," *Language Arts,* Vol. 55 (1978). Copyright © 1978 by the National Council of Teachers of English. Reprinted by permission of the publisher and the author.

Chapter 24, p. 431: From Jean Piaget, *The Moral Judgment of the Child* by Jean Piaget, translated by M. Gabain (New York: The Free Press, 1965). Reprinted by permission of Macmillan Publishing Co., Inc. and Routledge & Kegan Paul Ltd.

Chapter 27, pp. 286, 287: From L. P. Nucci and N. J. Gordon, "Educating Adolescents from a Piagetian Perspective," *Journal of Education,* 1979, 161(1), 87–99. Reprinted by permission.

Name Index

Subject Index

Operations Management

Sports/Gaming

*These represent page numbers found in the online bonus Chapter 17.

4TH EDITION

Data Analysis and Decision Making

S. Christian Albright
Kelley School of Business, Indiana University

Wayne L. Winston
Kelley School of Business, Indiana University

Christopher J. Zappe
Bucknell University

With cases by
Mark Broadie
Graduate School of Business, Columbia University

Peter Kolesar
Graduate School of Business, Columbia University

Lawrence L. Lapin
San Jose State University

William D. Whisler
California State University, Hayward

SOUTH-WESTERN
CENGAGE Learning

Australia • Brazil • Japan • Korea • Mexico • Singapore • Spain • United Kingdom • United States

Data Analysis and Decision Making, Fourth Edition

S. Christian Albright, Wayne L. Winston, Christopher J. Zappe

Vice President of Editorial, Business: Jack W. Calhoun

Publisher: Joe Sabatino

Sr. Acquisitions Editor: Charles McCormick, Jr.

Sr. Developmental Editor: Laura Ansara

Editorial Assistant: Nora Heink

Marketing Manager: Adam Marsh

Marketing Coordinator: Suellen Ruttkay

Sr. Content Project Manager: Tim Bailey

Media Editor: Chris Valentine

Frontlist Buyer, Manufacturing: Miranda Klapper

Sr. Marketing Communications Manager: Libby Shipp

Production Service: MPS Limited, A Macmillan company

Sr. Art Director: Stacy Jenkins Shirley

Cover Designer: Lou Ann Thesing

Cover Image: iStock Photo

For product information and technology assistance, contact us at **Cengage Learning Customer & Sales Support 1-800-354-9706**

For permission to use material from this text or product, submit all requests online at **www.cengage.com/permissions** Further permissions questions can be emailed to **permissionrequest@cengage.com**

Exam*View* ®is a registered trademark of eInstruction Corp. Microsoft® and Excel® spreadsheet software are registered trademarks of Microsoft Corporation used herein under license.

Library of Congress Control Number: 2010930495

Student Edition Package ISBN 13: 978-0-538-47612-6
Student Edition Package ISBN 10: 0-538-47612-5
Student Edition ISBN 13: 978-0-538-47610-2
Student Edition ISBN 10: 0-538-47610-9

South-Western Cengage Learning
5191 Natorp Boulevard
Mason, OH 45040
USA

Cengage Learning products are represented in Canada by Nelson Education, Ltd.

For your course and learning solutions, visit **www.cengage.com**

Purchase any of our products at your local college store or at our preferred online store **www.cengagebrain.com**

Printed in the United States of America
1 2 3 4 5 6 7 14 13 12 11 10

To my wonderful family

To my wonderful wife Mary—my best friend and constant companion; to Sam, Lindsay, and Teddy, our new and adorable grandson; and to Bryn, our wild and crazy Welsh corgi, who can't wait for Teddy to be able to play ball with her!   S.C.A

To my wonderful family   *W.L.W.*

To my wonderful family

Jeannie, Matthew, and Jack. And to my late sister, Jenny, and son, Jake, who live eternally in our loving memories.   C.J.Z.

S. Christian Albright got his B.S. degree in Mathematics from Stanford in 1968 and his Ph.D. in Operations Research from Stanford in 1972. Since then he has been teaching in the Operations & Decision Technologies Department in the Kelley School of Business at Indiana University (IU). He has taught courses in management science, computer simulation, statistics, and computer programming to all levels of business students: undergraduates, MBAs, and doctoral students. In addition, he has taught simulation modeling at General Motors and Whirlpool, and he has taught database analysis for the Army. He has published over 20 articles in leading operations research journals in the area of applied probability, and he has authored the books S*tatistics for Business and Economics, Practical Management Science, Spreadsheet Modeling and Applications, Data Analysis for Managers*, and *VBA for Modelers*. He also works with the Palisade Corporation on the commercial version, *StatTools*, of his statistical StatPro add-in for Excel. His current interests are in spreadsheet modeling, the development of VBA applications in Excel, and programming in the .NET environment.

On the personal side, Chris has been married for 39 years to his wonderful wife, Mary, who retired several years ago after teaching 7th grade English for 30 years and is now working as a supervisor for student teachers at IU. They have one son, Sam, who lives in Philadelphia with his wife Lindsay and their newly born son Teddy. Chris has many interests outside the academic area. They include activities with his family (especially traveling with Mary), going to cultural events at IU, power walking while listening to books on his iPod, and reading. And although he earns his livelihood from statistics and management science, his *real* passion is for playing classical piano music.

Wayne L. Winston is Professor of Operations & Decision Technologies in the Kelley School of Business at Indiana University, where he has taught since 1975. Wayne received his B.S. degree in Mathematics from MIT and his Ph.D. degree in Operations Research from Yale. He has written the successful textbooks *Operations Research: Applications and Algorithms, Mathematical Programming: Applications and Algorithms, Simulation Modeling Using @RISK, Practical Management Science, Data Analysis and Decision Making,* and *Financial Models Using Simulation and Optimization*. Wayne has published over 20 articles in leading journals and has won many teaching awards, including the schoolwide MBA award four times. He has taught classes at Microsoft, GM, Ford, Eli Lilly, Bristol-Myers Squibb, Arthur Andersen, Roche, PricewaterhouseCoopers, and NCR. His current interest is showing how spreadsheet models can be used to solve business problems in all disciplines, particularly in finance and marketing.

Wayne enjoys swimming and basketball, and his passion for trivia won him an appearance several years ago on the television game show *Jeopardy*, where he won two games. He is married to the lovely and talented Vivian. They have two children, Gregory and Jennifer.

Christopher J. Zappe earned his B.A. in Mathematics from DePauw University in 1983 and his M.B.A. and Ph.D. in Decision Sciences from Indiana University in 1987 and 1988, respectively. Between 1988 and 1993, he performed research and taught various decision sciences courses at the University of Florida in the College of Business Administration. From 1993 until 2010, Professor Zappe taught decision sciences in the Department of Management at Bucknell University, and in 2010, he was named provost at Gettysburg College. Professor Zappe has taught undergraduate courses in business statistics, decision modeling and analysis, and computer simulation. He also developed and taught a number of interdisciplinary Capstone Experience courses and Foundation Seminars in support of the Common Learning Agenda at Bucknell. Moreover, he has taught advanced seminars in applied game theory, system dynamics, risk assessment, and mathematical economics. He has published articles in scholarly journals such as *Managerial and Decision Economics, OMEGA, Naval Research Logistics, and Interfaces*.

Brief Contents

Contents

PART 4   REGRESSION ANALYSIS AND TIME SERIES FORECASTING 527

PART 5   OPTIMIZATION AND SIMULATION MODELING 743

Preface

With today's technology, companies are able to collect tremendous amounts of data with relative ease. Indeed, many companies now have more data than they can handle. However, the data are usually meaningless until they are analyzed for trends, patterns, relationships, and other useful information. This book illustrates in a practical way a variety of methods, from simple to complex, to help you analyze data sets and uncover important information. In many business contexts, data analysis is only the first step in the solution of a problem. Acting on the solution and the information it provides to make good decisions is a critical next step. Therefore, there is a heavy emphasis throughout this book on analytical methods that are useful in decision making. Again, the methods vary considerably, but the objective is always the same—to equip you with decision-making tools that you can *apply* in your business careers.

We recognize that the majority of students in this type of course are *not* majoring in a quantitative area. They are typically business majors in finance, marketing, operations management, or some other business discipline who will need to analyze data and make quantitative-based decisions in their jobs. We offer a hands-on, example-based approach and introduce fundamental concepts as they are needed. Our vehicle is spreadsheet software—specifically, Microsoft Excel. This is a package that most students already know and will undoubtedly use in their careers. Our MBA students at Indiana University are so turned on by the required course that is based on this book that *almost all* of them (mostly finance and marketing majors) take at least one of our follow-up elective courses in spreadsheet modeling. We are convinced that students see value in quantitative analysis when the course is taught in a practical and example-based approach.

Rationale for writing this book

Data Analysis and Decision Making is different from the many fine textbooks written for statistics and management science. Our rationale for writing this book is based on three fundamental objectives.

1. **Integrated coverage and applications.** The book provides a unified approach to business-related problems by integrating methods and applications that have been traditionally taught in separate courses, specifically statistics and management science.

2. **Practical in approach.** The book emphasizes realistic business examples and the processes managers actually use to analyze business problems. The emphasis is *not* on abstract theory or computational methods.

3. **Spreadsheet-based.** The book provides students with the skills to analyze business problems with tools they have access to and will use in their careers. To this end, we have adopted Excel and commercial spreadsheet add-ins.

Integrated coverage and applications

In the past, many business schools, including ours at Indiana University, have offered a required statistics course, a required decision-making course, and a required management science course—or some subset of these. One current trend, however, is to have only one required course that covers the basics of statistics, some regression analysis, some decision making under uncertainty, some linear programming, some simulation, and possibly others. Essentially, we faculty in the quantitative area get one opportunity to teach all business students, so we attempt to cover a *variety* of useful quantitative methods. We are not necessarily arguing that this trend is ideal, but rather that it is a reflection of the reality at our university and, we suspect, at many others. After several years of teaching this course, we have found it to be a great opportunity to attract students to the subject and more advanced study.

The book is also integrative in another important aspect. It not only integrates a number of analytical methods, but it also applies them to a wide variety of business problems—that is, it analyzes realistic examples from many business disciplines. We include examples, problems, and cases that deal with portfolio optimization, workforce scheduling, market share analysis, capital budgeting, new product analysis, and many others.

Practical in approach

We want this book to be very example-based and practical. We strongly believe that students learn best by working through examples, and they appreciate the material most when the examples are realistic and interesting. Therefore, our approach in the book differs in two important ways from many competitors. First, there is just enough conceptual development to give students an understanding and appreciation for the issues raised in the examples. We often introduce important concepts, such as multicollinearity in regression, in the context of examples, rather than discussing them in the abstract. Our experience is that students gain greater intuition and understanding of the concepts and applications through this approach.

Second, we place virtually no emphasis on hand calculations. We believe it is more important for students to understand why they are conducting an analysis and what it means than to emphasize the tedious calculations associated with many analytical techniques. Therefore, we illustrate how powerful software can be used to create graphical and numerical outputs in a matter of seconds, freeing the rest of the time for in-depth interpretation of the output, sensitivity analysis, and alternative modeling approaches. In our own courses, we move directly into a discussion of examples, where we focus almost exclusively on interpretation and modeling issues and let the software perform the number crunching.

Spreadsheet-based teaching

We are strongly committed to teaching spreadsheet-based, example-driven courses, regardless of whether the basic area is data analysis or management science. We have found tremendous enthusiasm for this approach, both from students and from faculty around the world who have used our books. Students learn and remember more, and they appreciate the material more. In addition, instructors typically enjoy teaching more, and they usually receive immediate reinforcement through better teaching evaluations. We were among the first to move to spreadsheet-based teaching almost two decades ago, and we have never regretted the move.

What we hope to accomplish in this book

Condensing the ideas in the above paragraphs, we hope to:

- Reverse negative student attitudes about statistics and quantitative methods by making these topics real, accessible, and interesting;

- Give students lots of hands-on experience with real problems and challenge them to develop their intuition, logic, and problem-solving skills;

- Expose students to real problems in many business disciplines and show them how these problems can be analyzed with quantitative methods;

- Develop spreadsheet skills, including experience with powerful spreadsheet add-ins, that add immediate value in students' other courses and their future careers.

New in the fourth edition

There are two major changes in this edition.

- We have completely rewritten and reorganized Chapters 2 and 3. Chapter 2 now focuses on the description of one variable at a time, and Chapter 3 focuses on relationships between variables. We believe this reorganization is more logical. In addition, both of these chapters have more coverage of categorical variables, and they have new examples with more interesting data sets.

- We have made major changes in the problems, particularly in Chapters 2 and 3. Many of the problems in previous editions were either uninteresting or outdated, so in most cases we deleted or updated such problems, and we added a number of brand-new problems. We also created a file, essentially a database of problems, that is available to instructors. This file, **Problem Database.xlsx**, indicates the context of each of the problems, and it also shows the correspondence between problems in this edition and problems in the previous edition.

Besides these two major changes, there are a number of smaller changes, including the following:

- Due to the length of the book, we decided to delete the old Chapter 4 (Getting the Right

Data) from the printed book and make it available online as Chapter 17. This chapter, now called "Importing Data into Excel," has been completely rewritten, and its section on Excel tables is now in Chapter 2. (The old Chapters 5–17 were renumbered 4–16.)

■ The book is still based on Excel 2007, but where it applies, notes about changes in Excel 2010 have been added. Specifically, there is a small section on the new slicers for pivot tables, and there are several mentions of the new statistical functions (although the old functions still work).

■ Each chapter now has 10–20 "Conceptual Questions" in the end-of-chapter section. There were a few "Conceptual Exercises" in some chapters in previous editions, but the new versions are more numerous, consistent, and relevant.

■ The first two linear programming (LP) examples in Chapter 13 (the old Chapter 14) have been replaced by two product mix models, where the second is an extension of the first. Our thinking was that the previous diet-themed model was overly complex as a first LP example.

■ Several of the chapter-opening vignettes have been replaced by newer and more interesting ones.

■ There are now many short "fundamental insights" throughout the chapters. We hope these allow the students to step back from the details and see the really important ideas.

Software

This book is based entirely on Microsoft Excel, the spreadsheet package that has become the standard analytical tool in business. Excel is an extremely powerful package, and one of our goals is to convert *casual* users into *power* users who can take full advantage of its features. If we accomplish no more than this, we will be providing a valuable skill for the business world. However, Excel has some limitations. Therefore, this book includes several Excel add-ins that greatly enhance Excel's capabilities. As a group, these add-ins comprise what is arguably the most impressive assortment of spreadsheet-based software accompanying any book on the market.

DecisionTools® add-in. The textbook Web site for *Data Analysis and Decision Making* provides a link to the powerful DecisionTools® Suite by Palisade Corporation. This suite includes seven separate add-ins, the first three of which we use extensively:

■ **@RISK**, an add-in for simulation

■ **StatTools**, an add-in for statistical data analysis

■ **PrecisionTree**, a graphical-based add-in for creating and analyzing decision trees

■ **TopRank**, an add-in for performing what-if analyses

■ **RISKOptimizer**, an add-in for performing optimization on simulation models

■ **NeuralTools®**, an add-in for finding complex, nonlinear relationships

■ **Evolver™**, an add-in for performing optimization on complex "nonsmooth" models

Online access to the DecisionTools® Suite, available with new copies of the book, is an academic version, slightly scaled down from the professional version that sells for hundreds of dollars and is used by many leading companies. It functions for two years when properly installed, and it puts only modest limitations on the size of data sets or models that can be analyzed. (Visit www.kelley.iu.edu/albrightbooks for specific details on these limitations.) We use @RISK and PrecisionTree extensively in the chapters on simulation and decision making under uncertainty, and we use StatTools throughout all of the data analysis chapters.

SolverTable add-in. We also include SolverTable, a supplement to Excel's built-in Solver for optimization. If you have ever had difficulty understanding Solver's sensitivity reports, you will appreciate SolverTable. It works like Excel's data tables, except that for each input (or pair of inputs), the add-in runs Solver and reports the *optimal* output values. SolverTable is used extensively in the optimization chapters. The version of SolverTable included in this book has been revised for Excel 2007. (Although SolverTable is available on this textbook's Web site, it is also available for free from the first author's Web site, www.kelley.iu.edu/albrightbooks.)

Possible sequences of topics

Although we use the book for our own required one-semester course, there is admittedly more material than can be covered adequately in one semester. We have tried to make the book as modular as possible, allowing an instructor to cover, say, simulation before optimization or vice versa, or to omit either of these topics. The one exception is statistics. Due to the natural progression of statistical topics, the basic topics in the early chapters should be covered before the more advanced topics (regression and time series analysis) in the later chapters. With this in mind, there are several possible ways to cover the topics.

- For a one-semester required course, with no statistics prerequisite (or where MBA students have forgotten whatever statistics they learned years ago): If data analysis is the primary focus of the course, then Chapters 2–5, 7–11, and possibly the online Chapter 17 (all statistics and probability topics) should be covered. Depending on the time remaining, any of the topics in Chapters 6 (decision making under uncertainty), 12 (time series analysis), 13–14 (optimization), or 15–16 (simulation) can be covered in practically any order.

- For a one-semester required course, with a statistics prerequisite: Assuming that students know the basic elements of statistics (up through hypothesis testing, say), the material in Chapters 2–5 and 7–9 can be reviewed quickly, primarily to illustrate how Excel and add-ins can be used to do the number crunching. Then the instructor can choose among any of the topics in Chapters 6, 10–11, 12, 13–14, or 15–16 (in practically any order) to fill the remainder of the course.

- For a two-semester required sequence: Given the luxury of spreading the topics over two semesters, the entire book can be covered. The statistics topics in Chapters 2–5 and 7–9 should be covered in order before other statistical topics (regression and time series analysis), but the remaining chapters can be covered in practically any order.

Custom publishing

If you want to use only a subset of the text, or add chapters from the authors' other texts or your own materials, you can do so through Cengage Learning Custom Publishing. Contact your local Cengage Learning representative for more details.

Student ancillaries

Textbook Web Site

Every new student edition of this book comes with an Instant Access Code (bound inside the book). The code provides access to the *Data Analysis and Decision Making, 4e* textbook Web site that links to all of the following files and tools:

- DecisionTools® Suite software by Palisade Corporation (described earlier)
- Excel files for the examples in the chapters (usually two versions of each—a template, or data-only version, and a finished version)
- Data files required for the problems and cases
- **Excel Tutorial.xlsx**, which contains a useful tutorial for getting up to speed in Excel 2007

Students who do not have a new book can purchase access to the textbook Web site at www.CengageBrain.com.

Student Solutions

Student Solutions to many of the odd-numbered problems (indicated in the text with a colored box on the problem number) are available in Excel format. Students can purchase access to Student Solutions files on www.CengageBrain.com. (ISBN-10: 1-111-52905-1; ISBN-13: 978-1-111-52905-5).

Instructor ancillaries

Adopting instructors can obtain the *Instructors' Resource CD* (IRCD) from your regional Cengage Learning Sales Representative. The IRCD includes:

- **Problem Database.xlsx** file (contains information about all problems in the book and the correspondence between them and those in the previous edition)
- Example files for all examples in the book, including annotated versions with additional explanations and a few extra examples that extend the examples in the book
- Solution files (in Excel format) for all of the problems and cases in the book and solution shells (templates) for selected problems in the modeling chapters
- PowerPoint® presentation files for all of the examples in the book

- Test Bank in Word format and now also in ExamView® Testing Software (new to this edition).

The book's password-protected instructor Web site, www.cengage.com/decisionsciences/albright, includes the above items (Test Bank in Word format only), as well as software updates, errata, additional problems and solutions, and additional resources for both students and faculty. The first author also maintains his own Web site at www.kelley.iu.edu/albrightbooks.

Acknowledgments

The authors would like to thank several people who helped make this book a reality. First, the authors are indebted to Peter Kolesar, Mark Broadie, Lawrence Lapin, and William Whisler for contributing some of the excellent case studies that appear throughout the book.

There are more people who helped to produce this book than we can list here. However, there are a few special people whom we were happy (and lucky) to have on our team. First, we would like to thank our editor Charles McCormick. Charles stepped into this project after two editions had already been published, but the transition has been smooth and rewarding. We appreciate his tireless efforts to make the book a continued success.

We are also grateful to many of the professionals who worked behind the scenes to make this book a success: Adam Marsh, Marketing Manager; Laura Ansara, Senior Developmental Editor; Nora Heink, Editorial Assistant; Tim Bailey, Senior Content Project Manager; Stacy Shirley, Senior Art Director; and Gunjan Chandola, Senior Project Manager at MPS Limited.

We also extend our sincere appreciation to the reviewers who provided feedback on the authors' proposed changes that resulted in this fourth edition:

Henry F. Ander, Arizona State University

James D. Behel, Harding University

Dan Brooks, Arizona State University

Robert H. Burgess, Georgia Institute of Technology

George Cunningham III, Northwestern State University

Rex Cutshall, Indiana University

Robert M. Escudero, Pepperdine University

Theodore S. Glickman, George Washington University

John Gray, The Ohio State University

Joe Hahn, Pepperdine University

Max Peter Hoefer, Pace University

Tim James, Arizona State University

Teresa Jostes, Capital University

Jeffrey Keisler, University of Massachusetts – Boston

David Kelton, University of Cincinnati

Shreevardhan Lele, University of Maryland

Ray Nelson, Brigham Young University

William Pearce, Geneva College

Thomas R. Sexton, Stony Brook University

Malcolm T. Whitehead, Northwestern State University

Laura A. Wilson-Gentry, University of Baltimore

Jay Zagorsky, Boston University

S. Christian Albright

Wayne L. Winston

Christopher J. Zappe

May 2010

Introduction to Data Analysis and Decision Making

George Doyle/Jupiter Images

HOTTEST NEW JOBS: STATISTICS AND MATHEMATICS

Much of this book, as the title implies, is about data analysis. The term *data analysis* has long been synonymous with the term *statistics*, but in today's world, with massive amounts of data available in business and many other fields such as health and science, data analysis goes beyond the more narrowly focused area of traditional statistics. But regardless of what we call it, data analysis is currently a hot topic and promises to get even hotter in the future. The data analysis skills you learn here, and possibly in follow-up quantitative courses, might just land you a very interesting and lucrative job.

This is exactly the message in a recent *New York Times* article, "For Today's Graduate, Just One Word: Statistics," by Steve Lohr. (A similar article, "Math Will Rock Your World," by Stephen Baker, was the cover story for

BusinessWeek. Both articles are available online by searching for their titles.) The statistics article begins by chronicling a Harvard anthropology and archaeology graduate, Carrie Grimes, who began her career by mapping the locations of Mayan artifacts in places like Honduras. As she states, "People think of field archaeology as Indiana Jones, but much of what you really do is data analysis." Since then, Grimes has leveraged her data analysis skills to get a job with Google, where she and many other people with a quantitative background are analyzing huge amounts of data to improve the company's search engine. As the chief economist at Google, Hal Varian, states, "I keep saying that the sexy job in the next 10 years will be statisticians. And I'm not kidding." The salaries for statisticians with doctoral degrees currently *start* at $125,000, and they will probably continue to increase. (The math article indicates that mathematicians are also in great demand.)

Why is this trend occurring? The reason is the explosion of digital data—data from sensor signals, surveillance tapes, Web clicks, bar scans, public records, financial transactions, and more. In years past, statisticians typically analyzed relatively small data sets, such as opinion polls with about 1000 responses. Today's massive data sets require new statistical methods, new computer software, and most importantly for you, more young people trained in these methods and the corresponding software. Several particular areas mentioned in the articles include (1) improving Internet search and online advertising, (2) unraveling gene sequencing information for cancer research, (3) analyzing sensor and location data for optimal handling of food shipments, and (4) the recent Netflix contest for improving the company's recommendation system.

The statistics article mentions three specific organizations in need of data analysts—and lots of them. The first is government, where there is an increasing need to sift through mounds of data as a first step toward dealing with long-term economic needs and key policy priorities. The second is IBM, which created a Business Analytics and Optimization Services group in April 2009. This group will use the more than 200 mathematicians, statisticians, and data analysts already employed by the company, but IBM intends to retrain or hire 4000 more analysts to meet its needs. The third is Google, which needs more data analysts to improve its search engine. You may think that today's search engines are unbelievably efficient, but Google knows they can be improved. As Ms. Grimes states, "Even an improvement of a percent or two can be huge, when you do things over the millions and billions of times we do things at Google."

Of course, these three organizations are not the only organizations that need to hire more skilled people to perform data analysis and other analytical procedures. It is a need faced by *all* large organizations. Various recent technologies, the most prominent by far being the Web, have given organizations the ability to gather massive amounts of data easily. Now they need people to make sense of it all and use it to their competitive advantage. ■

1.1 INTRODUCTION

We are living in the age of technology. This has two important implications for everyone entering the business world. First, technology has made it possible to collect huge amounts of data. Retailers collect point-of-sale data on products and customers every time a transaction occurs; credit agencies have all sorts of data on people who have or would like to obtain credit; investment companies have a limitless supply of data on the historical patterns of stocks, bonds, and other securities; and government agencies have data on economic trends, the environment, social welfare, consumer product safety, and virtually everything else imaginable. It has become relatively *easy* to collect the data. As a result, data are plentiful. However, as many organizations are now beginning to discover, it is quite a challenge to analyze and make sense of all the data they have collected.

A second important implication of technology is that it has given many more people the power and responsibility to analyze data and make decisions on the basis of quantitative analysis. People entering the business world can no longer pass all of the quantitative analysis to the "quant jocks," the technical specialists who have traditionally done the number crunching. The vast majority of employees now have a desktop or laptop computer at their disposal, access to relevant data, and training in easy-to-use software, particularly spreadsheet and database software. For these employees, statistics and other quantitative methods are no longer forgotten topics they once learned in college. Quantitative analysis is now an integral part of their daily jobs.

A large amount of data already exists, and it will only increase in the future. Many companies already complain of swimming in a sea of data. However, enlightened companies are seeing this expansion as a source of competitive advantage. By using quantitative methods to uncover the *information* in the data and then acting on this information—again guided by quantitative analysis—they are able to gain advantages that their less enlightened competitors are not able to gain. Several pertinent examples of this follow.

- Direct marketers analyze enormous customer databases to see which customers are likely to respond to various products and types of promotions. Marketers can then target different classes of customers in different ways to maximize profits—and give their customers what they want.

- Hotels and airlines also analyze enormous customer databases to see what their customers want and are willing to pay for. By doing this, they have been able to devise very clever pricing strategies, where different customers pay different prices for the same accommodations. For example, a business traveler typically makes a plane reservation closer to the time of travel than a vacationer. The airlines know this. Therefore, they reserve seats for these business travelers and charge them a higher price for the same seats. The airlines profit from clever pricing strategies, and the customers are happy.

- Financial planning services have a virtually unlimited supply of data about security prices, and they have customers with widely differing preferences for various types of investments. Trying to find a match of investments to customers is a very challenging problem. However, customers can easily take their business elsewhere if good decisions are not made on their behalf. Therefore, financial planners are under extreme competitive pressure to analyze masses of data so that they can make informed decisions for their customers.[1]

- We all know about the pressures U.S. manufacturing companies have faced from foreign competition in the past couple of decades. The automobile companies, for example, have had to change the way they produce and market automobiles to stay in business. They have had to improve quality and cut costs by orders of magnitude. Although the struggle continues, much of the success they have had can be attributed to data analysis and wise decision making. Starting on the shop floor and moving up through the organization, these companies now measure almost everything, analyze these measurements, and then act on the results of their analysis.

---

[1] For a great overview of how quantitative techniques have been used in the financial world, read the book *The Quants*, by Scott Patterson (Random House, 2010). It describes how quantitative models made millions for a lot of bright young analysts, but it also describes the dangers of relying totally on quantitative models, at least in the complex and global world of finance.

We talk about companies analyzing data and making decisions. However, *companies* don't really do this; *people* do it. And who will these people be in the future? They will be *you*! We know from experience that students in all areas of business, at both the undergraduate and graduate level, will soon be *required* to describe large complex data sets, run regression analyses, make quantitative forecasts, create optimization models, and run simulations. You are the person who will soon be analyzing data and making important decisions to help your company gain a competitive advantage. And if you are *not* willing or able to do so, there will be plenty of other technically trained people who will be more than happy to replace you.

Our goal in this book is to teach you how to use a variety of quantitative methods to analyze data and make decisions. We will do so in a very hands-on way. We will discuss a number of quantitative methods and illustrate their use in a large variety of realistic business situations. As you will see, this book includes many examples from finance, marketing, operations, accounting, and other areas of business. To analyze these examples, we will take advantage of the Microsoft Excel spreadsheet software, together with a number of powerful Excel add-ins. In each example we will provide step-by-step details of the method and its implementation in Excel.

This is *not* a "theory" book. It is also not a book where you can lean comfortably back in your chair, prop your legs up on a table, and read about how *other* people use quantitative methods. It is a "get your hands dirty" book, where you will learn best by actively following the examples throughout the book at your own PC. In short, you will learn by doing. By the time you have finished, you will have acquired some very useful skills for today's business world.

1.2 AN OVERVIEW OF THE BOOK

This book is packed with quantitative methods and examples, probably more than can be covered in any single course. Therefore, we purposely intend to keep this introductory chapter brief so that you can get on with the analysis. Nevertheless, it is useful to introduce the methods you will be learning and the tools you will be using. In this section we provide an overview of the methods covered in this book and the software that is used to implement them. Then in the next section we present a brief discussion of models and the modeling process. Our primary purpose at this point is to stimulate your interest in what is to follow.

1.2.1 The Methods

This book is rather unique in that it combines topics from two separate fields: statistics and management science. In a nutshell, statistics is the study of data analysis, whereas management science is the study of model building, optimization, and decision making. In the academic arena these two fields have traditionally been separated, sometimes widely. Indeed, they are often housed in separate academic departments. However, from a user's standpoint it makes little sense to separate them. Both are useful in accomplishing what the title of this book promises: data analysis and decision making.

Therefore, we do not distinguish between the statistics and the management science parts of this book. Instead, we view the entire book as a collection of useful quantitative methods that can be used to analyze data and help make business decisions. In addition, our choice of software helps to integrate the various topics. By using a single package, Excel, together with a number of add-ins, you will see that the methods of statistics and management science are similar in many important respects. Most importantly, their combination gives you the power and flexibility to solve a wide range of business problems.

Three important themes run through this book. Two of them are in the title: data analysis and decision making. The third is *dealing with uncertainty*.[2] Each of these themes has subthemes. Data analysis includes data description, data inference, and the search for relationships in data. Decision making includes *optimization* techniques for problems with no uncertainty, *decision analysis* for problems with uncertainty, and structured *sensitivity analysis*. Dealing with uncertainty includes measuring uncertainty and modeling uncertainty explicitly. There are obvious overlaps between these themes and subthemes. When you make inferences from data and search for relationships in data, you must deal with uncertainty. When you use *decision trees* to help make decisions, you must deal with uncertainty. When you use *simulation models* to help make decisions, you must deal with uncertainty, and then you often make inferences from the simulated data.

Figure 1.1 shows where you will find these themes and subthemes in the remaining chapters of this book. In the next few paragraphs we discuss the book's contents in more detail.

Figure 1.1

Themes and Subthemes

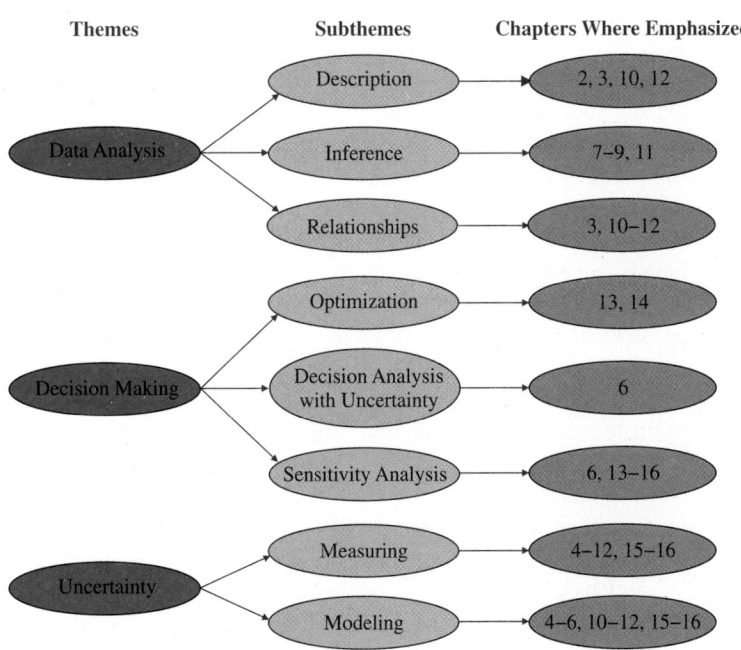

We begin in Chapters 2 and 3 by illustrating a number of ways to summarize the information in data sets. These include graphical and tabular summaries, as well as numerical summary measures such as means, medians, and standard deviations. The material in these two chapters is elementary from a mathematical point of view, but it is extremely important. As we stated at the beginning of this chapter, organizations are now able to collect huge amounts of raw data, but what does it all mean? Although there are very sophisticated methods for analyzing data sets, some of which we cover in later chapters, the "simple" methods in Chapters 2 and 3 are crucial for obtaining an initial understanding of the data. Fortunately, Excel and available add-ins now make what was once a very tedious task quite easy. For example, Excel's pivot table tool for "slicing and dicing" data is an analyst's

---

[2]The fact that the uncertainty theme did not find its way into the title of this book does not detract from its importance. We just wanted to keep the title reasonably short!

dream come true. You will be amazed at the complex analysis pivot tables enable you to perform—with almost no effort.[3]

Uncertainty is a key aspect of most business problems. To deal with uncertainty, you need a basic understanding of probability. We provide this understanding in Chapters 4 and 5. Chapter 4 covers basic rules of probability and then discusses the extremely important concept of probability distributions. Chapter 5 follows up this discussion by focusing on two of the most important probability distributions, the normal and binomial distributions. It also briefly discusses the Poisson and exponential distributions, which have many applications in probability models.

We have found that one of the best ways to make probabilistic concepts "come alive" and easier to understand is by using computer simulation. Therefore, simulation is a common theme that runs through this book, beginning in Chapter 4. Although the final two chapters of the book are devoted entirely to simulation, we do not hesitate to use simulation early and often to illustrate statistical concepts.

In Chapter 6 we apply our knowledge of probability to decision making under uncertainty. These types of problems—faced by all companies on a continual basis—are characterized by the need to make a decision *now*, even though important information (such as demand for a product or returns from investments) will not be known until later. The material in Chapter 6 provides a rational basis for making such decisions. The methods we illustrate do not guarantee perfect outcomes—the future could unluckily turn out differently than expected—but they do enable you to proceed rationally and make the best of the given circumstances. Additionally, the software used to implement these methods allows you, with very little extra work, to see how sensitive the optimal decisions are to inputs. This is crucial, because the inputs to many business problems are, at best, educated guesses. Finally, we examine the role of risk aversion in these types of decision problems.

In Chapters 7, 8, and 9 we discuss sampling and statistical inference. Here the basic problem is to estimate one or more characteristics of a population. If it is too expensive or time consuming to learn about the *entire* population—and it usually is—we instead select a random sample from the population and then use the information in the sample to *infer* the characteristics of the population. You see this continually on news shows that describe the results of various polls. You also see it in many business contexts. For example, auditors typically sample only a fraction of a company's records. Then they infer the characteristics of the entire population of records from the results of the sample to conclude whether the company has been following acceptable accounting standards.

In Chapters 10 and 11 we discuss the extremely important topic of regression analysis, which is used to study relationships between variables. The power of regression analysis is its generality. Every part of a business has variables that are related to one another, and regression can often be used to estimate possible relationships between these variables. In managerial accounting, regression is used to estimate how overhead costs depend on direct labor hours and production volume. In marketing, regression is used to estimate how sales volume depends on advertising and other marketing variables. In finance, regression is used to estimate how the return of a stock depends on the "market" return. In real estate studies, regression is used to estimate how the selling price of a house depends on the assessed valuation of the house and characteristics such as the number of bedrooms and square footage. Regression analysis finds perhaps as many uses in the business world as any method in this book.

From regression, we move to time series analysis and forecasting in Chapter 12. This topic is particularly important for providing inputs into business decision problems. For example, manufacturing companies must forecast demand for their products to make

---

[3]Users of the previous edition will notice that the old Chapter 4 (getting data into Excel) is no longer in the book. We did this to keep the book from getting even longer. However, an updated version of this chapter is available at this textbook's Web site. Go to www.cengage.com/decisionsciences/albright for access instructions.

sensible decisions about quantities to order from their suppliers. Similarly, fast-food restaurants must forecast customer arrivals, sometimes down to the level of 15-minute intervals, so that they can staff their restaurants appropriately. There are many approaches to forecasting, ranging from simple to complex. Some involve regression-based methods, in which one or more time series variables are used to forecast the variable of interest, whereas other methods are based on extrapolation. In an extrapolation method the historical patterns of a time series variable, such as product demand or customer arrivals, are studied carefully and are then *extrapolated* into the future to obtain forecasts. A number of extrapolation methods are available. In Chapter 12 we study both regression and extrapolation methods for forecasting.

Chapters 13 and 14 are devoted to spreadsheet optimization, with emphasis on linear programming. We assume a company must make several decisions, and there are constraints that limit the possible decisions. The job of the decision maker is to choose the decisions such that all of the constraints are satisfied and an objective, such as total profit or total cost, is optimized. The solution process consists of two steps. The first step is to build a spreadsheet model that relates the decision variables to other relevant quantities by means of logical formulas. In this first step there is no attempt to find the *optimal* solution; its only purpose is to relate all relevant quantities in a logical way. The second step is then to find the optimal solution. Fortunately, Excel contains a Solver add-in that performs this step. All you need to do is specify the objective, the decision variables, and the constraints; Solver then uses powerful algorithms to find the optimal solution. As with regression, the power of this approach is its generality. An enormous variety of problems can be solved by spreadsheet optimization.

Finally, Chapters 15 and 16 illustrate a number of computer simulation models. This is not your first exposure to simulation—it is used in a number of previous chapters to illustrate statistical concepts—but here it is studied in its own right. As we discussed previously, most business problems have some degree of uncertainty. The demand for a product is unknown, future interest rates are unknown, the delivery lead time from a supplier is unknown, and so on. Simulation allows you to build this uncertainty *explicitly* into spreadsheet models. Essentially, some cells in the model contain random values with given probability distributions. Every time the spreadsheet recalculates, these random values change, which causes "bottom-line" output cells to change as well. The trick then is to force the spreadsheet to recalculate many times and keep track of interesting outputs. In this way you can see which output values are most likely, and you can see best-case and worst-case results.

Spreadsheet simulations can be performed entirely with Excel's built-in tools. However, this is quite tedious. Therefore, we use a spreadsheet add-in to streamline the process. In particular, you will learn how the @RISK add-in can be used to run replications of a simulation, keep track of outputs, create useful charts, and perform sensitivity analyses. With the inherent power of spreadsheets and the ease of using such add-ins as @RISK, spreadsheet simulation is becoming one of the most popular quantitative tools in the business world.

1.2.2 The Software

The quantitative methods in this book can be used to analyze a wide variety of business problems. However, they are not of much practical use unless you have the software to do the number crunching. Very few business problems are small enough to be solved with pencil and paper. They require powerful software.

The software included in new copies of this book, together with Microsoft Excel, provides you with a powerful combination. This software is being used—and will continue to be used—by leading companies all over the world to analyze large, complex problems. We firmly believe that the experience you obtain with this software, through working the examples and problems in this book, will give you a key competitive advantage in the marketplace.

It all begins with Excel. All of the quantitative methods that we discuss are implemented in Excel. Specifically, in this edition, we use Excel 2007.[4] We cannot forecast the state of computer software in the long-term future, but Excel is currently *the* most heavily used spreadsheet package on the market, and there is every reason to believe that this state will persist for many years. Most companies use Excel, most employees and most students have been trained in Excel, and Excel is a *very* powerful, flexible, and easy-to-use package.

Built-in Excel Features

Virtually everyone in the business world knows the basic features of Excel, but relatively few know some of its more powerful features. In short, relatively few people are the "power users" we expect you to become by working through this book. To get you started, the file **Excel Tutorial.xlsx** explains some of the "intermediate" features of Excel—features that we expect you to be able to use (access this file on the textbook's Web site that accompanies new copies of this book). These include the SUMPRODUCT, VLOOKUP, IF, NPV, and COUNTIF functions. They also include range names, data tables, the Paste Special option, the Goal Seek tool, and many others. Finally, although we assume you can perform routine spreadsheet tasks such as copying and pasting, the tutorial includes many tips to help you perform these tasks more efficiently.

In the body of the book we describe several of Excel's advanced features in more detail. For example, we introduce pivot tables in Chapter 3. This Excel tool enables you to summarize data sets in an almost endless variety of ways. (Excel has many useful tools, but we personally believe that pivot tables are the most ingenious and powerful of all. We won't be surprised if you agree.) As another example, we introduce Excel's RAND and RANDBETWEEN functions for generating random numbers in Chapter 4. These functions are used in all spreadsheet simulations (at least those that do not take advantage of an add-in). In short, when an Excel tool is useful for a particular type of analysis, we provide step-by-step instructions on how to use it.

Solver Add-in

In Chapters 13 and 14 we make heavy use of Excel's Solver add-in. This add-in, developed by Frontline Systems (not Microsoft), uses powerful algorithms—all behind the scenes—to perform spreadsheet optimization. Before this type of spreadsheet optimization add-in was available, specialized (nonspreadsheet) software was required to solve optimization problems. Now you can do it all within a familiar spreadsheet environment.

SolverTable Add-in

An important theme throughout this book is sensitivity analysis: How do outputs change when inputs change? Typically these changes are made in spreadsheets with a data table, a built-in Excel tool. However, data tables don't work in optimization models, where we would like to see how the *optimal* solution changes when certain inputs change. Therefore, we include an Excel add-in called SolverTable, which works almost exactly like Excel's data tables. (This add-in was developed by Albright.) In Chapters 13 and 14 we illustrate the use of SolverTable.

Decision Tools Suite

In addition to SolverTable and built-in Excel add-ins, we also have included on the textbook's Web site an educational version of Palisade Corporation's powerful Decision Tools suite. All of the programs in this suite are Excel add-ins, so the learning curve isn't very steep. There are seven separate add-ins in this suite: @RISK,

---

[4]At the time we wrote this edition, Excel 2010 was in beta form and was about to be released. Fortunately, the changes, at least for our purposes, are not extensive, so users familiar with Excel 2007 will have no difficulty in moving to Excel 2010. Where relevant, we have pointed out changes in the new version.

StatTools, PrecisionTree, TopRank, RISKOptimizer, NeuralTools, and Evolver.[5] We will use only the first three in this book, but all are useful for certain tasks and are described briefly below.

@RISK

The simulation add-in @RISK enables you to run as many replications of a spreadsheet simulation as you like. As the simulation runs, @RISK automatically keeps track of the outputs you select, and it then displays the results in a number of tabular and graphical forms. @RISK also enables you to perform a sensitivity analysis, so that you can see which inputs have the most effect on the outputs. Finally, @RISK provides a number of spreadsheet functions that enable you to generate random numbers from a variety of probability distributions.

StatTools

Much of this book discusses basic statistical analysis. Here we needed to make an important decision as we developed the book. A number of excellent statistical software packages are on the market, including Minitab, SPSS, SAS, JMP, Stata, and others. Although there are user-friendly Windows versions of these packages, they are *not* spreadsheet-based. We have found through our own experience that students resist the use of nonspreadsheet packages, regardless of their inherent quality, so we wanted to use Excel as our "statistics package." Unfortunately, Excel's built-in statistical tools are rather limited, and the Analysis ToolPak (developed by a third party) that ships with Excel has significant limitations.

Fortunately, the Palisade suite includes a statistical add-in called StatTools. StatTools is powerful, easy to use, and capable of generating output quickly in an easily interpretable form. We do *not* believe you should have to spend hours each time you want to produce some statistical output. This might be a good learning experience the first time, but it acts as a strong incentive *not* to perform the analysis at all. We believe you should be able to generate output quickly and easily. This gives you the time to *interpret* the output, and it also allows you to try different methods of analysis.

A good illustration involves the construction of histograms, scatterplots, and time series graphs, discussed in Chapters 2 and 3. All of these extremely useful graphs can be created in a straightforward way with Excel's built-in tools. But by the time you perform all the necessary steps and "dress up" the charts exactly as you want them, you will not be very anxious to repeat the whole process again. StatTools does it all quickly and easily. (You still might want to "dress up" the resulting charts, but that's up to you.) Therefore, if we advise you in a later chapter, say, to look at several scatterplots as a prelude to a regression analysis, you can do so in a matter of seconds.

PrecisionTree

The PrecisionTree add-in is used in Chapter 6 to analyze decision problems with uncertainty. The primary method for performing this type of analysis is to draw a decision tree. Decision trees are inherently graphical, and they have always been difficult to implement in spreadsheets, which are based on rows and columns. However, PrecisionTree does this in a very clever and intuitive way. Equally important, once the basic decision tree has been built, it is easy to use PrecisionTree to perform a sensitivity analysis on the model's inputs.

TopRank

TopRank is a "what-if" add-in used for sensitivity analysis. It starts with any spreadsheet model, where a set of inputs, along with a number of spreadsheet formulas, leads to one or

---

[5] The Palisade suite has traditionally included two stand-alone programs, BestFit and RISKview. The functionality of both of these is now included in @RISK, so they are not included in the suite.

more outputs. TopRank then performs a sensitivity analysis to see which inputs have the largest effect on a given output. For example, it might indicate which input affects after-tax profit the most: the tax rate, the risk-free rate for investing, the inflation rate, or the price charged by a competitor. Unlike @RISK, TopRank is used when uncertainty is not *explicitly* built into a spreadsheet model. However, it considers uncertainty implicitly by performing sensitivity analysis on the important model inputs.

RISKOptimizer

RISKOptimizer combines optimization with simulation. There are often times when you want to use simulation to model some business problem, but you also want to optimize a summary measure, such as a mean, of an output distribution. This optimization can be performed in a trial-and-error fashion, where you try a few values of the decision variable(s) and see which provides the best solution. However, RISKOptimizer provides a more automatic (and time-intensive) optimization procedure.

NeuralTools

In Chapters 10 and 11, we show how regression can be used to find a linear equation that quantifies the relationship between a dependent variable and one or more explanatory variables. Although linear regression is a powerful tool, it is not capable of quantifying all possible relationships. The NeuralTools add-in mimics the working of the human brain to find "neural networks" that quantify complex nonlinear relationships.

Evolver

In Chapters 13 and 14, we show how the built-in Solver add-in can optimize linear models and even some nonlinear models. But there are some "non-smooth" nonlinear models that Solver cannot handle. Fortunately, there are other optimization algorithms for such models, including "genetic" algorithms. The Evolver add-in implements these genetic algorithms.

Software Guide

Figure 1.2 provides a guide to the use of these add-ins throughout the book. We don't show Excel explicitly in this figure for the simple reason that Excel is used extensively in *all* chapters.

Figure 1.2
Software Guide

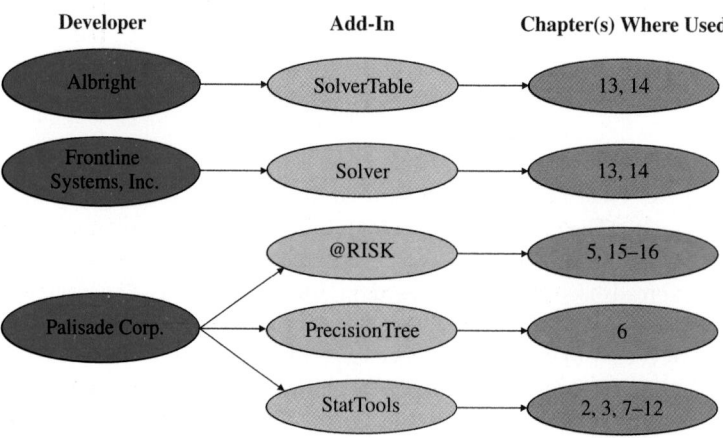

With Excel and the add-ins included in this book, you have a wealth of software at your disposal. The examples and step-by-step instructions throughout this book will help you become a power user of this software. Admittedly, this takes plenty of practice and a willingness to experiment, but it is certainly within your grasp. When you are finished, we will not be surprised if you rate "improved software skills" as the most valuable thing you have learned from this book.

1.3 MODELING AND MODELS

We have already used the term *model* several times in this chapter. Models and the modeling process are key elements throughout this book, so we explain them in more detail in this section.[6]

A model is an abstraction of a real problem. A model tries to capture the essence and key features of the problem without getting bogged down in relatively unimportant details. There are different types of models, and depending on an analyst's preferences and skills, each can be a valuable aid in solving a real problem. We briefly describe three types of models here: graphical models, algebraic models, and spreadsheet models.

1.3.1 Graphical Models

Graphical models are probably the most intuitive and least quantitative type of model. They attempt to portray graphically how different elements of a problem are related—what affects what. A very simple graphical model appears in Figure 1.3. It is called an *influence diagram*. (It can be constructed with the PrecisionTree add-in discussed in Chapter 6, but we will not use influence diagrams in this book.)

Figure 1.3
Influence Diagram

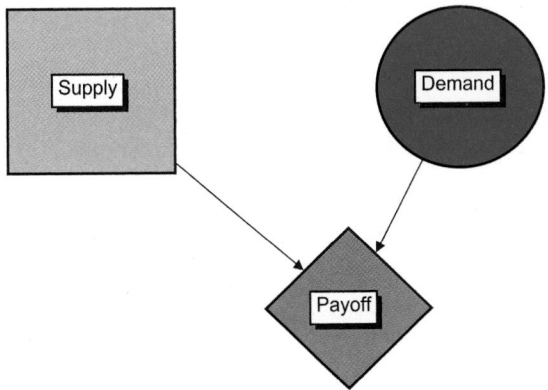

This particular influence diagram is for a company that is trying to decide how many souvenirs to order for the upcoming Olympics. The essence of the problem is that the company will order a certain supply, customers will request a certain demand, and the combination of supply and demand will yield a certain payoff for the company. The diagram indicates fairly intuitively what affects what. As it stands, the diagram does not provide enough quantitative details to "solve" the company's problem, but this is usually not the purpose of a graphical model. Instead, its purpose is usually to show the important elements of a problem and how they are related. For complex problems, this can be very helpful and enlightening information for management.

---

[6]Management scientists tend to use the terms *model* and *modeling* more than statisticians. However, many traditional statistics topics such as regression analysis and forecasting are clearly applications of modeling.

1.3.2 Algebraic Models

Algebraic models are at the opposite end of the spectrum. By means of algebraic equations and inequalities, they specify a set of relationships in a very precise way. Their preciseness and lack of ambiguity are very appealing to people with a mathematical background. In addition, algebraic models can usually be stated concisely and with great generality.

A typical example is the "product mix" problem in Chapter 13. A company can make several products, each of which contributes a certain amount to profit and consumes certain amounts of several scarce resources. The problem is to select the product mix that maximizes profit subject to the limited availability of the resources. *All* product mix problems can be stated algebraically as follows:

$$\max \sum_{j=1}^{n} p_j x_j \tag{1.1}$$

$$\text{subject to } \sum_{j=1}^{n} a_{ij} x_j \leq b_j, \quad 1 \leq i \leq m \tag{1.2}$$

$$0 \leq x_j \leq u_j, \quad 1 \leq j \leq n \tag{1.3}$$

Here x_j is the amount of product j produced, u_j is an upper limit on the amount of product j that can be produced, p_j is the unit profit margin for product j, a_{ij} is the amount of resource i consumed by each unit of product j, b_i is the amount of resource i available, n is the number of products, and m is the number of scarce resources. This algebraic model states very concisely that we should maximize total profit [expression (1.1)], subject to consuming no more of each resource than is available [inequality (1.2)], and all production quantities should be between 0 and the upper limits [inequality (1.3)].

Algebraic models appeal to mathematically trained analysts. They are concise, they spell out exactly which data are required (the values of the u_js, the p_js, the a_{ij}s, and the b_is would need to be estimated from company data), they scale well (a problem with 500 products and 100 resource constraints is just as easy to state as one with only five products and three resource constraints), and many software packages accept algebraic models in essentially the same form as shown here, so that no "translation" is required. Indeed, algebraic models were the preferred type of model for years—and still are by many analysts. Their main drawback is that they require an ability to work with abstract mathematical symbols. Some people have this ability, but many perfectly intelligent people do not.

1.3.3 Spreadsheet Models

An alternative to algebraic modeling is spreadsheet modeling. Instead of relating various quantities with algebraic equations and inequalities, you relate them in a spreadsheet with cell formulas. In our experience, this process is much more intuitive to most people. One of the primary reasons for this is the instant feedback available from spreadsheets. If you enter a formula incorrectly, it is often immediately obvious (from error messages or unrealistic numbers) that you have made an error, which you can then go back and fix. Algebraic models provide no such immediate feedback.

A specific comparison might help at this point. We already saw a general algebraic model of the product mix problem. Figure 1.4, taken from Chapter 13, illustrates a spreadsheet model for a specific example of this problem. The spreadsheet model should be fairly self-explanatory. All quantities in shaded cells (other than in rows 16 and 25) are inputs to

Figure 1.4 Optimal Solution for Product Mix Model

	A	B	C	D	E	F	G
1	**Assembling and testing computers**				**Range names used:**		
2					Hours_available	=Model!$D$21:$D$22	
3	Cost per labor hour assembling	$11			Hours_used	=Model!$B$21:$B$22	
4	Cost per labor hour testing	$15			Maximum_sales	=Model!$B$18:$C$18	
5					Number_to_produce	=Model!$B$16:$C$16	
6	Inputs for assembling and testing a computer				Total_profit	=Model!$D$25	
7		Basic	XP				
8	Labor hours for assembly	5	6				
9	Labor hours for testing	1	2				
10	Cost of component parts	$150	$225				
11	Selling price	$300	$450				
12	Unit margin	$80	$129				
13							
14	Assembling, testing plan (# of computers)						
15		Basic	XP				
16	Number to produce	560	1200				
17		<=	<=				
18	Maximum sales	600	1200				
19							
20	Constraints (hours per month)	Hours used		Hours available			
21	Labor availability for assembling	10000	<=	10000			
22	Labor availability for testing	2960	<=	3000			
23							
24	Net profit ($ this month)	Basic	XP	Total			
25		$44,800	$154,800	$199,600			

the model, the quantities in row 16 are the decision variables (they correspond to the x_js in the algebraic model), and all other quantities are created through appropriate Excel formulas. To indicate constraints, inequality signs have been entered as labels in appropriate cells.

Although a well-designed and well-documented spreadsheet model such as the one in Figure 1.4 is undoubtedly more intuitive for most people than its algebraic counterpart, the art of developing good spreadsheet models is not easy. Obviously, they must be *correct*. The formulas relating the various quantities must have the correct syntax, the correct cell references, and the correct logic. In complex models this can be quite a challenge.

However, we do not believe that correctness is enough. If spreadsheet models are to be used in the business world, they must also be well designed and well documented. Otherwise, no one other than you (and maybe not even you after a few weeks have passed) will be able to understand what your models do or how they work. The strength of spreadsheets is their flexibility—you are limited only by your imagination. However, this flexibility can be a liability in spreadsheet modeling unless you design your models carefully.

Note the clear design in Figure 1.4. Most of the inputs are grouped at the top of the spreadsheet. All of the financial calculations are done at the bottom. When there are constraints, the two sides of the constraints are placed next to each other (as in the range B21:D22). Colored backgrounds (which appear on the screen but not in this book) are used for added clarity, and descriptive labels are used liberally. Excel itself imposes none of these "rules," but you should impose them on yourself.

We have made a conscious effort to establish good habits for you to follow throughout this book. We have designed and redesigned our spreadsheet models so that they are as clear as possible. This does not mean that you have to copy everything we do—everyone tends to develop their own spreadsheet style—but our models should give you something to emulate. Just remember that in the business world, you typically start with a *blank* spreadsheet. It is then up to you to develop a model that is not only correct but is also intelligible to you and others. This takes a lot of practicing and a lot of editing, but it is a skill well worth developing.

1.3.4 A Seven-Step Modeling Process

Most of the modeling you will do in this book is only part of an overall modeling process typically done in the business world. We portray it as a seven-step process, as discussed here. But not all problems require all seven steps. For example, the analysis of survey data might entail primarily steps 2 (data analysis) and 5 (decision making) of the process, without the formal model building discussed in steps 3 and 4.

The Modeling Process

1. **Define the problem.** Typically, a company does not develop a model unless it believes it has a problem. Therefore, the modeling process really begins by identifying an underlying problem. Perhaps the company is losing money, perhaps its market share is declining, or perhaps its customers are waiting too long for service. Any number of problems might be evident. However, as several people have warned [see Miser (1993) and Volkema (1995), for example], this step is not always as straightforward as it might appear. The company must be sure that it has identified the *correct* problem before it spends time, effort, and money trying to solve it.

   For example, Miser cites the experience of an analyst who was hired by the military to investigate overly long turnaround times between fighter planes landing and taking off again to rejoin the battle. The military was convinced that the problem was caused by inefficient ground crews; if they were faster, turnaround times would decrease. The analyst nearly accepted this statement of the problem and was about to do classical time-and-motion studies on the ground crew to pinpoint the sources of their inefficiency. However, by snooping around, he found that the problem obviously lay elsewhere. The trucks that refueled the planes were frequently late, which in turn was due to the inefficient way they were refilled from storage tanks at another location. Once this latter problem was solved—and its solution was embarrassingly simple—the turnaround times decreased to an acceptable level without any changes on the part of the ground crews. If the analyst had accepted the military's statement of the problem, the *real* problem might never have been located or solved.

2. **Collect and summarize data.** This crucial step in the process is often the most tedious. All organizations keep track of various data on their operations, but these data are often not in the form an analyst requires. They are also typically scattered in different places throughout the organization, in all kinds of different formats. Therefore, one of the first jobs of an analyst is to gather exactly the right data and summarize the data appropriately—as we discuss in detail in Chapters 2 and 3—for use in the model. Collecting the data typically requires asking questions of key people (such as the accountants) throughout the organization, studying existing organizational databases, and performing time-consuming observational studies of the organization's

processes. In short, it entails a lot of legwork. Fortunately, many companies have understood the need for good clean data and have spent large amounts of time and money to build *data warehouses* for quantitative analysis.

3. **Develop a model.** This is the step we emphasize, especially in the latter chapters of the book. The form of the model varies from one situation to another. It could be a graphical model, an algebraic model, or a spreadsheet model. The key is that the model should capture the important elements of the business problem in such a way that it is understandable by all parties involved. This latter requirement is why we favor spreadsheet models, especially when they are well designed and well documented.

4. **Verify the model.** Here the analyst tries to determine whether the model developed in the previous step is an accurate representation of reality. A first step in determining how well the model fits reality is to check whether the model is valid for the current situation. This verification can take several forms. For example, the analyst could use the model with the company's current values of the input parameters. If the model's outputs are then in line with the outputs currently observed by the company, the analyst has at least shown that the model can duplicate the current situation.

   A second way to verify a model is to enter a number of input parameters (even if they are not the company's current inputs) and see whether the outputs from the model are reasonable. One common approach is to use extreme values of the inputs to see whether the outputs behave as they should. If they do, this is another piece of evidence that the model is reasonable.

   If certain inputs are entered in the model and the model's outputs are *not* as expected, there could be two causes. First, the model could simply be a poor representation of reality. In this case it is up to the analyst to refine the model so that it is more realistic. The second possible cause is that the model is fine but our intuition is not very good. In this case the fault lies with us, not the model.

   An interesting example of faulty intuition occurs with random sequences of 0s and 1s, such as might occur with successive flips of a fair coin. Most people expect that heads and tails will alternate and that there will be very few sequences of, say, four or more heads (or tails) in a row. However, a perfectly accurate simulation model of these flips will show, contrary to what most people expect, that fairly long runs of heads or tails are not at all uncommon. In fact, one or two long runs should be *expected* if there are enough flips.

   The fact that outcomes sometimes defy intuition is an important reason why models are important. These models prove that your ability to predict outcomes in complex environments is often not very good.

5. **Select one or more suitable decisions.** Many, but not all, models are decision models. For any specific decisions, the model indicates the amount of profit obtained, the amount of cost incurred, the level of risk, and so on. If the model is working correctly, as discussed in step 4, then it can be used to see which decisions produce the *best* outputs.

6. **Present the results to the organization.** In a classroom setting you are typically finished when you have developed a model that correctly solves a particular problem. In the business world a correct model, even a useful one, is not always enough. An analyst typically has to "sell" the model to management. Unfortunately, the people in management are sometimes not as well trained in quantitative methods as the analyst, so they are not always inclined to trust complex models.

   There are two ways to mitigate this problem. First, it is helpful to include relevant people throughout the company in the modeling process—from beginning to end—so that everyone has an understanding of the model and feels an ownership of it. Second, it helps to use a *spreadsheet* model whenever possible, especially if it is designed and documented properly. Almost everyone in today's business world is comfortable with spreadsheets, so spreadsheet models are more likely to be accepted.

7. **Implement the model and update it over time.** Again, there is a big difference between a classroom situation and a business situation. When you turn in a classroom assignment, you are typically finished with that assignment and can await the next one. In contrast, an analyst who develops a model for a company usually cannot pack up his bags and leave. If the model is accepted by management, the company will then need to implement it company-wide. This can be very time consuming and politically difficult, especially if the model's prescriptions represent a significant change from the past. At the very least, employees must be trained how to use the model on a day-to-day basis.

   In addition, the model will probably have to be updated over time, either because of changing conditions or because the company sees more potential uses for the model as it gains experience using it. This presents one of the greatest challenges for a model developer, namely, the ability to develop a model that *can* be modified as the need arises.

1.4 CONCLUSION

In this chapter we have tried to convince you that the skills in this book are important for *you* to know as you enter the business world. The methods we discuss are no longer the sole province of the "quant jocks." By having a PC on your desk that is loaded with powerful software, you incur a responsibility to use this software to analyze business problems. We have described the types of problems you will learn to analyze in this book, along with the software you will use to analyze them. We also discussed the modeling process, a theme that runs throughout this book. Now it is time for you to get started!

Cruise ship traveling has become big business. Many cruise lines are now competing for customers of all age groups and socioeconomic levels. They offer all types of cruises, from relatively inexpensive 3- to 4-day cruises in the Caribbean, to 12- to 15-day cruises in the Mediterranean, to several-month around-the-world cruises. Cruises have several features that attract customers, many of whom book six months or more in advance: (1) they offer a relaxing, everything-done-for-you way to travel; (2) they serve food that is plentiful, usually excellent, and included in the price of the cruise; (3) they stop at a number of interesting ports and offer travelers a way to see the world; and (4) they provide a wide variety of entertainment, particularly in the evening.

This last feature, the entertainment, presents a difficult problem for a ship's staff. A typical cruise might have well over 1000 passengers, including elderly singles and couples, middle-aged people with or without children, and young people, often honeymooners. These various types of passengers have varied tastes in terms of their after-dinner preferences in entertainment. Some want traditional dance music, some want comedians, some want rock music, some want movies, some want to go back to their cabins and read, and so on. Obviously, cruise entertainment directors want to provide the variety of entertainment their customers desire—within a reasonable budget—because satisfied customers tend to be repeat customers. The question is how to provide the right mix of entertainment.

On a cruise one of the authors and his wife took a few years ago, the entertainment was of high quality and there was plenty of variety. A seven-piece show band played dance music nightly in the largest lounge, two other small musical combos played nightly at two smaller lounges, a pianist played nightly at a piano bar in an intimate lounge, a group of professional singers and dancers played Broadway-type shows about twice weekly, and various professional singers and comedians played occasional single-night performances.[7] Although this entertainment was free to all of the passengers, much of it had embarrassingly low attendance. The nightly show band and musical combos, who were contracted to play nightly until midnight, often had less than a half dozen people in the audience— sometimes literally none. The professional singers, dancers, and comedians attracted larger audiences, but there were still plenty of empty seats. In spite of this, the cruise staff posted a weekly schedule, and they stuck to it regardless of attendance. In a short-term financial sense, it didn't make much difference. The performers got paid the same whether anyone was in the audience or not, the passengers had already paid (indirectly) for the entertainment as part of the cost of the cruise, and the only possible opportunity cost to the cruise line (in the short run) was the loss of liquor sales from the lack of passengers in the entertainment lounges. The morale of the entertainers was not great—entertainers love packed houses—but they usually argued, philosophically, that their hours were relatively short and they were still getting paid to see the world.

If you were in charge of entertainment on this ship, how would you describe the problem with entertainment: Is it a problem with deadbeat passengers, low-quality entertainment, or a mismatch between the entertainment offered and the entertainment desired? How might you try to solve the problem? What constraints might you have to work within? Would you keep a strict schedule such as the one followed by this cruise director, or would you play it more by ear? Would you gather data to help solve the problem? What data would you gather? How much would financial considerations dictate your decisions? Would they be long-term or short-term considerations? ∎

---

[7]There was also a moderately large onboard casino, but it tended to attract the same people every night, and it was always closed when the ship was in port.

PART 1

Exploring Data

Describing the Distribution of a Single Variable

Photo by Alex Wong/Newsmakers/Getty

RECENT PRESIDENTIAL ELECTIONS

Presidential elections in United States are scrutinized more than ever. It hardly seems that one is over before we start hearing plans and polls for the next. There is thorough coverage of the races leading up to the elections, but it is also interesting to analyze the results after the elections have been held. This is not difficult, given the many informative Web sites that appear immediately with election results. For example, a Web search for "2008 presidential election results" finds many sites with in-depth results, interactive maps, and more. In addition, the resulting data can often be imported into Excel rather easily for further analysis.

The file **Presidential Elections 2000–2008.xlsx** contains such down-loaded data for the 2000 (Bush versus Gore), 2004 (Bush versus Kerry), and 2008 (Obama versus McCain) elections. The results of the 2000 election are particularly interesting. As you probably remember, this was one of the closest elections of all time, with Bush defeating Gore by a very narrow margin in the electoral vote, 271 to 266, following a disputed recount in Florida. In fact, Gore actually beat Bush in the total count of U.S. votes, 50,999,897 to 50,456,002. However, because of the all-or-nothing nature of electoral votes in each state, Bush's narrow margin of victory in many closely contested states won him a lot of electoral votes. In contrast, Gore outdistanced Bush by a wide margin in several large states, winning him the same electoral votes he would have won even if these races had been much closer.

A closer analysis of the state-by-state results shows how this actually happened. In the Excel file, we created two new columns: **Bush Votes minus Gore Votes** and **Pct for Bush minus Pct for Gore**, with a value for each state (including the District of Columbia). We then created column charts of these two variables, as shown in Figures 2.1 and 2.2.

Figure 2.1   Chart of Vote Differences

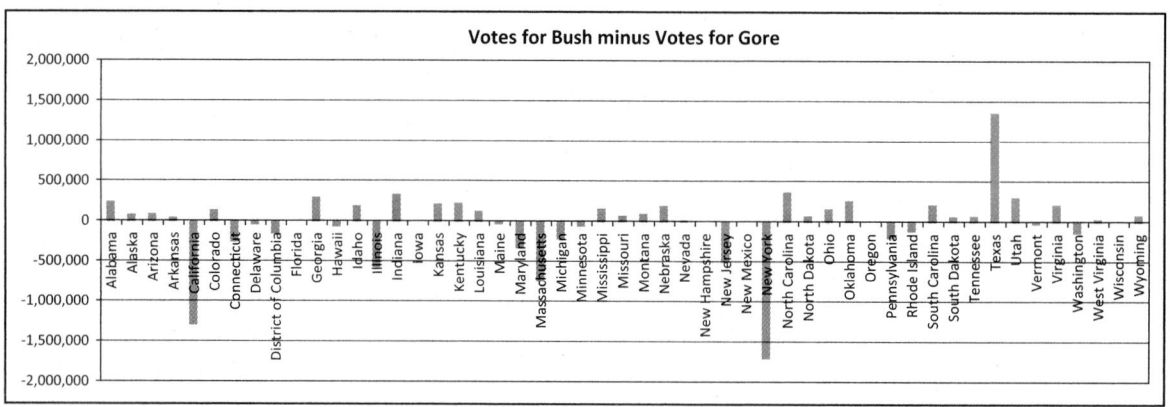

Figure 2.2   Chart of Percent Differences

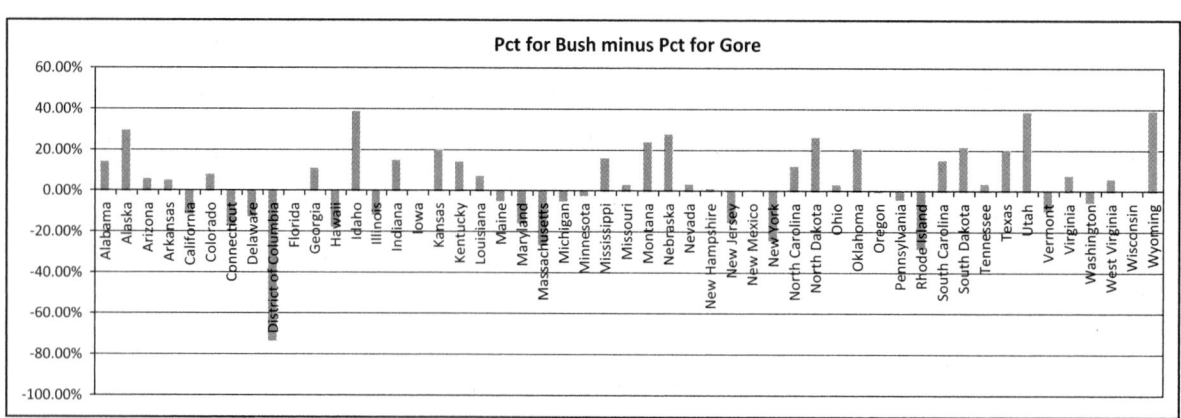

Each of these charts tells the same story, but in slightly different ways. From Figure 2.1, we see how Gore won big (large vote difference) in several large states, most notably California, Massachusetts, and New York. Bush's only comparable margin of victory was in his home state of Texas. However, Bush won a lot of close races in states with relatively few electoral votes—but enough to add up to an overall win. As Figure 2.2 indicates, many of these "close" races, such as Alaska and Idaho for Bush and District of Columbia for Gore, were not that close after all, at least not from a percentage standpoint. This is one case of many where multiple charts can be created to "tell a story." Perhaps an argument can be made that Figure 2.1 tells the story best, but Figure 2.2 is also interesting.

The bottom line is that the election could easily have gone the other way. With one more swing state, particularly Florida, Al Gore would have been president. On the other hand, Gore won some very close races as well, particularly in Iowa, Minnesota, New Mexico, and Oregon. If these had gone the other way, the popular vote would still have been very close, but Bush's victory in the electoral vote would have been more impressive. ■

2.1 INTRODUCTION

The goal of this chapter and the next is very simple: to make sense out of data by constructing appropriate summary measures, tables, and graphs. Our purpose here is to take a set of data that at first glance might have little meaning and to present the data in a form that makes sense to people. There are numerous ways to do this, limited only by your imagination, but there are several tools used most often: (1) a variety of graphs, including bar charts, pie charts, histograms, scatterplots, and time series graphs; (2) numerical summary measures such as counts, percentages, averages, and measures of variability; and (3) tables of summary measures such as totals, averages, and counts, grouped by categories. These terms might not all be familiar to you at this point, but you have undoubtedly seen examples of them in newspapers, magazine articles, and books.

The material in these two chapters is *simple, complex,* and *important.* It is simple because there are no difficult mathematical concepts. With the possible exception of variance, standard deviation, and correlation, all of the numerical measures, graphs, and tables are natural and easy to understand. It used to be a tedious chore to produce them, but with the advances in statistical software, including add-ins for spreadsheet packages such as Excel, they can now be produced quickly and easily.

It is customary to refer to the raw numbers as data and the output of a statistical analysis as information. You start with the data, and you hope to end with information that an organization can use for competitive advantage.

If it is so easy, why do you also claim that the material in this chapter is complex? The data sets available to companies in today's computerized world tend to be extremely large and filled with "unstructured" data. As you will see, even in data sets that are quite small in comparison to those that real companies face, it is a challenge to summarize the data so that the important *information* stands out clearly. It is easy to produce summary measures, graphs, and tables, but our goal is to produce the most *appropriate* ones.

The typical employees of today—not just the managers and technical specialists—have a wealth of easy-to-use tools at their disposal, and it is frequently up to them to summarize data in a way that is both meaningful and useful to their constituents: people within their company, their company's suppliers, and their company's customers. It takes some training and practice to do this effectively.

Because today's companies are inundated with data, and because virtually every employee in the company must summarize data to some extent, the material in this chapter and the next one is arguably the most important material in the book. There is sometimes a tendency to race through the "descriptive statistics" chapters to get to the more "interesting" material in later chapters as quickly as possible. We want to resist this tendency. The material covered in these two chapters deserves close examination, and this takes some time.

Data analysis in the real world is never done in a vacuum. It is done to solve a problem. Typically, there are four steps that are followed, whether the context is business, medical science, or any other field. The first step is to recognize a problem that needs to be solved. Perhaps a retail company is experiencing decreased sales in a particular region or for a particular product. Why is this happening? The second step is to gather data to help understand and then solve the problem. This might be done through a survey of customers, by assembling data from already-existing company systems, by finding relevant data on the Web, or other means. Once the data is gathered, the third step is to analyze the data using the tools you will learn in the book. The fourth step is to act on this analysis by changing policies, undertaking initiatives, publishing reports, and so on. Of course, the analysis can sometimes repeat steps. For example, once a given set of data is analyzed, it might be apparent that even more data needs to be collected.

Use your imagination to ask interesting questions about the many data sets available to you. We will supply you with the tools to answer these questions.

As we discuss the tools for analyzing data, we will often jump into the third step directly, providing you with a data set to analyze. Although this data set may not be directly connected to the goal of solving some company's problem, you should still strive to ask interesting questions of the data. (We have tried to include interesting data sets, often containing real data, that make this possible.) If the data set contains salaries, you might ask what drives these salaries. Does it depend on the industry a person is in? Does it depend on gender? Does it depend on educational background? Is the salary structure, whatever it is, changing over time? If the data set contains cost-of-living indexes, there are also a lot of interesting questions you can ask. How are the indexes changing over time? Does this behavior vary in different geographical regions? Does this behavior vary across different items such as housing, food, and automobiles? These early chapters provide you with many tools to answer such questions, but it is up to you to ask good questions—and then take advantage of the most appropriate tools to answer them.

The material in these chapters is organized as follows. In this chapter, we present a number of ways for analyzing one variable at a time. In the next chapter, we look at ways of discovering relationships between variables. In addition, there is a bonus Chapter 17 on importing data from external sources into Excel, a natural companion to Chapters 2 and 3. This bonus chapter is available on this textbook's Web site.

2.2 BASIC CONCEPTS

We begin with a short discussion of several important concepts: populations and samples, data sets, variables and observations, and types of data.

2.2.1 Populations and Samples

First, we distinguish between a population and a sample. A **population** includes all of the entities of interest, whether they be people, households, machines, or whatever. The following are three typical populations:

- All potential voters in a presidential election
- All subscribers to cable television
- All invoices submitted for Medicare reimbursement by nursing homes

In these situations and many others, it is virtually impossible to obtain information about all members of the population. For example, it is far too costly to ask all potential voters which presidential candidates they prefer. Therefore, we often try to gain insights into the characteristics of a population by examining a **sample**, or subset, of the population. In later chapters, we will examine populations and samples in some depth, but for now it is enough to know that we typically want samples to be *representative* of the population so that observed characteristics of the sample can be generalized to the population as a whole.

> A **population** includes all of the entities of interest in a study. A **sample** is a subset of the population, often randomly chosen and preferably representative of the population as a whole.

A famous example where a sample was *not* representative is the case of the *Literary Digest* fiasco of 1936. In the 1936 presidential election, subscribers to the *Literary Digest,* a highbrow literary magazine, were asked to mail in a ballot with their preference for president. Overwhelmingly, these ballots favored the Republican candidate, Alf Landon, over the Democratic candidate, Franklin D. Roosevelt. Despite this, FDR was a landslide winner. The discrepancy arose because the readers of the *Literary Digest* were not at all representative of most voters in 1936. Most voters in 1936 could barely make ends meet, let alone subscribe to a literary magazine. Thus, the typical lower-to-middle-income voter had almost no chance of being chosen in this sample.

Today, Gallup, Harris, and other pollsters make a conscious effort to ensure that their samples—which usually include about 1000 to 1500 people—are representative of the population. (It is truly remarkable, for example, that a sample of 1500 voters can almost surely predict a candidate's actual percentage of votes correctly to within 3%. We explain why this is possible in Chapters 7 and 8.) The important point is that a representative sample of reasonable size can provide a lot of important information about the population of interest.

We use the terms *population* and *sample* a few times in this chapter, which is why we have defined them here. However, the distinction is not really important until later chapters. Our intent in this chapter is to focus entirely on the data in a given data set, not to generalize beyond it. Therefore, the given data set could be a population or a sample from a population. For now, the distinction is largely irrelevant.

2.2.2 Data Sets, Variables, and Observations

We now discuss the types of data sets we will examine. Although the focus of this book is Excel, virtually all statistical software packages use the same concept of a data set: A **data set** is generally a rectangular array of data where the columns contain **variables**, such as height, gender, and income, and each row contains an **observation**. Each observation includes the attributes of a particular member of the population, whether it be a person, a company, a city, a machine, or other entity. This terminology is common, but other terms are often used. A variable (column) is often called a **field** or an **attribute**, and an observation (row) is often called a **case** or a **record**. Also, data sets are occasionally rearranged, so that the variables are in rows and the observations are in columns. However, the most common arrangement by far is to have variables in columns, with variable names in the top row, and observations in the remaining rows.

> A **data set** is usually a rectangular array of data, with variables in columns and observations in rows. A **variable** (or **field** or **attribute**) is a characteristic of members of a population, such as height, gender, or salary. An **observation** (or **case** or **record**) is a list of all variable values for a single member of a population.

EXAMPLE 2.1 Data from an Environmental Survey

The data set shown in Figure 2.3 represents 30 responses from a questionnaire concerning the president's environmental policies. (See the file **Questionnaire Data.xlsx**.) Identify the variables and observations.

Figure 2.3 Environmental Survey Data

	A	B	C	D	E	F	G
1	**Person**	**Age**	**Gender**	**State**	**Children**	**Salary**	**Opinion**
2	1	35	Male	Minnesota	1	$65,400	5
3	2	61	Female	Texas	2	$62,000	1
4	3	35	Male	Ohio	0	$63,200	3
5	4	37	Male	Florida	2	$52,000	5
6	5	32	Female	California	3	$81,400	1
7	6	33	Female	New York	3	$46,300	5
8	7	65	Female	Minnesota	2	$49,600	1
9	8	45	Male	New York	1	$45,900	5
10	9	40	Male	Texas	3	$47,700	4
11	10	32	Female	Texas	1	$59,900	4
12	11	57	Male	New York	1	$48,100	4
13	12	38	Female	Virginia	0	$58,100	3
14	13	37	Female	Illinois	2	$56,000	1
15	14	42	Female	Virginia	2	$53,400	1
16	15	38	Female	New York	2	$39,000	2
17	16	48	Male	Michigan	1	$61,500	2
18	17	40	Male	Ohio	0	$37,700	1
19	18	57	Female	Michigan	2	$36,700	4
20	19	44	Male	Florida	2	$45,200	3
21	20	40	Male	Michigan	0	$59,000	4
22	21	21	Female	Minnesota	2	$54,300	2
23	22	49	Male	New York	1	$62,100	4
24	23	34	Male	New York	0	$78,000	3
25	24	49	Male	Arizona	0	$43,200	5
26	25	40	Male	Arizona	1	$44,500	3
27	26	38	Male	Ohio	1	$43,300	1
28	27	27	Male	Illinois	3	$45,400	2
29	28	63	Male	Michigan	2	$53,900	1
30	29	52	Male	California	1	$44,100	3
31	30	48	Female	New York	2	$31,000	4

Objective To illustrate variables and observations in a typical data set.

Solution

This data set provides observations on 30 people who responded to the questionnaire. Each observation lists the person's age, gender, state of residence, number of children, annual salary, and opinion of the president's environmental policies. These six pieces of information represent the variables. It is customary to include a row (row 1 in this case) that lists variable names. These variable names should be concise but meaningful. Note that an index of the observation is often included in column A. If you start sorting on other variables, you can always sort on the index to get back to the original sort order.

As you will see shortly when we begin to use a very powerful statistical add-in for Excel called StatTools, the concept of a data set is crucial. Before you can perform any statistical analysis on a data set with StatTools, you must designate a rectangular range as a StatTools data set. This is easy, yet it must be done. As you will also see, StatTools allows several layouts for data sets, including one where the variables are in rows and the observations are in columns. However, the default layout, the one you will see over 99% of the time, is the one shown in Figure 2.3, where variables are in columns, observations are in rows, and the top row contains variable names. ∎

2.2.3 Types of Data

There are several ways to categorize data, as we explain in the context of Example 2.1. A basic distinction is between **numerical** and **categorical** data. The distinction here is whether you intend to do any arithmetic on the data. It makes sense to do arithmetic on numerical data, but not on categorical data. (Actually, there is a third data type, a **date** variable. As you may know, Excel stores dates as numbers, but for obvious reasons, dates are treated differently from typical numbers.)

Three variables that appear to be numerical but are usually treated as categorical are phone numbers, zip codes, and Social Security numbers. Do you see why? Can you think of others?

> A variable is **numerical** if meaningful arithmetic can be performed on it. Otherwise, the variable is **categorical**.

In the questionnaire data, Age, Children, and Salary are clearly numerical. For example, it makes perfect sense to sum or average any of these. In contrast, Gender and State are clearly categorical because they are expressed as text, not numbers.

The Opinion variable is less obvious. It is expressed numerically, on a 1-to-5 scale. However, these numbers are really only *codes* for the categories "strongly disagree," "disagree," "neutral," "agree," and "strongly agree." We never intend to perform arithmetic on these numbers; in fact, it is not really appropriate to do so. Therefore, it is most appropriate to treat the Opinion variable as categorical. Note, too, that there is a definite ordering of its categories, whereas there is no natural ordering of the categories for the Gender or State variables. When there is a natural ordering of categories, we classify the variable as **ordinal**. If there is no natural ordering, as with the Gender and State variables, we classify the variables as **nominal**. However, both ordinal and nominal variables are categorical.

> A categorical variable is **ordinal** if there is a natural ordering of its possible values. If there is no natural ordering, it is **nominal**.

Excel Tip *How do you remember, for example, that "1" stands for "strongly disagree" in the Opinion variable? You can enter a comment—a reminder to yourself and others—in any cell. To do so, right-click on a cell and select the Insert Comment item. A small red tag appears in any cell with a comment. Moving the cursor over that cell causes the comment to appear. You will see numerous comments in the files that accompany this book.*

Categorical variables can be coded numerically or left uncoded. In Figure 2.3, Gender has not been coded, whereas Opinion has been coded. This is largely a matter of taste—so long as you realize that coding a truly categorical variable does not make it numerical and open to arithmetic operations. An alternative way of displaying the data appears in Figure 2.4. Now Opinion has been replaced by text, and Gender has been coded as 1 for males and 0 for females. This 0–1 coding for a categorical variable is very common. Such a variable is called a **dummy variable**, and it often simplifies the analysis. You will see dummy variables often throughout the book.

> A **dummy variable** is a 0–1 coded variable for a specific category. It is coded as 1 for all observations in that category and 0 for all observations not in that category.

Figure 2.4   Environmental Data Using a Different Coding

	A	B	C	D	E	F	G	H	I	J	K	L
1	Person	Age	Gender	State	Children	Salary	Opinion					
2	1	Middle-aged	1	Minnesota	1	$65,400	Strongly agree					
3	2	Elderly	0	Texas	2	$62,000	Strongly disagree		Note the formulas I used in columns B, C,			
4	3	Middle-aged	1	Ohio	0	$63,200	Neutral		and G to get this recoded data. The formulas			
5	4	Middle-aged	1	Florida	2	$52,000	Strongly agree		in columns A and F are based on the lookup			
6	5	Young	0	California	3	$81,400	Strongly disagree					
7	6	Young	0	New York	3	$46,300	Strongly agree					
8	7	Elderly	0	Minnesota	2	$49,600	Strongly disagree					
9	8	Middle-aged	1	New York	1	$45,900	Strongly agree					
10	9	Middle-aged	1	Texas	3	$47,700	Agree					
11	10	Young	0	Texas	1	$59,900	Agree					
12	11	Middle-aged	1	New York	1	$48,100	Agree					
13	12	Middle-aged	0	Virginia	0	$58,100	Neutral					
14	13	Middle-aged	0	Illinois	2	$56,000	Strongly disagree		Age lookup table (range name AgeLookup)			
15	14	Middle-aged	0	Virginia	2	$53,400	Strongly disagree			0	Young	
16	15	Middle-aged	0	New York	2	$39,000	Disagree			35	Middle-aged	
17	16	Middle-aged	1	Michigan	1	$61,500	Disagree			60	Elderly	
18	17	Middle-aged	1	Ohio	0	$37,700	Strongly disagree					
19	18	Middle-aged	0	Michigan	2	$36,700	Agree		Opinion lookup table (range name OpinionLookup)			
20	19	Middle-aged	1	Florida	2	$45,200	Neutral			1	Strongly disagree	
21	20	Middle-aged	1	Michigan	0	$59,000	Agree			2	Disagree	
22	21	Young	0	Minnesota	2	$54,300	Disagree			3	Neutral	
23	22	Middle-aged	1	New York	1	$62,100	Agree			4	Agree	
24	23	Young	1	New York	0	$78,000	Neutral			5	Strongly agree	
25	24	Middle-aged	1	Arizona	0	$43,200	Strongly agree					
26	25	Middle-aged	1	Arizona	1	$44,500	Neutral					
27	26	Middle-aged	1	Ohio	1	$43,300	Strongly disagree					
28	27	Young	1	Illinois	3	$45,400	Disagree					
29	28	Elderly	1	Michigan	2	$53 900	Strongly disagree					
30	29	Middle-aged	1	California	1	$44,100	Neutral					
31	30	Middle-aged	0	New York	2	$31,000	Agree					

In addition, we have categorized the Age variable as "young" (34 years or younger), "middle-aged" (from 35 to 59 years), and "elderly" (60 years or older). This method of taking a numerical variable and making it categorical is called **binning** (putting the data into discrete bins), and it is also very common. (It is also called **discretizing**.) The purpose of the study dictates whether age should be treated numerically or should be binned; there is no absolute right or wrong way.

> A **binned** (or **discretized**) variable corresponds to a numerical variable that has been categorized into discrete categories. These categories are typically called **bins**.

Excel Tip *As Figure 2.4 indicates, we used lookup tables, along with the very important* **VLOOKUP** *function, to transform the data set from Figure 2.3 to Figure 2.4. Take a look at these functions in the questionnaire file. There is arguably no more important Excel function than VLOOKUP, so you should definitely learn how to use it.*

Numerical variables can be classified as **discrete** or **continuous**. The basic distinction is whether the data arise from counts or continuous measurements. The variable Children is clearly a count (that is, discrete), whereas the variable Salary is best treated as continuous. This distinction between discrete and continuous variables is sometimes important because it dictates the type of analysis that is most natural.

> A numerical variable is **discrete** if it results from a count, such as the number of children. A **continuous** variable is the result of an essentially continuous measurement, such as weight or height.

Finally, data sets can be categorized as cross-sectional or time series. The opinion data set in Example 2.1 is **cross-sectional**. A pollster evidently sampled a cross section of people at one particular point in time. In contrast, **time series** data occur when we track one or more variables through time. A typical example of a time series variable is the series of daily closing values of the Dow Jones Index. Very different types of analyses are appropriate for cross-sectional and time series data, as becomes apparent in this and later chapters.

> **Cross-sectional** data are data on a cross section of a population at a distinct point in time. **Time series** data are data collected over time.

A time series data set generally has the same layout—variables in columns and observations in rows—but now each variable is a time series. Also, one of the columns usually indicates the time period. A typical example appears in Figure 2.5. (See the file **Toy Revenues.xlsx**.)

Figure 2.5

Typical Time Series Data Set

	A	B	C	D	E	F
1	**Quarter**	**Revenue**				
2	Q1-2007	1026				
3	Q2-2007	1056		All monetary values are in		
4	Q3-2007	1182		thousands of dollars.		
5	Q4-2007	2861				
6	Q1-2008	1172				
7	Q2-2008	1249				
8	Q3-2008	1346				
9	Q4-2008	3402				
10	Q1-2009	1286				
11	Q2-2009	1317				
12	Q3-2009	1449				
13	Q4-2009	3893				
14	Q1-2010	1462				
15	Q2-2010	1452				
16	Q3-2010	1631				
17	Q4-2010	4200				

It has quarterly observations on revenues from toy sales over a four-year period in column B, with the time periods listed chronologically in column A. Of course, there could be other related time series variables to the right of column B.

2.3 DESCRIPTIVE MEASURES FOR CATEGORICAL VARIABLES

In this section we indicate methods for describing a categorical variable. Because it is not appropriate to perform arithmetic on the actual values of the variable, there are only a few possibilities for describing the variable, and these are all based on *counting*. First, you can count the *number* of categories. Many categorical variables such as Gender have only two categories. Others such as Region can have more than two categories. As you count the categories, you can also give the categories *names*, such as Male and Female. Keep in mind that categorical variables, such as Opinion in Example 2.1, can be coded numerically. In these cases, it is still a good idea to supply text descriptions of these categories, such as "strongly agree," and it is often useful to substitute these meaningful descriptions for the numerical codes, as in Figure 2.4. This is especially useful for statistical reports.

The only meaningful way to summarize categorical is with counts of observations in its categories.

Once you know the number of categories and their names, the only thing left to do is count the number of observations in each category.[1] The resulting counts can be reported as "raw counts" or they can be transformed into percentages. For example, if there are 1000 observations, you can report that there are 560 males and 440 females, or you can report that 56% of the observations are males and 44% are females. In fact, it is often useful to report the counts in both of these ways. Finally, once you have the counts, you can display them graphically, usually in a column chart or a pie chart. The following example illustrates how to do this in Excel.

EXAMPLE | **2.2 SUPERMARKET SALES**

The file **Supermarket Transactions.xlsx** contains over 14,000 transactions made by supermarket customers over a period of approximately two years. (The data are not real, but real supermarket chains have huge data sets just like this one.) A small sample of the data appears in Figure 2.6. Column B contains the date of the purchase, column C is a unique identifier for each customer, columns D–H contain information about the customer, columns I–K contain the location of the store, columns L–N contain information about the

---

Figure 2.6 Supermarket Data Set

	A	B	C	D	E	F	G	H	I	J	K	L	M	N	O	P
1	Transaction	Purchase Date	Customer ID	Gender	Marital Status	Home Owner	Children	Annual Income	City	State or Province	Country	Product Family	Product Department	Product Category	Units Sold	Revenue
2	1	12/18/2007	7223	F	S	Y		2	$30K - $50K	Los Angeles	CA	USA	Food	Snack Foods	Snack Foods	5	$27.38
3	2	12/20/2007	7841	M	M	Y		5	$70K - $90K	Los Angeles	CA	USA	Food	Produce	Vegetables	5	$14.90
4	3	12/21/2007	8374	F	M	N		2	$50K - $70K	Bremerton	WA	USA	Food	Snack Foods	Snack Foods	3	$5.52
5	4	12/21/2007	9619	M	M	Y		3	$30K - $50K	Portland	OR	USA	Food	Snacks	Candy	4	$4.44
6	5	12/22/2007	1900	F	S	Y		3	$130K - $150K	Beverly Hills	CA	USA	Drink	Beverages	Carbonated Bev	4	$14.00
7	6	12/22/2007	6696	F	M	Y		3	$10K - $30K	Beverly Hills	CA	USA	Food	Deli	Side Dishes	3	$4.37
8	7	12/23/2007	9673	M	S	Y		2	$30K - $50K	Salem	OR	USA	Food	Frozen Foods	Breakfast Foods	4	$13.78
9	8	12/25/2007	354	F	M	Y		2	$150K +	Yakima	WA	USA	Food	Canned Foods	Canned Soup	6	$7.34
10	9	12/25/2007	1293	M	M	Y		3	$10K - $30K	Bellingham	WA	USA	Non-Consuma	Household	Cleaning Supplie	1	$2.41
11	10	12/25/2007	7938	M	S	N		1	$50K - $70K	San Diego	CA	USA	Non-Consuma	Health and Hyg	Pain Relievers	2	$8.96

---

[1]Researchers have devised some very sophisticated tools for dealing with categorical variables. However, we plan to keep it simple by focusing solely on counts of categories.

product purchased, and the last two columns indicate the number of items purchased and the amount paid. Which of the variables are categorical, and how can these categorical variables be summarized?

Objective   To summarize categorical variables in a large data set.

Solution

Most of the variables in this data set are categorical. Only Children, Units Sold, and Revenue are numerical. Purchase Date is a date variable, and Customer ID is used only to identify customers. All of the others are categorical. This includes Annual Income, which has been binned into categories. Three of these categorical variables—Gender, Marital Status, and Homeowner—have only two categories. The others have more than two categories.

The first question is how you can discover all of the categories for a variable such as Product Department. Without good tools, this is not a trivial problem. One option is to sort on this variable and then manually go through the list, looking for the different categories. Fortunately, there are much easier ways, using Excel's built-in table and pivot table tools. We will postpone these for later and deal for now only with the "easy" categorical variables.

Figure 2.7 shows summaries of Gender, Marital Status, Homeowner, and Annual Income, along with several corresponding charts for Gender. Each of the **counts** in column S can be obtained with Excel's COUNTIF function. For example, the formula in cell S3 is **=COUNTIF($D$2:$D$14060,R3)**. This function takes two arguments, the data range and a criterion, so it is perfect for counting observations in a category. Then, to get the percentages in column T, each count is divided by the total number of observations. (As a check, it is a good idea to sum these percentages. They should sum to 100% for each variable, as they do here.)

Figure 2.7   Summaries of Categorical Variables

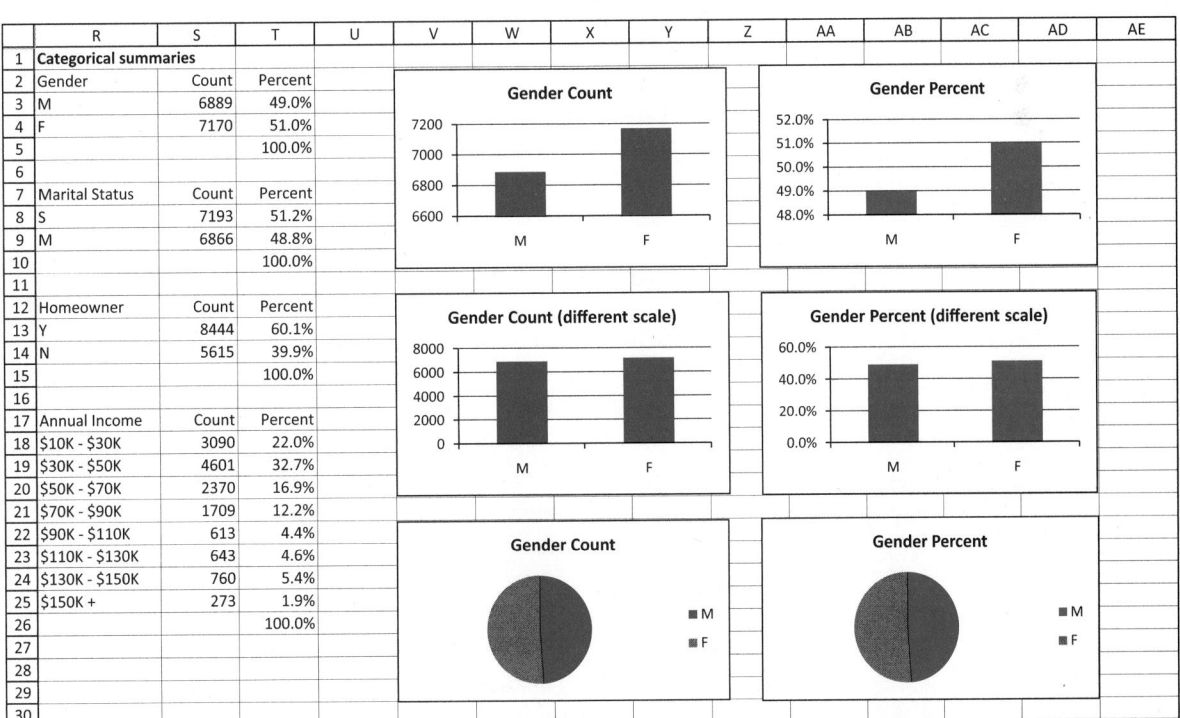

As the charts indicate, you get essentially the same chart regardless of whether you graph the counts or the percentages. However, be careful with misleading scales. If you highlight the range R2:S4 and then insert a column chart, you get the top left chart by default. Its vertical scale starts well above 6000, which makes it appear that there are *many* more females than males. By resetting the vertical scale to start at 0, as in the two middle charts, you see more accurately that there are almost as many males as females. Finally, which is preferable, a column chart or a pie chart? We tend to prefer column charts, but this is entirely a matter of taste. (We also tend to prefer column charts to horizontal bar charts, but this is again a matter of taste.) Our only recommendation in general is to keep charts *simple* so that the information they contain emerges as clearly as possible.

Excel Tip *If you are new to Excel charts, particularly in Excel 2007, you should try creating the charts in Figure 2.7 on your own. One way is to put your cursor in a blank cell, select a desired chart type from the Insert ribbon, and then designate the data to be included in the chart. However, it is usually more efficient to select the data to be charted and then insert the chart. For example, try highlighting the range R2:S4 and then inserting a column chart. Except for a little cleanup (deleting the legend, changing the chart title, and possibly changing the vertical scale), you get almost exactly what you want with little work.*

If this example of summarizing categorical variables appears to be overly tedious, be patient. As we indicated earlier, Excel has some powerful tools, especially pivot tables, that make this summarization much easier. We will discuss pivot tables in depth in the next chapter. For now, just remember that the only meaningful way to summarize a categorical variable is to count observations in each of its categories.

Before leaving this section, we mention one other efficient way to find the counts and percentages for a categorical variable. This method uses dummy (0–1) variables. To see how it works, focus on any category of some categorical variable, such as M for Gender. Recode the variable so that each M is replaced by a 1 and all other values are replaced by 0. (This can be done in Excel in a new column, using a simple IF formula. See column E of Figure 2.8.) Now you can find the count of males by *summing* the 0s and 1s, and you can

Figure 2.8

Summarizing a Category with a Dummy Variable

	A	B	C	D	E
1	Transaction	Purchase Date	Customer ID	Gender	Gender Dummy for M
2	1	12/18/2007	7223	F	0
3	2	12/20/2007	7841	M	1
4	3	12/21/2007	8374	F	0
5	4	12/21/2007	9619	M	1
6	5	12/22/2007	1900	F	0
7	6	12/22/2007	6696	F	0
8	7	12/23/2007	9673	M	1
9	8	12/25/2007	354	F	0
10	9	12/25/2007	1293	M	1
11	10	12/25/2007	7938	M	1
14055	14054	12/29/2009	2032	F	0
14056	14055	12/29/2009	9102	F	0
14057	14056	12/29/2009	4822	F	0
14058	14057	12/31/2009	250	M	1
14059	14058	12/31/2009	6153	F	0
14060	14059	12/31/2009	3656	M	1
14061				Count	6889
14062				Percent	49.0%

find the percentage of males by *averaging* the 0s and 1s. That is, the formulas in cells E14061 and E14062 use the SUM and AVERAGE functions on the data in column E. You should convince yourself why this works (for example, what arithmetic are you really doing when you average 0s and 1s?), and you should remember this method. It is one reason why dummy variables are used so frequently in spreadsheet data analysis. ■

PROBLEMS

Note: Student solutions for problems whose numbers appear within a color box are available for purchase at www.cengagebrain.com.

Level A

1. The file **P02_01.xlsx** indicates the gender and nationality of the MBA incoming class in two successive years at the Kelley School of Business at Indiana University.
  a. For each year, create tables of counts of gender and of nationality. Then create column charts of these counts. Do they indicate any noticeable change in the composition of the two classes?
  b. Repeat part **a** for nationality, but recode this variable so that all nationalities that have counts of 1 or 2 are classified as Other.

2. The file **P02_02.xlsx** contains information on over 200 movies that came out during 2006 and 2007.
  a. Create two column charts of counts, one of the different genres and one of the different distributors.
  b. Recode the Genre column so that all genres with count 10 or less are lumped into a category called Other. Then create a column chart of counts for this recoded variable. Repeat similarly for the Distributor variable.

3. The file **P02_03.xlsx** contains data from a survey of 399 people regarding a government environmental policy.
  a. Which of the variables in this data set are categorical? Which of these are nominal; which are ordinal?
  b. For each categorical variable, create a column chart of counts.
  c. Recode the data into a new data set, making four transformations: (1) change Gender to list "Male"

or "Female"; (2) change Children to list "No children" or "At least one child"; (3) change Salary to be categorical with categories "Less than $40K," "Between $40K and $70K," "Between $70K and $100K," and "Greater than $100K" (where you can treat the breakpoints however you like); and (4) change Opinion to be a numerical code from 1 to 5 for Strongly Disagree to Strongly Agree. Then create a column chart of counts for the new Salary variable.

4. The file **P02_04.xlsx** contains salary data on all Major League Baseball players for each year from 2002 to 2009. (The 2009 sheet is used for examples later in this chapter.) For each year, create a table of counts of the various positions, expressed as percentages of all players for the year. Then create a column chart of these percentages for each year. Do they remain fairly constant from year to year?

Level B

5. The file **DJIA Monthly Close.xlsx** contains monthly values of the Dow Jones Industrial Average from 1950 through 2009. It also contains the percentage changes from month to month. (This file will be used for an example later in this chapter.) Create a new column for recoding the percentage changes into six categories: Large negative ($<-3\%$), Medium negative ($<-1\%$, $\geqslant-3\%$), Small negative ($<0\%$, $\geqslant-1\%$), Small positive ($<1\%$, $\geqslant0\%$), Medium positive ($<3\%$, $\geqslant1\%$), and Large positive ($\geqslant3\%$). Then create a column chart of the counts of this categorical variable. Comment on its shape.

2.4 DESCRIPTIVE MEASURES FOR NUMERICAL VARIABLES

There are many ways to summarize numerical variables, both with numerical summary measures and with charts, and we will discuss the most common ways in this section. But before we get into details, it is important to understand the basic goal of this section. We begin with a numerical variable such as Salary, where there is one observation for each person. Our basic goal is to learn how these salaries are distributed across the different people. To do this, we can ask a number of questions, including the following. (1) What are the most "typical" salaries? (2) How spread out are the salaries? (3) What are the "extreme" salaries on either end? (4) Is a chart of the salaries symmetric about some middle value, or is it skewed in some direction? (5) Does the chart of salaries have any other peculiar features besides possible skewness? In the next chapter, we will explore methods for checking whether a variable such as Salary is related to *other* variables, but for now we simply want to explore the distribution of values in the Salary column.

As always in this book, our main tool is Excel. Excel has a number of built-in tools for summarizing numerical variables, and we will discuss these. However, even better tools are available in Excel add-ins, and in this section we will introduce a very powerful add-in from Palisade Corporation called **StatTools**. There are two important advantages of StatTools over other statistical software. First, it works inside Excel, which is an obvious advantage for the many users who prefer to work in Excel. Second, it is extremely easy to learn, with virtually no learning curve. However, keep in mind that StatTools is not part of Microsoft Office. You get the academic version of StatTools free with this book, but if you eventually want to use StatTools in your job, you will have to persuade your company to purchase it. (Many of our graduates have done exactly that.)

2.4.1 Numerical Summary Measures

Throughout this section, we will focus on a Salary variable. Specifically, we examine the 2009 salaries for Major League Baseball players, as described in the following example.

CHANGES IN EXCEL 2010

Microsoft modified many of the statistical functions and added a few new ones in Excel 2010. Although Microsoft advertises the superiority of the new functions, all of the old functions can still be used. When a modified or new function is relevant, we will indicate this in the text.

EXAMPLE 2.3 BASEBALL SALARIES

The file **Baseball Salaries 2009.xlsx** contains data on 818 Major League Baseball (MLB) players as of May 2009. There are four variables, as shown in Figure 2.9: the player's name, team, the position, and salary. How can these 818 salaries be summarized?

Figure 2.9
Baseball Salaries

	A	B	C	D
1	Player	Team	Position	Salary
2	Aardsma, Dave	Seattle Mariners	Pitcher	$419,000
3	Abreu, Bobby	Los Angeles Angels	Outfielder	$5,000,000
4	Adams, Mike	San Diego Padres	Pitcher	$414,800
5	Adenhart, Nick	Los Angeles Angels	Pitcher	$400,000
6	Affeldt, Jeremy	San Francisco Giants	Pitcher	$3,500,000
7	Albaladejo, Jon	New York Yankees	Pitcher	$403,075
8	Albers, Matt	Baltimore Orioles	Pitcher	$410,000
9	Amezaga, Alfredo	Florida Marlins	Shortstop	$1,300,000
10	Anderson, Brett	Oakland Athletics	Pitcher	$400,000
11	Anderson, Brian Nikoli	Chicago White Sox	Outfielder	$440,000
12	Anderson, Garret	Atlanta Braves	Outfielder	$2,500,000
13	Anderson, Josh	Detroit Tigers	Outfielder	$400,000
14	Anderson, Marlon	New York Mets	Second Baseman	$1,150,000

Objective   To learn how salaries are distributed across all 2009 MLB players.

Solution

The various numerical summary measures can be categorized into several groups: measures of central tendency; minimum, maximum, percentiles, and quartiles; measures of variability; and measures of shape. We will explain each of these in this extended example. ■

Measures of Central Tendency

There are three common measures of central tendency, all of which try to answer the basic question of which value is most "typical." These are the mean, the median, and the mode.

The **mean** is the average of all values of a variable. If the data set represents a sample from some larger population, we call this measure the **sample mean** and denote it by $\overline{X}$ (pronounced "X-bar"). If the data set represents the entire population, we call it the **population mean** and denote it by μ (the Greek letter *mu*). This distinction is not important in this chapter, but it will become relevant in later chapters when we discuss statistical inference. In either case, the formula for the mean is given by Equation (2.1).

Formula for the Mean

$$\text{Mean} = \frac{\sum_{i=1}^{n} X_i}{n} \qquad\qquad \textbf{(2.1)}$$

Here, n is the number of observations and X_i is the value of observation i. Equation (2.1) says to add all the observations and divide by n, the number of observations. The Σ (Greek capital *sigma*) symbol means to sum from $i = 1$ to $i = n$, that is, to sum over all observations.

For Excel data sets, you can calculate the mean with the **AVERAGE** function. This is shown for the baseball data (along with a lot of other summary measures we will discuss shortly) in Figure 2.10. Specifically, the average salary for all players is a whopping $3,260,059. Is this a typical salary? Keep reading.

Figure 2.10

Summary Measures of Baseball Salaries Using Excel Functions

	A	B	C	D	E	F
1	Measures of central tendency				Measures of variability	
2	Mean	$3,260,059			Range	$32,600,000
3	Median	$1,151,000			Interquartile range	$5,088,800
4	Mode	$400,000	70		Variance	19,045,050,733,784
5					Standard deviation	$4,364,064
6	Min, max, percentiles, quartiles				Mean absolute deviation	$3,205,753
7	Min	$400,000				
8	Max	$33,000,000			Measures of shape	
9	P01	$400,000	0.01		Skewness	2.0996
10	P05	$400,000	0.05		Kurtosis	5.1266
11	P10	$401,000	0.10			
12	P20	$411,200	0.20		Percentages of values less than given values	
13	P50	$1,151,000	0.50		Value	Percentage less than
14	P80	$5,500,000	0.80		$1,000,000	46.70%
15	P90	$10,000,000	0.90		$1,500,000	53.67%
16	P95	$13,000,000	0.95		$2,000,000	58.56%
17	P99	$18,707,500	0.99		$2,500,000	63.45%
18	Q1	$419,550	1		$3,000,000	67.85%
19	Q2	$1,151,000	2			
20	Q3	$4,237,500	3			

The **median** is the middle observation when the data are arranged from smallest to largest. If the number of observations is odd, the median is literally the middle observation. For example, if there are nine observations, the median is the fifth smallest (or fifth largest). If the number of observations is even, the median is usually defined as the average of the two middle observations (although there are some slight variations of this definition). For example, if there are 10 observations, the median is usually defined to be the average of the fifth and sixth smallest values.

In any case, the median can be calculated in Excel with the **MEDIAN** function. Figure 2.10 shows that the median salary is $1,151,000. In words, half of the players make less than this, and half make more. Why is the median in this example so much smaller than the mean, and which is more appropriate? These are important questions, and they are relevant for many real-world data sets. As you might expect, the vast majority of baseball players have relatively modest salaries that are dwarfed by the astronomical salaries of a few stars. Because it is an average, the mean is strongly influenced by these really large values, so it is quite high. In contrast, the median is completely unaffected by the magnitude of the really large salaries, so it is much smaller. (For example, the median would not change by a single cent if Alex Rodriguez made $33 *trillion* instead of his measly $33 million, but the mean would increase to more than $34 million.)

In many situations like this, where the data are skewed to the right (a few extremely large salaries not balanced by any extremely small salaries), most people would argue that the median is a more representative measure of central tendency than the mean. However, both are often quoted. And for variables that are *not* skewed in one direction or the other, the mean and median are often quite close to one another.

The **mode** is the value that appears most often, and it can be calculated in Excel with the **MODE** function. In most cases where a variable is essentially continuous, the mode is not very interesting because it is often the result of a few lucky ties. However, the mode for the salary data in Figure 2.10 is not a result of luck. Its value, $400,000, is evidently the minimum possible salary set by the league. As shown in cell C4 (with a COUNTIF formula), this value occurred 70 times. In other words, close to 10% of the players earn the minimum possible salary. This is a good example of learning something you probably didn't know simply by exploring the data.

For highly skewed data, the median is typically a better measure of central tendency. The median is unaffected by the extreme values, whereas the mean is very sensitive to extreme values.

CHANGES IN EXCEL 2010

There are two new versions of the MODE function in Excel 2010: MODE.MULT and MODE.SNGL. The latter is the same as the current MODE function. The MULT version returns multiple modes if there are multiple modes.

Minimum, Maximum, Percentiles, and Quartiles

As you look at the values of some variable, it is natural to ask how many values are lower than a particular value. For example, you might ask how many salaries are less than $1 million. In this subsection, you will come back to this question, but we first answer a slightly different question: Given a certain percentage such as 25%, what is the salary value such that this percentage of salaries is below it? This leads to **percentiles** and **quartiles**. Specifically, for any percentage p, the pth percentile is the value such that a percentage p of all values are less than it. Similarly, the first, second, and third quartiles are the percentiles corresponding to $p = 25\%$, $p = 50\%$, and $p = 75\%$. These three values divide the data into four groups, each with (approximately) a quarter of all observations.

(Note that the second quartile is equal to the median by definition.) To complete this group of descriptive measures, we add the **minimum** and **maximum** values, with the obvious meanings.

You are probably aware of percentiles from standardized tests. For example, if you learn that your score in the verbal SAT test was at the 93rd percentile, this means that you scored better than 93% of those taking the test.

The minimum and maximum can be calculated with Excel's **MIN** and **MAX** functions. For the percentiles and quartiles, you can use Excel's **PERCENTILE** and **QUARTILE** functions. The PERCENTILE function takes two arguments: the data range and a value of p between 0 and 1. (It has to be between 0 and 1. For example, if you want the 95th percentile, you must enter the second argument as 0.95, not as 95.) The QUARTILE function also takes two arguments: the data range and 1, 2, or 3, depending on which quartile you want. Figure 2.10 shows the minimum, maximum, the three quartiles, and several commonly requested percentiles for the baseball data. Note that at least 25% of the players make within $20,000 of the league minimum, and more than a quarter of all players make more than $4 million. In fact, more than 1% of the players make well over $18 million, with Alex Rodriguez topping the list at $33 million. And they say it's just a game!

Excel Tip *Note the values in column C of Figure 2.10 for percentiles and quartiles. These allow you to enter one formula for the percentiles and one for quartiles that can then be copied down. Specifically, the formulas in cells B9 and B18 are*

=PERCENTILE(Data!$D$2:$D$819,C9)

and

=QUARTILE(Data!$D$2:$D$819,C18).

(Here, Data! is a reference to the worksheet that contains the data.) Always look for ways to make your Excel formulas copyable. It saves time and it limits errors. And if you don't want the values in column C to be visible, just color them white.

CHANGES IN EXCEL 2010

Excel's PERCENTILE and QUARTILE functions can give strange results when there are only a few observations. For this reason, Microsoft added new functions in Excel 2010: PERCENTILE.EXC, PERCENTILE.INC, QUARTILE.EXC, and QUARTILE.INC, where EXC and INC stand for exclusive and inclusive. The INC functions work just like the old PERCENTILE and QUARTILE functions. The EXC versions are recommended especially for a small number of observations.

Before continuing, let's revisit the first question asked in this subsection. If you are given a certain salary figure such as $1 million, how can you find the percentage of all salaries less than this? This is essentially the opposite of a percentile question. In a percentile question, you are given a percentage and you want to find a value. Now you are given a value and you want to find a percentage. You can find this percentage in Excel by dividing a COUNTIF by the total number of observations. A few such values are shown in the bottom right of Figure 2.10. The typical formula in cell F14, which is then copied down, is

=COUNTIF(Data!$D$2:$D$819,"<"&E14)/COUNT(Data!$D$2:$D$819).

The following Excel tip explains this formula in more detail.

Excel Tip *The condition in this COUNTIF formula is a bit tricky. You literally want it to be "<1000000", but you want the formula to refer to the values in column E to enable copying. Therefore, you can **concatenate** (or string together) the literal part, "<", and the variable part, the reference to cell E14. The ampersand symbol (&) in the middle is the symbol used to concatenate in Excel. This use of concatenation to join literal and variable parts is especially useful in functions like COUNTIF that require a condition, so don't be afraid to use it.*

Measures of Variability

If you learn that the mean (or median) salary in some company is $100,000, this tells you something about the "typical" salary, but it tells you nothing about how spread out the salaries are, that is, their variability. The percentiles and quartiles discussed in the previous section certainly tell you something about variability. In fact, by knowing a lot of percentiles, you know almost exactly how the data are spread out. (Just look at the list of percentiles in Figure 2.10 and add a few more if you want to fill in the gaps.) In this sub-section, we list a few measures that summarize variability even more. These include the range, the interquartile range, the variance and standard deviation, and the mean absolute deviation. None of these says as much about variability as a complete list of percentiles, but they are very useful.

The **range** is a fairly crude measure of variability. It is defined as the maximum value minus the minimum value. For the baseball salaries, this range is $32.6 million. It certainly tells us how spread out the salaries are, but it is too sensitive to the extremes. For example, if Alex Rodriguez's salary increased to $43 million, the range would increase by $10 million—just because of one player. A less sensitive measure is the **interquartile range** (abbreviated **IQR**). It is defined as the third quartile minus the first quartile, so it is really the range of the middle 50% of the data. For the baseball data, the IQR is $3,817,950. If you excluded the 25% of players with the lowest salaries and the 25% with the highest salaries, this IQR would be the range of the remaining salaries.

The range or a modified range such as the IQR probably seems like a natural measure of variability, but there is another measure that is quoted much more frequently: the standard deviation. Actually, there are two totally related measures, variance and standard deviation, and we will begin with a definition of variance. The **variance** is essentially the average of the squared deviations from the mean, where if X_i is a typical observation, its squared deviation from the mean is $(X_i - \overline{X})^2$. As in our discussion of the mean, there is a **sample variance**, denoted by s^2, and a **population variance**, denoted by σ^2 (where σ is the Greek letter *sigma*). They are defined by the following formulas:

Formula for Sample Variance

$$s^2 = \frac{\sum_{i=1}^{n}(X_i - \text{mean})^2}{n - 1}$$

(2.2)

Formula for Population Variance

$$\sigma^2 = \frac{\sum_{i=1}^{n}(X_i - \text{mean})^2}{n}$$

(2.3)

Technical note *It is traditional to use the capital letter N for the population size and n for the sample size, but we won't worry about this distinction in this chapter. Furthermore, there is a technical reason why the sample variance uses n–1 in the denominator, not n, and this will be explained in a later chapter. However, the difference is negligible when n is large. Excel implements both of these formulas. You can use the **VAR** function to obtain the sample variance (denominator n–1), and you can use the **VARP** function to obtain the population variance (denominator n).*

To understand why the variance is indeed a measure of variability, look at either formula. If all of the observations are close to the mean, then their squared deviations from the mean will be relatively small, and the variance will be relatively small. On the other hand, if at least a few of the observations are far from the mean, then their squared deviations from the mean will be large, and this will cause the variance to be large. Note that because deviations from the mean are *squared*, an observation a certain amount *below* the mean contributes the same amount to variance as an observation that same amount *above* the mean.

There is a fundamental problem with variance as a measure of variability: It is hard to interpret the variance numerically because it is in *squared* units. For example, if the observations are measured in dollars, then variance is in squared dollars. To obtain a more natural measure, we take the square root of variance. The result is called **standard deviation**. Again, there are two versions of standard deviation. The **sample standard deviation**, denoted by *s*, is the square root of the quantity in Equation (2.2). The **population standard deviation**, denoted by σ, is the square root of the quantity in Equation (2.3).

To calculate either standard deviation in Excel, you can first find the variance with the VAR or VARP function and then take its square root, or you can find it directly with the **STDEV** (sample) or **STDEVP** (population) function.

CHANGES IN EXCEL 2010

The functions for variance and standard deviation have been renamed in Excel 2010 to VAR.S, VAR.P, STDEV.S, and STDEV.P. However, they work exactly like the old versions.

The data in Figure 2.11 should help clarify these concepts. It is in the file **Variability.xlsx**. (It will help if you open this file and look at its formulas as you read this.) The variable Diameter1 on the left has relatively low variability; its 10 values hover closely around its mean of approximately 100 (found in cell A16 with the AVERAGE function). To show how variance is calculated, we explicitly calculated the 10 squared deviations from the mean in column B. Then either variance, sample or population, can be calculated (in cells A19 and A22) as the sum of squared deviations divided by 9 or 10. Alternatively, they can be calculated more directly (in cells B19 and B22) with Excel's VAR and VARP functions. Then either standard deviation, sample or population, can be calculated as the square root of the corresponding variance or with Excel's STDEV or STDEVP functions.

The calculations are exactly the same for Diameter2 on the right. It also has mean approximately equal to 100, but its observations vary much more around 100 than the observations for Diameter1. As expected, this increased variability is obvious in a comparison of the variances and standard deviations.

This example also indicates why variability, along with measures of it, is important. Imagine that you are about to buy 10 parts from one of two suppliers, and you want each part's diameter to be close to 100 centimeters. Furthermore, suppose that Diameter1 in

Figure 2.11 Calculating Variance and Standard Deviation

	A	B	C	D	E	F
1	Low variability supplier				High variability supplier	
2						
3	Diameter1	Sq dev from mean			Diameter2	Sq dev from mean
4	102.61	6.610041			103.21	9.834496
5	103.25	10.310521			93.66	41.139396
6	96.34	13.682601			120.87	432.473616
7	96.27	14.205361			110.26	103.754596
8	103.77	13.920361			117.31	297.079696
9	97.45	6.702921			110.23	103.144336
10	98.22	3.308761			70.54	872.257156
11	102.76	7.403841			39.53	3665.575936
12	101.56	2.313441			133.22	1098.657316
13	98.16	3.530641			101.91	3.370896
14						
15	Mean				Mean	
16	100.039				100.074	
17						
18	Sample variance				Sample variance	
19	9.1098	9.1098			736.3653	736.3653
20						
21	Population variance				Population variance	
22	8.1988	8.1988			662.7287	662.7287
23						
24	Sample standard deviation				Sample standard deviation	
25	3.0182	3.0182			27.1361	27.1361
26						
27	Population standard deviation				Population standard deviation	
28	2.8634	2.8634			25.7435	25.7435

Variability is usually the enemy. Being close to a target value on average is not good enough if there is a lot of variability around this target.

the example represents 10 randomly selected parts from supplier 1, whereas Diameter2 represents 10 randomly selected parts from Supplier 2. You can see that both suppliers are very close to the target of 100 *on average*, but the increased variability for Supplier 2 makes this supplier much less attractive. There is a famous saying in operations management: Variability is the enemy. This example illustrates exactly what this saying means.

Empirical Rules for Interpreting Standard Deviation

Now you know how to *calculate* the standard deviation, but there is a more important question: How do you interpret its value? Fortunately, the standard deviation often has a very natural interpretation, which is why it is quoted so frequently. This interpretation can be stated as three **empirical rules**. Namely, if the values of this variable are approximately *normally* distributed (symmetric and bell-shaped), then the following rules hold:

(1) Approximately 68% of the observations are within one standard deviation of the mean, that is, within the interval $\overline{X} \pm s$.

(2) Approximately 95% of the observations are within two standard deviations of the mean, that is, within the interval $\overline{X} \pm 2s$.

(3) Approximately 99.7% of the observations—almost all of them—are within three standard deviations of the mean, that is, within the interval $\overline{X} \pm 3s$.

These empirical rules give a concrete meaning to standard deviation for symmetric, bell-shaped distributions. However, they tend to be much less accurate for skewed distributions.

Fortunately, many variables in real-world data are indeed approximately normally distributed, so these empirical rules correctly apply. (We will study the normal distribution in much more depth in Chapter 5.)

FUNDAMENTAL INSIGHT

Usefulness of Standard Deviation

Variability is clearly an important property of any numerical variable, and there are several measures for quantifying the amount of variability. However, standard deviation is by far the most popular such measure. It is measured in the same units as the variable, it has a long tradition, and, at least for many data sets, it obeys the empirical rules discussed here. These empirical rules give a very concrete meaning to a standard deviation.

As an example, if the parts supplied by the suppliers in Figure 2.11 have diameters that are approximately normally distributed, then the intervals in the empirical rules for supplier 1 are about 100 ± 3, 100 ± 6, and 100 ± 9. Therefore, about 68% of this supplier's parts should have diameters from 97 to 103, 95% should have diameters from 94 to 106, and almost none should have diameters below 91 or above 109. Obviously, the situation for supplier 2 is much worse. With a standard deviation slightly larger than 25, the second empirical rule implies that about 1 out of every 20 of this supplier's parts will be below 50 or above 150. It is clear that supplier 2 has to do something to reduce its variability. In fact, this is exactly what almost all suppliers are continuously trying to do: reduce variability.

Returning to the baseball data, Figure 2.10 indicates that the standard deviation of salaries is slightly above $4.36 million. (The variance is shown, but because it is in squared dollars, it is a huge value without a meaningful interpretation.) Can the empirical rules be applied to these baseball salaries? The answer is that you can always try, but if the salaries are not at least approximately normally distributed, the rules won't be very accurate. And because of obvious skewness in the salary data (due to the stars with astronomical salaries), the assumption of a normal distribution is not a good one.

Nevertheless, the rules are checked in Figure 2.12. For each of the three rules, the lower and upper endpoints of the corresponding interval are found in columns I and J. Right away there are problems. Because the standard deviation is *larger* than the mean, all three lower

---

Figure 2.12 Empirical Rules for Baseball Salaries

	H	I	J	K	L	M	N	O
1	Do empirical rules apply?							
2		Lower endpoint	Upper endpoint	# below lower	# above upper	% below lower	% above upper	% between
3	Rule 1	($1,104,004)	$7,624,123	0	120	0%	14.67%	85.33%
4	Rule 2	($5,468,068)	$11,988,186	0	61	0%	7.46%	92.54%
5	Rule 3	($9,832,131)	$16,352,249.96	0	16	0%	1.96%	98.04%

endpoints are *negative*, which automatically means that can be no salaries below them. But continuing, the COUNTIF was used (again with concatenation) to find the number of salaries above the upper endpoints in column L, and the corresponding percentages appear in column N. Finally, subtracting columns M and N from 100% gives the percentages between the endpoints in column O. These three percentages, according to the empirical rules, should be about 68%, 95%, and 99.7%. Rules 2 and 3 are not way off, but rule 1 isn't even close.

The point of these calculations is that even though the empirical rules give substantive meaning to the standard deviation for many variables, they should be applied with caution, especially when the data are clearly skewed.

Before leaving variance and standard deviation, you might ask why the deviations from the mean are *squared* in the definition of variance. Why not simply take the *absolute* deviation from the mean? For example, if the mean is 100 and two observations have values 95 and 105, then each has a *squared* deviation of 25, but each has an *absolute* deviation of only 5. Wouldn't this latter value be a more natural measure of variability? Intuitively, it would, but there is a long history in the field of statistics of using squared deviations. They have many nice theoretical properties that are not shared by absolute deviations. Still, some analysts quote the **mean absolute deviation** (abbreviated as **MAD**) as another measure of variability, particularly in time series analysis. It is defined as the average of the absolute deviations.

Formula for Mean Absolute Deviation

$$\text{MAD} = \frac{\sum_{i=1}^{n} |X_i - \overline{X}|}{n}$$

(2.4)

There is another empirical rule for MAD: For many (but not all) variables, the standard deviation is approximately 25% larger than MAD, that is, $s \approx 1.25\text{MAD}$. Fortunately, Excel has a little-known function, **AVEDEV**, that performs the calculation in Equation (2.4). Using it for the baseball salaries in Figure 2.10, you can see that MAD is slightly above $3.2 million. If this is multiplied by 1.25, the result is slightly over $4 million, which is indeed fairly close to the standard deviation.

Measures of Shape

There are two final measures of a distribution you will hear occasionally: **skewness** and **kurtosis**. Each of these has not only an intuitive meaning, but also a specific numeric measure. We have already mentioned skewness in terms of the baseball salaries. It occurs because of a lack of symmetry. A few stars have really large salaries, and no players have really small salaries. Alternatively, the largest salaries are much farther to the right of the mean than the smallest salaries are to the left of the mean. This lack of symmetry will be apparent from a histogram of the salaries in the next section. We say that these salaries are **skewed to the right** (or **positively skewed**) because the skewness is due to the really *large* salaries. If the skewness were due to really small values (as might occur if we were examining temperature lows in Antarctica), then we would call it **skewness to the left** (or **negatively skewed**).

In either case, there is a measure of skewness that can be calculated with Excel's **SKEW** function. For the baseball data, it is approximately 2.1, as shown in Figure 2.10. You don't need to know exactly what this value means. Simply remember that (1) it is positive when there is skewness to the right, (2) it is negative when there is skewness to the left, (3) it is approximately zero when there is no skewness (the symmetric case), and (4) its magnitude increases as the degree of skewness increases.

Kurtosis is all about extreme events—the kind that occurred in late 2008 and sent Wall Street into a panic.

The other measure, kurtosis, has to do with the "fatness" of the tails of the distribution relative to the tails of a normal distribution. Remember from the third empirical rule that a normal distribution has almost all of its observations within three standard deviations of the mean. In contrast, a distribution with high kurtosis has many more extreme observations.

Is this important in reality? It certainly is. For example, many researchers believe the Wall Street meltdown in late 2008 was at least partly due to financial analysts relying on the normal distribution, whereas in reality the actual distribution had much fatter tails. More specifically, financial analysts followed complex mathematical models that indicated really extreme events would virtually never occur. Unfortunately, a number of extreme events *did* occur, and they sent the economy into a deep recession.[2]

Although kurtosis can be calculated in Excel with the **KURT** function (it is about 5.1 for the baseball salaries), we won't have any use for this measure in the book. Nevertheless, when you hear the word kurtosis, think fat tails and extreme events. And if you plan to work on Wall Street, you should definitely learn more about kurtosis.

Numerical Summary Measures in the Status Bar

You might have noticed that summary measures sometimes appear automatically in the status bar at the bottom of your Excel window. The rule is that if you select multiple cells (in a single column or even in multiple columns), selected summary measures appear for the selected cells. (Nothing appears if only a single cell is selected.) These can be very handy for quick lookups. Also, you can control the summary measures that appear by right-clicking on the status bar and selecting your favorites.

2.4.2 Numerical Summary Measures with StatTools

In the previous subsection, we used Excel's built-in functions (AVERAGE, STDEV, and others) to calculate a number of summary measures. A much quicker way is to use Palisade's StatTools add-in. As we promised earlier, StatTools requires almost no learning curve. After you go through this section, you will know everything you need to know to continue using StatTools like a professional.

EXAMPLE | **2.3 BASEBALL SALARIES (CONTINUED)**

Use the StatTools add-in to generate the same summary measures that were calculated in the previous subsection.

Objective   To learn the fundamentals of StatTools and use this add-in to generate summary measures of baseball salaries.

Solution

Because this is your first exposure to StatTools, we must first explain how to get started. StatTools is part of the Palisade DecisionTools Suite, and you have the free academic version of this suite as a result of purchasing the book. The explanations and screenshots in the book are based on version 5.5 of the suite. (It is possible that by the time you are reading this, you might have a later version.) In any case, you must install the suite before you can use StatTools.

Once the suite is installed, you can load StatTools by double-clicking on the StatTools item in the list of programs on the Windows Start menu. (It is in the Palisade group.) If Excel is already running, this will load StatTools on top of Excel. If Excel isn't running,

---

[2]The popular book *The Black Swan*, by Nassim Nicholas Taleb (Random House, 2007), is all about extreme events and the trouble they can cause.

Figure 2.13 StatTools Ribbon

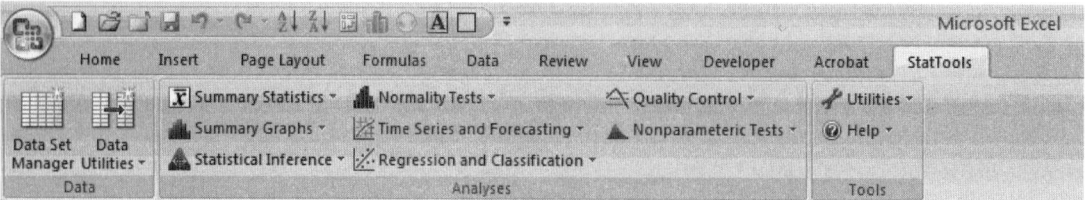

this will launch Excel and load StatTools as well. You will know that StatTools is loaded when you see the StatTools tab and ribbon, as shown in Figure 2.13.

The buttons in the Analyses group on this ribbon are for performing the various statistical analyses, many of which will be explained in the book. But before you can use these, you need to know a few basic features of StatTools. ∎

Basic StatTools Features

1. There is an Application Settings item on the Utilities dropdown list. When you click it, you get the dialog box in Figure 2.14. (All of the other add-ins in the Palisade suite have a similar Application Settings item.) This is where you can change overall settings of StatTools. You can experiment with these settings, but the only one you will probably ever need to change is the Reports Placement setting—where your results are placed. The dropdown list in Figure 2.14 shows the four possibilities. We tend to prefer

Figure 2.14

Application Settings Dialog Box

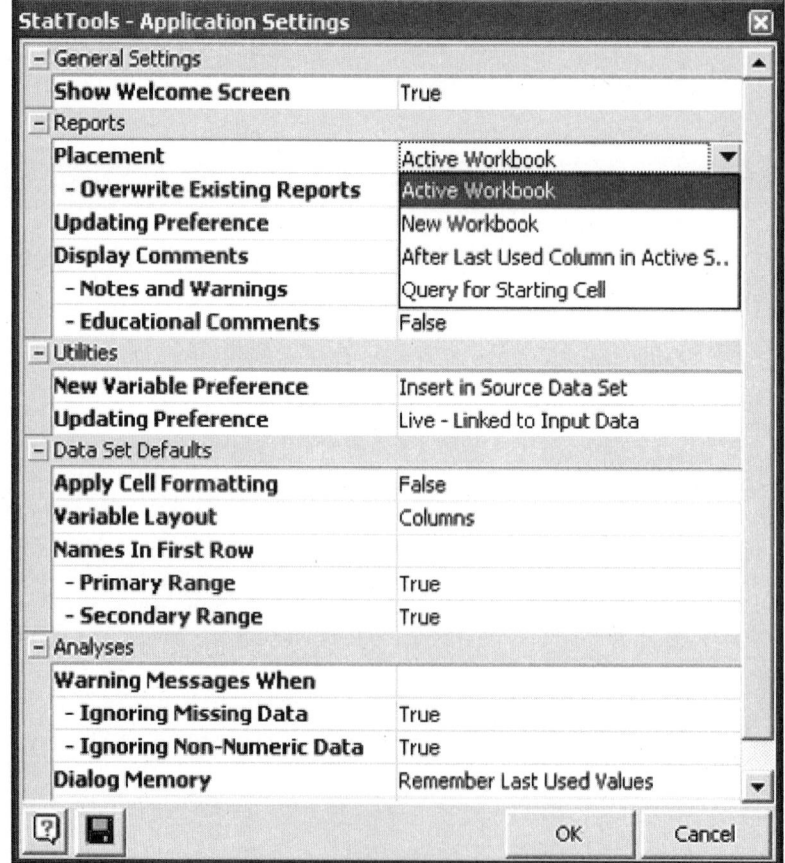

the Active Workbook option (this places the results on a new worksheet) or the Query for Starting Cell option (this lets you choose the cell where your results will start).

2. If you want to unload StatTools without closing Excel, you can choose the Unload StatTools Add-In item from the Utilities dropdown list.

3. Although you probably won't need it, there is plenty of online help, including example spreadsheets, on the Help dropdown list.

4. This is the important one. Before you can perform any statistical analysis, you must define a StatTools data set. You do this using the Data Set Manager button. Try it now. With the **Baseball Salaries 2009.xlsx** file open, make sure your cursor is *anywhere* within the data set, and click on the Data Set Manager button. You will first be asked whether you want to add the range $A$1:$D$819 as a new StatTools data set. Click on Yes. Then you will see the dialog box in Figure 2.15. StatTools makes several guesses about your data set. They are generally correct, but you can always override them. First, it gives your data set a generic name, such as Data Set #1. You can accept this or supply a more meaningful name. The latter is especially useful if your file contains more than one data set. Second, you can override the data range. (Note that this range *should* include the variable names in row 1.) Third, the default layout is that variables are in columns, with variable names in the top row. You should override these settings only in rare cases where your data set has the roles of rows and columns reversed. (The Multiple button is for very unusual cases. We will not discuss it here.) Finally, if you want to apply some color to your data set, you can check the Apply Cell Formatting option. (We generally don't.)

Figure 2.15
Data Set Manager
Dialog Box

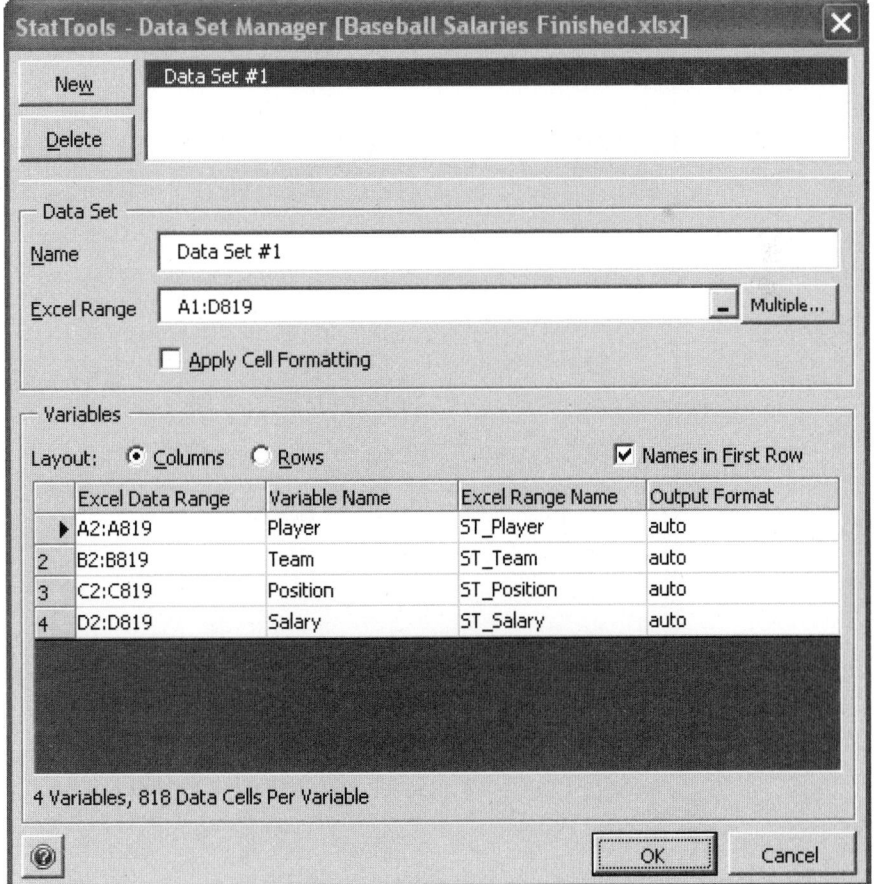

For now, simply click on OK. You now have a StatTools data set, and you can begin the analysis. Fortunately, this step has to be done only once. If you save the file and reopen it at a later date, StatTools still remembers this data set. So when we said that StatTools has a short learning curve, this is it—simply remember to designate a StatTools data set before you begin any analysis.

Now that the preliminaries are over, you can quickly get the summary measures for the Salary variable. To do so, select the One-Variable Summary item from the Summary Statistics dropdown list. You will see the dialog box in Figure 2.16. (If you see two columns of variables in the top pane, click on the Format button and select Stacked.) This is a typical StatTools dialog box. In the top section, you can select a StatTools data set and one or more variables. In the bottom section, you can select the measures you want. For this example, we have chosen all of the measures. (In addition, you can add other percentiles if you like.) Before you click on OK, click on the "double-check" button to the left of the OK button. This brings up the Application Settings dialog box already shown in Figure 2.14. This is your last chance to designate where you want to place the results. (We chose Active Workbook, which means that the results are placed in a new worksheet automatically named One Var Summary.)

Figure 2.16

One Variable Summary Dialog Box

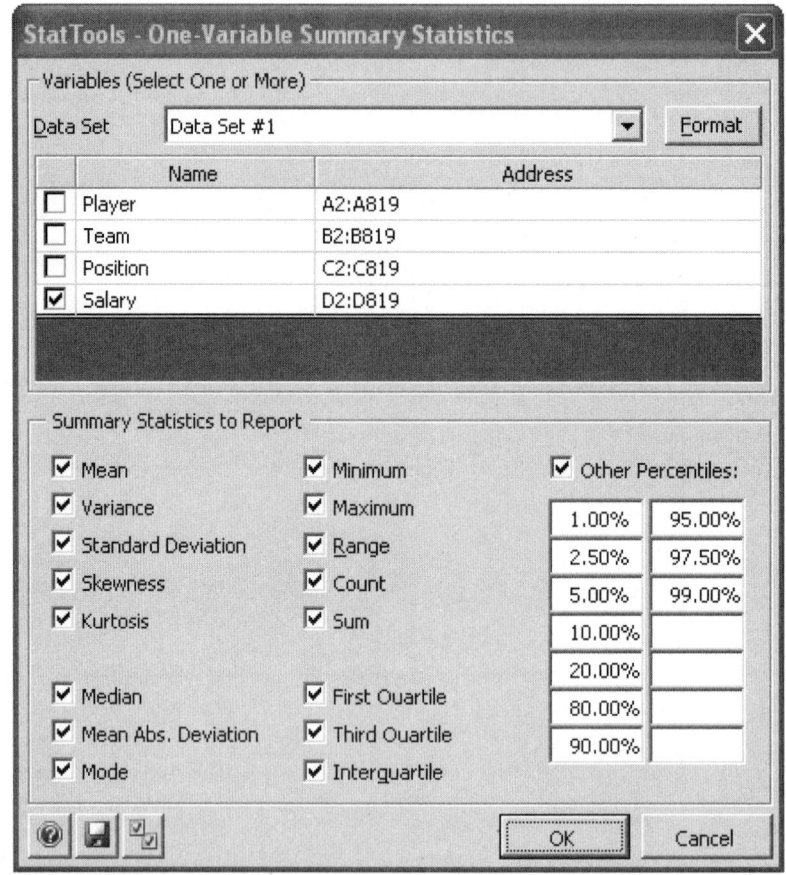

StatTools Tip *In general, you might want to choose only your favorite summary measures, such as mean, median, standard deviation, minimum, and maximum. This requires you to uncheck all of the others. To avoid all of this unchecking in future analyses, you can click on the Save button in the middle of the bottom left group. This saves your choices as the defaults from then on.*

The results appear in Figure 2.17. If you compare these to the measures from Excel functions in Figure 2.10, you will see some slight discrepancies in the percentiles and quartiles. (The kurtosis is also quite different.) When Palisade developed StatTools, it did not fully trust Excel's statistical functions, so it developed its own based on best practices from the statistical literature. In fact, if you click on any of the results, you will see functions such as StatMean, StatStdDev, StatPercentile, and so on. Don't be overly concerned that the percentiles and quartiles don't exactly match. Both sets provide the same basic picture of how the salaries are distributed.

Figure 2.17

Summary Measures for Salaries

	A	B
7		Salary
8	*One Variable Summary*	Data Set #1
9	Mean	$3260059.28
10	Variance	19045050733784.30
11	Std. Dev.	$4364063.56
12	Skewness	2.0996
13	Kurtosis	8.1266
14	Median	$1150000.00
15	Mean Abs.Dev.	$3205752.60
16	Minimum	$400000.00
17	Maximum	$33000000.00
18	Range	$32600000.00
19	Count	818
20	Sum	$2666728494.00
21	1st Quartile	$419400.00
22	3rd Quartile	$4250000.00
23	Interquartile Range	$3830600.00
24	1.00%	$400000.00
25	2.50%	$400000.00
26	5.00%	$400000.00
27	10.00%	$401000.00
28	20.00%	$411000.00
29	80.00%	$5500000.00
30	90.00%	$10000000.00
31	95.00%	$13000000.00
32	97.50%	$15000000.00
33	99.00%	$18750000.00

Technical Note *Why is there a discrepancy at all in the percentiles and quartiles? Suppose, for example, that you want the 75th percentile (3rd quartile) and there are 818 observations. By definition, the 75th percentile is the value such that 75% of the values are below it and 25% are above it. Now, 75% of 818 is 613.50. This suggests that you should sort the 818 observations in increasing order and locate the 613th and 614th smallest. For the baseball data, these salaries are $4,200,000 and $4,250,000. Excel reports the 75th percentile as $4,237,500, whereas StatTools reports it as $4,250,000. In words, Excel interpolates and StatTools doesn't, but either is reasonable. As for kurtosis, Excel provides an index that is 0 for a normal distribution, whereas StatTools returns a value 3 for a normal distribution. So the two indexes differ by 3. (For what it's worth, Wikipedia indicates that either definition of kurtosis is acceptable.)*

If you open a file with errors in StatTools outputs, close the file, load StatTools, and reopen the file.

There are three other things to note about the StatTools output. First, it formats the results according to its own rules. If you would like fewer or more decimals or any other formatting changes, you can certainly reformat in the usual way. Second, the fact that there are *formulas* in these result cells indicates that they are "live." If you go back to the data and change any of the salaries, the summary measures will update automatically. This is true for most, but not quite all, StatTools outputs. (Regression analysis, discussed in Chapters 10 and 11, is the most important situation where the StatTools results are not live.) Finally, if you open a file with StatTools outputs but StatTools is not loaded, you may see #VALUE! errors in the cells. These can be fixed by closing the file, loading StatTools, and opening the file again.

2.4.3 Charts for Numerical Variables

The term *distribution* refers to the way the data are distributed in the various categories. It is common to refer to a skewed distribution, say, rather than a skewed histogram. However, either term can be used.

There are many graphical ways to indicate the distribution of a numerical variable, but the two we prefer and will discuss in this subsection are **histograms** and **box plots** (also called **box-whisker plots**). Each of these is useful primarily for cross-sectional variables. If they are used for time series variables, the time dimension gets buried. Therefore, we will discuss **time series graphs** for time series variables separately in the next section.

FUNDAMENTAL INSIGHT

Histograms Versus Summary Measures

It is important to remember that each of the summary measures we have discussed for a numerical variable—the mean, the median, the standard deviation, and others—describes only one aspect of a numerical variable. In contrast, a histogram provides the complete picture. It indicates the "center" of the distribution, the variability, the skewness, and other aspects, all in one convenient chart.

Histograms

A histogram is the most common type of chart for showing the distribution of a numerical variable. It is based on binning the variable—that is, dividing it up into discrete categories. The histogram is then a column chart of the counts in the various categories (with no gaps between the bars). In general, a histogram is great for showing the shape of a distribution. We are particularly interested in whether the distribution is symmetric or is skewed in one direction. The concept is a simple one, as illustrated in the following example with the baseball salary data.

EXAMPLE	2.3 BASEBALL SALARIES (CONTINUED)

We have already mentioned that the baseball salaries are skewed to the right. How does this show up in a histogram of salaries?

Objective   To see the shape of the salary distribution through a histogram.

Solution

A histogram can be created with Excel tools only, but the process is quite tedious. It is much easier to use StatTools.

It is possible to create a histogram with Excel tools only—no add-ins—but it is a tedious process. First, the bins must be defined. If you do it yourself, you will probably choose "nice" bins, such as $400,000 to $800,000, $800,000 to $1,200,000, and so on. But there is also the question of *how many* bins there should be and what their endpoints should be, and these are not always easy choices. In any case, once the bins have been selected, the number of observations in each bin must be counted. This can be done in

Excel with the COUNTIF function. (You can also use the COUNTIFS and FREQUENCY functions, but we won't discuss them here.) The resulting table of counts is usually called a **frequency table**. Finally, a column chart of the counts must be created. If you are interested, we have indicated the steps in the Histogram sheet of the finished version of the baseball file.

It is much easier to create a histogram with StatTools, as we now illustrate. As with all StatTools analyses, the first step is to designate a StatTools data set, which has already been done for the salary data. To create a histogram, select the Histogram item from the Summary Graphs dropdown list to obtain the dialog box in Figure 2.18. At this point, all you really need to do is select the Salary variable and click on OK. This gives you the default bins, indicated by "auto" values. Essentially, StatTools checks your data and chooses "good" settings for the bins. The resulting histogram, along with the bin data it is based on, appears in Figure 2.19. StatTools has used 11 bins, with the endpoints indicated in columns B and C. The histogram is then a column chart (with no gaps between the bars) of the counts in column E. (These counts are also called *frequencies*.)

Figure 2.18
StatTools Histogram
Dialog Box

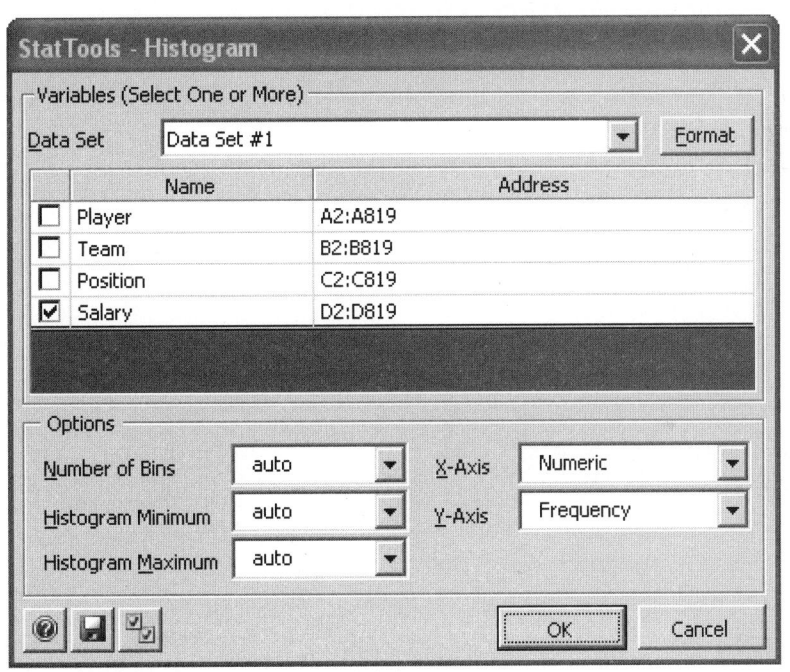

In many situations, you can accept the StatTools defaults for histogram bins. They generally show the big picture quite well, which is the main goal.

You could argue that the bins chosen by StatTools aren't very "nice." For example, the upper limit of the first bin is $3,363,636.36. If you want to fine-tune these, you can enter your own bins instead of the "auto" values in Figure 2.18. We will illustrate this in the next example, but it is largely beside the point for the main question about baseball salaries. The StatTools default histogram shows very clearly that the salaries are skewed to the right, and fine-tuning bins won't change this primary finding. The vast majority of the players are in the lowest two categories, and the salaries of the stars account for the long tail to the right. This big picture finding is all you typically want from a histogram.

When is it useful to fine-tune the StatTools histogram bins? One good example is when the values of the variable are integers, as illustrated next.

Figure 2.19   Histogram of Salaries

	A	B	C	D	E	F	G
7				Salary / Data Set #1			
8	*Histogram*	**Bin Min**	**Bin Max**	**Midpoint**	**Freq.**	**Rel. Freq.**	**Prb. Density**
9	Bin #1	$400000.00	$3363636.36	$1881818.18	574	0.7017	0.000000237
10	Bin #2	$3363636.36	$6327272.73	$4845454.55	102	0.1247	0.000000042
11	Bin #3	$6327272.73	$9290909.09	$7809090.91	49	0.0599	0.000000020
12	Bin #4	$9290909.09	$12254545.45	$10772727.27	43	0.0526	0.000000018
13	Bin #5	$12254545.45	$15218181.82	$13736363.64	32	0.0391	0.000000013
14	Bin #6	$15218181.82	$18181818.18	$16700000.00	8	0.0098	0.000000003
15	Bin #7	$18181818.18	$21145454.55	$19663636.36	7	0.0086	0.000000003
16	Bin #8	$21145454.55	$24109090.91	$22627272.73	2	0.0024	0.000000001
17	Bin #9	$24109090.91	$27072727.27	$25590909.09	0	0.0000	0.000000000
18	Bin #10	$27072727.27	$30036363.64	$28554545.45	0	0.0000	0.000000000
19	Bin #11	$30036363.64	$33000000.00	$31518181.82	1	0.0012	0.000000000

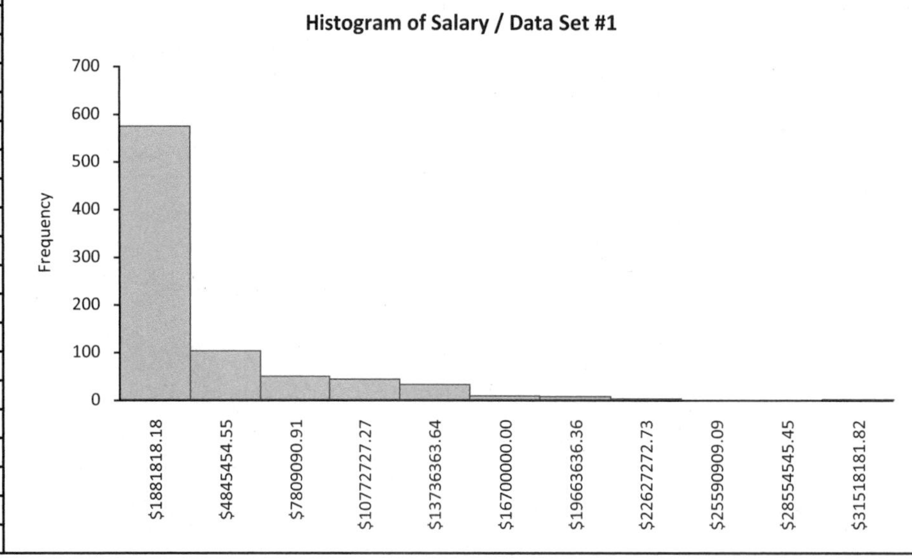

Histogram of Salary / Data Set #1

EXAMPLE | **2.4 LOST OR LATE BAGGAGE AT AIRPORTS**

The file **Late or Lost Baggage.xlsx** contains information on 456 flights into an airport. (This is not real data.) For each flight, it lists the number of bags that were either late or lost. A sample is shown in Figure 2.20. What is the most natural histogram for this data set?

Objective   To fine-tune a histogram for a variable with integer counts.

Solution

From a scan of the data (sort from lowest to highest), it is apparent that all flights had from 0 to 8 late or lost bags. Therefore, the most natural histogram is one that shows the count of each possible value. If you try using the default settings in StatTools, this is *not* what you will get. However, if you fill in the Histogram dialog box as shown in Figure 2.21, you

Figure 2.20

Data on Late or Lost Baggage

	A	B
1	**Flight**	**Bags late or lost**
2	1	0
3	2	3
4	3	5
5	4	0
6	5	2
7	6	2
8	7	1
9	8	5
10	9	1
11	10	3
12	11	3
13	12	4
14	13	5
15	14	4
16	15	3

Figure 2.21

Histogram Dialog Box with Desired Bins

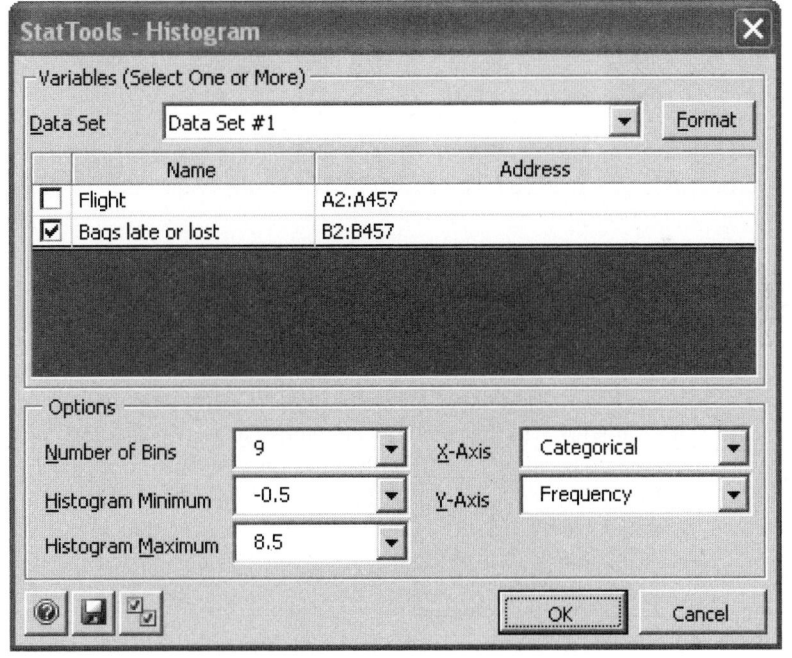

For a quick analysis, feel free to accept StatTools's automatic histogram options. However, don't be afraid to experiment with these options in defining your own bins. The goal is to make the histogram as meaningful and easy to read as possible.

will get exactly what you want. The resulting histogram appears in Figure 2.22. Do you see the trick? When you request 9 bins and set the min and max to −0.5 and 8.5, StatTools divides the range from −0.5 to 8.5 into 9 equal-length bins: −0.5 to 0.5, 0.5 to 1.5, and on up to 7.5 to 8.5. Of course, each bin contains only one possible value, the integer in the middle. So you get the count of 0s, the count of 1s, and so on. As an extra benefit, StatTools always labels the horizontal axis with the midpoints of the bins, which are exactly the integers you want. (For an even nicer look, we formatted these horizontal axis values with no decimals.)

Figure 2.22 Histogram of Counts

	A	B	C	D	E	F	G
7				Bags late or lost / Data Set #1			
8	*Histogram*	Bin Min	Bin Max	Bin Midpoint	Fred.	Rel. Fred.	Prb. Density
9	Bin #1	−0.500	0.500	0.000	16	0.0351	0.04
10	Bin #2	0.500	1.500	1.000	67	0.1469	0.15
11	Bin #3	1.500	2.500	2.000	113	0.2478	0.25
12	Bin #4	2.500	3.500	3.000	101	0.2215	0.22
13	Bin #5	3.500	4.500	4.000	77	0.1689	0.17
14	Bin #6	4.500	5.500	5.000	44	0.0965	0.10
15	Bin #7	5.500	6.500	6.000	23	0.0504	0.05
16	Bin #8	6.500	7.500	7.000	13	0.0285	0.03
17	Bin #9	7.500	8.500	8.000	2	0.0244	0.00
18							

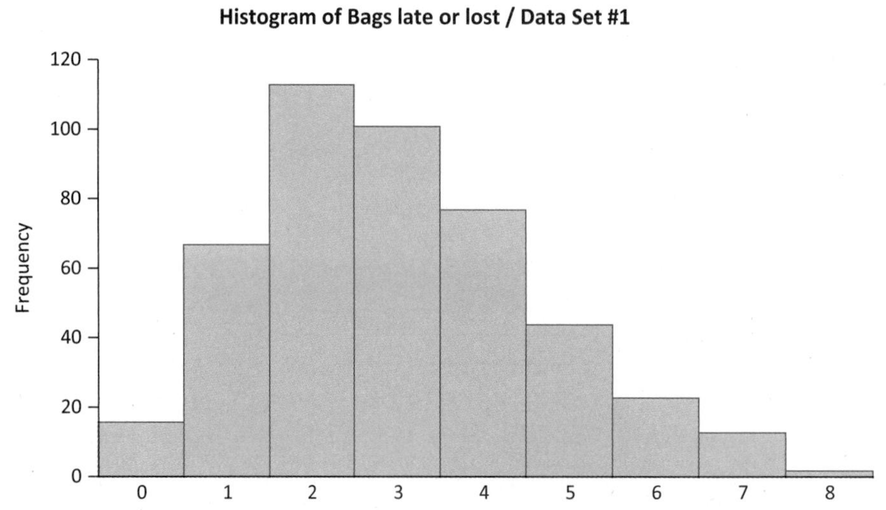

Histogram of Bags late or lost / Data Set #1

The point of this example is that you *do* have control over the histogram bins if you are not satisfied with the StatTools defaults. Just keep one technical detail in mind. If a bin extends, say, from 2.7 to 3.4, then its count is the number of observations greater than 2.7 and less than *or equal to* 3.4. In other words, observations equal to the right endpoint are counted, but observations equal to the left endpoint are not. (They would be counted in the *previous* bin.) So in this example, if we had designated the minimum and maximum as −1 and 8 in Figure 2.21, we would have gotten the same histogram. ∎

Box Plots

A box plot (also called a box-whisker plot) is an alternative type of chart for showing the distribution of a variable. For the distribution of a single variable, a box plot is not nearly as popular as a histogram, but as you will see in the next chapter, side-by-side box plots are very popular for comparing distributions, such as salaries for men versus salaries for women. As with histograms, box plots are "big picture" charts. They show you at a glance some of the key features of a distribution. We explain how they do this in the following continuation of the baseball salary example.

EXAMPLE 2.3 BASEBALL SALARIES (CONTINUED)

A histogram of the salaries clearly indicated the skewness to the right. Does a box plot of salaries indicate the same behavior?

Objective To illustrate the features of a box plot, particularly how it indicates skewness.

Solution

Excel has no built-in box plot chart type. In this case, you must rely on StatTools.

This time you *must* rely on StatTools. There is no easy way to create a box plot with Excel tools only. Fortunately, it is easy with StatTools. Select the Box-Whisker Plot item from the Summary Graphs dropdown list and fill in the resulting dialog box as in Figure 2.23—there are no other choices to make. The box plot appears in Figure 2.24. (StatTools also lists some mysterious values below the box plot. You can ignore these, but don't delete them. They are the basis for the box plot itself.)

Figure 2.23
StatTools Box-Whisker Plot Dialog Box

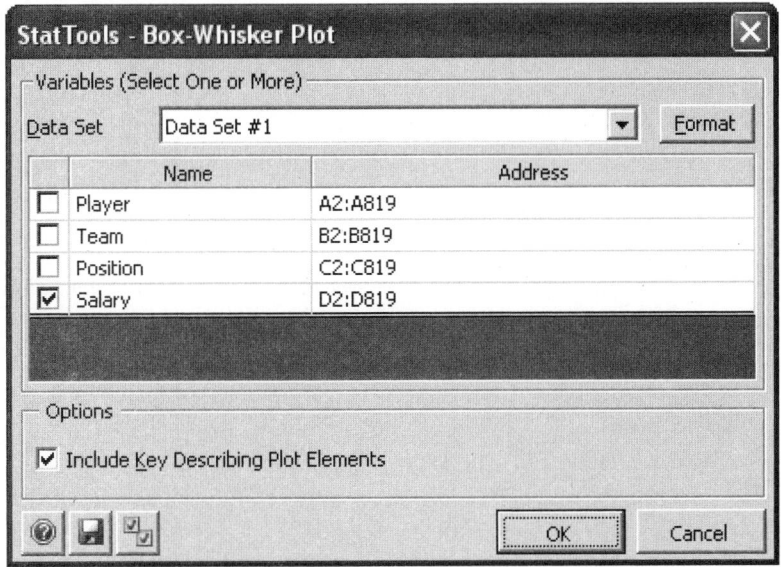

Figure 2.24
Box Plot of Salaries

Box Plot of Salary / Data Set #1

To help you understand the elements of a box plot, StatTools provides the generic box plot shown in Figure 2.25. (It is not drawn to scale.) You can get this by checking the Include Key Describing Plot Elements option in Figure 2.23, although you will probably want to do this only once or twice. As this generic diagram indicates, the box itself extends, left to right, from the 1st quartile to the 3rd quartile. This means that it contains the middle half of the data. The line inside the box is positioned at the median, and the x inside the box is positioned at the mean. The lines (whiskers) coming out either side of the box extend to 1.5 IQRs (interquartile ranges) from the quartiles. These generally include most of the data outside the box. More distant values, called outliers, are denoted separately with small squares. They are hollow for "mild" outliers, and solid for "extreme" outliers, as indicated in the explanation.

Figure 2.25

Elements of a Generic Box Plot

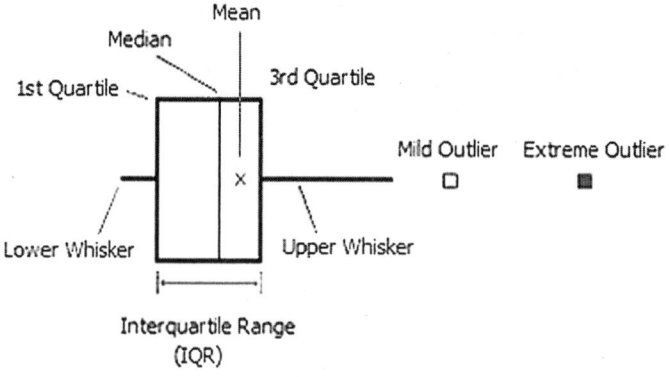

Whiskers extend to the furthest observations that are no more than 1.5 IQR from the edges of the box. Mild outliers are observations between 1.5 IQR and 3 IQR from the edges of the box. Extreme outliers are greater than 3 IQR from the edges of the box.

The box plot of salaries in Figure 2.24 should now make more sense. It is typical of an extremely right-skewed distribution. The mean is much larger than the median as we explained earlier; there is virtually no whisker out of the left side of the box (because the first quartile is barely above the minimum value—remember all the players earning $400,000?), and there are many outliers to the right (the stars). In fact, many of these outliers overlap one another. You can decide whether you prefer the histogram of salaries to this box plot or vice versa, but both are clearly telling the same story.

Box plots have been around for several decades, and they are probably more popular now than ever. The implementation of box plots in StatTools is just one version of what you might see. Some packages draw box plots vertically, not horizontally. Also, some vary the height of the box to indicate some other feature of the distribution. (The height of the box is irrelevant in StatTools's box plots.) Nevertheless, they all follow the same basic rules and provide the same basic information. ∎

FUNDAMENTAL INSIGHT

Box Plots Versus Histograms

Box plots and histograms are complementary ways of displaying the distribution of a numerical variable. Although histograms are much more popular and are arguably more intuitive, box plots are still informative. Besides, side-by-side box plots are very useful for comparing two or more populations.

PROBLEMS

Level A

6. The file **P02_06.xlsx** lists the average time (in minutes) it takes citizens of 379 metropolitan areas to travel to work and back home each day.
   a. Create a histogram of the daily commute times.
   b. Find the most representative average daily commute time across this distribution.
   c. Find a useful measure of the variability of these average commute times around the mean.
   d. The empirical rule for standard deviations indicates that approximately 95% of these average travel times will fall between which two values? For this particular data set, is this empirical rule at least approximately correct?

7. The file **P02_07.xlsx** includes data on 204 employees at the (fictional) company Beta Technologies.
   a. Indicate the data type for each of the six variables included in this data set.
   b. Create a histogram of the Age variable. How would you characterize the age distribution for these employees?
   c. What proportion of these full-time Beta employees are female?
   d. Find appropriate summary measures for each of the numerical variables in this data set.
   e. For the Salary variable, explain why the empirical rules for standard deviations do or do not apply.

8. The file **P02_08.xlsx** contains data on 500 shipments of one of the computer components that a company manufactures. Specifically, the proportion of items that are defective is listed for each shipment.
   a. Create a histogram that will help a production manager understand the variation of the proportion of defective components in the company's shipments.
   b. Is the mean or median the most appropriate measure of central location for this data set? Explain your reasoning.
   c. Discuss whether the empirical rules for standard deviations apply. Can you tell, or at least make an educated guess, by looking at the shape of the histogram? Why?

9. The file **P02_09.xlsx** lists the times required to service 200 consecutive customers at a (fictional) fast-foods restaurant.
   a. Create a histogram of the customer service times. How would you characterize the distribution of service times?
   b. Calculate the mean, median, and first and third quartiles of this distribution.
   c. Which measure of central tendency, the mean or the median, is more appropriate in describing this distribution? Explain your reasoning.
   d. Find and interpret the variance and standard deviation of these service times.
   e. Are the empirical rules for standard deviations applicable for these service times? If not, explain why. Can you tell whether they apply, or at least make an educated guess, by looking at the shape of the histogram? Why?

10. The file **P02_10.xlsx** contains midterm and final exam scores for 96 students in a corporate finance course.
    a. Create a histogram for each of the two sets of exam scores.
    b. What are the mean and median scores on each of these exams?
    c. Explain why the mean and median values are different for these data.
    d. Based on your previous answers, how would you characterize this group's performance on the midterm and on the final exam?
    e. Create a new column of differences (final exam score minus midterm score). A positive value means the student improved, and a negative value means the student did the opposite. What are the mean and median of the differences? What does a histogram of the differences indicate?

11. The file **P02_11.xlsx** contains data on 148 houses that were recently sold in a (fictional) suburban community. The data set includes the selling price of each house, along with its appraised value, square footage, number of bedrooms, and number of bathrooms.
    a. Which of these variables are continuous? Which are discrete?
    b. Create histograms for the appraised values and selling prices of the houses. How are these two distributions similar? How are they different?
    c. Find the maximum and minimum sizes (measured in square footage) of all sample houses.
    d. Find the house(s) at the 80th percentile of all sample houses with respect to appraised value. Find the house(s) at the 80th percentile of all sample houses with respect to selling price.
    e. What are the typical number of bedrooms and the typical number of bathrooms in this set of houses? How do you interpret the word "typical?"

12. The file **P02_12.xlsx** includes data on the 50 top graduate programs in the United States, according to a recent *U.S. News & World Report* survey.
    a. Indicate the type of data for each of the 10 variables considered in the formulation of the overall ranking.

b. Create a histogram for each of the numerical variables in this data set. Indicate whether each of these distributions is approximately symmetric or skewed. Which, if any, of these distributions are skewed to the right? Which, if any, are skewed to the left?

c. Identify the schools with the largest and smallest annual out-of-state tuition and fee levels.

d. Find the annual out-of-state tuition and fee levels at each of the 25th, 50th, and 75th percentiles for these schools. For Excel 2010 users only, find these percentiles using both the PERCENTILE.INC and PERCENTILE.EXE functions. Can you explain how and why they are different (if they are indeed different)?

f. Create a box plot to characterize this distribution of these MBA salaries. Is this distribution essentially symmetric or skewed? If there are any outliers on either end, which schools do they correspond to? Are these same schools outliers in box plots of any of the other numerical variables (from columns E to L)?

13. The file **P02_13.xlsx** contains the thickness (in centimeters) of 252 mica pieces. A piece meets specifications if its thickness is between 7 and 15 centimeters.

a. What fraction of mica pieces meets specifications?

b. Are the empirical rules for standard deviations at least approximately valid for these data? Can you tell, or at least make an educated guess, by looking at a histogram of the data?

c. If the histogram of the data is approximately bell-shaped and you want about 95% of the observations to meet specifications, is it sufficient for the average and standard deviation to be, at least approximately, 11 and 2 centimeters, respectively?

14. Recall that the file **Supermarket Transactions.xlsx** contains over 14,000 transactions made by supermarket customers over a period of approximately two years. Using these data, create a box plot to characterize the distribution of revenues earned from the given transactions. Is this distribution essentially symmetric or skewed? What if you restrict the box plot to transactions in the food product family?
(Hint: StatTools will not let you define a second data set that is a subset of an existing data set. But you can copy data for the second question to a second worksheet.)

15. Recall that the file **Baseball Salaries 2009.xlsx** contains data on 818 MLB players as of May 2009. Using these data, create a box plot to characterize the distribution of salaries of all pitchers. Do the same for non-pitchers. Summarize your findings. (See the hint in the previous problem.)

16. The file **P02_16.xlsx** contains traffic data from 256 weekdays on four variables. Each variable lists the number of vehicle arrivals to a tollbooth during a specific five-minute period of the day.

a. Create a histogram of each variable. How would you characterize and compare these distributions?

b. Find a table of summary measures for these variables that includes (at least) the means, medians, standard deviations, first and third quartiles, and 5th and 95th percentiles. Use these to compare the arrival process at the different times of day.

Level B

17. The file **P02_17.xlsx** contains salaries of 200 recent graduates from a (fictional) MBA program.

a. What salary level is most indicative of those earned by students graduating from this MBA program this year?

b. Do the empirical rules for standard deviations apply to these data? Can you tell, or at least make an educated guess, by looking at the shape of the histogram? Why?

c. If the empirical rules apply here, between which two numbers can you be about 68% sure that the salary of any one of these 200 students will fall?

d. If the MBA program wants to make a statement such as "Some of our recent graduates started out making X dollars or more, and almost all of them started out making at least Y dollars" for their promotional materials, what values of X and Y would you suggest they use? Defend your choice.

e. As an admissions officer of this MBA program, how would you proceed to use these findings to market the program to prospective students?

18. The file **P02_18.xlsx** contains daily values of the Standard & Poor's 500 Index from 1970 to 2009. It also contains percentage changes in the index from each day to the next.

a. Create a histogram of the percentage changes and describe its shape.

b. Check the percentage of these percentage changes that are more than k standard deviations from the mean for $k = 1, 2, 3, 4,$ and 5. Are these approximately what the empirical rules indicate or are there "fat" tails? Do you think this has any real implications for the financial markets? (Note that we have discussed the empirical rules only for $k = 1, 2,$ and 3. For $k = 4$ and 5, they indicate that only 0.006% and 0.0001% of the observations should be this distant from the mean.)

2.5 TIME SERIES DATA

If we are analyzing time series variables, summary measures such as means and standard deviations and charts such as histograms and box plots often don't make much sense. Our main interest in time series variables is how they change over time, and this information is lost in traditional summary measures and in histograms or box plots. Imagine, for example, that you are interested in daily closing prices of a stock that has historically been between 20 and 60. If you create a histogram with a bin such as 45 to 50, you will get a count of all daily closing prices in this interval—but you won't have a clue of when they occurred. The histogram is missing a key feature: time. Similarly, if you report the *mean* of a time series such as the monthly Dow Jones average over the past 40 years, you will get a measure that isn't very relevant for the current and future values of the Dow.

Therefore, we turn to a different but very intuitive type of chart called a **time series graph**. This is simply a graph of the values of one or more time series, using time on the horizontal axis, and it is always the place to start a time series analysis. We illustrate some possibilities in the following example.

EXAMPLE | **2.5 CRIME IN THE U.S.**

The file **Crime in US.xlsx** contains annual data on violent and property crimes for the years 1960 to 2007. Part of the data is listed in Figure 2.26. This shows the number of crimes. The rates per 100,000 population are not shown, but they also appear in the file. Are there any apparent trends in this data? If so, are the trends the same for the different types of crimes?

Figure 2.26   Crime Data

	A	B	C	D	E	F	G	H	I	J	K
1	Year	Population	Violent crime total	Murder and nonnegligent manslaughter	Forcible rape	Robbery	Aggravated assault	Property crime total	Burglary	Larceny-theft	Motor vehicle theft
2	1960	179,323,175	288,460	9,110	17,190	107,840	154,320	3,095,700	912,100	1,855,400	328,200
3	1961	182,992,000	289,390	8,740	17,220	106,670	156,760	3,198,600	949,600	1,913,000	336,000
4	1962	185,771,000	301,510	8,530	17,550	110,860	164,570	3,450,700	994,300	2,089,600	366,800
5	1963	188,483,000	316,970	8,640	17,650	116,470	174,210	3,792,500	1,086,400	2,297,800	408,300
6	1964	191,141,000	364,220	9,360	21,420	130,390	203,050	4,200,400	1,213,200	2,514,400	472,800
7	1965	193,526,000	387,390	9,960	23,410	138,690	215,330	4,352,000	1,282,500	2,572,600	496,900
8	1966	195,576,000	430,180	11,040	25,820	157,990	235,330	4,793,300	1,410,100	2,822,000	561,200
9	1967	197,457,000	499,930	12,240	27,620	202,910	257,160	5,403,500	1,632,100	3,111,600	659,800
10	1968	199,399,000	595,010	13,800	31,670	262,840	286,700	6,125,200	1,858,900	3,482,700	783,600

Excel Tip *Note the format of the variable names in row 1. If you have long variable names, one possibility is to align them vertically and check the Wrap Text option. (These are both available through the Format Cells command, which can be accessed by right-clicking any cell.) With these changes, the row 1 labels are neither too tall nor too wide.*

Objective   To see how time series graphs help to detect trends in crime data.

Solution

It is actually quite easy to create a time series graph with Excel tools only—no add-ins. We illustrate the process in the Time Series worksheet of the finished version of the crime file. But as usual, StatTools is a bit quicker and easier. We will illustrate a few of the many time series graphs you could create from this data set. As usual, start by designating a StatTools data set. Then select the Time Series Graph item from the Time Series and Forecasting dropdown list. (Note that this item is *not* in the Summary Graphs group.) The resulting dialog box appears in Figure 2.27. At the top, you can

Figure 2.27

StatTools Time Series Graph Dialog Box

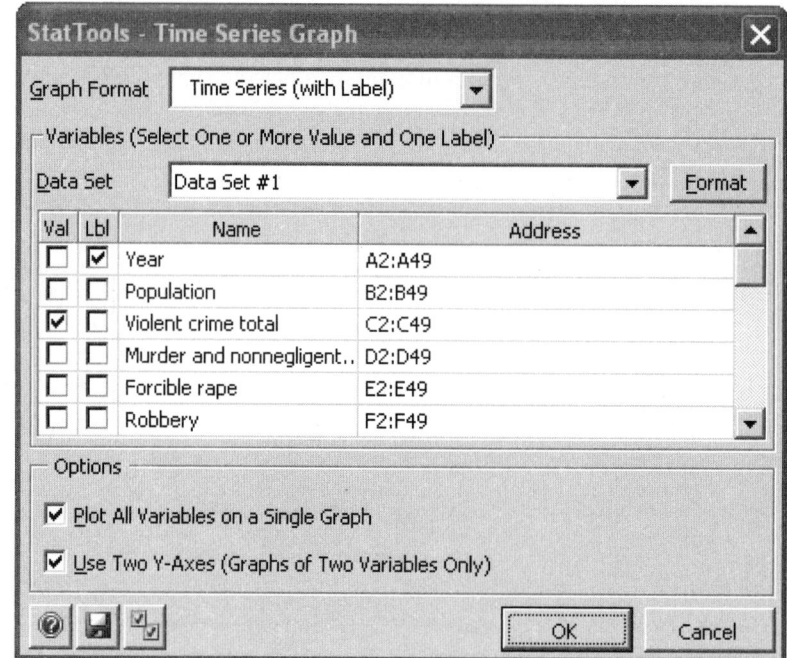

choose between a graph with a label and one without a label. The label is for time, so if you have a time variable (in this case, Year), choose the "with label" option. This leads to two columns of variables, one for the label (Lbl) and one for values (Val). Check Year in the Lbl column and select one or more variables in the Val column. For this first graph, we selected the Violent crime total and Property crime total variables to get started.

When you select multiple Val variables, the first option at the bottom lets you plot all variables in a single chart or create a separate chart for each. We chose the former. Furthermore, when you select *exactly two* Val variables, you can use two different Y-axis scales for the two variables. This is useful when they are of very different magnitudes, as is the case for violent and property crimes, so we checked this option. (This option isn't available if you select *more* than two Val variables. In this case, all are forced to share the same Y-axis scale.) The resulting time series graph appears in Figure 2.28. The graph shows that both types of crimes increased sharply until the early 1990s and have been gradually decreasing since then.

However, the time series population in Figure 2.29 indicates that the U.S. population has increased steadily since 1960, so it is possible that the trend in crime *rates* is different

The whole purpose of time series graphs is to detect historical patterns in the data. In this crime example, we are looking for broad trends.

Figure 2.28   Total Violent and Property Crimes

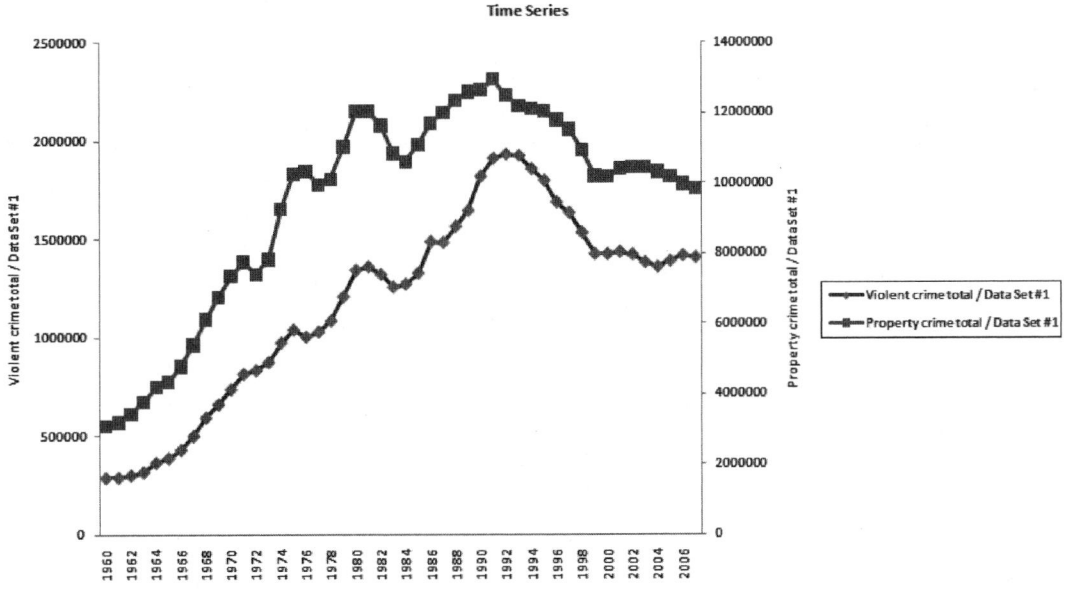

Figure 2.29   Population Totals

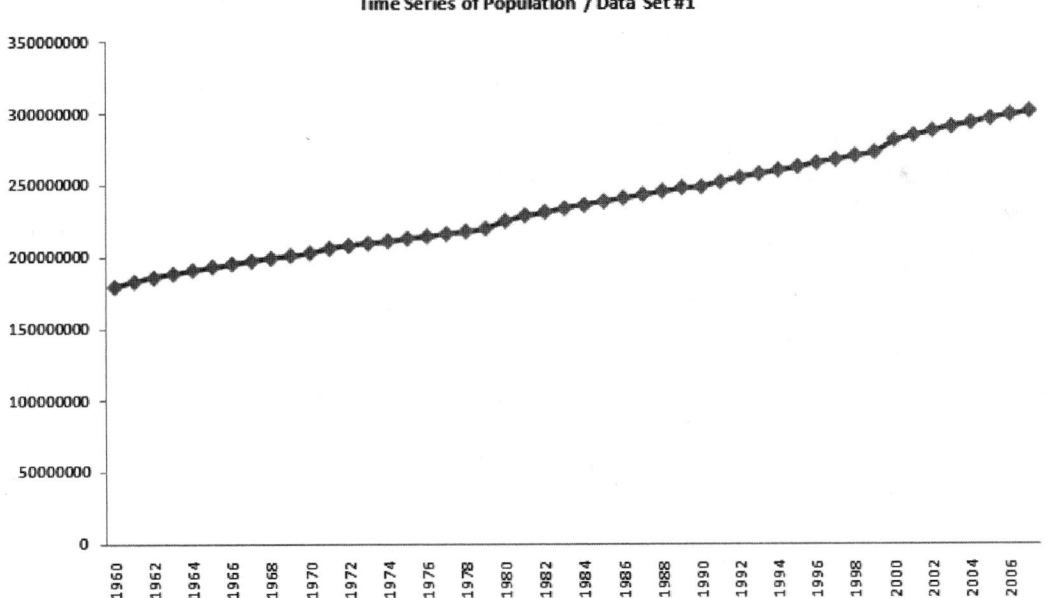

than the trends in Figure 2.28. This is indeed true, as seen in Figure 2.30. It shows the good news that the crime rate has been falling fairly rapidly since its peak in early 1990s.[3]

---

[3]Why did this occur? One compelling reason was suggested by Levitt and Dubner in their popular book *Freakonomics*. Read their somewhat controversial analysis to see if you agree.

Figure 2.30   Violent and Property Crime Rates

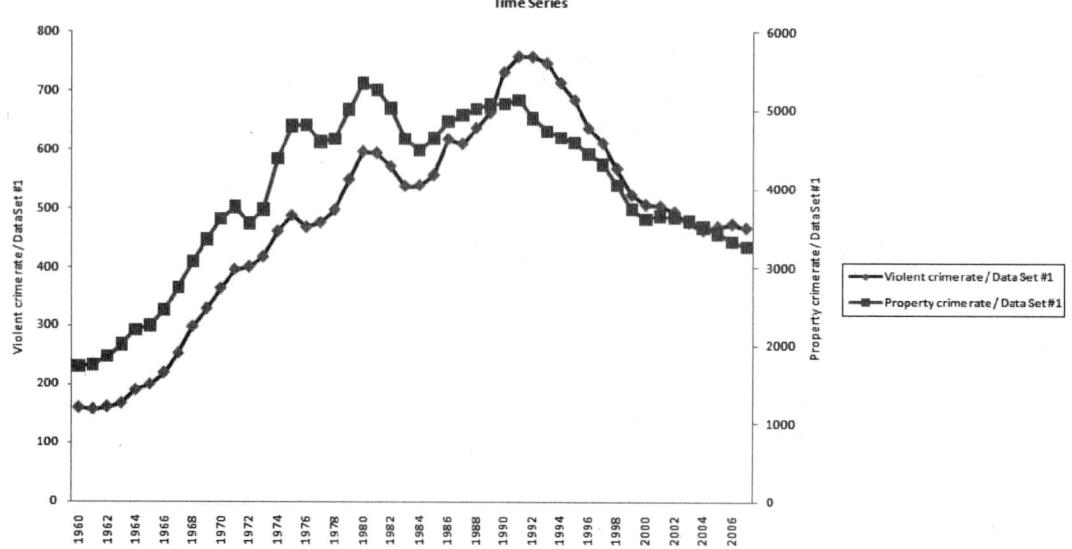

Think about interesting questions you might ask about crime in the U.S. These will lead naturally to particular time series graphs that help answer these questions.

StatTools Tip *StatTools remembers your previous choices for any particular type of analysis such as time series graphs. Therefore, if you run another analysis of the same type, make sure to uncheck variables you don't want in the current analysis.*

Because it is so easy, we also created two more time series graphs that appear in Figures 2.31 and 2.32. The first shows the crime rates for the various types of violent crimes, whereas the second does the same for property crimes. The patterns (up, then down) are similar for each type of crime, but they are certainly not identical. For example, the larceny-theft and motor vehicle theft rates both peaked in the early 1990s, but the burglary

Figure 2.31   Rates of Violent Crime Types

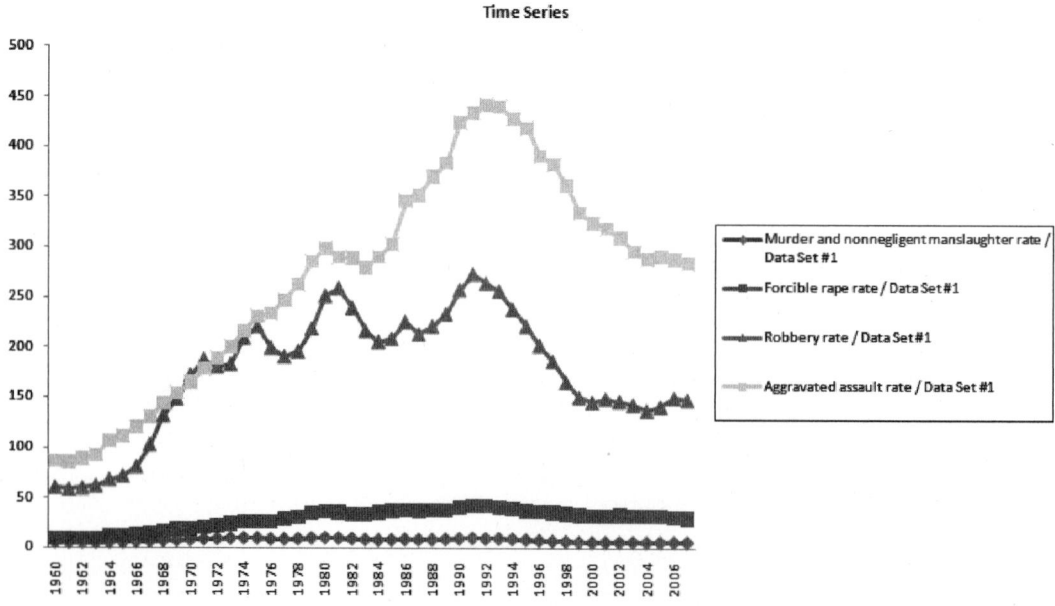

Figure 2.32   Rates of Property Crime Types

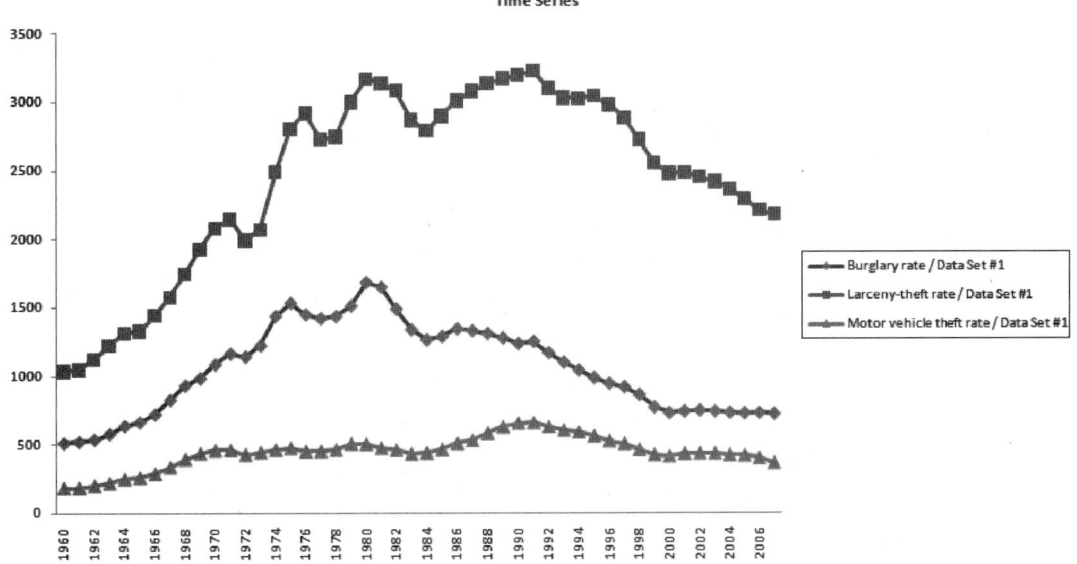

rate was well in decline by this time. Finally, Figure 2.31 indicates one problem with having multiple time series variables on a single chart—any variable with small values can become swamped by variables with much larger values. It might be a good idea to create two separate charts for these four variables, with murder and rape on one and robbery and aggravated assault on the other. Then you could see the murder and rape patterns more clearly. ■

CHANGES IN EXCEL 2010

One new feature in Excel 2010 is the *sparkline*. This is a mini-chart embedded in a cell. Although it applies to any kind of data, it is especially useful for time series data. Try the following. Open a file, such as the problem file **P03_30.xlsx**, that has multiple time series, one per column. Highlight the cell below the last time series value of the first time series, and click on the Line item in the Sparklines group on the Insert ribbon. In the resulting dialog box, highlight the data in the first time series. You will get a mini-time series graph in the cell. Now copy this cell across for the other time series, and increase the row height to expand the graphs. Change any of the time series values to see how the sparklines change automatically. We suspect that these instant-graph sparklines will become very popular.

As we mentioned earlier, traditional summary measures such as means, medians, and standard deviations are often not very meaningful for time series data, at least not for the original data. However, it is often useful to find differences or percentage changes in the data from period to period and then report traditional measures of these. The following example illustrates these ideas.

EXAMPLE   2.6 THE DJIA INDEX

The Dow Jones Industrial Average (DJIA or simply "the Dow") is an index of 30 large publicly traded U.S. stocks and is one of the most quoted stock indexes. The file **DJIA Monthly Close.xlsx** contains monthly values of the Dow from 1950 through 2009. What is a useful way to summarize the data in this file?

Objective   To find useful ways to summarize the monthly Dow data.

Figure 2.33 Summary Measures and Graph of the Dow

One Variable Summary	Closing Value Data Set #1
Mean	3222.12
Std.Dev.	3840.15
Median	952.39
1st Quartile	755.23
3rd Quartile	3913.42

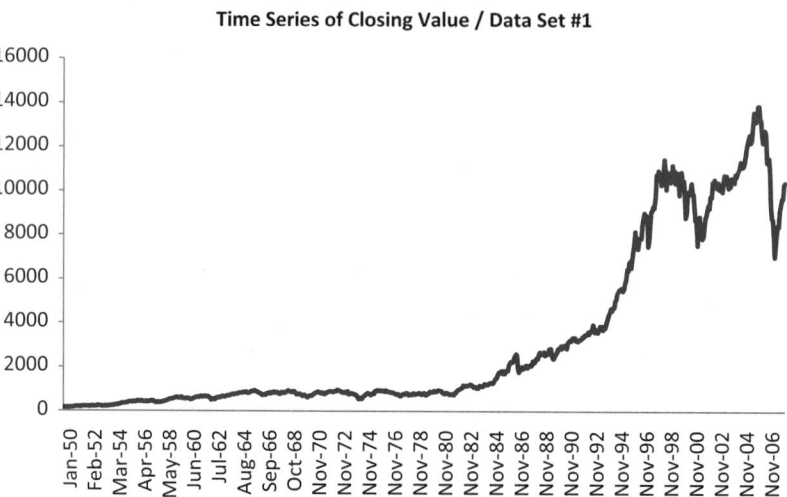

Solution

A time series graph and a few summary measures of the Dow appear in Figure 2.33. The graph clearly shows a gradual increase through the early 1990s (except for Black Monday in 1987), then a sharp increase through the rest of the 1990s, and finally huge swings in the past decade. The mean (3222), the median (952), and any of the other traditional summary measures are of historical interest at best.

In situations like this, it is useful to look at percentage changes in the Dow. These have been calculated in the file and have been used to create the summary measures and time series graph in Figure 2.34. The graph shows that these percentage changes have fluctuated around zero, sometimes with wild swings (like Black Monday). Actually, the mean and median of the percentage changes are slightly positive, about 0.64% and 0.85%, respectively.

Figure 2.34 Summary Measures and Graph of Percentage Changes of the Dow

One Variable Summary	Percentage Change Data Set #1
Mean	0.00638
Std.Dev.	0.04175
Median	0.00851
1st Quartile	-0.01648
3rd Quartile	0.03289

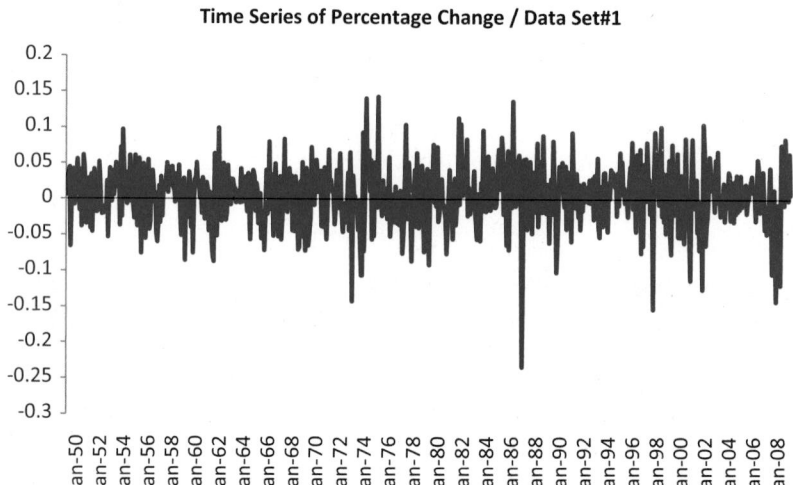

In addition, the quartiles show that 25% of the changes have been less than -1.65% and 25% have been greater than 3.29%. Finally, the empirical rules indicate, for example, that about 95% of the percentage changes over this period have been no more than two standard deviations (8.35%) from the mean. (You can check that the actual percentage within two standard deviations of the mean is 95.41%, so this empirical rule applies very well.)[4] ■

PROBLEMS

Level A

19. The file **P02_19.xlsx** lists annual percentage changes in the Consumer Price Index (CPI) from 1914 through 2008. Find and interpret the first and third quartiles and the interquartile range for these annual percentage changes. Discuss whether these are even meaningful summary measures for this time series data set. Suppose that the data set listed the actual CPI values, not percentage changes, for each year. Would the quartiles and interquartile range be meaningful in this case? Why or why not?

20. The Consumer Confidence Index (CCI) attempts to measure people's feelings about general business conditions, employment opportunities, and their own income prospects. Monthly average values of the CCI are listed in the file **P02_20.xlsx**.
  a. Create a time series graph of the CCI values.
  b. Have U.S. consumers become more or less confident through time?
  c. How would you explain recent variations in the overall trend of the CCI?

21. The file **P02_21.xlsx** contains monthly interest rates on 30-year fixed-rate mortgages in the United States from 1977 to 2009. The file also contains rates on 15-year fixed-rate mortgages from late 1991 to 2009. What conclusion(s) can you draw from a time series graph of these mortgage rates? Specifically, what has been happening to mortgage rates in general, and how does the behavior of the 30-year rates compare to the behavior of the 15-year rates?

22. The file **P02_22.xlsx** contains annual trade balances (exports minus imports) from 1980 to 2008.
  a. Create a times series graph for each of the three time series in this file.
  b. Characterize recent trends in the U.S. balance of trade figures using your time series graphs.

23. What has happened to the total number and average size of farms in the United States since the middle of the 20th century? Answer this question by creating a time series graph of the data from the U.S.

Department of Agriculture in the file **P02_23.xlsx**. Is the observed result consistent with your knowledge of the structural changes within the U.S. farming economy?

24. Is educational attainment in the United States on the rise? Explore this question by creating time series graphs for each of the variables in the file **P02_24.xlsx**. Comment on any observed trends in the annual educational attainment of the general U.S. population over the given period.

25. The monthly averages of the federal funds rate and the bank prime loan rate are listed in the file **P02_25.xlsx**.
  a. Describe the time series behavior of these two variables. Can you discern any cyclical or other patterns in the times series graphs of these key interest rates?
  b. Discuss whether it would make much sense, especially to a person at the present time, to quote traditional summary measures such as means or percentiles of these series.

Level B

26. In which months of the calendar year do U.S. gasoline service stations typically have their *lowest* retail sales levels? In which months of the calendar year do the service stations typically have their *highest* retail sales levels? Create time series graphs for the monthly data in the file **P02_26.xlsx** to respond to these two questions. There are really two series, one of actual values and one of seasonally adjusted values. The latter adjusts for any possible seasonality, such as higher values in June and lower values in January, so that any trends are more apparent.

27. The file **P02_27.xlsx** contains monthly data for total U.S. retail sales of building materials. There are really two series, one of actual values and one of seasonally adjusted values. The latter adjusts for any possible seasonality, such as higher values in June and lower values in January, so that any trends are more apparent.

[4]One of the problems asks you to check whether all three of the empirical rules apply to similar stock price data. The extreme tails are where there are some surprises.

a. Is there an observable trend in these data? That is, do the values of the series tend to increase or decrease over time?

b. Is there a seasonal pattern in these data? If so, what is the seasonal pattern?

28. The file **P02_28.xlsx** contains total monthly U.S. retail sales data for a number of years. There are really two series, one of actual sales and one of seasonally adjusted sales. The latter adjusts for any possible seasonality, such as higher sales in December and lower sales in February, so that any trends are more apparent.

a. Create a graph of both time series and comment on any observable trends, including a possible seasonal pattern, in the data. Does seasonal adjustment make a difference? How?

b. Based on your time series graph of actual sales, make a qualitative projection about the total retail sales levels for the next 12 months. Specifically, in which months of the subsequent year do you expect retail sales levels to be *highest?* In which months of the subsequent year do you expect retail sales levels to be *lowest?*

2.6 OUTLIERS AND MISSING VALUES

Most textbooks on data analysis, including this one, tend to use example data sets that are "cleaned up." Unfortunately, the data sets you are likely to encounter in your jobs are often not so clean. Two particular problems you will encounter are outliers and missing data, the topics of this section. There are no easy answers for dealing with these problems, but you should at least be aware of the issues.

2.6.1 Outliers

An **outlier** is literally a value or an entire observation that lies well outside of the norm. For the baseball data, Alex Rodriguez's salary of $33 million is definitely an outlier. This is indeed his correct salary—the number wasn't entered incorrectly—but it is way beyond what most players make. Actually, statisticians disagree on an exact definition of an outlier. Going by the third empirical rule, you might define an outlier as any value more than three standard deviations from the mean, but this is only a rule of thumb. Let's just agree to define outliers as *extreme* values, and then for any particular data set, you can decide how extreme a value needs to be to be labeled an outlier.

Sometimes an outlier is easy to detect and deal with. For example, this is often the case with data entry errors. Suppose a data set includes a Height variable, a person's height measured in inches, and you see a value of 720. This is certainly an outlier—and it is certainly an error. Once you spot it, you can go back and check this observation to see what the person's height should be. Maybe an extra 0 was accidentally appended and the true value is 72. In any case, this type of outlier can usually be fixed easily.

Sometimes a careful check of the variable values, one variable at a time, will not reveal any outliers, but there still might be unusual *combinations* of values. For example, it would be strange to find a person with Age equal to 10 and Height equal to 72. Neither of these values is unusual by itself, but the combination is certainly unusual. Again, this would probably be a result of a data entry error, but it would be harder to spot. (The scatterplots discussed in the next chapter are useful for spotting unusual combinations.)

It isn't always easy to detect outliers, but an even more important issue is what to do about them. Of course, if they are due to data entry errors, they can be fixed, but what if they are legitimate values like Alex Rodriguez's salary? One or a few wild outliers like this one can dominate a statistical analysis. For example, they can make a mean or standard deviation much different than if the outliers were not present.

For this reason, some people argue, rather naïvely, that outliers should be eliminated before running statistical analyses. However, it is *not* appropriate to eliminate outliers simply because the resulting analysis comes out "nicer" without them. There has to be a legitimate reason for eliminating outliers, and such a reason sometimes exists. For example, suppose you want to analyze salaries of "typical" managers at your company. Then it is probably appropriate to eliminate the CEO and possibly other high-ranking executives from the analysis, arguing that they aren't really part of the population of interest and would just throw off the results. Or if you are interested in the selling prices of "typical" homes in some community, it is probably appropriate to eliminate the few homes that sell for over $2 million, again arguing that these are not the types of homes you are interested in.

One good way of dealing with outliers is to report results with the outliers and without them.

Probably the best advice we can give for dealing with outliers is to run the analyses two ways: with the outliers and without them. This way, you can report the results both ways—and you are being honest.

2.6.2 Missing Values

There is no missing data in the baseball salary data set. All 818 observations have a value for each of the four variables. For real data sets, however, this is probably the exception rather than the rule. Most real data sets unfortunately have gaps in the data. This could be because a person didn't want to provide all the requested personal information (what business is it of yours how old I am or whether I drink alcohol?), it could be because data doesn't exist (stock prices in the 1990s for companies that went public after 2000), or it could be because some values are simply unknown. Whatever the reason, you will undoubtedly encounter data sets with varying degrees of **missing values**.

As with outliers, there are two issues: how to detect missing values and what to do about them. The first issue isn't as trivial as you might imagine. For an Excel data set, you might expect missing data to be obvious from blank cells. This is certainly one possibility, but there are others. Perhaps surprisingly, missing data are coded in a variety of strange ways. One common method is to code missing values with an unusual number such as –9999 or 9999. Another method is to code missing values with a symbol such as – or *. If you know the code (and it is often supplied in a footnote), then it is usually a good idea, at least in Excel, to perform a global search and replace, replacing all of the missing value codes with blanks.

The more important issue is what to do about missing values. One option is to simply ignore them. Then you will have to be aware of how the software deals with missing values. For example, if you use Excel's AVERAGE function on a column of data with some missing values, it will react the way you would hope and expect—it adds all the existing values and divides by the number of existing values. StatTools reacts in the same way for all of the measures discussed in this chapter (after alerting you that there are indeed missing values). We will say more about how StatTools deals with missing data for other analyses in later chapters. If you are using other statistical software such as SPSS or SAS, you should read its online help to learn how its various statistical analyses deal with missing data.

Because this is such an important topic in real-world data analysis, researchers have studied many ways of filling in the gaps so that the missing data problem goes away (or is at least disguised). One possibility is to fill in all of the missing values in a column with the average of the existing values in that column. Indeed, this is an option in some software packages, but we don't believe it is usually a very good option. (Is there any reason to believe that missing values would be average values if they were known? Probably not.) Another possibility is to examine the existing values in the *row* of any missing value. It is possible that they provide some information on what the missing value should be. For example, if a person is male, is 55 years old, has an MBA degree from Harvard, and has been a manager at an oil company for 25 years, this should probably help to predict his missing salary. (It probably isn't below $100,000.) We will not discuss this issue any further here because it is quite complex, and there are no easy answers. But be aware that you will undoubtedly have to deal with missing data at some point in your jobs, either by ignoring the missing values or by filling in the gaps in some way.

Level A

29. The file **P02_29.xlsx** contains monthly percentages of on-time arrivals at several of the largest U.S. airports and all of the major airlines from 1988 to 2008. The "By Airline" sheet contains a lot of missing data, presumably because some the airlines were not in existence in 1988 and some went out of business before 2008. The "By Airport" sheet contains missing data only for Atlantic City International Airport (and we're not sure why).
   a. Use StatTools to calculate summary measures (means, medians, standard deviations, and any other measures you would like to report) for each airline and each airport. How does it deal with missing data?
   b. Use StatTools to create histograms for a few of the airports and a few of the airlines, including Atlantic City International. How does it deal with missing data?
   c. Use StatTools to create time series graphs for a few of the airports and a few of the airlines, including Atlantic City International. How does it deal with missing data?
   d. Which airports and which airlines have done a good job? Which would you like to avoid?

30. *The Wall Street Journal CEO Compensation Study* analyzed CEO pay for many U.S. companies with fiscal year 2008 revenue of at least $5 billion that filed their proxy statements between October 2008 and March 2009. The data are in the file **P02_30.xlsx**. (Note: This data set is a somewhat different CEO compensation data set from the one used as an example in the next chapter.)
   a. Create a new variable that is the sum of salary and bonus, and create a box plot of this new variable.
   b. As the box plot key indicates, mild outliers are observations between 1.5 IQR (interquartile range) and 3.0 IQR from the edge of the box, whereas extreme outliers are greater than 3 IQR from the edge of the box. Use these definitions to identify the names of all CEOs who are mild outliers and all those who are extreme outliers.

Level B

31. There is no consistent way of defining an outlier that everyone agrees upon. For example, some people refer to an outlier that is any observation more than three standard deviations from the mean. Other people use the box plot definition, where an outlier (moderate or extreme) is any observation more than 1.5 IQR from the edges of the box, and some people care only about the extreme box plot-type outliers, those that are 3.0 IQR from the edges of the box. The file **P02_18.xlsx** contains daily percentage changes in the S&P 500 index over a four-year period. Identify outliers—days when the percentage change was unusually large in either a negative or positive direction—according to each of these three definitions. Which definition produces the most outliers?

32. Sometimes it is possible that missing data are predictive in the sense that rows with missing data are somehow different from rows without missing data. Check this with the file **P02_32.xlsx**, which contains blood pressures for 1000 (fictional) people, along with variables that can be related to blood pressure. These other variables have a number of missing values, presumably because the people didn't want to report certain information.
   a. For each of these other variables, find the mean and standard deviation of blood pressure for all people without missing values and for all people with missing values. Can you conclude that the presence or absence of data for any of these other variables has anything to do with blood pressure?
   b. Some analysts suggest filling in missing data for a variable with the *mean* of the nonmissing values for that variable. Do this for the missing data in the blood pressure data. In general, do you think this is a valid way of filling in missing data? Why or why not?

2.7 EXCEL TABLES FOR FILTERING, SORTING, AND SUMMARIZING[5]

In this section, we introduce a great tool that was introduced in Excel 2007: tables. Tables were somewhat available in previous versions of Excel, but they were never called tables before, and some of the really useful features of Excel 2007 tables are new.

It is useful to begin with some terminology and history. Earlier in this chapter, we discussed data arranged in a rectangular range of rows and columns, where each row is an observation and each column is a variable, with variable names at the top of each column.

---

[5]This section indicates how powerful the Excel 2007 table filtering tools are. However, if you are interested in more advanced filters or database ("D") functions, see Chapter 2's "Advanced Filter and Database Functions" on this textbook's Web site.

Informally, we refer to such a range as a data set. In fact, this is the technical term used by StatTools. In previous versions of Excel, data sets were called lists, and Excel provided several tools for dealing with lists. In Excel 2007, recognizing the importance of data sets, Microsoft made them much more prominent and provided even better tools for analyzing them. Specifically, you now have the ability to designate a rectangular data set as a table and then employ a number of new and powerful tools for analyzing tables. These tools include filtering, sorting, and summarizing.

We illustrate **Excel tables** in the following example. Before proceeding, however, we mention one important caveat. Some of the tools discussed in this section will not work on an Excel file in the old .xls format. Therefore, we purposely illustrate them on files saved in the new .xlsx format (new to Excel 2007).

EXAMPLE | 2.7 HYTEX'S CUSTOMER DATA

The file **Catalog Marketing.xlsx** contains data on 1000 customers of HyTex, a (fictional) direct marketing company, for the current year. A sample of the data appears in Figure 2.35. The variables are defined as follows.

Figure 2.35 HyTex Customer Data

	A	B	C	D	E	F	G	H	I	J	K	L	M	N	O
1	Person	Age	Gender	OwnHome	Married	Close	Salary	Children	History	Catalogs	Region	State	City	FirstPurchase	AmountSpent
2	1	1	0	0	0	1	$16,400	1	1	12	South	Florida	Orlando	10/23/2003	$218
3	2	2	0	1	1	0	$108,100	3	3	18	Midwest	Illinois	Chicago	5/25/2001	$2,632
4	3	2	1	1	1	1	$97,300	1	NA	12	South	Florida	Orlando	8/18/2007	$3,048
5	4	3	1	1	1	1	$26,800	0	1	12	East	Ohio	Cleveland	12/26/2004	$435
6	5	1	1	0	0	1	$11,200	0	NA	6	Midwest	Illinois	Chicago	8/4/2007	$106
7	6	2	0	0	0	1	$42,800	0	2	12	West	Arizona	Phoenix	3/4/2005	$759
8	7	2	0	0	0	1	$34,700	0	NA	18	Midwest	Kansas	Kansas City	6/11/2007	$1,615
9	8	3	0	1	1	0	$80,000	0	3	6	West	California	San Francisco	8/17/2001	$1,985
10	9	2	1	1	0	1	$60,300	0	NA	24	Midwest	Illinois	Chicago	5/29/2007	$2,091
11	10	3	1	1	1	0	$62,300	0	3	24	South	Florida	Orlando	6/9/2003	$2,644

- Age: coded as 1 for 30 or younger, 2 for 31 to 55, 3 for 56 or older

- Gender: coded as 1 for males, 0 for females

- OwnHome: coded as 1 if the customer owns a home, 0 otherwise

- Married: coded as 1 if the customer is currently married, 0 otherwise

- Close: coded as 1 if the customer lives reasonably close to a shopping area that sells similar merchandise, 0 otherwise

- Salary: combined annual salary of the customer and spouse (if any)

- Children: number of children living with the customer

- History: coded as "NA" if the customer had no dealings with HyTex before this year, 1 if the customer was a low-spending customer last year, 2 if medium-spending, 3 if high-spending

- Catalogs: number of catalogs sent to the customer this year

- FirstPurchase: date of the customer's first purchase with HyTex

- AmountSpent: total amount of purchases made by the customer this year

In addition, the variables Region, State, and City indicate where the customer resides. HyTex wants to find some useful and quick information about its customers by using an Excel table. How can it proceed?

Objective To illustrate Excel tables for analyzing the HyTex data.

Solution

The range A1:O1001 is in the form of a data set—it is a rectangular range bounded by blank rows and columns, where each row is an observation, each column is a variable, and variable names appear in the top row. Therefore, it is a candidate for an Excel table. However, it doesn't benefit from the new table tools until you actually *designate* it as a table. To do so, select *any* cell in the data set, click on the Table button in the left part of the Insert ribbon (see Figure 2.36), and accept the default options. (An alternative way to designate an Excel table is to select any of the options on the Format as Table dropdown list on the Home ribbon.) Two things happen. First, the data set is designated as a table, it is formatted nicely, and a dropdown arrow appears next to each variable name, as shown in Figure 2.37. Second a new Table Tools Design ribbon becomes available (see Figure 2.38). This ribbon is available any time the active cell is inside a table. Note that the table is named Table1 by default (if this is the first table). However, you can change this to a more descriptive name if you like.

Figure 2.36 Insert Ribbon with Table Button

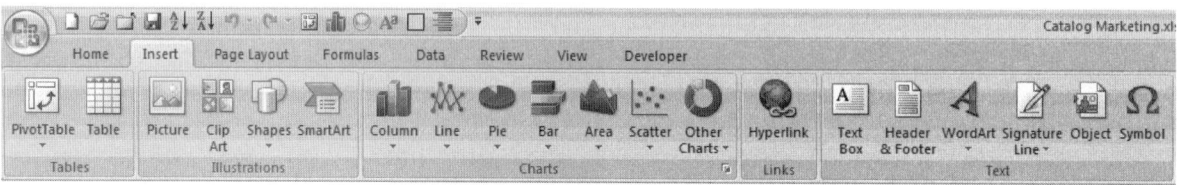

Figure 2.37 Table with Dropdown Arrows Next to Variable Names

	A	B	C	D	E	F	G	H	I	J	K	L	M	N	O
1	Perso	A	Gend	OwnHor	Marri	Clo	Sala	Childr	Histo	Catalo	Region	State	City	FirstPurcha	AmountSpe
2	1	1	0	0	0	1	$16,400	1	1	12	South	Florida	Orlando	10/23/2003	$218
3	2	2	0	1	1	0	$108,100	3	3	18	Midwest	Illinois	Chicago	5/25/2001	$2,632
4	3	2	1	1	1	1	$97,300	1	NA	12	South	Florida	Orlando	8/18/2007	$3,048
5	4	3	1	1	1	1	$26,800	0	1	12	East	Ohio	Cleveland	12/26/2004	$435
6	5	1	1	0	0	1	$11,200	0	NA	6	Midwest	Illinois	Chicago	8/4/2007	$106
7	6	2	0	0	0	1	$42,800	0	2	12	West	Arizona	Phoenix	3/4/2005	$759
8	7	2	0	0	0	1	$34,700	0	NA	18	Midwest	Kansas	Kansas City	6/11/2007	$1,615
9	8	3	0	1	1	0	$80,000	0	3	6	West	California	San Francisco	8/17/2001	$1,985
10	9	2	1	1	0	1	$60,300	0	NA	24	Midwest	Illinois	Chicago	5/29/2007	$2,091
11	10	3	1	1	1	0	$62,300	0	3	24	South	Florida	Orlando	6/9/2003	$2,644

Figure 2.38 Table Tools Design Ribbon

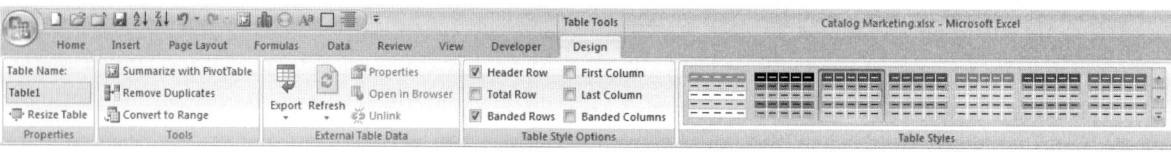

One handy feature of Excel tables is that the variable names remain visible even when you scroll down the screen. Try it to see how it works. When you scroll down far enough that the variable names would disappear, the column headers, A, B, C, and so on, change to the variable names. Therefore, you no longer need to freeze panes or split the screen to see the variable names. However, this works only when the active cell is within the table. If you click outside the table, the column headers revert back to A, B, C, and so on.

The dropdown arrows next to the variable names allow you to filter in many different ways. For example, click on the OwnHome dropdown list, uncheck the Select All option, and check the 1 option. This filters out all customers except those who own their own home. Filtering is discussed in much more detail later on, but at this point, just be aware that filtering does not *delete* any observations; it only hides them. There are three indications that the table has been filtered: (1) the row numbers are colored blue and some are missing; (2) a message appears at the bottom of the screen indicating that only 516 out of 1000 records are visible; and (3) there is a filter icon next to the OwnHome dropdown arrow. It is easy to remove this filter by opening the OwnHome dropdown list and selecting Clear Filter (but don't do so yet).

As illustrated in Figure 2.38, there are various options you can apply to tables, including the following:

- A number of table styles are available for making the table attractive. You can experiment with these, including the various table styles and table style options. Note the dropdown list in the Table Styles group. It gives you many more styles than the seven originally visible. In particular, at the top left of options, there is a "no color" style you might prefer.

- In the Tools group, you can click on Convert to Range. This undesignates the range as a table (and the dropdown arrows disappear).

- In the Properties group, you can change the name of the table. You can also click on the Resize Table button to expand or contract the table range.

- A particularly useful option is the Total Row in the Table Style Options group. If you check this, a new row is appended to the bottom of the table (see Figure 2.39). It creates a sum formula in the rightmost column.[6] This sum includes *only* the non-hidden rows. To prove this to youself, clear the OwnHome filter and check the sum. It increases to $1,216,768. This total row is quite flexible. First, you can summarize the last column by a number of summary measures, such as Average, Max, Min, Count, and others. To do so, select cell O1002 and click on the dropdown list that appears. Second, you can summarize any other column in the table in the same way. For example, if you select cell G1002, a dropdown list appears for Salary, and you can then summarize Salary with the same summarizing options.

The Total row in an Excel table summarizes only the visible data. The data that has been filtered out is ignored.

Figure 2.39 Total Row

	Children	History	Catalogs	Region	State	City	FirstPurchase	AmountSpent
994	0	3	18	Midwest	Ohio	Cincinnati	10/23/2004	$1,857
996	0	2	6	South	Florida	Miami	7/7/2005	$654
997	0	2	12	West	Washington	Seattle	8/14/2007	$843
999	0	3	18	East	Pennsylvania	Philadelphia	8/9/2005	$2,546
1001	1	3	24	West	Utah	Salt Lake City	3/9/2004	$2,464
1002								$796,260

[6]The actual formula is =**SUBTOTAL(109,[AmountSpent])**, where 109 is a code for summing. However, you never need to type any such formula; you can choose the summary function you want from the dropdown list.

Excel tables have a lot of built-in intelligence. Although there is not enough space here to give a full account, try the following to see what we mean:

- In cell R2 (or any cell in row 2 outside the table), enter a formula by typing an equals sign, pointing to cell O2, typing a divide sign (/), and pointing to cell G2. You do *not* get the usual formula =O2/G2. Instead you get =Table1[[#This Row],[AmountSpent]]/Table1[[#This Row],[Salary]]. This is certainly not the Excel syntax you are used to, and it is pretty ugly, but it makes perfect sense.

- Similarly, you can expand the table with a new variable, such as the ratio of AmountSpent to Salary. Start by typing the variable name Ratio in cell P1. Then in cell P2, enter a formula exactly as you did in the previous bullet. You will notice two things. First, as soon as you enter the Ratio label, column P becomes part of the table. Second, as soon as you enter the new formula in one cell, it is copied to all of column P. This is what we mean by table intelligence.

- We saved the best for last. Excel tables expand automatically as new rows are added to the bottom or new columns are added to the right. (You saw this latter behavior in the previous bullet.) To appreciate the benefit of this, suppose you have a monthly time series data set. You designate it as a table and then build a line chart from it to show the time series behavior. Later on, if you add new data to the bottom of the table, the chart will *automatically* update to include the new data. This is a great feature. In fact, when we discuss pivot tables in the next chapter, we will recommend always basing them on tables, not ranges. Then they too will update automatically when new data is added to the table. ∎

2.7.1 Filtering

We now discuss ways of filtering data sets—that is, finding records that match particular criteria. Before getting into details, there are two aspects of filtering you should be aware of. First, this section is concerned with the types of filters called AutoFilter in previous versions of Excel (2003 and earlier). The term AutoFilter implied that these were very simple filters, easily learned in a few minutes. If you wanted to do any complex filtering, you had to move beyond AutoFilter to Excel's Advanced Filter tool. Excel 2007 still has Advanced Filter. However, the term AutoFilter has been changed to Filter to indicate that these "easy" filters are now more powerful than the old AutoFilter. Fortunately, they are just as easy as AutoFilter.

Filtering is certainly possible without using Excel tables, but there are definitely advantages to filtering with Excel tables.

Second, one way to filter is to create an Excel table, as indicated in the previous subsection. This automatically provides the dropdown arrows next to the field names that allow you to filter. Indeed, this is the way we will filter in this section: on an existing table. However, a designated table is not required for filtering. You can filter on any rectangular data set with variable names. There are actually three ways to do so. For each method, the active cell should be a cell inside the data set.

(1) Use the Filter button from the Sort & Filter dropdown list on the Home ribbon.

(2) Use the Filter button from the Sort & Filter group on the Data ribbon.

(3) Right-click on any cell in the table and choose the Filter option. You get several options, the most popular of which is Filter by Selected Cell's Value. For example, if the selected cell has value 1 and is in the Children column, then only customers with a single child will remain visible. (This behavior should be familiar to Access users.)

The point is that Microsoft realizes how important filtering is to Excel users. Therefore, they have made filtering a very prominent and powerful tool in Excel 2007.

As far as we can tell, the two main advantages of filtering on a table, as opposed to the three options just listed, are the nice formatting (banded rows, for example) provided by tables, and, more importantly, the totals row. If this totals row is showing, it summarizes *only* the visible records; the hidden rows are ignored.

We now continue Example 2.7 to illustrate a number of filtering possibilities. Unlike some "how to" Excel books, we won't lead you through a lot of descriptions and screenshots. Once you know the possibilities that are available, you should find them extremely easy to use.

| EXAMPLE | **EXAMPLE 2.7 HyTex's Customer Data (Continued)** |

The HyTex company wants to analyze its customer data by applying one or more filters to the data. It has already designated the data set as an Excel table. What types of filters might be useful?

Objective   To investigate the types of filters that might be applied to the HyTex data.

Solution

There is almost no limit to the filters you can apply, but here are a few possibilities.

- **Filter on one or more values in a field.** Click on the Catalogs dropdown arrow. You will see five checkboxes, all checked: Select All, 6, 12, 18, and 24. To select one or more values, uncheck Select All and then check any values you want to filter on, such as 6 and 24. In this case, only customers who received 6 or 24 catalogs will remain visible. (In Excel 2003 and earlier, it wasn't possible to select more than one value this way. Now it's easy.)

- **Filter on more than one field.** With the Catalogs filter still in place, create a filter on some other field, such as customers with one child. When there are filters on multiple fields, only records that meet *all* of the criteria are visible, in this case customers with one child who received 6 or 24 catalogs.

- **Filter on a continuous numerical field.** The Salary and AmountSpent fields are basically continuous fields, so it would not make much sense to filter on one or a few particular values. However, it does make sense to filter on *ranges* of values, such as all salaries greater than $75,000. This is easy. Click on the dropdown arrow next to Salary and select Number Filters. You will see a number of obvious possibilities, including Greater Than.

- **Top 10 and Above/Below Average filters.** Continuing the previous bullet, the Number Filters include Top 10, Above Average, and Below Average options. These are particularly useful if you like to see the highs and the lows. The Above Average and Below Average filters do exactly what their names imply. The Top 10 filter is actually more flexible than its name implies. It can be used to select the top *n* items (where you can choose *n*), the bottom *n* items, the top *n* percent of items, or the bottom *n* percent of items. Note that if a Top 10 filter is used on a text field, the ordering is alphabetical. If it is used on a date field, the ordering is chronological.

- **Filter on a text field.** If you click on the dropdown arrow for a text field such as Region, you can choose one or more of its values, such as East and South, to filter on. You can also select the Text Filters item, which provides a number of choices, including Begins With, Ends With, Contains, and others. For example, if there were

The number of ways you can filter with Excel's newest tools is virtually unlimited. Don't be afraid to experiment. You can always clear filters to get back to where you started.

an Address field, you could use the Begins With option to find all addresses that begin with P.O. Box.

- **Filter on a date field.** Excel 2007 has great built-in intelligence for filtering on dates. If you click on the FirstPurchase arrow, you will see an item for each year in the data set with plus signs next to them. By clicking on the plus signs, you can drill down to months and then days for as much control as you need. Figure 2.40 shows one possibility, where we have filtered out all dates except the last part of July 2007. In addition, if you click on the Date Filters item, you get a number of possibilities, such as Yesterday, Next Week, Last Month, and many others. There aren't many possibilities regarding dates that Microsoft hasn't included.

Figure 2.40

Filtering on a Date Variable

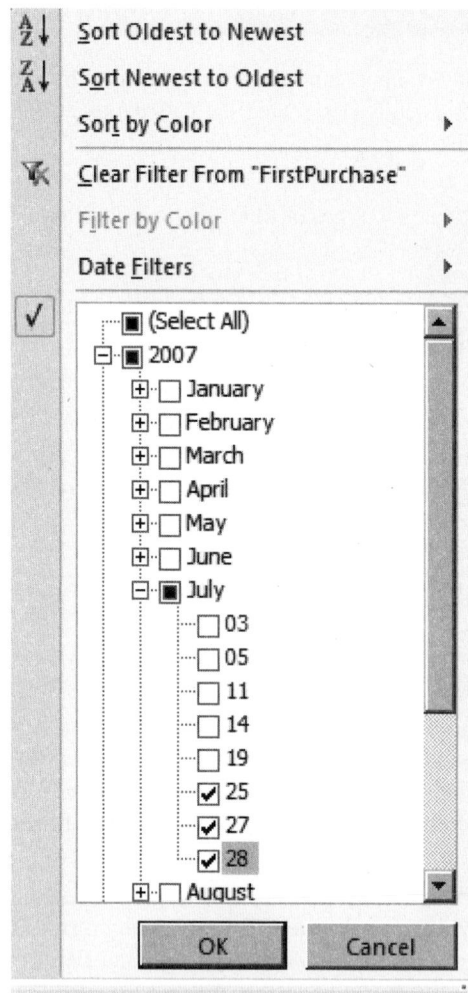

- **Filter on color or icon.** Excel 2007 has many ways to color cells or put icons in cells. Often the purpose is to denote the sizes of the numbers in the cells, such as red for small numbers and green for large numbers. We won't cover the possibilities in this book, but you can experiment with Conditional Formatting on the Home ribbon. The point is that cells are often colored in certain ways or contain certain icons. Therefore, Excel 2007 allows you to filter on background color, font color, or icon. For example, if certain salaries are colored yellow, you can isolate them by filtering on yellow. We are not sure how often this feature will be used, but it is available and easy to use.

- **Use a custom filter.** If nothing else works, you can try a custom filter, available at the bottom of the Number Filters, Text Filters, and Date Filters lists. Figures 2.41 and 2.42 illustrate two possibilities. The first of these filters out all salaries between $25,000 and $75,000. Without a custom filter, this wouldn't be possible. The second uses the * wildcard to find regions ending in *est* (West and Midwest). Admittedly, this is an awkward way to perform this filter, but it indicates how flexible custom filters can be.

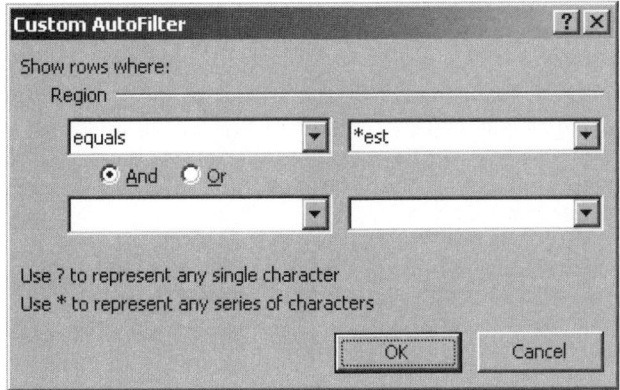

We remind you once again that if you filter on an Excel table and you have summary measures in a total row at the bottom of the table, these summary measures are based *only* on the filtered data; they ignore the hidden rows.

One final comment about filters is that when you click on the dropdown arrow for any variable, you always get three items at the top for *sorting,* not filtering (see Figure 2.40, for example). These allow you to perform the obvious sorts, from high to low or vice versa, and they even allow you to sort on color. As with filtering, you do not need to designate an Excel table to perform sorting (the popular A-Z and Z-A buttons work just fine without tables), but sorting is made even easier with tables.

Now that you know the possibilities, here is one particular filter you can try. Suppose HyTex wants information about all middle-aged married customers with at least two children who have above average salaries, own their own home, and live in Indiana or Kentucky. We imagine that you can run this filter in a few seconds. The result, sorted in decreasing order of AmountSpent and shown in Figure 2.43, indicates that the

Figure 2.43   Results from a Typical Filter

	A	B	C	D	E	F	G	H	I	J	K	L	M	N	O
1	Perso	A	Gend	OwnHor	Marri	Clo	Sala	Childr	Histc	Catalc	Region	State	City	FirstPurcha	AmountSpe
155	154	2	0	1	1	0	$96,800	3	NA		24	Midwest	Kentucky	Louisville	3/7/2007	$3,082
163	162	2	0	1	1	1	$62,200	3	NA		24	Midwest	Indiana	Indianapolis	6/17/2007	$2,119
245	244	2	1	1	1	0	$82,400	2	3		24	Midwest	Indiana	Indianapolis	11/25/2006	$2,035
370	369	2	1	1	1	0	$113,400	3	3		18	Midwest	Kentucky	Louisville	6/15/2006	$1,790
430	429	2	1	1	1	1	$113,000	2	2		18	Midwest	Kentucky	Louisville	3/3/2007	$1,554
570	569	2	1	1	1	1	$70,400	2	NA		12	Midwest	Indiana	Indianapolis	4/28/2007	$1,127
764	763	2	0	1	1	1	$85,500	2	2		18	Midwest	Kentucky	Louisville	6/7/2003	$895
790	789	2	1	1	1	1	$74,500	2	2		12	Midwest	Indiana	Indianapolis	4/12/2002	$824
804	803	2	0	1	1	1	$72,200	2	2		18	Midwest	Kentucky	Louisville	10/1/2003	$715
851	850	2	1	1	1	1	$77,100	2	2		6	Midwest	Indiana	Indianapolis	7/3/2006	$568
1002	Total						$84,750								$14,709

average salary for these 10 customers is $84,750, and their total amount spent at HyTex is $1,4709. (We summarized Salary by average and AmountSpent by sum in the totals row.) ∎

PROBLEMS

Level A

33. The file **P02_03.xlsx** contains data from a survey of 399 people regarding an environmental policy. Use filters for each of the following.
   a. Identify all respondents who are female, middle-aged, and have two children. What is the average salary of these respondents?
   b. Identify all respondents who are elderly and strongly disagree with the environmental policy. What is the average salary of these respondents?
   c. Identify all respondents who strongly agree with the environmental policy. What proportion of these individuals are young?
   d. Identify all respondents who are either (1) middle-aged men with at least one child and an annual salary of at least $50,000, or (2) middle-aged women with two or fewer children and an annual salary of at least $30,000. What are the mean and median salaries of the respondents who meet these conditions? What proportion of the respondents who satisfy these conditions agree or strongly agree with the environmental policy?

34. The file **P02_07.xlsx** includes data on 204 employees at the (fictional) company Beta Technologies. Use filters for each of the following.
   a. Identify all employees who are male and have exactly 4 years of post-secondary education. What is the average salary of these employees?
   b. Find the average salary of all female employees who have exactly 4 years of post-secondary education. How does this mean salary compare to the one obtained in part **a**?

   c. Identify all employees who have more than 4 years of post-secondary education. What proportion of these employees are male?
   d. Identify all full-time employees who are either (1) females between the ages of 30 and 50 (inclusive) with at least 5 years of prior work experience, at least 10 years of prior work experience at Beta, and at least 4 years of postsecondary education; or (2) males between the ages of 40 and 60 (inclusive) with at least 6 years of prior work experience, at least 12 years of prior work experience at Beta, and at least 4 years of postsecondary education.
   e. For those employees who meet the conditions specified in part **d**, compare the mean salary of the females with that of the males. Also, compare the median salary of the female employees with that of the male employees.
   f. What proportion of the full-time employees identified in part **d** earns less than $50,000 per year?

35. The file **P02_35.xlsx** contains (fictional) data from a survey of 500 randomly selected households. Use Excel filters to answer the following questions.
   a. What are the average monthly home mortgage payment, average monthly utility bill, and average total debt (excluding the home mortgage) of all homeowners residing in the southeast sector of the city?
   b. What are the average monthly home mortgage payment, average monthly utility bill, and average total debt (excluding the home mortgage) of all homeowners residing in the northwest sector of the city? How do these results compare to those found in part **a**?

c. What is the average annual income of the first household wage earners who rent their home (house or apartment)? How does this compare to the average annual income of the first household wage earners who own their home?

d. What proportion of the surveyed households contains a single person who owns his or her home?

36. Recall that the file **Supermarket Transactions.xlsx** contains over 14,000 transactions made by supermarket customers over a period of approximately two years. Use Excel filters to answer the following questions.

a. What proportion of these transactions are made by customers who are married?

b. What proportion of these transactions are made by customers who do not own a home?

c. What proportion of these transactions are made by customers who have at least one child?

d. What proportion of these supermarket customers are single and own a home?

Level B

37. The file **P02_35.xlsx** contains (fictional) data from a survey of 500 randomly selected households. Use Excel filters to answer the following questions.

a. Identify households that own their home and have a monthly home mortgage payment in the top quartile of the monthly payments for all households.

b. Identify households with monthly expenditures on utilities that are within two standard deviations of the mean monthly expenditure on utilities for all households.

c. Identify households with total indebtedness (excluding home mortgage) less than 10% of the household's primary annual income level.

2.8 CONCLUSION

The summary measures, charts, and tables we have discussed in this chapter are extremely useful for describing variables in data sets. We call the methods in this chapter (and the next chapter) *exploratory* methods because they allow you to explore the characteristics of the data and at least tentatively answer interesting questions. Most of these tools have been available for many years, but with the powerful software now accessible to virtually everyone, the tools can be applied quickly and easily to gain insights. We can promise that you will be using many if not all of these tools in your jobs. Indeed, the knowledge you gain from these early chapters is arguably the most valuable knowledge you will gain from the book.

To help you remember which analyses are appropriate for different questions and different data types, and which tools are useful for performing the various analyses, we have created the taxonomy in the file **Data Analysis Taxonomy.xlsx**. (It doesn't fit nicely on the printed page.) Feel free to refer back to the diagram in this file as you learn the tools in this chapter and the next chapter.

Summary of Key Terms

Term	Explanation	Excel	Pages	Equation
Population	Includes all objects of interest in a study— people, households, machines, etc.		24	
Sample	Representative subset of population, usually chosen randomly		24	
Variable (or field)	Attribute or measurement of members of a population, such as height, gender, or salary			
Observation (or record or case)	List of all variable values for a single member of a population		25	
Data set	(Usually) a rectangular array of data, with variables in columns, observations in rows, and variable names in the top row		25	

(continued)

Summary of Key Terms (*Continued*)

Term	Explanation	Excel	Pages	Equation
Data type	Several categorizations are possible: numerical versus categorical, discrete versus continuous, cross-sectional versus time series; categorical can be nominal or ordinal		25	
Dummy variable	A variable coded 1 or 0: 1 for observations in a category, 0 for observations not in the category		28	
Binned (or discretized) variable	Numerical variable that has been categorized into discrete categories called bins		28	
Counts of categories	Numbers of observations in various categories	COUNTIF function	30	
StatTools	Palisade add-in for data analysis in Excel	StatTools ribbon	34	
Mean	Average of observations	AVERAGE or StatTools	35	2.1
Median	Middle observation after sorting	MEDIAN or StatTools	35	
Mode	Most frequent observation	MODE	35	
Percentiles	Values that have specified percentages of observations below them	PERCENTILE or StatTools	36	
Quartiles	Values that have 25%, 50%, or 75% of observations below them	QUARTILE or StatTools	36	
Minimum	Smallest observation	MIN or StatTools	37	
Maximum	Largest observation	MAX or StatTools	37	
Concatenate	String together two or more pieces of text	& character (or CONCATENATE)	38	
Range	Difference between largest and smallest observations	MAX, MIN, or StatTools	38	
Interquartile range (IQR)	Difference between first and third quartiles	QUARTILE functions or StatTools	38	
Variance	Measure of variability; essentially the average of squared deviations from the mean	VAR (or VARP) or StatTools	38	2.2, 2.3
Standard deviation	Measure of variability in same units as observations; square root of variance	STDEV (or STDEVP) or StatTools	39	
Empirical rules	Rules that specify approximate percentage observations within one, two, or three standard deviations of mean for bell-shaped distributions		41	
Mean absolute Deviation (MAD)	Another measure of variability; average of absolute deviations from the mean	AVEDEV or StatTools	42	2.4
Skewness	When one tail of a distribution is longer than the other	SKEW or StatTools	42	
Kurtosis	Measure of "fatness" of tails of a distribution	KURT or StatTools	42	
Histogram	Chart of bin counts for a numerical variable; shows shape of the distribution	StatTools	48	

(*continued*)

Term	Explanation	Excel	Pages	Equation
Frequency table	Contains counts of observations in specified categories	COUNTIF or FREQUENCY	49	
Box plots	Alternative chart that shows the distribution of a numerical variable	StatTools	49	
Time series graph	Graph showing behavior through time of one or more time series variables	StatTools	48	
Outlier	Observation that lies outside of the general range of observations in a data set		64	
Missing values	Values that are not reported in a data set		65	
Excel tables	Rectangular ranges specified as *tables*; especially useful for sorting and filtering	Table from Insert ribbon	67	

PROBLEMS

Conceptual Questions

C.1. An airline analyst wishes to estimate the proportion of all American adults who are afraid to fly in light of the thwarted terrorist attack on a U.S. commercial airliner on December 25, 2009. To estimate this percentage, the analyst decides to survey 1500 Americans from across the nation. Identify the relevant sample and population in this situation.

C.2. The number of children living in each of a large number of randomly selected households is an example of which data type? Be specific.

C.3. Does it make sense to construct a histogram for the state of residence of randomly selected individuals in a sample? Explain why or why not.

C.4. Characterize the likely shape of a histogram of the distribution of scores on a midterm exam in a graduate statistics course.

C.5. A researcher is interested in determining whether there is a relationship between the number of room air-conditioning units sold each week and the time of year. What type of descriptive chart would be most useful in performing this analysis? Explain your choice.

C.6. Suppose that the histogram of a given income distribution is positively skewed. What does this fact imply about the relationship between the mean and median of this distribution?

C.7. "The midpoint of the line segment joining the first quartile and third quartile of any distribution is the median." Is this statement true or false? Explain your answer.

C.8. Explain why the standard deviation would likely *not* be a reliable measure of variability for a distribution of data that includes at least one extreme outlier.

C.9. Explain how a box plot can be used to determine whether the associated distribution of values is essentially symmetric.

C.10. Suppose that you collect a random sample of 250 salaries for the salespersons employed by a large PC manufacturer. Furthermore, assume that you find that two of these salaries are considerably higher than the others in the sample. In cleansing this data set, should you delete the unusual observations? Explain why or why not.

Level A

38. The file **P02_35.xlsx** contains (fictional) data from a survey of 500 randomly selected households.
   a. Indicate the type of data for each of the variables included in the survey.
   b. For each of the categorical variables in the survey, indicate whether the variable is nominal or ordinal. Explain your reasoning in each case.
   c. Create a histogram for each of the numerical variables in this data set. Indicate whether each of these distributions is approximately symmetric or skewed. Which, if any, of these distributions are skewed to the right? Which, if any, are skewed to the left?
   d. Find the maximum and minimum debt levels for the households in this sample.
   e. Find the indebtedness levels at each of the 25th, 50th, and 75th percentiles.
   f. Find and interpret the interquartile range for the indebtedness levels of these selected households.

39. The file **P02_39.xlsx** contains SAT test scores (two verbal components, a mathematical component, and the sum of these three) for each state and Washington

DC in 2009. It also lists the percentage of high school graduates taking the test in each of the states.

a. Create a histogram for each of the numerical variables. Are these distributions essentially symmetric or are they skewed?

b. Compare the distributions of the average verbal scores and average mathematical scores. In what ways are these distributions similar? In what ways are they different?

c. Find the mean, median, and mode of the set of percentages taking the test.

d. For each of the numerical variables, which is the most appropriate measure of central tendency? Explain the reasoning behind your choice.

e. How does the mean of the Combined variable relate to the means of the Critical Reading, Math, and Writing variables? Is the same true for medians?

40. *The Wall Street Journal CEO Compensation Study* analyzed CEO pay from many U.S. companies with fiscal year 2008 revenue of at least $5 billion that filed their proxy statements between October 2008 and March 2009. The data are in the file **P02_30.xlsx**. (Note: This data set is a somewhat different CEO compensation data set from the one used as an example in the next chapter.)

a. Create histograms to gain a clearer understanding of the distributions of annual base salaries and bonuses earned by the surveyed CEOs in fiscal 2008. How would you characterize these histograms?

b. Find the annual salary below which 75% of all given CEO salaries fall.

c. Find the annual bonus above which 55% of all given CEO bonuses fall.

d. Determine the range of the middle 50% of all given total direct compensation figures. For the 50% of the executives that do not fall into this middle 50% range, is there more variability in total direct compensation to the right than to the left? Explain.

41. The file **P02_41.xlsx** contains monthly returns on Barnes and Noble stock for several years. As the formulas in the file indicate, each return is the percentage change in the adjusted closing price from one month to the next. Do monthly stock returns appear to be skewed or symmetric? On average, do they tend to be positive, negative, or zero?

42. The file **P02_42.xlsx** contains monthly returns on Mattel stock for several years. As the formulas in the file indicate, each return is the percentage change in the adjusted closing price from one month to the next. Create a histogram of these returns and summarize what you learn from it. On average, do the returns tend to be positive, negative, or zero?

43. The file **P02_43.xlsx** contains U.S. Bureau of Labor Statistics data on the year-to-year percentage changes in the wages and salaries of workers in private industries, including both white-collar and blue-collar occupations.

a. Create box plots to summarize these distributions of annual percentage changes. Comparing the box plots for white-collar and blue-collar workers, discuss the similarities or differences you see.

b. Given that these are time series variables, what information is omitted from the box plots? Are box plots even relevant?

44. The file **P02_44.xlsx** contains annual data on the percentage of Americans under the age of 18 living below the poverty level.

a. In which years of the sample has the poverty rate for American children exceeded the rate that defines the third quartile of these data?

b. In which years of the sample has the poverty rate for American children fallen below the rate that defines the first quartile of these data?

c. What is the typical poverty rate for American children during this period?

d. Create and interpret a time series graph for these data. How successful have Americans been recently in their efforts to win "the war against poverty" for the nation's children?

e. Given that this data set is a time series, discuss whether the measures requested in parts **a-c** are very meaningful at the current time.

Level B

45. The file **P02_45.xlsx** contains the salaries of 135 business school professors at a (fictional) large state university.

a. If you increased every professor's salary by $1000, what would happen to the mean and median salary?

b. If you increased every professor's salary by $1000, what would happen to the sample standard deviation of the salaries?

c. If you increased every professor's salary by 5%, what would happen to the sample standard deviation of the salaries?

46. The file **P02_46.xlsx** lists the fraction of U.S. men and women of various heights and weights. Use these data to estimate the mean and standard deviation of the height of American men and women. (*Hint*: Assume all heights in a group are concentrated at the group's midpoint.) Do the same for weights.

47. Recall that the HyTex Company is a direct marketer of technical products and that the file **Catalog Marketing.xlsx** contains recent data on 1000 HyTex customers.

a. Identify all customers in the data set who are 55 years of age or younger, female, single, and who have had at least some dealings with HyTex before this year. Find the average number of catalogs sent to these customers and the average amount spent by these customers this year.

b. Do any of the customers who satisfy the conditions stated in part **a** have salaries that fall in the bottom 10% of all 1000 combined salaries in the data set? If so, how many?

c. Identify all customers in the sample who are more than 30 years of age or younger, male, homeowners, married, and who have had little if any dealings with HyTex before this year. Find the average combined household salary and the average amount spent by these customers this year.

d. Do any of the customers who satisfy the conditions stated in part **c** have salaries that fall in the top 10% of all 1000 combined salaries in the data set? If so, how many?

48. Recall that the file **Baseball Salaries 2009.xlsx** contains data on 818 MLB players as of May 2009. Using this data set, answer the following questions:

a. Find the mean and median of the salaries of all shortstops. Are any of these measures influenced significantly by one or more unusual observations?

b. Find the standard deviation, first and third quartiles, and 5th and 95th percentiles for the salaries of all shortstops. Are any of these measures influenced significantly by one or more unusual observations?

c. Create a histogram of the salaries of all shortstops. Are any of these measures influenced significantly by one or more unusual observations?

49. In 1969 and again in 1970, a lottery was held to determine who would be drafted and sent to Vietnam in the following year. For each date of the year, a ball was put into an urn. For example, in the first lottery, January 1 was number 305 and February 14 was number 4. Thus a person born on February 14 would be drafted before a person born on January 1. The file **P02_49.xlsx** contains the "draft number" for each date for the two lotteries. Do you notice anything unusual about the results of either lottery? What do you think might have caused this result? (*Hint*: Create a box plot for each month's numbers.)

50. The file **P02_50.xlsx** contains the average price of gasoline in each of the 50 states. (*Note*: You will need to manipulate the data to some extent before performing the analyses requested below.)

a. Compare the distributions of gasoline price data (one for each year) across states. Specifically, do you find the mean and standard deviation of these distributions to be changing over time? If so, how do you explain the trends?

b. In which regions of the country have gasoline prices changed the most?

c. In which regions of the country have gasoline prices remained relatively stable?

51. The file **P02_51.xlsx** contains data on U.S. home-ownership rates.

a. Employ numerical summary measures to characterize the changes in homeownership rates across the country during this period.

b. Do the trends appear to be uniform across the U.S. or are they unique to certain regions of the country? Explain.

52. Recall that the HyTex Company is a direct marketer of technical products and that the file **Catalog Marketing.xlsx** contains recent data on 1000 HyTex customers.

a. Identify all customers who are either (1) homeowners between the ages of 31 and 55 who live reasonably close to a shopping area that sells similar merchandise, and have a combined salary between $40,000 and $90,000 (inclusive) and a history of being a medium or high spender at HyTex; or (2) homeowners greater than the age of 55 who live reasonably close to a shopping area that sells similar merchandise and have a combined salary between $40,000 and $90,000 (inclusive) and a history of being a medium or high spender at HyTex.

b. Characterize the subset of customers who satisfy the conditions specified in part **a**. In particular, what proportion of these customers are women? What proportion of these customers are married? On average, how many children do these customers have? Finally, how many catalogs do these customers typically receive, and how much do they typically spend each year at HyTex?

c. In what ways are the customers who satisfy condition 1 in part **a** different from those who satisfy condition 2 in part **a**? Be specific.

53. Recall that the file **Supermarket Transactions.xlsx** contains data on over 14,000 transactions. There are two numerical variables, Units Sold and Revenue. The first of these is discrete and the second is continuous. For each of the following, do whatever it takes to create a bar chart of counts for Units Sold and a histogram of Revenue for the given subpopulation of purchases.

a. All purchases made during January and February of 2008.

b. All purchase made by married female homeowners.

c. All purchases made in the state of California.

d. All purchases made in the Produce product department.

54. The file **P02_54.xlsx** contains daily values of an EPA air quality index in Washington DC and Los Angeles from January 1980 through April 2009. For some unknown reason, the source provides slightly different dates for the two cities.

a. Starting in column G, create three new columns: Date, Wash DC Index, and LA Index. Fill the new date column with *all* dates from 1/1/1980 to 4/30/2009. Then use lookup functions to fill in the two new index columns, entering the observed index if available or a blank otherwise. (*Hint*: Use a combination of the VLOOKUP function with False as the last argument and the IFERROR function. Look up the latter in online help if you have never seen it before.)

b. Create a separate time series graph of each new index column. Because there are so many dates, it is difficult to see how the graph deals with missing data, but see if you can determine this (maybe by expanding the size of the graph or trying a smaller example). In spite of the few missing points, explain the patterns in the graphs and how Washington DC compares to Los Angeles. (*Note*: StatTools will not let you create a time series graph with missing data in the *middle* of the series, but you can create a line chart manually in Excel, without StatTools.)

55. The file **P02_55.xlsx** contains monthly sales (in millions of dollars) of beer, wine, and liquor. The data have not been seasonally adjusted, so there might be seasonal patterns that can be discovered. For any month in any year, define that month's seasonal index as the ratio of its sales value to the average sales value over all months of that year.

a. Calculate these seasonal indexes, one for each month in the series. Do you see a consistent pattern from year to year? If so, what is it?

b. To "deseasonalize" the data and get the seasonally adjusted series often reported, divide each monthly sales value by the corresponding seasonal index from part a. Then create a time series graph of both series, the actual sales and the seasonally adjusted sales. Explain how they are different and why the seasonally adjusted series might be of interest.

56. The file **P02_56.xlsx** contains monthly values of indexes that measure the amount of energy necessary to heat or cool buildings due to outside temperatures. (See the explanation in the Source sheet of the file.) These are reported for each state in the U.S. and also for several regions, as listed in the Locations sheet, from 1931 to 2000. Create summary measures and/or charts to see whether there is any indication of temperature changes (global warming?) through time, and report your findings.

57. The file **P02_57.xlsx** contains data on mortgage loans in 2008 for each state in the U.S. The file is different from similar ones in this chapter in that each state has its own sheet with the same data laid out in the same format. Each state sheet breaks down all mortgage applications by loan purpose, applicant race, loan type, outcome, and denial reason (for those that were denied). The question is how a *single* data set for all states can be created for analysis. The Typical Data Set sheet indicates a simple way of doing this, using the powerful but little-known INDIRECT function. This sheet is basically a template for bringing in any pieces of data from the state sheet you would like to examine.

a. Create histograms and summary measures for the example data given in the Typical Data Set sheet and write a short report on your findings.

b. Create a copy of the Typical Data Set sheet and repeat part **a** on this copy for at least one other set of variables (of your choice) from the state sheets.

CASE 2.1 CORRECT INTERPRETATION OF MEANS

A mean, as defined in this chapter, is a pretty simple concept—it is the average of a set of numbers. But even this simple concept can cause confusion if you aren't careful. The data in Table 2.1 are typical of data presented by marketing researchers for a type of product, in this case beer.

Each value is an average of the number of six-packs of beer purchased per customer during a month. For the individual brands, the value is the average only for the customers who purchased at least one six-pack of that brand. For example, the value for Miller is the average number of six-packs purchased of *all* of these brands for customers who purchased at least one six-pack of Miller. In contrast, the "Any" average is the average number of six-packs purchased of these brands for all customers in the population.

Is there a paradox in these averages? On first glance, it might appear unusual, or even impossible, that the "Any" average is less than each brand average. Make up your own (small) data set, where you list a number of customers, along with the number of six-packs of each brand of beer each customer purchased, and calculate the averages for your data that correspond to those in Table 2.1. Do you get the same result (that the "Any" average is lower than all of the others)? Are you *guaranteed* to get this result? Does it depend on the amount of brand loyalty in your population, where brand loyalty is greater when customers tend to stick to the same brand, rather than buying multiple brands? Write up your results in a concise report. ■

Table 2.1 Average Beer Purchases

	Q	R	S	T	U	V	W	X	Y	Z	AA	AB	AC	AD
1	Criteria range (starts in row 3)													
2														

The monthly closing values of the Dow Jones Industrial Average (DJIA) for the period beginning in January 1950 are given in the file **DJIA Monthly Close.xlsx**. According to Wikipedia (http://en.wikipedia.org/wiki/Dow_Jones_Industrial_Average), the Dow Jones Industrial Average, also referred to as the Industrial Average, the Dow Jones, the Dow 30, or simply the Dow, is one of several stock market indices created by *Wall Street Journal* editor and Dow Jones & Company co-founder Charles Dow. The average is named after Dow and one of his business associates, statistician Edward Jones. It is an index that shows how 30 large, publicly owned companies based in the U.S. have traded during a standard trading session in the stock market. It is the second oldest U.S. market index after the Dow Jones Transportation Average, which Dow also created. Currently, Dow Jones & Company, which regularly publishes the index, is a subsidiary of News Corporation.

The *Industrial* portion of the name is largely historical, as many of the modern 30 components have little or nothing to do with traditional heavy industry. The average is price-weighted, and to compensate for the effects of stock splits and other adjustments, it is currently a scaled average. The value of the Dow is not the actual average of the prices of its component stocks, but rather the sum of the component prices divided by a *divisor*, which changes whenever one of the component stocks has a stock split or stock dividend, so as to generate a consistent value for the index.

Along with the NASDAQ Composite, the S&P 500 Index, and the Russell 2000 Index, the Dow is among the most closely watched benchmark indices tracking targeted stock market activity. Although Dow compiled the index to gauge the performance of the industrial sector within the American economy, the index's performance continues to be influenced not only by corporate and economic reports, but also by domestic and foreign political events such as war and terrorism, as well as by natural disasters that could potentially lead to economic harm. Components of the Dow trade on both the NASDAQ OMX and the NYSE Euronext, two of the largest stock exchanges. Derivatives of the Dow trade on the Chicago Board Options Exchange and through the CME Group, the world's largest futures exchange company.

Using the summary measures and graphical tools from this chapter, analyze this important time series over the given period. Summarize in detail the behavior of the monthly closing values of the Dow and the associated monthly percentage changes in the closing values of the Dow. ∎

The file **Home Price Index.xlsx** contains an index of home prices and a seasonally adjusted (SA) version of this index for several large U.S. cities. It also contains a condo price index for several large cities and a national index. (The data are explained in the Source sheet.) Use the tools in this chapter to make sense out of these data, and write a report of your findings. Some important questions you can answer are the following: Are there trends over time? Are there differences across cities? Are there differences across months? Do condo prices mirror home prices? Why are seasonally adjusted indexes published? ■

Finding Relationships among Variables

© Mimal/Dreamstime.com

PREDICTORS OF SUCCESSFUL MOVIES

The movie industry is a high-profile industry with a highly variable revenue stream. In 1998, U.S. moviegoers spent close to $7 billion at the box office alone. Ten years later, the figure was slightly higher, despite the number of people watching DVDs at home. With this much money at stake, it is not surprising that movie studios are interested in knowing what variables are useful for predicting a movie's financial success. The article by Simonoff and Sparrow (2000) examines this issue for 311 movies released in 1998 and late 1997. (They obtained their data from a public Web site, www.imdb.com.) Although it is preferable to examine movie *profits*, the costs of making movies are virtually impossible to obtain. Therefore, the authors focused instead on revenues—specifically, the total U.S. domestic gross revenue for each film.

Simonoff and Sparrow obtained prerelease information on a number of variables that were thought to be possible predictors of gross revenue. (Prerelease means that this information is known about a film *before* the film is actually released.) These variables include: (1) the genre of the film, categorized as action, children's, comedy, documentary, drama, horror, science fiction, or thriller; (2) the Motion Picture Association of America (MPAA) rating of the film, categorized as G (general audiences), PG (parental guidance suggested), PG-13 (possibly unsuitable for children under 13), R (children not admitted unless accompanied by an adult), NC-17 (no one under 17 admitted), or U (unrated); (3) the country of origin of the movie, categorized as United States, English-speaking but non–United States, or non–English-speaking; (4) number of actors and actresses in the movie who were listed in *Entertainment Weekly's* lists of the 25 Best Actors and 25 Best Actresses, as of 1998; (5) number of actors and actresses in the movie who were among the top 20 actors and top 20 actresses in average box office gross per movie in their careers; (6) whether the movie was a sequel; (7) whether the movie was released before a holiday weekend; (8) whether the movie was released during the Christmas season; and (9) whether the movie was released during the summer season.

To get a sense of whether these variables are related to gross revenue, we could calculate a lot of summary measures and create numerous tables. However, we agree with Simonoff and Sparrow that the information is best presented in a series of *side-by-side box plots*. (See Figure 3.1.) These box plots are slightly different from the versions introduced in the previous chapter, but they accomplish exactly the same thing. (There are two differences: First, their box plots are vertical; ours are horizontal. Second, their box plots capture an extra piece of information—the *widths* of their boxes are proportional to the square roots of the sample sizes, so that wide boxes correspond to categories with more movies. In contrast, the *heights* of our boxes carry no information about sample size.) Basically, each box and the lines and points extending above and below it indicate the distribution of gross revenues for any category. Remember that the box itself, from bottom to top, captures the middle 50% of the revenues in the category, the line in the middle of the box represents the median revenue, and the lines and dots indicate possible skewness and outliers.

These particular box plots indicate some interesting and possibly surprising information about the movie business. First, almost all of the box plots indicate a high degree of variability and positive skewness, where there are a few movies that gross extremely large amounts compared to the "typical" movies in the category. Second, genre certainly makes a difference. There are more comedies and dramas (wider boxes), but they typically gross considerably less than action, children's, and science fiction films. Third, the same is true of R-rated movies compared to movies rated G, PG, or PG-13—there are more of them, but they typically gross much less. Fourth, U.S. movies do considerably better than foreign movies. Fifth, it helps to have stars, although there are quite a few "sleepers" that succeed without having big-name stars. Sixth, sequels do better, presumably reflecting the success of the earlier films. Finally, the release date makes a big difference. Movies released before holidays, during the Christmas season, or during the summer season tend to have larger gross revenues. Indeed, as Simonoff and Sparrow discuss, movie studios compete fiercely for the best release dates.

Are these prerelease variables sufficient to predict gross revenues accurately? As you might expect from the amount of variability in most of the box plots in Figure 3.1, the answer is "no." Many intangible factors evidently determine the ultimate success of a movie, so that some, such as *There's Something About Mary*, do much better than expected, and others, such as *Godzilla*, do worse than expected. We will revisit this movie data set in the chapter opener to Chapter 11. There, you will see how Simonoff and Sparrow use *multiple regression* to predict gross revenue—with limited success.

Figure 3.1 Box Plots of Domestic Gross Revenues for 1998 Movies

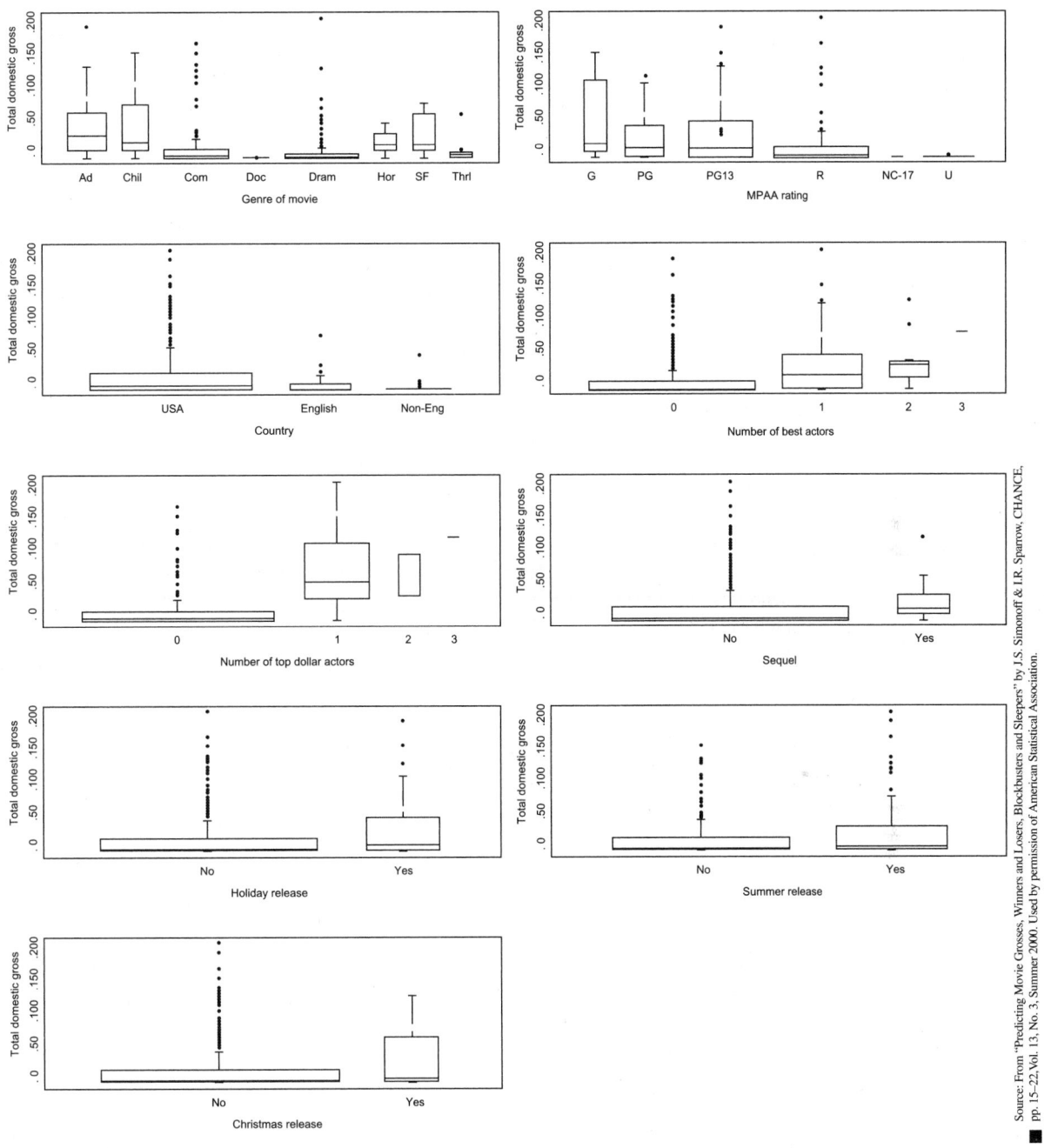

Source: From "Predicting Movie Grosses, Winners and Losers, Blockbusters and Sleepers" by J.S. Simonoff & I.R. Sparrow, CHANCE, pp. 15–22, Vol. 13, No. 3, Summer 2000. Used by permission of American Statistical Association.

3.1 INTRODUCTION

In the previous chapter, we introduced a number of summary measures, graphs, and tables to describe the distribution of a single variable. For a variable such as baseball salary, our entire focus was on how salaries were distributed over some range. This is an important first step in any exploratory data analysis—to look closely at variables one at a time—but it is almost never the *last* step. We are almost always interested in *relationships* between variables. For example, it is natural to ask what drives baseball salaries. Does it depend on qualitative factors, such as the player's team or position? Does it depend on quantitative factors, such as the number of hits the player gets or the number of strikeouts? To answer these questions, we have to examine relationships between various variables and salary.

A key issue in this chapter is that different tools should be used to examine relationships, depending on whether the variables involved are numerical or categorical.

In this chapter, we will again discuss several numerical summary measures, graphs, and tables, but they will now involve at least two variables at a time. The most useful numerical summary measure is correlation, a measure that applies primarily to *numerical* variables. The most useful graph is a scatterplot, which again applies primarily to numerical variables. For relationships involving categorical variables, we will introduce other tools. For example, to break down a numerical variable by a categorical variable, as in the chapter opener with movie gross revenues, it is often useful to create side-by-side box plots as in Figure 3.1. Finally, we will introduce Excel's arguably most powerful tool, pivot tables. Pivot tables allow you to break down one variable by others so that all sorts of relationships can be uncovered in a matter of minutes.

As you read this chapter, remember that the diagram in the file **Data Analysis Taxonomy.xlsx** is available. This diagram gives you the big picture of which analyses are appropriate for which data types and which tools are best for performing the various analyses.

3.2 RELATIONSHIPS AMONG CATEGORICAL VARIABLES

Consider a data set with at least two categorical variables, Smoking and Drinking. Each person is categorized into one of three smoking categories: nonsmoker (NS), occasional smoker (OS), and heavy smoker (HS). Similarly, each person is categorized into one of three drinking categories: nondrinker (ND), occasional drinker (OD), and heavy drinker (HD). We want to examine whether smoking and drinking habits are related. For example, do nondrinkers tend to be nonsmokers? Do heavy smokers tend to be heavy drinkers?

Use a crosstabs, a table of counts of joint categories, to discover relationships between two categorical variables.

As we discussed in the previous chapter, the most meaningful way to describe a categorical variable is with counts, possibly expressed as percentages, and corresponding charts of the counts. The same is true of examining relationships between two categorical variables. We can find the counts of the categories of either variable separately, and more importantly, we can find counts of the *joint* categories of the two variables, such as the count of all nondrinkers who are also nonsmokers. Again, corresponding percentages and charts help tell the story.

It is customary to display all such counts in a table called a **crosstabs** (for cross-tabulations). This is also sometimes called a **contingency table**. We illustrate these tables in the following example.

| EXAMPLE | 3.1 RELATIONSHIP BETWEEN SMOKING AND DRINKING |

The file **Smoking Drinking.xlsx** lists the smoking and drinking habits of 8761 adults. (This is not real data.) The categories have been coded so that "N," "O," and "H" stand for "Non," "Occasional," and "Heavy," and "S" and "D" stand for "Smoker" and "Drinker." Is there any indication that smoking and drinking habits are related? If so, how are they related?

Objective   To use a crosstabs to explore the relationship between smoking and drinking.

Solution

The first question is the data format. If you are lucky, you will be given a table of counts. However, it is also possible that you will have to create these counts. In the file for this example, the data are in long columns, a small part of which is shown in Figure 3.2. (Presumably, there could be other variables describing these people, but we are interested only in the Smoking and Drinking variables.)

Figure 3.2

Smoking and Drinking Data

	A	B	C
1	Person	Smoking	Drinking
2	1	NS	OD
3	2	NS	HD
4	3	OS	HD
5	4	HS	ND
6	5	NS	OD
7	6	NS	ND
8	7	NS	OD
9	8	NS	ND
10	9	OS	HD
11	10	HS	HD

To create the crosstabs, start by entering the category headings in Figure 3.3. The goal is to fill in the box with counts of joint categories, along with totals as row and column sums. If you are thinking about using the COUNTIF function to obtain the joint counts, you are close. Unfortunately, the COUNTIF function lets you specify only a single criterion, but there are now *two* criteria, one for smoking and one for drinking. Fortunately, Excel has a new function (new to Excel 2007) designed exactly for this: **COUNTIFS**. It allows you to specify any number of range-criterion pairs. In fact, you can fill in the entire table with a single formula entered in cell F4 and copied to the range F4:H6:

=COUNTIFS($B$2:$B$8762,F$3,$C$2:$C$8762,$E4)

The first two arguments are for the condition on smoking; the last two are for the condition on drinking. You can then sum across rows and down columns to get the totals.

Figure 3.3

Headings for Crosstabs

	E	F	G	H	I
1	Crosstabs from COUNTIFS formulas				
2					
3		NS	OS	HS	Total
4	ND				
5	OD				
6	HD				
7	Total				

The resulting counts appear in the top table in Figure 3.4. For example, among the 8761 people, 4912 are nonsmokers, 2365 are heavy drinkers, and 733 are nonsmokers *and* heavy drinkers. Because the totals are far from equal (there are many more non-smokers than heavy smokers, for example), any relationship between smoking and

Figure 3.4

Crosstabs of
Smoking and
Drinking

	E	F	G	H	I
1	Crosstabs from COUNTIFS formulas				
2					
3		NS	OS	HS	Total
4	ND	2118	435	163	2716
5	OD	2061	1067	552	3680
6	HD	733	899	733	2365
7	Total	4912	2401	1448	8761
8					
9	Shown as percentages of row				
10		NS	OS	HS	Total
11	ND	78.0%	16.0%	6.0%	100.0%
12	OD	56.0%	29.0%	15.0%	100.0%
13	HD	31.0%	38.0%	31.0%	100.0%
14					
15	Shown as percentages of column				
16		NS	OS	HS	
17	ND	43.1%	18.1%	11.3%	
18	OD	42.0%	44.4%	38.1%	
19	HD	14.9%	37.4%	50.6%	
20	Total	100.0%	100.0%	100.0%	

drinking is difficult to detect in these raw counts. Therefore, it is useful to express the counts as percentages of row in the middle table and as percentages of column in the bottom table.

Relationships between the two variables are usually more evident when the counts are expressed as percentages of row or percentages of column.

The latter two tables indicate, in complementary ways, that there is definitely a relationship between smoking and drinking. If there were no relationship, the rows in the middle table would be practically identical, as would the columns in the bottom table. (Convince yourself why this is true.) But they are far from identical. For example, the middle table indicates that only 6% of the nondrinkers are heavy smokers, whereas 31% of the heavy drinkers are heavy smokers. Similarly, the bottom table indicates that 43.1% of the nonsmokers are nondrinkers, whereas only 11.3% of the heavy smokers are nondrinkers. In short, these tables indicate that smoking and drinking habits tend to go with one another. These tendencies are reinforced by the column charts of the two percentage tables in Figure 3.5.

Figure 3.5   Column Charts of Smoking and Drinking Percentages

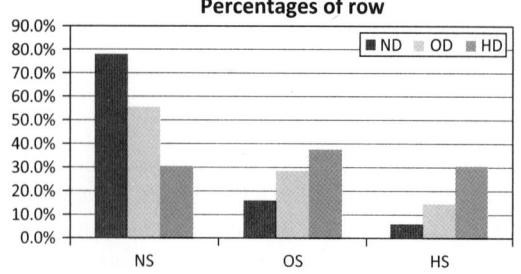
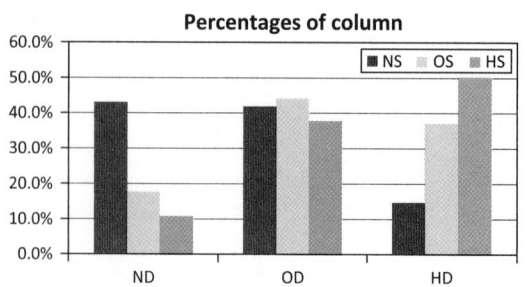

Counts Versus Percentages

There is no single correct way to display the data in a contingency table. Ultimately, the data are always counts, but they can be shown as raw counts, percentages of row totals, percentages of column totals, or even percentages of the overall total. However, when you are looking for relationships between two categorical variables, showing the counts as percentages of row totals or percentages of column totals usually makes any relationships stand out more clearly. Corresponding charts are also very useful.

Excel Tip *It takes almost no work to create these charts. To get the one on the left, highlight the range E10:H13 and insert a column chart from the Insert ribbon. Do the same with the range E16:H19 to get the chart on the right, except that it will have smoking on the horizontal axis and drinking in the legend. To reverse their roles, simply click on Switch Row/Column from the Chart Tools Design ribbon.*

Although this example illustrates that it doesn't take too much work to create crosstabs and corresponding charts, you will see a much quicker and easier way when pivot tables are discussed later in this chapter.

PROBLEMS

Note: Student solutions for problems whose numbers appear within a colored box are available for purchase at www.cengagebrain.com.

Level A

1. The file **P02_01.xlsx** indicates the gender and nationality of the MBA incoming class in two successive years at the Kelley School of Business at Indiana University.
   a. For each year separately, recode Nationality so that all nationalities with a count of 1 or 2 are listed as Other.
   b. For each year, create a crosstabs of Gender versus the recoded Nationality and an associated column chart. Does there seem to be any relationship between Gender and the recoded Nationality? Is the pattern about the same in the two years?

2. The file **P02_03.xlsx** contains data from a survey of 399 people regarding a government environmental policy.
   a. Create a crosstabs and an associated column chart for Gender versus Opinion. Express the counts as percentages so that for either gender, the percentages add to 100%. Discuss your findings. Specifically, do the two genders tend to differ in their opinions about the environmental policy?
   b. Repeat part **a** with Age versus Opinion.

   c. Recode Salary to be categorical with categories "Less than $40K", "Between $40K and $70K", "Between $70K and $100K", and "Greater than $100K" (where you can treat the breakpoints however you like). Then repeat part **a** with this new Salary variable versus Opinion.

3. The file **P02_02.xlsx** contains data about 211 movies released in 2006 and 2007.
   a. Recode Distributor so that all distributors except for Paramount Pictures, Buena Vista, Fox Searchlight, Universal, Warner Bros., 20th Century Fox, and Sony Pictures are listed as Other. (Those in Other released fewer than 16 movies.) Similarly, recode Genre so that all genres except for Action, Adventure, Thriller/Suspense, Drama, and Comedy are listed as Other. (Again, those in Other are genres with fewer than 16 movies.)
   b. Create a crosstabs and an associated column chart for these two recoded variables. Express the counts as percentages so that for any distributor, the percentages add to 100%. Discuss your findings.

4. Recall from Chapter 2 that the file **Supermarket Transactions.xlsx** contains over 14,000 transactions made by supermarket customers over a period of approximately two years. To understand which customers purchase which products, create a crosstabs

and an associated column chart for each of the following. For each, express the counts as percentages so that for any value of the first variable listed, the percentages add to 100%. Do any patterns stand out?
a. Gender versus Product Department
b. Marital Status versus Product Department
c. Annual Income versus Product Department

Level B

5. Recall from Chapter 2 that the HyTex Company is a direct marketer of technical products and that the file **Catalog Marketing.xlsx** contains recent data on 1000 HyTex customers. To understand these customers, first recode Salary and AmountSpent as indicated in part **a**, and then create each of the requested crosstabs and an associated column chart in parts **b** to **e**. Express each count as a percentage, so that for any value of the first variable listed, the percentages add to 100%. Do any patterns stand out?

a. Find the first, second, and third quartiles of Salary, and then recode Salary as 1 to 4, depending on which quarter of the data each value falls into. For example, the first salary, $16,400, is recoded as 1 because $16,400 is less than the first quartile, $29,975. Recode AmountSpent similarly, based on its quartiles. (*Hint*: The recoding can be done most easily with lookup tables.)
b. Age versus the recoded AmountSpent
c. OwnHome versus the recoded AmountSpent
d. History versus the recoded AmountSpent
e. The recoded Salary versus the recoded AmountSpent

6. In the smoking/drinking example in this section, we used the function COUNTIFS function (new to Excel 2007) to find the counts of the joint categories. Without using this function (or pivot tables), devise another way to get the counts. The raw data are in the file **Smoking Drinking.xlsx**. (*Hint*: One possibility is to concatenate the values in columns B and C into a new column D. But feel free to find the counts in any way you like.)

3.3 RELATIONSHIPS AMONG CATEGORICAL VARIABLES AND A NUMERICAL VARIABLE

This section describes a very common situation where you are interested in a numerical variable such as salary and you would like to "break it down" by category of some categorical variable such as gender. This is precisely what pivot tables were built for, as we will discuss later in the chapter, but for now we will discuss the numerical and graphical tools offered by StatTools to explore this problem. This general problem, typically referred to as the **comparison problem**, is one of the most important problems in data analysis. It occurs whenever you want to compare a numerical measure across two or more subpopulations. Here are some examples:

- The subpopulations are males and females, and the numerical measure is salary.
- The subpopulations are different regions of the country, and the numerical measure is the cost of living.

The comparison problem, where a numerical variable is compared across two or more sub-populations, is one of the most important problems faced by data analysts in all fields of study.

- The subpopulations are different days of the week, and the numerical measure is the number of customers going to a particular fast-food chain.
- The subpopulations are different machines in a manufacturing plant, and the numerical measure is the number of defective parts produced per day.
- The subpopulations are patients who have taken a new drug and those who have taken a placebo, and the numerical measure is the recovery rate from a particular disease.
- The subpopulations are undergraduates with various majors (business, English, history, and so on), and the numerical measure is the starting salary after graduating.

The list could go on and on. Our discussion of the comparison problem begins in this chapter, where we use exploratory methods to investigate whether there appear to be differences across the subpopulations on the numerical variable of interest. In later chapters, we will use inferential methods—confidence intervals and hypothesis tests—to see whether the differences we see in samples from the subpopulations can be generalized to the subpopulations as a whole.

Fundamental Insight

Breaking Down By Category

There is arguably no more powerful data analysis technique than breaking down a numerical variable by category. The methods in this chapter, especially side-by-side box plots and pivot tables, get you started with this general comparison problem. They allow you to see quickly, with charts and/or summary measures, how two or more categories compare. More sophisticated techniques for comparing across categories will be covered in later chapters.

3.3.1 Stacked and Unstacked Formats

The stacked format is by far the most common. There are one or more long numerical variables and another long variable that specifies which category each observation is in.

We begin by discussing two possible **data formats** you will see, stacked and unstacked. This concept is crucial for understanding how StatTools deals with comparison problems. Consider salary data on males and females. (There could be other variables in the data set, but we will ignore them for now.) Then the data are **stacked** if there are two "long" variables, Gender and Salary, as indicated in Figure 3.6. The idea is that the male salaries are stacked in with the female salaries. This is the format you will see in the vast majority of situations. However, you will occasionally see data in **unstacked** format, as shown in Figure 3.7. (Note that both tables list exactly the same data. See the file **Stacked Unstacked Data.xlsx**.) Now there are two "short" variables, Female Salary and Male Salary. In addition, it is very possible that the two variables have different lengths. This is the case here because there are more females than males.

Figure 3.6
Stacked Data

	A	B
1	Gender	Salary
2	Male	81600
3	Female	61600
4	Female	64300
5	Female	71900
6	Male	76300
7	Female	68200
8	Male	60900
9	Female	78600
10	Female	81700
11	Male	60200
12	Female	69200
13	Male	59000
14	Male	68600
15	Male	51900
16	Female	64100
17	Male	67600
18	Female	81100
19	Female	77000
20	Female	58800
21	Female	87800
22	Male	78900

Figure 3.7

Unstacked Data

	A	B
1	Female Salary	Male Salary
2	61600	81600
3	64300	76300
4	71900	60900
5	68200	60200
6	78600	59000
7	81700	68600
8	69200	51900
9	64100	67600
10	81100	78900
11	77000	
12	58800	
13	87800	

StatTools is capable of dealing with either stacked or unstacked format. (Not all statistical software can make this claim. Some packages require stacked format.) Nevertheless, there are a few times when you might want to convert from stacked to unstacked format or vice versa. StatTools has utilities for doing this. These utilities are found on the Data Utilities (*not* the Utilities) dropdown list on the StatTools ribbon. They are very simple to use, and we suggest that you try them on the data in Figures 3.6 and 3.7. (If you need help, open the finished version of the Stacked Unstacked Data.xlsx file, which includes instructions for using these data utilities.)

We now return to the baseball data to see which, if any, of the categorical variables makes a difference in player salaries.

EXAMPLE | 3.2 BASEBALL SALARIES

The file Baseball Salaries 2009 Extra.xlsx contains the same 2009 baseball data examined in the previous chapter. In addition, several extra categorical variables are included:

- Pitcher (Yes for all pitchers, No for the others)
- League (American or National)
- Division (National West, American East, and so on)
- Yankees (Yes if team is New York Yankees, No otherwise)
- Playoff Team 2008 (Yes for the eight teams that made it to the playoffs, No for the others)
- World Series Team 2008 (Yes for Philadelphia Phillies and Tampa Bay Rays, No for others)

Do pitchers (or any other positions) earn more than others? Does one league pay more than the other, or do any divisions pay more than others? How does the notoriously high Yankees payroll compare to the others? Do the successful teams from 2008 tend to have larger 2009 payrolls?

Objective   To learn methods in StatTools for breaking down baseball salaries by various categorical variables.

Solution

StatTools often lets you choose the stacked format. This allows you to choose a Cat (categorical) variable and a Val (value) variable for the analysis.

We first look at some numerical summary measures for salary. These are the same summary measures from the previous chapter, but now we want to break them down by position. Fortunately, StatTools makes this easy. (Imagine how you would have to do it without an add-in. It would not be fun!) To get started, designate the range as a StatTools data set in the usual way and then select One-Variable Summary from the Summary Statistics dropdown list. The key now is to click on the Format button (see Figure 3.8) and choose Stacked (if it isn't already selected). When you choose Stacked, you get two lists of variables to choose from. In the Cat (categorical) list, choose the variable that you want to categorize by, in this case Position. In the Val (value) list, choose the variable that you want to summarize, in this case Salary. Then select any of the summary measures you would like to see, such as those checked in Figure 3.8.

Figure 3.8
One-Variable
Summary Dialog
Box with Stacked
Format

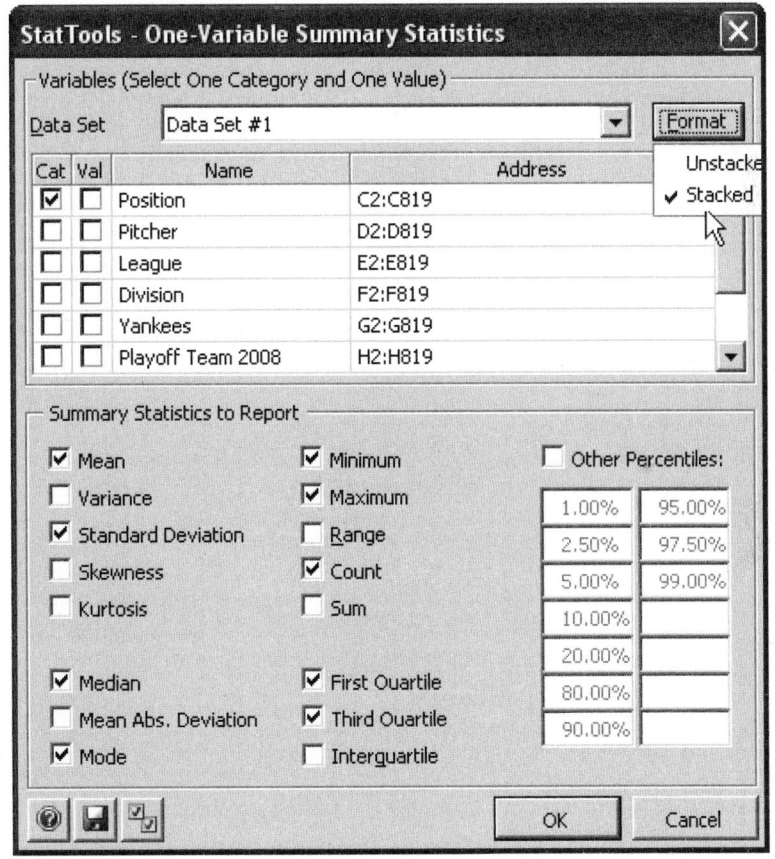

The results appear in Figure 3.9. This table lists each of the requested summary measures for each of the nine positions in the data set. If you want to see salaries broken down by team or any other categorical variable, you can easily run this analysis again and choose a different Cat variable.[1]

---

[1]For baseball fans, don't be fooled by the low mean for the Infielder position. There are only seven players in this category, evidently the "utility" infielders who can play several positions—and don't command high salaries.

Figure 3.9   Summary Measures of Salary for Various Positions

	A	B	C	D	E	F	G	H	I	J
7		Salary (Catcher)	Salary (Designated Hitter)	Salary (First Baseman)	Salary (Infielder)	Salary (Outfielder)	Salary (Pitcher)	Salary (Second Baseman)	Salary (Shortstop)	Salary (Third Baseman)
8	One Variable Summary	Data Set #1	Data Set #1	Data Set #1	Data Set #1	Data Set #1	Data Set #1	Data Set #1	Data Set #1	Data Set #1
9	Mean	$2,179,760	$6,633,875	$5,706,002	$667,143	$3,834,524	$2,887,334	$2,463,334	$3,113,541	$4,954,790
10	Std. Dev.	$2,660,154	$5,425,908	$5,824,204	$590,670	$5,042,623	$3,927,561	$2,478,960	$4,058,174	$6,333,443
11	Median	$950,000	$4,000,000	$3,125,000	$420,000	$1,500,000	$825,000	$1,400,000	$1,300,000	$2,400,000
12	Minimum	$400,000	$400,000	$400,000	$400,000	$400,000	$400,000	$400,000	$400,000	$400,000
13	Maximum	$13,100,000	$13,000,000	$20,625,000	$2,000,000	$23,854,494	$18,876,139	$11,285,714	$21,600,000	$33,000,000
14	Count	63	8	39	7	150	407	47	53	44
15	1st Quartile	$415,000	$421,000	$750,000	$400,000	$417,500	$414,800	$416,700	$425,000	$432,400
16	3rd Quartile	$2,800,000	$11,500,000	$11,600,000	$550,000	$5,000,000	$3,750,000	$3,500,000	$4,650,000	$7,050,000

Side-by-side box plots are our favorite way of comparing the distribution of a numerical variable across categories of some categorical variable.

There are a lot of numbers to digest in Figure 3.9, so it is difficult to get a clear picture of differences across positions. It is much more enlightening to see a graphical summary of this information. There are several types of graphs you can use. Our favorite way is to create side-by-side box plots (the same type of chart illustrated in the chapter opener), as we will discuss shortly. Another possibility is to create side-by-side histograms, with one histogram for each category. This is easy with StatTools, using the Stacked format option exactly as we did for summary measures. However, you should *not* accept the default bins because they will differ across categories and prevent a fair comparison. So make sure you enter your own bins. (See the finished version of the baseball file for an illustration of side-by-side histograms done with default bins and with specified bins.) A third possibility is to use pivot tables and corresponding pivot charts, as will be discussed later in this chapter.

For now, we illustrate side-by-side box plots. These are very easy to obtain. Select Box-Whisker Plot from the Summary Graphs dropdown list and fill in the resulting dialog box as shown in Figure 3.10. Again, the key is to select the Stacked format so that you can choose a Cat variable and a Val variable.

The results appear in Figure 3.11. There is a separate box plot for each category of the Position variable, and each has exactly the same interpretation that we discussed in the

Figure 3.10

Box Plot Dialog Box with Stacked Format

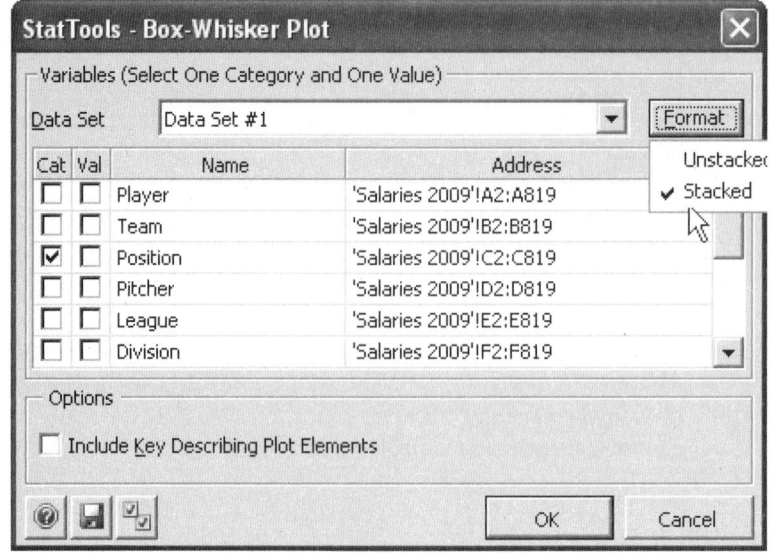

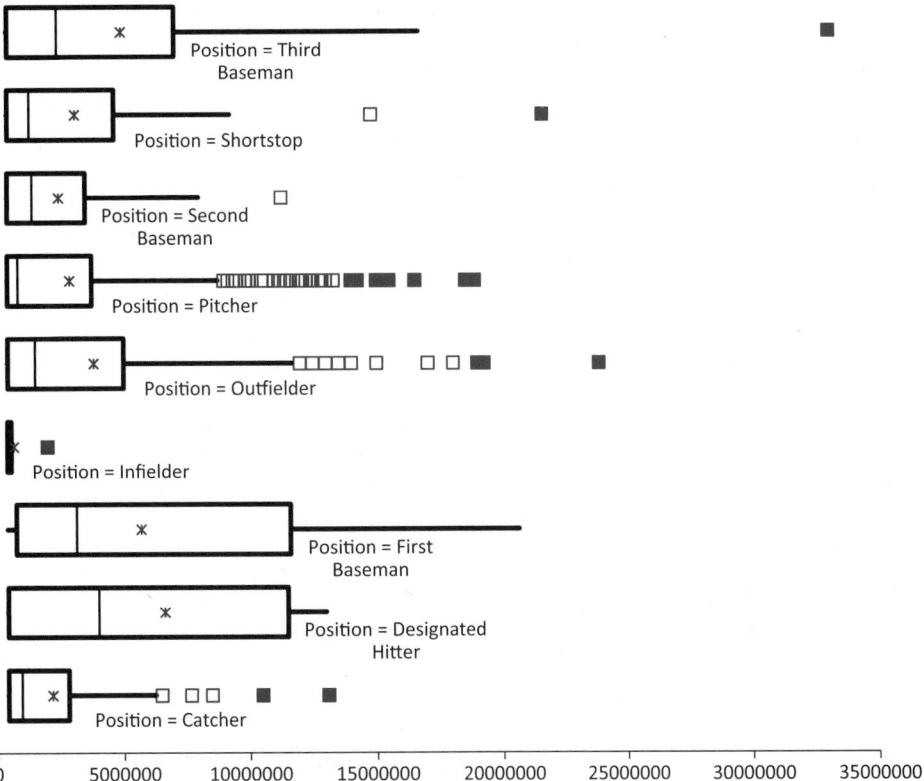

Figure 3.11

Box Plots of Salary by Position

Because these side-by-side box plots are so easy to obtain, you can generate a lot of them to provide insights into the salary data. Several interesting examples appear in Figures 3.12–3.14. From these box plots, we can conclude the following:

previous chapter. Now the differences between positions emerge fairly clearly. A few of the conclusions that can be made are the following.

- The salaries for all positions are skewed to the right (mean greater than median, long lines and outliers to the right).
- As a whole, first basemen tend to be the highest paid players, followed by third basemen. The designated hitters also make a lot, but there are only eight such players in the data set.
- As a whole, pitchers and outfielders don't make as much as first basemen and third basemen, but there are a lot of high-earning outliers at these two positions.
- Except for a few notable exceptions, catchers and second basemen don't get much respect.

Because these side-by-side box plots are so easy to obtain, you can generate a lot of them to provide insights into the salary data. Several interesting examples appear in Figures 3.12–3.14. From these box plots, we can conclude the following:

- Pitchers make somewhat less than other players, although there are many outliers in each group.
- The Yankees payroll is indeed *much* larger than the payrolls for the rest of the teams. In fact, it is so large that Alex Rodriguez's $33 million is considered only a *mild* outlier relative to the rest of the team.

- Aside from the many outliers, the playoff teams from 2008 tend to have larger payrolls than the non-playoff teams. The one question we cannot answer, however, at least not without additional data, is whether these larger payrolls are a cause or an effect of being successful.

Figure 3.12

Box Plots of Salary by Pitcher

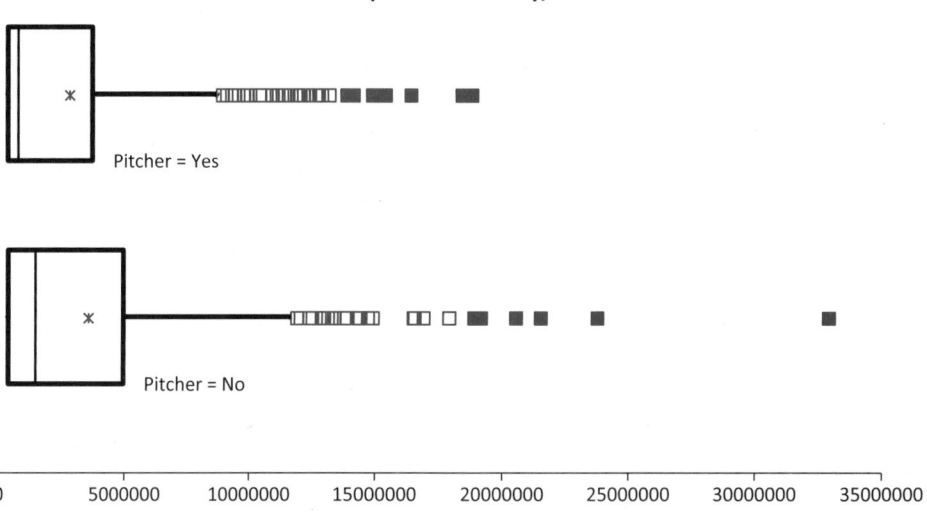

Figure 3.13

Box Plots of Salary by Yankees

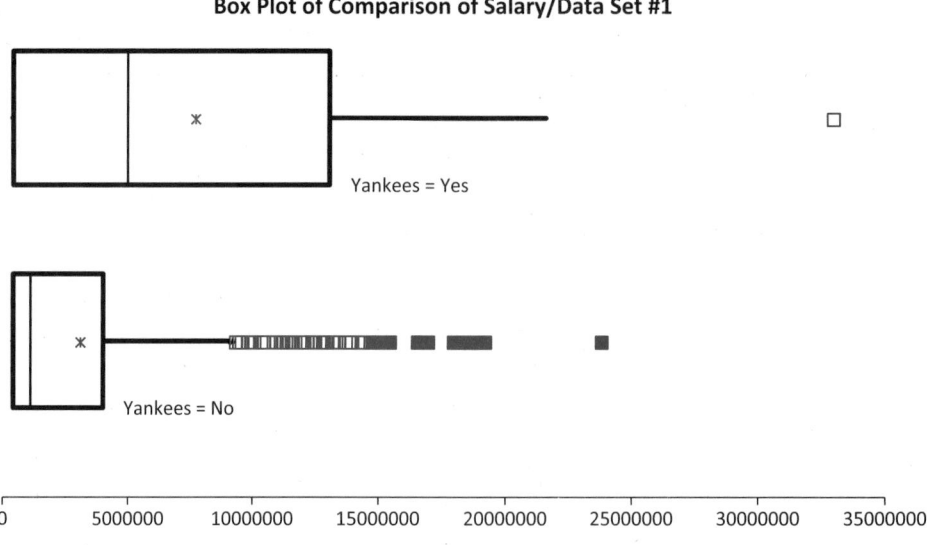

You can often create a categorical variable on the fly with an IF formula and then use it for side-by-side box plots. We did this with the Yankees.

There is one StatTools limitation you should be aware of. The academic version allows only 12 categories for box plots. Therefore, you can't choose Team as the Cat variable because there are 30 teams. However, it is possible to isolate one or more teams in a column and then base the box plots on this column, as we did for the Yankees. As another example, if you were interested in comparing the Yankees, the Red Sox, and all the others, you could create another column with three values: Yankees, Red Sox, and Other.

Figure 3.14

Box Plots of Salary by Playoff Team 2008

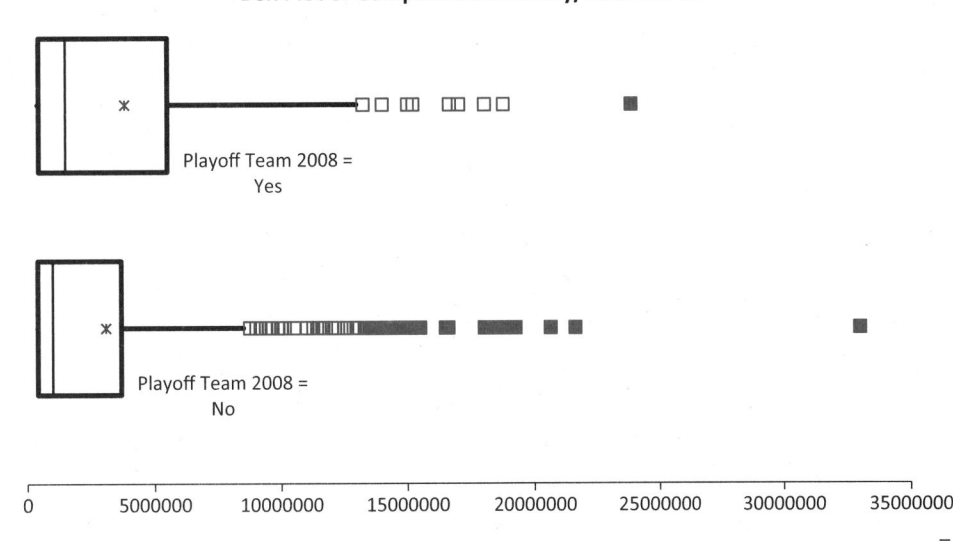

Box Plot of Comparison of Salary/Data Set #1

Playoff Team 2008 = Yes

Playoff Team 2008 = No

PROBLEMS

Level A

7. Recall that the file **Baseball Salaries 2009 Extra.xlsx** contains data on 818 Major League Baseball (MLB) players during the 2009 season. Use StatTools to find the mean, median, standard deviation, and first and third quartiles of Salary, broken down by each of the following categories. Comment on your findings.
   a. Team
   b. Division
   c. Whether they played for the Yankees
   d. Whether they were in the playoffs

8. The file **P02_07.xlsx** includes data on 204 employees at the (fictional) company Beta Technologies. Use StatTools to find the mean, median, and standard deviation of Annual Salary, broken down by each of the following categories. Comment on your findings.
   a. Gender
   b. A recoded version of Education, with new values 1 for Education less than 4, 2 for Education equal to 4, and 3 for Education greater than 4
   c. A recoded version of Age, with people aged less than 34 listed as Young, those aged at least 34 and less than 50 listed as Middle-aged, and those aged at least 50 listed as Older

9. The file **Golf Stats.xlsx** contains data on the 200 top golfers each year from 2003 to 2009. (This data set is used in an example in the next section.) Create a recoded Age variable, with values "Twenties,"

"Thirties," and "Forties," based on their ages in the 2009 sheet. Then use StatTools to calculate the mean, median, and standard deviation of the following 2009 variables, broken down by the recoded Age. Comment on whether it appears that golfers peak in their thirties.
   a. Earnings
   b. Yard/Drive and Driving Accuracy
   c. Greens in Regulation
   d. Putting Average (Golfers want this to be small.)

10. Recall from Chapter 2 that the HyTex Company is a direct marketer of technical products and that the file **Catalog Marketing.xlsx** contains recent data on 1000 HyTex customers. Use StatTools to find the mean, median, and standard deviation of AmountSpent, broken down by the following variables. Then create side-by-side box plots of AmountSpent, broken down by the same variables. Comment on how the box plots complement the summary measures.
   a. Age
   b. Gender
   c. Close
   d. Region
   e. Year of first purchase. (*Hint*: For this one, use the YEAR function to create a Year column.)
   f. The combination of Married and OwnHome. (For this one, create a code variable, with values from 1 to 4, for the four combinations of Married and OwnHome. Alternatively, create a text variable with values such as "Not married, Owns home.")

11. The file **P02_35.xlsx** contains data from a survey of 500 randomly selected households.

    a. Create a new column Has Second Income with values "Yes" and "No" depending on whether the household has a reported second income.

    b. Use StatTools to find the mean, median, and standard deviation of First Income, broken down by the variable you created in part **a.** Is there any indication that first income tends to be any larger or smaller, or has more or less variation, depending on whether there is a second income?

    c. Repeat part **b** for each of the Monthly Payment and Debt variables.

12. The file **P02_02.xlsx** contains data about 211 movies released in 2006 and 2007.

    a. Recode Genre so that all genres except for Action, Adventure, Thriller/Suspense, Drama, and Comedy are listed as Other. (Those in Other are genres with fewer than 16 movies.)

    b. Use StatTools to find the mean, median, and standard deviation of Total US Gross, broken down by the recoded Genre variable. Also, create side-by-side box plots of Total US Gross, again broken down by the recoded Genre variable. Comment on what the results say about the popularity of different genres.

13. *The Wall Street Journal CEO Compensation Study* analyzed chief executive officer (CEO) pay from many U. S. companies with fiscal year 2008 revenue of at least $5 billion that filed their proxy statements between October 2008 and March 2009. The data are in the file **P02_30.xlsx**. (Note: This data set contains somewhat different CEO compensation data from the data set used as an example later in this chapter.)

    a. Create a new variable Total 2008, the sum of Salary 2008 and Bonus 2008. (Actually, this is not "total" compensation because it omits the very lucrative compensation from stock options.) Also, recode Company Type so that the Technology and Telecommunications are collapsed into a Tech/Telecomm category.

    b. Use StatTools to find the mean, median, and standard deviation of Total 2008, broken down by the recoded Company Type. Also, create side-by-side box plots of Total 2008, again broken down by the recoded Company Type. What do the results tell you about differences in level or variability across company types?

14. The file **P02_55.xlsx** contains monthly sales (in millions of dollars) of beer, wine, and liquor. The data have not been seasonally adjusted, so there might be seasonal patterns that can be discovered.

    a. Create a new Month Name variable with values Jan, Feb, and so on. (Use Excel's MONTH function and then a lookup table.)

    b. Use StatTools to create side-by-side box plots of Total Sales, broken down by Month Name. Is there any evidence of differences across months for either the level of sales or the variability of sales?

15. The file **P03_15.xlsx** contains monthly data on the various components of the Consumer Price Index (CPI). The source claims that these data have been seasonally adjusted. The following parts ask you to check this claim.

    a. Create a new Month Name variable with values Jan, Feb, and so on. (Use Excel's MONTH function and then a lookup table.)

    b. Create side-by-side box plots of each component of the CPI (including the All Items variable), broken down by the Month Name variable from part **a.** What results would you expect for "seasonally adjusted" data? Are your results in line with this?

16. The file **P02_11.xlsx** contains data on 148 houses that were recently sold in a (fictional) suburban community. The data set includes the selling price of each house, along with its appraised value, square footage, number of bedrooms, and number of bathrooms.

    a. Create two new variables, Ratio1 and Ratio2. Ratio1 is the ratio of Appraised Value to Selling Price, and Ratio2 is the ratio of Selling Price to Square Feet. Identify any obvious outliers in these two Ratio variables.

    b. Use StatTools to find the mean, median, and standard deviation of each Ratio variable, broken down by Bedrooms. Also, create side-by-side box plots of each Ratio variable, again broken down by Bedrooms. Comment on the results.

    c. Repeat part **b** with Bedrooms replaced by Bathrooms.

    d. If you repeat parts **b** and **c** with any obvious outlier(s) from part **a** removed, do the conclusions change in any substantial way?

Level B

17. The file **P02_32.xlsx** contains blood pressures for 1000 people, along with variables that can be related to blood pressure. These other variables have a number of missing values, probably because some people didn't want to report certain information. For each of the Alcohol, Exercise, and Smoke variables, use StatTools to find the mean, median, and standard deviation of Blood Pressure, broken down by whether the data for that variable is missing. For example, there should be one set of statistics for people who reported their alcohol consumption and another for those who didn't report it. Based on your results, does it appear that there is any difference in blood pressure between those who reported and those who didn't?

18. The file **P03_18.xlsx** contains the times in the Chicago marathon for the top runners each year (the top 10,000 in 2006, the top 20,000 in 2007 and 2008).
   a. Merge the data in these three sheets into a single sheet named 2006-2008, and in the new sheet, create a variable Year that lists the year.
   b. The Time variable, shown as something like 2:16:12, is really stored as a time, the fraction of day starting from midnight. So 2:16:12, for example, which means 2 hours, 16 minutes, and 12 seconds, is stored as 0.0946, meaning that 2:16:12 AM is really 9.46% of the way from midnight to the next midnight. This isn't very useful. Do whatever it takes to recode the times into a new Minutes variable with two decimals, so that 2:16:12 becomes 136.20 minutes. (*Hint*: Look up Time functions in Excel's online help.)
   c. Create a new variable Nationality to recode Country as "KEN, ETH," "USA," or "Other," depending on whether the runner is from Kenya/Ethiopia (the usual winners), the USA, or some other country.
   d. Use StatTools to find the mean, median, standard deviation, and first and third quartiles of Minutes, broken down by Nationality. Also, create side-by-side box plots of Minutes, again broken down by Nationality. Comment on the results.
   e. Repeat part **d**, replacing Nationality by Gender.

19. The file **P02_18.xlsx** contains daily values of the S&P Index from 1970 to 2009. It also contains percentage changes in the index from each day to the next.
   a. Create a new variable President that lists the U.S. presidents Nixon through Obama on each date. You can look up the presidents and dates online.
   b. Use StatTools to find the mean, median, standard deviation, and first and third quartiles of % Change, broken down by President. Also, create side-by-side box plots of % Change, again broken down by President. Comment on the results.

20. The file **P02_56.xlsx** contains monthly values of indexes that measure the amount of energy necessary to heat or cool buildings due to outside temperatures. (See the explanation in the Source sheet of the file.) These are reported for each state in the U.S. and also for several regions, as listed in the Locations sheet, from 1931 to 2000.
   a. For each of the Heating Degree Days and Cooling Degree Days sheets, create a new Season variable with values "Winter," "Spring," "Summer," and "Fall." Winter consists of December, January, and February, Spring consists of March, April, and May, Summer consists of June, July, and August, and Fall consists of September, October, and November.
   b. Use StatTools to find the mean, median, and standard deviation of Heating Degree Days (HDD), broken down by Season, for the 48 contiguous states location (code 5999). (Ignore the first and last rows for the given location, the ones that contain -9999, the code for missing values.) Also, create side-by-side box plots of HDD, broken down by season. Comment on the results. Do they go in the direction you would expect? Do the same for Cooling Degree Days (which has no missing data).
   c. Repeat part **b** for California (code 0499).
   d. Repeat part **b** for the New England group of states (code 5801).

3.4 RELATIONSHIPS AMONG NUMERICAL VARIABLES

In this section, we discuss methods for finding relationships among numerical variables. For example, we might want to examine the relationship between heights and weights of people, or between salary and years of experience of employees. To study such relationships, we introduce two new summary measures, correlation and covariance, and a new type of chart called a scatterplot.

In general, don't use correlations that involve coded categorical variables such as 0-1 dummies. The methods from the previous two sections are more appropriate.

Note that these measures can be applied to *any* variables that are displayed numerically. However, they are appropriate only for truly numerical variables, not for categorical variables that have been coded numerically. In particular, many people create dummy (0–1) variables for categorical variables such as Gender and then include these dummies in a table of correlations. This is certainly possible, and we do not claim that it is wrong. However, if you want to investigate relationships involving categorical variables, it is better to employ the tools in the previous two sections.

3.4.1 Scatterplots

We first discuss scatterplots, a graphical method for detecting relationships between two numerical variables.[2] Then we will discuss the numerical summary measures, correlation and covariance, in the next subsection. (We do it in this order because correlation and covariance will make more sense once you understand scatterplots.) A **scatterplot** is a scatter of points, where each point denotes the values of an observation for two selected variables. The two variables are often labeled generically as X and Y, so a scatterplot is sometimes called an **X-Y chart**. The whole purpose of a scatterplot is to make a relationship (or the lack of it) apparent. Do the points tend to rise upward from left to right? Do they tend to fall downward from left to right? Does the pattern tend to be linear, nonlinear, or no particular shape? Do any points fall outside the general pattern? The answers to these questions provide information about the possible relationship between the two variables. We illustrate the process in the following example.

EXAMPLE | **3.3 GOLF STATS ON THE PGA TOUR**

For the past decade or so, the Professional Golf Association (PGA) has kept statistics on all PGA Tour players, and these stats are published on the Web. We imported yearly data from 2003–2009 into the file **Golf Stats.xlsx**. (The full 2009 data set wasn't available when we wrote this example, but it is now available in the file.) The file includes an observation for each of the top 200 earners for each year, including age, earnings, events played, rounds played, 36-hole cuts made (only the top scorers on Thursday and Friday get to play on the weekend; the others don't make the cut), top 10s, and wins. It also includes stats about efficiency in the various parts of the game (driving, putting, greens in regulation, and sand saves), as well as good holes (eagles and birdies) and bad holes (bogies). A sample of the data for 2008 appears in Figure 3.15, with the data sorted in decreasing order of earnings and a few variables not shown.[3] What relationships can be uncovered in these data for any particular year?

Figure 3.15 Golf Stats

	A	B	C	D	E	F	G	H	I	J	K
1	Player	Age	Events	Rounds	Cuts Made	Top 10s	Wins	Earnings	Yards/Drive	Driving Accuracy	Greens in Regulation
2	Vijay Singh	45	23	82	18	8	3	$6,601,095	298.7	59.5	65.1
3	Tiger Woods	32	6	23	6	6	4	$5,775,000			
4	Phil Mickelson	37	21	79	20	8	2	$5,188,875	296.5	55.3	65
5	Sergio Garcia	28	19	70	18	6	1	$4,858,224	294.6	59.4	67.1
6	Kenny Perry	47	26	97	24	7	3	$4,663,794	295.7	62	67.5
7	Anthony Kim	22	22	81	19	8	2	$4,656,266	301	58.3	65.8
8	Camilo Villegas	26	22	78	19	7	2	$4,422,641	293.6	58.2	64.6
9	Padraig Harrington	36	15	51	12	6	2	$4,313,551	297.6	59.4	59.5
10	Stewart Cink	35	23	85	19	7	1	$3,979,301	297.2	55.3	64.6
11	Justin Leonard	35	25	96	24	8	1	$3,943,542	282.5	67.7	65.9

Objective   To use scatterplots to search for relationships in the golf data.

Solution

This example is typical in that you are given many numerical variables, and it is up to you to search for possible relationships. A good first step is to ask some interesting questions

---

[2]Some people spell these plots as *scatterplots*, others *scatter plots*. We (and StatTools) prefer the one-word spelling.
[3]You might recall that Tiger Woods missed the rest of 2008 because of knee surgery, after winning the U.S. Open in June. This explains his missing values.

and then try to answer them with scatterplots. For example, do younger players play more events? Are earnings related to age? Which is related most strongly to earnings: driving, putting, or greens in regulation? Do the answers to these questions remain the same from year to year? This example is all about *exploring* the data, and we will answer only a few of the questions that could be asked. Fortunately, scatterplots are easy to create, especially with StatTools, so you can do a lot of exploring very quickly.

It is possible to create a scatterplot with Excel tools only—that is, without StatTools. To do so, highlight any two variables of interest and select a scatter chart of the top left type from the Insert ribbon. At this point, you will probably want to modify the chart by deleting the legend, inserting some titles, and possibly changing some formatting. Also, you might want to swap the roles of the *X* and *Y* variables. The point is that you can do it, but the process is a bit tedious, especially if you want to create a *lot* of scatterplots.

Excel Tip *How do you highlight two long variables such as Age and Earnings? Here are the steps that make it easy. (1) Highlight the Age label in cell B1. (2) With your finger on the Shift key, press the End key and then the down arrow key. This highlights the Age column. (3) With your finger on the Ctrl key, highlight the Earnings label in cell H1. (4) With your finger on the Shift key, press the End key and then the down arrow key. Now both columns are highlighted.*

It is much easier to use StatTools. Begin by designating a StatTools data set called Stats 2008 (to distinguish it from data sets you might want to create for the other years). Then select Scatterplot from the Summary Graphs dropdown list. This resulting dialog box appears in Figure 3.16. You *must* select at least one *X* variable and at least one *Y* variable. However, you are allowed to select multiple *X* variables and/or multiple *Y* variables. Then a scatterplot will be created for *each X-Y pair* selected. For example, if you want to see how a number of variables are related to Earnings, you can select Earnings as the *Y* variable and the others as *X* variables, as shown in the figure. Note that StatTools shows the associated correlation below each scatterplot if you check the Display Correlation Coefficient option. We will discuss correlations shortly.

Several scatterplots appear in Figures 3.17 through 3.20. (In a few of these, we modified the scale on the horizontal axis so that the scatter fills the chart.) The scatterplots in Figure 3.17 indicate the possibly surprising results that age is practically unrelated to the number of events played and earnings. Each scatter is basically a shapeless swarm of

Figure 3.16
StatTools Scatterplot Dialog Box

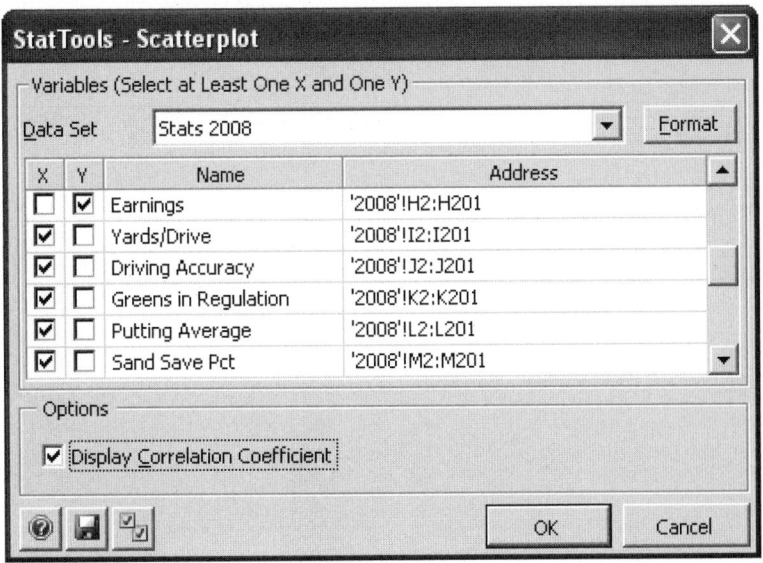

Figure 3.17 Scatterplots of Age Versus Events and Earnings

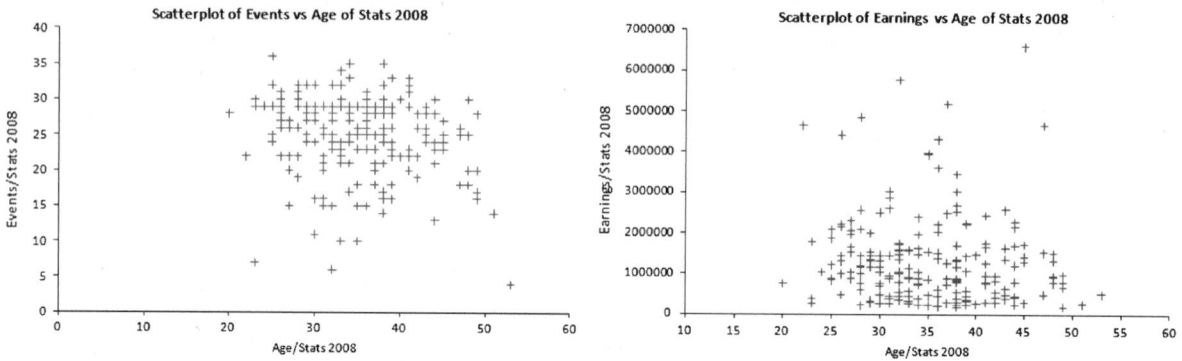

Remember that all StatTools charts are really Excel charts, so you can modify them as you like with the usual Excel chart tools.

points, and a shapeless swarm always indicates "no relationship." The scatterplots in Figure 3.18 confirm what we would expect. Specifically, players who play in more events tend to earn more, although there are a number of exceptions to this pattern. Also, players who make more 36-hole cuts tend to earn more. Note the outlier in both of these scatterplots: Tiger Woods. In spite of playing in only six events (and making the cut in all of them), he earned nearly $6 million!

Excel Tip *Unfortunately, there is no automatic way to enter a label such as "Tiger Woods" next to a point in a scatterplot. We wish there were, but there isn't, at least not without writing a macro. We had to insert the text boxes manually in Figure 3.18. If you click twice on a point (don't double-click, but slowly click twice), you can select this point. Then if you right-click, you have the option of adding a data label. However, this data label is always the value of the Y variable. In this case, it would be Tiger's earnings, not his name.*

Figure 3.18 Scatterplots of Earnings Versus Events and Cuts Made

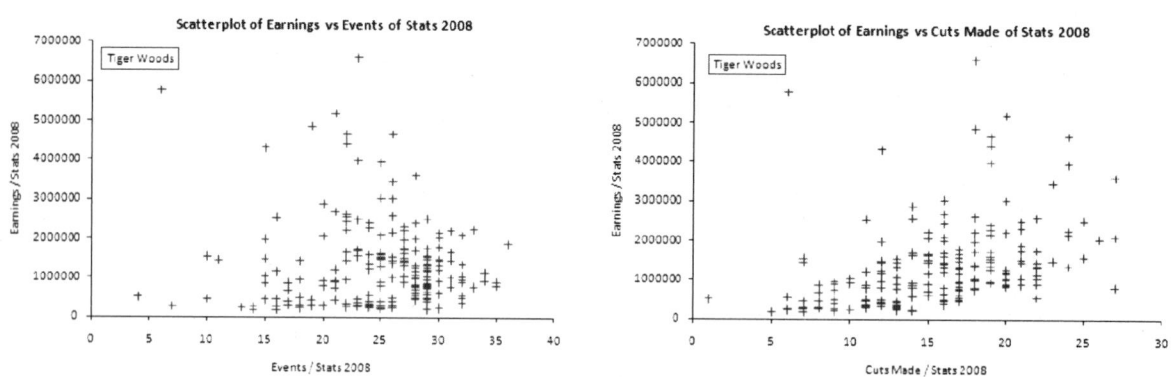

Golfers will be particularly interested in the scatterplots in Figures 3.19 and 3.20. First, the scatterplots in Figure 3.19 indicate almost no relationships between earnings and the two components of driving, length (yards per drive) and accuracy (percentage of fairways hit). At least in 2008, neither driving length nor driving accuracy seems to have much effect on earnings. In contrast, there is a reasonably strong upward relationship between

Figure 3.19   Scatterplots of Earnings Versus Driving Length and Driving Accuracy

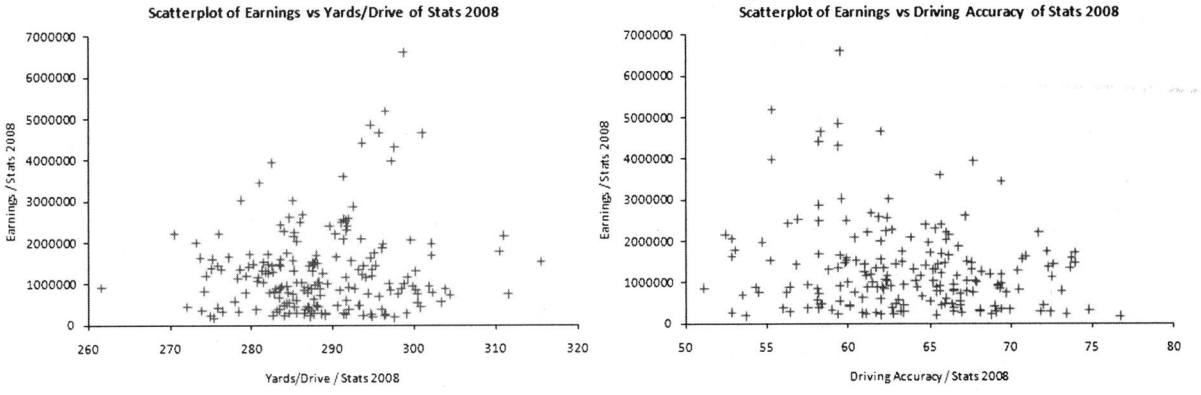

Figure 3.20   Scatterplots of Earnings Versus Putting and Greens in Regulation

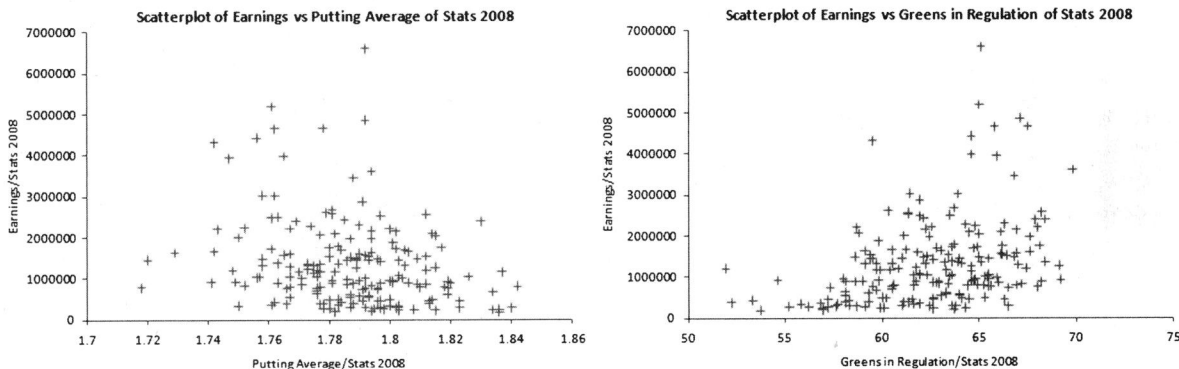

greens hit in regulation and earnings. We would expect players who hit a lot of greens in regulation to earn more, and this appears to be the case. Finally, there is a definite *downward* relationship between putting average and earnings. Does this mean that better putters earn less? Absolutely not! The putting stat is the average number of putts per hole, so that a *lower* value is better. Therefore, we expect the downward relationship indicated in the chart. In fact, the driving and putting scatterplots tend to confirm the old saying in golf: Drive for show, putt for dough.

We could obviously ask many more questions about the relationships in this golf data set and then attempt to answer them with scatterplots. For example, are the relationships (or lack of them) in the above scatterplots consistent through the years? Or should Earnings per Round be used instead of Earnings as the *Y* variable? You now have a powerful tool, scatterplots, for examining relationships, and the tool is easy to implement. We urge you to use it—a lot. ∎

Excel allows you to superimpose a trend line, linear or curved, on a scatterplot. It is an easy way to quantify the relationship apparent in the scatterplot.

Trend Lines in Scatterplots

In Chapters 10 and 11 we will discuss regression, a method for quantifying relationships between variables. We can provide a gentle introduction to regression at this point by discussing the very useful Trendline tool in Excel. Once you have a scatterplot, Excel enables you to superimpose one of several trend lines on the scatterplot. Essentially, a **trend line** is a line or curve that "fits" the scatter as well as possible. This could indeed be a straight line, or it could be one of several types of curves. (By the way, you can also superimpose a trend line on a time series graph, exactly as described here for scatterplots.)

To illustrate the Trendline option, we created the scatterplot of driving length versus driving accuracy in Figure 3.21. If you are a golfer, you are probably not surprised to see that the longest hitters tend to be less accurate. This scatterplot is definitely downward sloping, and it appears to follow a straight line reasonably well.

Figure 3.21

Scatterplots of Driving Length Versus Driving Accuracy

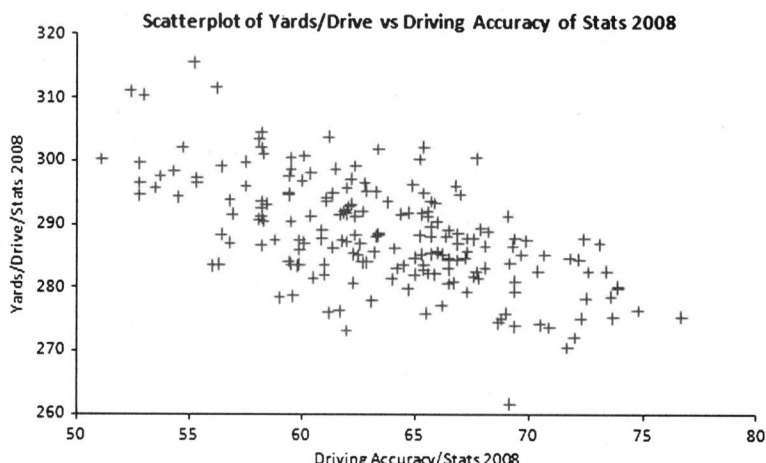

Therefore, it is reasonable to fit a linear trend line to this scatterplot. To do this, right-click on any point on the chart, select Add Trendline, and fill out the resulting dialog box as shown in Figure 3.22. Note that we have checked the Display Equation on Chart option. The result (after moving the equation to a blank part of the chart) appears in Figure 3.23. The equation you see is a regression equation. It states that driving length (y) is 350.89 minus 0.9829 times driving accuracy (x). This line is certainly not a perfect fit—there are many points well above the line and others below the line. Still, it quantifies the downward trend.

The tools in this subsection, scatterplots and trend lines superimposed on scatterplots, are among the most valuable tools you will learn in the book. When you are interested in a possible relationship between two numerical variables, these are the tools you should use first.

3.4.2 Correlation and Covariance

We discussed many numerical summary measures in Chapter 2, all of which involve a *single* variable. The two measures discussed in this section, correlation and covariance, involve *two* variables. Specifically, each measures the strength and direction of a *linear* relationship between two numerical variables. Intuitively, the relationship is "strong" if the points in a scatterplot cluster tightly around some straight line. If this straight line rises from left to right, the relationship is *positive* and the measures will be positive numbers. If it falls from left to right, the relationship is *negative* and the measures will be negative numbers.

To measure the covariance or correlation between two numerical variables X and Y—indeed, to form a scatterplot of X versus Y—X and Y must be "paired" variables. That is,

Figure 3.22
More Trendline
Options Dialog Box

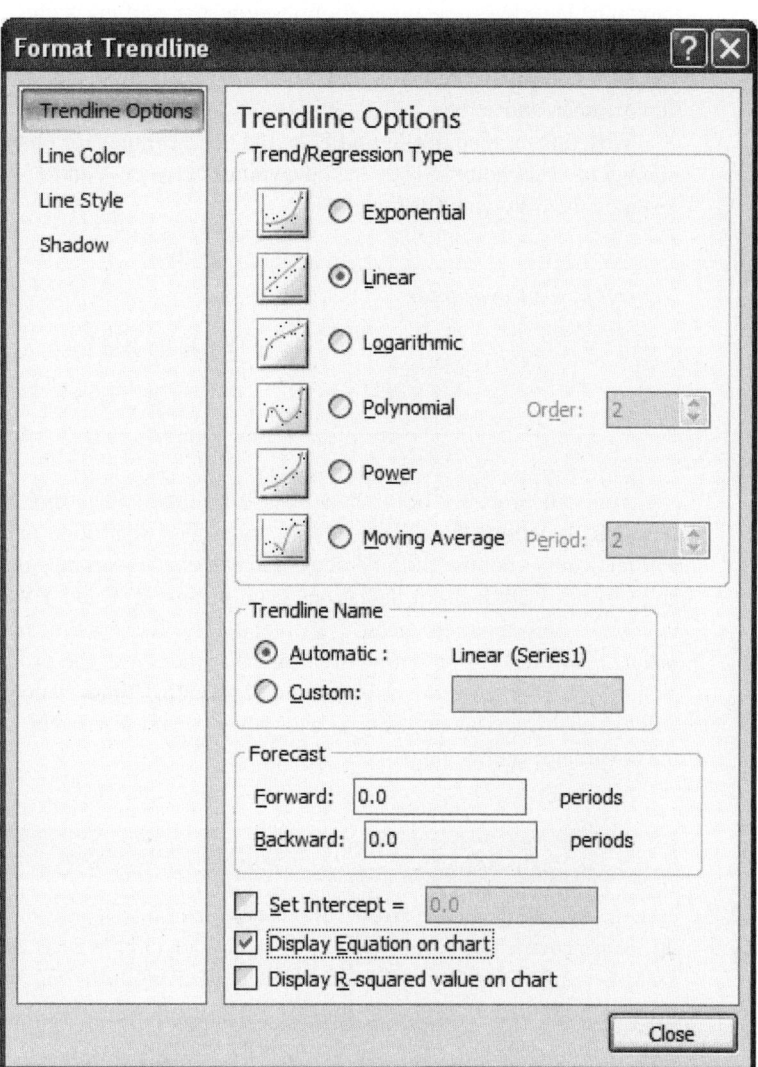

Figure 3.23
Scatterplot
with Trend Line
and Equation
Superimposed

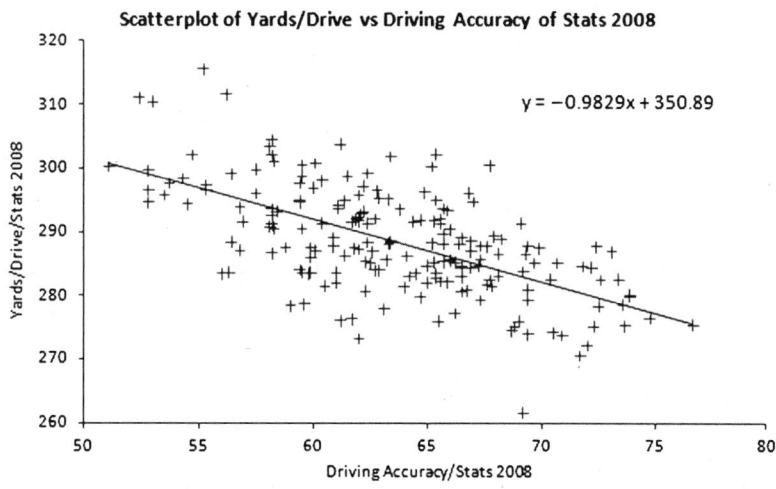

they must have the same number of observations, and the X and Y values for any observation should be naturally paired. For example, each observation could be the height and weight for a particular person, the time in a store and the amount purchased for a particular customer, and so on.

With this in mind, let X_i and Y_i be the paired values for observation i, and let n be the number of observations. Then the **covariance** between X and Y, denoted by Covar(X, Y), is given by the following formula.[4]

Formula for Covariance

$$\text{Covar}\,(X, Y) = \frac{\sum_{i=1}^{n}(X_i - \overline{X})(Y_i - \overline{Y})}{n - 1} \tag{3.1}$$

You will probably never have to use Equation (3.1) directly—Excel has a built-in **COVAR** function that does it for you, and StatTools also calculates covariance automatically—but the formula does indicate what covariance is all about. It is essentially an average of products of deviations from means. If X and Y vary in the *same* direction, then when X is above its mean, Y will tend to be above its mean, and when X is below its mean, Y will tend to be below its mean. In either case, the product of deviations will be positive—a positive times a positive or a negative times a negative—so the covariance will be positive. The opposite is true when X and Y vary in *opposite* directions. Then the covariance will be negative.

CHANGES IN EXCEL 2010

Excel's old COVAR function actually uses denominator n, so it gives the population covariance, not the sample covariance (denominator $n-1$) in Equation (3.1). In Excel 2010, both versions are available, named COVARIANCE.P (population) and COVARIANCE.S (sample).

Covariance is too sensitive to the measurement scales of X and Y to make it interpretable, so we rely much more on correlation, which is unaffected by measurement scales.

Covariance has a serious limitation as a descriptive measure because it is very sensitive to the *units* in which X and Y are measured. For example, the covariance can be inflated by a factor of 1000 simply by measuring X in dollars rather than thousands of dollars. This limits the usefulness of covariance as a descriptive measure, and we will use it very little in the book.[5]

In contrast, the **correlation**, denoted by Correl(X, Y), remedies this problem. It is a *unitless* quantity that is unaffected by the measurement scale. For example, the correlation is the same regardless of whether the variables are measured in dollars, thousands of dollars, or millions of dollars. The correlation is defined by Equation (3.2), where Stdev(X) and Stdev(Y) denote the standard deviations of X and Y. Again, you will probably never have to use this formula for calculations—Excel does it for you with the built-in **CORREL** function, and StatTools also calculates correlations automatically—but it does show how correlation and covariance are related to one another.

---

[4]Actually, Excel's COVAR function uses n in the denominator, whereas StatTools uses $n-1$. Fortunately, this is not an issue with correlation. Excel's CORREL function and StatTools produce exactly the same correlations.
[5]Don't write off covariance too quickly, however. If you plan to take a finance course in investments, you will see plenty of covariances.

> **Formula for Correlation**
>
> $$\text{Correl}\,(X, Y) = \frac{\text{Covar}(X, Y)}{\text{Stdev}(X) \times \text{Stdev}(Y)} \qquad \textbf{(3.2)}$$

Correlation is useful only for measuring the strength of a linear relationship. Strongly related variables could have correlation close to 0 if the relationship is nonlinear.

The correlation is not only unaffected by the units of measurement of the two variables, but it is *always* between -1 and $+1$. The closer it is to either of these two extremes, the closer the points in a scatterplot are to a straight line, either in the negative or positive direction. On the other hand, if the correlation is close to 0, then the scatterplot is typically a "cloud" of points with no apparent relationship. However, while it is not common, it is also *possible* that the points are close to a curve and have a correlation close to 0. This is because correlation is relevant only for measuring *linear* relationships.

When there are several numerical variables in a data set, it is useful to create a table of covariances and/or correlations. Each value in the table then corresponds to a particular pair of variables. StatTools allows you to do this easily, as illustrated in the following continuation of the golf example. However, we first make three important points about the roles of scatterplots, correlations, and covariances.

- **A correlation is a single-number summary of a scatterplot.** It never conveys as much information as the full scatterplot; it only summarizes the information in the scatterplot. However, it is often more convenient to report a table of correlations for many variables than to report an unwieldy number of scatterplots.

A correlation is only a single-number summary of a scatterplot, so it always contains less information than the full scatterplot

- **We are usually on the lookout for large correlations, those near -1 or $+1$.** But how large is "large"? There is no generally agreed-upon cutoff, but by looking at a number of scatterplots and their corresponding correlations, you will start to get a sense of what a correlation such as -0.5 or $+0.7$ really means in terms of the strength of the linear relationship between the variables. (In addition, we will attach a concrete meaning to the *square* of a correlation when we discuss regression in Chapters 10 and 11.)

- **Do not even try to interpret covariances numerically except possibly to check whether they are positive or negative.** For interpretive purposes, concentrate on correlations.

FUNDAMENTAL INSIGHT

Scatterplots Versus Correlations

It is important to remember that a correlation is a single-number measure of the linear relationship between two numerical variables. Although a correlation is a very useful measure, it is hard to imagine exactly what a correlation of 0.3 or 0.8, say, actually means. In contrast, a scatterplot of two numerical variables indicates the relationship between the two variables very clearly. In short, a scatterplot conveys *much* more information than the corresponding correlation.

EXAMPLE | **3.3 GOLF STATS (CONTINUED)**

In the previous subsection, we saw how relationships between several of the golf variables can be detected with scatterplots. What further insights do we get by looking at correlations between these variables?

Objective To use correlations to understand relationships in the golf data.

Solution

With the many numerical variables in the golf data set, it is indeed unwieldy to create scatterplots for all pairs of variables, but it is easy to create a table of correlations with StatTools.[6] (If you want only one correlation, you might instead use Excel's CORREL function.) As an example, we will create a table of correlations for the golf data in 2008. To do so, select Correlation and Covariance from the Summary Statistics dropdown list, and fill in the resulting dialog box as shown in Figure 3.24. There are several options. First, you can check as many numerical variables as you like. We checked a few but not all. Second, you can ask for a table of correlations and/or a table of covariances. We asked for correlations only. Finally, correlations (and covariances) are symmetric in that the correlation between any two variables X and Y is the same as the correlation between Y and X. Therefore, you can choose any of the three table structure options and receive exactly the same information. We tend to favor the Entries Below the Diagonal Only option.

Figure 3.24

StatTools Correlation and Covariance Dialog Box

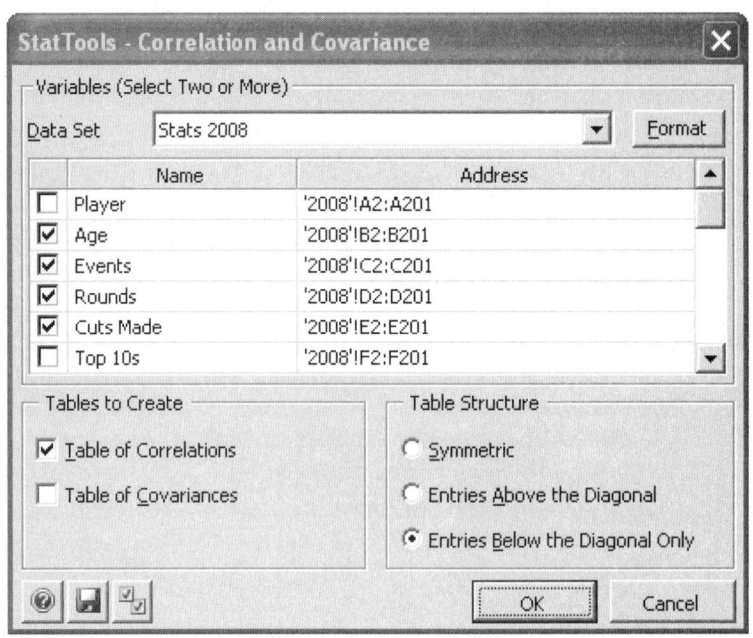

You typically scan a table of correlations for the large correlations, either positive or negative. Conditional formatting is useful, especially if the table is a large one.

The resulting table of correlations appears in Figure 3.25. You can ignore the 1.000 values along the diagonal because a variable is always perfectly correlated with itself. Besides these, we are looking for relatively large values, either positive or negative. When the table is fairly large, conditional formatting is useful. Although it doesn't show up on the printed page, we formatted all correlations between 0.6 and 0.999 as red and all correlations between -1.0 and -0.6 as green. (See the finished version of the golf file for instructions on how to create the conditional formatting.) There are three large positive values involving events, rounds, and cuts made. None of these should come as a surprise. There is only one large negative correlation, the one between driving length and driving accuracy, and we already saw the corresponding scatterplot in Figure 3.21. So if you want to know what a correlation of approximately -0.6 actually means, look at the scatterplot in this figure. It indicates a definite downward trend, but there is quite a lot of variability around the best-fitting straight line.

[6]Some statistical software packages provide a "matrix of scatterplots" option. This is essentially like a table of correlations between all pairs of variables except that each correlation is replaced by a scatterplot. StatTools does not provide this option, at least not yet.

Figure 3.25 Correlations for Golf Data

	A	B	C	D	E	F	G	H	I	J	K
7		Age	Events	Rounds	Cuts Made	Earnings	Yards/Drive	Driving Accuracy	Greens in Regulation	Putting Average	Sand Save Pct
8	Correlation Table	Stats 2008	Stats 2008	Stats 2008	Stats 2008	Stats 2008	Stats 2008	Stats 2008	Stats 2008	Stats 2008	Stats 2008
9	Age	1.000									
10	Events	-0.189	1.000								
11	Rounds	-0.185	0.941	1.000							
12	Cuts Made	-0.173	0.701	0.891	1.000						
13	Earnings	-0.102	-0.065	0.143	0.417	1.000					
14	Yards/Drive	-0.365	0.012	0.001	0.012	0.128	1.000				
15	Driving Accuracy	0.274	0.079	0.103	0.088	-0.186	-0.612	1.000			
16	Greens in Regulation	-0.037	0.261	0.418	0.527	0.356	0.271	0.092	1.000		
17	Putting Average	0.097	-0.098	-0.199	-0.262	-0.271	0.177	0.118	0.134	1.000	
18	Sand Save Pct	0.049	-0.175	-0.080	0.037	0.211	-0.271	-0.001	-0.123	-0.383	1.000

Again, a correlation is only a summary of a scatterplot. Therefore, you can learn more about any interesting-looking correlations by creating the corresponding scatterplot. For example, the scatterplot corresponding to the 0.891 correlation between Cuts Made and Rounds appears in Figure 3.26. (We also superimposed a trend line.) This chart shows the strong linear relationship between cuts made and rounds played, but it also shows that there is still considerable variability around the best-fitting straight line, even with a correlation as large as 0.891.

Figure 3.26

Scatterplot of Cuts Made Versus Rounds

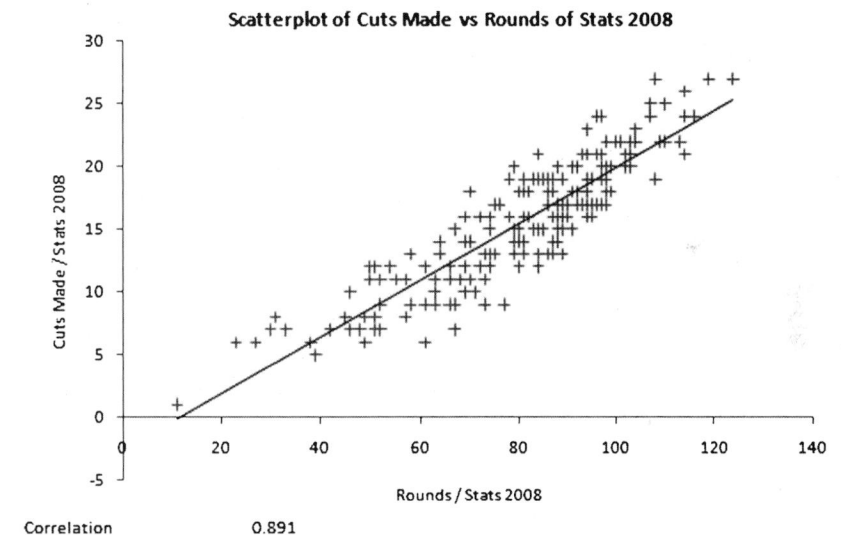

Scatterplot of Cuts Made vs Rounds of Stats 2008

Correlation   0.891

PROBLEMS

Level A

21. The file **P02_07.xlsx** includes data on 204 employees at the (fictional) company Beta Technologies.
  a. Create a table of correlations between the variables Age, Prior Experience, Beta Experience, Education, and Annual Salary. Which of the first four of these variables is most highly correlated (in a positive direction) with Annual Salary?
  b. Create scatterplots of Annual Salary (Y axis) versus each of Age, Prior Experience, Beta Experience, and Education.
  c. For the variable from part **a** most highly correlated with Annual Salary, create a (linear) trend line in its scatterplot with the corresponding equation shown in the chart. What does this equation imply about the relationship between the two variables? Be specific.

22. The file **P03_22.xlsx** lists financial data on movies released since 1980 with budgets at least $20 million.

a. Reduce the size of this data set by deleting all movies with a budget of more than $100 million. Also, delete all movies where US Gross and/or Worldwide Gross is listed as Unknown.

b. For the remaining movies, create a table of correlations between the variables Budget, US Gross, and Worldwide Gross. Comment on the results. Are there any surprises?

c. For the movies remaining after part **a**, create a scatterplot of Worldwide Gross (Y axis) versus US Gross and another scatterplot of US Gross (Y axis) versus Budget. Briefly explain any patterns you see in these scatterplots. Do they seem to be consistent with the corresponding correlations?

23. The file **P02_10.xlsx** contains midterm and final exam scores for 96 students in a corporate finance course.

a. Do the students' scores for the two exams tend to go together, so that those who do poorly on the midterm tend to do poorly on the final, and those who do well on the midterm tend to do well on the final? Create a scatterplot, along with a correlation, to answer this question.

b. Superimpose a (linear) trend line on the scatterplot, along with the equation of the line. Based on this equation, what would you expect a student with a 75 on the midterm to score on the final exam?

24. Recall that the file **Golf Stats.xlsx** contains data on the 200 top golfers each year from 2003 to 2009. The question to be explored in this problem is what drives earnings, and whether this is consistent from year to year.

a. For each year, create a new variable Earnings/Event. This is potentially a better measure of earnings because some players enter more events than others.

b. Create a separate table of correlations for each year that includes Earnings/Event, Yards/Drive, Driving Accuracy, Greens in Regulation, Putting Average, Sand Save Pct, and Birdies/Round. (StatTools will warn you about missing data, but don't worry about it.) Explain whether these correlations help answer the questions posed above.

c. There is a saying in golf: "Drive for show, putt for dough." Create a separate set of scatterplots for each year of Earnings/Event (Y axis) versus each of Yards/Drive, Driving Accuracy, and Putting Average. Discuss whether these scatterplots tend to support the saying.

25. The file **P02_02.xlsx** contains data about 211 movies released in 2006 and 2007. The question to be explored in this problem is whether the total gross for a movie can be predicted from how it does in its first week or two.

a. Create a table of correlations between the five variables 7-day Gross, 14-day Gross, Total US

Gross, International Gross, and US DVD Sales. (StatTools will warn you about missing data, but don't worry about it.) Does it appear that the last three variables are related to either of the first two?

b. Explore the basic question further by creating a scatterplot of each of Total US Gross, International Gross, and US DVD Sales (Y axis) versus each of 7-day Gross and 14-day Gross (X axis)—six scatterplots in all. Do these support the claim that you can tell how well a movie will do by seeing how it does in its first week or two?

26. The file **P02_39.xlsx** lists the average high school student scores on the SAT exam by state. There are three components of the SAT: critical reading, math, and writing. These components are listed, along with their sum. The percentage of all potential students who took the SAT is also listed by state. Create correlations and scatterplots to explore the following relationships and comment on the results.

a. The relationship between the combined score and the percentage taking the exam.

b. The relationship between the critical reading and writing components.

c. The relationship between a combined verbal component (the average of critical reading and writing) and the math component.

d. The relationship between each of critical reading, math, and writing with the combined score. Are these bound to be highly correlated because the sum of the three components *equals* the combined score?

27. The file **P02_16.xlsx** contains traffic data from 256 weekdays on four variables. Each variable lists the number of arrivals during a specific 5-minute period of the day.

a. What would it mean, in the context of traffic, for the data in the four columns to be positively correlated? Based on your observations of traffic, would you expect positive correlations?

b. Create a table of correlations and check whether these data behave as you would expect.

28. The file **P02_11.xlsx** contains data on 148 houses that were recently sold in a (fictional) suburban community. The data set includes the selling price of each house, along with its appraised value, square footage, number of bedrooms, and number of bathrooms.

a. Create a table of correlations between all of the variables. Comment on the magnitudes of the correlations. Specifically, which of the last three variables, Square Feet, Bedrooms, and Bathrooms, are highly correlated with Selling Price?

b. Create four scatterplots to show how the other four variables are related to Selling Price. In each, Selling Price should be on the Y axis. Are these in line with the correlations in part **a**?

c. You might think of the difference, Selling Price minus Appraised Value, as the "error" in the appraised value, in the sense that this difference is how much more or less the house sold for than the appraiser expected. Find the correlation between this difference and Selling Price, and find the correlation between the *absolute value* of this difference and Selling Price. If either of these correlations is reasonably large, what is it telling us?

Level B

29. The file **P03_29.xlsx** contains monthly prices of four precious metals: gold, silver, platinum, and palladium. The question to be explored here is whether changes in these commodities move together through time.

a. Create time series graphs of the four series. Do the series appear to move together?

b. Create four new difference variables, one for each metal. Each should list this month's price minus the previous month's price. Then create time series graphs of the differences. Note that there will be missing data for Jan-97 because the Dec-96 prices are not listed. Also, because the source for this data set listed prices for platinum and palladium through Nov-08 only, there will be missing data at the end of these series.

c. Create a table of correlations between the differences created in part **b**. Based on this table, comment on whether the changes in the prices of these metals tend to move together over time.

d. For all correlations in part **c** above 0.6, create the corresponding scatterplots of the differences (for example, gold differences versus silver differences). Do these, along with the time series graphs from parts **a** and **b**, provide a clearer picture of how these series move together over time? Discuss in some detail.

e. Check with your own formulas using Excel's CORREL function that StatTools uses data through Dec-09 for the correlation between gold and silver, but it uses data through Nov-08 for correlations between gold and platinum. That is, check that StatTools uses all of the available data for either correlation.

30. The file **P03_30.xlsx** contains monthly data on exchange rates of various currencies versus the U.S. dollar. It is of interest to financial analysts and economists to see whether exchange rates move together through time. You could find the correlations between the exchange rates themselves, but it is often more useful with time series data to check for correlations between *differences* from month to month.

a. Create a column of differences for each currency. For example, the difference corresponding to

Jan-06 will be blank for each currency because the Dec-05 value isn't listed, but the difference for euros in Feb-06 will be 0.8375 − 0.8247.

b. Create a table of correlations between all of the *original* variables. Then on the same sheet, create a second table of correlations between the difference variables. On this same sheet, enter two cutoff values, one positive such as 0.6 and one negative such as −0.5, and use conditional formatting to color all correlations (in both tables) above the positive cutoff green and all correlations below the negative cutoff red. Do it so that the 1s on the diagonal are not colored.

c. Based on the second table and your coloring, can you conclude that these currencies tend to move together in the same direction? If not, what can you conclude?

d. Can you explain how the correlation between two currencies like the Chinese yuan and British pound can be fairly highly negatively correlated, whereas the correlation between their differences is essentially zero? Would you conclude that these two currencies "move together?" (*Hint*: There is no easy answer, but scatterplots and time series graphs for these two currencies and their differences are revealing.)

31. The file **P02_35.xlsx** contains data from a survey of 500 randomly selected (fictional) households.

a. Create a table of correlations between the last five variables (First Income to Debt). On the sheet with these correlations, enter a "cutoff" correlation such as 0.5 in a blank cell. Then use conditional formatting to color green all correlations in the table at least as large as this cutoff, but don't color the 1s on the diagonal. The coloring should change automatically as you change the cutoff. This is always a good idea for highlighting the "large" correlations in any correlations table.

b. When you create the table of correlations, you are warned about the missing values for Second Income. Do some investigation to see how StatTools deals with missing values and correlations. There are two basic possibilities (and both of these are options in some software packages). First, it could delete all rows that have missing values for *any* variables and then calculate all of the correlations based on the remaining data. Second, when it creates the correlation for any pair of variables, it could (temporarily) delete only the rows that have missing data for these two variables and then calculate the correlation on what remains for these two variables. Why would you prefer the second option? How does StatTools do it?

32. We have indicated that if you have two categorical variables and you want to check whether they are related, the best method is to create a crosstabs, possibly with the counts expressed as percentages. But suppose both categorical variables have only two categories and these variables are coded as dummy 0–1 variables. Then there is nothing to prevent you from finding the correlation between them with the same Equation (3.2) from this section. However, if we let C(i,j) be the count of observations where the first variable has value i and the second variable has value j, there are only four joint counts that can have any bearing on the relationship between the two variables: C(0,0), C(0,1), C(1,0), and C(1,1). Let $C_1(1)$ be the count of 1s for the first variable and let $C_2(1)$ be the count of 1s for the second variable. Then it is clear that $C_1(1) = C(1,0) + C(1,1)$ and $C_2(1) = C(0,1) + C(1,1)$, so $C_1(1)$ and $C_2(1)$ are determined

by the joint counts. It can be shown algebraically that the correlation between the two 0–1 variables is

$$\frac{nC(1,\,1) - C_1(1)C_2(1)}{\sqrt{C_1(1)(n - C_1(1))}\,\sqrt{C_2(1)(n - C_2(1))}}$$

To illustrate this, the file **P03_32.xlsx** contains two 0–1 variables. (The values were generated fairly randomly.) Create a crosstabs to find the required counts, and use the above formula to calculate the correlation. Then use StatTools (or Excel's CORREL function) to find the correlation in the usual way. Do your two results match? (Nevertheless, we do not necessarily recommend finding correlations between 0–1 variables. A crosstabs is more meaningful and easier to interpret.)

3.5 PIVOT TABLES

We now look at one of Excel's most powerful—and easy-to-use—tools, the **pivot table**. This tool provides an incredible amount of useful information about a data set. Pivot tables allow you to "slice and dice" data in a variety of ways. That is, they break the data down by categories so that you can see, for example, average sales by gender, by region of country, by time of day, or any combination of these. Sometimes pivot tables are used to display counts, such as the number of customers broken down by gender and region of country. These tables of counts, which are often called crosstabs or contingency tables, have been used by statisticians for years. However, Excel provides more variety and flexibility with its pivot tables than most statistical software packages have traditionally provided with their crosstabs options. In particular, crosstabs typically list only counts, whereas pivot tables can list counts, sums, averages, and other summary measures.[7]

It is easiest to understand pivot tables by means of examples, so we illustrate several possibilities in the following example.

EXAMPLE | **3.4 EXAMINING CUSTOMER ORDERS AT ELECMART**

The file **Elecmart Sales.xlsx** (see Figure 3.27) contains data on 400 customer orders during a period of several months for Elecmart (a fictional company). This is a typical data set where pivot tables can be used to gain useful information. There are several categorical variables and several numerical variables. The categorical variables include the day of week, time of day, region of country, type of credit card used, gender of customer, and buy category of the customer (high, medium, or low) based on previous behavior. Even the date variable can be treated as a categorical variable. The numerical variables include the number of items ordered, the total cost of the order, and the price of the highest-priced item purchased. The manager of Elecmart wants to summarize the data so that she can understand the buying patterns of her customers. How can she use pivot tables to gain useful information?

Objective To use pivot tables to break down the customer order data by a number of categorical variables.

---

[7]To be fair, many other statistical software packages, such as SPSS and SAS, now emulate Excel pivot tables.

Figure 3.27 Elecmart Data

	A	B	C	D	E	F	G	H	I	J
1	Date	Day	Time	Region	CardType	Gender	BuyCategory	ItemsOrdered	TotalCost	HighItem
2	6-Mar	Mon	Morning	West	ElecMart	Female	High	4	$136.97	$79.97
3	6-Mar	Mon	Morning	West	Other	Female	Medium	1	$25.55	$25.55
4	6-Mar	Mon	Afternoon	West	ElecMart	Female	Medium	5	$113.95	$90.47
5	6-Mar	Mon	Afternoon	NorthEast	Other	Female	Low	1	$6.82	$6.82
6	6-Mar	Mon	Afternoon	West	ElecMart	Male	Medium	4	$147.32	$83.21
7	6-Mar	Mon	Afternoon	NorthEast	Other	Female	Medium	5	$142.15	$50.90
8	7-Mar	Tues	Evening	West	Other	Male	Low	1	$18.65	$18.65
9	7-Mar	Tues	Evening	South	Other	Male	High	4	$178.34	$161.93
10	7-Mar	Tues	Evening	West	Other	Male	Low	2	$25.83	$15.91
11	8-Mar	Wed	Morning	MidWest	Other	Female	Low	1	$18.13	$18.13
12	8-Mar	Wed	Morning	NorthEast	ElecMart	Female	Medium	2	$54.52	$54.38
13	8-Mar	Wed	Afternoon	South	Other	Male	Medium	2	$61.93	$56.32
14	9-Mar	Thurs	Morning	NorthEast	ElecMart	Male	High	3	$147.68	$96.64
15	9-Mar	Thurs	Afternoon	NorthEast	Other	Male	Low	1	$27.24	$27.24
16	10-Mar	Fri	Morning	West	Other	Female	Low	3	$46.18	$44.27
17	10-Mar	Fri	Afternoon	West	Other	Male	Low	5	$107.44	$91.64

Solution

Pivot tables are perfect for breaking down data by categories. We call this "slicing and dicing" the data.

Before we dive into the details, we first preview the results you can obtain. Pivot tables are useful for breaking down numerical variables by categories, or for counting observations in categories and possibly expressing the counts as percentages. So, for example, you might want to see how the average total cost for females differs from the similar average for males. Or you might simply want to see the percentage of the 400 sales made by females. Pivot tables allow you to find such averages and percentages easily.

Actually, you could find such averages or percentages without using pivot tables. For example, you could sort on gender and then find the average of the Female rows and the average of the Male rows. However, this takes time, and more complex breakdowns are even more difficult and time-consuming. They are all easy and quick with pivot tables. Besides that, the resulting tables can be accompanied with corresponding charts that require virtually no extra effort to create. Pivot tables are a manager's dream. Fortunately, with Excel they are also a manager's *reality*.[8]

We begin by building a pivot table to find the sum of TotalCost broken down by time of day and region of country. Although we show this in a number of screen shots, just to help beginners get the knack of it, the process takes only a few seconds after you gain some experience with pivot tables.

To start, click on the PivotTable button at the far left on the Insert ribbon (see Figure 3.28). This produces the dialog box in Figure 3.29. The top section allows you to specify the table or range that contains the data. (You can also specify an external data source, but we will not cover this option here.) The bottom section allows you to select the location where you want the results to be placed. If you start with the cursor inside the data set, Excel's guess for the table or range is usually correct, although you can override it if necessary. Make sure the range selected for this example is A1:J401. This selected range should

---

[8]One Excel 2007 book by Bill Jelen (known as "Mr. Excel") claims that although pivot tables have been around for years and represent Excel's arguably most powerful tool, they are used by only about 10% of business people. Fortunately, you will be in that 10%.

Figure 3.28 PivotTable Button on the Insert Ribbon

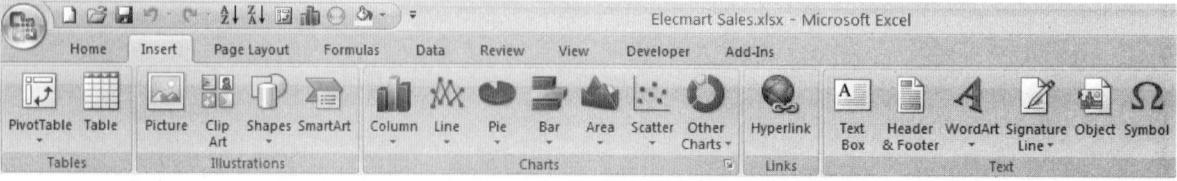

Figure 3.29

Create PivotTable
Dialog Box

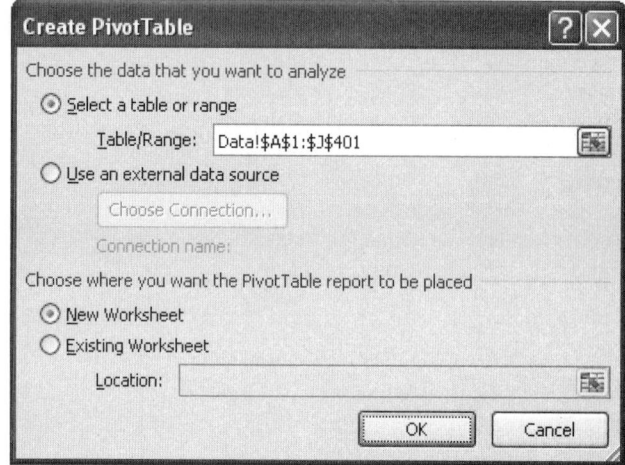

always include the variable names at the top of each column. Then click on OK. Note that with these settings, the pivot table will be placed in a new worksheet with a generic name such as Sheet1. We recommend that you rename it to something like PivotTable1.

This produces a blank pivot table, as shown in Figure 3.30. Also, assuming the cursor is within this blank pivot table, the PivotTable Tools "super tab" is selected. This super tab

Figure 3.30

Blank Pivot Table

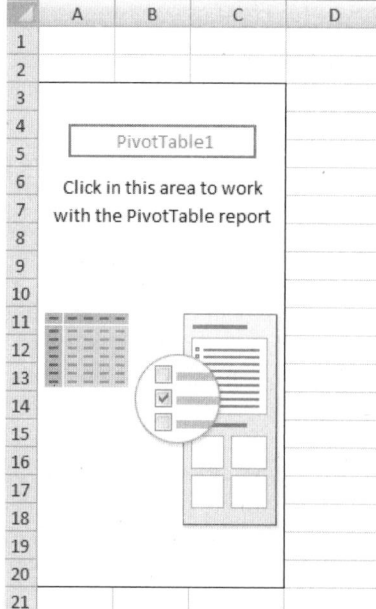

has two ribbons, Options and Design. The Options ribbon appears in Figure 3.31, and the Design ribbon appears in Figure 3.32. Each of these has a variety of buttons for manipulating pivot tables, some of which we will explore shortly. Finally, the PivotTable Field List window in Figure 3.33 is visible. By default, it is docked at the right of the screen, but you can move it if you like.

Figure 3.31 PivotTable Options Ribbon

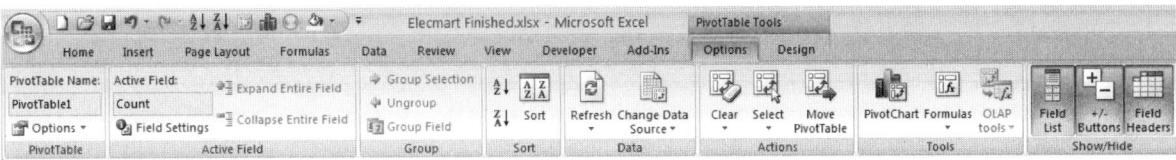

Figure 3.32 PivotTable Design Ribbon

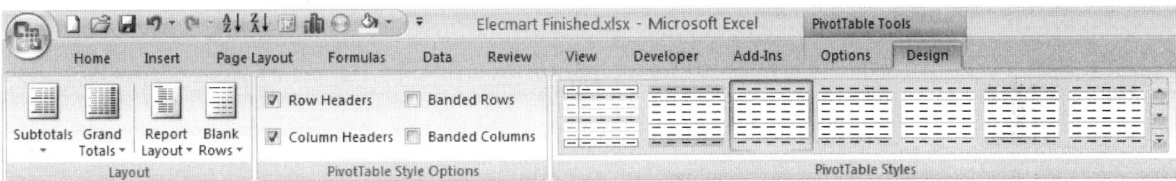

Figure 3.33

PivotTable Field List Window

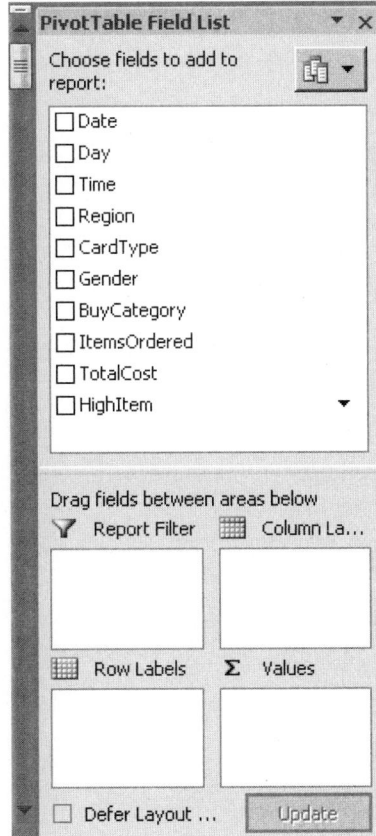

Note that the two pivot table ribbons and the pivot table field list window are visible only when the active cell is inside a pivot table. If you click outside the pivot table, say, in cell D1, all three of these will disappear. Don't worry. You can get them back by clicking anywhere inside the pivot table.

If you have used pivot tables in a previous version of Excel, the blank pivot table in Figure 3.30 will look different. Here are two things to be aware of. First, if you open a file in the old .xls format (Excel 2003 or earlier) and go through the same steps as above, you will get an "old style" pivot table, as shown in Figure 3.34. Second, if you prefer the old style, especially for dragging and dropping, Excel 2007 lets you revert back to it. To do so, right-click on the pivot table, select PivotTable Options, click on the Display tab, and check the Classic PivotTable layout option (see Figure 3.35). You can use the new layout or the old one,

The pivot table "look" changed considerably in Excel 2007, but the functionality is virtually the same.

Figure 3.34
Old-Style Blank
Pivot Table

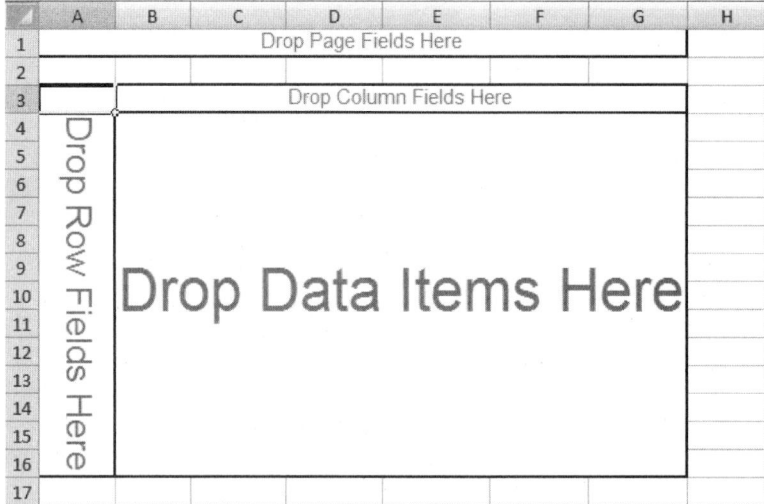

Figure 3.35
Switching to Classic
PivotTable Layout

whichever you prefer. We were perfectly happy with the old layout, but Microsoft evidently got enough complaints from users that they tried to make it more user friendly.

The Field List window indicates that a pivot table has four areas. These are for Report Filter, Row Labels, Column Labels, and Values. They correspond to the four areas in Figure 3.34 where you can put fields.[9] Note that the terminology is slightly different in Excel 2007. Here is the correspondence (old to new):

- Page Fields correspond to Report Filters.
- Row Fields correspond to Row Labels.
- Column Fields correspond to Column Labels.
- Data Fields correspond to Values.

Essentially, a Row field has categories that go down the left side of a pivot table, a Column field has categories that go across the top of a pivot table, a Report Filter field lets you filter the whole pivot table by its categories, and a Values field contains the data you want to summarize. Typically (but not always), you will place categorical variables in the Report Filter, Row, and/or Column areas, and you will place numerical variables in the Values area.

In the present example, select Time and Region for the Row fields and TotalCost for the Values field. To do this, check the Time, Region, and TotalCost boxes in the upper half of the Field List window. With no extra work whatsoever, you get the pivot table in Figure 3.36. It shows the sum of TotalCost, broken down by time of day and region of country. For example, the total cost of orders in the morning in the South was $3,835.86, and the total cost of orders in the morning (over all regions) was $18,427.31.

Figure 3.36

Sum of TotalCost by Time and Region (Compact Layout)

	A	B	C
1			
2			
3	Row Labels ▼	Sum of TotalCost	
4	⊟Afternoon	24265.6	
5	MidWest	3187.16	
6	NorthEast	8159.78	
7	South	5729.72	
8	West	7188.94	
9	⊟Evening	18834.3	
10	MidWest	2552.89	
11	NorthEast	5941.49	
12	South	3864.12	
13	West	6475.8	
14	⊟Morning	18427.31	
15	MidWest	3878.22	
16	NorthEast	5084.57	
17	South	3835.86	
18	West	5628.66	
19	Grand Total	61527.21	
20			

Excel applies two rules to variables checked at the top of the Field List window:

1. When you check a text variable or a date variable in the field list, it is added to the Row Labels area.

2. When you check a numerical variable in the field list, it is added to the Values area and summarized with the Sum function.

[9]In discussing pivot tables, Microsoft uses the term *field* rather than *variable*, so we will do so as well.

This is exactly what happens when you check Time, Region, and TotalCost. However, this is just the beginning. With very little work, you can do a lot more. Some of the possibilities are explained in the remainder of this example.

Starting with Excel 2007, there are three different layouts for pivot tables, but the differences are relatively minor. Ultimately, it is a matter of taste.

First, however, we discuss the new look of pivot tables in Excel 2007. Notice that the pivot table in Figure 3.36 has *both* row fields, Time and Region, in column A. This wasn't possible in old-style pivot tables, where the two row fields would have been in separate columns. Microsoft decided to offer this new layout because of its clean, streamlined look. In fact, you can now choose from three layouts: Compact, Outline, or Tabular. These are available from the Report Layout dropdown list on the Design ribbon. When you create a pivot table (in an .xlsx file), you get the compact layout by default. If you would rather have the tabular or outline layout, it is easy to switch to them. In particular, the tabular layout, shown in Figure 3.37, is closer to what was used in previous versions of Excel. (Outline layout, not shown here, is very similar to tabular layout except for the placement of its subtotals.)

Figure 3.37

Sum of TotalCost by Time and Region (Tabular Layout)

	A	B	C	D
1				
2				
3	**Time**	**Region**	**Sum of TotalCost**	
4	⊟Afternoon	MidWest	3187.16	
5		NorthEast	8159.78	
6		South	5729.72	
7		West	7188.94	
8	**Afternoon Total**		**24265.6**	
9	⊟Evening	MidWest	2552.89	
10		NorthEast	5941.49	
11		South	3864.12	
12		West	6475.8	
13	**Evening Total**		**18834.3**	
14	⊟Morning	MidWest	3878.22	
15		NorthEast	5084.57	
16		South	3835.86	
17		West	5628.66	
18	**Morning Total**		**18427.31**	
19	**Grand Total**		**61527.21**	
20				

One significant advantage to using tabular (or outline) layout instead of compact layout is that you can see which fields are in the row and column areas. Take another look at the pivot table in Figure 3.36. It is pretty obvious that categories such as afternoon and morning have to do with time of day and that categories such as Midwest and South have to do with region of country. However, there are no labels that explicitly name the row fields. In contrast, the tabular layout in Figure 3.37 names them explicitly. Still, you can choose the layout you prefer.

Hiding Categories (Filtering)

The pivot table in Figure 3.36 shows all times of day for all regions, but this is not necessary. You can filter out any of the times or regions you don't want to see. To understand how this works, make sure the Options ribbon is visible. In the Active Field group, you will notice that one of the fields is designated as the active field. The active field corresponds to the location of your cursor. If your cursor is on a Time category, such as Evening, then Time is the active field. If your cursor is on a Region category such as NorthEast, then Region is the active field. If your cursor is on any of the numbers, then Sum of TotalCost is the active field.

Once you understand the active field concept, then the way Excel implements filtering makes sense. If Time is the active field and you click on the Row Labels dropdown arrow, you see the dialog box in Figure 3.38. To see data only for Afternoon and Morning, for example, uncheck the Select All item and then check the Afternoon and Morning items. Similarly, if Region is the active field and you click on the Row Labels dropdown arrow, you can check which regions you want to filter on. (If you are in tabular layout, it is more straightforward, because each row field then has its own dropdown list.) For example, the pivot table in Figure 3.39 is obtained by filtering out the Evening and NorthEast categories. Note how the filter symbols replace the arrows in row 3 to indicate that some categories have been filtered out. Also, note that the updated subtotals for Morning and Afternoon and the updated grand total for all categories do *not* include the hidden categories.[10]

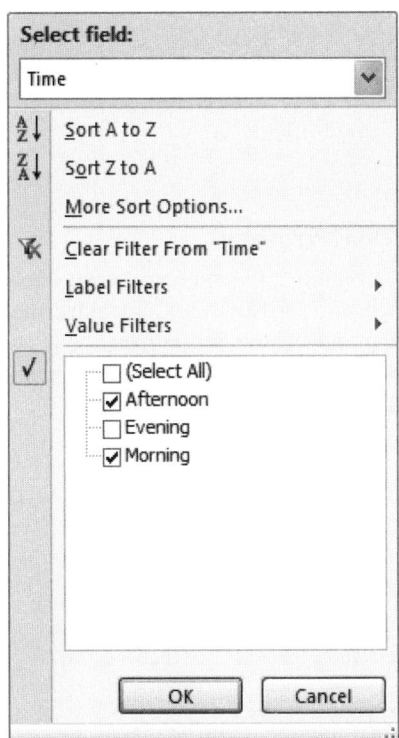

Figure 3.38
Filtering on Time

Figure 3.39
Pivot Table with
Hidden Categories

	A	B	C	D
1				
2				
3	Time ▾	Region ▾	Sum of TotalCost	
4	⊟Afternoon	MidWest	3187.16	
5		South	5729.72	
6		West	7188.94	
7	Afternoon Total		16105.82	
8	⊟Morning	MidWest	3878.22	
9		South	3835.86	
10		West	5628.66	
11	Morning Total		13342.74	
12	Grand Total		29448.56	
13				

[10]You have probably noticed that the dialog box in Figure 3.38 is exactly like the one for Excel tables discussed in the previous chapter. This is no accident. You already learned how to filter tables, so there is nothing new to learn for filtering pivot tables.

Sorting on Values or Categories

It is easy to sort in a pivot table, either by the numbers in the Values area of the table or by the labels in a Row or Column field. To sort by the numbers in the Values area, right-click on any number and choose the Sort item. If a simple A-Z or Z-A sort isn't enough, you can use the More Sort Options item. For example, this allows you to sort on the *column* of numbers that contains the selected cell or on the *row* of numbers that contains this cell.

To sort on the labels of a Row or Column field, you can again right-click on any of the categories such as Morning and select Sort. Alternatively, you can click on the dropdown arrow for the field, such as Time in Figure 3.39, and you will get the dialog box in Figure 3.38 that allows both sorting and filtering. However, be aware that sorting on labels is always in alphabetical or reverse alphabetical order. This is not always what you want. For example, suppose you want the natural sort order Morning, Afternoon, Evening. This isn't the A-Z or Z-A order, but it is still possible to sort *manually*. The trick is to select the cell of some label such as Morning and place the cursor on the border of the cell so that it becomes a four-sided arrow. Then you can drag the label up or down, or to the left or right. It takes a little practice, but it isn't difficult. ∎

Changing Locations of Fields (Pivoting)

Starting with the pivot table in Figure 3.39, you can choose where to place either Time or Region; it does *not* have to be in the Row area. To place the Region variable in the Column area, for example, drag the Region button from the Row Labels area of the Field List window to the Column Labels area. The pivot table changes automatically, as shown in Figure 3.40. (We removed the filters on Time and Region.)

Figure 3.40

Placing Region in the Column Labels Area

	A	B	C	D	E	F	G
1							
2							
3	Sum of TotalCost	Region ▼					
4	Time ▼	MidWest	NorthEast	South	West	Grand Total	
5	Afternoon	3187.16	8159.78	5729.72	7188.94	24265.6	
6	Evening	2552.89	5941.49	3864.12	6475.8	18834.3	
7	Morning	3878.22	5084.57	3835.86	5628.66	18427.31	
8	Grand Total	9618.27	19185.84	13429.7	19293.4	61527.21	
9							

Changing the locations of fields in pivot tables has always been easy, but the new user interface introduced in Excel 2007 makes it even easier. We favor dragging the fields to the various areas, but you can experiment with the various options.

Alternatively, you can categorize by a third field such as Day and locate it in a different area. As before, if you check Day in the Field List window, it goes to the Row area by default, but you can then drag it to another area. The pivot table in Figure 3.41 shows the result of placing Day in the Report Filter area. By clicking on the dropdown arrow in row 1, you can then show the pivot table for all days or any particular day. In fact, there is now a Show Multiple Items option you can check. (This option wasn't available before Excel 2007.) We checked this option and then selected Friday and Saturday to obtain the pivot table in Figure 3.41. It reports data only for Fridays and Saturdays.

This ability to categorize by multiple fields and rearrange the fields as you like is a big reason why pivot tables are so powerful and useful—and easy to use.

Changing Field Settings

Depending on which field is the active field, you can change various settings in the Field Settings dialog box. You can get to this dialog box in at least two ways. First, there is a Field Setting button on the Options ribbon. Second, you can right-click on any of the pivot

Figure 3.41 Placing Day in the Report Filter Area and Filtering on Day

	A	B	C	D	E	F	G
1	Day	(Multiple Items)					
2							
3	Sum of TotalCost	Region					
4	Time	MidWest	NorthEast	South	West	Grand Total	
5	Afternoon	1978.13	4230.5	1426.74	2818.51	10453.88	
6	Evening	1358.56	2584.97	665.98	1334.55	5944.06	
7	Morning	1786.67	2253.85	1507.69	2406.81	7955.02	
8	Grand Total	5123.36	9069.32	3600.41	6559.87	24352.96	
9							

The key to summarizing the data the way you want it summarized is the Value Field Settings dialog box. Get used to it because you will use it often.

table cells and select the Field Settings item. The field settings are particularly useful for fields in the Values area, as we now explain.

For now, right-click on any number in the pivot table in Figure 3.41 and select Value Field Settings to obtain the dialog box in Figure 3.42. This allows you to choose which way you want to summarize the TotalCost variable—by Sum, Average, Count, or several others. You can also click on the Number Format button to choose from the usual number formatting options, and you can click on the Show Values As tab to display the data in various ways (more on this later). If you choose Average and format as currency with two decimals, the resulting pivot table appears as in Figure 3.43. Now each number is the

Figure 3.42

Value Field Settings
Dialog Box

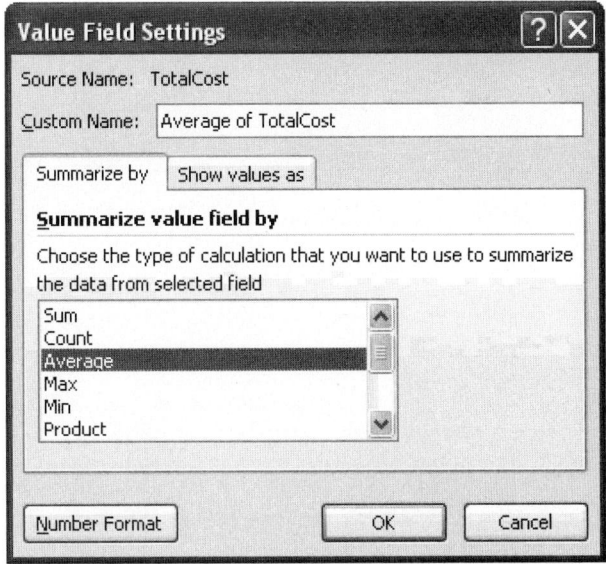

Figure 3.43

Pivot Table
with Average of
TotalCost

	A	B	C	D	E	F	G
1	Day	(Multiple Items)					
2							
3	Average of TotalCost	Region					
4	Time	MidWest	NorthEast	South	West	Grand Total	
5	Afternoon	$141.30	$192.30	$118.90	$156.58	$158.39	
6	Evening	$150.95	$161.56	$95.14	$111.21	$135.09	
7	Morning	$127.62	$150.26	$107.69	$150.43	$134.83	
8	Grand Total	$138.47	$171.12	$109.10	$142.61	$144.10	
9							

average of TotalCost for all orders in its category combination. For example, the average of TotalCost for all Friday and Saturday morning orders in the South is $107.69, and the average of *all* Friday and Saturday orders in the South is $109.10.

Pivot Charts

Pivot charts are a great extension of pivot tables. They not only "tell the story" graphically, but they update automatically when you rearrange the pivot table.

It is easy to accompany pivot tables with **pivot charts**. These charts are not just typical Excel charts; they adapt automatically to the underlying pivot table. If you make a change to the pivot table, such as pivoting the Row and Column fields, the pivot chart makes the same change automatically. To create a pivot chart, click anywhere inside the pivot table, select the PivotChart button on the Options ribbon (see Figure 3.31), and select a chart type. That's all there is to it. The resulting pivot chart (using the default column chart option) for the pivot table in Figure 3.43 appears in Figure 3.44. If you decide to pivot the Row and Column fields, the pivot chart changes automatically, as shown in Figure 3.45. Note that the categories on the horizontal axis are always based on the row field, and the categories in the legend are always based on the Column field.

Figure 3.44

Pivot Chart Based on Pivot Table

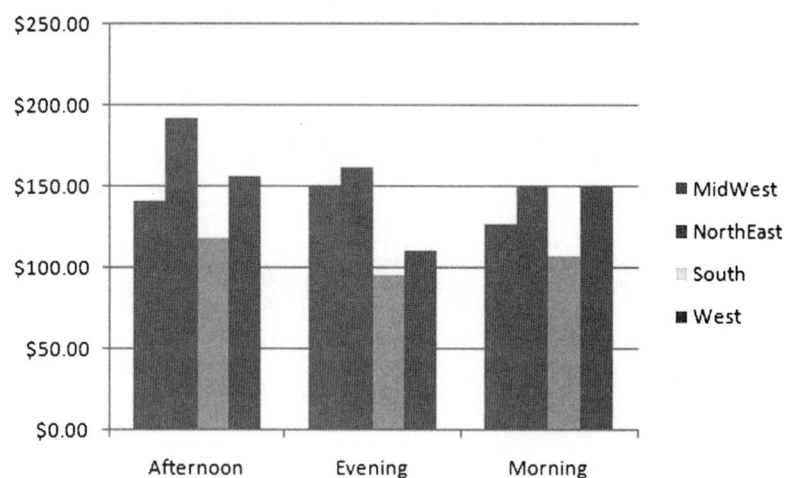

Figure 3.45

Pivot Chart after Pivoting Row and Column Fields

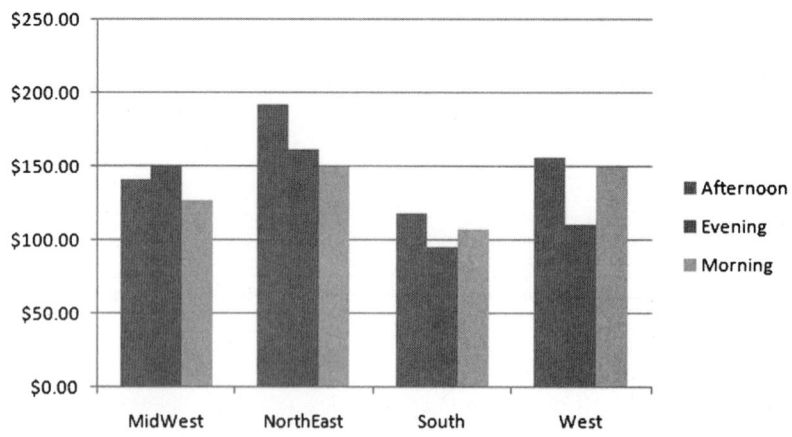

Note that when you activate a pivot chart, the PivotTable Tools "super tab" changes to PivotChart Tools. This super tab includes four ribbons for manipulating pivot charts: Design, Layout, Format, and Analyze (see Figure 3.46). There is not enough space here to discuss the many options on these ribbons, but they are intuitive and easy to use. As usual, don't be afraid to experiment.

Figure 3.46   PivotChart Tools Ribbons

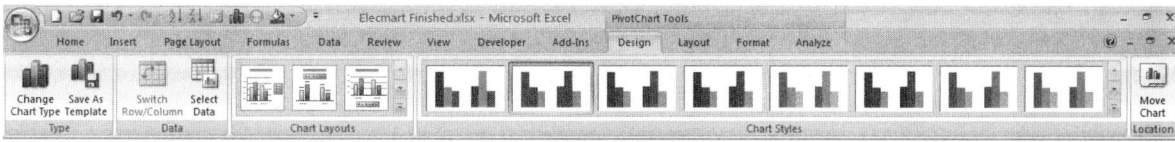

Multiple Variables in the Data Area

More than a single variable can be placed in the Values area. In addition, a given variable in the Values area can be summarized by more than one summarizing function. This can make for a rather busy pivot table, so we indicate our favorite way of doing it. Starting with the pivot table in Figure 3.43, drag the TotalCost item in the top of the Field List window (the item that is already checked) to the Values area. The bottom half of the Field List window should now appear as in Figure 3.47, and the pivot table should now appear as in Figure 3.48. Note in particular the Values button in the Column Labels area. This button controls the placement of the data in the pivot table. You have a number of options for this button: (1) leave it where it is, (2) drag it above the Time button, (3) drag it to the Row Labels area, below the Region button, or (4) drag it to the Row Labels area, above the

Figure 3.47

Field List Window with Two Values Fields

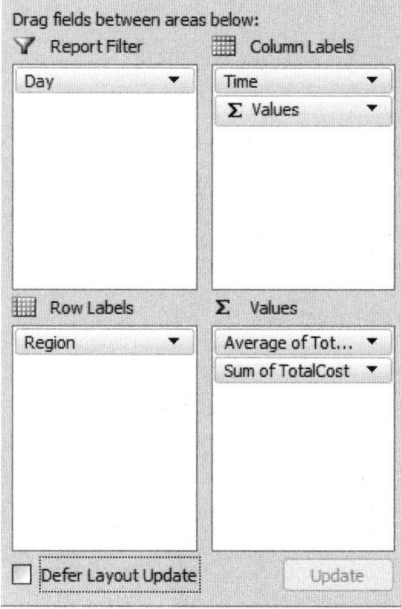

Figure 3.48   Pivot Table with Two Values Fields

	A	B	C	D	E	F	G	H	I	J
1	Day	(Multiple Items)								
2										
3		Time	Values							
4		Afternoon		Evening		Morning		Total Average of TotalCost	Total Sum of TotalCost	
5	Region	Average of TotalCost	Sum of TotalCost	Average of TotalCost	Sum of TotalCost	Average of TotalCost	Sum of TotalCost			
6	MidWest	$141.30	$1,978.13	$150.95	$1,358.56	$127.62	$1,786.67	$138.47	$5,123.36	
7	NorthEast	$192.30	$4,230.50	$161.56	$2,584.97	$150.26	$2,253.85	$171.12	$9,069.32	
8	South	$118.90	$1,426.74	$95.14	$665.98	$107.69	$1,507.69	$109.10	$3,600.41	
9	West	$156.58	$2,818.51	$111.21	$1,334.55	$150.43	$2,406.81	$142.61	$6,559.87	
10	Grand Total	$158.39	$10,453.88	$135.09	$5,944.06	$134.83	$7,955.02	$144.10	$24,352.96	
11										

Figure 3.49 Rearranged Pivot Table with Two Values Fields

	A	B	C	D	E	F	G	H	I	J
1	Day	(Multiple Items)								
2										
3		Values	Time							
4		Average of TotalCost			Sum of TotalCost			Total Average of TotalCost	Total Sum of TotalCost	
5	Region	Afternoon	Evening	Morning	Afternoon	Evening	Morning			
6	MidWest	$141.30	$150.95	$127.62	$1,978.13	$1,358.56	$1,786.67	$138.47	$5,123.36	
7	NorthEast	$192.30	$161.56	$150.26	$4,230.50	$2,584.97	$2,253.85	$171.12	$9,069.32	
8	South	$118.90	$95.14	$107.69	$1,426.74	$665.98	$1,507.69	$109.10	$3,600.41	
9	West	$156.58	$111.21	$150.43	$2,818.51	$1,334.55	$2,406.81	$142.61	$6,559.87	
10	Grand Total	$158.39	$135.09	$134.83	$10,453.88	$5,944.06	$7,955.02	$144.10	$24,352.96	
11										

Region button. You can experiment with these options, but we tend to prefer option (2), which leads to the pivot table in Figure 3.49.

In a similar manner, you can experiment with the buttons in the Values area. However, the effect here is less striking. If you drag the Sum of TotalCost button *above* the Average of TotalCost button in the field list, the effect is simply to switch the ordering of these summaries in the pivot table, as shown in Figure 3.50.

Figure 3.50 Another Rearrangement of the Pivot Table with Two Values Fields

	A	B	C	D	E	F	G	H	I	J
1	Day	(Multiple Items)								
2										
3		Values	Time							
4		Sum of TotalCost			Average of TotalCost			Total Sum of TotalCost	Total Average of TotalCost	
5	Region	Afternoon	Evening	Morning	Afternoon	Evening	Morning			
6	MidWest	$1,978.13	$1,358.56	$1,786.67	$141.30	$150.95	$127.62	$5,123.36	$138.47	
7	NorthEast	$4,230.50	$2,584.97	$2,253.85	$192.30	$161.56	$150.26	$9,069.32	$171.12	
8	South	$1,426.74	$665.98	$1,507.69	$118.90	$95.14	$107.69	$3,600.41	$109.10	
9	West	$2,818.51	$1,334.55	$2,406.81	$156.58	$111.21	$150.43	$6,559.87	$142.61	
10	Grand Total	$10,453.88	$5,944.06	$7,955.02	$158.39	$135.09	$134.83	$24,352.96	$144.10	
11										

Summarizing by Count

The variable in the Values area, whatever it is, can be summarized by the Count function. This is useful when you want to know, for example, how *many* of the orders were placed by females in the South. When summarizing by Count, the key is to understand that the actual variable placed in the Values area is irrelevant, so long as you summarize it by the Count function. To illustrate, start with the pivot table in Figure 3.50, where TotalCost is summarized with the Sum function. Now right-click on any number in the pivot table, select Value Field Settings, and select the Count function (see Figure 3.51). The default Custom Name you will see in this dialog box, Count of TotalCost, is misleading, because TotalCost has nothing to do with the counts obtained. Therefore, we like to change this Custom Name label to Count, as shown in the figure. The resulting pivot table, with values formatted as numbers with zero decimals, appears in Figure 3.52. For example, 27 of the 400 orders were placed in the morning in the South, and 115 of the 400 orders were placed in the NorthEast. (Do you now see why the counts have nothing to do with TotalCost?) This type of pivot table, with counts for various categories, is the same *crosstabs* that we discussed in Section 3.2. However, it has now been created much more easily with a pivot table.

Figure 3.51

Field Settings Dialog
Box with Count
Selected

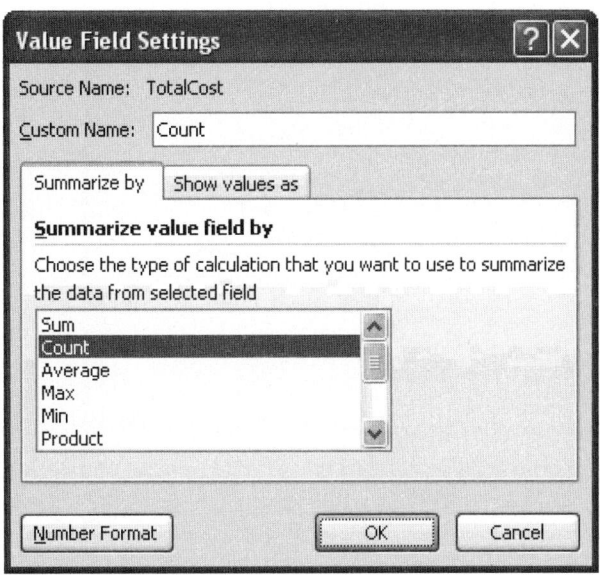

*Counts can be
displayed in a number
of ways. You should
choose the way that
best answers the
question you are
asking.*

When data are summarized by counts, there are a number of ways they can be displayed. The pivot table in Figure 3.52 shows "raw counts." Depending on the type of information you want, it might be more useful to display the counts as percentages. Three particular options are typically chosen: as percentages of total, as percentages of row, and as percentages of column. When shown as percentages of total, the percentages in the table sum to 100%; when shown as percentages of row, the percentages in *each* row sum to 100%; when shown as percentages of column, the percentages in *each* column sum to 100%. Each of these options can be useful, depending on the question you are trying to answer. For example, if you want to know whether the daily pattern of orders varies from region to region, showing the counts as percentages of column is useful so that you can compare columns. But if you want to see whether the regional ordering pattern varies by time of day, showing the counts as percentages of row is useful so that you can compare rows.

Figure 3.52

Pivot Table with
Counts.

	A	B	C	D	E	F
1						
2						
3	Count	Time				
4	Region	Afternoon	Evening	Morning	Grand Total	
5	MidWest	26	19	26	71	
6	NorthEast	48	34	33	115	
7	South	39	27	27	93	
8	West	41	42	38	121	
9	Grand Total	154	122	124	400	
10						

To display the counts as percentages of some type, display the Value Field Settings dialog box (remember how?), select the Show Values As tab, and select the appropriate option (see Figure 3.53). The resulting pivot table and corresponding pivot chart appear in Figure 3.54. As you can see, the pattern of regional orders varies somewhat by time of day.

Figure 3.53

Value Field Settings
Dialog Box with
"Show Values As"
Options

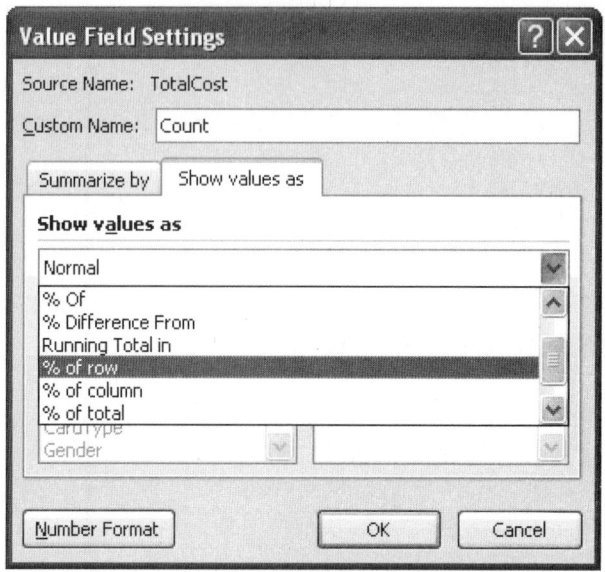

Figure 3.54 Pivot Table and Pivot Chart with Counts As Percentages of Rows

	A	B	C	D	E
3	**Count**	**Time**			
4	**Region**	**Afternoon**	**Evening**	**Morning**	**Grand Total**
5	MidWest	36.62%	26.76%	36.62%	100.00%
6	NorthEast	41.74%	29.57%	28.70%	100.00%
7	South	41.94%	29.03%	29.03%	100.00%
8	West	33.88%	34.71%	31.40%	100.00%
9	**Grand Total**	**38.50%**	**30.50%**	**31.00%**	**100.00%**

Sometimes it is useful to see the raw counts *and* the percentages. This can be done easily by dragging any variable to the Data area, summarizing it by Count, and displaying it as "Normal." Figure 3.55 shows one possibility, where we have changed the custom names of the two Count variables to make them more meaningful. Alternatively, the counts and percentages could be shown in two separate pivot tables.

Figure 3.55 Pivot Table with Percentages of Rows and Raw Counts

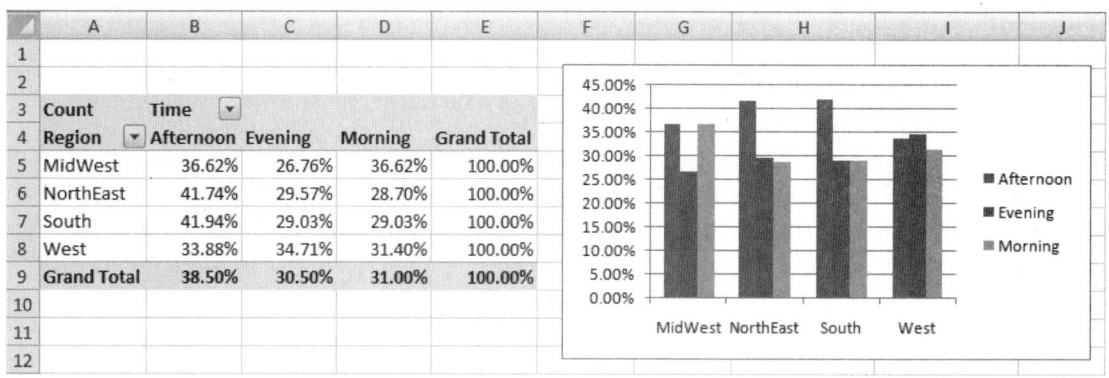

	A	B	C	D	E	F	G	H	I
3		**Time**	**Values**						
4		**Afternoon**		**Evening**		**Morning**		**Total Pct of Row**	**Total Raw Count**
5	**Region**	**Pct of Row**	**Raw Count**	**Pct of Row**	**Raw Count**	**Pct of Row**	**Raw Count**		
6	MidWest	36.62%	26	26.76%	19	36.62%	26	100.00%	71
7	NorthEast	41.74%	48	29.57%	34	28.70%	33	100.00%	115
8	South	41.94%	39	29.03%	27	29.03%	27	100.00%	93
9	West	33.88%	41	34.71%	42	31.40%	38	100.00%	121
10	**Grand Total**	**38.50%**	**154**	**30.50%**	**122**	**31.00%**	**124**	**100.00%**	**400**

Grouping

Finally, categories in a Row or Column variable can be grouped. This is especially useful when a Row or Column variable has many distinct values. Because a pivot table creates a row or column for each distinct value, the results can be unwieldy. We present two possibilities. First, suppose you want to break Sum of TotalCost down by Date. Starting with a blank pivot table, check both Date and TotalCost in the pivot table field list window. This creates a separate row for each distinct date in the data set—112 separate dates. This is too much detail, so it is useful to group on the Date variable. To do so, right-click on any date in column A and select the Group item. (Group options are also available on the Options ribbon.) Accept the default selections in the Grouping dialog box (see Figure 3.56) to obtain the pivot table in Figure 3.57.

Figure 3.56

Grouping Dialog Box

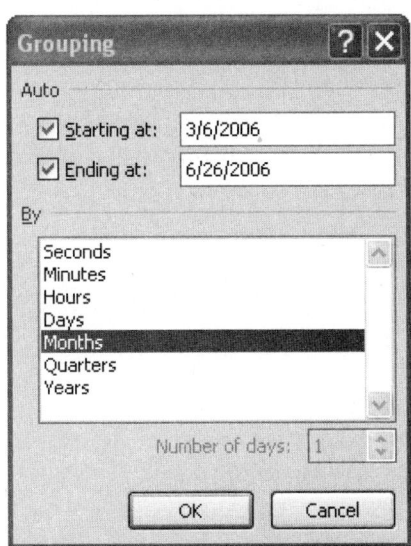

Figure 3.57

Pivot Table after Grouping by Month

	A	B	C
1			
2			
3	Date	Sum of TotalCost	
4	Mar	$9,383.26	
5	Apr	$14,589.91	
6	May	$19,468.11	
7	Jun	$18,085.93	
8	Grand Total	$61,527.21	
9			

Pivot Table Tip *Suppose you have multiple years of data and you would like a monthly grouping such as January 2007 through December 2009. If you simply select Months as in Figure 3.56, all of the Januaries, for example, will be lumped together. The trick is to select both Months and Years in the dialog box.*

As a second possibility for grouping, suppose you want to see how the average of TotalCost varies by the amount of the highest priced item in the order. Place TotalCost in the Data area, summarized by Average, and place HighItem in the Row area. Because HighItem has nearly 400 distinct values, the resulting pivot table is virtually worthless. Again, however, the trick is to group on the Row variable. This time there are no natural groupings as there are for a date variable, so it is up to you to create the groupings. Excel provides a suggestion, as shown in Figure 3.58, but you can override it. For example, changing the bottom entry to 50 leads to the pivot table in Figure 3.59. Some experimentation is typically required to obtain the grouping that presents the results in the most appropriate way.

Figure 3.58

Grouping Dialog Box for a Non-Date Variable

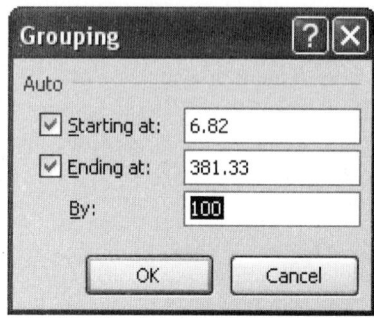

Figure 3.59

Pivot Table after Grouping by 50 on HighItem

	A	B	C
1			
2			
3	**HighItem**	**Sum of TotalCost**	
4	6.82-56.82	$7,496.40	
5	56.82-106.82	$22,903.94	
6	106.82-156.82	$11,225.99	
7	156.82-206.82	$9,634.78	
8	206.82-256.82	$3,891.15	
9	256.82-306.82	$2,960.29	
10	306.82-356.82	$2,169.15	
11	356.82-406.82	$1,245.51	
12	**Grand Total**	$61,527.21	
13			

By now, we have illustrated the pivot table features that are most commonly used. Be aware, however, that there are *many* more features available. These include (but are not limited to) the following:

- Showing/hiding subtotals and grand totals (check the Layout options on the Design ribbon)

- Dealing with blank rows, that is, categories with no data (right-click on any number, choose PivotTable Options, and check the options on the Layout & Format tab)

- Displaying the data behind a given number in a pivot table (double-click on the number to get a new worksheet)

- Formatting a pivot table with various styles (check the style options on the Design ribbon)

- Sorting pivot tables in various ways (check the Sort options on the Options ribbon)

- Moving or renaming pivot tables (check the PivotTable and Action options on the Options ribbon)

- Refreshing pivot tables as the underlying data changes (check the Refresh dropdown list on the Options ribbon)

- Creating pivot table formulas for calculated fields or calculated items (check the Formulas dropdown list on the Options ribbon)

- Basing pivot tables on external databases (not covered here,)

Not only are these (and other) features available, but Excel usually provides more than one way to implement them. The suggestions above are just some of the ways they can be implemented. The key to learning pivot table features is to *experiment*. There are entire books written on pivot tables, but we don't recommend them. You can learn a lot more, and a lot more quickly, by experimenting with data such as the Elecmart data. Don't be afraid to mess up. Pivot tables are very forgiving, and you can always start over.

We complete this section by providing one last quick example to illustrate how pivot tables can answer business questions very quickly.

| EXAMPLE | 3.5 FROZEN LASAGNA DINNERS |

The file **Lasagna Triers.xlsx** contains data on over 800 potential customers being tracked by a (fictional) company that has been marketing a frozen lasagna dinner. The file contains a number of demographics on these customers, as indicated in Figure 3.60: their age, weight, income, pay type, car value, credit card debt, gender, whether they live alone, dwelling type, monthly number of trips to the mall, and neighborhood. It also indicates whether they have tried the company's frozen lasagna. The company wants to understand why some potential customers are triers and others are not. Does gender make a difference? Does income make a difference? In general, what distinguishes triers from nontriers? How can the company use pivot tables to explore these questions?

Figure 3.60 Lasagna Trier Data

	A	B	C	D	E	F	G	H	I	J	K	L	M
1	Person	Age	Weight	Income	PayType	CarValue	CCDebt	Gender	LiveAlone	DwellType	MallTrips	Nbhd	HaveTried
2	1	48	175	65500	Hourly	2190	3510	Male	No	Home	7	East	No
3	2	33	202	29100	Hourly	2110	740	Female	No	Condo	4	East	Yes
4	3	51	188	32200	Salaried	5140	910	Male	No	Condo	1	East	No
5	4	56	244	19000	Hourly	700	1620	Female	No	Home	3	West	No
6	5	28	218	81400	Salaried	26620	600	Male	No	Apt	3	West	Yes
7	6	51	173	73000	Salaried	24520	950	Female	No	Condo	2	East	No
8	7	44	182	66400	Salaried	10130	3500	Female	Yes	Condo	6	West	Yes
9	8	29	189	46200	Salaried	10250	2860	Male	No	Condo	5	West	Yes
10	9	28	200	61100	Salaried	17210	3180	Male	No	Condo	10	West	Yes
11	10	29	209	9800	Salaried	2090	1270	Female	Yes	Apt	7	East	Yes
12	11	29	171	46600	Salaried	16350	5520	Male	Yes	Home	11	West	Yes
13	12	30	243	24500	Salaried	5410	300	Male	No	Home	3	West	Yes
14	13	62	246	110900	Salaried	8410	730	Male	Yes	Condo	7	West	Yes
15	14	29	228	37200	Salaried	6420	700	Male	Yes	Apt	3	East	Yes
16	15	40	230	21800	Hourly	3230	1650	Male	No	Home	4	East	Yes
17	16	61	185	28900	Hourly	1300	1030	Male	Yes	Apt	2	South	No

Objective   To use pivot tables to explore which demographic variables help to distinguish lasagna triers from nontriers.

Solution

Pivot tables, with counts in the Values area, are a great way to discover which variables have the largest effect on a Yes/No variable.

The key is to set up a pivot table that shows counts of triers and nontriers for different categories of any of the potential explanatory variables. For example, one such pivot table shows the percentages of triers and nontriers for males and females separately. If the percentages are different for males than for females, the company will know that gender has an effect. On the other hand, if the percentages for males and females are about the same, the company will know that gender does not make much of a difference.

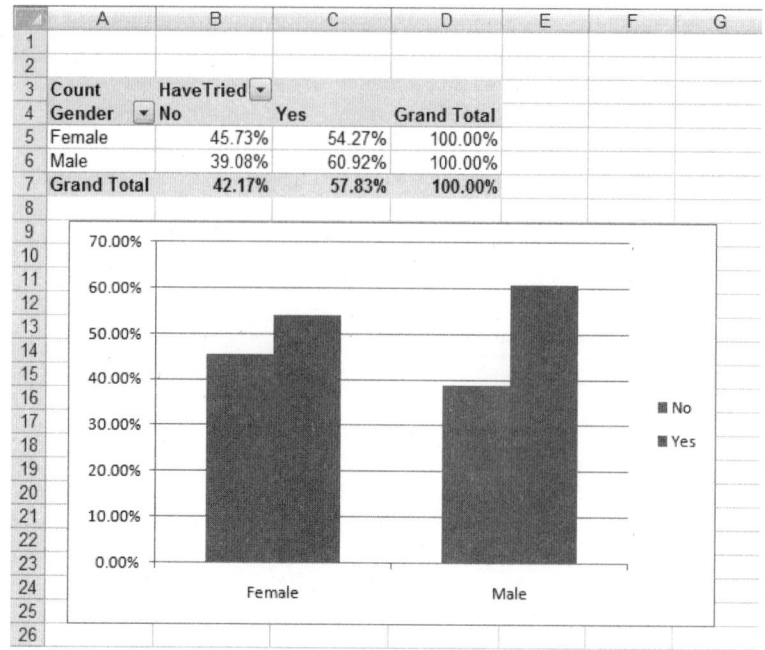

You should set up the typical pivot table as shown in Figure 3.61. The Row variable is any demographic variable you want to investigate, in this case, Gender. The Column variable is HaveTried (Yes or No). The Values variable can be *any* variable, so long as it is expressed as a count. Finally, it is useful to show these counts as percentage of row. This way you can easily look down column C to see whether the percentage in one category (Female) who have tried the product is any different from the percentage in another category (Male) who have tried the product. Specifically, males are somewhat more likely to try the product than females: 60.92% versus 54.27%. This is also apparent from the associated pivot chart.

Once this generic pivot table and associated pivot chart are set up, you can easily explore other demographic variables by swapping them for Gender. For example, Figure 3.62

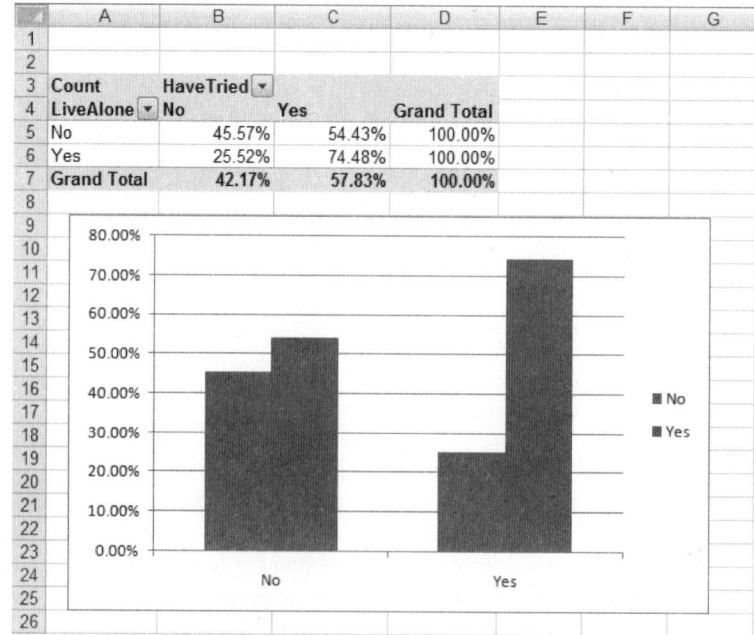

indicates that people who live alone are (not surprisingly) *much* more likely to try this frozen microwave product than people who don't live alone.

As another example, Figure 3.63 indicates that people with larger incomes are slightly more likely to try the product. There are two things to note about this income pivot table. First, because there are so many individual income values, grouping is useful. You can experiment with the grouping to get the most meaningful results. Second, you should be a bit skeptical about the last group, which has 100% triers. It is possible that there are only one or two people in this group. (It turns out that there are four.) For this reason, it is a good idea to show two pivot tables of the counts, one showing percentage of row and one showing the raw counts. This second pivot table is shown at the bottom of Figure 3.63.

Figure 3.63

Pivot Table and Pivot Chart for Examining the Effect of Income

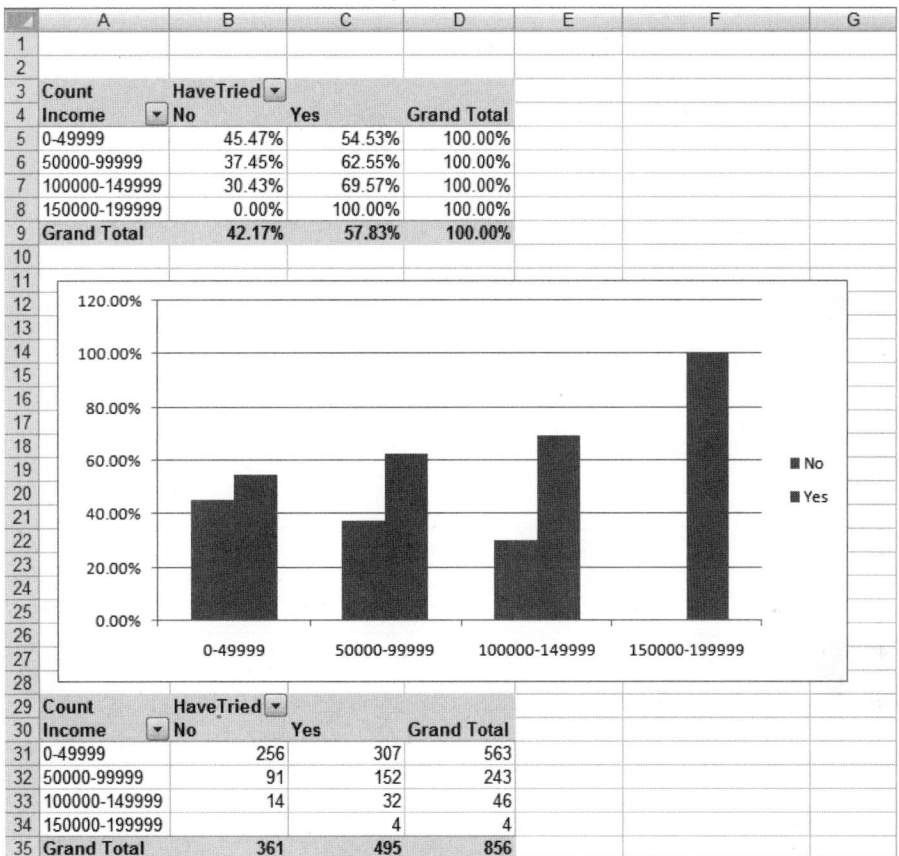

Count	HaveTried		
Income	No	Yes	Grand Total
0-49999	45.47%	54.53%	100.00%
50000-99999	37.45%	62.55%	100.00%
100000-149999	30.43%	69.57%	100.00%
150000-199999	0.00%	100.00%	100.00%
Grand Total	42.17%	57.83%	100.00%

Count	HaveTried		
Income	No	Yes	Grand Total
0-49999	256	307	563
50000-99999	91	152	243
100000-149999	14	32	46
150000-199999		4	4
Grand Total	361	495	856

The problem posed in this example is a common one in real business situations. One variable indicates whether people are in one group or another (triers or nontriers), and there are a lot of other variables that could potentially explain why some people are in one group and others are in the other group. There are a number of rather sophisticated techniques for attacking this *classification* problem, most of which are beyond the level of this book. However, you can go a long way toward understanding which variables are important by the simple pivot table method illustrated here.

CHANGES IN EXCEL 2010

Microsoft has made the already user-friendly pivot tables even friendlier in Excel 2010 with the addition of **slicers**. These are essentially lists of the distinct values of any variable, which you can then filter on. You add a slicer from the PivotTable Tools/Options ribbon. For example, in the

Elecmart sales data, you can choose Region as a slicer. You then see a list on the screen with a button for each possible value: Midwest, Northeast, South, and West. You can then click any combination of these buttons to filter on the chosen regions. Note that a slicer variable does *not* have to be part of the pivot table. For example, if you are showing sum of TotalCost, and Region is not part of the pivot table, a Region slicer will still filter sum of TotalCost for the regions selected. On the other hand, if Region is already in the row area, say, you can filter on it through the slicer. In this case, clicking on regions from the slicer is equivalent to filtering on the same regions in the row area. Basically, the slicers have been added as a convenience to users. They make filtering easier and more transparent.

As an example, Figure 3.64 shows a pivot table accompanied by two slicers. The row field is Time, which has been filtered in the usual way (through the dropdown list in the row area) to show only Afternoon and Evening. The two slicers appear next to the pivot table. The Region slicer has been filtered on Midwest and South, and the Gender slicer has been filtered on Male. So, for example, the sum of TotalCost for all sales in the evening by males in the Midwest and South is $3824.03.

Figure 3.64
Pivot Table with Slicers

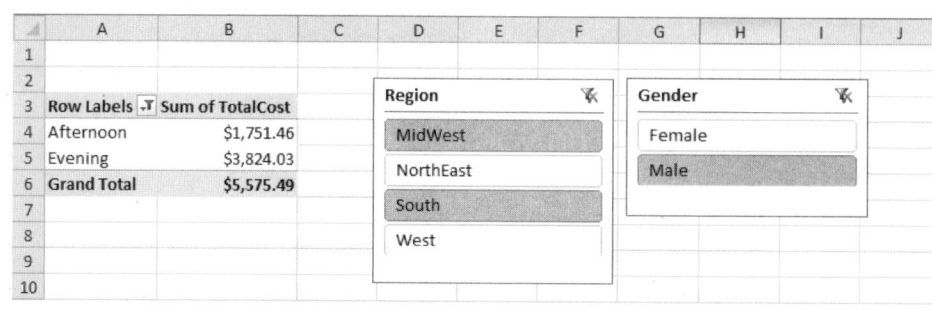

PROBLEMS

Level A

33. Solve problem 1 with pivot tables and create corresponding pivot charts. Express the counts as percentage of row. What do these percentages indicate about this particular data set? Then repeat, expressing the counts as percentages of column.

34. Solve problem 2 with pivot tables and create corresponding pivot charts. Express the counts as percentage of row. What do these percentages indicate about this particular data set? Then repeat, expressing the counts as percentages of column.

35. Solve problem 3 with pivot tables and create corresponding pivot charts. Express the counts as percentage of row. What do these percentages indicate about this particular data set? Then repeat, expressing the counts as percentages of column.

36. Solve problem 4 with pivot tables and create corresponding pivot charts. Express the counts as percentage

of row. What do these percentages indicate about this particular data set? Then repeat, expressing the counts as percentages of column.

37. Solve problem 7 with pivot tables and create corresponding pivot charts. However, find only means and standard deviations, not medians or quartiles. (This is one drawback of pivot tables. Medians, quartiles, and percentiles are not in the list of summary measures.)

38. Solve problem 8 with pivot tables and create corresponding pivot charts. However, find only means and standard deviations, not medians. (This is one drawback of pivot tables. Medians are not among their summary measures.)

39. Solve problem 9 with pivot tables and create corresponding pivot charts. However, find only means and standard deviations, not medians. (This is one drawback of pivot tables. Medians are not among their summary measures.)

40. The file **P03_40.xlsx** contains monthly data on the number of border crossings from Mexico into four southwestern states.
   a. Restructure this data set on a new sheet so that there are three long columns: Month, State, and Crossings. Essentially, you should stack the original columns B through E on top of one another to get the Crossings column, and you should also indicate which state each row corresponds to in the State column. The Month column should have four replicas of the original Month column.
   b. Create a pivot table and corresponding pivot table chart based on the restructured data. It should break down the average of Crossings by Year and State. Comment on any patterns you see in the chart.

41. *The Wall Street Journal CEO Compensation Study* analyzed CEO pay from many U.S. companies with fiscal year 2008 revenue of at least $5 billion that filed their proxy statements between October 2008 and March 2009. The data are in the file **P02_30.xlsx**. (Note: This data set is a somewhat different CEO compensation data set from the one used as an example in the next section.)
   a. Create a pivot table and a corresponding pivot chart that simultaneously shows average of Salary 2008 and average of Bonus 2008, broken down by Company Type. Comment on any striking results in the chart.
   b. In the Data sheet, create a new column, Total 2008, which is the sum of Salary 2008 and Bonus 2008. Then create two pivot tables and corresponding pivot charts on a single sheet. The first should show the counts of CEOs broken down by Company Type, and the second should simultaneously show the average of Total 2008, the minimum of Total 2008, and the maximum of Total 2008, all broken down by Company Type. Comment on any striking results in these charts.

42. One pivot table element we didn't explain is a **calculated item**. This is usually a new category for some categorical variable that is created from existing categories. It is easiest to learn from an example. Open the file **Elecmart Sales.xlsx** from this section, create a pivot table, and put Day in the row area. Proceed as follows to create two new categories, Weekday and Weekend.
   a. Select any day and select Calculated Item from the Formulas dropdown list on the PivotTable Tools Options ribbon. This will open a dialog box. Enter Weekend in the Name box and enter the formula **=Sat+Sun** in the formula box. (You can double-click on the items in the Items list to help build this formula.) When you click on OK, you will see Weekend in the pivot table.
   b. Do it yourself. Create another calculated item, Weekday, for Mon through Fri.

   c. Filter out all of the individual days from the row area, so that only Weekday and Weekend remain, and then find the sum of TotalCost for these two new categories. How can you check whether these sums are what you think they should be? (Notes about calculated items: First, if you have Weekend, Weekday, and some individual days showing in the row area, the sum of TotalCost will double-count these individual days, so be careful about this. Second, be aware that if you create a calculated item from some variable such as Day, you are no longer allowed to drag that variable to the Report Filter area. We are not sure why.)

43. Building on the previous problem, another pivot table element we didn't explain is a **calculated field**. This is usually a new numerical variable built from numerical variables that can be summarized in the Values area. It acts somewhat like a new column in the spreadsheet data, but there is an important difference. Again, it is easiest to learn from an example. Open the file **Elecmart Sales.xlsx** and follow the instructions below.
   a. Create a new column in the data, CostPerItem, which is TotalCost divided by ItemsOrdered. Then create a pivot table and find the average of CostPerItem, broken down by Region. You should find averages such as $50.41 for the MidWest. Explain exactly how this value was calculated. Would such an average be of much interest to a manager at Elecmart? Why or why not?
   b. Select any average in the pivot table and then select Calculated Field from the Formulas dropdown list on the PivotTable Tools Options ribbon. This will open a dialog box. Enter CF_CostPerItem in the name box (we added CF, for calculated field, because we are not allowed to use the CostPerItem name that already exists), enter the formula **=TotalCost/ItemsOrdered**, and click on OK. You should now see a new column in the pivot table, Sum of CF_CostPerItem, with *different* values than in the Average of CostPerItem column. For example, the new value for the MidWest should be $46.47. Do some investigation to understand how this "sum" was calculated. From a manager's point of view, does it make any sense? (Note on calculated fields: When you summarize a calculated field, it doesn't matter whether you express it as sum, average, max, or any other summary measure. It is calculated in exactly the same way in each case.)

44. The file **P02_18.xlsx** contains daily values of the S&P Index from 1970 to 2009. It also contains percentage changes in the index from each day to the next. Create a pivot table with average of % Change in the Values area and Date in the Row area. You will see every single date, with no real averaging taking place. This

problem lets you explore how you can group naturally on a date variable. For each part below, explain the result briefly.

a. Group by Month.

b. Group by Year.

c. Group by Month and Year (select both in the Group dialog box). Can you make it show the year averages from part **b**?

d. Group by Quarter.

e. Group by Month and Quarter. Can you make it show the averages from part **c**?

f. Group by Quarter and Year.

g. Group by Month, Quarter, and Year.

45. (For Excel 2010 users only) Using the **Elecmart Sales.xlsx** file from this section, experiment with slicers as follows.

a. Create a pivot table that shows the average of TotalCost, broken down by Region in the row area and Time in the column area. Then insert two slicers, one for Region and one for Time. Select the West and NorthEast buttons on the Region slicer and the Morning and Afternoon buttons on the Time slicer. Explain what happens in the pivot table.

b. Create a pivot table that shows the average of TotalCost, broken down by Region in the row area and Time in the column area. Insert a Day slicer and select the Sat and Sun buttons. Explain what averages are now showing in the pivot table. Verify this by deleting the slicer and instead making Day a report filter, with Sat and Sun selected.

46. (For Excel 2010 users only) We used the **Lasagna Triers.xlsx** file in this section to show how pivot tables can help explain which variables are related to the buying behavior of customers. Illustrate how the same information could be obtained with slicers. Specifically, set up the pivot table as in the example, but use a slicer instead of a row variable. Then set it up exactly as in the example, *with* a row variable, but include a slicer for some other variable. Comment on the type of results you obtain with these two versions. Do slicers appear to provide any advantage in this type of problem?

Level B

47. Solve problem 5 with pivot tables and create corresponding pivot charts. If you first find the quartiles of Salary and AmountSpent (by any method), is it possible to create the desired crosstabs by grouping, *without* recoding these variables?

48. Solve problem 17 with pivot tables. However, find only means and standard deviations, not medians. (This is one drawback of pivot tables. Medians are not among their summary measures.)

49. The file **P03_22.xlsx** lists financial data on movies released since 1980 with budgets at least $20 million.

a. Create three new variables, Ratio1, Ratio2, and Decade. Ratio1 should be US Gross divided by Budget, Ratio2 should be Worldwide Gross divided by Budget, and Decade should list 1980s, 1990s, or 2000s, depending on the year of the release date. If either US Gross or Worldwide Gross is listed as "Unknown," the corresponding ratio should be blank. (*Hint*: For Decade, use the YEAR function to fill in a new Year column. Then use a lookup table to populate the Decade column.)

b. Use a pivot table to find counts of movies by various distributors. Then go back to the data and create one more column, Distributor New, which lists the distributor for distributors with at least 30 movies and lists Other for the rest. (*Hint*: Use a lookup table to populate Distributor New, but also use an IF to fill in Other where the distributor is missing.)

c. Create a pivot table and corresponding pivot chart that shows average and standard deviation of Ratio1, broken down by Distributor New, with a report filter for Decade. Comment on any striking results.

d. Repeat part **c** for Ratio2.

50. The file **P03_50.xlsx** lists NBA salaries for five seasons. (Each NBA season straddles two calendar years.)

a. Merge all of the data into a single new sheet called All Data. In this new sheet, add a new column Season that lists the season, such as 2006–2007.

b. Note that many of the players list a position such as C-F or F-C. Presumably, the first means the player is primarily a center but sometimes plays forward, whereas the second means the opposite. Recode these so that only the primary position remains (C in the first case, F in the second). To complicate matters further, the source lists positions differently in 2007–2008 than in other years. It lists PG and SG (point guard and shooting guard) instead of just G, and it lists SF and PF (small forward and power forward) instead of just F. Recode the positions for this season to be consistent with the other seasons (so that there are only three positions: G, F, and C).

c. Note that many players have (p) or (t) in their Contract Thru value. The Source sheet explains this. Create two new columns in the All Data sheet, Years Remaining and Option. The Years Remaining column should list the years remaining in the contract. For example, if the season is 2004–2005 and the contract is through 2006–2007, years remaining should be 2. The Option column should list Player if there is a (p), Team if there is a (t), and blank if neither.

d. Use a pivot table to find the average Salary by Season. Change it to show average Salary by Team. Change it to show average Salary by Season and

Team. Change it to show average Salary by Primary Position. Change it to show average Salary by Team and Primary Position, with filters for Season, Contract Years, Years Remaining, and Option. Comment on any striking findings.

51. The files **P02_29.xlsx** contain monthly percentages of on-time arrivals at several of the largest U.S. airports.

a. Explain why the current format of either data set limits the kind of information you can obtain with a pivot table. For example, does it allow you find the average on-time arrival percentage by year for any selected subset of airports, such as the average for O'Hare, Los Angeles International, and La Guardia?

b. Restructure the data appropriately and then use a pivot table to answer the specific question in part **a.**

3.6 AN EXTENDED EXAMPLE

Now that you are equipped with a collection of tools for describing data, it is time to apply these tools to some serious data analysis. In this section we examine a very interesting data set that contains real data on CEO compensation in 2008. With a data set as rich as this one, there are always many summary measures that could be calculated, many tables that could be formed, and many charts that could be created. We illustrate some of the outputs that might be of interest, but you should realize that there are many other analyses you could perform. Given all the attention CEO compensation has received in the recent economic recession, you probably have your own questions you would like to answer. Therefore, we encourage you to take the analysis a few steps beyond what we present here.

EXAMPLE | **3.6 CEO COMPENSATION**

The file **CEO Compensation 2008 Forbes.xlsx** contains data on the 500 mostly highly compensated CEOs in 2008, according to a Forbes Web site. The data was gathered by going to Web sites such as www.forbes.com/lists/2009/12/best-boss-09_John-B-Hess_7YAE.html (one per CEO) and copying the data to Excel. A small subset of this data appears in Figures 3.65 and 3.66 (where the rows are sorted in decreasing order of total compensation, in millions of dollars, in column J). The data set includes some personal data about each CEO, the CEO's total compensation for 2008 and its components (columns K–N), the CEO's total 5-year compensation, and the value of company shares owned by the CEO. For those CEOs with tenure at least six years, it also shows some six-year values, including a performance versus pay ranking (1 is best) in column U. Finally, the last two columns indicate the CEO's total return versus tenure and how this compares to the market. (More details about the variables in this file can be found in the cell comments in row 1 and at the Web links in column A.) The file also includes median compensation

---

Figure 3.65 CEO Compensation (Columns A–L)

	A	B	C	D	E	F	G	H	I	J	K	L
1	CEO	Gender	Company	Ticker	Industry	Founder	Years as company CEO	Years with company	Age	Total 2008 compensation	2008 Salary	2008 Bonus
2	Lawrence J Ellison	M	Oracle	ORCL	Software & Services	Yes	32	32	64	556.98	1.00	10.78
3	Ray R Irani	M	Occidental Petroleum	OXY	Oil & Gas Operations	No	18	26	74	222.64	1.30	3.63
4	John B Hess	M	Hess	HES	Oil & Gas Operations	No	14	32	55	154.58	1.50	3.50
5	Michael D Watford	M	Ultra Petroleum	UPL	Oil & Gas Operations	No	10	10	55	116.93	0.60	1.75
6	Mark G Papa	M	EOG Resources	EOG	Oil & Gas Operations	No	11	28	62	90.47	0.94	1.00
7	William R Berkley	M	WR Berkley	WRB	Insurance	Yes	42	42	63	87.48	1.00	8.50
8	Matthew K Rose	M	Burlington Santa Fe	BNI	Transportation	No	8	16	50	68.62	1.18	1.68
9	Paul J Evanson	M	Allegheny Energy	AYE	Utilities	No	6	17	67	67.26	1.12	1.23
10	Hugh Grant	M	Monsanto	MON	Chemicals	No	6	28	51	64.60	1.29	3.33
11	Robert W Lane	M	Deere & Co	DE	Capital Goods	No	9	27	59	61.30	1.44	3.59

Figure 3.66   CEO Compensation (Columns M–W)

	M	N	O	P	Q	R	S	T	U	V	W
1	2008 Other	2008 Stock gains	5-year compensation total	Shares owned ($ millions)	6-year average compensation	6-year annual total return	6-year return relative to industry	6-year return relative to market	Performance vs pay rank	Total return during tenure	Relative to market
2	1.45	543.75	944.45	21987.4	164.26	9%	101	107	103	27%	118
3	33.32	184.39	743.55	394.3	128.82	28%	106	125	106	14%	106
4	36.66	112.92	234.83	2016.8	39.68	27%	106	125	115	10%	104
5	1.10	113.48	174.17	104.1	29.47	45%	120	142	28	48%	153
6	18.86	69.67	170.69	51.7	28.92	23%	102	120	92	23%	123
7	5.42	72.56	178.29	627.4	30.79	13%	118	111	67	14%	104
8	20.70	45.06	140.73	39.8	23.68	19%	114	117	40	13%	117
9	22.28	42.63	143.54	33.1						18%	119
10	9.32	50.67	135.30	28.0						44%	144
11	15.24	41.04	142.40	11.8	24.13	13%	100	111	109	9%	113

Figure 3.67   Industry Medians

	Y	Z	AA	AB	AC	AD
1	Lookup table for industry medians in 2008					
2	Industry	Total compensation	Salary	Bonus	Other	Stock Gains
3	Aerospace & Defense	14.29	1.20	2.46	4.74	2.99
4	Banking	2.29	0.90	0.00	0.37	0.00
5	Business Services & Supplies	2.47	0.94	0.45	1.09	0.00
6	Capital Goods	9.00	1.12	1.36	3.06	0.88
7	Chemicals	4.86	1.00	1.55	0.93	0.00
8	Conglomerates	12.21	1.16	2.69	8.34	0.00
9	Construction	7.66	0.99	1.20	1.91	1.45
10	Consumer Durables	3.38	1.23	0.00	1.78	0.00

values for the various industries, a few of which are shown in Figure 3.67, so that you can compare any CEO to these median values in his/her industry.

Objective   To use the tools in this chapter to explore the CEO compensation data.

Solution

We first present a short discussion on CEO compensation.

A Primer on CEO Compensation

If a normal person gets a salary of $80,000 in a given year, that's about the end of the story. However, CEO compensation is considerably more complex. Each CEO receives a base salary (column K) and an incentive bonus (column L), the latter decided by negotiation. A CEO can also receive "other compensation" (column M), including vested restricted stock grants, LTIP (long-term incentive plan) payouts, and perks. However, the big difference between CEOs and the rest of us is the granting of stock options. A stock option allows a CEO to purchase company stock at a fixed stated price during a certain period of time, often 10 years. If the price of the company stock increases during that period, the CEO can then *exercise* the stock options by buying the stock at the low fixed price and selling it at the high current price, thereby making a windfall. This explains the huge stock gains in column N for several of the CEOs at the top of the list. They evidently exercised at least some of their options in 2008.

In a sense, these huge stock gains for some CEOs overstate their compensation for 2008. They had been holding these valuable stock options for years, but their gains showed up only in 2008 when they exercised the options. This is essentially an accounting issue. When and how should stock options show up in compensation figures? The data in our file indicate one possibility. In particular, the total compensation in column J is relevant for tax purposes in 2008—this is the amount subject to 2008 taxes. However, it is not the value that appears on company financial statements. For example, if you visit other Forbes Web sites, such as http://people.forbes.com/profile/mark-g-papa/30517 for Mark Papa, number 5 on our list, you will see a much different total compensation, about $23.44 million rather than the $90.47 million we report. The difference can be explained by the way stock options are accounted for on corporate financial statements.

Obviously, accounting for CEO compensation is a complex issue, and much academic research has been devoted to it. However, now that you understand the basic issues, we will begin analyzing the data in the file.

With a data set this large and including so many variables, it is difficult to know where to start. Probably the best strategy is to ask some interesting questions and then find the best tools to answer them. Here are some possibilities.

Question Set 1: There are clearly very few female CEOs. How many are there? Do they tend to be in certain industries? Does their tenure tend to be shorter than that of their male counterparts? Do they tend to be younger than their male counterparts?

Answer Set 1: The pivot table in Figure 3.68 answers the first two questions. It shows the counts of males and females across industries. (See the finished version of the CEO file

Figure 3.68
CEOs by Gender and Industry

3	Count of CEO	Column Labels		
4	Row Labels	F	M	Grand Total
5	Aerospace & Defense		10	10
6	Banking		29	29
7	Business Services & Supplies	1	15	16
8	Capital Goods		12	12
9	Chemicals	1	15	16
10	Conglomerates		10	10
11	Construction		8	8
12	Consumer Durables		12	12
13	Diversified Financials	1	42	43
14	Drugs & Biotechnology		20	20
15	Food Drink & Tobacco	5	22	27
16	Food Markets		4	4
17	Health Care Equipment & Services	1	27	28
18	Hotels, Restaurants & Leisure		8	8
19	Household & Personal Products	1	14	15
20	Insurance		27	27
21	Materials		16	16
22	Media		19	19
23	Oil & Gas Operations	1	32	33
24	Retailing	2	30	32
25	Semiconductors		11	11
26	Software & Services	1	16	17
27	Technology Hardware & Equipment		20	20
28	Telecommunications Services		11	11
29	Transportation		14	14
30	Utilities		42	42
31	Grand Total	14	486	500

for detailed instructions on getting all of the results in this example.) There are only 14 female CEOs, and five of them are in the Food Drink & Tobacco industry. Note that if you double-click on the 5 count in this pivot table, you can "drill down" to the underlying data to see which five companies these female CEOs represent. (They are Archer Daniels, Sara Lee, Kraft Foods, Reynolds American, and Pepsico.)

One way to investigate age and tenure across gender is to use StatTools, with one-variable summary statistics broken down by gender. (Remember to use the Stacked format option.) Selected results appear in Figure 3.69. Although there are only 14 female CEOs, their tenure tends to be much lower than for men (and less spread out), whereas the differences in age are fairly minimal, with females being slightly younger than males on average.

Figure 3.69

CEO Tenure and Age by Gender

One Variable Summary	Years as company CEO (F) Data Set #1	Years as company CEO (M) Data Set #1
Mean	3.643	7.013
Std. Dev.	2.783	7.208
Median	3.000	5.000
One Variable Summary	Age (F) Data Set #1	Age (M) Data Set #1
Mean	54.643	56.062
Std. Dev.	4.162	6.393
Median	55.000	56.000

Question Set 2: How much do these CEOs make, and how is this allocated across the four different components of compensation?

Answer Set 2: Several tools, including numerical summary measures, histograms, box plots, and pivot tables, can be used to answer these questions. We illustrate only the first two of these. Figure 3.70 shows StatTools numerical summary measures of total

Figure 3.70   Summary Measures of CEO Compensation

One Variable Summary	Total 2008 compensation Full Data Set	2008 Salary Full Data Set	2008 Bonus Full Data Set	2008 Other Full Data Set	2008 Stock gains Full Data Set
Mean	11.43	1.0595	1.757	3.096	5.52
Std. Dev.	29.88	0.5310	2.285	4.726	27.87
Median	5.39	1.0000	1.300	1.440	0.00
Minimum	0.00	0.0000	0.000	0.000	0.00
Maximum	556.98	8.1000	18.500	36.660	543.75
1st Quartile	2.88	0.8400	0.400	0.350	0.00
3st Quartile	10.99	1.2000	2.250	3.730	2.80
1.00%	0.13	0.0000	0.000	0.000	0.00
2.50%	0.77	0.3200	0.000	0.000	0.00
5.00%	1.09	0.4500	0.000	0.010	0.00
10.00%	1.46	0.6000	0.000	0.050	0.00
20.00%	2.37	0.7800	0.000	0.200	0.00
80.00%	12.87	1.2800	2.530	4.790	4.22
90.00%	24.29	1.5000	3.700	7.650	14.18
95.00%	36.01	1.7500	5.000	11.690	25.04
97.50%	51.29	2.0000	8.280	18.800	39.52
99.00%	90.47	2.4300	13.950	25.240	72.56

compensation and its four components. (Note that these are not broken down by any categories, so the Unstacked format option in StatTools should be used.) Evidently, base salary varies through a fairly limited range, with the middle 90% of CEOs between $0.45 million and $1.75 million (see the 5th and 95th percentiles). The bonuses are spread out a bit more, but not much; the median bonus is $1.3 million, and 95% are no more than $5 million. Probably the most striking feature is the extreme skewness in the "other" and stock gains components. For example, at least a quarter of the CEOs had no stock gains, but at least 10% made more than $14 million in stock gains.

If you create histograms of these five variables, you will see that some of them have almost no shape, being totally dominated by outliers. For example, the histogram of total compensation in Figure 3.71 has only one bar of appreciable size. (This bar contains 489 of the 500 CEOs.) Even the histogram of base salary in Figure 3.72 is affected by outliers, although it is not nearly as skewed as the histogram of total compensation.

Figure 3.71

Histogram of Total Compensation

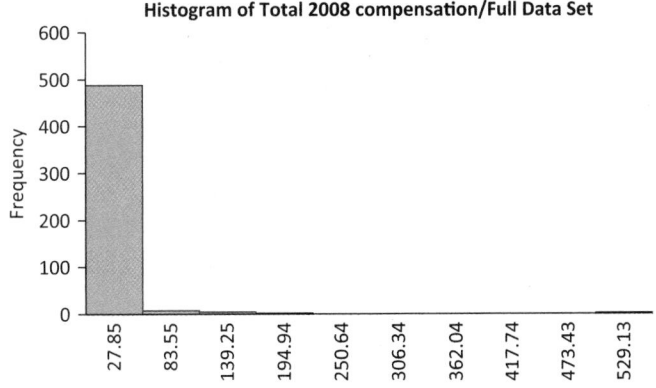

Figure 3.72

Histogram of Base Salary

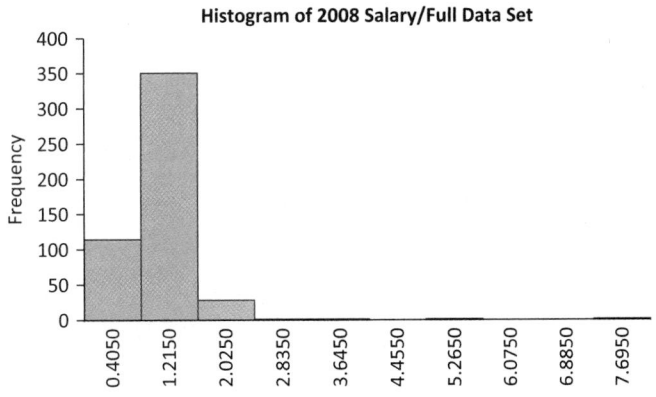

If you want to see more clearly how "most" of the CEO compensations are distributed, you can create a new StatTools data set with the outliers removed. (Here it is useful to copy the data to a new sheet and then work with the copy.) As an example, we sorted in increasing order of total compensation and then deleted the bottom 50, the ones with the largest compensations. A histogram of the remaining 450 appears in Figure 3.73. There is still skewness, but not nearly as pronounced as before.

Figure 3.73

Histogram of Total Compensation without Top 50 Earners

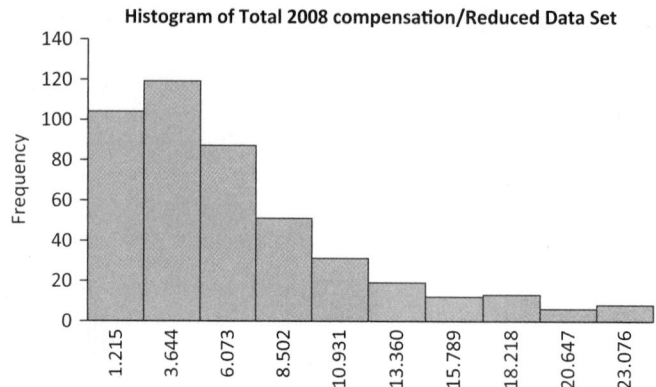

Histogram of Total 2008 compensation/Reduced Data Set

Question Set 3: How do CEO compensations vary by industry? Is the variability about the same in each industry?

Answer Set 3: The first question can be answered partly by the table in Figure 3.67, which we obtained directly from the Web site. However, it is easy to calculate additional results with one or more pivot tables and associated pivot charts. One such pivot chart appears in Figure 3.74. This summarizes total compensation in two ways, by average and by standard deviation, sorted on the averages. The smallest average compensation is for Consumer Durables and the largest is for Software & Services. But note that the two categories to the right have by far the largest standard deviations. Evidently, a few very highly paid CEOs in these two industries not only pulled up the averages but also the amount of variability. (The top five CEOs are in these two industries.)

Remember also that you can filter in pivot tables. Figure 3.74 shows all industries, but to see only a few, you can easily filter out the ones you want to hide. For example, Figure 3.75 shows a clearer picture of industries in the financial sector. It took almost no work to create this chart. After filtering out all but the three industries, the pivot chart in Figure 3.74 updated automatically.

Figure 3.74 Pivot Chart of Total Compensation by Industry

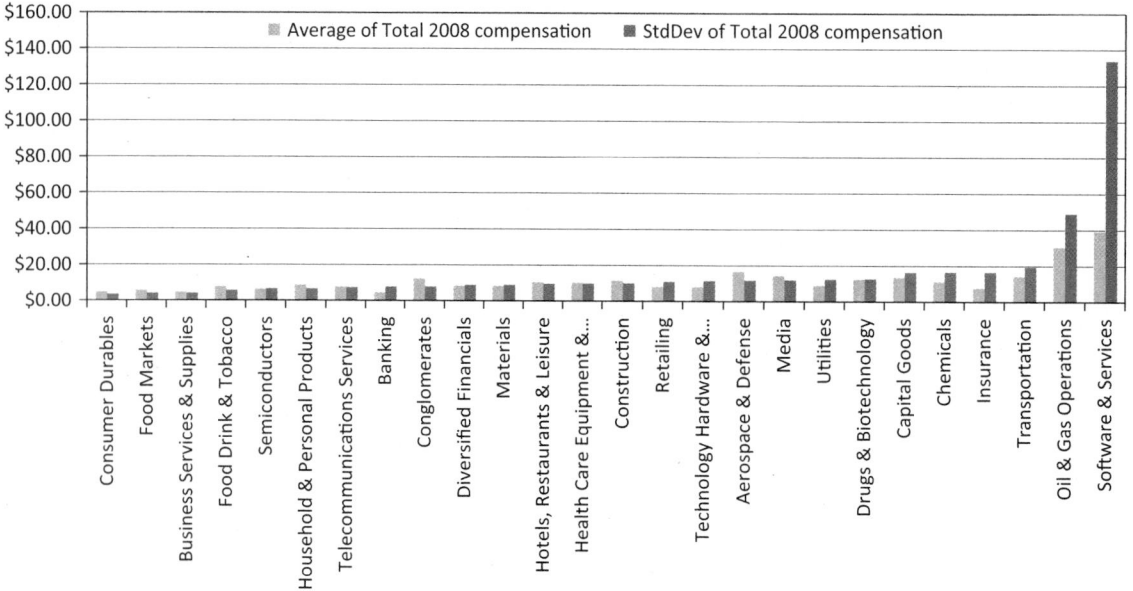

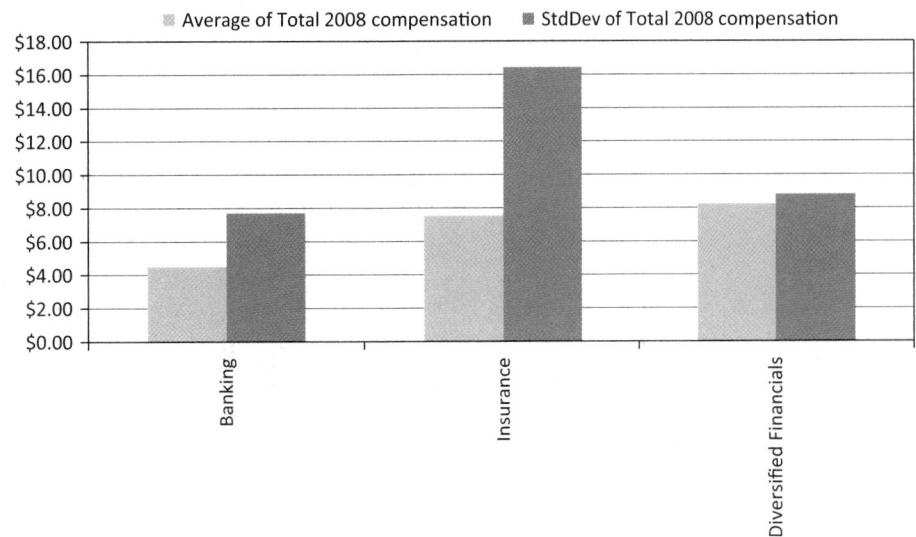

Figure 3.75

Pivot Chart of Total Compensation for Financial Industries

Question Set 4: An obvious question deals with the relationship, if any, between the size of the CEO's compensation and the performance of the company. We would hope there is a positive relationship, but is there one?

Answer Set 4: First, you need to be aware that any conclusions drawn from this data set are tentative at best. This is the area that has been researched most by academics: Are CEOs worth the huge compensations they are receiving? There are no easy answers, and we have to be very careful to use the most appropriate data, but we can take a look at the evidence here. It is probably best to look at long-term results rather than just a single year, so we focus on the data in columns Q–W in Figure 3.66, which is reported only for CEOs who have a six-year tenure and six-year compensation history. There are 179 such CEOs, so we created another StatTools data set called Six-year Data Set for these 179 CEOs. Column Q contains the six-year average compensation for the CEO. Columns R–T show the annualized stock returns (including dividends) for the company; columns S and T show this as an index relative to the industry and the market (S&P 500), respectively, where a score of 100 is par. Columns V and W are similar to columns R and T, except that they are for the CEO's entire tenure. Finally, column U lists Forbes's ranking of these 179 CEOs based on a performance versus pay score, with 1 being best, 179 being worst.[11]

Probably the best way to explore these data is with correlations and scatterplots. The correlations among the seven variables appear in Figure 3.76. As always, we are on the

Figure 3.76 Correlations among Pay and Performance Variables

	A	B	C	D	E	F	G	H
7		6-year average compensation	6-year annual total return	6-year return relative to industry	6-year return relative to market	Performance vs pay rank	Total return during tenure	Relative to market
8	Correlation Table	Six-year Data Set	Six-year Data Set	Six-year Data Set	Six-year Data Set	Six-year Data Set	Six-year Data Set	Six-year Data Set
9	6-year average compensation	1.000						
10	6-year annual total return	0.188	1.000					
11	6-year return relative to industry	0.111	0.629	1.000				
12	6-year return relative to market	0.188	1.000	0.630	1.000			
13	Performance vs pay rank	0.114	-0.668	-0.667	-0.668	1.000		
14	Total return during tenure	0.272	0.638	0.423	0.637	-0.589	1.000	
15	Relative to market	0.084	0.113	0.075	0.113	-0.093	0.197	1.000

[11]We are not told exactly how these rankings were made, but you can find more information at www.forbes.com/2009/04/22/compensation-chief-executive-salary-leadership-best-boss-09-ceo-intro.html.

Figure 3.77 Scatterplots of Pay Versus Performance Variables

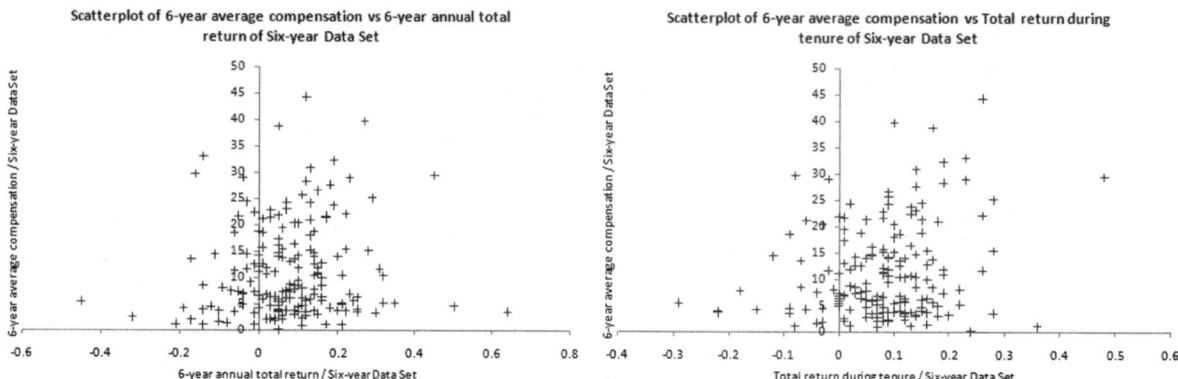

lookout for large correlations, but it is also interesting to look at small correlations for the *lack* of relationships. In this case, the six-year average compensation (which includes stock gains) has very small correlations with all other variables. There is a hint of a positive relationship in the 0.188 and 0.272 correlations between six-year average compensation and total return and total return during tenure, but these are certainly not large. This is apparent in the two corresponding scatterplots in Figure 3.77, where there is again a hint of a positive relationship between pay and performance, but certainly not a strong one. (We changed the scale of the vertical axis to a maximum of 50 so that the shapes of the scatters are clearer. This hides a few outliers.)

The correlations in Figures 3.76 and 3.77 are probably the best evidence we have, at least from this data set, that CEO compensation and company performance are at best weakly related. However, some other correlations are also interesting. Specifically, note the perfect correlation of 1.0 between six-year total return and six-year return relative to market. Although it is not clear from the Forbes footnotes, these two variables evidently express exactly the same information in different ways. But then why is the correlation between the last two variables not also 1.0? Its small value, 0.197, raises the question of whether we misinterpreted the last variable. The lesson here is that correlations in real data sets can sometimes lead to surprises—and further questions.

We have certainly not answered all of the questions that could be asked about the CEO data set, and we have not exploited all of the tools that could be used to answer such questions. With a data set as rich as this one, all you can hope to do is use the various data analysis tools in your arsenal to uncover as much interesting information as possible.

3.7 CONCLUSION

Finding relationships among variables is arguably the most important task in data analysis. This chapter has equipped you with some very powerful tools for detecting relationships. As we have discussed, the tools vary depending on whether the variables are categorical or numerical. (Again, refer to the diagram in the **Data Analysis Taxonomy.xlsx** file.) Tables and charts of counts are useful for relationships among categorical variables. Summary measures broken down by categories and side-by-side box plots (or side-by-side histograms) are useful for finding relationships between a categorical and a numerical variable. Scatterplots and correlations are useful for finding relationships among numerical variables. Finally, pivot tables are useful for all types of variables.

Summary of Key Terms

Term	Explanation	Excel	Pages	Equation
Crosstabs (or contingency table)	Table of counts of joint categories of two categorical variables	COUNTIFS function or pivot table	88	
Comparison problem	Comparing a numerical variable across two or more subpopulations		92	
Stacked or unstacked data formats	Stacked means long columns, one for categories and another for values, unstacked means a separate values column for each category		93	
Scatterplot (or X-Y chart)	Chart for detecting a relationship between two numerical variables; one point for each observation	Scatter from Insert ribbon or StatTools	93	
Trend line	Line or curve fit to scatterplot (or time series graph)	Right-click on chart point, select Add Trendline	105	
Covariance	Measure of linear relationship between two numerical variables, but affected by units of measurement	COVAR function or StatTools	108	3.1
Correlation	Measure of linear relationship between two numerical variables, always from -1 to $+1$	CORREL function or StatTools	108	3.2
Pivot table	Table for breaking down data by category; can show counts, averages, or other summary measures	PivotTable from Insert ribbon	114	
Pivot chart	Chart corresponding to a pivot table	PivotChart from PivotTable Tools Options ribbon	124	
Slicers	Graphical elements for filtering in pivot tables	New to Excel 2010	133	

PROBLEMS

Conceptual Questions

C.1. When you are trying to discover whether there is a relationship between two categorical variables, why is it useful to transform the counts in a crosstabs to percentages of row or column? Once you do this, how can you tell if the variables are related?

C.2. Suppose you have a crosstabs of two "Yes/No" categorical variables, with the counts shown as percentages of row. What will these percentages look like if there is absolutely no relationship between the variables? Besides this case, list all possible *types* of relationships that could occur. (There aren't many.)

C.3. If you suspect that a company's advertising expenditures in a given month affect its sales in *future* months, what correlations would you look at to confirm your suspicions? How would you find them?

C.4. Suppose you have customer data on whether they have bought your product in a given time period, along with various demographics on the customers. Explain how you could use pivot tables to see which demographics are the primary drivers of their "yes/no" buying behavior.

C.5. Suppose you have data on student achievement in high school for each of many school districts. In spreadsheet format, the school district is in column A, and various student achievement measures are in columns B, C, and so on. If you find fairly low correlations (magnitudes from 0 to 0.4, say) between the variables in these achievement columns, what exactly does this mean?

C.6. A supermarket transactions data set is likely to have "hierarchical" columns of data. For example, for the product sold, there might be columns like Product Family, Product Department, Product Category, and maybe even more. (See the file **Supermarket Transactions.xlsx** as an example.) Another hierarchy is for store location, where there might be columns for Country, State or Province, City, and possibly more. One more hierarchy is time, with the hierarchy Year, Quarter, Month, and so on. How could a supermarket manager use pivot tables to "drill down" through a hierarchy to examine revenues? For example, you might start at the Drink level, then drill down to Alcoholic Beverages, and then to Beer and Wine? Illustrate with the file mentioned.

C.7. Suppose you have a large data set for some sport. Each row might correspond to a particular team (as in the file **P03_57.xlsx** on football outcomes, for example) or it might even correspond to a given play. Each row contains one or more measures of success as well as many pieces of data that could be drivers of success. How might you find the most important drivers of success if the success measure is categorical (such as Win or Lose)? How might you find the most important drivers of success if the success measure is numerical and basically continuous (such as Points Scored in basketball)?

C.8. If two variables are highly correlated, does this imply that changes in one *cause* changes in the other? If not, give at least one example from the real world that illustrates what else could cause a high correlation.

C.9. Suppose there are two commodities A and B with strongly negatively correlated daily returns, such as a stock and gold. Is it possible to find another commodity with daily returns that are strongly negatively correlated with *both* A and B?

C.10. In checking whether several times series, such as monthly exchange rates of various currencies, move together, why do most analysts look at correlations between their *differences* rather than correlations between the original series?

Level A

52. Unfortunately, StatTools doesn't have a stacked option for its correlation procedure, which would allow you to get a separate table of correlations for each category of a categorical variable. The only alternative is to sort on the categorical variable, insert some blank rows between values of different categories, copy the headings to each section, create separate StatTools data sets for each, and then ask for correlations from each. Do this with the movie data in the file **P02_02.xlsx**. Specifically, separate the data into three data sets based on Genre: one for Comedy, one for Drama, and one for all the rest. For this problem, you can ignore the third group. For each of Comedy and Drama, create a table of correlations between 7-day Gross, 14-day Gross, Total US Gross,

International Gross, and US DVD Sales. Comment on whether the correlation structure is much different for these two popular genres.

53. The file **P03_53.xlsx** lists campaign contributions, by number of contributors and contribution amount, by state (including Washington DC) for the four leading contenders in the 2008 presidential race. Create a scatterplot and corresponding correlation between Dollar Amount (Y axis) and Contributors for each of the four contenders. For each scatterplot, superimpose a linear trend line and show the corresponding equation. Interpret each equation and compare them across candidates. Finally, identify the state for any points that aren't on or very close to the corresponding trend line.

54. The file **P03_54.xlsx** lists data for 539 movies released in 2009. Obviously, some movies are simply more popular than others, but success in 2009, measured by 2009 gross or 2009 tickets sold, could also be influenced by the release date. To check this, create a new variable, Days Out, which is the number of days the movie was out during 2009. For example, a movie released on 12/15 would have Days Out equal to 17 (which includes the release day). Create two scatterplots and corresponding correlations, one of 2009 Gross (Y axis) versus Days Out and one of 2009 Tickets Sold (Y axis) versus Days Out. Describe the behavior you see. Do you think a movie's success can be predicted very well just by knowing how many days it has been out?

55. The file **P03_55.xlsx** lists the average salary for each MLB team from 2004 to 2009, along with the number of team wins in each of these years.
   a. Create a table of correlations between the Wins columns. What do these correlations indicate? Are they higher or lower than you expected?
   b. Create a table of correlations between the Salary columns. What do these correlations indicate? Are they higher or lower than you expected?
   c. For each year, create a scatterplot and the associated correlations between Wins for that year (Y axis) and Salary for that year. Does it appear that teams are buying their way to success?
   d. The coloring in the Wins columns indicates the playoff teams. Create a new Yes/No column for each year, indicating whether the team made it to the playoffs that year. Then create a pivot table for each year showing average of Salary for that year, broken down by the Yes/No column for that year. Do these pivot tables indicate that teams are buying their way into the playoffs?

56. The file **P03_56.xlsx** lists the average salary for each NBA team from 2004 to 2009, along with the number of team wins each of these years. Answer the same questions as in the previous problem for this basketball data.

57. The file **P03_57.xlsx** lists the average salary for each NFL team from 2004 to 2009, along with the number of team wins each of these years. Answer the same questions as in the problem 55 for this football data.

58. The file **P03_58.xlsx** lists salaries of MLB players in the years 2007 to 2009. Each row corresponds to a particular player. As indicated by blank salaries, some players played in one of these years, some played in two of these years, and the rest played in all three years.
    a. Create a new Yes/No variable, All 3 Years, that indicates which players played all three years.
    b. Create two pivot tables and corresponding pivot charts. The first should show the count of players by position who played all three years. The second should show the average salary each year, by position, for all players who played all three years. (For each of these, put the All 3 Years variable in the Report Filter area.) Explain briefly what these two pivot tables indicate.
    c. Define a StatTools data set on only the players who played all three years. Using this data set, create a table of correlations of the three salary variables. What do these correlations indicate about player salaries?

59. The file **P03_59.xlsx** lists the results of about 20,000 runners in the 2008 New York Marathon.
    a. For all runners who finished in 3.5 hours or less, create a pivot table and corresponding pivot chart of average of Time by Gender. (To get a fairer comparison in the chart, change it so that the vertical axis starts at zero.) For the same runners, and on the same sheet, create another pivot table and pivot chart of counts by Gender. Comment on the results.
    b. For all runners who finished in 3.5 hours or less, create a pivot table and corresponding pivot chart of average of Time by Age. Group by Age so that the teens are in one category, those in their twenties are in another category, and so on. For the same runners, and on the same sheet, create another pivot table and pivot chart of counts of these age groups. Comment on the results.
    c. For all runners who finished in 3.5 hours or less, create a single pivot table of average of Time and of counts, broken down by Country. Then filter so that only the 10 countries with the 10 lowest average times appear. Finally, sort on average times so that the fastest countries rise to the top. Guess who the top two are! (*Hint*: Try the Value Filters for the Country variable.) Comment on the results.

60. The file **P02_12.xlsx** includes data on the 50 top graduate programs in the U.S., according to a recent *U.S. News & World Report* survey.
    a. Create a table of correlations between all of the numerical variables. Discuss which variables are highly correlated with which others.

    b. The Overall score is the score schools agonize about. Create a scatterplot and corresponding correlation of each of the other variables versus Overall, with Overall always on the Y axis. What do you learn from these scatterplots?

61. Recall from an example in the previous chapter that the file **Supermarket Transactions.xlsx** contains over 14,000 transactions made by supermarket customers over a period of approximately two years. Set up a single pivot table and corresponding pivot chart, with some instructions to a user (like the supermarket manager) in a text box, on how the user can get answers to any typical question about the data. For example, one possibility (of many) could be total revenue by product department and month, for any combination of gender, marital status, and homeowner. (The point is to get you to explain pivot table basics to a nontechnical user.)

62. The file **P03_15.xlsx** contains monthly data on the various components of the Consumer Price Index.
    a. Create differences for each of the variables. You can do this quickly with StatTools, using the Difference item in the Data Utilities dropdown list, or you can create the differences with Excel formulas.
    b. Create a times series graph for each CPI component, including the All Items component. Then create a time series graph for each difference variable. Comment on any patterns or trends you see.
    c. Create a table of correlations between the differences. Comment on any large correlations (or the lack of them).
    d. Create a scatterplot for each difference variable versus the difference for All Items (Y axis). Comment on any patterns or outliers you see.

Level B

63. The file **P03_63.xlsx** contains financial data on 85 U.S. companies in the Computer and Electronic Product Manufacturing sector (NAICS code 334) with 2009 earnings before taxes of at least $10,000. Each of these companies listed R&D (research and development) expenses on its income statement. Create a table of correlations between all of the variables and use conditional formatting to color green all correlations involving R&D that are strongly positive or negative. (Use cutoff values of your choice to define "strongly.") Then create scatterplots of R&D (Y axis) versus each of the other most highly correlated variables. Comment on any patterns you see in these scatterplots, including any obvious outliers, and explain why (or if) it makes sense that these variables are highly correlated with R&D. If there are highly correlated variables with R&D, can you tell which way the causality goes?

64. The file **P03_64.xlsx** lists monthly data since 1950 on the well-known Dow Jones Industrial Average (DJIA), as well as the less well-known Dow Jones Transportation Average (DJTA) and Dow Jones Utilities Average (DJUA). Each of these is an index based on 20 to 30 leading companies (which change over time).

   a. Create monthly differences in three new columns. The Jan-50 values will be blank because there are no Dec-49 values. Then, for example, the Feb-50 difference is the Feb-50 value minus the Jan-50 value. (You can easily calculate these with Excel formulas, but you might want to try the StatTools Difference procedure from its Data Utilities dropdown list.)

   b. Create a table of correlations of the three difference columns. Does it appear that the three Dow indexes tend to move together through time?

   c. It is possible (and has been claimed) that one of the indexes is a "leading indicator" of another. For example, a change in the DJUA in September might predict a similar change in the DJIA in the following December. To check for such behavior, create "lags" of the difference variables. To do so, select Lag from the StatTools Data Utilities dropdown list, select one of the difference variables, and enter the number of lags you want. For this problem, try four lags. Then press OK and accept the StatTools warnings. Do this for each of the three difference variables. You should end up with 12 lag variables. Explain in words what these lag variables contain. For example, what is the Dec-50 lag3 of the DJIA difference?

   d. Create a table of correlations of the three differences and the 12 lags. Use conditional formatting to color green all correlations greater than 0.5 (or any other cutoff you choose). Does it appear that any index is indeed a leading indicator of any other? Explain.

65. The file **P03_65.xlsx** lists a lot of data for each NBA team for the seasons 2004–2005 to 2008–2009. The variables are divided into groups: (1) Overall success, (2) Offensive, and (3) Defensive. The basic question all basketball fans (and coaches) ponder is what causes success or failure.

   a. Explore this question by creating a correlation matrix with the variable Wins (the measure of success) and all of the variables in groups (2) and (3). Based on these correlations, which five variables appear to be the best predictors of success? (Keep in mind that negative correlations can also be important.)

   b. Explore this question in a different way, using the Playoff Team column as a measure of success. Here, it makes sense to proceed as in the Lasagna Triers example in Section 3.5, using the variables

in groups (2) and (3) as the predictors. However, these predictors are all basically continuous, so grouping would be required for all of them in the pivot table, and grouping is always somewhat arbitrary. Instead, create a copy of the Data sheet. Then for each variable in groups (2) to (13), create a formula that returns 1, 2, 3, or 4, depending on which quarter of that variable the value falls in (1 if it is less than or equal to the first quartile, and so on). (This sounds like a lot of work, but a *single* copyable formula will work for the entire range.) Now use these discrete variables as predictors and proceed as in the Lasagna Triers example. List the five variables that appear to be the best (or at least good) predictors of making the playoffs.

66. The file **P03_66.xlsx** lists a lot of data for each NFL team for the years 2004 to 2009. The variables are divided into groups: (1) Overall success, (2) Team Offense, (3) Passing Offense, (4) Rushing Offense, (5) Turnovers Against, (6) Punt Returns, (7) Kick Returns, (8) Field Goals, (9) Punts, (10) Team Defense, (11) Passing Defense, (12) Rushing Defense, and (13) Turnovers Caused. The basic question all football fans (and coaches) ponder is what causes success or failure. Answer the same questions as in the previous problem for this football data, but use all of the variables in groups (2) to (13) as possible predictors.

67. The file **P02_57.xlsx** contains data on mortgage loans in 2008 for each state in the U.S. The file is different from others in this chapter in that each state has its own sheet with the same data in the same format. Each state sheet breaks down all mortgage applications by loan purpose, applicant race, loan type, outcome, and denial reason (for those that were denied). The question is how a *single* data set for all states can be created for analysis. The Typical Data Set sheet indicates a simple way of doing this, using the powerful but little-known INDIRECT function. This sheet is basically a template for bringing in any pieces of data from the state sheets you would like to examine.

   a. Do whatever it takes to populate the Typical Data Set sheet with information in the range B7:D11 and B14:D14 (18 variables in all) of each state sheet. Add appropriate labels in row 3, such as Asian Dollar Amount Applied For.

   b. Create a table of correlations between these variables. Color yellow all correlations between a given applicant race, such as those between Asian Mortgage Application, Asian Dollar Amount Applied For, and Asian Average Income. Comment on the magnitudes of these. Are there any surprises?

   c. Create scatterplots of White Dollar Amount Applied For (X axis) versus the similar variable for each of the other five applicant races. Comment on any patterns in these scatterplots, and identify any obvious outliers.

CASE 3.1 CUSTOMER ARRIVALS AT BANK98

Bank98 operates a main location and three branch locations in a medium-size city. All four locations perform similar services, and customers typically do business at the location nearest them. The bank has recently had more congestion—long waiting lines—than it (or its customers) would like. As part of a study to learn the causes of these long lines and to suggest possible solutions, all locations have kept track of customer arrivals during one-hour intervals for the past 10 weeks. All branches are open Monday through Friday from 9 A.M. until 5 P.M. and on Saturday from 9 A.M. until noon. For each location, the file **Bank98 Arrivals.xlsx** contains the number of customer arrivals during each hour of a 10-week period. The manager of Bank98 has hired you to make some sense of these data. Specifically, your task is to present charts and/or tables that indicate how customer traffic into the bank locations varies by day of week and hour of day. There is also interest in whether any daily or hourly patterns you observe are stable across weeks. Although you don't have full information about the way the bank currently runs its operations—you know only its customer arrival pattern and the fact that it is currently experiencing long lines—you are encouraged to append any suggestions for improving operations, based on your analysis of the data. ■

The best-selling book *The Millionaire Next Door* by Thomas J. Stanley and William D. Danko (Longstreet Press, 1996) presents some very interesting data on the characteristics of millionaires. We tend to believe that people with expensive houses, expensive cars, expensive clothes, country club memberships, and other outward indications of wealth are the millionaires. The authors define wealth, however, in terms of savings and investments, not consumer items. In this sense, they argue that people with a lot of expensive *things* and even large incomes often have surprisingly little wealth. These people tend to spend much of what they make on consumer items, often trying to keep up with, or impress, their peers.

In contrast, the real millionaires, in terms of savings and investments, frequently come from "unglamorous"

professions (particularly teaching), own unpretentious homes and cars, dress in inexpensive clothes, and otherwise lead rather ordinary lives.

Consider the (fictional) data in the file **Social Climbers.xlsx**. For several hundred couples, it lists their education level, their annual combined salary, the market value of their home and cars, the amount of savings they have accumulated (in savings accounts, stocks, retirement accounts, and so on), and a self-reported "social climber index" on a scale of 1 to 10 (with 1 being very unconcerned about social status and material items and 10 being very concerned about these). Prepare a report based on these data, supported by relevant charts and/or tables, that could be used in a book such as *The Millionaire Next Door*. Your conclusions can either support or contradict those of Stanley and Danko. ∎

The term "churn" is very important to managers in the cellular phone business. Churning occurs when a customer stops using one company's service and switches to another company's service. Obviously, managers try to keep churning to a minimum, not only by offering the best possible service, but by trying to identify conditions that lead to churning and taking steps to stop churning before it occurs. For example, if a company learns that customers tend to churn at the end of their two-year contract, they could offer customers an incentive to stay a month or two before the end of their two-year contract. The file Churn.xlsx contains data on over 2000 customers of a particular cellular phone company. Each row contains the activity of a particular customer for a given time period, and the last column indicates whether the customer churned during this time period. Use the tools in this chapter (and possibly the previous chapter) to learn (1) how these variables are distributed, (2) how the variables in columns B–R are related to each other, and (3) how the variables in columns B–R are related to the Churn variable in column S. Write a short report of your findings, including any recommendations you would make to the company to reduce churn. ■

PART

2

Probability and Decision Making under Uncertainty

Probability and Probability Distributions

© Viviolsen/Dreamstime.com

GAME AT MCDONALD'S

Several years ago, McDonald's ran a campaign in which it gave game cards to its customers. These game cards made it possible for customers to win hamburgers, french fries, soft drinks, and other fast-food items, as well as cash prizes. Each card had 10 covered spots that could be uncovered by rubbing them with a coin. Beneath three of these spots were "zaps." Beneath the other seven spots were names of prizes, two of which were identical. (Some cards had variations of this pattern, but we'll use this type of card for purposes of illustration.) For example, one card might have two pictures of a hamburger, one picture of a Coke, one of french fries, one of a milk shake, one of $5, one of $1000, and three zaps. For this card the customer could win a hamburger. To win on any card, the customer had to uncover the two matching spots (which showed the potential prize for that card) before uncovering a zap; any card with a zap uncovered was automatically void. Assuming that the two matches and the three zaps were arranged randomly on the cards, what is the probability of a customer winning?

We will label the two matching spots M_1 and M_2, and the three zaps Z_1, Z_2, and Z_3. Then the probability of winning is the probability of uncovering M_1 *and* M_2 before uncovering Z_1, Z_2, *or* Z_3. In this case the relevant set of outcomes is the set of all orderings of M_1, M_2, Z_1, Z_2, and Z_3, shown in the order they are uncovered. As far as the outcome of the game is concerned, the other five spots on the card are irrelevant. Thus, an outcome such as M_2, M_1, Z_3, Z_1, Z_2 is a winner, whereas M_2, Z_2, Z_1, M_1, Z_3 is a loser. Actually, the first of these would be declared a winner as soon as M_1 was uncovered, and the second would be declared a loser as soon as Z_2 was uncovered. However, we show the whole sequence of Ms and Zs so that we can count outcomes correctly. We then find the probability of winning using the argument of equally likely outcomes. Specifically, we divide the number of outcomes that are winners by the total number of outcomes. It can be shown that the number of outcomes that are winners is 12, whereas the total number of outcomes is 120. Therefore, the probability of a winner is 12/120 = 0.1.

This calculation, which showed that on the average, 1 out of 10 cards could be winners, was obviously important for McDonald's. Actually, this provides only an upper bound on the fraction of cards where a prize was awarded. The fact is that many customers threw their cards away without playing the game, and even some of the winners neglected to claim their prizes. So, for example, McDonald's knew that if they made 50,000 cards where a milk shake was the winning prize, somewhat less than 5000 milk shakes would be given away. Knowing approximately what their expected "losses" would be from winning cards, McDonald's was able to design the game (how many cards of each type to print) so that the expected extra revenue (from customers attracted to the game) would cover the expected losses. ■

4.1 INTRODUCTION

The world is full of uncertainty, and this is certainly true in business. A key aspect of solving real business problems is dealing appropriately with uncertainty. This involves recognizing explicitly that uncertainty exists and using quantitative methods to model uncertainty. If you want to develop realistic models of business problems, you should not simply act as if uncertainty doesn't exist. For example, if you don't know next month's demand, you shouldn't build a model that assumes next month's demand is a sure 1500 units. This is only wishful thinking. You should instead incorporate the uncertainty about demand explicitly into your model. To do this, you need to know how to deal quantitatively with uncertainty. This involves probability and probability distributions. We will introduce these topics in this chapter and then use them in a number of later chapters.

There are many sources of uncertainty. Demands for products are uncertain, times between arrivals to a supermarket are uncertain, stock price returns are uncertain, changes in interest rates are uncertain, and so on. In many situations, the uncertain quantity—demand, time between arrivals, stock price return, change in interest rate—is a numerical quantity. In the language of probability, such a numerical quantity is called a **random variable**. More formally, a random variable associates a numerical value with each possible random outcome.

Associated with each random variable is a *probability distribution* that lists all of the possible values of the random variable and their corresponding probabilities. A probability distribution provides very useful information. It not only indicates the possible values of the random variable, but it also indicates how likely they are. For example, it is useful to know that the possible demands for a product are, say, 100, 200, 300, and 400, but it is even more useful to know that the probabilities of these four values are, say, 0.1, 0.2, 0.4, and 0.3. Now we know, for example, that there is a 70% chance that demand will be at least 300.

It is often useful to summarize the information from a probability distribution with several well-chosen numerical summary measures. These include the mean, variance, and standard deviation, and, for distributions of more than one random variable, the covariance and correlation. As their names imply, these summary measures are much like the corresponding summary measures in Chapters 2 and 3. However, they are *not* identical. The summary measures in this chapter are based on probability distributions, not an observed data set. We will use numerical examples to explain the difference between the two—and how they are related.

The purpose of this chapter is to explain the basic concepts and tools necessary to work with probability distributions and their summary measures. We begin by briefly discussing the basic rules of probability, which we need in this chapter and in several later chapters. We also introduce *computer simulation,* an extremely useful tool for illustrating important concepts in probability and statistics.

Modeling uncertainty, as we will be doing in the next few chapters and later in Chapters 15 and 16, is sometimes difficult, depending on the complexity of the model, and it is easy to get so caught up in the details that you lose sight of the big picture. For this reason, the flow chart in Figure 4.1 is useful. (A colored version of this chart is available in the file **Modeling Uncertainty - Flow Chart.xlsx**.) Take a close look at the middle row of this chart. It indicates that we begin with inputs, some of which are uncertain quantities, use Excel formulas to incorporate the logic of the model, end with probability distributions of important outputs that we can summarize in various ways, and finally use this information to make decisions. (The abbreviation EMV stands for expected monetary value. It will be discussed extensively in Chapter 6.) The other boxes in the chart deal with implementation issues, particularly with software you can use to perform the analysis. Read this chart carefully, and return to it as you proceed through the next few chapters and Chapters 15 and 16.

Figure 4.1   Flow Chart for Modeling Uncertainty

Assess probability distributions of uncertain inputs:

1. If a lot of historical data is available, use software like @RISK to find the distribution that best fits the data.

2. Choose a probability distribution (normal? triangular?) that seems reasonable. Software like @RISK is helpful for exploring distributions.

3. Gather relevant information, ask experts, and do the best you can.

Two fundamental approaches:

1. Build an exact probability model that incorporates the rules of probability. (Pros: It is exact and amenable to sensitivity analysis. Cons: It is often difficult mathematically, maybe not even possible.)

2. Build a simulation model. (Pros: It is typically much easier, especially with an add-in like @RISK, and extremely versatile. Cons: It is only approximate and runs can be time consuming for complex models).

For simulation models, this can be done "manually" with data tables and built-in functions like AVERAGE, STDEV, etc. But an add-in like @RISK takes care of these bookkeeping details automatically.

Use decision trees (made easier with an add-in like Precision Tree) if the number of possible decisions and the number of possible outcomes are not too large.

Decide which inputs are important for the model.

1. Which are known with certainty?
2. Which are uncertain?

Model the problem.

Use Excel formulas to relate inputs to important outputs, i.e., enter the business logic.

Examine important outputs.

The result of these formulas should be probability distribution(s) of important output(s). Summarize these probability distributions with (1) histograms (risk profiles), (2) means and standard deviations, (3) percentiles, (4) possibly others.

Make decisions based on this information.

Criterion is usually EMV, but it could be something else, e.g., minimize the probability of losing money.

This is an overview of spreadsheet modeling with uncertainty. The main process is in red. The blue boxes deal with implementation issues.

For simulation models, random values for uncertain inputs are necessary.

1. They can sometimes be generated with built-in Excel functions. This often involves tricks and can be obscure.

2. Add-ins like @RISK provide functions (like RISKNORMAL, RISKTRIANG) that make it much easier.

Before proceeding, we discuss two terms you often hear in the business world: *uncertainty* and *risk*. They are sometimes used interchangeably, but they are not really the same. You typically have no control over uncertainty; it is something that simply exists. A good example is the uncertainty in exchange rates. You cannot be sure what the exchange rate between the U.S. dollar and the euro will be a year from now. All you can try to do is *measure* this uncertainty with a probability distribution.

In contrast, risk depends on your position. Even though you don't know what the exchange rate will be, it makes no difference to you—there is no risk—if you have no European investments, you aren't planning a trip to Europe, and you don't have to buy or sell anything in Europe. You might be interested in the exchange rate, but you have no risk. You have risk only when you stand to gain or lose money depending on the eventual exchange rate. Of course, the form of your risk depends on your position. If you are holding euros in a money market account, you are hoping that euros gain value relative to the dollar. But if you are planning a European vacation, you are hoping that euros lose value relative to the dollar.

Uncertainty and risk are inherent in many of the examples in this book. By learning about probability, you will learn how to measure uncertainty, and you will also learn how to measure the risks involved in various decisions. One important topic you will *not* learn much about is risk mitigation by various types of hedging. For example, if you know you have to purchase a large quantity of some product from Europe a year from now, you face the risk that the value of the euro could increase dramatically, thus costing you a lot of money. Fortunately, there are ways to hedge this risk, so that if the euro does increase relative to the dollar, your hedge minimizes your losses. Hedging risk is an extremely important topic, and it is practiced daily in the real world, but it is beyond the scope of this book.

4.2 PROBABILITY ESSENTIALS

We begin with a brief discussion of probability. The concept of probability is one that we all encounter in everyday life. When a weather forecaster states that the chance of rain is 70%, she is making a probability statement. When we hear that the odds of the Los Angeles Lakers winning the NBA Championship are 2 to 1, this is also a probability statement. The *concept* of probability is quite intuitive. However, the *rules* of probability are not always as intuitive or easy to master. We examine the most important of these rules in this section.

> A **probability** is a number between 0 and 1 that measures the likelihood that some event will occur. An event with probability 0 cannot occur, whereas an event with probability 1 is certain to occur. An event with probability greater than 0 and less than 1 involves uncertainty, and the closer its probability is to 1, the more likely it is to occur.

As the examples in the preceding paragraph illustrate, probabilities are sometimes expressed as percentages or odds. However, these can easily be converted to probabilities on a 0-to-1 scale. If the chance of rain is 70%, then the probability of rain is 0.7. Similarly, if the odds of the Lakers winning are 2 to 1, then the probability of the Lakers winning is 2/3 (or 0.6667).

There are only a few probability rules you need to know, and we will discuss them in the next few subsections. Surprisingly, these are the *only* rules you need to know. Probability is not an easy topic, and a more thorough discussion of it would lead to considerable mathematical complexity, well beyond the level of this book. However, it is all based on the few relatively simple rules discussed next.

4.2.1 Rule of Complements

The simplest probability rule involves the *complement* of an event. If A is any event, then the **complement of** A, denoted by $\overline{A}$ (or in some books by A^c), is the event that A does *not* occur. For example, if A is the event that the Dow Jones Industrial Average will finish the year at or above the 11,000 mark, then the complement of A is that the Dow will finish the year below 11,000.

If the probability of A is $P(A)$, then the probability of its complement, $P(\overline{A})$, is given by Equation (4.1). Equivalently, the probability of an event and the probability of its complement sum to 1. For example, if we believe that the probability of the Dow finishing at or above 11,000 is 0.25, then the probability that it will finish the year below 11,000 is $1 - 0.25 = 0.75$.

Rule of Complements
$$P(\overline{A}) = 1 - P(A) \qquad \textbf{(4.1)}$$

4.2.2 Addition Rule

We say that events are **mutually exclusive** if at most one of them can occur. That is, if one of them occurs, then none of the others can occur. For example, consider the following three events involving a company's annual revenue for the coming year: (1) revenue is less than \$1 million, (2) revenue is at least \$1 million but less than \$2 million, and (3) revenue is at least \$2 million. Clearly, only one of these events can occur. Therefore, they are mutually exclusive. They are also **exhaustive** events, which means that they exhaust all possibilities— one of these three events *must* occur. Let A_1 through A_n be any n events. Then the *addition rule* of probability involves the probability that at least one of these events will occur. In general, this probability is quite complex, but it simplifies considerably when the events are mutually exclusive. In this case the probability that at least one of the events will occur is the sum of their individual probabilities, as shown in Equation (4.2). Of course, when the events are mutually exclusive, "at least one" is equivalent to "exactly one." In addition, if the events A_1 through A_n are exhaustive, then the probability is 1. In this case we are certain that one of the events will occur.

Addition Rule for Mutually Exclusive Events
$$P(\text{at least one of } A_1 \text{ through } A_n) = P(A_1) + P(A_2) + \cdots + P(A_n) \qquad \textbf{(4.2)}$$

In a typical application, the events A_1 through A_n are chosen to partition the set of all possible outcomes into a number of mutually exclusive events. For example, in terms of a company's annual revenue, define A_1 as "revenue is less than \$1 million," A_2 as "revenue is at least \$1 million but less than \$2 million," and A_3 as "revenue is at least \$2 million." Then these three events are mutually exclusive and exhaustive. Therefore, their probabilities must sum to 1. Suppose these probabilities are $P(A_1) = 0.5$, $P(A_2) = 0.3$, and $P(A_3) = 0.2$. (Note that these probabilities *do* sum to 1.) Then the additive rule enables us to calculate other probabilities. For example, the event that revenue is at least \$1 million is the event that either A_2 or A_3 occurs. From the addition rule, its probability is

$$P(\text{revenue is at least \$1 million}) = P(A_2) + P(A_3) = 0.5$$

Similarly,

$$P(\text{revenue is less than \$2 million}) = P(A_1) + P(A_2) = 0.8$$

and

$$P(\text{revenue is less than \$1 million } or \text{ at least \$2 million}) = P(A_1) + P(A_3) = 0.7$$

Again, the addition rule works only for mutually exclusive events. If the events overlap, then the situation is more complex. For example, suppose you are dealt a bridge hand (13 cards from a 52-card deck). Let H, D, C, and S, respectively, be the events that you get at least 5 hearts, at least 5 diamonds, at least 5 clubs, and at least 5 spades. What is the probability that at least one of these four events occurs? It is not the sum of their individual probabilities because they are not mutually exclusive. For example, you could get 5 hearts and 5 spades. Probabilities such as this one are actually quite difficult to calculate, and we will not pursue them here. Just be aware that the addition rule does not apply unless the events are mutually exclusive.

4.2.3 Conditional Probability and the Multiplication Rule

Probabilities are always assessed relative to the information currently available. As new information becomes available, probabilities often change. For example, if you read that Kobe Bryant pulled a hamstring muscle, your assessment of the probability that the Lakers will win the NBA Championship would obviously change. A formal way to revise probabilities on the basis of new information is to use *conditional probabilities.*

Let A and B be any events with probabilities $P(A)$ and $P(B)$. Typically, the probability $P(A)$ is assessed without knowledge of whether B occurs. However, if you are *told* that B has occurred, then the probability of A might change. The new probability of A is called the **conditional probability** of A given B. It is denoted by $P(A|B)$. Note that there is still uncertainty involving the event to the left of the vertical bar in this notation; you do not know whether it will occur. However, there is no uncertainty involving the event to the right of the vertical bar; you *know* that it has occurred.

Conditional Probability

$$P(A|B) = \frac{P(A \text{ and } B)}{P(B)} \qquad\qquad \textbf{(4.3)}$$

The conditional probability formula enables you to calculate $P(A|B)$ as shown in Equation (4.3). The numerator in this formula is the probability that *both* A and B occur. This probability must be known to find $P(A|B)$. However, in some applications $P(A|B)$ and $P(B)$ are known. Then you can multiply both sides of the conditional probability formula by $P(B)$ to obtain the **multiplication rule** for $P(A \text{ and } B)$ in Equation (4.4).

Multiplication Rule

$$P(A \text{ and } B) = P(A|B)\,P(B) \qquad\qquad \textbf{(4.4)}$$

The conditional probability formula and the multiplication rule are both valid; in fact, they are equivalent. The one you use depends on which probabilities you know and which you want to calculate, as illustrated in the following example.

EXAMPLE | **4.1 ASSESSING UNCERTAINTY AT THE BENDER COMPANY**

The Bender Company supplies contractors with materials for the construction of houses. The company currently has a contract with one of its customers to fill an order by the end of July. However, there is some uncertainty about whether this deadline can be met, due to uncertainty about whether Bender will receive the materials it needs from one of its suppliers by the middle of July. Right now it is July 1. How can the uncertainty in this situation be assessed?

Objective   To apply several of the essential probability rules in determining the probability that Bender will meet its end-of-July deadline, given the information the company has at the beginning of July.

Solution

Let A be the event that Bender meets its end-of-July deadline, and let B be the event that Bender receives the materials from its supplier by the middle of July. The probabilities Bender is best able to assess on July 1 are probably $P(B)$ and $P(A|B)$. At the beginning of July, Bender might estimate that the chances of getting the materials on time from its supplier are 2 out of 3, that is, $P(B) = 2/3$. Also, thinking ahead, Bender estimates that *if* it receives the required materials on time, the chances of meeting the end-of-July deadline are 3 out of 4. This is a conditional probability statement, namely, that $P(A|B) = 3/4$. Then the multiplication rule implies that

$$P(A \text{ and } B) = P(A|B)P(B) = (3/4)(2/3) = 0.5$$

That is, there is a fifty-fifty chance that Bender will get its materials on time *and* meet its end-of-July deadline.

This uncertain situation is depicted graphically in the form of a **probability tree** in Figure 4.2. Note that Bender initially faces (at the leftmost branch of the tree diagram) the uncertainty of whether event B or its complement will occur. Regardless of whether event B takes place, Bender must next confront the uncertainty regarding event A. This uncertainty is reflected in the set of two parallel pairs of branches that model whether event A or its complement will occur next. Hence, there are four mutually exclusive outcomes regarding the two uncertain events, as shown on the right-hand side of Figure 4.2. Initially, we are

Figure 4.2

Probability Tree for Example 4.1

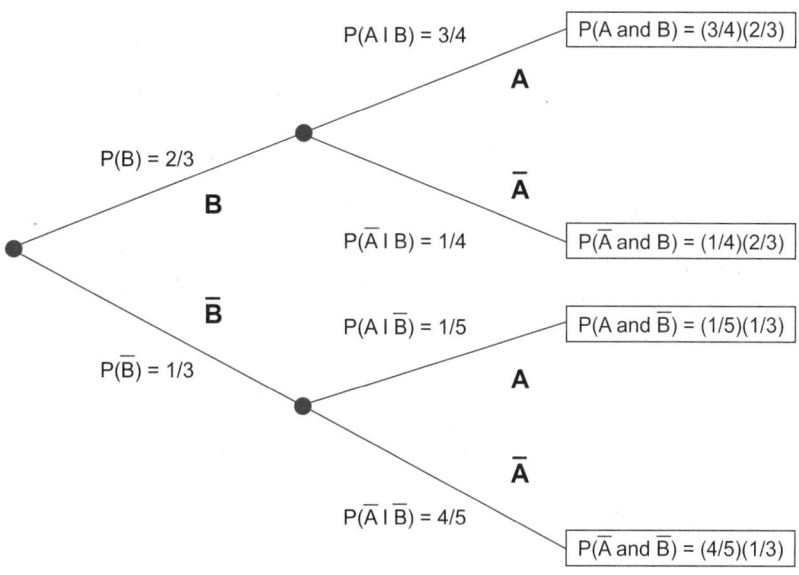

interested in the first possible outcome, the joint occurrence of events A and B, found at the top of the probability tree diagram. Another way to compute the probability of *both* events B and A occurring is to multiply the probabilities associated with the branches along the path from the root of the tree (on the left-hand side) to the desired terminal point or outcome of the tree (on the right-hand side). In this case, we multiply the probability of B, corresponding to the first branch along the path of interest, by the conditional probability of A given B, associated with the second branch along the path of interest.

There are several other probabilities of interest in this example. First, let $\overline{B}$ be the complement of B; it is the event that the materials from the supplier do *not* arrive on time. We know that $P(\overline{B}) = 1 - P(B) = 1/3$ from the rule of complements. However, we do not yet know the conditional probability $P(A|\overline{B})$, the probability that Bender will meet its end-of-July deadline, given that it does not receive the materials from the supplier on time. In particular, $P(A|\overline{B})$ is *not* equal to $1 - P(A|B)$. (Can you see why?) Suppose Bender estimates that the chances of meeting the end-of-July deadline are 1 out of 5 if the materials do not arrive on time, that is, $P(A|\overline{B}) = 1/5$. Then a second use of the multiplication rule gives

$$P(A \text{ and } \overline{B}) = P(A|\overline{B})P(\overline{B}) = (1/5)(1/3) = 0.0667$$

In words, there is only 1 chance out of 15 that the materials will not arrive on time *and* Bender will meet its end-of-July deadline.

Again, you can use the probability tree for Bender in Figure 4.2 to compute the probability of the joint occurrence of events A and $\overline{B}$. This outcome is the third (from the top of the diagram) terminal point of the tree. To find the desired probability, multiply the probabilities corresponding to the two branches included in this path from the left-hand side of the tree to the right-hand side. This confirms that the probability of interest is the product of the two relevant probabilities, namely 1/5 and 1/3. Simply stated, probability trees can be quite useful in modeling and assessing such uncertain outcomes in real-life situations.

The bottom line for Bender is whether it will meet its end-of-July deadline. After mid-July, this probability is either $P(A|B) = 3/4$ or $P(A|\overline{B}) = 1/5$ because by this time, Bender will *know* whether the materials arrived on time. But on July 1, the relevant probability is $P(A)$—there is still uncertainty about whether B or $\overline{B}$ will occur. Fortunately, you can calculate $P(A)$ from the probabilities you already know. The logic is that A consists of the two mutually exclusive events (A and B) and (A and $\overline{B}$). That is, if A is to occur, it must occur with B or with $\overline{B}$. Therefore, using the *addition* rule for mutually exclusive events, we obtain

$$P(A) = P(A \text{ and } B) + P(A \text{ and } \overline{B}) = 1/2 + 1/15 = 17/30 = 0.5667$$

The chances are 17 out of 30 that Bender will meet its end-of-July deadline, given the information it has at the beginning of July. ∎

4.2.4 Probabilistic Independence

A concept that is closely tied to conditional probability is *probabilistic independence.* You just saw how the probability of an event A can depend on whether another event B has occurred. Typically, the probabilities $P(A)$, $P(A|B)$, and $P(A|\overline{B})$ are all different, as in Example 4.1. However, there are situations where all of these probabilities are equal. In this case we say that the events A and B are independent. This does *not* mean they are mutually exclusive. Rather, **probabilistic independence** means that knowledge of one event is of no value when assessing the probability of the other.

The main advantage to knowing that two events are independent is that in that case the multiplication rule simplifies to Equation (4.5). This follows by substituting $P(A)$ for $P(A|B)$ in the multiplication rule, which is allowed because of independence. In words, the probability that both events occur is the product of their individual probabilities.

> **Multiplication Rule for Independent Events**
> $$P(A \text{ and } B) = P(A)P(B) \qquad (4.5)$$

How can you tell whether events *are* probabilistically independent? Unfortunately, this issue usually cannot be settled with mathematical arguments; typically, you need empirical data to decide whether independence is reasonable. As a simple example, let *A* be the event that a family's first child is male, and let *B* be the event that its second child is male. Are *A* and *B* independent? You could argue that they aren't independent if you believe, say, that a boy is more likely to be followed by another boy than by a girl. You could argue that they are independent if you believe the chances of the second child being a boy are the same, regardless of the gender of the first child. (Note that neither argument has anything to do with boys and girls being equally likely.)

In any case, the only way to settle the argument is to observe many families with at least two children. If you observe, say, that 55% of all families with first child male also have the second child male, and only 45% of all families with first child female have the second child male, then you can make a good case that *A* and *B* are *not* independent.

It is probably fair to say that most events in the real world are not truly independent. However, because of the simplified multiplication rule for independent events, many mathematical models assume that events are independent; the math is much easier with this assumption. The question is then whether the results from such a model are believable. All we can say in general is that it depends on how unrealistic the independence assumption really is.

4.2.5 Equally Likely Events

Much of what you know about probability is probably based on situations where outcomes are equally likely. These include flipping coins, throwing dice, drawing balls from urns, and other random mechanisms that are often discussed in introductory probability books. For example, suppose an urn contains 20 red marbles and 10 blue marbles. You plan to randomly select five marbles from the urn, and you are interested, say, in the probability of selecting at least three red marbles. To find this probability, you argue that because of randomness, every possible set of five marbles is equally likely to be chosen. Then you *count* the number of sets of five marbles that contain at least three red marbles, you count the total number of sets of five marbles that could be selected, and you set the desired probability equal to the ratio of these two counts.

Let us put this method of calculating probabilities into proper perspective. It is true that many probabilities, particularly in games of chance, *can* be calculated by using an equally likely argument. It is also true that probabilities calculated in this way satisfy all of the rules of probability, including the rules we have already discussed. However, many probabilities, especially those in business situations, *cannot* be calculated by equally likely arguments, simply because the possible outcomes are not equally likely. For example, just because you are able to identify five possible scenarios for a company's future, there is probably no reason whatsoever to conclude that each scenario has probability 1/5.

The bottom line is that we will have almost no need in this book to discuss complex counting rules for equally likely outcomes. If you dreaded learning about probability in terms of balls and urns, rest assured that you will *not* have to do so here.

4.2.6 Subjective Versus Objective Probabilities

We now ask a very basic question: Where do the probabilities in a probability distribution come from? A complete answer to this question could lead to a chapter by itself, so we only briefly discuss the issues involved. There are essentially two distinct ways to assess probabilities, objectively and subjectively. *Objective probabilities* are those that can be estimated from long-run proportions, whereas *subjective probabilities* cannot be estimated from long-run proportions. Some examples will make this distinction clearer.

Consider throwing two dice and observing the sum of the two sides that face up. What is the probability that the sum of these two sides is 7? You might argue as follows. Because there are $6 \times 6 = 36$ ways the two dice can fall, and because exactly 6 of these result in a sum of 7, the probability of a 7 is $6/36 = 1/6$. This is the equally likely argument we discussed previously. It reduces probability to counting.

What if the dice are weighted in some way? Then the equally likely argument is no longer valid. You can, however, toss the dice many times and record the proportion of tosses that result in a sum of 7. This proportion is called a *relative frequency*.

The **relative frequency** of an event is the proportion of times the event occurs out of the number of times the random experiment is run. A relative frequency can be recorded as a proportion or a percentage.

A famous result called the *law of large numbers* states that this relative frequency, in the long run, will get closer and closer to the "true" probability of a 7. This is exactly what we mean by an objective probability. It is a probability that can be estimated as the long-run proportion of times an event occurs in a sequence of many identical experiments.

If you are flipping coins, throwing dice, or spinning roulette wheels, objective probabilities are certainly relevant. You don't need a person's *opinion* of the probability that a roulette wheel, say, will end up pointing to a red number; you can simply spin it many times and keep track of the proportion of times it points to a red number. However, there are many situations, particularly in business, that cannot be repeated many times—or even more than once—under identical conditions. In these situations objective probabilities make no sense (and equally likely arguments usually make no sense either), so you must resort to subjective probabilities. A subjective probability is one person's assessment of the likelihood that a certain event will occur. We assume that the person making the assessment uses all of the information available to make the most rational assessment possible.

This definition of subjective probability implies that one person's assessment of a probability can differ from another person's assessment of the *same* probability. For example, consider the probability that the Indianapolis Colts will win the next Super Bowl. If you ask a casual football observer to assess this probability, you will get one answer, but if you ask a person with a lot of inside information about injuries, team cohesiveness, and so on, you might get a very different answer. Because these probabilities are *subjective*, people with different information typically assess probabilities in different ways.

Subjective probabilities are usually relevant for unique, one-time situations. However, most situations are not completely unique; you often have some history to guide you. That is, historical relative frequencies can be factored into subjective probabilities. For example, suppose a company is about to market a new product. This product might be quite different in some ways from any products the company has marketed before, but it might also share some features with the company's previous products. If the company wants to assess the probability that the new product will be a success, it will certainly analyze the unique features of this product and the current state of the market to obtain a subjective assessment. However, the company will also look at its past successes and failures with reasonably similar products. If the proportion of successes with past products was 40%, say, then this value might be a starting point in the assessment of *this* product's probability of success.

All of the "given" probabilities in this chapter and later chapters can be placed somewhere on the objective-to-subjective continuum, usually closer to the subjective end. An important implication of this placement is that these probabilities are not cast in stone; they are only educated guesses. Therefore, it is always a good idea to run a *sensitivity analysis* (especially on a spreadsheet, where this is easy to do) to see how any "bottom-line" answers depend on the given probabilities. Sensitivity analysis is especially important in Chapter 6, when we study decision making under uncertainty.

PROBLEMS

Note: Student solutions for problems whose numbers appear within a colored box are available for purchase at www.cengagebrain.com.

Level A

1. In a particular suburb, 30% of the households have installed electronic security systems.
   a. If a household is chosen at random from this suburb, what is the probability that this household has *not* installed an electronic security system?
   b. If two households are chosen at random from this suburb, what is the probability that *neither* has installed an electronic security system?

2. Several major automobile producers are competing to have the largest market share for sport utility vehicles (SUVs) in the coming quarter. A professional automobile market analyst assesses that the odds of General Motors *not* being the market leader are 6 to 1. The odds against Toyota and Ford having the largest market share in the coming quarter are similarly assessed to be 12 to 5 and 8 to 3, respectively.
   a. Find the probability that General Motors will have the largest market share for SUVs in the coming quarter.
   b. Find the probability that Toyota will have the largest market share for SUVs in the coming quarter.
   c. Find the probability that Ford will have the largest market share for SUVs in the coming quarter.
   d. Find the probability that some other automobile manufacturer will have the largest market share for SUVs in the coming quarter.

3. The publisher of a popular financial periodical has decided to undertake a campaign in an effort to attract new subscribers. Market research analysts in this company believe that there is a 1 in 4 chance that the increase in the number of new subscriptions resulting from this campaign will be less than 3000, and there is a 1 in 3 chance that the increase in the number of new subscriptions resulting from this campaign will be between 3000 and 5000. What is the probability that the increase in the number of new subscriptions resulting from this campaign will be less than 3000 *or* more than 5000?

4. Suppose that 18% of the employees of a given corporation engage in physical exercise activities during the lunch hour. Moreover, assume that 57% of all employees are male, and 12% of all employees are males who engage in physical exercise activities during the lunch hour.
   a. If you choose an employee at random from this corporation, what is the probability that this person is a female who engages in physical exercise activities during the lunch hour?
   b. If you choose an employee at random from this corporation, what is the probability that this person is a female who does not engage in physical exercise activities during the lunch hour?

5. In a study designed to gauge married women's participation in the workplace today, the data provided in the file **P04_05.xlsx** were obtained from a sample of 750 randomly selected married women. Consider a woman selected at random from this sample in answering the following questions.
   a. What is the probability that this randomly selected woman has a job outside the home?
   b. What is the probability that this randomly selected woman has at least one child?
   c. What is the probability that this randomly selected woman has a full-time job and no more than one child?
   d. What is the probability that this randomly selected woman has a part-time job or at least one child, but not both?

6. Suppose that you draw a single card from a standard deck of 52 playing cards.
   a. What is the probability that a diamond *or* club is drawn?
   b. What is the probability that the drawn card is not a 4?
   c. Given that a black card has been drawn, what is the probability that it is a spade?
   d. Let E_1 be the event that a black card is drawn. Let E_2 be the event that a spade is drawn. Are E_1 and E_2 independent events? Why or why not?

e. Let E_3 be the event that a heart is drawn. Let E_4 be the event that a 3 is drawn. Are E_3 and E_4 independent events? Why or why not?

Level B

7. In a large accounting firm, the proportion of accountants with MBA degrees and at least five years of professional experience is 75% as large as the proportion of accountants with no MBA degree and less than five years of professional experience. Furthermore, 35% of the accountants in this firm have MBA degrees, and 45% have fewer than five years of professional experience. If one of the firm's accountants is selected at random, what is the probability that this accountant has an MBA degree or at least five years of professional experience, but not both?

8. A local beer producer sells two types of beer, a regular brand and a light brand with 30% fewer calories. The company's marketing department wants to verify that its traditional approach of appealing to local white-collar workers with light beer commercials and appealing to local blue-collar workers with regular beer commercials is indeed a good strategy. A randomly selected group of 400 local workers are questioned about their beer-drinking preferences, and the data in the file **P04_08.xlsx** are obtained.

a. If a blue-collar worker is chosen at random from this group, what is the probability that he/she prefers light beer (to regular beer or no beer at all)?

b. If a white-collar worker is chosen at random from this group, what is the probability that he/she prefers light beer (to regular beer or no beer at all)?

c. If you restrict your attention to workers who like to drink beer, what is the probability that a randomly selected blue-collar worker prefers to drink light beer?

d. If you restrict your attention to workers who like to drink beer, what is the probability that a randomly selected white-collar worker prefers to drink light beer?

e. Does the company's marketing strategy appear to be appropriate? Explain why or why not.

9. Suppose that two dice are tossed. For each die, it is equally likely that 1, 2, 3, 4, 5, or 6 dots will turn up. Let S be the sum of the two dice.

a. What is the probability that S will be 5 or 7?

b. What is the probability that S will be some number other than 4 or 8?

c. Let E_1 be the event that the first die shows a 3. Let E_2 be the event that S is 6. Are E_1 and E_2 independent events?

d. Again, let E_1 be the event that the first die shows a 3. Let $E3$ be the event that S is 7. Are E_1 and E_3 independent events?

e. Given that S is 7, what is the probability that the first die showed 4 dots?

f. Given that the first die shows a 3, what is the probability that S is an even number?

4.3 DISTRIBUTION OF A SINGLE RANDOM VARIABLE

We now discuss the topic of most interest in this chapter, *probability distributions*. In this section we examine the probability distribution of a single random variable. In later sections we discuss probability distributions of two or more related random variables.

FUNDAMENTAL INSIGHT

Concept of Probability Distribution

A probability distribution is a way of describing the uncertainty of some numerical outcome. It is *not* based, at least not directly, on a data set of the type discussed in the previous two chapters. Instead, it is essentially a list of all possible outcomes and their corresponding probabilities.

There are really two types of random variables: discrete and continuous. A discrete random variable has only a finite number of possible values, whereas a continuous random variable has a continuum of possible values.[1] Usually a discrete distribution results from a count, whereas a continuous distribution results from a measurement. For example, the number of children in a family is clearly discrete, whereas the amount of rain this year in San Francisco is clearly continuous.

[1]Actually, a more rigorous discussion allows a discrete random variable to have an infinite number of possible values, such as all positive integers. The only time this occurs in this book is when we discuss the Poisson distribution in Chapter 5.

This distinction between counts and measurements is not always clear-cut. For example, what about the demand for refrigerators at a particular store next month? The number of refrigerators demanded is clearly an integer (a count), but it probably has many possible values, such as all integers from 0 to 100. In some cases like this, we often approximate in one of two ways. First, we might use a discrete distribution with only a few possible values, such as all multiples of 20 from 0 to 100. Second, we might approximate the possible demand as a continuum from 0 to 100. The reason for such approximations is to simplify the mathematics, and they are frequently used.

Mathematically, there is an important difference between discrete and continuous probability distributions. Specifically, a proper treatment of continuous distributions, analogous to the treatment we will provide in this chapter, requires calculus—which we do not presume for this book. Therefore, we discuss only discrete distributions in this chapter. In later chapters we often *use* continuous distributions, particularly the bell-shaped normal distribution, but we simply state their properties without trying to derive them mathematically.

The essential properties of a discrete random variable and its associated probability distribution are quite simple. We discuss them in general and then analyze a numerical example. Let X be a random variable. (Usually, capital letters toward the end of the alphabet, such as X, Y, and Z, are used to denote random variables.)

To specify the probability distribution of X, we need to specify its possible values and their probabilities. We assume that there are k possible values, denoted v_1, v_2, . . . , v_k. The probability of a typical value v_i is denoted in one of two ways, either $P(X = v_i)$ or $p(v_i)$. The first reminds you that this is a probability involving the random variable X, whereas the second is a simpler shorthand notation. Probability distributions must satisfy two criteria: (1) the probabilities must be nonnegative, and (2) they must sum to 1. In symbols, we must have

$$\sum_{i=1}^{k} p(v_i) = 1, \quad p(v_i) \geq 0$$

A discrete probability distribution is a set of possible values and a corresponding set of nonnegative probabilities that sum to 1.

This is basically all there is to it: a list of possible values and a list of associated probabilities that sum to 1. It is also sometimes useful to calculate *cumulative* probabilities. A **cumulative probability** is the probability that the random variable is *less than or equal to* some particular value. For example, assume that 10, 20, 30, and 40 are the possible values of a random variable X, with corresponding probabilities 0.15, 0.25, 0.35, and 0.25. Then a typical cumulative probability is $P(X \leq 30)$. From the addition rule it can be calculated as

$$P(X \leq 30) = P(X = 10) + P(X = 20) + P(X = 30) = 0.75$$

The point is that the cumulative probabilities are completely determined by the individual probabilities.

It is often convenient to summarize a probability distribution with two or three well-chosen numbers. The first of these is the *mean,* often denoted μ. It is also called the *expected value* of X and denoted $E(X)$ (for *e*xpected X). The mean is a weighted sum of the possible values, weighted by their probabilities, as shown in Equation (4.6). In much the same way that an average of a set of numbers indicates "central location," the mean indicates the center of the probability distribution. You will see this more clearly when we analyze a numerical example.

Mean of a Probability Distribution, μ

$$\mu = E(X) = \sum_{i=1}^{k} v_i p(v_i) \qquad (4.6)$$

To measure the variability in a distribution, we calculate its variance or standard deviation. The *variance*, denoted by σ^2 or Var(X), is a weighted sum of the squared deviations of the possible values from the mean, where the weights are again the probabilities. This is shown in Equation (4.7). As in Chapter 2, the variance is expressed in the *square* of the units of X, such as dollars squared. Therefore, a more natural measure of variability is the *standard deviation*, denoted by σ or Stdev(X). It is the square root of the variance, as indicated by Equation (4.8).

Variance of a Probability Distribution, σ^2

$$\sigma^2 = Var(X) = \sum_{i=1}^{k}(v_i - E(X))^2\, p(v_i) \qquad \textbf{(4.7)}$$

Standard Deviation of a Probability Distribution, σ

$$\sigma^2 = \text{Stdev}(X) = \sqrt{\text{Var}(X)} \qquad \textbf{(4.8)}$$

Equation (4.7) is useful for understanding variance as a weighted average of squared deviations from the mean. However, the following is an equivalent formula for variance and is somewhat easier to implement in Excel. (It can be derived with straightforward algebra.) In words, you find the weighted average of the squared values, weighted by their probabilities, and then subtract the square of the mean.

Variance (computing formula)

$$\sigma^2 = \sum_{i=1}^{k} v_i^2\, p(v_i) - \mu^2 \qquad \textbf{(4.9)}$$

We now consider a typical example.

| EXAMPLE | 4.2 MARKET RETURN SCENARIOS FOR THE NATIONAL ECONOMY |

In reality, there is a continuum of possible returns. Her assumption of only five possible returns is clearly an approximation to reality, but such an assumption is often useful.

An investor is concerned with the market return for the coming year, where the market return is defined as the percentage gain (or loss, if negative) over the year. The investor believes there are five possible scenarios for the national economy in the coming year: rapid expansion, moderate expansion, no growth, moderate contraction, and serious contraction. Furthermore, she has used all of the information available to her to estimate that the market returns for these scenarios are, respectively, 23%, 18%, 15%, 9%, and 3%. That is, the possible returns vary from a high of 23% to a low of 3%. Also, she has assessed that the probabilities of these outcomes are 0.12, 0.40, 0.25, 0.15, and 0.08. Use this information to describe the probability distribution of the market return.

Objective   To compute the mean, variance, and standard deviation of the probability distribution of the market return for the coming year.

Solution

To make the connection between the general notation and this particular example, let X denote the market return for the coming year. Then each possible economic scenario leads to a possible value of X. For example, the first possible value is $v_1 = 23\%$, and its probability is $p(v_1) = 0.12$. These values and probabilities appear in columns B and C of Figure 4.3.[2] (See the file **Market Return.xlsx**.) Note that the five probabilities sum to 1, as they should. This probability distribution implies, for example, that the probability of a market return at least as large as 18% is $0.12 + 0.40 = 0.52$ because it could occur as a result of rapid or moderate expansion of the economy. Similarly, the probability that the market return is 9% or less is $0.15 + 0.08 = 0.23$ because this could occur as a result of moderate or serious contraction of the economy.

Figure 4.3 Probability Distribution of Market Returns

	A	B	C	D	E	F	G	H
1	Mean, variance, and standard deviation of the market return					Range names Used		
2						Market_return	=Market!$C$4:$C$8	
3	Economic outcome	Probability	Market return	Sq dev from mean		Mean	=Market!$B$11	
4	Rapid Expansion	0.12	23%	0.005929		Probability	=Market!$B$4:$B$8	
5	Moderate Expansion	0.40	18%	0.000729		Sq_dev_from_mean	=Market!$D$4:$D$8	
6	No Growth	0.25	15%	0.000009		Stdev	=Market!$B$13	
7	Moderate Contraction	0.15	9%	0.003969		Variance	=Market!$B$12	
8	Serious Contraction	0.08	3%	0.015129				
9								
10	Summary measures of return							
11	Mean	15.3%						
12	Variance	0.002811	0.002811	←‑‑‑‑‑‑‑‑	Quick alternative formula			
13	Stdev	5.3%	5.3%					

The summary measures of this probability distribution appear in the range B11:B13. They can be calculated with the following steps. (Note that the formulas make use of the range names listed in the figure.)

PROCEDURE FOR CALCULATING SUMMARY MEASURES

① Mean return. Calculate the mean return in cell B11 with the formula

=SUMPRODUCT(Market_return,Probability)

Excel Tip *Excel's SUMPRODUCT function is a gem, and you should use it whenever possible. It takes (at least) two arguments, which must be ranges of exactly the same size and shape. It sums the products of the values in these ranges. For example, =SUMPRODUCT (A1:A3,B1:B3) is equivalent to the formula =A1*B1+A2*B2+A3*B3. If the ranges contain only a few cells, there isn't much advantage to using SUMPRODUCT, but when the ranges are large, such as A1:A100 and B1:B100, SUMPRODUCT is the only viable choice.*

This formula illustrates the general rule in Equation (4.6): The mean is the sum of products of possible values and probabilities.

② Squared deviations. To get ready to compute the variance from equation (4.7), calculate the squared deviations from the mean by entering the formula

=(C4-Mean)^2

in cell D4 and copying it down through cell D8.

---

[2]From here on, we often shade the given inputs in the spreadsheet figures blue so that you can immediately tell which cells contain inputs. This shading comes through clearly in the Excel files. On the printed page, the shading is a light blue.

3 **Variance.** Calculate the variance of the market return in cell B12 with the formula

=SUMPRODUCT(Sq_dev_from_mean,Probability)

This illustrates the general formula for variance in Equation (4.7): The variance is always a sum of products of squared deviations from the mean and probabilities. Alternatively, you can skip the calculation of the squared deviations from the mean and use Equation (4.9) directly. This is done in cell C12 with the formula

=SUMPRODUCT(Market_return,Market_return,Probability)-Mean^2

By entering the Market_return range twice in this SUMPRODUCT formula, you get the squares. From now on, we will use this simplified formula for variance and dispense with squared deviations from the mean. But regardless of how it is calculated, you should remember the essence of variance: it is a weighted average of squared deviations from the mean.

4 **Standard deviation.** Calculate the standard deviation of the market return in cell B13 with the formula

=SQRT(Variance)

You can see that the mean return is 15.3% and the standard deviation is 5.3%. What do these measures really mean? First, the mean, or *expected,* return does not imply that the most likely return is 15.3%, nor is this the value that the investor "expects" to occur. In fact, the value 15.3% is not even a possible market return (at least not according to the model). You can understand these measures better in terms of long-run averages. Specifically, if you could imagine the coming year being repeated many times, each time using the probability distribution in columns B and C to generate a market return, then the average of these market returns would be close to 15.3%, and their standard deviation— calculated as in Chapter 2—would be close to 5.3%.

Before leaving this section, we want to emphasize a key point, a point that is easy to forget with all the details. The whole point of discussing probability and probability distributions, especially in the context of business problems, is that uncertainty is often a key factor, and you cannot simply ignore it. For instance, you saw in Example 4.2 that the mean return is 15.3%. However, it would be far from realistic to treat the actual return as a sure 15.3%, with no uncertainty. If you did this, you would be ignoring the uncertainty completely, and it is often the uncertainty that makes business problems interesting—and difficult. Therefore, to model such problems in a realistic way, you are forced to deal with probability and probability distributions. ∎

As always, range names are not required, but they make the Excel formulas easier to read. You can use them or omit them, as you wish.

4.3.1 Conditional Mean and Variance

There are many situations where the mean and variance of a random variable depend on some external event. In this case, you can *condition* on the outcome of the external event to find the overall mean and variance (or standard deviation) of the random variable.

It is best to motivate this with an example. Consider the random variable X, representing the percentage change in the price of stock A from now to a year from now. This change is driven partly by circumstances specific to company A, but it is also driven partly by the economy as a whole. In this case, the outcome of the economy is the external event. Let's assume that the economy in the coming year will be awful, stable, or great with probabilities 0.20, 0.50, and 0.30, respectively. In addition, we make the following assumptions. (1) Given that the economy is awful, the mean and standard deviation of X are -20% and 30%; (2) given that the economy is stable, the mean and standard deviation of X are 5% and 20%; and (3) given that the economy is great, the mean and standard deviation of X are 25% and 15%. Each of these latter statements is a statement about X, conditional upon the economy. What can you say about the *unconditional* mean and standard deviation of X? That is, what are the mean and standard deviation of X *before* you learn the state of the economy? The answers come from Equations (4.10) and (4.11). In the context of the example, p_i is the probability of economy state i, and $E_i(X)$ and $\text{Var}_i(X)$ are the mean and variance of X, given that economy state i occurs.

Conditional Mean Formula

$$E(X) = \sum_{i=1}^{k} E_i(X)p_i \tag{4.10}$$

Conditional Variance Formula

$$\text{Var}(X) = \sum_{i=1}^{k}\left[\text{Var}_i(X) + [E_i(X)]^2\right]p_i - [E(X)]^2 \tag{4.11}$$

In the example, the mean percentage change in the price of stock A, from Equation (4.10), is

$$E(X) = 0.2(-20\%) + 0.5(5\%) + 0.3(25\%) = 6\%$$

To calculate the standard deviation of X, first use Equation (4.11) to calculate the variance and then take its square root. The variance is

$$\text{Var}(X) = \left[0.2[(30\%)^2 + (-20\%)^2] + 0.5[(20\%)^2 + (5\%)^2]\right.$$
$$\left. + 0.2[(15\%)^2 + (25\%)^2]\right] - (6\%)^2 = 0.06915$$

Taking the square root gives

$$\text{Stdev}(X) = \sqrt{0.06915} = 26.30\%$$

Of course, these calculations can be done easily in Excel. See the file **Stock Price and Economy.xlsx** for the details.

The point of this example is that it is often easier to assess the uncertainty of some random variable X by conditioning on every possible outcome of some external event like the economy. However, *before* that outcome is known, the relevant mean and standard deviation of X are those calculated from Equations (4.10) and (4.11). In this particular example, *before* you know the state of the economy, the relevant mean and standard deviation of the change in the price of stock A are 6% and 26.3%, respectively.

PROBLEMS

Level A

10. A fair coin (i.e., heads and tails are equally likely) is tossed three times. Let X be the number of heads observed in three tosses of this fair coin.
  a. Find the probability distribution of X.
  b. Find the probability that two or fewer heads are observed in three tosses.
  c. Find the probability that at least one head is observed in three tosses.

  d. Find the expected value of X.
  e. Find the standard deviation of X.

11. Consider a random variable with the following probability distribution: $P(X = 0) = 0.1$, $P(X = 1) = 0.2$, $P(X = 2) = 0.3$, $P(X = 3) = 0.3$, and $P(X = 4) = 0.1$.
  a. Find $P(X \leq 2)$.
  b. Find $P(1 < X \leq 3)$.
  c. Find $P(X > 0)$.

d. Find $P(X > 3 | X > 2)$.

e. Find the expected value of X.

f. Find the standard deviation of X.

12. A study has shown that the probability distribution of X, the number of customers in line (including the one being served, if any) at a checkout counter in a department store, is given by $P(X = 0) = 0.25$, $P(X = 1) = 0.25$, $P(X = 2) = 0.20$, $P(X = 3) = 0.20$, and $P(\geq 4) = 0.10$. Consider a newly arriving customer to the checkout line.

   a. What is the probability that this customer will not have to wait behind anyone?

   b. What is the probability that this customer will have to wait behind at least one customer?

   c. On average, behind how many other customers will the newly arriving customer have to wait?

13. A construction company has to complete a project no later than three months from now or there will be significant cost overruns. The manager of the construction company believes that there are four possible values for the random variable X, the number of months from now it will take to complete this project: 2, 2.5, 3, and 3.5. The manager currently thinks that the probabilities of these four possibilities are in the ratio 1 to 2 to 4 to 2. That is, $X = 2.5$ is twice as likely as $X = 2$, $X = 3$ is twice as likely as $X = 2.5$, and $X = 3.5$ is half as likely as $X = 3$.

   a. Find the probability distribution of X.

   b. What is the probability that this project will be completed in less than three months from now?

   c. What is the probability that this project will *not* be completed on time?

   d. What is the expected completion time (in months) of this project from now?

   e. How much variability (in months) exists around the expected value you found in part **d**?

14. Three areas of southern California are prime candidates for forest fires each dry season. You believe (based on historical evidence) that each of these areas, independently of the others, has a 30% chance of having a major forest fire in the next dry season.

   a. Find the probability distribution of X, the number of the three regions that have major forest fires in the next dry season.

   b. What is the probability that none of the areas will have a major forest fire?

   c. What is the probability that all of them will have a major forest fire?

   d. What is expected number of regions with major forest fires?

   e. Each major forest fire is expected to cause $20 million in damage and other expenses. What is

the expected amount of damage and other expenses in these three regions in the next dry season?

Level B

15. The National Football League playoffs are just about to begin. Because of their great record in the regular season, the Colts get a bye in the first week of the playoffs. In the second week, they will play the winner of the game between the Ravens and the Patriots. A football expert estimates that the Ravens will beat the Patriots with probability 0.45. This same expert estimates that if the Colts play the Ravens, the mean and standard deviation of the point spread (Colts points minus Ravens points) will be 6.5 and 10.5, whereas if the Colts play the Patriots, the mean and standard deviation of the point spread (Colts points minus Patriots points) will be 3.5 and 12.5. Find the mean and standard deviation of the point spread (Colts points minus their opponent's points) in the Colts game.

16. Because of tough economic times, the Indiana legislature is debating a bill that could have significant negative implications for public school funding. There are three possibilities for this bill: (1) it could be passed in essentially its current version; (2) it could be passed but with amendments that make it less harsh on public school funding; or (3) it could be defeated. The probabilities of these three events are estimated to be 0.4, 0.25, and 0.35, respectively. The estimated effect on percentage changes in salaries next year at Indiana University are estimated as follows. If the bill is passed in its current version, the mean and standard deviation of salary percentage change will be 0% and 1%. If the bill is passed with amendments, the mean and standard deviation will be 1.5% and 3.5%. Finally, if the bill is defeated, the mean and standard deviation will be 3.5% and 6%. Find the mean and standard deviation of the percentage change in salaries next year at Indiana University.

17. The "house edge" in any game of chance is defined as

$$\frac{E(\text{player's loss on a bet})}{\text{Size of player's loss on a bet}}$$

For example, if a player wins $10 with probability 0.48 and loses $10 with probability 0.52 on any bet, the house edge is

$$\frac{-[10(0.48) - 10(0.52)]}{10} = 0.04$$

Give an interpretation to the house edge that relates to how much money the house is likely to win on average. Which do you think has a larger house edge: roulette or sports gambling? Why?

4.4 AN INTRODUCTION TO SIMULATION

In the previous section, we asked you to imagine many repetitions of an event, with each repetition resulting in a different random outcome. Fortunately, you can do more than *imagine;* you can make it happen with computer simulation. **Simulation** is an extremely useful tool that can be used to incorporate uncertainty explicitly into spreadsheet models. A simulation model is the same as a regular spreadsheet model except that some cells include random quantities. Each time the spreadsheet recalculates, new values of the random quantities occur, and these typically lead to different bottom-line results. By forcing the spreadsheet to recalculate many times, a business manager is able to discover the results that are most likely to occur, those that are least likely to occur, and best-case and worst-case results. We will use simulation several places in this book to help explain difficult concepts in probability and statistics. We begin in this section by using simulation to explain the connection between summary measures of probability distributions and the corresponding summary measures from Chapter 2.

We continue to use the market return distribution in Figure 4.3. Because this is your first discussion of computer simulation in Excel, we proceed in some detail. Our goal is to simulate many returns (we arbitrarily choose 400) from this distribution and analyze the resulting returns. We want each simulated return to have probability 0.12 of being 23%, probability 0.40 of being 18%, and so on. Then, using the methods for summarizing data from Chapter 2, we calculate the average and standard deviation of the 400 simulated returns.

The method for simulating many market returns is straightforward once you know how to simulate a *single* market return. The key to this is Excel's RAND function, which generates a random number between 0 and 1. The RAND function has no arguments, so every time you call it, you must enter =RAND().[3] (Although there is nothing inside the parentheses next to RAND, the parentheses cannot be omitted.) That is, to generate a random number between 0 and 1 in any cell, enter the formula

=RAND()

in that cell. The RAND function can also be used as part of another function. For example, you can simulate the result of a single flip of a fair coin by entering the formula

=IF(RAND()<=0.5,"Heads","Tails")

Random numbers generated with Excel's RAND function are said to be uniformly distributed between 0 and 1 because all decimal values between 0 and 1 are equally likely. These uniformly distributed random numbers can then be used to generate numbers from any discrete distribution such as the market return distribution in Figure 4.3. To see how this is done, note first that there are five possible values in this distribution. Therefore, we divide the interval from 0 to 1 into five parts with lengths equal to the probabilities in the probability distribution. Then we see which of these parts the random number from RAND falls into and generate the associated market return. If the random number is between 0 and 0.12 (of length 0.12), we generate 23% as the market return; if the random number is between 0.12 and 0.52 (of length 0.40), we generate 18% as the market return; and so on. See Figure 4.4.

This procedure is accomplished most easily in Excel through the use of a lookup table. A lookup table is useful when you want to compare a particular value to a set of values and,

---

[3]Before Excel 2007, RAND was the only built-in function for generating random numbers. The RANDBETWEEN appeared in Excel 2007. (Actually, RANDBETWEEN was available in the Analysis Toolpak add-in, but most people weren't aware of it.) It generates uniformly distributed random integers within a given range. For example, =RANDBETWEEN(1,6) generates a random integer from 1 to 6, with all values equally likely. This could be used to simulate the roll of a single die, for example.

Figure 4.4

Associating RAND Values with Market Returns

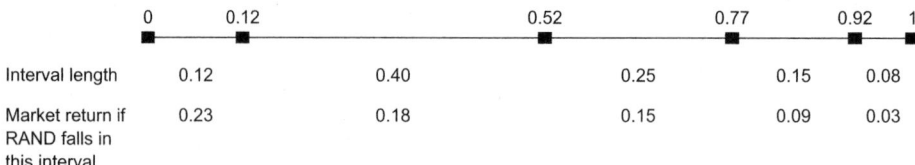

	0	0.12	0.52	0.77	0.92	1
Interval length	0.12	0.40	0.25	0.15	0.08	
Market return if RAND falls in this interval	0.23	0.18	0.15	0.09	0.03	

depending on where the particular value falls, assign a given "answer" or value from an associated list of values. In this case we want to compare a generated random number to values (between 0 and 1) falling in each of the five intervals shown in Figure 4.4, and then report the corresponding market return. This process is made relatively simple in Excel by applying the VLOOKUP function, as explained in the following steps.[4] (Refer to Figure 4.5 and the **Market Return.xlsx** file.)

Figure 4.5 Simulation of Market Returns

	A	B	C	D	E	F	G	H	I
1	Simulating market returns					Range names used			
2						LTable	=Simulation!$D$13:$E$17		
3	Summary statistics from simulation below					Simulated_market_return	=Simulation!$B$13:$B$412		
4	Average return	15.2%							
5	Stdev of returns	5.2%							
6									
7	Exact values from previous sheet (for comparison)								
8	Average return	15.3%							
9	Stdev of returns	5.3%							
10									
11	Simulation			Lookup table					
12	Random #	Simulated market return		Cum Prob	Return				
13	0.937678	3%		0	23%				
14	0.925121	3%		0.12	18%				
15	0.447876	18%		0.52	15%				
16	0.915249	9%		0.77	9%				
17	0.125884	18%		0.92	3%				
18	0.966630	3%							
19	0.614663	15%							
410	0.087177	23%							
411	0.576865	15%							
412	0.564437	15%							

PROCEDURE FOR GENERATING RANDOM MARKET RETURNS IN EXCEL

1 **Lookup table.** Copy the possible returns to the range E13:E17. Then enter the *cumulative* probabilities next to them in the range D13:D17. To do this, enter the value 0 in cell D13. Then enter the formula

=D13+Market!B4

in cell D14 and copy it down through cell D17. (Note that the Market!B4 in this formula refers to cell B4 in the Market sheet, that is, cell B4 in Figure 4.3.) Each value in column D is the current probability plus the previous value. The table in this range, D13:E17, becomes the lookup range. For convenience, we have named this range LTable.

[4]This could also be accomplished with nested IF functions, but the resulting formula would be much more complex.

2 **Random numbers.** Enter random numbers in the range A13:A412. An easy way to do this is to highlight the range, then type the formula

=**RAND()**

and finally press Ctrl-Enter. Note that these random numbers are "live." That is, each time you do any calculation in Excel or press the recalculation key (the F9 key), these random numbers change.

Excel Tip *A quick way to enter a formula (or value) into a range of cells is to highlight the range, type in the formula (or value), and press Ctrl-Enter (both keys at once). This is equivalent to entering the formula in the first cell of the range in the usual way and then copying it to the rest of the range.*

3 **Market returns.** Generate the random market returns by referring the random numbers in column A to the lookup table. Specifically, enter the formula

=**VLOOKUP(A13,LTable,2)**

in cell B13 and copy it down through cell B412. This formula compares the random number in cell A13 to the cumulative probabilities in the first column of the lookup table and sees where it "fits," as illustrated in Figure 4.4. Then it returns the corresponding market return in the second column of the lookup table. (It uses the second column because the third argument of the VLOOKUP function is 2.)

Excel Tip *In general, the VLOOKUP function takes three arguments: (1) the value to be compared, (2) a table of lookup values, with the values to be compared against always in the leftmost column, and (3) the column number of the lookup table that contains the "answer." (It also takes a fourth optional argument, not needed here. You can look it up in online help.)*

4 **Summary statistics.** Summarize the 400 market returns by entering the formulas

=**AVERAGE(Simulated_market_return)**

and

=**STDEV(Simulated_market_return)**

in cells B4 and B5. For comparison, copy the average and standard deviation from the Market sheet in Figure 4.3 to cells B8 and B9.

Now let's step back and see what has been accomplished. The following points are relevant.

- Simulations like this are very common, and we will continue to use them to illustrate concepts in probability and statistics.

- The numbers you obtain will be different from the ones in Figure 4.5 because of the nature of simulation. The results depend on the particular random numbers that happen to be generated.

- The way we entered cumulative probabilities and then used a lookup table is generally the best way to generate random numbers from a discrete probability distribution. However, there is an easier way if a simulation add-in is available. We will discuss this in Chapter 15.

- Each generated market return in the Simulated_market_return range is one of the five possible market returns. If you count the number of times each return appears and then divide by 400, the number of simulated values, you will see that the resulting fractions are approximately equal to the original probabilities. For example, the fraction of times the highest return 23% appears is about 0.12. This is the essence of what it means to simulate from a given probability distribution.

- The average and standard deviation in cells B4 and B5, calculated from the formulas in Chapter 2, are very close to the mean and standard deviation of the probability distribution in cells B8 and B9. Note, however, that these measures are calculated in entirely different ways. For example, the average in cell B4 is a simple average of 400 numbers, whereas the mean in cell B8 is a weighted sum of the possible market returns, weighted by their probabilities.

This last point allows you to interpret the summary measures of a probability distribution. Specifically, the mean and standard deviation of a probability distribution are approximately what you would obtain if you calculated the average and standard deviation, using the formulas from Chapter 2, of many simulated values from this distribution. In other words, the mean is the long-run average of the simulated values. Similarly, the standard deviation measures their variability.

You might ask whether this long-run average interpretation of the mean is relevant if the situation is going to occur only once. For example, the market return in the example is for "the coming year," and the coming year will occur only once. So what is the use of a long-run average? In this type of situation, the long-run average interpretation is probably not very relevant, but fortunately, there is another use of the expected value that we exploit in Chapter 6. Specifically, when a decision maker must choose among several actions that have uncertain outcomes, the preferred decision is often the one with the largest expected (monetary) value. This makes the expected value of a probability distribution extremely important in decision-making contexts.

FUNDAMENTAL INSIGHT

Role of Simulation

Spreadsheet simulation is one of the most important tools in an analyst's arsenal. For this reason, it will be discussed in much more depth in later chapters, particularly the last two chapters. Simulation doesn't show you what *will* occur; instead, it shows you many of the possible scenarios that *might* occur. By seeing a variety of scenarios, including those that are "normal" and those that are "extreme," you understand the situation much better and can make more informed decisions.

PROBLEMS

Level A

18. A quality inspector picks a sample of 15 items at random from a manufacturing process known to produce 10% defective items. Let X be the number of defective items found in the random sample of 15 items. Assume that the condition of each item is independent of that of each of the other items in the sample. The probability distribution of X is provided in the file **P04_18.xlsx**.
    a. Use simulation to generate 500 values of this random variable X.
    b. Calculate the mean and standard deviation of the simulated values. How do they compare to the mean and standard deviation of the given probability distribution?

19. A personnel manager of a large manufacturing plant is investigating the number of reported on-the-job

accidents at the facility over the past several years. Let X be the number of such accidents reported during a one-month period. Based on past records, the manager has established the probability distribution for X as shown in the file **P04_19.xlsx**.
    a. Use simulation to generate 1000 values of this random variable X.
    b. Is the simulated distribution indicative of the given probability distribution? Explain why or why not.

20. Let X be the number of heads when a fair coin is flipped four times.
    a. Find the distribution of X and then use simulation to generate 1000 values of X.
    b. Is the simulated distribution indicative of the given probability distribution? Explain why or why not.
    c. Calculate the mean and standard deviation of the simulated values. How do they compare to the

mean and standard deviation of the given probability distribution?

21. The probability distribution of X, the number of customers in line (including the one being served, if any) at a checkout counter in a department store, is given by $P(X = 0) = 0.25$, $P(X = 1) = 0.25$, $P(X = 2) = 0.20$, $P(X = 3) = 0.20$, and $P(X = 4) = 0.10$.

a. Use simulation to generate 500 values of this random variable X.

b. Is the simulated distribution indicative of the given probability distribution? Explain why or why not.

c. Calculate the mean and standard deviation of the simulated values. How do they compare to the mean and standard deviation of the given probability distribution?

d. Repeat parts **a** through **c** with 5000 simulated values rather than 500. Explain any differences you observe.

Level B

22. Betting on a football point spread works as follows. Suppose Michigan is favored by 17.5 points over Indiana. If you bet a "unit" on Indiana and Indiana loses by 17 or less, you win $10. If Indiana loses by 18 or more points, you lose $11. Find the mean and standard deviation of your winnings on a single bet. Assume that there is a 0.5 probability that you will win your bet and a 0.5 probability that you will lose your bet. Also simulate 1600 "bets" to estimate the average loss per bet. (*Note*: Do not be too disappointed if you are off by up to 50 cents. It takes many, say 10,000, simulated bets to get a really good estimate of the mean loss per bet. This is because there is a lot of variability on each bet.)

4.5 DISTRIBUTION OF TWO RANDOM VARIABLES: SCENARIO APPROACH[5]

We now turn to the distribution of two related random variables. In this section we discuss the situation where the two random variables are related in the sense that they both depend on which of several possible scenarios occurs. In the next section we discuss a second way of relating two random variables probabilistically. These two methods differ slightly in the way they assign probabilities to different outcomes. However, for both methods there are two summary measures, *covariance* and *correlation*, that measure the relationship between the two random variables. As with the mean, variance, and standard deviation, covariance and correlation are similar to the corresponding measures from Chapter 3, but they are conceptually different. In Chapter 3, correlation and covariance were calculated from data; here they are calculated from a probability distribution.

We denote the covariance and correlation between two random variables X and Y by Correl(X, Y) and Correl(X, Y). These are defined by equations (4.12) and (4.13). Here, $p(x_i, y_i)$ in Equation (4.12) is the probability that X and Y equal the values x_i and y_i, respectively; it is called a *joint probability*.

Covariance between X and Y

$$\text{Covar}(X, Y) = \sum_{i=1}^{k} (x_i - E(X))(y_i - E(Y))p(x_i, y_i) \qquad \textbf{(4.12)}$$

Correlation between X and Y

$$\text{Correl}(X, Y) = \frac{\text{Covar}(X, Y)}{\text{Stdev}(X) \times \text{Stdev}(Y)} \qquad \textbf{(4.13)}$$

---

[5]The rest of this chapter is optional. Although it is very useful for applied probability models, it is not used in the rest of the book.

As with variance, the following is an equivalent formula for covariance that is easier to implement in Excel because it avoids the need for deviations from the means. This formula says to find a weighted sum of all the products of xs and ys, weighted by their joint probabilities, and then subtract the product of the means.

Covariance between X and Y (computing formula)

$$\text{Covar}(X, Y) = \sum_{i=1}^{k} x_i y_i p(x_i, y_i) - E(X)E(Y) \qquad \textbf{(4.14)}$$

Although covariance and correlation based on a joint probability distribution are calculated differently than for known data, their interpretation is essentially the same as that discussed in Chapter 3. Each indicates the strength of a linear relationship between X and Y. That is, if X and Y tend to vary in the *same* direction, then both measures are positive. If they vary in *opposite* directions, both measures are negative. As before, the magnitude of the covariance is more difficult to interpret because it depends on the units of measurement of X and Y. However, the correlation is always between -1 and $+1$.

The following example illustrates the scenario approach, as well as covariance and correlation. Simulation is used to explain the relationship between the covariance and correlation as defined here and the corresponding measures from Chapter 3.

EXAMPLE | **4.3 ANALYZING A PORTFOLIO OF INVESTMENTS IN GM STOCK AND GOLD**

An investor plans to invest in General Motors (GM) stock and in gold. He assumes that the returns on these investments over the next year depend on the general state of the economy during the year. To keep things simple, he identifies four possible states of the economy: depression, recession, normal, and boom. Also, given the most up-to-date information he can obtain, he assesses the probabilities of these four states to be 0.05, 0.30, 0.50, and 0.15. For each state of the economy, he estimates the resulting return on GM stock and the return on gold. These appear in the shaded section of Figure 4.6. (See the file **GM vs Gold.xlsx**.) For example, if there is a depression, he estimates that GM stock will

---

Figure 4.6

Distribution of GM and Gold Returns

	A	B	C	D	E
1	Calculating covariance and correlation between two random variables				
2					
3	Economic outcome	Probability	GM Return	Gold Return	
4	Depression	0.05	-20%	5%	
5	Recession	0.30	10%	20%	
6	Normal	0.50	30%	-12%	
7	Boom	0.15	50%	9%	
8					
9		GM	Gold		
10	Means	24.5%	1.6%		
11	Variances	0.0275	0.0203		
12	Stdevs	16.6%	14.2%		
13					
14	Covariance	-0.0097			
15	Correlation	-0.410			

decrease by 20% and the price of gold will increase by 5%. The investor wants to analyze the joint distribution of returns on these two investments. He also wants to analyze the distribution of a portfolio of investments in GM stock and gold.

As in the previous example, this assumption of discreteness is clearly an approximation of reality.

Objective To obtain the relevant joint distribution and use it to calculate the covariance and correlation between returns on the two given investments, and also to analyze a portfolio containing these two investments.

Solution

To obtain the joint distribution, use the distribution of GM return, defined by columns B and C of the shaded region in Figure 4.6, and the distribution of gold return, defined by columns B and D. The scenario approach applies because a given state of the economy determines *both* GM and gold returns, so that only four pairs of returns are possible. For example, −20% is a possible GM return and 9% is a possible gold return, but they cannot occur simultaneously. The only possible *pairs* of returns, according to our assumptions, are −20% and 5%; 10% and 20%; 30% and −12%; and 50% and 9%. These possible pairs have the probabilities shown in column B.

To calculate means, variances, and standard deviations, GM and gold returns can be treated separately. For example, the formula for the mean GM return in cell B10 is

=SUMPRODUCT(C4:C7,$B$4:$B$7)

The only new calculations in Figure 4.6 involve the covariance and correlation between GM and gold returns. To obtain these, use the following steps.

PROCEDURE FOR CALCULATING THE COVARIANCE AND CORRELATION

We could again use range names, but there would be too many of them. Besides, it is usually easier to copy formulas when range names are not used.

1 **Covariance.** Calculate the covariance between GM and gold returns in cell B14 with the formula

=SUMPRODUCT(C4:C7,D4:D7,B4:B7)-B10*C10

Note the use of the SUMPRODUCT function in this formula. It usually takes two range arguments, but it can take more than two, all of which must have exactly the same dimension. This function multiplies corresponding elements from each of the three ranges and sums these products—exactly as prescribed by the summation in Equation (4.14). Then subtract the product of the means.

2 **Correlation.** Calculate the correlation between GM and gold returns in cell B15 with the formula

=B14/(B12*C12)

as prescribed by Equation (4.13).

The negative covariance indicates that GM and gold returns tend to vary in opposite directions, although it is difficult to judge the strength of the relationship between them by the magnitude of the covariance. The correlation of −0.410, on the other hand, is also negative and indicates a moderately negative relationship. You can't rely too much on this correlation, however, because the relationship between GM and gold returns is *not* linear. From the values in the range C4:D7, it is apparent that GM does better and better as the economy improves, whereas gold does better, then worse, then better.

This simulation is not necessary for the calculation of the covariance and correlation, but it provides some insight into their meanings.

A simulation of GM and gold returns sheds some light on the covariance and correlation measures. This simulation is shown in Figure 4.7. There are two keys to this simulation. First, we simulate the states of the economy, not—at least not directly—the GM and

Figure 4.7

Simulation of GM
and Gold Returns

	A	B	C	D	E	F	G
1	**Simulating GM and Gold returns**						
2							
3	**Summary measures from simulation below**						
4		GM	Gold				
5	Means	23.6%	2.5%				
6	Stdevs	16.4%	14.5%				
7							
8	Covariance	-0.0106					
9	Correlation	-0.448					
10							
11	**Exact results from previous sheet (for comparison)**						
12		GM	Gold				
13	Means	24.5%	1.6%				
14	Stdevs	16.6%	14.2%				
15							
16	Covariance	-0.0097					
17	Correlation	-0.410					
18							
19	**Simulation results**				Lookup table for generating returns		
20	Random #	GM return	Gold return		CumProb	GM return	Gold return
21	0.0100693	-20%	5%		0	-20%	5%
22	0.9107821	50%	9%		0.05	10%	20%
23	0.4105589	30%	-12%		0.35	30%	-12%
24	0.0385696	-20%	5%		0.85	50%	9%
25	0.9010982	50%	9%				
26	0.7536752	30%	-12%				
418	0.8730589	50%	9%				
419	0.1297612	10%	20%				
420	0.7331896	30%	-12%				

gold returns. For example, any random number between 0.05 and 0.35 implies a recession. The returns for GM and gold from a recession are then known to be 10% and 20%. You can implement this by entering a RAND function in cell A21 and then entering the formulas

=VLOOKUP(A21,LTable,2)

and

=VLOOKUP(A21,LTable,3)

in cells B21 and C21. Then copy these formulas down through row 420. This way, the *same* random number—hence the same scenario—is used to generate both returns in a given row, and the effect is that only four *pairs* of returns are possible.

Second, once you have the simulated returns in the range B21:C420, you can calculate the covariance and correlation of these numbers in cells B8 and B9 with the formulas[6]

=COVAR(B21:B420,C21:C420)

and

=CORREL(B21:B420,C21:C420)

---

[6]These formulas implement the covariance and correlation definitions from Chapter 3, not Equations (4.12) and (4.13) of this chapter, because these formulas are based on the simulated rows of data.

Here, COVAR and CORREL are the built-in Excel functions discussed in Chapter 3 for calculating the covariance and correlation between pairs of numbers. A comparison of cells B8 and B9 with B16 and B17 shows that there is a reasonably good agreement between the covariance and correlation of the probability distribution [from Equations (4.12) and (4.13)] and the measures based on the simulated values. This agreement is not perfect, but it typically improves as you simulate more pairs.

The final question in this example involves a portfolio consisting of GM stock and gold. The analysis appears in Figure 4.8. We assume that the investor has $10,000 to invest. He puts some fraction of this in GM stock (see cell B6) and the rest in gold. Of course, these fractions determine the total dollar values invested in row 7. The key to the analysis is the following. Because there are only four possible scenarios, there are only four possible portfolio returns. For example, if there is a recession, the GM and gold returns are 10% and 20%, so the portfolio return (per dollar) is a weighted average of these returns, weighted by the fractions invested:

$$\text{Portfolio return in recession} = 0.6(10\%) + 0.4(20\%) = 14\%$$

Figure 4.8 Distribution of Portfolio Return

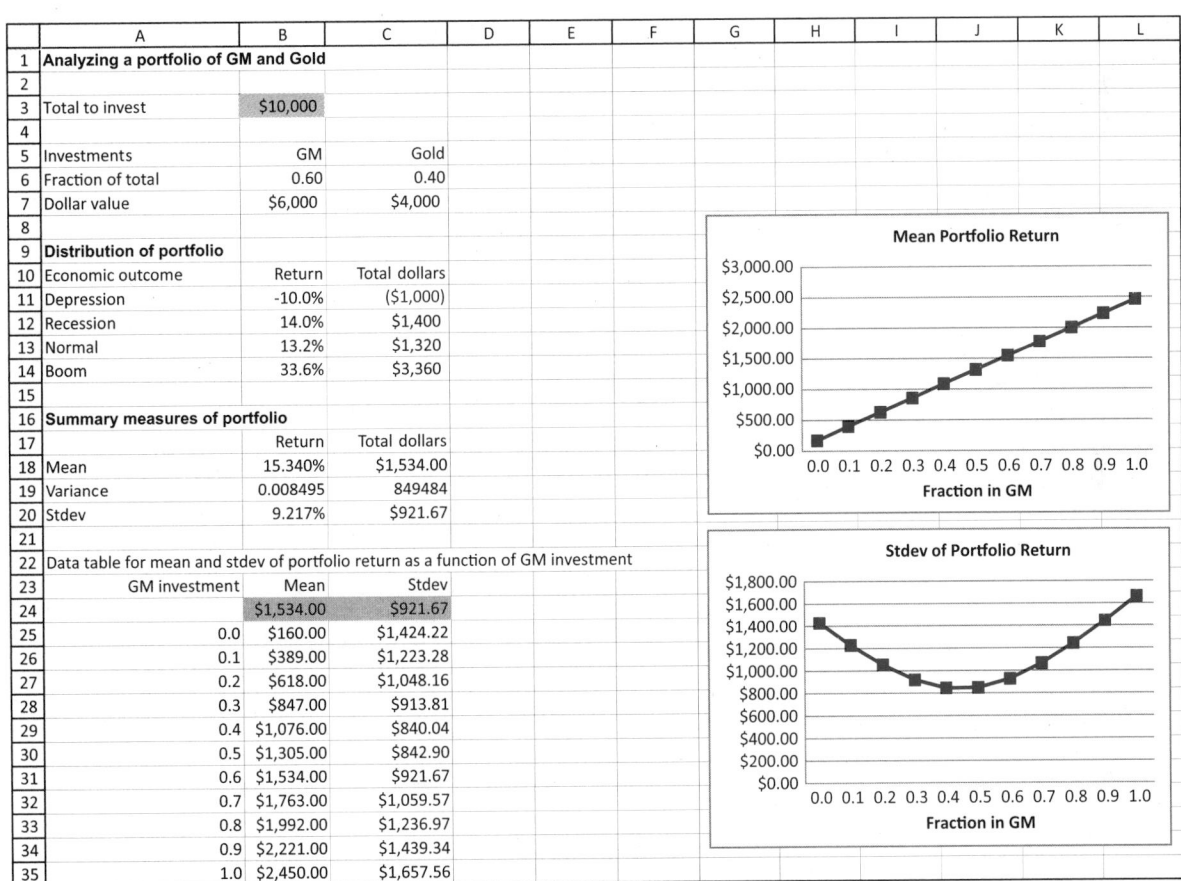

In this way, you can calculate the entire portfolio return distribution—either per dollar or total dollars—and then calculate its summary measures in the usual way. The details, which are similar to other spreadsheet calculations in this chapter, can be found in the **GM vs Gold.xlsx** file. In particular, the possible returns are listed in the ranges B11:B14 and

C11:C14 of Figure 4.8, and the associated probabilities are the same as those used previously in this example. These lead to the summary measures in the range B18:C20. In particular, the investor's expected return is 15.34% and the standard deviation is 9.217%. Based on a $10,000 investment, these translate to an expected total dollar return of $1534 and a standard deviation of $921.67.

Because an investor can choose the fractions to invest in GM and gold, it is important to see how the expected portfolio return and the standard deviation of portfolio return change as these fractions vary. To do this, make sure that the value in cell B6 is a constant and that *formulas* are entered in cells C6, B7, and C7. In this way, these last three cells update automatically when the value in cell B6 changes (and the total investment amount remains $10,000). Then form a data table in the range A24:C35 that calculates the mean and standard deviation of the total dollar portfolio return for each of several GM investment proportions in column A. (To do this, enter the formulas =**C18** and =**C20** in cells B24 and C24, highlight the range A24:C35, select Data Table from the What-If Analysis dropdown list on the Data ribbon, and enter cell B6 as the column input cell. No row input cell is necessary.)

The graphs of the means and standard deviations from this data table appear in Figure 4.8. They show that the expected portfolio return steadily increases as more and more is put into GM (and less is put into gold). However, the standard deviation, often used as a measure of risk, first decreases, then increases. This means there is a trade-off between expected return and risk as measured by the standard deviation. The investor could obtain a higher expected return by putting more of his money into GM, but past a fraction of approximately 0.4, the risk also increases. ∎

Recall that an Excel data table is used for "what-if" analysis. It allows you to vary an input over some range and see how one or more outputs change. For more details, refer to the Excel Tutorial.xlsx file.

PROBLEMS

Level A

23. The quarterly sales levels (in millions of dollars) of two U.S. retail giants are dependent on the general state of the national economy in the coming months. The file **P04_23.xlsx** provides the probability distribution for the projected sales volume of each of these two retailers in the next quarter.
  a. Find the mean and standard deviation of the quarterly sales volume for each of these two retailers. Compare these two sets of summary measures.
  b. Find the covariance and correlation for the given quarterly sales volumes. Interpret your results.

24. The possible annual percentage returns of the stocks of Alpha, Inc. and Beta, Inc. are distributed as shown in the file **P04_24.xlsx**.
  a. What is the expected annual return of Alpha's stock? What is the expected annual return of Beta's stock?
  b. What is the standard deviation of the annual return of Alpha's stock? What is the standard deviation of the annual return of Beta's stock?
  c. On the basis of your answers to the questions in parts **a** and **b**, which of these two stocks would you prefer to buy? Defend your choice.
  d. Are the annual returns of these two stocks positively or negatively associated with each other?

Answer by calculating the correlation between them. How might the answer to this question influence your decision to purchase shares of one or both of these companies?

25. The annual bonuses awarded to members of the management team and assembly-line workers of an automobile manufacturer depend largely on the corporation's sales performance during the preceding year. The file **P04_25.xlsx** contains the probability distribution of possible bonuses (measured in hundreds of dollars) awarded to white-collar and blue-collar employees at the end of the company's fiscal year.
  a. How much do a manager and an assembly-line worker expect to receive in their bonus check at the end of a typical year?
  b. For which group of employees within this organization does there appear to be more variability in the distribution of possible annual bonuses?
  c. How strongly associated are the bonuses awarded to the white-collar and blue-collar employees of this company at the end of the year? Answer by calculating the correlation between them. What are some possible implications of this result for the relations between members of the management team and the assembly-line workers in the future?

26. Consumer demand for small, economical automobiles depends somewhat on recent trends in the average price of unleaded gasoline. For example, consider the information given in the file **P04_26.xlsx** on the distributions of average annual sales of the Honda Civic and the Toyota Prius in relation to the trend of the average price of unleaded fuel over the past two years.

    a. Find the annual mean sales levels of the Honda Civic and the Toyota Prius.

    b. For which of these two models are sales levels more sensitive to recent changes in the average price of unleaded gasoline?

    c. Given the available information, how strongly associated are the annual sales volumes of these two popular compact cars? Answer by calculating the correlation between them. Provide a qualitative explanation of the results.

27. Upon completing their respective homework assignments, marketing majors and accounting majors at a large state university enjoy hanging out at the local tavern in the evenings. The file **P04_27.xlsx** contains the distribution of number of hours spent by these students at the tavern in a typical week, along with typical cumulative grade-point averages (on a 4-point scale) for marketing and accounting students with similar social habits.

    a. Compare the means and standard deviations of the grade-point averages of the two groups of students. Does one of the two groups consistently perform better academically than the other? Explain.

    b. Does academic performance, as measured by cumulative GPA, seem to be associated with the amount of time students typically spend at the local tavern? If so, characterize the observed relationship.

    c. Find the covariance and correlation between the typical grade-point averages earned by the two subgroups of students. What do these measures of association indicate in this case?

4.6 DISTRIBUTION OF TWO RANDOM VARIABLES: JOINT PROBABILITY APPROACH

The previous section illustrated one possibility, the scenario approach, for specifying the joint distribution of two random variables. You first identify several possible scenarios, next specify the value of each random variable that will occur under each scenario, and then assess the probability of each scenario. For people who think in terms of scenarios—and this includes many business managers—this is a very appealing approach.

In this section we illustrate an alternative method for specifying the probability distribution of two random variables X and Y. You first identify the possible values of X and the possible values of Y. Let x and y be any two such values. Then you *directly* assess the joint probability of the pair (x, y) and denote it by $P(X = x$ and $Y = y)$ or more simply by $p(x, y)$. This is the probability of the joint event that $X = x$ and $Y = y$ both occur. As always, the joint probabilities must be nonnegative and sum to 1.

A joint probability distribution, specified by all probabilities of the form $p(x, y)$, provides a tremendous amount of information. It indicates not only how X and Y are related, but also how each of X and Y is distributed in its own right. In probability terms, the joint distribution of X and Y determines the *marginal* distributions of both X and Y, where each marginal distribution is the probability distribution of a single random variable. (They are called marginal because they are usually displayed in the margins of a table.) The joint distribution also determines the conditional distributions of X given Y, and of Y given X. The conditional distribution of X given Y, for example, is the distribution of X, given that Y is known to equal a certain value.

These concepts are best explained by means of an example, as we do next.

EXAMPLE | **4.4 UNDERSTANDING THE RELATIONSHIP BETWEEN DEMANDS FOR SUBSTITUTE PRODUCTS**

A company sells two products, product 1 and product 2, that tend to be substitutes for one another. That is, if a customer buys product 1, she tends not to buy product 2, and vice versa. The company assesses the joint probability distribution of demand for the two products during the coming month. This joint distribution appears in the shaded region of

Figure 4.9. (See the Demand sheet of the file **Substitute Products.xlsx**.) Column B and row 4 of this table show the possible values of demand for the two products. Specifically, the company assumes that demand for product 1 can be from 100 to 400 in increments of 100, and demand for product 2 can be from 50 to 250 in increments of 50. Furthermore, each possible value of demand 1 can occur with each possible value of demand 2, with the joint probability given in the table. For example, the joint probability that demand 1 is 200 and demand 2 is 100 is 0.08. Given this joint probability distribution, describe more fully the probabilistic structure of demands for the two products.

Figure 4.9

Joint Probability
Distribution of
Demands

	A	B	C	D	E	F
1	Probability distribution of demands for substitute products					
2						
3				Demand for product 1		
4			100	200	300	400
5		50	0.015	0.040	0.050	0.035
6	Demand	100	0.030	0.080	0.075	0.025
7	for	150	0.050	0.100	0.100	0.020
8	product 2	200	0.045	0.100	0.050	0.010
9		250	0.060	0.080	0.025	0.010

Objective   To use the given joint probability distribution of demands to find the conditional distribution of demand for each product, given the demand for the other product, and to calculate the covariance and correlation between demands for these substitutes.

Solution

Let D_1 and D_2 denote the demands for products 1 and 2. You first find the marginal distributions of D_1 and D_2. These are the row and column sums of the joint probabilities in Figure 4.10. An example of the reasoning is as follows. Consider the probability $P(D_1 = 200)$. If demand for product 1 is to be 200, it must be accompanied by *some* value of D_2; that is, exactly one of the joint events ($D_1 = 200$ and $D_2 = 50$) through ($D_1 = 200$ and $D_2 = 250$) must occur. Using the addition rule for probability, find the total probability of these joint events by summing the corresponding joint probabilities. The result is $P(D_1 = 200) = 0.40$, the column sum corresponding to $D_1 = 200$. Similarly, marginal probabilities for D_2 such as $P(D_2 = 150) = 0.27$ are the row sums, calculated in column G in Figure 4.10. Note that the marginal probabilities, either those in row 10 or those in column G, sum to 1, as they should. These marginal probabilities indicate how the demand for either product behaves in its own right, aside from any considerations of the *other* product.

The marginal distributions indicate that "in-between" values of D_1 or of D_2 are most likely, whereas extreme values in either direction are less likely. However, these marginal distributions tell you nothing about the *relationship* between D_1 and D_2. After all, products 1 and 2 are supposedly *substitute* products. The joint probabilities spell out this relationship, but they are rather difficult to interpret. A better way is to calculate the conditional distributions of D_1 given D_2, or of D_2 given D_1. You can do this in rows 12 through 29 of Figure 4.10.

Focus on the conditional distribution of D_1 given D_2, shown in rows 12 through 19. In each row of this table (rows 15–19), you fix the value of D_2 at the value in column B and calculate the conditional probabilities of D_1 given this fixed value of D_2. The conditional probability is the joint probability divided by the marginal probability

Figure 4.10

Marginal and
Conditional
Distributions and
Summary Measures

	A	B	C	D	E	F	G
1	**Probability distribution of demands for substitute products**						
2							
3				Demand for product 1			
4			100	200	300	400	
5		50	0.015	0.040	0.050	0.035	0.140
6	Demand	100	0.030	0.080	0.075	0.025	0.210
7	for	150	0.050	0.100	0.100	0.020	0.270
8	product 2	200	0.045	0.100	0.050	0.010	0.205
9		250	0.060	0.080	0.025	0.010	0.175
10			0.20	0.40	0.30	0.10	
11							
12	Conditional distribution of demand for product 1, given demand for product 2						
13				Demand for product 1			
14			100	200	300	400	
15		50	0.11	0.29	0.36	0.25	1.00
16	Demand	100	0.14	0.38	0.36	0.12	1.00
17	for	150	0.19	0.37	0.37	0.07	1.00
18	product 2	200	0.22	0.49	0.24	0.05	1.00
19		250	0.34	0.46	0.14	0.06	1.00
20							
21	Conditional distribution of demand for product 2, given demand for product 1						
22				Demand for product 1			
23			100	200	300	400	
24		50	0.08	0.10	0.17	0.35	
25	Demand	100	0.15	0.20	0.25	0.25	
26	for	150	0.25	0.25	0.33	0.20	
27	product 2	200	0.23	0.25	0.17	0.10	
28		250	0.30	0.20	0.08	0.10	
29			1.00	1.00	1.00	1.00	
30							
31		Product 1	Product 2				
32	Means	230.00	153.25				
33	Variances	8100.00	4176.94				
34	Stdevs	90.00	64.63				
35							
36	Products of demands 1 and 2 (for covariance calculation)						
37			100	200	300	400	
38		50	5000	10000	15000	20000	
39		100	10000	20000	30000	40000	
40		150	15000	30000	45000	60000	
41		200	20000	40000	60000	80000	
42		250	25000	50000	75000	100000	
43							
44	Covariance	-1647.50					
45	Correlation	-0.283					

of D_2. For example, the conditional probability that D_1 equals 200, given that D_2 equals 150, is

$$P(D_1 = 200 | D_2 = 150) = \frac{P(D_1 = 200 \text{ and } D_2 = 150)}{P(D_2 = 150)} = \frac{0.10}{0.27} = 0.37$$

This formula follows from the general conditional probability formula in Section 4.2.3.

These conditional probabilities can be calculated all at once by entering the formula

=C5/$G5

in cell C15 and copying it to the range C15:F19. (Make sure you see why only column G, not row 5, is held absolute in this formula.) You can also check that each row of this table is a probability distribution in its own right by summing across rows. The row sums shown in column G are all equal to 1, as they should be.

Similarly, the conditional distribution of D_2 given D_1 is in rows 21 through 29. Here, each column represents the conditional probability distribution of D_2 given the fixed value of D_1 in row 23. These probabilities can be calculated by entering the formula

=C5/C$10

in cell C24 and copying it to the range C24:F28. Now the column sums shown in row 29 are 1, indicating that each column of the table represents a probability distribution.

Various summary measures can now be calculated. Some of these are shown in Figure 4.10. The following steps present the details.

PROCEDURE FOR CALCULATING SUMMARY MEASURES

1 Expected values. The expected demands in cells B32 and C32 follow from the marginal distributions. To calculate these, enter the formulas

=SUMPRODUCT(C4:F4,C10:F10)

and

=SUMPRODUCT(B5:B9,G5:G9)

in these two cells. Note that each of these is based on Equation (4.6) for an expected value, that is, a sum of products of possible values and their (marginal) probabilities.

2 Variances and standard deviations. These measures of variability are also calculated from the marginal distributions by appealing to Equation (4.9). For example, to find the variance of D_1, enter the formula

=SUMPRODUCT(C4:F4,C4:F4,C10:F10)-B32^2

in cell B33, and take its square root in cell B34.

3 Covariance and correlation. The formulas for covariance and correlation are the same as before [see Equations (4.14) and (4.13)]. However, unlike Example 4.3, a complete table of products of possible demands in the range C38:F42 is required.

Then calculate the covariance in cell B44 with the formula

=SUMPRODUCT(C38:F42,C5:F9)-B32*C32

Finally, calculate the correlation in cell B45 with the formula

=B44/(B34*C34)

Now let's step back and examine the results. If you are interested in the behavior of a single demand only, say, D_1, then the relevant quantities are the marginal probabilities in row 10 and the mean and standard deviation of D_1 in cells B32 and B34. However, you are often more interested in the joint behavior of D_1 and D_2. The best way to see this behavior is in the conditional probability tables. For example, compare the probability distributions in rows 15 through 19. As the value of D_2 increases, the probabilities for D_1 tend to shift to the left. That is, as demand for product 2 increases, demand for product 1 tends to decrease.

This is only a *tendency*. When D_2 equals its largest value, there is still some chance that D_1 will be large, but this probability is fairly small.

This behavior can be seen more clearly from the graph in Figure 4.11. Each line in this graph corresponds to one of the rows 15 through 19. The legend shows the different values of D_2. You can see that when D_2 is large, D_1 tends to be small, although again, this is only a tendency, not a perfect relationship. When economists say that the two products are substitutes for one another, this is the type of behavior they imply.

Figure 4.11

Conditional Distributions of Demand 1, Given Demand 2

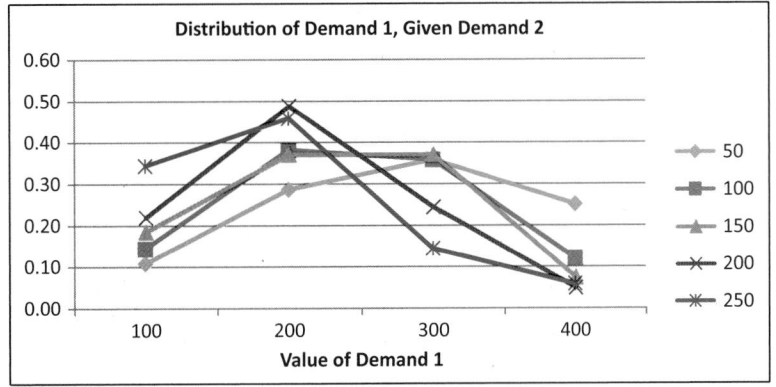

By symmetry, the conditional distribution of D_2 given D_1 shows the same type of behavior. This is illustrated in Figure 4.12, where each line represents one of the columns C through F in the range C24:F28 and the legend shows the different values of D_1.

Figure 4.12

Conditional Distributions of Demand 2, Given Demand 1

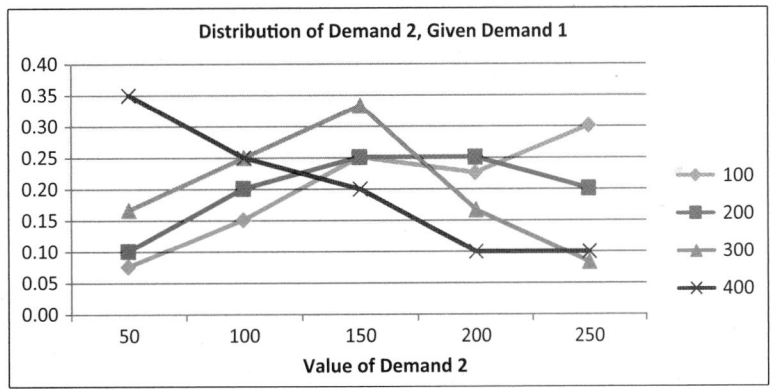

The information in these graphs is confirmed—to some extent, at least—by the covariance and correlation between D_1 and D_2. In particular, their negative values indicate that demands for the two products tend to move in opposite directions. Also, the rather small magnitude of the correlation, -0.283, indicates that the relationship between these demands is far from perfect. When D_1 is large, there is still a reasonably good chance that D_2 will be large, and when D_1 is small, there is still a reasonably good chance that D_2 will be small. ∎

4.6.1 How to Assess Joint Probability Distributions

In the scenario approach from Section 4.5, only one probability for each scenario has to be assessed. In the joint probability approach, a whole table of joint probabilities must be assessed. This can be quite difficult, especially when there are many possible values for each of the random variables. In Example 4.4 the approach requires $4 \times 5 = 20$ joint probabilities that not only sum to 1 but imply the desired "substitute product" behavior.

One approach is to proceed *backward* from the way illustrated in the example. Instead of specifying the joint probabilities and then deriving the marginal and conditional distributions, you can specify either set of marginal probabilities and either set of conditional probabilities, and then use these to *calculate* the joint probabilities. The reasoning is based on the multiplication rule for probability in the form given by Equation (4.15).

Assessing the joint probability distribution of two (or more) random variables is never easy for a manager, but the suggestions here are useful.

Joint Probability Formula
$$P(X = x \text{ and } Y = y) = P(X = x | Y = y)P(Y = y) \qquad \textbf{(4.15)}$$

In words, the joint probability on the left is the conditional probability that $X = x$ given $Y = y$, multiplied by the marginal probability that $Y = y$. The roles of X and Y can be reversed, yielding the alternative formula in Equation (4.16). In general, you would choose the formula that makes the probabilities on the right-hand side easiest to assess.

Alternative Joint Probability Formula
$$P(X = x \text{ and } Y = y) = P(Y = y | X = x)P(X = x) \qquad \textbf{(4.16)}$$

The advantage of this procedure over assessing the joint probabilities directly is that it is probably easier and more intuitive for a business manager. The manager has more control over the relationship between the two random variables, as determined by the conditional probabilities she assesses. Still, it is not easy, especially if these are *subjective* probabilities. The manager will need to make many assessments of the likelihoods of events, based on her knowledge of the business.

PROBLEMS

Level A

28. Let X and Y represent the number of Dell and HP laptop computers, respectively, sold per month from online sites. The file **P04_28.xlsx** contains the probabilities of various combinations of monthly sales volumes of these competitors.
   a. Find the marginal distributions of X and Y. Interpret your findings.
   b. Calculate the expected monthly laptop computer sales volumes for Dell and HP at these sites.
   c. Calculate the standard deviations of the monthly laptop computer sales volumes for Dell and HP at these sites.
   d. Find and interpret the conditional distribution of X given Y.
   e. Find and interpret the conditional distribution of Y given X.
   f. Find and interpret the correlation between X and Y. Are these random variables independent (or nearly so)?

29. The joint probability distribution of the weekly demand for two brands of diet soda is provided in the file **P04_29.xlsx**. In particular, let D_1 and D_2 represent the weekly demand (in hundreds of two-liter bottles) for brand 1 and brand 2, respectively, in a small town in central Indiana.
   a. Find the mean and standard deviation of this community's weekly demand for each brand of diet soda.
   b. What is the probability that the weekly demand for each brand will be at least one standard deviation above its mean?
   c. What is the probability that at least one of the two weekly demands will be at least one standard deviation above its mean?
   d. What is the correlation between the weekly demands for these two brands of diet soda? What does this measure of association tell you about the relationship between these two products?

30. A local pharmacy has two checkout stations available to its customers: a regular checkout station and an

express checkout station. Customers with six or fewer items are assumed to join the express line. Let X and Y be the numbers of customers in the regular checkout line and the express checkout line, respectively, at the busiest time of a typical day. Note that these numbers include the customer(s) being served, if any. The joint distribution for X and Y is given in the file **P04_30.xlsx**.

a. Find the marginal distributions of X and Y. What does each of these distributions tell you?

b. Find the conditional distribution of X given Y. What is the practical benefit of knowing this conditional distribution?

c. What is the probability that no one is waiting or being served in the regular checkout line?

d. What is the probability that no one is waiting or being served in the express checkout line?

e. What is the probability that no more than two customers are waiting in both lines combined?

f. On average, how many customers would you expect to see in each of these two lines during the busiest time of day at the pharmacy?

31. Suppose that the manufacturer of a particular product assesses the joint distribution of price P per unit and demand D for its product in the coming quarter as provided in the file **P04_31.xlsx**.

a. Find the expected price and the expected demand in the coming quarter.

b. What is the probability that the price of this product will be above its mean in the coming quarter?

c. What is the probability that the demand for this product will be below its mean in the coming quarter?

d. What is the probability that demand for this product will exceed 2500 units during the coming quarter, given that its price is less than \$40?

e. What is the probability that demand for this product will be fewer than 3500 units during the coming quarter, given that its price is greater than \$30?

f. Find the correlation between price and demand. Is the result consistent with your expectations? Explain.

Level B

32. The recent weekly trends of two particular stock prices can best be described by the joint probability distribution shown in the file **P04_32.xlsx**.

a. What is the probability that the price of stock 1 will not increase in the coming week?

b. What is the probability that the price of stock 2 will change in the coming week?

c. What is the probability that the price of stock 1 will not decrease, given that the price of stock 2 remains constant in the coming week?

d. What is the probability that the price of stock 2 will change, given that the price of stock 1 changes in the coming week?

e. Why is it impossible to find the correlation between the typical weekly movements of these two stock prices from the information given? Nevertheless, does it appear that they are positively or negatively related? Why? What are the implications of this result for choosing an investment portfolio that may or may not include these two particular stocks?

33. Two service elevators are used in parallel by employees of a three-story hotel building. At any point in time when both elevators are stationary, let X_1 and X_2 be the floor numbers at which elevators 1 and 2, respectively, are currently located. The joint probability distribution of X_1 and X_2 is given in the file **P04_33.xlsx**.

a. What is the probability that these two elevators are not stationed on the same floor?

b. What is the probability that elevator 2 is located on the third floor?

c. What is the probability that elevator 1 is not located on the first floor?

d. What is the probability that elevator 2 is located on the first floor, given that elevator 1 is not stationed on the first floor?

e. What is the probability that a hotel employee approaching the first-floor elevators will find at least one available for service?

f. Repeat part **e** for a hotel employee approaching each of the second- and third-floor elevators.

g. How might this hotel's operations manager respond to your findings in the previous questions?

4.7 INDEPENDENT RANDOM VARIABLES

A very important special case of joint distributions is when the random variables are **independent**. Intuitively, this means that any information about the values of any of the random variables is worthless in terms of predicting any of the others. In particular, if there are only two random variables X and Y, then information about X is worthless in terms of predicting Y, and vice versa. Usually, random variables in real applications are *not* independent; they are usually related in some way, in which case we say they are **dependent**.

However, we often make an assumption of independence in mathematical models to simplify the analysis.

The most intuitive way to express independence of X and Y is to say that their conditional distributions are equal to their marginals. For example, the conditional probability that X equals any value x, given that Y equals some value y, equals the marginal probability that X equals x—and this statement is true for *all* values of x and y. In words, knowledge of the value of Y has no effect on probabilities involving X. Similarly, knowledge of the value of X has no effect on probabilities involving Y.

An equivalent way of stating the independence property is that for all values x and y, the events $X = x$ and $Y = y$ are probabilistically independent, in the sense of Section 4.2.4. This leads to the important property that *joint probabilities equal the product of the marginals,* as shown in Equation (4.17). This follows from Equation (4.15) and also because conditionals equal marginals under independence. Equation (4.17) might not be as intuitive, but it is very useful, as illustrated in the following example.

Joint Probability Formula for Independent Random Variables
$$P(X = x \text{ and } Y = y) = P(X = x)P(Y = y)$$
(4.17)

EXAMPLE

4.5 ANALYZING THE SALES OF TWO POPULAR PERSONAL DIGITAL ASSISTANTS

A local office supply and equipment store, Office Station, sells several different brands of personal digital assistants (PDAs). One of the store's managers has studied the daily sales of its two most popular personal digital assistants, the Palm M505 and the Palm Vx, over the past quarter. In particular, she has used historical data to assess the joint probability distribution of the sales of these two products on a typical day. The assessed distribution is shown in Figure 4.13 (see the file **PDA Sales.xlsx**). The manager would like to use this distribution to determine whether there is support for the claim that the sales of the Palm Vx are often made at the expense of Palm M505 sales, and vice versa.

Figure 4.13

Joint Probability
Distribution of Sales

	A	B	C	D	E	F
1	Assessed probability distribution of sales of two popular PDAs					
2						
3				Daily sales of Palm Vx		
4			0	1	2	3
5		0	0.01	0.03	0.06	0.09
6	Daily sales of	1	0.02	0.06	0.12	0.09
7	Palm M505	2	0.03	0.12	0.06	0.09
8		3	0.04	0.09	0.06	0.03

Objective To use the assessed joint probability distribution to find the conditional distribution of daily sales of each PDA, given the sales of the other PDA, and to determine whether the daily sales of these two products are *independent* random variables.

Solution

As in the solution of Example 4.4, begin by applying the addition rule for probability to find the marginals for each of the two personal digital assistants, as shown in Figure 4.14.

Figure 4.14

Marginal and
Conditional
Distributions of
Sales

	A	B	C	D	E	F	G
1	**Assessed probability distribution of sales of two popular PDAs**						
2							
3				Daily sales of Palm Vx			
4			0	1	2	3	
5		0	0.01	0.03	0.06	0.09	0.19
6	Daily sales of	1	0.02	0.06	0.12	0.09	0.29
7	Palm M505	2	0.03	0.12	0.06	0.09	0.30
8		3	0.04	0.09	0.06	0.03	0.22
9			0.10	0.30	0.30	0.30	
10							
11	Conditional distribution of sales of Palm Vx, given sales of Palm M505						
12				Daily sales of Palm Vx			
13			0	1	2	3	
14		0	0.05	0.16	0.32	0.47	1
15	Daily sales of	1	0.07	0.21	0.41	0.31	1
16	Palm M505	2	0.10	0.40	0.20	0.30	1
17		3	0.18	0.41	0.27	0.14	1
18							
19	Conditional distribution of sales of Palm M505, given sales of Palm Vx						
20				Daily sales of Palm Vx			
21			0	1	2	3	
22		0	0.10	0.10	0.20	0.30	
23	Daily sales of	1	0.20	0.20	0.40	0.30	
24	Palm M505	2	0.30	0.40	0.20	0.30	
25		3	0.40	0.30	0.20	0.10	
26			1	1	1	1	

Before finding the conditional distribution of sales for each product, you can check whether these two random variables are independent. Let M and V denote the daily sales for the Palm M505 and Palm Vx, respectively. Equation (4.17) states that $P(M = m$ and $V = v) = P(M = m) P(V = v)$ for all values of m and v if M and V are independent. However, the marginal probabilities indicate that $P(M = 0) P(V = 0) = (0.19)(0.10) = 0.019$, whereas $P(M = 0$ and $V = 0) = 0.01$ from the table. Therefore, there is at least one case where the joint probability does *not* equal the product of the marginals. This inequality rules out the possibility that M and V are independent random variables. If you are not yet convinced of this conclusion, compare the products of other marginal probabilities with corresponding joint probabilities in Figure 4.14. You can verify that Equation (4.17) fails to hold for virtually all of the different combinations of sales levels.

The conditional distributions of V given M and M given V are shown in the ranges C14:F17 and C22:F25, calculated exactly as in Example 4.4. What can the Office Station manager infer from these conditional probability distributions? Observe in the first table that the likelihood of achieving the *highest* daily sales level of the Palm Vx *decreases* as the daily sales level of the Palm M505 increases. This same table reveals that the probability of experiencing the *lowest* daily sales level of the Palm Vx *increases* as the daily sales level of the Palm M505 increases. Furthermore, by closely examining the second table, you can see that the likelihood of achieving the *highest* daily sales level of the Palm M505 *decreases* as the daily sales level of the Palm Vx increases. This same table reveals that the probability of experiencing the *lowest* daily sales level of the Palm M505 *increases* as the daily sales level of the Palm Vx increases.

Therefore, there is considerable support for the claim that sales of the Palm Vx are often made at the expense of Palm M505 sales, and vice versa. This result makes sense from a business point of view, and it implies that the daily sales of these two products are not independent of one another. In other words, by knowing the sales level of one of these PDAs, the manager has a better understanding of the likelihood of achieving particular sales of the other product. ∎

PROBLEMS

Level A

34. The file **P04_34.xlsx** shows the conditional distribution of the daily number of accidents at a given intersection during the winter months, X_2, given the amount of snowfall (in inches) for the day, X_1. The marginal distribution of X_1 is provided in the bottom row of the table.
   a. Are X_1 and X_2 independent random variables? Explain why or why not.
   b. What is the probability of no accidents at this intersection on a winter day with no snowfall?
   c. What is the probability of no accidents at this intersection on a randomly selected winter day?
   d. What is the probability of at least two accidents at this intersection on a randomly selected winter day on which the snowfall is at least three inches?
   e. What is the probability of less than four inches of snowfall on a randomly selected day?

35. A sporting goods store sells two competing brands of exercise bicycles. Let X_1 and X_2 be the numbers of the two brands sold on a typical day at this store. Based on available historical data, the conditional probability distribution of X_1 given X_2 is assessed as shown in the file **P04_35.xlsx**. The marginal distribution of X_2 is given in the bottom row of the table.
   a. Are X_1 and X_2 independent random variables? Explain why or why not.
   b. What is the probability of observing the sale of exactly one brand 1 bicycle and exactly one brand 2 bicycle on the same day at this store?
   c. What is the probability of observing the sale of at least one brand 1 bicycle on a given day at this store?
   d. What is the probability of observing the sale of no more than two brand 2 bicycles on a given day at this store?
   e. Given that no brand 2 bicycles are sold on a given day, what is the likelihood of observing the sale of at least one brand 1 bicycle at this store?

36. The file **P04_28.xlsx** contains the probabilities of various combinations of monthly sales volumes of Dell (X) and HP (Y) laptop computers from online sites. Are the monthly sales of these two competitors independent of each other? Explain your answer.

37. Let D_1 and D_2 represent the weekly demand (in hundreds of two-liter bottles) for brand 1 diet soda and brand 2 diet soda, respectively, in a small central Indiana town. The joint probability distribution of the weekly demand for these two brands of diet soda is provided in the file **P04_29.xlsx**. Are D_1 and D_2 independent random variables? Explain why or why not.

38. The file **P04_31.xlsx** contains the joint probability distribution of price P per unit and demand D for a particular product in the coming quarter.
   a. Are P and D independent random variables? Explain your answer.
   b. If P and D are *not* independent random variables, which joint probabilities result in the same *marginal* probabilities for P and D as given in the file but make P and D independent of each other?

Level B

39. You know that in one year you are going to buy a house. (In fact, you have already selected the neighborhood, but right now you are finishing your graduate degree and you are engaged to be married this summer, so you are delaying the purchase for a year.) The annual interest rate for fixed-rate 30-year mortgages is currently 6.00%, and the price of the type of house you are considering is $120,000. However, things may change. Using your knowledge of the economy (and a crystal ball), you estimate that the interest rate might increase or decrease by as much as one percentage point. Also, the price of the house might increase by as much as $10,000—it certainly won't decrease. You assess the probability distribution of the interest rate change as shown in the file **P04_39.xlsx**. The probability distribution of the increase in the price of the house is also shown in this file. Finally, you assume that the two random events (change in interest rate, change in house price) are probabilistically independent. This means that the probability of any joint event, such as an interest increase of 0.50% and a price increase of $5000, is the product of the individual probabilities.

a. Using Excel's PMT function, find the expected monthly house payment (using a 30-year fixed-rate mortgage) if there is no down payment. Find the variance and standard deviation of this monthly payment.

b. Repeat part **a**, but assume that the down payment is 10% of the price of the house (so that you finance only 90%).

c. Is the independence assumption realistic?

4.8 WEIGHTED SUMS OF RANDOM VARIABLES

In this section we will analyze summary measures of weighted sums of random variables. An extremely important application of this topic is in financial investments. The example in this section illustrates such an application. However, there are many other applications of weighted sums of random variables, both in business and elsewhere. It is a topic well worth learning.

It is common (but not required) to use uppercase letters to denote random variables and lowercase letters to denote constants.

Before proceeding to the example, we lay out the main concepts and results. Let X_1, $X_2,..., X_n$ be any n random variables (which could be independent or dependent), and let a_1, $a_2,..., a_n$ be any n constants. We form a new random variable Y that is the weighted sum of the Xs:

$$Y = a_1 X_1 + a_2 X_2 + \cdots + a_n X_n$$

In general, it is too difficult to obtain the complete probability distribution of Y, so we will be content to obtain its mean $E(Y)$ and variance $\text{Var}(Y)$. Of course, $\text{Stdev}(Y)$ is then the square root of $\text{Var}(Y)$.

FUNDAMENTAL INSIGHT

Distributions of Weighted Sums

In general, it is difficult to find the distribution of a weighted sum of random variables. However, for some analyses, such as the portfolio analysis in the following example, it suffices to find means and standard deviations, and these can generally be found quite easily by using the formulas in this section.

The mean is the easy part. You substitute the mean of each X into the formula for Y to obtain E(Y). This result appears in Equation (4.18).

Expected Value of a Weighted Sum of Random Variables

$$E(Y) = a_1 E(X_1) + a_2 E(X_2) + \cdots + a_n E(X_n)$$ **(4.18)**

Using summation notation, this can be written more compactly as

$$E(Y) = \sum_{i=1}^{n} a_i E(X_i)$$

The variance is not as straightforward. Its value depends on whether the Xs are independent or dependent. If they are independent, then $\text{Var}(Y)$ is a weighted sum of the variances of the Xs, using the *squares* of the as as weights, as shown in Equation (4.19).

> **Variance of a Weighted Sum of Independent Random Variables**
> $$\text{Var}(Y) = a_1^2 \, \text{Var}(X_1) + a_2^2 \, \text{Var}(X_2) + \cdots + a_n^2 \, Var(X_n) \qquad \textbf{(4.19)}$$

Using summation notation, this becomes

$$\text{Var}(Y) = \sum_{i=1}^{n} a_i^2 \text{Var}(X_i)$$

If the Xs are not independent, the variance of Y is more complex and requires covariances. In particular, for every pair X_i and X_j, there is an extra term in Equation (4.19): $2 \, a_i a_j \text{Covar}(X_i, X_j)$. The general result is best written in summation notation, as shown in Equation (4.20).

> **Variance of a Weighted Sum of Dependent Random Variables**
> $$\text{Var}(Y) = \sum_{i=1}^{n} a_i^2 \text{Var}(X_i) + \sum_{i<j} 2 a_i a_j \text{Covar}(X_i, X_j) \qquad \textbf{(4.20)}$$

The first summation would be the variance if the Xs were independent. The second summation indicates that a covariance term must be added for all pairs of Xs that have nonzero covariances. Actually, this equation is always valid, regardless of independence, because the covariance terms are all zero if the Xs are independent. There are a number of special cases of Equation (4.20), which we list next.

Special Cases of Expected Value and Variance

- **Sum of independent random variables.** Here we assume the Xs are independent and the weights are all 1, that is,

$$Y = X_1 + X_2 + \cdots + X_n$$

Then the mean of the sum is the sum of the means, and the variance of the sum is the sum of the variances:

$$E(Y) = E(X_1) + E(X_2) + \cdots + E(X_n)$$
$$\text{Var}(Y) = \text{Var}(X_1) + \text{Var}(X_2) + \cdots + \text{Var}(X_n)$$

- **Difference between two independent random variables.** Here we assume X_1 and X_2 are independent and the weights are $a_1 = 1$ and $a_2 = -1$, so that Y can be written as

$$Y = X_1 - X_2$$

Then the mean of the difference is the difference between means, but the variance of the difference is the *sum* of the variances (because $a_2^2 = (-1)^2 = 1$):

$$E(Y) = E(X_1) - E(X_2)$$
$$\text{Var}(Y) = \text{Var}(X_1) + \text{Var}(X_2)$$

- **Sum of two dependent random variables.** In this case we make no independence assumption and set the weights equal to 1, so that $Y = X_1 + X_2$. Then the mean of the sum is again the sum of the means, but the variance of the sum includes a covariance term:

$$E(Y) = E(X_1) + E(X_2)$$
$$\text{Var}(Y) = \text{Var}(X_1) + \text{Var}(X_2) + 2\text{Covar}(X_1, X_2)$$

- **Difference between two dependent random variables.** This is the same as the second case except that the Xs are no longer independent. Again, the mean of the difference is the difference between means, but the variance of the difference now includes a covariance term, and because of the negative weight $a_2 = -1$, the sign of this covariance term is negative:

$$E(Y) = E(X_1) - E(X_2)$$
$$\text{Var}(Y) = \text{Var}(X_1) + \text{Var}(X_2) - 2\text{Covar}(X_1, X_2)$$

- **Linear Function of a Random Variable.** Suppose that Y can be written as

$$Y = a + bX$$

for some constants a and b. In this special case the random variable Y is called a *linear function* of the random variable X. Then the mean, variance, and standard deviation of Y can be calculated from the similar quantities for X with the following formulas:

$$E(Y) = a + bE(X)$$
$$\text{Var}(Y) = b^2\text{Var}(X)$$
$$\text{Stdev}(Y) = |b|\,\text{Stdev}(X)$$

In particular, if Y is a constant multiple of X (that is, if $a = 0$), then the mean and standard deviation of Y are the same multiple of the mean and standard deviation of X. (Note that the absolute value of b is used in the formula for Stdev(Y). This is because b could be negative, whereas a standard deviation cannot be negative.)

We now put these concepts to use in an investment example.

EXAMPLE	**4.6 DESCRIBING INVESTMENT PORTFOLIO RETURNS**

In fact, all of the correlations are positive, which probably indicates that each stock tends to vary in the same direction as some underlying economic indicator. Of course, the diagonal entries in the correlation matrix are all 1 because any stock return is perfectly correlated with itself.

An investor has $100,000 to invest, and she would like to invest it in a portfolio of eight stocks. She has gathered historical data on the returns of these stocks and has used the historical data to estimate means, standard deviations, and correlations for the stock returns. These summary measures appear in rows 12, 13, and 17 through 24 of Figure 4.15. (See the file **Portfolio Analysis.xlsx**.)

For example, the mean and standard deviation of stock 1 are 10.1% and 12.4%. These probably imply that the historical annual returns of stock 1 averaged 10.1% and the standard deviation of the annual returns was 12.4%, although they might not be based purely on historical data. Also, the correlation between the annual returns on stocks 1 and 2, for example, is 0.32 (see either cell C17 or B18, which necessarily contain the same value). This value, 0.32, probably indicates a moderate positive correlation between the historical annual returns of these stocks.

Figure 4.15 Input Data for Investment Example

	A	B	C	D	E	F	G	H	I	J	K	L	M
1	Calculating mean, variance, and stdev for a weighted sum of random variables										Range names used		
2											Covariances	=Model!$B$28:$I$35	
3			Assumptions:								Means	=Model!$B$12:$I$12	
4			1. Random variables are one-year returns from various stocks.								Stdevs	=Model!$B$13:$I$13	
5			2. Weights are amounts invested in stocks.								Variance	=Model!$B$39	
6			3. Weighted sum is return from portfolio.								Weights	=Model!$B$9:$I$9	
7	Given quantities												
8		Stock1	Stock2	Stock3	Stock4	Stock5	Stock6	Stock7	Stock8	Total			
9	Weights	$10,500	$16,300	$9,600	$9,300	$9,500	$15,400	$14,300	$15,100	$100,000			
10													
11		Stock1	Stock2	Stock3	Stock4	Stock5	Stock6	Stock7	Stock8				
12	Means	10.1%	7.3%	11.8%	9.9%	11.8%	9.1%	9.6%	12.3%				
13	Stdevs	12.4%	11.9%	13.4%	14.1%	15.8%	15.9%	11.3%	17.4%				
14													
15	Correlations between stock returns												
16		Stock1	Stock2	Stock3	Stock4	Stock5	Stock6	Stock7	Stock8				
17	Stock1	1.000	0.320	0.370	0.610	0.800	0.610	0.550	0.560				
18	Stock2	0.320	1.000	0.410	0.780	0.430	0.800	0.950	0.480				
19	Stock3	0.370	0.410	1.000	0.330	0.860	0.380	0.340	0.700				
20	Stock4	0.610	0.780	0.330	1.000	0.680	0.500	0.500	0.670				
21	Stock5	0.800	0.430	0.860	0.680	1.000	0.580	0.420	0.540				
22	Stock6	0.610	0.800	0.380	0.500	0.580	1.000	0.920	0.340				
23	Stock7	0.550	0.950	0.340	0.500	0.420	0.920	1.000	0.650				
24	Stock8	0.560	0.480	0.700	0.670	0.540	0.340	0.650	1.000				

Although these summary measures have probably been obtained from historical data, the investor believes they are relevant for predicting *future* returns. Now she would like to analyze a portfolio of these stocks, using the investment amounts shown in row 9. What is the mean annual return from this portfolio? What are its variance and standard deviation?

Objective To determine the mean annual return of the portfolio, and to quantify the risk associated with the total dollar return from the given weighted sum of annual stock returns.

Solution

This is a typical weighted sum model. The random variables are the annual returns from the stocks; the weights are the dollar amounts invested in the stocks; and the summary measures of the random variables are given in rows 12, 13, and 17 through 24 of Figure 4.15. Be careful about units, however. Each X_i (expressed as a percentage) represents the return on a *single* dollar invested in stock i, whereas Y, the weighted sum of the X's, represents the *total* dollar return. So a typical value of an X might be 10.5%, whereas a typical value of Y might be $10,500.

We can immediately apply Equation (4.18) to obtain the mean return from the portfolio. This appears in cell B38 of Figure 4.16, using the formula

=SUMPRODUCT(Weights,Means)

Figure 4.16 Calculations for Investment Example

	A	B	C	D	E	F	G	H	I
26	Covariances between stock returns (variances of stock returns are on the diagonal)								
27		Stock1	Stock2	Stock3	Stock4	Stock5	Stock6	Stock7	Stock8
28	Stock1	0.0154	0.0047	0.0061	0.0107	0.0157	0.0120	0.0077	0.0121
29	Stock2	0.0047	0.0142	0.0065	0.0131	0.0081	0.0151	0.0128	0.0099
30	Stock3	0.0061	0.0065	0.0180	0.0062	0.0182	0.0081	0.0051	0.0163
31	Stock4	0.0107	0.0131	0.0062	0.0199	0.0151	0.0112	0.0080	0.0164
32	Stock5	0.0157	0.0081	0.0182	0.0151	0.0250	0.0146	0.0075	0.0148
33	Stock6	0.0120	0.0151	0.0081	0.0112	0.0146	0.0253	0.0165	0.0094
34	Stock7	0.0077	0.0128	0.0051	0.0080	0.0075	0.0165	0.0128	0.0128
35	Stock8	0.0121	0.0099	0.0163	0.0164	0.0148	0.0094	0.0128	0.0303
36									
37	Summary measures of portfolio								
38	Mean	$10,056.40							
39	Variance	124992021							
40	Stdev	$11,179.98							

You cannot yet calculate the variance of the portfolio return. The reason is that the input data include standard deviations and correlations, not the variances and covariances required in Equation (4.18).[7] But the variances and covariances are related to standard deviations and correlations by

$$\text{Var}(X_i) = (\text{Stdev}(X_i))^2 \qquad (4.21)$$

and

$$\text{Covar}(X_i, X_j) = \text{Stdev}(X_i) \times \text{Stdev}(X_j) \times \text{Correl}(X_i, X_j) \qquad (4.22)$$

You can form a table of variances and covariances in the range B28:I35, using Equations (4.21) and (4.22), in one step with a careful use of the HLOOKUP (horizontal lookup) function. To do so, highlight the range B28:I35, type the formula

=HLOOKUP($A28,$B$11:$I$13,3,FALSE)*B17*HLOOKUP(B$27,$B$11:$I$13,3,FALSE)

and press Ctrl-Enter. (Be careful with relative and absolute addresses.) Note how the HLOOKUP functions find the appropriate standard deviations from row 13 for use in the covariance formula. Each diagonal element of the covariance range is a variance, and the elements off the diagonal are covariances.

Now you can use Equation (4.20) to calculate the portfolio variance in cell B39. Although Equation (4.20) looks intimidating, it can be implemented fairly easily with Excel's matrix multiplication function, MMULT, and its TRANSPOSE function. To do so, enter the following formula in cell B39 and then press Ctrl-Shift-Enter (all three keys at once):

=MMULT(Weights,MMULT(Covariances,TRANSPOSE(Weights)))

[7]This was intentional. It is often easier for an investor to assess standard deviations and correlations because they are more intuitive measures.

(This formula, called an array formula, is somewhat advanced, but it is a very handy short-cut for implementing Equation (4.20). Section 14.8.3 provides more information about matrix multiplication and the MMULT function in general. If you are interested, you can read that section now.) Finally, calculate the standard deviation of the portfolio return in cell B40 as the square root of the variance.

The results in Figure 4.16 indicate that the investor has an expected return of slightly more than $10,000 (or 10%) from this portfolio. However, the standard deviation of approximately $11,200 is sizable. This standard deviation is a measure of the portfolio's risk. Investors always want a large mean return, but they also want low risk. Moreover, they realize that the only way to obtain a higher mean return is usually to accept more risk. You can experiment with the spreadsheet for this example to see how the mean and standard deviation of portfolio return vary with the investment amounts. Just enter new weights in row 9 (keeping the sum equal to $100,000) and see how the values in B38 through B40 change. ∎

PROBLEMS

Level A

40. A typical consumer buys a random number (X) of polo shirts when he shops at a men's clothing store. The distribution of X is given by the following probability distribution: $P(X = 0) = 0.30$, $P(X = 1) = 0.30$, $P(X = 2) = 0.20$, $P(X = 3) = 0.10$, and $P(X = 4) = 0.10$.
  a. Find the mean and standard deviation of X.
  b. Assuming that each shirt costs $35, let Y be the total amount of money (in dollars) spent by a customer when he visits this clothing store. Find the mean and standard deviation of Y.
  c. Find the probability that a customer's expenditure will be more than one standard deviation above the mean expenditure level.

41. Based on past experience, the number of customers who arrive at a local gasoline station during the noon hour to purchase fuel is best described by the probability distribution given in the file **P04_41.xlsx**.
  a. Find the mean, variance, and standard deviation of this random variable.
  b. Find the probability that the number of arrivals during the noon hour will be within one standard deviation of the mean number of arrivals.
  c. Suppose that the typical customer spends $28 on fuel upon stopping at this gasoline station during the noon hour. Find the mean and standard deviation of the total gasoline revenue earned by this gas station during the noon hour.
  d. What is the probability that the total gasoline revenue will be less than the mean value found in part **c**?
  e. What is the probability that the total gasoline revenue will be more than two standard deviations above the mean value found in part **c**?

42. Let X be the number of defective items found by a quality inspector in a random batch of 15 items from a particular manufacturing process. The probability distribution of X is provided in the file **P04_18.xlsx**. This firm earns $500 profit from the sale of each *acceptable* item in a given batch. In the event that an item is found to be *defective,* it must be reworked at a cost of $100 before it can be sold, thus reducing its per-unit profit to $400.
  a. Find the mean and standard deviation of the profit earned from the sale of all items in a given batch.
  b. What is the probability that the profit earned from the sale of all items in a given batch is within two standard deviations of the mean profit level? Is this result consistent with the empirical rules from Chapter 2? Explain.

43. The probability distribution for the number of job applications processed at a small employment agency during a typical week is given in the file **P04_43.xlsx**.
  a. Assuming that it takes the agency's administrative assistant two hours to process a submitted job application, on average how many hours in a typical week will the administrative assistant spend processing incoming job applications?
  b. Find an interval with the property that the administrative assistant can be approximately 95% sure that the total amount of time he spends each week processing incoming job applications will be in this interval.

44. Consider a financial services salesperson whose annual salary consists of both a fixed portion of $25,000 and a variable portion that is a commission based on her sales performance. In particular, she estimates that her monthly sales commission can be represented by a random variable with mean $5000 and standard deviation $700.

a. What annual salary can this salesperson expect to earn?

b. Assuming that her sales commissions in different months are independent random variables, what is the standard deviation of her annual salary?

c. Between what two annual salary levels can this salesperson be approximately 95% sure that her true total earnings will fall?

45. A film-processing shop charges its customers 18 cents per print, but customers may refuse to accept one or more of the prints for various reasons. Assume that this shop does not charge its customers for refused prints. The number of prints refused per 24-print roll is a random variable with mean 1.5 and standard deviation 0.5.

a. Find the mean and standard deviation of the amount that customers pay for the development of a typical 24-print roll.

b. Assume that this shop processes 250 24-print rolls of film per week. Assuming the numbers of refused prints on these rolls are independent random variables, find the mean and standard deviation of the weekly film processing revenue of this shop.

c. Find an interval such that the manager of this film shop can be approximately 95% sure that the weekly processing revenue will be contained within the interval.

46. Suppose the monthly demand for Thomson televisions has a mean of 40,000 and a standard deviation of 20,000. Find the mean and standard deviation of the annual demand for Thomson TVs. Assume that demands in different months are probabilistically independent. (Is this assumption realistic?)

47. Suppose there are five stocks available for investment and each has an annual mean return of 10% and a standard deviation of 4%. Assume the returns on the stocks are independent random variables.

a. If you invest 20% of your money in each stock, find the mean and standard deviation of the annual dollar return on your investments.

b. If you invest $100 in a single stock, determine the mean and standard deviation of the annual return on your investment.

c. How do the answers to parts **a** and **b** relate to the phrase, "Don't put all your eggs in one basket"?

48. An investor puts $10,000 into each of four stocks, labeled A, B, C, and D. The file **P04_48.xlsx** contains the means and standard deviations of the annual returns of these four stocks. Assuming that the returns of these four stocks are independent, find the mean and standard deviation of the total amount that this investor earns in one year from these four investments.

Level B

49. Consider again the investment problem described in the previous problem. Now, assume that the returns of the four stocks are no longer independent. Specifically, the correlations between all pairs of stock returns are given in the file **P04_49.xlsx**.

a. Find the mean and standard deviation of the total amount that this investor earns in one year from these four investments. Compare these results to those you found in the previous problem. Explain the differences in your answers.

b. Suppose that this investor now decides to place $15,000 each in stocks B and D and $5000 each in stocks A and C. How do the mean and standard deviation of the total amount that this investor earns in one year change from the allocation used in part **a**? Provide an intuitive explanation for these changes.

50. A supermarket chain operates five stores of varying sizes in Bloomington, Indiana. Profits (represented as a percentage of sales volume) earned by these five stores are 2.75%, 3%, 3.5%, 4.25%, and 5%, respectively. The means and standard deviations of the daily sales volumes at these five stores are given in the file **P04_50.xlsx**. Assuming that the daily sales volumes are independent, find the mean and standard deviation of the total profit that this supermarket chain earns in one day from the operation of its five stores in Bloomington.

51. A manufacturing company constructs a 1-cm assembly by snapping together four parts that average 0.25 cm in length. The company would like the standard deviation of the length of the assembly to be 0.01 cm. Its engineer, Peter Purdue, believes that the assembly will meet the desired level of variability if each part has standard deviation $0.01/4 = 0.0025$ cm. Instead, show Peter that you can do the job by making each part have standard deviation $0.01/4 \sqrt{4} = 0.005$ cm. This could save the company a lot of money because not as much precision is needed for each part.

52. The weekly demand function for one of a given firm's products can be represented by $q = 200 - 5p$, where q is the number of units purchased (in hundreds) at price p (in dollars). Assume that the price of the product will be an integer value from $10 to $15, with probabilities 0.10, 0.15, 0.25, 0.30, 0.15, and 0.05.

a. Find the mean and standard deviation of p.

b. Find the mean and standard deviation of q.

c. Assuming that it costs this firm $10 to manufacture and sell each unit of the product, express the firm's weekly contribution to profit from the sale of this product (measured in dollars), as a function of the quantity purchased, q.

d. Find the mean and standard deviation of weekly contribution to the firm's profit from the sale of this product.

53. A retailer purchases a batch of 1000 fluorescent lightbulbs from a wholesaler at a cost of $2 per bulb. The wholesaler agrees to replace each defective bulb with one that is guaranteed to function properly for a charge of $0.20 per bulb. The retailer sells the bulbs at a price of $2.50 per bulb and gives his customers free replacements if they bring defective bulbs back to the store. Let X be the number of defective bulbs in a typical batch, and assume that the mean and standard deviation of X are 50 and 10, respectively.

a. Find the mean and standard deviation of the profit (in dollars) the retailer makes from selling a batch of lightbulbs.

b. Find an interval with the property that the retailer can be approximately 95% sure that his profit will be in this interval.

4.9 CONCLUSION

This chapter has introduced some very important concepts, including the basic rules of probability, random variables, probability distributions, and summary measures of probability distributions. We have also shown how computer simulation can be used to help explain some of these concepts. Many of the concepts presented in this chapter will be used in later chapters, so it is important to learn them now. In particular, we rely heavily on probability distributions in Chapter 6 when we discuss decision making under uncertainty. There you will learn how the expected value of a probability distribution is the primary criterion for making decisions. We will also continue to use computer simulation in later chapters to help explain difficult statistical concepts.

Summary of Key Terms

Term	Explanation	Excel	Pages	Equation
Random variable	Associates a numerical value with each possible outcome in a situation involving uncertainty		156	
Probability	A number between 0 and 1 that measures the likelihood that some event will occur		158	
Rule of complements	The probability of any event A and the probability of its complement sum to 1	Basic formulas	159	4.1
Mutually exclusive events	Events where only one of them can occur		200	
Exhaustive events	Events where at least one of them must occur		159	
Addition rule for mutually exclusive events	The probability that at least one of a set of mutually exclusive events will occur is the sum of their probabilities	Basic formulas	159	4.2
Conditional probability formula	Updates the probability of an event, given the knowledge that another event has occurred	Basic formulas	160	4.3
Multiplication rule	Formula for the probability that two events both occur	Basic formulas	160	4.4
Probability tree	A graphical representation of how events occur through time, useful for calculating probabilities		160	

(continued)

Term	Explanation	Excel	Pages	Equation
Probabilistic independence	Events where knowledge that one of them has occurred is of no value in assessing the probability that the other will occur		201	4.5
Relative frequency	The proportion of times the event occurs out of the number of times a random experiment is performed		201	
Cumulative probability	"Less than or equal to" probabilities associated with a random variable		167	
Mean (or expected value) of a probability distribution	A measure of central tendency—the weighted sum of the possible values, weighted by their probabilities	Basic formulas	167	4.6
Variance of a probability distribution	A measure of variability: the weighted sum of the squared deviations of the possible values from the mean, weighted by the probabilities	Basic formulas	168	4.7, 4.9
Standard deviation of a probability distribution	A measure of variability: the square root of the variance	Basic formulas	168	4.8
Simulation	An extremely useful tool that can be used to incorporate uncertainty explicitly into spreadsheet models		173	
Uniformly distributed random numbers	Random numbers such that all decimal values between 0 and 1 are equally likely	=RAND()	173	
Uniformly distributed random integers	Random integers such that all integers between two given values are equally likely	=RAND-BETWEEN(1,6), for example	173	
Covariance between two random variables	A measure of the relationship between two jointly distributed random variables	Basic formulas	177	4.12, 4.14
Correlation between two random variables	A measure of the relationship between two jointly distributed random variables, scaled to be between -1 and $+1$	Basic formulas	201	4.13
Multiplication rule for random variables	Formula for a joint probability as the product of a marginal probability and a conditional probability	Basic formulas	193	4.15, 4.16
Independent random variables	Random variables where information about one of them is no value in terms of predicting the others		189	
Multiplication rule for independent random variables	The joint probability is the product of the marginal probabilities.	Basic formulas	195	4.17
Expected value of a weighted sum of random variables	Useful for finding the expected value of Y, where $Y = a_1 X_1 + a_2 X_2 + \cdots + a_n X_n$	Basic formulas	193	4.18
Variance of a weighted sum of independent random variables	Useful for finding the variance of Y, where $Y = a_1 X_1 + a_2 X_2 + \cdots + a_n X_n$ and the Xs are independent	Basic formulas	194	4.19

(continued)

Summary of Key Terms   (*Continued*)

Term	Explanation	Excel	Pages	Equation
Variance of a weighted sum of dependent random variables	Useful for finding the variance of Y, where $Y = a_1X_1 + a_2X_2 + \cdots + a_nX_n$ and the Xs are not independent	Basic formulas	194	4.20
Covariance in terms of standard deviations and correlation	Used to calculate covariance when only information on correlations and standard deviations is given	Basic formulas	197	4.22

PROBLEMS

Conceptual Questions

C.1. Suppose that you want to find the probability that event A or event B will occur. If these two events are *not* mutually exclusive, explain how you would proceed.

C.2. "If two events are mutually exclusive, they must *not* be independent events." Is this statement true or false? Explain your choice.

C.3. Is the number of passengers who show up for a particular commercial airline flight a discrete or a continuous random variable? Is the time between flight arrivals at a major airport a discrete or a continuous random variable? Explain your answers.

C.4. Suppose that officials in the federal government are trying to determine the likelihood of a major smallpox epidemic in the United States within the next 12 months. Is this an example of an objective probability or a subjective probability? How might the officials assess this probability?

C.5. What is another term for the covariance between a random variable and itself? If this variable is measured in dollars, what are the units of this covariance?

C.6. Consider the statement, "When there are a finite number of outcomes, then all probability is just a matter of counting. Specifically, if n of the outcomes are favorable to some event E, and there are N outcomes total, then the probability of E is n/N." Is this statement always true? Is it always false?

C.7. If there is uncertainty about some monetary outcome and you are concerned about return and risk, then all you need to see are the mean and standard deviation. The entire distribution provides no extra useful information. Do you agree or disagree? Provide an example to back up your argument.

C.8. Choose at least one uncertain quantity of interest to you. For example, you might choose the highest price of gas between now and the end of the year, the highest point the Dow Jones Industrial Average will reach between now and the end of the year, the number of majors Tiger Woods will win in his career, and so on. Using all of the information and insight you have, assess the probability distribution of this uncertain quantity. Is there one "right answer"?

C.9. Historically, the most popular measure of variability has been the standard deviation, the square root of the weighted sum of *squared* deviations from the mean, weighted by their probabilities. Suppose analysts had always used an alternative measure of variability, the weighted sum of the *absolute* deviations from the mean, again weighted by their probabilities. Do you think this would have made a big difference in the theory and practice of probability and statistics?

C.10. Suppose a person flips a coin, but before you can see the result, the person puts her hand over the coin. At this point, does it make sense to talk about the *probability* that the result is heads? Is this any different from the probability of heads *before* the coin was flipped?

C.11. Consider an event that will either occur or not. For example, the event might be that California will experience a major earthquake in the next five years. You let p be the probability that the event will occur. Does it make any sense to have a probability distribution of p? Why or why not? If so, what might this distribution look like? How would you interpret it?

C.12. Suppose a couple is planning to have two children. Let B1 be the event that the first child is a boy, and let B2 be the event that the second child is a boy. You and your friend get into an argument about whether B1 and B2 are *independent* events. You think they are independent and your friend thinks they aren't. Which of you is correct? How could you settle the argument?

Level A

54. A business manager who needs to make many phone calls has estimated that when she calls a client, the probability that she will reach the client right away is 60%. If she does not reach the client on the first call, the probability that she will reach the client with a subsequent call in the next hour is 20%.
   a. Find the probability that the manager reaches her client in two or fewer calls.
   b. Find the probability that the manager reaches her client on the second call but not on the first call.
   c. Find the probability that the manager is unsuccessful on two consecutive calls.

55. Suppose that a marketing research firm sends questionnaires to two different companies. Based on historical evidence, the marketing research firm believes that each company, independently of the other, will return the questionnaire with probability 0.40.
   a. What is the probability that *both* questionnaires are returned?
   b. What is the probability that *neither* of the questionnaires is returned?
   c. Now, suppose that this marketing research firm sends questionnaires to *ten* different companies. Assuming that each company, independently of the others, returns its completed questionnaire with probability 0.40, how do your answers to parts **a** and **b** change?

56. Based on past sales experience, an appliance store stocks five window air conditioner units for the coming week. No orders for additional air conditioners will be made until next week. The weekly consumer demand for this type of appliance has the probability distribution given in the file **P04_56.xlsx**.
   a. Let X be the number of window air conditioner units left at the end of the week (if any), and let Y be the number of special stockout orders required (if any), assuming that a special stockout order is required each time there is a demand and no unit is available in stock. Find the probability distributions of X and Y.
   b. Find the expected value of X and the expected value of Y.
   c. Assume that this appliance store makes a $60 profit on each air conditioner sold from the weekly available stock, but the store loses $20 for each unit sold on a special stockout order basis. Let Z be the profit that the store earns in the coming week from the sale of window air conditioners. Find the probability distribution of Z.
   d. Find the expected value of Z.

57. Simulate 1000 weekly consumer demands for window air conditioner units with the probability distribution given in the file **P04_56.xlsx**. How does your simulated distribution compare to the given probability distribution? Explain any differences between these two distributions.

58. The probability distribution of the weekly demand for copier paper (in hundreds of reams) used in the duplicating center of a corporation is provided in the file **P04_58.xlsx**.
   a. Find the mean and standard deviation of this distribution.
   b. Find the probability that weekly copier paper demand is at least one standard deviation above the mean.
   c. Find the probability that weekly copier paper demand is within one standard deviation of the mean.

59. Consider the probability distribution of the weekly demand for copier paper (in hundreds of reams) used in a corporation's duplicating center, as shown in the file **P04_58.xlsx**.
   a. Use simulation to generate 500 values of this random variable.
   b. Find the mean and standard deviation of the simulated values.
   c. Use your simulated values to estimate the probability that weekly copier paper demand is within one standard deviation of the mean. Why is this only an estimate, not an exact value?

60. The probability distribution of the weekly demand for copier paper (in hundreds of reams) used in the duplicating center of a corporation is provided in the file **P04_58.xlsx**. Assuming that it costs the duplicating center $5 to purchase a ream of paper, find the mean and standard deviation of the weekly copier paper cost for this corporation.

61. The instructor of an introductory organizational behavior course believes that there might be a relationship between the number of writing assignments (X) she gives in the course and the final grades (Y) earned by students in this class. She has taught this course with varying numbers of writing assignments for many semesters and has compiled relevant historical data in the file **P04_61.xlsx**.
   a. Convert the given frequency table to a table of conditional probabilities of final grades (Y) earned by students in this class, given the number of writing assignments (X) in the course. Comment on the table of conditional probabilities. Generally speaking, what does this table tell you?
   b. Given that this instructor requires only one writing assignment in the course, what is the expected final grade earned by the typical student?
   c. How much variability exists around the conditional mean grade you found in part **b**? Also, what proportion of all relevant students earn final grades within two standard deviations of this conditional mean?
   d. Given that this instructor gives *more* than one writing assignment in the course, what is the expected final grade earned by the typical student?
   e. How much variability exists around the conditional mean grade you found in part **d**? What proportion

of all relevant students earn final grades within two standard deviations of this conditional mean?

f. Find the covariance and correlation between X and Y. What does each of these measures tell you? In particular, is this instructor correct in believing that there is a systematic relationship between the number of writing assignments made and final grades earned in her classes?

62. The file **P04_62.xlsx** contains the joint probability distribution of recent weekly trends of two particular stock prices, P_1 and P_2.
   a. Are P_1 and P_2 independent random variables? Explain why or why not.
   b. If P_1 and P_2 are *not* independent random variables, which joint probabilities result in the same *marginal* probabilities for P_1 and P_2 as given in the file but make P_1 and P_2 independent ?

63. Consider two service elevators used in parallel by employees of a three-story hotel building. At any point in time when both elevators are stationary, let X_1 and X_2 be the floor numbers at which elevators 1 and 2, respectively, are currently located. The file **P04_33.xlsx** contains the joint probability distribution of X_1 and X_2.
   a. Are X_1 and X_2 independent random variables? Explain your answer.
   b. If X_1 and X_2 are *not* independent random variables, which joint probabilities result in the same *marginal* probabilities for X_1 and X_2 as given in this file but make X_1 and X_2 independent?

64. A roulette wheel contains the numbers 0, 00, and 1 to 36. If you bet $1 on a single number coming up, you earn $35 if the number comes up and lose $1 otherwise. Find the mean and standard deviation of your winnings on a single bet. Then find the mean and standard deviation of your net winnings if you make 100 bets. You can assume (realistically) that the results of the 100 spins are independent. Finally, provide an interval such that you are 95% sure your net winnings from 100 bets will be inside this interval.

65. Assume that there are four equally likely states of the economy: boom, low growth, recession, and depression. Also, assume that the percentage annual return you obtain when you invest a dollar in gold or the stock market is shown in the file **P04_65.xlsx**.
   a. Find the covariance and correlation between the annual return on the market and the annual return on gold. Interpret your answers.
   b. Suppose you invest 40% of your available money in the market and 60% of your money in gold. Determine the mean and standard deviation of the annual return on your portfolio.
   c. Obtain your part **b** answer by determining the actual return on your portfolio in each state of the economy and then finding the mean and variance

directly, without using any formulas involving covariances or correlations.
   d. Suppose you invested 70% of your money in the market and 30% in gold. Without doing any calculations, determine whether the mean and standard deviation of your portfolio would increase or decrease from your answer in part **b**. Give an intuitive explanation to support your answers.

66. Suppose there are three states of the economy: boom, moderate growth, and recession. The annual return on Honda and Toyota stock in each state of the economy is shown in the file **P04_66.xlsx**.
   a. Calculate the mean and standard deviation of the annual return on each stock, assuming the probability of each state is 1/3.
   b. Calculate the mean and standard deviation of the annual return on each stock, assuming the probabilities of the three states are 1/4, 1/4, and 1/2.
   c. Calculate the covariance and correlation between the annual returns of the two companies' stocks, assuming the probability of each state is 1/3.
   d. Calculate the covariance and correlation between the annual returns of the two companies'stocks, assuming the probabilities of the three states are 1/4, 1/4, and 1/2.
   e. You have invested 25% of your money in Honda and 75% in Toyota. Assuming that each state is equally likely, find the mean and variance of your portfolio's return.
   f. Now check your answer to part **e** by directly calculating the return on your portfolio for each state and use the formulas for mean and variance of a random variable. For example, in the boom state, your portfolio earns 0.25(0.25) + 0.75(0.32).

67. Each year the employees at Zipco receive a $0, $2000, or $4500 salary increase. They also receive a merit rating of 0, 1, 2, or 3, with 3 indicating outstanding performance and 0 indicating poor performance. The joint probability distribution of salary increase and merit rating is listed in the file **P04_67.xlsx**. For example, 20% of all employees receive a $2000 increase and have a merit rating of 1. Find the correlation between salary increase and merit rating. Then interpret this correlation.

68. The return on a portfolio during a period is defined by

$$\frac{PV_{end} - PV_{beg}}{PV_{beg}}$$

where PV_{beg} is the portfolio value at the beginning of a period and PV_{end} is the portfolio value at the end of the period. Suppose there are two stocks in which you can invest, stock 1 and stock 2. During each year there is a 50% chance that each dollar invested in stock 1 will turn into $2 and a 50% chance that each dollar invested in stock 1 will turn into $0.50. During each year there is also a 50% chance that each dollar invested in stock 2 will turn into $2 and a 50% chance that each dollar invested in stock 2 will turn into $0.50.

    a. If you invest all your money in stock 1, find the expected value and standard deviation of your one-year return.

    b. Assume the returns on stocks 1 and 2 are independent random variables. If you put half your money into each stock, find the expected value and standard deviation of your one-year return.

    c. Can you give an intuitive explanation of why the standard deviation in part **b** is smaller than the standard deviation in part **a**?

    d. Use simulation to check your answers to part **b**. Use at least 1000 trials.

69. You are involved in a risky business venture where three outcomes are possible: (1) you will lose not only your initial investment ($5000) but an additional $3000; (2) you will just make back your initial investment (for a net gain of $0); or (3) you will make back your initial investment plus an extra $10,000.

The probability of (1) is half as large as the probability of (2), and the probability of (3) is one-third as large as the probability of (2).

    a. Find the individual probabilities of (1), (2), and (3). (They should sum to 1.)

    b. Find the expected value and standard deviation of your net gain (or loss) from this venture.

70. Suppose X and Y are independent random variables. The possible values of X are -1, 0, and 1; the possible values of Y are 10, 20, and 30. You are given that $P(X = -1 \text{ and } Y = 10) = 0.05$, $P(X = 0 \text{ and } Y = 30) = 0.20$, $P(Y = 10) = 0.20$, and $P(X = 0) = 0.50$. Determine the joint probability distribution of X and Y.

Level B

71. Equation (4.7) for variance indicates exactly what variance is: the weighted average of squared deviations from the mean, weighted by the probabilities. However, the computing formula for variance, Equation (4.9), is more convenient for spreadsheet calculations. Show algebraically that the two formulas are equivalent.

72. Equation (4.10) for covariance indicates exactly what covariance is: the weighted average of products of deviations from the means, weighted by the joint probabilities. However, the computing formula for covariance, Equation (4.12), is more convenient for spreadsheet calculations. Show algebraically that the two formulas are equivalent.

73. The basic game of craps works as follows. You throw two dice. If the sum of the two faces showing up is 7 or 11, you win and the game is over. If the sum is 2, 3, or 12, you lose and the game is over. If the sum is anything else (4, 5, 6, 8, 9, or 10), that value becomes

your "point." You then keep throwing the dice until the sum matches your point or equals 7. If your point occurs first, you win and the game is over. If 7 occurs first, you lose and the game is over. What is the probability that you win the game?

74. Imagine that you are trying to predict the price of gasoline (regular unleaded) and the price of natural gas for home heating during the next month. Assume you believe that the price of either will stay the same, go up by 5%, or go down by 5%. Assess the joint probabilities of these possibilities, that is, assess nine probabilities that sum to 1 and are "realistic." Do you believe it is easier to assess the marginal probabilities of one and the conditional probabilities of the other, or to assess the joint probabilities directly? (*Note*: There is no "correct" answer, but there are unreasonable answers—those that do not reflect reality.)

75. Consider an individual selected at random from a sample of 750 married women (see the data in the file **P04_05.xlsx**) in answering each of the following questions.

    a. What is the probability that this woman does not work outside the home, given that she has at least one child?

    b. What is the probability that this woman has no children, given that she works part time?

    c. What is the probability that this woman has at least two children, given that she does not work full time?

76. Suppose that 8% of all managers in a given company are African American, 13% are women, and 17% have earned an MBA degree from a top-10 graduate business school. Let A, B, and C be, respectively, the events that a randomly selected individual from this population is African American, is a woman, and has earned an MBA from a top-10 graduate business school.

    a. Do you believe that A, B, and C are independent events? Explain why or why not.

    b. Assuming that A, B, and C *are* independent events, find the probability that a randomly selected manager from this company is a white male and has earned an MBA degree from a top-10 graduate business school.

    c. If A, B, and C are *not* independent events, can you calculate the probability requested in part **b** from the information given? What further information would you need?

77. Consider again the supermarket chain described in Problem 50. Now, assume that the daily sales of the five stores are no longer independent of one another. In particular, the file **P04_77.xlsx** contains the correlations between all pairs of daily sales volumes.

    a. Find the mean and standard deviation of the total profit that this supermarket chain earns in one day from the operation of its five stores in Bloomington.

Compare these results to those you found in Problem 50. Explain the differences in your answers.

    b. Find an interval such that the regional sales manager of this supermarket chain can be approximately 95% sure that the total daily profit earned by its stores in Bloomington will be contained within the interval.

78. A manufacturing plant produces two distinct products, A and B. The cost of producing one unit of A is $18 and that of B is $22. Assume that this plant incurs a weekly setup cost of $24,000 regardless of the number of units of A or B produced. The means and standard deviations of the weekly production levels of A and B are given in the **P04_78.xlsx**.

    a. Assuming that the weekly production levels of A and B are independent, find the mean and standard deviation of this plant's total weekly production cost. Between which two total cost figures can you be about 68% sure that this plant's actual total weekly production cost will fall?

    b. How do your answers in part **a** change if you discover that the correlation between the weekly production levels of A and B is actually 0.29? Explain the differences in the two sets of results.

79. The typical standard deviation of the annual return on a stock is 20% and the typical mean return is about 12%. The typical correlation between the annual returns of two stocks is about 0.25. Mutual funds often put an equal percentage of their money in a given number of stocks. By choosing a large number of stocks, they hope to diversify away the risk involved with choosing particular stocks. How many stocks does an investor need to own to diversify away the risk associated with individual stocks? To answer this question, use the above information about "typical" stocks to determine the mean and standard deviation for the following portfolios:

- Portfolio 1: Half your money in each of 2 stocks
- Portfolio 2: 20% of your money in each of 5 stocks
- Portfolio 3: 10% of your money in each of 10 stocks
- Portfolio 4: 5% of your money in each of 20 stocks
- Portfolio 5: 1% of your money in each of 100 stocks

What do your answers tell you about the number of stocks a mutual fund needs to invest in to diversify adequately?

80. You are ordering milk for Mr. D's supermarket, and you are determined to please. Milk is delivered once a week (at midnight Sunday). The mean and standard deviation of the number of gallons of milk demanded each day are given in the file **P04_80.xlsx**. Find the mean and standard deviation of the weekly demand for milk. What assumption must you make to determine the weekly standard deviation? Presently you are ordering 1000 gallons per week. Is this a sensible order quantity? Assume all milk spoils after one week.

81. Two gamblers play a version of roulette with a wheel as shown in the file **P04_81.xlsx**. Each gambler places four bets, but their strategies are different, as explained below. For each gambler, use the rules of probability to find the distribution of their net winnings after four bets. Then find the mean and standard deviation of their net winnings. The file gets you started.

    a. Player 1 always bets on red. On each bet, he either wins or loses what he bets. His first bet is for $10. From then on, he bets $10 following a win, and he doubles his bet after a loss. (This is called a martingale strategy and is used frequently at casinos.) For example, if he spins red, red, not red, and not red, his bets are for $10, $10, $10, and $20, and he has a net loss of $10. Or if he spins not red, not red, not red, and red, then his bets are for $10, $20, $40, and $80, and he has a net gain of $10.

    b. Player 2 always bets on black and green. On each bet, he places $10 on black and $2 on green. If red occurs, he loses all $12. If black occurs, he wins a net $8 ($10 gain on black, $2 loss on green). If green occurs, he wins a net $50 ($10 loss on black, $60 gain on green).

82. Suppose the New York Yankees and Philadelphia Phillies (two Major League Baseball teams) are playing a best-of-three series. The first team to win two games is the winner of the series, and the series ends as soon as one team has won two games. The first game is played in New York, the second game is in Philadelphia, and if necessary the third game is in New York. The probability that the Yankees win a game in their home park is 0.55. The probability that the Phillies win a game in their home park is 0.53. You can assume that the outcomes of the games are independent.

    a. Find the probability that the Yankees win the series.

    b. Suppose you are a Yankees fan, so you place a bet on each game played where you win $100 if the Yankees win the game and you lose $105 if the Yankees lose the game. Find the distribution of your net winnings. Then find the mean and standard deviation of this distribution. Is this betting strategy favorable to you?

    c. Repeat part **a**, but assume that the games are played in Philadelphia, then New York, then Philadelphia. How much does this "home field advantage" help the Phillies?

    d. Repeat part **a**, but now assume that the series is a best-of-five series, where the first team that wins three games wins the series. Assume that games alternate between New York and Philadelphia, with the first game in New York.

83. The application at the beginning of this chapter describes the campaign McDonald's used several years ago, where customers could win various prizes.

a. Verify the figures that are given in the description. That is, argue why there are 10 winning outcomes and 120 total outcomes.

b. Suppose McDonald's had designed the cards so that each card had two zaps and three pictures of the winning prize (and again five pictures of other irrelevant prizes). The rules are the same as before: To win, the customer must uncover all three pictures of the winning prize before uncovering a zap. Would there be more or fewer winners with this design? Argue by calculating the probability that a card is a winner.

c. Going back to the original game (as in part **a**), suppose McDonald's printed one million cards, each of which was eventually given to a customer. Assume that the (potential) winning prizes on these were: 500,000 Cokes worth $0.40 each, 250,000 french fries worth $0.50 each, 150,000 milk shakes worth $0.75 each, 75,000 hamburgers worth $1.50 each, 20,000 cards with $1 cash as the winning prize, 4000 cards with $10 cash as the winning prize, 800 cards with $100 cash as the winning prize, and 200 cards with $1000 cash as the winning prize. Find the expected amount (the dollar equivalent) that McDonald's gave away in winning prizes, assuming everyone played the game and claimed the prize if they won. Also find the standard deviation of this amount.

84. A manufacturing company is trying to decide whether to sign a contract with the government to deliver an instrument to the government no later than eight weeks from now. Due to various uncertainties, the company isn't sure when it will be able to deliver the instrument. Also, when the instrument is delivered, there is a chance that the government will judge it as being of inferior quality. The company estimates that the probability distribution of the time it takes to deliver the instrument is as given in the file **P04_84.xlsx**. Independently of this, it estimates that the probability of rejection due to inferior quality is 0.15. If the instrument is delivered at least a week ahead of time and the government judges the quality to be inferior, the company will have time to fix the problem (with certainty) and still meet the deadline. However, if the delivery is late, or if it is exactly on time but of inferior quality, the government won't pay up. The company expects its cost of manufacturing the instrument to be $45,000. This is a sunk cost that will be incurred regardless of timing or the quality of the instrument. The company also estimates that the cost to fix an inferior instrument depends on the number of weeks left to fix it: $7,500 if there are three weeks left, $10,000 if there are two weeks left, and $15,000 if there is one week left. The government will pay $70,000 for an instrument of sufficient quality delivered on time, but it will pay nothing otherwise. Find the distribution of profit or loss to the company. Then find the mean and standard deviation of this distribution. Do you think the company should sign the contract?

85. Have you ever watched the odds at a horse race? You might hear that the odds against a given horse winning are 9 to 1, meaning that the horse has a probability $1/(1 + 9) = 1/10$ of winning. However, these odds, after being converted to probabilities, typically add to something greater than one. Why is this? Suppose you place a bet of $10 on this horse. It seems that it is a fair bet if you lose your $10 if the horse loses, but you win $90 if the horse wins. However, argue why this isn't really fair to you, that is, argue why your expected winnings are negative.

The results we obtain with conditional probabilities can be quite counterintuitive, even paradoxical. This case is similar to one described in an article by Blyth (1972), and is usually referred to as Simpson's paradox. [Two other examples of Simpson's paradox are described in articles by Westbrooke (1998) and Appleton et al. (1996).] Essentially, Simpson's paradox says that even if one treatment has a better effect than another on *each* of two separate subpopulations, it can have a *worse* effect on the population as a whole.

Suppose that the population is the set of managers in a large company. We categorize the managers as those with an MBA degree (the Bs) and those without an MBA degree (the $\bar{B}$s). These categories are the two "treatment" groups. We also categorize the managers as those who were hired directly out of school by this company (the Cs) and those who worked with another company first (the $\bar{C}$s). These two categories form the two "subpopulations." Finally, we use as a measure of effectiveness those managers who have been promoted within the past year (the As).

Assume the following conditional probabilities are given:

$$P(A|B \text{ and } C) = 0.10, P(A|\bar{B} \text{ and } C) = 0.05 \qquad (4.23)$$

$$P(A|B \text{ and}(\bar{C})) = 0.35, P(A|\bar{B} \text{ and } \bar{C}) = 0.20 \qquad (4.24)$$

$$P(C|B) = 0.90, P(C|\bar{B}) = 0.30 \qquad (4.25)$$

Each of these can be interpreted as a proportion. For example, the probability $P(A|B \text{ and } C)$ implies that 10% of all managers who have an MBA degree and were hired by the company directly out of school were promoted last year. Similar explanations hold for the other probabilities.

Joan Seymour, the head of personnel at this company, is trying to understand these figures. From the probabilities in Equation (4.23), she sees that among the subpopulation of workers hired directly out of school, those with an MBA degree are twice as likely to be promoted as those without an MBA degree. Similarly, from the probabilities in Equation (4.24), she sees that among the subpopulation of workers hired after working with another company, those with an MBA degree are *almost* twice as likely to be promoted as those without an MBA degree. The information provided by the probabilities in Equation (4.25) is somewhat different. From these, she sees that employees with MBA degrees are three times as likely as those without MBA degrees to have been hired directly out of school.

Joan can hardly believe it when a whiz-kid analyst uses these probabilities to show—correctly—that

$$P(A|B) = 0.125, P(A|\bar{B}) = 0.155 \qquad (4.26)$$

In words, those employees *without* MBA degrees are more likely to be promoted than those with MBA degrees. This appears to go directly against the evidence in equations (4.23) and (4.24), both of which imply that MBAs have an advantage in being promoted. Can you derive the probabilities in Equation (4.26)? Can you shed any light on this "paradox"? ∎

Normal, Binomial, Poisson, and Exponential Distributions

CHALLENGING CLAIMS OF *THE BELL CURVE*

One of the most controversial books in recent years is *The Bell Curve* (The Free Press, 1994). The authors are the late Richard Herrnstein, a psychologist, and Charles Murray, an economist, both of whom had extensive training in statistics. The book is a scholarly treatment of differences in intelligence, measured by IQ, and their effect on socioeconomic status (SES). The authors argue, by appealing to many past studies and presenting many statistics and graphs, that there are significant differences in IQ among different groups of people, and that these differences are at least partially responsible for differences in SES. Specifically, their basic claims are that (1) there is a quantity, intelligence, that can be measured by an IQ test; (2) the distribution of IQ scores is essentially a symmetric bell-shaped curve; (3) IQ scores are highly correlated with various indicators of success; (4) IQ is determined predominantly by genetic factors and less so by environmental factors; and (5) African Americans score significantly lower—about 15 points lower—on IQ than whites.

Although the discussion of this latter point takes up a relatively small part of the book, it has generated by far the most controversy. Many criticisms of the authors' racial thesis have been based on emotional arguments. However, it can also be criticized on entirely statistical grounds, as Barnett (1995) has done.[1] Barnett never states that the analysis by Herrnstein and Murray is *wrong*. He merely states that (1) the assumptions behind some of the analysis are at best questionable, and (2) some of the crucial details are not made as explicit as they should have been. As he states, "The issue is not that *The Bell Curve* is demonstrably wrong, but that it falls so far short of being demonstrably right. The book does not meet the burden of proof we might reasonably expect of it."

For example, Barnett takes issue with the claim that the genetic component of IQ is, in the words of Herrnstein and Murray, "unlikely to be smaller than 40 percent or higher than 80 percent." Barnett asks what it would mean if genetics made up, say, 60% of IQ. His only clue from the book is in an endnote, which implies this definition: If a large population of genetically identical newborns grew up in randomly chosen environments, and their IQs were measured once they reached adulthood, then the variance of these IQs would be 60% less than the variance for the entire population. The key word is *variance*. As Barnett notes, however, this statement implies that the corresponding drop in *standard deviation* is only 37%. That is, even if all members of the population were exactly the same genetically, differing environments would create a standard deviation of IQs 63% as large as the standard deviation that exists today. If this is true, it is hard to argue, as Herrnstein and Murray have done, that environment plays a minor role in determining IQ.

Because the effects of different racial environments are so difficult to disentangle from genetic effects, Herrnstein and Murray try at one point to bypass environmental influences on IQ by matching blacks and whites from similar environments. They report that blacks in the top decile of SES have an average IQ of 104, but that whites within that decile have an IQ one standard deviation higher. Even assuming that they have their facts straight, Barnett criticizes the vagueness of their claim. What standard deviation are they referring to: the standard deviation of the entire population or the standard deviation of only the people in the upper decile of SES? The latter is certainly much smaller than the former. Should we assume that the "top-decile blacks" are in the top decile of the black population or of the overall population? If the latter, then the matched comparison between blacks and whites is flawed because the wealthiest 10% of whites have far more wealth than the wealthiest 10% of blacks. Moreover, even if the reference is to the pooled national population, the matching is imperfect. It is possible that the blacks in this pool could average around the ninth percentile, whereas the whites could average around the fourth percentile, with a significant difference in income between the two groups.

The problem is that Herrnstein and Murray never state these details explicitly. Therefore, we have no way of knowing—without collecting and analyzing all of the data ourselves—whether their results are essentially correct. As Barnett concludes his article, "I believe that *The Bell Curve*'s statements about race would have been better left unsaid even if they were definitely true. And they are surely better left unsaid when, as we have seen, their meaning and accuracy [are] in doubt." ■

[1]Arnold Barnett is a professor in operations research at MIT's Sloan School of Management. He specializes in data analysis of health and safety issues.

5.1 INTRODUCTION

In the previous chapter we discussed probability distributions in general. In this chapter we investigate several specific distributions that commonly occur in a variety of business applications. The first of these is a continuous distribution called the *normal* distribution. It is characterized by a symmetric bell-shaped curve and is the cornerstone of statistical theory. The second distribution is a discrete distribution called the *binomial* distribution. It is relevant when we sample from a population with only two types of members or when we perform a series of independent, identical *experiments* with only two possible outcomes. The other two distributions we will discuss briefly are the *Poisson* and *exponential* distributions. These are often used when we are counting events of some type through time, such as arrivals to a bank. In this case, the Poisson distribution, which is discrete, describes the *number* of arrivals in any period of time, and the exponential distribution, which is continuous, describes the *times* between arrivals.

The main goals in this chapter are to present the properties of these distributions, give some examples of when they apply, and show how to perform calculations involving them. Regarding this last objective, analysts have traditionally used special tables to find probabilities or values for the distributions in this chapter. However, these tasks have been simplified with the statistical functions available in Excel. Given the availability of these Excel functions, the traditional tables are no longer necessary.

We cannot overemphasize the importance of these distributions. Almost all of the statistical results discussed in later chapters are based on either the normal distribution or the binomial distribution. The Poisson and exponential distributions play a less important role in this book, but they are nevertheless extremely important in many management science applications. Therefore, it is important for you to become familiar with these distributions before proceeding.

5.2 THE NORMAL DISTRIBUTION

The single most important distribution in statistics is the normal distribution. It is a continuous distribution and is the basis of the familiar symmetric bell-shaped curve. Any particular normal distribution is specified by its mean and standard deviation. By changing the mean, the normal curve shifts to the right or left. By changing the standard deviation, the curve becomes more or less spread out. Therefore, there are really many normal distributions, not just a single one. We say that the normal distribution is a *two-parameter family*, where the two parameters are the mean and standard deviation.

5.2.1 Continuous Distributions and Density Functions

We first take a moment to discuss continuous probability distributions in general. In the previous chapter we discussed discrete distributions, characterized by a list of possible values and their probabilities. The same basic idea holds for continuous distributions such as the normal distribution, but the mathematics is more complex. Now instead of a list of possible values, there is a *continuum* of possible values, such as all values between 0 and 100 or all values greater than 0. Instead of assigning probabilities to each individual value in the continuum, the total probability of 1 is spread over this continuum. The key to this spreading is called a *density function,* which acts like a histogram. The higher the value of the density function, the more likely this region of the continuum is.

Density Function

A **density function**, usually denoted by $f(x)$, specifies the probability distribution of a continuous random variable X. The higher $f(x)$ is, the more likely x is. Also, the total area between the graph of $f(x)$ and the horizontal axis, which represents the total probability, is equal to 1. Finally, $f(x)$ is nonnegative for all possible values of X.

As an example, consider the density function shown in Figure 5.1. (This is *not* a normal density function.) It indicates that all values in the continuum from 25 to 100 are possible, but that the values near 70 are most likely. (This density function might correspond to scores on an exam.) More specifically, because the height of the density at 70 is approximately twice the height of the curve at 84 or 53, a value near 70 is approximately twice as likely as a value near 84 or a value near 53. In this sense, the height of the density function indicates *relative* likelihoods.

Figure 5.1

A Skewed Density Function

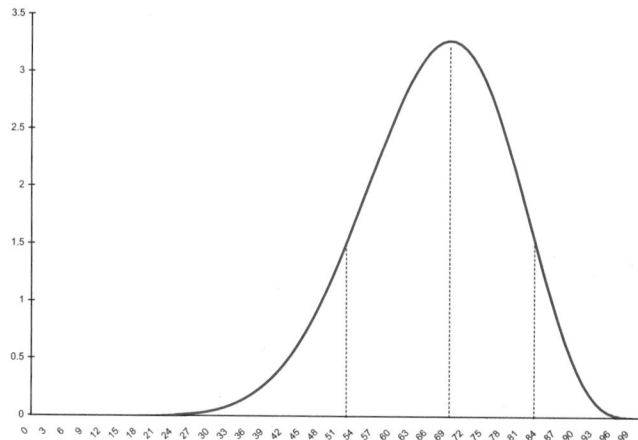

For continuous distributions, probabilities are areas under the density function. These probabilities can often be calculated with Excel functions.

Probabilities are found from a density function as areas under the curve. For example, the area of the designated region in Figure 5.2 represents the probability of a score between 65 and 75. Also, the area under the *entire* curve is 1 because the total probability of all possible values is always 1. Unfortunately, this is about as much as we can say without calculus. Integral calculus is required to find areas under curves. Fortunately, statistical tables have been constructed to find such areas for a number of well-known density functions, including the normal. Even better, Excel functions have been developed to find these

Figure 5.2

Probability as the Area Under the Density

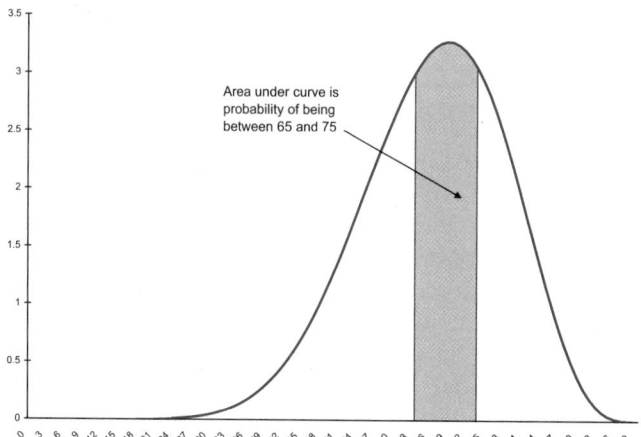

Area under curve is probability of being between 65 and 75

areas—without the need for bulky tables. We take advantage of these Excel functions in the rest of this chapter.

As in the previous chapter, the mean is a measure of central tendency of the distribution, and the standard deviation (or variance) measures the variability of the distribution. Again, however, calculus is generally required to calculate these quantities. We will simply list their values (which *were* obtained through calculus) for the normal distribution and any other continuous distributions where we need them. By the way, the mean for the (non-normal) density in Figure 5.1 is slightly *less* than 70—it is always to the left of the peak for a left-skewed distribution and to the right of the peak for a right-skewed distribution—and the standard deviation is approximately 15.

5.2.2 The Normal Density

The **normal distribution** is a continuous distribution with possible values ranging over the *entire* number line—from "minus infinity" to "plus infinity." However, only a relatively small range has much chance of occurring. The normal density function is actually quite complex, in spite of its "nice" bell-shaped appearance. For the sake of completeness, we list the formula for the normal density function in Equation (5.1). Here, μ and σ are the mean and standard deviation of the distribution.

Normal Density Function

$$f(x) = \frac{1}{\sqrt{2\pi}\sigma} e^{-(x-\mu)^2/(2\sigma^2)} \quad \text{for} \quad -\infty < x < +\infty \qquad \textbf{(5.1)}$$

The curves in Figure 5.3 illustrate several normal density functions for different values of μ and σ. The mean μ can be any number: negative, positive, or zero. As you can see, the effect of increasing or decreasing the mean μ is to shift the curve to the right or the left. On the other hand, the standard deviation σ must be a *positive* number. It controls the spread of the normal curve. When σ is small, the curve is more peaked; when σ is large, the curve is more spread out. For shorthand, we use the notation $N(\mu, \sigma)$ to refer to the normal distribution with mean μ and standard deviation σ. For example, $N(-2, 1)$ refers to the normal distribution with mean -2 and standard deviation 1.

Figure 5.3

Several Normal Density Functions

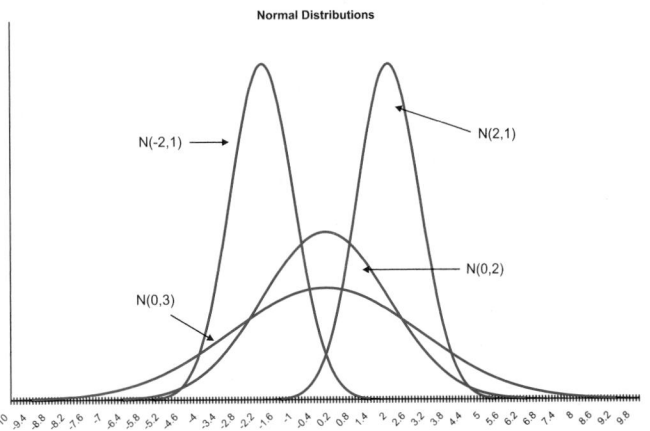

Why the Normal Distribution?

The normal density in Equation (5.1) is certainly not very intuitive, so why is the normal distribution the basis for so much of statistical theory? One reason is practical. Many histograms based on real data resemble the bell-shaped normal curve to a remarkable extent. Granted, not all histograms are symmetric and bell-shaped, but a surprising number are. Another reason is theoretical. In spite of the complexity of Equation (5.1), the normal distribution has many appealing properties that have enabled researchers to build the rich statistical theory that finds widespread use in business, the sciences, and other fields.

5.2.3 Standardizing: Z-Values

There are infinitely many normal distributions, one for each pair μ and σ. We single out one of these for special attention, the *standard* normal distribution. The **standard normal** distribution has mean 0 and standard deviation 1, so we denote it by $N(0,1)$. It is also referred to as the Z distribution. Suppose the random variable X is normally distributed with mean μ and standard deviation σ. We define the random variable Z by Equation (5.2). This operation is called *standardizing*. That is, to **standardize** a variable, you subtract its mean and then divide the difference by the standard deviation. When X is normally distributed, the standardized variable is $N(0, 1)$.

Standardizing a Normal Random Variable

$$Z = \frac{X - \mu}{\sigma}$$

(5.2)

One reason for standardizing is to measure variables with different means and/or standard deviations on a single scale. For example, suppose several sections of a college course are taught by different instructors. Because of differences in teaching methods and grading procedures, the distributions of scores in these sections might differ, possibly by a wide margin. However, if each instructor calculates his or her mean and standard deviation and then calculates a Z-value for each student, the distributions of the Z-values should be approximately the same in each section.

It is easy to interpret a Z-value. It is the number of standard deviations to the right or the left of the mean. If Z is positive, the original value (in this case, the original score) is to the *right* of the mean; if Z is negative, the original score is to the *left* of the mean. For example, if the Z-value for some student is 2, then this student's score is two standard deviations above the mean. If the Z-value for another student is -0.5, then this student's score is half a standard deviation below the mean. We illustrate Z-values in the following example.

EXAMPLE | **5.1 STANDARDIZING RETURNS FROM MUTUAL FUNDS**

The annual returns for 30 mutual funds appear in Figure 5.4. (See the file **Standardizing.xlsx**.) Find and interpret the Z-values of these returns.

Objective To use Excel to standardize annual returns of various mutual funds.

Figure 5.4 Mutual Fund Returns and *Z*-Values

	A	B	C	D	E	F	G	H
1	Standardizing mutual fund returns							
2								
3	Summary statistics from returns below					Calculated two different ways–the second with the Standardize		
4	Mean		0.091	0.000	0.000			
5	Stdev		0.047	1.000	1.000			
6								
7		Fund	Annual return	Z value	Z value		Range names used		
8		1	0.007	-1.8047	-1.8047		Mean	=Data!$B$4	
9		2	0.080	-0.2363	-0.2363		Stdev	=Data!$B$5	
10		3	0.082	-0.1934	-0.1934				
11		4	0.123	0.6875	0.6875				
12		5	0.022	-1.4824	-1.4824				
13		6	0.054	-0.7949	-0.7949				
32		25	0.088	-0.0645	-0.0645				
33		26	0.077	-0.3008	-0.3008				
34		27	0.125	0.7305	0.7305				
35		28	0.094	0.0645	0.0645				
36		29	0.078	-0.2793	-0.2793				
37		30	0.066	-0.5371	-0.5371				

Solution

The 30 annual returns appear in column B of Figure 5.4. Their mean and standard deviation are calculated in cells B4 and B5 with the AVERAGE and STDEV functions. The corresponding *Z*-values are calculated in column C by entering the formula

=(B8-Mean)/Stdev

in cell C8 and copying it down column C.

There is an equivalent way to calculate these *Z*-values in Excel. This is done in column D by using Excel's **STANDARDIZE** function directly. To use this function, enter the formula

=STANDARDIZE(B8,Mean,Stdev)

in cell D8 and copy it down column D.

The *Z*-values in Figure 5.4 range from a low of −1.80 to a high of 2.19. Specifically, the return for stock 1 is about 1.80 standard deviations below the mean, whereas the return for fund 17 is about 2.19 standard deviations above the mean. As you will see shortly, these values are typical: *Z*-values are usually in the range from −2 to +2 and values beyond −3 or +3 are very uncommon. (Recall the *empirical rules* for interpreting standard deviation first discussed in Chapter 2.) Also, the *Z*-values automatically have mean 0 and standard deviation 1, as you can see in cells C5 and C6 by using the AVERAGE and STDEV functions on the *Z*-values in column C (or D). ■

5.2.4 Normal Tables and Z-Values[2]

A common use for Z-values and the standard normal distribution is in calculating probabilities and percentiles by the traditional method. This method is based on a table of the standard normal distribution found in many statistics textbooks. Such a table is given in Figure 5.5. The body of the table contains probabilities. The left and top margins contain possible values. Specifically, suppose you want to find the probability that a standard normal random variable is less than 1.35. You locate 1.3 along the left and 0.05—the second decimal in 1.35—along the top, and then read into the table to find the probability 0.9115. In words, the probability is about 0.91 that a standard normal random variable is less than 1.35.

Figure 5.5 Normal Probabilities

z	0.00	0.01	0.02	0.03	0.04	0.05	0.06	0.07	0.08	0.09
0.0	0.5000	0.5040	0.5080	0.5120	0.5160	0.5199	0.5239	0.5279	0.5319	0.5359
0.1	0.5398	0.5438	0.5478	0.5517	0.5557	0.5596	0.5636	0.5675	0.5714	0.5753
0.2	0.5793	0.5832	0.5871	0.5910	0.5948	0.5987	0.6026	0.6064	0.6103	0.6141
0.3	0.6179	0.6217	0.6255	0.6293	0.6331	0.6368	0.6406	0.6443	0.6480	0.6517
0.4	0.6554	0.6591	0.6628	0.6664	0.6700	0.6736	0.6772	0.6808	0.6844	0.6879
0.5	0.6915	0.6950	0.6985	0.7019	0.7054	0.7088	0.7123	0.7157	0.7190	0.7224
0.6	0.7257	0.7291	0.7324	0.7357	0.7389	0.7422	0.7454	0.7486	0.7517	0.7549
0.7	0.7580	0.7611	0.7642	0.7673	0.7704	0.7734	0.7764	0.7794	0.7823	0.7852
0.8	0.7881	0.7910	0.7939	0.7967	0.7995	0.8023	0.8051	0.8078	0.8106	0.8133
0.9	0.8159	0.8186	0.8212	0.8238	0.8264	0.8289	0.8315	0.8340	0.8365	0.8389
1.0	0.8413	0.8438	0.8461	0.8485	0.8508	0.8531	0.8554	0.8577	0.8599	0.8621
1.1	0.8643	0.8665	0.8686	0.8708	0.8729	0.8749	0.8770	0.8790	0.8810	0.8830
1.2	0.8849	0.8869	0.8888	0.8907	0.8925	0.8944	0.8962	0.8980	0.8997	0.9015
1.3	0.9032	0.9049	0.9066	0.9082	0.9099	0.9115	0.9131	0.9147	0.9162	0.9177
1.4	0.9192	0.9207	0.9222	0.9236	0.9251	0.9265	0.9279	0.9292	0.9306	0.9319
1.5	0.9332	0.9345	0.9357	0.9370	0.9382	0.9394	0.9406	0.9418	0.9429	0.9441
1.6	0.9452	0.9463	0.9474	0.9484	0.9495	0.9505	0.9515	0.9525	0.9535	0.9545
1.7	0.9554	0.9564	0.9573	0.9582	0.9591	0.9599	0.9608	0.9616	0.9625	0.9633
1.8	0.9641	0.9649	0.9656	0.9664	0.9671	0.9678	0.9686	0.9693	0.9699	0.9706
1.9	0.9713	0.9719	0.9726	0.9732	0.9738	0.9744	0.9750	0.9756	0.9761	0.9767
2.0	0.9772	0.9778	0.9783	0.9788	0.9793	0.9798	0.9803	0.9808	0.9812	0.9817
2.1	0.9821	0.9826	0.9830	0.9834	0.9838	0.9842	0.9846	0.9850	0.9854	0.9857
2.2	0.9861	0.9864	0.9868	0.9871	0.9875	0.9878	0.9881	0.9884	0.9887	0.9890
2.3	0.9893	0.9896	0.9898	0.9901	0.9904	0.9906	0.9909	0.9911	0.9913	0.9916
2.4	0.9918	0.9920	0.9922	0.9925	0.9927	0.9929	0.9931	0.9932	0.9934	0.9936
2.5	0.9938	0.9940	0.9941	0.9943	0.9945	0.9946	0.9948	0.9949	0.9951	0.9952
2.6	0.9953	0.9955	0.9956	0.9957	0.9959	0.9960	0.9961	0.9962	0.9963	0.9964
2.7	0.9965	0.9966	0.9967	0.9968	0.9969	0.9970	0.9971	0.9972	0.9973	0.9974
2.8	0.9974	0.9975	0.9976	0.9977	0.9977	0.9978	0.9979	0.9979	0.9980	0.9981
2.9	0.9981	0.9982	0.9982	0.9983	0.9984	0.9984	0.9985	0.9985	0.9986	0.9986
3.0	0.9987	0.9987	0.9987	0.9988	0.9988	0.9989	0.9989	0.9989	0.9990	0.9990
3.1	0.9990	0.9991	0.9991	0.9991	0.9992	0.9992	0.9992	0.9992	0.9993	0.9993
3.2	0.9993	0.9993	0.9994	0.9994	0.9994	0.9994	0.9994	0.9995	0.9995	0.9995
3.3	0.9995	0.9995	0.9995	0.9996	0.9996	0.9996	0.9996	0.9996	0.9996	0.9997
3.4	0.9997	0.9997	0.9997	0.9997	0.9997	0.9997	0.9997	0.9997	0.9997	0.9998

[2]If you intend to rely on Excel functions for normal calculations, you can skip this subsection.

Alternatively, if you are given a probability, you can use the table to find the value with this much probability to the left of it under the standard normal curve. This is called a *percentile* calculation. For example, if the probability is 0.75, you can find the 75th percentile by locating the probability in the table closest to 0.75 and then reading to the left and up. With interpolation, the required value is approximately 0.675. In words, the probability of being to the left of 0.675 under the standard normal curve is approximately 0.75.

You can perform the same kind of calculations for *any* normal distribution if you first standardize. As an example, suppose that X is normally distributed with mean 100 and standard deviation 10. We will find the probability that X is less than 115 and the 85th percentile of this normal distribution. To find the probability that X is less than 115, first standardize the value 115. The corresponding Z-value is

$Z = (115 - 100)/10 = 1.5$

Now look up 1.5 in the table (1.5 row, 0.00 column) to obtain the probability 0.9332. For the percentile question, first find the 85th percentile of the standard normal distribution. Interpolating, a value of approximately 1.037 is obtained. Then set this value equal to a standardized value:

$Z = 1.037 = (X - 100)/10$

Finally, solve for X to obtain 110.37. In words, the probability of being to the left of 110.37 in the $N(100, 10)$ distribution is about 0.85.

There are some obvious drawbacks to using the standard normal table for probability calculations. The first is that there are holes in the table—interpolation is often necessary. A second drawback is that the standard normal table takes different forms in different textbooks. These differences are rather minor, but they can easily cause confusion. Finally, the table requires you to perform calculations. For example, you often need to standardize. More importantly, you often have to use the symmetry of the normal distribution to find probabilities that are not in the table. As an example, to find the probability that Z is less than -1.5, you must go through some mental gymnastics. First, by symmetry this is the same as the probability that Z is greater than 1.5. Then, because only left-tail ("less than") probabilities are tabulated, you must find the probability that Z is less than 1.5 and subtract this probability from 1. The chain of reasoning is

$P(Z < -1.5) = P(Z > 1.5) = 1 - P(Z < 1.5) = 1 - 0.9332 = 0.0668$

This is not too difficult, given a bit of practice, but it is easy to make a mistake. Excel functions make the whole procedure much easier and less error-prone.

5.2.5 Normal Calculations in Excel

Two types of calculations are typically made with normal distributions: finding probabilities and finding percentiles. Excel makes each of these fairly simple. The functions used for normal probability calculations are **NORMDIST** and **NORMSDIST**. The main difference between these is that the one with the "S" (for standardized) applies only to $N(0, 1)$ calculations, whereas NORMDIST applies to *any* normal distribution. On the other hand, percentile calculations that take a probability and return a value are often called *inverse* calculations. Therefore, the Excel functions for these are named **NORMINV** and **NORMSINV**. Again, the "S" in the second of these indicates that it applies to the standard normal distribution.

The NORMDIST and NORMSDIST functions return left-tail probabilities, such as the probability that a normally distributed variable is *less than* 35. The syntax for these functions is

=**NORMDIST**(x,μ,σ,1)

and

=NORMSDIST(x)

Here, x is a number you supply, and μ and σ are the mean and standard deviation of the normal distribution. The last argument in the NORMDIST function, 1, is used to obtain the *cumulative* normal probability, the type usually required. (This 1 is a nuisance to remember, but it is necessary.) Note that NORMSDIST takes only one argument (because μ and σ are known to be 0 and 1), so it is easier to use—when it applies.

The NORMINV and NORMSINV functions return values for user-supplied probabilities. For example, if you supply the probability 0.95, these functions return the 95th percentile. Their syntax is

=NORMINV(p,μ,σ)

and

=NORMSINV(p)

where p is a probability you supply. These are analogous to the NORMDIST and NORMS-DIST functions (except there is no fourth argument in the NORMINV function).

CHANGES IN EXCEL 2010

Many of the statistical functions have been revamped in Excel 2010, as we will point out throughout the next few chapters. Microsoft evidently wanted a more consistent naming convention that would make functions better match the ways they are used in statistical inference. All of the old functions, including the normal functions discussed here, are still available for compatibility, but Microsoft is hoping that users will switch to the new functions. The new normal functions are NORM.DIST, NORM.S.DIST, NORM.INV, and NORM.S.INV. These work exactly like the old normal functions except that NORM.S.DIST takes the same last "cumulative" argument, as was explained above for NORMDIST. The new and old functions are both shown in the file for the next example.

FUNDAMENTAL INSIGHT

Probability and Percentile Calculations

There are two basic types of calculations involving probability distributions, normal or otherwise. In a probability calculation, you provide a possible value, and you ask for the probability of being less than or equal to this value. In a percentile calculation, you provide a probability, and you ask for the value that has this probability to the left of it. Excel's statistical functions, especially with the new names in Excel 2010, use DIST in functions that perform probability calculations and INV (for inverse) in functions that perform percentile calculations.

We illustrate these Excel functions in the following example.[3]

EXAMPLE | 5.2 BECOMING FAMILIAR WITH NORMAL CALCULATIONS IN EXCEL

Use Excel to calculate the following probabilities and percentiles for the standard normal distribution: (a) $P(Z < -2)$, (b) $P(Z > 1)$, (c) $P(-0.4 < Z < 1.6)$, (d) the 5th percentile, (e) the 75th percentile, and (f) the 99th percentile. Then for the $N(75, 8)$ distribution, find the following probabilities and percentiles: (a) $P(X < 70)$, (b) $P(X > 73)$, (c) $P(75 < X < 85)$, (d) the 5th percentile, (e) the 60th percentile, and (f) the 97th percentile.

[3]Actually, we already illustrated the NORMSDIST function; it was used to create the body of Figure 5.5. In other words, you can use it to build your own normal probability table.

Objective   To calculate probabilities and percentiles for standard normal and general normal distributions in Excel.

Solution

The solution appears in Figure 5.6. (See the file **Normal Calculations.xlsx.**) The $N(0, 1)$ calculations are in rows 7 through 14; the $N(75, 8)$ calculations are in rows 23 through 30. For your convenience, the formulas used in column B are spelled out in column D (as labels). Note that the standard normal calculations use the normal functions with the "S" in the middle; the rest use the normal functions without the "S"—and require more arguments. (The Excel 2010 functions don't appear in this figure, but they are included in the file.)

Figure 5.6   Normal Calculations with Excel Functions

	A	B	C	D	E	F	G	H	I
1	**Normal probability calculations**								
2									
3	**Examples with standard normal**								
4									
5	**Probability calculations**								
6	Range	Probability		Formula					
7	Less than -2	0.0228		=NORMSDIST(-2)					
8	Greater than 1	0.1587		=1-NORMSDIST(1)					
9	Between -0.4and1.6	0.6006		=NORMSDIST(1.6)-NORMSDIST(-0.4)					
10									
11	**Percentiles**								
12	5th	-1.645		=NORMSINV(0.05)					
13	75th	0.674		=NORMSINV(0.75)					
14	99th	2.326		=NORMSINV(0.99)					
15									
16	**Examples with nonstandard normal**								
17				**Range names used:**					
18	Mean	75		Mean	=Normal!$B$18				
19	Stdev	8		Stdev	=Normal!$B$19				
20									
21	**Probability calculations**								
22	Range	Probability		Formula					
23	Less than 70	0.2660		=NORMDIST(70,Mean,Stdev,1)					
24	Greater than 73	0.5987		=1-NORMDIST(73,Mean,Stdev,1)					
25	Between 75 and 85	0.3944		=NORMDIST(85,Mean,Stdev,1) -NORMDIST(75,Mean,Stdev,1)					
26									
27	**Percentiles**								
28	5th	61.841		=NORMINV(0.05,Mean,Stdev)					
29	60th	77.027		=NORMINV(0.6,Mean,Stdev)					
30	97th	90.046		=NORMINV(0.97,Mean,Stdev)					

Note the following for normal *probability* calculations:

■   For "less than" probabilities, use NORMDIST or NORMSDIST directly. (See rows 7 and 23.)

- For "greater than" probabilities, subtract the NORMDIST or NORMSDIST function from 1. (See rows 8 and 24.)

- For "between" probabilities, subtract the two NORMDIST or NORMSDIST functions. For example, in row 9 the probability of being between −0.4 and 1.6 is the probability of being less than 1.6 minus the probability of being less than −0.4.

The percentile calculations are even more straightforward. In most percentile problems you want to find the value with a certain probability to the *left* of it. In this case you use the NORMINV or NORMSINV function with the specified probability as the first argument. See rows 12 through 14 and 28 through 30. ∎

There are a couple of variations of percentile calculations. First, suppose you want the value with probability 0.05 to the *right* of it. This is the same as the value with probability 0.95 to the left of it, so you use NORMINV or NORMSINV with probability argument 0.95. For example, the value with probability 0.4 to the right of it in the N(75, 8) distribution is 77.027. (See cell B29 in Figure 5.6.)

As a second variation, suppose you want to find an interval of the form −x to x, for some positive number x, with (1) probability 0.025 to the left of −x, (2) probability 0.025 to the right of x, and (3) probability 0.95 between −x and x. This is a very common problem in statistical inference. In general, you want a probability (such as 0.95) to be in the middle of the interval so that half of the remaining probability (0.025) is in each of the tails. (See Figure 5.7.) Then the required x can be found with NORMINV or NORMSINV, using probability argument 0.975, because there must be a total probability of 0.975 to the left of x.

For example, if the relevant distribution is the standard normal, the required value of x is 1.96, found with the function NORMSINV(0.975). Similarly, if you want probability 0.90 in the middle and probability 0.05 in each tail, the required x is 1.645, found with the function NORMSINV(0.95). Remember these two numbers, 1.96 and 1.645. They occur frequently in statistical applications.

Figure 5.7

Typical Normal Probabilities

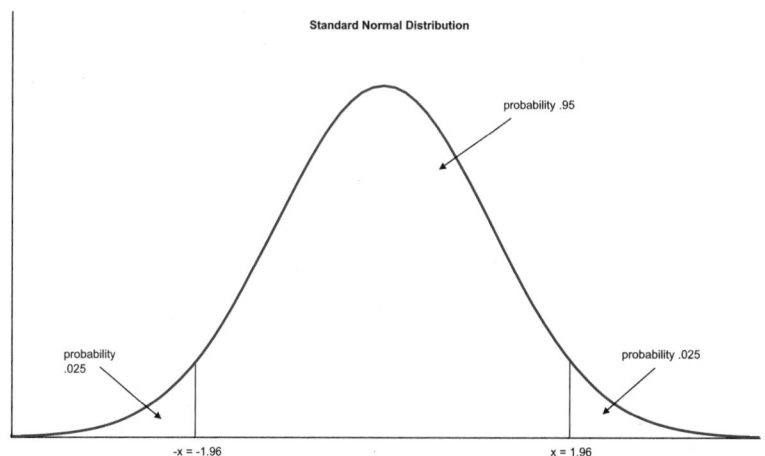

5.2.6 Empirical Rules Revisited

We introduced three empirical rules in Chapter 2 that apply to many data sets. Namely, about 68% of the data fall within one standard deviation of the mean, about 95% fall within two standard deviations of the mean, and almost all fall within three standard deviations of the mean. For these rules to hold with real data, the distribution of the data must be at least approximately symmetric and bell-shaped. Let's look at these rules more closely.

Let X be normally distributed with mean μ and standard deviation σ. To perform a probability calculation on X, we can first standardize X and then perform the calculation on the standardized variable Z. Specifically, we will find the probability that X is within k standard deviations of its mean for $k = 1$, $k = 2$, and $k = 3$. In general, this probability is $P(\mu - k\sigma < X < \mu + k\sigma)$. But by standardizing the values $\mu - k\sigma$ and $\mu + k\sigma$, we obtain the equivalent probability $P(-k < Z < k)$, where Z has a $N(0, 1)$ distribution. This latter probability can be calculated in Excel with the formula

=NORMSDIST(k)—NORMSDIST(—k)

The normal distribution is the basis for the empirical rules introduced in Chapter 2.

By substituting the values 1, 2, and 3 for k, we find the following probabilities:

$P(-1 < Z < 1) = 0.6827$

$P(-2 < Z < 2) = 0.9545$

$P(-3 < Z < 3) = 0.9973$

As you can see, there is virtually no chance of being beyond three standard deviations from the mean, the chances are about 19 out of 20 of being within two standard deviations of the mean, and the chances are about 2 out of 3 of being within one standard deviation of the mean. These probabilities are the basis for the empirical rules in Chapter 2. These rules more closely approximate reality as the histograms of observed data become more bell-shaped.

5.3 APPLICATIONS OF THE NORMAL DISTRIBUTION

In this section we apply the normal distribution to a variety of business problems.

EXAMPLE	5.3 PERSONNEL TESTING AT ZTEL

The personnel department of ZTel, a large communications company, is reconsidering its hiring policy. Each applicant for a job must take a standard exam, and the hire or no-hire decision depends at least in part on the result of the exam. The scores of all applicants have been examined closely. They are approximately normally distributed with mean 525 and standard deviation 55.

The current hiring policy occurs in two phases. The first phase separates all applicants into three categories: automatic accepts, automatic rejects, and maybes. The automatic accepts are those whose test scores are 600 or above. The automatic rejects are those whose test scores are 425 or below. All other applicants (the maybes) are passed on to a second phase where their previous job experience, special talents, and other factors are used as hiring criteria. The personnel manager at ZTel wants to calculate the percentage of applicants who are automatic accepts or rejects, given the current standards. She also wants to know how to change the standards to automatically reject 10% of all applicants and automatically accept 15% of all applicants.

Objective To determine test scores that can be used to accept or reject job applicants at ZTel.

Solution

Let X be the test score of a typical applicant. Then historical data suggest that the distribution of X is $N(525, 55)$. A probability such as $P(X \leq 425)$ can be interpreted as the probability that a typical applicant is an automatic reject, or it can be interpreted as the percentage of *all* applicants who are automatic rejects. Given this observation, the solution to ZTel's problem appears in Figure 5.8. (See the file **Personnel Decisions.xlsx**.) The probability that a typical applicant is automatically accepted is 0.0863, found in cell B10 with the formula

=1−NORMDIST(B7,Mean,Stdev,1)

Figure 5.8

Calculations for Personnel Example

	A	B	C	D	E	F
1	**Personnel Decisions**					
2				**Range names used:**		
3	Mean of test scores	525		Mean	=Model!$B$3	
4	Stdev of test scores	55		Stdev	=Model!$B$4	
5						
6	**Current Policy**					
7	Automatic accept point	600				
8	Automatic reject point	425				
9						
10	Percent accepted	8.63%		=1-NORMDIST(B7,Mean,Stdev,1)		
11	Percent rejected	3.45%		=NORMDIST(B8,Mean,Stdev,1)		
12						
13	**New Policy**					
14	Percent accepted	15%				
15	Percent rejected	10%				
16						
17	Automatic accept point	582		=NORMINV(1-B14,Mean,Stdev)		
18	Automatic reject point	455		=NORMINV(B15,Mean,Stdev)		

Similarly, the probability that a typical applicant is automatically rejected is 0.0345, found in cell B11 with the formula

=NORMDIST(B8,Mean,Stdev,1)

Therefore, ZTel automatically accepts about 8.6% and rejects about 3.5% of all applicants under the current policy.

To find new cutoff values that reject 10% and accept 15% of the applicants, we need the 10th and 85th percentiles of the $N(525, 55)$ distribution. These are 455 and 582 (rounded to the nearest integer), respectively, found in cells B17 and B18 with the formulas

=NORMINV(1-B14,Mean,Stdev)

and

=NORMINV(B15,Mean,Stdev)

To accomplish its objective, ZTel needs to raise the automatic rejection point from 425 to 455 and lower the automatic acceptance point from 600 to 582. ∎

EXAMPLE | 5.4 QUALITY CONTROL AT PAPERSTOCK COMPANY

The PaperStock Company runs a manufacturing facility that produces a paper product. The fiber content of this product is supposed to be 20 pounds per 1000 square feet. (This is typical for the type of paper used in grocery bags, for example.) Because of random variations in the inputs to the process, however, the fiber content of a typical 1000-square-foot roll varies according to a $N(\mu, \sigma)$ distribution. The mean fiber content (μ)

can be controlled—that is, it can be set to any desired level by adjusting an instrument on the machine. The variability in fiber content, as measured by the standard deviation σ, is 0.10 pound when the process is "good," but it sometimes increases to 0.15 pound when the machine goes "bad." A given roll of this product must be rejected if its actual fiber content is less than 19.8 pounds or greater than 20.3 pounds. Calculate the probability that a given roll is rejected, for a setting of $\mu = 20$, when the machine is "good" and when it is "bad."

Objective To determine the machine settings that result in paper of acceptable quality at PaperStock Company.

Solution

Let X be the fiber content of a typical roll. The distribution of X will be either $N(20, 0.10)$ or $N(20, 0.15)$, depending on the status of the machine. In either case, the probability that the roll must be rejected can be calculated as shown in Figure 5.9. (See the file **Paper Machine Settings.xlsx**.) The formula for rejection in the "good" case appears in cell B12:

=NORMDIST(B8,Mean,Stdev_good,1)+(1-NORMDIST(B9,Mean,Stdev_good,1))

Figure 5.9   Calculations for Paper Quality Example

	A	B	C	D	E	F	G	H	I	J
1	**Paper Machine Settings**			Range names used:						
2				Mean	=Model!$B$3					
3	Mean	20		Stdev_good	=Model!$B$4					
4	Stdev in good case	0.1		Stdev_bad	=Model!$B$5					
5	Stdev in bad case	0.15								
6										
7	Reject region									
8	Lower limit	19.8								
9	Upper limit	20.3								
10										
11	Probability of reject									
12	in good case	0.024		=NORMDIST(B8,Mean,Stdev_good,1)+(1-NORMDIST(B9,Mean,Stdev_good,1))						
13	in bad case	0.114		=NORMDIST(B8,Mean,Stdev_bad,1)+(1-NORMDIST(B9,Mean,Stdev_bad,1))						
14										
15	Data table of rejection probability as a function of the mean and good standard deviation									
16					Standard deviation					
17		0.024	0.10	0.11	0.12	0.13	0.14	0.15		
18		19.7	0.841	0.818	0.798	0.779	0.762	0.748		
19		19.8	0.500	0.500	0.500	0.500	0.500	0.500		
20		19.9	0.159	0.182	0.203	0.222	0.240	0.256		
21	Mean	20.0	0.024	0.038	0.054	0.072	0.093	0.114		
22		20.1	0.024	0.038	0.054	0.072	0.093	0.114		
23		20.2	0.159	0.182	0.203	0.222	0.240	0.256		
24		20.3	0.500	0.500	0.500	0.500	0.500	0.500		
25		20.4	0.841	0.818	0.798	0.779	0.762	0.748		

This is the sum of two probabilities: the probability of being to the left of the lower limit and the probability of being to the right of the upper limit. These probabilities of rejection are represented graphically in Figure 5.10. A similar formula for the "bad" case appears in cell B13, using Stdev_bad in place of Stdev_good.

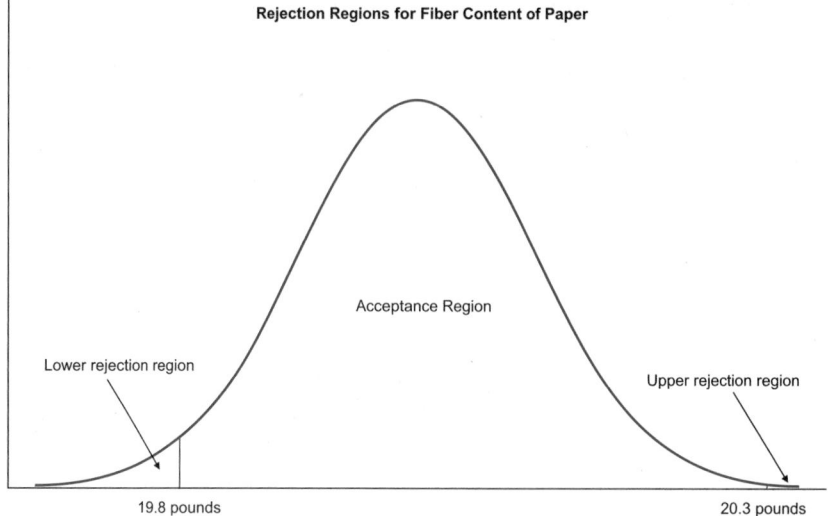

Figure 5.10

Rejection Regions for Paper Quality Example

Rejection Regions for Fiber Content of Paper

Acceptance Region

Lower rejection region

Upper rejection region

19.8 pounds

20.3 pounds

To form this data table, enter the formula =B12 in cell B17, highlight the range B17:H25, and create a data table with row input cell B4 and column input cell B3.

You can see that the probability of a rejected roll in the "good" case is 0.024; in the "bad" case it is 0.114. That is, when the standard deviation increases by 50% from 0.10 to 0.15, the percentage of rolls rejected more than quadruples, from 2.4% to 11.4%.

It is certainly possible that the true process mean and "good" standard deviation will not always be equal to the values in cells B3 and B4. Therefore, it is useful to see how sensitive the rejection probability is to these two parameters. You can do this with a two-way data table, as shown in Figure 5.9. The tabulated values show that the probability of rejection varies greatly even for small changes in the key inputs. In particular, a combination of a badly centered mean and a large standard deviation can make the probability of rejection quite large. ∎

EXAMPLE | **5.5 ANALYZING AN INVESTOR'S AFTER-TAX PROFIT**

Howard Davis invests $10,000 in a certain stock on January 1. By examining past movements of this stock and consulting with his broker, Howard estimates that the annual return from this stock, X, is normally distributed with mean 10% and standard deviation 4%. Here X (when expressed as a decimal) is the profit Howard receives per dollar invested. It means that on December 31, his $10,000 will have grown to $10,000(1 + X)$ dollars. Because Howard is in the 33% tax bracket, he will then have to pay the Internal Revenue Service 33% of his profit. Calculate the probability that Howard will have to pay the IRS at least $400. Also, calculate the dollar amount such that Howard's after-tax profit is 90% certain to be less than this amount; that is, calculate the 90th percentile of his after-tax profit.

Objective   To determine the after-tax profit Howard Davis can be 90% certain of earning.

Solution

Howard's before-tax profit is $10,000X$ dollars, so the amount he pays the IRS is $0.33(10,000X)$, or $3300X$ dollars. We want the probability that this is at least $400. Because $3300X > 400$ is the same as $X > 4/33$, the probability of this outcome can be found as in Figure 5.11. (See the file **Tax on Stock Return.xlsx**.) It is calculated with the formula

=1-NORMDIST(400/(Amount_invested*Tax_rate),Mean,Stdev,1)

in cell B8. As you can see, Howard has about a 30% chance of paying at least $400 in taxes.

To answer the second question, note that the after-tax profit is 67% of the before-tax profit, or $6700X$ dollars, and we want its 90th percentile. If this percentile is x, then we know that $P(6700X < x) = 0.90$, which is the same as $P(X < x/6700) = 0.90$. In words, we want the 90th percentile of the X distribution to be $x/6700$. From cell B10 of Figure 5.11, the 90th percentile is 15.13%, so the required value of x is $1,013. Note that the *mean* after-tax profit is $670 (67% of the mean before-tax profit of 0.10 multiplied by $10,000). Of course, Howard might get lucky and make more than this, but he is 90% certain that his after-tax profit will be no greater than $1013.

Figure 5.11   Calculations for Taxable Returns Example

	A	B	C	D	E	F	G	H	I
1	Tax on Stock Return								
2				Range names used:					
3	Amount invested	$10,000		Amount_invested	=Model!$B$3				
4	Mean	10%		Mean	=Model!$B$4				
5	Stdev	4%		Stdev	=Model!$B$5				
6	Tax rate	33%		Tax_rate	=Model!$B$6				
7									
8	Probability he pays at least $400 in taxes	0.298		=1-NORMDIST(400/(Amount_invested*Tax_rate),Mean,Stdev,1)					
9									
10	90th percentile of stock return	15.13%		=NORMINV(0.9,Mean,Stdev)					
11	90th percentile of after-tax return	$1,013		=(1-Tax_rate)*Amount_invested*B10					

It is sometimes tempting to model every continuous random variable with a normal distribution. This can be dangerous for at least two reasons. First, not all random variables have a *symmetric* distribution. Some are skewed to the left or the right, and for these the normal distribution can be a poor approximation to reality. The second problem is that many random variables in real applications must be *nonnegative*, and the normal distribution allows the possibility of negative values. The following example shows how assuming normality can get you into trouble if you aren't careful.

EXAMPLE

5.6 PREDICTING FUTURE DEMAND FOR MICROWAVE OVENS AT HIGHLAND COMPANY

The Highland Company is a retailer that sells microwave ovens. The company wants to model its demand for microwaves over the next 12 years. Using historical data as a guide, it assumes that demand in year 1 is normally distributed with mean 5000 and standard deviation 1500. It assumes that demand in each subsequent year is normally distributed with mean equal to the *actual* demand from the previous year and standard deviation 1500. For example, if demand in year 1 turns out to be 4500, then the *mean* demand in year 2 is 4500. This assumption is plausible because it leads to correlated demands. For example, if demand is high one year, it will tend to be high the next year. Investigate the ramifications of this model, and suggest models that might be more realistic.

Objective To construct and analyze a spreadsheet model for microwave oven demand over the next 12 years using Excel's NORMINV function, and to show how models using the normal distribution can lead to nonsensical outcomes unless they are modified appropriately.

Solution

To generate a random number from a normal distribution, use NORMINV with three arguments: RAND(), the mean, and the standard deviation.

The best way to analyze this model is with simulation, much as in Chapter 4. To do this, you must be able to simulate normally distributed random numbers in Excel. You can do this with the NORMINV function. Specifically, to generate a normally distributed number with mean μ and standard deviation σ, use the formula

=NORMINV(RAND(),μ,σ)

Because this formula uses the RAND function, it generates a *different* random number each time it is used—and each time the spreadsheet recalculates.[4]

    The spreadsheet in Figure 5.12 shows a simulation of yearly demands over a 12-year period. (See the file **Oven Demand Simulation.xlsx.**) To simulate the demands in row 15, enter the formula

=NORMINV(RAND(),B6,B7)

in cell B15. Then enter the formula

=NORMINV(RAND(),B15,$B$11)

Figure 5.12 One Set of Demands for Model 1 in the Microwave Example

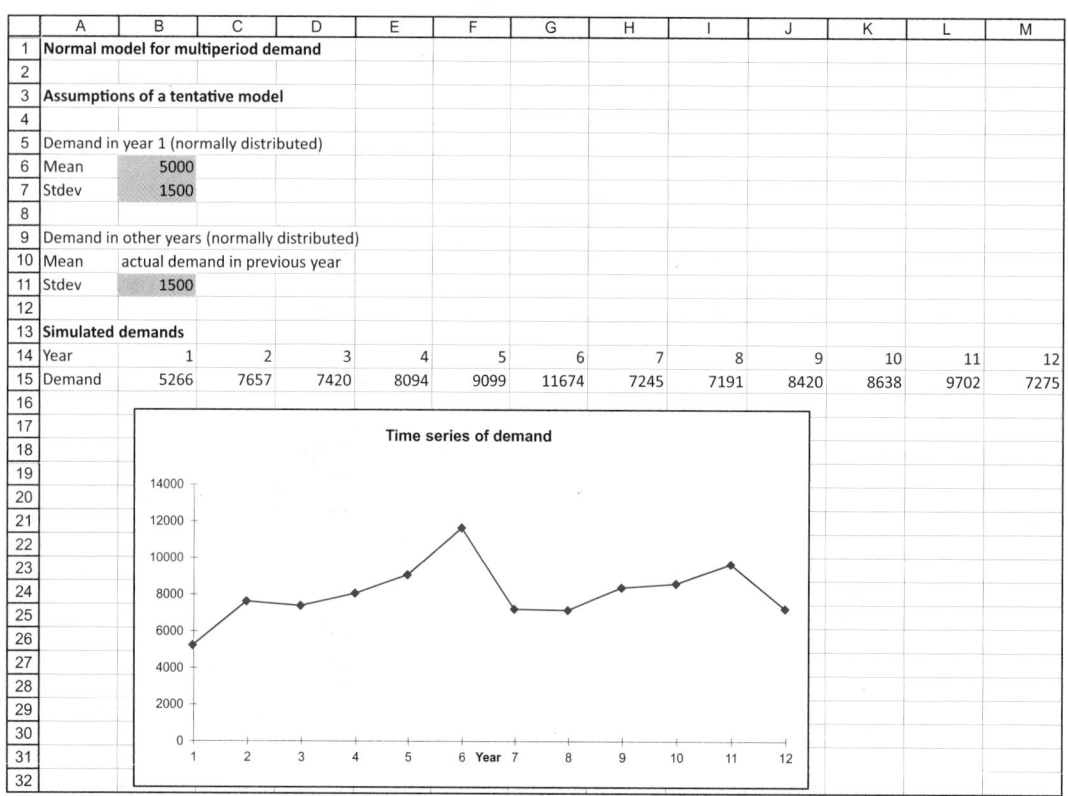

	A	B	C	D	E	F	G	H	I	J	K	L	M
1	Normal model for multiperiod demand												
2													
3	Assumptions of a tentative model												
4													
5	Demand in year 1 (normally distributed)												
6	Mean	5000											
7	Stdev	1500											
8													
9	Demand in other years (normally distributed)												
10	Mean	actual demand in previous year											
11	Stdev	1500											
12													
13	Simulated demands												
14	Year	1	2	3	4	5	6	7	8	9	10	11	12
15	Demand	5266	7657	7420	8094	9099	11674	7245	7191	8420	8638	9702	7275
16													

---

[4]To see why this formula makes sense, note that the RAND function in the first argument generates a uniformly distributed random value between 0 and 1. Therefore, the effect of the function is to generate a random *percentile* from the normal distribution.

in cell C15 and copy it across row 15. (Note how the mean demand in any year is the *simulated* demand from the previous year.) As the accompanying time series graph of these demands indicates, the model seems to be performing well.

However, the simulated demands in Figure 5.12 are only one set of possible demands. Remember that each time the spreadsheet recalculates, all of the random numbers change.[5] Figure 5.13 shows a different set of random numbers generated by the *same* formulas. Clearly, the model is not working well in this case—some demands are negative, which makes no sense. The problem is that if the actual demand is low in one year, there is a fairly good chance that the next normally distributed demand will be negative. You can check (by recalculating many times) that the demand sequence is *usually* all positive, but every now and then a nonsense sequence as in Figure 5.13 appears. We need a new model!

One way to modify the model is to let the standard deviation and mean move together. That is, if the mean is low, then the standard deviation will also be low. This minimizes the chance that the *next* random demand will be negative. Besides, this type of model is probably more realistic. If demand in one year is low, there could be less variability in next year's demand. Figure 5.14 illustrates one way (but not the only way) to model this changing standard deviation.

Figure 5.13   Another Set of Demands for Model 1 in the Microwave Example

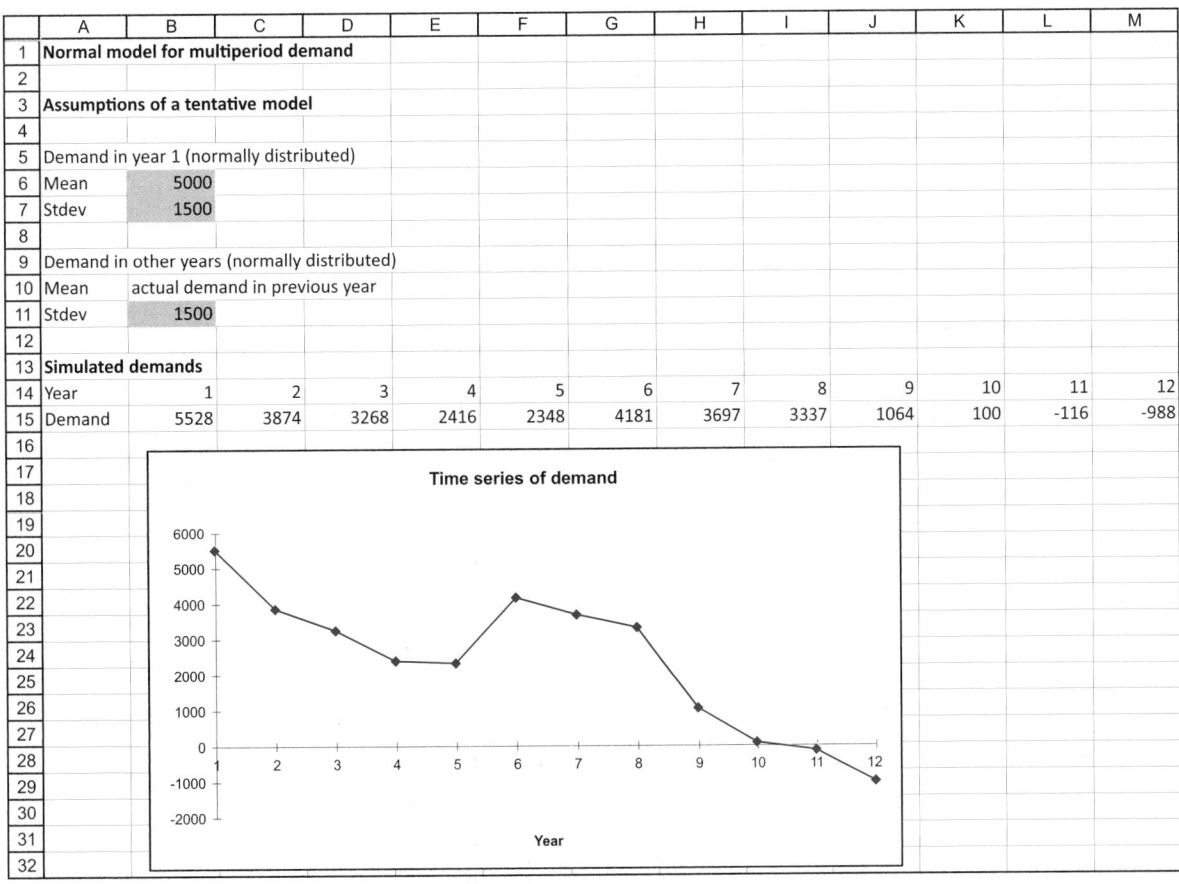

	A	B	C	D	E	F	G	H	I	J	K	L	M
1	Normal model for multiperiod demand												
2													
3	Assumptions of a tentative model												
4													
5	Demand in year 1 (normally distributed)												
6	Mean	5000											
7	Stdev	1500											
8													
9	Demand in other years (normally distributed)												
10	Mean	actual demand in previous year											
11	Stdev	1500											
12													
13	Simulated demands												
14	Year	1	2	3	4	5	6	7	8	9	10	11	12
15	Demand	5528	3874	3268	2416	2348	4181	3697	3337	1064	100	-116	-988
16													
17				Time series of demand									

[5]The usual way to get Excel to recalculate is to press the F9 key. However, this makes all of the data tables in the workbook recalculate, which can take significant time. Because there is a data table in another sheet of the **Oven Demand Simulation.xlsx** file, we suggest a different way to recalculate. Simply position the cursor on any blank cell and press the Delete key.

Figure 5.14   Generated Demands for Model 2 in Microwave Example

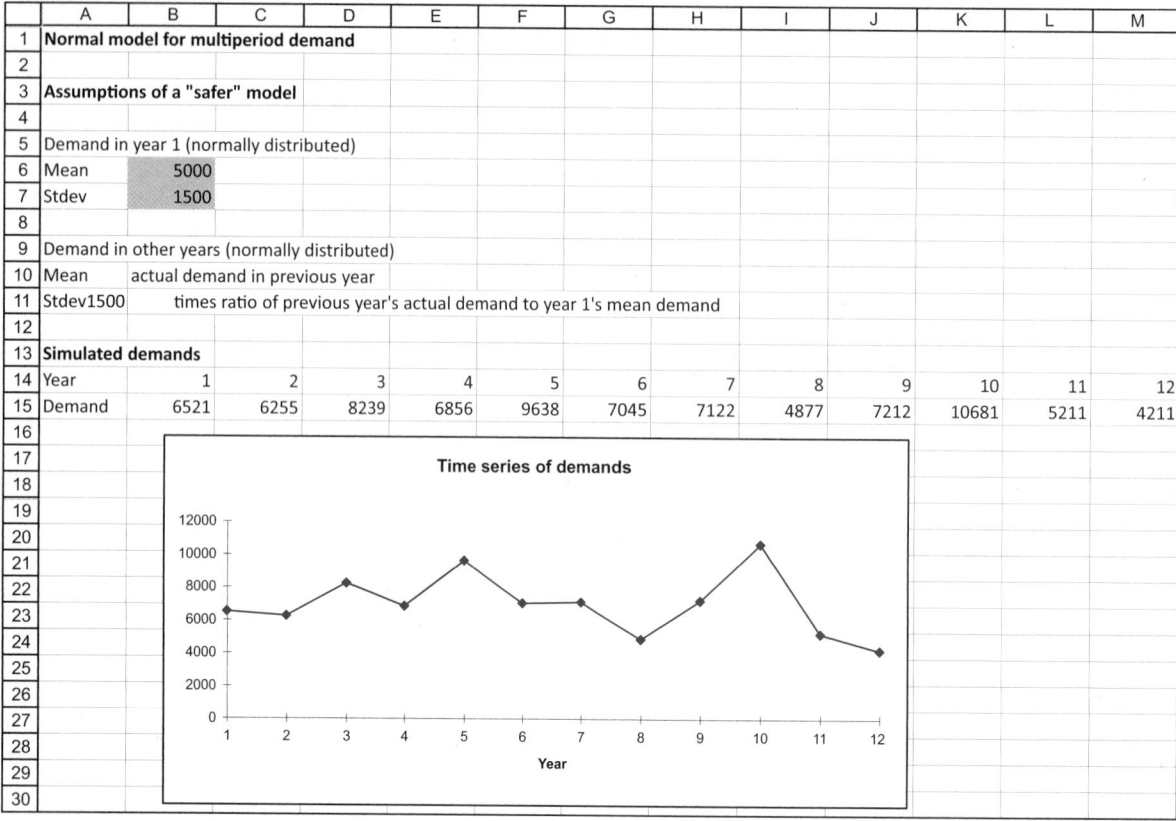

We let the standard deviation of demand in any year (after year 1) be the original standard deviation, 1500, multiplied by the ratio of the expected demand for this year to the expected demand in year 1. For example, if demand in some year is 500, the expected demand next year is 500, and the standard deviation of next year's demand is reduced to 1500(500/5000) = 150. The only change to the spreadsheet model is in row 15, where cell C15 contains the formula

=NORMINV(RAND(),B15,$B$7*B15/$B$6)

and is copied across row 15. Now the chance of a negative demand is practically negligible because this would require a value more than three standard deviations below the mean.

Unfortunately, the model in Figure 5.14 is still not foolproof. By recalculating many times, negative demands still appear occasionally. To be even safer, it is possible to *truncate* the demand distribution at some nonnegative value such as 250, as shown in Figure 5.15. Now a random demand is generated as in the previous model, but if this randomly generated value is below 250, it is replaced by 250. This is done with the formulas

=MAX(NORMINV(RAND(),B8,B9),D5)

and

=MAX(NORMINV(RAND(),B17,$B$9*B17/$B$8),$D$5)

in cells B17 and C17 and copying this latter formula across row 17. Whether this is the way the demand process works for Highland's microwaves is an open question, but at

Figure 5.15 Generated Demands for a Truncated Model in Microwave Example

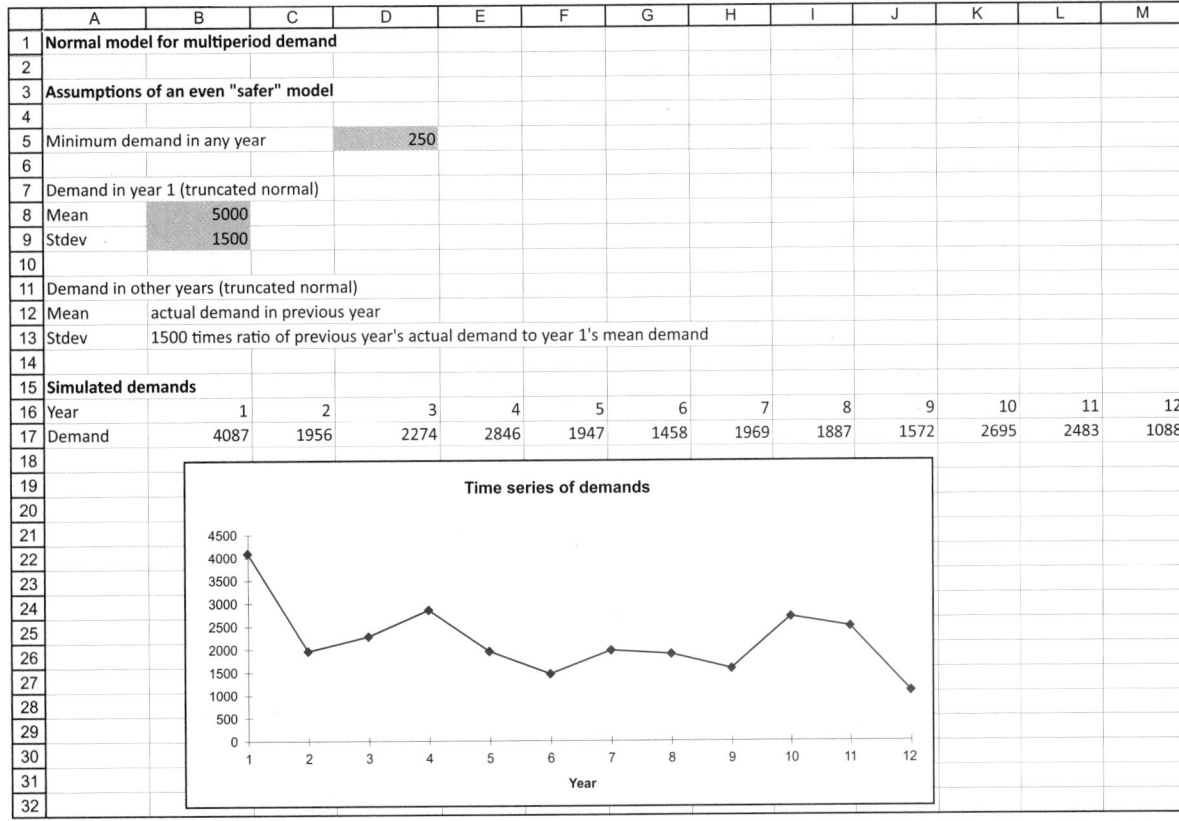

	A	B	C	D	E	F	G	H	I	J	K	L	M
1	Normal model for multiperiod demand												
2													
3	Assumptions of an even "safer" model												
4													
5	Minimum demand in any year			250									
6													
7	Demand in year 1 (truncated normal)												
8	Mean	5000											
9	Stdev	1500											
10													
11	Demand in other years (truncated normal)												
12	Mean	actual demand in previous year											
13	Stdev	1500 times ratio of previous year's actual demand to year 1's mean demand											
14													
15	Simulated demands												
16	Year	1	2	3	4	5	6	7	8	9	10	11	12
17	Demand	4087	1956	2274	2846	1947	1458	1969	1887	1572	2695	2483	1088
18													

least it prevents demands from becoming negative—or even falling below 250. Moreover, this type of truncation is a common way of modeling when you want to use a normal distribution but for physical reasons cannot allow the random quantities to become negative.

Before leaving this example, we challenge your intuition. In the final model in Figure 5.15, the demand in any year (say, year 6) is, aside from the truncation, normally distributed with a mean and standard deviation that depend on the previous year's demand. Does this mean that if you recalculate many times and keep track of the year 6 demand each time, the resulting histogram of these year 6 demands will be normally distributed? Perhaps surprisingly, the answer is a clear no. Evidence of this appears in Figures 5.16 and 5.17. In Figure 5.16 we use a data table to obtain 400 replications of demand in year 6 (in column B). Then we use StatTools's histogram procedure to create a histogram of these simulated demands in Figure 5.17. It is clearly skewed to the right and *nonnormal*.

What causes this distribution to be nonnormal? It is *not* the truncation. Truncation has a relatively minor effect because most of the demands don't need to be truncated. The real reason is that the distribution of year 6 demand is only normal *conditional* on the demand in year 5. That is, if we fix the demand in year 5 at any level and then replicate year 6 demand many times, the resulting histogram *is* normally shaped. But the year 5 demand is *not* fixed. It varies from replication to replication, and this variation causes the skewness in Figure 5.17. Admittedly, the reason for this skewness is not intuitively obvious, but simulation makes it easy to demonstrate.

Figure 5.16

Replication of Demand in Year 6

	A	B	C	D	E
36	Replication	Demand			
37		4476		Average	4916
38	1	1635		Stdev	3956
39	2	8229			
40	3	3582			
41	4	11282			
42	5	2845			
43	6	3942			
44	7	5700			
45	8	12273			
433	396	8919			
434	397	4587			
435	398	10003			
436	399	5012			
437	400	3944			

Figure 5.17

Histogram of Year 6 Demands

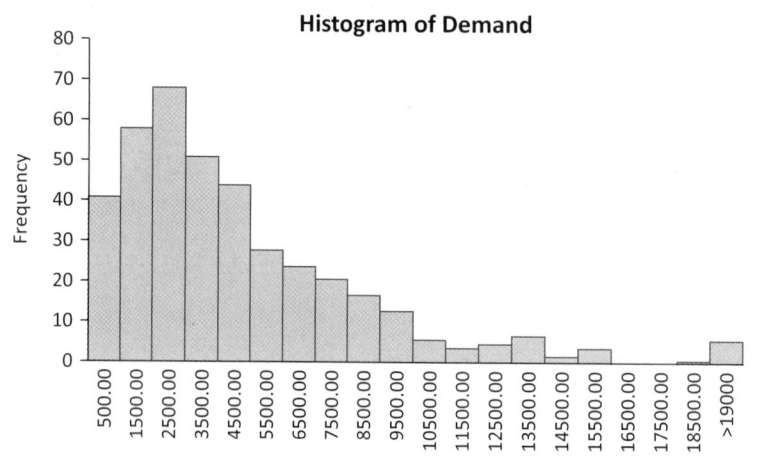

Histogram of Demand

PROBLEMS

Note: Student solutions for problems whose numbers appear within a colored box are available for purchase at www.cengagebrain.com.

Level A

1. The grades on the midterm examination given in a large managerial statistics class are normally distributed with mean 75 and standard deviation 9. The instructor of this class wants to assign an A grade to the top 10% of the scores, a B grade to the next 10% of the scores, a C grade to the next 10% of the scores, a D grade to the next 10% of the scores, and an F grade to all scores below the 60th percentile of this distribution. For each possible letter grade, find the lowest acceptable score within the established range.

For example, the lowest acceptable score for an A is the score at the 90th percentile of this normal distribution.

2. Suppose it is known that the distribution of purchase amounts by customers entering a popular retail store is approximately normal with mean $25 and standard deviation $8.

   a. What is the probability that a randomly selected customer spends less than $35 at this store?

   b. What is the probability that a randomly selected customer spends between $15 and $35 at this store?

   c. What is the probability that a randomly selected customer spends more than $10 at this store?

d. Find the dollar amount such that 75% of all customers spend no more than this amount.

e. Find the dollar amount such that 80% of all customers spend at least this amount.

f. Find two dollar amounts, equidistant from the mean, such that 90% of all customer purchases are between these values.

3. A machine used to regulate the amount of a certain chemical dispensed in the production of a particular type of cough syrup can be set so that it discharges an average of μ milliliters (ml) of the chemical in each bottle of cough syrup. The amount of chemical placed into each bottle of cough syrup is known to have a normal distribution with a standard deviation of 0.250 ml. If this machine discharges more than 2 ml of the chemical when preparing a given bottle of this cough syrup, the bottle is considered to be unacceptable by industry standards. Determine the setting for μ so that no more than 1% of the bottles of cough syrup prepared by this machine will be rejected.

4. Assume that the weekly demand for Ford car sales follows a normal distribution with mean 50,000 cars and standard deviation 14,000 cars.

a. There is a 1% chance that Ford will sell more than what number of cars during the next year?

b. What is the probability that Ford will sell between 2.4 and 2.7 million cars during the next year?

5. An investor has invested in nine different investments. The dollar returns on the different investments are probabilistically independent, and each return follows a normal distribution with mean $50,000 and standard deviation $10,000.

a. There is a 1% chance that the total return on the nine investments is less than what value? (Use the fact that the sum of independent normal random variables is normally distributed, with mean equal to the sum of the individual means and variance equal to the sum of the individual variances.)

b. What is the probability that the investor's total return is between $400,000 and $520,000?

6. Scores on an exam appear to follow a normal distribution with $\mu = 60$ and $\sigma = 20$. The instructor wishes to give a grade of D to students scoring between the 10th and 30th percentiles on the exam. For what range of scores should a D be given? What percentage of the students will get a D?

7. Suppose that the weight of a typical American male follows a normal distribution with $\mu = 180$ lb and $\sigma = 30$ lb. Also, suppose 91.92% of all American males weigh more than I weigh.

a. What fraction of American males weigh more than 225 pounds?

b. How much do I weigh?

c. If I weighed 20 pounds more than I do, what percentile would I be in?

8. Assume that the length of a typical televised baseball game, including all the commercial timeouts, is normally distributed with mean 2.45 hours and standard deviation 0.37 hour. Consider a televised baseball game that begins at 2:00 in the afternoon. The next regularly scheduled broadcast is at 5:00.

a. What is the probability that the game will cut into the next show, that is, go past 5:00?

b. If the game is over before 4:30, another half-hour show can be inserted into the 4:30–5:00 slot. What is the probability of this occurring?

9. The amount of a soft drink that goes into a typical 12-ounce can varies from can to can. It is normally distributed with an adjustable mean μ and a fixed standard deviation of 0.05 ounce. (The adjustment is made to the filling machine.)

a. If regulations require that cans have at least 11.9 ounces, what is the smallest mean μ that can be used so that at least 99.5% of all cans meet the regulation?

b. If the mean setting from part **a** is used, what is the probability that a typical can has at least 12 ounces?

10. Suppose that the demands for a company's product in weeks 1, 2, and 3 are each normally distributed. The means are 50, 45, and 65. The standard deviations are 10, 5, and 15. Assume that these three demands are probabilistically independent. This means that if you observe one of them, it doesn't help you to predict the others. Then it turns out that total demand for the three weeks is also normally distributed. Its mean is the sum of the individual means, and its variance is the sum of the individual variances. (Its standard deviation, however, is not the sum of the individual standard deviations; square roots don't work that way.)

a. Suppose that the company currently has 180 units in stock, and it will not be receiving any more shipments from its supplier for at least three weeks. What is the probability that stock will run out during this three-week period?

b. How many units should the company currently have in stock so that it can be 98% certain of not running out during this three-week period? Again, assume that it won't receive any more shipments during this period.

Level B

11. Matthew's Bakery prepares peanut butter cookies for sale every morning. It costs the bakery $0.50 to bake each peanut butter cookie, and each cookie is sold for $1.25. At the end of the day, leftover cookies are discounted and sold the following day at $0.40 per cookie. The daily demand (in dozens) for peanut butter cookies at this bakery is known to be normally distributed with mean 200 and standard deviation 60.

The manager of Matthew's Bakery is trying to determine how many dozen peanut butter cookies to make each morning to maximize the product's contribution to bakery profits. Use simulation to find a very good, if not optimal, production plan.

12. The manufacturer of a particular bicycle model has the following costs associated with the management of this product's inventory. In particular, the company currently maintains an inventory of 1000 units of this bicycle model at the beginning of each year. If X units are demanded each year and X is less than 1000, the excess supply, $1000 - X$ units, must be stored until next year at a cost of \$50 per unit. If X is greater than 1000 units, the excess demand, $X - 1000$ units, must be produced separately at an extra cost of \$80 per unit. Assume that the annual demand (X) for this bicycle model is normally distributed with mean 1000 and standard deviation 75.
   a. Find the expected annual cost associated with managing potential shortages or surpluses of this product. (*Hint*: Use simulation to approximate the answer. An exact solution using probability arguments is beyond the level of this book.)
   b. Find two annual total cost levels, equidistant from the expected value found in part **a**, such that 95% of all costs associated with managing potential shortages or surpluses of this product are between these values. (Continue to use simulation.)
   c. Comment on this manufacturer's annual production policy for this bicycle model in light of your findings in part **b**.

13. Suppose that a particular production process fills detergent in boxes of a given size. Specifically, this process fills the boxes with an amount of detergent (in ounces) that is adequately described by a normal distribution with mean 50 and standard deviation 0.5.
   a. Simulate this production process for the filling of 500 boxes of detergent. Find the mean and standard deviation of your simulated sample weights. How do your sample statistics compare to the theoretical population parameters in this case? How well do the empirical rules apply in describing the variation in the weights in your simulated detergent boxes?
   b. A box of detergent is rejected by quality control personnel if it is found to contain less than 49 ounces or more than 51 ounces of detergent. Given these quality standards, what proportion of all boxes are rejected? What step(s) could the supervisor of this production process take to reduce this proportion to 1%?

14. It is widely known that many drivers on interstate highways in the United States do not observe the posted speed limit. Assume that the actual rates of speed driven by U.S. motorists are normally distributed with mean μ mph and standard deviation 5 mph. Given this information, answer each of the following independent questions. (*Hint*: Use Goal Seek in parts **a** and **b**, and use the Solver add-in with no objective in part **c**. Solver is usually used to optimize, but it can also be used to solve equations with multiple unknowns.)
   a. If 40% of all U.S. drivers are observed traveling at 65 mph or more, what is the mean μ?
   b. If 25% of all U.S. drivers are observed traveling at 50 mph or less, what is the mean μ?
   c. Suppose now that the mean μ and standard deviation σ of this distribution are both unknown. Furthermore, it is observed that 40% of all U.S. drivers travel at less than 55 mph and 10% of all U.S. drivers travel at more than 70 mph. What must μ and σ be?

15. The lifetime of a certain manufacturer's washing machine is normally distributed with mean 4 years. Only 15% of all these washing machines last at least 5 years. What is the standard deviation of the lifetime of a washing machine made by this manufacturer?

16. You have been told that the distribution of regular unleaded gasoline prices over all gas stations in Indiana is normally distributed with mean \$2.95 and standard deviation \$0.075, and you have been asked to find two dollar values such that 95% of all gas stations charge somewhere between these two values. Why is each of the following an acceptable answer: between \$2.776 and \$3.081, or between \$2.803 and \$3.097? Can you find any other acceptable answers? Which of the many possible answers would you give if you are asked to obtain the *shortest* interval?

17. A fast-food restaurant sells hamburgers and chicken sandwiches. On a typical weekday the demand for hamburgers is normally distributed with mean 313 and standard deviation 57; the demand for chicken sandwiches is normally distributed with mean 93 and standard deviation 22.
   a. How many hamburgers must the restaurant stock to be 98% sure of not running out on a given day?
   b. Answer part **a** for chicken sandwiches.
   c. If the restaurant stocks 400 hamburgers and 150 chicken sandwiches for a given day, what is the probability that it will run out of hamburgers or chicken sandwiches (or both) that day? Assume that the demand for hamburgers and the demand for chicken sandwiches are probabilistically independent.
   d. Why is the independence assumption in part **c** probably not realistic? Using a more realistic assumption, do you think the probability requested in part **c** would increase or decrease?

18. Referring to the box plots introduced in Chapter 2, the sides of the "box" are at the first and third quartiles, and the difference between these (the length of the

box) is called the interquartile range (IQR). A *mild* outlier is an observation that is between 1.5 and 3 IQRs from the box, and an *extreme* outlier is an observation that is more than 3 IQRs from the box.

a. If the data are normally distributed, what percentage of values will be mild outliers? What percentage will be extreme outliers? Why don't the answers depend on the mean and/or standard deviation of the distribution?

b. Check your answers in part **a** with simulation. Simulate a large number of normal random numbers (you can choose any mean and standard deviation), and count the number of mild and extreme outliers with appropriate IF functions. Do these match, at least approximately, your answers to part **a**?

5.4 THE BINOMIAL DISTRIBUTION

The normal distribution is undoubtedly the most important probability distribution in statistics. Not far behind, however, is the *binomial* distribution. The **binomial distribution** is a discrete distribution that can occur in two situations: (1) when sampling from a population with only two types of members (males and females, for example), and (2) when performing a sequence of identical experiments, each of which has only two possible outcomes.

Imagine any experiment that can be repeated many times under identical conditions. It is common to refer to each repetition of the experiment as a *trial*. We assume that the outcomes of successive trials are probabilistically independent of one another and that each trial has only two possible outcomes. We label these two possibilities generically as *success* and *failure*. In any particular application the outcomes might be Democrat/Republican, defective/nondefective, went bankrupt/remained solvent, and so on. We label the probability of a success on each trial as p, and the probability of a failure as $1 - p$. We let n be the number of trials.

> ### FUNDAMENTAL INSIGHT
>
> **Why the Binomial Distribution?**
>
> Unlike the normal distribution, which can describe all sorts of random phenomena, the binomial distribution is relevant for a very common and specific situation: the number of *successes* in a fixed number of *trials*, where the trials are probabilistically independent and the probability of success remains constant across trials. Whenever this situation occurs, the binomial distribution is the relevant distribution.

> ### Binomial Distribution
>
> Consider a situation where there are n independent, identical trials, where the probability of a success on each trial is p and the probability of a failure is $1 - p$. Define X to be the random number of successes in the n trials. Then X has a **binomial** distribution with parameters n and p.

For example, the binomial distribution with parameters 100 and 0.3 is the distribution of the number of successes in 100 trials when the probability of success is 0.3 on each trial. A simple example that you can keep in mind throughout this section is the number of heads you would see if you flipped a coin n times. Assuming the coin is well balanced, the relevant distribution is binomial with parameters n and $p = 0.5$. This coin-flipping example is often used to illustrate the binomial distribution because of its simplicity, but you will see that the binomial distribution also applies to many important business situations.

To understand how the binomial distribution works, consider the coin-flipping example with $n = 3$. If X represents the number of heads in three flips of the coin, then the possible values of X are 0, 1, 2, and 3. You can find the probabilities of these values by considering the eight possible outcomes of the three flips: (T,T,T), (T,T,H), (T,H,T),

(H,T,T), (T,H,H), (H,T,H), (H,H,T), and (H,H,H). Because of symmetry (the well-balanced property of the coin), each of these eight possible outcomes must have the same probability, so each must have probability 1/8. Next, note that one of the outcomes has $X = 0$, three outcomes have $X = 1$, three outcomes have $X = 2$, and one outcome has $X = 3$. Therefore, the probability distribution of X is

$$P(X = 0) = 1/8, P(X = 1) = 3/8, P(X = 2) = 3/8, P(X = 3) = 1/8$$

This is a special case of the binomial distribution, with $n = 3$ and $p = 0.5$. In general, where n can be any positive integer and p can be any probability between 0 and 1, there is a rather complex formula for calculating $P(X = k)$ for any integer k from 0 to n. Instead of presenting this formula, we will discuss how to calculate binomial probabilities in Excel. You do this with the **BINOMDIST** function. The general form of this function is

$= \textbf{BINOMDIST}(k,n,p,cum)$

The middle two arguments are the number of trials n and the probability of success p on each trial. The first parameter k is an integer number of successes that you specify. The last parameter, *cum*, is either 0 or 1. It is 1 if you want the probability of *less than or equal to k* successes, and it is 0 if you want the probability of *exactly k* successes. We illustrate typical binomial calculations in the following example.

CHANGES IN EXCEL 2010

As with the new normal functions, there are new binomial functions in Excel 2010. The BINOMDIST and CRITBINOM functions in the following example have been replaced by BINOM.DIST and BINOM.INV, but the old functions still work fine. Both versions are indicated in the file for the following example.

EXAMPLE | 5.7 BATTERY LIFE EXPERIMENT

Suppose that 100 identical batteries are inserted in identical flashlights. Each flashlight takes a single battery. After eight hours of continuous use, a given battery is still operating with probability 0.6 or has failed with probability 0.4. Let X be the number of successes in these 100 trials, where a success means that the battery is still functioning. Find the probabilities of the following events: (a) exactly 58 successes, (b) no more than 65 successes, (c) less than 70 successes, (d) at least 59 successes, (e) greater than 65 successes, (f) between 55 and 65 successes (inclusive), (g) exactly 40 failures, (h) at least 35 failures, and (i) less than 42 failures. Then find the 95th percentile of the distribution of X.

Objective To use Excel's BINOMDIST and CRITBINOM functions for calculating binomial probabilities and percentiles in the context of flashlight batteries.

Solution

Figure 5.18 shows the solution to all of these problems. (See the file **Binomial Calculations.xlsx**.) The probabilities requested in parts (a) through (f) all involve the number of successes X. The key to these is the wording of phrases such as "no more than," "greater than," and so on. In particular, you have to be careful to distinguish between probabilities such as $P(X < k)$ and $P(X \le k)$. The latter includes the possibility of having $X = k$ and the former does not.

Figure 5.18 Typical Binomial Calculations

	A	B	C	D	E	F	G	H	I	J
1	**Binomial Probability Calculations**									
2				**Range names used:**						
3	Number of trials	100		NTrials	=BinomCalcs!$B$3					
4	Probability of success on each trial	0.6		PSuccess	=BinomCalcs!$B$4					
5										
6	**Event**	**Probability**		**Formula**						
7	Exactly 58 successes	0.0742		=BINOMDIST(58,NTrials,PSuccess,0)						
8	No more than 65 successes	0.8697		=BINOMDIST(65,NTrials,PSuccess,1)						
9	Less than 70 successes	0.9752		=BINOMDIST(69,NTrials,PSuccess,1)						
10	At least 59 successes	0.6225		=1-BINOMDIST(58,NTrials,PSuccess,1)						
11	Greater than 65 successes	0.1303		=1-BINOMDIST(65,NTrials,PSuccess,1)						
12	Between 55 and 65 successes (inclusive)	0.7386		=BINOMDIST(65,NTrials,PSuccess,1)-BINOMDIST(54,NTrials,PSuccess,1)						
13										
14	Exactly 40 failures	0.0812		=BINOMDIST(40,NTrials,1-PSuccess,0)						
15	At least 35 failures	0.8697		=1-BINOMDIST(34,NTrials,1-PSuccess,1)						
16	Less than 42 failures	0.6225		=BINOMDIST(41,NTrials,1-PSuccess,1)						
17										
18	**Finding the 95th percentile (trial and error)**									
19	Trial values	CumProb								
20	65	0.8697		=BINOMDIST(A20,NTrials,PSuccess,1)						
21	66	0.9087		(Copy down)						
22	67	0.9385								
23	68	0.9602								
24	69	0.9752								
25	70	0.9852								
26				Formula in cell A27:						
27	68	0.95		=CRITBINOM(NTrials,PSuccess,B27)						

With this in mind, the probabilities requested in (a) through (f) become:

a. $P(X = 58)$

b. $P(X \leq 65)$

c. $P(X < 70) = P(X \leq 69)$

d. $P(X \geq 59) = 1 - P(X < 59) = 1 - P(X \leq 58)$

e. $P(X > 65) = 1 - P(X \leq 65)$

f. $P(55 \leq X \leq 65) = P(X \leq 65) - P(X < 55) = P(X \leq 65) - P(X \leq 54)$

Note how we have manipulated each of these so that it includes only terms of the form $P(X = k)$ or $P(X \leq k)$ for suitable values of k. These are the types of probabilities that can be handled directly by the BINOMDIST function. The answers appear in the range B7:B12, and the corresponding formulas are shown (as labels) in column D. (The Excel 2010 functions do not appear in this figure, but they are included in the file.)

The probabilities requested in (g) through (i) involve *failures* rather than successes. But because each trial results in either a success or a failure, the number of failures is also binomially distributed, with parameters n and $1 - p = 0.4$. So in rows 14 through 16 the requested probabilities are calculated in exactly the same way, except that 1-PSuccess is substituted for PSuccess in the third argument of the BINOMDIST function.

Finally, to calculate the 95th percentile of the distribution of X, you can proceed by trial and error. For each value k from 65 to 70, the probability $P(X \leq k)$ is calculated in column B with the BINOMDIST function. Note that there is no value k such that $P(X \leq k) = 0.95$ exactly. Specifically, $P(X \leq 67)$ is slightly less than 0.95 and $P(X \leq 68)$ is slightly greater than 0.95. Therefore, the meaning of the "95th percentile" is somewhat ambiguous. If you want the largest value k such that $P(X \leq k) \leq 0.95$, then this k is 67. If instead you want the smallest value k such that $P(X \le k) \ge 0.95$, then this value is 68. The latter interpretation is the one usually accepted for binomial percentiles.

In fact, Excel has another built-in function, **CRITBINOM**, for finding this value of k. This function is illustrated in row 27 of Figure 5.18. Now you enter the requested probability, 0.95, in cell B27 and the formula

=**CRITBINOM**(NTrials,PSuccess,B27)

in cell A27. It returns 68, the smallest value k such that $P(X \le k) \ge 0.95$ for this binomial distribution. ∎

5.4.1 Mean and Standard Deviation of the Binomial Distribution

It can be shown that the mean and standard deviation of a binomial distribution with parameters n and p are given by the following equations.

$$E(X) = np \tag{5.3}$$

$$\text{Stdev}(X) = \sqrt{np(1 - p)} \tag{5.4}$$

The formula for the mean is quite intuitive. For example, if you observe 100 trials, each with probability of success 0.6, your best guess for the number of successes is clearly $100(0.6) = 60$. The standard deviation is less obvious but still very useful. It indicates how far the actual number of successes is likely to deviate from the mean. In this case the standard deviation is $\sqrt{100(0.6)(0.4)} = 4.90$.

Fortunately, the empirical rules discussed in Chapter 2 also apply, at least approximately, to the binomial distribution. That is, there is about a 95% chance that the actual number of successes will be within two standard deviations of the mean, and there is almost no chance that the number of successes will be more than three standard deviations from the mean. So for this example, it is very likely that the number of successes will be in the range of approximately 50 to 70, and it is very unlikely that there will be fewer than 45 or more than 75 successes.

This reasoning is extremely useful. It provides a rough estimate of the number of successes you are likely to observe. Suppose 1000 parts are sampled randomly from an assembly line and, based on historical performance, the percentage of parts with some type of defect is about 5%. Translated into a binomial model, each of the 1000 parts, independently of the others, has some type of defect with probability 0.05. Would it be surprising to see, say, 75 parts with a defect? The mean is $1000(0.05) = 50$ and the standard deviation is $\sqrt{1000(0.05)(0.95)} = 6.89$. Therefore, the number of parts with defects is 95% certain to be within $50 \pm 2(6.89)$, or approximately from 36 to 64. Because 75 is slightly beyond three standard deviations from the mean, it is highly unlikely that there would be 75 (or more) defective parts.

5.4.2 The Binomial Distribution in the Context of Sampling

We now discuss how the binomial distribution applies to sampling from a population with two types of members. Let's say these two types are men and women, although in applications they might be Democrats and Republicans, users of our product and nonusers, and so on. We assume that the population has N members, of whom N_M are men and N_W are women (where $N_M + N_W = N$). If you sample n of these randomly, you are typically interested in the composition of the sample. You might expect the number of men in the sample to be binomially distributed with parameters n and $p = N_M/N$, the fraction of men in the population. However, this depends on how the sampling is performed.

If sampling is done **without replacement**, each member of the population can be sampled only once. That is, once a person is sampled, his or her name is struck from the list and cannot be sampled again. If sampling is done **with replacement**, then it is possible, although maybe not likely, to select a given member of the population more than once. Most real-world sampling is performed *without* replacement. There is no point in obtaining information from the same person more than once. However, *the binomial model applies only to sampling with replacement.* Because the composition of the remaining population keeps changing as the sampling progresses, the binomial model provides only an approximation if sampling is done without replacement. If there is no replacement, the value of p, the proportion of men in this case, does *not* stay constant, a requirement of the binomial model. The appropriate distribution for sampling without replacement is called the *hypergeometric* distribution, a distribution we will not discuss here.[6]

If n is small relative to N, however, the binomial distribution is a very good approximation to the hypergeometric distribution and can be used even if sampling is performed without replacement. A rule of thumb is that if n is no greater than 10% of N, that is, no more than 10% of the population is sampled, then the binomial model can be used safely. Of course, most national polls sample considerably less than 10% of the population. In fact, they often sample only a few thousand people from the hundreds of millions in the entire population. The bottom line is that in most real-world sampling contexts, the binomial model is perfectly adequate.

5.4.3 The Normal Approximation to the Binomial

If n is large and p is not too close to 0 or 1, the binomial distribution is bell-shaped and can be approximated well by the normal distribution.

If you graph the binomial probabilities, you will see an interesting phenomenon—namely, the graph begins to look symmetric and bell-shaped when n is fairly large and p is not too close to 0 or 1. An example is illustrated in Figure 5.19 with the parameters $n = 30$ and $p = 0.4$. Generally, if $np > 5$ and $n(1 - p) > 5$, the binomial distribution can be approximated well by a normal distribution with mean np and standard deviation $\sqrt{np(1 - p)}$.

One practical consequence of the normal approximation to the binomial is that the empirical rules can be applied. That is, when the binomial distribution is approximately symmetric and bell-shaped, there is about a 68% chance that the number of successes will be within one standard deviation of the mean. Similarly, there is about a 95% chance that the number of successes will be within two standard deviations of the mean, and the

Figure 5.19

Bell-shaped Binomial Distribution

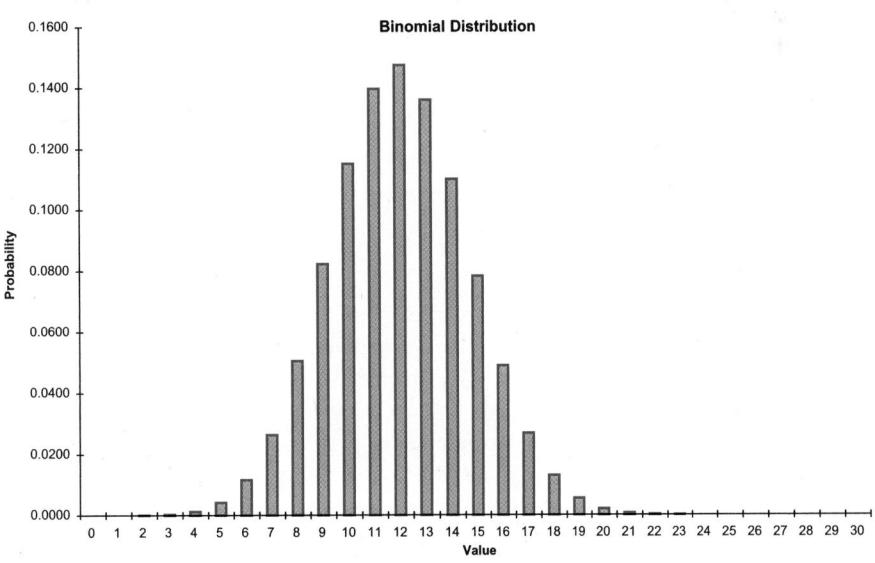

[6]Excel has a function HYPGEOMDIST for sampling without replacement that works much like the BINOMDIST function. You can look it up under the Statistical category of Excel functions.

number of successes will almost surely be within three standard deviations of the mean. Here, the mean is *np* and the standard deviation is $\sqrt{np(1-p)}$.

Technical Tip: *Continuity Correction*

Because the normal distribution is continuous and the binomial distribution is discrete, the normal approximation to the binomial can be improved slightly with a continuity correction. If you want to approximate a binomial probability such as P(36≤X≤45), expand the interval by 0.5 on each end in the normal approximation. That is, approximate with the normal probability P(35.5≤X≤45.5). Similarly, approximate binomial P(X≤45) with normal P(X≤4.5), or binomial P(X≥36) with normal P(X≥35.5).

5.5 APPLICATIONS OF THE BINOMIAL DISTRIBUTION

The binomial distribution finds many applications in the business world and elsewhere. We discuss a few typical applications in this section.

EXAMPLE | **5.8 IS THIS MUTUAL FUND REALLY A WINNER?**

An investment broker at the Michaels & Dodson Company claims that he has found a real winner. He has tracked a mutual fund that has beaten a standard market index in 37 of the past 52 weeks. Could this be due to chance, or has he *really* found a winner?

Objective   To determine the probability of a mutual fund outperforming a standard market index at least 37 out of 52 weeks.

Solution

The broker is no doubt tracking a lot of mutual funds, and he is probably reporting only the best of these. Therefore, we will check whether the best of *many* mutual funds could do at least this well purely by chance. To do this, we first specify what we mean by "purely by chance." This means that each week, a given fund has a fifty-fifty chance of beating the market index, independently of performance in other weeks. In other words, the number of weeks where a given fund outperforms the market index is binomially distributed with $n = 52$ and $p = 0.5$. With this in mind, cell B6 of Figure 5.20 shows the probability that a given fund does at least as well—beats the market index at least 37 out of 52 weeks— as the reported fund. (See the **Beating the Market.xlsx** file.) Because $P(X \geq 37) = 1 - P(X \leq 36)$, the relevant formula is

=1-BINOMDIST(B3-1,B4,0.5,1)

Obviously, this probability, 0.00159, is quite small. A single fund isn't likely to beat the market this often purely by chance.

Figure 5.20

Binomial
Calculations for
Investment Example

	A	B	C	D	E	F	G
1	**Beating the market**						
2							
3	Weeks beating market index	37					
4	Total number of weeks	52					
5							
6	Probability of doing at least this well by chance	0.00159		=1-BINOMDIST(B3-1,B4,0.5,1)			
7							
8	Number of mutual funds	400					
9	Probability of at least one doing at least this well	0.471		=1-BINOMDIST(0,B8,B6,1)			
10							
11	Two-way data table of the probability in B9 as a function of values in B3 and B8						
12			Number of weeks beating the market index				
13		0.471	36	37	38	39	40
14	Number of mutual funds	200	0.542	0.273	0.113	0.040	0.013
15		300	0.690	0.380	0.164	0.060	0.019
16		400	0.790	0.471	0.213	0.079	0.025
17		500	0.858	0.549	0.258	0.097	0.031
18		600	0.904	0.616	0.301	0.116	0.038

However, the probability that the *best* of many mutual funds does at least this well is much larger. To calculate this probability, assume that 400 funds are being tracked, and let Y be the number of these that beat the market at least 37 of 52 weeks. Then Y is also binomially distributed, with parameters $n = 400$ and $p = 0.00159$, the probability calculated previously. To see whether *any* of the 400 funds beats the market at least 37 of 52 weeks, calculate $P(Y \geq 1) = 1 - P(Y = 0)$ in cell B9 with the formula

=1-BINOMDIST(0,B8,B6,1)

(Can you see why the fourth argument could be 0 *or* 1?) The resulting probability is nearly 0.5—that is, there is nearly a fifty-fifty chance that at least one of 400 funds will do as well as the reported fund. This certainly casts doubt on the broker's claim that he has found a real winner. Perhaps his star fund just got lucky and will perform no better than average in succeeding weeks.

To see how the probability in cell B9 depends on the level of success of the reported fund (the value in cell B3) and the number of mutual funds being tracked (in cell B8), you can create a two-way data table in the range B13:G18. (The formula in cell B13 is **=B9**, the row input cell is B3, and the column input cell is B8.) As you saw, beating the market 37 times out of 52 is no big deal with 400 funds, but beating it 40 times out of 52, even with 600 funds, is something worth reporting. The probability of this happening purely by chance is only 0.038, or less than 1 out of 25. ∎

The next example requires a normal calculation to find a probability p, which is then used in a binomial calculation.

EXAMPLE	**5.9 ANALYZING DAILY SALES AT A SUPERMARKET**

Customers at a supermarket spend varying amounts. Historical data show that the amount spent per customer is normally distributed with mean $85 and standard deviation $30. If 500 customers shop in a given day, calculate the mean and standard deviation of the number who spend at least $100. Then calculate the probability that at least 30% of all customers spend at least $100.

Objective   To use the normal *and* binomial distributions to calculate the typical number of customers who spend at least $100 per day and the probability that at least 30% of all 500 daily customers spend at least $100.

Solution

Both questions involve the number of customers who spend at least $100. Because the amounts spent are normally distributed, the probability that a typical customer spends at least $100 is found with the NORMDIST function. This probability, 0.309, appears in cell B7 of Figure 5.21. (See the file **Supermarket Spending.xlsx.**) It is calculated with the formula

=1-NORMDIST(100,B4,B5,1)

This probability is then used as the parameter p in a binomial model. The mean and standard deviation of the number who spend at least $100 are calculated in cells B13 and B14 as np and $\sqrt{np(1-p)}$, using $n = 500$, the number of shoppers, and $p = 0.309$. The expected number who spend at least $100 is slightly greater than 154, and the standard deviation of this number is slightly greater than 10.

Figure 5.21   Calculations for Supermarket Example

	A	B	C	D	E	F
1	Supermarket spending					
2						
3	Amount spent per customer (normally distributed)					
4	Mean	$85				
5	StDev	$30				
6						
7	Probability that a customer spends at least $100	0.309		=1-NORMDIST(100,B4,B5,1)		
8						
9						
10	Number of customers	500				
11						
12	Mean and stdev of number who spend at least $100					
13	Mean	154.27		=B10*B7		
14	StDev	10.33		=SQRT(B10*B7*(1-B7))		
15						
16	Probability at least 30% spend at least $100	0.676		=1-BINOMDIST(0.3*B10-1,B10,B7,1)		

To answer the second question, note that 30% of 500 customers is 150 customers. Then the probability that at least 30% of the customers spend at least $100 is the probability that a binomially distributed random variable, with $n = 500$ and $p = 0.309$, is at least 150. This binomial probability, which turns out to be about 2/3, is calculated in cell B16 with the formula

=1-BINOMDIST(0.3*B10-1,B10,B7,1)

Note that the first argument calculates to 149. This is because the probability of *at least* 150 customers is one minus the probability of less than or equal to 149 customers. ∎

5.10 OVERBOOKING BY AIRLINES

This example presents a simplified version of calculations used by airlines when they overbook flights. They realize that a certain percentage of ticketed passengers will cancel at the last minute. Therefore, to avoid empty seats, they sell more tickets than there are seats, hoping that just about the right number of passengers show up. We assume that the no-show rate is 10%. In binomial terms, we assume that each ticketed passenger, independently of the others, shows up with probability 0.90 and cancels with probability 0.10.

For a flight with 200 seats, the airline wants to see how sensitive various probabilities are to the number of tickets it issues. In particular, it wants to calculate (a) the probability that more than 205 passengers show up, (b) the probability that more than 200 passengers show up, (c) the probability that at least 195 seats are filled, and (d) the probability that at least 190 seats are filled. The first two of these are "bad" events from the airline's perspective; they mean that some customers will be bumped from the flight. The last two events are "good" in the sense that the airline wants most of the seats to be occupied.

Objective   To assess the benefits and drawbacks of airline overbooking.

Solution

To solve the airline's problem, we use the BINOMDIST function and a data table. The solution appears in Figure 5.22. (See the file **Airline Overbooking.xlsx**.) For any number of tickets issued in cell B6, the required probabilities are calculated in row 10. For example, the formulas in cells B10 and D10 are

=1-BINOMDIST(205,NTickets,1-PNoShow,1)

and

=1-BINOMDIST(194,NTickets,1-PNoShow,1)

Note that the condition "more than" requires a slightly different calculation from "at least." The probability of more than 205 is one minus the probability of less than or equal to 205, whereas the probability of at least 195 is one minus the probability of less than or equal to 194. Also, note that a passenger who shows up is called a success. Therefore, the third argument of each BINOMDIST function is one minus the no-show probability.

To see how sensitive these probabilities are to the number of tickets issued, we create a one-way data table at the bottom of the spreadsheet. It is *one-way* because there is only one *input,* the number of tickets issued, even though four output probabilities are tabulated. (To create the data table, list several possible numbers of tickets issued along the side in column A and create links to the probabilities in row 10 in row 14. That is, enter the formula =B10 in cell B14 and copy it across row 14. Then form a data table using the range A14:E24, no row input cell, and column input cell B6.)

The results are as expected. As the airline issues more tickets, there is a larger chance of having to bump passengers from the flight, but there is also a larger chance of filling most seats. In reality, the airline has to make a trade-off between these two, taking its various costs and revenues into account. ∎

The following is another simplified example of a real problem that occurs every time you watch election returns on TV. This problem is of particular interest in light of the highly unusual events that took place during election night television coverage of the U.S. presidential election in 2000, where the networks declared Al Gore an early winner in at least one state that he eventually lost. The basic question is how soon the networks can

Figure 5.22 Binomial Calculations for Overbooking Example

	A	B	C	D	E	F
1	Airline overbooking			Range names used:		
2				NTickets	=Overbooking!$B$6	
3	Number of seats	200		PNoShow	=Overbooking!$B$4	
4	Probability of no-show	0.1				
5						
6	Number of tickets issued	215				
7						
8	Required probabilities					
9		More than 205 show up	More than 200 show up	At least 195 seats filled	At least 190 seats filled	
10		0.001	0.050	0.421	0.820	
11						
12	Data table showing sensitivity of probabilities to number of tickets issued					
13	Number of tickets issued	More than 205 show up	More than 200 show up	At least 195 seats filled	At least 190 seats filled	
14		0.001	0.050	0.421	0.820	
15	206	0.000	0.000	0.012	0.171	
16	209	0.000	0.001	0.064	0.384	
17	212	0.000	0.009	0.201	0.628	
18	215	0.001	0.050	0.421	0.820	
19	218	0.013	0.166	0.659	0.931	
20	221	0.064	0.370	0.839	0.978	
21	224	0.194	0.607	0.939	0.995	
22	227	0.406	0.802	0.981	0.999	
23	230	0.639	0.920	0.995	1.000	
24	233	0.822	0.974	0.999	1.000	

declare one of the candidates the winner, based on early voting returns. Our example is somewhat unrealistic because it ignores the possibility that early tabulations can be biased one way or the other. For example, the earliest reporting precincts might be known to be more heavily in favor of the Democrat than the population in general. Nevertheless, the example indicates why the networks are able to make early conclusions based on such seemingly small amounts of data.

EXAMPLE | 5.11 PROJECTING ELECTION WINNERS FROM EARLY RETURNS

We assume that there are N voters in the population, of whom N_R will vote for the Republican and N_D will vote for the Democrat. The eventual winner will be the Republican if $N_R > N_D$ and will be the Democrat otherwise, but we won't know which until all of the votes are tabulated. (To simplify the example, we assume there are only two candidates and that the election will *not* end in a tie.) Let's suppose that a small percentage of the votes have been counted and the Republican is currently ahead 540 to 460. On what basis can the networks declare the Republican the winner, especially if there are millions of voters in the population?

Objective   To use a binomial model to determine whether early returns reflect the eventual winner of an election between two candidates.

Solution

Let $n = 1000$ be the total number of votes that have been tabulated. If X is the number of Republican votes so far, we are given that $X = 540$. Now we pose the following question. If the Democrat were going to be the eventual winner, that is, $N_D > N_R$, and we randomly sampled 1000 voters from the population, how likely is it that at least 540 of these voters would be in favor of the Republican? If this is very *unlikely*, then the only reasonable conclusion is that the Democrat will *not* be the eventual winner. This is the reasoning the networks might use to declare the Republican the winner so early in the tabulation.

We use a binomial model to see how unlikely the event "at least 540 out of 1000" is, assuming that the Democrat will be the eventual winner. We need a value for p, the probability that a typical vote is for the Republican. This probability should be the proportion of voters in the entire population who favor the Republican. All we know is that this probability is less than 0.5, because we have *assumed* that the Democrat will eventually win. In Figure 5.23, we show how the probability of at least 540 out of 1000 varies with values of p less than, but close to, 0.5. (See the file **Election Returns.xlsx**.)

Figure 5.23   Binomial Calculations for Voting Example

	A	B	C	D	E	F
1	Election returns					
2						
3	Population proportion for Republican	0.49				
4						
5	Votes tabulated so far	1000				
6	Votes for Republican so far	540				
7						
8	Binomial probability of at least this many votes for Republican					
9		0.0009		=1-BINOMDIST(B6-1,B5,B3,1)		
10						
11	Data table showing sensitivity of this probability to population proportion for Republican					
12	Population proportion for Republican	Probability				
13		0.0009				
14	0.490	0.0009				
15	0.492	0.0013				
16	0.494	0.0020				
17	0.496	0.0030				
18	0.498	0.0043				
19	0.499	0.0052				

We enter a trial value of 0.49 for p in cell B3 and then calculate the required probability in cell B9 with the formula

=1-BINOMDIST(B6-1,B5,B3,1)

Then we use this to create the data table at the bottom of the spreadsheet. This data table tabulates the probability of the given lead (at least 540 out of 1000) for various values of p less than 0.5. As shown in the last few rows, even if the eventual outcome were going to be a virtual tie—with the Democrat slightly ahead—there would still be *very* little chance of the Republican being at least 80 votes ahead so far. But because the Republican *is* currently ahead by 80 votes, the networks feel safe in declaring the Republican the winner. Admittedly, the probability model they use is more complex than our simple binomial model, but the idea is the same. ∎

The final example in this section challenges the two assumptions of the binomial model. So far, we have assumed that the outcomes of successive trials have the same probability p of success and are probabilistically independent. There are many situations where either or both of these assumptions are questionable. For example, consider successive items from a production line, where each item either meets specifications (a success) or doesn't (a failure). If the process deteriorates over time, at least until it receives maintenance, the probability p of success will slowly decrease. But even if p remains constant, defective items could come in bunches (because of momentary inattentiveness on the part of a worker, say), which would invalidate the independence assumption.

If you believe that the binomial assumptions are invalid, then you must specify an alternative model that reflects reality more closely. This is not easy—all kinds of *nonbinomial* assumptions can be imagined. Furthermore, when you make such assumptions, there are probably no simple formulas to use, such as the BINOMDIST formulas we have been using. Simulation might be the only (simple) alternative, as illustrated in the following example.

| EXAMPLE | 5.12 STREAK SHOOTING IN BASKETBALL |

Do basketball players shoot in streaks? This question has been debated by thousands of basketball fans, and it has been studied statistically by academic researchers. Most fans believe the answer is yes, arguing that players clearly alternate between hot streaks where they can't miss and cold streaks where they can't hit the broad side of a barn. This situation does not fit a binomial model where, say, a "450 shooter" has a 0.450 probability of making each shot and a 0.550 probability of missing, independently of other shots. If the binomial model does not apply, what model is appropriate, and how could it be used to calculate a typical probability such as the probability of making at least 13 shots out of 25 attempts?[7]

Objective   To formulate a nonbinomial model of basketball shooting, and to use it to find the probability of a "450 shooter" making at least 13 out of 25 shots.

Solution

This example is quite open-ended. There are numerous alternatives to the binomial model that could capture the "streakiness" most fans believe in, and the one we suggest here is by no means the only possibility. We challenge you to develop others.

The model we propose assumes that this shooter makes 45% of his shots in the long run. The probability that he makes his first shot in a game is 0.45. In general, consider

[7]There are obviously a lot of extenuating circumstances surrounding any shot: the type of shot (layup versus jump shot), the type of defense, the score, the time left in the game, and so on. For this example, we focus on a pure jump shooter who is unaffected by the various circumstances in the game.

his nth shot. If he has made his last k shots, we assume the probability of making shot n is $0.45 + kd_1$. On the other hand, if he has missed his last k shots, we assume the probability of making shot n is $0.45 - kd_2$. Here, d_1 and d_2 are small values (0.01 and 0.02, for example) that indicate how much the shooter's probability of success increases or decreases depending on his current streak. The model implies that the shooter gets better the more shots he makes and worse the more he misses.

Figure 5.24 Simulation of Basketball Shooting Model

	A	B	C	D	E	F	G	H	I
1	Basketball shooting simulation								
2									
3	Long-run average	0.45							
4	Increment d1 after a make	0.015							
5	Increment d2 after a miss	0.015							
6									
7	Number of shots	25							
8									
9	Binomial probability of at least 13 out of 25	0.306							
10									
11	Summary statistics from simulation below			Compare these		Fraction of reps with at least 13 from table below			
12	Number of makes	14				0.272			
13	At least 13 makes?	1							
14									
15	Simulation of makes and misses using nonbinomial model					Data table to replicate 25 shots many times			
16		Shot	Streak	P(make)	Make?		Rep	At least 13?		
17		1	NA	0.45	0			1		
18		2	-1	0.435	0		1	0		
19		3	-2	0.42	0		2	1		
20		4	-3	0.405	1		3	1		
21		5	1	0.465	1		4	0		
37		21	-1	0.435	0		20	0		
38		22	-2	0.42	1		21	0		
39		23	1	0.465	0		22	1		
40		24	-1	0.435	0		23	1		
41		25	-2	0.42	1		24	0		
42							25	1		
43							26	0		
265							248	0		
266							249	0		
267							250	1		

To implement this model, we use simulation as shown in Figure 5.24 (with many hidden rows). (See the file **Basketball Simulation.xlsx**.) Actually, we first do a baseline binomial calculation in cell B9, using the parameters $n = 25$ and $p = 0.450$. The formula in cell B9 is

=1-BINOMDIST(12,B7,B3,1)

If the player makes each shot with probability 0.45, independently of the other shots, then the probability that he will make over half of his 25 shots is 0.306—about a 30% chance. (Remember that this is a binomial calculation for a situation where the binomial distribution probably does not apply.) The simulation in the range A17:D41 shows the results of 25 random shots according to the *nonbinomial* model we have assumed. Column B indicates the length of the current streak, where a negative value indicates a streak of misses and a positive value indicates a streak of makes. Column C indicates the probability of a make on the current shot, and column D contains 1s for makes and 0s for misses. Here are step-by-step instructions for developing this range.

1 First shot. Enter the formulas

=B3

and

=IF(RAND()<C17,1,0)

in cells C17 and D17 to determine the outcome of the first shot.

2 Second shot. Enter the formulas

=IF(D17=0,-1,1)

=IF(B18<0,$B$3+B18*$B$5,$B$3+B18*$B$4)

and

=IF(RAND()C18,1,0)

in cells B18, C18, and D18. The first of these indicates that by the second shot, the shooter will have a streak of one make or one miss. The second formula is the important one. It indicates how the probability of a make changes depending on the current streak. The third formula simulates a make or a miss, using the probability in cell C18.

3 Length of streak on third shot. Enter the formula

=IF(AND(B18<0,D18=0),B18-1, IF(AND(B18<0,D18=1),1,

IF(AND(B18>0,D18=0),−1,B18+1)))

in cell B19 and copy it down column B. This nested IF formula checks for all four combinations of the previous streak (negative or positive, indicated in cell B18) and the most recent shot (make or miss, indicated in cell D18) to see whether the current streak continues by 1 or a new streak starts.

4 Results of remaining shots. The logic for the formulas in columns C and D is the same for the remaining shots as for shot 2, so copy the formulas in cells C18 and D18 down their respective columns.

5 Summary of 25 shots. Enter the formulas

=SUM(D17:D41)

and

=IF(B12>=13,1,0)

in cells B12 and B13 to summarize the results of the 25 simulated shots. In particular, the value in cell B13 is 1 only if at least 13 of the shots are successes.

What about the *probability* of making at least 13 shots with this nonbinomial model? So far, we have simulated one set of 25 shots and have reported whether at least 13 of the shots are successes. We need to replicate this simulation many times and report the fraction of the replications where at least 13 of the shots are successes. We do this with a data table in columns F and G.

To create this table, enter the replication numbers 1 through 250 (you could use any number of replications) in column F. Then put a link to B13 in cell G17 by entering the formula = **B13** in this cell. Essentially, we are recalculating this value 250 times, each with different random numbers. To do this, highlight the range F17:G267, and create a data table with no row input cell and *any blank cell* (such as F17) as the column input cell. This causes Excel to recalculate the basic simulation 250 times, each time with different random numbers. (This trick of using a blank column input cell will be discussed in more detail in Chapter 15.) Finally, enter the formula

=AVERAGE(G18:G267)

in cell F12 to calculate the fraction of the replications with at least 13 makes out of 25 shots.

After finishing all of this, note that the spreadsheet is "live" in the sense that if you press the F9 recalculation key, all of the simulated quantities change with new random numbers. In particular, the estimate in cell F12 of the probability of at least 13 makes out of 25 shots changes. It is sometimes less than the binomial probability in cell B9 and sometimes greater. In general, the two probabilities are roughly the same. The bottom line? Even if the world doesn't behave exactly as the binomial model indicates, probabilities of various events can often be approximated fairly well by binomial probabilities—which saves you the trouble of developing and working with more complex models. ■

PROBLEMS

Level A

19. In a typical month, an insurance agent presents life insurance plans to 40 potential customers. Historically, one in four such customers chooses to buy life insurance from this agent. Based on the relevant binomial distribution, answer the following questions:
  a. What is the probability that exactly five customers will buy life insurance from this agent in the coming month?
  b. What is the probability that no more than 10 customers will buy life insurance from this agent in the coming month?
  c. What is the probability that at least 20 customers will buy life insurance from this agent in the coming month?
  d. Determine the mean and standard deviation of the number of customers who will buy life insurance from this agent in the coming month.
  e. What is the probability that the number of customers who buy life insurance from this agent in the coming month will lie within two standard deviations of the mean?
  f. What is the probability that the number of customers who buy life insurance from this agent in the coming month will lie within three standard deviations of the mean?

20. Continuing the previous exercise, use the normal approximation to the binomial to answer each of the questions posed in parts **a** through **f**. How well does the normal approximation perform in this case? Explain.

21. Many vehicles used in space travel are constructed with redundant systems to protect flight crews and their valuable equipment. In other words, backup systems are included within many vehicle components so that if one or more systems fail, backup systems will assure the safe operation of the given component and thus the entire vehicle. For example, consider one particular component of the U.S. space shuttle that has n duplicated systems (i.e., one original system and $n - 1$ backup systems). Each of these systems functions, independently of the others, with probability 0.98. This shuttle component functions successfully provided that *at least* one of the n systems functions properly.
  a. Find the probability that this shuttle component functions successfully if $n = 2$.
  b. Find the probability that this shuttle component functions successfully if $n = 4$.
  c. What is the minimum number n of duplicated systems that must be incorporated into this shuttle component to ensure at least a 0.9999 probability of successful operation?

22. Suppose that a popular hotel for vacationers in Orlando, Florida, has a total of 300 identical rooms. As many major airline companies do, this hotel has adopted an overbooking policy in an effort to maximize the usage of its available lodging capacity. Assume that each potential hotel customer holding a room reservation, independently of other customers, cancels the reservation or simply does not show up at the hotel on a given night with probability 0.15.

a. Find the largest number of room reservations that this hotel can book and still be at least 95% sure that everyone who shows up at the hotel will have a room on a given night.

b. Given that the hotel books the number of reservations found in part **a**, find the probability that at least 90% of the available rooms will be occupied on a given night.

c. Given that the hotel books the number of reservations found in part **a**, find the probability that at most 80% of the available rooms will be occupied on a given night.

d. How does your answer to part **a** change as the required assurance rate increases from 95% to 97%? How does your answer to part **a** change as the required assurance rate increases from 95% to 99%?

e. How does your answer to part **a** change as the cancellation rate varies between 5% and 25% (in increments of 5%)? Assume now that the required assurance rate remains at 95%.

23. A production process manufactures items with weights that are normally distributed with mean 15 pounds and standard deviation 0.1 pound. An item is considered to be defective if its weight is less than 14.8 pounds or greater than 15.2 pounds. Suppose that these items are currently produced in batches of 1000 units.

a. Find the probability that at most 5% of the items in a given batch will be defective.

b. Find the probability that at least 90% of the items in a given batch will be acceptable.

c. How many items would have to be produced in a batch to guarantee that a batch consists of no more than 1% defective items?

24. Past experience indicates that 30% of all individuals entering a certain store decide to make a purchase. Using (a) the binomial distribution and (b) the normal approximation to the binomial, find that probability that 10 or more of the 30 individuals entering the store in a given hour will decide to make a purchase. Compare the results obtained using the two different approaches. Under what conditions will the normal approximation to this binomial probability become even more accurate?

25. Suppose that the number of ounces of soda put into a soft-drink can is normally distributed with $\mu = 12.05$ ounces and $\sigma = 0.03$ ounce.

a. Legally, a can must contain at least 12 ounces of soda. What fraction of cans will contain at least 12 ounces of soda?

b. What fraction of cans will contain less than 11.9 ounces of soda?

c. What fraction of cans will contain between 12 and 12.08 ounces of soda?

d. One percent of all cans will weigh more than what value?

e. Ten percent of all cans will weigh less than what value?

f. The soft-drink company controls the mean weight in a can by setting a timer. For what mean should the timer be set so that only 1 in 1000 cans will be underweight?

g. Every day the company produces 10,000 cans. The government inspects 10 randomly chosen cans each day. If at least two are underweight, the company is fined $10,000. Given that $\mu = 12.05$ ounces and $\sigma = 0.03$ ounce, what is the probability that the company will be fined on a given day?

26. Suppose that 53% of all registered voters prefer Barack Obama to John McCain. (You can substitute the names of the current presidential candidates if you like.)

a. In a random sample of 100 voters, what is the probability that the sample will indicate that Obama will win the election (that is, there will be more votes in the sample for Obama)?

b. In a random sample of 100 voters, what is the probability that the sample will indicate that McCain will win the election?

c. In a random sample of 100 voters, what is the probability that the sample will indicate a dead heat (fifty-fifty)?

d. In a random sample of 100 voters, what is the probability that between 40 and 60 (inclusive) voters will prefer Obama?

27. Assume that, on average, 95% of all ticket holders show up for a flight. If a plane seats 200 people, how many tickets should be sold to make the chance of an overbooked flight as close as possible to 5%?

28. Suppose that 55% of all people prefer Coke to Pepsi. We randomly choose 500 people and ask them if they prefer Coke to Pepsi. What is the probability that our survey will (erroneously) indicate that Pepsi is preferred by more people than Coke? Does this probability increase or decrease as we take larger and larger samples? Why?

29. A firm's office contains 150 PCs. The probability that a given PC will not work on a given day is 0.05.

a. On a given day what is the probability that exactly one computer will not be working?

b. On a given day what is the probability that at least two computers will not be working?

c. What assumptions do your answers in parts **a** and **b** require? Do you think they are reasonable? Explain.

30. Suppose that 4% of all tax returns are audited. In a group of n tax returns, consider the probability that at most two returns are audited. How large must n be before this probability is less than 0.01?

31. Suppose that the height of a typical American female is normally distributed with $\mu = 64$ inches and $\sigma = 4$

inches. We observe the height of 500 American females.

    a. What is the probability that fewer than 35 of the 500 women will be less than 58 inches tall?

    b. Let X be the number of the 500 women who are less than 58 inches tall. Find the mean and standard deviation of X.

32. Consider a large population of shoppers, each of whom spends a certain amount during his or her current shopping trip; the distribution of these amounts is normally distributed with mean $55 and standard deviation $15. We randomly choose 25 of these shoppers. What is the probability that at least 15 of them spend between $45 and $75?

Level B

33. Many firms utilize sampling plans to control the quality of manufactured items ready for shipment. To illustrate the use of a sampling plan, suppose that a particular company produces and ships electronic computer chips in lots, each lot consisting of 1000 chips. This company's sampling plan specifies that quality control personnel should randomly sample 50 chips from each lot and accept the lot for shipping if the number of defective chips is four or fewer. The lot will be rejected if the number of defective chips is five or more.

    a. Find the probability of accepting a lot as a function of the actual fraction of defective chips. In particular, let the actual fraction of defective chips in a given lot equal any of 0.02, 0.04, 0.06, 0.08, 0.10, 0.12, 0.14, 0.16, 0.18. Then compute the lot acceptance probability for each of these lot defective fractions.

    b. Construct a graph showing the probability of lot acceptance for each of the lot defective fractions, and interpret your graph.

    c. Repeat parts **a** and **b** under a revised sampling plan that calls for accepting a given lot if the number of defective chips found in the random sample of 50 chips is five or fewer. Summarize any notable differences between the two graphs.

34. Suppose you play a game at a casino where your probability of winning each game is 0.49. On each game, you bet $10, which you either win or lose. Let $P(n)$ be the probability that you are ahead by at least $50 after n games. Graph this probability versus n for n equal to multiples of 50 up to 1000. Discuss the behavior of this function and why it behaves as it does.

35. Comdell Computer receives computer chips from Chipco. Each batch sent by Chipco is inspected as follows: 35 chips are tested and the batch passes inspection if at most one defective chip is found in the set of 35 tested chips. Past history indicates an average of 1% of all chips produced by Chipco are defective.

Comdell has received 10 batches this week. What is the probability that at least nine of the batches will pass inspection?

36. A standardized test consists entirely of multiple-choice questions, each with five possible choices. You want to ensure that a student who randomly guesses on each question will obtain an expected score of zero. How can you accomplish this?

37. In the current tax year, suppose that 5% of the millions of individual tax returns are fraudulent. That is, they contain errors that were purposely made to cheat the government.

    a. Although these errors are often well concealed, let's suppose that a thorough IRS audit will uncover them. If a random 250 tax returns are audited, what is the probability that the IRS will uncover at least 15 fraudulent returns?

    b. Answer the same question as in part **a**, but this time assume there is only a 90% chance that a given fraudulent return will be spotted as such if it is audited.

38. Suppose you work for a survey research company. In a typical survey, you mail questionnaires to 150 companies. Of course, some of these companies might decide not to respond. Assume that the nonresponse rate is 45%; that is, each company's probability of not responding, independently of the others, is 0.45.

    a. If your company requires at least 90 responses for a valid survey, find the probability that it will get this many. Use a data table to see how your answer varies as a function of the nonresponse rate (for a reasonable range of response rates surrounding 45%).

    b. Suppose your company does this survey in two "waves." It mails the 150 questionnaires and waits a certain period for the responses. As before, assume that the nonresponse rate is 45%. However, after this initial period, your company follows up (by telephone, say) on the nonrespondents, asking them to please respond. Suppose that the nonresponse rate on this second wave is 70%; that is, each original nonrespondent now responds with probability 0.3, independently of the others. Your company now wants to find the probability of obtaining at least 110 responses total. It turns out that this is a difficult probability to calculate directly. So instead, approximate it with simulation.

39. Suppose you are sampling from a large population, and you ask the respondents whether they believe men should be allowed to take paid paternity leave from their jobs when they have a new child. Each person you sample is equally likely to be male or female. The population proportion of females who believe males should be granted paid paternity leave is 56%, and the population proportion of males who favor it is 48%. If you sample 200 people and count the number who believe males should be granted paternity leave, is this number binomially distributed? Explain why or why not. Would your answer change if you knew your sample was going to consist of exactly 100 males and 100 females?

40. A woman claims that she is a fortune-teller. Specifically, she claims that she can predict the direction of the change (up or down) in the Dow Jones Industrial Average for the next 10 days (such as U, U, D, U, D, U, U, D, D, D). (You can assume that she makes all 10 predictions right now, although that does not affect your answer to the question.) Obviously, you are skeptical, thinking that she is just guessing, so you would be surprised if her predictions are accurate. Which would surprise you more: (1) she predicts at least 8 out of 10 correctly, or (2) she predicts at least 6 out of 10 correctly on each of four separate occasions? Answer by assuming that (1) she is really guessing and (2) each day the Dow is equally likely to go up or down.

5.6 THE POISSON AND EXPONENTIAL DISTRIBUTIONS

The final two distributions in this chapter are called the *Poisson* and *exponential* distributions. In most statistical applications, including those in the rest of this book, these distributions play a much less important role than the normal and binomial distributions. For this reason, we will not analyze them in as much detail. However, in many applied management science models, the Poisson and exponential distributions are key distributions. For example, much of the study of probabilistic inventory models, queuing models, and reliability models relies heavily on these two distributions.

5.6.1 The Poisson Distribution

The **Poisson distribution** is a discrete distribution. It usually applies to the *number* of events occurring within a specified period of time or space. Its possible values are all of the nonnegative integers: 0, 1, 2, and so on—there is no upper limit. Even though there is an infinite number of possible values, this causes no real problems because the probabilities of all sufficiently large values are essentially 0.

The Poisson distribution is characterized by a single parameter, usually labeled λ (Greek lambda), which must be positive. By adjusting the value of λ, we are able to produce different Poisson distributions, all of which have the same basic shape as in Figure 5.25. That is, they first increase and then decrease. It turns out that λ is easy to interpret. It is both the mean and the variance of the Poisson distribution. Therefore, the standard deviation is $\sqrt{\lambda}$.

Typical Examples of the Poisson Distribution

1. A bank manager is studying the arrival pattern to the bank. The events are customer arrivals, the number of arrivals in an hour is Poisson distributed, and λ represents the expected number of arrivals per hour.

2. An engineer is interested in the lifetime of a type of battery. A device that uses this type of battery is operated continuously. When the first battery fails, it is replaced by a second; when the second fails, it is replaced by a third, and so on. The events are battery failures, the number of failures that occur in a month is Poisson distributed, and λ represents the expected number of failures per month.

3. A retailer is interested in the number of customers who order a particular product in a week. Then the events are customer orders for the product, the number of customer orders in a week is Poisson distributed, and λ is the expected number of orders per week.

4. In a quality control setting, the Poisson distribution is often relevant for describing the number of defects in some unit of space. For example, when paint is applied to the body of a new car, any minor blemish is considered a defect. Then the number of defects on the hood, say, might be Poisson distributed. In this case, λ is the expected number of defects per hood.

These examples are representative of the many situations where the Poisson distribution has been applied. The parameter λ is often called a *rate*—arrivals per hour, failures per month, and so on. If the unit of time is changed, the rate must be modified accordingly. For example, if the number of arrivals to a bank in a single hour is Poisson distributed with rate $\lambda = 30$, then the number of arrivals in a half-hour period is Poisson distributed with rate $\lambda = 15$.

We can use Excel to calculate Poisson probabilities much as we did with binomial probabilities. The relevant function is the POISSON function. It takes the form

=**POISSON**(k,λ,cum)

The third argument *cum* works exactly as in the binomial case. If it is 0, the function returns $P(X = k)$; if it is 1, the function returns $P(X \le k)$. As examples, if $\lambda = 5$, =**POISSON(7,5,0)** returns the probability of exactly 7, =**POISSON(7,5,1)** returns the probability of less than or equal to 7, and =**1-POISSON(3,5,1)** returns the probability of greater than 3.

CHANGES IN EXCEL 2010

The POISSON function has been replaced in Excel 2010 by POISSON.DIST. Either version can be used, and they work exactly the same way. Both versions are shown in the file for the following example. (Curiously, there is still no POISSON.INV function.)

The following example shows how a manager or consultant could use the Poisson distribution.

EXAMPLE 5.13 MANAGING TV INVENTORY AT KRIEGLAND

Kriegland is a department store that sells various brands of flat-screen TVs. One of the manager's biggest problems is to decide on an appropriate inventory policy for stocking TVs. He wants to have enough in stock so that customers receive their requests right away, but he does not want to tie up too much money in inventory that sits on the storeroom floor.

Most of the difficulty results from the unpredictability of customer demand. If this demand were constant and known, the manager could decide on an appropriate inventory policy fairly easily. But the demand varies widely from month to month in a random manner. All the manager knows is that the historical average demand per month is approximately 17. Therefore, he decides to call in a consultant. The consultant immediately suggests using a probability model. Specifically, she attempts to find the probability distribution of demand in a typical month. How might she proceed?

Objective To model the probability distribution of monthly demand for flat-screen TVs with a particular Poisson distribution.

Solution

Let X be the demand in a typical month. The consultant knows that there are many possible values of X. For example, if historical records show that monthly demands have always been between 0 and 40, the consultant knows that almost all of the probability should be assigned to the values 0 through 40. However, she does not relish the thought of finding 41 probabilities, $P(X = 0)$ through $P(X = 40)$, that sum to 1 and reflect historical frequencies. Instead, she discovers from the manager that the histogram of demands from previous months is shaped much like the graph in Figure 5.25. That is, it rises to some peak and then falls.

Figure 5.25

Typical Poisson
Distribution

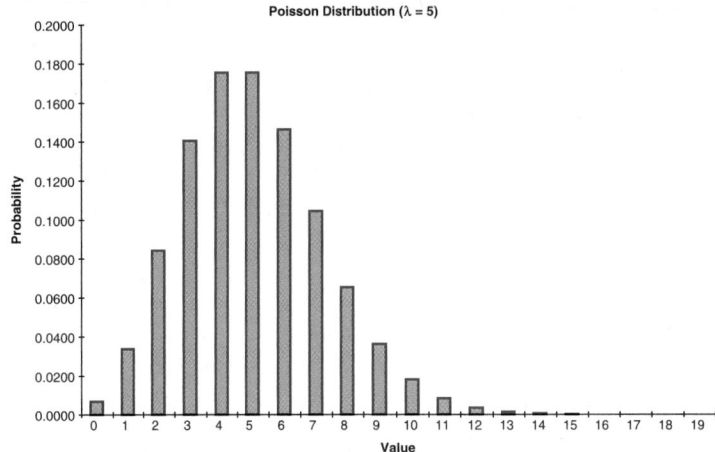

Knowing that a Poisson distribution has this same basic shape, the consultant decides to model the monthly demand with a Poisson distribution. To choose a particular Poisson distribution, all she has to do is choose a value of λ, the mean demand per month. Because the historical average is approximately 17, she chooses $\lambda = 17$. Now she can test the Poisson model by calculating probabilities of various events and asking the manager whether these probabilities are reasonable approximations to reality.

For example, the Poisson probability that monthly demand is less than or equal to 20, $P(X \leq 20)$, is 0.805 [using the Excel function **POISSON(20,17,1)**], and the probability that demand is between 10 and 15 inclusive, $P(10 \leq X \leq 15)$, is 0.345 [using **POISSON(15,17,1)-POISSON(9,17,1)**]. Figure 5.26 illustrates various probability calculations and shows the graph of the individual Poisson probabilities. (See the file **Poisson Demand Distribution.xlsx.**)

If the manager believes that these probabilities and other similar probabilities are reasonable, then the *statistical* part of the consultant's job is finished. Otherwise, she must try a different Poisson distribution—a different value of λ—or perhaps a different type of distribution altogether. ∎

5.6.2 The Exponential Distribution

Suppose that a bank manager is studying the pattern of customer arrivals at her branch location. As indicated previously in this section, the number of arrivals in an hour at a facility such as a bank is often well described by a Poisson distribution with parameter λ, where λ represents the expected number of arrivals per hour. An alternative way to view the uncertainty in the arrival process is to consider the *times* between customer arrivals. The most common probability distribution used to model these times, often called *interarrival times,* is the *exponential* distribution.

In general, the *continuous* random variable X has an **exponential** distribution with parameter λ (with $\lambda > 0$) if the density function of X has the form $f(x) = \lambda e^{-\lambda x}$ for $x > 0$. This density function has the shape shown in Figure 5.27. Because this density function decreases continuously from left to right, its most likely value is $x = 0$. Alternatively, if you collect many observations from an exponential distribution and draw a histogram of the observed values, then you should expect it to resemble the smooth curve shown in Figure 5.27, with the tallest bars to the left. The mean and standard deviation of this distribution are easy to remember. They are both equal to the *reciprocal* of the parameter λ. For example, an exponential distribution with parameter $\lambda = 0.1$ has mean and standard deviation both equal to 10.

Figure 5.26   Poisson Calculations for TV Example

	A	B	C	D	E	F	G	H	I	J	K
1	**Poisson distribution for monthly demand**										
2				Range name used:							
3	Mean monthly demand (λ)	17		Mean	=Sheet1!$B$3						
4											
5	Representative probability calculations										
6	Less than or equal to 20	0.805		=POISSON(20,Mean,1)							
7	Between 10 and 15 (inclusive)	0.345		=POISSON(15,Mean,1)-POISSON(9,Mean,1)							
8											
9	Individual probabilities										
10	Value	Prob									
11	0	0.000		=POISSON(A11,MeanDem,0)							
12	1	0.000									
13	2	0.000									
14	3	0.000									
15	4	0.000									
16	5	0.000									
17	6	0.001									
18	7	0.003									
19	8	0.007									
20	9	0.014									
21	10	0.023									
22	11	0.036									
23	12	0.050									
24	13	0.066									
25	14	0.080									
26	15	0.091									
27	16	0.096									
28	17	0.096									
29	18	0.091									
30	19	0.081									
31	20	0.069									
32	21	0.056									
33	22	0.043									
34	23	0.032									
35	24	0.023									
36	25	0.015									
37	26	0.010									
38	27	0.006									
39	28	0.004									
40	29	0.002									
41	30	0.001									
42	31	0.001									
43	32	0.000									
44	33	0.000									
45	34	0.000									
46	35	0.000									
47	36	0.000									
48	37	0.000									
49	38	0.000									
50	39	0.000									
51	40	0.000									

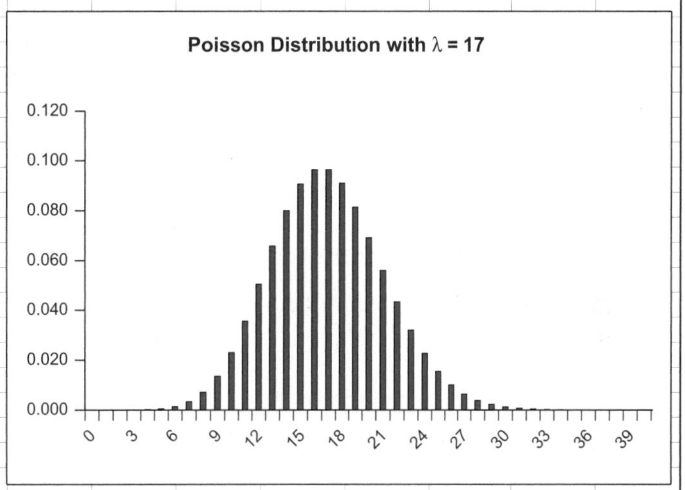

Poisson Distribution with λ = 17

As with the normal distribution, you usually want probabilities to the left or right of a given value. For any exponential distribution, the probability to the left of a given value $x > 0$ can be calculated with Excel's **EXPONDIST** function. This function takes the form

$$=\textbf{EXPONDIST}(x, \lambda, 1)$$

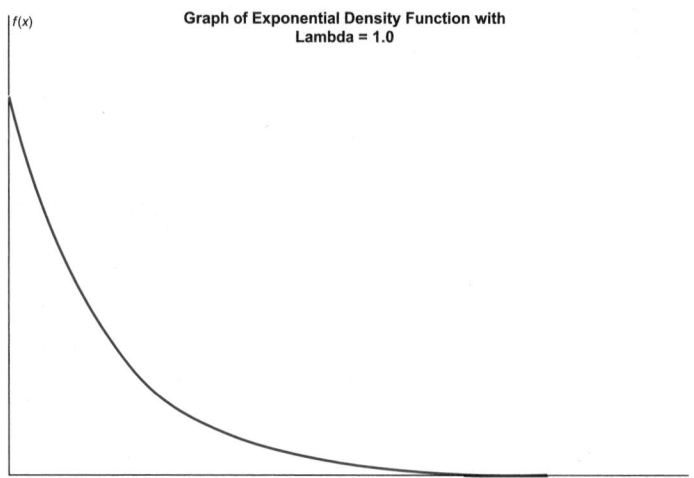

Figure 5.27
Exponential Density
Function

For example, if $x = 0.5$ and $\lambda = 5$ (so that the mean equals $1/5 = 0.2$), the probability of being less than 0.5 can be found with the formula

=EXPONDIST(0.5, 5, 1)

This returns the probability 0.918. Of course, the probability of being greater than 0.5 is then $1 - 0.918 = 0.082$.

CHANGES IN EXCEL 2010

The EXPONDIST function has been replaced in Excel 2010 by EXPON.DIST. Either version can be used, and they work exactly the same way. (As with the Poisson distribution, there is no EXPON.INV function.)

Returning to the bank manager's analysis of customer arrival data, when the times between arrivals are exponentially distributed, you sometimes hear that "arrivals occur according to a Poisson process." This is because there is a close relationship between the exponential distribution, which measures *times* between events such as arrivals, and the Poisson distribution, which counts the *number* of events in a certain length of time. The details of this relationship are beyond the level of this book, so we will not explore the topic further. But if you hear, for example, that customers arrive at a facility according to a Poisson process at the rate of six per hour, then the corresponding times between arrivals are exponentially distributed with mean 1/6 hour.

PROBLEMS

Level A

41. The annual number of industrial accidents occurring in a particular manufacturing plant is known to follow a Poisson distribution with mean 12.
    a. What is the probability of observing exactly 12 accidents during the coming year?
    b. What is the probability of observing no more than 12 accidents during the coming year?
    c. What is the probability of observing at least 15 accidents during the coming year?
    d. What is the probability of observing between 10 and 15 accidents (inclusive) during the coming year?

e. Find the smallest integer k such that we can be at least 99% sure that the annual number of accidents occurring will be less than k.

42. Suppose that the number of customers arriving each hour at the only checkout counter in a local pharmacy is approximately Poisson distributed with an expected arrival rate of 20 customers per hour.
    a. Find the probability that exactly 10 customers arrive in a given hour.
    b. Find the probability that at least five customers arrive in a given hour.
    c. Find the probability that no more than 25 customers arrive in a given hour.
    d. Find the probability that between 10 and 30 customers (inclusive) arrive in a given hour.
    e. Find the largest integer k such that we can be at least 95% sure that the number of customers arriving in a given hour will be greater than k.
    f. Recalling the relationship between the Poisson and exponential distributions, find the probability that the time between two successive customer arrivals is more then four minutes. Find the probability that it is less than two minutes.

43. Suppose the number of baskets scored by the Indiana University basketball team in one minute follows a Poisson distribution with $\lambda = 1.5$. In a 10-minute span of time, what is the probability that Indiana University scores exactly 20 baskets; at most 20 baskets? (Use the fact that if the rate per minute is λ, then the rate in t minutes is λt.)

44. Suppose that the times between arrivals at a bank during the peak period of the day are exponentially distributed with a mean of 45 seconds. If you just observed an arrival, what is the probability that you will need to wait for more than a minute before observing the next arrival? What is the probability you will need to wait at least two minutes?

Level B

45. Consider a Poisson random variable X with parameter $\lambda = 2$.
    a. Find the probability that X is within one standard deviation of its mean.
    b. Find the probability that X is within two standard deviations of its mean.
    c. Find the probability that X is within three standard deviations of its mean.
    d. Do the empirical rules we learned previously seem to be applicable in working with the Poisson distribution where $\lambda = 2$? Explain why or why not.
    e. Repeat parts **a** through **d** for the case of a Poisson random variable where $\lambda = 20$.

46. Based on historical data, the probability that a major league pitcher pitches a no-hitter in a game is about 1/1300.
    a. Use the binomial distribution to determine the probability that in 650 games 0, 1, 2, or 3 no-hitters will be pitched. (Find the separate probabilities of these four events.)
    b. Repeat part **a** using the Poisson approximation to the binomial. This approximation says that if n is large and p is small, a binomial distribution with parameters n and p is approximately the same as a Poisson distribution with $\lambda = np$.

5.7 FITTING A PROBABILITY DISTRIBUTION TO DATA WITH @RISK[8]

The normal, binomial, Poisson, and exponential distributions are four of the most commonly used distributions in real applications. However, many other discrete and continuous distributions are also used. These include the uniform, triangular, Erlang, lognormal, gamma, Weibull, and others. How do you know which to choose for any particular application? One way to answer this is to check which of several potential distributions fits a given set of data most closely. Essentially, you compare a histogram of the data with the theoretical probability distributions available and see which gives the best fit.

The @RISK add-in, part of the Palisade DecisionTools suite, makes this fairly easy, as we illustrate in the following example. (Many other features of @RISK are discussed in depth in Chapters 15 and 16.)

[8]In a previous edition, we showed how to do this with Palisade's stand-alone program BestFit. Because @RISK incorporates all the functionality of BestFit, and because BestFit is not included in the current version of the Palisade suite, you should now use @RISK.

EXAMPLE	**5.14 ASSESSING A DISTRIBUTION OF SUPERMARKET CHECKOUT TIMES**

A supermarket has collected checkout times on over 100 customers. (See the file **Checkout Times.xlsx**.) As shown in Figure 5.28, the times vary from 40 seconds to 279 seconds, with the mean and median close to 160 seconds.

Figure 5.28

Supermarket Checkout Times

	A	B	C	D	E	F	G
1	Customer	Time		**Summary measures for selected variables**			
2	1	131				Time	
3	2	101			Count	113.000	
4	3	178			Mean	159.239	
5	4	246			Median	155.000	
6	5	207			Standard deviation	52.609	
7	6	155			Minimum	40.000	
8	7	95			Maximum	279.000	
9	8	105					
10	9	168					
11	10	92					
12	11	112					
13	12	163					
111	110	138					
112	111	279					
113	112	90					
114	113	155					

The supermarket manager would like to check whether these data are normally distributed or whether some other distribution fits them better. How can he tell?

Objective To use @RISK to determine which probability distribution fits the given data best.

Solution

To open @RISK, click on the Windows Start button, find the Palisade group, and click on @RISK. If Excel is already open, this opens @RISK on top of it. If Excel isn't open, this launches Excel and @RISK. You will know that @RISK is open when you see the @RISK tab and the associated ribbon in Figure 5.29. For now, choose the Distribution Fitting item. From here, you can go in one of two ways. You can test the fit of a *given* distribution, or you can find the best-fitting distribution from a number of candidates. Both are now illustrated.

Because the supermarket manager wants to know whether the data could come from a normal distribution, check this possibility first. To do so, select Fit Manager from the Distribution Fitting dropdown menu. The first step is to define a data set, as in Figure 5.30.

Figure 5.29 @RISK Ribbon

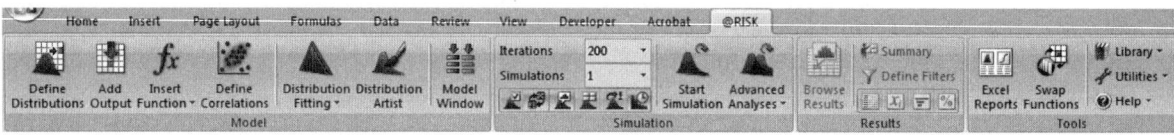

Figure 5.30

Defining a Data Set

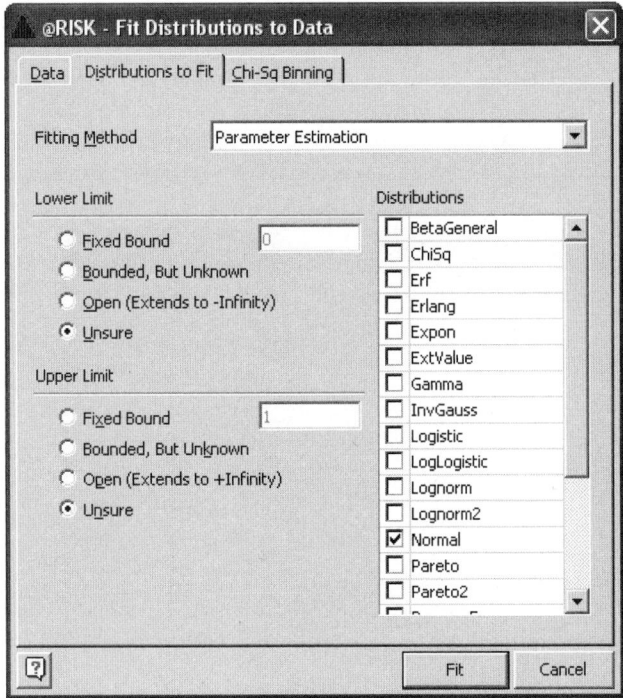

Figure 5.31

Selecting the
Distribution(s) to Fit

The second step is to click on the Distributions to Fit tab and select the Normal distribution, as shown in Figure 5.31. To see how well a normal distribution fits the data, click on the Fit button. This produces the output shown in Figure 5.32, with a normal curve superimposed on the histogram of the data. A visual examination of this graph is often sufficient to tell whether the fit is any "good." (This fit appears to be "fair," but not great.)

Figure 5.32

Normal Fit to the
Data

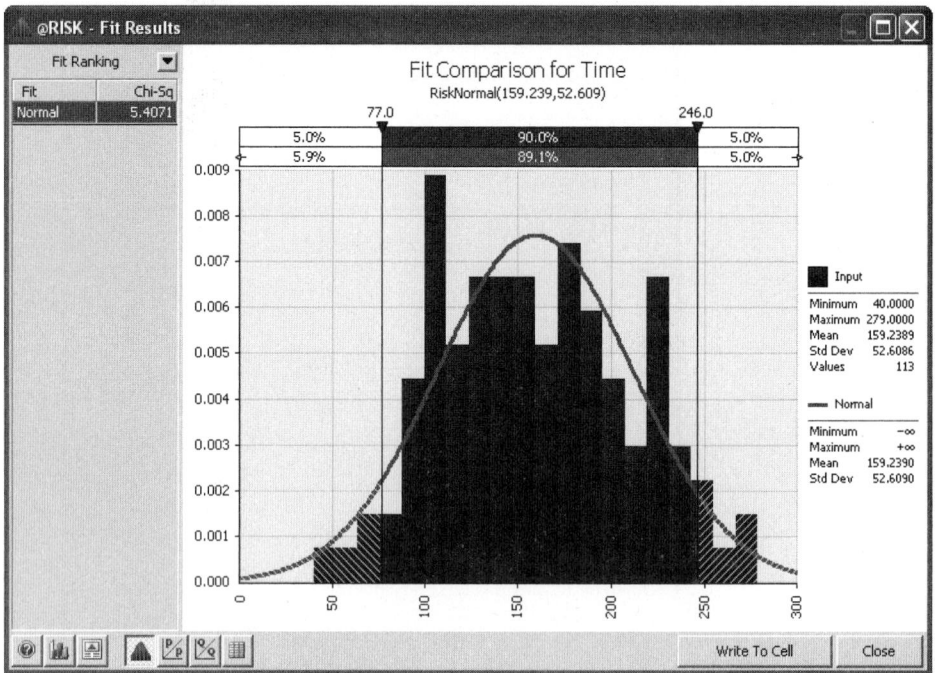

@RISK provides several numerical measures of the goodness of fit, which you can find by clicking on the dropdown arrow next to Fit Ranking at the top left in the figure. The details are rather technical, but each test value measures goodness of fit in a slightly different way. For each of these measures, the larger the test value is, the *worse* the fit is. They can then be used to compare fits; the distribution with the lowest test values is the winner.

To see which of several possible distributions fit the data best, go back to the Fit Distributions to Data dialog box and click on the Distributions to Fit tab. (See Figure 5.33.)

Figure 5.33

Selecting
Distributions to Fit

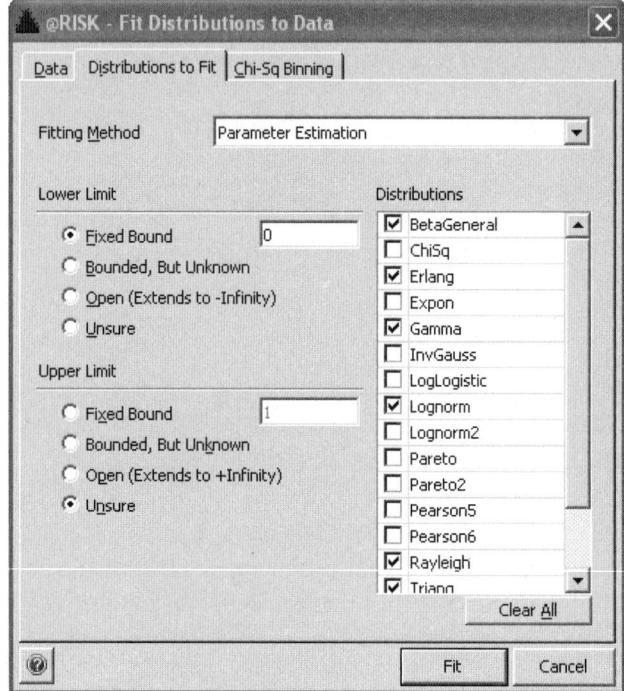

Some "reasonable" choices about the checkout data have been made on the left. The lowest possible checkout time is 0 but there is no obvious upper limit. When you make such choices, the set of possible distributions that are checked on the right changes. For example, the selected list here contains only distributions with a lower limit of 0. (Note that the normal distribution does *not* satisfy this condition.) You can then uncheck any distributions you do not want included in the search for the best fit. (For example, you might want to uncheck distributions you have never heard of.)

Once you specify these candidate distributions and click on Fit, @RISK performs a numerical algorithm to find the best-fitting distribution from each selected distribution family (the best gamma of all gamma distributions, for example) and displays them in ranked order, from best to worst. The best fit for these data is the beta general distribution, as shown in Figure 5.34. (The beta general family includes skewed distributions, although

Figure 5.34

Beta General Fit to the Data

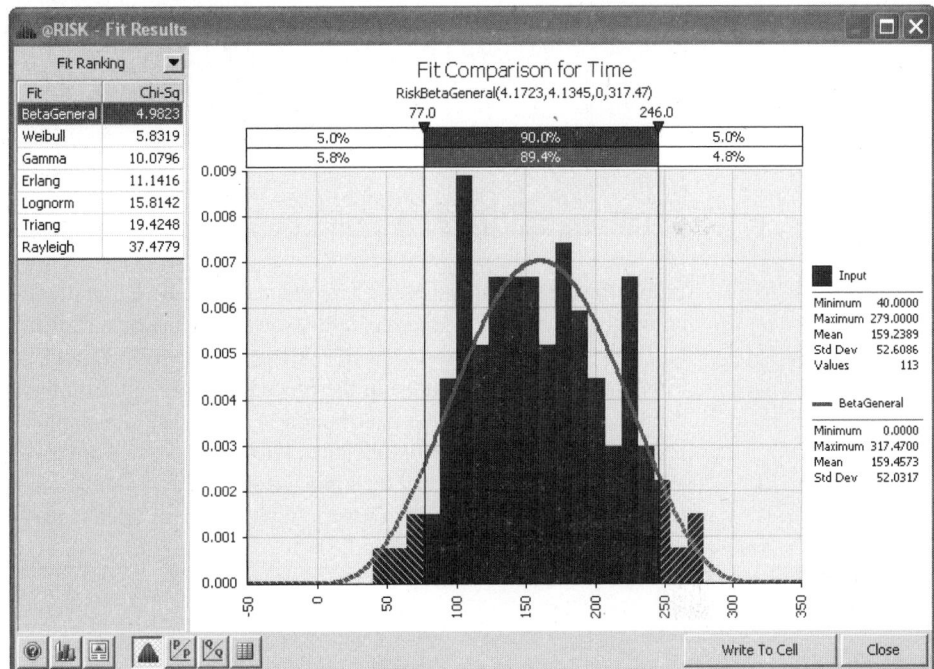

this one appears to be symmetric.) You can also click on any of the "runner-up" distributions to see how well they fit. For example, the triangular fit is shown in Figure 5.35. Obviously, this fit is not nearly as good as the beta general fit.

It is not always easy to look at these graphs and judge which fit is best. This is the reason for the goodness-of-fit measures. Comparing Figures 5.34 and 5.35, you can see that the triangular fit is considerably worse than the beta general—its test values (some not shown) are all much larger. By comparison, the test values for the normal fit in Figure 5.32 are quite comparable to those for the beta general. The only downside to the normal distribution, in this example, is that checkout times cannot possibly be negative, which the normal distribution allows. But the probability of a negative value for this particular normal distribution is so low that the manager might decide to use it anyway. ∎

At this point, you might wonder why we bother fitting a distribution to a set of data in the first place. The usual reason is given in the following scenario. Suppose a manager needs to make a decision, but there is at least one source of uncertainty. If the manager wants to develop a decision model or perhaps a simulation model to help solve his problem,

Figure 5.35
Triangular Fit to the Data

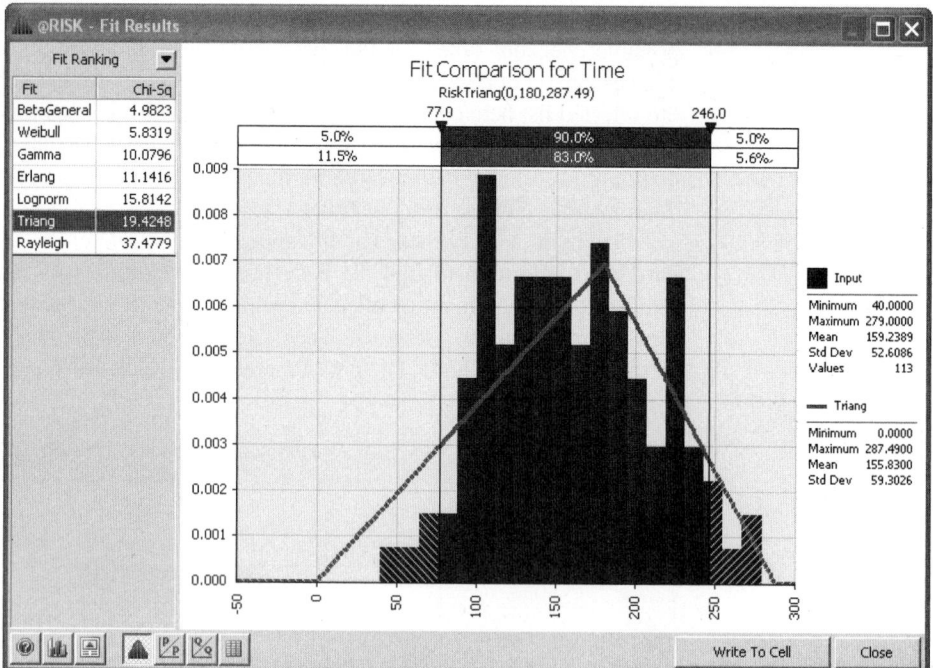

probability distributions of all uncertain outcomes are typically required. The manager could always choose one of the well-known distributions, such as the normal, for all uncertain outcomes, but these might not reflect reality well. Instead, the manager could gather historical data, such as those in the preceding example, find the distribution that fits these data best, and then use this distribution in the decision or simulation model. Of course, as this example has illustrated, it helps to know a few distributions other than the normal—the Weibull and the gamma, for example. Although we will not pursue these in this book, the more distributions you have in your tool kit, the more effectively you can model uncertainty.

PROBLEMS

Level A

47. A production manager is interested in determining the proportion of defective items in a typical shipment of one of the computer components that her company manufactures. The proportion of defective components is recorded for each of 250 randomly selected shipments collected during a one-month period. The data are in the file **P05_47.xlsx**. Use @RISK to determine which probability distribution best fits these data.

48. The manager of a local fast-food restaurant is interested in improving the service provided to customers who use the restaurant's drive-up window. As a first step in this process, the manager asks his assistant to record the time (in minutes) it takes to serve 200 different customers at the final window in the facility's drive-up system. The given 200 customer service times are all observed during the busiest hour of the day for this fast-food operation. The data are in the file

P05_48.xlsx. Use @RISK to determine which probability distribution best fits these data.

49. The operations manager of a tollbooth located at a major exit of a state turnpike is trying to estimate the average number of vehicles that arrive at the tollbooth during a one-minute period during the peak of rush-hour traffic. To estimate this average throughput value, he records the number of vehicles that arrive at the tollbooth over a one-minute interval commencing at the same time for each of 250 normal weekdays. The data are in the file **P05_49.xlsx**. Use @RISK to determine which probability distribution best fits these data.

50. A finance professor has just given a midterm examination in her corporate finance course and is interested in learning how her class of 250 students performed on this exam. The data are in the file **P05_50.xlsx**. Use @RISK to determine which probability distribution best fits these data.

5.8 CONCLUSION

We have covered a lot of ground in this chapter, and much of the material, especially that on the normal distribution, will be used in later chapters. The normal distribution is the cornerstone for much of statistical theory. As you will see in later chapters on statistical inference and regression, an assumption of normality is behind most of the procedures we use. Therefore, it is important for you to understand the properties of the normal distribution and how to work with it in Excel. The binomial, Poisson, and exponential distributions, although not used as frequently as the normal distribution in this book, are also extremely important. The examples we have discussed indicate how these distributions can be used in a variety of business situations.

Although we have attempted to stress *concepts* in this chapter, we have also described the details necessary to work with these distributions in Excel. Fortunately, these details are not too difficult to master once you understand Excel's built-in functions, especially NORMDIST, NORMINV, and BINOMDIST. Figures 5.6 and 5.18 provide typical examples of these functions. We suggest that you keep a copy of these figures handy.

Summary of Key Terms

Term	Explanation	Excel[9]	Page	Equation
Density function	Specifies the probability distribution of a continuous random variable		211	
Normal distribution	A continuous distribution with possible values ranging over the *entire* number line; its density function is a symmetric bell-shaped curve		213	5.1
Standardizing a normal random variable	Transforms any normal distribution with mean μ and standard deviation σ to the *standard* normal distribution with mean 0 and standard deviation 1	STANDARDIZE	214	5.2
Normal calculations in Excel	Useful for finding probabilities and percentiles for nonstandard and standard normal distributions	NORMDIST, NORMSDIST, NORMINV, NORMSINV	217	
Empirical rules for normal distribution	About 68% of the data fall within one standard deviation of the mean, about 95% of the data fall within two standard deviations of the mean, and almost all fall within three standard deviations of the mean.		221	
Binomial distribution	The distribution of the number of successes in n independent, identical trials, where each trial has probability p of success	BINOMDIST CRITBINOM	233	
Mean and standard deviation of a binomial distribution	The mean and standard deviation of a binomial distribution with parameters n and p are np and $\sqrt{np(1-p)}$, respectively.		236	5.3, 5.4
Sampling without replacement	Sampling where no member of the population can be sampled more than once		236	

(continued)

[9]See the text for the new versions of some of these Excel functions in Excel 2010.

Summary of Key Terms   (*Continued*)

Term	Explanation	Excel[9]	Page	Equation
Sampling with replacement	Sampling where any member of the population can be sampled more than once		236	
Normal approximation to the binomial distribution	If $np > 5$ and $n(1 - p) > 5$, the binomial distribution can be approximated well by a normal distribution with mean np and standard deviation $\sqrt{np(1 - p)}$.		237	
Poisson distribution	A discrete probability distribution that often describes the number of events occurring within a specified period of time or space; mean and variance both equal the parameter λ	POISSON	250	
Exponential distribution	A continuous probability distribution useful for measuring *times* between events, such as customer arrivals to a service facility; mean and standard deviation both equal $1/\lambda$	EXPONDIST	252	
Relationship between Poisson and exponential distributions	Exponential distribution measures *times* between events; Poisson distribution counts the *number* of events in a certain period of time.		254	
@RISK	An Excel add-in for finding how well a specified distribution fits a set of data, or for finding the distribution that best fits a set of data	Distribution Fitting item on @RISK ribbon	255	

PROBLEMS

Conceptual Questions

C.1. For each of the following uncertain quantities, discuss whether it is reasonable to assume that the probability distribution of the quantity is normal. If the answer isn't obvious, discuss how you could discover whether a normal distribution is reasonable.

a. The change in the Dow Jones Industrial Average between now and a year from now

b. The length of time (in months) a battery that is in continuous use lasts

c. The time between two successive arrivals to a bank

d. The time it takes a bank teller to service a random customer

e. The length (in yards) of a typical drive on a par 5 by Phil Michelson

f. The amount of snowfall (in inches) in a typical winter in Minneapolis

g. The average height (in inches) of all boys in a randomly selected seventh-grade middle school class

h. Your bonus from finishing a project, where your bonus is $1000 per day under the deadline if the project is completed before the deadline, your bonus is $500 if the project is completed right on the deadline, and your bonus is $0 if the project is completed after the deadline

i. Your gain on a call option on a stock, where you gain nothing if the price of the stock a month from now is less than or equal to $50 and you gain $(P–50)$ dollars if the price P a month from now is greater than $50

C.2. For each of the following uncertain quantities, discuss whether it is reasonable to assume that the probability distribution of the quantity is binomial. If you think it is, what are the parameters n and p. If you think it isn't, explain your reasoning.

a. The number of wins the Boston Red Sox baseball team has next year in its 81 home games

b. The number of free throws Kobe Bryant misses in his next 250 attempts

c. The number of free throws it takes Kobe Bryant to achieve 100 successes

d. The number out of 1000 randomly selected customers in a supermarket who have a bill of at least $150

e. The number of trading days in a typical year where Microsoft's stock price increases

f. The number of spades you get in a 13-card hand from a well-shuffled 52-card deck

g. The number of adjacent 15-minute segments during a typical Friday where at least 10 customers enter a McDonald's restaurant

h. The number of pages in a 500-page book with at least one misprint on the page

C.3. The Poisson distribution is often appropriate in the "binomial" situation of n independent and identical trials, where each trial has probability p of success, but n is very large and p is very small. In this case, the Poisson distribution is relevant for the number of successes, and its parameter (its mean) is np. Discuss some situations where such a Poisson model might be appropriate. How would you measure n and p, or would you measure only their product np? Here is one to get you started: the number of traffic accidents at a particular intersection in a given year.

C.4. One disadvantage of a normal distribution is that there is always some probability that a quantity is negative, even when this makes no sense for the uncertain quantity. For example, the time a light bulb lasts cannot be negative. In any particular situation, how would you decide whether you could ignore this disadvantage for all practical purposes?

C.5. Explain why probabilities such as $P(X < x)$ and $P(X \leq x)$ are equal for a continuous random variable.

C.6. State the major similarities and differences between the *binomial* distribution and the *Poisson* distribution.

C.7. You have a bowl with 100 pieces of paper inside, each with a person's name written on it. It turns out that 50 of the names correspond to males and the other 50 to females. You reach inside and grab five pieces of paper. If X is the random number of male names you choose, is X binomially distributed? Why or why not?

C.8. A distribution we didn't discuss is the Bernoulli distribution. It is essentially a binomial distribution with $n = 1$. In other words, it is the number of successes (0 or 1) in a single trial when the probability of success is p. What are the mean and standard deviation of a Bernoulli distribution? Discuss how a binomial random variable can be expressed in terms of n independent Bernoulli random variables, each with the same parameter p.

C.9. For real applications, the normal distribution has two potential drawbacks: (1) it can be negative, and (2) it isn't symmetric. Choose some continuous random numeric outcomes of interest to you. Are either potential drawbacks really drawbacks for your random outcomes? If so, which is the more serious drawback?

C.10. Many basketball players and fans believe strongly in the "hot hand." That is, they believe that players tend to shoot in streaks, either makes or misses. If this is the case, why does the binomial distribution not apply, at least not exactly, to the number of makes in a given number of shots? Which assumption of the binomial model is violated, the independence of successive shots or the constant probability of success on each shot? Or can you tell?

C.11. Suppose the demands in successive weeks for your product are normally distributed with mean 100 and standard deviation 20, and suppose your lead time for receiving a placed order is three weeks. A quantity of interest to managers is the lead-time demand, the total demanded over three weeks. Why does the formula for the standard deviation of lead-time demand include a square root of 3? What assumptions are behind this?

Level A

51. Suppose the annual return on XYZ stock follows a normal distribution with mean 0.12 and standard deviation 0.30.

a. What is the probability that XYZ's value will decrease during a year?

b. What is the probability that the return on XYZ during a year will be at least 20%?

c. What is the probability that the return on XYZ during a year will be between –6% and 9%?

d. There is a 5% chance that the return on XYZ during a year will be greater than what value?

e. There is a 1% chance that the return on XYZ during a year will be less than what value?

f. There is a 95% chance that the return on XYZ during a year will be between which two values (equidistant from the mean)?

52. Assume the annual mean return on ABC stock is around 15% and the annual standard deviation is around 25%. Assume the annual and daily returns on ABC stock are normally distributed.

a. What is the probability that ABC will lose money during a year?

b. There is a 5% chance that ABC will earn a return of at least what value during a year?

c. There is a 10% chance that ABC will earn a return of less than or equal to what value during a year?

d. What is the probability that ABC will earn at least 35% during a year?

e. Assume there are 252 trading days in a year. What is the probability that ABC will lose money on a given day? (*Hint*: Let Y be the annual return on ABC and X_i be the return on ABC on day i. Then (approximately) $Y = X_1 + X_2 + \ldots + X_{252}$. Use the fact that the sum of independent normal random variables is normally distributed, with mean equal to the sum of the individual means and variance equal to the sum of the individual variances.)

53. Suppose Comdell Computer receives its hard drives from Diskco. On average, 4% of all hard disk drives received by Comdell are defective.

a. Comdell has adopted the following policy. It samples 50 hard drives in each shipment and accepts the shipment if all hard drives in the sample are nondefective. What fraction of shipments will Comdell accept?

b. Suppose instead that the shipment is accepted if at most one hard drive in the sample is defective. What fraction of shipments will Comdell accept?

c. What is the probability that a sample of size 50 will contain at least 10 defectives?

54. A family is considering a move from a midwestern city to a city in California. The distribution of housing costs where the family currently lives is normal, with mean $105,000 and standard deviation $18,200. The distribution of housing costs in the California city is normal with mean $235,000 and standard deviation $30,400. The family's current house is valued at $110,000.

a. What percentage of houses in the family's current city cost less than theirs?

b. If the family buys a $200,000 house in the new city, what percentage of houses there will cost less than theirs?

c. What price house will the family need to buy to be in the same percentile (of housing costs) in the new city as they are in the current city?

55. The number of traffic fatalities in a typical month in a given state has a normal distribution with mean 125 and standard deviation 31.

a. If a person in the highway department claims that there will be at least m fatalities in the next month with probability 0.95, what value of m makes this claim true?

b. If the claim is that there will be no more than n fatalities in the next month with probability 0.98, what value of n makes this claim true?

56. It can be shown that a sum of independent normally distributed random variables is also normally distributed. Do *all* functions of normal random variables lead to normal random variables? Consider the following. SuperDrugs is a chain of drugstores with three similar-size stores in a given city. The sales in a given week for any of these stores is normally distributed with mean $15,000 and standard deviation $3000. At the end of each week, the sales figure for the store with the largest sales among the three stores is recorded. Is this maximum value normally distributed? To answer this question, simulate a weekly sales figure at each of the three stores and

calculate the maximum. Then replicate this maximum 500 times and create a histogram of the 500 maximum values. Does it appear to be normally shaped? Whatever this distribution looks like, use your simulated values to estimate its mean and standard deviation of the maximum.

57. In the game of baseball, every time a player bats, he is either successful (gets on base) or he fails (doesn't get on base). (This is all you need to know about baseball for this problem!) His on-base percentage, usually expressed as a decimal, is the percentage of times he is successful. Let's consider a player who is theoretically a 0.375 on-base batter. Specifically, assume that each time he bats, he is successful with probability 0.375 and unsuccessful with probability 0.625. Also, assume that he bats 600 times in a season. What can you say about his on-base percentage, (# of successes)/600, for the season? (*Hint*: Each on-base percentage is equivalent to a number of successes. For example, 0.380 is equivalent to 228 successes because 0.380*600 = 228.)

a. What is the probability that his on-base percentage will be *less than* 0.360?

b. What is the probability that his on-base percentage will be *greater than* 0.370?

c. What is the probability that his on-base percentage will be *less than or equal to* 0.400?

58. In the financial world, there are many types of complex instruments called derivatives that *derive* their value from the value of an underlying asset. Consider the following simple derivative. A stock's current price is $80 per share. You purchase a derivative whose value to you becomes known a month from now. Specifically, let P be the price of the stock in a month. If P is between $75 and $85, the derivative is worth nothing to you. If P is less than $75, the derivative results in a loss of $100*(75–P)$ dollars to you. (The factor of 100 is because many derivatives involve 100 shares.) If P is greater than $85, the derivative results in a gain of $100*(P–85)$ dollars to you. Assume that the distribution of the change in the stock price from now to a month from now is normally distributed with mean $1 and standard deviation $8. Let P(big loss) be the probability that you lose at least $1000 (that is, the price falls below $65), and let P(big gain) be the probability that you gain at least $1000 (that is, the price rises above $95). Find these two probabilities. How do they compare to one another?

Level B

59. When you sum 30 or more independent random variables, the sum of the random variables will usually be approximately normally distributed, even if each individual random variable is not normally distributed. Use this fact to estimate the probability that a casino will be behind after 90,000 roulette bets, given that it wins $1 or loses $35 on each bet with probabilities 37/38 and 1/38.

60. The daily demand for six-packs of Coke at Mr. D's supermarket follows a normal distribution with mean 120 and standard deviation 30. Every Monday the Coke delivery driver delivers Coke to Mr. D's. If Mr. D's wants to have only a 1% chance of running out of Coke by the end of the week, how many should Mr. D's order for the week? Assume orders are placed on Sunday at midnight. Also assume that demands on different days are probabilistically independent. (Use the fact that the sum of independent normal random variables is normally distributed, with mean equal to the sum of the individual means and variance equal to the sum of the individual variances.)

61. Many companies use sampling to determine whether a batch should be accepted. An (n, c) sampling plan consists of inspecting n randomly chosen items from a batch and accepting the batch if c or fewer sampled items are defective. Suppose a company uses a $(100, 5)$ sampling plan to determine whether a batch of 10,000 computer chips is acceptable.
   a. The "producer's risk" of a sampling plan is the probability that an acceptable batch will be rejected by the sampling plan. Suppose the customer considers a batch with 3% defectives acceptable. What is the producer's risk for this sampling plan?
   b. The "consumer's risk" of a sampling plan is the probability that an unacceptable batch will be accepted by the sampling plan. Our customer says that a batch with 9% defectives is unacceptable. What is the consumer's risk for this sampling plan?

62. Suppose that if a presidential election were held today, 53% of all voters would vote for Obama over McCain. (You can substitute the names of the current presidential candidates.) This problem shows that even if there are 100 million voters, a sample of several thousand is enough to determine the outcome, even in a fairly close election.
   a. If 1500 voters are sampled randomly, what is the probability that the sample will indicate (correctly) that Obama is preferred to McCain?
   b. If 6000 voters are sampled randomly, what is the probability that the sample will indicate (correctly) that Obama is preferred to McCain?

63. A soft-drink factory fills bottles of soda by setting a timer on a filling machine. It has generally been observed that the distribution of the number of ounces the machine puts into a bottle is normal, with standard deviation 0.05 ounce. The company wants 99.9% of all its bottles to have at least 16 ounces of soda. To what value should the mean amount put in each bottle be set? (Of course, the company does not want to fill any more than is necessary.)

64. The time it takes you to swim 100 yards in a race is normally distributed with mean 62 seconds and standard deviation 2 seconds. In your next five races, what is the probability that you will swim under a minute exactly twice?

65. A company assembles a large part by joining two smaller parts together. Assume that the smaller parts are normally distributed with a mean length of 1 inch and a standard deviation of 0.01 inch.
   a. What fraction of the larger parts are longer than 2.05 inches? (Use the fact that the sum of independent normal random variables is normally distributed, with mean equal to the sum of the individual means and variance equal to the sum of the individual variances.)
   b. What fraction of the larger parts are between 1.96 inches and 2.02 inches long?

66. (Suggested by Sam Kaufmann, Indiana University MBA, who runs Harrah's Lake Tahoe Casino.) A high roller has come to the casino to play 300 games of craps. For each game of craps played there is a 0.493 probability that the high roller will win $1 and a 0.507 probability that the high roller will lose $1. After 300 games of craps, what is the probability that the casino will be behind more than $10?

67. (Suggested by Sam Kaufmann, Indiana University MBA, who runs Harrah's Lake Tahoe Casino.) A high roller comes to the casino intending to play 500 hands of blackjack for $1 a hand. On each hand, the high roller will win $1 with probability 0.48 and lose $1 with probability 0.52. After the 500 hands, what is the probability that the casino has lost more than $40?

68. A soft-drink company produces 100,000 12-ounce bottles of soda per year. By adjusting a dial, the company can set the mean number of ounces placed in a bottle. Regardless of the mean, the standard deviation of the number of ounces in a bottle is 0.05 ounce. The soda costs 5 cents per ounce. Any bottle weighing less than 12 ounces will incur a $10 fine for being underweight. Determine a setting for the mean number of ounces per bottle of soda that minimizes the expected cost per year of producing soda. Your answer should be accurate within 0.001 ounce. Does the number of bottles produced per year influence your answer?

69. The weekly demand for TVs at Lowland Appliance is normally distributed with mean 400 and standard deviation 100. Each time an order for TVs is placed, it arrives exactly four weeks later. That is, TV orders have a four-week lead time. Lowland doesn't want to run out of TVs during any more than 1% of all lead times. How low should Lowland let its TV inventory drop before it places an order for more TVs? (*Hint*: How many standard deviations above the mean lead-time demand must the reorder point be for there to be

a 1% chance of a stockout during the lead time? Use the fact that the sum of independent normal random variables is normally distributed, with mean equal to the sum of the individual means and variance equal to the sum of the individual variances.)

70. An elevator rail is assumed to meet specifications if its diameter is between 0.98 and 1.01 inches. Each year a company produces 100,000 elevator rails. For a cost of $10/\sigma^2$ per year the company can rent a machine that produces elevator rails whose diameters have a standard deviation of σ. (The idea is that the company must pay more for a smaller variance.) Each such machine will produce rails having a mean diameter of one inch. Any rail that does not meet specifications must be reworked at a cost of $12. Assume that the diameter of an elevator rail follows a normal distribution.

   a. What standard deviation (within 0.001 inch) minimizes the annual cost of producing elevator rails? You do not need to try standard deviations in excess of 0.02 inch.

   b. For your answer in part **a**, one elevator rail in 1000 will be at least how many inches in diameter?

71. A 50-question true–false examination is given. Each correct answer is worth 10 points. Consider an unprepared student who randomly guesses on each question.
   a. If no points are deducted for incorrect answers, what is the probability that the student will score at least 350 points?
   b. If 5 points are deducted for each incorrect answer, what is the probability that the student will score at least 200 points?
   c. If 10 points are deducted for each incorrect answer, what is the probability that the student will receive a negative score?

72. The percentage of examinees who took the GMAT (Graduate Management Admission) exam from June 1992 to March 1995 and scored below each total score is given in the file **P05_72.xlsx**. For example, 96% of all examinees scored 690 or below. The mean GMAT score for this time period was 497 and the standard deviation was 105. Does it appear that GMAT scores can accurately be approximated by a normal distribution? (Source: 1995 GMAT Examinee Interpretation Guide)

73. What caused the crash of TWA Flight 800 in 1996? Physics professors Hailey and Helfand of Columbia University believe there is a reasonable possibility that a meteor hit Flight 800. They reason as follows. On a given day, 3000 meteors of a size large enough to destroy an airplane hit the earth's atmosphere. Approximately 50,000 flights per day, averaging two hours in length, have been flown from 1950 to 1996. This means that at any given point in time, planes in flight cover approximately two-billionths of the world's atmosphere. Determine the probability that at least one

plane in the last 47 years has been downed by a meteor. (*Hint*: Use the Poisson approximation to the binomial. This approximation says that if n is large and p is small, a binomial distribution with parameters n and p is approximately Poisson distributed with $\lambda = np$.)

74. In the decade 1982 through 1991, 10 employees working at the Amoco Company chemical research center were stricken with brain tumors. The average employment at the center was 2000 employees. Nationwide, the average incidence of brain tumors in a single year is 20 per 100,000 people. If the incidence of brain tumors at the Amoco chemical research center were the same as the nationwide incidence, what is the probability that at least 10 brain tumors would have been observed among Amoco workers during the decade 1982 through 1991? What do you conclude from your analysis? (Source: AP wire service report, March 12, 1994)

75. Claims arrive at random times to an insurance company. The daily amount of claims is normally distributed with mean $1570 and standard deviation $450. Total claims on different days each have this distribution, and they are probabilistically independent of one another.
   a. Find the probability that the amount of total claims over a period of 100 days is at least $150,000. (Use the fact that the sum of independent normally distributed random variables is normally distributed, with mean equal to the sum of the individual means and variance equal to the sum of the individual variances.)
   b. If the company receives premiums totaling $165,000, find the probability that the company will net at least $10,000 for the 100-day period.

76. A popular model for stock prices is the following. If p_0 is the current stock price, then the price k periods from now, p_k, (where a period could be a day, week, or any other convenient unit of time, and k is any positive integer) is given by

$$p_k = p_0 \exp((\mu - 0.5\sigma^2)k + sZ\sqrt{k})$$

Here, exp is the exponential function (EXP in Excel), μ is the mean percentage growth rate per period of the stock, σ is the standard deviation of the growth rate per period, and Z is a normally distributed random variable with mean 0 and standard deviation 1. Both μ and σ are typically estimated from actual stock price data, and they are typically expressed in decimal form, such as $\mu = 0.01$ for a 1% mean growth rate.
   a. Suppose a period is defined as a month, the current price of the stock (as of the end of December 2010) is $75, $\mu = 0.006$, and $\sigma = 0.028$. Use simulation to obtain 500 possible stock price changes from the end of December 2010 to the end of December 2013. Each simulated change will be the price at the

end of 2013 minus the price at the end of 2010. (Note that you can simulate a given change in one line and then copy it down.) Create a histogram of these changes to see whether the stock price change is at least approximately normally distributed. Also, use the simulated data to estimate the mean price change and the standard deviation of the change.

b. Use simulation to generate the ending stock prices for each month in 2011. (Use $k = 1$ to get January's price from December's, use $k = 1$ again to get February's price from January's, and so on.) Then use a data table to replicate the ending December 2011 stock price 500 times. Create a histogram of these 500 values. Do they appear to resemble a normal distribution?

77. Your company is running an audit on the Sleaze Company. Because Sleaze has a bad habit of overcharging its customers, the focus of your audit is on checking whether the billing amounts on its invoices are correct. Assume that each invoice is for too high an amount with probability 0.06 and for too low an amount with probability 0.01 (so that the probability of a correct billing is 0.93). Also, assume that the outcome for any invoice is probabilistically independent of the outcomes for other invoices.

a. If you randomly sample 200 of Sleaze's invoices, what is the probability that you will find at least 15 invoices that overcharge the customer? What is the probability you won't find any that undercharge the customer?

b. Find an integer k such that the probability is at least 0.99 that you will find at least k invoices that overcharge the customer. (*Hint*: Use trial and error with the BINOMDIST function to find k.)

78. Continuing the previous problem, suppose that when Sleaze overcharges a customer, the distribution of the amount overcharged (expressed as a percentage of the correct billing amount) is normally distributed with mean 15% and standard deviation 4%.

a. What percentage of overbilled customers are charged at least 10% more than they should pay?

b. What percentage of *all* customers are charged at least 10% more than they should pay?

c. If your auditing company samples 200 randomly chosen invoices, what is the probability that it will find at least five where the customer was overcharged by at least 10%?

79. Your manufacturing process makes parts such that each part meets specifications with probability 0.98. You need a batch of 250 parts that meet specifications. How many parts must you produce to be at least 99% certain of producing at least 250 parts that meet specifications?

80. Let X be normally distributed with a given mean and standard deviation. Sometimes you want to find two

values a and b such that $P(a < X < b)$ is equal to some specific probability such as 0.90 or 0.95. There are many answers to this problem, depending on how much probability you put in each of the two tails. For this question, assume the mean and standard deviation are $\mu = 100$ and $\sigma = 10$, and that you want to find a and b such that $P(a < X < b) = 0.90$.

a. Find a and b so that there is probability 0.05 in each tail.

b. Find a and b so that there is probability 0.025 in the left tail and 0.075 in the right tail.

c. The usual answer to the general problem is the answer from part a, that is, where you put equal probability in the two tails. It turns out that this is the answer that minimizes the length of the interval from a to b. That is, if you solve the following problem: minimize $(b - a)$, subject to $P(a < X < b) = 0.90$, you will get the same answer as in part **a**. Verify this by using Excel's Solver add-in.

81. As any credit-granting agency knows, there are always some customers who default on credit charges. Typically, customers are grouped into relatively homogeneous categories, so that customers within any category have approximately the same chance of defaulting on their credit charges. Here we will look at one particular group of customers. We assume each of these customers has (1) probability 0.07 of defaulting on his or her current credit charges, and (2) total credit charges that are normally distributed with mean $350 and standard deviation $100. We also assume that if a customer defaults, 20% of his or her charges can be recovered. The other 80% are written off as bad debt.

a. What is the probability that a typical customer in this group will default and produce a write-off of more than $250 in bad debt?

b. If there are 500 customers in this group, what are the mean and standard deviation of the number of customers who will meet the description in part **a**?

c. Again assuming there are 500 customers in this group, what is the probability that at least 25 of them will meet the description in part **a**?

d. Suppose now that nothing is recovered from a default—the whole amount is written off as bad debt. Show how to simulate the total amount of bad debt from 500 customers in just two cells, one with a binomial calculation, the other with a normal calculation.

82. The Excel functions discussed in this chapter are useful for solving a lot of probability problems, but there are other problems that, even though they are similar to normal or binomial problems, cannot be solved with these functions. In cases like this, simulation can often be used. Here are a couple of

such problems for you to simulate. For each example, simulate 500 replications of the experiment.

a. You observe a sequence of parts from a manufacturing line. These parts use a component that is supplied by one of two suppliers. Each part made with a component from supplier 1 works properly with probability 0.95, and each part made with a component from supplier 2 works properly with probability 0.98. Assuming that 100 of these parts are made, 60 from supplier 1 and 40 from supplier 2, you want the probability that at least 97 of them work properly.

b. Here we look at a more generic example such as coin flipping. There is a sequence of trials where each trial is a success with probability p and a failure with probability $1 - p$. A run is a sequence of consecutive successes or failures. For most of us, intuition says that there should not be long runs. Test this by finding the probability that there is at least one run of length at least six in a sequence of 15 trials. (The run could be of 0s or 1s.) You can use any value of p you like—or try different values of p.

83. You have a device that uses a single battery, and you operate this device continuously, never turning it off. Whenever a battery fails, you replace it with a brand new one immediately. Suppose the lifetime of a typical battery has an exponential distribution with mean 205 minutes. Suppose you operate the device continuously for three days, making battery changes when necessary. Find the probability that you will observe at least 25 failures. (*Hint*: The number of failures is Poisson distributed.)

84. In the previous problem, we ran the experiment for a certain number of days and then asked about the number of failures. In this problem, we take a different point of view. Suppose you operate the device, starting with a new battery, until you have observed 25 battery failures. What is the probability that at least 15 of these 25 batteries lived at least 3.5 hours? (*Hint*: Each lifetime is exponentially distributed.)

85. In the game of soccer, players are sometimes awarded a penalty kick. The player who kicks places the ball 12 yards from the 24-foot-wide goal and attempts to kick it past the goalie into the net. (The goalie is the only defender.) The question is where the player should aim. Make the following assumptions. (1) The player's kick is off target from where he aims, left or right, by a normally distributed amount with mean 0 and some standard deviation. (2) The goalie typically guesses left or right and dives in that direction at the moment the player kicks. If the goalie guesses wrong, he won't block the kick, but if he guesses correctly, he will be able to block a kick that would have gone into the net as long as the kick is within a distance d from the middle of the goal. The goalie is equally likely to guess left or right. (3) The player never misses high, but he can miss to the right of the goal (if he aims to the right) or to the left (if he aims to the left). For reasonable values of the standard deviation and d, find the probability that the player makes a goal if he aims at a point t feet inside the goal. (By symmetry, you can assume he aims to the right, although the goalie doesn't know this.) What value of t seems to maximize the probability of making a goal?

having a winning ticket, but is it assured of covering its costs? Calculate the expected net benefit (in terms of net present value) to the syndicate, using any reasonable values of n and R, to see whether the syndicate can expect to come out ahead.

Actually, the analysis suggested in the previous paragraph is not complete. There are at least two complications to consider. The first is the effect of taxes. Fortunately for the Australian syndicate, it did not have to pay federal or state taxes on its winnings, but a U.S. syndicate wouldn't be so lucky. Second, the jackpot from a $20 million jackpot, say, is actually paid in 20 annual $1 million payments. The Lottery Commission pays the winner $1 million immediately and then purchases 19 "strips" (bonds with the interest not included) maturing at 1-year intervals with face value of $1 million each. Unfortunately, the lottery prize does not offer the liquidity of the Treasury issues that back up the payments. This lack of liquidity could make the lottery less attractive to the syndicate. ■

Decision Making under Uncertainty

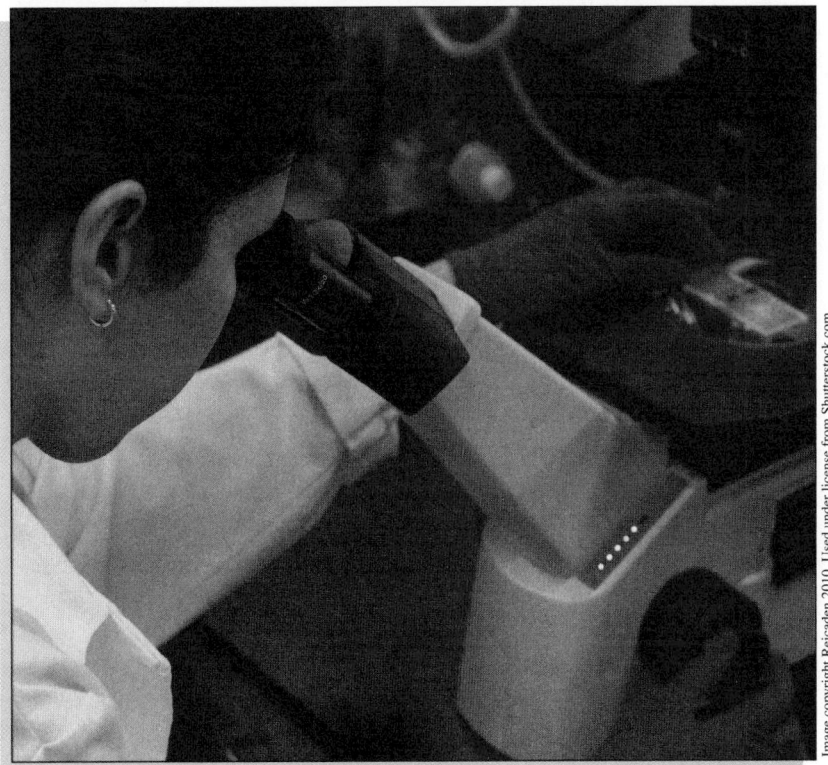

Image copyright Reicaden 2010. Used under license from Shutterstock.com

DECIDING WHETHER TO DEVELOP NEW DRUGS AT BAYER

The formal decision-making process discussed in this chapter is often used to make difficult decisions in the face of much uncertainty, large monetary values, and long-term consequences. Stonebraker (2002) chronicles one such decision-making process he performed for Bayer Pharmaceuticals in 1999. The development of a new drug is a time-consuming and expensive process that is filled with risks along the way. A pharmaceutical company must first get the proposed drug through preclinical trials, where the drug is tested on animals. Assuming this stage is successful (and only about half are), the company can then file an application with the Food and Drug Administration (FDA) to conduct clinical trials on humans. These clinical trials have three phases. Phase 1 is designed to test the safety of the drug on a small sample of healthy patients. Phase 2 is designed to identify the optimal dose of the new drug on patients with the disease. Phase 3 is a statistically designed study to prove the efficacy and safety of the new drug on a larger sample of patients with the disease. Failure at any one of these phases means that further testing stops and the drug is never brought to market. Of course, this means that all costs up to the failure point are lost. If the drug makes it through the clinical tests (and only about 25% of all drugs do so), the company can then apply to the FDA for permission to manufacture and market its drug in the United States. Assuming that FDA approves, the company is then free to launch the drug in the marketplace.

The study involved the evaluation of a new drug for busting blood clots called BAY 57-9602, and it commenced at a time just prior to the first decision point: whether to conduct preclinical tests. This was the company's first formal use of decision making for evaluating a new drug, so to convince the company of the worth of such a study, Stonebraker did exactly what a successful management science study should do. He formulated the problem and its objectives; he identified risks, costs, and benefits; he involved key people in the organization to help provide the data needed for the decision analysis; and, because much of the resulting data consisted of educated guesses at best, he performed a thorough sensitivity analysis on the inputs. Although we are not told in the article how everything turned out, the analysis did persuade Bayer management to proceed in January 2000 with preclinical testing of the drug.

The article provides a fascinating look at how such a study should proceed. Because there is so much uncertainty, the key is determining probabilities and probability distributions for the various inputs. First, there are uncertainties in the various phases of testing. Each of these can be modeled with a probability of success. For example, the chance of making it through preclinical testing was assessed to be about 65% for BAY 57-9602, although management preferred to use the more conservative benchmark of 50% (based on historical data on other drugs) for the decision analysis. Many of the other uncertain quantities, such as the eventual market share, are continuous random variables. Because the decision tree approach discussed in this chapter requires discrete random variables, usually with only a few possible values, Stonebraker used a popular three-point approximation for all continuous quantities. He asked experts to assess the 10th percentile, the 50th percentile, and the 90th percentile, and he assigned probabilities 0.3, 0.4, and 0.3 to these three values. [The validity of such an approximation is discussed in Keefer and Bodily (1983).]

After getting all such estimates of uncertain quantities from the company experts, the author examined the expected net present value (NPV) of all costs and benefits from developing the new drug. To see which of the various uncertain quantities affected the expected NPV most, he varied each such quantity, one at a time, from its 10th percentile to its 90th percentile, leaving the other inputs at their base 50th percentile values. This identified several quantities that the expected NPV was most sensitive to, including the peak product share, the price per treatment in the United States, and the annual growth rate. The expected NPV was not nearly as sensitive to other uncertain inputs, including the product launch date and the production process yield. Therefore, in the final decision analysis, Stonebraker treated the sensitive inputs as uncertain and the less sensitive inputs as certain at their base values. He also calculated the risk profile from developing the drug. This indicates the probability distribution of NPV, taking all sources of uncertainty into account. Although this risk profile was not exactly optimistic (90% chance of losing money using the conservative probabilities of success, 67% chance of losing money with the more optimistic product-specific probabilities of success), this risk profile compared favorably with Bayer's other potential projects. This evaluation, plus the rigor and defensibility of the study, led Bayer management to give the go-ahead on preclinical testing. ■

6.1 INTRODUCTION

This chapter provides a formal framework for analyzing decision problems that involve uncertainty. Our discussion includes the following:

- criteria for choosing among alternative decisions
- how probabilities are used in the decision-making process

- how early decisions affect decisions made at a later stage
- how a decision maker can quantify the value of information
- how attitudes toward risk can affect the analysis

Throughout, we employ a powerful graphical tool—a decision tree—to guide the analysis. A decision tree enables a decision maker to view all important aspects of the problem at once: the decision alternatives, the uncertain outcomes and their probabilities, the economic consequences, and the chronological order of events. We show how to implement decision trees in Excel by taking advantage of a very powerful and flexible add-in from Palisade called PrecisionTree.

Many examples of decision making under uncertainty exist in the business world, including the following:

- Companies routinely place bids for contracts to complete a certain project within a fixed time frame. Often these are sealed bids, where each company presents a bid for completing the project in a sealed envelope. Then the envelopes are opened, and the low bidder is awarded the bid amount to complete the project. Any particular company in the bidding competition must deal with the uncertainty of the other companies' bids, as well as possible uncertainty regarding their cost to complete the project if they win the bid. The trade-off is between bidding low to win the bid and bidding high to make a larger profit.

- Whenever a company contemplates introducing a new product into the market, there are a number of uncertainties that affect the decision, probably the most important being the customers' reaction to this product. If the product generates high customer demand, the company will make a large profit. But if demand is low—and, after all, the vast majority of new products do poorly—the company could fail to recoup its development costs. Because the level of customer demand is critical, the company might try to gauge this level by test marketing the product in one region of the country. If this test market is a success, the company can then be more optimistic that a full-scale national marketing of the product will also be successful. But if the test market is a failure, the company can cut its losses by abandoning the product.

- Whenever manufacturing companies make capacity expansion decisions, they face uncertain consequences. First, they must decide whether to build new plants. If they don't expand and demand for their products is higher than expected, they will lose revenue because of insufficient capacity. If they do expand and demand for their products is lower than expected, they will be stuck with expensive underutilized capacity. Of course, in today's global economy, companies also need to decide *where* to build new plants. This decision involves a whole new set of uncertainties, including exchange rates, labor availability, social stability, competition from local businesses, and others.

- Banks must continually make decisions on whether to grant loans to businesses or individuals. As we all know, many banks made many very poor decisions, especially on mortgage loans, during the years leading up to the financial crisis in 2008. They fooled themselves into thinking that housing prices would only increase, never decrease. When the bottom fell out of the housing market, banks were stuck with loans that could never be repaid.

- Utility companies must make many decisions that have significant environmental and economic consequences. For these companies it is not necessarily enough to conform to federal or state environmental regulations. Recent court decisions have found companies liable—for huge settlements—when accidents occurred, even though the companies followed all existing regulations. Therefore, when utility companies decide, say, whether to replace equipment or mitigate the effects of environmental pollution, they must take into account the possible environmental consequences (such as injuries to people) as well as economic consequences (such as lawsuits). An aspect of these situations that makes decision analysis particularly difficult is that the potential "disasters" are often extremely unlikely; hence, their probabilities are difficult to assess accurately.

■ Sports teams continually make decisions under uncertainty. Sometimes these decisions involve long-run consequences, such as whether to trade for a promising but as yet untested pitcher in baseball. Other times these decisions involve short-run consequences, such as whether to go for a fourth down or kick a field goal late in a close football game. You might be surprised at the level of quantitative sophistication in professional sports these days. Management and coaches typically do *not* make important decisions by gut feel. They employ many of the tools in this chapter and in other chapters of this book.

6.2 ELEMENTS OF DECISION ANALYSIS

Although decision making under uncertainty occurs in a wide variety of contexts, all problems have three common elements: (1) the set of decisions (or strategies) available to the decision maker, (2) the set of possible outcomes and the probabilities of these outcomes, and (3) a value model that prescribes monetary values for the various decision–outcome combinations. Once these elements are known, the decision maker can find an optimal decision, depending on the optimality criterion chosen.

Before moving on to realistic business problems, we discuss the basic elements of any decision analysis for a very simple problem. We assume that a decision maker must choose among three decisions, labeled *D*1, *D*2, and *D*3. Each of these decisions has three possible outcomes, labeled *O*1, *O*2, and *O*3.

6.2.1 Payoff Tables

At the time the decision must be made, the decision maker does *not* know which outcome will occur. However, once the decision is made, the outcome will eventually be revealed, and a corresponding payoff will be received. This payoff might actually be a cost, in which case it is indicated as a negative value. The listing of payoffs for all decision–outcome pairs is called the **payoff table**.[1] For our simple decision problem, this payoff table appears in Table 6.1. For example, if the decision maker chooses decision *D*2 and outcome *O*3 then occurs, a payoff of $30 is received.

> **A payoff table** lists the payoff for each decision–outcome pair. Positive values correspond to *rewards* (or gains) and negative values correspond to *costs* (or losses).

Table 6.1 Payoff Table for Simple Decision Problem

		Outcome		
		*O*1	*O*2	*O*3
Decision	*D*1	10	10	10
	*D*2	−10	20	30
	*D*3	−30	30	80

[1]In situations where all monetary consequences are costs, it is customary to list these costs in a *cost table*. In this case, all monetary values are shown as *positive* costs.

A decision maker gets
to decide which row of
the payoff table she
wants. However, she
does not get to choose
the column.

This table shows that the decision maker can play it safe by choosing decision $D1$. This provides a sure $10 payoff. With decision $D2$, rewards of $20 or $30 are possible, but a loss of $10 is also possible. Decision $D3$ is even riskier; the possible loss is greater, and the maximum gain is also greater. Which decision would you choose? Would your choice change if the values in the payoff table were measured in *thousands* of dollars? The answers to these questions are what this chapter is all about. There must be a criterion for making choices, and this criterion must be evaluated so that the *best* decision can be identified. As you will see, it is customary to use one particular criterion for decisions involving moderate amounts of money.

Before proceeding, there is one very important point we need to emphasize: the distinction between good *decisions* and good *outcomes*. In any decision-making problem where there is uncertainty, the "best" decision can have less than optimal results—that is, you can be unlucky. Regardless of which decision you choose, you might get an outcome that, in hindsight, makes you wish we had made a different decision. For example, if you make decision $D3$, hoping for a large reward, you might get outcome $O1$, in which case you will wish you had chosen decision $D1$ or $D2$. Or if you choose decision $D2$, hoping to limit possible losses, you might get outcome $O3$, in which case you will wish you had chosen decision $D3$. The point is that decision makers must make rational decisions, based on the information they have when the decisions must be made, and then live with the consequences. Second-guessing these decisions, just because of bad luck with the outcomes, is not appropriate.

FUNDAMENTAL INSIGHT

What Is a "Good" Decision?

In the context of decision making under uncertainty, a "good" decision is one that is based on the sound decision-making principles discussed in this chapter. Because the decision must usually be made before

uncertainty is resolved, a good decision might have unlucky consequences. However, decision makers should not be criticized for unlucky outcomes. They should be criticized only if their analysis *at the time the decision has to be made* is faulty.

6.2.2 Possible Decision Criteria

What do we mean when we call a decision the "best" decision? We will eventually settle on one particular criterion for making decisions, but we first explore some possibilities. With respect to Table 6.1, one possibility is to choose the decision that maximizes the *worst* payoff. This criterion, called the **maximin** criterion, is appropriate for a very conservative (or pessimistic) decision maker. The worst payoffs for the three decisions are the minimums in the three rows: 10, -10, and -30. The maximin decision maker chooses the decision corresponding to the best of these: decision $D1$ with payoff 10. Such a criterion tends to avoid large losses, but it fails to even consider large rewards. Hence, it is typically *too* conservative and is seldom used.

The **maximin** criterion finds the worst payoff in each row of the payoff table and chooses the decision corresponding to the best of these.

At the other extreme, the decision maker might choose the decision that maximizes the *best* payoff. This criterion, called the **maximax** criterion, is appropriate for a risk taker (or optimist). The best payoffs for the three decisions are the maximums in the three rows: 10, 30, and 80. The maximax decision maker chooses the decision corresponding to the best of these: decision *D3* with payoff 80. This criterion looks tempting because it focuses on large gains, but its very serious downside is that it ignores possible losses. Because this type of decision making could eventually bankrupt a company, the maximax criterion is also seldom used.

> The **maximax** criterion finds the best payoff in each row of the payoff table and chooses the decision corresponding to the best of these.

6.2.3 Expected Monetary Value (EMV)

We have introduced the maximin and maximax criteria because (1) they are occasionally used to make decisions, and (2) they illustrate that there are several "reasonable" criteria for making decisions. In fact, there are other possible criteria that we will not discuss (although a couple are explored in the problems). Instead, we now focus on a criterion that is generally regarded as the preferred criterion in most decision problems. It is called the **expected monetary value**, or **EMV**, criterion. To motivate the EMV criterion, we first note that the maximin and maximax criteria make no reference to how *likely* the various outcomes are. However, decision makers typically have at least some idea of these likelihoods, and they ought to use this information in the decision-making process. After all, if outcome *O1* in our problem is extremely unlikely, then the pessimist who uses maximin is being overly conservative. Similarly, if outcome *O3* is quite unlikely, then the optimist who uses maximax is taking an unnecessary risk.

The EMV approach assesses probabilities for each outcome of each decision and then calculates the *expected* payoff from each decision based on these probabilities. This expected payoff, or EMV, is a weighted average of the payoffs in any given row of the payoff table, weighted by the probabilities of the outcomes. You calculate the EMV for each decision, then choose the decision with the largest EMV. (Note that the terms *expected payoff* and *mean payoff* are equivalent. We will use them interchangeably.)

> The **expected monetary value**, or **EMV**, for any decision is a weighted average of the possible payoffs for this decision, weighted by the probabilities of the outcomes. Using the EMV criterion, you choose the decision with the largest EMV. This is sometimes called "playing the averages."

Where do the probabilities come from? This is a difficult question to answer in general because it depends on each specific situation. In some cases the current decision problem is similar to those a decision maker has faced many times in the past. Then the probabilities can be estimated from the knowledge of previous outcomes. If a certain type of outcome occurred, say, in about 30% of previous situations, an estimate of its current probability might be 0.30.

However, there are many decision problems that have no parallels in the past. In such cases, a decision maker must use whatever information is available, plus some intuition, to assess the probabilities. For example, if the problem involves a new product decision, and one possible outcome is that a competitor will introduce a similar product in the coming year, the decision maker will have to rely on any knowledge of the market and the competitor's situation to assess the probability of this outcome. It is important to note that this assessment can be very subjective. Two decision makers could easily assess the probability of the *same* outcome as 0.30 and 0.45, depending on their information and feelings, and neither could be considered "wrong." This is the nature of assessing probabilities subjectively in real business situations. Still, it is important for the decision maker to consult all relevant sources (historical data, expert opinions, government forecasts, and so on) when assessing these probabilities. As you will see, they are crucial to the decision-making process.

With this general framework in mind, let's assume that a decision maker assesses the probabilities of the three outcomes in Table 6.1 as 0.3, 0.5, and 0.2 if decision $D2$ is made, and as 0.5, 0.2, 0.3 if decision $D3$ is made.[2] Then the EMV for each decision is the sum of products of payoffs and probabilities:

$$\text{EMV for } D1: 10 \text{ (a sure thing)}$$

$$\text{EMV for } D2: -10(0.3) + 20(0.5) + 30(0.2) = 13$$

$$\text{EMV for } D3: -30(0.5) + 30(0.2) + 80(0.3) = 15$$

These calculations lead to the optimal decision: Choose decision $D3$ because it has the largest EMV.

It is important to understand what the EMV of a decision represents—and what it doesn't represent. For example, the EMV of 15 for decision $D3$ does *not* mean that you expect to gain $15 from this decision. The payoff table indicates that the result from $D3$ will be a loss of $30, a gain of $30, or a gain of $80; it will *never* be a gain of $15. The EMV is only a weighted average of the possible payoffs. As such, it can be interpreted in one of two ways. First, imagine that this situation can occur many times, not just once. If decision $D3$ is used each time, then *on average*, you will make a gain of about $15. About 50% of the time you will lose $30, about 20% of the time you will gain $30, and about 30% of the time you will gain $80. These average to $15. For this reason, using the EMV criterion is sometimes referred to as "playing the averages."

FUNDAMENTAL INSIGHT

What It Means to Be an EMV Maximizer

An EMV maximizer, by definition, is indifferent when faced with the choice between entering a gamble that has a certain EMV and receiving a sure dollar amount in the amount of the EMV. For example, consider a gamble where you flip a fair coin and win $0 or $1000 depending on whether you get a head or a tail. If you are an EMV maximizer, you are indifferent between entering this gamble, which has EMV $500, and receiving $500 for sure. Similarly, if the gamble is between losing $1000 and winning $500, based on the flip of the coin, and you are an EMV maximizer, you are indifferent between entering this gamble, which has EMV −$250, and *paying* a sure $250 to avoid the gamble. (This latter scenario is the basis of insurance.)

But what if the current situation is a one-shot deal that will *not* occur many times in the future? Then the second interpretation of EMV is still relevant. It states that the EMV is a "sensible" criterion for making decisions under uncertainty. This is actually a point that has been debated in intellectual circles for years—what is the best criterion for making decisions? However, researchers have generally concluded that EMV makes sense, even for one-shot deals, as long as the monetary values are not too large. For situations where the monetary values are extremely large, we will introduce an alternative criterion in the last section of this chapter. Until then, however, we will use EMV.

This is the gist of decision-making uncertainty. You develop a payoff table, assess probabilities of outcomes, calculate EMVs, and choose the decision with the largest EMV. However, before proceeding to examples, it is useful to introduce a few other concepts: *sensitivity analysis*, *decision trees*, and *risk profiles*.

---

[2]In a change from the previous edition of this book, we allow these probabilities to depend on the decision that is made, which is often the case in real decision problems.

6.2.4 Sensitivity Analysis

Some of the quantities in a decision analysis, particularly the probabilities, are often intelligent guesses at best. Therefore, it is important, especially in real-world business problems, to accompany any decision analysis with a sensitivity analysis. Here we systematically vary inputs to the problem to see how (or if) the outputs—the EMVs and the best decision—change. For our simple decision problem, this is easy to do in a spreadsheet. The spreadsheet model is shown in Figure 6.1. (See the file **Simple Decision Problem.xlsx**.)

Figure 6.1

Spreadsheet Model of a Simple Decision Problem

	A	B	C	D	E	F
1	Simple decision problem under uncertainty					
2						
3			Outcome			
4			O1	O2	O3	EMV
5	Decision	D1	10	10	10	10
6		D2	-10	20	30	13
7		D3	-30	30	80	15
8						
9	Probabilities					
10		D2	0.3	0.5	0.2	
11		D3	0.5	0.2	0.3	

Usually, the most important information from a sensitivity analysis is whether the optimal decision continues to be optimal as one or more inputs change.

After entering the payoff table and probabilities, calculate the EMVs in column F as a sum of products, using the formula

=SUMPRODUCT(C6:E6,C10:E10)

in cell F6 and copying it down. (A link to the sure 10 for *D*1 is entered in cell F5.) Then it is easy to change any of the inputs and see whether the optimal decision continues to be *D*3. For example, you can check that if the probabilities for *D*3 change only slightly to 0.6, 0.2, and 0.2, the EMV for *D*3 changes to 4. Now *D*3 is the worst decision and *D*2 is the best, so it appears that the optimal decision is quite sensitive to the assessed probabilities. As another example, if the probabilities remain the same but the last payoff for *D*2 changes from 30 to 45, then its EMV changes to 16, and *D*2 becomes the best decision.

Given a simple spreadsheet model, it is easy to make a number of ad hoc changes to inputs, as we have done here, to answer specific sensitivity questions. However, it is often useful to conduct a more systematic sensitivity analysis, as we will do this later in the chapter. The important thing to realize at this stage is that a sensitivity analysis is not an afterthought to the overall analysis; it is a key component of the analysis.

6.2.5 Decision Trees

The decision problem we have been analyzing is very basic. You make a decision, you then observe an outcome, you receive a payoff, and that is the end of it. Many decision problems are of this basic form, but many are more complex. In these more complex problems, you make a decision, you observe an outcome, you make a second decision, you observe a second outcome, and so on. A graphical tool called a **decision tree** has been developed to represent decision problems. Decision trees can be used for any decision problems, but they are particularly useful for the more complex types. They clearly show the sequence of events (decisions and outcomes), as well as probabilities and monetary values. The decision tree for the simple problem appears in Figure 6.2. This tree is based on one we drew and calculated by hand. We urge you to try this on your own, at least once. However, later in the chapter we will introduce an Excel add-in that automates the procedure.

Figure 6.2

Decision Tree for
Simple Decision
Problem

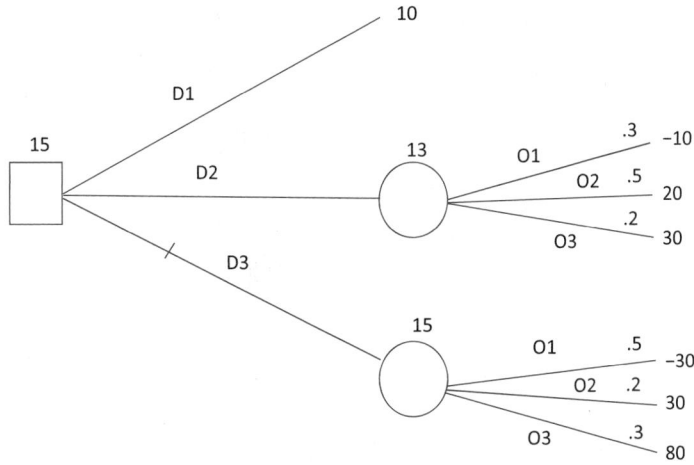

To explain this decision tree, we introduce a number of decision tree conventions that have become standard.

Decision Tree Conventions

1. Decision trees are composed of *nodes* (circles, squares, and triangles) and *branches* (lines).

2. The nodes represent points in time. A *decision node* (a square) represents a time when the decision maker makes a decision. A *probability node* (a circle) represents a time when the result of an uncertain outcome becomes known. An *end node* (a triangle) indicates that the problem is completed—all decisions have been made, all uncertainty has been resolved, and all payoffs and costs have been incurred. (When people draw decision trees by hand, they often omit the actual triangles, as we have done in Figure 6.2. However, we still refer to the right-hand tips of the branches as the end nodes.)

3. Time proceeds *from left to right*. This means that any branches leading into a node (from the left) have already occurred. Any branches leading out of a node (to the right) have not yet occurred.

4. Branches leading out of a decision node represent the possible decisions; the decision maker can choose the preferred branch. Branches leading out of probability nodes represent the possible outcomes of uncertain events; the decision maker has no control over which of these will occur.

5. Probabilities are listed on probability branches. These probabilities are *conditional* on the events that have already been observed (those to the left). Also, the probabilities on branches leading out of any probability node must sum to 1.

6. Monetary values are shown to the right of the end nodes. (As we discuss shortly, some monetary values are also placed under the branches where they occur in time.)

7. EMVs are calculated through a "folding-back" process, discussed next. They are shown above the various nodes. It is then customary to mark the optimal decision branch(es) in some way. We have marked ours with a small notch.

The decision tree in Figure 6.2 follows these conventions. The decision node comes first (to the left) because the decision maker must make a decision *before* observing the uncertain outcome. The probability nodes then follow the decision branches, and the probabilities appear above their branches. (Actually, there is no need for a probability node after the $D1$ branch because its monetary value is a sure 10.) The ultimate payoffs appear next to the end nodes, to the right of the probability branches. The EMVs above the probability nodes are for the various decisions. For example, the EMV for the $D2$ branch is 13. The maximum of the EMVs is for the D2 branch written above the decision node. Because it corresponds to $D3$, we put a notch on the $D3$ branch to indicate that this decision is optimal.

This decision tree is almost a direct translation of the spreadsheet model in Figure 6.1. Indeed, the decision tree is overkill for such a simple problem; the spreadsheet model provides all of the required information. However, decision trees are very useful in business problems. First, they provide a graphical view of the whole problem. This can be useful in its own right for the insights it provides, especially in more complex problems. Second, the decision tree provides a framework for doing all of the EMV calculations. Specifically, it allows you to use the following **folding-back procedure** to find the EMVs and the optimal decision.

Folding-Back Procedure

Starting from the right of the decision tree and working back to the left:

1. At each probability node, calculate an EMV—a sum of products of monetary values and probabilities.

2. At each decision node, take a maximum of EMVs to identify the optimal decision.

The folding-back process is a systematic way of calculating EMVs in a decision tree and thereby identifying the optimal decision strategy.

This is exactly what we did in Figure 6.2. At each probability node, we calculated EMVs in the usual way (sums of products) and wrote them above the nodes. Then at the decision node, we took the maximum of the three EMVs and wrote it above this node. Although this procedure entails more work for more complex decision trees, the same two steps—taking EMVs at probability nodes and taking maximums at decision nodes—are the only arithmetic operations required. In addition, the PrecisionTree add-in in the next section does the folding-back calculations for you.

6.2.6 Risk Profiles

In our small example each decision leads to three possible monetary payoffs with various probabilities. In more complex problems, the number of outcomes could be larger, maybe considerably larger. It is then useful to represent the probability distribution of the monetary values for any decision graphically. Specifically, we show a "spike" chart, where the spikes are located at the possible monetary values, and the heights of the spikes correspond to the probabilities. In decision-making contexts, this type of chart is called a **risk profile**. By looking at the risk profile for a particular decision, you can see the risks and rewards involved. By comparing risk profiles for different decisions, you can gain more insight into their relative strengths and weaknesses.

The **risk profile** for a decision is a "spike" chart that represents the probability distribution of monetary outcomes for this decision.

The risk profile for decision *D3* appears in Figure 6.3. It shows that a loss of $30 has probability 0.5, a gain of $30 has probability 0.2, and a gain of $80 has probability 0.3. The risk profile for decision *D2* is similar, except that its spikes are above the values −10, 20, and 30, and the risk profile for decision *D1* is a single spike of height 1 over the value 10. (The finished version of the **Simple Decision Problem.xlsx** file provides instructions for constructing such a chart with Excel tools.)

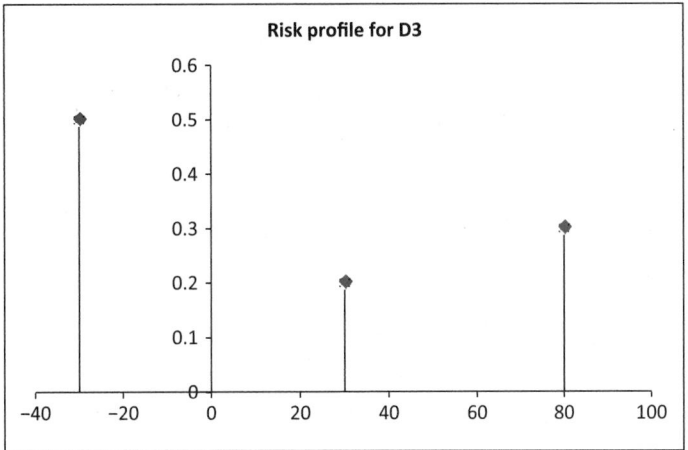

A risk profile shows the complete probability distribution of monetary outcomes, but you typically use only its mean, the EMV, for making decisions.

Note that the EMV for any decision is a summary measure of the complete risk profile—it is the *mean* of the corresponding probability distribution. Therefore, when you use the EMV criterion for making decisions, you are not using *all* of the information in the risk profiles; you are comparing only their means. Nevertheless, risk profiles can be useful as extra information for making decisions. For example, a manager who sees too much risk in the risk profile of the EMV-maximizing decision might choose to override this decision and instead choose a somewhat less risky alternative.

We now apply all of these concepts to the following example.

EXAMPLE | **6.1 BIDDING FOR A GOVERNMENT CONTRACT AT SciTools**

SciTools Incorporated, a company that specializes in scientific instruments, has been invited to make a bid on a government contract. The contract calls for a specific number of these instruments to be delivered during the coming year. The bids must be sealed, so that no company knows what the others are bidding, and the low bid wins the contract. SciTools estimates that it will cost $5000 to prepare a bid and $95,000 to supply the instruments if it wins the contract. On the basis of past contracts of this type, SciTools believes that the possible low bids from the competition, if there is any competition, and the associated probabilities are those shown in Table 6.2. In addition, SciTools believes there is a 30% chance that there will be *no* competing bids. What should SciTools bid to maximize its EMV?

Objective To develop a decision model that finds the EMV for various bidding strategies and indicates the best bidding strategy.

Table 6.2 Data for Bidding Example

Low Bid	Probability
Less than $115,000	0.2
Between $115,000 and $120,000	0.4
Between $120,000 and $125,000	0.3
Greater than $125,000	0.1

WHERE DO THE NUMBERS COME FROM?

The company has probably done a thorough cost analysis to estimate its cost to prepare a bid and its cost to manufacture the instruments if it wins the contract. (Actually, even if there is uncertainty in the manufacturing cost, the only value required for the decision problem is the *mean* manufacturing cost.) The company's estimates of whether, or how, the competition will bid are probably based on previous bidding experience and some subjectivity. This is discussed in more detail next.

Solution

Let's examine the three elements of SciTools's problem. First, SciTools has two basic strategies: submit a bid or do not submit a bid. If SciTools submits a bid, then it must decide how much to bid. Based on the cost to SciTools to prepare the bid and supply the instruments, there is clearly no point in bidding less than $100,000—SciTools wouldn't make a profit even if it won the bid. (Actually, this isn't totally true. Looking ahead to future contracts, SciTools might make a low bid just to "get in the game" and gain experience. However, we won't consider such a possibility here.) Although any bid amount over $100,000 might be considered, the data in Table 6.2 suggest that SciTools might limit its choices to $115,000, $120,000, and $125,000.[3]

The next element of the problem involves the uncertain outcomes and their probabilities. We have assumed that SciTools knows exactly how much it will cost to prepare a bid and how much it will cost to supply the instruments if it wins the bid. (In reality, these are probably only estimates of the actual costs, and a follow-up study could perform a sensitivity analysis on these quantities.) Therefore, the only source of uncertainty is the behavior of the competitors—will they bid, and if so, how much? From SciTools's standpoint, this is difficult information to obtain. The behavior of the competitors depends on (1) how many competitors are likely to bid and (2) how the competitors assess *their* costs of supplying the instruments. Nevertheless, we assume that SciTools has been involved in similar bidding contests in the past and can reasonably predict competitor behavior from past competitor behavior. The result of such prediction is the assessed probability distribution in Table 6.2 and the 30% estimate of the probability of no competing bids.

The last element of the problem is the value model that transforms decisions and outcomes into monetary values for SciTools. The value model is straightforward in this example. If SciTools decides not to bid, its monetary value is $0—no gain, no loss. If it makes a bid and is underbid by a competitor, it loses $5000, the cost of preparing the bid. If it bids B dollars and wins the contract, it makes a profit of B minus $100,000—that is, B dollars for winning the bid, minus $5000 for preparing the bid and $95,000 for supplying the instruments. For example, if it bids $115,000 and the lowest competing bid, if any, is greater than $115,000, then SciTools wins the bid and makes a profit of $15,000.

[3]The problem with a bid such as $117,000 is that the data in Table 6.2 make it impossible to calculate the probability of SciTools winning the contract if it bids this amount. Other than this, however, there is nothing that rules out such "in-between" bids.

Developing the Payoff Table

The corresponding payoff table, along with probabilities of outcomes, appears in Table 6.3. At the bottom of the table, the probabilities of the various outcomes are listed. For example, the probability that the competitors' low bid is less than $115,000 is 0.7 (the probability of at least one competing bid) multiplied by 0.2 (the probability that the lowest competing bid is less than $115,000).

Table 6.3 Payoff Table for SciTools Bidding Example

		No bid	<115	>115, <120	>120, <125	>125
SciTools' Bid ($1000s)	**No bid**	0	0	0	0	0
	115	15	−5	15	15	15
	120	20	−5	−5	20	20
	125	25	−5	−5	−5	25
Probability		0.3	0.7(0.2) = 0.14	0.7(0.4) = 0.28	0.7(0.3) = 0.21	0.7(0.1) = 0.07

Competitors' Low Bid ($1000s)

It is sometimes possible to simplify a payoff table to better understand the essence of the problem. In the present example, if SciTools bids, the only necessary information about the competitors' bid(s) is whether SciTools has the lowest bid. That is, SciTools really only cares whether it wins the contract. Therefore, an alternative way of presenting the payoff table is shown in Table 6.4. (See the file **SciTools Bidding Decision 1.xlsx** for these and other calculations. However, we urge you to work this problem on a piece of paper with a calculator, just for practice with the concepts.)

Table 6.4 Alternative Payoff Table for SciTools Bidding Example

		Monetary Value		Probability That SciTools Wins
		SciTools Wins	SciTools Loses	
SciTools' Bid ($1000s)	**No Bid**	NA	0	0.00
	115	15	−5	0.86
	120	20	−5	0.58
	125	25	−5	0.37

The Monetary Value columns of this table indicate the payoffs to SciTools, depending on whether it wins or loses the bid. The rightmost column shows the probability that SciTools wins the bid for each possible decision. For example, if SciTools bids $120,000, then it wins the bid if there are no competing bids (probability 0.3) *or* if there are competing bids and the lowest of these is greater than $120,000 [probability 0.7(0.3 + 0.1) = 0.28]. In this case the total probability that SciTools wins the bid is 0.3 + 0.28 = 0.58.

Developing the Risk Profiles

Table 6.4 contains all the required information to obtain a risk profile for each of SciTools's decisions. Again, each risk profile indicates all possible monetary values and their corresponding probabilities in a spike chart. For example, if SciTools bids $120,000, there are two monetary values possible, a profit of $20,000 and a loss of $5000, and their probabilities are 0.58 and 0.42, respectively. The corresponding risk profile, shown in Figure 6.4, is a spike chart with two spikes, one above −$5000 with height 0.42 and one above $20,000 with height 0.58. On the other hand, if SciTools decides not to bid, there is a sure monetary value of $0—no profit, no

Figure 6.4

Risk Profile for a Bid of $120,000

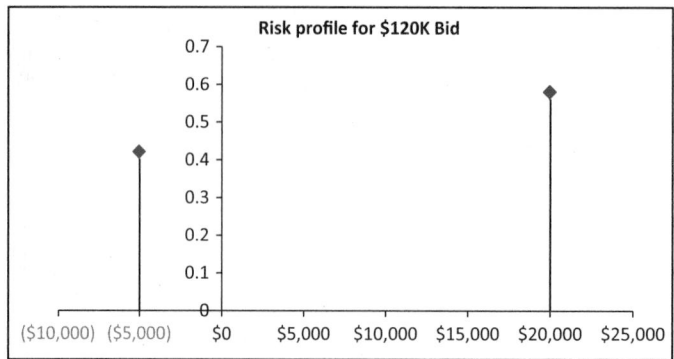

loss. Therefore, the risk profile for the "no bid" decision, not shown here, has a single spike above $0 with height 1.

Calculating EMVs

The EMVs for SciTools's problem are listed in Table 6.5. As always, each EMV (other than the EMV of $0 for not bidding) is a sum of products of monetary outcomes and probabilities. These EMVs indicate that if SciTools uses the EMV criterion for making its decision, it should bid $115,000. The EMV from this bid, $12,200, is the largest of the EMVs.

Table 6.5 EMVs for SciTools Bidding Example

Alternative	EMV Calculation	EMV
No bid	0(1)	$0
Bid $115,000	15,000(0.86) + (−5000)(0.14)	$12,200
Bid $120,000	20,000(0.58) + (−5000)(0.42)	$9500
Bid $125,000	25,000(0.37) + (−5000)(0.63)	$6100

As discussed previously, it is important to understand what an EMV implies and what it does not imply. If SciTools bids $115,000, its EMV is $12,200. However, SciTools will definitely *not* earn a profit of $12,200. It will earn $15,000 or it will lose $5000. The EMV of $12,200 represents only a weighted average of these two possible values. Nevertheless, it is the value that is used as the decision criterion. In words, if SciTools is truly an EMV maximizer, it considers this gamble equivalent to a sure return of $12,200.

Developing the Decision Tree

The corresponding decision tree for this problem is shown in Figure 6.5. This is a direct translation of the payoff table and EMV calculations. The company first makes a bidding

Figure 6.5

Decision Tree for SciTools Bidding Example

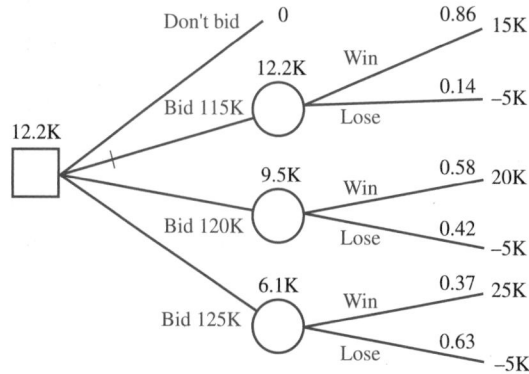

It is common to place monetary values below the branches where they occur in time.

decision, then observes what the competition bids, if anything, and finally receives a payoff. The folding-back process is equivalent to the calculations shown in Table 6.5.

There are often equivalent ways to structure a decision tree. One alternative for this example appears in Figure 6.6. This tree shows exactly how the problem unfolds. The company first decides whether to bid at all. If the company does not make a bid, the profit is a sure $0. Otherwise, the company then decides how much to bid. Note that if the company decides to bid, it incurs a sure cost of $5000, so this cost is placed under the Bid branch. It is a common procedure to place the monetary values on the branches where they occur in time, and we typically do so. Once the company decides how much to bid, it then observes whether there is any competition. If there isn't any, the company wins the bid for sure and makes a corresponding profit. Otherwise, if there is competition, the company eventually discovers whether it wins or loses the bid, with the corresponding probabilities and payoffs. Note that these payoffs are placed below the branches where they occur in time. Also, the *cumulative* payoffs are placed at the ends of the branches. Each cumulative payoff is the sum of all payoffs on branches that lead to that end node.

Figure 6.6

Equivalent Decision Tree for SciTools Bidding Example

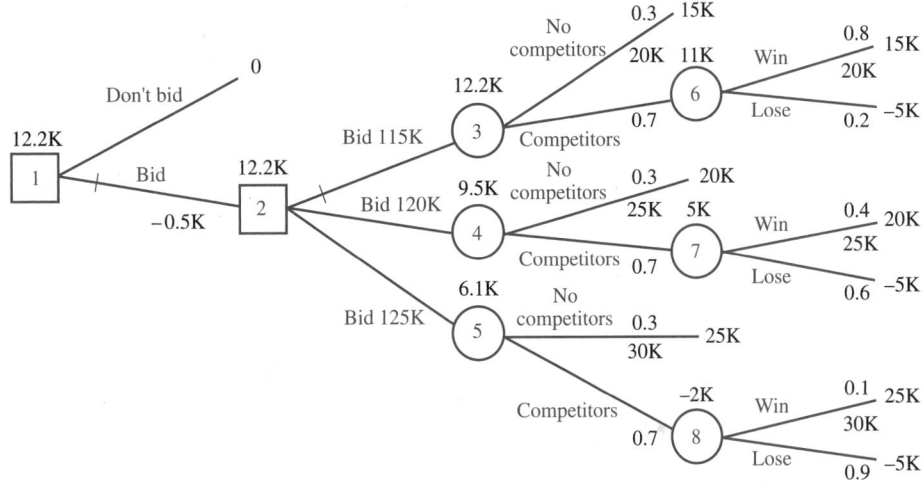

Folding Back the Decision Tree

The folding-back procedure is somewhat more complex than it was for the smaller tree in Figure 6.5. To illustrate, the nodes in Figure 6.6 have been numbered for reference. The EMVs above a selected few of these nodes are calculated as follows:

- Node 7: EMV = 20000(0.40) + (−5000)(0.60) = $5000 (uses monetary values from end nodes)

- Node 4: EMV = 20000(0.30) + (5000)(0.70) = $9500 (uses monetary value from an end node and the EMV from node 7)

- Node 2: EMV = max(12200, 9500, 6100) = $12,200 (uses EMVs from nodes 3, 4, and 5)

- Node 1: EMV = max(0, 12200) = $12,200 (uses monetary value from an end node and EMV from node 2)

The results are the same, regardless of whether you use the table of EMVs in Table 6.5, the decision tree in Figure 6.5, or the decision tree in Figure 6.6, because they all calculate the same EMVs in equivalent ways. In each case, the bottom line is that the company should bid $115,000, with a resulting EMV of $12,200. Of course, this decision is not *guaranteed* to produce a good outcome for the company. For example, the competition could bid less than

$115,000, in which case SciTools would lose $5000. Alternatively, the competition could bid more than $120,000, in which case SciTools would be kicking itself for not bidding $120,000 and gaining an extra $5000 in profit. Unfortunately, in problems with uncertainty, there is virtually never a guarantee that the optimal decision will produce the best result. The only guarantee is that the EMV-maximizing decision is the most rational decision, given the information known when the decision must be made.

Sensitivity Analysis

The next step in the SciTools decision analysis is to perform a sensitivity analysis. You will eventually see that PrecisionTree, an Excel add-in that helps automate the decision-making process, has some powerful sensitivity analysis tools. However, it is also possible to use Excel data tables. One example is shown in Figure 6.7. (See the finished version of the file **SciTools Bidding Decision 1.xlsx**.) The EMVs are calculated in column G, exactly as described previously. Then you can find the maximum of these in cell B21, and you can use the following nested IF formula in cell B22 to find the decision from column B that achieves this maximum:

=INDEX(B16:B19,MATCH(B21,G16:G19,0))

This formula checks which EMV in column G matches the maximum EMV in cell B21 and returns the corresponding decision from column B. (This combination of the INDEX and MATCH functions is often useful for finding the value that corresponds to a maximum or minimum. For an explanation of this combination, see the **Excel Tutorial.xlsx** file that accompanies this book.)

Figure 6.7   Sensitivity Analysis with a Data Table

	A	B	C	D	E	F	G
1	SciTools Bidding Example						
2							
3	Inputs						
4	Cost to prepare a bid	$5,000		Range names used:			
5	Cost to supply instruments	$95,000		BidCost	=Data!$B$4		
6				PrNoBid	=Data!$B$7		
7	Probability of no competing bid	0.3		ProdCost	=Data!$B$5		
8	Comp bid distribution (if they bid)						
9	<$115K	0.2					
10	$115K to $120K	0.4					
11	$120K to $125K	0.3					
12	>$125K	0.1					
13							
14	EMV analysis		Monetary outcomes		Probabilities		
15			SciTools wins	SciTools loses	SciTools wins	SciTools loses	EMV
16		No bid	NA	0	0	1	$0
17	SciTools' Bid	$115,000	$15,000	-$5,000	0.86	0.14	$12,200
18		$120,000	$20,000	-$5,000	0.58	0.42	$9,500
19		$125,000	$25,000	-$5,000	0.37	0.63	$6,100
20							
21	Maximum EMV	$12,200					
22	Best decision	$115,000					
23							
24	Data table for sensitivity analysis						
25	Probability of no competing bid	Maximum EMV	Best decision				
26		$12,200	$115,000				
27	0.2	$11,800	$115,000				
28	0.3	$12,200	$115,000				
29	0.4	$12,600	$115,000				
30	0.5	$13,000	$115,000				
31	0.6	$14,200	$125,000				
32	0.7	$16,900	$125,000				

Once the formulas in cells B21 and B22 have been entered, the data table is easy. In Figure 6.7 the probability of no competing bid is allowed to vary from 0.2 to 0.7. The data table shows how the optimal EMV increases over this range. Also, its third column shows that the $115,000 bid is optimal for small values of the input, but that a $125,000 bid becomes optimal for larger values. The main point here is that if you set up a spreadsheet model that links all of the EMV calculations to the inputs, it is easy to use data tables to perform sensitivity analyses on selected inputs. ∎

PROBLEMS

Note: Student solutions for problems whose numbers appear within a colored box are available for purchase at www.cengagebrain.com.

Level A

1. For the example in **Simple Decision Problem.xlsx**, are there any probabilities that make the EMV criterion equivalent to the maximin criterion? Are there any probabilities that make the EMV criterion equivalent to the maximax criterion? Explain.

2. Using a data table in Excel, perform a sensitivity analysis on the example in **Simple Decision Problem.xlsx**. Specifically, keep the probabilities in row 10 (for D2) as they are, but vary the probability in cell C11 from 0 to 1 in increments of 0.05, and keep the probabilities in cells D11 and E11 in the same ratio as they are currently (2 to 3).

3. In the SciTools example, make two changes: change all references to $115,000 to $110,000, and change all references to $125,000 to $130,000. Rework the EMV calculations and the decision tree. What is the best decision and its corresponding EMV?

4. In the SciTools example, which decision would a maximin decision maker choose? Which decision would a maximax decision maker choose? Would you defend either of these criteria for this particular example? Explain.

5. In the SciTools example, use a two-way data table to see how (or whether) the optimal decision changes as the bid cost and the company's production cost change simultaneously. Let the bid cost vary from $2000 to $8000 in increments of $1000, and let the production cost vary from $90,000 to $105,000 in increments of $2500. Explain your results.

6. In the SciTools example, the probabilities for the low bid of competitors, given that there is at least one competing bid, are currently 0.2, 0.4, 0.3, and 0.1. Let the second of these be p, and let the others sum to $1 - p$ but keep the same ratios to one another: 2 to 3 to 1. Use a one-way data table to see how (or whether) the optimal decision changes as p varies from 0.1 to 0.7 in increments of 0.05. Explain your results.

Level B

7. For the example in **Simple Decision Problem.xlsx**, we found that decision D3 is the EMV-maximizing decision for the given probabilities. See whether you can find probabilities that make decision D1 the best. If the probabilities in row 10 (for D2) are the same as the probabilities in row 11 (for D3), is it possible for D2 to be the best decision? What if these two rows are allowed to be different? Qualitatively, how can you explain the results? That is, which types of probabilities tend to favor the various decisions? (*Hint*: To search for probabilities where D2 is better than the other two decisions, given that rows 10 and 11 are the same, you can use Solver.)

8. A decision d is said to be *dominated* by another decision D if, for every outcome, the payoff from D is better than (or no worse than) the payoff from d.
   a. Explain why you would never choose a dominated decision using the maximin criterion, the maximax criterion, or the EMV criterion.
   b. Are any of the decisions in the example in **Simple Decision Problem.xlsx** dominated by any others? What about in the SciTools example?

9. Besides the maximin, maximax, and EMV criteria, there are other possible criteria for making decisions. One possibility involves *regret*. The idea behind regret is that if you make any decision and then some outcome occurs, you look at that outcome's column in the payoff table to see how much more you could have made if you had chosen the best payoff in that column. For example, if the decision you make and the outcome you observe lead to a $50 payoff, and if the highest payoff in this outcome's column is $80, then your regret is $30. You regret looking back and seeing how much more you could have made, if only you had made a different decision. Therefore, you calculate the regret for each cell in the payoff table (as the maximum payoff in that column minus the payoff in that cell), calculate the maximum regret in each row, and choose the row with the smallest maximum regret. This is called the *minimax regret criterion*.

a. Apply this criterion to the example in **Simple Decision Problem.xlsx**. Which decision do you choose?

b. Repeat part **a** for the SciTools example.

c. In general, discuss potential strengths and weaknesses of this decision criterion.

10. Referring to the previous problem, another possible criterion is called *expected regret*. Here you calculate the regret for each cell, take a weighted average of these regrets in each row, weighted by the probabilities of the outcomes, and choose the decision with the smallest expected regret.

a. Apply this criterion to the SciTools example. Which decision do you choose?

b. The expected regret criterion is actually *equivalent* to the EMV criterion, in that they always lead to the same decisions. Argue why this is true.

11. In the SciTools example, you might argue that there is a *continuum* of possible low competitor bids (given that there is at least one competing bid), not just four possibilities. In fact, assume the low competitor bid in this case is normally distributed with mean $118,000 and standard deviation $4500. Also, assume that SciTools will still either not bid or bid $115,000, $120,000, or $125,000. Use Excel's NORMDIST function to find the EMV for each alternative. Which is the best decision now? Why can't this be represented in a decision tree?

6.3 THE PRECISIONTREE ADD-IN

Decision trees present a challenge for Excel. We must somehow take advantage of Excel's calculating capabilities (to calculate EMVs, for example) and its graphical capabilities (to depict the decision tree). Fortunately, there is a powerful add-in, **PrecisionTree**, developed by Palisade Corporation, that makes the process relatively straightforward. This add-in not only enables you to draw and label a decision tree, but it performs the folding-back procedure automatically and then allows you to perform sensitivity analysis on key input parameters.

The first thing you must do to use PrecisionTree is to "add it in." We assume you have already installed the Palisade DecisionTools suite. Then to run PrecisionTree, you have two options:

- If Excel is not currently running, you can launch Excel *and* PrecisionTree by clicking on the Windows Start button and selecting the PrecisionTree item from the Palisade Decision Tools group in the list of Programs.

- If Excel is currently running, the first procedure will launch PrecisionTree on top of Excel.

You will know that PrecisionTree is ready for use when you see its tab and the associated ribbon (shown in Figure 6.8). If you want to unload PrecisionTree *without* closing Excel, you can do so from its Utilities dropdown list in the Tools group.

Figure 6.8   PrecisionTree Ribbon

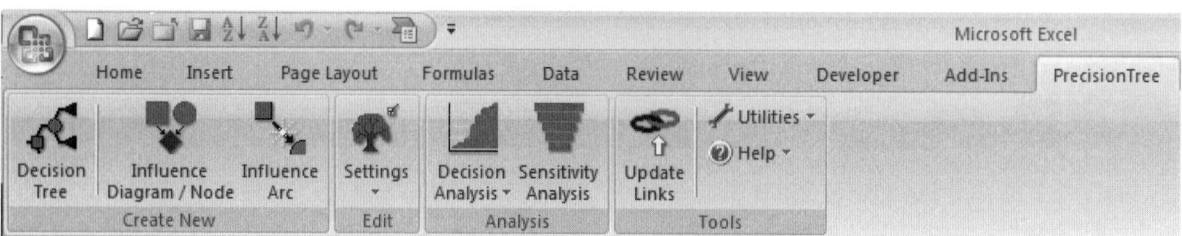

The Decision Tree Model

PrecisionTree is quite easy to use—at least its most basic items are. We will lead you through the steps for the SciTools example. Figure 6.9 shows the results of this procedure, just so that you can see what you are working toward. (See the file **SciTools Bidding Decision 2.xlsx**.)

However, we recommend that you work through the steps on your own, starting with a blank spreadsheet.

Figure 6.9 Completed Tree from PrecisionTree

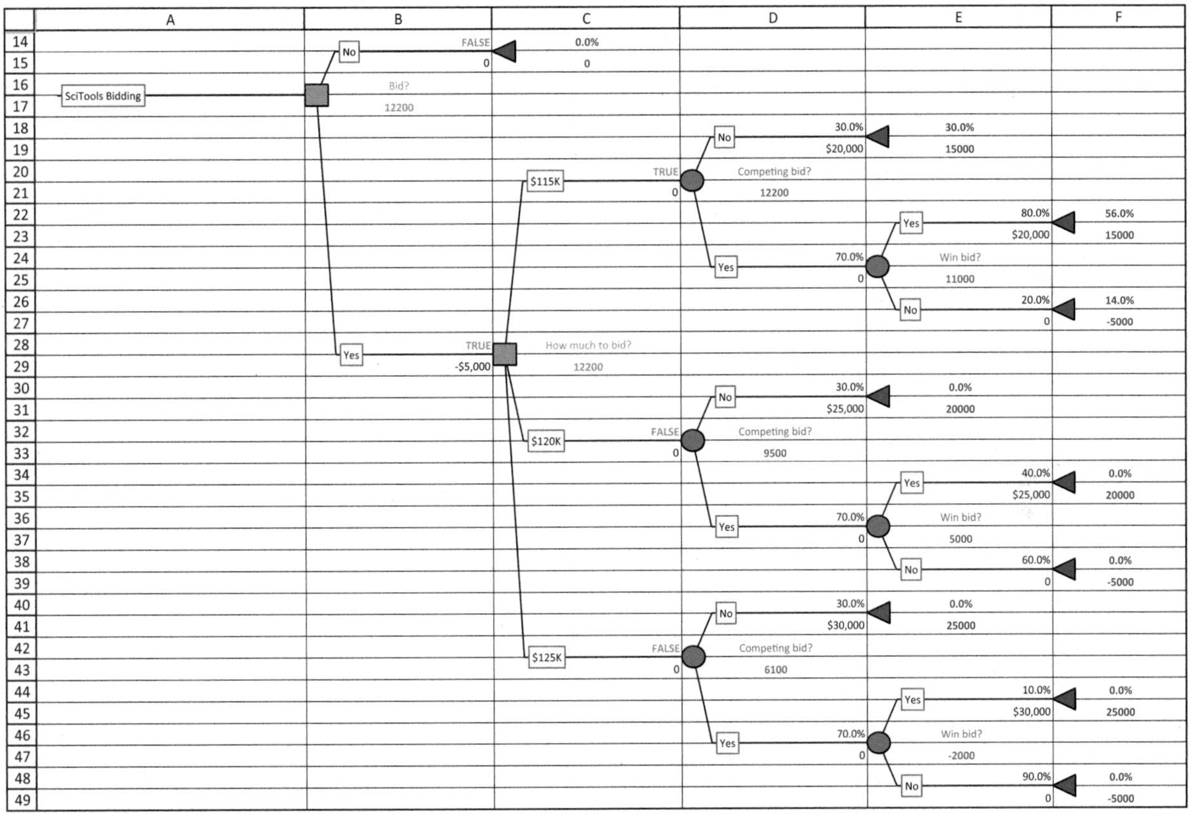

BUILDING THE DECISION TREE

1 **Inputs.** Enter the inputs shown in columns A and B of Figure 6.10. (We have listed the possible bids in column D so that they can be linked through formulas in the tree.)

Figure 6.10 Inputs for SciTools Bidding Example

	A	B	C	D	E
1	**SciTools Bidding Decision**				
2					
3	**Inputs**			**Range names used:**	
4	Cost to prepare a bid	$5,000		BidCost	=Model!$B$4
5	Cost to supply instruments	$95,000		PrNoBid	=Model!$B$7
6				ProductionCost	=Model!$B$5
7	Probability of no competing bid	0.3			
8	Comp bid distribution (if they bid)			SciTools's possible bids	
9	<$115K	0.2		$115,000	
10	$115K to $120K	0.4		$120,000	
11	$120K to $125K	0.3		$125,000	
12	>$125K	0.1			

② **New tree.** Click on the Decision Tree button on the PrecisionTree ribbon, and then select cell A14 below the input section to start a new tree. You will immediately see a dialog box where, among other things, you can name the tree. Enter a descriptive name for the tree, such as SciTools Bidding, and click on OK. You should now see the beginnings of a tree, as shown in Figure 6.11.

Figure 6.11   Beginnings of a New Tree

	A	B	C
14	SciTools Bidding	100.0%	
15		0	

③ **Decision nodes and branches.** From here on, keep the tree in Figure 6.9 in mind. This is the finished product you eventually want. To obtain decision nodes and branches, select the (only) triangle end node to open the dialog box in Figure 6.12. Click on the green square to indicate that you want a decision node, and fill in the dialog box as shown. Then click on the Branches (2) tab and supply labels for the branches under Name, as shown in Figure 6.13. By default, you get two branches, which is what you want in this case. However, if you wanted more than two branches, you would click on Add to get additional branches. The tree expands as shown in Figure 6.14. Under the "Yes" branch, enter the following link to the bid cost cell:

=-BidCost

(Note that it is negative to reflect a *cost.*)

Figure 6.12

Dialog Box for Adding a New Decision Node and Branches

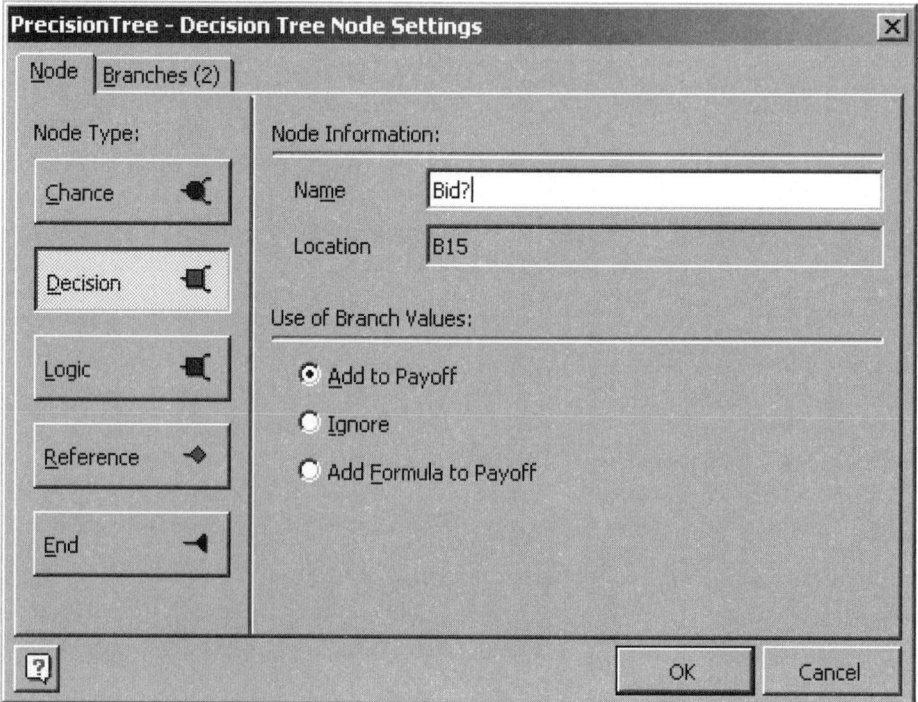

Figure 6.13 Dialog Box for Adding or Labeling Branches

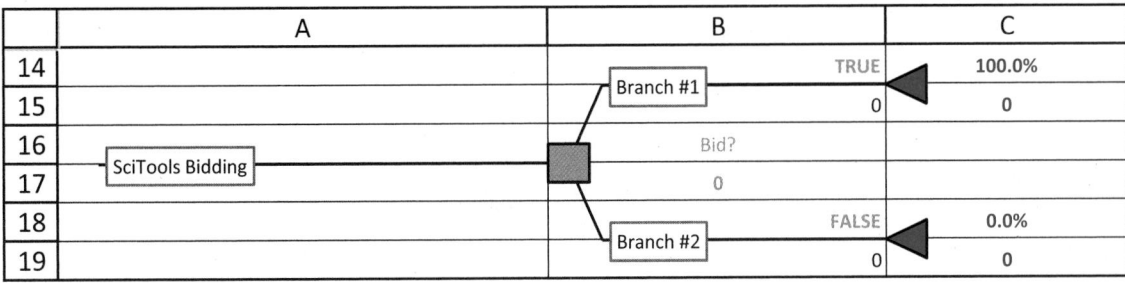

Figure 6.14 Decision Tree with Decision Branches Labeled

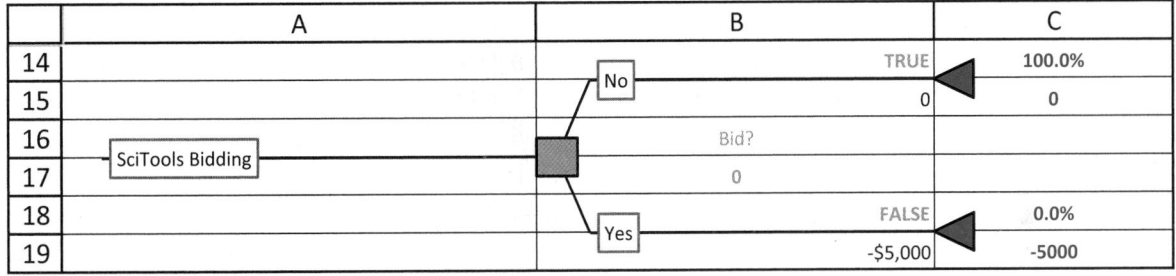

PrecisionTree Tip: *Allowable Entries*

On your computer screen, you will note the color-coding PrecisionTree uses. If you investigate any colored (nonblack) cells, you will see strange formulas that PrecisionTree uses for its own purposes. You should not modify these formulas. You should enter your own probabilities and monetary values only in the cells with black font.

4 **More decision branches.** The top branch is completed; if SciTools does not bid, there is nothing left to do. So click on the bottom end node (the triangle), following SciTools's decision to bid, and proceed as in the previous step to add and label the decision node and three decision branches for the amount to bid. (Again, refer to Figure 6.9.) The tree to this point should appear as in Figure 6.15. Note that there are no monetary values below these decision branches because no *immediate* payoffs or costs are associated with the bid amount decision.

Figure 6.15 Tree with All Decision Nodes and Branches

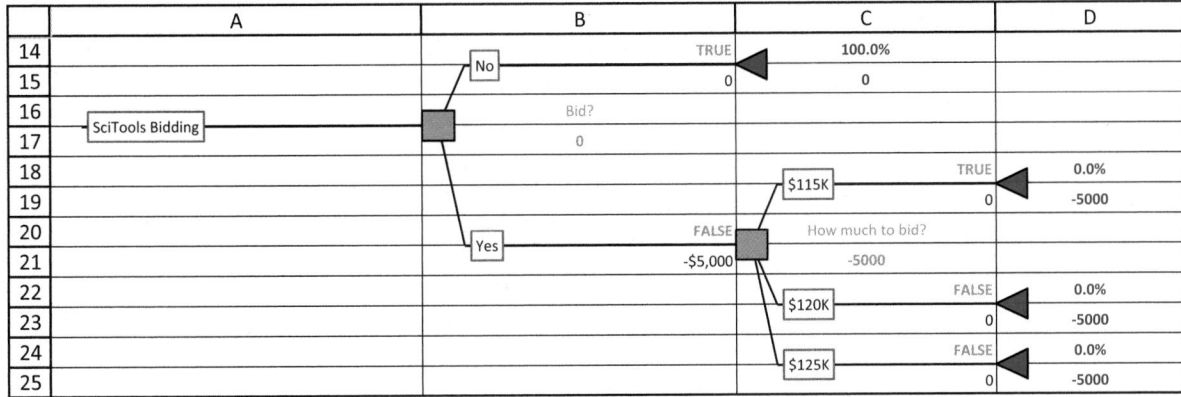

5 **Probability nodes and branches.** Using the same procedure (and using Figure 6.9 as a guide), create probability nodes extending from the "bid $115,000" decision. You should have the skeleton in Figure 6.16.

Figure 6.16   Decision Tree with One Set of Probability Nodes and Branches

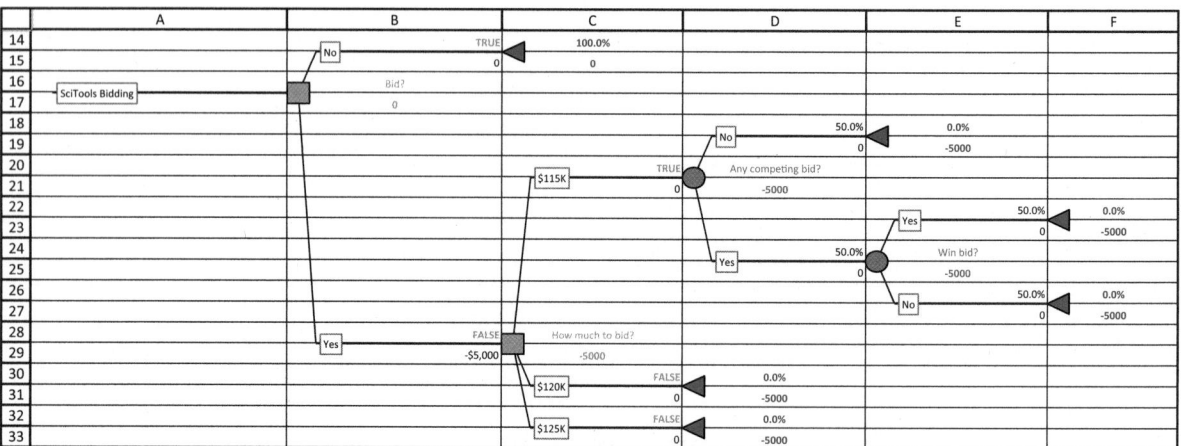

6 **Copying probability nodes and branches.** You could now repeat the same procedure from the previous step to build probability nodes and branches following the other bid amount decisions, but because they are structurally equivalent, you can save a lot of work by using PrecisionTree's copy and paste feature. Right-click on the leftmost probability node and click on Copy SubTree. Then right-click on either end node below it and click on Paste SubTree. Do this again with the other end node. Decision trees can get very "bushy," but this copy and paste feature can make them much less tedious to construct.

7 **Enter probabilities on probability branches.** You should now have the decision tree shown in Figure 6.17. It is structurally the same as the completed tree in Figure 6.9, but the probabilities and monetary values on the probability branches are incorrect. Note that each probability branch has a value above and below the branch. The value above is the probability (the default values make the branches equally likely), and the value below is the monetary value (the default values are 0). You can enter any values or formulas in these cells (remember, the cells with black font only), exactly as you do in typical Excel worksheets. As usual, it is a good practice to enter cell references, not numbers, whenever possible. In addition, range names can be used instead of cell addresses.

PrecisionTree Tip: *Sum of Probabilities*
PrecisionTree does not enforce the rule that probabilities on branches leading out of a node must sum to 1. You must enforce this rule with appropriate formulas.

PrecisionTree Tip: *Entering Monetary Values, Probabilities*
A good practice is to calculate all of the monetary values and probabilities that will be needed in the decision tree in some other area of the spreadsheet. Then the values needed next to the tree branches can be created with simple linking formulas.

We will get you started with the probability branches following the decision to bid $115,000. First, enter the probability of no competing bid in cell D18 with the formula

=PrNoBid

and enter its complement in cell D24 with the formula

=1-D18

Figure 6.17   Structure of Completed Tree

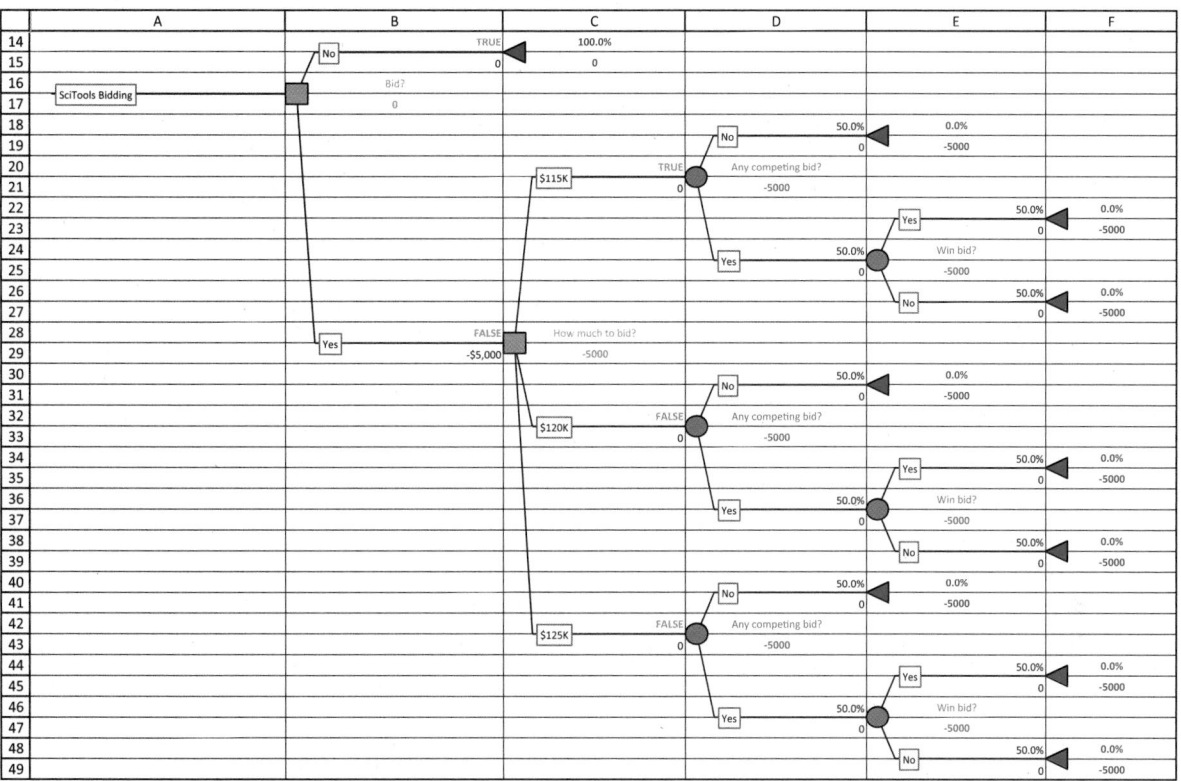

Next, enter the probability that SciTools wins the bid in cell E22 with the formula

=SUM(B10:B12)

and enter its complement in cell E26 with the formula

=1-E22

(Remember that SciTools wins the bid only if the competition bids higher, and in this part of the tree, SciTools is bidding $115,000.) For the monetary values, enter the formula

=D9-ProductionCost

in the two cells, D19 and E23, where SciTools wins the contract. Note that the cost of the bid was already subtracted in cell B29, so it should *not* be subtracted again. This would be double-counting, which you should always avoid in decision trees.

8 Enter the other formulas on probability branches. Using the previous step and Figure 6.9 as a guide, enter formulas for the probabilities and monetary values on the other probability branches, those following the decision to bid $120,000 or $125,000.

PrecisionTree Tip: *Copying Subtrees*

Before taking advantage of PrecisionTree's subtree copying capability , it is generally a good idea to fill the subtree as much as possible (with labels, probabilities, and monetary values). In this way, the copies will require less work. Note that formulas on the subtree are copied in the usual Excel way (in terms of relative and absolute references), so that the formulas on the copies often have to be adjusted slightly. In this example, you could have sped up the process slightly by completing step 7 before copying. Then step 8 would entail only a few formula adjustments on the copied subtrees.

Interpreting the Decision Tree

To find the optimal decision strategy in any PrecisionTree tree, follow the TRUE labels.

You are finished! The completed tree in Figure 6.9 shows the best strategy and its associated EMV, as we discussed previously. In fact, a comparison of the decision tree in Figure 6.6 that was created manually and the tree from PrecisionTree in Figure 6.9 indicates virtually identical results. The best decision strategy is now indicated by the TRUE and FALSE labels above the decision branches (rather than the notches we entered by hand). Each TRUE corresponds to the optimal decision out of a decision node, whereas each FALSE corresponds to a suboptimal decision. Therefore, you simply follow the TRUE labels. In this case, the company should bid, and its bid amount should be $115,000.

Note that you do *not* have to perform the folding-back procedure manually. PrecisionTree does this for you. Essentially, the tree is completed as soon as you finish entering the relevant inputs. In addition, if you change any of the inputs, the tree reacts automatically. For example, try changing the bid cost in cell B4 from $5000 to some large value such as $20,000. You will see that the tree calculations update automatically, and the best decision is then *not* to bid, with an associated EMV of $0.

PrecisionTree Tip: *Values at End Nodes*

You will notice that there are two values following each triangle end node. The bottom value is the sum of all monetary values on branches leading to this end node. The top value is the probability of getting to this end node when the optimal strategy is used. This explains why many of these probabilities are 0; the optimal strategy will never lead to these end nodes.

Policy Suggestion and Risk Profile for Optimal Strategy

The Policy Suggestion shows only the subtree corresponding to the optimal decision strategy.

Once the decision tree is completed, PrecisionTree has several tools you can use to gain more information about the decision analysis. First, you can see a subtree (called a Policy Suggestion) for the *optimal* decision. To do so, choose Policy Suggestion from the Decision Analysis dropdown list and fill in the resulting dialog box as shown in Figure 6.18. (You can experiment with other options.) The Policy Suggestion option shows only the part of the tree that corresponds to the best decision, as shown in Figure 6.19.

Figure 6.18

Dialog Box for Information about Optimal Decision

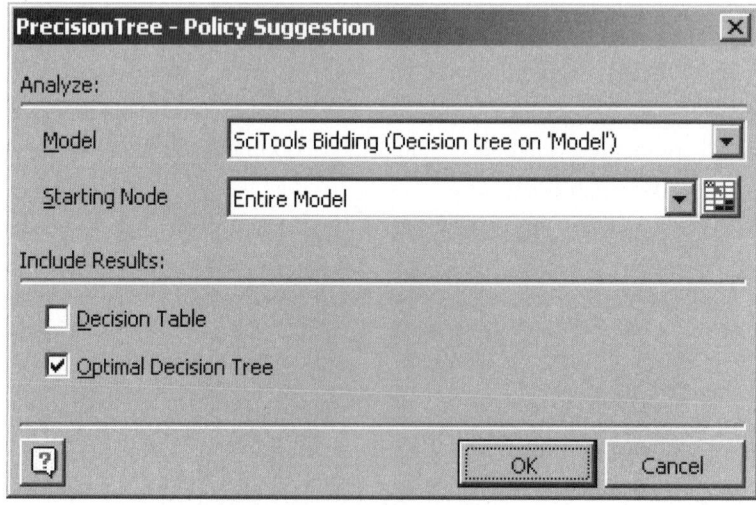

You can also obtain a graphical risk profile of the optimal decision by selecting Risk Profile from the Decision Analysis dropdown list and filling in the resulting dialog box as shown in Figure 6.20. (Again, you can experiment with the other options.) As the risk profile in Figure 6.21 indicates, there are only two possible monetary outcomes if SciTools bids $115,000. It either wins $15,000 or loses $5000, and the former is much more likely.

Figure 6.19   Subtree for Optimal Decision

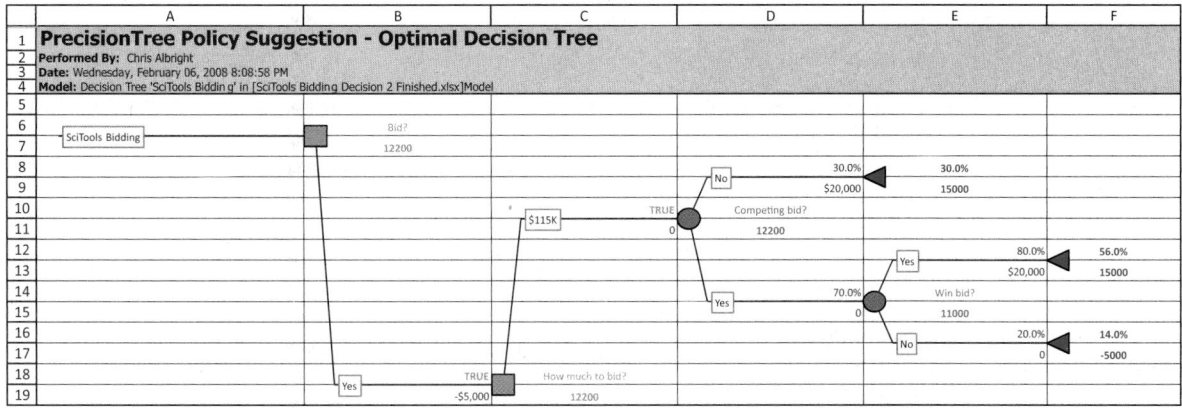

Figure 6.20

Risk Profile Dialog Box

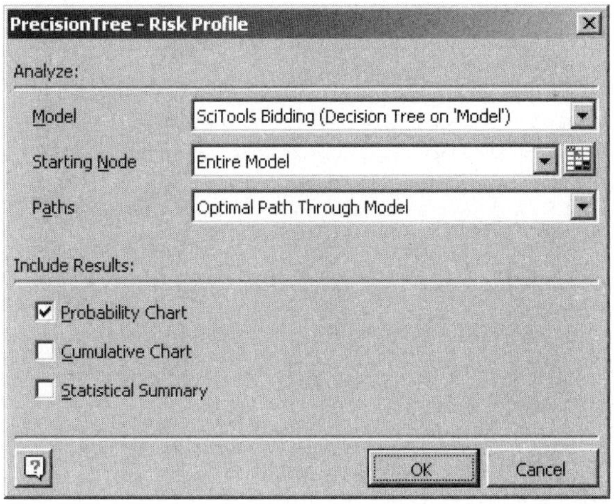

Figure 6.21

Risk Profile of Optimal Decision

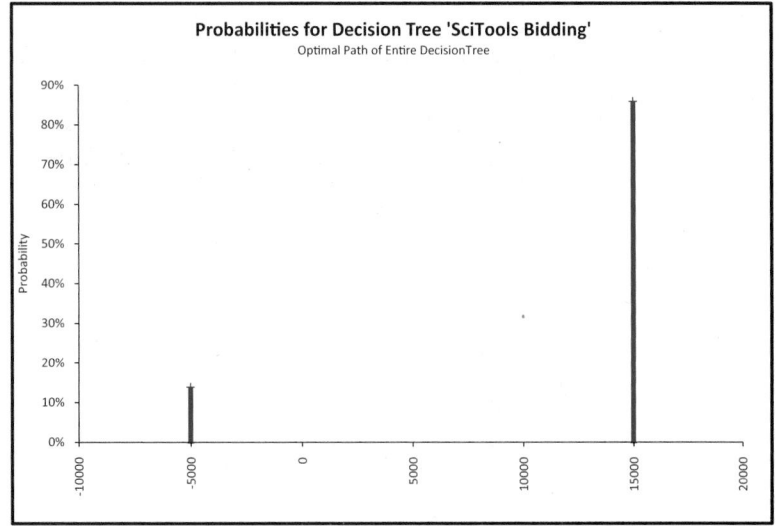

(The associated probabilities are 0.86 and 0.14, respectively.) This graphical information is even more useful when there are a larger number of possible monetary outcomes. You can see what they are and how likely they are.

Sensitivity Analysis

We have already stressed the importance of a follow-up sensitivity analysis to any decision problem, and PrecisionTree makes this relatively easy to perform. Of course, you can enter any values in the input cells and watch how the tree changes, but you can obtain more systematic information by clicking on PrecisionTree's Sensitivity Analysis button. This brings up the dialog box in Figure 6.22. Although it has a lot of options, it is easy to use once you understand the ideas behind it. Here are the main options and how to use them.

Figure 6.22

Sensitivity Analysis Dialog Box

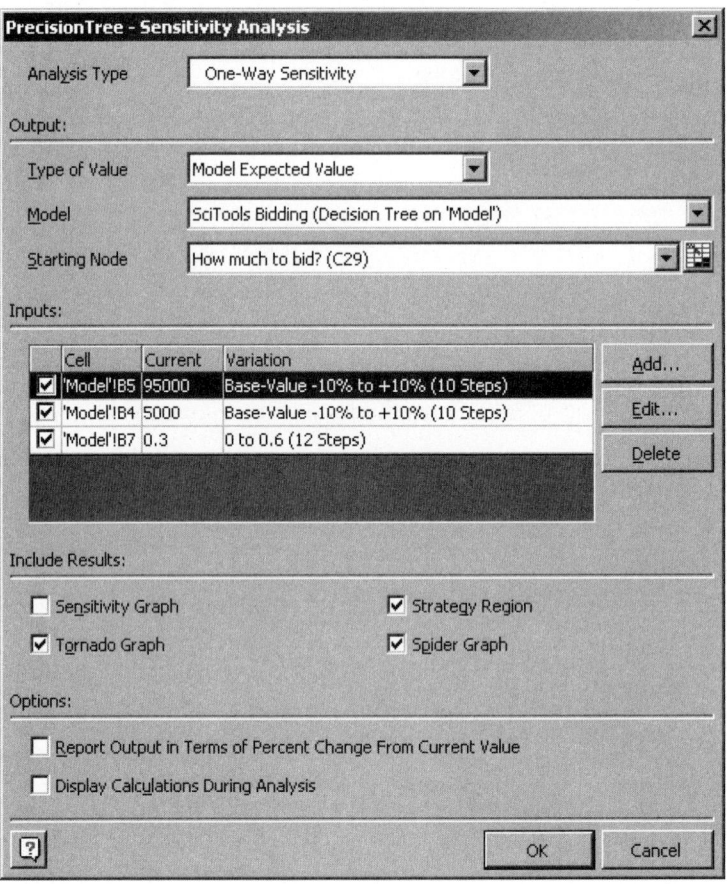

It takes some practice and experimenting to get used to PrecisionTree's sensitivity analysis tools. However, they are powerful and worth learning.

- The Analysis Type dropdown list allows you to vary one input (One-Way Sensitivity) or two inputs (Two-Way Sensitivity) simultaneously.

- The Starting Node dropdown list lets you choose any node in the tree, and the sensitivity analysis is then performed for the EMV *from that node to the right*. In other words, it assumes you have gotten to that node and are now interested in what will happen from then on. The node selected in the figure, C29, is the leftmost node, so by selecting it, the sensitivity analysis is on the EMV of the entire tree. This is the most common setting.

- You add inputs to vary in the Inputs section. You can add as many as you like, and all of the checked inputs are included in any particular sensitivity analysis. When you add an input to this section, you can specify the range over which you want it to vary. For example, you can vary it by plus or minus 10% in 10 steps from a selected base value, as we did for the production cost in cell B5, or you can vary it from 0 to 0.6 in 12 steps, as we did for the probability of no competing bids in cell B7.

■ The Include Results checkboxes allow you to select up to four types of charts, depending on the type of sensitivity analysis. (The bottom two options are disabled for a two-way sensitivity analysis.) You can experiment with these options, but we will illustrate our favorites shortly.

When you click on OK, PrecisionTree varies each of the checked inputs in the middle section, one at a time if you select the One-Way option, and presents the results in new worksheets. By default, these new worksheets are placed in a new workbook. If you would rather have them in the same workbook as the model, click on the PrecisionTree Utilities dropdown arrow, select Application Settings, and select Active Workbook from the Replace Reports In option. (This is a global setting. It will take effect for all future PrecisionTree analyses.)

Strategy Region Chart

In strategy region charts, the primary interest is in where (or whether) lines cross. This is where decisions change.

Figure 6.23 illustrates **a strategy region chart** from a one-way analysis. This chart shows how the EMV varies with the production cost for *both* of the original decisions (bid or don't bid). This type of chart is useful for seeing whether the optimal decision *changes* over the range of the input variable. It does so only if the two lines cross. In this particular graph it is clear that the "Bid" decision dominates the "No bid" decision over the selected production cost range.

Figure 6.23
EMV Versus Production Cost for Each of Two Decisions

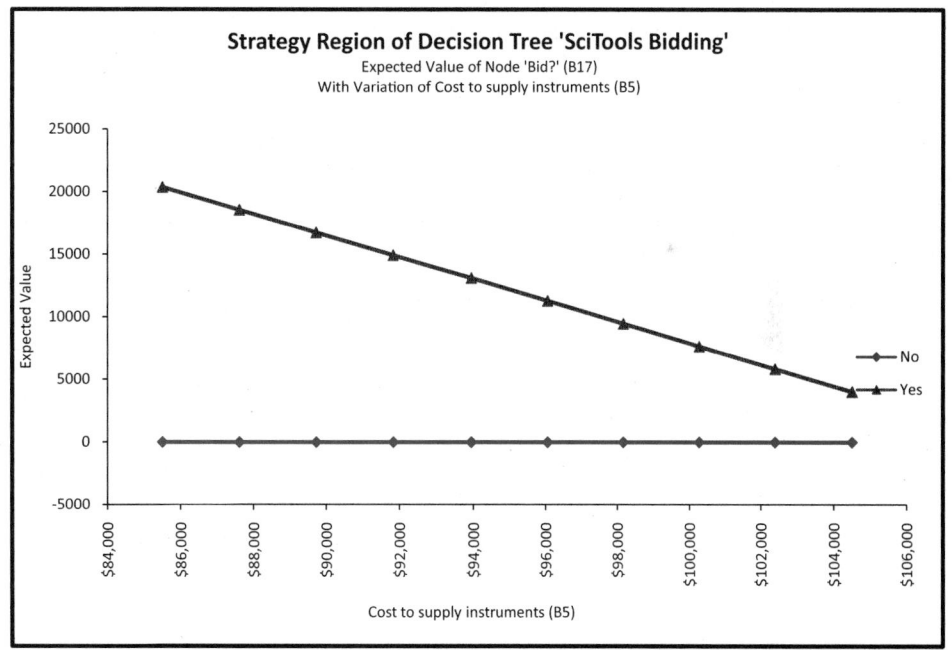

Tornado Chart

Tornado charts and spider charts indicate which inputs the selected EMV is most sensitive to.

A **tornado chart** shows how sensitive the EMV of the *optimal* decision is to each of the selected inputs over the specified ranges. (See Figure 6.24.) The length of each bar shows the change in the EMV in either direction, so inputs with longer bars have a greater effect on the selected EMV. (If you checked the next-to-bottom checkbox in Figure 6.22, the lengths of the bars would indicate *percentage* changes from the base value.) The bars are always arranged from longest on top to shortest on the bottom—hence the name *tornado* chart. Here it is apparent that production cost has the largest effect on EMV, and bid cost has the smallest effect.

Figure 6.24

Tornado Chart for
SciTools Example

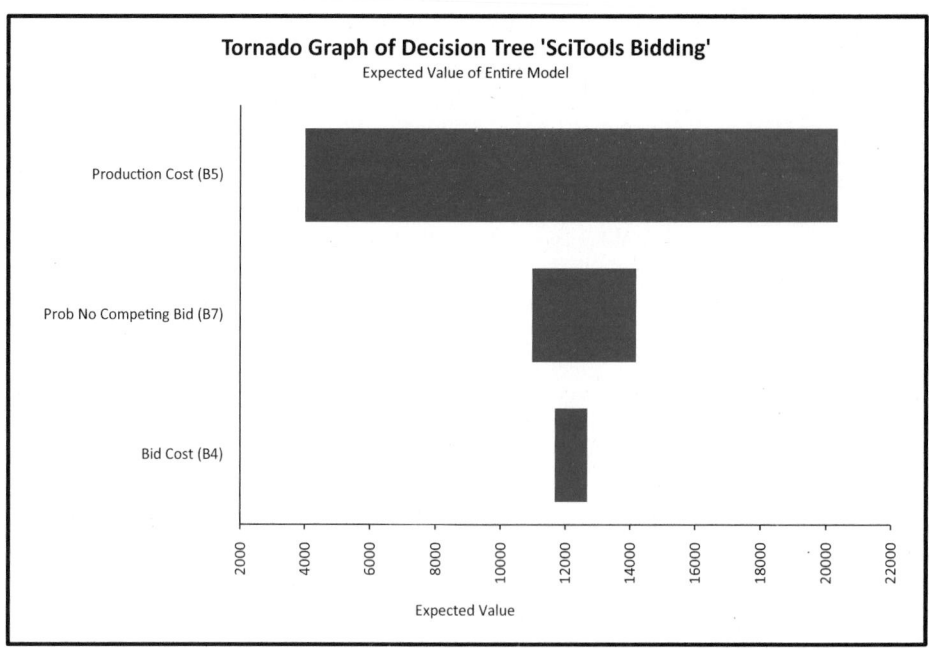

Spider Chart

Finally, a **spider chart** shows how much the optimal EMV varies in magnitude for various percentage changes in the input variables. (See Figure 6.25.) The steeper the slope of the line, the more the EMV is affected by a particular input. It is again apparent that the production cost has a relatively large effect, whereas the other two inputs have relatively small effects.

Figure 6.25

Spider Chart for
SciTools Example

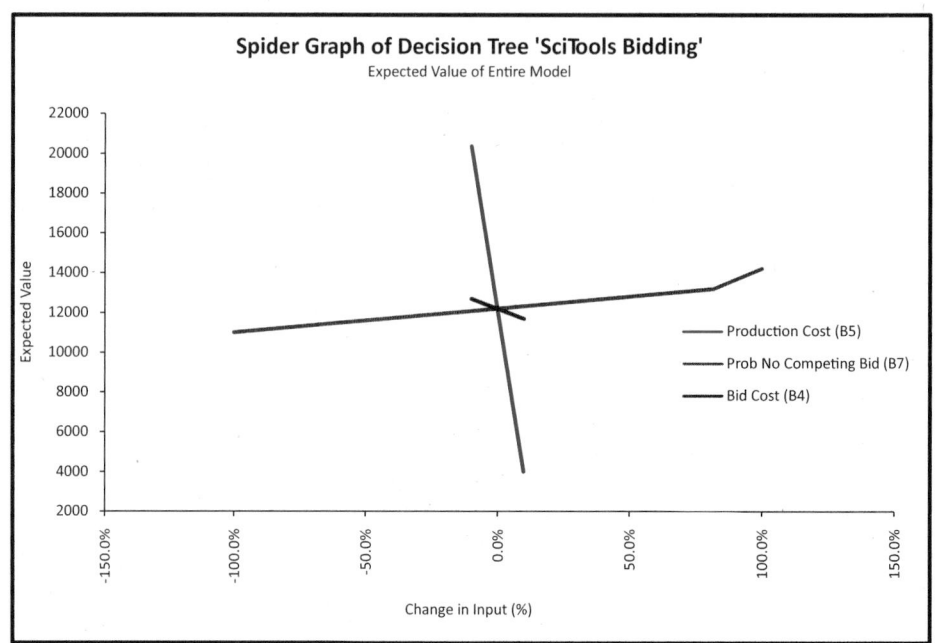

Another Sensitivity Chart

Each time you click on the Sensitivity Analysis button, you can run a different sensitivity analysis. For example, you might want to choose cell C29 as the cell to analyze. This is the optimal EMV for the problem, *given* that the company has decided to place a bid. One interesting chart from this analysis is the strategy region chart in Figure 6.26. It indicates how the EMV varies with the probability of no competing bid for *each* of the three bid amount decisions. The $115,000 bid is best for most of the range, but when the probability of no competing bid is sufficiently large (about 0.55), the $120,000 bid becomes best (by a small margin.)

Figure 6.26

Strategy Region Chart for Another EMV Cell

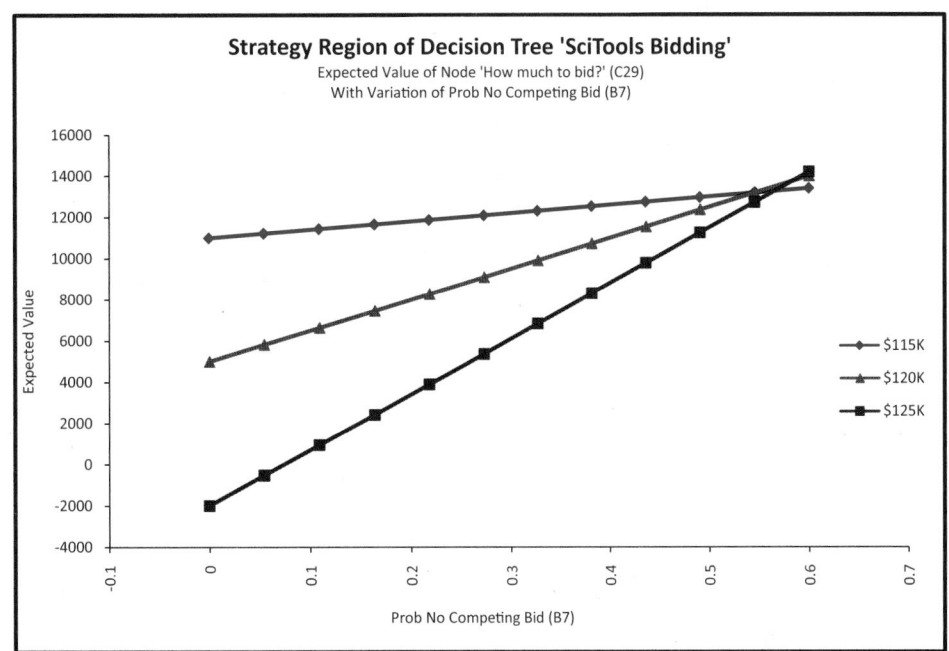

Two-Way Sensitivity Chart

A one-way sensitivity analysis varies only one input at a time. A two-way analysis varies two inputs simultaneously.

Another interesting option is to run a two-way analysis. This shows how the selected EMV varies as each *pair* of inputs varies simultaneously. We analyzed the EMV in cell C29 with this option, using the same inputs as before. A typical result is shown in Figure 6.27. For each of the possible values of production cost and the probability of no competitor bid, this chart indicates which bid amount is optimal. (By choosing cell C29, we are assuming SciTools will bid; the only question is how much.) As you can see, the optimal bid amount remains $115,000 unless the production cost *and* the probability of no competing bid are both large. Then it becomes optimal to bid $120,000 or $125,000. This makes sense intuitively. As the probability of no competing bid increases and a larger production cost must be recovered, it seems reasonable that SciTools should increase its bid.

We reiterate that a sensitivity analysis is always an important component of any real-world decision analysis. If you had to construct decision trees by hand—with paper and pencil—a sensitivity analysis would be very tedious, to say the least. You would have to recalculate everything each time through. Therefore, one of the most valuable features of the PrecisionTree add-in is that it enables you to perform sensitivity analyses in a matter of seconds.

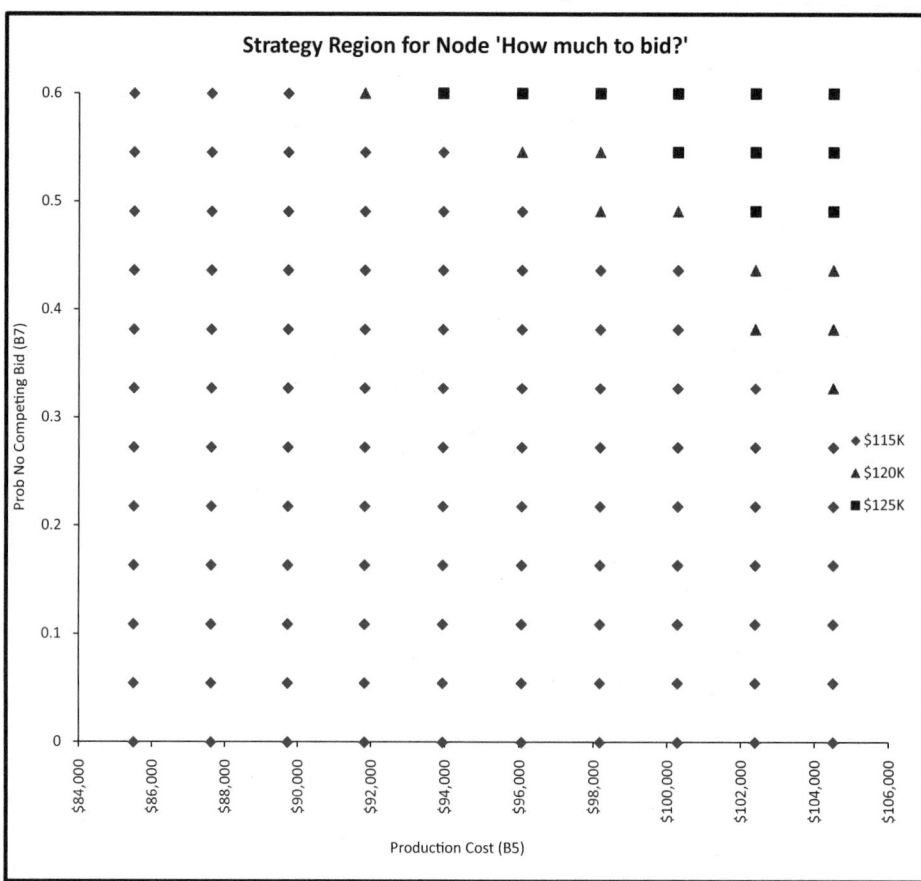

Figure 6.27
Two-Way Sensitivity
Analysis

PROBLEMS

Level A

12. In a tree built with PrecisionTree, there are two blue values at each end node, the top one of which is a probability. Why are so many of these probabilities 0 in the finished tree in Figure 6.9? What do the remaining (positive) probabilities represent?

13. In the SciTools example, there are two equivalent decision tree structures, shown in Figures 6.5 and 6.6. Use PrecisionTree to create the first of these, and verify that it yields the same EMVs and the same optimal decision as the tree developed in this section.

14. For the completed decision tree in Figure 6.9, the monetary values in black are those you enter. The monetary values in color are calculated automatically by PrecisionTree. For this particular example, explain exactly how these latter values are calculated (remember the folding-back process) and what they represent. These include the blue values at the end nodes, the red values at the probability nodes, and the green values at the decision nodes.

15. For the SciTools example, once you build the tree as in Figure 6.9 and then run a one-way sensitivity analysis with the dialog box filled in as in Figure 6.22, you obtain three strategy charts. (Try it.) Explain exactly what each of these charts represents. (For this problem, you can ignore the tornado and spider charts.)

16. The tornado chart in Figure 6.24 and the spider chart in Figure 6.25 show basically the same information in slightly different forms. Explain in words exactly what information they provide. (If necessary, consult PrecisionTree's online help.)

17. Explain in words what information a two-way sensitivity chart, such as the one in Figure 6.27, provides. Demonstrate how you could provide this same information without PrecisionTree's sensitivity tools, using only data tables. (You can still use the tree built with PrecisionTree.)

6.4 BAYES' RULE

The whole purpose of Bayes' rule is to revise probabilities as new information becomes available.

The examples to this point have required a single decision. We now examine multistage problems, where a decision maker must make at least two decisions that are separated in time, such as when a company must first decide whether to buy information that will help it make a second decision. In multistage decision problems there are typically alternating sets of decision nodes and probability nodes. The decision maker makes a decision, some uncertainty is resolved, the decision maker makes another decision, more uncertainty is resolved, and so on. Before analyzing such problems, we must discuss one important probability issue.

In a multistage decision tree, all probability branches at the *right* of the tree are conditional on outcomes that have occurred earlier, to their left. Therefore, the probabilities on these branches are of the form $P(A|B)$, read "A given B," where A is an event corresponding to a current probability branch, and B is an event that occurs *before* event A in time. However, when gathering data for the problem, it is sometimes more natural to *assess* conditional probabilities in the opposite order, that is, $P(B|A)$. Whenever this is the case, **Bayes' rule** must be used to obtain the probabilities needed on the tree. Essentially, Bayes' rule is a mechanism for revising probabilities as new information becomes available.

To develop Bayes' rule, let A_1 through A_n be any outcomes. Without any further information, we believe the probabilities of the As are $P(A_1)$ through $P(A_n)$. These are called **prior probabilities**. We then have the possibility of gaining some information. There are several information outcomes we might observe, a typical one of which is labeled B. We assume the probabilities of B, given that any of the As will occur, are known. These probabilities, labeled $P(B|A_1)$ through $P(B|A_n)$, are often called *likelihoods*. Because an information outcome might influence our thinking about the probabilities of the As, we need to find the conditional probability $P(A_i|B)$ for each outcome A_i. This is called the **posterior probability** of A_i. This is where Bayes' rule enters the picture. It states that we can calculate posterior probabilities from the following formula.

Bayes' rule

$$P(A_i|B) = \frac{P(B|A_i)P(A_i)}{P(B|A_1)P(A_1) + \cdots + P(B|A_n)P(A_n)} \qquad \textbf{(6.1)}$$

In words, Bayes' rule says that the posterior is the likelihood times the prior, divided by a sum of likelihoods times priors. As a side benefit, the denominator in Bayes' rule is also useful in multistage decision trees. It is the probability $P(B)$ of the information outcome.

Denominator of Bayes' rule (Law of Total Probability)

$$P(B) = P(B|A_1)P(A_1) + \cdots + P(B|A_1)P(A_n) \qquad \textbf{(6.2)}$$

This formula is important in its own right. For B to occur, it must occur along with one of the As. Formula 6.2) simply decomposes the probability of B into all of these possibilities. It is sometimes called the **law of total probability**.

In the case where there are only two *A*s, labeled as *A* and Not *A*, Bayes' rule takes the following form:

Bayes' rule for two outcomes

$$P(A|B) = \frac{P(B|A)P(A)}{P(B|A)P(A) + P(B|\text{Not } A)P(\text{Not } A_n)} \qquad \textbf{(6.3)}$$

We illustrate the mechanics of Bayes' rule in the following example. [See Feinstein (1990) for a real application of this example.]

EXAMPLE 6.2 DRUG TESTING COLLEGE ATHLETES

If an athlete is tested for a certain type of drug use (steroids, say), the test result will be either positive or negative. However, these tests are never perfect. Some drug-free athletes test positive, and some drug users test negative. The former are called *false positives*; the latter are called *false negatives*. Let's assume that 5% of all athletes use drugs, 3% of all tests on drug-free athletes yield false positives, and 7% of all tests on drug users yield false negatives. Suppose a typical athlete is tested. If this athlete tests positive, can you be sure that he is a drug user? If he tests negative, can you be sure he does not use drugs?

Objective To use Bayes' rule to revise the probability of being a drug user, given the positive or negative results of the test.

WHERE DO THE NUMBERS COME FROM?

The estimate that 5% of all athletes are drug users is probably based on a well-known national average. The error rates from the tests are undoubtedly known from extensive experience with the tests. (However, we are not claiming that the numbers used here match reality.)

Solution

Let *D* and *ND* denote that a randomly chosen athlete is or is not a drug user, and let $T+$ and $T-$ indicate a positive or negative test result. (The outcomes *D* and *ND* correspond to *A* and Not *A* in Equation (6.3), and either $T+$ or $T-$ corresponds to *B*.) The following probabilities are given. First, because 5% of all athletes are drug users, you know that $P(D) = 0.05$ and $P(ND) = 0.95$. These are the prior probabilities. They represent the chance that an athlete is or is not a drug user *prior* to the results of a drug test.

Second, from the information on the accuracy of the drug test, you know the conditional probabilities $P(T+|ND) = 0.03$ and $P(T-|D) = 0.07$. In addition, a drug-free athlete tests either positive or negative, and the same is true for a drug user. Therefore, you also know the probabilities $P(T-|ND) = 0.97$ and $P(T+|D) = 0.93$. These four conditional probabilities of test results given drug user status are the likelihoods of the test results.

Given these priors and likelihoods, you need to calculate posterior probabilities such as $P(D|T+)$, the probability that an athlete who tests positive is a drug user, and $P(ND|T-)$, the probability that an athlete who tests negative is drug free. They are called posterior probabilities because they are assessed *after* the drug test results.

Using Bayes' rule for two outcomes, Equation (6.3), you can calculate

$P(D|T+)$

$$= \frac{P(T+|D)P(D)}{P(T+|D)P(D) + P(T+|ND)P(ND)} = \frac{(0.93)(0.05)}{(0.93)(0.05) + (0.03)(0.95)} = 0.620$$

and

$P(ND|T-)$

$$= \frac{P(T-|ND)P(D)}{P(T-|D)P(D) + P(T-|ND)P(ND)} = \frac{(0.97)(0.95)}{(0.07)(0.05) + (0.97)(0.95)} = 0.996$$

In words, if the athlete tests positive, there is still a 38% chance that he is *not* a drug user, but if he tests negative, you are virtually sure he is not a drug user. The denominators of these two formulas are the probabilities of the test results. They can be calculated from Equation (6.2):

$$P(T+) = 0.93(0.05) + 0.03(0.95) = 0.075$$

and

$$P(T-) = 0.07(0.05) + 0.97(0.95) = 0.925$$

The first Bayes' rule result might surprise you. After all, the test is reasonably accurate, so if you observe a positive test result, you should be pretty sure that the athlete is a drug user, right? The reason the first posterior probability is "only" 0.620 is that very few athletes in the population are drug users—only 5%. Therefore, you need a lot of evidence to be convinced that a particular athlete is a drug user, and a positive test result from a somewhat inaccurate test is not enough evidence to be totally convincing. On the other hand, a negative test result simply adds confirmation to what you already suspected—that a typical athlete is *not* a drug user. This is why $P(ND|T-)$ is so close to 1.

A More Intuitive Calculation

If you have trouble understanding or implementing Bayes' rule, you are not alone. At least one study has shown that even trained medical specialists have trouble with this type of calculation (in the context of tests for cancer). Most of us do not think intuitively about conditional probabilities. However, there is an equivalent and more intuitive way to obtain the same result.

This alternative procedure, using counts instead of probabilities, is equivalent to Bayes' rule and is probably more intuitive.

Imagine that there are 100,000 athletes. Because 5% of all athletes are drug users, we assume that 5000 of these athletes use drugs and the other 95,000 do not. Now we administer the test to all of them. We expect 3%, or 2850, of the nonusers to test positive (because the false-positive rate is 3%), and we expect 93%, or 4650, of the drug users to test positive (because the false-negative rate is 7%). Therefore, we observe a total of 2850 + 4650 = 7500 positives. If one of these 7500 athletes is chosen at random, what is the probability that a drug user is chosen? It is clearly

$$P(D|T+) = 4650/7500 = 0.620$$

This is the same result we got using Bayes' rule! So if you have trouble with Bayes' rule using probabilities, you can use this alternative method of using *counts*. (By the way, the 100,000 value is irrelevant. We could have used 10,000, 50,000, 1,000,000, or any other convenient value.)

Spreadsheet Implementation of Bayes' Rule

It is fairly easy to implement Bayes' rule in a spreadsheet, as illustrated in Figure 6.28 for the drug example. (See the file **Bayes Rule.xlsx**.[4])

---

[4]The Bayes2 sheet in this file illustrates how Bayes' rule can be used when there are more than two possible test results and/or drug user categories.

Figure 6.28

Bayes' Rule for
Drug-Testing
Example

	A	B	C	D	E	F
1	Illustration of Bayes' rule using drug example					
2						
3	Prior probabilities of drug user status					
4		User	Non-user			
5		0.05	0.95	1		
6						
7	Likelihoods of test results, given drug user status					
8		User	Non-user			
9	Test positive	0.93	0.03			
10	Test negative	0.07	0.97			
11		1	1			
12						
13	Unconditional probabilities of test results (denominators of Bayes' rule)					
14	Test positive	0.075				
15	Test negative	0.925				
16		1				
17						
18	Posterior probabilities of drug user status (Bayes' rule)					
19		User	Non-user			
20	Test positive	0.620	0.380	1		
21	Test negative	0.004	0.996	1		

The given priors and likelihoods are listed in the ranges B5:C5 and B9:C10. You first use Equation (6.2) to calculate the denominators for Bayes' rule, the unconditional probabilities of the two possible test results, in the range B14:B15. Because each of these is a sum of products of priors and likelihoods, the formula in cell B14 is

=SUMPRODUCT($B$5:$C$5,B9:C9)

and this is copied to cell B15. Then you use Equation (6.1) to calculate the posterior probabilities in the range B20:C21. Because each of these is a product of a prior and a likelihood, divided by a denominator, the formula in cell B20 is

=B$5*B9/$B14

and this is copied to the rest of the B20:C21 range. The various 1s in the margins of Figure 6.28 are row sums or column sums that must equal 1. They are shown only as checks of the logic.

As we have noted, a positive drug test still leaves a 38% chance that the athlete is *not* a drug user. Is this a valid argument for not requiring drug testing of athletes? We explore this question in a continuation of the drug-testing example in the next section. ∎

PROBLEMS

Level A

18. For each of the following, use a one-way data table to see how the posterior probability of being a drug user, given a positive test, varies as the indicated input varies. Write a brief explanation of your results.

   a. Let the input be the prior probability of being a drug user, varied from 0.01 to 0.10 in increments of 0.01.

   b. Let the input be the probability of a false positive from the test, varied from 0 to 0.10 in increments of 0.01.

   c. Let the input be the probability of a false negative from the test, varied from 0 to 0.10 in increments of 0.01.

19. In the drug testing, assume there are three possible test results: positive, negative, and inconclusive. For a drug user, the probabilities of these outcomes are 0.65, 0.06, and 0.29. For a nonuser, they are 0.03, 0.72, and 0.25. Use Bayes' rule to find a table of all posterior probabilities. (The prior probability of being a drug user is still 0.05.) Then answer the following.

a. What is the posterior probability that the athlete is a drug user, (1) given that her test results are positive, (2) given that her test results are negative, and (3) given that her drug results are inconclusive?

b. What is the probability of observing a positive test result, a negative test result, or an inconclusive test result?

20. Referring to the previous problem, find the same probabilities through the counting argument explained in this section. Start with 100,000 athletes and divide them into the various categories.

21. Suppose you are a heterosexual white male and are going to be tested to see if you are HIV positive. Assume that if you are HIV positive, your test will always come back positive. Assume that if you are not HIV positive, there is still a 0.001 chance that your test will indicate that you are HIV positive. In reality, 1 of 10,000 heterosexual white males is HIV positive. Your doctor calls and says that you have tested HIV positive. He is sorry but there is a 99.9% $(1-0.001)$ chance that you have HIV. Is he correct? What is the actual probability that you are HIV positive?

Level B

22. The terms *prior* and *posterior* are relative. Assume that the drug test has been performed, and the outcome is positive, which leads to the posterior probabilities in row 20 of Figure 6.28. Now assume there is a *second* test, independent of the first, that can be used as a follow-up. Assume that its false-positive and false-negative rates are 0.02 and 0.06.

a. Use the posterior probabilities from row 20 as *prior* probabilities in a second Bayes' rule calculation. (Now *prior* means prior to the second test.) If the athlete also tests positive in this second test, what is the posterior probability that he is a drug user?

b. We assumed that the two tests are independent. Why might this not be realistic? If they are not independent, what kind of additional information would you need about the likelihoods of the test results?

23. In the OJ Simpson trial it was accepted that OJ had battered his wife. OJ's lawyer tried to negate the impact of this information by stating that in a one-year period, only 1 out of 2500 battered women are murdered, so the fact that OJ battered his wife does not give much evidence that he was the murderer. The prosecution (foolishly!) let this go unchallenged. Here are the relevant statistics: In a typical year 6.25 million women are battered, 2500 are battered and murdered, and 2250 of the women who were battered and murdered were killed by the batterer. How should the prosecution have refuted the defense's argument?

6.5 MULTISTAGE DECISION PROBLEMS

In this section we investigate multistage decision problems. In many such problems the first-stage decision is whether to purchase information that will help make a better second-stage decision. In this case the information, if obtained, typically changes the probabilities of later outcomes. To revise the probabilities once the information is obtained, you often need to apply Bayes' rule, as discussed in the previous section. In addition, you typically want to learn how much the information is worth. After all, information usually comes at a price, so you want to know whether the information is worth its price. This leads to an investigation of the value of information, an important theme of this section.

We begin with a continuation of the drug-testing example from the previous section. If drug tests are not completely reliable, should they be used? As you will see, it all depends on the "costs."[5]

| EXAMPLE | **6.3 DRUG TESTING COLLEGE ATHLETES** |

The administrators at State University are trying to decide whether to institute mandatory drug testing for athletes. They have the same information about priors and likelihoods as in Example 6.2, but they now want to use a decision tree approach to see whether the benefits outweigh the costs.[6]

---

[5]It might also depend on whether there is a second type of test that could help confirm the findings of the first test. However, we will not consider such a test.

[6]Again, see Feinstein (1990) for an enlightening discussion of this drug-testing problem at a real university.

Objective To use a multistage decision framework to see whether mandatory drug testing can be justified, given a somewhat unreliable test and a set of "reasonable" monetary values.

WHERE DO THE NUMBERS COME FROM?

We already discussed the source of the probabilities in Example 6.2. The monetary values we need are discussed in detail here.

Solution

We have already discussed the uncertain outcomes and their probabilities. Now we need to discuss the decision alternatives and the monetary values, the other two elements of a decision analysis. We will assume that there are only two alternatives: perform drug testing on all athletes or don't perform any drug testing. In the former case we assume that if an athlete tests positive, this athlete is barred from athletics.

Assessing the Monetary Values

The "monetary" values are more difficult to assess. They include

- the benefit B from correctly identifying a drug user and barring this person from athletics
- the cost $C1$ of the test itself for a single athlete (materials and labor)
- the cost $C2$ of falsely accusing a nonuser (and barring this person from athletics)
- the cost $C3$ of not identifying a drug user and allowing this person to participate in athletics
- the cost $C4$ of violating a nonuser's privacy by performing the test.

Real decision problems often involve nonmonetary benefits and costs. These must be assessed, relative to one another, before rational decisions can be made.

It is clear that only $C1$ is a direct monetary cost that is easy to measure. However, the other "costs" and the benefit B are real, and they must be compared on some scale to enable administrators to make a rational decision. We will do so by comparing everything to the cost $C1$, to which we assign value 1. (This does not mean that the cost of testing an athlete is necessarily \$1; it just means that all other monetary values are expressed as multiples of $C1$.) Clearly, there is a lot of subjectivity involved in making these comparisons, so sensitivity analysis on the final decision tree is a must.

Developing a Benefit–Cost Table

Before developing this decision tree, it is useful to form a benefit–cost table for both alternatives and all possible outcomes. Because we will eventually maximize expected net *benefit*, all benefits in this table have a positive sign and all costs have a negative sign. These net benefits are listed in Table 6.6. As before, let D and ND denote that a randomly chosen athlete is or is not a drug user, and let $T+$ and $T-$ indicate a positive or negative test result. The first two columns are relevant if no tests are performed; the last four are relevant when

Table 6.6 Net Benefit for Drug-Testing Example

Ultimate decision	Don't Test		Perform Test			
	D	ND	D and $T+$	ND and $T+$	D and $T-$	ND and $T-$
Bar from athletics	B	$-C_2$	$B-C_1$	$-(C_1+C_2+C_4)$	$B-C_1$	$-(C_1+C_2+C_4)$
Don't bar from athletics	$-C_3$	0	$-(C_1+C_3)$	$-(C_1+C_4)$	$-(C_1+C_3)$	$-(C_1+C_4)$

testing is performed. For example, if a positive test is obtained for a nonuser and this athlete is barred from athletics, there are three costs: the cost of the test (C_1), the cost of falsely accusing the athlete (C_2), and the cost of violating the athlete's privacy (C_4). The other entries are obtained similarly.

Developing the Decision Tree Model

The decision model, developed with PrecisionTree and shown in Figures 6.29 and 6.30, is now fairly straightforward. (See the file **Drug Testing Decision.xlsx**.) You first enter all of the benefits and costs in an input section. These, together with the Bayes' rule calculations from Example 6.2, appear at the top of Figure 6.29. Then you use PrecisionTree in the usual way to build the tree in Figure 6.30 and enter the links to the values and probabilities.

Figure 6.29 Inputs and Bayes' Rule Calculations for Drug-Testing Example

	A	B	C	D	E	F
1	Drug testing decision					
2						
3	Benefits			Given probabilities		
4	Identifying user	25		Prior probabilities		
5					User	Non-user
6	Costs				0.05	0.95
7	Test cost	1				
8	Barring non-user	50		Conditional probabilities of test results		
9	Not identifying user	20			User	Non-user
10	Violation of privacy	2		Positive	0.93	0.03
11				Negative	0.07	0.97
12	Key probabilities					
13	PrUser	0.05		Bayesian revision		
14	PrFalseNegative	0.07		Unconditional probabilities of test results		
15	PrFalsePositive	0.03		Positive	0.075	
16				Negative	0.925	
17						
18				Posterior probabilities		
19					User	Non-user
20				Positive	0.620	0.380
21				Negative	0.004	0.996

It is important to understand the timing (from left to right) in this decision tree. If drug testing is performed, the result of the drug test is observed first (a probability node). Each test result leads to an action (bar from sports or don't), and then the eventual benefit or cost depends on whether the athlete uses drugs (again a probability node). You might argue that the university never knows for certain whether the athlete uses drugs, but you must include this information in the tree to get the correct benefits and costs. On the other hand, if no drug testing is performed, there is no intermediate test result node or branch.

Bayes' rule is required because it yields exactly those probabilities that are needed in the decision tree.

Make sure you understand which probabilities are used in the tree. In the lower part, where no testing takes place, the probabilities are the prior probabilities. There is no test information in this case. In the upper part, where the test is performed, the probabilities for the user and nonuser branches are posterior probabilities, given the results of the test. The reason is that by the time we get to these nodes, the results of the test have already been observed. However, the probabilities for the test results are *unconditional* probabilities, the denominators in Bayes' rule. They are not conditional probabilities such as $P(T+|D)$ because you condition only on information to the *left* of any given branch. In other words, by the time you get to the test result branches, you do not yet know whether the athlete is a user.

Discussion of the Solution

Now we analyze the solution. First, we discuss the benefits and costs shown in Figure 6.29. These were chosen fairly arbitrarily, but with some hope of reflecting reality. The largest

Figure 6.30 Decision Tree for Drug-Testing Example

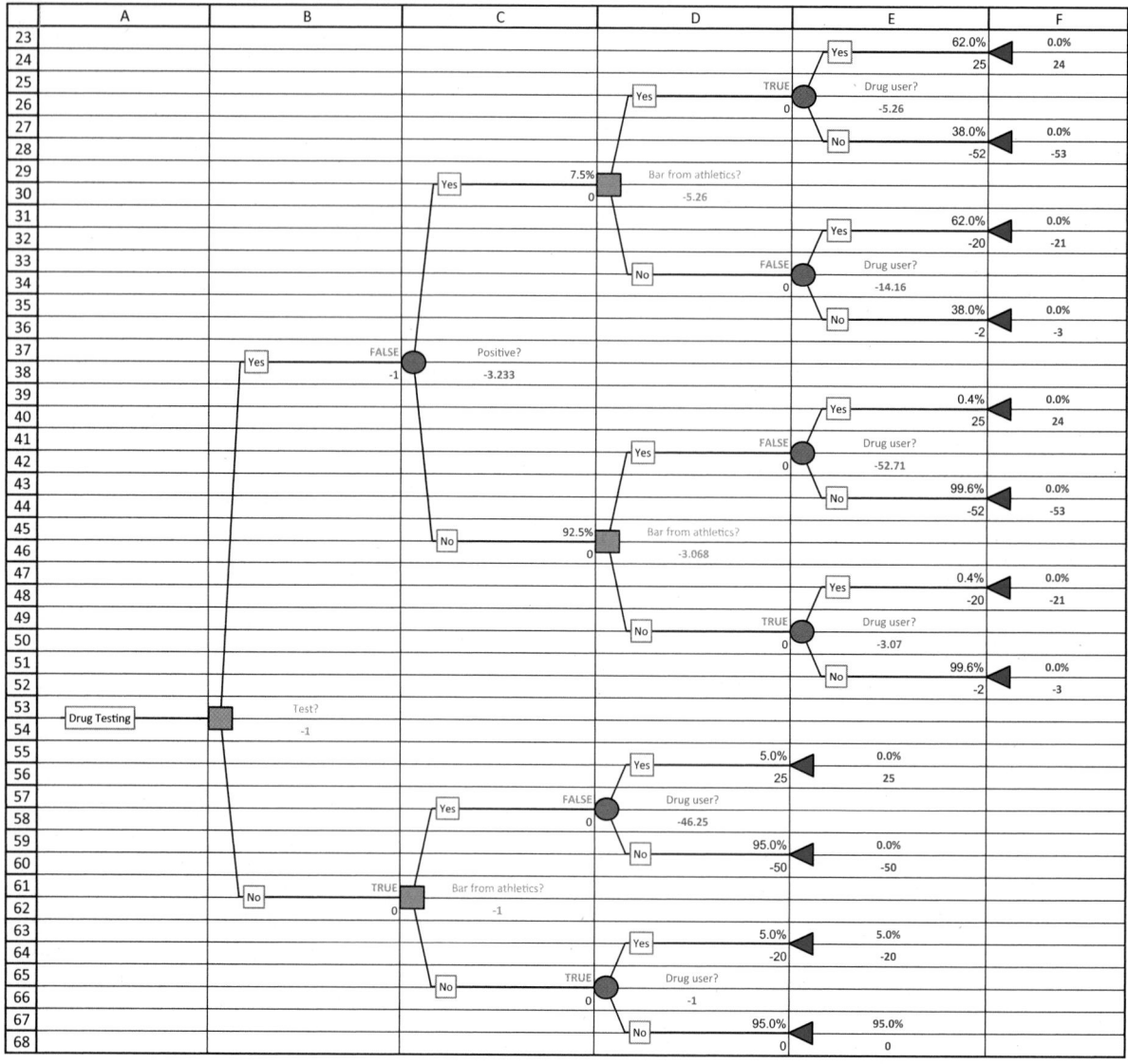

cost is falsely accusing (and then barring) a nonuser. This is 50 times as large as the cost of the test. The benefit of identifying a drug user is only half this large, and the cost of not identifying a user is 40% as large as barring a nonuser. The violation of the privacy of a nonuser is twice as large as the cost of the test. Based on these values, the decision tree implies that drug testing should *not* be performed (and no athletes should be barred). The EMVs for testing and for not testing are both negative, indicating that the costs outweigh the benefits for each, but the EMV for not testing is slightly *less* negative.[7]

Sensitivity Analysis

What would it take to change this decision? We begin with the assumption, probably accepted by most people in our society, that the cost of falsely accusing a nonuser (C_2) is the largest of the benefits and costs in the range B4:B10. In fact, because of possible legal

---

[7]The university in the Feinstein (1990) study came to the same conclusion.

costs, you might argue that C_2 is *more* than 50 times the cost of the test. But if C_2 increases, the scales are tipped even further in the direction of not testing. On the other hand, if the benefit B from identifying a user and the cost C_3 for not identifying a user increase, then testing might be the preferred alternative. We tried this, keeping C_2 constant at 50. When B and C_3 both had value 45, no testing was still optimal, but when they both increased to 50—the same magnitude as C_2—testing won out by a small margin. However, it would be difficult to argue that B and C_3 are of the same magnitude as C_2.

Other than the benefits and costs, the only other input you might vary is the accuracy of the test, measured by the error probabilities in cells B14 and B15. Presumably, if the test makes fewer false positives and false negatives, testing might be a more attractive alternative. We tried this, keeping the benefits and costs the same as those in Figure 6.29 but changing the error probabilities. Even when each error probability was decreased to 0.01, however, the no-testing alternative was still optimal—by a fairly wide margin.

In summary, based on a number of reasonable assumptions and parameter settings, this example has shown that it is difficult to make a case for mandatory drug testing. ∎

6.5.1 The Value of Information

The drug-testing decision problem represents a typical multistage decision problem. You first decide whether to obtain some information that could be useful—the results of a drug test. If you decide not to obtain the information, you make a decision right away (bar the athlete or don't), based on prior probabilities. If you do decide to obtain the information, then you first observe the information and *then* make the final decision, based on posterior probabilities.

The questions we ask now are: How much is the information worth, and if it costs a given amount, should you purchase it? Presumably, information that will help you make your ultimate decision should be worth something, but it might not be clear how much the information is worth. In addition, even if the information is worth something, it might not be worth as much as its actual price. Fortunately, the answers to these questions are embedded in the decision tree itself.

We will find the values of two types of information: sample information and perfect information. **Sample information** is the information from the experiment itself. For example, it is the information from the (less than perfect) drug test. (It has become customary to use the term *sample* information, and we will continue the practice here, but a more precise term would be *imperfect* information.) **Perfect information**, on the other hand, is information from a perfect test—that is, a test that will indicate with certainty which ultimate outcome will occur. In the drug example, this would correspond to a test that never makes mistakes. Admittedly, perfect information is almost never available at any price, but finding its value is still useful because it provides an upper bound on the value of *any* information. For example, if perfect information is valued at $2000, then *no* information can possibly be worth more than $2000.

We will find the **expected value of sample information**, or **EVSI**, and the **expected value of perfect information**, or **EVPI**. They are defined as follows:

The **EVSI** is the most you would be willing to pay for the sample information.

Formula for EVSI

EVSI = EMV with (free) sample information − EMV without information **(6.4)**

The **EVPI** is the most you would be willing to pay for perfect information.

We first make one important general point about the value of information. Suppose there is an ultimate decision to make. Before making this decision, you can obtain information, supposedly to help you make the ultimate decision. But suppose you make the *same* ultimate decision, regardless of the information you obtain—the same decision you would have made in the absence of information. Can you guess the value of this information? It is zero. The information cannot be worth anything if it never leads to a different decision than you would have made without the information. The moral is that if you plan to pay something for information, you are wasting your money unless this information influences your decision making.

FUNDAMENTAL INSIGHT

The Value of Information

The amount you should be willing to spend for information is the expected increase in EMV you can obtain from having the information. If the actual price of the information is less than or equal to this amount, you should purchase it; otherwise, the information is not worth its price. In addition, information that never affects your decision is worthless, and it should not be purchased at any price. Finally, the value of *any* information can never be greater than the value of perfect information that would eliminate all uncertainty.

We now see how Bayes' rule can be used and the value of information can be evaluated in a typical multistage decision problem.

EXAMPLE | 6.4 MARKETING A NEW PRODUCT AT ACME

The Acme Company is trying to decide whether to market a new product. As in many new-product situations, there is considerable uncertainty about whether the new product will eventually succeed. Acme believes that it might be wise to introduce the product in a regional test market before introducing it nationally. Therefore, the company's first decision is whether to conduct the test market.

Acme estimates that the net cost of the test market is $100,000. We assume this is mostly fixed costs, so that the same cost is incurred regardless of the test-market results. If Acme decides to conduct the test market, it must then wait for the results. Based on the results of the test market, it can then decide whether to market the product nationally, in which case it will incur a fixed cost of $7 million. On the other hand, if the original decision is *not* to run a test market, then the final decision—whether to market the product nationally—can be made without further delay. Acme's unit margin, the difference between its selling price and its unit variable cost, is $18. We assume this is relevant only for the national market.

Acme classifies the results in either the test market or the national market as great, fair, or awful. Each of these results in the national market is accompanied by a forecast of total units sold. These sales volumes (in 1000s of units) are 600 (great), 300 (fair), and 90 (awful). In the absence of any test market information, Acme estimates that probabilities of the three national market outcomes are 0.45, 0.35, and 0.20, respectively.

In addition, Acme has the following historical data from products that were introduced into both test markets and national markets.

- Of the products that eventually did great in the national market, 64% did great in the test market, 26% did fair in the test market, and 10% did awful in the test market.

- Of the products that eventually did fair in the national market, 18% did great in the test market, 57% did fair in the test market, and 25% did awful in the test market.
- Of the products that eventually did awful in the national market, 9% did great in the test market, 48% did fair in the test market, and 43% did awful in the test market.[8]

The company wants to use a decision tree approach to find the best strategy. It also wants to find the expected value of the information provided by the test market.

Objective To develop a decision tree to find the best strategy for Acme, to perform a sensitivity analysis on the results, and to find EVSI and EVPI.

WHERE DO THE NUMBERS COME FROM?

The fixed costs of the test market and the national market are probably accurate estimates, based on planned advertising and overhead expenses. The unit margin is just the difference between the anticipated selling price and the known unit cost of the product. The sales volume estimates are clearly approximations to reality, because the sales from any new product would form a continuum of possible values. Here, the company has "discretized" the problem into three possible outcomes for the national market, and it has estimated the sales for each of these discrete outcomes. The conditional probabilities of national-market results given test-market results are probably based on results from previous products that went through test markets and then national markets.

Solution

We begin by discussing the three basic elements of this decision problem: the possible strategies, the possible outcomes and their probabilities, and the value model. The possible strategies are clear. Acme must first decide whether to run a test market. Then it must decide whether to introduce the product nationally. However, it is important to realize that if Acme decides to run a test market, it can base the national market decision on the results of the test market. In this case its final strategy will be a **contingency plan**, where it conducts the test market, then introduces the product nationally if it receives sufficiently positive test-market results but abandons the product if it receives sufficiently negative test-market results. The optimal strategies from many multistage decision problems involve similar contingency plans.

> In a **contingency plan**, later decisions can depend on earlier decisions and information received.

FUNDAMENTAL INSIGHT

Making Sequential Decisions

Whenever you have a chance to make several sequential decisions and you will learn useful information between decision points, the decision you make initially depends on the decisions you plan to make in the future, and these depend on the information you will learn in the meantime. In other words, when you decide what to do initially, you should look ahead to see what your future options will be, and what your decision will be under each option. Such a contingency plan is typically superior to a *myopic* (short-sighted) plan that doesn't take into account future options in the initial decision making.

[8]You can question why the company ever marketed products nationally after awful test-market results, but we will assume that, for whatever reason, the company made a few such decisions—and that a few even turned out to be winners.

Regarding the uncertain outcomes and their probabilities, we note that the given prior probabilities of national-market results in the absence of test-market results will be needed in the part of the tree where Acme decides not to run a test market. However, the historical percentages we quoted are really likelihoods of test-market results, given national-market results. For example, one of these is P(Great test market | Great national market) = 0.64. Such probabilities are the opposite of those needed in the tree. This is because the event to the right of the given sign, "great national market," occurs in time *after* the event to the left of the given sign, "great test market." This is a sure sign that Bayes' rule is required.

The required posterior probabilities of national-market results, given test-market results, are calculated directly from Bayes' rule, Equation (6.1). For example, if *NG*, *NF*, and *NA* represent great, fair, and awful national-market results, respectively, and if *TG*, *TF*, and *TA* represent similar events for the test market, than one typical example of a posterior probability calculation is

$$P(NG|TF) = \frac{P(TF|NG)P(NG)}{P(TF|NG)P(NG) + P(TF|NF)P(NF) + P(TF|NA)P(NA)}$$

$$= \frac{0.26(0.45)}{0.26(0.45) + 0.57(0.35) + 0.48(0.20)} = \frac{0.117}{0.4125} = 0.2836$$

This is a reasonable result. In the absence of test market information, the probability of a great national market is 0.45. However, after a test market with only fair results, the probability of a great national market is revised down to 0.2836. The other posterior probabilities are calculated similarly. In addition, the denominator in this calculation, 0.4125, is the unconditional probability of a fair test market. Such test-market probabilities will be needed in the tree.

Finally, the monetary values in the tree are straightforward. There are fixed costs of test marketing or marketing nationally, which are incurred as soon as these go-ahead decisions are made. From that point, if the company markets nationally, it observe the sales volumes and multiplies them by the unit margin to obtain the selling profits.

Implementing Bayes' Rule

The inputs and Bayes' rule calculations are shown in Figure 6.31. (See file **Acme Marketing Decisions 1.xlsx.**) You perform the Bayes' rule calculations exactly as in the

Figure 6.31 Inputs and Bayes' Rule Calculations for Acme Marketing Example

	A	B	C	D	E	F	G	H	I	J	K	L	M	N
1	Acme marketing decisions													
2														
3	Inputs													
4	Fixed costs ($1000s)													
5	Test market	100												
6	National market	7000												
7														
8	Unit margin (either market)	$18												
9														
10	Possible quantities sold (1000s of units) in national market													
11	Great	600												
12	Fair	300												
13	Awful	90												
14						Bayes' rule calculations								
15	Prior probabilities of national market results					Unconditional probabilities of test mkt results (denominators of Bayes' rule)								
16		Great	Fair	Awful		Great	0.3690							
17		0.45	0.35	0.20		Fair	0.4125							
18						Awful	0.2185							
19	Likelihoods of test market results (along side), given national market results (along top) from historical data													
20		Great	Fair	Awful		Posterior probabilities of national mkt results (along top), given test mkt results (along side)								
21	Great	0.64	0.18	0.09			Great	Fair	Awful					
22	Fair	0.26	0.57	0.48		Great	0.7805	0.1707	0.0488					
23	Awful	0.10	0.25	0.43		Fair	0.2836	0.4836	0.2327					
24						Awful	0.2059	0.4005	0.3936					

drug example. To calculate the unconditional probabilities for test-market results, the denominators for Bayes' rule from Equation (6.2), enter the formula

=SUMPRODUCT($B$17:$D$17,B21:D21)

in cell G16 and copy it down to cell G18. To calculate the posterior probabilities from Equation (6.1), enter the formula

=B$17*B21/$G16

in cell G22 and copy it to the range G22:I24.

DEVELOPING THE DECISION TREE MODEL

The tree is now straightforward to build and label, as shown in Figure 6.32. Note that the fixed costs of test marketing and marketing nationally appear on the decision branches

Figure 6.32   Decision Tree for Acme Marketing Example

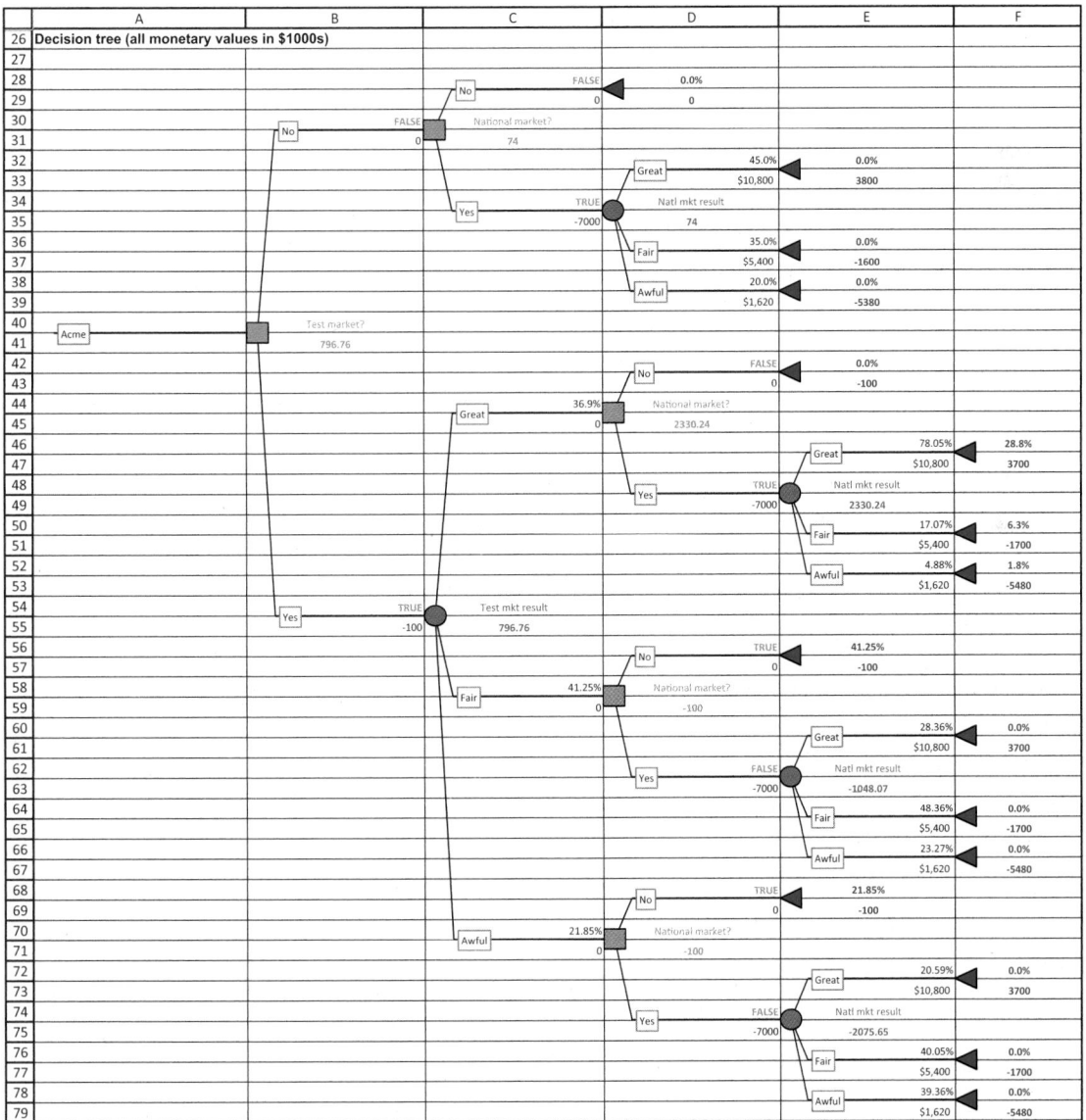

where they occur in time, so that only the selling profits need to be placed on the probability branches. For example, the formula for the selling profit in cell D33 is

=$B$8*$B$11

Pay particular attention to the probabilities on the branches. The top group are the prior probabilities from the range B17:D17. In the bottom group, the probabilities on the left are unconditional probabilities of test-market results from the range G16:G18, and those on the right are posterior probabilities of national-market results from the range G22:I24. Again, this corresponds to the standard decision tree convention, where all probabilities on the tree are conditioned on any events that have occurred to the left of them.

Discussion of the Solution

To interpret this tree, note that each value just below each node name is an EMV. (These are colored red or green in Excel.) For example, the 796.76 in cell B41 is the EMV for the entire decision problem. It means that Acme's best EMV from acting optimally is $796,760. As another example, the 74 in cell D35 means that if Acme ever gets to that point—there is no test market and the product is marketed nationally—the EMV is $74,000. Actually, this is the expected selling profit minus the $7 million fixed cost, so the expected selling profit, given that no information from a test market has been obtained, is $7,074,000.

Acme's optimal strategy is apparent by following the TRUE branches from left to right. Acme should first run a test market. If the test-market result is great, the product should be marketed nationally. However, if the test-market result is fair or awful, the product should be abandoned. In these cases the prospects from a national market look bleak, so Acme should cut its losses. (And there *are* losses. In these latter two cases, Acme has already spent $100,000 on the test market and has nothing to show for it.)

Once you have done the work to build the tree, you can reap the benefits of PrecisionTree's tools. For example, its policy suggestion and risk profile outputs are given in Figures 6.33 and 6.34. The policy suggestion shows only the part of the tree corresponding to the optimal strategy. Note that there are two values at each end node. The bottom number is the combined monetary value along this sequence of branches, and the top number is the probability of this sequence of branches. This information leads directly to probability distribution in the risk profile. For this optimal strategy, the only possible

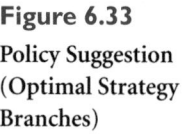

Figure 6.33

Policy Suggestion (Optimal Strategy Branches)

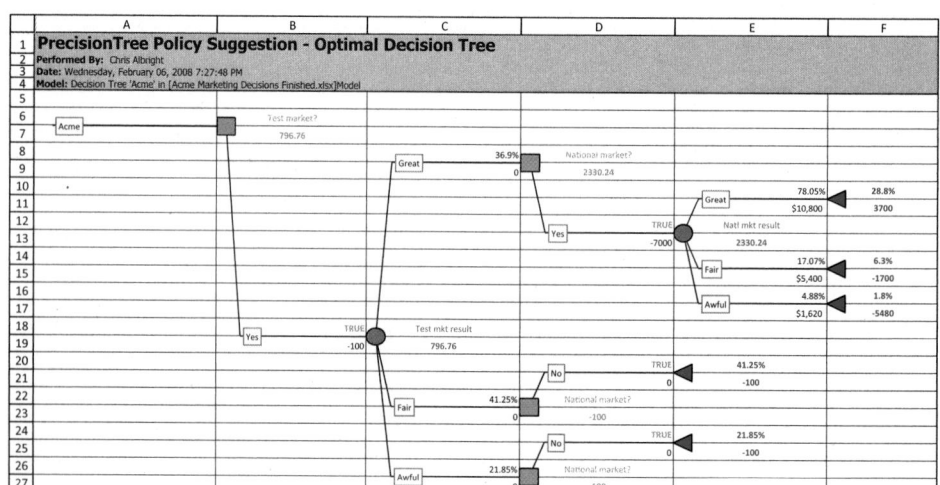

Figure 6.34

Risk Profile of
Optimal Strategy

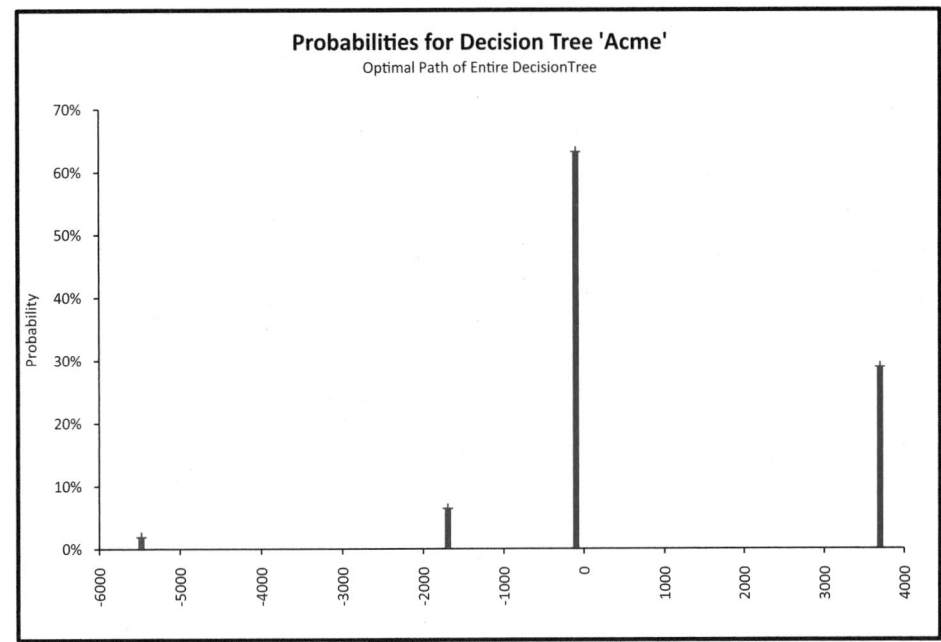

Probabilities for Decision Tree 'Acme'
Optimal Path of Entire DecisionTree

monetary outcomes are a gain of $3,700,000 and losses of $100,000, $1,700,000, and $5,480,000. Their respective probabilities are 0.288, 0.631, 0.063, and 0.018. Fortunately, the large possible losses are unlikely enough that the EMV is still positive, $796,760.

You might argue that the large potential losses and the slightly higher than 70% chance of *some* loss should persuade Acme to abandon the product right away—without a test market. However, this is what "playing the averages" with EMV is all about. Because the EMV of this optimal strategy is greater than 0, the EMV from abandoning the product right away, Acme should go ahead with this optimal strategy if the company is indeed an EMV maximizer. In Section 6.6 we will see how this reasoning can change if Acme is a risk-averse decision maker—as it might be with multimillion-dollar losses looming in the future.

Sensitivity Analysis

Sensitivity analysis is often important for the insights it provides. It makes you ask, "Why do these results occur?"

There are several sensitivity analyses that can performed on this model. We investigate how things change when the unit margin, currently $18, varies from $8 to $28. This could change the decision about whether to run a test market or to market nationally.

We first analyze the overall EMV in cell B41, setting up the sensitivity dialog box as in Figure 6.35. The resulting chart is shown in Figure 6.36. The chart indicates that for small unit margins, it is better *not* to run a test market. The top line, at value 0, corresponds to abandoning the product altogether, whereas the bottom line, at value -100, corresponds to running a test market and then abandoning the product regardless of the results. Similarly, for large unit margins, it is also best not to run a test market. Again, the top line is 100 above the bottom line. However, the reasoning now is different. For large unit margins, the company should market nationally *regardless* of test-market results, so there is no reason to spend money on a test market. Finally, for intermediate unit margins, as in the original model, the chart shows that it is best to run a test market. We hope you agree that this one single chart provides a lot of information and insight.

By changing the cell to analyze in Figure 6.35, we can gain additional insight. For example, if no test market is available, the EMV for deciding nationally right away, in cell C31, is

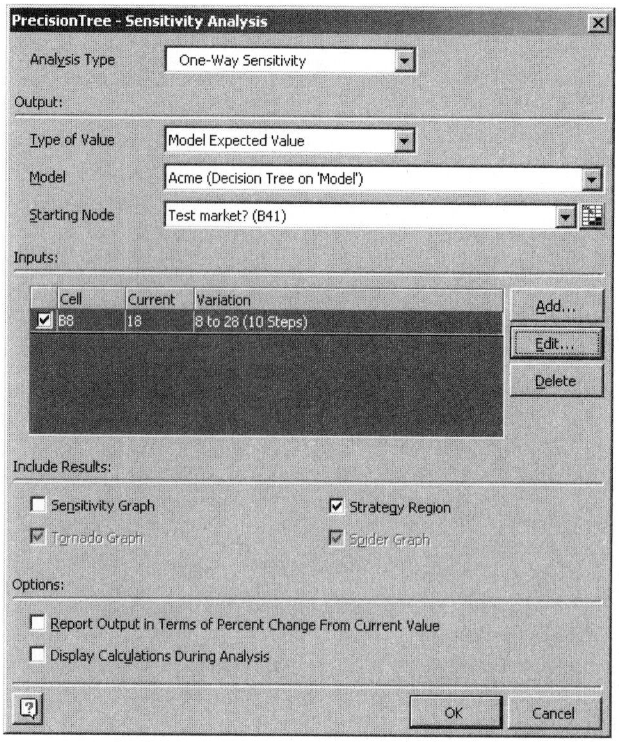

Figure 6.35

Dialog Box for Sensitivity

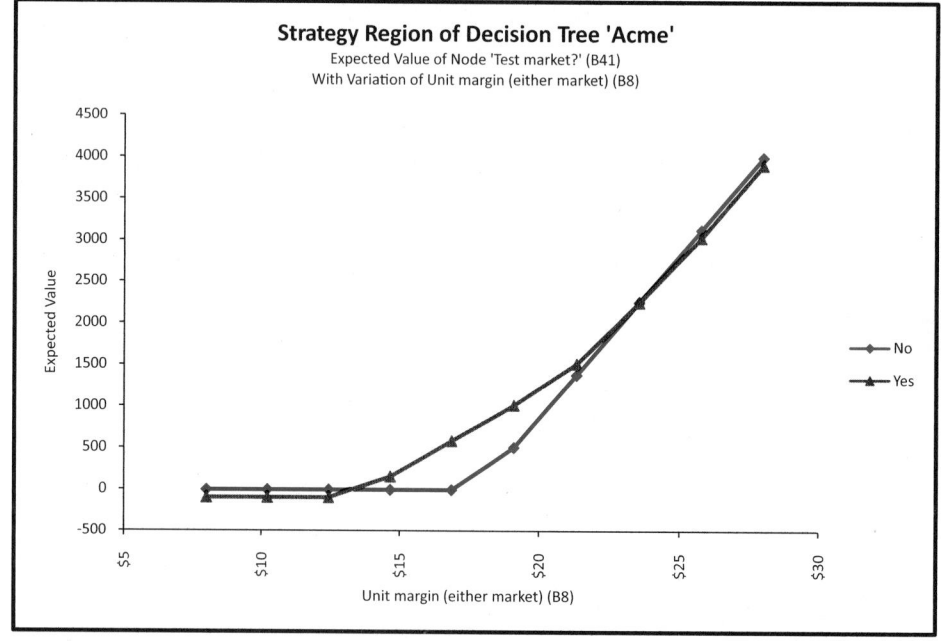

Figure 6.36

Sensitivity Analysis on Overall Profit

relevant. The resulting chart appears in Figure 6.37. Now it is a contest between getting zero profit from abandoning the product and getting a linearly increasing profit from marketing nationally. The breakpoint appears to be slightly below $18. If the unit margin is above this value, Acme should market nationally; otherwise, it should abandon the product.

Figure 6.37

Sensitivity Analysis
for Deciding
Nationally Right
Away

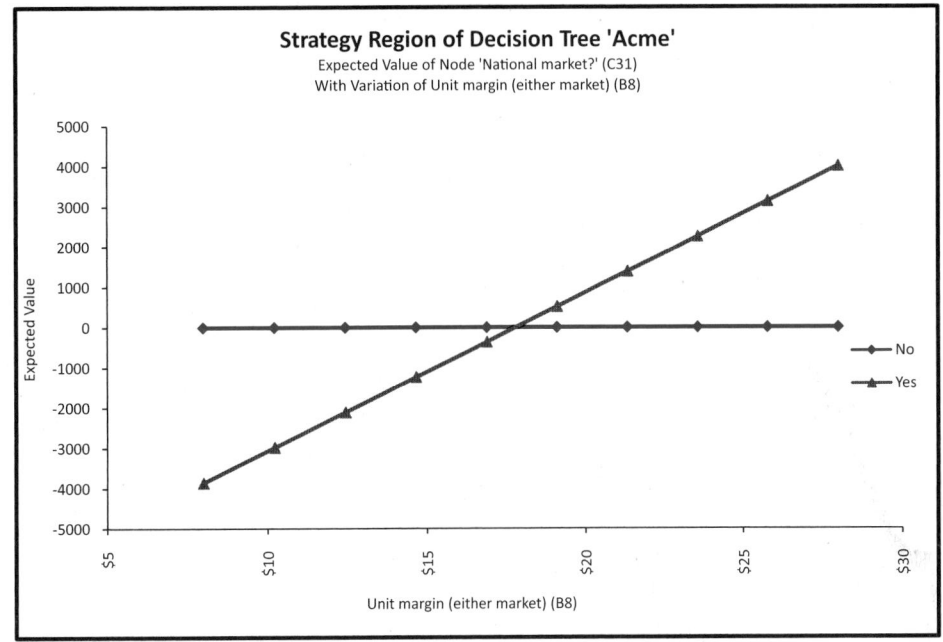

You can also choose to analyze any of the EMVs in cells D45, D59, or D71. Each of these is relevant in the case where the company has run the test market, has observed the test-market results, and is about to decide whether to market nationally. For example, if you choose D71 as the cell to analyze, you obtain the chart in Figure 6.38. It indicates that there are indeed situations—where the unit margin is about $26 or more—when the company should market nationally, even though the test market is awful. In contrast, the chart in

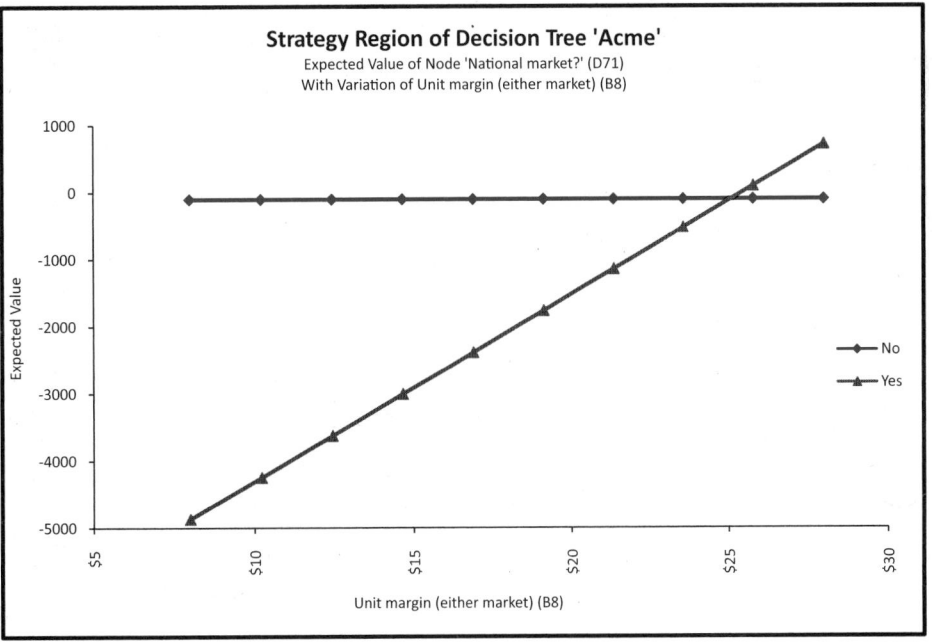

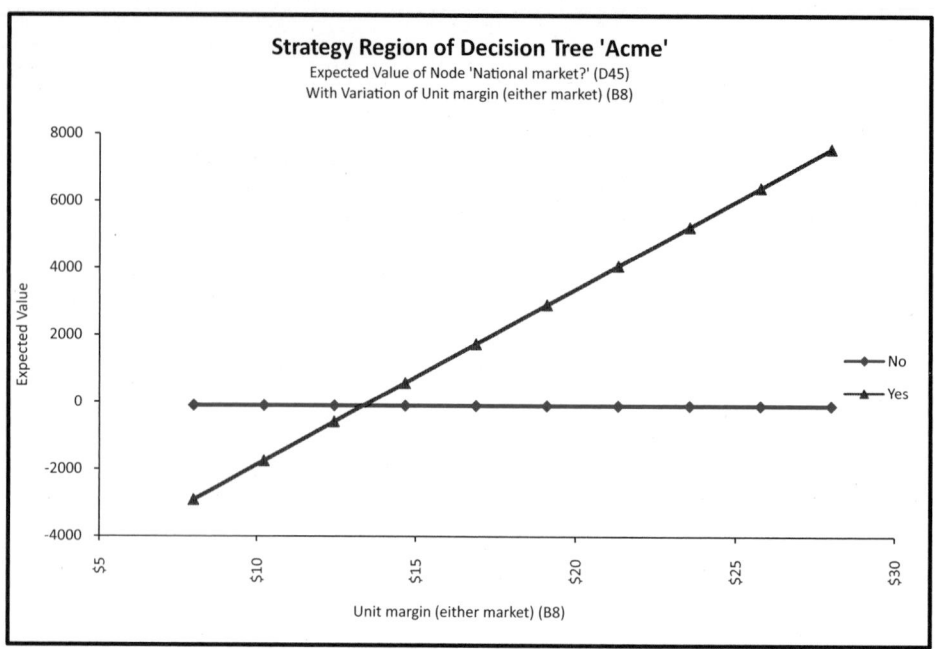

Figure 6.39, where we analyze cell D45, indicates the opposite behavior. It shows that if
the unit margin is low enough—about $13.50 or less—the company should abandon the
product nationally, even though the test-market results are great. These are again very useful
insights.

Expected Value of Sample Information

The role of the test market in this example is to provide information in the form of more
accurate probabilities of national-market results. Information usually costs something,
as it does in Acme's problem. Currently, the fixed cost of the test market is $100,000,
which is evidently not too much to pay because Acme's best strategy is to run the test
market. However, you might ask how much this test market is really worth. This is the
expected value of sample information, or EVSI, and it is easy to obtain from the tree.
From Figure 6.32, the EMV from test marketing is $796,760, $100,000 of which is the
cost of the test market. Therefore, if this test market were free, the expected profit would
be $896,760. On the other hand, the EMV from not running a test market is $74,000 (see
cell C31 in the tree). From Equation (6.4), the difference is EVSI:

$$\text{EVSI} = \$896{,}760 - \$74{,}000 = \$822{,}760$$

You can check that if you put any value less than 822.76 in the test-market fixed-cost cell
(cell B5), the decision to test-market will continue to be best.

Intuitively, running the test market is worth something because it changes the optimal
decision. With no test-market information, the best decision is to market nationally. (See
the top part of the tree in Figure 6.32.) However, with the test-market information, the ultimate decision depends on the test-market results. Specifically, Acme should market
nationally only if the test-market result is great. This is what makes information worth
something—its outcome affects the optimal decision.

Expected Value of Perfect Information

It took a lot of work to find EVSI. You had to assess various conditional probabilities, use Bayes' rule, and then build a fairly complex decision tree. In general, Acme might have many sources of information it could obtain that would help it make its national decision; the test market is just one of them. The question, then, is how much such information *could* be worth. This is answered by EVPI, the expected value of perfect information. It provides an upper bound on how much *any* information could be worth, and it is relatively easy to calculate.

This perfect information envelope is obviously a fiction, but it helps to explain how perfect information works.

Imagine that Acme could purchase an envelope that has the true national-market result—great, fair, or awful—written inside. Once opened, this envelope would remove all uncertainty, and Acme could make an easy decision. (We assume that Acme can open the envelope *before* having to make the national decision.) EVPI is what this envelope is worth. To calculate it, you build the tree in Figure 6.40. The key here is that the nodes are reversed in time. You first open the envelope to discover what is inside. This corresponds to the probability node. Then you make the final decision. Given the cost parameters, it is easy to see that Acme should market nationally only if the contents of the envelope reveal that the national market will be great. Otherwise, Acme should abandon the product right away.

Figure 6.40

Decision Tree for Evaluating EVPI

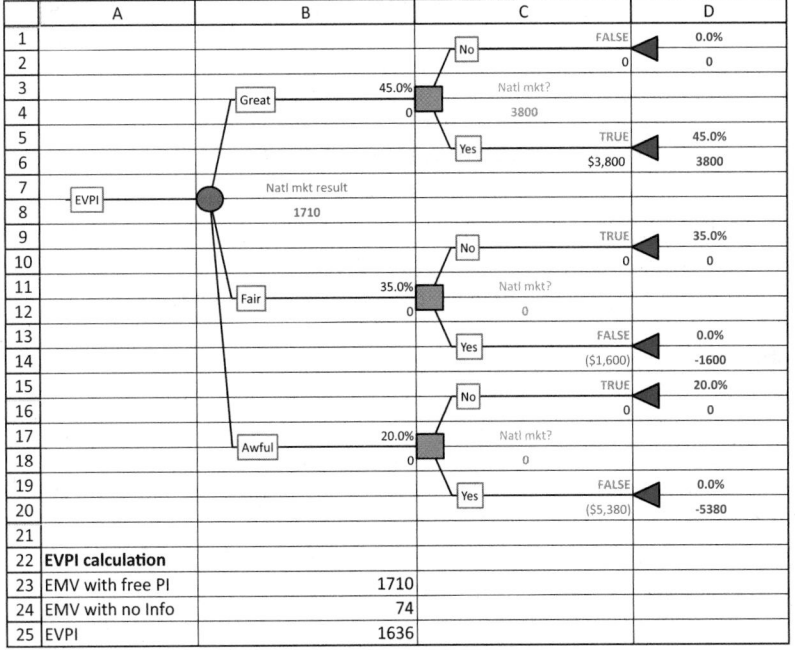

The EVPI calculation is now straightforward. If the envelope (perfect information) is free, the tree in Figure 6.40 indicates that the EMV is $1,710,000. If there is no information, the EMV is $74,000 (cell C31 of Figure 6.32). Therefore, from Equation (6.5),

$$\text{EVPI} = \$1,710,000 - \$74,000 = \$1,636,000$$

No sample information, test market or otherwise, could possibly be worth more than this. So if some hotshot market analyst offers to provide "extremely reliable" market information to Acme for, say, $1.8 million, Acme knows this information cannot be worth its cost. ■

PROBLEMS

Level A

24. In deciding whether to perform mandatory drug testing, we claimed that it is difficult to justify such testing under reasonable conditions. Check this yourself in the following questions.

   a. Drug testing ought to be more attractive if the test is more reliable. Keeping the costs the same as in the example, use PrecisionTree's two-way sensitivity tool to see whether the optimal decision (test or not test) changes as the probability of a false positive and the probability of a false negative both change. You can let them vary through some reasonable ranges. Explain the results.

   b. Repeat part **a**, but first double the two monetary values that make the test more attractive: the benefit of identifying a user and the cost of not identifying a user. How do your results differ from those in part **a**?

   c. In this part, keep the probabilities of false positives and false negatives the same, but let the benefits and costs vary. Specifically, let the benefit of identifying a user and the cost of not identifying a user be of the form 25*a* and 20*a*, where *a* is some factor that you can vary. Similarly, let the cost of barring a nonuser and the cost of violating privacy be of the form 50*b* and 2*b*. The cost of the test is still 1. (The idea is that large values of *a* and/or small values of *b* will make the testing more attractive.) Use PrecisionTree's two-way sensitivity tool to see whether the optimal decision (test or not test) changes for a reasonable range of values of *a* and *b*. Discuss your results.

25. In the drug testing decision, find and interpret EVSI and EVPI. Here, "sample" information refers to the information from the imperfect drug test, whereas "perfect" information refers to completely reliable information on whether the athlete uses drugs.

26. Explain in general why EVSI is the same, regardless of the actual cost of the information. For example, in the Acme problem EVSI is the same regardless of whether the actual cost of the test market is $100,000, $200,000, or any other value. Then explain how EVSI, together with the actual cost of the information, leads to the decision about whether to purchase the information.

27. Following up on the previous problem, the *expected net gain from information* is defined as the expected amount gained by having access to the information, at its given cost, as opposed to not having access to the information. Explain how you would calculate this in general. What is its value for the Acme problem?

28. Prior probabilities are often educated guesses at best, so it is worth performing a sensitivity analysis on their values. However, you must make sure that they are varied so that all probabilities are nonnegative and sum to 1. For the Acme problem, perform the following sensitivity analyses on the three prior probabilities and comment on the results.

   a. Vary the probability of a great national market in a one-way sensitivity analysis from 0 to 0.6 in increments of 0.1. Do this in such a way that the probabilities of the two other outcomes, fair and awful, stay in the same ratio as they are currently, 7 to 4.

   b. Vary the probabilities of a great and a fair national market independently in a two-way sensitivity analysis. You can choose the ranges over which these vary, but you must ensure that the three prior probabilities continue to be nonnegative and sum to 1. (For example, you couldn't choose ranges where the probabilities of great and fair are 0.6 and 0.5.)

29. In the Acme problem, perform a sensitivity analysis on the quantity sold from a great national market (the value in cell B11). Let this value vary over a range of values *greater than* the current value of 600, so that a great national market is even more attractive than before. Does this ever change the optimal strategy? If so, in what way?

30. Using trial and error on the prior probabilities in the Acme problem, find values of them that make EVSI equal to 0. These are values where Acme will make the same decision, regardless of the test-market results it observes. Comment on why the test market is worthless for your particular prior probabilities.

Level B

31. We related EVPI to the value of an envelope that contains the true ultimate outcome. This concept can be extended to "less than perfect" information. For example, in the Acme problem suppose that the company could purchase information that would indicate, with certainty, that one of the following two outcomes will occur: (1) the national market will be great, or (2) the national market will not be great. Note that outcome (2) doesn't say whether the national market will be fair or awful; it just says that it won't be great. How much should Acme be willing to pay for such information?

32. The concept behind EVPI is that you purchase perfect information (the envelope), then open the envelope to see which outcome occurs, and then make an easy decision. You do *not*, however, get to choose what

information the envelope contains. In contrast, sometimes a company can pay, not to obtain information, but to influence the outcome. Consider the following version of the Acme problem. There is no possibility of a test market, so that Acme must decide right away whether to market nationally. However, suppose Acme can pay to change the probabilities of the national market outcomes from their current values, 0.45, 0.35, and 0.20, to the new values p, $(7/11)(1 - p)$, and $(4/11)(1 - p)$, for some p. (In this way, the probabilities of fair and awful stay in the same ratio as before,

7 to 4, but by making p large, the probability of a great outcome increases.)

a. How much should Acme be willing to pay for the change if $p = 0.6$? If $p = 0.8$? If $p = 0.95$?

b. Are these types of changes realistic? Answer by speculating on the types of actions Acme might be able to take to make the probability of a great national market higher. Do you think such actions would cost more or less than what Acme should be willing to pay for them (from part **a**)?

6.6 INCORPORATING ATTITUDES TOWARD RISK

Rational decision makers are sometimes willing to violate the EMV maximization criterion when large amounts of money are at stake. These decision makers are willing to sacrifice some EMV to reduce risk. Are you ever willing to do so personally? Consider the following scenarios.

■ You have a chance to enter a lottery where you will win $100,000 with probability 0.1 or win nothing with probability 0.9. Alternatively, you can receive $5000 for certain. How many of you—truthfully—would take the certain $5000, even though the EMV of the lottery is $10,000? Or change the $100,000 to $1,000,000 and the $5000 to $50,000 and ask yourself whether you'd prefer the sure $50,000.

■ You can buy collision insurance on your expensive new car or not buy it. The insurance costs a certain premium and carries some deductible provision. If you decide to pay the premium, then you are essentially paying a certain amount to avoid a gamble: the possibility of wrecking your car and not having it insured. You can be sure that the premium is greater than the expected cost of damage; otherwise, the insurance company would not stay in business. Therefore, from an EMV standpoint you should not purchase the insurance. But how many of you drive without this type of insurance?

These examples, the second of which is certainly realistic, illustrate situations where rational people do not behave as EMV maximizers. Then how do they act? This question has been studied extensively by many researchers, both mathematically and behaviorally. Although there is still not perfect agreement, most researchers believe that if certain basic behavioral assumptions hold, people are **expected utility** maximizers—that is, they choose the alternative with the largest expected utility. Although we will not go deeply into the subject of expected utility maximization, the discussion in this section presents the main ideas.

FUNDAMENTAL INSIGHT

Risk Aversion

When large amounts of money are at stake, most of us are risk averse, at least to some extent. We are willing to sacrifice some EMV to avoid risk. The exact way this is done, using utility functions and expected utility, can be difficult to implement in real situations, but the idea is simple. If you are an EMV maximizer, you are indifferent between a gamble with a given EMV and a sure dollar amount equal to the EMV of the gamble. However, if you are risk averse, you prefer the sure dollar amount to the gamble. That is, you are willing to accept a sure dollar amount that is somewhat *less than* the EMV of the gamble, just to avoid risk. The more EMV you are willing to give up, the more risk averse you are.

6.6.1 Utility Functions

We begin by discussing an individual's **utility function**. This is a mathematical function that transforms monetary values—payoffs and costs—into *utility values*. Essentially, an individual's utility function specifies the individual's preferences for various monetary payoffs and costs and, in doing so, it automatically encodes the individual's attitudes toward risk. Most individuals are *risk averse*, which means intuitively that they are willing to sacrifice some EMV to avoid risky gambles. In terms of the utility function, this means that every extra dollar of payoff is worth slightly less to the individual than the previous dollar, and every extra dollar of cost is considered slightly more costly (in terms of utility) than the previous dollar. The resulting utility functions are shaped as shown in Figure 6.41. Mathematically, these functions are said to be *increasing* and *concave*. The increasing part means that they go uphill—everyone prefers more money to less money. The concave part means that they increase at a decreasing rate. This is the risk-averse behavior.

Figure 6.41

Risk-Averse Utility Function

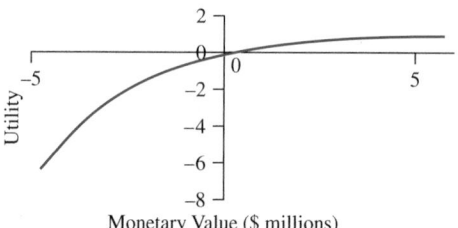

Monetary Value ($ millions)

There are two aspects of implementing utility maximization in a real decision analysis. First, an individual's (or company's) utility function must be assessed. This is a time-consuming task that typically involves many trade-offs. It is usually carried out by experts in the field, and we do not discuss the details of the process here. Second, the resulting utility function is used to find the best decision. This second step is relatively straightforward. You substitute utility values for monetary values in the decision tree and then fold back as usual. That is, you calculate expected *utilities* at probability branches and take maximums (of expected *utilities*) at decision branches. We will look at a numerical example later in this section.

6.6.2 Exponential Utility

As we have indicated, utility assessment is tedious. Even in the best of circumstances, when a trained consultant attempts to assess the utility function of a single person, the process requires the person to make a series of choices between hypothetical alternatives involving uncertain outcomes. Unless the person has some training in probability, these choices will probably be difficult to understand, let alone make, and it is unlikely that the person will answer *consistently* as the questioning proceeds. The process is even more difficult when a *company's* utility function is being assessed. Because different company executives typically have different attitudes toward risk, it can be difficult for these people to reach a consensus on a common utility function.

For these reasons, classes of ready-made utility functions have been developed. One important class is called **exponential utility** and has been used in many financial investment decisions. An exponential utility function has only one adjustable numerical parameter, called the **risk tolerance**, and there are straightforward ways to discover an appropriate value of this parameter for a particular individual or company. So the advantage of using an exponential utility function is that it is relatively easy to assess. The drawback is that exponential utility functions do not capture all types of attitudes toward risk. Nevertheless, their ease of use has made them popular.

An exponential utility function has the following form:

Exponential utility

$$U(x) = 1 - e^{-x/R} \tag{6.6}$$

Here x is a monetary value (a payoff if positive, a cost if negative), $U(x)$ is the utility of this value, and $R > 0$ is the risk tolerance. As the name suggests, the risk tolerance measures how much risk the decision maker will accept. The larger the value of R, the *less* risk averse the decision maker is. That is, a person with a large value of R is more willing to take risks than a person with a small value of R. In the limit, a person with an extremely large value of R is an EMV maximizer.

The **risk tolerance** for an exponential utility function is a single number that specifies an individual's aversion to risk. The higher the risk tolerance, the less risk averse the individual is.

To assess a person's (or company's) exponential utility function, only one number, the value of R, needs to be assessed. There are a couple of tips for doing this. First, it has been shown that the risk tolerance is approximately equal to that dollar amount R such that the decision maker is indifferent between the following two options:

- Option 1: Obtain no payoff at all.
- Option 2: Obtain a payoff of R dollars or a loss of $R/2$ dollars, depending on the flip of a fair coin.

For example, if you are indifferent between a bet where you win $1000 or lose $500, with probability 0.5 each, and not betting at all, your R is approximately $1000. From this criterion it certainly makes intuitive sense that a wealthier person (or company) ought to have a larger value of R. This has been found in practice.

Finding the appropriate risk tolerance value for any company or individual is not necessarily easy, but it is easier than assessing an entire utility function.

A second tip for finding R is based on empirical evidence found by Ronald Howard, a prominent decision analyst. Through his consulting experience with large companies, he discovered tentative relationships between risk tolerance and several financial variables: net sales, net income, and equity. [See Howard (1988).] Specifically, he found that R was approximately 6.4% of net sales, 124% of net income, and 15.7% of equity for the companies he studied. For example, according to this prescription, a company with net sales of $30 million should have a risk tolerance of approximately $1.92 million. Howard admits that these percentages are only guidelines. However, they do indicate that larger and more profitable companies tend to have larger values of R, which means that they are more willing to take risks involving large dollar amounts.

We illustrate the use of the expected utility criterion, and exponential utility in particular, in the following example.

EXAMPLE | **6.5 DECIDING WHETHER TO ENTER RISKY VENTURES AT VENTURE LIMITED**

Venture Limited is a company with net sales of $30 million. The company currently must decide whether to enter one of two risky ventures or invest in a sure thing. The gain from the latter is a sure $125,000. The possible outcomes for the less risky venture are a $0.5 million loss, a $0.1 million gain, and a $1 million gain. The probabilities of these outcomes are 0.25, 0.50, and 0.25, respectively. The possible outcomes of the more risky venture are a $1 million loss, a $1 million gain, and a $3 million gain. The probabilities of these outcomes are 0.35, 0.60, and 0.05, respectively. If Venture Limited must decide on exactly one of these alternatives, what should it do?

Objective   To see how the company's risk averseness, determined by its risk tolerance in an exponential utility function, affects its decision.

WHERE DO THE NUMBERS COME FROM?

The outcomes for each of the risky alternatives probably form a continuum of possible values. However, as in Example 6.4, the company has classified these into a few possibilities and made intelligent estimates of the monetary consequences and probabilities of these discrete possibilities.

Solution

Don't worry about the actual utility values (for example, whether they are positive or negative). Only the relative magnitudes matter in terms of decision making.

We assume that Venture Limited has an exponential utility function. Also, based on Howard's guidelines, we assume that the company's risk tolerance is 6.4% of its net sales, or $1.92 million. (A sensitivity analysis on this parameter will be performed later on.) You can substitute into Equation (6.6) to find the utility of any monetary outcome. For example, the gain from the riskless alternative (in $1000s) is 125, and its utility is

$$U(125) = 1 - e^{-125/1920} = 1 - 0.9370 = 0.0630$$

As another example, the utility of a $1 million loss is

$$U(-1000) = 1 - e^{-(-1000)/1920} = 1 - 1.6834 = -0.6834$$

These are the values we use (instead of monetary values) in the decision tree.

DEVELOPING THE DECISION TREE MODEL

The tree is built and labeled (with monetary values) exactly as before. PrecisionTree then takes care of calculating the expected utilities.

Fortunately, PrecisionTree takes care of the details. After building a decision tree and labeling it (with monetary values) in the usual way, click on the name of the tree (the box on the far left of the tree) to open the dialog box shown in Figure 6.42. Then fill in the information under the Utility Function tab as shown in the figure. This says to use an exponential utility function with risk tolerance 1920, the value in cell B5.[9] (As indicated in the spreadsheet, all monetary values are measured in $1000s.) It also indicates that expected utilities (as opposed to EMVs) should appear in the decision tree.

The completed tree for this example is shown in Figure 6.43. (See the file **Using Exponential Utility.xlsx**.) You build it in exactly the same way as usual and link probabilities and monetary values to its branches in the usual way. For example, there is a link in cell C22 to the monetary value in cell B12. However, the expected values shown in the tree (those shown in color on a computer screen) are expected *utilities*, and the optimal decision is the one with the largest expected utility. In this case the expected utilities for the riskless

---

[9]This is a definite improvement over the previous version of PrecisionTree. The "*R*" value is now linked to a cell, so that it is easy to perform sensitivity analysis on *R*.

Figure 6.42

Dialog Box for
Specifying the
Exponential Utility
Criterion

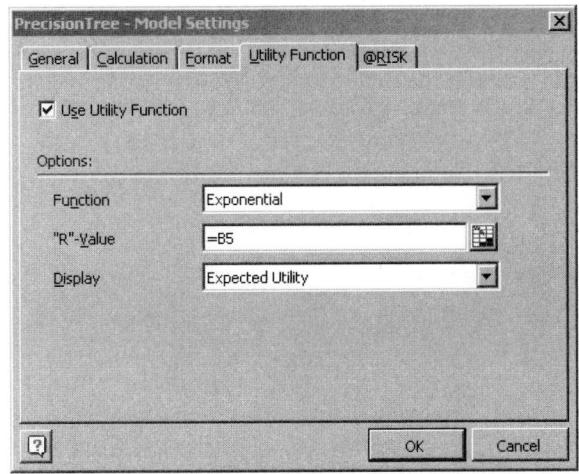

Figure 6.43

Decision Tree for
Risky Venture
Example

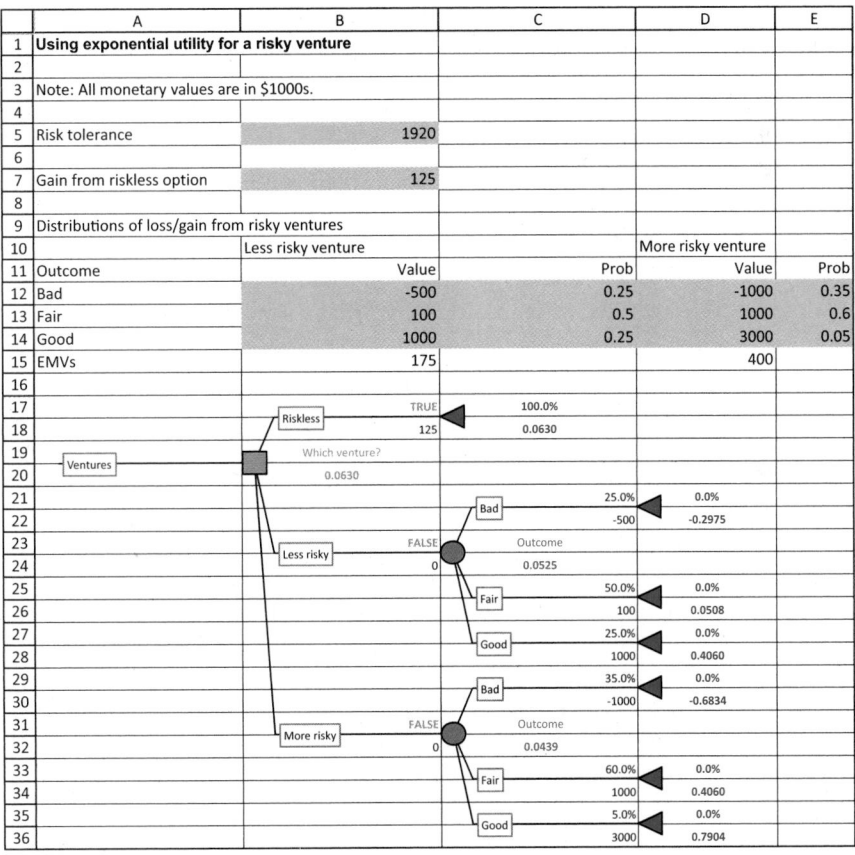

	A	B	C	D	E
1	**Using exponential utility for a risky venture**				
2					
3	Note: All monetary values are in $1000s.				
4					
5	Risk tolerance	1920			
6					
7	Gain from riskless option	125			
8					
9	Distributions of loss/gain from risky ventures				
10		Less risky venture		More risky venture	
11	Outcome	Value	Prob	Value	Prob
12	Bad	-500	0.25	-1000	0.35
13	Fair	100	0.5	1000	0.6
14	Good	1000	0.25	3000	0.05
15	EMVs	175		400	
16					
17			TRUE	100.0%	
18		Riskless	125	0.0630	
19			Which venture?		
20	Ventures		0.0630		
21				25.0%	0.0%
22			Bad	-500	-0.2975
23			FALSE	Outcome	
24		Less risky	0	0.0525	
25				50.0%	0.0%
26			Fair	100	0.0508
27				25.0%	0.0%
28			Good	1000	0.4060
29				35.0%	0.0%
30			Bad	-1000	-0.6834
31			FALSE	Outcome	
32		More risky	0	0.0439	
33				60.0%	0.0%
34			Fair	1000	0.4060
35				5.0%	0.0%
36			Good	3000	0.7904

option, investing in the less risky venture, and investing in the more risky venture are 0.0630, 0.0525, and 0.0439, respectively. Therefore, the optimal decision is to take the riskless option.

Discussion of the Solution

As indicated in the tree, the riskless option is best in terms of the expected utility criterion; it has the largest expected utility. However, note that the EMVs of the three

A risk-averse decision maker typically gives up EMV to avoid risk—when the stakes are large enough.

decisions are $125,000, $175,000, and $400,000. (The latter two of these are calculated in row 15 as the usual SUMPRODUCT of monetary values and probabilities.) So from an EMV point of view, the more risky venture is definitely best. In fact, the ordering of the three alternatives using the EMV criterion is exactly the *opposite* of the ordering using expected utility. But because Venture Limited is sufficiently risk averse and the monetary values are sufficiently large, the company is willing to sacrifice $275,000 of EMV to avoid risk.

Sensitivity Analysis

How sensitive is the optimal decision to the key parameter, the risk tolerance? You can answer this by changing the risk tolerance and watching how the decision tree changes. You can check that when the company becomes *more* risk tolerant, the more risky venture eventually becomes optimal. In fact, this occurs when the risk tolerance increases to approximately $2.210 million. In the other direction, of course, when the company becomes *less* risk tolerant, the riskless decision continues to be optimal. (The "middle" decision, the less risky alternative, is evidently not optimal for *any* value of the risk tolerance.) The bottom line is that the decision considered optimal depends entirely on the attitudes toward risk of Venture Limited's top management. ∎

6.6.3 Certainty Equivalents

Now let's change the problem slightly so that Venture Limited has only two options. It can either enter the less risky venture or receive a *certain* dollar amount x and avoid the gamble altogether. We want to find the dollar amount x so that the company is indifferent between these two options. If it enters the risky venture, its expected utility is 0.0525, calculated earlier. If it receives x dollars for certain, its utility is

$$U(x) = 1 - e^{-x/1920}$$

To find the value x where the company is indifferent between the two options, set $1 - e^{-x/1920}$ equal to 0.0525, or $e^{-x/1920} = 0.9475$, and solve for x. Taking natural logarithms of both sides and multiplying by 1920, the result is

$$x = -1920 \ln(0.9475) = 104$$

(Because of the units of measure, this is really $104,000.) This value is called the **certainty equivalent** of the risky venture. The company is indifferent between entering the less risky venture and receiving $104,000 to avoid it. Although the EMV of the less risky venture is $175,000, the company acts as if it is equivalent to a sure $104,000. In this sense, the company is willing to give up the difference in EMV, $71,000, to avoid a gamble.

By a similar calculation, the certainty equivalent of the more risky venture is approximately $86,000. That is, the company acts as if this more risky venture is equivalent to a sure $86,000, when in fact its EMV is a hefty $400,000. In this case, the company is willing to give up the difference in EMV, $314,000, to avoid this particular gamble. Again, the reason is that the company wants to avoid risk. You can see these certainty equivalents in PrecisionTree by changing the Display box in Figure 6.42 to show Certainty Equivalent. The resulting tree is shown in Figure 6.44. The certainty equivalents we just discussed appear in cells C24 and C32. (Note that we rounded the values in the text to the nearest $1000. The values in the figure are more exact.)

Figure 6.44 Certainty Equivalents in Tree

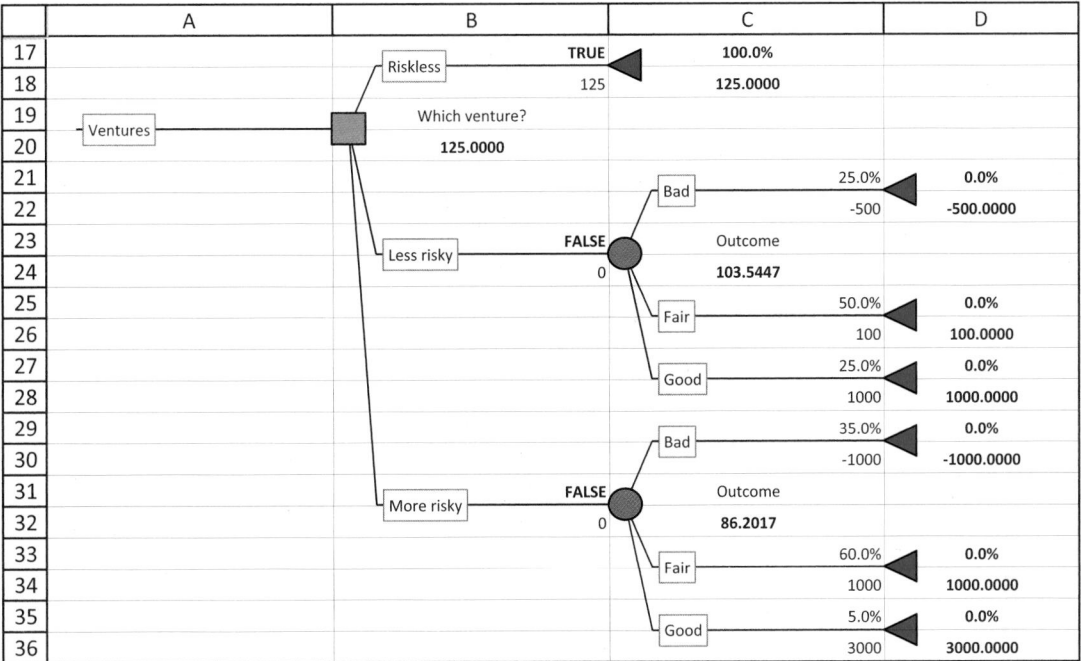

6.4 MARKETING A NEW PRODUCT AT ACME (CONTINUED)

Before concluding this section, we take a last look at the Acme marketing decision from the previous section. Suppose Acme decides to use expected utility as its criterion with an exponential utility function? Is the EMV-maximizing decision still optimal? Remember that this strategy first performed the test market and then marketed nationally only if the test-market results were great.

Objective   To see how risk aversion affects Acme's strategy.

Solution

There is very little work to do. You first enter a risk tolerance value in a blank cell. Then, starting with the tree from Figure 6.32, fill out the dialog box in Figure 6.42, with a link to the risk tolerance cell. (See the finished version of the file **Acme Marketing Decisions 2.xlsx** for the details.) It is then interesting to perform a sensitivity analysis on the risk tolerance. We tried this, letting the risk tolerance vary from 1000 to 10,000 (remember that these are in thousands of dollars) and seeing whether the decision to run a test market changes. The results appear in Figure 6.45.

Do you understand why it is better to run the test market only if the risk tolerance is sufficiently large? It is not really because of the cost of the test market. When the risk tolerance is small, the company is so risk averse that it never markets nationally—on *any* of the "National market?" decision nodes. So information from the test market is worthless. However, as *R* increases, the company becomes less risk averse and in some scenarios, its

Figure 6.45 Sensitivity to Risk Tolerance for Acme Decision

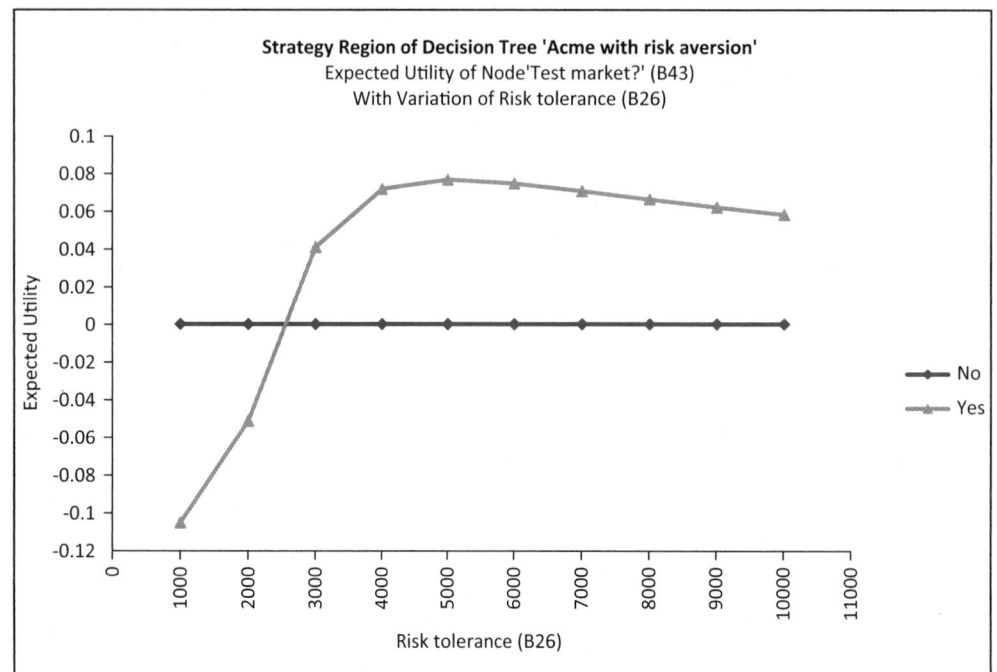

best decision is to market nationally. In these cases, the information from the test market can be worth its price. (If you don't follow this reasoning, open the finished version of the file, try large and small values of the risk tolerance, and see how the TRUEs and FALSEs on the decision tree change.) ∎

6.6.4 Is Expected Utility Maximization Used?

The previous discussion indicates that expected utility maximization is a fairly involved task. The question, then, is whether the effort is justified. Theoretically, expected utility maximization might be interesting to researchers, but is it really used in the business world? The answer appears to be: not very often. For example, one article on the practice of decision making [see Kirkwood (1992)] quotes Ronald Howard—the same person we quoted previously—as having found risk aversion to be of practical concern in only 5% to 10% of business decision analyses. This same article quotes the president of a Fortune 500 company as saying, "Most of the decisions we analyze are for a few million dollars. It is adequate to use expected value (EMV) for these."

PROBLEMS

Level A

33. For the risky venture example, create a line chart that includes three series—that is, three lines (or curves). Each line should show the expected utility of a particular decision for a sequence of possible risk tolerance values. This chart should make it clear when the more risky option becomes optimal and whether the less risky option is ever optimal.

34. In the risky venture example, the more risky alternative, in spite of its dominating EMV, is not preferred by a decision maker with a risk tolerance of $1.92 million. Now suppose everything stays the same except for the best monetary outcome of the more risky alternative (the value in cell D14). How much larger must this value be for the decision maker to prefer the more risky alternative? What is the corresponding EMV at that point?

35. In the risky venture example, suppose there is no riskless alternative; the only two possible decisions are the less risky venture and the more risky venture. Explore which of these is the preferred alternative for a range of risk tolerances. Can you find a cutoff point for the risk tolerance such that the less risky venture is preferred for risk tolerances below the cutoff and the more risky venture is preferred otherwise?

Level B

36. Do the absolute magnitudes of the monetary outcomes matter in the risky venture example? Consider the following two possibilities. In each case, multiply all monetary values in the example by a factor of A. (For example, double them if $A = 2$.) For each part, briefly explain your findings.

a. Currently, an EMV maximizer would choose the most risky venture. Would this continue to be the case for any factor A?

b. Currently, an expected utility maximizer with a risk tolerance of $1.92 million prefers the riskless alternative. Would this continue to be the case for any factor A greater than 1? What about when A is less than 1? You can answer by using trial and error on A.

c. Referring to the dialog box in Figure 6.42, there is a Display dropdown list with three options: expected value (EMV), expected utility, and certainty equivalent. The latter is defined for any gamble as the sure monetary amount a risk-averse person would take as a trade for the risky gamble. For example, you can check that the certainty equivalent for the more risky alternative is 86.2017 (in thousands of dollars). Explain what this really means by calculating the utility of 86.2017 manually and comparing it to the *expected* utility from the more risky venture (as shown on the tree). How does this explain why the decision maker prefers the riskless alternative to the more risky venture?

6.7 CONCLUSION

In this chapter we have discussed methods that can be used in decision-making problems where uncertainty is a key element. Perhaps the most important skill you can gain from this chapter is the ability to approach decision problems with uncertainty in a systematic manner. This systematic approach requires you to list all possible decisions or strategies, list all possible uncertain outcomes, assess the probabilities of these outcomes (possibly with the aid of Bayes' rule), calculate all necessary monetary values, and finally do the necessary calculations to obtain the best decision. If large dollar amounts are at stake, you might also need to perform a utility analysis, where the decision maker's attitudes toward risk are taken into account. Once the basic analysis has been completed, using best guesses for the various parameters of the problem, you should perform a sensitivity analysis to see whether the best decision continues to be best within a range of input parameters.

Summary of Key Terms

Term	Explanation	Excel	Page	Equation
Payoff (or cost) table	A table that lists the payoffs (or costs) for all combinations of decisions and uncertain outcomes		318	
Maximin criterion	The pessimist's criterion; find the worst possible payoff for each decision, and choose the decision with the best of these		277	

(continued)

Summary of Key Terms *(Continued)*

Term	Explanation	Excel	Page	Equation
Maximax criterion	The optimist's criterion; find the best possible payoff for each decision, and choose the decision with the best of these		278	
Expected monetary value (EMV)	The weighted average of the possible payoffs from a decision, weighted by their probabilities		278	
EMV criterion	Choose the decision with the maximum EMV		278	
Decision tree	A graphical device for illustrating all of the aspects of the decision problem and for finding the optimal decision (or decision strategy)		280	
Folding-back procedure	Calculation method for decision tree; starting at the right, take EMVs at probability nodes, maximums of EMVs at decision nodes		282	
Risk profile	Chart that represents the probability distribution of monetary outcomes for any decision		282	
PrecisionTree	Useful Excel add-in developed by Palisade for building and analyzing decision trees in Excel	Has its own ribbon	290	
PrecisionTree strategy region chart	Useful for seeing how the optimal decision changes as selected inputs vary	Use PrecisionTree Sensitivity Analysis button	299	
PrecisionTree tornado and spider charts	Useful for seeing which inputs affect a selected EMV the most	Use PrecisionTree Sensitivity Analysis button	299–00	
Bayes' rule	Formula for updating probabilities as new information becomes available; *prior probabilities* are transformed into *posterior probabilities*		303	6.1
Law of total probability	The denominator in Bayes' rule, for calculating the (unconditional) probability of an information outcome		303	6.2
Expected value of sample information (EVSI)	The most the (imperfect) *sample information* (such as the results of a test market) would be worth		311	6.4
Expected value of perfect information (EVPI)	The most *perfect information* on some uncertain outcome would be worth; represents an upper bound on *any* EVSI		311	6.5
Contingency plan	A decision strategy where later decisions depend on earlier decisions and outcomes observed in the meantime		313	
Expected utility maximization	Choosing the decision that maximizes the expected utility; typically sacrifices EMV to avoid risk when large monetary amounts are at stake		330	
Utility function	A mathematical function that encodes an individual's (or company's) attitudes toward risk		324	

(continued)

Term	Explanation	Excel	Page	Equation
Exponential utility function, risk tolerance	A popular class of utility functions, where only a single parameter, the risk tolerance, has to be specified		325	6.6
Certainty equivalent	The sure dollar value equivalent to the expected utility of a gamble		328	

PROBLEMS

Conceptual Questions

C.1. Your company needs to make an important decision that involves large monetary consequences. You have listed all of the possible outcomes and the monetary payoffs and costs from all outcomes and all potential decisions. You want to use the EMV criterion, but you realize that this requires probabilities and you see no way to find the required probabilities. What can you do?

C.2. If your company makes a particular decision in the face of uncertainty, you estimate that it will either gain $10,000, gain $1000, or lose $5000, with probabilities 0.40, 0.30, and 0.30, respectively. You (correctly) calculate the EMV as $2800. However, you distrust the use of this EMV for decision-making purposes. After all, you reason that you will never receive $2800; you will receive $10,000, $1000, or lose $5000. Discuss this reasoning.

C.3. In the previous question, suppose you have the option of receiving a check for $2700 instead of making the risky decision described. Would you make the risky decision, where you *could* lose $5000, or would you take the sure $2700? What would influence your decision?

C.4. In a classic oil-drilling example, you are trying to decide whether to drill for oil on a field that might or might not contain any oil. Before making this decision, you have the option of hiring a geologist to perform some seismic tests and then predict whether there is any oil or not. You assess that if there is actually oil, the geologist will predict there is oil with probability 0.85. You also assess that if there is no oil, the geologist will predict there is no oil with probability 0.90. Why will these two probabilities *not* appear on the decision tree? Which probabilities *will* be on the decision tree?

C.5. Your company has signed a contract with a good customer to ship the customer an order no later than 20 days from now. The contract indicates that the customer will accept the order even if it is late, but instead of paying the full price of $10,000, it will be allowed to pay 10% less, $9000, due to lateness. You estimate that it will take anywhere from 17 to 22

days to ship the order, and each of these is equally likely. You believe you are in good shape, reasoning that the expected days to ship is the average of 17 through 22, or 19.5 days. Because this is less than 20, you will get your full $10,000. What is wrong with your reasoning?

C.6. You must make one of two decisions, each with possible gains and possible losses. One of these decisions is much riskier than the other, having much larger possible gains but also much larger possible losses, and it has a larger EMV than the safer decision. Because you are risk averse and the monetary values are large relative to your wealth, you base your decision on expected utility, and it indicates that you should make the safer decision. It also indicates that the certainty equivalent for the risky decision is $210,000, whereas its EMV is $540,000. What do these two numbers mean? What do you know about the certainty equivalent of the safer decision?

C.7. A potentially huge hurricane is forming in the Caribbean, and there is some chance that it might make a direct hit on Hilton Head Island, South Carolina, where you are in charge of emergency preparedness. You have made plans for evacuating everyone from the island, but such an evacuation is obviously costly and upsetting for all involved, so the decision to evacuate shouldn't be made lightly. Discuss how you would make such a decision. Is EMV a relevant concept in this situation? How would you evaluate the consequences of uncertain outcomes?

C.8. It seems obvious that if you can purchase information before making an ultimate decision, this information should generally be worth something, but explain exactly why (and when) it is sometimes worth nothing.

C.9. Insurance companies wouldn't exist unless customers were willing to pay the price of the insurance and the insurance companies were making a profit. So explain how insurance is a win-win proposition for customers and the company.

C.10. You often hear about the trade-off between risk and reward. Is this trade-off part of decision making under uncertainty when the decision maker uses the EMV criterion? For example, how does this work in investment decisions?

C.11. Can you ever use the material in this chapter to help you make your own real-life decisions? Consider the following. You are about to take an important and difficult exam in one of your MBA courses, and you see an opportunity to cheat. Obviously, from an ethical point of view, you shouldn't cheat, but from a purely monetary point of view, could it also be the wrong decision? To model this, consider the long-term monetary consequences of all possible outcomes.

Level A

37. The SweetTooth Candy Company knows it will need 10 tons of sugar six months from now to implement its production plans. Jean Dobson, SweetTooth's purchasing manager, has essentially two options for acquiring the needed sugar. She can either buy the sugar at the going market price when she needs it, six months from now, or she can buy a futures contract now. The contract guarantees delivery of the sugar in six months but the cost of purchasing it will be based on today's market price. Assume that possible sugar futures contracts available for purchase are for five tons or ten tons only. No futures contracts can be purchased or sold in the intervening months. Thus, SweetTooth's possible decisions are to (1) purchase a futures contract for ten tons of sugar now, (2) purchase a futures contract for five tons of sugar now and purchase five tons of sugar in six months, or (3) purchase all ten tons of needed sugar in six months. The price of sugar bought now for delivery in six months is $0.0851 per pound. The transaction costs for five-ton and ten-ton futures contracts are $65 and $110, respectively. Finally, Ms. Dobson has assessed the probability distribution for the possible prices of sugar six months from now (in dollars per pound). The file **P06_37.xlsx** contains these possible prices and their corresponding probabilities.
  a. Given that SweetTooth wants to acquire the needed sugar in the least costly way, create a cost table that specifies the cost (in dollars) associated with each possible decision and possible sugar price in the future.
  b. Use PrecisionTree to identify the decision that minimizes SweetTooth's expected cost of meeting its sugar demand.
  c. Perform a sensitivity analysis on the optimal decision, letting each of the three currency inputs vary one at a time plus or minus 25% from its base value, and summarize your findings. In response to which of these inputs is the expected cost value most sensitive?

38. Carlisle Tire and Rubber, Inc., is considering expanding production to meet potential increases in the demand for one of its tire products. Carlisle's alternatives are to construct a new plant, expand the existing plant, or do nothing in the short run. The market for this particular tire product may expand, remain stable, or contract. Carlisle's marketing department estimates the probabilities of these market outcomes as 0.25, 0.35, and 0.40, respectively. The file **P06_38.xlsx** contains Carlisle's estimated payoff (in dollars) table.
  a. Use PrecisionTree to identify the strategy that maximizes this tire manufacturer's expected profit.
  b. Perform a sensitivity analysis on the optimal decision, letting each of the monetary inputs vary one at a time plus or minus 10% from its base value, and summarize your findings. In response to which monetary inputs is the expected profit value most sensitive?

39. A local energy provider offers a landowner $180,000 for the exploration rights to natural gas on a certain site and the option for future development. This option, if exercised, is worth an additional $1,800,000 to the landowner, but this will occur only if natural gas is discovered during the exploration phase. The landowner, believing that the energy company's interest in the site is a good indication that gas is present, is tempted to develop the field herself. To do so, she must contract with local experts in natural gas exploration and development. The initial cost for such a contract is $300,000, which is lost forever if no gas is found on the site. If gas is discovered, however, the landowner expects to earn a net profit of $6,000,000. The landowner estimates the probability of finding gas on this site to be 60%.
  a. Create a payoff table that specifies the landowner's payoff (in dollars) associated with each possible decision and each outcome with respect to finding natural gas on the site.
  b. Use PrecisionTree to identify the strategy that maximizes the landowner's expected net earnings from this opportunity.
  c. Perform a sensitivity analysis on the optimal decision, letting each of the inputs vary one at a time plus or minus 25% from its base value, and summarize your findings. In response to which model inputs is the expected profit value most sensitive?

40. Techware Incorporated is considering the introduction of two new software products to the market. In particular, the company has four options regarding these two proposed products: introduce neither product, introduce product 1 only, introduce product 2 only, or introduce both products. Research and development costs for products 1 and 2 are $180,000 and $150,000, respectively. Note that the first option entails no costs because research and development efforts have not yet begun. The success of these software products depends on the trend of the national economy in the coming year and on the consumers' reaction to these products. The company's revenues earned by introducing product 1 only, product 2 only, or both products in various states of the national economy are given in the file **P06_40.xlsx**. The probabilities of observing a strong, fair, or weak trend in the national economy in the coming year are assessed to be 0.30, 0.50, and 0.20, respectively.

a. Create a payoff table that specifies Techware's net revenue (in dollars) for each possible decision and each outcome with respect to the trend in the national economy.

b. Use PrecisionTree to identify the strategy that maximizes Techware's expected net revenue from the given marketing opportunities.

c. Perform a sensitivity analysis on the optimal decision, letting each of the inputs vary one at a time plus or minus 25% from its base value, and summarize your findings. In response to which model inputs is the expected net revenue value most sensitive?

41. Consider an investor with $10,000 available to invest. He has the following options regarding the allocation of his available funds: (1) he can invest in a risk-free savings account with a guaranteed 3% annual rate of return; (2) he can invest in a fairly safe stock, where the possible annual rates of return are 6%, 8%, or 10%; or (3) he can invest in a more risky stock, where the possible annual rates of return are 1%, 9%, or 17%. Note that the investor can place all of his available funds in any one of these options, or he can split his $10,000 into two $5000 investments in any two of these options. The joint probability distribution of the possible return rates for the two stocks is given in the file **P06_41.xlsx**.

a. Create a payoff table that specifies this investor's return (in dollars) in one year for each possible decision and each outcome with respect to the two stock returns.

b. Use PrecisionTree to identify the strategy that maximizes the investor's expected earnings in one year from the given investment opportunities.

c. Perform a sensitivity analysis on the optimal decision, letting the amount available to invest and the risk-free return both vary, one at a time, plus or minus 100% from their base values, and summarize your findings.

42. A buyer for a large department store chain must place orders with an athletic shoe manufacturer six months prior to the time the shoes will be sold in the department stores. In particular, the buyer must decide on November 1 how many pairs of the manufacturer's newest model of tennis shoes to order for sale during

the coming summer season. Assume that each pair of this new brand of tennis shoes costs the department store chain $45 per pair. Furthermore, assume that each pair of these shoes can then be sold to the chain's customers for $70 per pair. Any pairs of these shoes remaining unsold at the end of the summer season will be sold in a closeout sale next fall for $35 each. The probability distribution of consumer demand for these tennis shoes during the coming summer season has been assessed by market research specialists and is provided in the file **P06_42.xlsx**. Finally, assume that the department store chain must purchase these tennis shoes from the manufacturer in lots of 100 pairs.

a. Create a payoff table that specifies the contribution to profit (in dollars) from the sale of the tennis shoes by this department store chain for each possible purchase decision and each outcome with respect to consumer demand.

b. Use PrecisionTree to identify the strategy that maximizes the department store chain's expected profit earned by purchasing and subsequently selling pairs of the new tennis shoes.

c. Perform a sensitivity analysis on the optimal decision, letting the three monetary inputs vary one at a time over reasonable ranges, and summarize your findings. In response to which model inputs is the expected earnings value most sensitive?

43. Each day the manager of a local bookstore must decide how many copies of the community newspaper to order for sale in her shop. She must pay the newspaper's publisher $0.40 for each copy, and she sells the newspapers to local residents for $0.75 each. Newspapers that are unsold at the end of day are considered worthless. The probability distribution of the number of copies of the newspaper purchased daily at her shop is provided in the file **P06_43.xlsx**. Create a payoff table that lists the profit from each order quantity (multiples of 1000 only) and each demand, and use it to find the order quantity that maximizes expected profit. Why is this an easier approach than a decision tree for this particular problem?

44. Two construction companies are bidding against one another for the right to construct a new community center building in Bloomington, Indiana. The first construction company, Fine Line Homes, believes that its competitor, Buffalo Valley Construction, will place a bid for this project according to the distribution shown in the file **P06_44.xlsx**. Furthermore, Fine Line Homes estimates that it will cost $160,000 for its own company to construct this building. Given its fine reputation and long-standing service within the local community, Fine Line Homes believes that it will likely be awarded the project in the event that it and Buffalo Valley Construction submit exactly the same bids. Create a payoff table that lists the profit from each Fine Line bid and each competing bid, and use it

to find the bid that maximizes Fine Line's expected profit. Why is this an easier approach than a decision tree for this particular problem?

45. Suppose that you have sued your employer for damages suffered when you recently slipped and fell on an icy surface that should have been treated by your company's physical plant department. Specifically, your injury resulting from this accident was sufficiently serious that you, in consultation with your attorney, decided to sue your company for $500,000. Your company's insurance provider has offered to settle this suit with you out of court. If you decide to reject the settlement and go to court, your attorney is confident that you will win the case but is uncertain about the amount the court will award you in damages. He has provided his assessment of the probability distribution of the court's award to you in the file **P06_45.xlsx**. In addition, there are extra legal fees of $10,000 you will have to pay if you go to court. Let S be the insurance provider's proposed out-of-court settlement (in dollars). For which values of S will you decide to accept the settlement? For which values of S will you choose to take your chances in court? Assume that you are seeking to maximize the expected net payoff from this litigation.

46. One of your colleagues has $2000 available to invest. Assume that all of this money must be placed in one of three investments: a particular money market fund, a stock, or gold. Each dollar your colleague invests in the money market fund earns a virtually guaranteed 3% annual return. Each dollar he invests in the stock earns an annual return characterized by the probability distribution provided in the file **P06_46.xlsx**. Finally, each dollar he invests in gold earns an annual return characterized by the probability distribution given in the same file.
   a. If your colleague must place all of his available funds in a single investment, which investment should he choose to maximize his expected earnings over the next year?
   b. Suppose now that your colleague can place all of his available funds in one of these three investments as before, or he can invest $1000 in one alternative and $1000 in another. Assuming that he seeks to maximize his expected total earnings in one year, how should he allocate his $2000?

47. Consider a population of 2000 individuals, 800 of whom are women. Assume that 300 of the women in this population earn at least $60,000 per year, and 200 of the men earn at least $60,000 per year.
   a. What is the probability that a randomly selected individual from this population earns less than $60,000 per year?
   b. If a randomly selected individual is observed to earn less than $60,000 per year, what is the probability that this person is a man?

   c. If a randomly selected individual is observed to earn at least $60,000 per year, what is the probability that this person is a woman?

48. Yearly automobile inspections are required for residents of the state of Pennsylvania. Suppose that 18% of all inspected cars in Pennsylvania have problems that need to be corrected. Unfortunately, Pennsylvania state inspections fail to detect these problems 12% of the time. On the other hand, assume that an inspection never detects a problem when there is no problem. Consider a car that is inspected and is found to be free of problems. What is the probability that there is indeed something wrong that the inspection has failed to uncover?

49. Consider again the landowner's decision problem described in Problem 39. Suppose now that, at a cost of $90,000, the landowner can request that a soundings test be performed on the site where natural gas is believed to be present. The company that conducts the soundings concedes that 30% of the time the test will indicate that no gas is present when it actually is. When natural gas is not present in a particular site, the soundings test is accurate 90% of the time.
   a. Given that the landowner pays for the soundings test and the test indicates that gas is present, what is the landowner's revised estimate of the probability of finding gas on this site?
   b. Given that the landowner pays for the soundings test and the test indicates that gas is not present, what is the landowner's revised estimate of the probability of not finding gas on this site?
   c. Should the landowner request the given soundings test at a cost of $90,000? Explain why or why not. If not, at what price (if any) would the landowner choose to obtain the soundings test?

50. The chief executive officer of a firm in a highly competitive industry believes that one of her key employees is providing confidential information to the competition. She is 90% certain that this informer is the vice president of finance, whose contacts have been extremely valuable in obtaining financing for the company. If she decides to fire this vice president and he is the informer, she estimates that the company will gain $500,000. If she decides to fire this vice president but he is not the informer, the company will lose his expertise and still have an informer within the staff; the CEO estimates that this outcome would cost her company about $2.5 million. If she decides not to fire this vice president, she estimates that the firm will lose $1.5 million regardless of whether he actually is the informer (because in either case the informer is still with the company). Before deciding whether to fire the vice president for finance, the CEO could order lie detector tests. To avoid possible lawsuits, the lie detector tests would have to be administered to all company employees, at a total cost of $150,000. Another problem she must consider is that the available lie detector tests are not perfectly reliable. In particular, if a person is lying, the test will reveal that the person is lying 95% of the time. Furthermore, if a person is not lying, the test will indicate that the person is not lying 85% of the time.

a. To minimize the expected total cost of managing this difficult situation, what strategy should the CEO adopt?

b. Should the CEO order the lie detector tests for all of her employees? Explain why or why not.

c. Determine the maximum amount of money that the CEO should be willing to pay to administer lie detector tests.

d. How sensitive are the results to the accuracy of the lie detector test? Are there any "reasonable" values of the error probabilities that change the optimal strategy?

51. A customer has approached a bank for a $100,000 one-year loan at a 12% interest rate. If the bank does not approve this loan application, the $100,000 will be invested in bonds that earn a 6% annual return. Without additional information, the bank believes that there is a 4% chance that this customer will default on the loan, assuming that the loan is approved. If the customer defaults on the loan, the bank will lose $100,000. At a cost of $1000, the bank can thoroughly investigate the customer's credit record and supply a favorable or unfavorable recommendation. Past experience indicates that in cases where the customer did not default on the approved loan, the probability of receiving a favorable recommendation on the basis of the credit investigation was 0.80. Furthermore, in cases where the customer defaulted on the approved loan, the probability of receiving a favorable recommendation on the basis of the credit investigation was 0.25.

a. What strategy should the bank follow to maximize its expected profit?

b. Calculate and interpret the expected value of sample information (EVSI) for this decision problem.

c. Calculate and interpret the expected value of perfect information (EVPI) for this decision problem.

d. How sensitive are the results to the accuracy of the credit record recommendations? Are there any "reasonable" values of the error probabilities that change the optimal strategy?

52. A company is considering whether to market a new product. Assume, for simplicity, that if this product is marketed, there are only two possible outcomes: success or failure. The company assesses that the probabilities of these two outcomes are p and $1 - p$, respectively. If the product is marketed and it proves to be a failure, the company will have a net loss of $450,000. If the product

is marketed and it proves to be a success, the company will have a net gain of $750,000. If the company decides not to market the product, there is no gain or loss. The company is also considering whether to survey prospective buyers of this new product. The results of the consumer survey can be classified as favorable, neutral, or unfavorable. In similar cases where proposed products were eventually market successes, the fractions of cases where the survey results were favorable, neutral, or unfavorable were 0.6, 0.3, and 0.1, respectively. In similar cases where proposed products were eventually market failures, the fractions of cases where the survey results were favorable, neutral, or unfavorable were 0.1, 0.2, and 0.7, respectively. The total cost of administering this survey is C dollars.

a. Let $p = 0.4$. For which values of C, if any, would this company choose to conduct the consumer survey?

b. Let $p = 0.4$. What is the largest amount that this company would be willing to pay for perfect information about the potential success or failure of the new product?

c. Let $p = 0.5$ and $C = \$15,000$. Find the strategy that maximizes the company's expected earnings in this situation. Does the optimal strategy involve conducting the consumer survey? Explain why or why not.

53. The U.S. government is attempting to determine whether immigrants should be tested for a contagious disease. Assume that the decision will be made on a financial basis. Furthermore, assume that each immigrant who is allowed to enter the United States and has the disease costs the country $100,000. Also, each immigrant who is allowed to enter the United States and does not have the disease will contribute $10,000 to the national economy. Finally, assume that x percent of all potential immigrants have the disease. The U.S. government can choose to admit all immigrants, admit no immigrants, or test immigrants for the disease before determining whether they should be admitted. It costs T dollars to test a person for the disease, and the test result is either positive or negative. A person who does not have the disease *always* tests negative. However, 10% of all people who *do* have the disease test negative. The government's goal is to maximize the expected net financial benefits per potential immigrant.

a. If $x = 10$, what is the largest value of T at which the U.S. government will choose to test potential immigrants for the disease?

b. How does your answer to the question in part **a** change if x increases to 15?

c. If $x = 5$ and $T = \$500$, what is the government's optimal strategy?

d. If $x = 5$, calculate and interpret the expected value of perfect information (EVPI) for this decision problem.

54. The senior executives of an oil company are trying to decide whether to drill for oil in a particular field in the Gulf of Mexico. It costs the company $600,000 to drill in the selected field. Company executives believe that if oil is found in this field its estimated value will be $3,400,000. At present, this oil company believes that there is a 45% chance that the selected field actually contains oil. Before drilling, the company can hire a geologist at a cost of $55,000 to prepare a report that contains a recommendation regarding drilling in the selected field. In many similar situations in the past where this geologist has been hired, the geologist has predicted oil on 75% of all fields that have contained oil, and he has predicted no oil on 85% of all fields that have not contained oil.

a. Assuming that this oil company wants to maximize its expected net earnings, use a decision tree to determine its optimal strategy.

b. Calculate and interpret EVSI for this decision problem. Experiment with the accuracy probabilities of the geologist to see how EVSI changes as they change.

c. Calculate and interpret EVPI for this decision problem.

55. FineHair is developing a new product to promote hair growth in cases of male pattern baldness. If FineHair markets the new product and it is successful, the company will earn $1,000,000 in additional profit. If the marketing of this new product proves to be unsuccessful, the company will lose $350,000 in development and marketing costs. In the past, similar products have been successful 30% of the time. At a cost of $50,000, the effectiveness of the new restoration product can be thoroughly tested. In past tests on similar products, the test predicted success on 70% of products that were ultimately successful, and it predicted failure on 75% of products that were ultimately failures.

a. Identify the strategy that maximizes FineHair's expected net earnings in this situation.

b. Calculate and interpret EVSI for this decision problem.

c. Calculate and interpret EVPI for this decision problem.

56. A product manager at Clean & Brite (C&B) wants to determine whether her company should market a new brand of toothpaste. If this new product succeeds in the marketplace, C&B estimates that it could earn $1,800,000 in future profits from the sale of the new toothpaste. If this new product fails, however, the company expects that it could lose approximately $750,000. If C&B chooses not to market this new brand, the product manager believes that there would be little, if any, impact on the profits earned through sales of C&B's other

products. The manager has estimated that the new toothpaste brand will succeed with probability 0.50. Before making her decision regarding this toothpaste product, the manager can spend $75,000 on a market research study. Based on similar studies with past products, C&B believes that the study will predict a successful product, given that product would actually be a success, with probability 0.75. It also believes that the study will predict a failure, given that the product would actually be a failure, with probability 0.65.

a. To maximize expected profit, what strategy should the C&B product manager follow?

b. Calculate and interpret EVSI for this decision problem.

c. Calculate and interpret EVPI for this decision problem.

57. Ford is going to produce a new vehicle, the Pioneer, and wants to determine the amount of annual capacity it should build. Ford's goal is to maximize the profit from this vehicle over the next 10 years. Each vehicle will sell for $13,000 and incur a variable production cost of $10,000. Building one unit of annual capacity will cost $3000. Each unit of capacity will also cost $1000 per year to maintain, even if the capacity is unused. Demand for the Pioneer is unknown but marketing estimates the distribution of annual demand to be as shown in the file **P06_57.xlsx**. Assume that the number of units sold during a year is the minimum of capacity and annual demand.

a. Explain why a capacity of 1,300,000 is not a good choice.

b. Which capacity level should Ford choose?

58. Pizza King (PK) and Noble Greek (NG) are competitive pizza chains. PK believes there is a 25% chance that NG will charge $6 per pizza, a 50% chance NG will charge $8 per pizza, and a 25% chance that NG will charge $10 per pizza. If PK charges price p_1 and NG charges price p_2, PK will sell $100 + 25(p_2 - p_1)$ pizzas. It costs PK $4 to make a pizza. PK is considering charging $5, $6, $7, $8, or $9 per pizza. To maximize its expected profit, what price should PK charge for a pizza?

59. Many decision problems have the following simple structure. A decision maker has two possible decisions, 1 and 2. If decision 1 is made, a *sure* cost of c is incurred. If decision 2 is made, there are two possible outcomes, with costs c_1 and c_2 and probabilities p and $1 - p$. We assume that $c_1 < c < c_2$. The idea is that decision 1, the riskless decision, has a moderate cost, whereas decision 2, the risky decision, has a low cost c_1 or a high cost c_2.

a. Find the decision maker's cost table, that is, the cost for each possible decision and each possible outcome.

b. Calculate the expected cost from the risky decision.

c. List as many scenarios as you can think of that have this structure. (Here's an example to get you started. Think of insurance, where you pay a sure premium to avoid a large possible loss.)

60. A nuclear power company is deciding whether to build a nuclear power plant at Diablo Canyon or at Roy Rogers City. The cost of building the power plant is $10 million at Diablo and $20 million at Roy Rogers City. If the company builds at Diablo, however, and an earthquake occurs at Diablo during the next five years, construction will be terminated and the company will lose $10 million (and will still have to build a power plant at Roy Rogers City). Without further expert information the company believes there is a 20% chance that an earthquake will occur at Diablo during the next five years. For $1 million, a geologist can be hired to analyze the fault structure at Diablo Canyon. She will predict either that an earthquake will occur or that an earthquake will not occur. The geologist's past record indicates that she will predict an earthquake on 95% of the occasions for which an earthquake will occur and no earthquake on 90% of the occasions for which an earthquake will not occur. Should the power company hire the geologist? Also, calculate and interpret EVSI and EVPI.

61. Consider again Techware's decision problem described in Problem 40. Suppose now that Techware's utility function of net revenue x (measured in dollars), earned from the given marketing opportunities, is $U(x) = 1 - e^{-x/350000}$.

a. Find the decision that maximizes Techware's expected utility. How does this optimal decision compare to the optimal decision with an EMV criterion? Explain any difference between the two optimal decisions.

b. Repeat part **a** when Techware's utility function is $U(x) = 1 - e^{-x/50000}$.

62. Consider again the bank's customer loan decision problem in Problem 51. Suppose now that the bank's utility function of profit x (in dollars) is $U(x) = 1 - e^{-x/150000}$. Find the strategy that maximizes the bank's expected utility in this case. How does this optimal strategy compare to the optimal decision with an EMV criterion? Explain any difference between the two optimal strategies.

63. The Indiana University basketball team trails by two points with eight seconds to go and has the ball. Should it attempt a two-point shot or a three-point shot? Assume that the Indiana shot will end the game and that no foul will occur on the shot. Assume that a three-point shot has a 30% chance of success, and a two-point shot has a 45% chance of success. Finally,

assume that Indiana has a 50% chance of winning in overtime.

Level B

64. George Lindsey (1959) looked at box scores of more than 1000 baseball games and found the expected number of runs scored in an inning for each on-base and out situation to be as listed in the file **P06_64.xlsx**. For example, if a team has a man on first base with one out, it scores 0.5 run on average until the end of the inning. You can assume throughout this problem that the team batting wants to maximize the expected number of runs scored in the inning.

a. Use this data to explain why, in most cases, bunting with a man on first base and no outs is a bad decision. In what situation might bunting with a man on first base and no outs be a good decision?

b. Assume there is a man on first base with one out. What probability of stealing second makes an attempted steal a good idea?

65. One controversial topic in basketball (college or any other level) is whether to foul a player deliberately with only a few seconds left in the game. Specifically, consider the following scenario. With about 10 seconds left in the game, team A is ahead of team B by three points, and team B is just about to inbound the ball. Assume team A has committed enough fouls so that future fouls result in team B going to the free-throw line. If team A purposely commits a foul as soon as possible, team B will shoot two foul shots (a point apiece). The thinking is that this is better than letting team B shoot a three-point shot, which would be their best way to tie the game and send it into overtime. However, there is a downside to fouling. Team B could make the first free throw, purposely miss the second, get the rebound, and score a two-point shot to tie the game, or it even score a three-point shot to win the game. Examine this decision, using reasonable input parameters. It doesn't appear that this deliberate fouling strategy is used very often, but do you think it should be used?

66. The following situation actually occurred in a 2009 college football game between Washington and Notre Dame. With about 3.5 minutes left in the game, Washington had fourth down and one yard to go for a touchdown, already leading by two points. Notre Dame had just had two successful goal-line stands from in close, so Washington's coach decided not to go for the touchdown and the virtually sure win. Instead, Washington kicked a field goal, and Notre Dame eventually won in overtime. Use a decision tree, with some reasonable inputs, to see whether Washington made a wise decision or should have gone for the touchdown. Note the only "monetary" values here are 1 and 0. You can think of Washington getting $1 if they win and $0 if they lose. Then the EMV is $1*P(Win) + 0*P(lose) = P(Win)$, so maximizing EMV is equivalent to maximizing the probability of winning.

67. Mr. Maloy has just bought a new $30,000 sport utility vehicle. As a reasonably safe driver, he believes that there is only about a 5% chance of being in an accident in the coming year. If he is involved in an accident, the damage to his new vehicle depends on the severity of the accident. The probability distribution for the range of possible accidents and the corresponding damage amounts (in dollars) are given in the file **P06_67.xlsx**. Mr. Maloy is trying to decide whether he is willing to pay $170 each year for collision insurance with a $300 deductible. Note that with this type of insurance, he pays the *first* $300 in damages if he causes an accident and the insurance company pays the remainder.
  a. Create a cost table that specifies the cost (in dollars) associated with each possible decision and type of accident.
  b. Use PrecisionTree to identify the strategy that minimizes Mr. Maloy's annual expected cost.
  c. Perform a sensitivity analysis on the optimal decision with respect to the probability of an accident, the premium, and the deductible amount, and summarize your findings. (You can choose the ranges to test.) In response to which of these three inputs is the expected cost most sensitive?

68. The purchasing agent for a PC manufacturer is currently negotiating a purchase agreement for a particular electronic component with a given supplier. This component is produced in lots of 1000, and the cost of purchasing a lot is $30,000. Unfortunately, past experience indicates that this supplier has occasionally shipped defective components to its customers. Specifically, the proportion of defective components supplied by this supplier has the probability distribution given in the file **P06_68.xlsx**. Although the PC manufacturer can repair a defective component at a cost of $20 each, the purchasing agent learns that this supplier will now assume the cost of replacing defective components in excess of the first 100 faulty items found in a given lot. This guarantee may be purchased by the PC manufacturer prior to the receipt of a given lot at a cost of $1000 per lot. The purchasing agent wants to determine whether it is worthwhile to purchase the supplier's guarantee policy.
  a. Create a cost table that specifies the PC manufacturer's total cost (in dollars) of purchasing and repairing (if necessary) a complete lot of components for each possible decision and each outcome with respect to the proportion of defective items.

b. Use PrecisionTree to identify the strategy that minimizes the expected total cost of achieving a complete lot of satisfactory microcomputer components.
  c. Perform a sensitivity analysis on the optimal decision with respect to the number of components per lot and the three monetary inputs, and summarize your findings. (You can choose the ranges to test.) In response to which of these inputs is the expected cost most sensitive?

69. A home appliance company is interested in marketing an innovative new product. The company must decide whether to manufacture this product in house or employ a subcontractor to manufacture it. The file **P06_69.xlsx** contains the estimated probability distribution of the cost of manufacturing one unit of this new product (in dollars) if the home appliance company produces the product in house. This file also contains the estimated probability distribution of the cost of purchasing one unit of the product if from the subcontractor. There is also uncertainty about demand for the product in the coming year, as shown in the same file. The company plans to meet all demand, but there is a capacity issue. The subcontractor has unlimited capacity, but the home appliance company has capacity for only 5000 units per year. If it decides to make the product in house and demand is greater than capacity, it will have to purchase the excess demand from an external source at a premium: $225 per unit. Assuming that the company wants to minimize the expected cost of meeting demand in the coming year, should it make the new product in house or buy it from the subcontractor? Do you need a decision tree, or will a cost table with EMV calculations suffice? (You can assume that neither the company nor the subcontractor will ever produce *more* than demand.)

70. A grapefruit farmer in central Florida is trying to decide whether to take protective action to limit damage to his crop in the event that the overnight temperature falls to a level well below freezing. He is concerned that if the temperature falls sufficiently low and he fails to make an effort to protect his grapefruit trees, he runs the risk of losing his entire crop, which is worth approximately $75,000. Based on the latest forecast issued by the National Weather Service, the farmer estimates that there is a 60% chance that he will lose his entire crop if it is left unprotected. Alternatively, the farmer can insulate his fruit by spraying water on all of the trees in his orchards. This action, which would likely cost the farmer *C* dollars, would prevent total devastation but might not completely protect the grapefruit trees from incurring some damage as a result of the unusually cold overnight temperatures. The file **P06_70.xlsx** contains the assessed distribution of possible damages (in dollars) to the insulated fruit in light of the cold weather forecast. The farmer wants to minimize the expected total cost of coping with the threatening weather.

a. Find the maximum value of C below which the farmer should insulate his crop to limit the damage from the unusually cold weather.

b. Set C equal to the value identified in part **a**. Perform sensitivity analysis to determine under what conditions, if any, the farmer would be better off not spraying his grapefruit trees and taking his chances in spite of the threat to his crop.

c. Suppose that C equals $25,000, and in addition to this protection, the farmer can purchase insurance on the crop. Discuss possibilities for reasonable insurance policies and how much they would be worth to the farmer. You can assume that the insurance is relevant only if the farmer purchases the protection, and you can decide on the terms of the insurance policy.

71. A retired partner from a large brokerage firm has one million dollars available to invest in particular stocks or bonds. Each investment's annual rate of return depends on the state of the economy in the coming year. The file **P06_71.xlsx** contains the distribution of returns for these stocks and bonds as a function of the economy's state in the coming year. As this file indicates, the returns from stocks and bonds in a fair economy are listed as X and Y. This investor wants to allocate her one million dollars to maximize her expected value of the portfolio one year from now.

a. If $X = Y = 15\%$, find the optimal investment strategy for this investor. (*Hint*: You could try a decision tree approach, but it would involve a massive tree. It is much easier to find an algebraic expression for the expected final value of the investment when a percentage p is put in stocks and the remaining percentage is put in bonds. Given this expression, the best value of p should be obvious.)

b. For which values of X (where $10\% < X < 20\%$) and Y (where $12.5\% < Y < 17.5\%$), if any, will this investor prefer to place all of her available funds in stocks? Use the same method as in part **a** for each combination of X and Y.

72. A city in Ohio is considering replacing its fleet of gasoline-powered automobiles with electric cars. The manufacturer of the electric cars claims that this municipality will experience significant cost savings over the life of the fleet if it chooses to pursue the conversion. If the manufacturer is correct, the city will save about $1.5 million dollars. If the new technology employed within the electric cars is faulty, as some critics suggest, the conversion to electric cars will cost the city $675,000. A third possibility is that less serious problems will arise and the city will break even with the conversion. A consultant hired by the city estimates that the probabilities of these three outcomes are 0.30, 0.30, and 0.40, respectively. The city has an opportunity to implement a pilot program that would indicate the potential cost or savings resulting from a switch to electric cars. The pilot program involves renting a small number of electric cars for three months and running them under typical conditions. This program would cost the city $75,000. The city's consultant believes that the results of the pilot program would be significant but not conclusive; she submits the values in the file **P06_72.xlsx**, a compilation of probabilities based on the experience of other cities, to support her contention. For example, the first row of her table indicates that given that a conversion to electric cars actually results in a savings of $1.5 million, the conditional probabilities that the pilot program will indicate that the city saves money, loses money, and breaks even are 0.6, 0.1, and 0.3, respectively. What actions should the city take to maximize its expected savings? When should it run the pilot program, if ever? (Note: If you set up the input section of your spreadsheet in the right way, you will be able to perform all of the Bayes' rule calculations with a couple of *copyable* formulas.)

73. A manufacturer must decide whether to extend credit to a retailer who would like to open an account with the firm. Past experience with new accounts indicates that 45% are high-risk customers, 35% are moderate-risk customers, and 20% are low-risk customers. If credit is extended, the manufacturer can expect to lose $60,000 with a high-risk customer, make $50,000 with a moderate-risk customer, and make $100,000 with a low-risk customer. If the manufacturer decides not to extend credit to a customer, the manufacturer neither makes nor loses any money. Prior to making a credit extension decision, the manufacturer can obtain a credit rating report on the retailer at a cost of $2000. The credit agency concedes that its rating procedure is not completely reliable. In particular, the credit rating procedure will rate a low-risk customer as a moderate-risk customer with probability 0.10 and as a high-risk customer with probability 0.05. Similarly, the given rating procedure will rate a moderate-risk customer as a low-risk customer with probability 0.06 and as a high-risk customer with probability 0.07. Finally, the rating procedure will rate a high-risk customer as a low-risk customer with probability 0.01 and as a moderate-risk customer with probability 0.05. Find the strategy that maximizes the manufacturer's expected net earnings. (*Note*: If you set up the input section of your spreadsheet in the right way, you will be able to perform all of the Bayes' rule calculations with a couple of *copyable* formulas.)

74. A television network earns an average of $1.6 million each season from a hit program and loses an average of $400,000 each season on a program that turns out to be a flop. Of all programs picked up by this network in recent years, 25% turn out to be hits and 75% turn out to be flops. At a cost of C dollars, a market research firm will analyze a pilot episode of a prospective program and issue a report predicting whether the given program will end up being a hit. If the program is actually going to be a hit, there is a 90% chance that the market researchers will predict the program to be a hit. If the program is actually going to be a flop, there is only a 20% chance that the market researchers will predict the program to be a hit.

a. Assuming that $C = \$160,000$, find the strategy that maximizes the network's expected profit.

b. What is the maximum value of C that the network should be willing to pay the market research firm?

c. Calculate and interpret EVPI for this decision problem.

75. A publishing company is trying to decide whether to publish a new business law textbook. Based on a careful reading of the latest draft of the manuscript, the publisher's senior editor in the business textbook division assesses the distribution of possible payoffs earned by publishing this new book. The file **P06_75.xlsx** contains this probability distribution. Before making a final decision regarding the publication of the book, the editor can learn more about the text's potential for success by thoroughly surveying business law instructors teaching at universities across the country. Historical frequencies based on similar surveys administered in the past are also provided in this file.

a. Find the strategy that maximizes the publisher's expected payoff if the survey cost is $10,000.

b. What is the most that the publisher would be willing to pay to conduct a new survey of business law instructors?

c. Assuming that a survey could be constructed that provides perfect information to the publisher, how much would the company be willing to pay to acquire and implement such a survey?

76. Sharp Outfits is trying to decide whether to ship some customer orders now via UPS or wait until after the threat of another UPS strike is over. If Sharp Outfits decides to ship the requested merchandise now and the UPS strike takes place, the company will incur $60,000 in delay and shipping costs. If Sharp Outfits decides to ship the customer orders via UPS and no strike occurs, the company will incur $4000 in shipping costs. If Sharp Outfits decides to postpone shipping its customer orders via UPS, the company will incur $10,000 in delay costs regardless of whether UPS goes on strike. Let p represent the probability that UPS will go on strike and impact Sharp Outfits's shipments.

a. For which values of p, if any, does Sharp Outfits minimize its expected total cost by choosing to postpone shipping its customer orders via UPS?

b. Suppose now that, at a cost of $1000, Sharp Outfits can purchase information regarding the likelihood of a UPS strike in the near future. Based on similar strike threats in the past, the company assesses that if there will be a strike, the information will predict a strike with probability 0.75, and if there will not be a strike, the information will predict no strike with probability 0.85. Provided that $p = 0.15$, what strategy should Sharp Outfits pursue to minimize its expected total cost?

c. Use the tree from part **b** to find the EVSI when $p = 0.15$. Then use a data table to find EVSI for p from 0.05 to 0.30 in increments of 0.05, and chart EVSI versus p.

d. Continuing part **b**, compute and interpret the EVPI when $p = 0.15$.

77. A homeowner wants to decide whether he should install an electronic heat pump in his home. Given that the cost of installing a new heat pump is fairly large, the homeowner wants to do so only if he can count on being able to recover the initial expense over *five* consecutive years of cold winter weather. After reviewing historical data on the operation of heat pumps in various kinds of winter weather, he computes the expected annual costs of heating his home during the winter months with and without a heat pump in operation. These cost figures are shown in the file **P06_77.xlsx**. The probabilities of experiencing a mild, normal, colder than normal, and severe winter are $0.2(1 - x), 0.5(1 - x), 0.3(1 - x)$, and x, respectively. In words, we let the last probability vary, we let the other three be in the ratio 2 to 5 to 3, and we force them to sum to 1.

a. Given that $x = 0.1$, what is the most that the homeowner is willing to pay for the heat pump?

b. If the heat pump costs $500, how large must x be before the homeowner decides it is economically worthwhile to install the heat pump?

c. Given that $x = 0.1$, calculate and interpret EVPI when the heat pump costs $500.

d. Repeat part **c** when $x = 0.15$.

78. Sarah Chang is the owner of a small electronics company. In six months, a proposal is due for an electronic timing system for the next Olympic Games. For several years, Chang's company has been developing a new microprocessor, a critical component in a timing system that would be superior to any product currently on the market. However, progress in research and development has been slow, and Chang is unsure whether her staff can produce the microprocessor in time. If they succeed in developing the microprocessor (probability p_1), there is an excellent chance (probability p_2) that Chang's company will win the $1 million Olympic contract. If they do not, there is a small chance (probability p_3) that she will still be able to win the same contract with an

alternative but inferior timing system that has already been developed. If she continues the project, Chang must invest $200,000 in research and development. In addition, making a proposal (which she will decide whether to do after seeing whether the R&D is successful) requires developing a prototype timing system at an additional cost. This additional cost is $50,000 if R&D is successful (so that she can develop the new timing system), and it is $40,000 if R&D is unsuccessful (so that she needs to go with the older timing system). Finally, if Chang wins the contract, the finished product will cost an additional $150,000 to produce.

a. Develop a decision tree that can be used to solve Chang's problem. You can assume in this part of the problem that she is using EMV (of her net profit) as a decision criterion. Build the tree so that she can enter any values for p_1, p_2, and p_3 (in input cells) and automatically see her optimal EMV and optimal strategy from the tree.

b. If $p_2 = 0.8$ and $p_3 = 0.1$, what value of p_1 makes Chang indifferent between abandoning the project and going ahead with it?

c. How much would Chang benefit if she knew for certain that the Olympic organization would guarantee her the contract? (This guarantee would be in force only if she were successful in developing the product.) Assume $p_1 = 0.4$, $p_2 = 0.8$, and $p_3 = 0.1$.

d. Suppose now that this is a relatively big project for Chang. Therefore, she decides to use expected utility as her criterion, with an exponential utility function. Using some trial and error, see which risk tolerance changes her initial decision from "go ahead" to "abandon" when $p_1 = 0.4$, $p_2 = 0.8$, and $p_3 = 0.1$.

79. The Ventron Engineering Company has just been awarded a $2 million development contract by the U.S. Army Aviation Systems Command to develop a blade spar for its Heavy Lift Helicopter program. The blade spar is a metal tube that runs the length of and provides strength to the helicopter blade. Due to the unusual length and size of the Heavy Lift Helicopter blade, Ventron is unable to produce a single-piece blade spar of the required dimensions using existing extrusion equipment and material. The engineering department has prepared two alternatives for developing the blade spar: (1) sectioning or (2) an improved extrusion process. Ventron must decide which process to use. (Backing out of the contract at any point is not an option.) The risk report has been prepared by the engineering department. The information from this report is explained next.

The sectioning option involves joining several shorter lengths of extruded metal into a blade spar of sufficient length. This work will require extensive

testing and rework over a 12-month period at a total cost of $1.8 million. Although this process will definitely produce an adequate blade spar, it merely represents an extension of existing technology.

To improve the extrusion process, on the other hand, it will be necessary to perform two steps: (1) improve the material used, at a cost of $300,000, and (2) modify the extrusion press, at a cost of $960,000. The first step will require six months of work, and if this first step is successful, the second step will require another six months of work. If both steps are successful, the blade spar will be available at that time, that is, a year from now. The engineers estimate that the probabilities of succeeding in steps 1 and 2 are 0.9 and 0.75, respectively. However, if either step is unsuccessful (which will be known only in six months for step 1 and in a year for step 2), Ventron will have no alternative but to switch to the sectioning process—and incur the sectioning cost on top of any costs already incurred.

Development of the blade spar must be completed within 18 months to avoid holding up the rest of the contract. If necessary, the sectioning work can be done on an accelerated basis in a six-month period, but the cost of sectioning will then increase from $1.8 million to $2.4 million. The director of engineering, Dr. Smith, wants to try developing the improved extrusion process. He reasons that this is not only cheaper (if successful) for the current project, but its expected side benefits for future projects could be sizable. Although these side benefits are difficult to gauge, Dr. Smith's best guess is an additional $2 million. (These side benefits are obtained only if both steps of the modified extrusion process are completed successfully.)

a. Develop a decision tree to maximize Ventron's EMV. This includes the revenue from this project, the side benefits (if applicable) from an improved extrusion process, and relevant costs. You don't need to worry about the time value of money; that is, no discounting or net present values are required. Summarize your findings in words in the spreadsheet.

b. What value of side benefits would make Ventron indifferent between the two alternatives?

c. How much would Ventron be willing to pay, right now, for perfect information about both steps of the improved extrusion process? (This information would tell Ventron, right now, the ultimate success or failure outcomes of both steps.)

80. Suppose an investor has the opportunity to buy the following contract, a stock call option, on March 1. The contract allows him to buy 100 shares of ABC stock at the end of March, April, or May at a guaranteed price of $50 per share. He can exercise this option at most once. For example, if he purchases the stock at the end of March, he can't purchase more in April or May at the guaranteed price. The current price of the stock is $50. Each month, assume that the stock price either goes up by a dollar (with probability 0.55) or goes down by a dollar (with probability 0.45). If the investor buys the contract, he is hoping that the stock price will go up. The reasoning is that if he buys the contract, the price goes up to $51, and he buys the stock (that is, he exercises his option) for $50, he can then sell the stock for $51 and make a profit of $1 per share. On the other hand, if the stock price goes down, he doesn't have to exercise his option; he can just throw the contract away.

a. Use a decision tree to find the investor's optimal strategy (that is, when he should exercise the option), *assuming* he purchases the contract.

b. How much should he be willing to pay for such a contract?

81. [Based on Balson et al. (1992).] An electric utility company is trying to decide whether to replace its PCB transformer in a generating station with a new and safer transformer. To evaluate this decision, the utility needs information about the likelihood of an incident, such as a fire, the cost of such an incident, and the cost of replacing the unit. Suppose that the total cost of replacement as a present value is $75,000. If the transformer is replaced, there is virtually no chance of a fire. However, if the current transformer is retained, the probability of a fire is assessed to be 0.0025. If a fire occurs, the cleanup cost could be high ($80 million) or low ($20 million). The probability of a high cleanup cost, given that a fire occurs, is assessed at 0.2.

a. If the company uses EMV as its decision criterion, should it replace the transformer?

b. Perform a sensitivity analysis on the key parameters of the problem that are difficult to assess, namely, the probability of a fire, the probability of a high cleanup cost, and the high and low cleanup costs. Does the optimal decision from part **a** remain optimal for a wide range of these parameters?

c. Do you believe EMV is the correct criterion to use in this type of problem involving environmental accidents?

82. The ending of the game between the Indianapolis Colts and the New England Patriots (NFL teams) in Fall 2009 was quite controversial. With about two minutes left in the game, the Patriots were ahead 34 to 28 and had the ball on their *own* 28-yard line with fourth down and two yards to go. Their coach, Bill Belichick, decided to go for the first down rather than punt, contrary to conventional wisdom. They didn't make the first down, so that possession went to the Colts, who then scored a touchdown to win by a point. Belichick was harshly criticized by most of the media, but was his unorthodox decision really a bad one?

a. Use a decision tree to analyze the problem. You can make some simplifying decisions: (1) the game would essentially be over if the Patriots made a first down, and (2) at most one score would occur after a punt or a failed first down attempt. (Note that there are no monetary values. However, you can assume the Patriots receive $1 for a win and $0 for a loss, so that maximizing EMV is equivalent to maximizing the probability that the Patriots win.)

b. Show that the Patriots should go for the first down if $p > 1 - q/r$. Here, p is the probability the Patriots make the first down, q is the probability the Colts score a touchdown after a punt, and r is the probability the Colts score a touchdown after the Patriots fail to make a first down. What are your best guesses for these three probabilities? Based on them, was Belichick's decision a good one?

83. Suppose you believe that the price of a particular stock goes up each day with probability p and goes down with probability $1-p$. You also believe the daily price changes are independent of one another. However, you are not sure of the value of p. Based on your current information, you believe p could be 0.40, 0.45, 0.50, or 0.55, with probabilities 0.15, 0.25, 0.35, and 0.25, respectively. Then you watch the stock price changes for 25 days and observe 12 ups and 13 downs. Use Bayes' rule to find the posterior distribution of p. Based on this posterior distribution, calculate the probability that there will be at least 15 ups in the *next* 30 price changes. (*Hint*: Think in terms of the binomial distribution.)

The Jogger Shoe Company is trying to decide whether to make a change in its most popular brand of running shoes. The new style would cost the same to produce and be priced the same, but it would incorporate a new kind of lacing system that (according to its marketing research people) would make it more popular.

There is a fixed cost of $300,000 for changing over to the new style. The unit contribution to before-tax profit for either style is $8. The tax rate is 35%. Also, because the fixed cost can be depreciated and will therefore affect the after-tax cash flow, a depreciation method is needed. You can assume it is straight-line depreciation.

The current demand for these shoes is 190,000 pairs annually. The company assumes this demand will continue for the next three years if the current style is retained. However, there is uncertainty about demand for the new style, if it is introduced. The company models this uncertainty by assuming a normal distribution in year 1, with mean 220,000 and standard deviation 20,000. The company also assumes that this demand, whatever it is, will remain constant for the next three years. However, if demand in year 1 for the new style is sufficiently low, the company can always switch back to the current style and realize an annual demand of 190,000. The company wants a strategy that will maximize the expected net present value (NPV) of total cash flow for the next three years, where a 15% interest rate is used for the purpose of calculating NPV. ∎

The Westhouser Paper Company in the state of Washington currently has an option to purchase a piece of land with good timber forest on it. It is now May 1, and the current price of the land is $2.2 million. Westhouser does not actually need the timber from this land until the beginning of July, but its top executives fear that another company might buy the land between now and the beginning of July. They assess that there is a 5% chance that a competitor will buy the land during May. If this does not occur, they assess that there is a 10% chance that the competitor will buy the land during June. If Westhouser does not take advantage of its current option, it can attempt to buy the land at the beginning of June or the beginning of July, provided that it is still available.

Westhouser's incentive for delaying the purchase is that its financial experts believe there is a good chance that the price of the land will fall significantly in one or both of the next two months. They assess the possible price decreases and their probabilities in Table 6.7 and Table 6.8. Table 6.7 shows the probabilities of the possible price decreases during May. Table 6.8 lists the *conditional* probabilities of the possible price decreases in June, *given* the price decrease in May. For example, it indicates that if the price decrease in May is $60,000, then the possible price decreases in June are $0, $30,000, and $60,000 with respective probabilities 0.6, 0.2, and 0.2.

If Westhouser purchases the land, it believes that it can gross $3 million. (This does not count the cost of purchasing the land.) But if it does not purchase the land, Westhouser believes that it can make $650,000 from alternative investments. What should the company do?

Table 6.7   Distribution of Price Decrease in May

Price Decrease	Probability
$0	0.5
$60,000	0.3
$120,000	0.2

Table 6.8   Distribution of Price Decrease in June

Price Decrease in May					
$0			$60,000	$120,000	
June Decrease	Probability	June Decrease	Probability	June Decrease	Probability
$0	0.3	$0	0.6	$0	0.7
$60,000	0.6	$30,000	0.2	$20,000	0.2
$120,000	0.1	$60,000	0.2	$40,000	0.1

Biotechnical Engineering specializes in developing new chemicals for agricultural applications. The company is a pioneer in using the sterile-male procedure to control insect infestations. It operates several laboratories around the world that raise insects and expose them to extra-large doses of radiation, making them sterile. As an alternative to chlorinated hydrocarbon pesticides, such as DDT, the sterile-male procedure has been used frequently with a good track record of success, most notably with the Mediterranean fruit fly (or Medfly).

That pest was controlled in California through the release of treated flies on the premise that the sterile male flies would compete with fertile wild males for mating opportunities. Any female that has mated with a sterile fly will lay eggs that do not hatch. The California Medfly campaigns required about five successive releases of sterile males—at intervals timed to coincide with the time for newly hatched flies to reach adulthood—before the Medfly was virtually eliminated. (Only sterile flies were subsequently caught in survey traps.) The effectiveness of the sterile-male procedure was enhanced by the release of malathion poisonous bait just a few days before each release, cutting down on the number of viable wild adults.

More recently, Biotechnical Engineering has had particular success in using genetic engineering to duplicate various insect hormones and pheromones (scent attractants). Of particular interest is the application of such methods against the Gypsy Moth, a notorious pest that attacks trees. The company has developed synthetic versions of both hormones and pheromones for that moth. It has a synthetic sexual attractant that male moths can detect at great distances. Most promising is the synthetic juvenile hormone.

The juvenile hormone controls moth meta-morphosis, determining the timing for the transformation of a caterpillar into a chrysalis and then into an adult. Too much juvenile hormone wreaks havoc with this process, causing caterpillars to turn into freak adults that cannot reproduce.

Biotechnical Engineering has received a government contract to test its new technology in an actual eradication campaign. The company will participate in a small-scale campaign against the Gypsy Moth in the state of Oregon. Because the pest is so damaging, Dr. June Scribner, the administrator in charge, is considering using DDT as an alternative procedure. Of course, that banned substance is only available for government emergency use because of the environmental damage it may cause. In addition to spraying with DDT, two other procedures may be employed: (1) using Biotechnical's scent lure, followed by the release of sterile males, and (2) spraying with the company's juvenile hormone to prevent larvae from developing into adults. Dr. Scribner wants to select the method that yields the best expected payoff, described below.

Although both of the newer procedures are known to work under laboratory conditions, there is some uncertainty about successful propagation of the chemicals in the wild and about the efficacy of the sterile-male procedure with moths.

If the scent-lure program is launched at a cost of $5 million, Biotechnical claims that it will have a fifty-fifty chance of leaving a low number of native males versus a high number. Once the results of that phase are known, a later choice must be made to spray with DDT or to release sterile males; the cost of the sterilization and delivery of the insects to the countrside is an additional $5 million. But if this two-phase program is successful, the net present value of the worth of trees saved is $30 million, including the benefit of avoiding all other forms of environmental damage. The indigenous moth population would be destroyed, and a new infestation could occur only from migrants. Biotechnical's experience with other eradication programs indicates that if the scent lure leaves a small native male population, there is a 90% chance for a successful eradication by using sterile males; otherwise, there is only a 10% chance for success by using sterile males. A failure results in no savings.

[10]This case was written by Lawrence L. Lapin, San Jose State University.

The cost of synthesizing enough juvenile hormone is $3 million. Biotechnical maintains that the probability that the hormone can be effectively disseminated is only 0.20. If it works, the worth of the trees saved and environmental damage avoided will be $50 million. This greater level of savings is possible because of the permanent nature of the solution because a successful juvenile hormone can then be applied wherever the moths are known to exist, virtually eliminating the pest from the environment. But if the hormone does not work, the DDT must still be used to save the trees.

DDT constitutes only a temporary solution, and the worth of its savings in trees is far less than the worth of either of the esoteric eradication procedures—if they prove successful. To compare alternatives, Dr. Scribner proposes using the net advantage (crop and environmental savings, minus cost) relative to where she would be were she to decide to use DDT at the outset or were she to be forced to spray with it later. (Regardless of the outcome, Biotechnical will be reimbursed for all expenditures. The decision is hers, not the company's.)

Questions

1. Under Biotechnical's proposal, the selection of DDT without even trying the other procedures would lead to a neutral outcome for the government, having zero payoff. Discuss the benefits of Dr. Scribner's proposed payoff measure.

2. Construct Dr. Scribner's decision tree diagram, using the proposed payoff measure.

3. What action will maximize Dr. Scribner's expected payoff?

4. Dr. Scribner is concerned about the assumed fifty-fifty probability for the two levels of surviving native males following the scent-lure program.

   a. Redo the decision tree analysis to find what action will maximize Dr. Scribner's expected payoff when the probability of low native males is, successively, (1) 0.40 or (2) 0.60 instead.

   b. How is the optimal action affected by the probability level assumed for the low native male outcome?

5. Dr. Scribner is concerned about the assumed 0.20 probability for the dissemination success of the juvenile hormone.

   a. Keeping all other probabilities and cash flows at their original levels, redo the decision tree analysis to find what action will maximize Dr. Scribner's expected payoff when the probability of juvenile hormone success is, successively, (1) 0.15 or (2) 0.25 instead.

   b. How is the optimal action affected by the probability level assumed for the juvenile hormone's success?

6. Dr. Scribner is concerned about the assumed probability levels for the success of the sterile-male procedure.

   a. Keeping all other probabilities and cash flows at their original levels, redo the decision tree analysis to find what action will maximize Dr. Scribner's expected payoff when the sterile-male success probabilities are instead as follows:

      (1) 80% for a low number of native males and 5% for a high number of native males

      (2) 70% for a low number of native males and 15% for a high number of native males

   b. How is the optimal action affected by the probability level assumed for the success of the sterile-male procedure?

7. Dr. Scribner is concerned about the assumed levels for the net present value of the worth of trees saved and damage avoided. She believes these amounts are only accurate within a range of ±10%.

   a. Keeping all other probabilities and cash flows at their original levels, redo the decision tree analysis to find what action will maximize Dr. Scribner's expected payoff when the two net present values are instead, successively, (1) 10% lower or (2) 10% higher than originally assumed.

   b. How is the optimal action affected by the level assumed for the NPVs of the savings from using one of the two esoteric Gypsy Moth eradication procedures? ∎

Sampling and Sampling Distributions

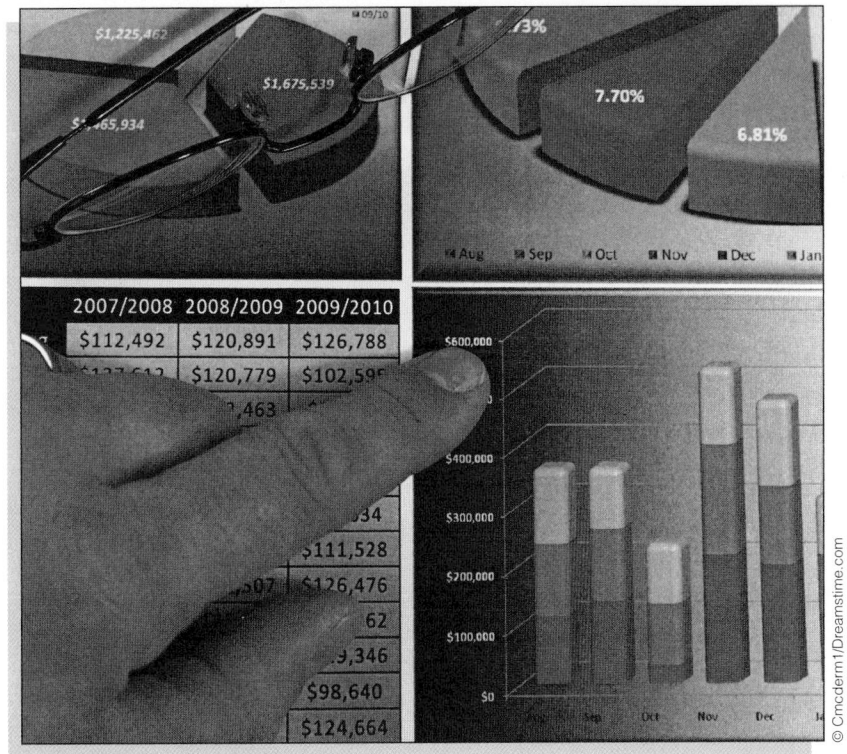

© Cmcderm1/Dreamstime.com

SAMPLE SIZE DETERMINATION IN A LEGAL CASE

This chapter introduces the important problem of estimating an unknown population quantity by randomly sampling from the population. Sampling is often expensive and/or time-consuming, so a key step in any sampling plan is to determine the sample size that produces a prescribed level of accuracy. Some of the issues in finding an appropriate sample size are discussed in Afshartous (2008). The author was involved as an expert statistical witness for the plaintiff in a court case. Over a period of several years, a service company had collected a flat "special service handling fee" from its client during any month in which a special service request was made. The plaintiff claimed that many of these fees had been charged erroneously and sought to recover all of the money collected from such erroneous fees. The statistical question concerns either the *proportion* of all monthly billing records that were erroneous or the *total number* of all erroneous billing records. Both sides had to agree on a sampling method for sampling through the very large population of billing records. They eventually agreed to simple random sampling, as discussed in this chapter. However, there was some contention (and confusion) regarding the appropriate sample size.

Their initial approach was to find a sample size n sufficiently large to accurately estimate p, the unknown proportion of all monthly billing records in error. Specifically, if they wanted to be 95% confident that the error in their estimate of p would be no more than 5%, then a standard sample size formula (provided in Chapter 8) requires n to be 385. (This number is surprisingly independent of the total number of billing records.) Then, for example, if the sample discovered 77 errors, or 20% of the sampled items, they would be 95% confident that between 15% and 25% (20% plus or minus 5%) of *all* billing records were in error.

The author argued that this "plus or minus 5%" does not necessarily provide the desired level of accuracy for the quantity of most interest, the total number of erroneously charged fees. A couple of numerical examples illustrate his point. Let's suppose that there were 100,000 billing records total and that 20%, or 20,000, were billed erroneously. Then the plus or minus 5% interval translates to an interval from 15,000 to 25,000 bad billings. That is, we are 95% confident that the estimate is not off by more than 5000 billing records on either side. The author defines the *relative error* in this case to be 0.25: the potential error, 5000, divided by the number to be estimated, 20,000. Now change the example slightly so that 60%, or 60,000, were billed erroneously. Then plus or minus 5% translates to the interval from 55,000 to 65,000, and the relative error is 5000/60,000, or 0.083. The point is that the same plus or minus 5% *absolute* error for p results in a much smaller *relative* error in the second example.

Using this reasoning, the author suggested that they should choose the sample size to achieve a prescribed *relative* error in the number of bad billings. This can change the magnitude of the sample size considerably. For example, the author shows by means of a rather complicated sample size formula that if a relative error of 0.10 is desired and the value of p is somewhere around 0.10, a sample size of about 3600 is required. On the other hand, if a relative error of 0.10 is still desired but the value of p is somewhere around 0.5, then the required sample size is only about 400.

Sample size formulas, and statistical arguments that lead to them, are far from intuitive. In this legal case, by keeping the math to a minimum and using simple terminology like *relative error*, the author eventually convinced the others to use his approach, even though it led to a considerably larger sample size than the 385 originally proposed. ■

7.1 INTRODUCTION

This chapter sets the stage for statistical inference, a topic that is explored in the following few chapters. In a typical statistical inference problem you want to discover one or more characteristics of a given population. For example, you might want to know the proportion of toothpaste customers who have tried, or intend to try, a particular brand. Or you might want to know the average amount owed on credit card accounts for a population of customers at a shopping mall. Generally, the population is large and/or spread out, and it is difficult, maybe even impossible, to contact each member. Therefore, you identify a sample of the population and then obtain information from the members of the sample.

There are two main objectives of this chapter. The first is to discuss the sampling schemes that are generally used in real sampling applications. We focus on several types of *random* samples and see why these are preferable to nonrandom samples. The second objective is to see how the information from a sample of the population—for example, 1% of the population—can be used to infer the properties of the entire population. The key here is the concept of a *sampling distribution*. In this chapter we focus on the sampling distribution of the sample mean, and we discuss the role of a famous mathematical result called the *central limit theorem*. Specifically, we discuss how the central limit theorem is the reason for the importance of the *normal* distribution in statistical inference.

7.2 SAMPLING TERMINOLOGY

We begin by introducing some terminology that is used in sampling. In any sampling problem there is a relevant *population*. A **population** is the set of all members about which a study intends to make inferences, where an *inference* is a statement about a numerical characteristic of the population, such as an average income or the proportion of incomes below $50,000. It is important to realize that a population is defined in relationship to any particular study. Any analyst planning a survey should first decide which population the conclusions of the study will concern, so that a sample can be chosen from *this* population.

> The relevant **population** contains all members about which a study intends to make inferences.

For example, if a marketing researcher plans to use a questionnaire to infer consumers' reactions to a new product, she must first decide which population of consumers is of interest—all consumers, consumers over 21 years old, consumers who do most of their shopping in shopping malls, or others. Once the relevant consumer population has been designated, a sample from this population can then be surveyed. However, inferences made from the study pertain only to this *particular* population.

Before you can choose a sample from a given population, you typically need a list of all members of the population. In sampling terminology, this list is called a **frame**, and the potential sample members are called **sampling units**. Depending on the context, sampling units could be individual people, households, companies, cities, or others.

> A **frame** is a list of all members, called **sampling units**, in the population.

It is customary in virtually all statistical literature to let uppercase N be the population size and lowercase n be the sample size. We follow this convention as well.

In this chapter we assume that the population is finite and consists of N sampling units. We also assume that a frame of these N sampling units is available. Unfortunately, there are situations where a complete frame is practically impossible to obtain. For example, if the purpose of a study is to survey the attitudes of all unemployed teenagers in Chicago, it is practically impossible to obtain a complete frame of them. In this situation the best alternative is to obtain is a partial frame, from which the sample can be selected. If the partial frame omits any significant segments of the population that a complete frame would include, then the resulting sample could be biased. For instance, if you use the Yellow Pages of a Los Angeles telephone book to choose a sample of restaurants, you automatically omit all restaurants that do not advertise in the Yellow Pages. Depending on the purposes of the study, this could be a serious omission.

There are two basic types of samples: *probability samples* and *judgmental samples*. A **probability sample** is a sample in which the sampling units are chosen from the population according to a random mechanism. In contrast, no formal random mechanism is used to select a **judgmental sample**. In this case the sampling units are chosen according to the sampler's judgment.

> The members of a **probability sample** are chosen according to a random mechanism, whereas the members of a **judgmental sample** are chosen according to the sampler's judgment.

Why Random Sampling?

One reason for sampling randomly from a population is to avoid biases (such as choosing mainly stay-at-home mothers because they are easier to contact). An equally important reason is that random sampling allows you to use probability to make inferences about unknown population parameters. If sampling were not random, there would be no basis for using probability to make such inferences.

We do not discuss judgmental samples. The reason is very simple—there is no way to measure the accuracy of judgmental samples because the rules of probability do not apply to them. In other words, if a population characteristic is estimated from the observations in a judgmental sample, there is no way to measure the accuracy of this estimate. In addition, it is very difficult to choose a representative sample from a population *without* using some random mechanism. Because our judgment is usually not as good as we think, judgmental samples are likely to contain our own built-in biases. Therefore, we focus exclusively on probability samples from here on.

7.3 METHODS FOR SELECTING RANDOM SAMPLES

In this section we discuss the types of random samples that are used in real sampling applications. Different types of sampling schemes have different properties. There is typically a trade-off between cost and accuracy. Some sampling schemes are cheaper and easier to administer, whereas others are more costly but provide more accurate information. We discuss some of these issues. However, anyone who intends to make a living in survey sampling needs to learn much more about the topic than we can cover here.

7.3.1 Simple Random Sampling

The simplest type of sampling scheme is appropriately called *simple random sampling.* Consider a population of size N and suppose you want to sample n units from this population. Then a **simple random sample** of size n has the property that every possible sample of size n has the same probability of being chosen. Simple random samples are the easiest to understand, and their statistical properties are fairly straightforward. Therefore, we will focus primarily on simple random samples in the rest of this book. However, as we discuss shortly, more complex random samples are often used in real applications.

> A **simple random sample** of size n is one where each possible sample of size n has the same chance of being chosen.

Let's illustrate the concept with a simple random sample for a small population. Suppose the population size is $N = 5$, and the five members of the population are labeled $a, b, c, d,$ and e. Also, suppose the sample size is $n = 2$. Then the possible samples are $(a, b), (a, c), (a, d), (a, e), (b, c), (b, d), (b, e), (c, d), (c, e),$ and (d, e). That is, there are 10 possible samples—the number of ways two members can be chosen from five members. Then a *simple* random sample of size $n = 2$ has the property that each of these 10 possible samples has the same probability, 1/10, of being chosen.

One other property of simple random samples can be seen from this example. If you focus on any member of the population, say, member b, you will see that b is a member of 4 of the 10 samples. Therefore, the probability that b is chosen in a simple random sample is 4/10, or 2/5. In general, any member has the same probability n/N of being chosen in a simple random sample. If you are one of 100,000 members of a population, then the probability that you will be selected in a simple random sample of size 100 is 100/100,000, or 1 out of 1000.

There are several ways simple random samples can be chosen, all of which involve random numbers. One approach that works well for the small example with $N = 5$ and $n = 2$ is to generate a single random number with the RAND function in Excel. You divide the interval from 0 to 1 into 10 equal subintervals of length 1/10 each and see which of these subintervals the random number falls into. You then choose the corresponding sample. For example, suppose the random number is 0.465. This is in the fifth subinterval, that is, the interval from 0.4 to 0.5, so you choose the fifth sample, (b, c).

This method is clearly consistent with simple random sampling—each of the samples has the same chance of being chosen—but it is prohibitive when n and N are large. In this case there are too many possible samples to list. Fortunately, there is another method that can be used. The idea is simple. You sort the N members of the population randomly, using Excel's RAND function to generate random numbers for the sort. Then you include the first n members from the sorted sequence in the random sample. This procedure is illustrated in the following example.

For those who have not yet covered the simulation sections of previous chapters: The RAND function in Excel generates numbers that are distributed randomly and uniformly between 0 and 1.

EXAMPLE **7.1 SELECTING A SAMPLE OF FAMILIES TO ANALYZE ANNUAL INCOMES**

Consider the frame of 40 families with annual incomes shown in column B of Figure 7.1. (See the file **Random Sampling.xlsm**. The extension is xlsm because this file contains a macro. When you open it, you will need to click on the Options button above the formula bar and elect to enable the macro.) We want to choose a simple random sample of size 10

Figure 7.1

Population Income Data

	A	B	C	D
1	Simple random sampling			
2				
3	Summary statistics			
4		Mean	Median	Stdev
5	Population	$39,985	$38,500	$7,377
6	Sample			
7				
8	Population			
9	Family	Income		
10	1	$43,300		
11	2	$44,300		
12	3	$34,600		
13	4	$38,000		
14	5	$44,700		
15	6	$45,600		
16	7	$42,700		
17	8	$36,900		
18	9	$38,400		
19	10	$33,700		
20	11	$44,100		
21	12	$51,500		
22	13	$35,900		
23	14	$35,600		
24	15	$43,000		
47	38	$46,900		
48	39	$37,300		
49	40	$41,000		

from this frame. How can this be done? And how do summary statistics of the chosen families compare to the corresponding summary statistics of the population?

Objective   To illustrate how Excel's random number function, RAND, can be used to generate simple random samples.

Solution

The idea is very simple. You first generate a column of random numbers in column F. Then you sort the rows according to the random numbers and choose the first 10 families in the sorted rows. The following procedure produces the results in Figure 7.2. (See the first sheet in the finished version of the file.)

Figure 7.2

Selecting a Simple Random Sample

	A	B	C	D	E	F
1	Simple random sampling					
2						
3	Summary statistics					
4		Mean	Median	Stdev		
5	Population	$39,985	$38,500	$7,377		
6	Sample	$41,490	$42,850	$5,323		
7						
8	Population			Random sample		
9	Family	Income		Family	Income	Random #
10	1	$43,300		1	$43,300	0.04545
11	2	$44,300		2	$44,300	0.1496768
12	3	$34,600		12	$51,500	0.23527
13	4	$38,000		7	$42,700	0.2746325
14	5	$44,700		13	$35,900	0.3003506
15	6	$45,600		15	$43,000	0.3197393
16	7	$42,700		6	$45,600	0.3610983
17	8	$36,900		3	$34,600	0.3852641
18	9	$38,400		9	$38,400	0.4427564
19	10	$33,700		14	$35,600	0.4447877
20	11	$44,100		5	$44,700	0.4505899
21	12	$51,500		40	$41,000	0.4597361
22	13	$35,900		11	$44,100	0.5621297
23	14	$35,600		4	$38,000	0.5860911
24	15	$43,000		38	$46,900	0.7192539
47	38	$46,900		39	$37,300	0.8644119
48	39	$37,300		8	$36,900	0.9059098
49	40	$41,000		10	$33,700	0.9637509

1 **Random numbers next to a copy.** Copy the original data to columns D and E. Then enter the formula

=RAND()

in cell F10 and copy it down column F.

2 **Replace with values.** To enable sorting, you must first "freeze" the random numbers—that is, replace their formulas with values. To do this, copy the range F10:F49 and select Paste Values from the Paste dropdown menu on the Home ribbon.

3 **Sort.** Sort on column F in ascending order. Then the 10 families with the 10 smallest random numbers are the ones in the sample. These are shaded in the figure. (Note that you could instead have chosen the 10 families with the 10 *largest* random numbers. This would be an equally valid method.)

4 **Means.** Use the AVERAGE, MEDIAN, and STDEV functions in row 6 to calculate summary statistics of the first 10 incomes in column E. Similar summary statistics for the population have already been calculated in row 5. (Cell D5 uses the STDEVP function because this is the *population* standard deviation.)

To obtain more random samples of size 10 (for comparison), you would need to go through this process repeatedly. To save you the trouble of doing so, we wrote a macro to automate the process. (See the Automated sheet in the **Random Samples.xlsm** file.) This sheet looks essentially the same as the sheet in Figure 7.2, except that there is a button to run the macro, and only the required data remain on the spreadsheet. Try clicking on this button. (Don't forget to enable the macro first.) Each time you do so, you will get a different random sample—and different summary measures in row 6. By doing this many times and keeping track of the sample summary data, you can see how the summary measures vary from sample to sample. We will have much more to say about this variation later in the chapter. ■

The procedure described in Example 7.1 can be used in Excel to select a simple random sample of any size from any population. All you need is a frame that lists the population values. Then it is just a matter of inserting random numbers, freezing them, and sorting on the random numbers.

Perhaps surprisingly, simple random samples are used infrequently in real applications. There are several reasons for this.

- Because each sampling unit has the same chance of being sampled, simple random sampling can result in samples that are spread over a large geographical region. This can make sampling extremely expensive, especially if personal interviews are used.

- Simple random sampling requires that all sampling units be identified prior to sampling. Sometimes this is infeasible.

- Simple random sampling can result in underrepresentation or overrepresentation of certain segments of the population. For example, if the primary—but not sole—interest is in the graduate student subpopulation of university students, a simple random sample of *all* university students might not provide enough information about the graduate students.

Despite this, most of the statistical analysis in this book assumes simple random samples. The analysis is considerably more complex for other types of random samples and is best left to more advanced books on sampling.

Using StatTools to Generate Simple Random Samples

The method described in Example 7.1 is simple but somewhat tedious, especially if you want to generate more than one random sample. (Even the macro described at the end of the example works only for that particular file.) Fortunately, a more general method is available in StatTools. This procedure generates any number of simple random samples of any specified sample size from a given data set. It can be found among the Data Utilities (not Utilities) on the StatTools ribbon.

EXAMPLE | **7.2 SAMPLING FROM ACCOUNTS RECEIVABLE AT SPRING MILLS COMPANY**

The file **Accounts Receivable.xlsx** contains 280 accounts receivable for the Spring Mills Company. There are three variables:

- Size: customer size, categorized as small, medium, or large depending on its volume of business with Spring Mills
- Days: number of days since the customer was billed
- Amount: amount of the bill

Generate 25 random samples of size 15 each from the small customers only, calculate the average amount owed in each random sample, and construct a histogram of these 25 averages.

Objective   To illustrate StatTools's method of choosing simple random samples and to demonstrate how sample means are distributed.

Solution

In most real-world applications, you would generate only a *single* random sample from a population, so why do we ask you to generate 25 random samples in this example? The reason is that we want to introduce the concept of a sampling distribution, in this case the sampling distribution of the sample mean. This is the distribution of *all possible* sample means you could generate from all possible samples (of a given size) from a population. By generating a fairly large number of random samples from the population of accounts receivable, you can begin to see what the sampling distribution of the sample mean looks like.

We proceed in several steps. First, because you want random samples of the small customers only and the data are already sorted on Size, you first create a StatTools data set of the small customers only. (It is the range A1:D151.) Then use the Random Sample item from StatTools Data Utilities dropdown menu to generate 25 samples of size 15 each of the Amount variable.[1] (The Random Sample dialog box should be filled out as shown in Figure 7.3.) These

Figure 7.3

Random Sample Dialog Box

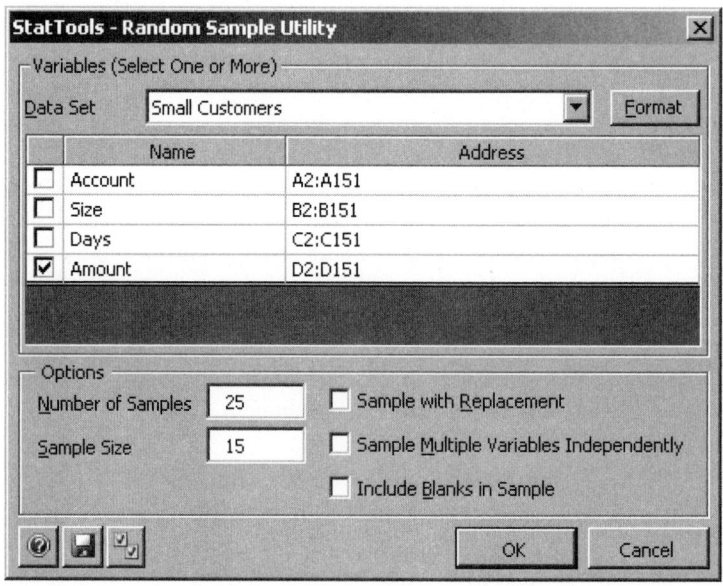

[1]Strictly speaking, the sampling distribution of the sample mean is the distribution of all possible sample means when sampling is done *with replacement*, where any member of the population can be sampled multiple times. However, real-world sampling is almost always done *without replacement*, so this is what we illustrate here.

Figure 7.4 Randomly Generated Samples		A	B	C	D	X	Y	Z
	1		Amount(1)	Amount(2)	Amount(3)	Amount(23)	Amount(24)	Amount(25)
	2		260	200	290	250	240	260
	3		230	240	260	220	210	290
	4		250	310	240	240	230	300
	5		280	250	290	260	220	240
	6		210	210	330	270	200	250
	7		310	270	210	280	220	270
	8		280	270	290	220	240	270
	9		260	190	260	290	410	250
	10		280	240	370	210	300	230
	11		240	190	290	260	260	240
	12		210	240	260	240	270	250
	13		270	240	260	210	210	150
	14		240	240	230	240	210	180
	15		220	300	240	250	250	310
	16		260	320	240	210	280	200
	17	Average	253.333	247.333	270.667	243.333	250.000	246.000

will appear on a new Random Sample sheet, as shown in Figure 7.4 (with many columns hidden). Each of these columns is a random sample of 15 Amount values.

Next, insert a new column A, as shown in Figure 7.4, and calculate the averages in row 17 for each sample with Excel's AVERAGE function. Finally, to obtain a histogram of the averages in row 17, define a second StatTools data set of the data in row 17 of Figure 7.4 but, for a change, specify that the only variable for this data set is in a *row,* not a column. (This is an option in the StatTools Data Set Manager.) You can then create a histogram of these 25 averages in the usual way. It appears in Figure 7.5.

The histogram in Figure 7.5 indicates the variability of sample means you might obtain by selecting many *different* random samples of size 15 from this particular population of small customer accounts. This histogram, which is approximately bell-shaped, approximates the sampling distribution of the sample mean. We will come back to this important idea when we discuss sampling distributions in Section 7.4.

Figure 7.5
Histogram of 25 Sample Averages

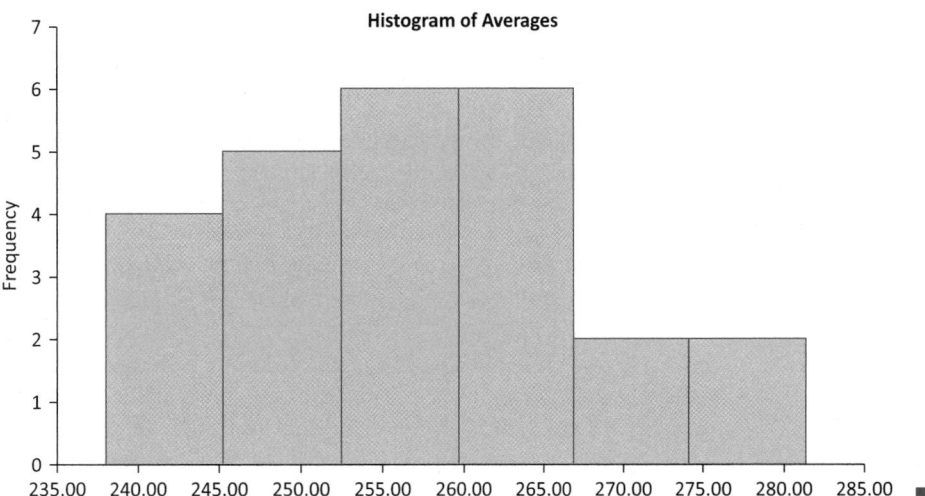

In the next several subsections we describe sampling plans that are often used. These plans differ from simple random sampling both in the way the samples are chosen and in the way the data analysis is performed. However, we will barely touch on this latter issue. The details are quite complicated and are better left to a book devoted entirely to sampling. [See, for example, the excellent book by Levy and Lemeshow (1999).]

FUNDAMENTAL INSIGHT

Types of Random Samples

There are actually many methods for choosing random samples, some described only briefly in this book, and they all have their advantages and disadvantages from practical and statistical standpoints. Surprisingly, the simplest of these, where each subset of the population has the same chance of being chosen, is *not* the most frequently used method in real applications. This is basically because other more complex methods can make more efficient use of a given sample size. Nevertheless, the *concepts* you learn here remain essentially the same, regardless of the exact sampling method used.

7.3.2 Systematic Sampling

Suppose you are asked to select a random sample of 250 names from the white pages of a telephone book. Let's also say that there are 55,000 names listed in the white pages. A **systematic sample** provides a convenient way to choose the sample. First, you divide the population size by the sample size: $55,000/250 = 220$. Conceptually, you can think of dividing the book into 250 "blocks" with 220 names per block. Next, you use a random mechanism to choose a number between 1 and 220. Suppose this number is 131. Then you choose the 131st name and every 220th name thereafter. So you would choose name 131, name 351, name 571, and so on. The result is a systematic sample of size $n = 250$.

In general, one of the first k members is selected randomly, and then every kth member after this one is selected. The value k is called the *sampling interval* and equals the ratio N/n, where N is the population size and n is the desired sample size.

Systematic sampling is quite different from simple random sampling because not every sample of size 250 has a chance of being chosen. In fact, there are only 220 different samples possible (depending on the first number chosen), and each of these is equally likely. Nevertheless, systematic sampling is generally similar to simple random sampling in its statistical properties. The key is the relationship between the ordering of the sampling units in the frame (the white pages of the telephone book in this case) and the purpose of the study.

Systematic random samples are typically chosen because of their convenience.

If the purpose of the study is to analyze personal incomes, then there is probably no relationship between the alphabetical ordering of names in the telephone book and personal income. However, there are situations where the ordering of the sampling units is *not* random, which could make systematic sampling more or less appealing. For example, suppose that a company wants to sample randomly from its customers, and its customer list is in decreasing order of order volumes. That is, the largest customers are at the top of the list and the smallest are at the bottom. Then systematic sampling might be more representative than simple random sampling because it guarantees a wide range of customers in terms of order volumes.

However, some type of cyclical ordering in the list of sampling units can lead to very *unrepresentative* samples. As an extreme, suppose a company has a list of daily transactions (Monday through Saturday) and it decides to draw a systematic sample with the sampling interval equal to 6. Then if the first sampled day is Monday, all other days in the sample will be Mondays. This could clearly bias the sample. Except for obvious examples like this one, however, systematic sampling can be an attractive alternative to simple random sampling and is often used because of its convenience.

7.3.3 Stratified Sampling

Suppose various subpopulations within the total population can be identified. These subpopulations are called *strata*. Then instead of taking a simple random sample from the entire population, it might make more sense to select a simple random sample from each stratum separately. This sampling method is called **stratified sampling**. It is a particularly useful approach when there is considerable variation *between* the various strata but relatively little variation *within* a given stratum.

> In **stratified sampling**, the population is divided into relatively homogeneous subsets called *strata*, and then random samples are taken from each stratum.

Stratified samples are typically chosen because they provide more accurate estimates of population parameters for a given sampling cost.

There are several advantages to stratified sampling. One obvious advantage is that separate estimates can be obtained within each stratum—which would not obtained with a simple random sample from the entire population. Even if the samples from the individual strata are eventually pooled, it cannot hurt to have the total sample broken down into separate samples initially.

A more important advantage of stratified sampling is that the accuracy of the resulting population estimates can be increased by using appropriately defined strata. The trick is to define the strata so that there is less variability *within* the individual strata than in the population as a whole. You want strata such that there is relative homogeneity within the strata, but relative heterogeneity across the strata, with respect to the variable(s) being analyzed. By choosing the strata in this way, you can generally obtain more accuracy for a given sampling cost than you could obtain from a simple random sample at the same cost. Alternatively, you can achieve the same level of accuracy at a lower sampling cost.

The key to using stratified sampling effectively is selecting the appropriate strata. Suppose a company that advertises its product on television wants to estimate the reaction of viewers to the advertising. Here the population consists of all viewers who have seen the advertising. But what are the appropriate strata? The answer depends on the company's objectives and its product. The company could stratify the population by gender, by income, by amount of television watched, by the amount of the product class consumed, and probably others. Without knowing more specific information about the company's objectives, it is impossible to say which of these stratification schemes is most appropriate.

Suppose that you have identified I nonoverlapping strata in a given population. Let N be the total population size, and let N_i be the population size of stratum i, so that

$$N = N_1 + N_2 + \cdots + N_I$$

To obtain a stratified random sample, you must first choose a total sample size n, and then choose a sample size n_i from each stratum i such that

$$n = n_1 + n_2 + \cdots + n_I$$

You can then select a simple random sample of the specified size from *each* stratum exactly as in Example 7.1.

However, how do you choose the individual sample sizes n_1 through n_I, given that the total sample size n has been chosen? For example, if you decide to sample 500 customers in total, how many should come from each stratum? There are many ways to choose sample sizes n_1 through n_I that sum to n, but probably the most popular method is to use

proportional sample sizes. The idea is very simple. If one stratum has, say, 15% of the total population, then you select 15% of the total sample from this stratum. For example, if the total sample size is $n = 500$, you select $0.15(500) = 75$ members from this stratum.

> With **proportional sample sizes**, the proportion of a stratum in the sample is the same as the proportion of that stratum in the population.

The advantage of proportional sample sizes is that they are very easy to determine. The disadvantage is that they ignore differences in variability among the strata. To illustrate, suppose that you are attempting to estimate the population mean amount paid annually per student for textbooks at a large university. You identify three strata: undergraduates, master's students, and doctoral students. Their population sizes are 20,000, 4000, and 1000, respectively. Therefore, the proportions of students in these strata are $20,000/25,000 = 0.80$, $4000/25,000 = 0.16$, and $1000/25,000 = 0.04$. If the total sample size is $n = 150$, then the sample should include 120 undergraduates, 24 master's students, and 6 doctoral students if proportional sample sizes are used.

However, let σ_i be the standard deviation of annual textbook payments in stratum i, and suppose that $\sigma_1 = \$50$, $\sigma_2 = \$120$, and $\sigma_3 = \$180$. That is, there is considerably more variation in the amounts paid by doctoral students than by undergraduates, with the master's students in the middle. If you are interested in estimating the mean amount spent per student, then despite its small sample size, the doctoral sample is likely to have a large effect on the accuracy of your estimate of the mean. This is because of its relatively large standard deviation. In contrast, you might not need to sample as heavily from the undergraduate population because of its relatively small standard deviation. In general, strata with less variability can afford to be sampled less heavily than proportional sampling calls for, and the opposite is true for strata with larger variability. In fact, there are *optimal* sample size formulas that take the σ_i's into account, but they are not presented here.

The following example illustrates how stratified sampling can be implemented in Excel.

EXAMPLE

7.3 STRATIFIED SAMPLING FROM THE MIDTOWN POPULATION OF SEARS CREDIT CARD HOLDERS

The file **Stratified Sampling.xlsx** contains a frame of all 50,000 people in the city of Midtown who have Sears credit cards. Sears is interested in estimating the average number of *other* credit cards these people own, as well as other information about their use of credit. The company decides to stratify these customers by age, select a stratified sample of size 200 with proportional sample sizes, and then contact these 200 people by phone. How might Sears proceed?

Objective   To illustrate how stratified sampling, with proportional sample sizes, can be implemented in Excel.

Solution

First, Sears has to decide exactly how to stratify by age. Their reasoning is that different age groups probably have different attitudes and behavior regarding credit. After some preliminary investigation, they decide to use three age categories: 18–30, 31–62, and 63–80. (We assume that no one in the population is younger than 18 or older than 80.)

Figure 7.6 shows how the calculations might then proceed. You begin with the following inputs: (1) the total sample size in cell B3, (2) the definitions of the strata in rows 6 through 8, and (3) the customer data in the range A11:B50010. To see which age category each customer is in, enter the formula

=IF(B11<=$D$6,1,IF(B11<=$D$7,2,3))

in cell C11 and then copy it down column C. Then sort on column C to put all of the customers in the same age groups together.

Figure 7.6   Selecting a Stratified Sample

	A	B	C	D	E	F	G	H
1	**Stratified sampling by Sears**							
2								
3	Total sample size	200						
4								
5	Strata based on age					Stratum	Count	Sample size
6	Stratum 1	18	to	30		1	10328	41
7	Stratum 2	31	to	62		2	25402	102
8	Stratum 3	63	to	80		3	14270	57
9								
10	Customer	Age	Stratum	Random #	Stratum index	In sample?		
11	23741	24	1	1.82E-05	1	Yes		
12	49746	21	1	0.0002263	2	Yes		
13	17423	29	1	0.00027	3	Yes		
14	10163	22	1	0.0002908	4	Yes		
15	44672	26	1	0.0005457	5	Yes		
16	46491	20	1	0.0007039	6	Yes		
17	15166	28	1	0.0007196	7	Yes		
18	10026	26	1	0.0007706	8	Yes		
19	39884	21	1	0.0008722	9	Yes		
20	4809	21	1	0.0009341	10	Yes		
21	37710	23	1	0.0009347	11	Yes		
22	12883	27	1	0.000977	12	Yes		
50007	8434	64	3	0.9997092	14267	No		
50008	43033	68	3	0.9998092	14268	No		
50009	35265	79	3	0.9999229	14269	No		
50010	28813	79	3	0.9999873	14270	No		

The next step is to find the proportional sample sizes. First, find the number of customers in stratum 1 with the formula

=COUNTIF($C$11:$C$50010,F6)

in cell G6 and copy it down to cell G8. Then find the required sample size for stratum 1 in cell H6 with the formula

=ROUND($B$3*G6/50000,0)

and copy it down to cell H8. Note that the ROUND function has been used to round to the nearest integer.

Finally, there are a number of ways the sampled members can be chosen. Here is one fairly simple procedure.

① Enter random numbers with the RAND function in column D and then freeze them.

② Do a custom sort, first on the strata in column C and then on the random numbers in column D.

③ Enter indexes, starting at 1 for each stratum, in column E by entering 1 in cell E11 and then entering the formula

=IF(C12=C11,E11+1,1)

in cell E12 and copying down.

④ Create a Yes/No column in column F by entering the formula

=IF(E11<=VLOOKUP(C11,$F$6:$H$8,3),"Yes","No")

in cell F11 and copying down.

If you want a different random sample, just repeat these four steps. The setup will appear (with many hidden rows) as in Figure 7.6. You can check that there are as many "Yes" entries for each stratum in column F as required by the proportional sample sizes in column H. ∎

7.3.4 Cluster Sampling

Suppose that a company is interested in various characteristics of households in a particular city. The sampling units are households. You could select a random sample of households by one of the sampling methods already discussed. However, it might be more convenient to proceed somewhat differently. You could first divide the city into city blocks and consider the city blocks as sampling units. You could then select a simple random sample of city blocks and then sample all of the households in the chosen blocks. In this case the city blocks are called *clusters* and the sampling scheme is called **cluster sampling**.

> In **cluster sampling**, the population is separated into clusters, such as cities or city blocks, and then a random sample of the clusters is selected.

Cluster analysis is typically more convenient and less costly than other random sampling methods.

The primary advantage of cluster sampling is sampling convenience (and possibly lower cost). If an agency is sending interviewers to interview heads of household, it is much easier for them to concentrate on particular city blocks than to contact households throughout the city. The downside, however, is that the inferences drawn from a cluster sample can be less accurate, for a given sample size, than from other sampling plans.

Consider the following scenario. A nationwide company wants to survey its salespeople with regard to management practices. It decides to randomly select several sales districts (the clusters) and then interview all salespeople in the selected districts. It is likely that in any particular sales district the attitudes toward management are somewhat similar. This overlapping information means that the company is probably not getting the maximum amount of information per sampling dollar spent. Instead of sampling 20 salespeople from a given district, all of whom have similar attitudes, it might be better to sample 20 salespeople from different districts who have a wider variety of attitudes. Nevertheless, the relative convenience of cluster sampling sometimes outweighs these statistical considerations.

Selecting a cluster sample is straightforward. The key is to define the sampling units as the *clusters*—the city blocks, for example. Then a simple random sample of clusters can be chosen exactly as in Example 7.1. Once the clusters are selected, it is typical to sample all of the population members in each selected cluster.

7.3.5 Multistage Sampling Schemes

The cluster sampling scheme just described, where a sample of clusters is chosen and then all of the sampling units within each chosen cluster are taken, is called a **single-stage** sampling scheme. Real applications are often more complex than this, resulting in **multistage** sampling schemes. For example, the Gallup organization uses multistage sampling in its nationwide surveys. A random sample of approximately 300 locations is chosen in the first stage of the sampling process. City blocks or other geographical areas are then randomly sampled from the first-stage locations in the second stage of the process. This is followed by a systematic sampling of households from each second-stage area. A total of about 1500 households comprise a typical Gallup poll.

We do not pursue the topic of multistage sampling schemes in this book. However, you should realize that real-world sampling procedures can be very complex.

PROBLEMS

Note: Student solutions for problems whose numbers appear within a colored box are available for purchase at www.cengagebrain.com.

Level A

1. The file **P02_07.xlsx** includes data on 204 employees at the (fictional) company Beta Technologies. For this problem, consider this data set as the population frame.
   a. Using the method in this section (not StatTools), generate a simple random sample of size 20 from this population.
   b. Use StatTools to generate 10 simple random samples of size 20 from this population.
   c. Calculate the population mean, median, and standard deviation of Annual Salary. Then calculate the sample mean, median, and standard deviation of Annual Salary for each of the samples in parts **a** and **b**. Comment briefly on how they compare to each other and the population measures.

2. The file **P07_02.xlsx** contains data on the 1995 students who have gone through the MBA program at State University. You can consider this the population of State University's MBA students.
   a. Find the mean and standard deviation for each of the numerical variables in this population. Also, find the following proportions: the proportion of students who are male, the proportion of students who are international (not from the USA), the proportion of students under 30 years of age, and the proportion of students with an engineering undergrad major.
   b. Using the method in this section (not StatTools), generate a simple random sample of 100 students from this population, and find the mean and

standard deviation of each numerical variable in the sample. Is there any way to know (without the information in part **a**) whether your summary measures for the sample are lower or higher than the (supposedly unknown) population summary measures?
   c. Use StatTools to generate 10 simple random samples of size 100. For each, find the mean of School Debt and its deviation from the population mean in part **a** (negative if it is below the population mean, positive if it is above the population mean). What is the average of these 10 deviations? What would you expect it to be?
   d. We want random samples to be representative of the population in terms of various demographics. For each of the samples in part **c**, find each of the proportions requested in part **a**. Do these samples appear to be representative of the population in terms of age, gender, nationality, and undergrad major? Why or why not? If they are not representative, is it because there is something wrong with the sampling procedure?

3. The file **P02_35.xlsx** contains data from a survey of 500 randomly selected households.
   a. Suppose you decide to generate a systematic random sample of size 25 from this population of data. How many such samples are there? What is the mean of Debt for each of the first three such samples, using the data in the order given?
   b. If you wanted to estimate the (supposedly unknown) population mean of Debt from a systematic random sample as in part **a**, why might it be a good idea to sort first on Debt? If you do so, what is the mean of Debt for each of the first three such samples?

4. Recall from Chapter 2 that the file **Supermarket Transactions.xlsx** contains over 14,000 transactions made by supermarket customers over a period of approximately two years. For this problem, consider this data set the population of transactions.

    a. If you were interesting in estimating the mean of Revenue for the population, why *might* it make sense to use a stratified sample, stratified by product family, to estimate this mean?

    b. Suppose you want to generate a stratified random sample, stratified by product family, and have the total sample size be 250. If you use proportional sample sizes, how many transactions should you sample from each of the three product families?

    c. Calculate the population standard deviations for each of the three product families. Given these and the discussion in the book, do you think the *optimal* sample sizes would be much different from the proportional sample sizes?

    d. Using the sample sizes from part **b**, generate a corresponding stratified random sample. What are the individual sample means from the three product families? What are the sample standard deviations?

Level B

5. This problem illustrates an interesting variation of simple random sampling.

    a. Open a blank spreadsheet and use the RAND() function to create a column of 1000 random numbers. Don't freeze them. This is actually a simple random sample from the uniform distribution between 0 and 1. Use the COUNTIF function to count the number of values between 0 and 0.1, between 0.1 and 0.2, and so on. Each such interval should contain about 1/10 of all values. Do they?

(Keep pressing the F9 key to see how the results change.)

    b. Repeat part **a**, generating a second column of random numbers, but now generate the first 100 as uniform between 0 and 0.1, the next 100 as uniform between 0.1 and 0.2, and so on, up to 0.9 to 1. (*Hint*: For example, to create a random number uniformly distributed between 0.5 and 0.6, use the formula =**0.5+0.1*RAND()**. (Do you see why?) Again, use COUNTIF to find the number of the 1000 values in each of the intervals, although there shouldn't be any surprises this time. Why might this type of random sampling be preferable to the random sampling in part **a**? (Note: The sampling in part **a** is called Monte Carlo sampling, whereas the sampling in part **b** is basically Latin Hypercube sampling, the form of sampling we advocate in Chapters 15 and 16 on simulation.)

6. Another type of random sample is called a *bootstrap sample*. (It comes from the expression "pulling yourself up by your own bootstraps.") Given a data set with n observations, a bootstrap sample, also of size n, is when you randomly sample from the data set *with replacement*. To do so, you keep choosing a random integer from 1 to n and include that item in the sample. The "with replacement" part means that you can sample the same item more than once. For example, if $n = 4$, the sampled items might be 1, 2, 2, and 4. Using the data in the file **Accounts Receivable.xlsx**, illustrate a simple method for choosing bootstrap samples with the RANDBETWEEN and VLOOKUP functions. For each bootstrap sample, find the mean and standard deviation of Days and Amount, and find the counts in the different size categories. How do these compare to the similar measures for the original data set? (For more on bootstrap sampling, do a Web search. Wikipedia has a nice overview.)

7.4 AN INTRODUCTION TO ESTIMATION

The purpose of any random sample, simple or otherwise, is to estimate properties of a population from the data observed in the sample. The following is a good example to keep in mind. Suppose a government agency wants to know the average household income over the population of all households in Indiana. Then this unknown average is the population parameter of interest, and the government is likely to estimate it by sampling several representative households in Indiana and reporting the average of their incomes.

The mathematical procedures appropriate for performing this estimation depend on which properties of the population are of interest and which type of random sampling scheme is used. Because the details are considerably more complex for more complex sampling schemes such as multistage sampling, we will focus on *simple* random samples, where the mathematical details are relatively straightforward. Details for other sampling schemes such as stratified sampling can be found in Levy and Lemeshow (1999).

However, even for more complex sampling schemes, the *concepts* are the same as those we discuss here; only the details change.

Throughout most of this section, we focus on the population mean of some variable such as household income. Our goal is to estimate this population mean by using the data in a randomly selected sample. We first discuss the types of errors that can occur.

7.4.1 Sources of Estimation Error

There are two basic sources of errors that can occur when you sample randomly from a population: *sampling error* and all other sources, usually lumped together as *nonsampling error*. Sampling error results from "unlucky" samples. As such, the term *error* is somewhat misleading. Suppose, for example, that the mean household income in Indiana is $58,225. (We assume this is the true value. It wouldn't actually be known without taking a census.) A government agency wants to estimate this mean, so it randomly samples 500 Indiana households and finds that their average household income is $60,495. If the agency then infers that the mean of *all* Indiana household incomes is $60,495, the resulting sampling error is the difference between the reported value and the true value: $60,495 - $58,225 = $2270. Note that the agency hasn't done anything wrong. This sampling error is essentially due to bad luck.

Sampling error is the inevitable result of basing an inference on a random sample rather than on the entire population.

We will soon discuss how to measure the *potential* sampling error involved. The point here is that the resulting estimation error is not caused by anything the government agency is doing wrong—it might just get unlucky.

Nonsampling error is quite different and can occur for a variety of reasons. We discuss a few of them.

- Perhaps the most serious type of nonsampling error is **nonresponse bias**. This occurs when a portion of the sample fails to respond to the survey. Anyone who has ever conducted a questionnaire, whether by mail, by phone, or any other method, knows that the percentage of nonrespondents can be quite large. The question is whether this introduces estimation error. If the nonrespondents *would* have responded similarly to the respondents, you don't lose much by not hearing from them. However, because the nonrespondents don't respond, you typically have no way of knowing whether they differ in some important respect from the respondents. Therefore, unless you are able to persuade the nonrespondents to respond—through a follow-up email, for example—you must guess at the amount of nonresponse bias.

- Another source of nonsampling error is **nontruthful responses**. This is particularly a problem when there are sensitive questions in a questionnaire. For example, if the questions "Have you ever had an abortion?" or "Do you regularly use cocaine?" are asked, most people will answer "no," regardless of whether the true answer is "yes" or "no."

  There is a way of getting at such sensitive information, called the *randomized response* technique. Here the investigator presents each respondent with two questions, one of which is the sensitive question. The other is innocuous, such as, "Were you born in the summer?" The respondent is asked to decide randomly which of the two questions to answer—by flipping a coin, say—and then answer the chosen question truthfully. The investigator sees only the answer (yes or no), not the result of the coin flip. That is, the investigator doesn't know which question is being answered. However, by using probability theory, it is possible for the investigator to infer from many such responses the percentage of the population whose truthful answer to the sensitive question is "yes."

- Another type of nonsampling error is **measurement error**. This occurs when the responses to the questions do not reflect what the investigator had in mind. It might result from poorly worded questions, questions the respondents don't fully understand, questions that require the respondents to supply information they don't have, and so on. Undoubtedly, there have been times when you were filling out a questionnaire and said to yourself, "OK, I'll answer this as well as I can, but I know it's not what they want to know."

- One final type of nonsampling error is **voluntary response bias**. This occurs when the subset of people who respond to a survey differ in some important respect from all potential respondents. For example, suppose a population of students is surveyed to see how many hours they study per night. If the students who respond are predominantly those who get the best grades, the resulting sample mean number of hours could be biased on the high side.

From this discussion and your own experience with questionnaires, you should realize that the potential for nonsampling error is enormous. However, unlike sampling error, it cannot be measured with probability theory. It can be controlled only by using appropriate sampling procedures and designing good survey instruments. We will not pursue this topic any further here. If you are interested, however, you can learn about methods for controlling nonsampling error, such as proper questionnaire design, from books on survey sampling.

7.4.2 Key Terms in Sampling

We now set the stage for the rest of this chapter, as well as for the next few chapters. Suppose there is some numerical population parameter you would like to know. This parameter could be a population mean, a population proportion, the difference between two population means, the difference between two population proportions, or many others. Unless you measure each member of the population—that is, you take a census—you cannot learn the exact value of this population parameter. Therefore, you instead take a random sample of some type and *estimate* the population parameter from the data in the sample.

You typically begin by calculating a **point estimate** (or, simply, an *estimate*) from the sample data. This is a "best guess" of the population parameter. The difference between the point estimate and the true value of the population parameter is called the **sampling error** (or **estimation error**). You then use probability theory to gauge the magnitude of the sampling error. The key to this is the **sampling distribution** of the point estimate, which is defined as the distribution of the point estimates you would see from *all* possible samples (of a given sample size) from the population. Often you report the accuracy of the point estimate with an accompanying *confidence interval*. A **confidence interval** is an interval around the point estimate, calculated from the sample data, that is very likely to contain the true value of the population parameter. (We will say much more about this in the next chapter.)

> A **point estimate** is a single numeric value, a "best guess" of a population parameter, based on the data in a random sample.

> The **sampling error** (or **estimation error**) is the difference between the point estimate and the true value of the population parameter being estimated.

> The **sampling distribution** of any point estimate is the distribution of the point estimates from *all* possible samples (of a given sample size) from the population.

> A **confidence interval** is an interval around the point estimate, calculated from the sample data, that is very likely to contain the true value of the population parameter.

Additionally, there are two other key terms you should know. First, consider the *mean* of the sampling distribution of a point estimate. It is the average value of the point estimates you would see from all possible samples. When this mean is equal to the true value of the population parameter, the point estimate is **unbiased**. Otherwise, it is *biased*. Naturally, unbiased estimates are preferred. Even if they sometimes miss on the low side and sometimes miss on the high side, they tend to be on target on average.

> An **unbiased estimate** is a point estimate such that the mean of its sampling distribution is equal to the true value of the population parameter being estimated.

Unbiased estimates are desirable because they average out to the correct value. However, this isn't enough. Point estimates from different samples should vary as little as possible from sample to sample. If they vary wildly, a point estimate from a *single* random sample isn't very reliable. Therefore, it is common to measure the standard deviation of the sampling distribution of the estimate. This indicates how much point estimates from different samples vary. In the context of sampling, this standard deviation is called the **standard error** of the estimate. Ideally, estimates should have *small* standard errors.

> The **standard error of an estimate** is the standard deviation of the sampling distribution of the estimate. It measures how much estimates vary from sample to sample.

The terms in this subsection are relevant for practically any population parameter you might want to estimate. In the following subsection we discuss them in the context of estimating a population mean.

7.4.3 Sampling Distribution of the Sample Mean

In this section we discuss the estimation of the population mean from some population. For example, you might be interested in the mean household income for all families in a particular city, the mean diameter of all parts from a manufacturing process, the mean amount of underreported taxes by all U.S. taxpayers, and so on. We label the unknown population mean by μ.

The point estimate of μ typically used, based on a sample from the population, is the sample mean $\overline{X}$, the average of the observations in the sample. There are *other* possible point estimates for a population mean besides the sample mean, such as the sample median, the *trimmed mean* (where all but the few most extreme observations are averaged), and others. However, it turns out that the "natural" estimate, the sample mean, has very good theoretical properties, so it is the point estimate used most often.

How accurate is $\overline{X}$ in estimating μ? That is, how large does the estimation error $\overline{X} - \mu$ tend to be? The sampling distribution of the sample mean $\overline{X}$ provides the key. Before describing this sampling distribution in some generality, we provide some insight into it by revisiting the population of 40 incomes in Example 7.1. There we showed how to generate a single random sample of size 10. For the particular sample we generated (see Figure 7.2), the sample mean was $41,490. Because the population mean of all 40 incomes is $39,985, the estimation error based on this particular sample is the difference $41,490 – $39,985, or $1505 on the high side.

However, this is only one of many possible samples. To see other possibilities, you can use StatTools's procedure for generating random samples to generate 100 random samples of size 10 from the population of 40 incomes. (You must do this by generating four groups of 25 samples each because the academic version of StatTools limits you to 25 random samples at a time.) You can then calculate the sample mean for each random sample and create a histogram of these sample means. We did this, with the result shown in Figure 7.7. Although this is not *exactly* the sampling distribution of the sample mean (because there are many more than 100 possible samples of size 10 from a population of size 40), it indicates how the possible sample means are distributed. They are most likely to be near the population mean ($39,985), very unlikely to be more than about $3000 from this population mean, and have an approximately bell-shaped distribution.

Figure 7.7
Approximate
Sampling
Distribution of
Sample Mean

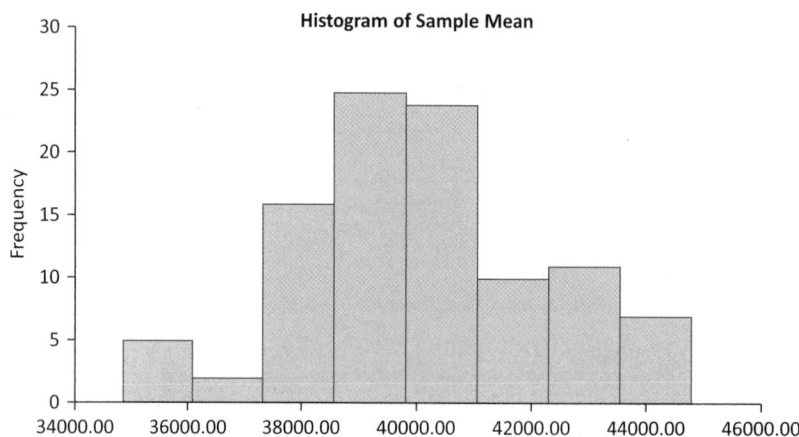

The insights in the previous paragraph can be generalized. It turns out that the sampling distribution of the sample mean has the following properties, regardless of the underlying population. First, it is an unbiased estimate of the population mean, as indicated in Equation (7.1). The sample means from some samples will be too low, and those from other samples will be too high, but on the average, they will be on target.

Unbiased Property of Sample Mean
$$E(\overline{X}) = \mu \tag{7.1}$$

The second property involves the variability of the $\overline{X}$ estimate. Recall that the standard deviation of an estimate, called the standard error, indicates how much the estimate varies from sample to sample. The standard error of $\overline{X}$ is given in Equation (7.2). Here, $\mathrm{SE}(\overline{X})$ is an abbreviation for the standard error of $\overline{X}$, σ is the standard deviation of the population, and n is the sample size. You can see that the standard error is large when the observations in the population are spread out (large σ), but that the standard error can be reduced by taking a larger sample.[2]

---

[2]This formula for $\mathrm{SE}(\overline{X})$ assumes that the sample size n is small relative to the population size N. As a rule of thumb, we assume that n is no more than 5% of N. Later we provide a "correction" to this formula when n is a larger percentage of N.

> **Standard Error of Sample Mean**
> $$\text{SE}(\overline{X}) = \sigma/\sqrt{n} \tag{7.2}$$

There is one problem with the standard error in Equation (7.2). Its value depends on another unknown population parameter, σ. Therefore, it is customary to approximate the standard error by substituting the *sample* standard deviation, s, for σ. This leads to Equation (7.3).

> **Approximate Standard Error of Sample Mean**
> $$\text{SE}(\overline{X}) = s/\sqrt{n} \tag{7.3}$$

As we discuss in the next subsection, the shape of the sampling distribution $\overline{X}$ of is approximately normal. Therefore, you can use the standard error exactly as you have used standard deviations in previous chapters to obtain confidence intervals for the population mean. Specifically, if you go two standard errors out on either side of the sample mean, as shown in Expression (7.4), you are 95% confident of capturing the population mean.[3] Alternatively, you are 95% confident that the estimation error will be no greater than two standard errors in magnitude.

> **(Approximate) Confidence Interval for Population Mean**
> $$\overline{X} \pm 2s/\sqrt{n} \tag{7.4}$$

FUNDAMENTAL INSIGHT

Sampling Distributions and Standard Errors

Any point estimate, such as the sample mean, is random because it depends on the random sample that happens to be chosen. The sampling distribution of the point estimate is the probability distribution of point estimates from all possible random samples. This distribution describes how the sample means would vary from one sample to another. The corresponding standard error is the standard deviation of the sampling distribution. These two concepts, sampling distribution and standard error, are the keys to statistical inference, as discussed in the next few chapters.

The following example illustrates a typical use of sample information.

EXAMPLE | **7.4 ESTIMATING THE MEAN OF ACCOUNTS RECEIVABLE FOR A FURNITURE RETAILER**

An internal auditor for a furniture retailer wants to estimate the average of all accounts receivable, where this average is taken over the population of all customer accounts. Because the company has approximately 10,000 accounts, an exhaustive enumeration of all accounts receivable is impractical. Therefore, the auditor randomly samples 100 of the accounts. The data from the sample appear in Figure 7.8. (See the file **Auditing Receivables.xlsx**.) What can the auditor conclude from this sample?

---

[3]Strictly speaking, as we discuss in the next chapter, this is an approximate 95% confidence interval for the mean.

Figure 7.8
Sampling in
Auditing Example

	A	B	C	D	E
1	Random sample of accounts receivable				
2					
3	Population size	10000			
4	Sample size	100			
5					
6	Sample of receivables			Summary measures from sample	
7	Account	Amount		Sample mean	$278.92
8	1	$85		Sample stdev	$419.21
9	2	$1,061		Std Error of mean	$41.92
10	3	$0			
11	4	$1,260		With fpc	$41.71
12	5	$924			
13	6	$129			
105	98	$657			
106	99	$86			
107	100	$0			

Objective To illustrate the meaning of standard error of the mean in a sample of accounts receivable.

Solution

The receivables for the 100 sampled accounts appear in column B. This is the only information available to the auditor, so he must base all conclusions on these sample data. Begin by calculating the sample mean and sample standard deviation in cells E7 and E8 with the formulas

=AVERAGE(B8:B107)

and

=STDEV(B8:B107)

Then use Equation (7.3) to calculate the (approximate) standard error of the mean in cell E9 with the formula

=E8/SQRT(B4)

The auditor should interpret these values as follows. First, the sample mean $279 is a point estimate of the unknown population mean. It provides a best guess for the average of the receivables from all 10,000 accounts. In fact, because the sample mean is an unbiased estimate of the population mean, there is no reason to suspect that $279 either underestimates or overestimates the population mean. Second, the standard error $42 provides a measure of accuracy of the $279 estimate. Specifically, there is about a 95% chance that the estimate differs by no more than two standard errors (about $84) from the true but unknown population mean. Therefore, the auditor can be 95% confident that the mean from all 10,000 accounts is within the interval $279 $\pm$ $84, that is, between $195 and $363. ∎

It is important to distinguish between the sample standard deviation s and the standard error of the mean, approximated by $s/\sqrt{n}$. The sample standard deviation in the auditing example, $419, measures the variability across *individual* receivables in the sample (or in the population). By scrolling down column B, you can see that there are some very low amounts (many zeros) and some fairly large amounts. This variability is indicated by the rather large sample standard deviation s. However, this value does not measure the accuracy of the sample mean as an estimate of the population mean. To judge *its* accuracy, you need to divide *s* by the square root of the sample size *n*. The resulting standard error, about $42, is much smaller than the sample standard deviation. It indicates that you can be about 95% confident that the sampling error is no greater than $84. In short, sample means vary much less than individual observations from a given population.

The Finite Population Correction

We mentioned that Equation (7.2) [or Equation (7.3)] for the standard error of $\overline{X}$ is appropriate when the sample size *n* is small relative to the population size *N*. Generally, "small" means that *n* is no more than 5% of *N*. In most realistic samples this is certainly true. For example, political polls are typically based on samples of approximately 1000 people from the entire U.S. population.

There are situations, however, when the sample size is greater than 5% of the population. In this case the formula for the standard error of the mean should be modified with a **finite population correction**, or *fpc*, factor. The modified standard error of the mean appears in Equation (7.5), where the *fpc* is given by Equation (7.6). Note that this factor is always less than 1 (when $n > 1$) and it decreases as *n* increases. Therefore, the standard error of the mean decreases—and the accuracy increases—as *n* increases.

Standard Error of Mean with Finite Population Correction Factor
$$\text{SE}(\overline{X}) = fpc \times (s/\sqrt{n}) \tag{7.5}$$

Finite Population Correction Factor
$$fpc = \sqrt{\frac{N-n}{N-1}} \tag{7.6}$$

To see how the *fpc* varies with *n* and *N*, consider the values in Table 7.1. Rather than listing *n*, we have listed the percentage of the population sampled, that is, $n/N \times 100\%$. It is clear that when 5% or less of the population is sampled, the *fpc* is very close to 1 and can safely be ignored. In this case you can use $s/\sqrt{n}$ as the standard error of the mean. Otherwise, you should use the modified formula in Equation (7.5).

Table 7.1 Finite Population Correction Factors

N	% Sampled	*fpc*
100	5	0.980
100	10	0.953
10,000	1	0.995
10,000	5	0.975
10,000	10	0.949
1,000,000	1	0.995
1,000,000	5	0.975
1,000,000	10	0.949

If less than 5% of the population is sampled, as is often the case, the fpc can safely be ignored.

In the auditing example, $n/N = 100/100{,}000 = 0.1\%$. This suggests that the *fpc* can safely be omitted. We illustrate this in cell E11 of Figure 7.8, which uses the formula from Equation (7.5):

=SQRT((B3-B4)/(B3-1))*E9

Clearly, it makes no practical difference in this example whether you use the *fpc* or not. The standard error, rounded to the nearest dollar, is $42 in either case.

Virtually all standard error formulas used in sampling include an *fpc* factor. However, because it is rarely necessary—the sample size is usually very small relative to the population size—we omit it from here on.

7.4.4 The Central Limit Theorem

Our discussion to this point has concentrated primarily on the mean and standard deviation of the sampling distribution of the sample mean. In this section we discuss this sampling distribution in more detail. Because of an important theoretical result called the *central limit theorem*, this distribution is approximately *normal* with mean μ and standard deviation $\sigma/\sqrt{n}$. This theorem is the reason why the normal distribution appears in so many statistical results. The theorem can be stated as follows.

> For any population distribution with mean μ and standard deviation σ, the sampling distribution of the sample mean $\overline{X}$ is approximately normal with mean μ and standard deviation $\sigma/\sqrt{n}$, and the approximation improves as n increases.

The important part of this result is the *normality* of the sampling distribution. We know, without any conditions placed upon the sample size n, that the mean and standard deviation are μ and $\sigma/\sqrt{n}$. However, the central limit theorem also implies normality, provided that n is reasonably large.

FUNDAMENTAL INSIGHT

The Central Limit Theorem

This important result states that when you sum or average n randomly selected values from *any* distribution, normal or otherwise, the distribution of the sum or average is approximately *normal*, provided that n is sufficiently large. This is the primary reason why the normal distribution is relevant in so many real applications.

How large must n be for the approximation to be valid? Most textbooks suggest $n \geq 30$ as a rule of thumb. However, this depends on the population distribution. If the population distribution is very *nonnormal*—extremely skewed or bimodal, for example—then the normal approximation might not be accurate unless n is considerably greater than 30. On the other hand, if the population distribution is already approximately symmetric, the normal approximation is quite good for n considerably less than 30. In fact, in the special case where the population distribution itself is normal, the sampling distribution of $\overline{X}$ is *exactly* normal for *any* value of n.

The central limit theorem is not a simple concept to grasp. To help explain it, we use simulation in the following example.

EXAMPLE | **7.5 Average Winnings from Spinning a Wheel of Fortune**

Suppose you have the opportunity to play a game with a "wheel of fortune" (similar to the one in a popular television game show). When you spin a large wheel, it is equally likely to stop in any position. Depending on where it stops, you win anywhere from $0 to $1000. Let's suppose your winnings are actually based on not one but the average of *n* spins of the wheel. For example, if *n* = 2, your winnings are based on the average of two spins. If the first spin results in $580 and the second spin results in $320, you win the average, $450. How does the distribution of your winnings depend on *n*?

Objective To illustrate the central limit theorem in the context of winnings in a game of chance.

Solution

First, what does this experiment have to do with random sampling? Here, the population is the set of all outcomes you could obtain from a *single* spin of the wheel—that is, all dollar values from $0 to $1000. Each spin results in one randomly sampled dollar value from this population. Furthermore, because we have assumed that the wheel is equally likely to land in any position, all possible values in the continuum from $0 to $1000 have the same chance of occurring. The resulting population distribution is called the *uniform distribution* on the interval from $0 to $1000. (See Figure 7.9, where the 1 on the horizontal axis corresponds to $1000.) It can be shown (with calculus) that the mean and standard deviation of this uniform distribution are μ = $500 and σ = $289.[4]

Figure 7.9
Uniform
Distribution

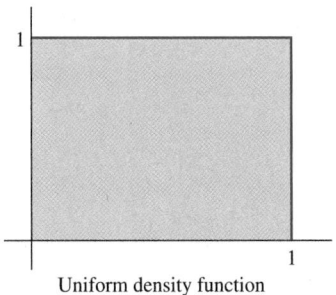

Uniform density function

Before we go any further, take a moment to test your own intuition. If you play this game once and your winnings are based on the average of *n* spins, how likely is that you will win at least $600 if *n* = 1? if *n* = 3? if *n* = 10? (The answers are 0.4, 0.27, and 0.14, respectively, where the last two answers are approximate and are based on the central limit theorem or the simulation. So you are much less likely to win big if your winnings are based on the average of many spins.)

Now we analyze the distribution of winnings based on the average of *n* spins. We do so by means of a sequence of simulations in Excel. (See the file **Wheel of Fortune Simulation.xlsx**, which is set up to work for any number of spins up to 10.) For each simulation, consider 1000 replications of an experiment. Each replication of the experiment simulates *n* spins of the wheel and calculates the average—that is, the winnings—from these *n* spins. Based on these 1000 replications, the average and standard deviation of winnings can be calculated, and a histogram of winnings can be formed, for any value of *n*. These will show clearly how the distribution of winnings depends on *n*.

The values in Figure 7.10 and the histogram in Figure 7.11 show the results for *n* = 1. Here there is no averaging—you spin the wheel once and win the amount shown. To replicate this experiment 1000 times and collect statistics, proceed as follows.

---

[4]In general, if a distribution is uniform on the interval from *a* to *b*, its mean is the midpoint (*a* + *b*)/2 and its standard deviation is (*b* − *a*)/$\sqrt{12}$.

Figure 7.10   Simulation of Winnings from a Single Spin

	A	B	C	D	E	F	G	H	I	J	K	L
1	Wheel of fortune simulation											
2												
3	Minimum winnings	$0									Summary measures of winnings	
4	Maximum winnings	$1,000									Mean	$503
5											Stdev	$291
6	Number of spins	1									P(>600)	0.411
7												
8	Simulation of spins											
9	Spin	1	2	3	4	5	6	7	8	9	10	
10	Replication	Outcome	Outcome	Outcome	Outcome	Outcome	Outcome	Outcome	Outcome	Outcome	Outcome	Winnings
11	1	$236										$236
12	2	$23										$23
13	3	$504										$504
14	4	$130										$130
15	5	$132										$132
16	6	$59										$59
17	7	$596										$596
18	8	$762										$762
19	9	$936										$936
20	10	$995										$995
21	11	$603										$603
22	12	$766										$766
23	13	$746										$746
24	14	$59										$59
25	15	$18										$18

Figure 7.11

Histogram of
Simulated Winnings
from a Single Spin

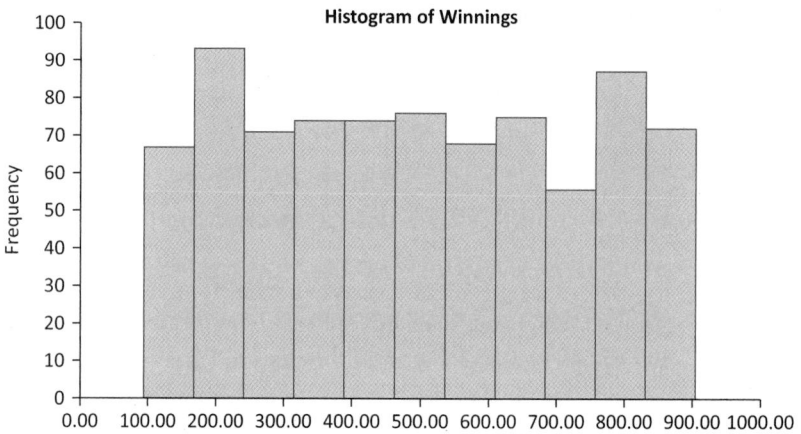

CALCULATING THE DISTRIBUTION OF WINNINGS BY SIMULATION

❶ Random outcomes. To generate outcomes uniformly distributed between $0 and $1000, enter the formula

=IF(B$9<=$B$6,$B$3+($B$4-$B$3)*RAND(), " ")

in cell B11 and copy it to the entire range B11:K1010. The effect of this formula, given the values in cells B3 and B4, is to generate a random number between 0 and 1 and multiply it by $1000. The effect of the IF part is to fill as many Outcome columns as there are spins in cell B6 and to leave the rest blank.

❷ Winnings. Calculate the winnings in each row in column L as the average of the outcomes of the spins in that row. (Note that the AVERAGE function ignores blanks.)

3 **Summary measures.** Calculate the average and standard deviation of the 1000 winnings in column L with the AVERAGE and STDEV functions. These values appear in cells L4 and L5.

4 **Histogram.** Use the StatTools Histogram procedure to create a histogram of the values in column L.

Note the following from Figures 7.10 and 7.11:

- The sample mean of the winnings (cell L4) is very close to the population mean, $500.
- The standard deviation of the winnings (cell L5) is very close to the population standard deviation, $289.
- The histogram is nearly flat.

These properties should come as no surprise. When $n = 1$, the sample mean is a single observation—that is, no averaging takes place. Therefore, the sampling distribution of the sample mean is *equivalent* to the flat population distribution in Figure 7.9.

But what happens when $n > 1$? Figure 7.12 shows the results for $n = 2$. All you need to do is change the number of spins in cell B6, and everything updates automatically. The average winnings is again very close to $500, but the standard deviation of winnings is much lower. In fact, it is close to $\sigma / \sqrt{2} = 289/\sqrt{2} = \$204$, exactly as the theory predicts. In addition, the histogram of winnings is no longer flat. It is triangularly shaped—symmetric, but not yet bell-shaped.

Figure 7.12

Histogram of Simulated Winnings from Two Spins

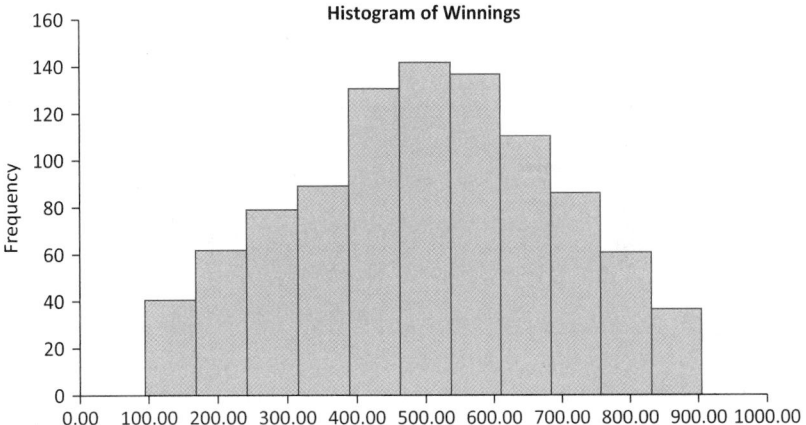

To develop similar simulations for $n = 3$, $n = 6$, $n = 10$, or any other n, simply change the number of spins in cell B6. The resulting histograms appear in Figures 7.13 through 7.15. They clearly show two effects of increasing n: (1) the histogram becomes more bell-shaped, and (2) there is less variability. However, the mean stays right at $500. This behavior is exactly what the central limit theorem predicts. In fact, because the population distribution is symmetric in this example—it is flat—you can see the effect of the central limit theorem for n much less than 30; it is already evident for n as low as 6.

Finally, it is easy to answer the question we posed previously: How does the probability of winning at least $600 depend on n? For any specific value of n, you can find the fraction of the 1000 replications where the average of n spins is greater than $600 with a COUNTIF formula in cell L6. (The value shown in Figure 7.10, 0.411, is only a point estimate of the true probability, which turns out to be very close to 0.4.)

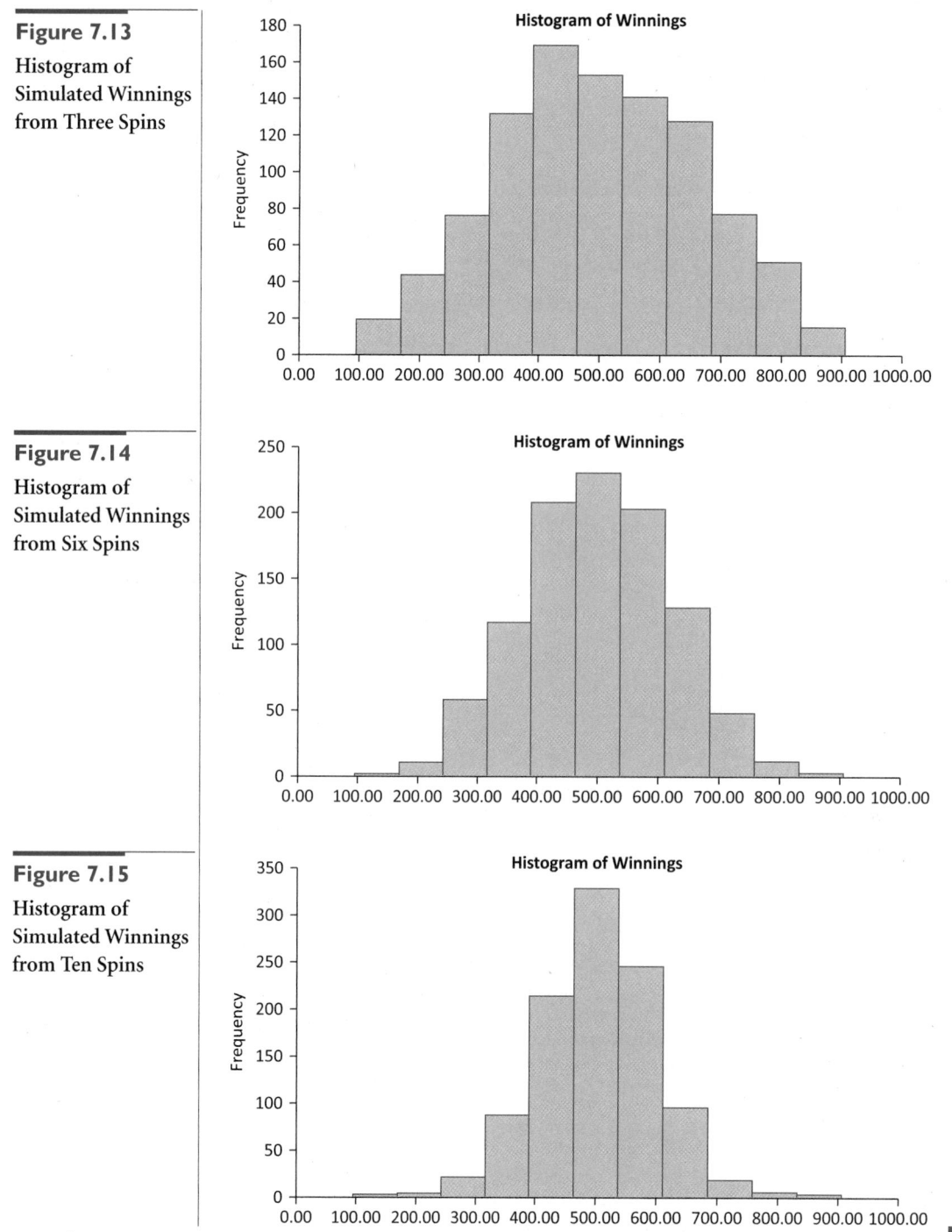

Figure 7.13

Histogram of Simulated Winnings from Three Spins

Figure 7.14

Histogram of Simulated Winnings from Six Spins

Figure 7.15

Histogram of Simulated Winnings from Ten Spins

What are the main lessons from this example? For one, you can see that the sampling distribution of the sample mean (winnings) is bell-shaped when n is reasonably large. This is in spite of the fact that the population distribution is flat—far from bell-shaped. Actually, the population distribution could have *any* shape, not just uniform, and the bell-shaped property would still hold (although n might have to be larger than in the example). This bell-shaped normality property allows you to perform probability calculations with the NORMDIST and NORMINV functions.

Equally important, this example demonstrates the *decreased variability* in the sample means as n increases. Why should an increased sample size lead to decreased variability? The reason is the averaging process. Think about winning $750 based on the average of two spins. All you need is two lucky spins. In fact, one really lucky spin and an average spin will do. But think about winning $750 based on the average of 10 spins. Now you need a *lot* of really lucky spins—and virtually no unlucky ones. The point is that you are much less likely to obtain a really large (or really small) sample mean when n is large than when n is small. This is exactly what we mean when we say that the variability of the sample means decreases with larger sample sizes.

This decreasing variability is predicted by the formula for the standard error of the mean, $\sigma/\sqrt{n}$. As n increases, the standard error decreases. This is what drives the behavior in Figures 7.12 through 7.15. In fact, using $\sigma = \$289$, the (theoretical) standard errors for $n = 2$, $n = 3$, $n = 6$, and $n = 10$ are $204, $167, $118, and $91, respectively.

Finally, what does this decreasing variability have to do with estimating a population mean with a sample mean? Very simply, it means that the sample mean tends to be a more *accurate* estimate when the sample size is large. Because of the approximate normality from the central limit theorem, you know from Chapter 5 that there is about a 95% chance that the sample mean will be within two standard errors of the population mean. In other words, there is about a 95% chance that the sampling error will be no greater than two standard errors in magnitude. Therefore, because the standard error decreases as the sample size increases, the sampling error is likely to decrease as well.

FUNDAMENTAL INSIGHT

The Averaging Effect

As you average more and more observations from a given distribution, the variance of the average decreases. This has a very intuitive explanation. For example, suppose you average only two observations. Then it is easy to get an abnormally large (or small) average. All it takes are two abnormally large (or small) observations. But if you average a much larger number of observations, you aren't likely to get an abnormally large (or small) average. The reason is that a few abnormally large observations will typically be cancelled by a few abnormally small observations. This cancellation produces the averaging effect. It also explains why a larger sample size tends to produce a more accurate estimate of a population mean.

To illustrate this, reconsider the auditor in Example 7.4. The standard error based on a sample of size $n = 100$ yielded a sample standard deviation of $419 and a standard error of about $42. Therefore, the sampling error has a 95% chance of being less than two standard errors, or $84, in magnitude. If the auditor believes that this sampling error is too large and therefore randomly samples 300 *more* accounts, the new standard error will be $419/\sqrt{400} \approx 21$. Now there is about a 95% chance that the sampling error will be no more than $42. Note that because of the square root, small standard errors come at a high price. To halve the standard error, the sample size must be quadrupled.

7.4.5 Sample Size Determination

The problem of determining the appropriate sample size in any sampling context is not an easy one (as illustrated in the chapter opener), but it must be faced in the planning stages, *before* any sampling is done. We focus here on the relationship between sampling error and sample size. As we discussed previously, the sampling error tends to decrease as the sample size increases, so the desire to minimize sampling error encourages us to select larger sample sizes. We should note, however, that several other factors encourage us to select *smaller* sample sizes. The ultimate sample size selection must achieve a trade-off between these opposing forces.

What are these other factors? First, there is the obvious cost of sampling. Larger samples are more costly. Sometimes, a company or agency might have a budget for a given sampling project. If the sample size required to achieve an acceptable sampling error is 500, but the budget allows for a sample size of only 300, budget considerations will probably prevail.

Another problem caused by large sample sizes is timely collection of the data. Suppose a retailer wants to collect sample data from its customers to decide whether to run an advertising blitz in the coming week. Obviously, the retailer needs to collect the data quickly if they are to be of any use, and a large sample could require too much time to collect.

Finally, a more subtle problem caused by large sample sizes is the increased chance of *nonsampling* error, such as nonresponse bias. As we discussed previously in this chapter, there are many potential sources of nonsampling error, and they are usually very difficult to quantify. However, they are likely to *increase* as the sample size increases. Arguably, the potential increase in *sampling* error from a smaller sample could be more than offset by a decrease in nonsampling error, especially if the cost saved by the smaller sample size is used to reduce the sources of nonsampling error—conducting more follow-up of nonrespondents, for example.

Nevertheless, the determination of sample size is usually driven by sampling error considerations. If you want to estimate a population mean with a sample mean, then the key is the standard error of the mean, given by

$$SE(\overline{X}) = \sigma/\sqrt{n}$$

The central limit theorem says that if n is reasonably large, there is about a 95% chance that the magnitude of the sampling error will be no more than two standard errors. Because σ is fixed in the formula for $SE(\overline{X})$, n can be chosen to make $2SE(\overline{X})$ acceptably small.

FUNDAMENTAL INSIGHT

Effect of Larger Sample Sizes

Accurate estimates of population parameters require small standard errors, and small standard errors require large sample sizes. However, standard errors are typically inversely proportional to the *square root* of the sample size (or sample sizes). The implication is that if you want to decrease the standard error by a given factor, you must increase the sample size by a much larger factor. For example, to decrease the standard error by a factor of 2, you must increase the sample size by a factor of 4. Accurate estimates are not cheap.

We postpone further discussion of sample size selection until the next chapter, where we will discuss in detail how it can be used to control confidence interval length.

7.4.6 Summary of Key Ideas for Simple Random Sampling

To this point, we have covered some very important concepts. Because we build on these concepts in later chapters, we summarize them here.

Key Concepts of Simple Random Sampling

- To estimate a population mean with a simple random sample, the sample mean is typically used as a "best guess." This estimate is called a *point estimate*. That is, $\overline{X}$ is a point estimate of μ.

- The accuracy of the point estimate is measured by its standard error. It is the standard deviation of the sampling distribution of the point estimate. The standard error of $\overline{X}$ is approximately $s/\sqrt{n}$, where s is the sample standard deviation.

- A *confidence interval* (with 95% confidence) for the population mean extends to approximately two standard errors on either side of the sample mean.
- From the *central limit theorem*, the sampling distribution of $\overline{X}$ is approximately normal when n is reasonably large.
- There is approximately a 95% chance that any particular $\overline{X}$ will be within two standard errors of the population mean μ.
- The sampling error can be reduced by increasing the sample size n. Appropriate sample size formulas for controlling confidence interval length are given in the next chapter.

PROBLEMS

Level A

7. A manufacturing company's quality control personnel have recorded the proportion of defective items for each of 500 monthly shipments of one of the computer components that the company produces. The data are in the file **P07_07.xlsx**. The quality control department manager does not have sufficient time to review all of these data. Rather, she would like to examine the proportions of defective items for a sample of these shipments. For this problem, you can assume that the population is the data from the 500 shipments.
   a. Use Excel to generate a simple random sample of size 25 from the data.
   b. Calculate a point estimate of the population mean from the sample selected in part **a**. What is the sampling error, that is, by how much does the sample mean miss the population mean?
   c. Calculate a good approximation for the standard error of the mean.
   d. Repeat parts **b** and **c** after generating a simple random sample of size 50 from the population. Is this estimate bound to be more accurate than the one in part **b**? Is its standard error bound to be smaller than the one in part **c**?

8. The manager of a local fast-food restaurant is interested in improving the service provided to customers who use the restaurant's drive-up window. As a first step in this process, the manager asks his assistant to record the time it takes to serve a large number of customers at the final window in the facility's drive-up system. The results are in the file **P07_08.xlsx**, which consists of nearly 1200 service times. For this problem, you can assume that the population is the data in this file.
   a. Use Excel to generate a simple random sample of size 30 from the data.
   b. Calculate a point estimate of the population mean from the sample selected in part **a**. What is the

sampling error, that is, by how much does the sample mean miss the population mean?
   c. Calculate a good approximation for the standard error of the mean.
   d. If you wanted to halve the standard error from part **c**, what approximate sample size would you need? Why is this only approximate?

9. The file **P02_16.xlsx** contains traffic data from 256 weekdays on four variables. Each variable lists the number of arrivals during a specific 5-minute period of the day. For this problem, consider this data set a simple random sample from all possible weekdays.
   a. For each of the four variables, find the sample mean. If each of these is used as an estimate from the corresponding (unknown) population mean, is there any reason to believe that they either underestimate or overestimate the population means? Why or why not?
   b. What are the (approximate) standard errors of the estimates in part **a**? How can you interpret these standard errors? Be as specific as possible.
   c. Is it likely that the estimates in part **a** are accurate to within 0.4 arrival? Why or why not? (Answer for each variable separately.)

10. The file **P02_35.xlsx** contains data from a survey of 500 randomly selected households. For this problem, consider this data set a simple random sample from all possible households, where the number of households in the population is well over 1,000,000.
   a. Create a new variable, Total Income, that is the sum of First Income and Second Income.
   b. For each of the four variables Total Income, Monthly Payment, Utilities, and Debt, find the sample mean. If each of these is used as an estimate from the corresponding (unknown) population mean, is there any reason to believe that they either underestimate or overestimate the corresponding population means? Why or why not?
   c. What are the (approximate) standard errors of the estimates in part **b**? How can you interpret these standard

errors? Be as specific as possible. Is the finite population correction required? Why or why not?

d. Is it likely that the estimate of Total Income in part **b** is accurate to within $1500? Why or why not?

11. The file **P02_10.xlsx** contains midterm and final exam scores for 96 students in a corporate finance course. For this problem, assume that these 96 students represent a sample of the 175 students taking the course, and that these 175 students represent the relevant population.

a. Assuming the same instructor is teaching all four sections of this course and that the 96 students are the students in two of these sections, is it fair to say that the 96 students represent a *random* sample from the population? Does it matter?

b. Find the sample mean and the standard error of the sample mean, based on the 96 students in the file. Should the finite population correction be used? What is the standard error without it? What is the standard error with it?

Level B

12. Create a simulation similar to the one in the **Wheel of Fortune Similation.xlsx** file. However, suppose that the outcome of each spin is no longer uniformly distributed between $0 and $1000. Instead, it is the number of 7s you get in 20 rolls of two dice. In other words, each spin results in a binomially distributed random number with parameters $n = 20$ and $p = 1/6$ (because the chance of rolling a 7 is 1 out of 6). The simulation should still allow you to vary the number

of "spins" from 1 to 10, and the "winnings" is still the average of the outcomes of the spins. What is fundamentally different from the simulation in the text? Does the central limit theorem still work? Explain from the results you obtain.

13. Suppose you plan to take a simple random sample from a population with N members. Specifically, you plan to sample a percentage p of the population. If p is 1%, is the finite population correction really necessary? Does the answer depend on N? Explain. Then answer the same questions when p is 5%, 10%, 25%, and 50%, respectively. In general, explain what goes wrong if the finite population correction is really necessary but isn't used.

14. The file **P07_14.xlsx** contains a very small population of only five members. For each member, the height of the person is listed. The purpose of this problem is to let you see exactly what a sampling distribution is. Find the *exact* sampling distribution of the sample mean with sample size 3. Verify that Equation (7.1) holds, that is, the mean of this sampling distribution is equal to the population mean. Also, verify that Equation (7.2) holds, that is, the standard deviation of this sampling distribution is equal to the population standard deviation divided by the square root of 3. (*Hint*: You will have to do this by brute force. There are 125 different samples of size 3 that could be drawn from this population. These include samples with duplicate members, and order counts. For example, they include (1,1,2), (1,2,1), (2,1,1), and (1,1,1). You will need to find the sample mean of each and then find the mean and standard deviation of these sample means.)

7.5 CONCLUSION

This chapter has provided the fundamental concepts behind statistical inference. We discussed ways to obtain random samples from a population; how to calculate a point estimate of a particular population parameter, the population mean; and how to measure the accuracy of this point estimate. The key idea is the sampling distribution of the estimate and specifically its standard deviation, called the standard error of the estimate. Due to the central limit theorem, the sampling distribution of the sample mean is approximately normal, which implies that the sample mean will be within two standard errors of the population mean in approximately 95% of all random samples. In the next two chapters we build on these important concepts.

Summary of Key Terms

Term	Symbol	Explanation	Excel	Page	Equation
Population		Contains all members about which a study intends to make inferences		353	
Frame		A list of all members of the population		353	

(continued)

Term	Symbol	Explanation	Excel	Page	Equation
Sampling units		Potential members of a sample from a population		353	
Probability sample		Any sample that is chosen by using a random mechanism		353	
Judgmental sample		Any sample that is chosen according to a sampler's judgment rather a random mechanism		353	
Simple random sample		A sample where each member of the population has the same chance of being chosen	StatTools/ Data Utilities	354	
Systematic sample		A sample where one of the first k members is selected randomly, and then every kth member after this one is selected		360	
Stratified sample		A sample in which the population is divided into relatively homogeneous subsets called *strata*, and then random samples are taken from each of the strata		361	
Proportional sample sizes (in stratified sampling)		The property of each stratum selected having the same proportion from stratum to stratum		362	
Cluster sampling		A sample where the population is separated into clusters, such as cities or city blocks, and then a random sample of the clusters is selected		364	
Sampling error		The inevitable result of basing an inference on a sample rather than on the entire population		367	
Nonsampling error		Any type of estimation error that is not sampling error, including nonresponse bias, nontruthful responses, measurement error, and voluntary response bias		367	
Point estimate		A single numeric value, a "best guess" of a population parameter, based on the data in a sample		368	
Sampling error (or estimation error)		Difference between the estimate of a population parameter and the true value of the parameter		368	
Sampling distribution		The distribution of the point estimates from *all* possible samples (of a given sample size) from the population		368	
Confidence interval		An interval around the point estimate, calculated from the sample data, where the true value of the population parameter is very likely to be		368	
Unbiased estimate		An estimate where the mean of its sampling distribution equals the value of the parameter being estimated		369	

(continued)

Summary of Key Terms (*Continued*)

Term	Symbol	Explanation	Excel	Page	Equation
Standard error of an estimate		The standard deviation of the sampling distribution of the estimate		369	
Mean of sample mean	$E(\overline{X})$	Indicates property of unbiasedness of sample mean		370	7.1
Standard error of sample mean	$SE(\overline{X})$	Indicates how sample means from different samples vary		371	7.2, 7.3
Confidence interval for population mean		An interval that is very likely to contain the population mean		371	7.4
Finite population correction	*fpc*	A correction for the standard error when the sample size is fairly large relative to the population size		373	7.5, 7.6
Central limit theorem		States that the distribution of the sample mean is approximately normal for sufficiently large sample sizes		374	

PROBLEMS

Note: Because the material in this chapter is more conceptual than calculation-based, we have included only conceptual questions here. You will get plenty of practice with calculations in the next two chapters, which build upon the concepts in this chapter.

Conceptual Questions

C.1. Suppose that you want to know the opinions of American secondary school teachers about establishing a national test for high school graduation. You obtain a list of the members of the National Education Association (the largest teachers' union) and mail a questionnaire to 3000 teachers chosen at random from this list. In all, 823 teachers return the questionnaire. Identify the relevant *population*. Do you believe there is a good possibility of nonsampling error? Why or why not?

C.2. A sportswriter wants to know how strongly the residents of Indianapolis, Indiana, support the local minor league baseball team, the Indianapolis Indians. He stands outside the stadium before a game and interviews the first 30 people who enter the stadium. Suppose that the newspaper asks you to comment on the approach taken by this sportswriter in performing the survey. How would you respond?

C.3. A large corporation has 4520 male and 567 female employees. The organization's equal employment opportunity officer wants to poll the opinions of a random sample of employees. To give adequate attention to the opinions of female employees, exactly how should the EEO officer sample from the given population? Be specific.

C.4. Suppose that you want to estimate the mean monthly gross income of all households in your local community. You decide to estimate this population parameter by calling 150 randomly selected residents and asking each individual to report the household's monthly income. Assume that you use the local phone directory as the frame in selecting the households to be included in your sample. What are some possible sources of error that might arise in your effort to estimate the population mean?

C.5. Provide an example of when you might want to take a stratified random sample instead of a simple random sample, and explain what the advantage of a stratified sample might be.

C.6. Provide an example of when you might want to take a cluster random sample instead of a simple random sample, and explain what the advantage of a cluster sample might be. Also, explain how you would choose the cluster sample.

C.7. Do you agree with the statement that nonresponse error can be overcome with larger samples? If you agree, explain why. If you disagree, provide an example that backs up your opinion.

C.8. When pollsters take a random sample of about 1000 people to estimate the mean of some quantity over a population of millions of people, how is it possible for them to gauge the accuracy of the sample mean?

C.9. Suppose you want to estimate the population mean of some quantity when the population consists of millions of members (such as the population of all U.S. households). How is it possible that you can obtain a fairly accurate estimate, using the sample mean of only about 1000 randomly selected members?

C.10. What is the difference between a *standard deviation* and a *standard error*? Be precise.

C.11. Explain as precisely as possible what it means that the sample mean is an *unbiased* estimate of the population mean (as indicated in Equation (7.1)).

C.12. Explain the difference between the standard error formulas in equations (7.2) and (7.3). Why is Equation (7.3) the one necessarily used in real situations?

C.13. Explain as precisely as possible what Equation (7.4) means, and the reason for the 2 in the formula.

C.14. Explain as precisely as possible the role of the finite population correction. In which types of situations is it necessary? Is it necessarily used in typical polls you see in the news?

C.15. In the wheel of fortune simulation with, say, three spins, many people mistakenly believe that the distribution of the average is the flat graph in Figure 7.9, that is, they believe the average of three spins is *uniformly* distributed between $0 and $1000. Explain intuitively why they are wrong.

C.16. Explain the difference between a point estimate for the mean and a confidence interval for the mean. Which provides more information?

C.17. Explain as precisely as possible what the central limit theorem says about averages.

C.18. Many people seem to believe that the central limit theorem "kicks in" only when n is at least 30. Why is this not necessarily true? When is such a large n necessary?

C.19. Suppose you are a pollster and are planning to take a sample that is very small relative to the population. In terms of estimating a population mean, can you say that a sample of size $9n$ is about 3 times as accurate as a sample of size n? Why or why not? Does the answer depend on the population size? For example, would it matter if the population size were 50 million instead of 10 million?

C.20. You saw in Equation (7.1) that the sample mean is an unbiased estimate of the population mean. However, some estimates of population parameters are biased. In such cases, there are two sources of error in estimating the population parameter: the bias and the standard error. To understand these, imagine a rifleman shooting at a bull's-eye. The rifleman could be aiming wrong and/or his shots could vary wildly from shot to shot. If he is aiming wrong but his shots are very consistent, what can you say about his bias and standard error? Answer the same question if he is correctly aiming at the bull's-eye but is very inconsistent. Can you say which of these two situations is worse?

The file **DVD Movies.xlsx** contains a large data set of 10,000 customer transactions for a fictional chain of video stores in the United States. Each row corresponds to a different customer and lists (1) a customer ID number (1–10,000), (2) the state where the customer lives, (3) the city where the customer lives, (4) the customer's gender, (5) the customer's favorite type of movie (drama, comedy, science fiction, or action), (6) the customer's next favorite type of movie, (7) the number of times the customer has rented movies in the past year, and (8) the total dollar amount the customer has spent on movie rentals during the past year. The data are sorted by state, then city, then gender. We assume that this data set represents the entire population of customers for this video chain. (Of course, national chains would have significantly larger customer populations, but this data set is large enough to illustrate the ideas.)

Imagine that only the data in columns A through D are readily available for this population. The company is interested in summary statistics of the data in columns E through H, such as the percentage of customers whose favorite movie type is drama or the average amount spent annually per customer, but it will have to do some work to obtain the data in columns E through H for any particular customer. Therefore, the company wants to perform sampling. The question is: What form—simple random sampling, systematic sampling, stratified sampling, cluster sampling, or even some type of multistage sampling—is most appropriate?

Your job is to investigate the possibilities and to write a report on your findings. For any sampling method, any sample size, and any quantity of interest (such as average dollar amount spent annually), you should be concerned with sampling cost and accuracy. One way to judge the latter is to generate several random samples from a particular method and calculate the mean and standard deviation of your point estimates from these samples. For example, you might generate 10 systematic samples, calculate the average amount spent (an $\overline{X}$) for each sample, and then calculate the mean and standard deviation of these 10 $\overline{X}$s. If your sampling method is accurate, the mean of the $\overline{X}$s should be close to the population average, and the standard deviation should be small. By doing this for several sampling methods and possibly several sample sizes, you can experiment to see what is most cost-efficient for the company. You can make any reasonable assumptions about the cost of sampling with any particular method. ■

Confidence Interval Estimation

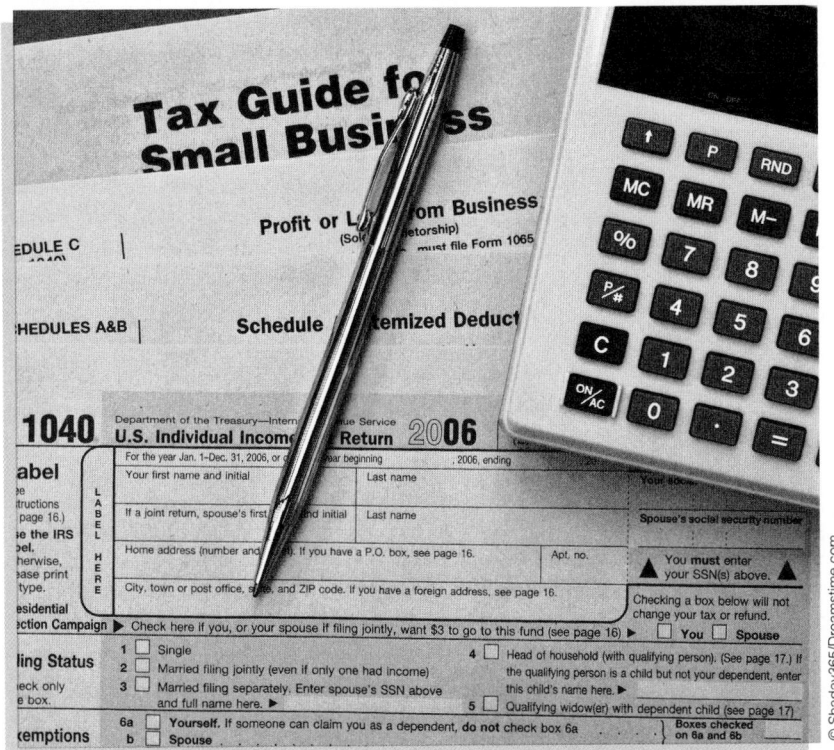

© Shaday365/Dreamstime.com

ESTIMATING A COMPANY'S TOTAL TAXABLE INCOME

In Example 7.4 in the previous chapter, we illustrated how sampling can be used in auditing. We see another illustration of sampling in auditing in Example 8.5 of this chapter. In both examples, the point of the sampling is to discover some property (such as a mean or a proportion) from a large population of a company's accounts by examining a small fraction of these accounts and projecting the results to the population. An article by Press (1995) offers an interesting variation on this problem. He poses the question of how a government revenue agency should assess a business taxpayer's income for tax purposes on the basis of a sample audit of the company's business transactions. A sample of the company's transactions will indicate a taxable income for each sampled transaction. The methods of this chapter will be applied to the sample information to obtain a confidence interval for the total taxable income owed by the company.

Suppose for the sake of illustration that this confidence interval extends from $1,000,000 to $2,200,000 and is centered at $1,600,000. In other words, the government's best guess of the company's taxable income is $1,600,000, and the government is fairly confident that the true taxable income is between $1,000,000 and $2,200,000. How much tax should it assess the company? Press argues that the agency would like to maximize its revenue while minimizing the risk that the company will be assessed more than it really owes. This last assumption, that the government does not want to *overassess* the company, is crucial. By making several reasonable assumptions, he is able to argue that the agency should base the tax on the *lower* limit of the confidence interval, in this case, $1,000,000.[1]

On the other hand, if the agency were indifferent between overcharging and undercharging, then it would base the tax on the midpoint, $1,600,000, of the confidence interval. Using this strategy, the agency would overcharge in about half the cases and undercharge in the other half. This would certainly be upsetting to companies—it would appear that the agency is flipping a coin to decide whether to overcharge or undercharge.

If the government agency does indeed decide to base the tax on the *lower* limit of the confidence interval, Press argues that it can still increase its tax revenue—by increasing the sample size of the audit. When the sample size increases, the confidence interval shrinks in width, and the lower limit, which governs the agency's tax revenue, almost surely increases. But there is some point at which larger samples are not warranted, for the simple reason that larger samples cost more money to obtain. Therefore, there is an optimal size that will balance the cost of sampling with the desire to obtain more tax revenue. ■

8.1 INTRODUCTION

This chapter expands on the ideas from the previous chapter. Given an observed data set, we want to make inferences to some larger population. Two typical examples follow:

■ A mail-order company has accounts with thousands of customers. The company would like to infer the average time its customers take to pay their bills, so it randomly samples a relatively small number of its customers, sees how long these customers take to pay their bills, and draws inferences about the entire population of customers.

■ A manufacturing company is considering two compensation schemes to implement for its workers. It believes that these two different compensation schemes might provide different incentives and hence result in different worker productivity. To see whether this is true, the company randomly assigns groups of workers to the two different compensation schemes for a period of three months and observes their productivity. Then it attempts to infer whether any differences observed in the experiment can be generalized to the overall worker population.

In each of these examples, there is an unknown population parameter a company would like to estimate. In the mail-order example, the unknown parameter is the mean length of time customers take to pay their bills. Its true value could be discovered only by learning how long *every* customer in the entire population takes to pay its bills. This is not really possible,

---

[1]In case this sounds overly generous on the government's part, the result is based on two important assumptions: (1) the confidence interval is a 90% confidence interval, and (2) the agency is 19 times more concerned about overassessing than about underassessing.

given the large number of customers. In the manufacturing example, the unknown parameter is a mean difference, the difference between the mean productivities with the two different compensation schemes. This mean difference could be discovered only by subjecting each worker to each compensation scheme and measuring their resulting productivities. This procedure would almost certainly be impossible from a practical standpoint. Therefore, the companies in these examples are likely to select random samples and base their estimates of the unknown population parameters on the sample data.

The inferences discussed in this chapter are always based on an underlying probability model, which means that some type of random mechanism must generate the data. Two random mechanisms are generally used. The first involves sampling randomly from a larger population, as we discussed in the previous chapter. This is the mechanism responsible for generating the sample of customers in the mail-order example. Regardless of whether the sample is a simple random sample or a more complex random sample, such as a stratified sample, the fact that it is *random* allows us to use the rules of probability to make inferences about the population as a whole.

The second commonly used random mechanism is called a *randomized experiment*. The compensation scheme example just described is a typical randomized experiment. Here the company selects a set of subjects (employees), randomly assign them to two different *treatment groups* (compensation schemes), and then compare some quantitative measure (productivity) across the groups. The fact that the subjects are *randomly* assigned to the two treatment groups is useful for two reasons. First, it allows us to rule out a number of factors that might have led to differences across groups. For example, assuming that males and females are randomly spread across the two groups, we can rule out gender as the cause of any observed group differences. Second, the random selection allows us to use the rules of probability to infer whether observed differences can be generalized to all employees.

We actually introduced 95% confidence intervals for the mean in the previous chapter. We generalize this method in the current chapter.

Generally, statistical inferences are of two types: *confidence interval estimation* and *hypothesis testing*. The first of these is the subject of the current chapter; hypothesis testing is discussed in the next chapter. They differ primarily in their point of view. For example, the mail-order company might sample 100 customers and find that they average 15.5 days before paying their bills. In confidence interval estimation, the data are used to obtain a point estimate and a **confidence interval** around this point estimate. In this example the point estimate is 15.5 days. It is a best guess for the mean bill-paying time in the entire customer population. Then, using the methods in this chapter, the company might find that a 95% confidence interval for the mean bill-paying time in the population is from 13.2 days to 17.8 days. The company is now 95% confident that the true mean bill-paying time in the population is within this interval.

Hypothesis testing takes a different point of view. Here we wish to check whether the observed data provide support for a particular hypothesis. In the compensation scheme example, suppose the manager believes that workers will have higher productivity if they are paid by salary than by an hourly wage. He runs the three-month randomized experiment described previously and finds that the salaried workers produce on average eight more parts per day than the hourly workers. Now he must make one of two conclusions. Either salaried workers are in general no more productive than hourly workers and the ones in the experiment just got lucky, or salaried workers really *are* more productive. The next chapter explains how to decide which of these conclusions is more reasonable.

There are only a few key ideas in this chapter, and the most important of these, *sampling distributions*, was introduced in the previous chapter. It is important to concentrate on these key ideas and not get bogged down in formulas or numerical calculations. Statistical software such as StatTools is generally available to take care of these calculations. The job of a businessperson is much more dependent on knowing which methods to use in which situations and how to interpret computer output than on memorizing and plugging into formulas.

8.2 SAMPLING DISTRIBUTIONS

As you will soon learn, most confidence intervals are of the form in Expression (8.1). For example, when estimating a population mean, the point estimate is the sample mean, the standard error is the sample standard deviation divided by the square root of the sample size, and the multiple is approximately equal to 2. To learn why it works this way, you must first learn a bit about sampling distributions. This knowledge will then be put to use in the next section.

Typical Form of Confidence Interval

$$\text{Point Estimate} \pm \text{Multiple} \times \text{Standard Error} \qquad \textbf{(8.1)}$$

In the previous chapter, we introduced the sampling distribution of the sample mean $\overline{X}$ and saw how it was related to the central limit theorem. In general, whenever you make inferences about one or more population parameters, such as a mean or the difference between two means, you always base this inference on the sampling distribution of a point estimate, such as the sample mean. Although the *concepts* of point estimates and sampling distributions are no different from those in the previous chapter, there are some new details to learn.

We again begin with the sample mean $\overline{X}$. The central limit theorem states that if the sample size n is reasonably large, then for *any* population distribution, the sampling distribution of $\overline{X}$ is approximately normally distributed with mean μ and standard deviation $\sigma/\sqrt{n}$, where μ and σ are the population mean and standard deviation. An equivalent statement is that the standardized quantity Z defined in Equation (8.2) is approximately normal with mean 0 and standard deviation 1.

Standardized Z-Value

$$Z = \frac{\overline{X} - \mu}{\sigma/\sqrt{n}} \qquad \textbf{(8.2)}$$

Typically, this fact is used to make inferences about an unknown population mean μ. There is one problem, however—the population standard deviation σ is almost always unknown. This parameter, σ, is called a *nuisance parameter*. Although it is typically not the parameter of primary interest, its value is needed for making inferences about the mean μ. The solution appears to be straightforward: Replace the nuisance parameter σ by its sample estimate s in the formula for Z and proceed from there. However, when σ is replaced by the sample standard deviation s, this introduces a new source of variability, and the sampling distribution is no longer normal. It is instead called the *t* **distribution**, a close relative of the normal distribution that appears in a variety of statistical applications.

8.2.1 The *t* Distribution

We first set the stage for this new sampling distribution. We are interested in estimating a population mean μ with a sample of size n. We assume the population distribution is normal with unknown standard deviation σ. We intend to base inferences on the standardized value of $\overline{X}$ from Equation (8.2), where σ is replaced by the sample standard deviation s, as shown in Equation (8.3). Then the standardized value in Equation (8.3) has a t distribution with $n - 1$ degrees of freedom.

$$t = \frac{\overline{X} - \mu}{s/\sqrt{n}} \qquad (8.3)$$

The *degrees of freedom* is a numerical parameter of the *t* distribution that defines the precise shape of the distribution. Each time we encounter a *t* distribution, we will specify its degrees of freedom. In this particular sampling context, where we are basing inferences about μ on the sampling distribution of $\overline{X}$, the degrees of freedom turns out to be 1 less than the sample size *n*.

The *t* distribution looks very much like the standard normal distribution. It is bell-shaped and centered at 0. The only difference is that it is slightly more spread out, and this increase in spread is greater for *small* degrees of freedom. In fact, when *n* is large, so that the degrees of freedom is large, the *t* distribution and the standard normal distribution are practically indistinguishable. This is illustrated in Figure 8.1. With 5 degrees of freedom, it is possible to see the increased spread in the *t* distribution. With 30 degrees of freedom, the *t* and standard normal curves are practically the same curve.

Figure 8.1

The *t* and Standard Normal Distributions

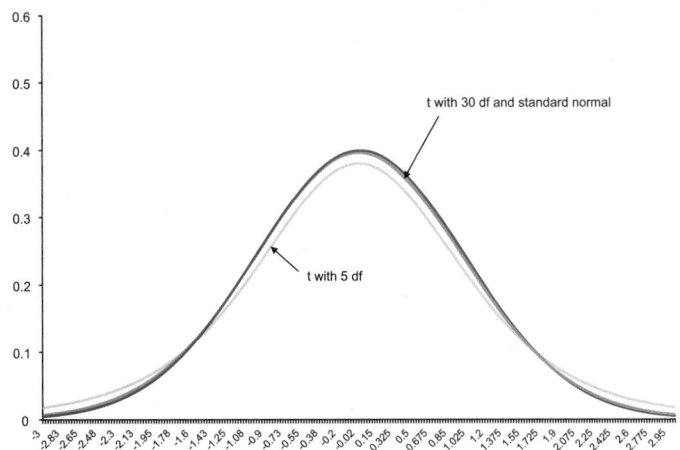

The t distribution and the standard normal distribution are practically the same when the degrees of freedom parameter is large.

The *t*-value in Equation (8.3) is very much like a typical *Z*-value such as in Equation (8.2). That is, the *t*-value represents the number of standard errors by which the sample mean differs from the population mean. For example, if a *t*-value is 2.5, the sample mean is 2.5 standard errors above the population mean. In contrast, if a *t*-value is −2.5, the sample mean is 2.5 standard errors below the population mean. Also, *t*-values greater in magnitude than 3 are quite unexpected because of the same property of the normal distribution: It is very unlikely for a random value to be more than three standard deviations from its mean. (In this case the random value is a sample mean, and the standard deviation is the standard error of the mean.)

A *t*-value indicates the number of standard errors by which a sample mean differs from a population mean.

Because of this interpretation, *t*-values are perfect candidates for the *multiple* term in Expression (8.1), as you will soon see. First, however, we briefly examine some Excel functions that are useful for working with the *t* distribution in Excel.

In Chapter 5 you learned how to use Excel's NORMSDIST and NORMSINV functions to calculate probabilities or percentiles from the standard normal distribution. There are similar Excel functions for the *t* distribution: TDIST and TINV. Unfortunately, these functions are somewhat more difficult to master than their normal counterparts. The file **t Calculations.xlsx** spells out the possibilities (see Figure 8.2). The top three examples use the TDIST function, which finds the probability to the left or right of a given value. The bottom three examples use the TINV function, which finds the value with a given probability beyond it in one or both tails.

Figure 8.2   Excel Functions for the *t* Distribution

	A	B	C	D	E	F	G	H	I	J
1	Calculations for the t distribution									
2										
3	Sample size	30								
4	Degrees of freedom	29								
5										
6	One-tailed probabilities									
7	t-value	-2		Formulas			Formulas in Excel 2010 (preferred)			
8	Probability in left tail	0.0275		=TDIST(-B7,B4,1)			=T.DIST(B7,B4,1)			
9										
10	t-value	2								
11	Probability in right tail	0.0275		=TDIST(B10,B4,1)			=T.DIST.RT(B10,B4)			
12										
13	Two-tailed probability									
14	t-value	2								
15	Probability in both tails	0.0549 ←		=TDIST(B14,B4,2)			=T.DIST.2T(B14,B4)			
16				Half of this probability is in each tail						
17	TINV calculations									
18	Probability in left tail	0.05								
19	t-value	-1.699		=-TINV(2*B18,B4)			=T.INV(B18,B4)			
20										
21	Probability in right tail	0.05								
22	t-value	1.699		=TINV(2*B15,B4)			=T.INV(1-B21,B4)			
23										
24	Probability in both tails	0.05 ←		Half of this probability is in each tail						
25	t-value	2.045		=TINV(B18,B4)			=T.INV.2T(B24,B4)			

CHANGES IN EXCEL 2010

In Chapter 5, we discussed new statistical functions in Excel 2010. Except possibly for the replacement of CRITBINOM by BINOM.INV, these changes don't really seem to make much difference. However, the latest changes definitely help with the *t* distribution. Before, the only available functions were TDIST and TINV, and because of the rather obscure way they work, everyone has had problems using them correctly. Therefore, Microsoft introduced five new functions in Excel 2010: T.DIST, T.DIST.RT, T.DIST.2T, T.INV, and T.INV.2T. As usual, a "DIST" function takes a value and returns a probability, whereas an "INV" function takes a probability and returns a value. Normally, these kinds of functions are written for left-hand tails ("<" problems), and this is the case for T.DIST and T.INV. However, T.DIST.RT lets you work with right-hand tails (">" problems), and T.DIST.2T and T.INV.2T let you work with both tails. Figure 8.2 shows both the old and the new functions, and the **t Calculations.xlsx** file provides more details on their use. We strongly recommend that you use the new functions if you have Excel 2010.

In general, here are the technical details for using the TDIST function properly. (These are the obscure rules for the *old* TDIST function only. You can ignore these if you are using the new Excel 2010 functions.)

- Its first argument must be nonnegative.

- Unlike the NORMSDIST function, TDIST returns the probability to the *right* of the first argument (if the third argument is 1).

- The third argument of the TDIST function is either 1 or 2 and indicates the number of tails. By using 1 for this argument, you get the probability in the right-hand tail only. If you use 2 for the third argument, you obtain the probability of greater than the first argument or less than its negative.

The technical details for using the TINV function properly are as follows. (Again, these are for the *old* TINV function only.)

- The first argument is the total probability you want in both tails—half of this goes in the right-hand tail and half goes in the left-hand tail.

- Unlike the TDIST function, there is no third argument for the TINV function.

We agree that these functions, old or new, are somewhat difficult to learn. Fortunately, the StatTools add-in simplifies the process for most statistical inference applications. It does the *t* distribution calculations for you.

8.2.2 Other Sampling Distributions

The *t* distribution, a close relative of the normal distribution, is used to make inferences about a population mean when the population standard deviation is unknown. Throughout this chapter (and later chapters) you will see other contexts where the *t* distribution appears. The theme is always the same—one or more means are of interest, and one or more standard deviations are unknown.

The *t* (and normal) distributions are not the only sampling distributions you will encounter. Two other close relatives of the normal distribution that appear in various contexts are the *chi-square* and *F distributions*. These are used primarily to make inferences about variances (or standard deviations), as opposed to means. We omit the details of these distributions for now, but you will see them in later sections.

PROBLEMS

Note: Student solutions for problems whose numbers appear within a colored box are available for purchase at www.cengagebrain.com.

Level A

1. Calculate the following probabilities using Excel. (If you have Excel 2010, we suggest using its new functions.)

  a. $P(t_{10} \geq 1.75)$, where t_{10} has a *t* distribution with 10 degrees of freedom.

  b. $P(t_{100} \geq 1.75)$, where t_{100} has a *t* distribution with 100 degrees of freedom. How do you explain the

difference between this result and the one obtained in part **a**?

  c. $P(Z \geq 1.75)$, where Z is a standard normal random variable. Compare this result to the results obtained in parts **a** and **b**. How do you explain the differences in these probabilities?

  d. $P(t_{20} \leq -0.80)$, where t_{20} has a *t* distribution with 20 degrees of freedom.

  e. $P(t_3 \leq -0.80)$, where t_3 has a *t* distribution with 3 degrees of freedom. How do you explain the difference between this result and the result obtained in part **d**?

2. Calculate the following quantities using Excel. (If you have Excel 2010, we suggest using its new functions.)

    a. $P(-2.00 \leq t_{10} \leq 1.00)$, where t_{10} has a t distribution with 10 degrees of freedom.

    b. $P(-2.00 \leq t_{100} \leq 1.00)$, where t_{100} has a t distribution with 100 degrees of freedom. How do you explain the difference between this result and the one obtained in part **a**?

    c. $P(-2.00 \leq Z \leq 1.00)$, where Z is a standard normal random variable. Compare this result to the results obtained in parts **a** and **b**. How do you explain the differences in these probabilities?

    d. Find the 68th percentile of the t distribution with 20 degrees of freedom.

    e. Find the 68th percentile of the t distribution with 3 degrees of freedom. How do you explain the difference between this result and the result obtained in part **d**?

3. Calculate the following quantities using Excel. (If you have Excel 2010, we suggest using its new functions.)

    a. Find the value of x such that $P(t_{10} > x) = 0.75$, where t_{10} has a t distribution with 10 degrees of freedom.

    b. Find the value of y such that $P(t_{100} > y) = 0.75$, where t_{100} has a t distribution with 100 degrees of freedom. How do you explain the difference between this result and the result obtained in part **a**?

    c. Find the value of z such that $P(Z > z) = 0.75$, where Z is a standard normal random variable. Compare this result to the results obtained in parts **a** and **b**. How do you explain the differences in the values of x, y, and z?

8.3 CONFIDENCE INTERVAL FOR A MEAN

We now come to the focal point of this chapter: using results about sampling distributions to construct confidence intervals. We assume that data have been generated by some random mechanism, either by observing a random sample from some population or by performing a randomized experiment. The goal is to infer the values of one or more population parameters such as the mean, the standard deviation, or a proportion from sample data. For each such parameter, you use the data to calculate a point estimate, which can be considered a best guess for the unknown parameter. You then calculate a confidence interval around the point estimate to gauge its accuracy.

We begin by deriving a confidence interval for a population mean μ, and we discuss its interpretation. Although the particular details pertain to a specific parameter, the mean, the same ideas carry over to other parameters as well, as will be described in later sections. As usual, the sample $\overline{X}$ is used as the point estimate of μ.

To obtain a confidence interval for μ, you first specify a **confidence level**, usually 90%, 95%, or 99%. You then use the sampling distribution of the point estimate to determine the *multiple* of the standard error (SE) to go out on either side of the point estimate to achieve the given confidence level. If the confidence level is 95%, the value used most frequently in applications, the multiple is approximately 2. More precisely, it is a t-value. That is, a typical confidence interval for μ is of the form in Expression (8.4), where $\text{SE}(\overline{X}) = s/\sqrt{n}$.

> *Confidence Interval for Population Mean*
> $$\overline{X} \pm t\text{-multiple} \times \text{SE}(\overline{X}) \tag{8.4}$$

To obtain the correct t-multiple, let α be one minus the confidence level (expressed as a decimal). For example, if the confidence level is 90%, then $\alpha = 0.10$. Then the appropriate t-multiple is the value that cuts off probability $\alpha/2$ in each tail of the t distribution with $n - 1$ degrees of freedom. For example, if $n = 30$ and the confidence level is 95%, cell

B25 of Figure 8.2 indicates that the correct t-value is 2.045. The corresponding 95% confidence interval for μ is then

$$\overline{X} \pm 2.045(s/\sqrt{n})$$

If the confidence level is instead 90%, the appropriate t-value is 1.699 (change the probability in cell B24 to 0.10 to see this), and the resulting 90% confidence interval is

$$\overline{X} \pm 1.699(s/\sqrt{n})$$

If the confidence level is 99%, the appropriate t-value is 2.756 (change the probability in cell B24 to 0.01 to see this), and the resulting 99% confidence interval is

$$\overline{X} \pm 2.756(s/\sqrt{n})$$

Confidence interval widths increase when you ask for higher confidence levels, but they tend to decrease when you use larger sample sizes.

Note that as the confidence level increases, the width of the confidence interval also increases. Because narrow confidence intervals are desirable, this presents a trade-off. You can either have less confidence and a narrow interval, or you can have more confidence and a wide interval. However, you can also take a larger sample. As n increases, the standard error $s/\sqrt{n}$ decreases, and the length of the confidence interval tends to decrease for *any* confidence level. (Why won't it decrease for sure? The larger sample *might* result in a larger value of s that could offset the increase in n.)

The following example illustrates confidence interval estimation for a population mean. It uses the One-Sample procedure in StatTools to perform the calculations. However, by examining the resulting Excel formulas, you can check that all it is really doing is (1) calculating the sample mean, (2) calculating the standard error of the sample mean, $s/\sqrt{n}$, (3) finding the appropriate t-multiple, and (4) combining these to form the confidence interval via Expression (8.4).

EXAMPLE | **8.1 CUSTOMER RESPONSE TO A NEW SANDWICH**

A fast-food restaurant recently added a new sandwich to its menu. To estimate the popularity of this sandwich, a random sample of 40 customers who ordered the sandwich were surveyed. Each of these customers was asked to rate the sandwich on a scale of 1 to 10, 10 being the best. The results of this survey appear in column B of Figure 8.4. (See the file **Satisfaction Ratings.xlsx**.) The manager wants to estimate the mean satisfaction rating over the entire population of customers by finding a 95% confidence interval. How should she proceed?

Objective   To use StatTools's One-Sample procedure to obtain a 95% confidence interval for the mean satisfaction rating of the new sandwich.

Solution

You need to use StatTools's One-Sample procedure on the Satisfaction variable. To do so, make sure a StatTools data set has been designated, select Confidence Interval from the StatTools Statistical Inference dropdown list, and select the Mean/Std. Deviation option. Fill in the resulting dialog box as shown in Figure 8.3. In particular, select One-Sample Analysis as the Analysis type. (Other types will be used later in the chapter.) You should

Figure 8.3

Dialog Box for
Confidence Interval
for Mean

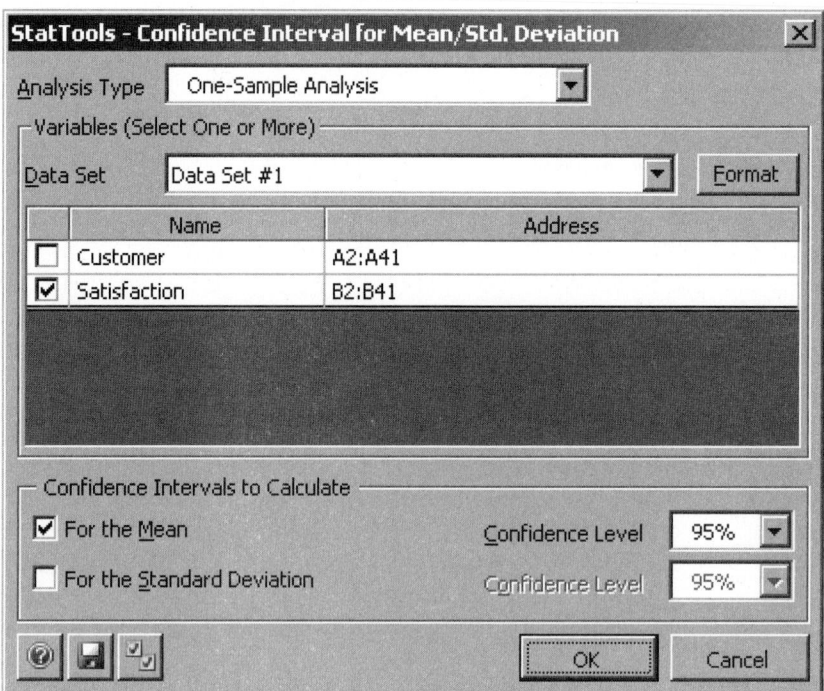

Figure 8.4

Analysis of New
Sandwich Data

	A	B	C	D	E
1	Customer	Satisfaction			Satisfaction
2	1	7		Conf. Intervals (One-Sample)	Data Set #1
3	2	5		Sample Size	40
4	3	5		Sample Mean	6.250
5	4	6		Sample Std Dev	1.597
6	5	8		Confidence Level (Mean)	95.0%
7	6	7		Degrees of Freedom	39
8	7	6		Lower Limit	5.739
9	8	7		Upper Limit	6.761
10	9	10			
11	10	7			
12	11	9			
13	12	5			
39	38	9			
40	39	5			
41	40	4			

obtain the output shown in Figure 8.4. (*Note*: To get the output to be next to the data, select Settings from the StatTools ribbon, and, in the Report group, select either of the last two Placement options.)

The principal results are that (1) the best guess for the population mean rating is 6.250, the sample average in cell E4, and (2) a 95% confidence interval for the population mean rating extends from 5.739 to 6.761, as seen in cells E8 and E9. The manager can be 95% confident that the true mean rating over all customers who might try the sandwich is within this confidence interval.

The degrees of freedom for the t distribution is one less than the sample size, as shown in cell E7. The formulas for the confidence interval limits, in cells E8 and E9, are

To understand where these numbers come from, take a look at the formulas in column E.

equivalent to the general formula in Expression (8.4), but they use special StatTools functions to calculate the *t*-multiples.

We stated previously that as the confidence level increases, the length of the confidence interval increases. You can convince yourself of this by entering different confidence levels such as 90% or 99% in cell E6. The lower and upper limits of the confidence interval in cells E8 and E9 will change automatically, getting closer together for the 90% level and farther apart for the 99% level. Just remember that you, the analyst, can choose the confidence level you favor, although 95% is the level most commonly chosen.

Before leaving this example, we discuss the assumptions that lead to the confidence interval. First, you might question whether the sample is really a *random* sample—or whether it matters. Perhaps the manager used some random mechanism to select the customers to be surveyed. More likely, however, she simply surveyed 40 consecutive customers who tried the sandwich on a given day. This is called a *convenience sample* and is not really a *random* sample. However, unless there is some reason to believe that these 40 customers differ in some relevant aspect from the entire population of customers, it is probably safe to treat them as a random sample.

A second assumption is that the population distribution is *normal*. We made this assumption when we introduced the *t* distribution. Obviously, the population distribution *cannot* be exactly normal because it is concentrated on the 10 possible satisfaction ratings, and the normal distribution describes a continuum. However, this is probably not a problem for two reasons. First, confidence intervals based on the *t* distribution are *robust* to violations of normality. This means that the resulting confidence intervals are valid for any populations that are *approximately* normal. Second, the normal population assumption is less crucial for larger sample sizes because of the central limit theorem. A sample size of 40 should be large enough.

Finally, it is important to recognize what this confidence interval implies and what it doesn't. In the entire population of customers who ordered this sandwich, there is a distribution of satisfaction ratings. Some fraction rate it as 1, some rate it as 2, and so on. All we are trying to determine here is the *average* of all these ratings. Based on the analysis, the manager can be 95% confident that this (still unknown) average is between 5.739 and 6.761. However, this confidence interval doesn't tell her other characteristics of the population of ratings that might be of interest, such as the proportion of customers who rate the sandwich 6 or higher. It only provides information about the *mean* rating. Later in this chapter, you will see how to find a confidence interval for a proportion, which allows you to analyze another important characteristic of a population distribution. ■

In the sandwich example we said that the manager can be 95% confident that the true mean rating is between 5.739 and 6.761. What does this statement really mean? Contrary to what you might expect, it does *not* mean that the true mean lies between 5.739 and 6.761 with probability 0.95. Either the true mean is inside this interval or it is not. The true meaning of a 95% confidence interval is based on the *procedure* used to obtain it. Specifically, if you use this procedure on a large number of random samples, all from the same population, then approximately 95% of the resulting confidence intervals will be "good" ones that include the true mean, and the other 5% will be "bad" ones that do not include the true mean. Unfortunately, when you have only a single sample, as in the sandwich example, you have no way of knowing whether your confidence interval is one of the good ones or one of the bad ones, but you can be 95% confident that you obtained one of the good intervals.

Because this is such an important concept, we illustrate it in Figure 8.5 with simulation. (See the file **Confidence Interval Simulation.xlsx.**) The data in column B are

Figure 8.5 Simulation Demonstration of Confidence Intervals

	A	B	C	D	E	F	G	H
1	Interpretation of a "95% confidence interval"							
2				This simulation uses a *normal* population for illustration. But you could generate the random				
3	Population mean	100		sample from another distribution (e.g., triangular) to see if the confidence intervals are still				
4	Population stdev	20		*valid*, i.e, if the % in cell H7 is about 95%.				
5								
6	Random sample			Random sample			Mean captured?	1
7	61.47		Conf. Intervals (One-Sample)	Data Set #1			% of CI's capturing mean	95.0%
8	90.67		Sample Size	30				
9	115.94		Sample Mean	103.94			Data table to replicate confidence interval	
10	128.39		Sample Std Dev	16.66			Replication	Mean captured?
11	101.11		Confidence Level (Mean)	95.0%				1
12	124.82		Degrees of Freedom	29			1	1
13	92.88		Lower Limit	97.72			2	1
14	121.72		Upper Limit	110.16			3	1
15	117.49						4	1
16	100.24		Graphical representation				5	1
17	115.04		Limit	Height			6	1
18	87.97		97.72	1			7	0
19	108.06		110.16	1			8	1
20	114.35						9	1
21	100.74		Mean	Height			10	1
22	90.80		100	1			11	1
23	83.30						12	1
24	121.87						13	1
25	84.70						14	1
26	82.66						15	1
27	110.82						16	1
28	110.04						17	1
29	84.71						18	1
30	111.35						19	1
31	117.51						20	1
32	138.46						21	1
33	99.58						22	1
34	103.16						23	1
35	94.50						24	1
36	103.79						25	1
37							26	1
38							27	1

This simulation is performed only to illustrate the true meaning of a "95% confidence interval." In any real situation, you obtain only a single random sample and the corresponding confidence interval.

generated randomly from a normal distribution with the *known* values of μ and σ in cells B3 and B4. Next, StatTools's One-Sample Confidence Interval procedure is used to calculate a 95% confidence interval for the true value of μ, exactly as in the sandwich example. However, because the true value of μ is known, it is possible to record a 1 in cell H6 if the true mean is inside the interval and a 0 otherwise. The appropriate formula is

=IF(AND(B3>=D13,B3<=D14),1,0)

Finally, a data table can be used to replicate the simulated results 1000 times.[2] Specifically, the formula in G11 is

=G6

Then to build the data table in the range G11:H1011, leave the row input cell box empty and specify any blank cell as the column input cell. Then the AVERAGE function can be used in cell H7 to find the fraction of 1s in the range G12:G1011.

[2]It can take quite a while to simulate 1000 samples of size 30 in this data table. Therefore, it is a good idea to set the recalculation mode to "automatic except tables." (You can find this option under the Calculation Options dropdown menu on the Formulas ribbon.) That way, the data table recalculates only if you explicitly tell it to (by pressing the F9 key).

You can see that 948 of the simulated confidence intervals (each based on a *different* random sample of size 30) contain the true mean 100. In theory, 950 of the 1000 intervals should cover the true mean, and this is almost exactly what occurred. Of course, in a particular application you might unluckily obtain the seventh sample (in row 18). However, without knowing that the true mean is 100, you would have no way of knowing that you obtained a "bad" interval.

We also show this graphically in the file. (See Figure 8.5.) The small square in this graph is positioned at the known mean and never changes. The blue line represents a particular confidence interval. Put your cursor below this chart in, say, cell C35, and press the Delete key. (This forces a recalculation without recalculating the whole data table.) The position of the blue line will change. About 95% of the time, the blue line will straddle the small square—the confidence interval will include the true mean—but about 1 time out of 20, it will not. This also illustrates the meaning of a "95% confidence interval."

FUNDAMENTAL INSIGHT

True Meaning of a 95% Confidence Interval

Given the data in a particular sample, a 95% confidence interval for the mean will either include the (unknown) population mean or it won't. The true meaning of a 95% confidence interval is that if the same *procedure* is used on many different random samples, about 95% of the resulting confidence intervals will include the population mean, and only about 5% won't. Therefore, you can be 95% confident that any particular confidence interval is a "good" one.

PROBLEMS

Level A

4. A manufacturing company's quality control personnel have recorded the proportion of defective items for each of 500 monthly shipments of one of the computer components that the company produces. The data are in the file **P07_07.xlsx**. The quality control department manager does not have sufficient time to review all of these data. Rather, she would like to examine the proportions of defective items for a sample of these shipments.
   a. Use StatTools to generate a simple random sample of size 25.
   b. Using the sample generated in part **a**, construct a 95% confidence interval for the mean proportion of defective items over all monthly shipments. Assume that the population consists of the proportion of defective items for each of the given 500 monthly shipments.
   c. Interpret the 95% confidence interval constructed in part **b**.
   d. Does the 95% confidence interval contain the actual population mean in this case? If not, explain why not. What proportion of many similarly constructed confidence intervals should include the true population mean?

5. The file **P08_05.xlsx** contains salary data on all NFL players in each of the years 2002 to 2009. Because this file contains all players for each of these years, you can calculate the *population mean* for each year if *population* is defined as all NFL players that year. However, proceed as in the previous chapter to select a random sample of size 50 from the 2009 population. Based on this random sample, calculate a 95% confidence interval for the mean NFL total salary in 2009. Does it contain the population mean? Repeat this procedure several times until you find a random sample where the population mean is *not* included in the confidence interval.

6. The file **P08_06.xlsx** contains data on repetitive task times for each of two workers. John has been doing this task for months, whereas Fred has just started. Each time listed is the time (in seconds) to perform a routine task on an assembly line. The times shown are in chronological order.
   a. Find a 95% confidence interval for the mean time it takes John to perform the task. Do the same for Fred.
   b. Do you believe both of the confidence intervals in part **a** are valid and/or useful? Why or why not? Which of the two workers would you rather have, assuming that task time is the only issue?

7. The manager of a local fast-food restaurant is interested in improving the service provided to customers who use the restaurant's drive-up window. As a first step in this process, the manager asks an assistant to record the time (in seconds) it takes to serve a large number of customers at the final window in the facility's drive-up system. The file **P08_07.xlsx**

contains a random sample of 200 service times during the busiest hour of the day.

a. Identify the relevant population.

b. Construct and interpret a 95% confidence interval for the mean service time of all customers arriving during the busiest hour of the day at this fast-food operation.

c. If the manager wants to improve service, at least during the busiest time of day, does this confidence interval provide useful information? What useful information does it *not* provide?

Level B

8. Continuing Problem 5, generate a random sample of 50 players for each of the eight years in the **P08_05.xlsx** file. For each of these samples, construct a 95% confidence interval for the mean total salary for that year. What is the confidence level that any particular one of these confidence intervals includes the population mean for that year? Is this the same confidence level that *all eight* of these confidence intervals include the respective population means? Why or why not?

9. The **Confidence Interval Simulation.xlsx** generates observations randomly from a *normal* population. Suppose instead that each observation in column A is exponentially distributed with mean 10. (Refer to Section 5.6 for a brief explanation of the exponential distribution.) Unlike a normal distribution, an exponential distribution is very skewed to the right. A value from this distribution can be generated with the formula $=-10*LN(RAND())$. Rerun the simulation, still with sample size 30, with this exponential distribution. Are 95% confidence intervals still *valid*? What does it mean for them to be valid?

10. Answer the questions in the previous problem when the population is a *mixture* of two normal distributions. Specifically, suppose each observation has a 65% chance of coming from a normal distribution with mean 100 and standard deviation 20, and a 35% chance of coming from a normal distribution with mean 200 and standard deviation 40. What is the mean of this mixture distribution? You will need it for the simulation.

8.4 CONFIDENCE INTERVAL FOR A TOTAL[3]

There are situations where a population mean is not the population parameter of most interest. A good example is the auditing example discussed in the previous chapter (Example 7.4). Rather than estimating the mean amount of receivables *per account,* the auditor might be more interested in the *total* amount of all receivables, summed over all accounts. In this section we provide a point estimate and a confidence interval for a population total.

First, we introduce some notation. Let T be a population total we want to estimate, such as the total of all receivables, and let $\hat{T}$ be a point estimate of T based on a simple random sample of size n from a population of size N. We first need a point estimate of T. For the population total T, it is reasonable to sum all of the values in the sample, denoted T_S, and then "project" this total to the population with Equation (8.5), where the second equality follows because the sample total T_S divided by the sample size n is the sample mean $\overline{X}$.

Point Estimate for Population Total

$$\hat{T} = \frac{N}{n} T_S = N\overline{X} \tag{8.5}$$

Equation (8.5) is quite intuitive. For example, suppose there are 1000 accounts in the population, you sample 50 of them, and you observe a sample total of $5000. Then, because only 1/20 of the population was sampled, a natural estimate of the population total is $20 \times \$5000 = \$100,000$.

Like the sample mean $\overline{X}$, the estimate $\hat{T}$ has a sampling distribution. The mean and standard deviation of this sampling distribution are given in Equations (8.6) and (8.7), where σ is again the population standard deviation.

---

[3]This section can be omitted without any loss of continuity.

> **Mean and Standard Error of Point Estimate for Population Total**
>
> $$E(\hat{T}) = T \tag{8.6}$$
>
> $$SE(\hat{T}) = N\sigma/\sqrt{n} \tag{8.7}$$

Because σ is usually unknown, s is used instead of σ to obtain the approximate standard error of $\hat{T}$ given in Equation (8.8). The second equality follows because $s/\sqrt{n}$ is the standard error of $\overline{X}$.

> **Approximate Standard Error of Point Estimate for Population Total**
>
> $$SE(\hat{T}) = Ns/\sqrt{n} = N \times SE(\overline{X}) \tag{8.8}$$

Note from Equation (8.6) that $\hat{T}$ is an unbiased estimate of the population total T. Therefore, it has no tendency to either overestimate or underestimate T.

From equations (8.5) and (8.8), the point estimate of T is the point estimate of the mean multiplied by N, and the standard error of this point estimate is the standard error of the sample mean multiplied by N. This has a very nice consequence. A confidence interval for T can be formed with the following two-step procedure:

1. Find a confidence interval for the sample mean in the usual way.

2. Multiply each endpoint of the confidence interval by the population size N.

We illustrate this procedure in the following example.

EXAMPLE | **8.2 ESTIMATING TOTAL TAX REFUNDS**

The Internal Revenue Service would like to estimate the total net amount of refund due to a particular set of 1,000,000 taxpayers. Each taxpayer will either receive a refund, in which case the net refund is positive, or will have to pay an amount due, in which case the net refund is negative. Therefore the *total* net amount of refund is a natural quantity of interest; it is the net amount the IRS will have to pay out (or receive, if negative). Find a 95% confidence interval for this total using the refunds from a random sample of 500 taxpayers in the file **IRS Refunds.xlsx**.

Objective   To use StatTools's One-Sample Confidence Interval procedure, with an appropriate modification, to find a 95% confidence interval for the total (net) amount the IRS must pay out to these 1,000,000 taxpayers.

Solution

The solution appears in Figure 8.6 (with only part of the sample shown). Although there is no explicit StatTools procedure for dealing with population totals, you can take advantage of the close relationship between the confidence interval for a mean and the confidence interval for a total. First use StatTools to find a 95% confidence interval for the population mean. This output appears in rows 5–11. The average refund per taxpayer in the sample is slightly less than $300 (cell E6), and the standard error of this sample mean (not shown explicitly) is about $26. The confidence interval for the mean (in cells E10 and E11) extends from $244 to $346. This part of the output analyzes the average refund per taxpayer.

Figure 8.6

Confidence Interval for Population Total

	A	B	C	D	E
1	Customer	Refund		Population size	1000000
2	1	$70			
3	2	$1,190			Refund
4	3	$220		*Conf. Intervals (One-Sample)*	Data Set #1
5	4	-$280		Sample Size	500
6	5	$260		Sample Mean	$294.98
7	6	$370		Sample Std Dev	$581.31
8	7	$450		Confidence Level (Mean)	95.0%
9	8	$210		Degrees of Freedom	499
10	9	$1,150		Lower Limit	$243.90
11	10	$270		Upper Limit	$346.06
12	11	$470			
13	12	-$10		Confidence interval for population total	
14	13	-$160		Confidence level	95.0%
15	14	$2,430		Point estimate	$294,980,000
16	15	$140		Standard error	$25,997,048
17	16	-$190		Lower limit	$243,902,836
18	17	-$810		Upper limit	$346,057,164
19	18	-$20			
500	499	$1,840			
501	500	-$20			

Next, project these results to the entire population. This is done in the range E15:E18 by multiplying each of the values in the previous paragraph by the population size, 1,000,000. The IRS can be 95% confident that it will need to pay out somewhere between 244 and 346 million dollars to these 1,000,000 taxpayers. ∎

PROBLEMS

Level A

11. The file **P02_16.xlsx** contains the number of arrivals at a turnpike tollbooth for each of four 5-minute intervals for each of 256 days. For this problem, assume that each column, such as arrivals from 8:00 AM to 8:05 AM, is a random sample of all arrivals from the corresponding hour of the day, such as 8:00 AM to 9:00 AM. Find a 95% confidence interval for the mean number of arrivals during each corresponding hour of the day, that is, one for 8:00 AM to 9:00 AM, one for 9:00 AM to 10:00 AM, and so on.

12. A lightbulb manufacturer wants to estimate the total number of defective bulbs contained in all of the boxes shipped by the company during the past week. Production personnel at this company have recorded the number of defective bulbs found in each of 50 randomly selected boxes shipped during the past week. These data are provided in the file **P08_12.xlsx**. Find a 95% confidence interval for the total number of defective bulbs contained in the 1000 boxes shipped by this company during the past week.

13. Auditors of a particular bank are interested in comparing the reported value of all 2265 customer savings account balances with their own findings regarding the actual value of such assets. Rather than reviewing the records of each savings account at the bank, the auditors decide to examine a representative sample of savings account balances. The population from which they will sample is given in the file **P08_13.xlsx**.
  a. Select 10 simple random samples, each consisting of 100 savings account balances from this population.
  b. For each sample generated in part **a**, construct a 95% confidence interval for the total value of all 2265 savings account balances within this bank. How many of them include the (known) population total?

Level B

14. Suppose you are gambling on a roulette wheel. Each time the wheel is spun, the result is one of the outcomes 0, 1, and so on through 36. Of these outcomes, 16 are red, 16 are black, and 1 is green. On each spin you bet $5 that a red outcome will occur and $1 that the green outcome will occur. If red occurs, you win a net $4. (You win $10 from red and nothing from green.) If green occurs, you win a net $24. (You win $30 from green and nothing from red.) If black occurs, you lose everything you bet for a loss of $6.

a. Use simulation to generate 20 plays from this strategy. Each play should indicate the net amount won or lost. Then, based on these 20 outcomes, find

a 95% confidence interval for the total net amount won or lost from 1000 plays of the game. Would you conclude that this strategy is a winning one for you?

b. Repeat part **a**, but with slightly changed rules. Now your betting strategy is the same, but if red occurs, your net gain is $5 (you win $11 from red, nothing from green). Comment on whether this slight change makes much of a difference in the mean total from 1000 bets.

8.5 CONFIDENCE INTERVAL FOR A PROPORTION

How often have you heard on the evening news a survey finding such as, "52% of the public agree with the president's handling of the economy, with a sampling error of plus or minus 3%"? Surveys are often used to estimate proportions, such as the proportion of the public who agree with the president's handling of the economy. We will now discuss how to form a confidence interval for any population proportion p.

The basic procedure is very similar to the procedure for a population mean. It requires a point estimate, the standard error of this point estimate, and a multiple that depends on the confidence level. Then the confidence level has the same form as in Expression (8.1):

$$\text{point estimate} \pm \text{multiple} \times \text{standard error}$$

In the news example the point estimate is 52% and the "multiple $\times$ standard error" is 3%. Therefore, the confidence interval extends from 49% to 55%. Although the news show doesn't state the confidence level explicitly, it is 95% by convention. In words, they are 95% confident that the percentage of the public who agree with the president's handling of the economy is somewhere between 49% and 55%.

The theory that leads to this result is fairly straightforward. Let A be any property that members of a population either have or do not have. As examples, A might be the property that

- a person agrees with the president's handling of the economy
- a person has purchased a company's product at least once in the past three months
- the diameter of a part is within specification limits
- a customer's account is at least two months overdue
- a customer's rating of a new sandwich is at least 6 on a 10-point scale.

In each of these examples, let p be the proportion of the population with property A. From a random sample of size n, let $\hat{p}$ be the sample proportion of members with property A. For example, if 10 out of 50 sampled members have property A, then $\hat{p} = 10/50 = 0.2$. Then $\hat{p}$ is used as a point estimate of p.

It can be shown that for sufficiently large n, the sampling distribution of $\hat{p}$ is approximately *normal* with mean p and standard error $\sqrt{p(1-p)/n}$. Because p is the unknown parameter, $\hat{p}$ is substituted for p in this standard error to obtain the following approximate standard error of $\hat{p}$:

Standard Error of Sample Proportion

$$\text{SE}(\hat{p}) = \sqrt{\frac{\hat{p}(1-\hat{p})}{n}} \tag{8.9}$$

Finally, the multiple used to obtain a confidence interval for p is a Z-value. It is the standard normal value that cuts off an appropriate probability in each tail. For example, the z-multiple for a 95% confidence interval is 1.96 because this value cuts off probability 0.025 in each tail of the standard normal distribution. In general, the confidence interval has the form in Expression (8.10):

Confidence Interval for a Proportion

$$\hat{p} \pm z\text{-multiple} \times \sqrt{\frac{\hat{p}(1 - \hat{p})}{n}} \qquad \qquad \textbf{(8.10)}$$

This confidence interval is based on the assumption of a large sample size. A rule of thumb for checking the validity of this assumption is the following. Let p_L and p_U be the lower and upper limits of the confidence interval. Then the sample size is sufficiently large—and the confidence interval is valid—if $np_L > 5$, $n(1 - p_L) > 5$, $np_U > 5$, and $n(1 - p_U) > 5$. Essentially, these mean that n should be reasonably large and the two values of p should not be too close to 0 or 1.

We illustrate the procedure in the following example.

EXAMPLE	**8.3 ESTIMATING THE RESPONSE TO A NEW SANDWICH**

The fast-food manager from Example 8.2 has already sampled 40 customers to estimate the population mean rating of the restaurant's new sandwich. Recall that each rating is on a 1-to-10 scale, 10 being the best. The manager would now like to use the same sample to estimate the proportion of customers who rate the sandwich at least 6. Her thinking is that these are the customers who are likely to purchase the sandwich on subsequent visits.

Objective   To illustrate the procedure for finding a confidence interval for the proportion of customers who rate the new sandwich at least 6 on a 10-point scale.

Solution

The solution appears in Figure 8.7.[4] (See the file **Satisfaction Ratings.xlsx**.) It is first useful to create a 0/1 column that indicates whether a customer's rating is at least 6. To do this, enter the formula

$=\text{IF}(\text{B2}>=6,1,0)$

Figure 8.7

Confidence Interval for Proportion

	A	B	C	D	E	F
1	Customer	Satisfaction	At least 6?		Confidence interval based on column C	
2	1	7	1			At least 6?
3	2	5	0		Conf. Interval (Proportion)	Data Set #2
4	3	5	0		Category	1
5	4	6	1		Sample Size	40
6	5	8	1		Sample Proportion	0.625
7	6	7	1		Confidence Level	95.0%
8	7	6	1		Standard Error of Proportion	0.077
9	8	7	1		Lower Limit	0.475
10	9	10	1		Upper Limit	0.775
11	10	7	1			
12	11	9	1			
13	12	5	0			

[4]The solution shown here is new. Starting in version 5.5, StatTools performs statistical inference on proportions, either a single proportion or the difference between two proportions.

in cell C2 and copy it down. Next, designate a StatTools data set that includes this new column. (It can include columns A and B, but they are not relevant for the confidence interval.) Finally, select Confidence Interval from the Statistical Inference dropdown list, and select Proportion. Then fill out the dialog box as shown in Figure 8.8. Specifically, check the 1 in the Categories to Analyze section to analyze the proportion of 1s, not the proportion of 0s.

Figure 8.8
StatTools Dialog Box
for Confidence
Interval for
Proportion

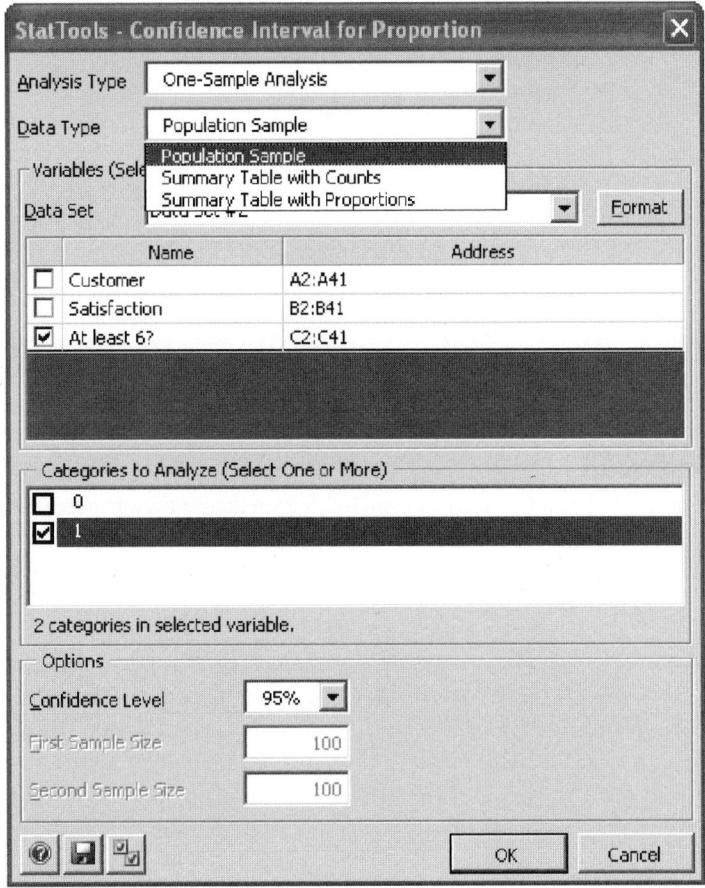

As the Data Type dropdown list indicates, the data for the confidence interval can be in three formats: (1) a sample of 0s and 1s, as in this example, (2) a summary table with counts, or (3) a summary table with proportions. These latter two options are also illustrated in the finished version of the **Satisfaction Ratings.xlsx** file. The reason for these options is that you could very easily start with a table of counts or proportions, rather than a long column of 0s and 1s. StatTools (version 5.5 and later) accommodates these possibilities.

Finally, using the confidence interval limits, $p_L = 0.475$ and $p_U = 0.775$, you can check the assumption of sufficiently large sample size. With $n = 40$, np_L, $n(1 - p_L)$, np_U, and $n(1 - p_U)$ are all well above 5, so that the validity of this confidence interval is established.

The output is fairly good news for the manager. Based on this sample of size 40, she can be 95% confident that the percentage of all customers who would rate the sandwich 6 or higher is somewhere between 47.5% and 77.5%. Of course, she realizes that this is a very wide interval, so there is still a lot of uncertainty about the *true* population proportion. To reduce the length of this interval, she would need to sample more customers—quite a few more customers. Typically, confidence intervals for proportions are fairly wide unless n is quite large. ■

We explore this final statement a bit more. Referring again to news shows, you have probably noticed that they almost always quote a sampling error of plus or minus 3%. In words, the "plus or minus" part of their 95% confidence interval is 3%, or 0.03. How large a sample size must they use to achieve this? The "plus or minus" part of the confidence interval is 1.96 times the standard error of $\hat{p}$, so we must have

$$1.96 \times \sqrt{\hat{p}(1 - \hat{p})/n} = 0.03$$

Now, the quantity $\hat{p}(1 - \hat{p})$ is fairly constant for values of $\hat{p}$ between 0 and 1, provided that $\hat{p}$ isn't too close to 0 or 1. To get a reasonable estimate of the required n, we use $\hat{p} = 0.5$. Then we have

$$1.96 \times \sqrt{(0.5)(0.5)/n} = 0.03$$

Solving for n, we obtain $n = [(1.96)(0.5)/0.03]^2 \approx 1067$.

This is a rather remarkable result. To obtain a 95% confidence interval of this length for a population proportion, where the population consists of millions of people, only about 1000 people need to be sampled. The remarkable fact is that this small a sample can provide such accurate information about such a large population.

FUNDAMENTAL INSIGHT

Sample Size for Estimating a Proportion

To obtain an estimate of a proportion that is accurate to within 3 percentage points with 95% confidence, it is sufficient to sample approximately 1000 members of the population, *regardless of the population size*. This remarkable fact allows news broadcasters to make such statements about various proportions on a nightly basis. By sampling only about 1000 people from the entire country, they can estimate very nearly what the entire population believes.

One of many business applications of confidence intervals for proportions is in auditing. Auditors typically use *attribute sampling* to check whether certain procedures are being followed correctly. The term "attribute" means that each item checked is done either correctly or incorrectly—there is no in-between. Examples of items not done correctly might include (1) an invoice copy that is not initialed by an accounting clerk, (2) an invoice quantity that does not agree with the quantity on the shipping document, (3) an invoice price that does not agree with the price on an authorized price list, and (4) an invoice with a clerical inaccuracy. Typically, an auditor focuses on one of these types of errors and then estimates the proportion of items with this type of error.

Because auditors are concerned primarily with how *large* the proportion of errors might be, they usually calculate *one-sided* confidence intervals for proportions. Instead of using sample data to find lower and upper limits p_L and p_U of a confidence interval, they automatically use $p_L = 0$ and then determine an upper limit p_U such that the 95% confidence interval is from 0 to p_U. A simple modification of the confidence interval in Expression (8.10) provides the result in Equation (8.11), where the z-multiple is chosen so that the entire probability (0.05 for a 95% interval) is in the right-hand tail. For a 95% confidence level, the relevant z-multiple is 1.645.

One further complication occurs, however. This formula for p_U relies on the large-sample approximation of the normal distribution to the binomial distribution. Auditors typically use an *exact* procedure to find p_U that is based directly on the binomial distribution. We illustrate how this is done in the following example.

Upper Limit of a One-Sided Confidence Interval for a Proportion

$$p_U = \hat{p} + z\text{-multiple} \times \sqrt{\hat{p}(1 - \hat{p})/n} \tag{8.11}$$

8.4 AUDITING FOR PRICE ERRORS

An auditor wants to check the proportion of invoices that contain price errors—that is, prices that do not agree with those on an authorized price list. He checks 93 randomly sampled invoices and finds that two of them include price errors. What can he conclude, in terms of a one-sided 95% confidence interval, about the proportion of all invoices with price errors?

Objective   To find the upper limit of a one-sided 95% confidence interval for the proportion of errors in the context of attribute sampling in auditing.

Solution

The results appear in Figure 8.9, where StatTools has *not* been used because it does not include a procedure for one-sided confidence intervals. (See the file **One-Sided Confidence Interval.xlsx**.) The sample proportion is p = 2/93 = 0.0215 and the upper confidence limit based on the large-sample approximation is 0.046. This latter value is calculated in cell B14 with the formula

=B7+B13*SQRT(B7*(1-B7)/B5)

However, note that $np_U = 93(0.046) = 4.278$, which is less than 5. This indicates that the large-sample approximation is not very accurate.

Figure 8.9

Analysis of Auditing Example

	A	B	C	D	E	F
1	An exact one-sided confidence interval in auditing					
2						
3	Confidence level	95%				
4	Number of errors	2				
5	Sample size	93				
6						
7	Sample proportion	0.0215				
8						
9	Exact upper confidence limit for p			Goal seek condition		
10	Upper limit	0.066		0.050	=	0.05
11						
12	Large-sample upper confidence limit for p					
13	z-multiple	1.645				
14	Upper limit	0.046				

A more accurate procedure, based on the binomial distribution, appears in row 10. It turns out that if p_U is the appropriate upper confidence limit, then p_U satisfies the equation

$$P(X \leq k) = \alpha \tag{8.12}$$

Here, X is binomially distributed with parameters n and p_U, k is the observed number of errors, and α is one minus the confidence level. There is no way to find p_U directly (by means of a formula) from Equation (8.12). However, you can use Excel's Goal Seek tool. First, enter *any* trial value of p_U in cell B10 and the binomial formula

=BINOMDIST(B4,B5,B10,1)

in cell D10. (This formula calculates $P(X \le k)$ from the trial value in cell B10.) Then use Goal Seek from the What-If Analysis dropdown menu on the Data ribbon, with cell D10 as the Set cell, 0.05 as the target value, and cell B10 as the Changing cell. (See Figure 8.10.)

Figure 8.10

Settings in Goal Seek Dialog Box

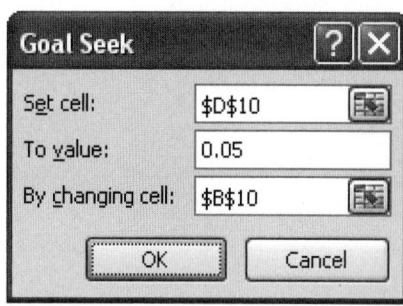

The resulting value of p_U is 0.066. This is considerably different (from the auditor's point of view) from the 0.046 value found from the large-sample approximation. It allows the auditor to state with 95% confidence that the percentage of invoices with price errors is no greater than 6.6%, based on the two errors out of 93 observed in the sample. ■

PROBLEMS

Level A

15. A drugstore manager needs to purchase adequate supplies of various brands of toothpaste to meet the ongoing demands of its customers. In particular, the company is interested in estimating the proportion of its customers who favor the country's leading brand of toothpaste, Crest. The Data sheet of the file **P08_15.xlsx** contains the toothpaste brand preferences of 200 randomly selected customers, obtained recently through a customer survey. Find a 95% confidence interval for the proportion of all of the company's customers who prefer Crest toothpaste. How might the manager use this confidence interval for purchasing decisions?

16. The same data as in the previous problem are stored in a different format in the last two sheets of the **P08_15.xlsx** file.
   a. Use StatTools to find a 95% confidence interval for the proportion who favor Crest from the data in the Counts sheet. Using this same data on counts, calculate the confidence interval directly from the appropriate formulas, without using StatTools.
   b. Use StatTools to find a 95% confidence interval for the proportion who favor Crest from the data in the proportions sheet. Using this same data on proportions, calculate the confidence interval directly from the appropriate formulas, without using StatTools.

17. The employee benefits manager of a large public university would like to estimate the proportion of full-time employees who prefer adopting the first (plan A) of three available health care plans in the next annual enrollment period. A random sample of the university's employees and their tentative health care preferences are given in the file **P08_17.xlsx**.
   a. Find a 90% confidence interval for the proportion of all the university's employees who favor plan A.
   b. The file also includes the classification of each employee (administrative staff, support staff, or faculty). Find a separate 90% confidence interval for each of these groups for the proportion who favor plan A. How do these confidence intervals compare to one another? How do their lengths compare to the confidence interval in part **a**? Is this what you would expect? Explain.

18. A market research consultant hired by a leading soft-drink company wants to determine the proportion of consumers who favor its low-calorie brand over the leading low-calorie competitor in a particular geographic region. A random sample of 250 consumers from the market under investigation is provided in **P08_18.xlsx**.
   a. Find a 90% confidence interval for the proportion of all consumers in this market who prefer the company's brand.
   b. The file contains the gender and age group for each customer in the sample. Find a separate 90% confidence for each gender for the proportion who prefer the company's brand. Then do the same for

each age group. Explain briefly how these confidence intervals compare to each other and to the confidence interval in part **a**.

Level B

19. Starting with the data from problem 17 in the file **P08_17.xlsx**, restructure the data so that you have a table of counts. Then use StatTools on the counts to answer the same questions as in problem 17.

20. Starting with the data from problem 18 in the file **P08_18.xlsx**, restructure the data so that you have a table of proportions. Then use StatTools on the proportions to answer the same questions as in problem 18.

8.6 CONFIDENCE INTERVAL FOR A STANDARD DEVIATION[5]

In Section 8.3 we focused primarily on estimation of a population *mean*. We had to deal with the population standard deviation σ in its role as a nuisance parameter. That is, we needed an estimate of σ to estimate the standard error of the sample mean. However, there are cases where the variability in the population, measured by σ, is of interest in its own right. We briefly describe a procedure for obtaining a confidence interval for σ in this section.

The theory is somewhat more complex than for the case of the mean. As you might expect, the sample standard deviation s is used as a point estimate of σ. However, the sampling distribution of s is not symmetric—in particular, it is not the normal distribution or the t distribution. Rather, the appropriate sampling distribution is a right-skewed distribution called the **chi-square distribution**. Like the t distribution, the chi-square distribution has a degrees of freedom parameter, which (for this procedure) is again $n - 1$.

Tables of the chi-square distribution, for selected degrees of freedom, appear in many statistics books, but the necessary information can be obtained more easily with Excel's CHIDIST and CHIINV functions. The CHIDIST function takes the form

=**CHIDIST**(v,df)

This function returns the probability to the *right* of value v when the degrees of freedom parameter is df. Similarly, the CHIINV function takes the form

=**CHIINV**(p,df)

This returns the value with probability p to the *right* of it when the degrees of freedom parameter is df.

CHANGES IN EXCEL 2010

These chi-square functions have been changed considerably in Excel 2010. There are now CHISQ.DIST and CHISQ.INV functions for *left* tails, and CHISQ.DIST has a last "cum" argument just like NORM.DIST and T.DIST. Also, there are two functions, CHISQ.DIST.RT and CHISQ.INV.RT, for *right* tails.

We do not present the rather complex confidence interval formulas for σ. However, we point out that because of the skewness of the sampling distribution of s, a confidence interval for σ is *not* centered at s. That is, the confidence interval is *not* the point estimate plus or minus a multiple of a standard error. Instead, s is always closer to the left endpoint of the confidence interval than to the right endpoint, as indicated in Figure 8.11.

---

[5]This section can be omitted without any loss of continuity.

Figure 8.11

Confidence Interval
for Standard
Deviation

Lower limit   Sample stdev *s*   Upper limit

The StatTools One-Sample Confidence Interval procedure enables you to obtain a confidence interval for a population standard deviation as easily as for a mean. We illustrate this in the following example.

EXAMPLE 8.5 ANALYZING VARIABILITY IN DIAMETERS OF MACHINE PARTS

A machine produces parts that are supposed to have diameter 10 centimeters. However, due to inherent variability, some diameters are greater than 10 and some are less. The production supervisor is concerned about two things. First, he is concerned that the mean diameter is not what it should be, 10 centimeters. Second, he is worried about the extent of variability in the diameters. Even if the mean is on target, excessive variability implies that many of the parts will fail to meet specifications. To analyze the process, he randomly samples 50 parts during the course of a day and measures the diameter of each part to the nearest millimeter. The results are shown in columns A and B of Figure 8.12. (See the file **Part Diameters.xlsx**.) Should the supervisor be concerned about the results from this sample?

Figure 8.12   Analysis of Parts Data

	A	B	C	D	E	F	G	H	I
1	Part	Diameter			**Diameter**				
2	1	10.031		*Conf. Intervals (One-Sample)*	Data Set #1				
3	2	10.011		Sample Size	50				
4	3	10.003		Sample Mean	9.996				
5	4	10.025		Sample Std Dev	0.034				
6	5	10.048		Confidence Level (Mean)	95.0%				
7	6	10.014		Degrees of Freedom	49				
8	7	10.030		Lower Limit	9.986				
9	8	10.008		Upper Limit	10.005				
10	9	10.049		Confidence Level (Std Dev)	95.0%				
11	10	9.995		Degrees of Freedom	49				
12	11	9.965		Lower Limit	0.029				
13	12	10.003		Upper Limit	0.043				
14	13	9.959							
15	14	10.013		**Proportion of unusable parts**					
16	15	10.012		Maximum deviation for usability	0.065				
17	16	10.005		Assumed mean	10				
18	17	9.921		Assumed standard deviation	0.043				
19	18	9.930		Proportion unusuable	0.131				
20	19	9.990							
21	20	9.948		**Twoway data table for finding proportion unusable as a function of mean and stdev**					
22	21	10.077			Assumed standard deviation				
23	22	9.959			0.131	0.029	0.034	0.043	
24	23	10.000		Assumed mean	9.986	0.041	0.080	0.149	
25	24	9.998			9.996	0.025	0.060	0.130	
26	25	9.983			10.005	0.026	0.061	0.131	
27	26	9.995							
49	48	10.009							
50	49	9.973							
51	50	9.970							

Objective To use StatTools's One-Sample Confidence Interval procedure to find a confidence interval for the standard deviation of part diameters, and to see how variability affects the proportion of unusable parts produced.

Solution

Because the manager is concerned about the mean *and* the standard deviation of diameters, it is useful to obtain 95% confidence intervals for both. This is easy to do with StatTools's One-Sample Confidence Interval procedure for Mean/Std. Deviation. Go through the same dialog box as before (see Figure 8.3), but now check the boxes for both confidence interval options—mean and standard deviation. The top part of the output in Figure 8.12 (through cell E9) provides a 95% confidence interval for the mean. This confidence interval extends from 9.986 cm to 10.005 cm. Therefore, there is probably not too much cause for concern about the mean. The supervisor can be fairly confident that the mean diameter of all parts is close to 10 cm.

The bottom part of the output (the range E10:E13) provides a 95% confidence interval for the standard deviation of diameters. This interval extends from 0.029 cm to 0.043 cm. Is this good news or bad news? It depends. Let's say that a part is unusable if its diameter is more than 0.065 cm from the target. Let's also assume that the true mean is right on target and that the standard deviation is at the *upper* end of the confidence interval, that is, $\sigma = 0.043$ cm. Finally, assume that the population distribution of diameters is normal. Then the calculation in cell E19 shows that 13.1% of the parts will be unusable. The formula in cell E19 is

=NORMDIST(10-E16,E17,E18,1)+(1-NORMDIST(10+E16,E17,E18,1))

It adds the normal probabilities of being below or above the usable range.

To pursue this analysis one step further, a two-way data table in the range E23:H26 is useful. The means used in column E are the lower confidence limit, the sample mean, and the upper confidence limit. Similarly, the assumed standard deviations used in row 23 are the lower confidence limit, the sample standard deviation, and the upper confidence limit. To form the table, enter the formula **=E19** in cell E23, highlight the range E23:H26, and create a data table with cells E18 and E17 as the row and column input cells.

Each value in the body of the data table is the resulting proportion of unusable parts. Obviously, a mean close to the target and a small standard deviation are best, but even this best-case scenario results in 2.5% unusable parts (see cell F25). However, a mean off target and a large standard deviation can lead to as many as 14.9% unusable parts (see cell H24). In any case, the message for the supervisor is clear—he must work to reduce the underlying variability in the process. This variability is hurting him much more than an off-target mean. ∎

PROBLEMS

Level A

21. Senior management of a large consulting firm is concerned about a growing decline in the organization's weekly number of billable hours. Ideally, the organization expects each professional employee to spend *at least* 40 hours per week on work. The file **P08_21.xlsx** contains the work hours reported by a random sample of employees in a typical week.
  a. Find a 95% confidence interval for the *mean* number of hours worked by the company's employees in a typical week.
  b. Find a 95% confidence interval for the *standard deviation* of the number of hours worked by the company's employees in a typical week.

c. Given the target range of 40 to 60 hours of work per week, should senior management be concerned about the number of hours their employees are currently devoting to work? Explain how the answers to *both* parts **a** and **b** help to answer this question.

Level B

22. The file **P08_06.xlsx** contains data on repetitive task times for each of two workers. John has been doing this task for months, whereas Fred has just started.

Each time listed is the time (in seconds) to perform a routine task on an assembly line. The times shown are in chronological order.

a. Find a 95% confidence interval for the standard deviation of times for John. Do the same for Fred. What do these indicate?

b. Given that these times are listed chronologically, how useful are the confidence intervals in part **a**? Specifically, is there any evidence that the variation in times is changing through time for either of the two workers?

8.7 CONFIDENCE INTERVAL FOR THE DIFFERENCE BETWEEN MEANS

One of the most important applications of statistical inference is the comparison of two population means. There are many applications to business, including the following.

Applications of Comparisons of Means in Business

- Men and women shop at a retail clothing store. The manager would like to know how much more (or less), on average, a woman spends on a typical purchase occasion than a man.

- Two airline companies fly similar routes. A consumer organization would like to check how much the average delay differs between the two airlines, where delay is defined as the actual arrival time at the destination minus the scheduled arrival time.

Statisticians call these general types of problems "comparison problems." They are among the most important types of problems tackled with statistical methods.

- A supermarket chain mails coupons for various products to a randomly selected subset of its customers in a particular city. Its other customers in this city receive no such coupons. The chain would like to check how much the average amount spent on these products differs between the two sets of customers over the next couple of months.

- A computer company has a customer service center that responds to customers' questions and complaints. The center employs two types of people: those who have had a recent course in dealing with customers (but little actual experience) and those with a lot of experience dealing with customers (but no formal course). The company would like to know how these two types of employees differ with respect to the average number of customer complaints of poor service in the last six months.

- A consulting company hires business students directly out of undergraduate school. The new hires all take a problem-solving test. They then go through an intensive three-month training program, after which they take another similar problem-solving test. The company wants to know how much the average test score improves after the training program.

- A car dealership often deals with husband–wife pairs shopping for cars. To check whether husbands react differently than their wives to the sales presentation, husbands and wives are asked (separately) to rate the quality of the sales presentation. The dealership wants to know how much husbands differ from their wives in terms of average ratings.

Each of these examples deals with a difference between means from two populations. However, the first four examples differ in one important respect from the last two. In the last two examples, there is a natural *pairing* across the two samples. In the first of these, each employee takes a test before a course and then a test after the course, so that each employee is naturally paired with himself or herself. In the final example, husbands and wives are naturally paired with one another. There is no such pairing in the first four examples. Instead, we assume that the samples in these first four examples are chosen *independently* of one another. For statistical reasons we need to distinguish these two cases, *independent samples* and *paired samples*, in the discussion that follows.

8.7.1 Independent Samples

The framework for this situation is the following. We are interested in some quantity, such as dollars spent or airplane delay, for each of two populations. The population means are μ_1 and μ_2, and the population standard deviations are σ_1 and σ_2. We take random samples of sizes n_1 and n_2 (which need not be equal) from the populations to estimate the difference between means, $\mu_1 - \mu_2$. A point estimate of this difference is the natural one, the difference between sample means, $\overline{X}_1 - \overline{X}_2$. Starting with this estimate, we want to form a confidence interval for the unknown population mean difference, $\mu_1 - \mu_2$.

It can be shown mathematically that the appropriate sampling distribution of the difference between sample means is again the t distribution, now with $n_1 + n_2 - 2$ degrees of freedom.[6] Therefore, a confidence interval for $\mu_1 - \mu_2$ is given by Expression (8.13). The t-multiple is the value that cuts off the appropriate probability (depending on the confidence level) in each tail of the t distribution with $n_1 + n_2 - 2$ degrees of freedom. For example, if the confidence level is 95% and $n_1 = n_2 = 30$, the appropriate t-multiple is 2.002, which can be found in Excel with the function **TINV(0.05,58)** (or **T.INV(0.025,58)** in Excel 2010).

Confidence Interval for Difference Between Means
$$\overline{X}_1 - \overline{X}_2 \pm t\text{-multiple} \times SE(\overline{X}_1 - \overline{X}_2) \tag{8.13}$$

The standard error, $SE(\overline{X}_1 - \overline{X}_2)$, is more involved. We must first make the assumption that the population standard deviations are equal, that is, $\sigma_1 = \sigma_2$. (We shortly present an alternative procedure for the situation where the population standard deviations are *not* equal.) Then an estimate of this common standard deviation is provided by the "pooled" estimate from both samples, labeled s_p.

Pooled Estimate of Common Standard Deviation
$$s_p = \sqrt{\frac{(n_1 - 1)s_1^2 + (n_2 - 1)s_2^2}{n_1 + n_2 - 2}}$$

Here, s_1 and s_2 are the sample standard deviations from the two samples. This pooled estimate is somewhere between s_1 and s_2, with the relative sample sizes determining its exact value. Then the standard error of $\overline{X}_1 - \overline{X}_2$ is given by Equation (8.14):

---

[6]This assumes that either the population distributions are normal or that the sample sizes are reasonably large, conditions that are at least approximately met in a wide variety of applications.

Standard Error of Difference Between Sample Means

$$\mathrm{SE}(\overline{X}_1 - \overline{X}_2) = s_{\mathrm{p}}\sqrt{\frac{1}{n_1} + \frac{1}{n_2}} \quad \textbf{(8.14)}$$

Fortunately, the StatTools Two-Sample Confidence Interval procedure takes care of these calculations, as illustrated in the following example.

EXAMPLE 8.6 Reliability of Treadmill Motors at the SureStep Company

The SureStep Company manufactures high-quality treadmills for use in exercise clubs. SureStep currently purchases its motors for these treadmills from supplier A. However, it is considering a change to supplier B, which offers a slightly lower cost. The only question is whether supplier B's motors are as reliable as supplier A's. To check this, SureStep installs motors from supplier A on 30 of its treadmills and motors from supplier B on another 30 of its treadmills. It then runs these treadmills under typical conditions and, for each treadmill, records the number of hours until the motor fails. The data from this experiment appear in Figure 8.13. (See the file **Treadmill Motors.xlsx**.) What can SureStep conclude?

Figure 8.13 Analysis of Treadmill Motors Data

	A	B	C	D	E	F
1	Supplier A	Supplier B			Supplier A	Supplier B
2	1358	658		*Sample Summaries*	Data Set #1	Data Set #1
3	793	404		Sample Size	30	30
4	587	735		Sample Mean	748.80	655.67
5	608	457		Sample Std Dev	283.88	259.99
6	472	431				
7	562	658			Equal	Unequal
8	879	453		*Conf. Intervals (Difference of Means)*	Variances	Variances
9	575	488		Confidence Level	95.0%	95.0%
10	1293	522		Sample Mean Difference	93.13	93.13
11	1457	1247		Standard Error of Difference	70.281	70.281
12	705	1095		Degrees of Freedom	58	58
13	623	430		Lower Limit	-47.549	-47.549
14	725	726		Upper Limit	233.815	233.815
15	569	793				
16	424	498				
17	436	502		*Equality of Variances Test*		
18	1250	589		Ratio of Sample Variances	1.1923	
19	493	975		p-Value	0.6390	
20	485	808				
21	462	456				
29	791	846				
30	684	732				
31	666	507				

Objective To use StatTools's Two-Sample Confidence Interval procedure to find a confidence interval for the difference between mean lifetimes of motors, and to see how this confidence interval can help SureStep choose the better supplier.

Solution

In any comparison problem it is a good idea to look initially at side-by-side box plots of the two samples. These appear in Figure 8.14. These show that (1) the distributions of times until failure are skewed to the right for each supplier, (2) the mean for supplier A is somewhat greater than the mean for supplier B, and (3) there are several mild outliers. There seems to be little doubt that supplier A's motors will last longer on average than supplier B's—or is there? A confidence interval for the mean difference allows you to see whether the differences apparent in the box plots can be generalized to *all* motors from the two suppliers.

Figure 8.14
Box Plots for
Treadmill Motors
Data

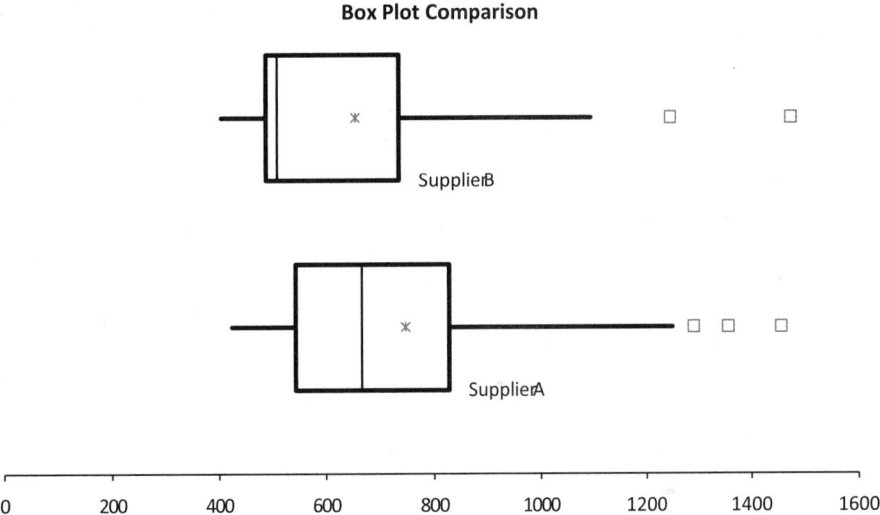

You can find this confidence interval by using the StatTools Two-Sample Confidence Interval procedure. To do so, select Confidence Interval and Mean/Std. Deviation from the StatTools Statistical Inference dropdown list, and fill in the resulting dialog box as shown in Figure 8.15. Specifically, make sure the Analysis Type dropdown list shows Two-Sample Analysis, and click on the Format button to make sure the Unstacked option is checked. You will then see the dialog box in Figure 8.16. By default, the difference analyzed will be "A minus B," but you can change it to "B minus A" by clicking on the Reverse Order button. For now, click on OK. This produces the output in Figure 8.13. The top part of the output summarizes the two samples. It shows that the sample means differ by approximately 93 hours and the sample standard deviations are of roughly the same magnitude.

StatTools Tip *The data are "unstacked" because there are separate columns for supplier A's times and supplier B's times. The Format button in the StatTools dialog box allows you to select the appropriate option: Stacked or Unstacked.*

The confidence interval calculations appear in the range E9:E14. The difference between sample means is 93.133 hours, the standard error of the sample mean difference is 70.281 hours, and a 95% confidence interval for the mean difference extends from

Figure 8.15

Dialog Box for Two-Sample Procedure

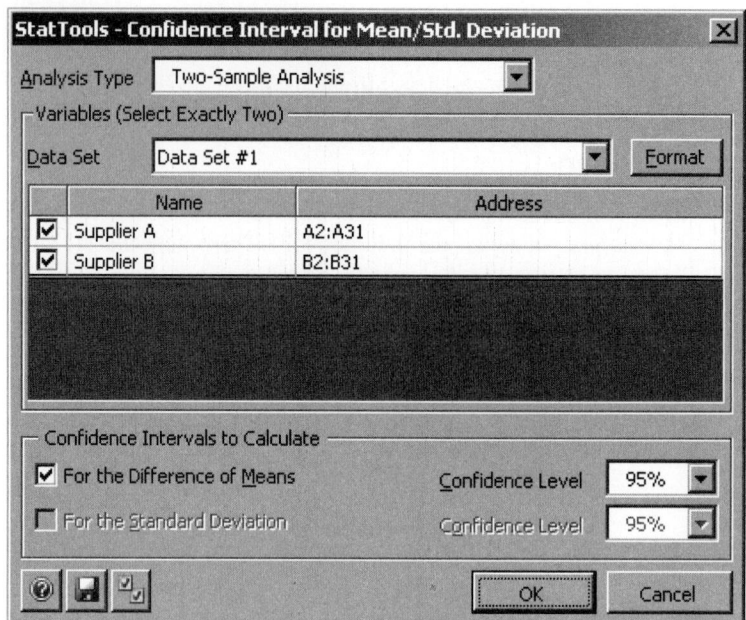

Figure 8.16

Dialog Box for Reversing the Difference

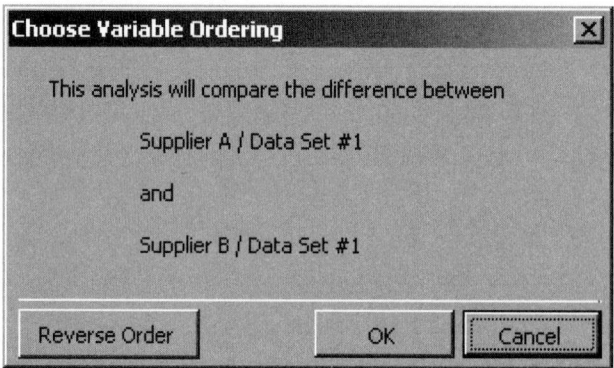

−47.549 to 233.815 hours. Not only is this interval quite wide, but it extends from a negative value to a positive value. If SureStep had to make a guess, it would say that supplier A's motors last longer on average than supplier B's. But because of the negative part of the confidence interval, there is still a possibility that the opposite is true.

Should SureStep continue with supplier A? This depends on the trade-off between the cost of the motors and warranty costs (and any other relevant costs). Because the warranty probably depends on whether a motor lasts a certain amount of time, warranty costs probably depend on a *proportion* (the proportion that fail before 500 hours, say) rather than a mean. Therefore, we postpone further discussion of this issue until we discuss differences between proportions in Section 8.8. ■

Equal-Variance Assumption

This two-sample analysis makes the strong assumption that the standard deviations (or variances) from the two populations are equal. How can you tell if they are equal, and what do you do if they are clearly *not* equal?

To check whether they are equal, first look at the two sample standard deviations. If they are of widely different magnitudes, this certainly casts doubt on the equal-variance assumption. The sample standard deviations in the treadmill example, 283.88 and 259.98, are of similar magnitudes and present no clear evidence of unequal population variances. However, a statistical test for equality of two population variances is automatically shown at the bottom of the StatTools Two-Sample output. Because we have not yet discussed hypothesis testing, we postpone the discussion of this test for now. Suffice it to say that the test presents no evidence of unequal variances for this example.

If there is reason to believe that the population variances are unequal, then a slightly different procedure can be used to calculate a confidence interval for the difference between means. The appropriate standard error of $\overline{X}_1 - \overline{X}_2$ is now

$$\text{SE}(\overline{X}_1 - \overline{X}_2) = \sqrt{s_1^2/n_1 + s_2^2/n_2}$$

and the degrees of freedom used to find the t-multiple is given by a complex expression not shown here.

StatTools always calculates the results in both columns. When they are nearly the same, as they often are, it makes no practical difference which you quote.

StatTools's Two-Sample procedure automatically calculates the confidence interval under this unequal-variance assumption. For the treadmill example the results are in the range F9:F14 of Figure 8.13. In this example they are exactly the same as the results (in column E), which makes the equal-variance assumption. This is a consequence of equal sample sizes and roughly equal sample variances. In general, the two results differ appreciably only when the sample sizes *and* the sample variances differ considerably across samples. In any case, the appropriate results to use are those on the right (column F) if there is reason to suspect unequal population variances and those on the left (column E) otherwise.

FUNDAMENTAL INSIGHT

Role of Variances in Estimating the Difference Between Means

It might be surprising that variances (or standard deviations) play such an important role in estimating the difference between means, but this is actually quite intuitive. If there is a lot of variability in the populations, it is more difficult to get accurate estimates of the population means, and hence the difference between the means. But if there is very little variability, it is much easier to estimate the means accurately.

We next examine customer waiting lines in a supermarket. We again make a comparison between two means, this time the mean number of customers in line during rush times versus normal times. There are two objectives in this example. First, it provides one more illustration of the two-sample procedure, now with unequal sample sizes. Perhaps more importantly, it illustrates that not all data sets come ready-made for performing a particular analysis. Some data manipulation is necessary before StatTools's Two-Sample procedure can be used. Indeed, this is sometimes the most time-consuming part of statistical analysis in real applications—getting the data ready for the analysis.

EXAMPLE | **8.7 ANALYZING CUSTOMER WAITING AT R&P SUPERMARKET**

The manager of the R&P Supermarket has collected a week's worth of data on customer arrivals, departures, and waiting. There are 48 observations per day, each taken at the end of a half-hour period. The data appear in the file **Customer Checkouts.xlsx**. The various times of day are listed in the TimeInterval variable. (See Figure 8.17.) They include Morning Rush, Morning, Lunch Rush, Afternoon, Afternoon Rush, Evening, and Night. (The comment in cell C3 explains exactly which time intervals these refer to.) There is also a variable, EndWaiting, that records the number of customers still being served or waiting in line at the end of each half-hour period.

Figure 8.17 Original Data for Supermarket Example

	A	B	C	D	E	F	G	H	I
1	Day	StartTime	TimeInterval	InitialWaiting	Arrivals	Departures	EndWaiting	Checkers	TotalCustomers
2	Mon	8:00 AM	Morning rush	2	21	22	1	3	23
3	Mon	8:30 AM	Morning rush	1	25	18	8	3	26
4	Mon	9:00 AM	Morning	8	27	28	7	3	35
5	Mon	9:30 AM	Morning	7	21	23	5	3	28
6	Mon	10:00 AM	Morning	5	20	23	2	5	25
7	Mon	10:30 AM	Morning	2	36	31	7	5	38
8	Mon	11:00 AM	Morning	7	30	36	1	5	37
9	Mon	11:30 AM	Lunch rush	1	34	29	6	5	35
10	Mon	12:00 PM	Lunch rush	6	56	48	14	7	62
11	Mon	12:30 PM	Lunch rush	14	58	64	8	7	72
12	Mon	1:00 PM	Lunch rush	8	53	52	9	7	61
13	Mon	1:30 PM	Afternoon	9	30	36	3	5	39
14	Mon	2:00 PM	Afternoon	3	34	31	6	5	37
15	Mon	2:30 PM	Afternoon	6	36	37	5	5	42
16	Mon	3:00 PM	Afternoon	5	30	28	7	5	35
17	Mon	3:30 PM	Afternoon	7	29	34	2	5	36
18	Mon	4:00 PM	Afternoon	2	35	33	4	5	37
19	Mon	4:30 PM	Afternoon rush	4	32	25	11	5	36

The manager would like to check whether the average value of EndWaiting differs during rush periods from normal, non-night periods. She is concerned that there might be excessive waiting during rush periods, in which case she might need to add more checkout people during these times. She plans to exclude the night period from the analysis because she knows from experience that customers very seldom need to wait during the night.

Objective   To use StatTools's Two-Sample Confidence Interval procedure to find a confidence interval for the difference between mean waiting times during the supermarket's rush periods versus its normal periods.

Solution

Starting with the data set in its original form, two main steps are required:

1 Rename the seven time intervals (Morning rush, Morning, and so on) so that there are only three: Rush, Normal, and Night.

2 Perform the statistical comparison between the EndWaiting variables for the Rush and Normal periods.

The finished version of the file contains the results of step 1 in the Renamed Data sheet and the results of step 2 in this same sheet (next to the renamed data). If you want to follow along, hands-on, with the step-by-step procedure, you should use the "data only" version of the **Customer Checkouts. xlsx** file and perform the following steps.

PERFORMING A STATISTICAL COMPARISON BETWEEN VARIABLES

1 **Copy sheet.** Create a copy of the Data sheet by pressing the Ctrl key and dragging the Data sheet tab to the right. Double-click on the new sheet tab and name it Renamed Data.

② **Rename time intervals.** To rename the time intervals on the Renamed Data sheet, use Excel's Find and Replace feature. Click on column C's tab to select the entire column, and then select Replace from the Find & Select dropdown menu on the Home ribbon. Type **Morning rush** in the "Find what:" box, type **Rush** in the "Replace with:" box, and click on the Replace All button. Repeat this for the other time intervals to be renamed. That is, replace Lunch rush and Afternoon rush by Rush, and replace Morning, Afternoon, and Evening by Normal. Figure 8.18 shows some of the results. (You could accomplish the same thing with a complex IF formula or a lookup table.)

Figure 8.18 Supermarket Data with Time Categories Renamed

	A	B	C	D	E	F	G	H	I
1	Day	StartTime	TimeInterval	InitialWaiting	Arrivals	Departures	EndWaiting	Checkers	TotalCustomers
2	Mon	8:00 AM	Rush	2	21	22	1	3	23
3	Mon	8:30 AM	Rush	1	25	18	8	3	26
4	Mon	9:00 AM	Normal	8	27	28	7	3	35
5	Mon	9:30 AM	Normal	7	21	23	5	3	28
6	Mon	10:00 AM	Normal	5	20	23	2	5	25
7	Mon	10:30 AM	Normal	2	36	31	7	5	38
8	Mon	11:00 AM	Normal	7	30	36	1	5	37
9	Mon	11:30 AM	Rush	1	34	29	6	5	35
10	Mon	12:00 PM	Rush	6	56	48	14	7	62
11	Mon	12:30 PM	Rush	14	58	64	8	7	72
12	Mon	1:00 PM	Rush	8	53	52	9	7	61
13	Mon	1:30 PM	Normal	9	30	36	3	5	39
14	Mon	2:00 PM	Normal	3	34	31	6	5	37
15	Mon	2:30 PM	Normal	6	36	37	5	5	42
16	Mon	3:00 PM	Normal	5	30	28	7	5	35
17	Mon	3:30 PM	Normal	7	29	34	2	5	36
18	Mon	4:00 PM	Normal	2	35	33	4	5	37
19	Mon	4:30 PM	Rush	4	32	25	11	5	36

③ **Create box plots.** Define a StatTools data set from the data on the Renamed Data sheet, and use StatTools's Box Plot procedure to create side-by-side box plots of the EndWaiting variable. Select the Stacked option, and select TimeInterval as the Cat variable and EndWaiting as the Val variable. See Figure 8.19 for the box plots.

Figure 8.19

Box Plots for Supermarket Example

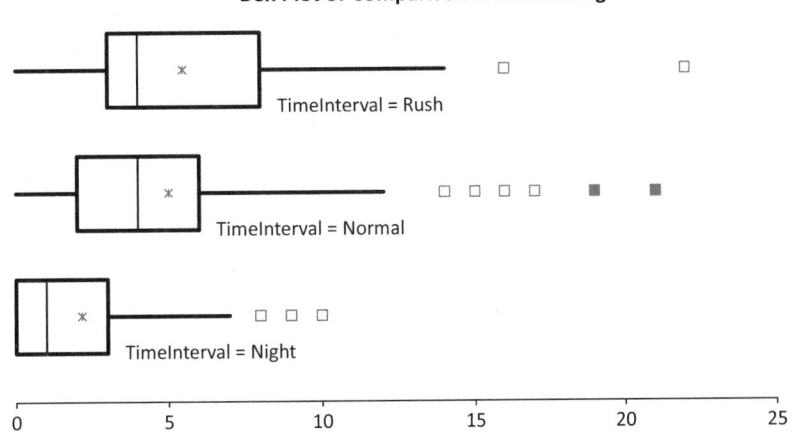

4 **Perform two-sample analysis.** Select Confidence Interval and Mean/Std. Deviation from the StatTools Statistical Inference dropdown list using the renamed data set. In the resulting dialog box, select the Stacked option, and again select TimeInterval as the Cat variable and EndWaiting as the Val variable. Because there are three categories for TimeInterval, StatTools will ask you which two of these you want to base the difference on. Select Normal and Rush. StatTools then analyzes the difference "Normal minus Rush." If you checked the Analyze in Reverse Order option, StatTools would analyze the opposite difference, "Rush minus Normal." (See the StatTools dialog boxes in Figures 8.20 and 8.21.)

Figure 8.20

Two-Sample Dialog Box

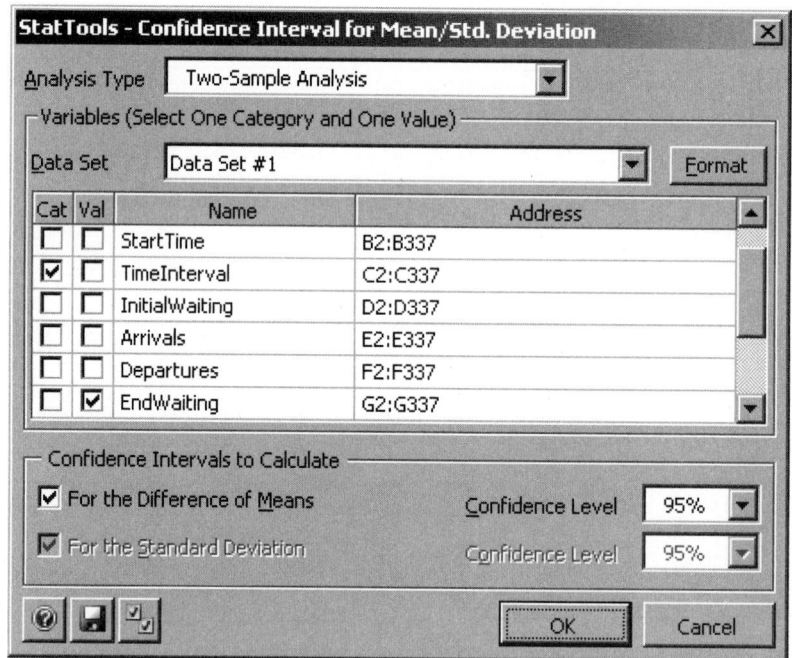

Figure 8.21

Dialog Box for Selecting Two Categories of Interest

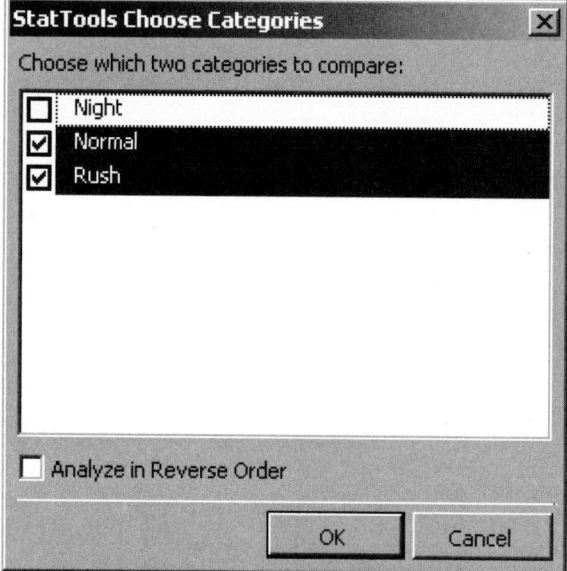

The side-by-side box plots in Figure 8.19 show that (1) the distribution of EndWaiting is skewed to the right for each time interval, with a number of outliers, and (2) the mean value of EndWaiting is slightly larger for Rush than for Normal, with Night a distant third. Given the nature of the data, it should not really be surprising that the data are skewed to the right with a number of outliers. When the supermarket gets busy, waiting lines can really build. All it takes are a few really long checkout times to produce an excessively large value of EndWaiting, and this is evidently what happened at R&P.

The output from the two-sample procedure appears in Figure 8.22. The sample means of EndWaiting are 5.480 and 5.014 for the Rush and Normal periods, the sample standard deviations are 4.284 and 4.293, and these are based on sample sizes of 98 and 140 half-hour periods. These summary statistics provide some evidence of a difference between population means but very little evidence of different population variances. This latter statement means that the results in column L, not column M, are relevant (although the two are practically identical). A point estimate for the mean difference (Normal minus Rush) is -0.465, and a 95% confidence interval for this mean difference extends from -1.578 to 0.648.

Figure 8.22

Analysis of Supermarket Data

	K	L	M
1		EndWaiting (Normal)	EndWaiting (Rush)
2	Sample Summaries	Data Set #1	Data Set #1
3	Sample Size	140	98
4	Sample Mean	5.014	5.480
5	Sample Std Dev	4.293	4.284
6			
7		Equal	Unequal
8	Conf. Intervals (Difference of Means)	Variances	Variances
9	Confidence Level	95.0%	95.0%
10	Sample Mean Difference	-0.465	-0.465
11	Standard Error of Difference	0.565	0.565
12	Degrees of Freedom	236	209
13	Lower Limit	-1.578	-1.579
14	Upper Limit	0.648	0.648
15			
16			
17	Equality of Variances Test		
18	Ratio of Sample Variances	1.0042	
19	p-Value	0.9912	

What can the manager conclude from this analysis? Should she add extra checkout people during rush periods? This is difficult to answer because it obviously involves a trade-off between the cost of extra checkout people and the "cost" of making customers wait in line. Also, there is no way of knowing, at least not from the present analysis, how much effect extra checkout people would have on waiting. However, the manager does know from this analysis that the mean difference between rush and normal periods is rather minor. Specifically, because the confidence interval extends from a negative value to a positive value, it is possible that the *true* mean difference is *positive*. That is, the mean for normal times could be *larger* than the mean for rush times. Therefore, the results of this analysis do not provide a strong incentive for the manager to change the current system. ∎

8.7.2 Paired Samples

When the samples to be compared are paired in some natural way, such as a pretest and posttest for each person, or husband–wife pairs, there is a more appropriate form of analysis than the two-sample procedure. Consider the example where each new employee takes a test, then receives a three-month training course, and finally takes another similar test.

There is likely to be a fairly strong correlation between the pretest and posttest scores. Employees who score relatively low on the first test are likely to score relatively low on the second test, and employees who score relatively high on the first test are likely to score relatively high on the second test. The two-sample procedure does not take this correlation into account and therefore ignores important information. The paired procedure described in this section, on the other hand, uses this information to advantage.

The procedure itself is very straightforward. You do not directly analyze two separate variables (pretest scores and posttest scores, say); you analyze their *differences*. For each pair in the sample, you calculate the difference between the two scores for the pair. Then you perform a *one*-sample analysis, as in Section 8.3, on these differences. Actually, StatTools's Paired-Sample procedure does the difference calculations *and* the ensuing one-sample analysis automatically, as described in the following example.

EXAMPLE	8.8 HUSBAND AND WIFE REACTIONS TO SALES PRESENTATIONS AT STEVENS HONDA-BUICK

The Stevens Honda-Buick automobile dealership often sells to husband-wife pairs. The manager would like to check whether the sales presentation is viewed any more or less favorably by the husbands than the wives. If it is, then some new training might be recommended for its salespeople. To check for differences, a random sample of husbands and wives are asked (separately) to rate the sales presentation on a scale of 1 to 10, 10 being the most favorable rating. The results appear in Figure 8.23. (See the **Sales Presentation Ratings.xlsx** file.) What can the manager conclude from these data?

Figure 8.23

Data for Sales Presentation Example

	A	B	C
1	Pair	Husband	Wife
2	1	6	3
3	2	7	8
4	3	8	5
5	4	6	4
6	5	8	5
7	6	7	6
8	7	8	5
9	8	6	7
10	9	7	8
31	30	7	3
32	31	7	5
33	32	5	1
34	33	7	5
35	34	7	4
36	35	10	5

Objective To use StatTools's Paired-Sample Confidence Interval procedure to find a confidence interval for the mean difference between husbands' and wives' ratings of sales presentations.

Solution

We illustrate two ways to perform the analysis. Normally, you would use only the second of these, but the first sheds some light on the procedure. For the first method, make a copy of the Data sheet and name it OneSample. Then manually form a new variable in column D called Difference by entering the formula

=B2-C2

in cell D2 and copying it down column D. (See Figure 8.24.) This new variable is, for each couple, the husband's rating minus the wife's rating. Next, with the cursor anywhere in the resulting data set, select Confidence Interval and Mean/Std. Deviation from the StatTools Statistical Inference dropdown list, select One-Sample Analysis as the Analysis Type, and select the Difference variable. This produces the output shown in Figure 8.24. The sample mean Husband minus Wife difference is 1.629 and a 95% confidence interval for this difference extends from 1.057 to 2.200.

Figure 8.24 One-Sample Analysis of Differences for Sales Presentation Data

	A	B	C	D	E	F	G
1	Pair	Husband	Wife	Difference			Difference
2	1	6	3	3		*Conf. Intervals (One-Sample)*	OneSampleData
3	2	7	8	-1		Sample Size	35
4	3	8	5	3		Sample Mean	1.629
5	4	6	4	2		Sample Std Dev	1.664
6	5	8	5	3		Confidence Level (Mean)	95.0%
7	6	7	6	1		Degrees of Freedom	34
8	7	8	5	3		Lower Limit	1.057
9	8	6	7	-1		Upper Limit	2.200
10	9	7	8	-1			
11	10	7	5	2			
34	33	7	5	2			
35	34	7	4	3			
36	35	10	5	5			

To perform this analysis more efficiently, again make a copy of the Data sheet and name it PairedSample. After creating a StatTools data set from the data on this sheet, select Confidence Interval and Mean/Std. Deviation from the StatTools Statistical Inference dropdown, and fill in the resulting dialog box as shown in Figure 8.25. Specifically, select Paired-Sample Analysis as the Analysis Type. (As usual, you will then get a chance to reverse the order of the difference, but don't do so; let it remain "Husband minus Wife.") The resulting output appears in Figure 8.26. The results are exactly the same as before. This is because StatTools's Paired-Sample procedure performs a one-sample analysis on the differences—and it saves you the work of creating the differences.

Figure 8.27 shows side-by-side box plots of the husband and wife scores. These box plots are not as useful here as in the two-sample procedure because you lose sight of which husbands are paired with which wives. A more useful box plot is of the differences, shown in Figure 8.28. Here it is apparent that the sample mean difference is positive, but even more importantly, the vast majority of husband scores are greater than the corresponding wife scores. There is little doubt that most husbands tend to react more favorably to the sales presentations than their wives. Perhaps the salespeople need to be somewhat more sensitive to their female customers.

Before leaving this example, let's see what would have happened if the two-sample procedure had been used on the Husband and Wife variables. The results appear in

Figure 8.25

Dialog Box for
Paired-Sample
Analysis

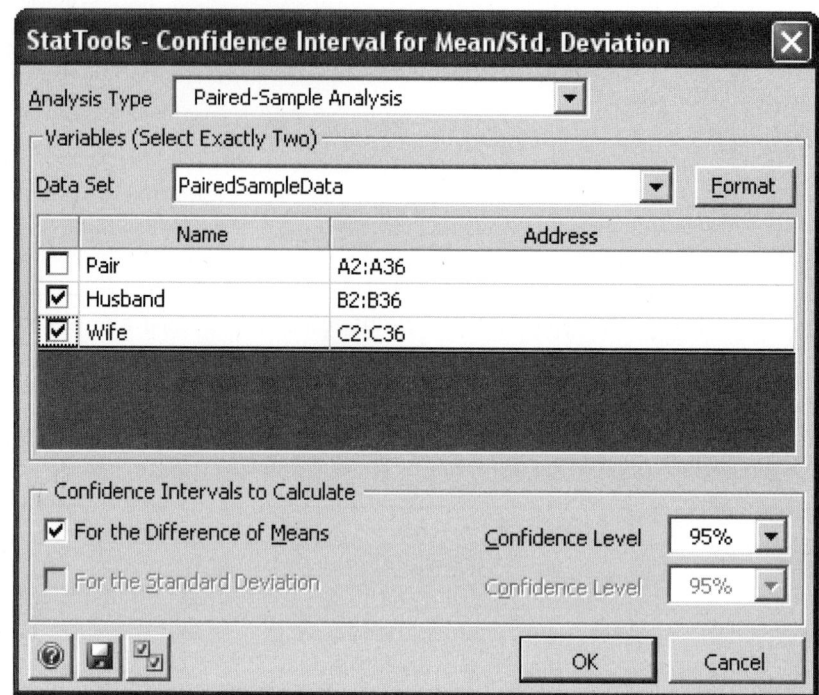

Figure 8.26

Paired-Sample
Analysis of Sales
Presentation Data

	A	B	C	D	E	F
1	Pair	Husband	Wife			
2	1	6	3		*Conf. Intervals (Paired-Sample)*	Husband - Wife
3	2	7	8		Sample Size	35
4	3	8	5		Sample Mean	1.629
5	4	6	4		Sample Std Dev	1.664
6	5	8	5		Confidence Level	95.0%
7	6	7	6		Degrees of Freedom	34
8	7	8	5		Lower Limit	1.057
9	8	6	7		Upper Limit	2.200
10	9	7	8			
11	10	7	5			
33	32	5	1			
34	33	7	5			
35	34	7	4			
36	35	10	5			

Figure 8.27

Side-by-Side Box
Plots for Sales
Presentation Data

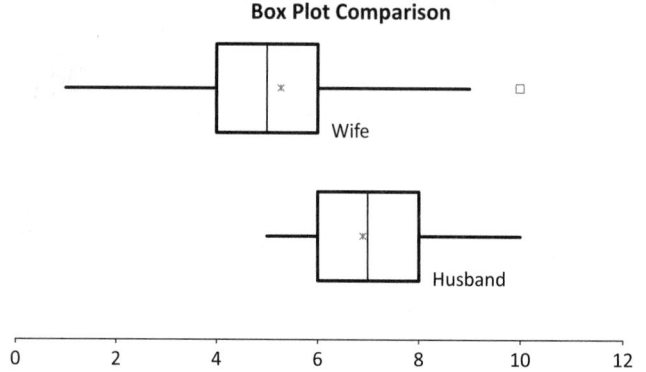

424 Chapter 8 Confidence Interval Estimation

Figure 8.28

Single Box Plot of Differences for Sales Presentation Data

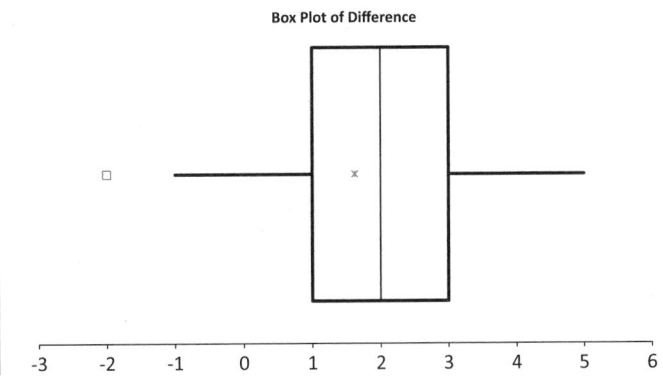

Box Plot of Difference

Figure 8.29 Two-Sample Analysis of Sales Presentation Data

	A	B	C	D	E	F	G
1	Pair	Husband	Wife			**Husband**	**Wife**
2	1	6	3		*Sample Summaries*	TwoSampleData	TwoSampleData
3	2	7	8		Sample Size	35	35
4	3	8	5		Sample Mean	6.914	5.286
5	4	6	4		Sample Std Dev	1.222	1.792
6	5	8	5				
7	6	7	6			Equal	Unequal
8	7	8	5		*Conf. Intervals (Difference of Means)*	Variances	Variances
9	8	6	7		Confidence Level	95.0%	95.0%
10	9	7	8		Sample Mean Difference	1.629	1.629
11	10	7	5		Standard Error of Difference	0.367	0.367
12	11	6	3		Degrees of Freedom	68	60
13	12	5	4		Lower Limit	0.897	0.895
14	13	8	5		Upper Limit	2.360	2.362
15	14	7	8				
16	15	7	5				
17	16	7	6		*Equality of Variances Test*		
18	17	6	5		Ratio of Sample Variances	0.4649	
19	18	5	4		p-Value	0.0285	
20	19	6	5				
34	33	7	5				
35	34	7	4				
36	35	10	5				

Figure 8.29. Because there is a considerable difference between the sample standard deviations, the confidence interval output in column G, not column F, is relevant, although there is not much difference between them. The important point is that the resulting confidence interval for the mean difference extends from 0.895 to 2.362, which is somewhat *wider* than the confidence interval from the paired-sample procedure. This is typical. When the two-sample procedure is used in a situation where the paired-sample procedure is more appropriate, the data are not used as efficiently. The effect is that the standard error of the difference tends to be larger, and the resulting confidence interval tends to be wider.

Why is the paired-sample procedure appropriate here? It is *not* just because husbands and wives naturally come in pairs. It is because they tend to react similarly to one another.

You can check that the correlation between the husbands' scores and their wives' scores is 0.442. (This can be found with Excel's CORREL function on the Husband and Wife variables.) This is far from a perfect correlation, but it is large enough to warrant using the paired-sample procedure. ∎

In general, the paired-sample procedure is appropriate when the samples are naturally paired in some way *and* there is a reasonably large positive correlation between the pairs. In this case the paired-sample procedure makes more efficient use of the data and generally results in narrower confidence intervals.

PROBLEMS

Level A

23. The director of a university's career development center is interested in comparing the starting annual salaries of male and female students who recently graduated from the university and commenced full-time employment. The director has formed pairs of male and female graduates with the same major and similar grade-point averages. Specifically, she has collected a random sample of 50 such pairs and has recorded the starting annual salary of each person. These data are provided in the file P08_23.xlsx. Find a 95% confidence interval for the mean difference between similar male and female graduates of this university. Interpret your result.

24. A real estate agent has collected a random sample of 75 houses that were recently sold in a suburban community. She is particularly interested in comparing the appraised value and recent selling price of the houses in this particular market. The data are provided in the file P08_24.xlsx. Using this sample data, find a 95% confidence interval for the mean difference between the appraised values and selling prices of the houses sold in this suburban community. Interpret the confidence interval for the real estate agent.

25. *The Wall Street Journal CEO Compensation Study* analyzed CEO pay from many U.S. companies with fiscal year 2008 revenue of at least $5 billion that filed their proxy statements between October 2008 and March 2009. The data are in the file P02_30.xlsx.
   a. Create a new column, Total, that is the sum of columns D and E.
   b. After combining Telecommunications and Technology into a single company type, there are nine company types. For each of these, find a 95% confidence interval for the difference between the mean of Total for that company type and mean of Total for all other company types. Comment on what these nine confidence intervals indicate about CEO pay in different industries.

Level B

26. The file P02_35.xlsx contains data from a survey of 500 randomly selected households.
   a. Separate the households in the sample by the location of their residence within the given community. For each of the four locations, use the sample information to find a 90% confidence interval for the mean annual income (sum of first income and second income) of all relevant households. Compare these four interval estimates. You might also consider generating box plots of the total income for households in each of the four locations.
   b. Find a 90% confidence interval for the difference between the mean annual income of all households in the first (i.e., SW) and second (i.e., NW) sectors of this community. Find similar 90% confidence intervals for the differences between the mean annual income levels of all households from all other pairs of locations (i.e., first and third, first and fourth, second and third, second and fourth, and third and fourth). Summarize your findings.

27. A company employs two shifts of workers. Each shift produces a type of gasket where the thickness is the critical dimension. The average thickness and the standard deviation of thickness for shift 1, based on a random sample of 30 gaskets, are 10.53 mm and 0.14 mm. The similar figures for shift 2, based on a random sample of 25 gaskets, are 10.55 mm and 0.17 mm. Let $\mu_1 - \mu_2$ be the mean difference in thickness between shifts 1 and 2.
   a. Using the formulas from this section, not StatTools, find a 95% confidence interval for $\mu_1 - \mu_2$.
   b. Based on your answer to part **a**, are you convinced that the gaskets from shift 2 are, on average, wider than those from shift 1? Why or why not?
   c. How would your answers to parts **a** and **b** change if the sample sizes were instead 300 and 250?

8.8 CONFIDENCE INTERVAL FOR THE DIFFERENCE BETWEEN PROPORTIONS

The final confidence interval we examine is a confidence interval for the difference between two population proportions. As in the previous section, this comparison procedure finds many real applications. Several potential business applications are the following:

Applications of Comparisons of Proportions in Business

- When an appliance store is about to have a sale, it sometimes sends selected customers a mailing to notify them of the sale. On other occasions it includes a coupon for 5% off the sale price in these mailings. The store's manager would like to know whether the inclusion of coupons affects the proportion of customers who respond.

- A manufacturing company has two plants that produce identical products. The company wants to know how much the proportion of out-of-spec products differs across the two plants.

- A pharmaceutical company has developed a new over-the-counter sleeping pill. To judge its effectiveness, the company runs an experiment where one set of randomly chosen people takes the new pill and another set takes a placebo. (Neither set knows which type of pill they are taking.) The company judges the effectiveness of the new pill by comparing the proportions of people who fall asleep within a certain amount of time with the new pill and with the placebo.

- An advertising agency would like to check whether men are more likely than women to switch TV channels when a commercial comes on. The agency runs an experiment where the channel-switching behavior of randomly chosen men and women can be monitored, and it collects data on the proportion of viewers who switch channels on at least half of the commercial times. The agency then compares these proportions across gender.

The basic form of analysis in each of these examples is the same as in the two-sample analysis for differences between means. However, instead of comparing two means, we now compare proportions.

Formally, let p_1 and p_2 represent the two unknown population proportions, and let $\hat{p}_1$ and $\hat{p}_2$ be the two sample proportions, based on samples of sizes n_1 and n_2. Then the point estimate of the difference between proportions, $p_1 - p_2$, is the difference between sample proportions, $\hat{p}_1 - \hat{p}_2$. If the sample sizes are reasonably large, then the sampling distribution of $\hat{p}_1 - \hat{p}_2$ is approximately normal.[7]

Therefore, a confidence interval for $p_1 - p_2$ is given by Expression (8.15). Here, the z-multiple is the usual value from the standard normal distribution that cuts off the appropriate probability in each tail (1.96 for a 95% confidence interval, for example). Also, the standard error of $\hat{p}_1 - \hat{p}_2$ is given by Equation (8.16).

Confidence Interval for Difference Between Proportions
$$\hat{p}_1 - \hat{p}_2 \pm z\text{-multiple} \times \text{SE}(\hat{p}_1 - \hat{p}_2) \tag{8.15}$$

---

[7]This large-sample assumption is valid as long as $n_i\hat{p}_i > 5$ and $n_i(1 - \hat{p}_i) > 5$ for $i = 1$ and $i = 2$.

Standard Error of Difference Between Sample Proportions

$$SE(\hat{p}_1 - \hat{p}_2) = \sqrt{\frac{\hat{p}_1(1 - \hat{p}_1)}{n_1} + \frac{\hat{p}_2(1 - \hat{p}_2)}{n_2}}$$

(8.16)

The following example illustrates this procedure and how it is implemented in StatTools. (As with the confidence interval for a proportion, the StatTools procedure for a difference between proportions is new in version 5.5.)

| EXAMPLE | 8.9 SALES RESPONSE TO COUPONS FOR DISCOUNTS ON APPLIANCES |

An appliance store is about to have a big sale. It selects 300 of its best customers and randomly divides them into two sets of 150 customers each. It then mails a notice of the sale to all 300 customers but includes a coupon for an extra 5% off the sale price to the second set of customers only. As the sale progresses, the store keeps track of which of these customers purchase appliances. The resulting data appear in Figure 8.30. They are shown in three equivalent ways, as discussed below. (See the file **Coupon Effectiveness.xlsx**.) What can the store's manager conclude about the effectiveness of the coupons?

Figure 8.30 Equivalent Setups for Coupon Data

	A	B	C	D	E	F	G
1	Customer	Received coupon	Purchased		**Table of counts**		
2	1	Yes	Yes				
3	2	Yes	Yes		Category	Received coupon	Didn't receive coupon
4	3	Yes	Yes		Purchased	55	35
5	4	Yes	Yes		Didn't purchase	95	115
6	5	Yes	Yes		Sample sizes	150	150
7	6	Yes	Yes				
8	7	Yes	Yes		**Table of proportions**		
9	8	Yes	Yes				
10	9		Yes		Category	Received coupon	Didn't receive coupon
11	10		Yes		Purchased	0.3667	0.2333
12	11	Yes	Yes		Didn't purchase	0.6333	0.7667
13	12	Yes	Yes		Sample sizes	150	150
14	13	Yes	Yes				
300	299	No	No				
301	300	No	No				

Objective   To illustrate how to find a confidence interval for the difference between proportions of customers purchasing appliances with and without 5% discount coupons.

Solution

First, keep in mind the overall objective. From Figure 8.30 (cells F11 and G11), you can see that 36.67% of customers who received a coupon purchased something, as opposed to only 23.33% of those who didn't receive a coupon. The difference, $36.67\% - 23.33\% = 13.33\%$ (or 0.1333), is the quantity of interest. Specifically, the sample difference is 13.33%, and the objective is to find a confidence interval for this difference. You could plug the data into Equations (8.15) and (8.16), but StatTools will do it for you. This is fairly simple once you understand how the difference between proportions procedure works in StatTools.

The data could be given as a table of counts (top right part of Figure 8.30), as a table of proportions (bottom right part of Figure 8.30), or as a long list of values (left part of Figure 8.30, with many hidden rows). StatTools allows all three setups, and they are discussed in detail in the finished version of the **Coupons Effectiveness.xlsx** file. For now, let's say the table of counts is available. Then the StatTools data set should be the top right shaded region in Figure 8.30. The Category variable indicates the two possible responses (purchased or didn't purchase), and the other two columns show how many customers purchased or didn't purchase in each of the two subpopulations (received coupon or didn't). Given this setup, the next step is to select Confidence Interval and Proportion from the Statistical Inference dropdown list and fill out the dialog box as shown in Figure 8.31. Once you click on OK, you will have the chance to reverse the difference (switch from "Received coupon minus Didn't receive coupon" to the opposite), but don't make this switch here. (Also, ignore the sample sizes at the bottom of this dialog box. With the table of counts option, StatTools figures out the correct sample sizes, in this case 150 for each subpopulation.)

Figure 8.31
Dialog Box for Difference Between Proportions

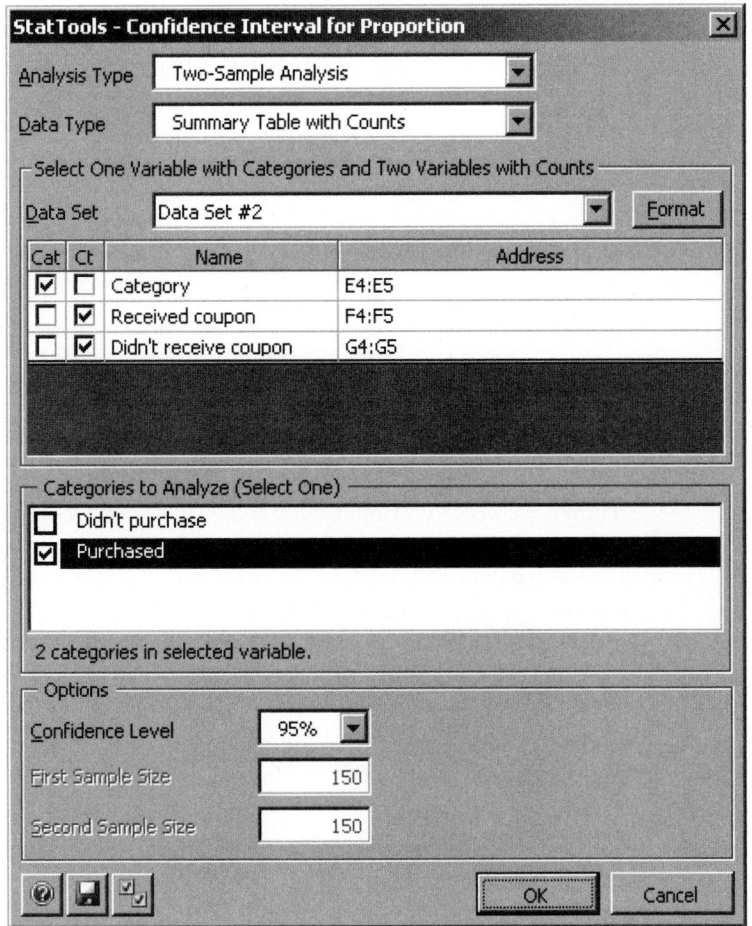

The output appears in Figure 8.32. It shows the sample difference between proportions, 0.133, and the standard error of this difference, 0.052. The 95% confidence interval for the difference is approximately plus or minus two standard errors from the sample difference. It extends from 0.031 to 0.236, or from 3.1 percentage points to 23.6 percentage points. This interval indicates how much higher the proportion of purchasers becomes when coupons are offered.

Figure 8.32
Confidence Interval
for Difference
Between
Proportions

	M	N	O
1			
2	*Analyzed Category*		
3	Proportion of Items in This Category	Purchased	
4			
5			
6		Received coupon	Didn't receive coupon
7	*Sample Summaries*	Data Set #2	Data Set #2
8	Sample Size	150	150
9	Sample Proportion	0.367	0.233
10			
11			
12	*Conf. Interval (Difference Between Proportions)*		
13	Confidence Level	95.0%	
14	Difference Between Proportions	0.133	
15	Standard Error of Difference	0.052	
16	Lower Limit	0.031	
17	Upper Limit	0.236	

This StatTools procedure is more complicated than the others in this book, because the StatTools developers wanted to accommodate different data setups. The finished version of the **Coupon Effectiveness.xlsx** file provides more details on how the procedure works. We suggest that you mimic this file when you do it on your own. ∎

We now revisit Example 8.6, where the SureStep Company is trying to decide which of two suppliers to buy its treadmill motors from. We now compare the two suppliers with regard to warranty costs by analyzing the difference between relevant proportions.

EXAMPLE | **8.10 ANALYZING WARRANTIES ON TREADMILL MOTORS AT SURESTEP COMPANY**

As before, the SureStep Company is trying to decide whether to switch from supplier A to supplier B for the motors in its treadmills. Let's suppose that each treadmill carries a three-month warranty on the motor. If the motor fails within three months, SureStep will supply the customer with a new motor at no cost. This includes installation of the new motor at SureStep's expense. Based on the normal usage at most exercise clubs, SureStep translates the three-month warranty period into approximately 500 hours of treadmill use. Therefore, using the data from Example 8.6 (in the **Treadmill Warranty.xlsx** file, the same data as in the **Treadmill Motors.xlsx** file), the company would like to compare the proportion of motors failing before 500 hours across the two suppliers.

Objective   To illustrate how to find a confidence interval for the difference between proportions of motors failing within the warranty period for the two suppliers.

Solution

The data and StatTools output appear in Figure 8.33. The data in column A and B are first transformed to Yes/No values in columns C and D to see which motors fail within warranty. The typical formula in cell C2 is

$=$IF(A2$<$500, "Yes","No")

Figure 8.33 Analysis of Treadmill Warranty Data

	A	B	C	D	E	F	G	H
1	Supplier A	Supplier B	Supplier A fail	Supplier B fail				
2	1358	658	No	No		*Analyzed Category*		
3	793	404	No	Yes		Proportion of Items in This Category	Yes	
4	587	735	No	No				
5	608	457	No	Yes				
6	472	431	Yes	Yes			Supplier B fail	Supplier A fail
7	562	658	No	No		*Sample Summaries*	Data Set #1	Data Set #1
8	879	453	No	Yes		Sample Size	30	30
9	575	488	No	Yes		Sample Proportion	0.367	0.200
10	1293	522	No	No				
11	1457	1247	No	No				
12	705	1095	No	No		*Conf. Interval (Difference Between Proportions)*		
13	623	430	No	Yes		Confidence Level	95.0%	
14	725	726	No	No		Difference Between Proportions	0.167	
15	569	793	No	No		Standard Error of Difference	0.114	
16	424	498	Yes	Yes		Lower Limit	-0.057	
17	436	502	Yes	No		Upper Limit	0.391	
18	1250	589	No	No				
19	493	975	Yes	No				
20	485	808	Yes	No				
21	462	456	Yes	Yes				
22	765	731	No	No				
23	854	491	No	Yes				
24	634	487	No	Yes				
25	1109	503	No	No				
26	800	465	No	Yes				
27	883	1475	No	No				
28	522	508	No	No				
29	791	846	No	No				
30	684	732	No	No				
31	666	507	No	No				

The StatTools data set should include columns C and D (but it can also include columns A and B). To obtain the confidence interval, select Confidence Interval and Proportion from the Statistical Inference dropdown list, and fill in the dialog box as shown in Figure 8.34. Note the Data Type is now Population Sample (long columns, not just counts), and the Format is Unstacked (one column for Supplier A, another for Supplier B). Then reverse the difference, so that the output shows "B minus A."

The output shows that the point estimate of the difference in proportions is 0.167 and a 95% confidence interval for this difference extends from −0.057 to 0.391. Keep in mind that this difference is the proportion for supplier B minus the proportion for supplier A.

This is fairly convincing, but not conclusive, evidence that a higher proportion of supplier B motors will fail under warranty. It says that if 100 motors from each supplier were tested, as many as 39 more B motors than A motors might fail before 500 hours—but as many as five or six more A motors than B motors might fail before 500 hours. In other words, there is still some uncertainty about which supplier makes the more reliable motors, even though the weight of the evidence favors supplier A.

What does this mean in terms of costs? And should SureStep change suppliers? The confidence interval implies that more motors are likely to fail under warranty if SureStep changes to supplier B, but B's motors cost less. A cost analysis might go as follows. Suppose that each motor from supplier A costs SureStep $500, whereas supplier B offers them for $475 apiece. Let's follow 100 motors sent to exercise clubs for a period of three months. If they are from supplier A, they cost $500 apiece, and approximately 20% (see cell H5 in Figure 8.33) will fail within the warranty period. Each failure costs SureStep another $500, so the expected cost to SureStep is

$$\$500(100) + \$500(20\%)(100) = \$60,000$$

Figure 8.34
Dialog Box for
Difference Between
Proportions

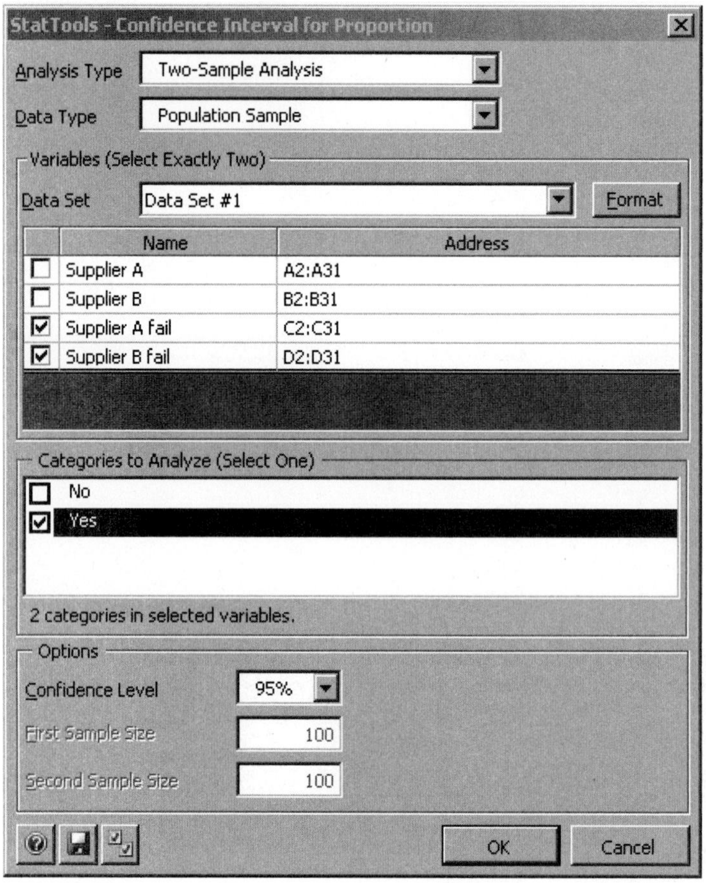

On the other hand, if these 100 motors come from supplier B, the unit cost is only $475, but approximately 36.7% of them will fail within the warranty period. Therefore, the expected cost is

$$= \$475(100) + \$475(36.7\%)(100) = \$64,933$$

Based on this analysis, the cheaper motors from supplier B are likely to cost more in the long run, so SureStep should probably not switch suppliers. (By the way, we omitted the cost of installing the motors from the analysis. This would have made supplier A look even better.) ∎

PROBLEMS

Level A

28. A company that advertises on the Web wants to know which search engine its customers prefer as their primary search engine: Google or Bing. Specifically, the company wants to know whether the preference depends on the browser being used. The

file **P08_28.xlsx** contains counts of 800 customers' favorite search engine, broken down by the browser used.

a. Find a 95% confidence interval for the difference between two proportions: the proportion of Internet Explorer users whose favorite search engine is Google and the similar proportion of Firefox users.

b. Repeat part **a**, replacing Google with Bing.

c. Interpret the results in parts **a** and **b**. Do the search engine preferences seem to depend on the browser used?

29. A market research consultant hired by a leading soft-drink company is interested in estimating the difference between the proportions of female and male consumers who favor the company's low-calorie brand over the leading competitor's low-calorie brand in a particular geographical region. A random sample of 250 consumers from the market under investigation is provided in the file **P08_18.xlsx**. After separating the 250 randomly selected consumers by *gender,* find a 95% confidence interval for the difference between these two proportions. Of what value might this interval estimate be to marketing managers at the company?

Level B

30. The file **P02_35.xlsx** contains data from a survey of 500 randomly selected households. Researchers would like to use the available sample information to see whether home ownership rates vary by household *location.* For example, is there a nonzero difference between the proportions of individuals who own their homes (as opposed to those who rent their homes) in households located in the first (i.e., SW) and second (i.e., NW) sectors of this community? Use the given sample to find a 95% confidence interval that estimates this difference between proportions in home ownership rates for each pair of locations. Interpret and summarize your results. (The solution should include six confidence intervals.)

31. Continuing problem 29, marketing managers at the soft-drink company have asked their market research consultant to explore further the difference between the proportions of women and men who prefer drinking their brand over the leading competitor. Specifically, the company's managers would like to know whether the difference between the proportions of female and male consumers who favor their brand varies by the *age* of the consumers. Use the same data as in problem 29 to assess whether estimates of this difference vary across the four given age categories: under 20, between 20 and 40, between 40 and 60, and over 60. Use a 95% confidence level for each of the *four* required confidence intervals. Summarize your findings. What recommendations would you make to the marketing managers in light of your findings?

8.9 CONTROLLING CONFIDENCE INTERVAL LENGTH

In this section we discuss the most widely used methods for achieving a confidence interval of a specified length. Confidence intervals are a function of three things: (1) the data in the sample, (2) the confidence level, and (3) the sample size(s). We briefly discuss the role of the first two in terms of their effect on confidence interval length and then discuss the effect of sample size in more depth.

The data in the sample directly affect the length of a confidence interval through their sample standard deviation(s). It might appear that because of *random* sampling, you have no control over the sample data, but this is not entirely true. In the case of surveys from a population, there are random sampling plans that can reduce the amount of variability in the sample and hence reduce confidence interval length. Indeed, this is the primary reason for using the stratified sampling procedure discussed in the previous chapter.

Variance reduction is also possible in randomized experiments. There is a whole area of statistics called *experimental design* that suggests how to perform experiments to obtain the most information from a given amount of sample data. Although this is often aimed at scientific and medical research, it is also appropriate in business contexts. For example, the automobile dealership in Example 8.8 was wise to use *paired* husband–wife data rather than two independent samples of men and women. The pairing leads to a potential reduction in variability and hence a narrower confidence interval.

The *confidence level* has a clear effect on confidence interval length. As the confidence level increases, the length of the confidence interval increases as well. For example, a 99% confidence interval is always longer than a 95% confidence interval, assuming that they are both based on the same data. However, the confidence level is rarely used to control the length of the confidence interval. Instead, the confidence level choice is usually based on convention, and 95% is by far the most commonly used value. In fact, it is the default level built into most software packages, including StatTools. You can override this default (by choosing 90% or 99%, for example), but it is not common to do so simply to control confidence interval length.

The most obvious way to control confidence interval length is to choose the sample size(s) appropriately. In the rest of this section, you will learn how this can be done. For each parameter we discuss, the goal is to make the length of a confidence interval sufficiently narrow. Because each confidence interval discussed so far (with the exception of the confidence interval for a standard deviation) is a point estimate plus or minus some quantity, we focus on the "plus or minus" part, called the *half-length* of the interval. (See Figure 8.35.) The usual approach is to specify the half-length B you would like to obtain. Then you find the sample size(s) necessary to achieve this half-length.

Figure 8.35
Half-Length of
Confidence Interval

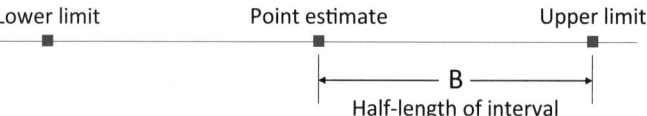

8.9.1 Sample Size for Estimation of the Mean

We begin with a confidence interval for the mean. From Section 8.3, the relevant formula is

$$\overline{X} \pm t\text{-multiple} \times s/\sqrt{n}$$

The goal is to make the half-length of this interval equal to some prescribed value B. For example, if you want the confidence interval to be of the form $\overline{X} \pm 5$, you use $B = 5$. Actually, it is not possible to achieve this half-length B *exactly*, but you can come close.

By setting

$$t\text{-multiple} \times s/\sqrt{n} = B$$

and solving for n, the appropriate sample size is

$$n = \left(\frac{t\text{-multiple} \times s}{B} \right)^2$$

Keep in mind that the sample size must be determined before the data are observed.

Unfortunately, sample size selection must be done *before* a sample is observed. Therefore, no value of s is yet available. Also, because the t-multiple depends on n (through the degrees of freedom parameter), it is not clear which t-multiple to use.

The usual solution is to replace s by some reasonable estimate σ_{est} of the population standard deviation σ, and to replace the t-multiple with the corresponding z-multiple from the standard normal distribution. The latter replacement is justified because z-values and t-values are practically equal unless n is very small. The resulting sample size formula is given in Equation (8.17). This formula generally results in a noninteger value of n, in which case the practice is to round n up to the next larger integer.

Sample Size Formula for Estimating a Mean

$$n = \left(\frac{z\text{-multiple} \times \sigma_{est}}{B} \right)^2$$

(8.17)

The following example, an extension of Example 8.1, shows how to implement Equation (8.17).

EXAMPLE **8.11 SAMPLE SIZE SELECTION FOR ESTIMATING REACTION TO A NEW SANDWICH**

The fast-food manager in Example 8.1 surveyed 40 customers, each of whom rated a new sandwich on a scale 1 to 10. Based on the data, a 95% confidence interval for the mean rating of all potential customers extended from 5.739 to 6.761, with a half-length of $(6.761 - 5.739)/2 = 0.511$. How large a sample would be needed to reduce this half-length to approximately 0.3?

Objective To find the sample size of customers required to achieve a sufficiently narrow confidence interval for the mean rating of the new sandwich.

Solution

Equation (8.17) for n uses three inputs: the z-multiple, which is 1.96 for a 95% confidence level; the prescribed confidence interval half-length B, which is 0.3 for this example; and an estimate σ_{est} of the standard deviation. This final quantity must be guessed, but based on the given sample of size 40, the observed sample standard deviation, 1.597, from Example 8.1 can be used. Therefore, Equation (8.17) yields

$$n = \left(\frac{1.96(1.597)}{0.3} \right)^2 = 108.86$$

which is rounded up to $n = 109$. The claim, then, is that if the manager surveys 109 customers, a 95% confidence interval will have approximate half-length 0.3. Its *exact* half-length will differ slightly from 0.3 because the standard deviation from the sample will almost surely not equal 1.597.

StatTools has a Sample Size Selection procedure that performs this sample size calculation and can be used anywhere in a spreadsheet. There doesn't even have to be a data set. Just select Sample Size Selection from the Statistical Inference dropdown list, select the parameter to analyze (in this case the mean), and enter the requested values. In this case the requested values are the confidence level (95%), the half-length of the interval (0.3), and an estimate of the standard deviation (1.597). (See Figure 8.36, where the choices on the

Figure 8.36
Sample Size
Selection Dialog Box

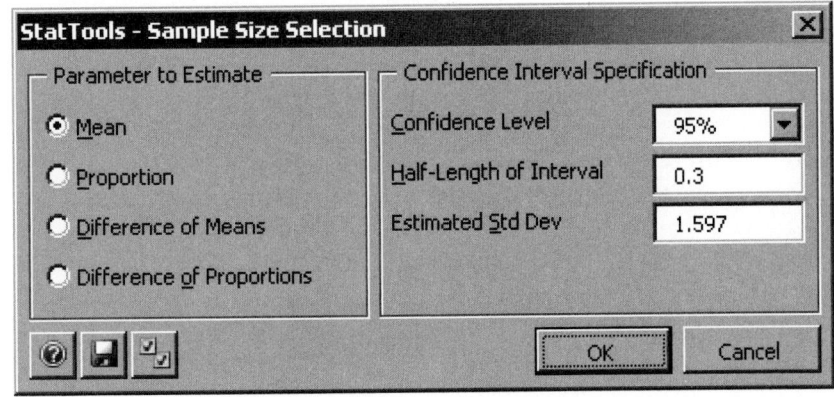

Figure 8.37
Sample Size for
Mean

	A	B
3	**Sample Size for Mean**	
4	Confidence Level	95.00%
5	Half-length of Interval	0.30
6	Std Dev (estimate)	1.5970
7	Sample Size	109

right depend on which parameter is selected on the left.) This produces the output shown in Figure 8.37, which indicates that a sample size of 109 is required.

What if the manager is at the planning stage and doesn't have a "preliminary" sample of size 40? What standard deviation estimate should she use for σ_{est} (because the value 1.597 is no longer available)? This is not an easy question to answer, but because of the role of σ_{est} in Equation (8.17), it is crucial for the determination of n. The manager basically has three choices: (1) she can base her estimate of the standard deviation on historical data, assuming relevant historical data are available; (2) she can take a small preliminary sample (of size 20, say) to get an estimate of the standard deviation; or (3) she can simply guess a value for the standard deviation. We do not recommend the third option, but there are cases in which it is the only feasible option available. ∎

We have demonstrated the use of Equation (8.17) for a sample mean. In the same way, it can also be used in the paired-sample procedure. In this case the resulting value of n refers to the number of *pairs* that should be included in the sample, and σ_{est} refers to an estimate of the standard deviation of the *differences* (Husband scores minus Wife scores, for example).

FUNDAMENTAL INSIGHT

Confidence Interval Length

The length of any confidence interval is influenced by three things: the sample size, the confidence level, and the variability in the population. The confidence level is typically set at 95%, and you have no control over the

variability in the population (except possibly by choosing an appropriate experimental design). Therefore, the best way to control confidence interval length is through the choice of the sample size.

8.9.2 Sample Size for Estimation of Other Parameters

The sample-size analysis for the mean carries over with very few changes to other parameters. We discuss three other parameters in this section: a *proportion*, the *difference between two means*, and the *difference between two proportions*. In each case the required confidence interval can be obtained by setting the half-length equal to a prescribed value B and solving for n.

There are two points worth mentioning. First, the confidence interval for the difference between means uses a t-multiple. As was done for the mean, this can be replaced by a z-multiple, which is perfectly acceptable in most situations. Second, the confidence intervals for differences between means or proportions require *two* sample sizes, one for each sample. The formulas below assume that each sample uses the *same* sample size, denoted by n.

The sample size formula for a proportion p is given by Equation (8.18). Here, p_{est} is an estimate of the population proportion p. A *conservative* value of n can be obtained by using $p_{est} = 0.5$. It is conservative in the sense that the sample size obtained by using $p_{est} = 0.5$ guarantees a confidence interval half-length no greater than B, regardless of the true value of p.

Sample Size Formula for Estimating a Proportion

$$n = \left(\frac{z\text{-multiple}}{B} \right)^2 p_{est}(1 - p_{est}) \tag{8.18}$$

The sample size formula for the difference between means is given by Equation (8.19). Here, σ_{est} is an estimate of the standard deviation of *each* population, where we make the assumption (as in Section 8.7.1) that the two populations have a *common* standard deviation σ.

Sample Size Formula for Estimating the Difference Between Means

$$n = 2\left(\frac{z\text{-multiple} \times \sigma_{est}}{B}\right)^2 \tag{8.19}$$

Finally, the sample size formula for the difference between proportions is given by Equation (8.20). Here, p_{1est} and p_{2est} are estimates of the two unknown population proportions p_1 and p_2. As in the case of a single proportion, a conservative value of n is obtained by using the estimates $p_{1est} = p_{2est} = 0.5$.

Sample Size Formula for Estimating the Difference Between Proportions

$$n = \left(\frac{z\text{-multiple}}{B}\right)^2 [p_{1est}(1 - p_{1est}) + p_{2est}(1 - p_{2est})] \tag{8.20}$$

EXAMPLE | **8.12 SAMPLE SIZE SELECTION FOR ESTIMATING THE PROPORTION WHO HAVE TRIED A NEW SANDWICH**

Suppose that the fast-food manager from the previous example wants to estimate the proportion of customers who have tried its new sandwich. She wants a 90% confidence interval for this proportion to have half-length 0.05. For example, if the sample proportion turns out to be 0.42, a 90% confidence interval should be (approximately) 0.42 ± 0.05. How many customers need to be surveyed?

Objective To find the sample size of customers required to achieve a sufficiently narrow confidence interval for the proportion of customers who have tried the new sandwich.

Solution

If the manager has no idea what the proportion is, she can use $p_{est} = 0.5$ in Equation (8.18) to obtain a conservative value of n. The appropriate z-multiple is now 1.645 because this value cuts off probability 0.05 in each tail of the standard normal distribution. (Remember that we are asking for a 90% confidence level, not the usual 95% level.) Therefore, the required value of n is

$$n = \left(\frac{1.645}{0.05}\right)^2 (0.5)(1 - 0.5) \approx 271$$

On the other hand, if the manager is fairly sure that the proportion who have tried the new sandwich is around 0.3, she can use $p_{est} = 0.3$ instead. This time, use StatTools and enter the values 90% (confidence level), 0.05 (desired half-length), and 0.3 (estimate of the proportion). The resulting output is shown in Figure 8.38.

Figure 8.38
Sample Size for
Proportion

	A	B
10	*Sample Size for Proportion*	
11	Confidence Level	90.00%
12	Half-length of Interval	0.05
13	Proportion (estimate)	0.3000
14	Sample Size	228

*Again, remember that
lower confidence levels
result in narrower
confidence intervals.*

These calculations indicate that if you have more specific information about the unknown proportion, you can use a smaller sample size—in this case 228 rather than 271. Also, note that we selected a 90% confidence level rather than the usual 95% level. There is a trade-off here. Using 90% rather than 95% obviously provides less confidence in the result, but it requires a smaller sample size. You can check that the required sample sizes for a 95% confidence level increase from the current values, 271 and 228, to 385 and 323, respectively. ∎

EXAMPLE

8.13 SAMPLE SIZE SELECTION FOR ANALYZING CUSTOMER COMPLAINTS ABOUT POOR SERVICE

A computer company has a customer service center that responds to customers' questions and complaints. The center employs two types of people: those who have had a recent course in dealing with customers (but little actual experience) and those with a lot of experience dealing with customers (but no formal course). The company wants to estimate the difference between these two types of employees in terms of the average number of customer complaints regarding poor service in the last six months. The company plans to obtain information on a randomly selected sample of each type of employee, using equal sample sizes. How many employees should be in each sample to achieve a 95% confidence interval with approximate half-length 2?

Objective To see how many employees in each experimental group must be sampled to achieve a sufficiently narrow confidence interval for the difference between the mean numbers of complaints.

Solution

Equation (8.19) should be used with z-multiple 1.96 and $B = 2$. However, this formula also requires a value for σ_{est}, an estimate of the (assumed) common standard deviation for each group of employees, and there is no obvious estimate available. The manager might use the following argument. Based on a brief look at complaint data, he believes that some employees receive as few as 6 complaints over a six-month period, whereas others receive as many as 36 (about six per month). Now he can estimate σ_{est} by arguing that all observations are likely to be within three standard deviations of the mean, so that the range of data—minimum to maximum—is about six standard deviations. Therefore, he sets

$$6\sigma_{est} = 36 - 6 = 30$$

and obtains $\sigma_{est} = 5$. Using this value in Equation (8.19), the required sample size is

$$n = 2\left(\frac{1.96(5)}{2}\right)^2 \simeq 49$$

Figure 8.39
Sample Size for Difference Between Means

	A	B
17	*Sample Size for Difference of Means*	
18	Confidence Level	95.00%
19	Half-length of Interval	2.00
20	Common Std Dev (estimate)	5.0000
21	Sample Size	49

The StatTools Sample Size Selection procedure confirms this value. Enter the values 95% (confidence level), 2 (desired half-length), and 5 (estimated standard deviation). The resulting output is shown in Figure 8.39.

Some analysts prefer the estimate

$$4\sigma_{est} = 36 - 6 = 30$$

that is, $\sigma_{est} = 7.5$, arguing that the quoted range (6 to 36) might not include "extreme" values and hence might extend to only two standard deviations on either side of the mean. By using this estimate of the standard deviation, you can check that the required sample size increases from 49 to 109. The important point here is that the estimate of the standard deviation can have a dramatic effect on the required sample size. (And don't forget that this size sample must be taken from *each* group of employees.) ∎

The final example in this section illustrates what can happen when you ask for extremely accurate confidence intervals.

EXAMPLE 8.14 SAMPLE SIZE SELECTION FOR ANALYZING PROPORTIONS OF OUT-OF-SPEC PRODUCTS

A manufacturing company has two plants that produce identical products. The production supervisor wants to know how much the proportion of out-of-spec products differs across the two plants. He suspects that the proportion of out-of-spec products in each plant is in the range of 3% to 5%, and he wants a 99% confidence interval to have approximate half-length 0.005 (or 0.5%). How many items should he sample from each plant?

Objective   To see how many products in each plant must be sampled to achieve a sufficiently narrow confidence interval for the difference between the proportions of out-of-spec products.

Solution

Equation (8.20) should be used with z-multiple 2.576 (the value that cuts off probability 0.005 in each tail of the standard normal distribution), $B = 0.005$, and $p_{1est} = p_{2est} = 0.05$. The reasoning for the latter is that the supervisor believes each proportion is around 3% to 5%, and the most conservative (largest) sample size corresponds to using the larger 5% value. Then the required sample size is

$$n = \left(\frac{2.576}{0.005}\right)^2 [0.05(0.95) + 0.05(0.95)] \simeq 25{,}213$$

This sample size (from *each* sample) is almost certainly prohibitive, so the supervisor realizes he must lower his goals. One way is to decrease the confidence level, say, from 99% to 95%. Another way is to increase the desired half-length from 0.005 to, say, 0.025. We implemented both of these changes in the StatTools Sample Size Selection procedure by

Figure 8.40
Sample Size for
Difference Between
Proportions

	A	B
24	**Sample Size for Difference of Proportions**	
25	Confidence Level	95.00%
26	Half-length of Interval	0.03
27	Proportion 1 (estimate)	0.0500
28	Proportion 2 (estimate)	0.0500
29	Sample Size	584

entering the values 95% (confidence level), 0.025 (desired half-length), and 0.05 and 0.05 (estimates of the proportions). The resulting output is shown in Figure 8.40. Even now each required sample size is 584. Obviously, narrow confidence intervals for differences between proportions can require very large sample sizes. ∎

PROBLEMS

Level A

32. Elected officials in a California city are preparing the annual budget for their community. They would like to estimate how much their constituents living in this city are typically paying each year in real estate taxes. Given that there are over 100,000 homeowners in this city, the officials have decided to sample a representative subset of taxpayers and study their tax payments.
  a. What sample size is required to generate a 95% confidence interval for the mean annual real estate tax payment with a half-length of $100? Assume that the best estimate of the population standard deviation σ is $535.
  b. If a random sample of the size from part **a** is selected and a 95% confidence interval for the mean is calculated from this sample, will the half-length of the confidence interval be equal to $100? Explain why or why not.
  c. Now suppose that the officials want to construct a 95% confidence interval with a half-length of $75. What sample size is required to achieve this objective? Again, assume that the best estimate of the population standard deviation σ is $535. Explain the difference between this result and the result from part **a**.

33. You have been assigned to determine whether more people prefer Coke or Pepsi. Assume that roughly half the population prefers Coke and half prefers Pepsi. How large a sample do you need to take to ensure that you can estimate, with 95% confidence, the proportion of people preferring Coke within 2% of the actual value?

34. You are trying to estimate the average amount a family spends on food during a year. In the past the standard deviation of the amount a family has spent on food during a year has been approximately $1000. If you

want to be 99% sure that you have estimated average family food expenditures within $50, how many families do you need to survey?

35. In past years, approximately 20% of all U.S. families purchased potato chips at least once a month. You are interested in determining the fraction of all U.S. families that currently purchase potato chips at least once a month. How many families must you survey if you want to be 99% sure that your estimate of the relevant proportion is accurate within 2%?

36. Continuing Problem 32, suppose that the officials in this city want to estimate the proportion of taxpayers whose annual real estate tax payments exceed $2000.
  a. What sample size is required to generate a 99% confidence interval for this proportion with a half-length of 0.10? Assume for now that the relevant population proportion p is close to 0.50.
  b. Assume now that officials discover another source that suggests that approximately 30% of all property owners in this community pay more than $2000 annually in real estate taxes. What sample size is now required to generate the 99% confidence interval requested in part **a**?
  c. Why is there a difference between your answers to parts **a** and **b**?
  d. If a random sample of the size from part **a** is selected and a 99% confidence for the proportion is calculated from this sample, will the half-length of the confidence interval be equal to 0.10? Explain why or why not.

Level B

37. Continuing the previous problem, suppose that the officials in this city want to estimate the difference between the proportions, labeled p_1 and p_2, of taxpayers living in neighborhood 1 whose annual real estate tax payments exceed $2000 and the similar proportion for taxpayers living in neighborhood 2.

a. What sample size (randomly selected from all taxpayers residing in each of neighborhoods 1 and 2) is required to generate a 90% confidence interval for this difference between proportions with a half-length of 0.10? Assume for now that p_1 and p_2 are both close to 0.5.

b. We assumed that the two population proportions in part **a** are both close to 0.5. Use a two-way data table to find the required (common) sample size when each of the population proportions is allowed to vary from 0.1 to 0.9 in increments of 0.1. Comment on the sensitivity of the required sample size to the magnitudes of the population proportions.

8.10 CONCLUSION

When you want to estimate a population parameter from sample data, one of the most useful ways to do so is to report a point estimate and a corresponding confidence interval. This confidence interval provides a quick sense of where the true parameter lies. It essentially quantifies the amount of uncertainty in the point estimate. Obviously, narrow confidence intervals are desired. You have seen that the length of a confidence interval is determined by the variability in the data, the confidence level, usually set at 95%, and the sample size(s). You have also seen how sample size formulas can be used at the planning stage to achieve confidence intervals that are sufficiently narrow. Finally, you have seen how confidence intervals can be calculated from mathematical formulas or with statistical software such as StatTools. The advantage of software is that it enables you to concentrate on the important issues for business applications: which confidence intervals are appropriate, how to interpret them, and how to control their length.

Summary of Key Terms

Term	Explanation	Excel	Pages	Equation
Confidence interval	An interval that, with a stated level of confidence, captures a population parameter		389	8.1
t distribution	The sampling distribution of the standardized sample mean when the sample standard deviation is used in place of the population standard deviation	=TDIST(*value, df,* 1 or 2) =TINV(*prob,df*)	390	8.2
Confidence level	Percentage (usually 90%, 95%, or 99%) that indicates how confident you are that the interval captures the true population parameter		394	
Confidence interval for a mean	Interval that is likely to capture a population mean	StatTools/ Statistical Inference/ Confidence Interval	394	8.4
Confidence interval for a total	Interval that is likely to capture the total of all observations in a population	Can be derived from StatTools/ Statistical Inference/ Confidence Interval	400	
Confidence interval for a proportion	Interval that is likely to capture the proportion of all population members that satisfy a specified property	StatTools/ Statistical Inference/ Confidence Interval	404	8.10

(continued)

Summary of Key Terms (*Continued*)

Term	Explanation	Excel	Pages	Equation
Confidence interval for a standard deviation	Interval that is likely to capture a population standard deviation	StatTools/ Statistical Inference/ Confidence Interval	409	
Chi-square distribution	Skewed distribution useful for estimating standard deviations	=CHIDIST(*value,df*) =CHIINV(*prob,df*)	409	
Confidence interval for difference between means with independent samples	Interval that is likely to capture the difference between two population means when the samples are independent	StatTools/ Statistical Inference/ Confidence Interval	413–414	8.13, 8.14
Confidence interval for difference between means with paired samples	Interval that is likely to capture the difference between two population means when the samples are paired in a natural way	StatTools/ Statistical Inference/ Confidence Interval	422	
Confidence interval for difference between proportions	Interval that is likely to capture the difference between similarly defined proportions from two populations	StatTools/ Statistical Inference/ Confidence Interval	427–428	8.15, 8.16
Sample size formulas	Formulas that specify the sample size(s) required to obtain sufficiently narrow confidence intervals	StatTools/ Statistical Inference/ Sample Size Selection	434–437	8.17–8.20

PROBLEMS

Conceptual Questions

C.1. Under what conditions, if any, is it *not* correct to assume that the sampling distribution of the sample mean is approximately normally distributed?

C.2. When, if ever, is it appropriate to use the standard normal distribution as a substitute for the t distribution with $n - 1$ degrees of freedom in estimating a population mean?

C.3. "Assuming that all else remains constant, the length of a confidence interval for a population mean increases whenever the confidence level and sample size increase simultaneously." Is this statement true or false? Explain your choice.

C.4. Assuming that all else remains constant, what happens to the length of a 95% confidence interval for a population parameter when the sample size is reduced by half? You can assume that the resulting sample size is still quite large. Justify your answer.

C.5. "The probability is 0.99 that a 99% confidence interval contains the true value of the relevant population parameter." Is this statement true or false? Explain your choice.

C.6. Suppose you have a list salaries of *all* professional athletes in a given sport in a given year. For example, you might have the salaries of all Major League Baseball players in 2010. Does it make sense to find a 95% confidence interval for the mean salary? If so, what is the relevant population?

C.7. Suppose that someone proposes a new way to calculate a 95% confidence interval for a mean. This could involve *any* arithmetic on the given data. For example, it *could* say to go out 1.75 interquartile ranges (IQRs) on either side of the median. What would it mean to say that this procedure produces *valid* 95% confidence intervals? How could you use simulation to check whether the procedure produces valid 95% confidence intervals?

C.8. The sample size formula for a confidence interval for the population mean requires an estimate of the population standard deviation. Intuitively, why is this the case? Specifically, why is the required sample size larger if the population standard deviation is larger?

C.9. Suppose a 95% confidence interval for a population mean has been calculated, and it extends from 123.7 to 155.2. Some people would then state,

"The probability that the population mean is between 123.7 and 155.2 is 0.95." Why is this, strictly speaking, an invalid statement? How would you rephrase it to make it a valid statement?

C.10. Researchers often create multiple 95% confidence intervals based on a given data set. For example, if the variable of interest is home price and there are five neighborhoods in the population, they might create 10 confidence intervals, one for each difference between mean home prices for a given pair of neighborhoods. (There are 10 pairs.) Can they then conclude that there is 95% confidence that *all* 10 of their confidence intervals will include the corresponding population mean differences? Why or why not?

C.11. Based on a given random sample, suppose you calculate a 95% confidence interval for the following difference: the mean test score for students under 25 years old minus the mean test score for students at least 25 years old, and the confidence interval extends from -14.3 to 1.2. How would you interpret these results? Would you claim that older students, on average, score higher on this test? Would you claim that, on average, it is possible that the younger students score higher on this test?

Level A

38. A sample of 15 quality control managers with more than 20 years experience have an average salary of $68,000 and a sample standard deviation of $19,000.
   a. You can be 95% confident that the mean salary for all quality managers with at least 20 years of experience is between what two numbers? What assumption are you making about the distribution of salaries?
   b. What size sample is needed to ensure that you can estimate the population mean salary of all quality managers with more than 20 years of experience and have only one chance in 100 of being off by more than $500?

39. Political polls typically sample randomly from the U.S. population to investigate the percentage of voters who favor some candidate or issue. The number of people polled is usually on the order of 1000. Suppose that one such poll asks voters how they feel about the President's handling of environmental issues. The results show that 575 out of the 1280 people polled say they either approve or strongly approve of the President's handling. Find a 95% confidence interval for the proportion of the entire voter population who approve or strongly approve of the President's handling. If the same sample proportion were found in a sample twice as large—that is 1150 out of 2560— how would this affect the confidence interval? How would the confidence interval change if the confidence level were 90% instead of 95%?

40. Referring to the previous problem, you often hear the results of such a poll in the news. In fact, the newscasters usually report something such as, "44.9% of the population approve or strongly approve of the President's handling of the environment. The margin of error in this result is plus or minus 3%." Where does this 3% comes from? If the pollsters want the margin of error to be plus or minus 3%, how does this lead to a sample size of approximately 1000?

41. The widths of 100 elevator rails have been measured. The sample mean and standard deviation of the elevator rails are 2.05 inches and 0.01 inch.
   a. Find a 95% confidence interval for the average width of an elevator rail. Do you need to assume that the widths of elevator rails are normally distributed?
   b. How large a sample of elevator rails would you have to measure to ensure that you could estimate, with 95% confidence, the average diameter of an elevator rail within 0.01 inch?

42. You want to determine the percentage of Fortune 500 CEOs who think Indiana University (IU) deserves its current *Business Week* rating. You mail a questionnaire to all 500 CEOs and 100 respond. Exactly half of the respondents believe IU does deserve its ranking.
   a. Find a 95% confidence interval for the fraction of Fortune 500 CEOs who believe IU deserves its ranking.
   b. Suppose again that you want to estimate the fraction of Fortune 500 CEOs who believe IU deserves its ranking. Your goal is to have only a 5% chance of having your estimate be in error by more than 0.02. What size sample would you need to take?

43. The SEC requires companies to file annual reports concerning their financial status. It is impossible to audit every account receivable. Suppose an auditor audits a random sample of 49 accounts receivable invoices and finds a sample average of $128 and a sample standard deviation of $53.
   a. Find a 99% confidence interval for the mean size of an accounts receivable invoice. Does your answer require the sizes of the accounts receivable invoices to be normally distributed?
   b. How large a sample is required for you to be 99% sure that the estimate of the mean invoice size is accurate within $5?

44. An opinion poll surveyed 900 people and reported that 36% believe a certain governor broke campaign financing laws in his election campaign.
   a. Find a 95% confidence interval for the population proportion of people who believe the governor broke campaign financing laws. Does the result of the poll convince you that fewer than 38% of all U.S. citizens favor that viewpoint?

b. Suppose 10,000 (not 900) people are surveyed and 36% believe that the governor broke campaign financing laws. Would you now be convinced that fewer than 38% of all U.S. citizens favor that viewpoint? Why is your answer different than in part **a**?

c. How many people would you have to survey to be 99% confident that you can estimate to within 1% the fraction of people who believe the governor broke campaign financing laws?

45. The file **P08_07.xlsx** contains a random sample of 200 service times during the busiest hour of the day at a particular fast-food restaurant. Find a 95% confidence interval for each of the following population parameters. Then explain how each result might be useful to the manager of the restaurant in terms of improving service.
  a. The mean service time
  b. The standard deviation of service times
  c. The proportion of service times longer than 90 seconds
  d. The proportion of service times shorter than 60 seconds

46. We know that IQs are normally distributed with a mean of 100 and standard deviation of 15. Suppose you want to verify this, so you take 100 random samples of size four each and, for each sample, find a 95% confidence interval for the mean IQ. You expect that approximately 95 of these intervals will contain the true mean IQ (100) and approximately five of these intervals will not contain the true mean. Use simulation in Excel to see whether this is the case.

47. In Section 8.9, we gave a sample size formula for confidence interval estimation of a mean. If the confidence level is 95%, then because the z-multiple is about 2, this formula is essentially

$$n = \frac{4\sigma^2}{B^2}$$

However, this formula is based on the assumption that the sample size n will be small relative to the population size N. If this is *not* the case, the appropriate formula turns out to be

$$n = \frac{N\sigma^2}{\sigma^2 + (N-1)B^2/4}$$

Now suppose you want to find a 95% confidence interval for a population mean. Based on preliminary (or historical) data, you believe that the population standard deviation is approximately 15. You want the confidence interval to have length 4. That is, you want the confidence interval to be of the form $\overline{X} \pm 2$. What sample size is required if $N = 400$? if $N = 800$? if $N = 10,000$? if $N = 100,000,000$? How would you summarize these findings in words?

48. The Ritter Manufacturing Company has kept track of machine hours and overhead costs at its main manufacturing plant for the past 52 weeks. The data appear in the file **P08_48.xlsx**. Ritter has studied these data to understand the relationship between machine hours and overhead costs. Although the relationship is far from perfect, Ritter believes a fairly accurate prediction of overhead costs can be obtained from machine hours through the equation

Estimated Overhead = 746.5078 + 3.3175*Machine Hours

By substituting any observed value of Machine Hours into this equation, Ritter obtains an estimated value of Overhead, which is always somewhat different from the true value of Overhead. The difference is called the prediction error.
  a. Find a 95% confidence interval for the mean prediction error. Do the same for the *absolute* prediction error. (*Hint:* For example, the prediction error in week 1, actual overhead minus predicted overhead, is –94.5303. The absolute prediction error is the absolute value, 94.5303.)
  b. A close examination of the data suggests that week 45 is a possible outlier. Illustrate this by creating a box plot of the prediction errors. In what sense is week 45 is an outlier? See whether week 45 has much effect on the confidence intervals from part **a** by recalculating these confidence intervals, this time with week 45 deleted. Discuss your findings briefly.

Problems 49 through 58 are related to the data in the file **P08_49.xlsx**. This file contains data on 400 customers' orders from ElecMart, a company that sells electronic appliances by mail order. (This same data set was used in Example 3.4 of Chapter 3.) You can consider the data as a random sample from all of ElecMart's orders.

49. Find a 95% confidence interval for the mean total cost of all customer orders. Then do this separately for each of the four regions. Create side-by-side box plots of total cost for the four regions. Does the positive skewness in these box plots invalidate the confidence interval procedure used?

50. Find a 95% confidence interval for the proportion of all customers whose order is for more than $100. Then do this separately for each of three times of day.

51. Find a 95% confidence interval for the proportion of all customers whose orders contain at least three items *and* cost at least $100 total.

52. Find a 95% confidence interval for the difference between the mean amount of the highest cost item purchased for the High customer category and the similar mean for the Medium customer category. Do the same for the difference between the Medium and Low customer categories. Because of the way these customer categories are defined, you would probably expect these mean differences to be positive. Is this what the data indicate?

53. Of the subpopulation of customers who order in the evening, consider the proportion who are female. Similarly, of the subpopulation of customers who order in the morning, consider the proportion who are female. Find a 95% confidence interval for the difference between these two proportions.

54. Find a 95% confidence interval for the difference between the following two proportions: the proportion of female customers who order during the evening and the proportion of male customers who order during the evening.

55. Find a 95% confidence interval for the difference between the following means: the mean total order cost for West customers and the mean total order cost of Northeast customers. Do the same for the other combinations: West versus Midwest, West versus South, Northeast versus South, Northeast versus Midwest, and South versus Midwest.

56. Find a 95% confidence interval for the difference between the mean cost per item for female orders and the similar mean for males.

Level B

57. Let $p_{E,F}$ be the proportion of female orders that are paid for with the ElecMart credit card, and let $p_{E,M}$ be the similar proportion for male orders.
  a. Find a 95% confidence interval for $p_{E,F}$; for $p_{E,M}$; for the difference $p_{E,F} - p_{E,M}$.
  b. Let $p_{E,F,Wd}$ be the proportion of female orders on weekdays that are paid for with the ElecMart credit card, and let $p_{E,F,We}$ be the similar proportion for weekends. Define $p_{E,M,Wd}$ and $p_{E,M,We}$ similarly for males. Find a 95% confidence interval for the difference $(p_{E,F,Wd} - p_{E,M,Wd}) - (p_{E,F,We} - p_{E,M,We})$. Interpret this difference in words. Why might it be of interest to ElecMart?

58. Suppose these 400 orders are a sample of the 4295 orders made during this time period, and suppose 2531 of these orders were placed by females. Find a 95% confidence interval for the total paid for all 4295 orders. Do the same for all 2531 orders placed by females. Do the same for all 1764 orders placed by males.

Problems 59 through 64 are related to the data in the file **P08_59.xlsx**. This file contains data on 91 billings from Rebco, a company that sells plumbing supplies to retailers. You can consider the data as a random sample from all of Rebco's billings.

59. Find a 95% confidence interval for the mean amount of all Rebco's bills. Do the same for each customer size separately.

60. Find a 95% confidence interval for the mean number of days it takes Rebco's customers (as a combined group) to pay their bills. Do the same for each customer size separately. Create a box plot for the variable Days, based on all 91 billings. Also, create side-by-side box plots for Days for the three separate customer sizes. Do any of these suggest problems with the validity of the confidence intervals?

61. Find a 95% confidence interval for the proportion of all large customers who pay bills of at least $1000 at least 15 days after they are billed.

62. Find a 95% confidence interval for the proportion of all bills paid within 15 days. Find a 95% confidence interval for the difference between the proportion of large customers who pay within 15 days and the similar proportion of medium-size customers. Find a 95% confidence interval for the difference between the proportion of medium-size customers who pay within 15 days and the similar proportion of small customers.

63. Suppose a bill is considered late if it is paid after 20 days. In this case its "lateness" is the number of days over 20. For example, a bill paid 23 days after billing has a lateness of 3, whereas a bill paid 18 days after billing has a lateness of 0. Find a 95% confidence interval for the mean amount of lateness for all customers. Find similar confidence intervals for each customer size separately. Why is the distribution of lateness certainly not normal? Do you think this matters for the validity of the confidence interval?

64. Suppose Rebco can earn interest at the rate of 0.011% daily on excess cash. The company realizes that it could earn extra interest if its customers paid their bills more promptly.
  a. Find a 95% confidence interval for the mean amount of interest it could gain if each of its customers paid exactly one day more promptly. Find similar confidence intervals for each customer class separately.
  b. Suppose these 91 billings represent a random sample of the 2792 billings Rebco generates during the year. Find a 95% confidence interval for the total amount of extra interest it could gain by getting each of these 2792 billings to be paid two days more promptly.

65. The file **P08_65.xlsx** contains data on the first 100 customers who entered a two-teller bank on Friday. All variables in this file are times, measured in minutes.
  a. Find a 95% confidence interval for the mean amount of time a customer spends in service with a teller.
  b. The bank is most interested in mean waiting times because customers get upset when they have to spend a lot of time waiting in line. Use the usual procedure to calculate a 95% confidence interval for the mean waiting time per customer.

c. Your answer in part **b** is not valid! (It is much too narrow. It makes you believe you have a much more accurate estimate of the mean waiting time than you really have.) We made two implicit assumptions when we stated the confidence interval procedure for a mean: (1) The individual observations come from the same distribution, and (2) the individual observations are probabilistically independent. Why are both of these, particularly (2), violated for the customer waiting times? [*Hint*: For (1), how do the first few customers differ from "typical" customers? For (2), if you are behind someone in line who has to wait a long time, what do you suspect about your own waiting time?]

d. Following up on assumption (2) of part **c**, you might expect waiting times of successive customers to be *autocorrelated*, that is, correlated with each other. Large waiting times tend to be followed by large waiting times, and small by small. Check this with StatTools's Autocorrelation procedure, under the Time Series & Forecasting/Autocorrelation menu item. An autocorrelation of a certain lag, say, lag 2, is the correlation in waiting times between a customer and the second customer behind her. Do these successive waiting times appear to be autocorrelated? (A *valid* confidence interval for the mean waiting time takes autocorrelations into account—but it is considerably more difficult to calculate.)

Problems 66 through 68 are related to the data in the file **P08_66.xlsx**. The SoftBus Company sells PC equipment and customized software to small companies to help them manage their day-to-day business activities. Although SoftBus spends time with all customers to understand their needs, the customers are eventually on their own to use the equipment and software intelligently. To understand its customers better, SoftBus recently sent questionnaires to a large number of prospective customers. Key personnel— those who would be using the software—were asked to fill out the questionnaire. SoftBus received 82 usable responses, as shown in the file. You can assume that these employees represent a random sample of all of SoftBus's prospective customers.

66. Construct a histogram of the PCKnowledge variable. [Because there are only five possible responses (1–5), this histogram should have only five bars.] Repeat this separately for those who own a PC and those who do not. Then find a 95% confidence interval for the mean value of PCKnowledge for all of SoftBus's prospective customers; of all its prospective customers who own PCs; of all its prospective customers who do not own PCs. The PCKnowledge variable obviously can't be exactly normally distributed because it has only five possible values. Do you think this invalidates the confidence intervals? Explain your choice.

67. SoftBus believes it can afford to spend much less time with customers who own PCs and score at least 4 on PCKnowledge. Let's call these the "PC-savvy" customers. On the other hand, SoftBus believes it will have to spend a lot of time with customers who do not own a PC and score 2 or less on PCKnowledge. Let's call these the "PC-illiterate" customers.
   a. Find a 95% confidence interval for the proportion of all prospective customers who are PC-savvy. Find a similar interval for the proportion who are PC-illiterate.
   b. Repeat part **a** twice, once for the subpopulation of customers who have at least 12 years of experience and once for the subpopulation who have less than 12 years of experience.
   c. Again repeat part **a** twice, once for the subpopulation of customers who have no more than a high school diploma and once for the subpopulation who have more than a high school diploma.
   d. Find a 95% confidence interval for the difference between two proportions: the proportion of all customers with some college education who are PC-savvy and the similar proportion of all customers with no college education. Repeat this, substituting "PC-savvy" with "PC-illiterate."
   e. Discuss any insights you gain from parts **a** through **d** that might be of interest to SoftBus.

68. Following up on the previous problem, SoftBus believes its profit from each prospective customer depends on the customer's level of PC knowledge. It divides the customers into three classes: PC-savvy, PC-illiterate, and all others (where the first two classes are as defined in the previous problem). As a rough guide, SoftBus figures it can gain profit P_1 from each PC-savvy customer, profit P_3 from each PC-illiterate company, and profit P_2 from each of the others.
   a. What values of P_1, P_2, and P_3 seem reasonable? For example, would you expect $P_1 < P_2 < P_3$ or the opposite?
   b. Using any reasonable values for P_1, P_2, and P_3, find a 95% confidence interval for the mean profit per customer that SoftBus can expect to obtain.

Problems 69 through 72 are related to the data in the file **P08_69.xlsx**. The Comfy Company sells medium-priced patio furniture through a mail-order catalog. It has operated primarily in the East but is now expanding to the Southwest. To get off to a good start, it plans to send potential customers a catalog with a discount coupon. However, Comfy is not sure how large a discount is needed to entice customers to buy. It experiments by sending catalogs to selected residents in six cities. Tucson and San Diego receive coupons for 5% off any furniture within the next two months, Phoenix and Santa Fe receive coupons for 10% off, and Riverside and Albuquerque receive coupons for 15% off.

69. Find a 95% confidence interval for the proportion of customers who will purchase at least one item if they receive a coupon for 5% off. Repeat for 10% off and for 15% off.

70. Find a 95% confidence interval for the proportion of customers who will purchase at least one item and pay at least $500 total if they receive a coupon for 5% off. Repeat for 10% off and for 15% off.

71. Comfy wonders whether the customers who receive larger discounts are buying more expensive items. Recalling that the value in the TotPaid column is *after* the discount, find a 95% confidence interval for the difference between the mean *original price per item* for customers who purchase something with the 5% coupon and the similar mean for customers who purchase something with the 10% coupon. Repeat with 5% and 10% replaced by 10% and 15%. What can you conclude?

72. Comfy wonders whether there are differences across pairs of cities that receive the *same* discount.
   a. Find a 95% confidence interval for the difference between the mean amount spent in Tucson and the similar mean in San Diego. (These means should include the "0 purchases.") Repeat this for the difference between Phoenix and Santa Fe and then between Riverside and Albuquerque. Does city appear to make a difference?
   b. Repeat part **a**, but instead of analyzing differences between means, analyze differences between proportions of customers who purchase something. Does city appear to make a difference?

Problems 73 through 76 are related to the data in the file **P08_73.xlsx**. The Niyaki Company sells Blu-ray disc players through a number of retail stores. On one popular model, there is a standard warranty that covers parts for the first six months and labor for the first year. Customers are always asked whether they wish to purchase an extended service plan for $50 that extends the original warranty two more years—that is, to 30 months on parts and 36 months on service. To get a better understanding of warranty costs, the company has gathered data on 70 Blu-ray units purchased. This data is listed in the Data1 sheet of the file **P08_73.xlsx**. The two costs in this sheet (columns D and E) are tracked only for repairs covered by warranty. [Otherwise, the customer bears the cost(s).]

73. Create a histogram of the time until first failure for this type of disc player. Then find a 95% confidence interval for the mean time until failure for this type of disc player. Does the shape of the histogram invalidate the confidence interval? Why or why not?

74. Find a 95% confidence interval for the proportion of customers who purchase the extended service plan. Find a 95% confidence interval for the proportion of all customers who would benefit by purchasing the extended service plan.

75. Find a 95% confidence interval for Niyaki's mean net warranty cost per unit sold (net of the $50 paid for the plan for those who purchase it). You can assume that this mean is for the *first* failure only; subsequent failures of the same units are ignored here.

76. This problem follows up on the previous two problems with the data in the Data2 sheet of the file. Here Niyaki did more investigation on the same 70 customers. It tracked subsequent failures and costs (if any) that occurred within the warranty period. (*Note:* Only two customers had three failures within the warranty period, and parts weren't covered for either on the third failure. Also, no one had more than three failures within the warranty period.)
   a. With these data, find the confidence intervals requested in the previous two problems.
   b. Suppose that Niyaki sold this Blu-ray model to 12,450 customers during the year. Find a 95% confidence interval for its total net cost due to warranties from all of these sales.

77. The file **P08_77.xlsx** contains data on 856 customers who have either tried or not tried a company's new frozen lasagna dinner. (This data set was used in Example 3.5 in Chapter 3.) The manager of the company would like to compare the proportion of customers who have tried the lasagna across various subpopulations. For each of the following, find a 95% confidence interval for the difference between the proportions who have tried the lasagna for the two specified subpopulations. Explain briefly how the results help the manager to understand his customers. (*Hint:* One approach is to use pivot tables to get the count data you need.)
   a. Those with weight under 190 versus those with weight at least 190
   b. Females versus males
   c. Those who live alone versus those who do not live alone
   d. Those who live in a home or condo versus those who live in an apartment
   e. Those who live in the South or West versus those who live in the East
   f. Those who average five or more trips to the mall per month versus those who average fewer than five trips to the mall per month.

78. The formula for a 95% confidence interval for a mean (sample mean plus or minus approximately two standard errors) is so well-rooted in statistical theory and practice that you might not even consider other possibilities. However, many researchers and even practitioners favor a totally different method of calculating a 95% confidence interval for the mean. It is called the *bootstrap* method. Starting with a sample of size n, they generate many "bootstrap samples," calculate the sample mean of each, and report the 2.5 and 97.5 percentiles of these sample means as the endpoints of the confidence interval. Each bootstrap sample is a random sample of size n, *with replacement*, from the given data. That is, each member of a bootstrap sample is equally likely to be any of the original n data points. Implement this in Excel, starting with the sample of 50 salaries in the file **P08_78.xlsx**. Create at least 100 bootstrap samples. Compare the resulting bootstrap confidence interval with the one from StatTools (the traditional one). (*Hint*: The bootstrap samples can be generated quickly with a combination of the RANDBETWEEN and VLOOKUP functions.)

Harrigan University is a liberal arts university in the Midwest that attempts to attract the highest-quality students, especially from its region of the country. It has gathered data on 178 applicants who were accepted by Harrigan (a random sample from all acceptable applicants over the past several years). The data are in the file **University Admissions.xlsx**. The variables are as follows:

- Accepted: whether the applicant accepts Harrigan's offer to enroll
- MainRival: whether the applicant enrolls at Harrigan's main rival university
- HSClubs: number of high school clubs applicant served as an officer
- HSSports: number of varsity letters applicant earned
- HSGPA: applicant's high school GPA
- HSPctile: applicant's percentile (in terms of GPA) in his or her graduating class
- HSSize: number of students in applicant's graduating class
- SAT: applicant's combined SAT score
- CombinedScore: a combined score for the applicant used by Harrigan to rank applicants.

The derivation of the combined score is a closely kept secret by Harrigan, but it is basically a weighted average of the various components of high school performance and SAT. Harrigan is concerned that it is not getting enough of the best students, and worse yet, that many of these best students are going to Harrigan's main rival. Solve the following problems and then, based on your analysis, comment on whether Harrigan appears to have a legitimate concern.

1. Find a 95% confidence interval for the proportion of all acceptable applicants who accept Harrigan's invitation to enroll. Do the same for all acceptable applicants with a combined score less than 330, with a combined score between 330 and 375, and then with a combined score greater than 375. (Note that 330 and 375 are approximately the first and third quartiles of the CombinedScore variable.)

2. Find a 95% confidence interval for the proportion of all acceptable students with a combined score less than the median (356) who choose Harrigan's rival over Harrigan. Do the same for those with a combined score greater than the median.

3. Find 95% confidence intervals for the mean combined score, the mean high school GPA, and the mean SAT score of all acceptable students who accept Harrigan's invitation to enroll. Do the same for all acceptable students who choose to enroll elsewhere. Then find 95% confidence intervals for the differences between these means, where each difference is a mean for students enrolling at Harrigan minus the similar mean for students enrolling elsewhere.

4. Harrigan is interested (as are most schools) in getting students who are involved in extracurricular activities (clubs and sports). Does it appear to be doing so? Find a 95% confidence interval for the proportion of all students who decide to enroll at Harrigan who have been officers of at least two clubs. Find a similar confidence interval for those who have earned at least four varsity letters in sports.

5. The combined score Harrigan calculates for each student gives some advantage to students who rank highly in a *large* high school relative to those who rank highly in a small high school. Therefore, Harrigan wonders whether it is relatively more successful in attracting students from large high schools than from small high schools. Develop one or more confidence intervals for relevant parameters to shed some light on this issue. ∎

Demand for systems analysts in the consulting industry is greater than ever. Graduates with a combination of business and computer knowledge—some even from liberal arts programs—are getting great offers from consulting companies. Once these people are hired, they frequently switch from one company to another as competing companies lure them away with even better offers. One consulting company, D&Y, has collected data on a sample of systems analysts with undergraduate degrees they hired several years ago. The data are in the file **Employee Retention.xlsx**. The variables are as follows:

- StartSal: employee's starting salary at D&Y
- OnRoadPct: percentage of time employee has spent on the road with clients
- StateU: whether the employee graduated from State University (D&Y's principal source of recruits)
- CISDegree: whether the employee majored in Computer Information Systems (CIS) or a similar computer-related area
- Stayed3Yrs: whether the employee stayed at least three years with D&Y
- Tenure: tenure of employee at D&Y (months) if he or she moved before three years

D&Y is trying to learn everything it can about retention of these valuable employees. You can help by solving the following problems and then, based on your analysis, presenting a report to D&Y.

1. Although starting salaries are in a fairly narrow band, D&Y wonders whether they have anything to do with retention.

   a. Find a 95% confidence interval for the mean starting salary of all employees who stay at least three years with D&Y. Do the same for those who leave before three years. Then find a 95% confidence interval for the difference between these means.

   b. Among all employees whose starting salary is below the median ($37,750), find a 95% confidence interval for the proportion who stay with D&Y for at least three years. Do the same for the employees with starting salaries above the median. Then find a 95% confidence interval for the difference between these proportions.

2. D&Y wonders whether the percentage of time on the road might influence who stays and who leaves. Repeat the previous problem, but now do the analysis in terms of percentage of time on the road rather than starting salary. (The median percentage of time on the road is 54%.)

3. Find a 95% confidence interval for the mean tenure (in months) of all employees who leave D&Y within three years of being hired. Why is it not possible with the given data to find a confidence interval for the mean tenure at D&Y among *all* systems analysts hired by D&Y?

4. State University's students, particularly those in its nationally acclaimed CIS area, have traditionally been among the best of D&Y's recruits. But are they relatively hard to retain? Find one or more relevant confidence intervals to help you make an argument one way or the other. ∎

The SnowPea Restaurant is a Chinese carryout/delivery restaurant. Most of SnowPea's deliveries are within a 10-mile radius, but it occasionally delivers to customers more than 10 miles away. SnowPea employs a number of delivery people, four of whom are relatively new hires. The restaurant has recently been receiving customer complaints about excessively long delivery times. Therefore, SnowPea has collected data on a random sample of deliveries by its four new delivery people during the peak dinner time. The data are in the file **Delivery Times.xlsx**. The variables are as follows:

- Deliverer: which person made the delivery
- PrepTime: time from when order was placed until delivery person started driving it to the customer
- TravelTime: time to drive from SnowPea to customer
- Distance: distance (miles) from SnowPea to customer

Solve the following problems and then, based on your analysis, write a report that makes reasonable recommendations to SnowPea management.

1. SnowPea is concerned that one or more of the new delivery people might be slower than others.

   a. Let μ_{Di} and μ_{Ti} be the mean delivery time and mean total time for delivery person i, where the total time is the sum of the delivery and prep times. Find 95% confidence intervals for each of these means for each delivery person. Although these might be interesting, give two reasons why they are not really fair measures for comparing the efficiency of the delivery people.

   b. Responding to the criticisms in part **a**, find a 95% confidence interval for the mean speed of delivery for each delivery person, where speed is measured as miles per hour during the trip from SnowPea to the customer. Then find 95% confidence intervals for the mean difference in speed between each pair of delivery people.

2. SnowPea would like to advertise that it can achieve a total delivery time of no more than M minutes for all customers within a 10-mile radius. On all orders that take more than M minutes, SnowPea will give the customers a $10 certificate on their next purchase.

   a. Assuming for now that the delivery people in the sample are representative of all of SnowPea's delivery people, find a 95% confidence interval for the proportion of deliveries (within the 10-mile limit) that will be on time if $M = 25$ minutes; if $M = 30$ minutes; if $M = 35$ minutes.

   b. Suppose SnowPea makes 1000 deliveries within the 10-mile limit. For each of the values of M in part **a**, find a 95% confidence interval for the total dollar amount of certificates it will have to pay for being late.

3. The policy in the previous problem is simple to state and simple to administer. However, it is somewhat unfair to customers who live close to SnowPea—they will never get $10 certificates. A fairer, but more complex, policy is the following. SnowPea first analyzes the data and finds that total delivery times can be predicted fairly well with the equation

   Predicted Delivery Time = 14.8 + 2.06*Distance

   (This is based on regression analysis, the topic of Chapters 10 and 11.) Also, most of these predictions are within 5 minutes of the actual delivery times. Therefore, whenever SnowPea receives an order over the phone, it looks up the customer's address in its computerized geographical database to find distance, calculates the predicted delivery time based on this equation, rounds this to the nearest minute, adds 5 minutes, and guarantees this delivery time or else a $10 certificate. It does this for *all* customers, even those beyond the 10-mile limit.

   a. Assuming again that the delivery people in the sample are representative of all of SnowPea's delivery people, find a 95% confidence interval for the proportion of all deliveries that will be within the guaranteed total delivery time.

   b. Suppose SnowPea makes 1000 deliveries. Find a 95% confidence interval for the total dollar amount of certificates it will have to pay for being late. ■

Ralph Butts, manager of Woodland Operations for Intergalactica Papelco's Southeastern Region, had to decide this morning whether to approve the Bodfish Lot logging contract that was sitting on his desk. Accompanying the contract was a cruise report that gave Mr. Butts the results of a sample survey of the timber on the Bodfish Lot. Was there enough timber to make logging operations worthwhile?

The Pluto Mill of Intergalactica Papelco is located on the River Styxx in Median, Michigan. The scale of operations at Pluto is enormous. Just one of its several $500 million, football-field-long, four-story-high paper machines has the capability to produce a 20-mile-long, 16-foot-wide, 20-ton reel of paper every hour. Such a machine is run nonstop 24 hours a day for as many of the 365 days in the year that mill maintenance can keep the machine running within specified quality levels. In total, the Pluto Mill produces about 400,000 tons of white paper a year. Because it takes about a ton of wood to produce a ton of paper, a huge quantity of cordwood logs suitable for chipping and pulping must be supplied continually to keep the mill operating. Intergalactica Papelco runs a large-scale logistics, planning, and procurement operation to provide the Pluto Mill with the requisite species, quantity, and quality of wood in a timely fashion.

The Pluto Mill sits on 500 acres of land in the midst of a region in which the huge Intergalactica Papelco owns over a quarter of a million acres of forest. Although this wholly owned forest is the single largest supplier of wood to the mill, more than 60% of the wood used at Pluto is purchased from independent landowners and loggers under contract. Supplying contract wood dependably on such an enormous scale involves frequent purchasing decisions by the Intergalactica Woodlands Operations as to which independent woodlots have sufficient wood volume and quality to support economical logging operations. A prospective seller enters into a tentative agreement with Intergalactica on the basis of market price and a visual scan of the woodlot. The final decision about whether to proceed with the logging is usually based on sampling estimates of the total wood volume on the lot.

A case in point was the Bodfish Lot in Henryville, Arkansas, whose owner approached Intergalactica with a proposal for logging during the 1991 to 1992 season. Aerial photographs indicated that the land was sufficiently promising to warrant a "cruise" to estimate the total volume of wood. (*Cruising* is a term used in the forestry industry to describe a systematic procedure for estimating the quantity, quality, variety, and value of the wood on a plot of land. Indeed, standard cruising methods have been developed and disseminated by the U.S. Department of Agriculture and Forestry Service.) Estimation based on limited sampling is essential. Even for the modest-size Bodfish Lot, with 586 acres of forested land, it would be practically impossible to measure every tree on the lot.

For the Bodfish Lot cruise, it was decided to sample 89 distinct 1/7-acre plots for actual measurement. Although the plots were chosen systematically, the sample was, Intergalactica hoped, still effectively "random." Indeed, *no* consistent attempt was made to select the plots from areas of heavy tree growth, large-diameter trees, heavy spruce concentration, and so on. In fact, the opposite was true: The regular spacing of the sampling grid more or less guaranteed a good cross section of the entire lot. This was what is called in forestry industry jargon a "standard line plot cruise." The total lot was 700 acres in area. The plots were spaced at 8-chain intervals apart on a rectangular grid drawn in advance at the Intergalactica Woodlands Field Office at One Rootmean Square in the town of Covariance, Illinois. The aerial photographs showed that, of the Bodfish Lot's 700 total acres, 586 acres were forested. The total volume estimate, to be done separately for each species, was to be based on the average for the 89 sampled plots on these 586 acres.

A circular area two-person cruise was then initiated. Typically, about 10 plots could be cruised in one

---

[8]This case was contributed by Peter Kolesar from Columbia University.

day. The foresters counted the entire number of cordwood trees over 6 inches in diameter within each 1/7-acre circle. Then, back in the office in Covariance, the number of trees on each plot was entered into a computer according to species, diameter, and possible end product. The file **Bodfish Trees.xlsx** contains this tabulation from the cruise notes of the counts for spruce, hard maple, and beech of the number of cordwood trees on the 89 sampled plots. (In the actual database, 13 different species of trees were recorded, and Intergalactica would have decided which trees were more suitable for lumber, plywood, or pulping applications.)

With these data, Intergalactica now had to decide whether to contract to log the lot. Ralph Butts, manager of Woodlands Operations, knew that even though Intergalactica would pay on the basis of the weight received at the mill, he needed at least 31,000 cordwood size trees on the lot to make operations economical. More detailed knowledge of the amount of timber by species would help the Pluto Mill make the crucial blending decisions that affect the cost and quality of the resulting wood pulp.

This was just one of several hundred similiar contracts to be made over the coming year. Butts was concerned with the rising cost of cruising in the Southeastern Region. Was the Bodfish Lot cruise excessive, he wondered? Could he get by in the future with considerably smaller samples? Suppose that only one-half or one-quarter of the plots on Bodfish had been cruised? ■

Hypothesis Testing

© Diademimages/Dreamstime.com

OFFICIAL SPONSORS OF THE OLYMPICS

Hypothesis testing is one of the most frequently used tools in academic research, including research in the area of business. Many studies pose interesting questions, stated as hypotheses, and then test these with appropriate statistical analysis of experimental data. One such study is reported in McDaniel and Kinney (1996). They investigate the effectiveness of "ambush marketing" in prominent sports events such as the Olympic Games. Many companies pay significant amounts of money, perhaps $10 million, to become official sponsors of the Olympics. Ambushers are their competitors, who pay no such fees but nevertheless advertise heavily during the Olympics, with the intention of linking their own brand image to the event in the minds of consumers. The question McDaniel and Kinney investigate is whether consumers are confused into thinking that the ambushers are the official sponsors.

At the time of the 1994 Winter Olympics in Lillehammer, Norway, the researchers ran a controlled experiment using 215 subjects ranging in age from 19 to 49 years old. Approximately half of the subjects—the "control group"—viewed a 20-minute tape of a women's skiing event in which several actual commercials for official sponsors in four product categories were interspersed. (The categories were fast food, automobile, credit card, and insurance; the official sponsors were McDonald's, Chrysler, VISA, and John Hancock.) The other half—the "treatment group"—watched the same tape but with commercials for competing ambushers. (The ambushers were Wendy's, Ford, American Express, and Northwestern Mutual, all of which advertised during the 1994 Olympics.) After watching the tape, each subject was asked to fill out a questionnaire. This questionnaire asked subjects to recall the official Olympics sponsors in each product category, to rate their attitudes toward the products, and to state their intentions to purchase the products.

McDaniel and Kinney tested several hypotheses. First, they tested the hypothesis that there would be *no* difference between the control and treatment groups in terms of which products they would recall as official Olympics sponsors. The experimental evidence allowed them to reject this hypothesis decisively. For example, the vast majority of the control group, who watched the McDonald's commercial, recalled McDonald's as being the official sponsor in the fast-food category. But a clear majority of the treatment group, who watched the Wendy's commercial, recalled Wendy's as being the official sponsor in this category. Evidently, Wendy's commercial was compelling.[1]

Because the ultimate objective of commercials is to increase purchases of a company's brand, the researchers also tested the hypothesis that viewers of official sponsor commercials would rate their intent to purchase that brand *higher* than viewers of ambusher commercials would rate their intent to purchase the ambusher brand. After all, isn't this why the official sponsors were paying large fees? However, except for the credit card category, the data did *not* support this hypothesis. VISA viewers did indeed rate their intent to use VISA higher than American Express viewers rated their intent to use American Express. But in the other three product categories, the ambusher brand came out *ahead* of the official brand in terms of intent to purchase (although the differences were not statistically significant).

There are at least two important messages this research should convey to business. First, if a company is going to spend a lot of money to become an official sponsor of an event such as the Olympic Games, it must create a more vivid link in the mind of consumers between its product and the event. Otherwise, the company might be wasting its money. Second, ambush marketing is very possibly a wise strategy. By seeing enough of the ambushers' commercials during the event, consumers get confused into thinking that the ambusher is an official sponsor. In addition, previous research in the area suggests that consumers do not view ambushers negatively for using an ambush strategy. ∎

9.1 INTRODUCTION

When you want to make inferences about a population on the basis of sample data, you can perform the analysis in either of two ways. You can proceed as in the previous chapter, where you calculate a point estimate of a population parameter and then form a confidence interval around this point estimate. In this way you bring no preconceived ideas to the analysis but instead let the data speak for themselves in telling you the parameter's true value.

In contrast, an analyst often has a particular theory, or hypothesis, that he or she would like to test. This hypothesis might be that a new packaging design will produce more sales than the current design, that a new drug will have a higher cure rate for a given disease than

---

[1]Whereas the McDonald's commercial featured the five-ringed Olympics logo and had an Olympics theme, the Wendy's commercial used a humorous approach built around the company's founder, Dave Thomas, and his dream of winning gold in the Olympics bobsled competition.

Hypothesis testing is a form of decision making under uncertainty, where you decide which of two competing hypotheses to accept, based on sample data. However, in contrast to the methods discussed in Chapter 6, it is performed in a very specific way, as described in this chapter.

any drug currently on the market, that people who smoke cigarettes are more susceptible to heart disease than nonsmokers, and so on. In this case the analyst typically collects sample data and checks whether the data provide enough evidence to support the hypothesis.

The hypothesis that the analyst is attempting to prove is called the **alternative hypothesis.** It is also frequently called the **research hypothesis.** The opposite of the alternative hypothesis is called the **null hypothesis.** It usually represents the current thinking or status quo. That is, the null hypothesis is usually the accepted theory that the analyst is trying to *disprove.* In the previous examples the null hypotheses are:

- The new packaging design is no better than the current design.

- The new drug has a cure rate no higher than other drugs on the market.

- Smokers are no more susceptible to heart disease than nonsmokers.

The burden of proof is traditionally on the alternative hypothesis. It is up to the analyst to provide enough evidence in support of the alternative; otherwise, the null hypothesis will continue to be accepted. A slight amount of evidence in favor of the alternative is usually not enough. For example, if a slightly higher percentage of people are cured with a new drug in a sequence of clinical tests, this still might not be enough evidence to warrant introducing the new drug to the market. In general, we reject the null hypothesis—and accept the alternative—only if the results of the hypothesis test are *statistically significant*, a concept we will explain in this chapter.

> The **null hypothesis** is usually the current thinking, or status quo. The **alternative, or research, hypothesis** is usually the hypothesis a researcher wants to prove. The burden of proof is on the alternative hypothesis.

As you will see in this chapter, confidence interval estimation and hypothesis testing use data in much the same way and they often report basically the same results, only from different points of view. There continues to be a debate (largely among academic researchers) over which of these two procedures is more useful. We believe that in a business context, confidence interval estimation is more useful and enlightening than hypothesis testing. However, hypothesis testing continues to be a key aspect of statistical analysis. Indeed, statistical software packages routinely include the elements of standard hypothesis tests in their outputs. You will see this, for example, when you study regression analysis in Chapters 10 and 11. Therefore, it is essential to understand the fundamentals of hypothesis testing so that you can interpret this output intelligently.

9.2 CONCEPTS IN HYPOTHESIS TESTING

Before we plunge into the details of specific hypothesis tests, it is useful to discuss the *concepts* behind hypothesis testing. There are a number of concepts and statistical terms involved, all of which lead eventually to the key concept of statistical significance. To make this discussion somewhat less abstract, we place it in the context of the following example.

EXAMPLE | 9.1 EXPERIMENTING WITH A NEW PIZZA STYLE AT THE PEPPERONI PIZZA RESTAURANT

The manager of the Pepperoni Pizza Restaurant has recently begun experimenting with a new method of baking pepperoni pizzas. He personally believes that the new method produces a better-tasting pizza, but he would like to base the decision whether to switch from the old method to the new method on customer reactions. Therefore, he performs an experiment. For 100 randomly selected customers who order a pepperoni pizza for home delivery, he includes both an old-style and a free new-style pizza in the order. All he asks is that these customers rate the *difference* between pizzas on a -10 to $+10$ scale, where -10 means that they strongly favor the old style, $+10$ means they strongly favor the new style, and 0 means they are indifferent between the two styles. Once he gets the ratings from the customers, how should he proceed?

We begin by stating that Example 9.1 is used primarily to explain hypothesis-testing concepts. We do *not* mean to imply that the manager would, or should, use a hypothesis-testing procedure to decide whether to switch from the old method to the new method. First, hypothesis testing does not take costs into account. If the new method of making pizzas uses more expensive cheese, for example, then hypothesis testing would ignore this important aspect of the decision problem. Second, even if the costs of the two pizza-making methods are equivalent, the manager might base his decision on a simple point estimate and possibly a confidence interval. For example, if the sample mean rating is 1.8 and a 95% confidence interval for the mean rating extends from 0.3 to 3.3, this in itself would probably be enough evidence to make the manager switch to the new method.

We come back to these ideas—basically, that hypothesis testing is not necessarily the best procedure to use in a business decision-making context—throughout this chapter. However, with these caveats in mind, we discuss how the manager *might* proceed by using hypothesis testing. ■

9.2.1 Null and Alternative Hypotheses

As we stated in the introduction to this chapter, the hypothesis the manager is trying to prove is called the alternative, or research, hypothesis, whereas the null hypothesis represents the status quo. In this example the manager would personally like to prove that the new method provides better-tasting pizza, so this becomes the alternative hypothesis. The opposite, that the old-style pizzas are at least as good as the new-style pizzas, becomes the null hypothesis. We assume he judges which of these is true on the basis of the mean rating over the entire customer population, labeled μ. If it turns out that $\mu \leq 0$, then the null hypothesis is true. Otherwise, if $\mu > 0$, the alternative hypothesis is true.

Hypotheses for Pizza Example

Null hypothesis: $\mu \leq 0$

Alternative hypothesis: $\mu > 0$

where μ is the mean population rating.

Usually, the null hypothesis is labeled H_0 and the alternative hypothesis is labeled H_a. Therefore, in our example they can be specified as $H_0: \mu \leq 0$ and $H_a: \mu > 0$. This is typical. The null and alternative hypotheses divide all possibilities into two nonoverlapping sets, exactly one of which must be true. In our case the mean rating is less than or equal to 0 or it is positive. Exactly one of these possibilities *must* be true, and the manager intends to use sample data to learn which it is.

Traditionally, hypothesis testing has been phrased as a decision-making problem, where an analyst decides either to accept the null hypothesis or reject it, based on the sample evidence. In our example, accepting the null hypothesis means deciding that the new-style pizza is not really better than the old-style pizza and presumably discontinuing the new style. In contrast, rejecting the null hypothesis means deciding that the new-style pizza is indeed better than the old-style pizza and presumably switching to the new style.

9.2.2 One-Tailed Versus Two-Tailed Tests

The form of the alternative hypothesis can be either *one-tailed* or *two-tailed,* depending on what the analyst is trying to prove. The pizza manager's alternative hypothesis is **one-tailed** because he is hoping to prove that the customers' ratings are, on average, greater than 0. The only sample results that can lead to rejection of the null hypothesis are those in a particular direction, namely, those where the sample mean rating is *positive.* On the other hand, if the manager sets up his rating scale in the reverse order, so that *negative* ratings favor the new-style pizza, then the test is still one-tailed, but now only negative sample means lead to rejection of the null hypothesis.

In contrast, a **two-tailed test** is one where results in either of two directions can lead to rejection of the null hypothesis. A slight modification of the pizza example where a two-tailed alternative might be appropriate is the following. Suppose the manager currently uses two methods for producing pepperoni pizzas. He is thinking of discontinuing one of these methods if it appears that customers, on average, favor one method over the other. Therefore, he runs the same experiment as before, but now the hypotheses he tests are $H_0: \mu = 0$ versus $H_a: \mu \neq 0$, where μ is again the mean rating across the customer population. In this case *either* a large positive sample mean *or* a large negative sample mean will lead to rejection of the null hypothesis—and presumably to discontinuing one of the production methods.

A **one-tailed alternative** is one that is supported only by evidence in a single direction.

A **two-tailed alternative** is one that is supported by evidence in either of two directions.

It is important to realize that the analyst, not the data, determines the type of alternative hypothesis. The hypothesis depends entirely on what the analyst wants to prove, and it should be formed before the data are collected.

Once the hypotheses are set up, it is easy to detect whether the test is one-tailed or two-tailed. One-tailed alternatives are phrased in terms of ">" or "<" whereas two-tailed alternatives are phrased in terms of "≠". The real question is whether to set up hypotheses for a particular problem as one-tailed or two-tailed. There is no *statistical* answer to this question. It depends entirely on what an analyst is trying to prove. If the pizza manager is trying to prove that the new-style pizza is better than the old-style pizza—only results on one side will lead to a switch—a one-tailed alternative is appropriate. However, if he is trying to decide whether to discontinue either of two existing production methods—where results on *either* side will lead to a switch—then a two-tailed alternative is appropriate.

9.2.3 Types of Errors

Regardless of whether the manager decides to accept or reject the null hypothesis, it *might* be the wrong decision. He might incorrectly reject the null hypothesis when it is true ($\mu \leq 0$), and he might incorrectly accept the null hypothesis when it is false ($\mu > 0$). In the tradition of hypothesis testing, these two types of errors have acquired the names *type I* and *type II errors.* In general, you commit a **type I error** when you incorrectly *reject* a null hypothesis that is true. You commit a **type II error** when you incorrectly *accept* a null hypothesis that is false. These ideas appear graphically in Figure 9.1.

The pizza manager commits a type I error if he concludes, based on sample evidence, that the new-style pizza is better (and switches to it) when in fact the entire customer

Figure 9.1

Types of Errors in Hypothesis Testing

		Truth	
		H_0 is true	H_a is true
Decision	Reject H_0	Type I error	No error
	Do not reject H_0	No error	Type II error

population would, on average, favor the old-style pizza. In contrast, he commits a type II error if he concludes, again based on sample evidence, that the new style is no better (and discontinues it) when in fact the entire customer population would, on average, favor the new style.

Possible Errors in Pizza Example

Type I error: Switching to new style when it is no better than old style

Type II error: Staying with old style when new style is better

---

The traditional hypothesis-testing procedure favors caution in terms of rejecting the null hypothesis. The thinking is that if you reject the null hypothesis and it is really true, then you commit a type I error—which is bad. Given this rather conservative way of thinking, you are inclined to accept the null hypothesis unless the sample evidence provides *strong* support for the alternative hypothesis. Unfortunately, you can't have it both ways. By accepting the null hypothesis, you risk committing a type II error.

Type I errors are usually considered more costly, although this can lead to conservative decision making.

This is exactly the dilemma the pizza manager faces. If he wants to avoid a type I error (where he switches to the new style but really shouldn't), then he will require fairly convincing evidence from the survey that he *should* switch. If he observes *some* evidence to this effect, such as a sample mean rating of $+1.5$ and a 95% confidence interval that extends from -0.3 to $+3.3$, this evidence might not be strong enough to make him switch. However, if he decides not to switch, he risks committing a type II error.

9.2.4 Significance Level and Rejection Region

The analyst gets to choose the significance level α. It is traditionally chosen to be 0.05, but it is occasionally chosen to be 0.01 or 0.10.

The real question, then, is how strong the evidence in favor of the alternative hypothesis must be to reject the null hypothesis. Two approaches to this problem are commonly used. In the first, you prescribe the probability of a type I error that you are willing to tolerate. This type I error probability is usually denoted by α and is most commonly set equal to 0.05, although $\alpha = 0.01$ and $\alpha = 0.10$ are also frequently used. The value of α is called the **significance level** of the test. Then, given the value of α, you use statistical theory to determine a *rejection region*. If the sample evidence falls in the **rejection region,** you reject the null hypothesis; otherwise, you accept it. The rejection region is chosen precisely so that the probability of a type I error is at most α. Sample evidence that falls into the rejection region is called **statistically significant at the α level.** For example, if $\alpha = 0.05$, the evidence is statistically significant at the 5% level.

The **rejection region** is the set of sample data that leads to the rejection of the null hypothesis.

The **significance level,** α, determines the size of the rejection region. Sample results in the rejection region are called **statistically significant** at the α level.

It is important to understand the effect of varying α. If α is small, such as 0.01, the probability of a type I error is small. Therefore, a lot of sample evidence in favor of the alternative hypothesis is required before the null hypothesis can be rejected. Equivalently, the rejection region in this case is small. In contrast, when α is larger, such as 0.10, the rejection region is larger, and it is easier to reject the null hypothesis.

9.2.5 Significance from *p*-values

A second approach, and one that is currently more popular, is to avoid the use of a significance level α and instead simply report *how significant* the sample evidence is. This is done by means of a *p-value*. The idea is quite simple—and very important. Suppose in the pizza example that the true mean rating (if it could be observed) is μ = 0. In other words, the customer population, on average, judges the two styles of pizza to be equal. Now suppose that the sample mean rating is +2.5. The manager has two options at this point. (Remember that he doesn't know that μ = 0; he observes only the sample.) He can conclude that (1) the null hypothesis is true—the new-style pizza is not preferred over the old style—and he just observed an unusual sample, or (2) the null hypothesis is *not* true—customers do prefer the new-style pizza—and the sample he observed is a typical one for such customers.

The *p*-value of the sample quantifies this. The **p-value** is the probability of seeing a random sample *at least as extreme as the observed sample*, given that the null hypothesis is true. Here, "extreme" is relative to the null hypothesis. For example, a sample mean rating of +3.5 from the pizza customers is more extreme evidence than a sample mean rating of +2.5. Each provides some evidence against the null hypothesis, but the former provides stronger, more extreme evidence.

> The **p-value** of a sample is the probability of seeing a sample with at least as much evidence in favor of the alternative hypothesis as the sample actually observed. The smaller the *p*-value, the more evidence there is in favor of the alternative hypothesis.

Let's suppose that the pizza manager collects data from the 100 sampled customers and finds that the *p*-value for the sample is 0.03. This means that *if* the entire customer population, on average, judges the two types of pizza to be approximately equal, then only three random samples out of 100 would provide as much evidence in support of the new style as the observed sample. So should he conclude that the null hypothesis is true and he just happened to observe an unusual sample, or should he conclude that the null hypothesis is *not* true? There is no clear *statistical* answer to this question; it depends on how convinced the manager must be before switching. But we can say in general that smaller *p*-values indicate more evidence in support of the alternative hypothesis. If a *p*-value is sufficiently small, then almost any analyst will conclude that rejecting the null hypothesis (and accepting the alternative) is the most reasonable decision.

How small is a "small" *p*-value? This is largely a matter of semantics, but Figure 9.2 indicates the attitude of many analysts. A *p*-value less than 0.01 is regarded as convincing evidence that the alternative hypothesis is true. After all, fewer than one sample out of 100 would provide such support for the alternative hypothesis if it weren't true. If the *p*-value is between 0.01 and 0.05, there is strong evidence in favor of the alternative hypothesis. Unless the consequences of making a type I error are really serious, this is typically enough evidence to reject the null hypothesis.

Figure 9.2

Evidence in Favor of the Alternative Hypothesis

The interval between 0.05 and 0.10 is a gray area. If a researcher is trying to prove a research hypothesis and observes a *p*-value between 0.05 and 0.10, she will probably be reluctant to publish her results as "proof" of the alternative hypothesis, but she will probably be encouraged to continue her research and collect more sample evidence. Finally, *p*-values larger than 0.10 are generally interpreted as weak evidence (or no evidence) in support of the alternative.

There is a strong connection between the α-level approach and the *p*-value approach. Specifically, the null hypothesis can be rejected at a specified significance level α only if the *p*-value from the sample is less than or equal to α. Equivalently, the sample evidence is statistically significant at a given α level only if its *p*-value is less than or equal to α. For example, if the *p*-value from a sample is 0.03, the null hypothesis can be rejected at the 10% and the 5% significance levels but not at the 1% level. The *p*-value essentially states *how* significant a given sample is.

If you remember only one thing from this chapter, remember that a p-value measures how unlikely the observed sample results are, given that the null hypothesis is true. Therefore, a low p-value provides evidence for rejecting the null hypothesis and accepting the alternative.

> Sample evidence is statistically significant at the α level only if the *p*-value is less than α.

The advantage of the *p*-value approach is that you don't have to choose a significance level α ahead of time. Because it is far from obvious what value of α to choose in any particular situation, this is certainly an advantage. Another compelling advantage is that *p*-values for standard hypothesis tests are routinely included in virtually all statistical software output. In addition, all *p*-values can be interpreted in basically the same way: A small *p*-value provides support for the alternative hypothesis.

FUNDAMENTAL INSIGHT

Key Role of *p*-values

The single most important thing to remember from this chapter is the role of *p*-values. This is especially important because *p*-values are listed in virtually all outputs from statistical software. If a *p*-value is small, the result is statistically significant, meaning that the null hypothesis can be rejected in favor of the alternative.

Analysts don't always agree on how "small" a *p*-value needs to be—some say less than 0.01, some say less than 0.05, and some say less than 0.10. But just about all analysts agree that if a *p*-value is greater than 0.10, the result is *not* statistically significant, which means that there is not enough evidence to reject the null hypothesis.

9.2.6 Type II Errors and Power

A type II error occurs when the alternative hypothesis is true but there isn't enough evidence in the sample to reject the null hypothesis. This type of error is traditionally considered less important than a type I error, but it can lead to serious consequences in real situations. For example, in medical trials on a proposed new cancer drug, a type II error occurs if the new drug is really superior to existing drugs but experimental evidence is not sufficiently conclusive to warrant marketing the new drug. For patients suffering from cancer, this is obviously a serious error.

As we stated previously, the alternative hypothesis is typically the hypothesis a researcher wants to prove. If it is in fact true, the researcher wants to be able to reject the null hypothesis and hence avoid a type II error. The probability that she is able to do so is called the **power** of the test—that is, the power is one minus the probability of a type II error. There are several ways to achieve high power, the most obvious of which is to increase sample size. By sampling more members of the population, you are better able to see whether the alternative is really true and hence avoid a type II error if the alternative is indeed true. As in the previous chapter, there are formulas that specify the sample size required to achieve a certain power for a given set of hypotheses. We will not pursue these in this book, but you should be aware that they exist.

> The **power** of a test is one minus the probability of a type II error. It is the probability of rejecting the null hypothesis when the alternative hypothesis is true.

9.2.7 Hypothesis Tests and Confidence Intervals

The results of hypothesis tests are often accompanied by confidence intervals. This provides two complementary ways to interpret the data. However, there is a more formal connection between the two, at least for two-tailed tests. Let α be the stated significance level of the test. We will state the connection for the most commonly used level, $\alpha = 0.05$, although it extends to any α value. The connection is that the null hypothesis can be rejected at the 5% significance level if and only if a 95% confidence interval does *not* include the hypothesized value of the parameter.

> *Using a Confidence Interval to Perform a Two-Tailed Hypothesis Test*
> Reject the null hypothesis if and only if the hypothesized value does *not* lie inside a confidence interval for the parameter.

As an example, consider the test of $H_0:\mu = 0$ versus $H_a:\mu \neq 0$. Suppose a 95% confidence interval for μ extends from 1.35 to 3.42, so that it does *not* include the hypothesized value 0. Then H_0 can be rejected at the 5% significance level, and the p-value from the sample must be less than 0.05. On the other hand, if a 95% confidence interval for μ extends, say, from -1.25 to 2.31 (negative to positive), the null hypothesis cannot be rejected at the 5% significance level, and the p-value must be greater than 0.05.

There is also a correspondence between one-tailed hypothesis tests and *one-sided* confidence intervals, but we will not pursue it here.

9.2.8 Practical Versus Statistical Significance

We have stated that statistically significant results are those that produce sufficiently small p-values. In other words, statistically significant results are those that provide strong evidence in support of the alternative hypothesis. You frequently hear about studies, particularly in the medical sciences, that produce statistically significant results. For example, you might hear that mice injected with one kind of drug develop significantly more cancer cells than mice injected with a second kind of drug.

The point of this section is that such results are not necessarily significant in terms of being *important*. They might be significant only in the statistical sense. An example of what could happen is the following. An education researcher wants to see whether quantitative SAT scores differ, on average, across gender. He sets up the hypotheses $H_0:\mu_M = \mu_F$ versus $H_a:\mu_M \neq \mu_F$, where μ_M and μ_F are the mean quantitative SAT scores for males and females, respectively. He then randomly samples scores from 4000 males and 4000 females and finds the male and female sample averages to be 521 and 524. He also finds that the sample standard deviation for each group is about 50. Based on these numbers, the p-value for the sample data is approximately 0.007. (You will learn how to make this calculation later in the chapter.) Therefore, he claims that the results are significant proof that males do score differently (lower) than females.

If you read these results in a newspaper, your immediate reaction might be, "Who cares?" After all, the difference between 521 and 524 is certainly not very large from a practical point of view. So why does the education researcher get to make his claim? The reasoning is as follows. In all likelihood, the means μ_M and μ_F are not *exactly* equal. There is bound to be some difference between genders over the entire population. If the researcher takes large enough samples—and 4000 is plenty large—he is almost certain to obtain enough evidence to "prove" that the means are not equal. That is, he will almost surely obtain *statistically* significant results. However, the difference he finds, as in the numbers we quoted, might be of little *practical* significance. No one really cares whether females score three points higher or lower than males. If the difference were on the order of 30 to 40 points, then the result would be more interesting.

Extremely large samples can easily lead to statistically significant results that are not practically important. In contrast, small samples can fail to produce statistically significant results that might indeed be practically important.

As this example illustrates, there is always a possibility of statistical significance but not practical significance with large sample sizes. To be fair, we should also mention the opposite case, which typically occurs with small sample sizes. Here the results are not statistically significant even though the truth about the population(s), if it were known, would be of practical significance. Let's assume that a medical researcher wants to test whether a new form of treatment produces a higher cure rate for a deadly disease than the best treatment currently on the market. Due to expenses, the researcher is able to run a controlled experiment on only a relatively small number of patients with the disease. Unfortunately, the results of the experiment are inconclusive. They show some evidence that the new treatment works better, but the *p*-value for the test is only 0.25.

In the scientific community these results would not be enough to warrant a switch to the new treatment. However, it is certainly possible that the new treatment, if it were used on a large number of patients, would provide a "significant" improvement in the cure rate—where "significant" now means *practical* significance. In this type of situation, the researcher could easily fail to discover practical significance because the sample sizes are not large enough to detect it statistically.

From here on, when we use the term "significant," we mean *statistically* significant. However, you should always keep the ideas in this section in mind. A statistically significant result is not necessarily of practical importance. Conversely, a result that fails to be statistically significant is not necessarily one that should be ignored.

9.3 HYPOTHESIS TESTS FOR A POPULATION MEAN

Now that we have covered the general concepts behind hypothesis testing and the principal sampling distributions, the mechanics of hypothesis testing are fairly straightforward. We discuss in some detail how the procedure works for a population mean. Then in later sections we illustrate similar hypothesis tests for other parameters.

As with confidence intervals, the key to the analysis is the sampling distribution of the sample mean. Recall that if you subtract the true mean μ from the sample mean and divide the difference by the standard error $s/\sqrt{n}$, the result has a t distribution with $n - 1$ degrees of freedom. In a hypothesis-testing context, the true mean to use is the null hypothesis value, specifically, the borderline value between the null and alternative hypotheses. This value is usually labeled μ_0, where the subscript indicates that it is based on the *null* hypothesis.

To run the test, you calculate the *test statistic* in Equation (9.1). This *t*-value indicates how many standard errors the sample mean is from the null value, μ_0. If the null hypothesis is true, or more specifically, if $\mu = \mu_0$, this test statistic has a t distribution with $n - 1$ degrees of freedom. The *p*-value for the test is the probability beyond the test statistic in both tails (for a two-tailed alternative) or in a single tail (for a one-tailed alternative) of the t distribution.

$$\text{Test Statistic for Test of Mean}$$

$$t\text{-value} = \frac{\overline{X} - \mu_0}{s/\sqrt{n}} \qquad (9.1)$$

We illustrate the procedure by continuing the pizza manager's problem in Example 9.1.

EXAMPLE

9.1 EXPERIMENTING WITH A NEW PIZZA STYLE AT THE PEPPERONI PIZZA RESTAURANT (CONTINUED)

Recall that the manager of the Pepperoni Pizza Restaurant is running an experiment to test the hypotheses $H_0: \mu \leq 0$ versus $H_a: \mu > 0$, where μ is the mean rating in the entire customer population. Here, each customer rates the difference between an old-style pizza and a new-style pizza on a scale from -10 to $+10$, where negative ratings favor the old style and positive ratings favor the new style. The ratings for 40 randomly selected customers and several summary statistics appear in Figure 9.3. (See the file **Pizza Ratings.xlsx**.) Is there sufficient evidence from these sample data for the manager to reject H_0?

Figure 9.3

Data and Summary Measures for Pizza Example

	A	B	C	D	E
1	Customer	Rating			Rating
2	1	-7		*One Variable Summary*	Data Set #1
3	2	7		**Mean**	2.100
4	3	-2		**Std. Dev.**	4.717
5	4	4		**Count**	40
6	5	7			
7	6	6			
8	7	0			
9	8	2			

Objective To use a one-sample t test to see whether consumers prefer the new-style pizza to the old style.

Solution

From the summary statistics, we see that the sample mean is $\overline{X} = 2.10$ and the sample standard deviation is $s = 4.717$. This positive sample mean provides some evidence in favor of the alternative hypothesis, but given the rather large value of s and the box plot of ratings in Figure 9.4, which indicates a lot of negative ratings, does it provide *enough* evidence to reject H_0?

To run the test, you calculate the test statistic, using the borderline null hypothesis value $\mu_0 = 0$, and report how much probability is beyond it in the right tail of the appropriate t distribution. The *right* tail is appropriate because the alternative is one-tailed of the "greater than" variety. The test statistic is

$$t\text{-value} = \frac{2.10 - 0}{4.717/\sqrt{40}} = 2.816$$

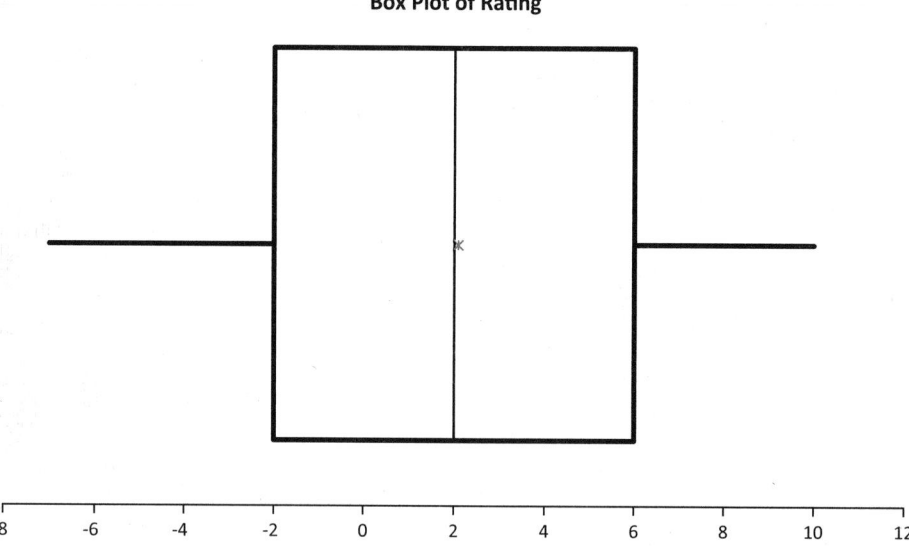

Figure 9.4

Box Plot for Pizza Data

Box Plot of Rating

This t-value indicates that the sample mean is slightly more than 2.8 standard errors to the right of the null value, 0. Intuitively, this provides a lot of evidence in favor of the alternative—it is quite unlikely to see a sample mean 2.8 standard errors to right of a "true" mean. The probability beyond this value in the right tail of a t distribution with $n - 1 = 39$ degrees of freedom is approximately 0.004, which can be found in Excel with the formula **=TDIST(2.816,39,1)**. (Recall that the first argument is the t-value, the second is the degrees of freedom, and the third is the number of tails. Better yet, recall that this value can be calculated in Excel 2010 with the more intuitive formula **=T.DIST.RT(2.816,39)**.)

This probability, 0.004, is the p-value for the test. It indicates that these sample results would be *very* unlikely if the null hypothesis were true. The manager has two choices at this point. He can conclude that the null hypothesis is true and he obtained a very unlikely sample, or he can conclude that the alternative hypothesis is true—and presumably switch to the new-style pizza. This second conclusion certainly appears to be the more reasonable of the two.

Another way of interpreting the results of the test is in terms of traditional significance levels. The null hypothesis can be rejected at the 1% significance level because the p-value is less than 0.01. Of course, it can also be rejected at the 5% level or the 10% level because the p-value is also less than 0.05 and 0.10. But the p-value is the preferred way to report the results because it indicates exactly *how* significant these sample results are.

The StatTools One-Sample Hypothesis Test procedure can be used to perform this analysis easily, with the results shown in Figure 9.5. To use it, create a StatTools data set and select Hypothesis Test and then Mean/Std. Deviation from the StatTools Statistical Inference dropdown list. Then fill out the resulting dialog box as shown in Figure 9.6. In particular, make sure the Analysis Type is One-Sample Analysis and the Alternative Hypothesis Type is the "Greater Than" choice.

Most of the output in Figure 9.5 should be familiar: It mirrors the calculations we just did, and you can check the formulas in the output cells to ensure that you understand the procedure. Note the following. First, the value in cell E13, 0, is the null hypothesis value μ_0 at the borderline between H_0 and H_a; it is the value specified in the dialog box in Figure 9.6. Second, look at the note entered in cell D9. (This note isn't visible in Figure 9.5,

Figure 9.5
Hypothesis Test for
the Mean for the
Pizza Example

	D	E
8		Rating
9	*Hypothesis Test (One-Sample)*	Data Set #1
10	Sample Size	40
11	Sample Mean	2.100
12	Sample Std Dev	4.717
13	Hypothesized Mean	0
14	Alternative Hypothesis	> 0
15	Standard Error of Mean	0.746
16	Degrees of Freedom	39
17	t-Test Statistic	2.8159
18	p-Value	0.0038
19	Null Hypoth. at 10% Significance	Reject
20	Null Hypoth. at 5% Significance	Reject
21	Null Hypoth. at 1% Significance	Reject

Figure 9.6
One-Sample
Hypothesis Test
Dialog Box

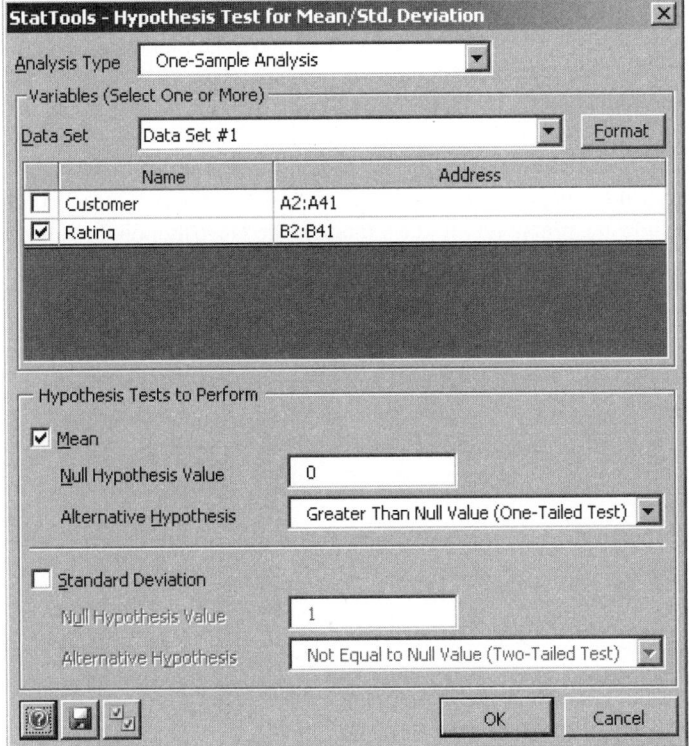

but it can be seen in the completed file.) It reminds you that this test is based on the normality of the underlying population distribution and/or a sufficiently large sample size. If these conditions are not satisfied (which is not a problem for this example), then other more appropriate tests are available. Finally, StatTools compares the p-value to the three traditional significance levels, 1%, 5%, and 10%, and interprets significance in terms of these. As indicated in cells E19, E20, and E21, the null hypothesis can be rejected in favor of the alternative at each of these three significance levels. ∎

Test Statistics and _p_-values

All hypothesis tests are implemented by calculating a test statistic from the data and seeing how far out this test statistic is in one of the tails of some well-known distribution. The details of this procedure might or might not be included in the output from statistical software, but the _p_-value is always included. The _p_-value specifies the probability in the tail (or tails) beyond the test statistic. In words, it measures how unlikely such an extreme value of the test statistic is if the null hypothesis is true.

Before leaving this example, we ask one last question. Should the manager switch to the new-style pizza on the basis of these sample results? We would probably recommend "yes." There is no indication that the new-style pizza costs any more to make than the old-style pizza, and the sample evidence is fairly convincing that customers, on average, prefer the new-style pizza. Therefore, unless there are reasons for not switching that we haven't mentioned here, we recommend the switch. However, if it costs more to make the new-style pizza (and its price is no higher), hypothesis testing is _not_ the best way to perform the decision analysis. We return to this theme throughout this chapter.

Example 9.1 illustrates how to run and interpret any one-tailed hypothesis for the mean, assuming the alternative is of the "greater than" variety. If the alternative is still one-tailed but of the "less than" variety, there is virtually no change. We illustrate this in Figure 9.7, where the ratings have been reversed in sign. That is, each rating was multiplied by -1, so that negative ratings now favor the new-style pizza. The hypotheses are now $H_0: \mu \geq 0$ versus $H_a: \mu < 0$ because a negative mean now supports the new style. The only difference in running the analysis with StatTools is that you select the "Less Than" choice for the Alternative Analysis Type in the dialog box shown in Figure 9.6. As Figure 9.7 indicates, the test statistic is now the negative of the previous test statistic, -2.816, and the _p_-value, 0.004, is exactly the same. This is now the probability in the _left_ tail of the t distribution, but the interpretation of the results is the same as before.

Figure 9.7

Hypothesis Test with Reverse Coding

	A	B	C	D	E
1	Customer	Rating			Rating
2	1	7		_Hypothesis Test (One-Sample)_	Data Set #2
3	2	-7		Sample Size	40
4	3	2		Sample Mean	-2.100
5	4	-4		Sample Std Dev	4.717
6	5	-7		Hypothesized Mean	0
7	6	-6		Alternative Hypothesis	< 0
8	7	0		Standard Error of Mean	0.746
9	8	-2		Degrees of Freedom	39
10	9	-8		t-Test Statistic	-2.8159
11	10	-2		p-Value	0.0038
12	11	-3		Null Hypoth. at 10% Significance	Reject
13	12	4		Null Hypoth. at 5% Significance	Reject
14	13	-8		Null Hypoth. at 1% Significance	Reject
15	14	5			
16	15	-7			
17	16	5			

The analysis of two-tailed tests for the mean is also quite similar to the analysis in Example 9.1. A typical two-tailed test is illustrated in the following example.

9.2 MEASURING STUDENT REACTION TO A NEW TEXTBOOK

A large required chemistry course at State University has been using the same textbook for a number of years. Over the years, the students have been asked to rate this textbook on 10-point scale, and the average rating has been stable at about 5.2. This year, the faculty decided to experiment with a new textbook. After the course, 50 randomly selected students were asked to rate this new textbook, also on a scale of 1 to 10. The results appear in column B of Figure 9.8. (See the file **Textbook Ratings.xlsx**.) Can we conclude that the students like this new textbook any more or less than the previous textbook?

Figure 9.8 Test of Two-Tailed Alternative

	A	B	C	D	E	F
1	Student	Rating		Mean rating of previous textbook (on a 1-10 scale)		5.2
2	1	6				
3	2	3			Rating	
4	3	6		*Hypothesis Test (One-Sample)*	Data Set #1	
5	4	7		Sample Size	50	
6	5	6		Sample Mean	5.680	
7	6	10		Sample Std Dev	1.953	
8	7	6		Hypothesized Mean	5.2	
9	8	8		Alternative Hypothesis	<> 5.2	
10	9	7		Standard Error of Mean	0 276	
11	10	10		Degrees of Freedom	49	
12	11	3		t-Test Statistic	1.738	
13	12	6		p-Value	0.088	
14	13	4		Null Hypoth. at 10% Significance	Reject	
15	14	6		Null Hypoth. at 5% Significance	Don't Reject	
16	15	8		Null Hypoth. at 1% Significance	Don't Reject	
17	16	10				
18	17	5			Rating	
19	18	4		*Conf. Intervals (One-Sample)*	Data Set #1	
20	19	6		Sample Size	50	
21	20	4		Sample Mean	5.680	
22	21	6		Sample Std Dev	1.953	
23	22	6		Confidence Level (Mean)	95.0%	
24	23	4		Degrees of Freedom	49	
25	24	5		Lower Limit	5 125	
26	25	7		Upper Limit	6.235	
27	26	8				
28	27	7				
29	28	5				

Objective To use a one-sample t test, with a two-tailed alternative, to see whether students like the new textbook any more or less than the old textbook.

Solution

The first question is whether the test should be one-tailed or two-tailed. Of course, the faculty have chosen the new textbook with the expectation that it will be preferred by the students, but it is very possible that students will like it *less* than the previous textbook.

(Students are notoriously unpredictable in their acceptance of textbooks.) Therefore, we set this up as a two-tailed test—that is, the alternative hypothesis is that the mean rating of the new textbook is either less than *or* greater than the mean rating of the previous textbook. Formally, we write the hypotheses as $H_0:\mu = 5.2$ versus $H_a:\mu \neq 5.2$.

The test is run (and the StatTools One-Sample Hypothesis Test procedure can be used) almost exactly as with a one-tailed test. The only difference is that you specify the "Not Equal" choice for the Alternative Hypothesis Type, and the Null Hypothesis Value is now 5.2, the historical average rating. (See Figure 9.9.) The *t*-distributed test statistic is calculated in the same way as before:

$$t\text{-value} = \frac{\overline{X} - 5.2}{s/\sqrt{n}} = \frac{5.680 - 5.2}{1.953/\sqrt{50}} = 1.738$$

The *p*-value is then the probability beyond -1.738 in the left tail *and* beyond $+1.738$ in the right tail of a *t* distribution with $n - 1 = 49$ degrees of freedom. The effect is to double the one-tailed *p*-value. From the output (cell E13) in Figure 9.8, you can see that the two-tailed *p*-value is 0.088.

Figure 9.9

Dialog Box for Two-Tailed Hypothesis Test

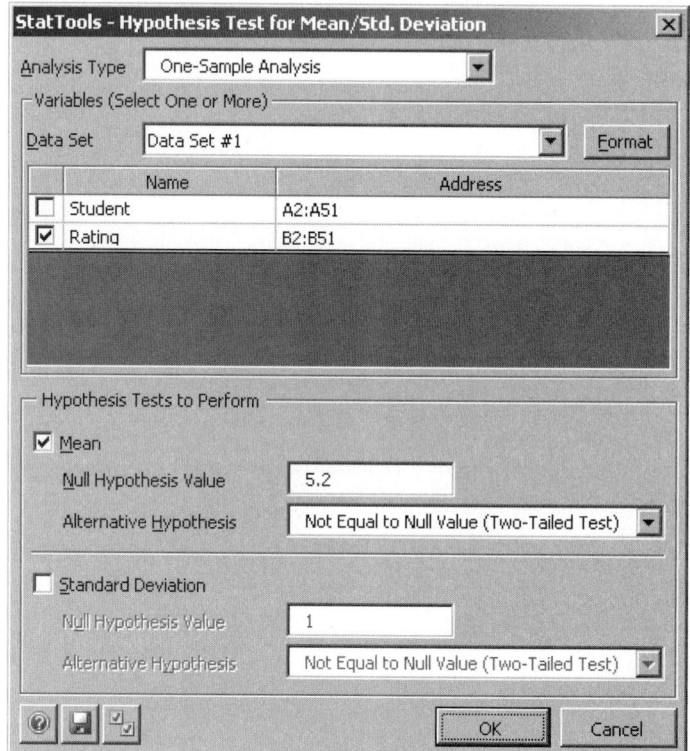

This moderately small *p*-value provides some evidence, but not absolutely convincing evidence, that the mean rating of the new textbook is different from the old mean rating of 5.2. Specifically, the output indicates that the null hypothesis can be rejected at the 10% level, but not at the 5% or 1% levels. If the *p*-value were lower (which might occur if more students were sampled), the evidence would be more conclusive. As in Example 9.1, we can now ask whether the faculty should continue to use the new textbook. Here again, it is probably not a decision that hypothesis testing, at least by itself, should determine. The students *appear* to favor the new textbook, if only by a small margin. If the faculty also favor it, we see no reason for not switching to it.

Because this is a two-tailed test, you could also perform the test by appealing to confidence intervals. A 95% confidence interval for the mean rating of the new textbook, also shown in Figure 9.8, extends from 5.125 to 6.235. Because this interval *does* include the old mean rating of 5.2, the null hypothesis cannot be rejected at the 5% significance level. This is in agreement with the *p*-value of the test, which is greater than 0.05. However, you can check that a 90% confidence interval for the mean does *not* include 5.2. Therefore, the null hypothesis can be rejected at the 10% level. This too is in agreement with the *p*-value, which is less than 0.10. ■

PROBLEMS

Note: Student solutions for problems whose numbers appear within a colored box are available for purchase at www.cengagebrain.com.

Level A

1. The file **P09_01.xlsx** contains a random sample of 100 lightbulb lifetimes. The company that produces these lightbulbs wants to know whether it can claim that its lightbulbs typically last more than 1000 burning hours.
   a. Identify the null and alternative hypotheses for this situation.
   b. Can this lightbulb manufacturer claim that its lightbulbs typically last more than 1000 hours at the 5% significance level? What about at the 1% significance level? Explain your answers.

2. A manufacturer is interested in determining whether it can claim that the boxes of detergent it sells contain, on average, more than 500 grams of detergent. The firm selects a random sample of 100 boxes and records the amount of detergent (in grams) in each box. The data are provided in the file **P09_02.xlsx**.
   a. Identify the null and alternative hypotheses for this situation.
   b. Is there statistical support for the manufacturer's claim? Explain.

3. A producer of steel cables wants to know whether the steel cables it produces have an average breaking strength of 5000 pounds. An average breaking strength of less than 5000 pounds would not be adequate, and to produce steel cables with an average breaking strength in excess of 5000 pounds would unnecessarily increase production costs. The producer collects a random sample of 64 steel cable pieces. The breaking strength for each of these cable pieces is recorded in the file **P09_03.xlsx**.
   a. Identify the null and alternative hypotheses for this situation.
   b. Using a 5% significance level, what statistical conclusion can the producer reach regarding the average breaking strength of its steel cables? Would the conclusion be any different at the 1% level? Explain your answers.

4. A U.S. Navy recruiting center knows from past experience that the heights of its recruits have traditionally been normally distributed with mean 69 inches. The recruiting center wants to test the claim that the average height of this year's recruits is greater than 69 inches. To do this, recruiting personnel take a random sample of 64 recruits from this year and record their heights. The data are provided in the file **P09_04.xlsx**.
   a. Identify the null and alternative hypotheses for this situation.
   b. On the basis of the available sample information, do the recruiters find support for the given claim at the 5% significance level? Explain.
   c. Use the sample data to construct a 95% confidence interval for the average height of this year's recruits. Based on this confidence interval, what conclusion should recruiting personnel reach regarding the given claim?

5. Suppose that you wish to test $H_0:\mu = 10$ versus $H_a:\mu > 10$ at the $\alpha = 0.05$ significance level. Furthermore, suppose that you observe values of the sample mean and sample standard deviation when $n = 40$ that do *not* lead to the rejection of H_0. Is it true that you might reject H_0 if you observed the same values of the sample mean and sample standard deviation from a sample with $n > 40$? Why or why not?

Level B

6. A study is performed in a large southern town to determine whether the average weekly grocery bill per four-person family in the town is significantly different from the national average. A random sample of the weekly grocery bills of four-person families in this town is given in the file **P09_06.xlsx**.
   a. Identify the null and alternative hypotheses for this situation.
   b. Assume that the national average weekly grocery bill for a four-person family is $100. Is the sample evidence statistically significant? If so, at what significance levels can you reject the null hypothesis?

c. For which values of the sample mean (i.e., average weekly grocery bill) would you reject the null hypothesis at the 1% significance level? For which values of the sample mean would you reject the null hypothesis at the 10% level?

7. An aircraft manufacturer needs to buy aluminum sheets with an average thickness of 0.05 inch. The manufacturer knows that significantly thinner sheets would be unsafe and considerably thicker sheets would be too heavy. A random sample of 100 sheets from a potential supplier is collected. The thickness of each sheet in this sample is measured (in inches) and recorded in the file **P09_07.xlsx**.

    a. Identify the null and alternative hypotheses for this situation.

b. Based on the results of an appropriate hypothesis test, should the aircraft manufacturer buy aluminum sheets from this supplier? Explain why or why not.

c. For which values of the sample mean (i.e., average thickness) would the aircraft manufacturer decide to buy sheets from this supplier? Assume a significance level of 5% in answering this question.

8. Suppose that you observe a random sample of size n from a normally distributed population. If you are able to reject $H_0: \mu = \mu_0$ in favor of a two-tailed alternative hypothesis at the 10% significance level, is it true that you can definitely reject H_0 in favor of the appropriate one-tailed alternative at the 5% significance level? Why or why not?

9.4 HYPOTHESIS TESTS FOR OTHER PARAMETERS

Just as we developed confidence intervals for a variety of parameters, we can develop hypothesis tests for other parameters. They are based on the same sampling distributions we discussed in the previous chapter, and they are run and interpreted exactly as the tests for the mean in the previous section. In each case the sample data are used to calculate a test statistic that has a well-known sampling distribution. Then a corresponding p-value measures the support for the alternative hypothesis. Beyond this, only the details change, as we illustrate in this section.

9.4.1 Hypothesis Tests for a Population Proportion

To test a population proportion p, recall that the sample proportion $\hat{p}$ has a sampling distribution that is approximately normal when the sample size is reasonably large. Specifically, the distribution of the standardized value

$$\frac{\hat{p} - p}{\sqrt{p(1 - p)/n}}$$

is approximately normal with mean 0 and standard deviation 1.

    Let p_0 be the borderline value of p between the null and alternative hypotheses. Then p_0 is substituted for p to obtain the test statistic in Equation (9.2). The p-value of the test is found by seeing how much probability is beyond this test statistic in the tail (or tails) of the standard normal distribution.[2] A rule of thumb for checking the large-sample assumption of this test is to check whether $np_0 > 5$ and $n(1 - p_0) > 5$.

Test Statistic for Test of Proportion

$$z\text{-value} = \frac{\hat{p} - p_0}{\sqrt{p_0(1 - p_0)/n}} \qquad (9.2)$$

We illustrate this test of proportion in the following example.

---

[2]Do not confuse the unknown proportion p with the p-value of the test. They are logically different concepts and just happen to share the same letter p.

9.3 CUSTOMER COMPLAINTS AT WALPOLE APPLIANCE COMPANY

The Walpole Appliance Company has a customer service department that handles customer questions and complaints. This department's processes are set up to respond quickly and accurately to customers who phone in their concerns. However, there is a sizable minority of customers who prefer to write letters. Traditionally, the customer service department has not been very efficient in responding to these customers.

Letter writers first receive a mailgram asking them to call customer service (which is exactly what letter writers wanted to avoid in the first place), and when they do call, the customer service representative who answers the phone typically has no knowledge of the customer's problem. As a result, the department manager estimates that 15% of letter writers have not obtained a satisfactory response within 30 days of the time their letters were first received. The manager's goal is to reduce this value by at least half, that is, to 7.5% or less.

To do so, she changes the process for responding to letter writers. Under the new process, these customers now receive a prompt and courteous form letter that responds to their problem. (This is possible because the vast majority of concerns can be addressed by one of several form letters.) Each form letter states that if the customer still has problems, he or she can call the department. The manager also files the original letters so that if customers do call back, the representative who answers will be able to find their letters quickly and respond intelligently. With this new process in place, the manager has tracked 400 letter writers and has found that only 23 of them are classified as "unsatisfied" after a 30-day period. Does it appear that the manager has achieved her goal?

Objective   To use a test for a proportion to see whether the new process of responding to complaint letters results in an acceptably low proportion of unsatisfied customers.

Solution

The manager's goal is to reduce the proportion of unsatisfied customers after 30 days from 0.15 to 0.075 or less. Because the burden of proof is on her to "prove" that she has accomplished this goal, we set up the hypotheses as $H_0{:}p \geq 0.075$ versus $H_a{:}\ p < 0.075$, where p is the proportion of all letter writers who are still unsatisfied after 30 days. The sample proportion she has observed is $\hat{p} = 23/400 = 0.0575$. This is obviously less than 0.075, but is it *enough* less to reject the null hypothesis?

The test can be run with StatTools, as shown in Figure 9.10 and the file **Customer Complaints.xlsx**. The trick is to arrange the data in one of the three formats for a StatTools proportions analysis, as described in section 8.5 of the previous chapter. (Refer to the finished version of the file **Satisfaction Ratings.xlsx** in the previous chapter for more details.) For this example, the data are arranged as shown in the range A5:B7. This is the StatTools data set, a table of counts. Then you run the test by selecting Hypothesis Test/Proportion from the Statistical Inference dropdown list and filling in the dialog box as shown in Figure 9.11. The results of the test appear in column E of Figure 9.10. Specifically, the sample proportion is $23/400 = 0.058$, its standard error is 0.013, the test statistic is -1.329, and the p-value for the test is 0.092.

The p-value might not be as low as you expected—or as low as the manager would like. In spite of the fact that the sample proportion appears to be well below the target proportion of 0.075, the evidence in support of the alternative hypothesis is not overwhelming. In statistical terminology, the results are significant at the 10% level, but not at the 5% or 1% levels.

Figure 9.10 also shows a 95% confidence interval for the unknown proportion p. This confidence interval extends from 0.035 to 0.080. It includes the target value, 0.075, but just

Figure 9.10 Analysis of New Process for Letter Writers

	A	B	C	D	E
1	**Test of a proportion: responding to customer complaint letters**				
2					
3	Target proportion with new procedure	0.075			**Count**
4				**Hypothesis Test (Proportion)**	**Data Set #1**
5	Category	Count		**Category**	Number of unsatisfied customers
6	Number of unsatisfied customers	23		**Sample Size**	400
7	Number of satisfied customers	377		**Sample Proportion**	0.058
8				**Hypothesized Proportion**	0.075
9				**Alternative Hypothesis**	< 0.075
10				**Standard Error of Sample Proportion**	0.013
11				**z-Test Statistic**	-1.3288
12				**p-Value**	0.0920
13				**Null Hypoth. at 10% Significance**	Reject
14				**Null Hypoth. at 5% Significance**	Don't Reject
15				**Null Hypoth. at 1% Significance**	Don't Reject
16					
17					**Count**
18				**Conf. Interval (Proportion)**	**Data Set #1**
19				**Category**	Number of unsatisfied customers
20				**Sample Size**	400
21				**Sample Proportion**	0.058
22				**Confidence Level**	95.0%
23				**Standard Error of Proportion**	0.012
24				**Lower Limit**	0.035
25				**Upper Limit**	0.080

Figure 9.11

Dialog Box for a Test of a Proportion

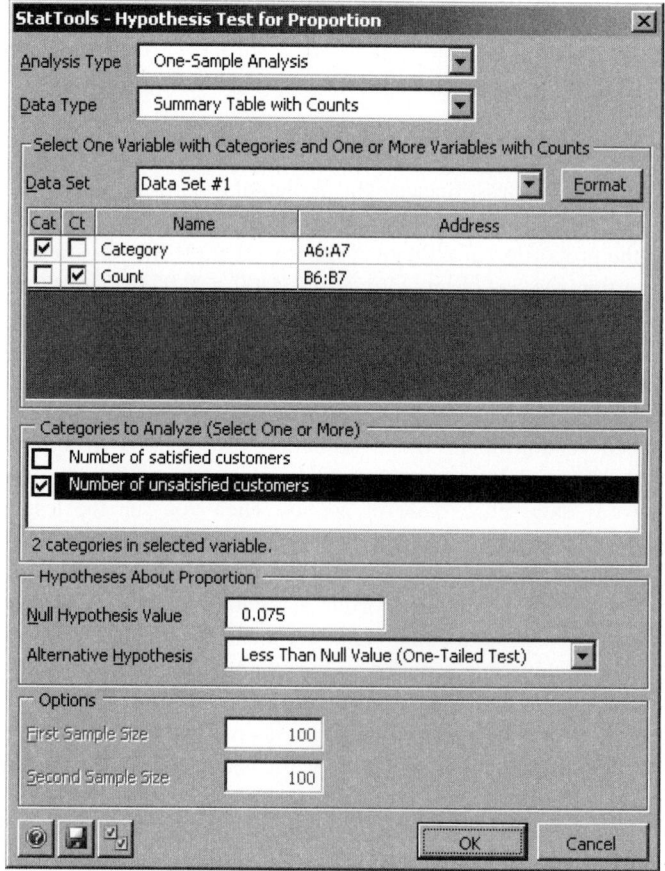

barely. In this sense it also provides some support for the argument that the manager has indeed achieved her goal.[3]

Analysts might disagree on whether a hypothesis test or a confidence interval is the more appropriate way to present these results. However, we see them as complementary and do not necessarily favor one over the other. The bottom line is that they both provide some, but not totally conclusive, evidence that the manager has achieved her goal. ■

9.4.2 Hypothesis Tests for Differences between Population Means

This comparison problem—comparing two population means—is one of the most important problems analyzed with statistical methods. It can be analyzed with confidence intervals, hypothesis tests, or both.

We now discuss the comparison problem, where the **difference between two population means** is tested. As in the previous chapter, the form of the analysis depends on whether the two samples are independent or paired. For variety, we begin with the paired case.

If the samples are paired, then the test proceeds exactly as in section 9.3, using the differences as the single variable of analysis. That is, if $\overline{D}$ is the sample mean difference between n pairs, D_0 is the hypothesized difference (the borderline value between H_0 and H_a), and s_D is the sample standard deviation of the differences, then the test is based on the test statistic in Equation (9.3). If D_0 is the true mean difference, this test statistic has a t distribution with $n - 1$ degrees of freedom. The validity of the test also requires that n be reasonably large and/or the population of *differences* be approximately normally distributed.

> **Test Statistic for Paired Samples Test of Difference Between Means**
> $$t\text{-value} = \frac{\overline{D} - D_0}{s_D/\sqrt{n}}$$
> (9.3)

If the samples are independent and the population standard deviations are equal, the two-sample theory discussed in section 8.7 is relevant. It leads to the test statistic in Equation (9.4). Here, $\overline{X}_1$ and $\overline{X}_2$ are the two sample means, D_0 is the hypothesized difference, n_1 and n_2 are the sample sizes, and s_p is the same pooled estimate of the common population standard deviation as in the previous chapter:

$$s_p = \sqrt{\frac{(n_1 - 1)s_1^2 + (n_2 - 1)s_2^2}{n_1 + n_2 - 2}}$$

If D_0 is the true mean difference, this test statistic has a t distribution with $n_1 + n_2 - 2$ degrees of freedom. The validity of this test again requires that the sample sizes be reasonably large and/or the populations be approximately normally distributed.

> **Test Statistic for Independent Samples Test of Difference Between Means**
> $$t\text{-value} = \frac{(\overline{X}_1 - \overline{X}_2) - D_0}{s_p\sqrt{1/n_1 + 1/n_2}}$$
> (9.4)

---

[3]Note that the standard error in cell E10 for the hypothesis test uses the target proportion 0.075. In contrast, the standard error for the confidence interval in cell E23 uses the sample proportion 0.0575. The sampling distribution for a hypothesis test always uses the borderline value between H_0 and H_a. But because confidence intervals are not connected to any hypotheses, their standard errors must rely on sample data. In most cases the two standard errors are practically the same.

Fortunately, these formulas are implemented automatically by StatTools's procedures. We begin by illustrating an example of the paired-sample t test.

EXAMPLE	9.4 MEASURING THE EFFECTS OF TRADITIONAL AND NEW STYLES OF SOFT-DRINK CANS

Beer and soft-drink companies have become very concerned about the style of their cans. There are cans with fluted and embossed sides and cans with six-color graphics and holograms. Coca-Cola has even introduced a contoured can, shaped like the old-fashioned Coke bottle minus the neck. Evidently, these companies believe the style of the can makes a difference to consumers, which presumably translates into higher sales.

Assume that a soft-drink company is considering a style change to its current can, which has been the company's trademark for many years. To determine whether this new style is popular with consumers, the company runs a number of focus group sessions around the country. At each of these sessions, randomly selected consumers are allowed to examine the new and traditional styles, exchange ideas, and offer their opinions. Eventually, they fill out a form where, among other questions, they are asked to respond to the following items, each on a scale of 1 to 7, 7 being the best:

- Rate the attractiveness of the traditional-style can (AO).
- Rate the attractiveness of the new-style can (AN).
- Rate the likelihood that you would buy the product with the traditional-style can (WBO).
- Rate the likelihood that you would buy the product with the new-style can (WBN).

(A and WB stand for "attractiveness" and "would buy," and O and N stand for "old" and "new.") What can the company conclude from these data? (See the file **Soft-Drink Cans.xlsx**.) Are hypothesis tests appropriate?

Objective   To use paired-sample t tests for differences between means to see whether consumers rate the attractiveness, and their likelihood to purchase, higher for a new-style can than for the traditional-style can.

Solution

First, it is a good idea to examine summary statistics for the data. The averages from each survey item are shown at the bottom of Figure 9.12. They indicate some support for the new-style can. Also, you might expect the ratings for a given consumer to be correlated. This turns out to be the case, as shown by the relatively large positive correlations in Figure 9.13. These large positive correlations indicate that if you want to examine differences between survey items, a paired-sample procedure will make the most efficient use of the data. Of course, a paired-sample procedure also makes sense because each consumer answers each item on the form. (If this is confusing, think about the following alternative setup, where there are four *separate* groups of consumers. The first group responds to item 1 only, the second group responds to item 2 only, and so on. Then the responses to the various items are in no way paired, and an *independent-sample* procedure would be used instead. However, this experimental design is not as efficient as the paired design in terms of making the best use of a given amount of data.)

There are several differences of interest. The two most obvious are the difference between the attractiveness ratings of the two styles and the difference between the likelihoods of buying the two styles—that is, column B minus column C and column D minus column E. A third difference of interest is the difference between the attractiveness ratings of the new

Figure 9.12

Data on Soft-Drink Cans

	A	B	C	D	E
1	Consumer	AO	AN	WBO	WBN
2	1	5	7	4	1
3	2	7	7	6	6
4	3	6	7	7	6
5	4	1	3	1	1
6	5	3	4	1	1
7	6	7	7	7	7
8	7	5	7	4	6
9	8	6	7	6	7
10	9	5	7	6	6
11	10	5	4	4	6
12	11	1	3	1	1
13	12	2	1	1	3
14	13	6	6	6	6
15	14	4	5	3	3
16	15	2	5	1	1
17	16	6	7	7	7
18	17	4	5	2	1
179	178	5	4	4	3
180	179	3	4	1	3
181	180	3	5	6	7
182					
183	Averages	4.41	4.95	3.86	4.34

Figure 9.13

Correlations for Soft-Drink Can Data

	A	B	C	D	E
7					
8	**Correlation Table**	AO	AN	WBO	WBN
9	AO	1.000			
10	AN	0.740	1.000		
11	WBO	0.746	0.595	1.000	
12	WBN	0.594	0.401	0.774	1.000

style and the likelihoods of buying the new can—that is, column C minus column E. This difference indicates whether *perceptions* of the new-style can are likely to translate into actual *sales*. Finally, a fourth difference that might be of interest is the difference between the third difference (column C minus column E) and the similar difference for the old style (column B minus column D). This checks whether the translation of perceptions into sales is any different for the two styles of cans.

All of these differences appear next to the original data in Figure 9.14. In terms of the original data, they are labeled as:

- Diff1: AO − AN
- Diff2: WBO − WBN
- Diff3: AN − WBN
- Diff4: AO − WBO
- Diff5: (AN − WBN) − (AO − WBO)

These differences have been calculated in columns F through J. (Actually, StatTools's Paired-Sample procedure generates the required differences internally when it tests

Figure 9.14 Original and Difference Variables for Soft-Drink Can Data

	A	B	C	D	E	F	G	H	I	J
1	Consumer	AO	AN	WBO	WBN	AO-AN	WBO-WBN	AN-WBN	AO-WBO	(AN-WBN)-(AO-WBO)
2	1	5	7	4	1	-2	3	6	1	5
3	2	7	7	6	6	0	0	1	1	0
4	3	6	7	7	6	-1	1	1	-1	2
5	4	1	3	1	1	-2	0	2	0	2
6	5	3	4	1	1	-1	0	3	2	1
7	6	7	7	7	7	0	0	0	0	0
8	7	5	7	4	6	-2	-2	1	1	0
9	8	6	7	6	7	-1	-1	0	0	0
10	9	5	7	6	6	-2	0	1	-1	2
11	10	5	4	4	6	1	-2	-2	1	-3
12	11	1	3	1	1	-2	0	2	0	2
13	12	2	1	1	3	1	-2	-2	1	-3

these differences. We manually inserted the differences in Figure 9.14 so that you can see them explicitly.)

For each of the differences, Diff1, Diff2, Diff3, and Diff5, you can test the mean difference over all potential consumers with a paired-sample analysis. (You actually run the one-sample procedure on the difference variables.) Exactly as in the previous chapter, each difference variable is treated as a *single* sample and the same t test as in section 9.3 is run on this sample. (This means that the differences in columns F through J of Figure 9.14 should be included in the StatTools data set.) In each case the hypothesized difference, D_0, is 0. The only question is whether to run one-tailed or two-tailed tests. We suggest that the tests for Diff1, Diff2, and Diff5 be two-tailed tests and that the test on Diff3 be a one-tailed test with the alternative of the "greater than" variety. The reasoning is that the company probably has little idea which way the differences Diff1, Diff2, and Diff5 will go (positive or negative), whereas it expects that Diff3 to be positive on average. That is, the company expects consumers' ratings of the attractiveness of the new design to be larger, on average, than their likelihoods of purchasing the product. However, any of these hypotheses could be run as one-tailed or two-tailed tests. It depends on the prior beliefs of the company. In any case, to change a one-tailed p-value to a two-tailed p-value, all you need to do is multiply by 2. Similarly, you can change two-tailed p-values to one-tailed p-values by dividing by 2.

The results from the four tests appear in Figures 9.15 and 9.16. (These outputs also include 99% confidence intervals for the corresponding mean differences.) You can obtain each output for Diff1, Diff2, and Diff3 by selecting Confidence Interval or Hypothesis Test from the StatTools Statistical Inference dropdown list, used on the appropriate difference variable and the One-Sample analysis type.[4]

Results of the analysis of soft-drink can style

■ From the output for the Diff1 variable (AO − AN) in Figure 9.15, there is overwhelming evidence that consumers, on average, rate the attractiveness of the new design higher than the attractiveness of the current design. The t-distributed test statistic is −5.351, calculated as

$$\frac{-0.539 - 0}{0.101} = -5.351$$

[4]Because this can be a source of confusion, we repeat again that when you want to run a paired-sample analysis in StatTools, you can do it by creating the differences manually and then using the One-Sample option, or you can choose the Paired-Sample option and select the two original variables you want to compare, in which case StatTools creates the difference variable internally for you. The results are identical.

Figure 9.15   Analysis of Diff1 and Diff2 Variables

	A	B	C	D	E
7		AO-AN			WBO-WBN
8	*Conf. Intervals (One-Sample)*	Data Set #1		*Conf. Intervals (One-Sample)*	Data Set #1
9	Sample Size	180		Sample Size	180
10	Sample Mean	-0.539		Sample Mean	-0.478
11	Sample Std Dev	1.351		Sample Std Dev	1.347
12	Confidence Level (Mean)	99.0%		Confidence Level (Mean)	99.0%
13	Degrees of Freedom	179		Degrees of Freedom	179
14	Lower Limit	-0.801		Lower Limit	-0.739
15	Upper Limit	-0.277		Upper Limit	-0.216
16					
17		AO-AN			WBO-WBN
18	*Hypothesis Test (One-Sample)*	Data Set #1		*Hypothesis Test (One-Sample)*	Data Set #1
19	Sample Size	180		Sample Size	180
20	Sample Mean	-0.539		Sample Mean	-0.478
21	Sample Std Dev	1.351		Sample Std Dev	1.347
22	Hypothesized Mean	0		Hypothesized Mean	0
23	Alternative Hypothesis	<> 0		Alternative Hypothesis	<> 0
24	Standard Error of Mean	0.1007		Standard Error of Mean	0.1004
25	Degrees of Freedom	179		Degrees of Freedom	179
26	t-Test Statistic	-5.3514		t-Test Statistic	-4.7578
27	p-Value	< 0.0001		p-Value	< 0.0001
28	Null Hypoth. at 10% Significance	Reject		Null Hypoth. at 10% Significance	Reject
29	Null Hypoth. at 5% Significance	Reject		Null Hypoth. at 5% Significance	Reject
30	Null Hypoth. at 1% Significance	Reject		Null Hypoth. at 1% Significance	Reject

Figure 9.16   Analysis of Diff3 and Diff5 Variables

	A	B	C	D	E
7		AN-WBN			(AN-WBN)-(AO-WBO)
8	*Conf. Intervals (One-Sample)*	Data Set #1		*Conf. Intervals (One-Sample)*	Data Set #1
9	Sample Size	180		Sample Size	180
10	Sample Mean	0.611		Sample Mean	0.061
11	Sample Std Dev	2.213		Sample Std Dev	2.045
12	Confidence Level (Mean)	99.0%		Confidence Level (Mean)	99.0%
13	Degrees of Freedom	179		Degrees of Freedom	179
14	Lower Limit	0.182		Lower Limit	-0.336
15	Upper Limit	1.041		Upper Limit	0.458
16					
17		AN-WBN			(AN-WBN)-(AO-WBO)
18	*Hypothesis Test (One-Sample)*	Data Set #1		*Hypothesis Test (One-Sample)*	Data Set #1
19	Sample Size	180		Sample Size	180
20	Sample Mean	0.611		Sample Mean	0.061
21	Sample Std Dev	2.213		Sample Std Dev	2.045
22	Hypothesized Mean	0		Hypothesized Mean	0
23	Alternative Hypothesis	> 0		Alternative Hypothesis	<> 0
24	Standard Error of Mean	0.1650		Standard Error of Mean	0.1524
25	Degrees of Freedom	179		Degrees of Freedom	179
26	t-Test Statistic	3.7046		t-Test Statistic	0.4010
27	p-Value	0.0001		p-Value	0.6889
28	Null Hypoth. at 10% Significance	Reject		Null Hypoth. at 10% Significance	Don't Reject
29	Null Hypoth. at 5% Significance	Reject		Null Hypoth. at 5% Significance	Don't Reject
30	Null Hypoth. at 1% Significance	Reject		Null Hypoth. at 1% Significance	Don't Reject

The corresponding p-value for a two-tailed test of the mean difference is (to three decimal places) 0.000. A 99% confidence interval for the mean difference extends from −0.801 to −0.277. Note that this 99% confidence interval does *not* include the hypothesized value 0. This is consistent with the fact that the two-tailed p-value is less than 0.01. (Recall the relationship between confidence intervals and two-tailed hypothesis tests from section 9.2.7.)

■ The results are basically the same for the difference between consumers' likelihoods of buying the product with the two styles. (See the output for the Diff2 variable, WBO–WBN, in Figure 9.15.) Again, consumers are definitely more likely, on average, to buy the product with the new-style can. A 99% confidence interval for the mean difference extends from −0.739 to −0.216, which is again all negative.

■ The company's hypothesis that consumers' ratings of attractiveness of the new-style can are greater, on average, than their likelihoods of buying the product with this style can is confirmed. (See the output for the Diff3 variable, AN–WBN, in Figure 9.16.) The test statistic for this one-tailed test is 3.705 and the corresponding p-value is 0.000. A 99% confidence interval for the mean difference extends from 0.182 to 1.041, which is all positive.

■ There is no evidence that the difference between attractiveness ratings and the likelihood of buying is any different for the new-style can than for the current-style can. (See the output for the Diff5 variable, (AN–WBN)–(AO–WBO), in Figure 9.16.) The test statistic for a two-tailed test of this difference is 0.401 and the corresponding p-value, 0.689, isn't even close to any of the traditional significance levels. Furthermore, a 99% confidence interval for the mean difference extends from a negative value, −0.336, to a positive value, 0.458.

These results are further supported by histograms of the difference variables, such as those shown in Figures 9.17 and 9.18. (Box plots could be used, but we prefer histograms when the variables include only a few possible integer values.) The histogram of the Diff1 variable in Figure 9.17 shows many more negative differences than positive differences. This leads to the large negative test statistic and the all-negative confidence interval. In contrast, the histogram of the Diff5 variable in Figure 9.18 is almost perfectly symmetric around 0 and hence provides no evidence that the mean difference is not zero.

Figure 9.17

Histogram of the Diff1 Variable

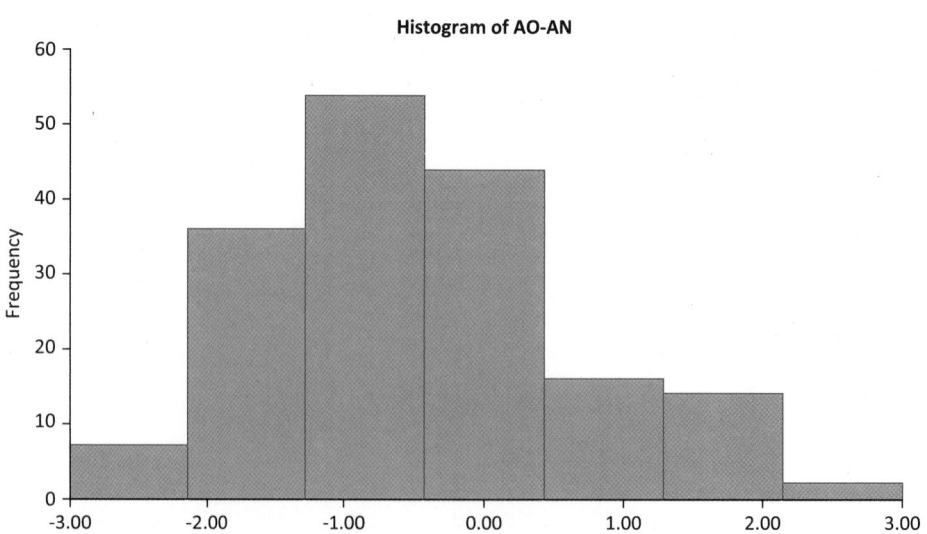

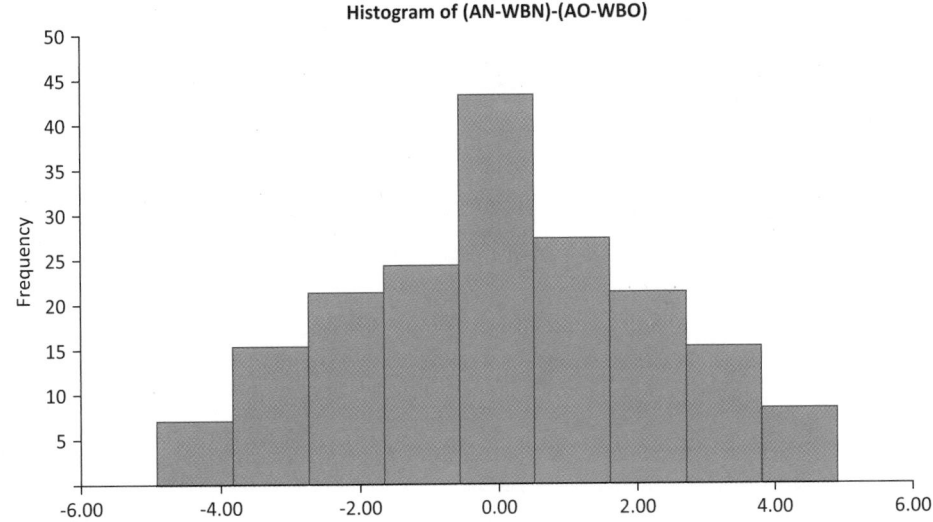

Figure 9.18
Histogram of the Diff5 Variable

This example illustrates once again how hypothesis tests and confidence intervals provide complementary information, although the confidence intervals are arguably more useful here. The hypothesis test for the first difference, for example, shows that the average rating for the new style is undoubtedly larger than for the current style. This is useful information, but it is even more useful to know *how much* larger the average for the new style is. A confidence interval provides this information.

We conclude this example by recalling the distinction between practical significance and statistical significance. Due to the extremely low *p*-values, the results in Figure 9.15, for example, leave no doubt as to statistical significance. But this could be due to the large sample size. That is, if the true mean differences are even slightly different from 0, large samples will almost surely discover this and report small *p*-values. The soft-drink company, on the other hand, is more interested in knowing whether the observed differences are of any practical importance. This is not a statistical question. It is a question of what differences are important for the *business*. We suspect that the company would indeed be quite impressed with the observed differences in the sample—and might very well switch to the new-style can. ■

FUNDAMENTAL INSIGHT

Signficance and Sample Size in Tests of Differences

The contrast between statistical and practical significance is especially evident in tests of differences between means. If the sample sizes are relatively small, it is likely that no *statistical* significance will be found, even though the real difference between means, if they could be estimated more accurately with more data, might be *practically* significant. On the other hand, if the sample sizes are very large, then just about any difference between sample means is likely to be *statistically* significant, even though the real difference between means might be of no *practical* importance.

The following example illustrates the independent two-sample *t* test. You can tell that a paired-sample procedure is not appropriate because there is no attempt to match the observations in the two samples in any way. Indeed, this is obvious because the sample sizes are not equal.

9.5 PRODUCTIVITY DUE TO EXERCISE AT INFORMATRIX SOFTWARE COMPANY

Many companies have installed exercise facilities at their plants. The goal is not only to provide a bonus (free use of exercise equipment) for their employees, but to make the employees more productive by getting them in better shape. One such (fictional) company, the Informatrix Software Company, installed exercise equipment on site a year ago. To check whether it has had a beneficial effect on employee productivity, the company gathered data on a sample of 80 randomly chosen employees, all between the ages of 30 and 40 and all with similar job titles and duties. The company observed which of these employees use the exercise facility regularly (at least three times per week on average). This group included 23 of the 80 employees in the sample. The other 57 employees were asked whether they exercise regularly elsewhere, and 6 of them replied that they do. The remaining 51, who admitted to being nonexercisers, were then compared to the combined group of 29 exercisers.

The comparison was based on the employees' productivity over the year, as rated by their supervisors. Each rating was on a scale of 1 to 25, 25 being the best. To increase the validity of the study, neither the employees nor the supervisors were told that a study was in progress. In particular, the supervisors did not know which employees were involved in the study or which were exercisers. The data from the study appear in Figure 9.19. (See the file **Exercise & Productivity.xlsx**.) Do these data support the company's (alternative) hypothesis that exercisers outperform nonexercisers on average? Can the company infer that any difference between the two groups is due to exercise?

Objective To use a two-sample t test for the difference between means to see whether regular exercise increases worker productivity.

Figure 9.19

Data for Study on Effectiveness of Exercise

	A	B	C
1	Employee	Exerciser	Rating
2	1	Yes	14
3	2	No	7
4	3	No	15
5	4	Yes	15
6	5	No	13
7	6	No	16
8	7	No	19
9	8	No	14
10	9	Yes	14
11	10	No	9
12	11	Yes	23
13	12	No	23
14	13	No	15
15	14	Yes	8
16	15	No	24
17	16	No	18
18	17	Yes	12
19	18	No	19
20	19	Yes	16
21	20	Yes	14

Solution

Side-by-side box plots are typically a good way to begin the analysis when comparing two populations.

To see whether there is any indication of a difference between the two groups, a good first step is to create side-by-side box plots of the Rating variable. These appear in Figure 9.20. Although there is a great deal of overlap between the two distributions, the distribution for the exercisers is somewhat to the right of that for the nonexercisers. Also, the variances of the two distributions appear to be roughly the same, although there is slightly more variation in the nonexerciser distribution.

Figure 9.20

Box Plots for Exercise Data

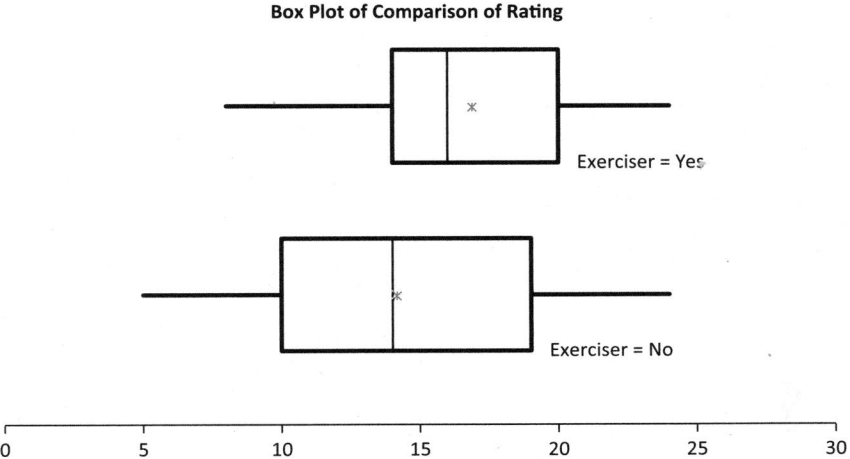

Box Plot of Comparison of Rating

A formal test of the mean difference uses the hypotheses $H_0: \mu_1 - \mu_2 \geq 0$ versus $H_a: \mu_1 - \mu_2 < 0$, where μ_1 and μ_2 are the mean ratings for the nonexerciser and exerciser populations. It makes sense to use a one-tailed test, with the alternative of the "less than" variety, because the company expects higher ratings, on average, for the exercisers. The output for this test, along with a 95% confidence interval for $\mu_1 - \mu_2$, appears in Figure 9.21. You can obtain the right part (the hypothesis test) by filling out the StatTools Hypothesis Test dialog box as shown in Figure 9.22. Specifically, select Two-Sample Analysis as the Analysis Type, click on the Format button and make sure the Stacked option is checked, select Exerciser as the "Cat" variable and Rating as the "Val" variable, and choose the "Less Than" Alternative Hypothesis Type.[5]

If the population standard deviations are at least approximately equal (and the values in cells B11 and C11 suggest that this assumption is plausible), the output in the range B37:B44 is relevant. It shows that the observed sample mean difference, -2.725, is indeed negative. That is, the exercisers in the sample outperformed the nonexercisers by 2.725 rating points on average. The output also shows that (1) the standard error of the sample mean difference is 1.142, (2) the test statistic is -2.387, and (3) the p-value for a one-tailed test is slightly less than 0.010. In words, the data provide enough evidence to reject the null hypothesis at the 1% significance level, as well as at the 5% and 10% levels. It is clear that exercisers perform better, in terms of mean ratings, than nonexercisers. A 95% confidence for this mean difference is all negative; it extends from -4.998 to -0.452.

This answers the first question we posed, but it doesn't answer the second. There is no way to be sure that the higher ratings for the exercisers are a direct result of exercise. It is

---

[5]The Stacked versus Unstacked issue is the same as you have seen before. The data in this file are stacked because there are two long columns that list a categorical variable, Exerciser, and a numeric variable, Rating.

Figure 9.21

Analysis of Exercise Data

	A	B	C
		Rating (No)	Rating (Yes)
7			
8	*Sample Summaries*	Data Set #1	Data Set #1
9	Sample Size	51	29
10	Sample Mean	14.137	16.862
11	Sample Std Dev	5.307	4.103
12			
13		Equal	Unequal
14	*Conf. Intervals (Difference of Means)*	Variances	Variances
15	Confidence Level	95.0%	95.0%
16	Sample Mean Difference	-2.725	-2.725
17	Standard Error of Difference	1.142	1.064
18	Degrees of Freedom	78	71
19	Lower Limit	-4.998	-4.847
20	Upper Limit	-0.452	-0.603
32			
33		Equal	Unequal
34	*Hypothesis Test (Difference of Means)*	Variances	Variances
35	Hypothesized Mean Difference	0	0
36	Alternative Hypothesis	< 0	< 0
37	Sample Mean Difference	-2.725	-2.725
38	Standard Error of Difference	1.142	1.064
39	Degrees of Freedom	78	70
40	t-Test Statistic	-2.387	-2.560
41	p-Value	0.0097	0.0063
42	Null Hypoth. at 10% Significance	Reject	Reject
43	Null Hypoth. at 5% Significance	Reject	Reject
44	Null Hypoth. at 1% Significance	Reject	Reject
45			
46			
47	*Equality of Variances Test*		
48	Ratio of Sample Variances	1.6725	
49	p-Value	0.1454	

possible that employees who exercise are naturally more ambitious and hard-working people, and that this extra drive is responsible for *both* their exercising and their higher ratings. This study is an *observational study*. The company observes two randomly selected groups of employees and analyzes the results. It does not explicitly control for other factors, such as personality, that might be responsible for differences in ratings. Therefore, the company can never be sure that there is a causal relationship between exercise and performance ratings. All the company can state is that exercisers appear, on average, to be more productive than nonexercisers—for whatever reason.

We are almost finished with this example, but not quite. What about the output in column C, and the test in rows 48 and 49? The test we just performed and the confidence interval we reported are based on the assumption of equal population standard deviations (or variances). As we discussed in section 8.7.1, if this assumption is violated, then a slightly different form of analysis should be performed, and its results are reported in column C. As you can see, the results are very similar to those in column B, although the p-value is slightly lower and the confidence interval is slightly narrower.

The test reported in rows 48 and 49 is a formal test of the hypothesis $H_0: \sigma_1^2/\sigma_2^2 = 1$ versus $H_a: \sigma_1^2/\sigma_2^2 \neq 1$, where the parameter being tested is the *ratio* of the two population variances. (The details behind this test are explained in the following subsection.) If this null hypothesis can be rejected on the basis of a low p-value in cell B49, then the equal-variance assumption is almost certainly *not* valid, and the output in column C should be

Figure 9.22

Dialog Box for Two-Sample Analysis

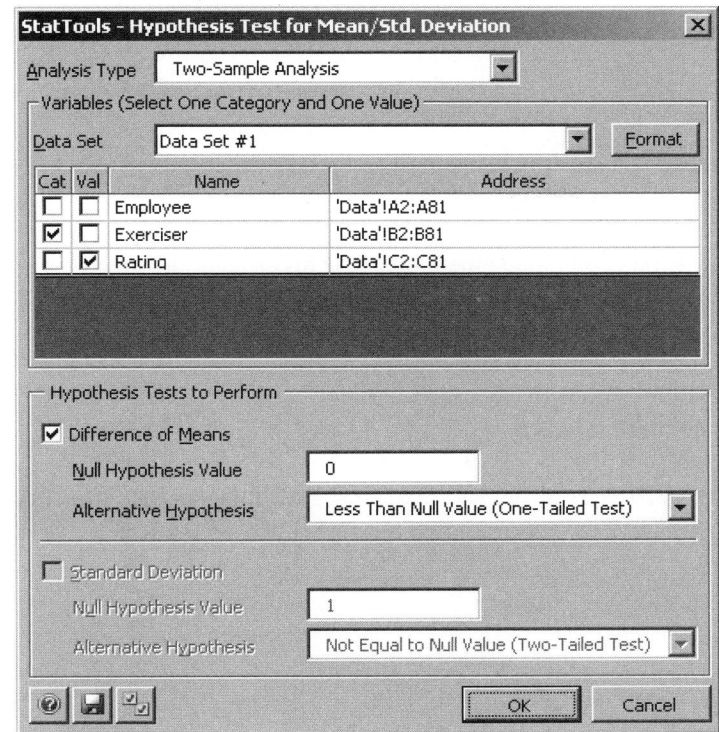

used. Otherwise, the output in column B should be used. The *p*-value in cell B49, 0.1454, suggests that the evidence *against* equal population variances is far from overwhelming. Of course, the similarity of the outputs in columns B and C implies, especially from a practical point of view, that it doesn't really make much difference. In other examples it could be more critical. ∎

StatTools Tip *If the p-value for the test of equal variances is small, use the right column (here column C) for testing the difference between means. Otherwise, use the (traditional) left column (here column B).*

9.4.3 Hypothesis Test for Equal Population Variances

As we just explained, the two-sample procedure for a difference between population means depends on whether population variances are equal.[6] Therefore, it is natural to test first for equal variances. This test is phrased in terms of the *ratio* of population variances, σ_1^2/σ_2^2. The null hypothesis is that this ratio is 1 (equal variances), whereas the alternative is that it is not 1 (unequal variances). The test statistic for this test is the ratio of sample variances:

$$F\text{-value} = s_1^2/s_2^2$$

Assuming that the population variances are equal, this test statistic has an *F* distribution with $n_1 - 1$ and $n_2 - 1$ degrees of freedom.

The **F distribution**, named after the famous statistician R. A. Fisher, is another sampling distribution that arises frequently in statistical studies. (It will appear again in the next

---

[6]The test in this section is traditionally stated in terms of variances, as we do here. It could also be stated in terms of standard deviations, because equal variances imply equal standard deviations and vice versa.

two chapters on regression.) Because it always describes a ratio, there are two degrees of freedom parameters, one for the numerator and one for the denominator, and the numerator degrees of freedom is always quoted first.

Tables of the F distribution, for selected degrees of freedom, appear in many statistics books, but the necessary information can be obtained more easily with Excel's FDIST and FINV functions. The FDIST function takes the form

$$=\text{FDIST}(v,df1,df2)$$

This function returns the probability to the *right* of value v when the degrees of freedom are $df1$ and $df2$. Similarly, the FINV function takes the form

$$=\text{FINV}(p,df1,df2)$$

It returns the value with probability p to the right of it when the degrees of freedom are $df1$ and $df2$.

CHANGES IN EXCEL 2010

These F functions have been changed considerably in Excel 2010. There are now F.DIST and F.INV functions for *left* tails, and F.DIST has a last "cum" argument just like NORM.DIST, T.DIST, and CHISQ.DIST. Also, there are two functions, F.DIST.RT and F.INV.RT, for *right* tails.

When StatTools tests for equal variances, it first calculates the ratio of variances. (See cell B48 in Figure 9.20.) It then implements the F test to calculate the corresponding p-value (in cell B49). For our purposes, the most important thing is the p-value from the test. A small p-value provides strong evidence that the population variances are *not* equal. Otherwise, an equal-variance assumption is reasonable. The p-value for the exercise data, 0.1454, provides *some* evidence of unequal variances, but the evidence is certainly not overwhelming.

9.4.4 Hypothesis Tests for Differences between Population Proportions

One of the most common uses of hypothesis testing is to test whether two population proportions are equal. Let p_1 and p_2 be the two population proportions, and let $\hat{p}_1$ and $\hat{p}_2$ be the corresponding sample proportions, based on sample sizes n_1 and n_2. The goal is to test whether the sample proportions differ enough to conclude that the *population* proportions are not equal. As usual, a test on the difference $\hat{p}_1 - \hat{p}_2$, requires a standard error. If the null hypothesis is true, so that $p_1 = p_2$, then it can be shown that the standard error of $\hat{p}_1 - \hat{p}_2$ is given by Equation (9.5), where $\hat{p}_c$ is the pooled proportion from the two samples combined. For example, if $\hat{p}_1 = 20/85$ and $\hat{p}_2 = 34/115$, then $\hat{p}_c = (20 + 34)/(85 + 115) = 54/200$. The reason for using this pooled estimate is that if the null hypothesis is true and the two population proportions are equal, it makes sense to base an estimate of this common proportion on the *combined* sample of data.

Standard Error for Difference between Sample Proportions

$$\text{SE}(\hat{p}_1 - \hat{p}_2) = \sqrt{\hat{p}_c(1 - \hat{p}_c)(1/n_1 + 1/n_2)} \qquad \textbf{(9.5)}$$

Given this standard error, the rest is straightforward. Assuming that the sample sizes are reasonably large, the test statistic in Equation (9.6) has (approximately) a standard normal distribution. The test can be run with StatTools, as illustrated in the next example.

Test Statistic for Difference between Proportions

$$z\text{-value} = \frac{\hat{p}_1 - \hat{p}_2}{SE(\hat{p}_1 - \hat{p}_2)} \qquad (9.6)$$

EXAMPLE 9.6 EMPLOYEE EMPOWERMENT AT ARMCO COMPANY

The ArmCo Company, a large manufacturer of automobile parts, has several plants in the United States. For years, ArmCo employees have complained that their suggestions for improvements in the manufacturing processes have been ignored by upper management. In the spirit of employee empowerment, ArmCo management at the Midwest plant decided to initiate a number of policies to respond to employee suggestions. For example, a mailbox was placed in a central location, and employees were encouraged to drop suggestions into this box. No such initiatives were taken at the other ArmCo plants. As expected, there was a great deal of employee enthusiasm at the Midwest plant shortly after the new policies were implemented, but the question was whether life would revert to normal and the enthusiasm would dampen with time.

To check this, 100 randomly selected employees at the Midwest plant and 300 employees from other plants were asked to fill out a questionnaire six months after the implementation of the new policies at the Midwest plant. Employees were instructed to respond to each item on the questionnaire by checking either a "yes" box or a "no" box. Two specific items on the questionnaire were the following:

- Management at this plant is generally responsive to employee suggestions for improvements in the manufacturing processes.

- Management at this plant is more responsive to employee suggestions now than it used to be.

The results of the questionnaire for these two items appear in rows 5 and 6 of Figure 9.23. (See the file **Empowerment 1.xlsx.**) Does it appear that the policies at the Midwest plant are appreciated? Should ArmCo implement these policies in its other plants?

Objective To use a test for the difference between proportions to see whether a program of accepting employee suggestions is appreciated by employees.

Solution

For either questionnaire item, let p_1 be the proportion of "yes" responses that would be obtained at the Midwest plant if the questionnaire were given to all of its employees, and define p_2 similarly for the other plants. Management certainly hopes to find a larger proportion of "yes" responses (to either item) at the Midwest plant than at the other plants, so the appropriate test is one-tailed, with the hypotheses set up as $H_0: p_1 - p_2 \le 0$ versus $H_a: p_1 - p_2 > 0$. (These could also be written as $H_0: p_1 \le p_2$ versus $H_0: p_1 > p_2$, but this has no effect on the test.)

Figure 9.23 Results for Employee Empowerment Example

	A	B	C	D	E	F	G
1	**Employee empowerment results**						
2			Note: The two StatTools data sets are in the ranges A4:C6 and E4:G6.				
3	**Item 1: Management responds**				**Item 2: Things have improved**		
4	Category	Midwest	Other		Category	Midwest	Other
5	Yes	39	93		Yes	68	159
6	No	61	207		No	32	141
7	Totals	100	300		Totals	100	300
8							
9							
10	*Analyzed Category*				*Analyzed Category*		
11	Proportion of Items in This Category	Yes			Proportion of Items in This Category	Yes	
12							
13							
14		Midwest	Other			Midwest	Other
15	*Sample Summaries*	Data Set #1	Data Set #1		*Sample Summaries*	Data Set #2	Data Set #2
16	Sample Size	100	300		Sample Size	100	300
17	Sample Proportion	0.390	0.310		Sample Proportion	0.680	0.530
18							
19							
20	*Hypothesis Test (Difference Between Proportions)*				*Hypothesis Test (Difference Between Proportions)*		
21	Pooled Proportion	0.330			Pooled Proportion	0.568	
22	Difference Between Proportions	0.080			Difference Between Proportions	0.150	
23	Hypothesized Difference	0			Hypothesized Difference	0	
24	Alternative Hypothesis	> 0			Alternative Hypothesis	> 0	
25	Standard Error of Difference	0.054			Standard Error of Difference	0.057	
26	Test Statistic	1.4734			Test Statistic	2.6221	
27	p-Value	0.0703			p -Value	0.0044	
28	Null Hypoth. at 10% Significance	Reject			Null Hypoth. at 10% Significance	Reject	
29	Null Hypoth. at 5% Significance	Don't Reject			Null Hypoth. at 5% Significance	Reject	
30	Null Hypoth. at 1% Significance	Don't Reject			Null Hypoth. at 1% Significance	Reject	
31							
43	*Conf. Interval (Difference Between Proportions)*				*Conf. Interval (Difference Between Proportions)*		
44	Confidence Level	95.0%			Confidence Level	95.0%	
45	Difference Between Proportions	0.080			Difference Between Proportions	0.150	
46	Standard Error of Difference	0.056			Standard Error of Difference	0.055	
47	Lower Limit	-0.029			Lower Limit	0.043	
48	Upper Limit	0.189			Upper Limit	0.257	

Using the counts in rows 5 and 6, StatTools can run the test for differences between proportions. As with the test for a single proportion, you should recall the three possible StatTools data setups that were discussed in section 8.8 of the previous chapter. (See the finished version of the file **Coupon Effectiveness.xlsx** from the previous chapter for more details.) For this example, the two relevant StatTools data sets are the tables of counts in the ranges A4:C6 and E4:G6. To run the test for the first item (whether management responds), select Hypothesis Test/Proportions from the Statistical Inference dropdown list and fill in the resulting dialog box as shown in Figure 9.24. This implies that the difference being tested is the difference between the proportion of "yes" votes in the Midwest and Other. When you click on OK, you will see the dialog box in Figure 9.25. As it now stands, the difference will be Midwest minus Other. This is fine for this example, so click on OK, but if you wanted Other minus Midwest, you would click on the Reverse Order button. Of course, the test for the second item (whether things have improved) is performed similarly.

As shown in Figure 9.23, the *p*-values for the two tests (row 27) are 0.070 and 0.004. These results should be fairly good news for management. There is moderate, but not over-whelming, support for the hypothesis that management at the Midwest plant is more responsive than at the other plants, at least as perceived by employees. There is convincing support for the hypothesis that things have improved more at the Midwest plant than at the other plants. Corresponding 95% confidence intervals for the differences between proportions appear in rows 47 and 48. Because they are almost completely positive, they support

Figure 9.24

Dialog Box for
Testing Difference
Between
Proportions

StatTools - Hypothesis Test for Proportion

Analysis Type: Two-Sample Analysis

Data Type: Summary Table with Counts

Select One Variable with Categories and Two Variables with Counts

Data Set: Data Set #2 | Format

Cat	Ct	Name	Address
☑	☐	Category	E5:E6
☐	☑	Midwest	F5:F6
☐	☑	Other	G5:G6

Categories to Analyze (Select One)

☐ No
☑ Yes

2 categories in selected variable.

Hypotheses About Difference Between Proportions

Null Hypothesis Value: 0

Alternative Hypothesis: Greater Than Null Value (One-Tailed Test)

Options

First Sample Size: 100

Second Sample Size: 100

OK | Cancel

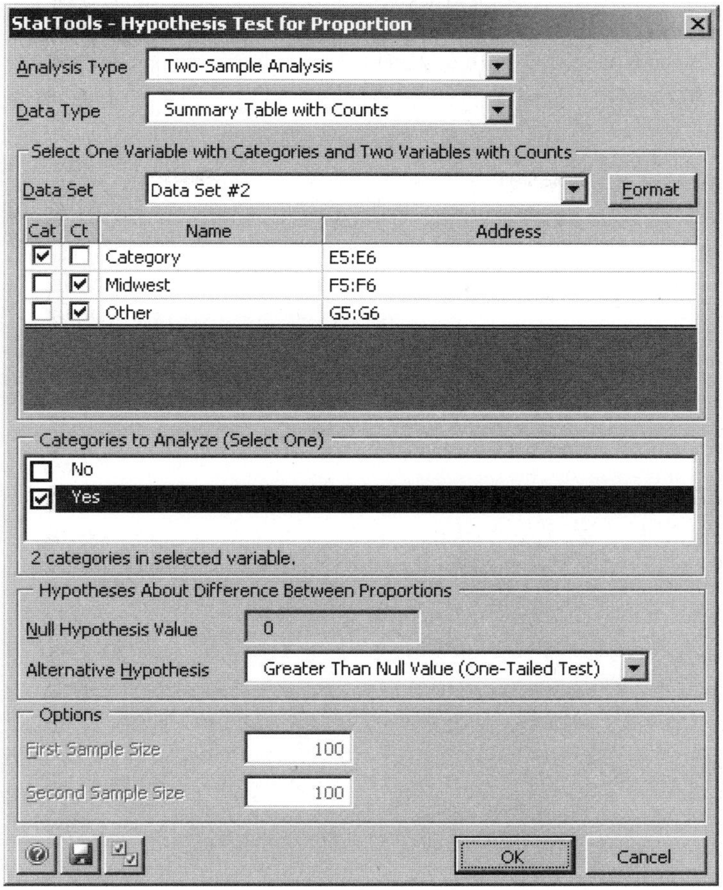

Figure 9.25

Dialog Box for
Reversing Difference

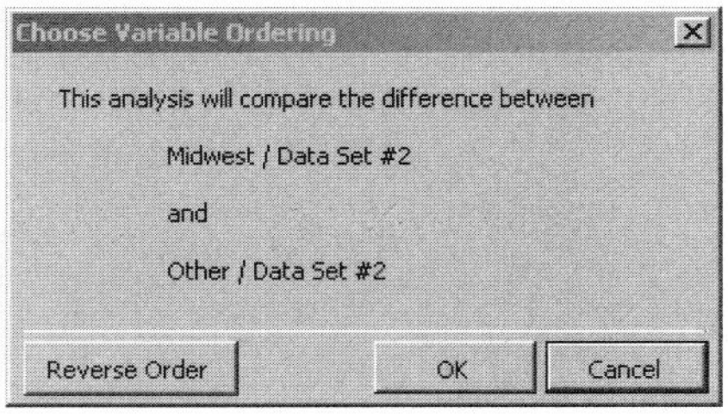

Choose Variable Ordering

This analysis will compare the difference between

Midwest / Data Set #2

and

Other / Data Set #2

Reverse Order | OK | Cancel

the hypothesis-test findings. Moreover, they provide a range of plausible values for the differences between the population proportions.

The only real downside to these findings, from Midwest management's point of view, is the sample proportion $\hat{p}_1$ for the first item. Only 39% of the sampled employees at the Midwest plant believe that management generally responds to their suggestions, even though 68% believe things are better than they used to be. A reasonable conclusion by ArmCo management is that they are on the right track at the Midwest plant, and the policies initiated there ought to be initiated at other plants, but more must be done at *all* plants. ■

PROBLEMS

Level A

9. In the past, 60% of all undergraduate students enrolled at State University earned their degrees within four years of matriculation. A random sample of 95 students from the class that matriculated in the fall of 2006 was recently selected to test whether there has been a change in the proportion of students who graduate within four years. Administrators found that 40 of these 95 students graduated in the spring of 2010 (i.e., four academic years after matriculation).

    a. Given the sample outcome, find a 95% confidence interval for the relevant population proportion. Does this interval estimate suggest that there has been in a change in the proportion of students who graduate within four years? Why or why not?

    b. Suppose now that State University administrators want to test the claim made by faculty that the proportion of students who graduate within four years at State University has fallen *below* the historical value of 60% this year. Use this sample proportion to test their claim. Report a *p*-value and interpret it.

10. Suppose a well-known baseball player states that, at this stage of his career, he is a "300 hitter" or better. That is, he claims that he gets a hit in at least 30% of his at-bats. Over the next month of the baseball season, this player has 105 at-bats and gets 33 hits.

    a. Identify the null and alternative hypotheses from the player's point of view.

    b. Is there enough evidence from this month's data to reject the null hypothesis at the 5% significance level?

    c. We might raise two issues with this test. First, does the data come from a *random* sample from some population? Second, what is the relevant population? Discuss these issues. Do you think the test in part **b** is valid? Is it meaningful?

11. The director of admissions of a distinguished (i.e., top-20) MBA program is interested in studying the proportion of entering students in similar graduate business programs who have achieved a composite score on the Graduate Management Admissions Test (GMAT) in excess of 630. In particular, the admissions director believes that the proportion of students entering top-rated programs with such composite GMAT scores is now 50%. To test this hypothesis, he has collected a random sample of MBA candidates entering his program in the fall of 2010. He believes that these students' GMAT scores are indicative of the scores earned by their peers in his program and in competitors' programs. The GMAT scores for these 125 individuals are given in the Data 2010 sheet of the file **P09_11.xlsx**. Test the admission

director's claim at the 5% significance level and report your findings. Does your conclusion change when the significance level is increased to 10%?

12. A market research consultant hired by a leading soft-drink company wants to determine the proportion of consumers who favor its low-calorie drink over the leading competitor's low-calorie drink in a particular urban location. A random sample of 250 consumers from the market under investigation is provided in the file **P08_18.xlsx**.

    a. Find a 95% confidence interval for the proportion of all consumers in this market who prefer this company's drink over the competitor's. What does this confidence interval tell us?

    b. Does the confidence interval in part **a** support the claim made by one of the company's marketing managers that more than half of the consumers in this urban location favor its drink over the competitor's? Explain your answer.

    c. Comment on the sample size used in this study. Specifically, is the sample unnecessarily large? Is it too small? Explain your reasoning.

13. The CEO of a medical supply company is committed to expanding the proportion of highly qualified women in the organization's staff of salespersons. He claims that the proportion of women in similar sales positions across the country in 2010 is less than 50%. Hoping to find support for his claim, he directs his assistant to collect a random sample of salespersons employed by his company, which is thought to be representative of sales staffs of competing organizations in the industry. These data are listed in the Data 2010 sheet of the file **P09_13.xlsx**. Test this manager's claim using the given sample data and report a *p*-value. Is there statistical support for his hypothesis that the proportion of women in similar sales positions across the country is less than 50%?

14. Management of a software development firm would like to establish a wellness program during the lunch hour to enhance the physical and mental health of its employees. Before introducing the wellness program, management must first be convinced that a sufficiently large majority of its employees are not already exercising at lunchtime. Specifically, it plans to initiate the program only if less than 40% of its personnel take time to exercise prior to eating lunch. To make this decision, management has surveyed a random sample of 100 employees regarding their midday exercise activities. The results of the survey are given in the Before sheet of the file **P09_14.xlsx**. Is there sufficient evidence at the 10% significance level for managers of this organization to initiate a corporate wellness program? Why or why not? What about at the 1% significance level?

15. The managing partner of a major consulting firm is trying to assess the effectiveness of expensive computer skills training given to all new entry-level professionals. In an effort to make such an assessment, she administers a computer skills test immediately before and after the training program to each of 40 randomly chosen employees. The pretraining and posttraining scores of these 40 individuals are recorded in the file **P09_15.xlsx**. Do the given sample data support the claim at the 10% significance level that the organization's training program is increasing the new employee's working knowledge of computing? What about at the 1% significance level?

16. A large buyer of household batteries wants to decide which of two equally priced brands to purchase. To do this, he takes a random sample of 100 batteries of each brand. The lifetimes, measured in hours, of the randomly chosen batteries are recorded in the file **P09_16.xlsx**.
   a. Using the given sample data, find a 95% confidence interval for the difference between the mean lifetimes of brand 1 and brand 2 batteries. Based on this confidence interval, which brand would you advise the buyer to purchase? Would you even need a confidence interval to make this recommendation? Explain.
   b. Repeat part **a** with a 99% confidence interval.
   c. How are your results in parts **a** and **b** related to hypothesis testing? Be specific.

17. The managers of a chemical manufacturing plant want to determine whether recent safety training workshops have reduced the weekly number of reported safety violations at the facility. The management team has randomly selected weekly safety violation reports for each of 25 weeks prior to the safety training and 25 weeks after the safety workshops. These data are provided in the file **P09_17.xlsx**. Given this evidence, is it possible to conclude that the safety workshops have been effective in reducing the number of safety violations reported per week? Report a *p*-value and interpret your findings for the management team.

18. A real estate agent has collected a random sample of 75 houses that were recently sold in a suburban community. She is particularly interested in comparing the appraised value and recent selling price of the houses in this particular market. The values of these two variables for each of the 75 randomly chosen houses are provided in the file **P08_24.xlsx**. Using these sample data, test whether there is a statistically significant mean difference between the appraised values and selling prices of the houses sold in this suburban community. Report a *p*-value. For which levels of significance is it appropriate to conclude that

no difference exists between these two values? Which is more appropriate, a one-tailed test or a two-tailed test? Explain your reasoning.

19. The owner of two submarine sandwich shops located in a particular city would like to know how the mean daily sales of the first shop (located in the downtown area) compares to that of the second shop (located on the southwest side of town). In particular, he would like to determine whether the mean daily sales levels of these two restaurants are essentially equal. He records the sales (in dollars) made at each location for 30 randomly chosen days. These sales levels are given in the file **P09_19.xlsx**. Find a 95% confidence level for the mean difference between the daily sales of restaurant 1 and restaurant 2. Based on this confidence interval, is it possible to conclude that there is a statistically significant mean difference at the 5% level of significance? Explain why or why not. Can you infer from this confidence interval whether there is a statistically significant mean difference at the 10% level? What about at the 1% level? Again, explain why or why not.

20. Suppose that an investor wants to compare the risks associated with two different stocks. One way to measure the risk of a given stock is to measure the variation in the stock's daily price changes. The investor obtains a random sample of 25 daily price changes for stock 1 and 25 daily price changes for stock 2. These data are provided in the file **P09_20.xlsx**. Explain why this investor can compare the risks associated with the two stocks by testing the null hypothesis that the variances of the stocks' price changes are equal. Perform this test, using a 10% significance level, and interpret the results.

21. A manufacturing company wants to determine whether there is a difference between the variance of the number of units produced per day by one machine operator and the similar variance for another machine operator. The file **P09_21.xlsx** contain the number of units produced by operator 1 and operator 2, respectively, on each of 25 days. Note that these two sets of days are not necessarily the same, so you can assume that the two samples are *independent* of one another.
   a. Identify the null and alternative hypotheses in this situation.
   b. Do these sample data indicate a statistically significant difference at the 10% level? Explain your answer. With your conclusion, which possible error could you be making, a type I or type II error?
   c. At which significance levels could you *not* reject the null hypothesis?

22. A large buyer of household batteries wants to decide which of two equally priced brands to purchase. To do this, he takes a random sample of 100 batteries of each brand. The lifetimes, measured in hours, of the batteries are recorded in the file **P09_16.xlsx**. Before testing for the difference between the mean lifetimes of these two batteries, he must first determine whether the underlying population variances are equal.

    a. Perform a test for equal population variances. Report a *p*-value and interpret its meaning.

    b. Based on your conclusion in part **a,** which test statistic should be used in performing a test for the difference between population *means*? Perform this test and interpret the results.

23. Do undergraduate business students who major in finance earn, on average, higher annual starting salaries than their peers who major in marketing? Before addressing this question through a statistical hypothesis test, you should determine whether the variances of annual starting salaries of the two types of majors are equal. The file **P09_23.xlsx** contains (hypothetical) starting salaries of 50 randomly selected finance majors and 50 randomly chosen marketing majors.

    a. Perform a test for equal population variances. Report a *p*-value and interpret its meaning.

    b. Based on your conclusion in part **a,** which test statistic should you use in performing a test for the existence of a difference between population means? Perform this test and interpret the results.

24. The CEO of a medical supply company is committed to expanding the proportion of highly qualified women in the organization's large staff of salespersons. Given the recent hiring practices of his human resources director, he claims that the company has increased the proportion of women in sales positions throughout the organization between 2005 and 2010. Hoping to find support for his claim, he directs his assistant to collect random samples of the salespersons employed by the company in 2005 and 2010. These data are listed in the file **P09_13.xlsx**. Test the CEO's claim using the sample data and report a *p*-value. Is there statistical support for the claim that his strategy is effective?

25. The director of admissions of a top-20 MBA program is interested in studying the proportion of entering students in similar graduate business programs who have achieved a composite score on the Graduate Management Admissions Test (GMAT) in excess of 630. In particular, the admissions director believes that the proportion of students entering top-rated programs with such composite GMAT scores is higher in 2010 than it was in 2000. To test this hypothesis, he has collected random samples of MBA candidates entering his program in the fall of 2010 and in the fall of 2000. He believes that these students' GMAT scores are indicative of the scores earned by their peers in his program and in competitors' programs. The GMAT scores for the randomly selected students entering in each year are listed in the file **P09_11.xlsx**. Test the admission director's claim at the 5% significance level and report your findings. Does your conclusion change when the significance level is increased to 10%?

26. Managers of a software development firm have established a wellness program during the lunch hour to enhance the physical and mental health of their employees. Now, they would like to see whether the wellness program has increased the proportion of employees who exercise regularly during the lunch hour. To make this assessment, the managers surveyed a random sample of 100 employees about their noontime exercise habits *before* the wellness program was initiated. Later, *after* the program was initiated, *another* 100 employees were independently chosen and surveyed about their lunchtime exercise habits. The results of these two surveys are given in the file **P09_14.xlsx**.

    a. Find a 95% confidence interval for the difference in the proportions of employees who exercise regularly during their lunch hour before and after the implementation of the corporate wellness program.

    b. Does the confidence interval found in part **a** support the claim that the wellness program has increased the proportion of employees who exercise regularly during the lunch hour? If so, at which levels of significance is this claim supported?

    c. Would your results in parts **a** and **b** differ if the *same* 100 employees surveyed before the program were also surveyed after the program? Explain.

27. An Environmental Protection Agency official asserts that more than 80% of the plants in the northeast region of the United States meet air pollution standards. An antipollution advocate is not convinced by the EPA's claim. She takes a random sample of 64 plants in the northeast region and finds that 56 meet the federal government's pollution standards.

    a. Does the sample information support the EPA's claim at the 5% level of significance?

    b. For which values of the sample proportion (based on a sample size of 64) would the sample data support the EPA's claim, using a 5% significance level?

    c. Would the conclusion found in part **a** change if the sample proportion remained constant but the sample size increased to 124? Explain why or why not.

Level B

28. A television network decides to cancel one of its shows if it is convinced that less than 14% of the viewing public are watching this show.

    a. If a random sample of 1500 households with televisions is selected, what sample proportion values will lead to this show's cancellation, assuming a 5% significance level?

b. What is the probability that this show will be cancelled if 13.4% of all viewing households are watching it? That is, what is the probability that a sample will lead to rejection of the null hypothesis? You can assume that 13.4% is the *population* proportion (even though it wouldn't be known to the network).

29. An economic researcher wants to know whether he can reject the null hypothesis, at the 10% significance level, that no more than 20% of the households in Pennsylvania make more than $70,000 per year.

    a. If 200 Pennsylvania households are chosen at random, how many of them would have to be earning more than $70,000 per year to allow the researcher to reject the null hypothesis?

    b. Assuming that the true proportion of *all* Pennsylvania households with annual incomes of at least $70,000 is 0.217, find the probability of *not* rejecting a *false* null hypothesis when the sample size is 200.

30. Senior partners of an accounting firm are concerned about recent complaints by some female managers that they are paid less than their male counterparts. In response to these charges, the partners ask their human resources director to record the salaries of female and male managers with equivalent education, work experience, and job performance. A random sample of these pairs of managers is provided in the file **P09_30.xlsx**. That is, each male-female pair is matched in terms of education, work experience, and job performance.

    a. Do these data support the claim made by the female managers? Report and interpret a *p*-value.

    b. Assuming a 5% significance level, which values of the sample mean difference between the female and male salaries would support the claim of discrimination against female managers?

31. Do undergraduate business students who major in finance earn, on average, higher annual starting salaries than their peers who major in marketing? Address this question through a statistical hypothesis test. The file **P09_23.xlsx** contains the starting salaries of 50 randomly selected finance majors and 50 randomly selected marketing majors.

    a. Is it appropriate to perform a paired-comparison *t* test with these data? Explain why or why not.

    b. Perform an appropriate hypothesis test with a 5% significance level. Summarize your findings.

    c. How large would the difference between the mean starting salaries of finance and marketing majors have to be before you could conclude that finance majors earn more on average? Employ a 5% significance level in answering this question.

32. The file **P02_35.xlsx** contains data from a survey of 500 randomly selected households. Test for the existence of a significant difference between the mean debt levels of the households in the first (i.e., SW) and second (i.e., NW) sectors of this community. Perform similar hypothesis tests for the differences between the mean debt levels of households from all other pairs of locations (i.e., first and third, first and fourth, second and third, second and fourth, and third and fourth). Summarize your findings.

33. Elected officials in a Florida city are preparing the annual budget for their community. They want to determine whether their constituents living across town are typically paying the same amount in real estate taxes each year. Given that there are over 20,000 homeowners in this city, they have decided to sample a representative subset of taxpayers and thoroughly study their tax payments. A randomly selected set of 170 homeowners is given in the file **P09_33.xlsx**. Specifically, the officials want to test whether there is a difference between the mean real estate tax bill paid by residents of the *first* neighborhood of this town and each of the remaining five neighborhoods. That is, each *pair* referenced below is from neighborhood 1 and one of the other neighborhoods.

    a. Before conducting any hypothesis tests on the difference between various pairs of mean real estate tax payments, perform a test for equal population variances for each pair of neighborhoods. For each pair, report a *p*-value and interpret its meaning.

    b. Based on your conclusions in part **a,** which test statistic should be used in performing a test for a difference between population means in each pair?

    c. Given your conclusions in part **b,** perform an appropriate test for the difference between mean real estate tax payments in each pair of neighborhoods. For each pair, report a *p*-value and interpret its meaning.

34. Suppose that you sample two normal populations independently. The variances of these two populations are σ_1^2 and σ_2^2. You take random samples of sizes n_1 and n_2 and observe sample variances of s_1^2 and s_2^2.

    a. If $n_1 = n_2 = 21$, how large must the fraction s_1/s_2 be before you can reject the null hypothesis that σ_1^2 is no greater than σ_2^2 at the 5% significance level?

    b. Answer part **a** when $n_1 = n_2 = 41$.

    c. If s_1 is 25% greater than s_2, approximately how large must n_1 and n_2 be if you are able to reject the null hypothesis in part **a** at the 5% significance level? Assume that n_1 and n_2 are equal.

35. Two teams of workers assemble automobile engines at a manufacturing plant in Michigan. Quality control personnel inspect a random sample of the teams' assemblies and judge each assembly to be acceptable or unacceptable. A random sample of 127 assemblies from team 1 shows 12 unacceptable assemblies. A similar random sample of 98 assemblies from team 2 shows 5 unacceptable assemblies.

a. Find a 95% confidence interval for the difference between the proportions of unacceptable assemblies from the two teams.

b. Based on the confidence interval found in part **a,** is there sufficient evidence to conclude, at the 5% significance level, that the two teams differ with respect to their proportions of unacceptable assemblies?

c. For which values of the difference between these two sample proportions could you conclude that a statistically significant difference exists at the 5% level?

36. A market research consultant hired by a leading soft-drink company is interested in determining whether there is a difference between the proportions of female and male consumers who favor the company's low-calorie brand over the leading competitor's low-calorie brand in a particular urban location. A random sample of 250 consumers from the market under investigation is provided in the file **P08_18.xlsx**.

a. After separating the 250 randomly selected consumers by *gender,* perform the statistical test and report a *p*-value. At which levels of α will the market research consultant conclude that there is essentially no difference between the proportions of female and male consumers who prefer this company's brand to the competitor's brand in this urban area?

b. Marketing managers at this company have asked their market research consultant to explore further the potential differences in the proportions of women and men who prefer drinking the company's brand to the competitor's brand. Specifically, the company's managers wants to know whether the potential difference between the proportions of female and male consumers who favor the company's brand varies by the *age* of the consumers. Using the same random sample of consumers as in part **a,** assess whether this difference varies across the four given age categories: under 20, between 20 and 40, between 40 and 60, and over 60. Specifically, run the test in part **a** four times, one

for each age group. Are the results the same for each age group?

37. The employee benefits manager of a large public university wants to determine whether differences exist in the proportions of various groups of full-time employees who prefer adopting the second (i.e., plan B) of three available health care plans in the coming annual enrollment period. A random sample of the university's employees and their tentative health care preferences is given in the file **P08_17.xlsx**.

a. Perform tests for differences in the proportions of employees within respective classifications who favor plan B in the coming year. For instance, the first such test should examine the difference between the proportion of administrative employees who favor plan B and the proportion of the support staff who prefer plan B.

b. Report a *p*-value for each of your hypothesis tests and interpret your results. How might the benefits manager use the information you have derived from these tests?

38. The file **P02_35.xlsx** contains data from a survey of 500 randomly selected households. Researchers would like to use the available sample information to test whether home ownership rates vary by household *location.* For example, is there a nonzero difference between the proportions of individuals who own their homes (as opposed to those who rent their homes) in households located in the first (i.e., SW) and second (i.e., NW) sectors of this community? Use the sample data to test for a difference in home ownership rates in these two sectors as well as for those of other pairs of household locations. In each test, use a 5% significance level. Interpret and summarize your results. (You should perform and interpret a total of six hypothesis tests.)

39. For testing the difference between two proportions, $\sqrt{\hat{p}_c(1 - \hat{p}_c)(1/n_1 + 1/n_2)}$ is used as the approximate standard error of $\hat{p}_1 - \hat{p}_2$, where $\hat{p}_c$ is the pooled sample proportion. Explain why this is reasonable when the null-hypothesized value of $p_1 - p_2$ is zero. Why would this not be a good approximation when the null-hypothesized value of $p_1 - p_2$ is a nonzero number? What would you recommend using for the standard error of $\hat{p}_1 - \hat{p}_2$ in that case?

9.5 TESTS FOR NORMALITY

In this section we discuss several **tests for normality**. As you have already seen, many statistical procedures are based on the assumption that population data are normally distributed. The tests in this section allow you to test this assumption. The null hypothesis is that the population is normally distributed, whereas the alternative is that the population distribution is not normal. Therefore, the burden of proof is on showing that the population distribution is *not* normal. Unless there is sufficient evidence to this effect, the normal assumption will continue to be accepted.

The first test we discuss is called a **chi-square goodness-of-fit test**. It is quite intuitive. A histogram of the sample data is compared to the *expected* bell-shaped histogram that would be observed if the data were normally distributed with the *same* mean and standard deviation as in the sample. If the two histograms are sufficiently similar, the null hypothesis of normality is accepted. Otherwise, it can be rejected.

The chi-square test for normality makes a comparison between the observed histogram and a histogram based on normality.

The test is based on a numerical measure of the difference between the two histograms. Let C be the number of categories in the histogram, and let O_i be the observed number of observations in category i. Also, let E_i be the expected number of observations in category i if the population were normal with the same mean and standard deviation as in the sample. Then the goodness-of-fit measure in Equation (9.7) is used as a test statistic. If the null hypothesis of normality is true, this test statistic has (approximately) a chi-square distribution with $C - 3$ degrees of freedom. Because *large* values of the test statistic indicate a poor fit—the O_i's do not match up well with the E_i's—the p-value for the test is the probability to the right of the test statistic in the chi-square distribution with $C - 3$ degrees of freedom.

Test Statistic for Chi-Square Test of Normality

$$\chi^2\text{-value} = \sum_{i=1}^{C} (O_i - E_i)^2 / E_i \qquad (9.7)$$

(Here, χ is the Greek letter chi.)

Although it is possible to perform this test manually, it is certainly preferable to use StatTools, as illustrated in the following example.

EXAMPLE | **9.7 DISTRIBUTION OF METAL STRIP WIDTHS IN MANUFACTURING**

A company manufactures strips of metal that are supposed to have width 10 centimeters. For purposes of quality control, the manager plans to run some statistical tests on these strips. However, realizing that these statistical procedures assume normally distributed widths, he first tests this normality assumption on 90 randomly sampled strips. How should he proceed?

Objective   To use the chi-square goodness-of-fit test to see whether a normal distribution of the metal strip widths is reasonable.

Solution

The sample data appear in Figure 9.26, where each width is measured to three decimal places. (See the file **Testing Normality.xlsx**.) A number of summary measures also appear.

To run the test, select Chi-square Test from the StatTools Normality Tests dropdown list, which leads to basically the same dialog box as in StatTools's Histogram procedure. As with the Histogram procedure, you can specify the bins, or you can accept StatTools's default bins. For now, do the latter.[7] The resulting histograms in

---

[7]You might try defining the bins differently and rerunning the test. The category definitions *can* make a difference in the results. This is a disadvantage of the chi-square test.

Figure 9.26

Data for Testing
Normality

	A	B	C	D	E
1	Part	Width			Width
2	1	9.990		*One Variable Summary*	Data Set #1
3	2	10.031		Mean	9.999
4	3	9.985		Std. Dev.	0.010
5	4	9.983		Median	9.998
6	5	10.004		Minimum	9.970
7	6	10.000		Maximum	10.031
8	7	9.992		Count	90
9	8	9.996		1st Quartile	9.993
10	9	9.997		3rd Quartile	10.006
11	10	9.993		5.00%	9.983
12	11	9.991		95.00%	10.014
13	12	9.991			
14	13	10.006			
15	14	9.998			
16	15	9.995			
17	16	9.989			
18	17	9.987			

Figure 9.27

Observed and
Normal Histograms

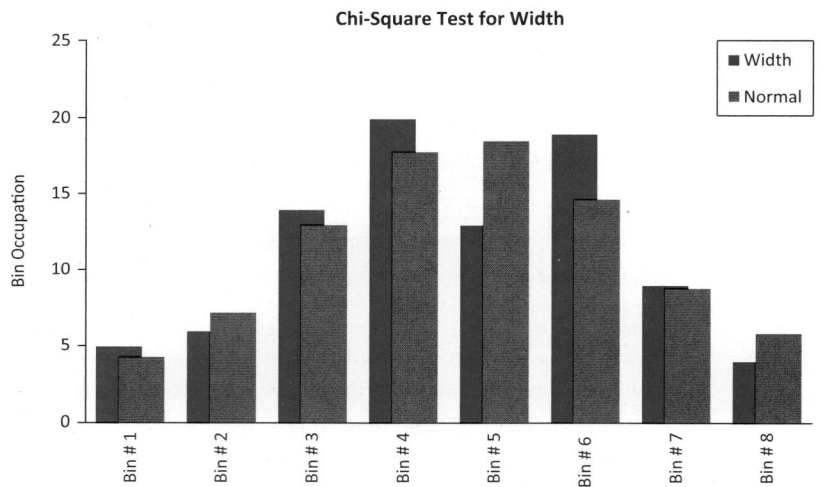

Figure 9.27 provide visual evidence of the goodness of fit. The left bars represent the observed frequencies (the O_is), and the right bars represent the expected frequencies for a normal distribution (the E_is). The normal fit to the data appears to be quite good.

The output in Figure 9.28 confirms this statistically. Each value in column E is an E_i, calculated as the total number of observations multiplied by the normal probability of being in the corresponding category. Column F contains the individual $(O_i - E_i)^2/E_i$ terms, and cell B11 contains their sum, the chi-square test statistic. The corresponding p-value in cell B12 is 0.5206.

This large p-value provides no evidence whatsoever of non-normality. It implies that if this procedure were repeated on many random samples, each taken from a population known to be normal, a fit at least this poor would occur in over 50% of the samples. Stated differently, fewer than 50% of the fits would be *better* than the one observed here. Therefore, the manager can feel comfortable in making a normal assumption for this population.

Figure 9.28   Chi-square Test of Normality

	A	B	C	D	E	F
7		Width				
8	*Chi-Square Test*	Data Set #1				
9	Mean	9.999256				
10	Std Dev	0.009728				
11	Chi-Square Stat.	4.2027				
12	P-Value	0.5206				
13						
14						
15	*Chi-Squared Bins*	BinMin	BinMax	Actual	Normal	Distance
16	Bin # 1	-Inf	9.983000	5	4.2630	0.1274
17	Bin # 2	9.983000	9.988167	6	7.1827	0.1948
18	Bin # 3	9.988167	9.993333	14	12.9751	0.0810
19	Bin # 4	9.993333	9.998500	20	17.7934	0.2736
20	Bin # 5	9.998500	10.003667	13	18.5249	1.6477
21	Bin # 6	10.003667	10.008833	19	14.6421	1.2970
22	Bin # 7	10.008833	10.014000	9	8.7859	0.0052
23	Bin # 8	10.014000	+Inf	4	5.8328	0.5759

We make three comments about this chi-square procedure. First, the test *does* depend on which (and how many) bins you use for the histogram. Reasonable choices are likely to lead to the same conclusion, but this is not guaranteed. Second, the test is not very effective unless the sample size is large, say, at least 80 or 100. Only then can you begin to see the true shape of the histogram and judge accurately whether it is normal. Finally, the test tends to be *too* sensitive if the sample size is really large. In this case any little "bump" on the observed histogram is likely to lead to a conclusion of non-normality. This is one more example of practical versus statistical significance. With a large sample size you might be able to reject normality with a high degree of certainty, but the practical difference between the observed and normal histograms could very well be unimportant.

The Lilliefors test is based on a comparison of the cdf from the data and a normal cdf.

The chi-square test of normality is an intuitive one because it is based on histograms. However, it suffers from the first two points discussed in the previous paragraph. In particular, it is not as *powerful* as other available tests. This means that it is often unable to distinguish between normal and non-normal distributions, and hence it often fails to reject the null hypothesis of normality when it should be rejected. A more powerful test is called the *Lilliefors test*.[8] This test is based on the *cumulative distribution function* (cdf), which shows the probability of being less than or equal to any particular value. Specifically, the **Lilliefors test** compares two cdfs: the cdf from a normal distribution and the cdf corresponding to the given data. This latter cdf, called the *empirical cdf*, shows the fraction of observations less than or equal to any particular value. If the data come from a normal distribution, the normal and empirical cdfs should be quite close. Therefore, the Lilliefors test compares the *maximum vertical distance* between the two cdfs and compares it to specially tabulated values. If this maximum vertical distance is sufficiently large, the null hypothesis of normality can be rejected.

To run the Lilliefors test for the Width variable in Example 9.7, select Lilliefors Test from the StatTools Normality Tests dropdown list. StatTools then shows the numerical outputs in Figure 9.29 and the corresponding graph in Figure 9.30 of the normal and

---

[8]This is actually a special case of the more general and widely known *Kolmogorov-Smirnoff* (or K-S) test.

Figure 9.29

Lilliefors Test
Results

	A	B
7		Width
8	*Lilliefors Test Results*	Data Set #1
9	Sample Size	90
10	Sample Mean	9.999256
11	Sample Std Dev	0.009728
12	Test Statistic	0.0513
13	CVal (15% Sig. Level)	0.0810
14	CVal (10% Sig. Level)	0.0856
15	CVal (5% Sig. Level)	0.0936
16	CVal (2.5% Sig. Level)	0.0998
17	CVal (1% Sig. Level)	0.1367

Figure 9.30

Normal and
Empirical
Cumulative
Distribution
Functions

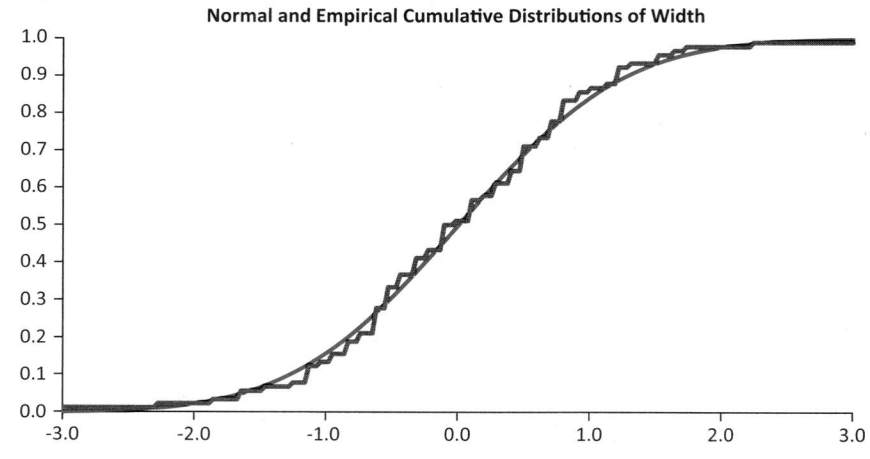

empirical cdfs. The numeric output indicates that the maximum vertical distance between the two curves is 0.0513. It also provides a number of "CVal" values for comparison. If the test statistic is larger than any of these, the null hypothesis of normality can be rejected at the corresponding significance level. In this case, however, the test statistic is relatively small—not nearly large enough to reject the normal hypothesis at any of the usual significance levels. This conclusion agrees with the one based on the chi-square goodness-of-fit test (as well as the closeness of the two curves in Figure 9.30). Nevertheless, you should be aware that the two tests do not agree on *all* data sets.

If data are normally distributed, the points on the corresponding Q-Q plot should be close to a 45° line.

We conclude this section with a popular, but informal, test of normality. This is based on a plot called a **quantile-quantile** (or **Q-Q) plot**. Although the technical details for forming this plot are somewhat complex, it is basically a scatterplot of the standardized values from the data set versus the values that would be expected if the data were perfectly normally distributed (with the same mean and standard deviation as in the data set). If the data are, in fact, normally distributed, the points in this plot tend to cluster around a 45° line. Any large deviation from a 45° line signals some type of non-normality. Again, however, this is not a *formal* test of normality. A Q-Q plot is usually used only to obtain a general idea of whether the data are normally distributed and, if they are not, what type of non-normality exists. For example, if points on the right of the plot are well *above* a 45° line, this is an indication that the largest observations in the data set are larger than would be expected from a normal distribution. Therefore, these points might be high-end outliers and/or a signal of positive skewness.

To obtain a Q-Q plot for the Width variable in Example 9.7, select Q-Q Normal Plot from the StatTools Normality Tests dropdown list and check each option at the bottom of the dialog box. The Q-Q plot for the Width data in Example 9.7 appears in Figure 9.31. Although the points in this Q-Q plot do not all lie *exactly* on a 45° line, they are about as close to doing so as can be expected from real data. Therefore, there is no reason to question the normal hypothesis for these data—the same conclusion as from the chi-square and Lilliefors tests. (Note that in the StatTools Q-Q plot dialog box, you can elect to plot *standardized* Q-values. This option was used in Figure 9.31. The plot with *unstandardized* Q-values, not shown here, provides virtually the same information. The only difference is in the scale of the vertical axis.)

Figure 9.31

Q-Q Plot with Standardized Q-Values

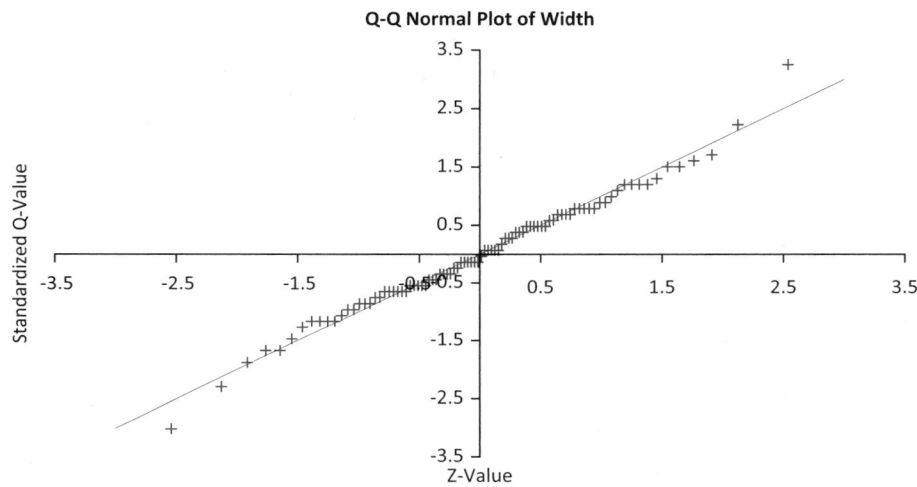

PROBLEMS

Level A

40. The file **P02_11.xlsx** contains data on 148 houses sold in a certain suburban region.

    a. Create a histogram of the selling prices. Is there any visual evidence that the distribution of selling prices is *not* normal?

    b. Test the selling prices for normality using the chi-square test. Is there enough evidence at the 5% significance level to conclude that selling prices are *not* normally distributed? If so, what is there about the distribution that is not normal?

    c. Use the Lilliefors test and the Q-Q plot to check for normality of selling prices. Do these suggest the same conclusion as in part **b**? Explain.

41. The file **P09_33.xlsx** contains real estate taxes paid by a sample of 170 homeowners in a Florida city.

    a. Create a histogram of the taxes paid. Is there any visual evidence that the distribution of taxes paid is *not* normal?

    b. Test the taxes paid for normality using the chi-square test. Is there enough evidence at the 5% significance level to conclude that taxes paid are *not* normally distributed? If so, what is there about the distribution that is not normal?

    c. Use the Lilliefors test and the Q-Q plot to check for normality of taxes paid. Do these suggest the same conclusion as in part **b**? Explain.

42. The file **P09_42.xlsx** contains many years of monthly percentage changes in the Dow Jones Industrial Average (DJIA). (This is the same data set that was used for Example 2.5 in Chapter 2.)

    a. Create a histogram of the percentage changes in the DJIA. Is there any visual evidence that the distribution of the Dow percentage changes is *not* normal?

    b. Test the percentage changes of the DJIA for normality using the chi-square test. Is there enough evidence at the 5% significance level to conclude that the Dow percentage changes are *not* normally distributed? If so, what is there about the distribution that is not normal?

c. Use the Lilliefors test and the Q-Q plot to check for normality of percentage changes. Do these suggest the same conclusion as in part **b**? Explain.

d. Repeat parts **a–c**, but use data only from the years 1990 to 2006. Do you get the same results as for the full data set?

Level B

43. Will the chi-square test ever conclude, at the 5% significance level, that data are not normally distributed when you know that they are? Check this with simulation. Specifically, generate *n* normally distributed numbers with mean 100 and standard deviation 15. You can do this with the formula **=NORMINV(RAND(),100,12)**. Do *not* freeze them; keep them random. Then run the chi-square normality test on the random numbers. Because the chi-square results are linked to the data, you will get new chi-square results every time you press F9 to recalculate.

a. Using *n* = 150, do you ever get a *p*-value less than 0.05? If so, what does such a *p*-value mean? Would you *expect* to get a few such *p*-values? Explain.

b. Repeat part **a** using *n* = 1000. Do the results change in any qualitative way?

c. Repeat parts **a** and **b**, but use the Lilliefors test instead of the chi-square test. Do you get the same basic results?

44. Repeat the previous problem but with a different nonnormal population. Specifically, generate *n* random numbers from a fifty-fifty mixture of two normal distributions with respective means 90 and 110 and common standard deviation 10. You can do this

with the formula **=IF(RAND()<0.5,NORMINV (RAND(),90,10),NORMINV(RAND(),110,10))** (This is *not* a normal distribution because it has two peaks.)

45. The file **P09_45.xlsx** contains measurements of ounces in randomly selected cans from a soft-drink filling machine. These cans reportedly contain 12 ounces, but because of natural variation, the actual amounts differ slightly from 12 ounces.

a. Can the company legitimately state that the amounts in cans are *normally* distributed?

b. *Assuming* that the distribution is normal with the mean and standard deviation found in this sample, calculate the probability that at least half of the *next* 100 cans filled will contain less than 12 ounces.

c. If the test in part **a** indicated that the data are *not* normally distributed, how might you calculate the probability requested in part **b**?

46. The chi-square test for normality discussed in this section is far from perfect. If the sample is too small, the test tends to accept the null hypothesis of normality for any population distribution even remotely bell-shaped; that is, it is not *powerful* in detecting non-normality. On the other hand, if the sample is very large, it will tend to reject the null hypothesis of normality for *any* data set.[9] Check this by using simulation. First, simulate data from a normal distribution using a large sample size. Is there a good chance that the null hypothesis will (wrongly) be rejected? Then simulate data from a non-normal distribution (uniform, say, or the mixture in Problem 44) using a small sample size. Is there is a good chance that the null hypothesis will (wrongly) not be rejected? Summarize your findings in a short report.

9.6 CHI-SQUARE TEST FOR INDEPENDENCE

The test we discuss in this section, like one of the tests for normality from the previous section, uses the name "chi-square." However, this test, called the **chi-square test for independence**, has an entirely different objective. It is used in situations where a population is categorized in two different ways. For example, people might be characterized by their smoking habits and their drinking habits. The question then is whether these two attributes are independent in a probabilistic sense. They are *independent* if information on a person's drinking habits is of no use in predicting the person's smoking habits (and vice versa). In this particular example, however, you might suspect that the two attributes are *dependent*. In particular, you might suspect that heavy drinkers are more likely (than non-heavy drinkers) to be heavy smokers, and you might suspect that nondrinkers are more likely (than drinkers) to be nonsmokers. The chi-square test for independence enables you to test this empirically.

Rejecting independence does not indicate the form of dependence. To see this, you must look more closely at the data.

The null hypothesis for this test is that the two attributes are independent. Therefore, statistically significant results are those that indicate some sort of dependence. As always,

[9]Actually, all of the tests for normality suffer from this latter problem.

this puts the burden of proof on the alternative hypothesis of dependence. In the smoking–drinking example, you will continue to believe that smoking and drinking habits are unrelated—that is, independent—unless there is sufficient evidence from the data that they are dependent. Furthermore, even if you are able to conclude that they are dependent, the test itself does not indicate the *form* of dependence. It could be that heavy drinkers tend to be nonsmokers, and nondrinkers tend to be heavy smokers. Although this is unlikely, it is definitely a form of dependence. The only way you can decide which form of dependence exists is to look closely at the data.

The data for this test consist of *counts* in various combinations of categories. These are usually arranged in a rectangular *contingency table*, also called a *cross-tabs*, or, using Excel terminology, a pivot table.[10] For example, if there are three smoking categories and three drinking categories, the table will have three rows and three columns, for a total of nine cells. The count in a cell is the number of observations in that particular combination of categories. We illustrate this data setup and the resulting analysis in the following example.

Chi-Square Test for Independence

The **chi-square test for independence** is based on the counts in a contingency (or cross-tabs) table. It tests whether the row variable is probabilistically independent of the column variable.

EXAMPLE | **9.8 RELATIONSHIP BETWEEN DEMANDS FOR DESKTOPS AND LAPTOPS AT BIG OFFICE**

Big Office, a chain of large office supply stores, sells an extensive line of desktop and laptop computers. Company executives want to know whether the demands for these two types of computers are related in any way. They might act as complementary products, where high demand for desktops accompanies high demand for laptops (computers in general are hot), they might act as substitute products (demand for one takes away demand for the other), or their demands might be unrelated. Because of limitations in its information system, Big Office does not have the exact demands for these products. However, it does have daily information on categories of demand, listed in aggregate (that is, over all stores). These data appear in Figure 9.32. (See the file **PC Demand.xlsx**.) Each day's demand for each type of computer is categorized as Low, MedLow (medium-low), MedHigh (medium-high), or High. The table is based on 250 days, so that the counts add

Figure 9.32
Counts of Daily Demands for Desktops and Laptops

	A	B	C	D	E	F	G
1	Counts on 250 days of demands at Big Office						
2							
3			Desktops				
4			Low	MedLow	MedHigh	High	
5	Laptops	Low	4	17	17	5	43
6		MedLow	8	23	22	27	80
7		MedHigh	16	20	14	20	70
8		High	10	17	19	11	57
9			38	77	72	63	250

---

[10]As discussed in Chapter 3, statisticians have long used the terms *contingency table* and *cross-tabs* (interchangeably) for the tables we are discussing here. Pivot tables are more general—they can contain summary measures such as averages and standard deviations, not just counts. But when they contain counts, they are equivalent to contingency tables and cross-tabs.

to 250. The individual counts show, for example, that demand was high for both desktops *and* laptops on 11 of the 250 days. For convenience, the row and column totals are provided in the margins. Based on these data, can Big Office conclude that demands for these two products are independent?

Objective   To use the chi-square test of independence to test whether demand for desktops is independent of demand for laptops.

Solution

The idea of the test is to compare the actual counts in the table with what would be *expected* under independence. If the actual counts are sufficiently far from the expected counts, the null hypothesis of independence can be rejected. The *distance* measure used to check how far apart they are, shown in Equation (9.8), is essentially the same chi-square statistic used in the chi-square test for normality. Here, O_{ij} is the actual count in cell i, j (row i, column j), E_{ij} is the expected count for this cell assuming independence, and the sum is over all cells in the table. If this test statistic is sufficiently large, the independence hypothesis can be rejected. (We provide more details of the test shortly.)

Test Statistic for Chi-Square Test for Independence

$$\text{Chi-square test statistic} = \Sigma_{ij}(O_{ij} - E_{ij})^2/E_{ij} \qquad \textbf{(9.8)}$$

What is expected under independence? The totals in row 9 indicate that demand for desktops was low on 38 of the 250 days. Therefore, if you had to estimate the probability of low demand for desktops, your estimate would be $38/250 = 0.152$. Now, if demands for the two products were independent, you should arrive at this *same* estimate from the data in any of rows 5 through 8. That is, a probability estimate for desktops should be the same regardless of the demand for laptops. The probability estimate of low desktop from row 5, for example, is $4/43 = 0.093$. Similarly, for rows 6, 7, and 8 it is $8/80 = 0.100$, $16/70 = 0.229$, and $10/57 = 0.175$, respectively. These calculations provide some evidence that desktops and laptops act as *substitute* products—the probability of low desktop demand is larger when laptop demand is medium-high or high than when it is low or medium-low.

This reasoning is the basis for calculating the E_{ij}s. Specifically, it can be shown that the relevant formula for E_{ij} is given by Equation (9.9), where R_i is the row total in row i, C_j is the total in column j, and N is the number of observations. For example, E_{11} for these data is $43(38)/250 = 6.536$, which is slightly larger than the corresponding observed count, $O_{11} = 4$.

Expected Counts Assuming Row and Column Independence

$$E_{ij} = R_iC_j/N \qquad \textbf{(9.9)}$$

Tables of counts expressed as percentages of rows or of columns are useful for judging the form (and extent) of any possible dependence.

You can perform the calculations for the test easily with StatTools. This is one StatTools procedure that does *not* require a data set to be defined. You simply select Chi-square Independence Test from the StatTools Statistical Inference dropdown list to obtain the dialog box shown in Figure 9.33. Here, you select the range of the contingency table. This range can include the row and column category labels (row 4 and column B), in which case you should check the top checkbox. The other two checkboxes, along with the titles, are used to provide labels for the resulting output.

The output appears in Figure 9.34. The top table repeats the counts from the original table. The next two tables show these counts as percentages of rows and percentages of

Figure 9.33

Dialog Box for
Chi-Square Test for
Independence

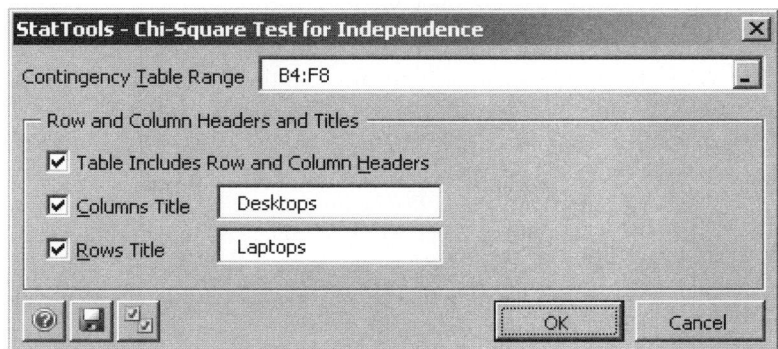

Figure 9.34 Output for Chi-square Test

	A	B	C	D	E	F
7				Rows: Laptops / Columns: Desktops		
8	*Original Counts*	Low	MedLow	MedHigh	High	Total
9	Low	4	17	17	5	43
10	MedLow	8	23	22	27	80
11	MedHigh	16	20	14	20	70
12	High	10	17	19	11	57
13	Total	38	77	72	63	250
14						
15				Rows: Laptops / Columns: Desktops		
16	*Percentage of Rows*	Low	MedLow	MedHigh	High	
17	Low	9.30%	39.53%	39.53%	11.63%	100.00%
18	MedLow	10.00%	28.75%	27.50%	33.75%	100.00%
19	MedHigh	22.86%	28.57%	20.00%	28.57%	100.00%
20	High	17.54%	29.82%	33.33%	19.30%	100.00%
21						
22				Rows: Laptops / Columns: Desktops		
23	*Percentage of Columns*	Low	MedLow	MedHigh	High	
24	Low	10.53%	22.08%	23.61%	7.94%	
25	MedLow	21.05%	29.87%	30.56%	42.86%	
26	MedHigh	42.11%	25.97%	19.44%	31.75%	
27	High	26.32%	22.08%	26.39%	17.46%	
28		100.00%	100.00%	100.00%	100.00%	
29						
30				Rows: Laptops / Columns: Desktops		
31	*Expected Counts*	Low	MedLow	MedHigh	High	
32	Low	6.5360	13.2440	12.3840	10.8360	
33	MedLow	12.1600	24.6400	23.0400	20.1600	
34	MedHigh	10.6400	21.5600	20.1600	17.6400	
35	High	8.6640	17.5560	16.4160	14.3640	
36						
37				Rows: Laptops / Columns: Desktops		
38	*Distance from Expected*	Low	MedLow	MedHigh	High	
39	Low	0.9840	1.0652	1.7206	3.1431	
40	MedLow	1.4232	0.1092	0.0469	2.3207	
41	MedHigh	2.7002	0.1129	1.8822	0.3157	
42	High	0.2060	0.0176	0.4067	0.7878	
43						
44						
45	*Chi-Square Statistic*					
46	Chi-Square	17.2420				
47	p-Value	0.0451				

columns, respectively. The expected counts and distances from actual to expected are shown next. They lead to the chi-square statistic and corresponding p-value at the bottom.

The p-value of the test, 0.045, can be interpreted in the usual way. Specifically, the null hypothesis of independence can be rejected at the 5% or 10% significance levels, but not at the 1% level. There is a fairly strong evidence that the demands for the two products are not independent.

If the alternative hypothesis of dependence is accepted, the output in Figure 9.34 can be used to examine its form. The two tables in rows 17 through 20 and rows 24 through 27 are especially helpful. If the demands *were* independent, the rows of this first table should be identical, and the columns of the second table should be identical. This is because each row in the first table shows the distribution of desktop demand for a given category of laptop demand, whereas each column in the second table shows the distribution of laptop demand for a given category of desktop demand. A close study of these percentages again provides some evidence that the two products act as substitutes, but the evidence is not overwhelming. ■

It is worth noting that the table of counts necessary for the chi-square test of independence can be a pivot table. For example, the pivot table in Figure 9.35 shows counts of the Married and OwnHome attributes. (For Married, 1 means married, 0 means unmarried, and for OwnHome, 1 means a home owner, 0 means not a home owner. This pivot table is based on the data in the **Catalog Marketing.xlsx** file from Chapter 2.) To see whether these two attributes are independent, the chi-square test would be performed on the table in the range B5:C6. You might want to check that the p-value for the test is 0.000 (to three decimals), so that Married and OwnHome are *definitely* not independent.

Figure 9.35
Using a Pivot Table for a Chi-Square Test

	A	B	C	D
3	Count	OwnHome ▾		
4	Married ▾	0	1	Grand Total
5	0	307	191	498
6	1	177	325	502
7	Grand Total	484	516	1000

PROBLEMS

Level A

47. The file **P08_49.xlsx** contains data on 400 orders placed to the ElecMart company over a period of several months. For each order, the file lists the time of day, the type of credit card used, the region of the country where the customer resides, and others. (This is the same data set used in Example 3.5 of Chapter 3.) Use a chi-square test for independence to see whether the following variables are independent. If the variables appear to be related, discuss the form of dependence you see.
   a. Time and Region
   b. Region and BuyCategory
   c. Gender and CardType

48. The file **P08_18.xlsx** categorizes 250 randomly selected consumers on the basis of their gender, their age, and their preference for our brand or a competitor's brand of a low-calorie soft drink. Use a chi-square test for independence to see whether the drink preference is independent of gender, and then whether it is independent of age. If you find any dependence, discuss its nature.

49. The file **P02_11.xlsx** contains data on 148 houses that were recently sold. Two variables in this data set are the selling price of the house and the number of bedrooms in the house. We want to use a chi-square test for independence to see whether these two variables are independent. However, this test requires

categorical variables, and Selling Price is essentially continuous. Therefore, to run the test, first divide the prices into several categories: less than 120, 120 to 130, 130 to 140, and greater than 140. Then run the test and report your results.

Level B

50. The file **P03_50.xlsx** contains annual salaries for all NBA basketball players in each of five seasons.
    a. Using only the data for the most recent season (2008–2009), check whether there is independence between position and salary. To do this, first change any hyphenated position such as C-F to the first listed, in this case C. (Presumably, this is the player's primary position.) Then make Salary categorical with four categories: the first is all salaries below the first quartile, the second is all salaries from the first quartile to the median, and so on. Explain your findings.
    b. Repeat part **a** but with a Yes/No playoff team categorization instead of position. The playoff teams in that season were Atlanta, Boston, Chicago, Cleveland, Dallas, Denver, Detroit, Houston, Los Angeles Lakers, Miami, New Orleans, Orlando, Philadelphia, Portland, San Antonio, and Utah.

51. The file **P09_51.xlsx** contains data on 1000 randomly selected Walmart customers. The data set includes demographic variables for each customer as well as their salaries and the amounts they have spent at Walmart during the past year.
    a. A lookup table in the file suggests a way to categorize the salaries. Use this categorization and chi-square tests of independence to see whether Salary is independent of (1) Age, (2) Gender, (3) Home, or (4) Married. Discuss any types of dependence you find.
    b. Repeat part **a,** replacing Salary with Amount Spent. First you must categorize Amount Spent. Create four categories for Amount Spent based on the four quartiles. The first category is all values of Amount Spent below the first quartile of Amount Spent, the second category is between the first quartile and the median, and so on.

52. The file **DVD Movies.xlsx** (the file that accompanies the case for Chapter 7) contains data on close to 10,000 customers from several large cities in the United States. The variables include the customers' gender and their first choice among several types of movies. Perform chi-square tests of independence to test whether the following variables are related. If they are, discuss the form of dependence you see.
    a. State and First Choice
    b. City and First Choice
    c. Gender and First Choice

9.7 ONE-WAY ANOVA

In sections 8.7.1 and 9.4.2, we discussed the two-sample procedure for analyzing the difference between two population means. A natural extension is to *more* than two population means. The resulting procedure is commonly called **one-way analysis of variance**, or **one-way ANOVA**. There are two typical situations where one-way ANOVA is used. The first is when there are several distinct populations. For example, consider recent graduates with BS degrees in one of three disciplines: business, engineering, and computer science. A random sample could be taken from each of these populations to discover whether there are any significant differences between them with respect to mean starting salary.

A second situation where one-way ANOVA is used is in randomized experiments. In this case a *single* population is treated in one of several ways. For example, a pharmaceutical company might select a group of people who suffer from allergies and randomly assign each person to a different type of allergy medicine currently being developed. Then the question is whether any of the treatments differ from one another with respect to the mean amount of symptom relief.

The data analysis in these two situations is identical; only the interpretation of the results differs. For the sake of clarity, we will phrase this discussion in terms of the first situation, where a random sample is taken from each of several populations. Let I be the number of populations, and denote the means of these populations by μ_1 through μ_I. The null hypothesis is that the I means are all equal, whereas the alternative is that they are not all equal. Note that this alternative admits many possibilities. With $I = 4$, for example, it is possible that $\mu_1 = \mu_2 = \mu_3 = 5$ and $\mu_4 = 10$, or that $\mu_1 = \mu_2 = 5$ and $\mu_3 = \mu_4 = 10$, or that $\mu_1 = 5$, $\mu_2 = 7$, $\mu_3 = 9$, and $\mu_4 = 10$. The alternative hypothesis simply specifies that *the means are not all equal.*

Hypotheses for One-Way ANOVA

Null hypothesis: All means are equal

Alternative hypothesis: At least one mean is different from the others

---

The one-way ANOVA procedure is usually run in two stages. In the first stage the null hypothesis of equal means is tested. Unless the resulting p-value is sufficiently small, there is not enough evidence to reject the equal-means hypothesis, and the analysis stops. However, if the p-value is sufficiently small, you can conclude with some assurance that the means are not all equal. Then the second stage attempts to discover which means are significantly different from which other means. This latter analysis is usually accomplished by examining confidence intervals.

One-way ANOVA is basically a test of differences between means, so why is it called analysis of *variance*? The answer to this question is the key to the procedure. Consider the box plot in Figure 9.36. It corresponds to observations from four populations with slightly

Figure 9.36

Samples with Large *Within* Variation

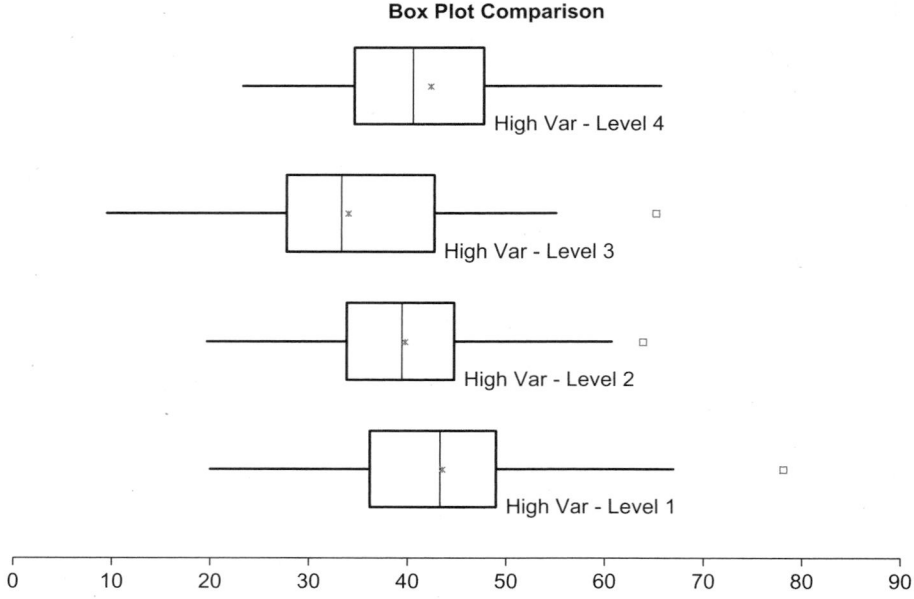

Box Plot Comparison

different means and fairly large variances. (The large variances are indicated by the relatively wide boxes and long lines extending from them.) From these box plots, can you conclude that the population means differ across the four populations? Does your answer change if the data are instead as in Figure 9.37? It probably does.

The sample means in these two figures are virtually the same, but the variances *within* each population in Figure 9.36 are quite large relative to the variance *between* the sample means. In contrast, there is very little variance within each population in Figure 9.37. In the first case, the large within variance makes it difficult to infer whether there are really any differences between population means, whereas the small within variance in the second case makes it easy to infer differences between population means.

Figure 9.37

Samples with Small
Within Variation

Box Plot Comparison

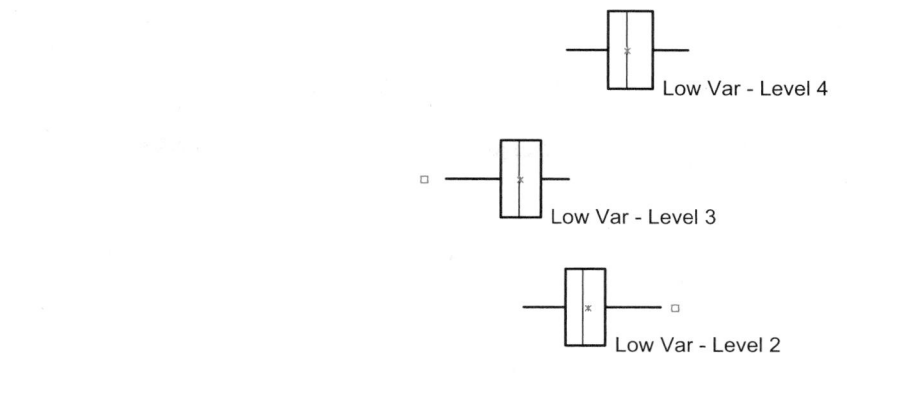

This is the essence of the ANOVA test. The variances *within* the individual samples are compared to variance *between* the sample means. Only if the between variance is large relative to the within variance can you conclude with any assurance that there are differences between population means—and reject the equal-means hypothesis.

The test itself is based on two assumptions: (1) the population variances are all equal to some common variance σ^2, and (2) the populations are normally distributed. These are analogous to the assumptions made for the two-sample t test. Although these assumptions are never satisfied exactly in any application, you should keep them in mind and check for gross violations whenever possible. Fortunately, the test we present is fairly robust to violations of these assumptions, particularly when the sample sizes are large and roughly the same.

A test is robust if its results are valid even when the assumptions behind it are not exactly true.

To understand the test, let $\overline{Y}_i$, s_i^2, and n_i be the sample mean, sample variance, and sample size from sample i. Also, let n and $\overline{Y}$ be the combined number of observations and the sample mean of all n observations. ($\overline{\overline{Y}}$ is called the *grand mean*.) Then a measure of the between variation is *SSB* (sum of squares between):

The between variation measures how much the sample means differ from one another.

$$SSB = \sum_{i=1}^{I} n_i(\overline{y}_i - \overline{\overline{y}})^2$$

Note that *SSB* is large if the individual sample means differ substantially from the grand mean $\overline{\overline{Y}}$, and this occurs only if they differ substantially from one another. A measure of the within variation is *SSW* (sum of squares within):

The within variation measures how much the observations within each sample differ from one another.

$$SSW = \sum_{i=1}^{I} (n_i - 1)s_i^2$$

This sum of squares is large if the individual sample variances are large. For example, *SSW* is much larger in Figure 9.36 than in Figure 9.37. However, *SSB* is the same in both figures.

Each of these sums of squares has an associated degrees of freedom, labeled *dfB* and *dfW:*

$$dfB = I - 1$$

and

$$dfW = n - I$$

When the sums of squares are divided by their degrees of freedom, the results are called *mean squares*, labeled *MSB* and *MSW:*

$$MSB = \frac{SSB}{dfB}$$

and

$$MSW = \frac{SSW}{dfW}$$

Actually, it can be shown that *MSW* is a weighted average of the individual sample variances, where the sample variance s_i^2 receives weight $(n_i - 1)/(n - I)$. In this sense *MSW* is a pooled estimate of the common variance σ^2, just as in the two-sample procedure.

Finally, the ratio of these mean squares, shown in Equation (9.10), is the test statistic used in the one-way ANOVA test. Under the null hypothesis of equal population means, this test statistic has an *F* distribution with *dfB* and *dfW* degrees of freedom. If the null hypothesis is *not* true, then *MSB* will tend to be large relative to *MSW*, as in Figure 9.37. Therefore, the *p*-value for the test is found by finding the probability to the *right* of the *F*-ratio in the *F* distribution with *dfB* and *dfW* degrees of freedom.

Test Statistic for One-Way ANOVA Test of Equal Means

$$F\text{-ratio} = \frac{MSB}{MSW} \qquad (9.10)$$

The elements of this test are usually presented in an *ANOVA table*, as you will see shortly. The bottom line in this table is the *p*-value. If it is sufficiently small, you can conclude that the population means are not all equal. Otherwise, you cannot reject the equal-means hypothesis.

If you can reject the equal-means hypothesis, then it is customary to examine confidence intervals for the differences between all pairs of population means. This can lead to quite a few confidence intervals. For example, if there are $I = 5$ samples, there are 10 pairs of differences (the number of ways two means can be chosen from five means). As usual, the confidence interval for any difference $\mu_i = \mu_j$ is of the form

$$\overline{Y}_i - \overline{Y}_j \pm \text{multiplier} \times \text{SE}(\overline{Y}_i - \overline{Y}_j)$$

The appropriate standard error is

$$\text{SE}(\overline{Y}_i - \overline{Y}_j) = s_p \sqrt{1/n_i + 1/n_j}$$

where s_p is the pooled standard deviation, calculated as $\sqrt{MSW}$.

If the confidence interval for a particular difference does not include 0, you can conclude that these two means are significantly different.

There are several forms of these confidence intervals, four of which are implemented in StatTools. In particular, the appropriate multiplier for the confidence intervals depends on which form is used. We will not pursue the technical details here, except to say that the multiplier is sometimes chosen to be its "usual" value near 2 and is sometimes chosen to be considerably larger, say, around 3.5. The reason for the latter is that if you want to conclude with 95% confidence that *each* of these confidence intervals includes its corresponding mean difference, you must make the confidence intervals somewhat wider than usual.

For any of these confidence intervals that does *not* include the value 0, you can infer that the corresponding means are not equal. Conversely, if a confidence interval does include 0, you cannot conclude that the corresponding means are unequal.

ANOVA and Experimental Design

This discussion of ANOVA is an introduction to the much larger topic of experimental design. Experimental design is extremely important in academic research, in the sciences, and in business. Indeed, large books have been written about it, and powerful statistical software, such as SPSS and SAS, implement many versions of experimental design, of which one-way ANOVA is probably the simplest. (Some packages use the acronym DOE, for design of experiments.) In general, the goal of experimental design is to discover which factors make a difference in some variable. This is done by carefully holding everything constant except for the factors being varied.

We have presented the formulas for one-way ANOVA to provide some insight into the procedure. However, StatTools's one-way ANOVA procedure takes care of all the calculations, as illustrated in the following example.

EXAMPLE | **9.9 EMPLOYEE EMPOWERMENT AT ARMCO COMPANY**

We discussed the ArmCo Company in Example 9.6. It initiated an employee empowerment program at its Midwest plant, and the reaction from employees was basically positive. Let's assume now that ArmCo has initiated this policy in all five of its plants—in the South, Midwest, Northeast, Southwest, and West—and several months later it wants to see whether the policy is being perceived equally by employees across the plants. Random samples of employees at the five plants have been asked to rate the success of the empowerment policy on a scale of 1 to 10, 10 being the most favorable rating. The data appear in Figure 9.38.[11] (See the file **Empowerment 2.xlsx**.) Is there any indication of mean differences across the plants? If so, which plants appear to differ from which others?

Objective   To use one-way ANOVA to test whether the empowerment initiatives are appreciated equally across Armco's five plants.

Solution

One-way ANOVA does not require equal sample sizes.

First, note that the sample sizes are not equal. This could be because some employees chose not to cooperate or it could be due to other reasons. Fortunately, equal sample sizes are not necessary for the ANOVA test. (Still, it is worth noting that when you create a StatTools data set as a first step in the ANOVA procedure, the data set range will extend to the longest of the data columns, in this case the Midwest column.)

To run one-way ANOVA with StatTools on these data, select One-Way ANOVA from the StatTools Statistical Inference dropdown and fill out the resulting dialog box as shown in Figure 9.39. In particular, click on the Format button and make sure the Unstacked option is selected, and then select the five variables. This dialog box indicates that there are several types of confidence intervals available. Each of these uses a slightly different multiplier in the general confidence interval formula. We will not pursue the differences between these confidence interval types, except to say that the default Tukey type is generally a good choice.

---

[11]StatTools's One-Way ANOVA procedure accepts the data in stacked or unstacked form. The data in this example are unstacked because there is a separate rating variable for each region.

Figure 9.38

Data for
Empowerment
Example

	A	B	C	D	E
1	South	Midwest	Northeast	Southwest	West
2	7	7	7	6	6
3	1	6	5	4	6
4	8	10	5	7	6
5	7	3	5	10	6
6	2	9	4	7	3
7	9	10	3	6	4
8	3	8	4	6	8
9	8	4	5	7	6
40	7	2	3	3	4
41	4	7	3	7	5
42		7	3	8	6
43		5	5	9	4
44		10	5	10	7
45		10		4	4
46		6		10	3
47		3		4	5
48		5		6	4
49		2			7
50		6			6
51		4			4
52		5			
53		2			
54		7			
55		8			
56		7			

Figure 9.39

One-Way ANOVA
Dialog Box

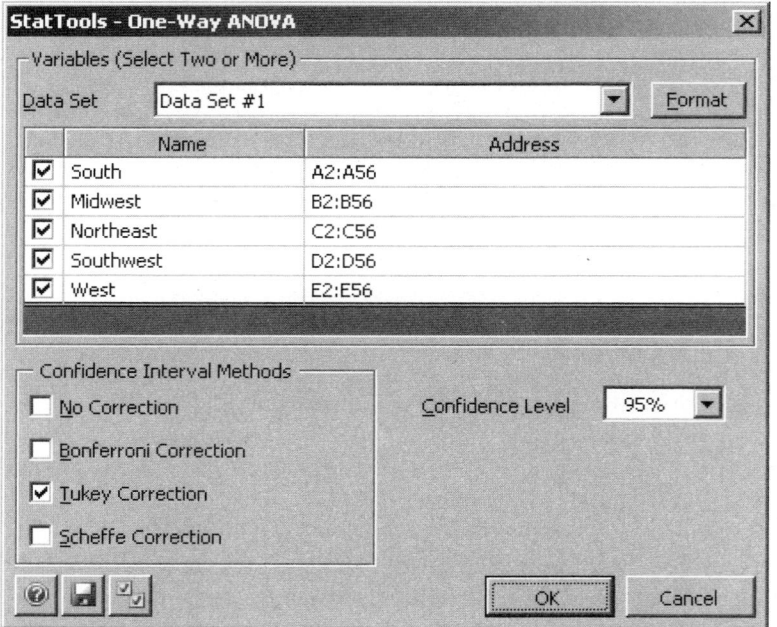

The main thing to remember from the ANOVA table is that a small p-value indicates that the population means are not all equal.

The resulting output in Figure 9.40 consists of three basic parts: summary measures and summary statistics, the ANOVA table, and confidence intervals. The summary statistics indicate that the Southwest has the largest mean rating, 6.745, and the Northeast has the smallest, 4.140, with the others in between. The sample standard deviations (or variances) vary somewhat across the plants, but not enough to invalidate

Figure 9.40 Analysis of Empowerment Data

	A	B	C	D	E	F
8	*ANOVA Summary*					
9	Total Sample Size	235				
10	Grand Mean	5.383				
11	Pooled Std Dev	1.976				
12	Pooled Variance	3.904				
13	Number of Samples	5				
14	Confidence Level	95.00%				
15						
16		South	Midwest	Northeast	Southwest	West
17	*ANOVA Sample Stats*	Data Set #1	Data Set #1	Data Set #1	Data Set #1	Data Set #1
18	Sample Size	40	55	43	47	50
19	Sample Mean	5.600	5.400	4.140	6.745	4.980
20	Sample Std Dev	2.073	2.469	1.820	1.687	1.635
21	Sample Variance	4.297	6.096	3.313	2.846	2.673
22	Pooling Weight	0.1696	0.2348	0.1826	0.2000	0.2130
23						
24		Sum of	Degrees of	Mean	F-Ratio	p-Value
25	*OneWay ANOVA Table*	Squares	Freedom	Squares		
26	Between Variation	163.653	4	40.913	10.480	< 0.0001
27	Within Variation	897.879	230	3.904		
28	Total Variation	1061.532	234			
29						
30		Difference		Tukey		
31	*Confidence Interval Tests*	of Means	Lower	Upper		
32	South-Midwest	0.200	-0.920	1.320		
33	South-Northeast	1.460	**0.276**	**2.644**		
34	South-Southwest	-1.145	-2.304	0.015		
35	South-West	0.620	-0.523	1.763		
36	Midwest-Northeast	1.260	**0.163**	**2.358**		
37	Midwest-Southwest	-1.345	**-2.415**	**-0.274**		
38	Midwest-West	0.420	-0.633	1.473		
39	Northeast-Southwest	-2.605	**-3.743**	**-1.468**		
40	Northeast-West	-0.840	-1.961	0.280		
41	Southwest-West	1.765	**0.670**	**2.860**		

the procedure. The side-by-side box plots in Figure 9.41 illustrate these summary measures graphically. However, there is too much overlap between the box plots to tell (graphically) whether the observed differences between plants are statistically significant.

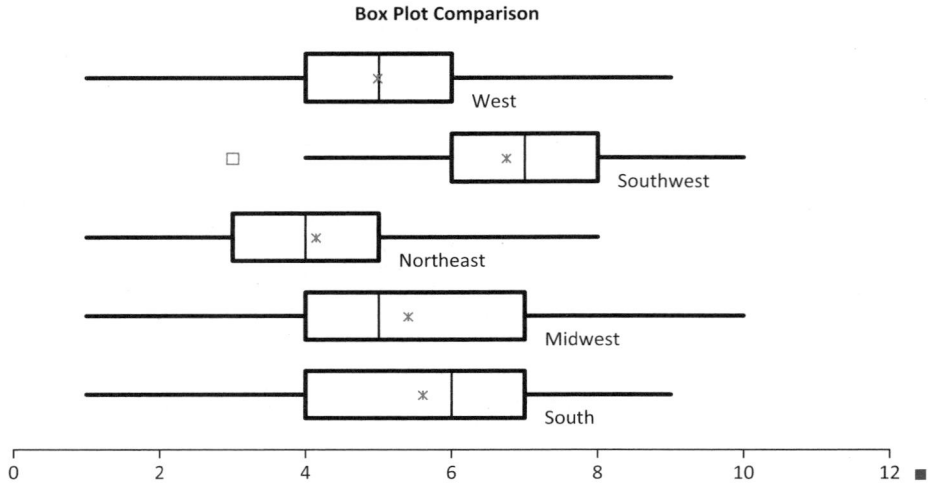

Figure 9.41
Box Plots for
Empowerment Data

The ANOVA table in rows 26 through 28 of Figure 9.40 displays the elements for the *F* test of equal means. All of it is based on the theory developed above. The only part we didn't discuss is the Total Variation in row 28. It is based on the total variation of all observations around the Grand Mean in cell B10, and is used mainly to check the calculations. Specifically, note that *SSB* and *SSW* in cells B26 and B27 add up to the total sum of squares in cell B28. Similarly, the degrees of freedom add up in column C. The *F*-ratio for the test is 10.480, in cell E26. Its corresponding *p*-value (to three decimal places) is 0.000. This leaves practically no doubt that the five population means are *not* all equal. Employees evidently do not perceive the empowerment policy equally across plants.

The 95% confidence intervals in rows 32 through 41 indicate which plants differ significantly from which others. For example, the mean for the Southwest plant is somewhere between 1.468 and 3.743 rating points above the mean for the Northeast plant. You can see that the Southwest plant is rated significantly higher than the Northeast, West, and Midwest plants, and the South and Midwest plants are also rated significantly higher than the Northeast plant. (StatTools boldfaces the significant differences.) Now it is up to ArmCo management to decide whether the magnitudes of these differences are *practically* significant, and, if so, what they can do to increase employee perceptions at the lower-rated plants.

PROBLEMS

Level A

53. An automobile manufacturer employs sales representatives who make calls on dealers. The manufacturer wishes to compare the effectiveness of four different call-frequency plans for the sales representatives. Thirty-two representatives are chosen at random from the sales force and randomly assigned to the four call plans (eight per plan). The representatives follow their plans for six months, and their sales for the six-month study period are recorded. These data are given in the file **P09_53.xlsx**.
   a. Do the sample data support the hypothesis that at least one of the call plans helps produce a higher average level of sales than some other call plan?

Perform an appropriate statistical test and report a *p*-value.
   b. If the sample data indicate the existence of mean sales differences across the call plans, which plans appear to produce different average sales levels? Use 95% confidence levels for the differences between all pairs of means to answer this question.

54. Consider a large chain of supermarkets that sells its own brand of potato chips in addition to many other name brands. Management would like to know whether the type of display used for the store brand has any effect on sales. Because there are four types of displays being considered, management decides to choose 24 similar stores to serve as experimental units.

A random six of these are instructed to use display type 1, another random six are instructed to use display type 2, a third random six are instructed to use display type 3, and the final six stores are instructed to use display type 4. For a period of one month, each store keeps track of the *fraction* of total potato chips sales that are of the store brand. The data for the 24 stores are shown in the file **P09_54.xlsx**. Note that one of the stores using display 3 has a blank cell. This store did not follow instructions properly, so its observation is disregarded.

a. Why do you think each store keeps track of the fraction of total potato chips sales that are of the store brand? Why do they not simply record the total amount of sales of the store brand potato chips?

b. Do the data suggest different mean proportions of store brand sales at the 10% significance level? If so, use 90% confidence intervals for the differences between all pairs of mean proportions to identify which of the display types are associated with higher fractions of sales.

55. National Airlines recently introduced a daily early-morning nonstop flight between Houston and Chicago. The vice president of marketing for National Airlines decided to perform a statistical test to see whether National's average passenger load on this new flight is different from that of each of its two major competitors. Ten early-morning flights were selected at random from each of the three airlines and the percentage of *unfilled* seats on each flight was recorded. These data are stored in the file **P09_55.xlsx**.

a. Is there evidence that National's average passenger load on the new flight is different from that of its

two competitors? Report a *p*-value and interpret the results of the statistical test.

b. Select an appropriate significance level and find confidence intervals for all pairs of differences between means. Which of these differences, if any, are statistically significant at the selected significance level?

Level B

56. How powerful is the ANOVA test in detecting differences between means when you are sure that there are differences? You can explore this question with simulation. Use the generic formula **=NORMINV(RAND(),mean,stdev)** to generate *n* random numbers in each of four columns. The numbers in any given column should have the same mean, but the means can vary across columns. The standard deviation should be the same in all columns. (Remember that this is an assumption behind the ANOVA test.) Do not freeze the random numbers; keep them random. You can choose the means and the common standard deviation. Run the ANOVA test on the randomly generated data. Because the ANOVA outputs are linked to the data, the results will change each time you recalculate with the F9 key. Try a number of settings for the means and report the results. For example, you could make all of the means different but very close to one another, you could make them all far apart from one another, you could make three of them equal and the fourth equal to some other value, and so on. Explain whether the results go in the direction you would expect. Is the ANOVA test very powerful in detecting mean differences?

9.8 CONCLUSION

The concepts and procedures in this chapter form a cornerstone in both applied and theoretical statistics. Of particular importance is the interpretation of a *p*-value, especially because *p*-values are outputs of all statistical software packages. A *p*-value summarizes the evidence in support of an alternative hypothesis, which is usually the hypothesis an analyst is trying to prove. Small *p*-values provide support for the alternative hypothesis, whereas large *p*-values provide little or no support for it.

Although hypothesis testing continues to be an important tool for analysts, it is important to note its limitations, particularly in business applications. First, given a choice between a confidence interval for some population parameter and a test of this parameter, we generally favor the confidence interval. For example, a confidence interval not only indicates whether a mean difference is 0, but it also provides a plausible range for this difference. Second, many business *decision* problems cannot be handled adequately with hypothesis-testing procedures. Either they ignore important cost information or they treat the consequences of incorrect decisions (type I and type II errors) in an inappropriate way. Finally, the *statistical* significance at the core of hypothesis testing is sometimes quite different from the *practical* significance that is of most interest to business managers.

Summary of Key Terms

Term	Explanation	Excel	Pages	Equation
Null hypothesis	Hypothesis that represents the current thinking or status quo		457	
Alternative hypothesis	Typically, the hypothesis the analyst is trying to prove or research hypothesis		457	
One-tailed test	Test where values in only one direction will lead to rejection of the null hypothesis		459	
Two-tailed test	Test where values in both directions will lead to rejection of the null hypothesis		459	
Type I error	Error committed when null hypothesis is true but is rejected		459	
Type II error	Error committed when null hypothesis is false but is not rejected		459	
Significance level	The probability of a type I error an analyst chooses			
Rejection region	Sample results that lead to rejection of null hypothesis		460	
Statistically significant results	Sample results that lead to rejection of null hypothesis		460	
p-value	Probability of observing a sample result at least as extreme as the one actually observed		461	
Power	Probability of correctly rejecting the null when it is false		462	
t test for a population mean	Test for a mean from a single population	StatTools/ Statistical Inference/ Hypothesis Test	465	9.1
Z test for a population proportion	Test for a proportion from a single population	StatTools/ Statistical Inference/ Hypothesis Test	472	9.2
t test for difference between means from paired samples	Test for the difference between two population means when samples are paired in a natural way	StatTools/ Statistical Inference/ Hypothesis Test	475	9.3
t test for difference between means from independent samples	Test for the difference between two population means when samples are independent	StatTools/ Statistical Inference/ Hypothesis Test	475	9.4
F test for equality of two variances	Test to check whether two population variances are equal, used to check an assumption of two-sample t test for difference between means	StatTools/ Statistical Inference/ Hypothesis Test	485	
F distribution	Skewed distribution useful for testing equality of variances	= FDIST(*value, df1, df2*) = FINV(*prob, df1, df2*)	485	
Z test for difference between proportions	Test for difference between similarly defined proportions from two populations	StatTools/ Statistical Inference/ Hypothesis Test	487	9.5, 9.6
Tests for normality	Tests to check whether a population is normally distributed; alternatives include chi-square test, Lilliefors test, and Q-Q plot	StatTools/ Normality Tests	494	9.7

(continued)

Term	Explanation	Excel	Pages	Equation
Chi-square test for independence	Test to check whether two attributes are probabilistically independent	StatTools/ Statistical Inference/ Chi-square Independence Test	500	9.8, 9.9
One-way ANOVA	Generalization of two-sample *t* test, used to test whether means from several populations are all equal, and if not, which are significantly different from which others	StatTools/ Statistical Inference/ One-Way ANOVA	505	9.10

PROBLEMS

Conceptual Questions

C.1. Suppose you are testing the null hypothesis that a mean equals 75 versus a two-tailed alternative. If the true (but unknown) mean is 80, what kind of error *might* you make? When will you *not* make this error?

C.2. Suppose you hear the claim that a given test, such as the chi-square test for normality, is not very *powerful*. What exactly does this mean? If another test, such as the Lilliefors test, is claimed to be more powerful, how is it better than the less powerful test?

C.3. Explain exactly what it means for a test statistic to fall in the rejection region.

C.4. Give an example of when a one-sided test on a population mean would make more sense than a two-tailed test. Give an example of the opposite. In general, why do we say that there is no *statistical* way to decide whether a test should be run as a one-tailed test or a two-tailed test?

C.5. For any given hypothesis test, that is, for any specification of the null and alternative hypotheses, explain why you could make only a type I error or a type II error, but not both. When would you make a type I error? When would you make a type II error? Answer as generally as possible.

C.6. What are the null and alternative hypotheses in the chi-square or Lilliefors test for normality? Where is the burden of proof? Might you argue that it goes in the wrong direction? Explain.

C.7. We didn't discuss the role of sample size in this chapter as thoroughly as we did for confidence intervals in the previous chapter, but more advanced books do include sample size formulas for hypothesis testing. Consider the situation where you are testing the null hypothesis that a population mean is less than or equal to 100 versus a one-tailed alternative. A sample size formula might indicate the sample size needed to make the power at least 0.90 when the true mean is 103. What are the trade-offs here? Essentially, what is the advantage of a larger sample size?

C.8. Suppose that you wish to test a researcher's claim that the mean height in meters of a normally distributed population of rosebushes at a nursery has increased from its commonly accepted value of 1.60. To carry out this test, you obtain a random sample of size 150 from this population. This sample yields a mean of 1.80 and a standard deviation of 1.30. What are the appropriate null and alternative hypotheses? Is this a one-tailed or two-tailed test?

C.9. Suppose that you wish to test a manager's claim that the proportion of defective items generated by a particular production process has decreased from its long-run historical value of 0.30. To carry out this test, you obtain a random sample of 300 items produced through this process. The test indicates a *p*-value of 0.01. What exactly is this *p*-value telling you? At what levels of significance can you reject the null hypothesis?

C.10. Suppose that a 99% confidence interval for the proportion *p* of all Lakeside residents whose annual income exceeds $80,000 extends from 0.10 to 0.18. The confidence interval is based on a random sample of 150 Lakeside residents. Using this information and a 1% significance level, you wish to test $H_0: p = 0.08$ versus $H_a: p \neq 0.08$. Based on the given information, are you able to reject the null hypothesis? Why or why not?

C.11. Suppose that you are performing a one-tailed hypothesis test. "Assuming that everything else remains constant, a decrease in the test's level of significance (α) leads to a higher probability of rejecting the null hypothesis." Is this statement true or false? Explain your reasoning.

C.12. Can pleasant aromas help people work more efficiently? Researchers conducted an investigation to answer this question. Fifty students worked a paper-and-pencil maze ten times. On five attempts, the students wore a mask with floral scents. On the other five attempts, they wore a mask with no scent. The 10 trials were performed in random order and each used a different maze. The researchers found that the subjects took less time to complete the maze when wearing the scented mask. Is this an example of an *observational study* or a *controlled experiment?* Explain.

C.13. Explain exactly what the one-way ANOVA test says about the various population means if the null hypothesis can be rejected. What does it imply if the null hypothesis cannot be rejected?

Level A

57. The file **P09_57.xlsx** contains the number of days 44 mothers spent in the hospital after giving birth (in the year 2005). Before health insurance rules were changed (the change was effective January 1, 2005), the average number of days spent in a hospital by a new mother was two days. For a 5% level of significance, do the data in the file indicate (the research hypothesis) that women are now spending less time in the hospital after giving birth than they were prior to 2005? Explain your answer in terms of the *p*-value for the test.

58. Eighteen readers took a speed-reading course. The file **P09_58.xlsx** contains the number of words that they could read before and after the course. Test the alternative hypothesis at the 5% significance level that reading speeds have increased, on average, as a result of the course. Explain your answer in terms of the *p*-value. Do you need to assume that reading speeds (before and after) are normally distributed? Why or why not?

59. Statistics have shown that a child 0 to 4 years of age has a 0.0002 probability of getting cancer in any given year. Assume that during each of the last seven years there have been 100 children ages 0 to 4 years whose parents work in a university's business school. Four of these children have gotten cancer. Use this evidence to test whether the incidence of childhood cancer among children ages 0 to 4 years whose parents work at this business school exceeds the national average. State your hypotheses and determine the appropriate *p*-value.

60. African Americans in a St. Louis suburb sued the city claiming they were discriminated against in schoolteacher hiring. Of the city's population, 5.7% were African American; of 405 teachers in the school system, 15 were African American. Set up appropriate hypotheses and determine whether African Americans

are underrepresented. Does your answer depend on whether you use a one-tailed or two-tailed test? In discrimination cases, the Supreme Court always uses a two-tailed test at the 5% significance level. (Source: U.S. Supreme Court Case, *Hazlewood v. City of St. Louis*)

61. In the past, monthly sales for HOOPS, a small software firm, have averaged $20,000 with standard deviation $4000. During the most recent year, sales averaged $22,000 per month. Does this indicate that monthly sales have changed (in a statistically significant sense at the 5% level)? Assume monthly sales are at least approximately normally distributed.

62. Twenty people have rated a new beer on a taste scale of 0 to 100. Their ratings are in the file **P09_62.xlsx**. Marketing has determined that the beer will be a success if the average taste rating exceeds 76. Using a 5% significance level, is there sufficient evidence to conclude that the beer will be a success? Discuss your result in terms of a *p*-value. Assume ratings are at least approximately normally distributed.

63. Twenty-two people were asked to rate a competitive beer on a taste scale of 0 to 100. Another 22 people were asked to rate our beer on the same taste scale. The file **P09_63.xlsx** contains the results. Do these data provide sufficient evidence to conclude, at the 1% significance level, that people believe our beer tastes better than the competitor's? Assume ratings are at least approximately normally distributed.

64. Callaway is thinking about entering the golf ball market. The company will make a profit if its market share is more than 20%. A market survey indicates that 140 of 624 golf ball purchasers will buy a Callaway golf ball.
   a. Is this enough evidence to persuade Callaway to enter the golf ball market?
   b. How would you make the decision if you were Callaway management? Would you use hypothesis testing?

65. Sales of a new product will be profitable if the average of sales per store exceeds 100 per week. The product was test-marketed for one week at 10 stores, with the results listed in the file **P09_65.xlsx**. Assume that sales at each store are at least approximately normally distributed.
   a. Is this enough evidence to persuade the company to market the new product?
   b. How would you make the decision if you were deciding whether to market the new product? Would you use hypothesis testing?

66. A recent study concluded that children born to mothers who take Prozac tend to have more birth defects than children born to mothers who do not take Prozac.
   a. What do you think the null and alternative hypotheses were for this study?

b. If you were a spokesperson for Eli Lilly (the company that produces Prozac), how might you rebut the conclusions of this study?

67. The file **P02_16.xlsx** contains traffic data from 256 weekdays on four variables. Each variable lists the number of arrivals during a specific five-minute period of the day. Use one-way ANOVA to test whether the mean numbers of arrivals for the four given time periods are equal. If you can conclude that there are significant differences at the 5% significance level, which means are significantly different from which others?

68. The file **P02_02.xlsx** contains data on over 200 popular movies in the years 2006 and 2007.

a. Run a one-way ANOVA to test whether there are significant differences in mean Total US Gross between different genres. Limit the genres to the six most common: Action, Adventure, Comedy, Drama, Horror, and Thriller/Suspense. If there are significant differences at the 5% level, indicate which genres have significantly different means from which others.

b. Is there any evidence that the equal-variance assumption of ANOVA has been violated? Explain.

c. Statistical inference is all about making inferences from a random sample to a population. Is this data a random sample from some population? What is the relevant population? Does it really matter?

Level B

69. Suppose that you are the state superintendent of Tennessee public schools. You want to know whether decreasing the class size in grades 1 through 3 will improve student performance. Explain how you would set up a test to determine whether decreased class size improves student performance. What hypotheses would you use in this experiment? (This was actually done and smaller class size did help, particularly with minority students.)

70. The file **P02_35.xlsx** contains data from a survey of 500 randomly selected households. Economic researchers would like to test for a significant difference between the mean annual income levels of the first household wage earners in the first (i.e., SW) and second (i.e., NW) sectors of this community. In fact, they intend to perform similar hypothesis tests for the differences between the mean annual income levels of the first household wage earners from all other pairs of locations (i.e., first and third, first and fourth, second and third, second and fourth, and third and fourth).

a. Before conducting any hypothesis tests on the difference between various pairs of mean income levels, perform a test for equal population variances in each pair of locations. For each pair, report a p-value and interpret its meaning.

b. Based on your conclusions in part **a,** which test statistic should be used in performing a test for the existence of a difference between population means?

c. Given your conclusions in part **b,** perform a test for the existence of a difference in mean annual income levels in each pair of locations. For each pair, report a p-value and interpret its meaning.

71. A group of 25 husbands and wives were chosen randomly. Each person was asked to indicate the most he or she would be willing to pay for a new car (assuming each had decided to buy a new car). The results are shown in the file **P09_71.xlsx**. Can you accept the alternative hypothesis that the husbands are willing to spend more, on average, than the wives at the 5% significance level? What is the associated p-value? Is it appropriate to use a paired-sample or independent-sample test? Does it make a difference? Explain your reasoning.

72. A company is concerned with the high cholesterol levels of many of its employees. To help combat the problem, it opens an exercise facility and encourages its employees to use this facility. After a year, it chooses a random 100 employees who claim they use the facility regularly, and another 200 who claim they don't use it at all. The cholesterol levels of these 300 employees are checked, with the results shown in the file **P09_72.xlsx**.

a. Is this sample evidence "proof" that the exercise facility, when used, tends to lower the mean cholesterol level? Phrase this as a hypothesis-testing problem and do the appropriate analysis. Do you feel comfortable that your analysis answers the question definitively (one way or the other)? Why or why not?

b. Repeat part **a,** but replace "mean cholesterol level" with "percentage with level over 215." (The company believes that any level over 215 is dangerous.)

c. What can you say about causality? Could you ever conclude from such a study that the exercise *causes* low cholesterol? Why or why not?

73. Suppose that you are trying to compare two populations on some variable (GMAT scores of men versus women, for example). Specifically, you are testing the null hypothesis that the means of the two populations are equal versus a two-tailed hypothesis. Are the following statements correct? Why or why not?

a. A given difference (such as five points) between sample means from these populations will probably not be considered statistically significant if the sample sizes are small, but it will probably be considered statistically significant if the sample sizes are large.

b. Virtually any difference between the population means will lead to statistically significant sample results if the sample sizes are sufficiently large.

74. Continuing the previous problem, analyze part **b** in Excel as follows. Start with hypothetical population mean GMAT scores for men and women, along with population standard deviations. Enter these at the top of a worksheet. You can make the two means as close as you like, but not identical. Simulate a sample of men's GMAT scores with your mean and standard deviation in column A. Do the same for women in column B. The sample sizes do not have to be the same, but you can make them the same. Then run the test for the difference between two means. (The point of this problem is that if the population means are fairly close and you pick relatively small sample sizes, the sample mean differences probably won't be significant. If you find this, generate new samples of a larger sample size and redo the test. Now they might be significant. If not, try again with a still larger sample size. Eventually, you should get statistically significant differences.)

75. This problem concerns course scores (on a 0–100 scale) for a large undergraduate computer programming course. The class is composed of both underclassmen (freshmen and sophomores) and upperclassmen (juniors and seniors). Also, the students can be categorized according to their previous mathematical background from previous courses as "low" or "high" mathematical background. The data for these students are in the file **P09_75.xlsx**. The variables are:
- Score: score on a 0–100 scale
- Upper Class: 1 for an upperclassman, 0 otherwise
- High Math: 1 for a high mathematical background, 0 otherwise

For the following questions, assume that the students in this course represent a random sample from all college students who might take the course. This latter group is the population.

  a. Find a 90% confidence interval for the population mean score for the course. Do the same for the mean of all upperclassmen. Do the same for the mean of all upperclassmen with a high mathematical background.

  b. The professor believes he has enough evidence to "prove" the research hypothesis that upperclassmen score at least five points better, on average, than lowerclassmen. Do you agree? Answer by running the appropriate test.

  c. If a "good" grade is one that is at least 80, is there enough evidence to reject the null hypothesis that the fraction of good grades is the same for students with low math backgrounds as those with high math backgrounds? Which do you think is more appropriate, a one-tailed or two-tailed test? Explain your reasoning.

76. A cereal company wants to see which of two promotional strategies, supplying coupons in a local newspaper or including coupons in the cereal package itself, is more effective. (In the latter case, there is a label on the package indicating the presence of the coupon inside.) The company randomly chooses 80 Kroger's stores around the country—all of approximately the same size and overall sales volume—and promotes its cereal one way at 40 of these sites, and the other way at the other 40 sites. (All are at different geographical locations, so local newspaper ads for one of the sites should not affect sales at any other site.) Unfortunately, as in many business experiments, there is a factor beyond the company's control, namely, whether its main competitor at any particular site happens to be running a promotion of its own. The file **P09_76.xlsx** has 80 observations on three variables:
- Sales: number of boxes sold during the first week of the company's promotion
- Promotion Type: 1 if coupons are in local paper, 0 if coupons are inside box
- Competitor Promotion: 1 if main competitor is running a promotion, 0 otherwise

  a. Based on all 80 observations, find (1) the difference in sample mean sales between stores running the two different promotional types (and indicate which sample mean is larger), (2) the standard error of this difference, and (3) a 90% confidence interval for the population mean difference.

  b. Test whether the population mean difference is zero (the null hypothesis) versus a two-tailed alternative. State whether you should accept or reject the null hypothesis, and why.

  c. Repeat part **b,** but now restrict the population to stores where the competitor is not running a promotion of its own.

  d. Based on data from all 80 observations, can you accept the (alternative) hypothesis, at the 5% level, that the mean company sales drop by at least 30 boxes when the competitor runs its own promotion (as opposed to not running its own promotion)?

  e. We often use the term *population* without really thinking what it means. For this problem, explain in words exactly what the population mean refers to. What is the relevant population?

77. There is a lot of concern about "salary compression" in universities. This is the effect of paying huge salaries to attract newly-minted Ph.D. graduates to university tenure-track positions and not having enough left in the budget to compensate tenured faculty as fully as they might deserve. In short, it is very possible for a new hire to make a larger salary than a person with many years of valuable experience. The file **P09_77.xlsx** contains (fictional but realistic) salaries for a sample of business school professors, some already tenured and some not yet through the tenure process. Formulate reasonable null and alternative hypotheses and then test them with this data set. Write a short report of your findings.

In Chapters 10 and 11, you will study regression, a method for relating one variable to other explanatory variables. However, the term *regression* has sometimes been used in a slightly different way, meaning "regression toward the mean." The example often cited is of male heights. If a father is unusually tall, for example, his son will typically be taller than average but not as tall as the father. Similarly, if a father is unusually short, the son will typically be shorter than average but not as short as the father. We say that the son's height tends to regress toward the mean. This case illustrates how regression toward the mean can occur.

Suppose a company administers an aptitude test to all of its job applicants. If an applicant scores below some value, he or she cannot be hired immediately but is allowed to retake a similar exam at a later time. In the interim the applicant can presumably study to prepare for the second exam. If we focus on the applicants who fail the exam the first time and then take it a second time, we would probably expect them to score better on the second exam. One plausible reason is that they are more familiar with the exam the second time. However, we will rule this out by assuming that the two exams are sufficiently different from one another. A second plausible reason is that the applicants have studied between exams, which has a beneficial effect. However, we will argue that even if studying has *no beneficial effect whatsoever*, these applicants will tend to do better the second time around. The reason is regression toward the mean. All of these applicants scored unusually low on the first exam, so they will tend to regress toward the mean on the second exam—that is, they will tend to score higher.

You can employ simulation to demonstrate this phenomenon, using the following model. Assume that the scores of *all* potential applicants are normally distributed with mean μ and standard deviation σ. Because we are assuming that any studying between exams has no beneficial effect, this distribution of scores is the *same* on the second exam as on the first. An applicant fails the first exam if his or her score is below some cutoff value L. Now, we would certainly expect scores on the two exams to be positively correlated, with some correlation ρ. That is, if everyone took both exams, then applicants who scored high on the first would tend to score high on the second, and those who scored low on the first would tend to score low on the second. (This isn't regression to the mean, but simply that some applicants are better than others.)

Given this model, you can proceed by simulating many pairs of scores, one pair for each applicant. The scores for each exam should be normally distributed with parameters μ and σ, but the trick is to make them correlated. You can use our Binormal_ function to do this. (Binormal is short for *bivariate normal*.) This function is supplied in the file **Regression Toward Mean.xlsx**. (Binormal_ is *not* a built-in Excel function.) It takes a pair of means (both equal to μ), a pair of standard deviations (both equal to σ), and a correlation ρ as arguments, with the syntax **=BINORMAL_(*means,stdevs,correlation*)**. To enter the formula, highlight two adjacent cells such as B5 and C5, type the formula, and press Ctrl-Shift-Enter. Then copy and paste to generate similar values for other applicants. (The Binormal_ Example sheet in this file illustrates the procedure. You should create another sheet in the same file to solve this case.)

Once you have generated pairs of scores for many applicants, you should ignore all pairs except for those where the score on the first exam is less than L. (Sorting is suggested here, but freeze the random numbers first.) For these pairs, test whether the mean score on the second exam is *higher* than on the first, using a paired-samples test. If it is, you have demonstrated regression toward the mean. As you will probably discover, however, the results will depend on the values of the parameters you choose for μ, σ, ρ, and L. You should experiment with these. Assuming that you are able to demonstrate regression toward the mean, can you explain intuitively why it occurs? ∎

Baseball has long been the sport of statistics. Probably more statistics—both relevant and completely obscure—are kept on baseball games and players than for any other sport. During the early 1990s, the first author of this book was able to acquire an enormous set of baseball data.[12] It includes data on every at-bat for every player in every game for the four-year period from 1987 to 1990. The bulk of the data are in eight files with names such as **89AL.exe**—for the 1989 American League. See the **BB_Readme.txt** file for detailed information about the files. The files include data for approximately 500 player-years during this period. Each text file contains data for a particular player during an entire year, such as Barry Bonds during 1989, provided that the player had at least 500 at-bats during that year. Each record (row) of such a file lists the information pertaining to a single at-bat,

such as whether the player got a hit, how many runners were on base, the earned run average (ERA) of the pitcher, and more.

The author analyzed these data to see whether batters tend to hit in "streaks," a phenomenon that has been debated for years among avid fans. [The results of this study are described in Albright (1993).] However, the data set is sufficiently rich to enable testing of any number of hypotheses. We challenge you to develop your own hypotheses and test them with these data. ∎

[12]The data were collected by volunteers of a group called Project Scoresheet. These volunteers attended each game and kept detailed records of virtually everything that occurred. Such detail is certainly not available in newspaper box scores, but it is becoming increasingly available on the Web.

Each year drinking and driving behavior are esti-mated to be responsible for approximately 24,000 traffic fatalities in the United States. Data show that a preponderance of this problem is due to the behavior of young males. Indeed, a dispropor-tionate number of traffic fatalities are young people between 15 and 24 years of age. Market research among young people has suggested that the perverse behavior of driving automobiles while under the influence of alcoholic beverages might be reduced by a mass media communications/advertising program based on an understanding of the "consumer psy-chology" of young male drinking and driving. There is some precedent for this belief. Reduction in cigarette smoking over the last 25 years is often attributed in part to mass antismoking advertising campaigns. There is also precedent for being less optimistic because past experimental campaigns against drunk driving have shown little success.

Between March and August of 1986, an anti–drinking and driving advertising campaign was conducted in the city of Wichita, Kansas. In this federally sponsored experiment, several carefully constructed messages were aired on television and radio and posted in newspapers and on billboards. Unlike earlier and largely ineffective campaigns that depended on donated talent and media time, this test was sufficiently funded to create impressive anti–drinking and driving messages, and to place them so that the targeted audience would be reached. The messages were pretested before the program and the final version won an OMNI advertising award.

To evaluate the effectiveness of this anti–drinking and driving campaign, researchers collected before and after data (preprogram and postprogram) of several types. In addition to data collection in Wichita, they also selected Omaha, Nebraska, as a control. Omaha, another midwestern city on the Great Plains, was arguably similar to Wichita, but was not subjected to such an advertising campaign. The following tables contain some of the data gathered by researchers to evaluate the impact of the program.

Table 9.1 contains background demographics on the test and control cities. Table 9.2 contains data obtained from telephone surveys of 18- to

24-year-old males in both cities. The surveys were done using a random telephone dialing technique. They had an 88% response rate during the prepro-gram survey and a 91% response rate during the post-program survey. Respondents were asked whether they had driven under the influence of four or more alcoholic drinks, or six or more alcoholic drinks, at least once in the previous month. The preprogram data were collected in September 1985, and the post-program data were collected in September 1986.

Table 9.1   Demographics for Wichita and Omaha

	Wichita	Omaha
Total population	411,313	483,053
Percentage 15–24 years	19.2	19.5
Race		
White	85	87
Black	8	9
Hispanic	4	2
Other	3	2
Percent high school graduates among those 18 years and older	75.4	79.9
Private car ownership	184,641	198,723

Table 9.2   Telephone Survey of 18- to 24-Year-Old Males

	Wichita		Omaha	
	Before Program	After Program	Before Program	After Program
Respondents	205	221	203	157
Drove after 4 drinks	71	61	77	69
Drove after 6 drinks	42	37	45	38

Table 9.3 contains counts of fatal or incapacitat-ing accidents involving young people gathered from the Kansas and Nebraska traffic safety departments during the spring and summer months of 1985

[13]This case was contributed by Peter Kolesar from Columbia University.

Table 9.3 Average Monthly Number of Fatal and Incapacitating Accidents, March to August

Driver Group	Accident Type	Wichita 1985	Wichita 1986	Omaha 1985	Omaha 1986
18- to 24-year-old males	Total	68	55	41	40
	Single	13	13	13	14
	Night	36	35	25	26
15- to 24-year-old	Total	117	97	59	57
males and females	Single	22	17	16	20
	Night	56	52	34	38

(before program) and 1986 (during the program). The spring and summer months were defined to be the period from March to August. These data were taken by the research team as indicators of driving under the influence of alcohol. Researchers at first proposed to also gather data on the blood alcohol content of drivers involved in fatal accidents. However, traffic safety experts pointed out that such data are often inconsistent and incomplete because police at the scene of a fatal accident have more pressing duties to perform than to gather such data. On the other hand, it is well established that alcohol is implicated in a major proportion of nighttime traffic fatalities, and for that reason, the data also focus on accidents at night among two classes of young people: the group of accidents involving 18- to 24-year-old males as a driver, and the group of accidents involving 15- to 24-year-old males and/or females as a driver.

The categories of accidents recorded were as follows:

- Total: total count of all fatal and incapacitating accidents in the indicated driver group

- Single vehicle: single vehicle fatal and incapacitating accidents in the indicated driver group

- Nighttime: nighttime (8 P.M. to 8 A.M.) fatal and incapacitating accidents in the indicated driver group

It was estimated that if a similar six-month advertising campaign were run nationally, it would cost about $25 million. The Commissioner of the U.S. National Highway Safety Commission had funded a substantial part of the study and needed to decide what, if anything, to do next. ∎

9.4 DECIDING WHETHER TO SWITCH TO A NEW TOOTHPASTE DISPENSER

John Jacobs works for the Fresh Toothpaste Company and has recently been assigned to investigate a new type of toothpaste dispenser. The traditional tube of toothpaste uses a screw-off cap. The new dispenser uses the same type of tube, but there is now a flip-top cap on a hinge. John believes this new cap is easier to use, although it is a bit messier than the screw-off cap—toothpaste tends to accumulate around the new cap. So far, the positive aspects appear to outweigh the negatives. In informal tests, consumers reacted favorably to the new cap. The next step was to introduce the new cap in a regional test market. The company has just conducted this test market for a six-month period in 85 stores in the Cincinnati region. The results, in units sold per store, appear in Figure 9.42. (See the file **Toothpaste.xlsx**.)

John has done his homework on the financial side. Figure 9.43 shows a break-even analysis for the new dispenser relative to the current dispenser. The analysis is over the entire U.S. market, which consists of 9530 stores (of roughly similar size) that stock the product. Based on several assumptions that we soon discuss, John figures that to break even with the new dispenser, the sales volume per store per six-month period must be 3622 units. The question is whether the test market data support a decision to abandon

the current dispenser and market the new dispenser nationally.

We first discuss the break-even analysis in Figure 9.43. The assumptions are listed in rows 4 through 8 and relevant inputs are listed in rows 11 through 17. In particular, the new dispenser involves an up-front investment of $1.5 million, and its unit cost is two cents higher than the unit cost for the current dispenser. However, the company doesn't plan to raise the selling price. Rows 22 through 26 calculate the net present value (NPV) for the next four years, assuming that the company does not switch to the new dispenser. Starting with *any* first-year sales volume in cell C30, rows 29 through 35 calculate the NPV for the next four years, assuming that the company does switch to the new dispenser. The goal of the break-even analysis is to find a value in cell C30 that makes the two NPVs (in cells B26 and B35) equal.

The trickiest part of the analysis concerns the depreciation calculations for the new dispenser. You find the before-tax contribution from sales in row 31 and subtract the depreciation each year (one-quarter of the investment) to figure the after-tax profit. For example, the formula in cell C33 is

$$=(C31-C32)*(1-\$C\$16)$$

Figure 9.42

Toothpaste
Dispenser Data from
Cincinnati Region

	A	B	C	D	E	F
1	Sales volumes in Cincinnati regional test market for 6 months					
2						
3	Store	Units sold				
4	1	4106				
5	2	2786				
6	3	3858				
7	4	3015				
8	5	3900				
9	6	3572				
10	7	4633				
11	8	4128				
12	9	3044				
13	10	2585				
85	82	1889				
86	83	6436				
87	84	4179				
88	85	3539				

Figure 9.43

Break-even Analysis for Toothpaste Example

	A	B	C	D	E	F
1	**Breakeven analysis for Stripe Toothpaste**					
2						
3	**Assumptions:**					
4	The planning horizon is 4 years					
5	Sales volume is expected to remain constant over the 4 years					
6	Unit selling prices and unit costs will remain constant over the 4 years					
7	Straight-line depreciation is used to depreciate the initial investment for the new dispenser					
8	Breakeven analysis is based on NPV for the four-year period					
9						
10	**Given data**					
11	Current volume (millions of units) using current dispenser		65.317			
12	Initial investment ($ millions) for new dispenser		1.5			
13	Unit selling price (either dispenser)		$1.79			
14	Unit cost (current dispenser)		$1.25			
15	Unit cost (new dispenser)		$1.27			
16	Tax rate		35%			
17	Discount rate		16%			
18						
19	**Note:** From here on, all sales volumes are in millions of units, monetary values are in $ millions					
20						
21	**Analysis of current dispenser**		Year 1	Year 2	Year 3	Year 4
22	Sales volume					
23	Before-tax contribution					
24	After-tax profit					
25	Cash flow					
26	NPV					
27						
28	**Analysis of new dispenser**		Year 1	Year 2	Year 3	Year 4
29	Initial investment	$1.5				
30	Sales volume					
31	Before-tax contribution					
32	Depreciation					
33	After-tax profit					
34	Cash flow					
35	NPV					
36						
37	Number of stores nationally	9530				
38	Breakeven sales volume per store per 6 months					

Then you add back the depreciation to obtain the cash flow, so that the formula in cell C34 is

=C33+C32

Finally, you can calculate the NPV for the new dispenser in cell B35 with the formula

=B34+NPV(C17,C34:F34)

Note that the initial investment, which is assumed to occur at the *beginning* of year 1, is not part of the NPV function, which includes only *end-of-year* cash flows.

You can then use Excel's Goal Seek tool to force the NPVs in cells B26 and B35 to be equal. Again, begin by entering any value for first-year sales volume with the new dispenser in cell C30. Then select Goal Seek from the What-If Analysis dropdown menu on the Data ribbon and fill out the dialog box as shown in Figure 9.44.

The file **Toothpaste.xlsx** does not yet contain the break-even calculations. Your first job is to enter

Figure 9.44
Goal Seek Dialog
Box

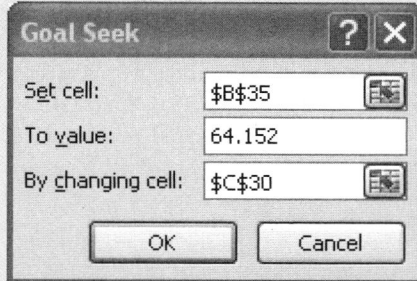

the appropriate formulas, using any year 1 sales volume figure in cell C30. Next, you should use Excel's Goal Seek tool to find the break-even point. Finally, you should test the alternative hypothesis that the mean sales volume over all stores (for a six-month period) will be large enough to warrant switching to the new dispenser. This hypothesis test should be based on the test-market data from Cincinnati. Do you recommend that the company should switch to the new dispenser? Discuss whether this decision should be based on the results of a hypothesis test. ■

For years, the drug Vioxx, developed and marketed by Merck, was one of the blockbuster drugs on the market. One of a number of so-called Cox-2 anti-inflammatory drugs, Vioxx was considered by many people a miracle drug for alleviating the pain from arthritis and other painful afflictions. Vioxx was marketed heavily on television, prescribed by most physicians, and used by an estimated two million Americans.

All of that changed in October 2004, when the results of a large study were released. The study, which followed approximately 2600 subjects over a period of about 18 months, concluded that Vioxx use over a long period of time caused a significant increase in the risk of developing serious heart problems. Merck almost immediately pulled Vioxx from the American market and doctors stopped prescribing it. On the basis of the study, Merck faced not only public embarrassment but the prospect of huge financial losses.

More specifically, the study had 1287 patients use Vioxx for an 18-month period, and it had another 1299 patients use a placebo over the same period. After 18 months, 45 of the Vioxx patients had developed serious heart problems, whereas only 25 patients on the placebo developed such problems.

Given these results, would you agree with the conclusion that Vioxx caused a *significant* increase in the risk of developing serious heart problems? First, answer this from a purely statistical point of view, where *significant* means statistically significant. What hypothesis should you test, and how should you run the test? When you run the test, what is the corresponding *p*-value? Next, look at it from the point of view of patients. If you were a Vioxx user, would these results cause you significant worry? After all, some of the subjects who took placebos also developed heart problems, and 45 might not be considered that much larger than 25. Finally, look at it from Merck's point of view. Are the results practically significant to the company? What does it stand to lose? Develop an estimate, no matter how wild it might be, of the financial losses Merck might incur. Just think of all of those American Vioxx users and what they might do. ■

Regression Analysis: Estimating Relationships

© Denkyw/Dreamstime.com

SITE LOCATION OF LA QUINTA MOTOR INNS

Regression analysis is an extremely flexible tool that can aid decision making in many areas. Kimes and Fitzsimmons (1990) describe how it has been used by La Quinta Motor Inns, a moderately priced hotel chain oriented toward serving the business traveler, to help make site location decisions. Location is one of the most important decisions for a lodging firm. All hotel chains search for ideal locations and often compete against each other for the same sites. A hotel chain that can select good sites more accurately and quickly than its competition has a distinct competitive advantage.

Kimes and Fitzsimmons, academics hired by La Quinta to model its site location decision process, used regression analysis. They collected data on 57 mature inns belonging to La Quinta during a three-year business cycle. The data included profitability for each inn (defined as operating margin percentage—profit plus depreciation and interest expenses, divided by the total revenue), as well as a number of potential explanatory variables that could be used to predict profitability. These explanatory variables fell into five categories: competitive characteristics (such as number of hotel rooms in the vicinity and average room rates); demand generators (such as hospitals and office buildings within a 4-mile radius that might attract customers to the area); demographic characteristics (such as local population, unemployment rate, and median family income); market awareness (such as years the inn has been open and state population per inn); and physical considerations (such as accessibility, distance to downtown, and sign visibility).

The analysts then determined which of these potential explanatory variables were most highly correlated (positively or negatively) with profitability and entered these variables into a regression equation for profitability. The estimated regression equation was

$$\text{Predicted Profitability} = 39.05 - 5.41\text{StatePop} + 5.81\text{Price}$$
$$- 3.09\sqrt{\text{MedIncome}} + 1.75\text{ColStudents}$$

where *StatePop* is the state population (in 1000s) per inn, *Price* is the room rate for the inn, *MedIncome* is the median income (in $1000s) of the area, *ColStudents* is the number of college students (in 1000s) within four miles, and all variables in this equation are standardized to have mean 0 and standard deviation 1. This equation predicts that profitability will increase when room rate and the number of college students *increase* and when state population and median income *decrease*. The R^2 value (to be discussed in this chapter) was a respectable 0.51, indicating a reasonable predictive ability. Using good statistical practice, the analysts validated this equation by feeding it explanatory variable data on a set of *different* inns, attempting to predict profitability for these new inns. The validation was a success—the regression equation predicted profitability fairly accurately for this new set of inns.

La Quinta management, however, was not as interested in predicting the exact profitability of inns as in predicting which would be profitable and which would be unprofitable. A cutoff value of 35% for operating margin was used to divide the profitable inns from the unprofitable inns. (Approximately 60% of the inns in the original sample were profitable by this definition.) The analysts were still able to use the regression equation they had developed. For any prospective site, they used the regression equation to predict profitability, and if the predicted value was sufficiently high, they predicted that site would be profitable. They selected a decision rule—that is, how high was "sufficiently high"—from considerations of the two potential types of errors. One type of error, a false positive, was predicting that a site would be profitable when in fact it was headed for unprofitability. The opposite type of error, a false negative, was predicting that a site would be unprofitable (and rejecting the site) when in fact it would have been profitable. La Quinta management was more concerned about false positives, so it was willing to be conservative in its decision rule and miss a few potential opportunities for profitable sites.

Since the time of the study, La Quinta has implemented the regression model in spreadsheet form. For each potential site, it collects data on the relevant explanatory variables, uses the regression equation to predict the site's profitability, and applies the decision rule on whether to build. Of course, the model's recommendation is only that—a recommendation. Top management has the ultimate say on whether any site is used. As Sam Barshop, then chairman of the board and president of La Quinta Motor Inns stated, "We currently use the model to help us in our site-screening process and have found that it has raised the 'red flag' on several sites we had under consideration. We plan to continue using and updating the model in the future in our attempt to make La Quinta a leader in the business hotel market." ■

10.1 INTRODUCTION

Regression analysis is the study of relationships between variables. It is one of the most useful tools for a business analyst because it applies to so many situations. Some potential uses of regression analysis in business include the following:

- How do wages of employees depend on years of experience, years of education, and gender?

- How does the current price of a stock depend on its own past values, as well as the current and past values of a market index?

- How does a company's current sales level depend on its current and past advertising levels, the advertising levels of its competitors, the company's own past sales levels, and the general level of the market?

- How does the total cost of producing a batch of items depend on the total quantity of items that have been produced?

- How does the selling price of a house depend on such factors as the appraised value of the house, the square footage of the house, the number of bedrooms in the house, and perhaps others?

Each of these questions asks how a single variable, such as selling price or employee wages, depends on other relevant variables. If we can estimate this relationship, then we can not only better understand how the world operates, but we can also do a better job of predicting the variable in question. For example, we can not only understand how a company's sales are affected by its advertising, but we can also use the company's records of current and past advertising levels to predict future sales.

The branch of statistics that studies such relationships is called **regression analysis**, and it is the subject of this chapter and the next. Because of its generality and applicability, regression analysis is one of the most pervasive of all statistical methods in the business world. There are several ways to categorize regression analysis. One categorization is based on the overall purpose of the analysis. As suggested previously, there are two potential objectives of regression analysis: to understand how the world operates and to make predictions. Either of these objectives could be paramount in any particular application. If the variable in question is employee salary and we are using variables such as years of experience, level of education, and gender to explain salary levels, then the purpose of the analysis is probably to understand how the world operates—that is, to explain how the variables combine in any given company to determine salaries. More specifically, the purpose of the analysis might be to discover whether there is any gender discrimination in salaries, after allowing for differences in work experience and education level.

Regression can be used to understand how the world operates, and it can be used for prediction.

On the other hand, the primary objective of the analysis might be prediction. A good example of this is when the variable in question is company sales, and variables such as advertising and past sales levels are used as explanatory variables. In this case it is certainly important for the company to know how the relevant variables impact its sales. But the company's primary objective is probably to predict *future* sales levels, given current and past values of the explanatory variables. A company could even use a regression model for a what-if analysis, where it predicts future sales for many conceivable patterns of advertising and then selects its advertising level on the basis of these predictions.

Fortunately, the same regression analysis enables us to solve both problems simultaneously. That is, it indicates how the world operates and it enables us to make predictions. So although the objectives of regression studies might differ, the same basic analysis always applies.

A second categorization of regression analysis is based on the type of data being analyzed. There are two basic types: cross-sectional data and time series data. *Cross-sectional data* are usually data gathered from approximately the same period of time from a population. The housing and wage examples mentioned previously are typical cross-sectional studies. The first concerns a sample of houses, presumably sold during a short period of time, such as houses sold in Florida during the first couple of months of 2010. The second concerns a sample of employees observed at a particular point in time, such as a sample of automobile workers observed at the beginning of 2011.

In contrast, *time series data* involve one or more variables that are observed at several, usually equally spaced, points in time. The stock price example mentioned previously fits this description. We observe the price of a particular stock and possibly the price of a market index at the beginning of every week, say, and then try to explain the movement of the stock's price through time.

Regression can be used to analyze cross-sectional data or time series data.

Regression analysis can be applied equally well to cross-sectional and time series data. However, there are technical reasons for treating time series data somewhat differently. The primary reason is that time series variables are usually related to their own past values. This property of many time series variables is called *autocorrelation*, and it adds complications to the analysis that we will discuss briefly.

A third categorization of regression analysis involves the number of explanatory variables in the analysis. First, we need to introduce some terms. In every regression study there is a single variable that we are trying to explain or predict, called the **dependent** variable (also called the **response** variable or the **target** variable). To help explain or predict the dependent variable, we use one or more **explanatory** variables (also called **independent** variables or **predictor** variables).[1] If there is a single explanatory variable, the analysis is called **simple regression**. If there are several explanatory variables, it is called **multiple regression**.

The **dependent** (or **response** or **target**) variable is the single variable being explained by the regression. The **explanatory** (or **independent** or **predictor**) variables are used to explain the dependent variable.

There are important differences between simple and multiple regression. The primary difference, as the name implies, is that simple regression is simpler. The calculations are simpler, the interpretation of output is somewhat simpler, and fewer complications can occur. We will begin with a simple regression example to introduce the ideas of regression. But simple regression is really just a special case of multiple regression, and there is little need to single it out for separate discussion—especially when computer software is available to perform the calculations in either case.

A **simple** regression analysis includes a single explanatory variable, whereas **multiple** regression can include any number of explanatory variables.

"Linear" regression allows you to estimate linear relationships as well as some nonlinear relationships.

A final categorization of regression analysis is of linear versus nonlinear models. The only type of regression analysis we study here is *linear* regression. Generally, this means that the relationships between variables are *straight-line* relationships, whereas the term *nonlinear* implies curved relationships. By focusing on linear regression, it might appear

---

[1]The traditional terms used in regression are *dependent* and *independent* variables. However, because these terms can cause confusion with probabilistic independence, a completely different concept, there has been an increasing use of the terms *response* and *explanatory* (or *predictor*) variables. We tend to prefer the terms *dependent* and *explanatory*, but this is largely a matter of taste.

that we are ignoring the many nonlinear relationships that exist in the business world. Fortunately, linear regression can often be used to estimate nonlinear relationships. As you will see, the term *linear regression* is more general than it appears. Admittedly, many of the relationships we study can be explained adequately by straight lines. But it is also true that many nonlinear relationships can be linearized by suitable mathematical transformations. Therefore, the only relationships we are ignoring in this book are those—and there are some—that cannot be transformed to linear. Such relationships can be studied, but only by advanced methods beyond the level of this book.

In this chapter we focus on line-fitting and curve-fitting; that is, on estimating equations that describe relationships between variables. We also discuss the interpretation of these equations, and we provide numerical measures that indicate the goodness of fit of the estimated equations. In the next chapter we extend the analysis to statistical inference of regression output.

10.2 SCATTERPLOTS: GRAPHING RELATIONSHIPS

A good way to begin any regression analysis is to draw one or more scatterplots. As discussed in Chapter 3, a scatterplot is a graphical plot of two variables, an *X* and a *Y*. If there is any relationship between the two variables, it is usually apparent from the scatterplot.

The following example, which we will continue through the chapter, illustrates the usefulness of scatterplots. It is a typical example of cross-sectional data.

EXAMPLE | **10.1 SALES VERSUS PROMOTIONS AT PHARMEX**

Pharmex is a chain of drugstores that operate around the country. To see how effective its advertising and other promotional activities are, the company has collected data from 50 randomly selected metropolitan regions. In each region it has compared its own promotional expenditures and sales to those of the leading competitor in the region over the past year. There are two variables:

- Promote: Pharmex's promotional expenditures as a percentage of those of the leading competitor
- Sales: Pharmex's sales as a percentage of those of the leading competitor

Note that each of these variables is an *index*, not a dollar amount. For example, if Promote equals 95 for some region, this tells us only that Pharmex's promotional expenditures in that region are 95% as large as those for the leading competitor in that region. The company expects that there is a positive relationship between these two variables, so that regions with relatively larger expenditures have relatively larger sales. However, it is not clear what the nature of this relationship is. The data are listed in the file **Drugstore Sales.xlsx**. (See Figure 10.1 for a partial listing of the data.) What type of relationship, if any, is apparent from a scatterplot?

Objective To use a scatterplot to examine the relationship between promotional expenses and sales at Pharmex.

Solution

First, recall from Chapter 3 that there are two ways to create a scatterplot in Excel. You can use Excel's Chart Wizard to create an X–Y chart, or you can use StatTools's Scatterplot

Figure 10.1

Data for Drugstore
Example

	A	B	C	D	E	F	G	H
1	Region	Promote	Sales					
2	1	77	85					
3	2	110	103					
4	3	110	102					
5	4	93	109					
6	5	90	85					
7	6	95	103					
8	7	100	110					
9	8	85	86					
10	9	96	92					
11	10	83	87					

Each value is a percentage of what the leading competitor did.

procedure. The advantages of the latter are that it is slightly easier to implement and it provides automatic formatting of the chart.

Which variable should be on the horizontal axis? It is customary to put the explanatory variable on the horizontal axis and the dependent variable on the vertical axis. In this example the store believes large promotional expenditures tend to "cause" larger values of sales, so Sales is on the vertical axis and Promote is on the horizontal axis. The resulting scatterplot appears in Figure 10.2.

Figure 10.2

Scatterplot of Sales Versus Promote

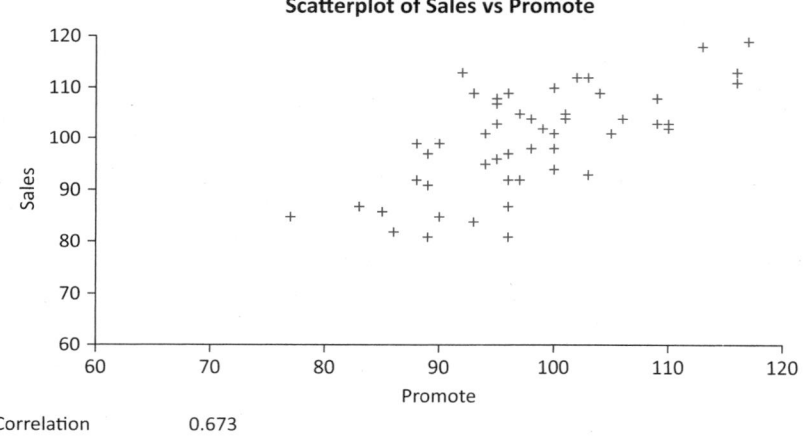

Correlation   0.673

Remember that a StatTools chart is really just an Excel chart. So you can manipulate it using Excel tools. For this scatterplot, we changed the scales of the axes so that the scatter filled up more of the chart area.

This scatterplot indicates that there is indeed a positive relationship between Promote and Sales—the points tend to rise from bottom left to top right—but the relationship is not perfect. If it were perfect, a given value of Promote would prescribe the value of Sales exactly. Clearly, this is not the case. For example, there are five regions with promotional values of 96 but all of them have different sales values. So the scatterplot indicates that while the variable Promote is helpful for predicting Sales, it does not lead to perfect predictions.

Note the correlation of 0.673 shown at the bottom of Figure 10.2. StatTools inserts this value automatically (if you request it) to indicate the strength of the linear relationship between the two variables. For now, just note that it is positive and its magnitude is moderately large. We will say more about correlations in the next section.

Finally, we briefly discuss causation. There is a tendency for an analyst (such as a drugstore manager) to say that larger promotional expenses *cause* larger sales values. However, unless the data are obtained in a carefully controlled experiment—which is certainly not the case here—you can never be absolutely sure about causation. One reason is that you can't always be sure which direction the causation goes. Does X cause Y, or does Y cause X? Another reason is that you can almost never rule out the possibility that some other variable is causing the variation in *both* of the observed variables. Although this is unlikely in this drugstore example, it is still a possibility. ∎

FUNDAMENTAL INSIGHT

Regression and Causation

A successful regression analysis does not necessarily imply that the the Xs *cause* Y to vary in a certain way. This is one possibility, but there are two others. First, even if a regression of Y versus X is promising, it could very easily be that Y is causing X; that is, the causality could go in the opposite direction. Second and more common, there could be other variables (not included in the regression) that are causing *both* Y and the Xs to vary.

The following example uses time series data to illustrate several other features of scatterplots. We will follow this example throughout the chapter as well.

EXAMPLE | 10.2 EXPLAINING OVERHEAD COSTS AT BENDRIX

The Bendrix Company manufactures various types of parts for automobiles. The manager of the factory wants to get a better understanding of overhead costs. These overhead costs include supervision, indirect labor, supplies, payroll taxes, overtime premiums, depreciation, and a number of miscellaneous items such as insurance, utilities, and janitorial and maintenance expenses. Some of these overhead costs are *fixed* in the sense that they do not vary appreciably with the volume of work being done, whereas others are *variable* and do vary directly with the volume of work. The fixed overhead costs tend to come from the supervision, depreciation, and miscellaneous categories, whereas the variable overhead costs tend to come from the indirect labor, supplies, payroll taxes, and overtime categories. However, it is not easy to draw a clear line between the fixed and variable overhead components.

The Bendrix manager has tracked total overhead costs for the past 36 months. To help explain these, he has also collected data on two variables that are related to the amount of work done at the factory. These variables are:

■ MachHrs: number of machine hours used during the month
■ ProdRuns: the number of separate production runs during the month

The first of these is a direct measure of the amount of work being done. To understand the second, we note that Bendrix manufactures parts in large batches. Each batch corresponds to a production run. Once a production run is completed, the factory must set up for the next production run. During this setup there is typically some downtime while the machinery is reconfigured for the part type scheduled for production in the next batch. Therefore, the manager believes that both of these variables could be responsible (in different ways) for variations in overhead costs. Do scatterplots support this belief?

Objective To use scatterplots to examine the relationships among overhead, machine hours, and production runs at Bendrix.

Solution

The data appear in Figure 10.3. (See the **Overhead Costs.xlsx** file.) Each observation (row) corresponds to a single month. The goal is to find possible relationships between the

Figure 10.3

Data for Bendrix
Overhead Example

	A	B	C	D
1	Month	MachHrs	ProdRuns	Overhead
2	1	1539	31	99798
3	2	1284	29	87804
4	3	1490	27	93681
5	4	1355	22	82262
6	5	1500	35	106968
7	6	1777	30	107925
8	7	1716	41	117287
9	8	1045	29	76868
10	9	1364	47	106001
11	10	1516	21	88738
35	34	1723	35	107828
36	35	1413	30	88032
37	36	1390	54	117943

Overhead variable and the MachHrs and ProdRuns variables, but because these are time series variables, you should also be on the lookout for any relationships between these variables and the Month variable. That is, you should also investigate any time series behavior in these variables.

This data set illustrates, even with a modest number of variables, how the number of potentially useful scatterplots can grow quickly. At the very least, you should examine the scatterplot between each potential explanatory variable (MachHrs and ProdRuns) and the dependent variable (Overhead). These appear in Figures 10.4 and 10.5. You can see

Figure 10.4

Scatterplot of
Overhead Versus
Machine Hours

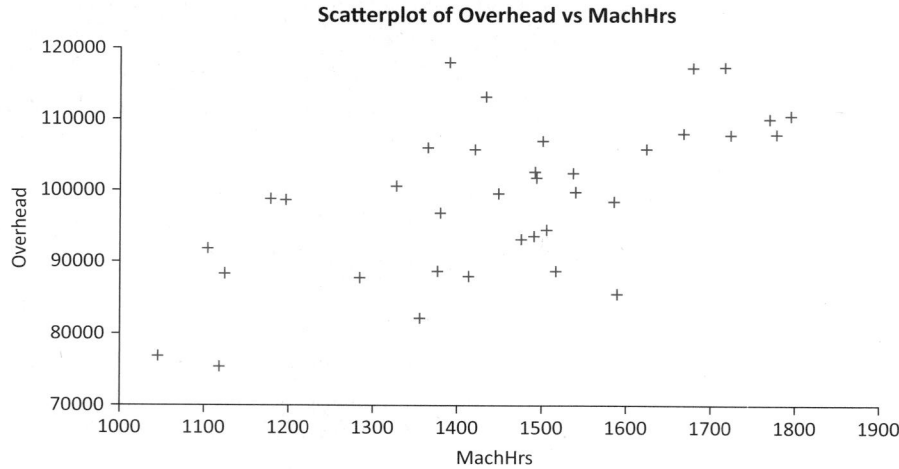

that Overhead tends to increase as either MachHrs increases or ProdRuns increases. However, both relationships are far from perfect.

To check for possible time series patterns, you can also create a time series graph for any of the variables. One of these, the time series graph for Overhead, is shown in Figure 10.6. It indicates a fairly random pattern through time, with no apparent upward trend or other obvious time series pattern. You can check that time series graphs of the MachHrs and ProdRuns variables also indicate no obvious time series patterns.

Finally, when there are multiple explanatory variables, you should check for relationships among them. The scatterplot of MachHrs versus ProdRuns appears in Figure 10.7. (Either variable could be chosen for the vertical axis.) This "cloud" of points indicates no relationship worth pursuing.

This is precisely the role of scatterplots: to provide a visual representation of relationships or the lack of relationships between variables.

Figure 10.5

Scatterplot of
Overhead Versus
Production Runs

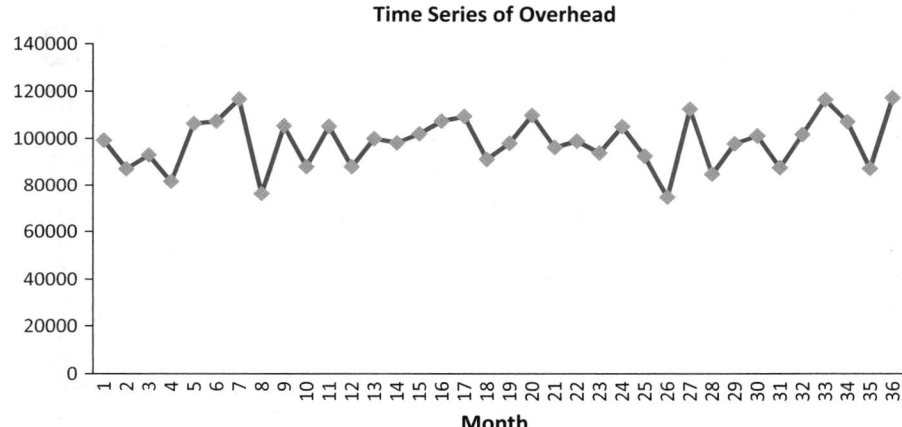

Scatterplot of Overhead vs ProdRuns

Figure 10.6

Time Series Graph
of Overhead Versus
Month

Time Series of Overhead

Figure 10.7

Scatterplot of
Machine Hours
Versus Production
Runs

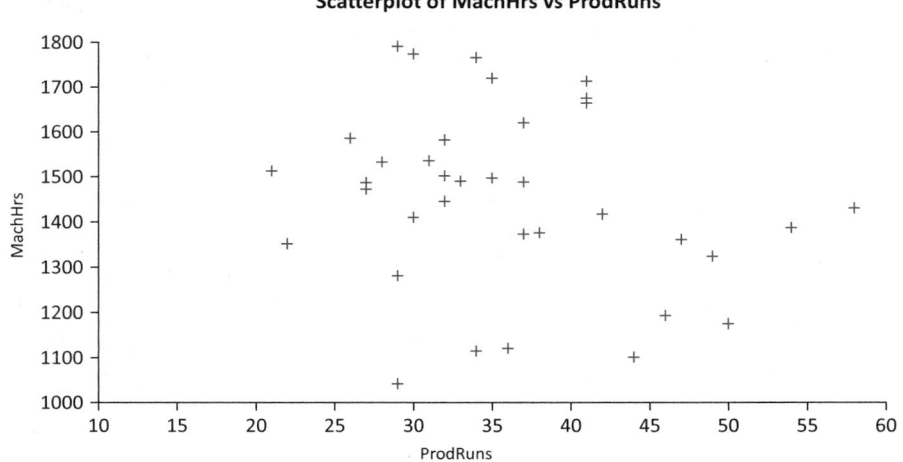

Scatterplot of MachHrs vs ProdRuns

In summary, the Bendrix manager should continue to explore the positive relationship between Overhead and each of the MachHrs and ProdRuns variables. However, none of the variables appears to have any time series behavior, and the two potential explanatory variables do not appear to be related to each other. ■

10.2.1 Linear Versus Nonlinear Relationships

Scatterplots are extremely useful for detecting behavior that might not be obvious otherwise. We illustrate some of these in the next few subsections. First, the typical relationship you hope to see is a straight-line, or *linear*, relationship. This doesn't mean that all points lie on a straight line—this is too much to expect in business data—but that the points tend to cluster around a straight line. The scatterplots in Figures 10.2, 10.4, and 10.5 all exhibit linear relationships. At least, there is no obvious curvature.

The scatterplot in Figure 10.8, on the other hand, illustrates a relationship that is clearly nonlinear. The data in this scatterplot are 1990 data on more than 100 countries. The variables listed are life expectancy (of newborns, based on current mortality conditions) and GNP per capita. The obvious curvature in the scatterplot can be explained as follows. For poor countries, a slight increase in GNP per capita has a large effect on life expectancy. However, this effect decreases for wealthier countries. A straight-line relationship is definitely not appropriate for these data. However, as discussed previously, *linear* regression—after an appropriate transformation of the data—might still be applicable.

Figure 10.8

Scatterplot of Life Expectancy Versus GNP per Capita

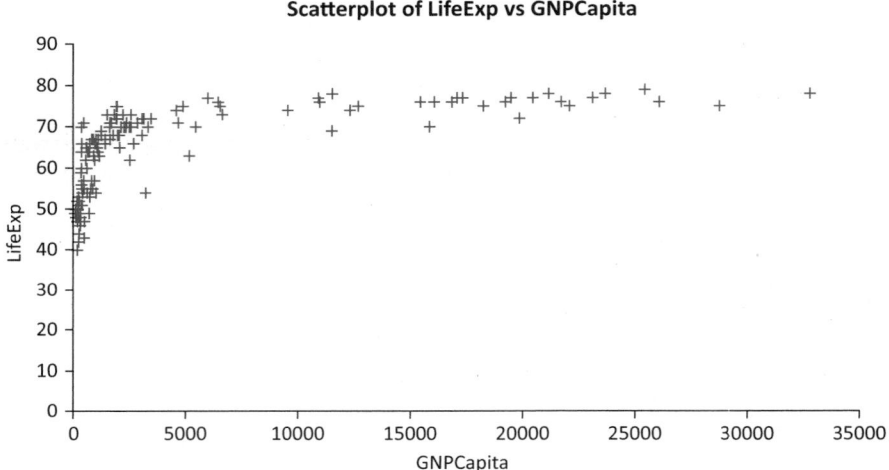

10.2.2 Outliers

Scatterplots are especially useful for identifying *outliers*, observations that lie outside the typical pattern of points. The scatterplot in Figure 10.9 shows annual salaries versus years of experience for a sample of employees at a particular company. There is a clear linear relationship between these two variables—for all employees except the point at the top right. Closer scrutiny of the data reveals that this one employee is the company CEO, whose salary is well above that of all the other employees.

> An **outlier** is an observation that falls outside of the general pattern of the rest of the observations.

Although scatterplots are good for detecting outliers, they do not necessarily indicate what you ought to do about any outliers you find. This depends entirely on the particular situation. If you are attempting to investigate the salary structure for typical employees at a company, then you should probably not include the company CEO. First, the CEO's salary is not determined in the same way as the salaries for typical employees. Second, if you do

Figure 10.9

Scatterplot of Salary
Versus Years of
Experience

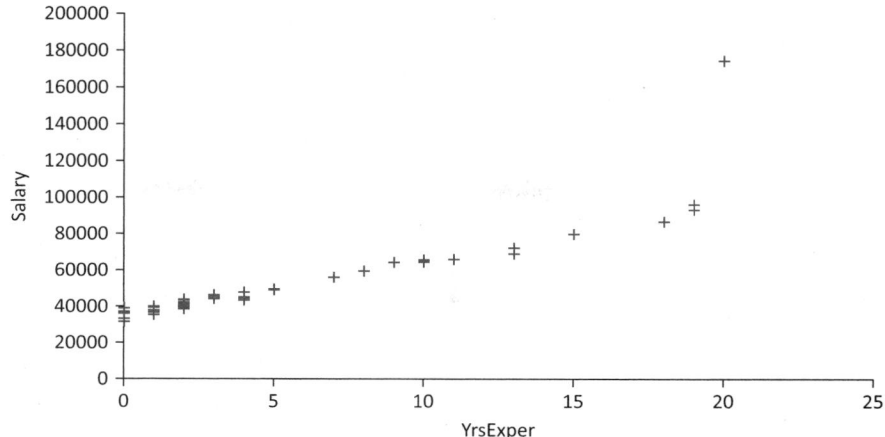

include the CEO in the analysis, it can greatly distort the results for the mass of typical employees. In other situations, however, it might *not* be appropriate to eliminate outliers just to make the analysis come out more nicely.

It is difficult to generalize about the treatment of outliers, but the following points are worth noting.

- If an outlier is clearly not a member of the population of interest, then it is probably best to delete it from the analysis. This is the case for the company CEO in Figure 10.9.

- If it isn't clear whether outliers are members of the relevant population, you can run the regression analysis with them and again without them. If the results are practically the same in both cases, then it is probably best to report the results with the outliers included. Otherwise, you can report both sets of results with a verbal explanation of the outliers.

10.2.3 Unequal Variance

Occasionally, there is a clear relationship between two variables, but the variance of the dependent variable depends on the value of the explanatory variable. Figure 10.10 illustrates a common example of this. It shows the amount spent at a mail-order company versus salary

Figure 10.10

Unequal Variance of
Dependent Variable
in a Scatterplot

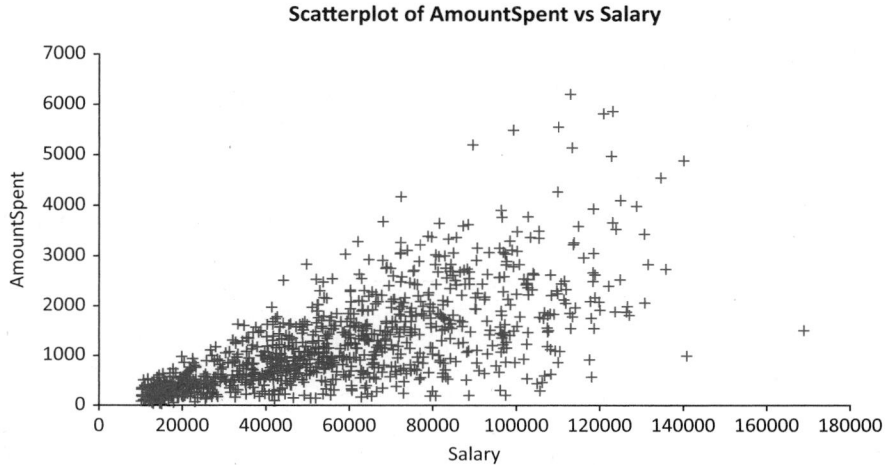

for the customers in the data set. There is a clear upward relationship, but the variability of amount spent increases as salary increases. This is evident from the *fan* shape. As you will see in the next chapter, this unequal variance violates one of the assumptions of linear regression analysis, and there are special techniques to deal with it.

10.2.4 No Relationship

A scatterplot can provide one other useful piece of information: It can indicate that there is *no* relationship between a pair of variables, at least none worth pursuing. This is usually the case when the scatterplot appears as a shapeless swarm of points, as illustrated in Figure 10.11. Here the variables are an employee performance score and the number of overtime hours worked in the previous month for a sample of employees. There is virtually no hint of a relationship between these two variables in this plot, and if these are the only two variables in the data set, the analysis can stop right here. Many people who use statistics evidently believe that a computer can perform magic on a set of numbers and find relationships that were completely hidden. Occasionally this is true, but when a scatterplot appears as in Figure 10.11, the variables are not related in any useful way, and that's all there is to it.

Figure 10.11

An Example of No Relationship

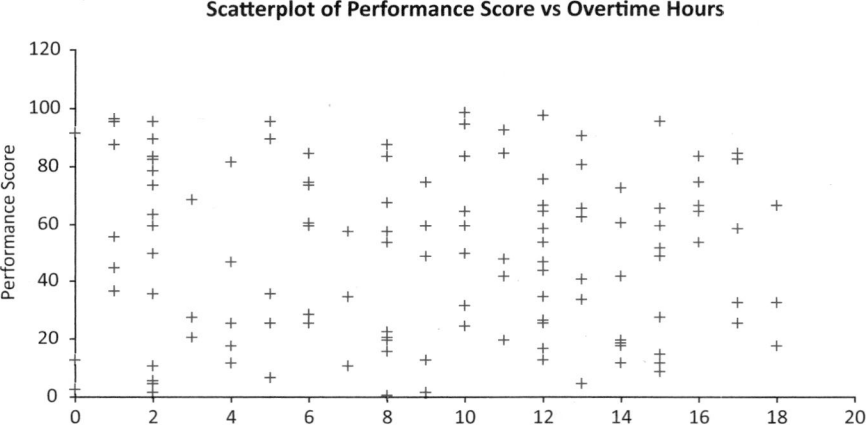

10.3 CORRELATIONS: INDICATORS OF LINEAR RELATIONSHIPS

Scatterplots provide graphical indications of relationships, whether they are linear, nonlinear, or essentially nonexistent. **Correlations** are numerical summary measures that indicate the strength of linear relationships between pairs of variables.[2] A correlation between a pair of variables is a single number that summarizes the information in a scatterplot. A correlation can be very useful, but it has an important limitation: It measures the strength of *linear* relationships only. If there is a nonlinear relationship, as suggested by a scatterplot, the correlation can be completely misleading. With this important limitation in mind, let's look a bit more closely at correlations.

The usual notation for a correlation between two variables X and Y is r_{XY}. (The subscripts can be omitted if the variables are clear from the context.) The formula for r_{XY} is given by Equation (10.1). Note that it is a sum of products in the numerator, divided by the

---

[2]This section includes some material from Chapter 3 that we repeat here for convenience.

product $s_X s_Y$ of the sample standard deviations of X and Y. This requires a considerable amount of computation, so correlations are almost always computed by software packages.

Formula for Correlation

$$r_{XY} = \frac{\Sigma(X_i - \overline{X})(Y_i - \overline{Y})/(n - 1)}{s_X s_Y}$$

(10.1)

The numerator of Equation (10.1) is also a measure of association between two variables X and Y, called the **covariance** between X and Y. Like a correlation, a covariance is a single number that measures the strength of the linear relationship between two variables. By looking at the sign of the covariance or correlation—plus or minus—you can tell whether the two variables are positively or negatively related. The drawback to a covariance, however, is that its magnitude depends on the units in which the variables are measured.

To illustrate, the covariance between Overhead and MachHrs in the Bendrix manufacturing data set is 1,333,138. (It can be found with Excel's COVAR function or with StatTools.) However, if each overhead value is divided by 1000, so that overhead costs are expressed in thousands of dollars, and each value of MachHrs is divided by 100, so that machine hours are expressed in hundreds of hours, the covariance decreases by a factor of 100,000 to 13.33138. This is in spite of the fact that the basic relationship between these variables has not changed and the revised scatterplot has exactly the same shape. For this reason it is difficult to interpret the magnitude of a covariance, and we concentrate instead on correlations.

Unlike covariances, correlations have the attractive property that they are completely unaffected by the units of measurement. The rescaling described in the previous paragraph has absolutely no effect on the correlation between Overhead and MachHrs. In either case the correlation is 0.632. All correlations are between -1 and $+1$, inclusive. The sign of a correlation, plus or minus, determines whether the linear relationship between two variables is positive or negative. In this respect, a correlation is just like a covariance. However, the strength of the linear relationship between the variables is measured by the absolute value, or magnitude, of the correlation. The closer this magnitude is to 1, the stronger the linear relationship is.

A correlation equal to 0 or near 0 indicates practically no linear relationship. A correlation with magnitude close to 1, on the other hand, indicates a strong linear relationship. At the extreme, a correlation equal to -1 or $+1$ occurs only when the linear relationship is perfect—that is, when all points in the scatterplot lie on a single straight line. Although such extremes practically never occur in business applications, large correlations greater in magnitude than 0.9, say, are not at all uncommon.

Looking back at the scatterplots for the Pharmex drugstore data in Figure 10.2, you can see that the correlation between Sales and Promote is positive—as the upward-sloping scatter of points suggests—and is equal to 0.673. This is a moderately large correlation. It confirms the pattern in the scatterplot, namely, that the points increase linearly from left to right but with considerable variation around any particular straight line.

Similarly, the scatterplots for the Bendrix manufacturing data in Figures 10.4 and 10.5 indicate moderately large positive correlations, 0.632 and 0.521, between Overhead and MachHrs and between Overhead and ProdRuns. However, the correlation indicated in Figure 10.7 between MachHrs and ProdRuns, -0.229, is quite small and indicates almost no relationship between these two variables.

You must be careful when interpreting the correlations in Figures 10.8 and 10.9. The scatterplot between life expectancy and GNP per capita in Figure 10.8 is obviously nonlinear, and correlations are relevant descriptors only for *linear* relationships. If anything, the correlation of 0.616 in this example tends to underestimate the true strength of the relationship—the nonlinear one—between life expectancy and GNP per capita. In contrast, the correlation between salary and years of experience in Figure 10.9 is large, 0.894, but it is not nearly as large as it would be if the outlier were omitted. (It is then 0.992.) This example illustrates the considerable effect a single outlier can have on a correlation.

An obvious question is whether a given correlation is "large." This is a difficult question to answer directly. Clearly, a correlation such as 0.992 is quite large—the points tend to cluster very closely around a straight line. Similarly, a correlation of 0.034 is quite small—the points tend to be a shapeless swarm. But there is a continuum of in-between values, as exhibited in Figures 10.2, 10.4, and 10.5. We give a more definite answer to this question when we examine the *square* of the correlation later in this chapter.

As for calculating correlations, there are two possibilities in Excel. To calculate a *single* correlation r_{XY} between variables X and Y, you can use Excel's CORREL function in the form

=**CORREL**(*X*-range,*Y*-range)

Alternatively, you can use StatTools to obtain a whole table of correlations between a set of variables.

Finally, we reiterate the important limitation of correlations (and covariances), namely, that they apply only to *linear* relationships. If a correlation is close to zero, you cannot automatically conclude that there is no relationship between the two variables. You should look at a scatterplot first. The chances are that the points are a shapeless swarm and that no relationship exists. But it is also possible that the points cluster around some curve. In this case the correlation is a misleading measure of the relationship.

10.4 SIMPLE LINEAR REGRESSION

Scatterplots and correlations are very useful for indicating linear relationships and the strengths of these relationships. But they do not actually *quantify* the relationships. For example, it is clear from the scatterplot of the Pharmex drugstore data that sales are related to promotional expenditures. But the scatterplot does not specify exactly what this relationship is. If the expenditure index for a given region is 95, what would you predict this region's sales index to be? Or if one region's expenditure index is 5 points higher than another's, how much larger would you predict sales of the former to be? To answer these questions, the relationship between the dependent variable Sales and the explanatory variable Promote must be quantified.

In this section we answer these types of questions for simple linear regression, where there is a *single* explanatory variable. We do so by fitting a straight line through the scatterplot of the dependent variable Y versus the explanatory variable X and then basing the answers to the questions on the fitted straight line. But which straight line? We address this issue next.

Remember that simple linear regression does not mean "easy"; it means only that there is a single explanatory variable.

10.4.1 Least Squares Estimation

The scatterplot between Sales and Promote, repeated in Figure 10.12, hints at a linear relationship between these two variables. It would not be difficult to draw a straight line through these points to produce a reasonably good fit. In fact, a possible linear fit is indicated in the graph. But we proceed more systematically than simply drawing lines freehand. Specifically, we choose the line that makes the vertical distances from the points to the line as small as possible, as explained next.

Figure 10.12

Scatterplot with Possible Linear Fit Superimposed

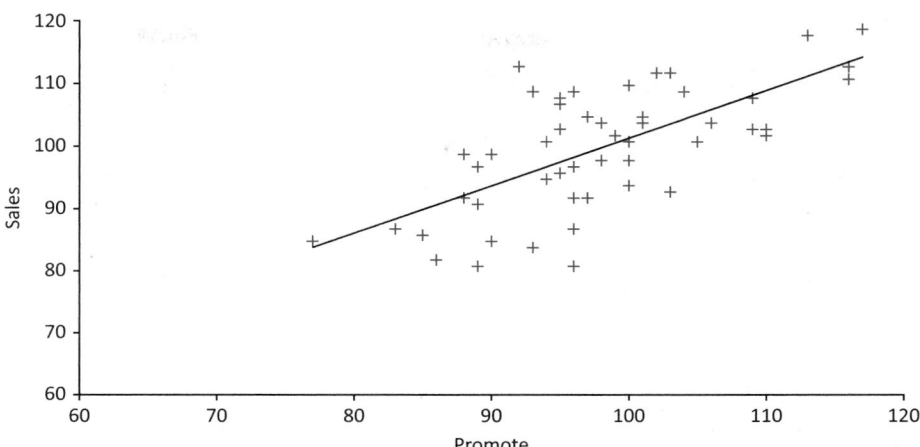

Consider the magnified graph in Figure 10.13. Several points in the scatterplot are shown, along with a line drawn through them. Note that the vertical distance from the horizontal axis to any point, which is just the value of Sales for that point, can be decomposed into two parts: the vertical distance from the horizontal axis to the line, and the vertical distance from the line to the point. The first of these is called the **fitted value**, and the second is called the **residual**. The idea is very simple. By using a straight line to reflect the relationship between Sales and Promote, you expect a given Sales to be at the height of the line above any particular value of Promote. That is, you expect Sales to equal the fitted value.

A **fitted value** is the predicted value of the dependent variable. Graphically, it is the height of the line above a given explanatory value. The corresponding **residual** is the difference between the actual and fitted values of the dependent variable.

Figure 10.13

Fitted Values and Residuals

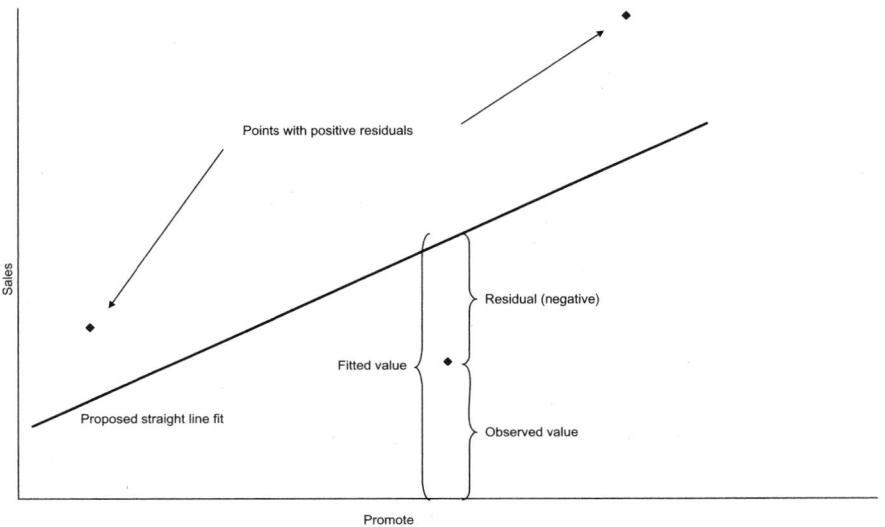

But the relationship is not perfect. Not all (perhaps not any) of the points lie exactly on the line. The differences are the residuals. They show how much the observed values differ from the fitted values. If a particular residual is positive, the corresponding point is above the line; if it is negative, the point is below the line. The only time a residual is zero is when the point lies directly on the line. The relationship between observed values, fitted values, and residuals is very general and is stated in Equation (10.2).

Fundamental Equation for Regression

$$\text{Observed Value} = \text{Fitted Value} + \text{Residual} \qquad \textbf{(10.2)}$$

We can now explain how to choose the best-fitting line through the points in the scatterplot. It is the line with the *smallest sum of squared residuals*. The resulting line is called the **least squares line**. Why do we use the sum of *squared* residuals? Why not minimize some other measure of the residuals? First, it is not appropriate to simply minimize the sum of the residuals. This is because the positive residuals would cancel the negative residuals. In fact, the least squares line has the property that the sum of the residuals is always exactly zero. To adjust for this, we could minimize the sum of the *absolute values* of the residuals, and this is a perfectly reasonable procedure. However, for technical and historical reasons, it is not the procedure usually chosen. The minimization of the sum of squared residuals is deeply rooted in statistical tradition, and it works well.

The **least squares line** is the line that minimizes the sum of the squared residuals. It is the line quoted in regression outputs.

The minimization problem itself is a calculus problem and is not discussed here. Virtually all statistical software packages perform this minimization automatically, so you do not need to be concerned with the technical details. However, we do provide the formulas for the least squares line.

Recall from basic algebra that the equation for any straight line can be written as

$$Y = a + bX$$

Here, a is the Y-intercept of the line, the value of Y when $X = 0$, and b is the slope of the line, the change in Y when X increases by one unit. Therefore, the least squares line is specified completely by its slope and intercept. These are given by equations (10.3) and (10.4).

Equation for Slope in Simple Linear Regression

$$b = \frac{\Sigma(X_i - \overline{X})(Y_i - \overline{Y})}{\Sigma(X_i - \overline{X})^2} = r_{XY}\frac{s_Y}{s_X} \qquad \textbf{(10.3)}$$

Equation for Intercept in Simple Linear Regression

$$a = \overline{Y} - b\overline{X} \qquad \textbf{(10.4)}$$

We have presented these formulas primarily for conceptual purposes, not for hand calculations—the software takes care of the calculations. From the right-hand formula for b, you can see that it is closely related to the correlation between X and Y. Specifically, if the standard deviations, s_X and s_Y, of X and Y are kept constant, then the slope b of the least squares line varies directly with the correlation between the two variables. The effect of the formula for a is not quite as interesting. It simply forces the least squares line to go through the point of sample means, $(\overline{X}, \overline{Y})$.

It is easy to obtain the least squares line in Excel with StatTools's Regression procedure. We illustrate this in the following continuations of Examples 10.1 and 10.2.

EXAMPLE | **10.1 SALES VERSUS PROMOTIONS AT PHARMEX (CONTINUED)**

Find the least squares line for the Pharmex drugstore data, using Sales as the dependent variable and Promote as the explanatory variable.

Objective To use StatTools's Regression procedure to find the least squares line for sales as a function of promotional expenses at Pharmex.

Solution

To perform the analysis, select Regression from the StatTools Regression and Classification dropdown list. Then fill in the resulting dialog box as shown in Figure 10.14. Specifically, select Multiple as the Regression Type (this type is used for both single and multiple regression in StatTools), and select Promote as the single I variable and Sales as the single D variable, where I and D stand for independent and dependent. (There is always a *single D* variable, but in multiple regression there can be several I variables.) Note that there is an option to create several scatterplots involving the fitted values and residuals. We suggest checking the third option, as shown. Finally, there is an Include Prediction option. We will explain it in a later section. You can leave it unchecked for now.

Figure 10.14
Regression Dialog
Box

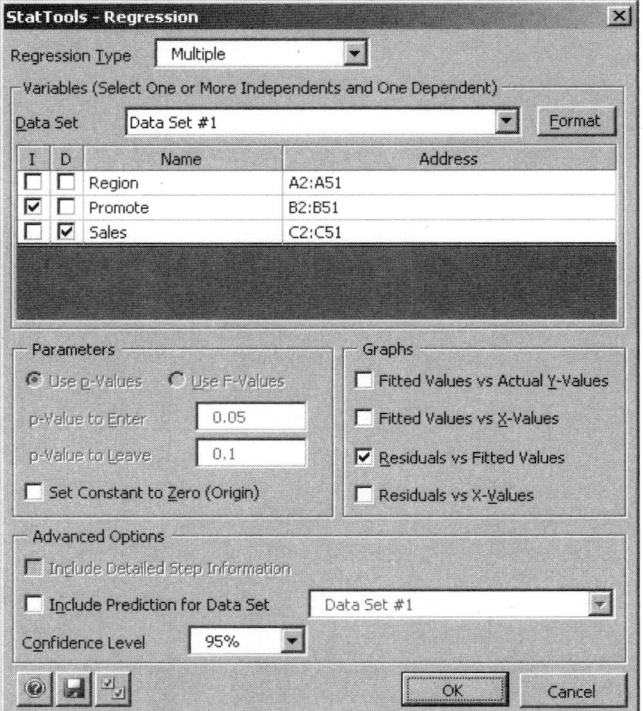

The regression output includes three parts. The first is the main regression output shown in Figure 10.15. The last two are a scatterplot of residuals and fitted values requested in the regression dialog box and a list of fitted values and residuals, a few of which are shown in Figure 10.16. (The list of fitted values and residuals is part of the output only if at least one of the optional scatterplots in the regression dialog box is selected.)

Figure 10.15

Regression Output for Drugstore Example

	A	B	C	D	E	F	G
7		Multiple			Adjusted	StErr of	
8	Summary	R	R-Square		R-Square	Estimate	
9		0.6730	0.4529		0.4415	7.3947	
10							
11		Degrees of	Sum of		Mean of		
12	ANOVA Table	Freedom	Squares		Squares	F-Ratio	p-Value
13	Explained	1	2172.8804		2172.8804	39.7366	< 0.0001
14	Unexplained	48	2624.7396		54.6821		
15							
16			Standard				Confidence Interval 95%
17	Regression Table	Coefficient	Error		t-Value	p-Value	Lower	Upper
18	Constant	25.1264	11.8826		2.1146	0.0397	1.2349	49.0180
19	Promote	0.7623	0.1209		6.3037	< 0.0001	0.5192	1.0054

Figure 10.16

Scatterplot and Partial List of Residuals Versus Fitted Values

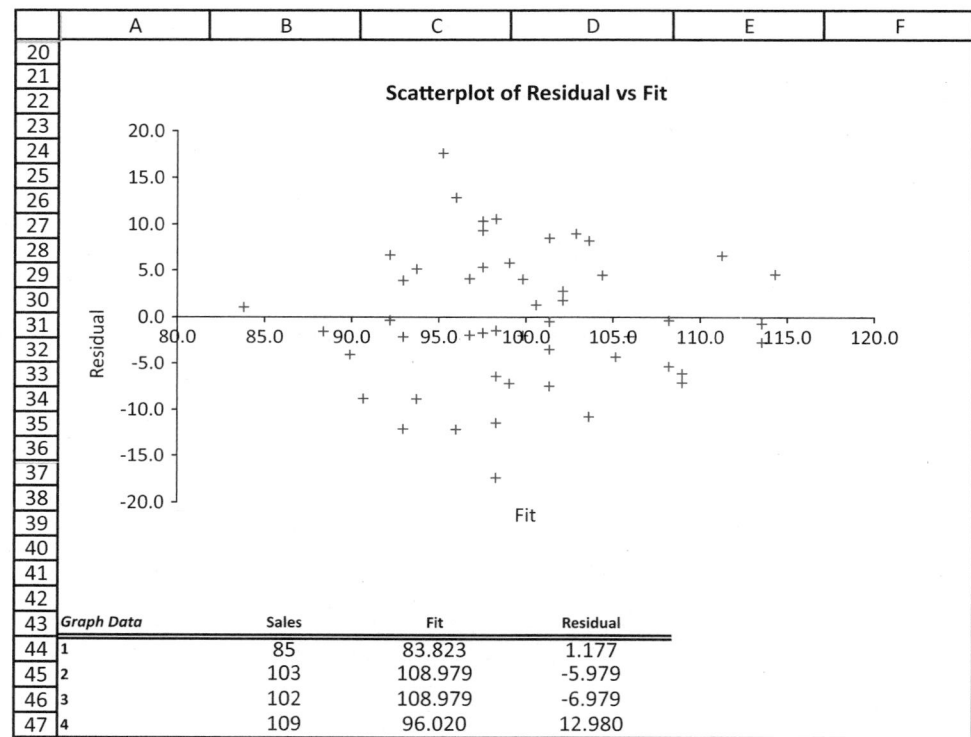

	A	B	C	D	E	F
43	Graph Data	Sales	Fit	Residual		
44	1	85	83.823	1.177		
45	2	103	108.979	-5.979		
46	3	102	108.979	-6.979		
47	4	109	96.020	12.980		

We will eventually interpret all of the output in Figure 10.15, but for now, we focus on only a small part of it. Specifically, the intercept and slope of the least squares line appear under the Coefficient label in cells B18 and B19. They imply that the equation for the least squares line is[3]

$$\text{Predicted Sales} = 25.1264 + 0.7623\text{Promote}$$

[3]We always report the left side of the estimated regression equation as the *predicted* value of the dependent variable. It is not the *actual* value of the dependent variable because the observations do not all lie on the estimated regression line.

Excel Tip *The Regression procedure for simple regression uses special StatTools functions to calculate all of the regression output. However, it can also be generated from several built-in statistical functions available in Excel. These include the CORREL, RSQ, STEYX, INTERCEPT, SLOPE, and LINEST functions. For example, the slope and intercept of the least squares line can be calculated directly with the formulas*

=SLOPE(Y-range,X-range)

and

=INTERCEPT(Y-range,X-range)

These formulas (with the appropriate X and Y ranges) can be entered anywhere in a spreadsheet to obtain the slope and intercept for a simple regression equation—no add-ins are necessary. The LINEST function can be used to find relevant output for a multiple regression. You can look up all of these functions in Excel's online help.

Excel Tip *As discussed in Chapter 3, you can also use superimpose a trendline on a scatterplot (by right-clicking on the chart and selecting the Trendline option). The line superimposed is indeed the least-squares regression line. In addition, you can ask for the equation of the trendline and its R^2 value (to be discussed shortly) to be added to the chart. However, this works only when there is a single X variable. There is no comparable trendline option for multiple regression.*

In many applications, it makes no sense to have the explanatory variable(s) equal to zero. Then the intercept term has no practical or economic meaning.

The regression equation for this example can be interpreted as follows. The slope, 0.7623, indicates that the sales index tends to increase by about 0.76 for each one-unit increase in the promotional expenses index. Alternatively, if two regions are compared, where the second region spends one unit more than the first region, the predicted sales index for the second region is 0.76 larger than the sales index for the first region. The interpretation of the intercept is less important. It is literally the predicted sales index for a region that does no promotions. However, no region in the sample has anywhere near a zero promotional value. Therefore, in a situation like this, where the range of observed values for the explanatory variable does not include zero, it is best to think of the intercept term as simply an "anchor" for the least squares line that enables predictions of Y values for the range of observed X values.

A shapeless swarm of points in a scatterplot of residuals versus fitted values is typically good news. It means that no regression assumptions are violated.

A useful graph in almost any regression analysis is a scatterplot of residuals (on the vertical axis) versus fitted values. This scatterplot for the Pharmex data appears in Figure 10.16 (along with a few of the residuals and fitted values used to create the chart). You typically examine such a scatterplot for any striking patterns. A good fit not only has small residuals, but it has residuals scattered *randomly* around zero with no apparent pattern. This appears to be the case for the Pharmex data. ∎

EXAMPLE | **10.2 EXPLAINING OVERHEAD COSTS AT BENDRIX (CONTINUED)**

The Bendrix manufacturing data set has two potential explanatory variables, MachHrs and ProdRuns. Eventually, we will estimate a regression equation with *both* of these variables included. However, if we include only one at a time, what do they tell us about overhead costs?

Objective To use StatTools's Regression procedure to regress overhead expenses at Bendrix against machine hours and then against production runs.

Solution

The regression output for Overhead with MachHrs as the single explanatory variable appears in Figure 10.17. The output when ProdRuns is the only explanatory variable appears in Figure 10.18. The two least squares lines are therefore

$$\text{Predicted Overhead} = 48621 + 34.7\text{MachHrs} \tag{10.5}$$

and

$$\text{Predicted Overhead} = 75606 + 655.1\text{ProdRuns} \tag{10.6}$$

Figure 10.17

Regression Output for Overhead versus MachHrs

	A	B	C	D	E	F	G
7		Multiple	R-Square	Adjusted	StErr of		
8	Summary	R		R-Square	Estimate		
9		0.6319	0.3993	0.3816	8584.739		
10							
11		Degrees of	Sum of	Mean of	F-Ratio	p-Value	
12	ANOVA Table	Freedom	Squares	Squares			
13	Explained	1	1665463368	1665463368	22.5986	< 0.0001	
14	Unexplained	34	2505723492	73697749.75			
15							
16		Coefficient	Standard	t-Value	p-Value	Confidence Interval 95%	
17	Regression Table		Error			Lower	Upper
18	Constant	48621.355	10725.333	4.5333	< 0.0001	26824.856	70417.853
19	MachHrs	34.702	7.300	4.7538	< 0.0001	19.867	49.537

Figure 10.18

Regression Output for Overhead versus ProdRuns

	A	B	C	D	E	F	G
7		Multiple	R-Square	Adjusted	StErr of		
8	Summary	R		R-Square	Estimate		
9		0.5205	0.2710	0.2495	9457.239		
10							
11		Degrees of	Sum of	Mean of	F-Ratio	p-Value	
12	ANOVA Table	Freedom	Squares	Squares			
13	Explained	1	1130247999	1130247999	12.6370	0.0011	
14	Unexplained	34	3040938861	89439378.26			
15							
16		Coefficient	Standard	t-Value	p-Value	Confidence Interval 95%	
17	Regression Table		Error			Lower	Upper
18	Constant	75605.516	6808.611	11.1044	< 0.0001	61768.754	89442.277
19	ProdRuns	655.071	184.275	3.5549	0.0011	280.579	1029.562

Clearly, these two equations are quite different, although each effectively breaks Overhead into a fixed component and a variable component. Equation (10.5) implies that the fixed component of overhead is about $48,621. Bendrix can expect to incur this amount even if zero machine hours are used. The variable component is the 34.7MachHrs term. It implies that the expected overhead increases by about $35 for each extra machine hour. Equation (10.6), on the other hand, breaks overhead down into a fixed component of $75,606 and a variable component of about $655 per each production run.

The difference between these two equations can be attributed to the fact that neither tells the whole story. If the manager's goal is to split overhead into a fixed component and a variable component, the variable component should include *both* of the measures of work activity (and maybe others) to give a more complete explanation of overhead. We will explain how to do this when this example is reanalyzed with *multiple* regression. ∎

10.4.2 Standard Error of Estimate

We now examine fitted values and residuals to see how they lead to a useful summary measure for a regression equation. In a typical simple regression model, the expression $a + bX$ is the fitted value of Y. Graphically, it is the height of the estimated line above the value X. The fitted value is often denoted as $\hat{Y}$ (pronounced Y-hat):[4]

$$\hat{Y} = a + bX$$

Then a typical residual, denoted by e, is the difference between the observed value Y and the fitted value $\hat{Y}$ [a restatement of Equation (10.2)]:

$$e = Y - \hat{Y}$$

Some of the fitted values and associated residuals for the Pharmex drugstore example are shown in Figure 10.19. (Recall that these columns are inserted automatically by StatTools's Regression procedure when you request the optional scatterplot of residuals versus fitted values.)

Figure 10.19

Fitted Values and Residuals for Pharmex Example

	A	B	C	D
43	Graph Data	Sales	Fit	Residual
44	1	85	83.823	1.177
45	2	103	108.979	-5.979
46	3	102	108.979	-6.979
47	4	109	96.020	12.980
48	5	85	93.733	-8.733
49	6	103	97.545	5.455
50	7	110	101.356	8.644
51	8	86	89.922	-3.922
52	9	92	98.307	-6.307
53	10	87	88.397	-1.397

The magnitudes of the residuals provide a good indication of how useful the regression line is for predicting Y values from X values. However, because there are numerous residuals, it is useful to summarize them with a single numerical measure. This measure, called the **standard error of estimate** and denoted s_e, is essentially the standard deviation of the residuals. It is given by Equation (10.7).

Formula for Standard Error of Estimate

$$s_e = \sqrt{\frac{\Sigma e_i^2}{n - 2}}$$

(10.7)

About two-thirds of the fitted $\hat{Y}$ values are typically within one standard error of the actual Y values. About 95% are within two standard errors.

Actually, because the average of the residuals from a least squares fit is always zero, this is identical to the standard deviation of the residuals except for the denominator $n - 2$, not the usual $n - 1$. As you will see in more generality later on, the rule is to subtract the number of parameters being estimated from the sample size n to obtain the denominator. Here there are two parameters being estimated: the intercept a and the slope b.

The usual empirical rules for standard deviations can be applied to the standard error of estimate. For example, about two-thirds of the residuals are typically within one

---

[4]We can also write Predicted Y instead of $\hat{Y}$, but the latter notation is common in the statistics literature.

standard error of their mean (which is zero). Stated another way, about two-thirds of the observed Y values are typically within one standard error of the corresponding fitted $\hat{Y}$ values. Similarly, about 95% of the observed Y values are typically within two standard errors of the corresponding fitted $\hat{Y}$ values.[5]

The standard error of estimate s_e is included in all StatTools regression outputs. Alternatively, it can be calculated directly with Excel's STEYX function (when there is only one X variable) in the form

=STEYX(Y-range,X-range)

In general, the standard error of estimate indicates the level of accuracy of predictions made from the regression equation. The smaller it is, the more accurate predictions tend to be.

The standard error for the Pharmex data appears in cell E9 of Figure 10.15. Its value, approximately 7.39, indicates the typical magnitude of error when using promotional expenses, via the regression equation, to predict sales. More specifically, if the regression equation is used to predict sales for many regions, about two-thirds of the predictions will be within 7.39 of the actual sales values, and about 95% of the predictions will be within two standard errors, or 14.78, of the actual sales values.

Is this level of accuracy good? One measure of comparison is the standard deviation of the sales variable, namely, 9.90. (This is obtained by the usual STDEV function applied to the observed sales values.) It can be interpreted as the standard deviation of the residuals around a *horizontal* line positioned at the mean value of Sales. This is the relevant regression line if there are no explanatory variables—that is, if Promote is ignored. In other words, it is a measure of the prediction error if the sample mean of Sales is used as the prediction for *every* region and Promote is ignored. Unfortunately, the standard error of estimate, 7.39, is not much less than 9.90. This means that the Promote variable adds a relatively small amount to prediction accuracy. Predictions with it are not much better than predictions without it. A standard error of estimate *well* below 9.90 would certainly be preferred.

The standard error of estimate can often be used to judge which of several potential regression equations is the most useful. In the Bendrix manufacturing example we estimated two regression lines, one using MachHrs and one using ProdRuns. From Figures 10.17 and 10.18, their standard errors are approximately \$8585 and \$9457. These imply that MachHrs is a slightly better predictor of overhead. The predictions based on MachHrs will tend to be slightly more accurate than those based on ProdRuns. Of course, the predictions based on *both* predictors should yield even more accurate predictions, as you will see when we discuss multiple regression for this example.

10.4.3 The Percentage of Variation Explained: R^2

We now discuss another important measure of the goodness of fit of the least squares line: R^2 (pronounced "R-square"). Along with the standard error of estimate s_e, it is the most frequently quoted measure in applied regression analysis. With a value always between 0 and 1, R^2 always has exactly the same interpretations: It is the *fraction of variation of the dependent variable explained by the regression line*. (It is often expressed as a percentage, so you hear about the *percentage* of variation explained by the regression line.)

> R^2 is the percentage of variation of the dependent variable explained by the regression.

To see more precisely what this means, we look briefly into the derivation of R^2. In the previous section we suggested that one way to measure the regression equation's ability to

---

[5]This requires that the residuals be at least approximately normally distributed, a requirement discussed in the next chapter.

predict is to compare the standard error of estimate, s_e, to the standard deviation of the dependent variable, s_Y. The idea is that s_e is (essentially) the standard deviation of the residuals, whereas s_Y is the standard deviation of the residuals from a horizontal regression line at height $\bar{Y}$, the sample mean of the dependent variable. Therefore, if s_e is small compared to s_Y (that is, if s_e/s_Y is small), the regression line is evidently doing a good job in explaining the variation of the dependent variable.

The R^2 measure is based on this idea. It is defined by Equation (10.8). (This value is obtained automatically with StatTools's regression procedure, or it can be calculated with Excel's RSQ function when there is a single X variable.) Equation (10.8) indicates that when the residuals are small, R^2 will be close to 1, but when they are large, R^2 will be close to 0.

Formula for R^2

$$R^2 = 1 - \frac{\Sigma e_i^2}{\Sigma (Y_i - \bar{Y})^2}$$

(10.8)

R^2 measures the goodness of a linear fit. The better the linear fit is, the closer R^2 is to 1.

You can see from cell C9 of Figure 10.15 that the R^2 measure for the Pharmex drugstore data is 0.453. In words, the single explanatory variable Promote is able to explain only 45.3% of the variation in the Sales variable. This is not particularly good—the same conclusion we made when we based goodness of fit on s_e. There is still 54.7% of the variation left unexplained. Of course, we would like R^2 to be as close to 1 as possible. Usually, the only way to increase it is to use better and/or more explanatory variables.

Analysts often compare equations on the basis of their R^2 values. You can see from Figures 10.17 and 10.18 that the R^2 values using MachHrs and ProdRuns as single explanatory variables for the Bendrix overhead data are 39.9% and 27.1%, respectively. These provide one more piece of evidence that MachHrs is a slightly better predictor of Overhead than ProdRuns. Of course, they also suggest that the percentage of variation of Overhead explained could be increased by including *both* variables in a single equation. This is true, as you will see shortly.

In simple linear regression, R^2 is the square of the correlation between the dependent variable and the explanatory variable.

There is a good reason for the notation R^2. It turns out that R^2 is the square of the correlation between the observed Y values and the fitted $\hat{Y}$ values. This correlation appears in all regression outputs as the *multiple R*. For the Pharmex data it is 0.673, as seen in cell B9 of Figure 10.15. Aside from rounding, the square of 0.673 is 0.453, which is the R^2 value right next to it. In the case of simple linear regression, when there is only a single explanatory variable in the equation, the correlation between the Y variable and the fitted $\hat{Y}$ values is the same as the absolute value of the correlation between the Y variable and the explanatory X variable. For the Pharmex data you already saw that the correlation between Sales and Promote is indeed 0.673.

This interpretation of R^2 as the square of a correlation helps to clarify the issue of when a correlation is "large." For example, if the correlation between two variables Y and X is ± 0.8, the regression of Y on X will have an R^2 of 0.64; that is, the regression with X as the only explanatory variable will explain 64% of the variation in Y. If the correlation drops to ± 0.7, this percentage drops to 49%; if the correlation increases to ± 0.9, the percentage increases to 81%. The point is that before a single variable X can explain a large percentage of the variation in some other variable Y, the two variables must be highly correlated—in *either* a positive or negative direction.

Note: Student solutions for problems whose numbers appear within a colored box are available for purchase at www.cengagebrain.com.

Level A

1. Explore the relationship between the selling prices (Y) and the appraised values (X) of the 148 homes in the file **P02_11.xlsx** by estimating a simple linear regression model. Interpret the standard error of estimate s_e and R^2 and the least squares line for these data.
   a. Is there evidence of a *linear* relationship between the selling price and appraised value? If so, characterize the relationship. Is it positive or negative? Is it weak or strong?
   b. For which of the three remaining variables, the size of the home, the number of bedrooms, and the number of bathrooms, is the relationship with the home's selling price *stronger*? Justify your choice with additional simple linear regression models.

2. The file **P02_10.xlsx** contains midterm and final exam scores for 96 students in a corporate finance course. Each row contains the two exam scores for a given student, so you might expect them to be positively correlated.
   a. Create a scatterplot of the final exam score (Y) versus the midterm score (X). Based on the visual evidence, would you say that the scores for the two exams are strongly related? Is the relationship a linear one?
   b. Superimpose a trend line on the scatterplot, and use the option to display the equation and the R^2 value. What does this equation indicate in terms of predicting a student's final exam score from his or her midterm score? Be specific.
   c. Run a regression to confirm the trend-line equation from part **b**. What does the standard error of estimate say about the accuracy of the prediction requested in part **b**?

3. A company produces electric motors for use in home appliances. One of the company's production managers is interested in examining the relationship between inspection costs in a month (X) and the number of motors produced that month that were returned by dissatisfied customers (Y). He has collected the data in the file **P10_03.xlsx** for the past 36 months. Estimate a simple linear regression equation using the given data and interpret it for this production manager. Also, interpret s_e and R^2 for these data.

4. The owner of the Original Italian Pizza restaurant chain wants to understand which variable most strongly influences the sales of his specialty deep-dish pizza. He has gathered data on the monthly sales of deep-dish pizzas at his restaurants and observations on other potentially relevant variables for each of his 15 outlets in central Indiana. These data are provided in the file **P10_04.xlsx**. Estimate a simple linear regression equation between the quantity sold (Y) and each of the following candidates for the best explanatory variable: average price of deep-dish pizzas, monthly advertising expenditures, and disposable income per household in the areas surrounding the outlets. Which variable is *most* strongly associated with the number of pizzas sold? Explain your choice.

5. The human resources manager of DataCom, Inc., wants to examine the relationship between annual salaries (Y) and the number of years employees have worked at DataCom (X). These data have been collected for a sample of employees and are given in columns B and C of the file **P10_05.xlsx**.
   a. Estimate the relationship between Y and X. Interpret the least squares line.
   b. How well does the estimated simple linear regression equation fit the given data? Provide evidence for your answer.

6. The file **P02_02.xlsx** contains information on over 200 movies that came out during 2006 and 2007.
   a. Create two scatterplots and corresponding correlations, one of Total US Gross (Y) versus 7-day Gross (X) and one of Total US Gross (Y) versus 14-day Gross (X). Based on the visual evidence, is it possible to predict the total U.S. gross of a movie from its first week's gross or its first two weeks' gross?
   b. Run two simple regressions corresponding to the two scatterplots in part **a**. Explain exactly what they tell you about the movie business. How accurate would the two predictions requested in part **a** tend to be? Be as specific as possible.

7. Examine the relationship between the average utility bills for homes of a particular size (Y) and the average monthly temperature (X). The data in the file **P10_07.xlsx** include the average monthly bill and temperature for each month of the past year.
   a. Use the given data to estimate a simple linear regression equation. Interpret the least squares line.
   b. How well does the estimated regression equation fit the given data? How might you do a better job of explaining the variation of the average utility bills for homes of a certain size?

8. The file **P10_08.xlsx** contains data on the top 200 professional golfers in 2009. (The same data set, covering multiple years, was used in Example 3.4 in Chapter 3.)
   a. Create a new variable, Earnings per Round, and the ratio of Earnings to Rounds. Then create five

scatterplots and corresponding correlations, each with Earnings per Round on the *Y* axis. The *X*-axis variables are those that most golf enthusiasts probably think are related to Earnings per Round: Yards/Drive, Driving Accuracy, Greens in Regulation, Putting Average, and Sand Save Pct. Comment on the results. Are any of these highly related to Earnings per Round? Do the correlations have the signs you would expect (positive or negative)?

b. For the two most highly correlated variables with Earnings per Round (positive or negative), run the regressions corresponding to the scatterplots. Explain exactly what they tell you about predicting Earnings per Round. How accurate do you think these predictions would be?

9. Management of a home appliance store wants to understand the growth pattern of the monthly sales of Blu-ray disc players over the past two years. The managers have recorded the relevant data in the file **P10_09.xlsx**. Have the sales of this product been growing linearly over the past 24 months? Using simple linear regression, explain why or why not.

10. Do the selling prices of houses in a given community vary systematically with their sizes (as measured in square feet)? Answer this question by estimating a simple regression equation where the selling price of the house is the dependent variable and the size of the house is the explanatory variable. Use the sample data given in the file **P10_10.xlsx**. Interpret your estimated equation and the associated R^2.

11. The file **P10_11.xlsx** contains annual observations of the American minimum wage since 1955. Has the minimum wage been growing at roughly a *constant* rate over this period? Use simple linear regression analysis to address this question. Explain the results you obtain. (You can ignore the data in column C for now.)

12. Based on the data in the file **P02_23.xlsx** from the U.S. Department of Agriculture, explore the relationship between the number of farms (*X*) and the average size of a farm (*Y*) in the United States.

Specifically, estimate a simple linear regression equation and interpret it.

13. Estimate the relationship between monthly electrical power usage (*Y*) and home size (*X*) using the data in the file **P10_13.xlsx**. Interpret your results. How well does a simple linear regression equation explain the variation in monthly electrical power usage?

14. The file **P02_12.xlsx** includes data on the 50 top graduate programs in the United States, according to a recent *U.S. News & World Report* survey. Columns B, C, and D contain ratings: an overall rating, a rating by peer schools, and a rating by recruiters. The other columns contain data that might be related to these ratings.

a. Find a table of correlations between all of the numerical variables. From these correlations, which variables in columns E–L are most highly correlated with the various ratings?

b. For the Overall rating, run a regression using it as the dependent variable and the variable (from columns E–L) most highly correlated with it. Interpret this equation. Could you have guessed the value of R^2 before running the regression? Explain. What does the standard error of estimate indicate?

c. Repeat part **b** with the Peers rating as the dependent variable. Repeat again with the Recruiters rating as the dependent variable. Discuss any differences among the three regressions in parts **b** and **c**.

Level B

15. If you haven't already done Problem 6 on 2006–2007 movies, do it now. The scatterplots of Total US Gross versus 7-day Gross or 14-day Gross indicate some possible outliers at the right—the movies that did great during their first week or two. Identify these outliers (you can decide how many qualify) and move them out of the data set. Then redo Problem 6 without the outliers. Comment on whether you get very different results. Specifically, do these outliers affect the slope of either regression line? Do they affect the standard error of estimate or R^2?

10.5 MULTIPLE REGRESSION

In general, there are two possible approaches to obtaining improved fits. The first is to examine a scatterplot of residuals for nonlinear patterns and then make appropriate modifications to the regression equation. We will discuss this approach later in the chapter. The second approach is much more straightforward: Add more explanatory variables to the regression equation. In the Bendrix manufacturing example, we deliberately included only a single explanatory variable in the equation at a time to keep the equations simple. But because scatterplots indicate that both explanatory variables are also related to Overhead, it makes sense to try including both in the regression equation. With any luck, the linear fit should improve.

When you include several explanatory variables in the regression equation, you move into the realm of *multiple* regression. Some of the concepts from simple regression carry over naturally to multiple regression, but some change considerably. The following list provides a starting point that we expand on throughout this section.

Characteristics of Multiple Regression

- Graphically, you are no longer fitting a *line* to a set of points. If there are exactly two explanatory variables, you are fitting a *plane* to the data in three-dimensional space. There is one dimension for the dependent variable and one for each of the two explanatory variables. Although you can imagine a flat plane passing through a swarm of points, it is difficult to graph this on a two-dimensional screen. If there are more than two explanatory variables, then you can only imagine the regression plane; drawing in four or more dimensions is impossible.

- The regression equation is still estimated by the least squares method—that is, by minimizing the sum of squared residuals. However, it is definitely not practical to implement this method by hand. A statistical software package such as StatTools is required.

- Simple regression is actually a special case of multiple regression—that is, an equation with a single explanatory variable can be considered a "multiple" regression equation. This explains why it is possible to use StatTools's Multiple Regression procedure for simple regression.

- There is a slope term for each explanatory variable in the equation. The interpretation of these slope terms is somewhat different than in simple regression, as explained in the following subsection.

- The standard error of estimate and R^2 summary measures are almost exactly as in simple regression, as explained in section 10.5.2.

- Many *types* of explanatory variables can be included in the regression equation, as explained in section 10.6. To a large part, these are responsible for the wide applicability of multiple regression in the business world. However, the burden is on you to choose the best set of explanatory variables. This is generally not easy.

10.5.1 Interpretation of Regression Coefficients

A typical slope term measures the expected change in Y when the corresponding X increases by one unit.

If Y is the dependent variable and X_1 through X_k are the explanatory variables, then a typical multiple regression equation has the form shown in Equation (10.9), where a is again the Y-intercept, and b_1 through b_k are the slopes. Collectively, a and the bs in Equation (10.9) are called the **regression coefficients**. The intercept a is the expected value of Y when all of the Xs equal zero. (Of course, this makes sense only if it is practical for all of the Xs to equal zero, which is seldom the case.) Each slope coefficient is the expected change in Y when this particular X increases by one unit *and the other Xs in the equation remain constant*. For example, b_1 is the expected change in Y when X_1 increases by one unit and the other Xs in the equation, X_2 through X_k, remain constant.

General Multiple Regression Equation

$$\text{Predicted } Y = a + b_1X_1 + b_2X_2 + \cdots + b_kX_k \qquad \textbf{(10.9)}$$

This extra proviso, "when the other Xs in the equation remain constant," is crucial for the interpretation of the regression coefficients. In particular, it means that the estimates of the bs depend on which other Xs are included in the regression equation. We illustrate these ideas in the following continuation of the Bendrix manufacturing example.

Estimate and interpret the equation for Overhead when both explanatory variables, MachHrs and ProdRuns, are included in the regression equation.

Objective To use StatTools's Regression procedure to estimate the equation for overhead costs at Bendrix as a function of machine hours and production runs.

Solution

To obtain the regression output, select Regression from the StatTools Regression and Classification dropdown list and fill out the resulting dialog box as shown in Figure 10.20. As before, choose the Multiple option, specify the single *D* variable and the two *I* variables, and check any optional graphs you want to see. (This time we have selected the first and third options.)

Figure 10.20
Multiple Regression
Dialog Box

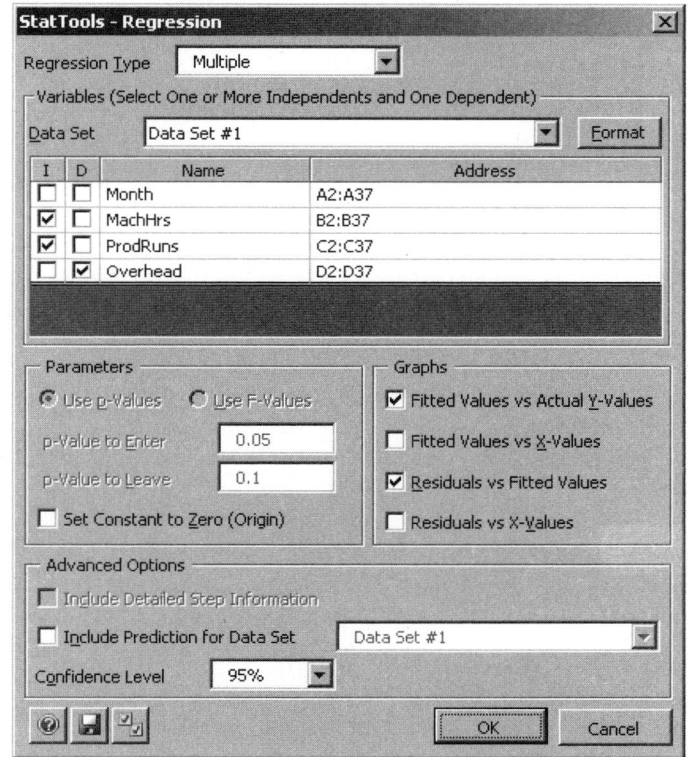

The main regression output appears in Figure 10.21. The coefficients in the range B18:B20 indicate that the estimated regression equation is

$$\text{Predicted Overhead} = 3997 + 43.54\text{MachHrs} + 883.62\text{ProdRuns} \qquad \textbf{(10.10)}$$

The interpretation of Equation (10.10) is that if the number of production runs is held constant, the overhead cost is expected to increase by \$43.54 for each extra machine hour, and if the number of machine hours is held constant, the overhead cost is expected to increase by \$883.62 for each extra production run. The Bendrix manager can interpret the intercept,

Figure 10.21

Multiple Regression Output for Bendrix Example

	A	B	C	D	E	F	G
7		Multiple	R-Square	Adjusted	StErr of		
8	Summary	R		R-Square	Estimate		
9		0.9308	0.8664	0.8583	4108.993		
10							
11		Degrees of	Sum of	Mean of	F-Ratio	p-Value	
12	ANOVA Table	Freedom	Squares	Squares			
13	Explained	2	3614020661	1807010330	107.0261	< 0.0001	
14	Unexplained	33	557166199.1	16883824.22			
15							
16			Standard			Confidence Interval 95%	
17	Regression Table	Coefficient	Error	t-Value	p-Value	Lower	Upper
18	Constant	3996.678	6603.651	0.6052	0.5492	-9438.551	17431.907
19	MachHrs	43.536	3.589	12.1289	< 0.0001	36.234	50.839
20	ProdRuns	883.618	82.251	10.7429	< 0.0001	716.276	1050.960

$3997, as the fixed component of overhead. The slope terms involving MachHrs and ProdRuns are the variable components of overhead.

It is interesting to compare Equation (10.10) with the separate equations for Overhead involving only a single variable each. From the previous section these are

$$\text{Predicted Overhead} = 48621 + 34.7\text{MachHrs}$$

and

$$\text{Predicted Overhead} = 75606 + 655.1\text{ProdRuns}$$

Note that the coefficient of MachHrs has increased from 34.7 to 43.5 and the coefficient of ProdRuns has increased from 655.1 to 883.6. Also, the intercept is now lower than either intercept in the single-variable equations. In general, it is difficult to guess the changes that will occur when more explanatory variables are included in the equation, but it is likely that changes *will* occur.

The reasoning is that when MachHrs is the only variable in the equation, ProdRuns constant is *not* being held constant—it is being ignored—so in effect the coefficient 34.7 of MachHrs indicates the effect of MachHrs *and* the omitted ProdRuns on Overhead. But when both variables are included, the coefficient 43.5 of MachHrs indicates the effect of MachHrs only, holding ProdRuns constant. Because the coefficients of MachHrs in the two equations have different *meanings*, it is not surprising that they result in different numerical estimates. ∎

The estimated coefficient of any explanatory variable typically depends on which other explanatory variables are included in the equation.

FUNDAMENTAL INSIGHT

Multiple Regression, Correlations, and Scatterplots

When there are multiple potential Xs for a regression on Y, it is useful to calculate correlations and scatterplots of Y versus each X. But remember that correlations and scatterplots are for *two variables only*; they do not necessarily tell the whole story. Sometimes, as in this overhead example, a multiple regression can turn out quite differently than might be expected from correlations and scatterplots alone. Specifically, the R^2 value for the multiple regression can be considerably smaller or larger than might be expected.

10.5.2 Interpretation of Standard Error of Estimate and R^2

The multiple regression output in Figure 10.21 is very similar to simple regression output. In particular, cells C9 and E9 again show R^2 and the standard error of estimate s_e. Also, the square root of R^2 appears in cell B9. The interpretation of these quantities is almost exactly the same as in simple regression. The standard error of estimate is essentially the standard deviation of residuals, but it is now given by Equation (10.11), where n is the number of observations and k is the number of explanatory variables in the equation.

Formula for Standard Error of Estimate in Multiple Regression

$$s_e = \sqrt{\frac{\sum e_i^2}{n - k - 1}}$$

(10.11)

Fortunately, you can interpret s_e exactly as before. It is a measure of the typical prediction error when the multiple regression equation is used to predict the dependent variable. In this example, about two-thirds of the predictions should be within one standard error, or $4109, of the actual overhead cost. By comparing this with the standard errors from the single-variable equations for Overhead, $8585 and $9457, you can see that the multiple regression equation will tend to provide predictions that are more than twice as accurate as the single-variable equations—a big improvement.

The R^2 value is again the percentage of variation of the dependent variable explained by the combined set of explanatory variables. In fact, it even has the same formula as before [see Equation (10.8)]. For the Bendrix data you can see that MachHrs and ProdRuns combine to explain 86.6% of the variation in Overhead. This is a big improvement over the single-variable equations that were able to explain only 39.9% and 27.1% of the variation in Overhead. Remarkably, the combination of the two explanatory variables explains a larger percentage than the *sum* of their individual effects. This is not common, but this example shows that it is possible.

R² is always the square of the correlation between the actual and fitted Y values—in both simple and multiple regression.

The square root of R^2 shown in cell B9 of Figure 10.21 (the multiple R) is again the correlation between the fitted values and the observed values of the dependent variable. For the Bendrix data the correlation between them is 0.931, quite high. A graphical indication of this high correlation can be seen in one of the requested scatterplots, the plot of fitted versus observed values of Overhead. This scatterplot appears in Figure 10.22. If the regression equation gave *perfect* predictions, all of the points in this plot would lie on a 45° line—each fitted value would *equal* the corresponding observed value. Although a perfect fit virtually never occurs, the closer the points are to a 45° line, the better the fit is, as indicated by R^2 or its square root.

Although the R^2 value is one of the most frequently quoted values from a regression analysis, it does have one serious drawback: R^2 can only *increase* when extra explanatory

Figure 10.22

Scatterplot of Fitted Values Versus Observed Values of Overhead

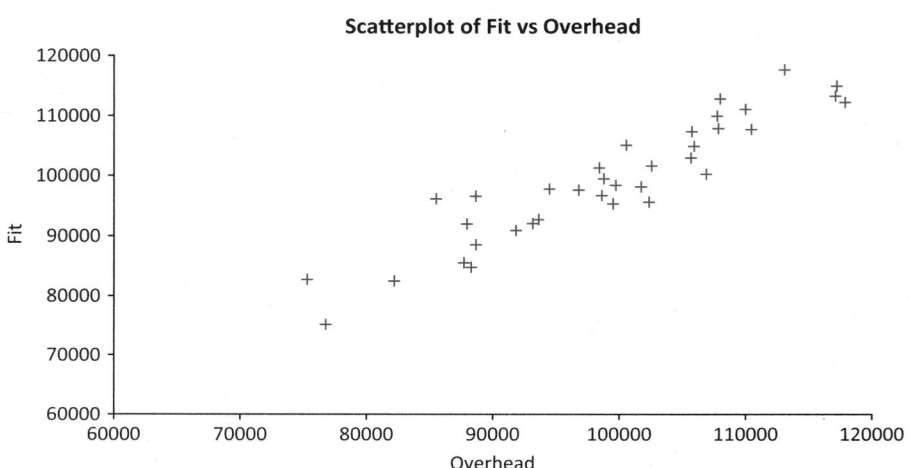

variables are added to an equation. This can lead to "fishing expeditions," where you keep adding variables to an equation, some of which have no conceptual relationship to the dependent variable, just to inflate the R^2 value. To avoid adding extra variables that do not really belong, an **adjusted R^2** value is typically listed in regression outputs. This adjusted value appears in cell D9 of Figure 10.21. Although it has no direct interpretation as "percentage of variation explained," it *can* decrease when unnecessary explanatory variables are added to an equation. Therefore, it serves as an index that you can monitor. If you add variables and the adjusted R^2 *decreases*, the extra variables are essentially not pulling their weight and should probably be omitted. We will say much more about this issue in the next chapter.

> The **adjusted R^2** is a measure that adjusts R^2 for the number of explanatory variables in the equation. It is used primarily to monitor whether extra explanatory variables really belong in the equation.

FUNDAMENTAL INSIGHT

R^2, Adjusted R^2, and Standard Error of Estimate

Sometimes a regression equation is "built" by successively adding explantory variables to an equation. As more variables are added, it is a mathematical fact that R^2 *must* increase; it cannot decrease. However, the standard error of estimate *can* increase, and the adjusted R^2 *can* decrease, each signaling that the extra variables are not useful and should probably be omitted from the equation. In fact, the only purpose of adjusted R^2 is to monitor whether the equation is getting better or worse as more variables are added.

PROBLEMS

Level A

16. A trucking company wants to predict the yearly maintenance expense (Y) for a truck using the number of miles driven during the year (X_1) and the age of the truck (X_2, in years) at the beginning of the year. The company has gathered the data given in the file **P10_16.xlsx**, where each observation corresponds to a particular truck.
   a. Estimate a multiple regression equation using the given data. Interpret each of the estimated regression coefficients. Why is the magnitude of the Miles Driven coefficient so much lower than the magnitude of the Age of Truck coefficient? Is it because Miles Driven is not as important in predicting Maintenance Expense?
   b. Interpret the standard error of estimate s_e and R^2 for these data.

17. DataPro is a small but rapidly growing firm that provides electronic data-processing services to commercial firms, hospitals, and other organizations. For each of the past 12 months, DataPro has tracked the number of contracts sold, the average contract price, advertising expenditures, and personal selling expenditures. These data are provided in **P10_17.xlsx**. Using the number of contracts sold as the dependent variable, estimate a multiple regression equation with three explanatory variables. Interpret each of the estimated regression coefficients, the standard error of estimate, and R^2.

18. An antique collector believes that the price received for a particular item increases with its age and with the number of bidders. The file **P10_18.xlsx** contains data on these three variables for 32 recently auctioned comparable items.
   a. Estimate a multiple regression equation using the given data. Interpret each of the estimated regression coefficients. Is the antique collector correct in believing that the price received for the item increases with its age and with the number of bidders?
   b. Interpret the standard error of estimate s_e and R^2. Does it appear that predictions of price from this equation will be very accurate?

19. Stock market analysts are continually looking for reliable predictors of stock prices. Consider the problem of modeling the price per share of electric utility stocks (Y). Two variables thought to influence this stock price are return on average equity (X_1) and annual dividend rate (X_2). The stock price, returns on equity, and dividend rates on a randomly selected day for 16 electric utility stocks are provided in the file **P10_19.xlsx**.

a. Estimate a multiple regression equation using the given data. Interpret each of the estimated regression coefficients.

b. Interpret the standard error of estimate s_e, R^2, and the adjusted R^2. Does it appear that predictions of price from this equation will be very accurate?

20. The manager of a commuter rail transportation system was recently asked by her governing board to determine which factors have a significant impact on the demand for rides in the large city served by the transportation network. The system manager collected data on variables thought to be possibly related to the number of weekly riders on the city's rail system. The file **P10_20.xlsx** contain these data.

a. What do you expect the signs of the coefficients of the explanatory variables in this multiple regression equation to be? Why? (Answer this *before* running the regression.)

b. Estimate a multiple regression equation using the given data. Interpret each of the estimated regression coefficients. Are the signs of the estimated coefficients consistent with your expectations in part **a**?

c. What proportion of the total variation in the number of weekly riders is *not* explained by this estimated multiple regression equation?

21. Consider the enrollment data for *Business Week*'s top U.S. graduate business programs in the file **P10_21.xlsx**. Use the data in the MBA Data sheet to estimate a multiple regression equation to assess whether there is a relationship between the total number of full-time students (Enrollment) and the following explanatory variables: (a) the proportion of female students, (b) the proportion of minority students, and (c) the proportion of international students enrolled at these business schools.

a. Interpret the coefficients of the estimated regression equation. Do any of these results surprise you? Explain.

b. How well does the estimated regression equation fit the given data?

22. A regional express delivery service company recently conducted a study to investigate the relationship between the cost of shipping a package (Y), the package weight (X_1), and the distance shipped (X_2). Twenty packages were randomly selected from among the large number received for shipment, and a detailed analysis of the shipping cost was conducted for each

package. These sample observations are given in the file **P10_22.xlsx**.

a. Estimate a simple linear regression equation involving shipping cost and package weight. Interpret the slope coefficient of the least squares line and the R^2 value.

b. Add another explanatory variable, distance shipped, to the regression model in part **a**. Estimate and interpret this expanded equation. How does the R^2 value for this multiple regression equation compare to that of the simple regression equation in part **a**? Explain any difference between the two R^2 values. Interpret the *adjusted R^2* value for the revised equation.

Level B

23. The owner of a restaurant in Bloomington, Indiana, has recorded sales data for the past 19 years. He has also recorded data on potentially relevant variables. The entire data set appears in the file **P10_23.xlsx**.

a. Estimate a simple linear regression equation involving annual sales (the dependent variable) and the size of the population residing within 10 miles of the restaurant (the explanatory variable). Interpret the R^2 value.

b. Add another explanatory variable—annual advertising expenditures—to the regression equation in part **a**. Estimate and interpret this expanded equation. How does the R^2 value for this equation compare to the equation in part **a**? Explain any difference between the two R^2 values. What, if anything, does the *adjusted R^2* value for the revised equation indicate?

c. Add one more explanatory variable to the multiple regression equation estimated in part **b**. In particular, estimate and interpret the coefficients of a multiple regression equation that includes the *previous* year's advertising expenditure. How does the inclusion of this third explanatory variable affect the R^2 and adjusted R^2 values, in comparison to the corresponding values for the equation of part **b**? Explain any changes in these values.

24. Continuing Problem 8 on the 2009 golfer data in the file **P10_08.xlsx**, the simple linear regressions for Earnings per Round were perhaps not as good as you expected. Explore several multiple regressions for Earnings per Round, using the variables in columns I–M and R. Proceed as follows.

a. Create a table of correlations for these variables.

b. Run a regression of Earnings per Round versus the most highly correlated variable (positive or negative) with Earnings per Round. Then run a second regression with the two most highly correlated variables with Earnings per Round. Then run a third with the three most highly correlated, and so on until all six explanatory variables are in the equation.

c. Comment on the changes you see from one equation to the next. Does the coefficient of a variable entered earlier change as you enter more variables? How much better do the equations get, in terms of standard error of estimate and R^2, as you enter more variables? Does adjusted R^2 ever indicate that an equation is *worse* than the one before it?

d. The bottom line is whether these variables, as a whole, do a very good job of predicting Earnings per Round. Would you say they do? Why or why not?

25. Using the sample data given in the file **P10_10.xlsx**, use multiple regression to predict the selling price of houses in a given community. Proceed as follows.

a. Add one explanatory variable at a time and estimate each regression equation along the way. Report and explain changes in the standard error of estimate s_e, R^2, and adjusted R^2 as each explanatory variable is added to the model. Does it matter which order you add the variables? Try at least two different orderings to answer this question.

b. Interpret each of the estimated regression coefficients in the full equation, that is, the equation with all explanatory variables included.

c. What proportion of the total variation in the selling price is explained by the multiple regression equation that includes all four explanatory variables?

10.6 MODELING POSSIBILITIES

Once you move from simple to multiple regression, the floodgates open. All types of explanatory variables are potential candidates for inclusion in the regression equation. In this section we examine several new types of explanatory variables. These include dummy variables, interaction variables, and nonlinear transformations. The techniques in this section provide you with many alternative approaches to modeling the relationship between a dependent variable and potential explanatory variables. In many applications these techniques produce much better fits than you could obtain without them.

FUNDAMENTAL INSIGHT

Modeling Possibilities

As the title of this section suggests, these techniques are modeling *possibilities*. They provide a wide variety of explanatory variables to choose from. However, this does not mean that it is wise to include all or even many of these new types of explanatory variables in any particular regression equation. The chances are that only a few, if any, will significantly improve the fit. Knowing which explanatory variables to include requires a great deal of practical experience with regression, as well as a thorough understanding of the data in its context. The material in this section should *not* be an excuse for a mindless fishing expedition.

10.6.1 Dummy Variables

Some potential explanatory variables are categorical and cannot be measured on a quantitative scale. However, these categorical variables are often related to the dependent variable, so you need a way to include them in a regression equation. The trick is to use **dummy** variables, also called **indicator** or **0–1** variables. Dummy variables are variables that indicate the category a given observation is in. If a dummy variable for a given category equals 1, the observation is in that category; if it equals 0, the observation is not in that category.

> A **dummy variable** is a variable with possible values 0 and 1. It equals 1 if the observation is in a particular category and 0 if it is not.

Categorical variables are used in two situations. The first and perhaps most common situation is when a categorical variable has only two categories. A good example of this is a gender variable that has the two categories "male" and "female." In this case only a *single* dummy variable is required, and you have the choice of assigning the 1s to either category. If the dummy variable is called Gender, you can code Gender as 1 for males and 0 for females, or you can code Gender as 1 for females and 0 for males. You just need to be consistent and specify explicitly which coding scheme you are using.

The other situation is when there are more than two categories. A good example of this is when you have quarterly time series data and you want to treat the quarter of the year as a categorical variable with four categories, 1 through 4. Then you can create four dummy variables, Q1 through Q4. For example, Q2 equals 1 for all second-quarter observations and 0 for all other observations. Although you can create four dummy variables, only three of them—*any* three—can be used in a regression equation, as will be explained shortly.

The following example illustrates how to create, use, and interpret dummy variables in regression analysis.

EXAMPLE	10.3 POSSIBLE GENDER DISCRIMINATION IN SALARY AT FIFTH NATIONAL BANK OF SPRINGFIELD

The Fifth National Bank of Springfield is facing a gender discrimination suit.[6] The charge is that its female employees receive substantially smaller salaries than its male employees. The bank's employee data are listed in the file **Bank Salaries.xlsx**. For each of its 208 employees, the data set includes the following variables:

- EducLev: education level, a categorical variable with categories 1 (finished high school), 2 (finished some college courses), 3 (obtained a bachelor's degree), 4 (took some graduate courses), 5 (obtained a graduate degree)

- JobGrade: a categorical variable indicating the current job level, the possible levels being 1 through 6 (6 is highest)

- YrsExper: years of experience with this bank

- Age: employee's current age

- Gender: a categorical variable with values "Female" and "Male"

- YrsPrior: number of years of work experience at another bank prior to working at Fifth National

- PCJob: a categorical yes/no variable depending on whether the employee's current job is computer-related

- Salary: current annual salary

Figure 10.23 lists a few of the observations. Do these data provide evidence that there is discrimination against females in terms of salary?

Objective   To use StatTools's Regression procedure to analyze whether the bank discriminates against females in terms of salary.

---

[6]This example and the accompanying data set are based on a real case from 1995. Only the bank's name has been changed.

Figure 10.23

Selected Data for Bank Example

	A	B	C	D	E	F	G	H	I
1	Employee	EducLev	JobGrade	YrsExper	Age	Gender	YrsPrior	PCJob	Salary
2	1	3	1	3	26	Male	1	No	$32,000
3	2	1	1	14	38	Female	1	No	$39,100
4	3	1	1	12	35	Female	0	No	$33,200
5	4	2	1	8	40	Female	7	No	$30,600
6	5	3	1	3	28	Male	0	No	$29,000
7	6	3	1	3	24	Female	0	No	$30,500
8	7	3	1	4	27	Female	0	No	$30,000
9	8	3	1	8	33	Male	2	No	$27,000
10	9	1	1	4	62	Female	0	No	$34,000
11	10	3	1	9	31	Female	0	No	$29,500
12	11	3	1	9	34	Female	2	No	$26,800
13	12	2	1	8	37	Female	8	No	$31,300
14	13	2	1	9	37	Female	0	No	$31,200
15	14	2	1	10	58	Female	6	No	$34,700
16	15	3	1	4	33	Female	0	No	$30,000

Solution

A naive approach to this problem is to compare the average female salary to the average male salary. This can be done with a pivot table, as in Chapter 3, or with a more formal hypothesis test, as in Chapter 9. Using these methods, you can check that the average of all salaries is $39,922, the female average is $37,210, the male average is $45,505, and the difference between the male and female averages is statistically significant at any reasonable level of significance. In short, the females definitely earn less. But perhaps there is a reason for this. They might have lower education levels, they might have been hired more recently, and so on. The question is whether the difference between female and male salaries is still evident after taking these other attributes into account. This is a perfect task for regression.

The first task is to create dummy variables for the various categorical variables. You can do this manually with IF functions or you can use StatTools's Dummy procedure. To do it manually, create a dummy variable Female based on Gender in column J by entering the formula

=IF(F45= "Female",1,0)

in cell J4 and copying it down. Note that females are coded as 1s and males as 0s. (Remember that the quotes are necessary when a text value is used in an IF function.)

StatTools's Dummy procedure is somewhat easier, especially when there are multiple categories. For example, to create five dummies for the education levels, select Dummy from the StatTools Data Utilities dropdown menu, select the Create One Dummy Variable for Each Distinct Category option, and select the EducLev variable to base the dummies on. This creates five dummy columns with variable names EducLev=1 through EducLev=5. You could follow the same procedure to create six dummies, JobGrade=1 through JobGrade=6, for the job grade categories.

It is also possible to add dummies to effectively collapse categories.

Sometimes you might want to collapse several categories. For example, you might want to collapse the five education categories into three categories: 1, (2,3), and (4,5). The new second category includes employees who have taken undergraduate courses or have completed a bachelor's degree, and the new third category includes employees who have taken graduate courses or have completed a graduate degree. It is easy to do this. You can again use IF functions, or you can simply add the EducLev=2 and EducLev=3 columns to get the dummy for the new second category. Similarly, you add the EducLev=4 and EducLev=5 columns for the new third category. (Do you see why this works?)

Once the dummies have been created, you can run a regression analysis with Salary as the dependent variable, using any combination of numerical and dummy explanatory variables. However, there are two rules you must follow:

1. You shouldn't use any of the *original* categorical variables, such as EducLev, that the dummies are based on.

2. You should always use *one fewer dummy* than the number of categories for any categorical variable.

Always include one fewer dummy than the number of categories. The omitted dummy corresponds to the reference category.

This second rule is a technical one. If you violate it, the statistical software (StatTools or any other package) will display an error message. For example, if you want to use education level as an explanatory variable, you should enter only four of the five dummies EducLev=1 through EducLev=5. *Any* four of these can be used. The omitted dummy then corresponds to the *reference* category. The interpretation of any dummy variable coefficient is relative to this reference category. When there are only two categories, as with the gender variable, the common procedure is to name the variable with the category, such as Female, that corresponds to the 1s. If you create the dummy variables manually, you probably will not even bother to create a dummy for males. In this case "Male" automatically becomes the reference category.

To explain dummy variables in regression, it is useful to proceed in several steps in this example. (After you get used to the procedure, you can combine all of these steps into a single step. Alternatively, you can use a stepwise procedure, as explained in the next chapter.) The first step is to estimate a regression equation with only one explanatory variable, Female. The output appears in Figure 10.24, and the resulting equation is

$$\text{Predicted Salary} = 45505 - 8296\text{Female} \qquad (10.12)$$

Figure 10.24
Output for Bank Example with a Single Explanatory Variable

	A	B	C	D	E	F	G
7		Multiple R	R-Square	Adjusted R-Square	StErr of Estimate		
8	*Summary*						
9		0.3465	0.1201	0.1158	10584.3		
10							
11		Degrees of Freedom	Sum of Squares	Mean of Squares	F-Ratio	p-Value	
12	*ANOVA Table*						
13	Explained	1	3149633845	3149633845	28.1151	< 0.0001	
14	Unexplained	206	23077473386	112026569.8			
15							
16		Coefficient	Standard Error	t-Value	p-Value	Confidence Interval 95%	
17	*Regression Table*					Lower	Upper
18	Constant	45505.4	1283.5	35.4533	< 0.0001	42974.9	48036.0
19	Female	-8295.5	1564.5	-5.3024	< 0.0001	-11380.0	-5211.0

To interpret regression equations with dummy variables, it is useful to rewrite the equation for each category.

To interpret this equation, recall that Female has only two possible values, 0 and 1. If you substitute Female=1 into Equation (10.12), you obtain

$$\text{Predicted Salary} = 45505 - 8296(1) = 37209$$

Because Female=1 corresponds to females, this equation simply indicates the average female salary. Similarly, if you substitute Female=0 into Equation (10.12), you obtain

$$\text{Predicted Salary} = 45505 - 8296(0) = 45505$$

Because Female=0 corresponds to males, this equation indicates the average male salary. Therefore, the interpretation of the −8296 coefficient of the Female dummy variable is straightforward. It is the average female salary relative to the reference (male) category. In short, females get paid $8296 less on average than males.

However, Equation (10.12) tells only part of the story. It ignores all information except for gender. The next step is to expand this equation by adding the experience variables

YrsPrior and YrsExper. The output with the Female dummy variable and these two experience variables appears in Figure 10.25. The corresponding regression equation is

$$\text{Predicted Salary} = 35492 + 988\text{YrsExper} + 131\text{YrsPrior} - 8080\text{Female} \quad \textbf{(10.13)}$$

Figure 10.25

Regression Output with Two Numerical Explanatory Variables Included

	A	B	C	D	E	F	G
7		Multiple	R-Square	Adjusted	StErr of		
8	Summary	R		R-Square	Estimate		
9		0.7016	0.4923	0.4848	8079.4		
10							
11		Degrees of	Sum of	Mean of	F-Ratio	p-Value	
12	ANOVA Table	Freedom	Squares	Squares			
13	Explained	3	12910668018	4303556006	65.9279	< 0.0001	
14	Unexplained	204	13316439212	65276662.81			
15							
16		Coefficient	Standard	t-Value	p-Value	Confidence Interval 95%	
17	Regression Table		Error			Lower	Upper
18	Constant	35491.7	1341.0	26.4661	< 0.0001	32847.6	38135.7
19	YrsExper	988.0	80.9	12.2083	< 0.0001	828.4	1147.6
20	YrsPrior	131.3	180.9	0.7259	0.4687	-225.4	488.1
21	Female	-8080.2	1198.2	-6.7438	< 0.0001	-10442.6	-5717.8

It is again useful to write Equation (10.13) in two forms: one for females (substituting Female=1) and one for males (substituting Female=0). After doing the arithmetic, they become

$$\text{Predicted Salary} = 27412 + 988\text{YrsExper} + 131\text{YrsPrior}$$

and

$$\text{Predicted Salary} = 35492 + 988\text{YrsExper} + 131\text{YrsPrior}$$

Except for the intercept term, these equations are identical. You can now interpret the coefficient -8080 of the Female dummy variable as the average salary disadvantage for females relative to males *after controlling for job experience*. Gender discrimination still appears to be a very plausible conclusion. However, note that the R^2 value is only 49.2%. Perhaps there is still more to the story.

The next step is to add education level to the equation by including four of the five education level dummies. Although *any* four could be used, we use EducLev=2 through EducLev=5, so that the lowest level becomes the reference category. (This should lead to *positive* coefficients for these dummies, which are easier to interpret.) The resulting output appears in Figure 10.26. The estimated regression equation is now

$$\text{Predicted Salary} = 26613 + 1033\text{YrsExper} + 362\text{YrsPrior} - 4501\text{Female}$$
$$+ 160\text{EducLev}=2 + 4765\text{EducLev}=3 + 7320\text{EducLev}=4 + 11770\text{EducLev}=5 \quad \textbf{(10.14)}$$

Figure 10.26

Regression Output with Education Dummies Included

	A	B	C	D	E	F	G
7		Multiple	R-Square	Adjusted	StErr of		
8	Summary	R		R-Square	Estimate		
9		0.8030	0.6449	0.6324	6824.4		
10							
11		Degrees of	Sum of	Mean of	F-Ratio	p-Value	
12	ANOVA Table	Freedom	Squares	Squares			
13	Explained	7	16912692100	2416098871	51.8787	< 0.0001	
14	Unexplained	200	9314415131	46572075.65			
15							
16		Coefficient	Standard	t-Value	p-Value	Confidence Interval 95%	
17	Regression Table		Error			Lower	Upper
18	Constant	26613.4	1794.1	14.8335	< 0.0001	23075.5	30151.2
19	YrsExper	1032.9	69.6	14.8404	< 0.0001	895.7	1170.2
20	YrsPrior	362.2	158.1	2.2908	0.0230	50.4	674.0
21	Female	-4501.3	1085.8	-4.1458	< 0.0001	-6642.3	-2360.3
22	EducLev = 2	160.2	1656.0	0.0968	0.9230	-3105.2	3425.7
23	EducLev = 3	4764.6	1473.4	3.2336	0.0014	1859.1	7670.0
24	EducLev = 4	7319.8	2694.2	2.7169	0.0072	2007.2	12632.5
25	EducLev = 5	11770.2	1510.2	7.7937	< 0.0001	8792.2	14748.2

Now there are two categorical variables involved, gender and education level. However, you can still write a separate equation *for each combination* of categories by setting the dummies to appropriate values. For example, the equation for females at education level 5 is found by setting Female and EducLev=5 equal to 1, and setting the other education dummies equal to 0. After combining terms, this equation is

$$\text{Predicted Salary} = 33882 + 1033\text{YrsExper} + 362\text{YrsPrior}$$

The intercept 33882 is the intercept from Equation (10.14), 26613, plus the coefficients of Female and EducLev=5.

Equation (10.14) can be interpreted as follows. For either gender and any education level, the expected increase in salary for one extra year of experience with Fifth National is $1033; the expected increase in salary for one extra year of prior experience with another bank is $362. The coefficients of the education dummies indicate the average increase in salary an employee can expect relative to the reference (lowest) education level. For example, an employee with education level 4 can expect to earn $7320 more than an employee with education level 1, all else being equal. Finally, the key coefficient, −$4501 for females, indicates the average salary disadvantage for females relative to males, given that they have the same experience levels *and* the same education levels. Note that the R^2 value is now 64.5%, quite a bit larger than when the education dummies were not included. We appear to be getting closer to the truth. In particular, you can see that there appears to be gender discrimination in salaries, even after accounting for job experience and education level.

One further explanation for gender differences in salary might be job grade. Perhaps females tend to be in lower job grades, which would help explain why they get lower salaries on average. One way to check this is with a pivot table, as in Figure 10.27, with job grade in the row area, gender in the column area, and counts, displayed as percentages of columns in the values area. Clearly, females tend to be concentrated at the lower job grades. For example, 28.85% of all employees are at the lowest job grade, but 34.29% of all females are at this grade and only 17.65% of males are at this grade. The opposite is true at the higher job grades. This certainly helps to explain why females get lower salaries on average.

Figure 10.27

Pivot Table of Job Grade Counts for Bank Data

	A	B	C	D
1				
2				
3	Count of Employee	Gender ▼		
4	JobGrade ▼	Female	Male	Grand Total
5	1	34.29%	17.65%	28.85%
6	2	20.71%	19.12%	20.19%
7	3	25.71%	10.29%	20.67%
8	4	12.14%	16.18%	13.46%
9	5	6.43%	17.65%	10.10%
10	6	0.71%	19.12%	6.73%
11	Grand Total	100.00%	100.00%	100.00%

It is possible to go one step further to see the effect of job grade on salary. As with the education dummies, the lowest job grade is used as the reference category and only the five dummies for the other categories are included. Two other potential explanatory variables can be added to the equation: Age and HasPCJob, a dummy based on the PCJob categorical variable. The regression output for this equation with all variables appears in Figure 10.28.

Figure 10.28

Regression Output with Other Variables Added

	A	B	C	D	E	F	G
7		Multiple R	R-Square	Adjusted R-Square	StErr of Estimate		
8	Summary						
9		0.8748	0.7652	0.7482	5648.1		
10							
11		Degrees of Freedom	Sum of Squares	Mean of Squares	F-Ratio	p-Value	
12	ANOVA Table						
13	Explained	14	20070250768	1433589341	44.9390	< 0.0001	
14	Unexplained	193	6156856463	31900810.69			
15							
16			Standard Error	t-Value	p-Value	Confidence Interval 95%	
17	Regression Table	Coefficient				Lower	Upper
18	Constant	29689.9	2490.0	11.9236	< 0.0001	24778.8	34601.1
19	YrsExper	515.6	98.0	5.2621	< 0.0001	322.3	708.8
20	Age	-9.0	57.7	-0.1553	0.8767	-122.8	104.8
21	YrsPrior	167.7	140.4	1.1943	0.2338	-109.3	444.7
22	Female	-2554.5	1012.0	-2.5242	0.0124	-4550.4	-558.5
23	EducLev = 2	-485.6	1398.7	-0.3472	0.7289	-3244.2	2273.1
24	EducLev = 3	527.9	1357.5	0.3889	0.6978	-2149.6	3205.4
25	EducLev = 4	285.2	2404.7	0.1186	0.9057	-4457.7	5028.1
26	EducLev = 5	2690.8	1620.9	1.6601	0.0985	-506.1	5887.7
27	JobGrade = 2	1564.5	1185.8	1.3194	0.1886	-774.2	3903.2
28	JobGrade = 3	5219.4	1262.4	4.1345	< 0.0001	2729.5	7709.2
29	JobGrade = 4	8594.8	1496.0	5.7451	< 0.0001	5644.2	11545.5
30	JobGrade = 5	13659.4	1874.3	7.2879	< 0.0001	9962.7	17356.1
31	JobGrade = 6	23832.4	2799.9	8.5119	< 0.0001	18310.1	29354.7
32	HasPCJob	4922.8	1473.8	3.3402	0.0010	2016.0	7829.7

As expected, the coefficients of the job grade dummies are all positive, and they increase as the job grade increases—it pays to be in the higher job grades. The effect of age appears to be minimal, and there appears to be a "bonus" of close to $5000 for having a PC-related job. The R^2 value has now increased to 76.5%, and the penalty for being a female has decreased to $2555—still large but not as large as before.

However, even if this penalty, the coefficient of Female in this last equation, is considered "small," is it convincing evidence against the argument for gender discrimination? We believe the answer is no. We have used variations in job grades to reduce the penalty for being female. But the question is why females are predominantly in the low job grades. Perhaps this is the real source of gender discrimination. Perhaps management is not advancing the females as quickly as it should, which naturally results in lower salaries for females. In a sense, JobGrade is not really an explanatory variable; it is a dependent variable.

We conclude this example for now, but we will say more about it in the next two subsections. ∎

The regression indicates that being in lower job grades implies lower salaries, but it doesn't explain why females are in the lower job grades in the first place.

10.6.2 Interaction Variables

Consider the following regression equation for a dependent variable Y versus a numerical variable X and a dummy variable D. If the estimated equation is of the form

$$\hat{Y} = a + b_1 X + b_2 D \qquad (10.15)$$

then, as in the previous section, this equation can be written as two separate equations:

$$\hat{Y} = (a + b_2) + b_1 X$$

and

$$\hat{Y} = a + b_1 X$$

The first corresponds to $D = 1$, and the second corresponds to $D = 0$. The only difference between these two equations is the intercept term; the slope for each is b_1. Geometrically, they correspond to two *parallel* lines that are a vertical distance b_2 apart. For example, if D corresponds to gender, there is a female line and a parallel male line. The effect of X on Y is the same for females and males. When X increases by one unit, Y is expected to change by b_1 units for males or females.

In effect, when you include *only* a dummy variable in a regression equation, as in Equation (10.15), you are allowing the intercepts of the two lines to differ (by an amount b_2), but you are *forcing* the lines to be parallel. To be more realistic, you might want to allow them to have different slopes, in addition to possibly different intercepts. You can do this by including an **interaction variable**. Algebraically, an interaction variable is the *product* of two variables. Its inclusion allows the effect of one of the variables on Y to depend on the value of the other variable.

> An **interaction variable** is the product of two explanatory variables. You can include such a variable in a regression equation if you believe the effect of one explanatory variable on Y depends on the value of another explanatory variable.

Suppose you create the interaction variable XD (the product of X and D) and then estimate the equation

$$\hat{Y} = a + b_1X + b_2D + b_3XD$$

As usual, this equation can be rewritten as two separate equations, depending on whether $D = 0$ or $D = 1$. If $D = 1$, terms can be combined to write

$$\hat{Y} = (a + b_2) + (b_1 + b_3)X$$

If $D = 0$, the dummy and interaction variables drop out and the equation becomes

$$\hat{Y} = a + b_1X$$

The notation is not important. The important part is that the interaction term, b_3XD, allows the slope of the regression line to differ between the two categories.

The following continuation of the bank discrimination example illustrates one possible use of interaction variables.

EXAMPLE

10.3 POSSIBLE GENDER DISCRIMINATION IN SALARY AT FIFTH NATIONAL BANK OF SPRINGFIELD (CONTINUED)

Earlier you estimated an equation for Salary using the numerical explanatory variables YrsExper and YrsPrior and the dummy variable Female. If you drop the YrsPrior variable from this equation (for simplicity) and rerun the regression, you obtain the equation

$$\text{Predicted Salary} = 35824 + 981\text{YrsExper} - 8012\text{Female} \qquad \textbf{(10.16)}$$

The R^2 value for this equation is 49.1%. If an interaction variable between YrsExper and Female is added to this equation, what is its effect?

Objective To use multiple regression with an interaction variable to see whether the effect of years of experience on salary is different across the two genders.

Solution

You first need to form an interaction variable that is the product of YrsExper and Female. This can be done in two ways in Excel. You can do it manually with an Excel formula that multiplies the two variables involved, or you can use the Interaction option from the StatTools Data Utilities dropdown menu. For the latter, select the Two Numeric Variables option in the Interaction Between dropdown list, and select Female and YrsExper as the variables to be used to create the interaction variable.[7]

Once the interaction variable has been created, you can include it in the regression equation in addition to the other variables in Equation (10.16). The multiple regression output appears in Figure 10.29. The estimated regression equation is

$$\text{Predicted Salary} = 30430 + 1528\text{YrsExper} + 4098\text{Female}$$
$$- 1248\text{Interaction(YrsExper,Female)}$$

where Interaction(YrsExper,Female) is StatTools's default name for the interaction variable. As before, it is useful to write this as two separate equations, one for females and one for males. The female equation (Female=1, so that Interaction(YrsExper,Female) = YrsExper) is

$$\text{Predicted Salary} = (30430 + 4098) + (1528 - 1248)\text{YrsExper}$$
$$= 34528 + 280\text{YrsExper}$$

and the male equation (Female=0, so that Interaction(YrsExper,Female) = 0) is

$$\text{Predicted Salary} = 30430 + 1528\text{YrsExper}$$

Figure 10.29

Regression Output with an Interaction Variable

	A	B	C	D	E	F	G
7		Multiple R	R-Square	Adjusted R-Square	StErr of Estimate		
8	Summary						
9		0.7991	0.6386	0.6333	6816.3		
10							
11		Degrees of Freedom	Sum of Squares	Mean of Squares	F-Ratio	p-Value	
12	ANOVA Table						
13	Explained	3	16748875071	5582958357	120.1620	< 0.0001	
14	Unexplained	204	9478232160	46461922.35			
15							
16		Coefficient	Standard Error	t-Value	p-Value	Confidence Interval 95%	
17	Regression Table					Lower	Upper
18	Constant	30430.0	1216.6	25.0129	< 0.0001	28031.4	32828.7
19	YrsExper	1527.8	90.5	16.8887	< 0.0001	1349.4	1706.1
20	Female	4098.3	1665.8	2.4602	0.0147	813.8	7382.7
21	Interaction(YrsExper,Female)	-1247.8	136.7	-9.1296	< 0.0001	-1517.3	-978.3

Graphically, these equations appear as in Figure 10.30. The Y-intercept for the female line is slightly higher—females with no experience with Fifth National tend to start out slightly higher than males—but the slope of the female line is much smaller. That is, males tend to move up the salary ladder much more quickly than females. Again, this provides another argument, although a somewhat different one, for gender discrimination against females. Notice that the R^2 value with the interaction variable has increased from 49.1% to 63.9%. The interaction variable has definitely added to the explanatory power of the equation.

---

[7]See the StatTools online help for this data utility. It explains the various options for creating interaction variables.

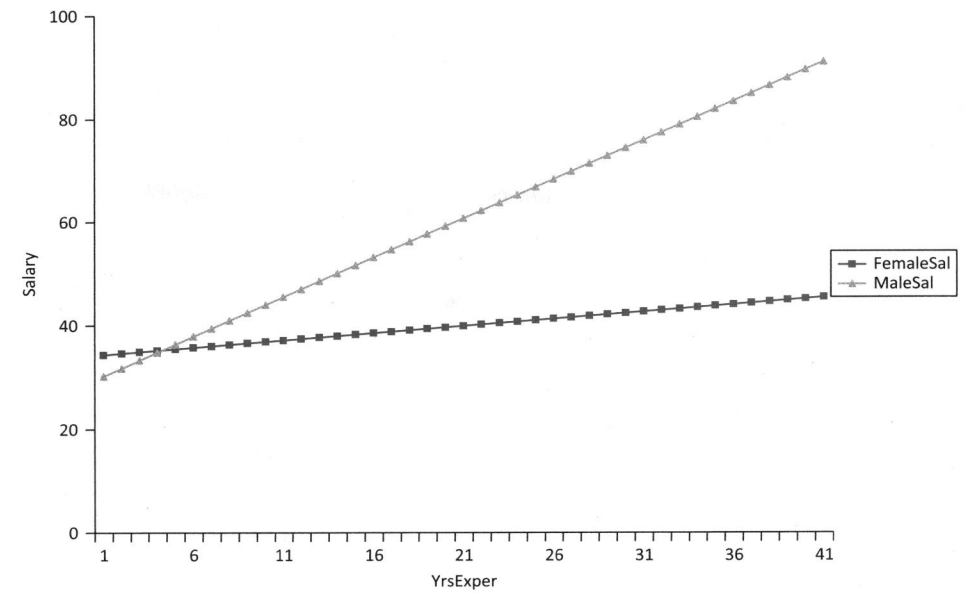

Figure 10.30
Nonparallel Female and Male Salary Lines

This example illustrates just one possible use of interaction variables. The product of *any* two variables, a numerical and a dummy variable, two dummy variables, or even two numerical variables, can be used. The trick is to interpret the results correctly, and the easiest way to do this is the way we have been doing it—by writing several separate equations and seeing how they differ. To illustrate one further possibility (among many), suppose you include the variables YrsExper, Female, and HighJob in the equation for Salary, along with interactions between Female and YrsExper and between Female and HighJob. Here, HighJob is a new dummy variable that is 1 for job grades 4 to 6 and is 0 for job grades 1 to 3. (It can be calculated as the sum of the dummies JobGrade=4 through JobGrade=6.) The resulting equation is

$$\text{Predicted Salary} = 28168 + 1261\text{YrsExper} + 9242\text{HighJob} + 6601\text{Female}$$
$$-1224\text{Interaction(YrsExper,Female)} + 1564\text{Interaction(Female,HighJob)} \quad \textbf{(10.17)}$$

and the R^2 value is now 76.6%.

The interpretation of Equation (10.17) is quite a challenge because it is really composed of four separate equations, one for each combination of Female and HighJob. For females in the high job category, the equation becomes

$$\text{Predicted Salary} = (28168 + 9242 + 6601 + 1564) + (1261 - 1224)\text{YrsExper}$$
$$= 45575 + 37\text{YrsExper}$$

and for females in the low job category it is

$$\text{Predicted Salary} = (28168 + 6601) + (1261 - 1224)\text{YrsExper}$$
$$= 34769 + 37\text{YrsExper}$$

Similarly, for males in the high job category, the equation becomes

$$\text{Predicted Salary} = (28168 + 9242) + 1261\text{YrsExper}$$
$$= 37410 + 1261\text{YrsExper}$$

and for males in the low job category it is

$$\text{Predicted Salary} = 28168 + 1261\,\text{YrsExper}$$

Putting this into words, the various coefficients can be interpreted as follows.

Interpretation of Regression Coefficients

- The intercept 28168 is the average *starting* salary (that is, with no experience at Fifth National) for males in the low job category.
- The coefficient 1261 of YrsExper is the expected increase in salary per extra year of experience for males (in either job category).
- The coefficient 9242 of HighJob is the expected salary premium for males starting in the high job category instead of the low job category.
- The coefficient 6601 of Female is the expected starting salary premium for females relative to males, given that they start in the low job category.
- The coefficient −1224 of Interaction(YrsExper,Female) is the penalty per extra year of experience for females relative to males—that is, male salaries increase this much more than female salaries each year.
- The coefficient 1564 of Interaction(Female,HighJob) is the extra premium (in addition to the male premium) for females starting in the high job category instead of the low job category.

FUNDAMENTAL INSIGHT

Interaction Variables

As this example indicates, interaction variables can make a regression quite difficult to interpret, and they are certainly not always necessary. However, without them, the effect of each *X* on *Y* is *independent* of the values of the other *X*s. If you believe, for example, that the effect of years of experience on salary is different for males than it is for females, the *only* way to capture this behavior is to include an interaction variable between years of experience and gender.

There are clearly pros and cons to adding interaction variables. On the plus side, they allow for more complex and interesting models, and they can lead to significantly better fits. On the minus side, they can become extremely difficult to interpret correctly. Therefore, we recommend that you add them only when there is good economic and statistical justification for doing so.

Postscript to Example 10.3

When regression analysis is used in a legal case, as it was in the bank gender discrimination example, it can uncover multiple versions of the "truth." That is, by including or omitting various variables, the resulting equations can imply quite different things about the issue in question, in this case, gender discrimination. If one side claims, for example, that the equation

$$\text{Predicted Salary} = 35492 + 988\,\text{YrsExper} + 131\,\text{YrsPrior} - 8080\,\text{Female}$$

is the true equation for explaining how salaries are determined at the bank, it is ludicrous for them to claim that the bank literally does it this way. No one believes that bank executives sit down and say: "We will start everyone at $35,492. Then we will add $988 for every year of experience with our bank and $131 for every year of prior work experience at another bank. Finally, we will subtract $8080 from this total if the person is female." All the analysts can claim is that the given regression equation is consistent, to a greater or lesser extent, with the observed data. If a number of regression equations, such as the ones estimated in this example, all point to lower salaries for females after controlling for other factors, then it doesn't matter whether management is deliberately discriminating against females according to some preconceived formula; the regression analysis indicates that females *are* compensated less than males with the same qualifications. Without a smoking gun, it is very difficult for either side to *prove* anything, but regression analysis permits either side to present evidence that is most consistent with the data.

10.6.3 Nonlinear Transformations

The general linear regression equation has the form

$$\text{Predicted } Y = a + b_1X_1 + b_2X_2 + \cdots + b_kX_k$$

You typically include nonlinear transformations in a regression equation because of economic considerations or curvature detected in scatterplots.

It is *linear* in the sense that the right side of the equation is a constant plus a sum of products of constants and variables. However, there is no requirement that the dependent variable Y or the explanatory variables X_1 through X_k be the *original* variables in the data set. Most often they are, but they can also be transformations of original variables. You already saw one example of this in the previous section with interaction variables. They are not original variables but are instead products of original (or even transformed) variables. The software treats them in the same way as original variables; only the interpretation differs. In this section we look at several possible **nonlinear transformations** of variables. These are often used because of curvature detected in scatterplots. They can also arise because of economic considerations. That is, economic theory often leads to particular nonlinear transformations.

You can transform the dependent variable Y or any of the explanatory variables, the Xs. You can also do both. In either case there are a few nonlinear transformations that are typically used. These include the natural logarithm, the square root, the reciprocal, and the square. The purpose of each of these is usually to "straighten out" the points in a scatterplot. If several different transformations straighten out the data equally well, the one that is easiest to interpret is preferred.

We begin with a small example where only the X variable needs to be transformed.

EXAMPLE | **10.4 DEMAND AND COST FOR ELECTRICITY**

The Public Service Electric Company produces different quantities of electricity each month, depending on the demand. The file **Cost of Power.xlsx** lists the number of units of electricity produced (Units) and the total cost of producing these (Cost) for a 36-month period. The data appear in Figure 10.31. How can regression be used to analyze the relationship between Cost and Units?

Figure 10.31

Data for Electric Power Example

	A	B	C
1	Month	Cost	Units
2	1	45623	601
3	2	46507	738
4	3	43343	686
5	4	46495	736
6	5	47317	756
7	6	41172	498
8	7	43974	828
9	8	44290	671
10	9	29297	305
11	10	47244	637
12	11	43185	499
13	12	42658	578

Objective To see whether the cost of supplying electricity is a nonlinear function of demand, and, if it is, what form the nonlinearity takes.

Solution

A good place to start is with a scatterplot of Cost versus Units. This appears in Figure 10.32. It indicates a definite positive relationship and one that is nearly linear. However, there is also some evidence of curvature in the plot. The points increase slightly less rapidly as Units increases from left to right. In economic terms, there might be economies of scale, so that the marginal cost of electricity decreases as more units of electricity are produced.

Figure 10.32

Scatterplot of Cost Versus Units for Electricity Example

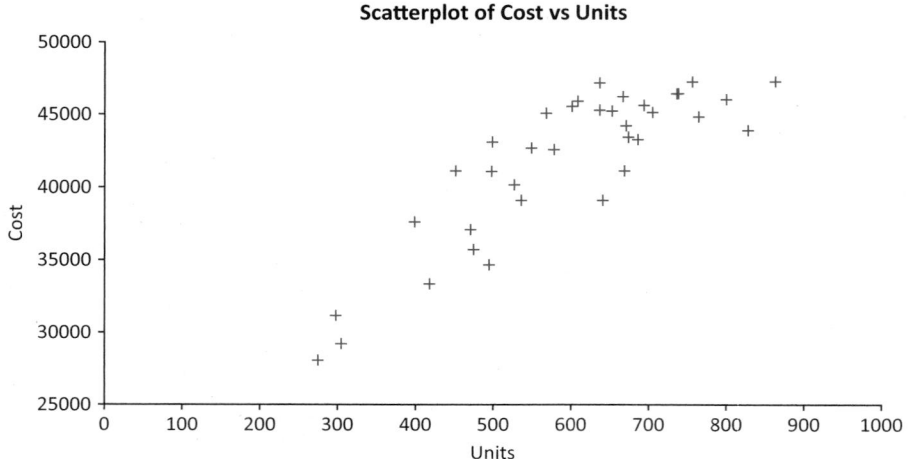

Nevertheless, you can first use regression to estimate a *linear* relationship between Cost and Units. The resulting regression equation is

$$\text{Predicted Cost} = 23651 + 30.53\text{Units}$$

The corresponding R^2 and s_e are 73.6% and $2734. It is always a good idea to request a scatterplot of the residuals versus the fitted values. This scatterplot is shown in Figure 10.33. Note that the residuals to the far left and the far right are all negative, whereas the majority of the residuals in the middle are positive. Admittedly, the pattern is far from perfect—there are several negative residuals in the middle—but this plot certainly suggests nonlinear behavior.

Figure 10.33

Residuals from a Straight-Line Fit

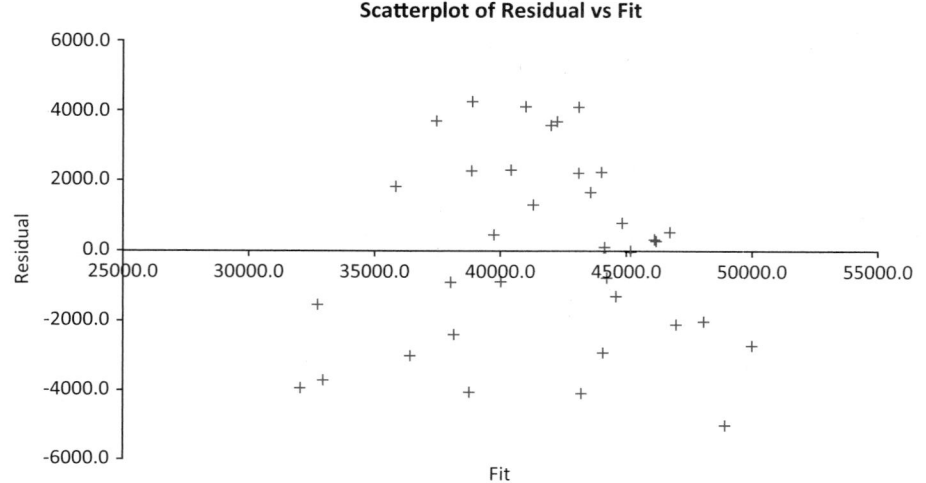

This negative–positive–negative behavior of residuals suggests a *parabola*—that is, a **quadratic** relationship with the *square* of Units included in the equation. The next step is to create a new variable (Units)^2 in the data set. You can do this manually (with the formula =C4^2 in cell D4, copied down) or with the Transform item in the StatTools Data Utilities dropdown menu.[8] This latter method has the advantage that it allows you to transform several variables simultaneously. Then you can use multiple regression to estimate the equation for Cost with *both* explanatory variables, Units and (Units)^2, included. The resulting equation, as shown in Figure 10.34, is

$$\text{Predicted Cost} = 5793 + 98.35\text{Units} - 0.0600(\text{Units})^2 \qquad \textbf{(10.18)}$$

Note that R^2 has increased to 82.2% and s_e has decreased to \$2281.

Figure 10.34

Regression Output with Squared Term Included

	A	B	C	D	E	F	G
7		Multiple		Adjusted	StErr of		
8	Summary	R	R-Square	R-Square	Estimate		
9		0.9064	0.8216	0.8108	2280.800		
10							
11		Degrees of	Sum of	Mean of			
12	ANOVA Table	Freedom	Squares	Squares	F-Ratio	p-Value	
13	Explained	2	790511518.3	395255759.1	75.9808	< 0.0001	
14	Unexplained	33	171667570.7	5202047.597			
15							
16			Standard			Confidence Interval 95%	
17	Regression Table	Coefficient	Error	t-Value	p-Value	Lower	Upper
18	Constant	5792.80	4763.06	1.2162	0.2325	-3897.72	15483.31
19	Units	98.350	17.237	5.7058	< 0.0001	63.282	133.419
20	(Units)^2	-0.0600	0.0151	-3.9806	0.0004	-0.0906	-0.0293

One way to see how this regression equation fits the scatterplot of Cost versus Units (in Figure 10.32) is to use Excel's Trendline option. To do so, activate the scatterplot, right-click on any point, select Add Trendline, and select the Polynomial type or order 2, that is, a quadratic. A graph of Equation (10.18) is superimposed on the scatterplot, as shown in Figure 10.35. It shows a reasonably good fit, plus an obvious curvature.

The main downside to a quadratic regression equation, as in Equation (10.18), is that there is no easy way to interpret the coefficients of Units and (Units)^2. For example, you can't conclude from the 98.35 coefficient of Units that Cost increases by 98.35 dollars when Units increases by one. The reason is that when Units increases by one, (Units)^2 doesn't

Figure 10.35

Quadratic Fit in Electricity Example

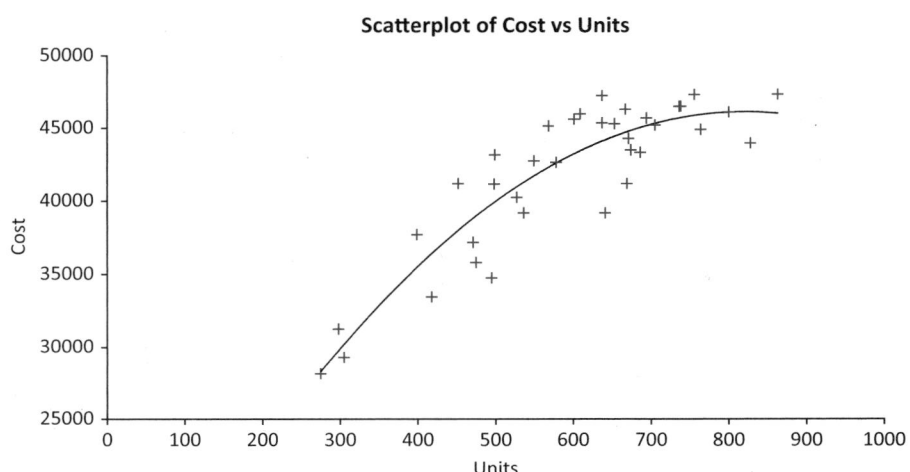

Scatterplot of Cost vs Units

[8]StatTools provides four nonlinear transformations: natural logarithm, square, square root, and reciprocal.

Excel's Trendline
option allows you
to superimpose a
number of different
curves on a
scatterplot.

stay constant; it *also* increases. All you can say is that the terms in Equation (10.18) combine to explain the nonlinear relationship between units produced and total cost.

Note that the coefficient of (Units)^2, −0.0600 is a small negative value. First, the fact that it is negative makes the parabola bend downward. This produces the decreasing marginal cost behavior, where every extra unit of electricity incurs a smaller cost. Actually, the curve described by Equation (10.18) eventually goes *downhill* for large values of Units, but this part of the curve is irrelevant because the company evidently never produces such large quantities. Second, you should not be fooled by the small magnitude of this coefficient. Remember that it is the coefficient of Units *squared*, which is a large quantity. Therefore, the effect of the product −0.0600(Units)^2 is sizable.

There is at least one other possibility you can examine. Rather than a quadratic fit, you can try a logarithmic fit. In this case you need to create a new variable, Log(Units), the natural logarithm of Units, and then regress Cost against the *single* variable Log(Units). To create the new variable, you can use a formula with Excel's LN function or you can use the Transform option from StatTools Data Utilities. Also, you can superimpose a logarithmic curve on the scatterplot of Cost versus Units by using Excel's Trendline feature with the logarithm option. This curve appears in Figure 10.36. To the naked eye, it appears to be similar, and about as good a fit, as the quadratic curve in Figure 10.35.

Figure 10.36

Logarithmic Fit to
Electricity Data

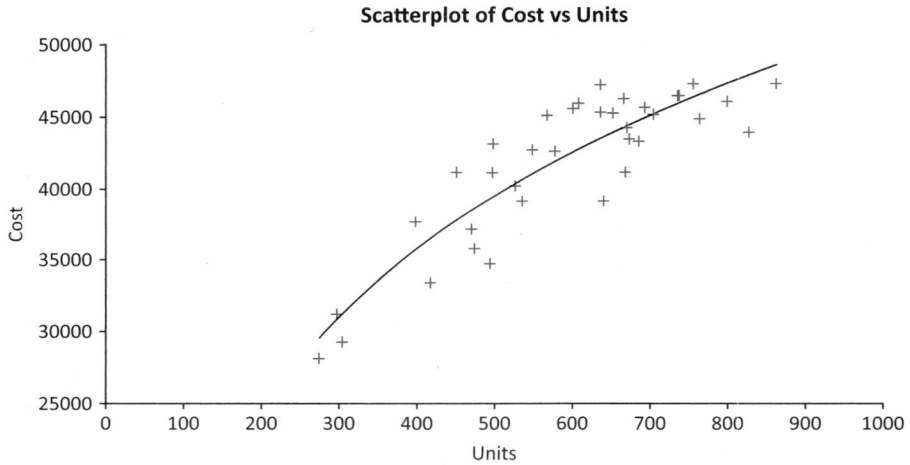

The resulting regression equation is

$$\text{Predicted Cost} = -63993 + 16654\text{Log(Units)} \qquad (10.19)$$

and the R^2 and s_e values are 79.8% and 2393. These latter values indicate that the logarithmic fit is not quite as good as the quadratic fit. However, the advantage of the logarithmic equation is that it is easier to interpret. In fact, one reason logarithmic transformations of variables are used so widely in regression analysis is that they are fairly easy to interpret.

In the present case, where the log of an *explanatory* variable is used, you can interpret its coefficient as follows. Suppose that Units increases by 1%, for example, from 600 to 606. Then Equation (10.19) implies that the expected Cost will increase by approximately 0.01(16654) = 166.54 dollars. In words, every 1% increase in Units is accompanied by an expected $166.54 increase in Cost. Note that for larger values of Units, a 1% increase represents a larger absolute increase (from 700 to 707 instead of from 600 to 606, say). But each such 1% increase entails the *same* increase in Cost. This is another way of describing the decreasing marginal cost property. ■

In general, if b is the
coefficient of the log
of X, then the
expected change in Y
when X increases by
1% is approximately
0.01 times b.

The electricity example has shown two possible nonlinear transformations of the *explanatory* variable (or variables) that you can use. All you need to do is create the transformed Xs and run the regression. The interpretation of statistics such as R^2 and s_e is exactly the same as before; only the interpretation of the coefficients of the transformed Xs changes. It is also possible to transform the dependent variable Y. Now, however, you must be careful when interpreting summary statistics such as R^2 and s_e, as explained in the following examples.

A logarithmic transformation of Y is often useful when the distribution of Y values is skewed to the right.

Each of these examples transforms the dependent variable Y by taking its natural logarithm and then using the log of Y as the new dependent variable. This approach has been used in a wide variety of business applications. Essentially, it is often a good option when the distribution of Y is skewed to the right, with a few very large values and many small to medium values. The effect of the logarithm transformation is to spread the small values out and squeeze the large values together, making the distribution more symmetric. This is illustrated in Figures 10.37 and 10.38 for a hypothetical distribution of household incomes. The histogram of incomes in Figure 10.37 is clearly skewed to the right. However, the histogram of the natural log of income in Figure 10.38 is much more nearly symmetric—and, for technical reasons, more suitable for use as the dependent variable in regression.

Figure 10.37
Skewed Distribution of Income

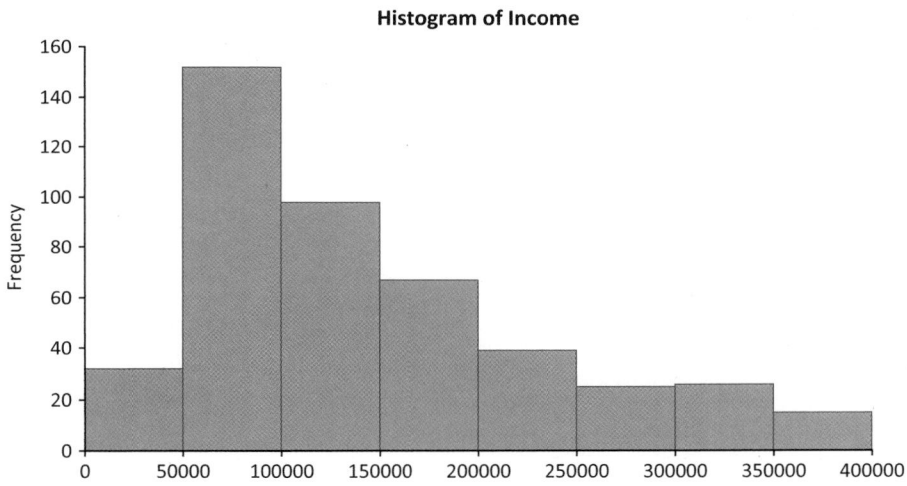

Figure 10.38
Symmetric Distribution of Log(Income)

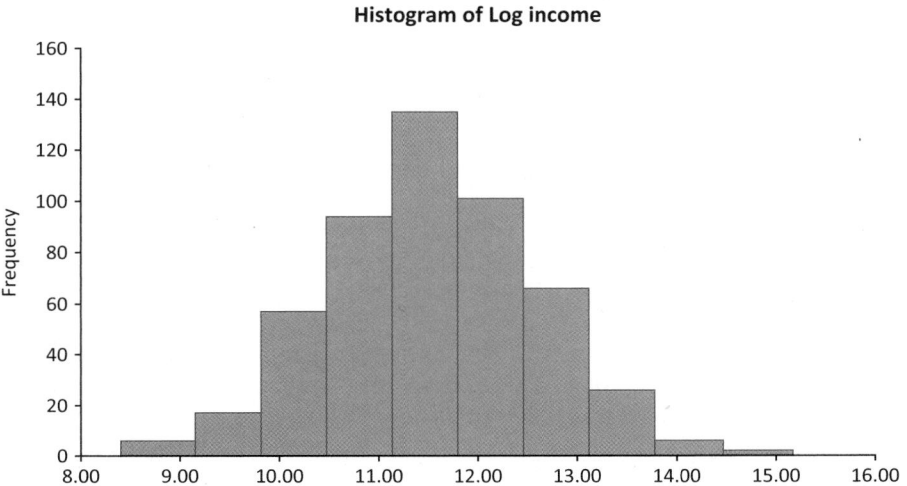

10.3 POSSIBLE GENDER DISCRIMINATION IN SALARY AT FIFTH NATIONAL BANK OF SPRINGFIELD (CONTINUED)

Returning to the bank discrimination example, a glance at the distribution of salaries of the 208 employees shows some skewness to the right—a few employees make substantially more than the majority of employees. Therefore, it might make more sense to use the natural logarithm of Salary as the dependent variable, not Salary. If you do this, how can you interpret the results?

Objective To reanalyze the bank salary data, now using the logarithm of salary as the dependent variable.

Solution

All of the previous analyses with this data set could be repeated with Log(Salary) as the dependent variable. For the sake of discussion, we look only at the regression equation with Female and YrsExper as explanatory variables. After creating the Log(Salary) variable and running the regression, the output in Figure 10.39 results. The estimated regression equation is

$$\text{Predicted Log(Salary)} = 10.4907 + 0.0188\text{YrsExper} - 0.1616\text{Female} \quad \textbf{(10.20)}$$

The R^2 and s_e values are 42.4% and 0.1794. For comparison, when this same equation was estimated with Salary as the dependent variable, R^2 and s_e were 49.1% and 8.070.

Figure 10.39
Regression Output with Log of Salary as Dependent Variable

	A	B	C	D	E	F	G
7		Multiple R	R-Square	Adjusted R-Square	StErr of Estimate		
8	Summary						
9		0.6514	0.4243	0.4187	0.1794		
10							
11		Degrees of Freedom	Sum of Squares	Mean of Squares	F-Ratio	p-Value	
12	ANOVA Table						
13	Explained	2	4.861326452	2.430663226	75.5556	< 0.0001	
14	Unexplained	205	6.59495595	0.032170517			
15							
16		Coefficient	Standard Error	t-Value	p-Value	Confidence Interval 95%	
17	Regression Table					Lower	Upper
18	Constant	10.4907	0.0280	374.8768	< 0.0001	10.4355	10.5458
19	YrsExper	0.0188	0.0018	10.5556	< 0.0001	0.0153	0.0224
20	Female	-0.1616	0.0265	-6.0936	< 0.0001	-0.2139	-0.1093

When the logarithm of Y is used in the regression equation, the interpretations of s_e and R^2 are different because the units of the dependent variable are completely different.

You must be careful when interpreting R^2 and s_e. Neither is directly comparable to the R^2 or s_e value with Salary as the dependent variable. Recall that R^2 in general is the percentage of the dependent variable explained by the regression equation. The problem here is that the two R^2 values are percentages explained of *different* dependent variables, Log(Salary) and Salary. The fact that one is smaller than the other (42.4% versus 49.1%) does not necessarily mean that it corresponds to a worse fit. They simply are not comparable.

The situation is even worse with s_e. Each s_e is a measure of a typical residual, but the residuals in the Log(Salary) equation are in log dollars, whereas the residuals in the Salary equation are in dollars. These units are completely different. For example, the log of $1000 is only 6.91. Therefore, it is no surprise that s_e for the Log(Salary) equation is *much* smaller than s_e for the Salary equation. If you want comparable standard error measures for the two equations, you should take antilogs of fitted values from the Log(Salary) equation to convert them back to dollars, subtract these from the original Salary values, and take the standard deviation of these "residuals." (The EXP function in Excel can be used to take antilogs.) You can check that the resulting standard deviation is 7774.[9] This is somewhat smaller than s_e from the Salary equation, an indication of a slightly better fit.

Finally, it is fairly easy to interpret Equation (10.20) itself. When the dependent variable is Log(Y) and a term on the right-hand side of the equation is of the form bX, then whenever X increases by one unit, the predicted value of Y changes by a constant *percentage*, and this percentage is approximately equal to b (written as a percentage). For example, if $b = 0.035$, then when X increases by one unit, the predicted value of Y increases by approximately 3.5%. Applied to Equation (10.20), this means that for each extra year of experience with Fifth National, an employee's salary can be expected to increase by about 1.88%. To interpret the Female coefficient, note that the only possible increase in Female is one unit (from 0 for male to 1 for female). When this occurs, the expected percentage *decrease* in salary is approximately 16.16%. In other words, Equation (10.20) implies that females can expect to make about 16% less than men for comparable years of experience. ∎

Any coefficient b can now be interpreted as the approximate percentage change in Y when the corresponding X increases by one unit.

We are not necessarily claiming that the bank data are fit better with Log(Salary) as the dependent variable than with Salary—it appears to be a virtual toss-up. However, the lessons from this example are important in general. They are as follows.

1. The R^2 values with Y and Log(Y) as dependent variables are not directly comparable. They are percentages explained of *different* variables.

2. The s_e values with Y and Log(Y) as dependent variables are usually of totally different magnitudes. To make the s_e from the log equation comparable, you need to go through the procedure described in the example so that the residuals are in *original* units.

3. To interpret any term of the form bX in the log equation, you should first express b as a percentage. For example, $b = 0.035$ becomes 3.5%. Then when X increases by one unit, the expected *percentage* change in Y is approximately this percentage b.

Remember these points, especially the third, when using the logarithm of Y as the dependent variable.

The log transformation of a dependent variable Y is used frequently. This is partly because it induces nice statistical properties (such as making the distribution of Y more symmetric). But an important advantage of this transformation is its ease of interpretation in terms of percentage changes.

Constant Elasticity Relationships

A particular type of nonlinear relationship that has firm grounding in economic theory is called a **constant elasticity relationship**. It is also called a **multiplicative relationship**. It has the form shown in Equation (10.21).

Formula for Multiplicative Relationship
$$\text{Predicted } Y = aX_1^{b_1} X_2^{b_2} \cdots X_k^{b_k} \tag{10.21}$$

One property of this type of relationship is that the effect of a one-unit change in any X on Y depends on the levels of the other Xs in the equation. This is not true for the *additive* relationships of the form

$$\text{Predicted } Y = a + b_1X_1 + b_2X_2 + \cdots + b_kX_k$$

[9]To make the two "standard deviations" comparable, we use the denominator $n - 3$ in each.

that we have been discussing. For additive relationships, when any X increases by one unit, the predicted value of Y changes by the corresponding b units, regardless of the levels of the other Xs. However, multiplicative relationships have the following nice property.

> In a **multiplicative** (or **constant elasticity**) **relationship**, the dependent variable is expressed as a *product* of explanatory variables raised to powers. When any explanatory variable X changes by 1%, the predicted value of the dependent variable changes by a constant *percentage*, regardless of the value of this X or the values of the other Xs.

The term *constant elasticity* comes from economics. Economists define the elasticity of Y with respect to X as the percentage change in Y that accompanies a 1% increase in X. Often this is in reference to a demand–price relationship. Then the *price elasticity* is the percentage decrease in demand when price increases by 1%. Usually, the elasticity depends on the current value of X. For example, the price elasticity when the price is \$35 might be different than when the price is \$50. However, if the relationship is of the form

$$\text{Predicted } Y = aX^b$$

then the elasticity is *constant*, the same for any value of X. In fact, it is approximately equal to the exponent b. For example, if Predicted $Y = 2X^{-1.5}$, the constant elasticity is approximately -1.5, so that when X increases by 1%, the predicted value of Y decreases by approximately 1.5%.

The constant elasticity for any X is approximately equal to the exponent of that X.

The constant elasticity property carries over to the multiple-X relationship in Equation (10.21). Then each exponent is the approximate elasticity for its X. For example, if Predicted $Y = 2X_1^{-1.5}X_2^{0.7}$, you can make the following statements:

- When X_1 increases by 1%, the predicted value of Y decreases by approximately 1.5%, regardless of the current values of X_1 and X_2.
- When X_2 increases by 1%, the predicted value of Y increases by approximately 0.7%, regardless of the current values of X_1 and X_2.

You can use linear regression to estimate the nonlinear relationship in Equation (10.21) by taking natural logarithms of *all* variables. Here two properties of logarithms are used: (1) the log of a product is the sum of the logs, and (2) the log of X^b is b times the log of X. Therefore, taking logs of both sides of Equation (10.21) gives

$$\text{Predicted Log}(Y) = \text{Log}(a) + b_1\text{Log}(X_1) + \cdots + b_k\text{Log}(X_k)$$

This equation is *linear* in the log variables $\text{Log}(X_1)$ through $\text{Log}(X_k)$, so you can estimate it in the usual way with multiple regression. You can then interpret the coefficients of the explanatory variables directly as elasticities. The following example illustrates the method.

10.5 FACTORS RELATED TO SALES OF DOMESTIC AUTOMOBILES

The file **Car Sales.xlsx** contains annual data (1970–1999) on domestic auto sales in the United States. The data are listed in Figure 10.40. The variables are defined as

- Sales: annual domestic auto sales (in number of units)
- PriceIndex: consumer price index of transportation
- Income: real disposable income
- Interest: prime rate of interest

Our goal is to estimate and interpret a multiplicative (constant elasticity) relationship between Sales and PriceIndex, Income, and Interest.

Objective To use logarithms of variables in a multiple regression to estimate a multiplicative relationship for automobile sales as a function of price, income, and interest rate.

Figure 10.40 Data for Automobile Demand Example

	A	B	C	D	E	F	G	H	I
1	Year	Sales	PriceIndex	Income	Interest				
2	1970	7,115,270	37.5	2630	7.91%				
3	1971	8,676,410	39.5	2745.3	5.72%	Sources: Automotive News, Market			
4	1972	9,321,310	39.9	2874.3	5.25%	Data Book (various issues) for column			
5	1973	9,618,510	41.2	3072.3	8.03%	B, from Economic Report of the			
6	1974	7,448,340	45.8	3051.9	10.81%	President, 2000, for columns C, D, E			
7	1975	7,049,840	50.1	3108.5	7.86%				
8	1976	8,606,860	55.1	3243.5	6.84%				
9	1977	9,104,930	59	3360.7	6.83%				
10	1978	9,304,250	61.7	3527.5	9.06%				
11	1979	8,316,020	70.5	3628.6	12.67%				
12	1980	6,578,360	83.1	3658	15.27%				
13	1981	6,206,690	93.2	3741.1	18.87%				
14	1982	5,756,610	97	3791.7	14.86%				
15	1983	6,795,230	99.3	3906.9	10.79%				
16	1984	7,951,790	103.7	4207.6	12.04%				
17	1985	8,204,690	106.4	4347.8	9.93%				
18	1986	8,222,480	102.3	4486.6	8.33%				
19	1987	7,080,890	105.4	4582.5	8.21%				
20	1988	7,526,334	108.7	4784.1	9.32%				
21	1989	7,014,850	114.1	4906.5	10.87%				
22	1990	6,842,733	120.5	5041.2	10.01%				
23	1991	6,072,255	123.8	5033	8.46%				
24	1992	6,216,488	126.5	5189.3	6.25%				
25	1993	6,674,458	130.4	5261.3	6.00%				
26	1994	7,181,975	134.3	5397.2	7.15%				
27	1995	7,023,843	139.1	5539.1	8.83%				
28	1996	7,139,884	143	5677.7	8.27%				
29	1997	6,907,992	144.3	5854.5	8.44%				
30	1998	6,756,804	141.6	6168.6	8.35%				
31	1999	6,987,208	144.4	6320	8.00%				

Solution

The first step is to take natural logs of all four variables. (You can do this in one step with the StatTools Transform utility or you can use Excel's LN function.) Then you can run a multiple regression, with Log(Quantity) as the dependent variable and Log(PriceIndex), Log(Income), and Log(Interest) as the explanatory variables. The resulting output is shown in Figure 10.41. The corresponding equation for Log(Quantity) is

$$\text{Predicted Log(Sales)} = 14.126 - 0.384\text{Log(PriceIndex)} + 0.388\text{Log(Income)}$$
$$- 0.070\text{Log(Interest)}$$

Figure 10.41 Regression Output for Multiplicative Relationship

	A	B	C	D	E	F	G
7		Multiple	R-Square	Adjusted	StErr of		
8	Summary	R		R-Square	Estimate		
9		0.6813	0.4642	0.4023	0.1053		
10							
11		Degrees of	Sum of	Mean of		F-Ratio	p-Value
12	ANOVA Table	Freedom	Squares	Squares			
13	Explained	3	0.249567775	0.083189258	7.5073	0.0009	
14	Unexplained	26	0.288107728	0.011081066			
15							
16		Coefficient	Standard	t-Value	p-Value	Confidence Interval 95%	
17	Regression Table		Error			Lower	Upper
18	Constant	14.1260	1.9838	7.1206	< 0.0001	10.0482	18.2037
19	Log(PriceIndex)	-0.3837	0.2091	-1.8351	0.0780	-0.8135	0.0461
20	Log(Income)	0.3881	0.3621	1.0720	0.2936	-0.3561	1.1324
21	Log(Interest)	-0.0698	0.0893	-0.7821	0.4412	-0.2534	0.1137

If you like, you can convert this back to original variables, that is, back to multiplicative form, by taking antilogs. The result is

$$\text{Predicted Sales} = 1364048\text{PriceIndex}^{-0.384}\text{Income}^{0.388}\text{Interest}^{-0.070}$$

The constant 1364048 is the antilog of 14.126 (and be calculated in Excel with the EXP function).

In either form the equation implies that the elasticities are approximately equal to -0.384, 0.388, and -0.070. When PriceIndex increases by 1%, the predicted value of Sales tends to decrease by about 0.384%; when Income increases by 1%, the predicted value of Sales tends to increase by about 0.388%; and when Interest increases by 1%, the predicted value of Sales tends to decrease by about 0.070%.

Does this multiplicative equation provide a better fit to the automobile data than an additive relationship? Without doing considerably more work, it is difficult to answer this question with any certainty. As discussed in the previous example, it is *not* sufficient to compare R^2 and s_e values for the two fits. Again, the reason is that one has Log(Sales) as the dependent variable, whereas the other has Sales, so the R^2 and s_e measures aren't comparable. We simply state that the multiplicative relationship provides a reasonably good fit (for example, a scatterplot of its fitted values versus residuals shows no unusual patterns), and it makes sense economically. But the additive equation is arguably just about as good.

Before leaving this example, we note that the results for this data set are not quite as clear as they might appear. (This is often the case with real data.) First, the correlation between Sales and Income, or between Log(Sales) and Log(Income), is negative, not positive. However, because of multicollinearity, a topic discussed in the next chapter, the regression coefficient of Log(Income) is positive. Second, most of the behavior appears to be driven by the early years. If you rerun the analysis from 1980 on, you will discover almost no relationship between Sales and the other variables. ∎

One final example of a multiplicative relationship is the *learning curve* model. A **learning curve** relates the unit production time (or cost) to the cumulative volume of output since that production process first began. Empirical studies indicate that production times tend to decrease by a relatively constant *percentage* every time cumulative output doubles. To model this phenomenon, let Y be the time required to produce a unit of output, and let X be the *cumulative* amount of output that has been produced so far. If we assume that the relationship between Y and X is of the constant elasticity form

$$\text{Predicted } Y = aX^b$$

then it can be shown that whenever X doubles, the predicted value of Y decreases to a *constant* percentage of its previous value. This constant is often called the *learning rate*. For example, if the learning rate is 80%, then each doubling of cumulative production yields a 20% reduction in unit production time. It can be shown that the learning rate satisfies the equation

$$b = \text{LN(learning rate)/LN(2)} \tag{10.22}$$

(where LN refers to the natural logarithm). So once you estimate b, you can use Equation (10.22) to estimate the learning rate.

The following example illustrates a typical application of the learning curve model.

EXAMPLE

10.6 THE LEARNING CURVE FOR PRODUCTION OF A NEW PRODUCT AT PRESARIO

The Presario Company produces a variety of small industrial products. It has just finished producing 22 batches of a new product (new to Presario) for a customer. The file **Learning Curve.xlsx** contains the times (in hours) to produce each batch. These data are listed in Figure 10.42. Clearly, the times have tended to decrease as Presario has gained more experience in making the product. Does the multiplicative learning model apply to these data, and what does it imply about the learning rate?

Objective   To use a multiplicative regression equation to estimate the learning rate for production time.

Solution

One way to check whether the multiplicative learning model is reasonable is to create the log variables Log(Time) and Log(Batch) in the usual way and then see whether a scatterplot of Log(Time) versus Log(Batch) is approximately *linear*. The multiplicative model implies that it should be. Such a scatterplot appears in Figure 10.43, along with a superimposed linear trend line. The fit appears to be quite good.

The relationship can be estimated by regressing Log(Time) on Log(Batch). The resulting equation is

$$\text{Predicted Log(Time)} = 4.834 - 0.155\text{Log(Batch)} \tag{10.23}$$

Figure 10.42

Data for Learning
Curve Example

	A	B
1	Batch	Time
2	1	125.00
3	2	110.87
4	3	105.35
5	4	103.34
6	5	98.98
7	6	99.90
8	7	91.49
9	8	93.10
10	9	92.23
11	10	86.19
12	11	82.09
13	12	82.32
14	13	87.67
15	14	81.72
16	15	83.72
17	16	81.53
18	17	80.46
19	18	76.53
20	19	82.06
21	20	82.81
22	21	76.52
23	22	78.45

Figure 10.43

Scatterplot of Log
Variables with
Linear Trend
Superimposed

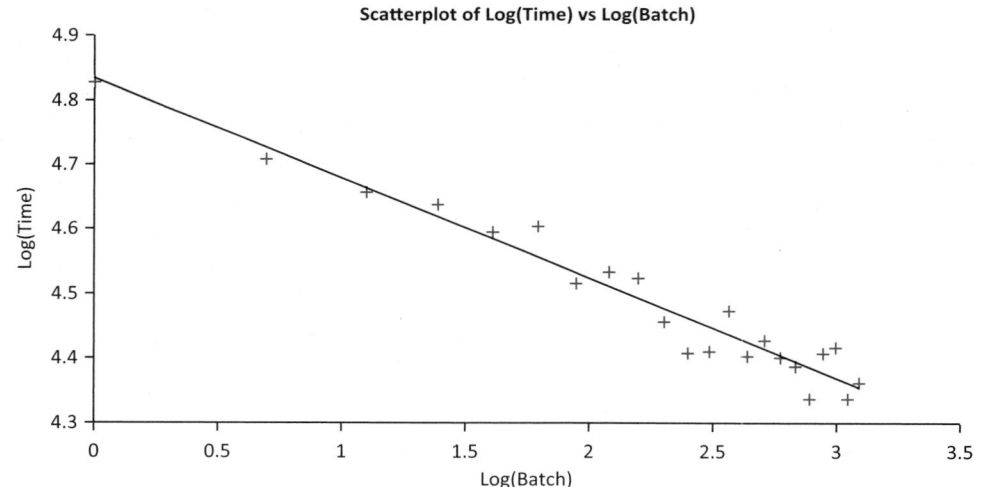

There are a couple of ways to interpret this equation. First, because it is a constant elasticity relationship, the coefficient -0.155 can be interpreted as an elasticity. That is, when Batch increases by 1%, Time tends to decrease by approximately 0.155%.

Although this interpretation is correct, it is not as useful as the "doubling" interpretation discussed previously. Equation (10.22) states that the estimated learning rate satisfies

$$-0.155 = LN(\text{learning rate})/LN(2)$$

Solving for the learning rate (multiply through by LN(2) and then take antilogs), you can see that it is 0.898, or approximately 90%. In words, whenever cumulative production doubles, the time to produce a batch decreases by about 10%.

Presario could use this regression equation to predict future production times. For example, suppose the customer places an order for 15 more batches of the same product. Note that Presario is already partway up the learning curve, that is, these batches are numbers 23 through 37, and the company already has experience producing the product. You can use Equation (10.23) to predict the log of production time for each batch. Then you can take their antilogs and sum them to obtain the total production time. The calculations are shown in rows 24 through 39 of Figure 10.44. You enter the batch numbers and calculate their logs in columns A and C. Then you substitute the values of Log(Batch) in column C into equation (10.23) to obtain the predicted values of Log(Time) in column E. Finally, you use Excel's EXP function to calculate the antilogs of these predictions in column B, and you calculate their sum in cell B39. The total predicted time to finish the order is about 1115 hours.

Figure 10.44

Using the Learning Curve Model for Predictions

	A	B	C	D	E	F
21	20	82.81	2.995732274	4.416548827		
22	21	76.52	3.044522438	4.337552145		
23	22	78.45	3.091042453	4.362461479		
24	23	77.324	3.135494216	4.348009995		
25	24	76.816	3.17805383	4.341413654		
26	25	76.332	3.218875825	4.335086627		
27	26	75.869	3.258096538	4.329007785		
28	27	75.426	3.295836866	4.323158388		
29	28	75.003	3.33220451	4.317521744		
30	29	74.596	3.36729583	4.312082919		
31	30	74.205	3.401197382	4.306828497		
32	31	73.829	3.433987204	4.301746382		
33	32	73.466	3.465735903	4.296825631		
34	33	73.117	3.496507561	4.292056313		
35	34	72.779	3.526360525	4.287429384		
36	35	72.453	3.555348061	4.282936587		
37	36	72.137	3.583518938	4.278570366		
38	37	71.832	3.610917913	4.274323782		
39		1115.183	⟵———	Predicted time for next 15 batches		

PROBLEMS

Level A

26. In a study of housing demand, a county assessor is interested in developing a regression model to estimate the selling price of residential properties within her jurisdiction. She randomly selects 15 houses and records the selling price in addition to the following values: the size of the house (in square feet), the total number of rooms in the house, the age of the house, and an indication of whether the house has an attached garage. These data are stored in the file **P10_26.xlsx**.

  a. Estimate and interpret a multiple regression equation that includes the four potential explanatory variables. How do you interpret the coefficient of the Attached Garage variable?

  b. Evaluate the estimated regression equation's goodness of fit.

  c. Use the estimated equation to predict the sales price of a 3000-square-foot, 20-year-old home that has seven rooms but no attached garage. How accurate is your prediction?

27. A manager of boiler drums wants to use regression analysis to predict the number of worker-hours needed to erect the drums in future projects. Data for 36 randomly selected boilers have been collected. In addition to worker-hours (Y), the variables measured include boiler capacity, boiler design pressure, boiler type, and drum type. All of these measurements are listed in the file **P10_27.xlsx**.
   a. Estimate an appropriate multiple regression equation to predict the number of worker-hours needed to erect boiler drums.
   b. Interpret the estimated regression coefficients.
   c. According to the estimated regression equation, what is the difference between the mean number of worker-hours required for erecting industrial and utility field boilers?
   d. According to the estimated regression equation, what is the difference between the mean number of worker-hours required for erecting boilers with steam drums and those with mud drums?
   e. Given the estimated regression equation, predict the number of worker-hours needed to erect a utility-field, steam-drum boiler with a capacity of 550,000 pounds per hour and a design pressure of 1400 pounds per square inch. How accurate is your prediction?
   f. Given the estimated regression equation, predict the number of worker-hours needed to erect an industrial-field, mud-drum boiler with a capacity of 100,000 pounds per hour and a design pressure of 1000 pounds per square inch. How accurate is your prediction?

28. Suppose that a regional express delivery service company wants to estimate the cost of shipping a package (Y) as a function of cargo type, where cargo type includes the following possibilities: fragile, semifragile, and durable. Costs for 15 randomly chosen packages of approximately the same weight and same distance shipped, but of different cargo types, are provided in the file **P10_28.xlsx**.
   a. Estimate an appropriate multiple regression equation to predict the cost of shipping a given package.
   b. Interpret the estimated regression coefficients. You should find that the estimated intercept and slope of the equation are sample means. Which sample means are they?
   c. According to the estimated regression equation, which cargo type is the *most* costly to ship? Which cargo type is the *least* costly to ship?
   d. How well does the estimated equation fit the given sample data? How do you think the model's goodness of fit could be improved?
   e. Given the estimated regression equation, predict the cost of shipping a package with semifragile cargo.

29. The file **P10_11.xlsx** contains annual observations (in column B) of the American minimum wage. The basic question here is whether the minimum wage has been growing at roughly a *constant* rate over this period.
   a. Create a time series graph for these data. Comment on the observed behavior of the minimum wage over time.
   b. Estimate a linear regression equation of the minimum wage versus time (the Year variable). What does the estimated slope indicate?
   c. Analyze the residuals from the equation in part **b**. Are they essentially random? If not, return to part **b** and revise your equation appropriately. Then interpret the revised equation.

30. Estimate a regression equation that *adequately* estimates the relationship between monthly electrical power usage (Y) and home size (X) using the data in the file **P10_13.xlsx**. Interpret your results. How well does your model explain the variation in monthly electrical power usage?

31. An insurance company wants to determine how its annual operating costs depend on the number of home insurance (X_1) and automobile insurance (X_2) policies that have been written. The file **P10_31.xlsx** contains relevant information for 10 branches of the insurance company. The company believes that a multiplicative model might be appropriate because operating costs typically increase by a constant percentage as the number of either type of policy increases by a given percentage. Use the given data to estimate a multiplicative model for this insurance company. Interpret your results. Does a multiplicative model provide a good fit with these data? Answer by calculating the appropriate standard error of estimate and R^2 value, based on *original* units of the dependent variable.

32. Suppose that an operations manager is trying to determine the number of labor hours required to produce the ith unit of a certain product. Consider the data provided in the file **P10_32.xlsx**. For example, the second unit produced required 517 labor hours, and the 600th unit required 34 labor hours.
   a. Use the given data to estimate a relationship between the total number of units produced and the labor hours required to produce the last unit in the total set. Interpret your findings.
   b. Use your estimated relationship to predict the number of labor hours that will be needed to produce the 800th unit.

Level B

33. The human resources manager of DataCom, Inc., wants to predict the annual salaries of given employees using the potential explanatory variables in the file **P10_05.xlsx**.

a. Estimate an appropriate multiple regression equation to predict the annual salary of a given DataCom employee using all of the data in columns C–H.
b. Interpret the estimated regression coefficients.
c. According to the estimated regression model, is there a difference between the mean salaries earned by male and female employees at DataCom? If so, how large is the difference? According to your equation, does this difference depend on the values of the other explanatory variables? Explain.
d. According to the estimated regression model, is there a difference between the mean salaries earned by employees in the sales department and those in the advertising department at DataCom? If so, how large is the difference? According to your equation, does this difference depend on the values of the other explanatory variables? Explain.
e. According to the estimated regression model, in which department are DataCom employees paid the *highest* mean salary (after controlling for other explanatory variables)? In which department are DataCom employees paid the *lowest* mean salary?
f. Given the estimated regression model, predict the annual salary of a female employee who served in a similar department at another company for 10 years prior to coming to work at DataCom. This woman, a graduate of a four-year collegiate business program, has been supervising 12 subordinates in the purchasing department since joining the organization five years ago.

34. Does the rate of violent crime acts vary across different regions of the United States? Answer this with the (somewhat old), 1999 data in the file **P10_34.xlsx** as requested below.
a. Estimate an appropriate regression model to explain the variation in violent crime rate across the four given regions of the United States. Interpret the estimated equation. Rank the four regions from highest to lowest according to their mean violent crime rate. Could you have done this without regression? Explain.
b. How would you modify the regression model in part **a** to account for possible differences in the violent crime rate across the various subdivisions of the given regions? Estimate your revised regression equation and interpret your findings. Rank the nine subdivisions from highest to lowest according to their mean violent crime rate.

35. Continuing Problems 6 and 15 on the 2006–2007 movie data in the file **P02_02.xlsx**, create a new variable Total Revenue that is the sum of Total US Gross, International Gross, and US DVD Sales. How well can this new variable be predicted from the data in columns C–F? For Distributor, relabel the categories so that there are only two: Large Distributor and Small Distributor. The former is any distributor that had at least 12 movies in this period, and the latter is all the rest. For Genre, relabel the categories to be Comedy, Drama, Adventure, Action, Thriller/Suspense, and Other. (Other includes Black Comedy, Documentary, Horror, Musical, and Romantic Comedy.) Interpret the coefficients of the estimated regression equation. How would you explain the results to someone in the movie business? Do you think that predictions of total revenue from this regression equation will be very accurate? Why?

36. Continuing Problem 18, suppose that the antique collector believes that the *rate of increase* of the auction price with the age of the item will be driven upward by a large number of bidders. How would you revise the multiple regression equation developed previously to model this feature of the problem?
a. Estimate your revised equation using the data in the file **P10_18.xlsx**.
b. Interpret each of the estimated coefficients in your revised model.
c. Does this revised model fit the given data better than the original multiple regression model? Explain why or why not.

37. Continuing Problem 19, revise the previous multiple regression equation to include an interaction term between the return on average equity (X_1) and annual dividend rate (X_2).
a. Estimate your revised equation using the data provided in the file **P10_19.xlsx**.
b. Interpret each of the estimated coefficients in your revised equation. In particular, how do you interpret the coefficient for the interaction term in the revised equation?
c. Does this revised equation fit the given data better than the original multiple regression equation? Explain why or why not.

38. Continuing Problem 22, suppose that one of the managers of this regional express delivery service company is trying to decide whether to add an interaction term involving the package weight (X_1) and the distance shipped (X_2) in the previous multiple regression equation.
a. Why would the manager want to add such a term to the regression equation?
b. Estimate the revised equation using the data given in the file **P10_22.xlsx**.
c. Interpret each of the estimated coefficients in your revised equation. In particular, how do you interpret the coefficient for the interaction term in the revised equation?
d. Does this revised equation fit the data better than the original multiple regression equation? Explain why or why not.

10.7 VALIDATION OF THE FIT

The fit from a regression analysis is often overly optimistic. When you use the least squares procedure on a given set of data, all of the idiosyncrasies of the particular data set are exploited to obtain the best possible fit. However, there is no guarantee that the fit will be as good when the estimated regression equation is applied to *new* data. In fact, it usually isn't. This is particularly important when the goal is to use the regression equation to predict new values of the dependent variable. The usual situation is that you use a given data set to estimate a regression equation. Then you gather new data on the *explanatory* variables and use these, along with the already-estimated regression equation, to predict the new (but unknown) values of the dependent variable.

> ### FUNDAMENTAL INSIGHT
>
> #### Training and Validation Sets
>
> This practice of *partitioning* a data set into a set for estimation and a set for validation is becoming much more common as larger data sets become available. It allows you to see how a given procedure such as regression works on a data set where you *know* the Ys. If it works well, you have more confidence that it will work well on a new data set where you do *not* know the Ys. This partitioning is a routine part of data mining, the exploration of large data sets. In data mining, the first data set is usually called the *training* set, and the second data set is called the *validation* or *testing* set.

One way to see whether this procedure will be successful is to split the original data set into two subsets: one subset for estimation and one subset for validation. A regression equation is estimated from the first subset. Then the values of explanatory variables from the second subset are substituted into this equation to obtain predicted values for the dependent variable. Finally, these predicted values are compared to the *known* values of the dependent variable in the second subset. If the agreement is good, there is reason to believe that the regression equation will predict well for new data. This procedure is called **validating the fit**.

This validation procedure is fairly simple to perform in Excel. We illustrate it for the Bendrix manufacturing data in Example 10.2. (See the file **Overhead Costs Validation.xlsx**.) There we used 36 monthly observations to regress Overhead on MachHrs and ProdRuns. For convenience, the regression output is repeated in Figure 10.45. In particular, it shows an R^2 value of 86.6% and an s_e value of $4109.

Now suppose that this data set is from one of Bendrix's two plants. The company would like to predict overhead costs for the other plant by using data on machine hours and production runs at the other plant. The first step is to see how well the regression from

Figure 10.45 Multiple Regression Output for Bendrix Example

	A	B	C	D	E	F	G
7		Multiple	R-Square	Adjusted	StErr of		
8	*Summary*	R		R-Square	Estimate		
9		0.9308	0.8664	0.8583	4108.993		
10							
11		Degrees of	Sum of	Mean of	F-Ratio	p-Value	
12	*ANOVA Table*	Freedom	Squares	Squares			
13	Explained	2	3614020661	1807010330	107.0261	< 0.0001	
14	Unexplained	33	557166199.1	16883824.22			
15							
16		Coefficient	Standard	t-Value	p-Value	Confidence Interval 95%	
17	*Regression Table*		Error			Lower	Upper
18	Constant	3996.678	6603.651	0.6052	0.5492	-9438.551	17431.907
19	MachHrs	43.536	3.589	12.1289	< 0.0001	36.234	50.839
20	ProdRuns	883.618	82.251	10.7429	< 0.0001	716.276	1050.960

Figure 10.45 fits data from the other plant. This validation on the 36 months of data is shown in Figure 10.46.

Figure 10.46
Validation of Bendrix Regression Results

	A	B	C	D	E	F
1	Validation data					
2						
3	Coefficients from regression equation (based on original data)					
4		Constant	MachHrs	ProdRuns		
5		3996.6782	43.5364	883.6179		
6						
7	Comparison of summary measures					
8		Original	Validation			
9	R-square	0.8664	0.7733			
10	StErr of Est	4108.99	5256.50			
11						
12	Month	MachHrs	ProdRuns	Overhead	Fitted	Residual
13	1	1374	24	92414	85023	7391
14	2	1510	35	92433	100663	-8230
15	3	1213	21	81907	75362	6545
16	4	1629	27	93451	98775	-5324
17	5	1858	28	112203	109629	2574
18	6	1763	40	112673	116096	-3423
19	7	1449	44	104091	105960	-1869
20	8	1422	46	104354	106552	-2198
45	33	1534	38	104946	104359	587
46	34	1529	29	94325	96189	-1864
47	35	1389	47	98474	105999	-7525
48	36	1350	34	90857	92814	-1957

To obtain the results in this figure, proceed as follows.

PROCEDURE FOR VALIDATING REGRESSION RESULTS

1 Copy old results. Copy the results from the original regression to the ranges B5:D5 and B9:B10.

2 Calculate fitted values and residuals. The fitted values are now the predicted values of overhead for the other plant, based on the original regression equation. Find these by substituting the new values of MachHrs and ProdRuns into the original equation. Specifically, enter the formula

=$B$5+SUMPRODUCT($C$5:$D$5,B13:C13)

in cell E13 and copy it down. Then calculate the residuals (prediction errors for the other plant) by entering the formula

=D13-E13

in cell F13 and copying it down.

3 Calculate summary measures. You can see how well the original equation fits the new data by calculating R^2 and s_e values. Recall that R^2 in general is the square of the correlation between observed and fitted values. Therefore, enter the formula

=CORREL(E13:E48,D13:D48)^2

in cell C9. The *se* value is essentially the average of the squared residuals, but it uses the denominator $n - 3$ (when there are two explanatory variables) rather than $n - 1$. Therefore, enter the formula

=SQRT(SUMSQ((F13:F48)/33)

in cell C10.

Excel's SUMSQ function is often handy. It sums the squares of values in a range.

The results in Figure 10.46 are typical. The validation results are usually not as good as the original results. The value of R^2 has decreased from 86.6% to 77.3%, and the value of s_e has increased from \$4109 to \$5257. Nevertheless, Bendrix might conclude that the original regression equation is adequate for making future predictions at either plant.

10.8 CONCLUSION

In this chapter we have illustrated how to fit an equation to a set of points and how to interpret the resulting equation. We have also discussed two measures, R^2 and s_e, that indicate the goodness of fit of the regression equation. Although the general technique is called *linear* regression, it can be used to estimate nonlinear relationships through suitable transformations of variables. We are not finished with our study of regression, however. In the next chapter we make some statistical assumptions about the regression model and then discuss the types of inferences that can be made from regression output. In particular, we discuss the accuracy of the estimated regression coefficients, the accuracy of predictions made from the regression equation, and the choice of explanatory variables to include in the regression equation.

Summary of Key Terms

Term	Symbol	Explanation	Excel	Page	Equation
Regression analysis		A general method for estimating the relationship between a dependent variable and one or more explanatory variables		531	
Dependent (or response) variable	Y	The variable being estimated or predicted in a regression analysis		532	
Explanatory (or independent) variables	X_1, X_2, and so on	The variables used to explain or predict the dependent variable		532	
Simple regression		A regression model with a single explanatory variable	StatTools/ Regression & Classification/ Regression	532	
Multiple regression		A regression model with any number of explanatory variables	StatTools/ Regression & Classification/ Regression	532	
Correlation	r_{XY}	A measure of the strength of the linear relationship between two variables X and Y	=CORREL (range1, range2), or StatTools/ Summary Statistics/ Correlation and Covariance	540	10.1

(continued)

Term	Symbol	Explanation	Excel	Page	Equation
Fitted value		The predicted value of the dependent variable, found by substituting explanatory values into the regression equation		543	10.2
Residual		The difference between the actual and fitted values of the dependent variable		543	10.2
Least squares line		The regression equation that minimizes the sum of squared residuals	StatTools/ Regression & Classification/ Regression	544	10.3, 10.4
Standard error of estimate	s_e	Essentially, the standard deviation of the residuals; indicates the magnitude of the prediction errors	StatTools/ Regression & Classification/ Regression	549	10.7, 10.11
R-square	R^2	The percentage of variation in the response variable explained by the regression model	StatTools/ Regression & Classification/ Regression	558	10.8
Adjusted R^2		A measure similar to R^2, but adjusted for the number of explanatory variables in the equation		558	
Regression coefficients	b_1, b_2, and so on	The coefficients of the explanatory variables in a regression equation	StatTools/ Regression & Classification/ Regression	554	10.9
Dummy (or indicator) variables		Variables coded as 0 or 1, used to capture categorical variables in a regression analysis	StatTools/ Data Utilities/ Dummy	560	
Interaction variables		Products of explanatory variables, used when the effect of one on the dependent variable depends on the value of the other	StatTools/ Data Utilities/ Interaction	567	
Nonlinear transformations		Variables created to capture nonlinear relationships in a regression model	StatTools/ Data Utilities/ Transform	571	
Quadratic model		A regression model with linear and squared explanatory variables	StatTools/ Regression & Classification/ Regression	573	
Model with logarithmic transformations		A regression model using logarithms of Y and/or Xs	StatTools/ Regression & Classification/ Regression	574	
Constant elasticity (or multiplicative relationship)		A relationship where predicted Y changes by a constant percentage when any X changes by 1%; requires logarithmic transformations	StatTools/ Regression & Classification/ Regression	577	10.21
Learning curve		A particular multiplicative relationship used to indicate how cost or time in production decreases over time	StatTools/ Regression & Classification/ Regression	581	10.22
Validation of fit		Checks how well a regression model based on one sample predicts a related sample	StatTools/ Regression & Classification/ Regression	586	

PROBLEMS

Conceptual Questions

C.1. Consider the relationship between yearly wine consumption (liters of alcohol from drinking wine, per person) and yearly deaths from heart disease (deaths per 100,000 people) in 19 developed countries. Suppose that you read a newspaper article in which the reporter states the following:

Researchers find that the correlation between yearly wine consumption and yearly deaths from heart disease is −0.84. Thus, it is reasonable to conclude that increased consumption of alcohol from wine causes fewer deaths from heart disease in industrialized societies.

Comment on the reporter's interpretation of the correlation in this situation.

C.2. "It is generally appropriate to delete all outliers in a data set that are apparent in a scatterplot." Do you agree with this statement? Explain.

C.3. How would you interpret the relationship between two numeric variables when the estimated least squares regression line for them is essentially *horizontal* (i.e., flat)?

C.4. Suppose that you generate a scatterplot of residuals versus fitted values of the dependent variable for an estimated regression equation. Furthermore, you find the correlation between the residuals and fitted values to be 0.829. Does this provide a good indication that the estimated regression equation is satisfactory? Explain why or why not.

C.5. Suppose that you have generated three alternative multiple regression equations to explain the variation in a particular dependent variable. The regression output for each equation can be summarized as follows:

	Equation 1	Equation 2	Equation 3
No. of Xs	4	6	9
R^2	0.76	0.77	0.79
Adjusted R^2	0.75	0.74	0.73

Which of these equation would you select as "best"? Explain your choice.

C.6. Suppose you want to investigate the relationship between a dependent variable Y and two potential explanatory variables X_1 and X_2. Is the R^2 value for the equation with both X variables included necessarily at least as large as the R^2 value from each equation with only a single X? Explain why or why not. Could the R^2 value for the equation with both X variables included be *larger* than the sum of the R^2 values from the separate equations, each with only a single X included? Is there any intuitive explanation for this?

C.7. Suppose you believe that two variables X and Y are related, but you have no idea which way the causality goes. Does X cause Y or vice versa (or maybe even neither)? Can you tell by regressing Y on X and then regressing X on Y? Explain. Also, provide at least one real example where the direction of causality would be ambiguous.

C.8. Suppose you have two columns of monthly data, one on advertising expenditures and one on sales. If you use this data set, as is, to regress sales on advertising, will it adequately capture the behavior that advertising in one month doesn't really affect sales in *that* month but only in *future* months? What should you do, in terms of regression, to capture this timing effect?

C.9. Suppose you want to predict reading speed using, among other variables, the device the person is reading from. This device could be a regular book, an iPhone, a Kindle, or others. Therefore, you create dummy variables for device. How, exactly, would you do it? If you use regular book as the reference category and another analyst uses, say, Kindle as the reference category, will you get the same regression results? Explain.

C.10. Explain the benefits of using natural logarithms of variables, either of Y or of the Xs, as opposed to other possible nonlinear functions, when scatterplots (or possibly economic considerations) indicate that nonlinearities should be taken into account. Explain exactly how you interpret regression coefficients if logs are taken only of Y, only of the Xs, or of both Y and the Xs.

C.11. The number of cars per 1000 people is known for virtually every country in the world. For many countries, however, per capita income is not known. How might you estimate per capita income for countries where it is unknown?

Level A

39. Many companies manufacture products that are at least partially produced using chemicals (e.g., paint, gasoline, and steel). In many cases, the quality of the finished product is a function of the temperature and pressure at which the chemical reactions take place. Suppose that a particular manufacturer wants to model the quality (Y) of a product as a function of the temperature (X_1) and the pressure (X_2) at which it is produced. The file **P10_39.xlsx** contains data obtained from a carefully designed experiment involving these variables. Note that the assigned quality score can range from a minimum of 0 to a maximum of 100 for each manufactured product.

    a. Estimate a multiple regression equation that includes the two given explanatory variables. Does the estimated equation fit the data well?

    b. Add an interaction term between temperature and pressure and run the regression again. Does the inclusion of the interaction term improve the model's goodness of fit?

    c. Interpret each of the estimated coefficients in the two equations. How are they different? How do you interpret the coefficient for the interaction term in the second equation?

40. A power company located in southern Alabama wants to predict the peak power load (i.e., the maximum amount of power that must be generated each day to meet demand) as a function of the daily high temperature (X). A random sample of 25 summer days is chosen, and the peak power load and the high temperature are recorded each day. The file **P10_40.xlsx** contains these observations.

    a. Create a scatterplot for these data. Comment on the observed relationship between Y and X.

    b. Estimate an appropriate regression equation to predict the peak power load for this power company. Interpret the estimated regression coefficients.

    c. Analyze the estimated equation's residuals. Do they suggest that the regression equation is adequate? If not, return to part **b** and revise your equation. Continue to revise the equation until the results are satisfactory.

    d. Use your final equation to predict the peak power load on a summer day with a high temperature of 100 degrees.

41. Management of a home appliance store would like to understand the growth pattern of the monthly sales of Blu-ray disc players over the past two years. Managers have recorded the relevant data in the file **P10_09.xlsx**.

    a. Create a scatterplot for these data. Comment on the observed behavior of monthly sales at this store over time.

    b. Estimate an appropriate regression equation to explain the variation of monthly sales over the given time period. Interpret the estimated regression coefficients.

    c. Analyze the estimated equation's residuals. Do they suggest that the regression equation is adequate? If not, return to part **b** and revise your equation. Continue to revise the equation until the results are satisfactory.

42. A small computer chip manufacturer wants to forecast monthly operating costs as a function of the number of units produced during a month. The company has collected the 16 months of data in the file **P10_42.xlsx**.

    a. Determine an equation that can be used to predict monthly production costs from units produced. Are there any outliers?

    b. How could the regression line obtained in part **a** be used to determine whether the company was efficient or inefficient during any particular month?

43. The file **P02_07.xlsx** includes data on 204 employees at the (fictional) company Beta Technologies.

    a. Create a recoded version of Education, where 0 or 2 is recoded as 1, 4 is recoded as 2, and 6 or 8 is recoded as 3. Then create dummy variables for these three categories.

    b. Use pivot tables to explore whether average salary depends on gender, and whether it depends on the recoded Education. Then use scatterplots to explore whether salary is related to age, prior experience, and Beta experience. Briefly state your results.

    c. Run a regression of salary versus gender, prior experience, Beta experience, and any two of the education dummies, and interpret the results.

    d. If any of the potential explanatory variables seems to be unrelated to salary, based on the results from part **b**, run one or more regressions without such a variable. Comment on whether it makes much of a difference in the regression outputs.

44. The file **P10_44.xlsx** contains data that relate the unit cost of producing a fuel pressure regulator to the cumulative number of fuel pressure regulators produced at an automobile production plant. For example, the 4000th unit cost \$13.70 to produce.

    a. Fit a learning curve to these data.

    b. You would predict that doubling cumulative production reduces the cost of producing a regulator by what amount?

45. The *beta* of a stock is found by running a regression with the monthly return on a market index as the explanatory variable and the monthly return on the stock as the dependent variable. The beta of the stock is then the slope of this regression line.

    a. Explain why most stocks have a positive beta.

    b. Explain why a stock with a beta with absolute value greater than one is more volatile than the market index and a stock with a beta less than one (in absolute value) is less volatile than the market index.

    c. Use the data in the file **P10_45.xlsx** to estimate the beta for each of the four companies listed: Caterpillar, Goodyear, McDonalds, and Ford. Use the S&P 500 as the market index.

    d. For each of these companies, what percentage of the variation in its returns is explained by the variation in the market index? What percentage is unexplained by variation in the market index?

e. Verify (using Excel's COVAR and VARP functions) that the beta for each company is given by

$$\frac{\text{Covariance between Company and Market}}{\text{Variance of Market}}$$

Also, verify that the correlation between each company's returns and the market's returns is the square root of R^2.

46. Continuing the previous problem, explore whether the beta for these companies changes through time. For example, are the betas based on 1990s data different from those based on 2000s data? Or are data based on only five years of data different from those based on longer time periods?

47. The file **Catalog Marketing.xlsx** contains recent data on 1000 HyTex customers. (This is the same data set used in Example 2.7 in Chapter 2.)

a. Create a pivot table of average amount spent versus the number of catalogs sent. Is there any evidence that these two variables are related? Would it make sense to enter Catalogs, as is, in a regression equation for AmountSpent, or should dummies be used? Explain.

b. Create a pivot table of average amount spent versus History. Is there any evidence that these two variables are related? Would it make sense to enter History, as is, in a regression equation for AmountSpent, or should dummies be used? Explain.

c. Answer part **b** with History replaced by Age.

d. Base on your results from parts **a** through **c**, estimate an appropriate regression equation for AmountSpent, using the appropriate forms for Catalogs, History, and Age, plus the variables Gender, OwnHome, Married, and Close. Interpret this equation and comment on its usefulness in predicting AmountSpent.

48. The file **P10_48.xlsx** contains monthly sales and price of a popular candy bar.

a. Describe the type of relationship between price and sales (linear/nonlinear, strong/weak).

b. What percentage of variation in monthly sales is explained by variation in price? What percentage is unexplained?

c. If the price of the candy bar is $1.05, predict monthly candy bar sales.

d. Use the regression output to determine the correlation between price and candy bar sales.

e. Are there any outliers?

49. The file **P10_49.xlsx** contains the amount of money spent advertising a product and the number of units sold for eight months.

a. Assume that the only factor influencing monthly sales is advertising. Fit the following three curves to these data: linear ($Y = a + bX$), exponential ($Y = ab^X$), and multiplicative ($Y = aX^b$). Which equation fits the data best?

b. Interpret the best-fitting equation.

c. Using the best-fitting equation, predict sales during a month in which $60,000 is spent on advertising.

50. A golf club manufacturer is trying to determine how the price of a set of clubs affects the demand for clubs. The file **P10_50.xlsx** contains the price of a set of clubs and the monthly sales.

a. Assume the only factor influencing monthly sales is price. Fit the following three curves to these data: linear ($Y = a + bX$), exponential ($Y = ab^X$), and multiplicative ($Y = aX^b$). Which equation fits the data best?

b. Interpret your best-fitting equation.

c. Using the best-fitting equation, predict sales during a month in which the price is $470.

51. The file **P03_55.xlsx** lists the average salary for each Major League Baseball (MLB) team from 2004 to 2009, along with the number of team wins in each of these years.

a. Rearrange the data so that there are four long columns: Team, Year, Salary, and Wins. There should be 6*30 values for each.

b. Create a scatterplot of Wins (Y) versus Salary (X). Is there any indication of a relationship between these two variables? Is it a linear relationship?

c. Run a regression of Wins versus Salary. What does it say, if anything, about teams buying their way to success?

52. Repeat the previous problem with the basketball data in the file **P03_56.xlsx**. (Now there will be 5*30 rows in the rearranged data set.)

53. Repeat Problem 51 with the football data in the file **P03_57.xlsx**. (Now there will be 8*32 rows in the rearranged data set.)

54. The Baker Company wants to develop a budget to predict how overhead costs vary with activity levels. Management is trying to decide whether direct labor hours (DLH) or units produced is the better measure of activity for the firm. Monthly data for the preceding 24 months appear in the file **P10_54.xlsx**. Use regression analysis to determine which measure, DLH or Units (or both), should be used for the budget. How would the regression equation be used to obtain the budget for the firm's overhead costs?

55. The auditor of Kiely Manufacturing is concerned about the number and magnitude of year-end adjustments that are made annually when the financial statements of Kiely Manufacturing are prepared. Specifically, the auditor suspects that the management of Kiely

Manufacturing is using discretionary write-offs to manipulate the reported net income. To check this, the auditor has collected data from 25 companies that are similar to Kiely Manufacturing in terms of manufacturing facilities and product lines. The cumulative reported third-quarter income and the final net income reported are listed in the file **P10_55.xlsx** for each of these 25 companies. If Kiely Manufacturing reports a cumulative third-quarter income of $2,500,000 and a preliminary net income of $4,900,000, should the auditor conclude that the relationship between cumulative third-quarter income and the annual income for Kiely Manufacturing differs from that of the 25 companies in this sample? Explain why or why not.

56. The file **P10_56.xlsx** contains some interesting data on the U.S. presidential elections from 1880 through 2008. The variable definitions are on the Source sheet. The question is whether the Vote variable can be predicted very well from the other variables.
    a. Create pivot tables and/or scatterplots to check whether Vote appears to be related to the other variables. Comment on the results.
    b. Run a regression of Vote versus the other variables (not including Year). Do the coefficients go in the direction (positive or negative) you would expect? If you were going to use the regression equation to predict Vote for the 2012 election and you had the relevant data for the explanatory variables for 2012, how accurate do you think your prediction would be?

Level B

57. We stated in the beginning of the chapter that regression can be used to understand the way the world works. That is, you can look at the regression coefficients (their signs and magnitudes) to see the effects of the explanatory variables on the dependent variable. However, is it possible that apparently small changes in the data can lead to very different-looking equations? The file **P10_57.xlsx** lets you explore this question. Columns K–R contain data on over 100 (fictional) homes that were recently sold. The regression equation for this original data set is given in the range T15:U21. (It was found with StatTools in the usual way.) Columns C–I contain slight changes to the original data, with the amount of change determined by the adjustable parameters in row 2. (Look at the formulas in columns C–I to see how the original data have been changed randomly.) The regression equation for the changed data appears in the range T6:U12. It has been calculated through special matrix functions (not StatTools), so that it changes automatically when the random data change. (These require the 1s in column B.) Experiment by pressing the F9 key or changing the adjustable parameters to see how much the two regression equations can differ.

After experimenting, briefly explain how you think housing pricing works—or can you tell?

58. The file **P02_35.xlsx** contains data from a survey of 500 randomly selected households. For this problem, use Monthly Payment as the dependent variable in several regressions, as explained below.
    a. Beginning with Family Size, iteratively add one explanatory variable and estimate the resulting regression equation to explain the variation in Monthly Payment. If adding any explanatory variable causes the *adjusted R^2* measure to fall, do not include that variable in subsequent versions of the regression model. Otherwise, include the variable and consider adding the next variable in the set. Which variables are included in the final version of your regression model? (Add dummies for Location in a single step, and use Total Income rather than First Income and Second Income separately.)
    b. Interpret the final estimated regression equation you obtained through the process outlined in part **a**. Also, interpret the standard error of estimate s_e, R^2, and the adjusted R^2 for the final estimated model.

59. (This problem is based on an actual court case in Philadelphia.) In the 1994 congressional election, the Republican candidate outpolled the Democratic candidate by 400 votes (excluding absentee ballots). The Democratic candidate outpolled the Republican candidate by 500 absentee votes. The Republican candidate sued (and won), claiming that vote fraud must have played a role in the absentee ballot count. The Republican's lawyer ran a regression to predict (based on past elections) how the absentee ballot margin could be predicted from the votes tabulated on voting machines. Selected results are given in the file **P10_59.xlsx**. Show how this regression could be used by the Republican to "prove" his claim of vote fraud.

60. In the world of computer science, Moore's law is famous. Although there are various versions of this law, they all say something to the effect that computing power *doubles* every two years. Several researchers estimated this law with regression using real data in 2006. Their paper can be found online at http://download.intel.com/pressroom/pdf/computer trendsrelease.pdf. For example, one interesting chart appears on page S1, backed up with regression results on another page. What exactly do these results say about doubling every two years (or do they contradict Moore's law)?

61. (The data for this problem are fictitious, but they are not far off.) For each of the top 25 business schools, the file **P10_61.xlsx** contains the average salary of a professor. Thus, for Indiana University (number 15 in the rankings), the average salary is $46,000. Use this information and regression to show that IU is doing a great job with its available resources.

62. Suppose the correlation between the average height of parents and the height of their firstborn male child is 0.5. You are also told that:

- The average height of all parents is 66 inches.
- The standard deviation of the average height of parents is 4 inches.
- The average height of all male children is 70 inches.
- The standard deviation of the height of all male children is 4 inches.

If a mother and father are 73 and 80 inches tall, respectively, how tall do you predict their son to be? Explain why this is called "regression toward the mean."

63. Do increased taxes increase or decrease economic growth? The file **P10_63.xlsx** lists tax revenues as a percentage of gross domestic product (GDP) and the average annual percentage growth in GDP per capita for nine countries during the years 1970 through 1994. Do these data support or contradict the dictum of supply-side economics?

64. For each of the four data sets in the file **P10_64.xlsx**, calculate the least squares line. For which of these data sets would you feel comfortable in using the least squares line to predict Y?

65. Suppose you run a regression on a data set of Xs and Ys and obtain a least squares line of $Y = 12 - 3X$.
   a. If you double each value of X, what is the new least squares line?
   b. If you triple each value of Y, what is the new least squares line?
   c. If you add 6 to each value of X, what is the new least squares line?
   d. If you subtract 4 from each value of Y, what is the new least squares line?

66. The file **P10_66.xlsx** contains monthly cost accounting data on overhead costs, machine hours, and direct material costs. This problem will help you explore the meaning of R^2 and the relationship between R^2 and correlations.
   a. Create a table of correlations between the individual variables.
   b. If you ignore the two explanatory variables Machine Hours and Direct Material Cost and predict each Overhead Cost as the *mean* of Overhead Cost, then a typical "error" is Overhead Cost minus the mean of Overhead Cost. Find the sum of squared errors using this form of prediction, where the sum is over all observations.
   c. Now run three regressions: (1) Overhead Cost (OHCost) versus Machine Hours, (2) OHCost versus Direct Material Cost, and (3) OHCost versus both Machine Hours and Direct Material Cost. (The first two are simple regressions, the third is a multiple regression.) For each, find the sum of squared residuals, and divide this by

the sum of squared errors from part **b**. What is the relationship between this ratio and the associated R^2 for that equation? (Now do you see why R^2 is referred to as the percentage of variation explained?)
   d. For the first two regressions in part **c**, what is the relationship between R^2 and the corresponding correlation between the dependent and explanatory variable? For the third regression it turns out that the R^2 can be expressed as a complicated function of all three correlations in part **a**. That is, the function involves not just the correlations between the dependent variable and each explanatory variable, but also the correlation between the explanatory variables. Note that this R^2 is not just the sum of the R^2 values from the first two regressions in part **c**. Why do you think this is true, intuitively? However, R^2 for the multiple regression is still the square of a correlation—namely, the correlation between the observed and predicted values of OHCost. Verify that this is the case for these data.

67. The file **P10_67.xlsx** contains hypothetical starting salaries for MBA students directly after graduation. The file also lists their years of experience prior to the MBA program and their class rank in the MBA program (on a 0–100 scale).
   a. Estimate the regression equation with Salary as the dependent variable and Experience and Class Rank as the explanatory variables. What does this equation imply? What does the standard error of estimate s_e tell you? What about R^2?
   b. Repeat part **a**, but now include the interaction term Experience*Class Rank (the product) in the equation as well as Experience and Class Rank individually. Answer the same questions as in part **a**. What evidence is there that this extra variable (the interaction variable) is worth including? How do you interpret this regression equation? Why might you expect the interaction to be present in real data of this type?

68. In a study published in 1985 in *Business Horizons*, Platt and McCarthy employed multiple regression analysis to explain variations in compensation among the CEOs of large companies. (Although the data set is old, we suspect the results would be similar with more current data.) Their primary objective was to discover whether levels of compensations are affected more by short-run considerations—"I'll earn more now if my company does well in the short run"—or long-run considerations—"My best method for obtaining high compensation is to stay with my company for a long time." The study used as its dependent variable the total compensation for each of the 100 highest paid CEOs in 1981. This variable was defined as the sum of salary, bonuses, and other benefits (measured in

$1000s). The following potential explanatory variables were considered. To capture short-run effects, the average of the company's previous five years' percentage changes in earnings per share (EPS) and the projected percentage change in next year's EPS were used. To capture the long-run effect, age and years as CEO, two admittedly correlated variables, were used. Dummy variables for the CEO's background (finance, marketing, and so on) were also considered. Finally, the researchers considered several nonlinear and interaction terms based on these variables. The best-fitting equation was the following:

$$\text{Total Compensation} = -3493 + 898.7 * \text{Years as CEO}$$
$$+ 9.28 * (\text{Years as CEO})^2 - 17.19 * \text{Years as CEO} * \text{Age}$$
$$+ 88.27 * \text{Age} + 867.4 * \text{Finance}$$

(The last variable is a dummy variable, equal to 1 if the CEO had a finance background, 0 otherwise.) The corresponding R^2 was 19.4%.

a. Explain what this equation implies about CEO compensations.

b. The researchers drew the following conclusions. First, it appears that CEOs should indeed concentrate on long-run considerations—namely, those that keep them on their jobs the longest. Second, the absence of the short-run company-related variables from the equations helps to confirm the conjecture that CEOs who concentrate on earning the quick buck for their companies may not be acting in their best self-interest. Finally, the positive coefficient of the dummy variable may imply that financial people possess skills that are vitally important, and firms therefore outbid one another for the best financial talent. Based on the data given, do you agree with these conclusions?

c. Consider a CEO (other than those in the study) who has been in his position for 10 years and has a financial background. Predict his total yearly compensation (in $1000s) if he is 50 years old and then if he is 55 years old. Explain why the difference between these two predictions is not 5(88.27), where 88.27 is the coefficient of the Age variable.

69. The Wilhoit Company has observed that there is a linear relationship between indirect labor expense and direct labor hours. Data for direct labor hours and indirect labor expense for 18 months are given in the file **P10_69.xlsx**. At the start of month 7, all cost categories in the Wilhoit Company increased by 10%, and they stayed at this level for months 7 through 12. Then at the start of month 13, another 10% across-the-board increase in all costs occurred, and the company operated at this price level for months 13 through 18.

a. Plot the data. Verify that the relationship between indirect labor expense and direct labor hours is approximately linear within each six-month period. Use regression (three times) to estimate the slope and intercept during months 1 through 6, during months 7 through 12, and during months 13 through 18.

b. Use regression to fit a straight line to all 18 data points simultaneously. What values of the slope and intercept do you obtain?

c. Perform a price level adjustment to the data and re-estimate the slope and intercept using all 18 data points. Assuming no cost increases for month 19, what is your prediction for indirect labor expense if there are 35,000 direct labor hours in month 19?

d. Interpret your results. What causes the difference in the linear relationship estimated in parts **b** and **c**?

70. The Bohring Company manufactures a sophisticated radar unit that is used in a fighter aircraft built by Seaways Aircraft. The first 50 units of the radar unit have been completed, and Bohring is preparing to submit a proposal to Seaways Aircraft to manufacture the next 50 units. Bohring wants to submit a competitive bid, but at the same time, it wants to ensure that all the costs of manufacturing the radar unit are fully covered. As part of this process, Bohring is attempting to develop a standard for the number of labor hours required to manufacture each radar unit. Developing a labor standard has been a continuing problem in the past. The file **P10_70.xlsx** lists the number of labor hours required for each of the first 50 units of production. Bohring accountants want to see whether regression analysis, together with the concept of learning curves, can help solve the company's problem.

The Firm Chair Company manufactures customized wood furniture and sells the furniture in large quantities to major furniture retailers. Jim Bolling has recently been assigned to analyze the company's pricing policy. He has been told that quantity discounts were usually given. For example, for one type of chair, the pricing changed at quantities of 200 and 400—that is, these were the price breaks, where the marginal cost of the next chair changed. For this type of chair, the file **Firm Chair.xlsx** contains the quantity and total price to the customer for 81 orders. Use regression to help Jim discover the pricing structure that Firm Chair evidently used. (*Note*: A linear regression of TotPrice versus Quantity will give you a "decent" fit, but you can do much better by introducing appropriate variables into the regression.) ■

Sales of single-family houses have been brisk in Mid City this year. This has especially been true in older, more established neighborhoods, where housing is relatively inexpensive compared to the new homes being built in the newer neighborhoods. Nevertheless, there are also many families who are willing to pay a higher price for the prestige of living in one of the newer neighborhoods. The file **Mid City.xlsx** contains data on 128 recent sales in Mid City. For each sale, the file shows the neighborhood (1, 2, or 3) in which the house is located, the number of offers made on the house, the square footage, whether the house is made primarily of brick, the number of bathrooms, the number of bedrooms, and the selling price. Neighborhoods 1 and 2 are more traditional neighborhoods, whereas neighborhood 3 is a newer, more prestigious neighborhood.

Use regression to estimate and interpret the pricing structure of houses in Mid City. Here are some considerations.

1. Do buyers pay a premium for a brick house, all else being equal?

2. Is there a premium for a house in neighborhood 3, all else being equal?

3. Is there an *extra* premium for a brick house in neighborhood 3, in addition to the usual premium for a brick house?

4. For purposes of estimation and prediction, could neighborhoods 1 and 2 be collapsed into a single "older" neighborhood? ∎

Howie's Bakery is one of the most popular bakeries in town, and the favorite at Howie's is French bread. Each day of the week, Howie's bakes a number of loaves of French bread, more or less according to a daily schedule. To maintain its fine reputation, Howie's gives away to charity any loaves not sold on the day they are baked. Although this occurs frequently, it is also common for Howie's to run out of French bread on any given day—more demand than supply. In this case, no extra loaves are baked that day; the customers have to go elsewhere (or come back to Howie's the next day) for their French bread. Although French bread at Howie's is always popular, Howie's stimulates demand by running occasional 10% off sales.

Howie's has collected data for 20 consecutive weeks, 140 days in all. These data are listed in the file **Howies Bakery.xlsx**. The variables are Day (Monday–Sunday), Supply (number of loaves baked that day), OnSale (whether French bread is on sale that day), and Demand (loaves actually sold that day). Howie's would like you to see whether regression can be used successfully to estimate Demand from the other data in the file. Howie reasons that if these other variables can be used to predict Demand, then he might be able to determine his daily supply (number of loaves to bake) in a more cost-effective way.

How successful is regression with these data? Is Howie correct that regression can help him determine his daily supply? Is any information missing that would be useful? How would you obtain it? How would you use it? Is this extra information *really* necessary? ■

CASE 10.4 INVESTING FOR RETIREMENT

Financial advisors offer many types of advice to customers, but they generally agree that one of the best things people can do is invest as much as possible in tax-deferred retirement plans. Not only are the earnings from these investments exempt from income tax (until retirement), but the investment itself is tax-exempt. This means that if a person invests, say, $10,000 of his $100,000 income in a tax-deferred retirement plan, he pays income tax that year on only $90,000 of his income. This is probably the best method available to most people for avoiding tax payments. However, which group takes advantage of this attractive investment opportunity: everyone, people with low salaries, people with high salaries, or who?

The file **Retirement Plan.xlsx** lets you investigate this question. It contains data on 194 (hypothetical) couples: number of dependent children, combined annual salary of husband and wife, current mortgage on home, average amount of other (non-mortgage) debt, and percentage of combined income invested in tax-deferred retirement plans (assumed to be limited to 15%, which is realistic). Using correlations, scatterplots, and regression analysis, what can you conclude about the tendency of this group of people to invest in tax-deferred retirement plans? ■

© Davecox78/Dreamstime.com

PREDICTING MOVIE REVENUES

In the opener for Chapter 3, we discussed the article by Simonoff and
Sparrow (2000) that examined movie revenues for 311 movies released
in 1998 and late 1997. We saw that movie revenues were related to several
variables, including genre, Motion Picture Association of America (MPAA)
rating, country of origin, number of stars in the cast, whether the movie was
a sequel, and whether the movie was released during a few choice times.
In Chapter 3, we were limited to looking at summary measures and charts
of the data. Now that we are studying regression, we can look further into
the analysis performed by Simonoff and Sparrow. Specifically, they examined
whether these variables, plus others, are effective in predicting movie
revenues.

The authors report the results from three multiple regression models.
All of these used the logarithm of the total U.S. gross revenue from the film
as the dependent variable. (They used the *logarithm* because the distribution
of gross revenues is very positively skewed.) The first model used only the

prerelease variables listed in the previous paragraph. The values of these variables were all known prior to the movie's release. Therefore, the purpose of this model was to see how well revenues could be predicted *before* the movie was released.

The second model used the variables from model 1, along with two variables that could be observed after the first week of the movie's release: the first weekend gross and the number of screens the movie opened on. (Actually, the logarithms of these latter two variables were used, again because of positive skewness. Also, the authors found it necessary to run two separate regressions at this stage—one for movies that opened on 10 or fewer screens, and another for movies that opened on more than 10 screens.) The idea here was that the success or failure of many movies depends to a large extent on how they do right after they are released. Therefore, it was expected that this information would add significantly to the predictive power of the regression model.

The third model built on the second by adding an additional explanatory variable: the number of Oscar nominations the movie received for key awards (Best Picture, Best Director, Best Actor, Best Actress, Best Supporting Actor, and Best Supporting Actress). This information is often not known until well after a movie's release, but it was hypothesized that Oscar nominations would lead to a significant increase in a movie's revenues, and that a regression model with this information could lead to very different predictions of revenue.

Simonoff and Sparrow found that the coefficients of the first regression model were in line with the box plots shown earlier in Figure 3.1 of Chapter 3. For example, the variables that measured the number of star actors and actresses were both positive and significant, indicating that star power tends to lead to larger revenues. However, the predictive power of this model was poor. Given its standard error of prediction (and taking into account that the *logarithm* of revenue was the dependent variable), the authors stated that "the predictions of total grosses for an individual movie can be expected to be off by as much as a multiplicative factor of 100 high or low." It appears that there is no way to predict which movies will succeed and which will fail based on prerelease data only.

The second model added considerable predictive power. The regression equations indicated that gross revenue is positively related to first weekend gross and negatively related to the number of opening screens, both of these variables being significant. As for prediction, the factor of 100 mentioned in the previous paragraph decreased to a factor of 10 (for movies with 10 or fewer opening screens) or 2 (for movies with more than 10 opening screens). This is still not perfect—predictions of total revenue made after the movie's first weekend can still be pretty far off—but this additional information about initial success certainly helps.

The third model added only slightly to the predictive power, primarily because so few of the movies (10 out of 311) received Oscar nominations for key awards. However, the predictions for those that did receive nominations increased considerably. For example, the prediction for the multiple Oscar nominee *Saving Private Ryan,* based on the second model, was 194.622 (millions of dollars). Its prediction based on the third model increased to a whopping 358.237. (Interestingly, the prediction for this movie from the first model was only 14.791, and its actual gross revenue was 216.119. Perhaps the reason *Saving Private Ryan* did not make as much as the third model predicted was that the Oscar nominations were announced about nine months after its release—too long after release to do much good.)

Simonoff and Sparrow then used their third model to predict gross revenues for 24 movies released in 1999—movies that were not in the data set used to estimate the regression model. They found that 21 out of 24 of the resulting 95% prediction intervals captured the actual gross revenues, which is about what would be expected. However, many of these prediction intervals were extremely wide, and several of the predictions were well above or below the actual revenues. The authors conclude by quoting Tim Noonan, a former movie executive: "Since predicting gross is extremely difficult, you have to serve up a [yearly] slate of movies and know that over time you'll have 3 or 4 to the left and 2 or 3 to the right. You must make sure you are doing things that mitigate your downside risk." ∎

11.1 INTRODUCTION

In the previous chapter you learned how to fit a regression equation to a set of points by using the least squares method. The purpose of this regression equation is to provide a good fit to the points in the sample so that you can understand the relationship between a dependent variable and one or more explanatory variables. The entire emphasis of the discussion in the previous chapter was on finding a regression model that fits the observations in the sample. In this chapter we take a slightly different point of view: We assume that the observations in the sample are taken from some larger population. For example, the sample of 50 regions from the Pharmex drugstore example could represent a sample of all the regions where Pharmex does business. In this case, we might be interested in the relationship between variables in the entire population, not just in the sample.

There are two basic problems we discuss in this chapter. The first has to do with a *population regression model*. We want to infer its characteristics—that is, its intercept and slope term(s)—from the corresponding terms estimated by least squares. We also want to know which explanatory variables belong in the equation. There are typically a large number of *potential* explanatory variables, and it is often not clear which of these do the best job of explaining variation in the dependent variable. In addition, we would like to infer whether there is any population regression equation worth pursuing. It is possible that the potential explanatory variables provide very little explanation of the dependent variable.

The second problem we discuss in this chapter is *prediction*. We touched on the prediction problem in the previous chapter, primarily in the context of predicting the dependent variable for part of the sample held out for validation purposes. In reality, we had the values of the dependent variable for that part of the sample, so prediction was not really necessary. Now we go beyond the sample and predict values of the dependent variable for *new* observations. There is no way to check the accuracy of these predictions, at least not right away, because the true values of the dependent variable are not yet known. However, it is possible to calculate prediction intervals to measure the accuracy of the predictions.

11.2 THE STATISTICAL MODEL

To perform statistical inference in a regression context, you must first make several assumptions about the population. Throughout the analysis these assumptions remain exactly that—they are only assumptions, not facts. These assumptions represent an idealization of reality, and as such, they are never likely to be entirely satisfied for the population in any real study. From a practical point of view, all you can ask is that they represent a close approximation to reality. If this is the case, then the analysis in this chapter is valid. But if the assumptions are grossly violated, statistical inferences that are based on these assumptions should be viewed with suspicion. Although you can never be entirely certain of the validity of the assumptions, there are ways to check for gross violations, and we discuss some of these.

Regression Assumptions

1. There is a population regression line. It joins the *means* of the dependent variable for all values of the explanatory variables. For any fixed values of the explanatory variables, the mean of the errors is zero.

2. For any values of the explanatory variables, the variance (or standard deviation) of the dependent variable is a constant, the same for all such values.

3. For any values of the explanatory variables, the dependent variable is normally distributed.

4. The errors are probabilistically independent.

Because these assumptions are so crucial to the regression analysis that follows, it is important to understand exactly what they mean. Assumption 1 is probably the most important. It implies that for some set of explanatory variables, there is an exact linear relationship in the population between the *means* of the dependent variable and the values of the explanatory variables.

These explanatory variables could be original variables or variables you create, such as dummies, interactions, or nonlinear transformations.

To be more specific, let Y be the dependent variable, and assume that there are k explanatory variables, X_1 through X_k. Let $\mu_{Y|X_1,\ldots,X_k}$ be the mean of all Ys for any fixed values of the Xs. Then assumption 1 implies that there is an exact linear relationship between the mean $\mu_{Y|X_1,\ldots,X_k}$ and the Xs. That is, it implies that there are coefficients α and β_1 through β_k such that the following equation holds for all values of the Xs:

Population Regression Line Joining Means

$$\mu_{Y|X_1,\ldots,X_k} = \alpha + \beta_1 X_1 + \cdots + \beta_k X_k \qquad \textbf{(11.1)}$$

We commonly use Greek letters to denote population parameters and regular letters for their sample estimates.

In the terminology of the previous chapter, α is the intercept term, and β_1 through β_k are the slope terms. We use Greek letters for these coefficients to denote that they are *unobservable* population parameters. Assumption 1 implies the existence of a population regression equation and the corresponding α and βs. However, it tells us nothing about the *values* of these parameters. They still need to be estimated from sample data, using the least squares method to do so.

Equation (11.1) says that the *means* of the Ys lie on the population regression line. However, it is clear from a scatterplot that most *individual* Ys do not lie on this line. The vertical distance from any point to the line is called an **error**. The error for any point, labeled ε, is the difference between Y and $\mu_{Y|X_1,\ldots,X_k}$, that is,

$$Y = \mu_{Y|X_1,\ldots,X_k} + \varepsilon$$

By substituting the assumed linear form for $\mu_{Y|X_1,\ldots,X_k}$, we obtain Equation (11.2). This equation states that each value of Y is equal to a fitted part plus an error. The fitted part is the linear expression $\alpha + \beta_1 X_1 + \cdots + \beta_k X_k$. The error ε is sometimes positive, in which case the point is above the regression line, and sometimes negative, in which case the point is below the regression line. The last part of assumption 1 states that these errors average to zero in the population, so that the positive errors cancel the negative errors.

Population Regression Line with Error

$$Y = \alpha + \beta_1 X_1 + \cdots + \beta_k X_k + \varepsilon \qquad \textbf{(11.2)}$$

Note that an error ε is not quite the same as a residual e. An error is the vertical distance from a point to the (unobservable) population regression line. A residual is the vertical distance from a point to the *estimated* regression line. Residuals can be calculated from observed data; errors cannot.

Assumption 2 concerns variation around the population regression line. Specifically, it states that the variation of the Ys about the regression line is the *same,* regardless of the values of the Xs. A technical term for this property is **homoscedasticity**. A simpler term is **constant error variance**. In the Pharmex example (Example 11.1), constant error variance implies that the variation in Sales values is the same regardless of the value of Promote. As another example, recall the Bendrix manufacturing example (Example 11.2). There we related overhead costs (Overhead) to the number of machine hours (MachHrs) and the number of production runs (ProdRuns). Constant error variance implies that overhead costs vary just as much for small values of MachHrs and ProdRuns as for large values—or any values in between.

There are many situations where assumption 2 is questionable. The variation in Y often increases as X increases—a violation of assumption 2. We presented an example of this in Figure 10.10 (repeated here in Figure 11.1), which is based on customer spending at a mail-order company. This scatterplot shows the amount spent versus salary for a sample of the company's customers. Clearly, the variation in the amount spent increases as salary increases, which makes intuitive sense. Customers with small salaries have little disposable income, so they all tend to spend small amounts for mail-order items. Customers with large salaries have more disposable income. Some of them spend a lot of it on mail-order items and some spend only a little of it—hence, a larger variation. Scatterplots with this "fan" shape are not at all uncommon in real studies, and they exhibit a clear violation of assumption 2.[1] We say that the data in this graph exhibit **heteroscedasticity**, or more simply, **nonconstant error variance**. These terms are summarized in the following box.

Homoscedasticity means that the variability of Y values is the same for all X values.

Heteroscedasticity means that the variability of Y values is larger for some X values than for others.

Figure 11.1

Illustration of Nonconstant Error Variance

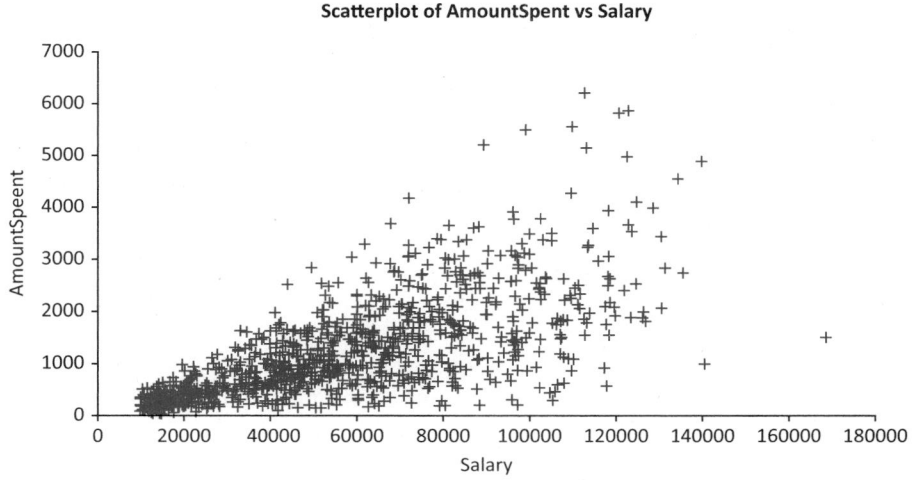

Scatterplot of AmountSpent vs Salary

---

[1]The fan shape in Figure 11.1 is probably the most common form of nonconstant error variance, but it is not the only possible form.

The easiest way to detect nonconstant error variance is through a visual inspection of a scatterplot. You create a scatterplot of the dependent variable versus an explanatory variable X and see whether the points vary more for some values of X than for others. You can also examine the residuals with a residual plot, where residual values are on the vertical axis and some other variable (Y or one of the Xs) is on the horizontal axis. If the residual plot exhibits a fan shape or other evidence of nonconstant error variance, this also indicates a violation of assumption 2.

Assumption 3 is equivalent to stating that the errors are normally distributed. You can check this by forming a histogram (or a Q-Q plot) of the residuals. If assumption 3 holds, the histogram should be approximately symmetric and bell-shaped, and the points in the Q-Q plot should be close to a 45° line.[2] But if there is an obvious skewness, too many residuals more than, say, two standard deviations from the mean, or some other nonnormal property, this indicates a violation of assumption 3.

Finally, assumption 4 requires probabilistic independence of the errors. Intuitively, this assumption means that information on some of the errors provides no information on the values of other errors. For example, if you are told that the overhead costs for months 1 through 4 are all above the regression line (positive residuals), you cannot infer anything about the residual for month 5 if assumption 4 holds.

Assumption 4 (independence of residuals) is usually in doubt only for time series data.

For cross-sectional data there is generally little reason to doubt the validity of assumption 4 unless the observations are ordered in some particular way. For cross-sectional data assumption 4 is usually taken for granted. However, for time series data, assumption 4 is often violated. This is because of a property called *autocorrelation.* For now, we simply mention that one output given automatically in many regression packages is the *Durbin–Watson statistic.* The Durbin–Watson statistic is one measure of autocorrelation and thus it measures the extent to which assumption 4 is violated. We briefly discuss this Durbin–Watson statistic toward the end of this chapter and in the next chapter.

One other assumption is important for numerical calculations. No explanatory variable can be an *exact* linear combination of any other explanatory variables. Another way of stating this is that there should be no exact linear relationship between any set of explanatory variables. This would be violated, for example, if one variable were an exact multiple of another, or if one variable were equal to the sum of several other variables. More generally, the violation occurs if one of the explanatory variables can be written as a weighted sum of several of the others. This is called *exact multicollinearity.*

Exact multicollinearity means that at least one of the explanatory variables is redundant and is not needed in the regression equation.

If exact multicollinearity exists, it means that there is *redundancy* in the data. One of the Xs could be eliminated without any loss of information. Here is a simple example. Suppose that MachHrs1 is machine hours measured in hours, and MachHrs2 is machine hours measured in *hundreds* of hours. Then it is clear that these two variables contain exactly the same information, and either of them could (and should) be eliminated.

As another example, suppose that Ad1, Ad2, and Ad3 are the amounts spent on radio ads, television ads, and newspaper ads. Also, suppose that TotalAd is the amount spent on radio, television, and newspaper ads combined. Then there is an exact linear relationship among these variables:

$$\text{TotalAd} = \text{Ad1} + \text{Ad2} + \text{Ad3}$$

In this case there is no need to include TotalAd in the analysis because it contains no information that is not already contained in the variables Ad1, Ad2, and Ad3. Therefore, TotalAd should be eliminated from the analysis.

---

[2]A Q-Q (quantile-quantile) plot is used to detect nonnormality. It is available in StatTools from the Normality Tests dropdown list. Nonnormal data often produce a Q-Q plot that is close to a 45° line in the middle of the plot but deviates from this line in one or both of the tails.

StatTools Tip *StatTools issues a warning if it detects an exact linear relationship between explanatory variables in a regression model.*

Generally, it is fairly simple to spot an exact linear relationship such as these, and then to eliminate it by excluding the redundant variable from the analysis. However, if you do *not* spot the relationship and try to run the regression analysis with the redundant variable included, regression packages will typically respond with an error message. If the package interrupts the analysis with an error message containing the words "exact multicollinearity" or "linear dependence," you should look for a redundant explanatory variable. The message from StatTools in this case is shown in Figure 11.2. We got it by deliberately entering dummy variables from *each* category of a categorical variable—something we have warned you *not* to do.

Figure 11.2
Error Message from StatTools Indicating Exact Multicollinearity

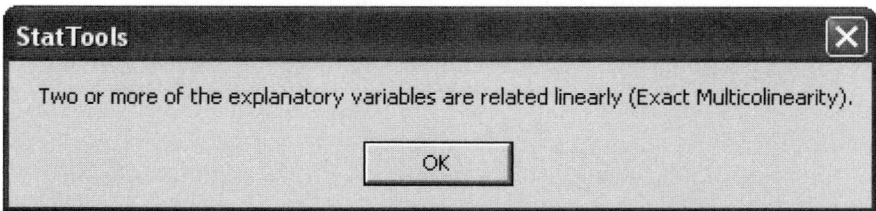

Although this problem can be a nuisance, it is usually caused by an oversight and can be fixed easily by eliminating a redundant variable. A more common and serious problem is *multicollinearity*, where explanatory variables are highly, but not exactly, correlated. A typical example is an employee's years of experience and age. Although these two variables are not equal for all employees, they are likely to be highly correlated. If they are both included as explanatory variables in a regression analysis, the software will not issue any error messages, but the estimates it produces can be unreliable and difficult to interpret. We will discuss multicollinearity in more detail later in this chapter.

11.3 INFERENCES ABOUT THE REGRESSION COEFFICIENTS

In this section we explain how to make inferences about the population regression coefficients from sample data. We begin by making the assumptions discussed in the previous section. In particular, the first assumption states that there is a population regression line. Equation (11.2) for this line is repeated here:

$$Y = \alpha + \beta_1 X_1 + \cdots + \beta_k X_k + \varepsilon$$

We refer to α and the βs collectively as the *regression coefficients*. Again, Greek letters are used to indicate that these quantities are unknown and unobservable. There is one other unknown constant in the model: the variance of the errors. Regression assumption 2 states that these errors have a constant variance, the same for all values of the Xs. We label this constant variance σ^2. Equivalently, the common standard deviation of the errors is σ.

This is how it looks in theory. There is a fixed set of explanatory variables, and given these variables, the problem is to estimate α, the βs, and σ. In practice, however, it is not usually this straightforward. In real regression applications the choice of relevant explanatory variables is almost never obvious. There are at least two guiding principles: relevance and data availability. You certainly want variables that are related to the dependent variable. The best situation is when there is an established economic or physical theory to guide you. For example, economic theory suggests that the demand for a product (dependent variable) is related to its price (possible explanatory variable). But there are not enough established theories to cover every situation. You often have to use the available data, plus some trial and error, to determine a *useful* set of explanatory variables. In this sense, it is usually pointless to search for one single "true" population regression equation. Instead, you typically estimate several competing models, each with a different set of explanatory variables, and ultimately select one of them as being the most useful.

Typically, the most challenging part of a regression analysis is deciding which explanatory variables to include in the regression equation.

Deciding which explanatory variables to include in a regression equation is probably the most difficult part of any applied regression analysis. Available data sets frequently offer an overabundance of potential explanatory variables. In addition, it is possible and often useful to create new variables from original variables, such as their logarithms. So where do you stop? Is it best to include every conceivable explanatory variable that might be related to the dependent variable? One overriding principle is **parsimony**—explaining the most with the least. For example, if a dependent variable can be explained just as well (or nearly as well) with two explanatory variables as with 10 explanatory variables, the principle of parsimony says to use only two. Models with fewer explanatory variables are generally easier to interpret, so they are preferred whenever possible.

The principle of **parsimony** is to explain the most with the least. It favors a model with fewer explanatory variables, assuming that this model explains the dependent variable almost as well as a model with additional explanatory variables.

Before you can determine which equation has the best set of explanatory variables, however, you must be able to estimate the unknown parameters for a given equation. That is, for a given set of explanatory variables X_1 through X_k, you must be able to estimate α, the βs, and σ. You learned how to find point estimates of these parameters in the previous chapter. The estimates of α and the βs are the least squares estimates of the intercept and slope terms. For example, the 36 months of overhead data in the Bendrix example were used to estimate the equation

$$\text{Predicted Overhead} = 3997 + 43.54\text{MachHrs} + 883.62\text{ProdRuns}$$

This implies that the least squares estimates of α, β_1, and β_2 are 3997, 43.54, and 883.62. Furthermore, because the residuals are really estimates of the errors, the standard error of estimate s_e is an estimate of σ. For the same overhead equation this estimate is $s_e = \$4109$.

You learned in Chapter 8 that there is more to statistical estimation than finding point estimates of population parameters. Each potential sample from the population typically leads to *different* point estimates. For example, if Bendrix estimates the equation for overhead from a different 36-month period (or possibly from another of its plants), the results will almost certainly be different. Therefore, we now discuss how these point estimates vary from sample to sample.

11.3.1 Sampling Distribution of the Regression Coefficients

The key idea is again sampling distributions. Recall that the sampling distribution of any estimate derived from sample data is the distribution of this estimate over all possible samples. This idea can be applied to the least squares estimate of a regression coefficient. For example, the sampling distribution of b_1, the least squares estimate of β_1, is the distribution of b_1s you would see if you observed many samples and ran a least squares regression on each of them.

Mathematicians have used theoretical arguments to find the required sampling distributions. We state the main result as follows. Let β be any of the βs, and let b be the least squares estimate of β. If the regression assumptions hold, the standardized value $(b - \beta)/s_b$ has a t distribution with $n - k - 1$ degrees of freedom. Here, k is the number of explanatory variables included in the equation, and s_b is the estimated standard deviation of the sampling distribution of b.

Sampling Distribution of a Regression Coefficient

If the regression assumptions are valid, the standardized value

$$ t = \frac{b - \beta}{s_b} $$

has a t distribution with $n - k - 1$ degrees of freedom.

This result has three important implications. First, the estimate b is *unbiased* in the sense that its mean is β, the true but unknown value of the slope. If bs were estimated from repeated samples, some would underestimate β and others would overestimate β, but on average they would be on target.

Second, the estimated standard deviation of b is labeled s_b. It is usually called the **standard error of b**. This standard error is related to the standard error of estimate s_e, but it is not the same. Generally, the formula for s_b is quite complicated, and it is not shown here, but its value is printed in all standard regression outputs. It measures how much the bs would vary from sample to sample. A small value of s_b is preferred—it means that b is a more accurate estimate of the true coefficient β.

Finally, the shape of the distribution of b is symmetric and bell-shaped. The relevant distribution is the t distribution with $n - k - 1$ degrees of freedom.

We have stated this result for a typical coefficient of one of the Xs. These are usually the coefficients of most interest. However, exactly the same result holds for the intercept term α. Now we illustrate how to use this result.

FUNDAMENTAL INSIGHT

Standard Errors in Regression

There are two quite different standard errors in regression outputs. The standard error of estimate, usually shown at the top of the output, is a measure of the error you are likely to make when you use the regression equation to predict a value of Y. In contrast, the standard errors of the coefficients measure the accuracy of the individual coefficients.

EXAMPLE 11.1 EXPLAINING OVERHEAD COSTS AT BENDRIX

This example is a continuation of the Bendrix manufacturing example from the previous chapter. As before, the dependent variable is Overhead and the explanatory variables are MachHrs and ProdRuns. What inferences can be made about the regression coefficients?

Objective To use standard regression output to make inferences about the regression coefficients of machine hours and production runs in the equation for overhead costs.

Solution

The output from StatTools's Regression procedure is shown in Figure 11.3. (See the file **Overhead Costs.xlsx**.) This output is practically identical to regression outputs from all

Figure 11.3 Regression Output for Bendrix Example

	A	B	C	D	E	F	G
7		Multiple	R-Square	Adjusted	StErr of		
8	*Summary*	R		R-Square	Estimate		
9		0.9308	0.8664	0.8583	4108.993		
10							
11		Degrees of	Sum of	Mean of	F-Ratio	p-Value	
12	*ANOVA Table*	Freedom	Squares	Squares			
13	Explained	2	3614020661	1807010330	107.0261	< 0.0001	
14	Unexplained	33	557166199.1	16883824.22			
15							
16		Coefficient	Standard	t-Value	p-Value	Confidence Interval 95%	
17	*Regression Table*		Error			Lower	Upper
18	Constant	3996.678	6603.651	0.6052	0.5492	-9438.551	17431.907
19	MachHrs	43.536	3.589	12.1289	< 0.0001	36.234	50.839
20	ProdRuns	883.618	82.251	10.7429	< 0.0001	716.276	1050.960

other statistical software packages. The estimates of the regression coefficients appear under the label Coefficient in the range B18:B20. These values estimate the true, but unobservable, population coefficients. The next column, labeled Standard Error, shows the s_b values. Specifically, 3.589 is the standard error of the coefficient of MachHrs, and 82.251 is the standard error of the coefficient of ProdRuns.

Each b represents a point estimate of the corresponding β, based on this particular sample. The corresponding s_b indicates the accuracy of this point estimate. For example, the point estimate of β_1, the effect on Overhead of a one-unit increase in MachHrs (when ProdRuns is held constant), is 43.536. You can be about 95% confident that the true β_1 is within two standard errors of this point estimate, that is, from approximately 36.357 to 50.715. Similar statements can be made for the coefficient of ProdRuns and the intercept (Constant) term. ■

As with any population parameters, the sample data can be used to obtain confidence intervals for the regression coefficients. For example, the preceding paragraph implies that an approximate 95% confidence interval for the coefficient of MachHrs extends from approximately 36.357 to 50.715. More precisely, a confidence interval for any β is of the form

$$b \pm t\text{-multiple} \times s_b$$

where the t-multiple depends on the confidence level and the degrees of freedom (here $n - k - 1$). StatTools always provides these 95% confidence intervals for the regression coefficients automatically, as shown in the bottom right of Figure 11.3.

11.3.2 Hypothesis Tests for the Regression Coefficients and p-Values

There is another important piece of information in regression outputs: the t-values for the individual regression coefficients. These are shown in the "t-Value" column of the regression output in Figure 11.3. Each t-value is the ratio of the estimated coefficient to its standard error, as shown in Equation (11.3). Therefore, it indicates how many standard errors the regression coefficient is from zero. For example, the t-value for MachHrs is about 11.13, so the regression coefficient of MachHrs, 43.536, is more than 12 of its standard errors to the right of zero. Similarly, the coefficient of ProdRuns is more than 10 of its standard errors to the right of zero.

> **t-value for Test of Regression Coefficient**
>
> $$t\text{-value} = b/s_b \qquad\qquad (11.3)$$

A t-value can be used in an important hypothesis test for the corresponding regression coefficient. To motivate this test, suppose that you want to decide whether a particular explanatory variable belongs in the regression equation. A sensible criterion for making this decision is to check whether the corresponding regression coefficient is zero. If a variable's coefficient is zero, there is no point in including this variable in the equation; the zero coefficient will cancel its effect on the dependent variable.

Therefore, it is reasonable to test whether a variable's coefficient is zero. This is usually tested versus a *two-tailed* alternative. The null and alternative hypotheses are of the form $H_0{:}\beta = 0$ versus $H_a{:}\beta \neq 0$. If you can reject the null hypothesis and conclude that this coefficient is *not* zero, you then have an argument for including the variable in the regression equation. Conversely, if you cannot reject the null hypothesis, you might decide to eliminate this variable from the equation.

The test for whether a regression coefficient is zero can be run by looking at the corresponding p-value: Reject the "equals zero" hypothesis if the p-value is small, say, less than 0.05.

The t-value for a variable allows you to run this test easily. You simply compare the t-value in the regression output with a tabulated t-value and reject the null hypothesis only if the t-value from the computer output is greater in magnitude than the tabulated t-value.

Most statistical packages, including StatTools, make this test even easier to run by reporting the corresponding p-value for the test. This eliminates the need for finding the tabulated t-value. The p-value is interpreted exactly as in Chapter 9. It is the probability (in both tails) of the relevant t distribution beyond the listed t-value. For example, referring again to Figure 11.3, the t-value for MachHrs is 12.13, and the associated p-value is less than 0.0001. This means that there is virtually no probability beyond the observed t-value. In words, you are still not exactly sure of the true coefficient of MachHrs, but you are virtually sure it is not zero. The same can be said for the coefficient of ProdRuns.

In practice, you typically run a multiple regression with several explanatory variables and scan their p-values. If the p-value of a variable is low, then this variable should be kept in the equation; if the p-value is high, you might consider eliminating this variable from the equation. In section 11.5, we will discuss this *include/exclude decision* in greater depth and provide rules of thumb for the meaning of "low" and "high" p-values.

11.3.3 A Test for the Overall Fit: The ANOVA Table

The t-values for the regression coefficients allow you to see which of the potential explanatory variables are useful in explaining the dependent variable. But it is conceivable that *none* of these variables does a very good job. That is, it is conceivable that the entire group of explanatory variables explains only an insignificant portion of the variability of the dependent variable. Although this is the exception rather than the rule in most real applications, it can certainly happen. An indication of this is that you obtain a very small R^2 value. Because R^2 is the square of the correlation between the observed values of the dependent variable and the fitted values from the regression equation, another indication of a lack of fit is that this correlation (the "multiple R") is small. In this section we state a formal procedure for testing the overall fit, or explanatory power, of a regression equation.

Suppose that the dependent variable is Y and the explanatory variables are X_1 through X_k. Then the proposed population regression equation is

$$Y = \alpha + \beta_1 X_1 + \cdots + \beta_k X_k + \varepsilon$$

To say that this equation has absolutely no explanatory power means that the same value of Y will be predicted regardless of the values of the Xs. In this case it makes no difference which values of the Xs are used, because they all lead to the same predicted value of Y. But the only way this can occur is if all of the βs are 0. So the formal hypothesis test in this section is $H_0{:}\beta_1 = \cdots = \beta_k = 0$ versus the alternative that at least one of the βs is not zero. If the null hypothesis can be rejected, as it can in the majority of applications, this means that the explanatory variables *as a group* provide at least some explanatory power. These hypotheses are summarized as follows.

> **Hypotheses for ANOVA Test**
>
> The null hypothesis is that all coefficients of the explanatory variables are zero. The alternative is that at least one of these coefficients is not zero.

At first glance it might appear that this null hypothesis can be tested by looking at the individual t-values. If they are all small (statistically insignificant), then the null hypothesis of no fit cannot be rejected; otherwise, it can be rejected. However, as you will see in the next section, it is possible, because of multicollinearity, to have small t-values even though the variables as a whole have *significant* explanatory power.

The alternative is to use an F test. This is sometimes referred to as the ANOVA (analysis of variance) test because the elements for calculating the required F-value are shown in an ANOVA table.[3] In general, an ANOVA table analyzes different sources of variation. In the case of regression, the variation in question is the variation of the dependent variable Y. The *total variation* of this variable is the sum of squared deviations about the mean and is labeled *SST* (sum of squares total).

$$SST = \sum(Y_i - \overline{Y})^2$$

The ANOVA table splits this total variation into two parts, the part *explained* by the regression equation, and the part left *unexplained*. The unexplained part is the sum of squared residuals, usually labeled *SSE* (sum of squared errors):

$$SSE = \sum e_i^2 = \sum(Y_i - \hat{Y}_i)^2$$

The explained part is then the difference between the total and unexplained variation. It is usually labeled *SSR* (sum of squares due to regression):

$$SSR = SST - SSE$$

The F test is a formal procedure for testing whether the explained variation is large compared to the unexplained variation. Specifically, each of these sources of variation has an associated degrees of freedom (*df*). For the explained variation, $df = k$, which is the number of explanatory variables. For the unexplained variation, $df = n - k - 1$, the sample size minus the total number of coefficients (including the intercept term). The ratio of either sum of squares to its degrees of freedom is called a mean square, or *MS*. The two mean squares in this case are *MSR* and *MSE*, given by

$$MSR = \frac{SSR}{k}$$

and

$$MSE = \frac{SSE}{n - k - 1}$$

[3]This ANOVA table is similar to the ANOVA table discussed in Chapter 9. However, we repeat the necessary material here for those who didn't cover that section.

Note that MSE is the square of the standard error of estimate, that is,

$$MSE = s_e^2$$

Finally, the ratio of these mean squares is the required F-ratio for the test:

$$F\text{-ratio} = \frac{MSR}{MSE}$$

When the null hypothesis of no explanatory power is true, this F-ratio has an F distribution with k and $n - k - 1$ degrees of freedom. If the F-ratio is small, the explained variation is small relative to the unexplained variation, and there is evidence that the regression equation provides little explanatory power. But if the F-ratio is large, the explained variation is large relative to the unexplained variation, and you can conclude that the equation does have some explanatory power.

As usual, the F-ratio has an associated p-value that allows you to run the test easily. In this case the p-value is the probability to the *right* of the observed F-ratio in the appropriate F distribution. This p-value is reported in most regression outputs, along with the elements that lead up to it. If it is sufficiently small, less than 0.05, say, then you can conclude that the explanatory variables as a whole have at least some explanatory power.

Reject the null hypothesis—and conclude that these X variables have at least some explanatory power—if the F-value in the ANOVA table is large and the corresponding p-value is small.

Although this test is run routinely in most applications, there is often little doubt that the equation has some explanatory power; the only questions are how much, and which explanatory variables provide the best combination. In such cases the F-ratio from the ANOVA table is typically "off the charts" and the corresponding p-value is practically zero. On the other hand, F-ratios, particularly large ones, should not necessarily be used to choose between equations with different explanatory variables included.

For example, suppose that one equation with three explanatory variables has an F-ratio of 54 with an extremely small p-value—very significant. Also, suppose that another equation that includes these three variables plus a few more has an F-ratio of 37 and also has a very small p-value. (When we say small, we mean *small*. These p-values are probably listed as <0.001.) Is the first equation better because its F-ratio is higher? Not necessarily. The two F-ratios imply only that both of these equations have a good deal of explanatory power. It is better to look at their s_e values (or adjusted R^2 values) and their t-values to choose between them.

The ANOVA table is part of the StatTools output for any regression run. It appeared for the Bendrix example in Figure 11.3, which is repeated for convenience in Figure 11.4. The ANOVA table is in rows 12 through 14. The degrees of freedom are in column B, the

---

Figure 11.4 Regression Output for Bendrix Example

	A	B	C	D	E	F	G
7		Multiple		Adjusted	StErr of		
8	*Summary*	R	R-Square	R-Square	Estimate		
9		0.9308	0.8664	0.8583	4108.993		
10							
11		Degrees of	Sum of	Mean of	F-Ratio	p-Value	
12	*ANOVA Table*	Freedom	Squares	Squares			
13	Explained	2	3614020661	1807010330	107.0261	< 0.0001	
14	Unexplained	33	557166199.1	16883824.22			
15							
16			Standard			Confidence Interval 95%	
17	*Regression Table*	Coefficient	Error	t-Value	p-Value	Lower	Upper
18	Constant	3996.678	6603.651	0.6052	0.5492	-9438.551	17431.907
19	MachHrs	43.536	3.589	12.1289	< 0.0001	36.234	50.839
20	ProdRuns	883.618	82.251	10.7429	< 0.0001	716.276	1050.960

sums of squares are in column C, the mean squares are in column D, the F-ratio is in cell E13, and its associated p-value is in cell F13. As predicted, this F-ratio is "off the charts," and the p-value is practically zero.

This information wouldn't be much comfort for the Bendrix manager who is trying to understand the causes of variation in overhead costs. This manager already *knows* that machine hours and production runs are related positively to overhead costs—everyone in the company knows that. What he really wants is a set of explanatory variables that yields a high R^2 and a low s_e. The low p-value in the ANOVA tables does not guarantee these. All it guarantees is that MachHrs and ProdRuns are of *some* help in explaining variations in Overhead.

As this example indicates, the ANOVA table can be used as a screening device. If the explanatory variables do not explain a significant percentage of the variation in the dependent variable, then you can either discontinue the analysis or search for an entirely new set of explanatory variables. But even if the F-ratio in the ANOVA table is extremely significant (as it usually is), there is no guarantee that the regression equation provides a good enough fit for practical uses. This depends on other measures such as s_e and R^2.

PROBLEMS

Note: Student solutions for problems whose numbers appear within a colored box are available for purchase at www.cengagebrain.com.

Level A

1. Explore the relationship between the selling prices (Y) and the appraised values (X) of the 148 homes in the file **P02_11.xlsx** by estimating a simple linear regression equation. Find a 95% confidence interval for the model's slope parameter (β_1). What does this confidence interval tell you about the relationship between Y and X for these data?

2. The owner of the Original Italian Pizza restaurant chain would like to predict the sales of his specialty, deep-dish pizza. He has gathered data on the monthly sales of deep-dish pizzas at his restaurants and observations on other potentially relevant variables for each of his 15 outlets in central Indiana. These data are provided in the file **P10_04.xlsx**.
   a. Estimate a multiple regression model between the quantity sold (Y) and the explanatory variables in columns C–E.
   b. Is there evidence of any violations of the key assumptions of regression analysis?
   c. Which of the variables in this equation have regression coefficients that are statistically different from zero at the 5% significance level?
   d. Given your findings in part **c**, which variables, if any, would you choose to remove from the equation estimated in part **a**? Why?

3. The file **P02_10.xlsx** contains midterm and final exam scores for 96 students in a corporate finance course.

Based on a regression equation for the final exam score as a function of the midterm exam score, find a 95% confidence interval for the slope of the population regression line. State exactly what this confidence interval indicates.

4. A trucking company wants to predict the yearly maintenance expense (Y) for a truck using the number of miles driven during the year (X_1) and the age of the truck (X_2, in years) at the beginning of the year. The company has gathered the information given in the file **P10_16.xlsx**. Each observation corresponds to a particular truck.
   a. Estimate a multiple regression equation using the given data.
   b. Does autocorrelation appear to be a problem? What about multicollinearity? What about heteroscedasticity?
   c. Find 95% confidence intervals for the regression coefficients of X_1 and X_2. Based on these interval estimates, which variable, if any, would you choose to remove from the equation estimated in part **a**? Why?

5. Based on the data in the file **P02_23.xlsx** from the U.S. Department of Agriculture, explore the relationship between the number of farms (X) and the average size of a farm (Y) in the United States.
   a. Use the given data to estimate a simple linear regression model.
   b. Test whether there is sufficient evidence to conclude that the slope parameter (β_1) is *less than* zero. Use a 5% significance level.

c. Based on your finding in part **b**, is it possible to conclude that a linear relationship exists between the number of farms and the average farm size during the given time period? Explain.

6. An antique collector believes that the price received for a particular item increases with its age and the number of bidders. The file **P10_18.xlsx** contains data on these three variables for 32 recently auctioned comparable items.
   a. Estimate an appropriate multiple regression model using the given data.
   b. Interpret the ANOVA table for this model. In particular, does this set of explanatory variables provide at least *some* power in explaining the variation in price? Report a *p*-value for this hypothesis test.

7. The file **P02_02.xlsx** contains information on over 200 movies that came out during 2006 and 2007. Run a regression of Total US Gross versus 7-day Gross, and then run a multiple regression of Total US Gross versus 7-day Gross and 14-day Gross. Report the 95% confidence interval for the coefficient of 7-day Gross in each equation. What exactly do these confidence intervals tell you about the effect of 7-day Gross on Total US Gross? Why are they not at all the same? What is the relevant population that this data set is a sample from?

8. The file **P10_10.xlsx** contains data on 150 homes that were sold recently in a particular community.
   a. Find a table of correlations between all of the variables. Do the correlations between Price and each of the other variables have the sign (positive or negative) you would expect? Explain briefly.
   b. Run a regression of Price versus Rooms. What does the 95% confidence interval for the coefficient of Rooms tell you about the effect of Rooms on Price for the entire population of such homes?
   c. Run a multiple regression of Price versus Home Size, Lot Size, Rooms, and Bathrooms. What is the 95% confidence interval for the coefficient of Rooms now? Why do you think it can be so different from the one in part **b**? Based on this regression, can you reject the null hypothesis that the population regression coefficient of Rooms is zero versus a two-tailed alternative? What does this mean?

9. Suppose that a regional express delivery service company wants to estimate the cost of shipping a package (Y) as a function of cargo type, where cargo type includes the following possibilities: fragile, semifragile, and durable. Costs for 15 randomly chosen packages of approximately the same weight and same distance shipped, but of different cargo types, are provided in the file **P10_28.xlsx**.

a. Estimate an appropriate multiple regression equation to predict the cost of shipping a given package.
b. Interpret the ANOVA table for this model. In particular, do the explanatory variables included in your equation in part **a** provide at least *some* power in explaining the variation in shipping costs? Report a *p*-value for this hypothesis test.

10. The file **P10_05.xlsx** contains salaries for a sample of DataCom employees, along with several variables that might be related to salary. Run a multiple regression of Salary versus Years Employed, Years Education, Gender, and Number Supervised. For each of these variables, explain exactly what the results in the Coefficient, Standard Error, t-Value, and p-Value columns mean. Based on the results, can you reject the null hypothesis that the population coefficient of any of these variables is zero versus a two-tailed alternative at the 5% significance level? If you can, what would you probably do next in the analysis?

Level B

11. A multiple regression with 36 observations and three explanatory variables yields the ANOVA table in Table 11.1.
   a. Complete this ANOVA table.
   b. Can you conclude at the 1% significance level that these three explanatory variables have *some* power in explaining variation in the dependent variable?

Table 11.1   ANOVA Table

	Degrees of Freedom	Sum of Squares
Explained		1211
Unexplained		
Total		2567

12. Suppose you find the ANOVA table shown in Table 11.2 for a simple linear regression.

Table 11.2   ANOVA Table

	Degrees of Freedom	Sum of Squares
Explained		52
Unexplained	87	
Total		1598

a. Find the correlation between X and Y, assuming that the slope of the least squares line is negative.
b. Find the *p*-value for the test of the hypothesis of no explanatory power at all. What does it tell you in this particular case?

11.4 MULTICOLLINEARITY

Recall that the coefficient of any variable in a regression equation indicates the effect of this variable on the dependent variable, provided that the other variables in the equation remain constant. Another way of stating this is that the coefficient represents the effect of this variable on the dependent variable *in addition to* the effects of the other variables in the equation. In the Bendrix example, if MachHrs and ProdRuns are included in the equation for Overhead, the coefficient of MachHrs indicates the *extra* amount MachHrs explains about variation in Overhead, in addition to the amount already explained by ProdRuns. Similarly, the coefficient of ProdRuns indicates the extra amount ProdRuns explains about variation in Overhead, in addition to the amount already explained by MachHrs. Therefore, the relationship between an explanatory variable X and the dependent variable Y is not always accurately reflected in the coefficient of X; it depends on which *other X*s are included or not included in the equation.

This is especially true when *multicollinearity* exists. By definition, **multicollinearity** is the presence of a fairly strong linear relationship between two or more explanatory variables, and it can make regression output difficult to interpret.

> **Multicollinearity** occurs when there is a fairly strong linear relationship among a set of explanatory variables.

Consider the following example. It is a rather contrived example, but it is useful for illustrating the potential effects of multicollinearity.

EXAMPLE | 11.2 HEIGHT AS A FUNCTION OF FOOT LENGTH

We want to explain a person's height by means of foot length. The dependent variable is Height, and the explanatory variables are Right and Left, the length of the right foot and the length of the left foot, respectively. What can occur when Height is regressed on *both* Right and Left?

Objective   To illustrate the problem of multicollinearity when both foot length variables are used in a regression for height.

Solution

Clearly, there is no need to include both Right and Left in an equation for Height—either one of them suffices—but we include them both to make a point. It is likely that there is a large correlation between height and foot size, so you would expect this regression equation to do a good job. For example, the R^2 value will probably be large. But what about the coefficients of Right and Left? Here there is a problem. The coefficient of Right indicates the right foot's effect on Height in addition to the effect of the left foot. This additional effect is probably minimal. That is, after the effect of Left on Height has been taken into account, the extra information provided by Right is probably minimal. But it goes the other way also. The extra effect of Left, in addition to that provided by Right, is probably also minimal.

To show what can happen numerically, we used simulation to generate a hypothetical data set of heights and left and right foot lengths. We did this so that, except for random error, height is approximately 31.8 plus 3.2 times foot length (all expressed in inches). (See Figure 11.5 and the file **Heights Simulation.xlsx**. You can check the formulas in

Suppose, for example, that you want to use regression to explain variations in salary. Three potentially useful explanatory variables are age, years of experience with the company, and years of experience in the industry. It is very likely that each of these is positively related to salary, and it is also very likely that they are very closely related to each other. However, it isn't clear which, if any, you should exclude from the regression equation. If you include all three, you are likely to find that at least one of them is insignificant (high p-value), in which case you might consider excluding it from the equation. If you do so, the s_e and R^2 values will probably not change very much—the equation will provide equally good predicted values—but the coefficients of the variables that remain in the equation could change considerably.

PROBLEMS

Level A

13. Using the data given in **P10_10.xlsx**, estimate a multiple regression equation to predict the price of houses in a given community. Employ all available explanatory variables. Is there evidence of multicollinearity in this model? Explain why or why not.

14. Consider the data for *Business Week's* top U.S. MBA programs in the MBA Data sheet of the file **P10_21.xlsx**. Use these data to estimate a multiple regression model to assess whether there is a relationship between the enrollment and the following explanatory variables: (a) the percentage of international students, (b) the percentage of female students, (c) the percentage of Asian American students, (d) the percentage of minority students, and (e) the resident tuition and fees at these business schools.

   a. Determine whether each of the regression coefficients for the explanatory variables in this model is statistically different from zero at the 5% significance level. Summarize your findings.

   b. Is there evidence of multicollinearity in this model? Explain why or why not.

15. The manager of a commuter rail transportation system was recently asked by her governing board to determine the factors that have a significant impact on the demand for rides in the large city served by the transportation network. The system manager has collected data on variables that might be related to the number of weekly riders on the city's rail system. The file **P10_20.xlsx** contains these data.

   a. Estimate a multiple regression model using all of the available explanatory variables. Perform a test

of significance for each of the model's regression coefficients. Are the signs of the estimated coefficients consistent with your expectations?

   b. Is there evidence of multicollinearity in this model? Explain why or why not. If multicollinearity is present, explain what you would do to remedy this problem.

Level B

16. The file **P10_05.xlsx** contains salaries for a sample of DataCom employees, along with several variables that might be related to salary.

   a. Estimate the relationship between Y (Salary) and X (Years Employed) using simple linear regression. (For this problem, ignore the other potential explanatory variables.) Is there evidence to support the hypothesis that the coefficient for the number of years employed is statistically different from zero at the 5% significance level?

   b. Estimate a multiple regression model to explain annual salaries of DataCom employees with X and X^2 as explanatory variables. Perform relevant hypothesis tests to determine the significance of the regression coefficients of these two variables. Summarize your findings.

   c. How do you explain your findings in part **b** in light of the results found in part **a**?

17. The owner of a restaurant in Bloomington, Indiana, has recorded sales data for the past 19 years. He has also recorded data on potentially relevant variables. The data appear in the file **P10_23.xlsx**.

   a. Estimate a multiple regression equation that includes annual sales as the dependent variable and the following explanatory variables: year, size of the population residing within 10 miles of the restaurant, annual advertising expenditures, and advertising expenditures in the *previous* year.

b. Which of the explanatory variables have significant effects on sales at the 10% significance level? Do any of these results surprise you? Explain why or why not.

c. Exclude all insignificant explanatory variables from the equation in part **a** and estimate the equation with the remaining variables. Comment on the significance of each remaining variable.

d. Based on your analysis of this problem, does multicollinearity appear to be present in the original or revised versions of the model? Explain.

11.5 INCLUDE/EXCLUDE DECISIONS

In this section we make further use of the *t*-values of regression coefficients. In particular, we explain how they can be used to make **include/exclude decisions** for explanatory variables in a regression equation. Section 11.3 explained how a *t*-value can be used to test whether a population regression coefficient is zero. But does this mean that you should automatically include a variable if its *t*-value is significant and automatically exclude it if its *t*-value is insignificant? The decision is not always this simple.

The bottom line is that you are always trying to get the best fit possible, and the principle of parsimony suggests using the fewest number of variables. This presents a trade-off, where there not always easy answers. On the one hand, more variables certainly increase R^2, and they usually reduce the standard error of estimate s_e. On the other hand, fewer variables are better for parsimony. To help with the decision, we present several guidelines. These guidelines are not hard and fast rules, and they are sometimes contradictory. In real applications there are often several equations that are equally good for all practical purposes, and it is rather pointless to search for a single "true" equation.

FUNDAMENTAL INSIGHT

Searching for the "True" Regression Equation

Finding the best *X*s (or the best form of the *X*s) to include in a regression equation is undoubtedly the most difficult part of any real regression analysis. We offer two important things to keep in mind. First, it is rather pointless to search for the "true" regression equation. There are often several equations that, for all practical purposes, are equally *useful* for describing how the world works or making predictions. Second, the guidelines provided here for including and excluding variables are not ironclad rules. They typically involve choices at the margin, that is, between equations that are very similar and equally useful. In short, there is usually no single "correct answer."

GUIDELINES FOR INCLUDING/EXCLUDING VARIABLES IN A REGRESSION EQUATION

1 Look at a variable's *t*-value and its associated *p*-value. If the *p*-value is above some accepted significance level, such as 0.05, this variable is a candidate for exclusion.

2 Check whether a variable's *t*-value is less than 1 or greater than 1 in magnitude. If it is less than 1, then it is a mathematical fact that s_e will decrease (and adjusted R^2 will increase) if this variable is excluded from the equation. If it is greater than 1, the opposite will occur. Because of this, some statisticians advocate excluding variables with *t*-values less than 1 and including variables with *t*-values greater than 1.

3 Look at *t*-values and *p*-values, rather than correlations, when making include/exclude decisions. An explanatory variable can have a fairly high correlation with the dependent variable, but because of *other* variables included in the equation, it might not be needed. This would be reflected in a low *t*-value and a high *p*-value, and this variable could possibly be excluded for reasons of parsimony. This often occurs in the presence of multicollinearity.

④ When there is a group of variables that are in some sense logically related, it is sometimes a good idea to include all of them or exclude all of them. In this case, their individual t-values are less relevant. Instead, a "partial F test" (discussed in section 11.7) can be used to make the include/exclude decision.

⑤ Use economic and/or physical theory to decide whether to include or exclude variables, and put less reliance on t-values and/or p-values. Some variables might really *belong* in an equation because of their theoretical relationship with the dependent variable, and their low t-values, possibly the result of an unlucky sample, should not necessarily disqualify them from being in the equation. Similarly, a variable that has no economic or physical relationship with the dependent variable might have a significant t-value just by chance. This does not necessarily mean that it should be included in the equation. You should not use a software package blindly to hunt for "good" explanatory variables. You should have some idea, before running the package, of which variables belong and which do not belong.

Again, these guidelines can give contradictory signals. Specifically, guideline 2 bases the include/exclude decision on whether the magnitude of the t-value is greater or less than 1. However, analysts who base the decision on statistical significance at the usual 5% level, as in guideline 1, typically exclude a variable from the equation unless its t-value is at least 2 (approximately). This latter approach is more stringent—fewer variables will be retained— but it is probably the more popular approach. However, either approach is likely to result in similar equations for all practical purposes.

In our experience, you should not agonize too much about whether to include or exclude a variable "at the margin." If you decide to exclude a variable that doesn't add much explanatory power, you get a somewhat cleaner equation, and you probably won't see any dramatic shifts in R^2 or s_e. On the other hand, if you decide to keep such a variable in the equation, the equation is less parsimonious and you have one more variable to interpret, but otherwise, there is no real penalty for including it.

We illustrate how these guidelines can be used in the following example.

EXAMPLE | **11.3 EXPLAINING SPENDING AMOUNTS AT HYTEX**

The file **Catalog Marketing.xlsx** contains data on 1000 customers who purchased mail-order products from the HyTex Company in the current year. (This is a slightly different version of the file that was used in Chapter 2.) HyTex is a direct marketer of stereo equipment, personal computers, and other electronic products. HyTex advertises entirely by mailing catalogs to its customers, and all of its orders are taken over the telephone. The company spends a great deal of money on its catalog mailings, and it wants to be sure that this is paying off in sales. For each customer there are data on the following variables:

- Age: age of the customer at the end of the current year
- Gender: coded as 1 for males, 0 for females
- OwnHome: coded as 1 if customer owns a home, 0 otherwise
- Married: coded as 1 if customer is currently married, 0 otherwise
- Close: coded as 1 if customer lives reasonably close to a shopping area that sells similar merchandise, 0 otherwise
- Salary: combined annual salary of customer and spouse (if any)
- Children: number of children living with customer
- PrevCust: coded as 1 if customer purchased from HyTex during the previous year, 0 otherwise

- PrevSpent: total amount of purchases made from HyTex during the previous year
- Catalogs: number of catalogs sent to the customer this year
- AmountSpent: total amount of purchases made from HyTex this year

Estimate and interpret a regression equation for AmountSpent based on all of these variables.

Objective To see which potential explanatory variables are useful for explaining current year spending amounts at HyTex with multiple regression.

Solution

With this much data, 1000 observations, it is possible to set aside part of the data set for validation, as discussed in section 10.7. Although any split can be used, we decided to base the regression on the first 750 observations and use the other 250 for validation. Therefore, you should select only the range through row 751 when defining the StatTools data set.

You can begin by entering all of the potential explanatory variables. The goal is then to exclude variables that aren't necessary, based on their *t*-values and *p*-values. The multiple regression output with all explanatory variables appears in Figure 11.7. It indicates a fairly good fit. The R^2 value is 74.7% and s_e is about $491. Given that the actual amounts spent in the current year vary from a low of under $50 to a high of over $5500, with a median of about $950, a typical prediction error of around $491 is decent but not great.

From the *p*-value column, you can see that there are four variables, Age, Gender, OwnHome, and Married, that have *p*-values well above 0.05. These are the obvious candidates for exclusion from the equation. You could rerun the equation with all three of these variables excluded, but it is a better practice to exclude one variable at a time. It is possible that when one of these variables is excluded, another one of them will become significant (the Right–Left foot phenomenon).

Figure 11.7 Regression Output with All Explanatory Variables Included

	A	B	C	D	E	F	G
7		Multiple R	R-Square	Adjusted R-Square	StErr of Estimate		
8	*Summary*						
9		0.8643	0.7470	0.7435	491.4513		
10							
11		Degrees of Freedom	Sum of Squares	Mean of Squares	F-Ratio	p-Value	
12	*ANOVA Table*						
13	Explained	10	526916948.1	52691694.81	218.1631	< 0.0001	
14	Unexplained	739	178486506.7	241524.3663			
15							
16		Coefficient	Standard Error	t-Value	p-Value	Confidence Interval 95%	
17	*Regression Table*					Lower	Upper
18	Constant	197.3915	85.8636	2.2989	0.0218	28.8259	365.9572
19	Age	0.6014	1.2596	0.4775	0.6332	-1.8715	3.0743
20	Gender	-57.4924	37.9022	-1.5169	0.1297	-131.9013	16.9165
21	OwnHome	23.3068	40.3559	0.5775	0.5638	-55.9191	102.5326
22	Married	8.6877	48.5435	0.1790	0.8580	-86.6119	103.9872
23	Close	-418.7341	45.2356	-9.2567	< 0.0001	-507.5397	-329.9284
24	Salary	0.0179	0.0012	15.5194	< 0.0001	0.0157	0.0202
25	Children	-161.4875	21.0032	-7.6887	< 0.0001	-202.7205	-120.2544
26	PrevCust	-546.0081	63.4794	-8.6013	< 0.0001	-670.6295	-421.3867
27	PrevSpent	0.2684	0.0528	5.0876	< 0.0001	0.1648	0.3719
28	Catalogs	43.9463	2.8618	15.3560	< 0.0001	38.3280	49.5646

Actually, this did not happen. We first excluded the variable with the largest p-value, Married, and reran the regression. At this point, Age, Gender, and OwnHome still had large p-values, so we excluded Age, the variable with the largest remaining p-value, and reran the regression. Next, we excluded OwnHome, the variable with the largest remaining p-value, and finally, we excluded Gender because its p-value was still large. The resulting output appears in Figure 11.8. The R^2 and s_e values of 74.6% and $491 are almost the same as they were with all variables included, and all of the p-values are very small.

Figure 11.8 Regression Output with Insignificant Variables Excluded

	A	B	C	D	E	F	G
7		Multiple	R-Square	Adjusted	StErr of		
8	Summary	R		R-Square	Estimate		
9		0.8636	0.7458	0.7438	491.2283		
10							
11		Degrees of	Sum of	Mean of	F-Ratio	p-Value	
12	ANOVA Table	Freedom	Squares	Squares			
13	Explained	6	526113683.9	87685613.98	363.3805	< 0.0001	
14	Unexplained	743	179289770.9	241305.2099			
15							
16		Coefficient	Standard	t-Value	p-Value	Confidence Interval 95%	
17	Regression Table		Error			Lower	Upper
18	Constant	205.0936	70.3152	2.9168	0.0036	67.0534	343.1338
19	Close	-416.2462	45.0846	-9.2326	< 0.0001	-504.7546	-327.7378
20	Salary	0.0180	0.0009	19.8773	< 0.0001	0.0162	0.0197
21	Children	-161.1577	20.4828	-7.8679	< 0.0001	-201.3688	-120.9466
22	PrevCust	-543.5948	63.2988	-8.5878	< 0.0001	-667.8606	-419.3290
23	PrevSpent	0.2724	0.0525	5.1844	< 0.0001	0.1692	0.3755
24	Catalogs	43.8067	2.8542	15.3481	< 0.0001	38.2034	49.4100

This final regression equation can be interpreted as follows:

Interpretation of Regression Equation

- The coefficient of Close implies that an average customer living close to stores with this type of merchandise spent about $416 less than an average customer living far from such stores.

- The coefficient of Salary implies that, on average, about 1.8 cents of every extra salary dollar was spent on HyTex merchandise.

- The coefficient of Children implies that about $161 *less* was spent for every extra child living at home.

- The PrevCust and PrevSpent terms are somewhat more difficult to interpret. First, both of these terms are zero for customers who didn't purchase from HyTex in the previous year. For those who did, the terms become $-544 + 0.27$PrevSpent. The coefficient 0.27 implies that each extra dollar spent the previous year can be expected to contribute an extra 27 cents in the current year. The -544 literally means that if you compare a customer who didn't purchase from HyTex last year to another customer who purchased only a tiny amount, the latter is expected to spend about $544 less than the former this year. However, none of the latter customers were in the data set. A look at the data shows that of all customers who purchased from HyTex last year, almost all spent at least $100 and most spent considerably more. In fact, the median amount spent by these customers last year was about $900 (the median of all positive values for the PrevSpent variable). If you substitute this median value into the expression −544 + 0.27PrevSpent, you obtain −298. Therefore, this "median" spender from last year can be expected to spend about $298 less this year than the previous year nonspender.

- The coefficient of Catalogs implies that each extra catalog can be expected to generate about $44 in extra spending.

We conclude this example with a couple of cautionary notes. First, if you validate this final regression equation on the other 250 customers, using the procedure from section 10.7, you will find R^2 and s_e values of 73.2% and $486. These are very promising. They are very close to the values based on the original 750 customers. Second, we haven't tried all possibilities yet. We haven't tried nonlinear or interaction variables, nor have we looked at different coding schemes (such as treating Catalogs as a categorical variable and using dummy variables to represent it). Also, we haven't checked for nonconstant error variance (Figure 11.1 is based on this data set) or looked at the potential effects of outliers. ■

PROBLEMS

Level A

18. The Undergraduate Data sheet of the file **P10_21.xlsx** contains information on 101 undergraduate business programs in the U.S., including various rankings by *Business Week*. Use multiple regression to explore the relationship between the median starting salary and the following set of potential explanatory variables: annual cost, full-time enrollment, faculty-student ratio, average SAT score, and average ACT score. Which explanatory variables should be included in a final version of this regression equation? Justify your choices. Is multicollinearity a problem? Why or why not?

19. A manager of boiler drums wants to use regression analysis to predict the number of worker-hours needed to erect the drums in future projects. Consequently, data for 36 randomly selected boilers were collected. In addition to worker-hours (*Y*), the variables measured include boiler capacity, boiler design pressure, boiler type, and drum type. All of these measurements are listed in the file **P10_27.xlsx**. Estimate an appropriate multiple regression model to predict the number of worker-hours needed to erect given boiler drums using all available explanatory variables. Which explanatory variables should be included in a final version of this regression model? Justify your choices.

20. The file **P02_35.xlsx** contains data from a survey of 500 randomly selected households.
  a. In an effort to explain the variation in the size of the monthly home mortgage or rent payment,

estimate a multiple regression equation that includes all of the potential household explanatory variables.
  b. Using the regression output, determine which of the explanatory variables should be excluded from the regression equation. Justify your choices.
  c. Do you obtain substantially different results if you combine First Income and Second Income into a Total Income variable and then use the latter as the only income explanatory variable?

21. The file **P02_07.xlsx** includes data on 204 employees at the (fictional) company Beta Technologies.
  a. Estimate a multiple regression equation to explain the variation in employee salaries at Beta Technologies using all of the potential explanatory variables.
  b. Using the regression output, determine which of the explanatory variables, if any, should be excluded from the regression equation. Justify your choices.
  c. Regardless of your answer to part **b**, exclude the *least* significant variable (not counting the constant) and estimate the resulting equation. Would you conclude that this equation and the one from part **a** are equally good? Explain.

22. Stock market analysts are continually looking for reliable predictors of stock prices. Consider the problem of modeling the price per share of electric utility stocks (*Y*). Two variables thought to influence such a stock price are return on average equity (X_1) and annual dividend rate (X_2). The stock price, returns on equity, and dividend rates on a randomly selected day for 16 electric utility stocks are provided in the file **P10_19.xlsx**.

a. Estimate a multiple regression model using the given data. Include linear terms as well as an interaction term involving the return on average equity (X_1) and annual dividend rate (X_2).

b. Which of the three explanatory variables (X_1, X_2, and X_1X_2) should be included in a final version of this regression model? Explain. Does your conclusion make sense in light of your knowledge of corporate finance?

11.6 STEPWISE REGRESSION[4]

Multiple regression represents an improvement over simple regression because it allows any number of explanatory variables to be included in the analysis. Sometimes, however, the large number of potential explanatory variables makes it difficult to know which variables to include. Many statistical packages provide some assistance by including automatic equation-building options. These options estimate a series of regression equations by successively adding (or deleting) variables according to prescribed rules. Generically, the methods are referred to as **stepwise regression**.

Before discussing how stepwise procedures work, consider a naive approach to the problem. You have already looked at correlation tables for indications of linear relationships. Why not simply include all explanatory variables that have large correlations with the dependent variable? There are two reasons for not doing this. First, although a variable is highly correlated with the dependent variable, it might also be highly correlated with other explanatory variables. Therefore, this variable might not be needed in the equation once the other explanatory variables have been included. Perhaps surprisingly, this happens frequently.

Second, even if a variable's correlation with the dependent variable is small, its contribution when it is included with a number of other explanatory variables can be greater than anticipated. Essentially, this variable can have something unique to say about the dependent variable that none of the other variables provides, and this fact might not be apparent from the correlation table. This behavior doesn't happen as often, but it is possible.

For these reasons it is sometimes useful to let the software discover the best combination of variables by means of a stepwise procedure. There are a number of procedures for building equations in a stepwise manner, but they all share a basic idea. Suppose there is an existing regression equation and you want to add another variable to this equation from a set of variables not yet included. At this point, the variables already in the equation have explained a certain percentage of the variation of the dependent variable. The residuals represent the part still unexplained. Therefore, in choosing the next variable to enter the equation, you should pick the one that is most highly correlated with the current residuals. If none of the remaining variables is highly correlated with the residuals, you might decide to quit. This is the essence of stepwise regression. However, besides adding variables to the equation, a stepwise procedure might delete a variable. This is sometimes reasonable because a variable entered early in the procedure might no longer be needed, given the presence of other variables that have entered subsequently.

Stepwise regression (and its variations) can be helpful in discovering a useful regression model, but it should not be used mindlessly.

Many statistical packages have three types of equation-building procedures: forward, backward, and stepwise. A *forward* procedure begins with no explanatory variables in the equation and successively adds one at a time until no remaining variables make a significant contribution. A *backward* procedure begins with *all* potential explanatory variables in the equation and deletes them one at a time until further deletion would do more harm than

---

[4]This section can be omitted without any loss of continuity.

good. Finally, a true *stepwise* procedure is much like a forward procedure, except that it also considers possible deletions along the way. All of these procedures have the same basic objective—to find an equation with a small s_e and a large R^2 (or adjusted R^2). There is no guarantee that they will all produce exactly the same final equation, but in most cases their final results are very similar. The important thing to realize is that the equations estimated along the way, including the final equation, are estimated exactly as before—by least squares. Therefore, none of these procedures produces any new results. They merely take the burden off the user of having to decide ahead of time which variables to include in the equation.

StatTools implements each of the forward, backward, and stepwise procedures. To use them, select the dependent variable and a set of *potential* explanatory variables. Then specify the criterion for adding and/or deleting variables from the equation. This can be done in two ways, with an *F*-value or a *p*-value. We suggest using *p*-values because they are easier to understand, but either method is easy to use. In the *p*-value method, select a *p*-value such as the default value of 0.05. If the regression coefficient for a potential entering variable would have a *p*-value less than 0.05 (if it were entered), then it is a candidate for entering (if the forward or stepwise procedure is used). The procedure selects the variable with the *smallest* *p*-value as the next entering variable. Similarly, if any currently included variable has a *p*-value greater than some value such as the default value of 0.10, then (with the stepwise and backward procedures) it is a candidate for leaving the equation. The methods stop when there are no candidates (according to their *p*-values) for entering or leaving the current equation.

The following continuation of the HyTex mail-order example illustrates these stepwise procedures.

EXAMPLE | **11.3 EXPLAINING SPENDING AMOUNTS AT HYTEX (CONTINUED)**

The analysis of the HyTex mail-order data (for the first 750 customers in the data set) resulted in a regression equation that included all potential explanatory variables except for Age, Gender, OwnHome, and Married. These were excluded because their *t*-values are large and their *p*-values are small (less than 0.05). Do forward, backward, and stepwise procedures produce the same regression equation for the amount spent in the current year?

Objective To use StatTools's Stepwise Regression procedure to analyze the HyTex data.

Solution

Each of these options is found in the StatTools Regression dialog box. It is just a matter of choosing the appropriate option from the Regression Type dropdown list. (See Figure 11.9.) In each, specify AmountSpent as the dependent variable and select all of the other variables (besides Customer) as *potential* explanatory variables. Once you choose one of the stepwise types, the dialog box changes, as shown in Figure 11.10, to include a Parameters section and an "advanced" option to Include Detailed Step Information. We suggest the choices in Figure 11.10 for stepwise regression.

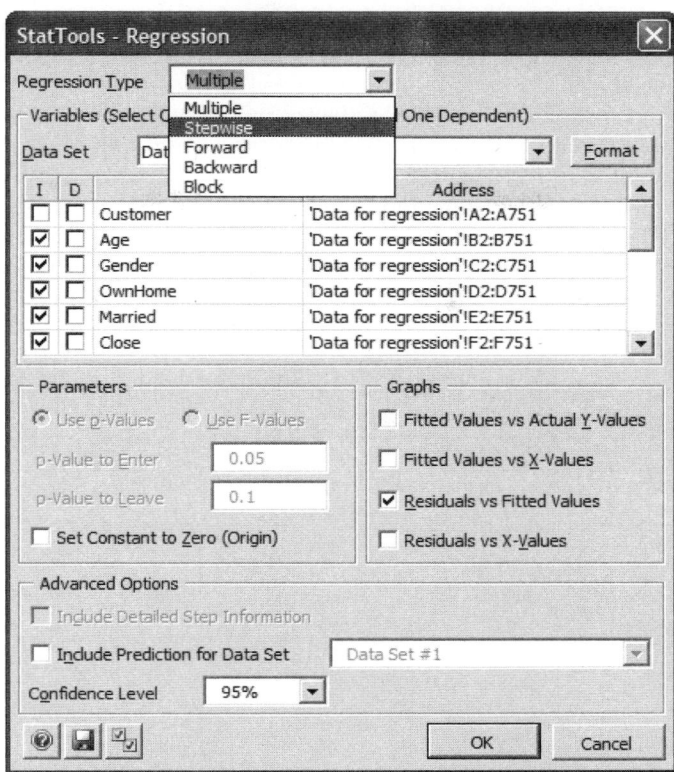

Figure 11.9
Regression Dialog
Box with Regression
Type Options

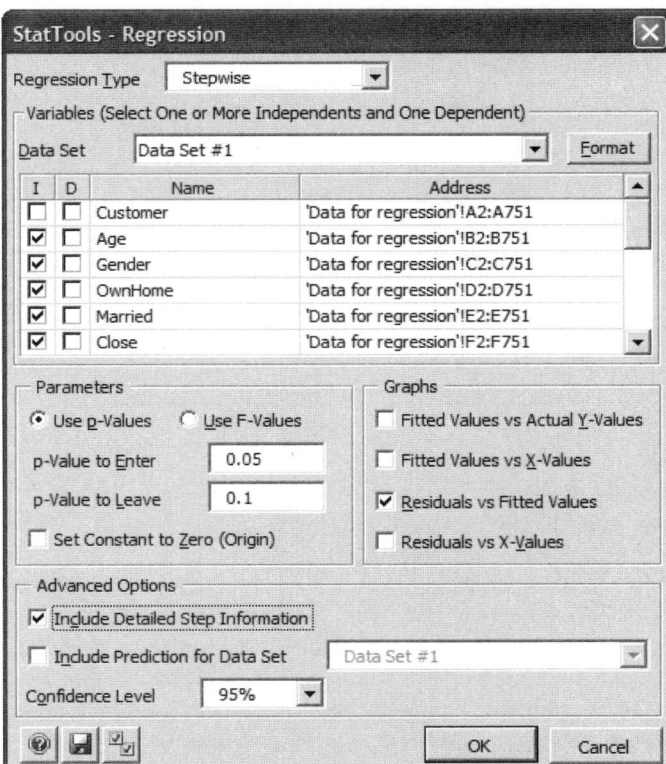

Figure 11.10
Dialog Box for
Stepwise Regression

It turns out that each stepwise procedure (stepwise, forward, and backward) produces the same *final* equation that we obtained previously, with all variables except Age, Gender, OwnHome, and Married included. This often happens, but not always. The stepwise and forward procedures add the variables in the order Salary, Catalogs, Close, Children, PrevCust, and PrevSpent. The backward procedure, which starts with *all* variables in the equation, eliminates variables in the order Age, Married, OwnHome, and Gender. A sample of the stepwise output appears in Figure 11.11. The variables that enter or exit the equation are listed at the bottom of the output. The usual regression output for the final equation also appears. Again, however, this final equation's output is *exactly* the same as when multiple regression is used with these particular variables.

Figure 11.11   Regression Output from Stepwise Procedure

	A	B	C	D	E	F	G
7		Multiple	R-Square	Adjusted	StErr of		
8	Summary	R		R-Square	Estimate		
9		0.8636	0.7458	0.7438	491.2283		
10							
11		Degrees of	Sum of	Mean of	F-Ratio	p-Value	
12	ANOVA Table	Freedom	Squares	Squares			
13	Explained	6	526113683.9	87685613.98	363.3805	< 0.0001	
14	Unexplained	743	179289770.9	241305.2099			
15							
16		Coefficient	Standard	t-Value	p-Value	Confidence Interval 95%	
17	Regression Table		Error			Lower	Upper
18	Constant	205.0936	70.3152	2.9168	0.0036	67.0534	343.1338
19	Salary	0.0180	0.0009	19.8773	< 0.0001	0.0162	0.0197
20	Catalogs	43.8067	2.8542	15.3481	< 0.0001	38.2034	49.4100
21	Close	-416.2462	45.0846	-9.2326	< 0.0001	-504.7546	-327.7378
22	Children	-161.1577	20.4828	-7.8679	< 0.0001	-201.3688	-120.9466
23	PrevCust	-543.5948	63.2988	-8.5878	< 0.0001	-667.8606	-419.3290
24	PrevSpent	0.2724	0.0525	5.1844	< 0.0001	0.1692	0.3755
25							
26		Multiple	R-Square	Adjusted	StErr of	Enter or	
27	Step Information	R		R-Square	Estimate	Exit	
28	Salary	0.6837	0.4674	0.4667	708.6821	Enter	
29	Catalogs	0.7841	0.6148	0.6138	603.0854	Enter	
30	Close	0.8192	0.6710	0.6697	557.7264	Enter	
31	Children	0.8477	0.7187	0.7171	516.1357	Enter	
32	PrevCust	0.8583	0.7366	0.7349	499.6982	Enter	
33	PrevSpent	0.8636	0.7458	0.7438	491.2283	Enter	

Stepwise regression or any of its variations can be very useful for narrowing down the set of all possible explanatory variables to a set that is useful for explaining a dependent variable. However, these procedures should not be used as a substitute for thoughtful analysis. With the availability of such procedures in statistical software packages, there is sometimes a tendency to turn the analysis over to the computer and accept its output. A good analyst does not just collect as much data as possible, throw it into a software package, and blindly report the results. There should always be some rationale, whether it is based on economic theory, business experience, or common sense, for the variables that are used to explain a given dependent variable. A thoughtless use of stepwise regression can sometimes capitalize on chance to obtain an equation with a reasonably large R^2 but no useful or practical interpretation. It is very possible that such an equation will not generalize well to new data.

Finally, keep in mind that if one stepwise procedure produces slightly different outputs than another (for example, one might include a variable, the other might exclude it), the differences are typically very small and are not worth agonizing about. The two equations typically have very similar R^2 values and standard errors of estimate, and they typically produce very similar predictions. If anything, most analysts prefer the smaller equation because of parsimony, but they realize that the differences are "at the margin."

PROBLEMS

Level A

23. The Undergraduate Data sheet of the file **P10_21.xlsx** contains information on 101 undergraduate business programs in the U.S., including various rankings by *Business Week*. Use forward, backward, and stepwise regression analysis to explore the relationship between the median starting salary and the following set of potential explanatory variables: annual cost, full-time enrollment, faculty-student ratio, average SAT score, and average ACT score. Do these three methods all lead to the same regression equation? If not, do you think any of the final equations are substantially better than any of the others?

24. The file **P10_08.xlsx** contains data on the top 200 professional golfers in each of the years 2003–2009. (The same data set was used in Example 3.4 in Chapter 3.)
  a. Create one large data set in a new sheet called All Years that has the data for all seven years stacked on top of one other. (This is possible because the variables are the same in each year.) In this combined data set, create a new column called Earnings per Round, the ratio of Earnings to Rounds. Similarly, create three other new variables, Eagles per Round, Birdies per Round, and Bogies per Round.
  b. Using the data set from part **a**, run a forward regression of Earnings per Round versus the following potential explanatory variables: Age, Yard/Drive, Driving Accuracy, Greens in Regulation, Putting Average, Sand Save Pct, Eagles per Round, Birdies per Round, and Bogies per Round. Given the results, comment on what seems to be important on the professional tour in terms of earnings per round. For any variable that does *not* end up in the equation, is it omitted because it is not related to Earnings per Round or because its effect is explained by other variables in the equation?
  c. Repeat part **b** with backward regression. Do you get the same, or basically the same, results?

25. In a study of housing demand, a county assessor is interested in developing a regression model to estimate the selling price of residential properties within her jurisdiction. She randomly selects 15 houses and records the selling price in addition to the following values: the size of the house (in hundreds of square feet), the total number of rooms in the house, the age of the house, and an indication of whether the house has an attached garage. These data are listed in the file **P10_26.xlsx**.
  a. Use stepwise regression to decide which explanatory variables should be included in the assessor's statistical model. Use the *p*-value method with a cutoff value of 0.05 for entering and leaving. Summarize your findings.
  b. How do the results in part **a** change when the critical *p*-value for entering and leaving is increased to 0.10? Explain any differences between the regression equation obtained here and the one found in part **a**.

26. Continuing Problem 2 with the data in the file **P10_04.xlsx**, employ stepwise regression to evaluate your conclusions regarding the specification of a regression model to predict the sales of deep-dish pizza by the Original Italian Pizza restaurant chain. Use the *p*-value method with a cutoff value of 0.05 for entering and leaving. Compare your conclusions in Problem 2 with those derived from a stepwise regression.

Level B

27. How sensitive are stepwise regression results to small changes in the data? This problem allows you to explore this. The file **P11_27.xlsm** can be used to generate 100 randomly chosen observations from a given population. It contains macros that help you do this. Specifically, the means, standard deviations, and correlations for the population of 10 *X*s and *Y* are given in rows 2–14. The macro has already been used to generate a "generic" row of data in row 16. It is done so that the *X*s and *Y* are normally distributed with the given means, standard deviations, and correlations. Press the F9 key a few times to see how the data in row 16 change. There is also a button you can click. When you do so, the generic row 16 is copied to rows 20–119 to generate new random data, and the new random data are frozen. Click on the button a few times to see how this works. Designate a StatTools data set in the range A19:L119 and run stepwise regression on the data. Then generate new data by clicking on the button and run stepwise regression again. Repeat this a few times. Then explain the results. Do all of the stepwise regressions produce

about the same results? Are they consistent with the parameters in the top section, particularly the correlations involving Y in row 14?

28. Repeat the previous problem at least once, using means, standard deviations, and correlations of your choice. The interesting thing you will discover is that you can't arbitrarily enter just any correlations between -1 and $+1$. For many choices, the generic row will exhibit #VALUE! errors. This means that no population could possibly have the correlations you entered. Try to find correlations that do *not* produce the #VALUE! errors.

11.7 THE PARTIAL F TEST[5]

There are many situations where a set of explanatory variables form a logical group. It is then common to include all of the variables in the equation or exclude all of them. An example of this is when one of the explanatory variables is categorical with more than two categories. In this case you model it by including dummy variables—one fewer than the number of categories. If you decide that the categorical variable is worth including, you might want to keep all of the dummies (except of course for the reference dummy). Otherwise, you might decide to exclude all of them. We look at an example of this type subsequently.

For now, consider the following general situation. You have already estimated an equation that includes the variables X_1 through X_j, and you are proposing to estimate a larger equation that includes X_{j+1} through X_k in addition to the variables X_1 through X_j. That is, the larger equation includes all of the variables from the smaller equation, but it also includes $k - j$ extra variables. These extra variables are the ones that form a group. We assume that it makes logical sense to include all of them or none of them.

The complete equation always contains all of the explanatory variables in the reduced equation, plus some more. In other words, the reduced equation is a subset of the complete equation.

In this section we describe a test to determine whether the extra variables provide enough *extra* explanatory power as a group to warrant their inclusion in the equation. The test is called the partial F test. The original equation is called the *reduced* equation, and the larger equation is called the *complete* equation. In simple terms, the partial F test tests whether the complete equation is significantly better than the reduced equation.[6]

The test itself is intuitive. The output from the ANOVA tables of the reduced and complete equations is used to form an F-ratio. This ratio measures how much the sum of squared residuals, *SSE, decreases* by including the extra variables in the equation. It *must* decrease by some amount because the sum of squared residuals cannot increase when extra variables are added to an equation. But if it does not decrease sufficiently, the extra variables might not explain enough to warrant their inclusion in the equation, and they should probably be excluded. The F-ratio measures this. If it is sufficiently large, the extra variables are worth including; otherwise, they can safely be excluded.

To state the test formally, let β_{j+1} through β_k be the coefficients of the extra variables in the complete equation. Then the null hypothesis is that these extra variables have no effect on the dependent variable, that is, $H_0:\beta_{j+1} = \cdots = \beta_k = 0$. The alternative is that at least one of the extra variables has an effect on the dependent variable, so that at least one of these βs is not zero. The hypotheses are summarized in the box.

---

[5]This section is somewhat more advanced and can be omitted without any loss of continuity.
[6]StatTools does not run the partial F test, but it provides all of the ingredients to do so.

> **Hypotheses for the Partial F Test**
>
> The null hypothesis is that the coefficients of all the extra explanatory variables in the complete equation are zero. The alternative is that at least one of these coefficients is not zero.

To run the test, estimate both the reduced and complete equations and look at the associated ANOVA tables. Let SSE_R and SSE_C be the sums of squared errors from the reduced and complete equations, respectively. Also, let MSE_C be the mean square error for the complete equation. All of these quantities appear in the ANOVA tables. Next, form the F-ratio in Equation (11.4).

> **Test Statistic for Partial F Test**
>
> $$F\text{-ratio} = \frac{(SSE_R - SSE_C)/(k - j)}{MSE_C} \qquad \textbf{(11.4)}$$

The numerator includes the reduction in sum of squared errors discussed previously. If the null hypothesis is true, this F-ratio has an F distribution with $k - j$ and $n - k - 1$ degrees of freedom. If it is sufficiently large, H_0 can be rejected. As usual, the best way to run the test is to find the p-value corresponding to this F-ratio. This is the probability beyond the calculated F-ratio in the F distribution with $k - j$ and $n - k - 1$ degrees of freedom. In words, you can reject the hypothesis that the extra variables have no explanatory power if this p-value is sufficiently small—less than 0.05, say.

This F-ratio and corresponding p-value are *not* part of the StatTools regression output. However, they are fairly easy to obtain. To do so, run two regressions, one for the reduced equation and one for the complete equation, and use the appropriate values from their ANOVA tables to calculate the F-ratio in Equation (11.4). Then use Excel's FDIST function in the form **FDIST(F-ratio, $k - j$, $n - k - 1$)** to calculate the corresponding p-value. The procedure is illustrated in the following example. It uses the bank discrimination data from Example 10.3 of the previous chapter.

EXAMPLE | **11.4 POSSIBLE GENDER DISCRIMINATION IN SALARY AT FIFTH NATIONAL BANK OF SPRINGFIELD**

Recall from Example 11.3 that Fifth National Bank has 208 employees. The data for these employees are stored in the file **Bank Salaries.xlsx**. In the previous chapter we ran several regressions for Salary to see whether there is convincing evidence of salary discrimination against females. We will continue this analysis here. First, we regress Salary versus the Female dummy, YrsExper, and the interaction between Female and YrsExper, Interaction(YrsExper,Female). This is the reduced equation. Then we will see whether the EducLev dummies, EducLev=2 to EducLev=5, add anything significant to the reduced equation. If so, we will then see whether the JobGrade dummies, JobGrade=2 to JobGrade=6, add anything significant to what we already have. If so, we will finally see whether the interactions between the Female dummy and the education dummies, Interaction(Female,EducLev=2) to Interaction(Female,EducLev=5), add anything significant to what we already have.

Objective To use several partial F tests to see whether various groups of explanatory variables should be included in a regression equation for salary, given that other variables are already in the equation.

Solution

First, it is possible to create all of the dummies and interaction variables with StatTools's Data Utilities procedures. These could be entered directly with Excel functions, but StatTools makes the process much quicker and easier. Also, note that there are three sets of dummies: for gender, job grade, and education level. When these are used in a regression equation, the dummy for one category of each should always be excluded; it is the reference category. The reference categories we have used are male, job grade 1, and education level 1.

The output for the "smallest" equation, the one using Female, YrsExper, and Interaction(YrsExper,Female) as explanatory variables, appears in Figure 11.12. (This output is in a sheet called Regression1.) These three variables already explain 63.9% of the variation in Salary.

Figure 11.12 Reduced Equation for Bank Example

	A	B	C	D	E	F	G
7		Multiple			Adjusted	StErr of	
8	*Summary*	R	R-Square		R-Square	Estimate	
9		0.7991	0.6386		0.6333	6816.298	
10							
11		Degrees of	Sum of		Mean of		
12	*ANOVA Table*	Freedom	Squares		Squares	F-Ratio	p-Value
13	Explained	3	16748875071		5582958357	120.1620	< 0.0001
14	Unexplained	204	9478232160		46461922.35		
15							
16			Standard				Confidence Interval 95%
17	*Regression Table*	Coefficient	Error		t-Value	p-Value	Lower	Upper
18	Constant	30430.028	1216.574		25.0129	< 0.0001	28031.356	32828.700
19	YrsExper	1527.762	90.460		16.8887	< 0.0001	1349.405	1706.119
20	Female	4098.252	1665.842		2.4602	0.0147	813.776	7382.727
21	Interaction(YrsExper,Female)	-1247.798	136.676		-9.1296	< 0.0001	-1517.277	-978.320

The output for the next equation, which adds the explanatory variables EducLev=2 to EducLev=5, appears in Figure 11.13. (This output is in a sheet called Regression2.) This equation appears to be much better. For example, R^2 has increased to 73.1%. You can check whether it is *significantly* better with the partial F test in rows 27 through 33. (This part of the output is not given by StatTools; you have to enter it manually.) The degrees of freedom in cell B28 is 4, the number of *extra* variables. The degrees of freedom in cell B29 is the same as the value in cell B14, the degrees of freedom for *SSE*. Then the F-ratio is calculated in cell B32 with the formula

=((Regression1!C13-C14)/B28)/D14

where Regression1!C13 refers to the *SSE* for the reduced equation from the Regression1 sheet. Finally, the corresponding p-value can be calculated in cell B33 with the formula

=FDIST(B30,B28,B29)

It is practically zero, so there is no doubt that the education dummies add significantly to the explanatory power of the equation.

Figure 11.13 Equation with Education Dummies Added

	A	B	C	D	E	F	G
7		Multiple	R-Square	Adjusted	StErr of		
8	Summary	R		R-Square	Estimate		
9		0.8552	0.7314	0.7220	5935.254		
10							
11		Degrees of	Sum of	Mean of	F-Ratio	p-Value	
12	ANOVA Table	Freedom	Squares	Squares			
13	Explained	7	19181659773	2740237110	77.7875	< 0.0001	
14	Unexplained	200	7045447458	35227237.29			
15							
16		Coefficient	Standard	t-Value	p-Value	Confidence Interval 95%	
17	Regression Table		Error			Lower	Upper
18	Constant	24780.996	1551.053	15.9769	< 0.0001	21722.480	27839.512
19	YrsExper	1456.388	79.761	18.2593	< 0.0001	1299.107	1613.669
20	Female	4898.656	1454.087	3.3689	0.0009	2031.347	7765.965
21	EducLev = 2	546.549	1418.139	0.3854	0.7004	-2249.874	3342.972
22	EducLev = 3	3587.341	1287.361	2.7866	0.0058	1048.798	6125.885
23	EducLev = 4	5862.894	2346.571	2.4985	0.0133	1235.700	10490.088
24	EducLev = 5	9428.090	1337.292	7.0501	< 0.0001	6791.089	12065.092
25	Interaction(YrsExper,Female)	-1029.858	121.924	-8.4467	< 0.0001	-1270.279	-789.437
26							
27	Partial F test for including EducLev dummies						
28	df numerator	4					
29	df denominator	200					
30	F ratio	68.863					
31	p-value	0.0000					

Do the job grade dummies add anything more? You can again use the partial F test, but now the previous *complete* equation becomes the new *reduced* equation, and the equation that includes the new job grade dummies becomes the new complete equation. The output for this new complete equation appears in Figure 11.14. (This output is in a sheet called Regression3.) The partial F test is performed in rows 32 through 36 exactly as before. For example, the formula for the F-ratio in cell B35 is

=(('Regression2'!C14-C14)/B33)/D14

Note how the SSE_R term in Equation (11.4) now comes from the Regression2 sheet because this sheet contains the current *reduced* equation. The terms *reduced* and *complete* are relative. The complete equation in one stage becomes the reduced equation in the next stage. In any case, the p-value in cell B36 is again extremely small, so there is no doubt that the job grade dummies add significantly to what was already in the equation. In fact, R^2 has increased from 73.1% to 81.5%.

Finally, you can add the interactions between Female and the education dummies. The resulting output is shown in Figure 11.15. (This output is in a sheet called Regression4.) Again, the terms *reduced* and *complete* are relative. This output now corresponds to the complete equation, and the previous output corresponds to the reduced equation. The formula in cell B39 for the F-ratio is now

=(('Regression3'!C14-C14)/B37)/D14

Its SSE_R value comes from the Regression3 sheet. Note that the increase in R^2 is from 81.5% to only 82.0%. Also, the p-value in cell B40 is *not* extremely small. According to the partial F test, it is not quite small enough to qualify for statistical significance at the 5% level. Based on this evidence, there is not much to gain from including the interaction terms in the equation, so you would probably elect to exclude them.

Figure 11.14 Regression Output with Job Dummies Added

	A	B	C	D	E	F	G
7		Multiple	R-Square	Adjusted	StErr of		
8	*Summary*	R		R-Square	Estimate		
9		0.9028	0.8150	0.8036	4988.127		
10							
11		Degrees of	Sum of	Mean of	F-Ratio	p-Value	
12	*ANOVA Table*	Freedom	Squares	Squares			
13	Explained	12	21375231697	1781269308	71.5904	< 0.0001	
14	Unexplained	195	4851875534	24881413			
15							
16		Coefficient	Standard	t-Value	p-Value	Confidence Interval 95%	
17	*Regression Table*		Error			Lower	Upper
18	Constant	25624.820	1450.166	17.6703	< 0.0001	22764.798	28484.843
19	YrsExper	1109.889	105.608	10.5096	< 0.0001	901.610	1318.169
20	Female	6066.112	1267.472	4.7860	< 0.0001	3566.399	8565.825
21	EducLev = 2	-675.106	1204.702	-0.5604	0.5759	-3051.024	1700.812
22	EducLev = 3	447.269	1147.751	0.3897	0.6972	-1816.330	2710.868
23	EducLev = 4	525.063	2109.284	0.2489	0.8037	-3634.875	4685.001
24	EducLev = 5	1946.144	1394.627	1.3955	0.1645	-804.344	4696.633
25	JobGrade = 2	2245.355	1034.406	2.1707	0.0312	205.295	4285.414
26	JobGrade = 3	5552.070	1098.504	5.0542	< 0.0001	3385.596	7718.543
27	JobGrade = 4	9970.290	1314.585	7.5844	< 0.0001	7377.659	12562.921
28	JobGrade = 5	13235.194	1631.437	8.1126	< 0.0001	10017.667	16452.720
29	JobGrade = 6	14928.127	2695.706	5.5377	< 0.0001	9611.644	20244.610
30	Interaction(YrsExper,Female)	-1002.905	119.060	-8.4235	< 0.0001	-1237.716	-768.094
31							
32	Partial F test for including JobGrade dummies						
33	df numerator	5					
34	df denominator	195					
35	F ratio	17.632					
36	p-value	0.0000					

Before leaving this example, we make several comments. First, the partial test is *the* formal test of significance for an extra set of variables. Many users look only at the R^2 and/or s_e values to check whether extra variables are doing a "good job." For example, they might cite that R^2 went from 81.5% to 82.0% or that s_e went from 4988 to 4965 as evidence that extra variables provide a "significantly" better fit. Although these are important indicators, they are not the basis for a *formal* hypothesis test.

Second, if the partial F test shows that a block of variables is significant, it does not imply that each variable in this block is significant. Some of these variables can have low t-values. Consider Figure 11.13, for example. The education dummies as a whole are significant, but one of these dummies, EducLev=2, is clearly not significant. Some analysts favor excluding the *individual* variables that aren't significant, whereas others favor keeping the whole block or excluding the whole block. We lean toward the latter but recognize that either approach is valid. Fortunately, the results are often nearly the same either way.

Third, producing all of these outputs and doing the partial F tests is a lot of work. Therefore, a Block option is included in StatTools to simplify the analysis. To run the analysis in this example in one step, select the Block option from the Regression Type dropdown list. The dialog box then changes, as shown in Figure 11.16. Select four blocks and then check which variables are in which blocks (B1 to B4). Block 1 has Female, YrsExper, and Interaction(YrsExper,Female), block 2 has the education dummies, block 3 has the job grade dummies, and block 4 has the interactions between

Figure 11.15 Regression Output with Interaction Terms Added

	A	B	C	D	E	F	G
7		Multiple	R-Square	Adjusted	StErr of		
8	Summary	R		R-Square	Estimate		
9		0.9058	0.8204	0.8054	4965.729		
10							
11		Degrees of	Sum of	Mean of	F-Ratio	p-Value	
12	ANOVA Table	Freedom	Squares	Squares			
13	Explained	16	21517339674	1344833730	54.5384	< 0.0001	
14	Unexplained	191	4709767556	24658468.88			
15							
16			Standard	t-Value	p-Value	Confidence Interval 95%	
17	Regression Table	Coefficient	Error			Lower	Upper
18	Constant	19845.279	3263.760	6.0805	< 0.0001	13407.637	26282.922
19	YrsExper	1166.782	109.100	10.6946	< 0.0001	951.586	1381.977
20	Female	12424.015	3457.402	3.5935	0.0004	5604.421	19243.609
21	EducLev = 2	3114.496	3666.760	0.8494	0.3967	-4118.048	10347.040
22	EducLev = 3	6991.038	3257.025	2.1464	0.0331	566.681	13415.395
23	EducLev = 4	6394.234	4312.345	1.4828	0.1398	-2111.702	14900.170
24	EducLev = 5	7550.157	3268.374	2.3101	0.0220	1103.414	13996.900
25	JobGrade = 2	2142.469	1038.726	2.0626	0.0405	93.621	4191.316
26	JobGrade = 3	5629.803	1096.800	5.1329	< 0.0001	3466.406	7793.200
27	JobGrade = 4	10092.551	1312.448	7.6899	< 0.0001	7503.796	12681.305
28	JobGrade = 5	13038.574	1636.716	7.9663	< 0.0001	9810.215	16266.934
29	JobGrade = 6	13672.521	2762.533	4.9493	< 0.0001	8223.528	19121.513
30	Interaction(YrsExper,Female)	-1069.576	122.680	-8.7184	< 0.0001	-1311.558	-827.594
31	Interaction(Female EducLev = 2)	-3923.850	3882.671	-1.0106	0.3135	-11582.270	3734.570
32	Interaction(Female,EducLev = 3)	-7533.870	3448.578	-2.1846	0.0301	-14336.060	-731.680
33	Interaction(Female,EducLev = 4)	-6471.909	4864.678	-1.3304	0.1850	-16067.301	3123.484
34	Interaction(Female,EducLev = 5)	-6178.817	3368.287	-1.8344	0.0681	-12822.635	465.000
35							
36	Partial F test for including EducLev/Female interactions						
37	df numerator	4					
38	df denominator	191					
39	F ratio	1.441					

Female and the education dummies. Finally, specify 0.05 as the p-value to enter, which in this case indicates how significant the block *as a whole* must be to enter (for the partial F test).

The regression calculations are then done in stages. At each stage, the partial F test checks whether a block is significant. If it is, the variables in this block enter and the procedure goes to the next stage. If it is not, the procedure ends; neither this block nor any later blocks enter.

The output from this procedure appears in Figure 11.17. The middle part of the output shows the final regression equation. The output in rows 34 through 37 indicates summary measures after successive blocks have entered. Note that the final block, the interactions between Female and the education dummies, is not in the final equation. This block did not pass the partial F test at the 5% level.

For comparison, we ran the block procedure a second time, changing the order of the blocks. Now block 2 includes the job grade dummies, block 3 includes the education dummies, and block 4 includes the interactions between Female and the education dummies. The regression output appears in Figure 11.18. Note that *neither* of the last two blocks enters the equation this time. Once the job grade dummies are in the equation, the terms including education are no longer needed. The implication is that the order of the blocks can make a difference.

Figure 11.16
Dialog Box for Block Regression Option

StatTools - Regression

Regression Type: Block   Number of Blocks: 4

Variables (Select Blocks and One Dependent)

Data Set: Data Set #1   Format

B1	B2	B3	B4	D	Name	Address
☐	☐	☑	☐	☐	JobGrade = 5	'Data'!T2:T209
☐	☐	☑	☐	☐	JobGrade = 6	'Data'!U2:U209
☐	☐	☐	☐	☐	HasPCJob	'Data'!V2:V209
☑	☐	☐	☐	☐	Interaction(YrsExper,Fe..	'Data'!W2:W209
☐	☐	☐	☐	☐	Interaction(Female,Educ..	'Data'!X2:X209
☐	☐	☐	☑	☐	Interaction(Female,Educ..	'Data'!Y2:Y209

Parameters
- ● Use p-Values   ○ Use F-Values
- p-Value to Enter: 0.05
- p-Value to Leave: 0.1
- ☐ Set Constant to Zero (Origin)

Graphs
- ☐ Fitted Values vs Actual Y-Values
- ☐ Fitted Values vs X-Values
- ☐ Residuals vs Fitted Values
- ☐ Residuals vs X-Values

Advanced Options
- ☑ Include Detailed Step Information
- ☐ Include Prediction for Data Set   Data Set #1
- Confidence Level: 95%

OK   Cancel

Figure 11.17   Block Regression Output

	A	B	C	D	E	F	G
7		Multiple	R-Square	Adjusted	StErr of		
8	Summary	R		R-Square	Estimate		
9		0.9028	0.8150	0.8036	4988.127		
10							
11		Degrees of	Sum of	Mean of	F-Ratio	p-Value	
12	ANOVA Table	Freedom	Squares	Squares			
13	Explained	12	21375231697	1781269308	70.1218	< 0.0001	
14	Unexplained	191	4851875534	25402489.71			
15							
16		Coefficient	Standard	t-Value	p-Value	Confidence Interval 95%	
17	Regression Table		Error			Lower	Upper
18	Constant	25624.820	1450.166	17.670	< 0.0001	22764.424	28485.217
19	YrsExper	1109.889	105.608	10.510	< 0.0001	901.582	1318.196
20	Female	6066.112	1267.472	4.786	< 0.0001	3566.072	8566.152
21	Interaction(YrsExper,Female)	-1002.905	119.060	-8.424	< 0.0001	-1237.747	-768.063
22	EducLev = 2	-675.106	1204.702	-0.560	0.5759	-3051.335	1701.123
23	EducLev = 3	447.269	1147.751	0.390	0.6972	-1816.626	2711.164
24	EducLev = 4	525.063	2109.284	0.249	0.8037	-3635.419	4685.545
25	EducLev = 5	1946.144	1394.627	1.395	0.1645	-804.704	4696.993
26	JobGrade = 2	2245.355	1034.406	2.171	0.0312	205.028	4285.681
27	JobGrade = 3	5552.070	1098.504	5.054	< 0.0001	3385.313	7718.826
28	JobGrade = 4	9970.290	1314.585	7.584	< 0.0001	7377.320	12563.260
29	JobGrade = 5	13235.194	1631.437	8.113	< 0.0001	10017.247	16453.141
30	JobGrade = 6	14928.127	2695.706	5.538	< 0.0001	9610.948	20245.306
31							
32		Multiple	R-Square	Adjusted	StErr of	Entry	
33	Step Information	R		R-Square	Estimate	Number	
34	Block 1	0.7991	0.6386	0.6333	6816.298	1	
35	Block 2	0.8552	0.7314	0.7220	5935.254	2	
36	Block 3	0.9028	0.8150	0.8036	4988.127	3	
37	Block 4	Did Not Enter					

Figure 11.18 Block Regression Output with Order of Blocks Changed

	A	B	C	D	E	F	G
7		Multiple	R-Square	Adjusted	StErr of		
8	Summary	R		R-Square	Estimate		
9		0.9005	0.8109	0.8033	4991.635		
10							
11		Degrees of	Sum of	Mean of	F-Ratio	p-Value	
12	ANOVA Table	Freedom	Squares	Squares			
13	Explained	8	21268738998	2658592375	104.5557	< 0.0001	
14	Unexplained	195	4958368233	25427529.4			
15							
16		Coefficient	Standard	t-Value	p-Value	Confidence Interval 95%	
17	Regression Table		Error			Lower	Upper
18	Constant	26104.223	1105.443	23.614	< 0.0001	23924.064	28284.381
19	YrsExper	1070.883	102.013	10.497	< 0.0001	869.692	1272.074
20	Female	6063.328	1266.322	4.788	< 0.0001	3565.883	8560.773
21	Interaction(YrsExper,Female)	-1021.051	118.726	-8.600	< 0.0001	-1255.202	-786.900
22	JobGrade = 2	2596.493	1010.122	2.570	0.0109	604.325	4588.660
23	JobGrade = 3	6221.394	998.177	6.233	< 0.0001	4252.784	8190.003
24	JobGrade = 4	11071.954	1172.588	9.442	< 0.0001	8759.371	13384.537
25	JobGrade = 5	14946.576	1340.249	11.152	< 0.0001	12303.332	17589.821
26	JobGrade = 6	17097.372	2390.671	7.152	< 0.0001	12382.481	21812.262
27							
28		Multiple	R-Square	Adjusted	StErr of	Entry	
29	Step Information	R		R-Square	Estimate	Number	
30	Block 1	0.7991	0.6386	0.6333	6816.298	1	
31	Block 2	0.9005	0.8109	0.8033	4991.635	2	
32	Block 3	Did Not Enter					
33	Block 4	Did Not Enter					

Finally, although we have concentrated on the partial F test and statistical significance in this example, we don't want you to lose sight of the bigger picture. Once you have decided on a "final" regression equation such as the one in Figure 11.14, you need to analyze its implications for the problem at hand. In this case the bank is interested in possible salary discrimination against females, so you should interpret this final equation in these terms. We will not go through this exercise again here—we did similar interpretations in the previous chapter. Our point is simply that you shouldn't get so immersed in the details of statistical significance that you lose sight of the original purpose of the analysis. ∎

PROBLEMS

Level A

29. A regional express delivery service company recently conducted a study to investigate the relationship between the cost of shipping a package (Y), the package weight (X_1), and the distance shipped (X_2). Twenty packages were randomly selected from among the large number received for shipment and a detailed analysis of the shipping cost was conducted for each package. These sample observations are given in the file **P10_22.xlsx**.
   a. Estimate a multiple regression equation involving the two given explanatory variables. What do the

results in the ANOVA table indicate about this regression?
   b. Is it worthwhile to add the terms X^2_1 and X^2_2 to the regression equation in part **a**? Base your decision here on a partial F test and a 5% significance level.
   c. Is it worthwhile to add the term X_1X_2 to the most appropriate reduced equation determined in part **b**? Again, perform a partial F test with a 5% significance level.
   d. What regression equation should this company use in predicting the cost of shipping a package? Defend your recommendation.

30. Continuing Problem 6 with the data in the file **P10_18.xlsx**, refer to the original multiple regression model (the one that includes the age of the auctioned item and the number of bidders as explanatory variables) as the *reduced* equation. Suppose now that the antique collector believes that the *rate of increase* of the auction price with the age of the item will be driven upward by a large number of bidders.

  a. Revise the reduced regression equation to model this additional feature of the problem. Estimate this larger regression equation, called the *complete* equation.

  b. Using a 5% significance level, perform a partial *F* test to check whether the complete equation is significantly better than the reduced equation. Briefly explain your findings.

31. Many companies manufacture products that are at least partially produced using chemicals (for example, paint, gasoline, and steel). In many cases, the quality of the finished product is a function of the temperature and pressure at which the chemical reactions take place. Suppose that a particular manufacturer wants to model the quality (Y) of a product as a function of the temperature (X_1) and the pressure (X_2) at which it is produced. The file **P10_39.xlsx** contains data obtained from a designed experiment involving these variables. Note that the quality score can range from a minimum of 0 to a maximum of 100 for each product.

  a. Estimate a multiple regression equation that includes the two given explanatory variables. What do the results in the ANOVA table indicate about this regression?

  b. Use a partial *F* test with a 5% significance level to decide whether it is worthwhile to add second-order terms (X_1^2, X_2^2, and X_1X_2) to the regression equation in part **a**.

  c. Which regression equation is the most appropriate one for modeling the quality of the product? Keep

in mind that a good statistical model is usually parsimonious.

Level B

32. Continuing Problem 27 with the simulated data in the file **P11_27.xlsm**, suppose the analyst believes that the variables $X4$ and $X6$ are the most important variables, $X2$, $X8$, and $X9$ are next most important, and the rest are of questionable importance. (Perhaps this is based on economic considerations.) Run stepwise regression on this data set. Then use the block regression procedure in StatTools, using the analyst's three blocks, and compare the block results to the stepwise results. Why are they different? Then repeat the whole comparison several more times, each time clicking on the button first to generate new data for the regressions. Do you get the same results (about which blocks enter and which don't) on each run?

33. The file **P02_35.xlsx** contains data from a survey of 500 randomly selected households.

  a. To explain the variation in the size of the Monthly Payment variable, estimate a multiple regression equation that includes the *numerical* variables Family Size, Total Income (sum of First Income and Second Income), Utilities, and Debt. What do the results in the ANOVA table indicate about this regression?

  b. Determine whether the *categorical* Location and Ownership variables add significantly to explaining Monthly Payment. Do this by using a partial *F* test, at the 5% significance level, for the group of extra variables that includes Ownership and the dummies corresponding to Location. Do the results depend on which Location dummy is used as the reference category? Experiment to find out.

11.8 OUTLIERS

In all of the regression examples so far, we have ignored the possibility of outliers. Unfortunately, outliers cannot be ignored in many real applications. They are often present, and they can often have a substantial effect on the results. In this section we briefly discuss outliers in the context of regression—how to detect them and what to do about them.

You probably tend to think of an **outlier** as an observation that has an extreme value for at least one variable. For example, if salaries in a data set are mostly in the $40,000 to $80,000 range, but one salary is $350,000, this observation is clearly an outlier with respect to salary. However, in a regression context outliers are not always this obvious. In fact, an observation can be considered an outlier for several reasons, and some types of outliers can be difficult to detect. An observation can be an outlier for one or more of the following reasons.

Potential Characteristics of an Outlier

Outliers can come in several forms, as indicated in this list.

1. It has an extreme value for one or more variables.

2. Its value of the dependent variable is much larger or smaller than predicted by the regression line, and its residual is abnormally large in magnitude. An example appears in Figure 11.19. The line in this scatterplot fits most of the points, but it misses badly on the one obvious outlier. This outlier has a large positive residual, but its Y value is not abnormally large. Its Y value is only large relative to points with the same X value that it has.

Figure 11.19   Outlier with a Large Residual

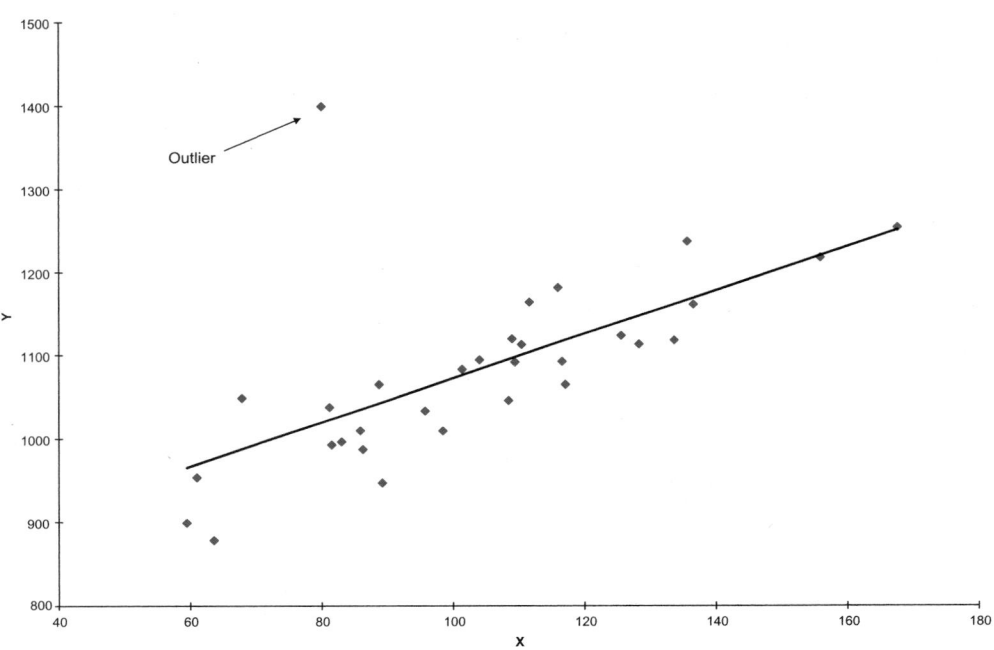

3. Its residual is not only large in magnitude, but this point "tilts" the regression line toward it. An example appears in Figure 11.20. The two lines shown are the regression lines with the outlier and without it. The outlier makes a big difference in the slope and intercept of the regression line. This type of outlier is called an **influential point**, for the obvious reason.

4. Its values of individual explanatory variables are not extreme, but they fall outside the general pattern of the other observations. An example appears in Figure 11.21. Here, we assume that the two variables shown, YrsExper (years of experience) and Rating (an employee's performance rating) are both explanatory variables for some other dependent variable (Salary) that isn't shown in the plot. The obvious outlier does not have an abnormal value of either YrsExper or Rating, but it falls well outside the pattern of most employees.

Once outliers have been identified, there is still the dilemma of what to do with them. In most cases the regression output will look "nicer" if you delete outliers, but this is not necessarily appropriate. If you can argue that the outlier isn't really a member of the relevant population, then it is appropriate and probably best to delete it. But if no such

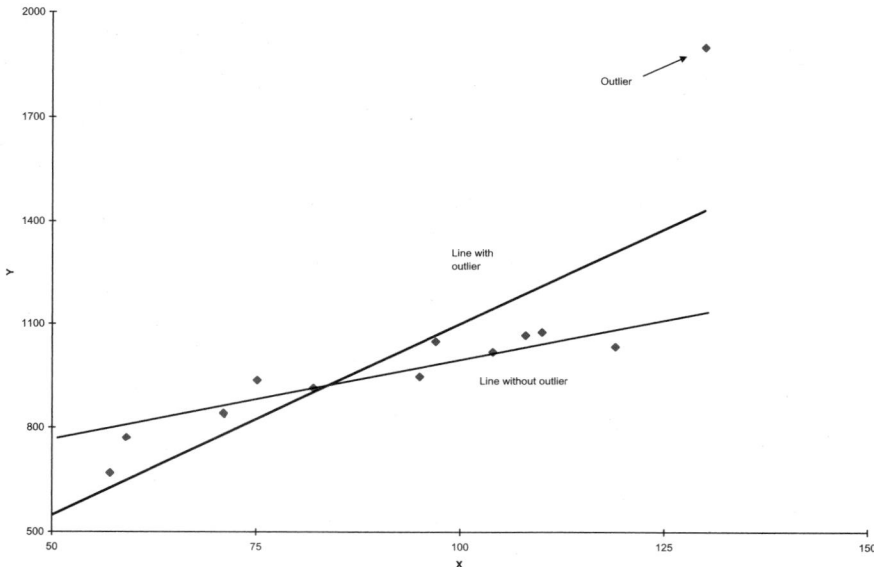

Figure 11.20
Outlier That Tilts the Regression Line

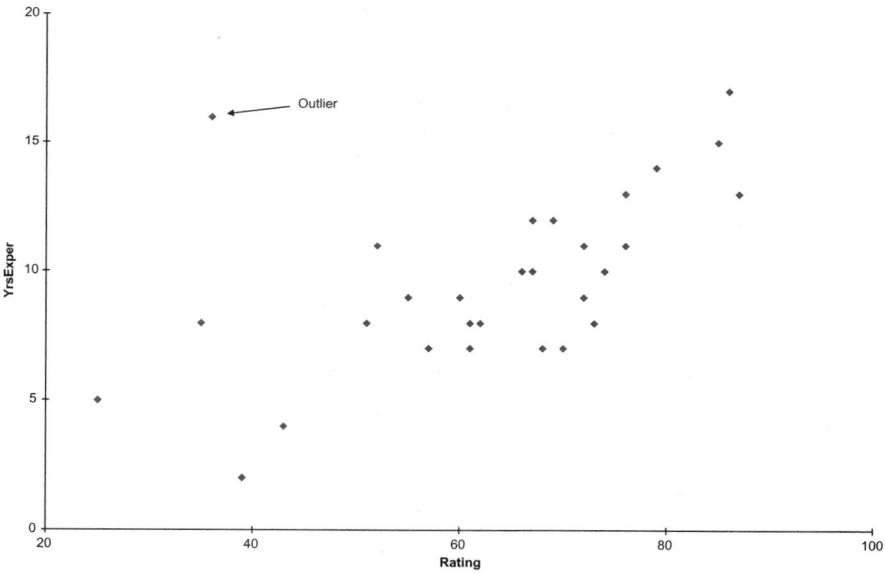

Figure 11.21
Outlier Outside the Pattern of Explanatory Variables

argument can be made, then it is not really appropriate to delete the outlier just to make the analysis come out better. Perhaps the best advice in this case is the advice we gave in the previous chapter: Run the analysis with the outliers and run it again without them. If the key outputs do not change much, then it does not really matter whether the outliers are included or not. If the key outputs change substantially, then report the results both with and without the outliers, along with a verbal explanation.

We illustrate this procedure in the following continuation of the bank discrimination example.

11.4 POSSIBLE GENDER DISCRIMINATION IN SALARY AT FIFTH NATIONAL BANK OF SPRINGFIELD (CONTINUED)

Of the 208 employees at Fifth National Bank, are there any obvious outliers? In what sense are they outliers? Does it matter to the regression results, particularly those concerning gender discrimination, whether the outliers are removed?

Objective   To locate possible outliers in the bank salary data, and to see to what extent they affect the regression model.

Solution

There are several places to look for outliers. An obvious place is the Salary variable. The box plot in Figure 11.22 shows that there are several employees making substantially more in salary than most of the employees. You could consider these outliers and remove them, arguing perhaps that these are senior managers who shouldn't be included in the discrimination analysis. We leave it to you to check whether the regression results are any different with these high-salary employees than without them.

Figure 11.22

Box Plot of Salaries for Bank Data

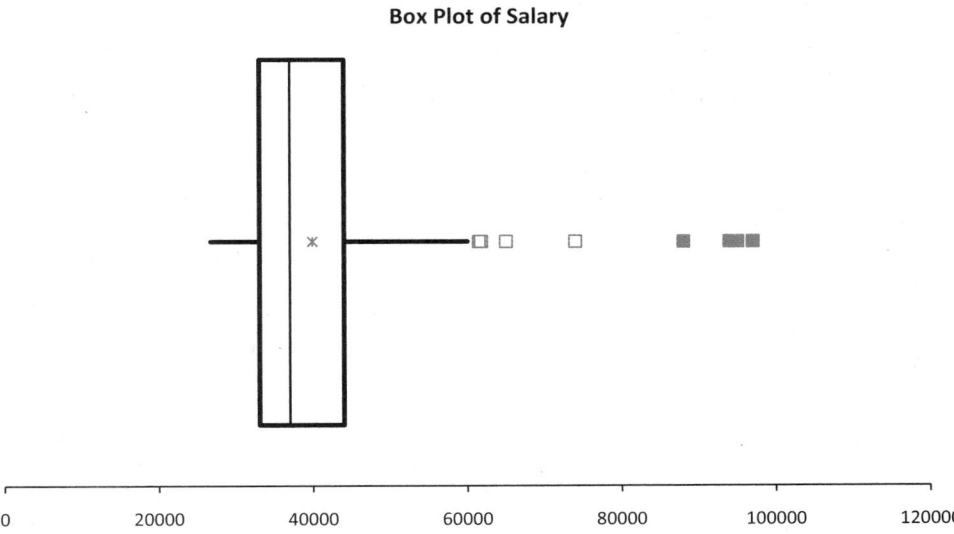

Another place to look is at a scatterplot of the residuals versus the fitted values. This type of plot (offered as an option by StatTools) shows points with abnormally large residuals. For example, we ran the regression with Female, YrsExper, Interaction(YrsExper,Female), and four education dummies, and we obtained the output and scatterplot in Figures 11.23 and 11.24. This scatterplot has several points that could be considered outliers, but we focus on the point identified in the figure. The residual for this point is approximately $-23{,}000$. Given that s_e for this regression is approximately 5900, this residual is about four standard errors below zero—quite a lot. If you examine this point more closely, you will see that it corresponds to employee 208, who is a 62-year-old female employee in the highest job grade. She has 33 years of experience with Fifth National, she has a graduate degree, and she earns only $30,000. She is clearly an unusual employee, and there are probably special circumstances that can explain her small salary, although we can only guess at what they are.

Figure 11.23 Regression Output with Outlier Included

	A	B	C	D	E	F	G
7		Multiple	R-Square	Adjusted	StErr of		
8	*Summary*	R		R-Square	Estimate		
9		0.8552	0.7314	0.7220	5935.254		
10							
11		Degrees of	Sum of	Mean of	F-Ratio	p-Value	
12	*ANOVA Table*	Freedom	Squares	Squares			
13	Explained	7	19181659773	2740237110	77.7875	< 0.0001	
14	Unexplained	200	7045447458	35227237.29			
15							
16		Coefficient	Standard	t-Value	p-Value	Confidence Interval 95%	
17	*Regression Table*		Error			Lower	Upper
18	Constant	24780.996	1551.053	15.9769	< 0.0001	21722.480	27839.512
19	YrsExper	1456.388	79.761	18.2593	< 0.0001	1299.107	1613.669
20	Female	4898.656	1454.087	3.3689	0.0009	2031.347	7765.965
21	EducLev = 2	546.549	1418.139	0.3854	0.7004	-2249.874	3342.972
22	EducLev = 3	3587.341	1287.361	2.7866	0.0058	1048.798	6125.885
23	EducLev = 4	5862.894	2346.571	2.4985	0.0133	1235.700	10490.088
24	EducLev = 5	9428.090	1337.292	7.0501	< 0.0001	6791.089	12065.092
25	Interaction(YrsExper,Female)	-1029.858	121.924	-8.4467	< 0.0001	-1270.279	-789.437

Figure 11.24

Scatterplot of
Residuals Versus
Fitted Values with
Outlier Identified

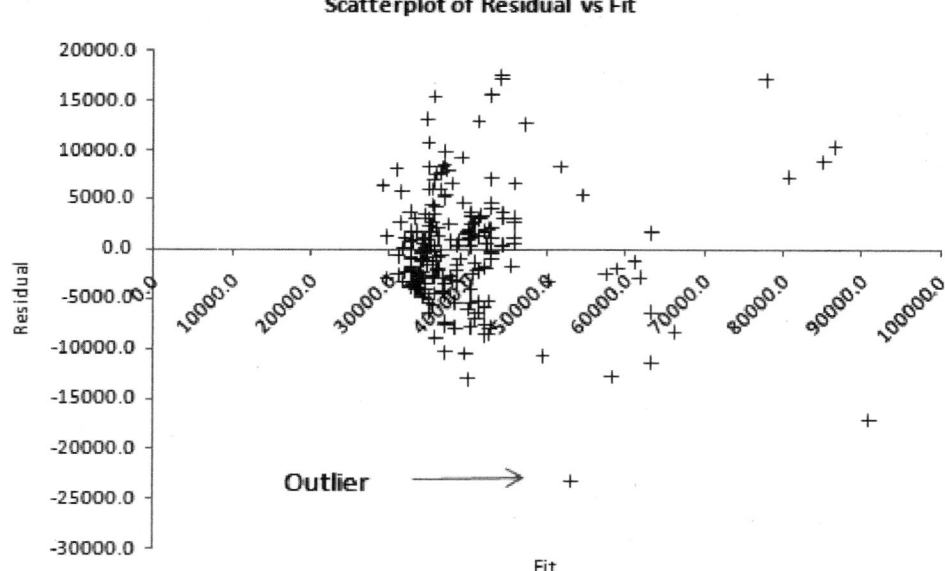

In any case, if you delete this employee and rerun the regression with the same variables, you will obtain the output in Figure 11.25.[7] Now, recalling that gender discrimination is the key issue in this example, you can compare the coefficients of Female and Interaction (YrsExper,Female) in the two outputs. The coefficient of Female has dropped from 4899 to 3774. In words, the *Y*-intercept for the female regression line used to be about $4900 higher than for the male line; now it is only about $3800 higher. More importantly, the coefficient of Interaction(YrsExper,Female) has changed from −1030 to −858. This

[7]As it turns out, this employee is the last observation in the data set. An easy way to run the regression (with StatTools) without this employee is to redefine the StatTools data set so that it doesn't include this last row.

Figure 11.25 Regression Output with Outlier Excluded

	A	B	C	D	E	F	G
7		Multiple	R-Square	Adjusted	StErr of		
8	**Summary**	R		R-Square	Estimate		
9		0.8690	0.7551	0.7465	5670.503		
10							
11		Degrees of	Sum of	Mean of	F-Ratio	p-Value	
12	**ANOVA Table**	Freedom	Squares	Squares			
13	Explained	7	19729421790	2818488827	87.6543	< 0.0001	
14	Unexplained	199	6398765306	32154599.53			
15							
16		Coefficient	Standard	t-Value	p-Value	Confidence Interval 95%	
17	**Regression Table**		Error			Lower	Upper
18	Constant	24056.616	1490.643	16.1384	< 0.0001	21117.132	26996.100
19	YrsExper	1449.596	76.218	19.0190	< 0.0001	1299.297	1599.896
20	Female	3774.315	1411.667	2.6737	0.0081	990.569	6558.060
21	EducLev = 2	777.542	1355.860	0.5735	0.5670	-1896.154	3451.239
22	EducLev = 3	4118.332	1235.623	3.3330	0.0010	1681.737	6554.926
23	EducLev = 4	6366.633	2244.711	2.8363	0.0050	1940.161	10793.105
24	EducLev = 5	10547.475	1301.794	8.1023	< 0.0001	7980.393	13114.556
25	Interaction(YrsExper,Female)	-858.202	122.613	-6.9993	< 0.0001	-1099.989	-616.415

coefficient indicates how much less steep the female line for Salary versus YrsExper is than the male line. So a change from -1030 to -858 indicates *less* discrimination against females now than before. In other words, this unusual female employee accounts for a good bit of the discrimination argument—although a strong argument still exists even without her. ■

PROBLEMS

Level A

34. The file **P11.34.xlsx** contains data on the top 40 golfers in 2008. (It is a subset of the data examined in earlier chapters.) This was the year when Tiger Woods won the U.S. Open in June and then had year-ending surgery directly afterward. Using all 40 golfers, run a forward stepwise regression of Earnings per Round versus the potential explanatory variables in columns B–G. (Don't use Earnings in column H.) Then create a second data set that omits Tiger Woods and repeat the regression on this smaller data set. Are the results about the same? Explain the effect, if any, of the Tiger Woods outlier on the regression.

35. The file **P02_07.xlsx** includes data on 204 employees at the (fictional) company Beta Technologies.
  a. Run a forward stepwise regression of Annual Salary versus Gender, Age, Prior Experience, Beta Experience, and Education. Would you say this equation does a good job of explaining the variation in salaries?

  b. Add a new employee to the end of the data set, a top-level executive. The values of Gender through Annual Salary for this person are, respectively, 0, 56, 10, 15, 6, and $500,000. Run the regression in part **a** again, including this executive. Are the results much different? Is it "fair" to exclude this executive when analyzing the salary structure at this company?

Level B

36. Statistician Frank J. Anscombe created a data set to illustrate the importance of doing more than just examining the standard regression output. These data are provided in the file **P10_64.xlsx**.
  a. Regress Y_1 on X. How well does the estimated equation fit the data? Is there evidence of a linear relationship between Y_1 and X at the 5% significance level?
  b. Regress Y_2 on X. How well does the estimated equation fit the data? Is there evidence of a linear

relationship between Y_2 and X at the 5% significance level?

c. Regress Y_3 on X. How well does the estimated equation fit the data? Is there evidence of a linear relationship between Y_3 and X at the 5% significance level?

d. Regress Y_4 on X_4. How well does the estimated equation fit the data? Is there evidence of a linear relationship between Y_4 and X_4 at the 5% significance level?

e. Compare these four simple linear regression equations (1) in terms of goodness of fit and (2) in terms of overall statistical significance.

f. How do you explain these findings, considering that each of the regression equations is based on a *different* set of variables?

g. What role, if any, do outliers have on each of these estimated regression equations?

11.9 VIOLATIONS OF REGRESSION ASSUMPTIONS

Much of the theoretical research in the area of regression has dealt with violations of the regression assumptions discussed in section 11.2. There are three issues: how to detect violations of the assumptions, what goes wrong if the violations are ignored, and what to do about them if they are detected. Detection is usually relatively easy. You can look at scatterplots, histograms, and time series graphs for visual signs of violations, and there are a number of numerical measures (many not covered here) that have been developed for diagnostic purposes. The second issue, what goes wrong if the violations are ignored, depends on the type of violation and its severity. The third issue is the most difficult to resolve. There are some relatively easy fixes and some that are well beyond the level of this book. In this section we briefly discuss some of the most common violations and a few possible remedies for them.

11.9.1 Nonconstant Error Variance

The second regression assumption states that the variance of the errors should be *constant* for all values of the explanatory variables. This is a lot to ask, and it is almost always violated to some extent. Fortunately, mild violations do not have much effect on the validity of the regression output, so you can usually ignore them.

A fan shape can cause an incorrect value for the standard error of estimate, so that confidence intervals and hypothesis tests for the regression coefficients are not valid.

However, one particular form of nonconstant error variance occurs fairly often and should be dealt with. This is the fan shape shown earlier in the scatterplot of AmountSpent versus Salary in Figure 11.1. As salaries increase, the variability of amounts spent also increases. Although this fan shape appears in the scatterplot of the dependent variable AmountSpent versus the explanatory variable Salary, it also appears in the scatterplot of residuals versus fitted values if you regress AmountSpent versus Salary. If you ignore this nonconstant error variance, the standard error of the regression coefficient of Salary is inaccurate, and a confidence interval for this coefficient or a hypothesis test concerning it can be misleading.

There are at least two ways to deal with this fan-shape phenomenon. The first is to use a different estimation method than least squares. It is called *weighted least squares,* and it is an option available in some statistical software packages. However, it is fairly advanced and it is not available with StatTools, so we will not discuss it here.

A logarithmic transformation of Y can sometimes cure the fan-shape problem.

The second method is simpler. When you see a fan shape, where the variability increases from left to right in a scatterplot, you can try a logarithmic transformation of the dependent variable. The reason this often works is that the logarithmic transformation squeezes the large values closer together and pulls the small values farther apart. The scatterplot of the log of AmountSpent versus Salary is in Figure 11.26. Clearly, the fan shape evident in Figure 11.1 is gone.

This logarithmic transformation is not a magical cure for all instances of nonconstant error variance. For example, it appears to have introduced some curvature into the plot in

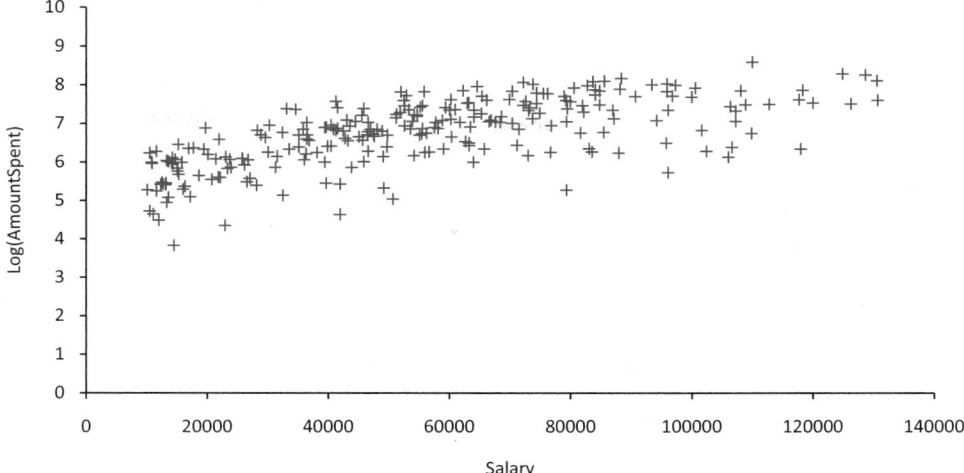

Figure 11.26

Scatterplot without Fan Shape

Scatterplot of Log(AmountSpent) vs Salary

Figure 11.26. However, as we discussed in the previous chapter, when the distribution of the dependent variable is heavily skewed to the right, as it often is, the logarithmic transformation is worth exploring.

11.9.2 Nonnormality of Residuals

The third regression assumption states that the error terms are normally distributed. You can check this assumption fairly easily by forming a histogram of the residuals. You can even perform a formal test of normality of the residuals by using the procedures discussed in section 9.5 of Chapter 9. However, unless the distribution of the residuals is severely nonnormal, the inferences made from the regression output are still approximately valid. In addition, one form of nonnormality often encountered is skewness to the right, and this can often be remedied by the same logarithmic transformation of the dependent variable that remedies nonconstant error variance.

11.9.3 Autocorrelated Residuals

The fourth regression assumption states that the error terms are probabilistically independent. This assumption is usually valid for cross-sectional data, but it is often violated for time series data. The problem with time series data is that the residuals are often correlated with nearby residuals, a property called **autocorrelation**. The most frequent type of autocorrelation is positive autocorrelation. For example, if residuals separated by one month are correlated—called **lag 1 autocorrelation**—in a positive direction, then an overprediction in January, say, will likely lead to an overprediction in February, and an underprediction in January will likely lead to an underprediction in February. If this autocorrelation is large, serious prediction errors can occur if it isn't dealt with appropriately.

A numerical measure has been developed to check for lag 1 autocorrelation. It is called the **Durbin–Watson statistic** (after the two statisticians who developed it), and it is quoted automatically in the regression output of many statistical software packages. The Durbin–Watson (DW) statistic is scaled to be between 0 and 4. Values close to 2 indicate very little lag 1 autocorrelation, values below 2 indicate positive autocorrelation, and values above 2 indicate negative autocorrelation.

A Durbin–Watson statistic below 2 signals that nearby residuals are positively correlated with one another.

Because *positive* autocorrelation is the usual culprit, the question becomes how much below 2 the DW statistic must be before you should react. There is a formal hypothesis test for answering this question, and a set of tables appears in some statistics texts. Without going into the details, we simply state that when the number of time series observations, n, is about 30 and the number of explanatory variables is fairly small, say, 1 to 5, then any DW statistic less than 1.2 should get your attention. If n increases to around 100, then you shouldn't be concerned unless the DW statistic is below 1.5.

If e_i is the ith residual, the formula for the DW statistic is

$$DW = \frac{\sum_{i=2}^{n}(e_i - e_{i-1})^2}{\sum_{i=1}^{n}e_i^2}$$

This is obviously not very attractive for hand calculation, so the StatDurbinWatson function is included in StatTools. To use it, run any regression and check the option to create a graph of residuals versus fitted values. This automatically creates columns of fitted values and residuals. Then enter the formula

=StatDurbinWatson(*ResidRange*)

in any cell, substituting the actual range of residuals for "ResidRange."

The following continuation of Example 11.1 with the Bendrix manufacturing data—the only time series data set we have analyzed with regression—checks for possible lag 1 autocorrelation.

EXAMPLE | **11.1 EXPLAINING OVERHEAD COSTS AT BENDRIX (CONTINUED)**

Is there any evidence of lag 1 autocorrelation in the Bendrix data when Overhead is regressed on MachHrs and ProdRuns?

Objective   To use the Durbin–Watson statistic to check whether there is any lag 1 autocorrelation in the residuals from the Bendrix regression model for overhead costs.

Solution

You should run the usual multiple regression and check that you want a graph of residuals versus fitted values. The results are shown in Figure 11.27. The residuals are listed in column D. Each represents how much the regression overpredicts (if negative) or underpredicts (if positive) the overhead cost for that month. You can check for lag 1 autocorrelation in two ways, with the DW statistic and by examining the time series graph of the residuals in Figure 11.28.

Figure 11.27   Regression Output with Residuals and DW Statistic

	A	B	C	D	E	F
44	Graph Data	Overhead	Fit	Residual		Durbin-Watson for residuals
45	1	99798	98391.35059	1406.649409		1.313
46	2	87804	85522.33322	2281.666779		
47	3	93681	92723.59538	957.4046174		
48	4	82262	82428.09201	-166.0920107		
49	5	106968	100227.9028	6740.097234		

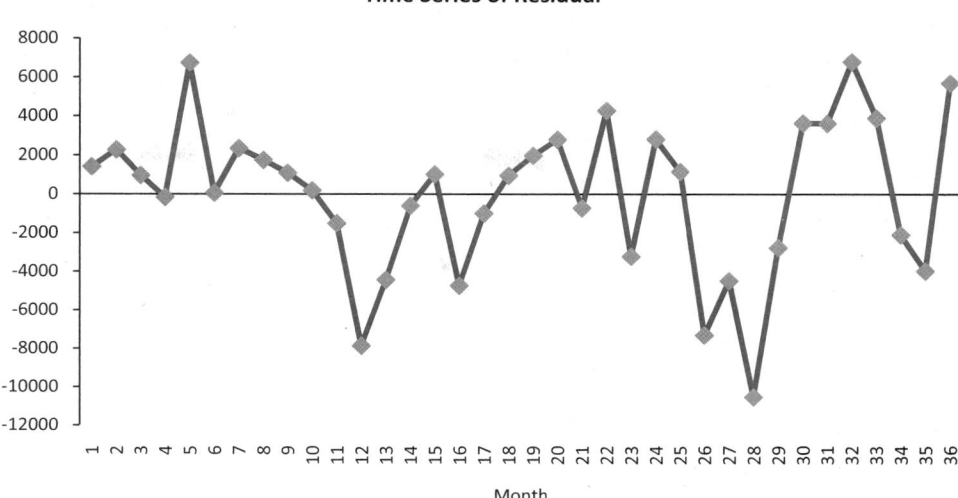

Figure 11.28

Time Series Graph of Residuals

Time Series of Residual

The DW statistic is calculated in cell F45 of Figure 11.27 with the formula

=StatDurbinWatson(D45:D80)

(Remember that StatDurbinWatson is *not* a built-in Excel function. It is available only if StatTools is loaded.) Based on our guidelines for DW values, 1.3131 suggests positive autocorrelation—it is less than 2—but not enough to cause concern.[8] This general conclusion is supported by the time series graph. Serious autocorrelation of lag 1 would tend to show longer runs of residuals alternating above and below the horizontal axis—positives would tend to follow positives, and negatives would tend to follow negatives. There is some indication of this behavior in the graph but not an excessive amount. ∎

What should you do if the DW statistic signals significant autocorrelation? Unfortunately, the answer to this question would take us much more deeply into time series analysis than we can go in this book. Suffice it to say that time series analysis in the context of regression can become very complex, and there are no easy fixes for the autocorrelation that often occurs.

PROBLEMS

Level A

37. A company produces electric motors for use in home appliances. One of the company's production managers is interested in examining the relationship between the dollars spent per month in inspecting finished motor products (X) and the number of motors produced during that month that were returned by dissatisfied customers (Y). He has collected the data in the file **P10_03.xlsx** to explore this relationship for the past 36 months.

a. Estimate a simple linear regression equation using the given data and interpret it. What does the ANOVA table indicate for this model?
b. Examine the residuals of the regression equation. Do you see evidence of any violations of the regression assumptions?
c. Conduct a Durbin–Watson test on the model's residuals. Interpret the result of this test.
d. In light of your result in part **c**, do you recommend modifying the original regression model? If so, how would you revise it?

---

[8]A more formal test, using Durbin–Watson tables, supports this conclusion.

38. Examine the relationship between the average utility bills for homes of a particular size (Y) and the average monthly temperature (X). The data in the file **P10_07.xlsx** include the average monthly bill and temperature for each month of the past year.

  a. Use the given data to estimate a simple linear regression equation. How well does the estimated regression model fit the given data? What does the ANOVA table indicate for this model?

  b. Examine the residuals of the regression equation. Do you see evidence of any violations of the regression assumptions?

  c. Conduct a Durbin–Watson test on the model's residuals. Interpret the result of this test.

  d. In light of your result in part **c**, do you recommend modifying the original regression model? If so, how would you revise it?

39. The manager of a commuter rail transportation system was recently asked by her governing board to predict the demand for rides in the large city served by the transportation network. The system manager has collected data on variables thought to be related to the number of weekly riders on the city's rail system. The file **P10_20.xlsx** contains these data.

  a. Estimate a multiple regression equation using all of the available explanatory variables. What does the ANOVA table indicate for this model?

  b. Is there evidence of autocorrelated residuals in this model? Explain why or why not.

11.10 PREDICTION

Once you have estimated a regression equation from a set of data, you might want to use this equation to predict the value of the dependent variable for *new* observations. As an example, suppose that a retail chain is considering opening a new store in one of several proposed locations. It naturally wants to choose the location that will result in the largest revenues. The problem is that the revenues for the new locations are not yet known. They can be observed only after stores are opened in these locations, and the chain cannot afford to open more than one store at the current time. An alternative is to use regression analysis. Using data from *existing* stores, the chain can run a regression of the dependent variable revenue on several explanatory variables such as population density, level of wealth in the vicinity, number of competitors nearby, ease of access given the existing roads, and so on.

Assuming that the regression equation has a reasonably large R^2 and, even more important, a reasonably small s_e, the chain can then use this equation to predict revenues for the proposed locations. Specifically, it will gather values of the explanatory variables for each of the proposed locations, substitute these into the regression equation, and look at the predicted revenue for each proposed location. All else being equal, the chain will probably choose the location with the highest predicted revenue.

As another example, suppose that you are trying to explain the starting salaries for undergraduate college students. You want to predict the *mean* salary of all graduates with certain characteristics, such as all male marketing majors from state-supported universities. To do this, you first gather salary data from a sample of graduates from various universities. Included in this data set are relevant explanatory variables for each graduate in the sample, such as the type of university, the student's major, GPA, years of work experience, and so on. You then use these data to estimate a regression equation for starting salary and substitute the relevant values of the explanatory variables into the regression equation to obtain the required prediction.

Regression can be used to predict Y for a single observation, or it can be used to predict the mean Y for many observations, all with the same X values.

These two examples illustrate two types of prediction problems in regression. The first problem, illustrated by the retail chain example, is the more common of the two. Here the objective is to predict the value of the dependent variable for one or more *individual* members of the population. In this specific example you are trying to predict the future revenue for several potential locations of the new store. In the second problem, illustrated by the salary example, the objective is to predict the *mean* of the dependent variable for all members of the population with certain values of the explanatory variables. In the first problem you are predicting an individual value; in the second problem you are predicting a mean.

The second problem is inherently easier than the first in the sense that the resulting prediction is bound to be more accurate. The reason is intuitive. Recall that the mean of the dependent variable for any fixed values of the explanatory variables lies on the population regression line. Therefore, if you can accurately estimate this line—that is, if you can accurately estimate the regression coefficients—you can accurately predict the required mean. In contrast, most individual points do *not* lie on the population regression line. Therefore, even if your estimate of the population regression line is perfectly accurate, you still cannot predict exactly where an individual point will fall.

Stated another way, when you predict a mean, there is a single source of error: the possibly inaccurate estimates of the regression coefficients. But when you predict an individual value, there are two sources of error: the inaccurate estimates of the regression coefficients and the inherent variation of individual points around the regression line. This second source of error often dominates the first.

We illustrate these comments in Figure 11.29. For the sake of illustration, the dependent variable is salary and the single explanatory variable is years of experience with the company. Let's suppose that you want to predict either the salary for a particular employee with 10 years of experience or the mean salary of all employees with 10 years of experience. The two lines in this graph represent the population regression line (which in reality is unobservable) and the estimated regression line. For each prediction problem the point prediction—the best guess—is the value above 10 on the estimated regression line. The error in predicting the mean occurs because the two lines in the graph are not the same—that is, the estimated line is not quite correct. The error in predicting the individual value (the point shown in the graph) occurs because the two lines are not the same and also because this point does not lie on the population regression line.

Figure 11.29
Prediction Errors for an Individual Value and a Mean

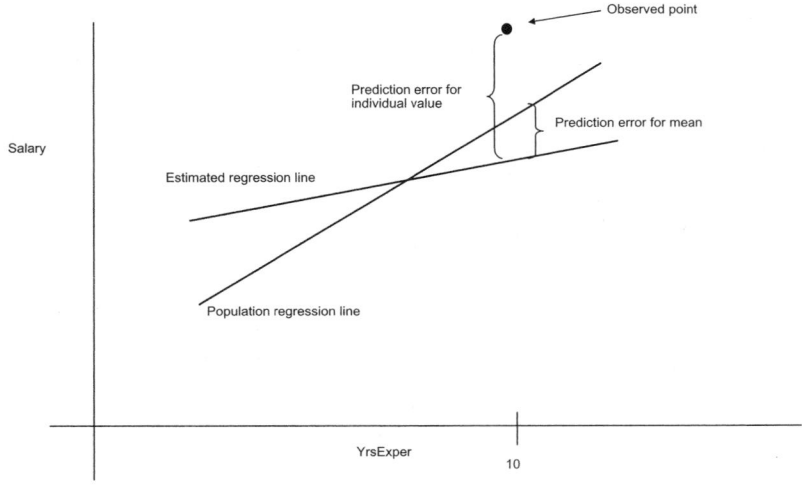

One general aspect of prediction becomes apparent by looking at this graph. If we let Xs denote the explanatory variables, predictions for values of the Xs close to their means are likely to be more accurate than predictions for Xs far from their means. In the graph, the mean of YrsExper is about 7. (This is approximately where the two lines cross.) Because the slopes of the two lines are different, they get farther apart as YrsExper gets farther away from 7 (on either side). As a result, predictions tend to become less accurate.

It is more difficult to predict for extreme Xs than for Xs close to the mean. Trying to predict for Xs beyond the range of the data set (extrapolation) is quite risky.

This phenomenon shows up as higher standard errors of prediction as the Xs get farther away from their means. However, for extreme values of the Xs, there is another problem. Suppose, for example, that all values of YrsExper in the data set are between 1 and 15, and you attempt to predict the salary for an employee with 25 years of experience. This is called *extrapolation*; you are attempting to predict beyond the limits of the sample.

The problem here is that there is no guarantee, and sometimes no reason to believe, that the relationship within the range of the sample is valid outside of this range. It is perfectly possible that the effect of years of experience on salary is considerably different in the 25-year range than in the range of the sample. If it is, then extrapolation is bound to yield inaccurate predictions. In general, you should avoid extrapolation whenever possible. If you really want to predict the salaries of employees with 25-plus years of experience, you should include some employees of this type in the original sample.

We now discuss how to make predictions and how to estimate their accuracy, both for individual values and for means. To keep it simple, we first assume that there is a single explanatory variable X. We choose a fixed "trial" value of X, labeled X_0, and predict the value of a single Y or the mean of all Ys when X equals X_0. For both prediction problems the **point prediction**, or best guess, is found by substituting into the right side of the estimated regression equation. Graphically, this is the height of the estimated regression line above X_0.

> To calculate a **point prediction**, substitute the given values of the Xs into the estimated regression equation.

The standard error of prediction for a single Y is approximately equal to the standard error of estimate.

To measure the accuracy of these point predictions, you calculate a standard error for each prediction. These standard errors can be interpreted in the usual way. For example, you are about 68% certain that the actual values will be within one standard error of the point predictions, and you are about 95% certain that the actual values will be within two standard errors of the point predictions. For the individual prediction problem, the standard error is labeled s_{ind} and is given by Equation (11.5). As indicated by the approximate equality on the right, when the sample size n is large and X_0 is fairly close to $\overline{X}$, the last two terms inside the square root are relatively small, and this standard error of prediction can be approximated by s_e, the standard error of estimate.

> **Standard Error of Prediction for a Single Y**
>
> $$s_{\text{ind}} = s_e\sqrt{1 + \frac{1}{n} + \frac{(X_0 - \overline{X})^2}{\sum_{i=1}^{n}(X_i - \overline{X})^2}} \simeq s_e \qquad \textbf{(11.5)}$$

For the prediction of the mean, the standard error is labeled s_{mean} and is given by Equation (11.6). Here, if X_0 is fairly close to $\overline{X}$, the last term inside the square root is relatively small, and this standard error of prediction is approximately equal to the expression on the right.

> **Standard Error of Prediction for the Mean Y**
>
> $$s_{\text{mean}} = s_e\sqrt{\frac{1}{n} + \frac{(X_0 - \overline{X})^2}{\sum_{i=1}^{n}(X_i - \overline{X})^2}} \simeq s_e/\sqrt{n} \qquad \textbf{(11.6)}$$

These standard errors can be used to calculate a 95% prediction interval for an individual value and a 95% confidence interval for a mean value. Exactly as in Chapter 8, you go out a t-multiple of the relevant standard error on either side of the point prediction. The t-multiple is the value that cuts off 0.025 probability in the right-hand tail of a t distribution with $n - 2$ degrees of freedom.

The term *prediction interval* (rather than confidence interval) is used for an individual value because an individual value of Y is not a population *parameter*; it is an individual point. However, the interpretation is basically the same. If you calculate a 95% prediction interval for many members of the population, you can expect their actual Y values to fall within the corresponding prediction intervals about 95% of the time.

To see how all of this can be implemented in Excel, we revisit the Bendrix example of predicting overhead expenses.

EXAMPLE 11.1 PREDICTING OVERHEAD AT BENDRIX (CONTINUED)

We have already used regression to analyze overhead expenses at Bendrix, based on 36 months of data. Suppose Bendrix expects the values of MachHrs and ProdRuns for the next three months to be 1430, 1560, 1520, and 35, 45, 40, respectively. What are their point predictions and 95% prediction intervals for Overhead for these three months?

Objective To predict Overhead at Bendrix for the next three months, given anticipated values of MachHrs and ProdRuns.

Solution

StatTools has the capability to provide predictions and 95% prediction intervals, but you must set up a second data set to capture the results. This second data set can be placed next to (or below) the original data set. It should have the same variable name headings, and it should include values of the explanatory variable to be used for prediction. (It can also have LowerLimit95 and UpperLimit95 headings, but these are optional and will be added by StatTools if they do not already exist.) For this example we called the original data set Original Data and the new data set Data for Prediction. The regression dialog box and results in Data for Prediction appear in Figures 11.30 and 11.31. In the dialog box, note that the Prediction option is checked, and the second data set is specified in the corresponding dropdown list.

The text box in Figure 11.31 explains how the second data set range should be set up. Initially, you should enter the given values in the Month, MachHrs, and ProdRuns columns. Then when the regression is run (with the Prediction option checked), the values in the Overhead, LowerLimit95, and UpperLimit95 columns will be filled in. (Again, if you do not create LowerLimit95 and UpperLimit95 columns as part of the second data set, StatTools will do it for you.)

The Overhead values in column I are the point predictions for the next three months, and the LowerLimit95 and UpperLimit95 values in column J and K indicate the 95% prediction intervals. You can see from the wide prediction intervals how much uncertainty remains. The reason is the relatively large standard error of estimate, s_e. If you could halve the value of s_e, the length of the prediction interval would be only half as large. Contrary to what you might expect, this is not a sample size problem. That is, a larger sample size would probably *not* produce a smaller value of s_e. The whole problem is that MachHrs and

Figure 11.30

Regression Dialog Box with Predictions Checked

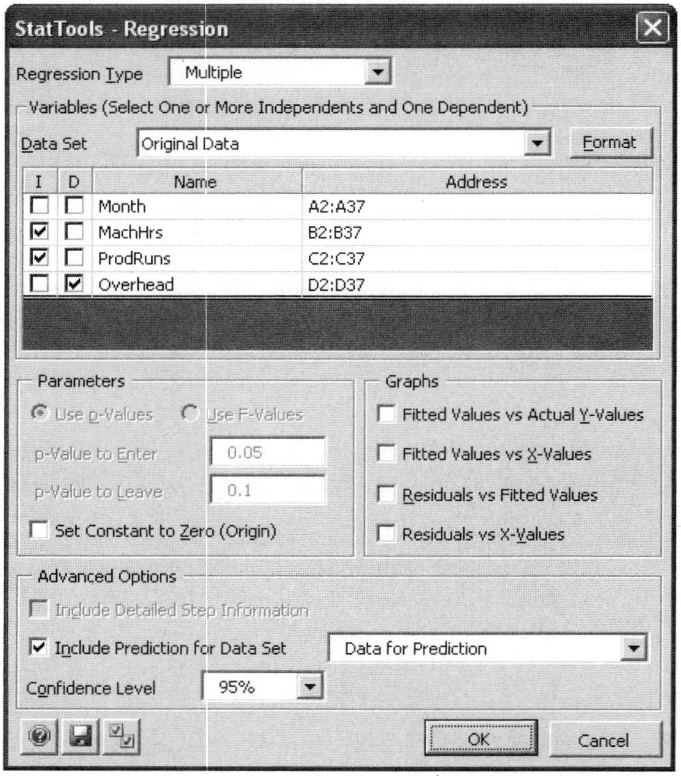

Figure 11.31

Prediction of Overhead

	F	G	H	I	J	K	L
1	Month	MachHrs	ProdRuns	Overhead	LowerLimit95	UpperLimit95	
2	37	1430	35	97180.35	88700.80	105659.91	
3	38	1560	45	111676.27	103002.95	120349.58	
4	39	1520	40	105516.72	96993.16	114040.28	
5							
6	Above is the data set for prediction. It is best to set this up ahead of time,						
7	entering all of the column headings, entering the values of the explanatory						
8	variables you want to test, and defining this entire range as a new StatTools data						
9	set. The values in the last three columns can be blank or have values, but when						
10	regression is run with the prediction options, they will be filled in or overwritten.						
11	Also, if you don't include the last two columns in your StatTools data set,						
12	StatTools will create them for you.						
13							

ProdRuns are not perfectly correlated with Overhead. The only way to decrease s_e and get more accurate predictions is to find other explanatory variables that are more closely related to Overhead. ∎

StatTools provides prediction intervals for individual values, as you have just seen, but it does not provide confidence intervals for the mean of Y, given a set of Xs. To obtain such a confidence interval, you can use Equation (11.6) to get the required standard error of prediction (for simple regression only), or you can approximate it by $s_e/\sqrt{n}$.

Level A

40. The file **P10_05.xlsx** contains salaries for a sample of DataCom employees, along with several variables that might be related to salary.

   a. Estimate an appropriate multiple regression equation to predict the annual salary of a given DataCom employee.

   b. Given the estimated regression model, predict the annual salary of a male employee who served in a similar department at another company for five years prior to coming to work at DataCom. This man, a graduate of a four-year collegiate business program, has been supervising six subordinates in the sales department since joining the organization seven years ago.

   c. Find a 95% prediction interval for the salary earned by the employee in part **b**.

   d. Find a 95% confidence interval for the mean salary earned by all DataCom employees sharing the characteristics provided in part **b**.

   e. How can you explain the difference between the widths of the intervals in parts **c** and **d**?

41. The owner of a restaurant in Bloomington, Indiana, has recorded sales data for the past 19 years. He has also recorded data on potentially relevant variables. The data appear in the file **P10_23.xlsx**.

   a. Estimate a regression equation for sales as a function of population, advertising in the current year, and advertising in the previous year. Can you expect predictions of sales in *future* years to be very accurate if they are based on this regression equation? Explain.

   b. The company would like to predict sales in the next year (year 20). It doesn't know what the population

will be in year 20, so it assumes no change from year 19. Its planned advertising level for year 20 is $30,000. Find a prediction and a 95% prediction interval for sales in year 20.

42. A power company located in southern Alabama wants to predict the peak power load (i.e., Y, the maximum amount of power that must be generated each day to meet demand) as a function of the daily high temperature (X). A random sample of 25 summer days is chosen, and the peak power load and the high temperature are recorded on each day. The file **P10_40.xlsx** contain these observations.

   a. Use the given data to estimate a simple linear regression equation. How well does the regression equation fit the given data?

   b. Examine the residuals of the estimated regression equation. Do you see evidence of any violations of the assumptions regarding the errors of the regression model?

   c. Calculate the Durbin–Watson statistic on the model's residuals. What does it indicate?

   d. Given your result in part **d**, do you recommend modifying the original regression model in this case? If so, how would you revise it?

   e. Use the final version of your regression equation to predict the peak power load on a summer day with a high temperature of 90 degrees.

   f. Find a 95% prediction interval for the peak power load on a summer day with a high temperature of 90 degrees.

   h. Find a 95% confidence interval for the *average* peak power load on all summer days with a high temperature of 90 degrees.

11.11 CONCLUSION

In these two chapters on regression, you have seen how useful regression analysis can be for a variety of business applications and how statistical software such as StatTools enables you to obtain relevant output—both graphical and numerical—with very little effort. However, you have also seen that there are many concepts that you must understand well before you can use regression analysis appropriately. Given that user-friendly software is available, it is all too easy to generate enormous amounts of regression output and then misinterpret or misuse much of it.

At the very least, you should (1) be able to interpret the standard regression output, including statistics on the regression coefficients, summary measures such as R^2 and s_e, and the ANOVA table, (2) know what to look for in the many scatterplots available, (3) know how to use dummy variables, interaction terms, and nonlinear transformations to improve a fit, and (4) be able to spot clear violations of the regression assumptions. However, we haven't covered everything. Indeed, many entire books are devoted exclusively to regression analysis. Therefore, you should recognize when you *don't* know enough to handle a regression problem such as nonconstant error variance or autocorrelation appropriately. In this case, you should consult a statistical expert.

Summary of Key Terms

Term	Symbol	Explanation	Excel	Page	Equation
Statistical model		A theoretical model including several assumptions that must be satisfied, at least approximately, for inferences from regression output to be valid		603	11.1
Error	ε	The difference between the actual Y value and the predicted value from the population regression line		604	
Homoscedasticity (and heteroscedasticity)		Equal (and unequal) variance of the dependent variable for different values of the explanatory variables		605	
Parsimony		The concept of explaining the most with the least		608	
Standard error of regression coefficient	s_b	Measures how much the estimates of a regression coefficient vary from sample to sample	StatTools/ Regression & Classification/ Regression	609	
Confidence interval for regression coefficient		An interval likely to contain the population regression coefficient	StatTools/ Regression & Classification/ Regression	610	
t-value for regression coefficient	t	The ratio of the estimate of a regression coefficient to its standard error, used to test whether the coefficient is 0	StatTools/ Regression& Classification/ Regression	611	11.3
Hypothesis test for regression coefficient		Typically, a two-tailed test, where the null hypothesis is that the regression coefficient is 0	StatTools/ Regression & Classification/ Regression	611	
ANOVA table for regression		Used to test whether the explanatory variables, as a whole, have any significant explanatory power	StatTools/ Regression & Classification/ Regression	612	
Multicollinearity		Occurs when there is a fairly strong linear relationship between explanatory variables		616	
Include/exclude decisions		Guidelines for deciding whether to include or exclude potential explanatory variables		620	
Stepwise regression		A class of automatic equation-building methods, where variables are added (or deleted) in order of their importance	StatTools/ Regression & Classification/ Regression	625	

(continued)

Term	Symbol	Explanation	Excel	Page	Equation
Partial F test		Tests whether a set of extra explanatory variables adds any explanatory power to an existing regression equation	Must be done manually, using StatTools regression outputs	631	11.4
Outliers		Observations that lie outside the general pattern of points and can have a substantial effect on the regression model		638	
Influential point		A point that can "tilt" the regression line		639	
Autocorrelation of residuals		Lack of independence in the series of residuals, especially relevant for time series data		645	
Durbin–Watson statistic		A measure of the autocorrelation between residuals, especially useful for time series data	**=StatDurbin Watson(range)**, a StatTools function	645	
Point prediction		The predicted value of Y from the regression equation		650	
Standard errors of prediction	s_{ind}, s_{mean}	Measures of the accuracy of prediction when predicting Y for an individual observation, or predicting the mean of all Y's, for fixed values of the explanatory variables	StatTools/ Regression & Classification/ Regression	650	11.5, 11.6

PROBLEMS

Conceptual Questions

C.1. Suppose a regression output produces the following 99% confidence interval for one of the regression coefficients: $[-32.47, -16.88]$. Given this information, should an analyst reject the null hypothesis that this population regression coefficient is equal to zero? Explain your answer.

C.2. Explain why it is not possible to estimate a linear regression model that contains *all* dummy variables associated with a particular categorical explanatory variable.

C.3. Suppose you have a data set that includes *all* of the professional athletes in a given sport over a given period of time, such as all NFL football players during the 2008–2010 seasons, and you use regression to estimate a variable of interest. Are the inferences discussed in this chapter relevant? Recall that we have been assuming that the data represent a random sample of some larger population. In this sports example, what is the larger population—or is there one?

C.4. Distinguish between the test of significance of an individual regression coefficient and the ANOVA

test. When, if ever, are these two statistical tests essentially equivalent?

C.5. Which of these intervals based on the same estimated regression equation with fixed values of the explanatory variables would be *wider*: (1) a 95% prediction interval for an individual value of Y or (2) a 95% confidence interval for the mean value of Y? Explain your answer. How do you interpret the wider of these two intervals in words?

C.6. Regression outputs from virtually all statistical packages look the same. In particular, the section on coefficients lists the coefficients, their standard errors, their t-values, their p-values, and (possibly) 95% confidence intervals for them. Explain how all of these are related.

C.7. If you are building a regression equation in a forward stepwise manner, that is, by adding one variable at a time, explain why it is useful to monitor the adjusted R^2 and the standard error of estimate. Why is it not as useful to monitor R^2?

C.8. You run a regression with two explanatory variables and notice that the p-value in the ANOVA table is extremely small but the *p*-values of both explanatory variables are larger than 0.10. What is the probable reason? Can you conclude that neither explanatory variable does a good job in predicting the dependent variable?

C.9. Why are outliers sometimes called *influential* observations? What *could* happen to the slope of a regression of *Y* versus a single *X* when an outlier is included versus when it is not included? Will this necessarily happen when a point is an outlier? Answer by giving a couple of examples.

C.10. The Durbin-Watson test is for detecting lag 1 autocorrelation in the residuals. Which values of DW signal *positive* autocorrelation? If you observe such a DW value but ignore it, what might go wrong with predictions based on the regression equation? Specifically, if the data are time series data, and your goal is to predict the next six months, what might go wrong with the predictions?

Level A

43. For 12 straight weeks you have observed the sales (in number of cases) of canned tomatoes at Mr. D's super-market. Each week you kept track of the following:
- Was a promotional notice placed in all shopping carts for canned tomatoes?
- Was a coupon given for canned tomatoes?
- Was a price reduction (none, 1, or 2 cents off) given?

The file **P11_43.xlsx** contains these data.
  a. Use multiple regression to determine how these factors influence sales.
  b. Discuss how you can tell whether autocorrelation, heteroscedasticity, or multicollinearity might be a problem.
  c. Predict sales of canned tomatoes during a week in which Mr. D's uses a shopping cart notice, a coupon, and a one-cent price reduction.

44. The file **P11_44.xlsx** contains quarterly data on pork sales. Price is in dollars per hundred pounds, quantity sold is in billions of pounds, per capita income is in dollars, U.S. population is in millions, and GDP is in billions of dollars.
  a. Use the data to develop a regression equation that could be used to predict the quantity of pork sold during future periods. Discuss how you can tell whether heteroscedasticity, autocorrelation, or multicollinearity might be a problem.
  b. Suppose that during each of the next two quarters, price is 45, U.S. population is 240, GDP is 2620, and per capita income is 10,000. (These are in the units described previously.) Predict the quantity of pork sold during each of the next two quarters.

45. The file **P11_45.xlsx** contains monthly sales for a photography studio and the price charged per portrait during each month. Use regression to estimate an equation for predicting the current month's sales from last month's sales and the current month's price.
  a. If the price of a portrait during month 21 is $30, predict month 21 sales.
  b. Discuss how you can tell whether autocorrelation, multicollinearity, or heteroscedasticity might be a problem.

46. The file **P11_46.xlsx** contains data on a motel chain's revenue and advertising. Note that column C is simply column B "pushed down" a row.
  a. If the goal is to get the best-fitting regression equation for Revenue, which of the Advertising variables should be used? Or is it better to use both?
  b. Using the best-fitting equation from part **a**, make predictions for the motel chain's revenues during the next four quarters. Assume that advertising during each of the next four quarters is $50,000.
  c. Does autocorrelation of the residuals from the best-fitting equation appear to be a problem?

47. The file **P11_47.xlsx** contains the quarterly revenues (in millions of dollars) of a utility company for a seven-year period. The goal is to use these data to build a multiple regression model that can be used to forecast future revenues.
  a. Which variables should be included in the regression? Explain your rationale for including or excluding variables. (Look at a time series graph for clues.)
  b. Interpret the coefficients of your final equation.
  c. Make a forecast for revenues during the next quarter, quarter 29. Also, estimate the probability that revenue in the next quarter will be at least $150 million. (*Hint*: Use the standard error of prediction and the fact that the errors are approximately normally distributed.)

48. The belief that larger majorities for a president in a presidential election help the president's party increase its representation in the House and Senate is called the *coattail* effect. The file **P11_48.xlsx** lists the percentage by which each president since 1948 won the election and the number of seats in the House and Senate gained (or lost) during each election by the elected president's party. Are these data consistent with the idea of presidential coattails?

49. When potential workers apply for a job that requires extensive manual assembly of small intricate parts, they are initially given three different tests to measure their manual dexterity. The ones who are hired are then periodically given a performance rating on a 0 to 100 scale that combines their speed and accuracy in performing the required assembly operations. The file **P11_49.xlsx** lists the test scores and performance ratings for a randomly selected group of employees. It also lists their seniority (months with the company) at the time of the performance rating.

a. Look at a matrix of correlations. Can you say with certainty (based only on these correlations) that the R^2 value for the regression will be at least 35%? Why or why not?

b. Is there any evidence (from the correlation matrix) that multicollinearity will be a problem? Why or why not?

c. Run the regression of Performance Rating versus all four explanatory variables. List the equation, the value of R^2, and the value of s_e. Do all of the coefficients have the signs (negative or positive) you would expect? Briefly explain.

d. Referring to the equation in part **c**, if a worker (outside of the 80 in the sample) has 15 months of seniority and test scores of 57, 71, and 63, find a prediction and an approximate 95% prediction interval for this worker's Performance Rating score.

e. One of the t-values for the coefficients in part **c** is less than 1. Explain briefly why this occurred. Does it mean that this variable is not related to Performance Rating?

f. Arguably, the three test measures provide overlapping (or redundant) information. For the sake of parsimony (explaining "the most with the least"), it might be sensible to regress Performance Rating versus only two explanatory variables, Seniority and Average Test, where Average Test is the average of the three test scores—that is, Average Test = (Test1 + Test2 + Test3)/3. Run this regression and report the same measures as in part **c**: the equation itself, R^2, and s_e. Can you argue that this equation is just as good as the equation in part **c**? Explain briefly.

50. Nicklaus Electronics manufactures electronic components used in the computer and space industries. The annual rate of return on the market portfolio and the annual rate of return on Nicklaus Electronics stock for the last 36 months are listed in the file **P11_50.xlsx**. The company wants to calculate the *systematic risk* of its common stock. (It is systematic in the sense that it represents the part of the risk that Nicklaus shares with the market as a whole.) The rate of return Y_t in period t on a security is hypothesized to be related to the rate of return m_t on a market portfolio by the equation

$$Y_t = \alpha + \beta m_t + \varepsilon_t$$

Here, α is the risk-free rate of return, β is the security's systematic risk, and ε_t is an error term. Estimate the systematic risk of the common stock of Nicklaus Electronics. Would you say that Nicklaus stock is a risky investment? Why or why not?

51. The auditor of Kaefer Manufacturing uses regression analysis during the analytical review stage of the firm's annual audit. The regression analysis attempts to uncover relationships that exist between various account balances. Any such relationship is subsequently used as a preliminary test of the reasonableness of the reported account balances. The auditor wants to determine whether a relationship exists between the balance of accounts receivable at the end of the month and that month's sales. The file **P11_51.xlsx** contains data on these two accounts for the last 36 months. It also shows the sales levels two months before month 1.

a. Is there any statistical evidence to suggest a relationship between the monthly sales level and accounts receivable?

b. Referring to part **a**, would the relationship be described any better by including this month's sales and the previous month's sales (called *lagged sales*) in the equation for accounts receivable? What about adding the sales from more than a month ago to the equation? For this problem, why might it make accounting sense to include lagged sales variables in the equation? How do you interpret their coefficients?

c. During month 37, which is a fiscal year-end month, the sales were $1,800,000. The reported accounts receivable balance was $3,000,000. Does this reported amount seem consistent with past experience? Explain.

52. A company gives prospective managers four separate tests for judging their potential. For a sample of 30 managers, the test scores and the subsequent job effectiveness ratings (Rating) given one year later are listed in the file **P11_52.xlsx**.

a. Look at scatterplots and the table of correlations for these five variables. Does it appear that a multiple regression equation for Rating, with the test scores as explanatory variables, will be successful? Can you foresee any problems in obtaining accurate estimates of the individual regression coefficients?

b. Estimate the regression equation that includes all four test scores, and find 95% confidence intervals for the coefficients of the explanatory variables. How can you explain the negative coefficient of Test3, given that the correlation between Rating and Test3 is positive?

c. Can you reject the null hypothesis that these test scores, as a whole, have no predictive ability for job effectiveness at the 1% level? Why or why not?

d. If a new prospective manager has test scores of 83, 74, 65, and 77, what do you predict his job effectiveness rating will be in one year? What is the standard error of this prediction?

53. Confederate Express is attempting to determine how its monthly shipping costs depend on the number of units shipped during a month. The file **P11_53.xlsx** contains the number of units shipped and total shipping costs for the last 15 months.

    a. Use regression to determine a relationship between units shipped and monthly shipping costs.

    b. Plot the errors for the predictions in order of time sequence. Is there any unusual pattern?

    c. You have now been told that there was a trucking strike during months 11 through 15, and you believe that this might have influenced shipping costs. How can the analysis in part **a** be modified to account for the effects of the strike? After accounting for the effects of the strike, does the unusual pattern in part **b** disappear?

54. The file **P11_54.xlsx** contains monthly data on fatal automobile crashes in the U.S. in each of eight three-hour intervals. Suppose you didn't have the data on the midnight to 3AM time interval. How well could multiple regression be used to predict the data for this interval? Which time intervals are most useful in this prediction? Is multicollinearity a problem?

Level B

55. You want to determine the variables that influence bus usage in major American cities. For 24 cities, the following data are listed in the file **P11_55.xlsx**:

- Bus travel (annual, in thousands of hours)
- Income (average per capita income)
- Population (in thousands)
- Land area (in square miles)

    a. Use these data to fit the multiplicative equation

$$\text{BusTravel} = \alpha \text{Income}^{\beta_1} \text{Population}^{\beta_2} \text{LandArea}^{\beta_3}$$

    b. Are all variables significant at the 5% level?

    c. Interpret the estimated values of β_1, β_2, and β_3.

56. The file **P11_56.xlsx** contains data on 80 managers at a large (fictitious) corporation. The variables are Salary (current annual salary), YrsExper (years of experience in the industry), YrsHere (years of experience with this company), and MglLevel (current level in the company, coded 1 to 4). You want to regress Salary on the potential explanatory variables. What is the best way to do so? Specifically, how should you handle Mg1Level? Should you include both YrsExper and YrsHere or only one of them, and if only one, which one? Present your results, and explain them and your reasoning behind them.

57. A toy company has assigned you to analyze the factors influencing the sales of its most popular doll. The number of these dolls sold during the last 23 years is given in the file **P11_57.xlsx**. The following factors are thought to influence sales of these dolls:

- Was there a recession?
- Were the dolls on sale at Christmas?
- Was there an upward trend over time?

    a. Determine an equation that can be used to predict annual sales of these dolls. Make sure that all variables in your equation are significant at the 10% level.

    b. Interpret the coefficients in your equation.

    c. Are there any outliers?

    d. Is heteroscedasticity or autocorrelation of residuals a problem?

    e. During the current year (year 24), a recession is predicted and the dolls will be put on sale at Christmas. There is a 1% chance that sales of the dolls will exceed what value? You can assume here that heteroscedasticity and autocorrelation are *not* a problem. (*Hint*: Use the standard error of prediction and the fact that the errors are approximately normally distributed.)

58. The file **P11_58.xlsx** shows the "yield curve" (at monthly intervals). For example, in January 1985 the annual rate on a three-month T-bill was 7.76% and the annual rate on a 30-year government bond was 11.45%. Use regression to determine which interest rates tend to move together most closely. (Source: *International Investment and Exchange Database. Developed by Craig Holden, Indiana University School of Business*)

59. The Keynesian school of macroeconomics believes that increased government spending leads to increased growth. The file **P11_59.xlsx** contains the following annual data:

- Government spending as percentage of GDP (gross domestic product)
- Percentage annual growth in annual GDP

Are these data consistent with the Keynesian school of economics? (Source: *Wall Street Journal*)

60. The June 1997 issue of *Management Accounting* gave the following rule for predicting your current salary if you are a managerial accountant. Take $31,865. Next, add $20,811 if you are top management, add $3604 if you are senior management, or subtract $11,419 if you are entry management. Then add $1105 for every year you have been a managerial accountant. Add $7600 if you have a master's degree or subtract $12,467 if you have no college degree. Add $11,257 if you have a professional certification. Finally, add $8667 if you are male.

    a. How do you think the journal derived this method of predicting an accountant's current salary? Be specific.

    b. How could a managerial accountant use this information to determine whether he or she is significantly underpaid?

61. A business school committee was charged with studying admissions criteria to the school. Until that time, only juniors were admitted. Part of the committee's task was to see whether freshman courses would be equally good predictors of success as freshman and sophomore courses combined. Here, we take "success" to mean doing well in I-core (the integrated core, a combination of the junior level finance, marketing, and operations courses, F301, M301, and P301). The file **P11_61.xlsx** contains data on 250 students who had just completed I-core. For each student, the file lists their grades in the following courses:

- M118 (freshman)—finite math
- M119 (freshman)—calculus
- K201 (freshman)—computers
- W131 (freshman)—writing
- E201, E202 (sophomore)—micro- and macroeconomics
- L201 (sophomore)—business law
- A201, A202 (sophomore)—accounting
- E270 (sophomore)—statistics
- I-core (junior)—finance, marketing, and operations

Except for I-core, each value is a grade point for a specific course (such as 3.7 for an A–). For I-core, each value is the average grade point for the three courses comprising I-core.

a. The I-core grade point is the eventual dependent variable in a regression analysis. Look at the correlations between all variables. Is multicollinearity likely to be a problem? Why or why not?

b. Run a multiple regression using all of the potential explanatory variables. Now, eliminate the variables as follows. (This is a reasonable variation of the procedures discussed in the chapter.) Look at 95% confidence intervals for their coefficients (as usual, not counting the intercept term). Any variable whose confidence interval contains the value zero is a candidate for exclusion. For all such candidates, eliminate the variable with the *t*-value lowest in magnitude. Then rerun the regression, and use the same procedure to possibly exclude another variable. Keep doing this until 95% confidence intervals of the coefficients of all remaining variables do *not* include zero. Report this final equation, its R^2 value, and its standard error of estimate s_e.

c. Give a quick summary of the properties of the final equation in part **b**. Specifically, (1) do the variables have the "correct" signs, (2) which courses tend to be the best predictors, (3) are the predictions from this equation likely to be much good, and (4) are there any obvious violations of the regression assumptions?

d. Redo part **b**, but now use as your potential explanatory variables only courses taken in the freshman year. As in part **b**, report the final equation, its R^2, and its standard error of estimate s_e.

e. Briefly, do you think there is enough predictive power in the freshman courses, relative to the freshman and sophomore courses combined, to change to a sophomore admit policy? (Answer only on the basis of the regression results; don't get into other merits of the argument.)

62. The file **P11_62.xlsx** has (somewhat old) data on several countries. The variables are listed here.

- Country: name of country
- GNPCapita: GNP per capita
- PopGrowth: average annual percentage change in population, 1980–1990
- Calorie: daily per capita calorie content of food used for domestic consumption
- LifeExp: average life expectancy of newborn given current mortality conditions
- Fertility: births per woman given current fertility rates

With data such as these, cause and effect are difficult to determine. For example, does low LifeExp cause GNPCapita to be low, or vice versa? Therefore, the purpose of this problem is to experiment with the following sets of dependent and explanatory variables. In each case, look at scatterplots (and use economic reasoning) to find and estimate the best form of the equation, using only linear and logarithmic variables. Then interpret precisely what each equation is saying.

a. Dependent: LifeExp; Explanatories: Calorie, Fertility

b. Dependent: LifeExp; Explanatories: GNPCapita, PopGrowth

c. Dependent: GNPCapita; Explanatories: PopGrowth, Calorie, Fertility

63. Suppose that an economist has been able to gather data on the relationship between demand and price for a particular product. After analyzing scatterplots and using economic theory, the economist decides to estimate an equation of the form $Q = aP^b$, where Q is quantity demanded and P is price. An appropriate regression analysis is then performed, and the estimated parameters turn out to be $a = 1000$ and $b = -1.3$. Now consider two scenarios: (1) the price increases from \$10 to \$12.50; (2) the price increases from \$20 to \$25.

a. Do you predict the percentage decrease in demand to be the same in scenario 1 as in scenario 2? Why or why not?

b. What is the predicted percentage decrease in demand in scenario 1? What about scenario 2? Be as exact as possible. (*Hint:* Remember from economics that an elasticity shows directly what happens for a "small" percentage change in price. These changes aren't that small, so you'll have to do some calculating.)

64. A human resources analyst believes that in a particular industry, the wage rate ($/hr) is related to seniority by an equation of the form $W = ae^{bS}$, where W equals wage rate and S equals seniority (in years). However, the analyst suspects that both parameters, a and b, might depend on whether the workers belong to a union. Therefore, the analyst gathers data on a number of workers, both union and nonunion, and estimates the following equation with regression:

$$\ln(W) = 2.14 + 0.027S + 0.12U + 0.006SU$$

Here $\ln(W)$ is the natural log of W, U is 1 for union workers and 0 for nonunion workers, and SU is the product of S and U.

  a. According to this model, what is the predicted wage rate for a nonunion worker with 0 years of seniority? What is it for a union worker with 0 years of seniority?

  b. Explain exactly what this equation implies about the predicted effect of seniority on wage rate for a nonunion worker and for a union worker.

65. A company has recorded its overhead costs, machine hours, and labor hours for the past 60 months. The data are in the file **P11_65.xlsx**. The company decides to use regression to explain its overhead hours linearly as a function of machine hours and labor hours. However, recognizing good statistical practice, it decides to estimate a regression equation for the first 36 months and then validate this regression with the data from the last 24 months. That is, it will substitute the values of machine and labor hours from the last 24 months into the regression equation that is based on the first 36 months and see how well it does.

  a. Run the regression for the first 36 months. Explain briefly why the coefficient of labor hours is not significant.

  b. For this part, use the regression equation from part **a** with both variables still in the equation (even though one was insignificant). Fill in the fitted and residual columns for months 37 through 60. Then do relevant calculations to see whether the R^2 (or multiple R) and the standard error of estimate s_e are as good for these 24 months as they are for the first 36 months. Explain your results briefly. (*Hint*: Remember the meaning of the multiple R and the standard error of estimate.)

66. Pernavik Dairy produces and sells a wide range of dairy products. Because most of the dairy's costs and prices are set by a government regulatory board, most of the competition between the dairy and its competitors takes place through advertising. The controller of Pernavik has developed the sales and advertising levels for the last 52 weeks. These appear in the file **P11_66.xlsx**. Note that the advertising levels for the three weeks prior to week 1 are also listed. The controller wonders whether Pernavik is spending too much money on advertising. He argues that the company's contribution-margin ratio is about 10%. That is, 10% of each sales dollar goes toward covering fixed costs. This means that each advertising dollar has to generate at least $10 of sales or the advertising is not cost-effective. Use regression to determine whether advertising dollars are generating this type of sales response. (*Hint*: It is very possible that the sales value in any week is affected not only by advertising this week, but also by advertising levels in the past one, two, or three weeks. These are called *lagged* values of advertising. Try regression models with lagged values of advertising included, and see whether you get better results.)

67. The Pierce Company manufactures drill bits. The production of the drill bits occurs in lots of 1000 units. Due to the intense competition in the industry and the correspondingly low prices, Pierce has undertaken a study of the manufacturing costs of each of the products it manufactures. One part of this study concerns the overhead costs associated with producing the drill bits. Senior production personnel have determined that the number of lots produced, the direct labor hours used, and the number of production runs per month might help to explain the behavior of overhead costs. The file **P11_67.xlsx** contains the data on these variables for the past 36 months.

  a. How well can you can predict overhead costs on the basis of these variables with a linear regression equation? Why might you be disappointed with the results?

  b. A production supervisor believes that labor hours and the number of production run setups affect overhead because Pierce uses a lot of supplies when it is working on the machines and because the machine setup time for each run is charged to overhead. As he says, "When the rate of production increases, we use overtime until we can train the additional people that we require for the machines. When the rate of production falls, we incur idle time until the surplus workers are transferred to other parts of the plant. So it would seem to me that there will be an additional overhead cost whenever the level of production changes. I would also say that because of the nature of this rescheduling process, the bigger the change in production, the greater the effect of the change in production on the increase in overhead." How might you use this information to find a better regression equation than in part **a**? (*Hint*: Develop a new explanatory variable, and assume that the number of lots produced in the month preceding month 1 was 5964.)

68. Danielson Electronics manufactures color television sets for sale in a highly competitive marketplace. Recently Ron Thomas, the marketing manager of Danielson Electronics, has been complaining that the company is losing market share because of a poor-quality image, and he has asked that the company's major product, the 25-inch console model, be redesigned to incorporate a higher quality level. The company general manager, Steve Hatting, is considering the request to improve the product quality but is not convinced that consumers will be willing to pay the additional expense for improved quality. As the company controller, you are in charge of determining the cost-effectiveness of improving the quality of the television sets. With the help of the marketing staff, you have obtained a summary of the average retail price of the company's television set and the prices of 29 competitive sets. In addition, you have obtained from *The Shoppers' Guide,* a magazine that evaluates and reports on various consumer products, a quality rating of the television sets produced by Danielson Electronics and its competitors. The file **P11_68.xlsx** summarizes these data. According to *The Shoppers' Guide,* the quality rating, which varies from 0 to 10 (10 being the highest level of quality), considers such factors as the quality of the picture, the frequency of repair, and the cost of repairs. Discussions with the product design group suggest that the cost of manufacturing this type of television set is $125 + Q^2$, where Q is the quality rating.

a. Regress Average Price versus Quality Rating. Does the regression equation imply that customers are willing to pay a premium for quality? Explain.

b. Given the results from part **a**, is there a preferred level of quality for this product? Assume that the quality level will affect only the price charged and not the level of sales of the product.

c. How might you answer part **b** if the level of sales is also affected by the quality level (or alternatively, if the level of sales is affected by price)?

69. The file **P11_69.xlsx** contains data on gasoline consumption and several economic variables. The variables are gasoline consumption for passenger cars (GasUsed), service station price excluding taxes (SSPrice), retail price of gasoline including state and federal taxes (RPrice), Consumer Price Index for all items (CPI), Consumer Price Index for public transportation (CPIT), number of registered passenger cars (Cars), average miles traveled per gallon (MPG), and real per capita disposable income (DispInc).

a. Regress GasUsed linearly versus CPIT, Cars, MPG, DispInc, and DefRPrice, where DefRPrice is the deflated retail price of gasoline (RPrice divided by CPI). What signs would you expect the coefficients to have? Do they have these signs? Which of the coefficients are statistically significant at the 5% significance level?

b. Suppose the government makes the claim that for every one cent of tax on gasoline, there will be a $1 billion increase in tax revenue. Use the estimated equation in part **a** to support or refute the government's claim.

70. On October 30, 1995, the citizens of Quebec went to the polls to decide the future of their province. They were asked to vote "Yes" or "No" on whether Quebec, a predominantly French-speaking province, should secede from Canada and become a sovereign country. The "No" side was declared the winner, but only by a thin margin. Immediately following the vote, however, allegations began to surface that the result was closer than it should have been. (Source: Cawley and Sommers (1996)). In particular, the ruling separatist Parti Québécois, whose job was to decide which ballots were rejected, was accused by the "No" voters of systematic electoral fraud by voiding thousands of "No" votes in the predominantly allophone and anglophone electoral divisions of Montreal. (An *allophone* refers to someone whose first language is neither English nor French. An *anglophone* refers to someone whose first language is English.)

Cawley and Sommers examined whether electoral fraud had been committed by running a regression, using data from the 125 electoral divisions in the October 1995 referendum. The dependent variable was REJECT, the percentage of rejected ballots in the electoral division. The explanatory variables were as follows:

- ALLOPHONE: percentage of allophones in the electoral division
- ANGLOPHONE: percentage of anglophones in the electoral division
- REJECT94: percentage of rejected votes from that electoral division during a similar referendum in 1994
- LAVAL: dummy variable equal to 1 for electoral divisions in the Laval region, 0 otherwise
- LAV_ALL: interaction (i.e., product) of LAVAL and ALLOPHONE

The estimated regression equation (with *t*-values in parentheses) is

$$\text{Prediced REJECT} = \underset{(5.68)}{1.112} + \underset{(4.34)}{0.020} \text{ ALLOPHONE}$$

$$+ \underset{(0.12)}{0.001} \text{ ANGLOPHONE} + \underset{(2.64)}{0.223} \text{ REJECT94}$$

$$- \underset{(-8.61)}{3.773} \text{ LAVAL} + \underset{(15.62)}{0.387} \text{ LAV\_ALL}$$

The R^2 value was 0.759. Based on this analysis, Cawley and Sommers state that, "The evidence presented here suggests that there were voting irregularities in the October 1995 Quebec referendum, especially in Laval." Discuss how they came to this conclusion.

71. Suppose you are trying to explain variations in salaries for technicians in a particular field of work. The file **P11_71.xlsx** contains annual salaries for 200 technicians.

It also shows how many years of experience each technician has, as well as his or her education level. There are four education levels, as explained in the comment in cell D1. Three suggestions are put forth for the relationship between Salary and these two explanatory variables:

- You should regress Salary linearly versus the two given variables, YrsExper and EducLev.
- All that really matters in terms of education is whether the person got a college degree or not. Therefore, you should regress Salary linearly versus YrsExper and a dummy variable indicating whether he or she got a college degree.
- Each level of education might result in different jumps in salary. Therefore, you should regress Salary linearly versus YrsExper and dummy variables for the different education levels.

a. Run the indicated regressions for each of these three suggestions. Then (1) explain what each equation is saying and how the three are different (focus here on the coefficients), (2) which you prefer, and (3) whether (or how) the regression results in your preferred equation contradict the average salary results shown in the Pivot Table sheet of the file.

b. Consider the four workers shown on the Prediction sheet of the file. (These are four new workers, not among the original 200.) Using your preferred equation, calculate a predicted salary and a 95% prediction interval for each of these four workers.

c. It turns out (you don't have to check this) that the interaction between years of experience and education level is *not* significant for this data set. In general, however, argue why you might expect an interaction between them for salary data of technical workers. What form of interaction would you suspect? (There is not necessarily one right answer, but argue convincingly one way or the other for a positive or a negative interaction.)

72. The file **P03_55.xlsx** contains baseball data on all MLB teams from during the years 2004–2009. For each year and team, the total salary and the number of (regular-season) wins are listed.

a. Rearrange the data so that there are six columns: Team, Year, Salary Last Year, Salary This Year, Wins Last Year, and Wins This Year. You don't need rows for 2004 rows, because the data for 2003 isn't available for Salary Last Year and Wins Last Year. Your ending data set should have 5*30 rows of data.

b. Run a multiple regression for Wins This Year versus the other variables (besides Team). Then run a forward stepwise regression with these same

variables. Compare the two equations, and explain exactly what the coefficients of the equation from the forward method imply about wins.

c. The Year variable *should* be insignificant. Is it? Why would it be contradictory for the "true" coefficient of Year to be anything other than zero?

d. Statistical inference from regression equations is all about inferring from the given data to a larger population. Does it make sense to talk about a larger population in this situation? If so, what is the larger population?

73. Do the previous problem, but use the basketball data on all NBA teams in the file **P03_56.xlsx**.

74. Do the previous problem, but use the football data on all NFL teams in the file **P03_57.xlsx**.

75. The file **P03_65.xlsx** contains basketball data on all NBA teams for five seasons. The SRS (simple rating system) variable is a measure of how good a team is in any given year. (It is explained in more detail in the comment in cell F3.)

a. Given the explanation of SRS, it makes sense to use multiple regression, with PTS and O_PTS as the explanatory variables, to predict SRS. Do you get a good fit?

b. Suppose instead that the goal is to predict Wins. Try multiple regression, using the variables in columns G–AH or variables calculated from them. For example, instead of FG and FGA, you could try FG/FGA, the fraction of attempted field goals made. You will have to guard against exact multi-collinearity. For example, PTS can be calculated exactly from FG, 3P, and FT. This is a good time to use some form of stepwise regression. How well is your best equation able to predict Wins?

76. Do the preceding problem, but now use the football data in the file **P03_66.xlsx**. (This file contains offensive and defensive ratings in the OSRS and DSRS variables, but you can ignore them for this problem. Focus only on the SRS rating in part **a**.)

77. The file **P03_63.xlsx** contains 2009 data on R&D expenses and many financial variables for 85 U.S. publicly traded companies in the computer and electronic product manufacturing industry. The question is whether R&D expenses can be predicted from any combination of the potential variables. Use scatterplots, correlations (possibly on nonlinear transformations of variables) to search for promising relationships. Eventually, find a regression that seems to provide the best explanatory power for R&D expenses. Interpret this best equation and indicate how good a fit it provides.

The Artsy Corporation has been sued in U.S. Federal Court on charges of sex discrimination in employment under Title VII of the Civil Rights Act of 1964.[10] The litigation at contention here is a class-action lawsuit brought on behalf of all females who were employed by the company, or who had applied for work with the company, between 1979 and 1987. Artsy operates in several states, runs four quite distinct businesses, and has many different types of employees. The allegations of the plaintiffs deal with issues of hiring, pay, promotions, and other "conditions of employment."

In such large class-action employment discrimination lawsuits, it has become common for statistical evidence to play a central role in the determination of guilt or damages. In an interesting twist on typical legal procedures, a precedent has developed in these cases that plaintiffs may make a prima facie case purely in terms of circumstantial statistical evidence. If that statistical evidence is reasonably strong, the burden of proof shifts to the defendants to rebut the plaintiffs' statistics with other data, other analyses of the same data, or nonstatistical testimony. In practice, statistical arguments often dominate the proceedings of such Equal Employment Opportunity (EEO) cases. Indeed, in this case the statistical data used as evidence filled numerous computer tapes, and the supporting statistical analysis comprised thousands of pages of printouts and reports. We work here with a typical subset that pertains to one contested issue at one of the company's locations.

The data in the file **Artsy Lawsuit.xlsx** relate to the pay of 256 employees on the hourly payroll at one of the company's production facilities. The data include an identification number (ID) that would identify the person by name or social security number; the person's gender (Gender), where 0 denotes female and 1 denotes male; the person's job grade in 1986 (Grade); the length of time (in years) the person had been in that job grade as of December 31, 1986 (TInGrade); and the person's weekly pay rate as of December 31, 1986 (Rate). These data permit a statistical examination of one of the issues in the case—fair pay for female employees. We deal with one of three pay classes of employees—those on the biweekly payroll at one of the company's locations at Pocahantas, Maine.

The plaintiffs' attorneys have proposed settling the pay issues in the case for this group of female employees for a "back pay" lump payment to female employees of 25% of their pay during the period 1979 to 1987. It is your task to examine the data statistically for evidence in favor of, or against, the charges. You are to advise the lawyers for the company on how to proceed. Consider the following issues as they have been laid out to you by the attorneys representing the firm:

1. Overall, how different is pay by gender? Are the differences in pay statistically significant? Does a statistical significance test have meaning in a case like this? If so, how should it be performed? Lay out as succinctly as possible the arguments that you anticipate the plaintiffs will make with this data set.

2. The company wishes to argue that a legitimate explanation of the pay-rate differences may be the difference in job grades. (In this analysis, we will tacitly assume that each person's job grade is, in fact, appropriate for him or her, even though the plaintiffs' attorneys have charged that females have been unfairly kept in the lower grades. Other statistical data, not available here, are used in that analysis.) The lawyers ask, "Is there a relatively easy way to understand, analyze, and display the pay differences by job grade? Is it easy enough that it could be presented to an average jury without confusing them?" Again, use the data to anticipate the possible arguments of the plaintiffs. To what extent does job grade appear to explain the pay-rate differences between the genders? Propose and carry out appropriate hypothesis tests or confidence intervals to check whether the difference in pay between genders is statistically significant within each of the grades.

---

[9]This case was contributed by Peter Kolesar from Columbia University.
[10]Artsy is an actual corporation, and the data given in this case are real, but the name has been changed to protect the firm's true identity.

3. In the actual case, the previous analysis suggested to the attorneys that differences in pay rates are due, at least in part, to differences in job grades. They had heard that in another EEO case, the dependence of pay rate on job grade had been investigated with regression analysis. Perform a simple linear regression of pay rate on job grade for them. Interpret the results fully. Is the regression significant? How much of the variability in pay does job grade account for? Carry out a full check of the quality of your regression. What light does this shed on the pay fairness issue? Does it help or hurt the company? Is it fair to the female employees?

4. It is argued that seniority within a job grade should be taken into account because the company's written pay policy explicitly calls for the consideration of this factor. How different are times in grade by gender? Are they enough to matter?

5. The Artsy legal team wants an analysis of the simultaneous influence of grade and time in grade on pay. Perform a multiple regression of pay rate versus grade and time in grade. Is the regression significant? How much of the variability in pay rates is explained by this model? Will this analysis help your clients? Could the plaintiffs effectively attack it? Consider residuals in your analysis of these issues.

6. Organize your analyses and conclusions in a brief report summarizing your findings for your client, the Artsy Corporation. Be complete but succinct. Be sure to advise them on the settlement issue. Be as forceful as you can be in arguing "the Artsy Case" without misusing the data or statistical theory. Apprise your client of the risks they face, by showing them the forceful and legitimate counterargument the female plaintiffs could make. ■

Dupree Fuels Company is facing a difficult problem. Dupree sells heating oil to residential customers. Given the amount of competition in the industry, both from other home heating oil suppliers and from electric and natural gas utilities, the price of the oil supplied and the level of service are critical in determining a company's success. Unlike electric and natural gas customers, oil customers are exposed to the risk of running out of fuel. Home heating oil suppliers therefore have to guarantee that the customer's oil tank will not be allowed to run dry. In fact, Dupree's service pledge is, "50 free gallons on us if we let you run dry." Beyond the cost of the oil, however, Dupree is concerned about the perceived reliability of his service if a customer is allowed to run out of oil.

To estimate customer oil use, the home heating oil industry uses the concept of a *degree-day*, equal to the difference between the average daily temperature and 68 degrees Fahrenheit. So if the average temperature on a given day is 50, the degree-days for that day will be 18. (If the degree-day calculation results in a negative number, the degree-day number is recorded as 0.) By keeping track of the number of degree-days since the customer's last oil fill, knowing the size of the customer's oil tank, and estimating the customer's oil consumption as a function of the number of degree-days, the oil supplier can estimate when the customer is getting low on fuel and then resupply the customer.

Dupree has used this scheme in the past but is disappointed with the results and the computational burdens it places on the company. First, the system requires that a consumption-per-degree-day figure be estimated for each customer to reflect that customer's consumption habits, size of home, quality of home insulation, and family size. Because Dupree has more than 1500 customers, the computational burden of keeping track of all of these customers is enormous. Second, the system is crude and unreliable. The consumption per degree-day for each customer is computed by dividing the oil consumption during the preceding year by the degree-days during the preceding year. Customers have tended to use less fuel than estimated during the colder months and more fuel than estimated during the warmer months. This means that Dupree is making more deliveries than necessary during the colder months and customers are running out of oil during the warmer months.

Dupree wants to develop a consumption estimation model that is practical and more reliable. The following data are available in the file **Dupree Fuels.xlsx**:

■ The number of degree-days since the last oil fill and the consumption amounts for 40 customers.

■ The number of people residing in the homes of each of the 40 customers. Dupree thinks that this might be important in predicting the oil consumption of customers using oil-fired water heaters because it provides an estimate of the hot-water requirements of each customer. Each of the customers in this sample uses an oil-fired water heater.

■ An assessment, provided by Dupree sales staff, of the home type of each of these 40 customers. The home type classification, which is a number between 1 and 5, is a composite index of the home size, age, exposure to wind, level of insulation, and furnace type. A low index implies a lower oil consumption per degree-day, and a high index implies a higher consumption of oil per degree-day. Dupree thinks that the use of such an index will allow them to estimate a consumption model based on a sample data set and then to apply the same model to predict the oil demand of each of his customers.

Use regression to see whether a statistically reliable oil consumption model can be estimated from the data. ■

---

[11]Case Studies 11.2 through 11.4 are based on problems from *Advanced Management Accounting*, 2nd edition, by Robert S. Kaplan and Anthony A. Atkinson, 1989, Upper Saddle River, NJ: Prentice Hall. We thank them for allowing us to adapt their problems.

CASE 11.3 DEVELOPING A FLEXIBLE BUDGET AT THE GUNDERSON PLANT

The Gunderson Plant manufactures the industrial product line of FGT Industries. Plant management wants to be able to get a good, yet quick, estimate of the manufacturing overhead costs that can be expected each month. The easiest and simplest method to accomplish this task is to develop a flexible budget formula for the manufacturing overhead costs. The plant's accounting staff has suggested that simple linear regression be used to determine the behavior pattern of the overhead costs. The regression data can provide the basis for the flexible budget formula. Sufficient evidence is available to conclude that manufacturing overhead costs vary with direct labor hours. The actual direct labor hours and the corresponding manufacturing overhead costs for each month of the last three years have been used in the linear regression analysis.

The three-year period contained various occurrences not uncommon to many businesses. During the first year, production was severely curtailed during two months due to wildcat strikes. In the second year, production was reduced in one month because of material shortages, and increased significantly (scheduled overtime) during two months to meet the units required for a one-time sales order. At the end of the second year, employee benefits were raised significantly as the result of a labor agreement. Production during the third year was not affected by any special circumstances. Various members of Gunderson's accounting staff raised some issues regarding the historical data collected for the regression analysis. These issues were as follows.

■ Some members of the accounting staff believed that the use of data from all 36 months would provide a more accurate portrayal of the cost behavior. While they recognized that any of the monthly data could include efficiencies and inefficiencies, they believed these efficiencies and inefficiencies would tend to balance out over a longer period of time.

■ Other members of the accounting staff suggested that only those months that were considered normal should be used so that the regression would not be distorted.

■ Still other members felt that only the most recent 12 months should be used because they were the most current.

■ Some members questioned whether historical data should be used at all to form the basis for a flexible budget formula.

The accounting department ran two regression analyses of the data—one using the data from all 36 months and the other using only the data from the last 12 months. The information derived from the two linear regressions is shown below (t-values shown in parentheses). The 36-month regression is

$$OH_t = 123{,}810 + 1.60\ DLH_t, \quad R^2 = 0.32$$
$$(1.64)$$

The 12-month regression is

$$OH_t = 109{,}020 + 3.00\ DLH_t, \quad R^2 = 0.48$$
$$(3.01)$$

Questions

1. Which of the two results (12 months versus 36 months) would you use as a basis for the flexible budget formula?

2. How would the four specific issues raised by the members of Gunderson's accounting staff influence your willingness to use the results of the statistical analyses as the basis for the flexible budget formula? Explain your answer. ■

Wagner Printers performs all types of printing, including custom work, such as advertising displays, and standard work, such as business cards. Market prices exist for standard work, and Wagner Printers must match or better these prices to get the business. The key issue is whether the existing market price covers the cost associated with doing the work. On the other hand, most of the custom work must be priced individually. Because all custom work is done on a job-order basis, Wagner routinely keeps track of all the direct labor and direct materials costs associated with each job. However, the overhead for each job must be estimated. The overhead is applied to each job using a predetermined (normalized) rate based on estimated overhead and labor hours. Once the cost of the prospective job is determined, the sales manager develops a bid that reflects both the existing market conditions and the estimated price of completing the job.

In the past, the normalized rate for overhead has been computed by using the historical average of overhead per direct labor hour. Wagner has become increasingly concerned about this practice for two reasons. First, it hasn't produced accurate forecasts of overhead in the past. Second, technology has changed the printing process, so that the labor content of jobs has been decreasing, and the normalized rate of overhead per direct labor hour has steadily been increasing. The file **Wagner Printers.xlsx** shows the overhead data that Wagner has collected for its shop for the past 52 weeks. The average weekly overhead for the last 52 weeks is $54,208, and the average weekly number of labor hours worked is 716. Therefore, the normalized rate for overhead that will be used in the upcoming week is about $76 (= 54208/716) per direct labor hour.

Questions

1. Determine whether you can develop a more accurate estimate of overhead costs.

2. Wagner is now preparing a bid for an important order that may involve a considerable amount of repeat business. The estimated requirements for this project are 15 labor hours, 8 machine hours, $150 direct labor cost, and $750 direct material cost. Using the existing approach to cost estimation, Wagner has estimated the cost for this job as $2040 (= 150 + 750 + (76 × 15)). Given the existing data, what cost would you estimate for this job? ■

Time Series Analysis and Forecasting

REVENUE MANAGEMENT AT HARRAH'S CHEROKEE CASINO & HOTEL

Real applications of forecasting are almost never done in isolation. They are typically one part—a crucial part—of an overall quantitative solution to a business problem. This is certainly the case at Harrah's Cherokee Casino & Hotel in North Carolina, as explained in an article by Metters et al. (2008). This particular casino uses revenue management (RM) on a daily basis to increase its revenue from its gambling customers. As customers call to request reservations at the casino's hotel, the essential problem is to decide which reservations to accept and which to deny. The idea is that there is an opportunity cost from accepting early requests from lower-valued customers because higher-valued customers might request the same rooms later on.

As the article explains, there are several unique features about casinos, and this casino in particular, that make a quantitative approach to RM successful. First, the detailed behaviors of customers can be tracked, via electronic cards they use while placing bets in the electronic gambling machines, so that the casino can create a large database of individual customers' gambling patterns. This allows the casino to segment the customers into different groups, based on how much they typically bet in a given night. For example, one segment might contain all customers who bet between $500 and $600 per night. When a customer calls for a room reservation and provides his card number, the casino can immediately look up his information in the database and see which segment he is in.

A second reason for the successful use of RM is that customers differ substantially in the price they are willing to pay for the same commodity, a stay at the casino's hotel. Actually, many don't pay anything for the room or the food—these are frequently complimentary from the casino—but they pay by losing money at gambling. Some customers typically gamble thousands of dollars per night while others gamble much less. (This is quite different from the disparities in other hotels or in air travel, where a business traveler might pay twice as much as a vacationer, but not much more.) Because some customers are much more valuable than others, there are real opportunity costs from treating all customers alike.

A third reason for the success of RM at this casino is that the casino can afford to hold out for the best-paying customers until the last minute. The reason is that a significant percentage of the customers from all segments wait until the last minute to make their reservations. In fact, they often make them while driving, say, from Atlanta to the casino. Therefore, the casino can afford to deny requests for reservations to lower-valued customers made a day or two in advance, knowing that last-minute reservations, very possibly from higher-valued customers, will fill up the casino's rooms. Indeed, the occupancy rate is virtually always 98% or above.

The overall RM solution includes (1) data collection and customer segmentation, as explained above, (2) forecasting demand for reservations from each customer segment, (3) a linear programming (LP) optimization model that is run frequently to decide which reservations to accept, and (4) a customer relationship management model to entice loyal customers to book rooms on nights with lower demand. The forecasting model is very similar to the Winters' exponential smoothing model discussed in this chapter. Specifically, the model uses the large volume of historical data to forecast customer demand by each customer segment for any particular night in the future. These forecasts include information about time-related or seasonal patterns (weekends are busier, for example) and any special events that are scheduled. Also, the forecasts are updated daily as the night in question approaches. These forecasts are then used in an LP optimization model to determine which requests to approve. For example, the LP model might indicate that, given the current status of bookings and three nights to go, requests for rooms on the specified night should be accepted only for the four most valuable customer segments. As the given night approaches and the number of booked rooms changes, the LP model is rerun many times and provides staff with the necessary information for real-time decisions. (By the way, a customer who is refused a room at the casino is often given a free room at another nearby hotel. After all, this customer can still be valuable enough to offset the price of the room at the other hotel.)

It is difficult to measure the effect of this entire RM system because it has always been in place since the casino opened. But there is no doubt that it is effective. Despite the fact that it serves no alcohol and has only electronic games, not the traditional gaming tables, the casino has nearly full occupancy and returns a 60% profit margin on gross revenue—double the industry norm. ■

12.1 INTRODUCTION

Many decision-making applications depend on a forecast of some quantity. Here are several examples.

Examples of Forecasting Applications

- When a service organization, such as a fast-food restaurant, plans its staffing over some time period, it must forecast the customer demand as a function of time. This might be done at a very detailed level, such as the demand in successive 15-minute periods, or at a more aggregate level, such as the demand in successive weeks.

- When a company plans its ordering or production schedule for a product it sells to the public, it must forecast the customer demand for this product so that it can stock appropriate quantities—neither too many nor too few.

- When an organization plans to invest in stocks, bonds, or other financial instruments, it typically attempts to forecast movements in stock prices and interest rates.

- When government officials plan policy, they attempt to forecast movements in macroeconomic variables such as inflation, interest rates, and unemployment.

Unfortunately, forecasting is a very difficult task, both in the short run and in the long run. Typically, forecasts are based on historical data. Analysts search for patterns or relationships in the historical data, and then make forecasts. There are two problems with this approach. The first is that it is not always easy to uncover historical patterns or relationships. In particular, it is often difficult to separate the noise, or random behavior, from the underlying patterns. Some forecasts can even overdo it, by attributing importance to patterns that are in fact random variations and are unlikely to repeat themselves.

The second problem is that there are no guarantees that past patterns will continue in the future. A new war could break out somewhere in the world, a company's competitor could introduce a new product into the market, the bottom could fall out of the stock market, and so on. Each of these shocks to the system being studied could drastically alter the future in a highly unpredictable way. This partly explains why forecasts are almost always wrong. Unless they have inside information to the contrary, analysts must assume that history will repeat itself. But we all know that history does *not* always repeat itself. Therefore, there are many famous forecasts that turned out to be way off the mark, even though the analysts made reasonable assumptions and used standard forecasting techniques. Nevertheless, forecasts are required throughout the business world, so fear of failure is no excuse for not giving it our best effort.

12.2 FORECASTING METHODS: AN OVERVIEW

There are many forecasting methods available, and all practitioners have their favorites. To say the least, there is little agreement among practitioners or academics as to the best forecasting method. The methods can generally be divided into three groups: (1) *judgmental* methods, (2) *extrapolation* (or *time series*) methods, and (3) *econometric* (or *causal*) methods. The first of these is basically nonquantitative and will not be discussed here; the last two are quantitative. In this section we describe extrapolation and econometric methods in some generality. In the rest of the chapter, we go into more detail, particularly about the extrapolation methods.

12.2.1 Extrapolation Methods

Extrapolation methods are quantitative methods that use past data of a time series variable—and nothing else, except possibly time itself—to forecast future values of the variable. The idea is that past movements of a variable, such as company sales or U.S. exports to Japan, can be used to forecast future values of the variable. Many extrapolation methods are available, including trend-based regression, autoregression, moving averages, and exponential smoothing. Some of these methods are relatively simple, both conceptually and in terms of the calculations required, whereas others are quite complex. Also, as the names imply, some of these methods use the same regression methods from the previous two chapters, whereas others do not.

All of these extrapolation methods search for *patterns* in the historical series and then extrapolate these patterns into the future. Some try to track long-term upward or downward trends and then project these. Some try to track the seasonal patterns (such as sales up in November and December, down in other months) and then project these. Basically, the more complex the method, the more closely it tries to track historical patterns. Researchers have long believed that good forecasting methods should be able to track the ups and downs—the zigzags on a graph—of a time series. This has led to voluminous research and increasingly complex methods. But is complexity always better?

Surprisingly, empirical evidence shows that complexity is *not* always better. This is documented in a quarter-century review article by Armstrong (1986) and an article by Schnarrs and Bavuso (1986). They document a number of empirical studies on literally thousands of time series forecasts where complex methods fared no better, and sometimes even worse, than simple methods. In fact, the Schnarrs and Bavuso article presents evidence that a naive forecast from a "random walk" model sometimes outperforms all of the more sophisticated extrapolation methods. This naive model forecasts that next period's value will be the same as this period's value. So if today's closing stock price is 51.375, it forecasts that tomorrow's closing stock price will be 51.375. This method is certainly simple, and it sometimes works quite well. We discuss random walks in more detail in section 12.5.

The evidence in favor of simpler models is not accepted by everyone, particularly not those who have spent years investigating complex models, and complex models continue to be studied and used. However, there is a very plausible reason why simple models can provide reasonably good forecasts. The whole goal of extrapolation methods is to extrapolate historical patterns into the future. But it is often difficult to determine which patterns are real and which represent noise—random ups and downs that are not likely to repeat themselves. Also, if something important changes (a competitor introduces a new product or there is an oil embargo, for example), it is certainly possible that historical patterns will change. A potential problem with complex methods is that they can track a historical series *too* closely. That is, they sometimes track patterns that are really noise. Simpler methods, on the other hand, track only the most basic underlying patterns and therefore can be more flexible and accurate in forecasting the future.

12.2.2 Econometric Models

Econometric models, also called **causal** or **regression-based** models, use regression to forecast a time series variable by using other explanatory time series variables. For example, a company might use a causal model to regress future sales on its advertising level, the population income level, the interest rate, and possibly others. In one sense, regression analysis involving time series variables is similar to the regression analysis discussed in the previous two chapters. The same least squares approach and the same multiple regression software can be used in many time series regression models. In fact, several examples and problems in the previous two chapters used time series data.

However, causal regression models for time series data present new mathematical challenges that go well beyond the level of this book. To get a glimpse of the potential difficulties, suppose a company wants to use a regression model to forecast its monthly sales for some product, using two other time series variables as predictors: its monthly advertising levels for the product and its main competitor's monthly advertising levels for a competing product. The resulting regression equation has the form

$$\text{Predicted } Y_t = a + b_1 X_{1t} + b_2 X_{2t} \tag{12.1}$$

Here, Y_t is the company's sales in month t, and X_{1t} and X_{2t} are, respectively, the company's and the competitor's advertising levels in month t. This regression model might provide some useful results, but there are some issues that must be faced.

One issue is that the appropriate "lags" for the regression equation must be determined. Do sales this month depend only on advertising levels *this* month, as specified in Equation (12.1), or also on advertising levels in the previous month, the previous two months, and so on? A second issue is whether to include lags of the *sales* variable in the regression equation as explanatory variables. Presumably, sales in one month might depend on the level of sales in previous months (as well as on advertising levels). A third issue is that the two advertising variables can be autocorrelated and cross-correlated. *Autocorrelation* means correlated with itself. For example, the company's advertising level in one month might depend on its advertising levels in previous months. *Cross-correlation* means being correlated with a lagged version of another variable. For example, the company's advertising level in one month might be related to the competitor's advertising levels in previous months, or the competitor's advertising in one month might be related to the company's advertising levels in previous months.

These are difficult issues, and the way in which they are addressed can make a big difference in the usefulness of the regression model. We will examine several regression-based models in this chapter, but we won't discuss situations such as the one just described, where one time series variable Y is regressed on one or more time series of Xs. [Pankratz (1991) is a good reference for these latter types of models. Unfortunately, the level of mathematics is considerably beyond the level in this book.]

12.2.3 Combining Forecasts

There is one other general forecasting method that is worth mentioning. In fact, it has attracted a lot of attention in recent years, and many researchers believe that it has potential for increasing forecast accuracy. The method is simple—it combines two or more forecasts to obtain the final forecast. The reasoning behind this method is also simple: The forecast errors from different forecasting methods might cancel one another. The forecasts that are combined can be of the same general type—extrapolation forecasts, for example—or they can be of different types, such as judgmental and extrapolation.

The *number* of forecasts to combine and the *weights* to use in combining them have been the subject of several research studies. Although the findings are not entirely consistent, it appears that the marginal benefit from each individual forecast after the first two or three is minor. Also, there is not much evidence to suggest that the simplest weighting scheme—weighting each forecast equally, that is, averaging them—is any less accurate than more complex weighting schemes.

12.2.4 Components of Time Series Data

In Chapter 2 we discussed time series graphs, a useful graphical way of displaying time series data. We now use these time series graphs to help explain and identify four important components of a time series. These components are called the *trend* component, the *seasonal* component, the *cyclic* component, and the *random* (or *noise*) component.

We start by looking at a very simple time series. This is a time series where every observation has the same value. Such a series is shown in Figure 12.1. The graph in this figure shows time (t) on the horizontal axis and the observed values (Y) on the vertical axis. We assume that Y is measured at regularly spaced intervals, usually days, weeks, months, quarters, or years, with Y_t being the value of the observation at time period t. As indicated in Figure 12.1, the individual observation points are usually joined by straight lines to make any patterns in the time series more apparent. Because all observations in this time series are equal, the resulting time series graph is a horizontal line. We refer to this time series as the *base* series. We will now illustrate more interesting time series built from this base series.

Figure 12.1

The Base Series

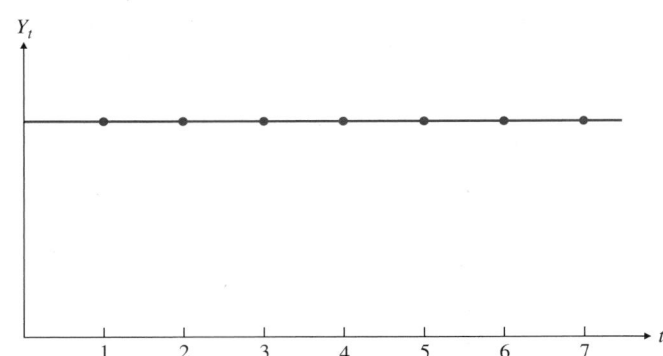

If the observations increase or decrease regularly through time, we say that the time series has a **trend**. The graphs in Figure 12.2 illustrate several possible trends. The *linear* trend in Figure 12.2a occurs if a company's sales increase by the same amount from period to period. This constant per period change is then the slope of the linear trend line. The curve in Figure 12.2b is an *exponential* trend. It occurs in a business such as the personal computer business, where sales have increased at a tremendous rate (at least during the 1990s, the boom years). For this type of curve, the *percentage* increase in Y_t from period to period remains constant. The curve in Figure 12.2c is an *S-shaped* trend. This type of trend is appropriate for a new product that takes a while to catch on, then exhibits a rapid increase in sales as the public becomes aware of it, and finally tapers off to a fairly constant

Figure 12.2   Series with Trends

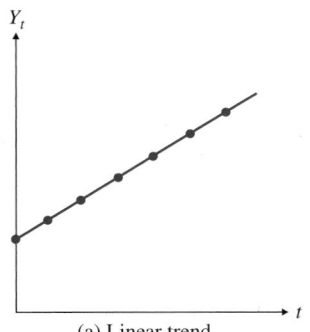

(a) Linear trend

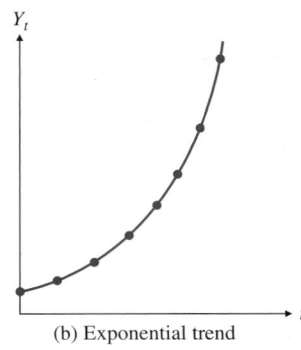

(b) Exponential trend

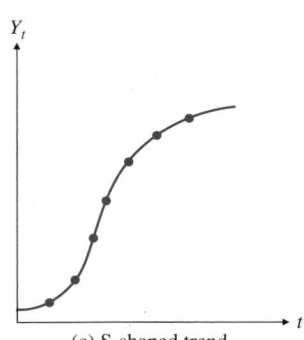

(c) S-shaped trend

level because of market saturation. The series in Figure 12.2 all represent *upward* trends. Of course, there are *downward* trends of the same types.

Many time series have a **seasonal** component. For example, a company's sales of swimming pool equipment increase every spring, then stay relatively high during the summer, and then drop off until next spring, at which time the yearly pattern repeats itself. An important aspect of the seasonal component is that it tends to be predictable from one year to the next. That is, the *same* seasonal pattern tends to repeat itself every year.

Figure 12.3 illustrates two possible seasonal patterns. In Figure 12.3a there is nothing but the seasonal component. That is, if there were no seasonal variation, the series would be the base series in Figure 12.1. Figure 12.3b illustrates a seasonal pattern superimposed on a linear trend line.

Figure 12.3

Series with Seasonality

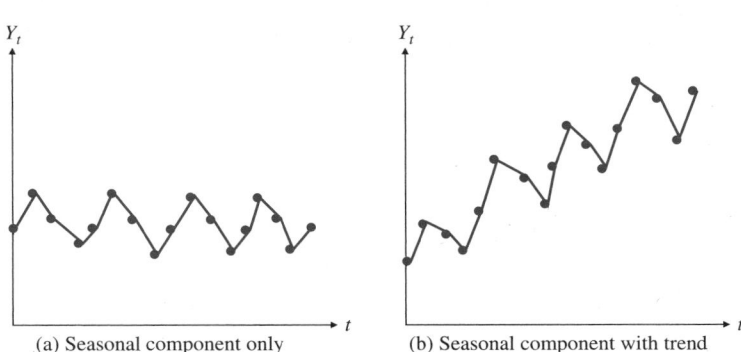

(a) Seasonal component only

(b) Seasonal component with trend

The third component of a time series is the **cyclic** component. By studying past movements of many business and economic variables, it becomes apparent that there are business cycles that affect many variables in similar ways. For example, during a recession housing starts generally go down, unemployment goes up, stock prices go down, and so on. But when the recession is over, all of these variables tend to move in the opposite direction. Unfortunately, the cyclic component is more difficult to predict than the seasonal component. The reason is that seasonal variation is much more regular. For example, swimming pool supplies sales *always* start to increase during the spring. Cyclic variation, on the other hand, is more irregular because the length of the business cycle varies, sometimes considerably. A further distinction is that the length of a seasonal cycle is generally one year; the length of a business cycle is generally longer than one year and its actual length is difficult to predict.

The graphs in Figure 12.4 illustrate the cyclic component of a time series. In Figure 12.4a cyclic variation is superimposed on the base series in Figure 12.1. In Figure 12.4b this same

Figure 12.4

Series with Cyclic Component

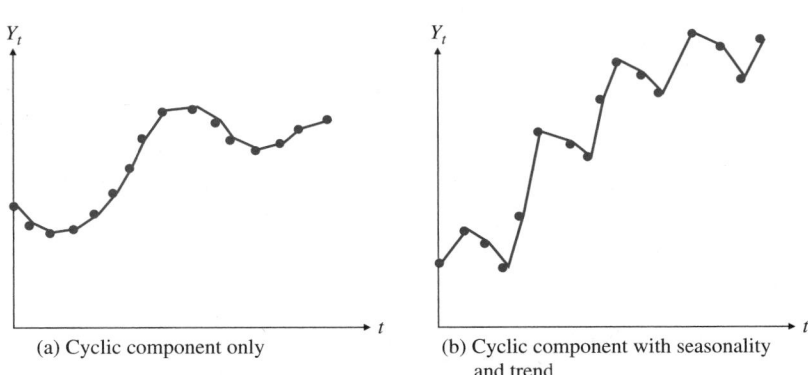

(a) Cyclic component only

(b) Cyclic component with seasonality and trend

cyclic variation is superimposed on the series in Figure 12.3b. The resulting graph has trend, seasonal variation, and cyclic variation.

The final component in a time series is called **random variation**, or simply **noise**. This unpredictable component gives most time series graphs their irregular, zigzag appearance. Usually, a time series can be determined only to a certain extent by its trend, seasonal, and cyclic components. Then other factors determine the rest. These other factors may be inherent randomness, unpredictable "shocks" to the system, the unpredictable behavior of human beings who interact with the system, and possibly others. These factors combine to create a certain amount of unpredictability in almost all time series.

Figures 12.5 and 12.6 show the effect that noise can have on a time series graph. The graph on the left of each figure shows the random component only, superimposed on the base series. Then on the right of each figure, the random component is superimposed on the trend-with-seasonal-component graph from Figure 12.3b. The difference between Figures 12.5 and 12.6 is the relative magnitude of the noise. When it is small, as in Figure 12.5, the other components emerge fairly clearly; they are not disguised by the noise. But if the noise is large in magnitude, as in Figure 12.6, the noise makes it very difficult to distinguish the other components.

Figure 12.5
Series with Noise

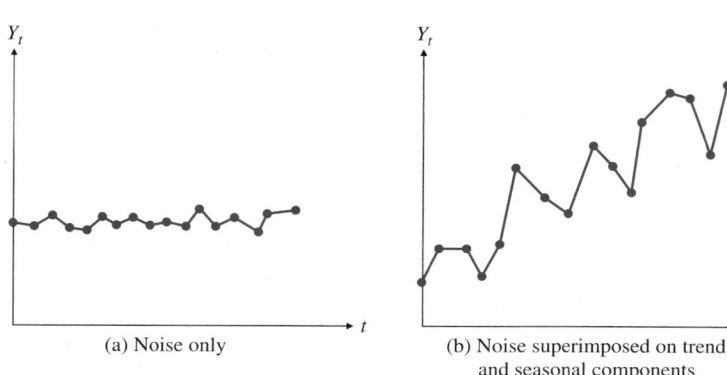

(a) Noise only

(b) Noise superimposed on trend and seasonal components

Figure 12.6
Series with More Noise

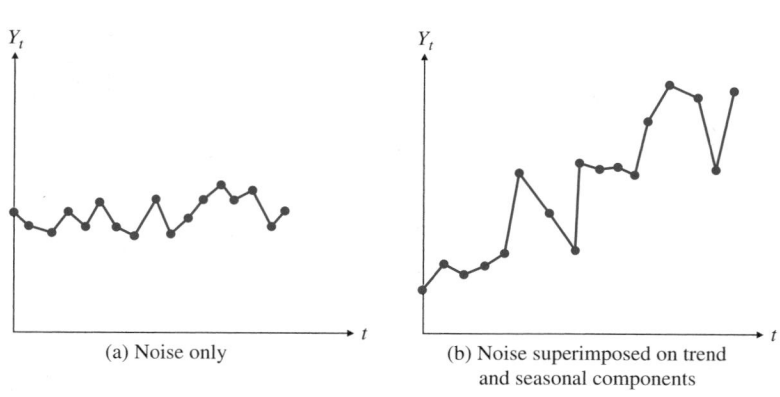

(a) Noise only

(b) Noise superimposed on trend and seasonal components

12.2.5 Measures of Accuracy

We now introduce some notation and discuss aspects common to most forecasting methods. In general, we let Y denote the variable of interest. Then Y_t denotes the observed value of Y at time t. Typically, the first observation (the most distant one) corresponds to period $t = 1$, and the last observation (the most recent one) corresponds to period $t = T$, where T denotes the number of historical observations of Y. The periods themselves might be days, weeks, months, quarters, years, or any other convenient unit of time.

Suppose that Y_{t-k} has just been observed and you want to make a "k-period-ahead" forecast; that is, you want to use the information through time $t-k$ to forecast Y_t. The resulting forecast is denoted by $F_{t-k,t}$. The first subscript indicates the period in which the forecast is made, and the second subscript indicates the period being forecast. As an example, if the data are monthly and September 2009 corresponds to $t = 67$, then a forecast of Y_{69}, the value in November 2009, would be labeled $F_{67,69}$. The **forecast error** is the difference between the actual value and the forecast. It is denoted by E with appropriate subscripts. Specifically, the forecast error associated with $F_{t-k,t}$ is

$$E_{t-k,t} = Y_t - F_{t-k,t}$$

This double-subscript notation is necessary to specify when the forecast is being made and which period is being forecast. However, the former is often clear from context. Therefore, to simplify the notation, we usually drop the first subscript and write F_t and E_t to denote the forecast of Y_t and the error in this forecast.

You first develop a model to fit the historical data. Then you use this model to forecast the future.

There are actually two steps in any forecasting procedure. The first step is to build a model that fits the historical data well. The second step is to use this model to forecast the future. Most of the work goes into the first step. For any trial model you see how well it "tracks" the known values of the time series. Specifically, the one-period-ahead forecasts, F_t (or more precisely, $F_{t-1,t}$) are calculated from the model, and these are compared to the known values, Y_t, for each t in the historical time period. The goal is to find a model that produces small forecast errors, E_t. Presumably, if the model tracks the *historical* data well, it will also forecast *future* data well. Of course, there is no guarantee that this is true, but it is often a reasonable assumption.

Forecasting software packages typically report several summary measures of the forecast errors. The most important of these are **MAE (mean absolute error)**, **RMSE (root mean square error)**, and **MAPE (mean absolute percentage error)**. These are defined in equations (12.2), (12.3), and (12.4). Fortunately, models that make any one of these measures small tend to make the others small, so you can choose whichever measure you want to minimize. In the following formulas, N denotes the number of terms in each sum. This value is typically slightly less than T, the number of historical observations, because it is usually not possible to provide a forecast for each historical period.

Mean Absolute Error

$$\text{MAE} = \left(\sum_{t=1}^{N} |E_t| \right) / N \tag{12.2}$$

Root Mean Square Error

$$\text{RMSE} = \sqrt{\left(\sum_{t=1}^{N} E_t^2 \right) / N} \tag{12.3}$$

Mean Absolute Percentage Error

$$\text{MAPE} = 100\% \times \left(\sum_{t=1}^{N} |E_t / Y_t| \right) / N \tag{12.4}$$

A model that makes any one of these error measures small tends to make the other two small as well.

RMSE is similar to a standard deviation in that the errors are squared; because of the square root, it is in the same units as those of the forecast variable. The MAE is similar to the RMSE, except that absolute values of errors are used instead of squared errors. The MAPE is probably the most easily understood measure because it does not depend on the units of the forecast variable; it is always stated as a percentage. For example, the statement that the forecasts are off on average by 2% has a clear meaning, even if you do not know the units of the variable being forecast.

Some forecasting software packages choose the best model from a given class (such as the best exponential smoothing model) by minimizing MAE, RMSE, or MAPE. However, small values of these measures guarantee only that the model tracks the *historical* observations well. There is still no guarantee that the model will forecast *future* values accurately.

One other measure of forecast errors is the *average* of the errors. (It is not reported by StatTools, but it is easy to calculate.) Recall from the regression chapters that the residuals from any regression equation, which are analogous to forecast errors, always average to zero. This is a mathematical property of the least-squares method. However, there is no such guarantee for forecasting errors based on nonregression methods. For example, it is very possible that most of the forecast errors, and the corresponding average, are *negative*. This would imply a *bias*, where the forecasts tend to be too high. Or the average of the forecast errors could be *positive* , in which case the forecasts tend to be too low. If you choose an "appropriate" forecasting method, based on the evidence from a time series graph, this type of bias is not likely to be a problem, but it is easy to check. Furthermore, if a company realizes that its forecasting method produces forecasts that are consistently, say, 5% below the actual values, it could simply multiply its forecasts by 1/0.95 to remove the bias.

We now examine a number of useful forecasting models. You should be aware that more than one of these models can be appropriate for any particular time series data. For example, a random walk model and an autoregression model could be equally effective for forecasting stock price data. (Remember also that forecasts from more than one model can be combined to obtain a possibly better forecast.) We try to provide some insights into choosing the best type of model for various types of time series data, but ultimately the choice depends on the experience of the analyst.

FUNDAMENTAL INSIGHT

Extrapolation and Noise

There are two important things to remember about extrapolation methods. First, by definition, all such methods try to extrapolate historical patterns into the future. If history doesn't essentially repeat itself, for whatever reason, these methods are doomed to fail. In fact, if you *know* that something has changed fundamentally, you probably should not use an extrapolation method. Second, it does no good to track noise and then forecast it into the future. For this reason, most extrapolation methods try to smooth out the noise, so that the underlying pattern is more apparent.

12.3 TESTING FOR RANDOMNESS

All forecasting models have the general form shown in Equation (12.5). The fitted value in this equation is the part calculated from past data and any other available information (such as the season of the year), and it is used as a forecast for Y. The residual is the forecast error, the difference between the observed value of Y and its forecast:

$$Y_t = \text{Fitted Value} + \text{Residual} \qquad \textbf{(12.5)}$$

In a time series context the terms residual *and* forecast error *are used interchangeably.*

For time series data, there is a residual for each historical period, that is, for each value of t. We want this time series of residuals to be random noise, as discussed in section 12.2.4. The reason is that if this series of residuals is not noise, it can be modeled further. For example, if the residuals trend upwardly, then the forecasting model can be modified to include this trend component in the *fitted* value. The point is that the fitted value should include all components of the original series that can possibly be forecast, and the leftover residuals should be unpredictable noise.

We now discuss ways to determine whether a time series of residuals is random noise (which we usually abbreviate to "random".) The simplest method, but not always a reliable one, is to examine time series graphs of residuals visually. Nonrandom patterns are sometimes easy to detect. For example, the time series graphs in Figures 12.7 through 12.11 illustrate some common nonrandom patterns. In Figure 12.7, there is an upward trend. In Figure 12.8, the variance increases through time (larger zigzags to the right). Figure 12.9 exhibits seasonality, where observations in certain months are consistently larger than those in other months. There is a meandering pattern in Figure 12.10, where large observations tend to be followed by other large observations, and small observations tend to be followed by other small observations. Finally, Figure 12.11 illustrates the opposite behavior, where there are *too many* zigzags—large observations tend to follow small observations and vice versa. None of the time series in these figures is random.

Figure 12.7

A Series with Trend

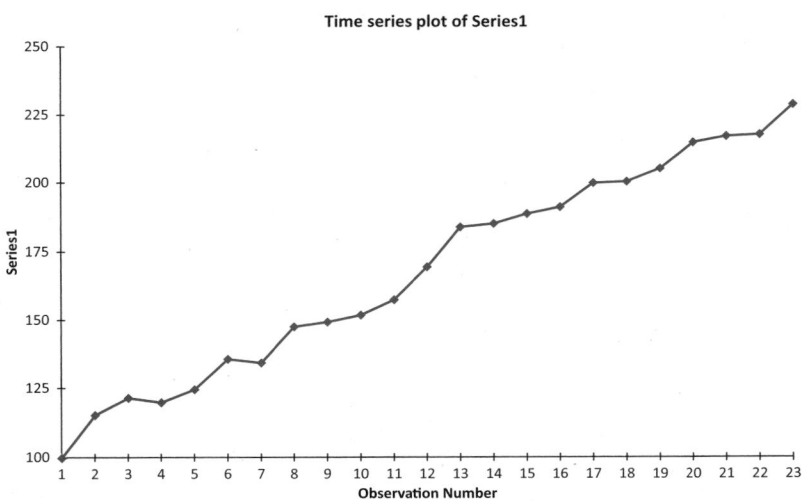

Figure 12.8

A Series with Increasing Variance Through Time

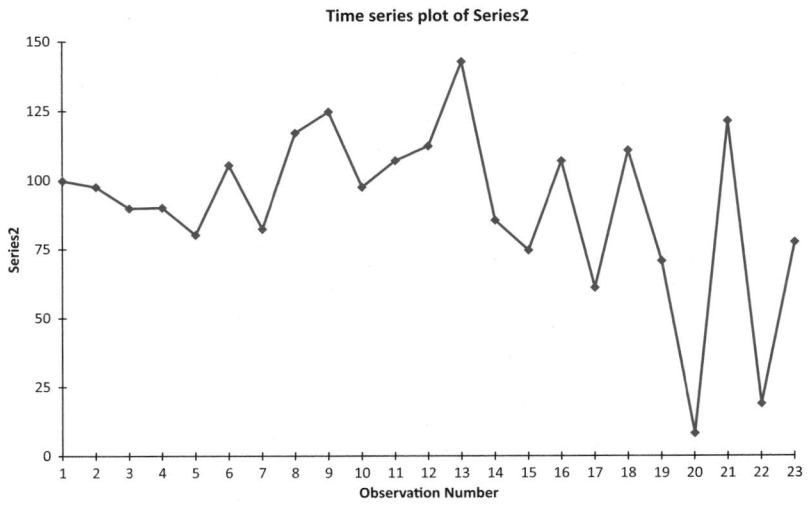

Figure 12.9

A Series with
Seasonality

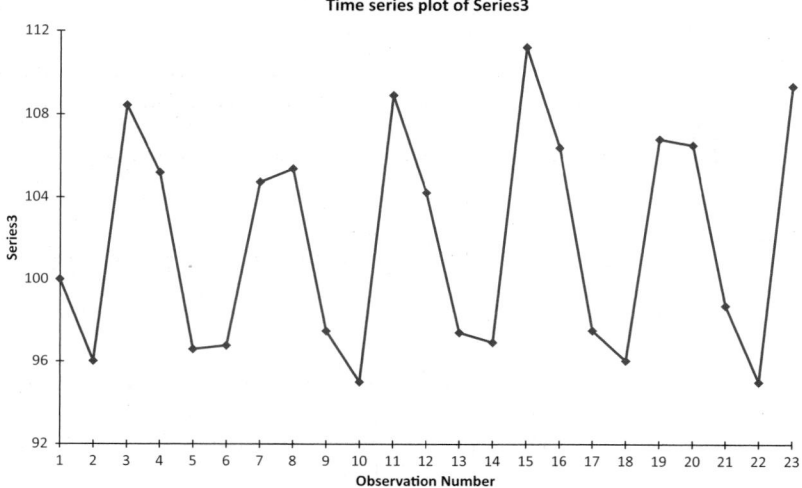

Figure 12.10

A Series That
Meanders

Figure 12.11

A Series That
Oscillates Frequently

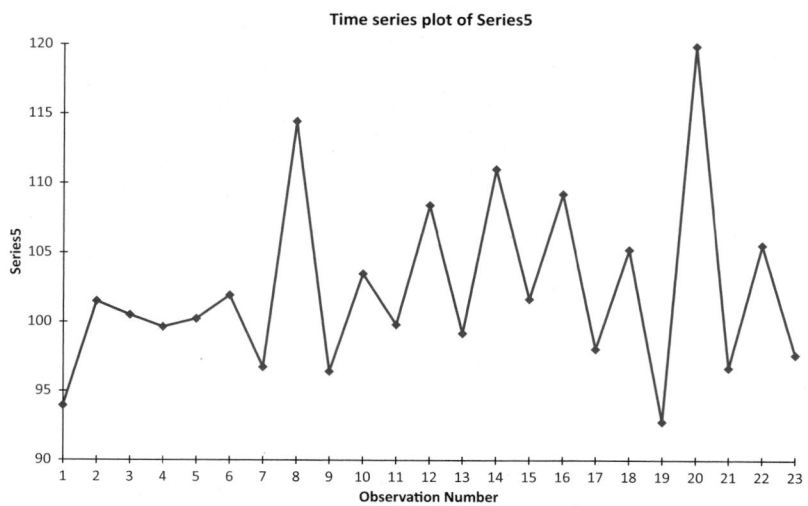

12.3.1 The Runs Test

It is not always easy to detect randomness or the lack of it from the visual inspection of a graph. Therefore, we discuss two quantitative methods that test for randomness. The first is called the *runs test*. You first choose a base value, which could be the average value of the series, the median value, or even some other value. Then a **run** is defined as a consecutive series of observations that remain on one side of this base level. For example, if the base level is 0 and the series is 1, 5, 3, –3, –2, –4, –1, 3, 2, there are three runs: 1, 5, 3; –3, –2, –4, –1; and 3, 2. The idea behind the runs test is that a random series should have a number of runs that is neither too large nor too small. If the series has too few runs, it could be trending (as in Figure 12.7) or it could be meandering (as in Figure 12.10). If the series has too many runs, it is zigzagging too often (as in Figure 12.11).

This runs test can be used on any time series, not just a series of residuals.

> The **runs test** is a formal test of the null hypothesis of randomness. If there are too many or too few runs in the series, the null hypothesis of randomness can be rejected.

We do not provide the mathematical details of the runs test, but we illustrate how it is implemented in StatTools in the following example.

EXAMPLE | **12.1 FORECASTING MONTHLY STEREO SALES**

Monthly sales for a chain of stereo retailers are listed in the file **Stereo Sales.xlsx**. They cover the period from the beginning of 2006 to the end of 2009, during which there was no upward or downward trend in sales and no clear seasonality. This behavior is apparent in the time series graph of sales in Figure 12.12. Therefore, a simple forecast model of sales is to use the *average* of the series, 182.67, as a forecast of sales for each month. Do the resulting residuals represent random noise?

Objective To use StatTools's Runs Test procedure to check whether the residuals from this simple forecasting model represent random noise.

Figure 12.12
Time Series Graph of Stereo Sales

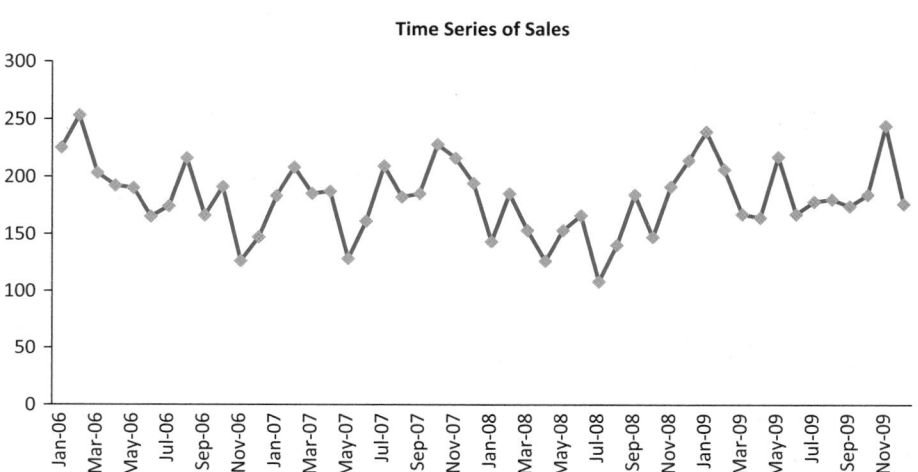

Solution

The residuals for this forecasting model are found by subtracting the average, 182.67, from each observation. Therefore, the plot of the residuals, shown in Figure 12.13, has exactly the same shape as the plot of sales. The only difference is that it is shifted down by 182.67 and has mean 0. The runs test can now be used to check whether there are too many or too few runs around the base value of 0 in this residual plot. To do so, select Runs Test for Randomness from the StatTools Time Series and Forecasting dropdown, choose Residual as the variable to analyze, and choose Mean of Series as the cutoff value. (This corresponds to the horizontal line at 0 in Figure 12.13.) The resulting output in shown in Figure 12.14.

Figure 12.13

Time Series Graph of Residuals

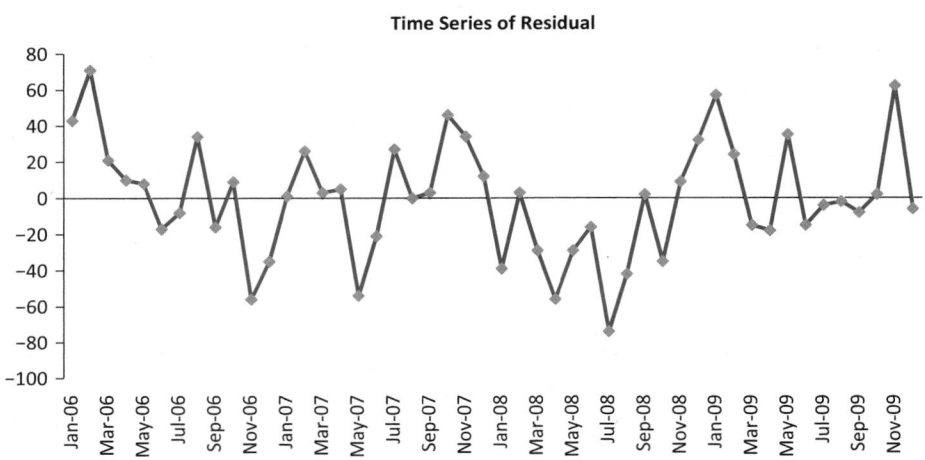

Figure 12.14

Runs Test for Randomness

	I	J
7		Residual
8	*Runs Test for Randomness*	Data Set #1
9	Observations	48
10	Below Mean	22
11	Above Mean	26
12	Number of Runs	20
13	Mean	0.00
14	E(R)	24.8333
15	StdDev(R)	3.4027
16	Z-Value	-1.4204
17	P-Value (two-tailed)	0.1555

The important elements of this output are the following:

- The number of observed runs is 20, in cell J12.

- The number of runs *expected* under an assumption of randomness is 24.833, in cell J14. (This follows from a probability argument not shown here.) Therefore, the series of residuals has too *few* runs. Positive values tend to follow positive values, and negative values tend to follow negative values.

A small p-value in the runs test provides evidence of nonrandomness.

- The z-value in cell J16, −1.42, indicates how many standard errors the observed number of runs is below the expected number of runs. The corresponding *p*-value indicates how extreme this z-value is. It can be interpreted just like other p-values for hypothesis tests. If it is small, say, less than 0.05, then the null hypothesis of randomness can be rejected. In this case, the conclusion is that the series of residuals is not random noise. However, the p-value for this example is only 0.1555. Therefore, there is not convincing evidence of nonrandomness in the residuals. In other words, it is reasonable to conclude that the residuals represent noise. ■

12.3.2 Autocorrelation

Like the runs test, autocorrelations can be calculated for any time series, not just a series of residuals.

In this section we discuss another way to check for randomness of a time series of residuals—we examine the **autocorrelations** of the residuals. The "auto" means that successive observations are correlated with one another. For example, in the most common form of autocorrelation, *positive* autocorrelation, large observations tend to follow large observations, and small observations tend to follow small observations. In this case the runs test is likely to pick it up because there will be fewer runs than expected. Another way to check for the same nonrandomness property is to calculate the autocorrelations of the time series.

> An **autocorrelation** is a type of correlation used to measure whether values of a time series are related to their own past values.

To understand autocorrelations, it is first necessary to understand what it means to *lag* a time series. This concept is easy to illustrate in a spreadsheet. We again use the monthly stereo sales data in the **Stereo Sales.xlsx** file. To lag by one month, you simply "push down" the series by one row. See column D of Figure 12.15. Note that there is a blank cell at the top of the lagged series (in cell D2). You can continue to push the series down one row at a time to obtain other lags. For example, the lag 3 version of the series appears in column F. Now there are three missing observations at the top. Note that in December 2006, say, the first, second, and third lags correspond to the observations in November 2006, October 2006, and September 2006, respectively. That is, lags are simply previous observations, removed by a certain number of periods from the present time. These lagged columns can be obtained by copying and pasting the original series or by selecting Lag from the StatTools Data Utilities dropdown menu.

Figure 12.15

Lags for Stereo Sales

	A	B	C	D	E	F
1	Month	Sales	Residual	Lag1(Residual)	Lag2(Residual)	Lag3(Residual)
2	Jan-06	226	43.333			
3	Feb-06	254	71.333	43.333		
4	Mar-06	204	21.333	71.333	43.333	
5	Apr-06	193	10.333	21.333	71.333	43.333
6	May-06	191	8.333	10.333	21.333	71.333
7	Jun-06	166	-16.667	8.333	10.333	21.333
8	Jul-06	175	-7.667	-16.667	8.333	10.333
9	Aug-06	217	34.333	-7.667	-16.667	8.333
10	Sep-06	167	-15.667	34.333	-7.667	-16.667
11	Oct-06	192	9.333	-15.667	34.333	-7.667
12	Nov-06	127	-55.667	9.333	-15.667	34.333
13	Dec-06	148	-34.667	-55.667	9.333	-15.667
14	Jan-07	184	1.333	-34.667	-55.667	9.333
15	Feb-07	209	26.333	1.333	-34.667	-55.667
16	Mar-07	186	3.333	26.333	1.333	-34.667

Then the autocorrelation of lag k, for any integer k, is essentially the correlation between the original series and the lag k version of the series. For example, in Figure 12.15 the lag 1 autocorrelation is the correlation between the observations in columns C and D. Similarly, the lag 2 autocorrelation is the correlation between the observations in columns C and E.[1]

We have shown the lagged versions of Sales in Figure 12.15, and we have explained autocorrelations in terms of these lagged variables, to help motivate the concept of autocorrelation. However, you can use StatTools's Autocorrelation procedure directly, *without* forming the lagged variables, to calculate autocorrelations. This is illustrated in the following continuation of Example 12.1.

EXAMPLE | **12.1 FORECASTING MONTHLY STEREO SALES (CONTINUED)**

The runs test on the stereo sales data suggests that the pattern of sales is not completely random. There is some tendency for large values to follow large values, and for small values to follow small values. Do autocorrelations support this evidence?

Objective To examine the autocorrelations of the residuals from the forecasting model for evidence of nonrandomness.

Solution

To answer this question, use StatTools's Autocorrelation procedure, found on the StatTools Time Series and Forecasting dropdown list. It requires you to specify the time series variable (Residual), the number of lags you want (the StatTools default value was accepted here), and whether you want a chart of the autocorrelations. This chart is called a **correlogram**. The resulting autocorrelations and correlogram appear in Figure 12.16. A typical autocorrelation of lag k indicates the relationship between observations k periods apart. For example, the autocorrelation of lag 3, 0.0814, indicates that there is very little relationship between residuals separated by three months.

How large is a "large" autocorrelation? Under the assumption of randomness, it can be shown that the standard error of any autocorrelation is approximately $1/\sqrt{T}$, in this case $1/\sqrt{48} = 0.1443$. (Recall that T denotes the number of observations in the series.) If the series is truly random, then only an occasional autocorrelation will be larger than two standard errors in magnitude. Therefore, any autocorrelation that *is* larger than two standard errors in magnitude is worth your attention. All significantly nonzero autocorrelations are boldfaced in the StatTools output. For this example, the only "large" autocorrelation for the residuals is the first, or lag 1, autocorrelation of 0.3492. The fact that it is *positive* indicates once again that there is some tendency for large residuals to follow large residuals and for small to follow small. The autocorrelations for other lags are less than two standard errors in magnitude and can safely be ignored.

[1]We ignore the exact details of the calculations here. Just be aware that the formula for autocorrelations that is usually used differs slightly from the correlation formula in Chapter 3. However, the difference is very slight and of no practical importance.

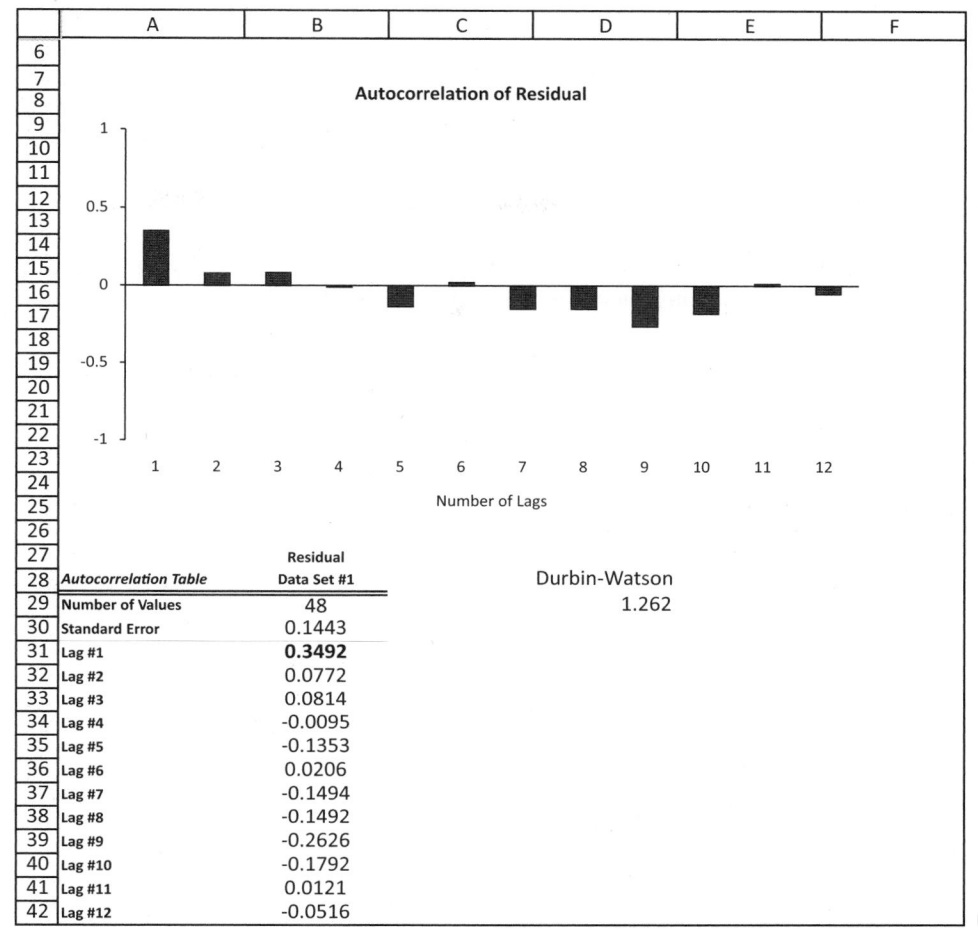

Figure 12.16

Correlogram and Autocorrelations of Residuals

	A	B	C	D	E	F
27		Residual				
28	*Autocorrelation Table*	Data Set #1		Durbin-Watson		
29	Number of Values	48		1.262		
30	Standard Error	0.1443				
31	Lag #1	**0.3492**				
32	Lag #2	0.0772				
33	Lag #3	0.0814				
34	Lag #4	-0.0095				
35	Lag #5	-0.1353				
36	Lag #6	0.0206				
37	Lag #7	-0.1494				
38	Lag #8	-0.1492				
39	Lag #9	-0.2626				
40	Lag #10	-0.1792				
41	Lag #11	0.0121				
42	Lag #12	-0.0516				

Typically, you can ask for autocorrelations up to as many lags as you like. However, there are several practical considerations to keep in mind. First, it is common practice to ask for no more lags than 25% of the number of observations. For example, if there are 48 observations, you should ask for no more than 12 autocorrelations (lags 1 to 12). (StatTools chooses this number of lags if you accept its Auto setting.)

Second, the first few lags are typically the most important. Intuitively, if there is any relationship between successive observations, it is likely to be between nearby observations. The June 2009 observation is more likely to be related to the May 2009 observation than to the October 2008 observation. Sometimes there is a fairly large spike in the correlogram at some large lag, such as lag 9. However, this can often be dismissed as a random blip unless there is some obvious reason for its occurrence. A similarly large autocorrelation at lag 1 or 2 is usually taken more seriously. The one exception to this is a *seasonal* lag. For example, an autocorrelation at lag 12 for monthly data corresponds to a relationship between observations a year apart, such as May 2009 and May 2008. If this autocorrelation is significantly large, it probably should not be ignored.

As discussed briefly in the previous chapter, one measure of the lag 1 autocorrelation, often the most important autocorrelation, is provided by the Durbin-Watson (DW) statistic. (See section 11.9.3.) This statistic can be calculated with the StatTools function StatDurbinWatson. Its value for the residuals in this example is 1.262, as shown in

Figure 12.16. The DW statistic is always between 0 and 4. A DW value of 2 indicates *no* lag 1 autocorrelation, a DW value less than 2 indicates *positive* autocorrelation, and a DW value greater than 2 indicates *negative* autocorrelation. The current DW value, 1.262, is considerably less than 2, another indication that the lag 1 autocorrelation of the residuals is positive and possibly significant. There are tables of significance levels for DW statistics (how much less than 2 must DW be to be significant?), but they are not presented here.

Autocorrelation analysis is somewhat advanced. However, it is the basis for many useful forecasting methods.

We will not examine autocorrelations much further in this book. However, many advanced forecasting techniques are based largely on the examination of the autocorrelation structure of time series. This autocorrelation structure indicates how a series is related to its own past values through time, which can be very valuable information for forecasting *future* values.

PROBLEMS

Note: Student solutions for problems whose numbers appear within a colored box are available for purchase at www.cengagebrain.com.

Level A

1. The file **P12_01.xlsx** contains the monthly number of airline tickets sold by a travel agency. Is this time series *random*? Perform a runs test and find a few autocorrelations to support your answer.

2. The file **P12_02.xlsx** contains the weekly sales at a local bookstore for each of the past 25 weeks. Is this time series *random*? Perform a runs test and find a few autocorrelations to support your answer.

3. The number of employees on the payroll at a food-processing plant is recorded at the start of each month. These data are provided in the file **P12_03.xlsx**. Perform a runs test and find a few autocorrelations to determine whether this time series is random.

4. The quarterly numbers of applications for home mortgage loans at a branch office of Northern Central Bank are recorded in the file **P12_04.xlsx**. Perform a runs test and find a few autocorrelations to determine whether this time series is random.

5. The number of reported accidents at a manufacturing plant located in Flint, Michigan, was recorded at the start of each month. These data are provided in the file **P12_05.xlsx**. Is this time series *random*? Perform a runs test and find a few autocorrelations to support your answer.

6. The file **P12_06.xlsx** contains the weekly sales at the local outlet of West Coast Video Rentals for each of the past 36 weeks. Perform a runs test and find a few autocorrelations to determine whether this time series is random.

Level B

7. Determine whether the RAND() function in Excel actually generates a random stream of numbers. Generate at least 100 random numbers to test their randomness with a runs test and with autocorrelations. Summarize your findings.

8. Use a runs test and calculate autorrelations to decide whether the random series explained in each part of this problem (**a–c**) are random. For each part, generate at least 100 random numbers in the series.
   a. A series of independent normally distributed values, each with mean 70 and standard deviation 5.
   b. A series where the first value is normally distributed with mean 70 and standard deviation 5, and each succeeding value is normally distributed with mean equal to the *previous* value and standard deviation 5. (For example, if the fourth value is 67.32, then the fifth value will be normally distributed with mean 67.32.)
   c. A series where the first value, Y_1, is normally distributed with mean 70 and standard deviation 5, and each succeeding value, Y_t, is normally distributed with mean $(1 + a_t)Y_{t-1}$ and standard deviation $5(1 + a_t)$, where the a_t values are independent and normally distributed with mean 0 and standard deviation 0.2. (For example, if $Y_{t-1} = 67.32$ and $a_t = -0.2$, then Y_t will be normally distributed with mean $0.8(67.32) = 53.856$ and standard deviation $0.8(5) = 4$.)

12.4 REGRESSION-BASED TREND MODELS

Many time series follow a long-term trend except for random variation. This trend can be upward or downward. A straightforward way to model this trend is to estimate a regression equation for Y_t, using time t as the *single* explanatory variable. In this section we discuss the two most frequently used trend models, *linear* trend and *exponential* trend.

12.4.1 Linear Trend

A linear trend means that the time series variable changes by a constant *amount* each time period. The relevant equation is Equation (12.6), where, as in previous regression equations, a is the intercept, b is the slope, and e_t is an error term.[2]

Linear Trend Model

$$Y_t = a + bt + e_t \qquad (12.6)$$

The interpretation of b is that it represents the expected change in the series from one period to the next. If b is positive, the trend is upward; if b is negative, the trend is downward. The intercept term a is less important. It literally represents the expected value of the series at time $t = 0$. If time t is coded so that the first observation corresponds to $t = 1$, then a is where the series was one period before the observations began. However, it is possible that time is coded in another way. For example, if the data are annual, starting in 1997, the first value of t might be entered as 1997, which means that the intercept a then corresponds to a period 1997 years earlier. Clearly, its value should not be taken literally in this case.

As always, a graph of the time series is a good place to start. It indicates whether a **linear trend** is likely to provide a good fit. Generally, the graph should rise or fall at approximately a constant rate through time, without too much random variation. But even if there is a lot of random variation—a lot of zigzags—a linear trend to the data might still be a good starting point. Then the *residuals* from this trend line, which should have no remaining trend, could possibly be modeled by some other method in this chapter.

EXAMPLE | **12.2 MONTHLY U.S. POPULATION**

The file **US Population.xlsx** contains monthly population data for the United States from January 1952 to October 2009 (in thousands). During this period, the population has increased steadily from about 156 million to about 308 million. The time series graph of these data appears in Figure 12.17. How well does a linear trend fit these data? Are the residuals from this fit random?

Objective   To fit a linear trend line to monthly population and examine its residuals for randomness.

---

[2]It is traditional in the regression literature to use Greek letters for population parameters and Roman letters for estimates of them. However, we decided to use only Roman letters in the regression sections of this chapter. For a book at this level, they are less intimidating.

Figure 12.17   Time Series Graph of U.S. Population

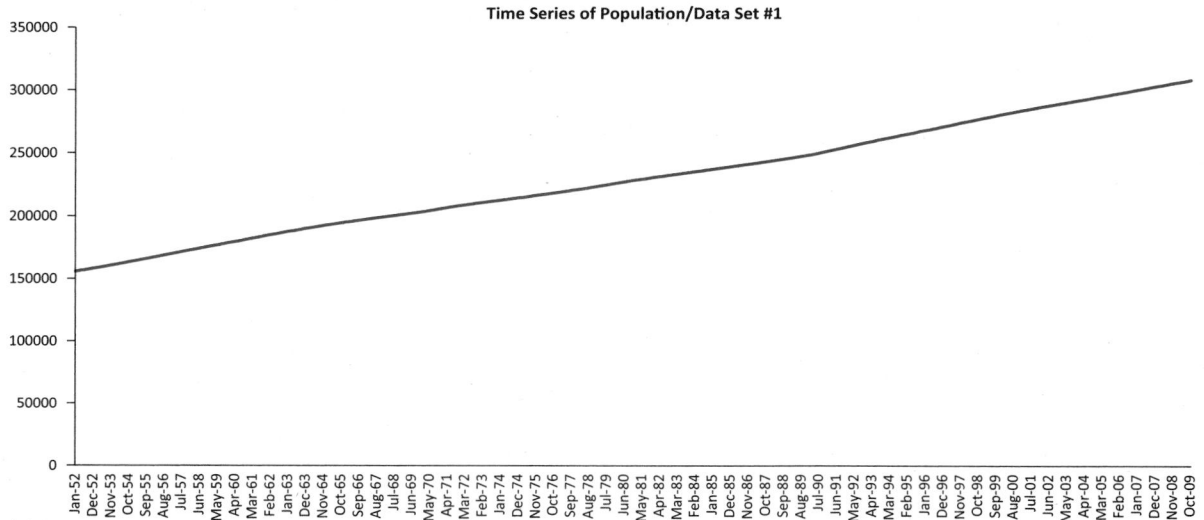

Solution

The graph in Figure 12.17 indicates a clear upward trend with little or no curvature. Therefore, a linear trend is certainly plausible. To estimate it with regression, a *numeric* time variable is needed—labels such as Jan-52 will not do. This time variable appears in column C of the data set, using the consecutive values 1 through 694. You can then run a simple regression of Population versus Time, with the results shown in Figure 12.18. The estimated linear trend line is

$$\text{Forecast Population} = 157003.69 + 211.55\,\text{Time}$$

Figure 12.18

Regression Output for Linear Trend

Summary	Multiple R	R-Square	Adjusted R-Square	StErr of Estimate		
	0.9982	0.9965	0.9965	2523.59		

ANOVA Table	Degrees of Freedom	Sum of Squares	Mean of Squares	F-Ratio	p-Value	
Explained	1	1.24664E+12	1.24664E+12	195750.8446	< 0.0001	
Unexplained	692	4406997370	6368493.309			

Regression Table	Coefficient	Standard Error	t-Value	p-Value	Confidence Interval 95% Lower	Upper
Constant	157003.69	191.80	818.6000	< 0.0001	156627.12	157380.26
Time	211.55	0.48	442.4374	< 0.0001	210.62	212.49

This equation implies that the population tends to increase by 211.55 thousand per month. (The 157003.69 value in this equation is the predicted population at time 0; that is, December 1951.) To use this equation to forecast future population values, substitute later values of Time into the regression equation, so that each future forecast is 211.55 larger than the previous forecast. For example, the forecast for January 2010 is

$$\text{Forecast Population Jan-2010} = 157003.69 + 211.55(697) = 304457$$

As described in Chapter 2, Excel provides an easier way to obtain this trend line. Once the graph in Figure 12.17 is constructed, you can use Excel's Trendline tool. To do so, right-click on any point on the chart and select Add Trendline. This provides several types of trend lines to choose from, and the linear option works well for this example. You can also check the options to show the regression equation and its R^2 value on the chart, as shown in Figure 12.19. This superimposed trend line indicates a very good fit.

Figure 12.19   Time Series Graph with Linear Trend Superimposed

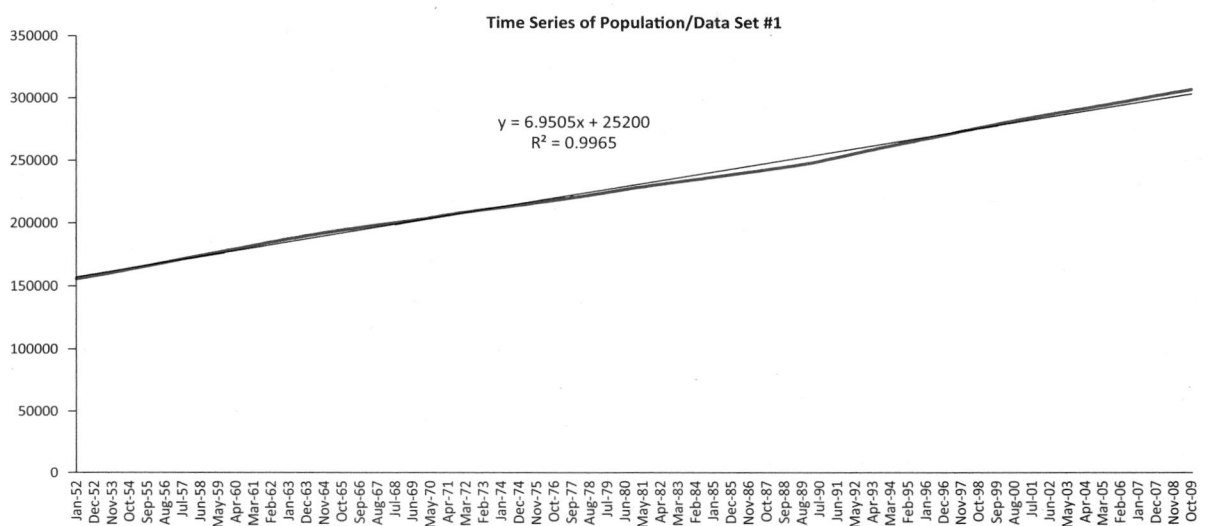

However, the fit is not perfect, as the plot of the residuals in Figure 12.20 indicates. These residuals tend to meander, staying negative for a while, then positive, then negative, and then positive. You can check that the runs test for these residuals produces a z-value of -26.13, with a corresponding p-value of 0.000, and that its first 32 autocorrelations are significantly positive. In short, these residuals are definitely *not* random noise, and they could be modeled further. However, we will not pursue this analysis here. In fact, it is not at all obvious how the autocorrelations of the residuals *could* be exploited to get a better forecast model.

Figure 12.20
Time Series Graph of Residuals

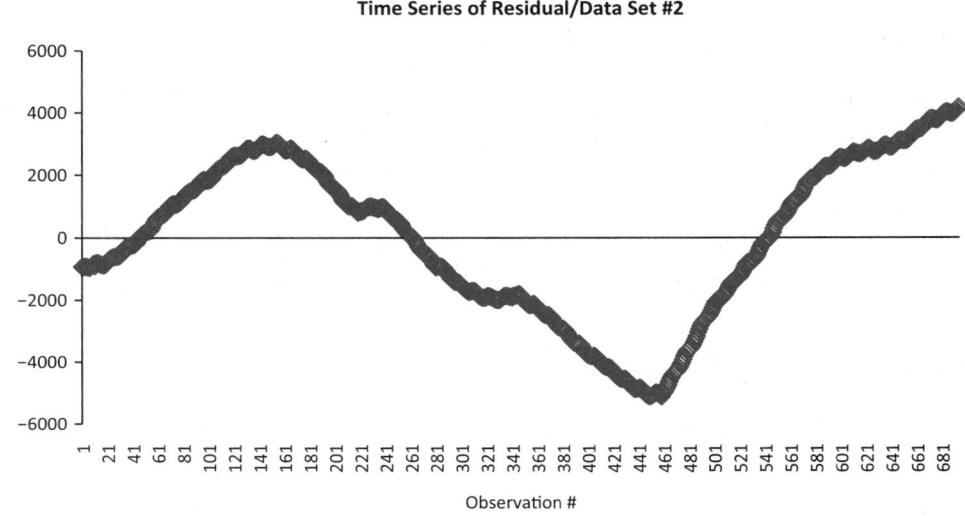

12.4.2 Exponential Trend

An exponential trend for Y is equivalent to a linear trend for the logarithm of Y.

In contrast to a linear trend, an exponential trend is appropriate when the time series changes by a constant *percentage* (as opposed to a constant dollar amount) each period. Then the appropriate regression equation is Equation (12.7), where c and b are constants, and u_t represents a *multiplicative* error term.

Exponential Trend Model

$$Y_t = ce^{bt}u_t \tag{12.7}$$

Equation (12.7) is useful for understanding how an exponential trend works, as we will discuss, but it is not useful for estimation. For that, a *linear* equation is required. Fortunately, you can achieve linearity by taking natural logarithms of both sides of Equation (12.7). (The key, as usual, is that the logarithm of a product is the sum of the logarithms.) The result appears in Equation (12.8), where $a = \ln(c)$ and $e_t = \ln(u_t)$. This equation represents a *linear* trend, but the dependent variable is now the logarithm of the original Y_t. This implies the following important fact: If a time series exhibits an exponential trend, then a plot of its logarithm should be approximately linear.

Equivalent Linear Trend for Logarithm of Y

$$\ln(Y_t) = a + bt + e_t \tag{12.8}$$

Because the software performs the calculations, your main responsibility is to interpret the final result. This is fairly easy. It can be shown that the coefficient b (expressed as a percentage) is approximately the percentage change per period. For example, if $b = 0.05$, the series is increasing by approximately 5% per period.[3] On the other hand, if $b = -0.05$, the series is decreasing by approximately 5% per period.

An exponential trend can be estimated with StatTools's Regression procedure, but only after the log transformation has been made on Y_t. We illustrate this in the following example.

EXAMPLE	12.3 QUARTERLY PC DEVICE SALES

The file **PC Device Sales.xlsx** contains quarterly sales data (in millions of dollars) for a large PC device manufacturer from the first quarter of 1995 through the fourth quarter of 2009. Are the company's sales growing exponentially through this entire period?

Objective To estimate the company's exponential growth and to see whether it has been maintained during the entire period from 1995 until the end of 2009.

Solution

We first estimate and interpret an exponential trend for the years 1995 through 2005. Then we see how well the projection of this trend into the future fits the data after 2005. The

---

[3]More precisely, this percentage change is $e^b - 1$. For example, when $b = 0.05$, this is $e^b - 1 = 5.13\%$.

time series graph through 2005 appears in Figure 12.21. You can use Excel's Trendline tool, with the Exponential option, to superimpose an exponential trend line and the corresponding equation on this plot. The fit is evidently quite good. Equivalently, Figure 12.22 illustrates the time series of log sales for this same period, with a *linear* trend line superimposed. Its fit is equally good.

Figure 12.21   Time Series Graph of Sales with Exponential Trend Superimposed

Time Series of Sales

$y = 61.376e^{0.0663x}$

Figure 12.22   Time Series Graph of Log Sales with Linear Trend Superimposed

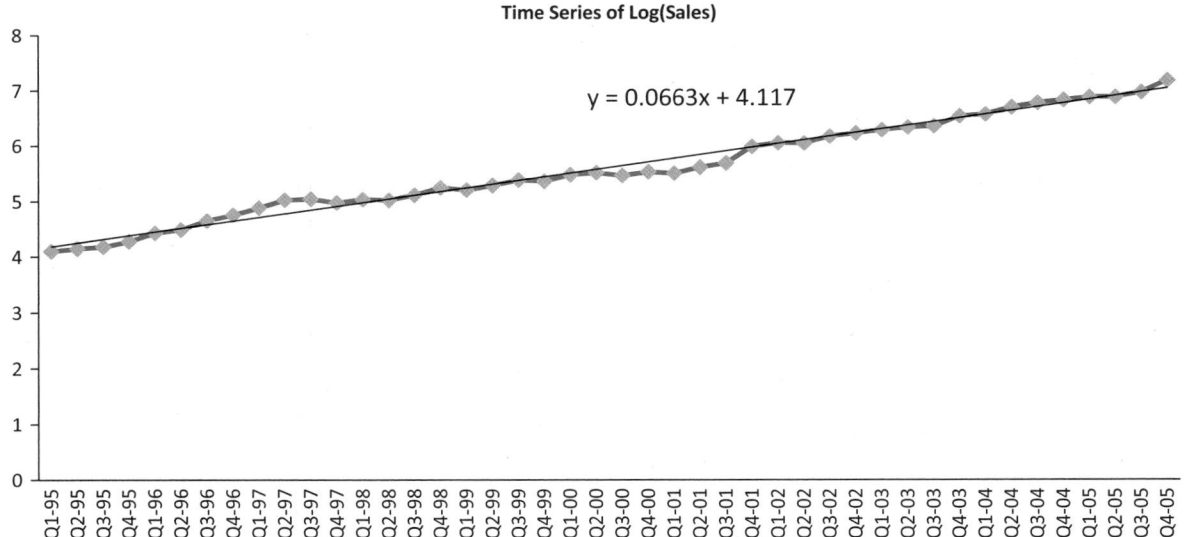

Time Series of Log(Sales)

$y = 0.0663x + 4.117$

You can also use StatTools's Regression procedure to estimate this exponential trend, as shown in Figure 12.23. To produce this output, you must first add a time variable in column C (with values 1 through 44) and make a logarithmic transformation of Sales in column D.

Then you can regress Log(Sales) on Time (using the data through 2005 only) to obtain the regression output. Note that its two coefficients in cells B18 and B19 are the same as those shown for the linear trend in Figure 12.22. If you take the antilog of the constant 4.117 (with the formula = EXP(B18)), you will obtain the constant *multiple* shown in Figure 12.21. It corresponds to the constant c in Equation (12.7).

Figure 12.23 Regression Output for Estimating Exponential Trend

	A	B	C	D	E	F	G
7		Multiple	R-Square	Adjusted	StErr of		
8	Summary	R		R-Square	Estimate		
9		0.9922	0.9844	0.9840	0.1086		
10							
11		Degrees of	Sum of	Mean of	F-Ratio	p-Value	
12	ANOVA Table	Freedom	Squares	Squares			
13	Explained	1	31.21992793	31.21992793	2645.6403	< 0.0001	
14	Unexplained	42	0.495621782	0.011800519			
15							
16		Coefficient	Standard	t-Value	p-Value	Confidence Interval 95%	
17	Regression Table		Error			Lower	Upper
18	Constant	4.1170	0.0333	123.5616	< 0.0001	4.0498	4.1843
19	Time	0.0663	0.0013	51.4358	< 0.0001	0.0637	0.0689

What does it all mean? The estimated Equation (12.7) is

$$\text{Forecast Sales} = 61.376 e^{0.0663t}$$

The most important constant in this equation is the coefficient of Time, $b = 0.0663$. Expressed as a percentage, this coefficient implies that the company's sales increased by approximately 6.63% per quarter throughout this 11-year period. (The constant multiple, $c = 61.376$, is the forecast of sales at time 0; that is, quarter 4 of 1994.) To use this equation for forecasting the future, substitute later values of Time into the regression equation, so that each future forecast is about 6.63% larger than the previous forecast. For example, the forecast of the second quarter of 2006 is

$$\text{Forecast Sales in Q2-06} = 61.376 e^{0.0663(46)} = 1295.72$$

Has this exponential growth continued beyond 2005? It has *not,* due possibly to slumping sales in the computer industry or increased competition from other manufacturers. You can check this by creating the Forecast column in Figure 12.24 (by substituting into the regression equation for the entire period through Q4−09). You can then use StatTools to create a time series graph of the two series Sales and Forecast, shown in Figure 12.25. It is clear that sales in the forecast period did not exhibit nearly the 6.63% growth observed in the estimation period. As the company clearly realizes, nothing this good lasts forever.

Before leaving this example, we comment briefly on the standard error of estimate shown in cell E9 of Figure 12.23. This value, 0.1086, is in *log* units, not original dollar units. Therefore, it is a totally misleading indicator of the forecast errors that might be made from the exponential trend equation. To obtain more meaningful measures, you should first obtain the forecasts of sales, as explained previously. Then you can easily obtain any of the three forecast error measures discussed previously. The results appear in Figure 12.26. The squared errors, absolute errors, and absolute percentage errors are first calculated with the formulas =(B2-E2)^2, =ABS(B2-E2), and =G2/B2 in cells F2, G2, and H2, which are then copied down. The error measures (for the data through 2005 only)

Figure 12.24

Creating Forecasts of Sales

	A	B	C	D
1	Quarter	Sales	Time	Log(Sales)
2	Q1-95	61.14	1	4.1131663
3	Q2-95	64.07	2	4.1599762
4	Q3-95	66.18	3	4.1923783
5	Q4-95	72.76	4	4.2871664
6	Q1-96	84.70	5	4.4391156
7	Q2-96	90.05	6	4.5003651
8	Q3-96	106.06	7	4.664005
9	Q4-96	118.21	8	4.7724627
10	Q1-97	134.38	9	4.9006716
11	Q2-97	154.67	10	5.0412938
12	Q3-97	157.41	11	5.0588539
13	Q4-97	147.16	12	4.9915204

Figure 12.25

Time Series Graph of Forecasts Superimposed on Sales for the Entire Period

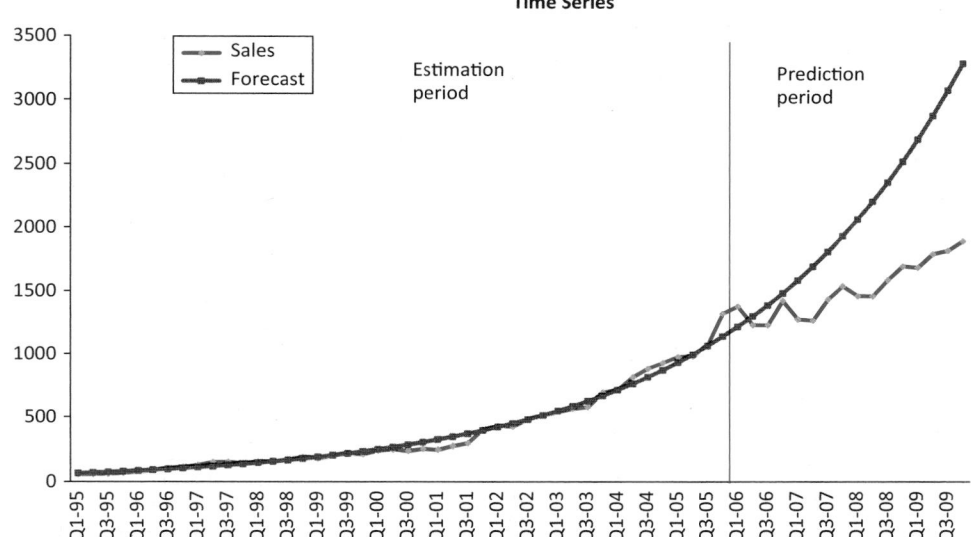

then appear in cells K2, K3, and K4. The corresponding formulas for RMSE, MAE, and MAPE are straightforward. RMSE is the square root of the average of the squared errors in column F, and MAE and MAPE are the averages of the values in columns G and H, respectively. The latter is particularly simple to interpret. Forecasts for the 11-year estimation period were off, on average, by 7.86%. (Of course, as you can check, forecasts for the quarters *after* 2005 were off by much more.)

Figure 12.26 Measures of Forecast Errors

	A	B	C	D	E	F	G	H	I	J	K	L
1	Quarter	Sales	Time	Log(Sales)	Forecast	SqError	AbsError	AbsPctError		Measures of forecast error		
2	Q1-95	61.14	1	4.1131663	65.58583	19.76541	4.445831	0.07271559		RMSE	41.86	
3	Q2-95	64.07	2	4.1599762	70.08398	36.16795	6.013979	0.09386576		MAE	25.44	
4	Q3-95	66.18	3	4.1923783	74.89063	75.87506	8.710629	0.13162027		MAPE	7.86%	
5	Q4-95	72.76	4	4.2871664	80.02694	52.8084	7.266939	0.09987547				
6	Q1-96	84.70	5	4.4391156	85.51552	0.66507	0.815518	0.00962831				
7	Q2-96	90.05	6	4.5003651	91.38053	1.770302	1.330527	0.01477542				
8	Q3-96	106.06	7	4.664005	97.64778	70.7654	8.412218	0.07931565				

Whenever you observe a time series that is increasing at an increasing rate (or decreasing at a decreasing rate), an exponential trend model is worth trying. The key to the analysis is to regress the *logarithm* of the time series variable versus time (or use Excel's Trendline tool). The coefficient of time, written as a percentage, is then the approximate percentage increase (if positive) or decrease (if negative) per period. ■

PROBLEMS

Level A

9. The file **P12_01.xlsx** contains the monthly number of airline tickets sold by a travel agency.
   a. Does a linear trend appear to fit these data well? If so, estimate and interpret the linear trend model for this time series. Also, interpret the R^2 and s_e values.
   b. Provide an indication of the typical forecast error generated by the estimated model in part **a**.
   c. Is there evidence of some seasonal pattern in these sales data? If so, characterize the seasonal pattern.

10. The file **P12_10.xlsx** contains the daily closing prices of Walmart stock for a one-year period. Does a linear or exponential trend fit these data well? If so, estimate and interpret the best trend model for this time series. Also, interpret the R^2 and s_e values.

11. The file **P12_11.xlsx** contains monthly values of the U.S. national debt (in dollars) from 1993 to early 2010. Fit an exponential growth curve to these data. Write a short report to summarize your findings. If the U.S. national debt continues to rise at the exponential rate you find, approximately what will its value be at the end of 2020?

12. The file **P12_12.xlsx** contains five years of monthly data on sales (number of units sold) for a particular company. The company suspects that except for random noise, its sales are growing by a constant *percentage* each month and will continue to do so for at least the near future.
   a. Explain briefly whether the plot of the series visually supports the company's suspicion.
   b. Fit the appropriate regression model to the data. Report the resulting equation and state explicitly what it says about the percentage growth per month.
   c. What are the RMSE and MAPE for the forecast model in part **b**? In words, what do they measure? Considering their magnitudes, does the model seem to be doing a good job?

   d. In words, how does the model make forecasts for future months? Specifically, given the forecast value for the last month in the data set, what simple arithmetic could you use to obtain forecasts for the next few months?

13. The file **P12_13.xlsx** contains quarterly data on GDP. (The data are expressed as an index where 2005 = 100, and they are seasonally adjusted.)
   a. Look at a time series plot of GDP. Does it suggest a linear relationship; an exponential relationship?
   b. Use regression to estimate a linear relationship between GDP and Time (starting with 1 for Q1-1966). Interpret the associated constant term and the slope term. Would you say that the fit is good?

Level B

14. The file **P03_30.xlsx** gives monthly exchange rates (units of local currency per U.S. dollar) for nine currencies. Technical analysts believe that by charting past changes in exchange rates, it is possible to predict future changes of exchange rates. After analyzing the autocorrelations for these data, do you believe that technical analysis has potential?

15. The unit sales of a new drug for the first 25 months after its introduction to the marketplace are recorded in the file **P12_15.xlsx**.
   a. Estimate a linear trend equation using the given data. How well does the linear trend fit these data? Are the residuals from this linear trend model *random*?
   b. If the residuals from this linear trend model are *not* random, propose another regression-based trend model that more adequately explains the long-term trend in this time series. Estimate the alternative model(s) using the given data. Check the residuals from the model(s) for randomness. Summarize your findings.
   c. Given the best estimated model of the trend in this time series, interpret R^2 and s_e.

12.5 THE RANDOM WALK MODEL

Random series are sometimes building blocks for other time series models. The model we now discuss, the **random walk model**, is an example of this. In a random walk model, the series itself is not random. However, its *differences*—that is, the changes from one period to the next—are random. This type of behavior is typical of stock price data (as well as various other time series data). For example, the graph in Figure 12.27 shows monthly closing prices for a tractor manufactor's stock from January 2003 through April 2009. (See the file **Tractor Closing Prices.xlsx**.) This series is not random, as can be seen from its gradual upward trend at the beginning and the general meandering behavior throughout. (Although the runs test and autocorrelations are not shown for the series itself, they confirm that the series is not random. There are significantly *fewer* runs than expected, and the autocorrelations are significantly *positive* for many lags.)

Figure 12.27   Time Series Graph of Tractor Stock Prices

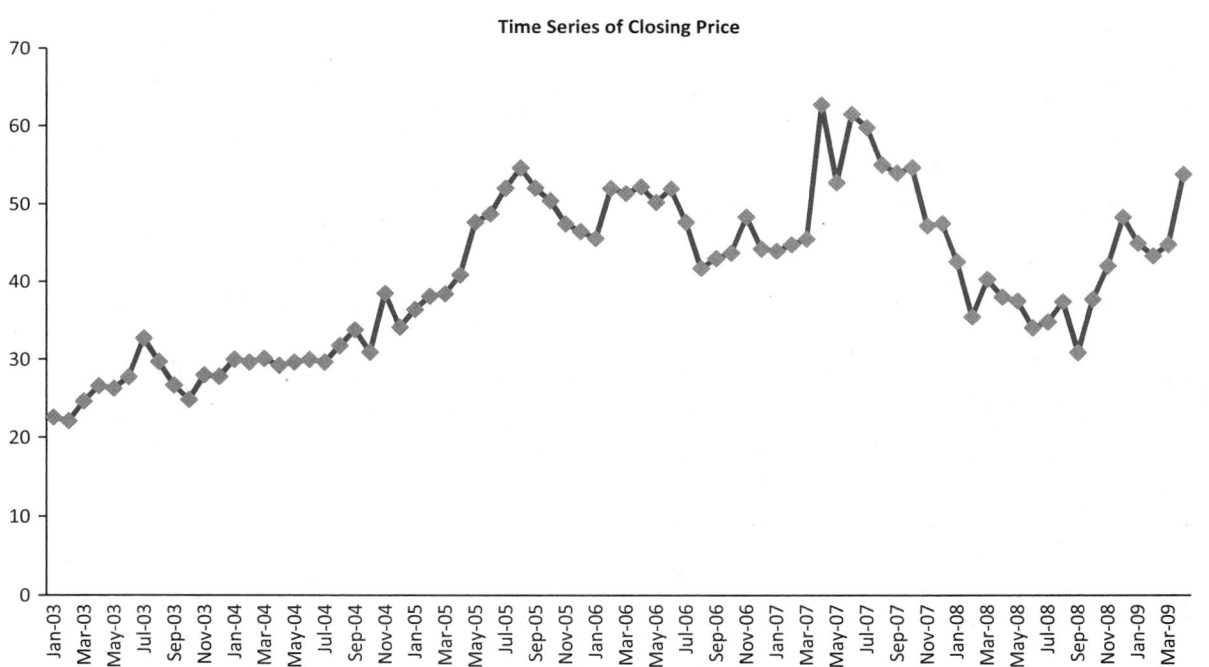

If it were April 2009, and you were asked to forecast the company's prices for the next few months, it is intuitive that you would not use the average of the historical values as your forecast. This forecast would tend to be too low because of the upward trend. Instead, you might base your forecast on the most recent observation. This is exactly what the random walk model does.

Equation (12.9) for the random walk model is given as follows, where m (for mean difference) is a constant and e_t is a random series (noise) with mean 0 and a standard deviation that remains *constant* through time.

$$Y_t = Y_{t-1} + m + e_t \qquad (12.9)$$

If we let $DY_t = Y_t - Y_{t-1}$, the change in the series from time t to time $t - 1$ (where D stands for difference), then the random walk model can be rewritten as in Equation (12.10). This implies that the differences form a random series with mean m and a constant standard deviation. An estimate of m is the average of the differences, labeled $\overline{Y}_D$, and an estimate of the standard deviation is the sample standard deviation of the differences, labeled s_D.

Difference Form of Random Walk Model

$$DY_t = m + e_t \qquad (12.10)$$

In words, a series that behaves according to this random walk model has random differences, and the series tends to trend upward (if $m > 0$) or downward (if $m < 0$) by an amount m each period. If you are standing in period t and want to forecast Y_{t+1}, then a reasonable forecast is given by Equation (12.11). That is, you add the estimated trend to the current observation to forecast the next observation.

One-Step-Ahead Forecast for Random Walk Model

$$F_{t+1} = Y_t + \overline{Y}_D \qquad (12.11)$$

We illustrate this method in the following example.

EXAMPLE | **12.4 RANDOM WALK MODEL OF STOCK PRICES**

The monthly closing prices of the tractor company's stock from January 2003 through April 2009, shown in Figure 12.27, indicate some upward trend. (See the file **Tractor Sales.xlsx**.) Does this series follow a random walk model with an upward trend? If so, how should future values of these stock prices be forecast?

Objective To check whether the company's monthly closing prices follow a random walk model with an upward trend and to see how future prices can be forecast.

Solution

We have already seen that the closing price series itself is not random, due to the upward trend. To check for the adequacy of a random walk model, a series of *differences* is required. Each value in the differenced series is that month's closing price minus the previous month's closing price. You can calculate this series easily with an Excel formula, or you can generate it automatically with the Difference item on the StatTools Data Utilities dropdown menu. (When asked for the *number* of difference variables, accept the default value of 1.) This differenced series appears in column C of Figure 12.28. This figure also shows the mean and standard deviation of the differences, 0.418 and 4.245, which are used in forecasting. Finally, this figure shows several autocorrelations of the differences, only one of which is (barely) significant. A runs test for the differences, not shown here, has a large p-value, which supports the conclusion that the differences are random.

Figure 12.28

Differences of
Closing Prices

	A	B	C	D	E	F
1	Month	Closing Price	Diff1(Closing Price)			Diff1(Closing Price)
2	Jan-03	22.595			*One Variable Summary*	Data Set #1
3	Feb-03	22.134	-0.461		Mean	0.418
4	Mar-03	24.655	2.521		Std. Dev.	4.245
5	Apr-03	26.649	1.994		Count	75
6	May-03	26.303	-0.346			
7	Jun-03	27.787	1.484			Diff1(Closing Price)
8	Jul-03	32.705	4.918		*Autocorrelation Table*	Data Set #1
9	Aug-03	29.745	-2.96		Number of Values	75
10	Sep-03	26.741	-3.004		Standard Error	0.1155
11	Oct-03	24.852	-1.889		Lag #1	**-0.2435**
12	Nov-03	28.050	3.198		Lag #2	0.1348
13	Dec-03	27.847	-0.203		Lag #3	-0.0049
14	Jan-04	30.040	2.193		Lag #4	-0.0507
15	Feb-04	29.680	-0.36		Lag #5	0.0696
16	Mar-04	30.139	0.459		Lag #6	0.0009
17	Apr-04	29.276	-0.863		Lag #7	-0.0630
18	May-04	29.703	0.427		Lag #8	-0.0295
19	Jun-04	30.017	0.314		Lag #9	0.0496
20	Jul-04	29.687	-0.33		Lag #10	-0.1728
21	Aug-04	31.765	2.078		Lag #11	-0.0334
22	Sep-04	33.788	2.023		Lag #12	-0.0554
23	Oct-04	30.942	-2.846			

The plot of the differences appears in Figure 12.29. A visual inspection of the plot also supports the conclusion of random differences, although these differences do not vary

Figure 12.29 Time Series Graph of Differences

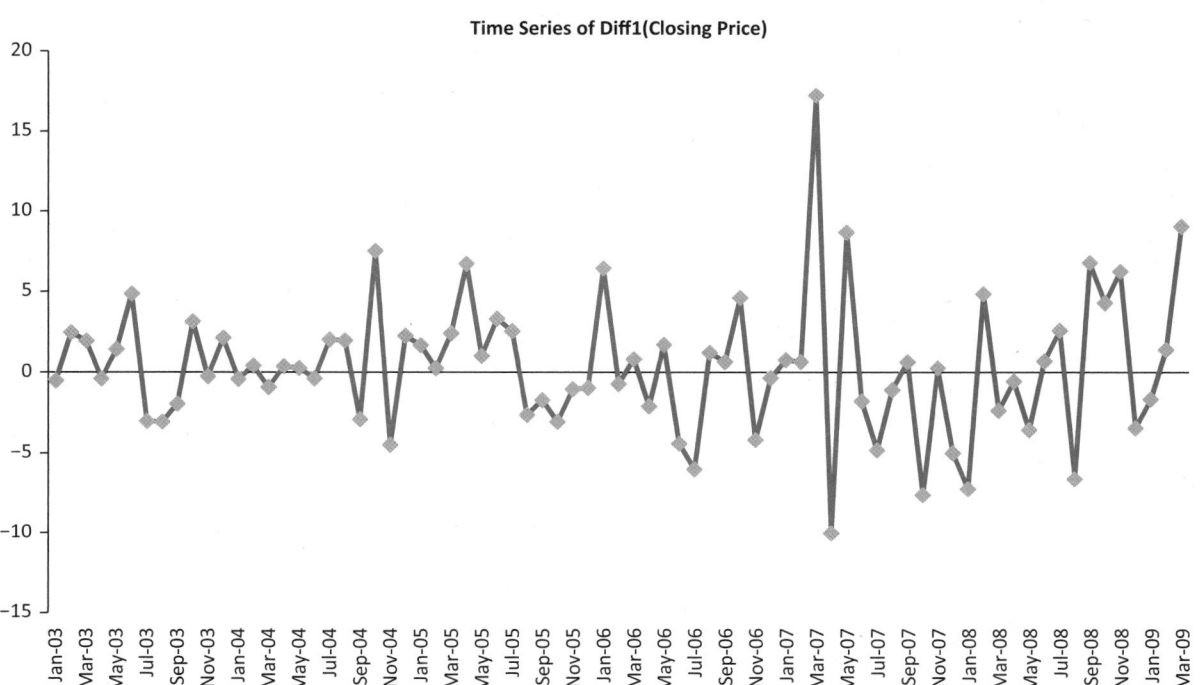

around a mean of 0. Rather, they vary around a mean of 0.418. This positive value measures the upward trend—the closing prices increase, on average, by 0.418 per month. Finally, the variability in this figure is fairly constant (except for the two wide swings in 2007). Specifically, the zigzags do not tend to get appreciably wider through time. Therefore, it is reasonable to conclude that the random walk model with an upward drift fits this series fairly well.

To forecast future closing prices, simply multiply the mean difference by the number of periods ahead, and add this to the final closing price (53.947 in April 2009). For example, a forecast of the closing price for September 2009 is:

$$\text{Forecast Closing Price for } 9/09 = 53.947 + 0.418(5) = 56.037$$

As a rough measure of the accuracy of this forecast, you can use the standard deviation of the differences, 4.245. Specifically, it can be shown that the standard error for forecasting k periods ahead is the standard deviation of the differences multiplied by the square root of k. In this case, the standard error is 9.492. As usual, you can be 95% confident that the actual closing price in September will be no more than two standard errors from the forecast. Unfortunately, this results in a wide interval—from about 37 to 75. This reflects the fact that it is very difficult to make accurate forecasts, especially long-range forecasts, for a series with this much variability. ■

PROBLEMS

Level A

16. The file **P12_16.xlsx** contains the daily closing prices of American Express stock for a one-year period.
    a. Use the random walk model to forecast the closing price of this stock on the next trading day.
    b. You can be about 95% certain that the forecast made in part **a** will be off by no more than how many dollars?

17. The closing value of the AMEX Airline Index for each trading day during a one-year period is given in the file **P12_17.xlsx**.
    a. Use the random walk model to forecast the closing price of this stock on the next trading day.
    b. You can be about 68% certain that the forecast made in part **a** will be off by no more than how many dollars?

18. The file **P12_18.xlsx** contains the daily closing prices of Chevron stock for a one-year period.
    a. Use the random walk model to forecast the closing price of this stock on the next trading day.
    b. You can be about 99.7% certain that the forecast made in part **a** will be off by no more than how many dollars?

19. The closing value of the Dow Jones Industrial Average for each trading day for a one-year period is provided in the file **P12_19.xlsx**.
    a. Use the random walk model to forecast the closing price of this index on the next trading day.

    b. Would it be wise to use the random walk model to forecast the closing price of this index for a trading day approximately *one month* after the next trading day? Explain why or why not.

20. Continuing the previous problem, consider the differences between consecutive closing values of the Dow Jones Industrial Average for the given set of trading days. Do these differences form a random series? Demonstrate why or why not.

21. The closing price of a share of J.P. Morgan's stock for each trading day during a one-year period is recorded in the file **P12_21.xlsx**.
    a. Use the random walk model to forecast the closing price of this stock on the next trading day.
    b. You can be about 68% certain that the forecast made in part **a** will be off by no more than how many dollars?

22. The purpose of this problem is to get you used to the concept of autocorrelation in a time series. You could do this with any time series, but here you should use the series of Walmart daily stock prices in the file **P12_10.xlsx**.
    a. First, do it the quick way. Use the Autocorrelation procedure in StatTools to get a list of autocorrelations and a corresponding correlogram of the closing prices. You can choose the number of lags.
    b. Now do it the more time-consuming way. Create columns of lagged versions of the Close variable—3 or 4 lags will suffice. Next, look at scatterplots of

Close versus its first few lags. If the autocorrelations are large, you should see fairly tight scatters—that's what autocorrelation is all about. Also, generate a correlation matrix to see the correlations between Close and its first few lags. These should be approximately the same as the autocorrelations from part **a**. (Autocorrelations are calculated slightly differently than regular correlations, which accounts for any slight discrepancies you might notice, but these discrepancies should be minor.)

c. Create the first differences of Close in a new column. (You can do this manually with formulas, or you can use StatTools's Difference procedure on the Data Utilities menu.) Now repeat parts **a** and **b** with the differences instead of the original closing prices—that is, examine the autocorrelations of the differences. They should be small, and the scatterplots of the differences versus lags of the differences should be shapeless swarms. This illustrates what happens when the differences of a time series variable have insignificant autocorrelations.

d. Write a short report of your findings.

Level B

23. Consider a random walk model with the following equation: $Y_t = Y_{t-1} + 500 + e_t$, where e_t is a normally distributed random series with mean 0 and standard deviation 10.

a. Use Excel to simulate a time series that behaves according to this random walk model.

b. Use the time series you constructed in part **a** to forecast the next observation.

24. The file **P12_24.xlsx** contains the daily closing prices of Procter & Gamble stock for a one-year period. Use only the 2003 data to estimate the trend component of the random walk model. Next, use the estimated random walk model to forecast the behavior of the time series for the 2004 dates in the series. Comment on the accuracy of the generated forecasts over this period. How could you improve the forecasts as you progress through the 2004 trading days?

12.6 AUTOREGRESSION MODELS[4]

We now discuss a regression-based extrapolation method that regresses the current value of the time series on past (lagged) values. This is called **autoregression**, where the *auto-* means that the explanatory variables in the equation are lagged values of the dependent variable, so that the dependent variable is regressed on lagged versions of *itself*. This procedure is fairly straightforward in Excel. You first create lags of the dependent variable and then use a regression procedure to regress the original series on the lagged series. Some trial and error is generally required to determine the appropriate number of lags in the regression equation. The following example illustrates the procedure.

EXAMPLE | **12.5 FORECASTING HAMMER SALES**

A retailer has recorded its weekly sales of hammers (units purchased) for the past 42 weeks. (See the file **Hammer Sales.xlsx**.) A graph of this time series appears in Figure 12.30. It reveals a meandering pattern of behavior. The values begin high and stay high awhile, then get lower and stay lower awhile, then get higher again. (This behavior could be caused by any number of things, including the weather, increases and decreases in building projects, and possibly others.) How useful is autoregression for modeling these data and how can it be used for forecasting?

Objective To use autoregression, with an appropriate number of lagged terms, to forecast hammer sales.

---

[4]This section can be omitted without any loss of continuity.

Figure 12.30 Time Series Graph of Sales of Hammers

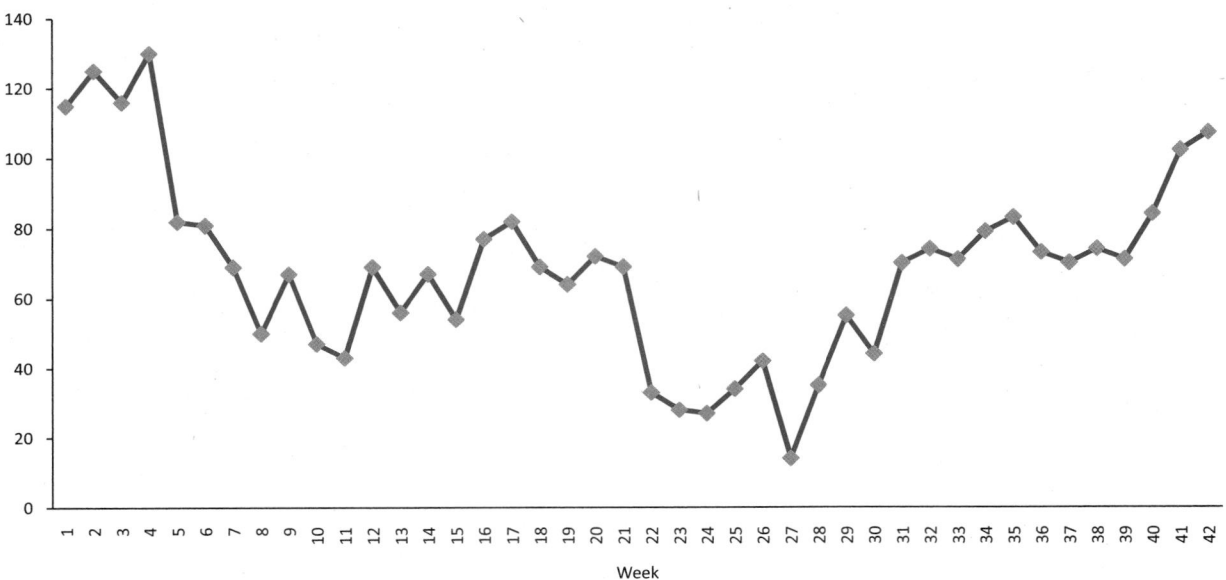

Time Series of Sales

Solution

It is generally best to begin with plenty of lags and then delete the higher numbered lags that aren't necessary.

A good place to start is with the autocorrelations of the series. These indicate whether the Sales variable is linearly related to any of its lags. The first six autocorrelations are shown in Figure 12.31. The first three of them are significantly positive, and then they decrease. Based on this information, create three lags of Sales and run a regression of Sales versus these three lags. The output from this regression appears in Figure 12.32. You can see that R^2 is fairly high, about 57%, and that s_e is about 15.7. However, the p-values for lags 2 and 3 are both quite large. It appears that once the first lag is included in the regression equation, the other two are not really needed.

Figure 12.31

Autocorrelations for Hammer Sales Data

	A	B
		Sales
27		**Sales**
28	*Autocorrelation Table*	Data Set #1
29	Number of Values	42
30	Standard Error	0.1543
31	Lag #1	**0.7523**
32	Lag #2	**0.5780**
33	Lag #3	**0.4328**
34	Lag #4	0.2042
35	Lag #5	0.1093
36	Lag #6	-0.0502

This suggests running another regression with only the first lag included. (Actually, we first omitted only the third lag. But the resulting output showed that the second lag was still insignificant, so we then deleted it.) The regression output with only the first lag

Figure 12.32 Autoregression Output with Three Lagged Variables

	A	B	C	D	E	F	G
7		Multiple	R-Square	Adjusted	StErr of		
8	Summary	R		R-Square	Estimate		
9		0.7573	0.5736	0.5370	15.7202		
10							
11		Degrees of	Sum of	Mean of	F-Ratio	p-Value	
12	ANOVA Table	Freedom	Squares	Squares			
13	Explained	3	11634.19978	3878.066594	15.6927	< 0.0001	
14	Unexplained	35	8649.38996	247.1254274			
15							
16		Coefficient	Standard	t-Value	p-Value	Confidence Interval 95%	
17	Regression Table		Error			Lower	Upper
18	Constant	15.4986	7.8820	1.9663	0.0572	-0.5027	31.5000
19	Lag1(Sales)	0.6398	0.1712	3.7364	0.0007	0.2922	0.9874
20	Lag2(Sales)	0.1523	0.1987	0.7665	0.4485	-0.2510	0.5556
21	Lag3(Sales)	-0.0354	0.1641	-0.2159	0.8303	-0.3686	0.2977

The two curves in this figure look pretty close to one another. However, a comparison of the vertical distances between pairs of points indicates that they are not that close after all.

included appears in Figure 12.33. In addition, a graph of the dependent and fitted variables, that is, the original Sales variable and its forecasts, appears in Figure 12.34. (This latter graph was formed from the Week, Sales, and Fitted columns.) The estimated regression equation is

$$\text{Forecast Sales}_t = 13.763 + 0.793\text{Sales}_{t-1}$$

The associated R^2 and s_e values are approximately 65% and 15.4. The R^2 value is a measure of the reasonably good fit evident in Figure 12.34, whereas s_e is a measure of the likely forecast error for short-term forecasts.[5] It implies that a short-term forecast could easily be off by as much as two standard errors, or about 31 hammers.

Figure 12.33 Autoregression Output with a Single Lagged Variable

	A	B	C	D	E	F	G
7		Multiple	R-Square	Adjusted	StErr of		
8	Summary	R		R-Square	Estimate		
9		0.8036	0.6458	0.6367	15.4476		
10							
11		Degrees of	Sum of	Mean of	F-Ratio	p-Value	
12	ANOVA Table	Freedom	Squares	Squares			
13	Explained	1	16969.97657	16969.97657	71.1146	< 0.0001	
14	Unexplained	39	9306.511237	238.6284932			
15							
16		Coefficient	Standard	t-Value	p-Value	Confidence Interval 95%	
17	Regression Table		Error			Lower	Upper
18	Constant	13.7634	6.7906	2.0268	0.0496	0.0281	27.4988
19	Lag1(Sales)	0.7932	0.0941	8.4329	< 0.0001	0.6029	0.9834

[5]If you are very observant, you may have noticed that R^2 increased when the two lag variables were omitted from the equation. Isn't R^2 always supposed to decrease when variables are omitted? Yes it is, but in this case the two equations are based on different data. When the second and third lags were included, weeks $1-3$ of the data set were omitted because of missing data in the lag columns. But when these lags were omitted, only the week 1 row had to be omitted because of missing data.

Figure 12.34 Forecasts from Autoregression

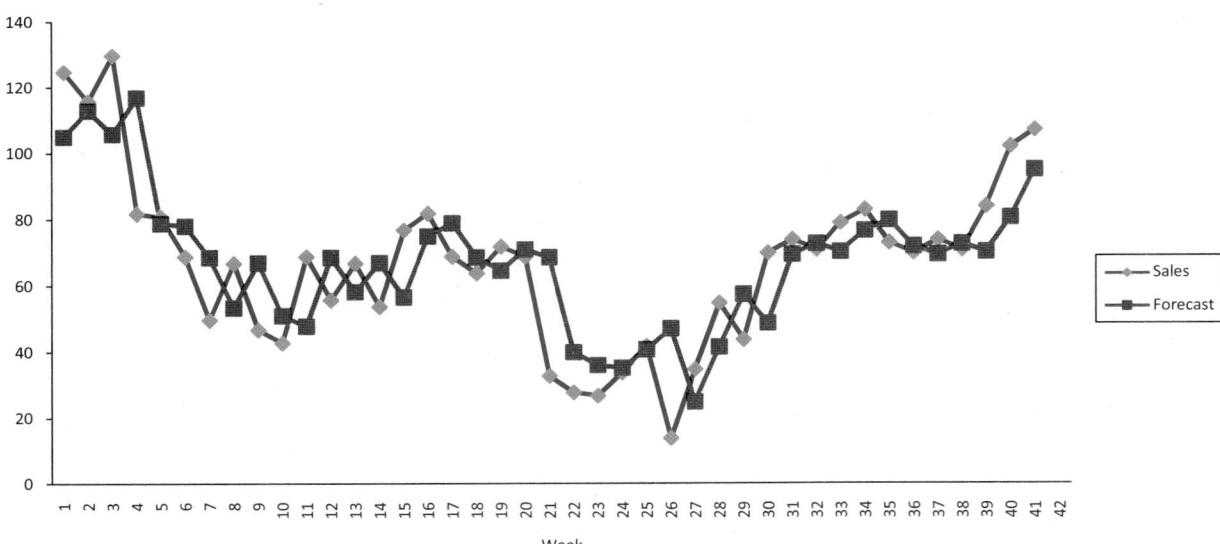

To use the regression equation for forecasting *future* sales values, you can substitute known or forecast sales values in the right-hand side of the equation. Specifically, the forecast for week 43, the first week after the data period, is

To forecast, substitute known values of Y into the regression equation if they are available. Otherwise, substitute forecast values.

$$\text{Forecast Sales}_{43} = 13.763 + 0.793\text{Sales}_{42} = 13.763 + 0.793(107) \simeq 98.6$$

Here the *known* value of sales in week 42 is used. However, the forecast for week 44 requires the *forecast* value of sales in week 43:

$$\text{Forecast Sales}_{44} = 13.763 + 0.793\text{Forecast Sales}_{43}$$
$$= 13.763 + 0.793(98.6) \simeq 92.0$$

Perhaps these two forecasts of future sales values are on the mark, and perhaps they are not. The only way to know for certain is to observe future sales values. However, it is interesting that in spite of the *upward* movement in the series in the last three weeks, the forecasts for weeks 43 and 44 are for *downward* movements. This is a combination of two properties of the regression equation. First, the coefficient of Sales_{t-1}, 0.793, is positive. Therefore, the equation forecasts that large sales will be followed by large sales, that is, positive autocorrelation. Second, however, this coefficient is less than 1, and this provides a dampening effect. The equation forecasts that a large will follow a large, but not *that* large. ■

Sometimes an autoregression model is virtually equivalent to another forecasting model. As an example, suppose you find that the following equation adequately models a time series variable *Y*:

$$Y_t = 75.65 + 0.976Y_{t-1}$$

The coefficient of the lagged term, 0.976, is nearly equal to 1. If this coefficient were 1, you could subtract the lagged term from both sides of the equation and write that the *difference* series is a constant—that is, a random walk model. As you can see, a random walk model is a special case of an autoregression model. However, autoregression models are much more general. Unfortunately, a more thorough study of them would take us into the realm of econometrics, which is well beyond the level of this book.

PROBLEMS

Level A

25. Consider the Consumer Price Index (CPI), which provides the annual percentage change in consumer prices. The data are in the file **P02_19.xlsx**.
  a. Find the first six autocorrelations of this time series.
  b. Use the results of part **a** to specify one or more promising autoregression models. Estimate each model with the available data. Which model provides the best fit to the data?
  c. Use the best autoregression model from part **b** to produce a forecast of the CPI in the next year. Also, provide a measure of the likely forecast error.

26. The Consumer Confidence Index (CCI) attempts to measure people's feelings about general business conditions, employment opportunities, and their own income prospects. The file **P02_20.xlsx** contains the annual average values of the CCI.
  a. Find the first six autocorrelations of this time series.
  b. Use the results of part **a** to specify one or more promising autoregression models. Estimate each model with the available data. Which model provides the best fit to the data?
  c. Use the best autoregression model from part **b** to produce a forecast of the CCI in the next year. Also, provide a measure of the likely forecast error.

27. Consider the proportion of Americans under the age of 18 living below the poverty level. The data are in the file **P02_44.xlsx**.
  a. Find the first six autocorrelations of this time series.
  b. Use the results of part **a** to specify one or more promising autoregression models. Estimate each model with the available data. Which model provides the best fit to the data?
  c. Use the best autoregression model from part **b** to produce a forecast of the proportion of American children living below the poverty level in the next year. Also, provide a measure of the likely forecast error.

28. The file **P02_25.xlsx** contains monthly values of two key interest rates, the federal funds rate and the prime rate.
  a. Specify one or more promising autoregression models based on autocorrelations of the federal funds rate series. Estimate each model with the available data. Which model provides the best fit to data?
  b. Use the best autoregression model from part **a** to produce forecasts of the federal funds rate in the next two years.
  c. Repeat parts **a** and **b** for the prime rate series.

29. The file **P02_24.xlsx** contains time series data on the percentage of the resident population in the United States who completed four or more years of college.
  a. Specify one or more promising autoregression models based on autocorrelations of this time series. Estimate each model with the available data. Which model provides the best fit to the data?
  b. Use the best autoregression model from part **a** to produce forecasts of higher education attainment (i.e., completion of four or more years of college) in the United States in the next three years.

30. Consider the average annual interest rates on 30-year fixed mortgages in the United States. The data are recorded in the file **P02_21.xlsx**.
  a. Specify one or more promising autoregression models based on autocorrelations of this time series. Estimate each model with the available data. Which model provides the best fit to the data?
  b. Use the best autoregression model from part **a** to produce forecasts of the average annual interest rates on 30-year fixed mortgages in the next three years.

31. The file **P12_31.xlsx** lists the monthly unemployment rates for several years. A common way to forecast time series is by using regression with lagged variables.
  a. Predict future monthly unemployment rates using some combination of the unemployment rates for the last four months. For example, you might use last month's unemployment rate and the unemployment rate from three months ago as explanatory variables. Make sure all variables that you decide to keep in your final equation are significant at the 15% significance level.
  b. Do the residuals in your equation exhibit any autocorrelation?
  c. Predict the next month's unemployment rate.
  d. There is a 5% chance that the next month's unemployment rate will be less than what value?
  e. What is the probability the next month's unemployment rate will be less than 6%, assuming normally distributed residuals?

Level B

32. The unit sales of a new drug for the first 25 months after its introduction to the marketplace are recorded in the file **P12_15.xlsx**. Specify one or more promising autoregression models based on autocorrelations of this time series. Estimate each model with the available data. Which model provides the best fit to the data? Use the best autoregression model you found to forecast the sales of this new drug in the 26th month.

33. The file **P12_02.xlsx** contains the weekly sales at a local bookstore for each of the past 25 weeks.

　a. Specify one or more promising autoregression models based on autocorrelations of this time series. Estimate each model with the available data. Which model provides the best fit to the data?

　b. What general result emerges from your analysis in part **a**? In other words, what is the most appropriate autoregression model for any given *random* time series?

　c. Use the best autoregression model from part **a** to forecast weekly sales at this bookstore for the next three weeks.

34. The file **P12_24.xlsx** contains the daily closing prices of Procter & Gamble stock for a one-year period.

　a. Use only the 2003 data to estimate an appropriate autoregression model.

　b. Next, use the estimated autoregression model from part **a** to forecast the behavior of this time series for the 2004 dates of the series. Comment on the accuracy of the forecasts over this period.

　c. How well does the autoregression model perform in comparison to the random walk model with respect to the accuracy of these forecasts? Explain any observed differences between the forecasting abilities of the two models.

12.7 MOVING AVERAGES

Perhaps the simplest and one of the most frequently used extrapolation methods is the **moving averages** method. To implement this method, you first choose a **span**, the number of terms in each moving average. Let's say the data are monthly and you choose a span of six months. Then the forecast of next month's value is the average of the values of the last six months. For example, you average January to June to forecast July, you average February to July to forecast August, and so on. This procedure is the reason for the term *moving* averages.

> A **moving average** is the average of the observations in the past few periods, where the number of terms in the average is the **span**.

A moving averages model with a span of 1 is a random walk model with a mean trend of 0.

The role of the span is important. If the span is large—say, 12 months—then many observations go into each average, and extreme values have relatively little effect on the forecasts. The resulting series of forecasts will be much smoother than the original series. (For this reason, the moving average method is called a *smoothing* method.) In contrast, if the span is small—say, three months—then extreme observations have a larger effect on the forecasts, and the forecast series will be much less smooth. In the extreme, if the span is 1, there is no smoothing effect at all. The method simply forecasts next month's value to be the same as the current month's value. This is often called the *naive* forecasting model. It is a special case of the random walk model with the mean difference equal to 0.

What span should you use? This requires some judgment. If you believe the ups and downs in the series are random noise, then you don't want future forecasts to react too quickly to these ups and downs, and you should use a relatively large span. But if you want to track every little zigzag—under the belief that each up or down is predictable—then you should use a smaller span. You shouldn't be fooled, however, by a plot of the (smoothed) forecast series superimposed on the original series. This graph will almost always look better when a small span is used, because the forecast series will appear to track the original series better. Does this mean it will always provide better future forecasts? Not necessarily. There is little point in tracking random ups and downs closely if they represent unpredictable noise.

The following example illustrates the use of moving averages.

12.6 HOUSES SOLD IN THE UNITED STATES

The file **House Sales.xlsx** contains monthly data on the number of new one-family houses sold in the U.S. (in thousands) from January 1991 through September 2009. (These data, available from the U.S. Census Bureau Web site, are listed as SAAR, seasonally adjusted at an annual rate.)[6] A time series graph of the data appears in Figure 12.35. Housing sales were steadily trending upward until about the beginning of 2006, but then the bottom fell out of the housing market. Does a moving averages model fit this series well? What span should be used?

Figure 12.35 Time Series Plot of Monthly House Sales

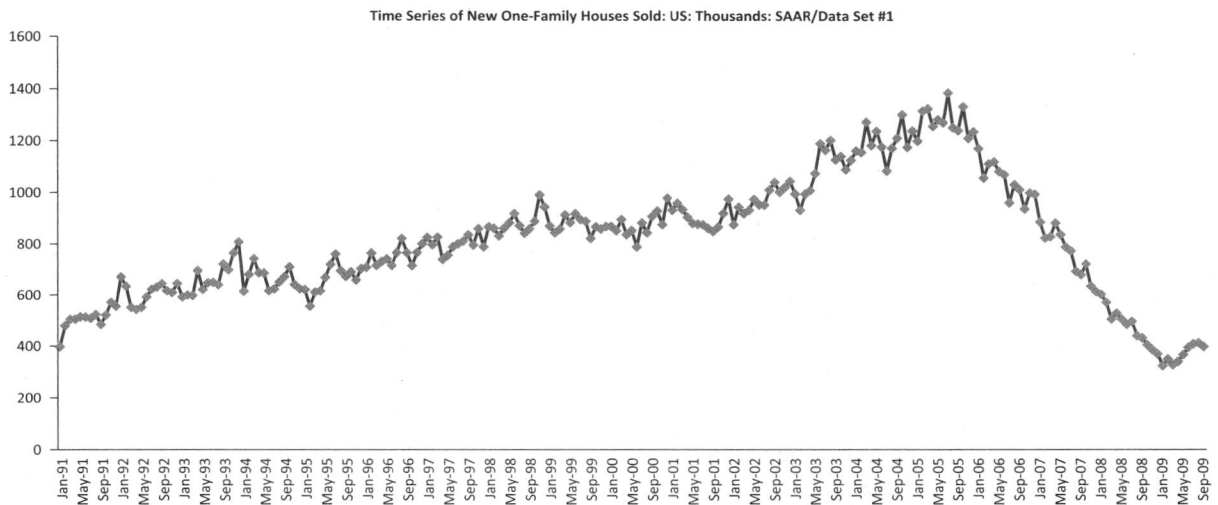

Objective To see whether a moving averages model with an appropriate span fits the housing sales data and to see how StatTools implements this method.

Solution

Although the moving averages method is quite easy to implement in Excel—you just form an average of the appropriate span and copy it down—it can be tedious. It is much easier to implement with StatTools. Actually, the StatTools forecasting procedure is fairly general in that it allows you to forecast with several methods, either with or without taking seasonality into account. Because this is your first exposure to this procedure, we will go through it in some detail in this example. In later examples, we will mention some of its other capabilities.

To use the StatTools Forecasting procedure, select Forecast from the StatTools Time Series and Forecasting dropdown list. This brings up the dialog box in Figure 12.36, which has three tabs in its bottom section. The Time Scale tab, shown in Figure 12.36, allows you to select the time period. The Forecast Settings tab, shown in Figure 12.37, allows you to select a forecasting method. Finally, the Graphs to Display tab, not shown here, allows you to select several optional time series graphs. For now, fill out the dialog box sections as

---

[6]We discuss seasonal adjustment in section 12.9. Government data are often reported in seasonally adjusted form, with the seasonality removed, to make any trends more apparent.

shown and select the Forecast Overlay option in the Graphs to Display tab. In particular, note from Figure 12.37 that the moving averages method is being used with a span of 3, and it will generate forecasts for the next 12 months.

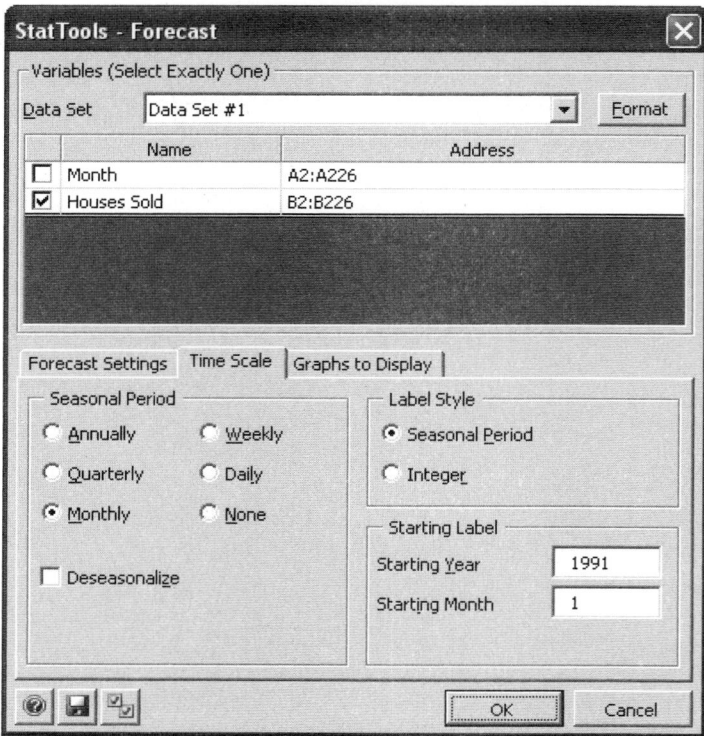

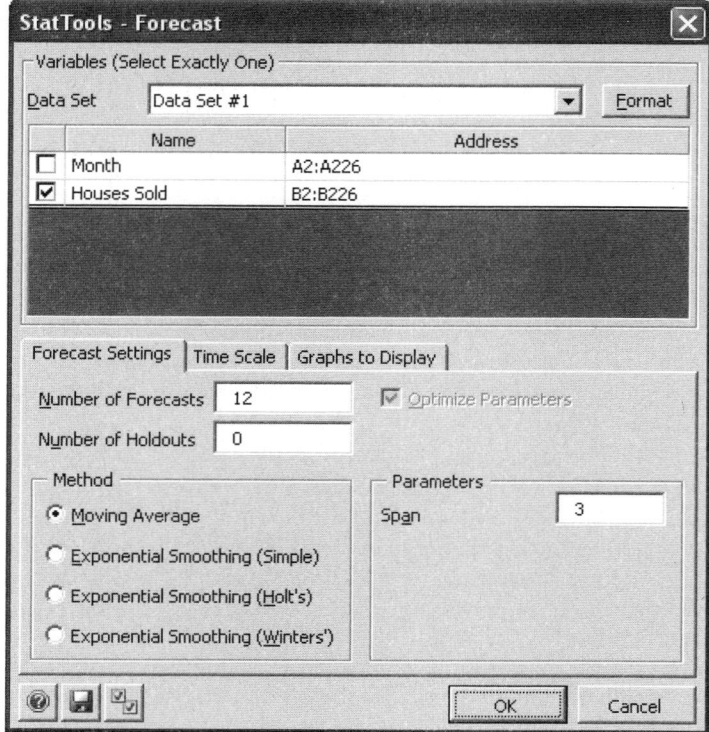

Another option in Figure 12.37 is that you can elect to "hold out" a subset of the series for validation purposes. If you hold out several periods at the end of the series for validation, any model that is built is estimated only for the non-holdout observations, and summary measures are reported for the non-holdout and holdout subsets separately. For now, don't use a holdout period.

The output consists of several parts, as shown in Figures 12.38 through 12.41. We actually ran the analysis twice, once for a span of 3 and once for a span of 12. These figures show the comparison. (We also obtained output for a span of 6, with results fairly similar to those for a span of 3.) First, the summary measures MAE, RMSE, and MAPE of the forecast errors are shown in Figure 12.38. As you can see, the forecasts using a span of 3 are considerably more accurate. For example, they are off by about 5.4% on average, whereas the similar measure with a span of 12 is 8.88%.

Figure 12.38 Moving Averages Summary Output

	A	B	C	D	E	F	G	H
8	*Forecasting Constant*						*Forecasting Constant*	
9	Span	3					Span	12
10								
11								
12	*Moving Averages*						*Moving Averages*	
13	Mean Abs Err	41.88					Mean Abs Err	66.29
14	Root Mean Sq Err	53.64					Root Mean Sq Err	85.45
15	Mean Abs Per% Err	5.37%					Mean Abs Per% Err	8.88%

Figure 12.39 Moving Averages Detailed Output

	A	B	C	D	E	F	G	H	I	J
40	*Forecasting Data*	Houses Sold	Forecast	Error			*Forecasting Data*	Houses Sold	Forecast	Error
41	Jan-1991	401.00					Jan-1991	401.00		
42	Feb-1991	482.00					Feb-1991	482.00		
43	Mar-1991	507.00					Mar-1991	507.00		
44	Apr-1991	508.00	463.33	44.67			Apr-1991	508.00		
45	May-1991	517.00	499.00	18.00			May-1991	517.00		
46	Jun-1991	516.00	510.67	5.33			Jun-1991	516.00		
47	Jul-1991	511.00	513.67	-2.67			Jul-1991	511.00		
48	Aug-1991	526.00	514.67	11.33			Aug-1991	526.00		
49	Sep-1991	487.00	517.67	-30.67			Sep-1991	487.00		
50	Oct-1991	524.00	508.00	16.00			Oct-1991	524.00		
51	Nov-1991	575.00	512.33	62.67			Nov-1991	575.00		
52	Dec-1991	558.00	528.67	29.33			Dec-1991	558.00		
53	Jan-1992	676.00	552.33	123.67			Jan-1992	676.00	509.33	166.67
54	Feb-1992	639.00	603.00	36.00			Feb-1992	639.00	532.25	106.75
55	Mar-1992	554.00	624.33	-70.33			Mar-1992	554.00	545.33	8.67
265	Sep-2009	402.00	409.67	-7.67			Sep-2009	402.00	380.75	21.25
266	Oct-2009		410.67				Oct-2009		377.92	
267	Nov-2009		409.89				Nov-2009		375.33	
268	Dec-2009		407.52				Dec-2009		374.10	
269	Jan-2010		409.36				Jan-2010		374.11	
270	Feb-2010		408.92				Feb-2010		377.87	
271	Mar-2010		408.60				Mar-2010		379.86	
272	Apr-2010		408.96				Apr-2010		383.85	
273	May-2010		408.83				May-2010		387.09	
274	Jun-2010		408.80				Jun-2010		388.43	
275	Jul-2010		408.86				Jul-2010		387.55	
276	Aug-2010		408.83				Aug-2010		385.43	
277	Sep-2010		408.83				Sep-2010		382.79	

The essence of the forecasting method is very simple and is captured in column C of Figure 12.39 for a span of 3 (with many hidden rows). Each value in the historical period in this column is an average of the three preceding values in column B. The forecast errors are then just the differences between columns B and C. For the future periods, the forecast

Figure 12.40

Moving Averages
Forecasts with
Span 3

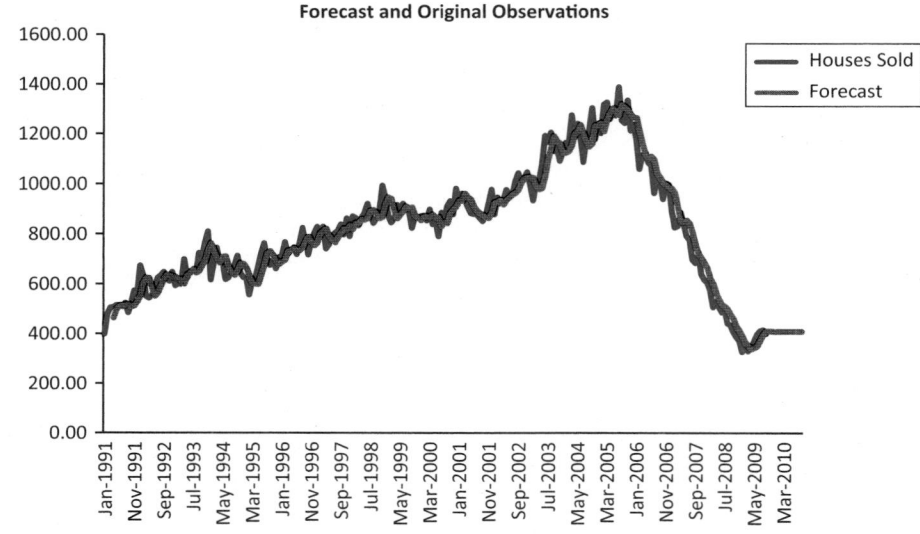

Figure 12.41

Moving Averages
Forecasts with
Span 12

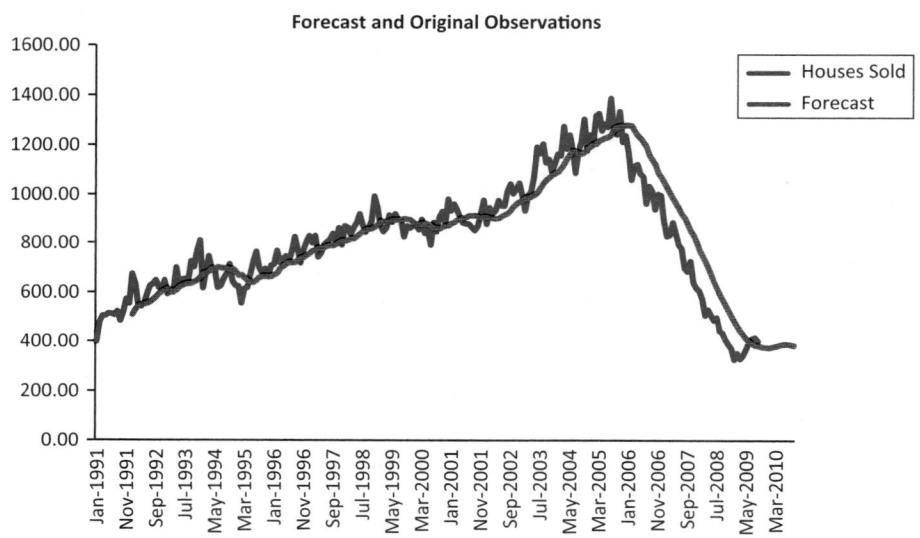

formulas in column C use observations when they are available. If they are not available, previous forecasts are used. For example, the value in cell C267, the forecast for November 2009, is the average of the *observed* values in August and September and the *forecast* value in October.

The graphs in Figures 12.40 and 12.41 show the behavior of the forecasts. The forecast series with span 3 follows the ups and downs of the actual series fairly closely, and when the series starts going down, the moving averages track the turnaround fairly well. In contrast, the 12-month moving average series is much smoother. This is probably a good feature when the series is trending upward—there is no sense in tracking the noise—but when the series suddenly starts downward, the moving averages consistently lag behind. That is, the forecasts in this latter period are consistently too high. (This same behavior occurs for a span of 6, but the forecasts are not as biased in the latter part of the series as with a span of 12.)

One interesting feature of the moving average method is that *future* forecasts tend to be quite flat. This is apparent in the last two figures, but you can check that if we had used only the data through 2008, where the series was still trending downward, the forecasts for 2009 would still be fairly constant; they would *not* continue to decrease. This is a basic property of moving average forecasts: *future* forecasts tend to be close to the last few values of the series. ■

The moving average method we have presented is the simplest of a group of moving average methods used by professional forecasters. We *smoothed* exactly once; that is, we took moving averages of several observations at a time and used these as forecasts. More complex methods smooth more than once, basically to get rid of random noise. They take moving averages, then moving averages of these moving averages, and so on for several stages. This can become quite complex, but the objective is quite simple—to smooth the data so that underlying patterns are easier to see.

PROBLEMS

Level A

35. The file **P12_16.xlsx** contains the daily closing prices of American Express stock for a one-year period.
  a. Using a span of 3, forecast the price of this stock for the next trading day with the moving average method. How well does this method with span 3 forecast the known observations in this series?
  b. Repeat part **a** with a span of 10.
  c. Which of these two spans appears to be more appropriate? Justify your choice.

36. The closing value of the AMEX Airline Index for each trading day during a one-year period is given in the file **P12_17.xlsx**.
  a. How well does the moving average method track this series when the span is 4; when the span is 12?
  b. Using the more appropriate span, forecast the closing value of this index on the next trading day with the moving average method.

37. The closing value of the Dow Jones Industrial Average for each trading day during a one-year period is provided in the file **P12_19.xlsx**.
  a. Using a span of 2, forecast the price of this index on the next trading day with the moving average method. How well does the moving average method with span 2 forecast the known observations in this series?
  b. Repeat part **a** with a span of 5; with a span of 15.
  c. Which of these three spans appears to be most appropriate? Justify your choice.

38. The file **P12_10.xlsx** contains the daily closing prices of Walmart stock during a one-year period. Use the moving average method with a carefully chosen span to forecast this time series for the next three trading days. Defend your choice of the span used.

39. The Consumer Confidence Index (CCI) attempts to measure people's feelings about general business conditions, employment opportunities, and their own income prospects. The file **P02_20.xlsx** contains the annual average values of the CCI. Use the moving average method with a carefully chosen span to forecast this time series in the next two years. Defend your choice of the span used.

Level B

40. The file **P02_28.xlsx** contains total monthly U.S. retail sales data. While holding out the final six months of observations for validation purposes, use the method of moving averages with a carefully chosen span to forecast U.S. retail sales in the next year. Comment on the performance of your model. What makes this time series more challenging to forecast?

41. Consider a random walk model with the following equation: $Y_t = Y_{t-1} + e_t$, where e_t is a random series with mean 0 and standard deviation 1. Specify a moving average model that is equivalent to this random walk model. In particular, what is the appropriate span in the equivalent moving average model? What is the smoothing effect of this span?

12.8 EXPONENTIAL SMOOTHING

There are two possible criticisms of the moving averages method. First, it puts equal weight on each value in a typical moving average. Many analysts would argue that if next month's forecast is to be based on the previous 12 months' observations, more weight should be placed on the more recent observations. The second criticism is that the moving averages method requires a lot of data storage. This is particularly true for companies that routinely make forecasts of hundreds or even thousands of items. If 12-month moving averages are used for 1000 items, then 12,000 values are needed for next month's forecasts. This may or may not be a concern, given today's inexpensive computer storage.

Exponential smoothing is a method that addresses both of these criticisms. It bases its forecasts on a weighted average of past observations, with more weight on the more recent observations, and it requires very little data storage. In addition, it is not difficult for most business people to understand, at least conceptually. Therefore, this method is used widely in the business world, particularly when frequent and automatic forecasts of many items are required.

There are many variations of exponential smoothing. The simplest is appropriately called *simple* exponential smoothing. It is relevant when there is no pronounced trend or seasonality in the series. If there is a trend but no seasonality, *Holt's* method is applicable. If, in addition, there is seasonality, *Winters'* method can be used. This does not exhaust the types of exponential smoothing models—researchers have invented many other variations—but these three models will suffice for us.

Exponential Smoothing Models

Simple exponential smoothing is appropriate for a series with no pronounced trend or seasonality. **Holt's** method is appropriate for a series with trend but no seasonality. **Winters'** method is appropriate for a series with seasonality (and possibly trend).

In this section we examine simple exponential smoothing and Holt's model for trend. Then in the next section we examine Winters' model for seasonal models.

12.8.1 Simple Exponential Smoothing

The level is an estimate of where the series would be if it were not for random noise.

We now examine simple exponential smoothing in some detail. We first introduce two new terms. Every exponential model has at least one **smoothing constant**, which is always a number between 0 and 1. Simple exponential smoothing has a single smoothing constant denoted by α. (Its role is discussed shortly.) The second new term is L_t, called the *level* of the series at time t. This value is not observable but can only be estimated. Essentially, it is an estimate of where the series would be at time t if there were no random noise. Then the simple exponential smoothing method is defined by the following two equations, where F_{t+k} is the forecast of Y_{t+k} made at time t:

Simple Exponential Smoothing Formulas

$$L_t = \alpha Y_t + (1 - \alpha)L_{t-1} \qquad \text{(12.12)}$$

$$F_{t+k} = L_t \qquad \text{(12.13)}$$

Even though you usually don't have to substitute into these equations manually, you should understand what they say. Equation (12.12) shows how to update the estimate of the level. It is a weighted average of the current observation, Y_t, and the previous level, L_{t-1}, with respective weights α and $1 - \alpha$. Equation (12.13) shows how forecasts are made. It says that the k-period-ahead forecast, F_{t+k}, made of Y_{t+k} in period t is the most recently estimated level, L_t. This is the *same* for any value of $k \geq 1$. The idea is that in simple exponential smoothing, you believe that the series is not really going anywhere. So as soon as you estimate where the series ought to be in period t (if it weren't for random noise), you forecast that this is where it will be in any future period.

The smoothing constant α is analogous to the span in moving averages. There are two ways to see this. The first way is to rewrite Equation (12.12), using the fact that the forecast error, E_t, made in forecasting Y_t at time $t - 1$ is $Y_t - F_t = Y_t - L_{t-1}$. Using algebra, Equation (12.12) can be rewritten as Equation (12.14).

Equivalent Formula for Simple Exponential Smoothing

$$L_t = L_{t-1} + \alpha E_t \qquad \textbf{(12.14)}$$

This equation says that the next estimate of the level is adjusted from the previous estimate by adding a multiple of the most recent forecast error. This makes sense. If the previous forecast was too high, then E_t is negative, and the estimate of the level is adjusted downward. The opposite is true if the previous forecast was too low. However, Equation (12.14) says that the method does not adjust by the entire magnitude of E_t, but only by a fraction of it. If α is small, say, $\alpha = 0.1$, the adjustment is minor; if α is close to 1, the adjustment is large. So if you want the method to react quickly to movements in the series, you should choose a large α; otherwise, you should choose a small α.

Another way to see the effect of α is to substitute recursively into the equation for L_t. By performing some algebra, you can verify that L_t satisfies Equation (12.15), where the sum extends back to the first observation at time $t = 1$.

Another Equivalent Formula for Simple Exponential Smoothing

$$L_t = \alpha Y_t + \alpha(1 - \alpha)Y_{t-1} + \alpha(1 - \alpha)^2 Y_{t-2} + \alpha(1 - \alpha)^3 Y_{t-3} + \cdots \quad \textbf{(12.15)}$$

Equation (12.15) shows how the exponentially smoothed forecast is a weighted average of previous observations. Furthermore, because $1 - \alpha$ is less than 1, the weights on the Ys decrease from time t backward. Therefore, if α is close to 0, then $1 - \alpha$ is close to 1 and the weights decrease very slowly. In other words, observations from the distant past continue to have a large influence on the next forecast. This means that the graph of the forecasts will be relatively smooth, just as with a large span in the moving averages method. But when α is close to 1, the weights decrease rapidly, and only very recent observations have much influence on the next forecast. In this case forecasts react quickly to sudden changes in the series. This is equivalent to a small span in moving averages.

Small smoothing constants provide forecasts that respond slowly to changes in the series. Large smoothing constants do the opposite.

What value of α should you use? There is no universally accepted answer to this question. Some practitioners recommend always using a value around 0.1 or 0.2. Others recommend experimenting with different values of α until a measure such as RMSE or MAPE is minimized. Some packages even have an optimization feature to find this optimal value of α. (This is the case with StatTools.) But just as we discussed in the moving averages section, the value of α that tracks the historical series most closely does not necessarily guarantee the most accurate *future* forecasts.

Smoothing Constants in Exponential Smoothing

All versions of exponential smoothing—and there are more than are discussed here—use one or more smoothing constants between 0 and 1. To make any such method produce smoother forecasts, and hence react less quickly to noise, use smaller smoothing constants, such as 0.1 or 0.2. When larger smoothing constants are used, the historical forecasts might appear to track the actual series fairly closely, but they might just be tracking random noise.

EXAMPLE | **12.6 HOUSES SOLD IN THE UNITED STATES (CONTINUED)**

Previously, we used the moving averages method to forecast monthly housing sales in the U.S. (See the **House Sales.xlsx** file.) How well does simple exponential smoothing work with this data set? What smoothing constant should be used?

Objective   To see how well a simple exponential smoothing model, with an appropriate smoothing constant, fits the housing sales data, and to see how StatTools implements this method.

Solution

You can use StatTools to implement the simple exponential smoothing model, specifically equations (12.12) and (12.13). You do this again with the Forecast item from the StatTools Time Series and Forecasting dropdown list. Specifically, you fill in the forecast dialog box essentially as with moving averages, except that you select the simple exponential smoothing option in the Forecast Settings tab (see Figure 12.42). You should also choose a

Figure 12.42

Forecast Settings for Exponential Smoothing

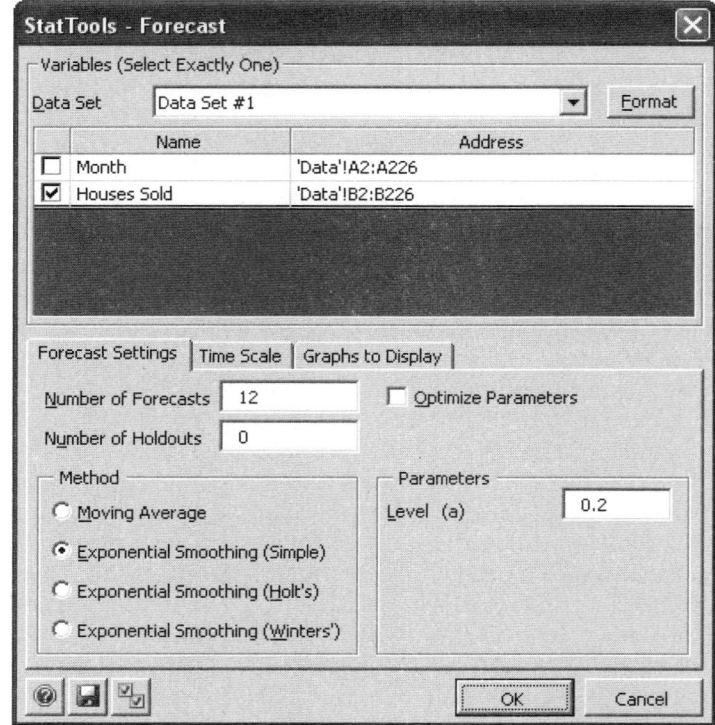

smoothing constant (0.2 was chosen here, but any other value could be chosen) or you can elect to find an optimal smoothing constant (we didn't optimize for this example, at least not yet).

The results appear in Figures 12.43 (with many hidden rows) and 12.44. The heart of the method takes place in columns C, D, and E of Figure 12.43. Column C calculates the smoothed levels (L_t) from Equation (12.12), column D calculates the forecasts (F_t) from Equation (12.13), and column E calculates the forecast errors (E_t) as the observed values minus the forecasts. Although the Excel formulas do not appear in the figure, you can examine them in the StatTools output.

Figure 12.43

Simple Exponential Smoothing Output

	A	B	C	D	E
8	*Forecasting Constant*				
9	Level (Alpha)	0.200			
10					
11					
12	*Simple Exponential*				
13	Mean Abs Err	54.81			
14	Root Mean Sq Err	69.91			
15	Mean Abs Per% Err	7.45%			
38					
39					
40	*Forecasting Data*	Houses Sold	Level	Forecast	Error
41	Jan-1991	401.00	401.00		
42	Feb-1991	482.00	417.20	401.00	81.00
43	Mar-1991	507.00	435.16	417.20	89.80
44	Apr-1991	508.00	449.73	435.16	72.84
45	May-1991	517.00	463.18	449.73	67.27
46	Jun-1991	516.00	473.75	463.18	52.82
47	Jul-1991	511.00	481.20	473.75	37.25
48	Aug-1991	526.00	490.16	481.20	44.80
263	Jul-2009	413.00	392.29	387.12	25.88
264	Aug-2009	417.00	397.24	392.29	24.71
265	Sep-2009	402.00	398.19	397.24	4.76
266	Oct-2009			398.19	
267	Nov-2009			398.19	
268	Dec-2009			398.19	
269	Jan-2010			398.19	
270	Feb-2010			398.19	
271	Mar-2010			398.19	
272	Apr-2010			398.19	
273	May-2010			398.19	
274	Jun-2010			398.19	
275	Jul-2010			398.19	
276	Aug-2010			398.19	
277	Sep-2010			398.19	

Every exponential smoothing method requires *initial* values, in this case the initial smoothed level in cell C41. There is no way to calculate this value, L_1, from Equation (12.12) because the *previous* value, L_0, is unknown. Different implementations of exponential smoothing initialize in different ways. StatTools initializes by setting L_1 equal to Y_1 (in cell B41). The effect of initializing in different ways is usually minimal because any effect of early data is usually washed out as forecast are made into the future. In the present example, values from 1991 have little effect on forecasts for 2009 and beyond.

Note that the 12 future forecasts (rows 266 down) are all equal to the last calculated smoothed level, the one for September 2009 in cell C265. The fact that these remain con-

Figure 12.44

Graph of Forecasts from Simple Exponential Smoothing

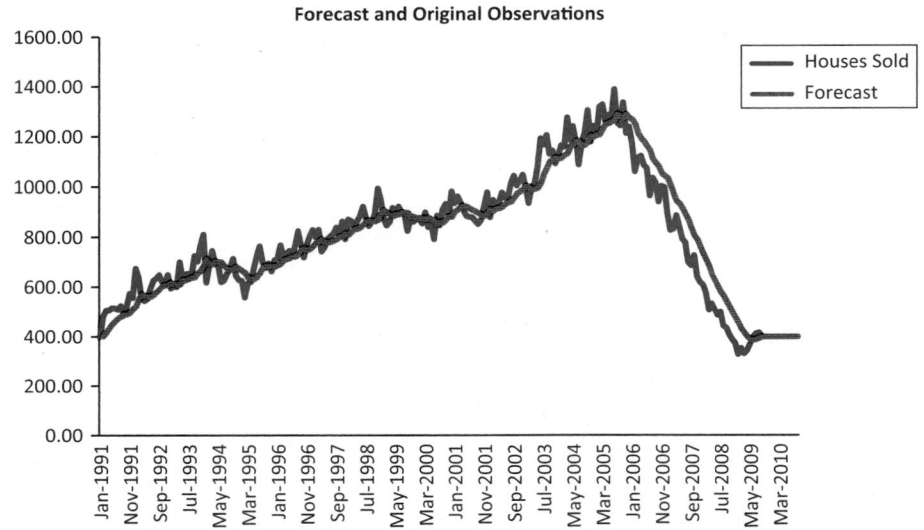

stant is a consequence of the assumption behind *simple* exponential smoothing, namely, that the series is not really going anywhere. Therefore, the last smoothed level is the best available indication of future values of the series.

Figure 12.44 shows the forecast series superimposed on the original series. You can see the obvious smoothing effect of a relatively small α level. The forecasts don't track the series very well, but if the various zigzags in the original series are really random noise, then perhaps the forecasts shouldn't try to track these random ups and downs too closely. That is, perhaps a forecast series that emphasizes the basic underlying pattern is preferred. However, notice that once the series starts going downhill, the forecasts never quite catch up. This is the same behavior you saw with a span of 12 for moving averages.

You can see several summary measures of the forecast errors in Figure 12.43. The RMSE and MAE indicate that the forecasts from this model are typically off by a magnitude of about 55 to 70 thousand, and the MAPE indicates that they are off by about 7.5%. (These are similar to the errors obtained earlier with moving averages with span 12.) These are fairly sizable errors. One way to reduce the errors is to use a different smoothing method. We will try this in the next subsection with Holt's method. Another way to reduce the errors is to use a different smoothing constant. There are two methods you can use. First, you can simply enter different values in the smoothing constant cell in the Forecast sheet. All formulas, including those for MAE, RMSE, and MAPE, will update automatically.

Second, you can check the Optimize Parameters option in the Forecast dialog box shown in Figure 12.42. This automatically runs an optimization algorithm (not Solver, by the way) to find the smoothing constant that minimizes RMSE. (StatTools is programmed to minimize RMSE. However, you could try minimizing MAPE, say, by using Excel's Solver add-in.) When this optimization option is used for the housing data, the results in Figure 12.45 are obtained (from a smoothing constant of 0.691). The corresponding MAE, RMSE, and MAPE are 39.6, 50.1, and 5.01%, respectively—better than before. This larger smoothing constant produces a less smooth forecast curve and slightly better error measures. However, there is no guarantee that *future* forecasts made with this optimal smoothing constant will be any better than with a smoothing constant of 0.2.

In the next subsection, Holt's method is used on this series to see whether it captures the trend better than simple exponential smoothing.

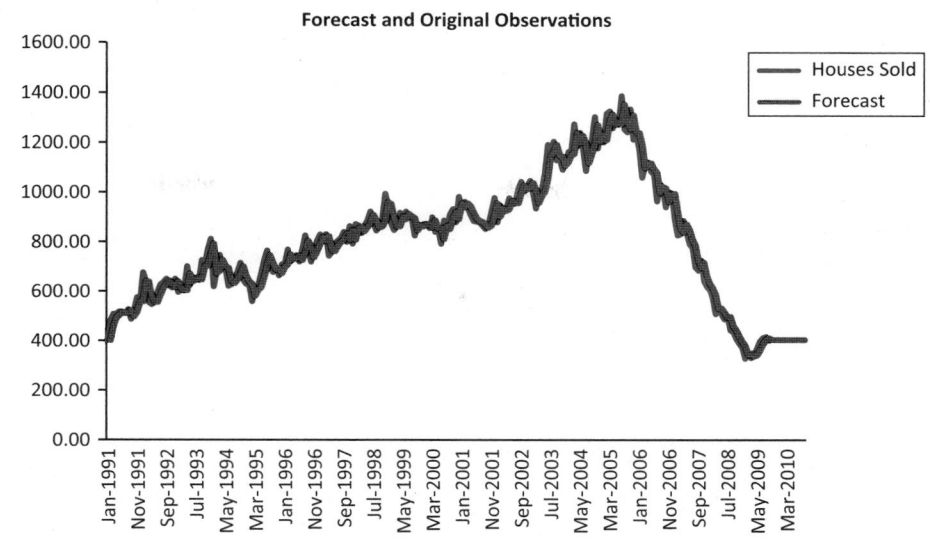

Forecast and Original Observations

12.8.2 Holt's Model for Trend

The trend term in Holt's method estimates the change from one period to the next.

The simple exponential smoothing model generally works well if there is no obvious trend in the series. But if there is a trend, this method consistently lags behind it. For example, if the series is constantly increasing, simple exponential smoothing forecasts will be consistently low. Holt's method rectifies this by dealing with trend explicitly. In addition to the level of the series, L_t, Holt's method includes a trend term, T_t, and a corresponding smoothing constant β. The interpretation of L_t is exactly as before. The interpretation of T_t is that it represents an estimate of the *change* in the series from one period to the next. The equations for Holt's model are as follows.

Formulas for Holt's Exponential Smoothing Method

$$L_t = \alpha Y_t + (1 - \alpha)(L_{t-1} + T_{t-1}) \qquad (12.16)$$

$$T_t = \beta(L_t - L_{t-1}) + (1 - \beta)T_{t-1} \qquad (12.17)$$

$$F_{t+k} = L_t + kT_t \qquad (12.18)$$

These equations are not as bad as they look. (And don't forget that the software does all of the calculations for you.) Equation (12.16) says that the updated level is a weighted average of the current observation and the previous level plus the estimated change. Equation (12.17) says that the updated trend is a weighted average of the difference between two consecutive levels and the previous trend. Finally, Equation (12.18) says that the k-period-ahead forecast made in period t is the estimated level plus k times the estimated change per period.

Everything we said about α for simple exponential smoothing applies to both α and β in Holt's model. The new smoothing constant β controls how quickly the method reacts to observed changes in the trend. If β is small, the method reacts slowly. If it is large, the method reacts more quickly. Of course, there are now two smoothing constants to select.

Some practitioners suggest using a small value of α (0.1 to 0.2, say) and setting β equal to α. Others suggest using an optimization option (available in StatTools) to select the optimal smoothing constants. We illustrate the possibilities in the following continuation of the housing sales example.

EXAMPLE	12.6 HOUSES SOLD IN THE UNITED STATES (CONTINUED)

We again examine the monthly data on housing sales in the U.S. In the previous subsection, we saw that simple exponential smoothing, even with an optimal smoothing constant, does only a fair job of forecasting housing sales. Given that there is an upward trend and then a downward trend in housing sales over this period, Holt's method might be expected to perform better. Does it? What smoothing constants are appropriate?

Objective To see whether Holt's method, with appropriate smoothing constants, captures the trends in the housing sales data better than simple exponential smoothing (or moving averages).

Solution

You implement Holt's method in StatTools almost exactly as you did for simple exponential smoothing. The only difference is that you can now choose *two* smoothing constants, as shown in Figure 12.46. They can have different values, but they have both been chosen to be 0.2 for this example.

Figure 12.46
Dialog Box for
Holt's Method

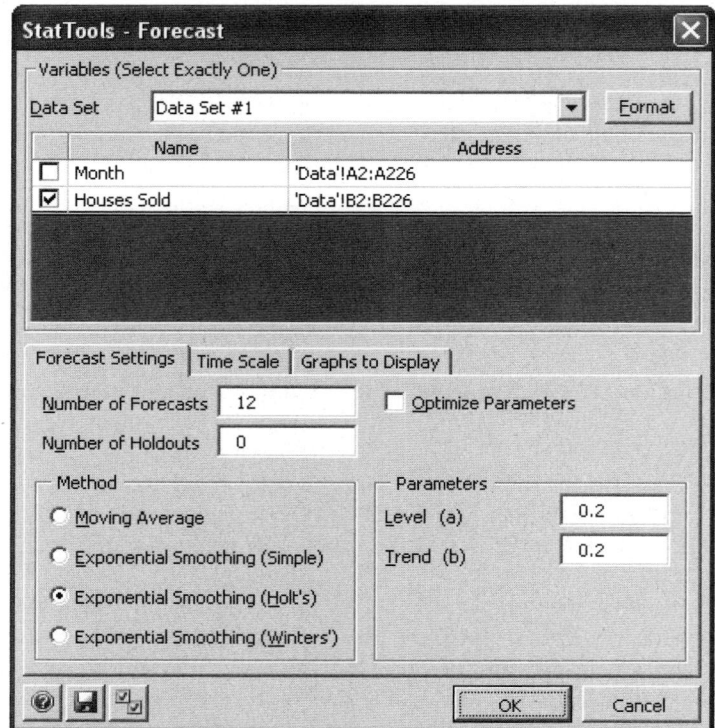

The StatTools outputs in Figures 12.47 and 12.48 are also very similar to the simple exponential smoothing outputs. The only difference is that there is now a trend column, column D, in the numerical output. You can check that the formulas in columns C, D, and E implement equations (12.16), (12.17), and (12.18). As before, an initialization is required in row 42. These require values of L_1 and T_1 to get the method started. Different implementations of Holt's method obtain these initial values in slightly different ways, but the effect is fairly minimal in most cases. (You can check cells C42 and D42 to see how StatTools does it.[7])

Figure 12.47

Output from Holt's Method

	A	B	C	D	E	F
8	*Forecasting Constants*					
9	Level (Alpha)	0.200				
10	Trend (Beta)	0.200				
11						
12						
13	*Holt's Exponential*					
14	Mean Abs Err	42.59				
15	Root Mean Sq Err	54.85				
16	Mean Abs Per% Err	5.57%				
40						
41	*Forecasting Data*	Houses Sold	Level	Trend	Forecast	Error
42	Jan-1991	401.00	401.00	0.00		
43	Feb-1991	482.00	417.20	3.24	401.00	81.00
44	Mar-1991	507.00	437.76	6.71	420.45	86.55
45	Apr-1991	508.00	457.17	9.25	444.46	63.54
46	May-1991	517.00	476.54	11.27	466.42	50.58
47	Jun-1991	516.00	493.45	12.40	487.81	28.19
48	Jul-1991	511.00	506.88	12.60	505.84	5.16
49	Aug-1991	526.00	520.78	12.87	519.48	6.52
50	Sep-1991	487.00	524.32	11.00	533.65	-46.65
264	Jul-2009	413.00	325.12	-4.21	303.15	109.85
265	Aug-2009	417.00	340.12	-0.37	320.91	96.09
266	Sep-2009	402.00	352.20	2.12	339.75	62.25
267	Oct-2009				354.32	
268	Nov-2009				356.44	
269	Dec-2009				358.56	
270	Jan-2010				360.68	
271	Feb-2010				362.80	
272	Mar-2010				364.92	
273	Apr-2010				367.03	
274	May-2010				369.15	
275	Jun-2010				371.27	
276	Jul-2010				373.39	
277	Aug-2010				375.51	
278	Sep-2010				377.63	

The error measures for this implementation of Holt's method are slightly better than for simple exponential smoothing, but these measures are fairly sensitive to the smoothing constants. Therefore, a second run of Holt's method was performed, using the Optimize Parameters option. This resulted in somewhat better results and the forecasts shown in Figure 12.49. The optimal smoothing constants are $\alpha = 0.691$ and $\beta = 0.000$, and the MAE, RMSE, and MAPE values are identical to those from simple exponential smoothing with an optimal smoothing constant. Note that the zero smoothing constant for trend

---

[7]The initial trend in cell D42 (the first period) is the final observation minus the initial observation, all divided by the number of observations. This is the average change over the entire time period. This is probably not the best way to initialize, as suggested by the literature, and StatTools will probably be rewritten in a future version to initialize with the average change over the first two years. This will give it a better chance to *learn* how a trend changes over time.

Figure 12.48

Forecasts from
Holt's Method with
Nonoptimal
Smoothing
Constants

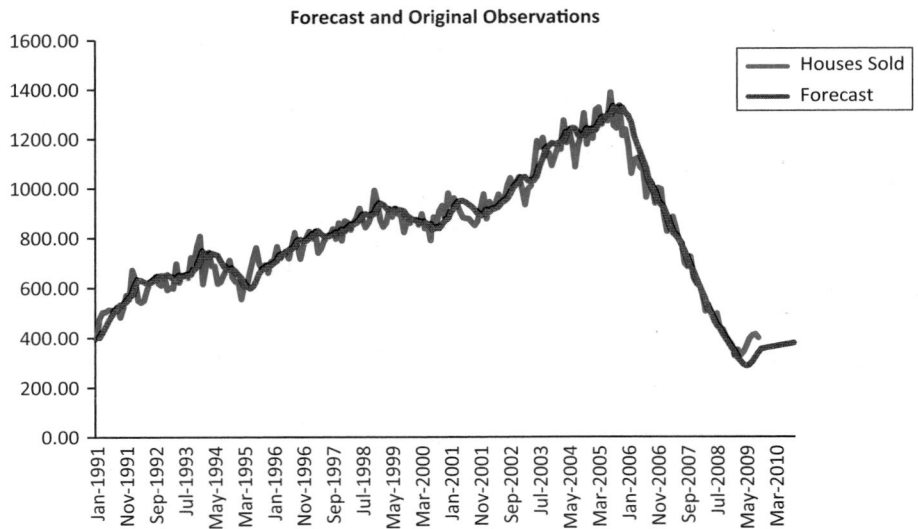

doesn't mean that there is no trend. It just means that the *initial* estimate of trend, the average change from the first time period to the last, is kept throughout. For this particular time series, despite the upward trend and the downward trend, the series ends very close to where it started. Therefore, the initial trend estimate is about zero, and future forecasts with the optimal smoothing constants are essentially flat. However, you can check that if a larger smoothing constant for trend is used, say 0.4, future forecasts will exhibit the same upward trend evident in the first nine months of 2009. Based on a look at the graph and common sense, we would suggest smoothing constants of about 0.2 for this series.

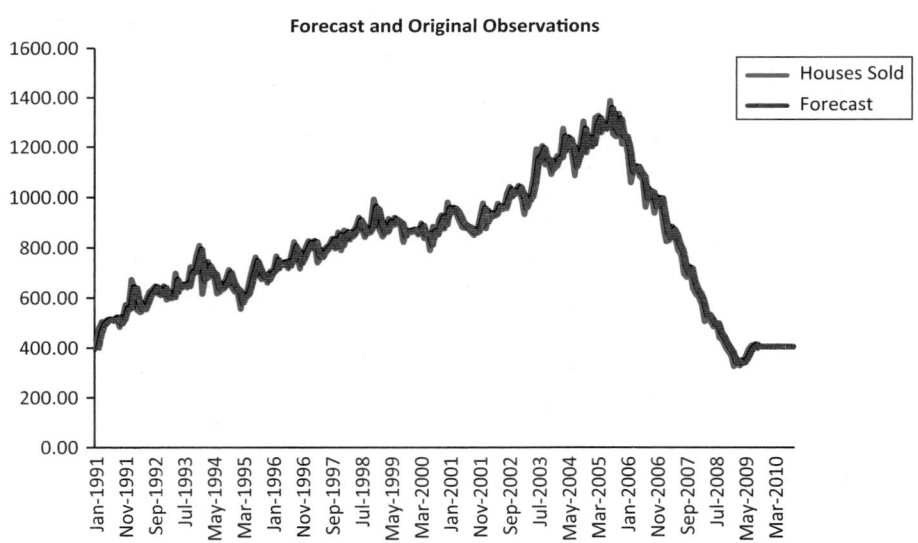

You should not conclude from this example that Holt's method is never superior to simple exponential smoothing. Holt's method is often able to react quickly to a sudden upswing or downswing in the data, whereas simple exponential smoothing typically has a delayed reaction to such a change. ∎

PROBLEMS

Level A

42. Consider the airline ticket data in the file **P12_01.xlsx.**
   a. Create a time series chart of the data. Based on what you see, which of the exponential smoothing models do you think should be used for forecasting? Why?
   b. Use simple exponential smoothing to forecast these data, using no holdout period and requesting 12 months of future forecasts. Use the default smoothing constant of 0.1.
   c. Repeat part **b**, optimizing the smoothing constant. Does it make much of an improvement?
   d. Write a short report to summarize your results.

43. Consider the applications for home mortgages data in the file **P12_04.xlsx.**
   a. Create a time series chart of the data. Based on what you see, which of the exponential smoothing models do you think should be used for forecasting? Why?
   b. Use simple exponential smoothing to forecast these data, using no holdout period and requesting four quarters of future forecasts. Use the default smoothing constant of 0.1.
   c. Repeat part **b**, optimizing the smoothing constant. Does it make much of an improvement?
   d. Write a short report to summarize your results.

44. Consider the American Express closing price data in the file **P12_16.xlsx.** Focus only on the closing prices.
   a. Create a time series chart of the data. Based on what you see, which of the exponential smoothing models do you think should be used for forecasting? Why?
   b. Use Holt's exponential smoothing to forecast these data, using no holdout period and requesting 20 days of future forecasts. Use the default smoothing constants of 0.1.
   c. Repeat part **b**, optimizing the smoothing constants. Does it make much of an improvement?
   d. Repeat parts **a** and **b**, this time using a holdout period of 50 days.
   e. Write a short report to summarize your results.

45. Consider the poverty level data in the file **P02_44.xlsx.**
   a. Create a time series chart of the data. Based on what you see, which of the exponential smoothing models do you think should be used for forecasting? Why?
   b. Use simple exponential smoothing to forecast these data, using no holdout period and requesting three years of future forecasts. Use the default smoothing constant of 0.1.

   c. Repeat part **b**, optimizing the smoothing constant. Make sure you request a chart of the series with the forecasts superimposed. Does the Optimize Parameters option make much of an improvement?
   d. Write a short report to summarize your results. Considering the chart in part **c**, would you say the forecasts are adequate?

Problems 46 through 48 ask you to apply the exponential smoothing formulas. These do not require StatTools. In fact, they do not even require Excel. You can do them with a calculator (or with Excel).

46. An automobile dealer is using Holt's method to forecast weekly car sales. Currently, the level is estimated to be 50 cars per week, and the trend is estimated to be six cars per week. During the current week, 30 cars are sold. After observing the current week's sales, forecast the number of cars three weeks from now. Use $\alpha = \beta = 0.3$.

47. You have been assigned to forecast the number of aircraft engines ordered each month from an engine manufacturing company. At the end of February, the forecast is that 100 engines will be ordered during April. Then during March, 120 engines are actually ordered.
   a. Using $\alpha = 0.3$, determine a forecast (at the end of March) for the number of orders placed during April and during May. Use simple exponential smoothing.
   b. Suppose that MAE = 16 at the end of March. At the end of March, the company can be 68% sure that April orders will be between what two values, assuming normally distributed forecast errors? (*Hint*: It can be shown that the standard deviation of forecast errors is approximately 1.25 times MAE.)

48. Simple exponential smoothing with $\alpha = 0.3$ is being used to forecast sales of SLR (single lens reflex) cameras at an appliance store. Forecasts are made on a monthly basis. After August camera sales are observed, the forecast for September is 100 cameras.
   a. During September, 120 cameras are sold. After observing September sales, what is the forecast for October camera sales? What is the forecast for November camera sales?
   b. It turns out that June sales were recorded as 10 cameras. Actually, however, 100 cameras were sold in June. After correcting for this error, what is the forecast for October camera sales?

Level B

49. Holt's method assumes an *additive* trend. For example, a trend of five means that the level will increase by five units per period. Suppose that there is actually a *multiplicative* trend. For example, if the current estimate of the level is 50 and the current estimate of the trend is 1.2, the forecast of demand increases by 20% per period. So the forecast demand for next period is 50(1.2) and forecast demand for two periods in the future is $50(1.2)^2$. If you want to use a multiplicative trend in Holt's method, you should use equations of the form:

$$L_t = \alpha Y_t + (1 - \alpha)(I)$$
$$T_t = \beta(II) + (1 - \beta)T_{t-1}$$

a. What should (*I*) and (*II*) be?

b. Suppose you are working with monthly data and month 12 is December, month 13 is January, and so on. Also suppose that $L_{12} = 100$ and $T_{12} = 1.2$, and you observe $Y_{13} = 200$. At the end of month 13, what is the forecast for Y_{15}? Assume $\alpha = \beta = 0.5$ and a multiplicative trend.

50. A version of simple exponential smoothing can be used to predict the outcome of sporting events. To illustrate, consider pro football. Assume for simplicity that all games are played on a neutral field. Before each day of play, assume that each team has a rating. For example, if the rating for the Bears is +10 and the rating for the Bengals is +6, the Bears are predicted to beat the Bengals by $10 - 6 = 4$ points. Suppose that the Bears play the Bengals and win by 20 points. For this game, the model underpredicted the Bears' performance by $20 - 4 = 16$ points. Assuming that the best α for pro football is 0.10, the Bears' rating will increase by $16(0.1) = 1.6$ points and the Bengals' rating will decrease by 1.6 points. In a rematch, the Bears will then be favored by $(10 + 1.6) - (6 - 1.6) = 7.2$ points.

a. How does this approach relate to the equation $L_t = L_{t-1} + \alpha E_t$?

b. Suppose that the home field advantage in pro football is three points; that is, home teams tend to outscore equally rated visiting teams by an average of three points a game. How could the home field advantage be incorporated into this system?

c. How might you determine the *best* α for pro football?

d. How could the ratings for each team at the beginning of the season be chosen?

e. Suppose this method is used to predict pro football (16-game schedule), college football (11-game schedule), college basketball (30-game schedule), and pro basketball (82-game schedule). Which sport do you think will have the smallest optimal α? Which will have the largest optimal α? Why?

f. Why might this approach yield poor forecasts for major league baseball?

12.9 SEASONAL MODELS

Some time series software packages have special types of graphs for spotting seasonality, but we won't discuss these here.

So far we have said practically nothing about seasonality. Seasonality is the consistent month-to-month (or quarter-to-quarter) differences that occur each year. (It could also be the day-to-day differences that occur each week.) For example, there is seasonality in beer sales—high in the summer months, lower in other months. Toy sales are also seasonal, with a huge peak in the months preceding Christmas. In fact, if you start thinking about time series variables that you are familiar with, the majority of them probably have some degree of seasonality.

How can you tell whether there is seasonality in a time series? The easiest way is to check whether a graph of the time series has a *regular* pattern of ups and/or downs in particular months or quarters. Although random noise can sometimes mask such a pattern, the seasonal pattern is usually fairly obvious.

As you saw with the housing sales data, government agencies often perform part of the second method for us—that is, they deseasonalize the data.

There are basically three methods for dealing with seasonality. First, you can use Winters' exponential smoothing model. It is similar to simple exponential smoothing and Holt's method, except that it includes another component (and smoothing constant) to capture seasonality. Second, you can *deseasonalize* the data, then use any forecasting method to model the deseasonalized data, and finally "reseasonalize" these forecasts. Finally, you can use multiple regression with dummy variables for the seasons. We discuss all three of these methods in this section.

Seasonal models are usually classified as *additive* or *multiplicative*. Suppose that the series contains monthly data, and that the average of the 12 monthly values for a typical year is 150. An **additive** model finds seasonal indexes, one for each month, that are *added* to the monthly average, 150, to get a particular month's value. For example, if the index for March is 22, then a typical March value is $150 + 22 = 172$. If the seasonal index for

September is -12, then a typical September value is $150 - 12 = 138$. A **multiplicative** model also finds seasonal indexes, but they are *multiplied* by the monthly average to get a particular month's value. Now if the index for March is 1.3, a typical March value is $150(1.3) = 195$. If the index for September is 0.9, then a typical September value is $150(0.9) = 135$.

In an **additive** seasonal model, an appropriate seasonal index is added to a base forecast. These indexes, one for each season, typically average to 0.

In a **multiplicative** seasonal model, a base forecast is multiplied by an appropriate seasonal index. These indexes, one for each season, typically average to 1.

Either an additive or a multiplicative model can be used to forecast seasonal data. However, because multiplicative models are somewhat easier to interpret (and have worked well in applications), we focus on them. Note that the seasonal index in a multiplicative model can be interpreted as a percentage. Using the figures in the previous paragraph as an example, March tends to be 30% above the monthly average, whereas September tends to be 10% below it. Also, the seasonal indexes in a multiplicative model typically average to 1. Software packages usually ensure that this happens.

12.9.1 Winters' Exponential Smoothing Model

We now turn to Winters' exponential smoothing model. It is very similar to Holt's model—it again has level and trend terms and corresponding smoothing constants α and β—but it also has seasonal indexes and a corresponding smoothing constant γ (gamma). This new smoothing constant controls how quickly the method reacts to observed changes in the seasonality pattern. If γ is small, the method reacts slowly. If it is large, the method reacts more quickly. As with Holt's model, there are equations for updating the level and trend terms, and there is one extra equation for updating the seasonal indexes. For completeness, we list these equations, but they are clearly too complex for hand calculation and are best left to the software. In Equation (12.21), S_t refers to the multiplicative seasonal index for period t. In equations (12.19), (12.21), and (12.22), M refers to the number of seasons ($M = 4$ for quarterly data, $M = 12$ for monthly data).

Formulas for Winters' Exponential Smoothing Model

$$L_t = \alpha \frac{Y_t}{S_{t-M}} + (1 - \alpha)(L_{t-1} + T_{t-1}) \qquad \textbf{(13.19)}$$

$$T_t = \beta(L_t - L_{t-1}) + (1 - \beta)T_{t-1} \qquad \textbf{(13.20)}$$

$$S_t = \gamma \frac{Y_t}{L_t} + (1 - \gamma)S_{t-M} \qquad \textbf{(13.21)}$$

$$F_{t+k} = (L_t + kT_t)S_{t+k-M} \qquad \textbf{(13.22)}$$

To see how the forecasting in Equation (12.22) works, suppose you have observed data through June and you want a forecast for the coming September, that is, a three-month-ahead forecast. (In this case t refers to June and $t + k = t + 3$ refers to September.) The method first adds 3 times the current trend term to the current level. This gives a forecast for September that would be appropriate if there were no seasonality. Next, it multiplies this forecast by the most recent estimate of September's seasonal index (the one from the previous September) to get the forecast for September. Of course, the software does all of the arithmetic, but this is basically what it is doing. We illustrate the method in the following example.

EXAMPLE | 12.7 QUARTERLY SOFT DRINK SALES

The data in the **Soft Drink Sales.xlsx** file represent quarterly sales (in millions of dollars) for a large soft drink company from quarter 1 of 1994 through quarter 4 of 2009. There has been an upward trend in sales during this period, and there is also a fairly regular seasonal pattern, as shown in Figure 12.50. Sales in the warmer quarters, 2 and 3, are consistently higher than in the colder quarters, 1 and 4. How well can Winters' method track this upward trend and seasonal pattern?

Figure 12.50

Time Series Graph of Soft Drink Sales

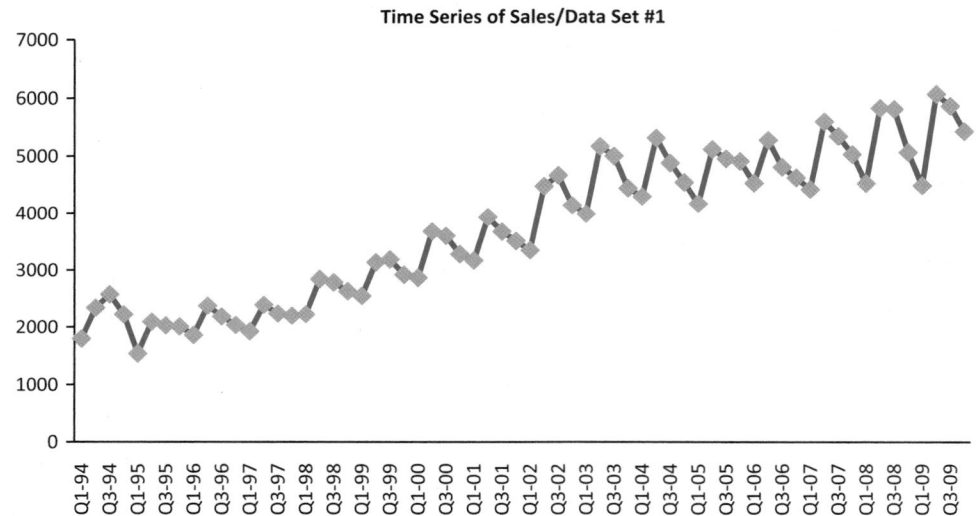

Objective To see how well Winters' method, with appropriate smoothing constants, can forecast the company's seasonal soft drink sales.

Solution

To use Winters' method with StatTools, you proceed exactly as with any of the other exponential smoothing methods. However, for a change (and because there are so many years of data), you can use StatTools's option of holding out some of the data for validation. Specifically, fill out the Time Scale tab in the Forecast dialog box as shown in Figure 12.51. Then fill in the Forecast Settings tab of this dialog box as shown in Figure 12.52, selecting Winters' method, basing the model on the data through Q4-2007, holding out eight quarters of data (Q1-2008 through Q4-2009), and forecasting four quarters into the future (all of 2010). Note that when you choose Winters' method in Figure 12.52, the Deseasonalize option in Figure 12.51 is automatically disabled. It wouldn't make sense to deseasonalize *and* use Winters' method; you do one or the other. Also, you can optimize the smoothing constants as is done here, but this is optional.

Figure 12.51
Time Scale Settings for Soft Drink Sales

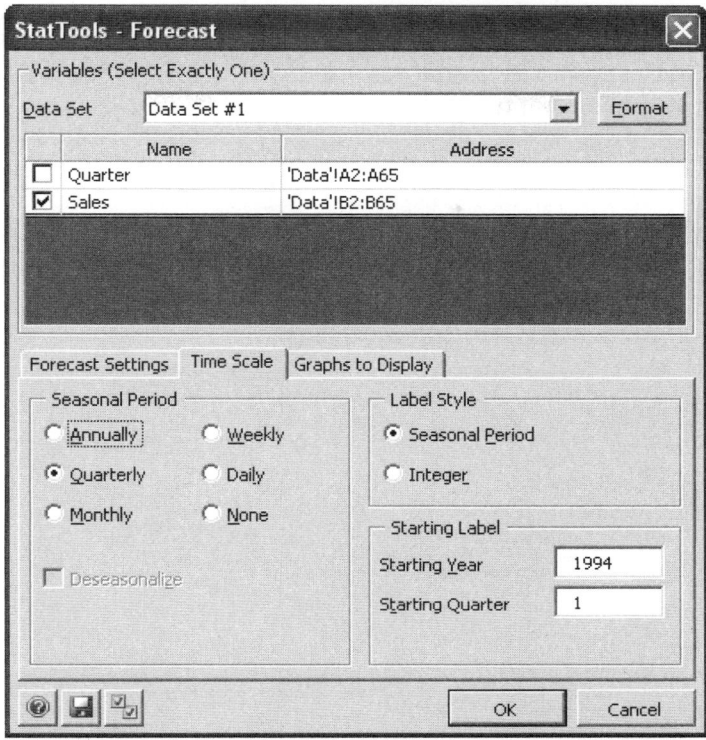

Figure 12.52
Forecast Settings for Soft Drink Sales

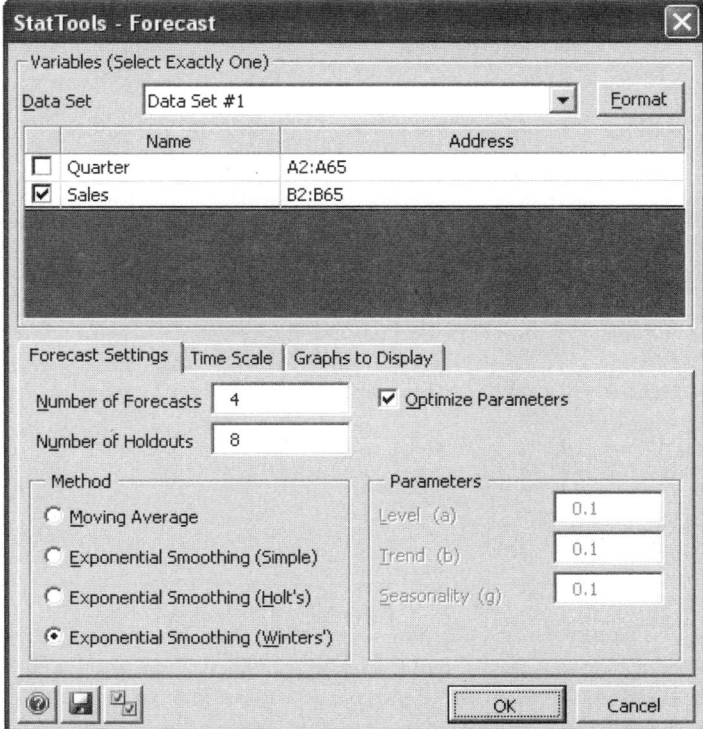

You can check that if three years of data are held out, the MAPE for the holdout period increases quite a lot. It is common for the fit to be considerably better in the estim-ation period than in the holdout period.

Parts of the output are shown in Figure 12.53. The following points are worth noting: (1) The optimal smoothing constants (those that minimize RMSE) are $\alpha = 1.0$, $\beta = 0.0$, and $\gamma = 0.0$. Intuitively, these mean that the method reacts immediately to changes in level, but it never reacts to changes in the trend or the seasonal pattern. (2) Aside from seasonality, the series is trending upward at a rate of 56.65 per quarter (see column D). This is the initial estimate of trend and, because β is 0, it never changes. (3) The seasonal pattern stays constant throughout this 14-year period. The seasonal indexes, shown in column E, are 0.88, 1.10, 1.05, and 0.96. For example, quarter 1 is 12% below the yearly average, and quarter 2 is 10% above the yearly average. (4) The forecast series tracks the actual series quite well during the non-holdout period. For example, MAPE is 3.86%, meaning that the forecasts are off by about 4% on average. Surprisingly, MAPE for the holdout period is even lower, at 2.48%.

Figure 12.53   Output from Winters' Method for Soft Drink Sales

	A	B	C	D	E	F	G
8	Forecasting Constants (Optimized)						
9	Level (Alpha)	1.000					
10	Trend (Beta)	0.000					
11	Season (Gamma)	0.000					
12							
13		Estimation	Holdouts				
14	Winters' Exponential	Period	Period				
15	Mean Abs Err	123.23	123.65				
16	Root Mean Sq Err	166.71	158.65				
17	Mean Abs Per% Err	3.86%	2.48%				
41							
42	Forecasting Data	Sales	Level	Trend	Season	Forecast	Error
43	Q1-1994	1807.37	2052.06	56.65	0.88		
44	Q2-1994	2355.32	2136.61	56.65	1.10	2324.57	30.75
45	Q3-1994	2591.83	2461.52	56.65	1.05	2309.37	282.46
46	Q4-1994	2236.39	2320.05	56.65	0.96	2427.36	-190.97
47	Q1-1995	1549.14	1758.87	56.65	0.88	2093.30	-544.16
48	Q2-1995	2105.79	1910.25	56.65	1.10	2001.37	104.42
49	Q3-1995	2041.32	1938.69	56.65	1.05	2071.03	-29.71
50	Q4-1995	2021.01	2096.62	56.65	0.96	1923.38	97.63
92	Q2-2006	5284.71	4793.98	56.65	1.10	5748.01	-463.30
93	Q3-2006	4817.43	4575.22	56.65	1.05	5107.42	-289.99
94	Q4-2006	4634.50	4807.88	56.65	0.96	4464.83	169.67
95	Q1-2007	4431.36	5031.31	56.65	0.88	4284.47	146.89
96	Q2-2007	5602.21	5082.00	56.65	1.10	5608.78	-6.57
97	Q3-2007	5349.85	5080.87	56.65	1.05	5410.69	-60.84
98	Q4-2007	5036.00	5224.40	56.65	0.96	4952.25	83.75
99	Q1-2008	4534.61				4651.32	-116.71
100	Q2-2008	5836.17				5884.09	-47.92
101	Q3-2008	5818.28				5679.93	138.35
102	Q4-2008	5070.42				5254.42	-184.00
103	Q1-2009	4497.47				4850.90	-353.43
104	Q2-2009	6075.52				6133.88	-58.36
105	Q3-2009	5868.67				5918.52	-49.85
106	Q4-2009	5432.24				5472.85	-40.61
107	Q1-2010					5050.47	
108	Q2-2010					6383.67	
109	Q3-2010					6157.11	
110	Q4-2010					5691.27	

The plot of the forecasts superimposed on the original series, shown in Figure 12.54, indicates that Winters' method clearly picks up the seasonal pattern and the upward trend and projects both of these into the future. In later examples, we will investigate whether other seasonal forecasting methods can do this well.

Figure 12.54

Graph of Forecasts from Winters' Method

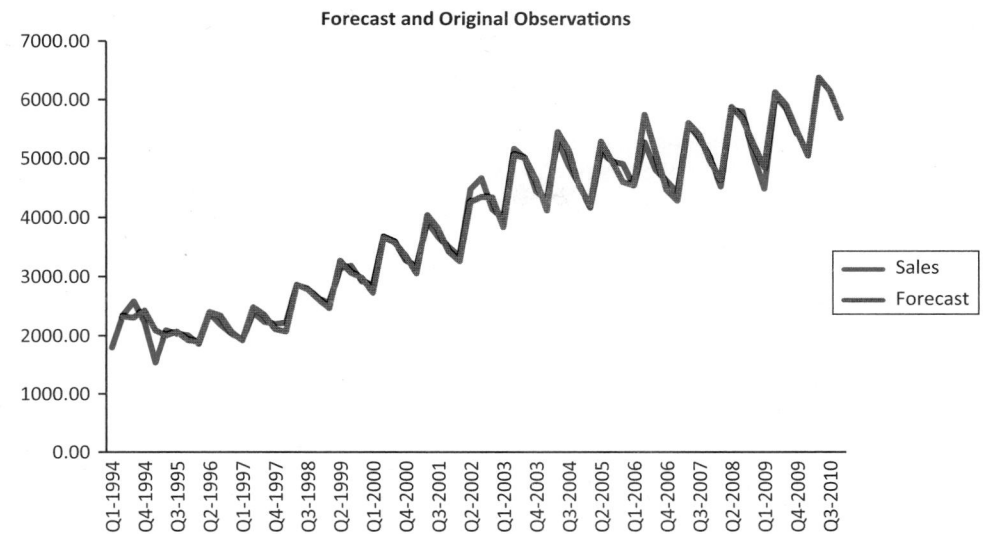

One final comment is that you are not obligated to find the *optimal* smoothing constants. Some analysts suggest using more "typical" values such as $\alpha = \beta = 0.2$ and $\gamma = 0.5$. (It is customary to choose γ larger than α and β because each season's seasonal index gets updated only once per year.) To see how these smoothing constants affect the results, you can substitute their values in the range B9:B11 of Figure 12.53. As expected, MAE, RMSE, and MAPE all get somewhat worse (they increase to 185, 236, and 5.78%, respectively, for the estimation period), but a plot of the forecasts superimposed on the original sales data still indicates a very good fit. ∎

The three exponential smoothing methods we have examined are not the only ones available. For example, there are linear and quadratic models available in some software packages. These are somewhat similar to Holt's model except that they use only a single smoothing constant. There are also adaptive exponential smoothing models, where the smoothing constants themselves are allowed to change over time. Although these more complex models have been studied thoroughly in the academic literature and are used by some practitioners, they typically offer only marginal gains in forecast accuracy over the models we have examined.

12.9.2 Deseasonalizing: The Ratio-to-Moving-Averages Method

You have probably seen references to time series data that have been **deseasonalized**. (Web sites often use the abbreviations SA and NSA for seasonally adjusted and nonseasonally adjusted.) The reason why data are often published in deseasonalized form is that readers can then spot trends more easily. For example, if you see a time series of sales that has not been deseasonalized, and it shows a large increase from November to December, you might not be sure whether this represents a real increase in sales or a seasonal phenomenon (Christmas sales). However, if this increase is really just a seasonal effect, the deseasonalized version of the series will show no such increase in sales.

Government economists and statisticians have a variety of sophisticated methods for deseasonalizing time series data, but they are typically variations of the **ratio-to-moving-averages** method described here. This method is applicable when seasonality is multiplicative, as described in the previous section. The goal is to find the seasonal indexes, which can then be used to deseasonalize the data. For example, if the estimated index for June is 1.3, this means that June's values are typically about 30% larger than the average for all months. Therefore, June's value is *divided* by 1.3 to obtain the (smaller) deseasonalized value. Similarly, if February's index is 0.85, then February's values are 15% below the average for all months, so February's value is divided by 0.85 to obtain the (larger) deseasonalized value.

To **deseasonalize** an observation (assuming a multiplicative model of seasonality), *divide* it by the appropriate seasonal index.

To find the seasonal index for June 2009 (or any other month) in the first place, you essentially divide June's observation by the average of the 12 observations surrounding June. (This is the reason for the term *ratio* in the name of the method.) There is one minor problem with this approach. June 2009 is not exactly in the middle of any 12-month sequence. If you use the 12 months from January 2009 to December 2009, June 2009 is in the *first* half of the sequence; if you use the 12 months from December 2008 to November 2009, June 2009 is in the *last* half of the sequence. Therefore, you can compromise by averaging the January-to-December and December-to-November averages. This is called a *centered* average. Then the seasonal index for June is June's observation divided by this centered average. The following equation shows more specifically how it works.

$$\text{Jun2009 index} = \frac{\text{June2009}}{\left(\dfrac{\text{Dec2010} + \cdots + \text{Nov2009}}{12} + \dfrac{\text{Jan2009} + \cdots + \text{Dec2009}}{12} \right)/2}$$

The only remaining question is how to combine all of the indexes for any specific month such as June. After all, if the series covers several years, the procedure produces several June indexes, one for each year. The usual way to combine them is to average them. This single average index for June is then used to deseasonalize *all* of the June observations.

Once the seasonal indexes are obtained, each observation is divided by its seasonal index to deseasonalize the data. The deseasonalized data can then be forecast by *any* of the methods we have described (other than Winters' method, which wouldn't make much sense). For example, Holt's method or the moving averages method could be used to forecast the deseasonalized data. Finally, the forecasts are "reseasonalized" by *multiplying* them by the seasonal indexes.

As this description suggests, the method is not meant for hand calculations. However, it is straightforward to implement in StatTools, as we illustrate in the following example.

EXAMPLE | **12.7 QUARTERLY SOFT DRINK SALES (CONTINUED)**

We return to the soft drink sales data. (See the file **Soft Drink Sales.xlsx**.) Is it possible to obtain the same forecast accuracy with the ratio-to-moving-averages method as with Winters' method?

Objective   To use the ratio-to-moving-averages method to deseasonalize the soft drink data and then forecast the deseasonalized data.

Solution

The answer to this question depends on which forecasting method is used to forecast the *deseasonalized* data. The ratio-to-moving-averages method only provides a means for deseasonalizing the data and providing seasonal indexes. Beyond this, any method can be used to forecast the deseasonalized data, and some methods typically work better than others. For this example, we actually compared two possibilities: the moving averages method with a span of four quarters, and Holt's exponential smoothing method optimized, but the results are shown only for the latter. Because the deseasonalized series still has a clear upward trend, Holt's method should do well, and the moving averages forecasts should tend to lag behind the trend. This is exactly what occurred. For example, the values of MAPE for the two methods are 6.11% (moving averages) and 3.86% (Holt's). (To make a fair comparison with the Winters' method output for these data, an eight-quarter holdout period was again used). The MAPE values reported are for the non-holdout period.)

To implement this latter method in StatTools, proceed exactly as before, but this time check the Deseasonalize option in the Time Scale tab of the Forecast dialog box. (See Figure 12.55.) Note that when the Holt's option is checked, this Deseasonalize option is enabled. When you check this option, you get a larger selection of optional charts in the Graphs to Display tab. You can ask to see charts of the deseasonalized data and/or the original "reseasonalized" data.

Figure 12.55
Checking the
Deseasonalizing
Option

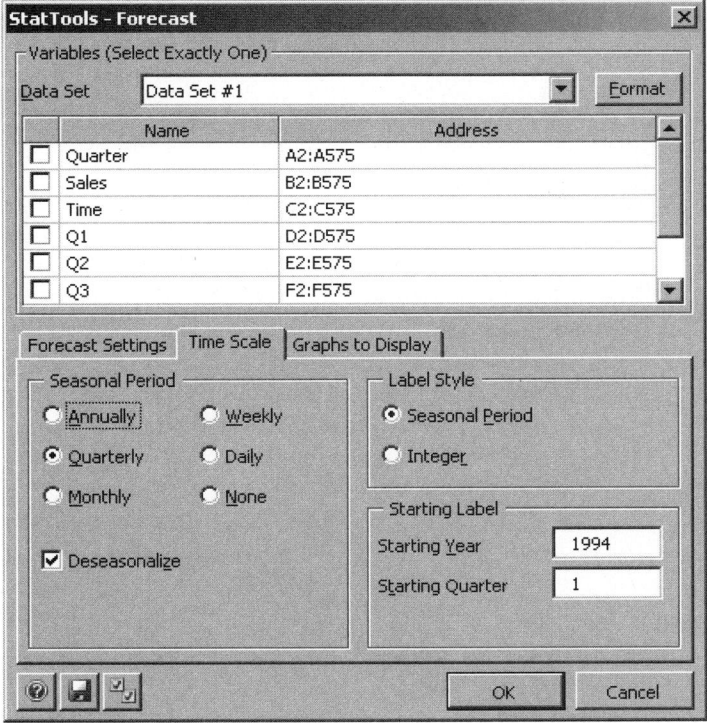

Selected outputs are shown in Figures 12.56 through 12.59. Figures 12.56 and 12.57 show the numerical output. In particular, Figure 12.57 shows the seasonal indexes from the ratio-to-moving averages method in column C. These are virtually identical to the seasonal indexes found with Winters' method, although the methods are mathematically different. Column D contains the deseasonalized sales (column B divided by column C), columns E through H implement Holt's method on the deseasonalized data, and columns I and J are the "reseasonalized" forecasts and errors.

Figure 12.56

Summary Measures
for Forecast Errors

	A	B	C	D	E
8	**Forecasting Constants (Optimized)**				
9	Level (Alpha)	1.000			
10	Trend (Beta)	0.000			
11					
12		Estimation	Holdouts	Deseason	Deseason
13	**Holt's Exponential**	Period	Period	Estimate	Holdouts
14	Mean Abs Err	123.23	123.65	124.26	130.24
15	Root Mean Sq Err	166.71	158.65	169.38	173.56
16	Mean Abs Per% Err	3.86%	2.48%	3.86%	2.48%

Figure 12.57   Ratio-to-Moving-Averages Output

	A	B	C	D	E	F	G	H	I	J
61			Season	Deseason	Deseason	Deseason	Deseason	Deseason	Season	Season
62	**Forecasting Data**	Sales	Index	Sales	Level	Trend	Forecast	Errors	Forecast	Errors
63	Q1-1994	1807.37	0.88	2052.06	2052.06	56.65				
64	Q2-1994	2355.32	1.10	2136.61	2136.61	56.65	2108.71	27.89	2324.57	30.75
65	Q3-1994	2591.83	1.05	2461.52	2461.52	56.65	2193.26	268.26	2309.37	282.46
66	Q4-1994	2236.39	0.96	2320.05	2320.05	56.65	2518.17	-198.11	2427.36	-190.97
67	Q1-1995	1549.14	0.88	1758.87	1758.87	56.65	2376.70	-617.83	2093.30	-544.16
68	Q2-1995	2105.79	1.10	1910.25	1910.25	56.65	1815.52	94.73	2001.37	104.42
69	Q3-1995	2041.32	1.05	1938.69	1938.69	56.65	1966.90	-28.21	2071.03	-29.71
70	Q4-1995	2021.01	0.96	2096.62	2096.62	56.65	1995.33	101.28	1923.38	97.63
112	Q2-2006	5284.71	1.10	4793.98	4793.98	56.65	5214.26	-420.28	5748.01	-463.30
113	Q3-2006	4817.43	1.05	4575.22	4575.22	56.65	4850.63	-275.41	5107.42	-289.99
114	Q4-2006	4634.50	0.96	4807.88	4807.88	56.65	4631.86	176.01	4464.83	169.67
115	Q1-2007	4431.36	0.88	5031.31	5031.31	56.65	4864.53	166.78	4284.47	146.89
116	Q2-2007	5602.21	1.10	5082.00	5082.00	56.65	5087.96	-5.96	5608.78	-6.57
117	Q3-2007	5349.85	1.05	5080.87	5080.87	56.65	5138.64	-57.78	5410.69	-60.84
118	Q4-2007	5036.00	0.96	5224.40	5224.40	56.65	5137.52	86.88	4952.25	83.75
119	Q1-2008	4534.61	0.88	5148.54			5281.05	-132.51	4651.32	-116.71
120	Q2-2008	5836.17	1.10	5294.23			5337.70	-43.47	5884.09	-47.92
121	Q3-2008	5818.28	1.05	5525.74			5394.35	131.40	5679.93	138.35
122	Q4-2008	5070.42	0.96	5260.11			5451.00	-190.89	5254.42	-184.00
123	Q1-2009	4497.47	0.88	5106.37			5507.64	-401.27	4850.90	-353.43
124	Q2-2009	6075.52	1.10	5511.35			5564.29	-52.94	6133.88	-58.36
125	Q3-2009	5868.67	1.05	5573.60			5620.94	-47.34	5918.52	-49.85
126	Q4-2009	5432.24	0.96	5635.46			5677.59	-42.13	5472.85	-40.61
127	Q1-2010		0.88				5734.24		5050.47	
128	Q2-2010		1.10				5790.89		6383.67	
129	Q3-2010		1.05				5847.54		6157.11	
130	Q4-2010		0.96				5904.19		5691.27	

Figure 12.58

Forecast Graph of
Deseasonalized
Series

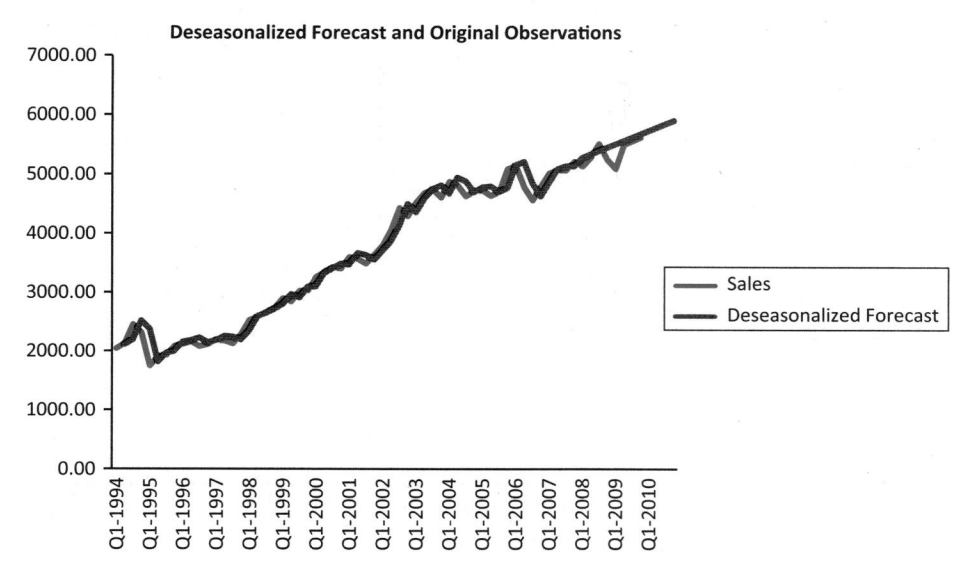

Deseasonalized Forecast and Original Observations

Figure 12.59

Forecast Graph of
Reseasonalized
(Original) Series

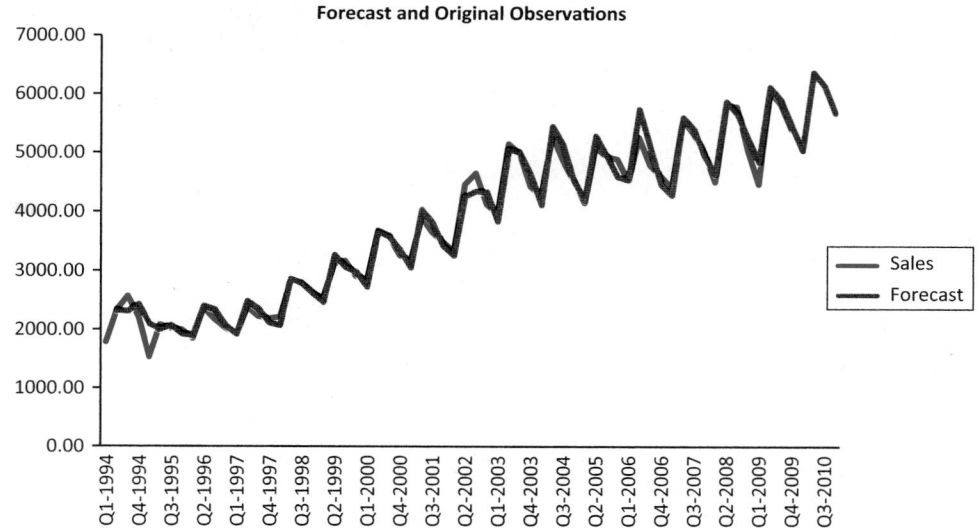

The deseasonalized data, with forecasts superimposed, appear in Figure 12.58. Here you see only the smooth upward trend with no seasonality, which Holt's method is able to track very well. Then Figure 12.59 shows the results of reseasonalizing. Again, the forecasts track the actual sales data very well. In fact, you can see that the summary measures of forecast errors (in Figure 12.56, range B14:B16) are quite comparable to those from Winters' method. The reason is that both arrive at virtually the same seasonal pattern. ∎

12.9.3 Estimating Seasonality with Regression

We now examine a regression approach to forecasting seasonal data that uses dummy variables for the seasons. Depending on how you write the regression equation, you can create either an additive or a multiplicative seasonal model.

As an example, suppose that the data are quarterly data with a possible linear trend. Then you can create dummy variables Q_1, Q_2, and Q_3 for the first three quarters (using quarter 4 as the reference quarter) and estimate the additive equation

$$\text{Forecast } Y_t = a + bt + b_1 Q_1 + b_2 Q_2 + b_3 Q_3$$

Then the coefficients of the dummy variables, b_1, b_2 and b_3, indicate how much each quarter differs from the reference quarter, quarter 4, and the coefficient b represents the trend.

For example, if the estimated equation is

$$\text{Forecast } Y_t = 130 + 25t + 15Q_1 + 5Q_2 - 20Q_3$$

the average increase from one quarter to the next is 25 (the coefficient of t). This is the trend effect. However, quarter 1 averages 15 units higher than quarter 4, quarter 2 averages 5 units higher than quarter 4, and quarter 3 averages 20 units lower than quarter 4. These coefficients indicate the seasonality effect.

As discussed in Chapter 10, it is also possible to estimate a *multiplicative* model using dummy variables for seasonality (and possibly time for trend). Then you would estimate the equation

$$\text{Forecast } Y_t = ae^{bt}e^{b_1 Q_1}e^{b_2 Q_2}e^{b_3 Q_3}$$

or, after taking logs,

$$\text{Forecast LN } Y_t = \text{LN } a + bt + b_1 Q_1 + b_2 Q_2 + b_3 Q_3$$

One advantage of this approach is that it provides a model with *multiplicative* seasonal factors. It is also fairly easy to interpret the regression output, as illustrated in the following continuation of the soft drink sales example.

| EXAMPLE | 12.7 QUARTERLY SOFT DRINK SALES (CONTINUED) |

Returning to the soft drink sales data (see the file **Soft Drink Sales.xlsx**), does a regression approach provide forecasts that are as accurate as those provided by the other seasonal methods in this chapter?

Objective To use a multiplicative regression equation, with dummy variables for seasons and a time variable for trend, to forecast soft drink sales.

Solution

We illustrate the multiplicative approach, although an additive approach is also possible. Figure 12.60 illustrates the data setup. Besides the Sales and Time variables, you need to create dummy variables for three of the four quarters and a Log(Sales) variable. You can then use multiple regression, with Log(Sales) as the dependent variable, and Time, Q1, Q2, and Q3 as the explanatory variables.

Figure 12.60

Data Setup for
Multiplicative Model
with Dummies

	A	B	C	D	E	F	G
1	Quarter	Sales	Time	Q1	Q2	Q3	Log(Sales)
2	Q1-94	1807.37	1	1	0	0	7.499628
3	Q2-94	2355.32	2	0	1	0	7.7644319
4	Q3-94	2591.83	3	0	0	1	7.8601195
5	Q4-94	2236.39	4	0	0	0	7.7126182
6	Q1-95	1549.14	5	1	0	0	7.3454552
7	Q2-95	2105.79	6	0	1	0	7.652446
8	Q3-95	2041.32	7	0	0	1	7.6213519
9	Q4-95	2021.01	8	0	0	0	7.6113527
10	Q1-96	1870.46	9	1	0	0	7.5339397
11	Q2-96	2390.56	10	0	1	0	7.7792829
12	Q3-96	2198.03	11	0	0	1	7.6953168
13	Q4-96	2046.83	12	0	0	0	7.6240475
14	Q1-97	1934.19	13	1	0	0	7.5674439
15	Q2-97	2406.41	14	0	1	0	7.7858913

The regression output appears in Figure 12.61. (Again, to make a fair comparison with previous methods, the regression is based only on the data through quarter 4 of 2007. That is, the last eight quarters are again held out. This means that the StatTools data set should extend only through row 57.) Of particular interest are the coefficients of the explanatory variables. Recall that for a log-dependent variable, these coefficients can be interpreted as *percentage* changes in the original sales variable. Specifically, the coefficient of Time means that deseasonalized sales increase by about 1.9% per quarter. Also, the coefficients of Q1, Q2, and Q3 mean that sales in quarters 1, 2, and 3 are, respectively, about 9.0% below, 14.0% above, and 9.1% above sales in the reference quarter, quarter 4. This pattern is quite comparable to the pattern of seasonal indexes you saw in previous models for these data.

Figure 12.61 Regression Output for Multiplicative Model

	A	B	C	D	E	F	G
7		Multiple	R-Square	Adjusted	StErr of		
8	Summary	R		R-Square	Estimate		
9		0.9628	0.9270	0.9218	0.102		
10							
11		Degrees of	Sum of	Mean of	F-Ratio	p-Value	
12	ANOVA Table	Freedom	Squares	Squares			
13	Explained	4	7.465	1.866	177.8172	< 0.0001	
14	Unexplained	56	0.588	0.010			
15							
16		Coefficient	Standard	t-Value	p-Value	Confidence Interval 95%	
17	Regression Table		Error			Lower	Upper
18	Constant	7.510	0.036	210.8236	< 0.0001	7.439	7.581
19	Time	0.019	0.001	25.9232	< 0.0001	0.018	0.021
20	Q1	-0.090	0.037	-2.4548	0.0172	-0.164	-0.017
21	Q2	0.140	0.037	3.7289	0.0005	0.065	0.215
22	Q3	0.091	0.037	2.4449	0.0177	0.017	0.166

To compare the forecast accuracy of this method to earlier models, you must perform several steps manually. (See Figure 12.62 for reference.) First, calculate the forecasts in column H by entering the formula

=EXP(Regression!$B$18+MMULT(Data!C2:F2,Regression!$B$19:$B$22))

in cell H2 and copying it down. (This formula assumes the regression output is in a sheet named Regression. It uses Excel's MMULT function to sum the products of explanatory values and regression coefficients. You can replace this by "writing out" the sum of products if you like. The formula then takes EXP of the resulting sum to convert the log sales value back to the original sales units.) Next, calculate the absolute errors, squared errors, and absolute percentage errors in columns I, J, and K, and summarize them in the usual way, both for the estimation period and the holdout period, in columns N and O.

Figure 12.62 Forecast Errors and Summary Measures

	A	B	C	D	E	F	G	H	I	J	K	L	M	N	O
1	Quarter	Sales	Time	Q1	Q2	Q3	Log(Sales)	Forecast	SqError	AbsError	PctAbsError		Error measures		
2	Q1-94	1807.37	1	1	0	0	7.499628	1701.137	11285.37	106.2326	0.05877746			Estimation	Holdout
3	Q2-94	2355.32	2	0	1	0	7.7644319	2182.866	29740.49	172.4543	0.07321906		RMSE	337.09	754.57
4	Q3-94	2591.83	3	0	0	1	7.8601195	2120.895	221779.5	470.9347	0.18169969		MAE	276.40	732.28
5	Q4-94	2236.39	4	0	0	0	7.7126182	1973.262	69236.44	263.1282	0.11765755		MAPE	8.05%	13.74%
6	Q1-95	1549.14	5	1	0	0	7.3454552	1837.876	83368.58	288.7362	0.18638482				
7	Q2-95	2105.79	6	0	1	0	7.652446	2358.326	63774.52	252.5362	0.11992467				
8	Q3-95	2041.32	7	0	0	1	7.6213519	2291.375	62527.28	250.0545	0.1224965				
9	Q4-95	2021.01	8	0	0	0	7.6113527	2131.874	12290.87	110.8642	0.05485584				
10	Q1-96	1870.46	9	1	0	0	7.5339397	1985.606	13258.63	115.1461	0.06156034				
11	Q2-96	2390.56	10	0	1	0	7.7792829	2547.89	24752.83	157.3303	0.06581317				

Note that these summary measures are considerably larger for this regression model than for the previous seasonality models, especially in the holdout period. You can get some idea why the holdout period does so poorly by looking at the plot of observations versus forecasts in Figure 12.63. The multiplicative regression model with Time included really implies *exponential* growth (as in section 12.4.2), with seasonality superimposed. However, this company's sales growth tapered off in the last couple of years and did not keep up with the exponential growth curve. In short, the dummy variables do a good job of tracking seasonality, but the underlying exponential trend curve outpaces actual sales. It is reasonable to conclude that this regression model is *not* as good for forecasting this company's sales as Winters' method or Holt's method on the deseasonalized data.

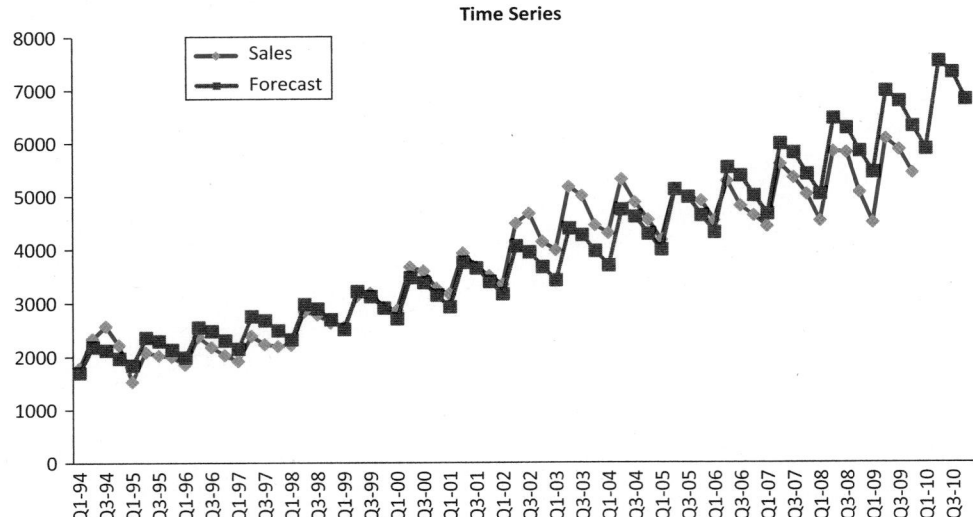

This method of detecting seasonality by using dummy variables in a regression equation is always an option. The other variables included in the regression equation could be time *t*, lagged versions of Y_t, and/or current or lagged versions of other explanatory variables. These variables would capture any time series behavior other than seasonality. Just remember that there is always one less dummy variable than the number of seasons. If the data are quarterly, then three dummies are needed; if the data are monthly, then 11 dummies are needed. If the coefficients of any of these dummies turn out to be statistically insignificant, they can be omitted from the equation. Then the omitted terms are effectively combined with the reference season. For example, if the Q_1 term were omitted, then quarters 1 and 4 would essentially be combined and treated as the reference season, and the other two seasons would be compared to them through their dummy variable coefficients. ■

PROBLEMS

Level A

51. The University Credit Union is open Monday through Saturday. Winters' method is being used (with $\alpha = \beta = \gamma = 0.5$) to predict the number of customers entering the bank each day. After incorporating the arrivals on Monday, October 16, the seasonal indexes are: Monday, 0.90; Tuesday, 0.70; Wednesday, 0.80; Thursday, 1.1; Friday, 1.2; Saturday, 1.3. Also, the current estimates of level and trend are 200 and 1. On Tuesday, October 17, 182 customers enter the bank. At the close of business on October 17, forecast the number of customers who will enter the bank on each of the next six business days.

52. A local bank is using Winters' method with $\alpha = 0.2$, $\beta = 0.1$, and $\gamma = 0.5$ to forecast the number of customers served each day. The bank is open Monday through Friday. At the end of the previous week, the following seasonal indexes have been estimated: Monday, 0.80; Tuesday, 0.90; Wednesday, 0.95; Thursday, 1.10; Friday, 1.25. Also, the current estimates of level and trend are 20 and 1. After observing that 30 customers are served by the bank on this Monday, forecast the number of customers who will be served on each of the next five business days.

53. Suppose that Winters' method is used to forecast quarterly U.S. retail sales (in billions of dollars). At the end of the first quarter of 2010, the seasonal indexes are: quarter 1, 0.90; quarter 2, 0.95; quarter 3, 0.95; quarter 4, 1.20. Also, the current estimates of level and trend are 300 and 30. During the second quarter of 2010, retail sales are $360 billion. Assume $\alpha = 0.2$, $\beta = 0.4$, and $\gamma = 0.5$.

a. At the end of the second quarter of 2010, develop a forecast for retail sales during the third and fourth quarters of 2010.

b. At the end of the second quarter of 2010, develop a forecast for the first and second quarter of 2011.

54. The file **P02_55.xlsx** contains monthly retail sales of beer, wine, and liquor at U.S. liquor stores.

a. Is seasonality present in these data? If so, characterize the seasonality pattern and then deseasonalize this time series using the ratio-to-moving-average method.

b. If you decided to deseasonalize this time series in part **a**, forecast the deseasonalized data for each month of the next year using the moving average method with an appropriate span.

c. Does Holt's exponential smoothing method, with optimal smoothing constants, outperform the moving average method employed in part **b**? Demonstrate why or why not.

55. Continuing the previous problem, how do your responses to the questions change if you employ Winters' method to handle seasonality in this time series? Explain. Which forecasting method do you prefer, Winters' method or one of the methods used in the previous problem? Defend your choice.

56. The file **P12_56.xlsx** contains monthly time series data for total U.S. retail sales of building materials (which includes retail sales of building materials, hardware and garden supply stores, and mobile home dealers).

a. Is seasonality present in these data? If so, characterize the seasonality pattern and then deseasonalize this time series using the ratio-to-moving-average method.

b. If you decided to deseasonalize this time series in part **a**, forecast the deseasonalized data for each month of the next year using the moving average method with an appropriate span.

c. Does Holt's exponential smoothing method, with optimal smoothing constants, outperform the moving average method employed in part **b**? Demonstrate why or why not.

57. The file **P12_57.xlsx** consists of the monthly retail sales levels of U.S. gasoline service stations.

a. Is there a seasonal pattern in these data? If so, how do you explain this seasonal pattern? Also, if necessary, deseasonalize these data using the ratio-to-moving-average method.

b. Forecast this time series for the first four months of the next year using the most appropriate method for these data. Defend your choice of forecasting method.

58. The number of employees on the payroll at a food processing plant is recorded at the start of each month. These data are provided in the file **P12_03.xlsx**.

a. Is there a seasonal pattern in these data? If so, how do you explain this seasonal pattern? Also, if necessary, deseasonalize these data using the ratio-to-moving-average method.

b. Forecast this time series for the first four months of the next year using the most appropriate method. Defend your choice of forecasting method.

59. The file **P12_59.xlsx** contains total monthly U.S. retail sales data. Compare the effectiveness of Winters' method with that of the ratio-to-moving-average method in deseasonalizing this time series. Using the deseasonalized time series generated by each of these two methods, forecast U.S. retail sales with the most appropriate method. Defend your choice of forecasting method.

60. Suppose that a time series consisting of six years (2005−2010) of quarterly data exhibits obvious seasonality. In fact, assume that the seasonal indexes turn out to be 0.75, 1.45, 1.25, and 0.55.

a. If the last four observations of the series (the four quarters of 2010) are 2502, 4872, 4269, and 1924, calculate the deseasonalized values for the four quarters of 2010.

b. Suppose that a plot of the deseasonalized series shows an upward linear trend, except for some random noise. Therefore, you estimate a linear regression equation for this series versus time and obtain the following equation:

Predicted deseasonalized value $= 2250 + 51$Quarter

Here the time variable Quarter is coded so that Quarter $= 1$ corresponds to first quarter 2005, Quarter $= 24$ corresponds to fourth quarter 2010, and the others fall in between. Forecast the actual (not deseasonalized) values for the four quarters of 2011.

61. The file **P12_61.xlsx** contains monthly data on the number of nonfarm hires in the U.S. since 2000.

a. What evidence is there that seasonality is important in this series? Find seasonal indexes (by any method you like) and state briefly what they mean.

b. Forecast the next 12 months by using a linear trend on the seasonally adjusted data. State briefly the steps you use to obtain this type of forecast. Then give the final RMSE, MAPE, and forecast for the next month. Show numerically how you could replicate this forecast (i.e., explain in words how the package uses its estimated model to get the next month's forecast).

62. Quarterly sales for a department store over a six-year period are given in the file **P12_62.xlsx**.
  a. Use multiple regression to develop an equation that can be used to predict future quarterly sales. (*Hint:* Use dummy variables for the quarters and a time variable for the quarter number, 1 to 24.)
  b. Letting Y_t be the sales during quarter t, discuss how to estimate the following equation for this series.

$$Y_t = ab_1^t b_2^{X_1} b_3^{X_2} b_4^{X_3}$$

Here X_1 is a dummy for first quarters, X_2 is a dummy for second quarters, and X_3 is a dummy for third quarters.
  c. Interpret the results from part **b**.
  d. Which model appears to yield better predictions for sales, the one in part **a** or the one in part **b**?

63. A shipping company is attempting to determine how its shipping costs for a month depend on the number of units shipped during a month. The number of units shipped and total shipping cost for the last 15 months are given in the file **P12_63.xlsx**.
  a. Determine a relationship between units shipped and monthly shipping cost.
  b. Plot the errors for the predictions in order of time sequence. Is there any unusual pattern?
  c. It turns out that there was a trucking strike during months 11 through 15, and you believe that this might have influenced shipping costs. How can the answer to part **a** be modified to account for the effect of the strike? After accounting for this effect, does the unusual pattern in part **b** disappear?

Level B

64. Consider a monthly series of air conditioner (AC) sales. In the discussion of Winters' method, a monthly seasonality of 0.80 for January, for example, means that during January, AC sales are expected to be 80% of the sales during an average month. An alternative approach to modeling seasonality, called an *additive model*, is to let the seasonality factor for each month represent how far above average AC sales are during the current month. For instance, if $S_{Jan} = -50$, then AC sales during January are expected to be 50 fewer than AC sales during an average month. (This is 50 ACs, not 50%.) Similarly, if $S_{July} = 90$, then AC sales during July are expected to be 90 more than AC sales during an average month. Let

S_t = Seasonality for month t after observing month t demand

L_t = Estimate of level after observing month t demand

T_t = Estimate of trend after observing month t demand

Then the Winters' method equations given in the text should be modified as follows:

$$L_t = \alpha(I) + (1 - \alpha)(L_{t-1} + T_{t-1})$$
$$T_t = \beta(L_t - L_{t-1}) + (1 - \beta)T_{t-1}$$
$$S_t = \gamma(II) + (1 - \gamma)S_{t-12}$$

  a. What should (*I*) and (*II*) be?
  b. Suppose that month 13 is January, $L_{12} = 30$, $T_{12} = -3$, $S_1 = -50$, and $S_2 = -20$. Let $\alpha = \gamma = \beta = 0.5$. Suppose 12 ACs are sold during month 13. At the end of month 13, what is the forecast for AC sales during month 14 using this additive model?

65. Winters' method assumes a multiplicative seasonality but an additive trend. For example, a trend of 5 means that the level will increase by five units per period. Suppose that there is actually a *multiplicative* trend. Then (ignoring seasonality) if the current estimate of the level is 50 and the current estimate of the trend is 1.2, the forecast of demand increases by 20% per period. So the forecast demand for the next period is 50(1.2) and forecast demand for two periods in the future is $50(1.2)^2$. If you want to use a multiplicative trend in Winters' method, you should use the following equations (assuming a period is a month):

$$L_t = \alpha\left(\frac{Y_t}{S_{t-12}}\right) + (1 - \alpha)(I)$$
$$T_t = \beta(II) + (I - \beta)T_{t-1}$$
$$S_t = \gamma\left(\frac{Y_t}{L_t}\right) + (1 - \gamma)S_{t-12}$$

  a. What should (*I*) and (*II*) be?
  b. Suppose that you are working with monthly data and month 12 is December, month 13 is January, and so on. Also, suppose that $L_{12} = 100$, $T_{12} = 1.2$, $S_1 = 0.90$, $S_2 = 0.70$, and $S_3 = 0.95$. If you have just observed $Y_{13} = 200$, what is the forecast for Y_{15} using $\alpha = \beta = \gamma = 0.5$ and a multiplicative trend?

66. Consider the file **P12_59.xlsx**, which contains total monthly U.S. retail sales data. Does a regression approach for estimating seasonality provide forecasts that are as accurate as those provided by (a) Winters' method and (b) the ratio-to-moving-average method? Compare the summary measures of forecast errors associated with each method for deseasonalizing this time series. Summarize the results of these comparisons.

67. The file **P12_56.xlsx** contains monthly time series data for total U.S. retail sales of building materials (which includes retail sales of building materials, hardware and garden supply stores, and mobile home dealers). Does a regression approach for estimating seasonality provide forecasts that are as accurate as those provided by (a) Winters' method and (b) the ratio-to-moving-average method? Compare the summary measures of forecast errors associated with each method for deseasonalizing the given time series. Summarize the results of these comparisons.

12.10 CONCLUSION

We have covered a lot of ground in this chapter. Because forecasting is such an important activity in business, it has received a tremendous amount of attention by both academics and practitioners. All of the methods discussed in this chapter—and more—are actually used, often on a day-to-day basis. There is really no point in arguing which of these methods is best. All of them have their strengths and weaknesses. The most important point is that when they are applied properly, they have all been found to be useful in real business situations.

Summary of Key Terms

Term	Explanation	Excel	Page	Equation
Extrapolation methods	Forecasting methods where only past values of a variable (and possibly time itself) are used to forecast future values		672	
Causal (or econometric) methods	Forecasting methods based on regression, where other time series variables are used as explanatory variables		672	
Trend	A systematic increase or decrease of a time series variable through time		674	
Seasonality	A regular pattern of ups and downs based onthe season of the year, typically months or quarters		675	
Cyclic variation	An irregular pattern of ups and downs caused by business cycles		675	
Noise (or random variation)	The unpredictable ups and downs of a time series variable		676	
Forecast error	The difference between the actual value and the forecast		677	
Mean absolute error (MAE)	The average of the absolute forecast errors	StatTools/ Time Series & Forecasting/ Forecast	677	12.2
Root mean square error (RMSE)	The square root of the average of the squared forecast errors	StatTools/ Time Series & Forecasting/ Forecast	677	12.3
Mean absolute percentage error (MAPE)	The average of the absolute percentage forecast errors	StatTools/ Time Series& Forecasting/ Forecast	677	12.4
Runs test	A test of whether the forecast errors are random noise	StatTools/ Time Series& Forecasting/ Runs Test for Randomness	681	
Autocorrelations	Correlations of a time series variable with lagged versions of itself	StatTools/ Time Series & Forecasting/ Autocorrelation	683	
Correlogram	A bar chart of autocorrelations at different lags	StatTools/ Time Series & Forecasting/ Autocorrelation	684	

(continued)

Summary of Key Terms *(Continued)*

Term	Explanation	Excel	Page	Equation
Linear trend model	A regression model where a time series variable changes by a constant amount each time period	StatTools/Regression & Classification/ Regression	687	12.6
Exponential trend model	A regression model where a time series variable changes by a constant percentage each time period	StatTools/ Regression & Classification/ Regression	690	12.7
Random walk model	A model indicating that the differences between adjacent observations of a time series variable are constant except for random noise		695	2.9−12.11
Autoregression model	A regression model where the only explanatory variables are lagged values of the dependent variable (and possibly other time series variables or their lags)	StatTools/ Regression & Classification/ Regression	699	
Moving averages model	A forecasting model where the average of several past observations is used to forecast the next observation	StatTools/ Time Series & Forecasting/ Forecast	704	
Span	The number of observations in each average of a moving averages model	StatTools/ Time Series & Forecasting/ Forecast	704	
Exponential smoothing models	A class of forecasting models where forecasts are based on weighted averages of previous observations, giving more weight to more recent observations	StatTools/ Time Series & Forecasting/ Forecast	710	
Smoothing constants	Constants between 0 and 1 that prescribe the weight attached to previous observations and hence the smoothness of the series of forecasts	StatTools/ Time Series & Forecasting/ Forecast	710	
Simple exponential smoothing	An exponential smoothing model useful for time series with no prominent trend or seasonality	StatTools/ Time Series & Forecasting/ Forecast	711	12.12−12.15
Holt's method	An exponential smoothing model useful for time series with trend but no seasonality	StatTools/ Time Series & Forecasting/ Forecast	715	12.16−12.18
Winters' method	An exponential smoothing model useful for time series with seasonality (and possibly trend)	StatTools/ Time Series & Forecasting/ Forecast	721	12.19−12.22
Deseasonalizing	A method for removing the seasonal component from a time series	StatTools/ Time Series& Forecasting/ Forecast	725	
Ratio-to-moving-averages method	A method for deseasonalizing a time series, so that some other method can then be used to forecast the deseasonalized series	StatTools/ Time Series & Forecasting/ Forecast	725	
Dummy variables for seasonality	A regression-based method for forecasting seasonality, where dummy variables are used for the seasons	StatTools/ Regression & Classification/ Regression	729	

PROBLEMS

Conceptual Questions

C.1. "A truly random series will likely have a very small number of runs." Is this statement true or false? Explain your choice.

C.2. Distinguish between a *correlation* and an *autocorrelation*. How are these measures similar? How are they different?

C.3. What is the relationship between the random walk model and an autoregression model, if any?

C.4. Under what conditions would you prefer a simple exponential smoothing model to the moving averages method for forecasting a time series?

C.5. Is it more appropriate to use an *additive* or a *multiplicative* model to forecast seasonal data? Summarize the difference(s) between these two types of seasonal models.

C.6. Explain why autocorrelations are so important in time series analysis. (Note that more advanced books on time series analysis investigate autocorrelations much more than we have done here.)

C.7. Suppose that monthly data on some time series variable exhibits a clear upward trend but no seasonality. You decide to use moving averages, with any appropriate span. Will there tend to be a systematic bias in your forecasts? Explain why or why not.

C.8. Suppose that monthly data on some time series variable exhibits obvious seasonality. Can you use moving averages, with any appropriate span, to track the seasonality well? Explain why or why not.

C.9. Suppose that quarterly data on some time series variable exhibits obvious seasonality, although the seasonal pattern varies somewhat from year to year. Which method do you believe will work best: Winters' method or regression with dummy variables for quarter (and possibly a time variable for trend)? Why?

C.10. Suppose you have three times series variables and you want to forecast the third one with an appropriate regression equation. You think that lagged values of all three variables might be useful explanatory variables in the regression equation. Explain how you could check the plausibility of this with appropriate correlations. If you find any fairly large correlations, explain how you would perform the appropriate regression with StatTools.

C.11. Most companies that use (any version of) exponential smoothing use fairly small smoothing constants such as 0.1 or 0.2. Explain why they don't tend to use larger values.

Level A

68. The file **P12_68.xlsx** contains monthly data on consumer revolving credit (in millions of dollars) through credit unions.
  a. Use these data to forecast consumer revolving credit through credit unions for the next 12 months. Do it in two ways. First, fit an exponential trend to the series. Second, use Holt's method with optimized smoothing constants.
  b. Which of these two methods appears to provide the best forecasts? Answer by comparing their MAPE values.

69. The file **P12_69.xlsx** contains net sales (in millions of dollars) for Procter & Gamble.
  a. Use these data to predict Procter & Gamble net sales for each of the next two years. You need consider only a linear and exponential trend, but you should justify the equation you choose.
  b. Use your answer from part **a** to explain how your predictions of Procter & Gamble net sales increase from year to year.
  c. Are there any outliers?
  d. You can be approximately 95% sure that Procter & Gamble net sales in the year following next year will be between what two values?

70. The file **P12_70.xlsx** lists annual revenues (in millions of dollars) for Nike. Forecast the company's revenue in each of the next two years with a linear or exponential trend. Are there any outliers in your predictions for the observed period?

71. The file **P11_44.xlsx** contains data on pork sales. Price is in dollars per hundred pounds sold, quantity sold is in billions of pounds, per capita income is in dollars, U.S. population is in millions, and GDP is in billions of dollars.
  a. Use these data to develop a regression equation that can be used to predict the quantity of pork sold during future periods. Is autocorrelation of residuals a problem?
  b. Suppose that during each of the next two quarters, price is $45, U.S. population is 240, GDP is 2620, and per capita income is $10,000. (All of these are expressed in the units described above.) Predict the quantity of pork sold during each of the next two quarters.
  c. Use Winters' method to develop a forecast of pork sales during the next two quarters. Does it appear to provide better (or different) predictions than the multiple regression in part **a**?

72. The file **P12_72.xlsx** contains data on a motel chain's revenue and advertising.
  a. Use these data and multiple regression to make predictions of the motel chain's revenues during

the next four quarters. Assume that advertising during each of the next four quarters is $50,000. (*Hint*: Try using advertising, lagged by one quarter, as an explanatory variable.)

   b. Use simple exponential smoothing to make predictions for the motel chain's revenues during the next four quarters.

   c. Use Holt's method to make forecasts for the motel chain's revenues during the next four quarters.

   d. Use Winters' method to determine predictions for the motel chain's revenues during the next four quarters.

   e. Which of these forecasting methods would you expect to be the most accurate for these data?

73. The file **P12_73.xlsx** contains data on monthly U.S. permits for new housing units (in thousands of houses).

   a. Using Winters' method, find values of α, β, and γ that yield an RMSE as small as possible. Does this method track the housing crash in recent years?

   b. Although we have not discussed autocorrelation for smoothing methods, good forecasts derived from smoothing methods should exhibit no substantial autocorrelation in their forecast errors. Is this true for the forecasts in part **a**?

   c. At the end of the observed period, what is the forecast of housing sales during the next few months?

74. Let Y_t be the sales during month t (in thousands of dollars) for a photography studio, and let P_t be the price charged for portraits during month t. The data are in the file **P11_45.xlsx**. Use regression to fit the following model to these data:

$$Y_t = a + b_1 Y_{t-1} + b_2 P_t + e_t$$

This equation indicates that last month's sales and the current month's price are explanatory variables. The last term, e_t, is an error term.

   a. If the price of a portrait during month 21 is $10, what would you predict for sales in month 21?

   b. Does there appear to be a problem with autocorrelation of the residuals?

Level B

75. The file **P12_75.xlsx** contains five years of monthly data for a particular company. The first variable is Time (1 to 60). The second variable, Sales1, contains data on sales of a product. Note that Sales1 increases linearly throughout the period, with only a minor amount of noise. (The third variable, Sales2, is discussed and used in the next problem.) For this problem use the Sales1 variable to see how the following forecasting methods are able to track a linear trend.

   a. Forecast this series with the moving average method with various spans such as 3, 6, and 12. What can you conclude?

   b. Forecast this series with simple exponential smoothing with various smoothing constants such as 0.1, 0.3, 0.5, and 0.7. What can you conclude?

   c. Now repeat part **b** with Holt's exponential smoothing method, again for various smoothing constants. Can you do significantly better than in parts **a** and **b**?

   d. What can you conclude from your findings in parts **a**, **b**, and **c** about forecasting this type of series?

76. The Sales2 variable in the file from the previous problem was created from the Sales1 variable by multiplying by monthly seasonal factors. Basically, the summer months are high and the winter months are low. This might represent the sales of a product that has a linear trend and seasonality.

   a. Repeat parts **a**, **b**, and **c** from the previous problem to see how well these forecasting methods can deal with trend *and* seasonality.

   b. Now use Winters' method, with various values of the three smoothing constants, to forecast the series. Can you do much better? Which smoothing constants work well?

   c. Use the ratio-to-moving-average method, where you first deseasonalize the series and then forecast (by any appropriate method) the deseasonalized series. Does this perform as well as, or better than, Winters' method?

   d. What can you conclude from your findings in parts **a**, **b**, and **c** about forecasting this type of series?

77. The file **P12_77.xlsx** contains monthly time series data on corporate bond yields. These are averages of daily figures, and each is expressed as an annual rate. The variables are:

   ■ Yield AAA: average yield on AAA bonds
   ■ Yield BAA: average yield on BAA bonds

If you examine either Yield variable, you will notice that the autocorrelations of the series are not only large for many lags, but that the lag 1 autocorrelation of the *differences* is significant. This is very common. It means that the series is not a random walk and that it is probably possible to provide a better forecast than the naive forecast from the random walk model. Here is the idea. The large lag 1 autocorrelation of the differences means that the differences are related to the first lag of the differences. This relationship can be estimated by creating the difference variable and a lag of it, then regressing the former on the latter, and finally using this information to forecast the original Yield variable.

   a. Verify that the autocorrelations are as described, and form the difference variable and the first lag of it. Call these DYield and L1DYield (where D means difference and L1 means first lag).

   b. Run a regression with DYield as the dependent variable and L1DYield as the single explanatory variable. In terms of the original variable Yield, this equation can be written as

$$\text{Yield}_t - \text{Yield}_{t-1} = a + b(\text{Yield}_{t-1} - \text{Yield}_{t-2})$$

Solving for Yield_t is equivalent to the following equation that can be used for forecasting:

$$\text{Yield}_t = a + (1 + b)\text{Yield}_{t-1} - b\text{Yield}_{t-2}$$

Try it—that is, try forecasting the next month from the known last two months' values. How might you forecast values two or three months from the last observed month? (*Hint*: If you do not have an *observed* value to use in the right side of the equation, use a forecast value.)

c. The autocorrelation structure led us to the equation in part **b**. That is, the autocorrelations of the original series took a long time to die down, so we looked at the autocorrelations of the differences, and the large spike at lag 1 led to regressing DYield on L1DYield. In turn, this ultimately led to an equation for Yield_t in terms of its first two lags. Now see what you would have obtained if you had tried regressing Yield_t on its first two lags in the first place—that is, if you had used regression to estimate the equation

$$\text{Yield}_t = a + b_1\text{Yield}_{t-1} + b_2\text{Yield}_{t-2}$$

When you use multiple regression to estimate this equation, do you get the same equation as in part **b**?

78. The file **P12_78.xlsx** lists monthly and annual values of the average surface air temperature of the earth (in degrees Celsius). (Actually, the data are indexes, relative to the period 1951−1980 where the average temperature was about 14 degrees Celsius. So if you want the actual temperatures, you can add 14 to all values.) A look at the time series shows a gradual upward trend, starting with negative values and ending with (mostly) positive values. This might be used to support the claim of global warming. For this problem, use only the annual averages in column N.

a. Is this series a random walk? Explain.

b. Regardless of your answer in part **a**, use a random walk model to forecast the next value (2010) of the series. What is your forecast, and what is an approximate 95% forecast interval, assuming normally distributed forecast errors?

c. Forecast the series in three ways: (i) simple exponential smoothing ($\alpha = 0.35$), (ii) Holt's method ($\alpha = 0.5$, $\beta = 0.1$), and (iii) simple exponential smoothing ($\alpha = 0.3$) on trend-adjusted data, that is, the residuals from regressing linearly versus time. (These smoothing constants are close to optimal.) For each of these, list the MAPE, the RMSE, and the forecast for next year. Also, comment on any "problems" with forecast errors from any of these three approaches. Finally, compare the qualitative features of the three forecasting methods. For example, how do their short-run or longer-run forecasts differ? Is any one of the methods clearly superior to the others?

d. Does your analysis predict convincingly that global warming has been occurring? Explain.

79. The file **P12_79.xlsx** contains data on mass layoff events in all industries in the U.S. (See the file for an explanation of how mass layoff events are counted.) There are two versions of the data: nonseasonally adjusted and seasonally adjusted. Presumably, seasonal factors can be found by dividing the nonseasonally adjusted values by the seasonally adjusted values. For example, the seasonal factor for April 1995 is 1431/1492=0.959. How well can you replicate these seasonal factors with appropriate StatTools analyses?

The Eastland Plaza Branch of the Indiana University Credit Union was having trouble getting the correct staffing levels to match customer arrival patterns. On some days, the number of tellers was too high relative to the customer traffic, so that tellers were often idle. On other days, the opposite occurred. Long customer waiting lines formed because the relatively few tellers could not keep up with the number of customers. The credit union manager, James Chilton, knew that there was a problem, but he had little of the quantitative training he believed would be necessary to find a better staffing solution. James figured that the problem could be broken down into three parts. First, he needed a reliable forecast of each day's number of customer arrivals. Second, he needed to translate these forecasts into staffing levels that would make an adequate trade-off between teller idleness and customer waiting. Third, he needed to translate these staffing levels into individual teller work assignments—who should come to work when.

The last two parts of the problem require analysis tools (queueing and scheduling) that we have not covered. However, you can help James with the first part—forecasting. The file **Credit Union Arrivals.xlsx** lists the number of customers entering this credit union branch each day of the past year. It also lists other information: the day of the week, whether the day was a staff or faculty payday, and whether the day was the day before or after a holiday. Use this data set to develop one or more forecasting models that James could use to help solve his problem. Based on your model(s), make any recommendations about staffing that appear reasonable. ■

Amanta Appliances sells two styles of refrigerators at more than 50 locations in the Midwest. The first style is a relatively expensive model, whereas the second is a standard, less expensive model. Although weekly demand for these two products is fairly stable from week to week, there is enough variation to concern management at Amanta. There have been relatively unsophisticated attempts to forecast weekly demand, but they haven't been very successful. Sometimes demand (and the corresponding sales) are lower than forecast, so that inventory costs are high. Other times the forecasts are too low. When this happens and on-hand inventory is not sufficient to meet customer demand, Amanta requires expedited shipments to keep customers happy—and this nearly wipes out Amanta's profit margin on the expedited units.[8] Profits at Amanta would almost certainly increase if demand could be forecast more accurately.

Data on weekly sales of both products appear in the file **Amanta Sales.xlsx**. A time series chart of the two sales variables indicates what Amanta management expected—namely, there is no evidence of any upward or downward trends or of any seasonality. In fact, it might appear that each series is an unpredictable sequence of random ups and downs. But is this really true? Is it possible to forecast either series, with some degree of accuracy, with an extrapolation method (where only past values of *that* series are used to forecast current and future values)? Which method appears to be best? How accurate is it? Also, is it possible, when trying to forecast sales of one product, to somehow incorporate current or past sales of the *other* product in the forecast model? After all, these products might be "substitute" products, where high sales of one go with low sales of the other, or they might be complementary products, where sales of the two products tend to move in the *same* direction. ∎

[8]Because Amanta uses expediting when necessary, its sales each week are equal to its customer demands. Therefore, the terms "demand" and "sales" are used interchangeably.

Introduction to Optimization Modeling

© Keith Dannemiller/Corbis

OPTIMIZING MANUFACTURING OPERATIONS AT GE PLASTICS

The General Electric Company (GE) is a global organization that must deliver products to its customers anywhere in the world in the right quantity, at the right time, and at a reasonable cost. One arm of GE is GE Plastics (GEP), a $5 billion business that supplies plastics and raw materials to such industries as automotive, appliance, computer, and medical equipment. (GEP has now been reorganized into GE Advanced Materials [GEAM].) As described in Tyagi et al. (2004), GEP practiced a "pole-centric" manufacturing approach, making each product in the geographic area (Americas, Europe, or Pacific) where it was to be delivered. However, it became apparent in the early 2000s that this approach was leading to higher distribution costs and mismatches in capacity as more of GEP's demand was originating in the Pacific region. Therefore, the authors of the article were asked to develop a global optimization model to aid GEP's manufacturing planning. Actually, GEP consists of seven major divisions, distinguished primarily by the capability of their products to withstand heat. The fastest growing of these divisions, the high performance polymer (HPP) division, was chosen as the pilot for the new global approach.

All GEP divisions operate as two-echelon manufacturing systems. The first echelon consists of resin plants, which convert raw material stocks into resins and ship them to the second echelon, the finishing plants. These latter plants combine the resins with additives to produce various grades of the end products. Each physical plant consists of several "plant lines" that operate independently, and each of these plant lines is capable of producing multiple products. All end products are then shipped to GE Polymerland warehouses throughout the world. GE Polymerland is a wholly owned subsidiary that acts as the commercial front for GEP. It handles all customer sales and deliveries from its network of distribution centers and warehouses in more than 20 countries. Because of its experience with customers, GE Polymerland is able to aid the GEP divisions in their planning processes by supplying forecasts of demands and prices for the various products in the various global markets. These forecasts are key inputs to the optimization model.

The optimization model itself attempts to maximize the total contribution margin over a planning horizon, where the contribution margin equals revenues minus the sum of manufacturing, material, and distribution costs. There are demand constraints, manufacturing capacity constraints, and network flow constraints. The decision variables include (1) the amount of resin produced at each resin plant line that will be used at each finishing plant line, and (2) the amount of each end product produced at each finishing plant line that will be shipped to each geographic region. The completed model has approximately 3100 decision variables and 1100 constraints and is completely linear. It was developed and solved in Excel (using LINGO, a commercial optimization solver, not Excel's Solver add-in), and execution time is very fast—about 10 seconds.

The demand constraints are handled in an interesting way. The authors of the study constrain manufacturing to produce no more than the forecasted demands, but they do not force manufacturing to meet these demands. Ideally, manufacturing would meet demands exactly. However, because of its rapid growth, capacity at HPP in 2002 appeared (at the time of the study) to be insufficient to meet the demand in 2005 and later years. The authors faced this challenge in two ways. First, in cases where demand exceeds capacity, they let their model of maximizing total contribution margin determine which demands to satisfy. The least profitable demands are simply not met. Second, the authors added a new resin plant to their model that would come on line in the year 2005 and provide much needed capacity. They ran the model several times for the year 2005 (and later years), experimenting with the location of the new plant. Although some of the details are withheld in the article for confidentiality reasons, the authors indicate that senior management approved the investment of a Europe-based plant that would cost more than $200 million in plant and equipment. This plant was planned to begin operations in 2005 and ramp up to full production capacity by 2007.

The decision support system developed in the study has been a success at the HPP division since its introduction in 2002. Although the article provides no specific dollar gains from the use of the model, it is noteworthy that the other GEP divisions are adopting similar models for their production planning. ∎

13.1 INTRODUCTION

In this chapter, we introduce spreadsheet optimization, one of the most powerful and flexible methods of quantitative analysis. The specific type of optimization we will discuss here is **linear programming** (LP). LP is used in all types of organizations, often on a daily basis, to solve a wide variety of problems. These include problems in labor scheduling, inventory management, selection of advertising media, bond trading, management of cash flows, operation of an electrical utility's hydroelectric system, routing of delivery vehicles, blending in oil refineries, hospital staffing, and many others. The goal of this chapter is to introduce the basic elements of LP: the types of problems it can solve, how LP problems can be modeled in Excel, and how Excel's powerful Solver add-in can be used to find optimal solutions. Then in the next chapter we will examine a variety of LP applications, and we will also look at applications of integer and nonlinear programming, two important extensions of LP.

13.2 INTRODUCTION TO OPTIMIZATION

Before we discuss the details of LP modeling, it is useful to discuss optimization in general. All optimization problems have several common elements. They all have *decision variables*, the variables whose values the decision maker is allowed to choose. Either directly or indirectly, the values of these variables determine such outputs as total cost, revenue, and profit. Essentially, they are the variables a company or organization must know to function properly; they determine everything else. All optimization problems have an *objective function* (**objective**, for short) to be optimized—maximized or minimized.[1] Finally, most optimization problems have **constraints** that must be satisfied. These are usually physical, logical, or economic restrictions, depending on the nature of the problem. In searching for the values of the decision variables that optimize the objective, only those values that satisfy all of the constraints are allowed.

Excel uses its own terminology for optimization, and we will use it as well. Excel refers to the decision variables as the **changing cells**. These cells must contain numbers that are allowed to change freely; they are *not* allowed to contain formulas. Excel refers to the objective as the **objective cell**. There can be only one objective cell, which could contain profit, total cost, total distance traveled, or others, and it must be related through formulas to the changing cells. When the changing cells change, the objective cell should change accordingly.

> The **changing cells** contain the values of the decision variables.
>
> The **objective cell** contains the objective to be minimized or maximized.
>
> The **constraints** impose restrictions on the values in the changing cells.

Finally, there must be appropriate cells and cell formulas that operationalize the constraints. For example, one constraint might indicate that the amount of labor used can be no more than the amount of labor available. In this case there must be cells for each of these two quantities, and typically at least one of them (probably the amount of labor used) will be related through formulas to the changing cells. Constraints can come in a variety of forms. One very common form is **nonnegativity**. This type of constraint states that changing cells must have nonnegative (zero or positive) values. Nonnegativity constraints are usually included for physical reasons. For example, it is impossible to produce a negative number of automobiles.

> **Nonnegativity** constraints imply that changing cells must contain nonnegative values.

Typically, most of your effort goes into the model development step.

There are basically two steps in solving an optimization problem. The first step is the *model development* step. Here you decide what the decision variables are, what the objective is, which constraints are required, and how everything fits together. If you are developing an algebraic model, you must derive the correct algebraic expressions. If you are developing a spreadsheet model, the main focus of this book, you must relate all variables with appropriate cell formulas. In particular, you must ensure that your model contains formulas that relate the changing cells to the objective cell and formulas that operationalize the constraints. This model development step is where most of your effort goes.

[1] Actually, some optimization models are *multicriteria* models that try to optimize several objectives simultaneously. However, we will not discuss multicriteria models in this book.

The second step in any optimization model is to *optimize*. This means that you must systematically choose the values of the decision variables that make the objective as large (for maximization) or small (for minimization) as possible and cause all of the constraints to be satisfied. Some terminology is useful here. Any set of values of the decision variables that satisfies all of the constraints is called a **feasible solution**. The set of all feasible solutions is called the **feasible region**. In contrast, an **infeasible solution** is a solution that violates at least one constraint. Infeasible solutions are disallowed. The desired feasible solution is the one that provides the best value—minimum for a minimization problem, maximum for a maximization problem—for the objective. This solution is called the **optimal solution**.

A **feasible solution** is a solution that satisfies all of the constraints.

The **feasible region** is the set of all feasible solutions.

An **infeasible solution** violates at least one of the constraints.

The **optimal solution** is the feasible solution that optimizes the objective.

An algorithm is basically a plan of attack. It is a prescription for carrying out the steps required to achieve some goal, such as finding an optimal solution. An algorithm is typically translated into a computer program that does the work.

Although most of your effort typically goes into the model development step, much of the published research in optimization has been about the optimization step. Algorithms have been devised for searching through the feasible region to find the optimal solution. One such algorithm is called the **simplex method**. It is used for *linear* models. There are other more complex algorithms used for other types of models (those with integer decision variables and/or nonlinearities).

We will not discuss the details of these algorithms. They have been programmed into the Excel's **Solver** add-in. All you need to do is develop the model and then tell Solver what the objective cell is, what the changing cells are, what the constraints are, and what type of model (linear, integer, or nonlinear) you have. Solver then goes to work, finding the best feasible solution with the appropriate algorithm. You should appreciate that if you used a trial-and-error procedure, even a clever and fast one, it could take hours, weeks, or even years to complete. However, by using the appropriate algorithm, Solver typically finds the optimal solution in a matter of seconds.

Before concluding this discussion, we mention that there is really a *third* step in the optimization process: **sensitivity analysis**. You typically choose the most likely values of input variables, such as unit costs, forecasted demands, and resource availabilities, and then find the optimal solution for these particular input values. This provides a single "answer." However, in any realistic situation, it is wishful thinking to believe that all of the input values you use are exactly correct. Therefore, it is useful—indeed, mandatory in most applied studies—to follow up the optimization step with what-if questions. What if the unit costs increased by 5%? What if forecasted demands were 10% lower? What if resource availabilities could be increased by 20%? What effects would such changes have on the optimal solution? This type of sensitivity analysis can be done in an informal manner or it can be highly structured. Fortunately, as with the optimization step itself, good software allows you to obtain answers to various what-if questions quickly and easily.

13.3 A TWO-VARIABLE PRODUCT MIX MODEL

We begin with a very simple two-variable example of a *product mix* problem. This is a type of problem frequently encountered in business where a company must decide its product mix—how much of each of its potential products to produce—to maximize its net profit. You will see how to model this problem algebraically and then how to model it in Excel.

You will also see how to find its optimal solution with Solver. Next, because it contains only two decision variables, you will see how it can be solved graphically. Although this graphical solution is not practical for most realistic problems, it provides useful insights into general LP models. The final step is then to ask a number of what-if questions about the completed model.

<table>
<tr><td>EXAMPLE</td><td>13.1 ASSEMBLING AND TESTING COMPUTERS</td></tr>
</table>

The PC Tech company assembles and then tests two models of computers, Basic and XP. For the coming month, the company wants to decide how many of each model to assembly and then test. No computers are in inventory from the previous month, and because these models are going to be changed after this month, the company doesn't want to hold any inventory after this month. It believes the most it can sell this month are 600 Basics and 1200 XPs. Each Basic sells for $300 and each XP sells for $450. The cost of component parts for a Basic is $150; for an XP it is $225. Labor is required for assembly and testing. There are at most 10,000 assembly hours and 3000 testing hours available. Each labor hour for assembling costs $11 and each labor hour for testing costs $15. Each Basic requires five hours for assembling and one hour for testing, and each XP requires six hours for assembling and two hours for testing. PC Tech wants to know how many of each model it should produce (assemble and test) to maximize its net profit, but it cannot use more labor hours than are available, and it does not want to produce more than it can sell.

Objective   To use LP to find the best mix of computer models that stays within the company's labor availability and maximum sales constraints.

Solution

Tables such as this one serve as a bridge between the problem statement and the ultimate spreadsheet (or algebraic) model.

In all optimization models, you are given a variety of numbers—the inputs—and you are asked to make some decisions that optimize an objective, while satisfying all constraints. We summarize this information in a table such as Table 13.1. We believe it is a good idea to create such a table before diving into the modeling details. In particular, you always need to identify the appropriate decision variables, the appropriate objective, and the constraints, and you should always think about the relationships between them. Without a clear idea of these elements, it is almost impossible to develop a correct algebraic or spreadsheet model.

Table 13.1   Variables and Constraints for Two-Variable Product Mix Model

Input variables	Hourly labor costs, labor availabilities, labor required for each computer, costs of component parts, unit selling prices, and maximum sales
Decision variables (changing cells)	Number of each computer model to produce (assemble and test)
Objective cell	Total net profit
Other calculated variables	Labor of each type used
Constraints	Labor used ≤ Labor available, Number produced ≤ Maximum sales

The decision variables in this product mix model are fairly obvious. The company must decide two numbers: how many Basics to produce and how many XPs to produce. Once these are known, they can be used, along with the problem inputs, to calculate the number of computers sold, the labor used, and the revenue and cost. However, as you will see with other models in this chapter and the next chapter, determining the decision variables is not always this obvious.

An Algebraic Model

In the traditional *algebraic* solution method, you first identify the decision variables.[2] In this small problem they are the numbers of computers to produce. We label these x_1 and x_2, although any other labels would do. The next step is to write expressions for the total net profit and the constraints in terms of the xs. Finally, because only nonnegative amounts can be produced, explicit constraints are added to ensure that the xs are nonnegative. The resulting **algebraic model** is

$$\text{Maximize } 80x_1 + 129x_2$$

subject to:

$$5x_1 + 6x_2 \leq 10000$$

$$x_1 + 2x_2 \leq 3000$$

$$x_1 \leq 600$$

$$x_2 \leq 1200$$

$$x_1, x_2 \geq 0$$

To understand this model, consider the objective first. Each Basic produced sells for $300, and the total cost of producing it, including component parts and labor, is $150 + 5(11) + 1(15) = \$220$, so the profit margin is $80. Similarly, the profit margin for an XP is $129. Each profit margin is multiplied by the number of computers produced and these products are then summed over the two computer models to obtain the total net profit.

The first two constraints are similar. For example, each Basic requires five hours for assembling and each XP requires six hours for assembling, so the first constraint says that the total hours required for assembling is no more than the number available, 10,000. The third and fourth constraints are the maximum sales constraints for Basics and XPs. Finally, negative amounts cannot be produced, so nonnegativity constraints on x_1 and x_2 are included.

For many years all LP problems were modeled this way in textbooks. In fact, many commercial LP computer packages are still written to accept LP problems in essentially this format. Since around 1990, however, a more intuitive method of expressing LP problems has emerged. This method takes advantage of the power and flexibility of spreadsheets. Actually, LP problems could always be *modeled* in spreadsheets, but now with the addition of Solver, spreadsheets have the ability to *solve*—that is, optimize—LP problems as well. We use Excel's Solver for all examples in this book.[3]

Many commercial optimization packages require, as input, an algebraic model of a problem. If you ever use one of these packages, you will be required to think algebraically.

A Graphical Solution

This graphical approach works only for problems with two decision variables.

When there are only two decision variables in an LP model, as there are in this product mix model, you can solve the problem graphically. Although this **graphical solution** approach is not practical in most realistic optimization models—where there are many more than two decision variables—the graphical procedure illustrated here still yields important insights for general LP models.

---

[2]This is not a book about algebraic models; the main focus is on *spreadsheet* modeling. However, we present algebraic models of the examples in this chapter for comparison with the corresponding spreadsheet models.

[3]The Solver add-in built into Microsoft Excel was developed by a third-party software company, Frontline Systems. This company develops much more powerful versions of Solver for commercial sales, but its standard version built into Office suffices for us. More information about Solver software offered by Frontline is given in a brief appendix to this chapter.

In general, if the two decision variables are labeled x_1 and x_2, then the steps of the method are to express the constraints and the objective in terms of x_1 and x_2, graph the constraints to find the feasible region [the set of all pairs (x_1, x_2) satisfying the constraints, where x_1 is on the horizontal axis and x_2 is on the vertical axis], and then move the objective through the feasible region until it is optimized.

To do this for the product mix problem, note that the constraint on assembling labor hours can be expressed as $5x_1 + 6x_2 \leq 10000$. To graph this, consider the associated equality (replacing $\leq$ with $=$) and find where the associated line crosses the axes. Specifically, when $x_1 = 0$, then $x_2 = 10000/6 = 1666.7$, and when $x_2 = 0$, then $x_1 = 10000/5 = 2000$. This provides the line labeled "assembling hour constraint" in Figure 13.1. It has slope $-5/6 = -0.83$. The set of all points that satisfy the assembling hour constraint includes the points on this line plus the points *below* it, as indicated by the arrow drawn from the line. (The feasible points are below the line because the point $(0, 0)$ is obviously below the line, and $(0, 0)$ clearly satisfies the assembly hour constraint.) Similarly, the testing hour and maximum sales constraints can be graphed as shown in the figure. The points that satisfy all three of these constraints and are nonnegative comprise the feasible region, which is below the dark lines in the figure.

Figure 13.1

Graphical Solution to Two-Variable Product Mix Problem

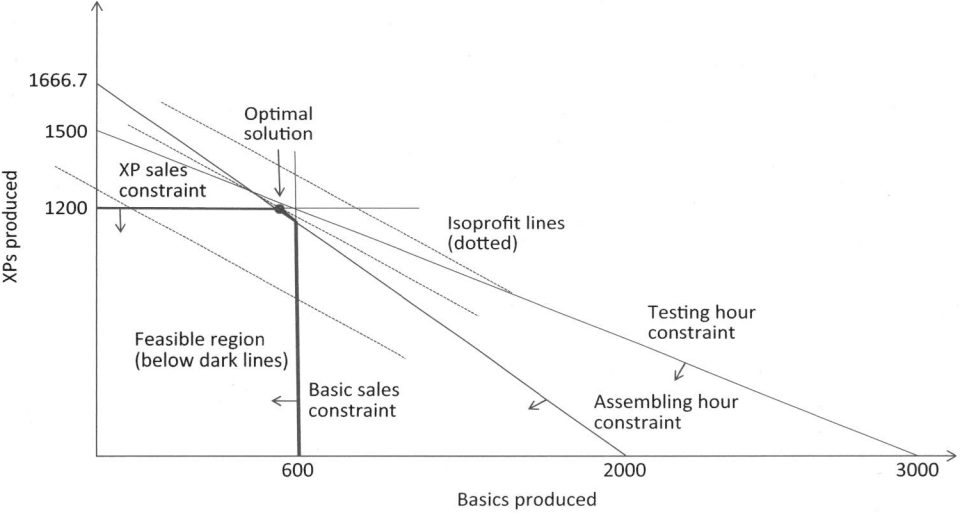

To see which feasible point maximizes the objective, it is useful to draw a sequence of lines where, for each, the objective is a constant. A typical line is of the form $80x_1 + 129x_2 = c$, where c is a constant. Any such line has slope $-80/129 = -0.620$, regardless of the value of c. This line is steeper than the testing hour constraint line (slope -0.5), but not as steep as the assembling hour constraint line (slope -0.83). The idea now is to move a line with this slope up and to the right, making c larger, until it just barely touches the feasible region. The last feasible point that it touches is the optimal point.

Several lines with slope -0.620 are shown in Figure 13.1. The middle dotted line is the one with the largest net profit that still touches the feasible region. The associated optimal point is clearly the point where the assembling hour and XP maximum sales lines intersect. You will eventually find (from Solver) that this point is (560,1200), but even if you didn't have the Solver add-in, you could find the coordinates of this point by solving two equations (the ones for assembling hours and XP maximum sales) in two unknowns.

Again, the graphical procedure illustrated here can be used only for the simplest of LP models, those with two decision variables. However, the type of behavior pictured in Figure 13.1 generalizes to *all* LP problems. In general, all feasible regions are (the multidimensional versions of) polygons. That is, they are bounded by straight lines (actually *hyperplanes*) that intersect at several *corner points*. There are five corner points in Figure 13.1, three of which are on the axes. (One of them is (0,0).) When the dotted objective line is moved as far as possible toward better values, the last feasible point it touches is one of the corner points. The actual corner point it last touches is determined by the slopes of the objective and constraint lines. Because there are only a finite number of corner points, it suffices to search among this finite set, not the infinite number of points in the entire feasible region.[4] This insight is largely responsible for the efficiency of the simplex method for solving LP problems.

FUNDAMENTAL INSIGHT

Geometry of LP Models and the Simplex Method

The feasible region in any LP model is always a multi-dimensional version of a polygon, and the objective is always a hyperplane, the multidimensional version of a straight line. The objective should always be moved as far as possible in the maximizing or minimizing direction until it just touches the edge of the feasible region.

Because of this geometry, the optimal solution is always a corner point of the polygon. The simplex method for LP works so well because it can search through the finite number of corner points extremely efficiently and recognize when it has found the best corner point. This rather simple insight, plus its clever implementation in software packages, has saved companies many, many millions of dollars in the past 50 years.

A Spreadsheet Model

We now turn our focus to *spreadsheet* modeling. There are many ways to develop an LP **spreadsheet model**. Everyone has his or her own preferences for arranging the data in the various cells. We do not provide exact prescriptions, but we do present enough examples to help you develop good habits. The common elements in all LP spreadsheet models are the inputs, changing cells, objective cell, and constraints.

- **Inputs.** All numerical inputs—that is, all numeric data given in the statement of the problem—should appear somewhere in the spreadsheet. Our convention is to color all of the input cells blue. We also try to put most of the inputs in the upper left section of the spreadsheet. However, we sometimes violate this latter convention when certain inputs fit more naturally somewhere else.

- **Changing cells.** Instead of using variable names, such as *xs*, spreadsheet models use a set of designated cells for the decision variables. The values in these changing cells can be changed to optimize the objective. The values in these cells must be allowed to vary freely, so there should *not* be any formulas in the changing cells. To designate them clearly, our convention is to color them red.

- **Objective cell.** One cell, called the objective cell, contains the value of the objective. Solver systematically varies the values in the changing cells to optimize the value in the objective cell. This cell must be linked, either directly or indirectly, to the changing cells by formulas. Our convention is to color the objective cell gray.[5]

---

[4]This is not entirely true. If the objective line is exactly parallel to one of the constraint lines, there can be *multiple optimal solutions*—a whole line segment of optimal solutions. Even in this case, however, at least one of the optimal solutions is a corner point.

[5]Our blue/red/gray color scheme shows up very effectively on a color monitor. For users of previous editions who are used to colored *borders*, we find that it is easier in Excel 2007 and Excel 2010 to color the cells rather than put borders around them.

1 **Inputs.** Enter all of the inputs from the statement of the problem in the shaded cells as shown.

2 **Range names.** Create the range names shown in columns E and F. Our convention is to enter enough range names, but not to go overboard. Specifically, we enter enough range names so that the setup in the Solver dialog box, to be explained shortly, is entirely in terms of range names. Of course, you can add more range names if you like (or you can omit them altogether). The following tip indicates a quick way to create range names.

Excel Tip *Shortcut for Creating Range Names*
Select a range such as A16:C16 that includes nice labels in column A and the range you want to name in columns B and C. Then, from the Formulas ribbon, select Create from Selection and accept the default. You automatically get the labels in cells A16 as the range name for the range B16:C16. This shortcut illustrates the usefulness of adding concise but informative labels next to ranges you want to name.

3 **Unit margins.** Enter the formula

=B11−B8*$B$3−B9*$B$4−B10

in cell B12 and copy it to cell C12 to calculate the unit profit margins for the two models. (Enter relative/absolute addresses that allow you to copy whenever possible.)

At this stage, it is pointless to try to outguess the optimal solution. Any values in the changing cells will suffice.

4 **Changing cells.** Enter any two values for the changing cells in the Number_to_produce range. Any trial values can be used initially; Solver eventually finds the optimal values. Note that the two values shown in Figure 13.2 cannot be optimal because they use more assembling hours than are available. However, you do not need to worry about satisfying constraints at this point; Solver takes care of this later on.

5 **Labor hours used.** To operationalize the labor availability constraints, you must calculate the amounts used by the production plan. To do this, enter the formula

=SUMPRODUCT(B8:C8,Number_to_produce)

in cell B21 for assembling and copy it to cell B22 for testing. This formula is a shortcut for the following fully written out formula:

=B8*B16+C8*C16

The "linear" in linear programming is all about sums of products. Therefore, the SUMPRODUCT function is natural and should be used whenever possible.

The SUMPRODUCT function is very useful in spreadsheet models, especially LP models, and you will see it often. Here, it multiplies the number of hours per computer by the number of computers for each model and then sums these products over the two models. When there are only two products in the sum, as in this example, the SUMPRODUCT formula is not really any simpler than the written-out formula. However, imagine that there are 50 models. Then the SUMPRODUCT formula is *much* simpler to enter (and read). For this reason, use it whenever possible. Note that each range in this function, B8:C8 and Number_to_produce, is a one-row, two-column range. It is important in the SUMPRODUCT function that the two ranges be exactly the same size and shape.

6 **Net profits.** Enter the formula

=B12*B16

in cell B25, copy it to cell C25, and sum these to get the total net profit in cell D25. This latter cell is the objective to maximize. Note that if you didn't care about the net profits for the two *individual* models, you could calculate the total net profit with the formula

=SUMPRODUCT(B12:C12,Number_to_produce)

As you see, the SUMPRODUCT function appears once again. It and the SUM function are the most used functions in LP models.

Experimenting with Possible Solutions

The next step is to specify the changing cells, the objective cell, and the constraints in a Solver dialog box and then instruct Solver to find the optimal solution. However, before you do this, it is instructive to try a few guesses in the changing cells. There are two reasons for doing so. First, by entering different sets of values in the changing cells, you can confirm that the formulas in the other cells are working correctly. Second, this experimentation can help you to develop a better understanding of the model.

For example, the profit margin for XPs is much larger than for Basics, so you might suspect that the company will produce only XPs. The most it can produce is 1200 (maximum sales), and this uses fewer labor hours than are available. This solution appears in Figure 13.3. However, you can probably guess that it is far from optimal. There are still many labor hours available, so the company could use them to produce some Basics and make more profit.

You can continue to try different values in the changing cells, attempting to get as large a total net profit as possible while staying within the constraints. Even for this small model with only two changing cells, the optimal solution is not totally obvious. You can only imagine how much more difficult it is when there are hundreds or even thousands of changing cells and many constraints. This is why software such as Excel's Solver is required. Solver uses a quick and efficient algorithm to search through all feasible solutions (or more specifically, all corner points) and eventually find the optimal solution. Fortunately, it is quite easy to use, as we now explain.

Figure 13.3   Two-Variable Product Mix Model with a Suboptimal Solution

	A	B	C	D	E	F	G
1	Assembling and testing computers				Range names used:		
2					Hours_available	=Model!$D$21:$D$22	
3	Cost per labor hour assembling	$11			Hours_used	=Model!$B$21:$B$22	
4	Cost per labor hour testing	$15			Maximum_sales	=Model!$B$18:$C$18	
5					Number_to_produce	=Model!$B$16:$C$16	
6	Inputs for assembling and testing a computer				Total_profit	=Model!$D$25	
7		Basic	XP				
8	Labor hours for assembly	5	6				
9	Labor hours for testing	1	2				
10	Cost of component parts	$150	$225				
11	Selling price	$300	$450				
12	Unit margin	$80	$129				
13							
14	Assembling, testing plan (# of computers)						
15		Basic	XP				
16	Number to produce	0	1200				
17		<=	<=				
18	Maximum sales	600	1200				
19							
20	Constraints (hours per month)	Hours used		Hours available			
21	Labor availability for assembling	7200	<=	10000			
22	Labor availability for testing	2400	<=	3000			
23							
24	Net profit ($ this month)	Basic	XP	Total			
25		$0	$154,800	$154,800			

Using Solver

To invoke Excel's Solver, select Solver from the Data ribbon. (If there is no such item on your PC, you need to *load* Solver. To do so, click on the Office button, then Excel Options, then Add-Ins, and then Go at the bottom of the dialog box. This shows you the list of available add-ins. If there is a Solver Add-in item in the list, check it to load Solver. If there is no such item, you need to rerun the Microsoft Office installer and elect to install Solver. It should be included in a typical install, but some people elect not to install it the first time around.) The dialog box in Figure 13.4 appears.[6] It has three important sections that you must fill in: the objective cell, the changing cells, and the constraints. For the product mix problem, you can fill these in by typing cell references or you can point, click, and drag the appropriate ranges in the usual way. Better yet, if there are any named ranges, these range names appear instead of cell addresses when you drag the ranges. In fact, for reasons of readability, our convention is to use only range names, not cell addresses, in this dialog box.

Figure 13.4
Solver Dialog Box (in Excel 2010)

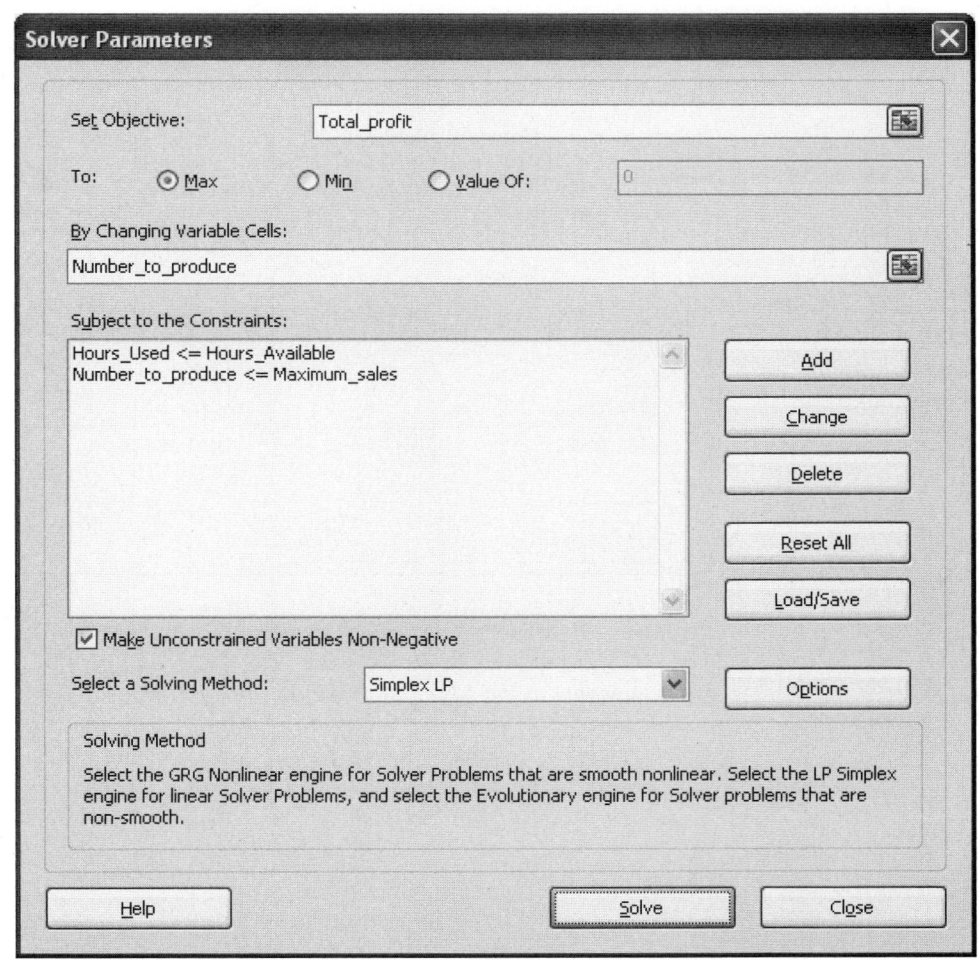

---

[6] This is the new Solver dialog box for Excel 2010. It is more convenient than similar dialog boxes in previous versions because the typical settings now all appear in a *single* dialog box. In previous versions you have to click on Options to complete the typical settings.

Excel Tip *Range Names in Solver Dialog Box*
Our usual procedure is to use the mouse to select the relevant ranges for the Solver dialog box. Fortunately, if these ranges have already been named, then the range names will automatically replace the cell addresses.

1 Objective. Select the Total_profit cell as the objective cell, and click on the Max option. (Actually, the default option is Max.)

2 Changing cells. Select the Number_to_produce range as the changing cells.

3 Constraints. Click on the Add button to bring up the dialog box in Figure 13.5. Here you specify a typical constraint by entering a cell reference or range name on the left, the type of constraint from the dropdown list in the middle, and a cell reference, range name, or numeric value on the right. Use this dialog box to enter the constraint

Number_to_produce<=Maximum_sales

(*Note:* You can type these range names into the dialog box, or you can drag them in the usual way. If you drag them, the cell addresses shown in the figure eventually change into range names if range names exist.) Then click on the Add button and enter the constraint

Hours_used ≤ Hours_available

Then click on OK to get back to the Solver dialog box. The first constraint says to produce no more than can be sold. The second constraint says to use no more labor hours than are available.

Figure 13.5
Add Constraint
Dialog Box

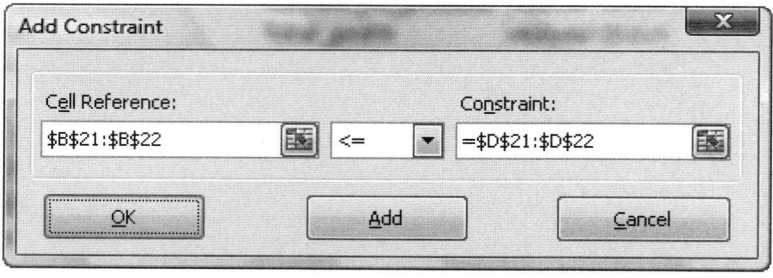

Excel Tip *Inequality and Equality Labels in Spreadsheet Models*
The <= signs in cells B17:C17 and C21:C22 (see Figure 13.2 or Figure 13.3) are not a necessary part of the Excel model. They are entered simply as labels in the spreadsheet and do not substitute for entering the constraints in the Add Constraint dialog box. However, they help to document the model, so we include them in all of the examples. In fact, you should try to plan your spreadsheet models so that the two sides of a constraint are in nearby cells, with "gutter" cells in between where you can attach labels like <=, >=, or =. This convention tends to make the resulting spreadsheet models much more readable.

Solver Tip *Entering Constraints in Groups*
Constraints typically come in groups. Beginners often enter these one at a time, such as B16 ≤ B18 and C16 ≤ C18, in the Solver dialog box. This can lead to a long list of constraints, and it is time-consuming. It is better to enter them as a group, as in B16:C16 ≤ B18:C18. This is not only quicker, but it also takes advantage of range names you have created. For example, this group ends up as Number_to_produce ≤ Maximum_Sales.

4 **Nonnegativity.** Because negative production quantities make no sense, you must tell Solver *explicitly* to make the changing cells nonnegative. To do this, check the Make Unconstrained Variables Non-Negative option shown in Figure 13.4. This automatically ensures that all changing cells are nonnegative. (In previous versions of Solver, you have to click on the Options button and then check the Assume Non-Negative option in the resulting dialog box.)

5 **Linear model.** There is one last step before clicking on the Solve button. As stated previously, Solver uses one of several numerical algorithms to solve various types of models. The models discussed in this chapter are all *linear* models. (We will discuss the properties that distinguish linear models shortly.) Linear models can be solved most efficiently with the simplex method. To instruct Solver to use this method, make sure Simplex LP is selected in the Select a Solving Method dropdown list in Figure 13.4. (In previous versions of Solver, you have to click on the Options button and then check the Assume Linear Model option in the resulting dialog box. In fact, from now on, if you are using a pre-2010 version of Excel and we instruct you to use the simplex method, you should check the Assume Linear Model option. In contrast, if we instruct you to use a nonlinear algorithm, you should uncheck the Assume Linear Model option.)

6 **Optimize.** Click on the Solve button in the dialog box in Figure 13.4. At this point, Solver does its work. It searches through a number of possible solutions until it finds the optimal solution. (You can watch the progress on the lower left of the screen, although for small models the process is virtually instantaneous.) When it finishes, it displays the message shown in Figure 13.6. You can then instruct it to return the values in the changing cells to their original (probably nonoptimal) values or retain the optimal values found by Solver. In most cases you should choose the latter. For now, click on the OK button to keep the Solver solution. You should see the solution shown in Figure 13.7.

Figure 13.6
Solver Results Message

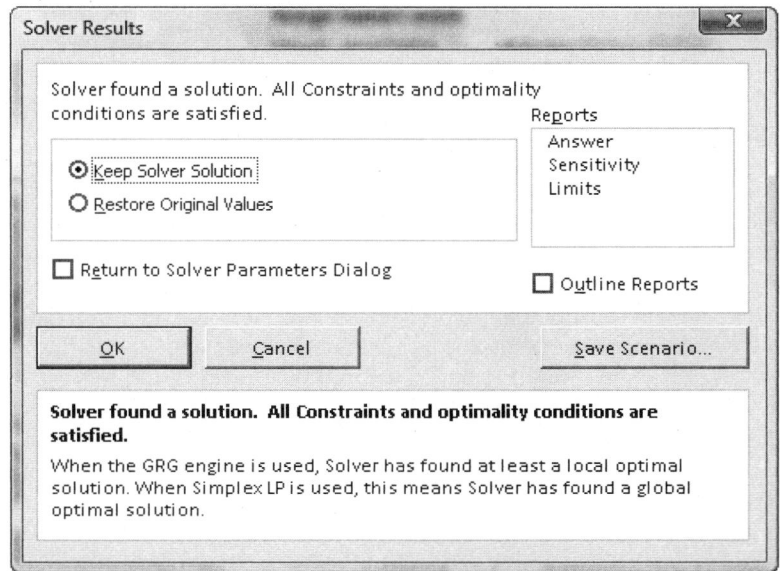

Solver Tip *Messages from Solver*
Actually, the message in Figure 13.6 is the one you hope for. However, in some cases Solver is not able to find an optimal solution, in which case one of several other messages appears. We discuss some of these later in the chapter.

Figure 13.7

Two-Variable Product Mix Model with the Optimal Solution

	A	B	C	D	E	F	G
1	**Assembling and testing computers**				**Range names used:**		
2					Hours_available	=Model!$D$21:$D$22	
3	Cost per labor hour assembling	$11			Hours_used	=Model!$B$21:$B$22	
4	Cost per labor hour testing	$15			Maximum_sales	=Model!$B$18:$C$18	
5					Number_to_produce	=Model!$B$16:$C$16	
6	Inputs for assembling and testing a computer				Total_profit	=Model!$D$25	
7		BasicXP					
8	Labor hours for assembly	5	6				
9	Labor hours for testing	1	2				
10	Cost of component parts	$150	$225				
11	Selling price	$300	$450				
12	Unit margin	$80	$129				
13							
14	Assembling, testing plan (# of computers)						
15		Basic	XP				
16	Number to produce	560	1200				
17		<=	<=				
18	Maximum sales	600	1200				
19							
20	Constraints (hours per month)	Hours used		Hours available			
21	Labor availability for assembling	10000	<=	10000			
22	Labor availability for testing	2960	<=	3000			
23							
24	Net profit ($ this month)	Basic	XP	Total			
25		$44,800	$154,800	$199,600			

Discussion of the Solution

This solution says that PC Tech should produce 560 Basics and 1200 XPs. This plan uses all available labor hours for assembling, has a few leftover labor hours for testing, produces as many XPs as can be sold, and produces a few less Basics than could be sold. No plan can provide a net profit larger than this one—that is, without violating at least one of the constraints.

The solution in Figure 13.7 is typical of solutions to optimization models in the following sense. Of all the inequality constraints, some are satisfied exactly and others are not. In this solution the XP maximum sales and assembling labor constraints are met exactly. We say that they are **binding**. However, the Basic maximum sales and testing labor constraints are **nonbinding**. For these nonbinding constraints, the differences between the two sides of the inequalities are called **slack**.[7] You can think of the binding constraints as bottlenecks. They are the constraints that prevent the objective from being improved. If it were not for the binding constraints on maximum sales and labor, PC Tech could obtain an even larger net profit.

> An inequality constraint is **binding** if the solution makes it an equality. Otherwise, it is **nonbinding**, and the positive difference between the two sides of the constraint is called the **slack**.

[7]Some analysts use the term *slack* only for ≤ constraints and the term *surplus* for ≥ constraints. We refer to both of these as *slack*—the absolute difference between the two sides of the constraint.

In a typical optimal solution, you should usually pay particular attention to two aspects of the solution. First, you should check which of the changing cells are *positive* (as opposed to 0). Generically, these are the "activities" that are done at a positive level. In a product mix model, they are the products included in the optimal mix. Second, you should check which of the constraints are binding. Again, these represent the bottlenecks that keep the objective from improving. ∎

FUNDAMENTAL INSIGHT

Binding and Nonbinding Constraints

Most optimization models contain constraints expressed as inequalities. In an optimal solution, each such constraint is either binding (holds as an equality) or nonbinding. It is extremely important to identify the binding constraints because they are the constraints that prevent the objective from improving.

A typical constraint is on the availability of a resource. If such a constraint is binding, the objective could typically improve by having more of that resource. But if such a resource constraint is nonbinding, more of that resource would not improve the objective at all.

13.4 SENSITIVITY ANALYSIS

Indeed, many analysts view the "finished" model as a starting point for all sorts of what-if questions. We agree.

Having found the optimal solution, it might appear that the analysis is complete. But in real LP applications the solution to a *single* model is hardly ever the end of the analysis. It is almost always useful to perform a sensitivity analysis to see how (or if) the optimal solution changes as one or more inputs vary. We illustrate systematic ways of doing so in this section. Actually, we discuss two approaches. The first uses an optional sensitivity report that Solver offers. The second uses an add-in called SolverTable that one of the authors (Albright) developed.

13.4.1 Solver's Sensitivity Report

When you run Solver, the dialog box in Figure 13.6 offers you the option to obtain a sensitivity report.[8] This report is based on a well-established theory of sensitivity analysis in optimization models, especially LP models. This theory was developed around algebraic models that are arranged in a "standardized" format. Essentially, all such algebraic models look alike, so the same type of sensitivity report applies to all of them. Specifically, they have an objective function of the form $c_1 x_1 + \cdots + c_n x_n$, where n is the number of decision variables, the cs are constants, and the xs are the decision variables, and each constraint can be expressed as $a_1 x_1 + \cdots + a_n x_n \leq b$, $a_1 x_1 + \cdots + a_n x_n \geq b$, or $a_1 x_1 + \cdots + a_n x_n = b$, where the as and bs are constants. **Solver's sensitivity report** performs two types of sensitivity analysis: (1) on the coefficients of the objective, the cs, and (2) on the right sides of the constraints, the bs.

---

[8]It also offers Answer and Limits reports. We don't find these particularly useful, so we will not discuss them here.

We illustrate the typical analysis by looking at the sensitivity report for PC Tech's product mix model in Example 13.1. For convenience, the algebraic model is repeated here.

$$\text{Maximize } 80x_1 + 129x_2$$

subject to:

$$5x_1 + 6x_2 \leq 10000$$
$$x_1 + 2x_2 \leq 3000$$
$$x_1 \leq 600$$
$$x_2 \leq 1200$$
$$x_1, x_2 \geq 0$$

On this Solver run, a sensitivity report is requested in Solver's final dialog box. (See Figure 13.6.) The sensitivity report appears on a new worksheet, as shown in Figure 13.8.[9] It contains two sections. The top section is for sensitivity to changes in the two coefficients, 80 and 129, of the decision variables in the objective. Each row in this section indicates how the optimal solution changes if one of these coefficients changes. The bottom section is for the sensitivity to changes in the right sides, 10000 and 3000, of the labor constraints. Each row of this section indicates how the optimal solution changes if one of these availabilities changes. (The maximum sales constraints represent a special kind of constraint—*upper bounds* on the changing cells. Upper bound constraints are handled in a special way in the Solver sensitivity report, as described shortly.)

Figure 13.8

Solver Sensitivity Results

	A	B	C	D	E	F	G	H
6		Variable Cells						
7				Final	Reduced	Objective	Allowable	Allowable
8		Cell	Name	Value	Cost	Coefficient	Increase	Decrease
9		$B$16	Number to produce Basic	560	0	80	27.5	80
10		$C$16	Number to produce XP	1200	33	129	1E+30	33
11								
12		Constraints						
13				Final	Shadow	Constraint	Allowable	Allowable
14		Cell	Name	Value	Price	R.H. Side	Increase	Decrease
15		$B$21	Labor availability for assembling Used	10000	16	10000	200	2800
16		$B$22	Labor availability for testing Used	2960	0	3000	1E+30	40

Now let's look at the specific numbers and their interpretation. In the first row of the top section, the *allowable increase* and *allowable decrease* indicate how much the coefficient of profit margin for Basics in the objective, currently 80, could change before the optimal product mix would change. If the coefficient of Basics stays within this allowable range, from 0 (decrease of 80) to 107.5 (increase of 27.5), the optimal product mix—the set of values in the changing cells—does not change at all. However, outside of these limits, the optimal mix between Basics and XPs *might* change.

[9]If your table looks different from ours, make sure you chose the simplex method (or checked Assume Linear Model in pre-2010 versions of Solver). Otherwise, Solver uses a nonlinear algorithm and produces a different type of sensitivity report.

To see what this implies, change the selling price in cell B11 from 300 to 299, so that the profit margin for Basics decreases to $79. This change is well within the allowable decrease of 80. If you rerun Solver, you will obtain the *same* values in the changing cells, although the objective value will decrease. Next, change the value in cell B11 to 330. This time, the profit margin for Basics increases by 30 from its original value of $300. This change is outside the allowable increase, so the solution might change. If you rerun Solver, you will indeed see a change—the company now produces 600 Basics and fewer than 1200 XPs.

The *reduced costs* in the second column indicate, in general, how much the objective coefficient of a decision variable that is currently 0 or at its upper bound must change before that variable changes (becomes positive or decreases from its upper bound). The interesting variable in this case is the number of XPs, currently at its upper bound of 1200. The reduced cost for this variable is 33, meaning that the number of XPs will stay at 1200 unless the profit margin for XPs decreases by at least $33. Try it. Starting with the original inputs, change the selling price for XPs to $420, a change of less than $33. If you rerun Solver, you will find that the optimal plan still calls for 1200 XPs. Then change the selling price to $410, a change of more than $33 from the original value. After rerunning Solver, you will find that *fewer* than 1200 XPs are in the optimal mix.

The **reduced cost** for any decision variable with value 0 in the optimal solution indicates how much better that coefficient must be before that variable enters at a positive level. The reduced cost for any decision variable at its upper bound in the optimal solution indicates how much worse its coefficient must be before it will decrease from its upper bound. The reduced cost for any variable between 0 and its upper bound in the optimal solution is irrelevant.

Now turn to the bottom section of the report in Figure 13.8. Each row in this section corresponds to a constraint, although upper bound constraints on changing cells are omitted in this section. To have this part of the report make economic sense, the model should be developed as has been done here, where the right side of each constraint is a numeric constant (not a formula). Then the report indicates how much these right-side constants can change before the optimal solution changes. To understand this more fully, the concept of a shadow price is required. A **shadow price** indicates the change in the objective when a right-side constant changes.

The term **shadow price** is an economic term. It indicates the change in the optimal value of the objective when the right side of some constraint changes by one unit.

A shadow price is reported for each constraint. For example, the shadow price for the assembling labor constraint is 16. This means that if the right side of this constraint increases by one hour, from 10000 to 10001, the optimal value of the objective will increase by $16. It works in the other direction as well. If the right side of this constraint *decreases* by one hour, from 10000 to 9999, the optimal value of the objective will decrease by $16. However, as the right side continues to increase or decrease, this $16 change in the objective might not continue. This is where the reported allowable increase and allowable decrease are relevant. As long as the right side increases or decreases within its allowable limits, the same shadow price of 16 still applies. Beyond these limits, however, a different shadow price might apply.

You can prove this for yourself. First, increase the right side of the assembling labor constraint by 200 (exactly the allowable increase), from 10000 to 10200, and rerun Solver. (Don't forget to reset other inputs to their original values.) You will see that the objective indeed increases by 16(200)=$3200, from $199,600 to $202,800. Now increase this right side by one more hour, from 10200 to 10201 and rerun Solver. You will observe that the objective doesn't increase at all. This means that the shadow price beyond 10200 is *less than* 16; in fact, it is zero. This is typical. When a right side increases beyond its allowable increase, the new shadow price is typically less than the original shadow price (although it doesn't always fall to zero, as in this example).

The idea is that a constraint "costs" the company by keeping the objective from being better than it would be. A shadow price indicates how much the company would be willing to pay (in units of the objective) to "relax" a constraint. In this example, the company would be willing to pay $16 for each extra assembling hour. This is because such a change would increase the net profit by $16. But beyond a certain point—200 hours in this example—further relaxation of the constraint does no good, and the company is not willing to pay for any further increases.

The constraint on testing hours is slightly different. It has a shadow price of zero. In fact, the shadow price for a nonbinding constraint is always zero, which makes sense. If the right side of this constraint is changed from 3000 to 3001, nothing at all happens to the optimal product mix or the objective value; there is just one more unneeded testing hour. However, the allowable decrease of 40 indicates that something *does* change when the right side reaches 2960. At this point, the constraint becomes binding—the testing hours used equal the testing hours available—and beyond this, the optimal product mix starts to change. By the way, the allowable increase for this constraint, shown as 1+E30, means that it is essentially infinite. The right side of this constraint can be increased above 3000 indefinitely and absolutely nothing will change in the optimal solution

13.4.2 SolverTable Add-In

The reason Solver's sensitivity report makes sense for the product mix model is that the spreadsheet model is virtually a direct translation of a standard algebraic model. Unfortunately, given the flexibility of spreadsheets, this is not always the case. We have seen many perfectly good spreadsheet models—and have developed many ourselves—that are structured quite differently from their standard algebraic-model counterparts. In these cases, we have found Solver's sensitivity report to be more confusing than useful. Therefore, Albright developed an Excel add-in called SolverTable. **SolverTable** allows you to ask sensitivity questions about any of the input variables, not just coefficients of the objective and right sides of constraints, and it provides straightforward answers.

The SolverTable add-in is on this textbook's Web site.[10] To install it, simply copy the SolverTable files to a folder on your hard drive. These files include the add-in itself (the .xlam file) and the online help files. To load SolverTable, you can proceed in one of two ways:

1. Open the **SolverTable.xlam** file just as you open any other Excel file.

2. Go to the add-ins list in Excel (click on the Office button, then Excel Options, then Add-Ins, then Go) and check the SolverTable item. If it isn't in the list, Browse for the **SolverTable.xlam** file.

The advantage of the second option is that if SolverTable is checked in the add-ins list, it will automatically open every time you open Excel, at least until you uncheck its item in the list.

The SolverTable add-in was developed to mimic Excel's built-in data table tool. Recall that data tables allow you to vary one or two inputs in a spreadsheet model and see instantaneously how selected outputs change. SolverTable is similar except that it runs Solver for every new input (or pair of inputs), and the newest version also provides automatic charts of the results. There are two ways it can be used.

1. **One-way table.** A one-way table means that there is a *single* input cell and *any number* of output cells. That is, there can be a single output cell or multiple output cells.

2. **Two-way table.** A two-way table means that there are *two* input cells and one or more output cells. (You might recall that an Excel two-way data table allows only *one* output. SolverTable allows more than one. It creates a separate table for each output as a function of the two inputs.)

We illustrate some of the possibilities for the product mix example. Specifically, we check how sensitive the optimal production plan and net profit are to (1) changes in the selling price of XPs, (2) the number of labor hours of both types available, and (3) the maximum sales of the two models.

We assume that the model has been formulated and optimized, as shown in Figure 13.7, and that the SolverTable add-in has been loaded. To run SolverTable, click on the Run SolverTable button on the SolverTable ribbon. You will be asked whether there is a Solver model on the active sheet. (Note that the *active* sheet at this point should be the sheet containing the model. If it isn't, click on Cancel and then activate this sheet.) You are then given the choice between a one-way or a two-way table. For the first sensitivity question, choose the one-way option. You will see the dialog box in Figure 13.9. For the sensitivity analysis on the XP selling price, fill it in as shown. Note that ranges can be entered as cell addresses or range names. Also, multiple ranges in the Outputs box should be separated by commas.

---

[10]It is also available from the Free Downloads link on the authors' Web site at www.kelley.iu.edu/albrightbooks. Actually, there are several versions of SolverTable available, each for a particular version of Solver. The one described in the text is for Solver in Excel 2007 or 2010. This Web site contains more information about these versions, as well as possible updates to SolverTable.

Figure 13.9

SolverTable One-Way Dialog Box

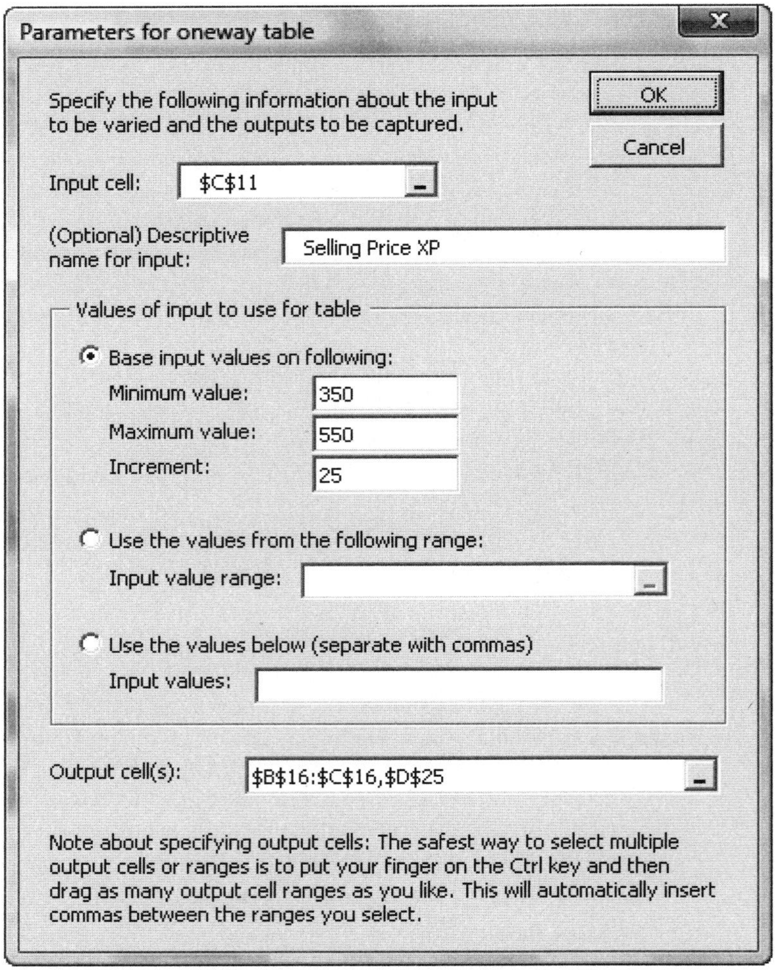

Parameters for oneway table

Specify the following information about the input to be varied and the outputs to be captured.

OK

Cancel

Input cell: $C$11

(Optional) Descriptive name for input: Selling Price XP

Values of input to use for table

○ Base input values on following:

Minimum value: 350

Maximum value: 550

Increment: 25

○ Use the values from the following range:

Input value range:

○ Use the values below (separate with commas)

Input values:

Output cell(s): $B$16:$C$16,$D$25

Note about specifying output cells: The safest way to select multiple output cells or ranges is to put your finger on the Ctrl key and then drag as many output cell ranges as you like. This will automatically insert commas between the ranges you select.

Figure 13.10

SolverTable Results for Varying XP Price

	A	B	C	D	E	F	G
1	Oneway analysis for Solver model in Model worksheet						
2							
3	Selling Price XP (cell $C$11) values along side, output cell(s) along top						
4		Number_to_produce_1	Number_to_produce_2	Total_profit			
5	$350	600	1166.667	$81,833			
6	$375	600	1166.667	$111,000			
7	$400	600	1166.667	$140,167			
8	$425	560	1200	$169,600			
9	$450	560	1200	$199,600			
10	$475	560	1200	$229,600			
11	$500	560	1200	$259,600			
12	$525	560	1200	$289,600			
13	$550	560	1200	$319,600			

Excel Tip *Selecting Multiple Ranges*

If you need to select multiple output ranges, the trick is to keep your finger on the Ctrl key as you drag the ranges. This automatically enters the separating comma(s) for you. Actually, the same trick works for selecting multiple changing cell ranges in Solver's dialog box.

When you click on OK, Solver solves a separate optimization problem for each of the nine rows of the table and then reports the requested outputs (number produced and net profit) in the table, as shown in Figure 13.10. It can take a while, depending on the speed of your computer and the complexity of the model, but everything is automatic. However, if you want to update this table—by using different XP selling prices in column A, for example—you must repeat the procedure. Note that if the requested outputs are included in named ranges, the range names are used in the SolverTable headings. For example, the label Number_to_produce_1 indicates that this output is the first cell in the Number_to_produce range. The label Total_profit indicates that this output is the *only* cell in the Total_profit range. (If a requested output is not part of a named range, its cell address is used as the label in the SolverTable results.)

Figure 13.11

Associated SolverTable Chart for Net Profit

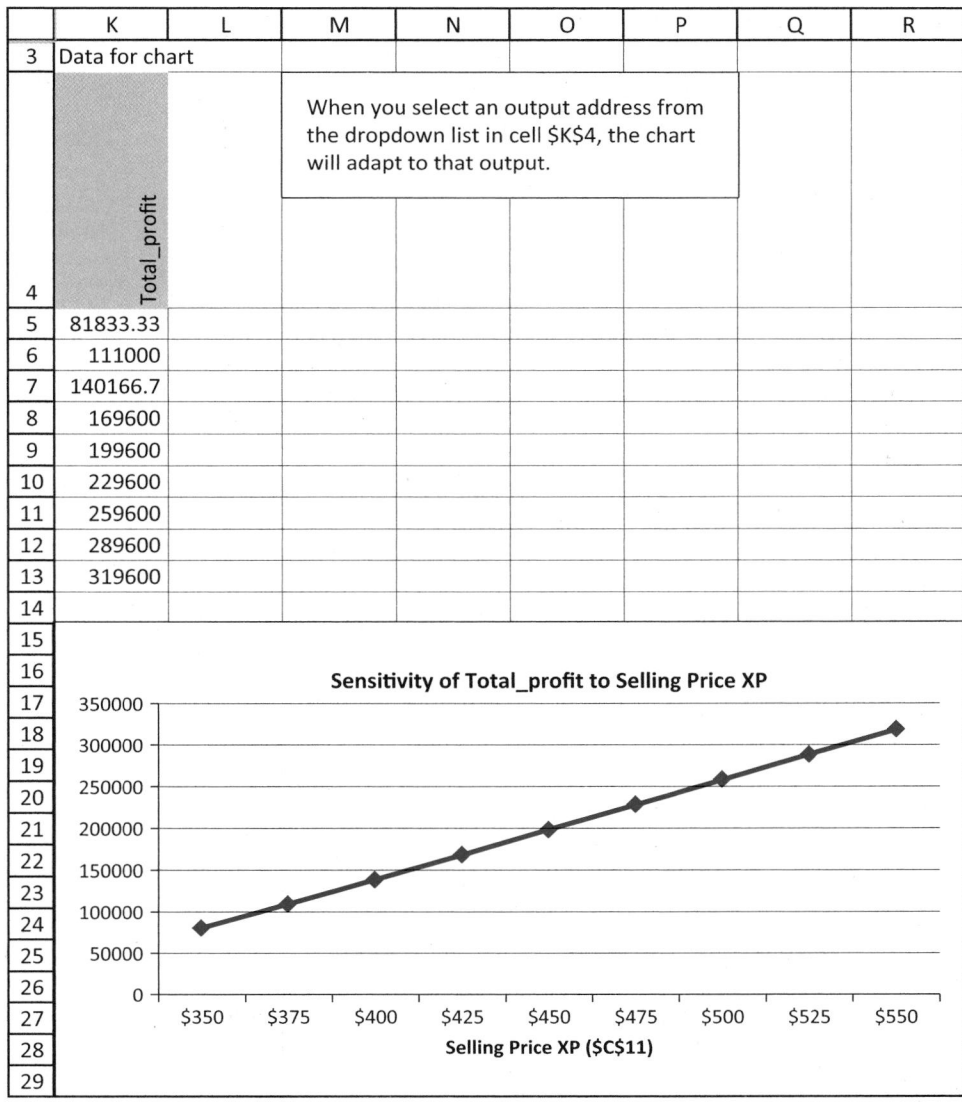

The outputs in this table show that when the selling price of XPs is relatively low, the company should make as many Basics as it can sell and a few less XPs, but when the selling price is relatively high, the company should do the opposite. Also, the net profit increases steadily through this range. You can calculate these changes (which are not part of the SolverTable output) in column E. The increase in net profit per every extra $25 in XP selling price is close to, but not always exactly equal to, $30,000.

SolverTable also produces the chart in Figure 13.11. There is a dropdown list in cell K4 where you can choose any of the SolverTable outputs. (We selected the net profit, cell D25.) The chart then shows the data for that column from the table in Figure 13.10. Here there is a steady increase (slope about $30,000) in net profit as the XP selling price increases.

The second sensitivity question asks you to vary two inputs, the two labor availabilities, simultaneously. This requires a two-way SolverTable, so fill in the SolverTable dialog box as shown in Figure 13.12. Here two inputs and two input ranges are specified, and multiple output cells are again allowed. An output table is generated for *each* of the output cells, as shown in Figure 13.13. For example, the top table shows how the optimal number of Basics varies as the two labor availabilities vary. Comparing the columns of this top table, it is apparent that the optimal number of Basics becomes increasingly sensitive to the available assembling hours as the number of available testing hours increases. The SolverTable output also includes two charts (not shown here) that let you graph any row or any column of any of these tables.

The third sensitivity question, involving maximum sales of the two models, reveals the flexibility of SolverTable. Instead of letting these two inputs vary independently in a two-way SolverTable, it is possible to let both of them vary according to a *single* percentage change. For example, if this percentage change is 10%, both maximum sales increase by

Figure 13.12
SolverTable Two-
Way Dialog Box

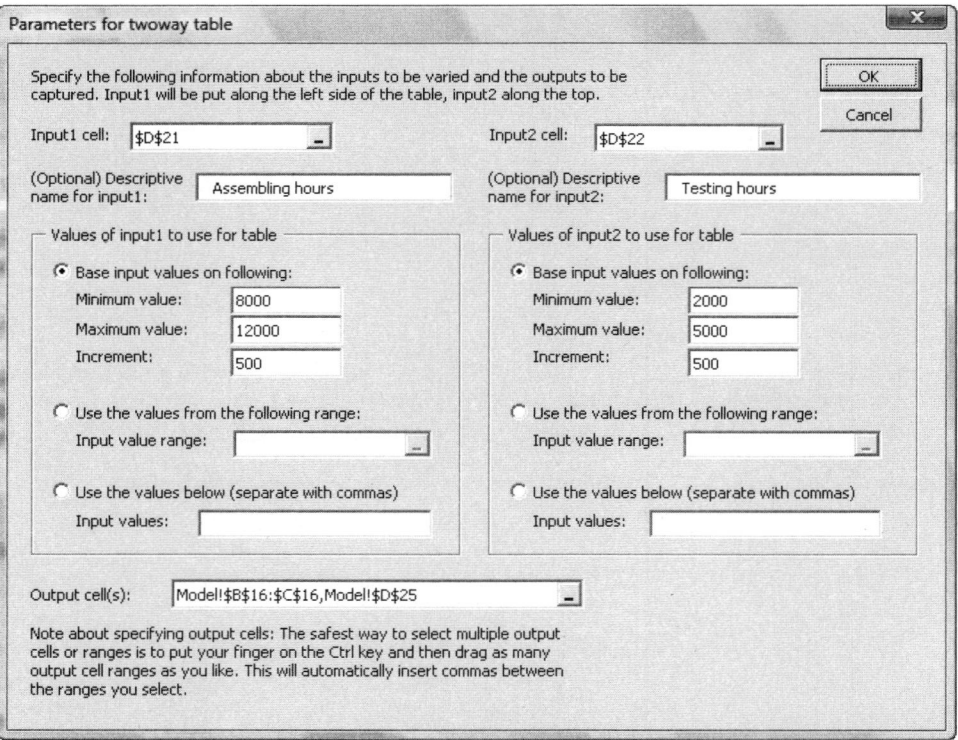

Figure 13.13

Two-Way SolverTable Results

	A	B	C	D	E	F	G	H	I
3	Assembling hours (cell $D$21) values along side, Testing hours (cell $D$22) values along top, output cell in corner								
4	Number_to_produce_1	2000	2500	3000	3500	4000	4500	5000	
5	8000	600	250	160	160	160	160	160	
6	8500	600	500	260	260	260	260	260	
7	9000	600	600	360	360	360	360	360	
8	9500	600	600	460	460	460	460	460	
9	10000	600	600	560	560	560	560	560	
10	10500	600	600	600	600	600	600	600	
11	11000	600	600	600	600	600	600	600	
12	11500	600	600	600	600	600	600	600	
13	12000	600	600	600	600	600	600	600	
14									
15	Number_to_produce_2	2000	2500	3000	3500	4000	4500	5000	
16	8000	700	1125	1200	1200	1200	1200	1200	
17	8500	700	1000	1200	1200	1200	1200	1200	
18	9000	700	950	1200	1200	1200	1200	1200	
19	9500	700	950	1200	1200	1200	1200	1200	
20	10000	700	950	1200	1200	1200	1200	1200	
21	10500	700	950	1200	1200	1200	1200	1200	
22	11000	700	950	1200	1200	1200	1200	1200	
23	11500	700	950	1200	1200	1200	1200	1200	
24	12000	700	950	1200	1200	1200	1200	1200	
25									
26	Total_profit	2000	2500	3000	3500	4000	4500	5000	
27	8000	$138,300	$165,125	$167,600	$167,600	$167,600	$167,600	$167,600	
28	8500	$138,300	$169,000	$175,600	$175,600	$175,600	$175,600	$175,600	
29	9000	$138,300	$170,550	$183,600	$183,600	$183,600	$183,600	$183,600	
30	9500	$138,300	$170,550	$191,600	$191,600	$191,600	$191,600	$191,600	
31	10000	$138,300	$170,550	$199,600	$199,600	$199,600	$199,600	$199,600	
32	10500	$138,300	$170,550	$202,800	$202,800	$202,800	$202,800	$202,800	
33	11000	$138,300	$170,550	$202,800	$202,800	$202,800	$202,800	$202,800	
34	11500	$138,300	$170,550	$202,800	$202,800	$202,800	$202,800	$202,800	
35	12000	$138,300	$170,550	$202,800	$202,800	$202,800	$202,800	$202,800	

10%. The trick is to modify the model so that one percentage-change cell drives changes in both maximum sales. The modified model appears in Figure 13.14. Starting with the original model, enter the original values, 600 and 1200, in new cells, E18 and F18. (Do *not* copy the range B18:C18 to E18:F18. This would make the right side of the constraint

Figure 13.14

Modified Model for Simultaneous Changes

	A	B	C	D	E	F	G	H
1	**Assembling and testing computers**							
2								
3	Cost per labor hour assembling	$11						
4	Cost per labor hour testing	$15						
5								
6	Inputs for assembling and testing a computer							
7		Basic	XP					
8	Labor hours for assembly	5	6					
9	Labor hours for testing	1	2					
10	Cost of component parts	$150	$225					
11	Selling price	$300	$450					
12	Unit margin	$80	$129					
13								
14	Assembling, testing plan (# of computers)							
15		Basic	XP					
16	Number to produce	560	1200					
17		<=	<=		Original values		% change in both	
18	Maximum sales	600	1200		600	1200	0%	
19								
20	Constraints (hours per month)	Hours used		Hours available				
21	Labor availability for assembling	10000	<=	10000				
22	Labor availability for testing	2960	<=	3000				
23								
24	Net profit ($ this month)	Basic	XP	Total				
25		$44,800	$154,800	$199,600				

E18:F18, which is not the desired behavior.) Then enter any percentage change in cell G18. Finally, enter the *formula*

=E18*(1+$G$18)

in cell B18 and copy it to cell C18. Now a one-way SolverTable can be used with the percentage change in cell G18 to drive two different inputs simultaneously. Specifically, the SolverTable dialog box should be set up as in Figure 13.15, with the corresponding results in Figure 13.16.

You should always scan these sensitivity results to see if they make sense. For example, if the company can sell 20% or 30% more of both models, it makes no more profit than if it can sell only 10% more. The reason is labor availability. By this point, there isn't enough labor to produce the increased demand.

It is always possible to run a sensitivity analysis by changing inputs manually in the spreadsheet model and rerunning Solver. The advantages of SolverTable, however, are that it enables you to perform a *systematic* sensitivity analysis for any selected inputs and outputs, and it keeps track of the results in a table and associated chart(s). You will see other applications of this useful add-in later in this chapter and in the next chapter.

13.4.3 Comparison of Solver's Sensitivity Report and SolverTable

Sensitivity analysis in optimization models is extremely important, so it is important that you understand the pros and cons of the two tools in this section. Here are some points to keep in mind.

Figure 13.15

SolverTable One-Way Dialog Box

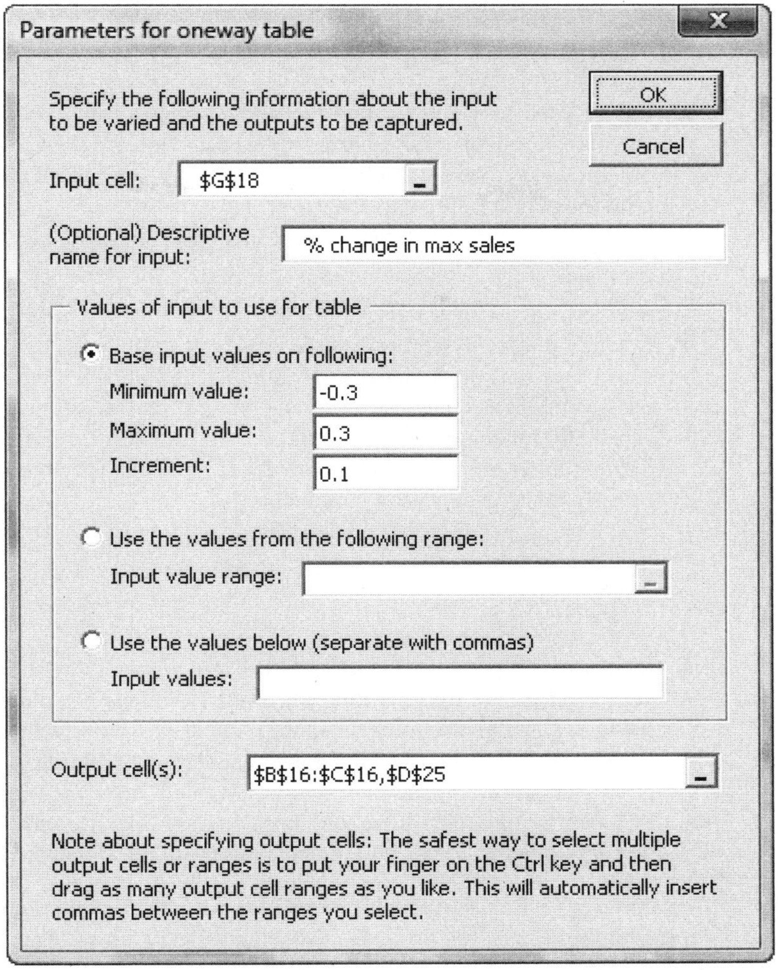

Parameters for oneway table [X]

Specify the following information about the input
to be varied and the outputs to be captured.

OK

Cancel

Input cell: | $G$18 | _

(Optional) Descriptive
name for input: | % change in max sales

Values of input to use for table

(•) Base input values on following:

Minimum value: | -0.3

Maximum value: | 0.3

Increment: | 0.1

( ) Use the values from the following range:

Input value range: | | _

( ) Use the values below (separate with commas)

Input values: | |

Output cell(s): | $B$16:$C$16,$D$25 | _

Note about specifying output cells: The safest way to select multiple
output cells or ranges is to put your finger on the Ctrl key and then
drag as many output cell ranges as you like. This will automatically insert
commas between the ranges you select.

Figure 13.16

Sensitivity to
Percentage Change
in Maximum Sales

	A	B	C	D	E	F	G
3	% change in max sales (cell $G$18) values along side, output cell(s) along top						
4		Number_to_produce_1	Number_to_produce_2	Total_profit	$B$12		
5	-30%	420	840	$141,960	$80		
6	-20%	480	960	$162,240	$80		
7	-10%	540	1080	$182,520	$80		
8	0%	560	1200	$199,600	$80		
9	10%	500	1250	$201,250	$80		
10	20%	500	1250	$201,250	$80		
11	30%	500	1250	$201,250	$80		

- Solver's sensitivity report focuses only on the coefficients of the objective and the right sides of the constraints. SolverTable allows you to vary *any* of the inputs.

- Solver's sensitivity report provides very useful information through its reduced costs, shadow prices, and allowable increases and decreases. This same information can be obtained with SolverTable, but it requires a bit more work and some experimentation with the appropriate input ranges.

- Solver's sensitivity report is based on changing only one objective coefficient or one right side at a time. This one-at-a-time restriction prevents you from answering certain questions directly. SolverTable is much more flexible in this respect.

- Solver's sensitivity report is based on a well-established mathematical theory of sensitivity analysis in linear programming. If you lack this mathematical background—as many users do—the outputs can be difficult to understand, especially for somewhat "nonstandard" spreadsheet formulations. In contrast, SolverTable's outputs are straightforward. You can vary one or two inputs and see directly how the optimal solution changes.

- Solver's sensitivity report is not even available for integer-constrained models, and its interpretation for nonlinear models is more difficult than for linear models. SolverTable's outputs have the same interpretation for any type of optimization model.

- Solver's sensitivity report comes with Excel. SolverTable is a separate add-in that is not included with Excel—but it is included with this book and is freely available from the Free Downloads link at the authors' Web site, www.kelley.iu.edu/albrightbooks. Because the SolverTable software essentially automates Solver, which has a number of its own idiosyncrasies, some users have had problems with SolverTable on their PCs. We have tried to document these on our Web site, and we are hoping that the revised Solver in Excel 2010 helps to alleviate these problems.

In summary, each of these tools can be used to answer certain questions. We tend to favor SolverTable because of its flexibility, but in the optimization examples in this chapter and the next chapter we will illustrate both tools to show how each can provide useful information.

13.5 PROPERTIES OF LINEAR MODELS

Linear programming is an important subset of a larger class of models called **mathematical programming models**.[11] All such models select the levels of various activities that can be performed, subject to a set of constraints, to maximize or minimize an objective such as total profit or total cost. In PC Tech's product mix example, the activities are the numbers of PCs to produce, and the purpose of the model is to find the levels of these activities that maximize the total net profit subject to specified constraints.

In terms of this general setup—selecting the optimal levels of activities—there are three important properties that LP models possess that distinguish them from general mathematical programming models: *proportionality*, *additivity*, and *divisibility*. We discuss these properties briefly in this section.

---

[11]The word *programming* in linear programming or mathematical programming has nothing to do with computer programming. It originated with the British term *programme*, which is essentially a plan or a schedule of operations.

13.5.1 Proportionality

Proportionality means that if the level of any activity is multiplied by a constant factor, the contribution of this activity to the objective, or to any of the constraints in which the activity is involved, is multiplied by the same factor. For example, suppose that the production of Basics is cut from its optimal value of 560 to 280—that is, it is multiplied by 0.5. Then the amounts of labor hours from assembling and from testing Basics are both cut in half, and the net profit contributed by Basics is also cut in half.

Proportionality is a perfectly valid assumption in the product mix model, but it is often violated in certain types of models. For example, in various *blending* models used by petroleum companies, chemical outputs vary in a nonlinear manner as chemical inputs are varied. If a chemical input is doubled, say, the resulting chemical output is not necessarily doubled. This type of behavior violates the proportionality property, and it takes us into the realm of *nonlinear* optimization, which we discuss briefly in the next chapter.

13.5.2 Additivity

The **additivity** property implies that the sum of the contributions from the various activities to a particular constraint equals the total contribution to that constraint. For example, if the two PC models use, respectively, 560 and 2400 testing hours (as in Figure 13.7), then the total number used in the plan is the *sum* of these amounts, 2960 hours. Similarly, the additivity property applies to the objective. That is, the value of the objective is the *sum* of the contributions from the various activities. In the product mix model, the net profits from the two PC models add up to the total net profit. The additivity property implies that the contribution of any decision variable to the objective or to any constraint is *independent* of the levels of the other decision variables.

13.5.3 Divisibility

The **divisibility** property simply means that both integer and noninteger levels of the activities are allowed. In the product mix model, we got integer values in the optimal solution, 560 and 1200, just by luck. For slightly different inputs, they could easily have been fractional values. In general, if you want the levels of some activities to be integer values, there are two possible approaches: (1) You can solve the LP model without integer constraints, and if the solution turns out to have fractional values, you can attempt to round them to integer values; or (2) you can explicitly constrain certain changing cells to contain integer values. The latter approach, however, takes you into the realm of *integer programming*, which we study briefly in the next chapter. At this point, we simply state that integer problems are *much* more difficult to solve than problems without integer constraints.

13.5.4 Discussion of Linear Properties

The previous discussion of these three properties, especially proportionality and additivity, is fairly abstract. How can you recognize whether a model satisfies proportionality and additivity? This is easy if the model is described algebraically. In this case the objective must be of the form

$$a_1 x_1 + a_2 x_2 + \cdots + a_n x_n$$

where n is the number of decision variables, the as are constants, and the xs are decision variables. This expression is called a *linear combination* of the xs. Also, each constraint must be equivalent to a form where the left side is a linear combination of the xs and the right side is a constant. For example, the following is a typical linear constraint:

$$3x_1 + 7x_2 - 2x_3 \leq 50$$

It is not quite so easy to recognize proportionality and additivity—or the lack of them—in a spreadsheet model, because the logic of the model is typically embedded in a series of cell formulas. However, the ideas are the same. First, the objective cell must ultimately (possibly through a series of formulas in intervening cells) be a sum of products of constants and changing cells, where a "constant" means that it does not depend on changing cells. Second, each side of each constraint must ultimately be either a constant or a sum of products of constants and changing cells. This explains why linear models contain so many SUM and SUMPRODUCT functions.

It is usually easier to recognize when a model is *not* linear. Two particular situations that lead to nonlinear models are when (1) there are products or quotients of expressions involving changing cells or (2) there are nonlinear functions, such as squares, square roots, or logarithms, that involve changing cells. These are typically easy to spot, and they guarantee that the model is nonlinear.

Whenever you model a real problem, you usually make some simplifying assumptions. This is certainly the case with LP models. The world is frequently *not* linear, which means that an entirely realistic model typically violates some or all of the three properties in this section. However, numerous successful applications of LP have demonstrated the usefulness of linear models, even if they are only *approximations* of reality. If you suspect that the violations are serious enough to invalidate a linear model, you should use an integer or nonlinear model, as we illustrate in the next chapter.

In terms of Excel's Solver, if the model is linear—that is, if it satisfies the proportionality, additivity, and divisibility properties—you should check the Simplex option (or the Assume Linear Model option in pre-2010 versions of Excel). Then Solver uses the simplex method, a very efficient method for a linear model, to solve the problem. Actually, you can check the Simplex option even if the divisibility property is violated—that is, for linear models with integer-constrained variables—but Solver then embeds the simplex method in a more complex algorithm (branch and bound) in its solution procedure.

Real-life problems are almost never exactly linear. However, linear approximations often yield very useful results.

13.5.5 Linear Models and Scaling[12]

In some cases you might be sure that a model is linear, but when you check the Simplex option (or the Assume Linear Model option) and then solve, you get a Solver message to the effect that the conditions for linearity are not satisfied. This can indicate a logical error in your formulation, so that the proportionality and additivity conditions are indeed not satisfied. However, it can also indicate that Solver erroneously *thinks* the linearity conditions are not satisfied, which is typically due to roundoff error in its calculations—not any error on your part. If the latter occurs and you are convinced that the model is correct, you can try *not* using the simplex method to see whether that works. If it does not, you should consult your instructor. It is possible that the non-simplex algorithm employed by Solver simply cannot find the solution to your problem.

In any case, it always helps to have a *well-scaled* model. In a well-scaled model, all of the numbers are roughly the same magnitude. If the model contains some very large numbers—100,000 or more, say—and some very small numbers—0.001 or less, say—it is *poorly scaled* for the methods used by Solver, and roundoff error is far more likely to be an issue, not only in Solver's test for linearity conditions but in all of its algorithms.

---

[12]This section might seem overly technical. However, when you develop a model that you are sure is linear and Solver then tells you it doesn't satisfy the linear conditions, you will appreciate this section.

If you believe your model is poorly scaled, there are three possible remedies. The first is to check the Use Automatic Scaling option in Solver. (It is found by clicking on the Options button in the main Solver dialog box.) This might help and it might not; we have had mixed success. (Frontline Systems, the company that develops Solver, has told us that the only drawback to checking this box is that the solution procedure can be slower.) The second option is to redefine the units in which the various quantities are defined. Finally, you can change the Precision setting in Solver's Options dialog box to a larger number, such 0.00001 or 0.0001. (The default has five zeros.)

Excel Tip *Rescaling a Model*
Suppose you have a whole range of input values expressed, say, in dollars, and you would like to reexpress them in thousands of dollars, that is, you would like to divide each value by 1000. There is a simple copy/paste way to do this. Enter the value 1000 in some unused cell and copy it. Then highlight the range you want to rescale, and from the Paste drop-down menu, select Paste Special and then the Divide option. No formulas are required; your original values are automatically rescaled (and you can then delete the 1000 cell). You can use this same method to add, subtract, or multiply by a constant.

13.6 INFEASIBILITY AND UNBOUNDEDNESS

In this section we discuss two of the things that can go wrong when you invoke Solver. Both of these might indicate that there is a mistake in the model. Therefore, because mistakes are common in LP models, you should be aware of the error messages you might encounter.

13.6.1 Infeasibility

The first problem is **infeasibility**. Recall that a solution is *feasible* if it satisfies all of the constraints. Among all of the feasible solutions, you are looking for the one that optimizes the objective. However, it is possible that there are no feasible solutions to the model. There are generally two reasons for this: (1) there is a mistake in the model (an input was entered incorrectly, such as a ≤ symbol instead of a ≥) or (2) the problem has been so constrained that there are no solutions left. In the former case, a careful check of the model should find the error. In the latter case, you might need to change, or even eliminate, some of the constraints.

A perfectly reasonable model can have no feasible solutions because of too many constraints.

To show how an infeasible problem could occur, suppose in PC Tech's product mix problem you change the maximum sales constraints to *minimum* sales constraints (and leave everything else unchanged). That is, you change these constraints from ≤ to ≥. If Solver is then used, the message in Figure 13.17 appears, indicating that Solver cannot find a feasible solution. The reason is clear: There is no way, given the constraints on labor hours, that the company can produce these minimum sales values. The company's only choice is to set at least one of the minimum sales values lower. In general, there is no fool-proof way to remedy the problem when a "no feasible solution" message appears. Careful checking and rethinking are required.

13.6.2 Unboundedness

A second type of problem is **unboundedness**. In this case, the model has been formulated in such a way that the objective is unbounded—that is, it can be made as large (or as small, for minimization problems) as you like. If this occurs, you have probably entered a wrong input or forgotten some constraints. To see how this could occur in the product mix problem,

Figure 13.17
No Feasible Solution
Message

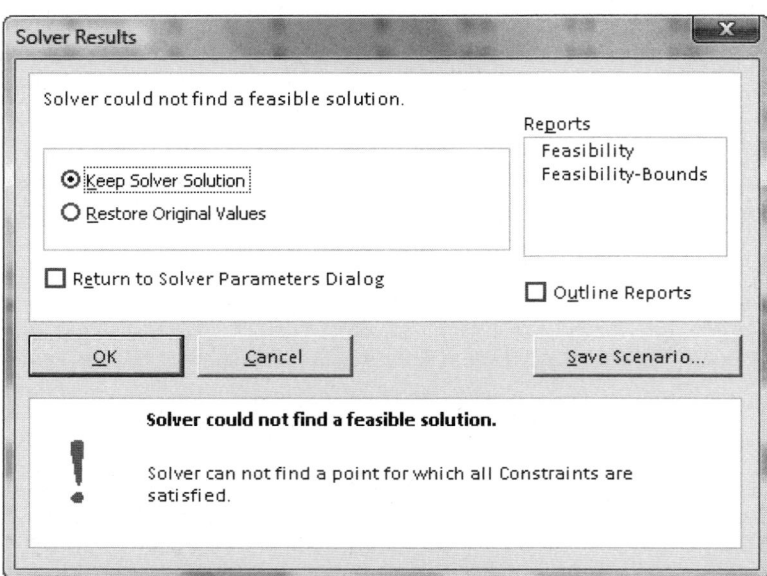

Figure 13.18
Unbounded
Solution Message

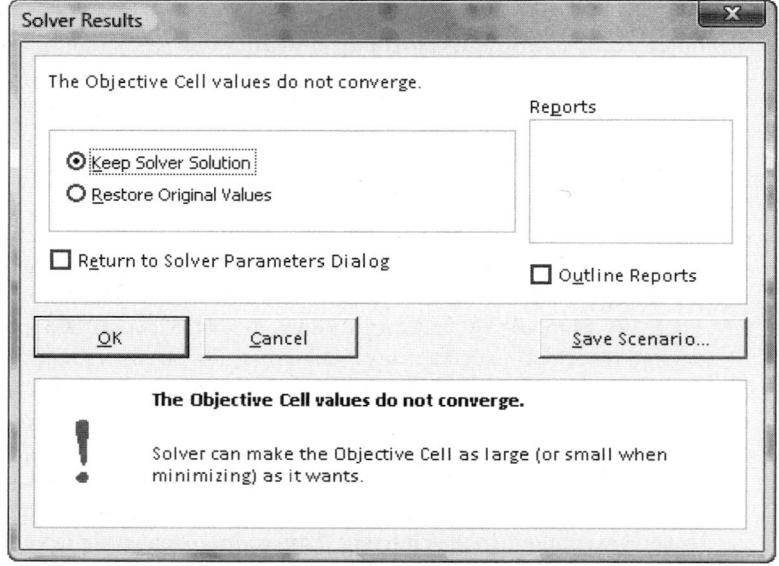

suppose that you change *all* constraints to be ≤ instead of ≥. Now there is no upper bound on how much labor is available or how many PCs the company can sell. If you make this change in the model and then use Solver, the message in Figure 13.18 appears, stating that the objective cell does not converge. In other words, the total net profit can grow without bound.

13.6.3 Comparison of Infeasibility and Unboundedness

Except in very rare situations, if Solver informs you that your model is unbounded, you have made an error.

Infeasibility and unboundedness are quite different in a practical sense. It is quite possible for a reasonable model to have no feasible solutions. For example, the marketing department might impose several constraints, the production department might add some more, the engineering department might add even more, and so on. Together, they might constrain the problem so much that there are no feasible solutions left. The only way out is to change or eliminate some of the constraints. An unboundedness problem is quite different. There is no way a realistic model can have an unbounded solution. If you get the message shown in Figure 13.18, then you must have made a mistake: You entered an input incorrectly, you omitted one or more constraints, or there is a logical error in your model.

PROBLEMS

Note: Student solutions for problems whose numbers appear within a colored box are available for purchase at www.cengagebrain.com.

Level A

1. Other sensitivity analyses besides those discussed could be performed on the product mix model. Use SolverTable to perform each of the following. In each case keep track of the values in the changing cells and the objective cell, and discuss your findings.
  a. Let the selling price for Basics vary from $220 to $350 in increments of $10.
  b. Let the labor cost per hour for assembling vary from $5 to $20 in increments of $1.
  c. Let the labor hours for testing a Basic vary from 0.5 to 3.0 in increments of 0.5.
  d. Let the labor hours for assembling and testing an XP vary independently, the first from 4.5 to 8.0 and the second from 1.5 to 3.0, both in increments of 0.5.

2. In PC Tech's product mix problem, assume there is another PC model, the VXP, that the company can produce in addition to Basics and XPs. Each VXP requires eight hours for assembling, three hours for testing, $275 for component parts, and sells for $560. At most 50 VXPs can be sold.
  a. Modify the spreadsheet model to include this new product, and use Solver to find the optimal product mix.
  b. You should find that the optimal solution is *not* integer-valued. If you round the values in the changing cells to the nearest integers, is the resulting solution still feasible? If not, how might you obtain a feasible solution that is at least close to optimal?

3. Continuing the previous problem, perform a sensitivity analysis on the selling price of VXPs. Let this price vary from $500 to $650 in increments of $10, and keep track of the values in the changing cells and the objective cell. Discuss your findings.

4. Again continuing problem 2, suppose that you want to force the optimal solution to be integers. Do this in Solver by adding a new constraint. Select the changing cells for the left side of the constraint, and in the middle dropdown list, select the "int" option. How does the optimal integer solution compare to the optimal noninteger solution in problem 2? Are the changing cell

values rounded versions of those in problem 2? Is the objective value more or less than in problem 2?

5. If all of the inputs in PC Tech's product mix problem are nonnegative (as they should be for any realistic version of the problem), are there any input values such that the resulting model has no feasible solutions? (Refer to the graphical solution.)

6. There are five corner points in the feasible region for the product mix problem. We identified the coordinates of one of them: (560, 1200). Identify the coordinates of the others.
  a. Only one of these other corner points has positive values for both changing cells. Discuss the changes in the selling prices of either or both models that would be necessary to make this corner point optimal.
  b. Two of the other corner points have one changing cell value positive and the other zero. Discuss the changes in the selling prices of either or both models that would be necessary to make either of these corner points optimal.

Level B

7. Using the graphical solution of the product mix model as a guide, suppose there are only 2800 testing hours available. How do the answers to the previous problem change? (Is the previous solution still optimal? Is it still feasible?)

8. Again continuing problem 2, perform a sensitivity analysis where the selling prices of Basics and XPs simultaneously change by the same percentage, but the selling price of VXPs remains at its original value. Let the percentage change vary from −25% to 50% in increments of 5%, and keep track of the values in the changing cells and the total profit. Discuss your findings.

9. Consider the graphical solution to the product mix problem. Now imagine that another constraint—*any* constraint—is added. Which of the following three things are possible: (1) the feasible region shrinks; (2) the feasible region stays the same; (3) the feasible region expands? Which of the following three things are possible: (1) the optimal value in objective cell decreases; (2) the optimal value in objective cell stays the same; (3) the optimal value in objective cell increases? Explain your answers. Do they hold just for this particular model, or do they hold in general?

13.7 A LARGER PRODUCT MIX MODEL

The problem we examine in this section is a direct extension of the product mix model in the previous section. There are two modifications. First, the company makes eight computer models, not just two. Second, testing can be done on either of two lines, and these two lines have different characteristics.

EXAMPLE | **13.2 PRODUCING COMPUTERS AT PC TECH**

As in the previous example, PC Tech must decide how many of each of its computer models to assemble and test, but there are now eight available models, not just two. Each computer must be assembled and then tested, but there are now two lines for testing. The first line tends to test faster, but its labor costs are slightly higher, and each line has a certain number of hours available for testing. Any computer can be tested on either line. The inputs for the model are same as before: (1) the hourly labor costs for assembling and testing, (2) the required labor hours for assembling and testing any computer model, (3) the cost of component parts for each model, (4) the selling prices for each model, (5) the maximum sales for each model, and (6) labor availabilities. These input values are listed in the file **Product Mix 2.xlsx**. As before, the company wants to determine the product mix that maximizes its total net profit.

Objective To use LP to find the mix of computer models that maximizes total net profit and stays within the labor hour availability and maximum sales constraints.

WHERE DO THE NUMBERS COME FROM?

The same comments as in Example 13.1 apply here.

Solution

Table 13.2 lists the variables and constraints for this model. You must choose the number of computers of each model to produce on each line, the sum of which cannot be larger than the maximum that can be sold. This choice determines the labor hours of each type used and all revenues and costs. No more labor hours can be used than are available.

Table 13.2 Variables and Constraints for Larger Product Mix Model

Input variables	Hourly labor costs, labor availabilities, labor required for each computer, costs of component parts, unit selling prices, and maximum sales
Decision variables (changing cells)	Numbers of computer of each model to test on each line
Objective cell	Total net profit
Other calculated variables	Number of each computer model produced, hours of labor used for assembling and for each line of testing
Constraints	Computers produced ≤ Maximum sales
	Labor hours used ≤ Labor hours available

It is probably not immediately obvious what the changing cells should be for this model (at least not before you look at Table 13.2). You might think that the company simply needs to decide how many computers of each model to produce. However, because of the two testing lines, this is not enough information. The company must also decide how many of each model to test *on each line*. For example, suppose they decide to test 100 model 4s on line 1 and 300 model 4s on line 2. This means they will need to assemble (and ultimately sell) 400 model 4s. In other words, given the detailed plan of how many to test on each line, everything else is determined. But without the detailed plan, there is not enough information to complete the model. This is the type of reasoning you must go through to determine the appropriate changing cells for any LP model.

An Algebraic Model

We will not spell out the algebraic model for this expanded version of the product mix model because it is so similar to the two-variable product mix model. However, we will say that it is larger, and hence probably more intimidating. Now we need decision variables of the form x_{ij}, the number of model j computers to test on line i, and the total net profit and each labor availability constraint will include a long SUMPRODUCT formula involving these variables. Instead of focusing on these algebraic expressions, we turn directly to the spreadsheet model.

DEVELOPING THE SPREADSHEET MODEL

The spreadsheet in Figure 13.19 illustrates the solution procedure for PC Tech's product mix problem. (See the file **Product Mix 2.xlsx**.) The first stage is to develop the spreadsheet model step by step.

1 **Inputs.** Enter the various inputs in the blue ranges. Again, remember that our convention is to color all input cells blue. Enter only *numbers*, not formulas, in input cells. They should always be numbers directly from the problem statement. (In this case, we supplied them in the spreadsheet template.)

2 **Range names.** Name the ranges indicated. According to our convention, there are enough named ranges so that the Solver dialog box contains only range names, no cell addresses. Of course, you can name additional ranges if you like. (Note that you can again use the range-naming shortcut explained in the Excel tip for the previous example. That is, you can take advantage of labels in adjacent cells, except for the Profit cell.)

3 **Unit margins.** Note that two rows of these are required, one for each testing line, because the costs of testing on the two lines are not equal. To calculate them, enter the formula

=B$13-$B$3*B$9-$B$4*B10-B$12

in cell B14 and copy it to the range B14:I15.

4 **Changing cells.** As discussed above, the changing cells are the red cells in rows 19 and 20. You do *not* have to enter the values shown in Figure 13.19. You can use any trial values initially; Solver will eventually find the *optimal* values. Note that the four values shown in Figure 13.19 cannot be optimal because they do not satisfy all of the constraints. Specifically, this plan uses more labor hours for assembling than are available. However, you do not need to worry about satisfying constraints at this point; Solver will take care of this later.

5 **Labor used.** Enter the formula

=SUMPRODUCT(B9:E9,Total_computers_produced)

in cell B26 to calculate the number of assembling hours used. Similarly, enter the formulas

=SUMPRODUCT(B10:I10,Number_tested_on_line_1)

Figure 13.19 Larger Product Mix Model with Infeasible Solution

	A	B	C	D	E	F	G	H	I	J
1	**Assembling and testing computers**									
2										
3	Cost per labor hour assembling	$11								
4	Cost per labor hour testing, line 1	$19								
5	Cost per labor hour testing, line 2	$17								
6										
7	Inputs for assembling and testing a computer									
8		Model 1	Model 2	Model 3	Model 4	Model 5	Model 6	Model 7	Model 8	
9	Labor hours for assembly	4	5	5	5	5.5	5.5	5.5	6	
10	Labor hours for testing, line 1	1.5	2	2	2	2.5	2.5	2.5	3	
11	Labor hours for testing, line 2	2	2.5	2.5	2.5	3	3	3.5	3.5	
12	Cost of component parts	$150	$225	$225	$225	$250	$250	$250	$300	
13	Selling price	$350	$450	$460	$470	$500	$525	$530	$600	
14	Unit margin, tested on line 1	$128	$132	$142	$152	$142	$167	$172	$177	
15	Unit margin, tested on line 2	$122	$128	$138	$148	$139	$164	$160	$175	
16										
17	Assembling, testing plan (# of computers)									
18		Model 1	Model 2	Model 3	Model 4	Model 5	Model 6	Model 7	Model 8	
19	Number tested on line 1	0	0	0	0	0	500	1000	800	
20	Number tested on line 2	0	0	0	1250	0	0	0	0	
21	Total computers produced	0	0	0	1250	0	500	1000	800	
22		<=	<=	<=	<=	<=	<=	<=	<=	
23	Maximum sales	1500	1250	1250	1250	1000	1000	1000	800	
24										
25	Constraints (hours per month)	Hours used		Hours available						
26	Labor availability for assembling	19300	<=	20000						
27	Labor availability for testing, line 1	6150	<=	5000						
28	Labor availability for testing, line 2	3125	<=	6000						
29										
30	Net profit ($ per month)	Model 1	Model 2	Model 3	Model 4	Model 5	Model 6	Model 7	Model 8	Totals
31	Tested on line 1	$0	$0	$0	$0	$0	$83,500	$172,000	$141,600	$397,100
32	Tested on line 2	$0	$0	$0	$184,375	$0	$0	$0	$0	$184,375
33										$581,475
34										
35	**Range names used:**									
36	Hours_available	=Model!$D$26:$D$28								
37	Hours_used	=Model!$B$26:$B$28								
38	Maximum_sales	=Model!$B$23:$I$23								
39	Number_tested_on_line_1	=Model!$B$19:$I$19								
40	Number_tested_on_line_2	=Model!$B$20:$I$20								
41	Total_computers_produce d	=Model!$B$21:$I$21								
42	Total_profit	=Model!$J$33								

and

=SUMPRODUCT(B11:I11,Number_tested_on_line_2)

in cells B27 and B28 for the labor hours used on each testing line.

Excel Tip *Copying formulas with range names*
When you enter a range name in an Excel formula and then copy the formula, the range name reference acts like an absolute reference. Therefore, it wouldn't work to copy the formula in cell B27 to cell B28. However, this would work if range names hadn't been used. This is one potential disadvantage of range names that you should be aware of.

6 **Revenues, costs, and profits.** The area from row 30 down shows the summary of monetary values. Actually, only the total profit in cell J33 is needed, but it is also useful to calculate the net profit from each computer model on each testing line. To obtain these, enter the formula

=B14*B19

in cell B31 and copy it to the range B31:I32. Then sum these to obtain the totals in column J. The total in cell J33 is the objective to maximize.

Experimenting with Other Solutions

Before going any further, you might want to experiment with other values in the changing cells. However, it is a real challenge to guess the optimal solution. It is tempting to fill up the changing cells corresponding to the largest unit margins. However, this totally ignores their use of the scarce labor hours. If you can guess the optimal solution to this model, you are better than we are!

USING SOLVER

The Solver dialog box should be filled out as shown in Figure 13.20. (Again, note that there are enough named ranges so that only range names appear in this dialog box.) Except that this model has two rows of changing cells, the Solver setup is identical to the one in Example 13.1.

Figure 13.20
Solver Dialog Box

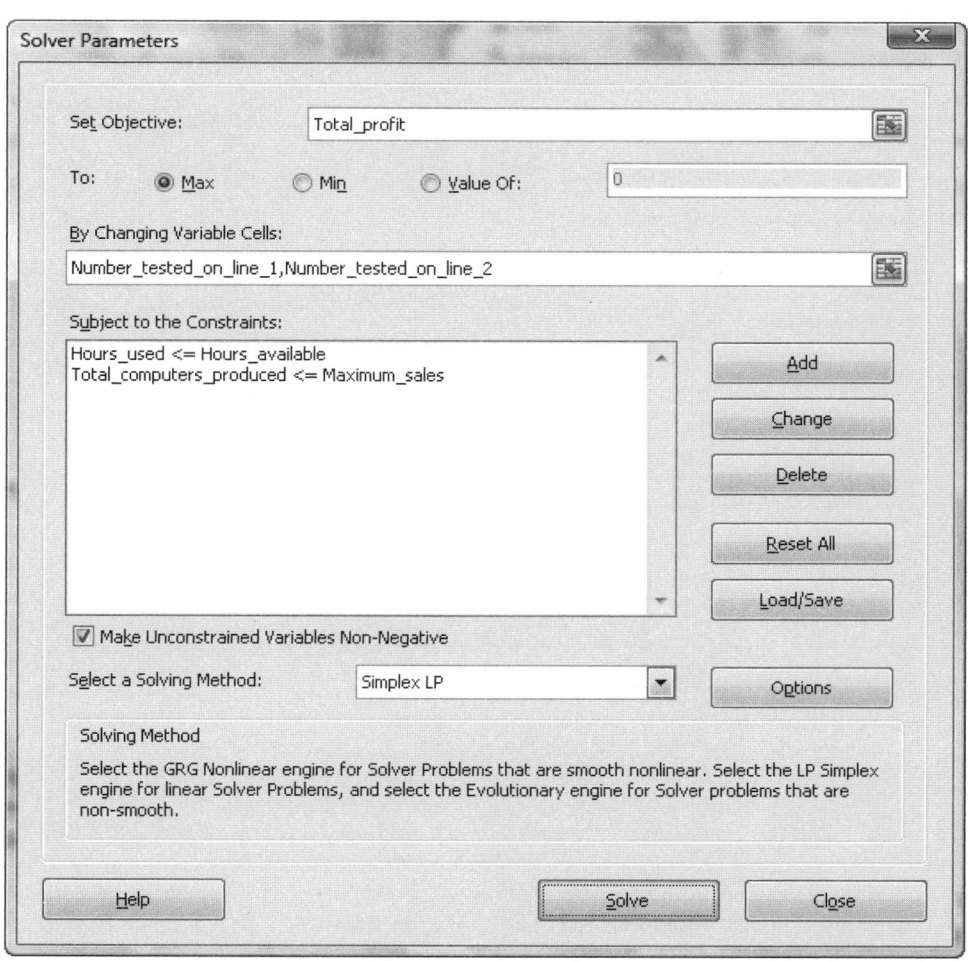

Discussion of the Solution

When you click on Solve, you obtain the optimal solution shown in Figure 13.21. The optimal plan is to produce computer models 1, 4, 6, and 7 only, some on testing line 1 and others on testing line 2. This plan uses all of the available labor hours for assembling and testing on line 1, but about 1800 of the testing line 2 hours are not used. Also, maximum sales are achieved only for computer models 1, 6, and 7. This is typical of an LP solution. Some of the constraints are met exactly—they are binding—whereas others contain a certain amount of slack. The binding constraints prevent PC Tech from earning an even higher profit.

Figure 13.21 Optimal Solution to Larger Product Mix Model

	A	B	C	D	E	F	G	H	I	J
1	Assembling and testing computers									
2										
3	Cost per labor hour assembling	$11								
4	Cost per labor hour testing, line 1	$19								
5	Cost per labor hour testing, line 2	$17								
6										
7	Inputs for assembling and testing a computer									
8		Model 1	Model 2	Model 3	Model 4	Model 5	Model 6	Model 7	Model 8	
9	Labor hours for assembly	4	5	5	5	5.5	5.5	5.5	6	
10	Labor hours for testing, line 1	1.5	2	2	2	2.5	2.5	2.5	3	
11	Labor hours for testing, line 2	2	2.5	2.5	2.5	3	3	3.5	3.5	
12	Cost of component parts	$150	$225	$225	$225	$250	$250	$250	$300	
13	Selling price	$350	$450	$460	$470	$500	$525	$530	$600	
14	Unit margin, tested on line 1	$128	$132	$142	$152	$142	$167	$172	$177	
15	Unit margin, tested on line 2	$122	$128	$138	$148	$139	$164	$160	$175	
16										
17	Assembling, testing plan (# of computers)									
18		Model 1	Model 2	Model 3	Model 4	Model 5	Model 6	Model 7	Model 8	
19	Number tested on line 1	1500	0	0	125	0	0	1000	0	
20	Number tested on line 2	0	0	0	475	0	1000	0	0	
21	Total computers produced	1500	0	0	600	0	1000	1000	0	
22		<=	<=	<=	<=	<=	<=	<=	<=	
23	Maximum sales	1500	1250	1250	1250	1000	1000	1000	800	
24										
25	Constraints (hours per month)	Hours used		Hours available						
26	Labor availability for assembling	20000	<=	20000						
27	Labor availability for testing, line 1	5000	<=	5000						
28	Labor availability for testing, line 2	4187.5	<=	6000						
29										
30	Net profit ($ per month)	Model 1	Model 2	Model 3	Model 4	Model 5	Model 6	Model 7	Model 8	Totals
31	Tested on line 1	$191,250	$0	$0	$19,000	$0	$0	$172,000	$0	$382,250
32	Tested on line 2	$0	$0	$0	$70,063	$0	$163,500	$0	$0	$233,563
33											$615,813

Excel Tip *Roundoff Error*

Because of the way numbers are stored and calculated on a computer, the optimal values in the changing cells and elsewhere can contain small roundoff errors. For example, the value that really appears in cell E20 on one of our Excel 2007 PCs is 475.000002015897, not exactly 475. For all practical purposes, this number can be treated as 475, and we have formatted it as such in the spreadsheet. (We have been told that roundoff in Solver results should be less of a problem in Excel 2010.)

Sensitivity Analysis

If you want to experiment with different inputs to this problem, you can simply change the inputs and then rerun Solver. The second time you use Solver, you do not have to specify the objective and changing cells or the constraints. Excel remembers all of these settings and saves them when you save the file.

You can also use SolverTable to perform a more systematic sensitivity analysis on one or more input variables. One possibility appears in Figure 13.22, where the number of available assembling labor hours is allowed to vary from 18,000 to 25,000 in increments of 1000, and the numbers of computers produced and profit are designated as outputs.

Figure 13.22 Sensitivity to Assembling Labor Hours

	A	B	C	D	E	F	G	H	I	J
3	Assembling labor (cell $D$26) values along side, output cell(s) along top									
4		Total_computers_produced_1	Total_computers_produced_2	Total_computers_produced_3	Total_computers_produced_4	Total_computers_produced_5	Total_computers_produced_6	Total_computers_produced_7	Total_computers_produced_8	Total_profit
5	18000	1500	0	0	200	0	1000	1000	0	$556,813
6	19000	1500	0	0	400	0	1000	1000	0	$586,313
7	20000	1500	0	0	600	0	1000	1000	0	$615,813
8	21000	1500	0	0	800	0	1000	1000	0	$645,313
9	22000	1500	0	0	1000	0	1000	1000	0	$674,813
10	23000	1500	0	0	1200	0	1000	1000	0	$704,313
11	24000	1500	0	700	1250	0	1000	500	0	$724,750
12	25000	1500	0	1250	1250	0	1000	60	0	$727,170

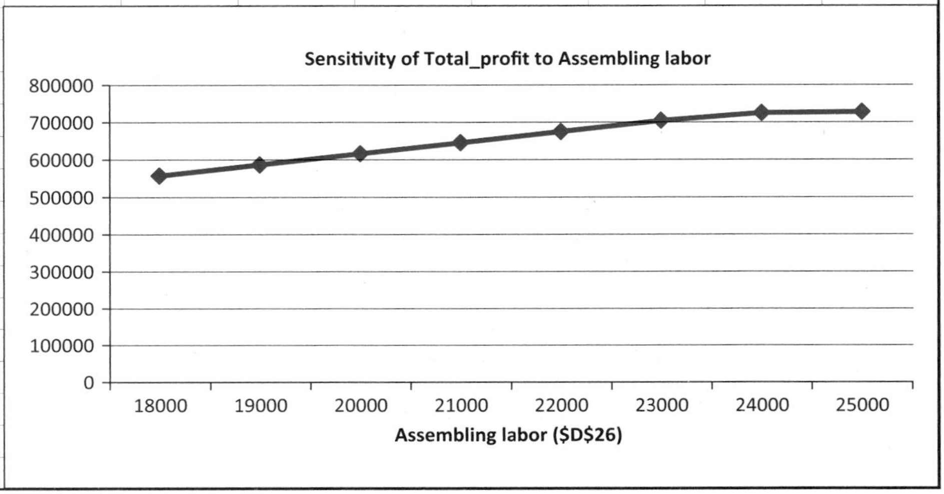

Sensitivity of Total_profit to Assembling labor

There are several ways to interpret the output from this sensitivity analysis. First, you can look at columns B through I to see how the product mix changes as more assembling labor hours become available. For assembling labor hours from 18,000 to 23,000, the only thing that changes is that more model 4s are produced. Beyond 23,000, however, the company starts to produce model 3s and produces fewer model 7s. Second, you can see how extra labor hours add to the total profit. Note exactly what this increased profit means. For example, when labor hours increase from 20,000 to 21,000, the model requires that the company must *pay* $11 apiece for these extra hours (if it uses them). But the *net* effect is that profit increases by $29,500, or $29.50 per extra hour. In other words, the labor cost increases by $11,000 [=$11(1000)], but this is more than offset by the increase in revenue that comes from having the extra labor hours.

As column J illustrates, it is worthwhile for the company to obtain extra assembling labor hours, even though it has to to pay for them, because its profit increases. However, the increase in profit per extra labor hour—the *shadow price* of assembling labor hours—is not constant. In the top part of the table, it is $29.50 (per extra hour), but it then decreases to $20.44 and then $2.42. The accompanying SolverTable chart of column J illustrates this decreasing shadow price through its decreasing slope.

SolverTable Technical Tip   *Charts and Roundoff*
As SolverTable makes all of its Solver runs, it reports and then charts the values found by Solver. These can include small roundoff errors and slightly misleading charts. For example, the chart in Figure 13.23 shows one possibility, where we varied the cost of testing on line 2 and charted the assembling hours used. Throughout the range, this output value was 20,000, but because of slight roundoff (19999.9999999292 and 20000.0000003259) in two of the cells, the chart doesn't appear to be flat. If you see this behavior, you can change it manually.

Figure 13.23

A Misleading SolverTable Chart

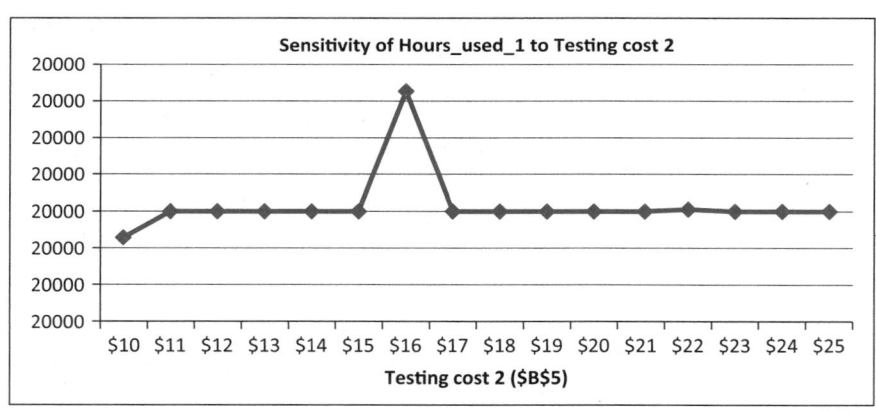

Finally, you can gain additional insight from Solver's sensitivity report, shown in Figure 13.24. However, you have to be very careful in interpreting this report. Unlike Example 13.1, there are no upper bound (maximum sales) constraints on the *changing cells*. The maximum sales constraints are on the total computers produced (row 21 of the model), not the changing cells. Therefore, the only nonzero reduced costs in the top part of the table are for changing cells currently at zero (not those at their upper bounds as in the previous example). Each nonzero reduced cost indicates how much the profit margin for this activity would have to change before this activity would be profitable.

Also, there is a row in the bottom part of the table for each constraint, *including* the maximum sales constraints. The interesting values are again the shadow prices. The first two indicate the amount the company would pay for an extra assembling or line 1 testing labor hour. (Does the 29.5 value look familiar? Compare it to the SolverTable results above.) The shadow prices for all *binding* maximum sales constraints indicate how much more profit the company could make if it could increase its demand by one computer of that model.

Figure 13.24 Solver's Sensitivity Report

	A	B	C	D	E	F	G	H
6		Variable Cells						
7				Final	Reduced	Objective	Allowable	Allowable
8		Cell	Name	Value	Cost	Coefficient	Increase	Decrease
9		$B$19	Number tested on line 1 Model 1	1500	0	127.5	1E+30	2.125
10		$C$19	Number tested on line 1 Model 2	0	-20	132	20	1E+30
11		$D$19	Number tested on line 1 Model 3	0	-10	142	10	1E+30
12		$E$19	Number tested on line 1 Model 4	125	0	152	2.833	1.7
13		$F$19	Number tested on line 1 Model 5	0	-25.875	142	25.875	1E+30
14		$G$19	Number tested on line 1 Model 6	0	-2.125	167	2.125	1E+30
15		$H$19	Number tested on line 1 Model 7	1000	0	172	1E+30	4.125
16		$I$19	Number tested on line 1 Model 8	0	-6.75	177	6.75	1E+30
17		$B$20	Number tested on line 2 Model 1	0	-2.125	122	2.125	1E+30
18		$C$20	Number tested on line 2 Model 2	0	-20	127.5	20	1E+30
19		$D$20	Number tested on line 2 Model 3	0	-10	137.5	10	1E+30
20		$E$20	Number tested on line 2 Model 4	475	0	147.5	1.136	2.083
21		$F$20	Number tested on line 2 Model 5	0	-23.75	138.5	23.75	1E+30
22		$G$20	Number tested on line 2 Model 6	1000	0	163.5	1E+30	1.25
23		$H$20	Number tested on line 2 Model 7	0	-6.375	160	6.375	1E+30
24		$I$20	Number tested on line 2 Model 8	0	-2.5	174.5	2.5	1E+30
25								
26		Constraints						
27				Final	Shadow	Constraint	Allowable	Allowable
28		Cell	Name	Value	Price	R.H. Side	Increase	Decrease
29		$B$26	Labor availability for assembling Hours used	20000	29.5	20000	3250	2375
30		$B$27	Labor availability for testing, line 1 Hours used	5000	2.25	5000	950	250
31		$B$28	Labor availability for testing, line 2 Hours used	4187.5	0	6000	1E+30	1812.5
32		$B$21	Total computers produced Model 1	1500	6.125	1500	166.667	812.5
33		$C$21	Total computers produced Model 2	0	0	1250	1E+30	1250
34		$D$21	Total computers produced Model 3	0	0	1250	1E+30	1250
35		$E$21	Total computers produced Model 4	600	0	1250	1E+30	650
36		$F$21	Total computers produced Model 5	0	0	1000	1E+30	1000
37		$G$21	Total computers produced Model 6	1000	1.25	1000	431.818	590.909
38		$H$21	Total computers produced Model 7	1000	4.125	1000	100	590.909
39		$I$21	Total computers produced Model 8	0	0	800	1E+30	800

The information in this sensitivity report is all relevant and definitely provides some insights if studied carefully. However, this really requires you to know the exact rules Solver uses to create this report. That is, it requires a fairly in-depth knowledge of the theory behind LP sensitivity analysis, more than we have provided here. Fortunately, we believe the same basic information—and more—can be obtained in a more intuitive way by creating several carefully chosen SolverTable reports. ■

PROBLEMS

Level A

Note: All references to the product mix model in the following problems are to the *larger* product mix model in this section.

10. Modify PC Tech's product mix model so that there is no maximum sales constraint. (This is easy to do in the Solver dialog box. Just highlight the constraint and click on the Delete button.) Does this make the problem unbounded? Does it change the optimal solution at all? Explain its effect.

11. In the product mix model it makes sense to change the maximum sales constraint to a "minimum sales" constraint, simply by changing the direction of the inequality. Then the input values in row 23 can be considered customer demands that must be met. Make this change and rerun Solver. What do you find? What do you find if you run Solver again, this time making the values in row 23 one-quarter of their current values?

12. Use SolverTable to run a sensitivity analysis on the cost per assembling labor hour, letting it vary from $5 to $20 in increments of $1. Keep track of the computers produced in row 21, the hours used in the range B26:B28, and the total profit. Discuss your findings. Are they intuitively what you expected?

13. Create a two-way SolverTable for the product mix model, where total profit is the only output and the two inputs are the testing line 1 hours and testing line 2 hours available. Let the former vary from 4000 to 6000 in increments of 500, and let the latter vary from 3000 to 5000 in increments of 500. Discuss the changes in profit you see as you look across the various rows of the table. Discuss the changes in profit you see as you look down the various columns of the table.

14. Model 8 has fairly high profit margins, but it isn't included at all in the optimal mix. Use SolverTable, along with some experimentation on the correct range, to find the (approximate) selling price required for model 8 before it enters the optimal product mix.

Level B

15. Suppose that you want to increase *all three* of the resource availabilities in the product mix model simultaneously by the same percentage. You want this percentage to vary from -25% to 50% in increments of 5%. Modify the spreadsheet model slightly so that this sensitivity analysis can be performed with a *one-way* SolverTable, using the percentage change as the single input. Keep track of the computers produced in row 21, the hours used in the range B26:B28, and the total profit. Discuss the results.

16. Some analysts complain that spreadsheet models are difficult to resize. You can be the judge of this. Suppose the current product mix problem is changed so that there is an extra resource, packaging labor hours, and two additional PC models, 9 and 10. What additional input data are required? What modifications are necessary in the spreadsheet model (including range name changes)? Make up values for any extra required input data and incorporate these into a modified spreadsheet model. Then optimize with Solver. Do you conclude that it is easy to resize a spreadsheet model? (By the way, it turns out that algebraic models are typically *much* easier to resize.)

17. In Solver's sensitivity report for the product mix model, the allowable decrease for available assembling hours is 2375. This means that something happens when assembling hours fall to $20,000 - 2375 = 17,625$. See what this means by first running Solver with 17,626 available hours and then again with 17,624 available hours. Explain how the two solutions compare to the original solution and to each other.

13.8 A MULTIPERIOD PRODUCTION MODEL

The product mix examples illustrate a very important type of LP model. However, LP models come in many forms. For variety, we now present a quite different type of model that can also be solved with LP. (In the next chapter we provide other examples, linear and otherwise.) The distinguishing feature of the following model is that it relates decisions made during several time periods. This type of problem occurs when a company must make a decision now that will have ramifications in the future. The company does not want to focus completely on the short run and forget about the long run.

EXAMPLE | **13.3 PRODUCING FOOTBALLS AT PIGSKIN**

The Pigskin Company produces footballs. Pigskin must decide how many footballs to produce each month. The company has decided to use a six-month planning horizon. The forecasted monthly demands for the next six months are 10,000, 15,000, 30,000, 35,000, 25,000, and 10,000. Pigskin wants to meet these demands on time, knowing that it currently has 5000 footballs in inventory and that it can use a given month's production to help meet the demand for that month. (For simplicity, we assume that production occurs during the month, and demand occurs at the end of the month.) During each month there is enough production capacity to produce up to 30,000 footballs, and there is enough storage capacity to store up to 10,000 footballs at the end of the month, after demand has occurred. The forecasted production costs per football for the next six months are $12.50, $12.55, $12.70, $12.80, $12.85, and $12.95, respectively. The holding cost per football held in inventory at the end of any month is figured at 5% of the production cost for that month. (This cost includes the cost of storage and also the cost of money tied up in inventory.) The selling price for footballs is not considered relevant to the production decision because Pigskin will satisfy all customer demand exactly when it occurs—at whatever the selling price is. Therefore, Pigskin wants to determine the production schedule that minimizes the total production and holding costs.

Objective To use LP to find the production schedule that meets demand on time and minimizes total production and inventory holding costs.

WHERE DO THE NUMBERS COME FROM?

The input values for this problem are not all easy to find. Here are some thoughts on where they might be obtained. (See Figure 13.25.)

- The initial inventory in cell B4 should be available from the company's database system or from a physical count.

- The unit production costs in row 8 would probably be estimated in two steps. First, the company might ask its cost accountants to estimate the current unit production cost. Then it could examine historical trends in costs to estimate inflation factors for future months.

- The holding cost percentage in cell B5 is typically difficult to determine. Depending on the type of inventory being held, this cost can include storage and handling, rent, property taxes, insurance, spoilage, and obsolescence. It can also include capital costs—the cost of money that could be used for other investments.

- The demands in row 18 are probably forecasts made by the marketing and sales department. They might be "seat-of-the-pants" forecasts, or they might be the result of a formal quantitative forecasting procedure as discussed in Chapter 12. Of course, if there are already some orders on the books for future months, these are included in the demand figures.

- The production and storage capacities in rows 14 and 22 are probably supplied by the production department. They are based on the size of the workforce, the available machinery, availability of raw materials, and physical space.

Solution

The variables and constraints for this model are listed in Table 13.3. There are two keys to relating these variables. First, the months cannot be treated independently. This is because the ending inventory in one month is the beginning inventory for the next month. Second, to ensure that demand is satisfied on time, the amount on hand after production in each month must be at least as large as the demand for that month. This constraint must be included explicitly in the model.

Table 13.3 Variables and Constraints for Production/Inventory Planning Model

Input variables	Initial inventory, unit holding cost percentage, unit production costs, forecasted demands, production and storage capacities
Decision variables (changing cells)	Monthly production quantities
Objective cell	Total cost
Other calculated variables	Units on hand after production, ending inventories, monthly production and inventory holding costs
Constraints	Units on hand after production $\geq$ Demand (each month)
	Units produced $\leq$ Production capacity (each month)
	Ending inventory $\leq$ Storage capacity (each month)

When you model this type of problem, you must be very specific about the *timing* of events. In fact, depending on the assumptions you make, there can be a variety of potential models. For example, when does the demand for footballs in a given month occur: at the beginning of the month, at the end of the month, or continually throughout the month? The same question can be asked about production in a given month. The answers to these two questions indicate how much of the production in a given month can be used to help satisfy the demand in that month. Also, are the maximum storage constraint and the holding cost based on the *ending* inventory in a month, the *average* amount of inventory in a month, or the *maximum* inventory in a month? Each of these possibilities is reasonable and could be implemented.

By modifying the timing assumptions in this type of model, alternative—and equally realistic—models with very different solutions can be obtained.

To simplify the model, we assume that (1) all production occurs at the beginning of the month, (2) all demand occurs *after* production, so that all units produced in a month can be used to satisfy that month's demand, and (3) the storage constraint and the holding cost are based on *ending* inventory in a given month. (You are asked to modify these assumptions in the problems.)

An Algebraic Model

In the traditional algebraic model, the decision variables are the *production quantities* for the six months, labeled P_1 through P_6. It is also convenient to let I_1 through I_6 be the corresponding *end-of-month inventories* (after demand has occurred).[13] For example, I_3 is the number of footballs left over at the end of month 3. Therefore, the obvious constraints are on production and inventory storage capacities: $P_j \leq 30000$ and $I_j \leq 10000$ for $1 \leq j \leq 6$.

In addition to these constraints, *balance* constraints that relate the Ps and Is are necessary. In any month the inventory from the previous month plus the current production equals the current demand plus leftover inventory. If D_j is the forecasted demand for month j, the balance equation for month j is

$$I_{j-1} + P_j = D_j + I_j$$

---

[13]This example illustrates a subtle difference between algebraic and spreadsheet models. It is often convenient in algebraic models to define "decision variables," in this case the Is, that are really determined by other decision variables, in this case the Ps. In spreadsheet models, however, we typically define the changing cells as the smallest set of variables that must be chosen—in this case the production quantities. Then values that are determined by these changing cells, such as the ending inventory levels, can be calculated with spreadsheet formulas.

The balance equation for month 1 uses the known beginning inventory, 5000, for the previous inventory (the I_{j-1} term). By putting all variables (Ps and Is) on the left and all known values on the right (a standard LP convention), these balance constraints can be written as

$$P_1 - I_1 = 10000 - 5000$$

$$I_1 + P_2 - I_2 = 15000$$

$$I_2 + P_3 - I_3 = 30000$$

$$I_3 + P_4 - I_4 = 35000$$

$$I_4 + P_5 - I_5 = 25000$$

$$I_5 + P_6 - I_6 = 10000 \qquad \textbf{(13.1)}$$

As usual, there are nonnegativity constraints: all Ps and Is must be nonnegative.

What about meeting demand on time? This requires that in each month the inventory from the preceding month plus the current production must be at least as large as the current demand. But take a look, for example, at the balance equation for month 3. By rearranging it slightly, it becomes

$$I_3 = I_2 + P_3 - 30000$$

Now, the nonnegativity constraint on I_3 implies that the right side of this equation, $I_2 + P_3 - 30000$, is also nonnegative. But this implies that demand in month 3 is covered—the beginning inventory in month 3 plus month 3 production is at least 30000. Therefore, the nonnegativity constraints on the Is *automatically* guarantee that all demands will be met on time, and no other constraints are needed. Alternatively, the constraint can be written directly as $I_2 + P_3 \geq 30000$. In words, the amount on hand after production in month 3 must be at least as large as the demand in month 3. The spreadsheet model takes advantage of this interpretation.

Finally, the objective to minimize is the sum of production and holding costs. It is the sum of unit production costs multiplied by Ps, plus unit holding costs multiplied by Is.

DEVELOPING THE SPREADSHEET MODEL

The spreadsheet model of Pigskin's production problem is shown in Figure 13.25. (See the file **Production Scheduling.xlsx**.) The main feature that distinguishes this model from the product mix model is that some of the constraints, namely, the balance equations (13.1), are built into the spreadsheet itself by means of formulas. This means that the only changing cells are the production quantities. The ending inventories shown in row 20 are *determined* by the production quantities and equations (13.1). As you see, the decision variables in an algebraic model (the Ps and Is) are not *necessarily* the same as the changing cells in an equivalent spreadsheet model. (The only changing cells in the spreadsheet model correspond to the Ps.)

To develop the spreadsheet model in Figure 13.25, proceed as follows.

1 **Inputs.** Enter the inputs in the blue cells. Again, these are all entered as *numbers* directly from the problem statement. (Unlike some spreadsheet modelers who prefer to put all inputs in the upper left corner of the spreadsheet, we enter the inputs wherever they fit most naturally. Of course, this takes some planning before diving in.)

2 **Name ranges.** Name the ranges indicated. Note that all but one of these (Total_cost) can be named easily with the range-naming shortcut, using the labels in column A.

Figure 13.25 Production Planning Model with a Suboptimal Solution

	A	B	C	D	E	F	G	H
1	**Multiperiod production model**							
2								
3	**Input data**							
4	Initial inventory (100s)	5000						
5	Holding cost as % of prod cost	5%						
6								
7	Month	1	2	3	4	5	6	
8	Production cost/unit	$12.50	$12.55	$12.70	$12.80	$12.85	$12.95	
9								
10	**Production plan (all quantities are in 100s of footballs)**							
11	Month	1	2	3	4	5	6	
12	Units produced	15000	15000	30000	30000	25000	10000	
13		<=	<=	<=	<=	<=	<=	
14	Production capacity	30000	30000	30000	30000	30000	30000	
15								
16	On hand after production	20000	25000	40000	40000	30000	15000	
17		>=	>=	>=	>=	>=	>=	
18	Demand	10000	15000	30000	35000	25000	10000	
19								
20	Ending inventory	10000	10000	10000	5000	5000	5000	
21		<=	<=	<=	<=	<=	<=	
22	Storage capacity	10000	10000	10000	10000	10000	10000	
23								
24	**Summary of costs (all costs are in hundreds of dollars)**							
25	Month	1	2	3	4	5	6	Totals
26	Production costs	$187,500.00	$188,250.00	$381,000.00	$384,000.00	$321,250.00	$129,500.00	$1,591,500.00
27	Holding costs	$6,250.00	$6,275.00	$6,350.00	$3,200.00	$3,212.50	$3,237.50	$28,525.00
28	Totals	$193,750.00	$194,525.00	$387,350.00	$387,200.00	$324,462.50	$132,737.50	$1,620,025.00
29								
30	**Range names used**							
31	Demand	=Model!$B$18:$G$18						
32	Ending_inventory	=Model!$B$20:$G$20						
33	On_hand_after_production	=Model!$B$16:$G$16						
34	Production_capacity	=Model!$B$14:$G$14						
35	Storage_capacity	=Model!$B$22:$G$22						
36	Total_Cost	=Model!$H$28						
37	Units_produced	=Model!$B$12:$G$12						

③ **Production quantities.** Enter *any* values in the range Units_produced as production quantities. As always, you can enter values that you believe are good, maybe even optimal. This is not crucial, however, because Solver eventually finds the *optimal* production quantities.

④ **On-hand inventory.** Enter the formula

=B4+B12

in cell B16. This calculates the first month's on-hand inventory after production (but before demand). Then enter the typical formula

=B20+C12

for on-hand inventory after production in month 2 in cell C16 and copy it across row 16.

⑤ **Ending inventories.** Enter the formula

=B16-B18

In multiperiod problems, there is often one formula for the first period and a slightly different (copyable) formula for all other periods.

for ending inventory in cell B20 and copy it across row 20. This formula calculates ending inventory in the current month as on-hand inventory before demand minus the demand in that month.

6 **Production and holding costs.** Enter the formula

=B8*B12

in cell B26 and copy it across to cell G26 to calculate the monthly production costs. Then enter the formula

=$B$5*B8*B20

in cell B27 and copy it across to cell G27 to calculate the monthly holding costs. Note that these are based on monthly ending inventories. Finally, calculate the cost totals in column H with the SUM function.

USING SOLVER

To use Solver, fill out the main dialog box as shown in Figure 13.26. The logic behind the constraints is straightforward. The constraints are that (1) the production quantities cannot exceed the production capacities, (2) the on-hand inventories after production must be at least as large as demands, and (3) ending inventories cannot exceed storage capacities. Check the Non-Negative option, and then click on Solve.

Figure 13.26
Solver Dialog Box for Production Planning Model

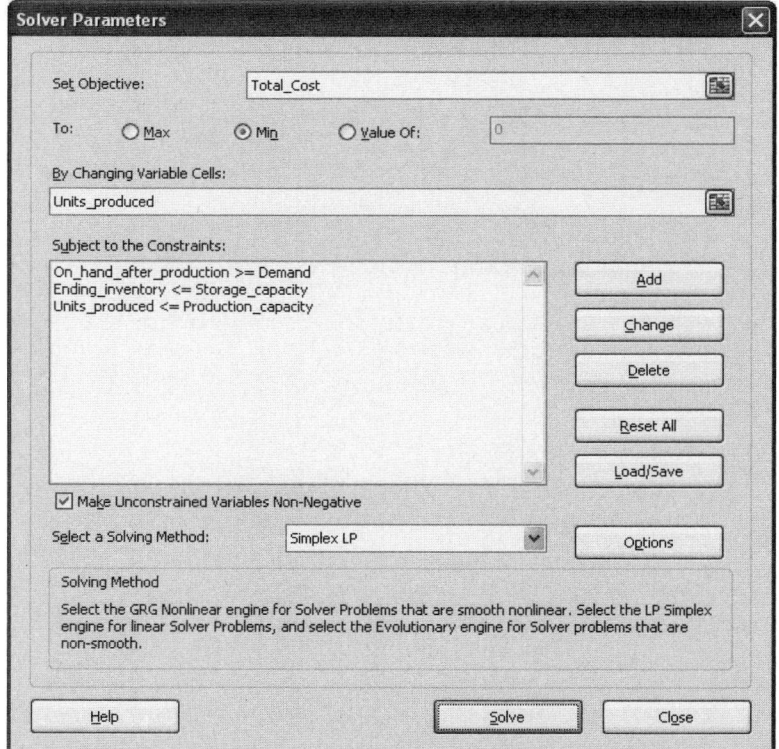

Discussion of the Solution

The optimal solution from Solver appears in Figure 13.27. The solution can be interpreted best by comparing production quantities to demands. In month 1, Pigskin should produce just enough to meet month 1 demand (taking into account the initial inventory of 5000). In month 2, it should produce 5000 more footballs than month 2 demand, and then in month 3 it should produce just enough to meet month 3 demand, while still carrying the extra 5000 footballs in inventory from month 2 production. In month 4, Pigskin should finally use these 5000 footballs, along with the maximum production amount, 30,000, to meet month 4 demand. Then in months 5 and 6 it should produce exactly enough to meet these months' demands. The total cost is $1,535,563, most of which is production cost.

Figure 13.27 Optimal Solution for Production Planning Model

	A	B	C	D	E	F	G	H
1	Multiperiod production model							
2								
3	Input data							
4	Initial inventory (100s)	5000						
5	Holding cost as % of prod cost	5%						
6								
7	Month	1	2	3	4	5	6	
8	Production cost/unit	$12.50	$12.55	$12.70	$12.80	$12.85	$12.95	
9								
10	Production plan (all quantities are in 100s of footballs)							
11	Month	1	2	3	4	5	6	
12	Units produced	5000	20000	30000	30000	25000	10000	
13		<=	<=	<=	<=	<=	<=	
14	Production capacity	30000	30000	30000	30000	30000	30000	
15								
16	On hand after production	10000	20000	35000	35000	25000	10000	
17		>=	>=	>=	>=	>=	>=	
18	Demand	10000	15000	30000	35000	25000	10000	
19								
20	Ending inventory	0	5000	5000	0	0	0	
21		<=	<=	<=	<=	<=	<=	
22	Storage capacity	10000	10000	10000	10000	10000	10000	
23								
24	Summary of costs (all costs are in hundreds of dollars)							
25	Month	1	2	3	4	5	6	Totals
26	Production costs	$62,500.00	$251,000.00	$381,000.00	$384,000.00	$321,250.00	$129,500.00	$1,529,250.00
27	Holding costs	$0.00	$3,137.50	$3,175.00	$0.00	$0.00	$0.00	$6,312.50
28	Totals	$62,500.00	$254,137.50	$384,175.00	$384,000.00	$321,250.00	$129,500.00	$1,535,562.50
29								
30	Range names used							
31	Demand	=Model!$B$18:$G$18						
32	Ending_inventory	=Model!$B$20:$G$20						
33	On_hand_after_production	=Model!$B$16:$G$16						
34	Production_capacity	=Model!$B$14:$G$14						
35	Storage_capacity	=Model!$B$22:$G$22						
36	Total_Cost	=Model!$H$28						
37	Units_produced	=Model!$B$12:$G$12						

You can often improve your intuition by trying to reason why Solver's solution is indeed optimal.

Could you have guessed this optimal solution? Upon reflection, it makes perfect sense. Because the monthly holding costs are large relative to the differences in monthly production costs, there is little incentive to produce footballs before they are needed to take advantage of a "cheap" production month. Therefore, the Pigskin Company produces footballs in the month when they are needed—when possible. The only exception to this rule is the 20,000 footballs produced during month 2 when only 15,000 are needed. The extra 5000 footballs produced in month 2 are needed, however, to meet the month 4 demand of 35,000, because month 3 production capacity is used entirely to meet the month 3 demand.

Thus month 3 capacity is not available to meet the month 4 demand, and 5000 units of month 2 capacity are used to meet the month 4 demand.

FUNDAMENTAL INSIGHT

Multiperiod Optimization Problems and Myopic Solutions

Many optimization problems are of a multiperiod nature, where a sequence of decisions must be made over time. When making the *first* of these decisions, the one for this week or this month, say, it is usually best to include future decisions in the model, as has been done here. If you ignore future periods and make the initial decision based only on the first period, the resulting decision is called *myopic* (short-sighted). Myopic decisions are occasionally optimal, but not very often. The idea is that if you act now in a way that looks best in the short run, it might lead you down a strategically unattractive path for the long run.

Sensitivity Analysis

If you want Solver Table to keep track of a quantity that is not in your model, you need to create it with an appropriate formula in a new cell.

SolverTable can now be used to perform a number of interesting sensitivity analyses. We illustrate two possibilities. First, note that the most inventory ever carried at the end of a month is 5000, although the storage capacity each month is 10,000. Perhaps this is because the holding cost percentage, 5%, is fairly large. Would more ending inventory be carried if this holding cost percentage were lower? Or would even less be carried if it were higher? You can check this with the SolverTable output shown in Figure 13.28. Now the single input cell is cell B5, and the *single* output is the maximum ending inventory ever held, which you can calculate in cell B31 with the formula

=MAX(Ending_inventory)

As the SolverTable results indicate, the storage capacity limit is reached only when the holding cost percentage falls to 1%. (This output doesn't indicate which month or how

Figure 13.28

Sensitivity of Maximum Inventory to Holding Cost

	A	B	C	D	E	F	G
3	Holding cost % (cell $B$5) values along side, output cell(s) along top						
4		Max_inventory					
5	1%	10000					
6	2%	5000					
7	3%	5000					
8	4%	5000					
9	5%	5000					
10	6%	5000					
11	7%	5000					
12	8%	5000					
13	9%	5000					
14	10%	5000					

many months the ending inventory is at the upper limit.) On the other hand, even when the holding cost percentage reaches 10%, the company still continues to hold a maximum ending inventory of 5000.

A second possible sensitivity analysis is suggested by the way the optimal production schedule would probably be implemented. The optimal solution to Pigskin's model specifies the production level for each of the next six months. In reality, however, the company would probably implement the model's recommendation only for the *first* month. Then at the beginning of the second month, it would gather new forecasts for the *next* six months, months 2 through 7, solve a new six-month model, and again implement the model's recommendation for the first of these months, month 2. If the company continues in this manner, we say that it is following a six-month **rolling planning horizon**.

The question, then, is whether the assumed demands (really, forecasts) toward the end of the planning horizon have much effect on the optimal production quantity in month 1. You would hope not, because these forecasts could be quite inaccurate. The two-way Solver table in Figure 13.29 shows how the optimal month 1 production quantity varies with the forecasted demands in months 5 and 6. As you can see, if the forecasted demands for months 5 and 6 remain fairly small, the optimal month 1 production quantity remains at 5000. This is good news. It means that the optimal production quantity in month 1 is fairly insensitive to the possibly inaccurate forecasts for months 5 and 6.

Figure 13.29 Sensitivity of Month 1 Production to Demand in Months 5 and 6

	A	B	C	D	E	F	G	H	I	J
3	Month 5 demand (cell $F$18) values along side, Month 6 demand (cell $G$18) values along top, output cell in corner									
4	Units_produced_1	10000	20000	30000						
5	10000	5000	5000	5000						
6	20000	5000	5000	5000						
7	30000	5000	5000	5000						

Solver's sensitivity report for this model appears in Figure 13.30. The bottom part of this report is fairly straightforward to interpret. The first six rows are for sensitivity to changes in the storage capacity, whereas the last six are for sensitivity to changes in the demand. (There are no rows for the production capacity constraints, because these are simple upper-bound constraints on the decision variables. Recall that Solver's sensitivity report handles this type of constraint differently from "normal" constraints.) In contrast, the top part of the report is virtually impossible to unravel. This is because the objective coefficients of the decision variables are each based on *multiple* inputs. (Each is a combination of unit production costs and the holding cost percentage.) Therefore, if you want to know how the solution will change if you change a single unit production cost or the holding cost percentage, this report does not answer your question. This is one case where a sensitivity analysis with SolverTable is much more straightforward and intuitive. It allows you to change *any* of the model's inputs and directly see the effects on the solution.

Modeling Issues

We assume that Pigskin uses a six-month planning horizon. Why six months? In multi-period models such as this, the company has to make forecasts about the future, such as the

Figure 13.30 Solver Sensitivity Report for Production Planning Model

	A	B	C	D	E	F	G	H
6		Variable Cells						
7				Final	Reduced	Objective	Allowable	Allowable
8		Cell	Name	Value	Cost	Coefficient	Increase	Decrease
9		$B$12	Units produced	5000	0	16.318	1E+30	0.575
10		$C$12	Units produced	20000	0	15.743	0.575	0.478
11		$D$12	Units produced	30000	-0.478	15.265	0.478	1E+30
12		$E$12	Units produced	30000	-1.013	14.730	1.013	1E+30
13		$F$12	Units produced	25000	0	14.140	1.603	0.543
14		$G$12	Units produced	10000	0	13.598	0.543	13.598
15								
16		Constraints						
17				Final	Shadow	Constraint	Allowable	Allowable
18		Cell	Name	Value	Price	R.H. Side	Increase	Decrease
19		$B$16	On hand after production <=	10000	0.575	10000	10000	5000
20		$C$16	On hand after production <=	20000	0	15000	5000	1E+30
21		$D$16	On hand after production <=	35000	0	30000	5000	1E+30
22		$E$16	On hand after production <=	35000	1.603	35000	5000	5000
23		$F$16	On hand after production <=	25000	0.543	25000	5000	20000
24		$G$16	On hand after production <=	10000	13.598	10000	10000	10000
25		$B$20	Ending inventory >=	0	0	10000	1E+30	10000
26		$C$20	Ending inventory >=	5000	0	10000	1E+30	5000
27		$D$20	Ending inventory >=	5000	0	10000	1E+30	5000
28		$E$20	Ending inventory >=	0	0	10000	1E+30	10000
29		$F$20	Ending inventory >=	0	0	10000	1E+30	10000
30		$G$20	Ending inventory >=	0	0	10000	1E+30	10000

level of customer demand. Therefore, the length of the planning horizon is usually the length of time for which the company can make reasonably accurate forecasts. Here, Pigskin evidently believes that it can forecast up to six months from now, so it uses a six-month planning horizon. ∎

PROBLEMS

Level A

18. Can you guess the results of a sensitivity analysis on the initial inventory in the Pigskin model? See if your guess is correct by using SolverTable and allowing the initial inventory to vary from 0 to 10,000 in increments of 1000. Keep track of the values in the changing cells and the objective cell.

19. Modify the Pigskin model so that there are eight months in the planning horizon. You can make up reasonable values for any extra required data. Don't forget to modify range names. Then modify the model

again so that there are only four months in the planning horizon. Do either of these modifications change the optimal production quantity in month 1?

20. As indicated by the algebraic formulation of the Pigskin model, there is no real need to calculate inventory on hand after production and constrain it to be greater than or equal to demand. An alternative is to calculate ending inventory directly and constrain it to be nonnegative. Modify the current spreadsheet model to do this. (Delete rows 16 and 17, and calculate ending inventory appropriately. Then add an *explicit* nonnegativity constraint on ending inventory.)

21. In one modification of the Pigskin problem, the maximum storage constraint and the holding cost are based on the *average* inventory (not ending inventory) for a given month, where the average inventory is defined as the sum of beginning inventory and ending inventory, divided by 2, and beginning inventory is *before* production or demand. Modify the Pigskin model with this new assumption, and use Solver to find the optimal solution. How does this change the optimal production schedule? How does it change the optimal total cost?

Level B

22. Modify the Pigskin spreadsheet model so that except for month 6, demand need not be met on time. The only requirement is that all demand be met eventually by the end of month 6. How does this change the optimal production schedule? How does it change the optimal total cost?

23. Modify the Pigskin spreadsheet model so that demand in any of the first five months must be met no later than a month late, whereas demand in month 6 must be met on time. For example, the demand in month 3 can be met partly in month 3 and partly in month 4. How does this change the optimal production schedule? How does it change the optimal total cost?

24. Modify the Pigskin spreadsheet model in the following way. Assume that the timing of demand and production are such that only 70% of the production in a given month can be used to satisfy the demand in that month. The other 30% occurs too late in that month and must be carried as inventory to help satisfy demand in later months. How does this change the optimal production schedule? How does it change the optimal total cost? Then use SolverTable to see how the optimal production schedule and optimal cost vary as the percentage of production usable for this month's demand (now 70%) is allowed to vary from 20% to 100% in increments of 10%.

13.9 A COMPARISON OF ALGEBRAIC AND SPREADSHEET MODELS

To this point you have seen three algebraic optimization models and three corresponding spreadsheet models. How do they differ? If you review the two product mix examples in this chapter, we believe you will agree that (1) the algebraic models are quite straightforward and (2) the spreadsheet models are almost direct translations into Excel of the algebraic models. In particular, each algebraic model has a set of *x*s that corresponds to the changing cell range in the spreadsheet model. In addition, each objective and each left side of each constraint in the spreadsheet model corresponds to a linear expression involving *x*s in the algebraic model.

However, the Pigskin production planning model is quite different. The spreadsheet model includes one set of changing cells, the production quantities, and everything else is related to these through spreadsheet formulas. In contrast, the algebraic model has *two* sets of variables, the *P*s for the production quantities and the *I*s for the ending inventories, and together these constitute the *decision variables*. These two sets of variables must then be related algebraically, and this is done through a series of *balance equations*.

This is a typical situation in algebraic models, where one set of variables (the production quantities) corresponds to the *real* decision variables, and other sets of variables, along with extra equations or inequalities, are introduced to capture the logic. We believe—and this belief is reinforced by many years of teaching experience—that this extra level of abstraction makes algebraic models much more difficult for typical users to develop and comprehend. It is the primary reason we have decided to focus almost exclusively on spreadsheet models in this book.

13.10 A DECISION SUPPORT SYSTEM

If your job is to develop an LP spreadsheet model to solve a problem such as Pigskin's production problem, then you will be considered the "expert" in LP. Many people who need to use such models, however, are *not* experts. They might understand the basic ideas behind LP and the types of problems it is intended to solve, but they will not know the details. In this case it is useful to provide these users with a **decision support system** (DSS) that can help them solve problems without having to worry about technical details.

We will not teach you in this book how to build a full-scale DSS, but we will show you what a typical DSS looks like and what it can do.[14] (We consider only DSSs built around spreadsheets. There are many other platforms for developing DSSs that we will not consider.) Basically, a spreadsheet-based DSS contains a spreadsheet model of a problem, such as the one in Figure 13.27. However, as a user, you will probably never even see this model. Instead, you will see a front end and a back end. The front end allows you to select input values for your particular problem. The user interface for this front end can include several features, such as buttons, dialog boxes, toolbars, and menus—the things you are used to seeing in Windows applications. The back end will then produce a report that explains the solution in nontechnical terms.

We illustrate a DSS for a slight variation of the Pigskin problem in the file **Decision Support.xlsm**. This file has three sheets. When you open the file, you see the Explanation sheet shown in Figure 13.31. It contains two buttons, one for setting up the problem (getting the user's inputs) and one for solving the problem (running Solver). When you click on the Set Up Problem button, you are asked for the inputs: the initial inventory, the forecasted demands for each month, and others. An example appears in Figure 13.32. These input boxes should be self-explanatory, so that all you need to do is enter the values you

Figure 13.31

Explanation Sheet for DSS

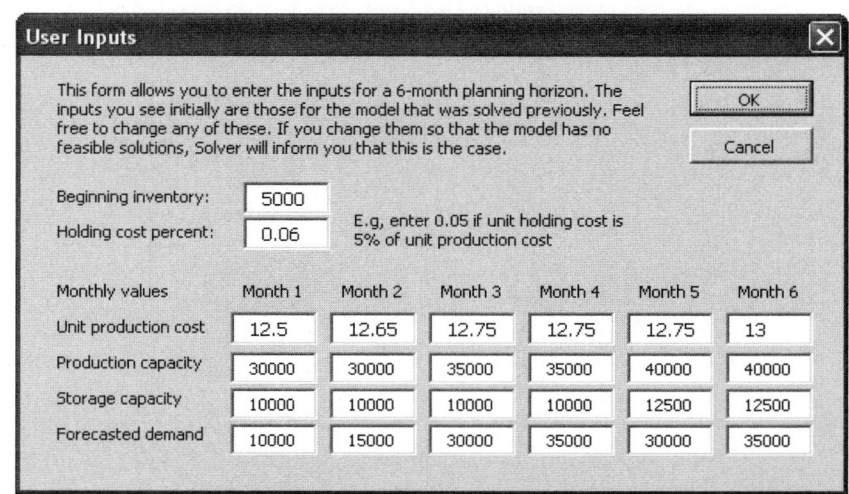

Pigskin Production Planning

This application solves a 6-month production planning model similar to Example 3 in the chapter. The only difference is that the production capacity and storage capacity are allowed to vary by month. To run the application, click on the left button to enter inputs. Then click on the right button to run Solver and obtain a solution report.

Set Up Problem   Find Optimal

Figure 13.32

Dialog Box for Obtaining User Inputs

User Inputs

This form allows you to enter the inputs for a 6-month planning horizon. The inputs you see initially are those for the model that was solved previously. Feel free to change any of these. If you change them so that the model has no feasible solutions, Solver will inform you that this is the case.

OK   Cancel

Beginning inventory: 5000

Holding cost percent: 0.06   E.g, enter 0.05 if unit holding cost is 5% of unit production cost

Monthly values	Month 1	Month 2	Month 3	Month 4	Month 5	Month 6
Unit production cost	12.5	12.65	12.75	12.75	12.75	13
Production capacity	30000	30000	35000	35000	40000	40000
Storage capacity	10000	10000	10000	10000	12500	12500
Forecasted demand	10000	15000	30000	35000	30000	35000

[14]For readers interested in learning more about this DSS, this textbook's Web site includes notes about its development in the file **Developing the Decision Support Application.docx** under Chapter 13 Example Files. If you are interested in learning more about spreadsheet DSSs in general, Albright has written the book *VBA for Modelers*, now in its third edition. It contains a primer on the VBA language and presents many applications and instructions for creating DSSs with VBA.

want to try. (To speed up the process, the inputs from the previous run are shown by default.) After you have entered all of these inputs, you can take a look at the Model sheet. This sheet contains a spreadsheet model similar to the one in Figure 13.27 but with the inputs you just entered.

Now go back to the Explanation sheet and click on the Find Optimal Solution button. This automatically sets up the Solver dialog box and runs Solver. There are two possibilities. First, it is possible that there is no feasible solution to the problem with the inputs you entered. In this case you see a message to this effect, as in Figure 13.33. In most cases, however, the problem has a feasible solution. In this case you see the Report sheet, which summarizes the optimal solution in nontechnical terms. Part of one sample output appears in Figure 13.34.

Figure 13.33

Indication of No Feasible Solutions

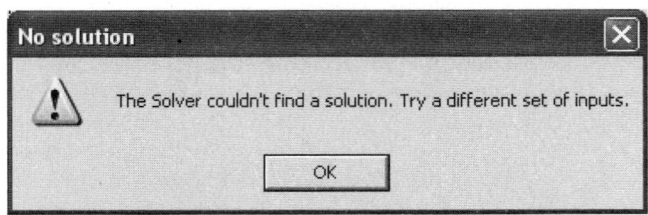

Figure 13.34

Optimal Solution Report

Monthly schedule

Month 1

Units		Dollars	
Start with	5000		
Produce	5000	Production cost	$62,500.00
Demand is	10000		
End with	0	Holding cost	$0.00

Month 2

Units		Dollars	
Start with	0		
Produce	15000	Production cost	$189,750.00
Demand is	15000		
End with	0	Holding cost	$0.00

Month 3

Units		Dollars	
Start with	0		
Produce	30000	Production cost	$382,500.00
Demand is	30000		
End with	0	Holding cost	$0.00

After studying this report, you can then click on the Solve Another Problem button, which takes you back to the Explanation sheet so that you can solve a new problem. All of this is done automatically with Excel macros. These macros use Microsoft's Visual Basic for Applications (VBA) programming language to automate various tasks. In most professional applications, nontechnical people need only to enter inputs and look at reports. Therefore, the Model sheet and VBA code will most likely be hidden and protected from end users.

13.11 CONCLUSION

This chapter has provided a good start to LP modeling—and to optimization modeling in general. You have learned how to develop three basic LP spreadsheet models, how to use Solver to find their optimal solutions, and how to perform sensitivity analyses with Solver's sensitivity reports or with the SolverTable add-in. You have also learned how to recognize whether a mathematical programming model satisfies the linear assumptions. In the next chapter you will see a variety of other optimization models, but the three basic steps of model development, Solver optimization, and sensitivity analysis remain the same.

Summary of Key Terms

Term	Explanation	Excel	Page
Linear programming model	An optimization model with a linear objective and linear constraints		746
Objective	The value, such as profit, to be optimized in an optimization model		747
Constraints	Conditions that must be satisfied in an optimization model		747
Changing cells	Cells that contain the values of the decision variables	Specify in Solver dialog box	747
Objective cell	Cell that contains the value of the objective	Specify in Solver dialog box	747
Nonnegativity constraints	Constraints that require the decision variables to be nonnegative, usually for physical reasons		747
Feasible solution	A solution that satisfies all of the constraints		748
Feasible region	The set of all feasible solutions		748
Optimal solution	The feasible solution that has the best value of the objective		748
Solver	Add-in that ships with Excel for performing optimization	Solver on Data ribbon	748
Simplex method	An efficient algorithm for finding the optimal solution in a linear programming model		748
Sensitivity analysis	Seeing how the optimal solution changes as various input values change		748
Algebraic model	A model that expresses the constraints and the objective algebraically		750
Graphical solution	Shows the constraints and objective graphically so that the optimal solution can be identified; useful only when there are two decision variables		750
Spreadsheet model	A model that uses spreadsheet formulas to express the logic of the model		752
Binding constraint	A constraint that holds as an equality		760

(continued)

Summary of Key Terms   *(Continued)*

Term	Explanation	Excel	Page
Nonbinding constraint, slack	A constraint where there is a difference, the slack, between the two sides of the inequality		760
Solver's sensitivity report	Report available from Solver that shows sensitivity to objective coefficients and right sides of constraints	Available in Solver dialog box after Solver runs	761
Reduced cost	Amount the objective coefficient of a variable currently equal to zero must change before it is optimal for that variable to be positive (or the amount the objective of a variable currently at its upper bound must change before that variable decreases from its upper bound)		763
Shadow price	The change in the objective for a change in the right side of a constraint; indicates amount a company would pay for more of a scarce resource		763
SolverTable	Add-in that performs sensitivity analysis to any inputs and reports results in tabular and graphical form	SolverTable ribbon	765
Selecting multiple ranges	Useful when changing cells, e.g., are in noncontiguous ranges	Pressing Ctrl key, drag ranges, one after the other	767
Mathematical programming model	Any optimization model, whether linear, integer, or nonlinear		772
Proportionality, additivity, divisibility	Properties of optimization model that result in a linear programming model		773
Infeasibility	Condition where a model has no feasible solutions		775
Unboundedness	Condition where there is no limit to the objective; almost always a sign of an error in the model		775
Rolling planning horizon	Multiperiod model where only the decision in the first period is implemented, and then a new multiperiod model is solved in succeeding periods		
Decision support system	User-friendly system where an end user can enter inputs to a model and see outputs, but need not be concerned with technical details		796

PROBLEMS

Conceptual Questions

C1. Suppose you use Solver to find the optimal solution to a maximization model. Then you remember that you omitted an important constraint. After adding the constraint and running Solver again, is the optimal value of the objective guaranteed to decrease? Why or why not?

C2. Consider an optimization model with a number of resource constraints. Each indicates that the amount of the resource used cannot exceed the amount available. Why is the shadow price of such a resource constraint always zero when the amount used in the optimal solution is *less than* the amount available?

C3. If you add a constraint to an optimization model, and the previously optimal solution satisfies the new constraint, will this solution still be optimal with the new constraint added? Why or why not?

C4. Why is it generally necessary to add nonnegativity constraints to an optimization model? Wouldn't Solver automatically choose nonnegative values for the changing cells?

C5. Suppose you have a *linear* optimization model where you are trying to decide which products to produce to maximize profit. What does the additive assumption imply about the profit objective? What does the proportionality assumption imply about the profit objective? Be as specific as possible. Can you think of any *reasonable* profit functions that would *not* be linear in the amounts of the products produced?

C6. In a typical product mix model, where a company must decide how much of each product to produce to maximize profit, discuss possible situations where there might not be any feasible solutions. Could these be realistic? If you had such a situation in your company, how might you proceed?

C7. In a typical product mix model, where a company must decide how much of each product to produce to maximize profit, there are sometimes customer demands for the products. We used upper-bound constraints for these: Don't produce more than you can sell. Would it be realistic to have lower-bound constraints instead: Produce at least as much as is demanded? Would it be realistic to have both (where the upper bounds are greater than the lower bounds)? Would it be realistic to have equality constraints: Produce exactly what is demanded?

C8. In a typical production scheduling model like Pigskin's, if there are no production capacity constraints—the company can produce as much as it needs in any time period—but there are storage capacity constraints and demand must be met on time, is it possible that there will be no feasible solutions? Why or why not?

C9. In a production scheduling problem like Pigskin's, suppose the company must produce *several* products to meet customer demands. Would it suffice to solve a separate model for each product, as we did for Pigskin, or would one big model for all products be necessary? If the latter, discuss what this big model might look like.

C10. In any optimization model such as those in this chapter, we say that the model is unbounded (and Solver will indicate as such) if there is no limit to the value of the objective. For example, if the objective is profit, then for any dollar value, no matter how large, there is a feasible solution with profit at least this large. In the real world, why are there never any unbounded models? If you run Solver on a model and get an "unbounded" message, what should you do?

Level A

25. A chemical company manufactures three chemicals: A, B, and C. These chemicals are produced via two production processes: 1 and 2. Running process 1 for an hour costs $400 and yields 300 units of A, 100 units of B, and 100 units of C. Running process 2 for an hour costs $100 and yields 100 units of A and 100 units of B. To meet customer demands, at least 1000 units of A, 500 units of B, and 300 units of C must be produced daily.

   a. Use Solver to determine a daily production plan that minimizes the cost of meeting the company's daily demands.

   b. Confirm graphically that the daily production plan from part **a** minimizes the cost of meeting the company's daily demands.

   c. Use SolverTable to see what happens to the decision variables and the total cost when the hourly processing cost for process 2 increases in increments of $0.50. How large must this cost increase be before the decision variables change? What happens when it continues to increase beyond this point?

26. A furniture company manufactures desks and chairs. Each desk uses four units of wood, and each chair uses three units of wood. A desk contributes $400 to profit, and a chair contributes $250. Marketing restrictions require that the number of chairs produced be at least twice the number of desks produced. There are 2000 units of wood available.

   a. Use Solver to maximize the company's profit.

   b. Confirm graphically that the solution in part **a** maximizes the company's profit.

   c. Use SolverTable to see what happens to the decision variables and the total profit when the availability of wood varies from 1000 to 3000 in 100-unit increments. Based on your findings, how much would the company be willing to pay for each extra unit of wood over its current 2000 units? How much profit would the company lose if it lost any of its current 2000 units?

27. A farmer in Iowa owns 450 acres of land. He is going to plant each acre with wheat or corn. Each acre planted with wheat yields $2000 profit, requires three workers, and requires two tons of fertilizer. Each acre planted with corn yields $3000 profit, requires two workers, and requires four tons of fertilizer. There are currently 1000 workers and 1200 tons of fertilizer available.

   a. Use Solver to help the farmer maximize the profit from his land.

   b. Confirm graphically that the solution from part **a** maximizes the farmer's profit from his land.

c. Use SolverTable to see what happens to the decision variables and the total profit when the availability of fertilizer varies from 200 tons to 2200 tons in 100-ton increments. When does the farmer discontinue producing wheat? When does he discontinue producing corn? How does the profit change for each 10-ton increment?

28. During the next four months, a customer requires, respectively, 500, 650, 1000, and 700 units of a commodity, and no backlogging is allowed (that is, the customer's requirements must be met on time). Production costs are \$50, \$80, \$40, and \$70 per unit during these months. The storage cost from one month to the next is \$20 per unit (assessed on ending inventory). It is estimated that each unit on hand at the end of month 4 can be sold for \$60. Assume there is no beginning inventory.
   a. Determine how to minimize the net cost incurred in meeting the demands for the next four months.
   b. Use SolverTable to see what happens to the decision variables and the total cost when the initial inventory varies from 0 to 1000 in 100-unit increments. How much lower would the total cost be if the company started with 100 units in inventory, rather than none? Would this same cost decrease occur for every 100-unit increase in initial inventory?

29. A company faces the following demands during the next three weeks: week 1, 2000 units; week 2, 1000 units; week 3, 1500 units. The unit production costs during each week are as follows: week 1, \$130; week 2, \$140; week 3, \$150. A holding cost of \$20 per unit is assessed against each week's ending inventory. At the beginning of week 1, the company has 500 units on hand. In reality, not all goods produced during a month can be used to meet the current month's demand. To model this fact, assume that only half of the goods produced during a week can be used to meet the current week's demands.
   a. Determine how to minimize the cost of meeting the demand for the next three weeks.
   b. Revise the model so that the demands are of the form $D_t + k\Delta_t$, where D_t is the original demand (from above) in month t, k is a given factor, and Δ_t is an amount of change in month t demand. (The Greek symbol *delta* is typically used to indicate change.) Develop the model in such a way that you can use SolverTable to analyze changes in the amounts produced and the total cost when k varies from 0 to 10 in 1-unit increments, for any fixed values of the Δ_ts. For example, try this when $\Delta_1 = 200$, $\Delta_2 = 500$, and $\Delta_3 = 300$. Describe the behavior you observe in the table. Can you find any reasonable Δ_ts that induce *positive* production levels in week 3?

30. Maggie Stewart loves desserts, but due to weight and cholesterol concerns, she has decided that she must plan her desserts carefully. There are two possible desserts she is considering: snack bars and ice cream. After reading the nutrition labels on the snack bar and ice cream packages, she learns that each serving of a snack bar weighs 37 grams and contains 120 calories and 5 grams of fat. Each serving of ice cream weighs 65 grams and contains 160 calories and 10 grams of fat. Maggie will allow herself no more than 450 calories and 25 grams of fat in her daily desserts, but because she loves desserts so much, she requires at least 120 grams of dessert per day. Also, she assigns a "taste index" to each gram of each dessert, where 0 is the lowest and 100 is the highest. She assigns a taste index of 95 to ice cream and 85 to snack bars (because she prefers ice cream to snack bars).
   a. Use Solver to find the daily dessert plan that stays within her constraints and maximizes the total taste index of her dessert.
   b. Confirm graphically that the solution from part **a** maximizes Maggie's total taste index.
   c. Use a two-way Solver table to see how the optimal dessert plan varies when the calories per snack bar and per ice cream vary. Let the former vary from 80 to 200 in increments of 10, and let the latter vary from 120 to 300 in increments of 10.

31. For a telephone survey, a marketing research group needs to contact at least 600 wives, 480 husbands, 400 single adult males, and 440 single adult females. It costs \$3 to make a daytime call and (because of higher labor costs) \$5 to make an evening call. The file **P13_31.xlsx** lists the results that can be expected. For example, 30% of all daytime calls are answered by a wife, 15% of all evening calls are answered by a single male, and 40% of all daytime calls are not answered at all. Due to limited staff, at most 40% of all phone calls can be evening calls.
   a. Determine how to minimize the cost of completing the survey.
   b. Use SolverTable to investigate changes in the unit cost of either type of call. Specifically, investigate changes in the cost of a daytime call, with the cost of an evening call fixed, to see when (if ever) *only* daytime calls or *only* evening calls will be made. Then repeat the analysis by changing the cost of an evening call and keeping the cost of a daytime call fixed.

32. A furniture company manufactures tables and chairs. Each table and chair must be made entirely out of oak or entirely out of pine. A total of 15,000 board feet of oak and 21,000 board feet of pine are available. A table requires either 17 board feet of oak or 30 board feet of pine, and a chair requires either 5 board feet of oak or 13 board feet of pine. Each table can be sold for \$800, and each chair for \$300.
   a. Determine how the company can maximize its revenue.

b. Use SolverTable to investigate the effects of simultaneous changes in the selling prices of the products. Specifically, see what happens to the total revenue when the selling prices of oak products change by a factor $1 + k_1$ and the selling prices of pine products change by a factor $1 + k_2$. Revise your model from the previous problem so that you can use SolverTable to investigate changes in total revenue as k_1 and k_2 both vary from -0.3 to 0.3 in increments of 0.1. Can you conclude that total revenue changes *linearly* within this range?

33. A manufacturing company makes two products. Each product can be made on either of two machines. The time (in hours) required to make each product on each machine is listed in the file **P13_33.xlsx**. Each month, 500 hours of time are available on each machine. Each month, customers are willing to buy up to the quantities of each product at the prices also given in the same file. The company's goal is to maximize the revenue obtained from selling units during the next two months.

a. Determine how the company can meet this goal. Assume that it will not produce any units in a month that it cannot sell in that month.

b. Use SolverTable to see what happens if customer demands for each product in each month simultaneously change by a factor $1 + k$. Revise the model so that you can use SolverTable to investigate the effect of this change on total revenue as k varies from -0.3 to 0.3 in increments of 0.1. Does revenue change in a linear manner over this range? Can you explain intuitively why it changes in the way it does?

34. There are three factories on the Momiss River. Each emits two types of pollutants, labeled P_1 and P_2, into the river. If the waste from each factory is processed, the pollution in the river can be reduced. It costs $1500 to process a ton of factory 1 waste, and each ton processed reduces the amount of P_1 by 0.10 ton and the amount of P_2 by 0.45 ton. It costs $1000 to process a ton of factory 2 waste, and each ton processed reduces the amount of P_1 by 0.20 ton and the amount of P_2 by 0.25 ton. It costs $2000 to process a ton of factory 3 waste, and each ton processed reduces the amount of P_1 by 0.40 ton and the amount of P_2 by 0.30 ton. The state wants to reduce the amount of P_1 in the river by at least 30 tons and the amount of P_2 by at least 40 tons.

a. Use Solver to determine how to minimize the cost of reducing pollution by the desired amounts. Are the LP assumptions (proportionality, additivity, divisibility) reasonable in this problem?

b. Use SolverTable to investigate the effects of increases in the minimal reductions required by the state. Specifically, see what happens to the amounts of waste processed at the three factories and the total cost if both requirements (currently 30 and 40 tons, respectively) are increased by the *same* percentage. Revise your model so that you can use SolverTable to investigate these changes when the percentage increase varies from 10% to 100% in increments of 10%. Do the amounts processed at the three factories and the total cost change in a linear manner?

Level B

35. A company manufactures two types of trucks. Each truck must go through the painting shop and the assembly shop. If the painting shop were completely devoted to painting type 1 trucks, 800 per day could be painted, whereas if the painting shop were completely devoted to painting type 2 trucks, 700 per day could be painted. If the assembly shop were completely devoted to assembling truck 1 engines, 1500 per day could be assembled, whereas if the assembly shop were completely devoted to assembling truck 2 engines, 1200 per day could be assembled. It is possible, however, to paint *both* types of trucks in the painting shop. Similarly, it is possible to assemble both types in the assembly shop. Each type 1 truck contributes $1000 to profit; each type 2 truck contributes $1500. Use Solver to maximize the company's profit. (*Hint:* One approach, but not the only approach, is to try a graphical procedure first and then deduce the constraints from the graph.)

36. A company manufactures mechanical heart valves from the heart valves of pigs. Different heart operations require valves of different sizes. The company purchases pig valves from three different suppliers. The cost and size mix of the valves purchased from each supplier are given in the file **P13_36.xlsx**. Each month, the company places an order with each supplier. At least 500 large, 300 medium, and 300 small valves must be purchased each month. Because of the limited availability of pig valves, at most 500 valves per month can be purchased from each supplier.

a. Use Solver to determine how the company can minimize the cost of acquiring the needed valves.

b. Use SolverTable to investigate the effect on total cost of increasing its minimal purchase requirements each month. Specifically, see how the total cost changes as the minimal purchase requirements of large, medium, and small valves all increase from their original values by the *same* percentage. Revise your model so that SolverTable can be used to investigate these changes when the percentage increase varies from 2% to 20% in increments of 2%. Explain intuitively what happens when this percentage is at least 16%.

37. A company that builds sailboats wants to determine how many sailboats to build during each of the next four quarters. The demand during each of the next four quarters is as follows: first quarter, 160 sailboats; second quarter, 240 sailboats; third quarter, 300 sailboats; fourth quarter, 100 sailboats. The company must meet demands on time. At the beginning of the first quarter, the company has an inventory of 40 sailboats. At the beginning of each quarter, the company must decide how many sailboats to build during that quarter. For simplicity, assume that sailboats built during a quarter can be used to meet demand for that quarter. During each quarter, the company can build up to 160 sailboats with regular-time labor at a total cost of $1600 per sailboat. By having employees work overtime during a quarter, the company can build additional sailboats with overtime labor at a total cost of $1800 per sailboat. At the end of each quarter (after production has occurred and the current quarter's demand has been satisfied), a holding cost of $80 per sailboat is incurred.

a. Determine a production schedule to minimize the sum of production and inventory holding costs during the next four quarters.

b. Use SolverTable to see whether any changes in the $80 holding cost per sailboat could induce the company to carry more or less inventory. Revise your model so that SolverTable can be used to investigate the effects on ending inventory during the four-quarter period of systematic changes in the unit holding cost. (Assume that even though the unit holding cost changes, it is still constant over the four-quarter period.) Are there any (nonnegative) unit holding costs that would induce the company to hold *more* inventory than it holds when the holding cost is $80? Are there any unit holding costs that would induce the company to hold *less* inventory than it holds when the holding cost is $80?

38. During the next two months an automobile manufacturer must meet (on time) the following demands for trucks and cars: month 1, 400 trucks and 800 cars; month 2, 300 trucks and 300 cars. During each month at most 1000 vehicles can be produced. Each truck uses two tons of steel, and each car uses one ton of steel. During month 1, steel costs $700 per ton; during month 2, steel is projected to cost $800 per ton. At most 2500 tons of steel can be purchased each month. (Steel can be used only during the month in which it is purchased.) At the beginning of month 1, 100 trucks and 200 cars are in the inventory. At the end of each month, a holding cost of $200 per vehicle is assessed. Each car gets 20 miles per gallon (mpg), and each truck gets 10 mpg. During each month, the vehicles produced by the company must average at least 16 mpg.

a. Determine how to meet the demand and mileage requirements at minimum total cost.

b. Use SolverTable to see how sensitive the total cost is to the 16 mpg requirement. Specifically, let this requirement vary from 14 mpg to 18 mpg in increments of 0.25 mpg. Explain intuitively what happens when the requirement is greater than 17 mpg.

39. A textile company produces shirts and pants. Each shirt requires two square yards of cloth, and each pair of pants requires three square yards of cloth. During the next two months the following demands for shirts and pants must be met (on time): month 1, 1000 shirts and 1500 pairs of pants; month 2, 1200 shirts and 1400 pairs of pants. During each month the following resources are available: month 1, 9000 square yards of cloth; month 2, 6000 square yards of cloth. In addition, cloth that is available during month 1 and is not used can be used during month 2. During each month it costs $8 to produce an article of clothing with regular-time labor and $12 with overtime labor. During each month a total of at most 2500 articles of clothing can be produced with regular-time labor, and an unlimited number of articles of clothing can be produced with overtime labor. At the end of each month, a holding cost of $3 per article of clothing is incurred.

a. Determine how to meet demands for the next two months (on time) at minimum cost. Assume that 100 shirts and 200 pairs of pants are already in inventory at the beginning of month 1.

b. Use a two-way SolverTable to investigate the effect on total cost of two *simultaneous* changes. The first change is to allow the ratio of overtime to regular-time production cost (currently $16/$8 = 2) to decrease from 20% to 80% in increments of 20%, while keeping the regular time cost at $8. The second change is to allow the production capacity *each* month (currently 2500) to decrease by 10% to 50% in increments of 10%. The idea here is that less regular-time capacity is available, but overtime becomes relatively cheaper. Is the net effect on total cost positive or negative?

40. Each year, a shoe manufacturing company faces demands (which must be met on time) for pairs of shoes as shown in the file **P13_40.xlsx**. Employees work three consecutive quarters and then receive one quarter off. For example, a worker might work during quarters 3 and 4 of one year and quarter 1 of the next year. During a quarter in which an employee works, he or she can produce up to 500 pairs of shoes. Each worker is paid $5000 per quarter. At the end of each quarter, a holding cost of $10 per pair of shoes is incurred.

a. Determine how to minimize the cost per year (labor plus holding) of meeting the demands for shoes. To simplify the model, assume that at the end of each year, the ending inventory is 0. (You can assume that a given worker gets the *same* quarter off during each year.)

b. Suppose the company can pay a flat fee for a training program that increases the productivity of all of its workers. Use SolverTable to see how much the company would be willing to pay for a training program that increases worker productivity from 500 pairs of shoes per quarter to P pairs of shoes per quarter, where P varies from 525 to 700 in increments of 25.

41. A small appliance manufacturer must meet (on time) the following demands: quarter 1, 3000 units; quarter 2, 2000 units; quarter 3, 4000 units. Each quarter, up to 2700 units can be produced with regular-time labor, at a cost of $40 per unit. During each quarter, an unlimited number of units can be produced with overtime labor, at a cost of $60 per unit. Of all units produced, 20% are unsuitable and cannot be used to meet demand. Also, at the end of each quarter, 10% of all units on hand spoil and cannot be used to meet any future demands. After each quarter's demand is satisfied and spoilage is accounted for, a cost of $15 per unit in ending inventory is incurred.

a. Determine how to minimize the total cost of meeting the demands of the next three quarters. Assume that 1000 usable units are available at the beginning of quarter 1.

b. The company wants to know how much money it would be worth to decrease the percentage of unsuitable items and/or the percentage of items that spoil. Write a short report that provides relevant information. Base your report on three uses of SolverTable: (1) where the percentage of unsuitable items decreases and the percentage of items that spoil stays at 10%, (2) where the percentage of unsuitable items stays at 20% and the percentage of items that spoil decreases, and (3) where both percentages decrease. Does the sum of the separate effects on total cost from the first two tables equal the combined effect from the third table? Include an answer to this question in your report.

42. A pharmaceutical company manufactures two drugs at Los Angeles and Indianapolis. The cost of manufacturing a pound of each drug depends on the location, as indicated in the file **P13_42.xlsx**. The machine time (in hours) required to produce a pound of each drug at each city is also shown in this table. The company must produce at least 1000 pounds per week of drug 1 and at least 2000 pounds per week of drug 2. It has 500 hours per week of machine time at Indianapolis and 400 hours per week at Los Angeles.

a. Determine how the company can minimize the cost of producing the required drugs.

b. Use SolverTable to determine how much the company would be willing to pay to purchase a combination of A extra hours of machine time at Indianapolis and B extra hours of machine time at Los Angeles, where A and B can be any positive multiples of 10 up to 50.

43. A company manufactures two products on two machines. The number of hours of machine time and labor depends on the machine and product as shown in the file **P13_43.xlsx**. The cost of producing a unit of each product depends on which machine produces it. These unit costs also appear in the same file. There are 200 hours available on each of the two machines, and there are 400 labor hours available total. This month at least 200 units of product 1 and at least 240 units of product 2 must be produced. Also, at least half of the product 1 requirement must be produced on machine 1, and at least half of the product 2 requirement must be produced on machine 2.

a. Determine how the company can minimize the cost of meeting this month's requirements.

b. Use SolverTable to see how much the "at least half" requirements are costing the company. Do this by changing *both* of these requirements from "at least half" to "at least x percent," where x can be any multiple of 5% from 0% to 50%.

APPENDIX   INFORMATION ON SOLVERS

Microsoft Office (or Excel) ships with a built-in version of Solver. This version and all other versions of Solver have been developed by Frontline Systems, not Microsoft. When you install Office (or Excel), you have the option of installing or not installing Solver. In most cases, a typical install should install Solver. To check whether Solver is installed on your system, open Excel, select the Office Button (or the File tab in Excel 2010), select Excel Options, select Add-Ins, and click on Go. If there is a Solver item in the list, Solver has been installed. (To actually add it in, make sure this item is checked.) Otherwise, you need to run the Office Setup program with the Add/Remove feature to install Solver. Users of previous versions of Excel (2003 or earlier) should note that the actual Solver add-in file is a different one in Excel 2007 or Excel 2010. In previous versions, it was Solver.xla; now it is Solver.xlam. However, the basic functionality is the same.

The built-in version of Solver is able to solve most problems you are likely to encounter. However, it does have one important limitation you should be aware of: it allows only 200 changing cells. This might sound like plenty, but many real-world problems go well beyond 200 changing cells. If you want to solve larger problems, you will need to purchase one of Frontline's commercial versions of Solver. For more information, check Frontline Systems' Web site at www.solver.com.

Shelby Shelving is a small company that manufactures two types of shelves for grocery stores. Model S is the standard model; model LX is a heavy-duty version. Shelves are manufactured in three major steps: stamping, forming, and assembly. In the stamping stage, a large machine is used to stamp (i.e., cut) standard sheets of metal into appropriate sizes. In the forming stage, another machine bends the metal into shape. Assembly involves joining the parts with a combination of soldering and riveting. Shelby's stamping and forming machines work on both models of shelves. Separate assembly departments are used for the final stage of production.

The file **Shelby Shelving.xlsx** contains relevant data for Shelby. (See Figure 13.35.) The hours required on each machine for each unit of product are shown in the range B5:C6 of the Accounting Data sheet. For example, the production of one model S shelf requires 0.25 hour on the forming machine. Both the stamping and forming machines can operate for 800 hours each month. The model S assembly department has a monthly capacity of 1900 units. The model LX assembly department has a monthly capacity of only 1400 units. Currently Shelby is producing and selling 400 units of model S and 1400 units of model LX per month.

Figure 13.35 Data for Shelby Case

	A	B	C	D	E	F	G	H	I
1	Shelby Shelving Data for Current Production Schedule								
2									
3	Machine requirements (hours per unit)					Given monthly overhead cost data			
4		Model S	Model LX	Available			Fixed	Variable S	Variable LX
5	Stamping	0.3	0.3	800		Stamping	$125,000	$80	$90
6	Forming	0.25	0.5	800		Forming	$95,000	$120	$170
7						Model S Assembly	$80,000	$165	$0
8		Model S	Model LX			Model LX Assembly	$85,000	$0	$185
9	Current monthly production	400	1400						
10						Standard costs of the shelves -- based on the current production levels			
11	Hours spent in departments						Model S	Model LX	
12		Model S	Model LX	Totals		Direct materials	$1,000	$1,200	
13	Stamping	120	420	540		Direct labor:			
14	Forming	100	700	800		Stamping	$35	$35	
15						Forming	$60	$90	
16	Percentages of time spent in departments					Assembly	$80	$85	
17		Model S	Model LX			Total direct labor	$175	$210	
18	Stamping	22.2%	77.8%			Overhead allocation			
19	Forming	12.5%	87.5%			Stamping	$149	$159	
20						Forming	$150	$229	
21	Unit selling price	$1,800	$2,100			Assembly	$365	$246	
22						Total overhead	$664	$635	
23	Assembly capacity	1900	1400			Total cost	$1,839	$2,045	

Model S shelves are sold for $1800, and model LX shelves are sold for $2100. Shelby's operation is fairly small in the industry, and management at Shelby believes it cannot raise prices beyond these levels because of the competition. However, the marketing department believes that Shelby can sell as much as it can produce at these prices. The costs of production are summarized in the Accounting Data sheet.

As usual, values in blue cells are given, whereas other values are calculated from these.

Management at Shelby just met to discuss next month's operating plan. Although the shelves are selling well, the overall profitability of the company is a concern. The plant's engineer suggested that the current production of model S shelves be cut back. According to him, "Model S shelves are sold for

$1800 per unit, but our costs are $1839. Even though we're selling only 400 units a month, we're losing money on each one. We should decrease production of model S." The controller disagreed. He said that the problem was the model S assembly department trying to absorb a large overhead with a small production volume. "The model S units are making a contribution to overhead. Even though production doesn't cover all of the fixed costs, we'd be worse off with lower production."

Your job is to develop an LP model of Shelby's problem, then run Solver, and finally make a recommendation to Shelby management, with a short verbal argument supporting the engineer or the controller.

Notes on Accounting Data Calculations

The fixed overhead is distributed using activity-based costing principles. For example, at current production levels, the forming machine spends 100 hours on model S shelves and 700 hours on model LX shelves. The forming machine is used 800 hours of the month, of which 12.5% of the time is spent on model S shelves and 87.5% is spent on model LX shelves. The $95,000 of fixed overhead in the forming department is distributed as $11,875 ($= 95,000 \times 0.125$) to model S shelves and $83,125 ($= 95,000 \times 0.875$) to model LX shelves. The fixed overhead per unit of output is allocated as $29.69 ($= 11,875/400$) for model S and $59.38 ($= 83,125/1400$) for model LX. In the calculation of the standard overhead cost, the fixed and variable costs are added together, so that the overhead cost for the forming department allocated to a model S shelf is $149.69 ($= 29.69 + 120$, shown in cell G20 rounded up to $150). Similarly, the overhead cost for the forming department allocated to a model LX shelf is $229.38 ($= 59.38 + 170$, shown in cell H20 rounded down to $229).

After graduating from business school, George Clark went to work for a Big Six accounting firm in San Francisco. Because his hobby has always been wine making, when he had the opportunity a few years later he purchased five acres plus an option to buy 35 additional acres of land in Sonoma Valley in Northern California. He plans eventually to grow grapes on that land and make wine with them. George knows that this is a big undertaking and that it will require more capital than he has at the present. However, he figures that if he persists, he will be able to leave accounting and live full time from his winery earnings by the time he is 40.

Because wine making is capital-intensive and because growing commercial-quality grapes with a full yield of five tons per acre takes at least eight years, George is planning to start small. This is necessitated by both his lack of capital and his inexperience in wine making on a large scale, although he has long made wine at home. His plan is first to plant the grapes on his land to get the vines started. Then he needs to set up a small trailer where he can live on weekends while he installs the irrigation system and does the required work to the vines, such as pruning and fertilizing. To help maintain a positive cash flow during the first few years, he also plans to buy grapes from other nearby growers so he can make his own label wine. He proposes to market it through a small tasting room that he will build on his land and keep open on weekends during the spring–summer season.

To begin, George is going to use $10,000 in savings to finance the initial purchase of grapes from which he will make his first batch of wine. He is also thinking about going to the Bank of Sonoma and asking for a loan. He knows that if he goes to the bank, the loan officer will ask for a business plan; so he is trying to pull together some numbers for himself first. This way he will have a rough notion of the profitability and cash flows associated with his ideas before he develops a formal plan with a pro forma income statement and balance sheet. He has decided to make the preliminary planning horizon two years and would like to estimate the profit over

that period. His most immediate task is to decide how much of the $10,000 should be allocated to purchasing grapes for the first year and how much to purchasing grapes for the second year. In addition, each year he must decide how much he should allocate to purchasing grapes to make his favorite Petite Sirah and how much to purchasing grapes to make the more popular Sauvignon Blanc that seems to have been capturing the attention of a wider market during the last few years in California.

In the first year, each bottle of Petite Sirah requires $0.80 worth of grapes and each bottle of Sauvignon Blanc uses $0.70 worth of grapes. For the second year, the costs of the grapes per bottle are $0.75 and $0.85, respectively.

George anticipates that his Petite Sirah will sell for $8.00 a bottle in the first year and for $8.25 in the second year, while his Sauvignon Blanc's price remains the same in both years at $7.00 a bottle.

Besides the decisions about the amounts of grapes purchased in the two years, George must make estimates of the sales levels for the two wines during the two years. The local wine-making association has told him that marketing is the key to success in any wine business; generally, demand is directly proportional to the amount of effort spent on marketing. Thus, since George cannot afford to do any market research about sales levels due to his lack of capital, he is pondering how much money he should spend to promote each wine each year. The wine-making association has given him a rule of thumb that relates estimated demand to the amount of money spent on advertising. For instance, they estimate that for each dollar spent in the first year promoting the Petite Sirah, a demand for five bottles will be created; and for each dollar spent in the second year, a demand for six bottles will result. Similarly, for each dollar spent on advertising for the Sauvignon Blanc in the first year, up to eight bottles can be sold; and for each dollar spent in the second year, up to ten bottles can be sold.

[15]This case was written by William D. Whisler, California State University, Hayward.

The initial funds for the advertising will come from the $10,000 savings. Assume that the cash earned from wine sales in the first year is available in the second year.

A personal concern George has is that he maintain a proper balance of wine products so that he will be well positioned to expand his marketing capabilities when he moves to the winery and makes it his full-time job. Thus, in his mind it is important to ensure that the number of bottles of Petite Sirah sold each year falls in the range between 40% and 70% of the overall number of bottles sold.

Questions

1. George needs help to decide how many grapes to buy, how much money to spend on advertising, how many bottles of wine to sell, and how much profit he can expect to earn over the two-year period. Develop a spreadsheet LP model to help him.
2. Solve the linear programming model formulated in Question 1.

The following questions should be attempted only after Questions 1 and 2 have been answered correctly.

3. After showing the business plan to the Bank of Sonoma, George learns that the loan officer is concerned about the market prices used in estimating the profits—recently it has been forecasted that Chile and Australia will be flooding the market with high-quality, low-priced white wines over the next couple of years. In particular, the loan officer estimates that the price used for the Sauvignon Blanc in the second year is highly speculative and realistically might be only half the price George calculated. Thus, the bank is nervous about lending the money because of the big effect such a decrease in price might have on estimated profits. What do you think?
4. Another comment the loan officer of the Bank of Sonoma has after reviewing the business plan is: "I see that you do have an allowance in your calculations for the carryover of inventory of unsold wine from the first year to the second year, but you do not have any cost associated with this. All companies must charge something for holding inventory, so you should redo your plans to allow for this." If the holding charges are $0.10 per bottle per year, how much, if any, does George's plan change?

5. The president of the local grape growers' association mentions to George that there is likely to be a strike soon over the unionization of the grape workers. (Currently they are not represented by any union.) This means that the costs of the grapes might go up by anywhere from 50% to 100%. How might this affect George's plan?
6. Before taking his business plan to the bank, George had it reviewed by a colleague at the accounting firm where he works. Although his friend was excited about the plan and its prospects, he was dismayed to learn that George had not used present value in determining his profit. "George, you are an accountant and must know that money has a time value; and although you are only doing a two-year planning problem, it still is important to calculate the present value profit." George replies, "Yes, I know all about present value. For big investments over long time periods, it is important to consider. But in this case, for a small investment and only a two-year time period, it really doesn't matter." Who is correct, George or his colleague? Why? Use an 8% discount factor in answering this question. Does the answer change if a 6% or 10% discount rate is used? Use a spreadsheet to determine the coefficients of the objective function for the different discount rates.
7. Suppose that the Bank of Sonoma is so excited about the prospects of George's wine-growing business that they offer to lend him an extra $10,000 at their best small business rate—28% plus a 10% compensating balance.[16] Should he accept the bank's offer? Why or why not?
8. Suppose that the rule of thumb George was given by the local wine-making association is incorrect. Assume that the number of bottles of Petite Sirah sold in the first and second years is at most four for each dollar spent on advertising. And likewise for the Sauvignon Blanc, assume that it can be at most only five in years 1 and 2.
9. How much could profits be increased if George's personal concerns (that Petite Sirah sales should account for between 40% and 70% of overall sales) are ignored?

[16]The compensating balance requirement means that only $9,000 of the $10,000 loan is available to George; the remaining $1,000 remains with the bank.

Optimization Models

© Bloomberg via Getty Images

PRODUCTION, INVENTORY, AND DISTRIBUTION AT KELLOGG

The Kellogg Company is the largest cereal producer in the world and is a leading producer of convenience foods. Its worldwide sales in 1999 were nearly $7 billion. Kellogg's first product in 1906 was Corn Flakes, and it developed a variety of ready-to-eat cereals over the years, including Raisin Bran, Rice Krispies, Corn Pops, and others. Although the company continues to develop and market new cereals, it has recently gone into convenience foods, such as Pop-Tarts and Nutri-Grain cereal bars, and has also entered the health-food market. Kellogg produces hundreds of products and sells thousands of stock-keeping units (SKUs). Managing production, inventory, and distribution of these—that is, the daily operations—in a cost-effective manner is a challenge.

By the late 1980s, Kellogg realized that the increasing scale and complexity of its operations required optimization methods to coordinate its daily operations in a centralized manner. As described in Brown et al. (2001), a team of management scientists developed an optimization software system called KPS (Kellogg Planning System). This system was originally intended for operational (daily and weekly) decisions, but it expanded into a system for making tactical (longer-range) decisions about issues such as plant budgets, capacity expansion, and consolidation. By the turn of the century, KPS had been in use for about a decade. Operational decisions made by KPS reduced production, inventory, and distribution costs by approximately $4.5 million per year. Better yet, the tactical side of KPS recently suggested a consolidation of production capacity that saved the company approximately $35–40 million annually.

Kellogg operates five plants in the United States and Canada, has seven distribution centers (DCs) in such areas as Los Angeles and Chicago, and has about 15 co-packers, companies that contract to produce or pack some of Kellogg's products. Customer demands are seen at the DCs and the plants. In the cereal business alone, Kellogg has to coordinate the packaging, inventorying, and distributing of 600 SKUs at about 27 locations with a total of about 90 production lines and 180 packaging lines. This requires a tremendous amount of day-to-day coordination to meet customer demand at a low cost. The KPS operational system that guides operational decisions is essentially a large linear programming (LP) model that takes as its inputs the forecasted customer demands for the various products and specifies what should be produced, held, and shipped on a daily basis. The resulting model is similar to the Pigskin model of football production discussed in the previous chapter, except that it is *much* larger.

Specifically, for each week of its 30-week planning horizon, the model specifies (1) how much of each product to make on each production line at each facility; (2) how much of each SKU to pack on each packaging line at each facility; (3) how much inventory of each SKU to hold at each facility; and (4) how much of each SKU to ship from each location to other locations. In addition, the model has to take constraints into account. For example, the production within a given plant in a week cannot exceed the processing line capacity in that plant. LP models such as Kellogg's tend to be very large— thousands of decision variables and hundreds or thousands of constraints—but the algorithms Kellogg uses are capable of optimizing such models very quickly. Kellogg runs its KPS model each Sunday morning and uses its recommendations in the ensuing week.

The KPS system illustrates a common occurrence when companies turn to management science for help. As stated earlier, the system was originally developed for making daily operational decisions. Soon, however, the company developed a tactical version of KPS for long-range planning on the order of 12 to 24 months. The tactical model is similar to the operational model except that time periods are now months, not days or weeks, and other considerations must be handled, such as limited product shelf lives. The point is, however, that when companies such as Kellogg become comfortable with management science methods in one part of their operations, they often look for other areas to apply similar methods. As with Kellogg, such methods can save the company millions of dollars. ■

14.1 INTRODUCTION

In a survey of Fortune 500 firms, 85% of those responding said that they use LP. In this chapter we discuss some of the LP models that are most often applied to real-world applications. Some typical examples include:

- scheduling bank clerks for check encoding
- optimizing the operation of an oil refinery

- planning dairy production at a creamery
- scheduling production of fiberglass products at Owens-Corning Fiberglass
- optimizing a Wall Street firm's bond portfolio.

Actually, these problems are just a sampling of the types of problems we will model in this chapter. There are two basic goals in this chapter. The first is to illustrate some of the many real applications that can take advantage of LP. You will see that these applications cover a wide range, from oil production to worker scheduling to cash management. The second goal is to increase your facility in modeling LP problems on a spreadsheet. We present a few principles that will help you model a wide variety of problems. The best way to learn, however, is to see many examples and work through numerous problems. In short, mastering the art of LP spreadsheet modeling takes hard work and practice. You will have plenty of opportunity to do both with the material in this chapter.

Although a wide variety of problems can be formulated as *linear* programming models, there are some that cannot. Either they require *integer* variables or they are *nonlinear* in the decision variables. We include examples of integer programming and nonlinear programming models in this chapter, just to give you a taste of what is involved.[1] You will see that the modeling process for these types of problems is not much different than for LP problems. Once the models are formulated, Excel's Solver can be used to solve them. Then SolverTable can be used to perform sensitivity analysis. However, we point out that these integer and nonlinear models are inherently more difficult to solve. Solver must use more complex algorithms and is not always guaranteed to find the optimal solution. As long as you are aware of this, you will see that Solver provides the power to solve a great variety of realistic business problems.

Although there is a tremendous amount of theory behind the *algorithms* that solve these problems, the modeling process itself is fairly straightforward and is learned best by seeing a variety of examples. Therefore, we proceed in this chapter by modeling (and then solving) a diverse class of problems that arise in business. The exercises scattered throughout the chapter provide even more examples of how LP and its integer and nonlinear extensions can be applied.

All of these models can benefit from sensitivity analysis, either done formally with the SolverTable add-in or informally by changing one or more inputs and rerunning Solver. To keep the chapter from getting too long, we present only a few of the many possible sensitivity analyses. However, we stress that in real applications, model development is just the beginning of the overall analysis. It is then usually followed by extensive sensitivity analysis.

14.2 WORKER SCHEDULING MODELS

Many organizations must determine how to schedule employees to provide adequate service. The following example illustrates how to use LP, possibly with integer constraints, to schedule employees on a daily basis.

---

[1]Besides the nonlinear models discussed in this chapter, which can be solved with Solver's GRG nonlinear algorithm, there is an even more difficult class of nonlinear models called *nonsmooth* models. Although we will not discuss nonsmooth models, we can recommend Solver's Evolutionary algorithm for these difficult models. (This is available only in Excel 2010's version of Solver.)

EXAMPLE | 14.1 POSTAL EMPLOYEE SCHEDULING

A post office requires different numbers of full-time employees on different days of the week. The number of full-time employees required each day is given in Table 14.1. Union rules state that each full-time employee must work five consecutive days and then receive two days off. For example, an employee who works Monday to Friday must be off on Saturday and Sunday. The post office wants to meet its daily requirements using only full-time employees. Its objective is to minimize the number of full-time employees on its payroll.

Table 14.1   Employee Requirements for Post Office

Day of Week	Minimum Number of Employees Required
Monday	17
Tuesday	13
Wednesday	15
Thursday	19
Friday	14
Saturday	16
Sunday	11

Objective   To develop an LP spreadsheet model that relates five-day shift schedules to daily numbers of employees available, and to use Solver on this model to find a schedule that uses the fewest number of employees and meets all daily workforce requirements.

WHERE DO THE NUMBERS COME FROM?

The only inputs needed for this problem are the minimum employee requirements in Table 14.1, but these are not easy to obtain. They would probably be obtained through a combination of two quantitative techniques: forecasting (Chapter 12) and queueing analysis (not covered in this book). The post office would first use historical data to forecast customer and mail arrival patterns throughout a typical week. It would then use queueing analysis to translate these arrival patterns into worker requirements on a daily basis. Actually, we have kept the problem relatively simple by considering only *daily* requirements. In a realistic setting, the organization might forecast worker requirements on an hourly or even a 15-minute basis.

Solution

The variables and constraints for this problem appear in Table 14.2. The trickiest part is identifying the appropriate decision variables. Many students believe the decision variables should be the numbers of employees working on the various days of the week. Clearly, these values must eventually be determined. However, it is not enough to specify, say, that 18 employees are working on Monday. The problem is that this doesn't indicate when these 18 employees start their five-day shifts. Without this knowledge, it is impossible to implement the five-consecutive-day, two-day-off requirement. (If you don't believe this, try developing your own model with the wrong decision variables. You will eventually reach a dead end.)

In real employee-scheduling problems, much of the work involves forecasting and queueing analysis to obtain worker requirements. This must be done before an optimal schedule can be found.

Table 14.2 Variables and Constraints for Postal Scheduling Problem

Input variables	Minimum required number of workers each day
Decision variables (changing cells)	Number of employees working each of the five-day shifts (defined by their first day of work)
Objective cell	Total number of employees on the payroll
Other calculated variables	Number of employees working each day
Constraints	Employees working ≥ Employees required

The key to this model is choosing the correct changing cells.

The trick is to define the decision variables as the numbers of employees working each of the seven possible five-day shifts. By knowing the values of these decision variables, the other output variables can be calculated. For example, the number working on Thursday is the sum of those who begin their five-day shifts on Sunday, Monday, Tuesday, Wednesday, and Thursday.

FUNDAMENTAL INSIGHT

Choosing the Changing Cells

The changing cells, which are really just the decision variables, should always be chosen so that their values determine all required outputs in the model. In other words, their values should tell the company exactly how to run its business. Sometimes the choice of changing cells is obvious, but in many cases (as in this worker scheduling model), the proper choice of changing cells takes some deeper thinking about the problem. An improper choice of changing cells typically leads to a dead end, where their values do not supply enough information to calculate required outputs or implement certain constraints.

Note that this is a "wraparound" problem. We assume that the daily requirements in Table 14.1 and the worker schedules continue week after week. So, for example, if eight employees are assigned to the Thursday through Monday shift, these employees always wrap around from one week to the next on their five-day shift.

DEVELOPING THE SPREADSHEET MODEL

The spreadsheet model for this problem is shown in Figure 14.1. (See the file **Worker Scheduling.xlsx**.) To form this spreadsheet, proceed as follows.

1 Inputs and range names. Enter the number of employees needed on each day of the week (from Table 14.1) in the blue cells, and create the range names shown.

2 Employees beginning each day. Enter *any* trial values for the number of employees beginning work on each day of the week in the Employees_starting range. These beginning days determine the possible five-day shifts. For example, the employees in cell B4 work Monday through Friday.

3 Employees on hand each day. The key to this solution is to realize that the numbers in the Employees_starting range—the changing cells—do not represent the number of workers who will show up each day. As an example, the number in cell B4 represent those who start on Monday work Monday through Friday. Therefore, enter the formula

=$B$4

Figure 14.1 Worker Scheduling Model with Optimal Solution

	A	B	C	D	E	F	G	H	I	J	K
1	Worker scheduling model								Range names used		
2									Employees_available	=Model!$B$23:$H$23	
3	Decision variables: number of employees starting their five-day shift on various days								Employees_required	=Model!$B$25:$H$25	
4	Mon	6.33							Employees_Starting	=Model!$B$4:$B$10	
5	Tue	5.00							Total_employees	=Model!$B$28	
6	Wed	0.33									
7	Thu	7.33									
8	Fri	0.00									
9	Sat	3.33									
10	Sun	0.00									
11											
12	Result of decisions: number of employees working on various days (along top) who started their shift on various days (along side)										
13		Mon	Tue	Wed	Thu	Fri	Sat	Sun			
14	Mon	6.33	6.33	6.33	6.33	6.33					
15	Tue		5.00	5.00	5.00	5.00	5.00				
16	Wed			0.33	0.33	0.33	0.33	0.33			
17	Thu	7.33			7.33	7.33	7.33	7.33			
18	Fri	0.00	0.00			0.00	0.00	0.00			
19	Sat	3.33	3.33	3.33			3.33	3.33			
20	Sun	0.00	0.00	0.00	0.00			0.00			
21											
22	Constraint on worker availabilities										
23	Employees available	17.00	14.67	15.00	19.00	19.00	16.00	11.00			
24		>=	>=	>=	>=	>=	>=	>=			
25	Employees required	17	13	15	19	14	16	11			
26											
27	Objective to maximize										
28	Total employees	22.33									

in cell B14 and copy it across to cell F14. Proceed similarly for rows 15–20, being careful to take "wraparounds" into account. For example, the workers starting on Thursday work Thursday through Sunday, plus Monday. Then calculate the total number who are available on each day by entering the formula

=SUM(B14:B20)

in cell B23 and copying it across to cell H23.

Excel Tip *CTRL-Enter Shortcut*
You often enter a typical formula in a cell and then copy it. One way to do this efficiently is to highlight the entire range, here B23:H23. Then enter the typical formula, here **=SUM(B14:B20)**, *and press* **Ctrl-Enter**. *This has the same effect as copying, but it is slightly quicker.*

4 **Total employees.** Calculate the total number of employees in cell B28 with the formula

=SUM(Employees_starting)

Note that there is no double-counting in this sum. For example, the employees in cells B4 and B5 are *not* the same people.

At this point, you might want to experiment with the numbers in the changing cell range to see whether you can guess an optimal solution (without looking at Figure 14.1). It is not that easy. Each worker who starts on a given day works the next four days as well, so when you find a solution that meets the minimal requirements for the various days, you usually have a few more workers available on some days than are needed.

Invoke Solver and fill out its main dialog box as shown in Figure 14.2. (You don't need to include the integer constraints yet. We will discuss them shortly.) Make sure you check the Non-Negative option and use the simplex method.

Figure 14.2

Solver Dialog Box
for Worker
Scheduling Model

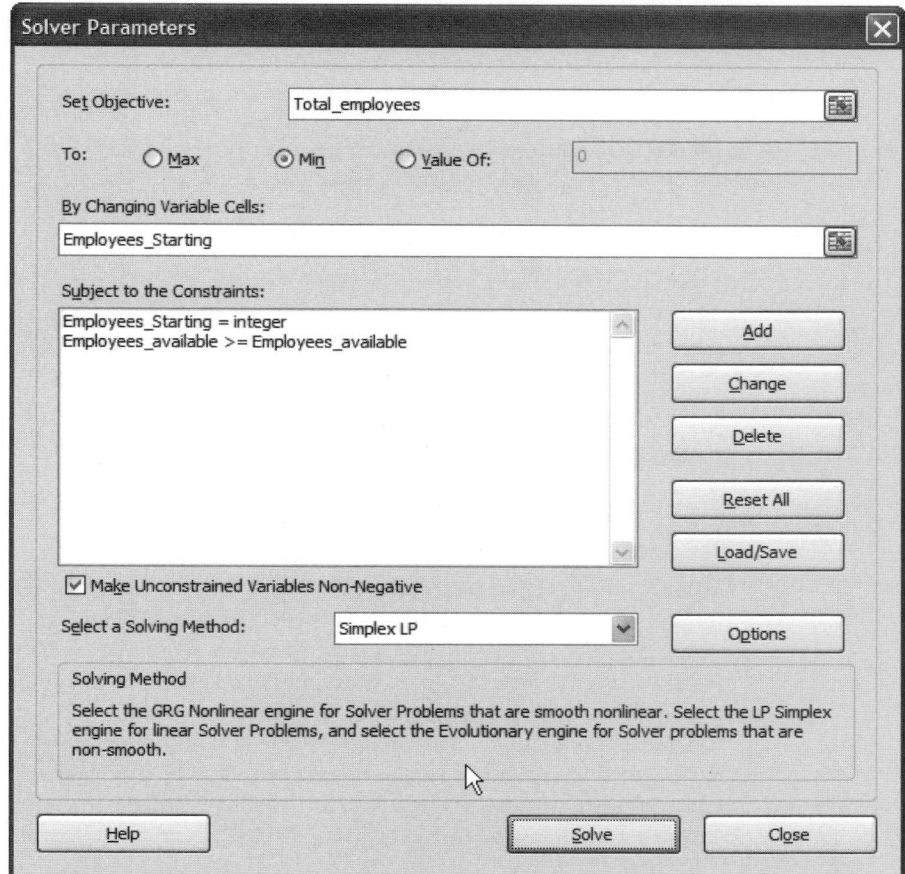

Discussion of the Solution

The optimal solution shown in Figure 14.1 has one drawback: It requires the number of employees starting work on some days to be a fraction. Because part-time employees are not allowed, this solution is unrealistic. However, it is simple to add an integer constraint on the changing cells. This integer constraint appears in Figure 14.2. (To create this integer constraint in Solver's Add Constraint dialog box, select the Employees_starting for the left side, and select Int in the middle dropdown list. The word "Integer" will automatically appear in the right side of the constraint.) With this integer constraint, the optimal solution appears in Figure 14.3.

The changing cells in the optimal solution indicate the numbers of workers who start their five-day shifts on the various days. You can then look at the *columns* of the B14:H20 range to see which employees are working on any given day. This optimal solution is typical in scheduling problems. Due to a labor constraint—each employee must work five

Figure 14.3 Optimal Integer Solution to Worker Scheduling Model

	A	B	C	D	E	F	G	H	I	J	K
1	Worker scheduling model								Range names used		
2									Employees_available	=Model!$B$23:$H$23	
3	Decision variables: number of employees starting their five-day shift on various days								Employees_required	=Model!$B$25:$H$25	
4	Mon	6							Employees_Starting	=Model!$B$4:$B$10	
5	Tue	6							Total_employees	=Model!$B$28	
6	Wed	0									
7	Thu	7									
8	Fri	0									
9	Sat	4									
10	Sun	0									
11											
12	Result of decisions: number of employees working on various days (along top) who started their shift on various days (along side)										
13		Mon	Tue	Wed	Thu	Fri	Sat	Sun			
14	Mon	6	6	6	6	6					
15	Tue		6	6	6	6	6				
16	Wed			0	0	0	0	0			
17	Thu	7			7	7	7	7			
18	Fri	0	0			0	0	0			
19	Sat	4	4	4			4	4			
20	Sun	0	0	0	0			0			
21											
22	Constraint on worker availabilities										
23	Employees available	17	16	16	19	19	17	11			
24		>=	>=	>=	>=	>=	>=	>=			
25	Employees required	17	13	15	19	14	16	11			
26											
27	Objective to maximize										
28	Total employees	23									

Multiple optimal solutions have different values in the changing cells, but they all have the same objective value.

consecutive days and then have two days off—it is typically impossible to meet the minimum employee requirements exactly. To ensure that there are enough employees available on busy days, it is necessary to have more than enough on hand on light days.

Another interesting aspect of this problem is that if you solve this problem on your own PC, you might get a *different* schedule that is still optimal—that is, a solution that still uses a total of 23 employees and meets all constraints. This is a case of **multiple optimal solutions,** not at all uncommon in LP problems. In fact, it is typically good news for a manager, who can then choose among the optimal solutions using other, possibly non-quantitative criteria.[2]

Technical Tip *Solver Tolerance Setting*

Set Solver's Tolerance to zero to ensure that you get the optimal integer solution. Be aware, however, that this can incur significant extra computing time for larger models.

When working with integer constraints, you should be aware of Solver's Tolerance setting. The idea is as follows. As Solver searches for the best integer solution, it is often able to find a "good" solution fairly quickly, but it often has to spend a lot of time finding slightly better solutions. A nonzero tolerance setting allows it to quit early. The default tolerance setting is 5 (percent). This means that if Solver finds a feasible solution that is guaranteed to have an objective value no more than 5% from the optimal value, it will quit and report this good solution (which might even be the optimal solution). Therefore, if you keep this default tolerance value, your integer solutions will sometimes not be optimal, but they will be close. If you want to ensure that you get an optimal solution, you can change the Solver tolerance value to zero. (In Excel 2010, this setting is directly under the Solver Options on the All Methods tab.)

---

[2] It is usually difficult to tell whether there are multiple optimal solutions. You typically discover this by rerunning Solver from different starting solutions.

Sensitivity Analysis

To run some sensitivity analyses with SolverTable, you need to modify the original model slightly to incorporate the effect of the input being varied.

The most obvious type of sensitivity analysis in this example is to analyze the effect of worker requirements on the optimal solution. Specifically, let's suppose the number of employees needed on each day of the week increases by two, four, or six. How does this change the total number of employees needed? You can answer this with SolverTable, but you must first modify the model slightly, as shown in Figure 14.4. The problem is that we want to increase *each* of the daily minimal required values by the same amount. The trick is to enter the original requirements in row 12, enter a trial value for the extra number required per day in cell K12, enter the formula **=B12+$K$12** in cell B27, and then copy this formula across to cell H27. Now you can use the one-way SolverTable option, using the Extra cell as the single input, letting it vary from 0 to 6 in increments of 2, and specifying the Total_employees cell as the single output cell.

Figure 14.4 Modified Worker Scheduling Model

	A	B	C	D	E	F	G	H	I	J	K
1	Worker scheduling model								Range names used		
2									Employees_available	=Model!$B$23:$H$23	
3	Decision variables: number of employees starting their five-day shift on various days								Employees_required	=Model!$B$25:$H$25	
4	Mon	2							Employees_Starting	=Model!$B$4:$B$10	
5	Tue	3							Total_employees	=Model!$B$28	
6	Wed	3									
7	Thu	7									
8	Fri	0									
9	Sat	4									
10	Sun	4									
11											
12	Employees required (original values)	17	13	15	19	14	16	11		Extra required each day	0
13											
14	Result of decisions: number of employees working on various days (along top) who started their shift on various days (along side)										
15		Mon	Tue	Wed	Thu	Fri	Sat	Sun			
16	Mon	2	2	2	2	2					
17	Tue		3	3	3	3	3				
18	Wed			3	3	3	3	3			
19	Thu	7			7	7	7	7			
20	Fri	0	0			0	0	0			
21	Sat	4	4	4			4	4			
22	Sun	4	4	4	4			4			
23											
24	Constraint on worker availabilities										
25	Employees available	17	13	16	19	15	17	18			
26		>=	>=	>=	>=	>=	>=	>=			
27	Employees required	17	13	15	19	14	16	11			
28											
29	Objective to maximize										
30	Total employees	23									

The results appear in Figure 14.5. When the requirement increases by two each day, only two extra employees are necessary (scheduled appropriately). However, when the requirement increases by four each day, *more* than four extra employees are necessary. The same is true when the requirement increases by six each day. This might surprise you at first, but there is an intuitive reason: Each extra worker works only five days of the week.

Note that we did not use Solver's sensitivity report here for two reasons. First, Solver does not offer a sensitivity report for models with integer constraints. Second, even if the integer constraints are deleted, Solver's sensitivity report does not answer questions about *multiple* input changes, as we have asked here. It is used primarily for questions about one-at-a-time changes to inputs, such as a change to a *specific* day's worker requirement. In this sense, SolverTable is a more flexible tool.

Figure 14.5 Sensitivity to Number of Extra Workers Required per Day

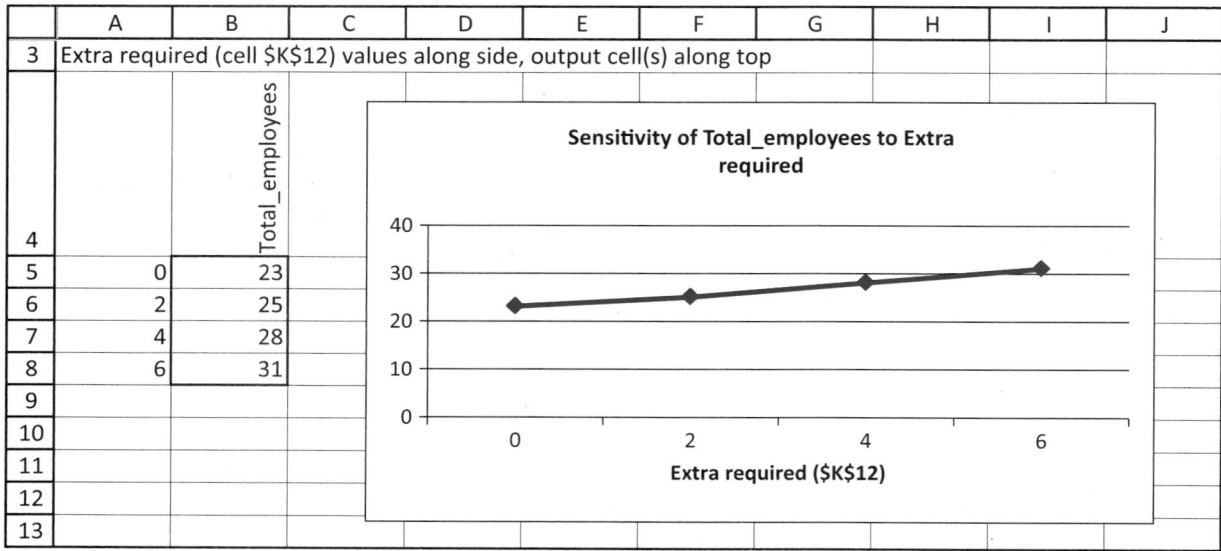

	A	B	C	D	E	F	G	H	I	J
3	Extra required (cell $K$12) values along side, output cell(s) along top									
4		Total_employees								
5	0	23								
6	2	25								
7	4	28								
8	6	31								
9										
10										
11										
12										
13										

MODELING ISSUES

1. The postal employee scheduling example is called a *static* scheduling model because we assume that the post office faces the same situation each week. In reality, demands change over time, workers take vacations in the summer, and so on, so the post office does not face the same situation each week. A *dynamic* scheduling model (not covered here) is necessary for such problems.

Heuristic solutions are often close to optimal, but they are never guaranteed to be optimal.

2. In a weekly scheduling model for a supermarket or a fast-food restaurant, the number of decision variables can grow quickly and optimization software such as Solver will have difficulty finding an optimal solution. In such cases, heuristic methods (essentially clever trial-and-error algorithms) have been used to find good solutions to the problem. Love and Hoey (1990) indicate how this was done for a particular staff scheduling problem.

3. Our model can easily be expanded to handle part-time employees, the use of overtime, and alternative objectives such as maximizing the number of weekend days off received by employees. You are asked to explore such extensions in the problems. ∎

PROBLEMS

Note: Student solutions for problems whose numbers appear within a colored box are available for purchase at www.cengagebrain.com.

Level A

1. Modify the post office model so that employees are paid $10 per hour on weekdays and $15 per hour on weekends. Change the objective so that you now minimize the weekly payroll. (You can assume that each employee works eight hours per day.) Is the previous optimal solution still optimal?

2. How much influence can the worker requirements for one, two, or three days have on the weekly schedule in the post office example? You are asked to explore this in the following questions.

a. Let Monday's requirements change from 17 to 25 in increments of 1. Use SolverTable to see how the total number of employees changes.

b. Suppose the Monday and Tuesday requirements can each, independently of one another, increase from 1 to 8 in increments of 1. Use a two-way SolverTable to see how the total number of employees changes.

c. Suppose the Monday, Tuesday, and Wednesday requirements each increase by the *same* amount, where this increase can be from 1 to 8 in increments of 1. Use a one-way SolverTable to investigate how the total number of employees changes.

3. In the post office example, suppose that each full-time employee works eight hours per day. Thus, Monday's requirement of 17 workers can be viewed as a requirement of $8(17) = 136$ hours. The post office can meet its daily labor requirements by using both full-time and part-time employees. During each week a full-time employee works eight hours a day for five consecutive days, and a part-time employee works four hours a day for five consecutive days. A full-time employee costs the post office $15 per hour, whereas a part-time employee (with reduced fringe benefits) costs the post office only $10 per hour. Union requirements limit part-time labor to 25% of weekly labor requirements.

a. Modify the model as necessary, and then use Solver to minimize the post office's weekly labor costs.

b. Use SolverTable to determine how a change in the part-time labor limitation (currently 25%) influences the optimal solution.

Level B

4. In the post office example, suppose the employees want more flexibility in their schedules. They want to be allowed to work five consecutive days followed by two days off *or* to work three consecutive days followed by a day off followed by two consecutive days followed by another day off. Modify the original model (with integer constraints) to allow this flexibility. Might this be a good deal for management as well as labor? Explain.

5. In the post office example, suppose that the post office can force employees to work one day of overtime each week on the day immediately following this five-day shift. For example, an employee whose regular shift is Monday to Friday can also be required to work on Saturday. Each employee is paid $100 a day for each of the first five days worked during a week and $124 for the overtime day (if any). Determine how the post office can minimize the cost of meeting its weekly work requirements.

6. Suppose the post office has 25 full-time employees and is not allowed to fire any of them or hire more. Determine a schedule that maximizes the number of weekend days off received by these employees.

14.3 BLENDING MODELS

In many situations, various inputs must be blended to produce desired outputs. In many of these situations, LP can find the optimal combination of outputs as well as the mix of inputs that are used to produce the desired outputs. The following are some typical examples of blending problems.

Inputs	**Outputs**
Meat, filler, water	Different types of sausage
Various types of oil	Heating oil, gasolines, aviation fuels
Carbon, iron, molybdenum	Different types of steels
Different types of pulp	Different kinds of recycled paper

The next example illustrates how to model a typical blending problem in Excel. Although this example is small relative to blending problems in real applications, it is probably too complex for you to guess the optimal solution.

EXAMPLE | **14.2 BLENDING AT CHANDLER OIL**

Chandler Oil has 5000 barrels of crude oil 1 and 10,000 barrels of crude oil 2 available. Chandler sells gasoline and heating oil. These products are produced by blending the two crude oils together. Each barrel of crude oil 1 has a "quality level" of 10 and each barrel of crude oil 2 has a quality level of 5.[3] Gasoline must have an average quality level of at least 8, whereas heating oil must have an average quality level of at least 6. Gasoline sells for $75 per barrel, and heating oil sells for $60 per barrel. We assume that demand for heating oil and gasoline is unlimited, so that all of Chandler's production can be sold. Chandler wants to maximize its revenue from selling gasoline and heating oil.

Objective To develop an LP spreadsheet model for finding the revenue-maximizing plan that meets quality constraints and stays within limits on crude oil availabilities.

WHERE DO THE NUMBERS COME FROM?

Most of the inputs for this problem should be easy to obtain.

- The selling prices for outputs are dictated by market pressures.
- The availabilities of inputs are based on crude supplies from the suppliers.
- The quality levels of crude oils are known from chemical analysis, whereas the required quality levels for outputs are specified by Chandler, probably in response to competitive or regulatory pressures.

Solution

In typical blending problems, the correct decision variables are the amounts of each input blended into each output.

The variables and constraints required for this blending model are listed in Table 14.3. The key is the selection of the appropriate decision variables. Many students, when asked what decision variables should be used, specify the amounts of the two crude oils used and the amounts of the two products produced. However, this is not enough. The problem is that this information doesn't tell Chandler how to *make* the outputs from the inputs. The company instead requires a blending plan: how much of each input to use in the production of a barrel of each output. Once you understand that this blending plan is the basic decision, all other output variables follow in a straightforward manner.

Table 14.3 Variables and Constraints for Blending Model

Input variables	Unit selling prices, availabilities of inputs, quality levels of inputs, required quality levels of outputs
Decision variables (changing cells)	Barrels of each input used to produce each output
Objective cell	Revenue from selling gasoline and heating oil
Other calculated variables	Barrels of inputs used, barrels of outputs produced (and sold), quality obtained and quality required for outputs
Constraints	Barrels of inputs used $\leq$ Barrels available Quality of outputs obtained $\geq$ Quality required

A secondary, but very important, issue in typical blending models is how to implement the quality constraints. (The constraints here are in terms of quality. In other blending problems they are often expressed in terms of percentages of some ingredient(s). For example, a typical quality constraint might be that some output can contain no more than 2% sulfur.) When we explain how to develop the spreadsheet model, we will discuss the preferred way to implement quality constraints.

---

[3]To avoid being overly technical, we use the generic term *quality level*. In real oil blending, qualities of interest might be octane rating, viscosity, and others.

DEVELOPING THE SPREADSHEET MODEL

The spreadsheet model for this problem appears in Figure 14.6. (See the file **Blending Oil.xlsx**.) To set it up, proceed as follows.

Figure 14.6 Oil Blending Model

	A	B	C	D	E	F	G	H
1	Chandler oil blending model					Range names used		
2						Barrels_available	=Model!$F$16:$F$17	
3	Monetary inputs	Gasoline	Heating oil			Barrels_sold	=Model!$B$18:$C$18	
4	Selling price/barrel	$75	$60			Barrels_used	=Model!$D$16:$D$17	
5						Blending_plan	=Model!$B$16:$C$17	
6	Quality level per barrel of crudes					Quality_points_obtained	=Model!$B$22:$C$22	
7	Crude oil 1	10				Quality_points_required	=Model!$B$24:$C$24	
8	Crude oil 2	5				Revenue	=Model!$B$27	
9								
10	Required quality level per barrel of product							
11		Gasoline	Heating oil					
12		8	6					
13								
14	Blending plan (barrels of crudes in each product)							
15		Gasoline	Heating oil	Barrels used		Barrels available		
16	Crude oil 1	3000	2000	5000	<=	5000		
17	Crude oil 2	2000	8000	10000	<=	10000		
18	Barrels sold	5000	10000					
19								
20	Constraints on quality							
21		Gasoline	Heating oil					
22	Quality points obtained	40000	60000					
23		>=	>=					
24	Quality points required	40000	60000					
25								
26	Objective to maximize							
27	Revenue	$975,000						

1 **Inputs and range names.** Enter the unit selling prices, quality levels for inputs, required quality levels for outputs, and availabilities of inputs in the blue cells. Then name the ranges as indicated.

2 **Inputs blended into each output.** As discussed, the quantities Chandler must specify are the barrels of each input used to produce each output. Enter *any* trial values for these quantities in the Blending_plan range. For example, the value in cell B16 is the amount of crude oil 1 used to make gasoline and the value in cell C16 is the amount of crude oil 1 used to make heating oil. The Blending_plan range contains the changing cells.

From here on, the solutions shown are optimal. However, remember that you can start with any solution. It doesn't even have to be feasible.

3 **Inputs used and outputs sold.** Calculate the row sums (in column D) and column sums (in row 18) of the Blending_plan range. There is a quick way to do this. Highlight both the row and column where the sums will go (highlight one, then hold down the Ctrl key and highlight the other), and click on the Summation (Σ) button on the Home ribbon. This creates SUM formulas in each highlighted cell.

4 **Quality achieved.** Keep track of the quality level of gasoline and heating oil in the Quality_points_obtained range as follows. Begin by calculating for each output the number of quality points (QP) in the inputs used to produce this output:

$$\text{QP in gasoline} = 10 * \text{Oil 1 in gasoline} + 5 * \text{Oil 2 in gasoline}$$
$$\text{QP in heating oil} = 10 * \text{Oil 1 in heating oil} + 5 * \text{Oil 2 in heating oil}$$

The gasoline quality constraint is then

$$QP \text{ in gasoline } \geq 8 * \text{Gasoline sold} \qquad (14.1)$$

Similarly, the heating oil quality constraint is

$$QP \text{ in heating oil } \geq 6 * \text{Heating oil sold} \qquad (14.2)$$

To implement inequalities (14.1) and (14.2), calculate the QP for gasoline in cell B22 with the formula

=SUMPRODUCT(B16:B17, $B$7:$B$8)

and copy this formula to cell C22 to generate the QP for heating oil.

⑤ Quality required. Calculate the required quality points for gasoline and heating oil in cells B24 and C24. Specifically, determine the required quality points for gasoline in cell B24 with the formula

=B12*B18

and copy this formula to cell C24 for heating oil.

⑥ Revenue. Calculate the total revenue in cell B27 with the formula

=SUMPRODUCT(B4:C4,B18:C18)

USING SOLVER

To solve Chandler's problem with Solver, fill out the main Solver dialog box as shown in Figure 14.7. As usual, check the Non-Negative option and specify the simplex algorithm before optimizing. You should obtain the optimal solution shown in Figure 14.6.

Discussion of the Solution

The optimal solution implies that Chandler should make 5000 barrels of gasoline with 3000 barrels of crude oil 1 and 2000 barrels of crude oil 2. The company should also make 10,000 barrels of heating oil with 2000 barrels of crude oil 1 and 8000 barrels of crude oil 2. With this blend, Chandler will obtain a revenue of $975,000. As stated previously, this problem is sufficiently complex to defy intuition. Clearly, gasoline is more profitable per barrel than heating oil, but given the crude availability and the quality constraints, it turns out that Chandler should sell twice as much heating oil as gasoline. This would have been very difficult to guess ahead of time.

Sensitivity Analysis

We perform two typical sensitivity analyses on this blending model. In each, we see how revenue and the amounts of the outputs produced (and sold) vary. In the first analysis, we use the unit selling price of gasoline as the input and let it vary from $50 to $90 in increments of $5. The SolverTable results appear in Figure 14.8. Two things are of interest. First, as the price of gasoline increases from $55 to $65, Chandler starts producing gasoline and less heating oil, exactly as you would expect. Second, the revenue can only increase or stay the same, as the changes in column E (calculated manually) indicate.

In the second sensitivity analysis, we vary the availability of crude 1 from 2000 barrels to 20,000 barrels in increments of 1000 barrels. The resulting SolverTable output appears in Figure 14.9. These results make sense if you analyze them carefully. First, the revenue increases, but at a decreasing rate, as more crude 1 is available. This is a common

Figure 14.7

Solver Dialog Box for Blending Model

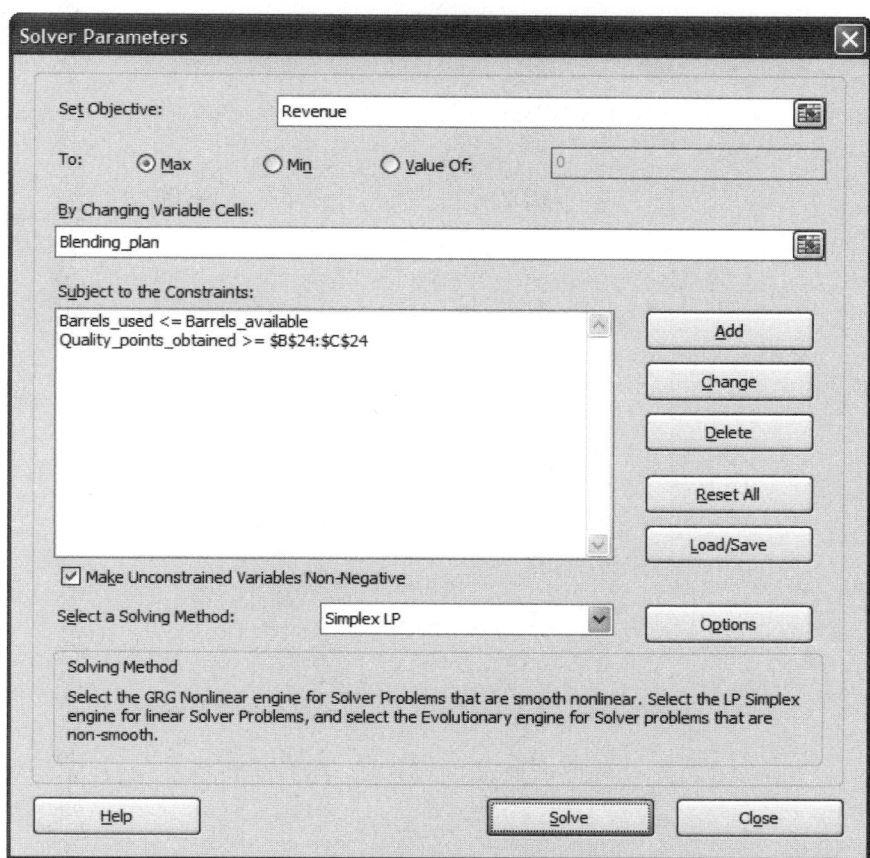

Figure 14.8

Sensitivity to the Selling Price of Gasoline

	A	B	C	D	E	F	G
1	Oneway analysis for Solver model in Model worksheet						
2							
3	Selling price gasoline (cell $B$4) values along side, output cell(s) along top						
4		Barrels_sold_1	Barrels_sold_2	Revenue	Increase		
5	$50	0	15000	$900,000			
6	$55	0	15000	$900,000	$0		
7	$60	5000	10000	$900,000	$0		
8	$65	5000	10000	$925,000	$25,000		
9	$70	5000	10000	$950,000	$25,000		
10	$75	5000	10000	$975,000	$25,000		
11	$80	5000	10000	$1,000,000	$25,000		
12	$85	5000	10000	$1,025,000	$25,000		
13	$90	5000	10000	$1,050,000	$25,000		

Figure 14.9

Sensitivity to the
Availability of
Crude 1

	A	B	C	D	E	F	G
1	Oneway analysis for Solver model in Model worksheet						
2							
3	Barrels available crude 1 (cell $F$16) values along side, output cell(s) along top						
4		Barrels_sold_1	Barrels_sold_2	Revenue	Increase		
5	2000	0	10000	$600,000			
6	3000	1000	12000	$795,000	$195,000		
7	4000	3000	11000	$885,000	$90,000		
8	5000	5000	10000	$975,000	$90,000		
9	6000	7000	9000	$1,065,000	$90,000		
10	7000	9000	8000	$1,155,000	$90,000		
11	8000	11000	7000	$1,245,000	$90,000		
12	9000	13000	6000	$1,335,000	$90,000		
13	10000	15000	5000	$1,425,000	$90,000		
14	11000	17000	4000	$1,515,000	$90,000		
15	12000	19000	3000	$1,605,000	$90,000		
16	13000	21000	2000	$1,695,000	$90,000		
17	14000	23000	1000	$1,785,000	$90,000		
18	15000	25000	0	$1,875,000	$90,000		
19	16000	26000	0	$1,950,000	$75,000		
20	17000	27000	0	$2,025,000	$75,000		
21	18000	28000	0	$2,100,000	$75,000		
22	19000	29000	0	$2,175,000	$75,000		
23	20000	30000	0	$2,250,000	$75,000		

occurrence in LP models. As more of a resource is made available, revenue can only increase or remain the same, but each extra unit of the resource produces less (or at least no more) revenue than the previous unit. Second, the amount of gasoline produced increases, whereas the amount of heating oil produced decreases. Here's why: Crude 1 has a higher quality than crude 2, and gasoline requires higher quality. Gasoline also sells for a higher price. Therefore, as more crude 1 is available, Chandler can produce more gasoline, receive more revenue, and still meet quality standards.

Could these sensitivity questions also be answered with Solver's sensitivity report, shown in Figure 14.10? Consider the sensitivity to the change in the price of gasoline. The first and third rows of the top table in this report are for sensitivity to the objective coefficients of decision variables involving gasoline. The problem is that when the price of gasoline changes, *both* of these coefficients change. The reason is that the objective includes the sum of these two decision variables, multiplied by the unit price of gasoline. However, Solver's sensitivity report is valid only for one-at-a-time coefficient changes. Therefore, it cannot answer our question.

In contrast, the first row of the bottom table in Figure 14.10 complements the SolverTable sensitivity analysis on the availability of crude 1. It shows that if the availability increases by no more than 10,000 barrels or decreases by no more than 2500 barrels, the shadow price remains $90 per barrel—that is, the same $90,000 increase in profit per 1000 barrels in Figure 14.9. Beyond that range, the sensitivity report indicates only that the shadow price will change. The SolverTable results indicate *how* it changes. For example, when crude 1 availability increases beyond 15,000 barrels, the SolverTable results indicate that the shadow price decreases to $75 per barrel.

Figure 14.10 Sensitivity Report for Blending Model

	A	B	C	D	E	F	G	H
6		Adjustable Cells						
7				Final	Reduced	Objective	Allowable	Allowable
8		Cell	Name	Value	Cost	Coefficient	Increase	Decrease
9		$B$16	Crude oil 1 Gasoline	3000	0	75	175	25
10		$C$16	Crude oil 1 Heating oil	2000	0	60	25	175
11		$B$17	Crude oil 2 Gasoline	2000	0	75	262.5	18.75
12		$C$17	Crude oil 2 Heating oil	8000	0	60	18.75	43.75
13								
14		Constraints						
15				Final	Shadow	Constraint	Allowable	Allowable
16		Cell	Name	Value	Price	R.H. Side	Increase	Decrease
17		$D$16	Crude oil 1 Barrels used	5000	90	5000	10000	2500
18		$D$17	Crude oil 2 Barrels used	10000	53	10000	10000	6666.666667
19		$B$22	Quality points obtained Gasoline	40000	-7	0	5000	20000
20		$C$22	Quality points obtained Heating oil	60000	-7	0	10000	6666.666667

A Caution About Blending Constraints

Blending models usually have various quality constraints, often expressed as required percentages of various ingredients. To keep these models linear (and avoid dividing by zero), it is important to clear denominators.

Before concluding this example, we discuss why the model is linear. The key is the implementation of the quality constraints, shown in inequalities (14.1) and (14.2). To keep a model linear, each side of an inequality constraint must be a constant, the product of a constant and a variable, or a sum of such products. If the quality constraints are implemented as in inequalities (14.1) and (14.2), the constraints are indeed linear. However, it is arguably more natural to rewrite this type of constraint by dividing through by the amount sold. For example, the modified gasoline constraint becomes

$$\frac{\text{QP in gasoline}}{\text{Gasoline sold}} \geq 8 \qquad \qquad \textbf{(14.3)}$$

Although this form of the constraint is perfectly valid—and is possibly more natural to many people—it suffers from two drawbacks. First, it makes the model nonlinear. This is because the left side is no longer a sum of products; it involves a quotient. We prefer linear models whenever possible. Second, suppose it turns out that Chandler's optimal solution calls for *no* gasoline at all. Then inequality (14.3) includes division by zero, and this causes an error in Excel. Because of these two drawbacks, it is best to "clear denominators" in all such blending constraints.

FUNDAMENTAL INSIGHT

Clearing Denominators

Some constraints, particularly those that arise in blending models, are most naturally expressed in terms of ratios. For example, the percentage of sulfur in a product is a ratio: (amount of sulfur in product)/(total amount of product). This ratio could then be constrained to be less than or equal to 6%, say.

This is a perfectly valid way to express the constraint, but it has the undesirable effect of making the model nonlinear. The fix is simple. To make the model linear, multiply through by the denominator of the ratio. This has the added benefit of ensuring that division by zero will not occur.

In reality, a company using a blending model would run the model periodically (each day, say) and set production on the basis of the current inventory of inputs and the current forecasts of demands and prices. Then the forecasts and the input levels would be updated, and the model would be run again to determine the next day's production. ■

PROBLEMS

Level A

7. Use SolverTable in Chandler's blending model to see whether, by increasing the selling price of gasoline, you can get an optimal solution that produces only gasoline, no heating oil. Then use SolverTable again to see whether, by increasing the selling price of heating oil, you can get an optimal solution that produces only heating oil, no gasoline.

8. Use SolverTable in Chandler's blending model to find the shadow price of crude oil 1—that is, the amount Chandler would be willing to spend to acquire more crude oil 1. Does this shadow price change as Chandler keeps getting more of crude oil 1? Answer the same questions for crude oil 2.

9. How sensitive is the optimal solution (barrels of each output sold and profit) to the required quality points? Answer this by running a two-way SolverTable with these three outputs. You can choose the values of the two inputs to vary.

10. In Chandler's blending model suppose there is a chemical ingredient called C1 that both gasoline and heating oil need. At least 3% of every barrel of gasoline must be C1, and at least 5% of every barrel of heating oil must be C1. Suppose that 4% of all crude

oil 1 is C1 and 6% of all crude oil 2 is C1. Modify the model to incorporate the constraints on C1, and then optimize. Don't forget to clear denominators.

11. In the current version of Chandler's blending model, a barrel of any input results in a barrel of output. However, in a real blending problem there can be losses. Suppose a barrel of input results in only a fraction of a barrel of output. Specifically, each barrel of either crude oil used for gasoline results in only 0.95 barrel of gasoline, and each barrel of either crude used for heating oil results in only 0.97 barrel of heating oil. Modify the model to incorporate these losses and then find the optimal solution.

Level B

12. We warned you about clearing denominators in the quality constraints. This problem indicates what happens if you don't do so.
   a. Implement the quality constraints as indicated in inequality (14.3). Then run Solver with the simplex algorithm. What happens? What if you run Solver with the GRG nonlinear algorithm?
   b. Repeat part **a**, but increase the selling price of heating oil to $120 per barrel. What happens now?

14.4 LOGISTICS MODELS

In many situations a company produces products at locations called *origins* and ships these products to customer locations called *destinations*. Typically, each origin has a limited capacity that it can ship, and each destination must receive a required quantity of the product. **Logistics models** can be used to determine the minimum-cost shipping method for satisfying customer demands.

14.4.1 Transportation Models

We begin by assuming that the only possible shipments are those directly from an origin to a destination. That is, no shipments between origins or between destinations are allowed. Such a problem has traditionally been called a *transportation problem*.

14.3 SHIPPING CARS FROM PLANTS TO REGIONS OF THE COUNTRY

The Grand Prix Automobile Company manufactures automobiles in three plants and then ships them to four regions of the country. The plants can supply the amounts listed in the right column of Table 14.4. The customer demands by region are listed in the bottom row of this table, and the unit costs of shipping an automobile from each plant to each region are listed in the middle of the table. Grand Prix wants to find the lowest-cost shipping plan for meeting the demands of the four regions without exceeding the capacities of the plants.

Table 14.4 Input Data for Grand Prix Example

	Region 1	Region 2	Region 3	Region 4	Capacity
Plant 1	131	218	266	120	450
Plant 2	250	116	263	278	600
Plant 3	178	132	122	180	500
Demand	450	200	300	300	

Objective   To develop a spreadsheet optimization model that finds the least-cost way of shipping the automobiles from plants to regions, staying within plant capacities and meeting regional demands.

WHERE DO THE NUMBERS COME FROM?

A typical transportation problem requires three sets of numbers: capacities (or supplies), demands (or requirements), and unit shipping (and possibly production) costs. We discuss each of these next.

- The *capacities* indicate the most each plant can supply in a given amount of time—a month, say—under current operating conditions. In some cases it might be possible to increase the "base" capacities, by using overtime, for example. In such cases the model could be modified to determine the amounts of additional capacity to use (and pay for).

- The customer *demands* are typically estimated from some type of forecasting model (as discussed in Chapter 12). The forecasts are often based on historical customer demand data.

- The *unit shipping costs* come from a transportation cost analysis—what does it really cost to send a single automobile from any plant to any region? This is not an easy question to answer, and it requires an analysis of the best mode of transportation (such as railroad, ship, or truck). However, companies typically have the required data. Actually, the unit "shipping" cost can also include the unit production cost at each plant. However, if this cost is the same across all plants, as we are tacitly assuming here, it can be omitted from the model.

Solution

The variables and constraints required for this model are listed in Table 14.5. The company must decide exactly the number of autos to send from each plant to each region—a shipping plan. Then it can calculate the total number of autos sent out of each plant and the total number received by each region.

Table 14.5 Variables and Constraints for Transportation Model

Input variables	Plant capacities, regional demands, unit shipping costs
Decision variables (changing cells)	Number of autos sent from each plant to each region
Objective cell	Total shipping cost
Other calculated variables	Number sent out of each plant, number sent to each region
Constraints	Number sent out of each plant $\leq$ Plant capacity
	Number sent to each region $\geq$ Region demand

Representing Transportation in a Network Model

In a transportation problem all flows go from left to right—from origins to destinations. You will see more complex network structures in the next subsection.

A network diagram of this model appears in Figure 14.11. This diagram is typical of network models. It consists of nodes and arcs. A *node*, indicated by a circle, generally represents a geographical location. In this case the nodes on the left correspond to plants, and the nodes on the right correspond to regions. An *arc*, indicated by an arrow, generally represents a route for getting a product from one node to another. Here, the arcs all go from a plant node to a region node—from left to right.

Figure 14.11

Network Representation of Transportation Model

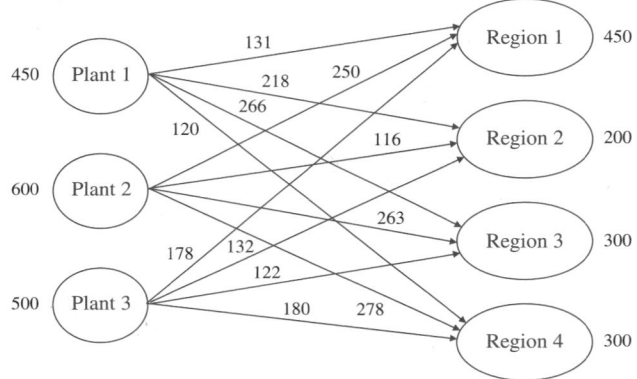

The problem data fit nicely on such a diagram. The capacities are placed next to the plant nodes, the demands are placed next to the region nodes, and the unit shipping costs are placed on the arcs. The decision variables are usually called *flows*. They represent the amounts shipped on the various arcs. Sometimes (although not in this problem), there are upper limits on the flows on some or all of the arcs. These upper limits, called *arc capacities*, can also be shown on the diagram.[4]

DEVELOPING THE SPREADSHEET MODEL

The spreadsheet model appears in Figure 14.12. (See the file **Transportation 1.xlsx**.) To develop this model, perform the following steps.

1 Inputs.[5] Enter the unit shipping costs, plant capacities, and region demands in the blue cells.

---

[4]There can even be lower limits, other than zero, on certain flows, but we don't consider any such models here.
[5]From here on, we might not remind you about creating range names, but we will continue to list our suggested range names on the spreadsheets.

Figure 14.12 Transportation Model

	A	B	C	D	E	F	G	H	I	J	K
1	Grand Prix transportation model								Range names used:		
2									Capacity	=Model!$I$13:$I$15	
3	Unit shipping costs								Demand	=Model!$C$18:$F$18	
4			To						Shipping_Plan	=Model!$C$13:$F$15	
5			Region 1	Region 2	Region 3	Region 4			Total_cost	=Model!$B$21	
6	From	Plant 1	$131	$218	$266	$120			Total_received	=Model!$C$16:$F$16	
7		Plant 2	$250	$116	$263	$278			Total_shipped	=Model!$G$13:$G$15	
8		Plant 3	$178	$132	$122	$180					
9											
10	Shipping plan, and constraints on supply and demand										
11			To								
12			Region 1	Region 2	Region 3	Region 4	Total shipped		Capacity		
13	From	Plant 1	150	0	0	300	450	<=	450		
14		Plant 2	100	200	0	0	300	<=	600		
15		Plant 3	200	0	300	0	500	<=	500		
16		Total received	450	200	300	300					
17			>=	>=	>=	>=					
18		Demand	450	200	300	300					
19											
20	Objective to minimize										
21	Total cost		$176,050								

2 **Shipping plan.** Enter any trial values for the shipments from plants to regions in the Shipping_plan range. These are the changing cells. Note that this rectangular range is exactly the same shape as the range where the unit shipping costs are entered. This is a natural model design, and it simplifies the formulas in the following steps.

3 **Numbers shipped from plants.** To calculate the amount shipped out of each plant in the range G13:G15, highlight this range and click on the summation (Σ) toolbar button.

4 **Amounts received by regions.** Similarly, calculate the amount shipped to each region in the range C16:F16 by highlighting the range and clicking on the summation button.

5 **Total shipping cost.** Calculate the total cost of shipping power from the plants to the regions in the Total_cost cell with the formula

=SUMPRODUCT(C6:F8,Shipping_plan)

This formula sums all products of unit shipping costs and amounts shipped. You now see the benefit of placing unit shipping costs and amounts shipped in similar-size rectangular ranges—you can then use the SUMPRODUCT function.

USING SOLVER

Invoke Solver with the settings shown in Figure 14.13. As usual, check the Non-Negative option and specify the simplex method before optimizing.

Discussion of the Solution

It is typical in transportation models, especially large models, that only a relatively few of the possible routes are used.

The Solver solution appears in Figure 14.12 and is illustrated graphically in Figure 14.14. The company incurs a total shipping cost of $176,050 by using the shipments listed in Figure 14.14. Except for the six routes shown, no other routes are used. Most of the shipments occur on the low-cost routes, but this is not always the case. For example, the route from plant 2 to region 1 is relatively expensive, and it is used. On the other hand, the route from plant 3 to region 2 is relatively cheap, but it is not used. A good shipping plan tries to use cheap routes, but it is constrained by capacities and demands.

Figure 14.13
Solver Dialog Box
for Transportation
Model

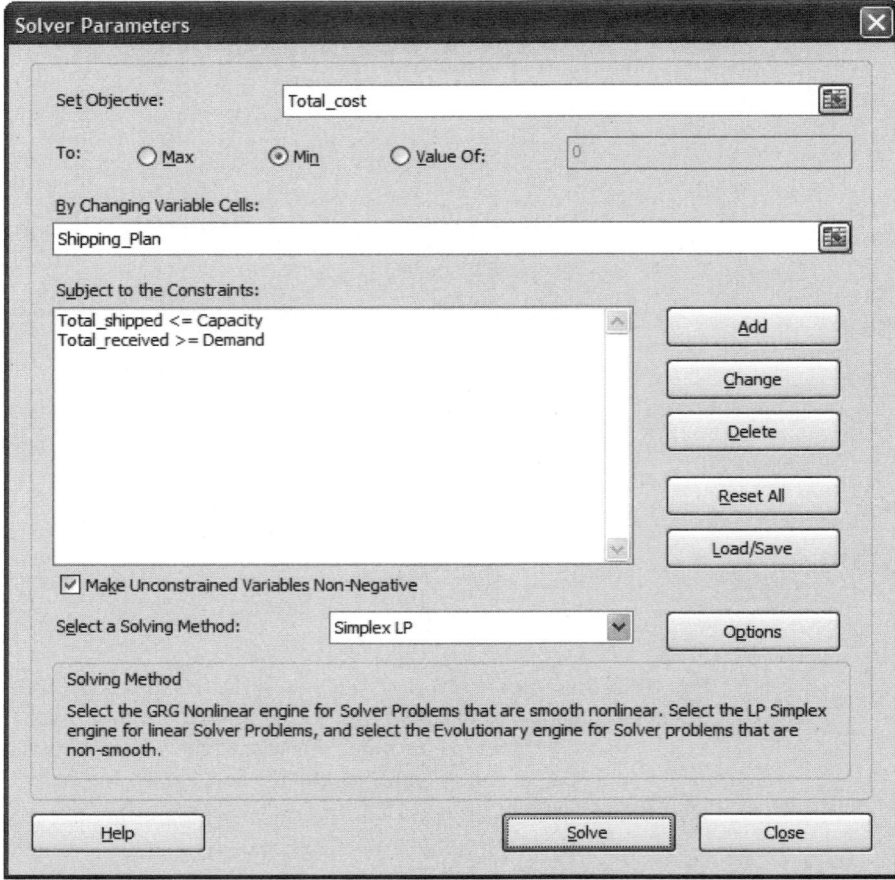

Figure 14.14
Graphical
Representation of
Optimal Solution

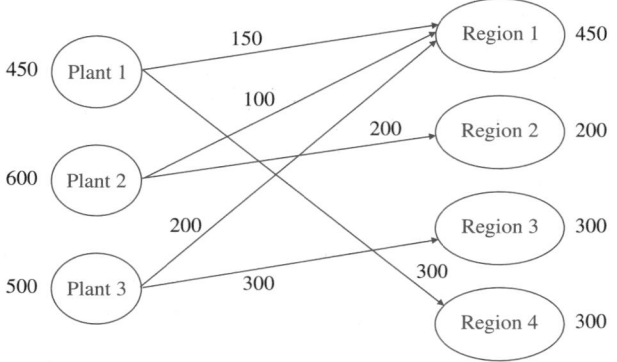

Note that the available capacity is not all used. The reason is that total capacity is 1550, whereas total demand is only 1250. Even though the demand constraints are of the "≥" type, there is clearly no reason to send the regions more than they request because it only increases shipping costs. Therefore, the optimal plan sends them the minimal amounts they request and no more. In fact, the demand constraints could have been modeled as "=" constraints, and Solver would have reached exactly the same solution.

Sensitivity Analysis

There are many sensitivity analyses you could perform on the basic transportation model. For example, you could vary any one of the unit shipping costs, capacities, or demands. The effect of any such change in a single input is captured nicely in Solver's sensitivity report, shown in Figure 14.15. The top part indicates the effects of changes in the unit shipping costs. The results here are typical. For all routes with positive flows, the corresponding reduced cost is zero, whereas for all routes not currently being used, the reduced cost indicates how much *less* the unit shipping cost would have to be before the company would start shipping along that route. For example, if the unit shipping cost from plant 2 to region 3 decreased by more than $69, this route would become attractive.

Figure 14.15

Solver's Sensitivity Report for Transportation Model

	A B	C	D	E	F	G	H
6	Adjustable Cells						
7			Final	Reduced	Objective	Allowable	Allowable
8	Cell	Name	Value	Cost	Coefficient	Increase	Decrease
9	$C$13	Plant 1 Region 1	150	0	131	119	13
10	$D$13	Plant 1 Region 2	0	221	218	1E+30	221
11	$E$13	Plant 1 Region 3	0	191	266	1E+30	191
12	$F$13	Plant 1 Region 4	300	0	120	13	239
13	$C$14	Plant 2 Region 1	100	0	250	39	72
14	$D$14	Plant 2 Region 2	200	0	116	88	116
15	$E$14	Plant 2 Region 3	0	69	263	1E+30	69
16	$F$14	Plant 2 Region 4	0	39	278	1E+30	39
17	$C$15	Plant 3 Region 1	200	0	178	13	69
18	$D$15	Plant 3 Region 2	0	88	132	1E+30	88
19	$E$15	Plant 3 Region 3	300	0	122	69	194
20	$F$15	Plant 3 Region 4	0	13	180	1E+30	13
21							
22	Constraints						
23			Final	Shadow	Constraint	Allowable	Allowable
24	Cell	Name	Value	Price	R.H. Side	Increase	Decrease
25	$G$13	Plant 1 Total shipped	450	-119	450	100	150
26	$G$14	Plant 2 Total shipped	300	0	600	1E+30	300
27	$G$15	Plant 3 Total shipped	500	-72	500	100	200
28	$C$16	Total received Region 1	450	250	450	300	100
29	$D$16	Total received Region 2	200	116	200	300	200
30	$E$16	Total received Region 3	300	194	300	200	100
31	$F$16	Total received Region 4	300	239	300	150	100

The bottom part of this report is useful because of its shadow prices. For example, plants 1 and 3 are currently shipping all of their capacity, so the company would benefit from having more capacity at these plants. In particular, the report indicates that each extra unit of capacity at plant 1 is worth $119, and each extra unit of capacity at plant 3 is worth $72. However, because the allowable increase for each of these is 100, you know that after an increase in capacity of 100 at either plant, further increases will probably be worth less than the current shadow prices.

The key to this sensitivity analysis is to modify the model slightly before running SolverTable.

One interesting analysis that cannot be performed with Solver's sensitivity report is to keep shipping costs and capacities constant and allow all of the demands to change by a certain percentage (positive or negative). To perform this analysis, use SolverTable, with the varying percentage as the single input. Then keep track of the total cost and any particular amounts shipped of interest. The key to doing this correctly is to modify the model slightly, as illustrated in the previous chapter and Example 14.1, before running SolverTable. The appropriate modifications appear in the third sheet of the finished

Transportation 1.xlsx file. Then run SolverTable, allowing the percentage change in all demands to vary from −20% to 30% in increments of 5%, and keep track of total cost. As the table in Figure 14.16 shows, the total shipping cost increases at an increasing rate as the demands increase. However, at some point the problem becomes infeasible. As soon as the total demand is greater than the total capacity, it is impossible to meet all demand.

Figure 14.16
Sensitivity Analysis to Percentage Changes in All Demands

	A	B	C	D	E	F	G
3	% change in demands (cell $I$10) values along side, output cell(s) along top						
4		Total_cost	Increase				
5	-20%	$130,850					
6	-15%	$140,350	$9,500				
7	-10%	$149,850	$9,500				
8	-5%	$162,770	$12,920				
9	0%	$176,050	$13,280				
10	5%	$189,330	$13,280				
11	10%	$202,610	$13,280				
12	15%	$215,890	$13,280				
13	20%	$229,170	$13,280				
14	25%	Not feasible					
15	30%	Not feasible					

An Alternative Model

The transportation model in Figure 14.12 is a very natural one. In the graphical representation in Figure 14.11, note that all arcs go from left to right, that is, from plants to regions. Therefore, the rectangular range of shipments allows you to calculate shipments out of plants as row sums and shipments into regions as column sums. In anticipation of later models in this chapter, however, where the graphical network can be more complex, we present an alternative model of the transportation problem. (See the file **Transportation 2.xlsx**.)

First, it is useful to introduce some additional network terminology. Recall that flows are the amounts shipped on the various arcs. The direction of the arcs indicates which way the flows are allowed to travel. An arc pointed into a node is called an *inflow*, whereas an arrow pointed out of a node is called an *outflow*. In the basic transportation model, all outflows originate from suppliers, and all inflows go toward demanders. However, general networks can have both inflows and outflows for any given node.

Although this model is possibly less natural than the original model, it generalizes better to other logistics models in this chapter.

With this general structure in mind, the typical network model has one changing cell per arc. It indicates how much (if any) to send along that arc in the direction of the arrow. Therefore, it is often useful to model network problems by listing all of the arcs and their corresponding flows in one long list. Then constraints can be indicated in a separate section of the spreadsheet. Specifically, for each node in the network, there is a **flow balance constraint**. These flow balance constraints for the basic transportation model are simply the supply and demand constraints already discussed, but they can be more general for other network models, as will be discussed in the next subsection.

The alternative model of the Grand Prix problem appears in Figure 14.17. The plant and region indexes and the associated unit shipping costs are entered manually in the range A5:C16. Each row in this range corresponds to an arc in the network. For example, row 12 corresponds to the arc from plant 2 to region 4, with unit shipping cost $278. Then the changing cells for the flows are in column D. (If there were arc capacities, they could be placed to the right of the flows.)

Figure 14.17 Alternative Form of Transportation Model

	A	B	C	D	E	F	G	H	I	J	K	L	M
1	Grand Prix transportation model: a more general network formulation										Range names used:		
2											Capacity	=Model!$I$6:$I$8	
3	Network structure and flows					Flow balance constraints					Demand	=Model!$I$12:$I$15	
4	Origin	Destination	Unit cost	Flow		Capacity constraints					Destination	=Model!$B$5:$B$16	
5	1	1	131	150		Plant	Outflow		Capacity		Flow	=Model!$D$5:$D$16	
6	1	2	218	0		1	450	<=	450		Inflow	=Model!$G$12:$G$15	
7	1	3	266	0		2	300	<=	600		Origin	=Model!$A$5:$A$16	
8	1	4	120	300		3	500	<=	500		Outflow	=Model!$G$6:$G$8	
9	2	1	250	100							Total_Cost	=Model!$B$19	
10	2	2	116	200		Demand constraints							
11	2	3	263	0		Region	Inflow		Demand				
12	2	4	278	0		1	450	>=	450				
13	3	1	178	200		2	200	>=	200				
14	3	2	132	0		3	300	>=	300				
15	3	3	122	300		4	300	>=	300				
16	3	4	180	0									
17													
18	Objective to minimize												
19	Total Cost	$176,050											

The flow balance constraints are conceptually straightforward. Each cell in the Outflow and Inflow ranges in column G contains the appropriate sum of flows. For example, cell G6, the outflow from plant 1, represents the sum of cells D5 through D8, whereas cell G12, the inflow to plant 1, represents the sum of cells D5, D9, and D13. Fortunately, there is an easy way to enter these summation formulas.[6] The trick is to use Excel's built-in SUMIF function, in the form =SUMIF(*CompareRange,Criteria,SumRange*). For example, the formula in cell G6 is

=SUMIF(Origin,F6,Flow)

This formula compares the plant number in cell F6 to the Origin range in column A and sums all flows where they are equal—that is, it sums all flows out of plant 1. This formula can be copied down to cell G8 to obtain the flows out of the other plants. For flows into regions, the similar formula in cell G12 for the flow into region 1 is

=SUMIF(Destination,F12,Flow)

and this can be copied down to cell G15 for flows into the other regions. In general, the SUMIF function finds all cells in the first argument that satisfy the criterion in the second argument and then sums the corresponding cells in the third argument. It is a very handy function—and not just for network modeling.

Excel Function *SUMIF*
*The SUMIF function is useful for summing values in a certain range if cells in a related range satisfy a given condition. It has the syntax =SUMIF (**compareRange,criterion, sumRange**), where compareRange and sumRange are similar-size ranges. This formula checks each cell in compareRange to see whether it satisfies the criterion. If it does, it adds the corresponding value in sumRange to the overall sum. For example, =SUMIF(A12: A23,1,D12:D23) sums all values in the range D12:D23 where the corresponding cell in the range A12:A23 has the value 1.*

This use of the SUMIF function, along with the list of origins, destinations, unit costs, and flows in columns A through D, is the key to the model. The rest is straightforward. The

---

[6]Try entering these formulas manually, even for a 3 × 4 transportation model, and you will see why the SUMIF function is so handy.

total cost is a SUMPRODUCT of unit costs and flows, and the Solver dialog box is set up as shown in Figure 14.18.

Figure 14.18
Solver Dialog Box for Alternative Transportation Model

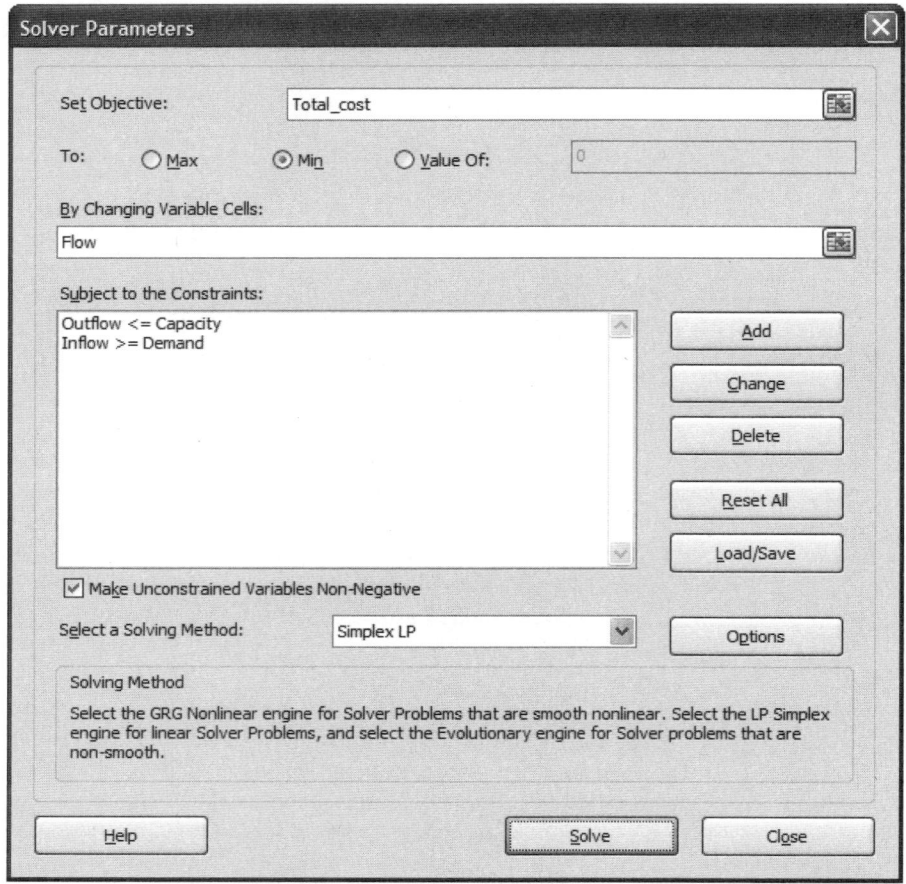

The alternative network model not only accommodates more general networks, but it is more efficient in that it has the fewest number of changing cells.

This alternative model generalizes nicely to other network problems. Essentially, it shows that all network models look alike. There is an additional benefit from this alternative model. Suppose that flows from certain plants to certain regions are not allowed. (Maybe no roads exist.) It is not easy to disallow such routes in the original model. The usual trick is to allow the "disallowed" routes but to impose extremely large unit shipping costs on them. This works, but it is wasteful because it adds changing cells that do not really belong in the model. However, the alternative network model simply omits arcs that are not allowed. For example, if the route from plant 2 to region 4 is not allowed, you simply omit the data in the range A12:D12. This creates a model with exactly as many changing cells as allowable arcs. This additional benefit can be very valuable when the number of potential arcs in the network is huge—even though the vast majority of them are disallowed—which is exactly the situation in many large network models.

We do not necessarily recommend this more general network model for simple transportation problems. In fact, it is probably less natural than the original model in Figure 14.12. However, it paves the way for the more complex network problems discussed next. ∎

Depending on how you treat the demand constraints, you can get several varieties of the basic transportation model.

1. The customer demands in typical transportation problems can be handled in one of two ways. First, you can think of these forecasted demands as minimal requirements that must be sent to the customers. This is how regional demands were treated here. Alternatively, you could consider the demands as maximal sales quantities, the most each region can sell. Then you would constrain the amounts sent to the regions to be less than or equal to the forecasted demands. Whether the demand constraints are expressed as "≥" or "≤" (or even "=") constraints depends on the context of the problem—do the dealers need at least this many, do they need exactly this many, or can they sell only this many?

2. If all the supplies and demands for a transportation problem are integers, the optimal Solver solution automatically has integer-valued shipments. Explicit integer constraints are not required. This is a very important benefit. It means that the "fast" simplex method can be used rather than much slower integer algorithms.

3. Shipping costs are often nonlinear (and "nonsmooth") due to quantity discounts. For example, if it costs $3 per item to ship up to 100 items between locations and $2 per item for each additional item, the proportionality assumption of LP is violated and the resulting transportation model is nonlinear. Shipping problems that involve quantity discounts are generally quite difficult to solve.

4. Excel's Solver uses the simplex method to solve transportation problems. There is a streamlined version of the simplex method, called the *transportation simplex method*, that is much more efficient than the ordinary simplex method for transportation problems. Large transportation problems are usually solved with the transportation simplex method. See Winston (2003) for a discussion of the transportation simplex method. ■

14.4.2 Other Logistics Models

The objective of many real-world network models is to ship goods from one set of locations to another at minimum cost, subject to various constraints. There are many variations of these models. The simplest models include a single product that must be shipped via one mode of transportation (truck, for example) in a particular period of time. More complex models—and much larger ones—can include multiple products, multiple modes of transportation, and/or multiple time periods. We discuss one such problem in this section.

Basically, the general logistics problem is like the transportation problem except for two possible differences. First, arc capacities are often imposed on some or all of the arcs. These become simple upper-bound constraints in the model. Second and more significant, there can be inflows *and* outflows associated with any node. Nodes are generally categorized as origins, destinations, and transshipment points. An *origin* is a location that starts with a certain supply (or possibly a capacity for supplying). A *destination* is the opposite; it requires a certain amount to end up there. A *transshipment point* is a location where goods simply pass through.

The best way to think of these categories is in terms of net inflow and net outflow. The *net inflow* for any node is defined as total inflow minus total outflow for that node. The *net outflow* is the negative of this, total outflow minus total inflow. Then an origin is a node with positive net outflow, a destination is a node with positive net inflow, and a transshipment point is a node with net outflow (and net inflow) equal to 0. It is important to realize that inflows are sometimes allowed to origins, but their *net* outflows are positive. Similarly, outflows from destinations are sometimes allowed, but their *net* inflows are positive. For example, if Cincinnati and Memphis are manufacturers (origins) and Dallas and Phoenix are retail locations (destinations), then it is possible that flow could go from Cincinnati to Memphis to Dallas to Phoenix.

There are typically two types of constraints in logistics models (besides nonnegativity of flows). The first type represents the arc capacity constraints, which are simple upper bounds on the arc flows. The second type represents the flow balance constraints, one for each node. For an origin, this constraint is typically of the form **Net Outflow = Capacity** or possibly **Net Outflow ≤ Capacity**. For a destination, it is typically of the form **Net Inflow >= Demand** or possibly **Net Inflow = Demand**. For a transshipment point, it is of the form **Net Inflow = 0** (which is equivalent to **Net Outflow = 0**, whichever you prefer).

It is easy to visualize these constraints in a graphical representation of the network by simply examining the flows on the arrows leading into and out of the various nodes. We illustrate a typical logistics model in the following example.

> ### FUNDAMENTAL INSIGHT
>
> #### Flow Balance Constraints
>
> All network optimization models have some form of flow balance constraints at the various nodes of the network. This flow balance relates the amount that enters the node to the amount that leaves the node. In many network models, the simple structure of these flow balance constraints guarantees that the optimal solutions have integer values. It also enables specialized network versions of the simplex method to solve the huge network models typically encountered in real logistics applications.

EXAMPLE | **14.4 PRODUCING AND SHIPPING TOMATO PRODUCTS AT REDBRAND**

The RedBrand Company produces a tomato product at three plants. This product can be shipped directly to the company's two customers or it can first be shipped to the company's two warehouses and then to the customers. Figure 14.19 is a network representation of RedBrand's problem. Nodes 1, 2, and 3 represent the plants (these are the origins, denoted by S for supplier), nodes 4 and 5 represent the warehouses (these are the transshipment points, denoted by T), and nodes 6 and 7 represent the customers (these are the destinations, denoted by D). Note that some shipments are allowed among plants, among warehouses, and among customers. Also, some arcs have arrows on both ends. This means that flow is allowed in either direction.

The cost of producing the product is the same at each plant, so RedBrand is concerned with minimizing the total shipping cost incurred in meeting customer demands. The production capacity of each plant (in tons per year) and the demand of each customer are

Figure 14.19

Graphical Representation of Logistics Model

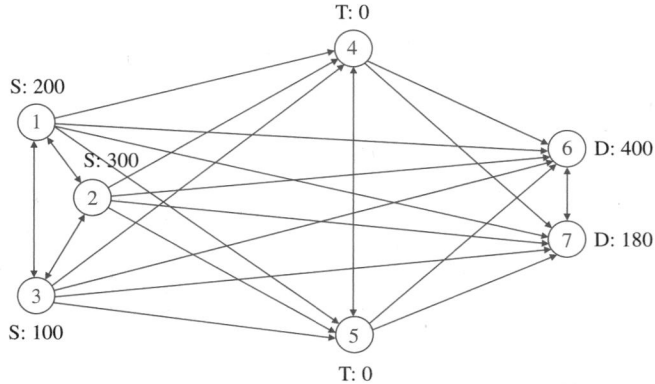

shown in Figure 14.19. For example, plant 1 (node 1) has a capacity of 200, and customer 1 (node 6) has a demand of 400. In addition, the cost (in thousands of dollars) of shipping a ton of the product between each pair of locations is listed in Table 14.6, where a blank indicates that RedBrand cannot ship along that arc. We also assume that at most 200 tons of the product can be shipped between any two nodes. This is the common arc capacity. RedBrand wants to determine a minimum-cost shipping schedule.

Table 14.6 Shipping Costs for RedBrand Example (in $1000s)

From node	To node						
	1	2	3	4	5	6	7
1		5.0	3.0	5.0	5.0	20.0	20.0
2	9.0		9.0	1.0	1.0	8.0	15.0
3	0.4	8.0		1.0	0.5	10.0	12.0
4					1.2	2.0	12.0
5				0.8		2.0	12.0
6							1.0
7						7.0	

Objective   To find the minimum-cost way to ship the tomato product from suppliers to customers, possibly through warehouses, so that customer demands are met and supplier capacities are not exceeded.

WHERE DO THE NUMBERS COME FROM?

The network configuration itself would come from geographical considerations—which routes are physically possible (or sensible) and which are not. The numbers would be derived as in the Grand Prix automobile example. (See Example 14.3 for further discussion.)

Solution

Other than arc capacity constraints, the only constraints are flow balance constraints.

The variables and constraints for RedBrand's model are listed in Table 14.7. The key to the model is handling the flow balance constraints. You will see exactly how to implement these when we give step-by-step instructions for developing the spreadsheet model. However, it is not enough, say, to specify that the flow out of plant 2 is less than or equal to the capacity of plant 2. The reason is that there might also be flow *into* plant 2 (from another plant). Therefore, the correct flow balance constraint for plant 2 is that the flow out of it must be less than or equal to its capacity plus any flow into it. Equivalently, the *net* outflow from plant 2 must be less than or equal to its capacity.

Table 14.7 Variables and Constraints for RedBrand Model

Input variables	Plant capacities, customer demands, unit shipping costs on allowable arcs, common arc capacity
Decision variables (changing cells)	Shipments on allowed arcs
Objective cell	Total cost
Other calculated variables	Flows into and out of nodes
Constraints	Flow on each arc ≤ Common arc capacity Flow balance at each node

Developing the Spreadsheet Model

To set up the spreadsheet model, proceed as follows. (See Figure 14.20 and the file **RedBrand Logistics 1.xlsx**. Also, refer to the network in Figure 14.19.)

Figure 14.20 Logistics Model

	A	B	C	D	E	F	G	H	I	J	K
1	RedBrand shipping model										
2											
3	Inputs										
4	Common arc capacity	200									
5											
6	Network structure, flows, and arc capacity constraints							Node balance constraints			
7		Origin	Destination	Unit Cost	Flow		Arc Capacity		Plant constraints		
8		1	2	5	0	<=	200	Node	Plant net outflow		Plant capacity
9		1	3	3	180	<=	200	1	180	<=	200
10		1	4	5	0	<=	200	2	300	<=	300
11		1	5	5	0	<=	200	3	100	<=	100
12		1	6	20	0	<=	200				
13		1	7	20	0	<=	200	Warehouse constraints			
14		2	1	9	0	<=	200	Node	Warehouse net outflow		Required
15		2	3	9	0	<=	200	4	0	=	0
16		2	4	1	120	<=	200	5	0	=	0
17		2	5	1	0	<=	200				
18		2	6	8	180	<=	200	Customer constraints			
19		2	7	15	0	<=	200	Node	Customer net inflow		Customer demand
20		3	1	0.4	0	<=	200	6	400	>=	400
21		3	2	8	0	<=	200	7	180	>=	180
22		3	4	1	80	<=	200				
23		3	5	0.5	200	<=	200	Range names used			
24		3	6	10	0	<=	200	Arc_Capacity	=Model!$F$8:$F$33		
25		3	7	12	0	<=	200	Customer_demand	=Model!$K$20:$K$21		
26		4	5	1.2	0	<=	200	Customer_net_inflow	=Model!$I$20:$I$21		
27		4	6	2	200	<=	200	Destination	=Model!$B$8:$B$33		
28		4	7	12	0	<=	200	Flow	=Model!$D$8:$D$33		
29		5	4	0.8	0	<=	200	Origin	=Model!$A$8:$A$33		
30		5	6	2	200	<=	200	Plant_capacity	=Model!$K$9:$K$11		
31		5	7	12	0	<=	200	Plant_net_outflow	=Model!$I$9:$I$11		
32		6	7	1	180	<=	200	Total_cost	=Model!$B$36		
33		7	6	7	0	<=	200	Unit_Cost	=Model!$C$8:$C$33		
34								Warehouse_net_outflow	=Model!$I$15:$I$16		
35	Objective to minimize										
36	Total cost	$3,260									

① Origins and destinations. Enter the node numbers (1 to 7) for the origins and destinations of the various arcs in the range A8:B33. Note that the disallowed arcs are not entered in this list.

② Input data. Enter the unit shipping costs (in thousands of dollars), the common arc capacity, the plant capacities, and the customer demands in the blue cells. Again, only the nonblank entries in Table 14.6 are used to fill the column of unit shipping costs.

③ Flows on arcs. Enter *any* initial values for the flows in the range D8:D33. These are the changing cells.

④ Arc capacities. To indicate a common arc capacity for all arcs, enter the formula

=$B$4

in cell F8 and copy it down column F.

We generally prefer positive numbers on the right sides of constraints. This is why we calculate net outflows for origins and net inflows for destinations.

⑤ Flow balance constraints. Nodes 1, 2, and 3 are supply nodes, nodes 4 and 5 are transshipment points, and nodes 6 and 7 are demand nodes. Therefore, set up the left sides of the flow balance constraints appropriately for these three cases. Specifically, enter the net *outflow* for node 1 in cell I9 with the formula

=SUMIF(Origin,H9,Flow)-SUMIF(Destination,H9,Flow)

and copy it down to cell I11. This formula subtracts flows into node 1 from flows out of node 1 to obtain net outflow for node 1. Next, copy this *same* formula to cells I15 and I16 for the warehouses. (Remember that, for transshipment nodes, the left side of the constraint can be net outflow *or* net inflow, whichever you prefer. The reason is that if net outflow is zero, net inflow must also be zero.) Finally, enter the net *inflow* for node 6 in cell I20 with the formula

=SUMIF(Destination,H20,Flow)-SUMIF(Origin,H20,Flow)

and copy it to cell I21. This formula subtracts flows out of node 6 from flows into node 6 to obtain the net inflow for node 6.

6 **Total shipping cost.** Calculate the total shipping cost (in thousands of dollars) in cell B36 with the formula

=SUMPRODUCT(Unit_cost,Flow)

USING SOLVER

The Solver dialog box should be set up as in Figure 14.21. The objective is to minimize total shipping costs, subject to the three types of flow balance constraints and the arc capacity constraints.

Figure 14.21

Solver Dialog Box for Logistics Model

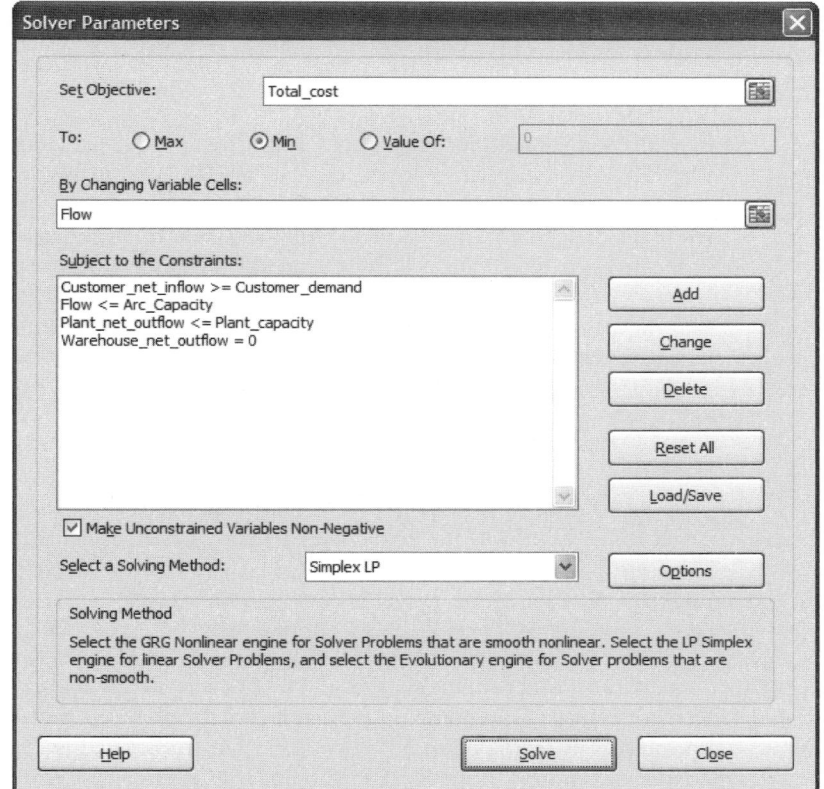

Discussion of the Solution

The optimal solution in Figure 14.20 indicates that RedBrand's customer demand can be satisfied with a shipping cost of $3,260,000. This solution appears graphically in Figure 14.22. Note in particular that plant 1 produces 180 tons (under capacity) and ships it all to plant 3,

Figure 14.22
Optimal Flows for Logistics Model

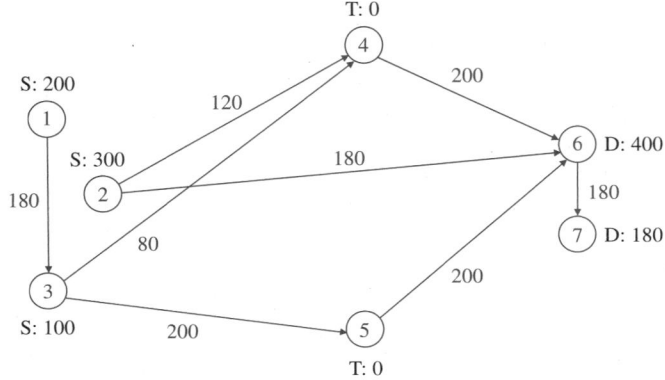

not directly to warehouses or customers. Also, note that all shipments from the warehouses go directly to customer 1. Then customer 1 ships 180 tons to customer 2. We purposely chose unit shipping costs (probably unrealistic ones) to produce this type of behavior, just to show that it *can* occur. As you can see, the costs of shipping from plant 1 directly to warehouses or customers are relatively large compared to the cost of shipping directly to plant 3. Similarly, the costs of shipping from plants or warehouses directly to customer 2 are prohibitive. Therefore, RedBrand ships to customer 1 and lets customer 1 forward some of its shipment to customer 2.

Sensitivity Analysis

How much effect does the arc capacity have on the optimal solution? Currently, three of the arcs with positive flow are at the arc capacity of 200. You can use SolverTable to see how sensitive this number and the total cost are to the arc capacity.[7] In this case the single input cell for SolverTable is cell B4, which is varied from 150 to 300 in increments of 25. Two quantities are designated as outputs: total cost and the number of arcs at arc capacity. As before, if you want to keep track of an output that does not already exist, you can create it with an appropriate formula in a new cell before running SolverTable. Specifically, you can enter the formula **=COUNTIF(Flow,B4)** in an unused cell. This formula counts the arcs with flow equal to arc capacity. (See the finished version of the file for a note about this formula.)

Excel Function *COUNTIF*
*The COUNTIF function counts the number of values in a given range that satisfy some criterion. The syntax is **=COUNTIF(range,criterion)**. For example, the formula **=COUNTIF(D8:D33,150)** counts the number of cells in the range D8:D33 that contain the value 150. This formula could also be entered as **=COUNTIF(D8:D33,"=150")**. Similarly, the formula **=COUNTIF(D8:D33,">=100")** counts the number of cells in this range with values greater than or equal to 100.[8]*

The SolverTable output in Figure 14.23 is what you would expect. As the arc capacity decreases, more flows bump up against it, and the total cost increases. But even when the arc capacity is increased to 300, two flows are constrained by it. In this sense, even this large an arc capacity costs RedBrand money.

---

[7]Note that Solver's sensitivity report would not answer our question. This report is useful only for one-at-a-time changes in inputs, and here we are simultaneously changing the upper limit for *each* flow. However, this report (its bottom section) can be used to assess the effects of changes in plant capacities or customer demands.

[8]The COUNTIF and SUMIF functions are limited in that they allow only one condition, such as ">=10". For this reason, Microsoft added two new functions in Excel 2007, COUNTIFS and SUMIFS, that allow multiple conditions. You can learn about them in online help.

Figure 14.23

Sensitivity to Arc Capacity

	A	B	C	D	E	F	G
3	Common arc capacity (cell $B$4) values along side, output cell(s) along top						
4		Total_cost	Arcs_at_capacity				
5	150	$4,120	5				
6	175	$3,643	6				
7	200	$3,260	3				
8	225	$2,998	3				
9	250	$2,735	3				
10	275	$2,473	3				
11	300	$2,320	2				

Variations of the Model

There are many variations of the RedBrand shipping problem that can be handled by a network model. We briefly consider two possible variations. First, suppose that RedBrand ships two products along the given network. We assume that the unit shipping costs are the same for both products (although this assumption could easily be relaxed), but the arc capacity, which has been changed to 300, represents the maximum flow of *both* products that can flow on any arc. In this sense, the two products are competing for arc capacity. Each plant has a separate production capacity for each product, and each customer has a separate demand for each product.

The spreadsheet model for this variation appears in Figure 14.24. (See the file **RedBrand Logistics 2.xlsx**.) Very little in the original model needs to be changed. You need to (1) have two columns of changing cells (columns D and E), (2) apply the previous logic to

There are endless variations of this basic minimum cost network flow model, corresponding to the many types of real-world logistics problems.

Figure 14.24 Logistics Model with Two Products

	A	B	C	D	E	F	G	H	I	J	K	L	M	N	O
1	RedBrand shipping model with two products competing for arc capacity														
2															
3	Inputs														
4	Common arc capacity	300													
5															
6	Network structure, flows, and arc capacity constraints									Node balance constraints					
7		Origin	Destination	Unit Cost	Flow product 1	Flow product 2	Total flow		Arc Capacity		Plant constraints				
8	1	2	5	0	0	0	<=	300		Node	Net outflow product 1	Net outflow product 2		Capacity product 1	Capacity product 2
9	1	3	3	160	140	300	<=	300		1	180	140	<=	200	200
10	1	4	5	20	0	20	<=	300		2	300	100	<=	300	100
11	1	5	5	0	0	0	<=	300		3	100	100	<=	100	100
12	1	6	20	0	0	0	<=	300							
13	1	7	20	0	0	0	<=	300		Warehouse constraints					
14	2	1	9	0	0	0	<=	300		Node	Net outflow product 1	Net outflow product 2		Required product 1	Required product 2
15	2	3	9	0	0	0	<=	300		4	0	0	=	0	0
16	2	4	1	100	0	100	<=	300		5	0	0	=	0	0
17	2	5	1	0	0	0	<=	300							
18	2	6	8	200	100	300	<=	300		Customer constraints					
19	2	7	15	0	0	0	<=	300		Node	Net inflow product 1	Net inflow product 2		Demand product 1	Demand product 2
20	3	1	0.4	0	0	0	<=	300		6	400	200	>=	400	200
21	3	2	8	0	0	0	<=	300		7	180	140	>=	180	140
22	3	4	1	0	180	180	<=	300							
23	3	5	0.5	240	60	300	<=	300							
24	3	6	10	0	0	0	<=	300							
25	3	7	12	20	0	20	<=	300							
26	4	5	1.2	0	0	0	<=	300							
27	4	6	2	120	180	300	<=	300							
28	4	7	12	0	0	0	<=	300							
29	5	4	0.8	0	0	0	<=	300							
30	5	6	2	240	60	300	<=	300							
31	5	7	12	0	0	0	<=	300							
32	6	7	1	160	140	300	<=	300							
33	7	6	7	0	0	0	<=	300							
34															
35	Objective to minimize														
36	Total cost	55,570													

both products separately in the flow balance constraints, and (3) apply the arc capacities to the *total* flows in column F (which are the sums of flows in columns D and E). The modified Solver dialog box is shown in Figure 14.25. Note that we have range-named blocks of cells for the flow balance constraints. For example, the ranges K9:L11 and N9:O11 are named Plant_net_outflow and Plant_capacity. These entire blocks can then be used to specify the capacity constraints for both products with the single entry **Plant_net_outflow <= Plant_capacity** in the Solver dialog box. This is another example of planning the spreadsheet layout so that the resulting model is as efficient and readable as possible.

Figure 14.25
Solver Dialog Box
for Two-Product
Logistics Model

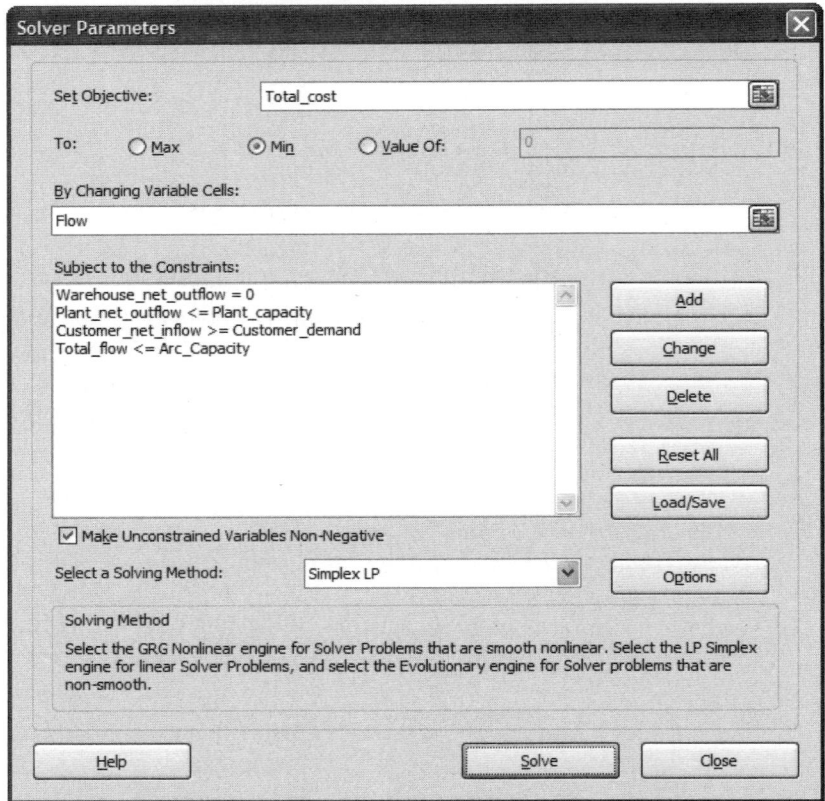

A second variation of the model is appropriate for perishable goods, such as fruit. (See the file **RedBrand Logistics 3.xlsx**.) We again assume that there is a single product, but some percentage of the product that is shipped to warehouses perishes and cannot be sent to customers. This means that the total inflow to a warehouse is *greater than* the total outflow from the warehouse. This behavior can be modeled as shown in Figure 14.26. (The corresponding Solver dialog box, not shown here, is the same as in the original RedBrand model.) The shrinkage factor in cell B5, the percentage that does *not* spoil in the warehouses, becomes a new input. It is then incorporated into the warehouse flow balance constraints by entering the formula

=SUMIF(Origin,H16,Flow)-$B$5*SUMIF(Destination,H16,Flow)

in cell I16 and copying to cell I17. This formula says that what goes out (the first term) is 90% of what goes in. The other 10% perishes. Of course, shrinkage results in a larger total cost—about 20% larger—than in the original RedBrand model.

Figure 14.26 Logistics Model with Shrinkage

	A	B	C	D	E	F	G	H	I	J	K
1	RedBrand shipping model with shrinkage at warehouses										
2											
3	Inputs										
4	Common arc capacity	200									
5	Shrinkage factor	90%									
6											
7	Network formulation							Node balance constraints			
8	Origin	Destination	Unit Cost	Flow		Arc Capacity		Plant constraints			
9	1	2	5	0	<=	200		Node	Plant net outflow		Plant capacity
10	1	3	3	200	<=	200		1	200	<=	200
11	1	4	5	0	<=	200		2	300	<=	300
12	1	5	5	0	<=	200		3	100	<=	100
13	1	6	20	0	<=	200					
14	1	7	20	0	<=	200		Warehouse constraints			
15	2	1	9	0	<=	200		Node	Warehouse net outflow		Required
16	2	3	9	0	<=	200		4	0	=	0
17	2	4	1	0	<=	200		5	0	=	0
18	2	5	1	100	<=	200					
19	2	6	8	200	<=	200		Customer constraints			
20	2	7	15	0	<=	200		Node	Customer net inflow		Customer demand
21	3	1	0.4	0	<=	200		6	400	>=	400
22	3	2	8	0	<=	200		7	180	>=	180
23	3	4	1	0	<=	200					
24	3	5	0.5	100	<=	200					
25	3	6	10	200	<=	200					
26	3	7	12	0	<=	200					
27	4	5	1.2	0	<=	200					
28	4	6	2	0	<=	200					
29	4	7	12	0	<=	200					
30	5	4	0.8	0	<=	200					
31	5	6	2	180	<=	200					
32	5	7	12	0	<=	200					
33	6	7	1	180	<=	200					
34	7	6	7	0	<=	200					
35											
36	Objective to minimize										
37	Total cost	$4,890									

Interestingly, however, some units are still sent to both warehouses, and the entire capacity of all plants is now used. Finally, you can check that a feasible solution exists even for a shrinkage factor of 0% (where everything sent to warehouses disappears). As you might guess, the solution then is to send everything directly from plants to customers—at a steep cost.

MODELING ISSUES

1. Excel's Solver uses the simplex method to solve logistics models. However, the simplex method can be simplified dramatically for these types of models. The simplified version of the simplex method, called the *network simplex method*, is much more efficient than the ordinary simplex method. Specialized computer codes have been written to implement the network simplex method, and all large logistics problems are solved by using the network simplex method. This is fortunate because real logistics models tend to be extremely large. See Winston (2003) for a discussion of this method.

2. If the given supplies and demands for the nodes are integers and all arc capacities are integers, the logistics model always has an optimal solution with all integer

flows. Again, this is very fortunate for large problems—you get integer solutions "for free" without having to use an integer programming algorithm. Note, however, that this "integers for free" benefit is guaranteed only for the basic logistics model, as in the original RedBrand model. When the model is modified in certain ways, such as by adding a shrinkage factor, the optimal solution is no longer guaranteed to be integer-valued. ■

ADDITIONAL APPLICATIONS

Distribution in Nu-kote International's Network

LeBlanc et al. (2002) used an LP transportation model similar to the one in section 14.3 to analyze distribution in Nu-kote International's network of vendors, manufacturing plants, warehouses, and customers. Nu-kote, a manufacturer of inkjet, laser, and toner cartridges, saves approximately $1 million annually as a result of this model. The LP model has nearly 6,000 variables and 2,500 constraints. The total time available for data collection and model development and verification was limited to only six weeks. It is a tribute to the efficiency and user-friendliness of Excel that everything was completed within this time frame. ■

PROBLEMS

Level A

13. In the original Grand Prix example, the total capacity of the three plants is 1550, well above the total customer demand. Would it help to have 100 more units of capacity at plant 1? What is the most Grand Prix would be willing to pay for this extra capacity? Answer the same questions for plant 2 and for plant 3. Explain why extra capacity can be valuable even though the company already has more total capacity than it requires.

14. The optimal solution to the original Grand Prix problem indicates that with a unit shipping cost of $132, the route from plant 3 to region 2 is evidently too expensive—no autos are shipped along this route. Use SolverTable to see how much this unit shipping cost would have to be reduced before some autos would be shipped along this route.

15. In the original RedBrand problem, suppose the plants cannot ship to each other and the customers cannot ship to each other. Modify the model appropriately, and rerun Solver. How much does the total cost increase because of these disallowed routes?

16. Modify the original RedBrand problem so that all flows must be from plants to warehouses and from

warehouses to customers. Disallow all other arcs. How much does this restriction cost RedBrand, relative to the original optimal shipping cost?

17. In the original RedBrand problem, the costs for shipping from plants or warehouses to customer 2 were purposely made high so that it would be optimal to ship to customer 1 and then let customer 1 ship to customer 2. Use SolverTable appropriately to do the following. Decrease the unit shipping costs from plants and warehouses to customer 1, all by the same amount, until it is no longer optimal for customer 1 to ship to customer 2. Describe what happens to the optimal shipping plan at this point.

18. In the original RedBrand problem the arc capacity is the same for all allowable arcs. Modify the model so that each arc has its own arc capacity. You can make up the arc capacities.

19. Continuing the previous problem, make the problem even more general by allowing upper bounds (arc capacities) *and* lower bounds for the flows on the allowable arcs. Some of the upper bounds can be very large numbers, effectively indicating that there is no arc capacity for these arcs, and the lower bounds can be zero or positive. If they are positive, they indicate that some positive flow must occur on these arcs. Modify the model appropriately to handle these upper and lower bounds. You can make up the upper and lower bounds.

20. Suppose in the original Grand Prix example that the routes from plant 2 to region 1 and from plant 3 to region 3 are not allowed. (Perhaps there are no railroad lines for these routes.) How would you modify the original model (Figure 14.12) to rule out these routes? How would you modify the alternative model (Figure 14.17) to do so? Discuss the pros and cons of these two approaches.

21. In the RedBrand two-product problem, we assumed that the unit shipping costs are the same for both products. Modify the spreadsheet model so that each product has its own unit shipping costs. You can assume that the original unit shipping costs apply to product 1, and you can make up new unit shipping costs for product 2.

Level B

22. Here is a problem to challenge your intuition. In the original Grand Prix example, reduce the capacity of plant 2 to 300. Then the total capacity is equal to the total demand. Rerun Solver on the modified model. You should find that the optimal solution uses all capacity and exactly meets all demands with a total cost of $176,050. Now increase the capacity of plant 1 and the demand at region 2 by one automobile each, and optimize again. What happens to the optimal total cost? How can you explain this "more for less" paradox?

23. Continuing the previous problem (with capacity 300 at plant 2), suppose you want to see how much extra capacity and extra demand you can add to plant 1 and region 2 (the same amount to each) before the total shipping cost stops decreasing and starts increasing. Use SolverTable appropriately to find out. (You will probably need to use some trial and error on the range of input values.) Can you explain intuitively what causes the total cost to stop decreasing and start increasing?

24. Modify the original Grand Prix example by increasing the demand at each regions by 200, so that total demand is well above total plant capacity. However, now interpret these "demands" as "maximum sales," the most each region can accommodate, and change the "demand" constraints to become "≤" constraints, not "≥" constraints. How does the optimal solution change? Does it make realistic sense? If not, how might you change the model to obtain a realistic solution?

25. Modify the original Grand Prix example by increasing the demand at each region by 200, so that total demand is well above total plant capacity. This means that some demands cannot be supplied. Suppose there is a unit "penalty" cost at each region for not supplying an automobile. Let these unit penalty costs be $600, $750, $625, and $550 for the four regions. Develop a model to minimize the sum of shipping costs and penalty costs for unsatisfied demands. (*Hint*: This requires a trick. Introduce a fourth plant with plenty of capacity, and set its unit shipping costs to the regions equal to the unit penalty costs. Then interpret an auto shipped from this fictitious plant to a region as a unit of demand not satisfied.)

26. How difficult is it to expand the original RedBrand model? Answer this by adding a new plant, two new warehouses, and three new customers, and modify the spreadsheet model appropriately. You can make up the required input data. Would you conclude that these types of spreadsheet models scale easily?

27. In the RedBrand problem with shrinkage, change the assumptions. Now instead of assuming that there is some shrinkage at the warehouses, assume that there is shrinkage in delivery along each *route*. Specifically, assume that a certain percentage of the units sent along each arc perish in transit—from faulty refrigeration, for example—and this percentage can differ from one arc to another. Modify the model appropriately to take this type of behavior into account. You can make up the shrinkage factors, and you can assume that arc capacities apply to the amounts originally shipped, not to the amounts after shrinkage. (Make sure your input data permit a *feasible* solution. After all, if there is too much shrinkage, it will be impossible to meet demands with available plant capacity. Increase the plant capacities if necessary.)

28. Consider a modification of the original RedBrand problem where there are N plants, M warehouses, and L customers. Assume that the only allowable arcs are from plants to warehouses and from warehouses to customers. If *all* such arcs are allowable—all plants can ship to all warehouses and all warehouses can ship to all customers—how many changing cells are in the spreadsheet model? Keeping in mind that Excel's Solver can handle at most 200 changing cells, provide some combinations of N, M, and L that barely stay within Solver's limit.

29. Continuing the previous problem, develop a sample model with your own choices of N, M, and L that barely stay within Solver's limit. You can make up any input data. The important point here is the layout and formulas of the spreadsheet model.

14.5 AGGREGATE PLANNING MODELS

In this section, we extend the production planning model discussed in Example 13.3 of the previous chapter to include a situation where the number of workers available influences the possible production levels. We allow the workforce level to be modified each period through the hiring and firing of workers. Such models, where we determine workforce levels and production schedules for a multiperiod time horizon, are called **aggregate planning models**. There are many variations of aggregate planning models, depending on the detailed assumptions made. We consider a fairly simple version and then ask you to modify it in the problems.

EXAMPLE | **14.5 WORKER AND PRODUCTION PLANNING AT SURESTEP**

During the next four months the SureStep Company must meet (on time) the following demands for pairs of shoes: 3000 in month 1; 5000 in month 2; 2000 in month 3; and 1000 in month 4. At the beginning of month 1, 500 pairs of shoes are on hand, and SureStep has 100 workers. A worker is paid $1500 per month. Each worker can work up to 160 hours a month before he or she receives overtime. A worker can work up to 20 hours of overtime per month and is paid $13 per hour for overtime labor. It takes four hours of labor and $15 of raw material to produce a pair of shoes. At the beginning of each month, workers can be hired or fired. Each hired worker costs $1600, and each fired worker costs $2000. At the end of each month, a holding cost of $3 per pair of shoes left in inventory is incurred. Production in a given month can be used to meet that month's demand. SureStep wants to use LP to determine its optimal production schedule and labor policy.

Objective To develop an LP spreadsheet model that relates workforce and production decisions to monthly costs, and to find the minimum-cost solution that meets forecasted demands on time and stays within limits on overtime hours and production capacity.

WHERE DO THE NUMBERS COME FROM?

There are a number of required inputs for this type of problem. Some, including initial inventory, holding costs, and demands, are similar to requirements for Example 13.3 in the previous chapter, so we won't discuss them again here. Others might be obtained as follows:

- The data on the current number of workers, the regular hours per worker per month, the regular hourly wage rates, and the overtime hourly rate, should be well known. The maximum number of overtime hours per worker per month is probably either the result of a policy decision by management or a clause in the workers' contracts.

- The costs for hiring and firing a worker are not trivial. The hiring cost includes training costs and the cost of decreased productivity due to the fact that a new worker must learn the job. The firing cost includes severance costs and costs due to loss of morale. Neither the hiring nor the firing cost would be simple to estimate accurately, but the human resources department should be able to estimate their values.

- The unit production cost is a combination of two inputs: the raw material cost per pair of shoes and the labor hours per pair of shoes. The raw material cost is the going rate from the supplier(s). The labor per pair of shoes represents the "production function"—the average labor required to produce a unit of the product. The operations managers should be able to supply this number.

Solution

The key to this model is choosing the correct changing cells—the decision variables that determine all outputs.

The variables and constraints for this aggregate planning model are listed in Table 14.8. As you see, there are a lot of variables to keep track of. In fact, the most difficult aspect of modeling this problem is knowing which variables the company gets to choose—the decision variables—and which variables are *determined* by these decisions. It should be clear that the company gets to choose the number of workers to hire and fire and the number of shoes to produce. Also, because management sets only an upper limit on overtime hours, it gets to decide how many overtime hours to use within this limit. But once it decides the values of these variables, everything else is determined. We will show how these are determined through detailed cell formulas, but you should mentally go through the list of "Other calculated variables" in the table and deduce how they are determined by the decision variables. Also, you should convince yourself that the three constraints listed are the ones, and the only ones, that are required.

Table 14.8   Variables and Constraints for Aggregate Planning Model

Input variables	Initial inventory of shoes, initial number of workers, number and wage rate of regular hours, maximum number and wage rate of overtime hours, hiring and firing costs, data for unit production and holding costs, forecasted demands
Decision variables (changing cells)	Monthly values for number of workers hired and fired, number of shoes produced, and overtime hours used
Objective cell	Total cost
Other calculated variables	Monthly values for workers on hand before and after hiring/firing, regular hours available, maximum overtime hours available, total production hours available, production capacity, inventory on hand after production, ending inventory, and various costs
Constraints	Overtime labor hours used $\leq$ Maximum overtime hours allowed Production $\leq$ Capacity Inventory on hand after production $\geq$ Demand

DEVELOPING THE SPREADSHEET MODEL

The spreadsheet model appears in Figure 14.27. (See the file **Aggregate Planning 1.xlsx**.) It can be developed as follows.

1 **Inputs and range names.** Enter the input data and create the range names listed.

2 **Production, hiring and firing plan.** Enter *any* trial values for the number of pairs of shoes produced each month, the overtime hours used each month, the workers hired each month, and the workers fired each month. These four ranges, in rows 18, 19, 23, and 30, comprise the changing cells.

3 **Workers available each month.** In cell B17 enter the initial number of workers available with the formula

=B5

This is common in multiperiod problems. You usually have to relate a beginning value in one period to an ending value from the previous period.

Because the number of workers available at the beginning of any other month (before hiring and firing) is equal to the number of workers from the previous month, enter the formula

=B20

Figure 14.27 Aggregate Planning Model

	A	B	C	D	E	F	G	H	I
1	SureStep aggregate planning model								
2									
3	Input data						Range names used:		
4	Initial inventory of shoes	500					Forecasted_demand	=Model!$B$36:$E$36	
5	Initial number of workers	100					Inventory_after_production	=Model!$B$34:$E$34	
6	Regular hours/worker/month	160					Maximum_overtime_labor_hours_available	=Model!$B$25:$E$25	
7	Maximum overtime hours/worker/month	20					Overtime_labor_hours_used	=Model!$B$23:$E$23	
8	Hiring cost/worker	$1,600					Production_capacity	=Model!$B$32:$E$32	
9	Firing cost/worker	$2,000					Shoes_produced	=Model!$B$30:$E$30	
10	Regular wages/worker/month	$1,500					Total_cost	=Model!$F$46	
11	Overtime wage rate/hour	$13					Workers_fired	=Model!$B$19:$E$19	
12	Labor hours/pair of shoes	4					Workers_hired	=Model!$B$18:$E$18	
13	Raw material cost/pair of shoes	$15							
14	Holding cost/pair of shoes in inventory/month	$3							
15									
16	Worker plan	Month 1	Month 2	Month 3	Month 4				
17	Workers from previous month	100	94	93	50				
18	Workers hired	0	0	0	0				
19	Workers fired	6	1	43	0				
20	Workers available after hiring and firing	94	93	50	50				
21									
22	Regular-time hours available	15040	14880	8000	8000				
23	Overtime labor hours used	0	80	0	0				
24		<=	<=	<=	<=				
25	Maximum overtime labor hours available	1880	1860	1000	1000				
26									
27	Total hours for production	15040	14960	8000	8000				
28									
29	Production plan	Month 1	Month 2	Month 3	Month 4				
30	Shoes produced	3760	3740	2000	1000				
31		<=	<=	<=	<=				
32	Production capacity	3760	3740	2000	2000				
33									
34	Inventory after production	4260	5000	2000	1000				
35		>=	>=	>=	>=				
36	Forecasted demand	3000	5000	2000	1000				
37	Ending inventory	1260	0	0	0				
38									
39	Monetary outputs	Month 1	Month 2	Month 3	Month 4	Totals			
40	Hiring cost	$0	$0	$0	$0	$0			
41	Firing cost	$12,000	$2,000	$86,000	$0	$100,000			
42	Regular-time wages	$141,000	$139,500	$75,000	$75,000	$430,500			
43	Overtime wages	$0	$1,040	$0	$0	$1,040			
44	Raw material cost	$56,400	$56,100	$30,000	$15,000	$157,500			
45	Holding cost	$3,780	$0	$0	$0	$3,780			
46	Totals	$213,180	$198,640	$191,000	$90,000	$692,820	← Objective to minimize		

in cell C17 and copy it to the range D17:E17. Then in cell B20 calculate the number of workers available in month 1 (after hiring and firing) with the formula

=B17+B18-B19

and copy this formula to the range C20:E20 for the other months.

4 Overtime capacity. Because each available worker can work up to 20 hours of overtime in a month, enter the formula

=$B$7*B20

in cell B25 and copy it to the range C25:E25.

5 Production capacity. Because each worker can work 160 regular-time hours per month, calculate the regular-time hours available in month 1 in cell B22 with the formula

=$B$6*B20

and copy it to the range C22:E22 for the other months. Then calculate the total hours available for production in cell B27 with the formula

=SUM(B22:B23)

In Example 13.3 from the previous chapter, production capacities were given inputs. Now they are based on the size of the workforce, which itself is a decision variable.

and copy it to the range C27:E27 for the other months. Finally, because it takes four hours of labor to make a pair of shoes, calculate the production capacity in month 1 with the formula

=B27/$B$12

in cell B32 and copy it to the range C32:E32.

6 **Inventory each month.** Calculate the inventory after production in month 1 (which is available to meet month 1 demand) with the formula

=B4+B30

in cell B34. For any other month, the inventory after production is the previous month's ending inventory plus that month's production, so enter the formula

=B37+C30

in cell C34 and copy it to the range D34:E34. Then calculate the month 1 ending inventory in cell B37 with the formula

=B34-B36

and copy it to the range C37:E37.

7 **Monthly costs.** Calculate the various costs shown in rows 40 through 45 for month 1 by entering the formulas

=$B$8*B18

=$B$9*B19

=$B$10*B20

=$B$11*B23

=$B$13*B30

=$B$14*B37

in cells B40 through B45. Then copy the range B40:B45 to the range C40:E45 to calculate these costs for the other months.

8 **Totals.** In row 46 and column F, use the SUM function to calculate cost totals, with the value in F46 being the overall total cost to minimize.

Excel Tip *Calculating Row and Column Sums Quickly*
A common operation in spreadsheet models is to calculate row and column sums for a rectangular range, as we did for costs in step 8. There is a very quick way to do this. Highlight the row and column where the sums will go (remember to press the Ctrl key to highlight nonadjacent ranges) and click on the summation (Σ) toolbar button. This enters all of the sums automatically. It even calculates the "grand sum" in the corner (cell F46 in the example) if you highlight this cell.

USING SOLVER

The Solver dialog box should be filled in as shown in Figure 14.28. Note that the changing cells include four separate named ranges. To enter these in the dialog box, drag the four ranges, keeping your finger on the Ctrl key. (Alternatively, you can drag a range, type a comma, drag a second range, type another comma, and so on.) As usual, you should also check the Non-Negative option and select the simplex method before optimizing.

Figure 14.28
Solver Dialog Box
for Aggregate
Planning Model

Figure 14.28 Solver Dialog Box for Aggregate Planning Model

Note that there are integer constraints on the numbers hired and fired. You could also constrain the numbers of shoes produced to be integers. However, integer constraints typically require longer solution times. Therefore, it is often best to omit such constraints, especially when the optimal values are fairly large, such as the production quantities in this model. If the solution then has noninteger values, you can usually round them to integers for a solution that is at least close to the optimal integer solution.

Discussion of the Solution

The optimal solution is given in Figure 14.27. Observe that SureStep should never hire any workers, and it should fire six workers in month 1, one worker in month 2, and 43 workers in month 3. Eighty hours of overtime are used, but only in month 2. The company produces over 3700 pairs of shoes during each of the first 2 months, 2000 pairs in month 3, and 1000 pairs in month 4. A total cost of $692,820 is incurred. The model will recommend overtime hours only when regular-time production capacity is exhausted. This is because overtime labor is more expensive.

Because integer constraints make a model more difficult to solve, use them sparingly—only when they are really needed.

Again, you would probably not force the number of pairs of shoes produced each month to be an integer. It makes little difference whether the company produces 3760 or 3761 pairs of shoes during a month, and forcing each month's shoe production to be an integer can greatly increase the time Solver needs to find an optimal solution. On the other hand, it is somewhat more important to ensure that the number of workers hired and fired each month is an integer, given the relatively small numbers of workers involved.

Finally, if you want to ensure that Solver finds the optimal solution in a problem where some or all of the changing cells must be integers, you should go into Options (in the Solver dialog box) and set the tolerance to zero. Otherwise, Solver might stop when it finds a solution that is only *close* to optimal.

Sensitivity Analysis

There are many possible sensitivity analyses for this SureStep model. We illustrate one of them with SolverTable, where we see how the overtime hours used and the total cost vary with the overtime wage rate.[9] The results appear in Figure 14.29. As you can see, when the wage rate is really low, the company uses considerably more overtime hours, whereas when it is sufficiently large, the company uses no overtime hours. It is not surprising that the company uses much more overtime when the overtime rate is $7 or $9 per hour. The *regular*-time wage rate is $9.375 per hour (= 1500/160). Of course, the company would never pay *less* per hour for overtime than for regular time.

Figure 14.29

Sensitivity to
Overtime Wage Rate

	A	B	C	D	E	F	G
3	Overtime rate (cell $B$11) values along side, output cell(s) along top						
4		Overtime_labor_hours_used_1	Overtime_labor_hours_used_2	Overtime_labor_hours_used_3	Overtime_labor_hours_used_4	Total_cost	
5	$7	1620	1660	0	0	$684,755	
6	$9	80	1760	0	0	$691,180	
7	$11	0	80	0	0	$692,660	
8	$13	0	80	0	0	$692,820	
9	$15	0	80	0	0	$692,980	
10	$17	0	80	0	0	$693,140	
11	$19	0	0	0	0	$693,220	
12	$21	0	0	0	0	$693,220	

The Rolling Planning Horizon Approach

In reality, an aggregate planning model is usually implemented via a rolling planning horizon. To illustrate, we assume that SureStep works with a four-month planning horizon. To implement the SureStep model in the rolling planning horizon context, we view the demands as forecasts and solve a four-month model with these forecasts. However, the company would implement only the month 1 production and work scheduling recommendation. Thus (assuming that the numbers of workers hired and fired in a month must be integers) the company would hire no workers, fire six workers, and produce 3760 pairs of shoes with regular-time labor in month 1. Next, the company would observe month 1's actual demand. Suppose it is 2950. Then SureStep would begin month 2 with 1310 (= 4260 − 2950) pairs of shoes and 94 workers. It would now enter 1310 in cell B4 and 94 in cell B5 (referring to Figure 14.27). Then it would replace the demands in the Demand

---

[9]Solver's sensitivity report isn't even available here because of the integer constraints.

range with the updated forecasts for the *next* four months. Finally, SureStep would rerun Solver and use the production levels and hiring and firing recommendations in column B as the production level and workforce policy for month 2.

Model with Backlogging Allowed

The term "backlogging" means that the customer's demand is met at a later date. The term "backordering" means the same thing.

In many situations, backlogging of demand is allowed—that is, customer demand can be met at a later date. We now show how to modify the SureStep model to include the option of backlogging demand. We assume that at the end of each month a cost of $20 is incurred for each unit of demand that remains unsatisfied at the end of the month. This is easily modeled by allowing a month's ending inventory to be negative. For example, if month 1's ending inventory is -10, a shortage cost of $200 (and no inventory holding cost) is incurred. To ensure that SureStep produces any shoes at all, we constrain the ending inventory in month 4 to be nonnegative. This implies that all demand is *eventually* satisfied by the end of the four-month planning horizon. We now need to modify the monthly cost calculations to incorporate costs due to backlogging.

There are actually several modeling approaches to this backlogging problem. We show the most natural approach in Figure 14.30. (See the file **Aggregate Planning 2.xlsx**.)

Figure 14.30   Nonlinear Aggregate Planning Model Using IF Functions

	A	B	C	D	E	F	G	H	I
1	SureStep aggregate planning model with backlogging: a nonsmooth model Solver might not handle correctly								
2									
3	Input data						Range names used:		
4	Initial inventory of shoes	500					Forecasted_demand_4	=Model!$E$37	
5	Initial number of workers	100					Inventory_after_production_4	=Model!$E$35	
6	Regular hours/worker/month	160					Maximum_overtime_labor_hours_available	=Model!$B$26:$E$26	
7	Maximum overtime hours/worker/month	20					Overtime_labor_hours_used	=Model!$B$24:$E$24	
8	Hiring cost/worker	$1,600					Production_capacity	=Model!$B$33:$E$33	
9	Firing cost/worker	$2,000					Shoes_produced	=Model!$B$31:$E$31	
10	Regular wages/worker/month	$1,500					Total_cost	=Model!$F$48	
11	Overtime wage rate/hour	$13					Workers_fired	=Model!$B$20:$E$20	
12	Labor hours/pair of shoes	4					Workers_hired	=Model!$B$19:$E$19	
13	Raw material cost/pair of shoes	$15							
14	Holding cost/pair of shoes in inventory/month	$3							
15	Shortage cost/pair of shoes/month	$20							
16									
17	Worker plan	Month 1	Month 2	Month 3	Month 4				
18	Workers from previous month	100	94	93	38				
19	Workers hired	0	0	0	0				
20	Workers fired	6	1	55	0				
21	Workers available after hiring and firing	94	93	38	38				
22									
23	Regular-time hours available	15040	14880	6080	6080				
24	Overtime labor hours used	0	0	0	0				
25		<=	<=	<=	<=				
26	Maximum overtime labor hours available	1880	1860	760	760				
27									
28	Total hours for production	15040	14880	6080	6080				
29									
30	Production plan	Month 1	Month 2	Month 3	Month 4				
31	Shoes produced	3760	3720	1520	1500				
32		<=	<=	<=	<=				
33	Production capacity	3760	3720	1520	1520				
34									
35	Inventory after production	4260	4980	1500	1000				
36					>=				
37	Forecasted demand	3000	5000	2000	1000				
38	Ending inventory	1260	-20	-500	0				
39									
40	Monetary outputs	Month 1	Month 2	Month 3	Month 4	Totals			
41	Hiring cost	$0	$0	$0	$0	$0			
42	Firing cost	$12,000	$2,000	$110,000	$0	$124,000			
43	Regular-time wages	$141,000	$139,500	$57,000	$57,000	$394,500			
44	Overtime wages	$0	$0	$0	$0	$0			
45	Raw material cost	$56,400	$55,800	$22,800	$22,500	$157,500			
46	Holding cost	$3,780	$0	$0	$0	$3,780			
47	Shortage cost	$0	$400	$10,000	$0	$10,400			
48	Totals	$213,180	$197,700	$199,800	$79,500	$690,180			

Note that we use IF functions in rows 46 and 47 to capture the holding and shortage costs. These IF functions make the model nonlinear (and "nonsmooth"), and Solver can't handle these functions in a predictable manner. We just got lucky here! Try changing the unit shortage cost in cell B15 to $40 and rerun Solver. Then you won't be so lucky -- Solver will converge to a solution that is pretty far from optimal.

(Row 48, cell F) ← Objective to minimize

To begin, enter the per-unit monthly shortage cost in cell B15. (A new row was inserted for this cost input.) Note in row 38 how the ending inventory in months 1 through 3 can be positive (leftovers) or negative (shortages). You can account correctly for the resulting costs with IF functions in rows 46 and 47. For holding costs, enter the formula

=IF(B38>0,$B$14*B38,0)

in cell B46 and copy it across. For shortage costs, enter the formula

=IF(B38<0,−$B$15*B38,0)

in cell B47 and copy it across. (The minus sign makes this a *positive* cost.)

Although these formulas accurately compute holding and shortage costs, the IF functions make the objective cell a *nonlinear* function of the changing cells, and Solver's GRG nonlinear algorithm must be used, as indicated in Figure 14.31.[10] (How do you know the model is nonlinear? Although there is a mathematical reason, it is easier to try running Solver with the simplex algorithm. Solver will then *inform* you that the model is nonlinear.)

We ran Solver with this setup from a variety of initial solutions in the changing cells, and it always found the solution shown in Figure 14.30. It turns out that this is indeed the optimal solution, but we were lucky. When certain functions, including IF, MIN, MAX,

Figure 14.31

Solver Dialog Box for the GRG Nonlinear Algorithm

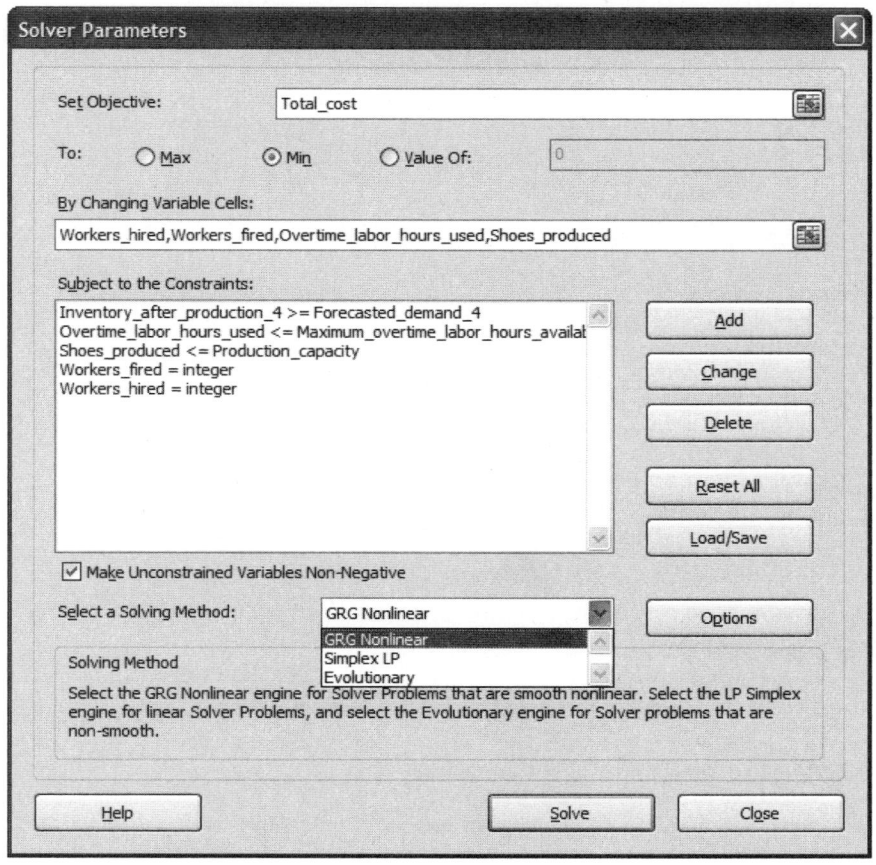

---

[10]GRG stands for generalized reduced gradient. This is a technical term for the mathematical algorithm used. The other algorithm available in Solver (starting with Excel 2010) is the Evolutionary algorithm. It can handle IF functions, but we will not discuss this algorithm here.

and ABS, are used to relate the objective cell to the changing cells, the resulting model becomes not only nonlinear but *nonsmooth*. Essentially, nonsmooth functions can have sharp edges or discontinuities. Solver's GRG nonlinear algorithm can handle "smooth" nonlinearities, as you will see in section 14.8, but it has trouble with nonsmooth functions. Sometimes it gets lucky, as it did here, and other times it finds a nonoptimal solution that is not even close to the optimal solution. For example, we changed the unit shortage cost from $20 to $40 and reran Solver. Starting from a solution where all changing cells contain zero, Solver stopped at a solution with total cost $726,360, even though the optimal solution has total cost $692,820. In other words, we weren't so lucky this time.

The moral is that you should avoid these nonsmooth functions in optimization models if at all possible. If you *do* use them, as we have done here, you should run Solver several times, starting from different initial solutions. There is still no guarantee that you will get the optimal solution, but you will see more evidence of how Solver is progressing. (Alternatively, you can use Frontline Systems's Evolutionary Solver, which became available in Excel's Solver in Excel 2010.)

Solver Tip *Nonsmooth Functions*
There is nothing inherently wrong with using IF, MIN, MAX, ABS, and other nonsmooth functions in spreadsheet optimization models. The problem is that Solver's GRG nonlinear algorithm cannot handle these functions in a predictable manner.

There are sometimes alternatives to using IF, MIN, MAX, and ABS functions that make a model linear. Unfortunately, these alternatives are often far from intuitive, and we will not cover them here. (If you are interested, we have included the "linearized" version of the backlogging model in the file **Aggregate Planning 3.xlsx**.) ∎

FUNDAMENTAL INSIGHT

Nonsmooth Functions and Solver

Excel's Solver, as well as most other commercial optimization software packages, has trouble with nonsmooth nonlinear functions. These nonsmooth functions typically have sharp edges or discontinuities that make them difficult to handle in optimization models, and (in Excel) they are typically implemented with functions such as IF, MAX, MIN, ABS, and a few others. There is nothing *wrong* with using such functions to implement complex logic in Excel optimization models. The problem is that Solver cannot handle models with these functions predictably. This is not really the fault of Solver. Such problems are inherently difficult.

PROBLEMS

Level A

30. Extend SureStep's original (no backlogging) aggregate planning model from four to six months. Try several different values for demands in months 5 and 6, and run Solver for each. Is your optimal solution for the *first* four months the same as the one in the example?

31. The current solution to SureStep's no-backlogging aggregate planning model does quite a lot of firing.

Run a one-way SolverTable with the firing cost as the input variable and the numbers fired as the outputs. Let the firing cost increase from its current value to double that value in increments of $400. Do high firing costs eventually induce the company to fire fewer workers?

32. SureStep is currently getting 160 regular-time hours from each worker per month. This is actually calculated from 8 hours per day times 20 days per month. For this, they are paid $9.375 per hour (=1500/160). Suppose workers can change their contract so that they have to work only 7.5 hours per day regular time—everything above this becomes overtime—and their regular-time wage rate increases to $10 per hour. They will still work 20 days per month. Does this change the optimal no-backlogging solution?

33. Suppose SureStep could begin a machinery upgrade and training program to increase its worker productivity. This program would result in the following values of labor hours per pair of shoes over the next four months: 4, 3.9, 3.8, and 3.8. How much would this new program be worth to SureStep, at least for this four-month planning horizon with no backlogging? How might you evaluate the program's worth *beyond* the next four months?

Level B

34. In the current no-backlogging problem, SureStep doesn't hire any workers, and it uses almost no overtime. This is evidently because of low demand. Change the demands to 6000, 8000, 5000, and 3000, and rerun Solver. Is there now any hiring and/or overtime? With this new demand pattern, explore the trade-off between hiring and overtime by running a two-way SolverTable. As inputs, use the hiring cost per worker and the maximum overtime hours allowed per worker per month, varied over reasonable ranges. As outputs, use the total number of workers hired

over the four months and the total number of overtime hours used over the four months. Discuss the results.

35. In the SureStep no-backlogging problem, change the demands so that they become 6000, 8000, 5000, and 3000. Also, change the problem slightly so that newly hired workers take six hours to produce a pair of shoes during their first month of employment. After that, they take only four hours per pair of shoes. Modify the model appropriately, and use Solver to find the optimal solution.

36. You saw that the "natural" way to model SureStep's backlogging problem, with IF functions, leads to a nonsmooth model that Solver has difficulty handling. There is another version of the problem that is also difficult for Solver. Suppose SureStep wants to meet all demands on time (no backlogging), but it wants to keep its employment level as constant over time as possible. To induce this, it charges a cost of $1000 each month on the absolute difference between the beginning number of workers and the number after hiring and firing—that is, the absolute difference between the values in rows 17 and 20 of the original spreadsheet model. Implement this extra cost in the model in the "natural" way, using the ABS function. Using demands of 6000, 8000, 5000, and 3000, see how well Solver does in solving this nonsmooth model. Try several initial solutions, and see whether Solver gets the same optimal solution from each of them.

14.6 FINANCIAL MODELS

The majority of optimization examples described in management science textbooks are in the area of operations: scheduling, blending, logistics, aggregate planning, and others. This is probably warranted, because many of the most successful management science applications in the real world have been in these areas. However, optimization and other management science methods have also been applied successfully in a number of financial areas, and they deserve recognition. In this section we begin the discussion with two typical applications of LP in finance. The first involves investment strategy. The second involves pension fund management.

EXAMPLE | **14.6 FINDING AN OPTIMAL INVESTMENT STRATEGY AT BARNEY-JONES**

At the present time, the beginning of year 1, the Barney-Jones Investment Corporation has $100,000 to invest for the next four years. There are five possible investments, labeled A through E. The timing of cash outflows and cash inflows for these investments is somewhat irregular. For example, to take part in investment A, cash must be invested at the beginning of year 1, and for every dollar invested, there are returns of $0.50 and $1.00 at the beginnings of years 2 and 3. Information for the other investments follows, where all returns are per dollar invested:

- Investment B: Invest at the beginning of year 2, receive returns of $0.50 and $1.00 at the beginnings of years 3 and 4

- Investment C: Invest at the beginning of year 1, receive return of $1.20 at the beginning of year 2

- Investment D: Invest at the beginning of year 4, receive return of $1.90 at the beginning of year 5

- Investment E: Invest at the beginning of year 3, receive return of $1.50 at the beginning of year 4

We assume that any amounts can be invested in these strategies and that the returns are the same for each dollar invested. However, to create a diversified portfolio, Barney-Jones wants to limit the amount put into any investment to $75,000. The company wants an investment strategy that maximizes the amount of cash on hand at the beginning of year 5. At the beginning of any year, it can invest only cash on hand, which includes returns from previous investments. Any cash not invested in any year can be put in a short-term money market account that earns 3% annually.

Objective To develop an LP spreadsheet model that relates investment decisions to total ending cash, and to use Solver to find the strategy that maximizes ending cash and invests no more than a given amount in any one investment.

WHERE DO THE NUMBERS COME FROM?

There is no mystery here. We assume that the terms of each investment are spelled out, so that Barney-Jones knows exactly when money must be invested and what the amounts and timing of returns will be. Of course, this would not be the case for many real-world investments, such as money put into the stock market, where considerable uncertainty is involved. We consider one such example of investing with uncertainty when we study portfolio optimization in section 14.8.

Solution

There are often multiple equivalent ways to state a constraint. You can choose the one that is most natural for you.

The variables and constraints for this investment model are listed in Table 14.9. On the surface, this problem appears to be very straightforward. You must decide how much to invest in the available investments at the beginning of each year, using only the cash available. If you try modeling this problem without our help, however, we suspect that you will have some difficulty. It took us a few tries to get a model that is easy to read and generalizes to other similar investment problems. Note that the second constraint in the

---

Table 14.9 Variables and Constraints for Investment Model

Input variables	Timing of investments and returns, initial cash, maximum amount allowed in any investment, money market rate on cash
Decision variables (changing cells)	Amounts to invest in investments
Objective cell	Ending cash at the beginning of year 5
Other calculated variables	Cash available at the beginning of years 2–4
Constraints	Amount in any investment ≤ Max investment amount
	Cash on hand after investing each year ≥ 0

table can be expressed in two ways. It can be expressed as shown, where the cash on hand *after* investing is nonnegative, or it can be expressed as "cash invested in any year must be less than or equal to cash on hand at the beginning of that year." These are equivalent. The one you choose is a matter of taste.

DEVELOPING THE SPREADSHEET MODEL

The spreadsheet model for this investment problem appears in Figure 14.32. (See the file **Investing.xlsx.**) To set up this spreadsheet, proceed as follows.

Figure 14.32 Investment Model

	A	B	C	D	E	F	G	H	I	J
1	Investments with irregular timing of returns							Range names used		
2								Cash_after_investing	=Model!$E$32:$E$35	
3	Inputs							Dollars_invested	=Model!$B$26:$F$26	
4	Initial amount to invest	$100,000						Final_cash	=Model!$B$38	
5	Maximum per investment	$75,000						Maximum_per_investment	=Model!$B$28:$F$28	
6	Interest rate on cash	3%								
7										
8	Cash outlays on investments (all incurred at beginning of year)									
9		Investment								
10	Year	A	B	C	D	E				
11	1	$1.00	$0.00	$1.00	$0.00	$0.00				
12	2	$0.00	$1.00	$0.00	$0.00	$0.00				
13	3	$0.00	$0.00	$0.00	$0.00	$1.00				
14	4	$0.00	$0.00	$0.00	$1.00	$0.00				
15										
16	Cash returns from investments (all incurred at beginning of year)									
17		Investment								
18	Year	A	B	C	D	E				
19	1	$0.00	$0.00	$0.00	$0.00	$0.00				
20	2	$0.50	$0.00	$1.20	$0.00	$0.00				
21	3	$1.00	$0.50	$0.00	$0.00	$0.00				
22	4	$0.00	$1.00	$0.00	$0.00	$1.50				
23	5	$0.00	$0.00	$0.00	$1.90	$0.00				
24										
25	Investment decisions									
26	Dollars invested	$64,286	$75,000	$35,714	$75,000	$75,000				
27		<=	<=	<=	<=	<=				
28	Maximum per investment	$75,000	$75,000	$75,000	$75,000	$75,000				
29										
30	Constraints on cash balance									
31	Year	Beginning cash	Returns from investments	Cash invested	Cash after investing					
32	1	$100,000	$0	$100,000	$0	>=	0			
33	2	$0	$75,000	$75,000	$0	>=	0			
34	3	$0	$101,786	$75,000	$26,786	>=	0			
35	4	$27,589	$187,500	$75,000	$140,089	>=	0			
36	5	$144,292	$142,500							
37										
38	Final cash	$286,792	←	Objective to maximize: final cash at beginning of year 5						

Note how the two input tables allow you to create copyable SUMPRODUCT formulas for cash outflows and inflows. Careful spreadsheet planning can often greatly simplify the necessary formulas.

1 **Inputs and range names.** As usual, enter the given inputs in the blue cells and name the ranges indicated. Pay particular attention to the two shaded tables. This is probably the first model you have encountered where model development is affected significantly by the way you enter the inputs, specifically, the information about the investments. We suggest separating cash outflows from cash inflows, as shown in the two ranges B11:F14 and B19:F23. The top table indicates when investments can be made, where $0.00 indicates no possible investment, and $1.00 indicates a dollar of investment. The bottom table then indicates the amounts and timing of returns per dollar invested.

2 **Investment amounts.** Enter *any* trial values in the Dollars_invested range. This range contains the changing cells. Also put a link to the maximum investment amount per investment by entering the formula

=$B$5

in cell B28 and copying it across.

3 **Cash balances and flows.** The key to the model is the section in rows 32 through 36. For each year, you need to calculate the beginning cash held from the previous year, the returns from investments that are due in that year, the investments made in that year, and cash balance after investments. Begin by entering the initial cash in cell B32 with the formula

=B4

Moving across, calculate the return due in year 1 in cell C32 with the formula

=SUMPRODUCT(B19:F19,Dollars_invested)

Admittedly, no returns come due in year 1, but this formula can be copied down column C for other years. Next, calculate the total amount invested in year 1 in cell D32 with the formula

=SUMPRODUCT(B11:F11,Dollars_invested)

Now find the cash balance after investing in year 1 in cell E32 with the formula

=B32+C32-D32

The only other required formula is the formula for the cash available at the beginning of year 2. Because any cash not invested earns 3% interest, enter the formula

=E32*(1+$B$6)

in cell B33. This formula, along with those in cells C32, D32, and E32, can now be copied down. (The zeros in column G are entered manually as a reminder of the nonnegativity constraint on cash after investing.)

4 **Ending cash.** The ending cash at the beginning of year 5 is the sum of the amount in the money market and any returns that come due in year 5. Calculate this sum with the formula

=SUM(B36:C36)

Always look at the Solver solution for signs of implausibility. This can often lead you to an error in your model.

in cell B38. (*Note*: Here is the type of error to watch out for. We originally failed to calculate the return in cell C36 and mistakenly used the beginning cash in cell B36 as the objective cell. We realized our error when the optimal solution called for no money in investment D, which is clearly an attractive investment. The moral is that you can often catch errors by looking at the *plausibility* of the outputs.)

Review of the Model

Take a careful look at this model and how it has been set up. There are undoubtedly many alternative ways to model this problem, but the attractive feature of this model is the way the tables of inflows and outflows in rows 11 through 14 and 19 through 23 create *copyable* formulas for returns and investment amounts in columns C and D of rows 32 through 35. In fact, this same model setup, with only minor modifications, will work for *any* set of investments, regardless of the timing of investments and their returns. This is a quality you should strive for in your spreadsheet models: generalizability.

USING SOLVER

To find the optimal investment strategy, fill in the main Solver dialog box as shown in Figure 14.33. Note that the explicit nonnegativity constraint in Figure 14.33 is necessary, even though the Non-Negative option is checked. Again, this is because the Non-Negative option covers only the changing cells. If you want other output cells to be nonnegative, you must add such constraints explicitly.

Figure 14.33
Solver Dialog Box
for Investment
Model

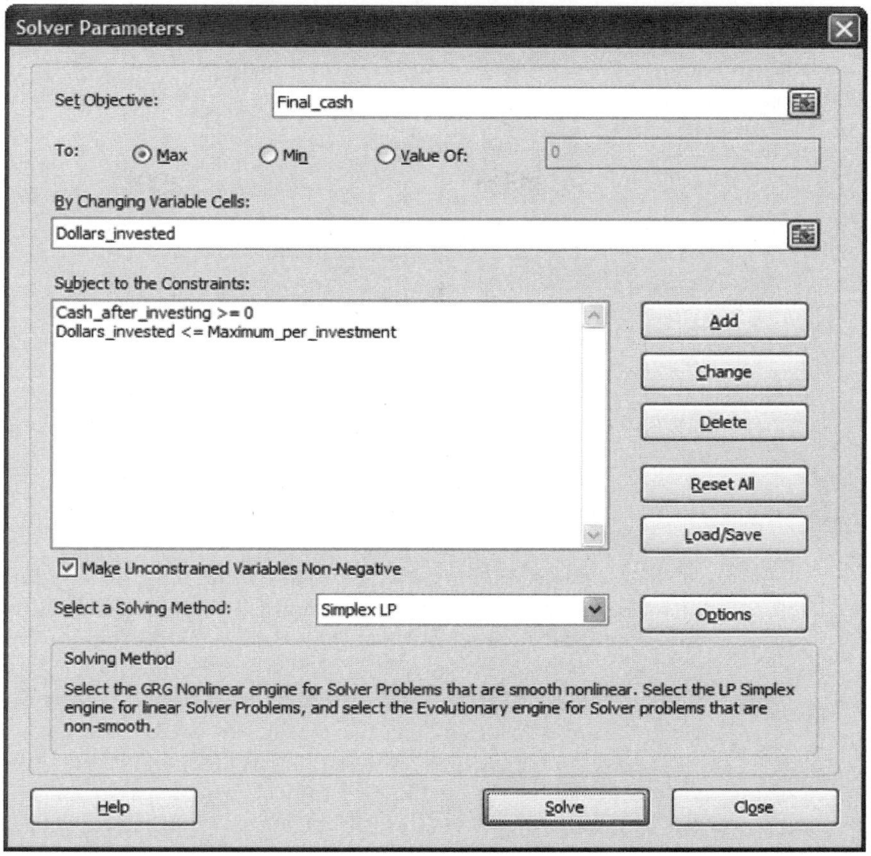

Discussion of the Results

The optimal solution appears in Figure 14.32. Let's follow the cash. The company spends all of its cash in year 1 on the two available investments, A and C ($64,286 in A, $35,714 in C). A total of $75,000 in returns from these investments is available in year 2, and all of this is invested in investment B. At the beginning of year 3, a total of $101,786 is available from investment A and B returns, and $75,000 of this is invested in investment E. This leaves $26,786 for the money market, which grows to $27,589 at the beginning of year 4. In addition, returns totaling $187,500 from investments B and E come due in year 4. Of this total cash of $215,089, $75,000 is invested in investment D, and the rest, $140,089, is put in the money market. The return from investment D, $142,500, plus the money available from the money market, $144,292, equals the final cash in the objective cell, $286,792.

Sensitivity Analysis

A close look at the optimal solution in Figure 14.32 indicates that Barney-Jones is penalizing itself by imposing a maximum of $75,000 per investment. This upper limit is forcing the company to put cash into the money market fund, despite this fund's low rate of return. Therefore, a natural sensitivity analysis is to see how the optimal solution changes as this maximum value changes. You can perform this sensitivity analysis with a one-way SolverTable, shown in Figure 14.34.[11] The maximum in cell B5 is the input cell, varied

[11]Because Solver's sensitivity reports do not help answer our specific sensitivity questions in this example or the next example, we discuss only SolverTable results.

Figure 14.34

Sensitivity of
Optimal Solution
to Maximum
Investment
Amount

	A	B	C	D	E	F	G
3	Max per investment (cell $B$5) values along side, output cell(s) along top						
4		Dollars_invested_1	Dollars_invested_2	Dollars_invested_3	Dollars_invested_4	Dollars_invested_5	Final_cash
5	$75,000	$64,286	$75,000	$35,714	$75,000	$75,000	$286,792
6	$100,000	$61,538	$76,923	$38,462	$100,000	$100,000	$320,731
7	$125,000	$100,000	$50,000	$0	$125,000	$125,000	$353,375
8	$150,000	$100,000	$50,000	$0	$150,000	$125,000	$375,125
9	$175,000	$100,000	$50,000	$0	$175,000	$125,000	$396,875
10	$200,000	$100,000	$50,000	$0	$200,000	$125,000	$418,625
11	$225,000	$100,000	$50,000	$0	$225,000	$125,000	$440,375

from $75,000 to $225,000 in increments of $25,000, and the optimal changing cells and objective cell are outputs. As you can see, the final cash (column G) grows steadily as the maximum allowable investment amount increases. This is because the company can take greater advantage of the attractive investments and put less in the money market account.

To perform sensitivity on an output variable not calculated explicitly in your spreadsheet model, calculate it in some unused portion of the spreadsheet before running SolverTable.

You can go one step further with the two-way SolverTable in Figure 14.35. Now both the maximum investment amount and the money market rate are inputs, and the maximum amount ever put in the money market fund is the single output. Because this latter amount is not calculated in the spreadsheet model, you need to calculate it with the formula **=MAX(Cash_after_investing)** in an unused cell before using it as the output cell for SolverTable. In every case, even with a large maximum investment amount and a low money

Figure 14.35 Sensitivity of Maximum in Money Market to Two Inputs

	A	B	C	D	E	F	G	H	I
3	Interest on cash (cell $B$6) values along side, Max per investment (cell $B$5) values along top, output cell in corner								
4	Maximum_in_money_market	$75,000	$100,000	$125,000	$150,000	$175,000	$200,000	$225,000	
5	0.5%	$139,420	$126,923	$112,500	$87,500	$62,500	$37,500	$12,500	
6	1.0%	$139,554	$126,923	$112,500	$87,500	$62,500	$37,500	$12,500	
7	1.5%	$139,688	$126,923	$112,500	$87,500	$62,500	$37,500	$12,500	
8	2.0%	$139,821	$126,923	$112,500	$87,500	$62,500	$37,500	$12,500	
9	2.5%	$139,955	$126,923	$112,500	$87,500	$62,500	$37,500	$12,500	
10	3.0%	$140,089	$126,923	$112,500	$87,500	$62,500	$37,500	$12,500	
11	3.5%	$140,223	$126,923	$112,500	$87,500	$62,500	$37,500	$12,500	
12	4.0%	$140,357	$126,923	$112,500	$87,500	$62,500	$37,500	$12,500	
13	4.5%	$140,491	$126,923	$112,500	$87,500	$62,500	$37,500	$12,500	

market rate, the company puts *some* money into the money market account. The reason is simple. Even when the maximum investment amount is $225,000, the company evidently has more cash than this to invest at some point (probably at the beginning of year 4). Therefore, it will have to put some of it in the money market. ■

The following example illustrates a common situation where fixed payments are due in the future and current funds must be allocated and invested so that their returns are sufficient to make the payments. We place this in a pension fund context.

EXAMPLE | 14.7 MANAGING A PENSION FUND AT ARMCO

James Judson is the financial manager in charge of the company pension fund at Armco Incorporated. James knows that the fund must be sufficient to make the payments listed in Table 14.10. Each payment must be made on the first day of each year. James is going to finance these payments by purchasing bonds. It is currently January 1, 2010, and three bonds are available for immediate purchase. The prices and coupons for the bonds are as follows. (All coupon payments are received on January 1 and arrive in time to meet cash demands for the date on which they arrive.)

■ Bond 1 costs $980 and yields a $60 coupon in the years 2011 through 2014 and a $1060 payment on maturity in the year 2015.

■ Bond 2 costs $970 and yields a $65 coupon in the years 2011 through 2020 and a $1065 payment on maturity in the year 2021.

■ Bond 3 costs $1050 and yields a $75 coupon in the years 2011 through 2023 and a $1075 payment on maturity in the year 2024.

James must decide how much cash to allocate (from company coffers) to meet the initial $11,000 payment and buy enough bonds to make future payments. He knows that any excess cash on hand can earn an annual rate of 4% in a fixed-rate account. How should he proceed?

Table 14.10 Payments for Pension Example

Year	Payment	Year	Payment	Year	Payment
2010	$11,000	2015	$18,000	2020	$25,000
2011	$12,000	2016	$20,000	2021	$30,000
2012	$14,000	2017	$21,000	2022	$31,000
2013	$15,000	2018	$22,000	2023	$31,000
2014	$16,000	2019	$24,000	2024	$31,000

Objective   To develop an LP model that relates initial allocation of money and bond purchases to future cash availabilities, and to minimize the initialize allocation of money required to meet all future pension fund payments.

WHERE DO THE NUMBERS COME FROM?

As in the previous financial example, the inputs are fairly easy to obtain. A pension fund has known liabilities that must be met in future years, and information on bonds and fixed-rate accounts is widely available.

Solution

Although it doesn't occur very often, it is perfectly acceptable to make the objective cell one of the changing cells. In fact, this is the key to the current model.

The variables and constraints required for this pension fund model are listed in Table 14.11. When modeling this problem, there is a new twist that involves the money James must allocate now for his funding problem. It is clear that he must decide how many bonds of each type to purchase now (note that no bonds are purchased in the *future*), but he must also decide how much money to allocate from company coffers. This allocated money has to cover the initial pension payment this year *and* the bond purchases. In addition, James wants to find the *minimum* allocation that will suffice. Therefore, this initial allocation serves two roles in the model. It is a decision variable *and* it is the objective to minimize. In terms of spreadsheet modeling, it is perfectly acceptable to make the objective cell one of the changing cells, and this is done here. You will not see this in many models—because the objective typically involves a linear combination of several decision variables—but it is occasionally the most natural way to proceed.

Table 14.11 Variables and Constraints for Pension Model

Input variables	Pension payments, information on bonds, fixed interest rate on cash
Decision variables (changing cells)	Money to allocate now, numbers of bonds to purchase now
Object cell	Money to allocate in now (minimize)
Other calculated variables	Cash available to meet pension payments each year
Constraints	Cash available for payments ≥ Payment amounts

FUNDAMENTAL INSIGHT

The Objective as a Changing Cell

In all optimization models, the objective cell has to be a function of the changing cells, that is, the objective value should change as values in the changing cells change. It is perfectly consistent with this requirement to have the objective cell *be* one of the changing cells. This doesn't occur in very many optimization models, but it is sometimes useful, even necessary.

DEVELOPING THE SPREADSHEET MODEL

The completed spreadsheet model is shown in Figure 14.36. (See the file **Pension Fund Management.xlsx.**) You can create it with the following steps.

1 Inputs and range names. Enter the given data and name the ranges as indicated. Note that the bond costs in the range B5:B7 have been entered as *positive* quantities. Some financial analysts might prefer that they be entered as negative numbers, indicating outflows. It doesn't really matter, however, as long as you are careful with the Excel formulas later on.

Always document your spreadsheet conventions as clearly as possible.

2 Money allocated and bonds purchased. As discussed previously, the money allocated in the current year and the numbers of bonds purchased now are both decision variables, so enter *any* values for these in the Money_allocated and Bonds_purchased ranges. Note that the color-coding convention for the Money_allocated cell have to be modified. Because it is both a changing cell and the objective cell, we colored it red but added a note to emphasize that it is the objective to minimize.

Figure 14.36 Pension Fund Management Model

	A	B	C	D	E	F	G	H	I	J	K	L	M	N	O	P
1	Pension fund management															
2																
3	Costs (now) and income (in other years) from bonds															
4	Year	2010	2011	2012	2013	2014	2015	2016	2017	2018	2019	2020	2021	2022	2023	2024
5	Bond 1	$980	$60	$60	$60	$60	$1,060									
6	Bond 2	$970	$65	$65	$65	$65	$65	$65	$65	$65	$65	$65	$1,065			
7	Bond 3	$1,050	$75	$75	$75	$75	$75	$75	$75	$75	$75	$75	$75	$75	$75	$1,075
8																
9	Interest rate	4%														
10																
11	Number of bonds (allowing fractional values) to purchase now															
12	Bond 1	73.69														
13	Bond 2	77.21														
14	Bond 3	28.84														
15																
16	Money allocated	$197,768	←		Objective to minimize, also a changing cell											
17																
18	Constraints to meet payments															
19	Year	2010	2011	2012	2013	2014	2015	2016	2017	2018	2019	2020	2021	2022	2023	2024
20	Amount available	$20,376	$21,354	$21,332	$19,228	$16,000	$85,298	$77,171	$66,639	$54,646	$41,133	$25,000	$84,390	$58,728	$31,000	$31,000
21		>=	>=	>=	>=	>=	>=	>=	>=	>=	>=	>=	>=	>=	>=	>=
22	Amount required	$11,000	$12,000	$14,000	$15,000	$16,000	$18,000	$20,000	$21,000	$22,000	$24,000	$25,000	$30,000	$31,000	$31,000	$31,000
23																
24	Range names used:															
25	Amount_available	=Model!$B$20:$P$20														
26	Amount_required	=Model!$B$22:$P$22														
27	Bonds_purchased	=Model!$B$12:$B$14														
28	Money_allocated	=Model!$B$16														

The value in cell B16 is the money allocated to make the current payment and buy bonds now. It is both a changing cell and the target cell to minimize.

③ Cash available to make payments. In the current year, the only cash available is the money initially allocated minus cash used to purchase bonds. Calculate this quantity in cell B20 with the formula

=Money_allocated-SUMPRODUCT(Bonds_purchased,B5:B7)

For all other years, the cash available comes from two sources: excess cash invested at the fixed interest rate the year before and payments from bonds. Calculate this quantity for 2011 in cell C20 with the formula

=(B20-B22)*(1+$B$9)+SUMPRODUCT(Bonds_purchased,C5:C7)

and copy it across row 20 for the other years.

As you can see, this model is fairly straightforward to develop once you understand the role of the amount allocated in cell B16. However, we have often given this problem as an assignment to our students, and many fail to deal correctly with the amount allocated. (They usually forget to make it a changing cell.) So make sure you understand what we have done, and why we have done it this way.

USING SOLVER

The main Solver dialog box should be filled out as shown in Figure 14.37. Once again, notice that the Money_allocated cell is both the objective cell and one of the changing cells.

Discussion of the Solution

The optimal solution appears in Figure 14.36. You might argue that the numbers of bonds purchased should be constrained to integer values. We tried this and the optimal solution changed very little: The optimal numbers of bonds to purchase changed to 74, 79, and 27, and the optimal money to allocate increased to $197,887. With this integer solution, shown in Figure 14.38, James sets aside $197,887 initially. Any less than this would not work— he couldn't make enough from bonds to meet future pension payments. All but $20,387 of this (see cell B20) is spent on bonds, and of the $20,387, $11,000 is used to make the

Figure 14.37
Solver Dialog Box
for Pension Fund
Model

Figure 14.37
Solver Dialog Box for Pension Fund Model

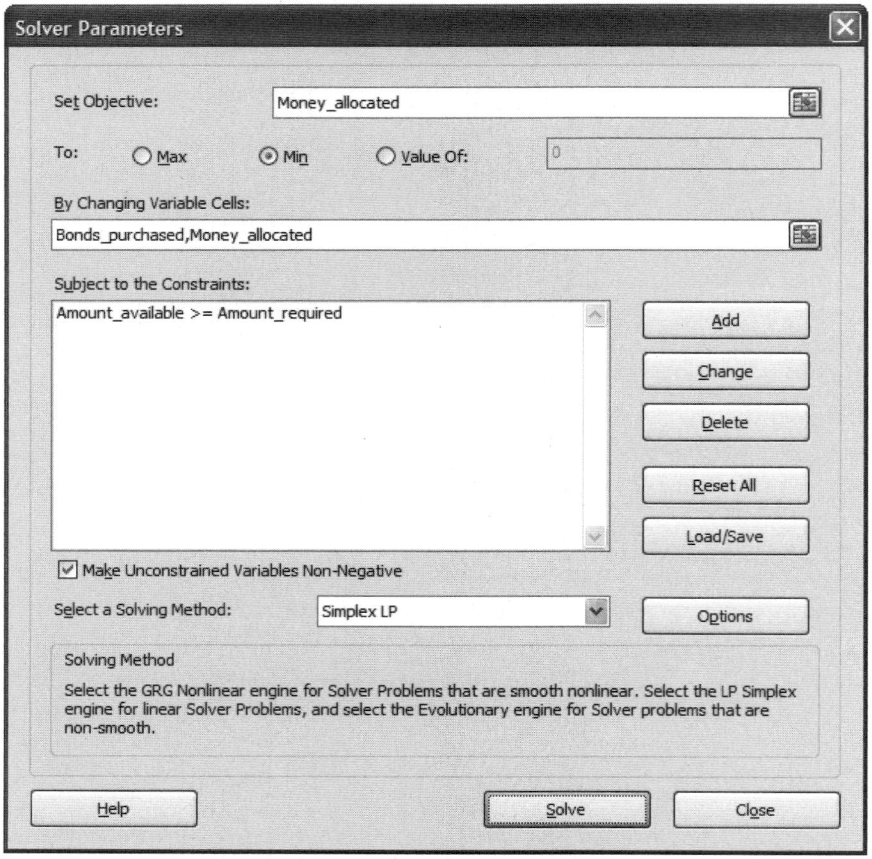

Figure 14.38   Optimal Integer Solution for Pension Fund Model

	A	B	C	D	E	F	G	H	I	J	K	L	M	N	O	P
1	Pension fund management															
2																
3	Costs (now) and income (in other years) from bonds															
4	Year	2010	2011	2012	2013	2014	2015	2016	2017	2018	2019	2020	2021	2022	2023	2024
5	Bond 1	$980	$60	$60	$60	$60	$1,060									
6	Bond 2	$970	$65	$65	$65	$65	$65	$65	$65	$65	$65	$65	$1,065			
7	Bond 3	$1,050	$75	$75	$75	$75	$75	$75	$75	$75	$75	$75	$75	$75	$75	$1,075
8																
9	Interest rate	4%														
10																
11	Number of bonds (allowing fractional values) to purchase now															
12	Bond 1	74.00														
13	Bond 2	79.00														
14	Bond 3	27.00														
15																
16	Money allocated	$197,887	←	Objective to minimize, also a changing cell												
17																
18	Constraints to meet payments															
19	Year	2010	2011	2012	2013	2014	2015	2016	2017	2018	2019	2020	2021	2022	2023	2024
20	Amount available	$20,387	$21,363	$21,337	$19,231	$16,000	$85,600	$77,464	$66,923	$54,919	$41,396	$25,252	$86,422	$60,704	$32,917	$31,019
21		>=	>=	>=	>=	>=	>=	>=	>=	>=	>=	>=	>=	>=	>=	>=
22	Amount required	$11,000	$12,000	$14,000	$15,000	$16,000	$18,000	$20,000	$21,000	$22,000	$24,000	$25,000	$30,000	$31,000	$31,000	$31,000

current pension payment. After this, the amounts in row 20, which are always sufficient to make the payments in row 22, are composed of returns from bonds and cash, with interest, from the previous year. Even more so than in previous examples, there is no way to guess this optimal solution. The timing of bond returns and the irregular pension payments make a spreadsheet optimization model absolute necessary.

Discussion of the Solution

The Solver solution in Figure 14.57 indicates that FPL should charge $70.31 per kwh during the peak-load period and $26.53 during the off-peak period. These prices generate demands of 27.5 (peak-load) and 20.5 (off-peak), so that a capacity of 27.5 kwh is required. The cost of this capacity is $275. When this is subtracted from the revenue of $2477.30, the daily profit becomes $2202.30.

Varying the changing cells slightly from their optimal values sometimes provides insight into the optimal solution.

To gain some insight into this solution, consider what happens if FPL changes the peak-load price slightly from its optimal value of $70.31. If FPL decreases the price to $70, say, you can check that the peak-load demand increases to 27.65 kwh and the off-peak demand decreases to 20.47 kwh. The net effect is that revenue increases slightly, to $2478.78. However, the peak-load demand is now greater than capacity, so FPL must increase its capacity from 27.50 to 27.65 kwh. This costs an extra $1.50, which more than offsets the increase in revenue. A similar chain of effects occurs if FPL increases the peak price to $71. In this case, peak-load demand decreases, off-peak demand increases, and total revenue decreases. Although FPL can get by with lower capacity, the net effect is slightly less profit. Fortunately, Solver evaluates all of these trade-offs when it finds the optimal solution.

Is the Solver Solution Optimal?

It is not difficult to show that the constraints for this model are linear and the objective is *concave*. This is enough to guarantee that there are no local maxima that are not globally optimal. In short, this guarantees that the Solver solution is optimal.

Sensitivity Analysis

To gain even more insight, SolverTable can be used to see the effects of changing the unit cost of capacity, which are allowed to vary from $5 to $15 in increments of $1. The results appear in Figure 14.59. They indicate that as the cost of capacity increases, the peak-load price increases, the off-peak price stays constant, the amount of capacity decreases, and profit decreases. The latter two effects are probably intuitive, but we challenge you to explain the effects on price. In particular, why does the peak-load price *increase*, and why doesn't the off-peak price increase as well?

Figure 14.59

Sensitivity to Cost of Capacity

	A	B	C	D	E	F
3	Capacity cost (cell $B$9) values along side, output cell(s) along top					
4		Prices_1	Prices_2	Capacity	Profit	
5	$5	$67.81	$26.53	28.75	$2,342.92	
6	$6	$68.31	$26.53	28.50	$2,314.30	
7	$7	$68.81	$26.53	28.25	$2,285.92	
8	$8	$69.31	$26.53	28.00	$2,257.80	
9	$9	$69.81	$26.53	27.75	$2,229.92	
10	$10	$70.31	$26.53	27.50	$2,202.30	
11	$11	$70.81	$26.53	27.25	$2,174.92	
12	$12	$71.31	$26.53	27.00	$2,147.80	
13	$13	$71.81	$26.53	26.75	$2,120.92	
14	$14	$72.31	$26.53	26.50	$2,094.30	
15	$15	$72.81	$26.53	26.25	$2,067.92	

14.8.3 Portfolio Optimization Models

Given a set of investments, how do financial analysts determine the portfolio that has the lowest risk and yields a high expected return? This question was answered by Harry Markowitz in the 1950s. For his work on this and other investment topics, he received the Nobel Prize in economics in 1991. The ideas discussed in this section are the basis for most methods of *asset allocation* used by Wall Street firms. Asset allocation models are used, for example, to determine the percentage of assets to invest in stocks, gold, and Treasury bills. Before proceeding, however, you need to learn about some important formulas involving the expected value and variance of sums of random variables.

Weighted Sums of Random Variables[16]

Let R_i be the (random) return earned during a year on a dollar invested in investment i. For example, if $R_i = 0.10$, a dollar invested at the beginning of the year grows to $1.10 by the end of the year, whereas if $R_i = -0.20$, a dollar invested at the beginning of the year decreases in value to $0.80 by the end of the year. We assume that n investments are available. Let x_i be the fraction of our money invested in investment i. We assume that $x_1 + x_2 + \cdots + x_n = 1$, so that all of our money is invested. (To prevent shorting a stock—that is, selling shares we don't own—we assume that $x_i \geq 0$.) Then the annual return on our investments is given by the random variable R_p, where

$$R_p = R_1 x_1 + R_2 x_2 + \cdots + R_n x_n$$

(The subscript p on R_p stands for "portfolio.")

Let μ_i be the expected value (also called the mean) of R_i, let σ_i^2 be the variance of R_i (so that σ_i is the standard deviation of R_i), and let ρ_{ij} be the correlation between R_i and R_j. To do any work with investments, you must understand how to use the following formulas, which relate the data for the individual investments to the expected return and the variance of return for a *portfolio* of investments.

$$\text{Expected value of } R_p = \mu_1 x_1 + \mu_2 x_2 + \cdots + \mu_n x_n \qquad \textbf{(14.7)}$$

$$\text{Variance of } R_p = \sigma_1^2 x_1^2 + \sigma_2^2 x_2^2 + \cdots + \sigma_n^2 x_n^2 + \Sigma_{ij} \rho_{ij} \sigma_i \sigma_j x_i x_j \qquad \textbf{(14.8)}$$

The latter summation in Equation (14.8) is over all pairs of investments. The quantities in equations (14.7) and (14.8) are extremely important in portfolio selection because of the risk–return trade-off investors need to make. All investors want to choose portfolios with high return, measured by the expected value in Equation (14.7), but they also want portfolios with low risk, usually measured by the variance in Equation (14.8).

Equation (14.8) can be rewritten slightly by using *covariances* instead of correlations. The covariance between two stock returns is another measure of the relationship between the two returns, but unlike a correlation, it is *not* scaled to be between -1 and $+1$. This is because covariances are affected by the units in which the returns are measured. Although a covariance is a somewhat less intuitive measure than a correlation, it is used so frequently by financial analysts that we use it here as well. If c_{ij} is the estimated covariance between stocks i and j, then $c_{ij} = r_{ij} s_i s_j$. (Here, r is an estimated correlation, and s is an estimated standard deviation.) Using this equation and the fact that the correlation between any stock and itself is 1, we can also write $c_{ii} = s_i^2$ for each stock i. Therefore, an equivalent form of Equation (14.8) is the following Equation (14.9):

$$\text{Estimated variance of } R_p = \Sigma_{i,j} c_{ij} x_i x_j \qquad \textbf{(14.9)}$$

This allows you to calculate the portfolio variance very easily with Excel's matrix functions, as explained next.

---

[16]The material was covered in Chapter 4, but it is included here for those who did not read Chapter 4.

constraints in the discussion of scheduling workers and aggregate planning. This section illustrates some of the tricks of the trade that are needed to formulate IP models of complex situations. You should be aware that Solver typically has a much harder time solving an IP problem than an LP problem. In fact, Solver is unable to solve some IP problems, even when they have an optimal solution. The reason is that these problems are inherently difficult, no matter what software package is used. However, as you will see in this section, your ability to model complex problems increases tremendously when you are able to use IP, particularly with 0–1 variables.

FUNDAMENTAL INSIGHT

Difficulty of Integer Programming Models

You might suspect that IP models would be *easier* to solve than LP models. After all, there are only a finite number of feasible integer solutions in an IP model, whereas there are infinitely many feasible (integer and noninteger) solutions in an LP model. However, exactly the opposite is true. As stated previously, IP models are *much* more difficult than LP models. All IP algorithms try to perform an efficient search through the typically huge number of feasible integer solutions. General-purpose algorithms such as branch and bound can be very effective for modest-size problems, but they can fail (or require extremely long computing times) on the large problems often faced in real applications. In such cases, analysts must develop special-purpose optimization algorithms, or perhaps even heuristics, to find "good," but not necessarily optimal, solutions.

14.7.1 Capital Budgeting Models

Perhaps the simplest IP model is the following **capital budgeting** example. It perfectly illustrates the go/no-go decisions inherent in many IP models.

EXAMPLE | 14.8 SELECTING INVESTMENTS AT TATHAM

The Tatham Company is considering seven investments. The cash required for each investment and the net present value (NPV) each investment adds to the firm are listed in Table 14.12. The cash available for investment is $15,000. Tatham wants to find the investment policy that maximizes its NPV. The crucial assumption here is that if Tatham wishes to take part in any of these investments, it must go all the way. It cannot, for example, go halfway in investment 1 by investing $2500 and realizing an NPV of $8000. In fact, if partial investments were allowed, LP could be used; IP wouldn't be necessary.

Table 14.12 Data for Capital Budgeting Example

Investment	Cash Required	NPV
1	$5000	$16,000
2	$2500	$8000
3	$3500	$10,000
4	$6000	$19,500
5	$7000	$22,000
6	$4500	$12,000
7	$3,000	$7,500

Objective To use a binary IP model to find the set of investments that stays within budget and maximizes total NPV.

WHERE DO THE NUMBERS COME FROM?

The initial required cash and the available budget are easy to obtain. It is undoubtedly harder to obtain the NPV for each investment. This requires a time sequence of anticipated cash inflows from the investments and a discount factor. Simulation might even be used to estimate these NPVs. In any case, this is exactly what many financial analysts do: estimate the NPVs for potential investments.

Solution

The variables and constraints required for this model are listed in Table 14.13. The most important part is that the decision variables must be binary, where a 1 means an investment is undertaken and a 0 means it is not. These variables cannot have fractional values such as 0.5, because partial investments are not allowed—the company has to go all the way or not at all. Note that the binary restriction is specified in the second row, not the last row. This is done throughout the chapter. However, when you set up the Solver dialog box, you need to add explicit binary constraints in the constraints section.

Table 14.13 Variables and Constraints for Capital Budgeting Model

Input variables	Initial cash required for investments, NPVs from investments, budget
Decision variables (changing cells)	Whether to invest (binary variables)
Objective cell	Total NPV
Other calculated variables	Total initial cash invested
Constraints	Total initial cash invested ≤ Budget

DEVELOPING THE SPREADSHEET MODEL

To form the spreadsheet model, which is shown in Figure 14.40, proceed as follows. (See the file **Capital Budgeting 1.xlsx**.)

1 **Inputs.** Enter the initial cash requirements, the NPVs, and the budget in the input cells.

2 **0–1 values for investments.** Enter *any* trial 0–1 values for the investments in the Investment_levels range. (Actually, you can even enter fractional values such as 0.5 in these cells. The Solver constraints will eventually force them to be 0 or 1.)

3 **Cash invested.** Calculate the total cash invested in cell B14 with the formula

=SUMPRODUCT(B5:H5,Investment_levels)

> A SUMPRODUCT formula, where one of the ranges consists of 0s and 1s, really just sums the values in the other range that "match up" with the 1s.

Note that this formula sums the costs *only* for those investments with binary variables equal to 1. To see this, think how the SUMPRODUCT function works when one of its ranges is a range of 0s and 1s. It effectively sums the cells in the other range corresponding to the 1s.

4 **NPV contribution.** Calculate the NPV contributed by the investments in cell B17 with the formula

=SUMPRODUCT(B6:H6,Investment_levels)

Again, this sums only the NPVs of the investments with binary variables equal to 1.

Figure 14.40   Capital Budgeting Model

	A	B	C	D	E	F	G	H
1	Tatham capital budgeting model							
2								
3	Input data on potential investments							
4	Investment	1	2	3	4	5	6	7
5	Investment cost	$5,000	$2,500	$3,500	$6,500	$7,000	$4,500	$3,000
6	NPV	$16,000	$8,000	$10,000	$19,500	$22,000	$12,000	$7,500
7	NPV per investment dollar	3.20	3.20	2.86	3.25	3.14	2.67	2.50
8								
9	Decisions: whether to invest							
10	Investment levels	1	1	0	0	1	0	0
11								
12	Budget constraints							
13		Amount invested			Budget			
14		$14,500	<=		$15,000			
15								
16	Objective to maximize							
17	Total NPV	$46,000						
18								
19	Range names used:							
20	Amount_invested	=Model!$B$14						
21	Budget	=Model!$D$14						
22	Investment_levels	=Model!$B$10:$H$10						
23	Total_NPV	=Model!$B$1						

USING SOLVER

Solver makes it easy to specify binary constraints, just by clicking on the "bin" option.

The Solver dialog box appears in Figure 14.41. The goal is to maximize the total NPV, subject to staying within the budget. However, the changing cells must be *constrained* to be binary. Fortunately, Solver makes this simple, as shown in the dialog box in Figure 14.42. You add a constraint with Investments in the left box and choose the "bin" option in the middle box. The "binary" in the right box is then added automatically. Note that if *all* changing cells are binary, you do not need to check Solver's Non-Negative option (because 0 and 1 are certainly nonnegative), but you should still choose the simplex algorithm.

Discussion of the Solution

The optimal solution in Figure 14.40 indicates that Tatham can obtain a maximum NPV of $46,000 by selecting investments 1, 2, and 5. These three investments consume only $14,500 of the available budget, with $500 left over. However, this $500 is not enough—because of the "investing all the way" requirement—to invest in any of the remaining investments.

If Tatham's investments are ranked on the basis of NPV per dollar invested (see row 7 of Figure 14.40), the ranking from best to worst is 4, 1, 2, 5, 3, 6, 7. Using your economic intuition, you might expect the investments to be chosen in this order—until the budget runs out. However, the optimal solution does not do this. It selects the second-, third-, and fourth-best investments, but it omits the best one. To understand why it does this, imagine investing in the order from best to worst, according to row 7, until the budget allows no more. By the time you have invested in investments 4, 1, and 2, you will have consumed $13,500 of the budget, and the remainder, $1500, is not sufficient to invest in any of the rest. This strategy provides an NPV of only $43,500. A smarter strategy, the optimal solution from Solver, gains you an extra $2500 in NPV.

Figure 14.41

Solver Dialog Box for Capital Budgeting Model

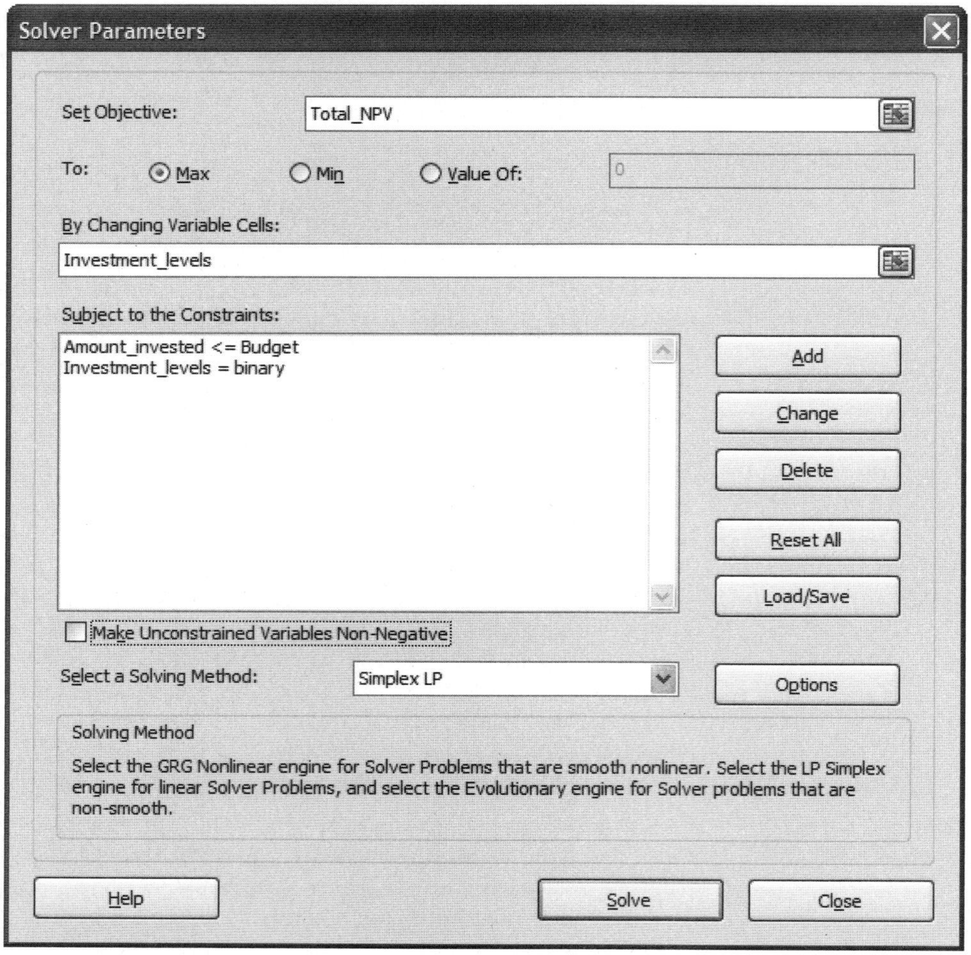

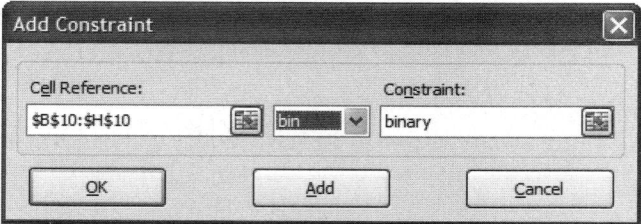

Figure 14.42

Specifying a Binary Constraint

Sensitivity Analysis

SolverTable can be used on models with binary variables exactly as in previous models. For example, to see how the total NPV varies as the budget increases, select the Budget cell as the single input cell, allow it to vary from $15,000 to $25,000 in increments of $1000, and designate the binary variables, the amount of the budget used, and the total NPV as outputs. The results are given in Figure 14.43. Clearly, Tatham can achieve a larger NPV with a larger budget, but as the numbers and the chart show, each extra $1000 of budget does *not* have the same effect on total NPV. The first $1000 increase to the budget adds $3500 to total NPV, the next two $1000 increases add $4000 each, the next two $1000 increases add $2000 each, and so on. Note also how the selected investments vary quite a lot as the budget increases. This somewhat strange behavior is due to the "lumpiness" of the inputs and the all-or-nothing nature of the problem.

Figure 14.43 Sensitivity to Budget

	A	B	C	D	E	F	G	H	I	J	K
3	Budget (cell $D$14) values along side, output cell(s) along top										
4		Investment_levels_1	Investment_levels_2	Investment_levels_3	Investment_levels_4	Investment_levels_5	Investment_levels_6	Investment_levels_7	Amount_invested	Total_NPV	Increase
5	$15,000	1	1	0	0	1	0	0	$14,500	$46,000	
6	$16,000	0	1	0	1	1	0	0	$15,500	$49,500	$3,500
7	$17,000	1	1	1	1	0	0	0	$17,000	$53,500	$4,000
8	$18,000	1	0	0	1	1	0	0	$18,000	$57,500	$4,000
9	$19,000	0	1	1	1	1	0	0	$19,000	$59,500	$2,000
10	$20,000	0	1	0	1	1	1	0	$20,000	$61,500	$2,000
11	$21,000	1	1	0	1	1	0	0	$20,500	$65,500	$4,000
12	$22,000	1	0	1	1	1	0	0	$21,500	$67,500	$2,000
13	$23,000	1	0	0	1	1	1	0	$22,500	$69,500	$2,000
14	$24,000	1	1	1	1	1	0	0	$24,000	$75,500	$6,000
15	$25,000	1	1	0	1	1	1	0	$25,000	$77,500	$2,000

Effect of Solver Tolerance Setting

When the Tolerance setting is 5% instead of 0%, Solver's solution might not be optimal, but it will be close.

To illustrate the effect of the Solver Tolerance setting, compare the SolverTable results in Figure 14.44 with those in Figure 14.43. Each is for the Tatham capital budgeting model, but Figure 14.44 uses Solver's default tolerance of 5%, whereas Figure 14.43 uses a tolerance of 0%. The three shaded cells in Figure 14.44 indicate *lower* total NPVs than the corresponding cells in Figure 14.43. In these three cases, Solver stopped short of finding the true optimal solutions because it found solutions within the 5% tolerance and then quit.

Figure 14.44
Results with Tolerance at 5%

	A	B	C	D	E	F	G	H	I	J
3	Budget (cell $D$14) values along side, output cell(s) along top									
4		Investment_levels_1	Investment_levels_2	Investment_levels_3	Investment_levels_4	Investment_levels_5	Investment_levels_6	Investment_levels_7	Amount_invested	Total_NPV
5	$15,000	1	1	0	0	1	0	0	$14,500	$46,000
6	$16,000	0	1	0	1	1	0	0	$15,500	$49,500
7	$17,000	1	1	1	1	0	0	0	$17,000	$53,500
8	$18,000	1	0	0	1	1	0	0	$18,000	$57,500
9	$19,000	0	1	1	1	1	0	0	$19,000	$59,500
10	$20,000	1	0	1	0	1	1	0	$20,000	$60,000
11	$21,000	1	1	0	1	1	0	0	$20,500	$65,500
12	$22,000	1	1	0	1	1	0	0	$20,500	$65,500
13	$23,000	0	1	0	1	1	1	1	$23,000	$69,000
14	$24,000	1	1	1	1	1	0	0	$24,000	$75,500
15	$25,000	1	1	0	1	1	1	0	$25,000	$77,500

Recognizing the Optimal Integer Solution

IP algorithms such as brand and bound often find a very good integer solution very quickly. So why do they sometimes run so long? This is due to the *implicit enumeration* aspect of the algorithms. They have difficulty ruling out large numbers of potential solutions until they have searched all regions of the solution space. In other words, they have difficulty recognizing that they might have found the optimal solution because there are many potential solutions they haven't yet explored. When you run Solver on a reasonably large IP model, watch the status bar. Often a very good *incumbent* solution, the best solution found so far, is found within seconds, but then Solver spins its wheels for minutes or even hours trying to verify that this solution is optimal. This is why the default tolerance setting in Solver is 5%, not 0%.

MODELING ISSUES

1. The following modifications of the capital budgeting example can be handled fairly easily. You are asked to explore similar modifications in the problems.

■ Suppose that at most two projects can be selected. In this case you can add a constraint that the sum of the binary variables for the investments is less than or equal to 2. This constraint is satisfied if 0, 1, or 2 investments are chosen, but it is violated if 3 or more investments are chosen.

■ Suppose that if investment 2 is selected, then investment 1 must also be selected. In this case you can add a constraint saying that the binary variable for investment 1 is greater than or equal to the binary variable for investment 2. This constraint rules out the one possibility that is not allowed—where investment 2 is selected but investment 1 is not.

■ Suppose that either investment 1 or investment 3 (or both) *must* be selected. In this case you can add a constraint that the sum of the binary variables for investments 1 and 3 must be greater than or equal to 1. This rules out the one possibility that is not allowed—where both of these binary variables are 0, so that neither investment is selected.

2. Capital budgeting models with multiple periods can also be handled. Figure 14.45 shows one possibility. (See the **Capital Budgeting 2.xlsx** file.) The costs in rows 5 and 6 are *both* incurred if any given investment is selected. Now there are two budget constraints, one in each year, but otherwise the model is exactly as before. Note that some investments could have a cost of 0 in year 1 and a positive cost in year 2. This would mean that these investments are undertaken in year 2 rather than year 1. Also, it would be easy to modify the model to incorporate costs in years 3, 4, and so on.

3. If Tatham could choose a *fractional* amount of an investment, then you could maximize its NPV by deleting the binary constraint. The optimal solution to the resulting LP model has a total NPV of $48,714. All of investments 1, 2, and 4, and 0.214 of investment 5 are chosen. Note that there is no way to round the changing cell values from this LP solution to obtain the optimal IP solution. Sometimes the solution to an IP model *without* the integer constraints bears little resemblance to the optimal IP solution.

Figure 14.45   A Two-Period Capital Budgeting Model

	A	B	C	D	E	F	G	H
1	Tatham two-period capital budgeting model							
2								
3	Input data on potential investments							
4	Investment	1	2	3	4	5	6	7
5	Year 1 cost	$5,000	$2,500	$3,500	$6,500	$7,000	$4,500	$3,000
6	Year 2 cost	$2,000	$1,500	$2,000	$0	$500	$1,500	$0
7	NPV	$16,000	$8,000	$10,000	$20,000	$22,000	$12,000	$8,000
8								
9	Decisions: whether to invest							
10	Investment levels	1	1	0	1	0	0	0
11								
12	Budget constraints							
13		Amount invested		Budget				
14		$14,000	<=	$14,000				
15		$3,500	<=	$4,500				
16								
17	Objective to maximize							
18	Total NPV	$44,000						
19								
20	Range names used:							
21	Amount_invested	=Model!$B$14:$B$15						
22	Budget	=Model!$D$14:$D$15						
23	Investment_levels	=Model!$B$10:$H$10						
24	Total_NPV	=Model!$B$18						

4. Any IP involving binary variables with only one constraint is called a *knapsack problem*. Think of the problem faced by a hiker going on an overnight hike. For example, imagine that the hiker's knapsack can hold only 34 pounds, and she must choose which of several available items to take on the hike. The benefit derived from each item is analogous to the NPV of each project, and the weight of each item is analogous to the cash required by each investment. The single constraint is analogous to the budget constraint—that is, only 34 pounds can fit in the knapsack. In a knapsack problem, the goal is to get the most value in the knapsack without overloading it. ∎

14.7.2 Fixed-Cost Models

In many situations a fixed cost is incurred if an activity is undertaken at *any positive* level. This cost is independent of the level of the activity and is known as a **fixed cost** (or fixed charge). Here are three examples of fixed costs:

- Construction of a warehouse incurs a fixed cost that is the same whether the warehouse is used at partial or full capacity.

- A cash withdrawal from a bank incurs a fixed cost, independent of the size of the withdrawal, due to the time spent at the bank.

- A machine that is used to make several products must be set up for the production of each product. Regardless of the number of units of a product the company produces, the same fixed cost (lost production due to the setup time) is incurred.

In these examples a fixed cost is incurred if an activity is undertaken at any positive level, and zero fixed cost is incurred if the activity is not undertaken at all. Although it might not be obvious, this feature makes the problem inherently *nonlinear*, which means that a straightforward application of LP is not possible. However, the following example illustrates how a clever use of binary variables results in a *linear* model.

Binary Variables for Modeling

Binary variables are often used to transform a non-linear model into a linear (integer) model. For example, a fixed cost is not a linear function of the level of some activity; it is either incurred or it isn't incurred. This type of all-or-nothing behavior is difficult for nonlinear algorithms to handle. However, this behavior can often be handled easily when binary variables are used to make the model linear. Still, large models with many binary variables can be difficult to solve. One approach is to solve the model without integer constraints and then round fractional values to the nearest integer (0 or 1). Unfortunately, this approach is typically not very good because the rounded solution is often infeasible. Even if it is feasible, its objective value can be considerably worse than the optimal objective value.

EXAMPLE | 14.9 TEXTILE MANUFACTURING AT GREAT THREADS

The Great Threads Company is capable of manufacturing shirts, shorts, pants, skirts, and jackets. Each type of clothing requires Great Threads to acquire the appropriate type of machinery. The machinery needed to manufacture each type of clothing must be rented at the weekly rates shown in Table 14.14. This table also lists the amounts of cloth and labor required per unit of clothing, as well as the sales price and the unit variable cost for each type of clothing. There are 4000 labor hours and 4500 square yards (sq yd) of cloth available in a given week. The company wants to find a solution that maximizes its weekly profit.

Table 14.14 Data for Great Threads Example

	Rental Cost	Labor Hours	Cloth (sq yd)	Sales Price	Unit Variable Cost
Shirts	$1500	2.0	3.0	$35	$20
Shorts	$1200	1.0	2.5	$40	$10
Pants	$1600	6.0	4.0	$65	$25
Skirts	$1500	4.0	4.5	$70	$30
Jackets	$1600	8.0	5.5	$110	$35

Objective To develop a linear model with binary variables that can be used to maximize the company's profit, correctly accounting for fixed costs and staying within resource availabilities.

WHERE DO THE NUMBERS COME FROM?

Except for the fixed costs, this is the same basic problem as the product mix problem (Examples 13.1 and 13.2) in Chapter 13. Therefore, the same discussion there about input variables applies here. As for the fixed costs, they are the given rental rates for the machinery.

Solution

The variables and constraints required for this model are listed in Table 14.15. Note that the cost of producing x shirts during a week is 0 if $x = 0$, but it is $1500 + 20x$ if $x > 0$. This cost structure violates the proportionality assumption (discussed in the previous chapter) that is needed for a linear model. If proportionality were satisfied, the cost of making, say, 10 shirts would be double the cost of making five shirts. However, because of the fixed cost, the total cost of making five shirts is $1600, and the cost of making 10 shirts is only $1700. This violation of proportionality requires you to resort to binary variables to obtain a *linear* model. Specifically, these binary variables model the fixed costs correctly, as explained in detail here.

Table 14.15 Variables and Constraints for Fixed-Cost Model

Input variables	Fixed rental costs, resource usages (labor hours, cloth) per unit of clothing, sales prices, unit variable costs, resource availabilities
Decision variables (changing cells)	Whether to produce any of each clothing (binary), how much of each clothing to produce
Objective cell	Profit
Other calculated variables	Resources used, upper limits on amounts to produce, total revenue, total variable cost, total fixed cost
Constraints	Amount produced $\leq$ Logical upper limit (capacity) Resources used $\leq$ Resources available

DEVELOPING THE SPREADSHEET MODEL

The spreadsheet model, shown in Figure 14.46, can now be developed as follows. (See the file **Fixed Cost Manufacturing.xlsx**.)

Figure 14.46 Fixed-Cost Clothing Model

	A	B	C	D	E	F	G	H	I	J	K
1	Great Threads fixed cost clothing model								Range names used:		
2									Logical_upper_limit	=Model!$B$18:$F$18	
3	Input data on products								Produce_any?	=Model!$B$14:$F$14	
4		Shirts	Shorts	Pants	Skirts	Jackets			Profit	=Model!$B$29	
5	Labor hours/unit	2	1	6	4	8			Resource_available	=Model!$D$22:$D$23	
6	Cloth (sq. yd.)/unit	3	2.5	4	4.5	5.5			Resource_used	=Model!$B$22:$B$23	
7									Units_produced	=Model!$B$16:$F$16	
8	Selling price/unit	$35	$40	$65	$70	$110					
9	Variable cost/unit	$20	$10	$25	$30	$35					
10	Fixed cost for equipment	$1,500	$1,200	$1,600	$1,500	$1,600					
11											
12	Production plan, constraints on capacity										
13		Shirts	Shorts	Pants	Skirts	Jackets					
14	Produce any?	0	1	0	0	1					
15											
16	Units produced	0	965.52	0	0	379.31					
17		<=	<=	<=	<=	<=					
18	Logical upper limit	0.00	1800.00	0.00	0.00	500.00					
19											
20	Constraints on resources										
21		Resource used		Available							
22	Labor hours	4000.00	<=	4000							
23	Cloth	4500.00	<=	4500							
24											
25	Monetary outputs										
26	Revenue	$80,345									
27	Variable cost	$22,931									
28	Fixed cost for equipment	$2,800									
29	Profit	$54,614	←	Objective to maximize							

1 **Inputs.** Enter the given inputs.

2 **Binary values for clothing types.** Enter *any* trial values for the binary variables for the various clothing types in the Produce_any? range. For example, a 1 in cell C14 implies that *some* shorts are produced. More importantly, it implies that the machinery for making shorts is rented and its fixed cost is incurred.

3 **Production quantities.** Enter *any* trial values for the numbers of the various clothing types produced in the Units_produced range. At this point you could enter "illegal" values, such as 0 in cell B14 and a positive value in cell B16. This is illegal because it implies that the company produces some shirts but avoids the fixed cost of the machinery for shirts. However, Solver will eventually disallow such illegal combinations.

4 **Labor and cloth used.** In cell B22 enter the formula

=SUMPRODUCT(B5:F5,Units_produced)

to calculate total labor hours, and copy this to cell B23 for cloth.

5 **Effective capacities.** Here is the tricky part of the model. You need to ensure that if any of a given type of clothing is produced, then its binary variable equals 1. This ensures that the model incurs the fixed cost of renting the machine for this type of clothing. You could easily implement these constraints with IF statements. For example, to implement the constraint for shirts, you could enter the following formula in cell B14:

=IF(B16>0,1,0)

However, Solver is unable to deal with IF functions predictably. Therefore, the fixed-cost constraints are modeled in a different way, as follows:

$$\text{Shirts produced} \leq \text{Maximum capacity} \times (0\text{--}1 \text{ variable for shirts}) \qquad \textbf{(14.4)}$$

There are similar inequalities for the other types of clothing.

Here is the logic behind inequality (14.4). If the 0–1 variable for shirts is 0, then the right side of the inequality is 0, which means that the left side must be 0—no shirts can be produced. That is, if the binary variable for shirts is 0, so that no fixed cost for shirts is incurred, then inequality (14.4) does not allow Great Threads to "cheat" and produce a positive number of shirts. On the other hand, if the binary variable for shirts is 1, the inequality is certainly true and is essentially redundant. It simply states that the number of shirts produced must be no greater than the *maximum* number that could be produced. Inequality (14.4) rules out the one case that needs to be ruled out—namely, that Great Threads produces shirts but avoids the fixed cost.

To implement inequality (14.4), a maximum capacity is required. To obtain this, suppose the company puts all of its resources into producing shirts. Then the number of shirts that can be produced is limited by the smaller of

$$\frac{\text{Available labor hours}}{\text{Labor hours per shirt}}$$

and

$$\frac{\text{Available square yards of cloth}}{\text{Square yards of cloth per shirt}}$$

Therefore, the smaller of these—the most limiting—can be used as the maximum needed in inequality (14.4).

To implement this logic, calculate the effective capacity for shirts in cell B18 with the formula

=B14*MIN($D$22/B5,$D$23/B6)

Then copy this formula to the range C16:F16 for the other types of clothing.[12] By the way, this MIN formula causes no problems for Solver because it does not involve *changing* cells, only input cells.

6 Monetary values. Calculate the total sales revenue and the total variable cost by entering the formula

=SUMPRODUCT(B8:F8,Units_produced)

in cell B26 and copying it to cell B27. Then calculate the total fixed cost in cell B28 with the formula

=SUMPRODUCT(B10:F10,Produce_any?)

Note that this formula sums the fixed costs only for those products with binary variables equal to 1. Finally, calculate the total profit in cell B29 with the formula

=B26-B27-B28

USING SOLVER

The Solver dialog box is shown in Figure 14.47. The goal is to maximize profit, subject to using no more labor hours or cloth than are available, and ensure that production is less

Figure 14.47
Solver Dialog Box for Fixed-Cost Model

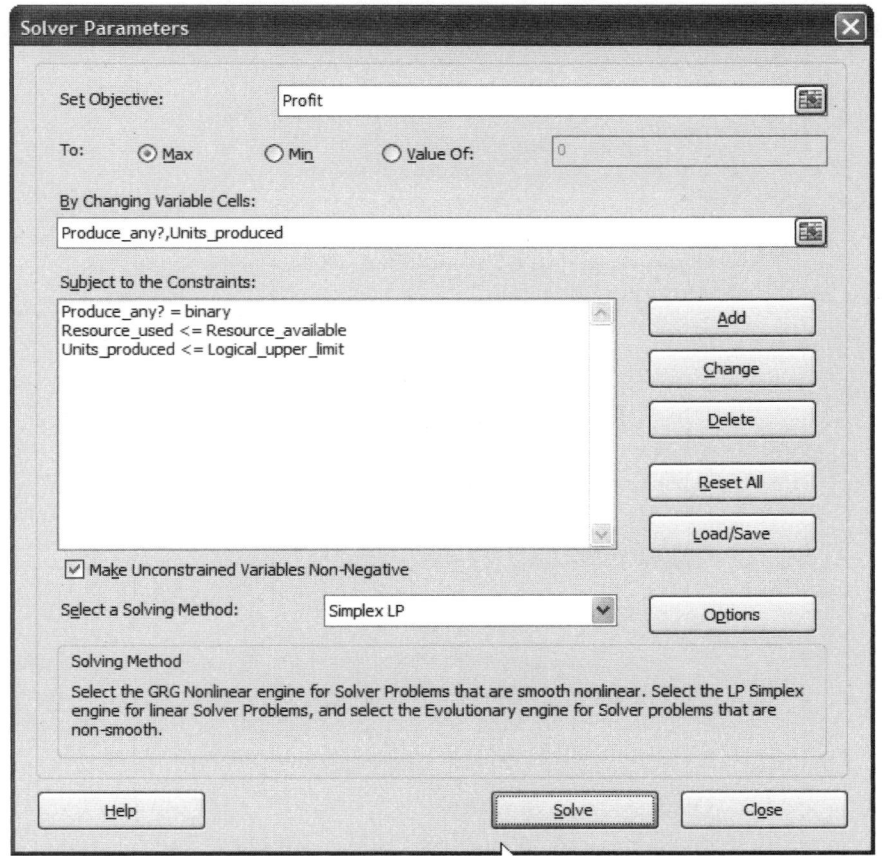

[12]Why not set the upper limit on shirts equal to a huge number like 1,000,000? The reason is that Solver works most efficiently when the upper limit is as tight—that is, as low—as possible. A tighter upper limit means fewer potential feasible solutions for Solver to search through. Here's an analogy. If you were trying to locate a criminal, which would be easier: (1) if you were told that he was somewhere in Texas, or (2) if you were told he was somewhere in Dallas?

than or equal to *effective* capacity. The key is that this effective capacity is zero if none of a given type of clothing is produced. As usual, check the Non-Negative option, and set the tolerance to zero (under the Options button). Importantly, note that by using binary changing cells, the resulting model is *linear*, which means that the simplex algorithm can be used.

Although Solver finds the optimal solution automatically, you should understand the effect of the logical upper-bound constraint on production. It rules out a solution such as the one shown in Figure 14.48. This solution calls for a positive production level of pants but does not incur the fixed cost of the pants equipment. The logical upper-bound constraint rules this out because it prevents a positive value in row 16 if the corresponding binary value in row 14 is 0. In other words, if the company wants to produce some pants, the constraint in inequality (14.4) forces the associated binary variable to be 1, thus incurring the fixed cost for pants.

Figure 14.48 An Illegal (and Nonoptimal) Solution

	A	B	C	D	E	F	G	H	I	J	K
1	Great Threads fixed cost clothing model								Range names used:		
2									Logical_upper_limit	=Model!$B$18:$F$18	
3	Input data on products								Produce_any?	=Model!$B$14:$F$14	
4		Shirts	Shorts	Pants	Skirts	Jackets			Profit	=Model!$B$29	
5	Labor hours/unit	2	1	6	4	8			Resource_available	=Model!$D$22:$D$23	
6	Cloth (sq. yd.)/unit	3	2.5	4	4.5	5.5			Resource_used	=Model!$B$22:$B$23	
7									Units_produced	=Model!$B$16:$F$16	
8	Selling price/unit	$35	$40	$65	$70	$110					
9	Variable cost/unit	$20	$10	$25	$30	$35					
10	Fixed cost for equipment	$1,500	$1,200	$1,600	$1,500	$1,600					
11											
12	Production plan, constraints on capacity										
13		Shirts	Shorts	Pants	Skirts	Jackets					
14	Produce any?	0	1	0	1	1					
15											
16	Units produced	0	965.52	450	0	379.31					
17		<=	<=	<=	<=	<=					
18	Logical upper limit	0.00	1800.00	0.00	1000.00	500.00					
19											
20	Constraints on resources										
21		Resource used		Available							
22	Labor hours	6700.00	<=	4000							
23	Cloth	6300.00	<=	4500							
24											
25	Monetary outputs										
26	Revenue	$109,595									
27	Variable cost	$34,181									
28	Fixed cost for equipment	$4,300									
29	Profit	$71,114	←	Objective to maximize							

Note that inequality (14.4) does *not* rule out the situation you see for skirts, where the binary value is 1 and the production level is 0. However, Solver will never choose this type of solution as optimal. Solver recognizes that the binary value in this case can be changed to 0, so that the fixed cost for skirt equipment is not incurred.

Discussion of the Solution

The optimal solution appears in Figure 14.46. It indicates that Great Threads should produce about 966 shorts and 379 jackets, but no shirts, pants, or skirts. The total profit is $54,614. Note that the binary variables for shirts, pants, and skirts are all 0, which forces production of these products to be 0. However, the binary variables for shorts and jackets, the products that are produced, are 1. This ensures that the fixed cost of producing shorts and jackets is included in the total cost.

It might be helpful to think of this solution as occurring in two stages. In the first stage Solver determines which products to produce—in this case, shorts and jackets only. Then in the second stage, Solver decides how *many* shorts and jackets to produce. If you knew that the company plans to produce shorts and jackets only, you could then ignore the fixed costs and determine the best production quantities with the same types of product mix models discussed in the previous chapter. Of course, these two stages—deciding which products to produce and how many of each to produce—are interrelated, and Solver considers both of them in its solution process.

As always, adding constraints can only make the objective worse. In this case, it means decreased profit.

The Great Threads management might not be very excited about producing shorts and jackets only. Suppose the company wants to ensure that at least three types of clothing are produced at positive levels. One approach is to add another constraint—namely, that the sum of the binary values in row 14 is greater than or equal to 3. You can check, however, that when this constraint is added and Solver is rerun, the binary variable for skirts becomes 1, but no skirts are produced. Shorts and jackets are more profitable than skirts, so only shorts and jackets are produced. (See Figure 14.49.) The new constraint forces Great Threads to rent an extra piece of machinery (for skirts), but it doesn't force the company to use it. To force the company to produce some skirts, you would also need to add a constraint on the value in E16, such as E16 >= 100. Any of these additional constraints will cost Great Threads money, but if, as a matter of policy, the company wants to produce more than two types of clothing, this is its only option.

Figure 14.49
Fixed-Cost Model with Extra Constraint

	A	B	C	D	E	F	G	H	I
1	Great Threads fixed cost clothing model								
2									
3	Input data on products								
4		Shirts	Shorts	Pants	Skirts	Jackets			
5	Labor hours/unit	2	1	6	4	8			
6	Cloth (sq. yd.)/unit	3	2.5	4	4.5	5.5			
7									
8	Selling price/unit	$35	$40	$65	$70	$110			
9	Variable cost/unit	$20	$10	$25	$30	$35			
10	Fixed cost for equipment	$1,500	$1,200	$1,600	$1,500	$1,600			
11									
12	Production plan, constraints on capacity								
13		Shirts	Shorts	Pants	Skirts	Jackets	Sum		Required
14	Produce any?	0	1	0	1	1	3	>=	3
15									
16	Units produced	0	965.52	0	0	379.31			
17		<=	<=	<=	<=	<=			
18	Logical upper limit	0.00	1800.00	0.00	1000.00	500.00			
19									
20	Constraints on resources								
21		Resource used		Available					
22	Labor hours	4000.00	<=	4000					
23	Cloth	4500.00	<=	4500					
24									
25	Monetary outputs								
26	Revenue	$80,345							
27	Variable cost	$22,931							
28	Fixed cost for equipment	$4,300							
29	Profit	$53,114	←	Objective to maximize					

Sensitivity Analysis

Because the optimal solution currently calls for only shorts and jackets to be produced, an interesting sensitivity analysis is to see how much incentive is required for other products to be produced. One way to model this is to increase the selling price for a nonproduced product such as skirts in a one-way SolverTable. The results of this, keeping track of all binary variables and profit, are shown in Figure 14.50. When the selling price for skirts is $85 or less, the company continues to produce only shorts and jackets. However, when the selling price is $90 or greater, the company stops producing shorts and jackets and produces *only* skirts. You can check that the optimal production quantity of skirts is 1000 when the selling price of skirts is any value $90 or above. The only reason that the profits in Figure 14.50 increase from row 9 down is that the revenues from these 1000 skirts increase.

Figure 14.50

Sensitivity of Binary Variables to Selling Price of Skirts

	A	B	C	D	E	F	G
3	Skirt price (cell $E$8) values along side, output cell(s) along top						
4		Produce_any?_1	Produce_any?_2	Produce_any?_3	Produce_any?_4	Produce_any?_5	Profit
5	$70	0	1	0	0	1	$54,614
6	$75	0	1	0	0	1	$54,614
7	$80	0	1	0	0	1	$54,614
8	$85	0	1	0	0	1	$54,614
9	$90	0	0	0	1	0	$58,500
10	$95	0	0	0	1	0	$63,500
11	$100	0	0	0	1	0	$68,500

A Model with IF Functions

In case you are still not convinced that the binary variable approach is required, and you think IF functions could be used instead, take a look at the last sheet in the finished version of the file. The resulting model *looks* the same as in Figure 14.46, but it incorporates the following changes:

- The binary range is no longer part of the changing cells range. Instead, the formula =IF(B16>0,1,0) is entered in cell B14 and copied across to cell F14. Logically, this probably appears more natural. If a production quantity is positive, a 1 is entered in row 14, which means that the fixed cost is incurred.

- The effective capacities are calculated in row 18 with IF functions. Specifically, the formula =IF(B16>0,MIN($D$22/B5,$D$23/B6),0) is entered in cell B18 and copied across to cell F18.

- The Solver dialog box is modified as shown in Figure 14.51. The Produce_any? range is not part of the changing cells range, and there is no binary constraint. The simplex method cannot be used because the IF functions make the model nonlinear.

When we ran Solver on this modified model, we found inconsistent results, depending on the initial production quantities entered in row 16. For example, when we entered initial values all equal to 0, the Solver solution was exactly that—all 0s. Of course, this solution is *terrible* because it leads to a profit of $0. However, when we entered initial production quantities all equal to 100, Solver found the correct optimal solution, the same as in Figure 14.46. Was this just lucky? To check, we tried another initial solution, where the production quantities for shorts and jackets were 0, and the production quantities for shirts, pants, and skirts were all 500. In this case Solver found a solution where only skirts are produced. Of course, we know this is not optimal.

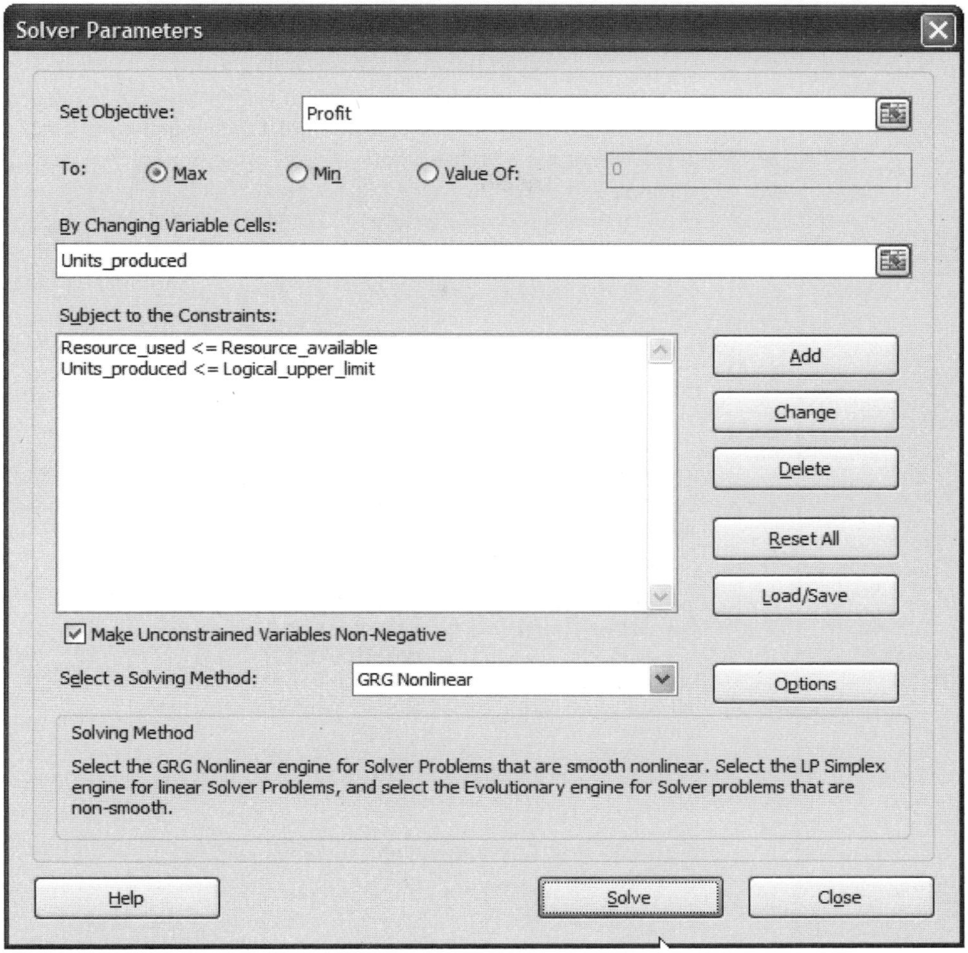

Figure 14.51

Solver Dialog Box
When IF Functions
Are Used

Solver Parameters

Se_t Objective: Profit

To: ⦿ _M_ax   ◯ Mi_n_   ◯ _V_alue Of: 0

_B_y Changing Variable Cells:

Units_produced

Su_b_ject to the Constraints:

Resource_used <= Resource_available
Units_produced <= Logical_upper_limit

[Add]
[_C_hange]
[_D_elete]
[_R_eset All]
[Load/Save]

☑ Ma_k_e Unconstrained Variables Non-Negative

Se_l_ect a Solving Method: GRG Nonlinear ▾   [O_p_tions]

Solving Method

Select the GRG Nonlinear engine for Solver Problems that are smooth nonlinear. Select the LP Simplex engine for linear Solver Problems, and select the Evolutionary engine for Solver problems that are non-smooth.

[_H_elp]   [_S_olve]   [Close]

The moral is that the IF-function approach is not the way to go. Its success depends strongly on the initial values in the changing cells, and this requires very good guesses. The binary approach ensures that Solver finds the correct solution. ∎

14.7.3 Set-Covering Models

In a set-covering model, each member of a given set (set 1) must be "covered" by an acceptable member of another set (set 2). The objective in a set-covering problem is to minimize the number of members in set 2 necessary to cover all the members in set 1. For example, set 1 might consist of all the cities in a county and set 2 might consist of the cities in which a fire station is located. A member of set 2 covers, or handles the needs of, a city in set 1 if the fire station is located within, say, 10 minutes of the city. The goal is to minimize the number of fire stations needed to cover all cities. Set-covering models have been applied to areas as diverse as airline crew scheduling, truck dispatching, political redistricting, and capital investment. The following is a typical set-covering model.

EXAMPLE | **14.10 HUB LOCATION AT WESTERN AIRLINES**

Western Airlines has decided that it wants to design a hub system in the United States. Each hub is used for connecting flights to and from cities within 1000 miles of the hub. Western runs flights among the following cities: Atlanta, Boston, Chicago, Denver, Houston, Los Angeles, New Orleans, New York, Pittsburgh, Salt Lake City, San Francisco, and Seattle. The company wants to determine the smallest number of hubs it will need to cover all of these cities, where a city is "covered" if it is within 1000 miles of at least one hub. Table 14.16 lists the cities that are within 1000 miles of other cities.

Table 14.16 Data for Western Airlines Set-Covering Example

	Cities Within 1000 Miles
Atlanta (AT)	AT, CH, HO, NO, NY, PI
Boston (BO)	BO, NY, PI
Chicago (CH)	AT, CH, NY, NO, PI
Denver (DE)	DE, SL
Houston (HO)	AT, HO, NO
Los Angeles (LA)	LA, SL, SF
New Orleans (NO)	AT, CH, HO, NO
New York (NY)	AT, BO, CH, NY, PI
Pittsburgh (PI)	AT, BO, CH, NY, PI
Salt Lake City (SL)	DE, LA, SL, SF, SE
San Francisco (SF)	LA, SL, SF, SE
Seattle (SE)	SL, SF, SE

Objective To develop a binary model to find the minimum number of hub locations that can cover all cities.

WHERE DO THE NUMBERS COME FROM?

Western has evidently made a policy decision that its hubs will cover cities within a 1000-mile radius. Then the cities covered by any hub location can be found from a map. (In a later sensitivity analysis, we explore how the solution changes when the allowable coverage distance varies.)

Solution

The variables and constraints for this set-covering model are listed in Table 14.17. The model is straightforward. There is a binary variable for each city to indicate whether a hub is located there. Then the number of hubs that cover each city is constrained to be at least one. There are no monetary costs in this version of the problem. The goal is to minimize the number of hubs.

Table 14.17 Variables and Constraints for Set-Covering Model

Input variables	Cities within 1000 miles of one another
Decision variables (changing cells)	Locations of hubs (binary)
Objective cell	Number of hubs
Other calculated variables	Number of hubs covering each city
Constraints	Number of hubs covering a city $\geq$ 1

DEVELOPING THE SPREADSHEET MODEL

The spreadsheet model for Western is shown in Figure 14.52. (See the file **Locating Hubs1.xlsx**.) It can be developed as follows.

Figure 14.52 Set-Covering Model

	A	B	C	D	E	F	G	H	I	J	K	L	M	N	O	P	Q
1	Western Airlines hub location model																
2																	
3	Input data: which cities are covered by which potential hubs														Range names used:		
4		Potential hub													Hubs_covered_by	=Model!$B$25:$B$36	
5	City	AT	BO	CH	DE	HO	LA	NO	NY	PI	SL	SF	SE		Total_hubs	=Model!$B$39	
6	AT	1	0	1	0	1	0	1	1	1	0	0	0		Used_as_hub?	=Model!$B$21:$M$21	
7	BO	0	1	0	0	0	0	0	1	1	0	0	0				
8	CH	1	0	1	0	0	0	1	1	1	0	0	0				
9	DE	0	0	0	1	0	0	0	0	0	1	0	0				
10	HO	1	0	0	0	1	0	1	0	0	0	0	0				
11	LA	0	0	0	0	0	1	0	0	0	1	1	0				
12	NO	1	0	1	0	1	0	1	0	0	0	0	0				
13	NY	1	1	1	0	0	0	0	1	1	0	0	0				
14	PI	1	1	1	0	0	0	0	1	1	0	0	0				
15	SL	0	0	0	1	0	1	0	0	0	1	1	1				
16	SF	0	0	0	0	0	1	0	0	0	1	1	1				
17	SE	0	0	0	0	0	0	0	0	0	1	1	1				
18																	
19	Decisions: which cities to use as hubs																
20		AT	BO	CH	DE	HO	LA	NO	NY	PI	SL	SF	SE				
21	Used as hub?	0	0	0	0	1	0	0	1	0	1	0	0				
22																	
23	Constraints that each city must be covered by at least one hub																
24	City	Hubs covered by		Required													
25	AT	2	>=	1													
26	BO	1	>=	1													
27	CH	1	>=	1													
28	DE	1	>=	1													
29	HO	1	>=	1													
30	LA	1	>=	1													
31	NO	1	>=	1													
32	NY	1	>=	1													
33	PI	1	>=	1													
34	SL	1	>=	1													
35	SF	1	>=	1													
36	SE	1	>=	1													
37																	
38	Objective to minimize																
39	Total hubs	3															

Note that there are multiple optimal solutions to this model, all of which require a total of 3 hubs. You might get a different solution from the one shown here.

1 **Inputs.** Enter the information from Table 14.16 in the input cells. A 1 in a cell indicates that the column city covers the row city, whereas a 0 indicates that the column city does not cover the row city. For example, the three 1s in row 7 indicate that Boston, New York, and Pittsburgh are the only cities within 1000 miles of Boston.

2 **Binary values for hub locations.** Enter *any* trial values of 0s or 1s in the Used_as_hub? range to indicate which cities are used as hubs. These are the changing cells.

3 **Cities covered by hubs.** Calculate the total number of hubs within 1000 miles of Atlanta in cell B25 with the formula

=SUMPRODUCT(B6:M6,Used_as_hub?)

For any binary values in the changing-cells range, this formula sums the number of hubs that cover Atlanta. Then copy this to the rest of the Hubs_covered_by range. Note that a value in the Hubs_covered_by range can be 2 or greater. This indicates that a city is within 1000 miles of multiple hubs.

4 Number of hubs. Calculate the total number of hubs used in cell B39 with the formula

=SUM(Used_as_hub?)

USING SOLVER

The completed Solver dialog box is shown in Figure 14.53. The goal is to minimize the total number of hubs, subject to covering each city by at least one hub and ensuring that the changing cells are binary.

Figure 14.53
Solver Dialog Box for Set-Covering Model

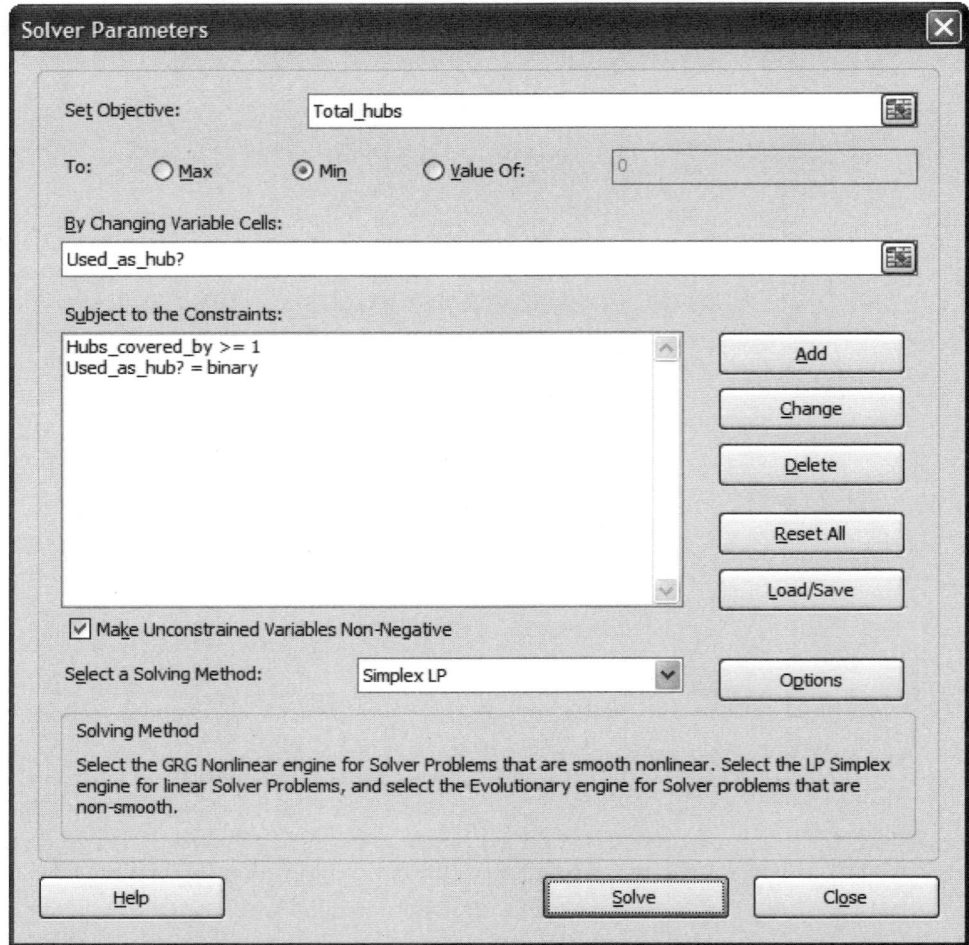

Discussion of the Solution

Figure 14.54 is a graphical representation of the optimal solution, where the double ovals indicate hub locations and the large circles indicate ranges covered by the hubs. (These large circles are not drawn to scale. In reality, they should be circles of radius 1000 miles centered at the hubs.) Three hubs—in Houston, New York, and Salt Lake City—are needed.[13] Would you have guessed this? The Houston hub covers Houston, Atlanta, and New Orleans. The New York hub covers Atlanta, Pittsburgh, Boston, New York, and Chicago. The Salt Lake City hub covers Denver, Los Angeles, Salt Lake City, San Francisco, and Seattle. Note that Atlanta is the only city covered by two hubs; it can be serviced by New York or Houston.

Figure 14.54
Graphical Solution to Set-Covering Model

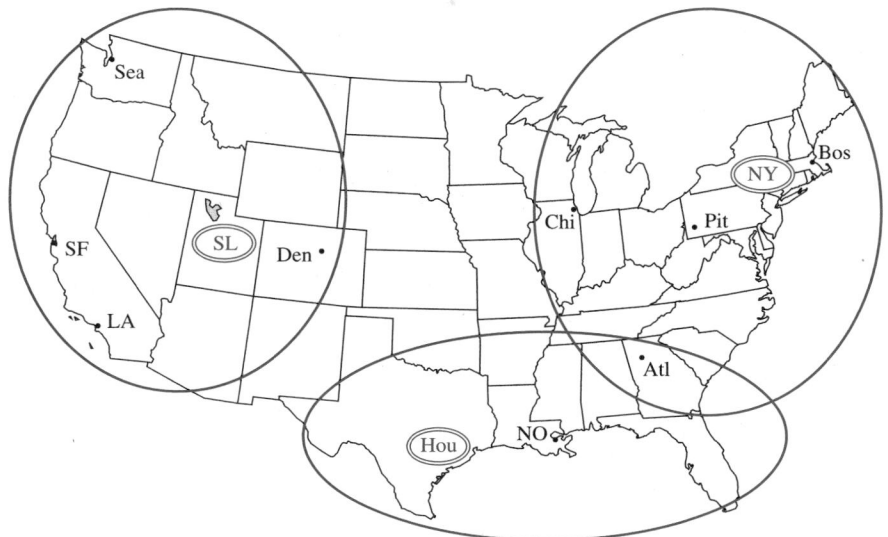

Sensitivity Analysis

An interesting sensitivity analysis for Western's problem is to see how the solution is affected by the mile limit. Currently, a hub can service all cities within 1000 miles. What if the limit were 800 or 1200 miles, say? To answer this question, you must first collect data on actual distances among all of the cities. Once you have a table of these distances, you can build the binary table, corresponding to the range B6:M17 in Figure 14.52, with IF functions. The modified model appears in Figure 14.55. (See the file **Locating Hubs 2.xlsx**.) The typical formula in B24 is =**IF(B8<=$B$4,1,0)**, which is then copied to the rest of the B24:M35 range.[14] You can then run SolverTable, selecting cell B4 as the single input cell, letting it vary from 800 to 1200 in increments of 100, and designating the hub locations and the number of hubs as outputs. The SolverTable results in Figure 14.56 show the effect of the mile limit. When this limit is lowered to 800 miles, four hubs are required, but when it is increased to 1100 or 1200, only two hubs are required. Note that the solution shown for the 1000-mile limit is different from the previous solution in Figure 14.52, but it still requires three hubs. (This is a case of multiple optimal solutions.)

[13]There are multiple optimal solutions for this model, all requiring three hubs, so you might obtain a different solution from ours.
[14]We have warned you about using IF functions in Solver models. However, the current use affects only the *inputs* to the problem, not quantities that depend on the changing cells. Therefore, it causes no problems.

Figure 14.55 Modified Hub Location Model

	A	B	C	D	E	F	G	H	I	J	K	L	M	N	O	P	Q
1	Western Airlines hub location model with distances														Range names used:		
2															Hubs_covered_by	=Model!$B$43:$B$54	
3	Input data														Total_hubs	=Model!$B$57	
4	Mile limit	1000													Used_as_hub?	=Model!$B$39:$M$39	
5																	
6	Distance from each city to each other city																
7		AT	BO	CH	DE	HO	LA	NO	NY	PI	SL	SF	SE				
8	AT	0	1037	674	1398	789	2182	479	841	687	1878	2496	2618				
9	BO	1037	0	1005	1949	1804	2979	1507	222	574	2343	3095	2976				
10	CH	674	1005	0	1008	1067	2054	912	802	452	1390	2142	2013				
11	DE	1398	1949	1008	0	1019	1059	1273	1771	1411	504	1235	1307				
12	HO	789	1804	1067	1019	0	1538	356	1608	1313	1438	1912	2274				
13	LA	2182	2979	2054	1059	1538	0	1883	2786	2426	715	379	1131				
14	NO	479	1507	912	1273	356	1883	0	1311	1070	1738	2249	2574				
15	NY	841	222	802	1771	1608	2786	1311	0	368	2182	2934	2815				
16	PI	687	574	452	1411	1313	2426	1070	368	0	1826	2578	2465				
17	SL	1878	2343	1390	504	1438	715	1738	2182	1826	0	752	836				
18	SF	2496	3095	2142	1235	1912	379	2249	2934	2578	752	0	808				
19	SE	2618	2976	2013	1307	2274	1131	2574	2815	2465	836	808	0				
20																	
21	Which cities are covered by which potential hubs with this mile limit																
22		Potential hub															
23	City	AT	BO	CH	DE	HO	LA	NO	NY	PI	SL	SF	SE				
24	AT	1	0	1	0	1	0	1	1	1	0	0	0				
25	BO	0	1	0	0	0	0	0	1	1	0	0	0				
26	CH	1	0	1	0	0	0	1	1	1	0	0	0				
27	DE	0	0	0	1	0	0	0	0	0	1	0	0				
28	HO	1	0	0	0	1	0	1	0	0	0	0	0				
29	LA	0	0	0	0	0	1	0	0	0	1	1	0				
30	NO	1	0	1	0	1	0	1	0	0	0	0	0				
31	NY	1	1	1	0	0	0	0	1	1	0	0	0				
32	PI	1	1	1	0	0	0	0	1	1	0	0	0				
33	SL	0	0	0	1	0	1	0	0	0	1	1	1				
34	SF	0	0	0	0	0	1	0	0	0	1	1	1				
35	SE	0	0	0	0	0	0	0	0	0	1	1	1				
36																	
37	Decisions: which cities to use as hubs																
38		AT	BO	CH	DE	HO	LA	NO	NY	PI	SL	SF	SE				
39	Used as hub?	0	0	0	0	1	0	0	1	0	1	0	0				
40																	
41	Constraints that each city must be covered by at least one hub																
42	City	Hubs covered by		Required													
43	AT	2	>=	1													
44	BO	1	>=	1													
45	CH	1	>=	1													
46	DE	1	>=	1													
47	HO	1	>=	1													
48	LA	1	>=	1													
49	NO	1	>=	1													
50	NY	1	>=	1													
51	PI	1	>=	1													
52	SL	1	>=	1													
53	SF	1	>=	1													
54	SE	1	>=	1													
55																	
56	Objective to minimize																
57	Total hubs	3															

Note: There are multiple optimal solutions to these problems, so don't be surprised if you don't get exactly the same hub locations as shown here.

Figure 14.56 Sensitivity to Mile Limit

	A	B	C	D	E	F	G	H	I	J	K	L	M	N
3	Mile limit (cell $B$4) values along side, output cell(s) along top													
4		Used_as_hub?_1	Used_as_hub?_2	Used_as_hub?_3	Used_as_hub?_4	Used_as_hub?_5	Used_as_hub?_6	Used_as_hub?_7	Used_as_hub?_8	Used_as_hub?_9	Used_as_hub?_10	Used_as_hub?_11	Used_as_hub?_12	Total_hubs
5	800	1	1	0	0	0	0	0	0	0	1	0	1	4
6	900	1	1	0	0	0	0	0	0	0	1	0	0	3
7	1000	1	1	0	0	0	0	0	0	0	1	0	0	3
8	1100	0	0	1	0	0	0	0	0	0	1	0	0	2
9	1200	0	0	1	0	0	1	0	0	0	0	0	0	2

PROBLEMS

Level A

48. Solve the following modifications of the capital budgeting model in Figure 14.40. (Solve each part independently of the others.)
   a. Suppose that at most two of projects 1 through 5 can be selected.
   b. Suppose that if investment 1 is selected, then investment 3 must also be selected.
   c. Suppose that at least one of investments 6 and 7 *must* be selected.
   d. Suppose that investment 2 can be selected only if *both* investments 1 and 3 are selected.

49. In the capital budgeting model in Figure 14.40, we supplied the NPV for each investment. Suppose instead that you are given only the streams of cash inflows from each investment shown in the file **P14_49.xlsx**. This file also shows the cash requirements and the budget. You can assume that (1) all cash outflows occur at the beginning of year 1; (2) all cash inflows occur at the ends of their respective years; and (3) the company uses a 10% discount rate for calculating its NPVs. Which investments should the company make?

50. Solve the previous problem using the input data in the file **P14_50.xlsx**.

51. Solve Problem 49 with the extra assumption that the investments can be grouped naturally as follows: 1–4, 5–8, 9–12, 13–16, and 17–20.
   a. Find the optimal investments when at most one investment from each group can be selected.
   b. Find the optimal investments when at least one investment from each group must be selected. (If the budget isn't large enough to permit this, increase the budget to a larger value.)

52. In the capital budgeting model in Figure 14.40, investment 4 has the largest ratio of NPV to cash requirement, but it is not selected in the optimal solution. How much NPV is lost if Tatham is *forced* to select investment 4? Answer by solving a suitably modified model.

53. As it currently stands, investment 7 in the capital budgeting model in Figure 14.40 has the lowest ratio of NPV to cash requirement, 2.5. Keeping this same ratio, can you change the cash requirement and NPV for investment 7 in such a way that it *is* selected in the optimal solution? Does this lead to any general insights? Explain.

54. Expand the capital budgeting model in Figure 14.40 so that there are now 20 possible investments. You can make up the data on cash requirements, NPVs, and the budget. However, use the following guidelines:

- The cash requirements and NPVs for the various investments can vary widely, but the ratio of NPV to cash requirement should be between 2.5 and 3.5 for each investment.
- The budget should allow somewhere between 5 and 10 of the investments to be selected.

55. Suppose in the capital budgeting model in Figure 14.40 that each investment requires $2000 during year 2 and only $5000 is available for investment during year 2.
   a. Assuming that available money uninvested at the end of year 1 cannot be used during year 2, what combination of investments maximizes NPV?
   b. Suppose that any uninvested money at the end of year 1 *can* be used for investment in year 2. Does your answer to part **a** change?

56. How difficult is it to expand the Great Threads model to accommodate another type of clothing? Answer by assuming that the company can also produce sweatshirts. The rental cost for sweatshirt equipment is $1100, the variable cost per unit and the selling price are $15 and $45, respectively, and each sweatshirt requires one labor hour and 3.5 square yards of cloth.

57. Referring to the previous problem, if it is optimal for the company to produce sweatshirts, use SolverTable to see how much larger the fixed cost of sweatshirt machinery would have to be before the company would *not* produce any sweatshirts. However, if the solution to the previous problem calls for no sweatshirts to be produced, use SolverTable to see how much lower the fixed cost of sweatshirt machinery would have to be before the company *would* start producing sweatshirts.

58. In the Great Threads model, the production quantities in row 16 were not constrained to be integers. Presumably, any fractional values could be safely rounded to integers. See whether this is true. Constrain these quantities to be integers and then run Solver. Are the optimal integer values the same as the rounded fractional values in Figure 14.46?

59. In the optimal solution to the Great Threads model, the labor hour and cloth constraints are both binding—the company is using all it has.
   a. Use SolverTable to see what happens to the optimal solution when the amount of available cloth increases from its current value. (You can choose the range of input values to use.) Capture all of the changing cells, the labor hours and cloth used, and the profit as outputs. The real issue here is whether the company can profitably use more cloth when it is already constrained by labor hours.

b. Repeat part **a**, but reverse the roles of labor hours and cloth. That is, use the available labor hours as the input for SolverTable.

60. In the optimal solution to the Great Threads model, no pants are produced. Suppose Great Threads has an order for 300 pairs of pants that *must* be produced. Modify the model appropriately and use Solver to find the new optimal solution. (Is it enough to put a lower bound of 300 on the production quantity in cell D16? Will this automatically force the binary value in cell D14 to be 1? Explain.) How much profit does the company lose because of having to produce pants?

61. In the original Western Airlines set-covering model in Figure 14.52, we assumed that each city must be covered by at least one hub. Suppose that for added flexibility in flight routing, Western requires that each city must be covered by at least two hubs. How do the model and optimal solution change?

62. In the original Western Airlines set-covering model in Figure 14.52, we used the number of hubs as the objective to minimize. Suppose instead that there is a fixed cost of locating a hub in any city, where these fixed costs can vary across cities. Make up some reasonable fixed costs, modify the model appropriately, and use Solver to find the solution that minimizes the sum of fixed costs.

63. Set-covering models such as the original Western Airlines model in Figure 14.52 often have multiple optimal solutions. See how many alternative optimal solutions you can find. Of course, each must use three hubs because we know this is optimal. (*Hint*: Use various initial values in the changing cells and then run Solver repeatedly.)[15]

64. How hard is it to expand a set-covering model to accommodate new cities? Answer this by modifying the model in Figure 14.55. (See the file **Locating Hubs 2.xlsx**.) Add several cities that must be served: Memphis, Dallas, Tucson, Philadelphia, Cleveland, and Buffalo. You can look up the distances from these cities to each other and to the other cities in a reference book (or on the Web), or you can make up approximate distances.
  a. Modify the model appropriately, assuming that these new cities must be covered *and* are candidates for hub locations.
  b. Modify the model appropriately, assuming that these new cities must be covered but are *not* candidates for hub locations.

Level B

65. The models in this section are often called *combinatorial* models because each solution is a combination of the various 0s and 1s, and there are only a finite number of such combinations. For the capital budgeting model in Figure 14.40, there are seven investments, so there are $2^7 = 128$ possible solutions (some of which are infeasible). This is a fairly large number, but not *too* large. Solve the model *without* Solver by listing all 128 solutions. For each, calculate the total cash requirement and total NPV for the model. Then manually choose the one that stays within the budget and has the largest NPV.

66. Make up an example, as described in Problem 54, with 20 possible investments. However, do it so that the ratios of NPV to cash requirement are in a very tight range, from 3.0 to 3.2. Then use Solver to find the optimal solution when the Solver tolerance is set to its default value of 5%, and record the solution. Next, solve again with the tolerance set to zero. Do you get the same solution? Try this on a few more instances of the model, where you keep tinkering with the inputs. The question is whether the tolerance matters in these types of narrow-range problems.

67. In the Great Threads model, we found an upper bound on production of any clothing type by calculating the amount that could be produced if *all* of the resources were devoted to this clothing type.
  a. What if you instead use a very large value such as 1,000,000 for this upper bound? Try it and see whether you get the same optimal solution.
  b. Explain why *any* such upper bound is required. Exactly what role does it play in the model?

68. In the last sheet of the finished version of the Fixed Cost Manufacturing file, we illustrated one way to model the Great Threads problem with IF functions, but saw that this approach doesn't work. Try a slightly different approach here. Eliminate the binary variables in row 14 altogether, and eliminate the upper bounds in row 18 and the corresponding upper bound constraints in the Solver dialog box. (The only constraints are now on resource availability.) However, use IF functions to calculate the total fixed cost of renting equipment, so that if the amount of any clothing type is positive, then its fixed cost is added to the total fixed cost. Is Solver able to handle this model? Does it depend on the initial values in the changing cells? (Don't forget to use Solver's nonlinear algorithm, not the simplex method.)

---

[15]One of our colleagues at Indiana University, Vic Cabot, now deceased, worked for years trying to develop a general algorithm (not just trial and error) for finding *all* alternative optimal solutions to optimization models. It turns out that this is a very difficult problem—and one that Vic never totally solved.

14.8 NONLINEAR PROGRAMMING MODELS

In many optimization models the objective and/or the constraints are nonlinear functions of the decision variables. Such an optimization model is called a **nonlinear programming** (NLP) model. In this section we discuss how to use Excel's Solver to find optimal solutions to NLP models. We then discuss a couple of interesting applications, including the important portfolio optimization model.

14.8.1 Basic Ideas of Nonlinear Optimization

When you solve an LP model with Solver, you are guaranteed that the solution obtained is an optimal solution. When you solve an NLP model, however, it is very possible that Solver will obtain a suboptimal solution. This is because a nonlinear function can have a *local* optimal solution that is not the *global* optimal solution. A **local** optimal solution is one that is better than all nearby points, whereas the **global optimum** is the one that beats all points in the entire feasible region. If there are indeed one or more local optimal solutions that are not globally optimal, then it is entirely possible that Solver will stop at one of them. Unfortunately, this is not what you want; you want the global optimum.

There are mathematical conditions that guarantee the Solver solution is indeed the global optimum. However, these conditions are difficult to understand, and they are often difficult to check. A much simpler approach is to run Solver several times, each time with different starting values in the changing cells. In general, if Solver obtains the same optimal solution in all cases, you can be fairly confident—but still not absolutely sure—that Solver has found the global optimal solution. On the other hand, if you try different starting values for the changing cells and obtain several different solutions, you should keep the best solution found so far. That is, you should keep the solution with the lowest objective value (for a minimization problem) or the highest objective value (for a maximization problem).

FUNDAMENTAL INSIGHT

Local Optimal Solution Versus Global Optimal Solution

Nonlinear objective functions can behave in many ways that make them difficult to optimize. In particular, they can have local optimal solutions that are not globally optimal, and nonlinear optimization algorithms can stop at such local optimal solutions. The important property of linear objectives that makes the simplex method so successful—namely, that the optimal solution is a corner point—doesn't hold for

nonlinear objectives. Now any point in the feasible region can conceivably be optimal. This not only makes the search for the optimal solution more difficult, but it also makes it much more difficult to recognize whether a promising solution (a local optimum) is indeed the global optimum. This is why researchers have spent so much effort trying to obtain conditions that, when true, guarantee that a local optimum must be a global optimum. Unfortunately, these conditions are often difficult to check.

14.8.2 Managerial Economics Models

Many problems in economics are nonlinear but can be solved with Solver. We illustrate one such peak-load pricing example in this section.

14.11 PEAK-LOAD PRICING AT FLORIDA POWER AND LIGHT

Florida Power and Light (FPL) faces demands during both peak-load and off-peak times. FPL must determine the price per kilowatt hour (kwh) to charge during both peak-load and off-peak periods. The daily demand for power during each period (in kwh) is related to price as follows:

$$D_p = 60 - 0.5P_p + 0.1P_o \tag{14.5}$$

$$D_o = 40 - P_o + 0.1P_p \tag{14.6}$$

Here, D_p and P_p are demand and price during peak-load times, and D_o and P_o are demand and price during off-peak times. Note that these demand functions are *linear* in the prices. Also, note from the signs of the coefficients that an increase in the peak-load price decreases the demand for power during the peak-load period but *increases* the demand for power during the off-peak period. Similarly, an increase in the price for the off-peak period decreases the demand for the off-peak period but *increases* the demand for the peak-load period. In economic terms, this implies that peak-load power and off-peak power are *substitutes* for one another. In addition, assume that it costs FPL $10 per day to maintain one kwh of capacity. The company wants to determine a pricing strategy and a capacity level that maximize its daily profit.

Objective To use a nonlinear model to determine prices and capacity when there are two different daily usage patterns, peak-load and off-peak.

WHERE DO THE NUMBERS COME FROM?

A cost accountant should be able to estimate the unit cost of capacity. The difficult task is to estimate the demand functions in equations (14.5) and (14.6). This requires either sufficient historical data on prices and demands (for both peak-load and off-peak periods) or educated guesses from management.

Solution

The variables and constraints for this model are listed in Table 14.18. The company must decide on two prices, and it must determine the amount of capacity to maintain. Because this capacity level, once determined, is relevant for peak-load and off-peak periods, it must be large enough to meet demands for both periods. This is the reasoning behind the constraint.

Table 14.18 Variables and Constraints for Peak-Load Pricing Model

Input variables	Parameters of demand functions, unit cost of capacity
Decision variables (changing cells)	Peak-load and off-peak prices, capacity
Objective cell	Profit
Other calculated variables	Peak-load and off-peak demands, revenue, cost of capacity
Constraints	Demands ≤ Capacity

Due to the relationships between the demand and price variables, it is not at all obvious what FPL should do. The pricing decisions determine demand, and larger demand requires larger capacity, which costs money. In addition, revenue is price multiplied by demand, so it is not clear whether price should be low or high to increase revenue.

The spreadsheet model appears in Figure 14.57. (See the file **Peak-Load Pricing.xlsx**.) It can be developed as follows.

Figure 14.57 Peak-Load Pricing Model

	A	B	C	D	E	F	G	H
1	**Florida Power & Light peak-load pricing model**					**Range names used:**		
2						Capacity	=Model!$B$15	
3	**Input data**					Common_Capacity	=Model!$B$21:$C$21	
4	Coefficients of demand functions					Demands	=Model!$B$19:$C$19	
5		Constant	Peak price	Off-peak price		Prices	=Model!$B$13:$C$13	
6	Peak-load demand	60	-0.5	0.1		Profit	=Model!$B$26	
7	Off-peak demand	40	0.1	-1				
8								
9	Cost of capacity/kwh	$10						
10								
11	**Decisions**							
12		Peak-load	Off-peak					
13	Prices	$70.31	$26.53					
14								
15	Capacity	27.50						
16								
17	**Constraints on demand**							
18		Peak-load	Off-peak					
19	Demand	27.50	20.50					
20		<=	<=					
21	Capacity	27.50	27.50					
22								
23	**Monetary summary**							
24	Revenue	$2,477.30						
25	Cost of capacity	$275.00						
26	Profit	$2,202.30						

1 **Inputs.** Enter the parameters of the demand functions and the cost of capacity in the input cells.

2 **Prices and capacity level.** Enter *any* trial prices (per kwh) for peak-load and off-peak power in the Prices range, and enter *any* trial value for the capacity level in the Capacity cell. These are the three values FPL has control over, so they are the changing cells.

3 **Demands.** Calculate the demand for the peak-load period by substituting into Equation (14.5). That is, enter the formula

=B6+SUMPRODUCT(Prices,C6:D6)

in cell B19. Similarly, enter the formula

=B7+SUMPRODUCT(Prices,C7:D7)

in cell C19 for the off-peak demand.

4 **Copy capacity.** To indicate the capacity constraints, enter the formula

=Capacity

in cells B21 and C21. The reason for creating these links is that the two demand cells in row 19 must be paired with two capacity cells in row 21, so that the Solver constraints can be specified appropriately. (Solver doesn't allow you to have a "two versus one" constraint like B19:C19 <= B15.)

⑤ Monetary values. Calculate the daily revenue, cost of capacity, and profit in the corresponding cells with the formulas

=SUMPRODUCT(Demands,Prices)

=Capacity*B9

and

=B24-B25

USING SOLVER

The complete Solver dialog box is shown in Figure 14.58. The goal is to maximize profit by setting appropriate prices and capacity and ensuring that demand never exceeds capacity. Most importantly, the simplex algorithm cannot be used; the GRG nonlinear algorithm must be used instead. This is because prices are multiplied by demands to calculate revenues, and demands are *functions* of prices. Therefore, profit is a nonlinear function of the prices.

Figure 14.58
Solver Dialog Box for Peak-Load Pricing Model

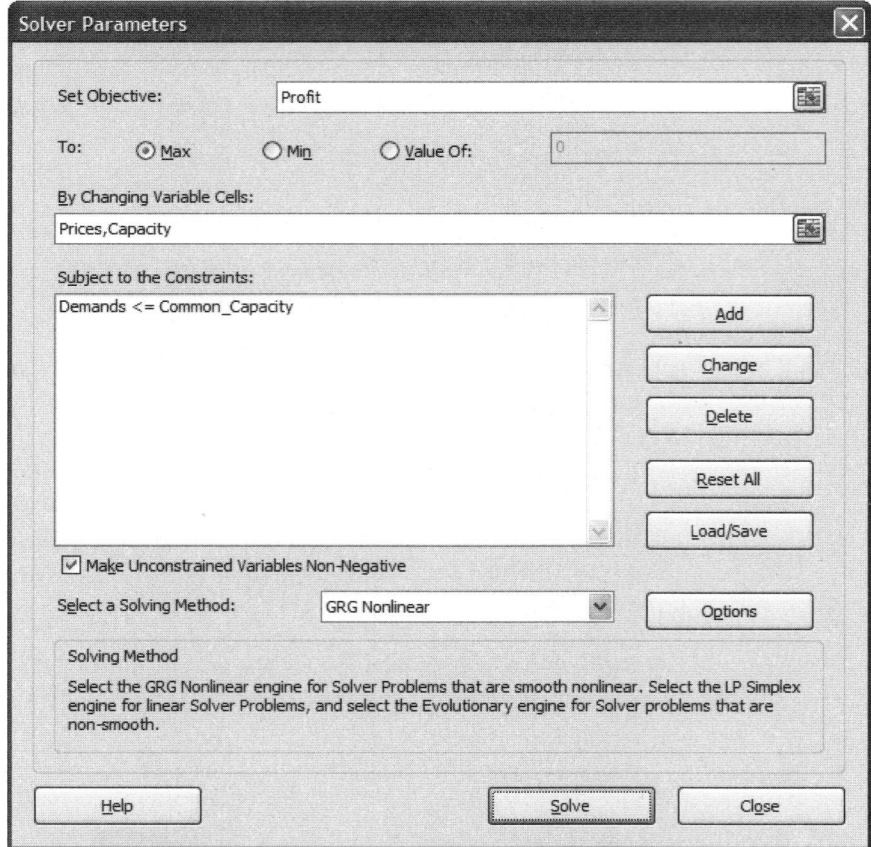

Matrix Functions in Excel

Equation (14.9) for the variance of portfolio return looks intimidating, particularly if there are many potential investments. Fortunately, two built-in Excel matrix functions, MMULT and TRANSPOSE, simplify the calculation. In this subsection we illustrate how to use these two functions. Then in the next subsection we use them in the portfolio selection model.

A *matrix* is a rectangular array of numbers. The matrix is an $i \times j$ matrix if it consists of i rows and j columns. For example,

$$A = \begin{pmatrix} 1 & 2 & 3 \\ 4 & 5 & 6 \end{pmatrix}$$

is a 2×3 matrix, and

$$B = \begin{pmatrix} 1 & 2 \\ 3 & 4 \\ 5 & 6 \end{pmatrix}$$

is a 3×2 matrix. If the matrix has only a single row, it is called a *row vector*. Similarly, if it has only a single column, it is called a *column vector*.

If matrix A has the same number of columns as matrix B has rows, it is possible to calculate the *matrix product* of A and B, denoted AB. The entry in row i, column j of the product AB is obtained by summing the products of the values in row i of A with the corresponding values in column j of B. If A is an $i \times k$ matrix and B is a $k \times j$ matrix, the product AB is an $i \times j$ matrix.

For example, if

$$A = \begin{pmatrix} 1 & 2 & 3 \\ 2 & 4 & 5 \end{pmatrix}$$

and

$$B = \begin{pmatrix} 1 & 2 \\ 3 & 4 \\ 5 & 6 \end{pmatrix}$$

then AB is the following 2×2 matrix:

$$AB = \begin{pmatrix} 1(1) + 2(3) + 3(5) & 1(2) + 2(4) + 3(6) \\ 2(1) + 4(3) + 5(5) & 2(2) + 4(4) + 5(6) \end{pmatrix} = \begin{pmatrix} 22 & 28 \\ 39 & 50 \end{pmatrix}$$

The Excel MMULT function performs matrix multiplication in a single step. The spreadsheet in Figure 14.60 indicates how to multiply matrices of different sizes. (See the file **Matrix Multiplication.xlsx**.) For example, to multiply matrix 1 by matrix 2 (which is possible because matrix 1 has three columns and matrix 2 has three rows), select the range B13:C14, type the formula

=MMULT(B4:D5,B7:C9)

and press Ctrl-Shift-Enter (all three keys at once). Note that you should select a range with two rows and two columns because matrix 1 has two rows and matrix 2 has two columns.

Figure 14.60 Examples of Matrix Multiplication in Excel

	A	B	C	D	E	F	G	H	I	J	K	L	M	N
1	Matrix multiplication in Excel													
2														
3	Typical multiplication of two matrices							Multiplication of a matrix and a column						
4	Matrix 1	1	2	3				Column 1	2					
5		2	4	5					3					
6									4					
7	Matrix 2	1	2											
8		3	4					Matrix 1 times Column 1, with formula =MMULT(B4:D5,I4:I6)						
9		5	6					Select range with 2 rows, 1 column, enter formula, press Ctrl-Shift-Enter						
10									20					
11	Matrix 1 times Matrix 2, with formula =MMULT(B4:D5,B7:C9)								36					
12	Select range with 2 rows, 2 columns, enter formula, press Ctrl-Shift-Enter.													
13		22	28					Multiplication of a row and a matrix						
14		39	50					Row 1	4	5				
15														
16	Multiplication of a quadratic form (row times matrix times column)							Row 1 times Matrix 1, with formula =MMULT(I14:J14,B4:D5)						
17	Matrix 3	2	1	3				Select range with 1 row, 3 columns, enter formula, press Ctrl-Shift-Enter						
18		1	-1	0					14	28	37			
19		3	0	4										
20								Multiplication of a row and a column						
21	Transpose of Column 1 times Matrix 3 times Column 1							Row 2	1	6	3			
22	Formula is =MMULT(TRANSPOSE(I4:I6),MMULT(B17:D19,I4:I6))													
23	Select range with 1 row, 1 column, enter formula, press Ctrl-Shift-Enter							Row 2 times Column 1, with formula =MMULT(I22:K22,I4:I6)						
24		123						Select range with 1 row, 1 column, enter formula, press Ctrl-Shift-Enter						
25									32					
26	Notes on quadratic form example:													
27	Two MMULT's are required because MMULT works on only two ranges at a time.													
28	TRANSPOSE is needed to change a column into a row.													

The matrix multiplication in cell B24 indicates that (1) it is possible to multiply three matrices together by using MMULT twice, and (2) the TRANSPOSE function can be used to convert a column vector to a row vector (or vice versa), if necessary. Here, you want to multiply Column 1 by the product of Matrix 3 and Column 1. However, Column 1 is 3×1, and Matrix 3 is 3×3, so Column 1 multiplied by Matrix 3 doesn't work. Instead, you must transpose Column 1 to make it 1×3. Then the result of multiplying all three together is a 1×1 matrix (a number). It can be calculated by selecting cell B24, typing the formula

=MMULT(TRANSPOSE(I4:I6),MMULT(B17:D19,I4:I6))

and pressing Ctrl-Shift-Enter. This formula uses MMULT twice because MMULT can multiply only *two* matrices at a time.

Excel Function   *MMULT*
The MMULT and TRANSPOSE functions are useful for matrix operations. They are called array functions because they return results to an entire range, not just a single cell. The MMULT function multiplies two matrices and has the syntax **=MMULT(range1,range2),** *where range1 must have as many columns as range2 has rows. To use this function, highlight a range that has as many rows as range1 and as many columns as range2, type the formula, and press Ctrl-Shift-Enter. The resulting formula will have curly brackets around it in the Excel formula bar. You should not type these curly brackets. Excel enters them automatically to remind you that this is an array formula.*

The Portfolio Selection Model

Most investors have two objectives in forming portfolios: to obtain a large expected return and to obtain a small variance (to minimize risk). The problem is inherently nonlinear because the portfolio variance is nonlinear in the investment amounts. The most common way of handling this two-objective problem is to specify a minimal required expected return and then minimize the variance subject to the constraint on the expected return. The following example illustrates how to do this.

EXAMPLE | **14.12 PORTFOLIO OPTIMIZATION AT PERLMAN & BROTHERS**

The investment company Perlman & Brothers intends to invest a given amount of money in three stocks. From past data, the means and standard deviations of annual returns have been estimated as shown in Table 14.19. The correlations between the annual returns on the stocks are listed in Table 14.20. The company wants to find a minimum-variance portfolio that yields an expected annual return of at least 0.12 (that is, 12%).

Table 14.19 Estimated Means and Standard Deviations of Stock Returns

Stock	Mean	Standard Deviation
1	0.14	0.20
2	0.11	0.15
3	0.10	0.08

Table 14.20 Estimated Correlations between Stock Return

Combination	Correlation
Stocks 1 and 2	0.6
Stocks 1 and 3	0.4
Stocks 2 and 3	0.7

Objective To use NLP to find the portfolio that minimizes the risk, measured by portfolio variance, subject to achieving an expected return of at least 12%.

WHERE DO THE NUMBERS COME FROM?

Financial analysts typically estimate the required means, standard deviations, and correlations for stock returns from historical data. However, you should be aware that there is no guarantee that these estimates, based on *historical* return data, are relevant for *future* returns. If analysts have new information about the stocks, they should incorporate this new information into their estimates.

Solution

The variables and constraints for this model are listed in Table 14.21. One interesting aspect of this model is that it is *not* necessary to specify the amount of money invested—it could be $100, $1000, $1,000,000, or any other amount. The model determines the *fractions* of this amount to invest in the various stocks, and these fractions are then relevant for any investment amount. The only requirement is that the fractions should sum to 1, so that all of the money is invested. Besides this, the fractions are constrained to be *nonnegative* to prevent shorting stocks.[17] Finally, the expected portfolio return is constrained to be at least as large as a specified expected return, such as 12%.

Table 14.21   Variables and Constraints for Portfolio Optimization Model

Input variables	Means, standard deviations, and correlations for stock returns, minimum required expected portfolio return
Decision variables (changing cells)	Fractions invested in the various stocks
Objective cell	Portfolio variance (minimize)
Other calculated variables	Covariances between stock returns, total fraction of money invested, expected portfolio return
Constraints	Total fraction invested = 1
	Expected portfolio return $\geq$ Minimum required expected portfolio return

DEVELOPING THE SPREADSHEET MODEL

The individual steps are now listed. (See Figure 14.61 and the file **Portfolio Selection.xlsx**.)

Figure 14.61   Portfolio Optimization Model

	A	B	C	D	E	F	G	H	I
1	Portfolio selection model					Range names used:			
2						Actual_return	=Model!$B$23		
3	Stock input data					Fractions_to_invest	=Model!$B$15:$D$15		
4		Stock 1	Stock 2	Stock 3		Portfolio_variance	=Model!$B$25		
5	Mean return	0.14	0.11	0.1		Required_return	=Model!$D$23		
6	StDev of return	0.2	0.15	0.08		Total_invested	=Model!$B$19		
7									
8	Correlations	Stock 1	Stock 2	Stock 3		Covariances	Stock 1	Stock 2	Stock 3
9	Stock 1	1	0.6	0.4		Stock 1	0.04	0.018	0.0064
10	Stock 2	0.6	1	0.7		Stock 2	0.018	0.0225	0.0084
11	Stock 3	0.4	0.7	1		Stock 3	0.0064	0.0084	0.0064
12									
13	Investment decisions								
14		Stock 1	Stock 2	Stock 3					
15	Fractions to invest	0.500	0.000	0.500					
16									
17	Constraint on investing everything								
18		Total invested		Required value					
19		1.00	=	1					
20									
21	Constraint on expected portfolio return								
22		Actual return		Required return					
23		0.12	>=	0.12					
24									
25	Portfolio variance	0.0148							
26	Portfolio stdev	0.1217							

❶ Inputs. Enter the inputs in the input cells. These include the estimates of means, standard deviations, and correlations, as well as the required expected return.

---

[17]If you want to allow shorting, do not check the Non-Negative option in the Solver dialog box.

2 Fractions invested. Enter *any* trial values in the Fractions_to_invest range for the fractions of Perlman's money placed in the three investments. Then sum these with the SUM function in cell B19.

3 Expected annual return. Use Equation (14.7) to calculate the expected annual return in cell B23 with the formula

=SUMPRODUCT(B5:D5,Fractions_to_invest)

4 Covariance matrix. Equation (14.9) is used to calculate the portfolio variance. To do this, you must first calculate a matrix of covariances. Using the general formula for covariance, $c_{ij} = r_{ij}s_i s_j$ (which holds even when $i = j$, because $r_{ii} = 1$), these can be calculated from the inputs by using lookups. Specifically, enter the formula

=HLOOKUP($F9,$B$4:$D$6,3)*B9*HLOOKUP(G$8,$B$4:$D$6,3)

in cell G9, and copy it to the range G9:I11. (This formula is a bit tricky, so take a close look at it. The term B9 captures the relevant correlation. The two HLOOKUP terms capture the appropriate standard deviations.)

5 Portfolio variance. Although the mathematical details are not presented here, it can be shown that the summation in Equation (14.9) is the product of three matrices: a row of fractions invested multiplied by the covariance matrix multiplied by a column of fractions invested. To calculate it, enter the formula

=MMULT(Fractions_to_invest,MMULT(G9:I11,TRANSPOSE(Fractions_to_invest)))

in cell B25 and press Ctrl-Shift-Enter. (Remember that Excel puts curly brackets around this formula. You should *not* type these curly brackets.) Note that this formula uses two MMULT functions. Again, this is because MMULT can multiply only two matrices at a time. The formula first multiplies the last two matrices and then multiplies this product by the first matrix.

6 Portfolio standard deviation. Most financial analysts talk in terms of portfolio *variance*. However, it is probably more intuitive to talk about portfolio *standard deviation* because it is in the same units as the returns. Calculate the standard deviation in cell B26 with the formula

=SQRT(Portfolio_variance)

Actually, either cell B25 or B26 can be used as the objective cell to minimize. Minimizing the square root of a function is equivalent to minimizing the function itself.

USING SOLVER

The completed Solver dialog box is shown in Figure 14.62. The constraints specify that the expected return must be at least as large as the minimal required return, and all of the company's money must be invested. The changing cells are constrained to be nonnegative (to avoid short selling), but because of the squared terms in the variance formula, the GRG nonlinear algorithm must be used.

Discussion of the Solution

The solution in Figure 14.61 indicates that the company should put half of its money in each of stocks 1 and 3, and it should not invest in stock 2 at all. This might be somewhat surprising, given that the ranking of riskiness of the stocks is 1, 2, 3, with stock 1 being the most risky but also having the highest expected return. However, the correlations play an important role in portfolio selection, so you can usually not guess the optimal portfolio on the basis of the means and standard deviations of stock returns alone.

Figure 14.62
Solver Dialog Box
for Portfolio Model

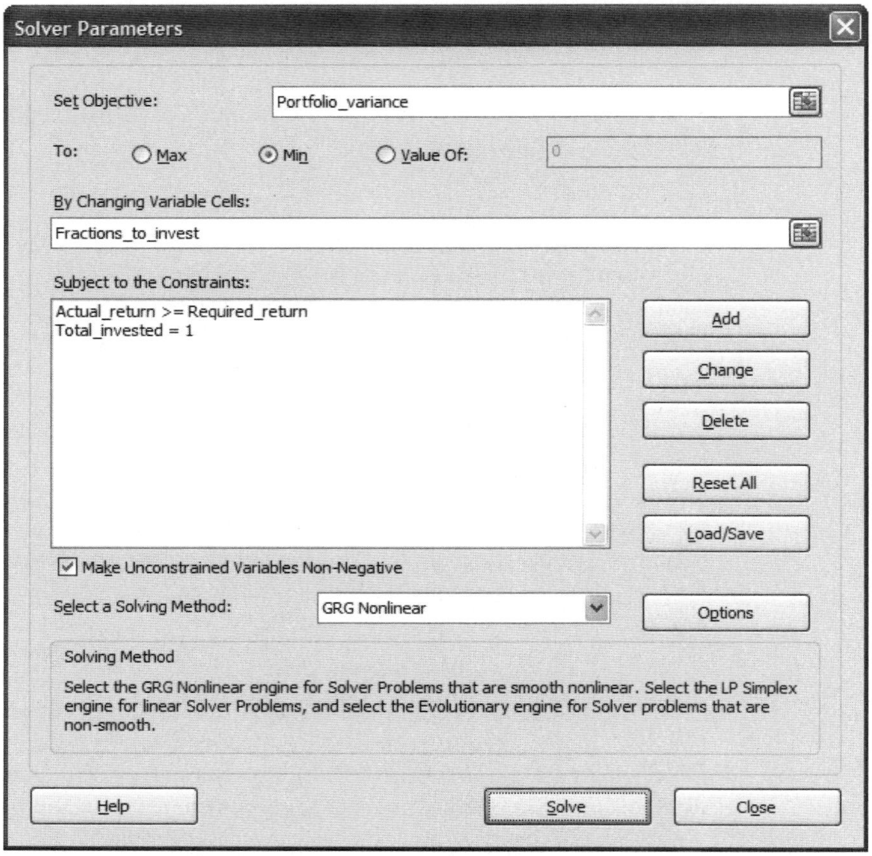

The portfolio standard deviation of 0.1217 can be interpreted in a probabilistic sense. Specifically, if stock returns are approximately *normally* distributed, the actual portfolio return will be within one standard deviation of the expected return with probability about 0.68, and the actual portfolio return will be within two standard deviations of the expected return with probability about 0.95. Given that the expected return is 0.12, this implies a lot of risk—two standard deviations below this mean is a *negative* return (or loss) of slightly more than 12%.

Is the Solver Solution Optimal?

The constraints for this model are linear, and it can be shown that the portfolio variance is a *convex* function of the investment fractions. This is sufficient to guarantee that the Solver solution is indeed optimal.

Sensitivity Analysis

This model begs for a sensitivity analysis on the minimum required return. When the company requires a larger expected return, it must assume a larger risk. This behavior is illustrated in Figure 14.63, where SolverTable has been used with cell D23 as the single input cell, varied from 0.10 to 0.14 in increments of 0.005. Note that values outside this range are of little interest. Stock 3 has the minimum expected return, 0.10, and stock 1 has the highest expected return, 0.14, so no portfolio can have an expected return outside of this range.

Figure 14.63

The Efficient
Frontier

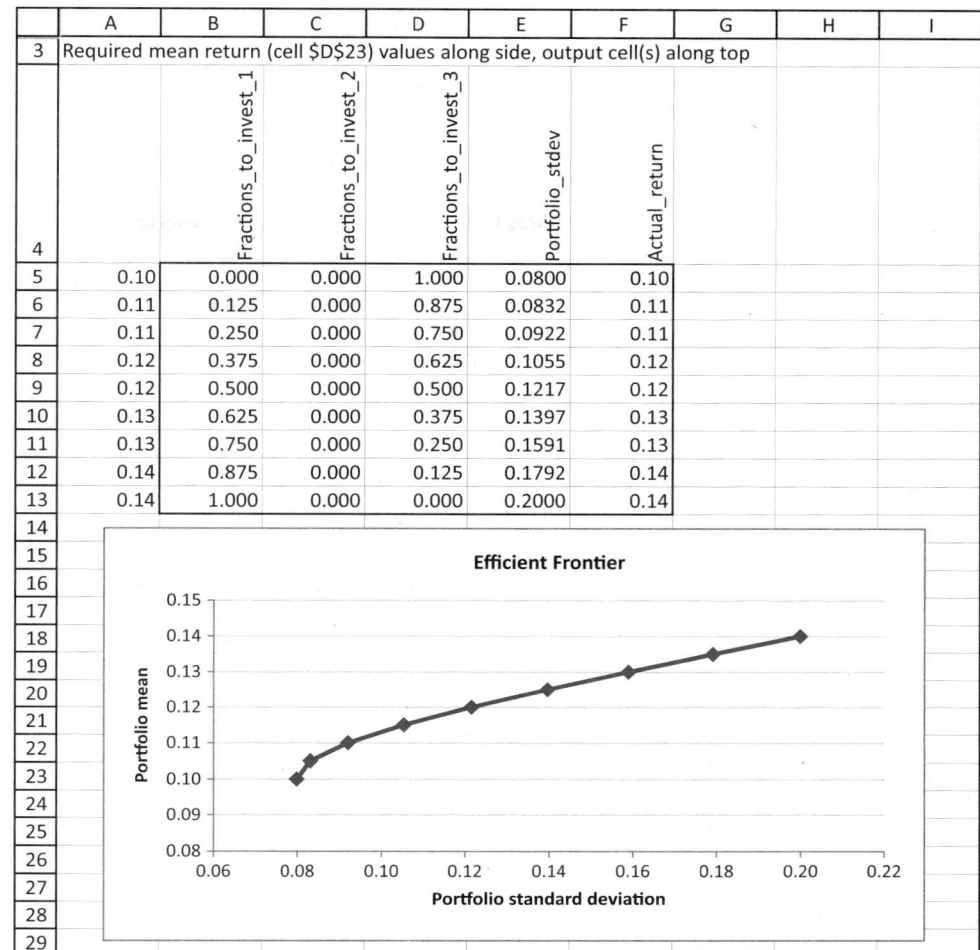

	A	B	C	D	E	F	G	H	I
3	Required mean return (cell $D$23) values along side, output cell(s) along top								
4		Fractions_to_invest_1	Fractions_to_invest_2	Fractions_to_invest_3	Portfolio_stdev	Actual_return			
5	0.10	0.000	0.000	1.000	0.0800	0.10			
6	0.11	0.125	0.000	0.875	0.0832	0.11			
7	0.11	0.250	0.000	0.750	0.0922	0.11			
8	0.12	0.375	0.000	0.625	0.1055	0.12			
9	0.12	0.500	0.000	0.500	0.1217	0.12			
10	0.13	0.625	0.000	0.375	0.1397	0.13			
11	0.13	0.750	0.000	0.250	0.1591	0.13			
12	0.14	0.875	0.000	0.125	0.1792	0.14			
13	0.14	1.000	0.000	0.000	0.2000	0.14			

The results indicate that the company should put more and more into risky stock 1 as the required return increases—and stock 2 continues to be unused. The accompanying scatter chart (with the option to "connect the dots") shows the risk–return trade-off. As the company assumes more risk, as measured by portfolio standard deviation, the expected return increases, but at a decreasing rate.

The curve in this chart is called the *efficient frontier*. Points on the efficient frontier can be achieved by appropriate portfolios. Points below the efficient frontier can be achieved, but they are not as good as points on the efficient frontier because they have a lower expected return for a given level of risk. In contrast, points above the efficient frontier are unachievable—the company cannot achieve this high an expected return for a given level of risk.

MODELING ISSUES

1. Typical real-world portfolio selection problems involve a large number of potential investments, certainly many more than three. This admittedly requires more input data, particularly for the correlation matrix, but the basic model does not change at all. In particular, the matrix formula for portfolio variance is exactly the same. This shows the power of using Excel's matrix functions. Without them, the formula for portfolio variance would be a long, involved sum.

2. If Perlman is allowed to short a stock, the fraction invested in that stock is allowed to be negative. To implement this, you can eliminate the nonnegativity constraints on the changing cells.

3. An alternative objective might be to minimize the probability that the portfolio loses money. This possibility is illustrated in one of the problems. ■

PROBLEMS

Level A

69. In the peak-load pricing model, the demand functions have positive and negative coefficients of prices. The negative coefficients indicate that as the price of a product increases, demand for *that* product decreases. The positive coefficients indicate that as the price of a product increases, demand for the *other* product increases.
  a. Increase the magnitudes of the negative coefficients from -0.5 and -1 to -0.7 and -1.2, and rerun Solver. Are the changes in the optimal solution intuitive? Explain.
  b. Increase the magnitudes of the positive coefficients from 0.1 and 0.1 to 0.3 and 0.3, and rerun Solver. Are the changes in the optimal solution intuitive? Explain.
  c. Make the changes in parts **a** and **b** simultaneously and rerun Solver. What happens now?

70. In the peak-load pricing model, we assumed that the capacity level is a decision variable. Assume now that capacity has already been set at 30 kwh. (Note that the cost of capacity is now a sunk cost, so it is irrelevant to the decision problem.) Change the model appropriately and run Solver. Then use SolverTable to see how sensitive the optimal solution is to the capacity level, letting it vary over some relevant range. Does it appear that the optimal prices will be set so that demand is always equal to capacity for at least one of the two periods of the day?

71. For each of the following, answer whether it makes sense to multiply the matrices of the given sizes. In each case where it makes sense, demonstrate an example in Excel, where you make up the numbers.
  a. AB, where A is 3×4 and B is 4×1
  b. AB, where A is 1×4 and B is 4×1
  c. AB, where A is 4×1 and B is 1×4
  d. AB, where A is 1×4 and B is 1×4
  e. ABC, where A is 1×4, B is 4×4, and C is 4×1
  f. ABC, where A is 3×3, B is 3×3, and C is 3×1
  g. $A^T B$, where A is 4×3 and B is 4×3, and A^T denotes the transpose of A

72. Add a new stock, stock 4, to the portfolio optimization model. Assume that the estimated mean and standard deviation of return for stock 4 are 0.125 and 0.175, respectively. Also, assume the correlations between stock 4 and the original three stocks are 0.3, 0.5, and 0.8. Run Solver on the modified model, where the required expected portfolio return is again 0.12. Is stock 4 in the optimal portfolio? Then run SolverTable as in the example. Is stock 4 in any of the optimal portfolios on the efficient frontier?

73. In the portfolio optimization model, stock 2 is not in the optimal portfolio. Use SolverTable to see whether it ever enters the optimal portfolio as its correlations with stocks 1 and 3 vary. Specifically, use a two-way SolverTable with two inputs, the correlations between stock 2 and stocks 1 and 3, each allowed to vary from 0.1 to 0.9 in increments of 0.1. Capture as outputs the three changing cells. Discuss the results. (*Note*: You will have to change the model slightly. For example, if you use cells B10 and C11 as the two SolverTable input cells, you will have to ensure that cells C9 and D10 change accordingly. This is easy. Just put formulas in these latter two cells.)

74. The stocks in the portfolio optimization model are all *positively* correlated. What happens when they are *negatively* correlated? Answer for each of the following scenarios. In each case, two of the three correlations are the negatives of their original values. Discuss the differences between the optimal portfolios in these three scenarios.
  a. Change the signs of the correlations between stocks 1 and 2 and between stocks 1 and 3. (Here, stock 1 tends to go in a different direction from stocks 2 and 3.)
  b. Change the signs of the correlations between stocks 1 and 2 and between stocks 2 and 3. (Here, stock 2 tends to go in a different direction from stocks 1 and 3.)
  c. Change the signs of the correlations between stocks 1 and 3 and between stocks 2 and 3. (Here, stock 3 tends to go in a different direction from stocks 1 and 2.)

75. The file **P14_75.xlsx** contains historical monthly returns for 28 companies. For each company, calculate the estimated mean return and the estimated variance of return. Then calculate the estimated correlations between the companies' returns. Note that "return" here means *monthly* return. (*Hint*: Use StatTools's Summary Statistics capabilities.)

76. This problem continues using the data from the previous problem. The file **P14_76.xlsx** includes all of the previous data. It also contains fractions in row 3 for creating a portfolio. These fractions are currently all equal to 1/28, but they can be changed to any values you like, so long as they continue to sum to 1. For any such fractions, find the estimated mean, variance, and standard deviation of the resulting portfolio return.

Level B

77. Continuing the previous problem, find the portfolio that achieves an expected monthly return of at least 0.01 (1%) and minimizes portfolio variance. Then use SolverTable to sweep out the efficient frontier. Create a chart of this efficient frontier from your SolverTable results. What are the relevant lower and upper limits on the required expected monthly return?

78. In many cases you can assume that the portfolio return is at least approximately *normally* distributed. Then you can use Excel's NORMDIST function as in Chapter 5 to calculate the probability that the portfolio return is negative. The relevant formula is **=NORMDIST(0,*mean*,*stdev*,1)**, where *mean* and *stdev* are the expected portfolio return and standard deviation of portfolio return, respectively.

a. Modify the portfolio optimization model slightly, and then run Solver to find the portfolio that achieves at least a 0.12 (12%) expected return and minimizes the probability of a negative return. Do you get the same optimal portfolio as before? What is the probability that the return from this portfolio will be negative?

b. Using the model in part **a**, create a chart of the efficient frontier. However, this time put the probability of a negative return on the horizontal axis.

14.9 CONCLUSION

This chapter has led you through spreadsheet optimization models of many diverse problems. No standard procedure can be used to model all problems. However, there are several keys to most models.

1. First, determine the changing cells. For example, in blending problems it is important to realize that the changing cells are the amounts of inputs used to produce outputs, and in worker scheduling problems such as the post office example, it is important to realize that the changing cells are the number of people who start their five-day shift each day of the week.

2. Set up the model so that you can easily calculate what you wish to maximize or minimize (usually profit or cost). For example, in the aggregate planning model it is a good idea to calculate total cost by calculating the monthly cost of the various activities in separate rows and then summing the subtotals.

3. Set up the model so that the relationships between the cells in the spreadsheet and the constraints of the problem are readily apparent. For example, in the post office scheduling model it is convenient to calculate the number of people working each day of the week adjacent to the minimum required number of people for each day of the week.

4. Optimization models do not always fall into ready-made categories. A model might involve a combination of the ideas discussed in the production scheduling, blending, and aggregate planning examples. In fact, many real applications are not strictly analogous to any of the models we have discussed. However, exposure to the models in this chapter should give you the insights you need to solve a wide variety of interesting problems.

Summary of Key Terms

Term	Explanation	Page
Worker scheduling models	Models for choosing the staffing levels to meet workload requirements	813
Multiple optimal solutions	Situation where several solutions obtain the same optimal objective value	818
Blending models	Models where inputs must be mixed in the right proportions to produce outputs	821
Logistics models	Models where goods must be shipped from one set of locations to another at minimal cost	828
Flow balance constraint	Constraint that relates the flow into a node and the flow out of the node	838
Aggregate planning models	Models where workforce levels and production levels must be set to meet customer demand	848
Integer programming models	Models where at least some of the decision variables must be integers	868
Binary variables	Integer variables that must be 0 or 1; used to indicate whether an activity takes place	868
Capital budgeting models	Models where a subset of investment activities is chosen from a set of possible activities	869
Fixed-cost models	Models where fixed costs are incurred for various activities if they are done at *any* positive level	875
Set-covering models	Models where members of one set must be selected to cover services to members of another set	883
Nonlinear programming models	Models where either the objective function or the constraints (or both) are nonlinear functions of the decision variables	890
Global optimum	Solution that is the best in the entire feasible region	891
Local optimum	Solution that is better than all nearby solutions (but might not be optimal globally)	891
Portfolio optimization models	Models that attempt to find the portfolio of securities that achieves the best balance between risk and return	896

PROBLEMS

Conceptual Exercises

C1. The worker scheduling model in this chapter was purposely made small (only seven changing cells). What would make a similar problem for a company like McDonald's much harder? What types of constraints would be required? How many changing cells (approximately) might there be?

C2. Explain why it is problematic to include a constraint such as the following in an LP model for a blending problem:

$$\frac{\text{Total octane in gasoline 1 blend}}{\text{Barrels of gasoline 1 blended daily}} \geq 10$$

C3. "It is essential to constrain all shipments in a transportation problem to have integer values to ensure that the optimal LP solution consists entirely of integer-valued shipments." Is this statement true or false? Why?

C4. What is the relationship between transportation models and more general logistics models? Explain how these two types of linear optimization models are similar and how they are different.

C5. Unlike the small logistics models presented here, real-world logistics problems can be huge. Imagine the global problem a company like FedEx faces each day. Describe as well as you can the types of decisions and constraints it has. How large (number of changing cells, number of constraints) might such a problem be?

C6. Suppose that you formulate and solve an integer programming model with a cost-minimization objective. Assume that the optimal solution yields an objective cell value of $500,000. Now, consider the same linear optimization model without the integer restrictions. That is, suppose that you drop the requirement that the changing cells be integer-valued and re-optimize with Solver. How does the optimal objective cell value for this modified model (called the *LP relaxation* of the IP model) compare to the original total cost value of $500,000? Explain your answer.

C7. The portfolio optimization model presented here is the standard model: minimize the variance (or standard deviation) of the portolio, as a measure of risk, for a given required level of expected return. In general, the goal is to keep risk low and expected return high. Can you think of other ways to model the problem to achieve these basic goals? Is high variability all *bad* risk?

Level A

79. A bus company believes that it will need the following numbers of bus drivers during each of the next five years: 60 drivers in year 1; 70 drivers in year 2; 50 drivers in year 3; 65 drivers in year 4; 75 drivers in year 5. At the beginning of each year, the bus company must decide how many drivers to hire or fire. It costs $4000 to hire a driver and $2000 to fire a driver. A driver's salary is $30,000 per year. At the beginning of year 1 the company has 50 drivers. A driver hired at the beginning of a year can be used to meet the current year's requirements and is paid full salary for the current year.
   a. Determine how to minimize the bus company's salary, hiring, and firing costs over the next five years.
   b. Use SolverTable to determine how the total number hired, total number fired, and total cost change as the unit hiring and firing costs *each* increase by the same percentage.

80. A pharmaceutical company produces the drug NasaMist from four chemicals. Today, the company must produce 1000 pounds of the drug. The three active ingredients in NasaMist are A, B, and C. By weight, at least 8% of NasaMist must consist of A, at least 4% of B, and at least 2% of C. The cost per pound of each chemical and the amount of each active ingredient in one pound of each chemical are given in the file **P14_80.xlsx**. It is necessary that at least 100 pounds of chemical 2 be used.
   a. Determine the cheapest way of producing today's batch of NasaMist.
   b. Use SolverTable to see how much the percentage of requirement of A is really costing the company. Let the percentage required vary from 6% to 12%.

81. A bank is attempting to determine where to invest its assets during the current year. At present, $500,000 is available for investment in bonds, home loans, auto loans, and personal loans. The annual rates of return on each type of investment are known to be the following: bonds, 6%; home loans, 8%; auto loans, 5%; personal loans, 10%. To ensure that the bank's portfolio is not too risky, the bank's investment manager has placed the following three restrictions on the bank's portfolio:
- The amount invested in personal loans cannot exceed the amount invested in bonds.
- The amount invested in home loans cannot exceed the amount invested in auto loans.
- No more than 25% of the total amount invested can be in personal loans.

Help the bank maximize the annual return on its investment portfolio.

82. A fertilizer company blends silicon and nitrogen to produce two types of fertilizers. Fertilizer 1 must be at least 40% nitrogen and sells for $70 per pound. Fertilizer 2 must be at least 70% silicon and sells for $40 per pound. The company can purchase up to 8000 pounds of nitrogen at $15 per pound and up to 10,000 pounds of silicon at $10 per pound.
   a. Assuming that all fertilizer produced can be sold, determine how the company can maximize its profit.
   b. Use SolverTable to explore the effect on profit of changing the minimum percentage of nitrogen required in fertilizer 1.
   c. Suppose the availabilities of nitrogen and silicon both increase by the same percentage from their current values. Use SolverTable to explore the effect of this change on profit.

83. LP models are used by many Wall Street firms to select a desirable bond portfolio. The following is a simplified version of such a model. A company is considering investing in four bonds; $1 million is available for investment. The expected annual return, the worst-case annual return on each bond, and the *duration* of each bond are given in the file **P14_83.xlsx**. (The duration of a bond is a measure of the bond's sensitivity to interest rates.) The company wants to maximize the expected return from its bond investments, subject to three constraints:
- The worst-case return of the bond portfolio must be at least 8%.
- The average duration of the portfolio must be at most 6. For example, a portfolio that invests $600,000 in bond 1 and $400,000 in bond 4 has an average duration of [600,000(3) + 400,000(9)]/1,000,000 = 5.4
- Because of diversification requirements, at most 40% of the total amount invested can be invested in a single bond.

Determine how the company can maximize the expected return on its investment.

84. At the beginning of year 1, you have $10,000. Investments A and B are available; their cash flows are shown in the file **P14_84.xlsx**. Assume that any money not invested in A or B earns interest at an annual rate of 8%.
   a. Determine how to maximize your cash on hand at the beginning of year 4.
   b. Use SolverTable to determine how a change in the year 2 return for investment A changes the optimal solution to the problem.
   c. Use SolverTable to determine how a change in the year 3 return of investment B changes the optimal solution to the problem.

85. An oil company produces two types of gasoline, G1 and G2, from two types of crude oil, C1 and C2. G1 is allowed to contain up to 4% impurities, and G2 is allowed to contain up to 3% impurities. G1 sells for $48 per barrel, whereas G2 sells for $72 per barrel. Up to 4200 barrels of G1 and up to 4300 barrels of G2 can be sold. The cost per barrel of each crude, their availability, and the level of impurities in each crude are listed in the file **P14_85.xlsx**. Before blending the crude oil into gas, any amount of each crude can be "purified" for a cost of $3.00 per barrel. Purification eliminates half of the impurities in the crude oil.
   a. Determine how to maximize profit.
   b. Use SolverTable to determine how an increase in the availability of C1 affects the optimal profit.
   c. Use SolverTable to determine how an increase in the availability of C2 affects the optimal profit.
   d. Use SolverTable to determine how a change in the profitability of G2 changes profitability and the types of gas produced.

86. The government is auctioning off oil leases at two sites: 1 and 2. At each site 10,000 acres of land are to be auctioned. Cliff Ewing, Blake Barnes, and Alexis Pickens are bidding for the oil. Government rules state that no bidder can receive more than 40% of the land being auctioned. Cliff has bid $10,000 per acre for site 1 land and $20,000 per acre for site 2 land. Blake has bid $9000 per acre for site 1 land and $22,000 per acre for site 2 land. Alexis has bid $11,000 per acre for site 1 land and $19,000 per acre for site 2 land.
   a. Determine how to maximize the government's revenue.
   b. Use SolverTable to see how changes in the government's rule on 40% of all land being auctioned affect the optimal revenue. Why can the optimal revenue not decrease if this percentage required increases? Why can the optimal revenue not increase if this percentage required decreases?

87. An automobile company produces cars in Los Angeles and Detroit and has a warehouse in Atlanta. The company supplies cars to customers in Houston and Tampa. The costs of shipping a car between various points are listed in the file **P14_87.xlsx**, where a blank means that a shipment is not allowed. Los Angeles can produce up to 1100 cars, and Detroit can produce up to 2900 cars. Houston must receive 2400 cars, and Tampa must receive 1500 cars.
   a. Determine how to minimize the cost of meeting demands in Houston and Tampa.
   b. Modify the answer to part **a** if shipments between Los Angeles and Detroit are not allowed.
   c. Modify the answer to part **a** if shipments between Houston and Tampa are allowed at a cost of $5 per car.

88. An oil company produces oil from two wells. Well 1 can produce up to 150,000 barrels per day, and well 2 can produce up to 200,000 barrels per day. It is possible to ship oil directly from the wells to the company's customers in Los Angeles and New York. Alternatively, the company could transport oil to the ports of Mobile and Galveston and then ship it by tanker to New York or Los Angeles, respectively. Los Angeles requires 160,000 barrels per day, and New York requires 140,000 barrels per day. The costs of shipping 1000 barrels between various locations are shown in the file **P14_88.xlsx**, where a blank indicates shipments that are not allowed. Determine how to minimize the transport costs in meeting the oil demands of Los Angeles and New York.

89. Based on Bean et al. (1987). Boris Milkem's firm owns six assets. The expected selling price (in millions of dollars) for each asset is given in the file **P14_89.xlsx**. For example, if asset 1 is sold in year 2, the firm receives $20 million. To maintain a regular cash flow, Milkem must sell at least $20 million of assets during year 1, at least $30 million worth during year 2, and at least $35 million worth during year 3. Determine how Milkem can maximize his total revenue from assets sold during the next three years.

90. Based on Sonderman and Abrahamson (1985). In treating a brain tumor with radiation, physicians want the maximum amount of radiation possible to bombard the tissue containing the tumors. The constraint is, however, that there is a maximum amount of radiation that normal tissue can handle without suffering tissue damage. Physicians must therefore decide how to aim the radiation so as to maximize the radiation that hits the tumor tissue subject to the constraint of not damaging the normal tissue. As a simple example of this situation, suppose there are six types of radiation beams (beams differ in where they are aimed and their intensity) that can be aimed at a tumor. The region containing the tumor has been divided into six regions: three regions contain tumors and three contain normal tissue. The amount of

radiation delivered to each region by each type of beam is shown in the file **P14_90.xlsx**. If each region of normal tissue can handle at most 60 units of radiation, which beams should be used to maximize the total amount of radiation received by the tumors?

91. A leading hardware company produces three types of computers: Pear computers, Apricot computers, and Orange computers. The relevant data are given in the file **P14_91.xlsx**. The equipment cost is a fixed cost; it is incurred if any of this type of computer is produced. A total of 30,000 chips and 12,000 hours of labor are available. The company wants to produce at least two types of computers.
    a. Determine how the company can maximize its profit.
    b. For any computer type *not* in the optimal product mix, use SolverTable to find how much larger its unit margin would have to be before it would enter the optimal product mix.

92. A food company produces tomato sauce at five different plants. The tomato sauce is then shipped to one of three warehouses, where it is stored until it is shipped to one of the company's four customers. All of the inputs for the problem are given in the file **P14_92.xlsx**, as follows:
    - The plant capacities (in tons)
    - The cost per ton of producing tomato sauce at each plant and shipping it to each warehouse
    - The cost of shipping a ton of sauce from each warehouse to each customer
    - The customer requirements (in tons) of sauce
    - The fixed annual cost of operating each plant and warehouse.

    The company must decide which plants and warehouses to open, and which routes from plants to warehouses and from warehouses to customers to use. All customer demand must be met. A given customer's demand can be met from more than one warehouse, and a given plant can ship to more than one warehouse.
    a. Determine the minimum-cost method for meeting customer demands.
    b. Use SolverTable to see how a change in the capacity of plant 1 affects the total cost.
    c. Use SolverTable to see how a change in the customer 2 demand affects the total cost.

93. You are given the following means, standard deviations, and correlations for the annual return on three potential investments. The means are 0.12, 0.15, and 0.20. The standard deviations are 0.20, 0.30, and 0.40. The correlation between stocks 1 and 2 is 0.65, between stocks 1 and 3 is 0.75, and between stocks 2 and 3 is 0.41. You have $100,000 to invest and can invest no more than half of your money in any single investment. Determine the minimum-variance

portfolio that yields an expected annual return of at least 0.14.

94. You have $50,000 to invest in three stocks. Let R_i be the random variable representing the annual return on $1 invested in stock i. For example, if $R_i = 0.12$, then $1 invested in stock i at the beginning of a year is worth $1.12 at the end of the year. The means are $E(R_1) = 0.14$, $E(R_2) = 0.11$, and $E(R_3) = 0.10$. The variances are $Var\ R_1 = 0.20$, $Var\ R_2 = 0.08$, and $Var\ R_3 = 0.18$. The correlations are $r_{12} = 0.8$, $r_{13} = 0.7$, and $r_{23} = 0.9$. Determine the minimum-variance portfolio that attains an expected annual return of at least 0.12.

Level B

95. The risk index of an investment can be obtained by taking the absolute values of percentage changes in the value of the investment for each year and averaging them. Suppose you are trying to determine the percentages of your money to invest in T-bills, gold, and stocks. The file **P14_95.xlsx** lists the annual returns (percentage changes in value) for these investments for the years 1968 through 1988. Let the risk index of a portfolio be the weighted average of the risk indices of these investments, where the weights are the fractions of the portfolio assigned to the investments. Suppose that the amount of each investment must be between 20% and 50% of the total invested. You would like the risk index of your portfolio to equal 0.15, and your goal is to maximize the expected return on your portfolio. Determine the maximum expected return on your portfolio, subject to the stated constraints. Use the average return earned by each investment during the years 1968 through 1988 as your estimate of expected return. (If you like, you can try this problem with more recent data, but the model will be exactly the same.)

96. Broker Sonya Wong is currently trying to maximize her profit in the bond market. Four bonds are available for purchase and sale at the bid and ask prices shown in the file **P14_96.xlsx**. Sonya can buy up to 1000 units of each bond at the ask price or sell up to 1000 units of each bond at the bid price. During each of the next three years, the person who sells a bond will pay the owner of the bond the cash payments listed in the same file. Sonya's goal is to maximize her revenue from selling bonds minus her payment for buying bonds, subject to the constraint that after each year's payments are received, her current cash position (due only to cash payments from bonds and not purchases or sales of bonds) is nonnegative. Note that her current cash position can depend on past coupons and that cash accumulated at the end of each year earns 2.5% annual interest. Determine how to maximize net profit

from buying and selling bonds, subject to the constraints previously described. Why do you think we limit the number of units of each bond that can be bought or sold?

97. A financial company is considering investing in three projects. If it fully invests in a project, the realized cash flows (in millions of dollars) will be as listed in the file **P14_97.xlsx**. For example, project 1 requires a cash outflow of $3 million today and returns $5.5 million three years from now. The company currently has $2 million in cash. At each time point (0, 6, 12, 18, 24, and 30 months from now), the company can, if desired, borrow up to $2 million at 3.5% interest (per six months). Leftover cash earns 3% interest (per six months). For example, if after borrowing and investing at the current time, the company has $1 million, it will receive $30,000 in interest six months from now. The company's goal is to maximize cash on hand after cash flows three years from now are accounted for. What investment and borrowing strategy should it use? Assume that the company can invest in a fraction of a project. For example, if it invests in one-half of project 3, it has cash outflows of −$1 million now and six months from now.

98. You are a CFA (chartered financial analyst). An overextended client has come to you because she needs help paying off her credit card bills. She owes the amounts on her credit cards listed in the file **P14_98.xlsx**. The client is willing to allocate up to $5000 per month to pay off these credit cards. All cards must be paid off within 36 months. The client's goal is to minimize the total of all her payments. To solve this problem, you must understand how interest on a loan works. To illustrate, suppose the client pays $5000 on Saks during month 1. Then her Saks balance at the beginning of month 2 is $20,000 − [5000 − 0.005(20,000)]$. This follows because she incurs $0.005(20,000)$ in interest charges on her Saks card during month 1. Help the client solve her problem. Once you have solved this problem, give an intuitive explanation of the solution found by Solver.

99. A food company produces two types of turkey cutlets for sale to fast-food restaurants. Each type of cutlet consists of white meat and dark meat. Cutlet 1 sells for $4 per pound and must consist of at least 70% white meat. Cutlet 2 sells for $3 per pound and must consist of at least 60% white meat. At most 500 pounds of cutlet 1 and 300 pounds of cutlet 2 can be sold. The two types of turkey used to manufacture the cutlets are purchased from a turkey farm. Each type 1 turkey costs $10 and yields five pounds of white meat and two pounds of dark meat. Each type 2 turkey costs $8 and yields three pounds of white meat and three pounds of dark meat. Determine how the company can maximize its profit.

100. Each hour from 10 A.M. to 7 P.M., a bank receives checks and must process them. Its goal is to process all checks the same day they are received. The bank has 13 check processing machines, each of which can process up to 500 checks per hour. It takes one worker to operate each machine. The bank hires both full-time and part-time workers. Full-time workers work 10 A.M. to 6 P.M., 11 A.M. to 7 P.M., or noon to 8 P.M. and are paid $160 per day. Part-time workers work either 2 P.M. to 7 P.M. or 3 P.M. to 8 P.M. and are paid $75 per day. The numbers of checks received each hour are listed in the file **P14_100.xlsx**. In the interest of maintaining continuity, the bank believes that it must have at least three full-time workers under contract. Develop a work schedule that processes all checks by 8 P.M. and minimizes daily labor costs.

101. An oil company has oil fields in San Diego and Los Angeles. The San Diego field can produce up to 500,000 barrels per day, and the Los Angeles field can produce up to 400,000 barrels per day. Oil is sent from the fields to a refinery, either in Dallas or in Houston. (Assume that each refinery has unlimited capacity.) To refine 100,000 barrels costs $700 at Dallas and $900 at Houston. Refined oil is shipped to customers in Chicago and New York. Chicago customers require 400,000 barrels per day, and New York customers require 300,000 barrels per day. The costs of shipping 100,000 barrels of oil (refined or unrefined) between cities are shown in the file **P14_101.xlsx**.
   a. Determine how to minimize the total cost of meeting all demands.
   b. If each refinery had a capacity of 380,000 barrels per day, how would you modify the model in part **a**?

102. An electrical components company produces capacitors at three locations: Los Angeles, Chicago, and New York. Capacitors are shipped from these locations to public utilities in five regions of the country: northeast (NE), northwest (NW), midwest (MW), southeast (SE), and southwest (SW). The cost of producing and shipping a capacitor from each plant to each region of the country is given in the file **P14_102.xlsx**. Each plant has an annual production capacity of 100,000 capacitors. Each year, each region of the country must receive the following number of capacitors: NE, 55,000; NW, 50,000; MW, 60,000; SE, 60,000; SW, 45,000. The company believes that shipping costs are too high, and it is therefore considering building one or two more production plants. Possible sites are Atlanta and Houston. The costs of producing a capacitor and shipping it to each region of the country are given in the same file. It costs $3 million (in current dollars) to build a new plant, and operating each plant incurs a fixed cost (in addition to variable shipping and production costs) of $50,000 per year. A plant at Atlanta or Houston will have the capacity to produce 100,000 capacitors per

year. Assume that future demand patterns and production costs will remain unchanged. If costs are discounted at a rate of 12% per year, how can the company minimize the net present value (NPV) of all costs associated with meeting current and future demands?

103. Based on Bean et al. (1988). The owner of a shopping mall has 10,000 square feet of space to rent and wants to determine the types of stores that should occupy the mall. The minimum number and maximum number of each type of store and the square footage of each type are given in the file **P14_103.xlsx**. The annual profit made by each type of store depends on the number of stores of that type in the mall. This dependence is given in the same file, where all profits are in units of $10,000. For example, if there are two department stores in the mall, each department store will earn $210,000 profit per year. Each store pays 5% of its annual profit as rent to the owner of the mall. Determine how the owner of the mall can maximize its rental income.

104. It is currently the beginning of 2010. A city (labeled C for convenience) is trying to sell municipal bonds to support improvements in recreational facilities and highways. The face values (in thousands of dollars) of the bonds and the due dates at which principal comes due are listed in the file **P14_104.xlsx**. (The due dates are the *beginnings* of the years listed.) An underwriting company (U) wants to underwrite C's bonds. A proposal to C for underwriting this issue consists of the following: (1) an interest rate, 3%, 4%, 5%, 6%, or 7%, for each bond, where coupons are paid annually, and (2) an up-front premium paid by U to C. U has determined the set of fair prices (in thousands of dollars) for the bonds listed in the same file. For example, if U underwrites bond 2 maturing in 2013 at 5%, it will charge C $444,000 for that bond. U is constrained to use at most three different interest rates. U wants to make a profit of at least $46,000, where its profit is equal to the sale price of the bonds minus the face value of the bonds minus the premium U pays to C. To maximize the chance that U will get C's business, U wants to minimize the total cost of the bond issue to C, which is equal to the total interest on the bonds minus the premium paid by U. For example, if the year 2012 bond (bond 1) is issued at a 4% rate, then C must pay two years of coupon interest: $2(0.04)(\$700{,}000) = \$56{,}000$. What assignment of interest rates to each bond and up-front premiums ensure that U will make the desired profit (assuming it gets the contract) and maximize the chance of U getting C's business? To maximize this chance, you can assume that U minimizes the net cost to C, that is, the cost of its coupon payments minus the premium from U to C.

This problem deals with strategic planning issues for a large company.[18] The main issue is planning the company's production capacity for the coming year. At issue is the overall level of capacity and the type of capacity—for example, the degree of *flexibility* in the manufacturing system. The main tool used to aid the company's planning process is a mixed integer programming model. A *mixed* integer program has both integer and continuous variables.

Problem Statement

The Giant Motor Company (GMC) produces three lines of cars for the domestic (U.S.) market: Lyras, Libras, and Hydras. The Lyra is a relatively inexpensive subcompact car that appeals mainly to first-time car owners and to households using it as a second car for commuting. The Libra is a sporty compact car that is sleeker, faster, and roomier than the Lyra. Without any options, the Libra costs slightly more than the Lyra; additional options increase the price further. The Hydra is the luxury car of the GMC line. It is significantly more expensive than the Lyra and Libra, and it has the highest profit margin of the three cars.

Retooling Options for Capacity Expansion

Currently GMC has three manufacturing plants in the United States. Each plant is dedicated to producing a single line of cars. In its planning for the coming year, GMC is considering the retooling of its Lyra and/or Libra plants. Retooling either plant would represent a major expense for the company. The retooled plants would have significantly increased production capacities. Although having greater *fixed* costs, the retooled plants would be more efficient and have lower *marginal* production costs—that is, higher *marginal* profit contributions. In addition, the retooled plants would be *flexible*: They would have the capability of producing more than one line of cars.

The characteristics of the current plants and the retooled plants are given in Table 14.22. The retooled Lyra and Libra plants are prefaced by the word *new*. The fixed costs and capacities in Table 14.22 are given on an annual basis. A dash in the profit margin section indicates that the plant cannot manufacture that line of car. For example, the new Lyra plant would be capable of producing both Lyras and Libras but not Hydras. The new Libra plant would be capable of producing any of the three lines of cars. Note, however, that the new Libra plant has a slightly lower profit margin for producing Hydras than the Hydra plant does. The flexible new Libra plant is capable of producing the luxury Hydra model but is not quite as efficient as the current Hydra plant that is dedicated to Hydra production.

The fixed costs are annual costs that are incurred by GMC independent of the number of cars that are produced by the plant. For the current plant configurations, the fixed costs include property taxes, insurance, payments on the loan that was taken out to construct the plant, and so on. If a plant is retooled, the fixed costs will include the previous fixed costs plus the additional cost of the renovation.

[18]The idea for this case came from Eppen, Martin, and Schrage, "A Scenario Approach to Capacity Planning." *Operations Research* 37, no. 4 (July–August 1989): 517–527.

Table 14.22 Plant Characteristics

	Lyra	Libra	Hydra	New Lyra	New Libra
Capacity (in 1000s)	1000	800	900	1600	1800
Fixed cost (in $millions)	2000	2000	2600	3400	3700
Profit Margin by Car Line (in $1000s)					
Lyra	2	—	—	2.5	2.3
Libra	—	3	—	3.0	3.5
Hydra	—	—	5	—	4.8

The additional renovation cost will be an annual cost representing the cost of the renovation amortized over a long period.

Demand for GMC Cars

Short-term demand forecasts have been very reliable in the past and are expected to be reliable in the future. (Longer-term forecasts are not so accurate.) The demand for GMC cars for the coming year is given in Table 14.23.

Table 14.23 Demand for GMC Cars

	Demand (in 1000s)
Lyra	1400
Libra	1100
Hydra	800

A quick comparison of plant capacities and demands in Tables 14.22 and 14.23 indicates that GMC is faced with insufficient capacity. Partially offsetting the lack of capacity is the phenomenon of *demand diversion*. If a potential car buyer walks into a GMC dealer showroom wanting to buy a Lyra but the dealer is out of stock, frequently the salesperson can convince the customer to purchase the better Libra car, which is in stock. Unsatisfied demand for the Lyra is said to be *diverted* to the Libra. Only rarely in this situation can the salesperson convince the customer to switch to the luxury Hydra model.

From past experience GMC estimates that 30% of unsatisfied demand for Lyras is diverted to demand for Libras and 5% to demand for Hydras. Similarly, 10% of unsatisfied demand for Libras is diverted to demand for Hydras. For example, if the demand for Lyras is 1,400,000 cars, then the unsatisfied demand will be 400,000 if no capacity is added. Out of this unsatisfied demand, 120,000 ($= 400,000 \times 0.3$) will materialize as demand for Libras, and 20,000 ($= 400,000 \times 0.05$) will materialize as demand for Hydras. Similarly, if the demand for Libras is 1,220,000 cars (1,100,000 original demand plus 120,000 demand diverted from Lyras), then the unsatisfied demand for Lyras would be 420,000 if no capacity is added. Out of this unsatisfied demand, 42,000 ($= 420,000 \times 0.1$) will materialize as demand for Hydras. All other unsatisfied demand is lost to competitors. The pattern of demand diversion is summarized in Table 14.24.

Table 14.24 Demand Diversion Matrix

	Lyra	Libra	Hydra
Lyra	NA	0.3	0.05
Libra	0	NA	0.10
Hydra	0	0.0	NA

Question

GMC wants to decide whether to retool the Lyra and Libra plants. In addition, GMC wants to determine its production plan at each plant in the coming year. Based on the previous data, develop a mixed integer programming model (some variables integer-constrained, some not) for solving GMC's production planning–capacity expansion problem for the coming year. According to the optimal solution, what should GMC do? How sensitive is the optimal solution to key inputs? The file **GMC Retooling.xlsx** gets you started. ∎

Kate Torelli, a security analyst for LionFund, has identified a gold-mining stock (ticker symbol GMS) as a particularly attractive investment. Torelli believes that the company has invested wisely in new mining equipment. Furthermore, the company has recently purchased mining rights on land that has high potential for successful gold extraction. Torelli notes that gold has underperformed the stock market in the last decade and believes that the time is ripe for a large increase in gold prices. In addition, she reasons that conditions in the global monetary system make it likely that investors may once again turn to gold as a safe haven in which to park assets. Finally, supply and demand conditions have improved to the point where there could be significant upward pressure on gold prices.

GMS is a highly leveraged company, so it is quite a risky investment by itself. Torelli is mindful of a passage from the annual report of a competitor, Baupost, which has an extraordinarily successful investment record: "Baupost has managed a decade of consistently profitable results despite, and perhaps in some respect due to, consistent emphasis on the avoidance of downside risk. We have frequently carried both high cash balances and costly market hedges. Our results are particularly satisfying when considered in the light of this sustained risk aversion." She would therefore like to *hedge* the stock purchase—that is, reduce the risk of an investment in GMS stock.

Currently GMS is trading at $100 per share. Torelli has constructed seven scenarios for the price of GMS stock one month from now. These scenarios and corresponding probabilities are shown in Table 14.25.

To hedge an investment in GMS stock, Torelli can invest in other securities whose prices tend to move in the direction opposite to that of GMS stock. In particular, she is considering over-the-counter put options on GMS stock as potential hedging instruments. The value of a put option increases as the price of the underlying stock decreases. For example, consider a put option with a strike price of $100 and a time to expiration of one month. This means that the owner of the put has the right to sell GMS stock at $100 per share one month in the future. Suppose that the price of GMS falls to $80 at that time. Then the holder of the put option can exercise the option and receive $20 (= 100 − 80). If the price of GMS falls to $70, the option would be worth $30 (= 100 − 70). However, if the price of GMS rises to $100 or more, the option expires worthless.

Torelli called an options trader at a large investment bank for quotes. The prices for three European-style put options are shown in Table 14.26. (A European put can be exercised only at the expiration date, not before.) Torelli wishes to invest $10 million in GMS stock and put options.

Table 14.25 Scenarios and Probabilities for GMS Stock in 1 Month

	Scenario 1	Scenario 2	Scenario 3	Scenario 4	Scenario 5	Scenario 6	Scenario 7
Probability	0.05	0.10	0.20	0.30	0.20	0.10	0.05
GMS stock price($)	150	130	110	100	90	80	70

Table 14.26 Put Option Prices (Today) for GMS Case Study

	Put Option A	Put Option B	Put Option C
Strike Price($)	90	100	110
Option Price($)	2.20	6.40	12.50

Questions

1. Based on Torelli's scenarios, what is the expected return of GMS stock? What is the standard deviation of the return of GMS stock?

2. After a cursory examination of the put option prices, Torelli suspects that a good strategy is to buy one put option A for each share of GMS stock purchased. What are the mean and standard deviation of return for this strategy?

3. Assuming that Torelli's goal is to minimize the standard deviation of the portfolio return, what is the optimal portfolio that invests all $10 million? (For simplicity, assume that fractional numbers of stock shares and put options can be purchased. Assume that the amounts invested in each security must be nonnegative. However, the number of options purchased need *not* equal the number of shares of stock purchased.) What are the expected return and standard deviation of return of this portfolio? How many shares of

GMS stock and how many of each put option does this portfolio correspond to?

4. Suppose that short selling is permitted—that is, the nonnegativity restrictions on the portfolio weights are removed. Now what portfolio minimizes the standard deviation of return?

(*Hint*: A good way to attack this problem is to create a table of security returns, as indicated in Table 14.27, where only a few of the table entries are shown. To correctly calculate the standard deviation of portfolio return, you will need to incorporate the scenario probabilities. If r_i is the portfolio return in scenario i, and p_i is the probability of scenario i, then the standard deviation of portfolio return is

$$\sqrt{\sum_{i=1}^{7} p_i(r_i - \mu)^2}$$

where $\mu = \Sigma^{7}_{i=1} p_i r_i$ is the expected portfolio return.)

Table 14.27	Table of Security Returns			
	GMS Stock	**Put Option A**	**Put Option B**	**Put Option C**
Scenario 1			−100%	
2	30%			
⋮				
7				220%

Photodisc/Getty Images

DEVELOPING BOARDING STRATEGIES AT AMERICA WEST

Management science often attempts to solve problems that we all experience. One such problem is the boarding process for airline flights. As customers, we all hate to wait while travelers boarding ahead of us store their luggage and block the aisles. But this is also a big problem for the airlines. Airlines lose money when their airplanes are on the ground, so they have a real incentive to reduce the turnaround time from when a plane lands until it departs on its next flight. Of course, the turnaround time is influenced by several factors, including passenger deplaning, baggage unloading, fueling, cargo unloading, airplane maintenance, cargo loading, baggage loading, and passenger boarding. Airlines try to perform all of these tasks as efficiently as possible, but passenger boarding is particularly difficult to shorten. Although the airlines want passengers to board as quickly as possible, they don't want to use measures that might antagonize their passengers.

One study by van den Briel et al. (2005) indicates how a combination of management science methods, including simulation, was used to make passenger boarding more efficient at America West Airlines. America West (which merged with US Airways in 2006) was a major U.S. carrier based in Phoenix, Arizona. It served more destinations nonstop than any other airline. The airline's fleet consisted of Airbus A320s, Airbus A319s, Boeing 757s, Boeing 737s, and Airbus A318s.

At the time of the study, airlines used a variety of boarding strategies, but the predominant strategy was the back-to-front (BF) strategy where, after boarding first-class passengers and passengers with special needs, the rest of the passengers are boarded in groups, starting with rows in the back of the plane. As the authors suspected (and most of us have experienced), this strategy still results in significant congestion. Within a given section of the plane (the back, say), passengers storing luggage in overhead compartments can block an aisle. Also, people in the aisle or middle seat often need to get back into the aisle to let window-seat passengers be seated. The authors developed an integer programming (IP) model to minimize the number of such aisle blockages. The decision variables determined which groups of seats should be boarded in which order. Of course, the BF strategy was one possible feasible solution, but it turned out to be a suboptimal solution. The IP model suggested that the best solution was an outside-in (OI) strategy, where groups of passengers in window seats board first, then groups in the middle seats, and finally groups in aisle seats, with all of these groups going essentially in a back-to-front order.

The authors recognized that their IP model was at best an idealized model of how passengers actually behave. Its biggest drawback is that it ignores the inherent randomness in passenger behavior. Therefore, they followed up their optimization model with a simulation model. As they state, "We used simulation to validate the analytical model and to obtain a finer level of detail." This validation of an approximate or idealized analytical model is a common use for simulation. To make the simulation as realistic as possible, they used two cameras, one inside the plane and one inside the bridge leading to the plane, to tape customer behavior. By analyzing the tapes, they were able to estimate the required inputs to their simulation model, such as the time between passengers, walking speed, blocking time, and time to store luggage in overhead compartments. After the basic simulation model was developed, it was used as a tool to evaluate various boarding strategies suggested by the IP model. It also allowed the authors to experiment with changes to the overall boarding process that might be beneficial. For example, reducing congestion *inside* the airplane is not very helpful if the gate agent at the entrance to the bridge processes passengers too slowly. Their final recommendation, based on a series of simulation experiments, was to add a second gate agent (there had been only one before) and to board passengers in six groups using an OI strategy. The simulation model suggested that this could reduce the boarding time by about 37%.

The authors' recommendations were implemented first as a pilot project and then systemwide. The pilot results were impressive, with a 39% reduction in boarding times. By September 2003, the new boarding strategies had been implemented in 80% of America West's airports, with a decrease in departure delays as much as 60.1%. Besides this obvious benefit to the airline, customers also appear to be happier. Now they can easily understand when to queue up for boarding, and they experience less blocking after they get inside the plane. ■

15.1 INTRODUCTION

A **simulation model** is a computer model that imitates a real-life situation. It is like other mathematical models, but it explicitly incorporates uncertainty in one or more input variables. When you run a simulation, you allow these random input variables to take on various values, and you keep track of any resulting output variables of interest. In this way, you are able to see how the outputs vary as a function of the varying inputs.

The fundamental advantage of a simulation model is that it provides an entire distribution of results, not simply a single bottom-line result. As an example, suppose an automobile manufacturer is planning to develop and market a new model car. The company is ultimately interested in the net present value (NPV) of the profits from this car over the next 10 years. However, there are many uncertainties surrounding this car, including the yearly customer demands for it, the cost of developing it, and others. The company could develop a spreadsheet model for the 10-year NPV, using its *best guesses* for these uncertain quantities. It could then report the NPV based on these best guesses. However, this analysis would be incomplete and probably misleading—there is no guarantee that the NPV based on best-guess inputs is representative of the NPV that will actually occur. It is much better to treat the uncertainty explicitly with a simulation model. This involves entering probability distributions for the uncertain quantities and seeing how the NPV varies as the uncertain quantities vary.

Each different set of values for the uncertain quantities can be considered a scenario. Simulation allows the company to generate many scenarios, each leading to a particular NPV. In the end, it sees a whole distribution of NPVs, not a single best guess. The company can see what the NPV will be on average, and it can also see worst-case and best-case results.

These approaches are summarized in Figures 15.1 and 15.2. Figure 15.1 indicates that the deterministic (non-simulation) approach, using best guesses for the uncertain inputs, is generally *not* the appropriate method. It leads to the "flaw of averages," as we will discuss later in the chapter. The problem is that the outputs from the deterministic model are often not representative of the true outputs. The appropriate method is shown in Figure 15.2. Here the uncertainty is modeled explicitly with random inputs, and the end result is a probability distribution for each of the important outputs.

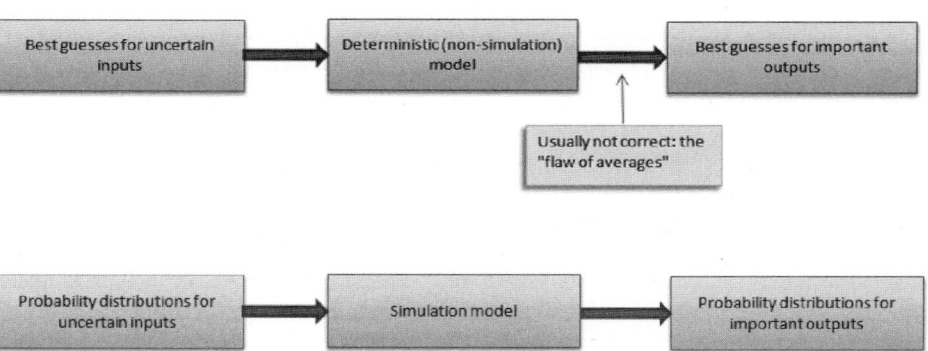

Figure 15.1
Inappropriate Deterministic Model

Figure 15.2
Appropriate Simulation Model

Simulation models are also useful for determining how sensitive a system is to changes in operating conditions. For example, the operations of a supermarket could be simulated. Once the simulation model has been developed, it could then be run (with suitable modifications) to ask a number of what-if questions. For example, if the supermarket experiences a 20% increase in business, what will happen to the average time customers must wait for service?

A huge benefit of computer simulation is that it enables managers to answer these types of what-if questions without actually changing (or building) a physical system. For example, the supermarket might want to experiment with the number of open registers to see the effect on customer waiting times. The only way it can *physically* experiment with more registers than it currently owns is to purchase more equipment. Then if it determines that this equipment is not a good investment—customer waiting times do not decrease appreciably—the company is stuck with expensive equipment it doesn't need. Computer simulation is a much less expensive alternative. It provides the company with an electronic replica of what would happen *if* the new equipment were purchased. Then, if the simulation indicates that the new equipment is worth the cost, the company can be confident that purchasing it is the right decision. Otherwise, it can abandon the idea of the new equipment *before* the equipment has been purchased.

Spreadsheet simulation modeling is quite similar to the other modeling applications in this book. You begin with input variables and then relate these with appropriate Excel formulas to produce output variables of interest. The main difference is that simulation uses *random* numbers to drive the whole process. These random numbers are generated with special functions that we will discuss in detail. Each time the spreadsheet recalculates, all of the random numbers change. This provides the ability to model the logical process once and then use Excel's recalculation ability to generate many different scenarios. By collecting the data from these scenarios, you can see the most likely values of the outputs and the best-case and worst-case values of the outputs.

In this chapter we begin by illustrating spreadsheet models that can be developed with built-in Excel functionality. However, because simulation is becoming such an important tool for analyzing real problems, add-ins to Excel have been developed to streamline the process of developing and analyzing simulation models. Therefore, we then introduce @RISK, one of the most popular simulation add-ins. This add-in not only augments the simulation capabilities of Excel, but it also enables you to analyze models much more quickly and easily.

The purpose of this chapter is to introduce basic simulation concepts, show how simulation models can be developed in Excel, and demonstrate the capabilities of the @RISK add-in. Then in the next chapter, armed with the necessary simulation tools, we will explore a number of interesting and useful simulation models.

Before proceeding, you might ask whether simulation is really used in the business world. The answer is a resounding "yes." The chapter opener described an airline example, and many other examples can be found online. For example, if you visit www.palisade.com, you will see descriptions of interesting @RISK applications from companies that regularly use this add-in. Simulation has always been a powerful tool, but it had limited use for several reasons. It typically required specialized software that was either expensive or difficult to learn, or it required a lot of tedious computer programming. Fortunately, in the past two decades, spreadsheet simulation, together with Excel add-ins such as @RISK, has put this powerful methodology in the hands of the masses—people like you and the companies you are likely to work for. Many businesses now understand that there is no longer any reason to ignore uncertainty; they can model it directly with spreadsheet simulation.

15.2 PROBABILITY DISTRIBUTIONS FOR INPUT VARIABLES

In spreadsheet simulation models, input cells can contain random numbers. Any output cells then vary as these random inputs change.

In this section we discuss the building blocks of spreadsheet simulation models. All spreadsheet simulation models are similar to the spreadsheet models from previous chapters. They have a number of cells that contain values of input variables. The other cells then contain formulas that embed the logic of the model and eventually lead to the output variable(s) of interest. The primary difference between the spreadsheet models you have developed so far and simulation models is that at least one of the input variable cells in a simulation model contains *random* numbers. Each time the spreadsheet recalculates, the random numbers change, and the new random values of the inputs produce new values of the outputs. This is the essence of simulation—it enables you to see how outputs vary as random inputs change.

Excel Tip: *Recalculation Key*

The easiest way to make a spreadsheet recalculate is to press the **F9 key**. *This is often called the "recalc" key.*

Technically speaking, input cells do not contain random numbers; they contain *probability distributions*. In general, a probability distribution indicates the possible values of a variable and the probabilities of these values. As a very simple example, you might indicate by an appropriate formula (to be described later) that you want a probability distribution with possible values 50 and 100, and corresponding probabilities 0.7 and 0.3. If you force the sheet to recalculate repeatedly and watch this input cell, you will see the value 50 about 70% of the time and the value 100 about 30% of the time. No other values besides 50 and 100 will appear.

When you enter a given probability distribution in a random input cell, you are describing the possible values and the probabilities of these values that you believe mirror reality. There are many probability distributions to choose from, and you should always attempt to choose an *appropriate* distribution for each specific problem. This is not necessarily an easy task. Therefore, we address it in this section by answering several key questions:

- What types of probability distributions are available, and why do you choose one probability distribution rather than another in an actual simulation model?

- Which probability distributions can you use in simulation models, and how do you invoke them with Excel formulas?

In later sections we address one additional question: Does the choice of input probability distribution really matter—that is, are the *outputs* from the simulation sensitive to this choice?

FUNDAMENTAL INSIGHT

Basic Elements of Spreadsheet Simulation

A spreadsheet simulation model requires three elements: (1) a method for entering random quantities from specified probability distributions in input cells, (2) the usual types of Excel formulas for relating outputs to inputs, and (3) the ability to make the spreadsheet recalculate many times and capture the resulting outputs for statistical analysis. Excel has some capabilities for performing these steps, but Excel add-ins such as @RISK provide much better tools for automating the process.

15.2.1 Types of Probability Distributions

Imagine a toolbox that contains the probability distributions you know and understand. As you obtain more experience in simulation modeling, you will naturally add probability distributions to your toolbox that you can then use in future simulation models. We begin by adding a few useful probability distributions to this toolbox. However, before adding any specific distributions, it is useful to provide a brief review of some important general characteristics of probability distributions.[1] These include the following distinctions:

- Discrete versus continuous
- Symmetric versus skewed

---

[1]This review is brief because the material was covered in Chapters 2, 4, and 5.

Choosing Probability Distributions for Uncertain Inputs

In simulation models, it is important to choose *appropriate* probability distributions for all uncertain inputs. These choices can strongly affect the results. Unfortunately, there are no "right answers." You need to choose the probability distributions that best encode your uncertainty, and this is not necessarily easy. However, the properties discussed in this section provide you with useful guidelines for making reasonable choices.

- Bounded versus unbounded
- Nonnegative versus unrestricted.

Discrete Versus Continuous

A probability distribution is *discrete* if it has a finite number of possible values.[2] For example, if you throw two dice and look at the sum of the faces showing, there are only 11 discrete possibilities: the integers 2 through 12. In contrast, a probability distribution is *continuous* if its possible values are essentially some continuum. An example is the amount of rain that falls during a month in Indiana. It could be any decimal value from 0 to, say, 15 inches.

The graph of a discrete distribution is a series of spikes, as shown in Figure 15.3.[3] The height of each spike is the probability of the corresponding value.

Figure 15.3

A Typical Discrete Probability Distribution

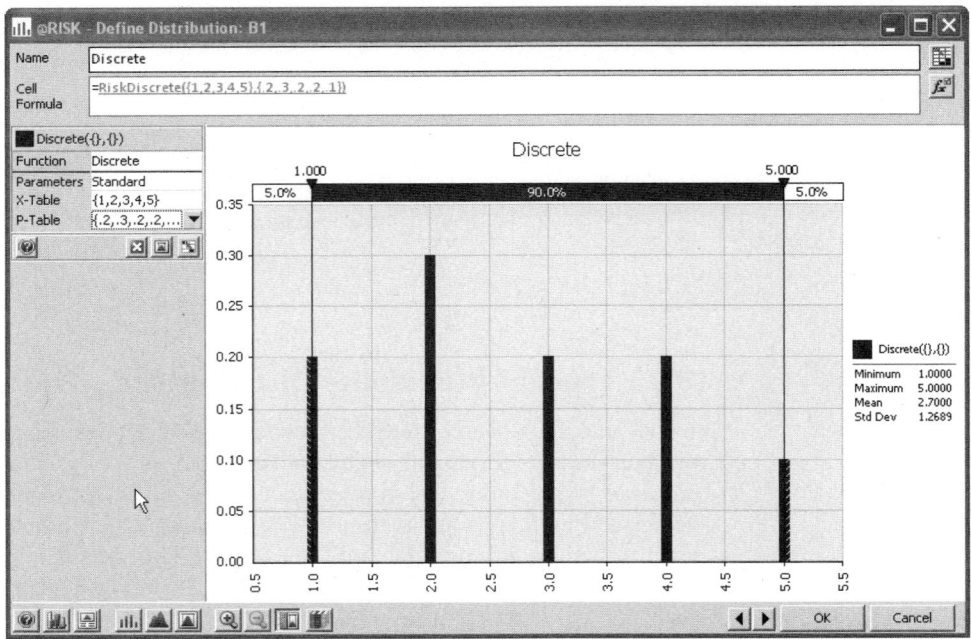

---

[2]Actually, it is possible for a discrete variable to have a *countably infinite* number of possible values, such as all the nonnegative integers 0, 1, 2, and so on. However, this is not an important distinction for practical applications.
[3]This figure and several later figures have been captured from Palisade's @RISK add-in.

The heights above a density function are not probabilities, but they still indicate relative likelihoods of the possible values.

In contrast, a continuous distribution is characterized by a *density function*, a smooth curve as shown in Figure 15.4. There are two important properties of density functions. Recall from Chapter 5 that the height of the density function above any value indicates the relative likelihood of that value, and probabilities can be calculated as areas under the curve.

Figure 15.4

A Typical Continuous Probability Distribution

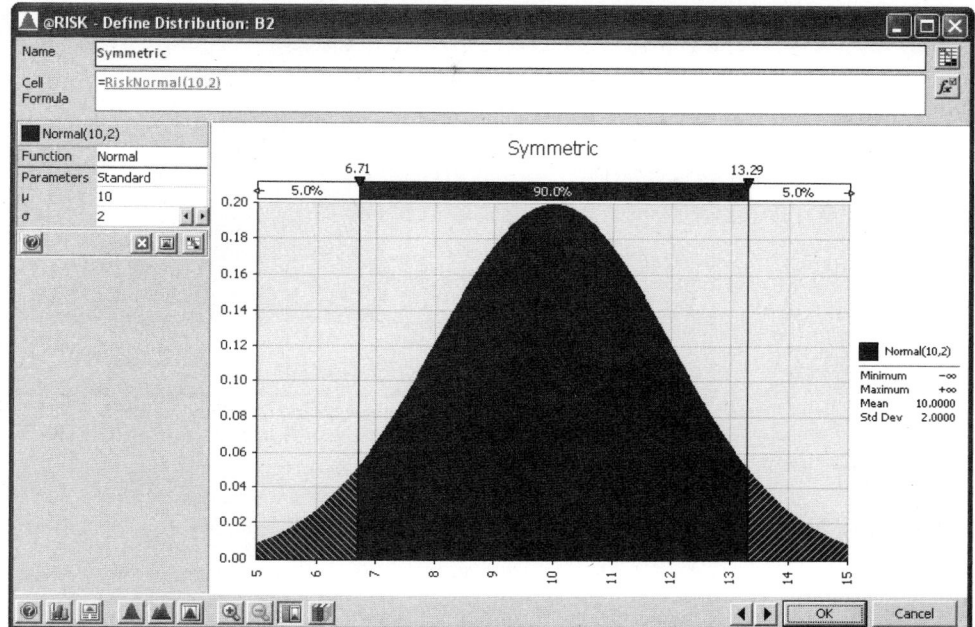

Sometimes it is convenient to treat a discrete probability distribution as continuous, and vice versa. For example, consider a student's random score on an exam that has 1000 possible points. If the grader scores each exam to the nearest integer, then even though the score is really discrete with many possible integer values, it is probably more convenient to model its distribution as a continuum. Continuous probability distributions are typically more intuitive and easier to work with than discrete distributions in cases such as this, where there are many possible values. In contrast, continuous distributions are sometimes *discretized* for simplicity.

Symmetric Versus Skewed

A probability distribution can either be symmetric or skewed to the left or right. Figures 15.4, 15.5, 15.6 provide examples of each of these. You typically choose between a symmetric and skewed distribution on the basis of realism. For example, if you want to model a student's score on a 100-point exam, you will probably choose a left-skewed distribution. This is because a few poorly prepared students typically "pull down the curve." On the other hand, if you want to model the time it takes to serve a customer at a bank, you will probably choose a right-skewed distribution. This is because most customers take only a minute or two, but a few customers take a long time. Finally, if you want to model the monthly return on a stock, you might choose a distribution symmetric around zero, reasoning that the stock return is just as likely to be positive as negative and there is no obvious reason for skewness in either direction.

Figure 15.5

A Positively Skewed Probability Distribution

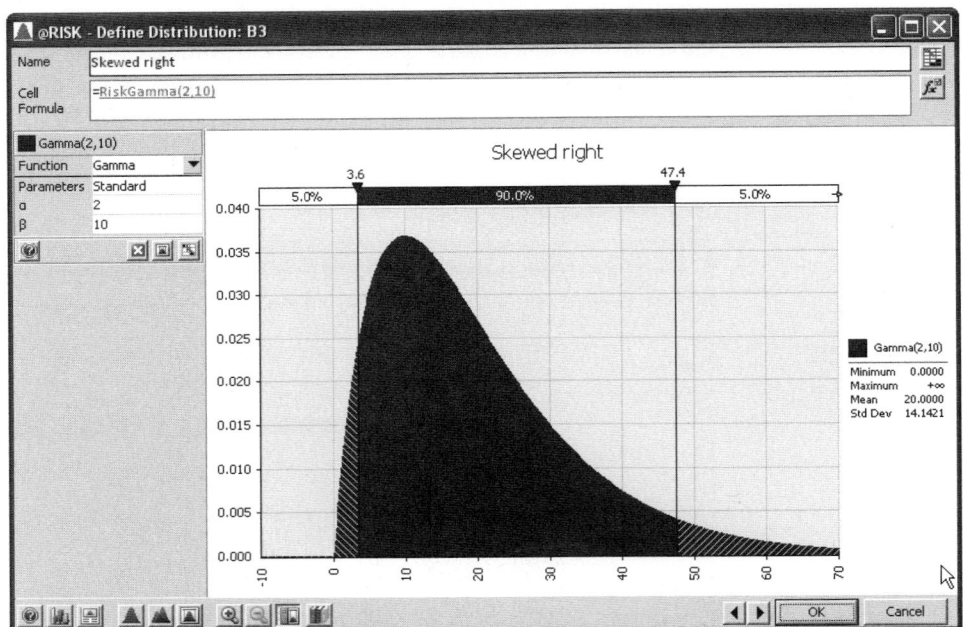

Figure 15.6

A Negatively Skewed Probability Distribution

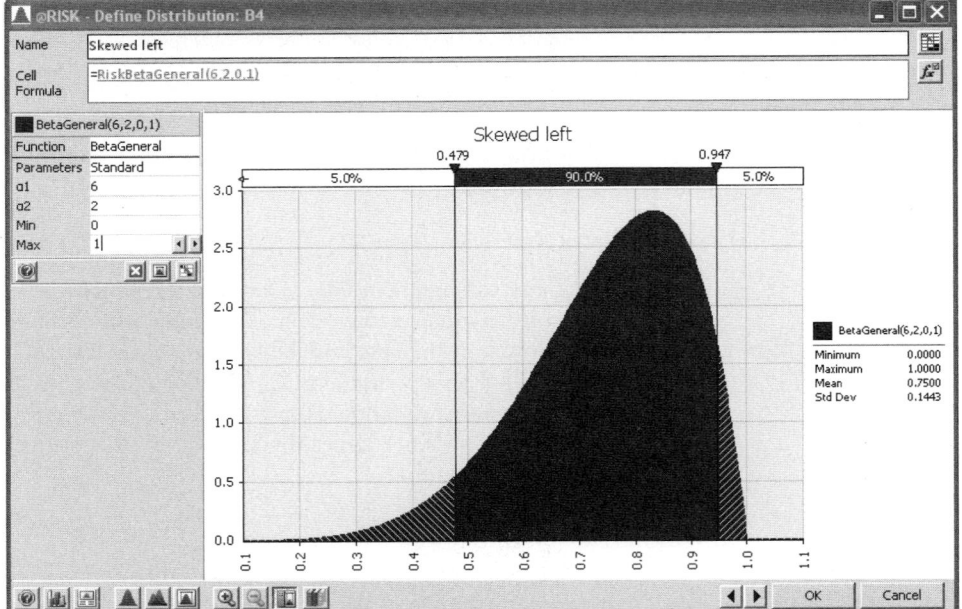

Bounded Versus Unbounded

A probability distribution is *bounded* if there are values A and B such that no possible value can be less than A or greater than B. The value A is then the *minimum* possible value, and the value B is the *maximum* possible value. The distribution is *unbounded* if there are no such bounds. Actually, it is possible for a distribution to be bounded in one direction but not the other. As an example, the distribution of scores on a 100-point exam is bounded between 0 and 100. In contrast, the distribution of the amount of damages Mr. Jones submits to his insurance company in a year is bounded on the left by 0, but there is no natural upper bound. Therefore, you might model this amount with a distribution that is bounded by 0 on the left but is unbounded on the right. Alternatively, if you believe that no damage amount larger than $20,000 can occur, you could model this amount with a distribution that is bounded in both directions.

Nonnegative Versus Unrestricted

One important special case of bounded distributions is when the only possible values are *nonnegative*. For example, if you want to model the random cost of manufacturing a new product, you know for sure that this cost must be nonnegative. There are many other such examples. In such cases, you should model the randomness with a probability distribution that is bounded below by 0. This rules out negative values that make no practical sense.

15.2.2 Common Probability Distributions

Think of the Probability Distributions.xlsx file as a "dictionary" of the most commonly used distributions. Keep it handy for reference.

Now that you know the *types* of probability distributions available, you can add some common probability distributions to your toolbox. The file **Probability Distributions.xlsx** was developed to help you learn and explore these. Each sheet in this file illustrates a particular probability distribution. It describes the general characteristics of the distribution, indicates how you can generate random numbers from the distribution either with Excel's built-in functions or with @RISK functions, and it includes histograms of these distributions from simulated data to illustrate their shapes.[4]

A family of distributions has a common name, such as "normal." Each member of the family is specified by one or more numerical parameters.

It is important to realize that each of the following distributions is really a *family* of distributions. Each member of the family is specified by one or more parameters. For example, there is not a *single* normal distribution; there is a normal distribution for each possible mean and standard deviation you specify. Therefore, when you try to find an appropriate input probability distribution in a simulation model, you first have to choose an appropriate family, and then you have to select the appropriate parameters for that family.

Uniform Distribution

The **uniform distribution** is the "flat" distribution illustrated in Figure 15.7. It is bounded by a minimum and a maximum, and all values between these two extremes are equally likely. You can think of this as the "I have no idea" distribution. For example, a manager might realize that a building cost is uncertain. If she can state only that, "I know the cost will be between $20,000 and $30,000, but other than this, I have no idea what the cost will be," then a uniform distribution from $20,000 to $30,000 is a natural choice. However, even though some people do use the uniform distribution in such cases, these situations are arguably not very common or realistic. If the manager really thinks about it, she can probably provide more information about the uncertain cost, such as, "The cost is more likely to be close to $25,000 than to either of the extremes." Then some distribution other than the uniform is more appropriate.

Regardless of whether the uniform distribution is an appropriate candidate as an input distribution, it is important for another reason. All simulation software packages, including Excel, are capable of generating random numbers uniformly distributed between 0 and 1. These are the building blocks of most simulated random numbers, in that random numbers from other probability distributions are generated from them.

---

[4]In later sections of this chapter, and all through the next chapter, we discuss much of @RISK's functionality. For this section, the only functionality we use is @RISK's collection of functions, such as RISKNORMAL and RISKTRIANG, for generating random numbers from various probability distributions. You can skim the details of these functions for now and refer back to them as necessary in later sections.

Figure 15.7
The Uniform
Distribution

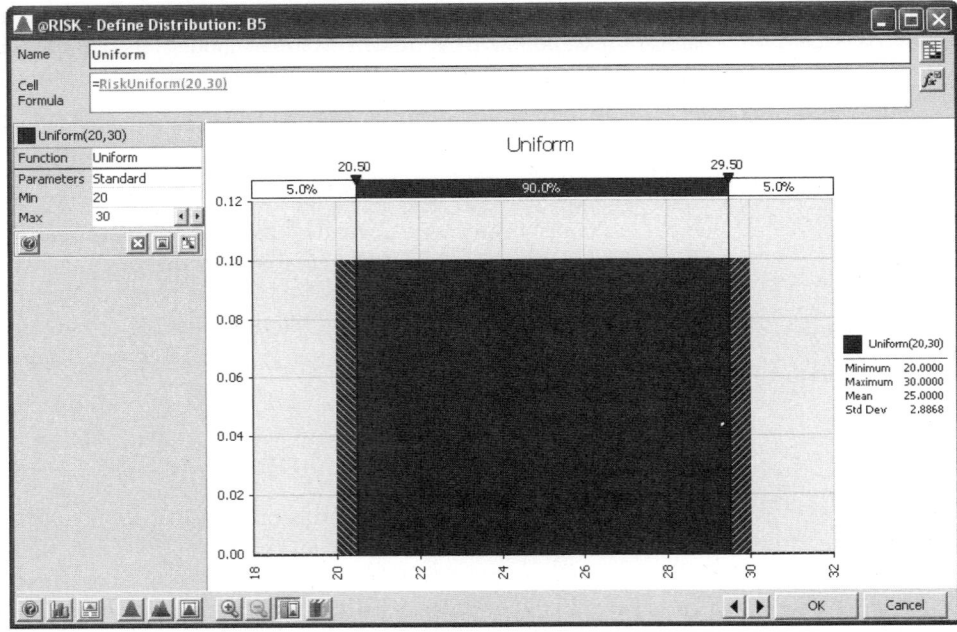

The RAND function is Excel's "building block" function for generating random numbers.

In Excel, you can generate a random number between 0 and 1 by entering the formula

=RAND()

in any cell. (The parentheses to the right of RAND indicate that this is an Excel function with no arguments. These parentheses must be included.)

Excel Function: *RAND*

To generate a random number equally likely to be anywhere between 0 and 1, enter the formula **=RAND()** *into any cell. Press the F9 key, or recalculate in any other way, to make it change randomly.*

In addition to being between 0 and 1, the numbers created by this function have two properties that you would expect "random" numbers to have.

1. **Uniform property.** Each time you enter the RAND function in a cell, all numbers between 0 and 1 have the same chance of occurring. This means that approximately 10% of the numbers generated by the RAND function will be between 0.0 and 0.1; 10% of the numbers will be between 0.65 and 0.75; 60% of the numbers will be between 0.20 and 0.80; and so on. This property explains why the random numbers are said to be *uniformly distributed* between 0 and 1.

2. **Independence property.** Different random numbers generated by **=RAND()** formulas are *probabilistically independent*. This implies that when you generate a random number in cell A5, say, it has no effect on the values of any other random numbers generated in the spreadsheet. For example, if one call to the RAND function yields a large random number such as 0.98, there is no reason to suspect that the next call to RAND will yield an abnormally small (or large) random number; it is unaffected by the value of the first random number.

Excel Tip *Besides the RAND function, there is one other function built into Excel that generates random numbers, the RANDBETWEEN function. It takes two integer arguments, as in* **=RANDBETWEEN(1,6)**, *and returns a random integer between these values* (including the endpoints) so that all such integers are equally likely. The function was introduced in Excel 2007. (It was actually available in previous versions of Excel, but only if the Analysis Toolpak add-in was loaded.)

To illustrate the RAND function, open a new workbook, enter the formula **=RAND()** in cell A4, and copy it to the range A4:A503. This generates 500 random numbers. Figure 15.8 displays a possible set of values. However, when you try this on your PC, you will undoubtedly obtain *different* random numbers. This is an inherent characteristic of simulation—no two answers are ever exactly alike. Now press the recalc (F9) key. All of the random numbers will change. In fact, each time you press the F9 key or do anything to make your spreadsheet recalculate, all of the cells containing the RAND function will change.

Figure 15.8

Uniformly Distributed Random Numbers Generated by the RAND Function

	A	B	C	D
1	500 random numbers from RAND function			
2				
3	Random #			
4	0.639741246			
5	0.977449085			
6	0.826336662			
7	0.794236038			
8	0.326052217			
9	0.540446013			
10	0.012582316			
501	0.868540879			
502	0.297930515			
503	0.960969187			

A histogram of the 500 random numbers appears in Figure 15.9. (Again, if you try this on your PC, the shape of your histogram will not be identical to the one shown in Figure 15.9, because it will be based on *different* random numbers.) From property 1, you would expect *equal* numbers of observations in the 10 categories. Obviously, the heights of the bars are *not* exactly equal, but the differences are due to chance—not to a faulty random number generator.

Figure 15.9

Histogram of the 500 Random Numbers Generated by the RAND Function

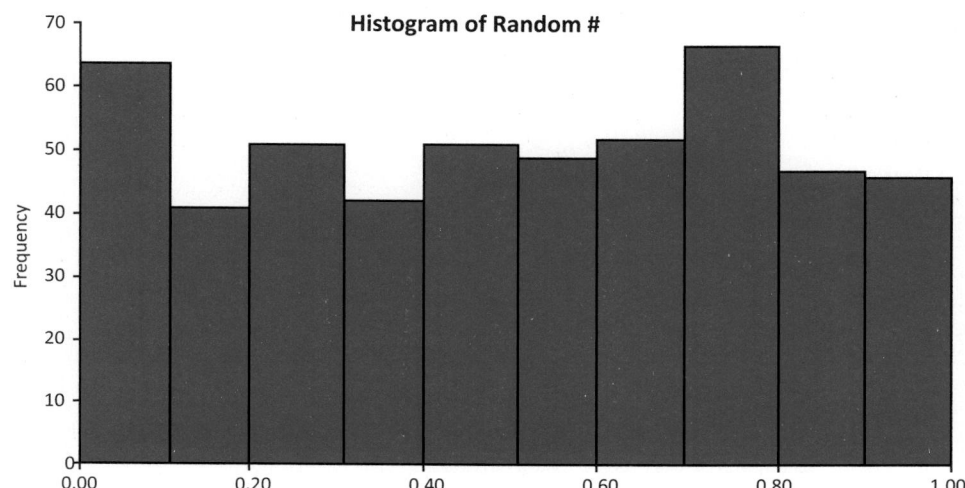

Histogram of Random #

Technical Note: *Pseudo-random Numbers*

The "random" numbers generated by the RAND function (or by the random number gener-ator in any simulation software package) are not really random. They are sometimes called pseudo-random numbers. Each successive random number follows the previous random number by a complex arithmetic operation. If you happen to know the details of this arithmetic operation, you can predict ahead of time exactly which random numbers will be generated by the RAND function. This is quite different from using a "true" random mech-anism, such as spinning a wheel, to get the next random number—a mechanism that would be impractical to implement on a computer. Mathematicians and computer scientists have studied many ways to produce random numbers that have the two properties we just discussed, and they have developed many competing random number generators such as the RAND function in Excel. The technical details need not concern you. The important point is that these random number generators produce numbers that appear to be random and are useful for simulation modeling.

It is simple to generate a uniformly distributed random number with a minimum and maximum other than 0 and 1. For example, the formula

=200+100*RAND()

generates a number uniformly distributed between 200 and 300. (Make sure you see why.) Alternatively, you can use the @RISK formula[5]

=RISKUNIFORM(200,300)

You can take a look at this and other properties of the uniform distribution on the Uniform sheet in the **Probability Distributions.xlsx** file. (See Figure 15.10.)

Figure 15.10   Properties of Uniform Distribution

	A	B	C	D	E	F	G	H
1	**Uniform distribution**							
2								
3	**Characteristics**			This is a flat distribution between two values, labeled here MinVal and MaxVal. Note that if MinVal=0 and MaxVal=1, then you can just use Excel's RAND function.				
4	Continuous							
5	Symmetric							
6	Bounded in both directions							
7	Not necessarily positive (depends on bounds)							
8								
9	**Parameters**							
10	MinVal	50						
11	MaxVal	100						
12								
13	**Excel**		**Example**					
14	=MinVal + (MaxVal-MinVal)*RAND()		96.105704					
15								
16	**@RISK**							
17	=RISKUNIFORM(MinVal,MaxVal)		96.880610					

[5]As we have done with other Excel functions, we capitalize the @RISK functions, such as RISKUNIFORM, in the text. However, this is not necessary when you enter the formulas in Excel.

> **@RISK Function: *RISKUNIFORM***
>
> *To generate a random number from any uniform distribution, enter the formula* **=RISKUNIFORM(MinVal,MaxVal)** *in any cell. Here,* MinVal *and* MaxVal *are the minimum and maximum possible values. Note that if* MinVal *is 0 and* MaxVal *is 1, this function is equivalent to Excel's RAND function.*

FREEZING RANDOM NUMBERS

The automatic recalculation of random numbers can be useful sometimes and annoying at other times. There are situations when you want the random numbers to stay fixed—that is, you want to *freeze* them at their current values. The following three-step method does this.

1. Select the range that you want to freeze, such as A4:A503 in Figure 15.8.

2. Press Ctrl-c to copy this range.

Random numbers that have been frozen do not change when you press the F9 key.

3. With the same range still selected, select the Paste Values option from the Paste dropdown menu on the Home ribbon. This procedure pastes a copy of the range onto itself, except that the entries are now numbers, not formulas. Therefore, whenever the spreadsheet recalculates, these numbers do not change.

Each sheet in the **Probability Distributions.xlsx** file has a list of 500 random numbers that have been frozen. The histograms in the sheets are based on the frozen random numbers. However, we encourage you to enter "live" random numbers in column B over the frozen ones and see how the histogram changes when you press F9.

15.2.3 Using @RISK to Explore Probability Distributions[6]

The **Probability Distributions.xlsx** file illustrates a few frequently used probability distributions, and it shows the formulas required to generate random numbers from these distributions. Another option is to use Palisade's @RISK add-in, which allows you to experiment with probability distributions. Essentially, it allows you to see the shapes of various distributions and to calculate probabilities for them, all in a user-friendly graphical interface.

To run @RISK, click on the Windows Start button, go to the Programs tab, locate the Palisades DecisionTools suite, and select @RISK. After a few seconds, you will see the welcome screen, which you can close. At this point, you should have an @RISK tab and corresponding ribbon. Select a blank cell in your worksheet, and then click on Define Distributions on left of the @RISK ribbon (see Figure 15.11). You will see one of several galleries of distributions, depending on the tab you select. For example, Figure 15.12

Figure 15.11 @RISK Ribbon

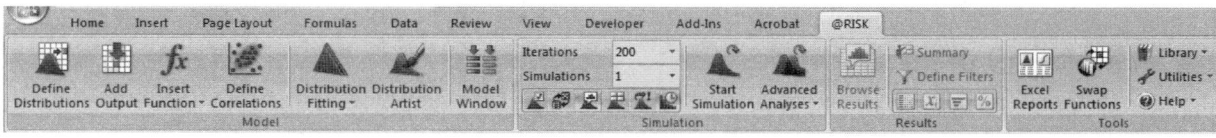

[6]Palisade previously offered a stand-alone program called RISKview for exploring probability distributions, and we discussed it in the previous edition. However, Palisade discontinued RISKview and instead incorporates its functionality in @RISK.

Figure 15.12

Gallery of
Continuous
Distributions

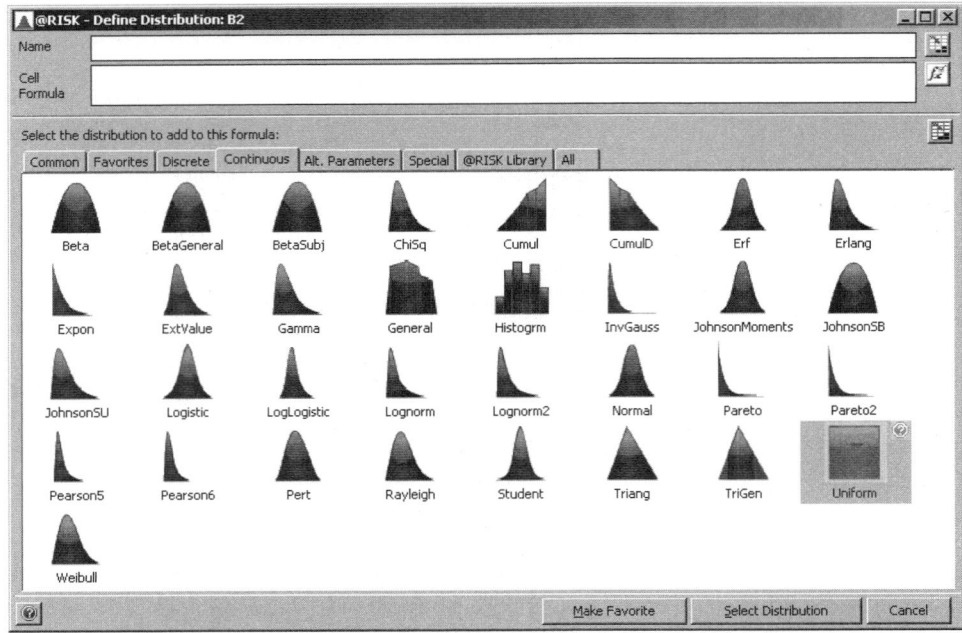

shows the gallery of continuous distributions. Highlight one of the distributions and click on Select Distribution. For example, choose the uniform distribution with minimum 75 and maximum 150. You will see the shape of the distribution and a few summary measures to the right, as shown in Figure 15.13. For example, it indicates that the mean and standard deviation of this uniform distribution are 112.5 and 21.65.

Everything in this window is interactive. Suppose you want to find the probability that a value from this distribution is less than 95. You can drag the left-hand "slider" in the diagram (the vertical line with the triangle at the top) to the position 95, as shown in Figure 15.13.

Figure 15.13

@RISK Illustration
of Uniform
Distribution

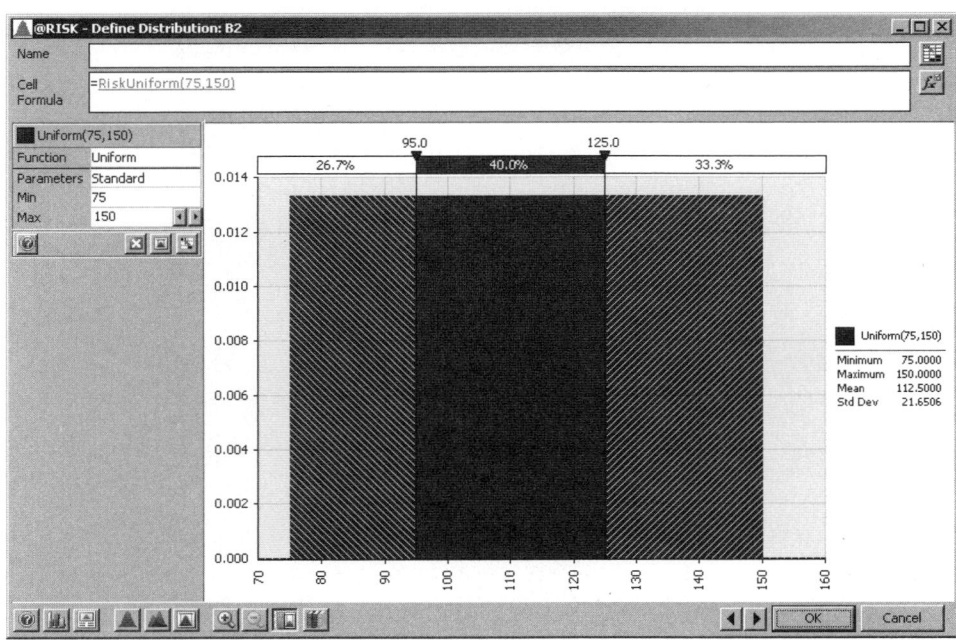

You see immediately that the left-hand probability is 0.267. Similarly, if you want the probability that a value from this distribution is greater than 125, you can drag the right-hand slider to the position 125 to see that the required probability is 0.3333. (Rather than sliding, you can enter the numbers, such as 95 and 125, directly into the areas above the sliders.)

You can also enter probabilities instead of values. For example, if you want the value such that there is probability 0.10 to the left of it—the 10th percentile—enter 10% in the left space above the chart. You will see that the corresponding value is 82.5. Similarly, if you want the value such that there is probability 0.10 to the right of it, enter 10% in the right space above the chart, and you will see that the corresponding value is 142.5.

The Define Distributions window in @RISK is quick and easy. We urge you to use it and experiment with some of its options. By the way, you can click on the third button from the left at the bottom of the window to copy the chart into an Excel worksheet. However, you then lose the interactive capabilities, such as moving the sliders.

Discrete Distribution

A **discrete distribution** is useful for many situations, either when the uncertain quantity is not really continuous (the number of televisions demanded, for example) or when you want a discrete approximation to a continuous variable. All you need to specify are the possible values and their probabilities, making sure that the probabilities sum to 1. Because of this flexibility in specifying values and probabilities, discrete distributions can have practically any shape.

As an example, suppose a manager estimates that the demand for a particular brand of television during the coming month will be 10, 15, 20, or 25, with respective probabilities 0.1, 0.3, 0.4, and 0.2. This typical discrete distribution is illustrated in Figure 15.14.

The interactive capabilities of @RISK's Define Distributions window, with its sliders, make it perfect for finding probabilities or percentiles for any given distribution.

Figure 15.14

Discrete Distribution (from @RISK)

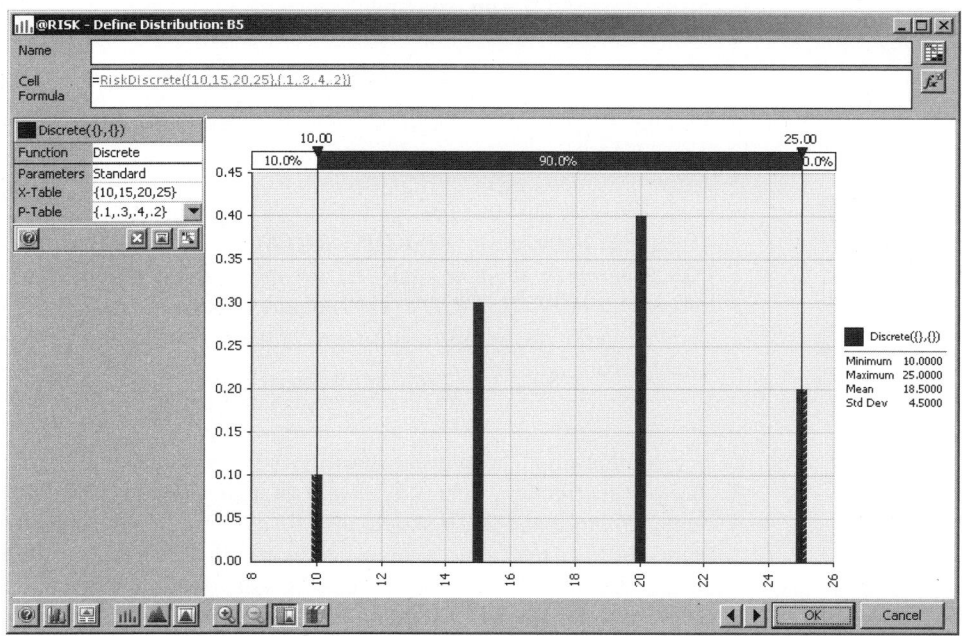

The Discrete sheet of the **Probability Distributions.xlsx** file indicates how to work with a discrete distribution. (See Figure 15.15.) As you can see, there are two quite different ways to generate a random number from this distribution. We discuss the Excel way in detail in section 15.4. For now, we simply mention that this is one case (of many) where it

Figure 15.15 Properties of a Discrete Distribution

	A	B	C	D	E	F	G	H	I
1	General discrete distribution								
2									
3	Characteristics								
4	Discrete				This can have any shape, depending				
5	Can be symmetric or skewed (or bumpy, i.e., basically any shape)				on the list of possible values and their				
6	Bounded in both directions				probabilities.				
7	Not necessarily positive (depends on possible values)								
8									
9	Parameters				Lookup table required for Excel method				
10		Values	Probabilities		CumProb	Value			
11		10	0.1		0	10			
12		15	0.3		0.1	15			
13		20	0.4		0.4	20			
14		25	0.2		0.8	25			
15									
16	Excel		Example						
17	=VLOOKUP(RAND(),LookupTable,2)		10						
18									
19	@RISK								
20	=RISKDISCRETE(Values,Probs)		20						

@RISK's way of generating a discrete random number is much simpler and more intuitive than Excel's method, which requires cumulative probabilities and a lookup function.

is much easier to generate random numbers with @RISK functions than with built-in Excel functions. Assuming that @RISK is loaded, all you need to do is enter the function RISKDISCRETE with two arguments, a list of possible values and a list of their probabilities, as in

=RISKDISCRETE(B11:B14,C11:C14)

The Excel way, which requires cumulative probabilities and a lookup table, takes more work and is harder to remember.

@RISK Function: *RISKDISCRETE*
*To generate a random number from any discrete probability distribution, enter the formula **=RISKDISCRETE(valRange,probRange)** into any cell. Here* valRange *is the range where the possible values are stored, and* probRange *is the range where their probabilities are stored.*

The selected input distributions for any simulation model reflect historical data and an analyst's best judgment as to what will happen in the future.

At this point, a relevant question is why a manager would choose this particular discrete distribution. First, it is clearly an approximation. After all, if it is possible to have demands of 20 and 25, it should also be possible to have demands between these values. Here, the manager approximates a discrete distribution with *many* possible values—all integers from 0 to 50, say—with a discrete distribution with a few well-chosen values. This is common in simulation modeling. Second, where do the probabilities come from? They are probably a blend of historical data (perhaps demand was near 15 in 30% of previous months) and the manager's subjective feelings about demand *next* month.

Normal Distribution

The *normal distribution* is the familiar bell-shaped curve that was discussed in detail in Chapter 5. (See Figure 15.16.) It is useful in simulation modeling as a continuous input

Figure 15.16

Normal Distribution
(from @RISK)

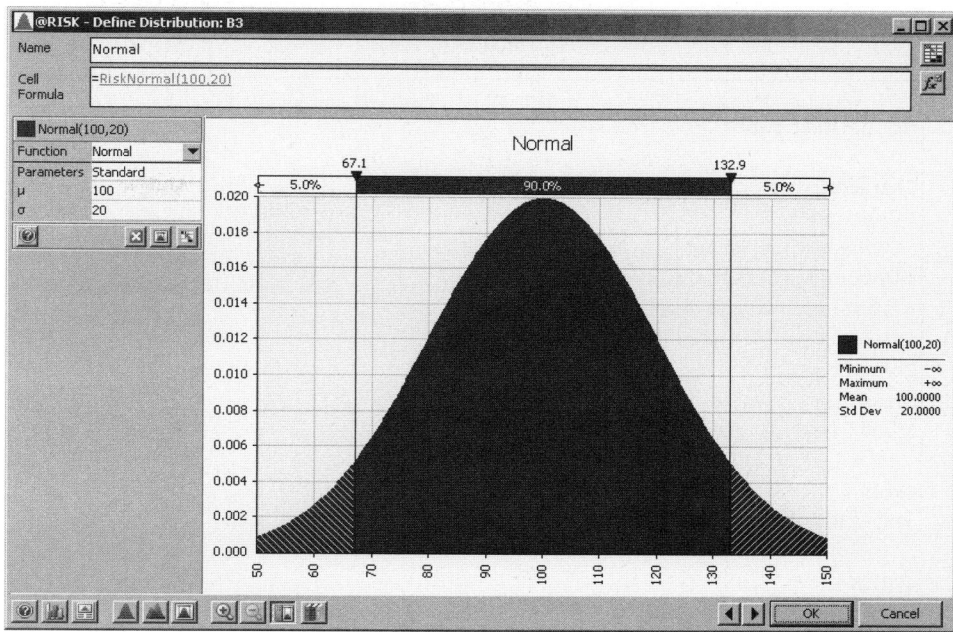

Normally distributed random numbers will almost certainly be within three standard deviations of the mean.

distribution. However, it is *not* always the most appropriate distribution. It is symmetric, which can be a drawback when a skewed distribution is more realistic. Also, it allows negative values, which are not appropriate in many situations. For example, the demand for televisions cannot be negative. Fortunately, this possibility of negative values is often not a problem. Suppose you generate a normally distributed random number with mean 100 and standard deviation 20. Then, as you should recall from Chapter 5, there is almost no chance of having values more than three standard deviations to the left of the mean, and this rules out negative values for all practical purposes.

A tip-off that a normal distribution might be an appropriate candidate for an input variable is a statement such as, "We believe the most likely value of demand is 100, and the chances are about 95% that demand will be no more than 40 units on either of side of this most likely value." Because a normally distributed value is within two standard deviations of its mean with probability 0.95, this statement translates easily to a mean of 100 and a standard deviation of 20. This does not imply that a normal distribution is the *only* candidate for the distribution of demand, but the statement naturally leads to this distribution.

The Normal sheet in the **Probability Distributions.xlsx** file indicates how you can generate normally distributed random numbers in Excel, either with or without @RISK. (See Figure 15.17.) This is one case where an add-in is not really necessary. The formula

=**NORMINV(RAND()**,*Mean,Stdev*)

always works. Still, this is not as easy to remember as @RISK's formula

=**RISKNORMAL**(*Mean,Stdev*)

@RISK Function: *RISKNORMAL*
To generate a normally distributed random number, enter the formula **=RISKNORMAL(Mean,Stdev)** *in any cell. Here,* Mean *and* Stdev *are the mean and standard deviation of the normal distribution.*

Figure 15.17 Properties of the Normal Distribution

	A	B	C	D	E	F	G	H
1	**Normal distribution**							
2								
3	**Characteristics**							
4	Continuous			This is the familiar bell-shaped curve, defined by				
5	Symmetric (bell-shaped)			two parameters: the mean and the standard				
6	Unbounded in both directions			deviation.				
7	Is both positive and negative							
8								
9	**Parameters**							
10	Mean	100						
11	Stdev	10						
12								
13	**Excel**		Example					
14	=NORMINV(RAND(),Mean,Stdev)		96.41946055					
15								
16	**@RISK**							
17	=RISKNORMAL(Mean,Stdev)		90.3093316					

Triangular Distribution

A triangular distribution is a good choice in many simulation models because it can have a variety of shapes and its parameters are easy to understand.

The **triangular distribution** is somewhat similar to the normal distribution in that its density function rises to some point and then falls, but it is more flexible and intuitive than the normal distribution. Therefore, it is an excellent candidate for many continuous input variables. The shape of a triangular density function is literally a triangle, as shown in Figure 15.18. It is specified by three easy-to-understand parameters: the minimum possible value, the most likely value, and the maximum possible value. The high point of the triangle

Figure 15.18

Triangular Distribution (from @RISK)

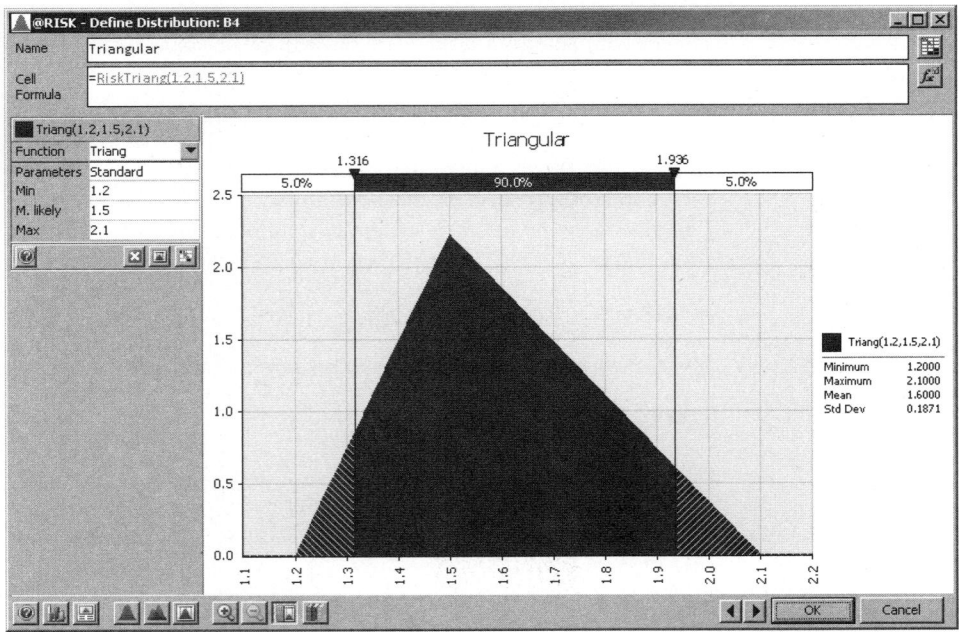

is above the most likely value. Therefore, if a manager states, "We believe the most likely development cost is $1.5 million, and we don't believe the development cost could possibly be less than $1.2 million or greater than $2.1 million," the triangular distribution with these three parameters is a natural choice. As in this numerical example, note that the triangular distribution can be skewed if the mostly likely value is closer to one extreme than another. Of course, it can also be symmetric if the most likely value is right in the middle.

The Triangular sheet of the **Probability Distributions.xlsx** file indicates how to generate random values from this distribution. (See Figure 15.19.) As you can see, there is no way to do it with native Excel (at least not without a macro). However, it is easy with @RISK, using the RISKTRIANG function, as in

=RISKTRIANG(B10,B11,B12)

This function takes three arguments: the minimum value, the most likely value, and the maximum value—in this order and separated by commas. You will see this function in many of our examples. Just remember that it has an abbreviated spelling: **RISKTRIANG**, not RISKTRIANGULAR.

Figure 15.19   Properties of the Triangular Distribution

	A	B	C	D	E	F	G	H	I	J
1	Triangular distribution									
2										
3	Characteristics			The density of this distribution is literally a triangle. The "top" of the triangle is above the most likely value, and the base of the triangle extends from the minimum value to the maximum value. It is intuitive for nontechnical people because the three parameters are meaningful.					
4	Continuous									
5	Can be symmetric or skewed in either direction									
6	Bounded in both directions									
7	Not necessarily positive (depends on bounds)									
8										
9	Parameters									
10	Min	50								
11	MostLikely	85								
12	Max	100								
13										
14	Excel									
15	There is no easy way to do it except by writing a macro.									
16										
17	@RISK		Example							
18	=RISKTRIANG(Min,MostLikely,Max)		62.61066937							

@RISK Function: *RISKTRIANG*

To generate a random number from a triangular distribution, enter the formula **=RISKTRIANG** *(**MinVal,MLVal,MaxVal**) in any cell. Here,* MinVal *is the minimum possible value,* MLVal *is the most likely value, and* MaxVal *is the maximum value.*

Binomial Distribution

The *binomial distribution* is a discrete distribution that was discussed extensively in Chapter 5. Recall that the binomial distribution applies to a very specific situation: when a number of independent and identical trials occur, and each trial results in a *success* or *failure*. Then the binomial random number is the number of successes in these trials. The two parameters of this distribution, n and p, are the number of trials and the probability of success on each trial.

A random number from a binomial distribution indicates the number of successes in a certain number of identical trials.

As an example, suppose an airline company sells 170 tickets for a flight and estimates that 80% of the people with tickets will actually show up for the flight. How many people will actually show up? It is tempting to state that *exactly* 80% of 170, or 136 people, will show up, but this neglects the inherent randomness. A more realistic way to model this situation is to say that each of the 170 people, independently of one another, will show up with probability 0.8. Then the number of people who actually show up is binomially distributed with $n = 170$ and $p = 0.8$. (This assumes independent behavior across passengers, which might not be the case, for example, if whole families either show up or don't.) This distribution is illustrated in Figure 15.20.

Figure 15.20

Binomial Distribution (from @RISK)

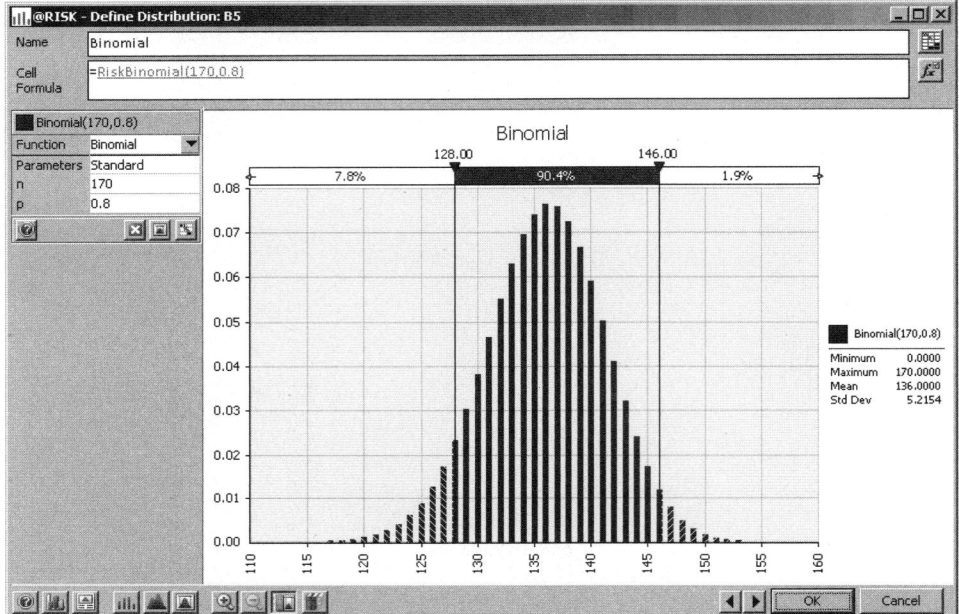

The Binomial sheet of the **Probability Distributions.xlsx** file indicates how to generate random numbers from this distribution. (See Figure 15.21.) Although it is possible to do this with Excel using the built-in CRITBINOM function and the RAND function, it is not very intuitive or easy to remember. Clearly, the @RISK way is preferable. In the airline example, you would generate the number who show up with the formula

=**RISKBINOMIAL(170,0.8)**

Note that the histogram in this figure is approximately bell-shaped. This is no accident. When the number of trials n is reasonably large and p isn't too close to 0 or 1, the binomial distribution can be well approximated by the normal distribution.

@RISK Function: *RISKBINOMIAL*
To generate a random number from a binomial distribution, enter the formula =***RISKBINOMIAL*(NTrials,PSuccess)** *in any cell. Here,* NTrials *is the number of trials, and* PSuccess *is the probability of a success on each trial.*

A common question asked by students is which distribution to use for a given uncertain quantity such as the price of oil, the demand for laptops, and so on. Admittedly, the

Figure 15.21 Properties of the Binomial Distribution

	A	B	C	D	E	F	G	H
1	**Binomial distribution**							
2								
3	**Characteristics**							
4	Discrete							
5	Can be symmetric or skewed							
6	Bounded below by 0, bounded above by Ntrials							
7	Nonnegative							
8								
9	**Parameters**							
10	NTrials	170						
11	PSuccess	0.8						
12								
13	**Excel**		Example					
14	=CRITBINOM(NTrials,PSuccess,RAND())		139					
15								
16	**@RISK**							
17	=RISKBINOMIAL(NTrials,PSuccess)		133					

(Cell note, rows 3–6): This distribution is of the number of "successes" in a given number of identical, independent trials, when the probability of success is constant on each trial.

choices we make in later examples are sometimes for convenience. However, in real business situations the choice is not always clear-cut, and it can make a difference in the results. Stanford professor Sam Savage and two of his colleagues discuss this choice in a series of two articles on "Probability Management." (These articles are available online at http://lionhrtpub.com/orms/orms-2-06/frprobability.html and http://lionhrtpub.com/orms/orms-4-06/frprobability.html.) They argue that with the increasing importance of simulation models in today's business world, input distributions should not only be chosen carefully, but they should be kept and maintained as important corporate assets. They shouldn't just be chosen in some ad hoc fashion every time they are needed. For example, if the price of oil is an important input in many of a company's decisions, then experts within the company should assess an appropriate distribution for the price of oil and modify it as necessary when new information arises. The authors even suggest a new company position, Chief Probability Officer, to control access to the company's probability distributions.

So as you are reading these final two chapters, keep Savage's ideas in mind. The choice of probability distributions for inputs is not easy, yet neither is it arbitrary. The choice *can* make a difference in the results. This is the reason why you want as many families of probability distributions in your toolbox as possible. You then have more flexibility to choose a distribution that is appropriate for your situation.

PROBLEMS

Note: Student solutions for problems whose numbers appear within a colored box are available for purchase at www.cengagebrain.com.

Level A

1. Use the RAND function and the Copy command to generate a set of 100 random numbers.
   a. What fraction of the random numbers are smaller than 0.5?
   b. What fraction of the time is a random number less than 0.5 followed by a random number greater than 0.5?
   c. What fraction of the random numbers are larger than 0.8?
   d. Freeze these random numbers. However, instead of pasting them over the original random numbers, paste them onto a new range. Then press the F9 recalculate key. The original random numbers

should change, but the pasted copy should remain the same.

2. Use Excel's functions (not @RISK) to generate 1000 random numbers from a normal distribution with mean 100 and standard deviation 10. Then freeze these random numbers.
   a. Calculate the mean and standard deviation of these random numbers. Are they approximately what you would expect?
   b. What fraction of these random numbers are within k standard deviations of the mean? Answer for $k = 1$; for $k = 2$; for $k = 3$. Are the answers close to what they should be (according to the empirical rules you learned in Chapters 2 and 5)?
   c. Create a histogram of the random numbers using 10 to 15 categories of your choice. Does this histogram have approximately the shape you would expect?

3. Use @RISK to draw a uniform distribution from 400 to 750. Then answer the following questions.
   a. What are the mean and standard deviation of this distribution?
   b. What are the 5th and 95th percentiles of this distribution?
   c. What is the probability that a random number from this distribution is less than 450?
   d. What is the probability that a random number from this distribution is greater than 650?
   e. What is the probability that a random number from this distribution is between 500 and 700?

4. Use @RISK to draw a normal distribution with mean 500 and standard deviation 100. Then answer the following questions.
   a. What is the probability that a random number from this distribution is less than 450?
   b. What is the probability that a random number from this distribution is greater than 650?
   c. What is the probability that a random number from this distribution is between 500 and 700?

5. Use @RISK to draw a triangular distribution with parameters 300, 500, and 900. Then answer the following questions.
   a. What are the mean and standard deviation of this distribution?
   b. What are the 5th and 95th percentiles of this distribution?
   c. What is the probability that a random number from this distribution is less than 450?
   d. What is the probability that a random number from this distribution is greater than 650?
   e. What is the probability that a random number from this distribution is between 500 and 700?

6. Use @RISK to draw a binomial distribution that results from 50 trials with probability of success 0.3

on each trial, and use it to answer the following questions.
   a. What are the mean and standard deviation of this distribution?
   b. You have to be more careful in interpreting @RISK probabilities with a discrete distribution such as this binomial. For example, if you move the left slider to 11, you find a probability of 0.139 to the left of it. But is this the probability of "less than 11" or "less than or equal to 11"? One way to check is to use Excel's BINOMDIST function. Use this function to interpret the 0.139 value from @RISK.
   c. Using part b to guide you, use @RISK to find the probability that a random number from this distribution will be greater than 17. Check your answer by using the BINOMDIST function appropriately in Excel.

7. Use @RISK to draw a triangular distribution with parameters 200, 300, and 600. Then superimpose a normal distribution on this drawing, choosing the mean and standard deviation to match those from the triangular distribution. (Click on the Add Overlay button and then choose the distribution to superimpose.)
   a. What are the 5th and 95th percentiles for these two distributions?
   b. What is the probability that a random number from the triangular distribution is less than 400? What is this probability for the normal distribution?
   c. Experiment with the sliders to answer questions similar to those in part b. Would you conclude that these two distributions differ most in the extremes (right or left) or in the middle? Explain.

8. We all hate to keep track of small change. By using random numbers, it is possible to eliminate the need for change and give the store and the customer a fair deal. This problem indicates how it could be done.
   a. Suppose that you buy something for $0.20. How could you use random numbers (built into the cash register system) to decide whether you should pay $1.00 or nothing?
   b. If you bought something for $9.60, how would you use random numbers to eliminate the need for change?
   c. In the long run, why is this method fair to both the store and the customers? Would you personally (as a customer) be willing to abide by such a system?

Level B

9. A company is about to develop and then market a new product. It wants to build a simulation model for the entire process, and one key uncertain input is the development cost. For each of the following scenarios,

choose an appropriate distribution together with its parameters, justify your choice in words, and use @RISK to draw your chosen distribution.

a. Company experts have no idea what the distribution of the development cost is. All they can state is "we are 95% sure it will be at least $450,000, and we are 95% sure it will be no more than $650,000."

b. Company experts can still make the same statement as in part **a**, but now they can also state: "We believe the distribution is symmetric, reasonably bell-shaped, and its most likely value is about $550,000."

c. Company experts can still make the same statement as in part **a**, but now they can also state: "We believe the distribution is skewed to the right, and its most likely value is about $500,000."

10. Continuing the preceding problem, suppose that another key uncertain input is the development time,

which is measured in an *integer* number of months. For each of the following scenarios, choose an appropriate distribution together with its parameters, justify your choice in words, and use @RISK to draw your chosen distribution.

a. Company experts believe the development time will be from 6 to 10 months, but they have absolutely no idea which of these will result.

b. Company experts believe the development time will be from 6 to 10 months. They believe the probabilities of these five possible values will increase linearly to a most likely value at 8 months and will then decrease linearly.

c. Company experts believe the development time will be from 6 to 10 months. They believe that 8 months is twice as likely as either 7 months or 9 months and that either of these latter possibilities is three times as likely as either 6 months or 10 months.

15.3 SIMULATION AND THE FLAW OF AVERAGES

To help motivate simulation modeling in general, we present a simple example in this section. It will clearly show the distinction between Figure 15.1 (a deterministic model with best-guess inputs) and Figure 15.2 (an appropriate simulation model). In doing so, it will illustrate a pitfall called the "flaw of averages" that you should always try to avoid.[7]

EXAMPLE | **15.1 ORDERING CALENDARS AT WALTON BOOKSTORE**

In August, Walton Bookstore must decide how many of next year's nature calendars to order. Each calendar costs the bookstore $7.50 and sells for $10. After January 1, all unsold calendars will be returned to the publisher for a refund of $2.50 per calendar. Walton believes that the number of calendars it can sell by January 1 follows some probability distribution with mean 200. Walton believes that ordering to the average demand, that is, ordering 200 calendars, is a good decision. Is it?

Objective To illustrate the difference between a deterministic model with a best guess for uncertain inputs and a simulation model that incorporates uncertainty explicitly.

WHERE DO THE NUMBERS COME FROM?

The monetary values are straightforward. The mean demand is probably an estimate based on historical demands for similar calendars.

Solution

A deterministic model appears in Figure 15.22. (See the file **Walton Bookstore 1.xlsx**. Assuming the best guess for demand, Walton orders to this average value, and it appears

[7]As far as we know, the term "flaw of averages" was coined by Sam Savage, the same Stanford professor quoted earlier.

Figure 15.22

Deterministic Model

	A	B	C	D	E	F
1	Walton's bookstore - deterministic model					
2						
3	Cost data					
4	Unit cost	$7.50				
5	Unit price	$10.00				
6	Unit refund	$2.50				
7						
8	Uncertain quantity					
9	Demand (average shown)	200				
10						
11	Decision variable					
12	Order quantity	200				
13						
14	Profit model					
15		Demand	Revenue	Cost	Refund	Profit
16		200	$2,000.00	$1,500.00	$0.00	$500.00

that the company's best guess for profit is $500. (The formulas in cells B16:F16 are straightforward. Anticipating that the order quantity and demand will not always be equal, they are **=B9**, **=B5*MIN(B9,B12)**, **=B4*B12**, **=B6*MAX(B12-B9,0)**, and **=C16-D16+E16**.) Before reading further, do you believe that the *average* profit will be $500 when uncertainty in demand is introduced explicitly (and the company still orders 200 calendars)? Think what happens to profit when demand is less than 200 and when it is greater than 200. Are these two cases symmetric?

We now contrast this with a simulation model where the demand in cell B9 is replaced by a random number. For this example, we assume that demand is *normally* distributed with mean 200 and standard deviation 40, although these specific assumptions are not crucial for the qualitative aspects of the example. All you need to do is enter the formula **=ROUND(RISKNORMAL(200,40),0)** in cell B9, where the ROUND function has been used to round to the nearest integer. Now the model appears as in Figure 15.23.

The random demand in cell B9 is now live, as are its dependents in row 16, so each time you press the F9 key, you get a new demand and associated profit. Do you get about

Figure 15.23

Simulation Model

	A	B	C	D	E	F
1	Walton's bookstore - simulation model					
2						
3	Cost data					
4	Unit cost	$7.50				
5	Unit price	$10.00				
6	Unit refund	$2.50				
7						
8	Uncertain quantity (assumed normal with mean 200, stdev 40)					
9	Demand (random)	263				
10						
11	Decision variable					
12	Order quantity	200				
13						
14	Profit model					
15		Demand	Revenue	Cost	Refund	Profit
16		263	$2,000.00	$1,500.00	$0.00	$500.00

$500 in profit on average? Absolutely not! The situation isn't symmetric. The *largest* profit you can get is $500, which occurs about half the time, whenever demand is greater than 200. A typical such situation appears in the figure, where the excess demand of 63 is simply lost. However, when demand is less than 200, the profit is *less than* $500, and it keeps decreasing as demand decreases.

We ran @RISK with 1000 iterations (which will be explained in detail in section 15.5) and found the resulting histogram of 1000 simulated profits shown in Figure 15.24. The large spike on the right is due to the cases where demand is 200 or more and profit is $500. All the little spikes to the left are where demand is less than 200 and profit is less than $500, sometimes considerably less. You can see on the right that the *mean* profit, the average of the 1000 simulated profits, is only about $380, well less than the $500 suggested by the deterministic model.

Figure 15.24

Histogram of
Simulated Profits

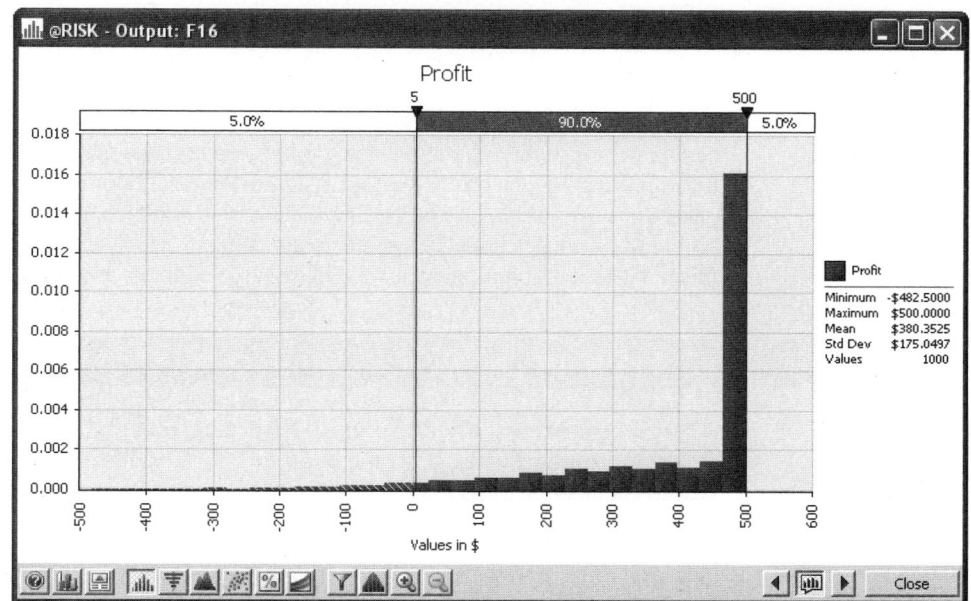

The point of this simple example is that a deterministic model can be very misleading. In particular, the output from a deterministic model that uses best guesses for uncertain inputs is *not* necessarily equal to, or even close to, the average of the output from a simulation. This is exactly what "the flaw of averages" means. ∎

FUNDAMENTAL INSIGHT

The Flaw of Averages

If a model contains uncertain inputs, it can be very misleading to build a deterministic model by using the *means* of the inputs to predict an output. The resulting output value can be considerably different—lower *or* higher—than the mean of the output values obtained from running a simulation with uncertainty incorporated explicitly.

15.4 SIMULATION WITH BUILT-IN EXCEL TOOLS

In this section, we show how spreadsheet simulation models can be developed and analyzed with Excel's built-in tools without using add-ins. As you will see, this is certainly possible, but it presents two problems. First, the @RISK functions illustrated in the **Probability Distributions.xlsx** file are not available. You are able to use only Excel's RAND function and transformations of it to generate random numbers from various probability distributions. Second, there is a bookkeeping problem. Once you build an Excel model with output cells linked to appropriate random input cells, you can press the F9 key as often as you like to see how the outputs vary. However, there is no quick way to keep track of these output values and summarize them. This bookkeeping feature is the real strength of a simulation add-in such as @RISK. It can be done with Excel, usually with data tables, but the summarization of the resulting data is completely up to the user—you. Therefore, we strongly recommend that you use the "Excel-only" method described in this section only if you don't have an add-in such as @RISK.

To illustrate the Excel-only procedure, we continue analyzing the calendar problem from Example 15.1. This general problem occurs when a company (such as a news vendor) must make a one-time purchase of a product (such as a newspaper) to meet customer demands for a certain period of time. If the company orders too few newspapers, it will lose potential profit by not having enough on hand to satisfy its customers. If it orders too many, it will have newspapers left over at the end of the day that, at best, can be sold at a loss. More generally, the problem is to match supply to an uncertain demand, a very common problem in business. In much of the rest of this chapter, we will discuss variations of this problem.

EXAMPLE | **15.2 SIMULATING WITH EXCEL ONLY AT WALTON BOOKSTORE**

Recall that Walton Bookstore must decide how many of next year's nature calendars to order. Each calendar costs the bookstore $7.50 and sells for $10. After January 1, all unsold calendars will be returned to the publisher for a refund of $2.50 per calendar. In this version, we assume that demand for calendars (at the full price) is given by the probability distribution shown in Table 15.1. Walton wants to develop a simulation model to help it decide how many calendars to order.

Table 15.1   Probability Distribution of Demand for Walton Example

Demand	Probability
100	0.30
150	0.20
200	0.30
250	0.15
300	0.05

Objective   To use built-in Excel tools—including the RAND function and data tables, but no add-ins—to simulate profit for several order quantities and ultimately choose the "best" order quantity.

WHERE DO THE NUMBERS COME FROM?

The numbers in Table 15.1 are the key to the simulation model. They are discussed in more detail next.

Solution

We first discuss the probability distribution in Table 15.1. It is a discrete distribution with only five possible values: 100, 150, 200, 250, and 300. In reality, it is clear that other values of demand are possible. For example, there could be demand for exactly 187 calendars. In spite of its apparent lack of realism, we use this discrete distribution for two reasons. First, its simplicity is a nice feature to get you started with simulation modeling. Second, discrete distributions are often used in real business simulation models. Even though the discrete distribution is only an *approximation* to reality, it can still provide important insights into the actual problem.

As for the probabilities listed in Table 15.1, they are typically drawn from historical data or (if historical data are lacking) educated guesses. In this case, the manager of Walton Bookstore has presumably looked at demands for calendars in previous years, and he has used any information he has about the market for next year's calendars to estimate, for example, that the probability of a demand for 200 calendars is 0.30. The five probabilities in this table *must* sum to 1. Beyond this requirement, they should be as reasonable and consistent with reality as possible.

It is important to realize that this is really a decision problem under uncertainty. Walton must choose an order quantity *before* knowing the demand for calendars. Unfortunately, Solver cannot be used because of the uncertainty.[8] Therefore, we develop a simulation model for any *fixed* order quantity. Then we run this simulation model with various order quantities to see which one appears to be best.

DEVELOPING THE SIMULATION MODEL

Now we discuss the ordering model. For any fixed order quantity, we show how Excel can be used to simulate 1000 replications (or any other number of replications). Each replication is an independent replay of the events that occur. To illustrate, suppose you want to simulate profit if Walton orders 200 calendars. Figure 15.25 illustrates the results obtained by simulating 1000 independent replications for this order quantity. (See the file **Walton Bookstore 2.xlsx**.) Note that there are many hidden rows in Figure 15.25. To develop this model, use the following steps.

1 Inputs. Enter the cost data in the range B4:B6, the probability distribution of demand in the range E5:F9, and the proposed order quantity, 200, in cell B9. Pay particular attention to the way the probability distribution is entered (and compare to the Discrete sheet in the **Probability Distributions.xlsx** file). Columns E and F contain the possible demand values and the probabilities from Table 15.1. It is also necessary (see step 2 for the reasoning) to have the cumulative probabilities in column D. To obtain these, first enter the value 0 in cell D5. Then enter the formula

=F5+D5

in cell D6 and copy it to the range D7:D9.

2 Generate random demands. The key to the simulation is the generation of the customer demands in the range B19:B1018 from the random numbers generated by the RAND function and the probability distribution of demand. Here is how it works. The interval from 0 to 1 is split into five segments: 0.0 to 0.3 (length 0.3), 0.3 to 0.5 (length 0.2), 0.5 to 0.8 (length 0.3), 0.8 to 0.95 (length 0.15), and 0.95 to 1.0 (length 0.05). Note that these lengths are the probabilities of the various demands. Then a demand is

---

[8]Palisade Corporation has another Excel add-in called RISKOptimizer that can be used for optimization in a simulation model. It is included in the suite that you own, but we will not discuss it here.

Figure 15.25 Walton Bookstore Simulation Model

	A	B	C	D	E	F	G	H	I	J
3	Cost data			Demand distribution				Range names used:		
4	Unit cost	$7.50		Cum Prob	Demand	Probability		LookupTable	=Model!$D$5:$F$9	
5	Unit price	$10.00		0.00	100	0.30		Order_quantity	=Model!$B$9	
6	Unit refund	$2.50		0.30	150	0.20		Unit_cost	=Model!$B$4	
7				0.50	200	0.30		Unit_price	=Model!$B$5	
8	Decision variable			0.80	250	0.15		Unit_refund	=Model!$B$6	
9	Order quantity	200		0.95	300	0.05				
10										
11	Summary measures for simulation below									
12	Average profit	$193.63		95% confidence interval for expected profit						
13	Stdev of profit	$331.68		Lower limit	$173.07					
14	Minimum profit	-$250.00		Upper limit	$214.18					
15	Maximum profit	$500.00								
16										
17	Simulation							Distribution of profit		
18	Replication	Demand	Revenue	Cost	Refund	Profit		Value	Frequency	
19	1	100	$1,000	$1,500	$250	-$250		-250	316	
20	2	150	$1,500	$1,500	$125	$125		125	185	
21	3	200	$2,000	$1,500	$0	$500		500	499	
22	4	100	$1,000	$1,500	$250	-$250				
23	5	100	$1,000	$1,500	$250	-$250				
1016	998	200	$2,000	$1,500	$0	$500				
1017	999	200	$2,000	$1,500	$0	$500				
1018	1000	200	$2,000	$1,500	$0	$500				

This rather cumbersome procedure for generating a discrete random number is not necessary when you use @RISK.

associated with each random number, depending on which interval the random number falls in. For example, if a random number is 0.5279, this falls in the third interval, so it is associated with the third possible demand value, 200.

To implement this procedure, you use a VLOOKUP function based on the range D5:F9 (named LookupTable). This table has the cumulative probabilities in column D and the possible demand values in column E. In fact, the whole purpose of the cumulative probabilities in column D is to allow the use of the VLOOKUP function. To generate the simulated demands, enter the formula

=VLOOKUP(RAND(),LookupTable,2)

in cell B19 and copy it to the range B20:B1018. This formula compares any RAND value to the values in D5:D9 and returns the appropriate demand from E5:E9. (In the file, you will note that random cells are colored green. This coloring convention is not required, but we use it consistently to identify the random cells.)

This step is the key to the simulation, so make sure you understand exactly what it entails. The rest is bookkeeping, as indicated in the following steps.

3 **Revenue.** Once the demand is known, the number of calendars sold is the smaller of the demand and the order quantity. For example, if 150 calendars are demanded, 150 will be sold. But if 250 are demanded, only 200 can be sold (because Walton orders only 200). Therefore, to calculate the revenue in cell C19, enter the formula

=Unit_price*MIN(B19,Order_quantity)

4 **Ordering cost.** The cost of ordering the calendars does not depend on the demand; it is the unit cost multiplied by the number ordered. Calculate this cost in cell D19 with the formula

=Unit_cost*Order_quantity

5 **Refund.** If the order quantity is greater than the demand, there is a refund of $2.50 for each calendar left over; otherwise, there is no refund. Therefore, calculate the refund in cell E19 with the formula

=Unit_refund*MAX(Order_quantity-B19,0)

For example, if demand is 150, then 50 calendars are left over, and this MAX is 50, the larger of 50 and 0. However, if demand is 250, then no calendars are left over, and this MAX is 0, the larger of −50 and 0. (This calculation could also be accomplished with an IF function instead of a MAX function.)

6 **Profit.** Calculate the profit in cell F19 with the formula

=C19+E19-D19

7 **Copy to other rows.** This is a "one-line" simulation, where all of the logic is captured in a single row, row 19. For one-line simulations, you can replicate the logic with new random numbers very easily by copying down. Copy row 19 down to row 1018 to generate 1000 replications.

8 **Summary measures.** Each profit value in column F corresponds to one randomly generated demand. You usually want to see how these vary from one replication to another. First, calculate the average and standard deviation of the 1000 profits in cells B12 and B13 with the formulas

=AVERAGE(F19:F1018)

and

=STDEV(F19:F1018)

Similarly, calculate the smallest and largest of the 1000 profits in cells B14 and B15 with the MIN and MAX functions.

9 **Confidence interval for mean profit.** Calculate a 95% confidence interval for the mean profit in cells E13 and E14 with the formulas

=B12−1.96*B13/SQRT(1000)

and

=B12+1.96*B13/SQRT(1000)

(See the next section on confidence intervals for details.)

10 **Distribution of simulated profits.** There are only three possible profits, −$250, $125, or $500 (depending on whether demand is 100, 150, or at least 200—see the following discussion). You can use the COUNTIF function to count the number of times each of these possible profits is obtained. To do so, enter the formula

=COUNTIF($F$19:$F$1018,H19)

in cell I19 and copy it down to cell I21.

Checking Logic with Deterministic Inputs

It can be difficult to check whether the logic in your model is correct, because of the random numbers. The reason is that you usually get different output values, depending on the particular random numbers generated. Therefore, it is sometimes useful to enter well-chosen *fixed* values for the random inputs, just to see whether your logic is correct. We call these *deterministic checks*. In the present example, you might try several fixed demands, at least one of which is *less than* the order quantity and at least one of which is *greater than* the order quantity. For example, if you enter a fixed demand of 150, the revenue, cost, refund, and profit should be $1500, $1500, $125, and $125, respectively. Or if you enter a fixed demand of 250, these outputs are $2000, $1500, $0, and $500. There is no randomness in these values; every correct model should get these same values. If your model doesn't get these values, there must be a logic error in your model that has nothing to do with random numbers or simulation. Of course, you should fix any such logical errors before reentering the *random* demand and running the simulation.

You can make a similar check by keeping the random demand, repeatedly pressing the F9 key, and watching the outputs for the different random demands. For example, if the refund is not $0 every time demand exceeds the order quantity, you know you have a logical error in at least one formula. The advantage of deterministic checks is that you can compare your results with those of other users, using *agreed-upon test values* of the random quantities. You should all get exactly the same outputs.

Discussion of the Simulation Results

At this point, it is a good idea to stand back and see what you have accomplished. First, in the body of the simulation, rows 19 through 1018, you randomly generated 1000 possible demands and the corresponding profits. Because there are only five possible demand values (100, 150, 200, 250, and 300), there are only five possible profit values: −$250, $125, $500, $500, and $500. Also, note that for the order quantity 200, the profit is $500 regardless of whether demand is 200, 250, or 300. (Make sure you understand why.) A tally of the profit values in these rows, including the hidden rows, indicates that there are 316 rows with profit equal to −$250 (demand 100), 185 rows with profit equal to $125 (demand 150), and 499 rows with profit equal to $500 (demand 200, 250, or 300). The average of these 1000 profits is $193.63, and their standard deviation is $331.68. (Again, however, remember that your answers will probably differ from these because of different random numbers.)

Typically, a simulation model should capture one or more output variables, such as profit. These output variables depend on random inputs, such as demand. The goal is to estimate the probability distributions of the outputs. In the Walton simulation the estimated probability distribution of profit is

For this particular model, the output distribution is also discrete: There are only three possible profits for an order quantity of 200.

$$P(\text{Profit} = -\$250) = 316/1000 = 0.316$$

$$P(\text{Profit} = \$125) = 185/1000 = 0.185$$

$$P(\text{Profit} = \$500) = 499/1000 = 0.499$$

The estimated mean of this distribution is $193.63 and the estimated standard deviation is $331.68. It is important to realize that if the entire simulation is run again with *different* random numbers (such as the ones you might have generated on your PC), the answers will probably be slightly different. This is the primary reason for the confidence interval in cells E13 and E14. This interval expresses the remaining uncertainty about the *mean* of the profit distribution. Your best guess for this mean is the average of the 1000 profits you happened to observe. However, because the corresponding confidence interval is somewhat wide, from $173.07 to $214.18, you are not at all sure of the *true* mean of the profit distribution. You are only 95% confident that the true mean is within this interval. If you run this simulation again with different random numbers, the average profit might be somewhat different from the average profit you observed, $193.63, and the other summary statistics will probably also be different. (For illustration, we pressed the F9 key five times and got the following average profits: $213.88, $206.00, $212.75, $219.50, and $189.50. So this is truly a case of "answers will vary.")

Notes about Confidence Intervals

The confidence interval provides a measure of accuracy of the mean profit, as estimated from the simulation.

It is common in computer simulations to estimate the mean of some distribution by the average of the simulated observations. The usual practice is then to accompany this estimate with a **confidence interval,** which indicates the accuracy of the estimate. You should recall from Chapter 8 that to obtain a confidence interval for the mean, you start with the estimated mean and then add and subtract a multiple of the *standard error* of the estimated mean. If the estimated mean (that is, the average) is $\overline{X}$, the confidence interval is given in the following formula.

Confidence Interval for the Mean

$$\overline{X} \pm (\text{Multiple} \times \text{Standard Error of } \overline{X})$$

We repeat these basic facts about confidence intervals from Chapter 8 here for your convenience.

The standard error of $\overline{X}$ is the standard deviation of the observations divided by the square root of n, the number of observations:

Standard Error of $\overline{X}$

$$s/\sqrt{n}$$

Here, s is the symbol for the standard deviation of the observations. You can obtain it with the STDEV function in Excel.

The *multiple* in the confidence interval formula depends on the confidence level and the number of observations. If the confidence level is 95%, for example, then the multiple is usually very close to 2, so a good guideline is to go out two standard errors on either side of the average to obtain an approximate 95% confidence interval for the mean.

Approximate 95% Confidence Interval for the Mean

$$\overline{X} \pm 2s/\sqrt{n}$$

To be more precise, if n is reasonably large, which is almost always the case in simulations, the central limit theorem implies that the correct multiple is the number from the standard normal distribution that cuts off probability 0.025 in each tail. This is a famous number in statistics: 1.96. Because 1.96 is very close to 2, it is acceptable for all practical purposes to use 2 instead of 1.96 in the confidence interval formula. (Note that you should use a different multiple if you want a 90% or a 99% confidence level rather than a 95% level.)

The idea is to choose the number of iterations large enough so that the resulting confidence interval will be sufficiently narrow.

Analysts often plan a simulation so that the confidence interval for the mean of some important output will be sufficiently narrow. The reasoning is that narrow confidence intervals imply more precision about the estimated mean of the output variable. If the confidence level is fixed at some value such as 95%, the only way to narrow the confidence interval is to simulate more replications. Assuming that the confidence level is 95%, the following value of n is required to ensure that the resulting confidence interval will have a half-length approximately equal to some specified value B:

Sample Size Determination

$$n = \frac{4 \times (\text{Estimated standard deviation})^2}{B^2}$$

This formula requires an estimate of the standard deviation of the output variable. For example, in the Walton simulation the 95% confidence interval with $n = 1000$ has half-length ($214.18 − $173.07)/2 = $20.56. Suppose that you want to reduce this half-length to $12.50—that is, you want $B = $12.50. You do not know the exact standard deviation of the profit distribution, but you can estimate it from the simulation as $331.68. Therefore, to obtain the required confidence interval half-length B, you need to simulate n replications, where

$$n = \frac{4(328.04)^2}{12.50^2} \approx 2755$$

(When this formula produces a noninteger, it is common to round upward.) The claim, then, is that if you rerun the simulation with 2817 replications rather than 1000 replications, the half-length of the 95% confidence interval for the mean profit will be close to $12.50.

Finding the Best Order Quantity

You are not yet finished with the Walton example. So far, the simulation has been run for only a single order quantity, 200. Walton's ultimate goal is to find the *best* order quantity. Even this statement must be clarified. What does "best" mean? As in Chapter 6, one possibility is to use the *expected* profit—that is, EMV—as the optimality criterion, but other characteristics of the profit distribution could influence the decision. You can obtain the required outputs with a data table. Specifically, you use a data table to rerun the simulation for other order quantities. This data table and a corresponding chart are shown in Figure 15.26. (This is still part of the finished version of the **Walton Bookstore 2.xlsx** file.)

Figure 15.26   Data Table for Walton Bookstore Simulation

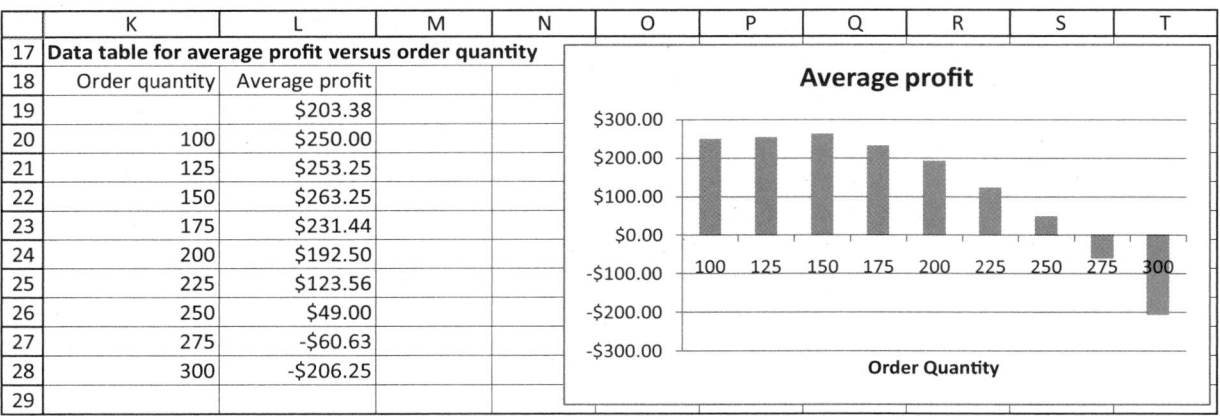

	K	L	M	N	O	P	Q	R	S	T
17	Data table for average profit versus order quantity									
18	Order quantity	Average profit								
19		$203.38								
20	100	$250.00								
21	125	$253.25								
22	150	$263.25								
23	175	$231.44								
24	200	$192.50								
25	225	$123.56								
26	250	$49.00								
27	275	-$60.63								
28	300	-$206.25								
29										

To optimize in simulation models, try various values of the decision variable(s) and run the simulation for each of them.

To create this table, enter the trial order quantities shown in the range K20:K28, enter the link **=B12** to the average profit in cell L19, and select the data table range K19:L28. Then select Data Table from the What-If Analysis dropdown list, specifying that the column input cell is B9. (See Figure 15.25.) Finally, construct a column chart of the average profits in the data table. Note that an order quantity of 150 appears to maximize the average profit. Its average profit of $263.25 is slightly higher than the average profits from nearby order quantities and much higher than the profit gained from an order of 200 or more calendars. However, again keep in mind that this is a simulation, so that all of these average profits depend on the particular random numbers generated. If you rerun the simulation with different random numbers, it is conceivable that some other order quantity could be best. (Did you notice in the data table that the average profits in cells L19 and L24 are both based on an order quantity of 200? They are different because they are based on different random numbers.)

Excel Tip: *Calculation Settings with Data Tables*
Sometimes you will create a data table and the values will be constant the whole way down. This could mean you did something wrong, but more likely it is due to a calculation setting. To check, go to the Formulas ribbon and click on the Calculation Options dropdown arrow. If it isn't Automatic (the default setting), you need to click on the Calculate Now (or Calculate Sheet) button or press the F9 key to make the data table calculate correctly. (The Calculate Now and F9 key recalculate everything in your workbook. The Calculate Sheet option recalculates only the active sheet.) Note that the Automatic Except for Data Tables setting is there for a reason. Data tables, especially those based on complex simulations, can take a lot of time to recalculate, and with the default setting, this recalculation occurs every time anything changes in your workbook. So the Automatic Except for Data Tables setting is handy to prevent data tables from recalculating until you force them to by pressing the F9 key or clicking on one of the Calculate buttons.

Using a Data Table to Repeat Simulations

The Walton simulation is a particularly simple one-line simulation model. All of the logic—generating a demand and calculating the corresponding profit—can be captured in a single row. Then to replicate the simulation, you can simply copy this row down as far as you like. Many simulation models are significantly more complex and require more than one row to capture the logic. Nevertheless, they still result in one or more output quantities (such as profit) that you want to replicate. We now illustrate another method of replicating with Excel only that is more general (still using the Walton example). It uses a data table to generate the replications. Refer to Figure 15.27 and the file **Walton Bookstore 3.xlsx**.

Through row 19, this model is exactly like the previous model. That is, it uses the given data at the top of the spreadsheet to construct a typical "prototype" of the simulation in row 19. This time, however, do not copy row 19 down. Instead, form a data table in the range A23:B1023 to replicate the basic simulation 1000 times. In column A, list the replication numbers, 1 to 1000. Next, enter the formula **=F19** in cell B23. This forms a link to the profit from the prototype row for use in the data table. Then create a data table and enter *any blank cell* (such as C23) as the column input cell. (No row input cell is necessary, so its box should be left empty.) This tricks Excel into repeating the row 19 calculations 1000 times, each time with a new random number, and reporting the profits in column B of the data table. (If you wanted to see other simulated quantities, such as revenue, for each replication, you could add extra output columns to the data table.)

Excel Tip: *How Data Tables Work*
To understand this procedure, you must understand exactly how data tables work. When you create a data table, Excel takes each value in the left column of the data table (here, column A), substitutes it into the cell designated as the column input cell, recalculates the spreadsheet, and returns the output value (or values) you have requested in the top row of the data table (such as profit). It might seem silly to substitute each replication number from column A into a blank cell such as cell C23, but this part is really irrelevant. The important part is the recalculation. Each recalculation leads to a new random demand and corresponding profit, and these profits are the quantities you want to keep track of.

The key to simulating many replications in Excel (without an add-in) is to use a data table with any blank cell as the column input cell.

Figure 15.27 Using a Data Table to Simulate Replications

	A	B	C	D	E	F	G	H	I	J
1	Simulation of Walton's bookstore									
2										
3	Cost data			Demand distribution				Range names used:		
4	Unit cost	$7.50		CumProb	Demand	Probability		LookupTable	=Model!$D$5:$F$9	
5	Unit price	$10.00		0.00	100	0.30		Order_quantity	=Model!$B$9	
6	Unit refund	$2.50		0.30	150	0.20		Unit_cost	=Model!$B$4	
7				0.50	200	0.30		Unit_price	=Model!$B$5	
8	Decision variable			0.80	250	0.15		Unit_refund	=Model!$B$6	
9	Order quantity	200		0.95	300	0.05				
10										
11	Summary measures from simulation below									
12	Average	$189.13		95% confidence interval for expected profit						
13	StDev	$327.89		Lower limit	$168.81					
14	Minimum	-$250.00		Upper limit	$209.45					
15	Maximum	$500.00								
16										
17	Simulation									
18		Demand	Revenue	Cost	Refund	Profit				
19		100	$1,000	$1,500	$250	-$250				
20										
21	Data table for replications, each shows profit from that replication									
22	Replication	Profit								
23		-$250								
24	1	-$250								
25	2	$500								
26	3	$500								
27	4	-$250								
1021	998	$500								
1022	999	$500								
1023	1000	$500								

Of course, this means that you should not freeze the quantity in cell B19 before forming the data table. The whole point of the data table is to use a different random number for each replication, and this will occur only if the random demand in row 19 is "live."

Using a Two-Way Data Table

You can carry this method one step further to see how the profit depends on the order quantity. Here you use a two-way data table with the replication number along the side and possible order quantities along the top. See Figure 15.28 and the file **Walton Bookstore 4.xlsx**. Now the data table range is A23:J1023, and the driving formula in cell A23 is again the link **=F19**. The column input cell should again be *any blank cell*, and the row input cell should be B9 (the order quantity). Each cell in the body of the data table shows a simulated profit for a particular replication and a particular order quantity, and each is based on a *different* random demand.

By averaging the numbers in each column of the data table (see row 14), you can see that 150 again appears to be the best order quantity. It is also helpful to construct a column chart of these averages, as in Figure 15.29. Now, however, assuming you have not frozen anything, the data table and the corresponding chart will change each time you press the F9 key. To see whether 150 is always the best order quantity, you can press the F9 key and see whether the bar above 150 continues to be the highest.

Figure 15.28   Using a Two-Way Data Table for the Simulation Model

	A	B	C	D	E	F	G	H	I	J
1	Simulation of Walton's bookstore									
2										
3	Cost data			Demand distribution				Range names used:		
4	Unit cost	$7.50		CumProb	Demand	Probability		LookupTable	=Model!$D$5:$F$9	
5	Unit price	$10.00		0.00	100	0.30		Order_quantity	=Model!$B$9	
6	Unit refund	$2.50		0.30	150	0.20		Unit_cost	=Model!$B$4	
7				0.50	200	0.30		Unit_price	=Model!$B$5	
8	Decision variable			0.80	250	0.15		Unit_refund	=Model!$B$6	
9	Order quantity	200		0.95	300	0.05				
10										
11	Summary measures of simulated profits for each order quantity									
12				Order quantity						
13		100	125	150	175	200	225	250	275	300
14	Average profit	$250.00	$261.13	$267.75	$237.44	$206.38	$118.69	$16.75	-$99.81	-$209.63
15	Stdev profit	$0.00	$83.67	$169.54	$243.62	$327.49	$361.44	$429.60	$432.34	$442.74
16										
17	Simulation									
18		Demand	Revenue	Cost	Refund	Profit				
19		100	$1,000	$1,500	$250	-$250				
20										
21	Data table showing profit for replications with various order quantities									
22	Replication			Order quantity						
23	($250.00)	100	125	150	175	200	225	250	275	300
24	1	$250	$313	$0	$250	-$250	375	625	125	375
25	2	$250	$313	$375	-$125	$125	0	-500	-250	-375
26	3	$250	$125	$375	$438	$500	375	250	-250	0
27	4	$250	$313	$0	$438	$500	375	250	-625	-750
1021	998	$250	$313	$375	$438	$125	375	625	-625	-375
1022	999	$250	$313	$0	$438	$500	375	250	500	375
1023	1000	$250	$313	$375	$438	$500	562.5	-500	500	375

Figure 15.29

Column Chart of Average Profits for Different Order Quantities

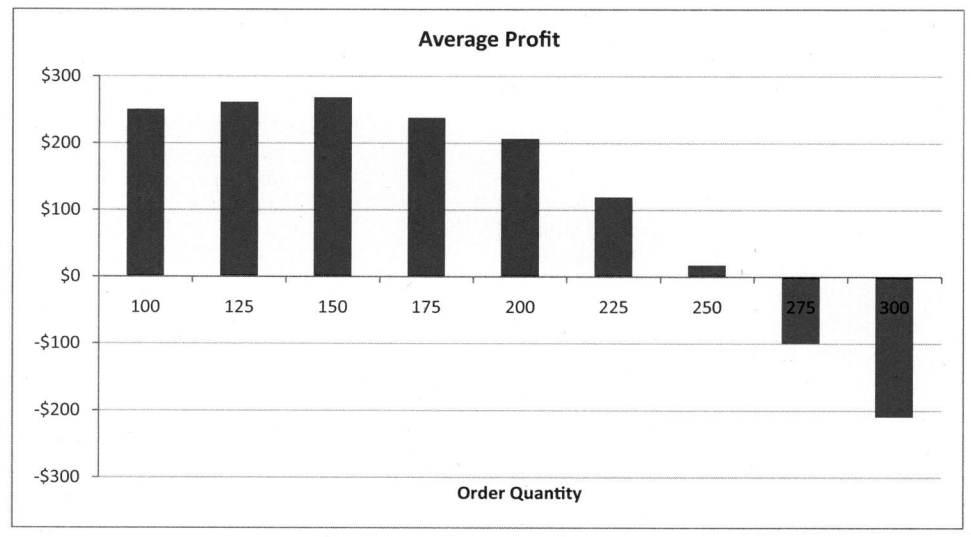

By now you should appreciate the usefulness of data tables in spreadsheet simulations. They allow you to take a prototype simulation and replicate its key results as often as you like. This method makes summary statistics (over the entire group of replications) and corresponding charts fairly easy to obtain. Nevertheless, it takes some work to create the data tables and charts. In the next section you will see how the @RISK add-in does a lot of this work for you.

PROBLEMS

Level A

11. Suppose you own an expensive car and purchase auto insurance. This insurance has a $1000 deductible, so that if you have an accident and the damage is less than $1000, you pay for it out of your pocket. However, if the damage is greater than $1000, you pay the first $1000 and the insurance pays the rest. In the current year there is probability 0.025 that you will have an accident. If you have an accident, the damage amount is normally distributed with mean $3000 and standard deviation $750.

   a. Use Excel to simulate the amount you have to pay for damages to your car. This should be a one-line simulation, so run 5000 iterations by copying it down. Then find the average amount you pay, the standard deviation of the amounts you pay, and a 95% confidence interval for the average amount you pay. (Note that many of the amounts you pay will be 0 because you have no accidents.)

   b. Continue the simulation in part **a** by creating a two-way data table, where the row input is the deductible amount, varied from $500 to $2000 in multiples of $500. Now find the average amount you pay, the standard deviation of the amounts you pay, and a 95% confidence interval for the average amount you pay for each deductible amount.

   c. Do you think it is reasonable to assume that damage amounts are *normally* distributed? What would you criticize about this assumption? What might you suggest instead?

12. In August of the current year, a car dealer is trying to determine how many cars of the next model year to order. Each car ordered in August costs $20,000. The demand for the dealer's next year models has the probability distribution shown in the file **P15_12.xlsx**. Each car sells for $25,000. If demand for next year's cars exceeds the number of cars ordered in August, the dealer must reorder at a cost of $22,000 per car. Excess cars can be disposed of at $17,000 per car.

Use simulation to determine how many cars to order in August. For your optimal order quantity, find a 95% confidence interval for the expected profit.

13. In the Walton Bookstore example, suppose that Walton receives no money for the first 50 excess calendars returned but receives $2.50 for every calendar after the first 50 returned. Does this change the optimal order quantity?

14. A sweatshirt supplier is trying to decide how many sweatshirts to print for the upcoming NCAA basketball championships. The final four teams have emerged from the quarterfinal round, and there is now a week left until the semifinals, which are then followed in a couple of days by the finals. Each sweatshirt costs $10 to produce and sells for $25. However, in three weeks, any leftover sweatshirts will be put on sale for half price, $12.50. The supplier assumes that the demand for his sweatshirts during the next three weeks (when interest in the tournament is at its highest) has the distribution shown in the file **P15_14.xlsx**. The residual demand, after the sweatshirts have been put on sale, has the distribution also shown in this file. The supplier, being a profit maximizer, realizes that every sweatshirt sold, even at the sale price, yields a profit. However, he also realizes that any sweatshirts produced but not sold (even at the sale price) must be thrown away, resulting in a $10 loss per sweatshirt. Analyze the supplier's problem with a simulation model.

Level B

15. In the Walton Bookstore example with a discrete demand distribution, explain why an order quantity other than one of the possible demands cannot maximize the expected profit. (*Hint*: Consider an order of 190 calendars, for example. If this maximizes expected profit, then it must yield a higher expected profit than an order of 150 or 100. But then an order of 200 calendars must also yield a larger expected profit than 190 calendars. Why?)

15.5 INTRODUCTION TO THE @RISK ADD-IN

Spreadsheet simulation modeling has become extremely popular in recent years, both in the academic and corporate communities. Much of the reason for this popularity is due to simulation add-ins such as @RISK. There are two primary advantages to using such an add-in. First, an add-in gives you easy access to many probability distributions you might want to use in your simulation models. You already saw in section 15.2 how the RISKDISCRETE, RISKNORMAL, and RISKTRIANG functions, among others, are easy to use and remember. Second, an add-in allows you to perform simulations much more easily than is possible with Excel alone. To replicate a simulation in Excel, you typically need to build a data table. Then you have to calculate summary statistics, such as averages, standard deviations, and percentiles, with built-in Excel functions. If you want graphs to enhance the analysis, you have to create them. In short, you have to perform a number of time-consuming steps for each simulation. Simulation add-ins such as @RISK perform much of this work automatically.

@RISK provides a number of functions for simulating from various distributions, and it takes care of all the bookkeeping in spreadsheet simulations. Excel simulations without @RISK require much more work for the user.

Although we will focus only on @RISK in this book, it is not the only simulation add-in available for Excel. Two worthy competitors are Crystal Ball, developed by Decisioneering (www.decisioneering.com) and Risk Solver Platform, developed by Frontline Systems, the developer of Solver (www.frontsys.com). Both Crystal Ball and Risk Solver Platform have much of the same functionality as @RISK. However, the authors have a natural bias for @RISK—we have been permitted by its developer, Palisade Corporation (www.palisade.com), to provide the academic version free with this book. If it were not included, you would have to purchase it from Palisade at a fairly steep price. Indeed, Microsoft Office does not include @RISK, Crystal Ball, Risk Solver Platform, or any other simulation add-in—you must purchase them separately.

15.5.1 @RISK Features

Here is an overview of some of @RISK's features. We will discuss all of these in more detail in this section.

1. @RISK contains a number of functions such as RISKNORMAL and RISKDISCRETE that make it easy to generate observations from a wide variety of probability distributions. You saw some of these in section 15.2.

2. You can designate any cell or range of cells in your simulation model as *output cells*. When you run the simulation, @RISK automatically keeps summary measures (averages, standard deviations, percentiles, and others) from the values generated in these output cells across the replications. It also creates graphs such as histograms based on these values. In other words, @RISK takes care of tedious bookkeeping operations for you.

3. @RISK has a special function, **RISKSIMTABLE**, that allows you to run the same simulation several times, using a different value of some key input variable each time. This input variable is often a decision variable. For example, suppose that you would like to simulate an inventory ordering policy (as in the Walton Bookstore example). Your ultimate purpose is to compare simulation outputs across a number of possible order quantities such as 100, 150, 200, 250, and 300. If you use an appropriate formula involving the RISKSIMTABLE function, the entire simulation is performed for each of these order quantities separately—with one click of a button. You can then compare the outputs to choose the best order quantity.

15.5.2 Loading @RISK

To build simulation models with @RISK, you need to have Excel open with @RISK added in. The first step, if you have not already done so, is to install the Palisade DecisionTools suite with the Setup program. Then you can load @RISK by clicking on the Windows Start button, selecting the Programs group, selecting the Palisade DecisionTools group, and finally selecting the @RISK item. If Excel is already open, this loads @RISK inside Excel. If Excel is not yet open, this launches Excel and @RISK simultaneously.[9] After @RISK is loaded, you see an @RISK tab and the corresponding @RISK ribbon in Figure 15.30.[10]

Figure 15.30 @RISK Ribbon

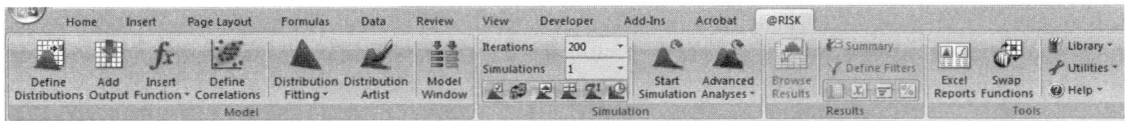

15.5.3 @RISK Models with a Single Random Input Variable

The majority of the work (and thinking) goes into developing the model. Setting up @RISK and then running it are relatively easy.

In the remainder of this section we illustrate some of @RISK's functionality by revisiting the Walton Bookstore example. The next chapter demonstrates the use of @RISK in a number of interesting simulation models. Throughout our discussion, you should keep one very important idea in mind. The development of a simulation model is basically a two-step procedure. The first step is to build the model itself. This step requires you to enter all of the logic that transforms inputs (including @RISK functions such as RISKDISCRETE) into outputs (such as profit). This is where most of the work and thinking go, exactly as in models from previous chapters, and @RISK cannot do this for you. It is *your* job to enter the formulas that link inputs to outputs appropriately. However, once this logic has been incorporated, @RISK takes over in the second step. It automatically replicates your model, with different random numbers on each replication, and it reports any summary measures that you request in tabular or graphical form. Therefore, @RISK greatly decreases the amount of busy work you need to do, but it is not a magic bullet.

We begin by analyzing an example with a single random input variable.

EXAMPLE	**15.3 USING @RISK AT WALTON BOOKSTORE**

Recall that Walton Bookstore buys calendars for $7.50, sells them at the regular price of $10, and gets a refund of $2.50 for all calendars that cannot be sold. In contrast to Example 15.2, assume now that Walton estimates a triangular probability distribution for demand, where the minimum, most likely, and maximum values of demand are 100, 175, and 300, respectively. The company wants to use this probability distribution, together with @RISK, to simulate the profit for any particular order quantity, with the ultimate goal of finding the best order quantity.

This is the same Walton Bookstore model as before, except that a triangular distribution for demand is used.

Objective To learn about @RISK's basic functionality by revisiting the Walton Bookstore problem.

---

[9]We have had the best luck when we (1) close other applications we are not currently using, and (2) launch Excel and @RISK together by starting @RISK. However, it is also possible to start @RISK *after* Excel is already running.
[10]If you have been using version 5.0 of @RISK, you will see only minor changes in the version 5.5 we are using here. However, if you have been using version 4.5, you will see *major* changes in the user interface.

WHERE DO THE NUMBERS COME FROM?

The monetary values are the same as before. The parameters of the triangular distribution of demand are probably Walton's best subjective estimates, possibly guided by its experience with previous calendars. As in many simulation examples, the triangular distribution has been chosen for simplicity. In this case, the manager would need to estimate only three quantities: the minimum possible demand, the maximum possible demand, and the most likely demand.

Solution

We use this example to illustrate important features of @RISK. We first show how it helps you to implement an appropriate input probability distribution for demand. Then we show how it can be used to build a simulation model for a specific order quantity and generate outputs from this model. Finally, we show how the RISKSIMTABLE function enables you to simultaneously generate outputs from several order quantities so that you can choose the optimal order quantity.

DEVELOPING THE SIMULATION MODEL

The spreadsheet model for profit is essentially the same model developed previously *without* @RISK, as shown in Figure 15.31. (See the file **Walton Bookstore 5.xlsx**.) There are only a few new things to be aware of.

Figure 15.31   Simulation Model with a Fixed Order Quantity

	A	B	C	D	E	F	G	H	I	J
1	Simulation of Walton's Bookstore using @RISK							Range names used:		
2								Order_quantity	=Model!$B$9	
3	Cost data			Demand distribution - triangular				Unit_cost	=Model!$B$4	
4	Unit cost	$7.50		Minimum	100			Unit_price	=Model!$B$5	
5	Unit price	$10.00		Most likely	175			Unit_refund	=Model!$B$6	
6	Unit refund	$2.50		Maximum	300					
7										
8	Decision variable									
9	Order quantity	200								
10										
11	Simulation									
12		Demand	Revenue	Cost	Refund	Profit				
13		187	$1,870	$1,500	$33	$403				
14										
15	Summary measures of profit from @RISK - based on 1000 iterations									
16	Minimum	-$235.00								
17	Maximum	$500.00								
18	Average	$337.50								
19	Standard deviation	$189.05								
20	5th percentile	-$47.50								
21	95th percentile	$500.00								
22	P(profit <= 300)	0.360								
23	P(profit > 400)	0.515								

---

1 Input distribution. To generate a random demand, enter the formula

=ROUND(RISKTRIANG(E4,E5,E6),0)

in cell B13 for the random demand. This uses the RISKTRIANG function to generate a demand from the triangular distribution. (As before, our convention is to color random input cells green.) Excel's ROUND function is used to round demand to the nearest integer. Recall from the discussion in section 15.3 that Excel has no built-in functions to generate random numbers from a triangular distribution, but this is easy with @RISK.

2 Output cell. When the simulation runs, you want @RISK to keep track of profit. In @RISK's terminology, you need to designate the Profit cell, F13, as an *output cell*. To do this, select cell F13 and then click on the Add Output button on the @RISK ribbon. (See Figure 15.30.) This adds **RISKOUTPUT(*"label"*)+** to the cell's formula. (Here, "label" is a label that @RISK uses for its reports. In this case it makes sense to use "Profit" as the label.) The formula in cell F13 changes from

=C13+E13-D13

to

=RISKOUTPUT("Profit")+C13+E13-D13

The RISKOUTPUT function indicates that a cell is an output cell, so that @RISK will keep track of its values throughout the simulation.

The plus sign following RISKOUTPUT does *not* indicate addition. It is simply @RISK's way of indicating that you want to keep track of the value in this cell (for reporting reasons) as the simulation progresses. Any number of cells can be designated in this way as output cells. They are typically the "bottom line" values of primary interest. Our convention is to color such cells gray for emphasis.

3 Summary functions. There are several places where you can store @RISK results. One of these is to use @RISK statistical functions to place results in your model worksheet. @RISK provides several functions for summarizing output values. Some of these are illustrated in the range B16:B23 of Figure 15.31. They contain the formulas

=RISKMIN(F13)

=RISKMAX(F3)

=RISKMEAN(F13)

=RISKSTDDEV(F13)

=RISKPERCENTILE(F13,0.05)

=RISKPERCENTILE(F13,0.95)

=RISKTARGET(F13,300)

These @RISK summary functions allow you to show simulation results on the same sheet as the model. However, they are totally optional.

and

=1-RISKTARGET(F13,400)

The values in these cells are not meaningful until you run the simulation (so do not be alarmed if they contain error symbols when you open the file). However, once the simulation runs, these formulas capture summary statistics of profit. For example, RISKMEAN calculates the average of the 1000 simulated profits, RISKPERCENTILE finds the value such that the specified percentage of simulated profits are less than or equal to this value, and RISKTARGET finds the percentage of simulated profits less than or equal to the specified value. Although these same summary statistics also appear in other @RISK reports, it is handy to have them in the same worksheet as the model.

Running the Simulation

After you develop the model, the rest is straightforward. The procedure is always the same: (1) specify simulation settings, (2) run the simulation, and (3) examine the results.

① Simulation settings. You must first choose some simulation settings. To do so, the buttons on the left in the Simulation group (see Figure 15.32) are useful. We typically do the following:

- Set Iterations to a number such as 1000. (@RISK calls "replications" iterations.) Any number can be used, but because the academic version of @RISK allows only 1000 uninterrupted iterations, we typically choose 1000.

- Set Simulations to 1. In a later section, we will explain why you might want to request multiple simulations.

- Click on the "dice" button so that it becomes orange. This button is actually a toggle for what appears in your worksheet. If it is orange, the setting is called "Monte Carlo" and all random cells appear random (they change when you press the F9 key). If it is blue, only the *means* appear in random input cells and the F9 key has no effect. We prefer the Monte Carlo setting, but both settings have exactly the same effect when you run the simulation.

- Many more settings are available by clicking on the button to the left of the "dice" button, but the ones we mentioned should suffice. In addition, more permanent settings can be chosen from Application Settings under Utilities on the @RISK ribbon. You can experiment with these, but the only one we like to change is the Place Reports In setting. The default is to place reports in a new workbook. If you like the reports to be in the same workbook as your model, you can change this setting to Active Workbook.

Figure 15.32
Simulation Group on @RISK Ribbon

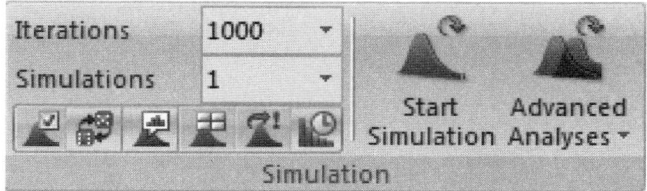

Leave Latin Hypercube sampling on. It produces more accurate results.

@RISK TECHNICAL ISSUES: *Latin Hypercube Sampling and Mersenne Twister Generator*

*Two settings you shouldn't change are the Sampling Type and Generator settings (available from the button to the left of the "dice" button and then the Sampling tab). They should remain at the default Latin Hypercube and Mersenne Twister settings. The Mersenne Twister is one algorithm, of many, for generating random numbers, and it has been shown to have very good statistical properties. (Not all random number generators do.) **Latin Hypercube sampling** is a more efficient way of sampling than the other option (Monte Carlo) because it produces a more accurate estimate of the output distribution. In fact, we were surprised how accurate it is. In repeated runs of this model, always using different random numbers, we virtually always got a mean profit within a few pennies of $337.50. It turns out that this is the true mean profit for this input distribution of demand. Amazingly, simulation estimates it correctly—almost exactly—on virtually every run. Unfortunately, this means that a confidence interval for the mean, based on @RISK's outputs and the usual confidence interval formula (which assumes Monte Carlo sampling), is much wider (more pessimistic) than it should be. Therefore, we do not even calculate such confidence intervals from here on.*

② **Run the simulation.** To run the simulation, simply click on the Start Simulation on the @RISK ribbon. When you do so, @RISK repeatedly generates a random number for each random input cell, recalculates the worksheet, and keeps track of all output cell values. You can watch the progress at the bottom left of the screen.

3 **Examine the results.** The big questions are (1) which results you want and (2) where you want them. @RISK provides a lot of possibilities, and we mention only our favorites.

- You can ask for summary measures in your model worksheet by using the @RISK statistical functions, such as RISKMEAN, discussed earlier.

For a quick histogram of an output or input, select the output or input cell and click on @RISK's Browse Results button.

- The quickest way to get results is to select an input or output cell (we chose the profit cell, F13) and then click on the Browse Results button on the @RISK ribbon. (See Figure 15.33.) This provides an interactive histogram of the selected value, as shown in Figure 15.34. You can move the sliders on this histogram to see probabilities of various outcomes. Note that the window you see from Browse Results is temporary—it goes away when you click on Close. You can make a permanent copy of the chart by clicking on the third button from the left (see the bottom of Figure 15.34) and choosing one of the copy options.

Figure 15.33

Results and Tools Groups on @RISK Ribbon

Figure 15.34

Interactive Histogram of Profit Output

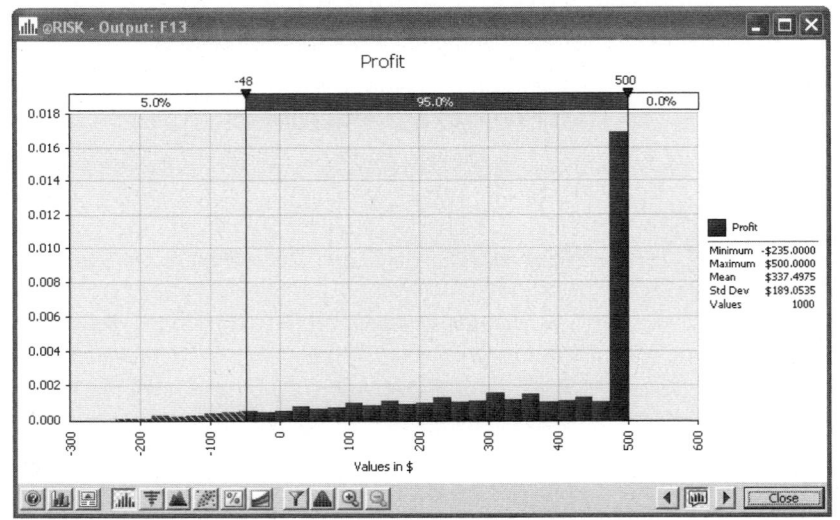

@RISK Tip: *Percentiles Displayed on Charts*
When we displayed the chart in Figure 15.34 the first time, it had the right slider on 500 but showed 5% to the right of it. By default, @RISK puts the sliders at the 5th and 95th percentiles, so that 5% is on either side of them. For this example, 500 is indeed the 95th percentile (why?), but the picture is a bit misleading because there is no chance of a profit greater than 500. When we manually moved the right slider away from 500 and back again, it displayed as in Figure 15.34, correctly indicating that there is no probability to the right of 500.

For a quick (and customizable) report of the results, click on @RISK's Summary button.

@RISK Tip: *Saving Graphs and Tables*

When you run a simulation with @RISK and then save your file, it asks whether you want to save your graphs and tables. We suggest that you save them. This makes your file slightly larger, but when you reopen it, the temporary graphs and tables, such as the histogram in Figure 15.34, are still available. Otherwise, you will have to rerun the simulation.

■ You can click on the Summary button (again, see Figure 15.33) to see the temporary window in Figure 15.35 with the summary measures for Profit. In general, this report shows the summary for *all* designated inputs and outputs. By default, this Results Summary window shows a mini histogram for each output and a number of numerical summary measures. However, it is easy to customize. If you right-click on this table and choose Columns for Table, you can check or uncheck any of the options. For most of the later screenshots in this book, we elected *not* to show the Graph and Errors columns, but instead to show median and standard deviation columns.

Figure 15.35   Summary Table of Profit Output

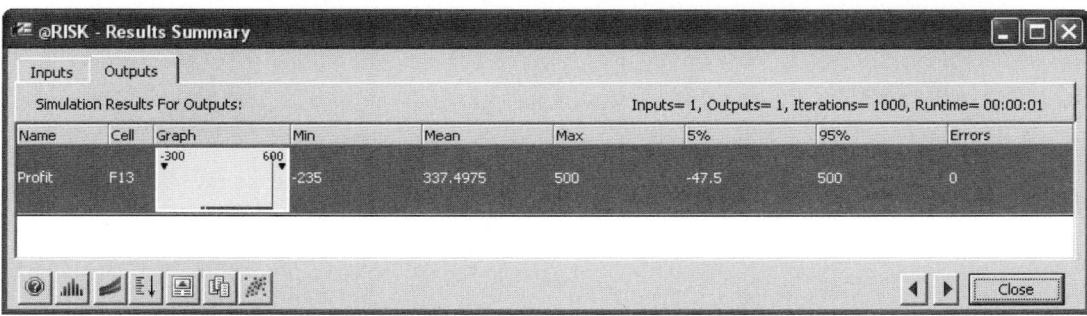

If you want permanent copies of the simulation results, click on @RISK's Excel Reports buttons and check the reports you want. They will be placed in new worksheets.

■ You can click on the Excel Reports button (again, see Figure 15.33) to choose from a number of reports that are placed on new worksheets. This is a good option if you want permanent (but non-interactive) copies of reports in your workbook. As an example, Figure 15.36 shows (part of) the Detailed Statistics report you can request. It has the same information as the summary report in Figure 15.35, plus a lot more.

Discussion of the Simulation Results

The strength of @RISK is that it keeps track of any outputs you designate and then allows you to show the corresponding results as graphs or tables, in temporary windows or in permanent worksheets. As you have seen, @RISK provides several options for displaying results, and we encourage you to explore the possibilities. However, don't lose sight of the overall goal: to see how outputs vary as random inputs vary, and to generate reports that tell the story most effectively. For this particular example, the results in Figures 15.31, 15.34, 15.35, and 15.36 allow you to conclude the following:

■ The smallest simulated profit (out of 1000) was −$235, the largest was $500, the average was $337.50, and the standard deviation of the 1000 profits was $189.05. Of all simulated profits, 5% were −$47.50 or below, 95% were $500 or above, 36% were less than or equal to $300, and 51.5% were larger than $400. (See Figure 15.31. These results are also available from the summary table in Figure 15.35 or the detailed statistics report in Figure 15.36. In particular, the bottom of the detailed statistics report, not shown in the figure, allows you to ask for any percentiles or target values.)

Figure 15.36

@RISK Detailed Statistics Report

	B	C	D
1	**@RISK Detailed Statistics**		
2	**Performed By:** Chris Albright		
3	**Date:** Tuesday, September 29, 2009 11:54:02 AM		
4			
5			
6	Name	Profit	Demand
7	Description	Output	RiskTriang(E4,E5,E6)
8	Cell	Model!F13	Model!B13
9	Minimum	-$235	102
10	Maximum	$500	295
11	Mean	$337	192
12	Std Deviation	$189	41
13	Variance	35741.22	1702.818
14	Skewness	-0.9485486	0.2346369
15	Kurtosis	2.796431	2.401627
16	Errors	0	0
17	Mode	$500	175
18	5% Perc	-$48	127
19	10% Perc	$43	139
20	15% Perc	$103	147
21	20% Perc	$163	155
22	25% Perc	$208	161
23	30% Perc	$253	167
24	35% Perc	$290	172

- The profit distribution for this particular order quantity is extremely skewed to the left, with a large bar at $500. (See Figure 15.34.) Do you see why? It is because profit is exactly $500 if demand is greater than or equal to the order quantity, 200. In other words, the probability that profit is $500 equals the probability that demand is at least 200. (This probability is 0.4.) Lower demands result in decreasing profits, which explains the gradual decline in the histogram from right to left.

Using RISKSIMTABLE

Walton's ultimate goal is to choose an order quantity that provides a large average profit. You could rerun the simulation model several times, each time with a different order quantity in the order quantity cell, and compare the results. However, this has two drawbacks. First, it takes a lot of time and work. The second drawback is more subtle. Each time you run the simulation, you get a *different* set of random demands. Therefore, one of the order quantities could win the contest just by luck. For a fairer comparison, it is better to test each order quantity on the *same* set of random demands.

The RISKSIMTABLE function allows you to run several simulations at once—one for each value of some variable (often a decision variable).

The RISKSIMTABLE function in @RISK enables you to obtain a fair comparison quickly and easily. This function is illustrated in Figure 15.37. (See the file **Walton Bookstore 6.xlsx**.) There are two modifications to the previous model. First, the order quantities to test are listed in row 9. (We chose these as representative order quantities. You could change, or add to, this list.) Second, instead of entering a *number* in cell B9, you enter the *formula*

=RISKSIMTABLE(D9:H9)

Note that the list does not need to be entered in the spreadsheet (although it is a good idea to do so). You could instead enter the formula

=RISKSIMTABLE({150,175,200,225,250})

Figure 15.37   Model with a RISKSIMTABLE Function

	A	B	C	D	E	F	G	H	I	J	K
1	Simulation of Walton's Bookstore using @RISK								Range names used:		
2									Order_quantity	=Model!$B$9	
3	Cost data			Demand distribution - triangular					Unit_cost	=Model!$B$4	
4	Unit cost	$7.50		Minimum	100				Unit_price	=Model!$B$5	
5	Unit price	$10.00		Most likely	175				Unit_refund	=Model!$B$6	
6	Unit refund	$2.50		Maximum	300						
7											
8	Decision variable			Order quantities to try							
9	Order quantity	150		150	175	200	225	250			
10											
11	Simulated quantities										
12		Demand	Revenue	Cost	Refund	Profit					
13		253	$1,500	$1,125	$0	$375					
14											
15	Summary measures of profit from @RISK - based on 1000 iterations for each simulation										
16	Simulation	1	2	3	4	5					
17	Order quantity	150	175	200	225	250					
18	Minimum	-$235.00	-$110.00	-$235.00	-$360.00	-$485.00					
19	Maximum	$500.00	$437.50	$500.00	$562.50	$625.00					
20	Average	$337.50	$367.20	$337.51	$270.32	$175.00					
21	Standard deviation	$189.05	$121.86	$189.05	$247.05	$286.96					
22	5th percentile	-$47.50	$77.50	-$47.50	-$172.50	-$297.50					
23	95th percentile	$500.00	$437.50	$500.00	$562.50	$625.00					

where the list of numbers must be enclosed in curly brackets. In either case, the worksheet displays the first member of the list, 150, and the corresponding calculations for this first order quantity. However, the model is now set up to run the simulation for *all* order quantities in the list.

To implement this, only one setting needs to be changed. As before, enter 1000 for the number of iterations, but also enter 5 for the number of simulations. @RISK then runs five simulations of 1000 iterations each, one simulation for each order quantity in the list, and it uses the *same* 1000 random demands for each simulation. This provides a fair comparison.

@RISK Function: *RISKSIMTABLE*

To run several simulations all at once, enter the formula **=RISKSIMTABLE** **(InputRange)** *in any cell. Here,* InputRange *refers to a list of the values to be simulated, such as various order quantities. Before running the simulation, make sure the number of simulations is set to the number of values in the* InputRange *list.*

You can again get results from the simulation in various ways. Here are some possibilities.

■ You can enter the same @RISK statistical functions in cells in the model worksheet, as shown in rows 18–23 of Figure 15.37. The trick is to realize that each such function has an optional last argument that specifies the simulation number. For example, the formulas in cells C20 and C22 are

=RISKMEAN($F$13,C16)

and

=RISKPERCENTILE($F$13,0.05,C16)

Remember that the results in these cells are meaningless (or show up as errors) until you run the simulation.

- You can select the profit cell and click on Browse Results to see a histogram of profits, as shown in Figure 15.38. By default, the histogram shown is for the *first* simulation, where the order quantity is 150. However, if you click on the red histogram button with the pound sign, you can select any of the simulations. As an example, Figure 15.39 shows the histogram of profits for the fifth simulation, where the order quantity is 250. (Do you see why these two histograms are so different? When the order quantity is 150, there is a high probability of selling out; hence the spike on the right is large. But the probability of selling out with an order quantity of 250 is much lower; hence its spike on the right is much less dominant.)

Figure 15.38

Histogram of Profit with Order Quantity 150

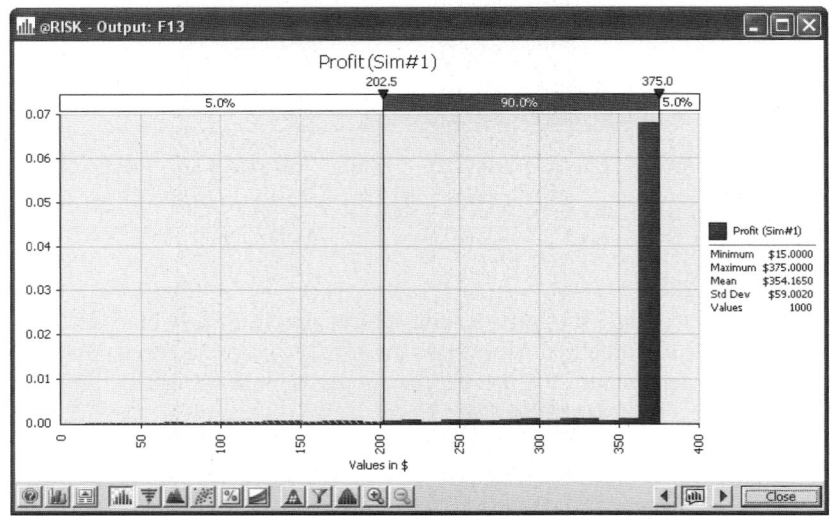

Figure 15.39

Histogram of Profit with Order Quantity 250

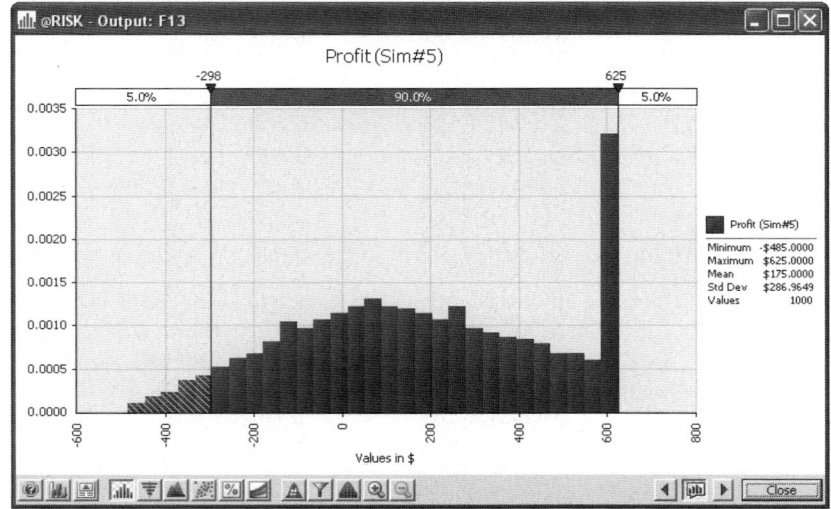

Figure 15.40 Summary Report for All Five Simulations

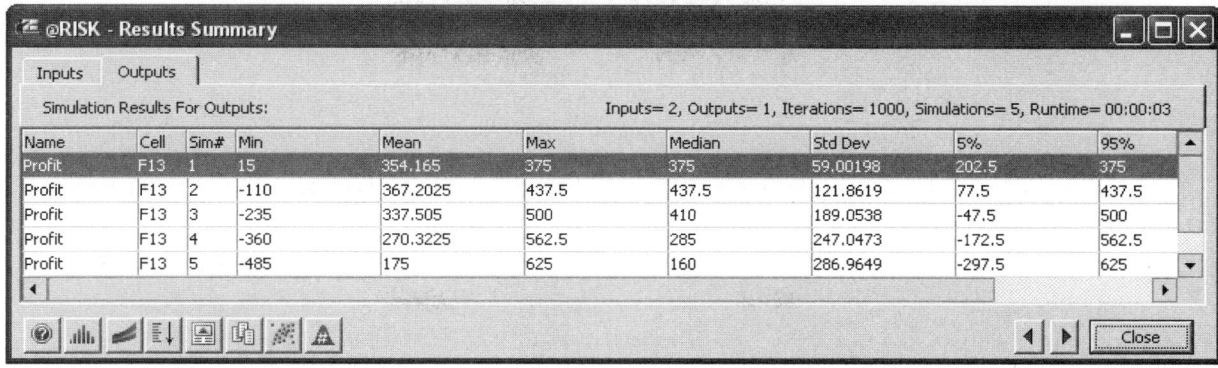

- You can click on the Summary button to get the results from all simulations shown in Figure 15.40. (These results match those in Figure 15.37.)
- You can click on Excel Reports to get any of a number of reports on permanent worksheets. Specifically, Quick Reports is a good choice. This produces several graphs and summary measures for each simulation, each on a different worksheet. This provides a lot of information with almost no work!

For this particular example, the results in Figures 15.37–15.40 are illuminating. You can see that an order quantity of 175 provides the largest *mean* profit. However, is this necessarily the optimal order quantity? This depends on the company's attitude toward risk. Certainly, larger order quantities incur more risk (their histograms are more spread out, their 5th and 95th percentiles are more extreme), but they also have more upside potential. On the other hand, a smaller order quantity, while having a somewhat smaller mean, might be preferable because of less variability. It is *not* an easy choice, but at least the simulation results provide plenty of information for making the decision. ∎

15.5.4 Some Limitations of @RISK

The academic version of @RISK included with the book has some limitations you should be aware of. (The commercial version of @RISK doesn't have these limitations. Also, the exact limitations could change as newer academic versions become available.)

- The simulation model must be contained in a single workbook with at most four worksheets, and each worksheet is limited to 300 rows and 100 columns.
- The number of @RISK input probability distribution functions, such as RISKNORMAL, is limited to 100.
- The number of unattended iterations is limited to 1000. You can request more than 1000, but you have to click a button after each 1000 iterations.
- All @RISK graphs contain a watermark.
- The Distribution Fitting tool can handle only 150 observations.

The first limitation shouldn't cause problems, at least not for the fairly small models discussed in this book. However, we strongly urge you to close all other workbooks when you are running an @RISK simulation model, *especially* if they also contain @RISK functions. @RISK does a lot of recalculation, both in your active worksheet and in all other worksheets or workbooks that are open. So if you are experiencing extremely slow simulations, this is probably the reason.

The second limitation can be a problem, especially in multiperiod problems. For example, if you are simulating 52 weeks of a year, and each week requires two random inputs, you are already over the 100-function limit. One way to get around this is to use built-in Excel functions for random inputs rather than @RISK functions whenever possible. For example, if you want to simulate the flip of a fair coin, the formula **=IF(RAND()<0.5,"Heads","Tails")** works just as well as the formula **=IF(RISKUNIFORM(0,1)<0.5,"Heads","Tails")**, but the former doesn't count against the 100-function limit.

15.5.5 @RISK Models with Several Random Input Variables

We conclude this section with another modification of the Walton Bookstore example. To this point, there has been a single random variable, demand. Often there are several random variables, each reflecting some uncertainty, and you want to include each of these in the simulation model. The following example illustrates how this can be done, and it also illustrates a very useful feature of @RISK, its sensitivity analysis.

EXAMPLE | **15.4 ADDITIONAL UNCERTAINTY AT WALTON BOOKSTORE**

As in the previous Walton Bookstore example, Walton needs to place an order for next year's calendar. We continue to assume that the calendars sell for $10 and customer demand for the calendars at this price is triangularly distributed with minimum value, most likely value, and maximum value equal to 100, 175, and 300. However, there are now two other sources of uncertainty. First, the maximum number of calendars Walton's supplier can supply is uncertain and is modeled with a triangular distribution. Its parameters are 125 (minimum), 200 (most likely), and 250 (maximum). Once Walton places an order, the supplier will charge $7.50 per calendar *if* he can supply the entire Walton order. Otherwise, he will charge only $7.25 per calendar. Second, unsold calendars can no longer be returned to the supplier for a refund. Instead, Walton will put them on sale for $5 apiece after January 1. At that price, Walton believes the demand for leftover calendars is triangularly distributed with parameters 0, 50, and 75. Any calendars *still* left over, say, after March 1, will be thrown away. Walton again wants to use simulation to analyze the resulting profit for various order quantities.

Objective To develop and analyze a simulation model with multiple sources of uncertainty using @RISK, and to introduce @RISK's sensitivity analysis features.

WHERE DO THE NUMBERS COME FROM?

As in Example 15.3, the monetary values are straightforward, and the parameters of the triangular distributions are probably educated guesses, possibly based on experience with previous calendars.

Solution

As always, the first step is to develop the model. Then you can run the simulation with @RISK and examine the results.

DEVELOPING THE SIMULATION MODEL

The completed model is shown in Figure 15.41. (See the file **Walton Bookstore 7.xlsx**.) The model itself requires a bit more logic than the previous Walton model. It can be developed with the following steps.

Figure 15.41 @RISK Simulation Model with Three Random Inputs

	A	B	C	D	E	F	G	H	I	J	K	L	M
1	Simulation of Walton's Bookstore using @RISK										Range names used:		
2											Order_quantity	=Model!$B$10	
3	Cost data			Demand distribution: triangular							Regular_price	=Model!$B$6	
4	Unit cost 1	$7.50			Regular price	Sale price		Supply distribution: triangular			Sale_price	=Model!$B$7	
5	Unit cost 2	$7.25		Minimum	100	0		Minimum	125		Unit_cost_1	=Model!$B$4	
6	Regular price	$10.00		Most likely	175	50		Most likely	200		Unit_cost_2	=Model!$B$5	
7	Sale price	$5.00		Maximum	300	75		Maximum	250				
8													
9	Decision variable			Order quantities to try									
10	Order quantity	150			150	175	200	225	250				
11													
12	Simulated quantities				At regular price			At sale price					
13		Maximum supply	Actual supply	Cost	Demand	Revenue	Left over	Demand	Revenue	Profit			
14		179	150	$1,125	164	$1,500	0	45	$0	$375			
15													
16	Summary measures of profit from @RISK - based on 1000 iterations for each simulation												
17	Simulation	1	2	3	4	5							
18	Order quantity	150	175	200	225	250							
19	Minimum	$50.00	-$137.50	-$325.00	-$421.75	-$421.75							
20	Maximum	$409.75	$478.50	$547.25	$616.00	$662.75							
21	Average	$361.37	$390.82	$395.94	$396.29	$398.96							
22	Standard deviation	$43.84	$92.83	$145.33	$176.12	$178.16							
23	5th percentile	$265.00	$178.00	$57.25	$13.00	$15.75							
24	95th percentile	$375.00	$459.25	$525.25	$577.50	$588.50							

1 **Random inputs.** There are three random inputs in this model: the maximum supply the supplier can provide Walton, the customer demand when the selling price is $10, and the customer demand for sale-price calendars. Generate these in cells B14, E14, and H14 (using the ROUND function to obtain integers) with the RISKTRIANG function. Specifically, the formulas in cells B14, E14, and H14 are

=ROUND(RISKTRIANG(I5,I6,I7),0)

=ROUND(RISKTRIANG (E5,E6,E7),0)

and

=ROUND(RISKTRIANG (F5,F6,F7),0)

Note that the formula in cell H14 generates the random *potential* demand for calendars at the sale price, even though there might not be any calendars left to put on sale.

2 **Actual supply.** The number of calendars supplied to Walton is the smaller of the number ordered and the maximum the supplier is able to supply. Calculate this value in cell C14 with the formula

=MIN(B14,Order_quantity)

3 **Order cost.** Walton gets the reduced price, $7.25, if the supplier cannot supply the entire order. Otherwise, Walton must pay $7.50 per calendar. Therefore, calculate the total order cost in cell D14 with the formula (using the obvious range names)

=IF(B14>=Order_quantity,Unit_cost_1,Unit_cost_2)*C14

④ Other quantities. The rest of the model is straightforward. Calculate the revenue from regular-price sales in cell F14 with the formula

=**Regular_price*MIN(C14,E14)**

Calculate the number left over after regular-price sales in cell G14 with the formula

=**MAX(C14-E14,0)**

Calculate the revenue from sale-price sales in cell I14 with the formula

=**Sale_price*MIN(G14,H14)**

Finally, calculate profit and designate it as an output cell for @RISK in cell J14 with the formula

=**RISKOUTPUT("Profit")+F14+I14-D14**

You could also designate other cells (the revenue cells, for example) as output cells.

⑤ Order quantities. As before, enter a RISKSIMTABLE function in cell B10 so that Walton can try different order quantities. Specifically, enter the formula

=**RISKSIMTABLE(D10:H10)**

in cell B10.

Running the Simulation

As usual, the next steps are to specify the simulation settings (we chose 1000 iterations and 5 simulations), and run the simulation. It is important to realize what @RISK does when it runs a simulation when there are several random input cells. In each iteration, @RISK generates a random value for each input variable *independently*. In this example, it generates a maximum supply in cell B14 from one triangular distribution, it generates a regular-price demand in cell E14 from another triangular distribution, and it generates a sale-price demand in cell H14 from a third triangular distribution. With these input values, it then calculates profit. For each order quantity, it then iterates this procedure 1000 times and keeps track of the corresponding profits.[11]

Discussion of the Simulation Results

Selected results are listed in Figure 15.41 (at the bottom), and the profit histogram for an order quantity of 200 is shown in Figure 15.42. (The histograms for the other order quantities are similar to what you have seen before, with more skewness to the left and a larger spike to the right as the order quantity decreases.) For this particular order quantity, the results indicate an average profit of about $396, a 5th percentile of $57, a 95th percentile of $525, and a distribution of profits that is again skewed to the left.

Sensitivity Analysis

We now demonstrate a feature of @RISK that is particularly useful when there are several random input cells. This feature lets you see which of these inputs is most related to, or *correlated* with, an output cell. To perform this analysis, select the profit cell, J14, and click on the Browse Results button. You will see a histogram of profit in a temporary window, as we have already discussed, with a number of buttons at the bottom of the window. Click on the red button with the pound sign to select a simulation. We chose #3, where the order quantity is 200. Then click on the "tornado" button (the fifth button from

---

[11]It is also possible to *correlate* the inputs, as we demonstrate in the next section.

966   Chapter 15   Introduction to Simulation Modeling

Figure 15.42

Histogram of Simulated Profits for Order Quantity 200

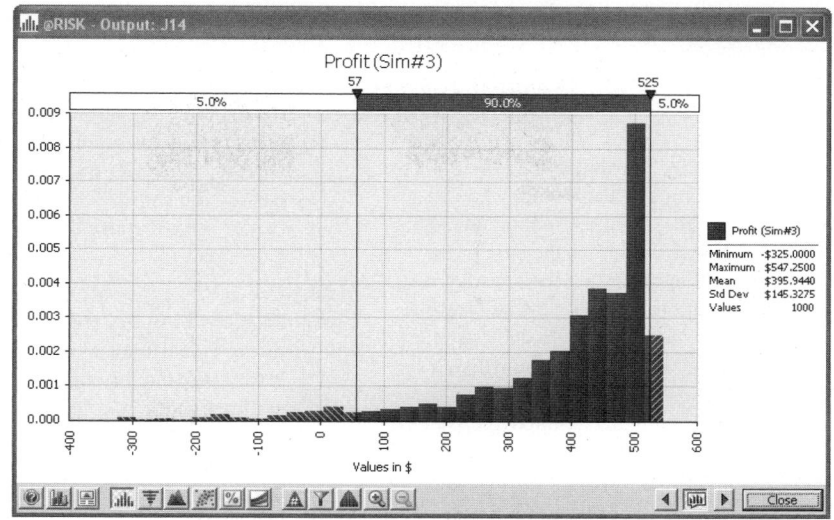

Figure 15.43

Tornado Graph for Sensitivity Analysis

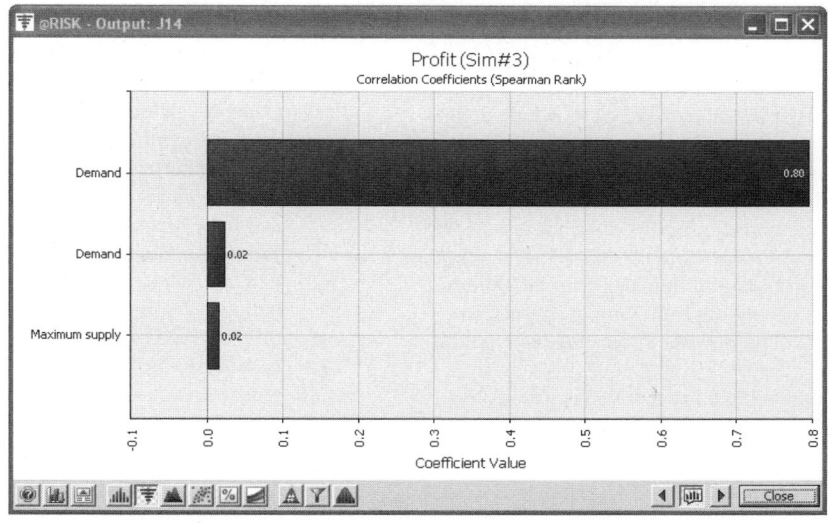

A tornado chart indicates which of the random inputs have large effects on an output.

the left) and choose Correlation Coefficients. This produces the chart in Figure 15.43. (The Regression option produces similar results, but we believe the Correlation option is easier to understand.)

This figure shows graphically and numerically how each of the random inputs correlates with profit: the higher the magnitude of the correlation, the stronger the relationship between that input and profit. In this sense, you can see that the regular-price demand has by far the largest effect on profit. The other two inputs, maximum supply and sale-price demand, are nearly uncorrelated with profit, so they are much less important. Identifying important input variables is important for real applications. If a random input is highly correlated with an important output, then it is probably worth the time and money to learn more about this input and possibly reduce the amount of uncertainty involving it. ■

PROBLEMS

Level A

16. If you add several normally distributed random numbers, the result is normally distributed, where the mean of the sum is the sum of the individual means, and the variance of the sum is the sum of the individual variances. (Remember that variance is the square of standard deviation.) This is a difficult result to prove mathematically, but it is easy to demonstrate with simulation. To do so, run a simulation where you add three normally distributed random numbers, each with mean 100 and standard deviation 10. Your single output variable should be the sum of these three numbers. Verify with @RISK that the distribution of this output is approximately normal with mean 300 and variance 300 (hence, standard deviation $\sqrt{300} = 17.32$).

17. In Problem 11 from the previous section, we stated that the damage amount is normally distributed. Suppose instead that the damage amount is triangularly distributed with parameters 500, 1500, and 7000. That is, the damage in an accident can be as low as $500 or as high as $7000, the most likely value is $1500, and there is definite skewness to the right. (It turns out, as you can verify in @RISK, that the mean of this distribution is $3000, the same as in Problem 11.) Use @RISK to simulate the amount you pay for damage. Run 5000 iterations. Then answer the following questions. In each case, explain how the indicated event would occur.
    a. What is the probability that you pay a positive amount but less than $750?
    b. What is the probability that you pay more than $600?
    c. What is the probability that you pay exactly $1000 (the deductible)?

18. Continuing the previous problem, assume, as in Problem 11, that the damage amount is *normally* distributed with mean $3000 and standard deviation $750. Run @RISK with 5000 iterations to simulate the amount you pay for damage. Compare your results with those in the previous problem. Does it appear to matter whether you assume a triangular distribution or a normal distribution for damage amounts? Why isn't this a totally fair comparison? (*Hint*: Use @RISK's Define Distributions tool to find the standard deviation for the triangular distribution.)

19. In Problem 12 of the previous section, suppose that the demand for cars is normally distributed with mean 100 and standard deviation 15. Use @RISK to determine the "best" order quantity—in this case, the one with the largest mean profit. Using the statistics and/or graphs from @RISK, discuss whether this order quantity would be considered best by the car dealer. (The point is that a decision maker can use more than just *mean* profit in making a decision.)

20. Use @RISK to analyze the sweatshirt situation in Problem 14 of the previous section. Do this for the discrete distributions given in the problem. Then do it for normal distributions. For the normal case, assume that the regular demand is normally distributed with mean 9800 and standard deviation 1300 and that the demand at the reduced price is normally distributed with mean 3800 and standard deviation 1400.

Level B

21. Although the normal distribution is a reasonable input distribution in many situations, it does have two potential drawbacks: (1) it allows negative values, even though they may be extremely improbable, and (2) it is a symmetric distribution. Many situations are modeled better with a distribution that allows only positive values and is skewed to the right. Two of these that have been used in many real applications are the gamma and lognormal distributions. @RISK enables you to generate observations from each of these distributions. The @RISK function for the gamma distribution is RISKGAMMA, and it takes two arguments, as in **=RISKGAMMA(3,10)**. The first argument, which must be positive, determines the shape. The smaller it is, the more skewed the distribution is to the right; the larger it is, the more symmetric the distribution is. The second argument determines the scale, in the sense that the product of it and the first argument equals the mean of the distribution. (The mean in this example is 30.) Also, the product of the second argument and the square root of the first argument is the standard deviation of the distribution. (In this example, it is $\sqrt{3}(10) = 17.32$.) The @RISK function for the lognormal distribution is RISKLOGNORM. It has two arguments, as in **=RISKLOGNORM(40,10)**. These arguments are the mean and standard deviation of the distribution. Rework Example 15.2 for the following demand distributions. Do the simulated outputs have any different qualitative properties with these skewed distributions than with the triangular distribution used in the example?
    a. Gamma distribution with parameters 2 and 85
    b. Gamma distribution with parameters 5 and 35
    c. Lognormal distribution with mean 170 and standard deviation 60

15.6 THE EFFECTS OF INPUT DISTRIBUTIONS ON RESULTS

In section 15.2, we discussed input distributions. The randomness in input variables causes the variability in the output variables. We now briefly explore whether the choice of input distribution(s) makes much difference in the distribution of an output variable such as profit. This is an important question. If the choice of input distributions doesn't matter much, then you do not need to agonize over this choice. However, if it *does* make a difference, then you have to be more careful about choosing the most appropriate input distribution for any particular situation. Unfortunately, it is impossible to answer the question definitively. The best we can say in general is, "It depends." Some models are more sensitive to changes in the shape or parameters of input distributions than others. Still, the issue is worth exploring.

We discuss two types of sensitivity analysis in this section. First, we check whether the shape of the input distribution matters. In the Walton Bookstore example, we assumed a triangularly distributed demand with some skewness. Are the results basically the same if a symmetric distribution such as the normal distribution is used instead? Second, we check whether the *independence* of input variables that have been assumed implicitly to this point is crucial to the output results. Many random quantities in real situations are *not* independent; they are positively or negatively correlated. Fortunately, @RISK enables you to build correlation into a model. We analyze the effect of this correlation.

15.6.1 Effect of the Shape of the Input Distribution(s)

We first explore the effect of the shape of the input distribution(s). As the following example indicates, if parameters that allow for a fair comparison are used, the shape can have a relatively minor effect.

EXAMPLE | **15.5 EFFECT OF DEMAND DISTRIBUTION AT WALTON'S**

We continue to explore the demand for calendars at Walton Bookstore. We keep the same unit cost, unit price, and unit refund for leftovers as in Example 15.3. However, in that example we assumed a triangular distribution for demand with parameters 100, 175, and 300. Assuming that Walton orders 200 calendars, is the distribution of profit affected if a *normal* distribution of demand is used instead?

Objective   To see whether a triangular distribution with some skewness gives the same profit distribution as a normal distribution for demand.

WHERE DO THE NUMBERS COME FROM?

The numbers here are the same as in Example 15.3. However, as discussed next, the parameters of the normal distribution are chosen to provide a fair comparison with the triangular distribution used earlier.

Solution

It is important in this type of analysis to make a fair comparison. When you select a normal distribution for demand, you must choose a mean and standard deviation for this distribution. Which values should you choose? It seems only fair to choose the *same* mean and

For a fair comparison of alternative input distributions, the distributions should have (at least approximately) equal means and standard deviations.

standard deviation that the triangular distribution has. To find the mean and standard deviation for a triangular distribution with given minimum, most likely, and maximum values, you can take advantage of @RISK's Define Distributions tool. Select any blank cell, click on the Define Distributions button, select the triangular distribution, and enter the parameters 100, 175, and 300. You will see that the mean and standard deviation are 191.67 and 41.248, respectively. Therefore, for a fair comparison you should use a normal distribution with mean 191.67 and standard deviation 41.248. In fact, @RISK allows you to see a comparison of these two distributions, as in Figure 15.44. To get this chart, click on the Add Overlay button, select the normal distribution from the gallery, and enter 191.67 and 41.248 as its mean and standard deviation.

Figure 15.44
Triangular and Normal Distributions for Demand

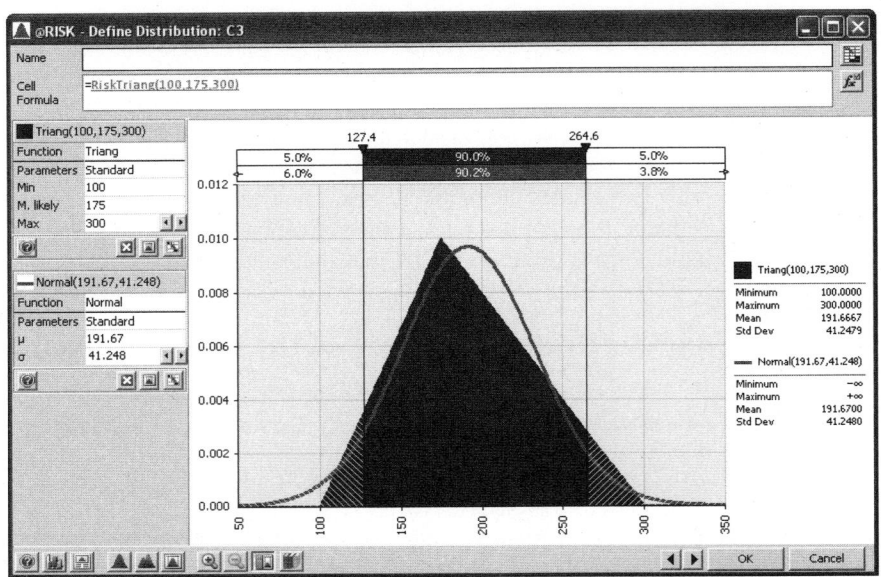

DEVELOPING THE SIMULATION MODEL

The logic in this model is almost exactly the same as before. (See Figure 15.45 and the file **Walton Bookstore 8.xlsx**.) However, a clever use of the RISKSIMTABLE function allows you to run two simulations at once, one for the triangular distribution and one for the corresponding normal distribution. The following two steps are required.

Look for ways to use the RISKSIMTABLE function. It can really improve efficiency because it runs several simulations at once.

1 RISKSIMTABLE function. It is useful to index the two distributions as 1 and 2. To indicate that you want to run the simulation with both of them, enter the formula

=RISKSIMTABLE({1,2})

in cell B11. Note that when you enter actual numbers in this function, rather than cell references, you must put curly brackets around the list.

2 Demand. When the value in cell B11 is 1, the demand distribution is triangular. When it is 2, the distribution is normal. Therefore, enter the formula

=ROUND(IF(B11=1,RISKTRIANG(E4,E5,E6),RISKNORMAL(H4,H5)),0)

in cell B15. The effect is that the first simulation will use the triangular distribution, and the second will use the normal distribution.

Figure 15.45 @RISK Model for Comparing Two Input Distributions

	A	B	C	D	E	F	G	H	I	J	K	L	M
1	Simulation of Walton's Bookstore using @RISK - two possible demand distributions										Range names used:		
2											Order_quantity	=Model!$B$9	
3	Cost data			Demand distribution 1 - triangular			Demand distribution 2 - normal				Unit_cost	=Model!$B$4	
4	Unit cost	$7.50		Minimum	100		Mean	191.67			Unit_price	=Model!$B$5	
5	Unit price	$10.00		Most likely	175		Stdev	41.248			Unit_refund	=Model!$B$6	
6	Unit refund	$2.50		Maximum	300								
7													
8	Decision variable												
9	Order quantity	200											
10													
11	Demand distribution to use	1	←——	Formula is =RiskSimtable({1,2})									
12													
13	Simulated quantities												
14			Demand	Revenue	Cost	Refund	Profit						
15			179	$1,790	$1,500	$53	$343						
16													
17	Summary measures of profit from @RISK - based on 1000 iterations for each simulation												
18	Simulation	1	2										
19	Distribution	Triangular	Normal										
20	Minimum	-$235.00	-$595.00										
21	Maximum	$500.00	$500.00										
22	Average	$337.48	$342.82										
23	Standard devia on	$189.10	$201.77										
24	5th percentile	-$47.50	-$70.00										
25	95th percentile	$500.00	$500.00										

Running the Simulation

The only @RISK setting to change is the number of simulations. It should now be set to 2, the number of values in the RISKSIMTABLE formula. Other than this, you run the simulation exactly as before.

Discussion of the Simulation Results

The comparison is shown numerically in Figure 15.46 and graphically in Figure 15.47. As you can see, there is more chance of really low profits when the demand distribution is normal, but each simulation results in the same maximum profit. Both of these statements make sense. The normal distribution, being unbounded on the left, allows for very low demands, and these occasional low demands result in very low profits. On the other side, Walton's maximum profit is $500 regardless of the input distribution (provided that it allows demands greater than the order quantity). This occurs when Walton's sells all it orders, in which case excess demand has no effect on profit. Note that the mean profits for the two distributions differ by only about $5.

Figure 15.46 Summary Results for Comparison Model

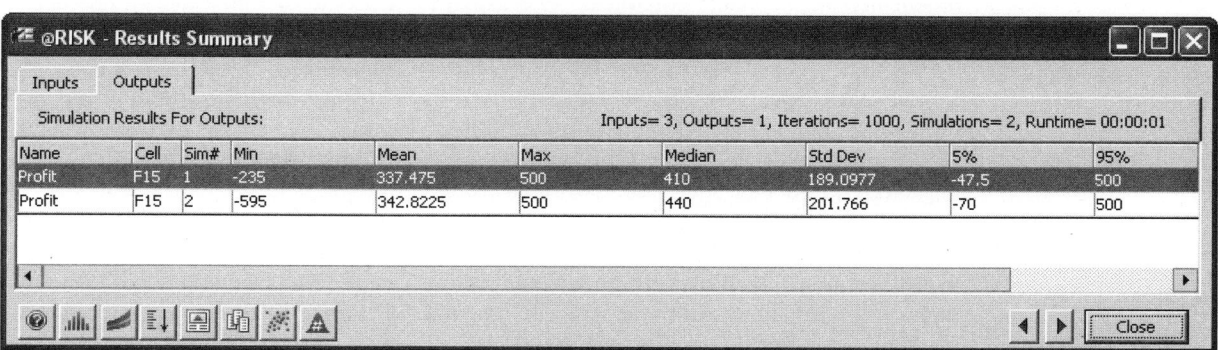

Figure 15.47 Graphical Results for Comparison Model

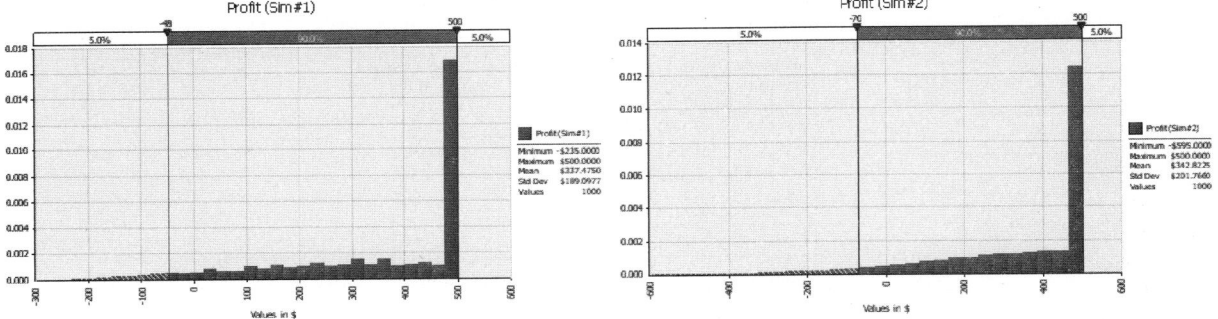

It is probably safe to conclude that the profit distribution in this model is not greatly affected by the choice of demand distribution, at least not when (1) the candidate input distributions have the same mean and standard deviation, and (2) their shapes are not *too* dissimilar. We would venture to guess that this general conclusion about insensitivity of output distributions to shapes of input distributions can be made in many simulation models. However, it is always worth checking, as we have done here, especially when there is a lot of money at stake. ■

FUNDAMENTAL INSIGHT

Shape of the Output Distribution

Predicting the shape of the output distribution from the shape(s) of the input distribution(s) is difficult. For example, normally distributed inputs don't necessarily produce normally distributed outputs. It is also difficult to predict how sensitive the shape of the output distribution is to the shape(s) of the input distribution(s).

For example, normally and triangularly distributed inputs (with the same means and standard deviations) are likely to lead to similar output distributions, but there could be differences, say, in the tails of the output distributions. In any case, you should examine the *entire* output distribution carefully, not just a few of its summary measures.

15.6.2 Effect of Correlated Input Variables

Input variables in real-world problems are often correlated, which makes the material in this section particularly important.

Until now, all of the random numbers generated with @RISK functions have been probabilistically independent. This means, for example, that if a random value in one cell is much larger than its mean, the random values in other cells are completely unaffected. They are no more likely to be abnormally large or small than if the first value had been average or below average. Sometimes, however, independence is unrealistic. In such cases, the random numbers should be correlated in some way. If they are positively correlated, then large numbers will tend to go with large numbers, and small with small. If they are negatively correlated, then large will tend to go with small and small with large. As an example, you might expect daily stock price changes for two companies in the same industry to be positively correlated. If the price of one oil company increases, you might expect the price of another oil company to increase as well. @RISK enables you to build in this correlated behavior with the RISKCORRMAT function, as we illustrate in the following continuation of the Walton example.

EXAMPLE | **15.6 CORRELATED DEMANDS FOR TWO CALENDARS AT WALTON'S**

$\mathbb{S}$uppose that Walton Bookstore must order two different calendars. To simplify the example, we assume that the calendars each have the same unit cost, unit selling price, and unit refund value as in previous examples. Also, we assume that each has a triangularly distributed demand with parameters 100, 175, and 300. However, we now assume they are "substitute" products, so that their demands are negatively correlated. This simply means that if a customer buys one, the customer is not likely to buy the other. Specifically, we assume a correlation of -0.9 between the two demands. How do these correlated inputs affect the distribution of profit, as compared to the situation where the demands are uncorrelated (correlation 0) or very *positively* correlated (correlation 0.9)?

Objective   To see how @RISK enables us to simulate correlated demands, and to see the effect of correlated demands on profit.

WHERE DO THE NUMBERS COME FROM?

The only new input here is the correlation. It is probably negative because the calendars are substitute products, but it is a difficult number to estimate accurately. This is a good candidate for a sensitivity analysis.

Solution

The key to building in correlation is @RISK's **RISKCORRMAT** (correlation matrix) function. To use this function, you must include a correlation matrix in the model, as shown in the range J5:K6 of Figure 15.48. (See the file **Walton Bookstore 9.xlsx**.)

Figure 15.48   Simulation Model with Correlations

	A	B	C	D	E	F	G	H	I	J	K
1	Simulation of Walton's Bookstore using @RISK - correlated demands										
2											
3	Cost data - same for each product			Demand distribution for each product- triangular					Correlation matrix between demands		
4	Unit cost	$7.50		Minimum	100					Product 1	Product 2
5	Unit price	$10.00		Most likely	175				Product 1	1	-0.9
6	Unit refund	$2.50		Maximum	300				Product 2	-0.9	1
7											
8	Decision variables						Note RISKSIMTABLE function in cell J6.		Possible correlations to try		
9	Order quantity 1	200								-0.9	0	0.9
10	Order quantity 2	200									
11									Range names used:		
12	Simulated quantities								Order_quantity_1	=Model!$B$9	
13		Demand	Revenue	Cost	Refund	Profit			Order_quantity_2	=Model!$B$10	
14	Product 1	190	$1,900	$1,500	$25	$425			Unit_cost	=Model!$B$4	
15	Product 2	177	$1,770	$1,500	$58	$328			Unit_price	=Model!$B$5	
16	Totals	367	$3,670	$3,000	$83	$753			Unit_refund	=Model!$B$6	
17											
18	Summary measures of profit from @RISK - based on 1000 iterations										
19	Simulation	1	2	3							
20	Correlation	-0.9	0	0.9							
21	Minimum	$272.50	-$245.00	-$425.00							
22	Maximum	$1,000.00	$1,000.00	$1,000.00							
23	Average	$675.04	$675.04	$675.04							
24	Standard deviation	$157.59	$262.33	$365.23							
25	5th percentile	$392.50	$205.00	-$80.00							
26	95th percentile	$925.00	$1,000.00	$1,000.00							

A correlation matrix must always have 1s along its diagonal (because a variable is always perfectly correlated with itself) and the correlations between variables elsewhere. Also, the matrix must be symmetric, so that the correlations above the diagonal are a mirror image of those below it. (You can enforce this by entering the *formula* **=J6** in cell K5. Alternatively, @RISK allows you to enter the correlations only below the diagonal, or only above the diagonal, and it then infers the mirror images.)

The RISKCORRMAT function is "tacked on" as an extra argument to a typical random @RISK function.

To enter random values in any cells that are correlated, you start with a typical @RISK formula, such as

=RISKTRIANG(E4,E5,E6)

Then you add an extra argument, the RISKCORRMAT function, as follows:

=RISKTRIANG(E4,E5,E6,RISKCORRMAT(J5:K6,1))

The first argument of the RISKCORRMAT function is the correlation matrix range. The second is an index of the variable. In this example, the first calendar demand has index 1 and the second has index 2.

@RISK Function: *RISKCORRMAT*

*This function enables you to correlate two or more input variables in an @RISK model. The function has the form **RISKCORRMAT(CorrMat,Index)**, where CorrMat is a matrix of correlations and Index is an index of the variable being correlated to others. For example, if there are three correlated variables, Index is 1 for the first variable, 2 for the second, and 3 for the third. The RISKCORRMAT function is not entered by itself. Rather, it is entered as the last argument of a random @RISK function, such as **=RISKTRIANG(10,15,30,RISKCORRMAT(CorrMat,2))**.*

DEVELOPING THE SIMULATION MODEL

Armed with this knowledge, the simulation model in Figure 15.48 is straightforward and can be developed as follows.

1 **Inputs.** Enter the inputs in the blue ranges in columns B and E.

2 **Correlation matrix.** For the correlation matrix in the range J5:H6, enter 1s on the diagonal, and enter the formula

=J6

in cell K5 (or leave cell K5 blank). Then enter the formula

=RISKSIMTABLE(I9:K9)

in cell J6. This allows you to simultaneously simulate negatively correlated demands, uncorrelated demands, and positively correlated demands.

3 **Order quantities.** Assume for now that the company orders the *same* number of each calendar, 200, so enter this value in cells B9 and B10. However, the simulation is set up so that you can experiment with any order quantities in these cells, including unequal values.

4 **Correlated demands.** Generate correlated demands by entering the formula

=ROUND(RISKTRIANG(E4,E5,E6,RISKCORRMAT(J5:K6,1)),0)

in cell B14 for demand 1 and the formula

=ROUND(RISKTRIANG(E4,E5,E6, RISKCORRMAT(J5:K6,2)),0)

in cell B15 for demand 2. The only difference between these is the index of the variable being generated. The first has index 1; the second has index 2.

5 **Other formulas.** The other formulas in rows 14 and 15 are identical to ones developed in previous examples, so they aren't presented again here. The quantities in row 16 are simply sums of rows 14 and 15. Also, the only @RISK output we designated is the total profit in cell F16, but you can designate others as output cells if you like.

Running the Simulation

You should set up and run @RISK exactly as before. For this example, set the number of iterations to 1000 and the number of simulations to 3 (because three different correlations are being tested).

Discussion of the Simulation Results

Selected numerical and graphical results are shown in Figures 15.49 and 15.50. You will probably be surprised to see that the *mean* total profit is the same, regardless of the correlation. This is no coincidence. In each of the three simulations, @RISK uses the *same* random numbers but "shuffles" them in different orders to get the correct correlations. This means that averages are unaffected. (The idea is that the average of the numbers 30, 26, and 48 is the same as the average of the numbers 48, 30, and 26.)

Figure 15.49 Summary Results for Correlated Model

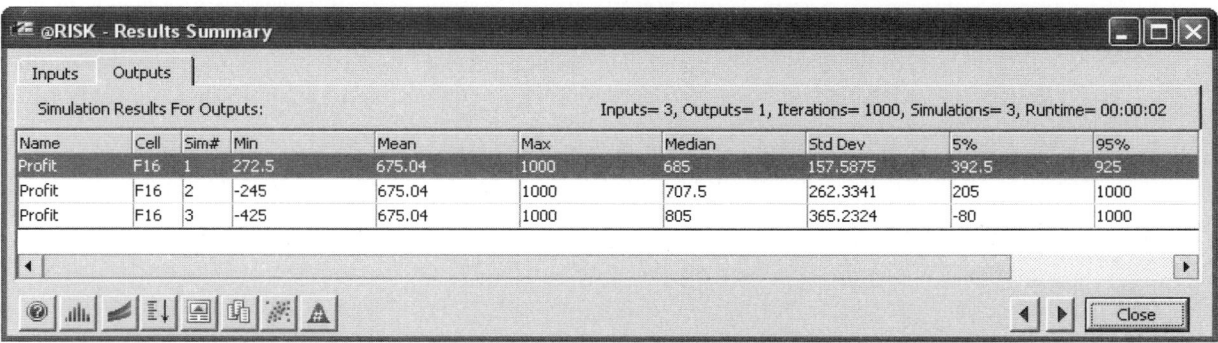

Figure 15.50 Graphical Results for Correlated Model

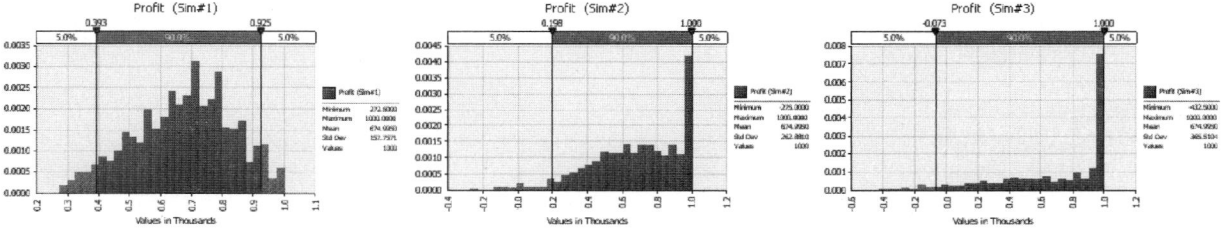

However, the correlation has a definite effect on the *distribution* of total profit. You can see this in Figure 15.49, for example, where the standard deviation of total profit increases as the correlation goes from negative to zero to positive. This same increase in variability is apparent in the histograms in Figure 15.50. Do you see intuitively why this increase in variability occurs? It is basically the "Don't put all of your eggs in one basket" effect. When the correlation is negative, high demands for one product tend to cancel low demands for the other product, so extremes in profit are rare. However, when the correlation is positive, high demands for the two products tend to go together, as do low demands. These make extreme profits on either end much more likely.

This same phenomenon would occur if you simulated an investment portfolio containing two stocks. When the stocks are positively correlated, the portfolio is much riskier (more variability) than when they are negatively correlated. Of course, this is the reason for diversifying a portfolio. ■

MODELING ISSUES

With the RISKCORRMAT function, you can correlate random numbers from any distributions.

We illustrated the RISKCORRMAT function for triangularly distributed values. However, it can be used with any of @RISK's distributions by tacking on RISKCORRMAT as a last argument. You can even mix them. For example, assuming CMat is the range name for a 2×2 correlation matrix, you could enter the formulas

=RISKNORMAL(10,2,RISKCORRMAT(CMat,1))

and

=RISKUNIFORM(100,200,RISKCORRMAT(CMat,2))

into any two cells. When you run the simulation, @RISK generates a sequence of normally distributed random numbers based on the first formula and another sequence of uniformly distributed random numbers based on the second formula. Then it shuffles them in some complex way until their correlation is approximately equal to the specified correlation in the correlation matrix. ■

FUNDAMENTAL INSIGHT

Correlated Inputs

When you enter random inputs in an @RISK simulation model and then run the simulation, each iteration generates *independent* values for the random inputs. If you know or suspect that some of the inputs are

positively or negatively correlated, you should build this correlation structure into the model explicitly with the RISKCORRMAT function. This function might not change the mean of an output, but it can definitely affect the variability and shape of the output distribution.

PROBLEMS

Level A

22. The Fizzy Company produces six-packs of soda cans. Each can is supposed to contain at least 12 ounces of soda. If the total weight in a six-pack is less than 72 ounces, Fizzy is fined $100 and receives no sales revenue for the six-pack. Each six-pack sells for $3.00. It costs Fizzy $0.02 per ounce of soda put in the cans. Fizzy can control the mean fill rate of its soda-filling machines. The amount put in each can

by a machine is normally distributed with standard deviation 0.10 ounce.
a. Assume that the weight of each can in a six-pack has a 0.8 correlation with the weight of the other cans in the six-pack. What mean fill quantity maximizes expected profit per six-pack? Try mean fill rates from 12.00 to 12.35 in increments of 0.05.
b. If the weights of the cans in the six-pack are probabilistically independent, what mean fill

quantity maximizes expected profit per six-pack? Try the same mean fill rates as in part **a**.

  c. How can you explain the difference in the answers to parts **a** and **b**?

23. When you use @RISK's correlation feature to generate correlated random numbers, how can you verify that they are correlated? Try the following. Use the RISKCORRMAT function to generate two normally distributed random numbers, each with mean 100 and standard deviation 10, and with correlation 0.7. To run a simulation, you need an output variable, so sum these two numbers and designate the sum as an output variable. Now run @RISK with 500 iterations. Click on @RISK's Excel Reports button and check the Simulation Data option to see the actual simulated data.

  a. Use Excel's CORREL function to calculate the correlation between the two input variables. It should be close to 0.7. Then create a scatterplot of these two input variables. The plot should indicate a definite positive relationship.

  b. Are the two input variables correlated with the output? Use Excel's CORREL function to find out. Interpret your results intuitively.

24. Repeat the previous problem, but make the correlation between the two inputs equal to –0.7. Explain how the results change.

25. Repeat Problem 23, but now make the second input variable triangularly distributed with parameters 50, 100, and 500. This time, verify not only that the correlation between the two inputs is approximately 0.7, but also that the shapes of the two input distributions are approximately what they should be: normal for the first and triangular for the second. Do this by creating histograms in Excel. The point is that you can use @RISK's RISKCORRMAT function to correlate random numbers from *different* distributions.

26. Suppose you are going to invest equal amounts in three stocks. The annual return from each stock is normally distributed with mean 0.01 (1%) and standard deviation 0.06. The annual return on your portfolio, the output variable of interest, is the average of the three stock returns. Run @RISK, using 1000 iterations, on each of the following scenarios.

  a. The three stock returns are highly correlated. The correlation between each pair is 0.9.

  b. The three stock returns are practically independent. The correlation between each pair is 0.1.

  c. The first two stocks are moderately correlated. The correlation between their returns is 0.4. The third stock's return is negatively correlated with the other two. The correlation between its return and each of the first two is −0.8.

  d. Compare the portfolio distributions from @RISK for these three scenarios. What do you conclude?

  e. You might think of a fourth scenario, where the correlation between each *pair* of returns is a large negative number such as −0.8. But explain intuitively why this makes no sense. Try to run the simulation with these negative correlations and see what happens.

27. The effect of the shapes of input distributions on the distribution of an output can depend on the output function. For this problem, assume there are 10 input variables. The goal is to compare the case where these 10 inputs each have a normal distribution with mean 1000 and standard deviation 250 to the case where they each have a triangular distribution with parameters 600, 700, and 1700. (You can check with @RISK's Define Distributions window that even though this triangular distribution is very skewed, it has the same mean and approximately the same standard deviation as the normal distribution.) For each of the following outputs, run two @RISK simulations, one with the normally distributed inputs and one with the triangularly distributed inputs, and comment on the differences between the resulting output distributions. For each simulation run 10,000 iterations.

  a. Let the output be the *average* of the inputs.

  b. Let the output be the *maximum* of the inputs.

  c. Calculate the average of the inputs. Then the output is the minimum of the inputs if this average is less than 1000; otherwise, the output is the maximum of the inputs.

Level B

28. The Business School at State University currently has three parking lots, each containing 155 spaces. Two hundred faculty members have been assigned to each lot. On a peak day, an average of 70% of all lot 1 parking sticker holders show up, an average of 72% of all lot 2 parking sticker holders show up, and an average of 74% of all lot 3 parking sticker holders show up.

  a. Given the current situation, estimate the probability that on a peak day, at least one faculty member with a sticker will be unable to find a spot. Assume that the number who show up at each lot is independent of the number who show up at the other two lots. Compare two situations: (1) each person can park only in the lot assigned to him or her, and (2) each person can park in any of the lots (pooling). (*Hint*: Use the RISKBINOMIAL function.)

  b. Now suppose the numbers of people who show up at the three lots are highly correlated (correlation 0.9). How are the results different from those in part **a**?

15.7 CONCLUSION

Simulation has traditionally not received the attention it deserves in management science courses. The primary reason for this has been the lack of easy-to-use simulation software. Now, with Excel's built-in simulation capabilities, plus powerful and affordable add-ins such as @RISK, simulation is receiving its rightful emphasis. The world is full of uncertainty, which is what makes simulation so valuable. Simulation models provide important insights that are missing in models that do not incorporate uncertainty explicitly. In addition, simulation models are relatively easy to understand and develop. Therefore, we suspect that simulation models (together with optimization models) will soon be the primary emphasis of many management science courses—if they are not already. In this chapter we have illustrated the basic ideas of simulation, how to perform simulation with Excel built-in tools, and how @RISK greatly enhances Excel's basic capabilities. In the next chapter we will build on this knowledge to develop and analyze simulation models in a variety of business areas.

Summary of Key Terms

Term	Explanation	Excel	Pages
Simulation model	Model with random inputs that affect one or more outputs, where the randomness is modeled explicitly		918
F9 key	The "recalc" key, used to make a spreadsheet recalculate	Press the F9 key	921
Probability distributions for input variables	Specification of the possible values and their probabilities for random input variables; these distributions must be specified in any simulation model		921
Uniform distribution	The flat distribution, where all values in a bounded continuum are equally likely		925
RAND function	Excel's built-in random number generator; generates uniformly distributed random numbers between 0 and 1	=RAND()	926
RANDBETWEEN function	Excel's built-in function for generating equally likely random integers over an indicated range	=RANDBETWEEN (*min,max*)	926
Freezing random numbers	Changing "volatile" random numbers into "fixed" numbers	Copy range, paste it onto itself with the Paste Values option	929
@RISK random functions	A set of functions, including RISKNORMAL and RISKTRIANG, for generating random numbers from various distributions	=RISKNORMAL (*mean,stdev*) or =RISKTRIANG (*min,mostlikely,max*), for example	929–936
Discrete distribution	A general distribution where a discrete number of possible values and their probabilities are specified		931
Triangular distribution	Literally a triangle-shaped distribution, specified by a minimum value, a most likely value, and a maximum value		934
Replicating with Excel only	Useful when an add-in such as @RISK is not available	Develop simulation model, use a data table with any blank column input cell to replicate one or more outputs	949

(continued)

Term	Explanation	Excel	Pages
@RISK	A useful simulation add-in developed by Palisade	@RISK ribbon	953
RISKSIMTABLE function	Used to run an @RISK simulation model for several values of some variable, often a decision variable	=RISKSIMTABLE (*list*)	953
RISKOUTPUT function	Used to indicate that a cell contains an output that will be tracked by @RISK	=RISKOUTPUT ("Profit") +Revenue-Cost, for example	956
Latin hypercube sampling	An efficient way of simulating random numbers for a simulation model, where the results are more accurate than with other sampling methods		957
Correlated inputs	Random quantities, such as returns from stocks in the same industry, that tend to go together (or possibly go in opposite directions from one another)		976
RISKCORRMAT function	Used to correlate two or more random input variables	=RISKNORMAL (100,10, RISKCORRMAT (*CorrMat,2*)), for example	976

PROBLEMS

Conceptual Questions

C.1. You are making several runs of a simulation model, each with a different value of some decision variable (such as the order quantity in the Walton calendar model), to see which decision value achieves the largest mean profit. Is it possible that one value beats another simply by random luck? What can you do to minimize the chance of a "better" value losing out to a "poorer" value?

C.2. If you want to replicate the results of a simulation model with Excel functions only, not @RISK, you can build a data table and let the column input cell be any blank cell. Explain why this works.

C.3. Suppose you simulate a gambling situation where you place many bets. On each bet, the distribution of your net winnings (loss if negative) is highly skewed to the left because there are some possibilities of really large losses but not much upside potential. Your only simulation output is the *average* of the results of all the bets. If you run @RISK with many iterations and look at the resulting histogram of this output, what will it look like? Why?

C.4. You plan to simulate a portfolio of investments over a multiyear period, so for each investment (which could be a particular stock or bond, for example), you need to simulate the change in its value for each of the years. How would you simulate these changes in a realistic way? Would you base it on historical

data? What about correlations? Do you think the changes for different investments in a particular year would be correlated? Do you think changes for a particular investment in different years would be correlated? Do you think correlations would play a significant role in your simulation in terms of realism?

C.5. Big Hit Video must determine how many copies of a new video to purchase. Assume that the company's goal is to purchase a number of copies that maximizes its expected profit from the video during the next year. Describe how you would use simulation to shed light on this problem. Assume that each time a video is rented, it is rented for one day.

C.6. Many people who are involved in a small auto accident do not file a claim because they are afraid their insurance premiums will be raised. Suppose that City Farm Insurance has three rates. If you file a claim, you are moved to the next higher rate. How might you use simulation to determine whether a particular claim should be filed?

C.7. A building contains 1000 lightbulbs. Each bulb lasts at most five months. The company maintaining the building is trying to decide whether it is worthwhile to practice a "group replacement" policy. Under a group replacement policy, all bulbs are replaced every T months (where T is to be determined). Also, bulbs are replaced when they burn out. Assume that it costs $0.05 to replace each bulb during a group replacement and $0.20 to replace each burned-out bulb if it is replaced individually. How would you use simulation to determine whether a group replacement policy is worthwhile?

C.8. Why is the RISKCORRMAT function necessary? How does @RISK generate random inputs by default, that is, when RISKCORRMAT is not used?

C.9. Consider the claim that normally distributed inputs in a simulation model are bound to lead to normally distributed outputs. Do you agree or disagree with this claim? Defend your answer.

C.10. It is very possible that when you use a correlation matrix as input to the RISKCORRMAT function in an @RISK model, the program will inform you that this is an invalid correlation matrix. Provide an example of an obviously invalid correlation matrix involving at least three variables, and explain why it is invalid.

C.11. When you use a RISKSIMTABLE function for a decision variable, such as the order quantity in the Walton model, explain how this provides a "fair" comparison across the different values tested.

C.12. Consider a situation where there is a cost that is either incurred or not. It is incurred only if the value of some random input is less than a specified cutoff value. Why might a simulation of this situation give a very different average value of the cost incurred than a deterministic model that treats the random input as *fixed* at its mean? What does this have to do with the "flaw of averages"?

Level A

29. Six months before its annual convention, the American Medical Association must determine how many rooms to reserve. At this time, the AMA can reserve rooms at a cost of $150 per room. The AMA believes the number of doctors attending the convention will be normally distributed with a mean of 5000 and a standard deviation of 1000. If the number of people attending the convention exceeds the number of rooms reserved, extra rooms must be reserved at a cost of $250 per room.
  a. Use simulation with @RISK to determine the number of rooms that should be reserved to minimize the expected cost to the AMA. Try possible values from 4100 to 4900 in increments of 100.
  b. Redo part **a** for the case where the number attending has a triangular distribution with minimum value 2000, maximum value 7000, and most likely value 5000. Does this change the substantive results from part **a**?

30. You have made it to the final round of the show *Let's Make a Deal*. You know that there is a $1 million prize behind either door 1, door 2, or door 3. It is equally likely that the prize is behind any of the three doors. The two doors without a prize have nothing behind them. You randomly choose door 2. Before you see whether the prize is behind door 2, host Monty Hall opens a door that has no prize behind it. Specifically, suppose that before door 2 is opened, Monty reveals that there is no prize behind door 3. You now have the opportunity to switch and choose door 1. Should you switch? Simulate this situation 1000 times. For each replication use an @RISK function to generate the door that leads to the prize. Then use another @RISK function to generate the door that Monty will open. Assume that Monty plays as follows: Monty knows where the prize is and will open an empty door, but he cannot open door 2. If the prize is really behind door 2, Monty is equally likely to open door 1 or door 3. If the prize is really behind door 1, Monty must open door 3. If the prize is really behind door 3, Monty must open door 1.

31. A new edition of a very popular textbook will be published a year from now. The publisher currently has 2000 copies on hand and is deciding whether to do another printing before the new edition comes out. The publisher estimates that demand for the book during the next year is governed by the probability distribution in the file **P15_31.xlsx**. A production run incurs a fixed cost of $10,000 plus a variable cost of $15 per book printed. Books are sold for $130 per book. Any demand that cannot be met incurs a penalty cost of $20 per book, due to loss of goodwill. Up to 500 of any leftover books can be sold to Barnes and Noble for $35 per book. The publisher is interested in maximizing expected profit. The following print-run sizes are under consideration: 0 (no production run) to 16,000 in increments of 2000. What decision would you recommend? Use simulation with 1000 replications. For your optimal decision, the publisher can be 90% certain that the actual profit associated with remaining sales of the current edition will be between what two values?

32. A hardware company sells a lot of low-cost, high-volume products. For one such product, it is equally likely that annual unit sales will be low or high. If sales are low (60,000), the company can sell the product for $10 per unit. If sales are high (100,000), a competitor will enter and the company will be able to sell the product for only $8 per unit. The variable cost per unit has a 25% chance of being $6, a 50% chance of being $7.50, and a 25% chance of being $9. Annual fixed costs are $30,000.
  a. Use simulation to estimate the company's expected annual profit.
  b. Find a 95% interval for the company's annual profit, that is, an interval such that about 95% of the actual profits are inside it.

c. Now suppose that annual unit sales, variable cost, and unit price are equal to their respective *expected* values—that is, there is no uncertainty. Determine the company's annual profit for this scenario.

d. Can you conclude from the results in parts **a** and **c** that the expected profit from a simulation is equal to the profit from the scenario where each input assumes its expected value? Explain.

33. W. L. Brown, a direct marketer of women's clothing, must determine how many telephone operators to schedule during each part of the day. W. L. Brown estimates that the number of phone calls received each hour of a typical eight-hour shift can be described by the probability distribution in the file **P15_33.xlsx**. Each operator can handle 15 calls per hour and costs the company $20 per hour. Each phone call that is not handled is assumed to cost the company $6 in lost profit. Considering the options of employing 6, 8, 10, 12, 14, or 16 operators, use simulation to determine the number of operators that minimizes the expected hourly cost (labor costs plus lost profits).

34. Assume that all of a company's job applicants must take a test, and that the scores on this test are normally distributed. The *selection ratio* is the cutoff point used by the company in its hiring process. For example, a selection ratio of 20% means that the company will accept applicants for jobs who rank in the top 20% of all applicants. If the company chooses a selection ratio of 20%, the average test score of those selected will be 1.40 standard deviations above average. Use simulation to verify this fact, proceeding as follows.

a. Show that if the company wants to accept only the top 20% of all applicants, it should accept applicants whose test scores are at least 0.842 standard deviation above average. (No simulation is required here. Just use the appropriate Excel normal function.)

b. Now generate 1000 test scores from a normal distribution with mean 0 and standard deviation 1. The average test score of those selected is the average of the scores that are at least 0.842. To determine this, use Excel's DAVERAGE function. To do so, put the heading Score in cell A3, generate the 1000 test scores in the range A4:A1003, and name the range A3:A1003 Data. In cells C3 and C4, enter the *labels* Score and >0.842. (The range C3:C4 is called the *criterion range*.) Then calculate the average of all applicants who will be hired by entering the formula **=DAVERAGE(Data, "Score", C3:C4)** in any cell. This average should be close to the theoretical average, 1.40. This formula works as follows. Excel finds all observations in the Data range that satisfy the criterion described in the range C3:C4 (Score>0.842). Then it averages the values in the Score column (the second argument of DAVERAGE) corresponding

to these entries. See online help for more about Excel's database "D" functions.

c. What information would the company need to determine an optimal selection ratio? How could it determine the optimal selection ratio?

35. Lemington's is trying to determine how many Jean Hudson dresses to order for the spring season. Demand for the dresses is assumed to follow a normal distribution with mean 400 and standard deviation 100. The contract between Jean Hudson and Lemington's works as follows. At the beginning of the season, Lemington's reserves x units of capacity. Lemington's must take delivery for at least $0.8x$ dresses and can, if desired, take delivery on up to x dresses. Each dress sells for $160 and Hudson charges $50 per dress. If Lemington's does not take delivery on all x dresses, it owes Hudson a $5 penalty for each unit of reserved capacity that is unused. For example, if Lemington's orders 450 dresses and demand is for 400 dresses, Lemington's will receive 400 dresses and owe Jean 400($50) + 50($5). How many units of capacity should Lemington's reserve to maximize its expected profit?

36. Dilbert's Department Store is trying to determine how many Hanson T-shirts to order. Currently the shirts are sold for $21, but at later dates the shirts will be offered at a 10% discount, then a 20% discount, then a 40% discount, then a 50% discount, and finally a 60% discount. Demand at the full price of $21 is believed to be normally distributed with mean 1800 and standard deviation 360. Demand at various discounts is assumed to be a multiple of full-price demand. These multiples, for discounts of 10%, 20%, 40%, 50%, and 60% are, respectively, 0.4, 0.7, 1.1, 2, and 50. For example, if full-price demand is 2500, then at a 10% discount customers would be willing to buy 1000 T-shirts. The unit cost of purchasing T-shirts depends on the number of T-shirts ordered, as shown in the file **P15_36.xlsx**. Use simulation to determine how many T-shirts the company should order. Model the problem so that the company first orders some quantity of T-shirts, then discounts deeper and deeper, as necessary, to sell all of the shirts.

Level B

37. The annual return on each of four stocks for each of the next five years is assumed to follow a normal distribution, with the mean and standard deviation for each stock, as well as the correlations between stocks, listed in the file **P15_37.xlsx**. You believe that the stock returns for these stocks in a given year are correlated, according to the correlation matrix given, but you believe the returns in different years are uncorrelated. For example, the returns for stocks 1 and 2 in year 1 have correlation 0.55, but the correlation between the return of stock 1 in year 1 and the return of stock 1 in year 2 is 0, and the correlation between the return of stock 1 in year 1 and the return of stock 2 in year 2 is also 0. The file has the formulas you might expect for this situation in the range C20:G23. You can check how the RISKCORRMAT function has been used in these formulas. Just so that there is an @RISK output cell, calculate the average of all returns in cell B25 and designate it as an @RISK output. (This cell is not really important for the problem, but it is included because @RISK requires at least one output cell.)

a. Using the model exactly as it stands, run @RISK with 1000 iterations. The question is whether the correlations in the simulated data are close to what they should be. To check this, go to @RISK's Report Settings and check the Input Data option before you run the simulation. This gives you all of the simulated returns on a new sheet. Then calculate correlations for all pairs of columns in the resulting Inputs Data Report sheet. (StatTools can be used to create a matrix of all correlations for the simulated data.) Comment on whether the correlations are different from what they should be.

b. Recognizing that this is a common situation (correlation within years, no correlation across years), @RISK allows you to model it by adding a *third* argument to the RISKCORRMAT function: the year index in row 19 of the **P15_37.xlsx** file. For example, the RISKCORRMAT part of the formula in cell C20 becomes **=RISKNORMAL ($B5,$C5, RISKCORRMAT($B$12:$E$15, $B20,C$19))**. Make this change to the formulas in the range C20:G23, rerun the simulation, and redo the correlation analysis in part **a**. Verify that the correlations between inputs are now more in line with what they should be.

38. It is surprising (but true) that if 23 people are in the same room, there is about a 50% chance that at least two people will have the same birthday. Suppose you want to estimate the probability that if 30 people are in the same room, at least two of them will have the same birthday. You can proceed as follows.

a. Generate random birthdays for 30 different people. Ignoring the possibility of a leap year, each person has a 1/365 chance of having a given birthday (label the days of the year 1 to 365). You can use the RANDBETWEEN function to generate birthdays.

b. Once you have generated 30 people's birthdays, how can you tell whether at least two people have the same birthday? One way is to use Excel's RANK function. (You can learn how to use this function in Excel's online help.) This function returns the rank of a number relative to a given group of numbers. In the case of a tie, two numbers are given the same rank. For example, if the set of numbers is 4, 3, 2, 5, the RANK function returns 2, 3, 4, 1. (By default, RANK gives 1 to the *largest* number.) If the set of numbers is 4, 3, 2, 4, the RANK function returns 1, 3, 4, 1.

c. After using the RANK function, you should be able to determine whether at least two of the 30 people have the same birthday. What is the (estimated) probability that this occurs?

39. United Electric (UE) sells refrigerators for $400 with a one-year warranty. The warranty works as follows. If any part of the refrigerator fails during the first year after purchase, UE replaces the refrigerator for an average cost of $100. As soon as a replacement is made, another one-year warranty period begins for the customer. If a refrigerator fails outside the warranty period, we assume that the customer immediately purchases another UE refrigerator. Suppose that the amount of time a refrigerator lasts follows a normal distribution with a mean of 1.8 years and a standard deviation of 0.3 year.

a. Estimate the average profit per year UE earns from a customer.

b. How could the approach of this problem be used to determine the optimal warranty period?

40. A Flexible Savings Account (FSA) plan allows you to put money into an account at the beginning of the calendar year that can be used for medical expenses. This amount is not subject to federal tax. As you pay medical expenses during the year, you are reimbursed by the administrator of the FSA until the money is exhausted. From that point on, you must pay your medical expenses out of your own pocket. On the other hand, if you put more money into your FSA than the medical expenses you incur, this extra money is lost to you. Your annual salary is $80,000 and your federal income tax rate is 30%.

a. Assume that your medical expenses in a year are normally distributed with mean $2000 and standard deviation $500. Build an @RISK model in which the output is the amount of money left to you after paying taxes, putting money in an FSA, and paying any extra medical expenses. Experiment with the amount of money put in the FSA, using a RISKSIMTABLE function.

b. Rework part **a**, but this time assume a gamma distribution for your annual medical expenses. Use 16 and 125 as the two parameters of this distribution. These imply the same mean and standard deviation as in part **a**, but the distribution of medical expenses is now skewed to the right, which is probably more realistic. Using simulation, see whether you should now put more or less money in an FSA than in the symmetric case in part **a**.

41. At the beginning of each week, a machine is in one of four conditions: 1 = excellent; 2 = good; 3 = average; 4 = bad. The weekly revenue earned by a machine in state 1, 2, 3, or 4 is $100, $90, $50, or $10, respectively. After observing the condition of the machine at the beginning of the week, the company has the option, for a cost of $200, of instantaneously replacing the machine with an excellent machine. The quality of the machine deteriorates over time, as shown in the file **P15_41.xlsx**. Four maintenance policies are under consideration:

- Policy 1: Never replace a machine.
- Policy 2: Immediately replace a bad machine.
- Policy 3: Immediately replace a bad or average machine.
- Policy 4: Immediately replace a bad, average, or good machine.

Simulate each of these policies for 50 weeks (using at least 250 iterations each) to determine the policy that maximizes expected weekly profit. Assume that the machine at the beginning of week 1 is excellent.

42. Simulation can be used to illustrate a number of results from statistics that are difficult to understand with nonsimulation arguments. One is the famous *central limit theorem*, which says that if you sample enough values from *any* population distribution and then average these values, the resulting average will be approximately normally distributed. Confirm this by using @RISK with the following population distributions (run a separate simulation for each): (a) discrete with possible values 1 and 2 and probabilities 0.2 and 0.8; (b) exponential with mean 1 (use the RISKEXPON function with the single argument 1); (c) triangular with minimum, most likely, and maximum values equal to 1, 9, and 10. (Note that each of these distributions is very skewed.) Run each simulation with 10 values in each average, and run 1000 iterations to simulate 1000 averages. Create a histogram of the averages to see whether it is indeed bell-shaped. Then repeat, using 30 values in each average. Are the histograms based on 10 values qualitatively different from those based on 30?

43. In statistics we often use observed data to test a hypothesis about a population or populations. The basic method uses the observed data to calculate a test statistic (a single number), as discussed in Chapter 9. If the magnitude of this test statistic is sufficiently large, the null hypothesis is rejected in favor of the research hypothesis. As an example, consider a researcher who believes teenage girls sleep longer than teenage boys on average. She collects observations on $n = 40$ randomly selected girls and $n = 40$ randomly selected boys. (Each observation is the average sleep time over several nights for a given person.) The averages are $\overline{X}_1 = 7.9$ hours for the girls and $\overline{X}_2 = 7.6$ hours for

the boys. The standard deviation of the 40 observations for girls is $s_1 = 0.5$ hour; for the boys it is $s_2 = 0.7$ hour. The researcher, consulting Chapter 9, then calculates the test statistic

$$\frac{\overline{X}_1 - \overline{X}_2}{\sqrt{s_1^2/40 + s_2^2/40}} = \frac{7.9 - 7.6}{\sqrt{0.25/40 + 0.49/40}} = 2.206$$

Based on the fact that 2.206 is "large," she claims that her research hypothesis is confirmed—girls do sleep longer than boys.

You are skeptical of this claim, so you check it out by running a simulation. In your simulation you assume that girls and boys have the *same* mean and standard deviation of sleep times in the entire population, say, 7.7 and 0.6. You also assume that the distribution of sleep times is normal. Then you repeatedly simulate observations of 40 girls and 40 boys from this distribution and calculate the test statistic. The question is whether the observed test statistic, 2.206, is "extreme." If it is larger than most or all of the test statistics you simulate, then the researcher is justified in her claim; otherwise, this large a statistic could have happened easily by chance, even if the girls and boys have identical population means. Use @RISK to see which of these possibilities occurs.

44. A technical note in the discussion of @RISK indicated that Latin Hypercube sampling is more efficient than Monte Carlo sampling. This problem allows you to see what this means. The file **P15_44.xlsx** gets you started. There is a single output cell, B5. You can enter any random value in this cell, such as **RISKNORMAL(500,100)**. There are already @RISK statistical formulas in rows 9–12 to calculate summary measures of the output for each of 10 simulations. On the @RISK ribbon, click on the button to the left of the "dice" button to bring up the Simulation Settings dialog box, click on the Sampling tab, and make sure the Sampling Type is Latin Hypercube. Run 10 simulations with at least 1000 iterations each, and then paste the results in rows 9–12 as *values* in rows 17–20. Next, get back in Simulations Settings and change the Sampling Type to Monte Carlo, run the 10 simulations again, and paste the results in rows 9–12 as values into rows 23–26. For each row, 17–20 and 23–26, summarize the 10 numbers in that row with AVERAGE and STDEV. What do you find? Why do we say that Latin Hypercube sampling is more efficient? (Thanks to Harvey Wagner at University of North Carolina for suggesting this problem.)

45. We are continually hearing reports on the nightly news about natural disasters—droughts in Texas, hurricanes in Florida, floods in California, and so on. We often hear that one of these was the "worst in over 30 years," or some such statement. Are natural disasters getting worse these days, or does it just appear so? How might you use simulation to answer this question? Here is one possible approach. Imagine that there are N areas of the country (or the world) that tend to have, to some extent, various types of weather phenomena each year. For example, hurricanes are always a potential problem for Florida, and fires are always a potential problem in southern California. You might model the severity of the problem for any area in any year by a normally distributed random number with mean 0 and standard deviation 1, where negative values are interpreted as good years and positive values are interpreted as bad years. (We suggest the normal distribution, but there is no reason other distributions couldn't be used instead.) Then you could simulate such values for all areas over a period of several years and keep track, say, of whether any of the areas have worse conditions in the current year than they have had in the past several years, where "several" could be 10, 20, 30, or any other number of years you want to test. What might you keep track of? How might you interpret your results?

Egress, Inc., is a small company that designs, produces, and sells ski jackets and other coats. The creative design team has labored for weeks over its new design for the coming winter season. It is now time to decide how many ski jackets to produce in this production run. Because of the lead times involved, no other production runs will be possible during the season. Predicting ski jacket sales months in advance of the selling season can be quite tricky. Egress has been in operation for only three years, and its ski jacket designs were quite successful in two of those years. Based on realized sales from the last three years, current economic conditions, and professional judgment, 12 Egress employees have independently estimated demand for their new design for the upcoming season. Their estimates are listed in Table 15.2.

Table 15.2 Estimated Demands

14,000	16,000
13,000	8000
14,000	5000
14,000	11,000
15,500	8000
10,500	15,000

To assist in the decision on the number of units for the production run, management has gathered the data in Table 15.3. Note that S is the price Egress charges retailers. Any ski jackets that do not sell during the season can be sold by Egress to discounters for V per jacket. The fixed cost of plant and equipment is F. This cost is incurred regardless of the size of the production run.

Table 15.3 Monetary Values

Variable production cost per unit (C):	$80
Selling price per unit (S):	$100
Salvage value per unit (V):	$30
Fixed production cost (F):	$100,000

Questions

1. Egress management believes that a normal distribution is a reasonable model for the unknown demand in the coming year. What mean and standard deviation should Egress use for the demand distribution?

2. Use a spreadsheet model to simulate 1000 possible outcomes for demand in the coming year. Based on these scenarios, what is the expected profit if Egress produces $Q = 7800$ ski jackets? What is the expected profit if Egress produces $Q = 12,000$ ski jackets? What is the standard deviation of profit in these two cases?

3. Based on the same 1000 scenarios, how many ski jackets should Egress produce to maximize expected profit? Call this quantity Q.

4. Should Q equal mean demand or not? Explain.

5. Create a histogram of profit at the production level Q. Create a histogram of profit when the production level Q equals mean demand. What is the probability of a loss greater than $100,000 in each case? ■

Management of Ebony, a leading manufacturer of bath soap, is trying to control its inventory costs. The weekly cost of holding one unit of soap in inventory is $30 (one unit is 1000 cases of soap). The marketing department estimates that weekly demand averages 120 units, with a standard deviation of 15 units, and is reasonably well modeled by a normal distribution. If demand exceeds the amount of soap on hand, those sales are *lost*—that is, there is no backlogging of demand. The production department can produce at one of three levels: 110, 120, or 130 units per week. The cost of changing the production level from one week to the next is $3000.

Management would like to evaluate the following production policy. If the current inventory is less than $L = 30$ units, they will produce 130 units in the next week. If the current inventory is greater than $U = 80$ units, they will produce 110 units in the next week. Otherwise, Ebony will continue at the previous week's production level.

Ebony currently has 60 units of inventory on hand. Last week's production level was 120.

Questions

1. Develop a simulation model for 52 weeks of operation at Ebony. Graph the inventory of soap over time. What is the total cost (inventory cost plus production change cost) for the 52 weeks?

2. Run the simulation for 500 iterations to estimate the average 52-week cost with values of U ranging from 30 to 80 in increments of 10. Keep $L = 30$ throughout.

3. Report the sample mean and standard deviation of the 52-week cost under each policy. Using the simulated results, is it possible to construct *valid* 95% confidence intervals for the average 52-week cost for each value of U? In any case, graph the average 52-week cost versus U. What is the best value of U for $L = 30$?

4. What other production policies might be useful to investigate? ∎

© AP Photo/Mary Altaffer

MERRILL LYNCH IMPROVES LIQUIDITY RISK MANAGEMENT FOR REVOLVING CREDIT LINES

The Merrill Lynch banking group comprises several Merrill Lynch affiliates, including Merrill Lynch Bank USA (ML Bank USA). (Its parent company is Bank of America.) ML Bank USA has assets of more than $60 billion (as of June 30, 2005 when the following article was written, closer to $70 billion by 2010). The bank acts as an intermediary, accepting deposits from Merrill Lynch retail customers and using the deposits to fund loans and make investments. One way ML Bank USA uses these assets is to provide revolving credit lines to institutional and large corporate borrowers. Currently, it has a portfolio of about $13 billion in credit-line commitments with more than 100 companies. When it makes these commitments, it must be aware of the liquidity risk, defined as the ability to meet all cash obligations when due. In other words, if a borrower asks for funds as part of its revolving credit-line agreement, the bank must have the funds available to honor the request, typically on the same day the request is made. This liquidity requirement poses a huge risk to the bank. The bank must keep enough cash or liquid investments (i.e., investments that can be converted to cash quickly) in reserve to honor its customers' requests whenever they occur. If the bank knew when, and in what quantities, these requests would occur, it could manage its cash reserves more prudently, essentially holding a smaller amount in liquid investments for credit requests and investing the rest in other more illiquid and profitable investments.

Duffy et al. (2005) discuss their role as members of Merrill Lynch's Banking Group and Management Science Group in developing a model to manage the liquidity risk for ML Bank USA's revolving credit lines. The revolving credit lines give borrowers access to a specified amount of cash on demand for short-term funding needs in return for a fee paid to the bank. The bank also earns an interest rate on advances that compensates it for the liquidity and other risks it takes. These credit lines are therefore profitable for the bank, but they are not the borrowers' primary sources of funding. Customers typically use these credit lines to retire maturing commercial paper (available at cheaper interest rates) during the process of rolling it over (i.e., attempting to reissue new commercial paper notes), and/or when their credit rating falls. The essence of the problem is that when a customer's credit ratings (measured by the Moody rating scale, for example) fall, the customers are less likely to obtain funds from cheaper sources such as commercial paper, so they then tend to rely on their credit lines from ML Bank USA and other banks. This poses problems for ML Bank USA. It must honor its commitments to the borrowers, as spelled out in the credit-line agreements, but customers with low credit ratings are the ones most likely to default on their loans.

Two other aspects of the problem are important. First, the credit-line agreements often have a "term-out" option, which allows the borrower to use funds for an additional period after expiration, typically for one year. A customer that is experiencing financial difficulties and has seen its credit rating fall is the type most likely to use its term-out option. Second, movements in credit ratings for customers in the same industry or even in different industries tend to be positively correlated because they can all be affected by movements in their industry or the overall economy. This increases the liquidity risk for ML Bank USA because it increases the chance that poor economic conditions will lead many customers to request additional credit.

The authors built a rather complex simulation model to track the demand for usage of these credit facilities. The model simulates monthly credit-line usage for each customer over a five-year period. During this period, some credit lines are renewed, some expire and are not renewed, and some customers exercise their term-out options. The model has several significant features: (1) It models the probabilistic changes in credit ratings for its customers, where a customer's credit rating can move from one level to another level in a given month with specified probabilities; (2) these probabilities are chosen in such a way that movements in credit ratings are positively correlated across customers; and (3) expert-system business rules are used to determine whether the company will renew or terminate expiring lines of credit and whether customers will exercise their term-out options. For example, a typical rule is that the bank does not renew a credit line if the borrower's credit rating is below a certain threshold.

The authors developed a user-friendly Excel-based system to run their model. It actually invokes and executes the simulation behind the scenes in a simulation package called Arena. Users of the system can change many of the parameters of the model, such as the business-rule cutoffs, to customize the simulation.

The model has helped ML Bank USA manage its revolving credit lines. The output of the model provides a scientific and robust measure of liquidity risk that the bank has confidence in—and therefore uses. The model has led to two tangible financial benefits. First, the model reduced the bank's liquidity requirement from 50% to 20% of outstanding commitments, thus freeing up about $4 billion of liquidity for other profitable illiquid investments. Second, during the first 21 months after the system was implemented, the bank's portfolio expanded from $8 billion in commitments and 80 customers to $13 billion and more than 100 customers. The bank continues to use the model for its long-range planning. ■

16.1 INTRODUCTION

In the previous chapter we introduced most of the important concepts for developing and analyzing spreadsheet simulation models. We also discussed many of the features available in the powerful simulation add-in, @RISK, that you receive with this book. Now we apply the tools to a wide variety of problems that can be analyzed with simulation. For convenience, we group the applications into four general areas: (1) operations models, (2) financial models, (3) marketing models, and (4) games of chance. The only overriding theme in this chapter is that simulation models can yield important insights in all of these areas. You do not need to cover all of the models in this chapter or cover them in any particular order. You can cover the ones of most interest to you in practically any order.

16.2 OPERATIONS MODELS

Whether we are discussing the operations of a manufacturing or a service company, there is likely to be uncertainty that can be modeled with simulation. In this section we look at examples of bidding for a government contract (uncertainty in the bids by competitors), warranty costs (uncertainty in the time until failure of an appliance), and drug production (uncertainty in the yield and timing).

16.2.1 Bidding for Contracts

In situations where a company must bid against competitors, simulation can often be used to determine the company's optimal bid. Usually the company does not know what its competitors will bid, but it might have an idea about the range of the bids its competitors will choose. In this section we show how to use simulation to determine a bid that maximizes the company's expected profit.

| EXAMPLE | 16.1 BIDDING FOR A GOVERNMENT CONTRACT |

The Miller Construction Company must decide whether to make a bid on a construction project. Miller believes it will cost the company $10,000 to complete the project (if it wins the contract), and it will cost $350 to prepare a bid. However, there is uncertainty about each of these. Upon further reflection, Miller assesses that the cost to complete the project has a triangular distribution with minimum, most likely, and maximum values $9000, $10,000, and $15,000. Similarly, Miller assesses that the cost to prepare a bid has a triangular distribution with parameters $300, $350, and $500. (Note the skewness in these distributions. Miller recognizes that cost overruns are much more likely than cost underruns.) Four potential competitors are going to bid against Miller. The lowest bid wins the contract, and the winner is then given the winning bid amount to complete the project. Based on past history, Miller believes that each potential competitor will bid, independently of the others, with probability 0.5. Miller also believes that each competitor's bid will be a multiple of its (Miller's) most likely cost to complete the project, where this multiple has a triangular distribution with minimum, most likely, and maximum values 0.9, 1.3, and 1.8, respectively. If Miller decides to prepare a bid, its bid amount will be a multiple of $500 in the range $10,500 to $15,000. The company wants to use simulation to determine which strategy to use to maximize its expected profit.

Objective   To simulate the profit to Miller from any particular bid, and to see which bid amount is best.

WHERE DO THE NUMBERS COME FROM?

We already discussed this type of bidding problem in Chapter 6. The new data required here are the parameters of the distributions of Miller's costs, those of the competitors' bids, and the probability that a given competitor will place a bid. Triangular distributions are chosen for simplicity, although Miller could try other types of distributions. The parameters of these distributions are probably educated guesses, possibly based on previous contracts and bidding experience against these same competitors. The probability that a given competitor will place a bid can be estimated from these same competitors' bidding history.

Solution

The logic is straightforward. You first simulate the number of competitors who will bid and then simulate their bids. Then for any bid Miller makes, you see whether Miller wins the contract, and if so, what its profit is.

DEVELOPING THE SIMULATION MODEL

The simulation model appears in Figure 16.1. (See the file **Contract Bidding.xlsx.**) It can be developed with the following steps. (Note that this model does not check the possibility of Miller not bidding at all. But this case is easy. If Miller opts not to bid, the profit is a certain $0.)

1 **Inputs.**   Enter the inputs in the blue cells.

2 **Miller's bid.**   You can test all of Miller's possible bids simultaneously with the RISKSIMTABLE function. To set up for this, enter the formula

=**RISKSIMTABLE(D16:M16)**

Recall that the RISKSIMTABLE function allows you to run a separate simulation for each value in its list.

in cell B16. As with all uses of this function, the spreadsheet shows the simulated values for the *first* bid, $10,500. However, when you run the simulation, you see outputs for all of the bids.

3 **Miller's costs.**   Generate Miller's cost to prepare a bid in cell B19 with the formula

=**RISKTRIANG(B5,C5,D5)**

Then copy this to cell B20 to generate Miller's cost to complete the project.

4 **Competitors and their bids.**   First, generate the random number of competitors who bid. This has a binomial distribution with four trials and probability of "success" equal to 0.5 for each trial, so enter the formula

=**RISKBINOMIAL(B8,B9)**

in cell B21. Then generate random bids for the competitors who bid in row 23 by entering the formula

Figure 16.1 Bidding Simulation Model

	A	B	C	D	E	F	G	H	I	J	K	L	M
1	**Bidding for a contract**												
2													
3	**Inputs**												
4	Miller's costs, triangular distributed	Min	Most likely	Max									
5	Cost to prepare a bid	$300	$350	$500									
6	Cost to complete project	$9,000	$10,000	$15,000									
7													
8	Number of potential competitors	4											
9	Probability a given competitor bids	0.5											
10													
11	Parameters of triangular distributions for each competitor's bid (expressed as multiple of Miller's most likely cost to complete project)												
12	Min	0.9											
13	Most likely	1.3											
14	Max	1.8											
15					Possible bids for Miller								
16	Miller's bid	$10,500			$10,500	$11,000	$11,500	$12,000	$12,500	$13,000	$13,500	$14,000	$14,500	$15,000
17													
18	**Simulation**												
19	Miller's cost to prepare a bid	$365											
20	Miller's cost to complete project	$10,332											
21	Number of competing bids	2											
22	Competitor index	1	2	3	4								
23	Competitors' bids	$13,130	$13,354										
24	Minimum competitor bid	$13,354											
25													
26	Miller wins bid? (1 if yes, 0 if no)	1											
27	Miller's profit	-$197											

=IF(B22<=$B$21,RISKTRIANG($B$12,$B$13,$B$14)*$C$6,"")

in cell B23 and copying across. This generates a random bid for all competitors who bid, and it enters a blank for those who don't. (Remember that the random value is the *multiple* of Miller's most likely cost to complete the project.) Calculate the smallest of these (if there are any) in cell B24 with the formula

=IF(B21>=1,MIN(B23:E23),"")

Of course, Miller will not see these other bids until it has submitted its own bid.

5 Win contract? See whether Miller wins the bid by entering the formula

=IF(OR(B16<B24,B21=0),1,0)

in cell B26. Here, 1 means that Miller wins the bid, and 0 means a competitor wins the bid. Of course, if there are no competing bids, Miller wins for sure. Then designate this cell as an @RISK output cell. Recall that to designate a cell as an @RISK output cell, you select the cell and then click on the Add Output button on @RISK's ribbon. You can then label this output appropriately. We used the label Wins Bid.

6 Miller's profit. If Miller submits a bid, the bid cost is lost for sure. Beyond that, the profit to Miller is the bid amount minus the cost of completing the project if the bid is won. Otherwise, Miller makes nothing. So enter the formula

=IF(B26=1,B16-B20,0)−B19

in cell B27. Then designate this cell as an additional @RISK output cell. (We named it Profit.)

Running the Simulation

Set the number of iterations to 1000, and set the number of simulations to 10 because there are 10 bid amounts Miller wants to test.

Discussion of the Simulation Results

The summary results appear in Figure 16.2. For each simulation—that is, each bid amount—there are two outputs: 1 or 0 to indicate whether Miller wins the contract and Miller's profit. The only interesting results for the 0–1 output are in the Mean column, which shows the fraction of iterations that resulted in 1s. So you can see, for example, that if Miller bids $12,000 (simulation #4), the probability of winning the bid is estimated to be 0.581. This probability clearly decreases as Miller's bid increases.

Figure 16.2 Summary Results for Bidding Simulation

Name	Cell	Sim#	Min	Mean	Max	Median	Std Dev	5%	95%
Wins Bid	B26	1	0	0.881	1	1	0.3239505	0	1
Wins Bid	B26	2	0	0.787	1	1	0.4096325	0	1
Wins Bid	B26	3	0	0.689	1	1	0.4631344	0	1
Wins Bid	B26	4	0	0.581	1	1	0.4936423	0	1
Wins Bid	B26	5	0	0.475	1	0	0.4996245	0	1
Wins Bid	B26	6	0	0.359	1	0	0.4799472	0	1
Wins Bid	B26	7	0	0.272	1	0	0.4452125	0	1
Wins Bid	B26	8	0	0.213	1	0	0.4096325	0	1
Wins Bid	B26	9	0	0.168	1	0	0.3740534	0	1
Wins Bid	B26	10	0	0.134	1	0	0.3408228	0	1
Profit	B27	1	-4764.677	-1109.27	1029.211	-747.65	1264.907	-3595.264	534.2583
Profit	B27	2	-4264.677	-640.0039	1529.211	-395.128	1178.434	-2933.573	1006.308
Profit	B27	3	-3764.677	-272.5675	2029.211	-353.8484	1100.608	-2392.814	1463.146
Profit	B27	4	-3264.677	-3.810187	2529.211	-346.4289	1058.958	-1805.828	1929.528
Profit	B27	5	-2764.677	149.7272	3029.211	-352.5558	1075.519	-1187.955	2332.889
Profit	B27	6	-2264.677	170.9912	3529.211	-359.0678	1108.717	-616.3383	2726.53
Profit	B27	7	-1764.677	166.7163	4029.211	-361.9686	1153.412	-464.5716	3058.364
Profit	B27	8	-1264.677	157.6586	4529.211	-364.9714	1225.319	-460.6413	3463.762
Profit	B27	9	-764.6771	119.4651	5029.211	-367.4769	1261.712	-459.4841	3558.395
Profit	B27	10	-496.554	84.26152	5529.211	-369.4244	1298.07	-458.998	3723.797

@RISK - Results Summary — Inputs / Outputs — Simulation Results For Outputs: — Inputs= 8, Outputs= 2, Iterations= 1000, Simulations= 10, Runtime= 00:00:04

In terms of net profit, if you concentrate only on the Mean column, a bid amount of $13,000 (simulation #6) is the best. But as the other numbers in this figure indicate, the mean doesn't tell the whole story. For example, if Miller bids $13,000, it could win the bid but still lose a considerable amount of money because of cost overruns. The histogram of profit in Figure 16.3 indicates this more clearly. It shows that in spite of the positive mean, most outcomes are negative.

So what should Miller do? If it doesn't bid at all, its profit is a certain $0. If Miller is an *expected* profit maximizer, then the fact that several of the means in Figure 16.2 are positive indicates that bidding is better than not bidding, with a bid of $13,000 being the best bid. However, potential cost overruns and the corresponding losses are certainly a concern. Depending on Miller's degree of risk aversion, the company might decide to (1) not bid at all, or (2) bid higher than $13,000 to minimize its worse loss. Still, we would caution Miller not to be *too* conservative. Rather than focusing on the Min (worst case) column in

Figure 16.3

Histogram of Profit
with $13,000 Bid

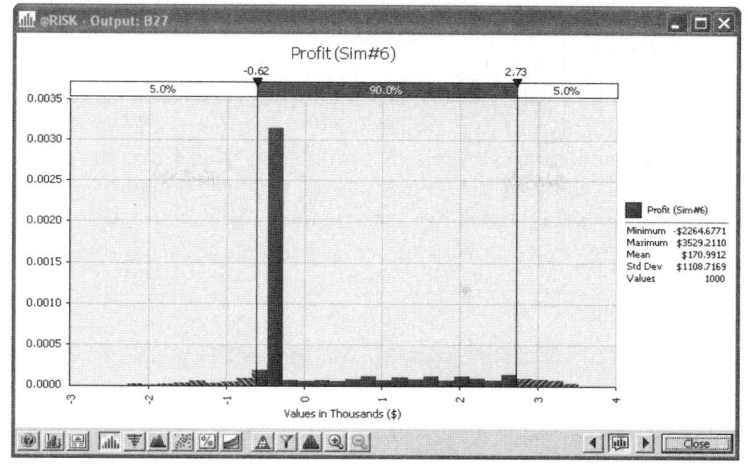

Figure 16.2, we would suggest focusing on the 5% column. This shows *nearly* how bad things could get (5% of the time it would be worse than this), and this 5th percentile remains fairly constant for higher bids. ■

16.2.2 Warranty Costs

When you buy a new product, it usually carries a warranty. A typical warranty might state that if the product fails within a certain period such as one year, you will receive a new product at no cost, and it will carry the *same* warranty. However, if the product fails after the warranty period, you have to bear the cost of replacing the product. Due to random lifetimes of products, we need a way to estimate the warranty costs (to the manufacturer) of a product. The next example illustrates how this can be accomplished with simulation.

EXAMPLE | **16.2 WARRANTY COSTS FOR A CAMERA**

The Yakkon Company sells a popular camera for $400. This camera carries a warranty such that if the camera fails within 1.5 years, the company gives the customer a new camera for free. If the camera fails after 1.5 years, the warranty is no longer in effect. Every replacement camera carries exactly the same warranty as the original camera, and the cost to the company of supplying a new camera is always $225. Use simulation to estimate, for a given sale, the number of replacements under warranty and the NPV of profit from the sale, using a discount rate of 8%.

Objective To use simulation to estimate the number of replacements under warranty and the total NPV of profit from a given sale.

WHERE DO THE NUMBERS COME FROM?

The warranty information is a policy decision made by the company. The hardest input to estimate is the probability distribution of the lifetime of the product. We discuss this next.

Solution

The gamma distribution is a popular distribution, especially when you want a right-skewed distribution of a nonnegative quantity.

The only randomness in this problem concerns the time until failure of a new camera. Yakkon could estimate the distribution of time until failure from historical data. This would probably indicate a right-skewed distribution, as shown in Figure 16.4. If you look through the list of distributions available in @RISK under Define Distributions, you will see several with this same basic shape. The one shown in Figure 16.4 is a commonly used distribution called the *gamma distribution*. We will use a gamma distribution in this example, although other choices such as the triangular are certainly possible.

Figure 16.4

Right-Skewed Gamma Distribution

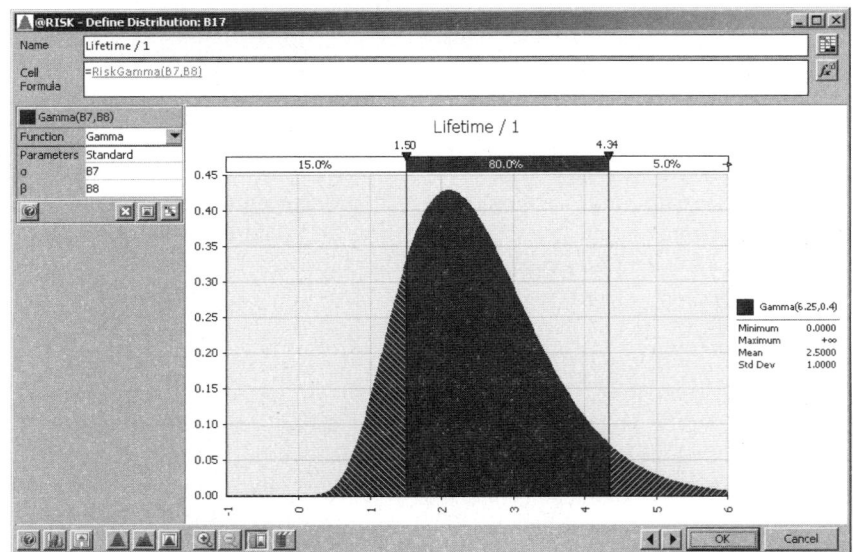

You can learn about distributions from @RISK's Define Distribution window.

Selecting a Gamma Distribution

The **gamma distribution** is characterized by two parameters, α and β. These determine its shape and location. It can be shown that the mean and standard deviation are $\mu = \alpha\beta$ and $\sigma = \sqrt{\alpha}\beta$. Alternatively, for any desired values of the mean and standard deviation, these equations can be solved for α and β, which leads to $\alpha = \mu^2/\sigma^2$ and $\beta = \sigma^2/\mu$. So, for example, if you want a gamma distribution with mean 2.5 and standard deviation 1 (which in this example would be based on camera lifetime data from the past), you should choose $\alpha = 2.5^2/1^2 = 6.25$ and $\beta = 1^2/2.5 = 0.4$. These are the values shown in Figure 16.4 and the ones used for this example. The values in the figure (from @RISK) imply that the probability of failure before 1.5 years is about 0.15, so that the probability of failure out of warranty is about 0.85.

DEVELOPING THE SIMULATION MODEL

The simulation model appears in Figure 16.5. (See the file **Warranty Costs.xlsx**.) The particular random numbers in this figure indicate an example (a rather unusual one) where there are two failures within warranty. However, because the lifetime of the second replacement (cell D17) is greater than 1.5, the company incurs only two replacement costs, as shown in cells B19 and C19. The model can be developed with the following steps.

Figure 16.5

Warranty
Simulation Model

	A	B	C	D	E	F
1	**Warranty costs for camera**					
2						
3	**Inputs**					
4	Parameters of time to failure distribution of any new camera (Gamma)					
5	Desired mean	2.5				
6	Desired stdev	1				
7	Implied alpha	6.250				
8	Implied beta	0.400				
9						
10	Warranty period	1.5				
11	Cost of new camera (to customer)	$400				
12	Replacement cost (to company)	$225				
13	Discount rate	8%				
14						
15	**Simulation of new camera and its replacements (if any)**					
16	Camera	1	2	3	4	5
17	Lifetime	1.330	0.850	2.674	NA	NA
18	Time of failure	1.330	2.180	4.854	NA	NA
19	Cost to company	225	225	0	0	0
20	Discounted cost	203.11	190.25	0.00	0.00	0.00
21						
22	Failures within warranty	2				
23	NPV of profit from customer	($218.35)				

1 **Inputs.** Enter the inputs in the blue cells.

2 **Parameters of gamma distribution.** As discussed previously, if you enter a desired mean and standard deviation (in cells B5 and B6), you have to calculate the parameters of the gamma distribution. Do this by entering the formulas

=B5^2/B6^2

and

=B6^2/B5

in cells B7 and B8.

3 **Lifetimes and times of failures.** Generate at most five lifetimes and corresponding times of failures. (Why only five? You could generate more, but it is extremely unlikely that this same customer would experience more than five failures within warranty, so five suffices.) As soon as a lifetime is greater than 1.5, the warranty period, no further lifetimes are required; instead, "NA" can be recorded in row 17. With this in mind, enter the formulas

=RISKGAMMA(B7,B8)

=IF(B17<B10,RISKGAMMA(B7,B8),"NA")

and

=IF(C17="NA","NA",IF(C17<$B$10,RISKGAMMA($B$7,$B$8), "NA"))

in cells B17, C17, and D17, and copy the latter formula to cells E17 and F17. These formulas guarantee that once "NA" is recorded in a cell, all cells to its right will also contain "NA." To get the actual times of failures, relative to time 0 when the customer originally purchases the camera, enter the formulas

=B17

and

=IF(C17="NA","NA",B18+C17)

in cells B18 and C18, and copy the latter across row 18. These values will be used for the NPV calculation because this requires the exact timing of cash flows.

@RISK Function: *RISKGAMMA*

*To generate a random number from the gamma distribution, use the RISKGAMMA function in the form =**RISKGAMMA(alpha,beta)**. The mean and standard deviation of this distribution are $\mu = \alpha\beta$ and $\sigma = \sqrt{\alpha}\beta$. Equivalently, $\alpha = \mu^2/\sigma^2$ and $\beta = \sigma^2/\mu$.*

4 **Costs and discounted costs.** In row 19, enter the replacement cost ($185) or 0, depending on whether a failure occurs within warranty, and in row 20 discount these costs back to time 0, using the failure times in row 18. To do this, enter the formulas

=IF(B17<B10,B12,0)

and

=IF(C17="NA",0,IF(C17<$B$10,$B$12,0))

in cells B19 and C19, and copy this latter formula across row 19. Then enter the formula

=IF(B19>0,B19/(1+$B$13)^B18,0)

in cell B20 and copy it across row 20. This formula uses the well-known fact that the present value of a cash flow at time t is the cash flow multiplied by $1/(1 + r)^t$, where r is the discount rate.

5 **Outputs.** Calculate two outputs, the number of failures within warranty and the NPV of profit, with the formulas

=COUNTIF(B19:F19,">0")

and

=B11–B12–SUM(B20:F20)

in cells B22 and B23. Then designate these two cells as @RISK output cells. Note that the NPV is the margin from the sale (undiscounted) minus the sum of the discounted costs from replacements under warranty.

Running the Simulation

The @RISK setup is typical. Run 1000 iterations of a *single* simulation (because there is no RISKSIMTABLE function).

Discussion of the Simulation Results

The @RISK summary statistics and histograms for the two outputs appear in Figures 16.6, 16.7, and 16.8. They show a fairly clear picture. About 85% of the time, there are no failures under warranty and the company makes a profit of $175, the margin from the camera sale. However, there is about a 12.9% chance of exactly one failure under warranty, in which case the company's NPV of profit will be an approximate $50 loss (before discounting). Additionally, there is about a 2.1% chance that there will be even more failures under warranty, in which case the loss will be even greater. Note that in our 1000 iterations, the maximum number of failures under warranty was three, and the maximum net loss was $416.44. On average, the NPV of profit was $138.43.

These results indicate that Yakkon is not suffering terribly from warranty costs. However, there are several ways the company could decrease the effects of warranty costs. First, it could increase the price of the camera. Second, it could decrease the warranty period, say, from 1.5 years to 1 year. Third, it could change the terms of the warranty. For example, it could stipulate

Excel's NPV function can be used only for cash flows that occur at the ends of the respective years. Otherwise, you have to discount cash flows manually.

Figure 16.6   Summary Statistics for Warranty Model

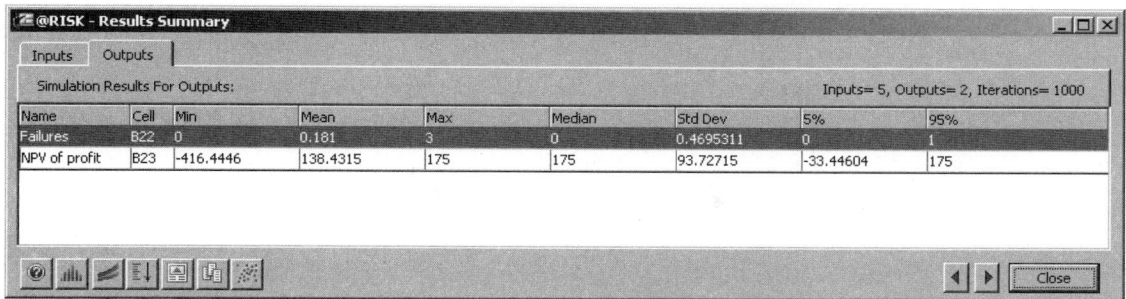

Figure 16.7

Histogram of
Number of Failures

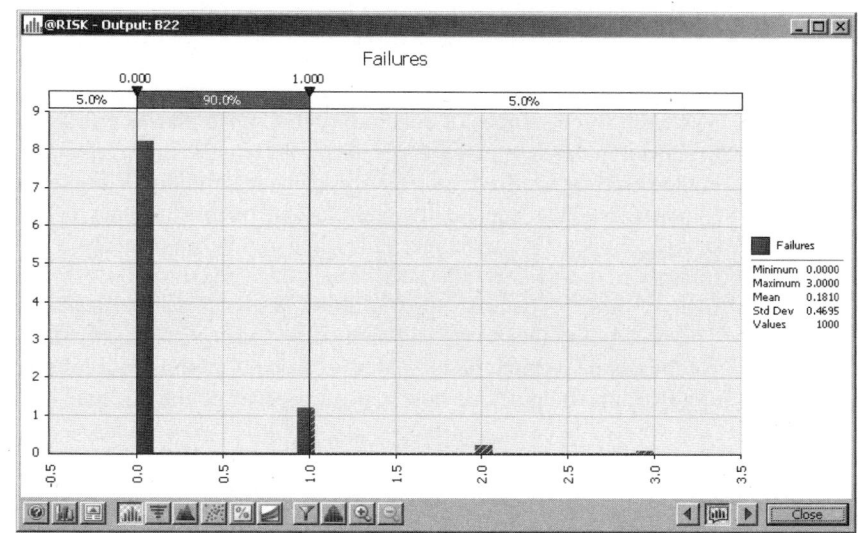

Figure 16.8

Histogram of
NPV of Profit

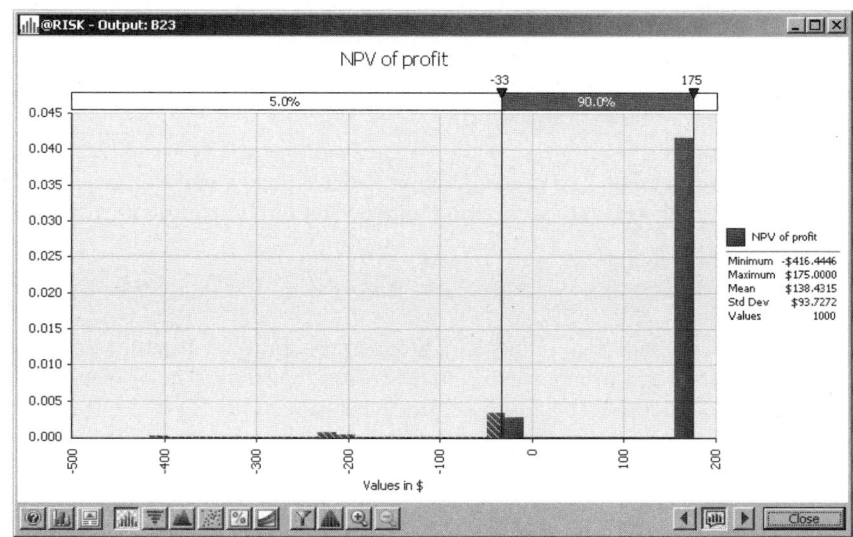

that if the camera fails within a year, the customer gets a new camera for free, whereas if the time to failure is between 1 and 1.5 years, the customer pays some pro rata share of the replacement cost. Finally, it could try to sell the customer an extended warranty—at a hefty price. We ask you to explore these possibilities in the problems. ■

16.2.3 Drug Production with Uncertain Yield

In many manufacturing settings, products are produced in batches, and the usable *yields* from these batches are uncertain. This is particularly true in the drug industry. The following example illustrates how a drug manufacturer can take this uncertainty into account when planning production.

| EXAMPLE | 16.3 TRYING TO MEET AN ORDER DUE DATE AT WOZAC |

The Wozac Company is a drug manufacturer. Wozac has recently accepted an order from its best customer for 8000 ounces of a new miracle drug, and Wozac wants to plan its production schedule to meet the customer's promised delivery date of December 1, 2010. There are three sources of uncertainty that make planning difficult. First, the drug must be produced in batches, and there is uncertainty in the time required to produce a batch, which could be anywhere from 5 to 11 days. This uncertainty is described by the discrete distribution in Table 16.1. Second, the yield (usable quantity) from any batch is uncertain. Based on historical data, Wozac believes the yield can be modeled by a triangular distribution with minimum, most likely, and maximum values equal to 600, 1000, and 1100 ounces, respectively. Third, all batches must go through a rigorous inspection once they are completed. The probability that a typical batch passes inspection is only 0.8. With probability 0.2, the batch fails inspection, and *none* of it can be used to help fill the order. Wozac wants to use simulation to help decide how many days prior to the due date it should begin production.

Table 16.1   Distribution of Days to Complete a Batch

Days	Probability
5	0.05
6	0.10
7	0.20
8	0.30
9	0.20
10	0.10
11	0.05

Objective   To use simulation to determine when Wozac should begin production for this order so that there is a high probability of completing it by the due date.

WHERE DO THE NUMBERS COME FROM?

The important inputs here are the probability distributions of the time to produce a batch, the yield from a batch, and the inspection result. The probabilities we have assumed would undoubtedly be based on previous production data. For example, the company might have observed that about 80% of all batches in the past passed inspection. Of course, a *discrete* distribution is natural for the number of days to produce a batch, and a *continuous* distribution is appropriate for the yield from a batch.

Solution

The idea is to simulate successive batches—their days to complete, their yields, and whether they pass inspection—and keep a running total of the usable ounces obtained so far. IF functions can then be used to check whether the order is complete or another batch is required. You need to simulate only as many as batches as are required to meet the order, and you should keep track of the days required to produce all of these batches. In this way you can "back up" to see when production must begin to meet the due date. For example, if the simulation indicates that the order takes 96 days to complete, then production must begin on August 27, 2010, 96 days before the due date. (For simplicity, you can assume that production occurs seven days a week.)

DEVELOPING THE SIMULATION MODEL

The completed model appears in Figure 16.9. (See the file **Drug Production.xlsx**.) It can be developed as follows.

Figure 16.9 Drug Production Simulation Model

	A	B	C	D	E	F	G	H	I	J	K	L
1	Planning production of a drug											
2												
3	Input section											
4	Amount required (ounces)	8000			Assumptions:							
5	Promised delivery date	12/01/10			The drug is produced in similar-sized batches, although the yield in each							
6					batch is random. Also, the number of days to produce a batch is							
7	Distribution of days needed to produce a batch (discrete)				random. Each batch is inspected, and if it doesn't pass inspection, none							
8			Days	Probability	of that batch can be used.							
9			5	0.05								
10			6	0.10								
11			7	0.20								
12			8	0.30								
13			9	0.20								
14			10	0.10								
15			11	0.05								
16												
17	Distribution of yield (ounces) from each batch (triangular)											
18			Min	Most likely	Max							
19			600	1000	1100							
20												
21	Probability of passing inspection	0.8										
22												
23	Simulation model							Summary measures				
24		Batch	Days	Yield	Pass?	CumYield	Enough?	Batches required	12			
25		1	7	805.7	Yes	805.7	Not yet	Days to complete	92			
26		2	6	913.6	Yes	1719.3	Not yet	Day to start	8/31/10			
27		3	6	938.9	Yes	2658.1	Not yet					
28		4	9	943.3	Yes	3601.4	Not yet	@Risk summary outputs				
29		5	8	743.1	Yes	4344.5	Not yet	Max batches reqd	20			
30		6	8	972.7	No	4344.5	Not yet					
31		7	8	700.0	Yes	5044.5	Not yet	Avg days reqd	94	8/29/10		
32		8	8	964.4	Yes	6008.8	Not yet	Min days reqd	59	10/3/10		
33		9	10	942.5	Yes	6951.3	Not yet	Max days reqd	160	6/24/10		
34		10	6	1030.5	No	6951.3	Not yet	5th perc days reqd	72	9/20/10		
35		11	9	766.9	Yes	7718.2	Not yet	95th perc days reqd	121	8/2/10		
36		12	7	882.0	Yes	8600.3	Yes					
37		13						Probability of meeting due date for several starting dates				
38		14						7/15/10	0.991			
39		15						8/1/10	0.954			
40		16						8/15/10	0.845			
41		17						9/1/10	0.469			
42		18						9/15/10	0.120			
43		19										
44		20										
45		21										
46		22										
47		23										
48		24										
49		25										

1 **Inputs.** Enter all of the inputs in the blue cells.

2 **Batch indexes.** You do not know ahead of time how many batches will be required to fill the order. There should be enough rows in the simulation to cover the worst case that is likely to occur. After some experimentation it is apparent that 25 batches are almost surely enough. Therefore, enter the batch indexes 1 through 25 in column A of the simulation section. (If 25 were not enough, you could always add more rows.) The idea, then, is to fill the *entire* range B25:F49 with formulas. However, you can use appropriate IF functions in these formulas so that if enough has already been produced to fill the order, blanks are inserted in the remaining cells. For example, the scenario shown in Figure 16.9 is one where 12 batches were required, so blanks appear below row 36.

3 **Days for batches.** Simulate the days required for batches in column B. To do this, enter the formulas

=**RISKDISCRETE(B9:B15,C9:C15)**

and

=**IF(OR(F25="Yes",F25=""),"",RISKDISCRETE($B$9:$B$15,$C$9:$C$15))**

in cell B25 and B26, and copy the latter formula down to cell B49. Note how the IF function enters a blank in this cell if either of two conditions is true: the order was just completed in the previous batch or it has been completed for some time. Similar logic appears in later formulas.

4 **Batch yields.** Simulate the batch yields in column C. To do this, enter the formulas

=**RISKTRIANG(B19,C19,D19)**

and

=**IF(OR(F25="Yes",F25=""),"",RISKTRIANG($B$19,$C$19,$D$19))'**

in cells C25 and C26, and copy the latter formula down to cell C49.

5 **Pass inspection?** Check whether each batch passes inspection with the formulas

=**IF(RAND()<B21,"Yes","No")**

and

=**IF(OR(F25="Yes",F25=""),"",IF(RAND()<$B$21,"Yes","No"))**

You can use Excel's RAND function inside an IF function to simulate whether some event occurs.

in cells D25 and D26, and copy the latter formula down to cell D49. Note that you could use @RISK's RISKUNIFORM(0,1) function instead of RAND(), but there is no real advantage to doing so. They are essentially equivalent. (Besides, the academic version of @RISK imposes an upper limit of 100 @RISK input functions per model, so it is often a good idea to substitute built-in Excel functions when possible.)

6 **Order filled?** To keep track of the cumulative usable production and whether the order has been filled in columns E and F, first enter the formulas

=**IF(D25="Yes",C25,0)**

and

=**IF(E25>=B4,"Yes","Not yet ")**

in cells E25 and F25 for batch 1. Then enter the general formulas

=**IF(OR(F25="Yes",F25=""),"",IF(D26="Yes",C26+E25,E25))**

and

=IF(OR(F25="Yes",F25=""),"",IF(E26>=$B$4, "Yes","Not yet "))

in cells E26 and F26, and copy them down to row 49. Note that the entry in column F is "Not enough" if the order is not yet complete. In the row that completes the order, it changes to "Yes," and then it is blank in succeeding rows.

7 **Summary measures.** Calculate the batches and days required in cells I24 and I25 with the formulas

=COUNT(B25:B49)

and

=SUM(B25:B49)

Date subtraction in Excel allows you to calculate the number of days between two given dates.

These are the two cells used as output cells for @RISK, so designate them as such. Also, calculate the day the order should be started to just meet the due date in cell I26 with the formula

=B5–I25

This formula uses date subtraction to find an elapsed time. (Again, the assumption is that production occurs every day of the week.)

This completes the simulation model development. The other entries in columns H through J are explained shortly.

FUNDAMENTAL INSIGHT

Dealing with Uncertain Timing

Many simulations that model a process over multiple time periods must deal with uncertain timing of events, such as when the manufacturing of an order will finish, which year sales of a new product will begin, and many others. Essentially, the spreadsheet model must generate random numbers that determine the timing and then play out the events. This can require tricky IF functions and possibly other functions. However, the hard work often involves getting the logic correct for the first period or two. Then this logic can be copied down for the other periods. In other words, some time spent on developing the first row or two can result in a very powerful model.

Running the Simulation

Set the number of iterations to 1000 and the number of simulations to 1, and then run the simulation as usual.

Discussion of the Simulation Results

After running the simulation, you can obtain the histograms of the number of batches required and the number of days required in Figures 16.10 and 16.11.

How should Wozac use this information? The key questions are (1) how many batches will be required and (2) when production should start. To answer these questions, it is helpful to use several of @RISK's statistical functions. Recall that these functions can be entered directly into the Excel model worksheet. (Also, recall that they provide useful information only *after* the simulation has been run.) These functions provide no new information you don't already have from other @RISK windows, but they allow you to see (and manipulate) this information directly in the spreadsheet.

Figure 16.10

Histogram of Batches Required

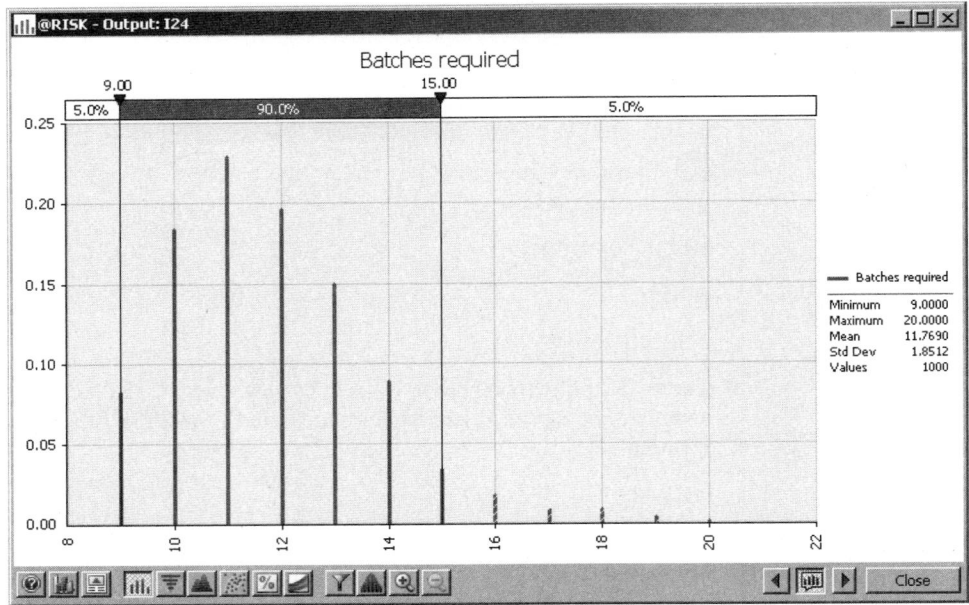

Figure 16.11

Histogram of Days Required

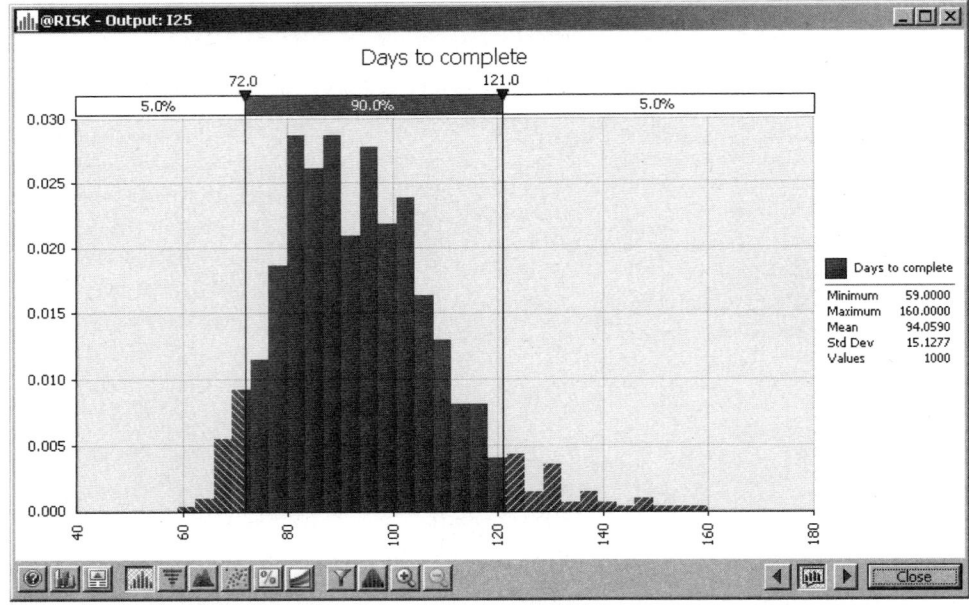

For the first question, enter the formula

=**RISKMAX(I24)**

in cell I29. (Refer to Figure 16.9.) It shows that the worst case from the 1000 iterations, in terms of batches required, is 20 batches. (If this maximum were 25, you would add more rows to the simulation model and run the simulation again.)

You can answer the second question in two ways. First, you can calculate summary measures for days required and then back up from the due date. This is done in the range I31:J35. The formulas in column I are

=INT(RISKMEAN(I25))

=RISKMIN(I25)

=RISKMAX(I25)

=RISKPERCENTILE(I25,0.05)

and

=RISKPERCENTILE(I25,0.95)

(The first uses the INT function to produce an integer.) You can then subtract each of these from the due date to obtain the potential starting dates in column J. Wozac should realize the pros and cons of these starting dates. For example, if the company wants to be 95% sure of meeting the due date, it should start production on August 2. In contrast, if Wozac starts production on September 20, there is only a 5% chance of meeting the due date.

Alternatively, you can get a more direct answer to the question by using @RISK's RISKTARGET function. This allows you to find the probability of meeting the due date for *any* starting date, such as the trial dates in the range H38:H42. To do it, enter the formula

=RISKTARGET(I25,$B$4–H38)

Using @RISK summary functions such as RISKMEAN, RISKPERCENTILE, and others enables you to capture simulation results in the same worksheet as the simulation model. These functions do not provide relevant results until the simulation is run.

in cell I38 and copy it down. This function returns the fraction of iterations where the (random) value in the first argument is less than or equal to the (fixed) value in the second argument. For example, you can see that 84.5% of the iterations have a value of days required less than or equal to 108, the number of days from August 15 to the due date.

What is our recommendation to Wozac? We suggest going with the 95th percentile—begin production on August 2. Then there is only a 5% chance of failing to meet the due date. But the table in the range H38:I42 also provides useful information. For each potential starting date, Wozac can see the probability of meeting the due date. ■

PROBLEMS

Note: Student solutions for problems whose numbers appear within a colored box are available for purchase at www.cengagebrain.com.

Level A

1. In Example 16.1, the possible profits vary from negative to positive for each of the 10 possible bids examined.
  a. For each of these, use @RISK's RISKTARGET function to find the probability that Miller's profit is positive. Do you believe these results should have any bearing on Miller's choice of bid?
  b. Use @RISK's RISKPERCENTILE function to find the 10th percentile for each of these bids. Can you explain why the percentiles have the values you obtain?

2. If the number of competitors in Example 16.1 doubles, how does the optimal bid change?

3. Referring to Example 16.1, if the average bid for each competitor stays the same, but their bids exhibit less variability, does Miller's optimal bid increase or decrease? To study this question, assume that each competitor's bid, expressed as a multiple of Miller's cost to complete the project, follows each of the following distributions.
  a. Triangular with parameters 1.0, 1.3, and 2.4
  b. Triangular with parameters 1.2, 1.3, and 2.2

c. Use @RISK's Define Distributions window to check that the distributions in parts **a** and **b** have the same mean as the original triangular distribution in the example, but smaller standard deviations. What is the common mean? Why is it not the same as the most likely value, 1.3?

4. In Example 16.2, the gamma distribution was used to model the skewness to the right of the lifetime distribution. Experiment to see whether the triangular distribution could have been used instead. Let its minimum value be 0, and choose its most likely and maximum values so that this triangular distribution has approximately the same mean and standard deviation as the gamma distribution in the example. (Use @RISK's Define Distributions window and trial and error to do this.) Then run the simulation and comment on similarities or differences between your outputs and the outputs in the example.

5. See how sensitive the results in Example 16.2 are to the following changes. For each part, make the change indicated, run the simulation, and comment on any differences between your outputs and the outputs in the example.
  a. The cost of a new camera is increased to $300.
  b. The warranty period is decreased to one year.
  c. The terms of the warranty are changed. If the camera fails within one year, the customer gets a new camera for free. However, if the camera fails between 1 year and 1.5 years, the customer pays a pro rata share of the new camera, increasing linearly from 0 to full price. For example, if it fails at 1.2 years, which is 40% of the way from

1 to 1.5, the customer pays 40% of the full price.
  d. The customer pays $50 up front for an extended warranty. This extends the warranty to three years. This extended warranty is just like the original, so that if the camera fails within three years, the customer gets a new camera for free.

6. In Example 16.3, we commented on the 95th percentile on days required in cell I35 and the corresponding date in cell J35. If the company begins production on this date, then it is 95% sure to complete the order by the due date. We found this date to be August 2. Do you always get this answer? Find out by (1) running the simulation 10 more times, each with 1000 iterations, and finding the 95th percentile and corresponding date in each, and (2) running the simulation once more, but with 10,000 iterations. Comment on the difference between simulations (1) and (2) in terms of accuracy. Given these results, when would you recommend that production should begin?

7. In Example 16.3, suppose you want to run five simulations, where the probability of passing inspection is varied from 0.6 to 1.0 in increments of 0.1. Use the RISKSIMTABLE function appropriately to do this. Comment on the effect of this parameter on the key outputs. In particular, does the probability of passing inspection have a large effect on when production should start? (*Note*: When this probability is low, it might be necessary to produce more than 25 batches, the maximum built into the model. Check whether this maximum should be increased.)

16.3 FINANCIAL MODELS

There are many financial applications where simulation can be applied. Future cash flows, future stock prices, and future interest rates are some of the many uncertain variables financial analysts must deal with. In every direction they turn, they see uncertainty. In this section we analyze a few typical financial applications that can benefit from simulation modeling.

16.3.1 Financial Planning Models

Many companies, such as GM, Eli Lilly, Procter & Gamble, and Pfizer, use simulation in their capital budgeting and financial planning processes. Simulation can be used to model the uncertainty associated with future cash flows. In particular, simulation can be used to answer questions such as the following:

- What are the mean and variance of a project's net present value (NPV)?
- What is the probability that a project will have a negative NPV?

- What are the mean and variance of a company's profit during the next fiscal year?
- What is the probability that a company will have to borrow more than $2 million during the next year?

The following example illustrates how simulation can be used to evaluate an investment opportunity.

<hr>

EXAMPLE **16.4 Developing a New Car at GF Auto**

General Ford (GF) Auto Corporation is developing a new model of compact car. This car is assumed to generate sales for the next five years. GF has gathered information about the following quantities through focus groups with the marketing and engineering departments.

- **Fixed cost of developing car.** This cost is assumed to $700 million. The fixed cost is incurred at the beginning of year 1, before any sales are recorded.

- **Margin per car.** This is the unit selling price minus the variable cost of producing a car. GF assumes that in year 1, the margin will be $4000. Every other year, GF assumes the margin will decrease by 4%.[1]

- **Sales.** The demand for the car is the uncertain quantity. In its first year, GF assumes sales—number of cars sold—will be triangularly distributed with parameters 50,000, 75,000, and 85,000. Every year after that, the company assumes that sales will decrease by some percentage, where this percentage is triangularly distributed with parameters 5%, 8%, and 10%. GF also assumes that the percentage decreases in successive years are independent of one another.

- **Depreciation and taxes.** The company will depreciate its development cost on a straight-line basis over the lifetime of the car. The corporate tax rate is 40%.

- **Discount rate.** GF figures its cost of capital at 10%.

Given these assumptions, GF wants to develop a simulation model that will evaluate its NPV of after-tax cash flows for this new car over the five-year time horizon.

Objective   To simulate the cash flows from the new car model, from the development time to the end of its life cycle, so that GF can estimate the NPV of after-tax cash flows from this car.

WHERE DO THE NUMBERS COME FROM?

There are many inputs to this problem. As we indicated, they are probably obtained from experts within the company and from focus groups of potential customers.

Solution

This model is like most financial multiyear spreadsheet models. The completed model extends several years to the right, but most of the work is for the first year or two. From that point, you can copy to the other years to complete the model.

<hr>

[1]The margin decreases because the company assumes variable costs tend to increase through time, whereas selling prices tend to remain fairly constant through time.

The simulation model for GF appears in Figure 16.12. (See the file **New Car Development.xlsx**.) It can be formed as follows.

Figure 16.12 GF Auto Simulation Model

	A	B	C	D	E	F	G
1	New car simulation						
2							
3	Inputs			Parameters of triangular distributions			
4	Fixed development cost	$700,000,000			Min	Most likely	Max
5	Year 1 contribution	$4,000		Year 1 sales	50000	75000	85000
6	Annual decrease in contribution	4%		Annual decay rate	5%	8%	10%
7	Tax rate	40%					
8	Discount rate	10%					
9							
10	Simulation						
11	End of year	1	2	3	4	5	
12	Unit sales	78474	72358	66813	61366	56351	
13	Unit contribution	$4,000	$3,840	$3,686	$3,539	$3,397	
14	Revenue minus variable cost	$313,896,351	$277,855,417	$246,300,063	$217,169,920	$191,445,402	
15	Depreciation	$140,000,000	$140,000,000	$140,000,000	$140,000,000	$140,000,000	
16	Before tax profit	$173,896,351	$137,855,417	$106,300,063	$77,169,920	$51,445,402	
17	After tax profit	$104,337,810	$82,713,250	$63,780,038	$46,301,952	$30,867,241	
18	Cash flow	$244,337,810	$222,713,250	$203,780,038	$186,301,952	$170,867,241	
19							
20	NPV of cash flows	$92,630,632					

1 **Inputs.** Enter the various inputs in the blue cells.

2 **Unit sales.** Generate first-year sales in cell B12 with the formula

=**RISKTRIANG(E5,F5,G5)**

Then generate the reduced sales in later years by entering the formula

=**B12*(1–RISKTRIANG($E$6,$F$6,$G$6))**

in cell C12 and copying it across row 12. Note that each sales figure is a random fraction of the *previous* sales figure.

3 **Contributions.** Calculate the unit contributions in row 13 by entering the formulas

=**B5**

and

=**B13*(1–$B$6)**

in cells B13 and C13, and copying the latter across. Then calculate the contributions in row 14 as the product of the corresponding values in rows 12 and 13.

Depreciation is subtracted to get before-tax profit, but it is then added back after taxes have been deducted.

4 **Depreciation.** Calculate the depreciation each year in row 15 as the development cost in cell B4 divided by 5. This is exactly what "straight-line depreciation" means.

5 **Before-tax and after-tax profits.** To calculate the before-tax profit in any year, subtract the depreciation from total contribution, so each value in row 16 is the difference between the corresponding values in rows 14 and 15. The reason is that depreciation isn't taxed. To calculate the after-tax profits in row 17, multiply each before-tax profit by one minus the tax rate in cell B7. Finally, each cash flow in row 18 is the sum of the corresponding values in rows 15 and 17. Here depreciation is added back to get the cash flow.

6 **NPV.** Calculate the NPV of cash flows in cell B20 with the formula

$$= -B4 + NPV(B8, B18:F18)$$

and designate it as an @RISK output cell (the only output cell). Here, we are assuming that the development cost is incurred right now, so that it isn't discounted, and that all other cash flows occur at the ends of the respective years. This allows the NPV function to be used directly.

Running the Simulation

Set the number of iterations to 1000 and the number of simulations to 1, and then run the simulation as usual.

Discussion of the Simulation Results

After running @RISK, you obtain the histogram in Figure 16.13. These results are somewhat comforting, but also a cause of concern for GF. On the bright side, the mean NPV is about $31.5 million, and there is some chance that the NPV could go well above that figure, even up to almost $150 million. However, there is also a dark side, as shown by the two sliders in the histogram. One slider has been placed over an NPV of 0. As the histogram indicates, there is about a 71% chance of a positive NPV, but there is about a 29% chance of it being negative. The second slider has been positioned at its default 5th percentile setting. Financial analysts often call this percentile the **value at risk at the 5% level**, or **VAR 5%**, because it indicates nearly the worst possible outcome. From this simulation, you can see that GF's VAR 5% is approximately a $67.6 million loss.

Figure 16.13
Histogram of NPV

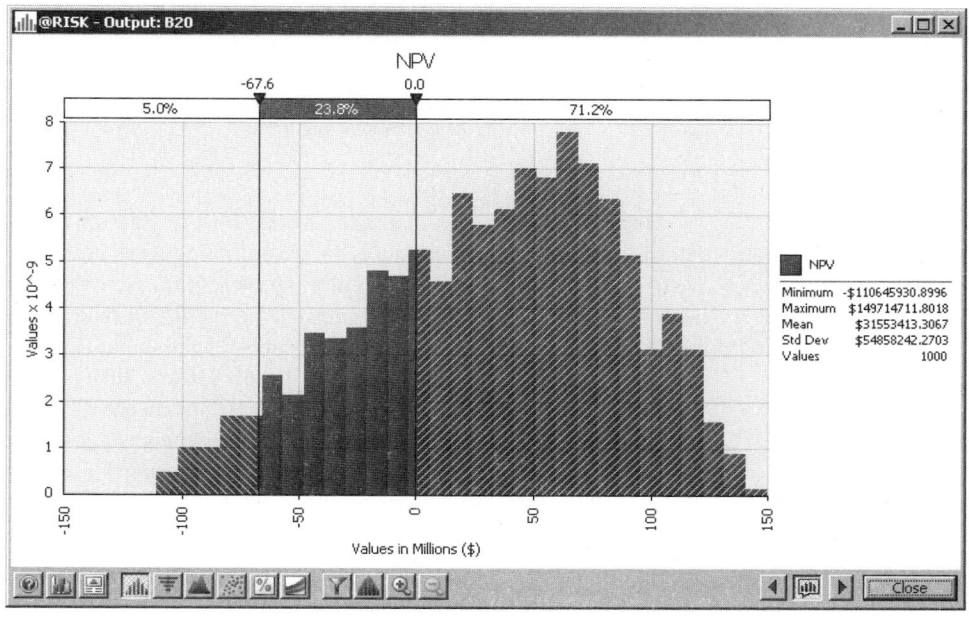

The **value at risk at the 5% level**, or **VAR 5%**, is the 5th percentile of a distribution, and it is often used in financial models. It indicates nearly the worst possible outcome.

What is most responsible for this huge variability in NPV, the variability in first-year sales or the variability in annual sales decreases? This can be answered with @RISK's tornado chart. (See Figure 16.14.) To get this chart, click on the tornado button below the histogram in Figure 16.13 and select the Correlation option. This chart answers the question emphatically. Variability in first-year sales is by far the largest influence on NPV. It correlates almost perfectly with NPV. The annual decreases in sales are not unimportant, but they have much less effect on NPV. If GF wants to get a more favorable NPV distribution, it should do all it can to boost first-year sales—and make the first-year sales distribution less variable.

Figure 16.14

Tornado Chart for NPV

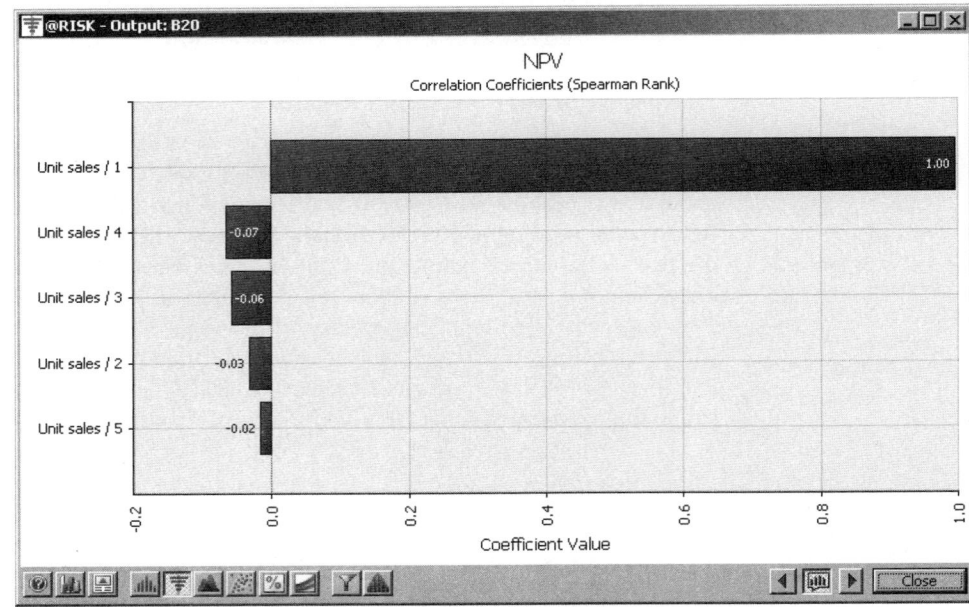

Before finishing this example, we revisit the flaw of averages. What if GF used a deterministic model to estimate NPV? Would the results match those from the simulation? We tried this two ways, once by entering the *most likely values* of the inputs instead of the random numbers, and once by entering the *means* instead of the random numbers. The results appear in Figure 16.15. (The mean of a triangular distribution is the average of its three parameters. These means appear in cells H5 and H6.) Now there are no random numbers in rows 12 and 24, only most likely values or means. The difference between the two NPVs is huge. In this case, the NPV by using means is very close to the mean NPV from the simulation, about $31 million. But if the company used most likely values for the inputs in its deterministic model, which certainly seems sensible, the NPV would be off by a factor of more than two, another variation of the flaw of averages. Besides this problem, neither deterministic model provides even a hint that the company has about a 29% chance of a negative NPV.[2]

---

[2]It turns out that the NPV in this model is *linear* in the two random inputs. When an output is linear in the inputs, the deterministic model using means of inputs *always* gives the correct mean output, so that the flaw of averages in the form from the previous chapter does not occur. Even so, a deterministic model still provides no indication of how bad or how good things could get.

Figure 16.15   Deterministic Models

	A	B	C	D	E	F	G	H
1	New car deterministic models							
2								
3	Inputs			Parameters of triangular distributions				
4	Fixed development cost	$700,000,000			Min	Most likely	Max	Mean
5	Year 1 contribution	$4,000		Year 1 sales	50000	75000	85000	70000
6	Annual decrease in contribution	4%		Annual decay rate	5%	8%	10%	7.67%
7	Tax rate	40%						
8	Discount rate	10%						
9								
10	Using most likely values for uncertain inputs							
11	End of year	1	2	3	4	5		
12	Unit sales	75000	69000	63480	58402	53729		
13	Unit contribution	$4,000	$3,840	$3,686	$3,539	$3,397		
14	Revenue minus variable cost	$300,000,000	$264,960,000	$234,012,672	$206,679,992	$182,539,769		
15	Depreciation	$140,000,000	$140,000,000	$140,000,000	$140,000,000	$140,000,000		
16	Before tax profit	$160,000,000	$124,960,000	$94,012,672	$66,679,992	$42,539,769		
17	After tax profit	$96,000,000	$74,976,000	$56,407,603	$40,007,995	$25,523,861		
18	Cash flow	$236,000,000	$214,976,000	$196,407,603	$180,007,995	$165,523,861		
19								
20	NPV of cash flows	$65,500,687						
21								
22	Using means for uncertain inputs							
23	End of year	1	2	3	4	5		
24	Unit sales	70000	64633	59678	55103	50878		
25	Unit contribution	$4,000	$3,840	$3,686	$3,539	$3,397		
26	Revenue minus variable cost	$280,000,000	$248,192,000	$219,997,389	$195,005,685	$172,853,040		
27	Depreciation	$140,000,000	$140,000,000	$140,000,000	$140,000,000	$140,000,000		
28	Before tax profit	$140,000,000	$108,192,000	$79,997,389	$55,005,685	$32,853,040		
29	After tax profit	$84,000,000	$64,915,200	$47,998,433	$33,003,411	$19,711,824		
30	Cash flow	$224,000,000	$204,915,200	$187,998,433	$173,003,411	$159,711,824		
31								
32	NPV of cash flows	$31,565,909						

FUNDAMENTAL INSIGHT

The Mean Isn't Everything

Many discussions of simulation focus on the *mean* of some output variable. This makes sense, given the importance of EMV for decision making, as discussed in Chapter 6. After all, EMV is just the mean of a monetary output. However, analysts in many areas, including finance, are often at least as interested in the extreme values of an output distribution. For example, the VAR 5% discussed in this example indicates nearly how bad things could get if unlucky outcomes

occur. If large amounts of money are at stake, particularly potential losses, companies might not want to play the averages by focusing only on the mean. They should be aware of potential disasters as well. Of course, simulation also shows the bright side, the extremes on the right that could occur if lucky outcomes occur. Managers shouldn't be so conservative that they focus only on the negative outcomes and ignore the upside potential.

16.3.2 Cash Balance Models

All companies track their cash balance over time. As specific payments come due, companies sometimes need to take out short-term loans to keep a minimal cash balance. The following example illustrates one such application.

EXAMPLE | 16.5 MAINTAINING A MINIMAL CASH BALANCE AT ENTSON

The Entson Company believes that its monthly sales during the period from November of the current year to July of next year are normally distributed with the means and standard deviations given in Table 16.2. Each month Entson incurs fixed costs of $250,000. In March taxes of $150,000 and in June taxes of $50,000 must be paid. Dividends of $50,000 must also be paid in June. Entson estimates that its receipts in a given month are a weighted sum of sales from the current month, the previous month, and two months ago, with weights 0.2, 0.6, and 0.2. In symbols, if R_t and S_t represent receipts and sales in month t, then

$$R_t = 0.2S_{t-2} + 0.6S_{t-1} + 0.2S_t \qquad \textbf{(16.1)}$$

The materials and labor needed to produce a month's sales must be purchased one month in advance, and the cost of these averages to 80% of the product's sales. For example, if sales in February are $1,500,000, then the February materials and labor costs are $1,200,000, but these must be paid in January.

Table 16.2 **Monthly Sales (in Thousands of Dollars) for Entson**

	Nov.	Dec.	Jan.	Feb.	Mar.	Apr.	May	Jun.	Jul.
Mean	1500	1600	1800	1500	1900	2600	2400	1900	1300
Standard Deviation	70	75	80	80	100	125	120	90	70

At the beginning of January, Entson has $250,000 in cash. The company wants to ensure that each month's ending cash balance never falls below $250,000. This means that Entson might have to take out short-term (one-month) loans. For example, if the ending cash balance at the end of March is $200,000, Entson will take out a loan for $50,000, which it will then pay back (with interest) one month later. The interest rate on a short-term loan is 1% per month. At the beginning of each month, Entson earns interest of 0.5% on its cash balance. The company wants to use simulation to estimate the maximum loan it will need to take out to meet its desired minimum cash balance. Entson also wants to analyze how its loans will vary over time, and it wants to estimate the total interest paid on these loans.

Objective   To simulate Entson's cash flows and the loans the company must take out to meet a minimum cash balance.

WHERE DO THE NUMBERS COME FROM?

Although there are many monetary inputs in the problem statement, they should all be easily accessible. Of course, Entson chooses the minimum cash balance of $250,000 as a matter of company policy.

Solution

There is a considerable amount of bookkeeping in this simulation, so it is a good idea to list the events in chronological order that occur each month. We assume the following:

- Entson observes its beginning cash balance.
- Entson receives interest on its beginning cash balance.

- Receipts arrive and expenses are paid (including payback of the previous month's loan, if any, with interest).
- If necessary, Entson takes out a short-term loan.
- The final cash balance is observed, which becomes next month's beginning cash balance.

DEVELOPING THE SIMULATION MODEL

The completed simulation model appears in Figure 16.16. (See the file **Cash Balance.xlsx**.) It requires the following steps.

1 **Inputs.** Enter the inputs in the blue cells. Note that loans are simulated (in row 42) only for the period from January to June of next year. However, sales figures are required (in row 28) in November and December of the current year to generate receipts for January and February. Also, July sales are required for next year to generate the material and labor costs paid in June.

2 **Actual sales.** Generate the sales in row 28 by entering the formula

=RISKNORMAL(B6,B7)

in cell B28 and copying across.

3 **Beginning cash balance.** For January of next year, enter the cash balance with the formula

=B19

in cell D31. Then for the other months enter the formula

=D43

in cell E31 and copy it across row 31. This reflects that the beginning cash balance for one month is the final cash balance from the previous month.

4 **Incomes.** Entson's incomes (interest on cash balance and receipts) are entered in rows 32 and 33. To calculate these, enter the formulas

=$B$24*D31

and

=SUMPRODUCT($B$14:$D$14,B28:D28)

in cells D32 and D33 and copy them across rows 32 and 33. This latter formula, which is based on Equation (16.1), multiplies the fixed weights in row 14 by the relevant sales and adds these products to calculate receipts.

5 **Expenses.** Entson's expenses (fixed costs, taxes and dividends, material and labor costs, and payback of the previous month's loan) are entered in rows 35 through 39. Calculate these by entering the formulas

=D9

=D10

=$B$17*E28

=D42

and

=D42*$B$23

Figure 16.16

Cash Balance
Simulation Model

	A	B	C	D	E	F	G	H	I	J
1	Entson cash balance simulation									
2										
3	Inputs			All monetary values are in $1000s.						
4	Distribution of monthly sales (normal)									
5		Nov	Dec	Jan	Feb	Mar	Apr	May	Jun	Jul
6	Mean	1500	1600	1800	1500	1900	2600	2400	1900	1300
7	St Dev	70	75	80	80	100	125	120	90	70
8										
9	Monthly fixed cost			250	250	250	250	250	250	
10	Tax, dividend expenses			0	0	150	0	0	100	
11										
12	Receipts in any month are of form: A*(sales from 2 months ago)+B*(previous month's sales)+C*(current month's sales), where:									
13		A	B	C						
14		0.2	0.6	0.2						
15										
16	Cost of materials and labor for next month, spent this month, is a percentage of product's sales from next month, where the percentage is:									
17		80%								
18										
19	Initial cash in January	250								
20	Minimum cash balance	250								
21										
22	Monthly interest rates									
23	Interest rate on loan	1.0%								
24	Interest rate on cash	0.5%								
25										
26	Simulation									
27		Nov	Dec	Jan	Feb	Mar	Apr	May	Jun	Jul
28	Actual sales	1572.558	1449.428	1862.074	1604.554	1777.390	2796.194	2290.963	1890.610	1274.369
29										
30	Cash, receipts									
31	Beginning cash balance			250.000	274.190	331.690	250.000	250.000	250.000	
32	Interest on cash balance			1.250	1.371	1.658	1.250	1.250	1.250	
33	Receipts			1556.583363	1728.040947	1690.625121	1946.583769	2491.387266	2311.938686	
34	Costs									
35	Fixed costs			250	250	250	250	250	250	
36	Tax, dividend expenses			0	0	150	0	0	100	
37	Material, labor expenses			1283.643	1421.912	2236.955	1832.770	1512.488	1019.495	
38	Loan payback (principal)				0.000	0.000	862.982	1006.548	286.465	0.000
39	Loan payback (interest)				0.000	0.000	8.630	10.065	2.865	0.000
40										
41	Cash balance before loan			274.190	331.690	-612.982	-756.548	-36.465	904.365	
42	Loan amount (if any)			0.000	0.000	862.982	1006.548	286.465	0.000	
43	Final cash balance			274.190	331.690	250.000	250.000	250.000	904.365	
44										
45	Maximum loan	1006.548								
46	Total intest on loans	21.560								

in cells D35, D36, D37, E38, and E39, respectively, and copying these across rows 35 through 39. (For the loan payback, we are assuming that no loan payback is due in January.)

The loan amounts are determined by the random cash inflows and outflows and the fact that Entson's policy is to maintain a minimum cash balance.

6 **Cash balance before loan.** Calculate the cash balance before the loan (if any) by entering the formula

=SUM(D31:D33)–SUM(D35:D39)

in cell D41 and copying it across row 41.

7 **Amount of loan.** If the value in row 41 is below the minimum cash balance ($250,000), Entson must borrow enough to bring the cash balance up to this minimum. Otherwise, no loan is necessary. Therefore, enter the formula

=MAX($B$20–D41,0)

in cell D42 and copy it across row 42. (You could use an IF function, rather the MAX function, to accomplish the same result.)

8 **Final cash balance.** Calculate the final cash balance by entering the formula

=D41+D42

in cell D43 and copying it across row 43.

9 **Maximum loan, total interest.** Calculate the maximum loan from January to June in cell B45 with the formula

=MAX(D42:I42)

Then calculate the total interest paid on all loans in cell B46 with the formula

=SUM(E39:J39)

⑩ Output range. In the usual way, designate cells B45 and B46 as output cells. Also, designate the entire range of loans, D42:I42, as an output range. To do this, highlight this range and click on the @RISK Add Output button. It will ask you for a name of the output. We suggest "Loans." Then a typical formula in this range, such as the formula for cell E42, will be

=RISKOUTPUT("Loans",2) + MAX($B$20–E41,0)

This indicates that cell E42 is the second cell in the Loans output range.

Running the Simulation

Set the number of iterations to 1000 and the number of simulations to 1. Then run the simulation in the usual way.

Discussion of the Simulation Results

After running the simulation, you will obtain the summary results in Figure 16.17. They indicate that the maximum loan varies considerably, from a low of about $461,000 to a high of about $1,534,000. The average is about $952,500. You can also see that Entson is spending close to $20,000 on average in interest on the loans, although the actual amounts vary considerably from one iteration to another.

Figure 16.17

Summary Measures for Cash Balance Simulation

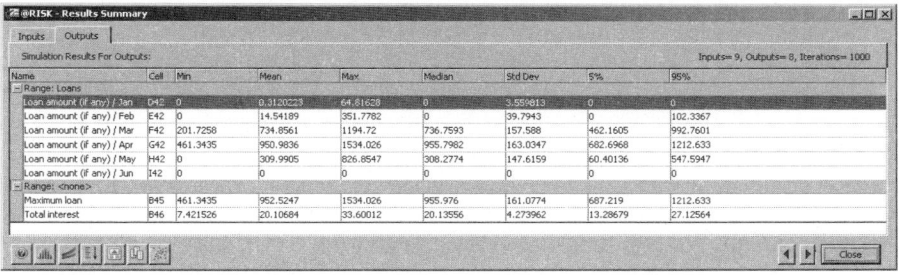

Name	Cell	Min	Mean	Max	Median	Std Dev	5%	95%
Range: Loans								
Loan amount (if any) / Jan	D42	0	9.3120223	64.81628	0	3.559813	0	0
Loan amount (if any) / Feb	E42	0	14.54189	351.7782	0	39.7943	0	102.3367
Loan amount (if any) / Mar	F42	201.7258	734.8561	1194.72	736.7593	157.588	462.1605	992.7601
Loan amount (if any) / Apr	G42	461.3435	950.9836	1534.026	955.7982	163.0347	682.6968	1212.633
Loan amount (if any) / May	H42	0	309.9905	826.8547	308.2774	147.6159	60.40136	547.5947
Loan amount (if any) / Jun	I42	0	0	0	0	0	0	0
Range: <none>								
Maximum loan	B45	461.3435	952.5247	1534.026	955.976	161.0774	687.219	1212.633
Total interest	B46	7.421526	20.10684	33.60012	20.13556	4.273962	13.28679	27.12564

You can also gain insights from the summary trend chart of the series of loans, shown in Figure 16.18. To obtain this chart, click on the third button at the bottom of the Results Summary window in Figure 16.17. (This button is also available in any histogram window.) This chart clearly shows how the loans vary through time. The middle line is the expected loan amount. The inner bands extend to one standard deviation on either side of the mean, and the outer bands extend to the 5th and 95th percentiles. (@RISK lets you customize these bands in a number of ways by right-clicking on the chart.) You can see that the largest loans are required in March and April.

Is it intuitively clear why the required loans peak in March and April? After all, why should Entson need money in months when its sales tend to be relatively high? There are two factors working here. First, Entson has to pay its costs early. For example, it has to pay 80% of its April sales for labor and material expenses in March. Second, most of its receipts arrive late. For example, 80% of its receipts from sales in March are not received until *after* March. Therefore, the answer to the question is that the timing and amounts of loans are fairly complex. Of course, this is why Entson goes to the trouble of building a simulation model.

Figure 16.18
Summary Chart of
Loans Through
Time

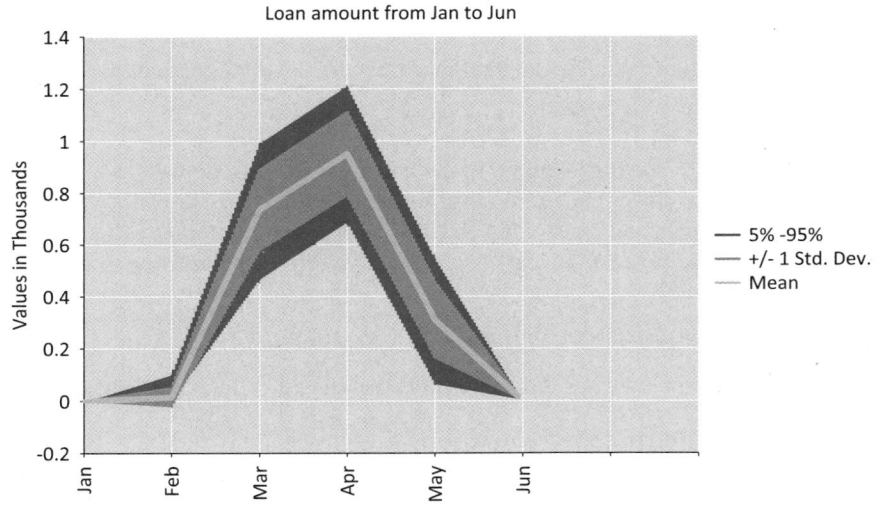

16.3.3 Investment Models

Individual investors typically want to choose investment strategies that meet some pre-specified goal. The following example is typical. Here, a person wants to meet a retirement goal, starting at an early age.

EXAMPLE | **16.6 INVESTING FOR RETIREMENT**

Attorney Sally Evans has just begun her career. At age 25, she has 40 years until retirement, but she realizes that now is the time to start investing. She plans to invest $1000 at the beginning of each of the next 40 years. Each year, she plans to put fixed percentages—the same each year—of this $1000 into stocks, Treasury bonds (T-bonds), and Treasury bills (T-bills). However, she is not sure which percentages to use. (We call these percentages *investment weights.*) She does have historical annual returns from stocks, T-bonds, and T-bills from 1946 to 2007. These are listed in the file **Retirement Planning.xlsx**. This file also includes inflation rates for these years. For example, for 1993 the annual returns for stocks, T-bonds, and T-bills were 9.99%, 18.24%, and 2.90%, respectively, and the inflation rate was 2.75%. Sally would like to use simulation to help decide what investment weights to use, with the objective of achieving a large investment value, in *today's* dollars, at the end of 40 years.

Objective To use simulation to estimate the value of Sally's future investments, in today's dollars, from several investment strategies in T-bills, T-bonds, and stocks.

WHERE DO THE NUMBERS COME FROM?

Historical returns and inflation rates, such as those quoted here, are widely available on the Web.

Solution

You can simulate future scenarios by randomly choosing past scenarios, giving higher probabilities to more recent scenarios.

The most difficult modeling aspect is settling on a way to use historical returns and inflation factors to generate *future* values of these quantities. We suggest using a *scenario* approach. You can think of each historical year as a possible scenario, where the scenario specifies the returns and inflation factor for that year. Then for any future year, you randomly choose one of these scenarios. It seems intuitive that more recent scenarios ought to have a greater chance of being chosen. To implement this idea, you can give a weight (not to be confused with the investment weights) to each scenario, starting with weight 1 for 2007. Then the weight for any year is a *damping factor* multiplied by the weight from the next year. For example, the weight for 1996 is the damping factor multiplied by the weight for 1997. To change these weights to probabilities, you can divide each weight by the sum of all the weights. The damping factor illustrated here is 0.98. Others could be used instead, and it is not clear which produces the most realistic results. (This is an important question for financial research.)

Without a package like RiskOptimizer, you cannot find the "best" set of investment weights, but the simulation model lets you experiment with various sets of weights.

The other difficult part of the solution is choosing "good" investment weights. This is really an optimization problem: find three weights that add to 1 and produce the largest mean final cash. Palisade has another software package, RiskOptimizer, that solves this type of optimization–simulation problem. However, the example illustrates several sets of weights, where some percentage is put into stocks and the remainder is split evenly between T-bonds and T-bills, and see which does best. You can try other sets if you like.

DEVELOPING THE SIMULATION MODEL

The historical data and the simulation model (each with some rows hidden) appear in Figures 16.19 and 16.20. (Again, see the **Retirement Planning.xlsx** file.) It can be developed as follows.

1 **Inputs.** Enter the data in the blue regions of Figures 16.19 and 16.20.

2 **Weights.** The investment weights used for the model are in rows 10 through 12. (For example, the first set puts 80% in stocks and 10% in each of T-bonds and T-bills.) You can simulate all three sets of weights simultaneously with a RISKSIMTABLE and VLOOKUP combination as follows. First, enter the formula

=RISKSIMTABLE({1,2,3})

in cell I16. Then enter the formula

=VLOOKUP($I$16,LTable1,2)

Figure 16.19

Historical Data, Inputs, and Probabilities

	A	B	C	D	E	F	G
3	Historical data and probabilities						
4	Year	T-Bills	T-Bonds	Stocks	Inflation	ProbWts	Probability
5	1946	0.0035	-0.0010	-0.0807	0.1817	0.2916	0.0082
6	1947	0.0050	-0.0263	0.0571	0.0901	0.2976	0.0083
7	1948	0.0081	0.0340	0.0550	0.0271	0.3036	0.0085
8	1949	0.0110	0.0645	0.1879	-0.0180	0.3098	0.0087
9	1950	0.0120	0.0006	0.3171	0.0579	0.3161	0.0089
58	1999	0.0439	-0.0825	0.2089	0.0270	0.8508	0.0238
59	2000	0.0537	0.1666	-0.0903	0.0340	0.8681	0.0243
60	2001	0.0573	0.0557	-0.1185	0.0160	0.8858	0.0248
61	2002	0.0180	0.1512	-0.2198	0.0159	0.9039	0.0253
62	2003	0.0180	0.0038	0.2841	0.0227	0.9224	0.0258
63	2004	0.0218	0.0449	0.1070	0.0268	0.9412	0.0264
64	2005	0.0431	0.0287	0.0485	0.0339	0.9604	0.0269
65	2006	0.0488	0.0196	0.1563	0.0324	0.9800	0.0274
66	2007	0.0548	0.0488	0.1021	0.0285	1.0000	0.0280
67					Sums -->	35.7115	1.0000

Figure 16.20 Retirement Simulation Model

	I	J	K	L	M	N	O	P	Q
3	Inputs								
4	Damping factor	0.98				Range names used			
5	Yearly investment	$1,000				LTable1	=Model!$I$10:$L$12		
6	Planning horizon	40	years			LTable2	=Model!$A$5:$E$66		
7						Weights	=Model!$J$16:$L$16		
8	Alternative sets of weights to test								
9	Index	T-Bills	T-Bonds	Stocks					
10	1	0.10	0.10	0.80					
11	2	0.20	0.20	0.60					
12	3	0.30	0.30	0.40					
13									
14	Weights used								
15	Index	T-Bills	T-Bonds	Stocks					
16	1	0.10	0.10	0.80					
17									
18	Output from simulation below								
19	Final cash (today's dollars)		$46,215						
20									
21						Column offset for lookup2			
22	Simulation model				2	3	4	5	
23	Future year	Beginning cash	Scenario	T-Bills	T-Bonds	Stocks	Inflation	Ending cash	Deflator
24	1	$1,000	1958	1.0154	0.9390	1.4336	1.0176	1342	0.983
25	2	2342	1991	1.0560	1.1930	1.3055	1.0306	2973	0.954
26	3	3973	1988	1.0635	1.0967	1.1681	1.0442	4571	0.913
27	4	5571	2003	1.0180	1.0038	1.2841	1.0227	6849	0.893
28	5	7849	1981	1.1471	1.0185	0.9509	1.0894	7671	0.820
29	6	8671	1976	1.0508	1.1675	1.2384	1.0481	10514	0.782
56	33	113803	1984	1.0985	1.1543	1.0627	1.0395	122389	0.246
57	34	123389	1995	1.0560	1.2348	1.3720	1.0250	163697	0.240
58	35	164697	1973	1.0693	0.9889	0.8534	1.0880	146340	0.220
59	36	147340	1990	1.0781	1.0618	0.9683	1.0611	145665	0.207
60	37	146665	1998	1.0516	1.1492	1.2834	1.0160	182862	0.204
61	38	183862	1988	1.0635	1.0967	1.1681	1.0442	211533	0.196
62	39	212533	1992	1.0351	1.0805	1.0767	1.0290	228031	0.190
63	40	229031	2007	1.0548	1.0488	1.1021	1.0285	250111	0.185

in cell J16 and copy it to cells K16 and L16. Then modify the formulas in these latter two cells, changing the last argument of the VLOOKUP to 3 and 4, respectively. For example, the formula in cell L16 should end up as

=VLOOKUP($I$16,LTable1,4)

The effect is that you can run three simulations, one for each set of weights in rows 10 through 12.

3 **Probabilities.** Enter value 1 in cell F66. Then enter the formula

=$J$4*F66

in cell F65 and copy it *up* to cell F5. Sum these values with the SUM function in cell F67. Then to convert them to probabilities (numbers that add to 1), enter the formula

=F5/$F$67

in cell G5 and copy it down to cell G66. Note how the probabilities for more recent years are considerably larger. When scenarios are selected randomly, recent years will have a greater chance of being chosen. (The SUM formula in cell G67 confirms that the probabilities sum to 1.)

4 **Scenarios.** Moving to the model in Figure 16.20, the goal is to simulate 40 scenarios in columns K through O, one for each year of Sally's investing. To do this, enter the formulas

=RISKDISCRETE($A$5:$A$66,$G$5:$G$66)

and

=1+VLOOKUP($K24,LTable2,L$22)

in cells K24 and L24, and copy this latter formula to the range M24:O24. Then copy all of these formulas down to row 63. Make sure you understand how the RISKDISCRETE and VLOOKUP functions combine to achieve the goal. (Also, check the list of range names used at the top of Figure 16.20.) The RISKDISCRETE randomly generates a year from column A, using the probabilities in column G. Then the VLOOKUP captures the data from this year. (You add 1 to the VLOOKUP to get a value such as 1.08, rather than 0.08.) This is the key to the simulation. (By the way, do you see why Excel's RANDBETWEEN function isn't used to generate the years in column K? The reason is that this function makes all possible years equally likely, and the goal is to make more recent years *more* likely.)

5 **Beginning, ending cash.** The bookkeeping part is straightforward. Begin by entering the formula

=J5

in cell J24 for the initial investment. Then enter the formulas

=J24*SUMPRODUCT(Weights,L24:N24)

and

=$J$5+P24

in cells P24 and J25 for ending cash in the first year and beginning cash in the second year. The former shows how the beginning cash grows in a given year. You should think it through carefully. The latter implies that Sally reinvests her previous money, plus she invests an additional $1000. Copy these formulas down columns J and P.

6 **Deflators.** You eventually need to deflate future dollars to today's dollars. The proper way to do this is to calculate deflators (also called deflation factors). Do this by entering the formula

=1/O24

in cell Q24. Then enter the formula

=Q24/O25

in cell Q25 and copy it down. The effect is that the deflator for future year 20, say, in cell Q43, is 1 divided by the product of all 20 inflation factors up through that year. (This is similar to discounting for the time value of money, but the relevant discount rate, now the inflation rate, varies from year to year.)

7 **Final cash.** Calculate the final value *in today's dollars* in cell K19 with the formula

=P63*Q63

Then designate this cell as an @RISK output cell.

Running the Simulation

Set the number of iterations to 1000 and the number of simulations to 3 (one for each set of investment weights to be tested). Then run the simulation as usual.

Discussion of the Simulation Results

Summary results appear in Figure 16.21. The first simulation, which invests the most heavily in stocks, is easily the winner. Its mean final cash, slightly more than $153,000 in today's dollars, is much greater than the means for the other two sets of weights. The first simulation also has a *much* larger upside potential (its 95th percentile is close to $360,000), and even its downside is slightly better than the others: Its 5th percentile is the best, and its minimum is only slightly worse than the minimum for the other sets of weights.

Figure 16.21
Summary Results
for Retirement
Simulation

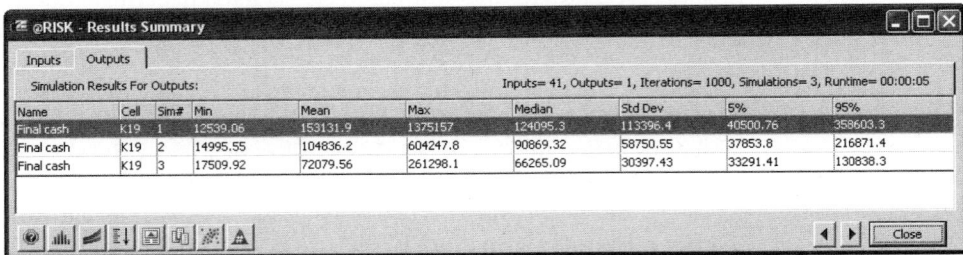

Nevertheless, the histogram for simulation 1 (put 80% in stocks), shown in Figure 16.22, indicates a lot of variability—and skewness—in the distribution of final cash. As in Example 16.4, the concept of value at risk (VAR) is useful. Recall that VAR 5% is defined as the 5th percentile of a distribution and is often the value investors worry about. Perhaps Sally should rerun the simulation with different investment weights, with an eye on the weights that increase her VAR 5%. Right now it is slightly more than $40,000—not too good considering that she invests $40,000 total. She might not like the prospect of a 5% chance of ending up with no more than this. We also encourage you to try running this simulation with other

Figure 16.22
Histogram of Final
Cash with 80% in
Stocks

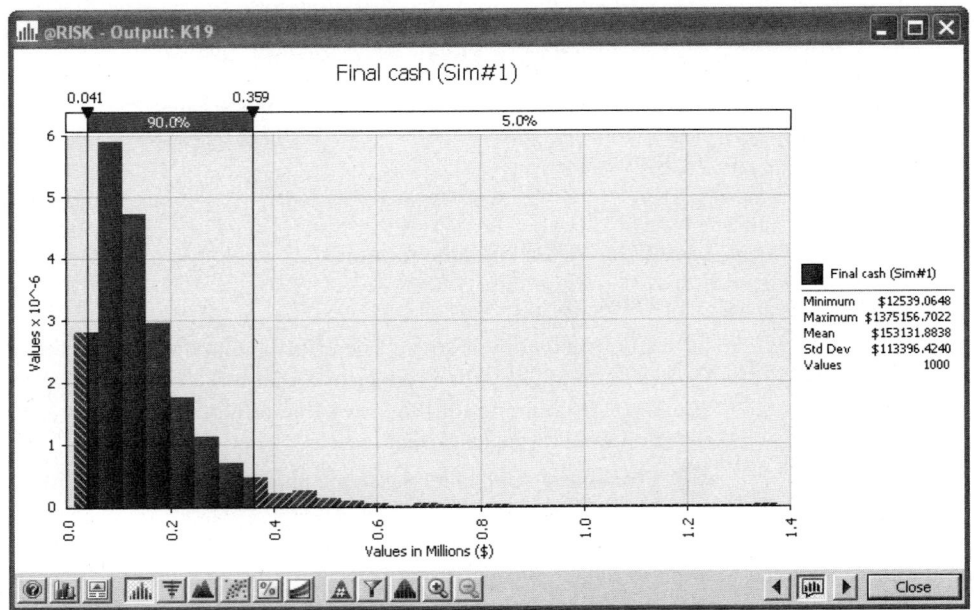

investment weights, both for the 40-year horizon and (after modifying the spreadsheet model slightly) for shorter time horizons such as 10 or 15 years. Even though the stock strategy appears to be best for a long horizon, it is not necessarily guaranteed to dominate for a shorter time horizon. ■

PROBLEMS

Level A

8. Rerun the new car simulation from Example 16.4, but now introduce uncertainty into the fixed development cost. Let it be triangularly distributed with parameters $600 million, $650 million, and $850 million. (You can check that the mean of this distribution is $700 million, the same as the cost given in the example.) Comment on the differences between your output and those in the example. Would you say these differences are important for the company?

9. Rerun the new car simulation from Example 16.4, but now use the RISKSIMTABLE function appropriately to simulate discount rates of 5%, 7.5%, 10%, 12.5%, and 15%. Comment on how the outputs change as the discount rate decreases from the value used in the example, 10%.

10. In the cash balance model from Example 16.5, the timing is such that some receipts are delayed by one or two months, and the payments for materials and labor must be made a month in advance. Change the model so that all receipts are received immediately, and payments made this month for materials and labor are 80% of sales *this* month (not next month). The period of interest is again January through June. Rerun the simulation, and comment on any differences between your outputs and those from the example.

11. In the cash balance model from Example 16.5, is the $250,000 minimum cash balance requirement really "costing" the company very much? Answer this by rerunning the simulation with minimum required cash balances of $50,000, $100,000, $150,000, and $200,000. Use the RISKSIMTABLE function to run all simulations at once. Comment on the outputs from these simulations. In particular, comment on whether the company appears to be better off with a lower minimum cash balance.

12. Run the retirement model from Example 16.6 with a damping factor of 1.0 (instead of 0.98), again using the same three sets of investment weights. Explain in words what it means, in terms of the simulation, to have a damping factor of 1. Then comment on the differences, if any, between your simulation results and those in the example.

13. The simulation output from Example 16.6 indicates that an investment heavy in stocks produces the best results. Would it be better to invest *entirely* in stocks? Answer this by rerunning the simulation. Is there any apparent downside to this strategy?

14. Modify the model from Example 16.6 so that you use only the years 1975 to 2007 of historical data. Run the simulation for the same three sets of investment weights. Comment on whether your results differ in any important way from those in the example.

15. Referring to the retirement example in Example 16.6, rerun the model for a planning horizon of 10 years; 15 years; 25 years. For each, which set of investment weights maximizes the VAR 5% (the 5th percentile) of final cash in today's dollars? Does it appear that a portfolio heavy in stocks is better for long horizons but not for shorter horizons?

Level B

16. Change the new car simulation from Example 16.4 as follows. It is the same as before for years 1 through 5, including depreciation through year 5. However, the car might sell through year 10. Each year *after* year 5, the company examines sales. If fewer than 45,000 cars were sold that year, there is a 50% chance the car won't be sold after that year. Modify the model and run the simulation. Keep track of two outputs: NPV (through year 10) and the number of years of sales.

17. Based on Kelly (1956). You currently have $100. Each week you can invest any amount of money you currently have in a risky investment. With probability 0.4, the amount you invest is tripled (e.g., if you invest $100, you increase your asset position by $300), and, with probability 0.6, the amount you invest is lost. Consider the following investment strategies:
    - Each week, invest 10% of your money.
    - Each week, invest 30% of your money.
    - Each week, invest 50% of your money.

    Use @RISK to simulate 100 weeks of each strategy 1000 times. Which strategy appears to be best in terms of the maximum growth rate? (In general, if you can multiply your investment by M with probability p and lose your investment with probability $q = 1 - p$, you should invest a fraction $[p(M - 1) - q]/(M - 1)$ of your money each week. This strategy maximizes the expected growth rate of your fortune and is known as the *Kelly criterion*.) (*Hint*: If an initial wealth of I dollars grows to F dollars in 100 weeks, the weekly growth rate, labeled r, satisfies $F = (1 + r)^{100} * I$, so that $r = (F/I)^{1/100} - 1$.)

18. Amanda has 30 years to save for her retirement. At the beginning of each year, she puts $5000 into her retirement account. At any point in time, all of Amanda's retirement funds are tied up in the stock market. Suppose the annual return on stocks follows a normal distribution with mean 12% and standard deviation 25%. What is the probability that at the end of 30 years, Amanda will have reached her goal of having $1,000,000 for retirement? Assume that if Amanda reaches her goal *before* 30 years, she will stop investing. (*Hint*: Each year you should keep track of Amanda's beginning cash position—for year 1, this is $5000—and Amanda's ending cash position. Of course, Amanda's ending cash position for a given year is a function of her beginning cash position and the return on stocks for that year. To estimate the probability that Amanda meets her goal, use an IF statement that returns 1 if she meets her goal and 0 otherwise.)

19. In the financial world, there are many types of complex instruments called derivatives that *derive* their value from the value of an underlying asset. Consider the following simple derivative. A stock's current price is $80 per share. You purchase a derivative whose value to you becomes known a month from now. Specifically, let P be the price of the stock in a month. If P is between $75 and $85, the derivative is worth nothing to you. If P is less than $75, the derivative results in a loss of $100*(75-P)$ dollars to you. (The factor of 100 is because many derivatives involve 100 shares.) If P is greater than $85, the derivative results in a gain of $100*(P-85)$ dollars to you. Assume that the distribution of the change in the stock price from now to a month from

now is normally distributed with mean $1 and standard deviation $8. Let EMV be the expected gain/loss from this derivative. It is a weighted average of all the possible losses and gains, weighted by their likelihoods. (Of course, any loss should be expressed as a negative number. For example, a loss of $1500 should be expressed as -$1500.) Unfortunately, this is a difficult probability calculation, but EMV can be estimated by an @RISK simulation. Perform this simulation with at least 1000 iterations. What is your best estimate of EMV?

20. Suppose you currently have a portfolio of three stocks, A, B, and C. You own 500 shares of A, 300 of B, and 1000 of C. The current share prices are $42.76, $81.33, and $58.22, respectively. You plan to hold this portfolio for at least a year. During the coming year, economists have predicted that the national economy will be awful, stable, or great with probabilities 0.2, 0.5, and 0.3. Given the state of the economy, the returns (one-year percentage changes) of the three stocks are independent and normally distributed. However, the means and standard deviations of these returns depend on the state of the economy, as indicated in the file **P16_20.xlsx**.

   a. Use @RISK to simulate the value of the portfolio and the portfolio return in the next year. How likely is it that you will have a negative return? How likely is it that you will have a return of at least 25%?

   b. Suppose you had a crystal ball where you could predict the state of the economy with certainty. The stock returns would still be uncertain, but you would know whether your means and standard deviations come from row 6, 7, or 8 of the **P16_20.xlsx** file. If you learn, with certainty, that the economy is going to be *great* in the next year, run the appropriate simulation to answer the same questions as in part **a**. Repeat this if you learn that the economy is going to be *awful*. How do these results compare with those in part **a**?

16.4 MARKETING MODELS

There are plenty of opportunities for marketing departments to use simulation. They face uncertainty in the brand-switching behavior of customers, the entry of new brands into the market, customer preferences for different attributes of products, the effects of advertising on sales, and so on. We examine some interesting marketing applications of simulation in this section.

16.4.1 Models of Customer Loyalty

What is a loyal customer worth to a company? This is an extremely important question for companies. (It is an important part of customer relationship management, or CRM, currently one of the hottest topics in marketing.) Companies know that if customers become dissatisfied with the company's product, they are likely to switch and never return. Marketers refer to this customer loss as **churn**. The loss in profit from churn can be large, particularly because long-standing customers tend to be more profitable in any given year than new customers. The following example uses a reasonable model of customer loyalty and simulation to estimate the worth of a customer to a company. It is based on the excellent discussion of customer loyalty in Reichheld (1996).

EXAMPLE	16.7 THE LONG-TERM VALUE OF A CUSTOMER AT CCAMERICA

CCAmerica is a credit card company that does its best to gain customers and keep their business in a highly competitive industry. The first year a customer signs up for service typically results in a loss to the company because of various administrative expenses. However, after the first year, the profit from a customer is typically positive, and this profit tends to increase through the years. The company has estimated the mean profit from a typical customer to be as shown in column B of Figure 16.23. For example, the company expects to lose $40 in the customer's first year but to gain $87 in the fifth year—provided that the customer stays loyal that long. For modeling purposes, we assume that the *actual* profit from a

Figure 16.23

Mean Profit as a Function of Years as Customer

	A	B
10	Year	Mean Profit(if still here)
11	1	($40.00)
12	2	$66.00
13	3	$72.00
14	4	$79.00
15	5	$87.00
16	6	$92.00
17	7	$96.00
18	8	$99.00
19	9	$103.00
20	10	$106.00
21	11	$111.00
22	12	$116.00
23	13	$120.00
24	14	$124.00
25	15	$130.00
26	16	$137.00
27	17	$142.00
28	18	$148.00
29	19	$155.00
30	20	$161.00
31	21	$161.00
32	22	$161.00
33	23	$161.00
34	24	$161.00
35	25	$161.00
36	26	$161.00
37	27	$161.00
38	28	$161.00
39	29	$161.00
40	30	$161.00

customer in the customer's nth year of service is *normally* distributed with mean shown in Figure 16.23 and standard deviation equal to 10% of the mean. At the end of each year, the customer leaves the company, never to return, with probability 0.15, the *churn rate*. Alternatively, the customer stays with probability 0.85, the *retention rate*. The company wants to estimate the NPV of the net profit from any such customer who has just signed up for service at the beginning of year 1, at a discount rate of 15%, assuming that the cash flow occurs in the middle of the year.[3] It also wants to see how sensitive this NPV is to the retention rate.

Objective   To use simulation to find the NPV of a customer and to see how this varies with the retention rate.

WHERE DO THE NUMBERS COME FROM?

The numbers in Figure 16.23 are undoubtedly averages, based on the historical records of many customers. To build in randomness for any *particular* customer, we need a probability distribution around the numbers in this figure. We arbitrarily chose a normal distribution centered on the historical average and a standard deviation of 10% of the average. These are educated guesses. Finally, the churn rate is a number very familiar to marketing people, and it can also be estimated from historical customer data.

Solution

The idea is to keep simulating profits (or a loss in the first year) for the customer until the customer churns. We simulate 30 years of potential profits, but this could be varied.

DEVELOPING THE SIMULATION MODEL

The simulation model appears in Figure 16.24. (See the file **Customer Loyalty.xlsx**.) It can be developed with the following steps.

1 **Inputs.** Enter the inputs in the blue cells.

2 **Retention rate.** Although an 85% retention rate was given in the statement of the problem, it is useful to investigate retention rates from 75% to 95%, as shown in column D. To run a separate simulation for each of these, enter the formula

=**RISKSIMTABLE(D4:D8)**

in cell B4.

3 **Timing of churn.** In column C, use simulation to discover when the customer churns. This column will contain a sequence of No values, followed by a Yes, and then a sequence of blanks (or all No values if the customer never churns). To generate these, enter the formulas

As usual, Excel's RAND function can be used inside an IF statement to determine whether a given event occurs.

=**IF(RAND()<1–B4,"Yes","No")**

and

=**IF(OR(C11="",C11="Yes"),"",IF(RAND()<1–$B$4,"Yes","No"))**

in cells C11 and C12, and copy the latter formula down column C. Study these formulas carefully to see how the logic works. Note that they do not rely on @RISK functions.

---

[3]This assumption makes the NPV calculation slightly more complex, but it is probably more realistic than the usual assumption that cash flows occur at the *ends* of the years.

Figure 16.24 Customer Loyalty Model

	A	B	C	D	E	F	G	H	I	J
1	Customer loyalty model in the credit card industry									
2										
3	Inputs			Retention rates to try						
4	Retention rate	0.75		0.75						
5	Discount rate	0.15		0.80						
6	Stdev as % of mean	10%		0.85						
7				0.90						
8				0.95						
9	Simulation						Outputs			
10	Year	Mean Profit(if still here)	Quits at end of year?	Actual profit	Discounted profit		NPV	$348.86		
11	1	($40.00)	No	($45.70)	($42.61)		Years loyal	10		
12	2	$66.00	No	$64.32	$52.15					
13	3	$72.00	No	$71.70	$50.55		Means			
14	4	$79.00	No	$86.56	$53.07		Simulation	Retention rate	NPV	Years loyal
15	5	$87.00	No	$86.34	$46.04		1	0.75	$101.47	4.08
16	6	$92.00	No	$100.87	$46.77		2	0.80	$129.03	4.86
17	7	$96.00	No	$101.92	$41.09		3	0.85	$185.57	6.80
18	8	$99.00	No	$99.72	$34.96		4	0.90	$251.28	9.59
19	9	$103.00	No	$123.92	$37.77		5	0.95	$365.89	15.77
20	10	$106.00	Yes	$109.67	$29.07					
21	11	$111.00		$0.00	$0.00					
38	28	$161.00		$0.00	$0.00					
39	29	$161.00		$0.00	$0.00					
40	30	$161.00		$0.00	$0.00					

Excel's RAND function can be used any time you want to simulate whether or not an event occurs.

④ **Actual and discounted profits.** Profits (or a loss in the first year) occur as long as there is not a blank in column C. Therefore, simulate the actual profits by entering the formula

=IF(C11<>"",RISKNORMAL(B11,$B$6*ABS(B11)),0)

Careful discounting is required if cash flows occur in the middle of a year.

in cell D11 and copying it down. (The absolute value function, ABS, is required in case any of the cash flows are negative. A normal distribution cannot have a *negative* standard deviation.) Then discount these appropriately in column E by entering the formula

=D11/(1+$B$5)^(A11−0.5)

in cell E11 and copying it down. Note how the exponent of the denominator accounts for the cash flow in the *middle* of the year.

⑤ **Outputs.** Keep track of two outputs, the total NPV and the number of years the customer stays with the company. Calculate the NPV in cell H10 by summing the discounted values in column E. (They have already been discounted, so the NPV function is not needed.) To find the number of years the customer is loyal, count the number of No values plus the number of Yes values, that is, all non-blanks. Calculate this in cell H11 with the formula

=COUNTIF(C11:C40,"No")+COUNTIF(C11:C40,"Yes")

Finally, designate both of cells H10 and H11 as @RISK output cells.

Running the Simulation

Set the number of iterations to 1000 and the number of simulations to 5 (one for each potential retention rate). Then run the simulation as usual. (Actually, we ran 5000 iterations for each simulation, just to get more stable results.)

Varying the retention rate can have a large impact on the value of a customer.

Discussion of the Simulation Results

Summary results for all five retention rates and the histogram for an 85% retention rate appear in Figures 16.25 and 16.26. The histogram indicates that there is a 14.4% chance that the NPV will be negative, whereas the chance that it will be above $300 is 27.3%. You can also see from the summary measures that the mean NPV and the mean number of years loyal are quite sensitive to the retention rate.

Figure 16.25 Summary Results for Customer Loyalty Model

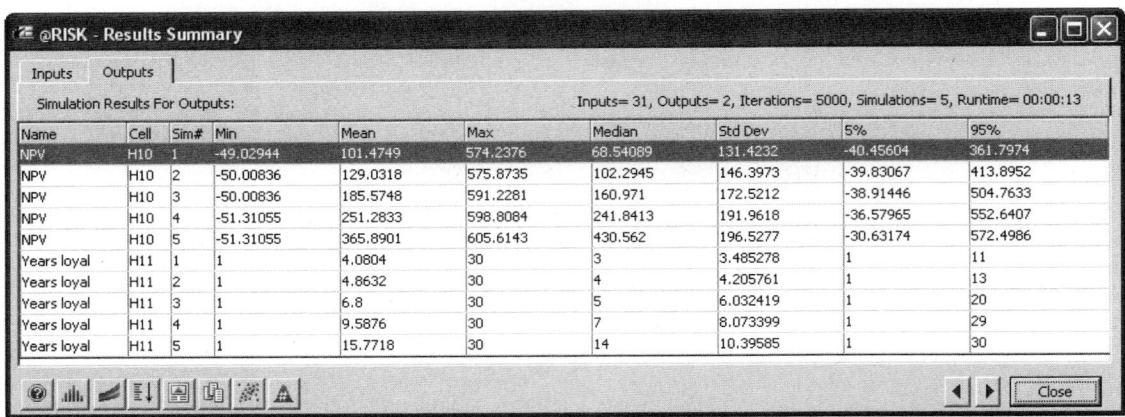

Figure 16.26

Histogram of NPV for an 85% Retention Rate

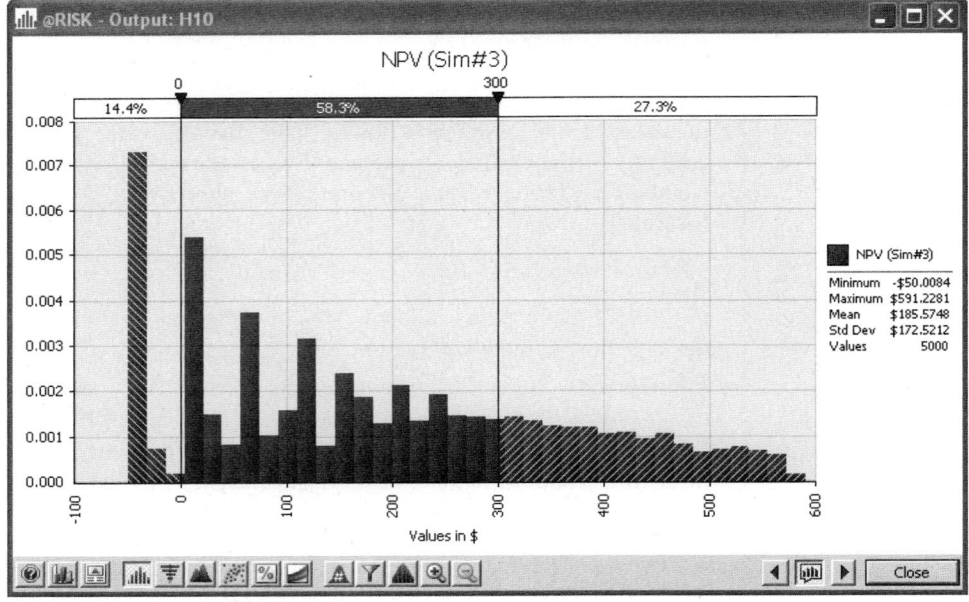

To follow up on this observation, you can use the RISKMEAN function to capture the means in columns I and J of the model sheet and then create a line chart of them as a function of the retention rate. (See Figure 16.27.) This line chart shows the rather dramatic effect the retention rate can have on the value of a customer. For example, if it increases from the current 85% to 90%, the mean NPV increases by about 35%. If it increases from

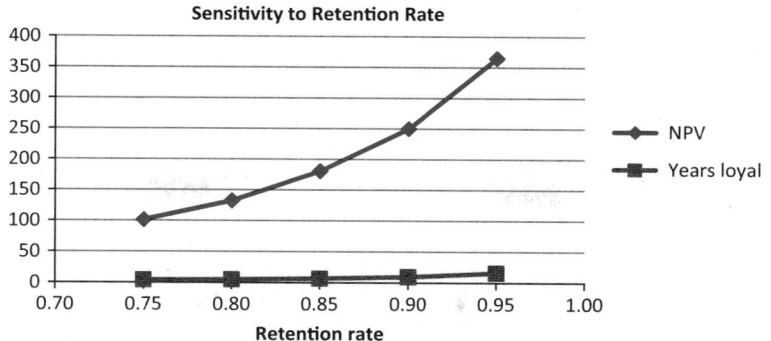

Figure 16.27
Sensitivity of
Outputs to the
Retention Rate

85% to 95%, the mean NPV increases by about 97%. In the other direction, if the retention rate decreases from 85% to 80%, the mean NPV decreases by about 30%. This is why credit card companies are so anxious to keep their customers. ■

The following example is a variation of the previous example. We now investigate the effect of offering a customer an incentive to remain loyal.

EXAMPLE | **16.8 THE VALUE OF A FREE MAINTENANCE AGREEMENT**

Companies value loyal customers, and they sometimes go to great lengths to keep their customers loyal. This example investigates whether one such plan is worth its cost. We consider a nationwide company called Jamesons, which sells electronic appliances. Specifically, we will focus on sales of DVD players. To attract customers, the company is considering giving customers a free maintenance agreement with each purchase of a DVD player. The unit profit without free maintenance is currently $20. The company believes this will decrease to $16 with free maintenance. Their thinking is that about 4% of customers will actually use the free maintenance, and for each such customer, the company will lose about $100. Hence the average decrease in profit per purchaser is about $4.

Prior to this year, 50,000 customers were loyal to Jamesons and 100,000 customers were loyal to their competitors. (Loyalty is defined in terms of where the customer bought his or her last DVD player.) There are a number of uncertain quantities, and we assume they are all triangularly distributed. Their parameters (minimum, most likely, and maximum) are as follows. (1) The percentage of the 150,000 customers who purchase a DVD player in any given year has parameters 20%, 25%, and 40%. (2) The annual percentage change in unit profit has parameters 3%, 5%, and 6%. (3) In any year, the percentage of Jamesons' loyal customers who remain loyal has parameters 56%, 60%, and 66% if there is no free maintenance, and they increase to 60%, 64%, and 70% with free maintenance. (4) Similarly, the percentage of the competitors' loyal customers who switch to Jamesons has parameters 27%, 30%, and 34% if there is no free maintenance, and they increase to 32%, 35%, and 39% with free maintenance. These inputs are listed in the file **Free Maintenance.xlsx** and are shown in Figure 16.28.

Jamesons is hoping that the decrease in unit profit from the free maintenance agreement will be more than offset by the higher loyalty percentages. Using a 15-year planning horizon, does the NPV of profits with a 10% discount rate confirm the company's hopes?

Objective   To use simulation to see whether it makes sense for Jamesons to give a free maintenance agreement to DVD player purchasers.

Figure 16.28

Inputs for Free
Maintenance
Example

	A	B	C	D	E	F
1	**Free maintenance agreement - is it worth it?**					
2						
3	**Common inputs**					
4	Loyal customers in previous year					
5	To our brand	50000				
6	To their brand	100000				
7						
8	Percentage of potential customers who purchase in any year (triangular distribution)					
9	Minimum	20%				
10	Most likely	25%				
11	Maximum	40%				
12						
13	Annual percentage growth in profit contribution (triangular distribution)					
14	Minimum	3%				
15	Most likely	5%				
16	Maximum	6%				
17						
18	Discount rate	10%				
19						
20	**Inputs that depend on policy**	Not free	Free			
21	Unit profit	$20	$16			
22						
23	Percentage of our loyal customers who remain loyal (triangular distribution)					
24	Minimum	56%	60%			
25	Most likely	60%	64%			
26	Maximum	66%	70%			
27						
28	Percentage of their loyal customers who switch to us (triangular distribution)					
29	Minimum	27%	32%			
30	Most likely	30%	35%			
31	Maximum	34%	39%			

WHERE DO THE NUMBERS COME FROM?

In the previous example we discussed the switching rates, which would be estimated from extensive customer data. The other data in the problem statement are straightforward to obtain.

Solution

The solution strategy is to compare two simulations, one without free maintenance and one with it. Because they are so similar, you can use RISKSIMTABLE to run both simulations. We make one assumption that is common in marketing but might not be intuitive. We assume that only *purchasers* in a given year have any chance of switching loyalty in the next year. For example, if a customer is loyal to Jamesons and doesn't purchase a DVD player in a given year, this customer is automatically loyal to Jamesons in the next year.

DEVELOPING THE SIMULATION MODEL

The completed simulation model appears in Figure 16.29. (Again, see the first finished version of the file **Free Maintenance.xlsx**.) It can be developed with the following steps.

Figure 16.29 Free Maintenance Simulation Model

A	B	C	D	E	F	G	H	I	J	K	L	M	N	O	P	Q
33 Simulation																
34 Index of simulation	1															
35																
36 Year	0	1	2	3	4	5	6	7	8	9	10	11	12	13	14	15
37 Percentage loyal to us who purchase	24.0%	25.7%	31.2%	25.8%	31.1%	29.7%	26.3%	25.0%	21.7%	30.0%	27.0%	23.4%	23.0%	31.5%	26.7%	22.1%
38 Percentage loyal to them who purchase	25.6%	30.7%	22.9%	22.6%	25.9%	33.4%	25.0%	34.5%	30.3%	34.3%	32.0%	23.3%	25.0%	28.6%	35.9%	21.0%
39 Percentage who stay loyal to us		63.8%	58.3%	59.3%	61.1%	59.7%	64.8%	56.8%	59.5%	59.3%	64.2%	58.2%	57.5%	58.4%	59.4%	61.8%
40 Percentage who switch loyalty to us		30.1%	30.1%	28.8%	29.6%	31.5%	27.6%	29.6%	29.5%	30.1%	30.9%	33.1%	30.4%	27.2%	32.4%	32.3%
41 Customers loyal to us	50000	53352	56564	55537	56292	56890	59521	59446	62649	65090	67113	68341	67329	66526	65739	68804
42 Customers loyal to them	100000	96648	93436	94463	93708	93110	90479	90554	87351	84910	82887	81659	82671	83474	84261	81196
43 Purchases of our product		13719	17672	14350	17506	16907	15645	14875	13611	19515	18092	15974	15461	20970	17532	15184
44 Percentage change in unit profit			4.93%	4.90%	4.43%	4.69%	5.27%	3.72%	3.61%	4.99%	4.76%	4.72%	4.64%	4.78%	4.74%	4.92%
45 Unit profit		$20.00	$20.99	$22.01	$22.99	$24.07	$25.34	$26.28	$27.23	$28.59	$29.95	$31.36	$32.82	$34.39	$36.02	$37.79
46 Profit contribution		$274,381	$370,853	$315,912	$402,460	$406,921	$396,411	$390,929	$370,609	$557,925	$541,845	$500,993	$507,420	$721,155	$631,471	$573,808
47																
48 NPV	$3,213,430															

1 **Inputs.** Enter the given data in the blue cells.

2 **Maintenance decision.** The current "no free maintenance" policy is labeled simulation #1 and the proposed "free maintenance" policy is labeled simulation #2, so enter the formula

=RISKSIMTABLE({1,2})

in cell B34.

3 **Percentages who purchase.** We assume that each year a random percentage of Jamesons' loyal customers and a random percentage of the competitors' loyal customers purchase a DVD player. Each of these is generated from the triangular distribution in rows 9–11 (see Figure 16.28), so enter the formula

=RISKTRIANG($B$9,$B$10,$B$11)

in the range B37:Q38.

4 **Percentage who stay or become loyal.** Each year a random percentage of the customers previously loyal to Jamesons remain loyal, and a random percentage of the competitors' previously loyal customers switch loyalty to Jamesons. Also, the distributions of these random percentages depend on the company's maintenance policy. Therefore, enter the formula

=IF($B$34=1,RISKTRIANG($B$24,$B$25,$B$26),RISKTRIANG($C$24,$C$25,$C$26))

in cell C39, enter the formula

=IF($B$34=1,RISKTRIANG($B$29,$B$30,$B$31),RISKTRIANG($C$29,$C$30,$C$31))

in cell C40, and copy these across their rows.

5 **Numbers of loyal customers.** Create links to cells B5 and B6 in cells B41 and B42. Then, remembering that only *purchasers* in a given year can switch loyalty, calculate the number of customers loyal to Jamesons in year 1 with the formula

=B41*((1-B37)+B37*C39)+B42*B38*C40

in cell C41 and copy it across row 41. Similarly, calculate the number of customers loyal to the competitors in year 1 with the formula

=B42*((1-B38)+B38*(1-C40))+B41*B37*(1-C39)

in cell C42 and copy it across row 42. These are basic bookkeeping formulas. Jamesons' loyal customers are those who (1) were loyal and didn't purchase, (2) were loyal, purchased, and stayed loyal, and (3) weren't loyal, purchased, and switched loyalty. Similar logic holds for the competitors' loyal customers.

6 **Purchasers at Jamesons.** Calculate the number of purchasers at Jamesons in year 1 with the formula

=C37*C41

in cell C43 and copy it across row 41.

7 **Monetary outcomes.** These are straightforward. Start by entering the formula

=IF($B$34=1,B21,C21)

for unit profit in year 1 in cell C45. Then enter the formulas

=RISKTRIANG($B$14,$B$15,$B$16)

=C45*(1+D44)

and

=C45*C43

in cells D44, D45, and C46, respectively, and copy them across their rows. Finally, calculate the NPV with the formula

=NPV(B18,C46:Q46)

in cell B48.

Running the Simulation

Set up @RISK to run 1000 iterations and 2 simulations, one for each maintenance decision to be tested. Then run the simulation as usual.

Discussion of the Simulation Results

The summary measures for the two simulations appear in Figure 16.30. Using the current inputs, the free maintenance initiative does not look good. Every measure, except possibly the standard deviation, is worse with the free maintenance agreement than without it. Evidently, the increase in loyal customers does *not* compensate for the decrease in unit profit. If Jamesons is reasonably confident about the inputs for this model, it should scrap the free maintenance idea. However, it might want to perform some sensitivity analysis on the decrease in unit profit or the increase in loyalty percentages (or both) to see when the free maintenance agreement starts looking attractive. We tried two possibilities. First, if the decrease in unit profit is only $2, not $4, and everything else remains the same, the two mean NPVs are very close, so the free maintenance agreement might be worth trying. Second, if the decrease in unit profit remains at $4, but all of the input percentages in the

Figure 16.30

Summary Measures for Comparing Two Decisions

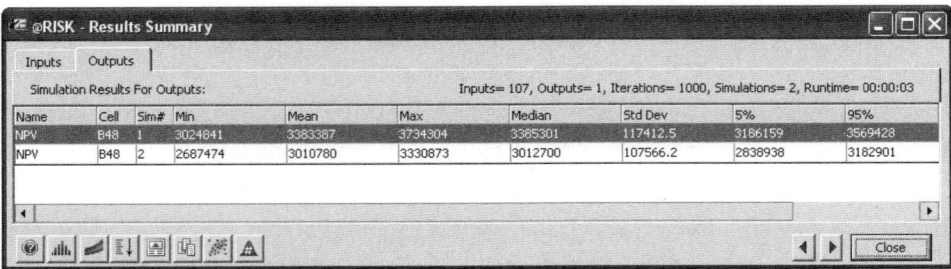

Name	Cell	Sim#	Min	Mean	Max	Median	Std Dev	5%	95%
NPV	B48	1	3024841	3383387	3734304	3385301	117412.5	3186159	3569428
NPV	B48	2	2687474	3010780	3330873	3012700	107566.2	2838938	3182901

Figure 16.31 Modified Simulation Model

	A	B	C	D	E	F	G	H	I	J	K	L	M	N	O	P	Q
33	Simulation																
34	Index of simulation	1															
35	Percentage loyal to us who purchase each year	23.3%															
36	Percentage not loyal to us who purchase each year	26.4%															
37	Percentage growth each year	5.7%															
38	Percentage who stay loyal each year	58.6%	63.6%														
39	Percentage who switch to us each year	30.1%	36.4%														
40																	
41	Year	0	1	2	3	4	5	6	7	8	9	10	11	12	13	14	15
42	Percentage loyal to us who purchase	23.3%	23.3%	23.3%	23.3%	23.3%	23.3%	23.3%	23.3%	23.3%	23.3%	23.3%	23.3%	23.3%	23.3%	23.3%	23.3%
43	Percentage loyal to them who purchase	26.4%	26.4%	26.4%	26.4%	26.4%	26.4%	26.4%	26.4%	26.4%	26.4%	26.4%	26.4%	26.4%	26.4%	26.4%	26.4%
44	Percentage who stay loyal to us		58.6%	58.6%	58.6%	58.6%	58.6%	58.6%	58.6%	58.6%	58.6%	58.6%	58.6%	58.6%	58.6%	58.6%	58.6%
45	Percentage who switch loyalty to us		30.1%	30.1%	30.1%	30.1%	30.1%	30.1%	30.1%	30.1%	30.1%	30.1%	30.1%	30.1%	30.1%	30.1%	30.1%
46	Customers loyal to us	50000	53119	55690	57808	59554	60992	62178	63155	63960	64623	65170	65620	65991	66297	66549	66757
47	Customers loyal to them	100000	96881	94310	92192	90446	89008	87822	86845	86040	85377	84830	84380	84009	83703	83451	83243
48	Purchases of our product		12376	12975	13469	13875	14210	14487	14714	14902	15056	15184	15289	15375	15446	15505	15554
49	Percentage change in unit profit			5.71%	5.71%	5.71%	5.71%	5.71%	5.71%	5.71%	5.71%	5.71%	5.71%	5.71%	5.71%	5.71%	5.71%
50	Unit profit		$20.00	$21.14	$22.35	$23.63	$24.98	$26.40	$27.91	$29.51	$31.19	$32.97	$34.86	$36.85	$38.95	$41.18	$43.53
51	Profit contribution		$247,522	$274,322	$301,022	$327,825	$354,921	$382,486	$410,686	$439,678	$469,613	$500,637	$532,891	$566,517	$601,653	$638,437	$677,011
52																	
53	NPV	$3,017,877															

ranges C24:C26 and C29:C31 increase by five percentage points, the mean NPV with the free maintenance agreement is still considerably lower than the mean NPV without it. Evidently, the company can't take this big a hit in its profit margin unless it can convince a *lot* more customers to stay or become loyal.

There is an interesting modeling issue in this example. For each of the random quantities, we have generated a new random value each year. Would it be better to generate one random number from each triangular distribution and use it for each year? Would it make a difference in the results? The modified simulation appears in Figure 16.31. (You can see the details in the second finished version of the **Free Maintenance.xlsx** file.) The only random quantities are in the range B35:B39. As is evident in the rows below, these random numbers are used for each of the years. The summary measures from this simulation appear in Figure 16.32. If we are interested in comparing the *mean* NPV with no free maintenance versus free maintenance, we get about the same comparison in either model. The main difference between Figures 16.30 and 16.32 is the variability. Are you surprised that the models with more random numbers in Figure 16.30 have much smaller standard deviations than those in Figure 16.32? Evidently, there is an averaging effect. When different random numbers are used for each year, the highs and lows tend to cancel out, resulting in lower variability in NPV.

Regardless of which version is more realistic (and an argument can be made for either), an advantage of the model with only a few random numbers is that you can use @RISK's tornado chart to see which source of randomness is most highly correlated with NPV. This tornado chart appears in Figure 16.33. (It is for simulation #2 with free maintenance agreement, but the chart for simulation #1 is virtually the same.) Perhaps surprisingly, it is not the

Figure 16.32

Summary Results for Modified Model

Name	Cell	Sim#	Min	Mean	Max	Median	Std Dev	5%	95%
NPV	B53	1	2392931	3358402	4871377	3325927	416418.7	2708514	4116711
NPV	B53	2	2154164	2989159	4131825	2966978	381162.1	2385595	3693195

@RISK - Results Summary

Inputs | Outputs

Simulation Results For Outputs: Inputs= 8, Outputs= 1, Iterations= 1000, Simulations= 2, Runtime= 00:00:01

Close

Figure 16.33
Tornado Chart
for NPV

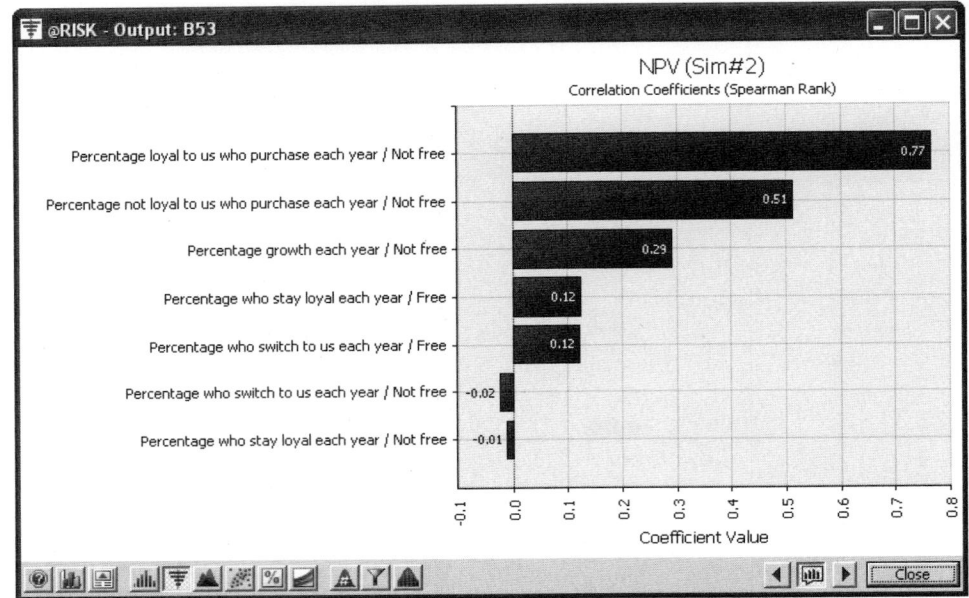

switching behavior that drives NPV; it is driven more by the percentage of customers who purchase. As this example illustrates, it is sometimes an advantage to keep the models simple. Key insights are then more apparent than when there is more complexity. ■

16.4.2 Marketing and Sales Models

We conclude this marketing section with a model of marketing and selling condos. The main issue is the timing of sales, and we demonstrate how a deterministic model of this timing can provide very misleading results.

EXAMPLE | **16.9 MARKETING AND SELLING CONDOS**

The Blackstone Development Company has just finished building 120 high-end condos, each priced at $300,000. Blackstone has hired another company, Pletcher Marketing, to market and sell these condos. Pletcher will incur all of the marketing and maintenance costs, assumed to be $800 per unsold condo per month, and it will receive a 10% commission ($30,000) from Blackstone at the time of each condo sale. Because Blackstone wants these condos to be sold in a timely manner, it has offered Pletcher a $200,000 bonus at the end of the first year if at least half of the condos have been sold, and an extra $500,000 bonus at the end of the second year if all of the condos have been sold. Pletcher estimates that it can sell five condos per month on average, so that it should be able to collect the bonuses. However, Pletcher also realizes that there is some uncertainty about the number of sales per month. How should this uncertainty be modeled, and will the resulting simulation model give different qualitative results than a deterministic model where exactly five condos are sold per month?

Objective   To develop a simulation model that allows us to see how the uncertain timing affects the monetary outcomes for Pletcher, and to compare this simulation model to a deterministic model with no uncertainty about the timing of sales.

The inputs are straightforward from Blackstone's agreement with Pletcher. The only difficulty is determining an appropriate probability model for the timing of sales, which we discuss next.

Solution

To make a fair comparison between a deterministic model with five sales per month and a simulation model with uncertainty in the timing of sales, we need a discrete distribution for monthly sales that has mean 5. One attractive possibility is to use the Poisson distribution discussed briefly in Chapter 5. It is discrete, and it has only one parameter, the mean. The Poisson distribution has one theoretical drawback in that it allows *all* nonnegative integers to occur, but this has no practical effect. As shown in Figure 16.34, the Poisson distribution with mean 5 has virtually no probability of values larger than, say, 15.

Figure 16.34

Poisson Distribution with Mean 5

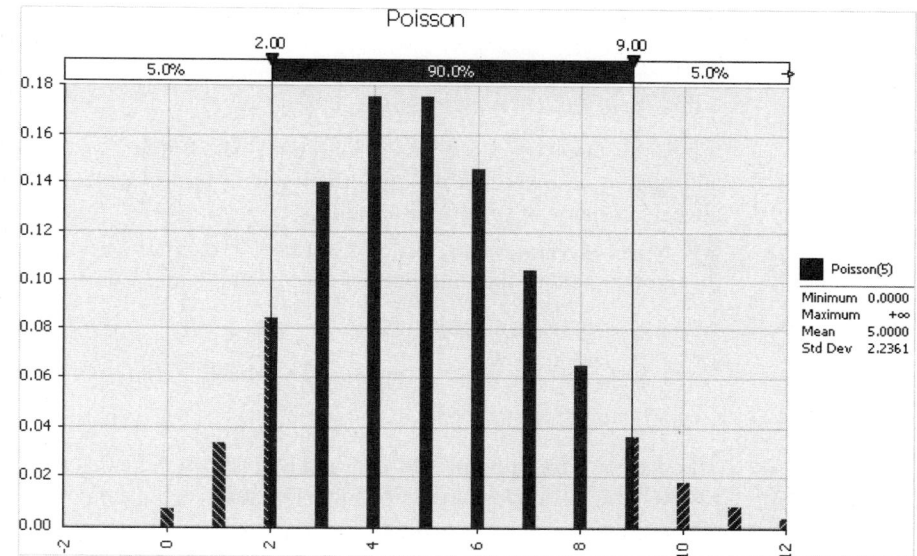

DEVELOPING THE SIMULATION MODEL

The deterministic model is very straightforward and is not shown here. By selling a *sure* five condos per month, Pletcher sells all condos by the end of year 2, receives both bonuses, and realizes an NPV (including bonuses) of $2,824,333. However, this is not very realistic. The steps for creating a more realistic simulation model follow. (See Figure 16.35, with several hidden columns, and the file **Selling Condos.xlsx**.) Note that because of the uncertain timing of sales, we cannot say when all 120 condos will be sold. It could be before 24 months or well after 24 months. Therefore, we model it through 40 months. By experimenting, we found that all 120 condos will almost surely be sold in 40 months.

1 **Inputs.** Enter the inputs in the blue ranges.

2 **Random demands.** Generate the random demands for condos (the number of people who would like to buy) by entering the formula

Figure 16.35 Condo Selling Simulation Model

	A	B	C	L	M	N	O	X	Y	Z	AA	AB	AO
1	Marketing and selling condos												
2													
3	Number to sell	120											
4	Monthly marketing maintenance cost	$800											
5	Commission per condo sale	$30,000											
6	Bonus if at least half sold in year 1	$200,000											
7	Extra bonus if all sold in 2 years	$500,000											
8	Discount rate (monthly)	0.8%											
9													
10	Simulation model												
11	Distribution of demand for condos each month (Poisson distributed)												
12	Mean demand per month	5											
13													
14	Month	1	2	11	12	13	14	23	24	25	26	27	40
15	Demand this month	5	3	8	4	2	6	1	12	5	4		
16	Number remaining to be sold	120	115	69	61	57	55	21	20	8	3	0	0
17	Number sold this month	5	3	8	4	2	6	1	12	5	3		
18	Maintenance cost	$92,000	$89,600	$48,800	$45,600	$44,000	$39,200	$16,000	$6,400	$2,400	$0		
19	Revenue from sales	$150,000	$90,000	$240,000	$120,000	$60,000	$180,000	$30,000	$360,000	$150,000	$90,000		
20	Bonus at end of year 1				$200,000								
21	Bonus at end of year 2									$0			
22	Net revenue	$58,000	$400	$191,200	$274,400	$16,000	$140,800	$14,000	$353,600	$147,600	$90,000		
23													
24	Months to sell out	26											
25	Total bonus	$200,000											

=IF(B16>0,RISKPOISSON($B$12),"")

in cell B15 and copying across to month 40. The IF function checks whether there are still any condos available in that month. If there aren't, a blank is recorded. Similar logic appears in many of the other formulas.

3 **Number remaining and sold.** In cell B16, enter a link to cell B3. In cell B17, find the number sold as the minimum of supply and demand with the formula

=IF(B16>0,MIN(B16,B15),"")

In cell C16, find the number remaining to be sold with the formula

=IF(B16>0,B16-B17,0)

Then copy the formulas in cells C16 and B17 across. Note that a 0, not a blank, is recorded in row 16 after all condos have been sold. This makes all the other IF functions work correctly.

4 **Monetary values.** Enter the formulas

=IF(B16>0,$B$4*(B16-B17),"")

=IF(B16>0,$B$5*B17,"")

and

=IF(B16>0,SUM(B19:B21)-B18,"")

in cells B18, B19, and B22, and copy these across. For the bonuses, enter the formulas

=IF(SUM(B17:M17)>=B3/2,B6,0)

and

=IF(SUM(B17:Y17)=B3,B7,0)

in cells M20 and Y21. These capture the all-or-nothing nature of the bonuses.

5 **Outputs.** Three interesting outputs are the number of months required to sell out, the total bonus earned, and the NPV of the cash flows, including bonuses. Calculate these in cells B24–B26 with the formulas

=COUNTIF(B16:AO16,">0")

=M20+Y21

and

=NPV($B$8,B22:AO22)

Then designate them as @RISK output cells.

Running the Simulation

Set @RISK to run 1000 iterations for a single simulation. Then run the simulation in the usual way.

Discussion of the Simulation Results

Recall that the deterministic model sells out in 24 months, receives both bonuses, and achieves an NPV of about $2.82 million. As you might guess, the simulation model doesn't do this well. The main problem is that there is a fairly good chance that one or both bonuses will not be received. Histograms of the three outputs appear in Figures 16.36 through 16.38. The first shows that although 24 months is the *most likely* number of months to sell out, there was at least one scenario where it took only 17 months and another where it took 32 months. The second histogram shows the four possibilities for bonuses: receive neither, receive one or the other, or receive both. Unfortunately for Pletcher, the first three possibilities are fairly likely; the probability of receiving both bonuses is only about 0.38. Finally, the shape of the NPV histogram, with three separate peaks, is influenced heavily by the bonuses or lack of them. On average, the NPV is only about $2.39 million, *much* less than estimated by the deterministic model. This is still one more example—a dramatic one—of the flaw of averages.

Figure 16.36
Histogram of
Months to Sell Out

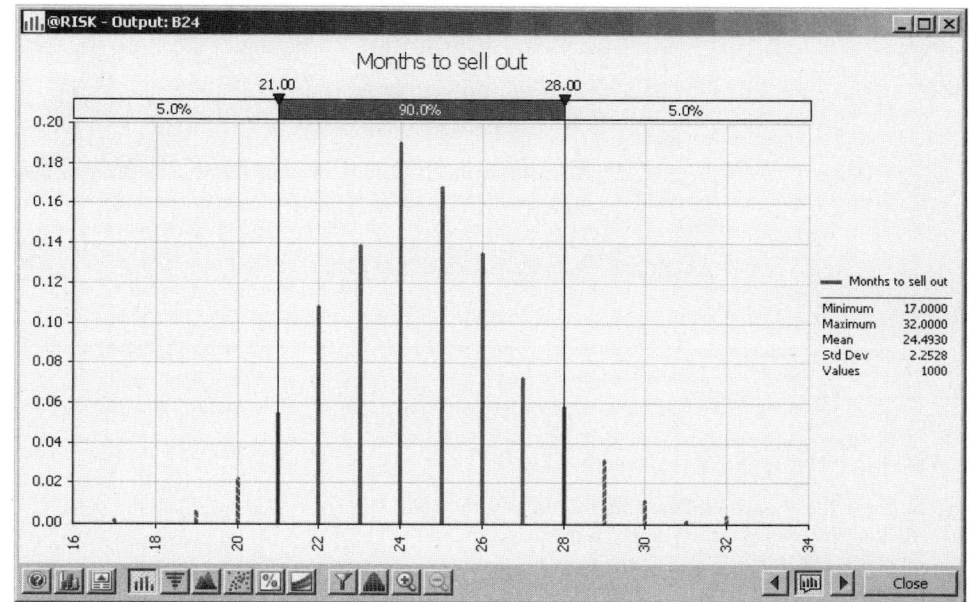

Figure 16.37
Histogram of Total
Bonus Received

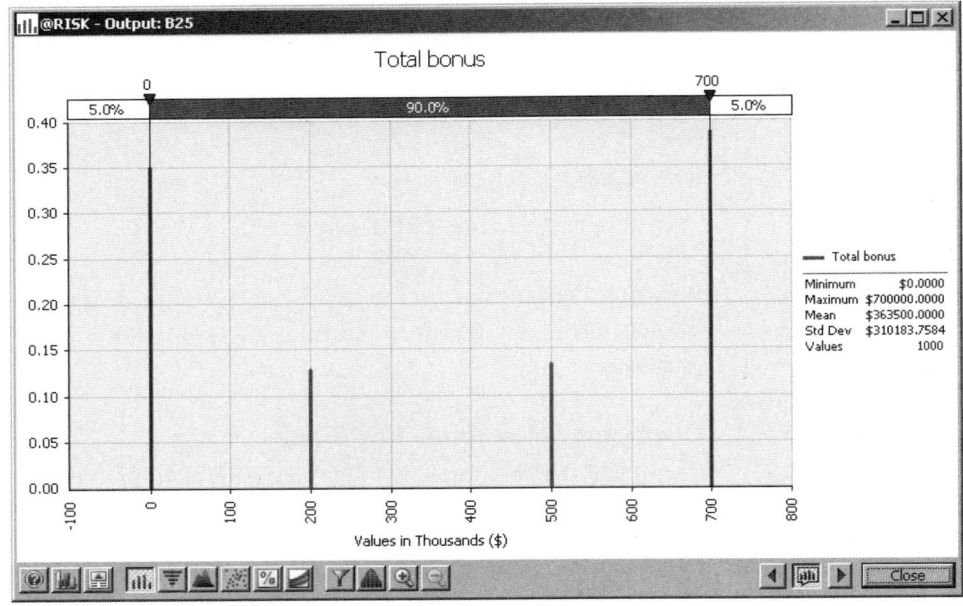

Figure 16.38
Histogram of NPV

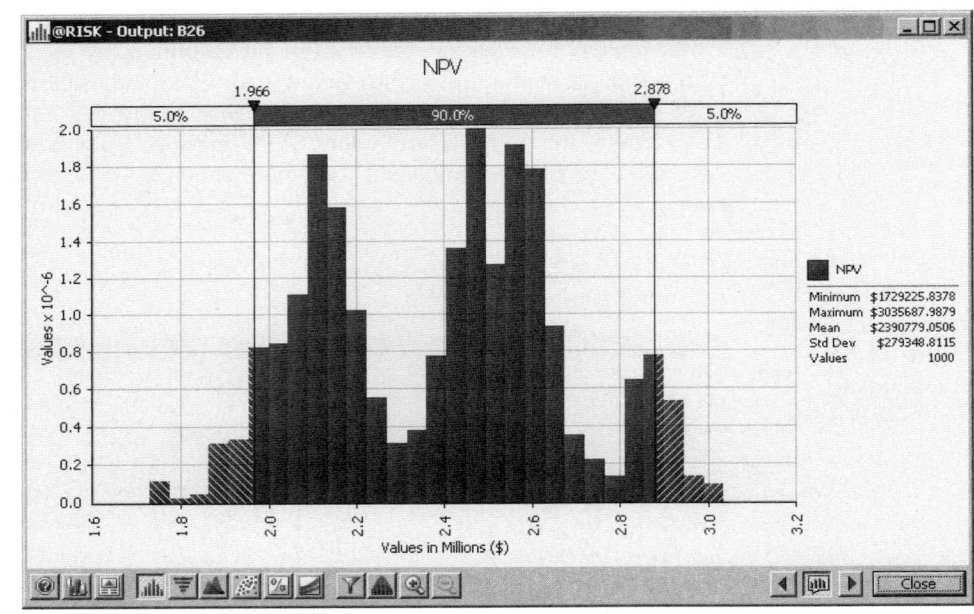

PROBLEMS

Level A

21. Suppose that Coke and Pepsi are fighting for the cola market. Each week each person in the market buys one case of Coke or Pepsi. If the person's last purchase was Coke, there is a 0.90 probability that this person's next purchase will be Coke; otherwise, it will be Pepsi. (You can assume that there are only two brands in the market.) Similarly, if the person's last purchase was Pepsi, there is a 0.80 probability that this person's next purchase will be Pepsi; otherwise, it will be Coke. Currently half of all people purchase Coke, and the other half purchase Pepsi. Simulate one year (52 weeks) of sales in the cola market and estimate each company's average weekly market share and each company's ending market share in week 52. Do this by assuming that the total market size is fixed at 100,000 customers. (*Hint*: Use the RISKBINOMIAL function. However, if your model requires more RISKBINOMIAL functions than the number allowed in the academic version of @RISK, remember that you can instead use the CRITBINOM function to generate binomially distributed random numbers. This takes the form **=CRITBINOM(*ntrials,psuccess*,RAND()).)**

22. Seas Beginning sells clothing by mail order. An important question is when to strike a customer from the company's mailing list. At present, the company strikes a customer from its mailing list if a customer fails to order from six consecutive catalogs. The company wants to know whether striking a customer from its list after a customer fails to order from four consecutive catalogs results in a higher profit per customer. The following data are available:

   ■ If a customer placed an order the last time she received a catalog, then there is a 20% chance she will order from the next catalog.
   ■ If a customer last placed an order one catalog ago, there is a 16% chance she will order from the next catalog she receives.
   ■ If a customer last placed an order two catalogs ago, there is a 12% chance she will order from the next catalog she receives.
   ■ If a customer last placed an order three catalogs ago, there is an 8% chance she will order from the next catalog she receives.
   ■ If a customer last placed an order four catalogs ago, there is a 4% chance she will order from the next catalog she receives.
   ■ If a customer last placed an order five catalogs ago, there is a 2% chance she will order from the next catalog she receives.

   It costs $2 to send a catalog, and the average profit per order is $30. Assume a customer has just placed an order. To maximize expected profit per customer, would Seas Beginning make more money canceling such a customer after six nonorders or four nonorders?

23. Based on Babich (1992). Suppose that each week each of 300 families buys a gallon of orange juice from company A, B, or C. Let p_A denote the probability that a gallon produced by company A is of unsatisfactory quality, and define p_B and p_C similarly for companies B and C. If the last gallon of juice purchased by a family is satisfactory, the next week they will purchase a gallon of juice from the same company. If the last gallon of juice purchased by a family is not satisfactory, the family will purchase a gallon from a competitor. Consider a week in which A families have

purchased juice A, B families have purchased juice B, and C families have purchased juice C. Assume that families that switch brands during a period are allocated to the remaining brands in a manner that is proportional to the current market shares of the other brands. For example, if a customer switches from brand A, there is probability $B/(B + C)$ that he will switch to brand B and probability $C/(B + C)$ that he will switch to brand C. Suppose that the market is currently divided equally: 10,000 families for each of the three brands.

   a. After a year, what will the market share for each firm be? Assume $p_A = 0.10$, $p_B = 0.15$, and $p_C = 0.20$. (*Hint*: You will need to use the RISKBINOMIAL function to see how many people switch from A and then use the RISKBINOMIAL function again to see how many switch from A to B and from A to C. However, if your model requires more RISKBINOMIAL functions than the number allowed in the academic version of @RISK, remember that you can instead use the CRITBINOM function to generate binomially distributed random numbers. This takes the form **=CRITBINOM(*ntrials,psuccess*,RAND()).)**

   b. Suppose a 1% increase in market share is worth $10,000 per week to company A. Company A believes that for a cost of $1 million per year it can cut the percentage of unsatisfactory juice cartons in half. Is this worthwhile? (Use the same values of p_A, p_B, and p_C as in part **a**.)

Level B

24. The customer loyalty model in Example 16.7 assumes that once a customer leaves (becomes disloyal), that customer never becomes loyal again. Assume instead that there are two probabilities that drive the model, the retention rate and the *rejoin* rate, with values 0.75 and 0.15, respectively. The simulation should follow a customer who starts as a loyal customer in year 1. From then on, at the end of any year when the customer was loyal, this customer remains loyal for the next year with probability equal to the retention rate. But at the end of any year the customer is disloyal, this customer becomes loyal the next year with probability equal to the rejoin rate. During the customer's nth loyal year with the company, the company's mean profit from this customer is the nth value in the mean profit list in column B. Keep track of the same two outputs as in the example, and also keep track of the number of times the customer rejoins.

25. We are all aware of the fierce competition by mobile phone service companies to get our business. For example, AT&T is always trying to attract Verizon's customers, and vice versa. Some even give away prizes to entice us to sign up for a guaranteed length of time.

This example is based on one such offer. We assume that a mobile provider named Syncit is willing to give a customer a free laptop computer, at a cost of $300 to Syncit, if the customer signs up for a guaranteed two years of service. During that time, the cost of service to the customer is a constant $60 per month, or $720 annually. After two years, we assume the cost of service increases by 2% annually. We assume that in any year after the guaranteed two years, the probability is 0.7 that the customer will stay with Syncit. This probability is the retention rate. We also assume that if a customer has switched to another mobile service, there is always a probability of 0.1 that the customer will (without any free laptop offer) willingly rejoin Syncit. The company wants to see whether this offer makes financial sense in terms of NPV, using a 10% discount rate. It also wants to see how the NPV varies with the retention rate. Simulate a 15-year time horizon, both with and without the free offer, to estimate the difference. (For the situation without the free offer, assume the customer has probability 0.5 of signing up with Syncit during year 1.)

26. Suppose that GLC earns a $2000 profit each time a person buys a car. We want to determine how the expected profit earned from a customer depends on the quality of GLC's cars. We assume a typical customer will purchase 10 cars during her lifetime. She will purchase a car now (year 1) and then purchase a car every five years—during year 6, year 11, and so on. For simplicity, we assume that Hundo is GLC's only competitor. We also assume that if the consumer is satisfied with the car she purchases, she will buy her next car from the same company, but if she is not satisfied, she will buy her next car from the other company. Hundo produces cars that satisfy 80% of its customers. Currently, GLC produces cars that also satisfy 80% of its customers. Consider a customer whose first car is a GLC car. If profits are discounted at 10% annually, use simulation to estimate the value of this customer to GLC. Also estimate the value of a

customer to GLC if it can raise its customer satisfaction rating to 85%, to 90%, or to 95%. You can interpret the satisfaction value as the probability that a customer will not switch companies.

27. The Mutron Company is thinking of marketing a new drug used to make pigs healthier. At the beginning of the current year, there are 1,000,000 pigs that could use the product. Each pig will use Mutron's drug or a competitor's drug once a year. The number of pigs is forecast to grow by an average of 5% per year. However, this growth rate is not a sure thing. Mutron assumes that each year's growth rate is an independent draw from a normal distribution, with probability 0.95 that the growth rate will be between 3% and 7%. Assuming it enters the market, Mutron is not sure what its share of the market will be during year 1, so it models this with a triangular distribution. Its worst-case share is 20%, its most likely share is 40%, and its best-case share is 70%. In the absence of any *new* competitors entering this market (in addition to itself), Mutron believes its market share will remain the same in succeeding years. However, there are three potential entrants (in addition to Mutron). At the beginning of each year, each entrant that has not already entered the market has a 40% chance of entering the market. The year after a competitor enters, Mutron's market share will drop by 20% for each *new* competitor who entered. For example, if two competitors enter the market in year 1, Mutron's market share in year 2 will be reduced by 40% from what it would have been with no entrants. Note that if all three entrants have entered, there will be no more entrants. Each unit of the drug sells for $2.20 and incurs a variable cost of $0.40. Profits are discounted by 10% annually.
   a. Assuming that Mutron enters the market, use simulation to find its NPV for the next 10 years from the drug.
   b. Again assuming that Mutron enters the market, it can be 95% certain that its *actual* NPV from the drug is between what two values?

16.5 SIMULATING GAMES OF CHANCE

We realize that this is a book about business applications. However, it is instructive (and fun) to see how simulation can be used to analyze games of chance, including sports contests. Indeed, many analysts refer to Monte Carlo simulation, and you can guess where that name comes from—the gambling casinos of Monte Carlo.

16.5.1 Simulating the Game of Craps

Most games of chance are great candidates for simulation because they are, by their very nature, driven by randomness. In this section we examine one such game that is extremely popular in the gambling casinos: the game of craps. In its most basic form, the game of craps is played as follows. A player rolls two dice and observes the sum of the two sides turned up. If this sum is 7 or 11, the player wins immediately. If the sum is 2, 3, or 12, the player loses immediately. Otherwise, if this sum is any other number (4, 5, 6, 8, 9, or 10), that number becomes the player's *point*. Then the dice are thrown repeatedly until the sum is the player's point or 7. In case the player's point occurs before a 7, the player wins. But if a 7 occurs before the point, the player loses. The following example uses simulation to determine the properties of this game.

EXAMPLE	16.10 ESTIMATING THE PROBABILITY OF WINNING AT CRAPS

Joe Gamble loves to play craps at the casinos. He suspects that his chances of winning are less than fifty-fifty, but he wants to find the probability that he wins a single game of craps.

Objective   To use simulation to find the probability of winning a single game of craps.

WHERE DO THE NUMBERS COME FROM?

There are no input numbers here, only the rules of the game.

Solution

The simulation is of a single game. By running this simulation for many iterations, you can find the probability that Joe wins a single game of craps. If his intuition is correct (and surely it must be, or the casino could not stay in business), this probability is less than 0.5.

DEVELOPING THE SIMULATION MODEL

The simulation model is for a single game. (See Figure 16.39 and the file **Craps.xlsx**.) There is a subtle problem here: The number of tosses of the dice necessary to determine the outcome of a single game is unknown. Theoretically, the game could continue forever, with the player waiting for his point or a 7. However, it is extremely unlikely that more than, say,

Figure 16.39   Simulation of Craps Game

	A	B	C	D	E	F	G	H	I	J
1	Craps Simulation									
2										
3	Simulated tosses									
4	Toss	Die 1	Die 2	Sum	Win on this toss?	Lose on this toss?	Continue?		Summary results from simulation	
5	1	6	2	8	0	0	Yes		Win? (1 if yes, 0 if no)	1
6	2	5	6	11	0	0	Yes		Number of tosses	8
7	3	4	2	6	0	0	Yes			
8	4	4	1	5	0	0	Yes		Pr(winning)	0.491
9	5	2	1	3	0	0	Yes		Expected number of tosses	3.364
10	6	5	4	9	0	0	Yes			
11	7	3	6	9	0	0	Yes			
12	8	6	2	8	1	0	No			
13	9	3	4	7						
14	10	6	3	9						
42	38	4	3	7						
43	39	2	6	8						
44	40	1	1	2						

40 tosses are necessary in a single game. (This can be shown by a probability argument not presented here.) Therefore, you can simulate 40 tosses and use only those that are necessary to determine the outcome of a single game. The steps required are as follows.

1 **Simulate tosses.** Simulate the results of 40 tosses in the range B5:D44 by entering the formula

=RANDBETWEEN(1,6)

in cells B5 and C5 and the formula

=SUM(B5:C5)

in cell D5. Then copy these to the range B6:D44. (Recall that the RANDBETWEEN function was new in Excel 2007. It generates a random integer between the two specified values such that all values are equally likely, so it is perfect for tossing a die. You could also use @RISK's RISKINTUNIFORM function, which works exactly like RANDBETWEEN.)

Excel Function: *RANDBETWEEN*
*The function RANDBETWEEN, in the form =**RANDBETWEEN(N1,N2),** generates a random integer from N1 to N2, with each possibility being equally likely.*

@RISK Function: *RISKINTUNIFORM*
*The @RISK function RISKINTUNIFORM in the form =**RISKINTUNIFORM(N1,N2)** works exactly like Excel's RANDBETWEEN function.*

As in many spreadsheet simulation models, the concepts in this model are simple. The key is careful bookkeeping.

2 **First toss outcome.** Determine the outcome of the first toss with the formulas

=IF(OR(D5=7,D5=11),1,0)

=IF(OR(D5=2,D5=3,D5=12),1,0)

and

=IF(AND(E5=0,F5=0),"Yes","No")

in cells E5, F5, and G5. Note that the OR condition checks whether Joe wins right away (in which case a 1 is recorded in cell E5). Similarly, the OR condition in cell F5 checks whether he loses right away. In cell G5, the AND condition checks whether both cells E5 and F5 are 0, in which case the game continues. Otherwise, the game is over.

3 **Outcomes of other tosses.** Assuming the game continues beyond the first toss, Joe's point is the value in cell D5. Then he is waiting for a toss to have the value in cell D5 or 7, whichever occurs first. To implement this logic, enter the formulas

=IF(OR(G5="No",G5=""),"",IF(D6=$D$5,1,0))

=IF(OR(G5="No",G5=""),"",IF(D6=7,1,0))

and

=IF(OR(G5="No",G5=""),"",IF(AND(E6=0,F6=0), "Yes","No"))

in cells E6, F6, and G6, and copy these to the range E7:G44. The OR condition in each formula checks whether the game just ended on the previous toss or has been over for some time, in which case blanks are entered. Otherwise, the first two formulas check whether Joe wins or loses on this toss. If both of these return 0, the third formula returns Yes (and the game continues). Otherwise, it returns No (and the game has just ended).

④ Game outcomes. Keep track of two aspects of the game in @RISK output cells: whether Joe wins or loses and how many tosses are required. To find these, enter the formulas

=SUM(E5:E44)

and

=COUNT(E5:E44)

in cells J5 and J6, and designate each of these as an @RISK output cell. Note that both functions, SUM and COUNT, ignore blank cells.

⑤ Simulation summary. Although you can get summary measures in the various @RISK results windows after you run the simulation, it is useful to see some key summary measures right on the model sheet. To obtain these, enter the formula

=RISKMEAN(J5)

in cell J8 and copy it to cell J9. As the labels indicate, the RISKMEAN in cell J8, being an average of 0s and 1s, is just the fraction of iterations where Joe wins. The average in cell J9 is the average number of tosses until the game's outcome is determined.

Recall that the mean (or average) of a sequence of 0s and 1s is the fraction of 1s in the sequence. This can typically be interpreted as a probability.

Running the Simulation

Set the number of iterations to 10,000 (partly for variety and partly to obtain a very accurate answer) and the number of simulations to 1. Then run the simulation as usual.

Discussion of the Simulation Results

Perhaps surprisingly, the probability of winning in craps is 0.493, only slightly less than 0.5.

After running @RISK, the summary results in cells J8 and J9 of Figure 16.39 (among others) are available. Our main interest is in the average in cell J8. It represents the best estimate of the probability of winning, 0.493. (It can be shown with a probability argument that the exact probability of winning in craps is indeed 0.493.) You can also see that the average number of tosses needed to determine the outcome of a game was about 3.4. (The maximum number of tosses ever needed on these 10,000 iterations was 39.) ∎

16.5.2 Simulating the NCAA Basketball Tournament

Each year the suspense reaches new levels as "March Madness" approaches, the time of the NCAA Basketball Tournament. Which of the 64 teams in the tournament will reach the "Sweet Sixteen," which will go on to the prestigious "Final Four," and which team will be crowned champion? The excitement at Indiana University is particularly high, given the strong basketball tradition here, so it has become a yearly tradition at IU (at least for the authors) to simulate the NCAA Tournament right after the 64-team field has been announced. We share that simulation in the following example. (We make two quick notes. First, everyone who watches basketball knows about IU's recent basketball problems. We hope the Hoosiers are now on the upswing. Second, we will have to change our simulation slightly in future years. It looks like the number of teams in the tournament will be significantly larger than 64.)

EXAMPLE	16.11 MARCH MADNESS

At the time this example was written, the most recent NCAA Basketball Tournament was the 2009 tournament, won by the University of North Carolina. Of course, on the Sunday evening when the 64-team field was announced, we did not know which team would win.[4] All we knew were the pairings (which teams would play which other teams) and the team ratings, based on Jeff Sagarin's nationally syndicated rating system. We show how to simulate the tournament and keep a tally of the winners.

Objective   To simulate the 64-team NCAA basketball tournament and keep a tally on the number of times each team wins the tournament.

WHERE DO THE NUMBERS COME FROM?

As soon as you learn the pairings for the *next* NCAA tournament, you can visit Sagarin's site at www.usatoday.com/sports/sagarin.htm#hoop for the latest ratings.

Solution

We model the point spread as normally distributed, with mean equal to the difference between the Sagarin ratings and standard deviation 10.

We need to make one probabilistic assumption. From that point, it is a matter of "playing out" the games and doing the required bookkeeping. To understand this probabilistic assumption, suppose team A plays team B and Sagarin's ratings for these teams are, say, 85 and 78. Then Sagarin predicts that the actual point differential in the game (team A's score minus team B's score) will be the difference between the ratings, or 7.[5] We take this one step further. We assume that the *actual* point differential is normally distributed with mean equal to Sagarin's prediction, 7, and standard deviation 10. (Why 10? This is an estimate based on an extensive analysis of historical data.) Then if the actual point differential is positive, team A wins. If it is negative, team B wins.

DEVELOPING THE SIMULATION MODEL

We provide only an outline of the simulation model. You can see the full details in the file **March Madness Men 2009.xlsm** (or the 2010 version). Remember that an .xlsm file that contains macros. When you open it, you need to enable the macros. (This file includes the data for the 2009 tournament, but you can easily modify it for future tournaments by following the directions on the sheet. We have also included the **March Madness Women 2009.xlsm** file (and the 2010 version). The women's tournament was won by the University of Connecticut both years.) The entire simulation is on a single Model sheet. Columns A through C list team indexes, team names, and Sagarin ratings. If two teams are paired in the first round, they are placed next to one another in the list. Also, all teams in a given region are listed together. (The regions are color-coded.) Columns K through Q contain the simulation. The first-round results are at the top, the second-round results are below these, and so on. Winners from one round are automatically carried over to the next round with appropriate formulas. Selected portions of the Model sheet appear in Figures 16.40 and 16.41. We now describe the essential features of the model.

1 **Teams and ratings.** We first enter the teams and their ratings, as shown in Figure 16.40. Most of the teams shown here were in the East region in the 2009 tournament. Pittsburgh played East Tennessee State in the first round, Oklahoma State played Tennessee, and so on.

---

[4]Actually, 65 teams are announced, and an early playoff game occurs to see which of two lowly rated teams gets to play a #1 seed. This has no effect on the simulation because neither lowly ranked team has much chance of winning against the #1 seed. Also, congratulations to Duke in the 2010 tournament.
[5]In general, there is also a home-court advantage, but we assume all games in the tournament are on "neutral" courts, so that there is no advantage to either team.

Figure 16.40 Teams and Sagarin Ratings

	A	B	C	D	E	F	G	H	I
1	Simulation of NCAA men's 2009 basketball tournament, using Sagarin ratings								
2									
3	Final Sagarin ratings of teams								
4	Index	Team	Rating						
5	1	Pittsburgh	92.78						
6	2	East Tenn. St.	73.94						
7	3	Oklahoma St.	85.04						
8	4	Tennessee	83.73						
9	5	Florida St.	85.35						
10	6	Wisconsin	84.78						
11	7	Xavier	86.19						
12	8	Portland St.	76.37						
13	9	UCLA	87.83		East regional				
14	10	VCU	79.97						
15	11	Villanova	88.23						
16	12	American	75.64						
17	13	Texas	85.15		Assumption: The actual point spread for				
18	14	Minnesota	84.52		each game is normally distributed with				
19	15	Duke	92.20		mean equal to difference between Sagarin				
20	16	Binghamton	72.73		ratings, standard deviation 10.				
21	17	North Carolina	93.48						
22	18	Radford	72.19						
23	19	LSU	83.59						
24	20	Butler	84.47						
25	21	Illinois	87.20						
26	22	Western Ky.	77.90						
27	23	Gonzaga	89.31						
28	24	Akron	80.25		South regional				
29	25	Arizona St.	87.26						

2 **Simulate rounds.** Jumping ahead to the fourth-round simulation in Figure 16.41, we capture the winners from the previous round 3 and then simulate the games in round 4. The key formulas are in columns N and O. For example, the formulas in cells N126 and O126 are

=VLOOKUP(L126,LTable,3)–VLOOKUP(L127,LTable,3)

and

=RISKNORMAL(N126,10)

The first of these looks up the ratings of the two teams involved (in this case, Pittsburgh and Duke) and subtracts them to get the predicted point spread. The second formula simulates a point spread with the predicted point spread as its mean. The rest of the formulas do the appropriate bookkeeping. You can view the details in the file.

3 **Outputs.** As shown by the boxed-in cells in Figure 16.41, seven cells have been designated as @RISK output cells: the index of the winner, the indexes of the two finalists, and the indexes of the four semifinalists (the Final Four teams). However, the results we

Figure 16.41 NCAA Basketball Simulation Model (Last Three Rounds Only)

	K	L	M	N	O	P	Q
124	**Results of Round 4**						
125	Game	Indexes	Teams	Predicted	Simulated	Index of winner	Winner
126	1	1	Pittsburgh	0.58	11.76	1	Pittsburgh
127		15	Duke				
128	1	19	LSU	1.36	23.13	19	LSU
129		26	Temple				
130	1	38	Arizona	-5.36	8.56	38	Arizona
131		43	Kansas				
132	1	49	Connecticut	3.43	-2.01	59	Missouri
133		59	Missouri				
134							
135	**Semifinals**						
136	Game	Indexes	Teams	Predicted	Simulated	Index of winner	Winner
137	1	1	Pittsburgh	9.19	4.51	1	Pittsburgh
138		19	LSU				
139	2	38	Arizona	-6.28	-20.66	59	Missouri
140		59	Missouri				
141							
142	**Finals**						
143	Game	Indexes	Teams	Predicted	Simulated	Index of winner	Winner
144	1	1	Pittsburgh	3.49	8.85	1	Pittsburgh
145		59	Missouri				
146							
147	**Winner**	1					

really want are tallies, such as the number of iterations where Pittsburgh (or any other team) wins the tournament. This takes some planning. In the @RISK Excel Reports dialog box, if you check the Simulation Data option, you get a sheet called Data that lists the values of all @RISK output cells for *each* of the iterations. (We used 1000 iterations.) Then COUNTIF functions can be used to tally the number of wins (or finalist or semifinalist appearances) for each team, right in the original Model sheet.

Some of these tallies appear in Figure 16.42. For example, the formula in cell U5 is

=COUNTIF('Data'!$I$8:$I$1007,S5)

The Simulation Data report in @RISK lists the outputs from each iteration of the simulation, which allows us to tally the winners.

In this case, the range I8:I1007 of the Data sheet contains the indexes of the 1000 winners, so this formula simply counts the number of these that are index 1.[6] As you can see, the top-rated team in the South region, North Carolina, won the tournament in 138 of the 1000 iterations and reached the Final Four 423 times. In contrast, the lowly rated East Tennessee State (and a few others) did not make the Final Four in any of the 1000 iterations.

---

[6]Unfortunately, each time you rerun the simulation, the Data sheet is deleted and then recreated, which invalidates the references in the tally formulas. Therefore, we created a macro to update these formulas. You can run the macro by clicking on the button at the top of the worksheet.

Figure 16.42 Tally of Tournament Winners

	S	T	U	V	W
3	**Tally of winners, finalists, and semifinalists**				
4	Index	Team	Winner	Finalist	Semifinalist
5	1	Pittsburgh	124	207	373
6	2	East Tenn. St.	0	0	0
7	3	Oklahoma St.	1	6	18
8	4	Tennessee	1	4	13
9	5	Florida St.	4	8	26
10	6	Wisconsin	2	9	26
11	7	Xavier	11	25	54
12	8	Portland St.	0	0	0
13	9	UCLA	16	35	88
14	10	VCU	0	0	2
15	11	Villanova	16	43	97
16	12	American	0	0	0
17	13	Texas	2	7	17
18	14	Minnesota	2	3	10
19	15	Duke	89	148	276
20	16	Binghamton	0	0	0
21	17	North Carolina	138	253	423
22	18	Radford	0	0	0

PROBLEMS

Level A

28. The game of Chuck-a-Luck is played as follows: You pick a number between 1 and 6 and toss three dice. If your number does not appear, you lose $1. If your number appears x times, you win $$x$. On the average, use simulation to find the average amount of money you will win or lose on each play of the game.

29. A *martingale* betting strategy works as follows. You begin with a certain amount of money and repeatedly play a game in which you have a 40% chance of winning any bet. In the first game, you bet $1. From then on, every time you win a bet, you bet $1 the next time. Each time you lose, you double your previous bet. Currently you have $63. Assuming you have unlimited credit, so that you can bet more money than you have, use simulation to estimate the profit or loss you will have after playing the game 50 times.

30. You have $5 and your opponent has $10. You flip a fair coin and if heads comes up, your opponent pays you $1. If tails comes up, you pay your opponent $1. The game is finished when one player has all the money or after 100 tosses, whichever comes first. Use simulation to estimate the probability that you end up with all the money and the probability that neither of you goes broke in 100 tosses.

Level B

31. Assume a very good NBA team has a 70% chance of winning in each game it plays. During an 82-game season what is the average length of the team's longest winning streak? What is the probability that the team has a winning streak of at least 16 games? Use simulation to answer these questions, where each iteration of the simulation generates the outcomes of all 82 games.

32. You are going to play the Wheel of Misfortune Game against the house. The wheel has 10 equally likely numbers: 5, 10, 15, 20, 25, 30, 35, 40, 45 ,and 50. The goal is to get a total as close as possible to 50 points without exceeding 50. You go first and spin the wheel. Based on your first spin, you can decide whether you want to spin again. (You can spin no more than twice.) After you are done, it is the house's turn. If your total is more than 50, the house doesn't need a turn; it wins automatically. Otherwise, the house spins the wheel. After its first spin, it can spin the wheel again if it wants. (The house can also spin no more than twice.) Then the winner is determined, where a tie goes to you. Use simulation to estimate your probability of winning the game if you and the house both use best strategies. What are the best strategies?

33. Consider the following card game. The player and dealer each receive a card from a 52-card deck. At the end of the game the player with the highest card wins; a tie goes to the dealer. (You can assume that Aces count 1, Jacks 11, Queens 12, and Kings 13.) After the player receives his card, he keeps the card if it is 7 or higher. If the player does not keep the card, the player and dealer swap cards. Then the dealer keeps his current card (which might be the player's original card) if it is 9 or higher. If the dealer does not keep his card, he draws another card. Use simulation with at least 1000 iterations to estimate the probability that the player wins. (*Hint*: See the file **Sampling Without Replacement.xlsx** to see a clever way of simulating cards from a deck so that the same card is never dealt more than once.)

34. Based on Morrison and Wheat (1984). When his team is behind late in the game, a hockey coach usually waits until there is one minute left before pulling the goalie out of the game. Using simulation, it is possible to show that coaches should pull their goalies much sooner. Suppose that if both teams are at full strength, each team scores an average of 0.05 goal per minute. Also, suppose that if you pull your goalie you score an average of 0.08 goal per minute and your opponent scores an average of 0.12 goal per minute. Suppose you are one goal behind with five minutes left in the game. Consider the following two strategies:

- Pull your goalie if you are behind at any point in the last five minutes of the game; put him back in if you tie the score.
- Pull your goalie if you are behind at any point in the last minute of the game; put him back in if you tie the score.

Which strategy maximizes your probability of winning or tying the game? Simulate the game using 10-second increments of time. Use the RISKBINOMIAL function to determine whether a team scores a goal in a given 10-second segment. This is reasonable because the probability of scoring two or more goals in a 10-second period is near zero.

35. You are playing Andy Roddick in tennis, and you have a 42% chance of winning each point. (You are *good!*)
  a. Use simulation to estimate the probability you will win a particular game. Note that the first player to score at least four points and have at least two more points than his or her opponent wins the game.
  b. Use simulation to determine your probability of winning a set. Assume that the first player to win six games wins the set if he or she is at least two games ahead; otherwise, the first player to win seven games wins the set. (We substitute a single game for the usual tiebreaker.)
  c. Use simulation to determine your probability of winning a match. Assume that the first player to win three sets wins the match.

16.6 AN AUTOMATED TEMPLATE FOR @RISK MODELS

As explained in the third edition of Albright's *VBA for Modelers* book, the macro language for Excel, VBA, can also be used to automate @RISK. We took advantage of this to create an automated template that you can use for any of your simulations. The template appears in Figure 16.43. (See the file **Simulation Template.xlsm**.) The text boxes provide the motivation and instructions. There are two basic ideas. First, you often have particular inputs you would like to vary in a sensitivity analysis. Once you specify these in the Inputs section, the program will run a separate simulation for each *combination* of the input values. In the example shown, it would run $1 \times 2 \times 3 = 6$ simulations. Second, you typically have outputs that you want to summarize in certain ways. The Outputs section lets you specify the summary measures you want for each of your outputs. The program then lists the results on separate worksheets.

This template is not a magic bullet. It is still up to you to develop the logic of the simulation. However, you no longer have to worry about RISKSIMTABLE functions or statistical functions such as RISKMEAN. The program takes care of these automatically, using your entries in the Inputs and Outputs sections. To see how the template can be used, we have included two simulations based on it. They are included in the files **World Series Simulation.xlsm** and **Newsvendor Simulation.xlsm**. (Again, remember that you must enable the macros when you open any of these .xlsm files.)

Figure 16.43 Simulation Template

	A	B	C	D	E	F	G	H	I	J	K
1	**Simulation Template**										
2											
3	**Number of iterations**										
4							Inputs:				
5	**Inputs**			Values to test			Enter as many inputs (with appropriate labels) as				
6	Input1			5			you'd like in column A, *any* values for them in				
7	Input2			A	B		column B, and values you'd like to test starting in				
8	Input3			0.50	0.75	1.00	column D. (Insert rows for more inputs if				
9	etc.						necessary.) The program will run a simulation for				
10							*each* combination of these input values.				
11				Tables requested							
12	**Outputs**			Mean	Stdev	Min	Max	Percentiles	Targets		
13	Output1			Yes	Yes	Yes	Yes	.05,.50,.95	5,6		
14	Output2			Yes	No	No	No	No	No		
15	Output3			Yes	Yes	No	No	0.05	4		
16	etc.										
17					Outputs:						
18					Enter as many outputs (with appropriate labels) as						
19	**Simulation**				you'd like in column A, and corresponding formulas						
20					(based on the simulation) in column B. (Insert rows						
21			Simulation model:		for more outputs if necessary.) Then request the						
22			Develop the simulation here. It should be		stats you'd like for the various outputs starting in						
23			dependent on the inputs above in column		column D.						
24			B, and the outputs above in column B								
25			should be dependent on it.		Overview:						
26					This file contains macros that run @RISK and generate requested tables						
27					of results for (1) any allowed number of iterations, (2) any number of						
28					(nonrandom) inputs in the blue cells, (3) any values of these inputs you						
29					want to test, and (4) any number of outputs in the gray cells. The Model						
30					sheet should be set up exactly as this. In particular, you shouldn't						
31					rename any of the bright yellow cells, and you should keep the headings						
32					in the light yellow cells right below the **Tables requested** label. To see						
33					completed versions of this template, open and run **World Series**						
34					**Simulation.xlsm** or **Newsvendor Simulation.xlsm**.						
35											

16.7 CONCLUSION

We claimed in the previous chapter that spreadsheet simulation, especially together with an add-in like @RISK, is a very powerful tool. After seeing the examples in this chapter, you should now appreciate how powerful and flexible simulation is. Unlike Solver optimization models, where you often make simplifying assumptions to achieve linearity, say, you can allow virtually anything in simulation models. All you need to do is relate output cells to input cells with appropriate formulas, where any of the input cells can contain probability distributions to reflect uncertainty. The results of the simulation then show the distribution of any particular output. It is no wonder that companies such as GM, Eli Lilly, and many others are increasingly relying on simulation models to analyze their corporate operations.

Summary of Key Terms

Term	Explanation	Excel	Page
Gamma distribution	Right-skewed distribution of nonnegative values useful for many quantities such as the lifetime of an appliance		994
RISKGAMMA function	Implements the gamma distribution in @RISK	=RISKGAMMA (*alpha,beta*)	996

(continued)

Summary of Key Terms   (*Continued*)

Term	Explanation	Excel	Page
Value at risk at the 5% level (VAR 5%)	Fifth percentile of distribution of some output, usually a monetary output; indicates nearly the worst possible outcome		1007
Churn	When customers stop buying a product or service and switch to a competitor's offering		1021
RANDBETWEEN function	Generates a random integer between two limits, where each is equally likely	=RANDBETWEEN (1,6), for example	1038

PROBLEMS

Conceptual Questions

C.1. We have separated the examples in this chapter into operations, finance, marketing, and sports categories. List at least one other problem in each of these categories that could be attacked with simulation. For each, identify the random inputs, possible probability distributions for them, and any outputs of interest.

C.2. Suppose you are an HR (human resources) manager at a big university, and you sense that the university is becoming too top-heavy with full professors. That is, there do not seem to be as many younger professors at the assistant and associate levels as there ought to be. How could you study this problem with a simulation model, using current and/or proposed promotions, hiring, firing, and retirement policies?

C.3. You are an avid basketball fan, and you would like to build a simulation model of an entire game so that you could compare two different strategies, such as man-to-man versus zone defense. Is this possible? What might make this simulation model difficult to build?

C.4. Suppose you are a financial analyst and your company runs many simulation models to estimate the profitability of its projects. If you had to choose just two measures of the distribution of any important output such as net profit to report, which two would you choose? Why? What information would be missing if you reported only these two measures? How could they be misleading?

C.5. Software development is an inherently risky and uncertain process. For example, there are many examples of software that couldn't be "finished" by the scheduled release date—bugs still remained and features weren't ready. (Many people believe this was the case with Office 2007.) How might you simulate the development of a software product? What random inputs would be required? Which outputs would be of interest? Which measures of the probability distributions of these outputs would be most important?

C.6. Health care is continually in the news. Can (or should) simulation be used to help solve, or at least study, some of the difficult problems associated with health care? Provide at least two examples where simulation might be useful.

Level A

36. You now have $3000. You will toss a fair coin four times. Before each toss you can bet any amount of your money (including none) on the outcome of the toss. If heads comes up, you win the amount you bet. If tails comes up, you lose the amount you bet. Your goal is to reach $6000. It turns out that you can maximize your chance of reaching $6000 by betting either the money you have on hand or $6000 minus the money you have on hand, whichever is smaller. Use simulation to estimate the probability that you will reach your goal with this betting strategy.

37. You now have $10,000, all of which is invested in a sports team. Each year there is a 60% chance that the value of the team will increase by 60% and a 40% chance that the value of the team will decrease by 60%. Estimate the mean and median value of your investment after 50 years. Explain the large difference between the estimated mean and median.

38. Suppose you have invested 25% of your portfolio in four different stocks. The mean and standard deviation of the annual return on each stock are shown in the file **P16_38.xlsx**. The correlations between the annual returns on the four stocks are also shown in this file.
   a. What is the probability that your portfolio's annual return will exceed 20%?
   b. What is the probability that your portfolio will lose money during the year?

39. A ticket from Indianapolis to Orlando on Deleast Airlines sells for $150. The plane can hold 100 people. It costs Deleast $8000 to fly an empty plane. Each person on the plane incurs variable costs of $30 (for food and fuel). If the flight is overbooked, anyone who cannot get a seat receives $300 in compensation. On average, 95% of all people who have a reservation show up for the flight. To maximize expected profit, how many reservations for the flight should Deleast book? (*Hint*: The function RISKBINOMIAL can be used to simulate the number who show up. It takes two arguments: the number of reservations booked and the probability that any ticketed person shows up.)

40. Based on Marcus (1990). The Balboa mutual fund has beaten the Standard and Poor's 500 during 11 of the last 13 years. People use this as an argument that you can beat the market. Here is another way to look at it that shows that Balboa's beating the market 11 out of 13 times is not unusual. Consider 50 mutual funds, each of which has a 50% chance of beating the market during a given year. Use simulation to estimate the probability that over a 13-year period the best of the 50 mutual funds will beat the market for at least 11 out of 13 years. This probability turns out to exceed 40%, which means that the best mutual fund beating the market 11 out of 13 years is not an unusual occurrence after all.

41. You have been asked to simulate the cash inflows to a toy company for the next year. Monthly sales are independent random variables. Mean sales for the months January through March and October through December are $80,000, and mean sales for the months April through September are $120,000. The standard deviation of each month's sales is 20% of the month's mean sales. Model the method used to collect monthly sales as follows:

- During each month a certain fraction of new sales will be collected. All new sales not collected become one month overdue.
- During each month a certain fraction of one-month overdue sales is collected. The remainder becomes two months overdue.
- During each month a certain fraction of two-month overdue sales is collected. The remainder is written off as bad debt.

You are given the information in the file **P16_41.xlsx** from past months. Using this information, build a simulation model that generates the total cash inflow for each month. Develop a simple forecasting model and build the error of your forecasting model into the simulation. Assuming that there are $120,000 of one-month-old sales outstanding and $140,000 of two-month-old sales outstanding during January, you are 95% sure that total cash inflow for the year will be between what two values?

42. Consider a device that requires two batteries to function. If either of these batteries dies, the device will not work. Currently there are two new batteries in the device, and there are three extra new batteries. Each battery, once it is placed in the device, lasts a random amount of time that is triangularly distributed with parameters 15, 18, and 25 (all expressed in hours). When any of the batteries in the device dies, it is immediately replaced by an extra if an extra is still available. Use @RISK to simulate the time the device can last with the batteries currently available.

43. Consider a drill press containing three drill bits. The current policy (called *individual replacement*) is to replace a drill bit when it fails. The firm is considering changing to a *block replacement* policy in which all three drill bits are replaced whenever a single drill bit fails. Each time the drill press is shut down, the cost is $100. A drill bit costs $50, and the variable cost of replacing a drill bit is $10. Assume that the time to replace a drill bit is negligible. Also, assume that the time until failure for a drill bit follows an exponential distribution with a mean of 100 hours. This can be modeled in @RISK with the formula =**RISKEXPON (100)**. Determine which replacement policy (block or individual replacement) should be implemented.

44. Appliances Unlimited (AU) sells refrigerators. Any refrigerator that fails before it is three years old is replaced for free. Of all refrigerators, 3% fail during their first year of operation; 5% of all one-year-old refrigerators fail during their second year of operation; and 7% of all two-year-old refrigerators fail during their third year of operation.
    a. Use simulation to estimate the fraction of all refrigerators that will have to be replaced.
    b. It costs $500 to replace a refrigerator, and AU sells 10,000 refrigerators per year. If the warranty period were reduced to two years, how much per year in replacement costs would be saved?

45. The annual demand for Prizdol, a prescription drug manufactured and marketed by the NuFeel Company, is normally distributed with mean 50,000 and standard deviation 12,000. Assume that demand during each of the next 10 years is an independent random number from this distribution. NuFeel needs to determine how large a Prizdol plant to build to maximize its expected profit over the next 10 years. If the company builds a plant that can produce x units of Prizdol per year, it will cost $16 for each of these x units. NuFeel will produce only the amount demanded each year, and each unit of Prizdol produced will sell for $3.70. Each unit of Prizdol produced incurs a variable production cost of $0.20. It costs $0.40 per year to operate a unit of capacity.
    a. Among the capacity levels of 30,000, 35,000, 40,000, 45,000, 50,000, 55,000, and 60,000 units per year, which level maximizes expected profit? Use simulation to answer this question.
    b. Using the capacity from your answer to part **a**, NuFeel can be 95% certain that *actual* profit for the 10-year period will be between what two values?

46. A company is trying to determine the proper capacity level for its new electric car. A unit of capacity provides the potential to produce one car per year. It costs $10,000 to build a unit of capacity and the cost is charged equally over the next five years. It also costs $400 per year to maintain a unit of capacity (whether or not it is used). Each car sells for $14,000 and incurs a variable production cost of $10,000. The annual demand for the electric car during each of the next five years is believed to be normally distributed with mean 50,000 and standard deviation 10,000. The demands during different years are assumed to be independent. Profits are discounted at a 10% annual interest rate. The company is working with a five-year planning horizon. Capacity levels of 30,000, 40,000, 50,000, 60,000, and 70,000 are under consideration. You can assume that the company never produces more than demand, so there is never any inventory to carry over from year to year.

    a. Assuming that the company is risk neutral, use simulation to find the optimal capacity level.

    b. Using the answer to part **a**, there is a 5% chance that the *actual* discounted profit will exceed what value, and there is a 5% chance that the *actual* discounted profit will be less than what value?

    c. If the company is risk averse, how might the optimal capacity level change?

47. The DC Cisco office is trying to predict the revenue it will generate next week. Ten deals may close next week. The probability of each deal closing and data on the possible size of each deal (in millions of dollars) are listed in the file **P16_47.xlsx**. Use simulation to estimate total revenue. Based on the simulation, the company can be 95% certain that its total revenue will be between what two numbers?

Level B

48. A common decision is whether a company should buy equipment and produce a product in house or outsource production to another company. If sales volume is high enough, then by producing in house, the savings on unit costs will cover the fixed cost of the equipment. Suppose a company must make such a decision for a four-year time horizon, given the following data. Use simulation to estimate the probability that producing in house is better than outsourcing.

    ■ If the company outsources production, it will have to purchase the product from the manufacturer for $18 per unit. This unit cost will remain constant for the next four years.

    ■ The company will sell the product for $40 per unit. This price will remain constant for the next four years.

    ■ If the company produces the product in house, it must buy a $400,000 machine that is depreciated

on a straight-line basis over four years, and its cost of production will be $7 per unit. This unit cost will remain constant for the next four years.

    ■ The demand in year 1 has a worst case of 10,000 units, a most likely case of 14,000 units, and a best case of 16,000 units.

    ■ The average annual growth in demand for years 2–4 has a worst case of 10%, a most likely case of 20%, and a best case of 26%. Whatever this annual growth is, it will be the same in each of the years.

    ■ The tax rate is 40%.

    ■ Cash flows are discounted at 12% per year.

49. Consider an oil company that bids for the rights to drill in offshore areas. The value of the right to drill in a given offshore area is highly uncertain, as are the bids of the competitors. This problem demonstrates the "winner's curse." The winner's curse states that the optimal bidding strategy entails bidding a substantial amount below the company's assumed value of the product for which it is bidding. The idea is that if the company does not bid under its assumed value, its uncertainty about the actual value of the product will often lead it to win bids for products on which it loses money (after paying its high bid). Suppose Royal Conch Oil (RCO) is trying to determine a profit-maximizing bid for the right to drill on an offshore oil site. The actual value of the right to drill is unknown, but it is equally likely to be any value between $10 million and $110 million. Seven competitors will bid against RCO. Each bidder's (including RCO's) estimate of the value of the drilling rights is equally likely to be any number between 50% and 150% of the actual value. Based on past history, RCO believes that each competitor is equally likely to bid between 40% and 60% of its value estimate. Given this information, what fraction (within 0.05) of RCO's estimated value should it bid to maximize its expected profit? (*Hint*: You can use the RISKUNIFORM function to model the actual value of the field and the competitors' bids.)

50. Suppose you begin year 1 with $5000. At the beginning of each year, you put half of your money under a mattress and invest the other half in Whitewater stock. During each year, there is a 50% chance that the Whitewater stock will double, and there is a 50% chance that you will lose half of your investment. To illustrate, if the stock doubles during the first year, you will have $3750 under the mattress and $3750 invested in Whitewater during year 2. You want to estimate your annual return over a 30-year period. If you end with F dollars, your annual return is $(F/5000)^{1/30} - 1$. For example, if you end with $100,000, your annual return is $20^{1/30} - 1 = 0.105$, or 10.5%. Run 1000 replications of an appropriate simulation. Based on the results, you can be 95% certain that your annual return will be between which two values?

51. Mary Higgins is a freelance writer with enough spare time on her hands to play the stock market fairly seriously. Each morning she observes the change in stock price of a particular stock and decides whether to buy or sell, and if so, how many shares to buy or sell. Assume that on day 1, she has $100,000 cash to invest and that she spends part of this to buy her first 500 shares of the stock at the current price of $50 per share. From that point on, she follows a fairly simple "buy low, sell high" strategy. Specifically, if the price has increased three days in a row, she sells 25% of her shares of the stock. If the price has increased two days in a row (but not three), she sells 10% of her shares. In the other direction, if the price has decreased three days in a row, she buys up to 25% more shares, whereas if the price has decreased only two days in a row, she buys up to10% more shares. The reason for the "up to" proviso is that she cannot buy more than she has cash to pay for. Assume a fairly simple model of stock price changes, as described in the file **P16_51.xlsx**. Each day the price can change by as much as $2 in either direction, and the probabilities depend on the previous price change: decrease, increase, or no change. Build a simulation model of this strategy for a period of 75 trading days. (You can assume that the stock price on each of the previous two days was $49.) Choose interesting @RISK output cells, and then run @RISK for at least 1000 iterations and report your findings.

52. You are considering a 10-year investment project. At present, the expected cash flow each year is $10,000. Suppose, however, that each year's cash flow is normally distributed with mean equal to *last* year's actual cash flow and standard deviation $1000. For example, suppose that the actual cash flow in year 1 is $12,000. Then year 2 cash flow is normal with mean $12,000 and standard deviation $1000. Also, at the end of year 1, your best guess is that each later year's expected cash flow will be $12,000.

    a. Estimate the mean and standard deviation of the NPV of this project. Assume that cash flows are discounted at a rate of 10% per year.

    b. Now assume that the project has an abandonment option. At the end of each year you can abandon the project for the value given in the file **P16_52.xlsx**. For example, suppose that year 1 cash flow is $4000. Then at the end of year 1, you expect cash flow for each remaining year to be $4000. This has an NPV of less than $62,000, so you should abandon the project and collect $62,000 at the end of year 1. Estimate the mean and standard deviation of the project with the abandonment option. How much would you pay for the abandonment option? (*Hint*: You can abandon a project at most once. So in year 5, for example, you abandon only if the sum of future

expected NPVs is less than the year 5 abandonment value *and* the project has not yet been abandoned. Also, once you abandon the project, the actual cash flows for future years are zero. So in this case the future cash flows after abandonment should be zero in your model.)

53. Play Things is developing a new Hannah Montana doll. The company has made the following assumptions:

- The doll will sell for a random number of years from 1 to 10. Each of these 10 possibilities is equally likely.
- At the beginning of year 1, the potential market for the doll is one million. The potential market grows by an average of 5% per year. The company is 95% sure that the growth in the potential market during any year will be between 3% and 7%. It uses a normal distribution to model this.
- The company believes its share of the potential market during year 1 will be at worst 20%, most likely 40%, and at best 50%. It uses a triangular distribution to model this.
- The variable cost of producing a doll during year 1 has a triangular distribution with parameters $8, $10, and $12.
- The current selling price is $20.
- Each year, the variable cost of producing the doll will increase by an amount that is triangularly distributed with parameters 4.5%, 5%, and 6.5%. You can assume that once this change is generated, it will be the same for each year. You can also assume that the company will change its selling price by the same percentage each year.
- The fixed cost of developing the doll (which is incurred right away, at time 0) has a triangular distribution with parameters $4, $6, and $12 million.
- Right now there is one competitor in the market. During each year that begins with four or fewer competitors, there is a 20% chance that a new competitor will enter the market.
- Year t sales (for $t > 1$) are determined as follows. Suppose that at the end of year $t - 1$, n competitors are present (including Play Things). Then during year t, a fraction $0.9 - 0.1n$ of the company's loyal customers (last year's purchasers) will buy a doll from Play Things this year, and a fraction $0.2 - 0.04n$ of customers currently in the market who did not purchase a doll last year will purchase a doll from Play Things this year. Adding these two provides the *mean* sales for this year. Then the *actual* sales this year is normally distributed with this mean and standard deviation equal to 7.5% of the mean.

    a. Use @RISK to estimate the expected NPV of this project.

b. Use the percentiles in @RISK's output to find an interval such that you are 95% certain that the company's *actual* NPV will be within this interval.

54. An automobile manufacturer is considering whether to introduce a new model called the Racer. The profitability of the Racer depends on the following factors:
   - The fixed cost of developing the Racer is triangularly distributed with parameters $3, $4, and $5, all in billions.
   - Year 1 sales are normally distributed with mean 200,000 and standard deviation 50,000. Year 2 sales are normally distributed with mean equal to actual year 1 sales and standard deviation 50,000. Year 3 sales are normally distributed with mean equal to actual year 2 sales and standard deviation 50,000.
   - The selling price in year 1 is $25,000. The year 2 selling price will be 1.05[year 1 price + $50 (% diff1)] where % diff1 is the number of percentage points by which actual year 1 sales differ from expected year 1 sales. The 1.05 factor accounts for inflation. For example, if the year 1 sales figure is 180,000, which is 10 percentage points below the expected year 1 sales, then the year 2 price will be 1.05[25,000 + 50(−10)] = $25,725. Similarly, the year 3 price will be 1.05[year 2 price + $50(% diff2)] where % diff2 is the percentage by which actual year 2 sales differ from expected year 2 sales.
   - The variable cost in year 1 is triangularly distributed with parameters $10,000, $12,000, and $15,000, and it is assumed to increase by 5% each year.

Your goal is to estimate the NPV of the new car during its first three years. Assume that the company is able to produce exactly as many cars as it can sell. Also, assume that cash flows are discounted at 10%. Simulate 1000 trials to estimate the mean and standard deviation of the NPV for the first three years of sales. Also, determine an interval such that you are 95% certain that the NPV of the Racer during its first three years of operation will be within this interval.

55. It costs a pharmaceutical company $40,000 to produce a 1000-pound batch of a drug. The average yield from a batch is unknown but the best case is 90% yield (that is, 900 pounds of good drug will be produced), the most likely case is 85% yield, and the worst case is 70% yield. The annual demand for the drug is unknown, with the best case being 22,000 pounds, the most likely case 18,000 pounds, and the worst case 12,000 pounds. The drug sells for $60 per pound and leftover amounts of the drug can be sold for $8 per pound. To maximize annual expected profit, how many batches of the drug should the company

produce? You can assume that it will produce the batches only once, *before* demand for the drug is known.

56. A truck manufacturer produces the Off Road truck. The company wants to gain information about the discounted profits earned during the next three years. During a given year, the total number of trucks sold in the United States is $500,000 + 50,000G - 40,000I$, where G is the number of percentage points increase in gross domestic product during the year and I is the number of percentage points increase in the consumer price index during the year. During the next three years, Value Line has made the predictions listed in the file **P16_56.xlsx**. In the past, 95% of Value Line's G predictions have been accurate within 6%, and 95% of Value Line's I predictions have been accurate within 5%. You can assume that the actual G and I values are normally distributed each year.

At the beginning of each year, a number of competitors might enter the trucking business. The probability distribution of the number of competitors that will enter the trucking business is also given in the same file. Before competitors join the industry at the beginning of year 1, there are two competitors. During a year that begins with n competitors (after competitors have entered the business, but before any have left, and not counting Off Road), Off Road will have a market share given by $0.5(0.9)^n$. At the end of each year, there is a 20% chance that any competitor will leave the industry. The selling price of the truck and the production cost per truck are also given in the file. Simulate 1000 replications of the company's profit for the next three years. Estimate the mean and standard deviation of the discounted three-year profits, using a discount rate of 10% and Excel's NPV function. Do the same if the probability that any competitor leaves the industry during any year increases to 50%.

57. Suppose you buy an electronic device that you operate continuously. The device costs you $300 and carries a one-year warranty. The warranty states that if the device fails during its first year of use, you get a new device for no cost, and this new device carries exactly the same warranty. However, if it fails after the first year of use, the warranty is of no value. You plan to use this device for the next six years. Therefore, any time the device fails outside its warranty period, you will pay $300 for another device of the same kind. (We assume the price does not increase during the six-year period.) The time until failure for a device is gamma distributed with parameters $\alpha = 2$ and $\beta = 0.5$. (This implies a mean of one year.) Use @RISK to simulate the six-year period. Include as outputs (1) your total cost, (2) the number of failures during the warranty period, and (3) the number of devices you own during the six-year period.

58. Rework the previous problem for a case in which the one-year warranty requires you to pay for the new device even if failure occurs during the warranty period. Specifically, if the device fails at time t, measured relative to the time it went into use, you must pay $300t$ for a new device. For example, if the device goes into use at the beginning of April and fails nine months later, at the beginning of January, you must pay $225. The reasoning is that you got 9/12 of the warranty period for use, so you should pay that fraction of the total cost for the next device. As before, however, if the device fails outside the warranty period, you must pay the full $300 cost for a new device.

59. Based on Hoppensteadt and Peskin (1992). The following model (the Reed–Frost model) is often used to model the spread of an infectious disease. Suppose that at the beginning of period 1, the population consists of five diseased people (called infectives) and 95 healthy people (called susceptibles). During any period there is a 0.05 probability that a given infective person will encounter a particular susceptible. If an infective encounters a susceptible, there is a 0.5 probability that the susceptible will contract the disease. An infective lives for an average of 10 periods with the disease. To model this, assume that there is a 0.10 probability that an infective dies during any given period. Use @RISK to model the evolution of the population over 100 periods. Use your results to answer the following questions. [*Hint:* During any period there is probability $0.05(0.50) = 0.025$ that an infective will infect a particular susceptible. Therefore, the probability that a particular susceptible is not infected during a period is $(1 - 0.025)^n$, where n is the number of infectives present at the end of the previous period.]

a. What is the probability that the population will die out?

b. What is the probability that the disease will die out?

c. On the average, what percentage of the population is infected by the end of period 100?

d. Suppose that people use infection "protection" during encounters. The use of protection reduces the probability that a susceptible will contract the disease during a single encounter with an infective from 0.50 to 0.10. Now answer parts **a** through **c** under the assumption that everyone uses protection.

60. Chemcon has taken over the production of Nasacure from a rival drug company. Chemcon must build a plant to produce Nasacure by the beginning of 2010. Once the plant is built, the plant's capacity cannot be changed. Each unit sold brings in $10 in revenue. The fixed cost (in dollars) of producing a plant that can produce x units per year of the drug is $5,000,000 + 10x$. This cost is assumed to be incurred at the end of 2010. In fact, you can assume that all cost and sales cash flows are incurred at the ends of the respective years. If a plant of capacity x is built, the variable cost of producing a unit of Nasacure is $6 - 0.1(x - 1,000,000)/100,000$. For example, a plant capacity of 1,100,000 units has a variable cost of $5.90. Each year a plant operating cost of $1 per unit of capacity is also incurred. Based on a forecasting sales model from the previous 10 years, Chemcon forecasts that demand in year t, D_t, is related to the demand in the previous year, D_{t-1}, by the equation $D_t = 67,430 + 0.985D_{t-1} + e_t$ where e_t is normally distributed with mean 0 and standard deviation 29,320. The demand in 2009 was 1,011,000 units. If demand for a year exceeds production capacity, all demand in excess of plant capacity is lost. If demand is less than capacity, the extra capacity is simply not used. Chemcon wants to determine a capacity level that maximizes expected discounted profits (using a discount rate of 10%) for the time period 2010 through 2019. Use simulation to help it do so.

61. The Tinkan Company produces one-pound cans for the Canadian salmon industry. Each year the salmon spawn during a 24-hour period and must be canned immediately. Tinkan has the following agreement with the salmon industry. The company can deliver as many cans as it chooses. Then the salmon are caught. For each can by which Tinkan falls short of the salmon industry's needs, the company pays the industry a $2 penalty. Cans cost Tinkan $1 to produce and are sold by Tinkan for $2 per can. If any cans are left over, they are returned to Tinkan and the company reimburses the industry $2 for each extra can. These extra cans are put in storage for next year. Each year a can is held in storage, a carrying cost equal to 20% of the can's production cost is incurred. It is well known that the number of salmon harvested during a year is strongly related to the number of salmon harvested the previous year. In fact, using past data, Tinkan estimates that the harvest size in year t, H_t (measured in the number of cans required), is related to the harvest size in the previous year, H_{t-1}, by the equation $H_t = H_{t-1}e_t$ where e_t is normally distributed with mean 1.02 and standard deviation 0.10.

Tinkan plans to use the following production strategy. For some value of x, it produces enough cans at the beginning of year t to bring its inventory up to $x + \hat{H}_t$, where $\hat{H}_t$ is the predicted harvest size in year t. Then it delivers these cans to the salmon industry. For example, if it uses $x = 100,000$, the predicted harvest size is 500,000 cans, and 80,000 cans are already in inventory, then Tinkan produces and delivers 520,000 cans. Given that the harvest size for the previous year was 550,000 cans, use simulation to help

Tinkan develop a production strategy that maximizes its expected profit over the next 20 years. Assume that the company begins year 1 with an initial inventory of 300,000 cans.

62. You are unemployed, 21 years old, and searching for a job. Until you accept a job offer, the following situation occurs. At the beginning of each year, you receive a job offer. The annual salary associated with the job offer is equally likely to be any number between $20,000 and $100,000. You must immediately choose whether to accept the job offer. If you accept an offer with salary x, you receive x per year while you work (assume you retire at age 70), including the current year. Assume that cash flows are discounted so that a cash flow received one year from now has a present value of 0.9. You decide to accept the first job offer that exceeds w dollars.

   a. Use simulation to determine the value of w (within $10,000) that maximizes the expected NPV of earnings you will receive the rest of your working life.

   b. Repeat part **a**, but now assume that you get a 3% raise in salary every year after the first year you accept the job.

63. A popular restaurant in Indianapolis does a brisk business, filling virtually all of its seats from 6 P.M. until 9 P.M. Tuesday through Sunday. Its current annual revenue is $2.34 million. However, it does not currently accept credit cards, and it is thinking of doing so. If it does, the bank will charge 4% on all receipts during the first year. (To keep it simple, you can ignore taxes and tips and focus only on the receipts from food and liquor.) Depending on receipts in year 1, the bank might then reduce its fee in succeeding years, as indicated in the file **P16_63.xlsx**. (This would be a one-time reduction, at the end of year 1 only.) This file also contains parameters of the two uncertain quantities, credit card usage (percentage of customers who will pay with credit cards) and increased spending (percentage increase in spending by credit card users, presumably on liquor but maybe also on more expensive food). The restaurant wants to simulate a five-year horizon. Its base case is not to accept credit cards at all, in which case it expects to earn $2.34 million in revenue each year. It wants to use simulation to explore other options, where it will accept credit cards in year 1 and then discontinue them in years 2–5 if the bank fee is less than or equal to

some cutoff value. For example, one possibility is to accept credit cards in year 1 and then discontinue them only if the bank fee is less than or equal to 3%. You should explore the cutoffs 2% to 4% in increments of 0.5%. Which policy provides with the largest mean *increase* in revenue over the five-year horizon, relative to never using credit cards?

64. The Ryder Cup is a three-day golf tournament played every other year with 12 of the best U.S. golfers against 12 of the best European golfers. They play 16 team matches (each match has two U.S. golfers against two European golfers) on Friday and Saturday, and they play 12 singles matches (each match has a single U.S. golfer against a European golfer) on Sunday. Each match is either won or tied. A win yields 1 point for the winning team and 0 points for the losing team. A tie yields 0.5 point for each team. A team needs 14.5 points to win the Cup. If each team gets 14 points, the tournament is a tie, but the preceding winner gets to keep the Cup. In 1999, the U.S. was behind 10 points to 6 after the team matches. To win the Cup, the U.S. needed at least 8.5 points on Sunday, a very unlikely outcome, but they pulled off the miracle and won. Use simulation to estimate the probability of the U.S. scoring at least 8.5 points in the 12 singles matches, assuming all golfers in the tournament are essentially equal. Proceed as follows.

   a. Use simulation to estimate the probability, call it h (for half), that a given match ends in a tie. To do this, you can assume that any of the 18 holes is tied with probability 0.475 and won with probability 0.525. (These are the historical fractions of holes that have been tied and won in singles matches in the past few Ryder Cups.) Note that each match is "match play," so the only thing that counts on each hole is whether a golfer has fewer strokes than the other golfer—winning a hole by one stroke is equivalent to winning the hole by two or more strokes in match play. The player winning the most holes wins the match, unless they tie.

   b. Run another simulation, using the estimated probability h as an input, to estimate the probability that the U.S. will score at least 8.5 points in the 12 singles matches.

Your next-door neighbor, Scott Jansen, has a 12-year-old daughter, and he intends to pay the tuition for her first year of college six years from now. The tuition for the first year will be $17,500. Scott has gone through his budget and finds that he can invest $200 per month for the next six years. Scott has opened accounts at two mutual funds. The first fund follows an investment strategy designed to match the return of the S&P 500. The second fund invests in short-term Treasury bills. Both funds have very low fees.

Scott has decided to follow a strategy in which he contributes a fixed fraction of the $200 to each fund. An adviser from the first fund suggested that in each month he should invest 80% of the $200 in the S&P 500 fund and the other 20% in the T-bill fund. The adviser explained that the S&P 500 has averaged much larger returns than the T-bill fund. Even though stock returns are risky investments in the short run, the risk should be fairly minimal over the longer six-year period. An adviser from the second fund recommended just the opposite: invest 20% in the S&P 500 fund and 80% in T-bills, because treasury bills are backed by the United States government. If you follow this allocation, he said, your average return will be lower, but at least you will have enough to reach your $17,500 target in six years.

Not knowing which adviser to believe, Scott has come to you for help.

Questions

1. The file **Investing for College.xlsx** contains 261 monthly returns of the S&P 500 and Treasury bills from January 1970 through September 1991. (If you can find more recent data on the Web, feel free to use it.) Suppose that in each of the next 72 months (six years), it is equally likely that any of the historical returns will occur. Develop a spreadsheet model to simulate the two suggested investment strategies over the six-year period. Plot the value of each strategy over time for a single iteration of the simulation. What is the total value of each strategy after six years? Do either of the strategies reach the target?

2. Simulate 1000 iterations of the two strategies over the six-year period. Create a histogram of the final fund values. Based on your simulation results, which of the two strategies would you recommend? Why?

3. Suppose that Scott needs to have $19,500 to pay for the first year's tuition. Based on the same simulation results, which of the two strategies would you recommend now? Why?

4. What other real-world factors might be important to consider in designing the simulation and making a recommendation? ∎

16.2 BOND INVESTMENT STRATEGY

An investor is considering the purchase of zero-coupon U.S. Treasury bonds. A 30-year zero-coupon bond yielding 8% can be purchased today for $9.94. At the end of 30 years, the owner of the bond will receive $100. The yield of the bond is related to its price by the following equation:

$$P = \frac{100}{(1 + y)^t}$$

Here, P is the price of the bond, y is the yield of the bond, and t is the maturity of the bond measured in years. Evaluating this equation for $t = 30$ and $y = 0.08$ gives $P = 9.94$.

The investor is planning to purchase a bond today and sell it one year from now. The investor is interested in evaluating the *return* on the investment in the bond. Suppose, for example, that the yield of the bond one year from now is 8.5%. Then the price of the bond one year later will be $9.39 $[=100/(1 + 0.085)^{29}]$. The time remaining to maturity is $t = 29$ because one year has passed. The return for the year is -5.54% $[= (9.39 - 9.94)/9.94]$.

In addition to the 30-year-maturity zero-coupon bond, the investor is considering the purchase of zero-coupon bonds with maturities of 2, 5, 10, or 20 years. All of the bonds are currently yielding 8.0%. (Bond investors describe this as a *flat yield curve*.) The investor cannot predict the future yields of the bonds with certainty. However, the investor believes that the yield of each bond one year from now can be modeled by a normal distribution with mean 8% and standard deviation 1%.

Questions

1. Suppose that the yields of the five zero-coupon bonds are all 8.5% one year from today. What are the returns of each bond over the period?
2. Using a simulation with 1000 iterations, estimate the expected return of each bond over the year. Estimate the standard deviations of the returns.
3. Comment on the following statement: "The expected yield of the 30-year bond one year from today is 8%. At that yield, its price would be $10.73. The return for the year would be 8% $[= (10.73 - 9.94)/9.94]$. Therefore, the average return for the bond should be 8% as well. A simulation isn't really necessary. Any difference between 8% and the answer in Question 2 must be due to simulation error." ■

REFERENCES

Aarvik, O., and P. Randolph. "The Application of Linear Programming to the Determination of Transmission Line Fees in an Electrical Power Network." *Interfaces* 6 (1975): 17–31.

Afshartous, D. "Sample Size Determination for Binomial Proportion Confidence Intervals: An Alternative Perspective Motivated by a Legal Case." *The American Statistician* 62, no. 1 (2008): 27–31.

Albright, S.C. "A Statistical Analysis of Hitting Streaks in Baseball." *Journal of the American Statistical Association* 88, no. 424 (1993): 1175–1196.

———. *VBA for Modelers*. 3rd ed. Mason, OH: South-Western Cengage Learning, 2010.

Altman, E. *Handbook of Corporate Finance*. New York: Wiley, 1986.

Appleton, D., J. French, and M. Vanderpump. "Ignoring a Covariate: An Example of Simpson's Paradox." *The American Statistician* 50 (1996): 340–341.

Armstrong, S. "Forecasting by Extrapolation: Conclusions from 25 Years of Research." *Interfaces* 14, no. 6 (1984): 52–66.

———. *Long-Range Forecasting*. New York: Wiley, 1985.

———. "Research on Forecasting: A Quarter-Century Review, 1960–1984." *Interfaces* 16, no. 1 (1986): 89–103.

Arntzen, B., G. Brown, T. Harrison, and L. Trafton. "Global Supply Chain Management at Digital Equipment Corporation." *Interfaces* 25, no. 1 (1995): 69–93.

Babich, P. "Customer Satisfaction: How Good Is Good Enough?" *Quality Progress* 25 (1992): 65–68.

Balson, W., J. Welsh, and D. Wilson. "Using Decision Analysis and Risk Analysis to Manage Utility Environmental Risk." *Interfaces* 22, no. 6 (1992): 126–139.

Barnett, A. "Genes, Race, IQ, and *The Bell Curve*." *ORMS Today* 22, no. 1 (1994): 18–24.

Bean, J., C. Noon, and G. Salton. "Asset Divestiture at Homart Development Company." *Interfaces* 17, no. 1 (1987): 48–65.

———, C. Noon, S. Ryan, and G. Salton. "Selecting Tenants in a Shopping Mall." *Interfaces* 18, no. 2 (1988): 1–10.

Benninga, S. *Numerical Methods in Finance*. Cambridge, MA: MIT Press, 1989.

Black, F., and M. Scholes. "The Pricing of Options and Corporate Liabilities." *Journal of Political Economy* 81 (1973): 637–654.

Blyth, C. "On Simpson's Paradox and the Sure-Thing Principle." *Journal of the American Statistical Association* 67 (1972): 364–366.

Borison, A. "Oglethorpe Power Corporation Decides about Investing in a Major Transmission System." *Interfaces* 25, no. 2 (1995): 25–36.

Boykin, R. "Optimizing Chemical Production at Monsanto." *Interfaces* 15, no. 1 (1985): 88–95.

Brigandi, A., D. Dargon, M. Sheehan, and T. Spencer. "AT&T's Call Processing Simulator (CAPS) Operational Design for Inbound Call Centers." *Interfaces* 24, no. 1 (1994): 6–28.

Brinkley, P., D. Stepto, J. Haag, K. Liou, K. Wang, and W. Carr. "Nortel Redefines Factory Information Technology: An OR-Driven Approach." *Interfaces* 28, no. 1 (1988): 37–52.

Brown, G., et al. "Real-Time Wide Area Dispatch of Mobil Tank Trucks." *Interfaces* 17, no. 1 (1987): 107–120.

Brown, G., J. Keegan, B. Vigus, and K. Wood. "The Kellogg Company Optimizes Production, Inventory, and Distribution." *Interfaces* 31, no. 6 (2001): 1–15.

Cawley, J., and P. Sommers, "Voting Irregularities in the 1995 Referendum on Quebec Sovereignty." *Chance* 9, no. 4 (Fall 1996): 29–30.

Cebry, M., A. DeSilva, and F. DiLisio. "Management Science in Automating Postal Operations: Facility and Equipment Planning in the United States Postal Service." *Interfaces* 22, no. 1 (1992): 110–130.

Charnes, A., and L. Cooper. "Generalization of the Warehousing Model." *Operational Research Quarterly* 6 (1955): 131–172.

Cox, J., S. Ross, and M. Rubenstein. "Option Pricing: A Simplified Approach." *Journal of Financial Economics* 7 (1979): 229–263.

Dantzig, G. "The Diet Problem." *Interfaces* 20, no. 4 (1990): 43–47.

Deming, E., *Out of the Crisis*. Cambridge, MA: MIT Center for Advanced Engineering Study, 1986.

DeWitt, C., L. Lasdon, A. Waren, D. Brenner, and S. Melhem. "OMEGA: An Improved Gasoline Blending System for Texaco." *Interfaces* 19, no. 1 (1989): 85–101.

Duffy, T., M. Hatzakis, W. Hsu, R. Labe, B. Liao, X. Luo, J. Oh, A. Setya, and L. Yang. "Merrill Lynch Improves Liquidity Risk Management for Revolving Credit Lines." *Interfaces* 35, no. 5 (2005): 353–369.

Eaton, D., et al. "Determining Emergency Medical Service Vehicle Deployment in Austin, Texas." *Interfaces* 15, no. 1 (1985): 96–108.

Efroymson, M., and T. Ray. "A Brand-Bound Algorithm for Plant Location." *Operations Research* 14 (1966): 361–368.

Engemann, K., and H. Miller. "Operations Risk Management at a Major Bank." *Interfaces* 22, no. 6 (1992): 140–149.

Eppen, G., K. Martin, and L. Schrage. "A Scenario Approach to Capacity Planning." *Operations Research* 37, no. 4 (1989): 517–527.

Fabian, T. "A Linear Programming Model of Integrated Iron and Steel Production." *Management Science* 4 (1958): 415–449.

Feinstein, C. "Deciding Whether to Test Student Athletes for Drug Use." *Interfaces* 20, no. 3 (1990): 80–87.

Fitzsimmons, J., and L. Allen. "A Warehouse Location Model Helps Texas Comptroller Select Out-of-State Audit Offices." *Interfaces* 13, no. 5 (1983): 40–46.

GeneHunter. Ward Systems Group, Frederick, Maryland, 1995.

Glover, F., G. Jones, D. Karney, D. Klingman, and J. Mote. "An Integrated Production, Distribution, and Inventory System." *Interfaces* 9, no. 5 (1979): 21–35.

———, et al. "The Passenger-Mix Problem in the Scheduled Airlines." *Interfaces* 12 (1982): 873–880.

Graddy, K. "Do Fast-Food Chains Price Discriminate on the Race and Income Characteristics of an Area?" *Journal of Business & Economic Statistics* 15, no. 4 (1997): 391–401.

Grossman, S., and O. Hart. "An Analysis of the Principal Agent Problem." *Econometrica* 51 (1983): 7–45.

Hauser, J., and S. Gaskin. "Application of the Defender Consumer Model." *Marketing Science* 3, no. 4 (1984): 327–351.

Herrnstein, R., and C. Murray. *The Bell Curve.* New York: The Free Press, 1994.

Hertz, D. "Risk Analysis in Capital Investment." *Harvard Business Review* 42 (Jan.–Feb. 1964): 96–108.

Hess, S. "Swinging on the Branch of a Tree: Project Selection Applications." *Interfaces* 23, no. 6 (1993): 5–12.

Holmer, M. "The Asset-Liability Management Strategy System at Fannie Mae." *Interfaces* 24, no. 3 (1994): 3–21.

Hoppensteadt, F., and C. Peskin. *Mathematics in Medicine and the Life Sciences.* New York: Springer-Verlag, 1992.

Howard, R. "Decision Analysis: Practice and Promise." *Management Science* 34, no. 6 (1988): 679–695.

———. "Heathens, Heretics, and Cults: The Religious Spectrum of Decision Aiding." *Interfaces* 22, no. 6 (1992): 15–27.

Huerter, J., and W. Swart. "An Integrated Labor-Management System for Taco Bell." *Interfaces* 28, no. 1 (1998): 75–91.

Jelen, B., and M. Alexander. *Pivot Table Data Crunching for Microsoft Office Excel 2007.* Indianapolis, IN: Que, 2007.

Kaplan, R. S., and A. A. Atkinson. *Advanced Management Accounting.* 2nd ed. Upper Saddle River, NJ: Prentice Hall, 1989.

Kauffman, J., B. Matsik, and K. Spencer. *Beginning SQL Programming.* Birmingham, UK: Wrox Press Ltd, 2001.

Keefer, D., and S. Bodily. "Three-Point Approximations for Continuous Random Variables." *Management Science* 29, no. 5 (1983): 595–609.

Kelly, J. "A New Interpretation of Information Rate." *Bell System Technical Journal* 35 (1956): 917–926.

Kimes, S., and J. Fitzsimmons. "Selecting Profitable Hotel Sites at La Quinta Motor Inns." *Interfaces* 20, no. 2 (1990): 12–20.

Kirkwood, C. "An Overview of Methods for Applied Decision Analysis." *Interfaces* 22, no. 6 (1992): 28–39.

Klingman, D., N. Phillips, D. Steiger, and W. Young. "The Successful Deployment of Management Science throughout Citgo Petroleum Corporation." *Interfaces* 17, no. 1 (1987): 4–25.

Kovar, M. "Four Million Adolescents Smoke: Or Do They?" *Chance* 13, no. 2 (2000): 10–14.

Krajewski, L., L. Ritzman, and P. McKenzie. "Shift Scheduling in Banking Operations: A Case Application." *Interfaces* 10, no. 2 (1980): 1–8.

Krumm, F., and C. Rolle. "Management and Application of Decision and Risk Analysis in DuPont." *Interfaces* 22, no. 6 (1992): 84–93.

Lancaster, L. "The Evolution of the Diet Model in Managing Food Systems." *Interfaces* 22, no. 5 (1992): 59–68.

Lanzenauer, C., E. Harbauer, B. Johnston, and D. Shuttleworth. "RRSP Flood: LP to the Rescue." *Interfaces* 17, no. 4 (1987): 27–40.

LeBlanc, L., J. Hill, G. Greenwell, and A. Czesnat. "Nu-kote's Spreadsheet Linear Programming Models for Optimizing Transportation." *Interfaces* 34, no. 2, (2004): 139–146.

Levitt, S., and S. Dubner. *Freakonomics.* New York: Harper Perennial, 2009.

Levy, P., and S. Lemeshow. *Sampling of Populations: Methods and Applications.* 3rd ed. New York: Wiley, 1999.

Littlechild, S. "Marginal Pricing with Joint Costs." *Economic Journal* 80 (1970): 323–334.

Love, R., and J. Hoey. "Management Science Improves Fast Food Operations." *Interfaces* 20, no. 2 (1990): 21–29.

Magoulas, K., and D. Marinos-Kouris. "Gasoline Blending LP." *Oil and Gas Journal* (July 1988): 44–48.

Marcus, A. "The Magellan Fund and Market Efficiency." *Journal of Portfolio Management* (Fall 1990): 85–88.

Martin, C., D. Dent, and J. Eckhart. "Integrated Production, Distribution, and Inventory Planning at Libbey-Owens-Ford." *Interfaces* 23, no. 3 (1993): 68–78.

McDaniel, S., and L. Kinney. "Ambush Marketing Revisited: An Experimental Study of Perceived Sponsorship Effects on Brand Awareness, Attitude Toward the Brand, and Purchase Intention." *Journal of Promotion Management* 3 (1996): 141–167.

Mellichamp, J., D. Miller, and O. Kwon. "The Southern Company Uses a Probability Model for Cost Justification of Oil Sample Analysis." *Interfaces* 23, no. 3 (1993): 118–124.

Metters, R., C. Queenan, M. Ferguson, L. Harrison, J. Higbie, S. Ward, B. Barfield, T. Farley, H. A. Kuyumcu, and A. Duggasani. "The Killer Application of Revenue Management: Harrah's Cherokee Casino & Hotel." *Interfaces* 38, no. 3 (2008): 161–175.

Miser, H., "Avoiding the Corrupting Lie of a Poorly Stated Problem." *Interfaces* 23, no. 6 (1993): 114–119.

Morrison, D., and R. Wheat. "Pulling the Goalie Revisited." *Interfaces* 16, no. 6 (1984): 28–34.

Mulvey, J. "Reducing the U.S. Treasury's Taxpayer Data Base by Optimization." *Interfaces* 10 (1980): 101–111.

Norton, R. "A New Tool to Help Managers." *Fortune* (May 30, 1994): 135–140.

Oliff, M., and E. Burch. "Multiproduct Production Scheduling at Owens-Corning Fiberglass." *Interfaces* 15, no. 5 (1985): 25–34.

Pankratz, A. *Forecasting with Dynamic Regression Models.* New York: Wiley, 1991.

Pass, S. "Digging for Value in a Mountain of Data." *ORMS Today* 24, no. 5 (1997): 24–28.

Patterson, S. *The Quants: How a New Breed of Math Whizzes Conquered Wall Street and Nearly Destroyed It.* New York: Random House, 2010.

Peterson, R., and E. Silver. *Decision Systems for Inventory Management and Production Planning.* 2nd ed. New York: Wiley, 1985.

Platt, H., and D. McCarthy. "Executive Compensation: Performance and Patience." *Business Horizons* 28, no. 1 (1985): 48–53.

Press, S.J. "Sample-Audit Tax Assessment for Businesses: What's Fair?" *Journal of Business & Economic Statistics* 13, no. 3 (1995): 357–359.

Ramsey, F., and D. Schafer. *The Statistical Sleuth: A Course in Methods of Data Analysis.* Belmont, CA: Duxbury Press, 1997.

Reichheld, F. *The Loyalty Effect.* Boston: Harvard Business School Press, 1996.

Robichek, A., D. Teichroew, and M. Jones. "Optimal Short-Term Financing Decisions." *Management Science* 12 (1965): 1–36.

Robinson, P., L. Gao, and S. Muggenborg. "Designing an Integrated Distribution System at DowBrands, Inc." *Interfaces* 23, no. 3 (1993): 107–117.

Rohn, E. "A New LP Approach to Bond Portfolio Management." *Journal of Financial and Quantitative Analysis* 22 (1987): 439–467.

Rothstein, M. "Hospital Manpower Shift Scheduling by Mathematical Programming." *Health Services Research* (1973).

Salkin, H., and C. Lin. "Aggregation of Subsidiary Firms for Minimal Unemployment Compensation Payments via Integer Programming." *Management Science* 25 (1979): 405–408.

Schindler, S., and T. Semmel. "Station Staffing at Pan American World Airways." *Interfaces* 23, no. 3 (1993): 91–106.

Schnarrs, S., and J. Bavuso. "Extrapolation Models on Very Short-Term Forecasts." *Journal of Business Research* 14 (1986): 27–36.

Silver, E., D. Pyke, and R. Peterson. *Inventory Management and Production Planning and Scheduling.* 3rd ed. New York: Wiley, 1998.

Simonoff, J., and I. Sparrow. "Predicting Movie Grosses: Winners and Losers, Blockbusters and Sleepers." *Chance* 13, no. 3 (2000): 15–24.

Smith, S. "Planning Transistor Production by Linear Programming." *Operations Research* 13 (1965): 132–139.

Sonderman, D., and P. Abrahamson. "Radiotherapy Design Using Mathematical Programming." *Operations Research* 33, no. 4 (1985): 705–725.

Stanley, T., and W. Danko. *The Millionaire Next Door.* Atlanta, GA: Longstreet Press, 1996.

Stonebraker, J. "How Bayer Makes Decisions to Develop New Drugs." *Interfaces* 32, no. 6 (2002): 77–90.

Strong, R. "LP Solves Problem: Eases Duration Matching Process." *Pension and Investment Age* 17, no. 26 (1989): 21.

Swart, W., and L. Donno. "Simulation Modeling Improves Operations, Planning and Productivity of Fast-Food Restaurants." *Interfaces* 11, no. 6 (1981): 35–47.

Taleb, N. N. *The Black Swan: The Impact of the Highly Improbable.* New York: Random House, 2007.

Tyagi, R., P. Kalish, K. Akbay, and G. Munshaw. "GE Plastics Optimizes the Two-Echelon Global Fulfillment Network at Its High Performance Polymers Division." *Interfaces* 34, no. 5 (2004): 359–366.

Ulvila, J. "Postal Automation (ZIP14) Technology: A Decision Analysis." *Interfaces* 17, no. 2 (1987): 1–12.

van den Briel, M., R. Villalobos, and G. Hogg. "America West Airlines Develops Efficient Boarding Strategies." *Interfaces* 35, no. 3 (2005): 191–201.

Volkema, R. "Managing the Process of Formulating the Problem." *Interfaces* 25, no. 3 (1995): 81–87.

Walkenbach, J. *Microsoft Excel 2000 Bible.* Foster City, CA: IDG Books Worldwide, Inc., 1999.

Walker, W. "Using the Set Covering Problem to Assign Fire Companies to Firehouses." *Operations Research* 22 (1974): 275–277.

Westbrooke, I. "Simpson's Paradox: An Example in a New Zealand Survey of Jury Composition." *Chance* 11, no. 2 (1998): 40–42.

Westerberg, C., B. Bjorklund, and E. Hultman. "An Application of Mixed Integer Programming in a Swedish Steel Mill." *Interfaces* 7, no. 2 (1977): 39–43.

Winston, W. L. *Operations Research: Applications and Algorithms.* 4th ed. Belmont, CA: Duxbury Press, 2003.

Zahavi, J. "Franklin Mint's Famous AMOS." *ORMS Today* 22, no. 5 (1995): 18–23.

Zangwill, W. "The Limits of Japanese Production Theory." *Interfaces* 22, no. 5 (1992): 14–25.